S0-BCT-653

CONGRESSIONAL QUARTERLY

Almanac

99th CONGRESS
2nd SESSION....1986

VOLUME XLII

Congressional Quarterly Inc.

1414 22nd St. N.W.
Washington, D.C. 20037

1986 Almanac

PUBLISHED BY

Congressional Quarterly Inc.

Congressional Quarterly Inc.

Congressional Quarterly Inc., an editorial research service and publishing company, serves clients in the fields of news, education, business and government. It combines Congressional Quarterly's specific coverage of Congress, government and politics with the more general subject range of an affiliated service, Editorial Research Reports.

Congressional Quarterly publishes the *Congressional Quarterly Weekly Report* and a variety of books, including college political science textbooks under the CQ Press imprint and public affairs paperbacks designed as timely reports to keep journalists, scholars and the public abreast of developing issues and events. CQ also publishes information directories and reference books on the federal government, national elections and politics, including the *Guide to Congress*, the *Guide to the U.S. Supreme Court*, the *Guide to U.S. Elections* and *Politics in America*. The *CQ Almanac*, a compendium of legislation for one session of Congress, is published each year. *Congress and the Nation*, a record of government for a presidential term, is published every four years.

CQ publishes *The Congressional Monitor*, a daily report on current and future activities of congressional committees, and several newsletters including *Congressional Insight*, a weekly analysis of congressional action, and *Campaign Practices Reports*, a semimonthly update on campaign laws.

An electronic online information system, the Washington Alert Service, provides immediate access to CQ's databases of legislative action, votes, schedules, profiles and analyses.

Printed in the United States of America

Library of Congress Catalog Number 47-41081

ISBN: 0-87187-418-0 ISSN: 0095-6007

"By providing a link between the local newspaper and Capitol Hill we hope Congressional Quarterly can help to make public opinion the only effective pressure group in the country. Since many citizens other than editors are also interested in Congress, we hope that they too will find Congressional Quarterly an aid to a better understanding of their government.

"Congressional Quarterly presents the facts in as complete, concise and unbiased form as we know how. The editorial comment on the acts and votes of Congress, we leave to our subscribers." Foreword, Congressional Quarterly, Vol. I, 1945.

Henrietta Poynter, 1901-1968
Nelson Poynter, 1903-1978

CQ

SUMMARY TABLE OF CONTENTS

TABLE OF CONTENTS

Chapter 1 — 99th Congress

Chapter 2 — Law/Judiciary

Chapter 3 — Environment/Energy

Chapter 4 — Appropriations

Chapter 5 — Health/Education/Welfare

Chapter 6 — Transportation/Commerce/Consumers

Chapter 7 — Agriculture

Chapter 8 — General Government

Chapter 9 — Trade Policy

Chapter 10 — Foreign Policy

Chapter 11 — Defense

Chapter 12 — Economic Policy

APPENDIXES

Supreme Court

Political Report

Voting Studies

Presidential Messages

Public Laws 3-E

Congress and Its Members

Roll-Call Charts

Index

Errata

1985 Almanac

Health Warning Labels, p. 301, col. 2: The story should have said that the Senate passed S 1574 on Dec. 16, 1985. Congress went on to clear the bill in 1986. The final version of the bill applied only to smokeless tobacco products. *(Story, p. 267)*

Presidents, Congress and the Budget, p. 440, box: Incorrect figures were given for the fiscal 1986 Reagan budget. The correct figures are as follows *(in billions of dollars)*: budget authority, $1,059.9; outlays, $973.7; revenues, $793.7; and deficit, -$180.0.

99th CONGRESS

CQ

Democrats in Full Control for 100th Congress

Dramatic changes produced by election results and retirements were evident as the members of the 100th Congress began to organize themselves late in 1986.

When the 99th Congress adjourned *sine die* Oct. 18, Republicans held control of the Senate and Thomas P. O'Neill Jr., D-Mass., was completing his 10th year as House Speaker.

An unexpectedly strong Democratic showing in the Nov. 4 elections converted a 53-47 Republican majority in the Senate into a 55-45 Democratic advantage. That restored Democrats to the dominance they had held for more than two decades before losing control to the GOP in 1980.

The shift in party power did not lead to major personnel changes in the Senate leadership; it simply converted minority posts into majority ones, and vice versa. But it did result in a number of other changes in the organization of the Senate, ranging from the partisan ratios on committees to the hiring of Senate staffers.

Democrats promised to adopt an assertive posture, particularly in dealing with President Reagan. "We are not going to wait three months in the president's waiting room," said newly elected Majority Leader Robert C. Byrd, D-W.Va. "The president has his schedule and we have ours."

But Robert Dole of Kansas, after being re-elected as Republican leader, insisted his diminished troops would not be "a helpless majority." "We're going to be a positive force," he said. "We may hold the balance of power more often than not."

In the House, the November elections produced only marginal additions to the solid Democratic majority — from a 253-180 margin at adjournment of the 99th Congress to 258-177 for the 100th Congress.

Instead, the major change was caused by the retirement of O'Neill, who had compiled the longest continuous period of service as House Speaker in the 200-year history of that office.

As expected, O'Neill was succeeded by Majority Leader Jim Wright of Texas. Wright's move up the ladder opened up a string of other leadership positions, although almost all of those who moved into top positions for the 100th Congress had already been serving in other leadership jobs.

Senate

Democrats: Old Team, New Titles

Byrd was elected without opposition Nov. 20 to the post he had held from 1977 to 1981. In the intervening years, Byrd served as minority leader.

The way for Byrd's unanimous election was cleared Nov. 11, when challenger J. Bennett Johnston, D-La., announced that he was dropping out of the race, citing Byrd's insurmountable lead. Johnston's leadership bid, announced in June, was the second time Byrd had faced a challenge — both times from moderate-to-conservative Southerners. In 1984, Lawton Chiles of Florida made an 11th-hour bid for the top Democratic post, but lost 11-36. *(1984 Almanac p. 4)*

Byrd was widely respected as a floor strategist, but critics argued that he was a weak party spokesman who lacked a telegenic image. However, neither Chiles nor Johnston managed to convert inchoate dissatisfaction with Byrd into strong support for their own candidacies.

Also re-elected by the Democratic caucus were Alan Cranston of California as majority whip and Daniel K. Inouye of Hawaii as secretary of the Democratic Conference, or caucus. John C. Stennis of Mississippi was named president pro tempore, who by tradition is the most senior member of the majority party.

A new addition to the Democratic leadership team was John Kerry of Massachusets, whom Byrd chose to succeed George J. Mitchell of Maine as chairman of the Democratic Senatorial Campaign Committee. Kerry's selection was somewhat controversial, because it brought to the key fund-raising post a man who had sharply criticized contributions from political action committees (PACs).

In tribute to Mitchell's role in helping Democrats regain the Senate, the caucus elected him to a previously

99th Congress Leadership

SENATE

President Pro Tempore — Strom Thurmond, R-S.C.
Majority Leader — Robert Dole, R-Kan.
Assistant Majority Leader — Alan K. Simpson, R-Wyo.
Republican Conference Chairman — John H. Chafee, R-R.I.
Republican Conference Secretary — Thad Cochran, R-Miss.

Minority Leader — Robert C. Byrd, D-W.Va.
Minority Whip — Alan Cranston, D-Calif.
Democratic Conference Secretary — Daniel K. Inouye, D-Hawaii

HOUSE

Speaker — Thomas P. O'Neill Jr., D-Mass.
Majority Leader — Jim Wright, D-Texas
Majority Whip — Thomas S. Foley, D-Wash.
Chairman of the Caucus — Richard A. Gephardt, D-Mo.

Minority Leader — Robert H. Michel, R-Ill.
Minority Whip — Trent Lott, R-Miss.
Chairman of the Conference — Jack F. Kemp, R-N.Y.
Republican Policy Committee Chairman — Dick Cheney, R-Wyo.

Public Laws

A total of 424 bills cleared by Congress in 1986 became public laws. Following is a list of the number of public laws enacted since 1969.

Year	Public Laws	Year	Public Laws
1986	424	1977	223
1985	240	1976	383
1984	408	1975	205
1983	215	1074	404
1082	328	1973	247
1981	145	1972	383
1980	426	1971	224
1979	187	1970	505
1978	410	1969	190

vacant leadership post revived for the occasion, deputy president pro tempore. The move kept Mitchell, a rising star among Democrats, as part of the elected leadership without displacing any of the incumbents. The deputy post was created in 1977, and filled only once — by Hubert H. Humphrey, after the Minnesota Democrat dropped out of a contest with Byrd to replace Mike Mansfield of Montana as majority leader. *(1977 Almanac p. 3)*

Other than questions about Kerry's appointment, the only source of contention in the Democratic caucus arose over the election of officers and the naming of the Senate chaplain.

The issue provoked controversy because some Democrats resented that the Republicans, after taking over the Senate in 1981, replaced the chaplain of 11 years and installed the Rev. Richard C. Halverson. The topic sparked lively debate, but Halverson was ultimately left in place.

Democrats did not hesitate, however, to replace three other Senate officials. Walter J. "Joe" Stewart, a Byrd protégé, was elected secretary of the Senate, the chief administrative officer. Henry K. Guigni, an aide to Inouye since 1957, was named sergeant-at-arms, to oversee the Capitol police and other Senate support personnel. David Pratt was named secretary for the majority, to supervise support services for Democrats. He had been secretary for the minority.

Caucus members also began struggling with the question of how to adjust the party lineup on committees. When they held a 53-47 majority, Republicans had enjoyed a one- or two-seat advantage in seats on each committee. With a larger majority, Democrats were seeking a two-seat edge in the 100th Congress.

At the same time, however, Senate leaders did not want to undo the hard-won changes made at the beginning of the 99th Congress, when the total number of seats on major committees was reduced from 231 to 214. As a result, some junior Republican members faced the prospect of being forced to give up some of the committee spots they had held previously.

In the end, Republicans did have to give up some committee seats. However, Senate leaders agreed to increase the total number of major committee seats to 224, allowing some members to stay on panels they might otherwise have been forced to leave.

Republicans: Also No Surprises

Republicans took even less time than the Democrats to re-elect their current leaders. Although some senators had questioned whether Dole would be able to balance his Senate responsibilities with his prospective 1988 presidential campaign, there was no resistance to his continuation as GOP leader.

Other familiar figures re-elected to their posts were: Alan K. Simpson of Wyoming as assistant minority leader; John H. Chafee of Rhode Island as conference chairman; Thad Cochran of Mississippi as conference secretary; and William L. Armstrong of Colorado as Policy Committee chairman.

Two new leaders were added to the bottom rungs:

Membership Changes, 99th Congress, 2nd Session

SENATE

Party	Member	Died	Successor	Party	Appointed	Elected	Sworn In
R	John P. East, N.C.	6/29/86	James T. Broyhill	R	7/3/86		7/14/86
R	James T. Broyhill, N.C. [1]		Terry Sanford [2]	D		11/4/86	12/10/86

HOUSE

Party	Member	Died	Resigned	Successor	Party	Elected	Sworn In
R	George M. O'Brien, Ill.	7/17/86					
R	John E. Grotberg, Ill.	11/15/86					
D	Cecil Heftel, Hawaii		7/11/86	Neil Abercrombie	D	9/20/86	9/23/86
R	James T. Broyhill, N.C.		7/13/86	Cass Ballenger [3]	R	11/4/86	
D	Joseph P. Addabbo, N.Y.	4/10/86		Alton R. Waldon Jr.	D	6/10/86	7/29/86

[1] *Rep. James T. Broyhill, R-N.C., was appointed to fill the seat of Sen. John P. East, R-N.C., on July 3, 1986. His appointment ran through Nov. 4, 1986.*
[2] *Terry Sanford, D-N.C., was elected to serve a full term and to fill a vacancy on the same day. While not officially sworn in until Dec. 10, 1986, he became a member of the U.S. Senate on Nov. 5, 1986.*
[3] *Cass Ballenger, R-N.C., was elected Nov. 4, 1986, to serve a full term and to fill a vacancy on the same day.*

Rudy Boschwitz of Minnesota was named chairman of the National Republican Senatorial Committee, which raises funds for party candidates, succeeding John Heinz of Pennsylvania. And Paul S. Trible Jr. of Virginia was named to chair the Committee on Committees, which makes GOP committee assignments.

House

The House Democratic Caucus chose Wright as Speaker by acclamation on Dec. 8; he faced no competition for the post he called the "apex of any lawmaker's ambition." He was elected formally by the full House when the 100th Congress convened Jan. 6, 1987.

Also by acclamation, Democrats elevated Majority Whip Thomas S. Foley of Washington to Wright's old job of majority leader.

Coelho Wins Whip's Post

In the only leadership contest, Tony Coelho of California trounced two rivals for the No. 3 job of majority whip. Coelho, who had been chairman of the Democratic Congressional Campaign Committee (DCCC) since 1981, easily defeated Charles B. Rangel, N.Y., and W. G. "Bill" Hefner, N.C. The vote, by secret ballot, was 167 for Coelho, 78 for Rangel and 15 for Hefner.

Three other contenders, Bill Alexander of Arkansas, Norman Y. Mineta of California and Martin Olav Sabo of Minnesota, dropped out of the whip's contest months before the balloting began.

Coelho, who was elected to Congress in 1978, brought to the leadership a voice of the younger generation of lawmakers who had come to the House in the preceding decade. A second such voice was added when Wright named David E. Bonior of Michigan to be chief deputy whip. Bonior, a member of the Rules Committee, had headed a whip's task force that handled the issue of aid to Nicaragua's contra rebels.

Bonior's appointment also helped allay concerns, most vocally expressed by Coelho's opponents in the whip's race, about the regional makeup of the new leadership team: None of the three top leaders came from east of the Mississippi River.

Also from west of the Mississippi was Richard A. Gephardt, Mo., who was re-elected chairman of the Caucus.

The one leadership post that was not filled at the caucus meetings was the chairmanship of the DCCC. Wright selected Beryl Anthony Jr. of Arkansas for the post on Dec. 18.

Wright's Acceptance Speech

In his acceptance speech, Wright made clear that unlike O'Neill, he would be deeply involved in the substance of the legislative agenda. He laid out an ambitious program for the early days of the 100th Congress.

Hoping to "move right into the batter's box," Wright said he wanted the House to pass legislation renewing the Clean Water Act, which Reagan vetoed earlier in the year. In addition, he urged action on a highway bill and on authorization of a select committee to conduct an inquiry into the administration's arms sales to Iran. *(Clean water, p. 136; highway bill, p. 284; Iran, p. 415)*

Wright insisted that he would not allow the Iran affair to divert attention from legislative issues. The investigation "will not preoccupy us or paralyze us or distract us from the major goals of this Congress," he said.

No More 'Other Body'

After 150 years of restraint, House members in 1987 could finally say the "S" word.

Representatives were permitted to refer directly to the Senate in floor debate, rather than resorting to talk of "the other body," after the House adopted a proposed rules change endorsed by the Democratic Caucus when it met the week of Dec. 8 to organize for the 100th Congress.

The existing ban on direct references to the Senate or its actions was supposed to help preserve comity between the two chambers. But senators abided by no comparable restriction.

"It's archaic not to be able to refer to the Senate," said Martin Frost, D-Texas, chairman of the Democratic Caucus' Committee on Organization, Study and Review, which called for the change.

The prohibition had its origin in Thomas Jefferson's "Manual of Parliamentary Practice," which was adopted by the House in 1837 and had the force of a House rule: "It is a breach of order in debate to notice what has been said on the same subject in the other House . . . because the opinion of each House should be left to its own independency, not to be influenced by the proceedings of the other. . . ."

The rules change allowed House members to mention actions taken by the Senate but still prohibited "references to individual members of the Senate, expressions of opinion concerning Senate action, or quotations from Senate proceedings."

Other issues cited by Wright as "achievable objectives" were trade legislation, welfare reform, moves to "restore the vitality of American agriculture" and measures to reduce the federal deficit.

In addition to urging a revision of the deficit-reduction targets set by the 1985 Gramm-Rudman-Hollings law (PL 99-177), and "stretching out" planned military expenditures, Wright suggested that new revenues could be raised by freezing the top tax rates on the wealthy at 1987 levels set by the tax overhaul law (PL 99-514), rather than allowing the rate to drop as scheduled in 1988. *(Tax overhaul law, p. 491)*

That suggestion drew criticism from other Democrats, who said that it was not supported by a majority of the caucus.

Steering Committee

Wright also moved quickly to create a more assertive role for the Democratic Steering and Policy Committee. Wright said he wanted the panel, which under O'Neill had been used almost solely to make committee assignments, to be a tool for developing Democratic policy positions.

The new Speaker also departed from O'Neill's practice of allowing the freshman class, Democratic members of the women's caucus and the Congressional Black Caucus to choose who would fill seats informally reserved for those groups on Steering and Policy. Wright made the choices himself.

Black Caucus members had written to Wright urging him to stick to O'Neill's policy. After consulting with black members, Wright appointed Harold E. Ford of Tennessee

Vetoes Cast by President Reagan

President Reagan vetoed 12 public bills and two private bills in 1986, bringing his total vetoes for the 99th Congress to 20.

Reagan had vetoed 39 bills during his first term in office (1981-84). Four of those vetoes were overridden. *(Previous vetoes, 1985 Almanac p. 6)*

Congress overrode one 1986 veto, of a bill imposing economic sanctions against South Africa. Two other override attempts failed: The Senate sustained Reagan's veto of a measure to block proposed arms sales to Saudi Arabia, and the House upheld Reagan's 1985 veto of legislation to restrict textile imports.

Seven of the 1986 bills were pocket-vetoed after Congress adjourned.

Under Article I, Section 7, of the Constitution, the president has 10 days (Sundays excepted) after receiving a bill passed by Congress to sign the measure into law or veto it, returning it to Congress with his objections. Congress can override a veto by a two-thirds vote of each chamber.

Any bill neither signed nor vetoed within those 10 days "shall be a law . . . unless the Congress by their adjournment prevent its return, in which case it shall not be a law."

The administration was challenging before the Supreme Court a lower court ruling that pocket vetoes could not be used between the same sessions of Congress. But the 1986 pocket vetoes would not be affected by that case because they were cast after final adjournment of the 99th Congress.

1985

40. HR 1096 (Farm Credit/African Famine Relief)
    Vetoed: March 6, 1985; no override attempt
41. HR 2409 (National Institutes of Health Research)
    Vetoed: Nov. 8, 1985
    Veto overridden Nov. 20*
    House: 380-32, Nov. 12
    Senate: 89-7, Nov. 20
42. HR 3036 (Treasury/Postal Service Appropriations)
    Vetoed: Nov. 15, 1985; no override attempt
43. HR 1562 (Textile Import Restrictions)
    Vetoed: Dec. 17, 1985
    House sustained Aug. 6, 1986: 276-149*
44. HR 1404 (Virginia Wildlife Refuge)
    Vetoed: Jan. 14, 1986; no override attempt
45. HR 3384 (Federal Employees' Health Benefits)
    Vetoed: Jan. 17, 1986; no override attempt

1986

46. HR 2466 (Coast Guard Laws)
    Vetoed: Feb. 14, 1986; no override attempt
47. S J Res 316 (Saudi Arms Sale)
    Vetoed: May 21, 1986
    Senate sustained June 5: 66-34*
48. HR 2316 (Private Bill)
    Vetoed: Sept. 25, 1986; no override attempt
49. HR 4868 (Anti-Apartheid Act)
    Vetoed: Sept. 26, 1986
    Veto overridden Oct. 2*
    House: 313-83, Sept. 29
    Senate: 78-21, Oct. 2
50. HR 3247 (Native American Programs)
    Vetoed: Sept. 26, 1986; no override attempt
51. HR 2787 (Small Business Pilot Programs)
    Vetoed: Oct. 7, 1986; no override attempt
52. H J Res 748 (Continuing Appropriations, FY 1987)
    Vetoed Oct. 9, 1986; no override attempt
53. S 593 (Private Bill)
    Pocket-vetoed: Oct. 25, 1986
54. HR 4175 (Maritime Authorization)
    Pocket-vetoed: Oct. 28, 1986†
55. HR 5465 (Appliance Energy Conservation)
    Pocket-vetoed: Nov. 1, 1986†
56. HR 4961 (Transportation Safety Board)
    Pocket-vetoed: Nov. 4, 1986†
57. S 2057 (Health Promotion Conference)
    Pocket-vetoed: Nov. 5, 1986
58. S 1128 (Clean Water Act)
    Pocket-vetoed: Nov. 6, 1986†
59. HR 5495 (NASA Authorization)
    Pocket-vetoed: Nov. 14, 1986†

* *Veto overrides require a two-thirds majority vote of both houses.*
† *President's memorandum of disapproval issued on this date.*

as the caucus' representative on Steering and Policy.

Wright's selection of a fellow Texan, Jim Chapman, to be the Steering and Policy representative for the Class of 1986 caused some grumbling among freshmen. Chapman actually had been elected in 1985, to fill the seat of Sam B. Hall Jr., who resigned to accept a federal judgeship. Meanwhile, Democratic freshmen chose Wayne Owens of Utah to be their class president. Republican newcomers picked Donald E. "Buzz" Lukens of Ohio. Both were former members of the House.

Wright selected Marcy Kaptur of Ohio to be the women's caucus representative on Steering and Policy.

As Speaker, Wright had the power to name eight members of Steering and Policy. The rest of the 31-member panel was made up of 12 members chosen by region and 11 who chaired committees or were in the leadership.

In addition to the representatives for women, blacks and freshmen, Wright's other choices were John D. Dingell, Mich., chairman of the Energy and Commerce Committee; Brian J. Donnelly, Mass.; Dave McCurdy, Okla.; Daniel A. Mica, Fla.; and James L. Oberstar, Minn.

Members elected to Steering and Policy as regional representatives were: Henry A. Waxman, Calif.; Norman D. Dicks, Wash.; Bob Traxler, Mich.; Marty Russo, Ill.; Dan Glickman, Kan.; Jack Brooks, Texas; Ronnie G. Flippo, Ala.; Butler Derrick, S.C.; Steny H. Hoyer, Md.; Louis Stokes, Ohio; Matthew F. McHugh, N.Y.; and Joseph D. Early, Mass.

Leadership members of the panel were Wright, Foley, Gephardt, Coelho, Bonior, and Mary Rose Oakar, Ohio, vice chairman of the caucus. The chairman of the DCCC also is a member of the committee.

Also serving were the following committee chairmen: Jamie L. Whitten, Miss., Appropriations; Claude Pepper, Fla., Rules; Dan Rostenkowski, Ill., Ways and Means; and William H. Gray III, Pa., Budget.

Whitten, Pepper, Rostenkowski and Gray were re-elected to their committee posts on Dec. 9. Also re-elected were Dante B. Fascell, Fla., Foreign Affairs, and James J. Howard, N.J., Public Works and Transportation. Other chairmen were to be selected in January.

Rules Changes

The most controversial rules change considered by the caucus affected the heated contest for the Armed Services chairmanship. Les Aspin, Wis., who was elected Armed Services chairman in 1985, faced opposition from Marvin Leath, Texas, and others.

Under existing caucus rules, Aspin's nomination as committee chairman by the Steering and Policy Committee was to be put first to the caucus for an up-or-down vote by secret ballot. If he was rejected, Steering and Policy would propose another nominee, but other nominations would be allowed from the floor.

Earl Hutto, Fla., proposed that the rules be changed to bar nominations from the floor. That would have required an up-or-down vote on each member of the committee below the chairman, in order of seniority.

Hutto agreed to withdraw his proposal after Martin Frost, Texas, chairman of the caucus panel that proposed rules changes, promised the idea would come before the caucus again in 1987.

Also withdrawn was a proposal backed by Wright to expand from 16 to 17 the number of members on the Select Committee on Intelligence — a panel whose Democratic members are chosen by the Speaker. Republicans opposed the change.

The caucus did endorse a few minor rules changes, which were to come before the full House for adoption. They included proposals to:

- Ease the requirement that members' financial disclosure reports list all gifts, including meals, whose value exceeds $35. Under a change proposed by John P. Murtha, Pa., the threshold was increased to $50.
- Lift the existing ban on direct references to the Senate during floor debate. The new rule allowed House members to mention Senate actions, but they still could not refer to individual senators, pass judgment on their actions or quote from Senate proceedings. *(Story, p. 5)*
- Change the name of the Science and Technology Committee to the Committee on Science, Space and Technology.
- Require one day's notice before a member of the Rules Committee could call up a rule governing consideration of a bill if it had not been brought up within seven legislative days of being reported by the Rules Committee.

GOP Leaders: Status Quo

There were no surprises at Republican meetings Dec. 8-10.

GOP members re-elected their current leaders: Robert H. Michel, Ill., minority leader; Trent Lott, Miss., GOP whip; Jack F. Kemp, N.Y., chairman of the Republican Conference; and Dick Cheney, Wyo., chairman of the Policy Committee.

In addition, Guy Vander Jagt, Mich., was re-elected as chairman of the National Republican Congressional Committee.

Lott named Edward R. Madigan, Ill., to be chief deputy whip, succeeding Tom Loeffler, Texas, who left the House for an unsuccessful bid for governor. Madigan remained ranking Republican on the Agriculture Committee and the Energy and Commerce Subcommittee on Health and the Environment, and said he would give up his leadership job if it conflicted with his committee duties.

Republicans approved several resolutions designed to clarify the obligations of GOP leaders, including ranking committee Republicans, to represent the conference. The resolutions built on the work of a study group, headed by Cheney, that was formed after Kemp in late 1985 backed passage of tax-overhaul legislation after the conference had voted to oppose the bill.

Some House Republicans complained that bills were being managed on the floor by ranking committee members whose views were different from the conference as a whole.

Cheney said his group's recommendations made clear that "elected leaders accept a certain obligation to the conference at large, and that they should try to the best of their ability to support the conference position." Although some members sought stronger language, the resolutions did not bind leaders and ranking members to stand by the conference position.

The conference also decided to designate the ranking Republican on each committee as "vice chairman." ∎

Members of the 99th Congress, Second Session . . .

As of Oct. 18, 1986

Representatives

D 253; R 180

2 Vacancies *

A

Abercrombie, Neil, D-Hawaii (1)
Ackerman, Gary L., D-N.Y. (7)
Akaka, Daniel K., D-Hawaii (2)
Alexander, Bill, D-Ark. (1)
Anderson, Glenn M., D-Calif. (32)
Andrews, Michael A., D-Texas (25)
Annunzio, Frank, D-Ill. (11)
Anthony, Beryl Jr., D-Ark. (4)
Applegate, Douglas, D-Ohio (18)
Archer, Bill, R-Texas (7)
Armey, Dick, R-Texas (26)
Aspin, Les, D-Wis. (1)
Atkins, Chester G., D-Mass. (5)
AuCoin, Les, D-Ore. (1)

B

Badham, Robert E., R-Calif. (40)
Barnard, Doug Jr., D-Ga. (10)
Barnes, Michael D., D-Md. (8)
Bartlett, Steve, R-Texas (3)
Barton, Joe L., R-Texas (6)
Bateman, Herbert H., R-Va. (1)
Bates, Jim, D-Calif. (44)
Bedell, Berkley, D-Iowa (6)
Beilenson, Anthony C., D-Calif. (23)
Bennett, Charles E., D-Fla. (3)
Bentley, Helen Delich, R-Md. (2)
Bereuter, Doug, R-Neb. (1)
Berman, Howard L., D-Calif. (26)
Bevill, Tom, D-Ala. (4)
Biaggi, Mario, D-N.Y. (19)
Bilirakis, Michael, R-Fla. (9)
Bliley, Thomas J. Jr., R-Va. (3)
Boehlert, Sherwood, R-N.Y. (25)
Boggs, Lindy (Mrs. Hale), D-La. (2)
Boland, Edward P., D-Mass. (2)
Boner, Bill, D-Tenn. (5)
Bonior, David E., D-Mich. (12)
Bonker, Don, D-Wash. (3)
Borski, Robert A., D-Pa. (3)
Bosco, Douglas H., D-Calif. (1)
Boucher, Frederick C., D-Va. (9)
Boulter, Beau, R-Texas (13)
Boxer, Barbara, D-Calif. (6)
Breaux, John B., D-La. (7)
Brooks, Jack, D-Texas (9)
Broomfield, William S., R-Mich. (18)
Brown, George E. Jr., D-Calif. (36)
Brown, Hank, R-Colo. (4)
Bruce, Terry L., D-Ill. (19)
Bryant, John, D-Texas (5)
Burton, Dan, R-Ind. (6)
Burton, Sala, D-Calif. (5)
Bustamante, Albert G., D-Texas (23)
Byron, Beverly B., D-Md. (6)

C

Callahan, Sonny, R-Ala. (1)
Campbell, Carroll A. Jr., R-S.C. (4)
Carney, William, R-N.Y. (1)
Carper, Thomas R., D-Del. (AL)
Carr, Bob, D-Mich. (6)
Chandler, Rod, R-Wash. (8)
Chapman, Jim, D-Texas (1)
Chappell, Bill Jr., D-Fla. (4)
Chappie, Gene, R-Calif. (2)
Cheney, Dick, R-Wyo. (AL)
Clay, William L., D-Mo. (1)
Clinger, William F. Jr., R-Pa. (23)
Coats, Dan, R-Ind. (4)
Cobey, Bill, R-N.C. (4)
Coble, Howard, R-N.C. (6)
Coelho, Tony, D-Calif. (15)
Coleman, E. Thomas, R-Mo. (6)
Coleman, Ronald D., D-Texas (16)
Collins, Cardiss, D-Ill. (7)
Combest, Larry, R-Texas (19)
Conte, Silvio O., R-Mass. (1)
Conyers, John Jr., D-Mich. (1)
Cooper, Jim, D-Tenn. (4)
Coughlin, Lawrence, R-Pa. (13)
Courter, Jim, R-N.J. (12)
Coyne, William J., D-Pa. (14)
Craig, Larry E., R-Idaho (1)
Crane, Philip M., R-Ill. (12)
Crockett, George W. Jr., D-Mich. (13)

D

Daniel, Dan, D-Va. (5)
Dannemeyer, William E., R-Calif. (39)
Darden, George "Buddy", D-Ga. (7)
Daschle, Thomas A., D-S.D. (AL)
Daub, Hal, R-Neb. (2)
Davis, Robert W., R-Mich. (11)
de la Garza, E. "Kika", D-Texas (15)
DeLay, Thomas D., R-Texas (22)
Dellums, Ronald V., D-Calif. (8)
Derrick, Butler, D-S.C. (3)
DeWine, Michael, R-Ohio (7)
Dickinson, William L., R-Ala. (2)
Dicks, Norman D., D-Wash. (6)
Dingell, John D., D-Mich. (16)
DioGuardi, Joseph J., R-N.Y. (20)
Dixon, Julian C., D-Calif. (28)
Donnelly, Brian J., D-Mass. (11)
Dorgan, Byron L., D-N.D. (AL)
Dornan, Bob, R-Calif. (38)
Dowdy, Wayne, D-Miss. (4)
Downey, Thomas J., D-N.Y. (2)
Dreier, David, R-Calif. (33)
Duncan, John J., R-Tenn. (2)
Durbin, Richard J., D-Ill. (20)
Dwyer, Bernard J., D-N.J. (6)
Dymally, Mervyn M., D-Calif. (31)
Dyson, Roy, D-Md. (1)

E

Early, Joseph D., D-Mass. (3)
Eckart, Dennis E., D-Ohio (11)
Eckert, Fred J., R-N.Y. (30)
Edgar, Bob, D-Pa. (7)
Edwards, Don, D-Calif. (10)
Edwards, Mickey, R-Okla. (5)
Emerson, Bill, R-Mo. (8)
English, Glenn, D-Okla. (6)
Erdreich, Ben, D-Ala. (6)
Evans, Cooper, R-Iowa (3)
Evans, Lane, D-Ill. (17)

F

Fascell, Dante B., D-Fla. (19)
Fawell, Harris W., R-Ill. (13)
Fazio, Vic, D-Calif. (4)
Feighan, Edward F., D-Ohio (19)
Fiedler, Bobbi, R-Calif. (21)
Fields, Jack, R-Texas (8)
Fish, Hamilton Jr., R-N.Y. (21)
Flippo, Ronnie G., D-Ala. (5)
Florio, James J., D-N.J. (1)
Foglietta, Thomas M., D-Pa. (1)
Foley, Thomas S., D-Wash. (5)
Ford, Harold E., D-Tenn. (9)
Ford, William D., D-Mich. (15)
Fowler, Wyche Jr., D-Ga. (5)
Frank, Barney, D-Mass. (4)
Franklin, Webb, R-Miss. (2)
Frenzel, Bill, R-Minn. (3)
Frost, Martin, D-Texas (24)
Fuqua, Don, D-Fla. (2)

G

Gallo, Dean A., R-N.J. (11)
Garcia, Robert, D-N.Y. (18)
Gaydos, Joseph M., D-Pa. (20)
Gejdenson, Sam, D-Conn. (2)
Gekas, George W., R-Pa. (17)
Gephardt, Richard A., D-Mo. (3)
Gibbons, Sam, D-Fla. (7)
Gilman, Benjamin A., R-N.Y. (22)
Gingrich, Newt, R-Ga. (6)
Glickman, Dan, D-Kan. (4)
Gonzalez, Henry B., D-Texas (20)
Goodling, Bill, R-Pa. (19)
Gordon, Bart, D-Tenn. (6)
Gradison, Bill, R-Ohio (2)
Gray, Kenneth J., D-Ill. (22)
Gray, William H. III, D-Pa. (2)
Green, Bill, R-N.Y. (15)
Gregg, Judd, R-N.H. (2)
Grotberg, John E., R-Ill. (14)
Guarini, Frank J., D-N.J. (14)
Gunderson, Steve, R-Wis. (3)

H

Hall, Ralph M., D-Texas (4)
Hall, Tony P., D-Ohio (3)
Hamilton, Lee H., D-Ind. (9)
Hammerschmidt, John Paul, R-Ark. (3)
Hansen, James V., R-Utah (1)
Hartnett, Thomas F., R-S.C. (1)
Hatcher, Charles, D-Ga. (2)
Hawkins, Augustus F., D-Calif. (29)
Hayes, Charles A., D-Ill. (1)
Hefner, W. G. "Bill", D-N.C. (8)
Hendon, Bill, R-N.C. (11)
Henry, Paul B., R-Mich. (5)
Hertel, Dennis M., D-Mich. (14)
Hiler, John, R-Ind. (3)
Hillis, Elwood, R-Ind. (5)
Holt, Marjorie S., R-Md. (4)
Hopkins, Larry J., R-Ky. (6)
Horton, Frank, R-N.Y. (29)
Howard, James J., D-N.J. (3)
Hoyer, Steny H., D-Md. (5)
Hubbard, Carroll Jr., D-Ky. (1)
Huckaby, Jerry, D-La. (5)
Hughes, William J., D-N.J. (2)
Hunter, Duncan L., R-Calif. (45)
Hutto, Earl, D-Fla. (1)
Hyde, Henry J., R-Ill. (6)

I, J

Ireland, Andy, R-Fla. (10)
Jacobs, Andrew Jr., D-Ind. (10)
Jeffords, James M., R-Vt. (AL)
Jenkins, Ed, D-Ga. (9)
Johnson, Nancy L., R-Conn. (6)
Jones, Ed, D-Tenn. (8)
Jones, James R., D-Okla. (1)
Jones, Walter B., D-N.C. (1)

K

Kanjorski, Paul E., D-Pa. (11)
Kaptur, Marcy, D-Ohio (9)
Kasich, John R., R-Ohio (12)
Kastenmeier, Robert W., D-Wis. (2)
Kemp, Jack F., R-N.Y. (31)
Kennelly, Barbara B., D-Conn. (1)
Kildee, Dale E., D-Mich. (7)
Kindness, Thomas N., R-Ohio (8)
Kleczka, Gerald D., D-Wis. (4)
Kolbe, Jim, R-Ariz. (5)
Kolter, Joe, D-Pa. (4)
Kostmayer, Peter H., D-Pa. (8)
Kramer, Ken, R-Colo. (5)

L

LaFalce, John J., D-N.Y. (32)
Lagomarsino, Robert J., R-Calif. (19)
Lantos, Tom, D-Calif. (11)
Latta, Delbert L., R-Ohio (5)
Leach, Jim, R-Iowa (1)
Leath, Marvin, D-Texas (11)
Lehman, Richard H., D-Calif. (18)
Lehman, William, D-Fla. (17)
Leland, Mickey, D-Texas (18)
Lent, Norman F., R-N.Y. (4)
Levin, Sander M., D-Mich. (17)
Levine, Mel, D-Calif. (27)
Lewis, Jerry, R-Calif. (35)
Lewis, Tom, R-Fla. (12)
Lightfoot, Jim, R-Iowa (5)
Lipinski, William O., D-Ill. (5)
Livingston, Bob, R-La. (1)
Lloyd, Marilyn, D-Tenn. (3)
Loeffler, Tom, R-Texas (21)
Long, Cathy (Mrs. Gillis), D-La. (7)
Lott, Trent, R-Miss. (5)
Lowery, Bill, R-Calif. (41)
Lowry, Mike, D-Wash. (7)
Lujan, Manuel Jr., R-N.M. (1)
Luken, Thomas A., D-Ohio (1)
Lundine, Stan, D-N.Y. (34)
Lungren, Dan, R-Calif. (42)

M

Mack, Connie, R-Fla. (13)
MacKay, Buddy, D-Fla. (6)
Madigan, Edward R., R-Ill. (15)
Manton, Thomas J., D-N.Y. (9)
Markey, Edward J., D-Mass. (7)
Marlenee, Ron, R-Mont. (2)
Martin, David O'B., R-N.Y. (26)
Martin, Lynn, R-Ill. (16)
Martinez, Matthew G., D-Calif. (30)
Matsui, Robert T., D-Calif. (3)
Mavroules, Nicholas, D-Mass. (6)
Mazzoli, Romano L., D-Ky. (3)
McCain, John, R-Ariz. (1)
McCandless, Al, R-Calif. (37)
McCloskey, Frank, D-Ind. (8)
McCollum, Bill, R-Fla. (5)
McCurdy, Dave, D-Okla. (4)
McDade, Joseph M., R-Pa. (10)
McEwen, Bob, R-Ohio (6)
McGrath, Raymond J., R-N.Y. (5)
McHugh, Matthew F., D-N.Y. (28)
McKernan, John R. Jr., R-Maine (1)
McKinney, Stewart B., R-Conn. (4)
McMillan, J. Alex, R-N.C. (9)
Meyers, Jan, R-Kan. (3)
Mica, Daniel A., D-Fla. (14)
Michel, Robert H., R-Ill. (18)
Mikulski, Barbara A., D-Md. (3)
Miller, Clarence E., R-Ohio (10)
Miller, George, D-Calif. (7)
Miller, John R., R-Wash. (1)
Mineta, Norman Y., D-Calif. (13)
Mitchell, Parren J., D-Md. (7)
Moakley, Joe, D-Mass. (9)
Molinari, Guy V., R-N.Y. (14)
Mollohan, Alan B., D-W.Va. (1)
Monson, David S., R-Utah (2)
Montgomery, G. V. "Sonny", D-Miss. (3)
Moody, Jim, D-Wis. (5)
Moore, W. Henson, R-La. (6)
Moorhead, Carlos J., R-Calif. (22)
Morrison, Bruce A., D-Conn. (3)
Morrison, Sid, R-Wash. (4)
Mrazek, Robert J., D-N.Y. (3)
Murphy, Austin J., D-Pa. (22)
Murtha, John P., D-Pa. (12)
Myers, John T., R-Ind. (7)

N

Natcher, William H., D-Ky. (2)
Neal, Stephen L., D-N.C. (5)
Nelson, Bill, D-Fla. (11)
Nichols, Bill, D-Ala. (3)
Nielson, Howard C., R-Utah (3)
Nowak, Henry J., D-N.Y. (33)

O

Oakar, Mary Rose, D-Ohio (20)
Oberstar, James L., D-Minn. (8)
Obey, David R., D-Wis. (7)
Olin, James R., D-Va. (6)
O'Neill, Thomas P. Jr., D-Mass. (8)
Ortiz, Solomon P., D-Texas (27)
Owens, Major R., D-N.Y. (12)
Oxley, Michael G., R-Ohio (4)

P

Packard, Ron, R-Calif. (43)
Panetta, Leon E., D-Calif. (16)
Parris, Stan, R-Va. (8)
Pashayan, Charles Jr., R-Calif. (17)
Pease, Don J., D-Ohio (13)
Penny, Timothy J., D-Minn. (1)
Pepper, Claude, D-Fla. (18)
Perkins, Carl C., D-Ky. (7)

. . . Governors, Supreme Court, Cabinet-rank Officers

Petri, Thomas E., R-Wis. (6)
Pickle, J. J., D-Texas (10)
Porter, John Edward, R-Ill. (10)
Price, Melvin, D-Ill. (21)
Pursell, Carl D., R-Mich. (2)

Q, R

Quillen, James H., R-Tenn. (1)
Rahall, Nick J. II, D-W.Va. (4)
Rangel, Charles B., D-N.Y. (16)
Ray, Richard, D-Ga. (3)
Regula, Ralph, R-Ohio (16)
Reid, Harry, D-Nev. (1)
Richardson, Bill, D-N.M. (3)
Ridge, Tom, R-Pa. (21)
Rinaldo, Matthew J., R-N.J. (7)
Ritter, Don, R-Pa. (15)
Roberts, Pat, R-Kan. (1)
Robinson, Tommy F., D-Ark. (2)
Rodino, Peter W. Jr., D-N.J. (10)
Roe, Robert A., D-N.J. (8)
Roemer, Buddy, D-La. (4)
Rogers, Harold, R-Ky. (5)
Rose, Charlie, D-N.C. (7)
Rostenkowski, Dan, D-Ill. (8)
Roth, Toby, R-Wis. (8)
Roukema, Marge, R-N.J. (5)
Rowland, J. Roy, D-Ga. (8)
Rowland, John G., R-Conn. (5)
Roybal, Edward R., D-Calif. (25)
Rudd, Eldon, R-Ariz. (4)
Russo, Marty, D-Ill. (3)

S

Sabo, Martin Olav, D-Minn. (5)
St Germain, Fernand J., D-R.I. (1)
Savage, Gus, D-Ill. (2)
Saxton, H. James, R-N.J. (13)
Schaefer, Dan L., R-Colo. (6)
Scheuer, James H., D-N.Y. (8)
Schneider, Claudine, R-R.I. (2)
Schroeder, Patricia, D-Colo. (1)
Schuette, Bill, R-Mich. (10)
Schulze, Richard T., R-Pa. (5)
Schumer, Charles E., D-N.Y. (10)
Seiberling, John F., D-Ohio (14)
Sensenbrenner, F. James Jr., R-Wis. (9)
Sharp, Philip R., D-Ind. (2)
Shaw, E. Clay Jr., R-Fla. (15)
Shelby, Richard C., D-Ala. (7)
Shumway, Norman D., R-Calif. (14)
Shuster, Bud, R-Pa. (9)
Sikorski, Gerry, D-Minn. (6)
Siljander, Mark D., R-Mich. (4)
Sisisky, Norman, D-Va. (4)
Skeen, Joe, R-N.M. (2)
Skelton, Ike, D-Mo. (4)
Slattery, Jim, D-Kan. (2)
Slaughter, D. French Jr., R-Va. (7)
Smith, Christopher H., R-N.J. (4)
Smith, Denny, R-Ore. (5)
Smith, Larry, D-Fla. (16)
Smith, Neal, D-Iowa (4)
Smith, Robert C., R-N.H. (1)
Smith, Robert F., R-Ore. (2)
Smith, Virginia, R-Neb. (3)
Snowe, Olympia J., R-Maine (2)
Snyder, Gene, R-Ky. (4)
Solarz, Stephen J., D-N.Y. (13)
Solomon, Gerald B. H., R-N.Y. (24)
Spence, Floyd, R-S.C. (2)
Spratt, John M. Jr., D-S.C. (5)
Staggers, Harley O. Jr., D-W.Va. (2)
Stallings, Richard H., D-Idaho (2)
Stangeland, Arlan, R-Minn. (7)
Stark, Fortney H. "Pete", D-Calif. (9)
Stenholm, Charles W., D-Texas (17)
Stokes, Louis, D-Ohio (21)
Strang, Mike, R-Colo. (3)
Stratton, Samuel S., D-N.Y. (23)
Studds, Gerry E., D-Mass. (10)
Stump, Bob, R-Ariz. (3)
Sundquist, Don, R-Tenn. (7)
Sweeney, Mac, R-Texas (14)
Swift, Al, D-Wash. (2)
Swindall, Pat, R-Ga. (4)
Synar, Mike, D-Okla. (2)

T

Tallon, Robin, D-S.C. (6)
Tauke, Tom, R-Iowa (2)
Tauzin, W. J. "Billy", D-La. (3)
Taylor, Gene, R-Mo. (7)
Thomas, Robert Lindsay, D-Ga. (1)
Thomas, William M., R-Calif. (20)
Torres, Esteban Edward, D-Calif. (34)
Torricelli, Robert G., D-N.J. (9)
Towns, Edolphus, D-N.Y. (11)
Traficant, James A. Jr., D-Ohio (17)
Traxler, Bob, D-Mich. (8)

U, V

Udall, Morris K., D-Ariz. (2)
Valentine, Tim, D-N.C. (2)
Vander Jagt, Guy, R-Mich. (9)
Vento, Bruce F., D-Minn. (4)
Visclosky, Peter J., D-Ind. (1)
Volkmer, Harold L., D-Mo. (9)
Vucanovich, Barbara F., R-Nev. (2)

W

Waldon, Alton R. Jr., D-N.Y. (6)
Walgren, Doug, D-Pa. (18)
Walker, Robert S., R-Pa. (16)
Watkins, Wes, D-Okla. (3)
Waxman, Henry A., D-Calif. (24)
Weaver, James, D-Ore. (4)
Weber, Vin, R-Minn. (2)
Weiss, Ted, D-N.Y. (17)
Wheat, Alan, D-Mo. (5)
Whitehurst, G. William, R-Va. (2)
Whitley, Charles, D-N.C. (3)
Whittaker, Bob, R-Kan. (5)
Whitten, Jamie L., D-Miss. (1)
Williams, Pat, D-Mont. (1)
Wilson, Charles, D-Texas (2)
Wirth, Timothy E., D-Colo. (2)
Wise, Bob, D-W.Va. (3)
Wolf, Frank R., R-Va. (10)
Wolpe, Howard, D-Mich. (3)
Wortley, George C., R-N.Y. (27)
Wright, Jim, D-Texas (12)
Wyden, Ron, D-Ore. (3)
Wylie, Chalmers P., R-Ohio (15)

X, Y, Z

Yates, Sidney R., D-Ill. (9)
Yatron, Gus, D-Pa. (6)
Young, C. W. Bill, R-Fla. (8)
Young, Don, R-Alaska (AL)
Young, Robert A., D-Mo. (2)
Zschau, Ed, R-Calif. (12)

Delegates

Blaz, Ben, R-Guam
de Lugo, Ron, D-Virgin Islands
Fauntroy, Walter E., D-D.C.
Sunia, Fofō I. F., D-American Samoa

Resident Commissioner

Fuster, Jaime B., Pop. Dem.-Puerto Rico

Senators

R 53; D 47

Abdnor, James, R-S.D.
Andrews, Mark, R-N.D.
Armstrong, William L., R-Colo.
Baucus, Max, D-Mont.
Bentsen, Lloyd, D-Texas
Biden, Joseph R. Jr., D-Del.
Bingaman, Jeff, D-N.M.
Boren, David L., D-Okla.
Boschwitz, Rudy, R-Minn.
Bradley, Bill, D-N.J.
Broyhill, James T., R-N.C.
Bumpers, Dale, D-Ark.
Burdick, Quentin N., D-N.D.
Byrd, Robert C., D-W.Va.
Chafee, John H., R-R.I.
Chiles, Lawton, D-Fla.
Cochran, Thad, R-Miss.
Cohen, William S., R-Maine
Cranston, Alan, D-Calif.
D'Amato, Alfonse M., R-N.Y.
Danforth, John C., R-Mo.
DeConcini, Dennis, D-Ariz.
Denton, Jeremiah, R-Ala.
Dixon, Alan J., D-Ill.
Dodd, Christopher J., D-Conn.
Dole, Robert, R-Kan.
Domenici, Pete V., R-N.M.
Durenberger, Dave, R-Minn.
Eagleton, Thomas F., D-Mo.
Evans, Daniel J., R-Wash.
Exon, J. James, D-Neb.
Ford, Wendell H., D-Ky.
Garn, Jake, R-Utah
Glenn, John, D-Ohio
Goldwater, Barry, R-Ariz.
Gore, Albert Jr., D-Tenn.
Gorton, Slade, R-Wash.
Gramm, Phil, R-Texas
Grassley, Charles E., R-Iowa
Harkin, Tom, D-Iowa
Hart, Gary, D-Colo.
Hatch, Orrin G., R-Utah
Hatfield, Mark O., R-Ore.
Hawkins, Paula, R-Fla.
Hecht, Chic, R-Nev.
Heflin, Howell, D-Ala.
Heinz, John, R-Pa.
Helms, Jesse, R-N.C.
Hollings, Ernest F., D-S.C.
Humphrey, Gordon J., R-N.H.
Inouye, Daniel K., D-Hawaii
Johnston, J. Bennett, D-La.
Kassebaum, Nancy Landon, R-Kan.
Kasten, Bob, R-Wis.
Kennedy, Edward M., D-Mass.
Kerry, John, D-Mass.
Lautenberg, Frank R., D-N.J.
Laxalt, Paul, R-Nev.
Leahy, Patrick J., D-Vt.
Levin, Carl, D-Mich.
Long, Russell B., D-La.
Lugar, Richard G., R-Ind.
Mathias, Charles McC. Jr., R-Md.
Matsunaga, Spark M., D-Hawaii
Mattingly, Mack, R-Ga.
McClure, James A., R-Idaho
McConnell, Mitch, R-Ky.
Melcher, John, D-Mont.
Metzenbaum, Howard M., D-Ohio
Mitchell, George J., D-Maine
Moynihan, Daniel Patrick, D-N.Y.
Murkowski, Frank H., R-Alaska
Nickles, Don, R-Okla.
Nunn, Sam, D-Ga.
Packwood, Bob, R-Ore.
Pell, Claiborne, D-R.I.
Pressler, Larry, R-S.D.
Proxmire, William, D-Wis.
Pryor, David, D-Ark.
Quayle, Dan, R-Ind.
Riegle, Donald W. Jr., D-Mich.
Rockefeller, John D. IV, D-W.Va.
Roth, William V. Jr., R-Del.
Rudman, Warren B., R-N.H.
Sarbanes, Paul S., D-Md.
Sasser, Jim, D-Tenn.
Simon, Paul, D-Ill.
Simpson, Alan K., R-Wyo.
Specter, Arlen, R-Pa.
Stafford, Robert T., R-Vt.
Stennis, John C., D-Miss.
Stevens, Ted, R-Alaska
Symms, Steven D., R-Idaho
Thurmond, Strom, R-S.C.
Trible, Paul S. Jr., R-Va.
Wallop, Malcolm, R-Wyo.
Warner, John W., R-Va.
Weicker, Lowell P. Jr., R-Conn.
Wilson, Pete, R-Calif.
Zorinsky, Edward, D-Neb.

Governors

D 34; R 16

Ala.—George C. Wallace, D
Alaska—Bill Sheffield, D
Ariz.—Bruce Babbitt, D
Ark.—Bill Clinton, D
Calif.—George Deukmejian, R
Colo.—Richard D. Lamm, D
Conn.—William A. O'Neill, D
Del.—Michael N. Castle, R
Fla.—Bob Graham, D
Ga.—Joe Frank Harris, D
Hawaii—George R. Ariyoshi, D
Idaho—John V. Evans, D
Ill.—James R. Thompson, R
Ind.—Robert D. Orr, R
Iowa—Terry E. Branstad, R
Kan.—John Carlin, D
Ky.—Martha Layne Collins, D
La.—Edwin W. Edwards, D
Maine—Joseph E. Brennan, D
Md.—Harry Hughes, D
Mass.—Michael S. Dukakis, D
Mich.—James J. Blanchard, D
Minn.—Rudy Perpich, D
Miss.—Bill Allain, D
Mo.—John Ashcroft, R
Mont.—Ted Schwinden, D
Neb.—Robert Kerrey, D
Nev.—Richard H. Bryan, D
N.H.—John H. Sununu, R
N.J.—Thomas H. Kean, R
N.M.—Toney Anaya, D
N.Y.—Mario M. Cuomo, D
N.C.—James G. Martin, R
N.D.—George Sinner, D
Ohio—Richard F. Celeste, D
Okla.—George Nigh, D
Ore.—Victor G. Atiyeh, R
Pa.—Dick Thornburgh, R
R.I.—Edward DiPrete, R
S.C.—Richard W. Riley, D
S.D.—William J. Janklow, R
Tenn.—Lamar Alexander, R
Texas—Mark White, D
Utah—Norman H. Bangerter, R
Vt.—Madeleine M. Kunin, D
Va.—Gerald L. Baliles, D
Wash.—Booth Gardner, D
W.Va.—Arch A. Moore Jr., R
Wis.—Anthony S. Earl, D
Wyo.—Ed Herschler, D

Supreme Court

Rehnquist, William H.—Ariz., Chief Justice
Blackmun, Harry A.—Minn.
Brennan, William J. Jr.—N.J.
Marshall, Thurgood—N.Y.
O'Connor, Sandra Day—Ariz.
Powell, Lewis F. Jr.—Va.
Scalia, Antonin—Va.
Stevens, John Paul—Ill.
White, Byron R.—Colo.

Cabinet

Baker, James A. III—Treasury
Baldrige, Malcolm—Commerce
Bennett, William J.—Education
Bowen, Otis—HHS
Brock, William E. III—Labor
Dole, Elizabeth Hanford—Transportation
Herrington, John S.—Energy
Hodel, Donald P.—Interior
Lyng, Richard E.—Agriculture
Meese, Edwin III—Attorney General
Pierce, Samuel R. Jr.—HUD
Shultz, George P.—State
Weinberger, Caspar W.—Defense

Other Officers With Cabinet Rank

Bush, George—Vice President
Casey, William J.—CIA Director
Miller, James C. III—OMB Director
Regan, Donald T.—Chief of Staff
Walters, Vernon A.—U.N. Representative
Yeutter, Clayton K.—U.S. Trade Representative

** Illinois 4th District, North Carolina 10th District*

The 99th Congress: A Mixed Record of Success

Luckily for members of the 99th Congress, they were not judged only against the goals of their leaders. If they had been, one of the most productive Congresses in years would have been considered a failure.

Deficit reduction was the top priority of the Senate majority leader, Robert Dole, R-Kan., when the Congress opened Jan. 3, 1985. But the expected deficit bequeathed to the next Congress remained about $180 billion.

House Speaker Thomas P. O'Neill Jr., D-Mass., vowed his chamber would transform trade policy. The House did pass a bill to boost exports and limit imports, but it died in the Senate.

Alongside those disappointments, however, the 99th Congress compiled an extraordinary record.

It revised the tax code more dramatically than at any time since World War II, rewrote immigration law, approved the most far-reaching environmental bills since the environmentally conscious 1970s, boosted student aid, reversed President Reagan's policy toward South Africa and joined him in openly seeking to overthrow Nicaragua's leftist government.

Major elements of Congress' legacy did not become clear until the end. When exhausted members finally quit Oct. 18, many seemed surprised at what they had wrought.

"When you consider the political divisions between the House and Senate, and given that you have a very important election coming up, it's not very short of a miracle what the Congress was able to accomplish," said Roger H. Davidson, a Congress expert at Georgetown University and the Congressional Research Service (CRS) of the Library of Congress.

Perhaps the biggest miracle was passage of the tax bill (HR 3838 — PL 99-514) after a two-year struggle, a feat that topped all lists of Congress' achievements. The president, who made tax revision the goal of his second term, signed the historic measure Oct. 22.

"Overhaul of the tax code! My God, I didn't think I'd see that in my lifetime," said Walter Kravitz, a former CRS senior specialist and an adjunct professor at the Catholic University of America. "I didn't like it, but you've got to consider it our biggest accomplishment," said Bill Frenzel, Minn., a senior Republican on the House Ways and Means Committee.

Still, even supporters' enthusiasm was tempered by fears of history's judgment. There was apprehension that many middle-class taxpayers would find the code neither simpler nor fairer, that higher business taxes would provoke a recession, and that revenues would decline, adding to deficits.

"The tax bill must be recognized as an extraordinary accomplishment," said Allen Schick, professor of public policy at the University of Maryland. "But it wouldn't surprise me if the verdict turns around in future years."

That sort of ambivalence also colored appraisals of the immigration bill (S 1200 — PL 99-603), which was second on many observers' congressional scorecards. Such legislation had eluded lawmakers as far back as the 1970s.

"I don't know whether immigration reform is going to work or not," said Rep. Leon E. Panetta, D-Calif., one who helped revive the bill from near death. "All I know is the present system wasn't working."

Second-Session Summary

The second session of the 99th Congress ended Oct. 18, 1986, when the House adjourned *sine die* at 9:34 p.m. The Senate had adjourned at 9:13 p.m.

Convened on Jan. 21, the session lasted 271 days — 81 days shorter than the first session. It ranked as the 43rd longest session in history. The third session of the 76th Congress, from Jan. 3, 1940, to Jan. 3, 1941, was the longest on record. *(CQ Guide to Congress Third Edition, p. 410)*

The Senate met for 143 days in 1986; the House for 129 days. There were 3,825 bills and resolutions introduced during the session, compared with 7,777 in 1985 and 3,764 in 1984.

A total of 424 bills cleared by Congress in 1986 became public laws, 184 more than in 1985 and 16 more than in 1984. President Reagan vetoed 12 public bills; one veto was overridden and the bill enacted into law without his signature.

During 1986, the House took 451 recorded votes, 12 more than in 1985. The Senate took 354 recorded votes, 27 fewer than in 1985. Following are the recorded vote totals between 1972 and 1986:

Year	House	Senate	Total
1986	451	354	805
1985	439	381	820
1984	408	275	683
1983	498	371	869
1982	459	465	924
1981	353	483	836
1980	604	531	1,135
1979	672	497	1,169
1978	834	516	1,350
1977	706	635	1,341
1976	661	688	1,349
1975	612	602	1,214
1974	537	544	1,081
1973	541	594	1,135
1972	329	532	861

Like immigration, environmental bills that had been perennial losers finally passed. Three years of work on "superfund," the toxic-waste cleanup program, paid off Oct. 8 when Congress cleared a bill (HR 2005 — PL 99-499) mandating a fivefold increase in funding.

The program, established in 1980, had expired in 1985 and was kept alive with such minimal funding that work was near a halt. Reagan threatened a veto, but relented Oct. 17.

Water Bills

On Oct. 16, Congress resolved a yearlong impasse and reauthorized the 1972 Clean Water Act (S 1128). The bill was the most extensive rewrite of landmark law in nine years. Its $18 billion for sewage and pollution treatment plants set up what was the second-largest public works project in history, next to the Interstate Highway System.

At the same time, the bill phased out federal funding for sewers by 1995. Although the bill passed both chambers unanimously, Reagan pocket-vetoed it Nov. 6.

He did sign, June 19, Congress' overhaul of the 1974 law regulating the nation's drinking water (S 124 — PL 99-339).

Another environmental bill, the first major water projects bill in a decade (HR 6 — PL 99-662), cleared in Congress' final hours. It authorized hundreds of dams, harbors, and recreational and flood control projects, but also required local users to pay more of the costs.

"We passed every environmental bill on our agenda," boasted Robert T. Stafford, R-Vt., chairman of the Senate Environment Committee.

"It was impressive that so many divisive environmental issues were settled in the end, issues that have been hanging around since the 1980s began," said CRS' Davidson.

Davidson and others ascribed the 1986 action to renewed interest in issues like toxic waste, nuclear-waste disposal and acid rain, and to the resonance of those issues in election races in 1986. Also, members up for re-election were anxious to tell voters back home about the new public works projects coming their way.

Election-year politics also contributed to an environmental setback. The search for a disposal site to bury high-level nuclear wastes was effectively blocked for a year when Congress withheld funds. The moratorium reflected Western lawmakers' resentment that their states were favored for the site. The issue was a big one in the Washington Senate race. *(Story, p. 5-B)*

A last-minute casualty was a bill to reauthorize and strengthen the law regulating pesticides (HR 2482). A variety of objections damned a hard-fought compromise.

Spending Bill Delays

Most of the environmental bills, among others, would have died if Congress had not stayed in session nearly two weeks past a scheduled Oct. 3 adjournment date to finish work on essential government spending bills.

Congress failed to complete action on any of the 13 separate appropriations bills that fund federal programs, so they were wrapped into an omnibus package (H Res 738 — PL 99-591). Typically, Congress is forced to combine unfinished bills, but the fiscal 1987 package was the first in 36 years to include all 13 measures.

The result was history's largest spending bill, $576 billion. At the same time, the overall increase was about 1 percent, smallest in a decade.

Gramm-Rudman Impact

Meanwhile, members all but ignored the 1985 Gramm-Rudman-Hollings budget-balancing law that members had predicted would rank as one of their top accomplishments.

Congress endorsed $11.7 billion in initial across-the-board cuts made March 1, but subsequently missed every deadline in the law's budget process and also its target for a $144 billion deficit in fiscal 1987. The Supreme Court declared the law's provision for automatic cuts unconstitutional in July, eliminating the hammer that was expected to force members to find sufficient cuts.

They took advantage of the law's $10 billion "fudge factor," moving the target to $154 billion. To meet that, they relied on $11 billion in extra first-year proceeds from the new tax law, an $11.7 billion deficit-reduction package (HR 5300 — PL 99-509) of federal asset sales and bookkeeping changes, and the freeze in many appropriations.

"It's clear Gramm-Rudman has not been a significant factor this year," said Schick, a budget expert. "There's been less, not more, deficit reduction and more, not less, budgetary gimmickry than ever before."

House Budget Committee Chairman William H. Gray III, D-Pa., said, "One could assume that the eulogy and benediction have been given to Gramm-Rudman. We haven't done the committal yet."

But Thomas E. Mann, executive director of the American Political Science Association, asked, "What were the alternatives? There were no better solutions proposed by the president. I'm impressed by how much spending will be held in line, and since you can't raise taxes without the president's support, it's hard to criticize Congress on that score."

Senate Budget Committee Chairman Pete V. Domenici, R-N.M., declared victory, based on the estimates of declining federal spending. "What a great testimonial to the impact of Gramm-Rudman-Hollings," he said.

Health, Education Initiatives

Among Congress' other products was a five-year education bill (S 1965 — PL 99-498) that raised the limits on loans and grants for college students.

"The Congress was an excellent one for education, notwithstanding the budgetary pressures and administration opposition," said Stafford, chairman of the Senate Education Subcommittee. "I only wish there could have been more money for it."

In both years of the 99th Congress, numerous cost-saving changes were made in the Medicare and Medicaid health programs, while benefits were extended to the poor. One of Congress' last acts was a bill to ensure a continued supply of vaccines against childhood diseases (S 1744 — PL 99-660).

In foreign policy, Congress voted to renew military aid to Nicaragua's rebels, and untied the CIA's hands there. Offsetting that presidential victory was Reagan's biggest foreign policy defeat, an override of his veto of sanctions against South Africa.

A major disappointment for members was the 1985 farm bill. They already had begun talking about revisiting the five-year law because the costs of farm programs were escalating out of control.

Other issues left to the next Congress were corrections in the tax law, pesticide regulations, product-liability law changes, arms control and, as usual, deficit reduction.

Whose Agenda?

As the immigration, environmental and South Africa bills showed, Congress continued to draw its own agenda, as it had since Reagan's second year in office. Still, in pressing for tax overhaul *without* increased revenues, Reagan had a pervasive influence.

Frenzel said Congress had "a love-hate relationship" with Reagan, forcing South Africa sanctions on him while embracing his tax-reform drive.

O'Neill, who retired after a decade as Speaker, was credited with leaving a more visible, national office. Davidson said he was impressed by the way O'Neill and his successor, Majority Leader Jim Wright, D-Texas, produced major legislation on drugs, terrorism and trade — acting as stern overseers for the many committees with jurisdiction, and expediting action.

The Senate in the 99th Congress finally allowed live broadcasts of its debates, seven years after the House. Mann declared Dole the biggest beneficiary. After a dismal bid for the presidency in 1980, "he's a much more serious candidate now," Mann said.

The record of the 99th Congress belied early predictions that it would dissolve in partisan rancor. In the House, Republicans were bitter about a contested Indiana seat that Democrats claimed, while in the Senate, Democrats saw the prospect of retaking control in the coming elections.

"Partisanship actually worked for the better," said Steven I. Hofman, executive director of the House Wednesday Group, whose members were moderate Republicans. The tax, drug and superfund bills all benefited, he said, "because both sides saw advantage in moving those forward, or political disadvantage in being seen as obstructionist. That, I think, is partisanship at its best."

Following is a summary of major legislative action in 1986:

Agriculture

Farm Bill. With the 1986 elections firmly in view, farm-state lawmakers took halting steps toward rewriting the 1985 farm bill (PL 99-198). But the five-year reauthorization law remained virtually untouched.

The only changes came in so-called "technical corrections." Despite nervous Senate Republicans clamoring for export-promotion and income-subsidy initiatives, the most substantive proposals fell by the wayside as Congress rushed to adjournment.

The first "corrections" bill (S 2036 — PL 99-253), cleared Feb. 7, revised the way planting histories were used to compute benefits for wheat and corn growers. It also softened "cross-compliance" requirements, allowing the agriculture secretary to let farmers who receive benefits on primary crops to avoid restrictions on planting secondary crops.

On March 6, Congress cleared a bill (HR 1614 — PL 99-260) to compensate wheat and feed grain farmers for reductions in income subsidies caused by the farm bill's new method of computing crop yields.

HR 1614 also spared some milk producers the most severe effects of fiscal 1986 cuts mandated by the Gramm-Rudman-Hollings deficit-reduction law (PL 99-177) by requiring higher assessments on all dairy farmers, rather than reducing price-support rates for those who turned surplus milk products over to the government.

To avoid a veto of HR 1614, lawmakers cut to $1 billion the farm bill's requirement to spend $2 billion over three years for farm export subsidies.

Democratic proponents of cutting supply to drive up farm prices were spurred by a non-binding summer poll that showed that 54 percent of wheat producers favored mandatory controls on production and marketing. However, strategists decided to wait until 1987 to press for passage.

To counter the Democrats, Senate Republicans, led by Majority Leader Robert Dole, Kan., floated a proposal for a "marketing loan" for wheat and corn, an export-oriented concept used successfully by cotton and rice farmers to compete on world markets. But Dole shelved the idea when its estimated $5 billion cost appeared too high.

Meanwhile, both sides discovered that the 1985 farm bill contained a new feature enabling Congress to pump billions of "off-budget" election-year dollars into farm country.

Negotiable certificates, redeemable for government-owned surplus commodities, were issued to farmers as a partial payment-in-kind (PIK) for federal benefits. These PIK certificates also moved surplus grain out of government storage, helping to forestall a storage crisis at election time.

Farm Exports. In a bow to farm-state Republicans seeking reelection, President Reagan Aug. 1 announced he would give substantial discounts on the sale of 4 million metric tons of U.S. wheat to the Soviet Union, enough to fulfill previous grain agreements through Sept. 30.

The Soviets never took up the offer.

The administration earlier had opposed export subsidies on the grounds that they would benefit communist governments at the expense of U.S. allies.

The Senate July 22 attached a measure to the Export-Import Bank reauthorization bill (HR 4510) allowing the Soviets to buy unlimited subsidized wheat, corn and soybeans by Sept. 30. But a conference was delayed, and the provision died.

House Agriculture Committee members in early August tried to bring to the floor a bill (HR 5242) that would require export subsidies to the Soviet Union and other nations for two years beyond Reagan's offer. But Foreign Affairs Committee members objected, arguing that the bill might harm U.S. allies who also depended heavily on grain sales to the Soviet Union.

Payment Limits. Congress placed a new cap on price-support payments to farmers that even its proponents conceded would touch few farmers and produce negligible savings. But in accepting a watered-down version of the payment limit, farm-state lawmakers had to agree to revisit the issue in 1987.

Southern senators representing powerful cotton and rice interests capitulated Oct. 16 to a House demand to place a $250,000 limit on the subsidies a farmer could get each year. The new ceiling was included in the fiscal 1987 catchall spending bill (H J Res 738 — PL 99-591).

The cap was aimed at cotton and rice farmers who legally avoided the existing $50,000 limit on farm program payments. But a major loophole allowed some farmers to continue to receive multimillion-dollar subsidies, to the extent that the $250,000 cap would save only $25 million over four years.

Crop subsidies amounted to $12.9 billion in 1986 alone.

Commodity Credit Corporation. The fiscal 1987 catchall spending bill (H J Res 738 — PL 99-591), cleared Oct. 17, included $19.8 billion for the Commodity Credit Corporation (CCC), the Agriculture Department agency that distributed price-support loans and income subsidies to farmers of major commodities.

The administration originally had said $16.8 billion would suffice for fiscal 1987, but ballooning costs of farm programs prompted Congress to add another $3 billion, subject to an administration request.

In fiscal 1986, the CCC received $24.9 billion, nearly half through supplemental appropriations.

On Feb. 6, Congress cleared an urgent supplemental appropriation (H J Res 520 — PL 99-243) of $1.5 billion, far short of the $8.8 billion requested by the administration.

A second supplemental (H J Res 534 — PL 99-263) stalled in the Senate over a conference amendment that effectively added $1 billion for Farmers Home Administration loans. But after the Senate dropped the funds, Congress cleared the $5 billion measure March 20.

Finally, June 26, Congress cleared a catchall supplemental appropriations bill (HR 4515 — PL 99-349) that included another $5.3 billion in CCC funds.

Commodity Futures Trading Commission. The Senate Oct. 17 cleared a three-year funding authorization (HR 4613 — PL 99-641) for the Commodity Futures Trading Commission (CFTC), after caving in to House demands to continue to permit so-called "leverage" contracts in precious metals — long-term installment contracts traded privately by only two authorized dealers.

The House bill limited the contracts to gold, silver and platinum, but also provided for other companies to enter the business after two years.

The Senate Oct. 6 had approved the commission's proposal to ban all leveraged transactions in two years. But floor action was permitted only after Pete Wilson, R-Calif., was assured a seat on the conference committee. There he successfully joined united House members in insisting on language protecting leverage.

The CFTC bill also combined a Senate floor amendment on grain quality and a similar House-passed bill (HR 5407), agreeing to prohibit exporters from adding dust and foreign material to grain at points of export.

Drought, Flood Aid. A summer-long drought in the Southeast, followed by autumn floods in the Midwest, prompted efforts to beef up relief programs for farmers whose crops were destroyed by natural disasters.

After repeated attempts to pass a relief measure bogged down for one reason or another, Congress attached a $400 million package to the fiscal 1987 omnibus spending bill (H J Res 738 — PL 99-591).

The measure required the administration to issue payment-in-kind certificates, redeemable for government-owned grain, to farmers in counties where crops were destroyed by drought, floods or hailstorms.

The House Aug. 6 unanimously passed a $530 million authorization bill (HR 5288) for relief to drought-stricken Southeastern farmers. The package, which would have required payments to farmers of government-owned surplus grain, was never considered by the Senate, but similar provisions were attached to a Senate measure (H J Res 668) to raise the ceiling on the federal debt. The debt measure died, however, over House disagreements on unrelated issues.

Despite delays in enacting the legislation, the administration acted on its own. Agriculture Secretary Richard E. Lyng announced disaster-relief steps allowed under existing law.

Farm Credit. A late-session proposal to loosen the regulatory grip on the Farm Credit System turned into a last-minute rush to bail out the beleaguered lending network.

System officials pleaded with Congress to let them set their own interest rates on loans without prior approval from the Farm Credit Administration. But with reports that the massive system was losing money at a suicidal rate, the debate quickly turned to how to cover 1986 losses of $1.7 billion to $2.9 billion.

Congress papered over the problem with a measure that loosened the accounting requirements for system banks and let the credit system stretch out over a 20-year period the heavy losses that system banks expected to incur over the next two and a half years. The provision was included in a House-passed bill (HR 5635) Oct. 6. A House-Senate conference committee attached the measure to a deficit-reduction bill (HR 5300 — PL 99-509), which cleared Oct. 17.

Farm Bankruptcy. As part of a bill to improve the efficiency of bankruptcy courts, a House-Senate conference included an amendment to permit small farmers to file for bankruptcy with less danger of losing their farms.

The bill (HR 5316 — PL 99-554), approved by the House Oct. 2 and the Senate Oct. 3, created a new Chapter 12 of the U.S. Bankruptcy Code to be used only by persons whose debts were at least 80 percent farm-connected, but did not exceed $1.5 million. The new chapter allowed farmers to reorganize debts without having to sell off their farms.

Tobacco Price Supports. A tactic that nearly backfired on Senate Agriculture Committee Chairman Jesse Helms, R-N.C., turned into a stunning victory March 20 when Congress cleared the fiscal 1986 reconciliation bill (HR 3128 — PL 99-272), which had been given up for dead.

HR 3128 included a new tobacco price-support program that allowed cigarette manufacturers to buy surplus tobacco at discounts and help set yearly quotas for growers. It also reduced price-support levels for tobacco and shifted half the cost of the program from farmers to manufacturers.

Helms, thinking the deficit-reduction measure had a better chance of passing than the then-pending 1985 farm bill, attached the provisions in late 1985 to the Senate's reconciliation measure, where they became a trade-off for extending permanently the 16-cents-a-pack cigarette tax.

Although the discounts on government-owned tobacco cost $1.1 billion, supporters of the package said it would reduce federal outlays for the tobacco program by more than $500 million over five years.

Appropriations

Spending Bills. Congress on Oct. 17 gave final approval to the conference agreement on a half-trillion-dollar appropriations bill for fiscal 1987, the largest in history.

The measure, known as a continuing resolution, funded about half the government; the remainder was sustained by permanent appropriations. It combined all 13 regular appropriations bills; none had been enacted by the Oct. 1 beginning of the fiscal year.

Four successive temporary funding measures kept the government going as Congress struggled with the yearlong bill (H J Res 738 — PL 99-591). The last of these stopgap measures (PL 99-434, PL 99-464, PL 99-465, PL 99-491) expired at midnight, Oct. 16. By then, both chambers and the Reagan administration had agreed on the major elements of H J Res 738, but a handful of relatively minor disputes held up final action.

At noon Oct. 17, non-essential federal workers were dismissed as the Reagan administration went through the motions of closing down the government. Later that day, the remaining disputes were settled and H J Res 738 cleared.

The comprehensive money bill appropriated $575.9 billion in fiscal 1987 budget authority, the amount that could be obligated under programs and activities covered in the bill. That, according to estimates, would yield $560 million in outlays, money actually disbursed. By both these gauges of spending, H J Res 738 fell below the budget limit derived from the fiscal 1987 budget resolution (S Con Res 120) and enforced by new procedures of the Gramm-Rudman-Hollings anti-deficit law (PL 99-177).

Each of the bills met specified allocations, except for foreign operations, which appeared to exceed its outlay limit by about $300 million.

Overall, H J Res 738 departed significantly from President Reagan's budget priorities, giving $30 billion less to defense and $2 billion less to foreign aid than he wanted and more to the domestic side of the ledger.

Preliminary estimates showed that H J Res 738 would increase fiscal 1987 outlays by just 1 to 2 percent, which would be the smallest year-to-year increase for programs covered by the omnibus measure in more than a decade, and probably not enough to keep pace with inflation.

Earlier in the year, Congress had cleared three fiscal 1986 supplemental appropriations measures, one (HR 4515 — PL 99-349) providing $1.7 billion for a variety of agencies, and two others (H J Res 520 — PL 99-243; H J Res 534 — PL 99-263) providing $6.5 billion for farm price-support payments.

Deferred Spending. A fight erupted in the spring over the Reagan administration's efforts to defer spending of certain funds appropriated the previous year for programs of which the administration disapproved. The struggle provoked bitter congressional complaints that the administration was improperly using its deferral power as a line-item veto; the administration responded that it was merely deferring the spending of what it viewed as unneeded funds.

A lawsuit, brought by several members of Congress and public interest groups, resulted in an August ruling by a federal district court in Washington, D.C., that the White House was wrong in deferring $5.1 billion in fiscal 1986 appropriations for housing programs and other aid to low-income individuals and neighborhoods.

The broad ruling also declared it improper for the president to use his deferral authority, as revised by the 1974 Congressional Budget and Impoundment Control Act (PL 93-344), to withhold funds for policy reasons; administration critics argued that Congress in 1974 had intended to allow the deferral power to be used only for management reasons.

The ruling was stayed, pending an appeal that was argued in November 1986.

Angry members also produced a flurry of amendments to a fiscal 1986 supplemental appropriations bill (HR 4515 — PL 99-349). As enacted, the measure overturned about $4.9 billion in deferred housing subsidies, although a House-passed amendment sharply restricting presidential deferral authority was dropped in conference, following White House veto threats.

Banking

Expanded Banking Powers. Legislation to expand the authority of financial institutions to offer new services and to do business across state lines continued to be stymied in the 99th Congress.

An omnibus banking bill (S 2592) that would have broadened banks' ability to enter new markets was abandoned Aug. 7 by its sponsor, Senate Banking Committee Chairman Jake Garn, R-Utah, because of lack of support. More-limited House legislation (HR 2707) to allow nationwide interstate banking remained blocked in the Rules Committee for more than a year.

Efforts to close the so-called "non-bank bank" loophole also failed in both the House and Senate. Non-bank banks avoided federal prohibitions on interstate banking by providing either checking accounts or commercial loans, but not both.

Sen. William Proxmire, D-Wis., was unable to attach amendments to ban non-bank banks to larger bills, and the House Rules Committee refused to act on a bill (HR 20) that would have prohibited the limited-service banks.

Bank Bailouts. Congress failed to pass legislation sought by the White House to help regulators deal with the growing number of problem banks and savings and loans (S&Ls).

The House Oct. 7 passed a banking bill (HR 5576) that contained two provisions the administration wanted: $15 billion for the under-funded Federal Savings and Loan Insurance Corporation (FSLIC), which guaranteed deposits at federally insured S&Ls, and expanded powers for bank regulators to arrange the sale of insolvent banks and S&Ls to healthy out-of-state financial institutions.

However, the bill also included two provisions strongly opposed by the administration: a reauthorization of all federal housing programs, and limits on the time that banks and S&Ls could hold customers' checks.

A bill (S 2752) approved by the Senate Banking Committee Aug. 13 contained only the FSLIC refinancing and bank regulatory powers. But threats of amendments and filibusters kept it from the floor.

Less than five hours before Congress adjourned Oct. 18, the Senate by voice vote passed legislation (S 2747, HR 2443) with substantially weaker provisions on FSLIC, bank regulatory powers and check holds than proposed by the House. But House Banking Committee Chairman Fernand J. St Germain, D-R.I., refused to accept the last-minute changes, and the legislation died.

Garn-St Germain. An important banking law expired in the closing days of the 99th Congress. The Garn-St Germain Act of 1982 (PL 97-320), which gave government regulators special powers to aid weak financial institutions through a series of paper transactions, and to find out-of-state buyers for troubled banks ran out Oct. 13.

It had been temporarily extended twice during the year (PL 99-452, PL 99-400). A long-term reauthorization of the law was contained in larger bank regulatory legislation that Congress failed to pass.

Truth in Savings. Inaction by the Senate killed a bill (HR 5613) that would have required uniform disclosure of interest rates paid by most savings and loans and banks, and charged by all credit card companies.

The House passed the bill Oct. 7 by voice vote, but the Senate did not consider it.

Bank Examiners. The Senate declined to act on a bill (HR 4917) that would have exempted federal bank regulatory agencies from automatic budget cuts under the Gramm-Rudman-Hollings deficit-control law (PL 99-177). The bill also would have increased the pay and training of federal bank examiners to stem their exodus to private industry. The House passed the bill Sept. 29.

Government Securities. Congress Oct. 9 cleared a bill (HR 2032 — PL 99-571) to tighten federal regulation of government-securities brokers and dealers. It was approved by the House Oct. 6 and cleared by the Senate Oct. 9. The measure placed previously unregulated securities dealers and brokers under the regulation of the Treasury Department and the Securities and Exchange Commission.

Commerce

Daylight-Saving Time. Congress capped a 10-year effort to expand daylight-saving time permanently by clearing a bill (S 2180 — PL 99-359) June 24 starting it three weeks earlier, on the first Sunday in April instead of the last Sunday.

The House had passed an extension (HR 2095) in October 1985, but rural- and Midwestern-state senators opposing the measure kept it bottled up in the Commerce, Science and Transportation Committee.

The breakthrough came when the Senate May 20 adopted a daylight-saving amendment by Slade Gorton, R-Wash., to an unrelated bill authorizing funding for federal firefighting programs, thereby bypassing the Commerce Committee. Gorton's proposal mirrored the House-passed bill, except that it dropped an extra week in the fall, the provision most irksome to opponents.

Product Liability. Legislation that would have set federal standards governing product liability lawsuits died in the Senate in late September after a brief filibuster by Ernest F. Hollings, D-S.C.

Prospects for the bill faded in June after the Senate Commerce Committee narrowly approved legislation (S 2760) that imposed limits on certain court awards to alleged victims of unsafe products. Critics said there should not be any monetary restrictions on recovery for damages.

Despite the bill's poor chances for success, proponents, including Bob Kasten, R-Wis., took their fight to the floor, hoping that would increase the odds of enacting legislation in 1987. Kasten said that a Senate vote of 84-13 in favor of a motion to proceed with floor consideration showed "tremendous support" for new legislation.

With Hollings prepared to filibuster a vote on the bill, Majority Leader Robert Dole, R-Kan., withdrew the measure.

Risk Retention. Congress enacted legislation (S 2129 — PL 99-563) intended to make it easier for businesses, municipal groups and professionals to band together to insure themselves.

The bill expanded on risk-retention legislation (PL 97-45) enacted in 1981 that allowed the formation of groups to provide product liability insurance.

The chief proponents of the measure, potential insurance purchasers, reached a compromise with state insurance regulators that would strengthen the powers of the regulators over risk groups.

The risk measure was the only legislation that managed to clear Congress in 1986 that addressed problems arising from the scarcity and rising cost of liability insurance.

Small Business Administration. Congress rebuffed the Reagan administration's proposal to transfer the functions of the Small Business Administration (SBA) to the Commerce Department.

Fiscal 1986 budget reconciliation legislation (HR 3128 — PL 99-272) authorized the SBA's independent existence for three years, while scaling back some programs.

Congress

Senate TV. The Senate joined the broadcast age July 29, giving permanent approval to live radio and television coverage of its proceedings. Like the House, which began gavel-to-gavel broadcasts in 1979, the Senate controlled the broadcast equipment, and its signals were picked up by public and commercial networks.

The July vote, 78-21, followed a test period of live radio coverage and closed-circuit TV broadcasts to legislative offices. The Senate actually voted for the resolution allowing radio-TV coverage (S Res 28) on Feb. 27, 67-21, but that measure required a second post-test vote to make TV a permanent fixture.

The presence of TV seemed to alter the Senate little, despite opponents' fears that it would require a faster pace and threaten the chamber's tradition of slow deliberation. A few senators complained that the pace had become too slow due to members' grandstanding. But generally, complaints were few. Majority Leader Robert Dole, R-Kan., was said to be a big winner, gaining daily exposure just as he was considering a bid for the presidency.

Ethics. Two House Democrats, Dan Daniel of Virginia and James Weaver of Oregon, were found in violation of federal ethics law and House rules after investigations by their colleagues, but they were spared any punishment. Congressional probes of two other House Democrats were left unresolved as the 99th Congress ended.

On Feb. 5, the House ethics committee reported that Daniel, a member of the Armed Services Committee, had accepted at least 68 and perhaps more than 200 free trips on a defense contractor's corporate jet. The panel concluded Daniel broke rules prohibiting gifts from parties with an interest in legislation, barring use of private funds to augment office allowances and requiring that members report certain gifts on annual financial statements. Concluding that Daniel misunderstood House rules, the committee recommended no punishment.

Weaver was cited Sept. 30 for spending campaign funds for other than "bona fide campaign purposes"; he used $81,667 to invest in commodities. The panel said he broke a second rule in failing to detail his commodity trading on his annual financial report. Again, the committee proposed no sanction, saying Weaver's errors were not intentional.

The ethics panel, formally known as the Committee on Standards of Official Conduct, did not complete a probe of reports that Fernand J. St Germain of Rhode Island, chairman of the House Banking Committee, used his position for personal enrichment. The panel suspended an inquiry into allegations of bribery and illegal use of campaign funds against Bill Boner, D-Tenn., at the request of the Justice Department, which was conducting its own investigation.

All four Democrats denied the allegations against them.

Congressional Mail. Budget limits forced Congress to reduce a subsidy covering members' free-mail privilege for a second year, after years of escalating costs. The fiscal 1987 omnibus spending bill (H J Res 738 — PL 99-591) included $91.4 million for mail, down from $95.7 million in fiscal 1986. Fiscal 1986 was the first in many years that members' costs for sending mail to constituents dropped in an election year.

The Senate Oct. 8 approved a measure (S Res 500) that committed its members to spending no more than half the amount, or $45.7 million. The House refused to adopt a similar constraint. Mail costs were included in a $1.6 billion appropriation to cover fiscal 1987 expenses of Congress and other legislative branch offices. The legislative branch total was $78.9 million over fiscal 1986 spending levels.

Honoraria. Both the House and Senate tried but failed in 1986 to alter the limits on members' ability to earn income other than their salaries.

The House April 22 approved a resolution (H Res 427) raising the cap on outside income from 30 percent to 40 percent of members' salary. But it reversed the action a day later, prodded by junior members who feared voters' political revenge.

Senators did the opposite. Having raised its outside earnings limit to 40 percent of salary in 1985, the Senate June 5 blocked an amendment to return it to 30 percent.

Campaign Finance. The Senate Aug. 11 voted to limit the amount of money that political action committees (PACs) could give each congressional candidate — and the amount that candidates could accept from all PACs together.

However, the bill (S 655) ended up mired in partisan maneuvering over who should get the credit (or blame) for reforming campaign finance guidelines, and which party would suffer the most under the proposed restrictions.

An amendment sponsored by David L. Boren, D-Okla., would have put caps on what a candidate could take from PACs overall and singly. It also would have closed loopholes on PAC giving that generally favored Republicans. Rudy Boschwitz, R-Minn., offered a countermeasure to stifle PAC contributions to party organizations, which Democrats relied on more heavily than the GOP.

Both amendments were approved, Boren's by a lopsided margin of 69-30, and Boschwitz' on a more partisan tally of 58-42. But the bill itself went no further.

Defense

Budget. Congress cut some $30 billion from President Reagan's $320 billion defense budget request for fiscal 1987, $2 billion more than was required by the congressional budget resolution (S Con Res 120).

The budget resolution, approved June 27 by the House and Senate, held new defense budget authority to $292 billion — the amount appropriated for defense in fiscal 1986. Defense outlays were held to $279 billion under the resolution.

The version of the annual defense authorization bill passed Aug. 9 by the Senate (S 2638 — PL 99-661) would have put defense budget authority at $295 billion and outlays at $285 billion.

However, the House authorization bill (HR 4428), passed Aug. 15, would have cut the overall defense budget to $285 billion in budget authority in order to meet the budget resolution ceiling of $279 billion on defense outlays.

In years past, the annual duel over the defense budget had been resolved purely in terms of the amount of new budget authority. But under the Gramm-Rudman-Hollings anti-deficit act (PL 99-177), the budget resolution's outlay ceiling became binding on fiscal 1987 appropriations bills.

Leading members of the Senate and House Armed Services committees — along with many observers — contended that it was technically impossible to produce a sensible defense budget that provided $292 billion in new budget authority but no more than $279 billion in outlays. So, the two panels resorted to what they frankly called "gimmicks" to work out a compromise version of the defense authorization bill that used nearly all the allowed budget authority while remaining under the outlay cap.

For instance, they proposed a one-day delay in military paydays during fiscal 1987. This would make the last payday of the year occur on the first day of fiscal 1988, thus trimming $2.9 billion from fiscal 1987 Pentagon outlays.

Conferees on the companion defense appropriations measure — one part of the omnibus continuing appropriations resolution (H J Res 738 — PL 99-591) — used all the reductions proposed by the Armed Services panels and made a few more cuts to bring fiscal 1987 Pentagon budget authority down to $290 billion.

Space Weapons. For the second year in a row, Congress sharply slowed the pace of research on President Reagan's nationwide anti-missile defense — the strategic defense initiative (SDI). Reagan requested $5.3 billion for the project in fiscal 1987. But Congress trimmed the program to $3.5 billion and came within a single vote of cutting the request even more deeply.

The $3.5 billion amount was roughly a split of the difference between the $3.125 billion authorized by the House for SDI and the $3.96 billion approved by the Senate. But on Aug. 5, the Senate rejected, by margins of only one vote, two amendments to the defense authorization bill that would have reduced SDI below the $3.96 billion recommended by the Senate Armed Services Committee, one to $3.24 billion and the other to $3.56 billion. Had either amendment been agreed to, the compromise SDI authorization would have been reduced accordingly.

The Senate and House also rehashed what had become their annual battle over whether to allow tests of the anti-satellite (ASAT) missile against targets in space. During debate on the annual defense authorization bill in 1984 and 1985, the House voted to ban such tests, so long as the Soviet Union continued its own moratorium on ASAT tests, while the Senate rejected similar proposals.

In 1985, conferees on the fiscal 1986 defense appropriations bill agreed to a moratorium through Sept. 30, 1986, the end of the fiscal year. The House approved and the Senate rejected amendments to the fiscal 1987 defense authorization bill (S 2638 — PL 99-661) to continue the moratorium through Sept. 30, 1987.

fense authorization bill an amendment that would have obligated the administration to continue observing three of the numerical limits on certain types of weapons contained in the unratified 1979 U.S.-Soviet strategic arms limitation treaty (SALT II).

The three limits specified included one that was violated late in the year when the Air Force modified one more B-52 bomber to carry cruise missiles than the limit allowed. Reagan announced on May 27 he would continue to deploy missile-armed bombers regardless of the SALT II limits because of alleged Soviet violations of other SALT II provisions.

On April 10, 52 senators signed a letter to Reagan urging him to continue compliance with the three specified SALT II sublimits. However, plans to offer such an amendment to the defense authorization bill were dropped when administration allies threatened to force a Senate vote on the entire SALT II treaty. Most observers believed the vote on the treaty would have been negative.

The Senate-House conference on the defense authorization measure deadlocked in late September over the nuclear testing and SALT compliance issues. The stalemate was broken by Reagan's surprise announcement that

e would meet Soviet leader Mikhail . Gorbachev in Iceland Oct. 11-12.

Under strong pressure from Rea-an to close ranks behind him on the ve of sensitive negotiations, House)emocratic leaders agreed to make he bill's call for SALT II compliance dvisory rather than mandatory. They ropped their insistence on a nuclear est ban in return for Reagan's pledge o seek Senate approval of the two test imitation pacts from the 1970s, with ertain conditions attached.

Chemical Weapons. In the lat-st round of a five-year-long battle, Congress lurched a half step closer to pproving President Reagan's plan to egin building new types of lethal hemical weapons — so-called binary nunitions.

During the debate on the defense uthorization bill (HR 4428), the House voted for the fifth year in a row to bar production of the new weapons through the end of the fiscal year. The Senate, with Vice President George Bush breaking a 50-50 tie, rejected an amendment that would have barred production of one of the proposed new weapons — an air-dropped bomb called Bigeye.

Authorization conferees approved all funds for production of a binary artillery shell, though they barred final assembly of any weapons until Oct. 1, 1987. They approved $35 million of the $72 million requested for Bigeye, and barred final assembly of bombs until Oct. 1, 1988.

Pentagon Reorganization. Despite vigorous opposition from the top Pentagon leadership, both houses overwhelmingly approved bills designed to shift bureaucratic power within the Defense Department from the separate armed services to the senior officials intended to coordinate the services: the chairman of the Joint Chiefs of Staff and the commanders in chief (or CINCs) of the combat forces in the field.

The reorganization effort followed the lead of several studies conducted in recent years, all of which concluded that the services' parochial viewpoints had undue influence on the Pentagon's budget, the CINCs' war plans and the Joint Chiefs' military advice to the president.

The House passed HR 3622, strengthening the role of the Joint Chiefs' chairman, on Nov. 20, 1985. A separate bill strengthening the CINCs was reported by the House Armed Services Committee as HR 4370, but its provisions were added to the defense authorization bill (HR 4428) Aug. 5 on a 406-4 vote.

The Senate included both the Joint Chiefs and CINCs portions of its reorganization package in its version of HR 3622.

A compromise version of the legislation (PL 99-433) was cleared for the president Sept. 17.

Economic Affairs

Budget Resolution. Congress adopted a fiscal 1987 budget resolution (S Con Res 120) just after midnight June 26 — more than two months after the April 15 deadline set by the Gramm-Rudman-Hollings anti-deficit law (PL 99-177). The resolution did meet the Gramm-Rudman target of a deficit no higher than $144 billion as it laid out a plan for more than $1 trillion in federal spending.

The budget was effective in keeping appropriations in check, since it imposed an enforceable ceiling on the half of the federal budget that was subject to annual spending decisions. The 1987 budget held defense expenditures to $292.2 billion in budget authority, compared with $320 billion requested by President Reagan. Most domestic programs were held to fiscal 1986 levels or trimmed, but no program was eliminated altogether. Almost all of the suggestions in the president's budget for heavy cuts in domestic programs were ignored.

Reagan did succeed in keeping congressional budget-makers from depending on new taxes to help close the budget gap. The measure called for only about $6 billion in new taxes against a revenue base of approximately $850 billion, the same amount proposed by Reagan.

The resolution proposed a contingency fund based on $4.8 billion in additional taxes, of which about $3 billion could go to defense — but only if Reagan requested the money. The president continued throughout the end of the year to block any action that could be labeled a tax increase, although he did allow some "user fees" to raise revenues.

Fiscal 1986 Reconciliation. The bill (HR 3128 — PL 99-272) to reconcile existing laws with the fiscal 1986 budget resolution (S Con Res 32) was a leftover from 1985. It started out as a deficit-reduction measure, but was considered dead at the end of the first session.

It sprang back to life in the first months of 1986, and was cleared March 20 after an unprecedented round of legislative pingpong between the House and Senate, because it also served as a major vehicle for revisions in tobacco subsidies and the Medicare and Medicaid programs. Many legislators from coastal states supported the measure because it divided approximately $6.4 billion from offshore drilling revenues between the states and the federal government.

By the end, estimates of its effect on the deficit had dwindled from savings of $74 billion over three years to $18.2 billion.

Fiscal 1987 Reconciliation. Congress pasted over the gap between official deficit projections and fiscal 1987 Gramm-Rudman targets Oct. 17 by clearing an $11.7 billion deficit-reduction measure (HR 5300 — PL 99-509). The "reconciliation" bill, designed to reconcile current laws with the fiscal 1987 budget resolution (S Con Res 120), was derided by members as a collection of "golden gimmicks" and a "massive yard sale" because it depended principally on accounting devices and one-shot asset sales, rather than long-term spending or tax changes.

The bill did contain some significant provisions, such as selling Conrail, the government-owned freight railroad; expanding Medicaid health coverage for the poor; imposing a customs fee; revising the Farm Credit System; and making Social Security cost-of-living increases automatic even if inflation was low.

Early versions of the measure, as reported by the Budget committees, fell short of deficit-reduction goals. But bipartisan, bicameral negotiations with the administration found ways to increase the package without addressing the stalemate between Congress and the administration over spending and taxing policy.

House negotiators pushed hard for a provision to assure welfare coverage for poor families when both parents live at home, but they dropped it in the face of adamant opposition from some senators and the administration.

Gramm-Rudman Developments. The Gramm-Rudman-Hollings anti-deficit law (PL 99-177) differed in practice from the heroic promises that accompanied its enactment in December 1985.

Assessments of Gramm-Rudman ranged from disgusted rejection to modest claims that its enforcement procedures had, for the first time, forced appropriators to respect spending limits set by the budget resolution.

In February, President Reagan submitted a fiscal 1987 budget that appeared to meet the statute's deficit goal. But critics discerned — and the administration later conceded — that it substantially understated defense spending and so exceeded the target. And the fiscal 1987 budget resolution (S Con Res 120) made none of the structural spending and revenue changes that budget experts said were essential to meet the law's declining annual deficit targets.

Then on July 7, the Supreme Court found Gramm-Rudman's automatic-spending-cut mechanism unconstitutional, thereby removing the device that was supposed to compel meaningful budget compromises as an alternative to across-the-board cuts.

Sen. Phil Gramm, R-Texas, and his original cosponsors were unsuccessful in reinstating the automatic procedure. They used a measure to increase the federal debt limit (H J Res 668) as a vehicle for the change, but it died when the House refused to take it up because of the provision.

After the high court acted, Congress swiftly affirmed an $11 billion first round of automatic cuts that had taken effect March 1 (PL 99-366).

As fall elections neared, members shied away from voting on a second round of across-the-board cuts, as envisioned by the statute's remaining fallback enforcement procedure. The Senate voted against the cuts (S J Res 412), after leaders said the deficit target would be met by pending legislation. The House never voted on them.

The combined effect of the $11.7 billion reconciliation bill (HR 5300 — PL 99-509) and an $11 billion revenue windfall from the mammoth tax overhaul bill (HR 3838 — PL 99-514) were said to bring the estimated fiscal 1987 deficit down below the $144 billion target set by Gramm-Rudman.

But the real deficit for fiscal 1987 would eventually go much higher, according to congressional budget leaders, who said the weak economy, soaring farm costs and other factors would yield a deficit of $160 billion or more. Moreover, they warned that revenue shortfalls from the tax overhaul bill in fiscal 1988 and 1989 would exacerbate the problem, making the task of meeting a fiscal 1988 deficit target of $108 billion nearly impossible.

Debt-Ceiling Increase. Congress voted to increase the ceiling on the federal debt to $2.3 trillion, with an expiration date on the increase of May 15, 1987, at which time the debt limit would revert to $2.111 trillion.

The provision was included in the fiscal 1987 reconciliation bill (HR 5300 — PL 99-509) after efforts failed to enact a yearlong increase in the debt ceiling (H J Res 668).

The yearlong measure, effectively passed by the House when it adopted the fiscal 1987 budget resolution (S Con Res 120) June 26, would have increased the debt limit to $2.323 trillion. When H J Res 668 got to the Senate, supporters of the Gramm-Rudman-Hollings anti-deficit act (PL 99-177) amended it to restore the automatic-spending-cut provisions of Gramm-Rudman stricken by the Supreme Court July 7.

The Senate added other riders and passed the measure Aug. 9. It died when the House would not accept the Senate's restoration of the automatic Gramm-Rudman cuts.

As the August recess approached, the House passed a bill (HR 5395 — PL 99-384) to increase the debt ceiling to $2.152 trillion, to carry the government through September. The Senate Aug. 15 added a one-year Gramm-Rudman fix and dropped the debt limit to $2.111 trillion, also expected to be sufficient through September.

The House then stripped off the Gramm-Rudman amendment and accepted the debt figure, and the Senate agreed. The Treasury managed to get by without a further debt increase until the reconciliation bill was enacted in mid-October.

Tax Reform. Congress in September cleared the most significant rewrite of the federal tax code since 1942.

The bill (HR 3838 — PL 99-514), which was the product of more than two years' work by Congress, the Treasury Department and the White House, dramatically reduced income tax rates for corporations and individuals and curtailed or eliminated dozens of tax breaks. It also, over the five years from 1987 through 1991, was expected to shift an estimated $120 billion of the total income tax burden from individuals to corporations, although the corporate share of total income tax collections was still projected to remain below the proportion that prevailed during the entire period 1940 through 1979.

The House version had passed in December 1985 after overcoming a Republican rebellion that threatened to kill the bill at the last minute. Only President Reagan's personal appeal salvaged enough GOP votes to keep the process alive.

The Senate Finance Committee initially started writing a bill that would have expanded the list of special tax breaks. In early May, however, Chairman Bob Packwood, R-Ore., junked that version and pushed through his committee a bill that so radically cut both rates and tax breaks that it passed the Senate 97-3 June 24.

The conference bill, ordered reported Aug. 16, reduced rates almost as much as the Senate version and considerably more than the House version. It also curtailed or eliminated more business breaks than the Senate bill and more individual breaks than the House bill.

After the House adopted the conference report Sept. 25 and the Senate followed suit Sept. 27, there was a final dispute over what was expected to be a routine resolution (H Con Res 395) correcting typographical and drafting errors in the bill.

Both chambers attempted to include in H Con Res 395 substantive changes to HR 3838, however, and members were never able to resolve their disagreements over these provisions. The tax bill thus went to the president for his signature full of acknowledged errors.

Balanced-Budget Constitutional Amendment. By a single vote March 25, the Senate killed a proposed constitutional amendment (S J Res 225) to require a balanced federal budget. The final tally was 66-34, one short of the two-thirds majority required for passage. Ten Republicans joined 24 Democrats in voting against the measure.

S J Res 225 was a compromise measure that would have required a balanced budget unless three-fifths of the House and Senate agreed to deficit spending, or in case of a declared war. A tax hike would have been allowed to balance the budget if a majority of both chambers agreed to the increase.

President Reagan supported the amendment and telephoned members to urge approval, but some sponsors said Reagan could have done more. Critics contended that the amendment would not work; it amounted to "subterfuge," according to Senate Appropriations Committee Chairman Mark O. Hatfield, R-Ore.

This was the second time since 1982 that Congress killed a balanced-budget amendment. The Senate passed one in 1982, but a similar proposal died in the House.

Social Security. In its only major action on Social Security, Congress repealed the "trigger" requirement that inflation reach at least 3 percent in a given year before a cost-of-living allowance (COLA) would be added to benefit payments. The provision was included in the fiscal 1987 reconciliation bill (HR 5300 — PL 99-509).

A proposal restricting the administration's ability to borrow — or "disinvest" — money from the Social Security trust funds in order to circumvent the statutory debt ceiling died when conflicting House and Senate versions proved unreconcilable.

The restrictive House provisions were contained in HR 5050, which contained a number of other elements relating to Social Security. The House passed HR 5050, but the Senate Finance Committee never considered the bill.

Lesser restrictions, which would have authorized some disinvestment, were put by the Senate into the reconciliation bill, as well as a measure (H J Res 668) that would have increased the ceiling on the federal debt through fiscal 1987. The provisions were dropped from reconciliation in conference, and the debt-limit bill died when a half-year increase was included in reconciliation.

"Disinvestment" of Social Security trust funds occurred in September and October 1984, and September, October and November 1985, when the government's debt was about to exceed the debt ceiling and Congress had not yet acted on an increase.

In addition to prohibiting trust fund disinvestment, HR 5050 would have made the Social Security Administration, which is part of the Department of Health and Human Services, an independent agency.

Education

Attorneys' Fees. Congress July 24 cleared legislation (S 415 — PL 99-372) that allowed courts to award attorneys' fees to parents who won legal disputes involving the education rights of handicapped children.

The law overturned a 1984 Supreme Court decision in the case of *Smith v. Robinson* that parents who prevailed in court could not be awarded legal fees under the Education for All Handicapped Children Act (PL 94-142).

College Aid. Congress Sept. 25 cleared a five-year higher education bill (S 1965 — PL 99-498) that reauthorized some of the government's most popular education programs, including subsidized student loans.

The bill tightened eligibility rules for Guaranteed Student Loans, but allowed those who did qualify to borrow more than was allowed under current loan limits. It cut interest subsidies paid to banks and made other changes to reduce student loan outlays by some $445 million over three years, as required by the fiscal 1987 budget resolution (S Con Res 120).

The bill also raised the limit on Pell Grants, which helped the poorest students pay for college, and made the grants available to students enrolled less than half time.

The bill authorized $10.2 billion in fiscal 1987 and allowed inflationary increases in 1988-91.

Handicapped Education. Congress Sept. 24 cleared a bill (S 2294 — PL 99-457) renewing handicapped-education programs, putting increased emphasis on helping disabled children in their preschool years.

Initially, the Senate June 6 passed a version of the bill that would have mandated that states provide special education services to all handicapped children beginning at age 3, instead of age 5, as was the case in many states.

But faced with stiff opposition from school boards and administrators, the House Sept. 22 approved a compromise that dropped the mandate. Instead, the compromise provided increased financial incentives for states to serve 3-to-5-year-olds. The compromise was approved without change by the Senate Sept. 24.

School Asbestos. Congress Oct. 3 cleared legislation (HR 5073 — PL 99-519) ordering schools around the nation to clean up hazardous asbestos and requiring the federal government to set standards for doing the job.

Staff negotiators reconciled differences between the versions of HR 5073 approved Sept. 10 by the Senate and Aug. 12 by the House.

The bill required the Environmental Protection Agency (EPA) to set standards for school inspections, and to spell out when asbestos was hazardous and what actions should be taken if a hazard was found. Schools would be required to inspect for asbestos and take remedial action if it was found.

The compromise was reached after negotiators agreed to drop controversial House provisions that would have limited the liability of asbestos-removal contractors and school boards. They also dropped House provisions that would have prohibited litigants in damage suits involving asbestos manufacturers from introducing as evidence requirements of the asbestos law or regulations issued under it.

Energy

Hydroelectric Power. President Reagan Oct. 16 signed a bill (S 426 — PL 99-495) setting guidelines to be used by the Federal Energy Regulatory Commission in renewing the licenses for hydroelectric power plants. The House had adopted the conference report (H Rept 99-934) Oct. 2 and the Senate Oct. 3.

Publicly and privately owned utilities had competed fiercely for hydropower because it was cheap, clean, safe, renewable and reliable. The 1920 Federal Power Act directed that public utilities were to be given a preference for hydropower licenses when all other factors were equal. But the law did not say whether the preference should apply when the licenses came up for renewal. In S 426, private utilities succeeded in getting Congress to disallow any re-licensing preference for public utilities.

Price-Anderson. Legislation (S 1225, HR 3653) renewing the nation's nuclear insurance law fell short of enactment, a victim perhaps of the April nuclear power accident at Chernobyl in the Soviet Union.

The legislation would have raised the amount of damages that U.S. nuclear utilities would pay in the event of an accident. Opponents charged that a good bill could not be written in the fearful public mood following the Chernobyl accident. Different versions moved through three House and two Senate committees in 1986, but did not reach the floor in either chamber.

All of the committee-approved bills to renew the 1957 Price-Anderson Act would have increased the current limit (about $650 million) on the amount that could be paid to victims of a nuclear accident. Three House committees and one in the Senate raised that to about $6.5 billion, but the Senate Energy Committee put the limit at about $2.4 billion.

Price-Anderson was to expire Aug. 1, 1987. Operating utilities would remain protected indefinitely from damage claims under existing terms. Nuclear generating plants starting up would not be able to get limitations on liability, but no new nuclear electric plants were currently being ordered. The expiration would most immediately affect federal contractors, who were also indemnified under the law.

Environment

Superfund. President Reagan Oct. 17 signed the "superfund" hazardous-waste cleanup bill (HR 2005 — PL 99-499), after veto threats from his advisers and pleas by congressional Republicans for him to sign.

The House had adopted the conference report (H Rept 99-962) Oct. 8, the Senate Oct. 3, both by wide margins. The bill funded the toxic-dump cleanup program at $8.5 billion for fiscal 1987-91. It had been funded at $1.6 billion for 1981-85.

Conferees on the tax portion of the bill chose to pay for the program with $2.75 billion from a tax on crude oil, $2.5 billion from a new tax on a broad base of businesses, $1.4 billion from the previous law's tax on raw chemicals, $1.25 billion from general revenues, and $600 million from other sources. It was the broad-based tax on business and the size of the program Reagan had objected to.

The bill set new schedules for the Environmental Protection Agency (EPA) to follow in cleaning up toxic-waste dump sites. The schedule required EPA to start work on 375 sites in five years, but set no timetable for completing the work. The bill also set cleanup standards aimed at destroying or detoxifying hazardous wastes rather than just burying them.

Drinking Water. President Reagan June 19 signed a major overhaul of the nation's drinking water law (S 124 — PL 99-339). The conference report, approved by the House May 13 and the Senate May 21, required the Environmental Protection Agency (EPA) to set maximum allowable limits for 83 toxic chemicals that could show up in household drinking water.

The amendments to the 1974 Safe Drinking Water Act gave EPA three years to set national limits for those contaminants. The bill authorized more than $800 million over five years for state grants and federal programs.

Harbors and Waterways. Just hours before adjournment, the Senate cleared for President Reagan's signature the first omnibus water projects authorization bill (HR 6 — PL 99-662) in at least 10 years.

The Senate adopted the conference report (H Rept 99-1013) by a vote of 84-2 Oct. 17. The House had done so earlier the same evening by a vote of 329-11.

The bill authorized the Army Corps of Engineers to build more than 260 new projects estimated to cost about $16.5 billion — of which about $7 billion would be paid by local users and beneficiaries. The bill established a new port use tax to pay for maintenance of ports; inland lock and dam projects would be paid for by increasing the current 10-cent tax on a gallon of barge fuel to 20 cents by 1995.

HR 6 authorized appropriations for hundreds of dam, port, waterway, flood control and recreation projects. Both environmentalists and Reagan administration budget-cutters supported it in 1986 because it reformed project funding to require that a greater share be paid by local beneficiaries and users.

Clean Water Act. Congress cleared an overhaul (S 1128) of the nation's water-pollution control law but President Reagan pocket-vetoed the bill. S 1128 languished in an inactive conference for most of the year. Both chambers passed the bill in mid-1985 and conferees met in March 1986, but they did not turn to the main issues until the final weeks of the session.

The bill authorized almost $20 billion in appropriations, $18 billion of that available through 1994 in grant and loan money to help communities build sewage treatment plants.

The House bill had contained $21 billion for sewers, and the Senate bill

$18 billion. The administration had complained that both bills would spend too much. Reagan wanted only $6 billion before an end to the program in fiscal 1989.

Conferees kept largely intact the formula in previous law for dividing the sewer funds among the states — which Sun Belt senators had complained favored the Northeast at their expense. The final bill gave an $18 million annual raise to Texas, taking the funds from all but the 10 smallest states.

Pesticide Control. Last-minute objections from Sen. Howard M. Metzenbaum, D-Ohio, and splinter environmental groups killed a bill (HR 2482) that would have reauthorized and dramatically strengthened the nation's pesticide law.

The bill had been passed in different forms by the House Sept. 19 and the Senate Oct. 6. Efforts to resolve differences, in informal discussions between House and Senate committee leaders, produced a compromise passed by the House Oct. 16. The Senate never took up that proposal and the bill died at adjournment.

Under existing law, the Federal Insecticide, Fungicide and Rodenticide Act (FIFRA — PL 92-516), the Environmental Protection Agency (EPA) had not required pesticide companies to test most of the pesticides in use to see if they presented a threat to human health.

HR 2482 set a nine-year schedule for completing such tests, and imposed a new fee on chemical companies to help pay EPA's costs in doing the work faster. The chemical companies agreed to this on the understanding that environmentalists would lift their objections to legislation to extend the life of pesticide patents, compensating for years lost in health testing before a company could sell a patented product.

That basic agreement was reached between a coalition of more than 40 environmental, consumer, public health and labor groups and a coalition of more than 90 agricultural chemical manufacturers. With the addition of language restricting farmer liability for damages from properly applied pesticides, the American Farm Bureau Federation and other farm groups also supported the bill.

Lobbyists for some environmental groups remained unsatisfied, however, and Metzenbaum objected to the patent-term extension language.

Foreign Policy

South Africa Sanctions. Handing President Reagan the most important foreign policy defeat of his presidency, Congress enacted into law a bill (HR 4868 — PL 99-440) imposing economic sanctions against South Africa. Reagan vetoed the bill on Sept. 26, saying it would hurt the South African blacks it was intended to help. But both houses voted overwhelmingly to override the veto, the House on Sept. 29 by a 313-83 vote, and the Senate on Oct. 2 by a 78-21 vote.

The bill barred imports of South African iron, steel, textiles, agricultural goods and other products, and ordered the suspension of direct air travel between the United States and South Africa. It also called for further sanctions in a year if the white minority government in Pretoria failed to move to dismantle the system of racial discrimination called apartheid. Proponents acknowledged that the bill would not, by itself, force an end to apartheid. But they said the bill would demonstrate to South African blacks that the United States actively opposed apartheid.

'Contra' Aid. After a battle of more than two years, President Reagan in 1986 persuaded Congress to renew military aid to the "contra" guerrillas who were battling to overthrow the leftist government of Nicaragua. The fiscal 1987 omnibus spending bill (H J Res 738 — PL 99-591) included $70 million in military aid and $30 million in non-military aid for the contras. It also included $300 million in economic aid for Central American nations other than Nicaragua.

The deadlock on contra aid was broken June 25, when the House voted for the $100 million 221-209.

Perhaps more important than the money itself, the bill lifted most restrictions that Congress had imposed in 1984-85 on direct U.S. involvement with the contras. Among other things, the bill allowed the CIA to resume management of the contra aid program. However, the separate fiscal 1987 intelligence authorization bill (HR 4759 — PL 99-569) barred the CIA from tapping into its multimillion-dollar contingency fund to give aid to the contras above the $100 million.

Foreign Aid. For the second year in a row, Congress made deep cuts in foreign aid — one of President Reagan's highest priorities. The fiscal 1987 omnibus appropriations bill (H J Res 738 — PL 99-591) cleared by Congress on Oct. 17 included $13.37 billion for foreign military, economic and development aid programs — $2.1 billion below Reagan's request and $1 billion below the fiscal 1986 level.

In spite of the cuts, the administration won more money for foreign aid — and under substantially better terms — than many observers had thought possible. One important element of the bill was its movement toward "concessional" terms for military aid, which was used to help allies buy weapons and defense services. The Senate had attempted to make all military aid in the form of grants, rather than the existing combination of loans and grants. House negotiators resisted that change, but did agree to a program under which all loans would carry below-market interest rates.

Intelligence Bill. After a one-year hiatus, Congress agreed to give the CIA and other intelligence agencies a real, after-inflation budget increase for fiscal 1987. Spending for the intelligence agencies had increased annually from 1978-1985, but dipped slightly in 1986 once inflation was taken into account. The secret intelligence budget was included in an authorization bill (HR 4759 — PL 99-569); actual appropriations were made in the defense portion of the omnibus spending bill for 1987 (H J Res 738 — PL 99-591).

Philippine Aid. Many members of Congress felt they had a personal stake in the almost-bloodless revolution that ousted Philippine President Ferdinand E. Marcos in February. Rep. Stephen J. Solarz, D-N.Y., long had been an unabashed supporter of the new president, Corazon Aquino, and in the closing days of the Marcos regime Sen. Richard G. Lugar, R-Ind., played a key role in persuading President Reagan to drop his backing for Marcos.

To encourage the new government and to bolster an economy that had suffered under years of Marcos-inspired "crony capitalism," Congress twice voted aid increases for the Philippines. First, in a fiscal 1986 supplemental appropriations bill (HR 4515 — PL 99-349), Congress voted a bonus for the Philippines of $100 million in economic aid and $50 million in military aid. That aid was in addition to about $230 million that already was allocated in 1986. Next, in the omnibus 1987 spending bill (H J Res 738 — PL 99-591), Congress set aside $200 million in "additional" economic aid for the Philippines.

Because of overall foreign aid cutbacks, it was uncertain what the fiscal 1987 final amount would be.

Angolan War. With little fanfare, Congress in 1986 gave the go-ahead for the Reagan administration to pursue a guerrilla war against the Marxist government of Angola. President Reagan in February approved a CIA "covert" operation to provide up to $15 million worth of weapons, ammunition and other supplies to a guerrilla faction called UNITA.

The Democratic members of the House Intelligence Committee, who had objected to the aid plan, failed in an attempt to kill it. They attached an amendment to the fiscal 1987 intelligence authorization bill (HR 4759) barring further aid to UNITA unless it was publicly debated and approved by Congress. In a major victory for Reagan, the full House deleted that amendment Sept. 17, 229-186.

Congress also went on record as opposing continued U.S. business dealings with the Angolan government. It included a provision in an Export-Import Bank authorization bill (HR 5548 — PL 99-472) deploring business support for the Angolan government and requesting the president to use his power under the 1979 Export Administration Act (PL 96-72) to restrict business dealings that were in conflict with U.S. security interests.

Saudi Arms Sale. President Reagan narrowly avoided an embarrassing defeat June 5 when the Senate upheld his plan to sell $265 million worth of weapons to Saudi Arabia.

Reagan had vetoed a measure (S J Res 316) that would have blocked the sale. The Senate — after some strong presidential arm-twisting — sustained his veto on a 66-34 vote, one short of the two-thirds majority required to override the president's action.

The Saudi arms deal started out as a much larger package, only to be whittled down by persistent critics on Capitol Hill. Before the veto vote, Reagan agreed to delete $89 million worth of Stinger anti-aircraft missiles.

Embassy Security. Congress Aug. 12 cleared legislation that authorized $2.4 billion over five years to strengthen and rebuild U.S. embassies and other diplomatic missions to protect them against terrorist attacks.

The money authorized in the measure (HR 4151 — PL 99-399) fell far short of the five-year, $4.4 billion program requested by the administration. The embassy security program grew out of recommendations of a blue-ribbon panel organized in the wake of attacks on U.S. Embassy and Marine posts in Lebanon in 1983-84.

The House originally agreed to authorize the president's full request. But the Senate — acting after the Foreign Relations Committee found that the State Department had trouble justifying the full amount — approved only $1.1 billion spread over two years. The compromise bill also included a variety of other anti-terrorist measures.

General Government

Federal Pensions. Congress May 22 cleared for the president legislation (HR 2672 — PL 99-335) creating a new federal retirement system for workers hired after Dec. 31, 1983.

The bill, the fruit of nearly three years' work and six months of House-Senate conference negotiations, established a three-tiered plan to provide retirement benefits to all civilian employees and postal workers hired on or after Jan. 1, 1984. Those workers, unlike their more senior colleagues, were covered by Social Security. Senior workers had the option of remaining in their current plan or joining the new plan.

The plan consisted of three main parts: Social Security; a required basic pension plan to supplement Social Security; and an optional tax-deferred savings plan similar to private-sector 401(k) plans. It was expected to cost the government about 23 percent of payroll — more than the 20 percent President Reagan wanted, but less than the 25 percent that the existing system cost.

Former Presidents. Congress May 13 cleared a bill to defray the cost to the government of future presidential libraries. But it failed to complete action on a second measure that would have limited Secret Service protection and office and staff allowances for former chief executives.

Under the bill (HR 1349 — PL 99-323) that cleared, private foundations that raised funds for construction of presidential libraries must establish an endowment equal to 20 percent of building costs to help cover operational expenses, which currently were paid entirely by the federal government. The measure also limited the size of libraries to 70,000 square feet, with costs for additional space to be picked up by private funding.

At President Reagan's insistence, the cost-sharing and size limits did not apply to his library, planned for Stanford University.

The Senate Aug. 15 passed a bill (S 1047 — S Rept 99-349) to curb the cost to the government of supporting former presidents. But companion legislation died in the House, where four committees shared jurisdiction over it.

The Senate bill would have ended the current guarantee of lifelong Secret Service protection, limiting it to five years in most cases, and would have placed a ceiling on former presidents' office and staff allowances.

OMB's Regulatory Power. As part of the omnibus fiscal 1987 continuing appropriations resolution (H J Res 738 — PL 99-591), Congress approved new curbs on the power of the Office of Management and Budget (OMB) to review and revise other agencies' regulatory actions.

Members of both parties had been angered by what they saw as overreaching by the Office of Information and Regulatory Affairs (OIRA), a unit of OMB established by the Paperwork Reduction Act of 1980 (PL 96-511). Under executive orders issued by President Reagan in 1981 and 1985, OIRA had been reviewing all major regulatory actions of other federal agencies to ensure that they met administration guidelines for cost effectiveness. Its reviews in many instances led to substantial revisions in health and environmental regulations.

The House, in passing a fiscal 1987 appropriations bill (HR 5294) for the Treasury Department, U.S. Postal Service, and Executive Office of the President, deleted all funding for OIRA. But the Senate Appropriations Committee refused to go along, providing $5.4 million for the office and voting to reauthorize it.

The compromise version of the omnibus fiscal 1987 spending bill reauthorized OIRA through fiscal 1989 at a funding level of $5.5 million annually. But it made future administrators of the office presidential appointees, subject to confirmation by the Senate. And it restricted OIRA's oversight functions to the "sole purpose" of reviewing information-collection requests contained in another agency's proposed rule or regulation.

Revolving-Door Bills. The lobbying activities of former White House aide Michael K. Deaver spurred conflict-of-interest legislation (S 2334, HR 5426) in both the House and Senate, but the bills died at adjournment.

The Senate Judiciary Committee June 26 approved S 2334 on a 17-1 vote, with Charles McC. Mathias Jr., R-Md., dissenting. It would have barred senior government officials and members of Congress from working for a foreign government for three years, and from lobbying any part of the government for 18 months.

On Aug. 7, the House Judiciary Subcommittee on Administrative Law by voice vote approved HR 5426, barring high-level officials and members of Congress from lobbying for foreign governments for four years. The full Judiciary Committee did not act on the measure.

An alliance of conservative Republicans and First Amendment activists argued that the measures would stifle the interest of competent persons to work for the government, and would conflict with rights of free speech and citizens' ability to petition the government.

Deaver gained notoriety by resigning as President Reagan's deputy chief of staff in May 1985 and immediately opening a lucrative public relations firm in Washington, with clients ranging from defense contractors to the governments of Canada, South Korea and Saudi Arabia. Questions arose about his lobbying contacts with former colleagues still in the White House, leading to the appointment of Whitney North Seymour Jr. as independent counsel to determine whether Deaver violated existing conflict-of-interest laws.

On Aug. 12, the House Energy and Commerce Subcommittee on Oversight and Investigations, climaxing a seven-month investigation, accused Deaver of lying during his May testimony before the panel. The subcommittee voted 17-0 to turn its evidence of "possible perjury" by Deaver over to the independent counsel.

Subcontractor Kickbacks. Congress took aim at bribery and kickbacks by defense subcontractors by clearing a bill (S 2250 — PL 99-634) Oct. 15 that sought to put teeth into a 40-year-old law governing contractor fraud.

While some kickbacks — illicit payments made in return for favored treatment — were illegal under current law, payoffs to prime contractors by subcontractors for improper purposes — such as gaining information about a competitor's bid — were not addressed. Congressional investigations found that subcontractors, particularly in the defense industry, were undeterred by the 1946 law that was seen as outdated and riddled with loopholes.

The bill increased criminal penalties for knowingly and willfully participating in kickbacks from a maximum of two years' imprisonment and a $10,000 fine to a maximum of 10 years' imprisonment and a $250,000 fine for individuals and a $500,000 fine for corporations. S 2250 also imposed civil penalties and allowed the government to withhold the amount of a kickback from money it owed to a contractor if the kickback occurred on that contract.

Health

Medicare, Medicaid. Again in 1986, Congress used the budget reconciliation process to make numerous substantive changes in Medicare, the federal health insurance program for the elderly, and Medicaid, the federal-state health care program for the poor.

The fiscal 1986 reconciliation measure (HR 3128 — PL 99-272), cleared March 20, sought to trim Medicare spending by extending through Dec. 31, 1986, a fee freeze for physicians, and by holding payment increases to hospitals at 0.5 percent. It also required that hospitals participating in the Medicare program provide emergency services for people in urgent need of care, regardless of their ability to pay.

The bill required states to provide Medicaid coverage for prenatal and postpartum care for low-income women in two-parent families in which the chief wage-earner was unemployed.

Fiscal 1987 budget reconciliation legislation (HR 5300 — PL 99-509), cleared Oct. 17, also made some major changes in Medicare and Medicaid.

In HR 5300, Congress allowed a 3.2 percent increase in physicians' fees beginning Jan. 1, 1987, and a 1.15 percent increase in Medicare payments to hospitals.

Congress changed the way to calculate the annual increase in the "deductible" that Medicare patients paid for each hospital stay. The deductible, based on the cost of one day in the hospital, rose from $400 in 1985 to $492 in 1986. Without congressional action, it would have reached $572 in 1987. Instead, Congress capped the 1987 deductible at $520 and based future increases on the percentage change that hospitals received each year.

And, HR 5300 provided one year of Medicare coverage for immunosuppressive drugs for organ transplant patients.

Congress also instituted a number of safeguards to ensure that the quality of care received by Medicare patients did not suffer because of cost-cutting incentives created by a 1983 Medicare overhaul bill (PL 98-21).

The bill required hospitals to have discharge planners to ensure that Medicare patients released from the hospital would continue to receive adequate care. It also required the secretary of health and human services (HHS) to submit legislation to modify Medicare's payment-by-diagnosis system to take into account illness severity and case complexity.

Finally, the bill permitted states to extend Medicaid coverage to the disabled, pregnant women and children up to age 5 who did not qualify for welfare but had incomes below the poverty line.

Health Insurance Continuation. Congress in 1986 took the first steps toward helping the estimated 35 million to 37 million Americans who did not have health insurance. Fiscal 1986 reconciliation legislation (HR 3128 — PL 99-272) required employers of 20 or more who offered group health insurance plans to allow laid-off workers, as well as spouses, widows and other dependents who would lose coverage due to death or divorce, to continue their coverage at the group rate.

The House, as part of its fiscal 1987 reconciliation bill (HR 5300 — PL 99-509), tried to extend the effort, voting to require states to set up "risk pools" to offer insurance to chronically ill and other traditionally uninsurable citizens. Under the plan, premiums could not exceed 150 percent of the average group premium for the state, and shortfalls in the pool would have to be made up by private employers of 20 or more people. Employers who refused to participate would have faced an excise tax of 5 percent of their gross payroll. The provision, however, was dropped in conference.

Tobacco Advertising, Labels. Congress cleared legislation to prohibit radio and television advertising of chewing tobacco and snuff. The bill (S 1574 — PL 99-252) also required manufacturers of such "smokeless tobacco" products to print health warning labels on their packages.

Alcohol Warning Labels. As part of its omnibus anti-drug bill (HR 5484 — PL 99-570), Congress ordered the Public Health Service to study the effect of health warning labels on alcoholic-beverage containers. The alcohol industry had mounted a major campaign to defeat proposed legislation requiring health warning labels on all alcoholic beverages.

The Senate Labor and Human Resources Committee voted May 20 to require such labels as part of a measure (S 2443) reauthorizing research activities of the National Institute on Alcohol Abuse and Alcoholism and the National Institute on Drug Abuse. The House version of the reauthorization bill (HR 5259) contained no warning-label language.

Vaccine Compensation. Congress approved an 11th-hour compromise Oct. 18 to ensure a continued, affordable supply of vaccines that prevent major childhood diseases.

The vaccine measure, part of an omnibus health package (S 1744 — PL 99-660) that was one of the last bills to clear the 99th Congress, created a no-fault compensation system for families of children who were injured or died as a result of adverse vaccine reactions. Families that chose not to accept an award under the compensation system were permitted to sue manufacturers on their own.

As passed by the House Oct. 14, the compensation provisions of the measure would not take effect until the 100th Congress approved a funding mechanism. The compensation bill approved by the Energy and Commerce Committee Sept. 18 (HR 5546) called for an excise tax on vaccines to finance a proposed trust fund, but the Ways and Means Committee failed to approve the tax and it was dropped during floor consideration.

Drug Exports. As part of an omnibus health bill package (S 1744 — PL 99-660), Congress moved to permit manufacturers to export drugs not yet approved by the Food and Drug Administration for use in this country.

The Senate May 14 passed a version of the measure (S 1848) that would have permitted U.S. drug manufacturers to export unapproved products to nations with their own sophisticated drug regulatory systems. But the bill's key proponent, the Pharmaceutical Manufacturers Association, withdrew its support after amendments to the bill were adopted toughening standards for the manufacture and sale of infant formula.

The version passed as part of S 1744, unlike S 1848, permitted drugs to be exported only to countries that had already approved their use, and required manufacturers to be "actively pursuing" FDA approval for use in this country.

Infant Formula. An omnibus anti-drug-abuse measure (HR 5484 — PL 99-570) contained provisions to toughen federal standards for infant formula. The measure required manufacturers to conduct quality-control testing and to post store notices when a batch of formula was recalled. It also increased record-keeping requirements for manufacturers.

The amendments to the 1980 Infant Formula Act (PL 96-359) were similar to ones attached May 14 to the drug export bill (S 1848), but they were not included when the drug export measure was rolled into omnibus health legislation (S 1744).

Housing/Community Development

Housing. Bills to reauthorize and to revamp federal housing programs died as Congress adjourned, despite an earlier agreement among key lawmakers on the general scope of the legislation. Housing programs, which had not been routinely reauthorized since 1980, would continue to operate without revision at their existing funding levels.

The agreement called for House Democrats to accept a spending freeze for housing programs, many of which President Reagan wanted to slash or eliminate, and an expansion of the Urban Development Action Grant economic development program in Republican areas of the South and West.

The Senate Banking, Housing and Urban Affairs Committee May 21 approved a bill embodying the compromise (S 2507), but the bill did not reach the floor because of filibuster threats from Phil Gramm, R-Texas, and William L. Armstrong, R-Colo.

The House passed its housing bill (HR 1) June 12, including a major policy shift toward renovation of existing public housing instead of construction. The measure also added incentives for public housing tenants to buy their units and grants for home construction in distressed areas.

As efforts in the Senate bogged down, the House tried to force action by including the text of HR 1 in an omnibus bank regulatory bill (HR 5576) that it passed Oct. 7. While Reagan wanted the bank regulatory changes, he threatened to veto HR 5576 if it retained the housing provisions. The Senate refused to accept the linkage, and housing and omnibus bank legislation died as Congress adjourned.

Revenue Sharing. Supporters of the general revenue sharing program failed in a last-ditch effort to keep the program alive.

Congress decided not to include a reauthorization of the program in its fiscal 1986 reconciliation bill (PL 99-272), allowing revenue sharing to die.

House Appropriations Committee Chairman Jamie L. Whitten, D-Miss., unsuccessfully tried to add $3.4 billion for revenue sharing to the omnibus fiscal 1987 spending bill (H J Res 738 — PL 99-591).

Federal Housing Administration (FHA). After approving seven short-term extensions, Congress Sept. 30 cleared a one-year reauthorization of the popular FHA home mortgage guarantee program and certain other community development programs.

The final bill (S J Res 353 — PL 99-430) reauthorized through Sept. 30, 1987: the FHA; the Government National Mortgage Association, which guaranteed securities backed by mortgages underwritten by FHA; the Farmers Home Administration; and federal flood insurance and crime insurance.

The mortgage guarantee program

had been caught in a larger battle between the House and Senate over housing programs.

Human Services

AFDC for Two-Parent Families. The 99th Congress adjourned without requiring states to provide welfare benefits under the Aid to Families with Dependent Children (AFDC) program to two-parent families in which the principal wage-earner was unemployed. The issue, however, produced lengthy deadlocks in House-Senate negotiations on two successive budget reconciliation bills.

AFDC coverage for two-parent families was optional under existing law, and only half the states provided it. Required coverage for two-parent families was included in versions of the fiscal 1986 reconciliation legislation (HR 3128 — PL 99-272) passed by both houses, but was dropped when President Reagan threatened to veto the entire bill unless it was removed.

House leaders, who claimed that Senate leaders had agreed to allow the requirement to remain in the fiscal 1987 reconciliation package (HR 5300 — PL 99-509), were not worried when they went to conference. But renewed veto threats and a desire to wrap up the bill and adjourn prevailed, and House conferees settled for a promise that the requirement would be considered in 1987 as part of an overall welfare reform package.

Anti-Poverty Programs. Congress Sept. 18 cleared for the president legislation reauthorizing for four years most of the federal government's non-entitlement anti-poverty human services programs, including Head Start, the Low Income Home Energy Assistance Program, and Community Services Block Grants.

The measure (HR 4421 — PL 99-425), which authorized more than $15 billion for the programs, also created a new program to help states fund scholarships for day care workers seeking a Child Development Associate job credential.

ACTION. Congress Oct. 8 cleared legislation (HR 4116 — PL 99-551) to reauthorize for three years the major domestic volunteer programs, including Volunteers in Service to America (VISTA) and the Older American Volunteer Programs.

In addition to authorizing more than $500 million for volunteer stipends and administrative costs, the legislation created a new literacy corps within VISTA to assist the needy illiterate.

Rehabilitation Act. A five-year reauthorization of popular vocational training programs for the handicapped was cleared by Congress Oct. 3. The legislation (HR 4021 — PL 99-506) extended programs created under the Rehabilitation Act of 1973 (PL 93-112).

Congress authorized $1.28 billion in fiscal 1986 for basic grants to states for rehabilitation programs, the largest program under the act.

The measure also provided some $200 million for other, smaller programs, such as research and special aid for disabled Indians and migrant workers.

The bill cleared Oct. 3 when the Senate adopted the conference report on the bill. The House had adopted the conference report Sept. 2.

Labor

Age Discrimination. In a flurry of last-minute activity, Congress Oct. 17 cleared legislation (HR 4154 — PL 99-592) to make it illegal for most employers to have mandatory retirement policies. Under existing law, workers could be forced to retire at age 70.

The final version of the bill included a seven-year exemption for firefighters, police and college faculty. During that time, the secretary of labor and the Equal Employment Opportunity Commission were to study the impact of eliminating mandatory retirement at universities and law enforcement institutions.

HR 4154 would also require that employers continue group health insurance for workers over the age of 70.

Polygraph Testing. Bills that would bar the use of polygraph, or lie detector, tests as a condition for employment were passed by the House and reported by the Senate Labor and Human Resources Committee. But there was no floor action in the Senate.

The Senate bill (S 1815) barred employers from requiring, requesting or suggesting that employees or prospective employees take lie detector tests for any purpose. It was approved by the committee June 25.

The House bill (HR 1524), passed March 12, was similar to the Senate measure, but included some exemptions. Under the bill, public utility workers, security guards at certain facilities, and workers at nursing homes and day-care centers could still be forced to take polygraphs.

EEOC Nominations. Clarence Thomas was confirmed by the Senate Aug. 12 for a second term as a member of the Equal Employment Opportunity Commission (EEOC). He had been chairman of the commission, which handled discrimination-in-employment complaints, since 1982 and continued in that post. His new term would expire in 1991.

On May 20, the Senate Labor and Human Resources Committee rejected, 5-10, the nomination of Jeffrey Zuckerman to be general counsel of the EEOC. Critics in the civil rights community said Zuckerman had no commitment to the enforcement of civil rights laws.

Law/Judiciary

Immigration. After five years of trying, Congress finally cleared legislation Oct. 17 transforming the nation's immigration laws. For the first time, employers would be subject to fines — and in repeat cases jail terms — for knowingly hiring illegal aliens. But the bill (S 1200 — PL 99-603) also included an amnesty program to give legal status to perhaps millions of illegals who could prove they had been in the United States prior to Jan. 1, 1982.

To allay the concerns of Western growers, who traditionally had relied on illegal aliens to harvest crops, the bill included a program to provide such workers. The bill granted temporary resident status to up to 350,000 foreigners who could prove they had worked in U.S. agriculture at least 90 days between May 1985 and May 1986.

As some of these people moved out of agricultural work, the bill provided a replenishment process that would terminate seven years after enactment.

The final bill was a delicate compromise forged by a host of competing interest groups that had fought out the issues in battles during the 97th and 98th Congresses. This time around, members were in a mood to reach the necessary compromises to pass a bill, and the way was cleared once Republicans and Democrats reached a compromise on the farm worker issue.

At the heart of the deal was a recognition on the one hand that Western growers needed an adequate labor force, and a willingness on the other to grant these workers protection from exploitation by giving them legal status within the United States.

Omnibus Anti-Drug Bill. On Oct. 17, Congress cleared omnibus anti-drug legislation (HR 5484 — PL 99-570) authorizing $1.7 billion in new funds for drug interdiction, eradication, enforcement, education, treatment and rehabilitation efforts. The measure also increased penalties for most federal drug crimes, created new penalties for money laundering and manufacture and distribution of so-called "designer drugs," and authorized $230 million annually for three years for grants to the states for drug-law enforcement.

HR 5484 contained the texts of several unrelated measures, including ones to establish nationwide licensing standards for commercial bus and truck drivers and to make the homeless eligible for federal welfare benefits and Medicaid.

Gun Control. Congress cleared legislation May 6 (S 49 — PL 99-308) that greatly eased federal gun control laws. The new law amended the 1968 Gun Control Act, enacted following the assassinations of the Rev. Dr. Martin Luther King Jr. and Sen. Robert F. Kennedy, D-N.Y.

The law lifted the ban on interstate sales of rifles and shotguns and limited the number of people who were required to get licenses to sell firearms. It also allowed gun owners to transport their firearms interstate, overriding state laws that barred residents from possessing firearms or transporting them in a vehicle.

The law also banned the future sales and possession of machine guns by private citizens. Shortly after the bill was enacted, this provision prompted new criticism from the National Rifle Association (NRA), which had lobbied hard for passage of the bill. The provision was enacted largely to appease law enforcement groups who were unhappy with parts of S 49, but the NRA vowed to overturn the ban in the 100th Congress.

To allay some of the police groups' concerns, Congress also enacted a separate bill (S 2414 — PL 99-360) that narrowed the circumstances under which a gun could be transported interstate.

Judicial Nominees. The Senate confirmed two members of the Supreme Court, Chief Justice William H. Rehnquist and Associate Justice Antonin Scalia.

Rehnquist was confirmed Sept. 17 by a 65-33 vote, the largest "nay" vote ever cast against a Supreme Court nominee who won confirmation. Scalia's confirmation was 98-0.

Two other disputed judicial nominations surfaced in the Senate.

A long controversy over the nomination of Indiana lawyer Daniel A. Manion to be a federal district judge came to an end July 23, when an effort to overturn an earlier vote confirming him failed, 49-50. Opponents charged that Manion was not qualified. His supporters said it was really his conservative credentials that were under attack.

The administration was less successful in winning support for Jefferson B. Sessions III, who became the first of President Reagan's judicial nominees to be rejected. He was nominated for a district court seat.

In dramatic roll calls June 5, the Judiciary Committee first voted 8-10 against sending Sessions' nomination to the Senate with a favorable recommendation. It then deadlocked 9-9 on a motion by Chairman Strom Thurmond, R-S.C., to send Sessions' name to the Senate without recommendation. The tie killed the nomination.

Critics had charged that Sessions was not qualified to sit on the bench and that several remarks he had made showed a "gross insensitivity" about racial issues. Sessions maintained that he was not a racist and that his remarks had been misconstrued or taken out of context.

Claiborne Impeachment. The Senate Oct. 9 removed imprisoned U.S. District Judge Harry E. Claiborne of Nevada from office after convicting him of "high crimes and misdemeanors" related to his 1984 conviction for tax fraud. An overwhelming majority voted to convict Claiborne on three articles, or charges, of impeachment; he was acquitted on a fourth.

Claiborne was the first official to be removed from office by impeachment in 50 years and the fifth in the history of the country. The last was Judge Halsted Ritter of Florida.

The House July 22 had voted 406-0 to impeach Claiborne, who was serving a two-year prison term for filing false income tax returns for 1979 and 1980. The amount of under-reported income was nearly $107,000.

The first two articles were based on the filing of false income tax returns; the third, on which he was acquitted, alleged that Claiborne should be removed from office because he was a convicted felon; the fourth alleged that he betrayed the trust of the people and brought disrepute on the federal judiciary.

A special 12-member committee — six Republicans and six Democrats — gathered evidence and made a report to the Senate, which then heard arguments on the record compiled by the panel. It was the first time such an impeachment procedure was used.

Claiborne and his lawyer, Oscar Goodman of Las Vegas, claimed that he was the victim of a vendetta by federal agents anxious to get him off the bench because he ruled against them in some controversial cases. Goodman said he intended to challenge the impeachment in court.

Electronic Privacy. Congress cleared legislation (HR 4952 — PL 99-508) Oct. 2 to extend privacy guarantees to communications transmitted by new forms of technology, including wireless phones that work by radio waves, computerized or "electronic" mail, and transmissions by private satellite and paging devices.

Violators could face fines and prison terms. And government officials would have to get court approval before intercepting these high-tech communications.

The bill was the product of two years of negotiations among privacy lawyers, the Justice Department and the electronics industry and was designed to close gaps in existing wiretap laws. Those provisions covered only conventional land-line phone systems and did not guarantee privacy protections for new forms of technology.

Privacy lawyers and the electronics industry said new legislation was necessary to protect individual rights and to help the industry grow. While the Justice Department was initially reluctant, it eventually supported the final product after requested modifications were made.

'Grove City' Legislation. For the third year in a row, Congress failed to pass legislation overturning a 1984 Supreme Court decision that had restricted the enforcement of four civil rights laws.

The legislation (HR 700), approved in differing forms by two House committees, was stalled in a dispute over abortion.

Sponsors did not push for floor action because of the abortion dispute, and intermittent negotiations throughout 1986 failed to bring a resolution to the problem.

The controversy centered on assertions by the U.S. Catholic Conference and anti-abortion groups that the measure could broaden abortion rights, forcing Catholic hospitals that receive federal aid, for example, to perform abortions.

Supporters of HR 700 rejected this claim and contended that the bill simply would restore to their previous scope of coverage the four civil rights laws: Title IX of the 1972 Education Amendments, Title VI of the 1964 Civil Rights Act, Section 504 of the Rehabilitation Act of 1973, and the Age Discrimination Act of 1975.

The court, in *Grove City College v. Bell,* ruled that Title IX barred sex discrimination only in a "program or activity" that received federal aid. Civil rights lawyers said an entire institution should be barred from discriminating if any part of it received aid.

The other three laws were affected because they contained the same "program or activity" language.

Science/Technology

NASA. President Reagan pocket-vetoed a $7.8 billion fiscal 1987 authorization for the National Aeronautics and Space Administration (NASA) that authorized a new orbiter to replace the space shuttle *Challenger,* which disintegrated during launch Jan. 28.

The bill (HR 5495), which was cleared for the president Oct. 18, also would have created a National Aeronautics and Space Council to advise and assist the president on space issues.

The White House strongly objected to an earlier version of the bill that would have given the council authority over both civilian and national security space issues; but Congress had revised the bill so that the council would be limited to civilian issues.

Although the authorization bill did not specify funding for a new orbiter, money was provided for that purpose by the fiscal 1987 omnibus spending bill (H J Res 738 — PL 99-591). An amendment added in conference to that measure transferred $2.4 billion in budget authority from the Defense Department to NASA for a new orbiter, with $100 million in outlays available after Aug. 15, 1987.

Trade

Omnibus Trade Bill. Alarmed by record trade deficits facing the United States, the House May 22 passed a sweeping bill (HR 4800) that would have toughened U.S. laws controlling imports, helped domestic industries obtain relief and taken steps to expand U.S. exports.

The bill was pushed heavily by Democratic leaders, who hoped the party's congressional candidates would benefit in November because of its trade stance. But the legislation, branded as protectionist by its foes, ran into stiff opposition from the Reagan administration and never got off the ground in the Senate.

Export-Import Bank. In another approach to rectifying the trade deficit, Congress approved a six-year reauthorization of the Export-Import Bank. The bank helped finance the purchase of U.S. goods, such as planes and other big-ticket items, by offering loans and loan guarantees to foreign purchasers.

A key feature of the legislation (HR 5548 — PL 99-472) was a $300 million trade "war chest" backed by the Reagan administration. The war chest would combine grants and direct loans to make U.S. exports more attractive to foreign customers. This "tied-aid" program was designed to offset similar subsidies provided by other trading nations, particularly Japan and France.

Final approval of the bill came Oct. 7 — too late to prevent the bank's charter from expiring Sept. 30, which resulted in a temporary halt of some Ex-Im operations. The delay was due in part to turf fights among committees.

Conferees on the fiscal 1987 omnibus spending bill (H J Res 738 — PL 99-591) dealt a blow to the tied-aid program. They provided that no more than $100 million of the bank's $900 million appropriation could be used for the tied-aid program, and linked it to certification by Ex-Im's chairman to Congress that the money was not needed for direct loans.

Textile Veto Override. In a key test of President Reagan's trade policies, the House failed Aug. 6 to override a veto of legislation (HR 1562) that would have sharply restricted textile and apparel imports.

Lawmakers from textile-producing states had been gearing up for the override attempt since Reagan vetoed the bill in December 1985. But strong White House lobbying, aided by new textile trade agreements with Hong Kong, Taiwan and South Korea, succeeded in sustaining Reagan's veto.

The margin — 276-149 — fell eight votes short of the two-thirds needed to override.

Transportation

Conrail. Legislation providing for a $2 billion stock offering to the public for the government's 85 percent share of Conrail cleared Congress as part of a reconciliation measure (HR 5300 — PL 99-509) to reduce the fiscal 1987 deficit.

The logjam over how to dispose of Conrail was broken when the Reagan administration abandoned its proposal to sell the railroad to the Norfolk Southern Corp. and embraced the plan of key House leaders for a public offering. The Senate in February had passed a bill (S 638) to implement the sale to Norfolk Southern, but met fierce opposition from House Energy and Commerce Committee members concerned that a merger would threaten jobs and competition in the rail industry.

House and Senate Budget committees pressed for Conrail's sale to raise revenue to sidestep budget cuts that might have been required by the Gramm-Rudman-Hollings anti-deficit law (PL 99-177).

An effort to amend the sale bill to increase federal regulation of the rail industry narrowly failed in the House Energy and Commerce Committee. The move was backed by Chairman John D. Dingell, D-Mich., who also was the chief House opponent to a Norfolk Southern merger.

Committee leaders did succeed in

tacking on an amendment supported by railroad unions that would have mandated labor protection for certain rail workers. But the provision met with strenuous opposition from Senate negotiators and was dropped in conference.

Amtrak, Mass Transit Cuts. The administration failed in its effort to eliminate subsidies to the Amtrak passenger railroad and to make deep cuts in mass transit funding.

The fiscal 1987 omnibus spending bill (H J Res 738 — PL 99-591) cleared Oct. 17 contained $602 million for Amtrak operating and capital expenses and $2 billion for mass transit formula grants. Funding for both programs was kept roughly at fiscal 1986 levels.

Congress did cut by 2.5 percent, or $21 million, funds for mass transit operating assistance for cities with more than 1 million people.

Lawmakers rejected an administration request to create a block grant for highway and transit programs that would have been funded by the Highway Trust Fund, which was made up of federal gasoline taxes and other road-related fees.

Highway, Mass Transit Authorizations. Congress did not pass legislation (HR 3129) to reauthorize billions of dollars for highway and mass transit programs, which expired when the fiscal year ended Sept. 30.

As a result, fiscal 1987 funding for highway programs would be limited to $6.3 billion in unobligated funds in the Highway Trust Fund, about half the level that would have been provided had the legislation been enacted.

The unobligated balances, however, were divided unevenly among states and among accounts in the trust funds. The Highway Users Federation, an umbrella organization for transportation groups, projected that many states would exhaust major funding categories by the end of 1986.

Congress also did not pass, as an alternative to a multi-year reauthorization bill, an emergency measure (S 2951) backed by the Reagan administration that would have allowed states to spread the $6.3 billion freely over trust fund accounts.

Despite agreement on many items, such as the level of funding for major programs, House and Senate conferees on HR 3129 could not resolve disputes over such controversial provisions as relaxing the 55 mph speed limit and whether to fund special "demonstration" projects.

Rep. James J. Howard, D-N.J., chairman of the House Public Works and Transportation Committee, repeatedly said the Senate's plan to allow states to raise the speed limit to 65 mph on rural Interstates would result in an unacceptable number of traffic fatalities. Senate negotiators refused to accept conditions Howard said states should meet before raising the speed limit — such as banning the use of radar detectors by motorists.

Senate leaders, especially Lloyd Bentsen, D-Texas, criticized the roughly 100 demonstration projects, funded at $1.2 billion, in the House bill. Bentsen said the "integrity" of the highway program was threatened by "pork-barrel" spending projects.

Airports Lease. Congress passed legislation backed by the Reagan administration to ease federal control over two metropolitan Washington, D.C., airports.

The plan, included in the fiscal 1987 omnibus spending bill (H J Res 738 — PL 99-591), called for a 50-year lease of Washington-Dulles International Airport and National Airport to a regional authority at an annual rate of $3 million, plus adjustments for inflation. Assuming a 4 percent annual inflation rate, the lease would cost $460 million. A congressional review board could veto decisions of the regional authority.

The bill also extended the legal range of non-stop flights to and from National Airport from 1,000 miles to 1,250 miles. Non-stop flights would be permitted to Dallas and Houston, as sought by House Majority Leader Jim Wright, D-Texas.

Truck Licensing. Concerned about the safety threat that some drivers of big trucks and buses pose on the nation's highways, Congress passed legislation to establish national licensing standards for commercial truckers. The licensing provisions were included in an omnibus anti-drug bill (HR 5484 — PL 99-570) cleared Oct. 17.

The plan called for states to issue "classified" licenses specifying the type of vehicle a driver would be eligible to operate. A driver applying for a new license would have to take a road test with the type of vehicle he or she intended to drive — a requirement currently maintained by only a dozen states.

The legislation also made it illegal for a driver to hold more than one commercial license, outlawing the practice of drivers getting licenses in several states.

States not complying by Oct. 1, 1993, with the licensing standards set by the transportation secretary would lose 5 percent of their federal highway aid otherwise due; aid would be cut by 10 percent for subsequent years of non-compliance.

House and Senate negotiators compromised on a drunken-driving standard for commercial drivers. The plan called for a 0.04 blood-alcohol standard within two years after enactment — unless the transportation secretary set a weaker standard.

Veterans

Disability COLA. Congress Oct. 8 cleared omnibus legislation (HR 5299 — PL 99-576) providing a 1.5 percent cost-of-living allowance in Veterans Administration (VA) disability and survivors' benefits, effective Dec. 1, 1986, to veterans with service-connected disabilities, and their widows and children.

The bill also exempted certain veterans' benefits and programs from automatic, across-the-board cuts triggered by the Gramm-Rudman-Hollings anti-deficit law (PL 99-177). VA life insurance accounts, two revolving funds and several other benefits were exempted permanently from Gramm-Rudman cuts; education aid programs for disabled veterans, their survivors and their dependents were exempted for one year.

HR 5299 included a number of other veterans' bills that had been passed by one chamber but not yet cleared by the other. One of those bills extended the federal "veterans' readjustment appointment" (VRA) authority from Sept. 30, 1986, to Dec. 31, 1989. The VRA was a hiring preference that allowed Vietnam-era veterans to win federal jobs without taking competitive exams.

In addition, the bill reauthorized for three years programs for state veterans' home construction. It also contained a three-year reauthorization for contracts and grants for medical care for U.S. veterans in the Philippines.

Also included was a prohibition on hiring discrimination against a member of the National Guard or reserves. ▮

The O'Neill Era Comes to an End in the House

When he left office at the end of the 99th Congress, Speaker Thomas P. O'Neill Jr. turned over to his successor a House of Representatives far different from the one whose gavel he assumed a decade earlier.

The extent of the change might not have been obvious to those who thought of the 1977-87 period as a time of relative stability in the House, compared with the period that preceded it. In the 10 years before O'Neill became Speaker, the institution underwent a surge of democracy, with the seniority system successfully challenged and power made available to the most junior members.

Nothing that dramatic happened in the O'Neill years. The changes were more gradual and more subtle. But a combination of forces — the Speaker himself, the Reagan administration, the budget process and economic austerity — created an institution that the proverbial traveler, returning after a 10-year absence, might have found difficult to comprehend.

O'Neill's House was an institution in which the media and public opinion became a common preoccupation both of the leadership and of much of the rank and file in both parties. At the same time, it was one in which real legislative power was quietly concentrating itself in a relatively small number of hands.

It was a place where Democrats and Republicans argued noisily against each other on the floor, and minor issues quickly became politicized beyond either side's apparent control. But it was a place where, beneath the veneer of partisanship, the two parties cooperated more than at any point in recent times.

Media Show

O'Neill's predecessor as Speaker, Carl Albert of Oklahoma, met quietly with a handful of reporters prior to each day's session of the House, answering a few perfunctory questions about the upcoming schedule. Few things that he said were printed or broadcast anywhere; none of them was calculated to influence the media.

An O'Neill press conference, however, was a media event, not only because dozens of print and broadcast reporters crowded into his office to hear him, but because much of what he said was designed for their benefit.

O'Neill often began with a prepared statement challenging one or another aspect of Reagan administration policy, drafted for him by press secretary Christopher J. Matthews, a glib wordsmith and specialist in one-liners. Often, O'Neill's comments were repeated on the evening news that night; even more often, they were printed in *The New York Times* and *The Washington Post* the next day.

A decade earlier, and for most of its history before that, the House was a relatively insular place outside the circle of national publicity and attention. Its members responded to each other, and to their constituents.

In the 1980s, with Republicans in control of the presidency and the Senate, the House was the one visible outpost of Democratic strength. The words of its leaders took on an importance far beyond the walls of the Capitol; they helped shape public opinion on all the important issues of the day. And they were uttered for that purpose.

"Ten years ago, nobody paid any attention to us," said Tony Coelho of California, who became House majority whip, the third-ranking Democratic leader, in the 100th Congress. "The Reagan years have forced the House into the spotlight. The question is whether we can go back anymore. I don't think the press is going to let the House go back to where it was. It's a goldfish bowl."

'Backroom Operator' in Goldfish Bowl

In the center of the bowl swam the largest and unlikeliest goldfish, a septuagenarian Speaker who spent a quarter-century in the House not only failing to attract media attention but actively avoiding it.

"I'm a backroom operator, no question about it," O'Neill told a television interviewer from the Cable-Satellite Public Affairs Network (C-SPAN) in August 1986, and his long career left little room for doubt about the issue. *(Profile, p. 30)*

Before he took over as Speaker, O'Neill had few dealings with the national press and virtually none with network television. He was a rank-and-file Massachusetts Democrat who arrived in Washington on Tuesday mornings, returned home on Thursday afternoons, and conducted his congressional business over poker, golf and dinner at Duke Zeibert's restaurant at Connecticut Avenue and L Street in downtown Washington.

Even as a national figure, O'Neill consistently avoided the Sunday TV interview programs, insisting that his Sabbath was reserved for church, golf and family.

Nevertheless, in the glare of attention the House commanded during the Reagan years, it was O'Neill who became the first media celebrity in the history of the speakership. None of his recent predecessors was the subject of endless cartoon caricature in newspapers across the country, and none provided material for monologues on late-night TV talk shows.

Some House Democrats, acknowledging this ironic development, took pains to point out that little of it was O'Neill's doing. The media needed a symbol for the Democratic Party, and the Republicans helped out by choosing O'Neill as the symbol of what they hoped to portray as an obsolete political generation.

For the House, though, what was important was that the speakership had worked its way out of its historic low profile, and nearly all members seemed to agree with Coelho that it would not return there.

"Sam Rayburn could have walked down the streets of Spokane, Wash., without anybody noticing him," said Majority Whip Thomas S. Foley of Washington, who moved up to majority leader in January 1987.

"Tip O'Neill couldn't do that," Foley said. "And it is very unlikely that any future Speaker will be anonymous to the country. The Speaker is going to join the vice president, the chief justice and a few Cabinet members in the fore-

After a Decade Full of Ups and Downs . . .

Colleagues had a right to feel some apprehension when Thomas P. O'Neill Jr. took over in 1977 as the 47th Speaker of the House. After 12 terms, he was a familiar and popular member, but one without any real reputation as a legislator.

He had been a compromise choice for Democratic whip in 1971, acceptable to liberals because of his anti-war record, and he had simply moved up the ladder after that. Even during the previous four years, as majority leader under Speaker Carl Albert of Oklahoma, O'Neill had worked a short week in Washington, continuing to focus on life and politics in Boston and playing little role in the day-to-day management of the House.

Some of "Tip" O'Neill's contemporaries knew that he had been Speaker of the Massachusetts House in the late 1940s, and that he had been considered a strong one. But there was nothing in his easygoing congressional career to suggest much of an appetite for leadership.

Setting the Tone: Crucial First Test

The first few months seemed to bear out contentions that O'Neill as Speaker would be like the man who had run the Massachusetts House, not the one who had coasted through 12 terms in Washington. "Power is when people assume you have power," he told a reporter in 1977. O'Neill began his speakership by convincing people that he had it.

Confronted with the challenge of enacting President Carter's energy package, he came up with a novel and successful idea, appointing an ad hoc committee to take up the bills on an emergency basis and thus bypass the parochial jealousies of the existing committee structure. Carter unveiled his proposals in April; by Aug. 5, O'Neill had moved them through the House. *(1977 Almanac p. 711)*

By the fall of 1977, there were stories claiming that O'Neill was the strongest congressional leader since Sam Rayburn. That early reputation was crucial, because he had to live off its capital for a long time. It was five years before O'Neill was able to win as impressively as he did the summer he took office.

The Frustrating Years

By 1978, the perceived failures of the Carter administration had taken their toll on the Democratic Party in Congress, and given O'Neill a Democratic majority that was increasingly reluctant to follow him. In November of that year, the midterm election brought in a belligerent crop of youthful Republicans, sensitive to the public relations potential of the House floor, and skillful at linking the Democratic leadership to the Carter White House and to overall economic decline.

The last two years of Carter's presidency marked the low point in O'Neill's personal management of the House. The leadership was embarrassed on issue after issue — energy, budget, foreign policy — by a coalition of Republicans and nervous conservative Democrats who thought it prudent to keep their distance from O'Neill as well as Carter.

"I've got a lot of good friends out there," the Speaker said one frustrating night in 1980, "who won't even give me a vote to adjourn."

Those frustrations, however, proved to be only a mild foreshadowing of what took place a year later, with President Reagan in the White House. Given Reagan's popular-

front of public recognition."

Winning the Nation at Large

If the only impact of the heightened media coverage were to give future Speakers a familiar face and more quotes in *The New York Times*, the significance for life in the House would be limited.

In reality, something more was going on. The media were not only using House leaders as a political symbol and source of news — House leaders were coming to use the media to accomplish their legislative goals.

A decade earlier, nearly all influential House members would have said that legislative arguments were won on the floor, by the tireless personal cultivation of colleagues.

By the late 1980s, however, many believed that floor fights were won by orchestrating a campaign aimed over the heads of the members, at the country at large.

"The idea is growing more and more," said a leadership aide, "that you have to have a media strategy to win an important vote."

The passage of President Reagan's 1981 economic program convinced leading House Democrats that an important legislative battle was a media engagement, not just a lobbying effort. When Reagan used national television to promote his budget-reduction plan in May 1981, O'Neill found himself unable to hold the support of nervous Democrats whose constituents liked the president's speech.

"Am I lobbying?" O'Neill said at one point. "The answer is yes. Am I getting commitments? The answer is no." He said Reagan had done "the greatest selling job I've ever seen."

Thereafter, House leaders operated on the assumption that traditional inside tactics were no longer enough. "Sometimes to pass a bill," Foley said, "you have to change the attitude of the country."

During the rest of the Reagan era, nearly any showdown on a major issue — a budget resolution, an arms control proposal, aid to the Nicaraguan anti-government contras — was preceded by a House leadership media effort orchestrated to match whatever campaign the administration was waging. That meant, among other things, floor speeches by Democratic members intended for inclusion on TV news programs, and articles in national newspapers by senior members of key committees.

Taking the Pulse

In the 99th Congress, developing a media and public opinion strategy moved beyond the ad hoc stage and became a year-round element of leadership thinking.

At least twice a week, a core group of House Democrats led by Californian Don Edwards met over breakfast to talk about using media to help them win on the floor. "When

. . . O'Neill Ends His Speakership on the Rise

ity and the Republican gain of 33 House seats in the fall of 1980, there may never have been much chance for O'Neill's Democrats to derail the president's economic program.

But O'Neill's handling of the 1981 economic debate did not particularly reinforce his image as a leader.

In April, while other Democrats were struggling to stave off a Reagan budget victory, the Speaker took his usual springtime foreign tour, this one to Australia. On his return, he announced that Reagan could not be beaten, an observation that struck some Democratic colleagues as an abdication of responsibility.

A few months later, he seemed to switch to the other extreme, fighting aggressively to win passage of a Democratic tax bill that had been laced with special interest concessions in an effort to hold Southern Democratic votes. Reagan won easily on the tax issue; the simple fact was that the Democratic leadership did not have control of the chamber.

The Turning of the Tide

Had O'Neill chosen to retire in 1982, his speakership would have had an aura of failure about it. But he opted to stay on, and his final years in office brought a gradual revival, not only in his public reputation but in his ability to lead.

By early 1982, recession had ended the Southern Democratic infatuation with Reagan policies, and there were no more Republican victories on major economic policy issues. That fall, GOP candidates throughout the country campaigned by attacking the Speaker as an obsolete hack, and they failed spectacularly. With national unemployment cresting above 10 percent on Election Day, Democrats regained 26 of the seats they had lost in 1980, reclaiming political control of the House in addition to the nominal control they never lost.

The two Congresses after that witnessed no landmark legislative initiatives from the Democratic side. But they established O'Neill as a Speaker who nearly always had the votes to prevail when he wanted to.

The key committees were packed with enough leadership loyalists to make most key votes predictable. Budget resolutions drafted in large part by the leadership won wide approval on the House floor, with Republicans offering only halfhearted opposition. The Republican strategy of making O'Neill their national campaign villain was a failure for the second time in 1984, and polls showed the Speaker's popularity rising among the American people in the closing months of his career.

Tip O'Neill will not be remembered as a great legislator — his casual attitude toward detail was too well documented for that. "I don't know the depth of every piece of legislation that goes around here," he told a television interviewer in August. "The important stuff, I understand it."

But like the Republican president who was his antagonist for the final six years of his speakership, O'Neill persuaded skeptics that there were elements of leadership that went beyond the mastery of facts.

"Tip is not a man who is interested in substance," said John D. Dingell, the veteran Michigan Democrat. "But he has the ability to reduce complicated issues down to a few simple, easily understood points. That's not a weakness. It's an unbelievable political strength."

you don't put public pressure on your colleagues," said Edwards, "just enough of them succumb to the other side for you to lose. That's what happened to us on the contras."

In 1986, Edwards and the Democratic leadership fell narrowly short (221-209) in their bid to block Reagan from sending $100 million in U.S. aid to the contra forces fighting Nicaragua's leftist regime. *(Contra aid, p. 394)*

Members of the media group regularly called producers of TV talk shows to suggest House Democrats as guests. On Sundays, if a national newspaper had not given space to the Democratic response to the president's Saturday radio address, they called an editor to complain.

Competing for Prime Time

But House leaders were not the only ones who had turned the House into a media-minded institution. In fact, they were several steps behind some of their more enterprising rank-and-file colleagues.

The House of 1986 — as opposed to the one of 1976 — was a place where any member who wanted to publicize his issues or himself could do it with relatively little effort.

This did not mean that the average U.S. representative was a television star. It remained true that the average member had virtually no continuing name recognition outside his district. But it was also true that the opportunity for coverage existed on a day-to-day basis, and even the most junior members realized it and sought to take advantage of it.

"If you want to reach your colleagues," said Thomas J. Downey, D-N.Y., "sometimes the best way is to let them see you on TV or read your name in the paper. If you say something pithy or clever, you can find yourself on the national news in a matter of hours.... News management by members through the electronic media is a more viable option than it ever was."

Opportunities for media exposure multiplied in the 1980s.

To start with, there was C-SPAN. Since the cable network began televising House proceedings in 1979, the number of people able to receive the broadcasts had grown to 25 million. Only a tiny fraction of those people were watching the House at a given moment, of course, but nearly every member returned home on weekend trips to find at least a few constituents who saw him perform recently on the House floor. *(TV in Congress, p. 43)*

One day-to-day consequence of C-SPAN was the thinning out of House floor attendance. Members who used to spend part of each afternoon on the floor to follow debate instead watched TV in their offices. In a broader way, though, C-SPAN sensitized members to the importance of TV in their work. There was always the chance that something they said in debate might turn up on a news program — or even in the campaign commercials of their opponents many months down the road.

C-SPAN was only the beginning. Cable News Network went on the air in 1980; its non-stop broadcasting gave members of Congress who wanted to be interviewed a 24-hour target to shoot at. Three years later, public television's highly regarded MacNeil-Lehrer show expanded its nightly public affairs program from 30 minutes to a full hour. Instead of dealing with one subject each evening, it tackled as many as four, and its need for credible spokesmen on major issues neatly matched the entrepreneurship of articulate members of the House.

"You have members talking on the floor all the time about how they are using the media," said Democrat Dan Glickman of Kansas, a 10-year House veteran. "And the media encourage us to do that — especially the electronic media. The media have found Congress to be a lot more interesting than they used to."

Basking in the Glow of the Tube

There was no evidence that either newspapers or TV were focusing more on how the House worked as an institution than they used to. *The Washington Post*, which maintained a full-time reporter for routine institutional House coverage until about 1980, had since then used a series of people to perform that job more selectively.

But at the same time, there was unprecedented opportunity for individual members to present themselves as analysts, commentators, polemicists and specialists in quick reaction to events around the world.

Some of the more traditional members found this disturbing. "You've got a bunch of verbalizers who have a smattering of the jargon and who have natural media ability," said Illinois Republican Henry J. Hyde. "A lot of them have been touched by the aphrodisiac of seeing their name in the papers or going on the evening news. It's a heady experience for them."

Matthews, O'Neill's press secretary, was just as critical. "You ask these guys why they want to be on TV," he said, "and it's like asking a moth why he likes a light bulb. It's why they're there."

But not all of them seemed to be in it simply for self-gratification. New York Democrat Charles E. Schumer, elected in 1980, made himself a significant force on a variety of issues with a media offensive that was both relentless and brilliant in its understanding of media needs.

A typical year for Schumer almost always included op-ed articles in *The Washington Post*, *The New York Times* and *The Wall Street Journal*, and so many MacNeil-Lehrer appearances that it was sometimes hard to tell whether he was a guest or a host.

The Foreign Affairs Committee became a media gold mine for newly elected members. Some attracted national news coverage remarkably soon after their arrival.

Robert G. Torricelli of New Jersey, elected as a Democrat in 1982, was on national news programs a few months later when he traveled to El Salvador and returned with the body of an American journalist murdered there. Later that year, he drew publicity for arranging a papal audience for a 97-year-old constituent. "Great television," he called the latter episode.

The Foreign Affairs Committee, in fact, offered a revealing clue to the ways the House changed in the O'Neill years.

It was not primarily a legislative committee. Its only regular legislative responsibility was an annual foreign aid authorization, which in most years did not clear both chambers and become law, if it passed the House at all. The Foreign Affairs Committee was a debating society.

And yet, it evolved in the 1980s from a backwater committee with a lackluster membership to a prize assignment that drew some of the best legislative talent arriving in any given year.

What the Foreign Affairs Committee offered its members was the unparalleled chance to talk, and to be listened to, not only by colleagues but by the media and the public.

The freedom to talk was precious in the House, and growing more important all the time. That was because the freedom to legislate, for many of the members, was disappearing.

"If I had been free to choose a time in the last 25 years to become Speaker," Jim Wright of Texas said, "I wouldn't have chosen this moment. I'm coming to the office at a time when Congress is circumscribed."

Power Shifts

It was easy to see what Wright meant. The combination of $200 billion deficits and an anti-government Republican president made it all but futile for House members to think about launching new programs to solve society's social problems.

That was the work that had been drawing Democratic members of Congress to Washington since Franklin D. Roosevelt's time. Blocked from performing it in the 1980s, many of them had gradually come to the conclusion that there was little for them to do in the House.

Democrats were not alone in this feeling. Even the conservative Republicans who used to fight to scale back programs acquired a sense of irrelevance when there were no new programs even to argue about. "Some of the younger members," said GOP leader Robert H. Michel of Illinois, "don't really know what it's like to be in the position of working on legislation with the thought that it might become law someday."

It could not be said that the 99th Congress was an unimportant one. Any Congress that overhauled the entire U.S. tax code and mandated a balanced federal budget was clearly passing landmark laws.

But tax revision and the Gramm-Rudman-Hollings budget law were only two pieces of legislation, and a relatively small number of House members worked on them. The rest, unable to create programs and spend money the way they used to, were left on the sidelines.

"When major changes are made," admitted Henry A. Waxman, D-Calif., one of the most effective current legislators, "they are made with limited input."

'Four Bill' System

Many members referred to the current legislative process in the House as the "four bill" system. What they meant was that in an average year, there were often only four important domestic legislative vehicles — the budget resolution, continuing appropriations, supplemental appropriations, and the reconciliation package of spending cuts that the budget dictated. Sometimes legislation to raise the federal debt limit was another.

"The only way to get things done in recent years," said Leon E. Panetta, a California Democrat, "has been to attach them to bills the Senate and the president cannot refuse."

Return to Oligarchy

Those who were in a position to influence one of the "must pass" bills could count on being important players in the process. Those who were not could count on being spectators.

As a result, one of the most common clichés about the modern House — its open, democratic character — was ceasing to be accurate. The House of the 1980s was democratic in the sense that all members, even the most junior ones, were part of the debate. But when it came to making decisions, democracy was the wrong word to use.

"The natural tendency of this institution is toward oligarchy," said Democrat Philip R. Sharp of Indiana, a six-term veteran. "What we have now is a technique for returning to a closed system where a few people make all the decisions."

This frustrated members not only in Washington but at home. Two decades earlier, most of them could return to their districts and explain that the restrictions of the seniority system made it difficult to accomplish what they wanted to do. By 1986, that explanation would not do, at least among sophisticated constituents.

In the mid-1980s, an honest explanation of why something could not be accomplished was likely to involve parliamentary distinctions and power relationships so complex that few members wanted to attempt it.

The return to oligarchy generally escaped notice because it bore so little resemblance to the form of oligarchy that prevailed before the reform wave of the early 1970s.

In the old days, power was vested in seniority; committee chairmen were the oligarchs. The modern system concentrated power not in the chairmen of many committees, as before, but in virtually all the members of a few elite committees.

Granting Favors

Appropriations was a power committee largely because it wrote the continuing resolution, which funded all programs for which regular appropriation bills had not cleared Congress when the new fiscal year began Oct. 1.

In the 1980s, that meant most government programs, so the continuing resolution became a budget unto itself, all but certain of presidential approval and so massive that there was little chance to question any item someone from the Appropriations Committee was able to place in it.

Increasingly, the continuing resolution also moved beyond the funding process to authorize programs on its own. Given the budget-cutting mentality of the Reagan administration, dozens of federal programs, from legal services for the poor to environmental protection grants, could not be reauthorized by Congress and avoid a presidential veto.

But the Appropriations Committee could fund them and could even make decisions about the way the programs should be structured.

There was still a significant difference in legislative influence between the Appropriations chairman, Jamie L. Whitten, a Democrat from Mississippi, and those at the bottom of Whitten's committee. But there was even more difference between anybody on Appropriations and most of the other members of the House.

When the fiscal 1987 Transportation Department appropriations bill passed the House in late July, it specifically included money for two projects in the district represented by one of the panel's lowest-ranking members, Democrat Robert J. Mrazek of New York. Projects like those were supposed to be authorized by the Public Works and Transportation Committee, but increasingly, Appropriations more often than not simply did that work on its own.

Even the most senior member of Public Works would have found it difficult to accomplish what Mrazek could do simply by having a seat at the Appropriations table.

The result of this situation was that members of the less fortunate committees spent much of their time trying to persuade those on the more fortunate committees to help them out.

"What you do," said Democrat Thomas A. Daschle of South Dakota, a member of the Agriculture Committee, "is you find a couple of people on Appropriations that you can rely on, and they are willing to do their homework for you."

Taxes and Spending

The Ways and Means Committee remained powerful not only because it wrote tax bills but because of its role in reconciliation. Ways and Means had jurisdiction over hundreds of billions of dollars in spending for health, Social Security and a variety of other social needs.

It therefore had leverage over reductions made in these areas, and in making its cuts, it had the ability to reshape the programs themselves in important ways.

Democrat Fortney H. "Pete" Stark of California became a major player on numerous issues largely because he chaired the Ways and Means Health Subcommittee. When budget priorities called for massive cuts in health spending, as happens nearly every year, Stark could help structure the cuts, and quietly change the programs themselves at the same time.

In 1986, when the LTV Corp. faced bankruptcy and refused to pay health benefits to the workers who lost their jobs, House members representing those workers struggled for a way to force payment of the benefits. As it turned out, there was one way: Approach Stark and persuade him to add language requiring such benefit payments to an upcoming reconciliation bill. Stark obliged.

The Energy and Commerce Committee possessed similar leverage, partly because so much spending was under its control, and partly because of the legislative skills of its most influential members, led by Chairman John D. Dingell of Michigan and by Waxman, the Health Subcommittee chairman.

Waxman, unsuccessful in 1980 in his effort to enact a new child health entitlement program, in the six years thereafter managed to slip nearly all its provisions into law through the reconciliation process.

Reconciliation was such an important legislative outlet that even those members who were not well-positioned to take advantage of it were reluctant to place limits on its use. In 1986, when Budget Chairman William H. Gray III, D-Pa., considered changing the rules to make it harder to attach new legislative language to reconciliation bills, a cross-section of members lobbied Speaker O'Neill to tell Gray to drop the idea, which Gray did.

At a time when there were only a handful of legislative trains leaving the station, few wanted to see any of them derailed.

'Irrelevant' Players

With a few important exceptions, the committees mentioned above pretty much delineated the power structure of the House in the important areas of domestic policy. And the people on the inside knew it.

"The budget system has made many of the committees

irrelevant," said Matthew F. McHugh, D-N.Y., who had been on Appropriations since 1978. "Over a period of time, it distorts the legislative process in a way that creates tension and frustration.... Some of the members don't have anything to do. So they have to look for ways to express themselves."

"In the retrenchment of the state, power is being concentrated," agreed Vic Fazio, D-Calif., an Appropriations colleague. "There's a certain amount of resentment among members who thought they had achieved power and find it's a blind alley. They are presiding over the dissolution of the empire."

Where Budget fit on the ranking of committee power was open to debate. There was no doubt that it was a glamour committee of the 1980s. Seats on it were prestigious and hard to get, and members had an advantage in visibility over most of their colleagues.

On the other hand, the rank-and-file Budget Committee Democrats did not necessarily have much control over the resolution that was approved each year (Republicans had none), and the resolution itself often bore little resemblance to the spending that eventually took place under its supposed guidelines. There was a substantial bloc in the House that believed the Budget Committee belonged to the talk-and-media region of current House life, not the region of legislative power.

"I've never taken the budget process very seriously," said David E. Bonior, D-Mich., who studied the whole system from his Rules Committee perch. "You go through the whole long process of passing the resolution and the numbers get changed later anyway. It's a mathematical game. The Budget Committee is a talker's shop."

Some of those who had served there said similar things, if less bluntly. "The Budget Committee has been put here to be a debating forum," said Fazio. "It's become symbolic to a lot of people, and less important.... Being on the Budget Committee is a source of external power. People think you're important, so they listen to you. The media wants to hear from members of the Budget Committee."

A top House leader, asked if he wanted to challenge that assertion, instead supported it. "There's a feeling among an increasing number of members," he said, "that the entire budget process is a waste of time."

Tight Reins at Rules

In the past, a House member who felt shut out of the important action in committee could count on virtually absolute freedom to make his case on the floor. That began changing in the 1980s.

The O'Neill years saw the floor evolve into a much more efficient legislative machine, with most major bills brought there under procedures barring more than a handful of amendments.

In 1983, a nuclear-freeze bill generated dozens of amendments and 40 hours of debate over a two-month period, and created an embarrassing atmosphere of chaos for the Democratic majority. After that, House leaders and the Rules Committee kept the terms of debate and amendment under tight control. Rarely did discussion of even the most controversial bill take more than a couple of days. Few sessions lasted past 7 p.m.

In 1978, thanks to a profusion of floor amendments, there were 834 roll calls on the House floor. By 1984, the figure was down to 408. In 1979, there were 30 amendments to the budget resolution, and debate stretched on for more than two weeks. In 1986, there were three amendments, and consideration of the entire issue was finished in 24 hours.

One result of the change was a feeling of pride among some members that their institution, unlike the disorganized and haphazard Senate, did its work in a competent, orderly way that did not embarrass them when people saw it on television. "This place operates like a Swiss watch compared with 10 years ago," said Downey, who arrived in 1975.

At the same time, though, the new efficiency was a further obstacle to members who did not have a place on the power committees and would have liked some freedom to legislate on the floor.

"If you are an activist member, it is a frustrating experience," said Glickman. "It makes a member seem impotent at home when a bill comes to the floor and he can't offer an amendment."

Partisanship

One common perception about floor debate — and about the House in general in the O'Neill years — was that it had become considerably more partisan.

Beneath the surface, though, the situation was different. All the talk about the 1980s as a time of rampant partisanship was badly misplaced.

The key bills that kept the government operating each year passed with a minimum of partisan controversy. Reconciliation, continuing resolutions and most appropriation bills moved through the House with relative ease. When they came up for debate, the main argument seemed to be between the House as a whole and the Reagan administration.

"To the extent we have been able to work out our differences in a bipartisan way," said Fazio, "it's because of Reagan. Reagan has cut off our running room in Congress to the point where we are driven together."

On this point, leaders of both parties seemed to be in agreement. "The Congress is not riven with disputes about basic policies," said Foley. "Because we are so restrained in our spending," said Michel, "we all have to talk the same tune around here."

In the 1970s, any major appropriations bill generated serious Republican alternatives calling for substantially less spending. These were discussed at length and drew roughly as many votes as there were Republicans in the House. In the 1980s, bipartisan consensus moved these bills through to final passage with a minimum of dissent.

Michel had that lesson reinforced for him in the summer of 1986, when he tried to scale back the appropriations for the Departments of Labor, Health and Human Services, and Education.

The bill increased funds for the National Institutes of Health by about 15 percent. Michel offered an amendment to cut that figure. There were 12 members on the floor, and he lost on an 8-4 vote. There was no roll call. Later, Michel was decisively beaten on a proposal to cut the entire bill by $2.7 billion. Then the bill passed by a vote of 328-86.

Nearly all of the significant legislative changes enacted through reconciliation in the past two Congresses — such as approval of Waxman's child health program and decisions about the use of oil revenue from the Outer Continental Shelf — provoked no real partisan dispute.

Some major legislation did produce Republican amendments closely tied to media efforts being promoted by the party campaign committee. But even this was more difficult than it used to be — it now required a complicated parliamentary maneuver for a member to add language to an appropriations bill placing limits on the ways its money could be used.

More and more, members regarded the periodic flashes of House partisanship as a kind of show that obscured the working cooperation that governed the real institution in the closing months of the O'Neill era.

"Partisanship is a game that's being played for media and the campaign committees," said Sharp. "We have reached a sort of *modus vivendi* in which each side knows it can't score any real political victories."

"You look at issues," said Panetta, "and you try to play them for political effect. But on the major bills, everyone knows they have to pass. Nobody is willing to throw themselves in front of these trains. What they want is to get on board.

"On stage, they are throwing things at each other, and sword fights are going on. But behind the curtain there's basic cooperation. Otherwise, there would be a huge embarrassment to all incumbents. Incumbency still drives this place." ∎

—By Alan Ehrenhalt

House Incumbents Enjoy Record Success Rate

More than ever before, the voters in 1986 verified an old political truism: They may not like Congress, but they like their congressman.

A record 98 percent of the House members who sought re-election were victorious. That topped the previous record from 1968, when 96.8 percent kept their seats. *(House elections, p. 11-B; table, next page)*

Perhaps more remarkable, however, was the record percentage of incumbents in the Nov. 4 general election who had what could be considered safe seats: 85 percent either won at least 60 percent of the vote or had no major-party opposition at all. That broke the 1978 record of 78 percent.

"It was truly an extraordinary year for House incumbents," said Thomas E. Mann, executive director of the American Political Science Association.

The new record marked the success of members who spent unprecedented amounts of time and money to win. But experts said it also reflected the overwhelming advantages of incumbency, the safety of political districts drawn by state legislators' partisan hands and the generally stable, nonpartisan tenor of 1986 politics.

Less Security in the Senate

In contrast with the House, a relatively low 75 percent of senators seeking re-election kept their seats, or 21 of the 28 who ran. All seven losers were Republicans, accounting in large part for Democrats' takeover of that chamber with a 55-45 majority. *(Senate elections, p. 5-B)*

The number of Senate losers was just one less than for the House, although all House seats and only one-third of Senate seats were up for grabs. Of the 393 House members who ran for re-election, two lost in the primaries and six in the general election.

The disparity between the electoral success of senators and House members was not unusual. For the four postwar decades, senators' average rate of success was 74.9 percent — almost exactly the 1986 rate — while the re-election average of House incumbents for 1946-84 was 90.9 percent.

"There's no question that Senate and House elections are very different now," Mann said. "For some years now, Senate elections have been more competitive.... There are just very few competitive races in the House."

David R. Mayhew, a political science professor at Yale University who studied the decline of competitive congressional elections, pointed out that more than 100 House members would lose their seats every election year if the results followed the pattern typical of Senate elections.

The experts said senators tended to be more vulnerable for a variety of reasons. A senator's constituency, covering an entire state rather than a single district, was usually more populous and diverse — socially, economically *and* politically. "We just simply have a lot of one-party [House] districts," said Roger H. Davidson, senior government specialist at the Library of Congress.

Mayhew suggested that "Senate elections are very salient to voters and important, and hence good candidates want them. So it's common to get two good candidates for the seat, both of whom are well-publicized."

Senators generally drew more media coverage, observers agreed, but this meant they were more likely to be held accountable on controversial issues. House members often had to generate their own publicity, but that meant laudatory press releases, videotapes and newsletters. They fostered closer contacts with voters through constituent services that transcended partisan politics — such as helping a veteran get a disability check.

The Incumbents' Edge

Taxpayer-financed mailings and assiduous attention to constituents were just two advantages of incumbency that made House service a career for many members.

Allowances for travel to the district were instituted in the mid-1960s, and had steadily risen. So had accounts for other office-related expenses, such as district-office leases, computers, stationery and staff.

Meanwhile, incumbents constantly raised money, much of it from groups whose interests were affected by the members' committee work. Even members who had not had a tough race in years continually replenished campaign chests as a deterrent to would-be rivals.

The incumbent's edge was such that Mayhew said that "if everybody retired — all of them — probably more than half the House seats would become competitive in a hurry."

For example, he cited Texas' 1st District. When Rep. Sam B. Hall Jr. resigned in 1985 to become a federal judge, Republicans stormed the longtime Democratic bastion. But their candidate lost by a hair (50.9 percent to 49.1 percent) to Democrat Jim Chapman, ending the district's brief fling with two-party competition. In 1986, in his first run for a full term, Chapman had no Republican rival.

The advantage of incumbency explained in general the security of House seats. But experts said the factor that best explained why the 1986 elections set a record for safe incumbents was the lack of a national theme. The economy was good, except for pockets in farm, oil and manufacturing centers. "There was no desire to throw the bums out," Mann said.

"Even with all the advantages of incumbency, when a national tide is running against those in office and there is widespread discontent and economic problems, you can get enough of a shift to knock incumbents out," he said. "It's not a massive shift, but it's something."

The recent examples were the general elections in 1974, when Watergate and recession cost 36 Republicans their seats; 1980, when 27 Democratic members lost in the wake of President Reagan's victory; and 1982, when 26 Republican incumbents were defeated in the midst of a recession.

Even in those swing years, however, at least 87 percent of House incumbents on the ballot won re-election.

In 1986, another reason for members' safety was Republicans' failure to capture many House seats in 1984, on the coattails of Reagan's landslide re-election. As a result, there were relatively few weak Republican freshmen for Democrats to pick off.

They did claim four: Fred J. Eckert of New York, Mike Strang of Colorado, Bill Hendon and Bill Cobey, both of North Carolina. Two other Republicans were defeated: Webb Franklin of Mississippi, serving his second term, and Mark D. Siljander of Michigan, who lost in the GOP primary.

Democrat Alton R. Waldon Jr. of New York lost in the primary after winning a special election this year. Among the other 232 Democrats who sought re-election, five-term Rep. Robert A. Young of Missouri had the unwanted distinction of being the sole loser.

Safe Districts by Design

To frustrated Republicans, who had not been the House majority since 1954, the main reason for the success of House incumbents — most of them Democrats — was the fact that political boundaries had been drawn by state legislators — most of them Democrats. But outside experts disputed that.

"Overall, redistricting supplies a bit of an advantage to the Democrats, especially in California," Mayhew said. "But my guess is that if you appointed a neutral panel to draw the lines, Democrats would have less advantage, but not much less."

In California, all 42 incumbents who ran were re-elected, and none received less than 57 percent of the vote.

Texas and Florida were other states commonly cited for their politically weighted maps. In Texas, all 26 incumbents who sought re-election won. Ten had no major party opponent, and 13 won at least 62 percent of the vote. Eight of Florida's 18 incumbents had no major-party foe, and the other 10 got 65 percent or more of the vote.

Of Massachusetts' 10 members who ran, seven Democrats had no GOP rival. But as Mann said, "That's a function of a moribund Republican Party, not redistricting. Most of the research on redistricting says it's greatly exaggerated. You can point to states where it's important. California is the obvious example. But Indiana is a counterexample."

Indiana's Republican Legislature drew a congressional map five years ago with the idea of assuring seven seats for Republicans and three for Democrats. But Democrats won six in the 1986 elections; five incumbents won with margins ranging from 53 percent to 74 percent, and a sixth Democrat captured an open seat. Of the four Republican incumbents who won, John Hiler barely got over 50 percent.

Advantage of Incumbency, 1946-86

	Seeking Re-election		Percent Re-elected	
Year	**House**	**Senate**	**House**	**Senate**
1946	398	30	82.4	56.7
1948	400	25	79.2	60.0
1950	400	32	90.5	68.8
1952	389	31	91.0	64.5
1954	407	32	93.1	75.0
1956	411	29	94.6	86.2
1958	396	28	89.9	64.3
1960	405	29	92.6	96.6
1962	402	35	91.5	82.9
1964	397	33	86.6	84.8
1966	411	32	88.1	87.5
1968	409	28	96.8	71.4
1970	401	31	94.5	77.4
1972	390	27	93.6	74.1
1974	391	27	87.7	85.2
1976	384	25	95.8	64.0
1978	382	25	93.7	60.0
1980	398	29	90.7	55.2
1982	396	30	90.6	93.3
1984	410	29	95.1	89.7
1986	393	28	98.0	75.0
Average *	**399**	**29.4**	**90.9**	**74.9**

** Does not include 1986 results.*

Is Success a Good Thing?

Despite the apparent safety of a House seat, many members felt anything but secure and campaigned full time to keep their seats. "I'm not worried about individual congressmen becoming insensitive to their districts," said Mann, whose 1978 article on nervous incumbents was titled "Unsafe at Any Margin."

Even the most entrenched members remembered colleagues who lost, like Al Ullman, D-Ore. (1957-81), a 12-term veteran and chairman of the Ways and Means Committee, and House Majority Whip John Brademas, D-Ind. (1959-81), an 11-term member.

Mann was concerned not by incumbents' near-perfect record of re-election, but by a related phenomenon.

"One of the unhealthy aspects of our politics today ... is this uninterrupted control of the House by the Democrats," he said. "I am much less concerned about the advantages of incumbency ... than I am by the fact that Republicans seem mired in permanent minority status."

Davidson recalled a time in the 1970s, when students of Congress worried that House turnover was getting too high, that expertise was being lost as veterans were defeated or choosing retirement.

"Overall, it's a good thing to encourage careerism among House and Senate members, to give them enough time to master legislative and policy areas," he said. "As long as they're doing an adequate job — at least as their constituents see it — there's no reason to look askance at that."

Then, pondering a moment more on the 98 percent re-election rate in the election just held, Davidson joked, "Maybe we ought to worry again about trying to get rid of people." ∎

No Changes Made in Outside Earnings Limits

Politically sensitive votes were taken in both the House and Senate to change the limits on members' outside earnings, but the status quo prevailed.

The House April 22 unexpectedly approved a resolution (H Res 427) raising the cap on outside earnings to an amount equal to 40 percent of a member's salary, up from 30 percent. However, fearing political fallout — especially in an election year — members quickly reversed themselves, voting the next day to restore the 30 percent cap (H Res 432).

The limit on senators' honoraria earnings had been raised to 40 percent of salary in late 1985, as part of the fiscal 1986 continuing appropriations resolution (PL 99-190). Although that change applied to the House as well, it could not take effect until and unless the House voted to alter a 1981 House rule limiting members' honoraria to 30 percent. *(1985 Almanac pp. 34, 360)*

During Senate debate on the fiscal 1986 supplemental appropriations bill (HR 4515 — PL 99-349), William Proxmire, D-Wis., offered an amendment to return the Senate cap to 30 percent. His amendment was blocked June 5, however, by a 68-30 vote on a procedural motion. *(Vote 114, p. 22-S)*

The House Tries for More

The resolution to raise the House cap to 40 percent of salary was offered April 22 by John P. Murtha, D-Pa., when only a few members were on the floor.

When Rep. John Hiler, R-Ind., asked "to be enlightened as to what the gentleman's resolution is about," Murtha said that it merely "changes the rules to bring them into closer compliance with the Senate rules" and had "been cleared by the leadership on both sides."

Hiler, satisfied, sat down, and the resolution was approved by voice vote.

But when members discovered what they had done, many were distressed. Even though some in Congress felt they were not adequately compensated, at an annual salary of $75,100 in 1986, few were willing to vote for increased pay or benefits.

"They don't give themselves a proper salary," said Speaker Thomas P. O'Neill Jr., D-Mass., who supported the hike in outside earning limits. "They haven't got the guts and the courage to say, 'We need a pay raise.' "

Confusion About Scope

The outside earnings cap, $22,530 in 1986 for the average House member, covered honoraria for speeches and articles, plus income from activities such as law practices. Increasing it to 40 percent of salary would have allowed maximum earnings of $30,040.

Because House members typically were less known than senators, few commanded enough in speaking fees to breach the limit. Only 39 of the 435 voting members, or 9 percent, earned $25,000 or more in outside income in 1985. In the Senate, 38 of the 100 members earned that much. In both chambers, those whose earnings exceeded the honoraria cap had to donate the excess to charity.

Backers said Murtha's plan would simply put the House on an equal footing with the Senate. However, opponents said it would do more.

H Res 427 deleted the House rule setting the 30 percent limit, and specified that the only limit on outside income would be that fixed by law — in other words, the 40 percent limit imposed by PL 99-190.

Critics charged this would eliminate limits on outside income from sources other than honoraria. They noted that under the House rule, the 30 percent limit applied to all outside income, including professional fees; the 40 percent limit established by law applied only to honoraria.

James H. Quillen of Tennessee, ranking Republican on the Rules Committee, argued that limits on outside income relegated House members to the status of "second-class citizens."

"I don't see what's wrong with our free-enterprise system," he said.

But others warned against increasing members' dependence on outside sources of income, saying that any added remuneration should come from a salary hike.

Richard J. Durbin, D-Ill., who urged reinstatement of the 30 percent limit, argued that Congress should not be boosting its own earnings at a time when federal budget cuts were forcing others to make do with less.

"This is the wrong thing to do, the wrong time to do it and the wrong way to approach it," said Durbin.

Murtha Replays 1981 Maneuver

The April 22 maneuver was a replay of action in 1981, when the House raised the ceiling on outside income from 15 percent of a member's salary to 30 percent. *(1981 Almanac p. 400)*

Murtha, who had close ties with the Democratic leadership, brought up the 1981 measure without notice before a virtually empty chamber, and pushed it through in seconds.

Similarly, after Murtha introduced H Res 427 April 22, he brought it to the floor under expedited procedures that circumvented committee consideration. The resolution was approved by unanimous consent.

O'Neill was presiding at the time, but he later claimed that he had been taken by surprise by the move, as did Minority Leader Robert H. Michel, R-Ill., and Majority Whip Thomas S. Foley, D-Wash.

"This was so inside, even the insiders didn't know about it," said Charles E. Schumer, D-N.Y.

However, Minority Whip Trent Lott, R-Miss., who was on the floor at the time, said House leaders knew such a measure would come up "at some point," even if they were unaware of the exact timing. O'Neill said there had been "common talk" about lifting the earnings cap ever since the Senate raised its limit.

The fast-track consideration of the resolution drew fire from Robert S. Walker, R-Pa., who came to the floor after the measure was approved and called Murtha's maneuver an "end run on the committee process."

Responding to criticisms of the procedure, O'Neill told reporters, "It is the only way I think you can get something of that nature through. If you have to stand for a roll call, it's going to lose."

Undoing the Deed

Democratic leaders came under heavy attack from party members during an April 23 meeting of the majority whip's organization. Faced with angry complaints about the Murtha resolution and the way it was handled, O'Neill agreed to give members the opportunity to vote on overturning it.

That apparently helped derail a strategy Walker had devised to undo the previous day's vote. Walker urged members to vote against approval of the April 22 *Journal* — thus opening it to amendments. He then hoped to nullify the House's action on the Murtha resolution. However, the House approved the *Journal*, 215-178. *(Vote 86, p. 28-H)*

Durbin then brought up a measure (H Res 431) vacating the proceedings by which the Murtha resolution had been approved, thereby restoring prior restrictions on outside income. Taking a page from Murtha's book, Durbin tried to bring his resolution directly to the floor by unanimous consent. That was blocked by Lott, sending the matter to the Rules Committee.

The committee met that afternoon, approved by voice vote a similar measure (H Res 432) to reverse the Murtha resolution, and sent it to the floor.

In a key procedural move, members voted 333-68 to consider the new measure, and thus reimpose the old limit. *(Vote 89, p. 28-H)*

The resolution itself, like the one lifting the cap, was then approved by voice vote.

Off the floor, members voiced anger and embarrassment at the way the boost in the earnings limit had been approved April 22.

"If they want to increase members' compensation, it should be done through the front door" — by increasing salaries — said David R. Obey, D-Wis., who was the principal author of the original 1977 rule limiting members' outside income. "Our primary responsibility is to represent taxpayers, not the people who provide speaking fees." *(Background, 1977 Almanac p. 763)*

Lott said the roll-call vote sent members "running for the bushes like whipped pups."

"I hope some day members have the courage to stand up and confront these issues," he said.

Outside Earnings Grow in 1985

House members collected almost one-third more in speaking fees and other honoraria in 1985 than they did the year before, according to a study by Common Cause, the self-styled citizens' lobby.

Based on an analysis of House members' financial disclosure forms, Common Cause calculated that the 420 House members who filed the documents had received a total of $4.6 million in honoraria. In 1984, members reported receiving $3.5 million.

In the Senate, Common Cause said, honoraria earnings hit a total of $2.4 million — up 20 percent from the year before.

Of that total, some $723,038 was donated to charity, leaving about $1.7 million in senators' pockets.

Top Earners: House

Party leaders, committee chairmen and members of the tax-writing committees were top earners of honoraria in both chambers.

In the House, Ways and Means Committee Chairman Dan Rostenkowski, D-Ill., who received $137,500, and O'Neill, who drew $88,000 in honoraria, led the list.

Twenty of the 39 members who earned $25,000 or more served on the Ways and Means Committee, which in 1985 wrote a major tax overhaul bill (HR 3838); 11 others were either committee chairmen or held top party leadership posts. *(Tax bill, p. 491)*

For the average House member, however, the speaking circuit was far less lucrative. About half the House (217 members) received less than $7,000 apiece in honoraria.

And only about one-fifth of House members (94 lawmakers) reported receiving at least $20,000 in honoraria, compared with about two-thirds of all senators.

Fourteen House members had not completed their 1985 disclosure forms and were granted extensions of the May 15 filing deadline. One House seat was vacant.

House rules prohibit members from keeping outside earned income, including honoraria, in excess of an amount equal to 30 percent of their salaries. In 1985, the cap was $22,467. A member's salary was $75,100, but because of bookkeeping practices, the amount actually disbursed in calendar year 1985 was $74,891.

Members of the leadership could keep more in outside income because they received higher salaries: The Speaker earned $97,900 and the majority and minority leaders earned $85,000.

Members whose earnings from honoraria exceeded the 30 percent cap had to donate the surplus to charity. Of the $4.6 million in honoraria received by House members, $847,834 was donated to charity.

Top Earners: Senate

In the Senate, the top earner was Robert Dole, R-Kan., who was both the majority leader and a member of the Finance Committee. He received $127,993 in honoraria, and gave all but $21,375 to charity.

Three senators did not file disclosure reports by the May 15 deadline — Lawton Chiles, D-Fla.; Jeff Bingaman, D-N.M.; and Malcolm Wallop, R-Wyo. They were granted filing extensions.

In its study of financial disclosure forms, Common Cause found that 65 senators — roughly two-thirds of the entire membership — reported keeping at least $20,000 in honoraria.

Ten senators accepted no honoraria in 1985 and two others — William L. Armstrong, R-Colo., and John Heinz, R-Pa. — gave all they collected to charity.

Thirteen senators received honoraria totaling $40,000 or more. Five of the top earners were committee chairmen, and the list included six members of the Finance Committee in addition to Dole: John H. Chafee, R-R.I.; Charles E. Grassley, R-Iowa; Bill Bradley, D-N.J.; Daniel Patrick Moynihan, D-N.Y.; Steven D. Symms, R-Idaho; and William V. Roth Jr., R-Del. ∎

Gramm-Rudman Hits Home

Under the 1985 Gramm-Rudman-Hollings anti-deficit law (PL 99-177), the legislative branch on March 1 suffered the same 4.3 percent across-the-board budget cut as most federal programs and agencies.

That amounted to a $62 million reduction in outlays from the $1.4 billion appropriated for Congress and legislative agencies for fiscal 1986.

Lawmakers responded to the mandated cuts in a variety of ways, some of which were cheered and others jeered.

When Democratic leaders announced in April that the House of Representatives would no longer hold late-night sessions, some members viewed it as a silver lining in the cloud of Gramm-Rudman budget-cutting.

Less Talk, Less Mail

House leaders said April 10 that they wanted to finish legislative business by 7 p.m. daily to avoid paying overtime to Capitol police and other personnel. Majority Whip Thomas S. Foley, D-Wash., said the new policy would not only save money but also provide a "degree of welcome predictability in the affairs of the House."

Minority Whip Trent Lott, R-Miss., said, "Frankly, I think it is an excellent idea that we not stay in past 7 o'clock, because we usually mess things up when we do."

However, members were less sanguine about other changes taking place as federal budget-cutting hit Congress where it hurt. The most politically sensitive pinch was felt in Congress' mailing budget, as members confronted a huge shortfall in funding for their cherished postal privileges. *(Mail cuts, p. 40)*

Other Types of Cuts

There were numerous other ways in which Congress got a taste of its own fiscal medicine, as cuts mandated by Gramm-Rudman-Hollings forced new curbs on congressional services and staff. For example:

- Sharp restrictions were imposed on the printing and distribution of congressional documents. Starting June 2, the general public had to pay if they wanted more than one copy of a document. Only members and congressional staff could continue to get bills and reports for free.
- Personnel cuts in the House resulted in delays of more than three weeks in getting members' newsletters into the mail.
- Many members, committees and congressional officers cut salary expenses through hiring freezes, layoffs and furloughs. Offices sought additional savings by such moves as limiting long-distance phone calls and halting staff travel.

Curbing Public Access?

The Government Printing Office (GPO) had to absorb a $3 million cut in its fiscal 1986 budget for congressional publications.

Some members and aides said the new austerity measures would limit the public's access to Congress and undermine lawmakers' ability to respond to constituents. "All these things are going to make it impossible for Congress to do what it is supposed to do for the American people," said one senior House committee official.

Others, however, said that constraints on spending for publications, office expenses and other aspects of congressional life provided a useful opportunity to eliminate waste.

"There are a lot of hearings printed, reports printed for which there is no demand," said Garner J. Cline, staff director of the House Judiciary Committee. "Maybe we should stop, look around and see whether this ill-designed Gramm-Rudman law can be a blessing in disguise and make the organization more efficient."

GPO set up an office in the Senate Document Room where the public could buy publications previously distributed free by the House and Senate document rooms — bills, public laws and reports accompanying legislation sent to the floor.

Sharp limits were imposed on the printing and distribution of other committee publications, such as hearing transcripts and investigative reports. As of April 14, no more than 300 copies of any document were printed for a committee — down from the current 1,000 cap. It was up to each committee to decide how to regulate distribution of its own document supply.

The 300-copy cap on committee documents was likely to have the greatest effect on non-legislative panels, such as the Senate Special Committee on Aging, whose principal products were reports that in the past had been widely distributed.

Sens. John Heinz, R-Pa., and John Glenn, D-Ohio, chairman and ranking Democrat of the Senate Aging panel, urged the Joint Committee on Printing to give special consideration to non-legislative committees.

"Special and select committees are set up by the House and Senate ... to fulfill an information and oversight need not supplied by the legislative committees," Heinz and Glenn said in an April 9 letter to the joint committee. Such panels had "a compelling need for adequate quantities of those documents which we believe ought to be distributed widely."

In other changes affecting congressional publications:

- The number of *Congressional Records* distributed to members and committees was cut.
- Congressional committees were urged to reduce or eliminate overtime hours for GPO printers who were detailed to work with them.
- The format of the House business calendar, which provided information on the status of pending legislation, was revised. The new format provided full legislative information only once a week, with abbreviated updates provided on other days.

Mail Backlogs

In an area of particular interest to members in an election year, staff reductions slowed the job of getting mail into and out of the Capitol.

House members were warned of significant — and lengthening — delays in the processing of newsletters and other outgoing mail. The Publications Distribution Service, which folded and prepared certain items for mailing, in early April faced a backlog of 18 million pieces.

The problem arose, officials said, because the distribution service could not hire the extra staff needed during an election year.

Staffing restrictions in the House Postmaster's Office also slowed the movement of mail. House Postmaster Robert V. Rota reported a two-day delay after mail arrived at the Capitol before it was delivered to members' offices. To free more personnel for sorting mail, deliveries to members' offices were cut from four to three times a day.

Clerks, Computers, Pages

In other areas, the Office of the House Clerk laid off about 15 employees and imposed a hiring freeze.

Staffing at the Senate computer center dropped from 206 to 183 between March 1 and mid-April, mostly due to resignations, according to Victor Ferreros, director of the office. "Some of those vacancies are not going to be filled because of budget cuts," he said.

Officials in both the House and Senate considered reductions in the summer page program. An aide to the House Administration Committee said that the idea of eliminating the summer program entirely was floated earlier in the year, but was not well received by members.

"These are patronage jobs. A lot of commitments already have been made," said the aide.

In another money-saving move, the House suspended an internship program, named after Lyndon B. Johnson, which provided stipends for an intern in each member's office.

Committee Savings

Senate and House committees also scrambled to accommodate cuts in their operating budgets.

The House Foreign Affairs Committee put each staff member on furlough one day a month. The panel also limited each subcommittee's long-distance phone budget to $45 a month, eliminated domestic travel and sharply cut back its newspaper subscriptions.

The Senate Foreign Relations Committee reduced its staff by about five people by attrition in the first quarter of the year, a spokesman said. The staff was encouraged to make long-distance telephone calls only after 5 p.m., when the rates went down.

Like many other offices, the House Judiciary Committee decided not to fill vacancies that opened up. That policy created a stir early in 1986, when the Republican counsel to the Subcommittee on Civil and Constitutional Rights left. The hiring freeze prevented F. James Sensenbrenner Jr., R-Wis., ranking minority member on the panel, from hiring a replacement. In protest, Sensenbrenner led a Republican boycott of subcommittee meetings until he was authorized in March to hire a new subcommittee counsel.

In another austerity move, the Judiciary Committee stopped paying witnesses' expenses for traveling to Washington for hearings. Cline, the staff director, said the policy had not prevented anyone from testifying.

"People will be forthcoming — they'll come to the mountain," said Cline. However, he acknowledged that the policy might eventually cause difficulties in areas such as civil rights legislation, where some potential witnesses "are not in a financial posture to spend a good deal of money to come to Washington."

"That could be a problem," said Cline, "but we'll face it when the time comes."

Caucus Cuts

Some lawmakers turned a cold eye on the dues they paid to congressional caucuses devoted to special interests ranging from the arts to women's issues.

Rep. James M. Jeffords, R-Vt., for example, saved $8,400 by dropping memberships in seven caucuses, including groups associated with the environment, arms control and rural issues.

"I didn't want to do it because I find them very valuable," Jeffords said, "but it was a choice between that and closing one of the district offices, or relieving more people on the staff."

Caucus financing came largely from dues and other contributions from members' office accounts.

"I'm not sure what the future holds for this kind of group," said William A. Connelly, executive director of the Congressional Sun Belt Council, a caucus of Southern members. "We'll know more by the end of the year, but I guess we're an endangered species."

The House Administration Committee certified 35 caucuses, officially called "legislative service organizations."

There was no official Senate count, because caucuses there did not need to be certified, but the "1985 Congressional Staff Directory" listed 13.

Some members were glad to see the caucuses in a bind. "These caucuses are financed by the federal Treasury and are by their nature lobbies," said Rep. Charles E. Bennett, D-Fla. "And I don't think the federal Treasury ought to be financing lobbying groups." ∎

Senate Moves to Curb Its Own Mailing Costs

Congress included $91.4 million for its own mailing costs in the continuing appropriations resolution (H J Res 738 — PL 99-591) for fiscal 1987, after dropping a Senate-passed provision that would have divided the funds equally between the two chambers.

All year, members stewed and squabbled over the likelihood that they would exceed the $95.7 million in fiscal 1986 funding available to support the franking privilege, which allowed senators and House members to send mail to constituents at taxpayers' expense.

In the end, though, restraints imposed formally in the Senate — and by informal methods in the House — kept the postal budget within bounds. And the Senate decided to continue its curbs in fiscal 1987.

Bid for Fiscal 1986 Supplemental

A move by the House Appropriations Committee to provide added money for congressional mail in fiscal 1986, when many other government programs were being cut, renewed a simmering controversy over Congress' postal privileges.

The Appropriations Committee included $42.2 million for Congress' mail in a $1.7 billion omnibus supplemental spending bill (HR 4515 — H Rept 99-510) it approved March 20. That was a 42 percent increase over the $100 million originally appropriated for fiscal 1986, and it would have more than offset a $4.3 million cut made in February as part of the across-the-board reductions required by the new Gramm-Rudman-Hollings anti-deficit law (PL 99-177). That cut had dropped the total appropriation to $95.7 million. *(Legislative budget cuts, p. 38)*

Without an increase, the postal account could run out in May, warned James S. Stanford, manager of the Postal Service's official-mail branch. Since 1986 was an election year, members did not want their mailing fund to dry up.

The franking privilege allowed members of Congress to send their constituents newsletters, press releases, meeting notices, calendars and other mail simply by stamping their signatures on the envelope.

In theory, the practice was limited by the size of Congress' annual appropriation for reimbursing the Postal Service, but members typically increased the account as it was depleted.

Election-Year Maneuvers

Congress purposely underestimated its mailing expenses when it approved fiscal 1986 appropriations for the legislative branch in 1985. Although staff projected that franked mail would cost $144.4 million, Congress voted only $100 million to help keep its overall budget ostensibly frozen at 1985 levels. Several members denounced the move at the time. Rep. Bill Frenzel, R-Minn., called it a "shell game," adding with considerable prescience, "Instead of finding a pea under the shell, you find a supplemental [spending bill]." *(1985 Almanac p. 326)*

In February, Stanford's office notified members that, unless they cut back, Congress would spend $146.2 million in fiscal 1986, $50.5 million more than appropriated.

That would have handily broken the $111 million record set in election-year 1984, which in turn broke 1982's record of $100 million. Since the 1982 elections, there had been only one postal rate increase, in February 1985.

The Appropriations Committee approved the $42.2 million franking increase by voice vote, along with several related changes in House franking rules that Vic Fazio, D-Calif., chairman of the Subcommittee on the Legislative Branch, said could save $8.25 million.

The rules changes were negotiated by a bipartisan House group named by Speaker Thomas P. O'Neill Jr., D-Mass. They included proposals for 1986 that reduced the number of mass-mailing newsletters from six to four, limited town-meeting notices to one per household, required certain materials without time value (such as calendars) to be mailed at the lowest postal rate, and required members to submit mailings to Congress' franking commission for possible advice on cost-saving measures.

The negotiators included both Republicans and Democrats who served on the franking commission and the Post Office and Civil Service Committee. The Republicans — Frenzel, Gene Taylor, Mo., and Jerry Lewis, Calif. — "have agreed to support the supplemental," a House Republican aide said, "but I'm not too sure there is widespread support among other House Republicans."

Fazio, acknowledging criticism from the Senate and potential complaints from House Republicans, suggested in a March 27 interview, "I'm not sure we're going to proceed [with the $42.2 million supplemental appropriation].... I have no desire to be set up by a couple people who are demagoguing the issue."

A Ban on Newsletters?

On March 27, Sens. Pete Wilson, R-Calif., David L. Boren, D-Okla., and John C. Danforth, R-Mo., introduced a bill (S 2255) to eliminate funding for congressional newsletters.

They estimated 75 percent of the Senate's mailing costs was due to unsolicited newsletters, which Wilson denounced as "campaigning at taxpayers' expense," while 23 percent was for town-meeting notices and only 2 percent for press releases and responses to constituents.

House members, and some senators, claimed a rise in constituent mail was responsible for higher franking costs. But because the House kept no data on types of mail sent out, or on individual members' mailing costs, the claim was impossible to prove. Opponents of franking increases said House costs of replying to constituents, like the Senate's, were small compared with the newsletters' expense.

Backing Off

After reports of the attempt to boost the free-mail subsidy received widespread publicity, Fazio and the Appropriations Committee decided to back off.

The House Rules Committee April 10 adopted a rule governing floor action on HR 4515 that included, at Fazio's request, language deleting the added mail appropriation upon adoption of the rule.

The House approved the rule April 15, thereby ending the fight over appropriating more funds for fiscal 1986, and shifting the focus to conserving the remaining funds. *(Fiscal 1986 supplemental, p. 153)*

Making Do

The Senate Rules and Administration Committee April 16 approved a measure (S Res 374) to limit each senator's mailing allowance for the rest of the fiscal year.

The measure, approved by voice vote, allotted each senator a fixed sum for remaining fiscal 1986 mailing expenses, under a formula designed to keep overall mail costs within the $95.7 million appropriated for the year.

The resolution approved by the Senate panel did not apply to the House. Committee members acknowledged that without similar action by the House, the Senate measure alone would not solve the immediate mail funding problem facing Congress.

The committee also debated, but then laid aside, a revised version of S 2272, whose principal sponsor was Dan Quayle, R-Ind. The revision represented a compromise between Quayle and Wilson, who had introduced a bill (S 2255) to cut off federal funding for mailing congressional newsletters.

The compromise prohibited unsolicited mass mailings, but imposed no restrictions on what members could send to constituents who had communicated with them.

The bill also set up permanently a rationing mechanism, similar to the one included in S Res 374, to give both House members and senators a set mail budget each year rather than having the frank operate essentially as an open-ended entitlement.

The committee laid aside S 2272 after some members said they wanted more time to consider what Charles McC. Mathias Jr., R-Md., described as a "serious change in procedure."

The Frank a Blank Check?

The franking debate was given a new twist by a May 2 ruling by the U.S. comptroller general, who interpreted the franking law as effectively giving Congress a blank check.

In response to a query from three senators, the comptroller general said that whatever Congress appropriated for its mail had to be accepted as payment in full by the U.S. Postal Service. If funding fell short, the Postal Service had to swallow the loss.

The ruling appeared to undermine any incentive for Congress to bring its postal spending under control, but it fanned the fury of those seeking new restrictions on the frank.

"We have created such a marvel — perhaps such a monster — that we can spend the whole additional $42 million without ever having to appropriate one nickel," said Quayle.

Senate Passes Curb on Own Mail

The Senate finally decided not to risk such a move. On May 14, it approved S Res 374 by voice vote.

The measure, sponsored by Mathias and Wendell H. Ford, D-Ky., took effect in the Senate upon adoption. It was approved by the Rules Committee on April 16 (S Rept 99-285).

Although the Senate passed a second resolution (S Con Res 139) that would have imposed a similar system for rationing mail funds on both chambers, that plan went nowhere.

"The whole House is up for re-election this year, and only one-third of the Senate," said one House aide. "A lot of those guys can afford to be above the fray" and propose limits on the frank, the staffer added.

S Res 374 imposed a seven-day moratorium on mass

mailings while Senate officials determined how much money remained for fiscal 1986 — an amount estimated at about $20 million as of May 15. Half the money was assumed to be available to the Senate. Funds were divided among senators based on their states' populations.

Members' allotments for the rest of fiscal 1986 ranged from $10,154 for each of the senators from Wyoming to $525,943 for the senators from California.

By the end of July, congressional officials said the funding shortfall would be far smaller than expected.

Fiscal 1987 Funding Bill

On Aug. 13, the Senate approved an amendment to the fiscal 1987 legislative branch appropriations bill (HR 5203) to set up separate appropriations accounts for House and Senate mail.

The amendment, offered by Ford, split the postal funds for fiscal 1987 equally between the 435-member House and the 100-member Senate. Historically, the House had spent considerably more than half of the mailing allowance.

"The Senate has proved it can live within its means," said Ford. "This amendment is designed to ensure that the House of Representatives does the same."

The Ford amendment also required Congress to appropriate enough money each year to cover its full mailing costs — to avoid the "blank check" problem cited by the comptroller general.

As expected, the proposed 50-50 funding split did not sit well with the House. The Ford amendment was dropped from the compromise version of HR 5203 (H Rept 99-805) that was drafted Aug. 15 by a conference committee. It thus did not survive in the final legislative appropriations included in the continuing resolution for fiscal 1987.

Senate Allocates Fiscal 1987 Funds

By voice vote, the Senate Oct. 8 approved a resolution (S Res 500) allocating funds to pay for senators' official mail in fiscal 1987, which began Oct. 1.

Ford, who sponsored the resolution, said it would continue the cost-saving steps first implemented in fiscal 1986 under S Res 374.

Ford told senators Oct. 8 the earlier resolution had successfully cut costs. In entreating them to pass the new one for fiscal 1987, he asked, "Are we going to go back to the days when we treated our mail like a 'sacred cow'? Or are we going to continue to accept the same kind of fiscal restraint that the American people are demanding?"

Under S Res 500, senators from states with small populations were allotted $100,000 apiece for mailing costs, while California's two senators received the top allocation — $2,100,478 each.

S Res 500, like the earlier resolution, covered only senators' mail costs. The House continued to resist Senate pleas that it adopt a similar measure. ▮

PAC Spending Limits

The Senate Aug. 11 went on record twice in favor of strict new controls on campaign fund raising, but in the end failed to pass legislation to that effect.

On a 69-30 vote, the Senate approved a proposal by David L. Boren, D-Okla., to limit the amount of money that political action committees (PACs) could give congressional candidates.

Then, on a 58-42 roll call, the Senate approved a GOP countermeasure by Rudy Boschwitz, Minn., to stifle PAC contributions to political parties and force party operations to disclose all hidden sources of their funds. *(Votes 209, 210, p. 37-S)*

Both amendments were attached to an unrelated bill (S 655) that had been stripped of its other provisions in 1985.

Republican leaders were willing to press for passage of S 655, and Boren and other Democrats were ready to go along. But Boschwitz blocked a final vote on the grounds that the issues had become lost in partisan gamesmanship.

Boren seemed content with the recorded vote in favor of his proposal. "This is not a vote they could cast without it coming back to haunt them," Boren said afterward. "This cause has a momentum now. It's not going to be stopped."

Boren Proposal

Boren had been pressing for Senate action on his PAC-limitation measure since January. The Senate had sidestepped a definitive vote on the issue in December 1985, but Boren was promised a floor vote in 1986. *(Previous action, 1985 Almanac p. 33)*

The Boren proposal would have:

- Limited overall PAC contributions to $100,000 for House candidates and between $175,000 and $750,000 for Senate candidates, depending on the populations in their states. Increases would have been permitted to allow for contested primaries and runoff elections.
- Reduced from $5,000 to $3,000 the ceiling on individual PAC contributions, while increasing the limit on maximum individual gifts to $1,500 from $1,000.
- Closed a loophole in existing campaign finance law that allowed a PAC to exceed existing limits by "bundling" further donations from individuals and passing those on to candidates in the PAC's name.
- Required television and radio broadcasters to provide free response time to candidates opposed by groups operating "independent expenditure" campaigns.

Boren and other supporters of PAC limits repeatedly invoked statistics that showed PAC spending on congressional campaigns had risen nearly tenfold in the past decade. In 1974, 608 PACs gave candidates for Congress a total of $12.5 million. In the 1984 campaigns, House and Senate candidates received $104 million from 4,000 registered PACs.

The rise in the number of PACs and their influence in political campaigns had put lawmakers on the defensive against a public perception that special-interest groups had undue influence on politicians.

"We have formalized and legalized political corruption," said Sen. William Proxmire, D-Wis.

Senate Minority Leader Robert C. Byrd, D-W.Va., complained bitterly that legislators had become obsessed with raising money for their re-election campaigns. "It's going to kill this institution," he said.

Boschwitz Countermeasure

Opponents of the proposed limits insisted that Boren's bill would do little to contain the flow of PAC money into campaigns, because PACs would merely funnel their funds into more negative advertising and other forms of "independent" expenditures.

"The Boren plan will only worsen the problems that he seeks to resolve," Boschwitz said, adding that PACs were formed in the post-Watergate era of the mid-1970s as a result of campaign reforms that sought to control the influence of wealthy individuals.

Boschwitz became the point man for Republican opposition to the Boren plan when Dole appointed him to head a special GOP task force to come up with an alternative.

Boschwitz came back with a countermeasure to prohibit PAC contributions to national political parties, which included the partisan campaign committees run by leaders of the House and Senate.

Boschwitz' amendment also would have required political parties to disclose the so-called "soft money" they accepted from corporations, unions and other donors that currently went unreported.

Soft money was used for general "party-building" purposes, such as paying for campaign headquarters or bolstering the coffers of state party organizations, rather than for a particular candidate's campaign. The practice allowed wealthy donors to exceed limits on individual contributions and allowed party organizations to provide indirect support for candidates with money that would be illegal if given directly to a candidate.

Boschwitz' amendment was assailed as a blatantly partisan attempt to embarrass Democrats, who traditionally relied more heavily on PAC contributions to party organizations than did Republicans, who got most of their donations from individuals.

In the 1984 congressional elections, national Democratic Party organizations, such as the Democratic Senatorial Campaign Committee (DSCC) and the Democratic Congressional Campaign Committee (DCCC), received $6.5 million in contributions from PACs, compared with $58.3 million from individuals, according to the Federal Election Commission (FEC).

Republican organizations, including the National Republican Senatorial Committee (NRSC) and the National Republican Congressional Committee (NRCC), received only $1.7 million from PACs, compared with $262 million from individual contributors.

Sen. George J. Mitchell of Maine, chairman of the DSCC, called the Boschwitz amendment a "plainly, openly, cynically partisan" attempt to give Republicans an even bigger edge in campaign fund raising. "If those figures were reversed, there would be no attempt to offer this amendment," Mitchell said.

Boschwitz acknowledged that his amendment was crafted with a political strategy in mind. The amendment and the rules governing the two votes were designed to give Republicans a way to vote successively for the Boren amendment and the Boschwitz alternative, working on the assumption that the Democratic-controlled House would probably not want to act on a bill that contained both measures. ▮

Senate TV Coverage

Following a successful two-month test period, the Senate July 29 decided to permit permanent live television coverage of its floor proceedings.

The 78-21 vote to allow gavel-to-gavel live coverage came seven years after the House began broadcasting its floor action and five months after the Senate first agreed to experiment with publicly televised debates.

Foes of live broadcasts bemoaned to the end what they foresaw as the demise of their body's historic role as the slower, more deliberative chamber of Congress. "My fundamental objection to television is rooted in my deep concern that television in the Senate will result in an increase in political expediency at the expense of statesmanship," said Russell B. Long, D-La., on July 29. No one had fought TV in the Senate longer or harder than Long.

Albert Gore Jr., D-Tenn., sought to allay such fears with release of a Library of Congress study of the test period concluding, "Television coverage has changed the patterns of Senate floor activity very little." The study, which surveyed 20 types of floor activity, found that the only change clearly traceable to TV was a 250 percent increase in the number of "special orders," or speeches that senators made on a variety of subjects, before the start of regular business.

"Television has not disrupted the institution of the Senate," Gore said. "If anything, television has helped to keep the Senate on its toes."

The Test Period

The Senate first approved a resolution (S Res 28) allowing radio and television broadcasts on Feb. 27. But the measure required a two-step test and a second vote July 29 before TV coverage could become permanent.

The test started May 1 with closed-circuit transmissions to legislative offices. On June 2 public broadcasts began. Cameras were supposed to be turned off for two weeks before the final vote, so senators could assess the results, but the Senate agreed July 15 to reduce the blackout to three days.

By its 78-21 vote on July 29, the Senate affirmed that radio and television coverage of the Senate should continue permanently, in effect giving final approval to S Res 28. The vote also made permanent several rules changes tentatively adopted as part of that resolution. The major change reduced to 30 hours, from 100, the time allowed for debate after senators voted to invoke cloture to halt a filibuster.

The Final Step

The decision to continue live radio and TV broadcasts of the Senate was the "final step of a long journey," said Charles McC. Mathias Jr., R-Md. Rep. Claude Pepper, D-Fla., had first proposed broadcasting proceedings of Congress when he was a senator in 1947.

The successful drive dated to an effort begun by then-Majority Leader Howard H. Baker Jr., R-Tenn. (1967-85), in 1981. The Senate failed to overcome filibusters against broadcasting measures in 1981, 1982 and 1984. *(1984 Almanac p. 209; 1982 Almanac p. 540; 1981 Almanac p. 391)*

The House began televising its proceedings in 1979. *(Congress and the Nation Vol. V, p. 919)*

As in the House, the Senate broadcast signal was controlled by congressional staff and made available to public and commercial stations. Most stations used excerpts on newscasts, but the Cable Satellite Public Affairs Network (C-SPAN) provided live satellite signals to its 2,300 cable TV affiliates. Though 25.5 million households could watch House proceedings, the potential Senate audience was about one-third that size, mainly because many cable stations lacked the extra channel space required for coverage of both chambers.

Action on S Res 28

Following 11 days of debate on S Res 28, the Senate Feb. 27 agreed to allow radio and television broadcasts of

Senate Cloture Votes, 1985-86

Following is a list of all cloture votes taken by the Senate during the 99th Congress. Motions to limit debate by invoking cloture required a three-fifths majority of the total Senate (60 if there were no vacancies), under a revised version of the Senate filibuster rule (Rule 22) adopted in 1975.

That revision applied to any matter except proposed rules changes, for which the previous requirement of a two-thirds majority of senators present and voting still applied.

The 14 cloture votes taken in 1986 brought to 229 the total number of cloture votes taken since 1917, when Rule 22 was adopted; 80 of the votes were successful. Successful 1985-86 cloture votes are indicated in **boldface type.** *(Previous votes, 1985 Almanac p. 27, 1977 Almanac p. 813)*

Issue	Date	Vote	Yeas Needed
Anti-Apartheid	**July 10, 1985**	**88-8**	**60**
Line-item Veto	July 18, 1985	57-42	60
Line-item Veto	July 23, 1985	57-41	60
Line-item Veto	July 24, 1985	58-40	60
Anti-Apartheid	Sept. 9, 1985	53-34	60
Anti-Apartheid	Sept. 11, 1985	57-41	60
Anti-Apartheid	Sept. 12, 1985	11-88	60
Debt Limit/Balanced Budget	Oct. 6, 1985	57-38	64†
Debt Limit/Balanced Budget	Oct. 9, 1985*	53-39	62†
Conrail Sale	**Jan. 23, 1986**	**90-7**	**60**
Conrail Sale	**Jan. 30, 1986**	**70-27**	**60**
Fitzwater Nomination	**March 18, 1986**	**64-33**	**60**
Washington Airports Transfer	March 21, 1986	50-39	60
Washington Airports Transfer	**March 25, 1986**	**66-32**	**60**
Hobbs Act Amendments	April 16, 1986	44-54	60
Defense Authorization, Fiscal 1987	Aug. 6, 1986	53-46	60
Military Construction Appropriations, Fiscal 1987 (Aid to Contras)	Aug. 13, 1986	59-40	60
South Africa Sanctions	**Aug. 13, 1986**	**89-11**	**60**
Military Construction Appropriations, Fiscal 1987 (Aid to Contras)	**Aug. 13, 1986**	**62-37**	**60**
Rehnquist Nomination	**Sept. 17, 1986**	**68-31**	**60**
Product Liability Reform	**Sept. 25, 1986**	**97-1**	**60**
Omnibus Drug Bill	Oct. 15, 1986	58-38	60
Immigration Reform	**Oct. 17, 1986**	**69-21**	**60**

** Vote was taken after midnight in the session that began Oct. 8.*
† Senate rules change; two-thirds majority required.

its floor debates on a test basis. S Res 28, which was approved on a 67-21 vote, had been reported (S Rept 99-190) by the Senate Rules and Administration Committee in 1985. *(Vote 24, p. 5-S; committee action, 1985 Almanac p. 31)*

As approved by the Senate, the resolution provided that radio and TV broadcasting begin no later than May 1. While radio service would be live and publicly available from the start, television would be limited to Senate offices until June 1.

From June 1 through July 15, live TV could be broadcast to the public. On July 15, both radio and TV would cease for two weeks. On July 29, the Senate would vote on whether to make broadcasting permanent, or to extend test coverage another 30 days before a final vote.

Cameras would be operated by Senate staff and would be fixed on the speaker — a senator, the presiding officer, chaplain or clerks. During roll-call votes, but only then, the camera could pan the chamber. Coverage was prohibited during closed sessions and during quorum calls, which were used to stall while senators conferred on or off the floor.

Earlier versions of the resolution provided for closed-circuit TV coverage only. The change allowing public coverage was added after private negotiations among several senators, including Majority Leader Robert Dole, R-Kan., who argued that a real test should include such coverage.

Also, the resolution initially had required a vote on broadcasting on the last day of the test period. The two-week waiting period was a last-minute amendment from a TV opponent, David L. Boren, D-Okla.

Boren offered that amendment, and said he had several others in hand, just as Senate leaders thought they were prepared for a final vote on S Res 28 late Feb. 27. Fearing an unexpected filibuster, Minority Leader Robert C. Byrd, D-W.Va., the resolution's sponsor, offered to accept the waiting-period blackout and implored Boren to drop his other demands. Boren agreed, clearing the way for approval.

Rules Change Proposals

Members shied away from making several sweeping rules changes that had been proposed to quicken the pace and sharpen the focus of Senate proceedings for listeners and viewers. In the end, only one significant rules change was adopted — a reduction to 30 hours, from 100, in the time allowed for debate, procedural moves and roll calls after the Senate had voted to invoke "cloture," thereby ending a filibuster.

The Senate also decided to make non-debatable a motion to approve the *Journal* to date. That step was designed to permit Senate leaders to override, by a fast majority vote, demands that the *Journal* be read aloud, a time-consuming tactic often used by senators seeking to stall action on legislation.

As introduced by Byrd in 1985, the resolution included a number of Senate rules changes, but they were stripped by the Rules Committee after several senators warned that those proposals could sink the radio-TV plan.

When S Res 28 came to the floor Feb. 3, however, it became clear that many members would not support the measure unless it was linked to rules changes that would force the Senate to accommodate the faster pace of television.

Compromise Rules Package. On Feb. 20, the Senate added to the resolution a compromise rules package that would have made the most far-reaching changes in Senate practices since the 1970s. The vote was 81-9. *(Vote 18, p. 4-S)*

One rules change would have ended filibusters on motions to take up legislation by limiting debate to two hours, a change that Dole particularly wanted.

Another, pushed by Long, would have required amendments to be germane to a bill if three-fifths of the Senate so decided.

A third change would have raised from 60 votes to two-thirds of those present and voting (67 if all members were present) the votes required to invoke cloture. In exchange, it would have slashed to 20 hours the time allotted for debate after cloture had been invoked. *(1985-86 cloture votes, box, p. 44)*

Byrd said the rules changes were needed not only to make the Senate more efficient and telegenic, but also to win the votes of senators who would not otherwise support the radio-TV plan. Byrd and Dole introduced the package after extensive private negotiations with a bipartisan group of senators.

Changes Dropped. On Feb. 26, the Senate voted 60-37 for a motion by William L. Armstrong, R-Colo., to drop the germaneness provision that Long wanted. *(Vote 20, p. 5-S)*

The vote followed no clear partisan or ideological lines. But many of those who voted with Armstrong to maintain the Senate policy of allowing unrelated amendments on bills were the Senate's most liberal or conservative members, who would be unable to force floor votes on pet measures such as anti-abortion bills unless those bills could be offered as amendments to unrelated legislation. (Under existing Senate rules, amendments had to be germane only after cloture was invoked.)

"I am willing to vote on their issues, be it abortion or gun control or whatever," Long said. "But to have to vote on various versions of that proposal on different bills many, many times during a session is really asking too much.... They do not have a right to have the amendment voted on every bill that passes the Senate."

But Armstrong countered, "It comes down to a very simple proposition of whether or not the majority of the Senate should deny, or have the power to deny, the minority the right to offer an amendment. I think the answer to that question is ... no."

The next day, Feb. 27, sponsors voluntarily dropped the provision limiting debate on motions to begin consideration of a measure.

They also scrapped the move to raise the threshold for invoking cloture, keeping the existing 60-vote requirement. Armstrong said the retreat came because "Common Cause hot-boxed the Democrats."

President Fred Wertheimer of Common Cause, the self-described citizens' lobby, acknowledged that his group opposed the change as a "disastrous step backwards.... We've been for TV in the Senate for years, but we'd rather have no television than go back to that."

Throughout the 1950s and 1960s, Senate liberals had fought to lower the number of votes needed to shut off filibusters, which in those years were waged primarily by Southerners seeking to block civil rights legislation. In 1975, after bitter battles, they succeeded in cutting the requirement from two-thirds of those present and voting to a flat 60 votes. *(Congress and the Nation Vol. IV, p. 773)*

The Senate voted 30-61 against an amendment by J. Bennett Johnston, D-La., allowing television only by unanimous consent. By 28-60, it rejected a Long amendment to allow TV only when senators by majority vote specified what debates could be covered and for how long. *(Votes 21, 23, p. 5-S)*

Daniel J. Evans, R-Wash., proposed that senators vote from their seats during roll calls. But that was tabled (killed), 49-43. *(Vote 22, p. 5-S)*

Final Vote

Satisfied by its two-month experiment with live television, the Senate July 29 voted 78-21 to keep the cameras rolling permanently. *(Vote 165, p. 31-S)*

In the end, opposition to TV crossed party and generational lines. Foes included Republican Dan Quayle of Indiana, 39, a telegenic freshman, and 84-year-old Democrat John C. Stennis of Mississippi, the Senate's longest-serving member.

Opponents also included two Republicans who had supported TV as an experiment — Jake Garn of Utah and Alan K. Simpson of Wyoming, the assistant majority leader.

Among supporters were three Republicans who had opposed TV in February — Mitch McConnell, Ky.; Rudy Boschwitz, Minn.; and Robert T. Stafford, Vt. ▮

Committee Finishes Two of Four Ethics Probes

After a probe of nearly five months, the House ethics committee in February found that Rep. Dan Daniel, D-Va., had wrongly accepted numerous free plane rides from a defense contractor and had billed the government as though he had made some of the trips by car. But the panel recommended no punishment.

The Committee on Standards of Official Conduct, as the ethics committee was formally entitled, also concluded in October that Rep. James Weaver, D-Ore., violated House rules when he borrowed campaign funds to speculate in the commodities market. Again, it recommended that he should not be punished.

Ethics committee probes of two other members, Reps. Fernand J. St Germain, D-R.I., chairman of the House Banking Committee, and Bill Boner, D-Tenn., were unresolved at year's end. The committee had suspended its probe of Boner in April to avoid interfering with a separate Justice Department investigation.

Daniel Probe

In a 343-page report released Feb. 10, the ethics committee concluded that Daniel misunderstood federal laws and House rules against taking certain gifts, failing to

Disclosure Rules Tightened by House Ethics Committee

The House ethics committee, responding to continuing controversy over the way some members reported their personal finances, revised disclosure forms and clarified its policies in time for the May 15 deadline for 1985 reports.

In an April 23 packet sent by Chairman Julian C. Dixon, D-Calif., and senior Republican Floyd Spence, S.C., the committee notified members of a new requirement: All interest in individual retirement accounts (IRAs) or so-called Keogh retirement plans had to be reported. The Senate and executive branch already required such information under their interpretations of the 1978 Ethics in Government Act (PL 95-521). *(1978 Almanac p. 835)*

On the redesigned disclosure forms, the first item was one that used to be last — a checkoff for members claiming an exemption from reporting income of spouses and dependent children. A note said that exemptions were proper only in "RARE CIRCUMSTANCES" where the member neither knew about nor benefited from the spouse's or child's assets.

Failure to report a spouse's assets was at the heart of past investigations of former Reps. George Hansen, R-Idaho (1965-69, 1975-85), and Geraldine A. Ferraro, D-N.Y. (1979-85). *(1984 Almanac p. 210)*

In 1984, Hansen was convicted of a felony violation of the ethics law and was reprimanded by the House; the Supreme Court March 3, 1986, refused to review that verdict. *(Story, p. 48)*

The House ethics committee found that Ferraro, the Democratic vice presidential nominee in 1984, technically had violated the same law. But the Justice Department took no action against her.

In other revisions, members were told to include separate listings for gifts and reimbursements of expenses for speaking engagements or fact-finding events, which formerly were combined, and to report earned and unearned income under separate headings. Subheadings for various types of assets were introduced by brief guidelines about federal law.

The ethics committee, formally known as the Committee on Standards of Official Conduct, also scrapped what had become a controversial policy on accepting late changes to financial forms. In February, the panel exonerated Dan Daniel, D-Va., for failing to report at least 68 free flights on a defense contractor's corporate jet, noting that during the investigation he amended past years' forms to reflect the gifts.

Under the new policy, the committee decided to require members to change their forms within the year they were filed, and to explain why they were late. Changes would not be deemed proper if they were "clearly intended to 'paper over' an earlier mis/non filing," the panel's letter said.

---

report others, using private help to offset official expenses and embezzling government funds.

The report said Daniel flew at Beech Aircraft Corp.'s expense at least 68 and perhaps more than 200 times, most often to his hometown of Danville but also to other cities in Virginia and to golf games outside the state. But it noted that Daniel later repaid both Beech and the Treasury, and that he had amended his financial disclosure statements to report Beech's gifts.

The committee also found no improper relationship between the nine-term lawmaker, a member of the Armed Services Committee and chairman of its Subcommittee on Readiness, and the defense contractor. It did express "concern regarding at least an appearance of impropriety."

"I'm pleased that this now has been resolved," said Daniel in a prepared statement Feb. 10. "Certainly there was no conscious attempt to circumvent House rules, and any technical violations were unintentional."

The ethics committee approved its report on Daniel by an 11-0 vote in private session Feb. 5 (H Rept 99-470). The report capped an inquiry begun more than four months earlier, on Sept. 19, in reaction to stories in the Richmond *News-Leader.*

Daniel's Gift Flights

The committee determined that 47 of the 68 Beech flights that it could document Daniel took from 1977-85 were gifts unrelated to his official responsibilities. By accepting them, Daniel violated a House rule prohibiting members from taking any gifts with aggregate value of $100 or more from sources with a direct interest in legislation, the ethics panel found.

Daniel made the other 21 trips at least partly for official reasons. But that, according to the panel, violated another House rule barring members from using private sources to augment their government allowance, which covered such expenses as travel.

And the panel found Daniel broke a third rule requiring members to disclose any gifts, including transportation, with a total value of at least $250 a year. All three rules were based on the 1978 Ethics in Government Act (PL 95-521). *(1978 Almanac p. 835)*

During its investigation, the committee also discovered that after 19 Beech flights on which he was a passenger, Daniel submitted vouchers seeking reimbursement for auto mileage. But the committee said it was satisfied by Daniel's testimony that he had not violated federal criminal statutes against submitting false claims and embezzling from the government.

Daniel testified that his wife or aides sometimes drove his car between Washington, D.C., and his district while he flew, because long drives aggravated injuries suffered in a 1982 auto accident. Daniel said he mistakenly thought he was entitled to repayment even if he was not in the car.

The ethics committee's findings were limited to the 68 documented flights. It reported, but drew no conclusions about, an affidavit by Beech executive William G. Rutherford saying that Daniel "could have" taken an additional 72 to 144 trips from 1977-82. "The committee considered it inappropriate, in the absence of supporting documentation, to use such trips as the basis" for recommendations of punishment or reimbursement, the report said.

Under law, a member who knowingly filed a false financial statement or made a false claim against the government could be subject to a maximum penalty of $10,000 and five years in prison. And embezzlement against the government was punishable by up to $10,000 and 10 years' imprisonment.

No Punishment Needed

However, for each of the "initial violations," as the committee called Daniel's actions, the panel decided no sanctions were necessary because Daniel subsequently complied by repaying Beech and the government and by updating his annual financial-disclosure statements, which were required of all federal officeholders.

Regarding laws against embezzlement, the committee concluded that Daniel's "apparent confusion" ruled out prosecution. "Rep. Daniel's actions do not indicate violations of the cited statutes, which require an element of 'knowing' improper action," the report said.

Similarly, in discussing Daniel's violations of the 1978 ethics law and House rules, the committee cited his sworn statement that "at the time, I believed the trips to be neither prohibited nor subject to disclosure, being that they did not individually exceed the $250 threshold for disclosure, or the $100 threshold in the House rules."

The panel did find it "troubling" that Daniel's statement proved that he was aware of the law and House rules, but that he "was not aware of the clear language thereof" holding that the thresholds were aggregate amounts, not individual amounts, for gifts received in a year.

"Nevertheless," the report continued, "the committee has decided to accept his response and explanation, particularly in the light that his assertion was submitted under penalty of perjury, coupled with the absence of any indication of bad faith by the congressman."

According to the report, Daniel had repaid the government $1,343.29, covering the $1,199.37 value of the 19 mileage vouchers, plus 12 percent interest.

He reimbursed Beech $7,663. His first $1,127 repayment was made a few days before the inquiry began in September, and covered 23 flights in 1983-85. When committee investigators later told Daniel they had evidence of 68 trips since 1977, he wrote a second check to Beech for $6,536.

He also updated his financial-disclosure reports — first shortly before the investigation began, and again when the committee uncovered the additional flights.

The committee said it began its inquiry based on Daniel's own recollection, and soon expanded the scope when Beech submitted evidence of more trips between Danville and Washington.

However, neither Daniel nor Beech voluntarily disclosed trips taken to other destinations, including Miami and Tampa, Fla. They did so only after the committee requested the information and issued subpoenas.

In a footnote to its report, the committee said it did not consider Beech's previously incomplete information to be proof of the company's "intent to deceive." The committee did not address that issue in regard to Daniel.

Appearance of Impropriety

In dismissing the suggestion of an improper relationship between Daniel and Beech, the committee stressed that the free flights were authorized not by Beech's corporate management, but by Daniel's longtime friend and golf partner, Rutherford.

Rutherford, the committee report said, "acted independently in response to his concern that Rep. Daniel may have been physically unable to regularly drive to and from his congressional district. Thus, without evidence that the flights were actually provided to influence Daniel's official actions or in appreciation for favorable actions, the committee concluded that an improper relationship did not exist in this situation."

The committee report did not mention Daniel's senior position on Armed Services. For years, the Virginia Democrat had been the leading advocate there for mandating that the Pentagon purchase Beech's C-12 transport planes. In 1985, however, Congress required that any contracts let in fiscal 1986 be subject to competitive bidding.

Daniel, 71, was first elected to the House in 1968 and had no Republican opposition since 1970 — a situation that was not altered by the House ethics investigation. In part, that reflected Republican satisfaction with Daniel's record; Congressional Quarterly's annual vote studies showed he had never supported his own party's position on issues more than 46 percent of the time, and he had supported Republican presidents, including Ronald Reagan, more than any other House Democrat.

Former Rep. Hansen Protests Ruling

Former Rep. George Hansen, R-Idaho (1965-69, 1975-85), reprimanded by the House in 1984 after he was convicted of violating the 1978 Ethics in Government Act, wrote the House ethics committee Feb. 18 to complain that its Feb. 5 clearance of Daniel demonstrated the committee employed "conflicting standards" in investigating members.

Hansen notified both the House clerk's office and the ethics committee that he was withdrawing all his required financial disclosure forms for 1978-81. The point, Hansen said, was to show that he would have been subject to a lesser civil penalty had he never filed the required forms than he suffered as a result of his conviction under criminal law for having omitted certain information from the forms he did file. Hansen's appeal from his conviction was rejected March 3 by the Supreme Court. *(Story, p. 48)*

The ethics committee exonerated Daniel in large part because it said he had willingly amended his disclosure form after the press and then committee investigators found the omissions. The committee's report on Daniel noted that Hansen, in contrast, never volunteered to amend his reports.

"I have been betrayed," Hansen wrote. He claimed he had sought and followed the ethics committee's advice in filing his forms. To amend later would have been an admission of his and the committee's error, Hansen said. *(1984 Almanac p. 210)*

The ethics committee refused to comment.

Weaver Investigation

In a unanimous decision, the ethics committee found that Rep. Weaver erred both in borrowing $81,667 from campaign funds in 1981-84 for commodity market trades and in failing to detail the trading on annual financial statements that members must file by law.

But because Weaver had reported his borrowings and made partial disclosure of his investments on his campaign and financial-worth reports, the committee ruled out sanctions.

"There was no evidence of an intent to avoid public notice" of the loans, the panel's report said. As for the commodities trading, it added, "disclosure was attempted — albeit inadequately."

The committee's 258-page report (H Rept 99-933),

which was approved Sept. 30 but not released until Oct. 7, ended an eight-month probe. During that period, Weaver won Oregon's Democratic nomination for the Senate and then abruptly dropped out in August, citing the cloud of the unresolved ethics case. He retired from the House in January after six terms.

"The report exonerated me completely," Weaver said. "I've always said that everything I did was legal and ethical."

The Weaver Loans

The committee reported that Weaver lent his campaign a total of $35,432 in 1974 and 1984. From 1981-1984, he borrowed $81,667.

By Weaver's reckoning, applying a 14 percent interest rate to both amounts, his committee owed him money. But the ethics panel concluded that he owed his campaign account $113,169.

Weaver variously described the $81,667 in borrowings either as repayment to him for his earlier loans to the campaign, or as loans he meant to repay — with interest and, if lucky, profits from his investments.

According to a transcript, Weaver told the ethics panel Aug. 14 that he hoped his market profits would free him from having to ask for campaign donations, which "revolted" him. But he "lost every penny," he admitted.

The committee said Weaver violated a House rule against spending campaign funds for anything other than "bona fide campaign purposes." His reports on commodity trading, listed only in broad summaries, violated a second rule requiring details of each transaction, the panel said.

The committee ruled that "any use of campaign funds which personally benefit the member rather than to exclusively and solely benefit the campaign is *not* a 'bona fide campaign purpose.' "

Fred Wertheimer, president of the self-styled citizens' group Common Cause, lauded that definition as "a very strong standard ... a very valuable precedent." But having found Weaver in violation, he added, "they do not have a rationale for not imposing sanctions."

Unresolved Probes

The ethics committee at year's end still had not acted on allegations against Reps. St Germain and Boner. The committee had launched its investigations of both men on Feb. 5.

St Germain

St Germain was the focus of stories in the Sept. 11 and Nov. 18, 1985, editions of *The Wall Street Journal* alleging he had become a millionaire, largely through investments made with the help of financial firms that had business before his Banking Committee.

The paper also said St Germain had traveled between Washington and Florida in the executive jet of a Florida savings and loan institution without properly reporting the cost on his financial disclosure forms. Meanwhile, the Journal reported, the Internal Revenue Service was probing whether St Germain invested in "abusive tax shelters."

"As I have said from the beginning, I have properly and fully reported all of my financial affairs on the disclosure forms filed with the ethics committee," St Germain said. "I have met both the spirit and the letter of the rules of the House."

The negative publicity did not hurt St Germain at the polls; he defeated John A. Holmes Jr., chairman of the state Republican Party, by 58-42 percent.

Boner

In Boner's case, the Nashville *Tennessean* reported in a series of stories that he improperly built a fortune from about $10,000 when he took office in 1979 to at least $2 million; that Boner and his wife used campaign funds for such personal benefits as a trip to Hong Kong, a car and pickup truck, $5,000 in furniture, and entertainment and gifts worth thousands of dollars more; and that Boner used his position as chairman of the House Travel and Tourism Caucus for hotel investments and free use of a boat for two years.

Another charge against Boner involved a claim by a defense contractor, who was a former friend of the Boners, that he paid what amounted to a $50,000 bribe by employing the congressman's wife, Betty, over two years for work that she never performed.

Boner denied wrongdoing. He said the questioned expenses and purchases were for legitimate political or office-related purposes. House rules allowed use of campaign funds only for "bona fide campaign expenditures."

Like Daniel and St Germain, Boner suffered no ill effects at the polls as a result of the committee's investigation. He was re-elected Nov. 4 by a 59-41 margin. ▮

Hansen Appeal Rejected

The Supreme Court March 3 refused to review the 1984 felony conviction of former Rep. George Hansen, R-Idaho (1965-69, 1975-85), for violating financial disclosure provisions of the 1978 Ethics in Government Act (PL 95-521).

Without comment, the court declined to consider Hansen's appeal of his conviction for failing to report nearly $334,000 in loans and profits for 1978-81. The decision freed federal prosecutors to force Hansen, 55, to serve his sentence of five to 15 months in prison and to pay a $40,000 fine. He was the first person to be convicted of criminal charges involving the law's disclosure provisions. *(1984 Almanac p. 210)*

Hansen was convicted April 2, 1984, while serving his seventh term, and was only narrowly beaten by Democrat Richard H. Stallings in the general election that year. Hansen's wife, Connie, unsuccessfully sought the Republican nomination to run for his old seat in 1986.

In 1985, a federal appeals court rejected Hansen's argument that Congress did not intend violations of the ethics law to be treated as criminal acts. The Supreme Court let the appeals court's ruling stand.

This was Hansen's second unsuccessful appeal to the Supreme Court. After his 1983 indictment, but before the case went to trial, Hansen argued that he could not be criminally prosecuted because the charges involved legislative activities protected under the Constitution's speech and debate clause. The court rejected his appeal. ▮

Fiedler Charges Dropped

The Los Angeles district attorney dropped political corruption charges against Rep. Bobbi Fiedler, R-Calif., on

Feb. 19, saying that the evidence was "not sufficient" to pursue the case.

Fiedler, who unsuccessfully sought the GOP nomination for the U.S. Senate seat held by Democrat Alan Cranston, had been indicted Jan. 23, along with an aide, on charges of violating an obscure California law by offering a rival candidate money to withdraw from the GOP primary.

The indictment was returned by the Los Angeles County grand jury after an investigation that began in November 1985. It charged Fiedler and Paul Clarke, her fiancé and chief aide, with violating an obscure state election statute that made it a felony to offer money to a candidate in an attempt to persuade him not to enter or to withdraw from a political contest. The statute, passed in 1893, apparently had never been used in criminal proceedings.

According to published accounts, the investigation began after a Fiedler supporter told a backer of state Sen. Ed Davis that he had heard Davis was considering dropping out, and that the Fiedler campaign might be willing to help him retire his campaign debt. Fiedler's own involvement reportedly came in a Jan. 12 meeting with Davis' campaign manager to discuss the matter.

Fiedler responded to the indictment by saying, "This whole thing is ridiculous. I've done nothing wrong, and I don't believe that anyone in my campaign has done anything wrong. We are the victims."

In the end, the entire flap probably harmed both Fiedler and Davis.

The Republican nomination was won by Rep. Ed Zschau, who went on to lose to Cranston in November. *(Senate elections, p. 5-B)* ▮

High Court Weighs New Legislative Veto Issue

Three years after it declared the legislative veto unconstitutional, the Supreme Court agreed to decide how much of a law containing a veto must fall with it.

The Supreme Court's ruling in the case of *Alaska Airlines v. Brock* was expected to clarify the status of laws that still contained legislative vetoes, a device that the court in 1983 ruled was in violation of the separation of powers between Congress and the president.

At the time of that decision in *Immigration and Naturalization Service v. Chadha,* there were about 110 laws in effect with similar provisions. *(1983 Almanac p. 565)*

Since *Chadha,* Congress had amended some of those laws, and repealed a few, but many of them remained on the books. *(Box, next page)*

What Did Congress Intend?

Sometimes the intent of Congress was clear. In writing the Gramm-Rudman-Hollings anti-deficit law (PL 99-177) in 1985, Congress — aware that a key mechanism of that measure would be challenged as unconstitutional — wrote into the act a fallback procedure for use if the preferred version was struck down — as it was July 7. Such a backup was compelling evidence that Congress did not intend the entire law to fall with this one provision. *(Gramm-Rudman, p. 579)*

More often, Congress left conflicting clues as to its intent. Sometimes it included a "severability clause" in a law, stating that whatever provisions were found to be unconstitutional or otherwise invalid were to be severed from the rest of the bill. But even then, the intent of Congress was sometimes debatable.

Appeals Court Judge Abner J. Mikva told a Senate Judiciary subcommittee in 1984 that "Congress puts in a severability clause almost mindlessly. It goes . . . at the end of the statute, sort of to signify that it *is* the end of the statute."

Mikva knew whereof he spoke. The Illinois Democrat served almost four terms in the House before President Jimmy Carter named him to the U.S. Court of Appeals for the District of Columbia in 1979.

In these cases, noted David Vladeck of the Public Citizen Litigation Group, a "court has to make a retrospective prophecy. It has to decide, 'What would Congress have done if they'd known what they didn't know?' " — that is, that some single provision of the law they were passing would be held unconstitutional.

The New Challenges

At issue in *Alaska Airlines v. Brock* was the Airline Deregulation Act of 1978 (PL 95-504). On Dec. 1, the court heard attorneys for the government and the airline industry argue over how much of one part of that law should survive the demise of its accompanying legislative veto. *(1978 Almanac p. 496)*

The justices were expected to rule on that case sometime in 1987.

A second law under challenge was the 1974 Congressional Budget and Impoundment Control Act (PL 93-344). That law gave the president the power to defer spending appropriated funds for a specific program, subject to a one-house legislative veto.

On Jan. 20, 1987, the U.S. Circuit Court of Appeals for the District of Columbia ruled that without the veto provision, this grant of deferral power was void. In the case of *City of New Haven v. United States, National League of Cities v. Pierce, City of Chicago v. Department of Housing and Urban Development,* city officials represented by Vladeck had argued that Congress in 1974 would never have granted President Richard M. Nixon this power without the veto. *(Deferrals, p. 576)*

Looking Back

The first legislative veto, written into the fiscal 1933 legislative branch appropriations act, was used to veto President Herbert Hoover's proposal for reorganizing the executive branch.

The device became increasingly popular in the 1970s and 1980s. Congress was legislating on complex and often technical subjects at the same time that it was becoming more and more distrustful of the executive branch. The veto provided a way for Congress to delegate authority to executive branch agencies while retaining for itself the right to veto misuse of that authority.

Over the years, Congress approved many varieties of legislative veto. One type permitted either chamber to block an agency plan or rule; another required passage of a concurrent resolution of disapproval by both chambers. A third permitted one or more congressional committees to

Congress Changes Only Selected Laws . . .

Following is a list of some of the major laws of the past 25 years that included legislative veto provisions and the changes — if any — made in them by Congress since the Supreme Court struck down the veto device in its 1983 ruling in *Immigration and Naturalization Service v. Chadha.*

Foreign Affairs and National Security

• **Act for International Development of 1961 (PL 87-195).** Act's foreign assistance funds may be terminated by a resolution approved by both chambers.

• **War Powers Resolution, 1973 (PL 93-148).** Absent a declaration of war, the president may be directed by a resolution approved by both chambers to remove U.S. armed forces engaged in foreign hostilities.

• **Department of Defense Appropriation Authorization Act, 1974 (PL 93-155).** National defense contracts obligating the United States for any amount in excess of $25 million may be disapproved by a resolution of either chamber.

• **Department of Defense Appropriation Authorization Act, 1975 (PL 93-365).** Applications for export of defense goods, technology or techniques may be disapproved by a resolution approved by both chambers.

• **House Joint Resolution 683, 1975 (PL 94-110).** Assignment of civilian personnel to the Sinai may be disapproved by a resolution approved by both chambers.

• **International Development and Food Assistance Act of 1975 (PL 94-161).** Foreign assistance to countries not meeting human rights standards may be terminated by a resolution approved by both chambers.

• **International Security Assistance and Arms Control Act of 1976 (PL 94-329).** The president's letter of an offer to sell major defense equipment may be disapproved by a resolution approved by both chambers. In 1986 Congress amended this (PL 99-247) to provide for disapproval through a joint resolution submitted to the president for his signature. *(Story, p. 374)*

• **National Emergencies Act, 1976 (PL 94-412).** Presidentially declared national emergency may be terminated by a resolution approved by both chambers. Amended in 1985 (PL 99-93) to provide for termination by a joint resolution submitted to the president for his signature. *(1985 Almanac p. 104)*

• **International Navigational Rules Act of 1977 (PL 95-75).** Presidential proclamation of International Regulations for Preventing Collisions at Sea may be disapproved by a resolution approved by both chambers.

• **International Security Assistance Act of 1977 (PL 95-92).** President's proposed transfer of arms to a third country may be disapproved by a resolution of both chambers. In 1986 Congress amended this (PL 99-247) to provide for disapproval through a joint resolution submitted to the president for his signature.

• **Act of December 28, 1977 (PL 95-223).** A presidentially declared national emergency and exercise of conditional powers may be terminated by a resolution of both chambers. This provision was effectively amended by the change Congress made in 1985 in the National Emergencies Act, above.

• **Nuclear Non-Proliferation Act of 1978 (PL 95-242).** Cooperative agreements concerning storage and disposition of spent nuclear fuel, proposed export of nuclear facilities, materials or technology and proposed agreements for international cooperation in nuclear reactor development may be disapproved by a resolution passed by both chambers. In 1985 Congress amended this (PL 99-64) to provide for disapproval through a joint resolution sent to the president for his signature. *(1985 Almanac p. 259)*

Budget

• **Congressional Budget and Impoundment Control Act of 1974 (PL 93-344).** The president's proposed deferral of budget authority provided for a specific project may be disapproved by a resolution passed by either chamber. This section had not been amended and was the subject of litigation in 1986. *(Story, p. 576)*

Rulemaking

• **Education Amendments of 1974 (PL 93-380).** Department of Education regulations may be disapproved by a resolution passed by both chambers.

• **Federal Election Campaign Act Amendments of 1979 (PL 96-187).** Proposed rules and regulations of the Federal Election Commission may be disapproved by a resolution of either chamber.

• **Act of January 2, 1975 (PL 93-595).** Proposed amendments to federal evidence rules by Supreme Court may be disapproved by resolution of either chamber.

• **Act of August 9, 1975 (PL 94-88).** Social Security standards proposed by the health, education and welfare secretary may be disapproved by a resolution passed by either chamber.

• **Airline Deregulation Act of 1978 (PL 95-504).** Rules or regulations governing employee protection programs may be disapproved by a resolution of either chamber. This law was the subject of a case before the Supreme Court in 1986. *(Alaska Airlines v. Brock)*

• **Education Amendments of 1978 (PL 95-561).** Rules and regulations proposed under the act may be disapproved by a resolution passed by both chambers.

• **Federal Trade Commission Improvements Act of 1980 (PL 96-252).** Federal Trade Commission rules may be disapproved by a resolution passed by both chambers. The Supreme Court July 6, 1983, affirmed an appeals court ruling striking down these provisions as unconstitutional.

• **Department of Education Organization Act, 1979 (PL 96-88).** Rules and regulations promulgated for various programs transferred by the act may be disapproved by a resolution passed by both chambers.

• **Multiemployer Pension Plan Amendments Act of 1980 (PL 96-364).** Schedules proposed by the Pension Benefit Guaranty Corporation (PBGC) that require an increase in premiums must be approved by a resolution passed by both chambers. Revised premium schedules for voluntary supplemental coverage proposed by the PBGC may be disapproved by a resolution passed by both chambers. Congress amended these provisions in 1986 to substitute a joint resolution rather than a concurrent resolution (PL 99-272).

• **Farm Credit Act Amendments of 1980 (PL 96-592).** Certain Farm Credit Administration regulations may be delayed by resolution of either chamber.

• **Comprehensive Environmental Response, Compensation and Liability Act of 1980 (PL 96-510).** Environmental Protection Agency regulations concerning hazardous-substances releases, liability and compensation may be disapproved by a resolution approved by both chambers or by the

. . . In Wake of 1983 Legislative Veto Ruling

adoption by either chamber of a concurrent resolution that is not disapproved by the other chamber.

• **National Historic Preservation Act Amendments of 1980 (PL 96-515).** Regulation proposed by the secretary of the interior may be disapproved by a resolution approved by both chambers.

• **Coastal Zone Management Improvement Act of 1980 (PL 96-464).** Rules proposed by the commerce secretary may be disapproved by a resolution of either chamber.

• **Act of December 17, 1980 (PL 96-539).** Rules or regulations promulgated by the administrator of the Environmental Protection Agency under the Federal Insecticide, Fungicide and Rodenticide Act may be disapproved by a resolution passed by both chambers.

• **Omnibus Budget Reconciliation Act of 1981 (PL 97-35).** The education secretary's schedule of expected family contributions for Pell Grant recipients may be disapproved by resolution of either chamber. Specified rules promulgated by the transportation secretary may be disapproved by resolution of either chamber. Amendments to Amtrak's route and service criteria may be disapproved by resolution of either chamber. Consumer Product Safety Commission regulations may be disapproved by a resolution approved by both chambers or by a concurrent resolution of disapproval by either chamber that is not disapproved by the other chamber.

Energy

• **Act of November 16, 1973 (PL 93-153).** Continuation of oil exports being made pursuant to the president's finding that such exports are in the national interest may be disapproved by a resolution approved by both chambers.

• **Federal Nonnuclear Energy Research and Development Act of 1974 (PL 93-577).** Rules or orders proposed by the president about allocation or acquisition of essential materials may be disapproved by resolution of either chamber.

• **Energy Policy and Conservation Act, 1975 (PL 94-163).** Certain presidentially proposed "energy actions" involving fuel economy and pricing may be disapproved by resolution of either chamber.

• **Naval Petroleum Reserves Production Act of 1976 (PL 94-258).** The president's extension of the production period for naval petroleum reserves may be disapproved by resolution of either chamber.

• **Department of Energy Act of 1978 (PL 95-238).** International agreements and expenditures by the secretary of energy of appropriations for foreign spent nuclear fuel storage must be approved by a resolution passed by both chambers, if not agreed to by legislation. Plans for such use of appropriated funds may be disapproved by either chamber. Financing in excess of $50 million for demonstration facilities must be approved by resolution in both chambers.

• **Outer Continental Shelf Lands Act Amendments of 1978 (PL 95-372).** Establishment by the secretary of energy of oil and gas lease bidding system may be disapproved by resolution of either chamber. Export of oil and gas may be disapproved by a resolution passed by both chambers.

• **Natural Gas Policy Act of 1978 (PL 95-621).** Presidential reimposition of natural gas price controls may be disapproved by a resolution passed by both chambers. Congress may reimpose natural gas price controls by a resolution passed by both chambers. A Federal Energy Regulatory Commission amendment to pass through incremental costs of natural gas, and exemptions from this rule, may be disapproved by resolution of either chamber. The Supreme Court July 6, 1983, affirmed an appeals court decision holding this latter veto provision unconstitutional.

• **Export Administration Act of 1979 (PL 96-72).** The president's proposal for domestic production of crude oil must be approved by a resolution passed by both chambers. Action by the commerce secretary to prohibit or curtail export of agricultural commodities may be disapproved by a resolution approved by both chambers. Congress in 1985 amended this law (PL 99-64) to substitute a joint resolution of approval, to be sent to the president for his signature, for the concurrent resolutions concerning agricultural commodities. *(1985 Almanac p. 259)*

• **Energy Security Act, 1980 (PL 96-294).** Loan guarantees by the Departments of Defense, Energy and Commerce in excess of specified amounts may be disapproved by resolution of either chamber. The president's proposal to provide loans or guarantees in excess of established amounts may be disapproved by resolution of either chamber. A proposed award by the president of individual contracts for purchase of 75,000 barrels per day of crude oil may be disapproved by resolution of either chamber. Certain actions of the Synthetic Fuels Corporation are subject to disapproval by a resolution of one chamber or both, as specified in the act.

International Trade

• **Trade Expansion Act of 1962 (PL 87-794).** Tariff or duties recommended by the Tariff Commission may be imposed by a resolution of approval passed by both chambers.

• **Trade Act of 1974 (PL 93-618).** Proposed presidential actions on import relief and actions concerning certain countries may be disapproved by a resolution passed by both chambers. Various presidential proposals for waiver extensions and for extension of non-discriminatory treatment of products of foreign countries may be disapproved either by a resolution of one chamber or a resolution approved by both chambers. Congress in 1984 amended the provisions concerning import relief to permit them to take effect unless Congress passed a joint resolution of disapproval within 90 days of receiving the proposal (PL 98-573). Congress in 1985 amended this law to require the president to report a proposal to extend non-discriminatory treatment to products of Afghanistan 30 days before he did so (PL 99-190).

Miscellaneous

• **Federal Land Policy and Management Act of 1976 (PL 94-579).** Sale of public lands larger than 2,500 acres and withdrawal of public lands totaling at least 5,000 acres may be disapproved by a resolution passed by both chambers.

• **National Aeronautics and Space Act of 1958 (PL 85-568).** President's transfer to NASA of functions of other departments and agencies may be disapproved by a resolution passed by both chambers.

• **Emergency Unemployment Compensation Extension Act of 1977 (PL 95-19).** The president's recommendations on rates of salary payment may be disapproved by a resolution of either chamber. Congress in 1985 amended this law to substitute a joint resolution for the one-house veto (PL 99-190).

• **Civil Service Reform Act of 1978 (PL 95-454).** Continuation of the Senior Executive Service (S.E.S.) may be disapproved by a resolution approved by both chambers. Congress in 1984 approved the indefinite continuation of the SES, negating this provision (PL 98-615).

block an agency action; still another required one or both chambers, or one or more committees, to adopt a resolution of approval before a given plan or rule could take effect.

All these provisions had one feature in common: They permitted Congress to block executive action without the president's approval. It was this feature that the court found unconstitutional.

Some Laws Modified

"The remarkable thing after *Chadha,*" said Vladeck, "is how little attention Congress has paid to trying to straighten out the dilemma it caused. There were a number of hearings, but there has been no concerted effort to fix up the problem. It is indeed striking how inattentive Congress has been, particularly since the veto is a device to maintain congressional control."

When Congress amended a legislative veto provision, it usually replaced language permitting Congress to veto some executive action by a concurrent resolution with a provision permitting a veto by joint resolution.

The difference was crucial: A joint resolution had to be sent to the president for his signature; a concurrent resolution did not.

Two of the most important laws changed in this fashion involved U.S. arms sales and the export of nuclear materials. In 1986 Congress substituted a joint resolution of disapproval for a concurrent resolution in the Arms Export Control Act (PL 99-247), permitting Congress to object to major arms sales by the president. A year earlier, it made a similar change (PL 99-64) in the law governing the export of nuclear materials. *(Arms sales, p. 374; nuclear exports, 1985 Almanac p. 259)*

Adaptation, Accommodation

More common than these forthright changes in existing law have been informal accommodations to the court's ruling.

"We should not be too surprised or disconcerted if, after the court has closed the door to the legislative veto, we hear a number of windows being raised and perhaps new doors constructed, making the executive-legislative structure as accommodating as before for shared power," wrote Louis Fisher, a specialist in American government at the Congressional Research Service, after *Chadha.*

Indeed, the response of Congress and the executive branch to the *Chadha* ruling testified to the flexibility and resilience of their relationship. The attitudes of conciliation and cooperation between executive agency and legislative body once mandated by the existence of the legislative veto generally remained in place. Informal arrangements replaced statutory arrangements; the results were usually the same.

Despite its dubious legality, for example, the committee veto remained alive and well. The fiscal 1987 continuing appropriations resolution (H J Res 738 — PL 99-591) contained a provision requiring the approval of the House and Senate Appropriations committees before the Treasury Department could transfer funds between its programs to provide more for Secret Service travel with the president than was specified in the bill. *(Continuing resolution, p. 219)*

Frederick Kaiser of the Congressional Research Service, who had kept a close eye on the use of committee vetoes and other alternatives, said that executive agencies were generally happy to cooperate with committees on this type of "reprogramming" veto.

"Otherwise, they would lose a great amount of agency discretion," Kaiser said, if they had to come back for supplemental appropriations bills or further legislative authorization to transfer funds.

In a special 1985 issue of the *Public Administration Review,* Fisher recounted an episode that illustrated the sort of informal arrangements that had replaced the legislative veto — and the gap between White House rhetoric opposing such arrangements and executive agency willingness to participate in them.

In 1984, a year after *Chadha,* Congress sent to Reagan a HUD-Independent Agencies appropriation bill (PL 98-371) that contained eight committee vetoes. In signing it, President Reagan declared that "the time has come ... to make clear that legislation containing legislative veto devices that comes to me for my approval or disapproval will be implemented in a manner consistent with ... *Chadha.*"

It was clear that Reagan did not feel bound by the committee veto requirements. In response, the House Appropriations Committee moved to repeal a standing agreement with the National Aeronautics and Space Administration under which NASA, with approval from both Appropriations committees, was permitted to exceed the "caps" set by the appropriations bill on certain of its programs.

NASA Administrator James M. Beggs quickly wrote the committees suggesting that "the present legislative procedure ... be converted by this letter into an informal agreement by NASA not to exceed amounts for committee-designated programs without the approval of the Committee on Appropriations." The committees agreed.

Such informal vetoes, Fisher wrote, were "not legal in effect. They are, however, in effect legal. Agencies are aware of the penalties that can be invoked by Congress if they decide to violate understandings and working relationships with their review committees."

A leading advocate of the legislative veto, Sen. Carl Levin, D-Mich., said that *"Chadha* didn't lessen the need for clearly stated arrangements of shared power between the executive and legislative branches on certain issues. It only significantly reduced our options for crafting those arrangements. The solutions to *Chadha* have been and will continue to be fashioned on a case-by-case basis. They will depend upon the importance of the issue involved and the degree of executive-legislative cooperation in the past. There really can be no overall quick fix."

Alan B. Morrison, the director of the Public Citizen Litigation Group and the attorney who won the *Chadha* decision, said he was not particularly concerned about the informal arrangements that Congress had devised to take the place of the veto. "They may chip away at the principle of the decision," he said, "but there is a big difference between these informal arrangements and the existence of a legislative veto."

Other Alternatives

In addition to the joint resolution and the committee veto, there were other alternatives to the one-house or two-house legislative veto.

Some were authorized by specific statutes. The War Powers Resolution (PL 93-148) provided an example. One section of that law was clearly a legislative veto left useless by *Chadha.* That was the section that allowed Congress by concurrent resolution to force withdrawal of U.S. troops engaged in hostilities overseas without specific congressional authorization. It was never exercised and had not been amended since *Chadha.*

Another section, however, forbade the president to keep U.S. forces in hostile situations overseas for more than 90 days unless Congress had declared war, expressly authorized the president's action or extended the deadline. That had the effect — but not the form — of a legislative veto.

Not only did this section survive *Chadha;* it was invoked for the first time a few months after that ruling when Congress passed a measure (PL 98-119) authorizing U.S. Marines who were in Lebanon as part of a multinational peacekeeping force to remain there for up to 18 months. *(1983 Almanac p. 113)*

Another alternative found in various laws was the "report and wait" provision, which gave Congress an opportunity to block proposed action by legislation.

The arms export law required the president to report to Congress 30 days in advance of each proposed arms sale of more than $14 million for a single item or $50 million for a package of arms. The purpose was to give lawmakers a chance to pass a joint resolution blocking the sale.

Congress also could deny funds to the executive for a specific activity, thereby nullifying an executive decision to engage in that activity.

In 1983, Congress disagreed with the administration's position on price-fixing in a major antitrust case before the Supreme Court. Congress included in the Justice Department appropriations bill for fiscal 1984 (PL 98-166) language specifically forbidding the use of funds in the bill for advocating that position. As a result, when the Justice Department attorney appeared before the court to argue in that case, he omitted any mention of that disputed issue. *(1983 Almanac p. 472; 1984 Almanac p. 12-A)*

Congress could always pass a law directly revoking or overruling executive action. It could also place certain matters beyond the reach of a particular agency or exempt them from regulation altogether, as it did repeatedly in prohibiting the Food and Drug Administration from banning the marketing and sale of saccharin. The most recent of these prohibitions was enacted in 1985 (PL 99-46). *(1985 Almanac p. 289)*

The Pending Case

While Congress found ways to work around the *Chadha* decision, other parties affected by laws containing legislative vetoes were less willing to look the other way.

In *Alaska Airlines v. Brock,* the case argued before the Supreme Court on Dec. 1, 14 airlines challenged as unconstitutional a provision of the 1978 airline deregulation law that set up an employee protection plan for airline workers who lost their jobs as a result of deregulation.

The airlines convinced Judge Gerhard A. Gesell of the U.S. District Court in Washington, D.C., that Congress would not have given the secretary of labor such broad power to administer the plan if it had known that the veto would be deleted. Gesell in May 1984 struck down the employee protection plan as invalid in its entirety.

Gesell said that the question was "not whether Congress would have enacted *some* type of employee protection plan in the absence of a legislative veto provision ... [but] whether Congress would have enacted the *same* statute. If not, the court cannot enforce the remainder of the statute merely because it might be an approximation of what Congress would have enacted."

"The task of determining the most preferable alternative to an unconstitutional statute belongs not to the courts, but to Congress itself," Gesell added.

The U.S. Circuit Court of Appeals for the District of Columbia disagreed with Gesell, and reversed his ruling in July 1985.

The appeals court said that the employee protection plan remained valid, even without the veto.

The appeals court applied a different test from Gesell's. The question, the court said, was whether Congress would have preferred the statute it enacted, minus the legislative veto, to none at all. Finding a clear intent of Congress to provide an employee protection program, the court upheld it — without the veto.

The Arguments

The airlines appealed, warning that the standard used by the appeals court would have implications "far beyond the confines of this case."

Indeed, warned attorney William T. Coleman, a former secretary of transportation, this test "would require the courts to rewrite acts of Congress by excising certain provisions."

Coleman framed his argument as a call for "judicial restraint." He warned that the appeals court approach "creates the same risks of intrusion on another branch of the government as does the legislative veto provision that caused the severability issue to arise here in the first place."

"The courts," he said, "will be creating laws that Congress would not have created, because the courts will presume that Congress would rather have something than nothing.

"If Congress wishes to reinstate a statute, it can do so. But Congress should not have to be constantly vigilant for judicially redrafted statutes and bear the burden of having to ... repeal or amend ... statutory provisions which, as revised, no longer comport with legislative intent."

Coleman insisted that "Congress emphatically wished to reserve for itself" ultimate authority over the manner in which the Labor Department implemented the employee protection program. Had Congress known that it would be unable to control the program's destiny through the veto power, it would have had to "confront the questions it deliberately left unanswered, rather than delegate that responsibility. The result, in all probability, would have been a different type of employee protection program," Coleman said.

'No Stopping Place'

The brief filed by Solicitor General Charles Fried on behalf of Labor Secretary William E. Brock III contended that "there is no stopping place" if one accepted the argument put forward by Coleman on behalf of the airlines.

"The evidence unmistakably shows that the EPP [Employee Protection Plan] was more essential to the passage of the entire Deregulation Act than the legislative veto was to the passage of the EPP," Fried said.

"The EPP was described, again and again in the legislative debates, as an important 'insurance' feature of deregulation; the veto provision, on the other hand, appears to have been a reflexive addition to the bill, added almost without comment."

Under the standard for which the airlines argued, "it is hard to see why the balance of the Deregulation Act should not be invalidated along with the EPP," Fried said.

Courts should presume that they should preserve what they can of a statute unless it is obvious that the legislature would not wish such a result, he argued. ■

State of the Union Postponed

Sharing the nation's shock and grief over the space shuttle explosion Jan. 28, President Reagan postponed his State of the Union address, which had been scheduled for 9 o'clock that night, and Congress abandoned legislative activities for the day.

"Today is a day for mourning and remembering," President Reagan said in a televised speech a few hours after the *Challenger* shuttle tragedy. "This is truly a national loss." *(Shuttle disaster, p. 326)*

The unprecedented postponement of the State of the Union address, until Feb. 4, also pushed back delivery of the president's fiscal 1987 budget and his legislative message for the year. The budget was released Feb. 5, the legislative message Feb. 6. *(Budget, p. 525)*

Stunned by news of the explosion, the House and Senate shelved their legislative agenda Jan. 28, and adjourned after passing resolutions (H Res 361, S Res 299) honoring the space shuttle crew.

The shuttle tragedy was particularly poignant for three congressional veterans of space travel — Sen. Jake Garn, R-Utah, who flew on a shuttle mission in April 1985; Rep. Bill Nelson, D-Fla., who was part of the crew of a shuttle flight that returned Jan. 18, 1986, and Sen. John Glenn, D-Ohio, who was the first American to orbit the Earth.

"Let me thank you all for paying tribute to my friends," Garn told his colleagues on the Senate floor. "It is especially hard because I trained with most of them."

"Sometimes triumph is accompanied by tragedy," said Glenn. "We hoped to push this day back forever, but that was not to be."

For Rep. Steny H. Hoyer, D-Md., the death of Christa McAuliffe, the New Hampshire teacher who had been part of the shuttle crew, had a personal meaning.

"She was my friend," said Hoyer, who had employed McAuliffe's husband as a law clerk for two years. "She embodied all of the qualities we would hope for in the very best of our teachers."

The White House announced the postponement of the State of the Union address after consulting with congressional leaders, including House Speaker Thomas P. O'Neill Jr., D-Mass., and Senate Majority Leader Robert Dole, R-Kan., who advised Reagan to defer the speech.

According to the Senate Historian's Office, the State of the Union had never before been canceled or postponed. There had, however, been years when the president has chosen not to deliver the address in person. ∎

Senate Committee Funding

The Senate March 13 by voice vote approved a resolution (S Res 353) authorizing $43.9 million for its 19 standing, select and special committees for the year that began March 1.

Members adopted an amendment by voice vote to boost allotments for the Finance and Armed Services committees over the levels approved Feb. 27 by the Rules and Administration Committee. The amendment, by John W. Warner, R-Va., provided a total of $335,000 more for the two panels.

Rules had drafted S Res 353 to spread equally among all committees the cuts in fiscal 1986 appropriations mandated by the Gramm-Rudman-Hollings deficit-reduction law (PL 99-177). It approved authorizations totaling $43.6 million, about $1.3 million below the previous year's level. However, the two committees said they needed more staff to deal with pending tax overhaul legislation and the president's defense budget request.

The Senate rejected, 27-69, an amendment by Ted Stevens, R-Alaska, to set up a $1.5 million reserve fund to help committees that run into unexpected expenses. *(Vote 36, p. 7-S)*

Also approved was an amendment by Gordon J. Humphrey, R-N.H., to authorize $200,000 from a contingency fund to investigate a November 1985 incident in which a Ukranian seaman fled from a Soviet grain freighter in an apparent effort to defect, and then was returned by U.S. authorities.

The amendment called for the investigation to be conducted by the Commission on Security and Cooperation in Europe, which monitored compliance with the 1975 Helsinki accords on human rights. ∎

Congressional Immunity

A three-judge federal panel April 25 ruled that a House stenographer could not go to court to challenge her dismissal as racially discriminatory.

At issue was the scope and application of the "speech and debate" clause of the Constitution, which shielded members of Congress from lawsuits related to their legislative activities.

In a 1984 decision, another three-judge panel concluded that Anne W. Walker, former manager of the House restaurant service, could pursue a court challenge of her June 1982 dismissal because her job was too remote from legislative activity to be covered by the "speech and debate" clause.

The latest case involved Betty G. Browning, who claimed she was fired from her stenographer's job in 1984 because she was black. Her right to sue had been upheld by U.S. District Court Judge Thomas P. Jackson, who cited the Walker case. On appeal, however, House lawyers argued that stenographers were an integral part of the legislative process because the House was informed through their work, which involved taking down hearing testimony and other congressional proceedings.

The U.S. Court of Appeals for the District of Columbia agreed. "The standard for determining the speech or debate clause immunity is best expressed as whether the employee's duties were directly related to the due functioning of the legislative process," said Judges George E. McKinnon, Laurence H. Silberman and Patricia M. Wald.

House Counsel Steven R. Ross said the decision "is not a license for members to discriminate," because House rules barred employment bias. ∎

Drug Testing of Hill Staff

The Senate Rules and Administration Committee said May 21 that Paula Hawkins, R-Fla., could not dip into her official expense account to pay for drug testing of her staff.

The committee, by voice vote, denied Hawkins' request for reimbursement for $483 in drug-testing expenses, amid concerns about the legal implications of government officials imposing such a requirement on their employees. Chairman Charles McC. Mathias Jr., R-Md., said a staff analysis of related court rulings indicated that mandatory drug testing of federal employees might be considered an "unreasonable search" unless there was "probable cause" for suspecting an individual was using drugs.

Hawkins in March announced she was requiring all 50 of her staff members to undergo tests to detect use of marijuana, cocaine and other illicit drugs.

All of the staffers agreed to undergo the tests, which were administered on April 14. However, one person not on the payroll but working with Hawkins' staff on a fellowship quit over the issue.

Hawkins sought the advice of the Rules Committee after questions were raised about whether she could, as planned, use her office expense account to pay for drug testing. "Drug testing of my office staff was based on my particular need to ensure the public trust and sense of effectiveness toward my work" as chairman of a Senate caucus and a subcommittee that handled drug abuse issues, Hawkins said in a May 20 letter to Mathias.

Senate rules allowed the use of office expense allowances for "ordinary and necessary expenses incurred by a senator and his staff in the discharge of their official duties."

Some members of the Senate committee voiced concern that approving Hawkins' request for reimbursement would be seen as an official Senate sanction of employee drug testing.

Based on a similarly worded rule, the House Administration Committee prohibited Rep. E. Clay Shaw Jr., R-Fla., from using his official allowance to pay for staff drug testing. ∎

Sen. East a Suicide Victim

Republican Sen. John P. East of North Carolina, who had been in ill health, took his own life June 29. He was 55.

East had planned to retire from the Senate when his term expired at the end of 1986.

On July 3, Republican Gov. James G. Martin appointed GOP Rep. James T. Broyhill to succeed East for the remainder of the 99th Congress. Broyhill was sworn in July 14.

East was found by an aide the morning of June 29 in the garage of his Greenville, N.C., home, an apparent suicide by carbon monoxide poisoning. According to local press reports, a note found alongside him mentioned health problems. East had used crutches or a wheelchair since the age of 24 as a result of polio, and he was hospitalized several times in 1985 for a thyroid gland disorder and urinary tract blockage.

He was the first U.S. senator to commit suicide since 1954, when Wyoming Democrat Lester C. Hunt shot himself in his Washington office after learning that he suffered from a terminal illness. A Republican House member, William O. Mills of Maryland, committed suicide in 1973, apparently because of anxiety over his reported involvement in a minor campaign finance scandal. ∎

More Security at Capitol

In the fiscal 1986 supplemental funding bill (HR 4515 — PL 99-349), Congress appropriated $14.3 million for improved security at the U.S. Capitol, possibly including the construction of a fence around the building.

Also appropriated was $1 million for added security personnel in the House and Senate, and $250,000 for the Architect of the Capitol to study new security systems.

The funds had been added to the supplemental by the Senate Appropriations Committee when it approved HR 4515 on May 15 (S Rept 99-301). The final version was cleared by Congress June 26. *(Supplemental, p. 153)*

Task Force Report

Amid heightened concern about terrorism, a congressional task force the week of April 28 proposed new security precautions at the Capitol, including a wrought-iron fence around the grounds and guard checkposts at the gates.

Other proposals called for increased electronic surveillance, elimination of 850 of the parking spaces currently available around the building, and restrictions on deliveries to the Capitol, possibly including a search at the Hart Senate Office Building loading dock.

"The question is how far you can go to reduce the risk" without inhibiting the public's movement around a building that symbolizes open, democratic government, said House Majority Whip Thomas S. Foley, D-Wash.

Security already was fairly tight around the Capitol. Guards and metal detectors were stationed at Capitol doors, the public was restricted to certain entrances, and staff, lobbyists and press had to wear color-coded badges for freer movement.

The task force developing the new proposals included Foley; House Minority Whip Trent Lott, R-Miss.; Senate Assistant Majority Leader Alan K. Simpson, R-Wyo.; and Senate Minority Whip Alan Cranston, D-Calif. It began work in late 1985.

Reaction

House Speaker Thomas P. O'Neill Jr., D-Mass., conceded he was "not that enthusiastic" about the proposals, but said he would not block legislation needed to implement them.

The anti-terrorist proposals were a topic at the House Democrats' caucus May 1. O'Neill said, "Some people are overly concerned; some think it's a waste of money."

Task force members defended the proposals. "All the experts recommended more than we are now proposing," at costs of up to $100 million, Cranston said.

Foley said the task force rejected more extreme ideas, such as barring traffic on Constitution and Independence avenues, which flanked the Capitol on the north and south, respectively. Simpson said ideas ranged from "reasonable to bizarre"; among the latter, he said, was installation of an anti-missile defense system atop the Russell Senate Office Building.

At an April 30 hearing of the House Public Works and Transportation Subcommittee on Public Buildings and Grounds, members voiced grudging support for the plans as needed to protect millions of tourists. ∎

LAW/JUDICIARY

CQ

Law/Judiciary

In the sixth year of Ronald Reagan's presidency, the administration, the House and Senate Judiciary committees and the civil rights community continued the uneasy coexistence that had characterized Reagan's term in office.

It was a year of accomplishment but also bitter confrontation. And the final tally was essentially a draw.

Political currents played a large part in driving two major pieces of legislation — a bill that substantially revised the nation's immigration laws and another hailed as a long overdue federal crackdown on drugs.

In the former, there was a feeling in Congress that something had to be done and a frustration that the problem might never go away. It was now or never, sponsors said.

On the latter, there was a rush to claim credit for launching a war on drugs, and a pre-election bandwagon developed that could not be stopped.

The confrontations in 1986 came mostly in fights over federal judgeships and particularly over civil rights issues that surfaced during the nomination debates. Reagan found himself in two bruising fights over judicial nominees — one was confirmed, the other rejected by the Judiciary Committee.

There was also a months-long confrontation in the House over gun control. The redoubtable National Rifle Association, which pushed legislation to ease federal gun regulations, found itself with a new political enemy — the nation's law enforcement groups, who were adamantly opposed to the NRA-backed legislation.

While Congress did pass a law that relaxed many of the existing controls covering guns and ammunition, the police groups held the line on some major issues and forced compromises on others.

Drugs, Immigration

On Oct. 17 Congress cleared both the drug and immigration bills. But the measures had widely disparate histories. The drug legislation, which authorized $1.7 billion in new funds for drug interdiction, eradication, enforcement, education and treatment, was pieced together in a matter of months.

The immigration bill, by contrast, had been around for five years in one form or another, and the issue had loomed over Capitol Hill even longer.

The heart of the bill was a new system of penalties against employers who knowingly hired illegal aliens. The penalties were designed to curb the flow of illegal aliens into the country.

The bill also established a program to provide legal status for illegal aliens who could prove they met certain criteria.

The most contentious part of the legislation was a section that granted legal residence to foreign farm laborers who could prove they had worked in U.S. agriculture for at least 90 days between May 1985 and May 1986.

This last provision was a compromise between Western growers, who contended they needed to have some mechanism for getting foreign workers, and organized labor and civil liberties advocates, who were concerned about exploitation of foreign labor.

While Reagan was highly visible on the drug effort, he was a silent partner on the immigration bill. The president hardly lobbied on the legislation, yet he was a critical element of the equation. House Judiciary Committee Chairman Peter W. Rodino Jr., D-N.J., refused to go ahead with work on the bill until he had assurances that Reagan would back it. And every step of the way in 1986, House members insisted on getting regular reports of the president's position. They did not want to go through a difficult exercise only to have the measure vetoed.

Judicial Politics

The president ended 1986 having deepened his imprint on the federal judiciary. By the end of the 99th Congress, Reagan had appointed a total of 299 judges to the federal bench, including the specialized courts that dealt with patent and trade issues.

Reagan's allies in conservative interest groups, such as the Free Congress Foundation, made no secret of the fact that they were pushing the administration to seek judicial candidates who shared the president's conservative philosophy.

An unintended byproduct of their aggressive efforts was an energized Senate Democratic caucus, whose members decided they needed to play a larger role in the advice and consent process.

One of the central dilemmas for the senators was whether a nominee's ideology was fair game for questioning and for confirmation or rejection.

There were four difficult confirmation fights, but Reagan lost only one of them. Jefferson B. Sessions III, a U.S. attorney from Alabama, was rejected as a district court judge by the Judiciary Committee. Members were concerned about his alleged insensitivity on racial matters.

Another kind of controversy erupted over the impeachment of a sitting judge — Harry E. Claiborne of Nevada, who became the first judge in office to go to prison. Claiborne, who was convicted of income tax fraud, refused to resign, and he battled his impeachment all the way to the Senate floor.

The Senate ultimately convicted him on three articles, or charges, stemming from the tax convictions. It acquitted him on a fourth.

The Claiborne impeachment was the first to use a streamlined committee process for gathering evidence. And, at year's end, it appeared as though the Claiborne case may have been a warmup for two other judicial impeachments.

One involved Florida federal District Judge Alcee L. Hastings, who was acquitted in 1983 on bribery charges. At the close of 1986, his case was before the U.S. Judicial Conference, the policy-making arm of the federal judiciary. The other case involved Mississippi federal District Judge Walter L. Nixon Jr., who was convicted on misconduct charges. At the end of 1986 his case was on appeal.

Other Matters

While some issues erupted into noisy fights, the work on an electronic privacy bill proceeded smoothly. With little fanfare, Congress enacted legislation that extended privacy protections to new forms of communication, such as computer mail, satellite transmissions and telephones that operated by radio waves. The smooth voyage of this bill was largely attributable to two years of quiet negotiations among privacy lawyers, business groups, members, staffers and administration officials.

The social issues were quiet as well, with no protracted fights on subjects like abortion or school prayer.

Although interest groups supporting these causes remained in evidence, they could not generate any legislative activity. Debate over abortion and school prayer, however, did surface in some of the investigations of judicial nominees.

—By Nadine Cohodas

Congress Clears Overhaul of Immigration Law

After five years of trying, Congress Oct. 17 cleared legislation (S 1200 — PL 99-603) that transformed the nation's immigration laws.

For the first time, employers faced fines — and in flagrant cases jail terms — for knowingly hiring foreigners who were in the country illegally. These sanctions were designed to stem the tide of illegal aliens entering the United States, and they addressed an anomaly in existing law: While it was illegal to enter the country without proper papers and illegal to work here, it was not a violation of the law for an employer to hire so-called "undocumented workers."

But the bill also created a mechanism for giving legal status, or amnesty, to perhaps millions of illegal aliens who could prove they had resided continuously in the United States since before Jan. 1, 1982. Sponsors hoped this program would end "the shadow society" of illegal aliens living in poverty, subject to exploitation and in fear of deportation.

And it included a controversial program designed to assure Western growers — who had historically relied on an illegal work force — that they would have an adequate supply of labor to harvest crops. The program would provide temporary resident status for up to 350,000 foreigners who could prove they had worked at least 90 days in American agriculture between May 1985 and May 1986.

The final bill was a delicate compromise forged by a host of competing interests that had fought out the issues in battles during the 97th and 98th Congresses. This time, members were in a mood to reach the necessary compromises to pass a bill, and the way was cleared once Republicans and Democrats reached a compromise on the farm worker issue.

At the heart of the deal was a recognition on the one hand that Western growers needed an adequate labor force, and a willingness on the other to grant these workers protection from exploitation by giving them legal status in the United States.

Provisions

As signed into law Nov. 6, S 1200 (PL 99-603):

Employer Sanctions

- Made it unlawful for any person knowingly to hire, recruit or refer for a fee any alien not authorized to work in the United States.
- Required employers to verify all newly hired people by examining either a U.S. passport, a certificate of U.S. citizenship, a certificate of naturalization or a resident alien card. If these documents were not available, verification could be established by a combination of papers showing identity and authority to work. For example, a person could show a driver's license in addition to either a U.S. birth certificate or a Social Security card.
- Required each employer to attest in writing under penalty of perjury that he saw such documentation before any hiring.
- Required the employee to attest in writing before being hired that he was authorized to work in the United States.
- Permitted the president to implement a more secure verification system upon notice and approval of Congress. The appropriate agencies were directed to study the feasibility of a system, like the one already used to check credit cards, where employers could telephone a central number to get documents verified.
- Established civil and criminal penalties for hiring illegal aliens but provided a six-month education period during which employers would not be subject to penalties. During the subsequent 12-month period, a violator would be given a warning citation for the first offense.
- Established the following fines for violations after the citation period:

First offense — a civil fine of not less than $250 nor more than $2,000 per each illegal alien found to be hired.

Second offense — a civil fine of not less than $2,000 nor more than $5,000 per illegal alien.

Third offense — a civil fine of not less than $3,000 nor more than $10,000 per illegal alien.

- Authorized criminal penalties of up to six months' imprisonment and/or a $3,000 fine for a "pattern or practice" of knowingly hiring an illegal alien.
- Required employers, recruiters and those who refer for employment to keep records. The bill established a civil fine of not less than $100 nor more than $1,000 for failure to keep records.
- Allowed employers charged with violating the law to defend themselves by showing that they had complied in good faith with the verification procedure.
- Required the attorney general to notify alleged violators of the infractions and, upon request, grant a hearing within 30 days before imposing any penalty.
- Required administrative law judges to conduct the hearings "at the nearest practicable place" to where alleged violators lived and the infractions occurred.
- Required the judge to use a "preponderance of the evidence" as the standard for finding that a violation had occurred.
- Made the decision of the judge final unless the attorney general modified or vacated the order within 30 days.
- Gave a violator 45 days from the time the order became final to challenge his penalty in a federal appeals court.
- Relieved employers from verifying a worker's credentials when a state employment agency had done so and the worker retained a certification of such verification.
- Terminated sanctions after three years if the comptroller general determined that sanctions resulted in discrimination in employment or had unduly burdened employers, and Congress enacted a joint resolution adopting that determination.
- Provided expedited procedures for Congress to consider a joint resolution terminating sanctions.

Anti-Discrimination Measures

- Created an Office of Special Counsel in the Justice Department to investigate and prosecute any charges of discrimination stemming from unlawful immigration-related employment practices.
- Barred employers from discriminating against legal residents simply because they were not full-fledged citizens. However, this provision would cover only those permanent or temporary residents who had shown an intention to become citizens.
- Made clear that an employer could not be sued if,

between two equally qualified people, he chose the U.S. citizen over the legal resident who was not yet a citizen.

• Exempted employers of three or fewer workers from coverage.

• Authorized an administrative law judge, after a hearing, to order a violator to hire the aggrieved person, to award limited back pay if appropriate and to pay a penalty of $1,000 for each individual discriminated against.

• Terminated the anti-discrimination provisions if the employer sanctions were lifted. The anti-bias mechanism also could be ended if Congress, by joint resolution, determined that sanctions had not resulted in discrimination or that the process had "created an unreasonable burden on employers."

Increased Enforcement and Service

• Provided a two-year authorization for the Immigration and Naturalization Service (INS) providing an additional $422 million in fiscal 1987 and $419 million in fiscal 1988. The bill also authorized $12 million in fiscal 1987 and $15 million in fiscal 1988 for the Executive Office of Immigration Review to carry out added duties for the INS imposed by the bill.

• Beefed up criminal penalties for smuggling aliens into the United States. A violator could be imprisoned for up to five years per smuggled alien and could be fined in accordance with fines specified in the federal criminal code.

• Authorized a contingency fund of $35 million for use in immigration emergencies, such as the 1980 boat lift from Cuba.

• Required states to verify the status of non-citizens applying for public assistance, such as food stamps, welfare programs, public housing and unemployment compensation. Under the bill, states would be reimbursed 100 percent for the implementation costs of this provision. However, the secretaries of the appropriate departments, such as Agriculture, Health and Human Services, and Labor, could waive this verification rule.

• Required a search warrant for INS officers to enter outdoor agricultural operations to enforce the immigration laws.

Legalization

• Provided temporary resident status for aliens who had resided continuously in the United States since before Jan. 1, 1982, and who could not be excluded for reasons specified in the immigration law.

• Allowed these temporary residents to become permanent residents after 18 months if they could show a minimal understanding of English and knowledge of history and government of the United States or were pursuing a course of instruction to gain such knowledge.

• Barred newly legalized aliens from most forms of public assistance for five years. Exceptions would be made for emergency medical care, aid to the aged, blind or disabled, for serious injury, or assistance that would be in the interest of public health.

• Provided permanent resident status for specified Cubans and Haitians who entered the United States prior to Jan. 1, 1982.

• Provided for administrative and judicial review of a denial of an application for legalization.

• Ensured the confidentiality of records by barring use of information in an application for any purpose other than determining the merits of the application or to determine whether fraud was involved.

• Allowed the attorney general to grant legal status to aliens who could show they had been in the United States prior to January 1972 and had lived in the country continuously since then. Under existing law, the attorney general could grant legal status to those who could show they had been in the country since June 30, 1948.

• Required appropriations of $1 billion in each of the four fiscal years after enactment to reimburse states for the public assistance, health and education costs resulting from legalizing aliens. Unspent money from one year could be carried over to the next year. In addition, any of the unspent $4 billion at the end of fiscal 1991 could be carried over an additional three fiscal years. States would have to apply for the aid and the money would be allotted according to a detailed formula specified in the bill. The money paid to the states would be reduced by the Social Security and Medicaid that went to newly legalized aliens.

• Reimbursed states for the costs of incarcerating certain aliens.

H-2 Workers

• Revised and expanded an existing temporary foreign worker program known as H-2. This program predominantly applied to farm workers.

• Required an employer to apply to the secretary of labor no more than 60 days in advance of needing foreign workers, and then required the employer to try to recruit domestic workers for the jobs that needed to be filled. Existing law required an 80-day advance request.

• Required the labor secretary to decide on the request for labor no later than 20 days in advance of an employer's need.

• Provided an expedited procedure for getting workers if the labor secretary had determined that U.S. workers would be available at the time needed but the employer subsequently found that the workers were not qualified and available.

• Guaranteed agricultural H-2 workers certain benefits such as housing and worker compensation (if not available under a state program), travel and subsistence costs.

• Allowed H-2 workers to get help from the federally funded Legal Services Corporation in disputes over wages, hours and working conditions.

Special Seasonal Agricultural Workers

• Provided temporary resident status for up to 350,000 aliens who could prove they had lived in the United States for at least three years and who could prove they had worked at least 90 days in American agriculture in each of those years. They could adjust to permanent resident status after an additional year or within three years of enactment, whichever was later.

• Provided temporary status for aliens who had worked 90 days in agriculture between May 1985 and May 1986. They could become permanent residents two years after they received their temporary status or three years after enactment, whichever was later. Workers in both of these groups would not have to remain in agricultural jobs once they received their temporary status.

• Disqualified these workers from receiving welfare benefits.

• Provided for "replenishment" farm labor to replace those who left agriculture and allowed these new workers to enter the United States as temporary residents. They would have to work at least 90 days in agriculture for three years; after three years, they could apply to become permanent residents. They would be barred from receiving most public aid.

- Terminated the replenishment worker program seven years after enactment.
- Established a commission to study the availability of domestic farm labor and that industry's need for foreign workers.

Miscellaneous

- Increased the legal immigration ceilings for colonies from 600 to 5,000. This provision was designed to help immigrants from Hong Kong, which was to become part of China in 1990.
- Provided special immigrant status to certain officers and employees of international organizations such as the United Nations and the World Bank and their immediate family members. This designation allowed these people to remain if they were the surviving spouse or dependent of a covered employee and had been in the United States for a specified period.
- Authorized the attorney general and secretary of state to establish a three-year pilot program for up to eight countries allowing tourists from these countries to enter the United States without first obtaining a visa.
- Allowed a father to petition the government to bring his illegitimate child into the United States as an immediate relative.
- Made clear that an alien's "brief, casual and innocent" trips outside of the United States would not constitute a failure to maintain a continuous physical presence in the United States, thereby subjecting him to deportation.
- Stated the sense of Congress that political prisoners from Cuba should be admitted to the United States.
- Required the expeditious deportation of convicted illegal aliens and required the government to list facilities available to incarcerate those aliens who were going to be deported.

Reports

- Required the president to submit several reports to Congress, including three studies on legal immigration, the program for granting visas. Among the other reports: one on the factors that caused illegal immigration, two on the legalization program established in the bill, and two on employer sanctions.
- Required the administration to submit reports on the H-2 program every two years.
- Required a report on the three-year visa waiver program.
- Required the attorney general to tell Congress the resources required to improve the INS.
- Stated a sense of Congress that Mexico should be consulted on the implementation of the immigration legislation.

Background

S 1200 represented the first comprehensive overhaul of the nation's immigration laws since enactment of the McCarran-Walter Act (PL 82-414) in 1952. *(Congress and the Nation Vol. I, p. 222)*

Spurred by growing political pressure from Southern and Western states, Congress had been grappling with proposals to revamp the immigration laws since 1981. Building on a report issued that year by a select commission on immigration, the Senate in August 1982 passed an overhaul of the immigration laws. A similar measure was approved in September 1982 by the House Judiciary Committee, but the House measure died in the closing hours of a lame-duck session. *(1981 Almanac p. 422; 1982 Almanac p. 405)*

In May 1983, the Senate again passed an immigration bill, and 13 months later the House, after slogging through seven days of debate, passed its own bill. Conferees met in the closing weeks of the 98th Congress but were unable to agree, and the measure died. *(1983 Almanac p. 287; 1984 Almanac p. 229)*

The Senate easily passed an immigration bill (S 1200) for the third time in September 1985. In response to vigorous lobbying by growers, the Senate added — over the objection of bill sponsor Alan K. Simpson, R-Wyo. — a three-year "guest worker" program to allow foreigners into the country temporarily to harvest perishable crops. House Judiciary Committee members balked at that plan, however, and when the Immigration, Refugees and International Law Subcommittee considered the bill in November 1985, members bypassed the issue. *(1985 Almanac p. 223)*

House Committee Action

The House version of the immigration bill was reported by the Judiciary Committee July 16 (HR 3810 — H Rept 99-682, Part I). The committee approved the bill late June 25 after a difficult seven-hour markup. The vote was 25-10.

Despite the 15-vote margin, support for the bill was lukewarm. Romano L. Mazzoli, D-Ky., chairman of the Subcommittee on Immigration, Refugees and International Law, and Dan Lungren, Calif., the panel's ranking Republican, said their backing was "qualified" because of a provision that would grant legal status to foreign farm workers.

The farm worker amendment was adopted by a much closer 19-16 vote. It would give permanent resident status to farm workers who had worked 60 days in American agriculture between May 1985 and May 1986. It was part of a compromise to appease Western growers who had demanded a large foreign guest worker program to guarantee them adequate labor for harvesting crops.

As reported, one section of HR 3810 imposed penalties against employers who knowingly hired illegal aliens. Another created a program to give legal status, as temporary United States residents, to illegal aliens who could prove they were in the country prior to Jan. 1, 1982.

In these areas, HR 3810 was similar to the Senate-passed bill, although the Senate legalization program would start within three years of enactment rather than immediately. In addition, under the Senate bill, legal status would be available only to those who could prove they were in the country prior to Jan. 1, 1980.

While both bills dealt with foreign farm workers, they did so in very different ways. Bowing to pressure from Western growers who traditionally had relied on illegal aliens to harvest crops, the Senate bill included a large guest worker program. It would allow up to 350,000 workers in the country at any one time, and these workers could stay for up to nine months each year. They could travel to different growers within specified agricultural regions.

The House provision grew out of seven months of efforts by Judiciary Committee members Charles E. Schumer, D-N.Y., and Howard L. Berman, D-Calif., and Agriculture Committee member Leon E. Panetta, D-Calif., to come up with an alternative to the Senate plan. Commit-

Marriage Fraud

Congress Oct. 17 cleared legislation (HR 3737 — PL 99-639) increasing the penalties for sham marriages used to gain entry into the United States.

Final action came when the Senate passed a bill that the House had approved Sept. 29. The legislation established a fine of up to $250,000 and up to a five-year prison term for those who committed marriage fraud. It also made a fraud conviction grounds for deportation.

In addition, the bill created a two-year conditional permanent resident status for alien spouses and their immediate relatives. Near the end of the two years, spouses would have to file a petition stating, under penalty of perjury, that their marriage had been legal, was still intact and was not aimed at evading the immigration law.

The bill, sponsored by Bill McCollum, R-Fla., was reported by the Judiciary Committee Sept. 26 (H Rept 99-906). McCollum, calling marriage fraud "a thriving cottage industry," noted that while total immigration to the United States dropped 9.6 percent from 1978 to 1984, the percentage of immigrants acquiring status as the spouse of U.S. citizens increased 43 percent during that period.

tee markups of the bill had been postponed repeatedly while the negotiations continued.

Schumer and Berman responded to criticism of the farm worker proposal by asserting that without it there would be no immigration bill in 1986. They argued that their compromise would help avoid a fight with the House Agriculture Committee, which had forced a massive guest worker program onto the 1984 immigration bill.

Details of Compromise

The main ingredient of the Schumer proposal was permanent resident status for farm workers who met the 60-day requirement. These workers would not have to remain in agricultural work once they obtained their permanent resident papers, or "green card," from the Immigration and Naturalization Service (INS).

To assure adequate farm workers in case a large number of these laborers left agriculture, the proposal provided for "replenishment" workers. They would also be admitted as permanent residents, but would have to work 60 days in agriculture for each of two years or be sent home. If they wanted to become citizens they would have to work another 60 days in agriculture for each of an additional three years.

The bill would establish a formula setting a cap on the number of farm workers who could be admitted under the permanent resident program. The cap would decline by 5 percent each year and was designed to encourage growers to use a domestic labor force.

The farm labor compromise also would revise and expand the existing H-2 program, under which employers petitioned the Labor Department for foreign workers for a specified time and type of work.

This part of the proposal was hammered out by Berman and Frederick C. Boucher, D-Va., along with labor lobbyists and representatives of growers in the Northeast and Southeast.

In general, the Berman-Boucher provisions made it easier for growers to use the H-2 program by streamlining application requirements. The compromise gave the attorney general the authority to administer the program, in consultation with the secretaries of labor and agriculture. The existing program was run by the Labor Department.

H-2 employers would have to provide workers either with housing at the work site or rental housing elsewhere. An earlier version of the proposal had a more stringent housing requirement.

The compromise also preserved an existing regulation governing the use of domestic labor. This regulation required H-2 employers to use domestic employees during 50 percent of the period for which they requested H-2 workers, even if that meant releasing foreign H-2 workers already on the job. However, the compromise exempted specified small employers from this provision.

In defending his package, Schumer contended the permanent resident proposal was "the only way to assure workers that they will be able to have the freedom of movement and bargaining power that is enjoyed by every other worker in every other industry in this nation." The proposal, he added, "is an attempt to get the free market principle into agriculture."

But Lungren, Mazzoli, and Bill McCollum, R-Fla., were sharply critical. Mazzoli called it a "rolling legalization" program, a "rolling enticement" for people to come into the country — the exact opposite of the bill's goal.

Hamilton Fish Jr., N.Y., the committee's ranking Republican, and two key Southern Democrats, John Bryant, Texas, and Larry Smith, Fla., disagreed. They sided with Schumer and Berman in arguing that the bill would die without the compromise.

Lungren offered an amendment to strike all provisions except the Berman-Boucher H-2 provisions. But his proposal was rejected 16-19. Berman cautioned members that Lungren's proposal would simply guarantee the addition of a guest worker program by the Agriculture Committee.

Mazzoli said he was troubled by the fact that permanent resident farm workers would be eligible for all forms of public assistance, such as food stamps and welfare, while aliens given legal status under the legalization provisions would be barred from most forms of aid for five years. He sought to change the bill so that the stricter legalization restrictions also applied to permanent resident workers, but his amendment was rejected 17-18.

But the panel adopted a Smith amendment providing that no worker could be given permanent resident status if government officials determined he would be a "public charge."

Mazzoli was successful on another amendment, adopted 33-2, that struck a provision barring INS raids on growers in the first 18 months after enactment. Schumer defended the provision, saying it would allow growers to get used to the new program without disruptions caused by raids.

Other Issues

During earlier markup sessions, June 17-18, the Judiciary Committee worked its way through other major sections of HR 3810.

Opponents of the bill's legalization program, led by McCollum and F. James Sensenbrenner Jr., R-Wis., argued that it was inappropriate and unfair. McCollum said it was a "slap in the face to those who are waiting legally to get into the country." McCollum sought to strike the legalization provisions, but his amendment was rejected 6-26.

Lungren offered a proposal to make the legalization program two-tiered, with permanent resident status available to those who were in the country prior to Jan. 1, 1977, and temporary resident status provided for those who arrived before Jan. 1, 1980. Fish amended the proposal to set the permanent resident date at Jan. 1, 1979, and the temporary resident date at Jan. 1, 1982, but the proposal ultimately was rejected 16-18.

An amendment by William J. Hughes, D-N.J., to provide a triggered legalization program was rejected by voice vote. Under Hughes' proposal, a legalization program would not begin until a commission determined that employer sanctions and beefed-up border patrols had cut down the number of illegals entering the United States.

One of the issues swirling around the legalization debate was the social services costs to the states if millions of aliens came forward. HR 3810 would provide for 100 percent reimbursement, but it would be up to the Appropriations committees to approve the money. A Lungren amendment to set a $1 billion-per-year cap was rejected 13-18.

The committee considered several other amendments over the two-day session. Two important proposals were adopted, but neither altered the structure of the bill.

One amendment, sponsored by Sensenbrenner and Barney Frank, D-Mass., deleted the requirement that the Immigration and Naturalization Service (INS) obtain a warrant before searching an open field. It was adopted 20-11.

The INS had vigorously objected to the warrant requirement, contending that it would hamper its ability to round up illegal aliens. INS officials noted that the Supreme Court had ruled that warrants were not required for "open field" searches. Frank said the INS told him the warrant requirement would "cripple their operations more than anything else we might do." But Lungren countered that getting a warrant was not difficult, and that one could even be obtained by phone.

By voice vote the committee adopted another Frank amendment to add procedural protections to the Systematic Alien Verification for Entitlements program, or SAVE. That program was designed to prevent illegal aliens from getting federal benefits, such as public housing and Aid to Families with Dependent Children (AFDC), the basic welfare program. It required states to verify that a benefit recipient was a legal U.S. resident.

In cases where an applicant was denied a benefit, the Frank amendment would require the recipient to have a "reasonable" opportunity to present additional documentation to prove that he or she was entitled to the aid.

The committee also agreed to set a maximum $1,000 penalty and a minimum $250 penalty for violating the requirement to keep employment records showing that an employer checked papers to verify that a worker was in the United States legally. The original bill had set a flat $1,000 penalty.

These amendments were rejected:

- By Sensenbrenner, to delete anti-discrimination provisions designed to protect legalized aliens who might face employment discrimination because they were not yet citizens, 15-20.
- By Lungren, stating that an employer could not be sued for discrimination for preferring a citizen over a permanent resident if both were equally qualified, 15-16.
- By Lungren, to exempt from sanctions those who employed three or fewer workers. He said it would be "a waste for the INS to concentrate on these employers."

But Bryant said the amendment sent the wrong signal. "The philosophy of the bill is to stop illegal immigration, to say it is pointless to come here because there will not be a job for you. The message must go out without equivocation."

Action by Other Committees

After the Judiciary Committee completed work on the bill, several other panels reviewed the measure. Additional reports were filed Aug. 5 by the Committees on Education and Labor (H Rept 99-682, Part II), Ways and Means (Part III), Energy and Commerce (Part IV) and Agriculture (Part V).

None of the committees altered the carefully negotiated farm worker compromise. However, Ways and Means insisted on a chance to offer a floor amendment giving some of these workers a right to welfare and other benefits once they were in the United States.

House Rejects Rule

The House Sept. 26 rejected, 180-202, ground rules for consideration of HR 3810 that would have limited floor amendments to the measure. Only 13 Republicans voted for the rule (H Res 559), with 145 against. Among Democrats 167 voted for it; 57 were opposed. *(Vote 385, p. 110-H)*

Just minutes earlier the House, in a procedural move, had agreed to leave the rule unchanged. That vote was 196-189. *(Vote 384, p. 110-H)*

Republicans complained bitterly that the rule denied them the right to change or eliminate the Schumer group's compromise farm worker proposal.

Peter W. Rodino Jr., D-N.J., said after the votes there was no way politically to resurrect the bill. He and Schumer blamed Republicans for killing the bill, noting the big GOP margins against the rule in the two votes. "I've always said we needed bipartisan support to pass this legislation," Rodino said. "Today, obviously, it wasn't there."

Lungren, who led the Republican charge against the rule, said Rodino was wrong. He said he only wanted a chance to offer a substitute for the farm worker amendment, which he said was unacceptable and not workable.

Lungren and a handful of other Republicans also complained that the Rules Committee inserted provisions in the bill to give temporary legal status to Salvadorans and Nicaraguans who had illegally entered the United States. The rule did not permit a motion to strike these provisions, which the Reagan administration opposed.

Refusing to concede outright defeat, Schumer resumed negotiations immediately after the Sept. 26 vote to redraft the farm compromise and resurrect the bill. A new agreement — drafted with Lungren, Fish, Panetta, Berman, Mazzoli and Rodino — emerged Oct. 7. And a day later, after meetings with Simpson, chief sponsor of S 1200, the House and Senate principals reached agreement on the package.

House Passage

In a stunning reversal, the House passed HR 3810 Oct. 9. The late-evening vote was 230-166, a much larger margin than when a similar measure passed the House in 1984. *(Vote 421, p. 118-H)*

Members narrowly rejected an amendment that would have stripped out one of the major elements of the legislation — the program to grant legal status to millions of illegal aliens already in the country. McCollum's move to strike this provision was rejected 192-199, after a seesaw vote that showed McCollum prevailing at several points during the roll call. *(Vote 419, p. 118-H)*

HR 3810 immediately went to conference with the Senate.

The Second Try

The new agriculture deal approved Oct. 9 included these elements:

- Provided temporary resident status for up to 350,000 foreigners who had resided in the United States for three years and who could prove they worked at least 90 days in agriculture in each of those years.

They would have to apply to the Justice Department to enter the program. If they received temporary status, they could become permanent residents after an additional year or three years after enactment, whichever was later.

- Provided temporary resident status for alien workers who had worked 90 days in agriculture between May 1985 and May 1986. They could become permanent residents two years after they received their temporary status or three years after enactment, whichever was later.

Workers in both of these groups would not have to remain in farm jobs once they received their legal status.

- Created a third category of "replenishment" workers to replace those workers who had left agriculture. These workers would be given temporary resident status and would have to work in agriculture for at least 90 days for three years following their admission into the program.

They could become citizens only if they worked in agriculture for at least 90 days for an additional two years, for a total of five years in agricultural work.

- Ended the replenishment program seven years after enactment.

This agreement was considerably more stringent than the original Schumer proposal, but more limited than provisions in the Senate bill.

Other Action

The Rules Committee crafted a rule for consideration (H Res 580) that, by consent, incorporated several changes into the bill before any debate. The amendments that were allowed all had strict time limits. The longest was 20 minutes, and that was reserved for the most controversial proposals, particularly McCollum's motion to strike legalization.

During the debate, the House also rejected, 197-199, a Fish motion to strike provisions inserted by the Rules Committee granting temporary legal residence to Nicaraguans and Salvadorans who had made their way into the United States. *(Vote 420, p. 118-H)*

These provisions incorporated a bill (HR 822 — H Rept 99-755, Parts I and II) sponsored by Rules member Joe Moakley, D-Mass., to grant "extended voluntary departure" (EVD) to the Salvadorans. HR 822 had been reported by the Judiciary Committee Aug. 6 and by Rules Sept. 16. The protections for Nicaraguans were added by Rules Chairman Claude Pepper, D-Fla.

The theory behind these provisions was that these aliens should be given refuge in the United States until conditions in their homelands improved.

The administration strongly opposed the EVD section, contending that the Central Americans were "economic migrants" seeking a better life in the United States and not refugees fleeing political persecution.

The House also adopted, 221-170, an amendment by E. "Kika" de la Garza, D-Texas, to require Immigration and Naturalization Service officials to have warrants before searching "open fields" for illegal aliens. The administration opposed this provision, arguing that it was too cumbersome for law enforcement. *(Vote 417, p. 118-H)*

Following passage of HR 3810, the House substituted its text for that of S 1200, clearing the way for a conference.

Conference

Conferees began meeting Oct. 10 and wrapped up their negotiations four days later. Most differences were resolved in private sessions. They filed their report Oct. 14 (H Rept 99-1000).

The House backed off the automatic end to sanctions in exchange for Senate provisions requiring Congress to review the program within three years. The program would be terminated by joint resolution if the comptroller general determined that sanctions had resulted in discrimination.

The House also agreed to give up Moakley's provisions on Salvadorans and Nicaraguans. But conferees said the administration had pledged not to deport any Salvadorans to areas stricken by an earthquake Oct. 10. In addition, Rodino promised to consider a bill on the subject early in the 100th Congress, and Simpson said if the House passed a measure, he would not prevent consideration in the Senate.

The Senate agreed to accept the Frank anti-discrimination provisions, and in modified form, agreed to free legal representation for H-2 workers. However, such legal work could apply only to job-related problems, such as wages, hours and work conditions.

On the funding issue, conferees agreed to require $1 billion in appropriations for each of the next four fiscal years, with unspent money in one year available in the following year. Any unused money at the end of fiscal 1990 could be carried over through fiscal 1994.

Another element of the agreement provided that the amount the government paid for Social Security supplements and Medicaid would be deducted from the $1 billion each year.

The Senate agreed to the House legalization date: Jan. 1, 1982.

Bill Cleared

Final action on S 1200 came Oct. 17 when the Senate adopted the conference report 63-24. The House had adopted the report Oct. 15, 238-173. *(Senate vote 352, p. 57-S; House vote 433, p. 122-H)*

The Senate had hoped to complete work Oct. 16, but Phil Gramm, R-Texas, prompted a delay with a long speech criticizing the bill's farm worker provisions, and complaining that the measure was too costly.

He forced members to vote on waiving the budget act because the legalization program would amount to a new "entitlement" and there was no budget provision covering that expenditure. Members agreed 75-21 to the waiver. *(Vote 343, p. 56-S)*

To make sure there was no extended debate, the Senate voted 69-21 Oct. 17 to invoke cloture — a move that cleared the way for the final vote hours later. *(Vote 350, p. 57-S)*

Despite misgivings in some administration quarters, President Reagan said Oct. 16 he would sign the bill. Reagan made that promise after Simpson said he and Rodino agreed to make floor statements clarifying some provisions in the bill aimed at protecting the rights of minority workers.

Simpson conceded that parts of the immigration legislation concerned him. But citing the sanctions on the one hand and the amnesty on the other, he said, "On balance you have the very absolute quintessential immigration reform."

Hispanic members had been the most vigorous opponents of the bill, arguing that employers, worried about the new penalties, would not hire anyone who looked or sounded foreign.

But five of the 11 voting members of the Hispanic Caucus supported the final measure, noting that it was the best that had emerged in the five-year effort. "I think this bill is better than nothing," said Bill Richardson, D-N.M. "It was the last gasp for legalization to take place in a humane way."

Reagan Statement

In a statement issued when he signed S 1200 Nov. 6, Reagan triggered a controversy over the bill's anti-discrimination provisions.

Reagan said he believed that a non-citizen who charged that he had been unfairly denied a job could prevail in a lawsuit only if he could prove an employer acted with "discriminatory intent." Without a showing by the plaintiff of a discriminatory intent, Reagan said, "the employer need not offer any explanation for his employee selection procedures."

Reagan's interpretation was challenged by members of Congress who had been involved in drafting the bill, and civil rights lawyers expressed concern over the enforcement of the provision because of the administration's interpretation of it. ■

Rehnquist, Scalia Win Senate Confirmation

After five days of debate, the Senate Sept. 17 confirmed Associate Justice William Hubbs Rehnquist as the 16th chief justice of the United States.

Antonin Scalia was then confirmed as an associate justice of the Supreme Court to fill the seat vacated by Rehnquist.

Both Rehnquist and Scalia were sworn in Sept. 26.

Rehnquist, who observed his 62nd birthday on Oct. 1, succeeded Warren E. Burger, who stepped down from the nation's highest judicial post to devote full time to his work as chairman of the commission planning the nation's celebration of the bicentennial of the Constitution. That celebration was to begin in 1987.

The Senate vote to confirm Rehnquist was 65-33. Republicans Charles McC. Mathias Jr., R-Md., and Lowell P. Weicker Jr., R-Conn., joined 31 Democrats in opposing Rehnquist's elevation to chief justice. *(Vote 266, p. 45-S)*

Hours before the confirmation roll call, the Senate voted 68-31 to invoke cloture and limit debate on the Rehnquist nomination. A minimum of 60 votes was needed. On that critical vote, 16 Democrats joined 52 Republicans to approve the cloture petition filed by Senate Majority Leader Robert Dole, R-Kan. The only absentee was Jake Garn, R-Utah, who was recuperating from surgery to donate a kidney to his daughter. *(Vote 265, p. 45-S)*

Those who opposed Rehnquist's confirmation did so because of concern about his 15-year record on the high court, his views on minority and individual rights, and his candor in testifying to the Judiciary Committee. Civil rights groups had mounted an all-out effort to persuade the Senate to reject the nomination.

The 33 votes against Rehnquist were the largest number ever cast by the Senate against a Supreme Court nominee who won confirmation. In 1971, when he won confirmation as an associate justice on a 68-26 vote, Rehnquist tied for the second-highest number of "nay" votes received by a 20th-century Supreme Court nominee who won confirmation. *(Background, Congress and the Nation Vol. III, p. 300)*

In 1930, the Senate confirmed Charles Evans Hughes by 52-26. Hughes, who like Rehnquist previously had served as an associate justice, went on to become one of the nation's most respected chief justices.

The Senate had refused to confirm a high court nominee five times since 1900.

Scalia, 50, a judge on the U.S. Court of Appeals for the District of Columbia, was confirmed 98-0. He was the second justice to be put on the court by President Reagan. The first was Sandra Day O'Connor in 1981. *(Vote 267, p. 45-S; O'Connor nomination, 1981 Almanac p. 409)*

In sharp contrast to the hours of floor debate over Rehnquist's nomination, there were only a few moments of speeches about the equally conservative Scalia before he was confirmed.

Scalia became the 103rd person to serve as a member of the Supreme Court. He also was the first justice of Italian-American descent.

Background

President Reagan on June 17 had announced the retirement of Burger, then 78, and the selection of Rehnquist and Scalia.

In making his selections, Reagan sought to transform the Supreme Court's conservative wing into a conservative center. A Rehnquist court, Reagan hoped, might yet halt or reverse the liberal trends in American law that began under his predecessor, Chief Justice Earl Warren, and continued during Burger's tenure. *(Burger's legacy, box, p. 70)*

O'Connor, Reagan's first nominee, in 1981 brought a strong new voice and generally conservative vote to the court. For a time in 1984 the court seemed to shift to the right, approving administration initiatives on affirmative action, the rights of criminal suspects, and questions of church and state. But more recent liberal decisions on abortion and school prayer highlighted the court's basically moderate character and underscored the significance of any additional Reagan appointments.

Scalia was more adamantly conservative than Burger on such politically sensitive subjects as abortion, affirmative action and freedom of the press. And Reagan clearly hoped that by promoting Rehnquist to chief justice, he would enhance the influence of the court's most conservative member.

Chief Justices of the United States

John Jay

Born: Dec. 12, 1745, New York, N.Y. **Died:** May 17, 1829.
Education: King's College (now Columbia University).
Position Held at Time of Appointment: Secretary of Foreign Affairs.
Appointment: By Washington, 1789. **Resigned:** 1795.

John Rutledge

Born: September 1739, Charleston, S.C. **Died:** June 21, 1800.
Education: Inns of Court (London).
Position Held at Time of Appointment: Chief justice, South Carolina Supreme Court. (Had served as associate justice, U.S. Supreme Court, 1789-91.)
Appointment: By Washington, 1795. Recess appointment; Senate rejected confirmation in December of same year.

Oliver Ellsworth

Born: April 29, 1745, Windsor, Conn. **Died:** Nov. 26, 1807.
Education: Princeton University.
Position Held at Time of Appointment: U.S. senator.
Appointment: By Washington, 1796. **Resigned:** 1800.

John Marshall

Born: Sept. 24, 1755, Germantown, Va. **Died:** July 6, 1835.
Education: Self-taught.
Position Held at Time of Appointment: Secretary of State.
Appointment: By Adams, 1801; died in office.

Roger Brooke Taney

Born: March 17, 1777, Calvert County, Md. **Died:** Oct. 12, 1864.
Education: Dickinson College.
Position Held at Time of Appointment: Secretary of the Treasury.
Appointment: By Jackson, 1835, confirmed in 1836; died in office.

Salmon Portland Chase

Born: Jan. 13, 1808, Cornish, N.H. **Died:** May 7, 1873.
Education: Dartmouth College.
Position Held at Time of Appointment: Secretary of the Treasury.
Appointment: By Lincoln, 1864; died in office.

Morrison Remick Waite

Born: Nov. 29, 1816, Lyme, Conn. **Died:** March 23, 1888.
Education: Yale College.
Position Held at Time of Appointment: President, Ohio constitutional convention.
Appointment: By Grant, 1874; died in office.

Melville Weston Fuller

Born: Feb. 11, 1833, Augusta, Maine. **Died:** July 4, 1910.
Education: Bowdoin College, Harvard Law School.
Position Held at Time of Appointment: Attorney in Chicago.
Appointment: By Cleveland, 1888; died in office.

Edward Douglass White

Born: Nov. 3, 1845, Lafourche Parish, La. **Died:** May 19, 1921.
Education: Mount St. Mary's College, Georgetown College.
Position Held at Time of Appointment: Associate justice, U.S. Supreme Court.
Appointment: By Taft, 1910; died in office.

William Howard Taft

Born: Sept. 15, 1857, Cincinnati, Ohio. **Died:** March 8, 1930.
Education: Yale University, Cincinnati Law School.
Previous Positions: President (1909-13); joint chairman of the National War Labor Board (1918-19).
Appointment: By Harding, 1921. **Resigned:** 1930.

Charles Evans Hughes

Born: April 11, 1862, Glens Falls, N.Y. **Died:** Aug. 27, 1948.
Education: Colgate University, Brown University, Columbia University Law School.
Position Held at Time of Appointment: Judge, Permanent Court of International Justice. (Had served as associate justice, U.S. Supreme Court, 1910-16.)
Appointment: By Hoover, 1930. **Resigned:** 1941.

Harlan Fiske Stone

Born: Oct. 11, 1872, Chesterfield, N.H. **Died:** April 22, 1946.
Education: Amherst College, Columbia University.
Position Held at Time of Appointment: Associate justice, U.S. Supreme Court.
Appointment: By Roosevelt, 1941; died in office.

Frederick Moore Vinson

Born: Jan. 22, 1890, Louisa, Ky. **Died:** Sept. 8, 1953.
Education: Centre College.
Position Held at Time of Appointment: Secretary of the Treasury.
Appointment: By Truman, 1946; died in office.

Earl Warren

Born: March 19, 1891, Los Angeles. **Died:** July 9, 1974.
Education: University of California.
Position Held at Time of Appointment: Governor of California.
Appointment: By Eisenhower, 1953. **Resigned:** 1969.

Warren Earl Burger

Born: Sept. 17, 1907, St. Paul, Minn.
Education: University of Minnesota, St. Paul College of Law (now Mitchell College of Law).
Position Held at Time of Appointment: Judge, U.S. Court of Appeals for the District of Columbia.
Appointment: By Nixon, 1969. **Resigned:** 1986.

Rehnquist: A Consistent Course

Like Burger, Rehnquist was named to the court by President Richard M. Nixon. Aged 47 when he was appointed in 1971, he was both the youngest and the most conservative of Nixon's four Supreme Court appointees.

Born in Milwaukee and raised in one of its suburbs, Rehnquist received his B.A. degree from Stanford University in 1948, and an M.A. in political science from Harvard University in 1950. He won his law degree in 1952 from Stanford University Law School, where one of his classmates was O'Connor.

After clerking for Supreme Court Justice Robert H. Jackson during the 1952-53 term, Rehnquist left Washington for Phoenix, Ariz., where he practiced law and became active in Republican politics. There he met Richard G. Kleindienst, who later became deputy attorney general and then attorney general. In 1969, Kleindienst invited Rehnquist to return to Washington as assistant attorney general, Office of Legal Counsel. He was serving in that post when Nixon named him to the court; he was confirmed by the Senate on a 68-26 vote.

An ardent advocate of judicial restraint, Rehnquist felt that the court should simply call a halt to unconstitutional policies — and stop at that. Innovation in public policy, he believed, is the prerogative of elected officials, not appointed judges.

Rehnquist often spoke for the court when it deferred to its partners in the federal system — Congress, the president and the states. He wrote its 1981 opinion upholding the decision of Congress to exclude women from the military draft, its 1981 opinion endorsing President Jimmy Carter's deal with Iran that freed 52 Americans held hostage by that country, and a 1984 opinion backing Reagan administration curbs on travel to Cuba. In all three, he emphasized the broad powers of the elected branches — and the narrow scope of judicial review.

Rehnquist took a literal approach to individual rights. Because he found no specific right of privacy in the Constitution, for example, he consistently dissented from the court's rulings protecting a woman's privacy-based right to have an abortion.

He was the only justice completely comfortable with the argument of Attorney General Edwin Meese III that the original intent of the men who wrote the Constitution and the Bill of Rights is the proper standard for interpreting those documents today.

Rehnquist consistently sided with police and prosecutors on questions of criminal law. He shared the administration's views that a number of decisions handed down by the court under Chief Justice Earl Warren had protected the rights of criminal suspects at too high a cost to society.

On controversial issues, Rehnquist usually agreed with Chief Justice Burger and Justices O'Connor and Lewis F. Powell Jr. However, he was far more likely to dissent than his allies, in recent years casting twice as many dissenting votes as Burger.

During his first 15 years on the court, Rehnquist was unchallenged in his role as the court's most conservative member. But although his opinions were praised for their intellectual character, they did not often attract a majority of the votes. That did not appear to concern Rehnquist, who, unlike Burger, seemed as much at home in dissent as in the majority.

Rehnquist expressed little interest in the sort of extra-judicial role played by Burger, who used his position to press for improvements in the structure and operations of the court system. The chief justice chairs the Judicial Conference of the United States, which governs administration of the federal courts. He is board chairman of the Federal Judicial Center, the research, training and planning arm of the courts. And he supervises the Administrative Office of the United States Courts, the court system's "housekeeping" and statistical arm.

Rehnquist was well liked by his colleagues, and some court observers suggested that he might prove a more effective coalition-builder than Burger — especially with Scalia, noted for his charm and persuasiveness, at his side. Some legal scholars attributed the fragmentation that characterized the court's opinions on particularly difficult issues during Burger's tenure as evidence of his failure to develop consensus among his colleagues.

Scalia: Conservative Favorite

Scalia, whom Reagan named to the U.S. Court of Appeals for the District of Columbia in 1982, had cast enough judicial votes and written enough opinions to give the president and his advisers confidence that his views were compatible with theirs. At 50, Scalia became the youngest member of the court, likely to serve well into the next century.

Because Scalia took a very restrictive view of the role of the courts, he had become a favorite of conservative lawyers and activists, who applauded his selection.

Scalia, a Roman Catholic, had nine children and had said he personally opposed abortion. Before joining the Court of Appeals, Scalia also expressed opposition to "affirmative action" preferences for minorities — another longstanding target of the Reagan administration.

The president was a strong advocate of deregulation, a subject of considerable interest to Scalia, a specialist in administrative law. Scalia was for a time editor of the magazine *Regulation*, published by the American Enterprise Institute, a Washington-based think tank.

Born in Trenton, N.J., on March 11, 1936, Scalia grew up in Queens, N.Y. He graduated from Georgetown University in 1957 and from Harvard Law School in 1960.

He first tried his hand at private practice, spending six years at the firm of Jones, Day in Cleveland before leaving for a teaching post at the University of Virginia Law School. There he taught contracts, commercial and comparative law.

In the 1970s, Scalia took time off from teaching to serve as general counsel of the White House Office of Telecommunications Policy in 1971-72. He then headed the Administrative Conference of the United States, a group that advises the government on questions of administrative law and procedure.

In 1974, he became head of the Office of Legal Counsel in the Justice Department, a post held only three years earlier by Rehnquist. After serving in that position through the Ford administration, Scalia returned to academia, accepting a position at the University of Chicago Law School. He maintained a Washington presence, however, as an active critic of the legislative veto — which the Supreme Court held unconstitutional in 1983 — and as editor of *Regulation*. In 1982, Reagan brought him back to the nation's capital as a member of the appeals court.

In his relatively brief appellate court career, Scalia showed himself a hard worker, an aggressive interrogator and an articulate advocate.

He was impatient with what he saw as regulatory or judicial over-reaching.

Burger Legacy Included Landmark Opinions

Named chief justice of the United States in May 1969 by President Richard M. Nixon and confirmed the following month, Warren E. Burger served longer than all but three of his predecessors — John Marshall (1801-35), Roger B. Taney (1836-64) and Melville Fuller (1888-1910). *(Chief justices, p. 68)*

Burger's career was in many respects the mirror image of the career of Earl Warren, the man who preceded him as chief justice (1953-69).

Burger was as conservative as Warren was liberal.

He made his strongest mark as chief justice outside the court, through his administrative reform efforts. Warren's most notable achievements came behind the closed doors of the cou·t's conference room, where he lobbied the justices themselves to win coherent and effective majorities on the liberal side of issue after issue.

Burger spent most of his adult life as a federal judge. Warren was a prosecutor and politician for more than 30 years before he was named chief justice in 1953.

Burger was the Supreme Court's spokesman in a number of landmark cases — including the unanimous July 24, 1974, ruling that forced Nixon to turn over White House tape recordings that led to his resignation in the Watergate scandal.

Ironically, it was Burger's outspoken criticism of liberal Warren court rulings on criminal law that had brought him to Nixon's attention in the first place. It was consistent with those views that Burger would not allow Nixon to withhold evidence sought for use in a criminal trial.

But Burger's basic respect for the presidency and for the principle of the separation of powers was also reflected in the Watergate opinion. There, for the first time, the Supreme Court recognized a constitutional privilege protecting the confidentiality of communications between a president and his advisers — even though it found that the need for the evidence in this case outweighed the privilege.

Burger, white-haired, handsome and portly, was the very image of a chief justice. He presided graciously over the court's public proceedings, but remained quiet during most of the arguments before the court.

Although a conservative, Burger disliked the role of dissenter. Observers of the court suspected that he sometimes voted with the majority primarily to retain the privilege of deciding who wrote the opinion.

When the chief justice dissents, the most senior member of the majority — usually William J. Brennan Jr., the court's leading liberal — decides who writes the court's opinion. When Burger assigned opinions, he tended to choose a justice who would couch a decision in narrow terms; Brennan preferred opinions that swept more broadly, and he assigned cases accordingly.

Burger often wrote the court's opinion in major cases. Sometimes he authored a "liberal" decision — such as the 1983 decision upholding the Internal Revenue Service's policy of denying tax-exempt status to racially discriminatory schools — an 8-1 decision from which Rehnquist dissented.

But Burger was more comfortable on the conservative side of issues. He favored limiting the reach of many of the Warren court landmarks, particularly those excluding illegally obtained evidence from criminal trials.

And in his final court term he moved into dissent from one of the court's most important rulings during his own tenure as chief. On June 11, the court by 5-4 reaffirmed its 1973 *Roe v. Wade* ruling legalizing abortion. But Burger, who had been part of the majority in that landmark ruling, shifted sides this time, declaring his fellow justices had gone to the point of endorsing "abortion on demand" — something he never supported.

In the area of religious freedoms, Burger viewed the First Amendment as requiring the government to "take pains not to compel people to act in the name of any religion," but he felt that the contemporary court required too high a wall of separation between church and state. On this point, Rehnquist agreed.

The Constitution, Burger wrote in 1984, does not "require complete separation of church and state; it affirmatively mandates accommodation, not merely tolerance, of all religions and forbids hostility toward any."

When the court in 1985 struck down Alabama's "moment-of-silence" law permitting voluntary silent prayer in public schools, Burger dissented. This law "does not remotely threaten religious liberty," he wrote. "It accommodates the purely private, voluntary religious choices of the individual pupils who wish to pray."

Burger objected to the idea that First Amendment freedoms give certain persons or groups, such as the press, special privileges. In 1985, he spoke for the court to reject the claim that the right of petition could shield the petitioner against a libel suit. "The right to petition is guaranteed," he wrote. "The right to commit libel with impunity is not."

In similar fashion, Burger not only agreed with the court in 1985 when it refused to expand the First Amendment's protection for libel defendants, but he also urged the court to reconsider earlier rulings and narrow that protection. "The great rights guaranteed by the First Amendment," he wrote, "carry with them certain responsibilities as well."

Burger had a strong sense of the limits of judicial power. In 1982, he dissented when the court told Texas that it could not refuse to educate the children of illegal aliens. The court, he said, had no authority "to strike down laws because they do not meet our standards of desirable social policy. We trespass on the assigned function of the political branches . . . when we assume a policy-making role."

Burger took a fairly strict view of the separation of powers set forth by the framers of the Constitution. He wrote the opinion in *Immigration and Naturalization Service v. Chadha,* when the court in 1983 ruled that the legislative veto was unconstitutional.

The veto, which permitted either or both chambers of Congress to nullify an executive branch regulation or order, was "a convenient shortcut," Burger conceded. But, he cautioned, "convenience and efficiency are not the primary objectives — or the hallmarks — of democratic government."

"The condemned prisoner executed by injection is no more the 'consumer' of the drug than is the prisoner executed by firing squad a consumer of the bullets," he wrote in 1983, dissenting from an appeals court ruling requiring the Food and Drug Administration (FDA) to consider whether drugs used for lethal injections met FDA standards as safe and effective. The Supreme Court agreed, reversing the appeals court in 1985.

In similar fashion, Scalia dissented forcefully when the appeals court held that the First Amendment's guarantee of free speech protected the right of demonstrators to sleep in Lafayette Park across from the White House. Again the Supreme Court agreed with Scalia, reversing the appeals court by 7-2 in 1984.

Scalia was thought to be the principal author of an unsigned decision early in 1986 by a three-judge panel that declared key portions of the Gramm-Rudman-Hollings anti-deficit act unconstitutional, a violation of the separation of powers. The Supreme Court affirmed that decision July 7. *(Story, p. 579)*

Committee Action

The Senate Judiciary Committee approved the two nominations Aug. 14. The vote to elevate Rehnquist to chief justice was 13-5. The vote to put Scalia on the high court was 18-0.

Those voting against Rehnquist were all Democrats: ranking member Joseph R. Biden Jr., Del.; Edward M. Kennedy, Mass.; Patrick J. Leahy, Vt.; Howard M. Metzenbaum, Ohio; and Paul Simon, Ill.

They expressed concern about a variety of matters — particularly Rehnquist's candor in answering questions about his political activities before going on the bench in 1971 and his sensitivity to civil rights as demonstrated by his court opinions arguing against minority rights.

They pointed specifically to Rehnquist's denial of charges that he had harassed minority voters in Phoenix 24 years earlier and testimony contradicting that denial.

Although the committee result was not in doubt, there was an element of drama to the proceedings. All 18 senators — 10 Republicans and eight Democrats — were present and all looked unusually solemn as they explained their votes.

There was some partisan jibing, with GOP members Paul Laxalt, Nev., Orrin G. Hatch, Utah, and Alan K. Simpson, Wyo., chiding the Democrats for grilling Rehnquist so rigorously during two days of hearings July 30-31.

"Justice Rehnquist came out of the hearings stronger than when he came in," Laxalt asserted. "Rehnquist had everything but the kitchen sink thrown at him at this hearing."

And Simpson charged that the hearings were "a puerile exercise in justice bashing."

Although the focus was on Rehnquist, senators spoke about both of the nominees. On Scalia, all senators, even those who said they were concerned about his conservative views — like Kennedy, Metzenbaum and Biden — praised his skills.

The biggest complaint from both Democrats and Republicans was that Scalia was more evasive than necessary in answering questions during his daylong committee appearance on Aug. 5.

Scalia declined to give specific responses to many questions, telling senators that the issues involved were either pending in cases before the Court of Appeals on which he then served, or were likely to come before him on the Supreme Court.

Arlen Specter, R-Pa., suggested that the committee work with the administration and the American Bar Association to develop better guidelines for confirmation hearings, or, he said, it might be necessary someday to reject a nominee for refusing to answer questions.

Rehnquist Controversies

A trio of Democrats — Biden, Kennedy and Metzenbaum — had grilled Rehnquist during the confirmation hearings about his views on civil rights; allegations that he harassed Phoenix voters in the 1960s; and the fact that two of his homes included restrictive covenants, or property agreements, barring sales to non-whites and people of "the Hebrew race."

Rehnquist steadfastly denied that he was biased against minorities or that he had engaged in voter intimidation while he was a lawyer in Phoenix.

He said he had not known his deeds contained restrictive covenants, and noted they were unenforceable.

But on Aug. 1, five men offered testimony that contradicted his assertions that he had not harassed voters. And at the end of the day, it was clear their testimony had reinforced Democrats' concerns over the nomination.

Throughout his many hours in the witness chair July 30-31, Rehnquist seemed unflappable, thoughtful, easygoing and, on occasion, firm in his refusal to answer questions he deemed inappropriate for a sitting justice.

When asked to explain some of his court opinions, Rehnquist said he believed he was being "called to account" for a judicial act and he declined to answer.

After Rehnquist was excused by the committee, Democrats tangled with Justice Department officials who refused to turn over memos Rehnquist wrote while he was a top department official during the Nixon administration.

Rehnquist said he had no objection to releasing the memos, but department officials claimed executive privilege and refused to provide the documents, which dealt with civil rights, civil liberties, wiretapping and surveillance of radical groups. After several days of negotiations, the department agreed Aug. 5 to let selected committee staff members and senators review the materials.

Voter Harassment. The voter harassment charges first surfaced at the end of Rehnquist's confirmation hearings in 1971. He was asked to respond in writing to allegations that he had intimidated or challenged Phoenix voters. In response, he wrote James O. Eastland, D-Miss. (1943-78), then Judiciary chairman, that "in none of these years [1958-68] did I personally engage in challenging the qualifications of any voters."

Rehnquist repeated his assertions July 30 when Kennedy and Metzenbaum questioned him about allegations made in the past month by 10 people who said they witnessed harassment. Rehnquist repeatedly denied the charges and told Kennedy the witnesses were wrong. "I think they're mistaken. I just can't offer any other explanation," he said.

Some of the most damaging testimony against Rehnquist came August 1.

James J. Brosnahan, an assistant U.S. attorney in Phoenix in 1962, said he was with FBI agents who were called to one polling station after voters complained they had been intimidated. Brosnahan said Rehnquist was there and some voters accused him of challenging their right to vote. Brosnahan told the committee Rehnquist did not deny being a vote "challenger." However, Brosnahan added, he did not actually see Rehnquist challenge anyone's credentials.

Later William Turner said he was with Rehnquist on Election Day in 1962, and added, "At no time in our presence did Bill Rehnquist assume the role of challenger."

Racial Bias. Democrats questioned Rehnquist closely on his civil rights views, particularly those he held as a young man working as a law clerk for Justice Jackson.

Biden grilled him about a memo he had written to Jackson when the Supreme Court was first considering the landmark 1954 *Brown v. Board of Education* decision, which held that official segregation of schools was unconstitutional.

In the memo, Rehnquist argued in favor of the doctrine that it was permissible to have separate but equal facilities for blacks and whites. That doctrine was upheld in an 1890 case, *Plessy v. Ferguson.*

Rehnquist said in 1971 that the memo represented Justice Jackson's views, not his own, but Metzenbaum challenged that, and Biden demanded to know how Rehnquist felt about both the *Plessy* decision and what conclusion he came to when the *Brown* case was being decided.

Rehnquist said he believed the *Plessy* decision was wrong and that "it was not a good interpretation of the equal protection clause to say that when you segregate people by race there's no denial of equal protection."

And he told Biden he had never completely decided what the court should do on *Brown.* "I had ideas on both sides. I don't think I truly decided in my own mind," he said.

When Biden pressed him, Rehnquist said, "Senator, I don't think I reached a conclusion. Law clerks don't have to vote." "No," Biden retorted, "but they surely think."

When Laxalt told Rehnquist there was concern among women and blacks about his civil rights views, Rehnquist conceded that some of his opinions resulted in "less favorable rulings for women and blacks than would a broader reading of the equal protection [clause of the Constitution]." But Rehnquist insisted he treated all parties equally: "It is the same with respect to corporations," he said. "I give the best interpretation I know how."

"Are women going to be prejudiced by your being chief justice?" Laxalt then asked. "I don't believe so, Senator," Rehnquist replied.

Restrictive Covenants. It was Leahy who asked Rehnquist July 30 about a property deed to a Vermont home that contained the covenant barring sales to Jews. Rehnquist said he had not known of the covenant until the FBI uncovered it in a routine screening investigation. He said he could not recall reading the deed. (In a subsequent letter to committee Chairman Strom Thurmond, R-S.C., Rehnquist said that in 1974 he had been given a copy of a letter referring to the restrictive language but did not recall the letter or its contents at the time he testified.)

Rehnquist added that the language was meaningless because it could not be enforced in a court, but that he considered it "obnoxious." At first Rehnquist said he saw no point in having the clause removed, but after Leahy raised the issue of appearances, Rehnquist said he would take steps to remove it.

A day later, Kennedy told Rehnquist that records showed a home he had owned in Phoenix included a covenant barring sales to non-whites. Rehnquist, who no longer owned the property, said he did not know of that restrictive language either.

Health. Senators avoided all but the most general questions about Rehnquist's health. However, the evening of July 31, Thurmond announced that the committee had appointed an independent physician to review Rehnquist's medical records and interview the justice's doctors, if necessary.

(After a survey of Rehnquist's medical records, but without examining the nominee, the doctor reportedly told the committee Rehnquist appeared to be in good health. Simon urged that the medical records be made public, but Thurmond refused to do so.)

Concern about Rehnquist's health stemmed from chronic, low-back problems that required hospitalization in January 1982 because of an adverse reaction to a drug prescribed for pain.

In response to questions from Howell Heflin, D-Ala., Rehnquist said he "certainly would not have accepted the nomination" as chief justice if he did not believe he was in good health. ■

Manion Confirmation

After months of controversy, Indiana lawyer Daniel A. Manion won a seat on the 7th U.S. Circuit Court of Appeals. Manion's confirmation became final July 23 when the Senate rejected, 49-50, a Democratic move to reconsider an earlier confirmation vote. *(Vote 162, p. 30-S)*

The July 23 vote brought to a close a dispute that began when the Senate Judiciary Committee received Manion's nomination Feb. 21. Critics claimed that Manion was not qualified to serve on the bench because he had a limited legal practice, had poor writing skills, and had, through his statements, called into question his willingness to follow Supreme Court rulings.

Joseph R. Biden Jr., D-Del., the leader of the anti-Manion effort, repeated those allegations July 23, adding that it was up to Manion's supporters to show he was qualified to serve. The burden on those supporting the nominee, Biden asserted, was to show "excellence, not mediocrity."

But Manion supporters, led by Indiana Republican Dan Quayle and Judiciary Committee Chairman Strom Thurmond, R-S.C., charged that much of the opposition to Manion was based on his reputation as a conservative, not his qualifications.

Manion, 44, was the son of the late Clarence Manion, a founder of the John Birch Society and one of the leaders of the modern conservative movement.

A 1973 graduate of Indiana University School of Law, the younger Manion was a lawyer in a South Bend law firm handling commercial work that involved litigation. He had served as Indiana deputy attorney general in 1973-74 and as a member of the Indiana Senate from 1978-82.

Manion appeared regularly from 1971-79 with his father, former dean of the University of Notre Dame law school, on the "Manion Forum," a radio and television program promoting conservative ideology.

The fight over the Manion nomination activated liberal and conservative lobbying groups. People for the American Way, the individual-rights organization founded by television producer Norman Lear, launched a newspaper and radio campaign against the nomination.

Phyllis Schlafly, head of the conservative Eagle Forum, brought her group into the fray, urging supporters to write senators on Manion's behalf. In her letter supporting

Reagan's Conservative Imprint on Courts

By the end of the 99th Congress, President Reagan had appointed nearly 30 percent of all federal judges then serving. Because these appointments were for life, Reagan had virtually assured that his conservative imprint would remain on the nation's judiciary long after he left the White House.

Reagan's conservative appointments provoked unaccustomed conflict in the Senate confirmation process in 1986. As civil rights groups intensified their criticism of several judicial nominees, senators were forced to take a much harder look at the president's appointments. That resulted in several bitter confirmation fights, including one that Reagan lost. *(Sessions nomination, p. 75)*

"I think both sides take their interest in judgeships very seriously, and rightly so," said Orrin G. Hatch, R-Utah, a Judiciary Committee member who had been one of the administration's chief defenders in the Senate. "I don't think that the animosities or the ideological infighting is going to end."

The Numbers

By Oct. 30, 1986, Reagan had appointed a total of 299 judges. Eight of the appointments were to specialized courts — three to the Court of Appeals for the Federal Circuit, which handled patent cases, and five to the U.S. Trade Court.

The remaining 291 appointments broke down this way: three to the Supreme Court — Associate Justices Antonin Scalia and Sandra Day O'Connor and the elevation of Justice William H. Rehnquist to chief justice; 63 appointments to the 12 regional appeals courts; and 225 appointments to the federal district courts.

As of Oct. 30, there were 734 judges actually hearing cases in the district courts, and 215, or 29.3 percent, were appointed by Reagan. (The total included 528 judges carrying full caseloads and another 206 in a semi-retired status that still allowed them to try cases.)

In all, Reagan had appointed 225 district court judges, but 10 of them had been elevated to the appeals courts.

Of the 212 appeals court judges handling cases, 61, or 28.8 percent, were Reagan appointees. (The total included 147 full-time judges and another 65 in a semi-retired status.)

Reagan made 63 appeals court appointments, but Scalia was elevated to the Supreme Court, and Emory Sneeden, who had been on the 4th U.S. Circuit Court of Appeals, resigned.

Reagan's appointments to the appeals courts were particularly important because most of the decisions made by these judges are final. They review federal district court decisions, and only a small fraction of their rulings are considered by the Supreme Court.

After filling the existing vacancies, Reagan would have appointed at least half of the judges on seven of the 12 appeals court circuits: 2d (Connecticut, New York, Vermont); 5th (Texas, Louisiana, Mississippi); 6th (Kentucky, Michigan, Ohio, Tennessee); 7th (Illinois, Indiana, Wisconsin); 8th (Arkansas, Iowa, Minnesota, Missouri, Nebraska, North Dakota, South Dakota); 10th (Colorado, Kansas, New Mexico, Oklahoma, Utah, Wyoming); and the District of Columbia.

Reagan's impact on the judiciary was especially apparent when matched against President Jimmy Carter's 258 appointments — a record until Reagan's administration. Carter was given 152 new judgeships to fill as a result of the 1978 Omnibus Judgeship Act, and the expectation was that he would be the president who left a lasting stamp on the judiciary because he had the chance to put so many people on the bench. *(Omnibus Judgeship Act, 1978 Almanac p. 173; Carter's judicial appointments, 1981 Almanac p. 410)*

In one regard Carter did, putting more women, blacks and Hispanics on the judiciary than any other president. But five years into his presidency, Reagan, through vacancies and new judgeships, had made enough appointments to dilute Carter's impact.

And as of Oct. 30, Reagan still had another 56 vacancies to fill — nine on the appeals courts and 47 on the district courts, according to the Administrative Office of the U.S. Courts.

Dozens more could be expected over the next two years as judges assumed semi-retired status or left the bench altogether.

Justice Department officials expected that by the time Reagan left office, he would have appointed at least 45 percent of the entire judiciary.

Daniel Manion, Schlafly said of his father: "His years of weekly radio programs were one of the factors that kept conservatism alive in those lean years before Ronald Reagan came along."

Committee Action

In a heated session May 8, the Senate Judiciary Committee voted 11-6 to send the Manion nomination to the Senate without recommendation.

A motion to send the nomination to the floor with a favorable recommendation died on a 9-9 tie. Republicans Arlen Specter, Pa., and Charles McC. Mathias Jr., Md., voted with seven of the panel's eight Democrats against the nomination. The eighth Democrat, Howell Heflin, Ala., voted for it.

Manion's backers contended that the Democrats opposed him because he was too conservative. The Democrats, in a report prepared for the Senate debate, countered that they had approved several avowedly conservative nominees. But these nominees, the Democrats said, "were either experienced federal practitioners, eminent jurists or respected academics."

During his confirmation hearings, Manion said he had abandoned some of his conservative views and could not recall certain statements attributed to him. He also said that as a judge he would abide by Supreme Court rulings.

The American Bar Association's Federal Courts Committee, which reviews and rates federal judicial candidates, gave Manion a split rating: A majority found him qualified; a minority found him unqualified.

The Republicans noted that other judges whom the committee had approved received the same ABA rating.

The Chicago Council of Lawyers, an organization of 1,000 attorneys who practiced regularly before the 7th Circuit, which includes Illinois and Indiana, found him not qualified to serve on the bench. After reviewing five of his legal briefs, the council concluded that Manion "has not demonstrated the level of legal skill necessary for appointment for the 7th Circuit."

The council said the briefs were poorly written and organized and riddled with misspelled words.

Manion's supporters were critical of the Chicago group's report. In a nine-page briefing paper on the nominee, the Justice Department described the council as a liberal organization founded in the aftermath of the riots at the 1968 Democratic National Convention in Chicago.

The Democrats pointed out that Manion had never argued a case before the 7th Circuit and described his practice as consisting "primarily of representation of clients in small personal and commercial claims, in state court."

The Republicans said his practice had been varied and sufficiently complex to qualify him for the federal bench. And a Justice Department briefing paper asserted that "it would be an insult to the qualifications of thousands of lawyers to suggest that only attorneys whose experience has been constitutional litigation in federal courts are fit to hold federal judgeships."

June 26 Vote

Senate Democrats took a high-stakes gamble June 26 to defeat the nomination, but their plan went awry when Republican Slade Gorton, Wash., unexpectedly voted for Manion. The Senate voted 48-46 to confirm Manion. *(Vote 152, p. 28-S)*

But that vote did not reflect Manion's actual support because of absentees, confusion and parliamentary maneuvering — including a move by Minority Leader Robert C. Byrd, D-W.Va., who abruptly switched his position from "nay" to "yea" so he could block the vote from becoming final by moving to reconsider it.

The maneuvering began when Biden, leader of the anti-Manion forces, told Majority Leader Robert Dole, R-Kan., he was ready to call off an expected filibuster and vote immediately on Manion's nomination.

Biden, his vote counters and allied lobbying groups knew that support for a filibuster was thin, and they felt they had the votes to defeat Manion that afternoon.

Dole expressed concern because of the absence of two Republican senators who were likely to vote for Manion: Paula Hawkins, Fla., and Bob Packwood, Ore. Dole said he was not willing to "gamble" on Manion's future with two absent senators, but he relented following a complicated series of maneuvers in which three votes against Manion were "paired" with, and thus canceled out by, the votes of three absent senators: Hawkins, Packwood and Barry Goldwater, R-Ariz. Packwood and Goldwater later said they had not yet decided how to vote, and Democrats charged that they had been misled.

The Democrats had expected Gorton to vote against confirmation. But less than a minute into the roll call, Gorton received a phone call from the White House and then announced he was voting for Manion. Gorton switched after the administration agreed to press action on the proposed nomination of Washington state lawyer William L. Dwyer for a district court judgeship. (Dwyer's nomination was sent to the Senate Sept. 26, but the Senate did not act on it.)

In the wake of the June 26 proceedings, the Democrats claimed to have captured the moral high ground by agreeing to vote quickly on Manion, and they accused the Republicans of reneging on agreements — an accusation strongly contested by spokesmen for Dole and Gorton.

Final Vote

Further action was delayed until after Congress' Independence Day recess, and the Senate did not take up Byrd's motion to reconsider the June 26 vote until July 23. Manion opponents again fell short.

When time ran out on the procedural vote, the count stood at 49-49. Under Senate rules, a tie is enough to defeat a motion, but Vice President George Bush, who was presiding, chose to cast his vote against Byrd's motion, making the final count 49-50. *(Vote 162, p. 30-S)*

There was only one vote switch between June 26 and July 23, and that made the difference. In the initial test, Daniel J. Evans, R-Wash., voted against Manion. But on July 23, he voted against Byrd's motion to reconsider — a position that, in effect, meant a vote for Manion.

Evans said in an interview that he believed opponents had had one chance to defeat Manion and a second vote would have meant going back over the same ground.

There had been speculation that Evans switched to help Gorton, his home-state colleague, who was facing a difficult re-election bid, and whose defeat Nov. 4 helped the Democrats take control of the Senate in 1987.

Democrats, who had expected Gorton to vote against Manion, subsequently accused him of selling his vote in return for administration assurances on the Dwyer nomination.

Gorton acknowledged dealing with the White House, but denied telling Democrats he would oppose Manion. He reiterated that view July 23 at a news conference.

But Howard M. Metzenbaum, D-Ohio, kept hammering away at Gorton. On the Senate floor July 23 he charged that the first vote had been "tainted," and then, in a pointed reference to Gorton and the White House, asserted, "Judges should not be traded like pork bellies or common stock."

Gorton said he had no regrets about his decision to vote for Manion and said he did not push Evans to vote against reconsideration. "Dan and I studiously avoided discussing this subject for three straight weeks," he said. Evans confirmed that he had not been pressured by Gorton.

Two of the absentees on the earlier vote, Hawkins and Packwood, were present for the July 23 tally; Packwood voted for Byrd's motion to reconsider, and Hawkins voted against it. Goldwater again was absent, however. He suddenly became ill the evening of July 22 and had to be hospitalized with what his office said was a badly upset stomach.

For a few hours it appeared as though his absence would cause another delay. But the vote proceeded after Goldwater made a deal with his Arizona colleague, Democrat Dennis DeConcini. According to Robert W. Maynes, DeConcini's press secretary, Goldwater called DeConcini from his hospital bed, said he had planned to vote against reconsideration, and asked DeConcini if he would withhold his planned vote in favor of reconsideration — in effect nullifying Goldwater's absence. Maynes said DeConcini agreed to Goldwater's request as "a personal favor." ∎

Sessions Nomination Blocked

The Senate Judiciary Committee June 5 rejected the nomination of Jefferson B. Sessions III, a U.S. attorney in Alabama, to be a federal district court judge. It was only the second time in 48 years that the committee had refused to send a judicial nominee to the full Senate.

In two dramatic roll calls, the committee first voted 8-10 against recommending that Sessions be confirmed. Then, on a 9-9 vote, the committee killed a motion by Chairman Strom Thurmond, R-S.C., to send the nomination to the Senate floor without any recommendation.

Critics had charged that Sessions was not qualified to sit on the bench and that several remarks he had made showed a "gross insensitivity" about racial issues.

The ranking Democrat on the committee, Joseph R. Biden Jr., Del., said the rejection of Sessions was a signal that "the burden is on any nominee to demonstrate that he is qualified. It is not the burden of the committee to prove that he is not qualified."

But Attorney General Edwin Meese III blasted the committee's action, calling it "an appalling surrender to the politics of ideology." He described Sessions as an "excellent nominee."

The Sessions vote marked the second time within a month that the committee had voted against recommending one of President Reagan's nominees. On May 8, the committee voted 9-9 against Daniel Manion of Indiana, who was nominated to become a federal appeals court judge. However, the committee then voted 11-6 to send Manion's nomination to the full Senate without a recommendation. Manion was confirmed July 23. *(Story, p. 72)*

Committee Action

During committee consideration June 5, Sessions' critics, led by Howard M. Metzenbaum, D-Ohio, and Edward M. Kennedy, D-Mass., asserted that he was not fit to be a federal judge. Citing statements he had made disparaging civil rights organizations and the American Civil Liberties Union, Metzenbaum said, "This is a nominee who is hostile to civil rights organizations and their causes."

Metzenbaum also said Sessions had only "marginal qualifications" for the lifetime appointment.

Jeremiah Denton, R-Ala., Sessions' principal supporter, charged that Sessions' record had been distorted by the media and by his enemies in Alabama. He said Sessions was the victim of a political conspiracy that grew out of his unsuccessful effort to prosecute blacks for voter fraud.

Denton charged that the press "chronicled only the inflammatory" statements attributed to Sessions and none of the explanations, denials or "recantations" by witnesses and by the nominee himself.

"I can't believe there is anything left anyone can hold validly against Mr. Sessions," Denton said.

But Democrat Howell Heflin, the other Alabama senator, opposed Sessions, and that was a pivotal factor. In remarks before the roll call, Heflin told the packed committee room that while it was difficult to vote against one of his constituents, it was his only choice.

"The question is, 'Will Jeff Sessions be a fair and impartial judge?' The answer is, 'I don't know.' " Heflin said that as long as he had a "reasonable doubt" about Sessions, he had to vote against him. "I regret that I cannot vote for confirmation," Heflin added, "but my duty to uphold the Constitution and my duty to the justice system is greater than any duty to any individual."

On the motion to give Sessions a favorable recommendation, Republicans Charles McC. Mathias Jr., Md., and Arlen Specter, Pa., voted "no" along with the panel's eight Democrats: Biden; Robert C. Byrd, W.Va.; Dennis DeConcini, Ariz.; Heflin; Kennedy; Patrick J. Leahy, Vt.; Metzenbaum; and Paul Simon, Ill.

Voting for Sessions were Republicans Thurmond; Paul Laxalt, Nev.; Orrin G. Hatch, Utah; Alan K. Simpson, Wyo.; John P. East, N.C.; Charles E. Grassley, Iowa; Denton; and Mitch McConnell, Ky.

On the second vote, to send the nomination forward without a recommendation, Specter joined the other eight Republicans in voting "aye." Specter said that while he opposed Sessions, he supported full Senate consideration because the Senate debates were now being televised and it would be "instructive for the country" to watch a debate on the nomination. ∎

Claiborne Impeached, Stripped of Judgeship

The Senate Oct. 9 removed imprisoned U.S. District Judge Harry E. Claiborne from office after convicting him of "high crimes and misdemeanors" related to his 1984 conviction for tax fraud.

An overwhelming majority of senators voted to convict Claiborne on three articles of impeachment. He was acquitted on a fourth.

The House on July 22 had voted the four articles of impeachment against the 69-year-old Claiborne — all stemming from his conviction for filing false income tax returns. The first two articles alleged that Claiborne willfully under-reported his income by $18,741 in 1979 and by $87,912 in 1980. The third alleged that he should be removed from office because of the 1984 conviction, and the fourth asserted that he betrayed the trust of the people and brought disrepute on the federal judiciary. *(Text of impeachment articles, box, p. 77)*

On Article I, the Senate found Claiborne guilty 87-10, with Ted Stevens, R-Alaska, voting present. This was 21 more than the two-thirds required to convict. *(Vote 335, p. 55-S)*

On Article II, 90 voted guilty and seven voted not guilty, with Stevens voting present. *(Vote 336, p. 55-S)*

On Article III, the vote was 46 guilty, 17 not guilty, with 35 voting present. Claiborne was acquitted on this article. *(Vote 337, p. 55-S)*

On Article IV, there were 89 guilty votes and eight not-guilty votes, with Stevens again voting present. *(Vote 338, p. 55-S)*

Several senators said after the proceedings they had voted against conviction on Article III because it would set a bad precedent. Sam Nunn, D-Ga., said senators worried that removing Claiborne simply because he had been convicted could be interpreted to mean that conviction is the equivalent of impeachment and an acquittal would mean a person could not be impeached.

Claiborne was automatically removed from office as soon as he was convicted on the first article. Shortly after the final vote was cast, the former judge was hustled out of the chamber by U.S. marshals.

Appointed to the bench in 1978 by President Jimmy Carter, the Nevada federal judge had been imprisoned since May following his 1984 conviction on tax evasion. Claiborne was the first sitting federal judge to be imprisoned. Federal court appeals of the conviction had been exhausted, although two procedural appeals were still pending.

Claiborne was the first federal official to be impeached and removed from office in 50 years, the fifth in the history of the nation. All of those removed were judges; the last was Halsted L. Ritter of Florida, who was removed from office in 1936 after being accused of corruption and filing false income tax returns. *(Previous impeachments, p. 78; background, CQ Guide to Congress Third Edition, p. 256)*

Because Claiborne could be removed from office only through the impeachment process and was immune under the Constitution from a pay cut, he continued to draw his $78,700 yearly salary. Had he not been removed from office, he could have returned to the bench when he was released from prison and could later have retired with full benefits.

Claiborne and his lawyers contended that he was the victim of a vendetta by federal officials who were angry because of rulings he made against them from the bench and because he had represented unsavory characters as a prominent Las Vegas defense attorney.

House: Articles Drafted

The House Judiciary Committee voted unanimously June 26 to seek the impeachment of Claiborne.

The committee agreed 35-0 on a resolution of impeachment (H Res 461) that included the four articles which were subsequently approved by the House. The first three articles were approved unanimously. The fourth, the general charge alleging that Claiborne brought "disrepute on the federal court," was adopted 28-7. Critics said they had no disagreement with that article's substance, but argued it was unnecessary.

The impeachment resolution was formally reported July 16 (H Rept 99-688).

Impeachment Articles

The Judiciary Subcommittee on Courts, Civil Liberties and Administration of Justice had approved the impeachment articles June 24.

Articles I and II of the resolution recounted Claiborne's tax evasions in 1979 and 1980. Each stated that because he knowingly filed false income tax returns, he was "guilty of misbehavior and was and is guilty of a high crime and misdemeanor, and by such conduct, warrants impeachment and trial and removal from office."

Article III stated that Claiborne should be impeached because he was convicted on the tax evasion charges.

Article IV asserted that Claiborne's actions had brought disrepute on the federal judiciary and therefore he should be impeached.

The subcommittee version of Article IV also charged that Claiborne had violated his oath of office. But several members, particularly Bruce A. Morrison, D-Conn., and Michael DeWine, R-Ohio, said they believed this language was unwise. Morrison said the entire article was unnecessary and argued it would be better to rely on just the first three articles to make clear that conviction of a felony was enough to warrant removing a judge from office.

But Robert W. Kastenmeier, D-Wis., chairman of the Courts Subcommittee, argued strongly for inclusion of the article, saying it alleged conduct that was an impeachable offense. Kastenmeier said it was premised on the fact that Claiborne had violated the canons of judicial ethics.

After some discussion, the committee agreed to a DeWine amendment striking language referring to the oath of office and adding language asserting that Claiborne had "betrayed the trust of the people of the United States." The article was subsequently adopted.

Moving for Impeachment

The last time the Judiciary Committee considered an impeachment was in 1974, when it recommended removing President Richard M. Nixon from office. But Nixon resigned before a House vote. *(Congress and the Nation Vol. IV, p. 935)*

Judiciary Chairman Peter W. Rodino Jr., D-N.J., who presided over those proceedings, told colleagues June 26 that judges "simply cannot act in a way that violates the public trust and undermines the integrity of the judicial office. Once public confidence in the courts erodes, our tripartite system of government fails."

Kastenmeier, briefing colleagues on a daylong hearing June 19, noted that Claiborne's attorney, Oscar Goodman, sought to "rationalize Judge Claiborne's behavior. But in the judgment of the subcommittee," Kastenmeier said, "Mr. Goodman's arguments, even when considered in their best light, could not adequately explain the conduct."

If Claiborne's conviction ultimately were overturned through procedural claims, Kastenmeier added, "the facts relating to Judge Claiborne's behavior cannot be reversed. The conduct remains the same."

The Defendant's Case

During a two-hour presentation June 19 to Kastenmeier's subcommittee before the panel drew up articles of impeachment, Goodman, Claiborne's principal lawyer, repeated his allegations that Claiborne's trial was tainted by government misconduct.

But members said they believed such assertions were irrelevant. Kastenmeier said the allegations did not change the facts — that Claiborne was found by a Nevada jury to have filed false income tax returns in 1979 and 1980.

Former Sen. Howard W. Cannon, D-Nev. (1959-83), who helped convince President Carter to appoint Claiborne in 1978 and who was advising Goodman during the impeachment action, said July 24 that Claiborne wanted to use the Senate trial to publicize the misconduct charges. "His objective is to try this matter of prosecutorial and government misconduct. He wants the opportunity to present that full-blown someplace. The only place, obviously, is before the Senate."

In drafting the impeachment articles, the Judiciary Committee tried to stick closely to the jury findings on tax evasion and to the conviction itself. Committee members wanted to avoid general charges that could give Goodman an opening for going beyond the findings of the Nevada jury.

House: Impeachment Voted

The House July 22 adopted H Res 461, voting to impeach Claiborne on a 406-0 roll call. *(Vote 212, p. 62-H)*

Claiborne became the 14th federal official to be im-

Impeachment Articles on Federal Judge Claiborne

Following is the text of the articles of impeachment of federal Judge Harry E. Claiborne of Nevada, as approved June 26 by the House Judiciary Committee.

Article I

That Judge Harry E. Claiborne, having been nominated by the President of the United States, confirmed by the Senate of the United States, and while serving as a judge of the United States District Court for the District of Nevada, was and is guilty of misbehavior and of high crimes and misdemeanors in office in a manner and form as follows:

On or about June 15, 1980, Judge Harry E. Claiborne did willfully and knowingly make and subscribe a United States Individual Income Tax Return for the calendar year 1979, which return was verified by a written declaration that the return was made under penalties of perjury; which return was filed with the Internal Revenue Service; and which return Judge Harry E. Claiborne did not believe to be true and correct as to every material matter in that the return reported total income in the amount of $80,227.04 whereas, as he then and there well knew and believed, he received and failed to report substantial income in addition to that stated on the return in violation of section 7206(1) of title 26, United States Code.

The facts set forth in the foregoing paragraph were found beyond a reasonable doubt by a twelve person jury in the United States District Court for the District of Nevada.

Wherefore, Judge Harry E. Claiborne was and is guilty of misbehavior and was and is guilty of a high crime and misdemeanor and, by such conduct, warrants impeachment and trial and removal from office.

Article II

That Judge Harry E. Claiborne, having been nominated by the President of the United States, confirmed by the Senate of the United States, and while serving as a judge of the United States District Court for the District of Nevada, was and is guilty of misbehavior and of high crimes and misdemeanors in office in a manner and form as follows:

On or about June 15, 1981, Judge Harry E. Claiborne did willfully and knowingly make and subscribe a United States Individual Income Tax Return for the calendar year 1980, which return was verified by a written declaration that the return was made under penalties of perjury; which return was filed with the Internal Revenue Service; and which return Judge Harry E. Claiborne did not believe to be true and correct as to every material matter in that the return reported total income in the amount of $54,251 whereas, as he then and there well knew and believed, he received and failed to report substantial income in addition to that stated on the return in violation of section 7206(1) of title 26, United States Code.

The facts set forth in the foregoing paragraph were found beyond a reasonable doubt by a twelve person jury in the United States District Court for the District of Nevada.

Wherefore, Judge Harry E. Claiborne was and is guilty of misbehavior and was and is guilty of a high crime and misdemeanor and, by such conduct, warrants impeachment and trial and removal from office.

Article III

That Judge Harry E. Claiborne, having been nominated by the President of the United States, confirmed by the Senate of the United States, and while serving as a judge of the United States District Court for the District of Nevada, was and is guilty of misbehavior and of high crimes in office in a manner and form as follows:

On August 10, 1984, in the United States District Court for the District of Nevada, Judge Harry E. Claiborne was found guilty by a twelve-person jury of making and subscribing a false income tax return for the calendar years 1979 and 1980 in violation of section 7206(1) of title 26, United States Code.

Thereafter, a judgment of conviction was entered against Judge Harry E. Claiborne for each of the violations of section 7206(1) of title 26, United States Code, and a sentence of two years imprisonment for each violation was imposed, to be served concurrently, together with a fine of $5,000 for each violation.

Wherefore, Judge Harry E. Claiborne was and is guilty of misbehavior and was and is guilty of high crimes.

Article IV

That Judge Harry E. Claiborne, having been nominated by the President of the United States, confirmed by the Senate of the United States, and while serving as a judge of the United States District Court for the District of Nevada, was and is guilty of misbehavior and of misdemeanors in office in a manner and form as follows:

Judge Harry E. Claiborne took the oath for the office of judge of the United States and is required to discharge and perform all the duties incumbent on him and to uphold and obey the Constitution and laws of the United States.

Judge Harry E. Claiborne, by virtue of his office, is required to uphold the integrity of the judiciary and to perform the duties of his office impartially.

Judge Harry E. Claiborne, by willfully and knowingly falsifying his income on his Federal tax returns for 1979 and 1980, has betrayed the trust of the people of the United States and reduced confidence in the integrity and impartiality of the judiciary, thereby bringing disrepute on the Federal courts and the administration of justice by the courts.

Wherefore, Judge Harry E. Claiborne was and is guilty of misbehavior and was and is guilty of misdemeanors and, by such conduct, warrants impeachment and trial and removal from office.

peached, or formally charged, by the House and the first to be impeached on a unanimous roll-call vote.

While Claiborne's impeachment was historic, there was little drama to the House debate. In fact, the final action July 22 was anticlimactic. There was no question that Claiborne would be impeached, and little doubt that it would be unanimous. The only unknown was how many members would show up for the roll call.

"Judge Claiborne is more than a mere embarrassment," said Hamilton Fish Jr., R-N.Y., the ranking Republican on the Judiciary Committee. "He is a disgrace — an affront — to the judicial office and the judicial branch he was appointed to serve."

Rodino said the House must act to safeguard the judicial system. "If we fail to act," he said, "the confidence of the people in that system will be gravely jeopardized."

And Kastenmeier said the House had "a responsibility to the public. The purpose of impeachment is not to punish the individual but to protect the institution."

Following the impeachment vote, the House selected nine Judiciary Committee members, led by Rodino, to manage, or try, the case against Claiborne in the Senate.

13 Senate Impeachment Trials Since 1798

Between 1798 and 1986 the Senate sat as a court of impeachment 13 times, as follows:

Year	Official	Position	Outcome
1798-99	William Blount	U.S. senator	Charges dismissed
1803-04	John Pickering	District court judge	Removed from office
1804-05	Samuel Chase	Supreme Court justice	Acquitted
1830-31	James H. Peck	District court judge	Acquitted
1862	West H. Humphreys	District court judge	Removed from office
1868	Andrew Johnson	President	Acquitted
1876	William W. Belknap	Secretary of war	Acquitted
1904-05	Charles Swayne	District court judge	Acquitted
1912-13	Robert W. Archbald	Commerce Court judge	Removed from office
1926	George W. English	District court judge	Charges dismissed
1933	Harold Louderback	District court judge	Acquitted
1936	Halsted L. Ritter	District court judge	Removed from office
1986	Harry E. Claiborne	District court judge	Removed from office

Note: The House in 1873 adopted a resolution of impeachment against District Judge Mark H. Delahay, but Delahay resigned before articles of impeachment were prepared, so there was no Senate action.

Source: *Congressional Directory*

The chief House prosecutor was William J. Hughes, D-N.J., chairman of the Crime Subcommittee and a lawyer who served for more than 10 years as a New Jersey prosecutor.

The other House managers were Kastenmeier; Romano L. Mazzoli, D-Ky.; Dan Glickman, D-Kan.; Fish; Henry J. Hyde, R-Ill.; Thomas N. Kindness, R-Ohio; and DeWine.

Senate: Setting the Stage

The House Aug. 6 formally presented the Senate with the four articles of impeachment against Claiborne, setting the stage for the first Senate impeachment trial in 50 years.

Rodino, flanked by eight other House managers, read each of the articles to an unusually somber Senate. About 40 senators were in their seats listening.

Procedures Set

The Senate Aug. 14 established a timetable and procedures for conducting the trial, the first ever to make use of a special 12-member committee to collect evidence.

In a brief ceremony with Vice President George Bush presiding, members of the Senate took a special oath for the impeachment trial. The only one absent was Barry Goldwater, R-Ariz., who was ill.

Although the special committee mechanism was added to the Senate impeachment rules in 1935, all previous impeachment trials had been conducted before the full Senate. The Senate's decision to use the special committee in 1986 was dictated in large part by the press of other business and the lateness of the session. The Republican and Democratic leadership concluded there was not enough time for the full Senate to hear all the testimony and felt they could not postpone the trial to a lame-duck session or until the next Congress.

Under Senate impeachment rules, the committee could gather evidence and present a report to the full Senate. However, the committee could not make a recommendation on whether to convict the impeached official. In addition, the Senate had the right to summon witnesses and to hear testimony.

The committee was made up of six Republicans named by Majority Leader Robert Dole, R-Kan., and six Democrats named by Minority Leader Robert C. Byrd, W.Va. All were lawyers.

The Republicans were: Orrin G. Hatch, Utah; Charles McC. Mathias Jr., Md.; Mitch McConnell, Ky.; Larry Pressler, S.D.; Warren B. Rudman, N.H.; and John W. Warner, Va. Hatch, Mathias and McConnell were members of the Judiciary Committee. Rudman was a former state attorney general.

The Democrats were: Jeff Bingaman, N.M.; Dennis DeConcini, Ariz.; Albert Gore Jr., Tenn.; Howell Heflin, Ala.; David Pryor, Ark.; and Paul S. Sarbanes, Md. Heflin was a former chief justice of the Alabama Supreme Court. Bingaman was a former state attorney general. Sarbanes served on the House Judiciary Committee in 1974 when it voted articles of impeachment against Nixon.

The Senate's decision to use the committee was controversial. "This is a very questionable or arguable procedure," said Hyde, one of the House managers. "It gives Judge Claiborne an entirely new direction to attack the impeachment."

Senate advocates of the committee procedure maintained that it was perfectly proper, arguing that the Senate did not have to operate by the same standards or traditions as a federal court.

Senate: Gathering Evidence

The special Senate committee, chaired by Mathias, began taking testimony Sept. 15. The panel met in the Russell Office Building's stately Caucus Room, the same room used by the special Watergate committee in 1973 for the investigation that eventually led to the resignation of Nixon.

While the Watergate hearings were very much in the legislative tradition, the Claiborne sessions were more in keeping with a judicial proceeding. The House managers, or prosecutors, were on one side of the room, and Claiborne, flanked by his lawyers and escorted each day by federal marshals, was on the other. The presentation of evidence followed the procedures used in a courtroom, and Mathias tried to follow the rules of evidence used in a trial.

At first, senators submitted their questions to Mathias and he put them to the witnesses. But on Sept. 17, the full Senate hastily adopted a rule permitting each senator to ask his own questions. That was the only obvious departure from courtroom procedure.

The committee finished gathering evidence Sept. 23 after taking testimony for seven days — nearly two of them devoted to questioning Claiborne. The committee's proceedings were compiled in a voluminous report to the Senate (Senate hearing 99-812, Parts I-IV and addendum).

Claiborne Defense

Claiborne told the panel he had been "chased" from the bench by ambitious federal agents. And he insisted that he had been wrongly convicted in 1984 of willfully filing false income tax returns for 1979 and 1980.

"They have been pursuing me like a pack of wolves would pursue a sick caribou," Claiborne asserted Sept. 23. "I know what they have done to my family. I know what they have done to my life. I am innocent," he contended. "I don't feel innocent merely. I am innocent."

While he acknowledged that his 1979 and 1980 income was under-reported, he blamed his tax preparers for "brutal errors" in his returns and said he was guilty only of "neglecting my personal affairs terribly."

During his testimony, Claiborne was asked repeatedly how he had his taxes prepared and how much he knew about tax law, particularly since he had ruled as a judge in tax cases.

Nicholas D. Chabraja, special House counsel for the Claiborne trial, and Warner, who said he had read all of Claiborne's opinions involving tax cases, were skeptical of Claiborne's claims that he did not know much about tax law. But Claiborne insisted that was correct. He said when he was in private practice, he never handled tax cases and never filled out his own returns, and he contended that some of the cases he presided over as a judge may have had tax issues but in fact rested on other legal principles.

The main issue concerning the 1979 tax return was whether Claiborne had informed his accountant, Joseph Wright, that his legal fee income for that year was $41,073.93. The return reported $22,332.87 in fee income.

Claiborne insisted that on April 11, 1980, he directed his secretary, Judy Ahlstrom, to deliver a letter to Wright using the higher amount as his fee income. Ahlstrom said she dropped the letter off at Wright's office.

Wright and his wife, Connie, who helped manage the office, testified they never got the letter, but Claiborne said he remembered seeing it on Wright's desk.

It was on this point that Goodman produced a surprise witness, Ellen M. Arthur, who said in an affidavit submitted Sept. 23 that while she was working for Wright she received an envelope from Ahlstrom containing tax papers from Claiborne. However, Arthur's affidavit did not say that she opened the envelope and actually saw what was in it.

Concerning 1980, senators said they did not understand why Claiborne switched tax preparers after sticking with Wright for more than 30 years. Claiborne's new tax preparer was Jerry Watson, owner of Creative Tax and Business Planning.

Senators said they found it hard to believe that a man as skilled as Claiborne would let Watson do his return and sign it without even looking at the document — which had been filled out in pencil.

"It strikes me as being so stupid," Warner said.

Under repeated questioning from Chabraja and the senators, Claiborne said that while he had "an impression" something was wrong with his 1980 return, he did not really look at it until he was indicted in 1983. He said he was not particularly surprised to see that Watson had found a way to reduce substantially the taxable income from the $725,000 sale of his house in 1980. Nor, he said, was he surprised to see that he would get a refund of $20,927.

A few months earlier, Claiborne estimated he would still owe the government $25,000 for 1980 and he sent a check for that amount when he applied for an extension to file his 1980 return. The $25,000 was returned along with the $20,927 refund.

Several senators, Pressler in particular, said they could not understand why in 1978 Claiborne began cashing fee checks at casinos, particularly checks as large as $37,000 and $42,000. They wondered aloud how that amount of cash fits into one's pockets.

Claiborne said cashing checks at casinos was a common practice in Las Vegas, and that he did it because he needed cash for repairs on a new home he had bought.

He said he did not use the money for gambling or carousing, and maintained that although he had been described as flamboyant, he was not. "I think I'm about as colorful and flamboyant as a cold mashed potato sandwich," he said.

The most dramatic exchange came Sept. 22 when Chabraja sought to find a motive for Claiborne's under-reporting of taxes in 1980. Chabraja suggested that it was greed, prompting an angry reply from the judge.

He whirled in his seat and told Chabraja that there was nothing to indicate in "my whole professional life or my personal life that I have been greedy."

Claiborne added, "I will tell you sir, your remark wounds me and I am sorry for that. Because I think you are a very fine lawyer, and it is regrettable that you would engage in such conduct, particularly in view of the fact that I have been a good judge."

When McConnell asked why the Senate should not remove Claiborne from office, the judge said the independence of the federal judiciary was at stake. "The biggest danger I can see to the federal court is if ever there be created a buddy relationship between the federal judiciary and the executive branch."

Senate: Trial and Conviction

Claiborne's trial was a departure from the usual order of Senate business in a number of ways. The "well," or front of the chamber, was set up to resemble a courtroom. On one side of the podium was a table for Claiborne and his lawyers. On the other side was a table for the nine House managers, or prosecutors, and their special counsel, Chabraja. Between the tables was a speaker's stand, where Goodman and the House managers made their arguments.

Normally there are only a few senators on the floor when legislation is pending, and they often visit with one another. The atmosphere is informal. During the impeachment trial, however, there were between 40 and 50 senators on the floor and even more during the final deliberations.

The senators were unusually attentive and several took

notes. "Everybody takes this assignment seriously," said Donald W. Riegle Jr., D-Mich. "I think we all feel an obligation to make an independent judgment."

Claiborne listened intently as the roll was called Oct. 9, whispering once or twice with his two lawyers, Goodman and Cannon, who were keeping tallies.

Instead of answering "aye" or "no," the traditional response during a vote, the senators were instructed to stand and say "guilty," "not guilty" or "present."

Senate President Pro Tempore Strom Thurmond, R-S.C., put the question before each roll call: "Senators, how say you: Is the respondent, Harry E. Claiborne, guilty or not guilty?"

In a gesture that underscored the solemnity and importance of the occasion, even John C. Stennis, D-Miss., who had lost a leg to cancer two years earlier, pulled himself to a standing position each time his name was called.

Full Trial Sought

Last-minute court appeals Oct. 8-9 to block the final Senate vote were unsuccessful. Claiborne and his attorneys argued that by using the special committee, the Senate had denied Claiborne his constitutional right to a full trial before the entire Senate. But a federal district judge and an appeals court panel in Washington, D.C., said they had no authority to tell the Senate how to conduct an impeachment trial. And two hours before the final vote, Chief Justice William H. Rehnquist denied Claiborne's request for a stay.

The decision to rely on the special committee's report came in a critical vote Oct. 8, when the Senate decided 61-32 not to question any witnesses directly. *(Vote 334, p. 55-S)*

After the conviction, Goodman said, "Harry Claiborne is no longer the fight. The fight is whether the Constitution is worth the paper it's written on." The Constitution, he said, "is a fragile document. Today it was bruised if not broken."

Goodman criticized senators — whom he declined to name — for not being informed about Claiborne's case. He said it appeared to him that many members had not touched the committee transcripts.

Pryor, who voted to acquit Claiborne on all the articles, told reporters later that he believed Claiborne got a fair trial. However, Pryor, who served on the special committee, said senators had little time to master the facts and issues in the case.

"I truly feel time was running against Judge Claiborne," he said, but then added, "Under the circumstances, they gave him the best trial they knew how."

During the Oct. 7 debate on whether to hold a full trial, Rep. Hughes contended that the Senate had the right to try Claiborne the way it wanted to. He said delegating to the committee was "wise, prudent and constitutional."

"The only conduct that is relevant in these proceedings," Hughes concluded, "is the defendant's conduct."

The Senate deliberated in closed session for nearly three hours Oct. 8 on Goodman's motion for a full trial.

When the deliberations concluded, Majority Leader Dole told colleagues the Senate had to decide whether it wanted to get on with the trial and then he offered a motion barring any other witnesses.

After the 61-32 vote on Dole's motion, several senators who had voted against it expressed unhappiness. "We weren't satisfied with just having a bunch of books handed to us," said J. James Exon, D-Neb.

Carl Levin, D-Mich., and Daniel J. Evans, R-Wash., said the chance to see and question witnesses was particularly important for Articles I and II, which specifically referred to Claiborne's state of mind. Evans voted to acquit Claiborne on all the articles; Levin voted for acquittal on Articles I and II.

But Dale Bumpers, D-Ark., said the committee had compiled a good record. "When you look at what the witnesses said," Bumpers added, "it doesn't matter to me whether they were frowning or smiling."

Goodman's Motions

The request for a full Senate trial was only one of several motions presented by Goodman when the proceedings began Oct. 7.

After the arguments, the Senate went into closed session for several hours. (By precedent, Senate impeachment deliberations are private.)

Goodman asked the Senate to postpone the trial until procedural claims Claiborne had filed in the 9th U.S. Circuit Court of Appeals had been decided. The Senate rejected that motion by voice vote.

He also asked the Senate to adopt a "guilty beyond a reasonable doubt" standard of proof for conviction.

Vice President Bush, who was presiding, ruled that each senator could decide for himself what the standard should be.

Orrin G. Hatch, R-Utah, asked for a vote on Claiborne's motion; it failed 17-75. *(Vote 333, p. 55-S)*

Goodman contended that the "beyond a reasonable doubt" standard was appropriate for an impeachment trial, and he was convinced his client would have been acquitted had it been used.

He and Claiborne maintained that the judge did not intentionally or willfully under-report his taxes. They blamed his tax preparers.

When Goodman and the House managers had completed their arguments Oct. 7, Claiborne made a dramatic address to the Senate. He said he wanted to speak to the members "primarily, I think, to let you see me."

Referring to the preceding arguments, Claiborne said, "I kind of feel like a piece of meat that is thrown out to a couple of dogs, jerked back and forth for possession ... between the House managers and my lawyers."

Claiborne again said he was innocent of wrongdoing. "I am not fighting for a judgeship. That may be forever gone," he said. "I am not fighting for my freedom because I have given up a large part of that.... What is involved is a sense of honesty and decency and what is involved is the independence of the American judiciary."

Vendetta Charges

Claiborne had contended since his indictment in 1983 that he was the victim of a vendetta by federal officials who wanted to force him off the bench.

And some senators expressed concern about the conduct of federal officials.

Pryor said he voted to acquit Claiborne "because of the long and abusive arm of the federal government." Citing the FBI and the Internal Revenue Service, Pryor asserted that "without their involvement, without their targeting, without their harassment, I have great doubt that he would have been convicted in the first place." Pryor said he would introduce a resolution calling for an investigation in 1987 of FBI strike force activities. ∎

Hastings Challenge

As Congress pursued impeachment proceedings against District Judge Harry E. Claiborne, the U.S. Judicial Conference was weighing impeachment recommendations against a second federal judge.

The conference, the policy-making arm of the federal judiciary, Sept. 19 decided to invite U.S. District Judge Alcee L. Hastings of Florida to respond in writing to a recommendation that he be impeached.

On Sept. 2, the governing council of the 11th U.S. Circuit Court of Appeals in Atlanta voted to recommend that Hastings be impeached for allegedly conspiring to solicit a bribe. Hastings was acquitted of the charges in a 1983 trial, but the governing council said he should have been convicted.

Should the Judiciary Conference agree with the 11th Circuit recommendation, the conference would forward its report to the House, which could begin an impeachment investigation.

Hastings, 50, was put on the bench in 1979 by President Jimmy Carter, and became the first black to serve in Florida's federal courts.

"A core group of members of the federal judiciary have conspired to seek my removal from office," said Hastings in a Sept. 4 interview. "... I certainly feel there is some personal animus involved."

Discipline Law Questioned

The judges were acting under a 1980 law (PL 96-458) that gave the judiciary a process for investigating complaints against members, taking some limited disciplinary actions and recommending that Congress impeach a judge.

Hastings' lawyers claimed the law was unconstitutional, and they filed a lawsuit in federal court in Washington, D.C., seeking to halt the process. Their principal claim was that the law improperly delegated congressional powers to the federal judiciary because under the Constitution only Congress could impeach a judge. *(1980 Almanac p. 391)*

A district judge dismissed the lawsuit Sept. 12, but Hastings appealed that decision.

Charges Against Hastings

In 1981, Hastings and Washington, D.C., lawyer William A. Borders Jr. were accused of conspiring to solicit a $150,000 bribe from an undercover FBI agent posing as a representative of two convicted racketeers allegedly seeking a reduction in prison terms and fines Hastings had imposed. Borders, who had met with the FBI agent, was convicted and jailed, but Hastings argued that the evidence against him was all circumstantial and he was acquitted.

The 11th Circuit recommended impeachment after a special investigating committee made a report on the Hastings case to the court's governing body. The investigating committee, according to Terence Anderson, a University of Miami law professor who represented the judge, alleged that Hastings should have been convicted and that he fabricated his defense in order to beat the charges.

Fitzwater Confirmation

Senate Republicans March 18 pushed through the controversial nomination of Sidney A. Fitzwater to be a federal judge for the northern district of Texas.

At 32, Fitzwater became the youngest federal district judge. His confirmation came after the Senate voted 64-33 to invoke cloture, or cut off debate, on the nomination. The vote to confirm Fitzwater was 52-42. *(Votes 40, 41, p. 8-S)*

Led by Edward M. Kennedy, D-Mass., Democrats contended that Fitzwater lacked the temperament to be a federal judge because during the 1982 elections, he posted signs in black-majority districts warning people they could be prosecuted for various types of election fraud. Fitzwater, a state judge, was running for re-election on the Republican ticket.

Kennedy and other critics contended the signs did not accurately reflect Texas law and were posted to intimidate blacks from voting.

But Phil Gramm, R-Texas, who had pressed the White House to nominate Fitzwater, said there was nothing wrong with the signs. He praised Fitzwater as a "brilliant jurist" and a man of "keen intellect" who would make a good federal judge.

The Judiciary Committee had approved Fitzwater's nomination Feb. 27 on a 10-5 vote. ∎

Judges' Survivor Benefits

Congress increased benefits for surviving spouses and children of deceased federal judges in legislation cleared May 22 (HR 3570 — PL 99-336).

Final action came when the House accepted the Senate version of HR 3570. The House originally passed the bill Dec. 16, 1985 (H Rept 99-423, Part I). The Senate passed a revised version April 11, 1986.

The bill addressed concerns expressed by members of the federal judiciary that the existing survivor benefits program was inadequate. Rep. Robert W. Kastenmeier, D-Wis., chief sponsor of the House bill, said the benefits program had not kept up with increases in judicial salaries.

As cleared by Congress May 22, HR 3570 provided that a survivor of a judge who served a minimum of 18 months on the federal bench would receive at least 25 percent of the judge's annual salary. The maximum survivor benefit would be 50 percent. District judges at the time made $78,700 per year; appeals judges made $83,200; and Supreme Court justices made $104,100, except for the chief justice, who made $108,400.

Previously, there was no minimum survivor benefit, and the maximum was 40 percent of salary. The original House bill had set a floor of 30 percent and a maximum of 55 percent of a judge's salary.

To help pay for survivor benefits, HR 3570 increased judges' contributions to a survivor fund from 4.5 percent of salary to 5 percent. The bill also provided that the government's contribution to the survivor fund should not exceed 9 percent of a judge's salary or retirement income.

When the judicial survivor benefit program was first enacted in 1956, judges contributed 3 percent of their salaries to the benefit fund, and the government matched the contribution. When the program was revised in 1976 (PL 94-554), judges' contributions were raised to 4 percent. ∎

Congress Relaxes Federal Gun Control Laws

Federal gun control laws were significantly eased by legislation signed by President Reagan May 19. Enactment of the bill (S 49 — PL 99-308) was a major victory for the National Rifle Association (NRA), which had worked for years to win relaxation of the landmark Gun Control Act of 1968.

Congress completed action on S 49 May 6, when the Senate accepted the version of the bill passed by the House April 10. As cleared, S 49 was very similar to the bill passed by the Senate in 1985.

Before passing its version in 1986, the House substituted NRA-backed provisions for a more limited measure reluctantly reported by the House Judiciary Committee. The Judiciary panel had long resisted moves to weaken existing gun controls but relented when it appeared that the House would take up gun legislation even if the committee declined to act.

The major provisions of S 49 lifted the existing ban on interstate sales of rifles and shotguns and limited the number of people who were required to get licenses to sell firearms. In addition, the bill allowed gun owners to transport their firearms interstate, overriding state laws that barred residents from possessing firearms or transporting them in a vehicle.

An existing ban on interstate sales of handguns was retained, despite NRA efforts to repeal it.

Law enforcement groups vigorously opposed S 49, contending that the bill would make it more difficult for police to trace guns used in crimes.

To appease these groups, the Senate May 6 passed a separate measure revising three sections of S 49. The House passed the revision measure without change June 24, and President Reagan signed it July 8 (S 2414 — PL 99-360).

Provisions

As signed into law, S 49 (PL 99-308) included the following provisions *(changes made by S 2414 appear in italics)*:

- Made legal the interstate sale of rifles and shotguns as long as the sale was over-the-counter and legal in the state of the buyer and seller.

Previous law barred the interstate sale of rifles, shotguns and handguns, although residents of one state could buy long guns in a contiguous state.

- Relieved ammunition dealers of record-keeping requirements.
- Narrowed the definition of who had to get a license to sell guns to cover only those people who "regularly" imported, manufactured and dealt in guns with the "principal objective of livelihood and profit."

S 2414 stipulated that licensing and record-keeping requirements also applied to anyone who engaged in the regular purchase and disposition of firearms for criminal purposes or terrorism, regardless of whether it was done for profit.

- Allowed licensed dealers to conduct business at gun shows and provided that records of gun show transactions could be inspected.
- Maintained existing record-keeping requirements for firearm transactions, while prohibiting the Treasury Department's Bureau of Alcohol, Tobacco and Firearms (BATF) from issuing any regulation requiring centralized dealer records.

The law also barred the establishment of any firearms registration plan.

A dealer would not be required to keep a record of any transaction involving his personal collection unless the gun was disposed of within one year of being transferred from the dealer's business inventory to his personal collection.

S 2414 altered this provision to require dealers to keep records for gun transactions involving their personal collection, no matter how long the guns were in the dealer's collection. The records had to include the name, place of residence and date of birth of the buyer.

Previous law required the dealer to record all firearm and handgun ammunition transactions, including those involving guns from a personal collection, and to maintain such records indefinitely.

- Allowed federal officials to make one unannounced inspection of a dealer's premises each year. Previous law allowed federal officials to make unannounced inspections of dealers' premises at "reasonable" times.
- Allowed federal officials to inspect a dealer's premises without a warrant during a criminal investigation of someone other than the dealer or when tracing firearms.
- Barred federal officials from denying or revoking a dealer's license because he allegedly violated provisions in the law if the dealer was acquitted or the case was terminated prior to trial.

If denied a license or if a license was revoked for another reason, the dealer would have the right to a full trial on the denial in federal court.

Previous law allowed federal officials to deny a dealer a license for failing to meet certain statutory criteria or for a "willful" violation of any provision of the gun control law or BATF regulation. Judicial review of the denial was limited.

- Made clear that the Treasury secretary could not deny import permits for firearms and ammunition meeting statutory requirements for importation.
- Barred the importation of barrels for firearms that did not meet the criteria for "sporting purposes." This provision was aimed at "Saturday night specials" — small handguns not suitable for sporting purposes but frequently used in the commission of crimes. The 1968 gun law banned the importation of most firearms, but not of gun parts.

Previous law gave the Treasury secretary greater discretion.

- Kept the current mandatory penalties for using a firearm during the commission of a federal crime of violence and added drug felonies and carrying a handgun loaded with armor-piercing bullets to the crimes covered by this provision.

A separate bill to ban the manufacture, importation and sale of such "cop-killer" bullets cleared Congress Aug. 13. *(Story, p. 85)*

The law set a mandatory five-year prison term for a first offense and 10 years for a subsequent offense.

- Imposed new penalties of 10 years for a first offense and 20 years for a subsequent offense for carrying or using a machine gun or a gun equipped with a silencer during commission of a federal crime of violence.

• Incorporated into the Gun Control Act provisions of the 1968 Omnibus Crime Control and Safe Streets Act (PL 90-351) that barred categories of people, such as those convicted of certain crimes, from transporting or owning a firearm. *(Congress and the Nation Vol. II, p. 323)*

• Specified that state law governed in determining whether a person, by reason of a previous conviction, was barred from handling or possessing firearms. This was similar to previous law.

• Allowed all persons barred from handling or possessing firearms because of a prior conviction to get their eligibility restored by BATF. This included persons with previous convictions involving the use of a firearm.

A state pardon for a crime would automatically carry with it a restoration of eligibility. An individual denied a restoration of eligibility was entitled to a full trial on the issues in federal district court.

Previous law automatically barred anyone from a restoration of eligibility if the offense involved use of a firearm. And a state pardon did not automatically mean that the person could once again own or deal in firearms.

• Restricted the circumstances under which federal officials could seize firearms or ammunition as a result of a violation of the Gun Control Act. S 49 barred such seizures unless the government could prove by "clear and convincing evidence" that the person intended to violate the law and that the violation involved specified crimes, such as crimes of violence, drug felonies and illegal exportation of firearms.

Previous law allowed federal officials to seize any firearm or ammunition involved in any violation of the gun control law.

• Required the government to return property to the alleged violator if he was acquitted of the criminal charges on which the seizure of property was based. Previous law contained no similar provision.

• Required the government to prove that a person "willfully" violated certain provisions of the law, such as failing to obtain a dealer's license. For other violations, such as selling a gun to a person not eligible to own one, the government would have to prove only that the person knew he was violating the law. The bill also reduced to a misdemeanor violations involving record keeping.

Previous law did not require the government to prove that a person "willfully" violated the law, and that all violations were felonies.

• Permitted a person to travel interstate with a firearm as long as the gun was not loaded and not readily accessible. This provision would override state and local laws that might bar possession or transportation of a firearm. However, the provision would not block a state from enforcing its own gun laws on its own citizens.

S 2414 narrowed this provision by allowing the interstate transportation of a gun only when it was legal for the person to own a gun in the states in which he began and ended his journey. Further, S 2414 specified that during travel the gun must be placed somewhere other than the passenger compartment of the vehicle.

• Barred the future possession or transfer of machine guns. Persons lawfully owning machine guns prior to the date the president signed S 49 were not affected. They could sell or swap their machine guns after the date of enactment as long as the machine gun was lawfully owned at that time.

• Allowed a court to award "reasonable" attorneys' fees to a person who prevailed against the government in getting his seized property returned. Previous law had no such provision.

• Made the bill effective within 180 days of enactment, except for the machine gun provision, which took effect upon enactment.

Background

The 1968 gun control law (PL 90-618) was enacted following the assassinations that year of the Rev. Dr. Martin Luther King Jr. and Sen. Robert F. Kennedy (D-N.Y.).

The law barred mail-order or interstate shipment of firearms and ammunition and established licensing procedures for those who manufactured, imported, sold or collected guns and ammunition. It also required licensed dealers to keep records of all firearms transactions and authorized federal authorities to inspect a licensee's firearms inventory and records at any "reasonable" time without advance notice. *(Congress and the Nation Vol. II, p. 328)*

Western members of Congress, encouraged by the NRA, sought relaxation of the 1968 law almost from the day it was enacted. They argued that overzealous federal officials used the law to harass law-abiding gun owners and dealers.

After years of relentless efforts by the NRA, the Senate in 1985 bypassed Judiciary Committee action and approved S 49 by a 79-15 vote. *(1985 Almanac p. 228)*

While the Senate-passed bill generally resembled the final version, it differed in three major respects. The Senate bill would have lifted the existing ban on interstate sales of handguns and barred unannounced inspections at any reasonable time. It did not include the final bill's ban on possession or transfer of machine guns.

House Committee Action

In a rare display of unity March 11, the House Judiciary Committee approved a gun control bill by a 35-0 vote. The bill, which had been unanimously approved by the Crime Subcommittee March 6, allowed interstate sales only for rifles and shotguns. While it revised some record-keeping requirements, it stuck more closely to existing law than the Senate measure. It was formally reported March 24 (HR 4332 — H Rept 99-495).

The committee's unusually quick action was in part an effort to beat a "discharge petition" circulated by Harold L. Volkmer, D-Mo., to force House votes on S 49, the Senate-passed gun bill, and a companion measure sponsored by Volkmer. Angry that Judiciary Chairman Peter W. Rodino Jr., D-N.J., had stymied gun legislation for nearly seven years, Volkmer had circulated his petition to get the legislation to the floor without a committee vote. Volkmer needed 218 signatures on the petition, and he obtained them March 13. The last successful discharge petition in the House was in 1983. *(1983 Almanac p. 261)*

NRA spokesmen immediately blasted HR 4332, contending it did not address problems in existing law and would create new ones for the nation's sportsmen. The NRA wrote House members March 13 opposing the bill "in the strongest possible terms." The group said it would work to defeat HR 4332 and to get the House to pass a bill along the lines of S 49.

However, HR 4332 was praised by law enforcement organizations which, along with Handgun Control, a Washington-based advocacy group, had been battling the NRA for months to protect gun restrictions in the 1968 law.

Attorney General Edwin Meese III told Judiciary members at a hearing March 12 that HR 4332 was "the kind of bill I'd feel comfortable with." Meese also had said he supported S 49.

Controversial Provisions

While HR 4332 and S 49 had some similar provisions, there were important differences.

The House bill allowed interstate sales of rifles and shotguns, and a new type of record check for anyone buying a handgun. The Senate bill allowed interstate sales of all types of guns, including handguns, as long as the transaction was over-the-counter and the purchase was legal in the state of the buyer and seller. The Senate bill also did not include a special record check for handgun purchases.

The House bill required dealers to notify law enforcement authorities when a handgun purchase was made to determine whether the purchaser was legally entitled to own a gun. Checks would be made by local authorities as well as the FBI, and if no problems with the purchaser turned up, the information would be destroyed within 90 days of receipt. Unlike a waiting period, which would come between the purchase and actual receipt of the gun, these background checks would come after the buyer purchased a gun.

S 49 barred unannounced inspections of dealers' records — a change from existing law, which allowed inspections at any "reasonable" time. The House bill allowed three unannounced inspections in any 18-month period. More would be allowed only if approved by the secretary of the Treasury or the director of Treasury's Bureau of Alcohol, Tobacco and Firearms.

S 49 also revised existing law to limit the number of people who were required to get licenses to sell guns. The House bill did not change the law. A Judiciary aide contended the Senate provision would provide too big a loophole for people to transfer firearms without a license.

Both bills made violations of certain record-keeping provisions misdemeanors instead of felonies. However, S 49 also revised the 1968 law so that certain technical violations would require a higher standard of proof by the government in order to secure a conviction under the law.

House Floor Action

The House passed HR 4332 April 10 by a 292-130 vote after substituting the text of Volkmer's bill for the provisions of the Judiciary Committee measure. *(Vote 69, p. 22-H)*

The Judiciary bill was never directly considered by the House. Instead, members voted 286-136 April 10 to adopt the Volkmer substitute. *(Vote 68, p. 22-H)*

As passed by the House, the bill was very similar to the measure passed by the Senate in 1985. The House bill made it easier to buy and sell rifles and shotguns and to transport them interstate. However, the House refused to lift the existing prohibition on interstate sales of handguns.

On two key votes April 9, the NRA demonstrated its political power by crushing a highly visible and determined effort by national law enforcement groups to keep the 1968 gun law basically intact.

The police groups and their ally, Handgun Control, prevailed only on the handgun sale issue, and while police spokesmen said that was an important victory, it was far less than they had hoped for.

Debate

For Volkmer, passage of HR 4332 was a personal triumph. He had pushed since 1979 to amend the 1968 law, and on April 10 he pronounced himself "very pleased." The bill, he said, "protects many of our citizens" from abuses by federal agents.

That argument — that law-abiding citizens had suffered under the 1968 law — was at the heart of the NRA's effort. The organization had contended for more than a decade that the law was too broad and subjected innocent gun owners to harassment by federal agents.

Volkmer, his congressional allies and the NRA sought to frame the House debate in terms of civil and constitutional rights. Their arguments centered on the Second Amendment to the Constitution, which says "the right of the people to keep and bear arms shall not be infringed."

During debate April 9, Volkmer called consideration of his bill the "second most important step in the history of American gun owners. The first was the Second Amendment to the U.S. Constitution."

Crime Subcommittee Chairman William J. Hughes, D-N.J., tried to portray the issue as one of law enforcement and safety. He claimed Volkmer's legislation "would elevate gun dealers to a special level of privilege never before seen in the law." By contrast, he said, the Judiciary Committee bill sought a balance between the interests of sportsmen and hunters and the interests of police and citizens.

Amendments

While Volkmer's discharge petition did not directly affect HR 4332, it played an important political role. With the backing of half the members of the House, Volkmer could virtually dictate the terms under which his substitute and HR 4332 would be considered by the full House.

On March 19 the Rules Committee approved a rule that foreclosed a clear yes-or-no vote on HR 4332. Instead, Volkmer was given the chance to offer his bill as a replacement for the Judiciary bill. In addition, Rules allowed only five hours of debate on the legislation, including the time required for roll-call votes. This had the effect of limiting the number of amendments that could be offered.

Hughes and his allies decided then that their best hope was to try to amend Volkmer's bill to meet police concerns.

On April 9 Hughes offered a package of law enforcement amendments to the Volkmer bill. Chief among them was the ban on interstate sales of handguns, a ban on interstate transportation of handguns and tighter record-keeping requirements.

The interstate transportation provision prompted the most debate, particularly from Westerners and longtime NRA members such as John D. Dingell, D-Mich., who contended that hunters should be able to travel interstate with their guns without fear of prosecution by local authorities. They pointed out that 37 states allowed hunting with handguns.

Hughes and Dan Lungren, R-Calif., another Judiciary member, said they had no objection to interstate transportation of rifles and shotguns for sporting purposes. But they said they could see no reason for taking handguns interstate.

Dingell retorted that if a sportsman from Maryland or Virginia wanted to go bear hunting in Maine, he risked prosecution on his way through New Jersey because it was "presumably illegal for him to have a firearm or handgun" in that state. Volkmer's bill would correct that problem, Dingell said, but Hughes' proposal would make "criminals every day out of law-abiding sportsmen and citizens."

Hughes' package was rejected by a 176-248 vote — a margin that was a sobering disappointment to the law-enforcement groups. *(Vote 64, p. 22-H)*

They had hoped their aggressive lobbying in the previous weeks and their presence April 9 around the House chamber would make a difference. During the voting, groups of state and local police officers stood at parade rest in full dress uniform at the doors of the chamber, staring silently at members as they filed in to vote.

After Hughes' package was defeated, he offered the interstate transportation provision separately. It also was handily rejected, 177-242. *(Vote 65, p. 22-H)*

Hughes then tried to offer another amendment, to ban the interstate sale of handguns. But he was interrupted by Speaker Thomas P. O'Neill Jr., D-Mass., who said he wanted to end work for the evening to keep the House from having to pay overtime to Capitol workers. "We have got to start watching pennies around here" because the Gramm-Rudman-Hollings anti-deficit law had forced spending cuts across the board, O'Neill said.

When the House reconvened April 10, members took up the amendment that retained the ban on interstate handgun sales.

It was adopted 233-184. *(Vote 66, p. 22-H)*

The House adopted a fourth amendment offered by Hughes in the closing minutes of debate. Adopted by voice vote, the amendment would bar all future sales and possession of machine guns by private citizens. It would not affect existing machine guns.

Following passage of HR 4332, the House-approved provisions were substituted for the text of S 49.

Lobbying Battle

For six weeks the looming fight on the gun measure was billed as a showdown between the police and the NRA. It turned out to be a rather mismatched affair. While the police groups were able to get more than 100 uniformed officers to Washington, they were, in the words of some members, too little too late.

"The police misunderstood the force of lobbying," said Buddy Roemer, D-La. "Lobbying is not standing in long lines at the door. Lobbying is good information early; it is a presence when minds are being made up. Minds were already made up yesterday," he said, referring to the April 9 vote.

Butler Derrick, D-S.C., said he thought the police leaders did not accurately represent rank-and-file police officers, who were NRA supporters.

Hughes and other members had attributed the NRA's success to the millions of dollars it had poured into congressional campaigns. But an equally important factor was the organization's ability to generate broad grass-roots support.

Some members from the South and Midwest said privately that while they supported Hughes, they could not afford to vote against the NRA.

"This is one vote where I have to be representational," said one Southerner, calling his district a "frontier" area where guns were a fact of life.

A Congressional Quarterly analysis of the key vote on Hughes' law enforcement package showed that Southerners voted overwhelmingly — 83 percent — against it. In the West, 59 percent of members were opposed. Midwestern members split 50-50, while in the East, Hughes got backing from 62 percent of the members.

Final Senate Action

The Senate May 6 approved by voice vote the House-passed version of S 49, clearing the measure for the president's signature. It then went on to pass S 2414, which made three changes in the newly cleared bill.

The brief Senate action on both bills belied the controversy that lay beneath them. The only clue to the delicate negotiations preceding floor action came in the congratulatory remarks senators made to one another just before passage.

Ever since the House passed its version of S 49 April 10, Sens. James A. McClure, R-Idaho, and Orrin G. Hatch, R-Utah, chief sponsors of S 49, had been talking with Sen. Howard M. Metzenbaum, D-Ohio, a chief opponent of the bill who was representing the concerns of police groups and gun control advocates unhappy with S 49.

While these organizations were pleased that S 49 retained the existing ban on interstate sales of handguns, they opposed lifting the ban on interstate sales of long guns, and they contended that easing the licensing requirements would make it more difficult to trace firearms used in a crime.

A coalition of police groups drafted a package of amendments they wanted the Senate to consider. For nearly three weeks, their efforts bore little fruit, but when police spokesmen were able to speak to Judiciary Committee Chairman Strom Thurmond, R-S.C. — a longtime law enforcement supporter — Thurmond set about trying to bring McClure, Hatch and Metzenbaum together.

Finally, on the afternoon of May 6, Thurmond got the three into a room and they hammered out S 2414, with language similar to what the police groups wanted. The full Senate passed S 2414 later that day, and the House cleared the bill June 24.

One provision of S 2414 made clear that any gun transported across state lines must be unloaded and locked away in something other than the passenger compartment of the vehicle. Another section made it easier for the federal government to trace guns supplied to terrorists. The third restored record-keeping requirements, deleted from existing law by S 49, for dealers who sold guns from their personal collections. ∎

Armor-Piercing Bullet Ban

Congress Aug. 13 cleared legislation (HR 3132 — PL 99-408) to ban most importation, manufacture or sale of "cop-killer" bullets that could pierce the protective vests of police officers. Bullets made for specified sporting purposes and industrial use were exempted from the bill's restrictions.

National law enforcement organizations had urged Congress for years to enact a law to protect officers from armor-piercing bullets, but previous bills had run into opposition from the politically powerful National Rifle Association (NRA), which viewed them as "a foot in the door" to gun control. In 1984, House leaders had blocked floor action on an earlier cop-killer bullet bill in the face of NRA opposition. The NRA did not actively oppose HR 3132. *(Background, 1984 Almanac p. 226; gun control, p. 82)*

Major Provisions

As signed into law Aug. 28, HR 3132 (PL 99-408):

- Prohibited the importation, manufacture or sale of armor-piercing ammunition, except in certain limited circumstances.
- Defined the banned ammunition as bullets that "may be used in a handgun," made of specific hard metals: tungsten alloys, steel, brass, bronze, iron, beryllium copper or depleted uranium. Standard ammunition is made from lead.
- Exempted bullets made to meet specified federal and state environmental regulations for hunting; also exempted ammunition used for industrial purposes, such as perforating devices involving oil and gas wells.
- Stipulated that the bullets could be produced only for use by federal or state government agencies, for export, or for testing or experimenting authorized by the secretary of the Treasury.
- Required manufacturers and importers to mark ammunition and label packages of armor-piercing ammunition.
- Provided a mandatory five-year penalty for anyone possessing armor-piercing ammunition when the individual committed a crime with a firearm capable of firing the ammunition.
- Provided that ammunition dealers who "willfully" violated the law could have their licenses revoked.

Legislative History

The House originally passed its version of the bill (H Rept 99-360) Dec. 17, 1985, on a 400-21 vote. A similar measure was reported by the Senate Judiciary Committee (S 104) in mid-1985, but floor action was blocked in the closing days of the session. *(1985 Almanac p. 232)*

On March 6, 1986, the Senate passed a version of HR 3132 that differed slightly from the House-passed measure. Passage came on a 97-1 roll call, with Steven D. Symms, R-Idaho, casting the sole dissenting vote. *(Vote 28, p. 6-S)*

By voice vote, the Senate adopted two amendments designed to limit the coverage of the bill. One, offered by Texas Democrat Lloyd Bentsen, exempted ammunition used in perforation devices for oil and gas wells. The other, offered by Symms, revised the definition of armor-piercing bullets to cover only those that could be used in a handgun.

The House proposed further amendments Aug. 11, and the Senate agreed Aug. 13, completing congressional action.

The final version of the bill deleted a Senate provision exempting from the bill's restrictions armor-piercing bullets already in ammunition dealers' inventories. ∎

Congress Puts More Teeth in Anti-Fraud Law

Congress Oct. 7 cleared legislation hailed by sponsors as a major weapon to fight anti-government fraud, particularly by defense contractors.

The bill (S 1562 — PL 99-562) amended the 123-year-old False Claims Act, the main statute for fighting fraud against the government, by making four major changes: It increased penalties against those who defraud the government, clarified the standards and procedures for bringing fraud suits, provided new incentives for private citizens to report suspected fraud and protected "whistleblowers" who report fraud.

Additional provisions establishing a streamlined, administrative process to handle small-dollar fraud were originally contained in the House version of the bill, but were deleted from the cleared version because of complaints that the proposed administrative procedure would deny due process. However, at the urging of Sen. William S. Cohen, R-Maine, the provisions were added to HR 5300 — PL 99-509, the fiscal 1987 deficit-reduction bill, and eventually enacted. The provisions apply if the fraud in question amounts to less than $150,000.

Final action on S 1562 came Oct. 7 when the House accepted Senate amendments to the bill. The Senate had passed it Oct. 3.

The False Claims Act had not been amended in any major way since it was enacted in 1863 to curb defense contractor fraud during the Civil War. Because of ambiguous language in the statute, government lawyers said they had a difficult time using the law effectively to bring suits for alleged fraud.

In addition, the key sponsors — Reps. Dan Glickman, D-Kan., Howard L. Berman, D-Calif., Andy Ireland, R-Fla, and Sen. Charles E. Grassley, R-Iowa — said the $2,000 fraud penalty was woefully out of date. S 1562, Glickman said Oct. 8, "allows us to recoup potentially millions of dollars lost through fraud each year."

The defense industry lobbied vigorously against the bill, contending that existing law was strong enough to discourage fraud. But the sponsors disagreed. "I have consistently voted to strengthen and upgrade our military might over the last few years in the effort to provide for our national security," Ireland said. "But all the increases in military spending aren't worth a nickel if waste, abuse and specifically fraud rob us of our efforts."

And Grassley said passage of the legislation was "one more sign that the American people have had enough of those who exploit taxpayers and erode national security for their own profit."

Provisions

As cleared, S 1562 included the following major provisions:

- Raised the fine for violations from $2,000 to between $5,000 and $10,000.
- Allowed a judge to require defendants to pay triple the amount of damages sustained by the government.
- Allowed a judge to reduce the award to double the government's damages if the defendant could prove that he cooperated fully with the government once the fraud was detected.
- Raised the term of imprisonment for a criminal violation from five years to 10 years and increased the criminal fine from $10,000 for individuals and corporations to $250,000 for individuals and $500,000 for corporations.

A criminal prosecution would occur when the Justice Department determined that the fraud was too serious for civil penalties only. An example would be a conspiracy to commit fraud against the government.

- Clarified the standard of knowledge a person must have before the government could pursue a case against that person. The bill specified that a person must have actual knowledge of information involving fraud or act in deliberate ignorance or reckless disregard for the truth or falsity of the information.

- Allowed an individual who uncovered fraud to bring a lawsuit seeking to recover damages for the fraud.
- Authorized a judge to limit the participation of the individual in the lawsuit if the government decided to join the litigation.
- Provided the individual who initiated the suit with a damage award of between 15 percent and 25 percent if the government entered the case. The individual could receive at least 25 percent of the damage award but not more than 30 percent if the government did not enter the case.

Under the old law, there was a cap of 10 percent on the individual's award if the government entered the case and 25 percent if the government did not.

- Required the offender to pay attorneys' fees to a citizen who prevailed in a suit.
- Provided "whistleblowers" with protection from harassment, firing, demotion or suspension by allowing them "all relief necessary to make the employee whole." Such relief could include reinstatement with seniority, twice the back pay owed, and compensation for any special damages sustained, such as the cost of litigation to get his job back.
- Authorized the attorney general to issue "civil investigative demands," which are requests for documentary material or information, in advance of filing a lawsuit under the act.
- Barred the attorney general from delegating the authority to issue such demands.
- Required any civil investigative demand to state the conduct allegedly in violation of the false claims law and to describe with specificity the material sought.

House Action

The House Judiciary Committee voted 35-0 June 10 to report legislation (HR 4827 — H Rept 99-660) to beef up the government's main anti-fraud statute after rejecting an amendment that would have undercut new powers proposed for the Justice Department.

The bill increased the penalties for fraud, provided the Justice Department with new pretrial investigative tools and included new definitions spelling out the standard of proof needed for the government to win a case and the degree of knowledge a defendant must have before he can be found liable. The new definitions were designed to clear up ambiguities in the old statute and to make it easier for the government to prosecute a wider range of fraud cases.

To help protect whistleblowers the bill provided broad relief to an employee who suffers discrimination after charging fraud. The bill allowed for reinstatement with full seniority rights, double back pay, attorneys' fees and, in egregious cases, punitive damages.

The bill also included a new, streamlined administrative process designed for small-dollar fraud cases.

Kindness Amendment

At the June 10 markup, the committee rejected an amendment by Thomas N. Kindness, R-Ohio, that would have barred the Justice Department from sending written questionnaires to individuals or companies suspected of defrauding the government.

Kindness said this pretrial investigative tool was unnecessary and could be abused. He said giving the government this authority was tantamount to letting officials engage in "fishing expeditions" for fraud.

But Glickman argued that Kindness' amendment would "take the guts out" of the bill and the amendment was rejected 15-19.

By voice vote the committee adopted an amendment by Jack Brooks, D-Texas, to restore current law allowing the government to recover double the damages it can prove. A version of the bill approved earlier by the Judiciary Subcommittee on Administrative Law and Governmental Relations had provided for a triple recovery.

The committee also adopted an amendment by Barney Frank, D-Mass., that would require the Justice Department to get court approval before it could share with other agencies any information it gathered during a pretrial investigation. The amendment provided that a judge would have to find that the information was "relevant to an investigation" conducted by the agency seeking the information.

By voice vote the committee adopted another Frank amendment clarifying the administrative remedies when the alleged fraud involves beneficiaries of federal programs like food stamps and Medicare, the health care program for the elderly.

Under the amendment the government must prove that the suspect actually knew he was not entitled to a benefit he accepted. In addition, at least $15,000 in fraud would have to be involved before the government could proceed under the administrative provisions of the bill.

A Glickman amendment requiring the attorney general, rather than any designee, to approve pretrial demands for documents or oral testimony also was adopted by voice vote.

Floor Action

The House Sept. 9 passed HR 4827, but first dropped the provisions that would have given federal officials a streamlined administrative process to go after small-dollar fraud.

The deleted provisions were aimed at fraudulent claims of less than $100,000. They were similar to a separate Senate bill (S 1134 — S Rept 99-212) that ran into strong opposition from defense contractors and groups representing recipients of federal programs like food stamps. These opponents said the proposed administrative enforcement scheme would deny contractors and individuals the constitutional right to a trial. Supporters contended that the administrative procedure was needed for fraud involving relatively small amounts because those cases were going unattended due to the time and cost of going to court.

Glickman, said that HR 4827, even without the small-dollar fraud provisions, was an important and effective anti-fraud tool. "I didn't view the administrative provisions as all that critical," he said, "because any case of any magnitude would go to the federal courts anyway."

Judiciary Committee Chairman Peter W. Rodino Jr., D-N.J., also hailed the bill, insisting that the old law was seriously out-of-date. "While fraud has become more sophisticated," said Rodino, "the law through which the government prosecutes fraud and recoups its losses has not followed the same pattern."

Rep. Howard L. Berman, D-Calif., one of those who helped draft the House bill, said it was especially important to beef up anti-fraud laws during this time of growing budget deficits. "The U.S. taxpayers are being bilked," he said, "and we need all the resources we can obtain to address the problem."

Senate Action

By voice vote Aug. 11, the Senate passed anti-fraud legislation (S 1562 — S Rept 99-345) similar to the measure passed by the House.

The bill had been reported by the Judiciary Committee on July 28.

Like the anti-fraud bill passed by the House, the Senate measure clarified ambiguous language in the original law that made it difficult for the government to win cases. It also increased fraud penalties, allowing a judge to impose double or triple the amount involved in the fraud, in addition to a penalty of between $5,000 and $10,000.

Previous law set the penalty at $2,000 and it had never been changed.

Amendment Adopted

The Senate made one important change before adopting S 1562 by voice vote.

As reported by the Judiciary Committee, S 1562 created a new standard for the degree of knowledge about fraudulent activity a person must have before the government can pursue a case against that person. The bill, as reported, made a person liable if he knew a statement was false or if he acted in "gross negligence of the duty" to inquire about fraud.

But business groups opposed this language, contending it was too broad, and the Senate modified it to resemble a provision in the House bill.

The House bill defined knowledge for purposes of the law as "deliberate ignorance of the truth or falsity of information or reckless disregard for the truth or falsity of the information."

Grassley, the chief Senate sponsor, said Aug. 11 he would use the House standard so long as it was clear the government did not have to prove that an alleged violator had a "specific intent" to defraud.

The revision, Grassley said, "is only to assure that mere negligence, mistake and inadvertence are not actionable under the False Claims Act." ∎

Child Abuse Bill Cleared

By agreeing to House amendments, the Senate Aug. 12 cleared legislation (S 140 — PL 99-401) aimed at helping states deal with child abuse — especially sexual abuse. The bill established a grant program to states to improve the prosecution, treatment and prevention of child abuse and to protect the victims. The president signed the bill Aug. 27.

The Senate originally passed S 140 Aug. 1, 1985. The bill was sponsored by Paula Hawkins, R-Fla., who was a strong advocate for improving the judicial system's handling of child abuse cases. *(1985 Almanac p. 308)*

The House passed a slightly different version of the measure by voice vote Aug. 4, 1986. Rep. Pat Williams, D-Mont., chairman of the Education and Labor Subcommittee on Select Education, said that due to deficiencies in existing law, victims were "being traumatized unnecessarily by the process" of investigating and prosecuting child abuse cases. He said sexual abuse cases that should have been prosecuted successfully were "being dropped or lost because of certain states' policies, practices or procedures."

The bill authorized the secretary of health and human services to issue grants to states that set up a task force to make recommendations on how to improve the investigation and prosecution of child abuse cases. The task forces also would look at ways to reduce emotional damage to victims of abuse. To remain eligible for grants, a state would have to adopt the task force's recommendations or come up with comparable alternatives.

Grants would be financed out of the Crime Victims Fund. Upon enactment, $2.7 million from the fund would be made available for child abuse grants, with the amount increasing in subsequent years to a $10 million cap. The fund was made up of bond forfeitures, fines and penalties paid by criminals. ∎

New Child Pornography Law

Legislation cleared Oct. 16 to strengthen federal laws against child pornography by increasing penalties for repeat offenders and providing victims an opportunity to get compensation from those who exploit them.

The measure was rolled into the massive continuing appropriations resolution (H J Res 738 — PL 99-591) that President Reagan signed Oct. 30.

Its inclusion in the spending bill was largely attributable to Sen. Charles E. Grassley, R-Iowa, who personally lobbied House members.

The measure raised the penalty for a second child pornography conviction from two to five years.

In addition, it gave victims who are minors the right to sue for damages anyone who entices or forces them into helping produce pornographic materials. The minor is entitled to a minimum of $50,000 and attorneys' fees.

Finally, the bill directed the attorney general to report within a year on courtroom procedures for child witnesses forced to testify against accused pornographers. ∎

Communications Privacy

Congress Oct. 2 cleared legislation (HR 4952 — PL 99-508) that provided privacy protection to communications transmitted with new forms of technology.

The measure extended existing privacy guarantees for conventional telephones to communications involving cellular telephones that operated by high-frequency radio waves, transmissions by private satellite, paging devices and messages transmitted and stored in computers — known as "electronic mail."

Violators were subject to fines and prison terms. Government officials would have to get court approval before intercepting these high-tech communications.

HR 4952 was the product of two years' negotiations among the American Civil Liberties Union (ACLU), the electronics industry, the Justice Department and members of Congress.

The ACLU argued that protections were needed to prevent eavesdropping and abuse. Industry leaders feared that without privacy protections, consumers would lose interest in high-tech forms of communication. The Justice Department at first opposed the legislation, fearing it would tie the hands of law enforcement officials. But members eventually were able to negotiate a compromise that met the concerns of the administration.

The House passed HR 4952 (H Rept 99-647) June 23. The Senate passed it Oct. 1, amending it to conform with an almost identical bill (S 2575 — S Rept 99-541). The House then accepted the Senate version. All approvals came on voice votes.

The new legislation expanded and updated a 1968 law (PL 90-351) that specified when and how the government could wiretap conventional telephones. *(1968 Almanac p. 225)*

Major Provisions

As cleared by Congress, the Electronic Communications Privacy Act (HR 4952 — PL 99-508) included the following major provisions:

- **Definitions and Exemptions.** Rewrote the 1968 wiretap law to protect "electronic communications" and "electronic communications systems."
- Defined electronic communications to include "any transfer of signs, signals, writing, images, sounds, data or intelligence of any nature" that was transmitted "in whole or in part by wire, radio, electromagnetic, photoelectronic or photo-optical system that affects interstate or foreign commerce."
- Defined electronic communications system to mean any wire, radio, electromagnetic, photo-optical or photoelectronic facilities for the transmission of electronic communications, and any computer facilities or related electronic equipment for the electronic storage of such communications.
- Exempted from coverage — and thus left unprotected from intrusion — any radio communication that was "readily accessible to the general public."

Also exempted were the radio portion of a cordless telephone communication, which was transmitted between the cordless telephone handset and the base unit, any communication made through a tone-only paging device, communications between amateur radio operators, general mobile radio services, marine and aeronautical communications systems, police, fire, civil defense and other public safety radio communications systems and specified satellite transmissions.

- Protected radio signals in several instances: if the signal were scrambled or put into code, that is "encrypted"; if the signal's frequency were changed to one withheld from general use by the Federal Communications Commission; if the signal were transmitted through a common carrier, like a cellular telephone company, that served the public; or if the signal were transmitted via specific radio frequencies set out in the bill.
- **Private Interception.** Made it illegal for individuals intentionally to intercept electronic communications as defined in the bill.
- Made the offense a felony with a penalty of a fine, a prison term of up to five years or both when the interception was for any illegal purpose, such as gathering stock information for insider trading, was for direct or indirect commercial gain or was an interception of a scrambled or encrypted signal. Fines could range up to $10,000 if the interception was for commercial advantage.
- **Government Interception.** Allowed the government to intercept electronic communications after obtaining a court order. A judge could grant the order after he had determined that the interception "may provide or has provided" evidence of any federal felony.
- Made it a felony for any person to divulge information about a possible communication interception by the government in order to obstruct, impede or prevent such interception.
- **Stored Communications.** Protected the privacy of stored communications, either before or after delivery if a copy was kept.
- Made it a misdemeanor to break into any electronic system holding copies of messages either before or after delivery or to exceed authorized access in the system to alter or obtain the stored messages.
- Provided a fine for a first offense of up to $250,000, a maximum one-year prison term or both, if the offense were committed for commercial advantage or "malicious destruction or damage." There would be a two-year prison term for a second offense.
- Provided a maximum fine of $5,000 or imprisonment of up to six months for an offense that was not for commercial gain or for malicious destruction or damage.
- Allowed the government to require disclosure of copies of electronic mail under certain conditions.
- **Pen Registers, Trap and Trace.** Generally barred government use of "pen registers" and "trap and trace devices" except pursuant to a court order.
- Defined a pen register as a device that recorded or decoded numbers dialed or otherwise transmitted by telephone. Devices used to monitor calls involving billing were not covered.
- Defined a trap and trace device as one that captured an incoming electronic or other impulse and could identify the number from which a call was made.
- Provided a penalty for knowingly violating this section of a fine and imprisonment of up to one year or both.
- Required a government agency seeking a court order to use a pen register or trap and trace device to certify that the information "likely to be obtained is relevant to an ongoing criminal investigation being conducted by the applying government agency."

Patent Process Protection

Despite last-minute efforts in the House, the 99th Congress failed to clear legislation that would have extended U.S. patent protections to some products manufactured abroad.

The House passed the bill (HR 4899 — H Rept 99-807) Sept. 16 by voice vote. On Oct. 3, the Senate amended the measure in a manner opposed by the Reagan administration and returned it to the House. On Oct. 16, the House approved a compromise version that had the administration's support, but the revised bill was never considered by the Senate.

The legislation would have created patent infringement liability for goods made abroad by a process patented in the United States. Process patents protect the technique, art or methods of creating a product. They have become especially important to the pharmaceutical and biotechnology industries and to the development of solid-state electronics.

A similar provision was approved by the House in 1984, only to be blocked at the last minute in the Senate. *(1984 Almanac p. 260)*

The main opposition to the legislation came from importers of generic drugs, who contended that the bill would lead to a flood of frivolous, time-consuming lawsuits filed by brand-name drug manufacturers.

The Senate bill made it more difficult than the original House bill to file an infringement suit against someone who unknowingly imported or sold products manufactured abroad under a process patent. It also allowed anyone selling or using a drug to request information on what patented processes were involved.

The compromise House bill provided that patent infringement would occur only after the alleged infringer knew or was on notice that the goods he obtained were made in violation of a process patent.

Inventions in Space

The Senate did not act on another House-passed patent bill that would have extended U.S. patent laws into outer space.

As passed by voice vote Sept. 16, the House bill (HR 4316 — H Rept 99-788) would have amended the U.S. patent code to make it apply to activities on all space vehicles under the jurisdiction of the United States. That would mean anything invented, used or sold in outer space would be covered by U.S. patent law. ■

Bankruptcy Court Expansion

The Senate Oct. 3 cleared the conference report on a bill (HR 5316 — PL 99-554) designed to improve the efficiency of bankruptcy courts and to make it easier for small farmers to avoid liquidation. The House had approved the report Oct. 2.

The bill authorized 52 new federal bankruptcy judges to help eliminate a backlog, which ran several months. That brought the total to 284. The measure also expanded a pilot bankruptcy "trustee" program, operated by the Justice Department, which was established in 1978 to speed up handling of cases. The trustees in the program oversaw the administration of bankruptcy cases.

The Judicial Conference, the policy-making arm of the federal judiciary, opposed the expansion of the trustee program, contending that the bankruptcy courts, and not the Justice Department, should supervise bankruptcy cases.

The bill also amended the bankruptcy laws to permit small farmers to reorganize without the consent of their creditors, as required under existing law. Rep. Mike Synar, D-Okla., said the effect of the change would be to grant family farmers the same rights enjoyed by small-business men.

He predicted it would save many farmers from having to liquidate.

Legislative History

The House Judiciary Committee reported the bill Aug. 7 (H Rept 99-764). The House passed the bill without amendment Aug. 12. The Senate passed HR 5316, amended, Aug. 16. The House agreed to the conference report (H Rept 99-958) Oct. 2 and the Senate followed suit Oct. 3.

The House had passed similar legislation (HR 2211) in 1985. As passed by the House, the bill did not increase the number of bankruptcy judges. *(1985 Almanac p. 545)*

The Senate passed HR 2211 by voice May 8. The Senate version increased the number of judges to 49. As passed by the House, HR 5316 provided for 52 new judges — the number eventually agreed upon in conference. ■

Bankruptcy Law Change

Congress failed to pass legislation clarifying bankruptcy law and labor union contracts in the 99th Congress.

The House Sept. 29 passed legislation (HR 5490 — H Rept 99-917) to make clear that companies filing for bankruptcy could not unilaterally terminate a retiree's benefits. The Senate Oct. 3 passed an amended version of the bill but the two houses failed to reconcile differences and the bill died.

HR 5490 was an outgrowth of a 1984 law (PL 98-353) that restructured the bankruptcy courts and included provisions establishing special criteria for determining when bankrupt companies could terminate labor contracts. *(1984 Almanac p. 263)*

Members of Congress said the 1984 legislation was meant to cover former as well as current employees. However, on July 17, 1986, LTV Corp. filed a petition to reorganize under the bankruptcy laws and decided to stop paying for retirees' medical and life insurance benefits as of that date.

The company contended that it could not pay these benefits without express approval from a bankruptcy judge and that these former employees were not covered by the 1984 law.

HR 5490 would have ensured that the former employees were covered.

After LTV canceled the benefits, employees responded with a strike. Subsequently, on July 30, a bankruptcy judge authorized a resumption in benefit payments. ■

Computer Tampering

Congress Oct. 6 completed action on a bill (HR 4718 — PL 99-474) to expand and clarify laws prohibiting computer fraud.

The legislation was designed to stop those who illegally gained access to computer files in order to defraud the government. It also clarified provisions in a 1984 computer fraud law (PL 98-473) that critics said were too broad and infringed on individual rights. *(1984 Almanac p. 215)*

The House passed HR 4718 (H Rept 99-612) June 3 by voice vote, and the Senate passed a slightly different version (S 2281 — S Rept 99-432) Oct. 1. The bill cleared Oct. 6 when the House accepted the Senate provisions.

As cleared, the measure made it a felony, punishable by five years in prison, to "access," or enter, a "federal interest" computer without authorization in order to alter or damage information stored there, or to obtain anything of value. Federal interest computers were defined as those owned or used by the federal government or a federally insured financial institution, or used in interstate communication. The provision covered computers used by stockbrokers registered with the Securities and Exchange Commission.

A second felony was created for illegally entering and maliciously damaging a federal interest computer. There would have to be at least $1,000 worth of damage over the course of a year before the federal government could prosecute.

HR 4718 also made it a felony to tamper with computerized medical records.

The bill established a misdemeanor to stop "pirate

bulletin boards" on which computer pirates displayed the passwords to computers for others to use. The government could prosecute only when the passwords were to federal computers or computers that "affect" interstate or foreign commerce. ▮

Refugee Program Authorized

Congress cleared legislation (HR 1452 — PL 99-605) Oct. 18 reauthorizing refugee resettlement programs for two years.

Final action came when the House adopted the Senate version of the measure, which had passed the same day.

The resettlement programs, run primarily through the Department of Health and Human Services, provide medical, educational and social services to foreigners who were admitted to the United States as refugees. (A refugee was defined under the immigration laws as a person fleeing his homeland because of a well-founded fear of persecution.)

The bill provided $74.8 million for social services in fiscal 1987 and 1988 and $8.8 million for health screening each year.

The original House bill, which passed June 13, 1985, would have provided more money in fiscal 1987 and 1988 for social services and health screening. It also would have provided $50 million for states with large refugee populations. *(1985 Almanac p. 240)*

That last provision was strongly opposed by the Reagan administration and was deleted from the final bill. However, House aides said the basic 1980 refugee law (PL 96-212) authorized special aid to areas with high concentrations of refugees.

The original House bill also would have made all refugees eligible for Medicaid the first year they were in the country. But this provision also was opposed by the administration and deleted.

The cleared bill required social service agencies that help refugees resettle to submit detailed reports on the number of refugees placed, how much money was spent and the refugees' progress.

The Senate Judiciary Committee reported a bill (S 1262 — S Rept 99-154) June 13, 1985, but it was not considered by the full Senate. Instead, the Senate Oct. 18, 1986, amended the House bill. ▮

Lobbying Restrictions

An unusual alliance of conservative Republicans and First Amendment activists joined forces to soften the impact of a lobbying restriction bill that was approved June 26 by the Senate Judiciary Committee.

Conservatives Orrin G. Hatch, R-Utah, Paul Laxalt, R-Nev., and Jeremiah Denton, R-Ala., working in concert with the American Civil Liberties Union (ACLU), challenged the sweeping nature of proposed prohibitions on lobbying by former government officials and members of Congress.

Hatch said the original bill (S 2334), sponsored by committee Chairman Strom Thurmond, R-S.C., would have affected 40,000 employees and could have stifled the interest of competent persons to work for the government.

Hatch also echoed the ACLU's contention that the measure could pose a conflict with Bill of Rights protections of free speech and the ability to petition the government.

Thurmond grudgingly accepted a scaled-back measure proposed by Hatch in order to win bipartisan committee approval. "Frankly, it's not as strong as I would like," Thurmond said.

The panel voted 17-1 to send the substitute version to the full Senate, with only Charles McC. Mathias Jr., R-Md., opposed. However, the Senate never acted on the bill.

The legislation was spurred by publicity surrounding former White House aide Michael K. Deaver, who was under investigation for possible conflict-of-interest violations.

Deaver gained notoriety when after resigning as President Reagan's deputy chief of staff in May 1985, he immediately opened a lucrative public relations firm in Washington, with clients ranging from defense contractors to the governments of Canada, South Korea and Saudi Arabia. Questions arose about his lobbying contacts with former colleagues still in the White House, leading to the appointment of an independent counsel, Whitney North Seymour Jr., to determine whether he violated conflict-of-interest laws.

Applies to Members of Congress

As approved by Senate Judiciary, S 2334 barred senior government officials and members of Congress from working for a foreign government for three years and from lobbying any part of the government for 18 months.

The bill also barred all government officials at the $61,000 salary level or higher from lobbying on behalf of a foreign entity for two years after leaving office and from lobbying their own agencies for one year.

Unlike existing law, which covered only senior officials in the executive branch, the new ban applied to judiciary and legislative branch employees, as well. Committee staff members said that would affect about 10,000 employees.

The bill included stiffer penalties for "willful" violations, increasing the maximum prison sentence from two to five years and adding forfeiture of any financial gains to a maximum $250,000 fine.

The bill also added new disclosure rules for government employees who go to work for foreign entities, requiring lobbyists to itemize periodically with their former agencies the money they were paid, the government contacts they make and the names of any employees who assisted in lobbying.

Thurmond had wanted to place a lifetime ban on senior officials and members of Congress working as foreign agents. He later proposed reducing that to 10 years for specified Cabinet-level officials and senior White House advisers, and to five years for members of Congress, but dropped that plan after continued opposition.

Committee members agreed that the biggest roadblock to passage was the provision restricting the future lobbying activities of members of Congress.

Members of Congress and higher-paid staff would, for the first time, be subject to the post-employment conflict-of-interest section of the Ethics in Government Act, as amended in 1982 (PL 97-409). *(1982 Almanac p. 386)*

Internal Senate rules, which do not have the force of law, placed a one-year restriction on members lobbying the Senate, and on staff members lobbying former offices or committees.

House Panel Also Acts

The day of the Senate Judiciary vote, June 26, Rep.

Dan Glickman, D-Kan., introduced a similar bill (HR 5426) in the House.

By voice vote Aug. 7, Glickman's House Judiciary Subcommittee on Administrative Law approved HR 5426, barring high-level officials and members of Congress from lobbying for foreign governments for four years. However, the full Judiciary Committee did not act on the measure.

On Aug. 12 the House Energy Subcommittee on Oversight and Investigations, climaxing a seven-month investigation, accused Deaver of lying during May testimony before the panel. The subcommittee voted 17-0 to turn its evidence of "possible perjury" over to the independent counsel. ∎

Congress Clears Massive Anti-Drug Measure

Responding to an apparent growth in voter concern over illegal-drug abuse, Congress cleared a massive anti-drug measure Oct. 17, less than three weeks before the mid-term congressional elections. President Reagan signed the $1.7 billion bill (HR 5484 — PL 99-570) Oct. 27.

The measure increased penalties for drug offenses and — despite concerns over controlling the federal budget deficit — authorized new funds in fiscal 1987 for drug enforcement, eradication and interdiction efforts, and for education, treatment and rehabilitation programs.

It also became a vehicle for various unrelated riders, ranging from a measure setting nationwide licensing standards for commercial bus and truck drivers to provisions strengthening infant formula regulations.

While members agreed they wanted to "get tough" on drugs, each chamber seemed determined to see the final version reflect its own ideas of how to achieve that goal. The drug bill very nearly derailed in the final days of the 99th Congress, as the chambers batted the measure back and forth, narrowly avoiding a threatened Senate filibuster over a provision authorizing the death penalty for certain drug-related crimes. But with the "war on drugs" such a prominent part of many election campaigns, neither house wanted the measure to die on its doorstep.

In the end, House and Senate sponsors, meeting at an informal conference, crafted a bipartisan, bicameral compromise that allowed both death penalty advocates and opponents to claim victory — or at least to save face.

The House Oct. 17 approved the compromise measure by a 378-16 vote, and the Senate followed suit later that day, clearing the bill by voice vote. *(Vote 448, p. 126-H)*

Full funding for the anti-drug crusade was provided in the fiscal 1987 continuing appropriations resolution (H J Res 738 — PL 99-591), even though addition of the money pushed the bill over the budget for the year. *(Appropriations bill, p. 219)*

Final Compromise

While the death penalty was the most emotional issue on which the two chambers were at odds, the House and Senate versions of the bill differed on other matters as well.

At an Oct. 16 meeting, it took nine senators and some two dozen House members more than two hours to iron out differences on issues ranging from federal penalties for receiving "laundered" money to the imposition of blood-alcohol standards for bus and truck drivers.

The final package authorized nearly $500 million in new funds for fiscal 1987 for drug interdiction, $275 million for drug enforcement, $230 million for grants for state and local law enforcement, $241 million for rehabilitation and treatment, and $200 million for drug abuse education and prevention programs.

The bill was touted by many members as an attack on major drug pushers, but it contained a number of provisions aimed at small-scale users. One, for example, imposed a mandatory $1,000 minimum fine for simple possession of a small amount of illegal drugs.

Dropped along the way, in addition to the death penalty provision, were controversial proposals that would have weakened the exclusionary rule that prohibited illegally obtained evidence from being used in court, ordered the military to intercept and arrest suspected drug smugglers, and required drug testing for federal employees in sensitive positions.

The American Civil Liberties Union (ACLU), in particular, had fought those provisions in a no-holds-barred lobbying effort during the weeks between passage of the first House version Sept. 9 and final clearing of the measure.

Background

Reagan and congressional leaders from both parties competed for credit in a race to combat drug abuse. The issue gained political momentum throughout the summer, spurred by publicity over the cocaine-related deaths of two popular athletes, University of Maryland basketball star Len Bias and Cleveland Browns football player Don Rogers.

But agreement in Congress was strained by differences over how much and what kind of government effort would work best. The House got a head start on the issue July 23, when Speaker Thomas P. O'Neill Jr., D-Mass., announced a major, bipartisan anti-drug initiative, to be coordinated by Majority Leader Jim Wright, D-Texas.

Under the Speaker's timetable, House committees with jurisdiction over drug-related issues were to report legislation or make recommendations to Wright no later than Aug. 12. During the August recess, the bills and recommendations were to be rolled into a single omnibus drug measure and presented to the Rules Committee Sept. 9 after Congress returned.

President Reagan jumped into the fray Aug. 4, with a nationally televised speech calling for a "mobilization" in "what we hope will be the final stage in our national strategy to eradicate drug abuse."

Reagan outlined plans to seek drug-free work places and schools, improved drug treatment for abusers, international cooperation to eradicate drugs in source countries, strengthened law enforcement and expanded public awareness. But it was clear the administration would not seek major new federal expenditures for the anti-drug crusade.

Reagan put emphasis instead on drug testing in both the private and public sectors. To set an example, Vice President George Bush, along with several dozen presidential assistants, agreed to submit to tests Aug. 11. Reagan took his test Aug. 9 during a checkup at the Bethesda Naval Hospital.

A day after Reagan spoke, a group of Senate Democrats, led by Lawton Chiles, Fla., and Joseph R. Biden Jr.,

Del., announced the formation of a nine-member Democratic Working Group on Substance and Narcotics Abuse.

Chiles, Biden and John D. Rockefeller IV, W.Va., unveiled the group's first legislative efforts — two bills (S 2715, S 2716) that increased penalties for users of a lethal type of cocaine called "crack," authorized funds for drug abuse awareness in schools, and established a Cabinet-level "drug czar" to oversee the myriad of federal agencies dealing with drug enforcement and prevention, a provision the administration strongly opposed.

House Committee Action

Omnibus Bill

House committees completed work Aug. 13 on their package to help the nation fight its battle against illegal drugs.

The legislation was a compilation of proposals from 12 standing committees and was aimed at stemming the flow of illegal drugs into the United States, stepping up enforcement of drug laws, increasing penalties for narcotics trafficking and improving drug abuse education, prevention and treatment programs.

The measure was compiled under the direction of Majority Leader Wright with help from Minority Leader Robert H. Michel, R-Ill. Although Democratic leaders seized the initiative on the drive for anti-drug legislation, they tried to be careful to pull GOP members along.

Seven House committees — Foreign Affairs, Government Operations, Energy and Commerce, Ways and Means, Education and Labor, Judiciary, and Merchant Marine — reported legislation in early August for inclusion in the drug package.

Four others — Armed Services, Interior, Post Office and Civil Service, and Public Works — submitted titles for the bill without formal markups. The Banking Committee's main contribution, legislation (HR 5176 — H Rept 99-746) to crack down on drug traffickers who laundered illegal profits through financial institutions, was reported Aug. 5.

As the committees began to mark up their packages for inclusion in the omnibus bill, the bipartisan alliance claimed by the House leadership often showed signs of strain.

The overriding issue threatening the bipartisan harmony was money. The committees authorized what was estimated to be a total of $1.92 billion for fiscal 1987 and more than $3.75 billion over three years. Such figures in a time of massive budget deficits drew the wrath of a number of Republicans who accused Democrats of trying to solve the drug problem by throwing money at it.

Separate House committee actions included the following:

Government Operations

The Government Operations Committee Aug. 5 ordered reported by voice vote a bill (HR 5266 — H Rept 99-786) that would require a president within six months of enactment to submit legislation reorganizing the executive branch to coordinate efforts to combat drug trafficking and abuse.

While stopping short of seeking the creation of a Cabinet-level drug czar, the bill sought to reduce infighting among agencies with jurisdiction over drug abuse and enforcement programs.

Energy and Commerce

The Energy and Commerce Committee voted Aug. 6 to create a new agency to oversee federal drug abuse prevention and treatment efforts.

The proposed Agency for Substance Abuse Prevention (ASAP), was to take over the prevention efforts then carried out by the National Institute on Drug Abuse (NIDA) and the National Institute on Alcohol Abuse and Alcoholism (NIAAA).

The bill creating ASAP (HR 5334 — H Rept 99-792, Part 1) was introduced by Committee Chairman John D. Dingell, D-Mich., and Health Subcommittee Chairman Henry A. Waxman, D-Calif. It was approved by voice vote, but not until the end of a fractious three-and-a-half-hour markup.

Before approving the package, the committee narrowly rejected, on a straight party-line show of hands, a substitute offered by Edward R. Madigan, R-Ill., ranking member of the Health Subcommittee, that would have deleted the provisions creating ASAP.

In addition to creating ASAP, the Dingell-Waxman package:

- Authorized a total of $180 million for ASAP for fiscal 1987: $30 million to be used for administrative costs, $100 million to be given as grants to states for drug abuse treatment and rehabilitation, and $50 million in grants for developing and administering community-based substance abuse prevention programs.
- Called on the president to convene a White House Conference on Drug Abuse and Trafficking Control, to increase public awareness, pool information and assist in the formulation of a national drug strategy.
- Closed a loophole to make so-called "designer drugs" illegal.
- Authorized $400,000 in each of fiscal years 1987-89 for a demonstration project to rehabilitate Navaho Indians suffering from alcohol abuse.
- Created a Congressional Advisory Commission on the Comprehensive Education of Intercollegiate Athletes and authorized up to $650,000 to pay the commission's expenses.
- Classified as a drug alkyl nitrites, better known as poppers.

By voice vote, the committee adopted an amendment by Doug Walgren, D-Pa., to require states to give preference, if possible, to youths between the ages of 15 and 24 in the spending of new funds for treatment.

After nearly an hour of debate, the committee refused, by a vote of 11-15, to strike the commission on college athletics.

Finally, by a vote of 11-17, the committee rejected a William E. Dannemeyer, R-Calif., amendment to prohibit ASAP funds from going to states that refused to close bathhouses "or other public establishments known to facilitate AIDS."

Ways and Means

After a four-hour debate Aug. 7, the Ways and Means Committee by voice vote approved its contribution to the omnibus drug package.

The committee agreed to give the U.S. Customs Service broader authority to stop drugs from entering the country and to authorize nearly $1 billion to beef up a Customs Service air interdiction program. The measure also would deny trade benefits to uncooperative "drug source nations."

Foreign Affairs

The Foreign Affairs Committee approved its portion (HR 5352 — H Rept 99-798) of the omnibus bill by voice vote Aug. 6. Key provisions:

- Repealed the so-called "Mansfield amendment" that prohibited American law enforcement officials from being present when drug traffickers were apprehended in foreign nations.
- Earmarked $10 million from military assistance programs to purchase aircraft for interdiction and eradication efforts. Half of that money had to be used for the creation of a regional South American fleet in Colombia.
- Withheld $1 million of narcotics aid from Mexico pending an investigation and prosecution of those responsible for the February 1985 murder of a U.S. narcotics agent and his pilot.

Armed Services

The bill contained a bare-bones title from the Armed Services Committee that authorized $213 million for purchase of advanced radar and other drug-detection hardware. The committee was unable to complete a markup that began Aug. 12 because of House floor action on a defense authorization bill (HR 4428).

Judiciary Committee

The most costly portion of the drug package was approved Aug. 13 by the Judiciary Committee. The committee July 29 had approved five other drug-related proposals, including one (HR 5217 — H Rept 99-855, Part I) to make it harder for drug dealers to launder their profits through banks and other financial institutions.

The two new bills (HR 5393 — H Rept 99-847; HR 5394 — H Rept 99-845, Part I), approved by voice vote after a six-hour markup, provided increased authorizations for drug enforcement and construction of new federal prisons, and stronger penalties for those convicted of drug-related offenses.

As approved by the Crime Subcommittee Aug. 11, HR 5393 increased the authorization for the Drug Enforcement Administration by $60 million for fiscal 1987, adding 543 new positions. It also created a new grant program to aid state and local drug enforcement efforts. The bill authorized $100 million for the grant program in fiscal 1987 and $200 million in 1988.

By the time the full committee had completed its work, it had added well over $1 billion to the package, largely to fund prison construction and salaries for fiscal 1987 and 1988.

HR 5394 imposed minimum mandatory prison sentences of five years for first-time "serious traffickers" and 10 years for "major traffickers." It increased sentences for other offenses and imposed fines of up to $10 million. It also made it a federal crime to use children to manufacture or distribute drugs, and imposed a new penalty of 20 years to life imprisonment if a death resulted from drug trafficking activities.

Debate was surprisingly restrained over an amendment offered by George W. Gekas, R-Pa., to allow the death penalty to be imposed on individuals who knowingly caused the death of another individual during the course of "a continuing criminal enterprise." Allowing capital punishment, argued Gekas, was "a natural extension of the war on drugs we are waging."

But committee Democrats, many of whom said they generally supported capital punishment, said they worried that the amendment could end up derailing the entire drug package. Gekas' amendment was ultimately rejected 16-19.

On a straight party-line vote, the committee also refused, 14-21, to adopt an amendment to permit plea bargaining after conviction in exchange for information that could lead to the conviction of a higher-up in a drug organization.

Merchant Marine

The Merchant Marine Committee Aug. 13 approved a bill (HR 5406 — H Rept 99-973, Part I) authorizing $150 million in each of fiscal years 1987 and 1988 for Coast Guard drug enforcement activities.

The $300 million package authorized $132 million for operating expenses — including the addition of 1,500 military personnel, the bulk of whom would be used to augment shore station crews — and $168 million for drug interdiction equipment. The equipment would be used primarily to allow the Coast Guard to carry out air surveillance operations over the high seas.

Education and Labor

By voice vote, the Education and Labor Committee Aug. 12 ordered reported HR 5378 (H Rept 99-808), its contribution to the omnibus drug package.

As approved by the committee, the bill:

- Allowed states receiving grant money to award funds to local educational agencies for the development of drug abuse education and prevention curriculums; counseling programs; drug abuse treatment referral; in-service training for teachers, counselors, law enforcement officials and community leaders; and community education programs for parents.
- Required the education secretary to establish a drug education and prevention program that included a national media campaign; programs involving sports and entertainment figures, medical professionals and former drug users; and community education for parents.
- Required the education secretary to establish a clearinghouse to collect and disseminate information to educational agencies on successful drug education and prevention programs and to provide technical assistance on the selection and implementation of such programs.
- Authorized $350 million for each of fiscal years 1987-89.

Other amendments adopted by the committee:

- Created a National Advisory Council on Drug Abuse Education and Prevention to "attract and focus national attention on drug-related problems."
- Required the secretary of labor to conduct a two-year study on the incidence of drug abuse in the work place and efforts to assist workers.

Other Proposals

Three other committees — Post Office and Civil Service, Public Works and Transportation, and Interior — also sent recommendations to Wright for inclusion in the omnibus bill.

The Post Office Committee proposed requiring the Office of Personnel Management to develop prevention, treatment and rehabilitation programs for all federal employees, and to establish a governmentwide education program on the health hazards of alcohol and drug abuse, symptoms of abuse, and availability of services. It also proposed to make the mailing of drugs a separate criminal offense.

The Public Works Committee suggested a number of changes in the Federal Aviation Act, including one that would allow state and local law enforcement officials to inspect the registrations of all aircraft.

The Interior Committee called for inclusion of provisions to help control alcohol and drug abuse among Indian tribes.

House Floor Action

Despite continued budget-deficit problems, the House Sept. 11 overwhelmingly approved legislation to authorize more than $6 billion to combat narcotics trafficking and discourage the use of illegal drugs.

The vote on passage of HR 5484 was 392-16, with all but one of the "nays" cast by Democratic liberals who said the House was being stampeded by political considerations into approving provisions that threatened civil liberties. The lone Republican to oppose the bill was Philip M. Crane of Illinois. *(Vote 348, p. 98-H)*

Most other members vociferously supported the measure, approving amendment after amendment that stiffened penalties against drug dealers and added money to programs. Indeed, every amendment offered that authorized more funds or expanded anti-drug efforts in any way was approved, and every amendment that would have cut authorizations or programs was rejected.

"In football there's a thing called piling on," said Patricia Schroeder, D-Colo. "I think we're seeing political piling on right before the election."

Before passing the bill, the House adopted amendments increasing authorization levels by more than $1.2 billion. The Congressional Budget Office had estimated the cost of the earlier version at a total of $4.799 billion over three years, $3.943 billion of it for new programs and personnel.

By wide margins, the House also adopted three controversial, Republican-backed amendments that authorized the death penalty for certain drug traffickers, gave military personnel authority to pursue and arrest drug smugglers in U.S. territory, and provided an exception for the so-called exclusionary rule, which prohibited evidence obtained illegally from being offered in court.

Those amendments, which were allowed to be offered as a result of negotiations between Wright and Michel, angered some liberals. Several Democrats criticized the leadership for putting them in the position of having to choose between long-held philosophical views and running the risk of "looking soft on drugs."

Several members expressed concerns that the addition of such controversial amendments had turned a consensus bill into one that could prompt a Senate filibuster and potentially doom the legislation.

Only minutes after the House approved the death penalty amendment, ACLU Director Morton H. Halperin pledged all of the organization's resources toward stopping the bill in the Senate.

The military amendment, offered by Duncan L. Hunter, R-Calif., and Tommy F. Robinson, D-Ark., was approved by a 237-177 vote. It required the Department of Defense to use existing funds to "deploy equipment and personnel of the armed forces sufficient to halt the unlawful penetration of U.S. borders by aircraft and vessels carrying narcotics." For the first time, the military would be given authority to pursue suspected drug smugglers into U.S. territory and make arrests. *(Vote 337, p. 96-H)*

The exclusionary rule amendment, offered by Dan Lungren, R-Calif., and adopted 259-153, created an exception to the rule. It permitted evidence gathered in an illegal search to be offered in court "if the search or seizure was undertaken in a reasonable, good-faith belief that it was in conformity with the Fourth Amendment to the Constitution," which prohibited unreasonable search and seizure. *(Vote 343, p. 98-H)*

The day's most heated debate came on an amendment offered by Pennsylvania Republican Gekas that allowed the death penalty to be imposed on drug traffickers involved in a "continuing criminal enterprise" who knowingly caused the death of an individual.

Opponents said that the death penalty was inappropriate in a consensus bill, and pointed repeatedly to a statement by Reagan that "the drug issue is too important" to let it become "embroiled in a side issue such as the death penalty."

"This is one of the most tragic days of my life when in our hatred of drugs, we trample the Constitution," said Parren J. Mitchell, D-Md. Nevertheless, the amendment was adopted on a 296-112 vote. *(Vote 344, p. 98-H)*

Other Amendments

Other major amendments adopted:

- Allowed the military to assist drug enforcement officials in searches, seizures and arrests outside the United States, by 359-52. It was further amended by the Hunter-Robinson amendment. *(Vote 338, p. 96-H)*
- Established a sentence of life imprisonment without parole for a second conviction of an individual over age 21 for selling drugs to a child or teenager or selling drugs at or near a school; by 355-54. *(Vote 340, p. 96-H)*
- Increased new funds for the Drug Enforcement Administration from $60 million to $114 million and earmarked the additional money for cooperative narcotics interdiction efforts in the Bahamas.
- Increased by $1.055 billion the authorization for grants for state and local law enforcement, to reduce the state and local matching requirement from 50 percent to 10 percent, and to permit the funds to be used for non-federal prison construction; by 242-171. *(Vote 341, p. 96-H)*
- Increased the authorization of funds for drug abuse treatment from $180 million to $280 million, by voice.

The House rejected a number of amendments, including one to mandate transfer of aliens arrested for illegal entry or violation of other federal laws from state and local jails to federal prisons.

On Sept. 25, the House voted to fund the drug initiatives through a 0.34 percent across-the-board cut from discretionary funding in the fiscal 1987 continuing appropriations resolution (H J Res 738 — PL 99-591). *(Continuing resolution, p. 219)*

Reagan Plan

On Sept. 15, President Reagan sent to Congress the "Drug-Free America Act of 1986," the administration's legislative proposals to deal with the drug problem.

The night before, in a televised address from their living quarters in the White House, the president and his wife, Nancy, called on the nation to "mobilize for a national crusade against drugs."

His legislative proposal called for $889 million for drug enforcement, interdiction, research, prevention and education for fiscal 1987.

The most controversial proposal in the White House package was funding to carry out an executive order, issued Sept. 15, requiring drug testing of selected civilian federal employees. (Military personnel already were routinely tested for drugs.)

The order required the heads of each executive agency to establish a testing program for employees in "sensitive positions." Decisions on who was to be tested were to be based on the agency's mission, the employees' duties and the potential consequences of employee drug use to public health and safety or to national security.

The order provided that persons found to be using illegal drugs could obtain treatment or counseling, but if they refused to enter into a treatment program, or tested positive after completing a treatment program, they could be fired.

On Sept. 16, the day after the executive order was signed, the National Treasury Employees Union filed suit in federal court to block its implementation, charging that testing without probable cause to suspect illegal activity violated the Fourth Amendment to the Constitution prohibiting unreasonable searches and seizures.

The suit also charged that the program violated the Civil Service Reform Act of 1978 (PL 95-454), which courts had interpreted to prohibit disciplinary actions against federal employees unless the actions in question affected their job performance.

A federal district judge in New Orleans ruled Nov. 12 that a drug testing program run by the Customs Service was unconstitutional. The issue was expected to go to the Supreme Court, delaying actual implementation of the federal testing program.

Senate Proposals

The Senate Democratic Caucus announced its own $1.65 billion anti-drug package at a Sept. 9 press conference led by Minority Leader Robert C. Byrd, D-W.Va.

Billed as a complement to the House bill, it established a Cabinet-level "drug czar" to coordinate federal drug control policy, increased penalties for drug-related offenses, and authorized funds for stepped-up drug enforcement, interdiction at the border, eradication in drug-source nations, education, and treatment and rehabilitation.

Senate Republicans joined the anti-drug campaign 10 days later when Majority Leader Robert Dole, R-Kan., unveiled a GOP drug package that incorporated many of Reagan's proposals. Dole met with Senate Democrats later that day to seek a bipartisan compromise.

The Senate Republican package consisted of three major parts. The first part included several of the proposals contained in the administration package, with some alterations.

The second part contained seven drug-related measures previously approved by the Senate. Some of these, such as a bill prohibiting manufacture and sale of "designer drugs," and another intended to curb "money laundering," were covered in the House omnibus bill.

The final part of the GOP proposal contained new initiatives, including a tax refund checkoff to help pay for the anti-drug campaign. Dole estimated the voluntary checkoff could raise $500 million in 1987.

The Senate package, like the House bill, authorized the death penalty for certain federal crimes and would have relaxed the exclusionary rule.

The package did not contain a House provision that ordered the president to use the military to halt the flow of illegal drugs coming over the border and authorized armed forces personnel to make arrests. It did, however, permit the military to track and chase suspected drug smugglers — with arrests to be made by civilian authorities.

Dole said his bill called for about $1.3 billion in new spending for fiscal 1987. However, unlike the House measure, which authorized more than $2 billion in new funding for fiscal 1987 according to a Congressional Budget Office (CBO) estimate, both Reagan's proposal and the Senate package were "revenue neutral."

All new money devoted to the anti-drug effort was to be offset by reductions elsewhere, including proposed cuts in student aid, the National Institutes of Health and health care for the needy.

Senate Floor Action

The Senate Sept. 26 adopted an amendment to the House-passed measure substituting the provisions of S 2878, introduced a day earlier by Dole and Byrd.

The measure authorized about $1.5 billion for drug interdiction, eradication, prevention, education and treatment efforts. It also authorized grants to state and local governments to aid in drug law enforcement.

The Dole-Byrd bill did not contain several controversial provisions of earlier versions introduced Sept. 23 by Senate Republicans (S 2850) and Sept. 9 by Senate Democrats (S 2798).

Omitted, for example, was a Democratic proposal to create a Cabinet-level "drug czar" to oversee and coordinate federal enforcement efforts. The Reagan administration had long opposed that idea.

Also dropped were provisions from the Republican bill that would have authorized the death penalty for several federal crimes, including murder committed in the course of a continuing drug enterprise, and that would have weakened the exclusionary rule.

The consensus measure also dropped from the GOP bill provisions, included at President Reagan's request, to make clear that the government could implement a mandatory drug-testing program for federal workers in "sensitive" positions.

The compromise Senate bill contained GOP provisions increasing the military's involvement in the drug war. The measure, however, did not contain House language authorizing military personnel to make arrests.

The bill's price tag for fiscal 1987 was expected to fall between the $1.3 billion of the Republican version and the $1.6 billion cost of the Democratic measure.

The Senate consensus bill included a controversial plan offered by Dole to allow federal taxpayers to check off a box on their tax form to forgo a portion of any refund owed and earmark it instead for anti-drug efforts. Taxpayers not receiving refunds could use the checkoff to make contributions to anti-drug efforts.

Extra Cargo

As one of the last legislative vehicles considered fairly certain to reach the White House during the year, the bill picked up a good deal of unrelated cargo during a 10-hour amending session that began Sept. 27 and ended after 2 a.m. the next day. All told, the Senate adopted 43 amendments, about one-fourth of which were only loosely related, if at all, to the anti-drug bill.

The Senate refused to table an amendment by Mack

Mattingly, R-Ga., containing the House death penalty language. The provision would have authorized capital punishment for anyone who, during the course of a "continuing criminal enterprise ... knowingly causes the death of any other individual."

However, after the 25-60 vote, Mattingly withdrew the amendment to avoid a filibuster by a group of moderate Republicans led by Charles McC. Mathias Jr., Md. Mattingly said, "The Senate has sent a very strong signal" to its own conferees that they "should accept the House provision on the death penalty." *(Vote 300, p. 50-S)*

Another problem was how to finance the "war on drugs" authorized by HR 5484.

Lowell P. Weicker Jr., R-Conn., vowed to bar passage of the bill until he was assured that funding for it would not be taken from other programs, especially those within his jurisdiction as chairman of the Appropriations subcommittee handling health and welfare programs.

After prolonged negotiations, the Senate by voice vote Sept. 30 adopted a non-binding amendment stating that funding for the bill would not come from other programs. (On Oct. 3, the Senate added $1.5 billion in budget authority to the continuing resolution to fund the bill, in effect adding $642 million to the deficit for the year.)

Funding was not the only contentious issue in the Senate debate. Members debated at length the role that the armed forces should play in combating drug smuggling.

Sam Nunn, Ga., ranking Democrat on the Senate Armed Services Committee, described the House-passed amendment calling for sufficient military involvement to halt the influx of drugs over U.S. borders as "the equivalent of passing a law saying the president shall, by Thanksgiving, devise a cure for the common cold."

Alan J. Dixon, D-Ill., also a member of Armed Services, offered a modified version of the House-passed amendment. Like that measure, Dixon's amendment would have permitted military personnel to pursue aircraft and vessels into U.S. territory, force them to land, and arrest their crews. But instead of ordering the president to seal the borders against drug smugglers within 45 days, the amendment required only that border penetration be halted "to the extent possible."

After extended debate, the amendment was tabled and thus killed, 72-14. *(Vote 299, p. 50-S)*

By a vote of 83-4, the Senate did adopt an amendment offered by Dennis DeConcini, D-Ariz., to require that the secretary of defense, within 90 days, complete an inventory of military equipment, intelligence and personnel that could be made available to civilian drug agencies for interdiction efforts and develop a plan for making such assistance available. The amendment would require House and Senate Armed Services and Appropriations committees to approve or disapprove the plans. *(Vote 297, p. 50-S)*

Among the amendments adopted by the Senate, all by voice vote, were the following proposals:

- To prevent drug traffickers and other criminals from obtaining information about ongoing government probes by invoking the Freedom of Information Act (FOIA, PL 89-487).
- To permit up to 500 Forest Service personnel to carry firearms, and to authorize them to eradicate marijuana and make arrests within the National Forest System.
- To authorize $9 million for the purchase of secure voice radios (to prevent eavesdropping) for the FBI and Secret Service, and to earmark $7 million for secure radios for the Drug Enforcement Administration.
- To authorize reimbursement of state and local drug enforcement agencies for investigative expenses if they provided to the Internal Revenue Service information that led to IRS recovery of federal tax dollars. Reimbursement could not exceed 10 percent of the tax money recovered.
- To increase by $50 million the authorization for drug treatment programs.
- To set a mandatory minimum sentence of one year in prison for anyone convicted of selling drugs to children, using children to distribute drugs, or manufacturing or distributing drugs near schools.

The bill passed Sept. 30 by a vote of 97-2. *(Vote 302, p. 50-S)*

House-Senate Negotiations

By an overwhelming 391-23 vote, House members Oct. 8 approved a substitute to the Senate version of the omnibus bill, even though few if any of them had seen the language they were voting on. *(Vote 404, p. 114-H)*

The substitute increased authorization levels from the Senate-passed version, stripped several unrelated riders from the bill and reinstated a controversial House-passed provision authorizing the death penalty for certain drug-related crimes.

House Democratic leaders flirted with the idea of accepting the Senate version of the bill, which did not contain the death penalty language, minus some unrelated provisions added in the Senate. But they quickly acknowledged that House Republicans had more than enough votes to thwart any such attempt, which would have wasted precious time in the waning days of the 99th Congress.

House liberals who opposed the death penalty admitted they were relieved that the leaders who drafted the amendment to the Senate bill did not include a host of other controversial amendments passed by the House, including one to weaken the exclusionary rule and another mandating the use of the military to stop drug smugglers at U.S. borders.

During the hour-long debate Oct. 8, no House members complained about not having seen the bill on which they were being asked to vote. The House amendment, introduced separately as HR 5664, was brought up under a procedure whereby approval of the rule (H Res 576) for floor consideration was deemed approval of the House amendment to the Senate version of the bill.

In addition to adding the death penalty language, the House substitute also increased authorization levels in the bill for drug interdiction, eradication, enforcement, education, prevention and rehabilitation efforts. The Senate bill authorized a total of $1.4 billion in new funds to fight the nation's drug war; the House amendment increased that total to just over $1.7 billion in new budget authority.

The House stripped from the Senate version a number of unrelated amendments, including one to deny to nations that imported sugar from Cuba the right to sell sugar in the United States, and another to ban so-called "dial-a-porn" operations.

However, in fashioning the amendment, House leaders left untouched several other Senate-attached riders — including provisions toughening federal standards for the sale of infant formula, extending federal welfare benefits to the homeless, banning ballistic knives, creating federal licensing standards for bus and truck drivers, and updating federal privacy laws in light of new communications technologies.

Senate Response

The addition of the death penalty language all but ensured that the bill would face a filibuster in the Senate, where even before the House acted, 11 moderate Republicans and 14 Democrats sent letters to their respective leaders warning that inclusion of such a provision would "make it extremely difficult, if not impossible, to complete action" on the bill.

Late Oct. 10, Senate Majority Leader Dole offered several amendments to the drug bill, most of which restored earlier Senate provisions that had been deleted by the House. Noting the threat of "extended debate" over the death penalty, he also filed a cloture petition to cut off the impending filibuster.

The Senate death penalty impasse was broken after the motion to invoke cloture (and thus limit debate) — on the Senate amendment to the House amendment to the Senate version of the original House bill — failed Oct. 15, 58-38. Three-fifths of the Senate (60 votes) were needed to invoke cloture. *(Vote 341, p. 56-S)*

Immediately following the cloture vote, a negotiating session between death penalty advocates and opponents was held in Dole's office to see if a compromise could be struck.

Senate death penalty advocates, led by Orrin G. Hatch, R-Utah, finally agreed to replace the death penalty language in the bill with a mandatory minimum life sentence with no parole for those convicted of drug-related murders. Dole also was forced to drop his provision for a tax-checkoff.

The package was then approved by voice vote and sent back to the House.

Death Penalty Sidestep

Since the House never officially appointed conferees, a formal conference could not be convened. However, nine senators and about two dozen House members finally met informally Oct. 16 to try to resolve the differences between the two chambers. The death penalty provision threatened to bring down the entire bill.

House death penalty proponents, led by Gekas, vowed not to permit a bill to leave that chamber without the death penalty. But on the Senate side, some 25 Democrats and moderate Republicans, led by Mathias and Carl Levin, D-Mich., threatened to filibuster a bill containing such a provision.

Finally, it was agreed that the Senate provision replacing the death penalty with a mandatory life sentence should be dropped, after House members complained it would make life sentences more difficult to obtain.

Members also agreed to an unprecedented House rule under which a single House vote for approval would send to the Senate two measures: the compromise bill without the death penalty language and a resolution (H Con Res 415) mandating that the death penalty be added to the bill.

The Senate thus had the choice of taking up one or both measures. To avoid a filibuster, Majority Leader Dole opted to ignore the resolution.

Although the compromise left the cleared bill without a death penalty, House supporters said they were satisfied. Those on the other side of the issue were satisfied as well.

"Everybody shrugged and said it was a lousy way to do it, but it's the only way we're going to get a drug bill," said Rep. Don Edwards, D-Calif., a leading death penalty opponent.

Meanwhile, House and Senate conferees on the continuing resolution Oct. 15 dropped the across-the-board spending reduction passed in the House to fund the legislation and agreed instead to a new $1.7 billion appropriation.

Provisions

As signed into law, HR 5484:

Increased Penalties

- Stiffened penalties under the Controlled Substances Act (PL 91-513) for the manufacture, distribution or possession with intent to manufacture or distribute controlled substances.
- Established fines of up to $4 million for an individual and $10 million for an organization, and a minimum mandatory sentence of at least 10 years in prison, for those convicted of major drug trafficking offenses. Set a mandatory minimum prison term of 20 years if death or serious bodily injury resulted. These were offenses involving at least 5 kilograms of cocaine or 1 kilogram of heroin, among other substances.
- For second convictions of major offenses, established fines of up to $8 million for an individual and $20 million for an organization, and mandatory minimum sentences of 20 years, with mandatory life imprisonment if death or bodily injury resulted.
- Established fines of up to $2 million for individuals and $5 million for organizations, and mandatory minimum sentences of five years, for those convicted of certain serious drug offenses, with maximum prison terms rising to 40 years. These were offenses involving 100 grams of heroin, 500 grams of cocaine, or 5 grams of cocaine freebase, known as "crack," among other substances.
- For second convictions of serious offenses, established fines of up to $4 million for individuals and $10 million for organizations, and mandatory minimum sentences of 10 years rising to life imprisonment, in cases in which death or serious bodily injury resulted.
- Increased penalties for most other violations of the Controlled Substances Act, and set a mandatory minimum sentence of 20 years in prison for offenses resulting in death or serious injury.
- Prohibited probation or suspension of sentence for anyone given a mandatory minimum prison sentence for narcotics offenses.
- Authorized courts, upon motion of the prosecution, to impose less than a minimum mandatory sentence if a defendant provided "substantial assistance" in the investigation or prosecution of another person for a narcotics offense.
- Similarly stiffened penalties under the Controlled Substance Import and Export Act (PL 91-513), which barred the unlawful importing of controlled substances into the United States, or possession of such substances on the high seas with intent to import them unlawfully.
- Set minimum mandatory fines for simple unlawful possession of a controlled substance at $1,000 for a first offense and $2,500 for a second offense; and set a minimum fine of $5,000 and a minimum sentence of at least 90 days in prison for all offenses after the second.
- Subjected owners or operators of so-called "crack houses" or other dwellings used for the unlawful manufacture, storage, distribution or use of illegal drugs to penalties of up to 20 years in prison and fines of up to $500,000.
- Prohibited the use of minors in drug dealing and set a minimum sentence of one year in prison for anyone aged 18

or older convicted of using a minor under age 18 in the commission of a drug offense. Such persons could be sentenced to twice the maximum prison term or fine normally imposed for the offense in question, with penalties to be tripled for a second conviction of using a minor to carry out a drug offense.

- Provided for sentences of up to five years and fines of up to $50,000 for anyone convicted of selling drugs to a minor or using a minor aged 14 or less in commission of a drug offense.
- Prohibited probation or suspension of sentence for anyone convicted of using minors in drug trafficking or of selling drugs to minors.
- Prohibited the manufacture, as well as distribution, of controlled substances within 1,000 feet of a school, and extended the ban to colleges as well as elementary and secondary schools.
- Authorized courts to confiscate substitute assets of comparable value if a defendant had placed illegally obtained assets out of the court's reach.
- Provided that "controlled substance analogues" — drugs that are not chemically identical to controlled substances but produce similar reactions — be treated as controlled substances for purposes of law enforcement. These substances were better known as "designer drugs."
- Increased from $100,000 to $2 million the fine for an individual convicted of a first offense of engaging in "a continuing criminal enterprise," and increased from $200,000 to $4 million the fine for a second or subsequent offense.
- Required mandatory life sentences for "principal administrators, organizers or leaders" of continuing criminal enterprises, defined as those receiving $10 million in gross receipts during a 12-month period.
- Added serious drug offenses to those triggering mandatory minimum sentences under the "armed career criminal" provisions of the 1984 omnibus anti-crime law (PL 98-473). *(1984 Almanac p. 221)*
- Prohibited the interstate sale, transportation, import, export or use of the U.S. Postal Service for drug paraphernalia, and provided penalties for violators of up to three years in prison and up to $100,000 in fines.
- Defined drug paraphernalia to include water pipes, bongs, roach clips, spoons with level capacities of one-tenth cubic centimeter or less and cocaine freebase kits.

Money Laundering

- Prohibited completed or attempted financial transactions involving the proceeds of unlawful activity if the intent was to promote such activity, conceal the source of the funds or to evade reporting requirements, and set penalties up to $500,000 or twice the amount of the transaction involved and prison sentences up to 20 years for violations.
- Made it a crime, subject to the same penalties above, to transport or attempt to transport funds or a monetary instrument knowingly obtained through the commission of a crime or intended for use in a crime.
- Made it a crime to structure financial transactions in order to evade federal reporting requirements for cash transactions and authorized civil penalties up to the amount of the transaction.
- Authorized civil penalties for money laundering offenses of $10,000 or the value of property or funds involved in the transaction.
- Authorized seizure and forfeiture of cash or other property derived from criminal activity.
- Increased the authority of the secretary of the Treasury to investigate cases of suspected money laundering.
- Exempted from liability under all federal laws a financial institution or its employees who disclose information on money laundering transactions to law enforcement officials.
- Increased record-keeping requirements for financial institutions and authorized the imposition of civil fines for failure to comply with such requirements.
- Ordered federal bank regulatory agencies to prescribe regulations requiring insured banks to establish and maintain procedures for monitoring compliance with the money laundering law and reporting requirements.
- Ordered the Treasury secretary, in consultation with the Board of Governors of the Federal Reserve System, to propose to central banks of other countries an information exchange system to combat the international flow of money from drug enterprises.

Funds for Drug Enforcement

- Authorized an additional $60 million for fiscal 1987 for the Drug Enforcement Administration (DEA).
- Authorized an additional $124.5 million for the federal prison system for fiscal 1987 — $96.5 million for new prison construction and $28 million for salaries and expenses.
- Authorized an additional $18 million for federal public defenders for fiscal 1987.
- Authorized an additional $7.5 million in fiscal 1987 for fees and expenses for federal jurors and commissioners.
- Authorized $5 million for the Justice Department's Office of Justice Assistance for a pilot program on prison capacity.
- Authorized an additional $31 million for U.S. attorneys in fiscal 1987.
- Authorized $17 million for fiscal 1987 for the U.S. Marshals Service.
- Authorized $5 million for fiscal 1987 to support the cost of federal prisoners incarcerated in non-federal prisons.
- Authorized $5 million for the U.S. Secret Service and $2 million for the FBI for the purchase of "secure" voice radios to prevent eavesdropping.
- Authorized $230 million per year for each of fiscal 1987, 1988 and 1989 for grants to states for state and local drug enforcement efforts.
- Required states to match federal grants on a 25-75 basis.
- Provided that 80 percent of the funds be distributed to states applying for grants on the basis of population (with each participating state guaranteed at least $500,000), and the remaining 20 percent be distributed at the discretion of the director of the Bureau of Justice Assistance. States need not match funds received from the discretionary fund.

Illegal Aliens, New Studies, Reward

- Required the Department of Defense to conduct a study of the feasibility of converting surplus federal buildings for use as prisons.
- Required law enforcement officials to notify the Immigration and Naturalization Service (INS) when they arrested on drug charges any individual suspected of being in the United States illegally.
- Directed the establishment of a pilot program to establish or improve the computer capabilities of the local INS offices and of local law enforcement agencies to respond to inquiries concerning aliens who had been arrested or con-

victed or were under investigation on drug-related charges.

- Required the attorney general to conduct a study of the need for legislation or regulation to prevent the diversion of legitimate chemicals for use in the manufacture of illegal drugs.
- Established a White House Conference for a Drug Free America, whose purpose was to review and develop recommendations concerning the effectiveness of drug law enforcement at all levels of government, the impact of drug abuse on the nation's educational system (including the relationship between drug abuse by student athletes and college athletic policies), and the impact of current laws on efforts to control international and domestic trafficking of illicit drugs.
- Required the conference to prepare and transmit to the president within six months a final report containing findings and recommendations, and authorized $2 million for fiscal 1988 for the conference.
- Authorized the attorney general to make payments of up to $100,000 to any individual who provided original information leading to the arrest and conviction of a person who killed or kidnapped a federal drug law enforcement agent.

Freedom of Information Act

- Provided limited exemptions from the Freedom of Information Act (PL 89-487) for certain records that "could reasonably be expected to interfere with enforcement proceedings, would deprive a person of a right to a fair trial or impartial adjudication, could reasonably be expected to disclose the identity of a confidential source, or could reasonably be expected to endanger the life or physical safety of any individual."
- Provided for fee waivers or fee reductions when disclosure of the information at issue "is in the public interest because it is likely to contribute significantly to public understanding of the operations or activities of the government and is not primarily in the commercial interest of the requester."

Driving Under Influence

- Imposed penalties of up to five years in prison and up to $10,000 in fines for anyone who operated or directed the operation of a common carrier — including a rail carrier, bus, ship or airplane — while under the influence of alcohol or drugs.
- Provided that a person should be conclusively presumed to be under the influence of alcohol with a blood alcohol level of 0.10 and under the influence of drugs if the quantity of the drug in the individual's system "would be sufficient to impair the perception, mental processes or motor functions of the average individual."

International Assistance

- Authorized an additional $62.9 million for fiscal 1987 for international narcotics control assistance.
- Specified that $45 million of that amount be made available only after the president presented a detailed plan as to how he would promote regional cooperation on narcotics control matters; that not less than $10 million be available to provide helicopters or other aircraft to Latin American countries already receiving U.S. narcotics control aid for fiscal 1987.
- Stipulated that title to any aircraft made available to a foreign country for drug control, eradication or interdiction be retained by the U.S. government, and required the secretary of state to maintain detailed records of the use of aircraft made available to other countries.
- Earmarked $2 million in foreign assistance funds for education and training in the operation and maintenance of aircraft used in narcotics control interdiction and eradication efforts.
- Required the withholding from major illicit drug-producing or drug-transit countries of half the U.S. assistance funds otherwise allocated unless the president certified that the country had cooperated with the United States or had taken adequate steps of its own to stop the production or transport of illegal drugs. The president could also allocate all of the funds if he certified that the "vital national interests" of the United States required such assistance. Congress could disapprove such presidential certification by passage of a joint resolution within 30 days of the certification's receipt.
- Required the president to deny preferential tariff treatment to major drug-producing or drug-transit nations unless the president certified to Congress that the country had cooperated fully with the United States or had taken adequate steps on its own to disrupt drug production or traffic.
- Prohibited the president from allocating quotas for the sale of sugar in the United States to any country whose government was involved in the trade of illicit narcotics or had failed to cooperate with the United States in narcotics enforcement.
- Beginning March 1, 1987, directed the secretary of the Treasury to instruct the U.S. executive directors of the multilateral development banks to vote against any loans to major illicit-drug-producing or drug-transit nations.
- Required the secretary of state to use at least $1 million in foreign aid funds for fiscal 1987 to finance research, development, and testing of safe and effective herbicides for use in the aerial eradication of coca, from which cocaine was derived.
- Required the comptroller general to report to Congress by March 1, 1988, the results of an investigation to determine the effectiveness of foreign assistance relating to international narcotics control.
- Amended the so-called Mansfield amendment, which prohibited U.S. law enforcement agents from being present at narcotics arrests outside the United States, to permit them to be present when arrests were being made if they were assisting foreign officers. Also permitted U.S. officers to take "direct action to protect life or safety" if circumstances posed "an immediate threat to U.S. officers or employees, officers or employees of a foreign government, or members of the public."
- Provided that U.S. officers could not be present during interrogation of U.S. citizens arrested on narcotics charges in a foreign country without that person's written consent.
- Required the president to establish expeditiously a comprehensive information system so that known foreign drug traffickers could be denied visas to enter the United States. Establishment of such a system had been required under the fiscal 1986-87 State Department authorization act (PL 99-93). *(1985 Almanac p. 104)*
- Applauded Bolivia's 1986 cooperative drug interdiction effort with the United States and authorized half the foreign assistance appropriated for Bolivia to be allocated as soon as the president certified to Congress that Bolivia had met certain targets with respect to disrupting its illicit coca industry. The remainder was to be allocated upon certification by the president that Bolivia had either met

its 1986 eradication targets or had entered into a new agreement with the United States for achieving numerical eradication targets in 1987.

- Directed the president to send Congress, within six months after enactment, a list of major illicit-drug-producing or drug-transit countries that had failed to cooperate in drug interdiction efforts, or in which U.S. drug agents had suffered violence by or with the complicity of local authorities.
- Directed the president to collect information on the links between narcotics traffickers and acts of terrorism abroad, and to develop an effective and coordinated means of responding to the threat those links posed.
- Permitted the secretary of state to use existing funds to assist Colombia or other Latin American countries in protecting judicial or other officials who could be targets of "narco-terrorist" attacks.
- Expressed the sense of Congress that a $500,000 reward should be established for information leading to the arrest or conviction of Jorge Luis Ochoa Vasquez, a Nicaraguan indicted in 1984 in Miami for drug smuggling.
- Directed the secretary of state to increase efforts to negotiate with foreign countries procedures to facilitate U.S. Coast Guard interdiction of vessels of foreign registry suspected of carrying illegal drugs.
- Required the president to take "appropriate actions" against countries that refused to negotiate such procedures, including denying access to U.S. ports of vessels registered in those nations.
- Directed the president to study narcotics trafficking in Africa and to determine whether to provide increased narcotics control training for African nations.
- Directed the secretary of state to instruct the U.S. executive directors of the multilateral development banks to propose increases in the amount of lending for drug eradication programs in major illicit-drug-producing countries, and for crop substitution programs that provided economic alternatives for the cultivation or production of drugs.
- Declared drugs a national security problem and directed the president to explore the possibility of engaging the North Atlantic Treaty Organization (NATO) and other security-oriented organizations in cooperative anti-drug programs.
- Declared congressional support for United Nations efforts related to narcotics control and called on the president to ensure U.S. participation in a planned 1987 U.N. conference on drug abuse and illicit trafficking.
- Urged the president to direct the secretary of state to enter into negotiations to establish a Mexico-United States Intergovernmental Commission on Narcotics and Psychotropic Drug Abuse and Control.
- Expressed the sense of Congress that unless Mexico made "substantial progress" toward the resolution of numerous drug-related issues discussed during an August 1986 meeting between President Reagan and Mexican President Miguel de la Madrid, Reagan should consider taking actions against that nation, including imposing a mandatory travel advisory for all of Mexico, denying favorable tariff treatment for Mexican products, and denying Mexico favorable U.S. votes in multilateral development banks.
- Required that $1 million in foreign aid funds for Mexico be withheld until its government prosecuted those responsible for the 1985 murders of DEA agent Enrique Camarena Salazar and his pilot, Alfredo Zavala Avelar. Before those funds could be released, Mexico also had to bring to trial and effectively prosecute those responsible for the 1986 detention and torture of DEA agent Victor Cortez Jr.

Interdiction Activities

- Authorized $138 million in fiscal 1987 for the Navy to refurbish for drug interdiction purposes four E-2C Hawkeye surveillance aircraft or better-suited craft that the secretary of the Navy designated, and to purchase four replacement aircraft; $99.5 million for the purchase of radar aerostat surveillance balloons; and $40 million for the purchase of eight Blackhawk helicopters.
- Directed that two of the refurbished aircraft be loaned to the U.S. Customs Service and the other two to the U.S. Coast Guard, the two agencies with primary drug interdiction jurisdiction; and that the balloons and helicopters be available for loan to agencies as determined by the National Drug Enforcement Policy Board.
- Authorized transfer of $15 million appropriated for the Navy in fiscal 1987 to pay for the placement of Coast Guard personnel trained in law enforcement on naval vessels to assist with drug interdiction.
- Increased the Coast Guard's active duty military strength by 500 and mandated that the extra personnel be assigned to naval vessels.
- Authorized $45 million for the Department of Defense in fiscal 1987 for the installation of 360-degree radar systems on Coast Guard long-range surveillance aircraft.
- In addition to any other amounts, authorized for the Coast Guard an additional $128 million for fiscal 1987, $39 million of which was to be used to increase the Coast Guard's active duty strength for fiscal 1987 to 39,220.
- Expanded provisions allowing Defense Department personnel to assist in the operation or maintenance of equipment being used by U.S. drug enforcement agents by allowing such equipment to be used as a base of operations outside the United States in emergency situations and to be used to transport law enforcement officials in connection with such operations.
- Permitted such equipment to be used to intercept vessels and aircraft outside U.S. territory, and in U.S. territory in cases involving a pursuit that began outside the borders, but only if the secretary of defense, the secretary of state, and the attorney general jointly determined that an emergency circumstance existed and that law enforcement would be "seriously impaired" if such use of equipment were not permitted.
- Defined an emergency to exist when the size or scope of the suspected criminal activity posed "a serious threat to the interest of the United States" and the military assistance in question "would significantly enhance the enforcement" of the law in question.
- Required that the secretary of defense, within 90 days of enactment, complete an inventory of military equipment, intelligence and personnel that could be made available to civilian drug agencies for interdiction efforts and develop a plan for making such assistance available.

Upon receipt of the inventory and plan, the House and Senate Armed Services committees would have 30 days to approve or disapprove them.

- Authorized the Department of Defense to use $7 million of any fiscal 1987 unobligated and uncommitted appropriations to acquire equipment for use by the Civil Air Patrol for drug interdiction surveillance and reporting missions.

• Established a United States-Bahamas drug interdiction task force and authorized $15 million for its implementation — $9 million for three pursuit helicopters, $1 million to enhance communications capabilities for task force operations, and $5 million for planning construction of a drug interdiction docking facility in the Bahamas.

Anti-Smuggling Provisions

• Required the master of any vessel arriving from a foreign port, any foreign vessel, or any vessel carrying foreign merchandise, upon arrival in the United States, to report the vessel's arrival to U.S. Customs Service officials within 24 hours.

• Stipulated that vehicles could arrive in the United States only at designated crossing points.

• Authorized civil penalties of up to $10,000 for failure to comply with arrival reporting requirements and provided criminal penalties, including up to one year in prison, for anyone in charge of a vessel, vehicle, or aircraft found to have carried illegal drugs into the United States.

• Increased penalties for departure before report of entry and for unauthorized unloading of passengers.

• Required individuals arriving in the United States on foot to enter only at designated border crossing points and to report immediately to customs, and increased civil and imposed criminal penalties for violations.

• Provided that individuals caught trying to smuggle controlled substances be subject to a penalty of twice the price for which that substance was likely to be illegally sold to a consumer; and directed the attorney general to establish a method for determining that value.

• Increased penalties for falsifying cargo manifests and for unlawful unloading of cargo.

• Made smuggling by air a separate offense, as well as the unauthorized transfer of prohibited merchandise from an aircraft to a ship, and imposed civil and criminal penalties of up to $250,000 and 20 years in prison for violations involving illegal drugs.

• Authorized the forfeiture and sale of any vessel, vehicle, or aircraft whose owner, operator, or other person in charge was subject to a penalty for violation of customs law.

• Exempted from that provision common carriers unless the person in charge participated in, had knowledge of, or was "grossly negligent" in preventing or discovering the violation.

• Authorized the payment of rewards for persons who provided original information leading to the recovery of customs fines, penalties or the forfeiture of property. Awards could amount to 25 percent of the funds recovered or 25 percent of the appraised value of forfeited property, but could not in any case exceed $250,000.

• Authorized the exchange of information between U.S. customs officers and foreign customs and law enforcement agencies in certain situations.

• Authorized stationing of U.S. customs officers in foreign countries to examine persons and merchandise prior to arrival in the United States. Also authorized agreements permitting foreign customs officials to be stationed in the United States, but only if the country allowed U.S. customs officials to be stationed there.

• Authorized the Customs Service to buy property, establish businesses and take other steps needed to carry out undercover investigations.

• Extended the Customs Service forfeiture fund through fiscal 1991 and increased the ceiling on authorized appropriations from the fund from $10 million to $20 million.

• Authorized U.S. customs officers to demand the assistance of any person in making an arrest, search or seizure.

Made refusal to render such assistance a misdemeanor, subject to a fine of up to $1,000, and provided that no one be held liable for civil damages as a result of rendering such assistance.

• Created a separate crime of knowingly or intentionally manufacturing or distributing, or possessing with intent to manufacture or distribute, controlled substances on board a vessel of the United States or one subject to U.S. jurisdiction. Violators were subject to the same penalties as if they were in U.S. territory.

• Allowed states to impose criminal penalties, including forfeiture or seizure of an aircraft, for the use or attempted use of forged or altered aircraft registrations.

• Authorized state and local law enforcement officials to inspect aircraft registrations.

• Made it a federal offense, in conjunction with a drug offense, to operate an unregistered aircraft or to serve as an airman without a valid airman's certificate or knowingly to employ such a person; to operate an aircraft without use of required navigation or anti-collision lights, or knowingly to operate an aircraft whose fuel tank or system has been unlawfully modified.

• Provided that violators be subject to forfeiture of the aircraft as well as penalties of up to $25,000 in fines or up to five years in jail.

• Authorized for the Department of Justice an additional $7 million for fiscal 1987 for the purchase of special radar-equipped helicopters for drug interdiction operations in Hawaii.

• Authorized the Federal Communications Commission (FCC) to revoke the private operator's license of any person found willfully to have used that license to distribute or assist in the distribution of illegal drugs.

• Validated the standards set forth by the Interstate Commerce Commission (ICC) with respect to the consideration of applications by rail carriers to purchase trucking companies. The purchase of North American Van Lines by Norfolk Southern Corp., which was approved by the ICC but rejected by the courts, would be allowed.

Also, the ICC would be permitted to base a decision on the application of Union Pacific Corp. to buy Overnite Transportation Co. on the same standards that it used in the Norfolk Southern case.

Treatment and Rehabilitation

• Authorized $241 million for fiscal 1987 for alcohol abuse and drug abuse treatment and rehabilitation programs.

• Stipulated that 4.5 percent of that amount be made available to transfer to the administrator of veterans' affairs to be used for outpatient treatment, rehabilitation and counseling of veterans for alcohol or drug abuse dependence or disabilities.

• Also stipulated that 1 percent of the funds be used by the administrator of the Alcohol, Drug Abuse, and Mental Health Administration (ADAMHA) to develop and evaluate alcohol and drug abuse treatment programs to determine the most effective forms of treatment.

• Stipulated that the remaining funds be allotted to the states, with 45 percent to be distributed on the basis of population (although no state could receive less than $50,000) and 55 percent to be distributed on the basis of need.

• Established within ADAMHA an Office of Substance Abuse Prevention (ASAP) to sponsor regional workshops on drug and alcohol abuse prevention, coordinate federal research findings on the prevention of substance abuse, develop effective substance abuse prevention literature and public service announcements, and establish a national clearinghouse for alcohol and drug abuse information.

• Authorized $20 million of the $241 million total for ASAP administrative expenses for fiscal 1987.

• Directed ASAP to make grants to public and private non-profit organizations for projects to demonstrate effective models for prevention, treatment and rehabilitation of drug and alcohol abuse among high-risk youth.

ADAMHA Research

• Authorized $69 million for research activities for fiscal 1987 for the National Institute of Alcohol Abuse and Alcoholism (NIAAA) and $129 million for research activities of the National Institute of Drug Abuse (NIDA).

• Authorized the secretary of health and human services (HHS) to expedite research on "public health emergencies," which were to be determined by the secretary in conjunction with the commissioner of food and drugs or the director of the Centers for Disease Control (CDC).

• Ordered the director of the National Institute of Mental Health (NIMH) to develop and publish information regarding the causes of suicide and means to prevent it, with special emphasis on suicides among individuals under age 21.

• Ordered a study on alkyl nitrites (over-the-counter substances better known as "poppers") to determine the extent and nature of their use, the extent to which that use conformed to the advertised uses of the products, and the extent to which their abuse presented a health risk.

• Ordered a study on the effect that health warning labels on alcoholic beverage containers would have in reducing health problems associated with alcohol.

• Expressed the sense of Congress that the Motion Picture Association of America should develop a new rating to identify films that depict alcohol abuse and drug use.

• Extended to ADAMHA research animal care provisions mandated for the National Institutes of Health in 1985 (PL 99-158). *(1985 Almanac p. 287)*

• Ordered a study by the National Academy of Sciences of alternative approaches and mechanisms for the provision of alcoholism and alcohol abuse treatment and rehabilitative services.

Infant Formula

• Amended the Infant Formula Act of 1980 (PL 96-359) to require that each batch of infant formula be tested for each essential nutrient before distribution and to ensure purity. *(1980 Almanac p. 418)*

• Required infant formula manufacturers periodically to test samples throughout the formula's shelf life.

• Required manufacturers to retain production records for one year after the formula's expiration date, and to keep a file of complaints concerning the product.

• Gave the Food and Drug Administration increased authority to order recall of defective formula, including authority to order the posting of recall notices at points of sale.

Drug-Free Schools

• Authorized $200 million for fiscal 1987 and $250 million for each of fiscal 1988 and 1989 for grants for drug abuse education and prevention programs.

• Set aside 1 percent of the total for grants to U.S. territories; 0.2 percent for Hawaiian natives; 8 percent for higher education institutions; 3.5 percent for federal activities and 4.5 percent for regional centers.

• Allocated the remaining funds to the states, with grants to be allotted on the basis of each state's school-age population, except that no state would receive less than 0.5 percent of the funds.

• Provided that 70 percent of the funds allotted to each state be used by the state educational agency to make grants to local and intermediate education agencies for the development and implementation of drug abuse education programs.

• Provided that 30 percent of the funds be available to the governor of each state for discretionary grants to local public and private non-profit organizations to develop and implement community-based drug and alcohol abuse prevention programs. At least half of those grants had to be for programs to help youths at high risk to become drug or alcohol abusers.

• Authorized the secretary of education to make competitive grants to colleges and universities to provide teacher training in drug and alcohol abuse education and prevention; training programs for law enforcement officials, judicial officials, community leaders and government officials; and to develop, implement, operate and improve drug abuse prevention programs for college and university students.

• Directed the secretary of education to provide information on drug abuse education and prevention to the HHS secretary for dissemination by a clearinghouse for alcohol and drug abuse information.

Also directed the education secretary to develop, publicize and widely disseminate audio-visual and other drug abuse education materials; provide technical assistance to state, local and intermediate education agencies; and identify research and development priorities with regard to school-based drug abuse education and prevention.

• Stipulated that any materials produced or distributed with funds under this section should "reflect the message that illicit drug use is wrong and harmful."

• Established a National Trust for Drug Free Youth to encourage private gifts to assist in carrying out drug-abuse prevention educational programs.

• Established a Presidential Media Commission on Alcohol and Drug Abuse Prevention to examine existing programs and assist the implementation of new programs and national strategies for the dissemination via the media of information intended to prevent alcohol and drug abuse.

Indians and Substance Abuse

• Directed the secretary of the interior and the secretary of HHS to determine and define the scope of substance abuse problems among Indian tribes, and to identify the resources and programs of the Bureau of Indian Affairs (BIA) and the Indian Health Service.

• Authorized the governing body of an Indian tribe to establish a resolution detailing a Tribal Action Plan to coordinate available resources and programs in an effort to combat alcohol and substance abuse among its members.

• Authorized $1 million for each of fiscal 1987, 1988 and 1989 for the secretary of the interior to make grants to Indian tribes to provide technical assistance in the development of Tribal Action Plans.

• Established within the BIA an Office of Alcohol and

Substance Abuse, which would be responsible for monitoring the performance and compliance of BIA regarding drug and alcohol abuse programs and would serve as a point of contact within BIA for Indian tribes interested in such programs.

- Established within the Office of Alcohol and Substance Abuse an Indian youth programs officer to advise the director of the office.
- Directed the secretaries of HHS and interior to make available for community use federal facilities, property and equipment.
- Directed the secretary of the interior, in cooperation with the HHS and education secretaries, to publish a quarterly newsletter reporting on Indian alcohol and substance abuse projects and programs. The newsletter was to be distributed free of charge to schools, tribal offices, BIA agency and area offices, Indian Health Service area and service unit offices, and Indian Health Service alcohol programs.
- Authorized such sums as necessary for fiscal 1987, 1988 and 1989 for the establishment of a pilot program in selected schools to determine the effectiveness of summer youth programs in curbing Indian alcohol and substance abuse.
- Authorized $8 million annually for fiscal 1987 through 1989 for grants to tribes whose Tribal Action Plans provided for emergency shelters or halfway houses for Indian youths who were alcohol or substance abusers, including youths who had been arrested for offenses directly or indirectly related to alcohol or substance abuse.
- Directed the interior secretary to ensure that all BIA and tribal law enforcement and judicial personnel had training in the investigation and prosecution of offenses relating to illegal narcotics and in alcohol and substance abuse prevention and treatment. Authorized $1.5 million for each of fiscal 1987 through 1989 to provide such training.
- Authorized $15 million for each of fiscal 1987 through 1989 for the construction or renovation and staffing of tribal juvenile detention and rehabilitation centers for Indian tribes.
- Directed the Indian Health Service to provide a program of comprehensive alcohol and substance abuse prevention and treatment, including acute detoxification and treatment, and community-based rehabilitation.
- Authorized $9 million for each of fiscal 1987 through 1989 for the construction or renovation and staffing of Indian youth regional treatment centers, and an additional $3 million per year for each of fiscal 1987 through 1989 for the renovation of existing federal buildings to house such treatment centers.
- Authorized $9 million for each of fiscal 1987 through 1989 to provide community-based rehabilitation services.
- Authorized $300,000 for each of fiscal 1987 through 1989 for a demonstration program in Gallup, N.M., to rehabilitate adult Navaho Indians suffering from alcoholism or alcohol abuse.

Federal Lands, Employees, Organization

- For drug interdiction in U.S. territories, authorized for fiscal 1987: $7.8 million for Puerto Rico; $4 million for the U.S. Virgin Islands; $700,000 for American Samoa; $1 million for Guam; and $250,000 for the Northern Mariana Islands.
- Authorized law enforcement officers of American Samoa and the Northern Mariana Islands, with approval of the attorney general, to serve warrants and subpoenas, make arrests and seize property as needed to enforce federal anti-drug laws.
- Authorized $1 million for fiscal 1987 for the employment and training of additional U.S. Park Police to improve federal law enforcement activities relating to the use of illegal drugs in the National Park System.
- Directed the Office of Personnel Management (OPM) to develop appropriate drug and alcohol abuse prevention, treatment and rehabilitation programs for federal employees, and directed the heads of all executive branch agencies to establish such programs pursuant to OPM's guidelines.
- Directed OPM to report to Congress within six months of enactment, and annually thereafter, descriptions of all agency programs, levels of participation, training and qualifications of personnel involved, and recommendations for legislation if warranted.
- Directed OPM to establish governmentwide programs to inform federal workers about health hazards associated with alcohol and drug abuse; symptoms of such abuse; availability of prevention, treatment and rehabilitation programs; confidentiality protections afforded in connection with such programs; penalties for substance abuse provided under law, rule or regulation; and about possible administrative actions against those who failed to seek or receive appropriate treatment or rehabilitation services.
- Ordered an Institute of Medicine study of the extent to which the cost of drug abuse treatment was covered by private insurance, public programs and other sources of payment, and the adequacy of such coverage for the rehabilitation of drug abusers.
- Required the president, within six months of enactment, to submit to Congress recommendations for legislation to reorganize the executive branch to combat more effectively international drug traffic and drug abuse.

National Forest System

- Authorized $10 million for fiscal 1987 for the secretary of agriculture to designate and train up to 500 U.S. Forest Service officers and employees to carry out anti-drug efforts within the National Forest System.
- Authorized the designated personnel to carry firearms, to conduct investigations of drug law violations relating to substances manufactured, distributed or dispensed on National Forest System lands, to make arrests with or without a warrant for misdemeanors, to serve warrants, and to make searches and seizures.
- Created a new offense of placing a booby trap on federal property where a controlled substance was being manufactured, distributed or dispensed, with penalties of up to 10 years in jail and $10,000 for a first offense, and up to 20 years and $20,000 for a second or greater offense.
- Defined "booby trap" as any concealed or camouflaged device designed to cause bodily injury when triggered by an unsuspecting person making contact with the device.

Ballistic Knife Prohibition

- Prohibited the manufacture, sale, importation and mailing of ballistic knives, which had spring-loaded, detachable blades that could be shot like a gun.
- Provided penalties of up to 10 years in prison for the use of a ballistic knife in the commission of a violent crime.

Eligibility of Homeless for Welfare

- Extended eligibility for food stamps to homeless individuals with no fixed address if they would otherwise meet eligibility requirements.

• Authorized homeless individuals who qualified for food stamps to use them to purchase prepared meals at soup kitchens or homeless shelters. (Previously, food stamps could be used only to purchase groceries.)

• Ordered the HHS secretary to devise a method of making Supplemental Security Income (SSI) payments to homeless individuals. SSI was the federal welfare program for the needy aged, blind and disabled.

• Designated the homeless as a target group for employment training under the Job Training Partnership Act (PL 97-300). *(1982 Almanac p. 39)*

• Extended Medicaid health coverage to otherwise eligible homeless individuals and ordered the HHS secretary to devise a method of providing eligibility cards to homeless beneficiaries.

• Ordered the HHS secretary to issue guidelines to the states for providing benefits to homeless children under the Aid to Families with Dependent Children (AFDC) program.

• Ordered the HHS secretary, with the secretary of agriculture, to develop a system allowing individuals to apply for SSI benefits and food stamps prior to discharge or release from a public institution such as a mental hospital or prison.

• Specified that a homeless individual could not be denied veterans' benefits because of the lack of a fixed address.

Wrongful Cyanide Use

• Ordered a study by the administrator of the Environmental Protection Agency (EPA) of the manufacturing and distribution process of cyanide to determine ways to safeguard the public from cyanide's wrongful use. The study was to examine the feasibility and desirability of a number of options, including requiring cyanide to be dyed a distinctive color and requiring increased record-keeping for those who manufactured and sold the chemical.

• Authorized such sums as necessary to carry out the study.

Miscellaneous

• Authorized $6 million for each of fiscal 1987 and 1988 for the director of the ACTION domestic volunteer agency to use to mobilize and initiate private-sector efforts to increase volunteer activity aimed at preventing drug abuse.

• Authorized $3 million for fiscal 1987-88 combined for the secretary of labor to collect information concerning the incidence of drug abuse in the work place.

Funding Intent

• Expressed the sense of the Senate that funds to carry out the new drug initiatives should be provided as new budget authority for fiscal 1987 and not through transfers from or reductions in amounts appropriated for other programs.

Truck, Bus Driver Licensing

• Required the transportation secretary to issue regulations by July 15, 1988, establishing minimum standards for state testing and licensing of operators of commercial vehicles. Regulations had to include a requirement for a driving test on the type of vehicle that the person operated or would operate. Also, the state license had to specify the type of vehicle the operator was eligible to drive.

For drivers of vehicles carrying hazardous materials, regulations had to ensure that the operator had a working knowledge of the handling of such material and the appropriate response in an emergency.

Licensing standards had to apply to trucks weighing more than 26,000 pounds and to vehicles, such as buses, designed to carry more than 15 passengers. They could apply to commercial vehicles of more than 10,000 pounds at the discretion of the transportation secretary.

• Banned a driver of a commercial motor vehicle from having more than one license, subject to certain limited exceptions, effective July 1, 1987.

• Required a commercial driver who violated a traffic law in a state other than the one in which his or her license was issued to notify the license-issuing state of the violation within 30 days. The driver also had to notify his or her employer of a traffic violation and of a severe restriction on his license imposed by a state, such as a suspension.

• Prohibited employers from knowingly allowing an employee to drive a big truck or bus if the employee had more than one license or had had his license suspended or otherwise seriously restricted by a state.

• Required the transportation secretary to establish an information system to serve as a clearinghouse to enable states and employers to share data on safety violations by commercial drivers, or to contract with states or private entities for the use of an existing system. At a minimum, the system had to include data on whether an operator had had his license suspended or otherwise restricted by a state. Federal funds of $2 million annually through fiscal 1989 were authorized for the Department of Transportation (DOT) operation of this program.

• Required the secretary to set fees to be charged for use of the system.

• Required, as a general rule, license suspension for one year for any commercial driver who committed a first violation of driving under the influence of alcohol or a controlled substance; leaving the scene of an accident; or using his vehicle in the commission of a felony. If the felony was committed with a vehicle carrying hazardous materials, the suspension had to be for at least three years. If the felony involved controlled substances, then suspension had to be for life.

• Required, as a general rule, lifetime license suspension for commercial drivers who committed a second offense of driving under the influence of alcohol or drugs; leaving the scene of an accident; or using their vehicles in the commission of a felony.

The transportation secretary could establish guidelines under which a lifetime suspension for any of these second offenses could be reduced to a period of not less than 10 years.

• Set mandatory federal penalties against commercial drivers who committed serious traffic violations, such as excessive speeding, as defined by the transportation secretary by regulation. A driver who committed two serious violations within a three-year period had to have his license suspended for at least 60 days. Suspension would rise to at least 120 days for a driver who committed three serious violations within a three-year period.

• Set new sanctions against drivers who violated a current federal regulation prohibiting them from drinking within four hours of reporting to work. The drivers would be placed out of service immediately for a 24-hour period.

• Set civil penalties of fines up to $2,500 against drivers for violations such as carrying more than one license and failing to notify employers or the license-issuing state of safety violations.

• Set criminal penalties of up to $5,000 or 90 days in jail, or both, for "knowingly and willfully" violating such requirements as notifying employers and the state of safety violations.

• Required a study within one year by the National Academy of Sciences on the appropriateness of shifting the standard for determining drunken driving from 0.10 percent blood-alcohol content to 0.04 percent blood-alcohol content.

No later than one year after enactment, the transportation secretary had to begin preparing a rule to determine whether the standard should be reduced from 0.10 percent to 0.04 percent, or to some percentage less than 0.10 percent.

No later than two years after enactment, the secretary had to issue a rule setting the standard at 0.10 percent or a lesser percentage. The standard was to become 0.04 percent if no rule was issued during this period.

• Set sanctions against states that failed to comply with the licensing standards and other requirements imposed by the legislation. States not "substantially" in compliance by Oct. 1, 1993, would lose 5 percent of their federal highway aid otherwise due; highway aid would be reduced by 10 percent for subsequent years of non-compliance.

• Authorized grants to states to set up drivers' testing programs and the information-sharing system, among other purposes. Grants would total $10 million in fiscal 1987, $10 million in 1988, $15 million in 1989 and $13 million in fiscal 1990 and 1991.

To be eligible in fiscal years 1987-89, a state had to have in effect a standard of 0.10 blood-alcohol content or less for determining drunkenness. To be eligible after fiscal 1989, a state also had to operate a drivers' testing and licensing program that conformed to minimal federal standards.

• Authorized separate grants to states for safety inspections of commercial vehicles of $45 million in fiscal 1987 and fiscal 1988; and $47 million in fiscal years 1989-91.

• Allowed the transportation secretary to waive any provisions of the legislation or any regulation issued under the legislation with respect to a particular class of drivers or class of vehicles. However, the secretary had to determine that the waiver was not contrary to the public interest and would not diminish the safe operation of commercial vehicles.

The transportation secretary could decide, for example, that drivers who had demonstrated safe driving records over the years on big trucks or buses did not have to take a road test.

• Mandated a change in federal regulations to require trucks and truck tractors manufactured after July 24, 1980, to have brakes operating on all wheels. ∎

ENVIRONMENT/ENERGY

CQ

Environment/Energy

Congress in 1986 accomplished as much significant environmental legislation as it had in any year since the "environmental decade" of the 1970s.

Lawmakers broke new ground in overhauling several major environmental laws — a job long overdue — but at the same time, they failed to find agreement on several other issues.

With energy legislation it was a different story. Although a yearlong slide in oil prices caused drastic changes in the nation's energy economy, Congress did little to address the situation and stuck largely to fine-tuning existing energy laws.

Perhaps the major legislative accomplishment of the year in the energy and environment field was renewal of the "superfund" hazardous-waste cleanup law. The House and Senate actually passed superfund bills in 1985, but it took most of 1986 to settle the differences in a bitterly contested conference.

The superfund bill was only one of several that started new environmental protection programs or dramatically strengthened or enlarged existing ones. Not only was the size of the superfund program expanded from $2.4 billion in its first five years to $8.5 billion in its second five years, but the "right to know" about potentially harmful activities was granted to communities around industrial plants making or using hazardous chemicals.

Two catastrophes loomed over Congress as it legislated on energy and the environment in 1986: the December 1984 chemical accident at Bhopal, India, and the April 1986 nuclear accident at Chernobyl in the Soviet Union — both of which caused thousands of casualties. Environmental concerns that had been dismissed as unrealistic doomsaying took on a new credibility as the public was inundated with media coverage of those events.

The Bhopal incident, in which thousands of unprepared residents near a chemical plant were killed or injured by toxic fumes, helped cause Congress to assert the right of communities to know what dangerous chemicals were being used nearby and to require local and state planning on how to respond to such emergencies.

Such expansion of federal requirements for environmental protection was typical of other legislation enacted — or nearly enacted — during the year. The stricter requirements took on greater significance because they ran opposite to the policies of the Reagan administration.

Reagan came into office in 1981 riding high on a wave of deregulatory fervor, applauded by businesses for his plans to roll back health and environmental rules they considered burdensome. By 1983, however, he was facing a steady drumbeat of criticism from some in Congress who thought he had gone too far. It was charges that the Environmental Protection Agency (EPA) was dragging its feet in carrying out the 1980 superfund law that eventually led to the ouster of EPA Administrator Anne M. Burford in 1983.

During the early years of the Reagan administration, she had testified that EPA was not sure the superfund program needed to be reauthorized. Congress answered in 1986, after several years of struggle, by not only reauthorizing but vastly expanding it. Reagan signed the bill reluctantly Oct. 17 after Republican members warned a veto would be a liability in the November election.

Congress followed a similar pattern in reauthorizing the Safe Drinking Water Act of 1974. More than a decade after enactment of the law, which required EPA to set limits on the impurities allowed in public drinking water, the agency had yet to regulate most of the hundreds of toxic chemicals found in household tap water. The new bill set a timetable for regulating 83 chemicals within three years — almost four times the number regulated since 1974.

Equally important was the omnibus water projects bill passed by the 99th Congress and signed by the president. It had been a decade or more since Congress passed a large bill authorizing new construction of the locks, dams and harbors so important to some local economies. The delay had largely been caused by disagreement over whether to raise the share of costs paid by local project users and beneficiaries in light of growing deficits in the federal budget. That issue was finally settled with a substantial increase in the local share and other reforms sought by environmentalists.

Legislation that was stopped just short of completion in 1986 was possibly as significant as that finally enacted.

The Clean Water Act reauthorization, for example, set the nation's underlying water pollution control policy for the next decade. It was settled — as far as Congress was concerned — in 1986, although a pocket veto kept it from becoming law until early in 1987. The bill, passed unanimously in both chambers, confirmed congressional backing for the basic federal program to regulate wastewater going into lakes and streams. It also pledged another $18 billion in federal aid to state and local governments for sewage plant construction over the decade.

Another major legislative accomplishment — short of final enactment — was a breakthrough agreement between environmentalists and chemical companies on pesticide control legislation. The agreement broke years of stalemate and yielded legislation dramatically strengthening health protections. Both chambers passed bills based on that agreement, amending and reauthorizing the Federal Insecticide, Fungicide and Rodenticide Act (FIFRA). Most provisions were identical in both House and Senate versions, but disagreements over a comparatively small number of controversial items could not be settled before Congress adjourned.

Energy

The drop in oil prices that occurred during 1986 was as dramatic as the rises that took place during the "energy crisis" of the 1970s. Typical crude oil prices dropped from around $27 a barrel in late 1985 to under $10 a barrel in the summer of 1986, before easing back up to about $18 by the end of the year. Oil companies, fearing they could not make profits with prices so low, simply stopped drilling for new oil. While part of the industry, dependent on drilling for its livelihood, went bankrupt, the refining companies enjoyed an increase in margins as crude costs dropped faster than the price of refined products.

The oil industry's pleas for relief went to a large extent unheeded by Congress in 1986. Member after member from the Sun Belt introduced relief bills as the November elections neared, but they went nowhere. Northeastern members, whose constituents suffer when oil prices go up, were facing election, too. Typical proposals included an oil import fee and a repeal of the Windfall Profits Tax that came with oil price deregulation of the 1970s. The oil industry did preserve cherished tax breaks like the "percentage depletion allowance" — despite the broad effort to sweep away similar breaks for other industries in the tax reform bill. Oil companies still condemned the tax bill, saying that overall it would increase their taxes.

The year 1986 also stood as a crossroads for nuclear energy in the United States. The Soviet nuclear accident at Chernobyl deepened the already serious questions about the industry's future. More than a dozen died in that accident, and thousands more were expected to die in future years from cancer and other diseases caused by fallout blown across much of Europe.

Even before the accident, House and Senate committees had begun work on renewing the Price-Anderson Act, which functioned as the nation's insurance policy against nuclear accidents. All sides agreed the coverage should be raised from the $650 million per-accident level set three decades earlier; the issue was how much. The law limited what nuclear electric utilities must pay in case of an accident — with public damage above that level left uncovered and potentially uncompensated.

Work on the bill stopped after the Chernobyl accident.

Although environmental and consumer groups wanted to go ahead, nuclear industry and utility groups saw no rush to proceed, hoping that public concern would die down as Chernobyl became last year's news.

— by Joe Davis

Reagan Signs 'Superfund' Waste-Cleanup Bill

President Reagan signed the "superfund" hazardous-waste cleanup bill (HR 2005 — PL 99-499) Oct. 17, ending more than a week of congressional pleas for a signature and White House threats of a veto.

The legislation reauthorized for five years, through fiscal 1991, the government's program to clean up the nation's most dangerous abandoned chemical dumps. Congress cleared HR 2005 Oct. 8, when the House adopted the conference report (H Rept 99-962) on the bill by a 386-27 vote. The Senate had adopted the conference report Oct. 3, 88-8. Both chambers originally passed the bill in 1985. *(House vote 408, p. 116-H; Senate vote 329, p. 54-S)*

As cleared, the measure provided for a fivefold increase, to $8.5 billion, in the amount available for the program and represented a broad expansion of the original superfund law. The measure set strict standards for cleaning up sites and required the Environmental Protection Agency (EPA) to begin work at 375 sites within five years. It stressed the use of permanent cleanup methods, calling for detoxifying wastes whenever possible, rather than burying them in landfills.

The bill also added new requirements that industry provide local communities with information on what chemicals they handled and dumped, and it gave victims of toxic dumping a longer opportunity to sue those responsible.

Attached to the bill was an additional $500 million program to clean up gasoline storage tanks that corroded and were leaking into groundwater.

Reagan had threatened to veto the measure because of its cost and the additional taxes it imposed. The administration objected to funding the $8.5 billion cleanup measure with a new, broad-based tax on business that would raise $2.5 billion over fiscal 1987-91. It also objected to the way the bill's $2.75 billion tax on crude oil was written. The bill taxed imported oil at a higher rate than domestically produced oil — which Treasury officials said amounted to an oil import fee, something the administration opposed.

The president signed the bill on Air Force One en route to North Dakota to campaign for Sen. Mark Andrews, R-N.D. "I signed the superfund legislation to accelerate the cleanup of the nation's hazardous-waste sites," Reagan said.

EPA Administrator Lee M. Thomas had strongly urged the president to sign the measure. Thomas wrote congressional leaders Sept. 22 saying funds for the program had run out, and that he was starting to end contracts and would soon be furloughing workers if Congress adjourned with no bill. "While it will take only a few months to dismantle the program, it will take years and many millions of dollars to rebuild it," he said.

"We now face a situation which threatens the very existence of the superfund program," Thomas wrote. "Now, we have reached the end."

Pressures on Reagan

Senate Majority Leader Robert Dole, R-Kan., said he thought the president had been swayed by a letter signed by more than 40 senators, circulated by Dole himself, promising not to expand the taxes in the bill during future years.

Equally persuasive, however, may have been an earlier letter to Dole from 57 senators, urging him to keep the Senate in session in case a veto override was necessary. In still another letter, 81 senators had urged the president to sign.

Meanwhile, House Speaker Thomas P. O'Neill Jr., D-Mass., and Majority Leader Jim Wright, D-Texas, had promised that they would keep the House in session long enough to override a veto or prevent a "pocket veto." If Congress is not in session 10 days after a president receives a bill and the president has still not signed it, it fails to become law. This is known as a pocket veto.

More than 120 members had urged O'Neill and Minority Leader Robert H. Michel, R-Ill., to keep the House in session.

The president had until midnight Oct. 21 to act on the bill, according to the House parliamentarian's office. If he had not signed the bill by then, and Congress were in session, it would have become law.

Background

The Senate passed a $7.5 billion, five-year superfund reauthorization Sept. 26, 1985. The House passed its own $10 billion version Dec. 10. But the chambers differed sharply on how to finance expansion of the superfund program, which was created in 1980 (PL 96-510) and funded at $1.6 billion for its first five years. *(1985 action, 1985 Almanac p. 191; PL 96-510, 1980 Almanac p. 584))*

The Reagan administration said both the Senate and House bills were too expensive. It requested five-year funding of $5.3 billion. Reagan also threatened to veto a new broad-based business tax in the Senate bill.

Senate-House conferees held their first meeting Feb. 26, 1986. The conference then broke up into two subgroups — one on the cleanup program itself and one on tax measures for funding it.

Conferees were under pressure to reach a speedy compromise. Taxing authority for the superfund expired Sept. 30, 1985, and EPA Administrator Thomas said he would have to start shutting down the program if Congress did not enact new funding authority by April 1.

At a March 20 meeting, the conferees acknowledged they could not meet the April 1 deadline. That evening, a two-month extension bill was whisked through the House and the next morning, March 21, the Senate accepted it. Both chambers passed it by voice vote.

The bill (H J Res 573 — PL 99-270) made available $150 million, with the proviso that none of it could be spent after May 31. That was designed to keep the pressure on superfund conferees, and Senate Assistant Majority Leader Alan K. Simpson, R-Wyo., vowed to get a bill out of conference by the new deadline "if we have to pull some teeth . . . or some other things" to do it.

The stopgap resolution did not actually appropriate new money. Rather, it unlocked funds Congress had appropriated as part of EPA's regular fiscal 1986 appropriation. That bill (PL 99-160) had prohibited EPA from spending superfund money until Congress passed legislation reauthorizing the program and taxes to pay for it. The stopgap resolution was fashioned as an advance from the general Treasury, to be repaid from taxes that Congress had yet to enact. *(PL 99-160, 1985 Almanac p. 317)*

Congress Aug. 15 cleared a second stopgap extension

bill (H J Res 713 — PL 99-411) providing a further $48 million advance to keep the program going through September.

Conference Agreement

The conference report on HR 2005 was not filed until Oct. 3 (H Rept 99-962).

The bitterly divisive conference had been moving at a snail's pace since February. At times, differences among Democratic House conferees were greater than differences between the two chambers. Dissident House conferees, who felt too many concessions were being made to the Senate, threatened to challenge the final agreement on the floor.

A major milestone was reached July 31 when conferees agreed on all issues except how to pay for the program. Conferees from both parties and both chambers lined up behind the proposal, calling it an improvement over existing law. Lobby groups expressed reservations about the final compromise, but most said they could live with it.

House Ways and Means and Senate Finance Committee members, working as a separate conference group, had delayed a decision on financing provisions until other conferees could settle conflicts on how the program would operate. But the tax group now faced pressure to act soon or see the dismantling of the program.

"We need money by the first of September," said EPA Administrator Thomas, noting that cleanup contractors were beginning to lay off employees. "I just need some money."

The tax-writing was complicated by Reagan administration objections to the size of the program and the two main proposals for funding it. A letter from Treasury Secretary James A. Baker III to the bill's managers said he would recommend a presidential veto of a bill funding a program larger than $5.3 billion, if it were funded by a hike in the tax on oil and chemicals, as proposed by the House, or a new broad-based business tax, as favored by the Senate.

Conferees announced agreement on a tax package Oct. 2. They settled the dispute over whether all businesses or just petrochemical companies would bear the burden by taxing both.

Standards and Schedules

The five-year reauthorization represented a broad expansion of the original 1980 law. The bill approved by the conference committee set strict standards for cleaning up sites and required EPA to begin work at 375 sites within five years. It stressed the use of permanent cleanup methods, calling for detoxifying wastes whenever possible, rather than burying them in landfills.

The measure added new requirements that industry provide local communities with information on what toxic chemicals companies routinely emitted into the environment and what chemicals they produced, stored or handled. Another expansion on existing law was a $500 million program to clean up gasoline storage tanks that had corroded and were leaking into groundwater.

The compromise bill retained the existing standard of "strict, joint and several liability" under which a single non-negligent dumper could be held responsible for all cleanup costs at a site; he must then go after other dumpers to recover costs. The House bill kept that liability standard, but the Senate bill weakened it.

Conferees voted to give victims of toxic dumping a longer opportunity to sue those responsible. Under the conference agreement, statutes of limitations set by state governments would begin to run only after a victim discovered his illness might have been caused by hazardous substances, rather than starting at the time he was exposed to the substances.

Under both bills and the conference report, citizens could sue EPA or private parties for violation of the superfund law. But the conferees followed the Senate bill and left out a House-passed provision allowing citizens to sue private parties to stop imminent threats to health or the environment.

Since Congress began working on superfund reauthorization in 1984, the issue of how much leeway to allow EPA had been central to the debate. As a reaction to the agency's slow performance from 1980 to 1983 — a factor behind the firing of superfund program administrator Rita M. Lavelle — House members wanted to hold EPA to a stringent timetable. The Senate bill had no timetables. *(Lavelle, 1983 Almanac p. 333)*

While the compromise bill required EPA to start a minimum number of cleanups over the next five years, it set no deadlines for EPA to finish work.

Conferees agreed to sever controversial House oil spill provisions from HR 2005. The House-passed measure would have limited liability and set up a $300 million fund to compensate victims of oil spills. The Senate bill had no such provision. Conferees dropped the House provisions with the understanding that oil pollution legislation would be considered separately. *(Oil Spill Liability, p. 146)*

Tax Provisions

Tax conferees chose to pay for the $8.5 billion program as follows: $2.75 billion from a tax on petroleum, $1.4 billion from a tax on chemical feedstocks, $2.5 billion from a broad-based tax, $1.25 billion from general revenues, and $0.6 billion from interest and cost recovery from companies responsible for toxic dumps.

The bill contained no tax on hazardous-waste disposal. Such a "waste-end" tax had been sought by the House and resisted by the Senate at the urging of oil-state senators.

The broad-based tax would be imposed on the income base defined in the tax reform bill (HR 3838) for collection of the "alternative minimum tax" — a mechanism to make sure corporations did not escape taxes entirely through loopholes. Corporations would have to pay $12 for each $10,000 of taxable income above $2 million. They would not be taxed if their income was under $2 million. *(Tax bill, p. 491)*

The broad-based tax drew fire from the Grocery Manufacturers Association (GMA), which had led a coalition of some 500 corporations and trade associations that opposed such a tax. "Only the polluters should pay for their cleanup," said GMA spokesman Jeffrey Nedelman. He said the broad tax "taxes all companies equally whether they pollute or not, whether they create large volumes of waste or no waste at all."

The key new feature of the oil tax, the one that seemed to cause agreement to click into place, was that it taxed imported oil at a higher rate (11.7 cents per barrel) than domestically produced oil (8.2 cents per barrel). Of the revenue produced by the plan, $1.25 billion would come from domestic oil and $1.5 billion from imported oil.

That "differential," as its sponsors called it, looked suspiciously like an oil import fee to its opponents at the Treasury Department.

"The proposal is such that the secretary of the Treasury will be unable to recommend that the president sign the measure," said a spokesman Oct. 2.

But the higher rate for imported oil was just what made the tax look good to domestic oil producers, the independent "wildcat" drillers who found much of the country's oil and were one of the most politically important segments of the industry.

At least that was how it looked to Sen. Lloyd Bentsen, D-Texas, a key tax conferee who had publicly declared his readiness to stop the superfund bill on the floor if it hurt his state's oil industry, already suffering from the collapse in oil prices. He had originally opposed any increase in the tax on oil.

"What I've been able to do is get it down to where it's not a burden on the domestic producer," Bentsen said, calling that a "major victory."

He invited reporters from Texas to his office to tell them that the tax could actually help domestic producers. The 11.7 cent tax on a barrel of imported oil, Bentsen and others said, would likely be passed on, producing a corresponding rise in the price of all oil. The 8.2 cents taken from domestic producers by the new tax would be offset by the 11.7 cents given to them as a price increase, according to the theory, and they could keep the difference.

The situation looked different to the big multinational oil companies who got much of their oil from abroad, who had interests in refining and distribution as well as drilling and who were not hurting nearly as badly as domestic producers.

The American Petroleum Institute (API), whose lobbying positions tended to reflect big oil's views, called the superfund tax agreement "totally unjustified and unfair in its treatment of the petroleum industry."

"The petroleum industry's share of such wastes is very small," an API statement said, "yet the new financing proposal would hit it with tax costs as high as all the rest of industry combined."

Final Action

The Senate Oct. 3 adopted the conference report on the bill by an 88-8 vote, with Republicans telling President Reagan he should sign it. *(Vote 329, p. 54-S)*

"I hope that the president and the president's advisers would study this bill carefully and I would hope that it would be signed," Majority Leader Dole said at the end of debate.

Senate Environment Committee Chairman Robert T. Stafford, R-Vt., said that a veto with no chance for Congress to override "would be a disaster for Senate Republicans."

The Senate votes against the conference report came from Sens. David L. Boren, D-Okla.; Phil Gramm, R-Texas; Jesse Helms, R-N.C.; James A. McClure, R-Idaho; Don Nickles, R-Okla.; Steven D. Symms, R-Idaho; Malcolm Wallop, R-Wyo.; and Edward Zorinsky, D-Neb.

The House adopted the conference report Oct. 8, 386-27, completing congressional action. *(Vote 408, p. 116-H)*

The superfund issue excited enough interest that more than 50 members rose to speak during the House debate. The opposition was led by Philip M. Crane, R-Ill., who urged members to sign a big card saying that they would "take the pledge of no new taxes."

The debate began with a procedural skirmish on a motion by Butler Derrick, D-S.C., to order the previous question on the rule (H Res 577) for the superfund conference report. The motion had the effect of cutting off any amendment to the rule. Hal Daub, R-Neb., had said that if the motion was defeated, he would offer an amendment allowing the House to take up separately the tax title of the bill and possibly amend it.

While an effort to change the tax title on the floor was unlikely to succeed, it might have opened the door to an effort to split the bill in two — allowing the president to veto the tax title and sign the rest. That scenario was being pushed by the White House and by House Republican leaders.

The vote on Derrick's motion was really a vote on whether to give Reagan a way out — and the House decided not to, 311-104. *(Vote 405, p. 114-H)*

Major Provisions

As signed into law Oct. 17, HR 2005 (PL 99-499):

Definitions

- Specified that responsibility for carrying out most provisions in the bill belonged to the president. (In practice, the president had delegated most of this authority to EPA.)
- Expanded the definition of a "release" of pollutants to include the abandonment of barrels or other containers, regardless of whether they had broken open or leaked.
- Changed the definition of "remedial action" — a long-term cleanup — to include specifically the off-site transport and storage of hazardous substances.
- Changed the definition of "owner or operator" of a hazardous-waste facility so that states and local governments would not be financially penalized if they acquired ownership of such facilities involuntarily and without contributing to the pollution problem. Under existing law, the state or local share of cleanup costs jumped from 10 percent to 50 percent when a state or local government owned or operated the facility.
- Redefined "alternative water supplies" to include household water as well as drinking water. This meant that when wells were closed under superfund because of a health threat, EPA was required to provide water for residents to shower with as well as water to drink.
- Specified that most provisions in the bill took effect on the date of enactment.

Schedules

- Established a timetable for cleanup progress that was a compromise between the "mandatory schedule" in the House bill and the lack of any schedule in the Senate bill.
- Established as a "goal" of the act that, to the extent practical, EPA should have completed preliminary assessment of all the possible hazardous-waste sites of which it had been notified — those in its computerized Comprehensive Environmental Response, Compensation, Liability and Information System (CERCLIS). By Jan. 1, 1988, EPA should have decided whether it needed to inspect each site on the list at the time of enactment. By Jan. 1, 1989, EPA should have actually inspected all those sites it decided it needed to inspect.
- Within four years of enactment, each facility on the CERCLIS list should, as a goal, have been evaluated, if EPA felt an evaluation was needed on the basis of the preliminary assessment and site inspection.
- If EPA failed to achieve the above goals, it was re-

quired to publish an explanation of why it could not do so.

- Set a schedule for EPA to begin studies ("remedial investigations and feasibility studies," or RI/FS) of how to clean up a site on the National Priorities List (the list of the worst sites). Beyond those studies already started at enactment, EPA must have started another 275 within 36 months after enactment. If it failed to meet that schedule, then it must have begun studies on an additional 175 sites within four years after enactment and an additional 200 by five years after enactment — for a total of 650 sites within five years of enactment. The bill did not specify when studies were to be finished.
- Set a schedule for EPA to begin physically new remedial cleanup actions: 175 sites during the first three years after enactment and another 200 sites during the next two years. The bill set no schedule for completing work.

Cleanup Standards

- Required EPA generally, in choosing a cleanup method for remedial action, to choose a method that was cost-effective in both the short term and long term and that protected human health.
- Stated that EPA should prefer methods of treatment that permanently reduced the volume, toxicity or mobility of the hazardous wastes, rather than non-permanent methods. The bill stated that off-site transport and disposal of hazardous substances or contaminated materials without such treatment, when it was available, should be EPA's least-favored alternative. If EPA did not follow these preferences, it must explain why.
- Required EPA, in choosing a method, to consider the long-term uncertainties of land disposal; the goals and requirements of the Solid Waste Disposal Act; the persistence, toxicity, mobility and tendency to bioaccumulate of the substances involved; the short-term and long-term threats to human health; long-term maintenance costs; the potential for future cleanup costs if the remedy were to fail; and the potential threat to health and the environment associated with excavation, transportation, redisposal or containment.
- Required EPA, if it chose a method that left any hazardous substances at the site, to review the remedial action at least every five years to ensure protection of health and the environment. EPA was required to report such sites to Congress. EPA was to take further action if it judged any necessary after the prescribed review.
- Set the protection of human health, in all cases, as a minimum standard for EPA in choosing the degree of cleanup or control of further release. The cleanup method must also have been relevant and appropriate under the circumstances at the site.

On-Site Cleanup Standards

- Required, in cases where pollutants were left on-site and where federal or more stringent state standards applied, that the cleanup method met the most stringent requirement.

Such requirements must have been met either when they were legally applicable or when they were relevant and appropriate under the circumstances. Federal environmental laws specifically mentioned were the Toxic Substances Control Act; the Safe Drinking Water Act; the Clean Air Act; the Clean Water Act; the Marine Protection, Research and Sanctuaries Act; and the Solid Waste Disposal Act. The provision also specifically required that cleanups meet the Maximum Contaminant Level Goals under the Safe Drinking Water Act and the water quality criteria under the Clean Water Act, when relevant and appropriate. In determining whether the water quality criteria were relevant and appropriate, EPA must have considered the designated or potential use of the water body or groundwater.

The bill also sharply limited cases under which EPA could base less stringent cleanups on a "point of exposure" beyond the boundaries of the site — i.e., clean up a site less thoroughly because there were few or no people around it.

- Allowed EPA to choose an on-site cleanup method that did not meet the other laws and requirements when it found that the action was part of a larger one that would meet such requirements, compliance would threaten health and the environment more than the alternatives, compliance was "technically impractical from an engineering perspective," the chosen method would achieve the same results, a state had not applied its requirement consistently, or a remedy would be so costly as to drain the fund of money needed to protect public health at other sites.
- Provided that no state, federal or local permit should be required for an on-site cleanup.

Off-Site Cleanup Standards

- Required, in cases where pollutants were transported off-site, that the material must be taken only to a facility operating in compliance with the Solid Waste Disposal Act and other applicable state and federal laws and requirements.
- Allowed off-site disposal only when two conditions were met: The unit of the facility where the hazardous materials were disposed of was not releasing pollutants, and all releases from other units at the same facility were being controlled in accordance with the Solid Waste Disposal Act.

Health Protection

- Required a series of health-related studies and programs to be carried out by the Agency for Toxic Substances and Disease Registry (ATSDR) and EPA.
- Required ATSDR and EPA to prepare a list of the hazardous substances most commonly found at superfund sites. Within six months of enactment, ATSDR must list at least 100 such substances. Within 24 months after enactment, ATSDR must list an additional 100 substances, and in each of the following three years, it must add another 25 substances to the list.

ATSDR must prepare toxicological profiles on all the listed substances. If information on the toxic properties of a substance was inadequate, this must be noted and the two agencies must ensure that research was started to determine the risk.

- Required ATSDR to perform a health assessment for each site or release on the National Priorities List. The assessments must be done by Dec. 10, 1988, for each site proposed for the list as of enactment and within one year after enactment for all sites proposed later.
- If the results of the assessment warranted, ATSDR was then authorized to go ahead with pilot or full-scale epidemiological studies and the establishment of a registry of exposed persons. If the health risk was significant enough, the ATSDR was supposed to start a health surveillance program for the site, to screen various groups for disease and refer them for treatment.
- If the health studies showed a significant risk to health, EPA or the federal government must take the steps necessary to reduce human exposure and eliminate or

"substantially mitigate" the risk. Such steps could include provision of alternative water supplies and permanent or temporary relocation of individuals. If the agencies judged the information on health risk to be inconclusive, they could take what action they judged necessary. It was not necessary for the agencies to wait for the results of any health studies before they acted to abate an imminent hazard.

EPA Procedures

● Authorized EPA to allow cleanup action to be carried out by a dumper or the owner or operator of a hazardous-waste site if EPA determined the party was qualified and would do the work properly and promptly. EPA still had to supervise the work.

● Directed EPA to give primary attention to those releases of hazardous substances that it believed might threaten public health.

● Required that any short-term (or "removal") cleanup action undertaken should, to the extent practical, contribute to an effective long-term ("remedial") cleanup.

● Prohibited EPA from undertaking superfund cleanups for releases of naturally occurring substances in unaltered form, releases from products that were part of the structure of buildings or releases into a drinking water system that resulted from normal deterioration of the system. This would exclude, for example, fraying asbestos insulation in a school building or certain kinds of mine drainage.

● Raised the spending and time limits on short-term removal actions from $1 million and six months to $2 million and 12 months. As under existing law, EPA could spend more than this if needed to deal with health emergencies.

● Strengthened federal authority to gather information about hazardous-waste threats. Authorized federal or state representatives to require that any person disclose information about chemicals at a facility or about a possible release if there was reason to believe a release was threatened. Authorities could enter premises, inspect and copy pertinent documents and obtain samples.

EPA or the courts could compel compliance unless the demand for information was unlawful, abusive, arbitrary or capricious. Federal administrative orders and civil suits were authorized as a means of compelling compliance, and courts could impose civil penalties of up to $25,000 per day of non-compliance. In order to withhold information, for example, on the basis that it constituted a trade secret, companies would have to demonstrate that it met specific criteria. Health and safety information could not be withheld.

● Authorized EPA, at its own discretion, to acquire real property for a limited time if necessary to carry out a cleanup action.

● Required EPA to revise, within 18 months, the National Contingency Plan to change the Hazard Ranking System. (The National Contingency Plan was the chief body of regulations under which the superfund program was carried out. The Hazard Ranking System was a system of criteria for choosing which sites went on the National Priorities List.) The Hazard Ranking System was to be revised to assure that it accurately reflected the relative degree of risk to human health and the environment posed by sites.

State and Local Governments

● Authorized a state to sue EPA in federal court to force it to choose a remedial action that complied with any applicable federal or state requirement under the superfund law.

● Required EPA to issue regulations providing for state involvement in the cleanup process beginning with site assessment and ranging through selection and carrying out the remedial action. EPA must also notify and involve the state in any negotiations with potentially responsible parties over the scope of a cleanup. EPA retained the right to settle with potentially responsible parties without state agreement.

● Allowed states, if a federal court ruled that a stricter cleanup method was not legally required, to pay the extra costs and have the stricter method used.

● Set rules for state participation in selection of cleanup methods at federal facilities. If EPA chose a method that did not meet other legal requirements, a state got 30 days to review the decision, which was carried out if the state agreed or was silent. If the state disagreed, it could take EPA to federal court.

If the state failed in court to show that EPA's decision was not supported by substantial evidence, it could pay the extra costs of the stricter remedy and have it carried out. If the state failed to pay within 60 days, EPA could carry out the remedy.

● Expanded the circumstances under which states or local governments must pay 50 (instead of 10) percent of cleanup costs to include cases where the state or local government operated the waste site through a contractor.

● Directed EPA to grant states a credit against their share of cleanup costs for money they may have spent before EPA put the site on the National Priorities List, the list of sites that would get federal funding aid for long-term cleanup. The credit would be subject to certain conditions. After enactment, EPA would have to approve any such state spending in advance for it to qualify.

● Authorized EPA to reimburse local authorities for expenses in responding to hazardous-substance emergencies. The reimbursement would be limited to $25,000 for each response.

● Delayed for up to 10 years the time when states would have to pay 100 percent of costs for the operation of cleanup measures.

While the federal government shared costs of cleanup measures, states must assume costs of operating them. In cases where groundwater must be pumped and treated for many years, operating costs could be significant.

Public Participation

● Required EPA or the states to allow public participation in selection of a remedial action and in any settlement of an enforcement action at a National Priorities List site.

● Before choosing a remedial action, EPA or the state had to give notice, which included an explanation of its proposed cleanup plan, and provide opportunity for written and oral comments, including a meeting near the site, of which a transcript must be kept. Before remedial action started, EPA must publish a final cleanup plan, together with discussion of how it might differ from the proposed plan and the reasons those changes were made, and responses to each of the significant public comments. At a minimum, the notice must include publication in a general circulation local newspaper.

● Authorized EPA, subject to appropriations and regulations, to make grants to public groups that might be affected by a threatened release at a National Priorities List site. The grants were to help groups obtain technical assistance in interpreting information and decisions related to the site. Generally, the grant amount could not exceed $50,000 and the local group had to pay 20 percent of the costs, although those requirements could be waived.

Federal Facilities

● Established the general principle that all requirements for assessing sites under the superfund law would apply to sites or facilities owned or operated by the federal government, with exceptions related to insurance and timetables. For sites not on the National Priorities List, state laws would also generally apply.

● Required EPA to establish a Federal Agency Hazardous Waste Compliance Docket to contain in a central repository all information submitted to it by various agencies under various laws about federal facilities handling hazardous substances.

● Required EPA, within 18 months of enactment, to assure that a preliminary assessment was conducted for each federal facility on the docket, and where appropriate, conduct further evaluation and place facilities on the National Priorities List.

● Required the agency operating any federal facility placed on the list to start a cleanup study (RI/FS) within six months of its listing. EPA and the states were required to set and publish deadlines for the studies. Facilities already on the list at the time of enactment had to begin studies within a year.

● Required EPA to review the results of agency cleanup studies. The bill required the agency operating the facility to enter into an interagency agreement for remedial action with EPA within 180 days after that review. The remedial action must start within 15 months of the study's completion. Public participation and participation by state and local officials in this process was required.

● Stated that federal agency remedial actions "shall be completed as expeditiously as practicable."

● Authorized the president to issue orders granting exemptions from superfund requirements at a specific site for up to one year, if necessary to protect national security. The president must notify Congress of such exemptions and state reasons for them. Exemptions could be renewed.

● Established an "Environmental Restoration Program" within the Department of Defense, to clean up hazardous pollution, dispose of unexploded shells, and demolish unsafe buildings at military sites. The program was to be carried out in consultation with EPA.

● Required the Defense Department to notify the Department of Health and Human Services and ATSDR of the 25 most common unregulated hazardous substances found at defense facilities, so that the latter agency could develop toxicological profiles of those substances.

● Required the Defense Department to notify EPA promptly of any releases of hazardous substances it discovered and any response actions it proposed.

Underground Storage Tanks

● Authorized EPA to require that owners of underground storage tanks maintain sufficient funds or insurance to cover damages in case of accidental releases from such tanks. The amount would depend on size, type, location, storage and handling capacity of the tank; the likelihood of release and the potential extent of damage; the economic impact of the limits on the owner; and the availability of insurance or other funds. The minimum amount of coverage required by EPA would be no less than $1 million for each accident, except for petroleum facilities not involving production, refining or marketing.

● Authorized EPA to require that the owner or operator of an underground storage tank undertake corrective action with respect to any accidental release, if the owner or operator was able to do the work properly.

● Authorized EPA to take corrective action on its own if it was necessary to protect human health and the environment, if the owner or operator could not be found or could not perform the corrective action or if the situation required a prompt response. These actions might include the temporary or permanent relocation of residents and alternative household water supplies. A separate fund was set up for this purpose.

● The owner or operator would be held liable for the costs of corrective actions up to the established limit of liability.

Penalties

● Provided increased penalties for civil and criminal violations of the superfund law and new authority for EPA to assess civil penalties administratively. Maximum criminal penalties were three years' imprisonment for first offenses and five years for subsequent offenses. EPA could impose civil penalties of up to $25,000 per violation after giving notice and opportunity for a hearing. EPA could impose penalties of up to $25,000 per day after formal hearing under the Administrative Procedures Act. These penalties could be reviewed by federal courts.

Liability

● Empowered EPA explicitly to collect from dumpers its enforcement costs as well as its cleanup costs.

● Protected from liability for cleanup, under specific conditions, landowners who acquired property without knowing of a hazardous-waste pollution problem there. To qualify for protection, the landowner must exercise reasonable due care.

● Overrode state time limits on when a person could sue for injury caused by hazardous substances. The statutes of limitation under state tort laws varied, but typically required a person to sue within several years of the time the injury occurred. With long-latency diseases like cancer, the injury might not be discovered for decades. The bill stated that time periods established in state laws would begin to run at the time when the injured party knew, or had reason to know, that the injury was caused by the hazardous substance, not when the damage occurred.

● Specified that the costs of health studies authorized under the law could be recovered, with interest, from parties found liable for a site.

● Provided that state and local governments were not liable for non-negligent emergency actions to deal with a release of a hazardous substance by another person.

● Required the federal government to issue, within six months of enactment, regulations for assessing damage to natural resources from releases of hazardous substances. The bill set out procedures for determining which state or federal agency was the trustee of such resources. It provided that the trustee, not EPA, get any funds recovered from responsible parties to pay for such damages.

● Provided that the United States should have an automatic lien on the appropriate property of an individual who was liable to the United States for costs and damages under the superfund law.

• Provided that insurance companies were liable for no more than the amount of liability specified in the insurance policies they wrote. (Insurance companies complained that courts had held them responsible for higher amounts.)

• Specified that liability for releases under the superfund law applied to releases from foreign vessels.

Litigation

• Set a time limit of six years from the date a response action was completed for claims against the fund. For natural resource damages, the limit was three years from discovery of loss or issuance of EPA regulations, whichever was later.

• Stated explicitly that any person who was being sued by the federal or state governments for recovery of response or cleanup costs could seek contribution from any other person who was potentially liable. Such contribution claims could be brought during or after the original suit under the Federal Rules of Civil Procedure (standard rules under which federal civil court cases are conducted). The court could allocate costs among liable parties as it deemed equitable.

• Provided that any person whose liability to the federal or state governments for response costs had been resolved through an administrative or judicially approved settlement would not be liable for contribution claims regarding matters addressed in the settlement. Such a settlement reduced the potential liability of the other parties involved by the amount of the settlement. If the government recovered less than its full costs in such a settlement, it could sue any non-settling party for the remainder. A party who had agreed to pay some or all of the response costs in a settlement could sue any non-settling party for a contribution.

• Set a time limit for parties bringing contribution suits of three years from the date of judgment or settlement or from the date of administrative order in *de minimis* (small) settlements.

• Prohibited persons from challenging in court an EPA decision on what cleanup remedy to use, except in a limited set of circumstances, generally after EPA had carried out the decision. The purpose of the provision was to avoid the delay of a cleanup action as a result of suits from potentially responsible parties claiming it was too costly, while protecting responsible parties from extravagant cleanup costs. If the remedy was later found too costly, the responsible parties must still pay the part of the cost that was reasonable. The burden was on the party objecting to a remedy to prove that it was arbitrary, capricious or unlawful.

• Required the government to allow public participation in selection of removal and remedial cleanup measures.

• Prohibited the government or other parties from suing gas station operators for costs or damages resulting from release of recycled oil that was not mixed with other hazardous substances, if they were following the regulations and law for handling such oil.

Settlements

• Authorized EPA explicitly to negotiate settlements with parties potentially responsible for a hazardous-waste site instead of suing them in court to force them to clean up or pay cleanup costs. The bill set procedures designed to encourage settlements rather than long and costly lawsuits, while at the same time protecting the public interest in effective cleanups and cost recovery.

• Authorized use of "mixed funding" in settlements — when companies settling agreed to pay some of the cleanup costs and EPA agreed to pay the remainder from the superfund. The purpose was to encourage settlement when some companies were willing to pay their share and others were not willing or not able.

• Required any agreement reached by EPA to be approved by the attorney general and entered in the appropriate U.S. district court as a consent decree. The proposed judgment must be filed 30 days before a final judgment was entered. During that time, the attorney general must provide opportunity for the public to comment on it. The final agreement could be enforced by the court.

• Authorized EPA, when it decided that a period of negotiation could speed agreement on a cleanup action, to notify potentially responsible parties of the names and addresses of all others involved and the amount of each pollutant contributed by each.

• Established a moratorium on further EPA action toward a cleanup for 120 days after such notice. The moratorium did not prohibit EPA from acting against any significant threat to health or the environment.

• Authorized EPA to prepare a "non-binding preliminary allocation of responsibility" under certain guidelines when EPA believed this would promote agreement. In collecting information for this allocation, EPA could issue court-enforceable subpoenas for witnesses and documents. The allocation did not establish any legal grounds for allocating liability, was not admissible as evidence and could not be reviewed by courts.

• Required EPA to provide its reasons in writing when it rejected a substantial offer from a company following a preliminary allocation. The rejection was not subject to court review. If EPA decided that a company had not made a good faith offer within 60 days of the notice, EPA could go ahead and sue in court for cleanup or costs.

• Authorized EPA and the Justice Department, at their discretion, to release companies from specific further liability as part of a settlement. The release would take the form of a covenant not to sue. The covenant must be in the public interest and must expedite responsive action consistent with the law. The responsive action must be approved by EPA and the company must comply fully with the settlement agreement. The covenant could not take effect until EPA certified that the remedial action was completed.

• Authorized the use of arbitration as a method of settling federal claims under superfund where the total response costs for the facility did not exceed $500,000, excluding interest. The arbitration would be conducted under rules issued by the agency after consultation with the attorney general.

Citizen Suits

• Authorized any citizen to sue in federal court any person who was in violation of the superfund law or requirements under it. This included suits against the U.S. government for failure to carry out its duties under an interagency agreement to clean up a federal facility. It included suits against the president or administrator of EPA for failure to carry out non-discretionary acts or duties under the superfund law. It also included suits against a state or local government, to the extent allowed by the 11th Amendment to the Constitution.

• Provided that the court, in such cases, had power to enforce any requirement under the law or agreement, to order such action as might be necessary to correct the violation and to impose any civil penalty provided for the violation.

- Required the plaintiff, in such cases, to give notice to the federal government, the state and any alleged violator. The plaintiff must wait 60 days after giving such notice before bringing suit. No such action could be brought if the federal government had begun and was diligently prosecuting an action of its own to obtain compliance with the requirement of law.
- Provided some protection from liability for companies performing cleanup or response actions for federal or state governments at hazardous-waste sites under superfund. The bill provided that such contractors were not liable except for their own negligent actions under the superfund law or any other federal law for damages related to release of any pollutant for which it was a contractor. Any liability under state law remained unchanged.

Pollution Insurance

- Authorized companies to form "risk retention groups" or purchasing groups as a way of insuring themselves when they were unable to get commercial pollution liability insurance. The bill exempted such groups of companies, when they met certain conditions, from state laws that prohibited or hindered their operation. Other state insurance laws would still apply.

Emergencies and Right to Know

- Required the governor of each state to appoint a state emergency response commission within six months of enactment. That commission must designate local emergency planning districts within nine months and must appoint local emergency planning committees within 10 months for all the districts. Both state commissions and local committees must devise procedures for handling public information requests.
- Required EPA to publish within 30 days a list of extremely hazardous substances specified in the bill and to begin drawing up rules establishing a "threshold planning quantity" for each. If EPA did not act, the law set the quantity at two pounds. If the threshold quantity was present at a facility, the facility would be subject to the bill's emergency planning requirements.
- Required owners or operators of plants or facilities subject to the requirements to notify the state commission within seven months. Governors or commissions could decide to subject other facilities to the requirements as well. States must notify EPA of such facilities.
- Required each local committee to complete an emergency plan within two years and to review it once a year thereafter. The plan was to identify facilities covered; methods to be followed by site operators and local emergency and medical personnel in response to a release; site and community coordinators; procedures for notification of emergency personnel or the public of a release; evacuation plans; training programs; and other items. Site operators were required to provide the committees with information needed to develop and carry out the plan. The plans were to be reviewed by the state commissions and superfund regional response teams.
- Required plant or facility operators to give immediate notice of a release of a listed extremely hazardous substance in certain circumstances. The release need not be reported immediately if it was a federally permitted release, it did not exceed the amount set by EPA as the level requiring reporting and it did not occur in a manner that would require notification under superfund "reportable quantities" provisions. Until EPA set rules dictating otherwise, releases of more than one pound of an extremely hazardous substance must be reported.
- Required plant operators, when immediate reporting was required, to notify local and state emergency coordinators by telephone or radio. The notification must include the identity of the chemicals involved; whether they were extremely hazardous; the estimated amount, time, duration and location of the release; known acute health effects; and health precautions.
- Authorized training for hazardous-substance emergencies to be included in existing federal emergency training programs. Also authorized appropriations for the Federal Emergency Management Agency to make grants to state, local and university programs to improve emergency preparedness, totaling $5 million annually for fiscal 1987-90.
- Set further requirements for plants and facilities to report the presence of substances in addition to those listed as extremely hazardous. These were the hazardous substances that must currently be reported on "material safety data sheets" (MSDS) under the Occupational Safety and Health Act of 1970.
- Required plant operators within 12 months to submit the MSDS form or a list of such chemicals to the local committee, the state commission and the local fire department. EPA could establish thresholds below which no such reporting was required.
- Required the local committee to make the MSDS form available upon request by any person.
- Exempted from the definition of hazardous chemicals certain food additives, coloring agents, drugs, cosmetics, solids contained in manufactured products, products sold to the general public, substances used in research and medical facilities, fertilizers and substances used in routine farming operations.
- Required any plant operator who was required to submit an MSDS form also to submit an "emergency and hazardous-chemical inventory form" to the state commission and the local committee and fire department. The chemicals that must be listed on the inventory form were those for which an MSDS was required.
- Required industries to report routine releases into the environment of substances that might cause chronic health problems like cancer. The information would go on a "toxic chemical release form." The list of substances for which such reporting was required was specified in the bill, and EPA could add or delete substances on its own initiative or on petition, if they met certain criteria. If a state governor made the petition to add a chemical (but not to delete one), the burden shifted to EPA to state why it would not do so.
- Specified that the release form was required for chemicals known or reasonably expected to cause cancer or cancerlike effects or to cause serious or irreversible reproductive or neurological disorders, heritable genetic mutations or other chronic health effects. The form was also required for chemicals that, because of toxicity, persistence, and tendency to bioaccumulate, were expected to cause serious environmental harm — and to do so beyond the boundaries of the plant site.
- Required such chemicals to be reported only if present in amounts above certain thresholds. For chemicals simply used at a facility, the threshold was 10,000 pounds per year. For chemicals manufactured or processed at a facility, the threshold was 75,000 pounds until July 1, 1988; 50,000 pounds until July 1, 1989; and 25,000 pounds thereafter.

• Allowed companies or facilities to base their reports on data already available, without undertaking new monitoring just to meet this requirement, and to estimate the amount released annually into the environment from information such as inventories. Companies were to report by July 1, 1988, and annually thereafter. EPA had authority to set and change these reporting requirements by regulation, but could not require reporting more often than annually. EPA was to maintain a computer database of the nation's toxic chemical inventory based on this information.

Companies subject to all the reporting requirements under this section of the bill could withhold information on the specific chemical identity of a substance (but not information on its generic class or category) if they established that the information was a trade secret. To do so a company must submit to EPA a statement of the reasons for its claim, and must show that it had not already disclosed the information, that it was not required to be disclosed under any other law, that disclosure was likely to cause the company substantial harm and that competitors could not determine the chemical's identity for themselves through reverse engineering.

Any person could petition EPA for disclosure of the identity of such a substance. EPA was to issue regulations for procedures in determining whether the information could be withheld as a trade secret. In a rulemaking procedure subject to court review, EPA made the determination of whether the information could be withheld.

Regardless of the determination, companies could not withhold such information from health professionals, including government public health officials. Health professionals who got such information must sign agreements to keep it confidential.

• Required that except for such withholding, each emergency response plan, material safety data sheet, list, inventory form, release form and follow-up emergency notice must be made available to the general public during normal working hours at designated government offices. Each local committee must annually publish notices in local newspapers that such information was available.

• Provided a system of administrative, civil and criminal penalties for enforcing the emergency planning and right-to-know provisions. Judicially imposed penalties could range as high as $75,000 per day of violation for repeated violations of requirements to provide information. The bill also provided penalties for improper disclosure of trade secrets and for frivolous claims of trade secrecy. Health professionals were given standing to sue in court for access to information.

• Gave any citizen the right to sue plant or facility operators for failure to meet right-to-know requirements of the act and to sue federal or state officials for failure to carry out its provisions. Local and state governments could sue facility operators to get compliance. The United States could intervene as a party in such suits, as could other persons whose interests were adversely affected.

Revenues and Taxes

• Renamed the Hazardous Substance Response Trust Fund officially as the "Hazardous Substances Superfund." The fund, to be used to pay for cleanups and other purposes specified in the bill, would come from appropriations and a series of taxes.

The $8.5 billion the fund would receive over five years would include $2.75 billion from a tax on petroleum, $1.4 billion from a tax on raw chemicals, $2.5 billion from a broad-based tax, $1.25 billion from general revenues, $0.3 billion from interest, and $0.3 billion from government recoveries of cleanup costs from companies responsible for dumps. The bill provided that the taxes to fund the superfund would generally take effect after Dec. 31, 1986, and end before Jan. 1, 1992.

• Provided two trigger mechanisms that would stop collection of all superfund taxes if the fund reached a certain size. If the unobligated balance in the fund exceeded $3.5 billion on Dec. 31, 1989, or Dec. 31, 1990, and EPA determined that the balance would stay above that level for the year following that date, then no taxes would be collected during 1990 or 1991, as the case might be. If the secretary of the Treasury estimated that the total amount of superfund taxes collected would exceed $6.65 billion by Jan. 1, 1992, authority to collect the taxes would terminate when that amount is collected.

• Reimposed and increased the tax on crude petroleum under the old superfund law from 0.79 cent per barrel to 8.2 cents per barrel for domestically produced petroleum and 11.2 cents per barrel for imported petroleum or petroleum products.

• Reimposed the old tax on 42 organic and inorganic raw industrial chemicals ("feedstocks"). The same chemicals would be taxed at the same rates, except for xylene.

• Increased the tax levied under the old superfund law on xylene, a raw chemical similar in some respects to benzene and derived from petroleum, from $4.87 to $10.13 per ton.

• Established a new tax on imported chemical derivatives of the feedstocks subject to the superfund tax. The bill listed 47 of them initially. The secretary of the Treasury was to add chemicals to the list if taxable feedstocks made up more than 50 percent by weight of the raw materials used to make the derivatives. The tax was to be the amount of tax that would have been imposed on the taxable feedstocks going into the derivative if they had been sold in the United States. If the importer did not provide enough information to compute the tax that way, the tax was 5 percent of the customs value of the imported derivative.

• Established a new broad-based tax on corporate income. The base amount that would be taxed would be a company's taxable income as defined under the provisions for an alternative minimum tax in the tax reform bill (HR 3838). The tax would be 0.12 percent ($12 per $10,000 of alternative minimum taxable income). The first $2 million of such income would be exempt, and the tax would be paid only on the excess above that amount. Companies would have to pay the tax whether or not they had to pay the alternative minimum tax.

• Financed the Leaking Underground Storage Tank Trust Fund by establishing an additional tax of 0.1 cent per gallon on gasoline; diesel fuel; special motor fuels; liquid fuels used in motor vehicles, boats and trains; liquid aviation fuels; and fuels used in commercial transportation on inland waterways. The tax would be in addition to excise taxes on these fuels under existing law. The tax expired on Dec. 31, 1991, or when net revenues exceeded $500 million.

• Repealed the Post-closure Liability Trust Fund and tax, set up under the Solid Waste Disposal Act to pay, from a tax on hazardous-waste disposal, possible pollution damage claims after a legally permitted landfill had closed and gone out of business. Repeal would be effective Oct. 1, 1983, the original effective date of the tax. Persons who had paid the tax could file claims for refunds, plus interest.

• Authorized appropriations of $250 million annually to the superfund for fiscal years 1987-91.

Miscellaneous

• Authorized "potentially responsible parties" (owners or operators of a site where a hazardous-substance release had occurred, companies whose wastes had been deposited at the site and certain others) to be reimbursed from the superfund for response costs in certain circumstances. One was when the party, under an EPA abatement order, paid cleanup costs for which it was not liable. Another was when the party could prove that EPA's choice of a response action was arbitrary, capricious or unlawful.

• Required an annual audit of superfund program activities and a report to Congress by the inspectors general of the agencies involved.

• Specified that Indian tribes had substantially the same rights as states did under many provisions of the superfund law.

• Required the comptroller general to conduct a study of the availability of insurance for persons who generated and handled hazardous substances, and to report to Congress in 12 months. ▮

Pesticide Bill Stalls at Session's End

The 99th Congress failed to complete action on legislation to reauthorize and dramatically strengthen the nation's pesticide control law.

The bill (HR 2482) was passed in different forms by the House Sept. 19 and the Senate Oct. 6. Efforts to resolve differences, in informal discussions between House and Senate committee leaders, produced a compromise measure that the House approved Oct. 16. But Senate action on the compromise was blocked by last-minute objections, and the bill died when Congress adjourned Oct. 18.

The measure would have amended and reauthorized through fiscal 1991 the Federal Insecticide, Fungicide and Rodenticide Act (FIFRA, PL 92-516), which prohibited the sale of pesticides unless they were registered with the Environmental Protection Agency (EPA). FIFRA had been overdue for reauthorization since 1981, but efforts to revamp the law had been stalled by bitter quarreling between environmentalists and chemical companies.

The basic outline of the 1986 legislation resulted from more than a year of negotiations between the National Agricultural Chemicals Association (made up of 92 chemical companies) and the Campaign for Pesticide Reform (an array of 41 environmental, consumer, public health and labor organizations). The bill also had the support of the National Farm Bureau Federation and other farm groups.

Major provisions of the bill would have speeded up pesticide testing of the hundreds of pesticides already in use even though their health effects were still unknown, increased public access to health and safety information, given EPA new authority to protect groundwater from pesticide contamination, regulated for the first time some hazardous pesticide ingredients previously classified as "inert," and strengthened existing requirements for certifying pesticide applicators and for protecting farm workers from exposure. Legislation that was eventually folded into the pesticide bill also would have given agrichemical firms extensions of pesticide patents to compensate for years spent on health testing.

Background

Although federal pesticide laws had been on the books much earlier, FIFRA largely took its existing shape in 1972. Amendments to the law that year sought to ensure that pesticides marketed in the United States did not pose a hazard to public health or the environment. But they also left leeway for farmers to keep using many of the pesticides they said were vital to the nation's food production. *(FIFRA enactment, Congress and the Nation Vol. III, p. 800; previous reauthorization action, 1983 Almanac p. 386)*

The law required all pesticides to be registered with EPA, which was to regulate their use and apply restrictions to pesticides that could have "substantial adverse effects" on the environment.

By 1986, an estimated 35,000 pesticide formulations were sold in the United States, using some 1,400 different registered active ingredients. Most of the pesticides in use were registered before 1972, under a less stringent version of the law. Since then, EPA had re-registered, after full testing, less than 20 of over 600 active ingredients in use.

In 1984, the government had sufficient data to assess health risks for only 10 percent of the pesticides in use, according to the National Academy of Sciences.

House Committee Action

The House Agriculture Committee approved HR 2482 June 17 by a 42-1 vote. Its report was filed July 18 (H Rept 99-695).

The first draft of that bill began as a text put forth jointly by the Campaign for Pesticide Reform and the National Agricultural Chemicals Association. Even after extensive debate, its main features remained essentially the same.

The panel's Subcommittee on Department Operations had approved the bill May 14, 13-0. In a change that helped win farm groups' support for the measure, the subcommittee added language limiting a farmer's liability for damage caused by his use of a pesticide if he could show he had followed label instructions.

While HR 2482 reflected a near-consensus among the scores of interest groups involved on most issues, some remaining disputes led to close votes during full committee consideration.

The bill set new deadlines for EPA to finish "re-registration" of some 600 pesticides that were in use when the law was passed in 1971 but had yet to be fully tested for their health effects.

The speedup in processing of re-registrations by EPA would theoretically be paid for by a new $150,000 fee on the manufacturers of each active ingredient seeking re-registration. But under the bill, the fee for 127 of those ingredients would be only $100,000. They were the ones for which EPA had already issued re-registration standards, or rules stating what information EPA needed to determine their safety.

Despite threatened administration opposition unless

more money was raised to pay for the speedup, the committee rejected, 20-21, an amendment by Arlan Stangeland, R-Minn., that would have made those 127 ingredients subject to the additional $50,000 fee. That would have raised another $6 million for EPA work.

The committee also rejected, on a 9-10 show of hands, another amendment by Stangeland that would have reduced the amount of money raised by the bill. The amendment would have lowered fees charged to producers of pesticides not used on food or feed products, even further than they were already reduced by the bill.

Manufacturers of these pesticides had claimed the fees would be a financial hardship. They had joined with certain agricultural interests to form what was called the "FIFRA Coalition," and that coalition supported both of Stangeland's amendments.

Data Compensation

Not only did the bill split the chemical industry between agricultural and non-agricultural pesticide manufacturers, but it also split the industry between the big companies whose research brought pesticides onto the market and the smaller companies who might later try to enter the market and produce the same pesticides at a lower cost to farmers.

The issue that caused the division was called "data compensation." Innovators, under patent law, got a 17-year exclusive right to reap the rewards of their research. But because a company had to cite health research to register a proposed product with EPA, health data had come to have a commercial value as well. Under existing law, companies later seeking to enter the market with a pesticide on which the patent had expired had to pay the pioneering companies more than five times their cost of generating health data in order to get the right to use it.

Small companies had sought relief, backing an amendment put before the committee by Jerry Huckaby, D-La., that would have limited data compensation to two times a fair share of costs. But Huckaby's amendment was defeated on a 19-23 vote.

Instead, the committee adopted an alternative by Charlie Rose, D-N.C., favored by the large chemical companies. It would limit the data compensation awards only in cases where the pioneering companies had the time periods of their patents extended under legislation then pending in the Judiciary Committee.

Other Issues

In other action, the committee:

- Rejected, by a 19-22 vote, an amendment by Ron Marlenee, R-Mont., that would have prohibited judges from awarding attorneys' fees to groups that went to court to try to force EPA to meet the new deadlines. Normally, when citizen groups win such lawsuits, they can get reimbursed for legal expenses.
- Adopted by voice vote an amendment by Sid Morrison, R-Wash., overhauling worker health and safety provisions approved in subcommittee. The Morrison amendment kept language in the subcommittee bill requiring EPA to issue regulations to protect employees who mixed, loaded and applied pesticides and agricultural employees who worked in pesticide-treated areas. Dropped from the subcommittee bill was language requiring the establishment of a separate office for worker health and safety within EPA.
- Approved language offered by Harold L. Volkmer, D-Mo., overhauling subcommittee provisions on certification and training of persons who applied pesticides as part of their jobs. The Volkmer language kept subcommittee provisions strengthening existing legal requirements for the training of commercial applicators — but eased the pinch of those requirements on farmers and those, such as janitors, who used pesticides only occasionally.
- Approved general language urging EPA to use its existing authority to protect groundwater from pesticides. The subcommittee bill had strengthened federal regulatory authority over groundwater, but the provisions had drawn fire from EPA.
- Avoided jurisdictional claims by the House Energy and Commerce Committee, which could have stalled prompt floor action on the bill. The committee did that by reversing an earlier vote on an amendment by Pat Roberts, R-Kan., that would have encouraged nationally uniform limits on the amount of pesticide residue allowed on foods. The Roberts amendment was first approved, 30-9, but later it was removed from the bill by a voice vote.

Senate Committee Action

The Senate Agriculture Committee approved its version of the pesticide bill Aug. 13 by voice vote. The Senate measure (S 2792 — S Rept 99-424), which was reported Sept. 3, was modeled in most respects on the House bill.

The panel's three-week markup culminated with a compromise between big chemical companies holding pesticide patents and small companies seeking to enter the market with generic versions once those patents expired.

On July 30, the Senate panel adopted an amendment establishing arbitration procedures for settling disputes over the use of health data, with provisions for court review if either party was not happy with the arbitration decision. But that amendment, by Richard G. Lugar, R-Ind., left the small companies unsatisfied. They felt they had been forced to pay unreasonably high compensation in the past, and they wanted specific limits written into the law.

Two weeks of negotiation followed, and on Aug. 13 the committee adopted another amendment, offered by Edward Zorinsky, D-Neb., that was aimed at pleasing both the large and small companies. The amendment did not reopen the compensation issue but dealt with two related questions: patent extensions and the timing of new tests on patented pesticides.

To the delight of large companies, the amendment allowed patents on new pesticide products to be extended for up to five years, depending on how long the product had been undergoing regulatory review at EPA. But it also gave small companies a head start in bringing their generic products to market. Under existing law, it was considered a patent infringement if a company began pre-marketing health tests on a patented product before the patent had actually expired. The amendment changed that, allowing companies that so desired to begin their own testing up to two years before the patent expired.

States' Rights

Another key issue — whether states could set their own pesticide limits — was tentatively decided Aug. 7, when the committee approved an amendment by Chairman Jesse Helms, R-N.C. Under the Helms amendment, states would be prohibited from setting pesticide residue limits that were more stringent than federal limits.

On a related issue, the committee decided at an Aug.

13 markup not to specifically prohibit local pesticide regulations.

Some cities and counties had begun adopting their own regulations restricting pesticides — for example, laws requiring warning signs to be posted on lawn areas that had recently been treated with pesticides.

Thad Cochran, R-Miss., had offered an amendment in the Senate committee to prohibit local regulations of the sale and use of pesticides. But he withdrew that amendment after being assured that the committee's report would include language frowning on such rules.

The measure reported by the House Agriculture Committee left intact the right of states to write their own laws.

Groundwater

In other action, the Senate committee adopted an amendment giving EPA more authority to prevent and correct contamination of groundwater by pesticides. The amendment was offered by Paula Hawkins, R-Fla., whose state was highly dependent on groundwater and had problems with pesticide contamination.

Her amendment would require EPA to set voluntary "guidance levels" suggesting what amount of contamination was dangerous and giving EPA authority to control contamination at specific sites. The authority granted went well beyond that in existing law and the House committee bill.

House Floor Action

The House Sept. 19 overwhelmingly passed HR 2482, 329-4. *(Vote 367, p. 104-H)*

But the Reagan administration threatened to veto the bill, which was supported by a coalition of farmers, environmentalists and chemical companies, as well as by committee leaders from both parties.

The administration wanted pesticide manufacturing companies to pay a greater share of the government's costs for evaluating health tests and issuing new registrations allowing the pesticides to be used.

In three days of work Sept. 17-19, the House left largely intact the bill approved by the Agriculture Committee.

Residues on Food

In the only real test of strength during floor consideration, farm-state members won an amendment that would prohibit states from setting stricter standards (or "tolerances") than the federal government for the amount of pesticides that could be left on food going to market.

The amendment, by Roberts and Charles W. Stenholm, D-Texas, was approved 214-121. *(Vote 366, p. 104-H)*

Some states wanted to set tolerances that were more protective than those set by EPA and the Food and Drug Administration. But the Grocery Manufacturers Association said the marketplace would be thrown into chaos if states set their own tolerances. They said it would be too difficult for a national manufacturer to meet a different standard in every state.

The Roberts-Stenholm amendment prohibiting state standards would apply only to pesticides registered after EPA's 1985 health standards took effect, or those that met those standards. States would nonetheless be able to set their own tolerances to deal with an imminent health threat and could petition EPA to allow a different tolerance if they could show their circumstances were unique.

The challenge to Roberts-Stenholm came as an amendment by Leon E. Panetta, D-Calif., which spelled out procedures to give states a hearing before EPA set the uniform national tolerances. Under Panetta's proposal, the burden of proof would be on EPA to show that uniform standards were needed to protect interstate commerce. The Panetta amendment was rejected 157-183. *(Vote 365, p. 104-H)*

Re-registration Fees

Less than 20 of the roughly 600 pesticide active ingredients registered for use had been completely tested for their effects on human health, and at the rate EPA had been reviewing them for re-registration, it would take until the year 2010 to do them all.

The House bill set a schedule for finishing that work within about nine years, and EPA estimated that it would cost $206 million to do it. The agency's existing budget levels would provide only $110 million during that period. Some of the remainder would come from chemical companies.

The bill reported by the Agriculture Committee imposed a $150,000 fee on the producers of each active ingredient to be re-registered. If more than one manufacturer produced the chemical, the fee would be split among the manufacturers in proportion to their market share. The fee in the bill as reported would have brought in another $45 million, leaving a shortfall of about $50 million. The Office of Management and Budget warned that the measure would be vetoed if that shortfall were not made up.

The bill's floor manager, Berkley Bedell, D-Iowa, offered an amendment that would have increased the fee for some pesticides to make up $6 million of the shortfall. Then Steve Gunderson, R-Wis., offered an amendment to Bedell's amendment that would have raised the fee still higher to make up the rest.

Roberts warned that the administration had specifically stated it would oppose the bill unless the Gunderson amendment were adopted. But Bedell opposed it, saying the chemical companies and bill sponsors had conceded enough, and that the public interest in speedy testing justified public spending to accomplish it. The Gunderson amendment was rejected on a 6-13 standing vote and Bedell's amendment adopted by voice vote.

Senate Floor Action

The Senate passed its version of the bill Oct. 6 by voice vote, after striking a provision prohibiting states from setting stricter limits than the federal government on the amount of pesticide residue allowed on food products. The amendment to strike, which was offered by Dave Durenberger, R-Minn., was approved by voice vote after the Senate rejected, 34-45, a motion to table it. *(Vote 332, p. 54-S)*

The Senate substituted the text of its own amended version for that of the House bill, and passed the latter, as a technical move to allow a conference.

Patent Extension

The Senate bill also contained language extending the life of pesticide patents. This was to compensate for time that was lost from the normal 17-year life of a patent because testing required for EPA registration could take several years.

In previous years, environmental groups had succeeded in blocking separate patent legislation, which was prized by the chemical companies; in 1986, they were able to use it to force manufacturers to the negotiating table. The eventual result was agreement by both sides on a pesticide bill — and an understanding that the patent legislation would be included in it.

Similar patent legislation (HR 5536) was passed by the House Oct. 6 separately from the pesticide bill, but Congress took no further action on that measure.

Although it received little floor time, the patent legislation was critical to passage of the pesticide bill. "It was the key that unlocked this thing," said Rep. Bedell, chairman of the House Agriculture Subcommittee on Department Operations.

Before passing the bill, the Senate approved 13 amendments, all by voice vote.

Food Residue Limits

The most controversial amendment was that striking the provision pre-empting states' rights to set their own food residue limits. The provision, also contained in the House-passed bill, was added to the Senate measure by Helms during the Agriculture Committee's markup.

The Helms amendment authorized EPA to set uniform national limits on the amount of pesticide allowed to remain on food. Under the Helms amendment, if EPA had completed all health tests and set a national tolerance, states would have been prohibited from setting a stricter tolerance unless the state faced an imminent hazard or successfully petitioned EPA.

The Grocery Manufacturers Association and other food producing groups favored the uniform tolerance provision, saying that marketing food was too difficult when each state had different requirements. The National Governors' Association and health groups, however, argued that each state has the right to protect the health of its citizens.

Farmer Liability

Splitting with the House, the Senate struck a provision that had been the key to winning the support of farm groups for the bill. The provision protected farmers from lawsuits for pesticide damages when they had followed instructions on the pesticide label. The amendment to strike — which again was offered by Durenberger — was adopted by voice vote.

Although he argued to strike the provision, Durenberger said that under the "polluter pays" theory, some kind of liability might be needed to help prevent or compensate real injury, and that farmers could be injured by pesticides as much as anyone else. He said the House had moved in the right direction when it adopted an amendment that shifted the liability from the farmer to the pesticide manufacturer.

Liability provisions normally fall within the jurisdiction of the Judiciary Committee, but if that panel had sought referral, there might not have been time to pass the bill. Durenberger said his amendment "resolves certain jurisdictional concerns," and was part of "an arrangement that has been carefully worked out."

Groundwater

Durenberger, chairman of the Environment Subcommittee on Toxic Substances, also offered a major amendment dealing with groundwater protection. He could have claimed jurisdiction for his subcommittee and held the bill up, but instead had informal talks with the Agriculture Committee in an effort to strengthen the groundwater provisions added by the Hawkins amendment.

Hawkins' amendment would set up a whole new program at EPA for addressing groundwater contamination. It would require EPA to set "Groundwater Residue Guidance Levels" (GRGLs) if it determined that a pesticide presented a threat to groundwater.

When such contamination occurred, pesticide companies would have to notify EPA, and EPA could require them to do further monitoring of the groundwater in other representative areas where the pesticide is used.

EPA would have to set GRGLs when it registered or re-registered a pesticide that it determined could leak into the groundwater. EPA would also have to issue a GRGL if contamination by a pesticide had been detected in three different geographical areas or found in drinking-water wells serving more than 500 people. If EPA had already set drinking-water health standards (called "Maximum Contaminant Levels") for that pesticide, then it would have to set the GRGL at the same level. Otherwise, it would be set at a level that would protect health with an adequate margin of safety.

If EPA found a pesticide in a drinking-water well at a level higher than the GRGL, it must notify the governor, who must within 90 days initiate action aimed at reducing the contamination below the GRGL. If the state failed to do so, and the contamination appeared to be from normal and widespread use, then EPA after Jan. 1, 1989, could ban use of the well or take other action.

EPA must also amend the registration of the pesticide as a preventive measure if it determined there was a reasonable likelihood that the GRGL would be exceeded in different areas. Such amendments could include restrictions on the purposes and location of its use; time or frequency of use; methods of handling, application or disposal; or other restrictions.

The amendment Durenberger offered was cosponsored by Hawkins and billed as a "consensus amendment," and it made only relatively technical changes within the basic structure of the original Hawkins amendment. One example was changing the level of pesticides in the water — from 25 percent to 30 percent of the GRGL — that triggered a registration amendment.

In hearings on the groundwater question, Durenberger made it clear he would have preferred stronger provisions, but he agreed to compromise when he was warned that insisting on more stringent language would upset the bill's delicate balance and might bring its defeat. But Durenberger said he would introduce new groundwater legislation early in 1987.

Food Stamp Eligibility

Another amendment adopted had little to do with the pesticide bill. Offered by Pete V. Domenici, R-N.M., it made homeless persons eligible for food stamps. The amendment had previously been attached to pending drug legislation (HR 5484), but Domenici said he needed to attach it to another vehicle since the drug bill might not be enacted. *(Drug bill, p. 92)*

House Compromise

Struggling to complete action on the bill before adjournment, the House Oct. 16 approved a compromise measure developed in informal discussions among House and Senate committee leaders. The Senate never voted on the House-proposed compromise, however. Action was blocked by Howard M. Metzenbaum, D-Ohio, who objected to the language extending patent terms. Other objections came from John Melcher, D-Mont., who sought data compensation provisions more favorable to generic pesticide manufacturers.

Further objections had come from Durenberger and several other senators favoring changes sought by environmentalists. They said they wanted to amend the bill sent them by the House. As the 99th Congress wound down to its last dozen hours, the Senate floor was jammed with bills, and any measure without consensus was doomed. As a result, the bill died when Congress adjourned Oct. 18.

The House compromise proposal had been agreed to by members speaking for a variety of contending factions in negotiations that had gone on for several days during the week of Oct. 13. The two main parties were the Agriculture Committee, reflecting farmers' views, and the Energy Committee, reflecting both environmentalist and chemical industry views.

The revisions were approved on the House floor in an unusual unanimous consent procedure that could have been blocked by objections from a single member. No one objected.

The House took the Senate-passed version of HR 2482 and attached the compromise proposal as an amendment. It also included legislation that would give agrichemical firms extensions of pesticide patents to compensate for years spent on health testing.

Lobbyists for the Audubon Society, the Sierra Club and some other environmental groups remained unhappy with the bill, saying the measure gave away too much of a state's right to protect its citizens' health, which the Senate had already voted to uphold.

Addressing the Disputes

The revised legislation addressed two key issues that had divided the House and Senate on overhauling FIFRA.

One was whether states should be allowed to set stricter tolerances than the federal government governing how much pesticide residue should be allowed on food. The other was whether farmers should be liable for damages caused by pesticides if they applied the chemical according to label instructions.

The House proposal protected farmers from liability for properly applied pesticides, but it left vague the question of who would be responsible for damages in such cases.

The original House bill had exempted farmers from liability and put the responsibility on companies registered to make or sell the pesticide. The Senate bill had taken out the language on farmer liability, leaving both farmers and businesses potential targets of damage suits.

The House compromise provided that if farmers were not liable, then "other responsible parties" would be responsible "to the extent provided under other environmental statutes," according to an Agriculture Committee explanation.

Under the revised bill, a farmer could escape damages if he showed that he used the pesticide according to label instructions. But if the claimant could show the farmer had acted negligently, recklessly or with intent to misuse it, the farmer could be liable.

The proposed settlement on food residues ended up with a more even balance between federal and state authority on setting tolerance levels than there had been in the original House bill, members and lobbyists on both sides said. The original House bill had imposed uniform federal tolerances, while the Senate struck that language altogether, making it possible for states to set stricter tolerances than the federal government.

The House compromise required tolerances to be uniform nationally — *if* the pesticide met the latest EPA health-testing requirements. But it gave states a chance to influence EPA's decision to set a tolerance beforehand by requiring EPA to follow a rulemaking process that would include the states.

And it gave states an opportunity, after EPA had made its decision, to petition for different tolerances if they could demonstrate a local need.

The states could set stricter tolerances for old pesticides that had not met new EPA health-testing requirements. But food producers and distributors would be protected against economic loss for food in the "pipeline," if the pesticide was legally applied when the food was being produced. States could override the pipeline provision if they found an unreasonable risk to health.

Major Provisions

Certain features were common to both the House and Senate versions of the FIFRA bill.

The heart of FIFRA was a prohibition on the sale and distribution of any pesticide which was not registered with EPA. In order to get a registration, the manufacturer had to submit scientific testing data to EPA. EPA then decided whether to register it on the basis of whether it would perform its intended function without unreasonable adverse effects on the environment. Pesticides were only registered for particular uses, and the registration included requirements for labeling the pesticide to specify proper methods of use and safety precautions.

As passed by the House and Senate, both bills would have:

Re-registration

- Set a five-step schedule by which EPA must "re-register" pesticides currently on the market without complete health testing. The schedule would cover active ingredients in pesticides registered before Nov. 1, 1984.

In phase one, EPA would publish a priority list of the active ingredients needing to be re-registered. Priority would be given to those used on food or feed that might leave residues after harvest; those that could significantly contaminate drinkable groundwater, fish or shellfish; those with major gaps in health data; and those to which field workers were most exposed.

In phase two, companies with registrations would notify EPA whether they intended to seek re-registration of a pesticide.

In phase three, applicants would summarize existing data on their ingredients, put it into a standard form for EPA to use, and promise to fill data gaps.

In phase four, EPA would review information so far submitted and determine whether companies had identified all the data gaps. EPA would then issue data requirements for re-registration of each active ingredient. Companies would have four years to work up and submit that data.

In phase five, EPA would review all the data and decide if the pesticide was safe enough to re-register. If more data were needed for the different specific products using an ingredient, EPA could ask for it and the companies would have to supply it. EPA would have to make a final decision within one year of getting all required data.

• Set a timetable for re-registering all active ingredients by approximately 8 years and 10 months from enactment, except for unusual circumstances. In order to spread out EPA's workload in processing the re-registrations, they would be divided into three groups of approximately 150 ingredients, and the deadlines for each group to finish each phase of the process would be staggered.

• Established a fee to be paid by companies seeking to re-register an active ingredient. Its purpose would be to help pay for the faster pace of work by EPA. The fee would be up to $150,000 for each ingredient, to be split among the companies seeking re-registration according to market share.

For food and feed pesticides, the first $50,000 would be paid when companies notified EPA they wanted to re-register, and the remaining $100,000 would be paid under phase three. For pesticides for which EPA had already issued the data requirements before enactment, the companies would pay only $100,000.

For non-food pesticides, EPA could reduce the fee as low as $75,000, or $50,000 if data requirements had already been issued. Fees could be reduced for pesticides registered only for minor uses, those produced by small businesses, or for certain low-volume, low-value, anti-microbial pesticides.

Inert Ingredients

• Required EPA to begin regulating so-called "inert" ingredients — those not claimed as having pesticidal action by manufacturers, many of which were known to be toxic to humans.

• Required EPA to establish within 90 days a priority list of 50 to 75 inert ingredients for immediate further action. They would be those appearing to cause unreasonable adverse effects to the environment, chemicals suspect because of their structural similarity to chemicals known to be harmful, and pesticides to which people were exposed in quantities large enough to make them a special concern.

• Required EPA to decide within one year whether additional data were needed on a listed inert ingredient, and required registrants to submit the additional data within four years. EPA would then have to take appropriate regulatory action within one year.

• Required pesticide labels to give the names and concentrations of inert ingredients which EPA had found to be dangerous, or for which it had required additional data because of an apparent danger.

Disclosure

• Allowed public access, effectively blocked under previous law, to health and safety data on a pesticide *before* it was registered. Access would be allowed to data submitted for registration of a new active ingredient or the first use of an active ingredient on food crops or products. People getting the information would have to affirm they were not working for other pesticide companies. The information could only be used for public comment on the proposed registration, on pain of criminal penalties.

• Established a "public right to know" what chemicals were being used at pesticide production plants. Producers would have to prepare a fact sheet for each active ingredient manufactured or used at the plant, giving the identity of the chemical and a summary of relevant health, safety and environmental data on it. The producer must keep copies of the fact sheet at the plant and furnish them to anyone requesting them.

• Gave EPA authority to decide what information must be included on the fact sheets and to require a producer to change its fact sheet if it did not meet the requirements. Generally, though, they would be similar to the "Material Safety Data Sheets" already required under the Occupational Safety and Health Act.

• Required producers to report to EPA annually on ingredients requiring a fact sheet, the location of the plant, and to include a copy of the fact sheet. This information would be public.

• Required EPA to disclose to the states information it acquired under FIFRA — if the state law protected the companies as well as the federal law did against improper disclosure or use of the information and allowed companies to sue for damages resulting from wrongful disclosure.

Review and Cancellation

• Provided new procedures for deciding, on the basis of new information about its safety, to cancel registration of a pesticide that had already been registered. This process was called "interim administrative review" or "special review." Such cases had dragged on for years under the old law, and the new procedures were intended to provide definite time limits. The new rules would apply to reviews started after Jan. 1, 1987.

• Required EPA to publish the criteria it would use in deciding whether to start a special review. The criteria must be based on levels of risk and could include consideration of currently available data on human exposure. EPA would, in effect, need validated test results or other solid new data to start a review. EPA would have to notify the registrant and the Agriculture Department when the process started.

• Required EPA to publish rules under which it would conduct the reviews, providing for a preliminary and final determination and for public comment. Participants would have 90 days to disclose all information uniquely available to them that was relevant to the review. EPA's administrator would have to make a final decision within 18 months on what regulatory action, if any, it should take.

• Limited the right to hearings to appeal the EPA administrator's final decision to persons adversely affected by the decision (including a person without an economic interest in the pesticide) who had submitted comments during the review and requested the hearing within 30 days. The hearings, to be conducted by an administrative law judge, would be conducted under a timetable set in the bill, but the EPA administrator would have to make a final decision based on the hearings within 300 days.

• Authorized EPA to review labeling requirements and change them by a less formal procedure than special reviews, as long as the labeling change did not have the effect of canceling the pesticide by making it unmarketable.

• Authorized EPA to suspend immediately a registration once it had determined that it was based on false or invalid data. At the same time, EPA could issue notice of intent to cancel the registration. The old law did not allow such action once the registration had been issued, even in cases where laboratory results had been fraudulently altered. EPA would have the choice of requiring the registrant to supply new, valid data as a way of avoiding cancellation. If the registrant willfully submitted data known to be false,

EPA must begin cancellation proceedings. The suspension or cancellation would automatically take place in 30 days, unless the registrant asked for a hearing, in which case there was a 75-day time limit on the hearing.

Export/Import

- Required pesticides shipped for export to bear, in the appropriate language, the same label warnings that would be required in the United States. EPA would have to notify the foreign government 30 days before shipment if it were restricted, suspended, canceled or not registered in this country.
- Required EPA to stop allowing any residue of a pesticide on foods once it took the pesticide out of use in this country. The effect of the provision would be to prevent importation of crops on which foreign growers had used pesticides banned in the United States. When any pesticide registration was withdrawn, suspended or canceled, EPA must withdraw the tolerance, or allowable minimum amount of residue, for the pesticide or any exemption from the requirement for a tolerance.

Certification, Training and Record-Keeping

- Established generally stricter rules and procedures for making sure than the more dangerous pesticides were applied only by persons qualified to use them safely. Existing law required that the more dangerous (or "restricted use") pesticides be applied only by, or under the supervision of, a certified applicator. The bill created new requirements for training and registration of persons applying the pesticide under the certified applicator's supervision. It also created a new requirement that all commercial applicators be certified or registered, whether the pesticide used was for restricted or general use.
- Outlined in the law the training requirements for both commercial and private applicators. EPA and the Agriculture Department must develop training materials and EPA must issue minimum standards for trainer competency and training programs. Certified commercial applicators would have to take refresher training and be recertified every five years. State agencies would continue to administer certification and training under EPA supervision.
- Required commercial applicators to keep records of the pesticides they applied for two years, including the chemical, amount, location, and date. Private applicators would not be required to do so.
- Required pesticide dealers to keep records of sales or distribution of restricted use and other dangerous pesticides, including the chemical, amount, date and person to whom it was distributed, for three years.

Enforcement

- Authorized EPA to take enforcement action in response to a complaint or information it received, if the state did not promptly begin investigative or enforcement action within 90 days from the time EPA referred the matter to the state.
- Increased the penalties for violation of various FIFRA requirements. The top civil penalty for a violation by a registrant, registration applicant or testing facility would be $25,000 per offense or $50,000 for subsequent violations. For knowing (i.e. criminal) violations, the penalty could be up to $50,000 and a year in jail.

For commercial applicators, dealers or distributors, the top civil penalty would be $10,000 for each offense and $20,000 for subsequent ones. For knowing violations, the penalty could be up to $25,000 or a year in jail.

For private applicators EPA would normally give a written warning for the first offense, followed by penalties of $1,000 for the first and $2,000 for subsequent violations.

- Stated explicitly that authorized U.S. and state agents could enter and inspect pesticide testing, sales and distribution facilities, or any other place where they had reason to believe the act was being violated, by any person other than a private applicator, execute warrants, copy and obtain records and other evidence, and seize any pesticide or device violating the law.

Miscellaneous

- Authorized appropriations for carrying out programs under FIFRA of $88 million for fiscal 1987, $97 million for 1988, $101 million for 1989, $108 million for 1990 and $116 million for 1991.
- Prohibited "conditional" amendments of an existing registration to add allowable uses of a pesticide unless EPA found it to be in the public interest. Under the old law, manufacturers did not have to demonstrate their product's safety and effectiveness as rigorously for a conditional amendment as for a regular registration. The bill added other restrictions on the granting of conditional amendments to those already in the law, but made them less stringent for minor uses.
- Required EPA to issue regulations defining the conditions under which EPA could disapprove state actions to register additional uses of a pesticide to meet special local needs.
- Required EPA to issue regulations to protect the health of workers who mixed, loaded or applied pesticides and agricultural workers who worked in pesticide-treated areas. EPA would also have to issue regulations for training of workers who mixed, loaded or applied pesticides and who were not covered by other sections of the law. EPA would have to issue the regulations as soon as practical but not later than three years from enactment. Before EPA's proposed regulations could be made final, the Agriculture Department would have to submit to EPA a report on their effectiveness, cost and impact on the agricultural community. EPA would have to submit the final regulations to Congress and wait 120 days before they could become effective. ∎

Garrison Diversion Project

Congress in 1986 approved compromise legislation (HR 1116 — PL 99-294) to reshape the Garrison Diversion water project in North Dakota. The controversial project involved a billion-dollar system of canals and reservoirs for irrigation and water supply.

HR 1116 was intended to settle a controversy that had plagued the Garrison project since well before it was authorized in 1965 (PL 89-108). It was one of the water projects on President Carter's "hit list" in 1977, and had been subject to frequent challenges on the floor of the House since then. *(1965 Almanac p. 740; Congress and the Nation Vol. V, p. 541)*

The compromise bill drew vocal support from Rep. Silvio O. Conte, R-Mass., who had led previous floor fights against the project. "Under this legislation, everyone wins," Conte told the House. "The people of North Dakota, the federal taxpayers, the Canadians and the wildlife resources of North Dakota."

Provisions

As signed into law May 12, HR 1116 (PL 99-294):

- Authorized a multipurpose water resources project that would ultimately cost approximately $1.18 billion, including $275 million already spent. The bill specifically authorized $679,840,000 in spending. Further authorizations would be needed to finish the project.
- Authorized works to irrigate 130,940 acres of North Dakota land.
- Repealed previous authorization of works to irrigate some 923,000 additional acres.
- Authorized a $200 million federal grant program for construction by North Dakota of municipal, rural and industrial water supply facilities.
- Authorized construction of the Sykeston Canal to replace the controversial Lonetree Dam and Reservoir project, which was postponed pending further study.
- Required farmers to pay 10 percent of the full cost of irrigation waters used to grow surplus crops.
- Set aside up to $12 million in federal funds to establish a Wetlands Trust to acquire land and water rights and manage wetlands and wildlife habitats.
- Authorized $39,545,000 in funds for enhancement of and mitigation of damage to fish and wildlife habitats.
- Prohibited construction of James River Valley irrigation works until 60 days after Congress received a report on their environmental impact.

Background

North Dakota allowed a half-million acres of its land to be flooded as part of the mammoth 1944 Pick-Sloan program to reduce flooding in lower Missouri River basin states. In return for the lost acreage, North Dakota officials were promised that water impounded behind the Garrison Dam would eventually be used to irrigate the northern half of the state.

But the plan quickly ran into trouble. Canadians objected that its drainage could bring harmful fish and pollutants to their waterways. Environmentalists said it would destroy too much of the wetlands in which waterfowl breed. And taxpayer groups objected to the cost.

Congress stopped work on the Garrison Diversion project, with construction only 15 percent complete, in 1984, while a 12-member commission sought ways to redesign it. But when the commission's plan was presented in February 1985, few rushed to embrace it.

Congress appropriated $41.3 million for the Garrison Diversion in fiscal 1986, but barred expenditure of the money until passage of authorizing legislation to redesign the project. *(1985 Almanac p. 323)*

Legislative History

House. The House Interior Committee approved HR 1116 (H Rept 99-525, Parts I and II) March 19. George Miller, D-Calif., chairman of the Interior Subcommittee on Water and Power Resources, was credited with fostering negotiations that produced the compromise embodied in the bill.

The compromise cut the size of the project from 250,000 to 130,000 acres and reduced its estimated cost to $1.2 billion. The original plan, with inflation and other changes factored in, would have cost about $2 billion.

The House passed the bill April 23 on a 254-154 vote after rejecting, by a slim 199-203 margin, a controversial amendment by Berkley Bedell, D-Iowa. The amendment would have canceled subsidies for farmers who used irrigated water to grow surplus crops. Managers of the bill said the Bedell proposal would have unraveled the delicate compromise. *(Votes 88, 87, p. 28-H)*

Bedell argued it was a mistake to provide federal subsidies in the form of irrigation waters to farmers growing surplus crops. "I cannot understand," Bedell said, "how anybody in this body could say that it makes sense today, with the problems we face, to pay farmers to grow more crops at the same time we are paying farmers not to grow those very same crops."

Opponents of Bedell's amendment, who included Miller, Byron L. Dorgan, D-N.D., and Mike Strang, R-Colo., argued it was not fair to single out North Dakota farmers when similar provisions did not apply to most other Bureau of Reclamation projects.

Strang said, "You cannot resolve all the surplus problems in agriculture in the United States on the backs of the citizens of North Dakota."

Senate. The Senate passed HR 1116 without change April 28, completing congressional action on the bill. ▮

Congress Clears Omnibus Water Projects Bill

In one of its final acts before adjournment, the 99th Congress completed action Oct. 17 on a dams and harbors bill (HR 6 — PL 99-662) that dramatically increased the share of construction costs paid by project users. President Reagan signed the legislation Nov. 17.

Congress completed action on HR 6 late in the evening of Oct. 17 when the Senate approved the conference report (H Rept 99-1013) on the bill by an 84-2 vote. The House had approved it earlier in the evening, 329-11. The water project votes were the last roll-call votes in either chamber for the 99th Congress. *(Vote 354, p. 57-S; vote 451, p. 126-H)*

The final bill authorized construction of 262 new projects by the U.S. Army Corps of Engineers. The corps had played a role in building and running civil works for navigation, mostly at federal expense, since the 19th century.

Included in the bill were 41 port development projects, seven major inland lock-and-dam projects, 113 new flood control projects and a variety of other projects for water supply, recreation, beach erosion control, and improvement of habitat for fish and wildlife. Most of those projects required appropriations before construction could start.

Leaders in both chambers viewed 1986 as possibly the last chance to get such a massive authorization bill through Congress because of the new mood of fiscal austerity.

HR 6 required that a far greater share of project costs be paid by users and local governments, some $4.3 billion of the $16.3 billion in projects in the bill. Although amounts varied with projects, a local share of 5 or 10 percent of the costs had been typical in the past.

The measure established two new user fees as a major source of funding for the projects. One, a national port user tax, was to be levied at a rate of 4 cents per $100 on the value of most cargo loaded or unloaded at U.S. ports. It was expected to produce about $140 million a year for a separate fund reserved for port construction. The other, an increase in the existing 10-cent per gallon tax on barge fuel, was to go into a fund for inland waterways.

The House originally passed its $20 billion version of the bill Nov. 13, 1985. The Senate Environment and Public Works Committee reported a $12 billion bill (S 1567 — S Rept 99-126) Aug. 1, 1985. The Senate Finance Committee, which had jurisdiction over revenue provisions, reported the measure (S Rept 99-228) Jan. 8, 1986. The Senate, after amending S 1567, substituted its text for HR 6 and passed it March 26. Following lengthy negotiations, conferees reached agreement late Oct. 17 and rushed the pact to the floor. *(1985 action, 1985 Almanac p. 198)*

Authorizations for water projects, sometimes referred to as "pork-barrel" projects, were once a regular staple of Congress, especially in election years. But a long debate over whether local users and beneficiaries of projects should bear a greater share of costs had kept any major water projects authorization bill from getting through Congress since 1976. Congress came close to passing an omnibus bill in 1984, but the measure died in the closing days of the session. *(1976 Almanac p. 202; 1984 Almanac p. 320)*

Senate Floor Action

The Senate passed its version of the water projects bill by voice vote March 26.

The Senate bill, which authorized more than 180 new projects, contained cost-sharing reforms long sought by the Reagan administration, environmentalists and taxpayer groups. Under the new financing formula, the federal government would pay only about three-quarters of the bill for water projects, instead of almost all of it.

Sen. James Abdnor, R-S.D., chairman of the Environment and Public Works Subcommittee on Water Resources, said the new cost-sharing measures were necessary to keep the program viable. "We just can't build these projects in the future without having a larger share from local sponsors," Abdnor said.

Among the cost-sharing measures in the Senate bill was an increase in the barge fuel tax to pay for construction of inland waterways. It would be raised gradually from 10 cents per gallon in 1985 to 20 cents per gallon in 1997. Half of the construction cost for six new inland projects would come from fuel tax revenues and half from the general Treasury.

The Senate bill would also limit the federal share of port and harbor construction costs. For channels less than 20 feet deep, local authorities would have to pay 10 percent of the costs. They would have to pay 25 percent of the incremental costs for channel depths between 21 and 45 feet, and 50 percent of incremental costs for deepening them beyond 45 feet.

Those amounts would have to be paid "up front," or during construction, but local authorities would be able to collect their own user fees to recover their share of these costs.

To help pay for operating and maintaining harbors and channels, the bill would impose a federal user fee at coastal and Great Lakes ports of .04 percent (4¢ per $100) of the value of cargoes loaded or unloaded.

By voice vote, the Senate accepted an amendment by Slade Gorton, R-Wash., that exempted from the user fee cargo passing through U.S. ports on its way to or from a foreign country. The exemption, designed to prevent the diversion of cargo from U.S. ports to Canada and Mexico, would stand until a study authorized in the bill determined the economic impact of the user fee.

The Senate also accepted by voice vote an amendment by Ted Stevens, R-Alaska, that exempted all cargo going to or from Alaska, except crude oil.

After finishing all amendments to its bill, S 1567, the Senate substituted its text for that of HR 6, clearing the way for a conference.

Before passing the bill, the Senate had to overcome objections from Minority Leader Robert C. Byrd, D-W.Va., who sought to soften the effect of the new cost-sharing requirements on the Tug Fork flood control project in West Virginia and Kentucky. Byrd dropped his opposition after receiving assurances that certain parts of the Tug Fork project would be exempted because they would already be under construction.

Managers of the Senate bill were extremely reluctant to add specific language exempting any particular project for fear it would trigger a rush of similar requests.

Major Water Projects

Included in the Senate bill were six major lock-and-dam projects for inland navigation, with a total federal and non-federal cost of nearly $1 billion: Oliver lock replacement, Black Warrior-Tombigbee rivers, Ala. ($147 million); Gallipolis lock-and-dam replacement, Ohio River, Ohio and W.Va. ($256 million); improvements and an additional lock at Bonneville Dam, Columbia River, Ore. and Wash. ($191 million); and replacement of lock-and-dam units 7 and 8, Monongahela River, Pa. ($163 million).

Also included were more than 32 port and harbor construction projects with total costs of about $3 billion. Major items included: Mobile Harbor, Ala. ($388 million); Mississippi River Ship Channel, Gulf to Baton Rouge, La. ($456 million); Kill Van Kull and Newark Bay channels, N.Y. and N.J. ($248 million); Norfolk Harbor and channels, Va. ($538 million).

Major Senate Provisions

As passed by the Senate, HR 6:

- Limited the amount of money the secretary of the Army could obligate for the Corps of Engineers' general construction and Mississippi River flood control programs. The ceiling, set at $1.3 billion annually for fiscal 1987-91, covered both new construction and work already under way.
- Automatically deauthorized any corps project on which construction had not begun within 10 years of its authorization, unless the secretary of the Army, in consultation with the states, notified Congress the project was still justified. The provision would deauthorize some 675 projects worth $26.4 billion, beginning a year after enactment.
- Prohibited construction from beginning on any project in the bill until it had been favorably reviewed by the chief of engineers, who judged whether a project was economically and environmentally justified.
- Required the federal government to acquire before or during construction of a project any lands needed to offset fish and wildlife damage the project might cause.
- Authorized a new research and development program on the depletion of the Ogallala Aquifer, a huge geologic formation holding groundwater that supported irrigated agriculture in Colorado, Kansas, Nebraska, New Mexico,

Oklahoma and Texas. The bill authorized $9.5 million annually for fiscal 1987-91.

- Set up a two-step corps study process requiring local sponsors to pay half the costs of a project feasibility study after an initial reconnaissance study.
- Imposed an increase in the existing barge fuel tax of 10 cents per gallon to pay for construction of inland waterway projects. The tax would be raised 1 cent per year until it reached 20 cents per gallon in 1997.
- Provided that half of the costs of building new inland navigation projects would come from the Inland Waterways Trust Fund, which received revenues from the federal tax on barge fuel. The other half would come from the general Treasury.
- Imposed new charges for port and harbor projects so the federal government would no longer have to pay the full cost of dredging silt-filled shipping channels to depths sufficient for deep-draft ocean vessels.

For construction costs, local port authorities would have to pay 10 percent for channels less than 20 feet deep. They would have to pay, during construction, 25 percent of the incremental costs for channel depths between 21 and 45 feet, and 50 percent of incremental costs for deepening them beyond 45 feet. Local authorities would also have to pay an additional 10 percent of total costs, plus interest, over 30 years, although much of that amount could be paid in lands, easements, or rights of way.

- Authorized local authorities to collect their own user fees to recover their share of these costs.
- Imposed a new port user fee to help pay federal costs of operating and maintaining harbors and channels at U.S. coastal and Great Lakes ports. The fee would amount to .04 percent (4 cents per $100) of the value of cargoes loaded or unloaded at those ports.
- Exempted from the port user fee freshly caught fish and seafood. Also exempt were cargoes shipped between the mainland and Alaska, Hawaii and U.S. possessions — unless those cargoes were being transshipped to and from foreign ports. The fee would apply to Alaskan crude oil.
- Exempted from the port user fee cargo passing through U.S. ports on its way to or from a foreign country. The exemption, aimed at preventing cargo diversion to Canada and Mexico, would stand until a study of the economic effects of the fee was completed.
- Set the non-federal share of costs for flood control projects at 5 percent cash during construction, plus all lands, easements and rights of way — up to a total of 25-35 percent. The secretary of the Army could waive the requirements if he found that a local sponsor could not afford to meet the cost-sharing provisions.
- Set new higher requirements for sharing of project costs by non-federal interests. For hydroelectric projects non-federal interests would pay 100 percent; they would also pay 100 percent for municipal and industrial water supplies; for agricultural water supplies, the non-federal share would be 35 percent; for recreation projects, it would be 50 percent.
- Authorized over 180 major projects, including lock-and-dam construction for inland navigation, port and harbor construction, flood control measures and beach erosion control projects.

Conference Action

Conferees on the omnibus water projects bill were slow to convene, and even slower to make much headway.

Because of a jurisdictional dispute, it took the House almost two months just to appoint conferees and it was June before the conference was even organized. The real problem, however, was that key conferees and key staffers were faced with conflicting demands on their time. Most were tied up in the conference on the controversial "superfund" hazardous-waste bill, which had been given a higher priority.

The delay gave the Corps of Engineers time to lobby heavily for the bill. Robert K. Dawson, assistant secretary of the Army for civil works and the head of the corps, warned that HR 6 was the last chance to approve a comprehensive water projects program for at least a decade. Others warned that without a bill, individual water projects would start popping up in appropriations bills without regard for environmental concerns and without the necessary cost-sharing provisions. And the administration kept warning of a veto if the higher-costing House bill was adopted.

Progress was first reported in late July when House conferees offered to accept most of the Senate language on cost sharing. By late August, there were predictions that an agreement was imminent, but failure to reach agreement on superfund repeatedly postponed work on HR 6.

The expected agreement (H Rept 99-1013) did not come until just before adjournment.

The final version of the bill authorized construction of 262 new projects at an estimated cost of $16.3 billion — of which about $4.3 billion would be paid by local users and beneficiaries. The Senate version had authorized more than 180 major projects at a cost of about $12 billion. The House version had 360 projects and a price tag of $20 billion.

Conferees accepted a modified Senate provision that would double barge fuel taxes by 1995 to pay for inland lock-and-dam projects. The increase, which was not included in the House bill, was part of a compromise on cost sharing worked out in 1985 negotiations between Senate leaders and the Reagan administration. Both chambers had approved another cost-sharing measure that established a new port use tax to pay for maintenance of ports.

Major Provisions

As signed into law, HR 6:

Revenues

- Imposed a new Harbor Maintenance Tax on the value of cargoes loaded or unloaded at U.S. ports. The tax was .04 percent of the value of the cargo ($4 per $10,000). It was to be paid by the importer, exporter or shipper. It would generally apply to any channel or harbor open to public navigation that was not an inland waterway, with certain exemptions. It was to take effect April 1, 1987.

Exempted from the tax would be harbors that had not received federal funds for construction, operation or maintenance since 1977 or that had been deauthorized before 1985. On the Columbia River, Washington and Oregon, it would apply only up to the downstream side of Bonneville lock and dam.

The tax would apply generally to any commercial cargo, including passengers carried for hire (in which case the value taxed would be the fare). Scheduled ferries between U.S. points or between the United States and contiguous countries would be exempt. Catches of fish or other aquatic animals not previously landed would not be subject to the tax. Also exempt would be bunker fuel and ship's stores.

The tax would not be imposed on cargoes going from the U.S. mainland for ultimate use and consumption in Alaska, Hawaii or any U.S. possession — nor on cargoes going from those places for use on the mainland. It would, however, be imposed on crude oil going to or from Alaska.

The tax would not be applied to bonded commercial cargo entering the United States for direct exportation to another country. Cargoes transshipped to Canada or Mexico would have to pay the tax if that country imposed a similar tax. The tax could also be imposed on particular Canadian and Mexican transshipments if a federal study, mandated by the bill, found that taxing a particular transaction would not divert an economically significant amount of cargo from U.S. ports.

The tax could be imposed only once on the loading or unloading of a cargo from a single vessel (thus protecting coastal traffic from double taxation). The tax would not be imposed, subject to Treasury Department regulations, on mere movement of cargo within a port.

- Established a Harbor Maintenance Trust Fund and appropriated to it all revenue from the Harbor Maintenance Tax. Subject to annual appropriation, the fund would pay up to 40 percent of the eligible operations and maintenance costs for U.S. harbors and 100 percent of the operations and maintenance costs of the parts of the St. Lawrence Seaway operated by the St. Lawrence Seaway Development Corporation.
- Raised the existing 10-cent-per-gallon tax on barge fuel, created under PL 95-502. The Inland Waterways Tax, imposed on fuel used in commercial transportation on inland waterways, would be 11 cents per gallon on fuel used during 1990, 13 cents during 1991, 15 cents during 1992, 17 cents during 1993, 19 cents during 1994 and 20 cents thereafter.

The bill applied the tax to the portion of the Tennessee-Tombigbee Waterway from its confluence with the Tennessee River to the Warrior River at Demopolis, Ala. It had been exempt from the tax and ineligible to use its revenues.

- Created the Inland Waterways Trust Fund and appropriated to it revenues from the barge fuel tax. Subject to appropriations, the fund could be spent for certain projects for construction and rehabilitation of inland waterways. Certain projects authorized under the bill could receive up to 50 percent of costs from the fund. No such limit was applied by the bill to funds for projects authorized in PL 95-502.

Cost Sharing

- Established new requirements for determining the portion of project construction costs to be paid by non-federal interests. The requirements varied according to the type of project. For multipurpose projects, costs were allocated among purposes.
- Required non-federal interests to enter into a binding agreement with the secretary of the Army — before construction started — to pay the appropriate share of the operation, maintenance, replacement and rehabilitation costs and to pay the non-federal share of construction costs specified in the bill. Requirements for agreements to repay costs of hydroelectric projects were subject to a series of other federal laws and not subject to this provision.
- Required non-federal interests to provide all land, easements, rights-of-way and disposal areas for dredged materials and, in most cases, to perform all necessary relocations (e.g., for a road to be routed around a project). The value of these contributions was to be counted toward the non-federal share of project costs, as described below.
- For harbor projects, required non-federal interests to pay 10 percent of the cost of construction for the portion of the project that had a depth of up to 20 feet; 25 percent of the incremental costs for depths more than 20 feet and less than 45 feet; and 50 percent of the incremental costs for depths more than 45 feet. These costs were to be paid during construction.
- For harbor projects, required non-federal interests to pay an additional 10 percent of construction costs over a 30-year period, with interest. The costs of lands, easements and rights-of-way provided by non-federal sponsors could be credited toward this amount.
- For harbor projects, required the federal government to pay 100 percent of operation and maintenance costs (as it does now), except for deep-draft harbors (those deeper than 45 feet). Non-federal interests would have to pay 50 percent of incremental operation and maintenance costs for depths of more than 45 feet.
- For inland waterway projects, authorized 50 percent of construction costs to be paid from the general fund of the federal Treasury. The other 50 percent would come from amounts appropriated by Congress out of the Inland Waterways Trust Fund. Planning, engineering, land acquisition and relocation costs were considered construction costs.
- For inland waterway projects, required the federal government to pay 100 percent of operation and maintenance costs, as it did under existing law.
- For flood control projects, required non-federal interests to pay a minimum of 25 percent and a maximum of 50 percent of the project costs. Non-federal interests must provide all lands, easements and rights-of-way for the project and for dredge-spoil disposal and relocations (the value of which could be counted toward the non-federal share). Non-federal interests must pay at least 5 percent of the project costs during construction. If the value of lands contributed was less than 25 percent of project costs, the non-federal interests must pay the remainder required to complete a 25 percent share during construction. If the amount the non-federal interests must contribute exceeded 30 percent of the total, the excess could be paid over 15 years, with interest, to the federal government. For non-structural projects, the non-federal share was 25 percent, but there was no requirement for a cash payment during construction.
- Required non-federal sponsors to pay 100 percent of project costs for hydroelectric power, 100 percent for municipal and industrial water supply, 35 percent for agricultural water supply, 50 percent for recreation, 35 percent for hurricane and storm damage reduction, and 50 percent of operational costs for aquatic plant control. For hydroelectric projects, the appropriate federal power marketing administration must comment on whether all of the project's power-related costs could be recovered from power revenues in the time allotted.
- Applied the new cost-sharing requirements to any project, or separable element thereof, on which physical construction began after April 30, 1986. Specific projects in the Yazoo Basin, Miss., and Harlan and Barbourville, Ky., were exempt from the new requirements. A "separable element" was defined as one that was physically separable from other portions of the project and that achieved hydro-

logic effects or produced physical or economic benefits separately identifiable from other parts of the project. (The definition was expected to exempt most unbuilt elements of the Mississippi River and Tributaries project, authorized in 1928 and still being enlarged.)

- Required non-federal interests to pay 50 percent of the costs of future project feasibility studies, except for inland waterways projects.
- Required non-federal interests to pay 50 percent of the cost of project planning and engineering during those phases of the project. Costs for design would be shared in the same way as construction costs.
- Authorized the secretary of the Treasury to determine the interest rate that would be paid by non-federal sponsors whose share of costs was being paid in installments. The secretary must take into account the average market yields of similar federal obligations, plus a premium of one-eighth of 1 percent. The provision did not apply to hydroelectric projects, which were covered under a series of other federal laws.

Harbor Development Projects

- Authorized the following deep-draft harbor development projects: (The numbers following individual project listings are the estimated total cost of the project in millions of dollars, followed in parentheses by the estimated first federal cost in millions of dollars. The amount authorized to be spent on a project could exceed the total estimated cost, because allowances were made for an escalation of expenses. The first federal cost was an estimate of the amount of federal funds or revenues that would need to be appropriated for a project, including amounts that non-federal interests might be required to pay back. Only projects over $10 million are listed.)

  Mobile Harbor, Ala.: $451 ($255)
  Mississippi River Ship Channel, Gulf to Baton Rouge, La.: $471 ($178)
  Texas City Channel, Texas: $200 ($130)
  Norfolk Harbor and Channels, Va.: $551 ($256)

- Authorized the following deep-draft harbor development projects, subject to a favorable report by the U.S. Army Corps of Engineers:

  Los Angeles and Long Beach Harbors, San Pedro Bay, Calif.: $620 ($310)
  New York Harbor and Adjacent Channels, N.Y. and N.J.: $326 ($156)

- Authorized the following shallow draft or general cargo harbor development projects:

  Kodiak Harbor, Alaska: $15 ($13.4)
  St. Paul Island, Alaska: $24.8 ($11.8)
  Oakland Outer Harbor, Calif.: $45.9 ($30.1)
  Oakland Inner Harbor, Calif.: $28.1 ($17.1)
  Richmond Harbor, Calif.: $43.8 ($26.5)
  Sacramento Deep Water Ship Channel, Calif.: $125 ($76)
  New Haven Harbor, Conn.: $26.5 ($19)
  Palm Beach Harbor, Fla. (annual maintenance cost of $86,000)
  Manatee Harbor, Fla.: $16.4 ($9.5)
  Tampa Harbor, East Bay Channel, Fla.: ($471,000 average annual cost)
  Savannah Harbor, Ga.: $14.7 ($7.1)
  Grand Haven Harbor, Mich.: $17.6 ($10.3)
  Monroe Harbor, Mich.: $142 ($55.5)
  Duluth-Superior, Minn. and Wis.: $12.5 ($6.71)
  Pascagoula Harbor, Miss.: $59.1 ($35.5)
  Gulfport Harbor, Miss.: $81.7 ($61.1)
  Portsmouth Harbor and Piscataqua River, N.H.: $22.2 ($16.7)
  Kill Van Kull, N.Y. and N.J.: $325 ($167)
  Cleveland Harbor, Ohio: $36 ($27)
  Charleston Harbor, S.C.: $88.5 ($58.2)
  Brazos Island Harbor, Texas-Brownsville Channel: $31.9 ($22.7)
  Blair and Sitcum Waterways, Tacoma Harbor, Wash.: $38.2 ($26.2)
  Grays Harbor, Wash.: $95.7 ($63.1)
  East, West and Duwamish Waterways, Wash.: $60.2 ($30.3)
  Saipan Harbor, Commonwealth of the Northern Mariana Islands: $14 (not available)
  San Juan Harbor, Puerto Rico: $72.3 ($52.7)

- Authorized the following shallow draft or general cargo harbor development projects, subject to a favorable report by the Corps of Engineers:

  Fresh Kills in Carteret, N.J.: $26 ($19.5)
  Arthur Kill, N.Y. and N.J.: $42.6 ($27.5)
  New York Harbor and Adjacent Channels, N.Y. and N.J.: $45.7 ($32.3)

Inland Waterways

- Established an Inland Waterway Users Board, consisting of 11 members named by the secretary of the Army, representing waterway user and shipper interests from various regions, to make recommendations on priorities for construction and rehabilitation of inland waterways and on spending for that purpose.
- Authorized improvements at the following inland waterway projects:

  Oliver Locks and Dam Replacement, Black Warrior-Tombigbee River, Ala.: $150 ($150)
  Disposition of Locks and Dams 5 through 14, Kentucky River, Ky.: (no construction costs authorized)
  Gallipolis Locks and Dam Replacement, Ohio River, Ohio and W.Va.: $285 ($285)
  New lock, Bonneville Lock and Dam, Columbia River and Tributaries, Ore. and Wash.: $191 ($191)
  Lock and Dam 7 Replacement, Monongahela River, Pa.: $123 ($123)
  Lock and Dam 8 Replacement, Monongahela River, Pa.: $82.9 ($82.9)
  Second lock, Locks and Dam 26, Mississippi River, Alton, Ill., and Mo. $220 ($200)

- Authorized the following inland waterway project, subject to a favorable report by the Corps of Engineers:

  Winfield Locks and Dam, Kanawha River, W.Va.: $153 ($153)

Flood Control

- Required local sponsors of all flood control projects authorized in the bill to agree to comply with applicable federal flood plain management and flood insurance programs.
- Redefined terms in existing law to make flood damages caused by groundwater eligible for federal flood protection aid.
- Authorized the following flood control projects:

  Village Creek, Jefferson Co., Ala.: $31.6 ($23.6)
  Threemile Creek, Mobile, Ala.: $19.1 ($13.4)
  Little Colorado River, Holbrook, Ariz.: $11.9 ($8.94)
  Eight Mile Creek, Paragould, Ark.: $16.1 ($11.2)

Fourche Bayou Basin, Little Rock, Ark.: $33.4 ($25.1)
Helena and Vicinity, Ark.: $15 ($11.2)
West Memphis and Vicinity, Ark.: $21.9 ($15.4)
Cache Creek Basin, Calif.: $28.5 ($19)
Redbank and Fancher Creeks, Calif.: $84.6 ($64.9)
Santa Ana River Mainstem (including Santiago Creek), Calif.: $1,090 ($809)
Metropolitan Denver and South Platte River and Tributaries, Colo., Wyo. and Neb.: $10.8 ($8.1)
Oates Creek, Ga.: $13.7 ($9.6)
Rock River, Rockford and Vicinity, Ill.: $31.3 ($23.5)
South Quincy Drainage and Levee District, Ill.: $11.9 ($8.9)
North Branch of Chicago River, Ill.: $22.7 ($15)
O'Hare System of the Chicago Underflow Plan, Ill.: $18.4 ($14.8)
Little Calumet River, Ind.: $87.1 ($65.3)
Little Calumet River Basin (Cady Marsh Ditch), Ind.: $11.2 ($6.6)
Perry Creek, Iowa: $44.6 ($31.2)
Des Moines River Basin, Iowa and Minn.: $15.2 ($10.9)
Upper Little Arkansas River Watershed, Kan.: $12.4 ($9.3)
Arkansas City, Kan.: $14.5 ($10.88)
Bushley Bayou, La.: $45.7 ($32.8)
Louisiana State Penitentiary Levee, Mississippi River, La.: $23.4 ($17.6)
Quincy Coastal Streams, Mass.: $24.7 ($20.6)
South Fork Zumbro River Watershed, Rochester, Minn.: $61.5 ($46)
Sowashee Creek, Meridian, Miss.: $17.5 ($12.3)
Maline Creek, Mo.: $62.9 ($43.7)
St. Johns Bayou and New Madrid Floodway, Mo.: $112 ($78.5)
Ste. Genevieve, Mo.: $34.4 ($25.8)
Brush Creek and Tributaries, Mo. and Kan.: $16.1 ($12.1)
Cape Girardeau, Mo.: $25.1 ($18.7)
Rahway River and Van Winkles Brook, Springfield, N.J.: $17.5 ($12.5)
Robinson's Branch, Rahway River, at Clark, Scotch Plains and Rahway, N.J.: $26.6 ($20)
Green Brook Subbasin, Raritan River Basin, N.J.: $203 ($151)
Molly Ann's Brook, N.J.: $21.6 ($16.2)
Lower Saddle River, N.J.: $36.5 ($25.8)
Middle Rio Grande Flood Protection, Bernalillo to Belen, N.M.: $44.9 ($33.7)
Mamaroneck, Sheldrake and Byram River Basins, N.Y. and Conn. (including flood protection for the town of Mamaroneck): $68.5 ($51.4)
Sugar Creek Basin, N.C. and S.C.: $29.7 ($19.5)
Sheyenne River, N.D.: $56.3 ($39.5)
Park River, Grafton, N.D.: $19.1 ($14.3)
Scioto River at North Chillicothe, Ohio: $10.7 ($8.08)
Miami River, Fairfield, Ohio: $14.4 ($9.4)
Mingo Creek, Tulsa, Okla.: $134 ($94)
Fry Creeks, Okla.: $13.2 ($9.4)
Harrisburg, Pa.: $133 ($99.8)
Lock Haven, Pa.: $82.2 ($61.7)
Wyoming Valley, Pa.: $241 ($181)
Nonconnah Creek and Johns Creek, Tenn. and Miss.: $28 ($19.5)
Boggy Creek, Austin, Texas: $24 ($16.5)
Buffalo Bayou and Tributaries (Upper White Oak Bayou), Texas: $92.1 ($69.1)
Lake Wichita, Holliday Creek, Texas: $39 ($27.3)
Lower Rio Grande Basin, Texas: $196 ($137)
Sims Bayou, Texas: $126 ($94.7)
James River Basin, Richmond, Va.: $91.8 ($68.9)
Roanoke River Upper Basin, Va.: $21 ($12.6)
Chehallis River at South Aberdeen and Cosmopolis, Wash.: $22.4 ($16.8)
Chehallis River and Tributaries, Centralia, Wash.: $19.9 ($15)
Island Creek Basin, Logan, W.Va.: $86 ($62.2)
Rio Puerto Nuevo, Puerto Rico: $234 ($151)
Pearl River Basin (including Carthage, Jackson, Monticello, Columbia and Leake County), Miss.: $80.1 ($56.07)
Tony's Creek and Marine Creek, Tarrant County, Texas: $20 ($15)

• Authorized the following flood control projects, subject to a favorable report from the Corps of Engineers:

Guadalupe River, San Jose, Calif.: $32.6 ($22.8)
Muscatine Island Levee District and Muscatine-Louisa County Drainage District No. 13, Iowa: $14.4 ($10.5)
Pearl River Basin, St. Tammany Parish, La.: $33.3 ($25)
West Bank Hurricane Protection Levee, Jefferson Parish, La.: $61.5 ($40)
James River, S.D.: $20 ($15)

Shoreline Protection

• Authorized the following projects for shoreline protection:

Panama City Beaches, Fla.: $48.5 ($22.8)
St. Johns County, Fla.: $18.2 ($11.1)
Indian River County, Fla.: $11.1 ($6.8)
North of Haulover Beach Park, Dade County, Fla.: $21.6 ($12)
Sarasota County, Fla.: $30.1 ($17.4)
Atlantic Coast (Ocean City), Md., and Assateague Island, Va.: $58.2 ($26.7)
Rockaway Inlet to Norton Point (New York City), N.Y.: $22.5 ($11.9)
Hereford Inlet to Cape May Canal, Delaware Bay, N.J.: $177 ($104)
Maumee Bay (southeast shore of Maumee Bay State Park), Lake Erie, Ohio: $15.9 ($7.95)
Presque Isle Peninsula, Erie, Pa.: $34.8 ($18.9)
Virginia Beach, Va.: $42.4 ($27.6)

• Authorized the following shoreline protection projects, pending a favorable report by the Corps of Engineers:

Pinellas County, Fla.: $52.6 ($32.7)
Illinois Beach State Park, Ill.: $13.4 ($9.39)

Other Projects

• Authorized the following other projects for various water resources conservation and development purposes:

Passaic, Pompton, Pequannock and Ramapo Rivers and tributaries, N.J. Clearing, snagging and channel rectification: $33.3 ($25)
Passaic River, near Beatties Dam in Little Falls, N.J. Flood control: $20 ($15)
Atlantic coast, Barnegat Inlet to Longport, N.J. Beach erosion control, navigation and storm protection: $106.29 ($59.505)
Warrior River, Fort Toulouse National Historic Landmark and Taskigi Indian Mound, Ala. Erosion con-

trol: $16 ($12)

Tennessee-Tombigbee Waterway, Ala. and Miss. Acquisition of 88,000 acres to mitigate wildlife losses: $60.2 (not available)

Bethel, Alaska. Bank stabilization: $19.4 ($14.6)

Helena Harbor, Phillips County, Ark. Navigation and mitigation of fish and wildlife habitat: $59 ($35.8)

White River Navigation to Batesville, Ark. Navigation and mitigation of habitat of the Fat Pocketbook Pearly Mussel and other benefits to aquatic habitat: $29.3 ($20.5)

Richard B. Russell Dam and Lake, Savannah River, Ga. and S.C. Mitigation of fish and wildlife losses: $20.2 ($20.15)

Metropolitan Atlanta area, Ga. Re-regulating dam for water supply on the Chattahoochee River downstream of Buford Dam and additional measures: $28 ($7)

Atchafalaya Basin Floodway System, La. Flood control, with fish and wildlife benefits: $250 ($223)

Yazoo Backwater Area, Miss. Mitigation of fish and wildlife losses: $17.7 ($17.7)

Greenville Harbor, Miss. Navigation: $43.7 ($28)

Vicksburg Harbor, Miss. Navigation: $79.2 ($55.9)

St. Louis Harbor, Mo. and Ill. Navigation: $31 ($10.4)

Project for mitigation of fish and wildlife losses, Mo. River Bank Stabilization and Navigation Project, Mo., Kan., Iowa and Neb.: $51.9 ($51.9)

Olcott Harbor, N.Y. Navigation, study and possible additional measures to mitigate fish and wildlife effects: $12.6 ($6.3)

Muddy Boggy Creek, Parker Lake, Okla. Flood control and water supply: $46 ($3.41)

Fort Gibson Lake, Okla.: $24.6 ($24.6)

Blue River Lake, Willamette River Basin, Ore. Hydroelectric power: $30.7 ($30.7)

Big River Reservoir, R.I. Flood control, including fish and wildlife mitigation and study: $86.7 ($8.36)

Gregory County, S.D. Hydroelectric pumped storage, stages I and II, and additional multipurpose water supply and irrigation features: $1,390 ($1,390)

Memphis Harbor, Memphis, Tenn. Navigation, including fish and wildlife mitigation: $110 ($38.4)

Cooper Lake and Channels, Texas. Fish and wildlife mitigation. $14.8 ($8.16)

McNary Lock and Dam, Columbia River, Wash. and Ore. Second Powerhouse, Phase I, general design: $667 ($667)

Bush River Watershed, Va. Runoff and erosion control (project carried out by Soil Conservation Service): $13.7 ($13.7)

Cottonwood-Walnut Creek Watershed, N.M. Runoff and erosion control (project carried out by Soil Conservation Service): $28.063 ($28.063)

Seal Beach Naval Weapons Station at Sunset Beach Harbor, Bolsa Chica Bay, Calif.: $89.6 ($44.8)

- Authorized the following projects pending a favorable report by the Corps of Engineers:

Rillito River, Tucson, Ariz. Bank erosion control: $26 ($19.5)

Wailua Falls, Wailua River, Kauai, Hawaii. Hydroelectric power: $13.5 ($13.5)

Trinity River, Texas. Fish and wildlife mitigation. $10.4 ($10)

Yazoo River, Miss. Dredging and other measures: $200,000 annually.

Miscellaneous

- Required the corps to undertake any necessary mitigation of fish and wildlife losses before or during construction of any newly authorized projects on which construction had not already started.
- Authorized the corps to undertake fish and wildlife mitigation measures for any of its projects, whether finished, under construction or not started yet. The bill prohibited condemnation by the corps as a way of acquiring interests in land when construction was at least 10 percent complete as of enactment, or as a way of acquiring any water rights. (Congress, however, could approve such condemnations upon corps recommendation.) The bill set a limit of $30 million per year on funds the corps could obligate under this authority (and a limit per project of $7.5 million or 10 percent of project cost).
- Established a new federal program to promote development of state dam safety programs. Annual appropriations of $13 million were authorized during fiscal 1988-92 for matching grants to states for up to 50 percent of the costs of carrying out dam safety programs. The bill included criteria the states must meet to qualify for the grants. It established a national Dam Safety Review Board to review state programs. It authorized additional appropriations of $500,000 annually for 1988-92 for federal training of state dam safety inspectors, $2 million annually for research on inspection methods and safety monitoring devices, and $500,000 for the corps to update an inventory of dams.
- Authorized modifications of approximately 71 previously authorized projects.
- Deauthorized approximately 300 projects that had been authorized by Congress in previous years but never built. The bill also provided for automatic deauthorization of any project authorized in the bill, if no funds had been obligated for its construction after five years. It also required the corps to submit a list of authorized but unbuilt projects (or separable elements) for which no funds had been obligated in 10 years.
- Set a timetable and procedures for the corps to follow in deciding on those projects that the bill authorized "subject to a favorable report." The corps must report and the secretary of the Army must comment on one-third of them in each of the first three years after enactment. If the corps had not acted by then, the project was considered authorized. If a proposed project's benefits did not exceed its costs, the non-federal sponsors must agree to pay, during construction, the difference necessary to ensure that the rest of the project had a favorable benefit/cost ratio.
- Required the corps, in evaluating a project, to include both the quantifiable and the unquantifiable costs and benefits, and to consider benefits from national and some regional economic development, environmental quality, social well-being, prevention of the loss of life and the preservation of cultural and historic values.
- Authorized non-federal interests to undertake study and construction of projects on their own, without congressional authorization, as long as they obtained all necessary federal and state permits. Non-federal interests could pay the Corps of Engineers to do the studies. They were authorized to go ahead and build the project once the corps had finished the studies. The corps was authorized to reimburse non-federal entities for the federal share of such a project if the corps found the project to be economically justified and environmentally acceptable and approved of the plans before construction starts and the non-federal

entities entered into a cost-sharing agreement.

- Authorized non-federal interests to levy port or harbor dues (in the form of tonnage duties or fees) on vessels or cargoes to finance the non-federal share of construction, operation and maintenance costs and to finance emergency services. Such fees could be imposed only for use of facilities that were complete. Fees to pay for the cost of making a project deeper could not be imposed on vessels not needing the deeper draft. The bill specified a number of requirements that local port authorities must meet in collecting such fees. They included limitations on which parties must pay the fee and how it was to be formulated, a public notice and hearing process before the fee was levied, filing of the fee schedule with the Federal Maritime Commission for public inspection, audit by the comptroller general, provisions for court review and provisions for enforcement in case of non-compliance by a vessel operator.
- Authorized the Corps of Engineers to make grants to non-federal entities for emergency services in a harbor, totaling up to $5 million annually for fiscal 1987-92. ▮

Congress Strengthens Safe Drinking Water Act

Congress in 1986 strengthened public health protections for the nation's drinking water as part of a five-year reauthorization of the 1974 Safe Drinking Water Act.

The reauthorization (S 124 — PL 99-339) cleared May 21 when the Senate adopted the conference report on the measure by a 94-0 vote. The House had approved the conference compromise May 13, 382-21. *(Senate vote 106, p. 20-S; House vote 110, p. 34-H)*

The Senate originally passed the bill May 16, 1985, and the House passed its own version (HR 1650) a month later. But conferees did not sit down to resolve their differences until Jan. 30, 1986. The conference report (H Rept 99-575) was filed May 5. *(Senate, House action, 1985 Almanac p. 207)*

As cleared, the bill forced the Environmental Protection Agency (EPA) to set national standards limiting contaminants in water supplies and to see that states used the "best available technology" to meet the standards.

The bill also required protection of underground water supplies, provided technical assistance to small water systems and established criminal penalties for anyone who willfully tampered with water supplies.

The groundwater provisions were the most controversial. The Reagan administration opposed new federal requirements on groundwater, traditionally a state concern. There were also objections from members representing Western states, where access to groundwater often made the difference between economic life and death.

The Senate version of the bill contained no groundwater provisions, but the House bill required states to draw up plans for protecting underground drinking water sources and to submit them to EPA for approval. Conferees compromised on the issue by restricting the area affected by the planning requirement.

Despite administration opposition to the groundwater provisions and to new deadlines for regulating contaminants, President Reagan signed the bill June 19.

Supporters of S 124 described it as a major environmental achievement. Dennis E. Eckart, D-Ohio, said the groundwater provisions would help deal with "the most fundamental environmental problem of the decade."

About half of the country gets its drinking water from underground sources. Once groundwater is contaminated, it is difficult to clean up because it must be pumped out of the ground before it can be treated.

The bill required EPA to set standards limiting 83 contaminants in drinking water within three years. Since enactment of the Safe Drinking Water Act (PL 93-523) in 1974, EPA had regulated only about two dozen of more than 600 contaminants found in drinking water. *(1974 act, Congress and the Nation Vol. IV, p. 293)*

Although both House and Senate bills provided four-year reauthorizations of the 1974 act, conferees approved a five-year reauthorization with a funding ceiling that increased in steps from $138 million in fiscal 1986 to $179 million in 1990. Funding authorization had expired in 1982, but the program had been kept alive through annual appropriations.

The conferees added one set of provisions not in either of the bills originally passed by the House and Senate. The provisions banned lead in pipes or solder in most drinking water systems. The provisions would apply to homes and commercial establishments if they were hooked up to public water systems. Existing pipes could be left in place; the ban applied only to installation or repairs.

Provisions

As signed into law June 19, S 124 (PL 99-339):

- Required EPA to set maximum contaminant level (MCL) goals. These standards were to be set at levels that would cause no adverse health effects and that allowed an adequate margin of safety.
- Required EPA to set national primary drinking water regulations (the enforceable standards) as close to the MCL goal as was feasible, taking costs into account and using the best available water treatment technology under field conditions.
- Required EPA to set MCL goals and issue primary regulations for 83 contaminants it had already listed in the *Federal Register* (Vol. 47, p. 9352; Vol. 44, p. 45502). EPA would have to regulate nine of them within a year of enactment, another 40 within two years, and the rest within three years. However, EPA would have the option of substituting up to seven other contaminants for those on the list if the agency found that doing so would achieve greater health protection.
- Declared that granular activated carbon was feasible as one "best available technology" for removing synthetic organic chemicals. Other technology of equal effectiveness also could be used.
- Required EPA, within 18 months of enactment, to issue regulations specifying when filtration was required for systems using surface water.
- Required EPA, within 36 months of enactment, to issue regulations requiring disinfection of public drinking water and specifying conditions under which variances would be allowed.

• Allowed EPA to forgo an MCL and simply require a treatment technique if it found that measuring the contaminant was not economically or technically feasible.

• Required EPA to publish a priority list of contaminants found in public drinking water systems that might harm human health. EPA would have to publish the list by Jan. 1, 1988, and every three years after that. The agency would have to propose regulations for 25 of the contaminants on that list within 24 months of its publication.

• Required EPA to issue, within 18 months of enactment, regulations requiring public water systems to test for contaminants not yet regulated by the federal government. The regulations would establish the frequency of testing, which could vary according to the number of persons served, the source of supply, and the contaminants likely to be found. After the rules were issued, public systems would have to test their water at least once every five years.

• Required EPA to list the unregulated contaminants to be monitored. States to which EPA had delegated enforcement authority could delete contaminants from the list if EPA approved. States could add to the list without EPA approval.

• Allowed small systems (those supplying less than 150 service connections) to meet the monitoring requirement simply by submitting a water sample to the state or EPA, or allowing them to take their own sample.

• Added a new enforcement mechanism, the administrative order, that EPA could use in minor cases instead of going to court to force a water system to comply with regulations. EPA would be able to assess penalties of up to $5,000 for failure to comply with an administrative order.

• Removed EPA's option under previous law to ignore violations of primary health-based regulations, or to allow states to ignore them. When EPA had delegated enforcement authority to a state, and a violation went on for 30 days without state action, EPA would have to bring a civil action or issue an administrative order for compliance. When the state did not have enforcement authority, EPA was required to act immediately upon finding a violation.

• Increased the maximum civil penalty courts could impose for violation of drinking water regulations from $5,000 to $25,000 per day.

• Removed an existing requirement that the government show a violation to be "willful" before civil penalties could be imposed.

• Required EPA to revise rules on how public water systems must notify their customers when they violated requirements for water purity or water testing. For violations EPA believed threatened health, notice must be given within 14 days. When the violation did not involve an MCL, notice must be given every three months to one year, depending on its seriousness.

• Required water systems notifying their customers of violations to use newspapers, radio, television or individual mailings. Notification must include a clear explanation of the violation, any possible harm to health, steps being taken to correct it and any need to use alternative water supplies.

• Tightened conditions under which states with enforcement authority could grant variances to primary drinking water regulations. Such states could grant variances only to systems that, because of the raw water sources available to them, could not comply with the regulations even when using the best available technology. But EPA's rulings as to the best technology available must take into account the size of the system and the costs of compliance.

• Tightened deadlines for compliance by water systems exempted from health-based regulations because of economic hardship. Previous law allowed EPA or the state to wait for a year after granting an exemption before setting a schedule for compliance. The bill required the schedule to be set when the exemption was granted. Systems would have to comply with existing regulations within one year of enactment. Systems would have to comply with new regulations within one year of issuance. (Previous law gave them seven years.) EPA could extend that deadline for another three years if a water system showed it was unable to meet requirements.

• Made it a federal offense to "tamper" with a public water system — that is, to introduce a contaminant into the system or otherwise interfere with its operation with the intent of harming persons. The bill set maximum criminal penalties of five years in jail and a $50,000 fine and a maximum civil fine of $50,000.

• Prohibited the use of pipes, solder and fluxes containing lead in the installation or repair of public water systems or plumbing systems connected to them. Required the states to carry out the ban through local plumbing codes or other means within two years of enactment. Public water systems would have to provide customers with information on health hazards caused by lead and ways to reduce them. New housing would not be eligible for guaranteed or insured mortgages from the Veterans Administration or the Department of Housing and Urban Development unless it was in compliance.

• Authorized $10 million annually during fiscal 1987-91 for technical assistance to small public water systems so they could comply with EPA regulations.

• Increased EPA's authority to enforce regulations for controlling underground injection of wastes that could contaminate groundwater. The bill allowed EPA to use two laws to enforce the ban on injection of hazardous or radioactive wastes above an underground drinking water source (class IV wells). It required EPA to issue rules within 18 months for monitoring of wells injecting wastes below a drinking water source (class II wells). It required EPA to begin enforcement action within 30 days of a violation if a state did not do so.

The bill raised maximum civil penalties from $5,000 to $25,000 per day, raised top penalties for willful violations from $10,000 to $50,000 per day, and added new authority for prison terms. It gave EPA new authority to issue administrative orders and to impose administrative fines up to $10,000 per day. (Oil or gas well operators, however, would face a lower ceiling of $5,000 per day.) It set the ceiling on all administrative fines at $125,000.

• Required each state to develop a program for protecting areas around wells supplying public drinking water systems from contamination that could harm health. EPA could provide grants to a state for 50 to 90 percent of program development and implementation costs. The bill authorized $20 million annually in fiscal 1987-88 and $35 million annually in 1989-91 for these grants.

• Gave states three years to develop these groundwater programs and submit them to EPA. Programs would be considered adequate unless EPA rejected them within nine months. States would be expected to implement their programs within two years after submitting them. EPA would have to reject a state's program if it did not meet requirements in the bill for protecting water systems.

• Required state wellhead protection to spell out responsibilities of state and local governments and water systems, to define wellhead areas under EPA technical guidance, to identify possible contamination, to describe a protection program and to meet other requirements.

- Authorized EPA to give grants of up to 50 percent of costs for demonstration programs to protect aquifers that were a community's "sole source" of drinking water. For those grants, the bill authorized $10 million in fiscal 1987, $15 million in 1988, and $17.5 million annually during 1989-91.
- Authorized appropriations for programs already in existence. For emergency federal technical assistance and grants, the bill authorized $7.65 million annually in 1987-88 and $8.02 million annually during 1989-91. For research technical assistance, information and training, it authorized $35.6 million annually during 1987-88 and $38.02 million during 1989-91.

For grants to states for supervision of public water systems, it authorized $37.2 million annually during 1987-88 and $40.15 million during 1989-91. For grants to support state programs for underground injection control, it authorized $19.7 million annually during 1987-88 and $20.85 million during 1989-91. ▮

Reagan Vetoes $20 Billion Clean Water Bill

President Reagan Nov. 6 pocket-vetoed a water pollution control bill (S 1128) that had been approved unanimously by both houses in the final days of the 1986 session.

The president was able to make the veto stick only because Congress had adjourned for the year. Had the House and Senate been able to vote on the veto, the two-thirds majority required for an override seemed assured.

Early in 1987, the 100th Congress overrode a second Reagan veto and a clean water bill was enacted into law.

In a memorandum explaining his 1986 pocket veto, Reagan said the legislation cost too much. "This administration remains committed to the act's objectives," Reagan stated. "Unfortunately, this bill so far exceeds acceptable levels of intended budgetary commitments that I must withhold my approval." *(Text, p. 35-D)*

At issue was $18 billion in federal money to help local governments build sewage treatment plants over fiscal 1987-94. The bill, containing $20 billion in all, amended and reauthorized the Clean Water Act, which funded sewer construction and required cities and industries to get a permit and clean up their wastewater before discharging it into lakes and streams. Although it had been amended many times, the law took its existing form in 1972 (PL 92-500) and underwent its last major overhaul in 1977 (PL 95-217). *(1977 Almanac p. 697)*

The Money Issue

In his fiscal 1986 budget, Reagan proposed terminating existing federal construction grants after spending $6 billion over fiscal 1986-89. The bill Congress sent him would have spent three times that in a longer phase-out, with direct federal grants gradually giving way to a state-run program of revolving loan funds for local governments. Federal grants would help get the funds started.

Congress had already scaled down the sewage plant construction program once at the behest of Reagan budget-cutters. PL 97-117, enacted in 1981, reduced the program's annual authorization from $5 billion to $2.4 billion. *(1981 Almanac p. 515)*

Other programs under the Clean Water Act had been carried out routinely without authorizations for several years, with funding provided in the annual appropriations bills.

The veto had little immediate effect because the sewer program had a $2 billion cushion of money to run on in fiscal 1987. Of that, some $800 million was carryover money from previous fiscal years. The fiscal 1987 omnibus appropriations measure (PL 99-500) appropriated another $1.2 billion to be available immediately, with an additional $1.2 billion subject to enactment of authorizing legislation (further Appropriations Committee action was also needed to release the funds).

Strong Support

The clean water measure pleased environmentalists by tightening some regulatory provisions of the law. At the same time, it extended for several years various unmet cleanup deadlines that had been imposed on the Environmental Protection Agency (EPA) and industry in the 1977 act.

The bill was politically popular not only as an environmental cleanup measure, but because it gave members of Congress a chance to send federal project dollars back to their home districts less than a month before the Nov. 4 elections.

The Senate originally passed its version of S 1128 in June 1985 and the House passed a similar measure (HR 8) the following month. *(1985 Almanac p. 204)*

Congress completed action on S 1128 Oct. 16, 1986, when the Senate adopted a conference report on the bill by a 96-0 vote. The House had adopted the conference report by a 408-0 vote Oct. 15. *(Senate vote 342, p. 56-S; House vote 434, p. 122-H)*

Because S 1128 did not reach the White House until Oct. 25, Reagan was spared the risk of a pre-election veto of the politically popular bill. The president has 10 days, excluding Sundays, in which to sign or veto a bill after he receives it. If Congress has adjourned, preventing return of the bill, the president can kill — or pocket veto — the measure by withholding his signature.

Conference Action

Conferees were appointed in 1985, but they did not meet until March 1986 and did not turn to the main issues until the final weeks of the session. Their report (H Rept 99-1004) was filed Oct. 15.

Highlights of conference action:

Sewer Funds

The House bill had authorized $21 billion for sewage treatment through 1994, while the Senate version authorized only $18 billion — the number conferees agreed on.

EPA Administrator Lee M. Thomas and other administration officials had threatened a presidential veto if Congress exceeded the administration's request for a final $6 billion in funding over 1986-89.

Conferees agreed to gradually shift the burden of financing sewers entirely to state and local governments, which under existing law paid less than half the construction costs. States paid all operating costs.

Federal funds increasingly would go to capitalize revolving loan funds administered by the states. Those funds, among other things, could lend money to a local government to build a sewage plant, and after the loan was repaid with interest, finance further projects.

For direct construction grants, the final bill authorized $2.4 billion annually for fiscal 1986-88 and $1.2 billion annually for 1989-90. No money would go to the revolving loan funds in fiscal 1986-88. After that, federal funding for the loan funds would increase from $1.2 billion annually in fiscal 1989-90 to a maximum of $2.4 billion in 1991. Then it would taper down to $1.8 billion in 1992, $1.2 billion in 1993 and finally $600 million in 1994.

State Allocations

A big difference between the House and Senate bills was the formula for dividing the fixed pot of federal sewer grant money among the states. The House bill kept the existing allocation formula while the Senate revised it.

The formula was the subject of a bitter floor fight in 1985, when Sun Belt senators claimed the previous formula shorted their states because it ignored their growth since 1970. Northern, Eastern and California senators protested that the revisions robbed them, and they eventually won some concessions.

Conferees settled the issue with little debate, using the House formula based on the old law, but giving Texas an additional $18 million per year, with the funds obtained by reducing the allocation to some other states.

Geographic rivalries also were cooled by the conference agreement, which funded special programs dealing with regionally significant bodies of water, such as the Great Lakes and Chesapeake Bay, or types of water bodies, such as estuaries or lakes.

Pollution Controls

Other major pollution control provisions included an authorization of $400 million over the life of the bill to help control so-called "non-point source" pollution, which is caused by diffuse runoff from farm land, construction sites or city streets.

States would have to come up with plans for controlling such pollution, but there would be no mandatory controls as there were for discharges from point sources, such as pipes.

The bill also set up a new program for attacking "toxic hot spots" — water bodies that still failed to meet standards after cities and industries had installed the "best available" cleanup technology that existing law required.

It kept the existing law's requirement that discharge permits be renewed and updated every five years — rather than 10 years, as the House bill would have mandated. ▮

Acid Rain Bill Stalls

Legislation to reduce acid rain pollution went further in 1986 than it ever had before, but still fell far short of enactment.

President Reagan gave the effort a boost on March 19 when he softened his long-held opposition to controls and called for a $5 billion dollar joint Canadian-American program to reduce acid rain, which is caused by emissions of sulfur and nitrogen oxides — largely from coal-fired plants — that are changed chemically as they fall through the atmosphere back to earth.

The issue had traditionally split Congress along regional lines. Members from the Northeast, where acid rain was worst, favored strict controls, but members from the Midwest, the area that produced the pollution, were leery of the economic costs. *(Background, 1984 Almanac p. 339)*

Legislation designed to bridge the gap (HR 4567) was introduced in the House by a bipartisan coalition, led by Henry A. Waxman, D-Calif. The measure would have required a phased reduction in emissions, with states free to decide what method should be used to reach the new limits. To limit the financial burden in the Midwest, a national fee would have been imposed on electricity.

Waxman's Energy Subcommittee on Health and the Environment approved the bill May 20 by a 16-9 margin, but it was bottled up in the full committee by Chairman John D. Dingell, D-Mich, and other opponents. Dingell objected to the bill on a number of grounds, including how it would affect the automobile industry.

A similar measure (S 2203) was introduced in the Senate, and Environment Committee Chairman Robert T. Stafford, R-Vt., said he would move it as soon as the House passed its bill, but that never happened.

Waxman and other acid rain control supporters vowed to try again in the 100th Congress and predicted a better chance of passage with Democrats controlling both chambers. But first they had to win over Senate Majority Leader Robert C. Byrd, D-W.Va., who was concerned about the bill's impact on his state's coal industry. ▮

Wilderness Protection

In the closing weeks of the session Congress approved a number of environmental measures aimed at preserving wilderness and park areas and protecting plant and animal life. Following is a summary of major action.

Georgia Wilderness

The Senate Oct. 9 cleared a bill (HR 5496 — PL 99-555) more than doubling the amount of federal wilderness in Georgia. The House passed the measure (H Rept 99-898, Part I) Sept. 30.

The bill set aside five areas totaling 42,258 acres, bringing the total national forest area in the state protected from development to 74,746 acres. The five were all in the Chattahoochee National Forest: Raven Cliffs Wilderness (8,562 acres), Brasstown Wilderness (11,405 acres), Tray Mountain Wilderness (9,702 acres), Rich Mountain Wilderness (9,649 acres) and an addition (2,940 acres) to the Cohutta Wilderness. The bill was supported by the Reagan administration and the Georgia delegation.

Nebraska Wilderness

Congress completed action Oct. 3 on a Nebraska wilderness bill (S 816 — PL 99-504). The bill cleared when the Senate by voice vote accepted a compromise version (H Rept 99-854, Part I) passed by the House Sept. 23. The Senate originally passed its version (S Rept 99-122) Aug. 1, 1985.

The measure established an 8,100-acre Soldier Creek National Wilderness and a 6,600-acre Pine Ridge recreation area, both in the Nebraska National Forest.

Tennessee Wilderness

A Tennessee wilderness bill (HR 5166 — PL 99-490) was cleared by the Senate Oct. 3. It (H Rept 99-853, Part I) was approved by the House Sept. 22.

The bill established six wilderness areas totaling 33,735 acres in the Cherokee National Forest. They were the Pond Mountain Wilderness Addition (6,665 acres), the Big Laurel Branch Wilderness (6,251 acres), the Unaka Mountain Wilderness (4,700 acres), the Sampson Mountain Wilderness (8,319 acres), the Little Frog Mountain Wilderness (4,800 acres) and the Big Frog Wilderness Extension (3,000 acres).

Sipsey Wilderness Bill Fails

The House Sept. 29 by voice vote passed a bill (HR 5508 — H Rept 99-899, Part I) to add 15,900 acres of national forest land to the existing Sipsey Wilderness in Alabama. The Senate did not act on the bill, which also would have added approximately 60 miles of the Sipsey River to the National Wild and Scenic Rivers System.

The House twice before had passed larger Sipsey Wilderness bills only to have them die in the Senate. House bills in 1982 and 1983 set aside 29,500 acres. The administration had recommended that 10,700 acres be added to the Sipsey Wilderness.

Great Basin Park

The Senate Oct. 9 cleared a bill (S 2506 — PL 99-565) to establish a 44,000-acre Great Basin National Park in easternmost Nevada. The measure (S Rept 99-458), which passed the House Oct. 6, was supported by the administration and Nevada's two Republican senators, Paul Laxalt and Chic Hecht.

The park to be established was smaller than one in a bill (HR 3302 — H Rept 99-427) passed April 30 by the House. That bill would have created a 129,000-acre park adjoined by a 45,000-acre preserve, as well as 592,000 acres of national forest wilderness. It was sponsored by Harry Reid, D-Nev., a candidate for that state's Senate seat.

Endangered Plants and Animals

The House Oct. 6 cleared a bill (S 1917 — PL 99-529) authorizing various special foreign aid programs and requiring steps aimed at slowing the pace at which plant and animal species were becoming extinct. Those provisions were first introduced as separate bills, but were later attached to S 1917, which the Senate approved Oct. 3.

In a purely procedural move intended to clarify the legislative history, the two bills were passed earlier by the Senate as separate measures.

On Sept. 29 the Senate approved HR 2958 (S Rept 99-482, H Rept 99-478) amending the Foreign Assistance Act of 1961, specifically sections added by the International Environmental Protection Act of 1983. The bill added to that law's existing provisions for protecting biological diversity in developing countries. It required the Agency for International Development (AID), in drawing up plans for boosting development in those countries, to take a number of environmental considerations into account. The Senate bill amended HR 2958 as originally passed by the House June 3.

On Sept. 30 the Senate passed HR 2957 (S Rept 99-481, H Rept 99-476), which directed the president and AID to give high priority, in giving aid to developing countries, to encouraging conservation of tropical forests. It directed the executive branch to deny aid for any logging unless it was done in an environmentally sound manner.

River Fish Stocks

The Senate Oct. 3 cleared a bill (HR 4712 — PL 99-552) aimed at restoring salmon and steelhead fish stocks in the Klamath and Trinity River basins in northern California. The House passed HR 4712 (H Rept 99-894, Part I) Sept. 30.

The bill authorized federal appropriations of $21 million over the next 20 years. States and other non-federal entities would have to match the federal money with an equal amount.

Stocks of salmon and steelhead in northern California, which were important to sport and commercial fishermen and Indian tribes, had dropped an estimated 80 percent in recent decades as a result of fishing and development, including construction of a federal dam.

The bill gave the secretary of the interior responsibility for developing a 20-year restoration program. To advise the secretary, it set up a Klamath River Basin Fisheries Task Force, representing sport and commercial fishermen, Indians, and state and local governments. It also set up a Klamath Fishery Management Council, similar in makeup, to offer non-binding recommendations on rules governing how many fish could be caught. The actual rules would be enforced under a cooperative agreement by the Interior Department and the California Department of Fish and Game. ▮

Wild and Scenic Rivers

Without much fanfare, Congress in 1986 enacted a wild and scenic rivers protection bill (HR 4350 — PL 99-590) that environmentalists hailed as a major step forward.

Under the National Wild and Scenic Rivers System Act of 1968 (PL 90-542), rivers named by Congress or the interior secretary were protected from commercialization, pollution or incompatible water resource development, including dams that would spoil their free flow. The federal government could also acquire land along their shores to prevent construction. *(Congress and the Nation Vol. II, p. 472)*

After a slow start in naming rivers for protection under the law, Congress in recent years had been adding to the system more rapidly. The 98th Congress added five new rivers in 1984. *(1984 Almanac p. 317)*

In HR 4350 and other smaller measures, Congress in 1986 named six new wild and scenic rivers, bringing the nation's total to 72. In addition, a number of other rivers were put under different forms of protection.

Named for wild and scenic status by the 99th Congress were segments of the Cache la Poudre River in Colorado, the Saline Bayou in Louisiana, Black Creek in Mississippi, the Klickitat River and White Salmon River in Washington and the Horsepasture River in North Carolina.

Named for study as possible wild and scenic rivers were segments of the Great Egg Harbor River in New Jersey, the Farmington River in Connecticut, and additional segments of the Klickitat and White Salmon rivers in Washington. They were protected while under study, a process that usually lasted two to five years.

Further protection came from bans on certain kinds of hydroelectric development on the 61 miles of the Henry's Fork of the Snake River in Idaho and on parts of several other Northwestern rivers.

The Henry's Fork ban was attached to another bill (S 426 — PL 99-495) that river conservationists considered a major accomplishment. That bill, which set rules for reissuing federal licenses for hydroelectric power projects, canceled much of the previous tilt in federal law favoring power development over river conservation. *(Hydroelectric power licenses, p. 142)*

The only major legislative floor battle over river protection came on Oct. 16, when the House debated a bill (HR 5705 — PL 99-663) to create a National Scenic Area along 85 miles of the Columbia River Gorge along the border between Oregon and Washington. Protection measures for other stream reaches in Oregon and Washington were included in that bill.

Omnibus Bill

HR 4350, which was signed by President Reagan Oct. 30, rolled up protection for several rivers into one legislative package. It was first passed by the House April 8 (H Rept 99-503). The Senate Sept. 12 approved its own version of the bill and on Oct. 8 the House added amendments to the Senate version. The Senate countered on Oct. 15 with additional amendments. House agreement to those amendments on Oct. 16 cleared the bill.

The rivers and streams protected by the bill were:

Black Creek. This was a "blackwater" stream that took its color from abundant organic matter. The low-lying channel, located within the DeSoto National Forest in Mississippi, meandered slowly through cypress, magnolia, various gum trees and bottomland hardwoods. Its wildlife included many waterfowl, turkey, black bear, the threatened American alligator and the red-cockaded woodpecker.

The U.S. Forest Service studied 41 miles of Black Creek and found that all of it qualified for designation as a wild and scenic river, but it recommended protection for only 21 miles (the length designated in the bill) because of conflicts with private landowners.

Saline Bayou. Popular for float trips, this Louisiana stream was characterized by a "placid moving flow, meandering route, murky water and moss-draped cypress trees," according to the House committee report. The diverse wildlife it supported included beaver, bobcat, grey fox, turkey, cormorant, wood duck and blue heron.

The bill designated as wild and scenic a 19-mile segment of the bayou from Saline Lake upstream to Kisatchie National Forest.

Cache la Poudre River. This was the largest stretch of undeveloped river east of the Rocky Mountains. It began at the Continental Divide in Rocky Mountain National Park and flowed eastward to the South Platte River through the Colorado cities of LaPorte, Fort Collins and Greeley.

In 1980, under President Jimmy Carter, the Interior Department recommended 83 miles of the upper part of the river for protection. In 1985 the Reagan administration reduced that to 62 miles. The final bill designated 75 miles.

Great Egg Harbor. Flowing through the New Jersey Pinelands National Reserve, this slow-moving, densely vegetated stream was considered one of the top canoe streams in the Mid-Atlantic area. It began in Berlin Township in Camden County and flowed south for 60 miles to Great Egg Harbor. Its entire length was to be studied for possible designation as a wild and scenic river, and protected while the study was under way.

Farmington River. The West Branch of the Farmington River, which began in Massachusetts, supported Connecticut's largest trout fishery and was part of the federal Atlantic Salmon Restoration Program. It also offered Class IV white water for canoeists and kayakers. Although the river ran through farm land, it also flowed through two state parks, five state forests and some remote natural areas.

An 18-mile segment would be studied by the Interior Department, with help from an advisory committee of 17 members appointed by the interior secretary.

Two California rivers that were included in the bill originally passed by the House were stripped from the final version. One was a 78-mile reach of the North Fork Kern River and the other was a 72.5-mile reach of the South Fork Kern River.

Horsepasture River Bill

The 99th Congress also added to the Wild and Scenic Rivers System a small stretch of the Horsepasture River, which tumbled down from the Blue Ridge Mountains in North Carolina.

The river was known for waterfalls, swimming holes and fishing holes. It came out of the Blue Ridge in rugged rocky gorges with high and steep walls, plunging 1,700 feet in four miles. That produced a whole series of cascades, the most spectacular being the 200-foot Rainbow Falls.

"For generations," James T. Broyhill, R-N.C., told the Senate, "the river has been a favorite of hikers, swimmers, fishermen, campers and picnickers." Fishermen went there for trout, and hunters for bear, among the many other species it supported.

In August 1984, the Federal Energy Regulatory Commission gave preliminary approval to an application by the Carrasan Power Co. to dam the river and divert its flow from certain waterfalls to a powerhouse.

Congress responded in the same year by naming the river for wild and scenic study — thus temporarily blocking further development. In 1985, Congress appropriated $1 million to buy 435 acres of private land along the river.

In 1986, the protection became permanent when President Reagan signed a bill (HR 2826 — PL 99-530) adding a 4.25-mile segment of the Horsepasture to the Wild and Scenic Rivers System. The House had passed the measure July 28 (H Rept 99-671), and the Senate followed suit Oct. 15.

Columbia Gorge Bill

The Columbia River Gorge bill (HR 5705) was cleared for the president's signature when the Senate passed it Oct. 17. He signed it reluctantly Nov. 17 (PL 99-663).

As the Columbia River, which defined much of the border between Oregon and Washington states, cut through the Cascade Mountains, it formed giant cliffs. The gorge, 60 to 70 miles long, was explored by Lewis and Clark in 1805-06. Indians had hunted and fished there for thousands of years before that.

The gorge was made up of a unique series of ecosystems ranging from sagebrush and grasslands in the East to rain forest in the West. Not only did it support salmon and steelhead fisheries, but some 800 plant species. Of these, 58 were considered rare or endangered and nine were found only within the gorge.

At the same time, the Columbia River was one of the hardest working rivers in the United States. It supported hydropower, navigation and industrial development, as well as a busy tourist industry.

The bill that emerged in 1986, after more than six years of negotiations, set up a National Scenic Area along the gorge between the Sandy River and the Deschutes River, taking in roughly 250,000 acres. That would afford some protection, but not as much as if the area had been put in one of the other federal land categories — such as wild and scenic rivers or national parks.

The problem of conservation in the gorge was especially complicated. Within its range lived some 41,000 people, mostly in 13 urban areas totaling some 19,000 acres. There were nearly 50 units of local government.

The bill as it cleared Congress had broad support from both Oregon and Washington. Washington's Democratic governor, Booth Gardner, and Oregon's Republican governor, Victor G. Atiyeh, favored the bill, as did the four Republican senators from the two states. All eight members of Washington's House delegation supported it, and of the five members from Oregon, only Robert F. Smith and Denny Smith, both Republicans, opposed it.

"This is federal land use control," said Robert Smith, who led the opposition. "I believe in local control."

The Justice Department had objected to parts of the bill on the grounds that it amounted to taking over private property. But the arguments of Republican senators persuaded Reagan to sign the bill despite "grave doubts as to the constitutionality" of certain parts.

Bitter feelings by opponents were stirred by the way the rule (H Res 596) providing for its House floor consideration was approved by the Rules Committee.

The panel had first met late in the afternoon of Oct. 15, when it rejected the pleas of the bill's sponsors for a closed rule. But the committee met again near midnight that same evening and approved a rule that allowed only three amendments — denying the chance for delay that could kill legislation so close to adjournment.

One opponent, Mike Strang, R-Colo., called the bill "a slimy travesty," one "which has slithered through the process here during the dark of night."

The rule was approved by 252-138, overcoming the stiffest challenge opponents managed to mount. The House passed the bill itself 290-91. *(Votes 443, 445, p. 124-H)*

The National Scenic Area established by the bill had three parts. The most sensitive and valuable resources in the gorge were placed in four special management areas totaling about 112,000 acres, for the most direct federal management by the U.S. Forest Service. Another 113,000 acres were included in the scenic area, but not in the special management areas. And the 13 incorporated urban enclaves were largely left to continue operating under their current laws.

A 12-member bi-state commission was to oversee management of the scenic area, developing a management plan in consultation with the affected counties and the Forest Service. Six of the members would be appointed by those counties and three by the governor of each state. One of each governor's three appointees would have to live in the scenic area.

The counties were: Clark, Skamania and Klickitat in Washington and Multnomah, Hood River and Wasco in Oregon.

The bill authorized federal acquisition of land to be included in the special management areas. If landowners were unwilling to sell, the government could condemn some land, but it could not condemn land used for single-family homes, agriculture or grazing, or for educational, religious or charitable institutions or Indian tribes.

Once a county had adopted a land-use ordinance that the Forest Service agreed was consistent with the management plan, federal condemnation authority would expire.

The bill also would protect several streams that were tributaries of the Columbia in the gorge. It designated segments of the lower Klickitat River (10 miles) and lower White Salmon River (9 miles), both on the Washington side, as National Wild and Scenic Rivers. Other segments of those rivers were designated for wild and scenic study.

The bill also included a ban on hydroelectric development (under various conditions) on three other specific tributaries. The bans applied to segments of the Wind River, Wash.; Hood River, Ore.; and the Little White Salmon, Wash. ∎

Disagreements Block Nuclear Insurance Bills

Committees in both the House and Senate approved legislation in 1986 overhauling the nation's basic nuclear insurance law, but disagreements over liability limits kept the measure from reaching the floor of either chamber.

The 1957 Price-Anderson Act (PL 85-256), enacted to help get the fledgling nuclear power industry off the ground, set up a no-fault claims system for nuclear accidents and limited the liability of electric utilities using nuclear power. *(Congress and the Nation Vol. I, p. 932)*

The law set a limit of about $650 million on the amount that could be paid to victims of a single nuclear accident. Legislators were agreed that the limit was far out of date, but they were not in agreement on how much to raise it.

Three House committees and one in the Senate voted to set the ceiling at about $6.5 billion per accident, but a fifth committee — Senate Energy — voted for a limit of $2.4 billion.

The Senate Energy Committee was the first to complete work on a Price-Anderson bill, voting 19-1 on April 23 to report a measure (S 1225 — S Rept 99-310) with the $2.4 billion dollar limit. That was just two days before a major nuclear accident at a Soviet nuclear power plant in Chernobyl. The Soviet accident had a big impact on the debate in the United States and contributed to the adoption of higher limits when other congressional committees took up Price-Anderson bills.

Senate Consideration

The bill reported by the Senate Energy and Natural Resources Committee was sponsored by James A. McClure, R-Idaho, and Alan K. Simpson, R-Wyo.

In a markup that spanned two months, the Energy Committee voted to make several other changes in the nuclear insurance law, in addition to raising the liability limit.

The committee voted, on March 6, to abolish the 20-year statute of limitations on suits by victims of nuclear accidents.

The Price-Anderson Act said individuals who claimed injury from a major nuclear accident — as designated by the Nuclear Regulatory Commission (NRC) — must have filed suit within three years of discovering the injury and in no case more than 20 years after the accident occurred.

The committee approved by voice vote an amendment offered by Daniel J. Evans, R-Wash., to eliminate the 20-year limit, but it left the three-year discovery rule intact.

Evans and other advocates of the change argued that the 20-year limit was inadequate because many of the injuries associated with exposure to radiation, including cancer, have long latency periods.

The federal limits applied only when the NRC declared an "extraordinary nuclear occurrence." Otherwise state tort law applied.

In other action March 6, the committee adopted by voice vote an amendment drafted by Pete V. Domenici, R-N.M., and Jeff Bingaman, D-N.M, that spelled out reimbursement rules for precautionary evacuations. The amendment said expenses for precautionary evacuations would be reimbursed under the Price-Anderson Act when they were "reasonable." If the secretary of energy and state and local officials disagreed on whether an evacuation was reasonable, the amendment authorized the establishment of a neutral three-member panel to decide.

On March 26, the Energy Committee decisively rejected efforts to make Energy Department contractors liable for nuclear accidents they might cause through negligence.

Contractors working for the Energy Department conducted activities that included refining nuclear materials, building weapons and handling nuclear waste. Under Price-Anderson, the contractors were largely shielded from lawsuits lodged by citizens claiming injury in a nuclear incident involving the contractor. The federal government did this, in essence, by assuming the liability itself.

Sen. Howard M. Metzenbaum, D-Ohio, offered an amendment that would have allowed the secretary of energy to recover damages from contractors found guilty of gross negligence or willful misconduct. The amendment would have allowed the government to recover only those amounts it had already paid to persons claiming injury, and only those amounts attributed to the contractor's negligence or misconduct.

The amendment was defeated 3-13.

A key opponent of the Metzenbaum amendment was ranking Democrat J. Bennett Johnston, La., who said the action would harm the nuclear industry and was "kind of like reconquering Grenada.... I mean the nuclear industry is already down — why kick it again? ... This would just make a whole new genus of lawsuits."

Metzenbaum denied that, saying only the government would have the right to sue to recover damages.

After defeating Metzenbaum's proposal, the committee voted 13-4 for an amendment offered by Johnston. That amendment prohibited courts from awarding punitive damages to victims of a nuclear accident covered by Price-Anderson.

Also adopted March 27, by voice vote, was a package of amendments that drew no vocal opposition.

One spelled out congressional intent that Price-Anderson compensation rules cover nuclear incidents arising from acts of theft, sabotage or terrorism.

Another required inflation adjustments in the annual contributions paid by nuclear electric utilities. The contributions would be used to help pay damage claims in the event of an accident at one of the utilities.

Environment Committee Action

After the Energy Committee completed its work on S 1225, the bill was referred to the Environment Committee's Subcommittee on Nuclear Regulations.

There, as part of a compromise negotiated by subcommittee Chairman Simpson and full committee Chairman Robert T. Stafford, R-Vt., the liability limit was raised to $4.3 billion.

In the full committee, however, Gary Hart, D-Colo., succeeded in overturning the compromise and a $6.5 billion ceiling was approved.

House Consideration

The Chernobyl accident came just as Republicans and Democrats on the House Interior Committee were bracing for a showdown over liability limits in a markup of a bill (HR 3653 — H Rept 99-636, Part I) reauthorizing the Price-Anderson Act.

As introduced by Morris K. Udall, D-Ariz., the bill raised the liability limit for a nuclear accident from $650 million to about $10 billion. Nuclear industry supporters succeeded Dec. 10, 1985, in cutting that to about $2.5 billion in the Subcommittee on Energy and the Environment, but Udall got a rematch in full committee on April 23, and by a 21-20 vote succeeded in bringing the limit back up to $8.2 billion.

Udall's opponents then regrouped and rallied behind an amendment offered by Ron Marlenee, R-Mont., to cut the limit back again, and claimed the voting strength to succeed. It was at this point, on the eve of a showdown on the Marlenee amendment, that news of the Chernobyl accident broke.

When the committee met on April 30 — just a few days after Chernobyl — members from both parties agreed that in view of the situation it would be better to adjourn for a few weeks.

Ranking Republican Don Young, Alaska, one of those wanting to lower the liability limit, said: "I am very concerned at the hysterical attitude of many members of this Congress over the events that supposedly have happened in Russia."

When the committee did meet, on May 21, it voted for a compromise that increased the liability limit to $6.5 billion.

Shared Liability

The Price-Anderson Act and HR 3653 required all nuclear utilities to help pay damage claims if one of them had an accident. But there was considerable controversy over whether the innocent utilities should eventually be reimbursed.

The committee compromise dropped hotly contested "subrogation" provisions that would have given innocent utilities the right to sue for reimbursement from the utility where a nuclear accident occurred. The provisions also would have allowed the Energy Department to sue contractors when accidents were caused by their negligence.

Environmental and consumer groups wanted subrogation language because they believed utilities would take more precautions if they had more at risk.

Nuclear utilities, suppliers and contractors, however, argued that unless protected from lawsuits, they would not take part in nuclear activities at all — even those involving nuclear weapons.

Other Provisions

The compromise proposal, offered as a package of amendments by Jerry Huckaby, D-La., and adopted by voice vote, required utilities to carry $200 million worth of private insurance, with the remaining $6.3 billion to be covered by a "deferred premium" mechanism under which all utilities would pitch in to help pay damages from an accident.

Each utility would be responsible for a maximum deferred premium of about $63 million per reactor for a worst-case accident, but could stretch out payment over several years.

The committee also dropped language from the previous version of the bill that allowed the Nuclear Regulatory Commission to adjust for inflation every five years the amount of required liability coverage.

John F. Seiberling, D-Ohio, an advocate of higher liability limits, called that "an enormous concession," saying it would reduce the real value of the coverage by 45 percent over a decade.

Science Committee

HR 3653 was also referred to the Science and Technology Committee, which approved the measure (H Rept 99-636 Part II) by voice vote July 29.

The Science Subcommittee on Energy Research and Production had approved a set of amendments July 24 — including a measure making permanent the Energy Department's authority to indemnify its nuclear contractors.

The Science Committee also eliminated from the Interior Committee bill the provision providing unlimited federal liability for accidents at Energy Department contract facilities. It was replaced with the same $6.5 billion ceiling that the bill applied to commercial power reactors. The committee also prohibited the recovery of punitive damages from the federal government.

Energy Committee

HR 3653 was approved Aug. 12 by the House Energy and Commerce Committee (H Rept 99-636, Part III), with the liability limit of $6.5 billion left intact.

The Energy Committee had adjourned Aug. 6 in a nervous 21-21 standoff over an amendment by Carlos J. Moorhead, R-Calif., to lower the limit from $6.5 billion to $2.5 billion.

When the committee resumed work, it debated and then rejected the Moorhead amendment by voice vote.

The committee then agreed, by a bare 21-20 margin, to accept an amendment by Edward J. Markey, D-Mass., which tied the liability formula to the index for inflation. That could have increased significantly the actual value of the liability in future years.

Other Amendments Considered

In addition to the liability limit, the committee resolved a number of other issues.

It rejected by voice vote an amendment offered by Markey that would have allowed "subrogation" — essentially a chain of lawsuits in which utilities paying for an accident through the post-accident assessments could seek to recover their money. The Markey amendment would have allowed utilities to turn around and sue the party they felt was really at fault for the accident — whether it was the utility that had the accident or a designer, contractor or supplier for that utility.

The committee approved by voice vote an amendment by Ralph M. Hall, D-Texas, that gave courts the power to limit attorneys' fees in nuclear damage cases to reasonable levels.

The committee also approved without controversy an amendment by Al Swift, D-Wash., that removed certain legal defenses available to the federal government under the Federal Tort Claims Act. For example, under the Swift amendment, if there were a nuclear accident involving federal activities, the government would not be able to defend itself by claiming it was performing a duty under its discretion.

The committee voted 25-17, along party lines, to adopt an amendment by Ron Wyden, D-Ore., that closed what he called a "hole" in the Interior Committee's version of the bill allowing the Energy Department to escape liability. The amendment removed the exclusion of Energy Department nuclear production activities when performed directly by the government and not by a contractor.

Defeated, however, was an amendment by Moorhead that would have overturned language put into the bill by the Interior Committee making the federal government subject to unlimited liability for its nuclear activities. Wyden argued that the federal government did not need to be encouraged to use nuclear energy, as had been the case with private companies when Price-Anderson was enacted. ∎

Hydroelectric Power Licenses

Congress cleared legislation (S 426 — PL 99-495) Oct. 3 ending a long and bitter dispute between public and private utilities over rules for renewing federal hydroelectric power licenses.

The legislation marked a major victory for the privately owned companies because their municipal counterparts were unable to convince Congress that they should be given an edge in the competition for expiring licenses.

Utilities generally were eager to use hydropower when they could get it, because it was cheaper, cleaner and safer than power from most other sources.

Much of the hydroelectric power generating capacity in the United States was owned and run by the federal government. When private companies wanted to build a dam and generate electricity from it, they had to get a license, good for 50 years, from the Federal Energy Regulatory Commission (FERC). When two utilities applied for a license to build on the same site, the Federal Water Power Act of 1920 required that FERC give the license to the one best serving the public interest. When they showed equal merit, the law gave a "preference" to state and municipally owned utilities.

The law was ambiguous, however, on whether public utilities got a preference when the original license expired — and that was the issue that S 426 was drafted to address.

The battle began early in the 99th Congress and included major lobbying efforts by both the public and private utilities, with the public companies arguing that the preference should extend to renewals and the private companies saying it should not.

Private companies currently holding hydropower licenses argued that rates for their customers would jump if they lost the hydropower; the public utilities said the benefits would simply go to other users. The private companies countered that they had more customers and could spread the benefits among more people. They noted that public utilities already held a portion of the licensed hydroelectric capacity that was much greater than their share of customers.

In the end, Congress came down on the side of the private utilities.

Major Provisions

As cleared by Congress, S 426:

- Gave no preference in re-licensing decisions to public power companies or incumbent license holders. However, in a concession to those who sought a preference for incumbents, the bill specified that insignificant differences between competing applications shall not result in transfer of a project.
- Required FERC, in awarding licenses, to take into account energy conservation, fish and wildlife and environmental quality, as well as power and development, and to give these other factors "equal consideration."
- Required FERC, in issuing licenses, to require protection, damage mitigation and enhancement of fish and wildlife habitat. Those conditions would generally be based on recommendations from the National Marine Fisheries Service, the U.S. Fish and Wildlife Service and state fish and wildlife agencies, received pursuant to the Fish and Wildlife Coordination Act.
- Required that FERC give the recommendations due weight and try to resolve any inconsistencies with the Federal Power Act. If it does not adopt the recommendations, it must publish its findings that they are inconsistent and that its license is protective of wildlife.
- Required FERC, in awarding licenses, to consider a range of other criteria for measuring the public interest, including the license applicant's ability to comply with the license and the law, to manage the project safely and to provide efficient and reliable electric service, as well as the applicant's existing and planned transmission services.
- Required FERC, in awarding licenses, to consider also the applicant's need for the project's electricity (including the cost of substitute supplies or doing without it) and the effect on communities to be served by the project. When the applicant is an industry, FERC must consider the effect on the operation and efficiency of the industrial facility or related operations, its workers and the related community.
- Required FERC to include in licenses conditions to prevent or minimize violation of the policies expressed in antitrust laws. If it is impossible to minimize adequately such violations, FERC shall deny or revoke the license or take appropriate action.
- Set terms for compensation to be paid to a previous license holder by an applicant who has challenged and won the license to operate a dam. As in current law and the Senate bill, the compensation would be the net investment plus severance damages incurred by the old licensee. Because of the effects of depreciation over a 50-year period, those amount to a small fraction of what it would cost to build such a dam or a replacement power source today.
- Eliminated major incentives to promote hydroelectric development established in the Public Utilities Regulatory Policies Act of 1978 (PURPA — PL 95-617), except where the environment is not harmed. The major incentive is a requirement that utilities buy power from hydroelectric facilities at "avoided cost," or the cost of generating or buying it themselves. New dams could not get such benefits unless FERC found they would have "no substantial adverse effects" on the environment, including recreation and water quality. Automatically disqualified would be stream segments protected under federal or state wild and scenic river programs. To qualify, the new projects would also have to meet terms set by fish and wildlife agencies under the law.
- Permitted hydroelectric projects to continue to qualify for the old PURPA benefits if they used only existing dam structures, or if the application for a license or exemption was filed before enactment or if the applicant demonstrated that it had, before enactment, committed substantial monetary resources to developing the project.
- Established procedures for settling re-licensing disputes for the Pacific Power and Light Company's Merwin Dam in Washington and nine other hydroelectric facilities. The Merwin case, now in the federal courts, would be settled according to the old law, however the courts ultimately interpret it. In the other cases, the bill would encourage negotiated settlement by allowing the existing licensee to pay the challenger to withdraw its application. If the licensee chose not to negotiate, then existing law (considered less favorable to investor-owned incumbents) would apply. If the challenger chose not to negotiate, then the new law would apply. If the parties did not agree on compensation, FERC would decide.
- Limited licenses to 30 years instead of the current 50, except when substantial construction or redevelopment was involved.
- Stiffened FERC's power to enforce license provisions, authorizing it to revoke licenses or exemptions for significant violations of license conditions or to go to court seeking compliance.

House Action

The hydroelectric re-licensing bill was introduced as HR 44 on Jan. 3, 1985, by Rep. Richard C. Shelby, D-Ala. It was referred to the Energy and Commerce Subcommittee on Energy Conservation and Power and eventually approved by voice vote on Jan. 29, 1986. It was approved by the full committee (H Rept 99-507) Feb. 6, also by voice vote.

HR 44 eliminated any preference for public utilities when a hydroelectric power license came up for renewal and sponsors said this would allow private utilities to compete on an even basis with public utilities.

The legislation was a compromise drafted by subcommittee Chairman Edward J. Markey, D-Mass., that ultimately won the support of both the private power community and environmentalists, two groups that had often been opposed in the past.

In exchange for the support of environmentalists, HR 44 provided several environmental safeguards that were lacking in existing law.

For example, existing law did not explicitly require FERC to look at effects on fish, wildlife and recreation when weighing competing hydroproject applications. The Markey bill did.

The Markey bill also corrected what environmentalists saw as flaws in a 1978 law (PL 95-617) meant to encourage more use of small and abandoned dams to produce energy. They feared those incentives have been too successful — producing a "hydro gold rush" to build new dams on small streams, often harming their environmental value.

The Markey bill prohibited FERC from accepting applications for new small hydro dams until the agency conducted a study of whether the power gained from these projects outweighs their environmental impacts. The bill set no deadline for completing the study.

Part of the compromise package was a formula for the compensation of losing license-holders by successful challengers. The winner would pay the depreciated value ("net investment") of the loser's generating facilities — plus an amount set by FERC to compensate for any demonstrated harm from the loss of power. Losers would have to allow use of their power lines to transmit power generated by the winner to its customers.

The Markey bill also included language beefing up FERC's power to enforce the conditions it places on licenses, and allowing FERC to consider a utility's compliance record when it applies for license renewal.

The House approved HR 44 by voice vote on Apr. 21.

Senate Action

The Senate version of the hydroelectric bill, S 426, was passed April 17, on a vote of 83-14. *(Vote 75, p. 14-S)*

It had been reported by the Senate Energy and Natural Resources Committee Oct. 22, 1985 (S Rept 99-161).

Unlike the House bill, which granted no preference on the renewal of hydroelectric power licenses, S 426 granted a preference to the existing license-holder when expiration time came — a rule that clearly worked to the advantage of the private companies, who held a large majority of the existing licenses.

One public-power supporter, John Melcher, D-Mont., eventually won a concession on the procedures by which small public utilities can win access to the transmission lines of big private companies, but it was a small concession.

Gary Hart, D-Colo., forced a debate on what he called the "underlying philosophy" of the bill. But the Senate voted 80-18 to table (kill) a Hart amendment giving the federal government control of hydropower plants when private licenses expired. *(Vote 66, p. 13-S)*

Hart's Amendment

Hart's amendment shifted the debate away from the technical, but economically important, questions that had dominated most of the Senate's consideration of the bill and focused it squarely on a basic conflict between two political philosophies.

Hart invoked the example of President Theodore Roosevelt who, as a progressive and a conservationist, laid the foundation for much of American natural resources law.

Men like Roosevelt, Hart said, "believed in private ownership and profit making. But they also shared a profound belief that America's natural resources were national assets, the property of the people and a legacy to be willed to future generations. They feared that assigning these assets to private concerns would interpose profit and the interests of shareholders between the resources and the people."

Hart said the Senate bill reversed this "presumption that the ownership of national assets should be as close to the people as possible."

His amendment made federal "recapture" of hydroelectric facilities automatic upon the expiration of private licenses, unless Congress authorized extension of the expiring license. Facilities held by public utilities would not have been subject to recapture. Current law allows the federal government to recapture projects, but it has never done so.

One opponent of the amendment was J. Bennett Johnston, D-La., ranking minority member on the Energy and Natural Resources Committee. "What this amendment does," Johnston said, "is to seek to unscramble an egg that has been scrambled now for over 30 years, and unscramble it in a most unfair way.

"The issue here," Johnston said, "is which consumers get the power and which consumers lose the power. There is nothing intrinsically right or wrong ... about one set of consumers being chosen over another."

The bill, he said, required FERC to examine each case and award expiring licenses to whoever would do "the greatest good for the most people" under specific economic, service, efficiency and environmental criteria.

Melcher's Stand

Melcher tied up the Senate for several days over a more technical issue of importance to small and public utilities — their ability to get power "wheeled" to them across the transmission lines of larger private utilities.

Without wheeling, small utilities located in the middle of private utility service areas would have to generate their own power, buy it from their competitor, or build expensive transmission lines to an outside source. The Public Utilities Regulatory Policy Act (PURPA) of 1978 (PL 95-617) gave FERC authority to order utilities to wheel power for others, at a reasonable price, when they had extra transmission capacity and it did not disrupt their own service. *(Congress and the Nation Vol. V, p. 516)*

Melcher, arguing for a coalition of rural cooperatives and municipal utilities, said PURPA had not solved the problem, and that FERC had yet to issue any mandatory orders.

He offered several amendments aimed at expanding the right of a utility to get a wheeling order from FERC by changing the procedures under which it could seek one of the criteria FERC must apply in granting one.

The amendments were opposed by the private utilities, by Johnston and by Energy Committee Chairman James A. McClure, R-Idaho. They said wheeling was a complicated subject that needed separate treatment.

They pointed to the fact that some 1,380 voluntary wheeling agreements had been filed with FERC during the last decade, and that only five requests for mandatory wheeling orders had been filed in that time.

Melcher raised the wheeling issue as soon as the Senate began work on the bill April 11 and eventually offered several amendments.

Talks on the issue broke down April 16, and a minor power struggle ensued. McClure and Johnston forced votes on Melcher's amendments and repeatedly tabled them. Melcher was never able to muster more than 22 votes, but he blocked progress on the bill by offering even more amendments, each broadening the PURPA wheeling provisions in a slightly different way, and asking for quorum calls. McClure and Johnston countered by speeding up the roll calls and moving to instruct the sergeant-at-arms to request the attendance of absent senators. *(Votes 68, 69, p. 13-S; votes 70, 71, 72, 73, 74, p. 14-S)*

Behind the Hydro Battle: More Than Money

Passage of S 426 marked a major victory for private power companies, which had fought a long lobbying war against public power advocates. The battle included thousands of dollars in campaign contributions, nationwide letter-writing campaigns and expensive public relations efforts.

In the heat of the debate, some public utility supporters accused the private utilities of buying cosponsors for their bill in order to ensure victory. But a Congressional Quarterly analysis of political action committees (PACs) run by private utilities found that campaign contributions were not the decisive factor.

Money was certainly part of the atmosphere in which Congress considered hydro re-licensing — private utility PACs gave House members more than half a million dollars in 1985 — but there were far more important influences shaping members' positions.

The private utilities' success seemed to be the result of compromise, coalition-building and old-fashioned convincing. Shaping members' decisions was the geography and politics of their states and districts, their philosophies about the role of government in people's lives and the ability of the private utilities to sell Congress on the importance of one fact: Private utilities serve three times as many electric customers as public utilities.

Utility PAC Gifts

Congressional Quarterly attempted to study the effect, if any, of private utility campaign contributions by analyzing data on file with the Federal Election Commission.

The analysis covered all 1985 campaign contributions to incumbent House members from 78 PACs affiliated with private electric utilities. Municipal utilities generally are prohibited from operating PACs and were not included in the CQ analysis. But public power interests did make campaign contributions through association PACs, rural cooperative PACs and donations from individuals.

Cosponsors of HR 44 did, on average, get more in campaign contributions from private utility PACs than non-cosponsors — but the relationship of utility giving to cosponsorship was less dramatic than its relationship to other variables such as geographic region or committee membership.

Utility companies with a lot of FERC-licensed hydropower did not give more to bill cosponsors than did utilities with modest amounts or none at all, suggesting that the hydropower issue was only one of many factors motivating their giving.

Nor did bill cosponsors, on the average, seem to get utility contributions very soon before or after they signed onto the bill. In fact, members who signed onto the bill during 1985 got less than those who began the year as original cosponsors — not what would be expected if the PACs were using contributions to induce members to come over to their side.

The average member of the House received $1,223 in 1985 from the private utility PACs. That includes 136 members who received nothing. Contributions of that magnitude would not constitute a large portion of the several hundred thousand dollars it takes to run a typical House campaign — and are far short of the maximum of $5,000 per election that members can, and sometimes do, receive legally from a single PAC.

The 253 members who did not cosponsor the bill got, on average, $960; the 59 original cosponsors averaged almost twice that, $1,826. The 123 members who signed on during the year got an average of $1,476. As a group, all cosponsors averaged $1,589 in gifts.

The analysis turned up little linkage between time of cosponsorship and time of PAC donations. Only 71 of the 1,391 contributions counted were given to cosponsors within 30 days before or after cosponsorship.

While cosponsorship does seem to have a statistically significant relationship to PAC donations, what seemed to influence PACs more was committee membership — especially a berth on the Energy Subcommittee on Energy Conservation and Power, the one that marked up the re-licensing bill. Members of that panel averaged $4,804 in utility PAC donations.

Members of the key Interior subcommittee, which had influence but not direct jurisdiction over HR 44, also fared well. Members of Interior's Water and Power Resources Subcommittee averaged $3,132.

What region a member came from also seemed to be more important than cosponsorship of HR 44. Members in the Southwest averaged the highest amount of donations ($3,135), while those in the Northeast were lowest ($689).

While there were many reasons for regional variations, one was heavy giving by particular PACs. Several especially active Texas utility PACs — including four from the Texas Utilities Co. group and one from the Houston Lighting and Power Co. — helped boost contributions received by the average Texas member to $4,224 and pulled up the score for the whole Southwest region.

For the sake of comparison, CQ also examined utility PAC donations to a 35-member elite defined as the House "leadership." It included members holding party leadership positions and the chairmen of relevant committees and subcommittees. In the CQ analysis, leaders averaged $1,853 in contributions.

Statistical inquiries like this one can neither prove nor disprove assertions that PAC giving causes members to support a particular bill, or that their support of a bill causes PACs to give. There remains the possibility that members supported the bill because they were already inclined to be sympathetic to the concerns of private utilities, and that utilities simply give more to their known friends.

In sum, while the analysis shows there was a considerable amount of private utility PAC money being distributed while the hydropower bill was being debated, it does not uphold the charge of some public utility supporters that cosponsors of HR 44 were being systematically bought with private utility PAC contributions.

When neither side prevailed with those tactics, off-the-floor talks resumed.

The concession Melcher finally won was, by his own admission, "a small step." It allowed a utility to file an application for a wheeling order before determination of a rate schedule — a procedural obstacle that sometimes prevents utilities from filing. The amendment did not change the standards that FERC applies when deciding whether to issue an order.

Other Provisions

As passed by the Senate, S 426 also:

- Added new criteria for FERC to consider when deciding which utility would win an expiring license. They included the cost to customers if a hydropower project was taken away from a utility.
- Required that FERC evaluate plans for offsetting the harm a dam may do to fish and wildlife.
- Eliminated financial incentives established under PURPA to encourage more small hydropower projects, unless they met conditions specified by state fish and wildlife agencies.
- Limited to 50 years the term for which FERC could grant an exemption from the hydroelectric licensing process for small projects at existing dams. PURPA allowed such exemptions for an unlimited time.
- Gave FERC authority it lacked to revoke licenses and exemptions for significant violations of the conditions under which they were granted.

Conference Agreement

House-Senate conferees reached agreement on S 426 on Sept. 30. The conference report was adopted by voice vote in the House Oct. 2 and the Senate Oct. 3.

One of the principal disagreements between the House and Senate was whether incumbents — utilities that now hold hydroelectric power licenses — would be favored to retain those licenses when they came due for renewal. The Senate bill favored incumbents; the House did not. Conferees agreed that incumbents would not be favored, but that a utility seeking to take over a hydroelectric dam would have to show that the public would benefit from the change in license-holders. The majority of the licenses coming due in the next 10 years are held by private utilities.

Another key sticking point was how much a successful challenger would have to compensate a utility that lost its license. Members agreed that payment would be an amount equal to net investment and severance costs as provided for in current law and the Senate bill.

The House did give up language requiring "equitable treatment" for fish and wildlife concerns in comparison with power development, which Senate conferees worried would be too rigid. Instead, the conference required "equal consideration," which environmentalists feared would leave FERC too free to make decisions adverse to their concerns. ∎

Oil Spill Liability

The House and Senate passed oil spill liability bills in 1986, but conferees were unable to resolve differences and the legislation died.

The Senate passed its bill (S 2799) Sept. 28. The House passed oil spill legislation twice in the 99th Congress — one time as part of the superfund bill (HR 2005), the other as part of reconciliation (HR 5300).

The two chambers agreed to limit the liability of oil companies and shippers and to impose a 1.3-cent-per-barrel tax on petroleum to create a $350 million fund to cover cleanup costs and damages that exceed those liability limits, but they were unable to agree on another key issue — whether federal law should pre-empt stricter state laws.

The House favored a uniform national system of liability and compensation for oil spills that would supersede individual state statutes. Oil companies, the insurance industry and shippers contended that would reduce uncertainty and increase the availability of insurance.

But senators from coastal states — led by George J. Mitchell, D-Maine — adamantly opposed any weakening of state authority, and the Senate bill made it clear that state law could not be pre-empted by federal law. ∎

Appliance Bill Pocket Veto

President Reagan Nov. 1 announced his pocket veto of a bill to set nationwide energy efficiency standards for major household appliances. *(Text, p. 34-D)*

Both the House and Senate passed the bill (HR 5465) by voice vote Oct. 15. It had been supported by a broad coalition that included both conservationists and appliance manufacturers concerned that state-by-state standards could disrupt their marketing.

The bill required most new household appliances to achieve a 15-25 percent increase over 1985 levels of efficiency by 1990. That standard was tougher than any state standards in effect at the time and would have pre-empted state and local laws.

In a memorandum explaining his veto of the bill, Reagan said: "The bill intrudes unduly on the free market, limits the freedom of choice available to consumers who would be denied the opportunity to purchase low-cost appliances and constitutes a substantial intrusion into traditional state responsibilities and prerogatives."

The measure's prime sponsor, Rep. Edward J. Markey, D-Mass., called the veto "a triumph of extreme right-wing ideology over practicality and common sense." ∎

Floor for Federal Oil Prices

Congress cleared a bill (HR 4843 — PL 99-413) Aug. 16 that established a floor price for the sale of oil produced at federally owned fields. The measure, approved by voice vote by the House Aug. 13 and by the Senate three days later, represented a compromise between Energy Department officials and members concerned that the government was losing millions of dollars by dumping oil on a glutted market.

HR 4843 banned the sale of oil from the Naval Petroleum Reserve at Elk Hills, Calif., for less than 90 percent of the market value or less than the purchase price, minus the cost of transporting the oil. The energy secretary could vary production rates, which were required to be set at the maximum.

President Reagan decided to sell the oil to help reduce the deficit. But because production at Elk Hills was kept at maximum capacity and demand for oil was low, the government received as little as $4.90 per barrel — about $7 below the market price. ∎

Fiscal '86 Deficit Bill Issues

Energy and environmental issues were some of the most contentious in Senate-House negotiations on the fiscal 1986 deficit-reduction bill (HR 3128 — PL 99-272), cleared March 20. Known as a "reconciliation" bill, HR 3128 was designed to bring Congress into compliance with its fiscal 1986 budget targets.

A dispute over how to finance the superfund hazardous-waste cleanup program kept the bill from clearing in 1985. Senate Finance Committee Chairman Bob Packwood, R-Ore., wanted to include the broad-based business tax approved by the Senate, while the House insisted on a tax formula that put more of the burden on the oil and chemical industries.

Only when both sides agreed to drop the superfund issue altogether did the bill begin to move forward again. The superfund tax dispute was left for settlement in the conference on the superfund reauthorization bill (HR 2005). *(Fiscal 1986 deficit-reduction bill, p. 555; superfund, p. 111)*

Another issue that held up reconciliation was how the states and the federal government should divide certain offshore oil and gas revenues from coastal areas that straddled the boundary between state and federal territory.

Louisiana, Texas and California eventually got most of the funds they had demanded. Although the administration protested the loss of revenue, in the end it dropped its objections. In return, Congress agreed to the administration's request to drop from the bill Buy American requirements for offshore rigs, and a House-proposed change to section 19 of the Outer Continental Shelf Lands Act (PL 95-372) that would have increased the states' say in federal offshore leasing decisions.

The reconciliation measure added revenue to the Treasury by establishing several new or increased user fees, including a fee for pipeline safety and a fee for nuclear-electric utilities. But it dropped a House-passed proposal for the Federal Energy Regulatory Commission to collect other fees from pipelines and utilities.

Provisions

As signed into law April 7, the energy and environment provisions of HR 3128:

- **Offshore Oil Revenue.** Settled a dispute between coastal states and the federal government over how to split revenues from offshore oil and gas formations that straddled federal-state boundaries. More than $6 billion had piled up in an escrow fund under section 8(g) of the Outer Continental Shelf Lands Act since 1978 because the two sides had disagreed over how to share it. *(Background, 1985 Almanac p. 203)*

Under a complex formula, seven states would get more than $2 billion of the escrow money and the federal Treasury more than $4 billion. Louisiana, California and Texas would get the largest shares, with smaller amounts going to Alaska, Alabama, Mississippi and Florida.

Ninety percent of the escrow funds were to be paid to the states immediately, with the rest paid over 15 years.

In the future, states would get 27 percent of all bonuses, rents, royalties and other revenues from the tracts.

That and other provisions related to the outer continental shelf would produce federal savings and revenue in 1986 of $4.9 billion, according to CBO estimates. But because those immediate revenues were traded off against future revenues, the "savings" for 1986-89 was tallied at only $1.1 billion.

- **Strategic Petroleum Reserve.** Authorized appropriations to fill the Strategic Petroleum Reserve for fiscal 1986-88 and set a minimum for how fast it must be filled. The Energy Department would have to maintain an average annual fill rate of 35,000 barrels per day, until there were at least 527 million barrels of crude oil stored in the reserve. If the department failed to meet the minimum fill rate, it would be barred from selling oil from the Elk Hills, Calif., Naval Petroleum Reserve. *(Background, 1985 Almanac p. 211)*

- Authorized spending, to buy and pump the oil into reservoirs, of $358 million for fiscal 1986, $334 million for 1987 and $357 million for 1988. To operate and expand the reservoirs, the bill authorized $136 million for 1986, $359 million for 1987 and $157 million for 1988. That would be enough to continue construction of the reservoir at Big Hill, Texas, and to build storage capacity of 750 million barrels.

- **Conservation.** Authorized federal agencies to conserve energy through an innovative kind of contract with private consultants. Under these "shared savings" contracts, the private company would install energy-saving equipment in a federal building at its own expense, in return for a share of the energy savings achieved. Previously, legal limitations on the use of long-term contracts had prevented federal agencies from using this method.

- **Uranium Enrichment.** Reauthorized through 1988 the federal program to enrich uranium for nuclear-electric utilities, other civilian users and some defense projects. Appropriations would be limited to the amount collected in payments from users of enrichment services, but if revenues exceeded appropriations, the difference would be used to pay back some of the money borrowed from the Treasury in previous years.

The program would pay back each year an amount to be determined by the secretary of energy. The General Accounting Office had estimated the unrecovered federal investment at $7.5 billion, but the nuclear industry disputed the figure, putting it as low as $350 million.

- **Nuclear Plant License Fees.** Required the Nuclear Regulatory Commission (NRC) to collect fees from its licensees amounting, with other charges, to as much as 33 percent of the NRC's budget. The new charges would, it was estimated, produce an additional $80 million per year for the Treasury.

- **Pipeline User Fees.** Established a user fee to collect costs of carrying out the Natural Gas Pipeline Safety Act (PL 94-447) and the Hazardous Liquid Pipeline Safety Act (PL 97-468). The fee would begin in fiscal 1986, and the bill authorized $9.3 million for that fiscal year.

The fees would be set by the secretary of transportation, who could base them on pipeline volume, transportation distance, pipeline revenues, or a combination of these. The federal government could collect enough in fees to recover all costs for running the pipeline safety program, but no more than that. ▮

APPROPRIATIONS

CQ

Appropriations

The appropriations process featured several firsts in 1986 and reprised a heated fight, with Nixon-era echoes, over presidential power to halt the spending of appropriated funds.

For the first time and with mixed results, congressional appropriators operated under the tightened budget constraints of the 1985 Gramm-Rudman-Hollings anti-deficit law (PL 99-177). Congress produced the largest-ever omnibus spending bill, known as a "continuing resolution," which nevertheless reflected the lowest increase in government spending — compared with the previous year — in more than a decade.

In both chambers, budget-minded members repeatedly invoked the new Gramm-Rudman rule that individual appropriations bills must conform to spending limits derived from the budget resolution. The continuing resolution was said to be comparatively free of the myriad amendments customary in an election year.

Critics complained that the new restraint effectively blocked them from offering floor amendments, but did not hamper the favored few on Appropriations committees, who could insert their politically useful projects into the bill before it came to the floor.

Gramm-Rudman's ambitious timetable for timely appropriations action was frustrated by congressional habits of delay, and the anti-deficit law paradoxically became another powerful reason to put off action until late in the year. Members were reluctant to face unpleasant spending-cut decisions before a mid-August report, mandated by Gramm-Rudman, showing how much they had to prune to reach the law's deficit target.

In the end, all 13 regular appropriations bills, in various states of completion, were combined into a record-sized continuing resolution, appropriating $576 billion, compared with the $570.9 billion requested by President Reagan for the programs funded by the bill. It was the first time such an omnibus measure included all the regular money bills.

Estimates were that the budget authority appropriated by the continuing resolution would result in about $560 billion in outlays — money actually spent. This figure was newly important because Gramm-Rudman compliance was calculated in outlays.

The continuing resolution elicited presidential veto threats, in part because the individual bills had exceeded certain of Reagan's spending plans. The most bitter dispute, however, was not over money but over sweeping arms control amendments, added by Congress, which the administration found intolerable. These were excised when the White House argued that the limits would undercut Reagan in his October meeting with Soviet leader Mikhail S. Gorbachev in Iceland.

Large as it was, the continuing resolution encompassed a little more than half the government's expenditures. An estimated $400 billion more in outlays would be required for Social Security, interest payments on the federal debt, the bulk of Medicare spending and other activities that were funded on a permanent basis.

The sheer size of the bill all but masked the fact that it marked an unusual moment of federal thrift. Between 1966 and 1986, federal spending had grown at an average rate of 11 percent a year. Between 1986 and 1987, according to initial estimates by the Congressional Budget Office (CBO), the increase would be less than 1 percent. (The CBO calculations covered both programs funded by the continuing resolution and those with permanent funding.)

CBO analysts said the decreased growth rate was probably artificially depressed by the impact of asset sales and certain other very short-term savings measures ordered by Congress. Absent those sales, the congressional agency estimated that the 1986 to 1987 growth rate would be 4 percent to 5 percent.

Deferral Fight

Early in the year, Reagan stirred angry protests and a lawsuit when he deferred the spending of more than $24 billion in funds that had already been appropriated for fiscal 1986. Most of the deferrals reflected uncontroversial decisions that, for assorted administrative reasons, the money should be spent more slowly.

But four members of the House and a group of cities went to court to force release of about $5 billion appropriated for housing subsidies and related programs for the urban poor. A deferral of strategic petroleum reserve funding also sparked objections.

Members complained that Reagan had imposed these deferrals a year earlier, and that subsequent negotiations and congressional action had released the money. In reimposing the deferrals, critics said, Reagan was ignoring negotiated agreements and improperly substituting his own policies for those set by law.

Two courts ruled (one ruling came early in 1987) that the president did not have legal authority to impose the so-called "policy" deferrals. Presidential authority to delay spending for legitimate management reasons, such as construction delays, was not in dispute. The deferrals themselves were also overturned in a supplemental appropriations bill (PL 99-349).

Indirectly, Gramm-Rudman contributed to the vehemence of congressional reactions because the law's stress on holding down spending discouraged supplemental appropriations bills, which had been the routine vehicles for overturning presidential deferrals of recent years.

—By Elizabeth Wehr

Fiscal 1987
Status of Appropriations
99th Congress, Second Session

(as of Oct. 18, 1986)

Appropriation Bills	House	Senate	Conference	Full-Year Funding Under PL 99-591
Continuing Resolution (HJ Res 738 — PL 99-591)	Passed 9/25/86	Passed 10/3/86	Cleared 10/17/86	$576 billion*
Agriculture and related agencies (HR 5177)	Passed 7/24/86	Reported 9/11/86		$45.2 billion
Commerce, Justice, State, Judiciary (HR 5161)	Passed 7/17/86	Committee reported 9/3/86		$12.9 billion
Defense (HR 5438, S 2827)	Committee reported 8/14/86	Committee reported 9/17/86		$273.9 billion
District of Columbia (HR 5175)	Passed 7/24/86	Passed 9/16/86		$560.4 million
Energy and Water Development (HR 5162)	Passed 7/23/86	Committee reported 9/15/86		$15.0 billion
Foreign Operations (HR 5339, S 2824)	Committee reported 8/5/86	Committee reported 9/16/86		$13.4 billion
Housing and Urban Development, Independent Agencies (HR 5313)	Passed 9/12/86	Passed 10/3/86	Conference report filed 10/7/86	$56.0 billion
Interior and related agencies (HR 5234)	Passed 7/31/86	Passed 9/16/86		$8.3 billion
Labor, Health and Human Services, Education (HR 5233)	Passed 7/31/86	Passed 9/10/86	Conference report filed 10/2/86	$114.8 billion
Legislative Branch (HR 5203)	Passed 7/29/86	Passed 8/13/86	Conference report filed 8/15/86	$1.6 billion
Military Construction (HR 5052)	Passed 6/25/86	Passed 8/13/86		$8.7 billion
Transportation and related agencies (HR 5205)	Passed 7/30/86	Passed 9/17/86	Conference report filed 10/7/86	$10.4 billion
Treasury, Postal Service, General Government (HR 5294)	Passed 8/6/86	Committee reported 8/14/86		$13.8 billion

* *Total does not add due to rounding.*

$1.7 Billion Fiscal 1986 Supplemental Cleared

After untangling several last-minute snags, Congress June 26 completed action on a $1.7 billion supplemental spending bill (HR 4515 — PL 99-349) to carry dozens of federal programs through Sept. 30, the end of the 1986 fiscal year. President Reagan, who had threatened to veto earlier versions of HR 4515, signed the measure into law July 2.

HR 4515 was the first major appropriations bill to be passed under the strictures of the 1985 Gramm-Rudman-Hollings deficit-control law (PL 99-177), which required new spending to be offset by corresponding reductions in other areas. *(Gramm-Rudman, p. 579)*

The bill actually appropriated $9.7 billion in new budget authority for fiscal 1986. To partially offset that figure, it provided $7 billion in rescissions, which permanently canceled previously enacted appropriations. Through an internal bookkeeping transaction it also provided $1 billion to pay off agency debt for the Great Plains Coal Gasification Project. That left the bill's net cost at $1.7 billion.

The largest appropriation in the bill was $5.4 billion for the Commodity Credit Corporation (CCC), to reinstate price support and subsidy payments to farmers that had run out earlier in June. *(Previous CCC supplemental, p. 161)*

Other major funding items included $702 million to improve security at U.S. diplomatic posts abroad, $531 million to redesign the space shuttle in the wake of the Jan. 28 *Challenger* explosion and $340 million to prevent a major disruption of the Internal Revenue Service. *(Highlights, box, p. 154)*

Lawmakers made several concessions demanded by the president, primarily by dropping a House provision that would have sharply restricted his power to defer, or delay, spending money appropriated by Congress. Members in both chambers and parties had charged that Reagan was improperly using spending deferrals to kill or curb programs he disliked. While deleting restrictions on the president's deferral authority, Congress disapproved about $4.9 billion in specific deferrals Reagan had proposed. *(Deferrals, p. 576)*

Members limited a potentially expensive bailout for rural utility cooperatives, refused to expand unemployment benefits for laid-off oil and gas workers, and released $6.3 billion in Defense Department funds hung up by jurisdictional disputes in Congress.

Additional provisions blocked regulatory attempts to limit Medicare reimbursements for hospital capital costs, and froze White House plans to sell any of the four government-owned power marketing administrations in the lower 48 states.

As orginally passed by the House May 8, net funding in the bill totaled $1.7 billion. The Senate, in passing the measure June 6, increased the total to $3.9 billion. Conferees kept most of the Senate additions but increased rescissions for housing programs to bring the net total close to the original House figure.

Final Provisions

As signed into law July 2, HR 4515 (PL 99-349) included the following major provisions *(funding is for fiscal 1986 unless otherwise indicated)*:

Agriculture

- Appropriated $36.7 million for Soil Conservation Service emergency flood relief.
- Appropriated $5 million for the Agriculture Stabilization and Conservation Service emergency conservation program.
- Transferred to the Agricultural Research Service $11.1 million for control of citrus canker, and $11.1 million to build a National Soil Tilth Center in Ames, Iowa.
- Appropriated $3.7 million to prevent Food Safety and Inspection Service staff furloughs.
- Appropriated $8 million to compensate dairy farmers in Arkansas, Missouri and Oklahoma whose herds were contaminated by pesticides, and earmarked an additional $1 million in previously appropriated funds for testing for milk contamination in the Midwest.
- Reduced Farmers Home Administration (FmHA) low-income housing repair direct loans by $3 million, to $11.3 million, and increased loan insurance authority by $1 million.
- Appropriated $1 million for site loans for mutual and self-help housing.
- Disapproved a $700 million deferral for rural housing programs.
- Provided $2 million for very-low-income elderly-housing repair grants.
- Appropriated $20 million for the Women, Infants and Children (WIC) feeding program, and directed that current distribution formulas be maintained through fiscal 1986.
- Appropriated $2.4 million for the Temporary Emergency Food Assistance Program and $8.5 million for feeding programs for the elderly.
- Provided, by transfer from the Commodity Credit Corporation, $71.6 million for salaries and expenses at the Agricultural Stabilization and Conservation Service, and directed the Agriculture Department to restore $3.9 million it had transferred from the Commodity Supplemental Food Program.
- Allowed farmers to keep advance deficiency payments for the 1986 crop year for wheat, feed grains, upland cotton and rice, if floods or other natural disasters prevented planting. Normally, farmers had to return the payments if they did not plant, even if stopped by natural disaster. The conference report expanded coverage to farmers who were prevented from planting by drought and required that deficiency payments a farmer received under this provision be deducted from any crop insurance indemnity payments he might be due.
- Eliminated the prepayment penalty for public utility cooperatives that used private-sector financing to pay off more expensive loans from the Rural Electrification Administration (REA). The co-op had to certify the refinancing would result in substantial savings to customers or lessen the threat of bankruptcy. The Treasury Department could veto any applications to ensure that only needy co-ops were granted the prepayment waiver. REA would still guarantee the loans.
- Appropriated $5.3 billion for farm programs funded by the CCC, and deleted Senate language earmarking $4 million for research and development of external combustion engines.
- Exempted certain farm lands in Alaska from a provi-

Highlights

Following are some major items in new budget authority contained in the fiscal 1986 supplemental appropriations bill (HR 4515) cleared by Congress June 26:

CCC	$ 5,300,000,000
Embassy Security	702,104,000
NASA	531,000,000
IRS	340,000,000
VA Compensation and Pensions	272,000,000
FEMA Disaster Relief	250,000,000
Compact of Free Association	210,840,000
National Forest System Firefighting	165,700,000
Philippine Aid	150,000,000
Student Aid Pell Grants	146,000,000

sion of the 1985 farm bill (PL 99-198) denying farm aid to those who created land by draining swamps.

• Provided, by transfer, $5 million for the control of avian influenza, and another $5 million in matching funds for development of an international trade center at Oklahoma State University.

• Prohibited foreign aid from being used to produce farm commodities for export that would compete with U.S. commodities.

Commerce, Justice, State, Judiciary

• Disapproved the deferral of $40 million for the Economic Development Administration.

• Appropriated $10.8 million for the National Oceanic and Atmospheric Administration. Of that amount, $4.4 million was earmarked for increased hurricane reconnaissance flights, partly due to the loss of the GOES-G weather satellite destroyed during a launch malfunction on May 3.

• Provided $2.6 million for salaries and expenses of the U.S. Marshals Service.

• Provided $3 million for the cost of federal prisoners housed in state or local jails.

• Appropriated $18 million for salaries and expenses of the Federal Prison System.

• Extended the availability of $10 million for relocating the Washington, D.C., field office of the FBI.

• Appropriated $3 million for salaries and expenses of the Immigration and Naturalization Service for detaining Mariel Cubans who had entered the United States following Fidel Castro's 1980 decision to allow virtually unlimited migration from that island. Directed the attorney general to provide Congress by Sept. 1, 1986, with a detailed strategy for the investigation, apprehension and deportation of criminal aliens.

• Transferred $500,000 for investigations by the Justice Department independent counsel.

• Directed the attorney general to develop a model state statute to halt drug trafficking in "rock" and "crack" cocaine.

• Appropriated $702 million for staff and construction to improve security at State Department posts around the world, most of it starting in fiscal 1987. That amount included $10 million for anti-terrorism research and development. Use of the funds would be governed by diplomatic security authorizing legislation (HR 4151) that had been passed by the House and Senate. *(Story, p. 377)*

• Provided $2 million to the Asia Foundation to promote democratic institutions in the Philippines.

• Appropriated $46,000 for the electric bill at the Supreme Court; $1.2 million for salaries at the federal court system; $3.8 million for juror fees at U.S. courts; and $1.3 million for a study of a new federal judicial center in Washington, D.C. Approved up to $11 million in transfers from maintenance and operations to salary and facility accounts.

• Permitted part-time federal bankruptcy judges in Oklahoma and Michigan to continue serving through the end of 1986.

• Disapproved a $1.7 million deferral of Maritime Administration funds for operations and training.

• Provided $18.8 million to Radio Free Europe and Radio Liberty.

• Transferred $2 million for loan-making activities of the Small Business Administration related to natural disasters.

• Transferred $3.9 million from construction accounts to salaries and expenses of the U.S. Information Agency, and to initiate a cultural exchange with the Soviet Union.

Defense, Energy Departments

• Authorized $6.3 billion previously appropriated for numerous Defense Department accounts, settling a dispute between the Senate Armed Services Committee and the Senate Appropriations Subcommittee on Defense.

• Lowered the limit for Marine Corps property maintenance from $238 million to $223.2 million.

• Extended through fiscal 1987 the availability of $8 million for the 10th International Pan American Games.

• Rescinded $114.5 million from three military procurement accounts to offset extra aid to the Philippines.

• Transferred $21.3 million from the Defense Department to the Coast Guard and mandated that it be used to purchase defense-related equipment, not for operations.

• Transferred $345.4 million in Defense Department funds for 13 Air Force Titan 34-D7 unmanned rockets to launch satellites into orbit.

• Transferred $84.4 million from the Navy's aircraft procurement account to Air Force research and development.

• Transferred $316.9 million for the Air Force's expendable-launch-vehicle program, which included $28 million for a classified project and $56.4 million for repairs to the Air Force Titan launch pad in Vandenberg, Calif.

• Extended the availability of $100 million to improve the procurement of computer services for the Defense Department.

• Earmarked $5 million in Department of Defense funds for property loss claims from an explosion at the Army munitions center near Checotah, Okla.

• Earmarked $3 million "and ammunition as necessary" for operating the National Rifle Matches at Camp Perry, Ohio. This consolidated federal costs from various accounts, which had averaged about $3 million a year, to run the Civilian Marksmanship Program.

• Earmarked $260 million for medical services under the Civilian Health and Medical Program of the Uniformed Services (CHAMPUS).

• Earmarked $38 million for a new drug interdiction program to be conducted by the Defense Department, including $12 million for a new radar system in the Bahamas.

• Directed the U.S. Army Corps of Engineers to use $8.2 million in existing funds to build the Cooper River seismic modification project in South Carolina, in addition to $1.4 million for a sediment retention structure at Mount St. Helens in Washington.

• Transferred $3 million within the Corps of Engineers to eliminate a 5 percent pay cut proposed by the administration in fiscal 1986.

• Appropriated $25 million for Corps of Engineers flood control and authorized $1 million for development of an emergency plan to control flooding along the Great Lakes.

• Transferred $62 million for research on the strategic defense initiative space-based anti-missile system.

• Earmarked $55.6 million for defense research at Syracuse University, Iowa State University, Wichita State University, University of Kansas, University of Nevada-Las Vegas, Northeastern University in Boston, Oregon Graduate Center, Oklahoma State University and the Rochester Institute of Technology in New York.

• Earmarked, by transfer, $50 million in foreign aid for Northern Ireland.

• Transferred $2.7 million for anti-terrorism aid.

• Earmarked $21.7 million for economic aid and $750,000 for military aid to Haiti.

• Appropriated $100 million for economic assistance and $50 million in military aid to the Philippines.

• Extended direct loan authority of the Export-Import Bank through fiscal 1987.

Housing, Urban Development

• Rescinded unobligated housing program budget authority totaling $6.7 billion in fiscal 1986 and $6 billion in fiscal 1987, to offset additional spending included elsewhere in the bill. The 1986 rescissions included $5.3 billion in assisted housing, $1.2 billion in rent supplements and $283.6 million in rental housing assistance.

• Extended the loan guarantee authority of the Federal Housing Administration (FHA) from June 6, 1986, to July 25, 1986. Separate legislation cleared by Congress June 24 (PL 99-345) reauthorized FHA and other federal housing programs through fiscal 1986.

• Raised the FHA loan guarantee ceiling from $74.4 billion to $132 billion and transferred $30 million within FHA for salaries and expenses.

• Raised the limit on guarantees of mortgage-backed securities by the Government National Mortgage Association (Ginnie Mae) from $126 billion to $175 billion.

• Disapproved all deferrals for assisted housing, housing for the elderly or handicapped, rehabilitation loans and Community Development Block Grants, totaling $3.4 billion.

• Dropped Senate language that would have changed the distribution formula of the Urban Development Action Grant program (UDAG). Similar language revising the UDAG formula was contained in separate housing authorization legislation passed by the House and pending in the Senate (HR 1, S 2507). *(Housing, p. 585)*

• Appropriated $1.6 million for salaries and expenses of the American Battle Monuments Commission.

• Transferred $3 million from research and development in the Environmental Protection Agency (EPA) for salaries and expenses, and restated the intent that EPA apply budget cuts to its programs evenly under the Gramm-Rudman-Hollings deficit-control law.

• Released an additional $1.2 billion for water pollution control grants.

• Appropriated $250 million for disaster relief by the Federal Emergency Management Agency (FEMA) and transferred $2.9 million within FEMA for salaries and expenses.

• Appropriated $431 million for the National Aeronautics and Space Administration (NASA) for recovery and redesign costs to the space shuttle, with an additional $100 million provided in fiscal 1987 if the NASA administrator certified that it was implementing recommendations of the Rogers commission, which investigated the Jan. 28 explosion that destroyed the space shuttle *Challenger*. Also, $5 million was transferred for research and development of a robot to service the space station. The conference report directed NASA to find a "second source" contractor for solid-fuel rocket boosters for the space shuttle; currently, only one company (Morton Thiokol Inc.) manufactured the boosters. Failure of a solid-fuel rocket booster caused the *Challenger* explosion. *(Rogers commission, p. 328)*

• Provided $272 million for Veterans Administration (VA) compensation and pensions and $91 million for readjustment benefits for Vietnam veterans.

• Transferred between $25 million and $30 million for VA medical care, up to $6 million for general operating expenses and $35 million for the Veterans Job Training program.

• Permitted payment for VA loan guarantee contract services (mostly for default appraisals) from the revolving fund rather than general operating expenses, a move that would free money to hire extra staff to reduce the backlog in VA mortgage guarantee applications.

• Provided $3.4 million for more bank examiners at the Federal Home Loan Bank Board to improve supervision of financially troubled banks.

Interior Department

• Deferred $3 million for land acquisition under the Bureau of Land Management.

• Earmarked $2.4 million to complete acquisition of 15,000 acres in the Atchafalaya National Wildlife Refuge in Alabama.

• Appropriated $13.5 million to the National Park Service for park operations and $3.9 million for reconstruction of the C&O Canal between Harpers Ferry, W.Va., and Washington, D.C.; and approved reprogramming of $1.4 million for a loan to repair the Filene Center at Wolf Trap Farm Park near Washington, D.C.

• Rescinded $28.7 million in contract authority for the Land and Water Conservation Fund.

• Prohibited closure of the National Park Service's Pacific Northwest regional office in Seattle, and restricted drainage of lakes in the Delaware Water Gap National Recreation Area in Pennsylvania and New Jersey.

• Appropriated $1.4 million for the U.S. Geological Survey.

• Provided $29.2 million for the Bureau of Indian Affairs, most of it for firefighting.

• Appropriated $210.8 million for implementing the Compact of Free Association with Micronesia in the Pacific. *(1985 Almanac p. 99)*

• Cleared title to 55 acres of land to be transferred to Brantley County, Ga., for an industrial development park.

• Appropriated for the Forest Service $161,000 for spraying the Western spruce budworm in the Carson National Forest, N.M.; $165.7 million to replenish forest fire funds; $1.7 million for flood damage rehabilitation in various parks; and $4.4 million for land acquisition at Lake

Tahoe, in Nevada and California.

• Disapproved $3.2 million of a proposed $22.7 million deferral for the Forest Service Timber Salvage Sale fund.

• Approved $210,000 out of a proposed $710,000 rescission for the Office of Surface Mining Enforcement.

Energy Department

• Barred the administration from selling to the private sector any of the four hydroelectric Power Marketing Administrations in the lower 48 states or the Tennessee Valley Authority without authorization by Congress.

• Disapproved deferral of $23.2 million for energy research and development.

• Disapproved deferral of $14.9 million for energy conservation.

• Disapproved deferrals of $41.2 million for construction of new capacity and $577.5 million for oil acquisition for the Strategic Petroleum Reserve.

• Appropriated $1 billion to enable the Energy Department to repay notes issued to the Treasury to pay off the Federal Financing Bank debt on the Great Plains Coal Gasification Project. This was an internal bookkeeping transaction that involved no outlays.

Health, Human Services, Education

• Appropriated $2 million for Public Health Service emergency medical services for children.

• Blocked, until the end of fiscal 1987, rule changes proposed by the Department of Health and Human Services that would include hospital capital costs in the Medicare prospective payment system.

• Delayed, for 60 days, new rules by the Office of Management and Budget limiting the amount of overhead universities could charge to federal research grants.

• Allowed health planning agencies to continue operating as long as their unobligated fiscal 1986 funds lasted, providing for a more orderly phase-out if Congress killed funding for the program in fiscal 1987. *(Health planning story, p. 238)*

• Appropriated $6 million for the National Cancer Institute.

• Mandated that nurses at the National Institutes of Health Clinical Center receive the same rate of pay as nurses employed by the Veterans Administration.

• Provided $13.5 million for Indian health services and deferred $11.7 million for facilities.

• Directed the Department of Health and Human Services to give a federally owned building in Washington, D.C., to the city government for use as a shelter for the homeless, and appropriated $1.5 million for repairs.

• Appropriated $20 million for disaster assistance to local schools.

• Prohibited the implementation of new regulations that would reduce the amount of impact aid to school districts that had large numbers of students from military families, and directed that the formula for calculating impact aid payments use the actual number of children in average daily attendance at a school, as opposed to a different formula being used by the Department of Education.

• Earmarked $27.9 million for demonstration projects for the severely disabled.

• Provided $146 million for college student financial aid, restoring assistance to an estimated 100,000 students who would otherwise lose their Pell Grants.

• Prohibited closure of any of the 106 Job Corps centers until July 1, 1987.

Congress

• Appropriated $26 million for the legislative branch, of which $14.3 million was for improved security at the Capitol, including probable construction of a fence around the Capitol, $1 million for additional security personnel in the House and Senate, and $250,000 for the Architect of the Capitol to study new security systems. Also appropriated $8 million to replace 36 PCB electrical transformers on the Capitol grounds; $350,000 for the House ethics committee; and $912,000 for the Joint Committee on Taxation.

• Deleted a Senate-passed requirement that appropriations for congressional mail accurately reflect costs. (A ruling by the General Accounting Office allowed Congress to avoid a specific appropriation for mail costs.) The conference report recommended a joint committee be formed to improve congressional mailing procedures for the next Congress. *(Mail, p. 40)*

• Increased the clerk-hire allowance for senators from Alabama and Florida to reflect population growth, and permitted greater flexibility in transferring funds within Senate office accounts.

• Appropriated $1.6 million for the Capitol Power Plant and $867,000 for the Library of Congress, directing that $247,000 of that amount be used to reopen the library's public reading room on evenings and Sundays.

Transportation Department

• Appropriated $35.5 million for the Coast Guard, augmented by another $10.4 million in transfers.

• Directed that $750,000 in savings from reconstruction of the Great Point Lighthouse on Nantucket Island, Mass., be used for maintenance and preservation of other lighthouses in Massachusetts.

• Appropriated $80 million for the Federal Aviation Administration (FAA) and provided $4.2 million by transfer.

• Mandated that the FAA have a minimum of 14,480 air traffic controllers on staff by the end of the fiscal year on Sept. 30. As of March 31, the FAA work force was 14,028.

• Transferred $72.2 million from the Airport and Airway Trust Fund for FAA research and development for the Advanced Automation System of air traffic control.

• Authorized $5 million for protecting Interstate 80 from flooding by the Great Salt Lake in Utah.

• Eliminated a change in mass transit formula grants that adversely affected 92 newly designated urban areas.

• Appropriated $18.3 million for Panama Canal Commission operating expenses and vessel accident claims.

Treasury Department

• Appropriated $340 million for the Internal Revenue Service for processing tax returns, examinations and collections.

• Appropriated $30.8 million for the U.S. Customs Service for drug interdiction efforts and $3.2 million for the Air Interdiction program.

• Appropriated $3.5 million for construction of a new post office and courthouse annex in Charleston, S.C., and raised the cost ceiling for the project to $8.9 million. The post office was approved in 1981 at a cost of $5.4 million, but encountered delays.

• Raised the ceiling for transportation audit contract administration from $5.2 million to $7.6 million through Sept. 30, 1989. The program was designed to catch overcharges on transportation bills paid by the government.

• Directed the Federal Election Commission to exhaust all money-saving options short of cutting staff before cutting public information programs.

- Mandated that the federal government's charity fund-raising program operate under the same format as the last two years and not exclude advocacy organizations.
- Required the Department of Transportation to continue highway payments to New York City, despite a local anti-apartheid statute that could interfere with federal competitive bidding requirements.

House Committee Action

HR 4515 was reported by the House Appropriations Committee March 25 (H Rept 99-510). The bill, which contained $1.7 billion in new funding, was heavily amended in committee before being approved by voice vote March 20.

The committee bill provided new funds for disaster relief, air safety, flood control, Congress' mail, the Internal Revenue Service, the Coast Guard and the Customs Service.

Also, $150 million was to be released for short-term operation of the "superfund" hazardous-waste cleanup program. The program had nearly run out of money because a House-Senate impasse had prevented passage of a separate bill (HR 2005) reauthorizing the superfund. *(Story, p. 111)*

Transfers and Blocked Deferrals

By voice vote, the committee endorsed an amendment by Sidney R. Yates, D-Ill., repealing the president's deferral authority.

The committee disapproved a total of $9.4 billion of Reagan's $24.7 billion in deferral proposals. Nearly $8 billion of that was for housing and community development programs. Also restored were $512.9 million for the Strategic Petroleum Reserve, $40 million for the Economic Development Administration, $23.1 million for energy programs and $9.35 million for maritime programs.

The bill made a $702 million first installment on anti-terrorist improvements to U.S. diplomatic posts, not through new spending but by transferring money from existing accounts.

Of the $702 million, $454 million was for construction, $237 million for salaries and expenses and $10 million for various counterterrorism efforts.

The transfer was approved by voice vote, after the committee adopted, 22-20, an amendment by David R. Obey, D-Wis., requiring the administration to transfer the money from defense or foreign aid accounts.

HR 4515 included other transfers from approved appropriations, as members sought sources other than new money to stay within deficit limits mandated by Gramm-Rudman-Hollings.

'Urgent' Funding

The bill had started out as an "urgent" supplemental appropriations measure providing $449.5 million in new budget authority and $36.5 million in fund transfers.

Committee amendments raised the total to $1.7 billion. In addition to new spending, the bill included $996.5 million in transfers, most of that for the embassy security program.

Much of the original bill was devoted to relief for areas hit by disasters, particularly Western states flooded in February. Of $382 million related to disaster aid, $250 million was for the Federal Emergency Management Agency, $52 million for loans to small businesses, $20 million for school repairs, $35 million for soil conservation in flooded rural areas and $25 million for flood-control projects.

The committee approved $85 million to prevent furloughs at the Federal Aviation Administration (FAA) and pay for air traffic controllers and airline safety inspections. The FAA funding would offset a $96 million cut made in the agency budget March 1 as part of the first across-the-board reductions under the Gramm-Rudman-Hollings law. Other provisions intended to allay that law's impact included $3.7 million for meat inspections, and language barring the closing of a court in Mississippi, home state of Appropriations Chairman Jamie L. Whitten, D.

Other amendments, approved by voice votes, added $340 million for computers and staffing at the IRS; $35.5 million for the Coast Guard; $30.8 million for Customs Service agents' salaries and drug-interdiction efforts; and $20 million for the WIC nutrition program for poor women, infants and children.

The committee bill appropriated $50 million for economic aid to Northern Ireland, the first payment of a $250 million package (HR 4329) that the House authorized March 11 at the urging of Speaker Thomas P. O'Neill Jr., D-Mass. *(Story, p. 379)*

Since Congress was about to exceed its $95 million mailing budget for fiscal 1986, the bill provided another $42.2 million.

House Floor Action

The House passed HR 4515 May 8, on its third try. Floor action on the measure had been sidetracked twice during the previous month.

On April 16, Democratic leaders halted action on the bill after Republicans stymied a key vote on aid to Nicaraguan rebels, known as "contras."

On April 22, action was blocked when jurisdictional disputes between the Appropriations and Agriculture committees caused the defeat of a rule governing debate on the bill.

Contra Aid

The Democratic leadership first brought HR 4515 to the House floor April 15 under a convoluted rule (H Res 415), adopted 212-208, that linked the supplemental bill to contra aid. But the supplemental was pulled from the floor the following day after Republicans staged a surprise parliamentary maneuver that resulted in separation of the two issues. *(Vote 72, p. 24-H; details, contra aid, p. 394)*

Jurisdictional Disputes

On April 22, HR 4515 was sidetracked again, when the House by a 187-220 vote rejected a second rule (H Res 425) for debating the measure, thereby preventing the bill from being considered. *(Vote 82, p. 26-H)*

The setback was caused largely by rebellious Democrats, particularly members of the Agriculture and Armed Services committees, who charged that they were bypassed by the restrictive procedures used to draft and debate the bill.

Sixty Democrats joined 160 Republicans in opposition, providing a majority vote to defeat the rule. All but eight Republicans voted against the rule, primarily because of a provision in the bill that would have repealed Reagan's power to defer spending money previously appropriated by Congress.

Members of the Agriculture Committee especially complained that they had no say in numerous farm policy changes written by the Appropriations Committee — a procedure that violated a House prohibition against allowing legislative language in an appropriations bill.

Also, several Democrats on the Armed Services Committee were angry at the Rules Committee for allowing a nuclear test ban amendment to be offered. The House Feb. 26 had passed a non-binding resolution (H J Res 3) calling for a test ban, but the Armed Services Committee had not acted on test ban legislation. *(Story, p. 461)*

If H Res 425 had been adopted, no objections could have been raised against the violations of House procedures because of waivers contained in the rule. Eight major amendments to HR 4515 that House rules normally would have banned also would have been protected.

Of the 60 Democrats who voted against the rule on HR 4515, fully one-third — 20 votes — came from majority members of the Agriculture Committee. Ten Armed Services Democrats also opposed the rule.

Leadership Concessions

In their third attempt to pass the supplemental, Democratic leaders satisfied rural and conservative members by making compromises in the rule governing floor consideration of the bill (H Res 448 — H Rept 99-586).

First, they gave Agriculture Committee Chairman E. "Kika" de la Garza, D-Texas, the procedural right to challenge about half of the bill's farm provisions, which had been written by Appropriations Committee Chairman Jamie L. Whitten, D-Miss.

Next, they dropped a nuclear test ban amendment opposed by conservative members of the Armed Services Committee. Patricia Schroeder, D-Colo., sponsor of the amendment and a committee member, said she would offer it later to a different measure. Her proposal would have barred U.S. nuclear weapons testing unless the Soviet Union resumed tests.

Finally, the Rules Committee cut from eight to five the number of amendments granted special protection from procedural challenges.

The committee also dropped an amendment by Minority Leader Robert H. Michel, R-Ill., to establish a new deferral process that would restrict the president less than the original language and a "Buy American" requirement for offshore oil rigs proposed by Douglas H. Bosco, D-Calif.

The rule automatically dropped two controversial sections of the bill: $42.2 million for congressional mailing costs and a provision rewriting a section of the 1985 farm bill (PL 99-198) aimed at stopping soil erosion.

Republicans renewed their complaints about the new rule May 8, with Minority Whip Trent Lott, R-Miss., describing it as "patched together with sealing wax, chewing gum and a charm." He appealed to conservative Democrats again to vote it down, saying: "Let's form another coalition."

But this time the Democratic leadership had done its homework, and the rule passed 212-189, allowing the House to take up the bill. *(Vote 103, p. 32-H)*

House Passage

After making concessions to rural and conservative members, the House May 8 passed the $1.7 billion bill by a comfortable 110-vote margin. The vote was 242-132. *(Vote 108, p. 34-H)*

Democrats beat back two GOP attempts to eliminate or weaken a provision in HR 4515 aimed at repealing much of Reagan's power to defer spending funds appropriated by Congress. Reagan had threatened to veto the bill because of its deferral language and its cost.

As passed by the House, the bill specifically overturned more than $5 billion in deferrals Reagan had proposed for fiscal 1986, including $3.3 billion for subsidized housing and $700 million for rural housing programs.

The House adopted amendments adding $10 million to compensate dairy farmers whose herds had been poisoned by pesticide-contaminated feed, and $21.7 million in foreign aid for Haiti. However, half a dozen farm provisions were knocked out on procedural grounds.

The administration's $2.1 billion supplemental appropriations request had included $702 million for improved embassy security and anti-terrorism programs. As approved by the House, the security and anti-terrorism programs were to be funded instead by transferring money from the Department of Defense and certain foreign aid programs to the State Department. That reduction was partially offset by $305 million in new appropriations, mostly for domestic programs, not requested by the administration.

The bill brought total discretionary spending to within about $256 million of the limit set by the fiscal 1986 budget resolution (S Con Res 32). *(1985 Almanac p. 441)*

Lott maintained that "the majority of this bill [the supplemental] is not urgent.... It's a lead balloon that's going down sooner or later."

But other members, including Silvio O. Conte, R-Mass., ranking minority member of the Appropriations Committee, argued that most of the funds were desperately needed — especially for the IRS, which would have to delay mailing taxpayers' refunds if pending staff cuts took place.

"What we are seeing is the reaction to Gramm-Rudman-Hollings," Conte said. "A lot of the Gramm-Rudman cuts are disastrous and should be restored."

Agriculture Provisions. Because of the jurisdictional dispute between de la Garza and Whitten, 11 farm provisions in HR 4515 became a crucial factor.

As provided for by the Rules Committee, and with de la Garza's approval, money for five popular programs was kept in the bill: new funding of $20 million for the WIC feeding program; and transfers of $14 million for citrus canker control and compensation, $10 million for control of avian influenza, $35 million for Department of Agriculture flood relief activities and $3.7 million for meat and poultry inspection.

Also retained was language blocking a $700 million deferral for the Farmers Home Administration (FmHA) Rural Housing Insurance Fund loan program, and transferring $71.6 million for salaries and expenses at the Agriculture Stabilization and Conservation Service.

Six provisions were struck from the bill on parliamentary points of order raised by Conte, mainly because they violated a rule prohibiting legislative language in an appropriations bill.

Amendments. Besides rejecting deferral amendments offered by Dick Armey, R-Texas, and Lott, the House rejected, 157-241, a proposal by Robert S. Walker, R-Pa., to cut $30 million in aid for Northern Ireland, reducing the appropriation to $20 million. *(Vote 104, p. 32-H)*

Among the amendments adopted by voice votes were those by:

• John Paul Hammerschmidt, R-Ark., adding $10 million for the dairy indemnity program to compensate farmers in Arkansas, Missouri and Oklahoma.

• Daniel A. Mica, D-Fla., restricting the expenditure of embassy security funds to the terms spelled out in the House-passed Omnibus Diplomatic Security and Anti-Terrorism Act (HR 4151).

• Walter E. Fauntroy, D-D.C., adding $21.7 million in economic aid to Haiti.

• Vic Fazio, D-Calif., barring the administration from selling to the private sector any of the four Power Marketing Administrations in the lower 48 states or the Tennessee Valley Authority, which controlled most of the nation's hydroelectric power facilities. A Conte amendment also was accepted, limiting to $400,000 the amount of money the Department of Energy could spend on studies of the proposed sale.

• Dan Rostenkowski, D-Ill., blocking the Department of Health and Human Services from issuing regulations governing the reimbursement of hospital capital costs, to give the Ways and Means Committee time to legislate on the issue.

• Conte, adding $6 million for the National Cancer Institute.

• Edward P. Boland, D-Mass., striking a short-term extension of the superfund program, which already had been extended by earlier legislation passed in March.

• Mike Strang, R-Colo., prohibiting the Labor Department from closing six Job Corps centers in Colorado, Oregon, Missouri, Kentucky and Oklahoma.

The Labor Department, in announcing the closures May 8, referred to the six Job Corps centers as the nation's worst. Closing them would save about $20 million and eliminate about 1,200 training positions, officials said. The Job Corps currently operated 106 training centers for the disadvantaged. The 21-year-old program had been targeted for cuts by Reagan.

Senate Committee Action

The Senate Appropriations Committee reported HR 4515 (S Rept 99-301) May 15. The Senate version appropriated $3.9 billion — more than twice the amount voted earlier by the House.

But the panel agreed to about $4.7 billion in rescissions not included by the House, mostly in housing programs. The Senate measure also overturned about $4.9 billion in deferrals proposed by Reagan for fiscal 1986 in such areas as the Economic Development Administration and community development grants.

While noting that it "shares in the frustration" over Reagan's use of deferrals, the Senate panel eliminated the House curbs on the practice. The administration had threatened to veto the House bill largely because of its provisions weakening the deferral process.

Both House and Senate versions of HR 4515 included funding for Reagan's plans to step up security at embassies and other diplomatic posts. However, the Senate panel included only $660 million of the $702 million requested for fiscal 1986 and specified that the money could not be spent until after the fiscal year ended Sept. 30.

The House version would provide immediately the full $702 million sought by Reagan for fiscal 1986 but would do so by transferring funds from other accounts. The Senate committee recommended new budget authority, as the president requested.

The panel also granted the administration's April 23 request for $150 million for the Philippines. The total, to be transferred from Pentagon appropriations, included $100 million in economic aid and $50 million in military assistance.

Closer to home, the Senate committee agreed to include $13 million to improve security around the Capitol. The panel said the funds could not be used until a detailed plan was approved by the appropriate authorizing committees.

The Senate committee also agreed to:

• Provide $526 million for the National Aeronautics and Space Administration for restoring the three existing space shuttles, which had been grounded since the Jan. 28 explosion of the *Challenger.*

• Provide $5.3 billion for the Commodity Credit Corporation for farm price support payments.

• Appropriate $146 million for Pell Grants to needy college students, to make up partially for a shortfall in funding for the $3.4 billion program.

Senators' Honoraria

The committee killed a proposal by William Proxmire, D-Wis., to lower the ceiling on senators' honoraria earnings — from an amount equal to 40 percent of members' income to 30 percent.

The Senate raised the cap to 40 percent in 1985 as part of an omnibus continuing appropriations resolution (PL 99-190). The change did not apply to the House. *(1985 Almanac p. 360)*

"This is a very unfortunate way for senators to increase their compensation," said Proxmire. "We ought to stand up and vote on it." Proxmire's proposal failed a second time on the Senate floor June 5.

The House April 22 had voted to raise the limit on its outside income to the 40 percent cap. The next day, fearing political fallout, representatives reversed themselves and restored the 30 percent limit. *(Details, p. 37)*

Pentagon Pork

Proxmire also lost an effort to delete what he called pork-barrel funding of university research facilities. He proposed eliminating provisions earmarking $80.6 million in defense funds for specified universities in the home states of key senators.

Defense Secretary Caspar W. Weinberger and some academic organizations had objected to the increasingly frequent congressional practice of earmarking funding for university projects that had not been subjected to the scrutiny of fellow scientists.

Ted Stevens, R-Alaska, chairman of the Appropriations Subcommittee on Defense, supported the projects but said the committee would not consider future requests to earmark defense research funds for unauthorized projects.

Proxmire's amendment to strike the funding was rejected 7-17.

Senate Floor Action

The Senate passed its $3.9 billion version of HR 4515 June 6 by a 71-8 vote. *(Vote 123, p. 23-S)*

The bill took on new urgency when the Agriculture Department announced June 4 that once again it had run out of borrowing authority for farm price support programs financed through the Commodity Credit Corporation. The Senate bill included $5.3 billion to reimburse the CCC through Sept. 30, the end of fiscal 1986. *(Earlier CCC supplementals, p. 161)*

Also, the Federal Housing Administration's authority to insure new home loans expired June 6. The Senate by voice vote approved an amendment to HR 4515 to extend that authority to July 25. *(FHA extension, p. 587)*

Deficit Spending Waivers

During consideration of the measure, the Senate twice voted to suspend the requirement of the Gramm-Rudman-Hollings prohibition on additions to the deficit.

The first Gramm-Rudman vote came June 5 when members voted 65-33 to waive the deficit restrictions and order the Internal Revenue Service not to impose new record-keeping requirements on taxpayers who deducted automobile expenses. The prohibition on record-keeping was then adopted 81-17. *(Votes 115, 116, p. 22-S)*

The second waiver was approved June 6 after Phil Gramm, R-Texas, objected to an amendment by J. Bennett Johnston, D-La., to add $44 million for trade adjustment aid for job retraining for unemployed oil and gas workers. Members voted 55-40 to waive the requirements, and agreed by voice vote to the amendment. *(Vote 118, p. 22-S; trade adjustment aid, p. 351)*

Other Amendments

Senators agreed by voice vote June 5 to remove a prepayment penalty for rural utilities that refinanced loans through the Rural Electrification Administration and to let farmers keep advance subsidies on crops even though bad weather prevented planting.

Earlier, the amendment was held germane on a 62-36 vote. *(Vote 112, p. 21-S)*

Also approved by voice vote was a proposal to prevent the administration from selling government-owned power-generating operations. An amendment by Gordon J. Humphrey, R-N.H., to let the administration study the feasibility of such "privatization" was tabled, 73-25. *(Vote 113, p. 21-S)*

Proxmire's second attempt to limit the amount of honoraria senators could receive for making speeches was blocked on a procedural vote, 68-30. *(Vote 114, p. 22-S)*

The Senate knocked out of the bill a committee provision that would have earmarked $80.6 million in defense funds for specific universities in the states of key senators. An amendment to drop the provision was adopted by voice vote after an attempt to table it failed, 40-58. *(Vote 117, p. 22-S)*

In other action, the Senate:

- On a 40-52 vote, ruled non-germane a Wilson, R-Calif., amendment to prohibit members of Congress from using franking privileges for mass mailings of unsolicited material. *(Vote 119, p. 22-S)*
- On a 48-47 vote, tabled an Exon, D-Neb., amendment to prevent the Federal Energy Regulatory Commission from deregulating the price structure of old natural gas. *(Vote 120, p. 22-S)*
- On a 46-44 procedural vote, found non-germane an Abdnor, R-S.D., amendment to permit debt-stressed farmers to participate in the interest rate reduction program for guaranteed Farmers Home Administration loans. *(Vote 121, p. 23-S)*
- On a 45-47 vote, ruled non-germane a Kennedy, D-Mass., amendment to transfer $62 million from Reagan's strategic defense initiative to certain nutrition programs. *(Vote 122, p. 23-S)*

Defense Dispute

During a late-night meeting June 5, leaders of the Armed Services Committee and the Appropriations Subcommittee on Defense reached a truce in a running turf battle over spending allocations for the Defense Department.

Leaders of the two committees had clashed repeatedly over which panel had final authority over Pentagon appropriations for specific programs that had not been authorized. The agreement hammered out June 5 settled the immediate dispute by authorizing upwards of $6 billion that had been appropriated previously.

It also provided for more cooperation between the two panels in the future.

The defense feud involved the Appropriations panel's language to repeal Armed Services' control over unauthorized Pentagon appropriations.

At issue was funding for various defense programs that the Appropriations panel in 1985 had included in the fiscal 1986 continuing appropriations resolution (PL 99-190). That money, which the Armed Services Committee said totaled $6.5 billion, exceeded amounts authorized for specific programs in the companion defense authorization bill (PL 99-145) produced by the Armed Services Committee. The continuing resolution included a requirement that the excess funds not be spent unless authorized by a subsequent law. *(1985 Almanac pp. 138, 377)*

After clashing briefly on the floor, Stevens, chairman of the Appropriations Subcommittee on Defense, and Barry Goldwater, R-Ariz., his counterpart on Armed Services, retired to a back room and spent four hours negotiating a settlement.

Goldwater and Nunn eventually agreed to approve most of the defense money that Stevens wanted to spend in fiscal 1986.

The committees' leaders drafted a document that included a pledge from Stevens not to continue putting funds in appropriations measures that exceeded the authorizing limits already set by Armed Services.

The treaty also gave the chairman and senior minority members of each panel the right to sit as informal members of the other group when each was marking up its major annual bill.

"We've now agreed that we'll allow each other into the committee process," Stevens said. "It's really a new beginning for a better relationship between the two committees."

Conference Action

The conference report (H Rept 99-649) was filed June June 19.

The House June 24 adopted the conference report by a 355-52 vote. The Senate cleared it by voice vote June 25, after abandoning a last-ditch effort to provide $7 million for trade adjustment assistance for laid-off oil and gas workers. *(Vote 174, p. 54-H)*

Conferees had settled a number of major disputes, largely in the administration's favor. But before adopting the conference report on the bill, Congress made further concessions to Reagan by restricting a bailout for rural utility cooperatives.

Even after the White House had given its blessing, a few last-minute sticking points developed between lawmakers on such issues as urban development grants, unemployment assistance for laid-off oil and gas workers, university research funding and aid to Northern Ireland. Those were resolved only hours before Congress adjourned for the Fourth of July recess.

House Agreements

The House agreed to drop its provision repealing the president's power to defer spending for policy reasons after receiving a promise from the administration that no further deferrals would be made during the rest of the 1986 calendar year.

Another controversy involved allowing utility cooperatives to escape a prepayment penalty if they refinanced their loans from the Rural Electrification Administration (REA). The administration claimed this would cost taxpayers up to $20 billion in lost interest over the life of the loans.

In addition to the concessions made by conferees to limit refinancing REA loans, the House June 25 agreed by voice vote to a new proposal that gave the Treasury Department power to block individual applications if the refinancing exposed the government to excessive losses. The Senate concurred June 26.

Lawmakers cited estimates from the Congressional Budget Office that even with the Treasury veto power, at least $300 million in REA loan refinancing was expected in fiscal 1986.

The House refused to accept two major items sponsored by the Senate.

By voice vote June 25, it struck a Senate plan to expand the awards formula for economic development aid under the Urban Development Action Grant program.

An identical UDAG formula change, designed to benefit newer and smaller cities in the South and West, was contained in separate housing legislation (HR 1) that passed the House June 12. In order to keep pressure on the Senate to pass a housing bill, House members balked at granting the UDAG changes in the funding bill. *(Housing bill, p. 585)*

Also June 25, the House deleted a Senate provision that would have blocked IRS record-keeping requirements for vehicles used for business. According to the Joint Committee on Taxation, passage of the amendment would have cost the Treasury an estimated $200 million in lost revenue in fiscal 1987.

Senate Action

On June 26, the Senate by voice vote agreed to the compromise language on deferrals, REA, UDAG and the IRS regulations. Three other issues were resolved as follows:

- The Senate voted 56-42 to retain a conference provision targeting $55.6 million in defense research funds to specific universities. This reversed a June 5 decision, when the Senate agreed to drop the targeting provision. *(Vote 153, p. 28-S)*
- On a 65-31 vote, the Senate retained $50 million in economic aid to Northern Ireland. *(Vote 154, p. 28-S)*
- Senators tried unsuccessfully to restore funding for trade adjustment assistance for unemployed oil and gas workers, which conferees had deleted because of White House opposition. The Senate agreed to waive Gramm-Rudman-Hollings rules and add a scaled-down $7 miilion appropriation.

But the House knocked it out on a parliamentary point of order, and the Senate concurred, clearing HR 4515 for the president. ∎

CCC Supplemental Funds

Congress completed action March 20 on an emergency funding bill (H J Res 534 — PL 99-263) providing an additional $5 billion in fiscal 1986 appropriations for the Commodity Credit Corporation (CCC).

The CCC, an Agriculture Department agency that distributes price- and income-support benefits to farmers, had run out of money two weeks earlier after conferees on H J Res 534 effectively added nearly $1 billion for Farmers Home Administration (FmHA) loans.

The Senate killed that additional funding, which the White House insisted would violate the spending restrictions of the Gramm-Rudman-Hollings deficit-reduction law (PL 99-177).

The final version of the bill directed the administration to use the full $1.7 billion previously appropriated for farm loans. Conferees said "other funds" should be found if that amount proved inadequate.

H J Res 534 was the second supplemental appropriation for the CCC to be approved in 1986. On Feb. 6, both chambers had passed an urgent supplemental measure (H J Res 520 — PL 99-243) providing $1.5 billion to cover expenses of the CCC through the end of the month.

That was in addition to the $13.3 billion appropriated by the fiscal 1986 continuing resolution (PL 99-190), cleared Dec. 19, 1985. The administration had asked for about $8.8 billion to meet CCC's needs through Sept. 30, 1986, the end of the fiscal year.

Congress voted an additional $5.3 billion for CCC programs in a catchall fiscal 1986 supplemental appropriations bill cleared June 26 (HR 4515 — PL 99-349). *(Story, p. 161)*

Background

The CCC was authorized to borrow up to $25 billion from the Treasury to distribute to farmers in the form of crop loans, income subsidies and other farm price supports. Congress reimbursed the agency for losses incurred when farmers defaulted on loans and surrendered the crops offered as collateral rather than repay the principal and interest.

Bumper 1985 harvests of corn and other grains resulted in lower prices, which forced more crops into the loan program instead of the marketplace. Furthermore, the Agriculture Department planned to distribute more money than usual in fiscal 1986 by giving partial income subsidies to farmers in advance of the planting season.

Legislative History

H J Res 534 was passed by the House Feb. 26 on a 321-86 vote. The Senate passed it by voice vote March 5. *(Vote 25, p. 10-H)*

Before passing the bill, the Senate stripped out a House-passed requirement that crop insurance and conservation reserve programs be funded on a line-item basis, instead of the existing method of paying for them out of the general CCC account.

The initial conference report was filed March 12 (H Rept 99-493). House conferees, led by Jamie L. Whitten, D-Miss., chairman of the Appropriations Subcommittee on Agriculture, agreed March 11 to drop their previous demand to restrict funding on soil conservation programs. But in return, Whitten insisted on language reflecting the spending levels for FmHA loans in the fiscal 1986 continuing appropriations resolution (PL 99-190).

That resolution, signed Dec. 19, 1985, was superseded Dec. 23 by the 1985 farm programs authorization bill (PL 99-198), which cut direct FmHA loans in fiscal 1986 by nearly $1 billion.

The administration had held to the lower amount in estimating spending for 1986. Adding the money back would push spending over the limits set by Gramm-Rudman-Hollings. *(Appropriations, 1985 Almanac p. 395; authorization, 1985 Almanac p. 517; Gramm-Rudman-Hollings, 1985 Almanac p. 459)*

Administration officials also maintained that the money was not needed. President Reagan March 12 released $750 million from other contingency funds for farm loans. The White House promised a veto if Congress cleared any more spending for farm loans.

The House nonetheless approved the conference agreement by a 272-141 vote March 13. *(Vote 45, p. 14-H)*

But after hours of arguing, Senate Republican leaders won a key vote that knocked out the additional funds. In a confrontation reminiscent of the 1985 farm bill debates, conservative demands for deficit reduction were pitted against liberal pleas for dispensation for struggling farmers.

A pivotal scene in a late-night Senate session March 13 again positioned nervous farm-state Republicans at the fulcrum. As before, urban Democrats gave the Republican leadership enough weight to offset the election-year jitters of rural GOP senators.

In a surprisingly lopsided 61-33 vote, the Senate killed an effort to exempt the loan amendment from the restrictions of the Gramm-Rudman-Hollings law. Ten Republicans, most from Midwestern farm states, voted with Democratic proponents of the higher loan authority. But 21 Democrats voted with the Republican leadership to keep the lower spending amount. *(Vote 38, p. 8-S)*

A second conference March 18-19 settled on language requiring the agriculture secretary to make loans up to the $1.7 billion previously appropriated. If that ran out, conferees said in their report (H Rept 99-499), "other funds" should be found.

The Senate approved the compromise bill by voice vote March 19, and the House cleared it on a 352-71 vote the following day. *(Vote 59, p. 20-H)* ▮

Foreign Aid Cutbacks: Minimizing the Pain

In spite of election-year politics, Congress approved a surprisingly large foreign aid program for fiscal 1987, as part of the governmentwide appropriations bill (H J Res 738 — PL 99-591) cleared Oct. 17.

The foreign aid portion of the bill, known as a continuing resolution, totaled $13.4 billion — $2 billion below Reagan's request and $1 billion below the 1986 level. As a result, nearly all foreign aid programs faced cuts — but not of the meat-ax variety that had been predicted earlier in the year by many members of Congress and administration officials. *(Funding, chart, next page; continuing resolution, p. 219)*

As in the past, foreign aid was spared even deeper cuts partly because Congress acted on it behind closed doors. A handful of members from the House and Senate Appropriations committees — each of whom was sympathetic to at least some aid programs — negotiated the final spending figures in those private meetings. With members from each chamber seeking to protect their favored programs, foreign aid benefited from old-fashioned horse-trading.

In addition, the House, where opposition to foreign aid traditionally was strongest, never took separate votes on those programs.

When conference committee negotiations on foreign aid broke down Oct. 10, Rep. David R. Obey, D-Wis., chairman of the Appropriations Subcommittee on Foreign Operations, threatened to take foreign aid disagreements to the full House for votes. Fellow Democratic leaders balked, fearing a fight over foreign aid could tie up the entire bill and result in massive cuts — especially if members saw political advantage in voting to slash foreign aid just weeks before an election.

House and Senate staff aides went back to work Oct. 14 and produced an agreement that took the bite out of the deepest cuts that each chamber's bill had made. The final product was an uneasy balance among the kinds of programs favored by various members for ideological and other reasons. At the Senate's insistence, the bill provided more generous terms for foreign military-related aid programs than Obey had wanted. And pressure by House members resulted in substantially greater contributions to the international development banks than the Senate had proposed.

For political reasons, a few programs escaped any cuts. Most important were U.S. donations to Israel and Egypt — linked together in the aid program since those countries signed a peace treaty in 1979. Congress mandated Reagan's military and economic requests for both countries: $3 billion for Israel and $2.1 billion for Egypt. That combined total was nearly half of all direct U.S. aid to foreign governments.

Among the other politically popular programs that received all Reagan requested or more were: aid to Cyprus ($15 million), subsidies for American schools and hospitals abroad ($30 million), the Export-Import Bank ($900 million) and international disaster assistance ($70 million).

Because Congress "earmarked" minimum aid for some countries — such as Israel and Egypt — while cutting back on the overall total, the Reagan administration was forced to make extra-deep cuts in donations to countries not protected by Congress. In the three military aid programs, for example, Congress cut Reagan's total request by 26 percent; once money was set aside for earmarked countries, military aid to all other countries had to be cut an average of nearly 50 percent.

The State Department and the Agency for International Development next had to determine how much to give to individual countries after the earmarks were taken into account.

For the second year in a row, foreign aid was the center of a dispute between the congressional Appropriations and authorizations committees.

The appropriations conferees included in their bill several provisions that conflicted with the existing 1986-87 foreign aid authorizations bill (PL 99-83) approved by Congress in 1985. For example, the bill appropriated $900 million for the Military Assistance Program — $95 million more than the authorizations law supposedly permitted.

Foreign Aid Appropriations, Fiscal 1987

The following chart shows President Reagan's request, the House- and Senate-approved amounts, and the final amounts, in new budget authority, for foreign aid appropriations in fiscal 1987. Foreign aid programs were included in a continuing resolution (PL 99-591).

(Figures in parentheses show program limitations that do not count as new budget authority. The figures for individual development banks include only paid-in capital and direct contributions.)

Program	Request	House-Passed Amount	Senate-Passed Amount	Final Amount
Inter-American Development Bank	$ 130,500,983	$ 67,397,000	$ 0	$ 33,680,000
Inter-American Investment Corporation	13,000,000	0	0	0
World Bank	182,845,991	94,805,000	0	55,805,000
International Development Association	750,000,000	604,844,000	622,623,251	622,623,251
Special Facility for Sub-Saharan Africa	0	64,805,000	0	64,805,000
International Finance Corporation	35,033,000	25,125,000	0	0
Multilateral Investment Guarantee Agency	44,403,116	0	0	0
Asian Development Bank and Fund	143,232,676	96,697,000	122,133,200	104,638,676
African Development Fund	75,000,000	53,788,000	62,827,225	53,788,000
African Development Bank	17,986,359	13,988,000	0	13,988,000
Total callable capital for development banks	(3,819,092,476)	(2,103,662,869)	(251,367,220)	(2,093,170,995)
International organizations and programs	186,000,000	238,995,000	236,074,000	237,264,000
Subtotal, multilateral aid	**$ 1,578,002,125**	**$ 1,260,444,000**	**$ 1,043,657,676**	**$ 1,186,591,927**
Agriculture aid	709,900,000	619,839,000	649,500,000	639,613,000
Population aid	250,000,000	239,250,000	230,000,000	234,625,000
Health aid	150,843,000	173,525,000	160,000,000	166,762,000
Child survival fund	25,000,000	50,000,000	75,000,000	75,000,000
Education, human resources aid	179,789,000	146,847,000	155,000,000	155,000,000
Energy, selected development aid	217,210,000	135,657,000	145,000,000	140,328,500
Science and technology aid	14,258,000	9,323,000	10,000,000	9,661,500
Private sector revolving fund	(13,500,000)	(15,553,000)	(13,500,000)	(15,553,000)
American schools and hospitals abroad	10,000,000	33,495,000	35,000,000	35,000,000
International disaster aid	25,000,000	19,441,000	20,000,000	70,000,000
Sahel development	80,000,000	69,557,000	70,000,000	70,000,000
Foreign service retirement and disability fund	45,492,000	45,492,000	45,492,000	45,492,000
Deobligation/reobligation authority for Agency for International Development (AID)	0	100,000,000	100,000,000	100,000,000
AID operating expenses	388,900,000	340,600,000	340,600,000	340,600,000
AID inspector general	21,750,000	18,189,000	21,750,000	21,000,000
African Development Foundation	6,500,000	3,872,000	6,500,000	6,500,000
Inter-American Foundation	10,800,000	11,800,000	10,800,000	11,800,000
Trade and development program	18,000,000	16,331,000	20,000,000	20,000,000
Peace Corps	126,200,000	130,000,000	130,000,000	130,000,000
International narcotics control	65,445,000	65,445,000	65,445,000	65,445,000
Anti-drug initiative	0	38,000,000	48,000,000	56,000,000
Migration and refugee aid	347,525,000	347,525,000	346,856,000	346,856,000
Emergency refugee and migration aid	25,000,000	25,000,000	0	25,000,000
Anti-terrorism aid	9,840,000	9,840,000	9,840,000	9,840,000
Peace-keeping operations	39,000,000	29,378,000	34,000,000	31,689,000
Economic Support Fund	4,093,800,000	3,196,798,000	3,900,000,000	3,550,000,000
Subtotal, bilateral aid	**$ 6,860,252,000**	**$ 5,875,204,000**	**$ 6,628,783,000**	**$ 6,345,212,500**
Military Assistance Program grants	1,046,450,000	675,697,000	0	900,000,000
International military education and training	68,830,000	47,082,000	65,000,000	56,000,000
Foreign Military Sales loans and credits	5,611,000,000	4,264,744,284	4,922,523,284	4,040,441,284
Defense Acquisition Fund	(350,000,000)	(280,820,000)	(350,000,000)	(315,820,000)
Subtotal, military aid	**$ 6,726,280,000**	**$ 4,987,523,284**	**$ 4,987,523,284**	**$ 4,996,441,284**
Housing Guaranty program	10,000,000	(145,464,000)	(145,464,000)	(145,464,000)
Overseas Private Investment Corporation	(165,000,000)	(223,000,000)	(165,000,000)	(223,000,000)
Export-Import Bank total limitation	(12,019,175,000)	(12,267,568,000)	(12,919,175,000)	(12,273,371,500)
Export-Import Bank direct loans	0	900,000,000	900,000,000	900,000,000
Fair Export Financing Program	300,000,000	0	0	0
GRAND TOTAL	**$ 15,474,534,125**	**$ 13,023,171,284**	**$ 13,559,963,960**	**$ 13,428,245,711**

(Authorizations bill, 1985 Almanac p. 41)

Although some members and staff aides of the two authorizing committees, House Foreign Affairs and Senate Foreign Relations, complained about the changes made by the appropriations bill, there was little they could do. The appropriations bill simply declared that its earmarks, ceilings and limitations on funding overrode previous laws.

Conference Compromise

'Security Assistance'

By far the most controversial part of the foreign aid program was what the Reagan administration called "security assistance" to friendly allies. That included two programs to help countries buy weapons, ammunition and military services: the Military Assistance Program (MAP), which made grants, and the Foreign Military Sales program (FMS), which made both loans and grants.

A third major military aid program was International Military Education and Training, which subsidized training at U.S. installations for foreign officers. Also counted as security assistance was the Economic Support Fund (ESF), which provided loans and grants to bolster the economies of key allies.

In fiscal 1986, the security assistance programs spent $9.2 billion. Reagan requested $10.8 billion for 1987 — by far the biggest increase he asked for any aspect of foreign aid.

In writing their bills, the House and Senate subcommittees on Foreign Operations handled the security aid issues in almost totally opposite ways.

Accepting Chairman Obey's call for budget "fairness," the House panel cut all aid programs according to a complicated series of formulas. The result was $4.99 billion for military aid programs and $3.2 billion for the Economic Support Fund — producing an $8.2 billion total far below both the fiscal 1986 level and Reagan's request.

The Senate Foreign Operations Subcommittee, under Bob Kasten, R-Wis., decided to use the 1987 budget to "reform" the military aid programs. Kasten argued that the United States had been forcing foreign nations to take out massive loans so they could modernize their armies. Egypt, Turkey and several other financially strapped countries were currently struggling to repay past loans.

The solution, Kasten said, was to give, rather than lend, those countries the money to buy military goods from the United States. As proposed by Kasten, the Senate-passed bill allowed Reagan to convert into grants up to $3.5 billion in previously appropriated but unused loans. The Senate bill also proposed abolishing the grant Military Assistance Program. In its place, the bill would have put the entire Foreign Military Sales program into the grant category; the practical effect would have been to convert about $1.9 billion worth of proposed loans into grants.

In conference negotiations, Obey adamantly refused to accept the conversion of military loans into grants, saying foreign countries "should not get a better deal than American farmers." Kasten, however, held out for military aid reforms.

In their compromise, conference negotiators settled for about the same total of military aid that each bill had proposed: $4.99 billion. However, they boosted the Military Assistance Program to $900 million and required that all of the $4 billion Foreign Military Sales program would have to be either grants or low-interest loans. That compromise reduced the interest rate on about $666 million worth of loans from 8 percent to 5 percent.

In their report (H Rept 99-1005), the foreign aid conferees said the Senate's military aid reform proposals had "merit," and they asked the administration to submit a reform plan to Congress along with the 1988 budget early in 1987.

The other major security aid issue was the size of the Economic Support Fund. The House and Senate bills were $700 million apart; conferees just about split the difference at $3.55 billion.

In a move to reduce the impact of actual budget outlays during 1987, the bill allowed the administration to spend the $3.55 billion during both fiscal years 1987-88.

The bill earmarked minimum security aid amounts for the following countries and regions:

- **Israel.** $1.8 billion in military aid and $1.2 billion in economic aid for Israel — all in grants. To increase its value to Israel, the bill continued a past requirement that all $1.2 billion of the economic money be given to Israel within 30 days of enactment.

The bill set aside $450 million of Israel's military aid for development of the new Lavi fighter plane. Since 1984, Congress had earmarked $1.8 billion for the plane. Conferees said the Pentagon must release money for the Lavi as soon as it found that contracts met "technical standards." That provision was aimed at thwarting the Pentagon's past practice of holding up payments on the Lavi as a way of pressuring Israel to consider dropping the program.

The final bill also included a Senate provision allowing the United States to lease military equipment to an ally — and to lease equipment from that country in exchange. The United States already leased military equipment both from and to other countries. But in the past there was no provision for one lease in exchange for another.

The main purpose of the provision was to allow a cross-lease between the United States and Israel. The Pentagon had leased Kfir fighters from Israel for training, and Israel, in exchange, reportedly wanted to lease Cobra antitank helicopters from the Army.

- **Egypt.** $1.3 billion in military aid and $815 million in economic aid. Of the latter amount, at least $115 million must be an outright grant with no strings attached, and another $200 million must be for subsidies of U.S. exports to Egypt.
- **Pakistan.** $312.5 million in arms aid and $250 million in economic aid.
- **Greece, Turkey.** $343 million in military aid for Greece and $490 million in military aid for Turkey — amounts equivalent to a traditional 7-10 ratio in military aid to the two countries. Reagan had sought another $150 million in economic aid for Turkey.
- **Central America.** $300 million in ESF aid was earmarked in the military construction part of PL 99-591 for Central American countries other than Nicaragua. Reagan had requested about $600 million.
- **Philippines.** A minimum of $200 million in ESF aid. Reagan had requested $95 million in ESF aid, plus $100 million in military aid and $30 million in development aid for the Philippines. Because of overall cuts, it was uncertain what the final total for the Philippines would be. The bill also repealed a provision of the 1986-87 foreign aid authorizations law (PL 99-83) that limited military aid to the Philippines to $50 million annually. Congress wrote the limit in 1985 to protest the authoritarian regime of President Ferdinand E. Marcos. Aid conferees said the provision "is no longer needed" since the coming to power of a new

government headed by Corazon Aquino. *(Philippines, p. 392)*

• **Ireland.** $35 million in ESF aid for both Northern Ireland (a part of the United Kingdom) and the Republic of Ireland.

• **Cyprus.** $15 million in ESF funds for scholarships and other programs, five times Reagan's request.

International Banks

Among the hardest hit programs were U.S. contributions to the World Bank and other international development banks. The bill included $949 million for cash payments to those banks — $443 million below Reagan's request. When added to about $250 million that Congress cut from the banks in previous years, the reduction meant that the United States had fallen $690 million behind on payments that Reagan had promised.

Rep. Matthew F. McHugh, D-N.Y., a leading congressional proponent of the banks, said the cuts "mean that the U.S. commitments to the banks are damaged significantly. We have been behind and we are now falling further behind."

Obey, another longtime proponent of the banks, charged that the Reagan administration failed to lobby Congress on their behalf. Treasury Department officials — responsible for handling U.S. contributions to the banks — rejected the charge but acknowledged that "lead responsibility" for lobbying on foreign aid was taken by the State Department, which emphasized its own programs instead.

The $949 million approved by Congress was almost exactly the same amount that Treasury informally had set as a "minimum" total for the banks. However, the appropriated figure included $64.8 million for one contribution the administration did not want: a donation to the World Bank's Special Facility for Sub-Saharan Africa. The facility was an emergency program to promote development in countries struck by famine, drought and other disasters.

Cuts of about $127 million each were made in the two major arms of the World Bank.

The most controversial arm of the bank, the International Development Association (IDA), made no-interest loans to the world's poorest countries. Reagan sought $750 million for the last of a three-year payment to IDA; the bill cut that to $622 million.

The largest arm of the bank, the International Bank for Reconstruction and Development, made subsidized loans to middle-income countries such as Mexico and Turkey. Reagan's request for $182.8 million in direct contributions was cut to $55.8 million. Using a standard formula, Congress also reduced the "callable capital" contribution, which was similar to a loan guarantee, to $688 million, from Reagan's $2.1 billion request.

Congress also slashed funding for operations of the Inter-American Development Bank. But it approved most of Reagan's requests for development banks serving Africa and Asia.

In one provision of potential significance, Congress barred "indirect" U.S. aid to Angola, Cambodia, Cuba, Iraq, Libya, Vietnam, South Yemen or Syria — unless the president certified to Congress that such a ban was "contrary to the national interests of the United States." If the president did not exercise his waiver power, that ban could stop all U.S. contributions to the development banks, which had said they could not take money with such strings attached.

The provision was inserted in the bill during conference negotiations by Obey, who complained that he and other Democrats were being attacked by Republicans for giving aid to communist countries.

At Kasten's initiative, the bill included several provisions pressuring the development banks to give serious consideration to environmental issues when they made their loans. Kasten and other critics had said the banks funded power plants, road networks and other projects without any regard for their impact on the environment.

For the first time in recent years, the foreign aid bill made only marginal increases over Reagan's requests for several United Nations programs that were widely supported in Congress. For example, the bill allocated $107.5 million to the United Nations Development Program — only $5 million above Reagan's request. In most recent years Congress added $20 million-$40 million for that agency.

Development Aid

Congress made relatively small cuts in U.S. programs aimed at developing the economies of and improving the quality of life in poor countries. Most of those programs — in agriculture, health, education and other areas — were run by the Agency for International Development.

In total, the "bilateral" development programs were cut by 2 percent below the fiscal 1986 amount and by 10 percent below Reagan's 1987 request. Those percentage cuts were among the smallest inflicted on any major foreign aid category.

As in past years, Congress substantially increased funding for several of the small aid programs. Among the most dramatic increases was the tripling of money for the Child Survival Fund, which paid for vaccinations and other preventive medicine programs for children in poor countries. Reagan requested $25 million, and Congress approved $75 million.

The bill protected both Central America and sub-Saharan Africa against wholesale cuts in development aid — especially in comparison with other regions of the world. It said that both regions must receive at least the same percentages of the total development aid budget in 1987 as in 1985.

The bill included language from the past two years that the Reagan administration had used to withhold U.S. contributions to the United Nations Fund for Population Activities. That language barred aid to any group that "participates in the management of a program of coercive abortion or involuntary sterilization." The administration had withheld funds from the U.N. program because it operated in China, which required abortions and sterilizations as part of its "one-family-one-child" policy.

In a related provision, the bill appeared to lay down conflicting guidelines on the awarding of U.S. grants to groups that offered family planning services for foreign countries.

The bill allowed funding only of groups that offered a "broad range of family planning methods and services" — a provision intended by sponsors to rule out grants to groups that advocated only "natural" family planning practices such as the rhythm method.

However, the bill said no group should be discriminated against because of its "religious or conscientious commitment to offer only natural family planning." Yet a third guideline reaffirmed the demand that groups must offer the broad range of services — effectively undermining the exemption for religious or conscientious reasons.

Ex-Im Bank

The foreign aid bill delivered a major blow to the Reagan administration's plan to replace the direct loan program of the Export-Import Bank with a $300 million trade "war chest" of cut-rate financing.

The Ex-Im Bank promoted foreign purchases of U.S. goods, primarily big-ticket items such as airplanes and power plants, by providing direct loans and loan guarantees to buyers overseas. The administration had tried for several years to end the bank's most popular program, which directly lent money to foreign purchasers of American goods.

The administration's alternative called for a $300 million war chest to subsidize U.S. exports. Also known as "tied aid" or "mixed credits," the program would encourage foreign countries to buy U.S. products by giving them a combination of subsidized loans and grants. The Ex-Im Bank had been giving highly subsidized loans in recent years but had been unable to offer outright grants.

Conferees on the foreign aid portion of the omnibus spending bill rejected the administration proposal, giving the Ex-Im Bank $900 million for its direct loans, just $160 million less than in fiscal 1986. Of the $900 million, up to $100 million could be used for a tied-aid program — if the chairman of the bank certified to Congress that the money was not needed for direct loans. *(Ex-Im authorization, p. 348)*

Other Provisions

The omnibus spending bill also:

- Appropriated "humanitarian" aid to two guerrilla groups widely favored by members of Congress: paramilitary groups battling the Soviet occupation of Afghanistan ($30 million) and the Vietnamese occupation of Cambodia (not less than $1.5 million and not more than $5 million). The aid to the Afghan guerrillas was on top of several hundred million dollars in annual CIA "covert" support.
- Barred any aid to the Sudan or Liberia unless the administration notified the Appropriations and Foreign Affairs committees in advance.

Until a military coup in April 1985, the Sudan was a close U.S. ally and the recipient of a rapidly expanding military and economic aid program. Since the coup, Sudanese leaders had tried to accommodate both Western interests and those of Libya and other radical states. Reagan requested $223 million in aid for the Sudan in fiscal 1987, an amount likely to be sharply reduced.

Congress also had soured on aiding Liberia since controversial elections were held there in October 1985. Several opposition candidates were excluded from the ballot, and the government of Samuel Doe refused to allow scrutiny of its counting of the votes. In response, both houses of Congress had passed resolutions (H Res 367, S Res 271) calling for suspension of aid to Liberia. Reagan had requested $75.9 million for Liberia in 1987.

- Barred economic aid to Chile and called on the administration to oppose all loans by international development banks to Chile, until the government there had ended human rights abuses and taken "significant steps" to restore democracy, including establishment of a "precise timetable" for elections. The State Department had said it would oppose new loans to Chile by the World Bank and the Inter-American Development Bank.
- Set aside $50 million in disaster aid for relief in El Salvador following an Oct. 10 earthquake that killed hundreds and caused massive damage.

The bill also continued the process of phasing out congressional restrictions on aid to the Salvadoran government. In the early 1980s, Congress attached strings to virtually every aspect of U.S. aid to El Salvador. That practice had diminished since the 1984 election of President José Napoleón Duarte.

Among the remaining requirements were that the administration notify Congress before giving military aid to law enforcement agencies and aircraft to the armed forces of El Salvador. The bill also withheld $5 million in military aid until the administration certified that the Salvadoran government had "substantially concluded" action in the case of Mark Pearlman and Michael Hammer, two U.S. land-reform consultants who were murdered in January 1981. Another provision required strict accounting of economic aid, to guard against misuse.

- Earmarked $37 million for development assistance to Haiti, including job creation, rural development, health care and reforestation.
- Included several new programs to encourage foreign countries to reduce illegal production of narcotics. Among them were a $20 million bonus fund to be divided among countries making "substantial progress" in curtailing illicit drugs, and a special authority for the administration to transfer extra aid to those countries.
- Barred aid to any country whose "duly elected" head of government was deposed by a military coup or decree. Congress drafted this provision in 1984 and applied it only to El Salvador; since then, the provision had been extended worldwide.
- Prohibited use of U.S. foreign aid to promote development of manufactured or agricultural items that would compete with American products.

House Committee Action

The House Appropriations Committee July 31 approved a $12.9 billion fiscal 1987 foreign aid spending bill. The committee reported the measure (HR 5339 — H Rept 99-747) Aug. 5, but the full House never considered it. Instead, the foreign aid funding was folded into the House version of the omnibus spending bill, passed Sept. 25.

Priorities, Cutbacks

The committee made deep slashes in all types of programs, even those preferred by its Democratic leaders. Obey, whose Foreign Operations Subcommittee had approved the bill July 24, said he tried to be "evenhanded in distributing the pain" of cutbacks.

However, several countries and programs heavily favored in Congress escaped some or all of the pain. Four countries were exempted from any cut: Israel (scheduled to receive $3 billion in economic and military aid); Egypt ($2.3 billion), Pakistan ($670 million) and Northern Ireland ($50 million).

By protecting those countries, which accounted for nearly half the total amount in the aid bill, the committee ensured that other countries and programs would face even more sharp cuts than the overall 13 percent reduction in the measure would seem to indicate. The three major economic and military aid programs — collectively called "security assistance" by the administration — would be cut 41 percent for the unprotected countries.

Protected Programs

The committee protected from substantial cuts several

programs that were politically popular on Capitol Hill but that were yearly targets of the Reagan administration's budget ax:

- The United Nations Childrens Fund (UNICEF), kept at the fiscal 1986 level of $51.1 million. Reagan sought $34.2 million for fiscal 1987.
- The Child Survival Fund, which financed immunization and other short-term health programs for children in low-income countries, set at $50 million, the amount originally appropriated for fiscal 1986 before the cuts required by the Gramm-Rudman-Hollings deficit-reduction law. Reagan had requested $25 million.
- The World Bank's "Special Facility" for Sub-Saharan Africa, pegged at $64.8 million. Reagan had requested no money for the program, which was intended to aid long-term economic development. Congress in 1985 authorized a three-year, $225 million contribution to the facility — over Reagan's opposition — and appropriated $71 million for the first year.

The committee complained that under Reagan, such programs "have consistently taken a back seat" to military and economic aid programs that helped pro-U.S. governments.

- American Schools and Hospitals Abroad, funded at $30 million. This State Department account included overseas institutions such as the American University of Beirut. Reagan had requested $10 million.
- The Peace Corps, for which the committee approved $130 million. Reagan had requested $126 million.
- The International Fund for Agricultural Development (IFAD), a United Nations agency that promoted long-term agricultural improvement in poor countries, especially in Africa, set at $28.7 million. Reagan had requested no money for 1987.

The committee gave a different kind of priority to several other programs, approving the full amount Reagan requested. Most were programs on which Congress and the administration agreed. Among those programs were: anti-terrorism aid for foreign countries ($9.8 million); the United Nations Development Program ($102.5 million); the International Atomic Energy Agency ($20.5 million).

Drug-Control Programs

Acting in response to a request by Speaker Thomas P. O'Neill Jr., D-Mass., for House initiatives on drug control, the committee approved several provisions to combat narcotics production overseas. The panel said that the threat to the United States "caused by illicit drug production is equal to or greater than most security threats" to the countries that got U.S. aid. Those provisions:

- Approved Reagan's $65.4 million request for the State Department's International Narcotics Control program. That was a $10.4 million increase over fiscal 1986. The program gave training and equipment for foreign countries to battle narcotics production. *(Drug legislation, p. 92)*
- Set aside $10 million of the narcotics program to buy aircraft for surveillance and eradication of narcotics crops such as coca.
- Set aside $20 million under the Economic Support Fund for bonus aid to countries that made "serious progress" in eliminating drug production.
- Authorized the president to take foreign aid money away from countries that did not take "adequate steps" against drugs, and to give that money to other countries that did.
- Retained fiscal 1986 appropriations provisions withholding 50 percent of economic aid to Jamaica and Peru until the president reported to Congress that they had been "sufficiently responsive" to U.S. concerns on drug control. The bill contained a similar provision on Bolivia, withholding half of its economic aid until the government achieved its 1985 coca eradication targets. In spite of that provision, the panel backed the July campaign in which U.S. military personnel helped Bolivian authorities attack drug production centers.

Noting the difficulty of getting foreign countries to make serious efforts to eradicate crops of narcotic substances, the committee called on the State Department to put more emphasis on disrupting narcotics production laboratories. The committee ordered the State Department to prepare a plan for closing down foreign drug labs, most of which were located in remote places over which local authorities had little control. The committee also ordered the department to give Congress an analysis by Feb. 1, 1987, on drug eradication programs in countries that received aid.

Development Banks

The committee approved $1.26 billion for direct contributions to the seven international development banks, a cut of $322 million from Reagan's request. Although Obey and other Democrats on the Foreign Operations Subcommittee had been strong supporters of the banks, they were forced to make the sharp cuts to keep the overall bill within the budget limits.

The biggest cut was $145 million from Reagan's $750 million request for the International Development Association.

The panel also cut $88 million in the donation to the World Bank.

The committee noted that the United States fell $277 million short of meeting its fiscal 1986 promises to the banks. That figure would increase "significantly" in 1987, the panel said.

While expressing regret at that shortage, the committee attacked the administration for its failure to ask Congress for the money to make up the difference. By not even asking for the money, it said, the administration violated its promise to the banks that it would make a "best effort" to get Congress to act.

The panel contrasted that failure with the administration's determined effort to get Congress to appropriate the full requests for military and economic aid to countries where U.S. bases were located. That was a "startling and inappropriate" inconsistency on the administration's part, the panel said.

Country Issues

The committee included provisions aimed at individual countries that received U.S. aid. Most focused on promoting political and economic reforms. Among them:

- **Liberia**. The bill required the administration to notify Congress before giving any assistance to Liberia. In its report, the panel said it would object to any such aid until the Liberian government made significant political reforms, and it demanded semiannual reports from the administration on the status of those reforms. Protesting fraud-plagued elections in 1985, both houses of Congress had passed resolutions (S Res 271, H Res 367) calling for suspension of aid to Liberia until it released all political prisoners and made democratic reforms.
- **Haiti.** Saying the new Haitian government was "seriously committed" to moving toward elections, the panel

earmarked $37 million in development assistance for Haiti, along with $1 million to be funneled through the Inter-American Foundation. The real need for U.S. aid could be as high as $80 million, the committee said, but it refused to embrace that amount because of conflicting information about Haiti's balance of payments and because of the needs of other countries.

- **South Korea.** Objecting to the administration's reluctance to criticize the government of South Korea, the panel said the United States publicly should advocate political and human rights reforms. Growing political turmoil there, the committee said, "could lead to instability which could harm the interests of the United States."

El Salvador

Once the major focus of attention, El Salvador received only secondary notice in the 1987 foreign aid measure. The Foreign Operations Subcommittee rejected amendments to put stiff conditions on that country's aid, but the full committee vented concerns about political developments in El Salvador.

While praising President Duarte, the committee pointed to El Salvador's deteriorating economy, the ongoing war against leftist guerrillas, and continuing human rights abuses as evidence that $2 billion in U.S. aid since 1981 had not produced a paradise.

Reagan had sought $514 million for El Salvador in 1987, an amount the committee implied was unrealistic. "Continued high levels of military, economic and development aid to El Salvador will be extremely difficult to maintain within dramatically reduced foreign aid levels and pressures on domestic programs," the committee said. The panel kept previous conditions barring aid to El Salvador in the event of a military coup, and requiring advance approval by congressional committees for the use of U.S. aid to buy aircraft for the Salvadoran armed forces.

Senate Committee Action

The Senate Appropriations Committee Sept. 16 reported a $13 billion foreign aid bill (S 2824 — S Rept 99-443) that shared the cost-cutting emphasis of the House version.

Even though the House and Senate funding totals were nearly the same, the Senate bill took a huge swipe out of various foreign aid programs that escaped such treatment in the House measure. At the same time, Senate drafters included much more money for bilateral economic aid than did their House counterparts.

Still, the end result was a bill that was more than $2.4 billion below Reagan's foreign aid request. It was also nearly $1.5 billion below the fiscal 1986 appropriations level. The committee made no changes in the spending levels approved by Kasten's subcommittee Sept. 11.

As a way of stretching out the available dollars, the Senate committee proposed to change existing foreign aid procedures. Chief among them was the elimination of the Military Assistance Program in favor of funneling all military aid through the Foreign Military Credit Sales program. Because of varying budget accounting procedures in the two programs, the change was designed to save on federal outlays — money that the government actually spent in a given year.

Obey charged that the Senate approach defied normal budget accounting procedures, but Senate Budget Committee Chairman Pete V. Domenici, R-N.M., said the bill met budget-cutting targets without resorting to "funny money," a term often used to describe questionable budget-saving devices.

Other significant changes included making foreign aid funds available over two years rather than one and setting a limit on how much aid could be disbursed during fiscal 1987.

In contrast to the House committee, sponsors of the Senate appropriations measure rejected across-the-board cuts, instead choosing to slash some programs more severely in order to reserve scarce funds for other preferred programs.

"While the committee does believe that all of the programs in the legislation serve U.S. interests, some have a more direct role and are, therefore, more important in the conduct of U.S. foreign policy," said the panel's report.

Multilateral Banks

A dramatic example of that approach could be seen in the committee's treatment of the World Bank and other international lending agencies that assisted lesser-developed nations.

No money was included for direct U.S. contributions to the World Bank's lending resources, compared with $94.8 million in the House bill and $182.8 million in Reagan's request.

Similarly, the Senate panel recommended no money for the Inter-American Development Bank and the African Development Bank, two regionally based lending agencies. Besides citing budget constraints, the panel also noted various policy disagreements with the international banks.

For example, the committee report complained about the banks' alleged lack of concern over the environmental effects of various projects that they financed. The report called on the Treasury secretary to emphasize environmental concerns when issuing instructions to U.S. officials at the various banks.

Partly in response to congressional concerns, World Bank officials said they had put in place a "major extension" of existing environmental policies. These included guidelines for ecological preservation and better staff training to assess the environmental effects of projects funded by the bank.

"The bank's policy is to seek to achieve a balance between preserving the environmental values of the world's most important remaining wild lands and converting some to more intensive human uses," read a portion of the World Bank's 1986 annual report released Sept. 22.

The Senate committee also took a shot at the Washington-based World Bank over what it considered excessive salaries paid to its officials. The panel said the bank's salaries and benefits "are higher than what is needed and reasonable, and out of touch with the willingness and ability of the United States to finance these institutions at a time of fiscal restraint within the United States." According to the report, a senior World Bank official could earn $89,800 while a comparable position in the private sector might command an average salary of $66,800.

The Senate legislation also painted a gloomy picture of the United States' financial ability to continue making sizable contributions to the IDA. The measure called for a fiscal 1987 appropriation of $622.6 million, compared with a House figure of $604.8 million and a White House request of $750 million.

The fiscal 1987 IDA appropriation marked the United States' third contribution in a three-year "replenishment"

'Security Aid' Totals, Fiscal 1986-87

Following are the amounts for major "security assistance" programs for key countries in fiscal years 1986-87. Security assistance includes Foreign Military Sales (FMS) loans, Military Assistance Program (MAP) grants and Economic Support Fund (ESF) loans and grants. Not included are military training aid, development aid, food aid and other programs. Fiscal 1986 appropriations were made in an omnibus appropriations bill (PL 99-190), and the 1987 "preliminary" figures are the administration's allocations of the appropriations made in that year's omnibus bill (PL 99-591). *(Figures are in millions of dollars; numbers may not add due to rounding; country totals are in boldface type; fiscal 1985 amounts, 1985 Almanac p. 375)*

	Fiscal 1986		Fiscal 1987	
Country	**Request**	**Final**	**Preliminary**	**Supplemental Request**
Egypt	**$ 2,365.0**	**$ 2,212.5**	**$ 2,115.0**	**$ 0**
FMS [1]	1,300.0	1,244.1	1,300.0	0
ESF	1,065.0	1,068.4 [2]	815.0	0
Israel	**3,750.0**	**3,621.0**	**3,000.0**	**0**
FMS [1]	1,800.0	1,722.6	1,800.0	0
ESF	1,950.0	1,898.4 [2]	1,300.0	0
Jordan	**195.0**	**176.3**	**53.9**	**0**
FMS [1]	95.0	81.3	0	0
MAP	0	0	39.9	0
ESF	100.0	95.0 [2]	14.0	0
Lebanon	**10.0**	**15.9**	**.5**	**0**
ESF	10.0	15.9	.5	0
Oman	**73.3**	**28.7**	**15.0**	**5**
FMS	58.3	9.1	0	0
ESF	15.0	19.6	15.0	5
Pakistan	**575.0**	**550.2**	**562.5**	**0**
FMS [1]	325.0	311.0	312.5	0
ESF	250.0	239.2	250.0	0
Turkey	**935.0**	**734.9**	**590.0**	**125**
FMS [1]	555.0	409.5	177.9	0
MAP	230.0	305.8	312.1	125
ESF	150.0	119.6	100.0	0
Greece	**500.0**	**430.6**	**343.0**	**0**
FMS [1]	500.0	430.6	343.0	0
Cyprus	**3.0**	**14.4**	**15.0**	**0**
ESF	3.0	14.4	15.0	0
Spain	**412.0**	**394.3**	**110.0**	307
FMS [1]	400.0	382.8	105.0	300
ESF	12.0	11.5	5.0	7
Portugal	**215.0**	**186.6**	**144.8**	**45**
FMS [1]	65.0	43.1	0	0
MAP	70.0	67.0	80.0	30
ESF	80.0	76.5	64.8	15
South Korea	**228.0**	**162.7**	**0**	**0**
FMS	228.0	162.7	0	0

	Fiscal 1986		Fiscal 1987	
Country	**Request**	**Final**	**Preliminary**	**Supplemental Request**
Philippines	**345.0**	**402.7**	**300.0**	**50**
FMS [1]	50.0	14.4	0	0
MAP	100.0 [2]	88.3 [2]	50.0	50
ESF	195.0 [2]	300.0 [2]	250.0	0
Morocco	**72.5**	**51.0**	**44.0**	**20**
FMS [1]	5.0	1.0	2.0	0
MAP	45.0	33.5	32.0	10
ESF	22.5	16.5	10.0	10
Tunisia	**81.5**	**86.7**	**48.7**	**0**
FMS [1]	43.0	25.8	0	0
MAP	16.0	38.3	32.5	0
ESF	22.5	22.6	16.2	0
Somalia	**75.0**	**41.1**	**25.0**	**3**
MAP	40.0	19.1	7.5	3
ESF	35.0	22.0	17.5	0
Sudan	**173.5**	**26.1**	**5.0**	**0**
MAP	58.5	16.1	5.0	0
ESF	115.0	10.0	0	0
Zaire	**25.4**	**31.2**	**14.0**	**0**
MAP	10.4	6.7	4.0	0
ESF	15.0	24.5	10.0	0
Costa Rica	**152.5**	**123.0**	**89.2**	**40**
MAP	2.5	2.4	1.5	0
ESF	150.0	120.6	87.7	40
El Salvador	**341.0**	**297.4**	**296.7**	**172**
MAP	131.0	120.4	115.0	17
ESF	210.0	177.0	181.7	55
Guatemala	**35.0**	**52.8**	**60.8**	**45**
FMS	10.0	0	0	0
MAP	0	5.0	2.0	5
ESF	25.0	47.8	58.8	40
Honduras	**167.0**	**121.3**	**131.4**	**82**
MAP	87.0	60.1	60.0	17
ESF	80.0	61.2	71.4	65

[1] *All or part of the FMS aid to these countries was in "concessional" loans carrying below-market interest rates. Egypt and Israel were not required to repay their FMS loans.*

[2] *Includes special supplemental aid in fiscal 1986. Economic aid supplementals for Egypt, Israel and Jordan were originally appropriated during fiscal 1985 (PL 99-88). Economic and military aid supplementals for the Philippines were appropriated during fiscal 1986 (PL 99-349).*

of IDA resources. With a new replenishment cycle set to begin in 1988, increased U.S. funding was "simply not possible" because of budget pressures, according to the committee.

The United States had been contributing more than 30 percent of IDA's total resources during the past several years. And the administration had agreed to a new three-year commitment for the United States to make annual contributions of $950 million, a figure jeopardized by the cost-cutting mood on Capitol Hill.

International Programs

In contrast to cutting money for the banks, the Senate bill matched or exceeded the House measure in funding other international programs. Among them:

- The Child Survival Fund, which paid for child immunization and other health programs in impoverished countries, would receive $75 million. The House measure would provide $50 million while the administration recommended $25 million.
- The Peace Corps, which was celebrating its 25th anniversary, would receive $130 million. The House bill provided the same amount, while the administration requested $126.2 million.
- The United Nations Childrens Fund (UNICEF) would receive $51 million. The House would provide $51.1 million, and the administration recommended $34.2 million.

Adding its voice to Congress' clamor for action against illicit drugs, the committee approved Reagan's $65.4 million request for the International Narcotics Control Program run by the State Department. The House foreign aid bill would provide the same amount, which was $10.4 million above the fiscal 1986 level.

More than half of the drug control funds would be targeted toward Latin American countries, such as Colombia and Mexico, that were the source of much of the drugs brought into the United States. The program provided training and equipment for other countries to fight narcotics production.

Like the House bill, the Senate measure singled out some countries for special treatment, though not the same ones in all cases. Both bills guaranteed identical levels of aid to Israel ($3 billion) and Egypt ($2.1 billion). In addition, the Senate committee earmarked $490 million for Turkey and $343 million for Greece, complying with a 10-7 ratio that Congress had traditionally applied to those adversary nations. The Senate bill earmarked $15 million in economic aid for Cyprus, where Turkish troops occupied a portion of the island.

In order to promote democracy in Ecuador, the Senate committee urged the administration to allocate $20 million in economic aid to that nation.

The Senate bill also included specific provisions aimed at other countries whose policies had prompted concerns in the United States. These involved:

- El Salvador, with a requirement that economic aid to that country be kept in a separate account to avoid mixing it with funds for military or other purposes. The bill also earmarked up to $1 million in U.S. aid for a unit of the Salvadoran government set up to prosecute those responsible for murdering American citizens there.
- Jordan, by earmarking up to $15 million in economic aid for the West Bank Development Project, established by Jordan's King Hussein. The program was designed to improve the living standards of Palestinians in the West Bank and Gaza.
- Cambodia, by earmarking $5 million in economic and military aid for non-communist resistance forces battling that country's government.
- Chile, by urging the United States to oppose international bank loans to that country because of human rights violations. The provision would exempt loans that provided assistance "in support of basic human needs." The regime of Chilean President Augusto Pinochet had come under increasing criticism, particularly since the July 2 killing in Santiago of Rodrigo Rojas de Negri, a 19-year-old Chilean exile.
- South Korea, saying the committee would be more receptive to future aid requests if that country "proceeds toward full democratic freedoms" that included national elections in 1988.
- Jamaica, where committee members expressed concern that the existing government was doing little to solve the country's persistent economic problems.
- Mozambique, where the committee restricted economic aid for use by private-sector groups in that country. The committee said it questioned the government's "desire to move away from a socialist system."

Central America

The Senate bill cited budget pressures in rejecting Reagan's request for a $400 million increase for aid to four Central American countries — Costa Rica, El Salvador, Guatemala and Honduras — and other regional programs.

In the case of El Salvador, the United States had provided more than $2 billion in economic and military aid since 1981. Reagan had proposed $514 million in additional aid in fiscal 1987.

The Senate panel said the U.S. deficit and "urgent domestic needs" precluded approval of Reagan's requested increase for Central America. But it added that the administration nonetheless should shield those countries from sharp cuts, "recognizing that not only is that region a top priority of the administration, but also of Congress."

Export Assistance

Again citing budget constraints, the committee turned down the administration's centerpiece request for boosting U.S. exports: a $300 million "war chest" to subsidize the sale of U.S. goods overseas.

The committee acknowledged that U.S. companies were losing business to foreign competitors because of subsidized export financing available in other countries.

In rejecting the war chest, the appropriations bill was at odds with separate legislation (HR 5548) that would authorize $300 million for the export financing scheme. That measure would extend the life of the Export-Import Bank through September 1992. *(Story, p. 348)*

The foreign aid appropriations measure, however, would allow the Ex-Im Bank to use up to $150 million in its direct loan program for export financing offers.

The committee recommended a total of $900 million for Ex-Im's direct loan program. The administration had been trying to replace the loan program with an interest-subsidy plan known as I-Match. But the committee rejected that approach because of disagreements over the way the new program would be treated in the budget.

Conference

A bitterly partisan dispute over foreign aid was resolved late on Oct. 14 with an agreement forcing a second year of cutbacks in the Reagan administration's program of "security assistance" to foreign allies.

The agreement among foreign aid conferees on the fiscal 1987 omnibus appropriations bill provided $13.37 billion for foreign aid — $2.1 billion less than President Reagan's request and almost exactly $1 billion below the fiscal 1986 amount. That agreement was ratified Oct. 15 by the full conference committee on the measure (H Rept 99-1005).

The conference had been held up by a feud between the chairmen of the two foreign aid Appropriations subcommittees, Rep. Obey and Sen. Kasten. Kasten was up for re-election in 1986 and Obey was helping his opponent. Obey also had been angered by campaign tactics of his own Republican opponent, who allegedly had criticized Obey for supporting aid to communist countries.

In addition, Obey had been trying for months to force the Reagan administration to keep its foreign aid program within limits of the Gramm-Rudman budget law, which the administration had supported and Obey had opposed. But the administration and the Senate resisted cuts, saying foreign aid, like defense spending, contributed to the national security and should be given special priority.

Although Obey threatened repeatedly to take the foreign aid issues back to the House in disagreement, eventually he agreed to compromises that undermined several positions he had taken earlier during conference negotiations.

In spite of the cuts, the bill provided substantially more for military aid than Obey had wanted.

Obey acknowledged that he was pressured by the House leadership to reach agreement, to avoid holding up the entire spending bill. "There are other things going on besides foreign aid," he said. "People did not want to be hanging here on foreign aid."

Another key House negotiator said the bill satisfied no one but was the best possible, given overall budget pressures. Under the circumstances, said Rep. Matthew F. McHugh, D-N.Y., "it was virtually impossible to write a responsible bill."

Aid Specifics

For more than a week, the negotiations on foreign aid had stalled on the issues of the amounts and terms of economic and military aid to friendly countries.

The most difficult issue was the total for the Economic Support Fund, which boosted the economies of Israel, Egypt and other key allies. The House and Senate bills were $700 million apart on that program: $3.2 billion in the House bill and $3.9 billion in the Senate measure. After extensive negotiations, conferees settled on $3.55 billion, permitting agreement on other issues.

Although each bill provided about $5 billion for military aid to U.S. allies, the two measures were fundamentally at odds over how the money was to be spent. The House bill was based on the traditional military aid program, mixing grants and loans to help friendly countries buy U.S. weapons and supplies. The Senate bill converted all loans — about $1.9 billion — into outright grants, on the grounds that many poor countries were having trouble paying back the United States. The Senate measure also proposed giving the administration the right to convert to grants $3.5 billion in loans from previous years.

In the compromise, the House conferees agreed to increase substantially the grant Military Assistance Program, but they refused to accept the transfer of all loans into grants. The final bill provided $900 million for MAP grants, $4 billion for grants and loans under the Foreign Military Sales program and $56 million for the international military training program. That total of nearly $5 billion was $1.7 billion less than Reagan had requested. Because a substantial portion of military aid was earmarked for Israel, Egypt and other countries, the cut amounted to about 50 percent for everybody else. However, the bill mandated that all loans must carry low interest rates, thus making them more valuable. ▮

HUD/Agency Funding Set at $56 Billion

The funding for the Department of Housing and Urban Development (HUD) and several independent agencies included in the fiscal 1987 continuing appropriations resolution (H J Res 738 — PL 99-591) was about 4 percent below the 1985 level, down to $56 billion.

The total was $9.5 billion more in budget authority than requested by President Reagan, who had threatened to veto the House- and Senate-passed measures.

The final figure included the transfer of $2.4 billion in budget authority from the Department of Defense (DOD) to the National Aeronautics and Space Administration (NASA) to replace the space shuttle *Challenger*, which was destroyed during launch Jan. 28. However, only $100 million could be spent in fiscal 1987 to begin construction. *(Challenger, p. 326)*

The omnibus spending bill incorporated a conference report on the regular fiscal 1987 HUD/Independent Agencies appropriations bill (HR 5313 — H Rept 99-977). HR 5313 had been passed by the House Sept. 12 and by the Senate Oct. 3. The only major amendment added by H J Res 738 was the extra money for a new orbiter. *(Funding levels, chart, p. 173)*

The final legislation provided $9.5 billion in budget authority for HUD housing programs; $3.3 billion for HUD community planning and development programs; $4.2 billion for the Environmental Protection Agency (EPA); $10.4 billion for NASA, including money for the new orbiter; $1.6 billion for the National Science Foundation (NSF); and $26 billion for the Veterans Administration (VA).

No grants were provided for the popular general revenue sharing program. Revenue sharing, which in 1985 distributed about $4 billion to some 39,000 local governments to use as they saw fit, expired when Congress adjourned. Only $5.6 million was allowed in fiscal 1987 for salaries and expenses required to close down the program.

Major Provisions

Funds in H J Res 738 included:

- **HUD.** The bill provided $7.8 billion in new budget authority for annual contributions for assisted housing. That was expected to support about 98,000 additional units.

It included $1.4 billion to modernize public housing; $138 million for 2,000 new units for Indian public housing;

$1.2 billion for 53,500 housing vouchers, which tenants used like cash toward rent for housing that they found on their own; $791 million for the Section 8 rental assistance program for low-income tenants; and $716 million for the moderate rehabilitation of 7,500 rental dwellings.

In addition, the measure provided $1.4 billion to operate low-income housing projects; $508 million for housing for the elderly and handicapped; and $3.4 million for local housing agencies and non-profit sponsors to provide meals and other supportive services to certain tenants.

In a significant policy change, the legislation directed HUD to give public housing authorities "maximum flexibility" either to rehabilitate existing unoccupied housing projects or to build new units. In fiscal 1986, housing authorities could use no more than 20 percent of their construction funds for rehabilitation; that restriction was dropped entirely for fiscal 1987.

The House June 12 passed a housing authorization bill (HR 1) that would have mandated a shift from construction of public housing to the repair and rehabilitation of existing dwellings. However, that measure died when Congress adjourned. *(Housing, p. 585)*

The continuing appropriations resolution set the fiscal 1987 mortgage loan guarantee limit for the Federal Housing Administration (FHA) at $100 billion, down $41.5 billion from fiscal 1986.

And the fiscal 1987 loan limit for the Government National Mortgage Association (Ginnie Mae) was set at $150 billion — a $25 billion reduction. Congress had to raise the loan limits for both organizations in 1986 because of record-setting mortgage activity caused by low interest rates.

• **Community Development.** Community Development Block Grants (CDBGs) were funded at $3 billion, a $9.6 million increase over fiscal 1986. Urban Development Action Grants (UDAG) received $225 million, a $91 million cut.

• **Fair Housing.** The Fair Housing Assistance program to combat racial discrimination in housing received $6.3 million, no change from fiscal 1986. Congress deferred Reagan's $7 million request for a Fair Housing Initiative to increase anti-discrimination enforcement.

• **Consumer Product Safety Commission (CPSC).** Two of the five seats on the commission were eliminated, and funding was set at $34.1 million — a $352,000 reduction.

• **EPA.** The agency received $507 million less than fiscal 1986. The largest cut was in new budget authority for the wastewater treatment grant program, which lost $574 million, going down to $1.8 billion. However, $600 million was rolled over from unused fiscal 1986 funds, bringing funding for sewer grants in fiscal 1987 to $2.4 billion.

A total of $1.4 billion was provided for the "superfund" hazardous-waste cleanup program, an increase of $550 million over fiscal 1986.

• **Disaster Relief.** The Federal Emergency Management Agency (FEMA) received $576 million, a $249 million cut from fiscal 1986. That included a reduction of $226 million in disaster relief, bringing that category to $120 million for fiscal 1987.

A $70 million emergency food and shelter program for the homeless was retained under FEMA, and $15 million was added for a new program under HUD to house the homeless.

• **NASA.** A total of $10.4 billion was provided for the space agency, $2.7 billion more than fiscal 1986. The bulk of that increase — $2.4 billion — was the transfer of budget authority from DOD for a new orbiter and related equipment to replace the *Challenger.*

However, because only $100 million in outlays was approved for work on the new orbiter in fiscal 1987, actual spending for NASA in fiscal 1987 would be $8.1 billion — about 5 percent more than fiscal 1986.

Of the $2.4 billion transfer, $2.1 billion was earmarked for construction of the orbiter, $36 million for replacement of the inertial upper-stage cradle equipment that was lost when *Challenger* blew up, and $33 million to build a new tracking and data relay satellite also lost on *Challenger.*

• **National Science Foundation (NSF).** The agency received $1.6 billion — $165 million or 11 percent more than fiscal 1986. That was the largest increase in fiscal 1987 for any major category contained in the HUD/Independent Agencies portion of the legislation.

• **VA.** The VA received $26 billion for fiscal 1987, a reduction of about $106 million. Most cuts came in readjustment benefits and construction.

Some $9.4 billion was provided for the medical care at 172 VA hospitals and nursing homes, an increase of $274 million, about 3 percent, from fiscal 1986.

Funds were included for four projects not requested by the administration: an outpatient addition at the New York City VA medical center; site acquisition for a medical center in Palm Beach, Fla.; and design work for a medical center in Pittsburgh, Pa., and a nursing home in New Orleans, La.

House Committee Action

After rejecting an attempt to continue funding for federal revenue sharing, the House Appropriations Committee July 31 approved a $54 billion fiscal 1987 spending bill (HR 5313 — H Rept 99-731) for HUD and the agencies.

The panel defeated, 8-38, an amendment by John P. Murtha, D-Pa., to provide $3.425 billion for revenue sharing, which was not reauthorized for fiscal 1987.

Although Chairman Jamie L. Whitten, D-Miss., backed the proposal, Edward P. Boland, D-Mass., chairman of the Subcommittee on HUD/Independent Agencies, noted it would put the bill over the budget resolution (S Con Res 120) ceiling for outlays.

The bill's $54 billion budget authority total exceeded the administration request by about $10.8 billion, largely because of housing subsidies the administration wanted to drop. The bill was about $4 billion less than fiscal 1986.

Funding highlights included:

• $26.1 billion for the VA.

• $13.3 billion for HUD, including $8.1 billion for subsidized housing. No public housing units would be constructed.

The measure contained $3 billion for community development grants, $875 million more than requested, and $275 million for UDAGs.

• $7.7 billion for NASA, including $410 million for work on a space station. No funds were included for a new space shuttle.

• $4.7 billion for the EPA, including $861 million for the superfund toxic-waste cleanup program and $2.4 billion for sewer construction grants.

Additional Detail

Assisted Housing. The committee recommended supporting 98,000 units of subsidized housing. Citing a

Fiscal 1987 HUD/Agency Funds

Following is the new budget authority for fiscal 1987 for the Department of Housing and Urban Development (HUD) and independent agencies requested by President Reagan, and included in a regular appropriations bill (HR 5313) approved by the House Sept. 12 and by the Senate Oct. 3, and contained in the fiscal 1987 omnibus continuing appropriations resolution (H J Res 738 — PL 99-591) as cleared by Congress Oct. 17. The resolution was amended to include an additional $2.4 billion for the National Aeronautics and Space Administration (NASA) for construction of a new space shuttle orbiter, but fiscal 1987 spending was limited to $100 million.

	Budget Request	House-Passed	Senate-Passed	Final Amount
Department of Housing and Urban Development				
Housing Programs	$ 3,410,464,000	$ 9,619,846,000	$ 9,184,163,500	$ 9,445,276,000
Community Development	2,636,800,000	3,287,000,000	3,337,000,000	3,252,000,000
Policy Development and Research	18,900,000	16,173,000	18,000,000	17,000,000
Fair Housing Assistance	5,000,000	6,341,300	6,341,300	6,341,300
Management and Administration	314,056,000	342,123,000	327,049,000	340,423,000
Limitation on Guaranteed Loans				
Federal Housing Administration	(90,000,000,000)	(80,000,000,000)	(120,000,000,000)	(100,000,000,000)
Government National Mortgage Association	(125,000,000,000)	(132,500,000,000)	(160,000,000,000)	(150,000,000,000)
TOTAL, HUD	$ 6,385,220,000	$ 13,271,483,300	$ 12,872,553,800	$ 13,061,040,300
Independent Agencies				
American Battle Monuments Commission	11,673,000	11,673,000	11,673,000	11,673,000
Consumer Product Safety Commission	33,000,000	34,452,000	33,000,000	34,100,000
Cemeterial Expenses, Army	15,783,000	6,701,000	15,783,000	15,783,000
Environmental Protection Agency	4,226,466,000	4,697,397,000	4,347,026,000	4,155,092,000
Council on Environmental Quality	820,000	670,000	800,000	800,000
Office of Science and Technology Policy	1,671,000	1,671,000	2,217,000	1,900,000
Federal Emergency Management Agency	469,250,000	614,250,000	517,800,000	576,000,000
GSA Consumer Information Center	1,272,000	1,272,000	1,272,000	1,272,000
HHS Office of Consumer Affairs	400,000	1,000,000	1,750,000	1,750,000
National Aeronautics and Space Administration	7,966,400,000	7,650,000,000	8,345,400,000	10,434,000,000
National Science Foundation	1,685,700,000	1,550,000,000	1,695,700,000	1,622,850,000
Neighborhood Reinvestment Corporation	15,285,000	18,669,000	19,000,000	19,000,000
Selective Service System	27,474,000	26,128,400	27,000,000	26,128,400
Treasury Department				
General Revenue Sharing	—	—	—	—
Salaries and Expenses	5,560,000	5,560,000	5,560,000	5,560,000
Veterans Administration	25,642,073,000	26,115,242,000	25,781,505,000	26,044,854,000
TOTAL, Independent Agencies	$ 40,102,827,000	$ 40,734,685,400	$ 40,805,486,000	$ 42,950,762,400
GRAND TOTAL	**$ 46,488,047,000**	**$ 54,006,168,700**	**$ 53,678,039,800**	**$ 56,011,802,700**

SOURCE: House Appropriations Committee

"dramatic contraction" of housing aid during the Reagan administration, the panel noted that 1981 subsidies totaled nearly $25 billion, while the 1986 appropriation, as adjusted by the March 1 automatic spending cuts required by the Gramm-Rudman-Hollings anti-deficit law (PL 99-177), was $9.5 billion.

"This dramatic decline is accentuated by the fact that a 1986 housing dollar buys approximately 15 percent less than a 1981 dollar," the committee report said.

The committee proposed 53,500 housing vouchers in fiscal 1987, compared with about 30,000 currently in use, a committee aide said. The remaining units would be subsidized by a direct payment by the government to the owner of the dwelling or a public housing agency.

The panel recommended that $225 million for grants to develop approximately 10,000 new rental units be reserved for areas with very low vacancy rates. Currently, cities with vacancy rates as high as 13 percent could qualify for the so-called HODAG grants. The committee proposed that areas with a vacancy rate of 8 percent or more, and with 4 percent or more of the housing remaining empty for more than two months, not be eligible for the grants.

Noting that the House-passed housing authorization restricted public housing construction, the panel recommended no funding for public housing construction other than $366 million for 2,000 units designated for Indians.

However, it provided $1.44 billion for public housing modernization, virtually doubling current funding, a committee staffer explained.

The committee also provided for 12,000 new units for

the elderly and handicapped; 17,500 units under the Section 8 rental assistance program; and rehabilitation of 35,000 rental units.

Public housing operating subsidies were set at $1.3 billion, up $128.5 million over the president's request.

Fair Housing. Another $6.3 million was allocated for fair housing assistance programs, but members deferred consideration of $7 million requested by the administration for a new fair housing initiative pending authorization.

CPSC. Calling the commission form of management "top-heavy" and prone to internal conflicts, the panel provided funds for only three of the five commission seats, for a total of $34.5 million for CPSC.

In 1985, a similar proposal was dropped because of opposition. *(1985 Almanac p. 281)*

EPA. For salaries, abatement and buildings, the committee allocated $1.2 billion, a slight increase over 1986. It maintained funding for the superfund program at the 1986 level of $861 million but made release of the money contingent on enactment of another appropriations bill after the committee evaluated pending reauthorizing legislation (HR 2005). *(Story, p. 111)*

Funding of $2.4 billion for wastewater grants also was made contingent on the committee's review of the authorizing legislation.

Disaster Relief. The committee approved $175 million for FEMA's relief activities, almost twice the president's request. A total of $668.8 million was provided for the agency, including $70 million for an emergency food and shelter program.

NASA. The panel recommended $3 billion for research and development, with $410 million for a manned space station.

However, it withheld the release of $150 million until certain requirements were met, including sufficient capability to provide early access to the station for commercial enterprises.

In connection with the *Challenger* accident, the committee urged a swift decision on building a fourth shuttle and ordered that none of the funds in the bill be spent for a new orbiter without a formal budget amendment or supplemental request being sent to Congress.

VA. The recommendation included $14.4 billion for compensation and pensions, but the committee pointed out that legislation (HR 5299 — H Rept 99-730) reported July 31 by the Veterans' Affairs Committee proposed a 3.7 percent cost-of-living increase and additional funds might be needed.

Another $9.5 billion was provided for medical care and treatment, $403 million more than requested. The increase was primarily due to rejecting staff reductions proposed by the administration.

Construction for major projects was set at $377.4 million and $77 million for minor projects.

Miscellaneous. Funding for other agencies included $11.7 million for the American Battle Monuments Commission; $6.7 million, Army cemeterial expenses; $1.6 billion, NSF; $2.3 million, Executive Office of the President, Office and Council on Environmental Quality, and Office of Science and Technology Policy; $1.3 million, General Services Administration Consumer Information Center; $1 million, Health and Human Services Office of Consumer Affairs; $18.7 million, Neighborhood Reinvestment Corporation; $26.1 million, Selective Service; and $5.6 million, to close down the Treasury Department's Office of Revenue Sharing.

House Floor Action

As passed Sept 12 by the House by a vote of 295-46, HR 5313 provided $13.3 billion for HUD, an increase of about $366 million over fiscal 1986. It included $8.1 billion for assisted housing programs, providing for 81,500 additional subsidized dwellings, mostly through rehabilitation of existing housing stock instead of new construction. *(Vote 353, p. 100-H)*

For the first time, the House did not request new funds to build non-Indian public housing, which was owned and operated by a public housing authority for low-income tenants. It directed instead that existing public housing be modernized. The bill provided $1.3 billion for public housing operating subsidies.

The measure called for 50,000 housing vouchers; 12,000 Section 202 units for the elderly and handicapped; 2,000 Indian public housing units; 17,500 Section 8 existing and moderate rehabilitation assisted housing units; and $225 million for about 10,000 rental development units.

The FHA loan guarantee ceiling, currently at $141.5 billion, was dropped to $80 billion in fiscal 1987. Ginnie Mae's guarantee limit was cut from $175 billion to $132.5 billion.

Community development grants were funded at $3 billion.

EPA was allocated $4.7 billion, about $36 million above fiscal 1986 appropriations; superfund was funded at its current $861.3 million. The VA would receive $26.1 billion, a decrease of about $115 million from fiscal 1986.

The bill set aside for FEMA, $614.3 million, $145 million above the president's request. A total of $70 million was added to continue the Emergency Food and Shelter Program at its current rate, and $75 million was added for disaster relief.

Senate Action

The Senate Appropriations Committee Sept. 25 reported the bill (S Rept 99-487) with the only major change to its subcommittee's Sept. 18 recommendation being the addition of $30 million for a HUD program for the homeless.

The committee approved a $53.4 billion fiscal 1987 appropriations bill that shifted funds from housing, veterans' and wastewater grant programs to NASA.

The bill was $591 million below the $54 billion level approved by the House Sept. 12. Both measures exceeded the president's request, the House by $7.5 billion and the Senate by about $6.9 billion.

Both bills also contained funding for programs the administration tried to eliminate or cut, such as UDAG grants, which under the committee's version would receive $225 million.

Most of the $591 million cut by the panel from the House bill came from HUD's assisted housing program, EPA wastewater treatment grants and the VA.

The committee recommended for NASA a total of $8.3 billion in new budget authority — $695 million more than the House-passed $7.7 billion. The space agency's fiscal 1986 budget was $7.8 billion.

Most of the additional funds for NASA would cover payments that would not be made by the Department of Defense because of the two-year suspension of space shuttle flights in the wake of the *Challenger* disaster.

The committee included no extra funds to begin construction of a new orbiter to replace the *Challenger.* Panel members said an agreement had been reached to pay the $3 billion cost of a new orbiter out of DOD's budget, as provided in the fiscal 1987 defense appropriations bill (S 2827). *(Defense appropriations, p. 206)*

Other major portions of the Senate version of HR 5313 included:

Assisted Housing. The panel provided $7.3 billion for subsidized housing, $535 million less than the House. The House version would support about 98,000 units, and the Senate about 89,000 units.

In addition, the committee provided $1.4 billion for payments to operate low-income housing projects, $100 million more than the House.

Both versions provided $508 million for housing for the elderly and handicapped, which would create about 12,000 new units.

The committee funded more housing vouchers than the House (60,000 compared with 53,500).

The FHA ceiling was set at $120 billion, which was $40 billion more than the House-passed amount but $21.5 billion below the current cap. Ginnie Mae's limit was $160 billion — $27.5 billion more than the House but $15 billion below current levels.

Community Development. Both House and Senate committee versions provided the same amount for CDBGs, $3 billion, about $9.6 million more than the current amount.

Fair Housing. Both versions provided $6.3 million for fair housing assistance programs and both turned down Reagan's request for an additional $7 million for a new fair housing initiative.

CPSC. The House voted to freeze CPSC funding at the current level ($34.5 million), but the Senate committee cut that by $1.45 million.

EPA. Funding was set at $4.3 billion, $358 million below the House-passed level.

Major changes proposed by the panel included a $600 million cut in wastewater treatment grants, but immediate release of an equal amount held over from prior years; the House version maintained restrictions on the prior-year funds.

The superfund program would get $1 billion from the Senate committee, $189 million more than the House approved.

NASA. As in the House version, no funds were provided for construction of a new orbiter to replace the *Challenger.*

For NASA, the Senate committee measure provided $8.3 billion, $695 million more than the House. Most of that would cover $531 million in lost reimbursements that would have been made to NASA by the Pentagon if shuttle flights had not been suspended because of the *Challenger* accident.

NSF. The panel voted $1.7 billion for NSF, an increase of $146 million over the House figure, all of it for research.

VA. The Senate panel recommended $25.8 billion, $334 million less than the House. Most of the cut came in funding for medical care (down $248 million from the House amount), which staff said could be made because of savings and increased efficiency within the agency.

The Senate passed the bill by voice vote in a session that began Oct. 2 and concluded Oct. 3. The only change was the adoption of an amendment by Patrick J. Leahy, D-Vt., and Frank R. Lautenberg, D-N.J., to ensure that funds for the superfund toxic-waste cleanup program would be available.

Conference Action

Conferees Oct. 7 agreed on a total of $53.6 billion for HUD and the agencies, $428 million below the House level and $100 million below the Senate version.

Assisted Housing. For HUD's subsidized housing programs, conferees provided $7.8 billion — $510 million more than approved by the Senate and $289 million less than the House. According to congressional staffers, that would support about 98,000 housing units, close to the House-passed level.

Conferees also provided $1.35 billion to operate low-income public housing projects, splitting the difference between $1.4 billion approved by the Senate and $1.3 billion voted by the House.

Also approved was the House-passed amount of $716.3 million for 7,500 units of moderately rehabilitated dwellings under the Section 8 rental assistance program. Conferees accepted the Senate's figure of $138 million for 2,000 new Indian housing units.

Housing for the elderly and handicapped was funded at $508 million — the figure contained in both versions of the bill — which would create an estimated 12,000 new units.

The conference agreement allowed for about 50,000 housing vouchers, less than the 60,000 sought by the House and the 53,000 provided by the Senate, but about 20,000 more than currently in use. Tenants could use vouchers toward rent for housing they found on their own.

Federal Housing Administration mortgage loan guarantees would be capped at $100 billion, down $41.5 billion from the fiscal 1986 level. And the guarantee limit for the Government National Mortgage Association, which underwrote mortgage-backed securities, would be set at $150 billion — $25 billion below the fiscal 1986 cap.

Community Development. CDBGs were funded at $3 billion, the amount approved by both chambers. The total would be $9.6 million more than fiscal 1986. UDAGs were allocated the Senate figure, $225 million, $50 million less than the House-passed level. About $6.3 million was provided for fair housing assistance programs to combat housing discrimination.

CPSC. Conferees recommended eliminating two of the five seats on the commission and cutting the commission's budget to $34.1 million, down $352,000 from the fiscal 1986 amount.

EPA. For the superfund program, $600 million in restricted and unused money from fiscal 1986 would be released for immediate use, bringing superfund's fiscal 1987 budget to $1.7 billion. The House-passed version withheld availability of the unused funds.

Another $600 million in unspent prior-year funding for wastewater treatment grants also would be rolled over to fiscal 1987. Funding for EPA wastewater construction grants would total $1.8 billion, $600 million less than the House-passed amount.

Disaster Relief. The $576 million for FEMA included $120 million for disaster relief. In addition, the conference agreement provided $70 million for an emergency food and shelter program for the homeless under FEMA and $15 million for housing and emergency shelter grants under HUD. The House originally included no funding at all for the HUD-operated program.

NASA. The $8 billion for the agency was $345 million less than the Senate approved but $350 million more than the House provided.

Neither chamber had approved funds for construction of a new orbiter to replace the space shuttle *Challenger*. Conferees said they would accept provisions in the pending fiscal 1987 defense appropriations bill, which would finance the $3 billion cost of a new orbiter by trimming other programs within the Department of Defense.

NSF. The foundation funding of $1.6 billion was $46 million more than provided by the House but $100 million less than approved by the Senate.

VA. Conferees allowed $26.4 billion for the Veterans Administration (VA), $333 million more than the House and $666 million more than the Senate.

Conferees accepted the House's higher figures for hospital staffing and added $90.5 million for four VA construction projects that the administration had not requested: an addition to a hospital in New York City; site acquisition for a new medical center in Palm Beach, Fla.; design of a replacement medical center in Pittsburgh, Pa.; and design of a nursing home and parking garage in New Orleans, La. ∎

Transportation Funding Set at $10.38 Billion

Spurning a White House call for funding cuts, Congress approved a fiscal 1987 transportation appropriations package that exceeded the administration's request by $3.37 billion, or nearly 50 percent.

The package, incorporated in a $576 billion omnibus spending bill (H J Res 738 — PL 99-591), provided $10.38 billion in new budget authority for the Department of Transportation (DOT) and related agencies.

A separate transportation measure (HR 5205) passed by the House in July called for $10.28 billion, while the Senate version passed in September provided $10.20 billion. The final funding level spilled over those earlier totals primarily because of extra money provided for the Coast Guard's drug interdiction effort.

The administration, which requested $7.01 billion for all the programs in the bill, repeatedly threatened to veto any bill that substantially exceeded its request.

But Congress did not clear the separate transportation measure. Instead, a conference agreement (H Rept 99-976) on transportation spending was wrapped into the omnibus funding resolution. The White House supported the final version of the continuing appropriations resolution.

Air Controllers

As sought by the White House, conference negotiators removed a controversial provision contained in the transportation package that would have lifted the ban against rehiring air traffic controllers fired by President Reagan during a strike in 1981. The president had dismissed more than 11,000 controllers, about 500 of whom successfully had pursued appeals to win back their jobs.

The administration contended that the morale of the current work force would be sapped by the return of strikers. Those calling for doing away with the ban argued that the employees, as well as the traveling public, could benefit from the return of experienced controllers.

Negotiators for the full conference on the continuing resolution inserted language calling for the Federal Aviation Administration (FAA) to bring the controllers' work force up from 14,803 at the end of fiscal 1986 to 15,000 by the end of fiscal 1987. Seventy percent of the workers also must have graduated from training programs and reached so-called full-performance status.

Also included was $2 million for an Air Safety Commission to study the adequacy of federal air safety efforts.

Conferees added $128 million for Coast Guard drug interdiction work. The Coast Guard's $2.54 billion appropriation represented a $300 million, or 13 percent, increase over 1986 funding adjusted for cuts required by the Gramm-Rudman-Hollings anti-deficit law (PL 99-177).

In floor action on the continuing resolution, the House adopted an amendment — subsequently agreed to by the Senate — to ease federal control over two Washington, D.C., metropolitan airports. The amendment modified a Senate plan to lease Washington-Dulles International Airport and National Airport to a regional authority. *(Story, p. 293)*

Trust Funds Capped

The final package set a cap of $15.29 billion on expenditures from trust funds and other authorized accounts — including a $13 billion ceiling on road programs financed by the Highway Trust Fund and a $1 billion limit on grants to airports from the Airport and Airway Trust Fund. Mass transit spending from the Highway Trust Fund was limited to $1 billion.

Congress adjourned without completing action on separate legislation (HR 3129) to reauthorize trust fund spending on highway and transit programs. States currently had available $7.4 billion in fiscal 1987 funds, most of which represented unobligated trust fund allocations. *(Story, p. 284)*

The resolution included $80 million for 14 previously unauthorized road and bridge "demonstration" projects targeted at particular states and districts. A dispute over funding of demonstration projects contributed to blocking HR 3129. In the past, leaders of the House Public Works and Transportation Committee had objected to the authorization of highway programs in the appropriations process. But protests were muted in 1986.

The final bill also included $2 billion for mass transit formula grants, which were funded by the Treasury and not by the trust fund. The administration did not request new budget authority for mass transit, asking instead for a block grant combining highway and transit programs that would be financed by the trust fund.

Lawmakers did cut by 2.5 percent, or $21 million, funds for mass transit operating assistance for cities with populations of more than 1 million.

Language was included stating that the Urban Mass Transportation Administration (UMTA) should not restrict the ability of recipients to determine for themselves whether to contract with private operators to provide services.

UMTA was an enthusiastic supporter of "privatization" efforts in the transit area. Conferees cited concerns that the agency had "overstepped its legal authority" by conditioning the release of formula grants on a given level of private-sector involvement in providing mass transit services.

Fiscal 1987 Transportation Funds

Following are the amounts of fiscal 1987 budget authority for the Transportation Department and related agencies requested by President Reagan, approved by the House July 30, passed by the Senate Sept. 17 and cleared Oct. 17 as part of the omnibus continuing resolution (H J Res 738 — PL 99-591):

	Budget Request	House-Passed	Senate-Passed	Final Amount
Department of Transportation				
Office of the Secretary	$ 56,540,000	$ 73,443,000	$ 84,349,000	$ 84,349,000
Coast Guard	2,391,600,000	2,396,607,000	2,500,200,000	2,542,400,000
Federal Aviation Administration	3,800,880,000	3,836,647,000	3,761,784,000	3,807,084,000
Federal Highway Administration	26,515,000	121,234,000	66,515,000	122,421,000
National Highway Traffic Safety Administration	83,930,000	88,600,000	81,448,000	84,222,000
Federal Railroad Administration	46,777,000	691,712,000	663,902,000	683,259,000
Urban Mass Transportation Administration	—	2,465,839,000	2,433,400,000	2,449,519,500
St. Lawrence Seaway	—	2,000,000	—	2,000,000
Research and Special Programs Administration	20,024,000	20,800,000	19,950,000	19,950,000
Office of the Inspector General	27,630,000	27,770,000	27,000,000	27,200,000
Subtotal	$6,453,896,000	$9,724,652,000	$9,638,548,000	$9,822,404,500
Related Agencies				
Architectural and Transportation Review Board	1,975,000	1,975,000	1,890,000	1,890,000
Aviation Safety Commission	—	—	—	2,000,000
National Transportation Safety Board	21,430,000	22,240,000	22,240,000	22,240,000
Interstate Commerce Commission	48,300,,000	47,900,000	46,802,000	46,802,000
Panama Canal Commission	437,250,000	434,173,000	434,403,000	434,173,000
U.S. Railway Association	0	2,297,000	2,200,000	2,200,000
Washington Metropolitan Area Transit Authority	51,663,569	51,663,569	51,663,569	51,663,569
Subtotal	$ 560,618,569	$ 560,248,569	$ 559,198,569	$ 560,968,569
GRAND TOTAL	**$7,014,514,569**	**$10,284,900,569**	**$10,197,746,569**	**$10,383,373,069**

Source: House and Senate Appropriations Committees

A statement by transportation conferees accompanying their report said, "There should be no quotas affecting local programs," and "the conferees firmly believe that the final decision regarding provision of service rests with the grantee."

Amtrak Subsidies

The package provided $602 million for Amtrak operating and capital expenses. As it did in 1985, the administration had requested the elimination of federal subsidies to the passenger railroad.

New budget authority for the Federal Highway Administration also substantially exceeded the administration's request. Congress provided $122 million; the administration asked for $27 million.

Congress allowed $2 million for repair of the Eisenhower Lock operated by the St. Lawrence Seaway Development Corporation; the administration had not requested any funding.

The administration also did not request new funds for the U.S. Railway Association, for which Congress provided $2.2 million.

On the other hand, lawmakers provided less funding than the administration requested for some programs.

These included DOT's Research and Special Programs Administration and its Inspector General's Office, the Architectural and Transportation Review Board, the Interstate Commerce Commission and the Panama Canal Commission.

House Committee Action

In defiance of the administration, the House Appropriations Committee July 17 approved a bill (HR 5205 — H Rept 99-696) providing $10.28 billion for fiscal 1987 transportation appropriations — 47 percent more than the president requested.

Although the funding exceeded Reagan's target, it was

only $138 million more than the level of fiscal 1986 spending, as cut by the Gramm-Rudman-Hollings law (PL 99-177).

Demonstration Projects

No major changes were made in the bill that the Appropriations Subcommittee on Transportation approved June 25. However, the full committee at the urging of Bob Livingston, R-La., added $5 million for an underpass in connection with a runway extension at the New Orleans International Airport.

The committee package included a number of similar "demonstration" projects — special projects that purported to highlight some new technology or engineering principle. The inclusion of such projects in appropriations legislation had in the past raised the hackles of the House Public Works and Transportation Committee, which authorized programs financed by the Highway Trust Fund — the revenues that flowed to the federal government from gasoline taxes and other road-related user fees.

Rebuffs to Administration

As was the case in 1986, the panel rejected the administration's request for the elimination of federal assistance to Amtrak and deep cuts in mass transit programs.

The bill contained $613 million for fiscal 1987 Amtrak operating and capital expenses.

It provided $2 billion for mass transit formula grants, a cut of $57.5 million from fiscal 1986 spending adjusted for Gramm-Rudman cuts.

The Reagan administration was concerned about language in the bill addressing South Africa. One provision would deny U.S. landing rights to aircraft owned or operated by South Africa. A second would bar the Transportation Department from withholding funds from municipalities that prohibited contracting with companies that did business in South Africa.

Until recently, DOT had withheld funds from New York City on grounds that that city's anti-apartheid ordinance violated federal procurement rules requiring that contracts go to the lowest bidder. *(South Africa, p. 359)*

Funding Totals

Funding for DOT and related agencies included the following:

- **Office of the Secretary.** For DOT administration, the committee provided $49.09 million, nearly $2.5 million less than sought by Reagan.
- **Coast Guard.** The committee provided $2.41 billion for Coast Guard activities, $10 million more than the administration's request.

The panel estimated that an additional $69.75 million would be available through Department of Defense appropriations.

- **Federal Aviation Administration.** The FAA would receive $4.9 billion in new budget authority, which would be $94.3 million more than spending adjusted for Gramm-Rudman and $392.4 million more than requested. In fiscal 1986, the panel recommended cuts in FAA programs.

The bill also set limits of $15.5 billion on fiscal 1987 expenditures from the highway, transit and aviation trust funds.

Highway safety programs would be funded at $233.8 million, $5.4 million below fiscal 1986 spending adjusted for Gramm-Rudman.

House Floor Action

The House July 30 overwhelmingly passed HR 5205 by a 329-87 vote. The $10.28 billion transportation spending bill exceeded the administration request by nearly 50 percent.

Sponsors defeated all major amendments, including a bitterly contested proposal to require the administration to rehire at least 1,000 of the air traffic controllers fired by Reagan in 1981. *(Vote 246, p. 72-H)*

Also rejected was a proposal by Dick Armey, R-Texas, for a 1.23 percent, or $312 million, cut in discretionary spending — the only proposal for across-the-board reductions offered in the 10 hours of debate. While acknowledging that the bill's total fell within the spending ceiling of the fiscal 1987 budget resolution (S Con Res 120), Armey argued that cuts were necessary to avoid reductions that would be required by the Gramm-Rudman-Hollings law.

Opponents countered that funds were vitally needed for air safety and the Coast Guard's drug interdiction effort, and the amendment was rejected 143-270. *(Vote 245, p. 70-H)*

The Office of Management and Budget had threatened a veto because of the bill's spending total.

Air Controllers' Debate

The most emotional debate surfaced over an amendment by Guy V. Molinari, R-N.Y., to mandate the rehiring in each of fiscal years 1987 and 1988 of at least 500 air traffic controllers who were fired during the 1981 air traffic controllers' strike.

Backers of the amendment said that the current work force was inexperienced and the FAA had added only 30 controllers in fiscal 1986, far behind its goal of adding 482.

They also pointed out that more than 500 of the strikers already had been reinstated through the government's appeals process and that the military had rehired some of them.

The package sent to the floor by the Appropriations Committee included a provision that would lift the ban on the reinstatement of controllers, but Molinari said that the White House was unlikely to take any action.

Rising in opposition, Gene Snyder, R-Ky., called the fired controllers "outlaws" for breaking an oath never to strike and said that the morale of the current controllers would be adversely affected by the return of the dismissed employees.

"If we mandate the rehiring of these strikers, we can expect a disruption of the air traffic control work force," Snyder said. "Numerous air traffic controllers including pre- and post-strike employees have voiced strenuous opposition against rehiring the strikers."

Countered Richard J. Durbin, D-Ill.: "It will be no consolation to the families of those who may be injured or killed in an air crash due to controller error to be told that the administration had stood firm in its opposition to the ... rehirings."

The amendment was rejected 193-226. *(Vote 243, p. 70-H)*

Other Action

In other action, the House rejected 115-299 an amendment by Robert S. Walker, R-Pa., to shift $315,000 in Department of Transportation funds for the enforcement of the 55 mph speed limit to the Coast Guard for the interdiction of drug traffic. *(Vote 238, p. 70-H)*

By 169-248, members rejected an amendment by Hank Brown, R-Colo., to cut Amtrak funds by 10 percent, or $22.3 million, to restore the fiscal 1986 funding level. *(Vote 241, p. 70-H)*

Senate Committee Action

The Senate Appropriations Committee Aug. 7 approved its version of HR 5205 (S Rept 99-423), which provided $10.2 billion in new budget authority for DOT and related agencies — $87 million less than the version the House approved July 30 and nearly $3.2 billion more than the president's request.

The Senate measure set a cap of $15.28 billion — $200 million less than the House bill — on expenditures from trust funds and other previously authorized accounts. The ceiling included a $1 billion limit on grants to airports from the Airport and Airway Trust Fund and a $13 billion limit on road programs financed by the Highway Trust Fund.

The bill cut a House grant to the Washington, D.C., Metro subway by $32 million, to $185 million, and reduced Amtrak funding by $22 million to provide $591 million — a freeze on fiscal 1986 spending.

Both the Senate panel and the House rejected an administration proposal to create a block grant for highway and transit programs that would be funded by the Highway Trust Fund. Both bills continued formula grant funding, on the order of $2 billion.

The Senate committee followed the lead of the House in boosting funds for Coast Guard activities and accepted the latter's appropriation of $373 million for drug interdiction.

Unlike the House bill, the Senate measure contained no special highway demonstration projects. However, several committee members, including Alfonse M. D'Amato, R-N.Y., and Thad Cochran, R-Miss., said that they would like projects in their states to be considered in conference.

Veto Threatened

In a letter to Senate leaders, James C. Miller III, director of the Office of Management and Budget, threatened a White House veto of the committee bill. The administration objected both to the funding level and the controller rehiring provision.

Administration lawyers contended that the provision was carefully worded to restrict the discretion of the FAA in considering applications for re-employment from dismissed controllers.

In a letter to Appropriations Chairman Mark O. Hatfield, R-Ore., Transportation Secretary Elizabeth Hanford Dole said that the morale and dedication of the current work force "would be demonstrably harmed" by the return of strikers.

Jake Garn, R-Utah, agreed not to offer an amendment to delete the provision after Mark Andrews, R-N.D., chairman of the Subcommittee on Transportation, indicated that prior to floor action, he would insert compromise report language to clarify the FAA's latitude in rehiring fired controllers.

Frank R. Lautenberg, D-N.J., attacked the administration's position on the controller rehiring issue, saying, "I think current policy is not morale-driven; it's vengeance-driven."

Lautenberg said that the FAA was "extremely hard-pressed" to fulfill its mandate of maintaining air safety and could benefit from the return of experienced workers.

Senate Floor Action

Defying a White House call for funding cuts, the Senate Sept. 17 passed HR 5205 by an 87-11 vote. The bill provided $10.2 billion in new budget authority, $87 million less than the version of HR 5205 the House approved July 30. *(Vote 264, p. 45-S)*

The Senate adopted by voice vote a White House-backed amendment that stripped the provision on rehiring air traffic controllers fired in 1981.

While Phil Gramm, R-Texas, said that removing the ban would repudiate the president's "courageous" decision to fire the strikers, Lautenberg argued that the existing work force was stretched dangerously thin and that "the ones we punish are the traveling public." ∎

Interior Funding Exceeds Reagan Request

Congress appropriated far more money than President Reagan requested for the Interior Department and related agencies in fiscal 1987, but it acceded to the White House on most policy items that had prompted veto threats.

For the Interior section of the continuing appropriations bill (H J Res 738 — PL 99-591), the $8.3 billion Congress approved was well above the $6.6 billion Reagan wanted — with most of the excess for fossil energy research, energy conservation and reservoirs for the Strategic Petroleum Reserve (SPR). *(Chart, next page)*

The final amount was also higher than either of the separate Interior bills approved earlier. The House passed an $8.19 billion bill (HR 5234) July 31, and the Senate passed an $8.04 billion version Sept. 16. The conference report (H Rept 99-1005) on the continuing resolution, including Interior funds, cleared Oct. 17. *(Story, p. 219)*

Forest Road-Building

House and Senate conferees came close to splitting their differences on the national forest road-building.

The House had voted to cut the National Forest Service's road-building budget from 1986 levels, heeding arguments from conservation groups that the agency was spoiling potential wilderness by building too many roads too fast. But the Senate had increased the road-building budget, heeding arguments of key timber-state members that wilderness would not be harmed and that the roads were needed to give logging companies access to federal timber.

Among those members were Sens. Mark O. Hatfield, R-Ore., chairman of the Appropriations Committee, and James A. McClure, R-Idaho, chairman of the Interior Subcommittee.

Senate staffers said the final bill provided $180 million for timber road-building. That was less than the $202.5 million first passed by the Senate, but more than the $99.8 million provided by the House. Reagan had requested $143.8 million.

The bill provided for a timber sales program of 11.2 billion board feet (bbf) — close to historic levels, but 0.2 bbf less than in the original Senate committee bill.

Fiscal 1987 Interior Appropriations

Following are budget authority totals in the fiscal 1987 continuing resolution (H J Res 738 — PL 99-591), the House-passed appropriations bill, the Senate-passed measure and the Reagan budget for the Department of the Interior and related agencies *(figures in thousands of dollars)*:

	Budget Request	House Bill	Senate Bill	Final Amount
Interior Department				
Bureau of Land Management	$ 550,246	$ 555,481	$ 653,566	$ 663,502
Fish and Wildlife Service	295,385	369,483	394,936	396,275
National Park Service	714,184	846,164	768,321	818,902
U.S. Geological Survey	395,500	423,220	402,933	418,665
Minerals Management Service	161,100	162,893	155,187	160,697
Bureau of Mines	107,100	126,429	130,965	138,162
Office of Surface Mining	291,400	331,798	283,150	303,723
Bureau of Indian Affairs	924,700	984,546	965,744	997,335
Territorial Affairs	112,499	129,384	170,923	147,861
Departmental Offices	80,600	80,721	78,315	80,680
Subtotal	**$ 3,632,714**	**$ 4,010,119**	**$ 4,004,040**	**$ 4,125,802**
Related Agencies				
Forest Service	$ 1,286,994	$ 1,424,637	$ 1,636,734	$ 1,665,845
Energy Department	336,853	1,179,752	848,065	935,350
Indian Health	722,378	891,257	894,026	907,364
Smithsonian Institution	215,240	212,377	201,208	205,490
National Endowment for the Arts	144,900	165,661	159,950	165,081
National Endowment for the Humanities	126,440	138,641	136,700	138,490
Other Agencies	151,456	167,702	160,758	164,983
Subtotal	**$ 2,984,261**	**$ 4,180,027**	**$ 4,037,441**	**$ 4,182,603**
TOTAL	**$ 6,616,975**	**$ 8,190,146**	**$ 8,041,481**	**$ 8,308,405**

SOURCE: *Congressional Record*

Reagan's Objections

Conferees yielded to the administration on all three of the items on the White House's so-called "A-List" of provisions that could have triggered a veto.

The most controversial required half the material and labor going into offshore drilling rigs to be of U.S. origin. After conferees failed to agree on this "Buy American" proviso, the Senate struck it from the measure Oct. 16 and the House finally concurred Oct. 17.

Congress also yielded to Reagan on a House-passed provision that forbade the administration from deferring spending in the Interior bill for policy reasons. That prohibition was dropped from the continuing resolution.

The provision had touched off a hot legal dispute between the administration and Congress over how to interpret the 1974 budget act (PL 93-344). The law allowed a president to delay spending money for management reasons — for example, if a flood stopped a road-building project.

But members such as Rep. Sidney R. Yates, D-Ill., chairman of the Appropriations Subcommittee on Interior, argued that once Congress had clearly rejected a deferral and directed the spending, the president could not keep deferring it only because he disagreed with the need for the spending. *(Deferrals, p. 576)*

The administration also objected to House language requiring that the SPR be filled at a minimum rate of 75,000 barrels per day.

The final bill appropriated no funds to fill the SPR, but that might have no practical effect because $550 million in unspent funds would be carried over from fiscal 1986. That should allow the SPR to be filled at up to 90,000 barrels per day, assuming crude-oil cost no more than $16.45 per barrel.

Policy Provisions

The bill authorized a one-year expansion of National Park System entrance fees — the first major hike since 1972. The Reagan administration had proposed such an increase in its 1987 budget, but separate authorizing legislation did not advance to the floor in 1986.

The Park Service had been limited by law since 1979 from charging more than 50 cents per person or $3 per vehicle for entrance fees, and then only at 63 of the 337 park system units. The one-year fee approved in the appropriations bill would have a top limit of $5 per vehicle or $3 per person. (Each vehicle would pay a single price, regardless of how many occupants. People entering a park by other means would pay the per-person rate.)

The fees could not be collected at urban recreational parks.

One item that helped boost the final bill amount above either the House or Senate total was the addition of $83 million for firefighting on federal lands — an expense usually added in supplemental appropriations.

As in previous years, the House sought to spend more on acquisition of park, refuge and recreation lands than did the administration or the Senate. But unlike previous years during the Reagan administration, the final result came out higher than even the House had proposed. That happened because of various extra sums becoming available and a tendency to include all lands sought by differing members.

The conference allotted $188 million for acquisition under the Land and Water Conservation Fund — compared with $178 million favored by the House, almost $140 million by the Senate and $20 million requested by the president. The final amount consisted of $35 million for state aid, $52.3 million for the Park Service, $6.5 million for the Bureau of Land Management, $42.4 million for the Fish and Wildlife Service and $52.2 million for the Forest Service.

The bill also included language ratifying a temporary cease-fire in the controversy over oil and gas drilling off the coast of California. The House Appropriations Committee included the language after the Interior Department and negotiators for the California delegation reached agreement in July. The plan put off any California offshore lease sales until 1989 and set up a new process for resolving state-federal disputes.

The conferees dropped language in the House bill that would have restricted implementation of an out-of-court settlement between the Interior Department and the Westlands Water District in California. Rep. George Miller, D-Calif., who originally offered the language, said the agreement gave subsidized water to some of the nation's richest corporate farmers while ignoring toxic pollution at the Kesterson Wildlife Refuge in California, where water draining from the irrigation district ended up. But Interior Secretary Donald P. Hodel said the settlement would bring in money for the Treasury and head off future lawsuits.

The bill did, however, include Senate language aimed at delaying the implementation of a settlement on oil shale claims in Colorado for 180 days. Sen. Gary Hart, D-Colo., who had offered the amendment, voiced concern that the Interior Department was giving private companies too generous a settlement.

The final bill included $296 million for fossil energy research and development, instead of $315 million as proposed by the House and $242 million as proposed by the Senate.

Another major difference between the two chambers was on energy conservation. The final bill appropriated $280 million for those programs, closer to the $286 million figure in the House bill than the Senate's $246 million.

But important strings were attached to much of that money. The $112 million account for weatherization of schools and hospitals was to be appropriated only if those programs reaped less than $200 million from court settlements. Courts had been awarding the programs money paid back by oil companies that overcharged customers in the late 1970s, customers hard to identify individually in 1986.

The administration had said the oil company refunds made it possible to cut appropriations to the conservation programs.

The final bill came out almost neutral on the question of selling off the Naval Petroleum Reserves, such as that at Elk Hills, Calif.

The Reagan administration proposed doing so as a revenue-raising measure. But congressional critics warned that by selling the oil at a time when world oil prices were in a deep slump, the Treasury would get only a fraction of what it should get.

The House bill prohibited the Energy Department from even studying a complete sell-off of the reserves. The Senate bill took the opposite tack, assuming the sell-off would take place and that it would generate $200 million in additional revenue. The final bill did not call for a sell-off, but neither did it prohibit one.

Another restriction in the bill prohibited the eviction of Navajo Indians living on lands partitioned for use by Hopis unless they had been provided with a new or replacement home. Some Navajos had been protesting a congressionally mandated program, run by the Navajo and Hopi Indian Relocation Commission, for settling a dispute between the two tribes over certain lands. *(Background, Congress and the Nation Vol. IV, p. 809)*

House Committee Action

As reported by the House Appropriations Committee July 24, HR 5234 (H Rept 99-714) appropriated $8.19 billion.

The committee accepted a compromise plan delaying the federal sale of oil and gas leases off the California coast until 1989. The compromise avoided a close and bitter vote on whether to accept another one-year moratorium — the fifth in six years — on California offshore leasing as part of the appropriations bill. Rejecting pleas from the administration, the Subcommittee on Interior Appropriations July 16 had approved another moratorium. *(1985 Almanac p. 340)*

Interior Secretary Hodel, who had negotiated with California members on the issue during much of the past year, said the administration was "greatly relieved" at the committee's decision "not to impose a blanket moratorium."

Environmental groups also welcomed the compromise, but the American Petroleum Institute objected, issuing a statement calling the arrangement "the same old moratorium against leasing except it is under a new label and the delay is three years instead of one."

The compromise set up a new process for resolving disputes over leases and gave California and Congress a say in the final decision.

Other Spending

The Appropriations Committee made only a few other changes in the subcommittee bill.

Yates said the measure was under the target for budget authority set in the budget resolution (S Con Res 120). And to bring it under the ceiling for outlays, Yates successfully offered an amendment lowering the required minimum fill rate for the Strategic Petroleum Reserve from 100,000 to 85,000 barrels per day. The amount of money in the bill for filling the reserve — $331 million — remained the same, but the move gave the Energy Department more leeway should the price of oil start to rise.

The only change in spending adopted by the committee was a $13 million cut in construction of National Forest roads and trails from the $168.6 million reported by the subcommittee. That subcommittee figure was already down from the $183.5 million President Reagan requested and the $195.2 million appropriated in fiscal 1986. The timber industry wanted roads to promote logging, but environmentalists said that would destroy wilderness areas.

As in previous years, the committee increased Reagan's request in the areas of park land acquisition ($178 million vs. $20 million) and fossil energy research and development ($315 million vs. $83 million).

The committee bill included $231 million for energy conservation programs — compared with enacted fiscal 1986 spending of $428 million. The committee expected the difference would be made up with court-ordered refunds to the states resulting from overcharges by the oil companies during the 1970s.

Courts had ordered the money to be paid back through government programs that benefited broad groups of energy consumers. Several billion dollars had already been paid to state-federal energy aid programs.

House Floor Action

Avoiding all potential controversy, the House July 31 passed its $8.19 billion Interior appropriations bill by a 359-51 vote. *(Vote 252, p. 72-H)*

The bill denied President Reagan most of the cuts he had asked for in natural resource protection, energy conservation and fossil fuel research — a pattern that had been repeated since Reagan took office in 1981. The bill was about $1.6 billion over Reagan's request.

An amendment offered by Yates reduced outlays in the bill below 1986 levels. It was approved by voice vote. That headed off an amendment by Bill Frenzel, R-Minn., who had been proposing across-the-board cuts in most appropriations bills to reduce the deficit.

Fee Controversy Settled

Westerners won a fight against a hike in federal grazing fees — the one major policy issue threatening smooth passage — before the bill even reached the floor.

The Appropriations Committee had decided to raise the fees the government charged ranchers to graze their cattle and sheep on lands administered by the Bureau of Land Management and the Forest Service.

Yates sought a rule waiving points of order objecting to the grazing fee hike as part of the appropriations bill. But the Rules Committee July 29 denied the waiver on a 5-4 vote.

The losers mounted no further resistance when the rule came before the House. Once adopted, 315-93, it made the grazing fee hike indefensible, and when Joe Skeen, R-N.M., raised the point of order, Yates conceded with no debate. *(Vote 251, p. 72-H)*

The previous law setting grazing fees — the Public Rangelands Improvement Act of 1978 (PL 95-514) — expired at the end of 1985. And negotiations since then had failed to produce an agreement. *(1978 act, Congress and the Nation Vol. V, p. 561)*

When the law expired, authority to set the fee reverted to the executive branch, and the Reagan administration decided to keep the fee at $1.35 per animal unit month (AUM) — the amount of forage needed to feed a mature cow for a month.

The Appropriations Subcommittee on Interior voted to raise the fee to $1.80 in 1987 and eventually to $4.68, with the increase limited to 33 percent in any one year.

Westlands Settlement Opposed

The House adopted by voice vote, and without prolonged debate, an amendment offered by California Rep. Miller aimed at blocking settlement of the lawsuit between the Westlands Water District and the Interior Department.

The settlement provided 900,000 acre-feet of water to the district at 1963 prices — far less than it cost the government to provide it and less than the market price.

Miller called Interior's agreement to the settlement a "capitulation" to "perhaps the wealthiest federal irrigation district in the country," consisting mostly of large corporate farms. Miller also criticized the agreement for failing to address toxic-pollution problems resulting from the irrigation — such as selenium contamination at the Kesterson Wildlife Refuge.

Senate Committee Action

The Senate Appropriations Committee Aug. 13 approved HR 5234 (S Rept 99-397) by voice vote.

The committee met its budget targets, but only by mandating a sell-off of the Naval Petroleum Reserve at Elk Hills, Calif. — creating some $200 million in revenue to offset what would have been a $150 million overrun on outlays during fiscal 1987.

The committee bill included approximately $7.96 billion in new budget authority and about $8.7 billion in outlays, putting it under its budget allocations in both categories. The committee reduced the $8.19 billion in budget authority passed by the House, but came in well above the $6.62 billion requested by Reagan.

As in previous years, the Senate committee's bill shifted spending in the House bill away from conservation and toward development, but not to the extent Reagan wanted. For example, the House bill provided $178 million for park land acquisition. The Senate bill cut that to $137 million, but Reagan wanted only $20 million.

The Senate committee bill also mandated an increase in National Park user fees — a change perennially sought by the Reagan administration and, until 1986, staunchly resisted by Congress. But the entire $50 million increase would have to be spent within the park system, rather than being partly used to offset the deficit as the president proposed.

The Elk Hills sale, proposed by Reagan as a deficit-cutting action, had met with skepticism and resistance on a number of fronts. Critics had questioned whether the Treasury would get an adequate return for oil sold quickly at a time when prices had already dropped steeply. The House passed a bill (HR 4843) Aug. 13 setting a floor price for the federal oil. *(Story, p. 146)*

Northeast vs. Northwest

The Appropriations Committee bill included a compromise involving competing interests in different regions of the country.

Before the bill was approved Aug. 7 by the Interior Subcommittee, a coalition of Northeasterners and environmentalists, led by Warren B. Rudman, R-N.H., succeeded in shifting money from forest road construction to energy conservation programs. Rudman's amendment, cosponsored by Patrick J. Leahy, D-Vt., was an insurrection against subcommittee Chairman McClure and committee Chairman Hatfield. Both McClure and Hatfield came from states where production of timber from national forests was a mainstay of the local economy.

Rudman and Leahy carried their amendment by an 8-7 vote in subcommittee. But by the time the full committee met, the compromise had been negotiated. The Northeast got much of what it sought; the Northwest got all of what it sought.

The Interior appropriations bill contained money for a variety of energy conservation programs — including insulating and weatherstripping homes of low-income families — a program that had proved politically popular in areas like New England where winters can be bitter.

The bill McClure proposed to the subcommittee contained $24 million in budget authority for weatherization and $253 million for national-forest road construction. Rudman's amendment changed those figures to $182 million for weatherization and $180 million for roads. In the full committee bill, the two sides finally agreed on $253 million for road construction and $110 million for weatherization.

"I'll be damned if people in New Hampshire are going to continue to have cold and drafty houses," Rudman declared.

Forest road construction funding had been under attack in recent years from a coalition of environmentalists and fiscal conservatives. They said the Forest Service was needlessly building roads in wilderness areas and that some were built to bring to market federal timber that was then sold at below market prices. McClure and other Northwesterners responded that the timber sales were needed to stave off economic disaster in specific lumbering communities and to promote the health of the forests.

Rudman was one of the original sponsors of the Gramm-Rudman-Hollings deficit-reduction legislation, which had forced the Appropriations committees to struggle to cut spending. Rudman's original amendment would have increased budget authority in the bill, but Rudman argued that because of peculiarities in the spending rate of the two programs, his amendment would not have put the bill over its Gramm-Rudman target on outlays.

Senate Floor Action

After adopting a controversial provision on forest roads, the Senate Sept. 16 passed HR 5234, appropriating $8.04 billion. The vote was 89-8. *(Vote 262, p. 45-S)*

Approval of the bill came after the Senate reversed an earlier stand and voted to back increased funding for road building in national forests. That 53-42 vote was a victory for Hatfield and McClure. *(Vote 261, p. 45-S)*

On Sept. 9, the Senate had handed McClure and Hatfield a surprise defeat, voting 43-51 to reject a motion to table an amendment to cut $90 million in road-building funds from the bill. The amendment was offered by William Proxmire, D-Wis., with support from environmental groups. Following that defeat, McClure pulled the bill from the floor abruptly. *(Vote 258, p. 44-S)*

The bill recommended by McClure's subcommittee included $254 million for road construction. The House-passed bill included $148 million; President Reagan requested $178 million and Congress in fiscal 1986 appropriated $188 million (before Gramm-Rudman adjustments) for fiscal 1986. These direct costs did not include credits given timber companies for roads they built and paid for.

On Sept. 16, McClure softened opposition to the road-building provisions by offering an amendment to Proxmire's amendment that made some concessions to environmental groups. It reduced the amount of timber the National Forest Service could sell in fiscal 1987 from 11.4 billion board feet to 11.2 billion board feet. It cut the amount appropriated for administering the sales by $7 million and the amount for road construction by $8 million — and applied that $15 million to land acquisition for national parks, wildlife refuges and forests.

Proxmire called that only a "token gesture," but it was enough to change the outcome.

The reversal hinged on eight senators who switched their votes from "no" on the tabling motion to "aye" on the McClure amendment. They were: William L. Armstrong, R-Colo.; Daniel K. Inouye, D-Hawaii; William S. Cohen, R-Maine; George J. Mitchell, D-Maine; Daniel Patrick Moynihan, D-N.Y.; Don Nickles, R-Okla.; David L. Boren, D-Okla.; and Larry Pressler, R-S.D.

No senators switched from "aye" on the first vote to "no" on the second. (The remaining difference in the two tallies was due to the absence of different members at each vote.)

Oil Shale Amendment

The Senate also adopted an amendment designed to force the administration to wait for 180 days before carrying out an Aug. 4 settlement of a court case involving Western oil shale claims.

Under the agreement, the Interior Department would transfer to private companies for $2.50 an acre the ownership of some 82,000 acres of public land. The case stemmed from longstanding mineral development claims staked on those lands under the 1872 Mining Act.

The amendment was offered by Hart and John Melcher, D-Mont. They said comparable land and mineral rights were worth thousands of dollars per acre, and they feared the legal precedent set could require the government to hand over another 280,000 acres on similar terms. They wanted the legal process put on hold so that Congress could review the matter and enact any legislative response it found necessary. ▮

$15 Billion Appropriated for Energy, Water

Congress appropriated just over $15 billion for energy and water development projects in the continuing appropriations resolution (H J Res 738 — PL 99-591), while smoothing over, at least for the moment, several major nuclear power controversies.

The troubled domestic uranium industry won a partial hold on Energy Department enrichment rules it had opposed. And Western states, upset with the Reagan administration's nuclear-waste repository decisions, won a short-term freeze on their implementation.

Congress significantly trimmed President Reagan's request for nuclear weapons — which constituted nearly half the spending in the bill. The president had asked for $8.23 billion, but Congress appropriated $7.48 billion.

That cut alone would have accounted for much of the reduction Congress made in the president's overall $15.87 billion budget request. But cuts in other categories and a reshuffling of priorities allowed members to put in money for things they wanted.

A separate 1987 energy and water appropriations bill (HR 5162) was passed by the House July 23 and approved by the Senate Appropriations Committee Aug. 13. As time

Fiscal 1987 Energy/Water Funding

Following are budget authority amounts requested by President Reagan, approved by the full House and the Senate Appropriations Committee and included in the continuing resolution (H J Res 738 — PL 99-591) for the Energy Department, Corps of Engineers, Bureau of Reclamation and related agencies *(in thousands of dollars)*:

	Budget Request	House Bill	Senate Committee	Final Amount
Energy Department				
Energy Supply, R&D	$ 1,254,162	$ 1,316,326	$ 1,318,798	$ 1,347,048
Uranium Enrichment:				
Budget Authority	1,286,400	1,256,400	1,286,400	1,210,400
Offsetting Revenues	(−1,286,400)	(−1,286,400)	(−1,286,400)	(−1,286,400)
General Science/Research	773,400	738,400	677,400	708,400
Nuclear Waste Disposal	769,349	677,649	380,000	499,000
Atomic Energy Defense	8,230,000	7,693,900	7,261,600	7,477,750
Other	456,190	450,771	449,719	448,719
Total Energy Department	**$11,483,101**	**$10,847,046**	**$10,087,517**	**$10,404,917**
Corps of Engineers				
Construction	1,072,500	1,187,734	1,061,260	1,152,150
Operations & Maintenance	1,420,000	1,417,447	1,369,418	1,389,846
Flood Control, Mississippi River & Tributaries	298,000	319,460	300,369	310,797
Other	279,000	301,411	261,240	273,287
Total Corps of Engineers	**$ 3,069,500**	**$ 3,226,052**	**$ 2,992,287**	**$ 3,126,080**
Bureau of Reclamation				
Construction	576,759	592,359	577,059	602,158
Operations & Maintenance	150,000	140,000	150,000	140,000
Other	124,441	131,571	123,009	125,489
Total Bureau of Reclamation	**$ 851,200**	**$ 863,930**	**$ 850,068**	**$ 867,647**
Independent Agencies	466,342	610,972	599,383	608,633
GRAND TOTAL	**$15,870,143**	**$15,548,000**	**$14,529,255**	**$15,007,277**

SOURCE: *Congressional Record*

ran short near the end of the 99th Congress, however, the bill was overtaken by the continuing resolution. Conferees on the big catchall funding measure essentially resolved (H Rept 99-1005) the differences between the two earlier versions of the bill. *(Continuing resolution legislative action, p. 219)*

The bill included funds for water projects by the Army Corps of Engineers ($3.1 billion) and the Bureau of Reclamation ($868 million) and for nuclear weapons production and other activities by the Defense Department.

The bill also contained fiscal 1987 appropriations for many independent agencies such as the Nuclear Regulatory Commission, the Tennessee Valley Authority and the Federal Energy Regulatory Commission.

Much of the water funding in the bill went to operate projects that had already been built. Among the projects getting the largest shares of money for actual construction were the second lock at Lock and Dam 26, on the Mississippi River at Alton, Ill. ($85 million); the Red River Waterway, Mississippi River to Shreveport, La. ($68 million); and the deepening to 50 feet of Baltimore Harbor and channels, Md. ($54 million).

Nuclear Waste Furor

Many Westerners in Congress protested loudly when the Energy Department announced in May that it was going to stop looking for a permanent nuclear-waste site in the East, while continuing to look for one in the West.

The understanding that there would be one site in each half of the country was what allowed Congress to suppress sectional rivalry long enough to legislate a solution to the nation's nuclear-waste problem in the first place. The Nuclear Waste Policy Act of 1982 (PL 97-425) set a timetable for establishing a permanent underground repository by the mid-1990s. *(1982 Almanac p. 304)*

Few states regarded as homes for possible sites liked the idea. The states under consideration were already charging that the Department of Energy (DOE) selection process was based more on politics than geology when the department announced it would not seek an Eastern site.

Resentment came from many parts of the West but was strongest among legislators from Washington, Nevada and Texas — the three states DOE was looking at for a Western site.

The House, when it considered HR 5162, rejected an

amendment by James Weaver, D-Ore., that would have cut out the $291 million DOE needed to go forward with site selection.

But the Senate Appropriations Committee, whose chairman, Mark O. Hatfield, R-Ore., also objected, cut $239 million from the $677 million the House had included for the Nuclear Waste Disposal Fund. That committee wanted a one-year moratorium while the issue was being settled.

The final bill provided $499 million, a $178 million cut from the House level. Of the amount provided, $420 million would be released immediately, but $79 million would be available only after approval by the relevant appropriations subcommittees of the House and Senate.

The bill managers said the secretary of energy would have to certify that he had consulted with the states involved and would have to "provide a detailed explanation of his efforts" before he would get the extra money.

Furthermore, the bill prohibited use of funds to drill any exploratory shafts during the fiscal year — without which a detailed characterization of underground rock formations would be difficult.

The report on the bill said the "conferees believe that the surest course for the department lies in the careful implementation of the Nuclear Waste Policy Act in close consultation with the affected parties, in particular the affected states.... It seems obvious that a restoration of consensus is required before significant progress can be made and that many of the original deadlines of the act will not be met."

Uranium Enrichment

The bill also addressed several related disputes in DOE's uranium enrichment program.

The minerals from which uranium was derived were scattered widely across the globe, but could be used for nuclear fuel or weapons only after the useful isotope of uranium, U-235, had been enriched — that is, concentrated into a final product.

Over the decades, the U.S. government had maintained control of enrichment in this country as a way of controlling the proliferation of technology that could lead to nuclear weapons.

But the U.S. government no longer held a monopoly on enrichment services in the Western world. Competition from two European consortia, plentiful supplies and lower prices had made it difficult for domestic producers of raw uranium to stay in business.

The ore was found in states such as Colorado, New Mexico, Texas, Utah and Wyoming. The Reagan administration caused a stir in these states when it announced plans to revamp the federal enrichment program.

On July 24, DOE sent Congress a set of new proposed rules (or "criteria") for the program. Although those rules technically had taken effect, Congress used the appropriations bill to hobble the administration's effort.

In his fiscal 1987 budget, the president proposed the eventual "privatization" of uranium enrichment, but the appropriations bill restricted spending to study that idea to no more than $250,000 in fiscal 1987. It required DOE to report to Congress on how the public interest would be served by privatization of enrichment and to include a legislative proposal and an estimate of the enterprise's fair market value.

It also specified that the administration's proposals must consider the "viability" of the entire domestic supply and enrichment industry "as a single enterprise and not propose dissolution of various components individually."

Domestic producers wanted DOE's enrichment criteria to restrict the amount of foreign uranium ore that could be enriched. DOE's new criteria did not do so.

The question of uranium import restrictions was the subject of a lawsuit pending before the 10th U.S. Circuit Court of Appeals, and the bill managers said the bill carefully avoided meddling in that case.

But the conference report did address another controversy. It concerned how much the U.S. nuclear-electric utilities that used uranium fuel owed for the enrichment services the government provided. Estimates of the amount owed the Treasury for services ranged from $350 million to $7.5 billion. The administration's new criteria set it at about $3.4 billion.

The conference report blocked DOE from requiring any further repayment by forbidding the use of funds in the bill to make any determination as to how much was owed to the Treasury.

In a statement accompanying the measure, the managers of the bill said: "This is a matter that the conferees believe should be determined by the Congress after full opportunity to inquire into the matter, rather than be determined unilaterally by DOE."

A resolution (H J Res 699) disapproving the DOE enrichment criteria was reported to the House by the Energy and Commerce Committee (H Rept 99-926, Part I) in September, but was not acted on by the full House.

House Committee Action

Despite budget pressures, the House Appropriations Committee June 20 approved an energy and water spending bill for fiscal 1987 that was bigger than that for the previous year.

The bill, traditionally the first approved by the Appropriations Committee each year, contained funds for hundreds of dams, levees and energy projects members would be able to claim credit for in the November elections.

It also contained money for nuclear warheads. But the committee took much of the increase President Reagan had proposed for national defense and used it instead to raise spending over levels he had proposed for local energy and water projects.

The $15.6 billion overall level of budget authority in the bill (HR 5162 — H Rept 99-670) was more than either the $15.3 billion in the bill as enacted for fiscal 1986 or the $14.8 billion adjusted 1986 level that resulted from the first round of cuts under the Gramm-Rudman budget-balancing law (PL 99-177). The committee's bill fell within its tentative allocation under the House budget resolution. *(Gramm-Rudman, 1985 Almanac p. 323)*

Compared with the House committee, however, President Reagan was a big spender: He proposed total budget authority of $15.9 billion for the bill — which included a hefty billion-dollar increase for atomic energy defense activities.

The bill contained funds for the Energy Department and certain independent agencies such as the Appalachian Regional Commission, the Tennessee Valley Authority, the Nuclear Regulatory Commission, and the Federal Energy Regulatory Commission.

More for Water Projects

Spending on politically popular water projects by the Army Corps of Engineers and the Interior Department's

Bureau of Reclamation would increase dramatically from 1986 spending. For the Corps of Engineers, it jumped from an adjusted 1986 level of $2.7 billion to $3.2 billion for 1987. For the Bureau of Reclamation, it jumped from $744 million to $864 million. Most of those increases came in the accounts for new project construction and for flood control work on the Mississippi River and tributaries.

To pay for those water projects and still keep the bill under the budget ceiling, the committee took money from Reagan's proposed increase in atomic energy defense activities, conducted by the Department of Energy. Reagan proposed $8.2 billion for such activities, compared with $7.2 billion (adjusted) for 1986. The committee set it at $7.7 billion.

The two main policy issues debated by the committee both had to do with atomic energy. Bill Green, R-N.Y., offered an amendment prohibiting the use of funds for testing of nuclear weapons as long as the Soviet Union continued the testing moratorium begun in August 1985. The amendment was rejected 26-29.

The committee also defeated by voice vote an amendment by Les AuCoin, D-Ore., that would have deleted spending to develop a long-term nuclear-waste storage site at Hanford, Wash., and a similar amendment by Ronald D. Coleman, D-Texas, applying to a site in Deaf Smith County, Texas.

The committee also defeated by a 7-20 show of hands an amendment by Lawrence Coughlin, R-Pa., that would have deleted funds for the Cliff Dam in Arizona.

House Floor Action

The House July 23 passed HR 5162 by a 329-82 vote after rejecting, 167-241, an amendment by Bill Frenzel, R-Minn., that would have applied an across-the-board 4.62 percent cut. *(Vote 222, p. 66-H; vote 221, p. 64-H)*

As passed by the House, the $15.5 billion spending bill was $792 million more than the fiscal 1986 appropriation, adjusted for the Gramm-Rudman cuts, although it was $320 million less than President Reagan had requested. The cuts in Reagan's budget came largely in the nuclear weapons research area.

The $15.5 billion appropriation was within the target for budget authority Congress set for itself in the budget resolution, according to Tom Bevill, D-Ala., chairman of the Appropriations Subcommittee on Energy and Water Development.

"Contrary to what you have heard, we are right on the House-passed budget," added the subcommittee's ranking Republican, John T. Myers, Ind.

But Frenzel argued that without his cut, outlays (the money actually spent during the year) would be above the House budget resolution.

The administration opposed both the appropriations bill and Frenzel's effort to cut it. A June 16 policy statement said the administration opposed the bill because Reagan's request for nuclear weapons programs had been cut $536 million and domestic programs increased $316 million. But Bevill said Reagan was opposing Frenzel's amendment because the across-the-board cut would take in some "very sensitive weapons research."

The House also rejected, 106-315, an amendment by Robert S. Walker, R-Pa., that would have cut funds for eight research projects not yet authorized by Congress. He criticized approval of such projects without a full review of their scientific value as "hog heaven pork-barrel science." But Bevill argued that other factors besides pure scientific merit should be taken into account. *(Vote 216, p. 64-H)*

Nuclear Issues

Much of the House debate on the bill, which lasted about nine hours, centered on nuclear issues. Members rejected, 68-351, an amendment by Weaver that would have cut $291 million from the Energy Department's budget. The effect would have been to halt the department's study of sites for a permanent nuclear-waste repository. Members from the Northwest were unhappy with the selection of Washington, Nevada and Texas as finalists in the process. Weaver said the department's methods of selection were more political than scientific. *(Vote 217, p. 64-H)*

The House also rejected by voice vote another Weaver amendment cutting $20 million to force the Energy Department to shut down the "N-Reactor" at the Hanford Nuclear Reservation in Washington state. That weapons-production reactor used a graphite-based technology similar in some ways to that used by the Soviet reactor at Chernobyl that exploded April 26.

Senate Committee Action

The Senate Appropriations Committee Aug. 13 approved a funding cut that amounted to a one-year moratorium in the search for a national nuclear-waste site. The cut was included in the committee's version of HR 5162 (S Rept 99-441), reported Sept. 15.

The measure, which provided $14.5 billion in budget authority and $14.9 billion in outlays, remained within budget resolution guidelines.

The bill included funds for water projects of the Army Corps of Engineers ($2.99 billion) and Bureau of Reclamation ($850 million) and for nuclear weapons production and other activities by the Department of Energy ($10.1 billion). It also contained funding for a host of independent agencies.

Waste-Site Controversy

The freeze on further study of a nuclear-waste repository site kept alive a storm of controversy over the way the Reagan administration had handled the program, which was established under the 1982 Nuclear Waste Policy Act (PL 97-425). The act set a timetable for establishing a permanent underground repository for high-level nuclear waste by the mid-1990s.

The Energy Department kicked off the current fuss when it announced in May that it was going to stop studying sites in the East, but keep looking at sites in Washington state, Nevada and Texas.

The resulting Western resentment made it a "highly charged issue," according to Sen. J. Bennett Johnston, D-La. The moratorium, he said, "depoliticizes it and deregionalizes it." Johnston sponsored the moratorium along with committee Chairman Hatfield.

The measure cut $239 million in budget authority from the $619 million in the bill for the Nuclear Waste Disposal Fund, which Hatfield and Johnston said would not dismantle the site study program, but put it in a holding pattern for a year. The House had rejected a similar amendment, 68-351.

Reagan's Requests Cut

The Senate bill contained approximately $7.26 billion in budget authority for atomic energy defense activities, less than the $7.69 billion passed by the House and the $8.23 billion requested by President Reagan. It amounted to a virtual freeze at the 1986 level.

For water projects, the Senate bill hewed to a policy of not funding any new construction starts. The House bill included 30 new Corps of Engineers projects, 19 of them requested by the Reagan administration.

Both the Senate and House bills overturned Reagan's budget plan to shift Energy Department research funds from civilian to military programs. For example, the Senate bill included $341 million for programs under Reagan's strategic defense initiative, or "star wars" program, compared with a $600 million request. In contrast, it provided $1.28 billion for energy supply research, up from Reagan's request of $1.25 billion.

Solar energy research and development made further gains in the Senate committee bill, getting $126 million. Reagan had requested $72 million, but the House had raised it to $113 million. Fiscal 1986 appropriations were $145 million.

Legislative Branch Funding Totals $1.6 Billion

Congress appropriated $1.635 billion for the legislative branch in fiscal 1987 as part of the omnibus continuing resolution (H J Res 738 — PL 99-591) cleared Oct. 17.

The omnibus bill incorporated provisions of a compromise legislative branch appropriations measure (HR 5203 — H Rept 99-805) approved by House and Senate conferees Aug. 15. The House originally passed HR 5203 July 29, and the Senate passed an amended version Aug. 13.

The conference report was filed after negotiators agreed to drop controversial Senate provisions intended to curb the cost of congressional mail. The provisions would have set up separate appropriations accounts for the two chambers' mail budgets. *(Mailing costs, p. 40)*

The compromise bill included $1.1 billion for congressional operations and $530 million for other legislative agencies such as the Library of Congress and the General Accounting Office.

The bill's total represented an increase of 5 percent over fiscal 1986 spending of $1.56 billion for the legislative branch. It included a $29 million increase for Senate operations and a $35 million increase for the House. *(Chart, p. 188)*

The bill also included a provision giving the House and Senate more leeway in deciding how to absorb cuts in their budgets that might be mandated by the Gramm-Rudman-Hollings anti-deficit law (PL 99-177). Gramm-Rudman called for across-the-board cuts in most government activities if Congress failed to meet specified deficit targets.

House Committee Action

The House Appropriations Committee July 17 approved a $1.3 billion bill to finance the operations of the House and related congressional agencies for fiscal 1987 — a 3.7 percent increase over fiscal 1986 spending. The action came by voice vote.

As approved by the committee (H Rept 99-693), HR 5203 included $775 million for House operations and $530 million for related agencies. The Senate later added funding for its own operations.

The House bill's $1.3 billion total was 12 percent less than the $1.48 billion that had been requested by the House and other legislative agencies for their fiscal 1987 budgets. But the total was up from the $1.26 billion available in fiscal 1986 after appropriations were reduced by the across-the-board cuts mandated by Gramm-Rudman-Hollings.

Anticipating the controversy that typically surrounded the annual debate over how much money Congress should spend on itself, Jerry Lewis of California urged committee members to stand by the bill on the floor.

"This is the easiest [appropriations bill] to target when you want to demagogue spending around here," said Lewis, who was ranking Republican on the Legislative Branch Subcommittee.

The subcommittee had approved the bill June 19, and the full committee accepted its recommendations without change.

Mail Money

HR 5203 included $95 million for House and Senate mailing costs, a touchy area of congressional spending. One of the members' most prized perquisites was the ability to send mail to constituents at taxpayers' expense.

Subcommittee Chairman Vic Fazio, D-Calif., said the $95 million should be enough to pay anticipated mail expenses in fiscal 1987, but left unresolved the question of whether or how Congress would make up a major shortfall expected in fiscal 1986 funding. Congress appropriated $95.7 million for its fiscal 1986 mailings, but its postal bill was expected to exceed $140 million. The Senate had taken some steps to curb its mail expenses, but the House had not followed suit.

Gramm-Rudman Leeway

The bill would give the House more leeway in absorbing reductions in its own budget if cuts were mandated by the Gramm-Rudman-Hollings law.

The House's discretion in absorbing such cuts was limited, because its activities were financed through about a dozen subaccounts. So, for example, Congress could not protect personal staff payrolls by making deeper cuts in committee staff, because the two payrolls were financed through separate accounts that must be cut equally. HR 5203 would allow those kinds of trade-offs by specifying that, for Gramm-Rudman purposes, all House subaccounts would count as one.

Library's Wrist Slapped

While the bill would generally freeze and squeeze legislative branch spending, there were exceptions. One would provide a 6 percent increase, to about $40 million, for the Congressional Research Service, an affiliate of the Library of Congress.

It provided an increase of more than 5 percent for the rest of the Library of Congress, where budget cuts had been loudly denounced by Librarian Daniel J. Boorstin and reductions in reading-room hours had prompted public outcry and protests.

That budget boost, to $183 million, was provided despite grumbling from some subcommittee members that, while other agencies had quietly borne their share of bud-

Legislative Branch Appropriations, FY '87

Following are the amounts in budget authority appropriated under the continuing resolution (H J Res 738 — PL 99-591) for legislative branch operations in fiscal 1987:

Congressional Operations	House	Senate	Conference
Senate	—	$ 307,658,014	$ 307,658,014
House of Representatives	$ 463,832,100	463,907,200	463,907,200
Joint Items	106,324,000	106,531,000	103,136,000
Office of Technology Assessment	15,532,000	15,532,000	15,532,000
Biomedical Ethics Board	—	2,500,000	150,000
Congressional Budget Office	17,251,000	17,251,000	17,251,000
Architect of the Capitol	70,297,000	95,620,000	95,553,000
Congressional Research Service	39,602,000	39,602,000	39,602,000
Government Printing Office (congressional printing)	62,000,000	64,200,000	62,000,000
Subtotal	**$ 774,838,100**	**$ 1,112,801,214**	**$ 1,104,789,214**
Related Agencies			
Botanic Garden	2,062,000	2,062,000	2,062,000
Library of Congress	182,970,000	184,570,000	183,670,000
Architect of the Capitol (library buildings)	6,080,000	6,080,000	6,080,000
Copyright Royalty Tribunal	123,000	123,000	123,000
Government Printing Office (non-congressional printing)	33,681,000	35,056,000	32,956,000
General Accounting Office	304,910,000	306,910,000	304,910,000
Railroad Accounting Principles Board	600,000	600,000	600,000
Subtotal	**$ 530,426,000**	**$ 535,401,000**	**$ 530,401,000**
TOTAL	**$ 1,305,264,100**	**$ 1,648,202,214**	**$ 1,635,190,214**

SOURCE: House Appropriations Committee

get cuts, the library and its supporters had resorted to extravagant rhetoric and tactics in opposing the cuts.

"I think the Library operated in a manner conducive to getting attention . . . but we didn't take vengeance," said Fazio.

However, the committee agreed to put in the report on the bill language by Lewis expressing "displeasure with those who have engaged in excessive hyperbole regarding their special interest programs."

House Floor Action

The House July 29 passed HR 5203 by a 266-146 vote, after rejecting an amendment to hold spending to fiscal 1986 levels. *(Vote 236, p. 68-H)*

The bill's $1.3 billion total was unchanged from the amount approved by the Appropriations Committee.

The amendment to cut the bill to fiscal 1986 levels was introduced by Bill Frenzel, R-Minn., who argued that Congress should take the same bitter budget-cutting medicine it was prescribing for others. But Fazio defended the bill and said it was within the outlay target set by the fiscal 1987 budget resolution (S Con Res 120). Frenzel's amendment was rejected, 199-209. *(Vote 235, p. 68-H)*

The House also rejected, 168-238, an amendment by Pat Swindall, R-Ga., to phase out the jobs of 14 House employees who operated automatic elevators. Fazio said the operators were needed to speed elevators when members needed to get to the House floor for roll-call votes. *(Vote 234, p. 68-H)*

An amendment by Bill Cobey, R-N.C., to cut $4.3 million from the $48 million budget for committee staff was rejected, 172-237. *(Vote 233, p. 68-H)*

Mailing Maneuver

Relatively little was said about the touchy subject of congressional mail costs, for which the bill contained $94.8 million. But without debate, the House sustained a point of order by Cobey and dropped a provision that would have allowed some of the fiscal 1987 mail money to be used to make up a shortfall in fiscal 1986.

Fazio said the provision, which would have allowed use of the money upon enactment of the bill, had been a standard feature of the appropriation measure in past years. But it was a fat target this time in light of controversy over the cost of the franking privilege. Members for months had been warned that fiscal 1986 mailing costs were likely to exceed the $95.7 million appropriated.

However, Fazio said the shortfall might end up smaller than earlier predicted, as members had taken steps to reduce their mailing. The Senate in May approved a resolution (S Res 374) to ration its mail budget among members; officials said that through less-publicized voluntary efforts, House members had substantially reduced their use of the frank.

Senate Action

As approved by the Senate Appropriations Committee Aug. 7, HR 5203 (S Rept 99-384) provided $1.65 billion for the legislative branch in fiscal 1987. The panel added $307,558,014 for the Senate operations to the $1.3 billion House-passed measure.

Alfonse M. D'Amato, R-N.Y., chairman of the Legislative Branch Subcommittee, said the Senate amount was 9.5 percent below President Reagan's budget request and 1.5 percent above the level of the past two years. Dale Bumpers, Ark., the subcommittee's senior Democrat, called it "a very conservative bill."

Like the House bill, the Senate measure included language specifying that, for Gramm-Rudman purposes, all Senate funding should be consolidated into one account.

Floor Action

The Senate Aug. 13 passed its version of HR 5203 by voice vote, after adopting an amendment intended to curb congressional mailing costs.

The $1.635 billion measure included $1.1 billion for congressional operations and $530 million for other legislative agencies.

The total, which represented an increase of almost 6 percent over fiscal 1986 levels, included a $29 million increase for Senate operations and a $35 million increase for the House.

Sen. Don Nickles, R-Okla., said Congress should be holding the line on its own budget. "If we're going to be asking other groups and appropriations bills to make reductions, this sets a bad example," Nickles protested. But Appropriations Chairman Mark O. Hatfield, R-Ore., responded that Congress had absorbed cuts in fiscal 1986 and that the proposed fiscal 1987 funding was only a 3 percent increase over fiscal 1985 levels.

The franking amendment, introduced by Wendell H. Ford of Kentucky, ranking Democrat on the Senate Rules and Administration Committee, would set up separate appropriations accounts for House and Senate mail. The two chambers currently drew from a single appropriations fund to pay postal costs.

"The Senate has proved it can live within its means," said Ford. "This amendment is designed to ensure that the House of Representatives does the same."

The amendment would divide the $94.8 million appropriated for mail in HR 5203 equally between the 435-member House and the 100-member Senate, although historically the House had spent more than half of the annual appropriation for mail.

The Ford amendment also would require Congress to appropriate enough money each year to cover its full mailing costs. It would do so by striking a part of existing law that required the U.S. Postal Service to accept as full payment whatever Congress chose to appropriate for mailing.

If costs exceeded the appropriation, the Postal Service had to make up the loss, according to a May 2 ruling by the U.S. comptroller general. ∎

Commerce, Justice, State Get $12.9 Billion

The omnibus spending bill (H J Res 738 — PL 99-591) approved by Congress Oct. 17 included $12.9 billion for the Commerce, Justice and State departments, the federal judiciary and several related agencies.

The House passed a separate bill for these departments and agencies (HR 5161) July 17. The Senate Appropriations Committee reported the bill Sept. 3, but it never reached the floor. Instead, final appropriations levels were set as part of the conference on the omnibus bill, known as a continuing resolution. The resolution cleared (H Rept 99-1005) Oct. 17. *(Story, p. 219)*

The total appropriated in the Commerce-Justice-State section of the omnibus measure — $12,908,785,000 — was $3,049,830,000 less than the administration's final request of $15,958,615,000. *(Chart, next page)*

Within the Justice Department's appropriation was $579 million earmarked for a variety of anti-drug law enforcement activities. This money was authorized in an omnibus anti-drug bill President Reagan signed Oct. 27 (HR 5484 — PL 99-570). The president's request, as reported by the Appropriations committees, did not include the anti-drug money. *(Drug bill, p. 92)*

The largest single area of difference was in the Small Business Administration (SBA). The administration requested $2.8 billion, but the final bill provided for only $481.7 million.

The administration said it needed the extra money in order to buy back SBA loans that had been transferred to another federal agency. Congress decided not to go along, however, because members disagreed that the funding was necessary for the transaction.

Civil Rights Commission

PL 99-591 also substantially reduced the funding for the U.S. Civil Rights Commission. The appropriation was cut from $11.7 million in fiscal 1986 to $7.5 million for fiscal 1987. In addition, Congress put restrictions on how the money could be spent, limiting the pay commissioners could receive, the number of employees they could hire and the amount of money that could be spent for consulting contracts. The restrictions were designed to make the commission part time.

The appropriation for the commission included $700,000 for activities to monitor civil rights and $2 million for the commission's regional offices.

The provision on the commission was a compromise between the House, which wanted to delete all funding for the commission, and some members of the Senate, who wanted to keep it alive. Critics said the commission had failed to meet its mandate over the past three years.

The commission, which was created in 1957 as an independent agency to monitor the progress of civil rights in the United States, had been controversial since it was reauthorized in 1983. After a prolonged congressional fight,

Funding Breakdown for Commerce/Justice/State

Following are the fiscal 1987 appropriations, in budget authority, for the Commerce, Justice and State departments, the federal judiciary and related agencies, as cleared by Congress Oct. 17 *(in thousands of dollars)*:

	Final Budget Request	Final Appropriation
Commerce Department		
General Administration	$ 39,250	$ 36,300
Bureau of the Census	277,230	262,780
Economic and Statistical Analysis	31,005	30,000
Economic Development Administration	—	203,867
International Trade Administration	179,170	189,400
Minority Business Development Agency	45,369	39,675
U.S. Travel and Tourism Administration	4,023	11,500
National Oceanic and Atmospheric Administration	917,779	1,072,138
Patent and Trademark Office	109,632	98,000
National Bureau of Standards	123,953	122,000
National Telecommunications and Information Administration	13,916	33,500
Subtotal	**$ 1,741,327**	**$ 2,099,160**
Related Agencies		
Federal Communications Commission	97,242	95,000
Federal Maritime Commission	11,940	11,600
Federal Trade Commission	69,045	65,000
International Trade Commission	33,700	33,900
Marine Mammal Commission	848	900
Maritime Administration	58,843	67,500
Office of the U.S. Trade Representative	12,216	13,300
Securities and Exchange Commission	110,050	110,500
Small Business Administration	2,803,621	481,742
Subtotal	**$ 3,197,505**	**$ 879,442**
Justice Department		
General Administration	73,708	67,000
U.S. Parole Commission	10,420	10,300
Legal Activities	979,591	990,822
Federal Bureau of Investigation	1,278,410	1,262,000
Drug Enforcement Administration	411,329	479,500
Immigration and Naturalization Service	609,393	593,000
Federal Prison System	767,454	854,818
Office of Justice Programs	74,400	415,650
Subtotal	**$ 4,204,705**	**$ 4,673,090**
Related Agencies		
Christopher Columbus Jubilee Commission	$ 220	$ 220
Civil Rights Commission	12,576	7,500
Commission on the Bicentennial of the Constitution	12,000	13,200
Equal Employment Opportunity Commission	167,691	165,000
Legal Services Corporation[1]	305,500	305,500
State Justice Institute	9,834	7,200
Subtotal	**$ 507,821**	**$ 498,620**
State Department		
Administration of Foreign Affairs	3,381,774	2,121,337
International Organizations and Conferences	493,221	419,860
International Commissions	29,700	29,200
U.S. Bilateral Science and Technology Agreements	2,000	1,900
The Asia Foundation	9,500	8,800
Soviet-East European Research and Training	4,000	4,600
Subtotal	**$ 3,920,195**	**$ 2,585,697**
Related Agencies		
Arms Control and Disarmament Agency	31,000	29,000
Board for International Broadcasting	167,509	140,000
Commission on Security and Cooperation in Europe	625	526
Japan-United States Trust Fund	1,550	1,408
U.S. Information Agency	959,195	809,250
Subtotal	**$ 1,159,879**	**$ 980,184**
The Judiciary[1]		
Supreme Court	17,086	16,879
U.S. Court of Appeals for the Federal Circuit	7,290	6,800
U.S. Court of International Trade	7,546	7,000
Court of Appeals, District Courts, other services	1,144,935	1,116,013
Administrative Office of the U.S. Courts	32,100	29,500
Federal Judicial Center	10,226	9,600
U.S. Sentencing Commission	6,500	5,800
Bicentennial Expenses	1,500	1,000
Subtotal	**$ 1,227,183**	**$ 1,192,592**
GRAND TOTAL	**$ 15,958,615**	**$ 12,908,785**

[1] *Request submitted directly to Congress.*

SOURCE: Senate and House Appropriations committees

the commission was reconstituted, and President Reagan appointed people opposed to school busing and affirmative action, angering members and civil rights lobbyists who thought they had worked out an agreement on commission appointments. *(1983 Almanac p. 292)*

Bucking Reagan

As in previous years, Congress approved funding for several items the administration had sought to abolish.

It appropriated $305.5 million for the Legal Services Corporation (LSC), which provided free legal help to the nation's poor; $205.4 million for the Economic Development Administration (EDA), which provided money to hard-pressed communities to help them spur private development projects; and $70.3 million for a Justice Department program to help states combat juvenile delinquency.

State Department Funding

The bill approved by the House Appropriations Committee had reduced the United States' mandatory contribution to international organizations by $17.6 million, to $405 million, and that amount was subsequently reduced to $385 million because of a 5 percent across-the-board cut the House adopted.

The administration had requested $432.9 million, with $298.2 million earmarked for the United Nations and such specialized agencies as the World Health Organization.

Conferees accepted the House's $385 million figure and left it up to the State Department to allocate the money. However, Congress did specify that $130 million should be deferred until fiscal 1988.

The measure also provided $440 million for maintenance and acquisition of buildings abroad. The conference report included a detailed section providing $1 million for the National Bureau of Standards and instructing the bureau to analyze how the U.S. Embassy office building in Moscow was being constructed.

The embassy, which was being built by the Soviets, was running several years behind schedule and was considerably over budget.

The measure required the secretary of state, starting Feb. 1, 1987, to report to the House and Senate every six months "on any failures of Soviet agencies to perform obligations to United States diplomats or missions and the actions taken by the State Department to redress these failures."

Of the $440 million provided for buildings abroad, $227 million was earmarked for "diplomatic security" in five places: Istanbul, Turkey, at $14.8 million; Lima, Peru, at $68.6 million; Bogota, Colombia, at $57.5 million; Pretoria, South Africa, at $33.3 million; and Cairo, Egypt, at $46,100. An additional $6.6 million was provided for project support. Congress had authorized the embassy security program earlier in the year. *(Embassy security, p. 377)*

House Committee Action

The House Appropriations Committee reported HR 5161 (H Rept 99-669) July 15, providing $12.9 billion for the Departments of Commerce, State and Justice, the federal judiciary and related agencies.

The appropriations measure, approved by voice vote, included $2.2 billion for the Commerce Department; $4.2 billion for Justice; $2.8 billion for State; $1.2 billion for the federal judiciary; and $2.4 billion for related agencies such as the Maritime Administration, Equal Employment Opportunity Commission, Federal Communications Commission, Federal Trade Commission, Legal Services Corporation, Securities and Exchange Commission, Small Business Administration and the U.S. Information Agency (USIA). The measure contained funds for a number of programs that the administration had proposed to eliminate.

Before approving the bill June 26, the committee voted 27-16 to eliminate funding for the Civil Rights Commission after Dec. 31, 1986. It left $11.8 million for the commission in the bill but said it could be used only for costs associated with closing down.

The amendment was offered by Julian C. Dixon, D-Calif., who said it was endorsed by the Leadership Conference on Civil Rights, an umbrella group for many civil rights organizations. He cited a General Accounting Office report to back his assertion that the commission was a "sorely mismanaged agency."

Harold Rogers, R-Ky., argued against the amendment, saying, "It doesn't make sense to burn down the church just because you don't like the preacher."

Other actions taken during the markup included:

- Rejection, on a mostly party-line vote of 15-21, of a proposal by Bob Livingston, R-La., to require that the USIA study the feasibility of establishing a special radio broadcast service directed at Nicaragua.
- Approval, by voice vote, of report language urging the Justice Department to pursue more actively investigations of violence at family planning and abortion clinics, including bomb threats, physical or verbal harassment, vandalism and sit-ins.

House Floor Action

The House passed HR 5161 the evening of July 17 by a 269-66 vote. *(Vote 211, p. 62-H)*

Before passing the bill, the House adopted an amendment to reduce virtually all discretionary spending in the bill by 5 percent. Only the FBI and the Drug Enforcement Administration (DEA) were exempted from the cut.

Bill Frenzel, R-Minn., who sponsored the budget-cutting amendment, said it would keep fiscal 1987 spending authority from exceeding 1986 levels and would hold the deficit closer to the target set in the Gramm-Rudman-Hollings anti-deficit law (PL 99-177).

As approved by the Appropriations Committee, the bill was $1 billion over the outlay target set by the budget resolution (S Con Res 120). Frenzel's amendment, adopted 213-125, cut $500 million in outlays. *(Vote 209, p. 62-H)*

While the Appropriations subcommittees figured their bills in "budget authority" — the amount of money that may be obligated — the deficit, and therefore the Gramm-Rudman-Hollings targets, were calculated in outlays, the amount of money actually disbursed.

The $12.2 billion appropriated for the departments and agencies compared with $15.96 billion requested by President Reagan.

Over administration objections, the bill included funding for the Legal Services Corporation at $305.5 million; the Economic Development Administration at $216 million; and a Justice Department program to combat juvenile delinquency at $70.3 million.

The bill ran contrary to administration wishes in two other noteworthy areas. The White House had requested $1.09 billion to beef up security at U.S. embassies and consulates overseas, but the House, agreeing with the

Appropriations Committee, cut that amount by $862 million to $227 million. The House also approved new procedures governing the expenditure of the money, requiring State Department officials to let Congress review each project before funds were committed.

The House also rejected an administration request to provide $2.3 billion that would be required to finance the sale of outstanding loans held by the Small Business Administration.

EDA vs. DEA

The most prolonged debate during nine hours of deliberations on the bill July 17 was over funding for EDA, which provided money to local communities to help them raise private funds for economic development. The program had not been authorized — that is, given formal congressional approval for its operations — since 1982.

Opponents of the program contended it was wasteful and unproductive, while defenders claimed it had helped beleaguered communities come up with the necessary seed money to create projects and jobs.

EDA opponents tried to use growing national concern about drug abuse to persuade colleagues to cut EDA. They suggested that the money would be better spent on drug enforcement efforts.

David S. Monson, R-Utah, sought to offer a two-part amendment cutting $50 million from EDA and transferring it to DEA. But Neal Smith, D-Iowa, chairman of the Appropriations Subcommittee on Commerce, Justice, State and Judiciary, objected to considering the proposals together.

Monson then offered an amendment to cut $190 million from EDA, with the understanding that some of that money would then be put into DEA, but his amendment was rejected 108-302. *(Vote 203, p. 60-H)*

During the debate, Robert S. Walker, R-Pa., who strongly supported Monson's effort, said Congress should use HR 5161 to set its priorities in favor of curbing drug abuse. "I submit that if we can take [money] away from EDA and give it to DEA, we will have a good reversal of the alphabet in favor of what taxpayers want."

Sherwood Boehlert, R-N.Y., an EDA advocate, disagreed. "We should not be pitting DEA against EDA," he said. "That is absolutely ludicrous."

Boehlert, like Smith and several other members, noted that HR 5161 provided DEA with a $48.3 million increase over fiscal 1986 levels and $671,000 above the administration request. The DEA total was $412 million.

Walker sought to trim $50 million from EDA, but his amendment was rejected 150-256. *(Vote 204, p. 60-H)*

Other Amendments

After the EDA/DEA debate, the House turned to discussion of U.S. contributions to the United Nations. By voice vote, the House agreed to an amendment that cut $17.6 million from the $423 million earmarked for international organizations. Of that $17.6 million reduction, $7.57 million would come from funds that went to the United Nation's Department of Public Information.

Pat Swindall, R-Ga., said the public information office had a history of disseminating materials with a bias against the United States. He noted that a General Accounting Office report reviewing 90 media pieces found that 40 were in opposition to U.S. positions, while only one was supportive.

By voice vote the House adopted an amendment by Bob Dornan, R-Calif., barring the Justice Department from using funds to pay for abortions for female inmates in federal prisons or for providing facilities for abortion, unless the life of the pregnant woman would be endangered by carrying the fetus to term.

Sen. Jesse Helms, R-N.C., had sought to attach a similar amendment to the fiscal 1986 bill, but it was rejected after senators cited constitutional problems. *(1985 Almanac pp. 346, 349)*

The House rejected these amendments:

- By Larry Combest, R-Texas, to delete funding for LSC, 103-278. *(Vote 205, p. 60-H)*
- By Dan Lungren, R-Calif., to cut LSC funding by half, to $153 million, by voice vote.
- By Combest, to trim LSC funding $25.5 million, to $280 million, 161-204. *(Vote 206, p. 62-H)*
- By John Hiler, R-Ind., to delete funding for SBA's direct loan program, except for $39 million for loans to minority businesses and $15 million for handicapped assistance, 118-243. *(Vote 207, p. 62-H)*
- By John Conyers Jr., D-Mich., to delete funding for the National Endowment for Democracy, an organization created in 1983 to provide grants to private organizations to explain the U.S. political system to people in foreign countries, 121-228. *(Vote 208, p. 62-H)*

Senate Committee Action

The Senate Appropriations Committee Aug. 14 approved its version of HR 5161 (S Rept 99-425) providing $11.93 billion for the departments and agencies covered by the bill.

The measure was just $41,000 under the outlay target set by the budget resolution. It was $378.9 million under the House-passed bill of $12.31 billion and $4.02 billion under the Reagan administration budget request of $15.96 billion.

Despite about two hours of debate, the committee made no changes in the total amount of money approved Aug. 12 by the Subcommittee on Commerce, Justice, State, the Judiciary and Related Agencies.

At that session and at the full committee, subcommittee Chairman Warren B. Rudman, R-N.H., highlighted funds in the bill for drug enforcement. He said about $900 million, spread over several agencies, was earmarked for the anti-drug campaign.

Civil Rights Commission Cut

The appropriations bill cut funding for the Civil Rights Commission almost in half. The commission was given $6 million under an amendment by Frank R. Lautenberg, D-N.J., that also placed a number of restrictions on the commissioners' activities.

Lautenberg said the amendment was designed to make the advisory panel part time. It would limit the pay commissioners could receive, the number of employees they could hire and the number of consulting contracts they could approve.

The House version of the bill provided $11.8 million for the commission, but specified that the money could be used only to phase out the commission by the end of the year.

Senate Republicans and Democrats said the House action was too strong and that it was important to preserve the commission. But several senators expressed strong disapproval of the panel.

Water Pact Added

At the subcommittee session Aug. 12, members agreed to a request by Paul Laxalt, R-Nev., to add a controversial water compact to HR 5161. At the full committee, that decision led to a long debate over the compact and the propriety of adding it to an appropriations bill.

The pact between the states of California and Nevada divided water rights without expressly protecting the rights of the federal government and Indian tribes in the affected area.

The tribes, the Reagan administration and many environmental groups opposed the agreement. They contended it would infringe upon the Indians' rights and the rights of the federal government to protect endangered species in the areas affected.

Laxalt defended the agreement, contending that there was nothing in it to prevent Indians from pursuing their claims in court.

Dennis DeConcini, D-Ariz., offered an amendment protecting the rights of the Indians and the government, but Laxalt said it would doom the pact and it was defeated, 12-12. ∎

Treasury, Postal Service Funding: $13.8 Billion

Lawmakers appropriated some $13.8 billion for the Treasury Department, the U.S. Postal Service and a variety of other federal agencies for fiscal 1987, as part of the omnibus spending bill (H J Res 738 — PL 99-591) that cleared at the end of the 99th Congress.

The funds for those agencies, among them the Executive Office of the President, totaled about $1 billion more than the Reagan administration requested and $800 million more than was appropriated in fiscal 1986. In its largest change in the president's requests, Congress provided $650 million for postal subsidies that President Reagan had sought to eliminate.

The funding was incorporated into the omnibus measure, known as a continuing resolution, after lawmakers resolved disputes over such diverse issues as standards for imported liquor, federal building projects, and a controversial regulatory unit within the Office of Management and Budget (OMB).

The House had passed a $13.7 billion fiscal 1987 Treasury-Postal Service bill (HR 5294) Aug. 6. The Senate's companion bill providing $13.3 billion was approved by the Appropriations Committee Aug. 14 but never sent to the floor as a distinct measure. Each chamber folded its version of HR 5294, with few changes, into the continuing resolution and worked out House-Senate differences during the conference on the omnibus measure (H Rept 99-1005). *(Continuing resolution, p. 219)*

The compromise $13.8 billion total for the Treasury-Postal Service portion of the spending bill included some $165 million added for anti-drug activities of the White House and Treasury Department authorized by a new drug abuse prevention law (HR 5484 — PL 99-570). *(Drug bill, p. 92)*

The total included $6.4 billion for the Treasury Department, $650 million for the Postal Service, $101 million for the Executive Office of the President and $6.7 billion for 11 independent agencies. *(Chart, next page)*

Beer and Buildings

One Senate controversy was defused before the bill went to conference. Faced with a filibuster threat during floor debate on H J Res 738, the Senate dropped a committee-passed proposal providing some antitrust protections to beer distributors.

The final bill also dropped an unrelated but controversial House provision that would have required imported wine, beer and distilled liquor to be certified as meeting U.S. purity standards. Advocates of this provision, proposed in Appropriations Committee debate on H J Res 738 by Robert J. Mrazek, D-N.Y., said it was a health and safety measure designed to protect Americans against adulterated foreign liquor.

But critics charged that the measure would give monopoly control to authorized distributors, because only those firms designated by the manufacturer would have easy access to the required ingredient information needed to meet U.S. standards. Among the most vocal critics were members from states such as Washington and Pennsylvania with controlled liquor sales, who believed the measure would jeopardize their states' ability to purchase cheaper liquor from independent exporters.

After House and Senate conferees failed to resolve the issue, the House on Oct. 15 voted 297-113 to back down and drop the liquor import restriction. *(Vote 438, p. 122-H)*

One of the last issues to be resolved on the continuing resolution involved a House provision allotting funds for new federal buildings and related projects, including some that had not been authorized. Critics viewed some of the projects as expensive "pork barrel" that took funds away from higher-priority building projects. Most controversial was $32 million provided for site selection and design costs for a building in Chicago that had the backing of Rep. Dan Rostenkowski, D, and other Illinois lawmakers.

After conferees failed to resolve the dispute, the House Oct. 15 approved, 301-106, and sent to the Senate a modified proposal that provided for the Chicago building and another project to be acquired through a lease rather than direct federal purchase. *(Vote 437, p. 122-H)*

The new proposal still met opposition from Senate critics, who wanted to finance only authorized projects, but eventually the House provisions were accepted by voice vote.

After Congress adjourned, however, the hard-fought issue hit another snag. Through what aides said was a clerical error, the provisions authorizing the federal building projects were not included in the copy of the massive continuing resolution sent to the president for his signature.

If Congress were in session it could have passed a resolution correcting the error, which affected not only the contested projects but all of the General Services Administration's authority to operate federal buildings. With Congress adjourned, the problem was solved by having President Reagan sign a new, complete copy of the bill.

IRS, Regulatory Review

Plagued in the past by tax return mishaps, the Internal Revenue Service (IRS) got $4.2 billion under H J Res 738 — the amount included in the House version. The Senate had included $313 million less for the IRS, citing budget

Fiscal 1987 Treasury, Postal Funding

Following are the amounts in new budget authority requested by President Reagan, approved by the House and Senate, and included in the continuing resolution (H J Res 738 — PL 99-591) for the Treasury Department, U.S. Postal Service and other agencies in fiscal 1987:

	Budget Request	House Amount	Senate Amount	Final Amount
Treasury Department				
Departmental offices	$ 80,084,000	$ 52,642,000	$ 76,000,000	$ 52,642,000
International Affairs	—	22,442,000	—	22,442,000
Federal Law Enforcement Training Center	20,899,000	29,499,000	23,000,000	29,499,000
Financial Management Service	251,117,000	251,117,000	240,117,000	240,117,000
Bureau of Alcohol, Tobacco and Firearms	178,463,000	190,463,000	193,463,000	193,463,000
U.S. Customs Service	747,700,000	863,200,000	847,819,000	1,001,070,000
Bureau of the Mint	48,502,000	44,202,000	43,202,000	43,202,000
Bureau of the Public Debt	218,564,000	218,564,000	198,564,000	198,564,000
Internal Revenue Service	4,097,792,000	4,247,792,000	3,935,000,000	4,247,792,000
U.S. Secret Service	307,140,000	316,800,000	318,000,000	323,000,000
Payment to the Government of Puerto Rico	—	—	—	7,800,000
Subtotal	**$ 5,950,261,000**	**$ 6,236,721,000**	**$ 5,875,165,000**	**$ 6,359,591,000**
Payment to the U.S. Postal Service	**$ 40,049,000**	**$ 690,049,000**	**$ 650,000,000**	**$ 650,000,000**
Executive Office of the President				
President's compensation	$250,000	$250,000	$250,000	$250,000
Office of administration	16,238,000	16,238,000	15,700,000	15,700,000
White House office	25,179,000	25,179,000	24,450,000	24,450,000
Executive residence	4,942,000	4,942,000	4,700,000	4,700,000
Vice president's residence	211,000	211,000	211,000	211,000
Vice president's staff	1,849,000	1,849,000	1,790,000	1,790,000
Council of Economic Advisers	2,346,000	2,346,000	2,275,000	2,275,000
Office of Policy Development	2,665,000	2,665,000	2,600,000	2,600,000
National Security Council	4,627,000	4,627,000	4,550,000	4,550,000
National Critical Materials Council	250,000	250,000	100,000	175,000
Office of Management and Budget	39,682,000	34,274,000	37,000,000	37,000,000
Office of Federal Procurement Policy	1,660,000	1,660,000	1,600,000	1,600,000
Unanticipated needs	1,000,000	1,000,000	500,000	1,000,000
Conference on Drug Abuse and Control	—	—	—	5,000,000
Subtotal	**$ 100,899,000**	**$ 95,491,000**	**$ 95,726,000**	**$ 101,301,000**
Independent Agencies				
Administrative Conference of the United States	$ 1,559,000	$ 1,559,000	$ 1,369,000	$ 1,469,000
Advisory Commission on Intergovernmental Relations	2,090,000	1,045,000	1,953,000	1,750,000
Advisory Committee on Federal Pay	229,000	229,000	201,000	201,000
Committee for Purchase From the Blind and Other Severely Handicapped	778,000	778,000	699,000	778,000
Federal Election Commission	12,800,000	12,000,000	12,800,000	12,800,000
General Services Administration	390,183,000	395,125,000	369,512,800	375,620,000
National Archives	101,321,000	105,321,000	100,321,000	100,321,000
Office of Personnel Management	6,188,568,000	6,188,568,000	6,112,250,000	6,120,250,000
Merit Systems Protection Board	24,891,000	24,891,000	23,536,000	23,536,000
Federal Labor Relations Authority	17,064,000	17,064,000	16,330,000	16,330,000
U.S. Tax Court	25,538,000	25,538,000	25,000,000	25,538,000
Subtotal	**$ 6,765,021,000**	**$ 6,772,118,000**	**$ 6,663,971,800**	**$ 6,678,593,000**
General reduction*	—	−142,622,000	—	—
GRAND TOTAL	**$ 12,856,230,000 †**	**$ 13,651,757,000**	**$ 13,284,862,800**	**$ 13,789,485,000**

* *General reduction reflects the total that would be cut under a House-passed amendment making a 9.75 percent reduction in certain accounts.*
† *Does not include president's request for anti-drug initiative.*

constraints. However, its Appropriations Committee warned that the reduced sum "may not be enough to fund planned enhancement of revenue collection efforts."

The Senate went along with the higher House figure — an investment in IRS staffing that Congress was counting on to help reduce the deficit. The fiscal 1987 budget "reconciliation" bill (HR 5300 — PL 99-509) assumed that the additional personnel would result in $2.4 billion in increased revenues in fiscal 1987. *(Fiscal 1987 reconciliation, p. 559)*

The final version of H J Res 738 included funding and new restrictions on the controversial OMB unit, the Office of Information and Regulatory Affairs, which had been criticized for overstepping its authority to review other agencies' regulations. The House bill had cut off all funds for the office.

Negotiators restored the funding and renewed the office for three years, authorizing $5.5 million annually through fiscal 1989 under the Paperwork Reduction Act of 1980 (PL 96-511). But the legislation restricted the use of those funds to regulatory oversight solely for review of agency requests to collect information from the public. The office could perform other regulatory reviews, but not with funds from the Paperwork Reduction Act.

In other areas, the spending bill also made changes in the Brooks Act of 1965 (PL 89-306), which gave the General Services Administration (GSA) responsibility for coordinating procurement of automatic data processing in the federal government. The changes were designed to clarify the limits of OMB's role in administering the act and to ensure that it covered procurement not only of equipment but also computer software, telecommunications and related services.

House Committee Action

The House Appropriations Committee approved HR 5294 on a voice vote July 30 without an effort to restore OMB funds removed earlier by the Subcommittee on Treasury-Postal Service-General Government.

In marking up the bill July 17, the subcommittee had denied $5.4 million requested for the OMB Office of Information and Regulatory Affairs. The office had come under increasingly heavy attack from House committee chairmen who charged that it frequently overruled decisions by federal agencies in order to please business interests.

But Silvio O. Conte, R-Mass., warned that OMB would recommend a presidential veto of the appropriations bill unless the funds were restored. The bill stated that OMB could not use other money to pay for the regulatory office.

As reported by the Appropriations Committee (H Rept 99-723), the bill was $938.2 million above the $12.9 billion recommended in President Reagan's fiscal 1987 budget. The chief reason for the difference was $650 million in the bill for the Postal Service to subsidize cheaper rates for non-profit mailers. The White House wanted Congress to end the postal subsidy.

The House measure also contained $4.2 billion for the Internal Revenue Service, $150 million above the amount requested by Reagan. Sponsors said the added amount was needed to avert future delays in processing tax returns.

In addition, the committee had recommended $860.2 million for the U.S. Customs Service, which was $112.5 million above Reagan's request. Most of the additional money would be used to hire nearly 2,400 new Customs employees to bolster anti-drug smuggling operations.

For the past several years, Congress had skirmished with the White House over funding for the IRS and Customs. Reagan vetoed a fiscal 1986 spending bill for the Treasury Department and other agencies, contending it was too expensive. Funds in the measure later were included in a continuing appropriations resolution. *(1985 Almanac p. 329)*

House Floor Action

The House passed HR 5294 Aug. 6 on a 302-118 vote. Before passing the $13.7 billion spending measure, the House rejected an across-the-board trim of nearly $700 million. *(Vote 271, p. 78-H)*

An amendment to cut discretionary spending by 8.94 percent, amounting to $690 million, was offered by Bill Frenzel, R-Minn., who frequently called for reductions in spending measures. But his amendment, offered as a substitute to a more moderate spending cut by Bruce A. Morrison, D-Conn., failed on a 7-19 division vote.

The House then voted 269-152 to approve Morrison's amendment, which reduced the bill's total by about $143 million. *(Vote 268, p. 76-H)*

Morrison's proposal cut 9.75 percent from many agencies in the bill. But it exempted the big-ticket items such as the IRS, Customs Service, Postal Service and Bureau of Alcohol, Tobacco and Firearms.

Some House members urged against cutting the budgets at the IRS and Customs because they help to produce federal revenues by collecting taxes and tariffs. The bill provided $4.2 billion for the IRS, $150 million above the amount proposed by Reagan. Customs would receive $863.2 million in the bill, compared with $747.7 million recommended by the White House.

In another section of the bill, Andrew Jacobs Jr., D-Ind., renewed his annual effort to strip nearly $1 million from the office and staff expenses accorded to former U.S. presidents. But the House turned aside Jacobs' amendment, instead voting 356-61 to substitute one by Joe Skeen, R-N.M., to reduce the allowance for ex-presidents by $58,000, a 5 percent cut. *(Vote 266, p. 76-H)*

The House voted a second time to approve a block of amendments by Robert S. Walker, R-Pa., to transfer $3 million from the Treasury secretary's office to the Customs Service. The second vote was taken so that members who were not present during the first, 254-109 vote Aug. 1, a Friday, could record their position. This time the amendments passed 387-30. *(Votes 256, 270, pp. 74-H, 78-H)*

The House went along with the committee's denial of funds for OMB's regulatory office. Edward R. Roybal, D-Calif., described the office as a "rogue agency, trampling on the authorities and responsibilities of Cabinet agencies."

Senate Committee Action

As approved by the Senate Appropriations Committee Aug. 14, HR 5294 (S Rept 99-406) provided $13.3 billion for the departments and agencies covered by the bill.

The committee cut nearly $313 million from the House-approved appropriation for the Internal Revenue Service, plagued in the past by tax return mishaps. The Senate bill included $3.9 billion for the IRS, compared with $4.2 billion provided by the House measure and $4.1 billion requested by the administration.

In recommending less spending for the IRS than the

House, the Senate panel cited budget constraints and the fact that the tax-collecting agency already commanded nearly 60 percent of the discretionary spending in the bill.

The committee said its funding level for the IRS "should be adequate" to cover increased costs due to inflation. But it warned that the money "may not be enough to fund planned enhancement of revenue collection efforts." As a result, the committee directed IRS officials to give top priority to activities during the busy January-April filing season.

Despite that instruction, the Senate bill provided $117.9 million less than the House for processing tax returns. The Senate panel recommended $1.21 billion compared with $1.33 billion in the House. The House had increased the money in this area to add 1,700 positions. The Senate bill also reduced the House level for tax examinations and appeals by $93.2 million. The Senate committee provided $1.53 billion while the House bill included $1.62 billion.

The Senate committee provided $5.4 million, the amount requested by the administration but denied by the House, for the OMB Office of Information and Regulatory Affairs.

The Customs Service received $856.2 million in the Senate bill, only slightly below the $863.2 million in the House legislation. Both versions were substantially higher than the $747.7 million requested. Legislators in both chambers said the extra funds were needed to maintain positions recommended for cutting by the White House.

One point of controversy in the Senate bill was the addition of unrelated legislation to provide some antitrust protections to beer distributors. That measure, however, was subsequently deleted during Senate debate on the continuing resolution. ▮

Congress Votes $114.78 Billion for Labor-HHS

As part of an omnibus fiscal 1987 funding bill, Congress voted $114.784 billion for the Departments of Labor, Health and Human Services (HHS), Education and related agencies.

More than two-thirds of the funding — about $79.1 billion — was for entitlement programs, including the nation's major welfare aid, unemployment compensation and Medicare. Under the programs, benefits must be paid to anyone who meets eligibility criteria.

But the $35.67 billion provided for discretionary programs still represented an increase of more than $3 billion over available funding for fiscal 1986, and more than $6 billion over what President Reagan requested in his fiscal 1987 budget. *(Funding chart, p. 198)*

The funding was included in the fiscal 1987 continuing appropriations resolution (H J Res 738 — PL 99-591). *(Story, p. 219)*

The House had passed a separate $103.7 billion Labor-HHS appropriations bill (HR 5233) on July 31. The Senate passed its version of HR 5233, providing $113.69 billion, Sept. 10.

The two bills were not as far apart as they seemed, because the House bill did not include funding for a number of major programs, including Head Start and Low Income Home Energy Assistance, that had not yet been reauthorized. Some $9.82 billion was later added for those programs.

The final amount reflected a conference agreement on HR 5233 reached Oct. 1 (H Rept 99-960), plus funding added to H J Res 738 for three purposes: $468 million for drug-abuse education, prevention and treatment programs; $361 million for refugee assistance and $7.1 million for Follow Through.

Health, Education Increases

The bill's biggest increases were for health and other needs-based programs. For example, the measure provided $396.4 million for research and treatment of acquired immune deficiency syndrome (AIDS), up from $224.3 million in fiscal 1986. AIDS funds were distributed across various institutes and agencies of HHS.

The National Institutes of Health (NIH) also received a large boost — from $5.27 billion in fiscal 1986 to $6.18 billion. The president asked for $5.08 billion for NIH. The added money was to be used to fund at least 6,200 new research projects, according to the conference report.

The Centers for Disease Control (CDC) also received a large funding increase, to $539.1 million, from $441.1 million in fiscal 1986. Reagan had proposed $425.26 million for the CDC. Within CDC, the childhood-disease vaccine program received an increase of more than $30 million, from $56.9 million to $87.35 million.

Education programs aimed at the poor and handicapped also received large increases.

The Chapter One program, which provided grants to schools to help pay for remedial education for disadvantaged students, received an increase from $3.53 billion for fiscal 1986 to $3.94 billion for fiscal 1987. The president wanted to increase the program to $3.69 billion.

Similarly, programs to aid education for the handicapped were increased significantly, from $1.35 billion in fiscal 1986 to $1.74 billion for fiscal 1987. Reagan had wanted to cut the programs to $1.3 billion.

By and large, needs-based programs received increases while other programs were frozen at fiscal 1986 levels. But there were exceptions.

One was the Work Incentive Program (WIN), which helped provide job training for welfare recipients. The Reagan administration had sought to terminate the program since 1981, but Congress had refused.

For fiscal 1987, the House bill included $200 million for the program, down from $210 million in fiscal 1986. The Senate Appropriations Committee, at an Aug. 15 markup, decided to delete the WIN funding to help the bill reach a budget outlay target mandated under the Gramm-Rudman-Hollings anti-deficit law (PL 99-177).

Conferees finally agreed to continue the program in fiscal 1987 at $110 million.

House Committee Action

The House Appropriations Committee July 24 approved a fiscal 1987 Labor-HHS spending bill providing more than $103.7 billion.

The bill (HR 5233 — H Rept 99-711), approved by voice vote, increased funding more than $6.6 billion over fiscal 1986 appropriations, and more than $5.9 billion over President Reagan's request.

About $78.8 billion — more than three-quarters of the total — was for entitlement programs.

The bill provided $24.9 billion for discretionary programs, more than $4.1 billion over Reagan's request and $2.2 billion over the amount available in fiscal 1986.

The committee deferred action on a number of major programs that had not yet been reauthorized. The administration requested $8.4 billion for the programs, which included most college student loan programs, Head Start, Low Income Home Energy Assistance and the Community Services Block Grant.

More for NIH, AIDS Research

The National Institutes of Health (NIH) would receive a major increase in funding under the bill. Spurning an administration proposal to cut funding, the committee gave NIH $6.1 billion, up more than $890 million over 1986 funding and more than $1 billion over the administration request.

For the second straight year, the panel dramatically increased funding for research on AIDS. The bill would provide $336.8 million for research, prevention and treatment activities, an increase of $112.5 million over 1986 funding. AIDS research funding had more than tripled since fiscal 1985.

Education, Labor Funding

The bill provided $13.3 billion for the Education Department, up more than $990 million from 1986 funding and more than $1.4 billion from the administration request. Much of that increase would go to remedial education services for the disadvantaged under the Chapter One program. The program would receive $4 billion, $469 million more than 1986 funding and $311 million more than Reagan asked.

The bill also provided $1.5 billion for handicapped education programs, up $144 million from 1986 and $191 million over Reagan's request.

The bill would cut Labor Department funding from $6.3 billion in 1986 to $5.5 billion in 1987, but some programs within the department would get increases. The bill provided $3.5 billion for training and employment services, most of which were authorized by the Job Training Partnership Act. That was an increase of $633 million over Reagan's request, and $206 million over 1986 funding.

The bill also provided $815 million for various independent agencies, including the Corporation for Public Broadcasting and the National Labor Relations Board. That was $9.9 million more than the fiscal 1986 funding, and $215 million more than the administration requested.

Liability Amendment Rejected

By 14-27, the committee rejected an amendment by John Edward Porter, R-Ill., designed to "send a message to the states" on liability insurance. The amendment would have required the HHS secretary to withhold 1 percent of the funds states received under the Social Services Block Grant program from any state that did not enact legislation to exempt unpaid volunteers from personal liability.

Because many charitable organizations could not obtain affordable liability insurance, Porter said, volunteers were resigning or not coming forward for fear of losing their personal assets should the organization lose a lawsuit. "Volunteers ought to be liable only for willful and wanton misconduct," Porter said.

But other members warned that the amendment, if adopted, would be subject to a point of order on the House floor because it would impermissibly legislate on an appropriations measure.

House Floor Action

After fending off Republican-led efforts to make across-the-board cuts, the House July 31 approved HR 5233 by a 328-86 vote. As passed, the bill appropriated $103.7 billion. *(Vote 250, p. 72-H)*

Before passing the bill, the House by voice vote adopted amendments hailed by sponsors as the first shots in a bipartisan war on drug abuse. One amendment would deny federal funds to any school that did not operate a drug-abuse prevention program.

Appropriations Committee members, led by Labor-HHS-Education Subcommittee Chairman William H. Natcher, D-Ky., and ranking subcommittee Republican Silvio O. Conte, Mass., hotly denied that the bill was a "budget buster."

"I firmly believe that this is a balanced bill, balanced between fiscal responsibility and concern for the needs of the American people," said Conte.

Natcher pointed out that the funding levels were well below the limits for budget authority under the fiscal 1987 budget resolution, even allowing for some expensive programs — including Head Start and the Low Income Home Energy Assistance Program — for which no funds were provided because they had not yet been reauthorized.

Funding levels for discretionary programs were $11 billion less than the limit under the budget resolution; the administration had requested a total of $8.4 billion in new budget authority for the unauthorized programs.

Minority Leader Robert H. Michel, R-Ill., and Bill Frenzel, R-Minn., offered amendments to cut bill totals.

"This is a seriously overfunded bill," said Frenzel, who had been offering similar amendments to other fiscal 1987 appropriations measures.

By a 4-8 show of hands, those present in the chamber first rejected a Michel amendment to cap increases for the National Institutes of Health at 3 percent over funding available for fiscal 1986. The bill increased NIH funding by approximately 15 percent.

Later, the House turned back, 164-253, a Michel amendment to cap all increases in the bill at 3 percent, and a Frenzel substitute to eliminate all funding increases in the bill, which would have cut $2.76 billion from the total for discretionary programs. The Frenzel substitute was rejected 99-321. *(Votes 249, 248, p. 72-H)*

Senate Committee Action

The Senate Appropriations Committee Aug. 15 approved its $113.6 billion version of HR 5233 (S Rept 99-408) by voice vote, but not without complaints from some members about constraints imposed by the Gramm-Rudman-Hollings law.

The House version of the bill, passed July 31, totaled $103.71 billion. But it did not include funds for a number of major programs, including Head Start and Low Income Home Energy Assistance, which had not yet been reauthorized. The Senate committee appropriated $9.9 billion for those programs, $1.5 billion more than the Reagan administration requested in its fiscal 1987 budget.

The committee was forced to pare $253 million in budget outlays from the version approved Aug. 5 by its Labor, HHS and Education Subcommittee in order to meet its $118 billion outlay target under the budget resolution.

To reach the outlay target, the committee had to cut $292 million in budget authority. It terminated the Department of Labor's WIN job training program for welfare recipients. It also cut $72 million from the Department of Education, including $65 million from impact aid, which went to school districts that educated large numbers of children of federal employees.

"Our hands have been tied by an arbitrary budget law," railed Labor-HHS Subcommittee Chairman Lowell P. Weicker Jr., R-Conn. "I want to place the blame exactly where it belongs — on Gramm-Rudman-Hollings. I want the American people to know that these cuts are forced upon us."

By voice vote, the committee adopted an amendment offered by Dennis DeConcini, D-Ariz., to prohibit the use of funds appropriated in the bill for abortions unless the life of the mother would be endangered if the fetus were carried to term. Such language was already in the House bill, and had been part of the annual measure since 1977.

Weicker, however, succeeded in amending DeConcini's amendment to allow exclusions for cases of rape and incest. The vote on Weicker's amendment was 14-12.

Senate Floor Action

After a backroom deal helped avoid a messy floor fight over abortion, the Senate Sept. 10 passed its $113.7 billion bill by an 83-12 vote. *(Vote 260, p. 44-S)*

Abortion Fight Averted

Early fears that the bill could be held up over language relating to abortion turned out to be unfounded.

A number of senators, led by Jesse Helms, R-N.C., were angry about the committee-approved language that would have allowed federal funds to be used to pay for abortions in cases of rape or incest.

In what Weicker's staff described as a major victory, Appropriations Committee Chairman Mark O. Hatfield, R-Ore., negotiated a deal between Weicker and Helms in which Weicker agreed to drop the rape/incest language. In exchange, Helms agreed not to seek to delete or otherwise restrict $145 million provided in the bill for federal family planning programs.

As part of the agreement, Helms also permitted Weicker to strike from the bill longstanding language concerning busing and school prayer. The busing language would have prohibited federal funds from being used to force busing of students or teachers "to overcome racial imbalance in any school or school system" or "to carry out a plan of racial desegregation." The prayer language would have prohibited schools or school systems from being denied federal funds because they have instituted voluntary prayer programs.

Senate Amendments

The Senate adopted a number of amendments to the bill on the floor, including one offered by Weicker to provide an additional $50 million to allow AIDS patients to receive a promising new drug. Because the bill's outlay total was already at the limit set by the budget resolution, Weicker made the money available by transferring funds from the Low Income Home Energy Assistance Program.

"I wish we did not cut any specific program to help those with AIDS," Weicker said. "However, under the budget [resolution] we have no choice."

The addition brought the bill total for AIDS research, prevention and treatment to $405 million. The House bill contained $336.8 million.

Over Weicker's objections, the Senate adopted an amendment offered by Pete V. Domenici, R-N.M., and Lawton Chiles, D-Fla., to provide an additonal $57 million to the Department of Education for math and science education. The $57 million would be raised by cutting $11 million in budget authority from the National Institutes of Health. Because of different spending rates, the change would keep outlays at the established limit for fiscal 1987, but over the course of several years, the amendment would produce a net increase in spending.

Weicker's motion to table the amendment failed on a 30-66 vote. *(Vote 259, p. 44-S)*

The Senate adopted several amendments by voice vote, including:

- By Bill Bradley, D-N.J., to provide $1 million to the Education Department for programs related to the bicentennial of the Constitution.
- By Christopher J. Dodd, D-Conn., to provide $1 million for the Child Development Associate Scholarship Program, which helped train workers for child-care facilities.
- By Robert C. Byrd, D-W.Va., to provide an additional $1.5 million to hire eight administrative law judges and support personnel to reduce the backlog of claims from those suffering from black lung disease.

Final Provisions, Fiscal 1987 Labor-HHS Funding Bill

Following are the amounts of fiscal 1987 budget authority for the Departments of Labor, Health and Human Services, Education and related agencies requested by President Reagan, approved by the House and Senate, and appropriated in the omnibus continuing appropriations resolution (H J Res 738 — PL 99-591) *(in thousands of dollars)*:

	Budget Request [1]	House-Passed Bill [2]	Senate-Passed Bill	Final Amount [4,5,6]
Labor				
Employment and training administration				
Program administration	$ 62,959	$ 67,363	$ 66,017	$ 67,363
Training and employment services	2,909,608	3,543,121	3,778,214	3,685,913

Labor (Continued)	Budget Request [1]	House-Passed Bill [2]	Senate-Passed Bill	Final Amount [4,5,6]
Community Service Employment for Older Americans	326,000	326,000	326,000	326,000
Federal and State Unemployment Benefits	141,400	145,300	141,400	141,400
Labor Management Services	62,275	62,275	62,275	62,275
Employment Standards Administration	688,603	692,603	693,103	693,103
Occupational Safety and Health Administration	225,811	225,811	225,811	225,811
Mine Safety and Health Administration	156,480	156,480	158,680	156,480
Bureau of Labor Statistics	160,726	166,589	168,330	167,925
Departmental Management	138,752	138,752	138,368	141,732 [4]
Total, Labor Department	**$4,872,614**	**$5,524,294**	**$5,758,198**	**$5,668,002**
Department of Health and Human Services (HHS)				
Health Resources and Services	1,162,670	1,250,368	1,499,753	1,470,763
Medical Facilities Guarantee and Loan Fund	20,000	20,000	20,000	20,000
Centers for Disease Control	425,255	518,254	541,862	539,067
National Institutes of Health				
Cancer	1,158,089	1,346,751	1,397,250	1,402,837
Heart, Lung, and Blood	785,697	921,410	921,502	930,001
Dental Research	96,482	116,275	116,553	117,945
Diabetes, Digestive, and Kidney Diseases	418,971	515,455	502;628	511,124
Neurological and Communicative Disorders and Stroke	399,351	491,085	487,218	490,233
Allergy and Infectious Diseases	330,551	403,853	541,343	545,523
General Medical Sciences	471,533	576,562	565,271	570,916
Child Health and Human Development	309,119	368,509	362,866	366,780
Eye	179,201	219,091	214,080	216,637
Environmental Health Sciences	187,995	209,872	208,067	209,294
Aging	145,829	174,279	179,582	176,931
Arthritis and Musculoskeletal and Skin Diseases	106,733	140,225	129,475	138,713
Research Resources	234,192	317,826	319,924	322,860
National Center for Nursing Research	(0)	16,700	20,000	19,000
John E. Fogarty Center	11,305	11,443	11,420	11,420
National Library of Medicine	56,408	61,588	62,088	61,838
Office of the Director	179,691	246,651 [3]	56,708	56,708
Undistributed Reduction	—	—	(−11,000)	—
Buildings and Facilities	8,000	31,900	31,900	31,900
Alcohol, Drug Abuse, and Mental Health Administration	905,973	893,434	1,099,113	1,324,365 [4]
St. Elizabeths Hospital	36,353	36,353	36,353	36,353
Office of the Assistant Secretary for Health	202,692	185,553	203,738	203,408
Health Care Financing Administration	38,649,655	40,290,892	40,681,396	40,681,396
(Fiscal 1988 advance)	(7,100,000)	(7,100,000)	(7,100,000)	(7,100,000)
Social Security Administration				
Payments to Social Security Trust Funds	500,555	500,555	500,555	500,555
Black Lung Payments	693,437	693,437	693,437	693,437
(Fiscal 1988 advance)	(252,450)	(252,450)	(252,450)	(252,450)
Supplemental Security Income	8,230,068	8,230,068	8,230,068	8,230,068
(Fiscal 1988 advance)	(2,765,000)	(2,765,000)	(2,765,000)	(2,765,000)
Assistance payments	6,009,478	7,023,420	7,025,376	7,024,398
(Fiscal 1988 advance)	(2,293,615)	(2,293,615)	(2,293,615)	(2,293,615)

Appropriations

HHS (Continued)	Budget Request [1]	House-Passed Bill [2]	Senate-Passed Bill	Final Amount [4,5,6]
Low-Income Energy Assistance	2,100,000	(defer)	1,825,000	1,825,000
Refugee and Entrant Assistance	(defer)	(defer)	(defer)	361,600 [5]
Child Support Enforcement	599,633	599,633	599,633	599,633
(Fiscal 1988 advance)	(187,000)	(187,000)	(187,000)	(187,000)
Assistant Secretary for Human Development	5,496,215	4,830,240	5,680,735	5,847,202
Community Services	3,612	(defer)	378,900	369,851
Community Food and Nutrition	(0)	(0)	2,500	2,500
Departmental Management	158,320	161,820	180,020	175,320
Total, HHS	**$70,273,063**	**$71,403,502**	**$75,315,314**	**$76,085,576**
(Fiscal 1988 advance)	(12,598,065)	(12,598,065)	(12,598,065)	(12,598,065)
Education Department				
Compensatory Education	3,688,163	3,999,163	3,896,663	3,951,663
Impact Aid	548,000	700,000	650,000	717,500
Special Programs	678,909	710,943	736,537	934,891[4,6]
Bilingual Education	142,951	179,637	138,955	173,095
Handicapped Education	1,303,100	1,494,420	1,741,900	1,741,900
Rehabilitation Services	1,225,400	1,152,656	1,484,758	1,484,758
Vocational and Adult Education	504,974	1,016,433	943,163	980,800
Student Financial Assistance	3,812,568	(defer)	5,196,000	5,196,000
Guaranteed Student Loans	3,460,250	3,394,000	3,004,000	3,004,000
Higher Education	261,578	29,500	454,428	479,128
Higher Education Facilities Loans	19,205	(defer)	19,205	19,205
Education Research and Statistics	70,231	8,747	63,578	63,578
Libraries	(0)	130,000	132,500	132,500
Special Institutions	254,797	268,477	261,670	269,730
Departmental management	295,755	296,255	295,070	294,070
Total, Education Department	**$16,265,881**	**$13,380,231**	**$19,018,427**	**$19,442,818**
Related Agencies				
ACTION	149,865	(defer)	153,287	156,287 [4]
Commission on Education of the Deaf	(0)	(0)	1,000	750
Corporation for Public Broadcasting (Fiscal 1989 advance)	(130,000)	(214,000)	(238,000)	(228,000)
Federal Mediation and Conciliation Service	23,220	22,656	24,390	23,523
Federal Mine Safety and Health Review Commission	3,919	3,651	3,919	3,785
National Commission on Libraries and Information Science	690	660	690	660
National Council on the Handicapped	850	732	850	850
National Labor Relations Board	130,865	129,055	130,865	129,960
National Mediation Board	6,540	6,401	6,540	6,401
Occupational Safety and Health Review Commission	5,750	5,647	5,750	5,750
Railroad Retirement Board	258,980	383,100	383,100	383,100
Soldiers' and Airmen's Home	38,507	49,022	50,263	50,263
U.S. Institute of Peace	1,250	(defer)	1,250	625
Total, Related Agencies	**$ 620,436**	**$ 600,924**	**$ 761,904**	**$ 761,954**
(Fiscal 1989 advance)	(130,000)	(214,000)	(238,000)	(228,000)
TOTAL, Fiscal 1987	**$ 92,031,994**	**$ 90,908,951**	**$ 100,853,843**	**$ 101,958,350**
(Fiscal 1988 advance)	(12,598,065)	(12,598,065)	(12,598,065)	(12,598,065)
(Fiscal 1989 advance)	(130,000)	(214,000)	(238,000)	(228,000)
GRAND TOTAL	**$104,760,059 [1]**	**$103,721,016 [2]**	**$113,689,908**	**$114,784,415 [4,5,6]**

[1] *Does not include anti-drug funding requests.*
[2] *The House bill deferred funding unauthorized programs.*
[3] *Includes funding for AIDS later redistributed elsewhere within NIH.*
[4] *Includes funding added for anti-drug initiative under HR 5484 (PL 99-570).*
[5] *Includes funding added for refugee assistance.*
[6] *Includes funding added for Follow Through.*

Agriculture Appropriations Total $45.2 Billion

Congress appropriated $45.2 billion for agriculture programs in fiscal 1987, an amount expected to fall far short of what farm and nutrition programs would require.

The omnibus continuing appropriations measure (H J Res 738 — PL 99-591) cleared by Congress Oct. 17 reduced total spending authority for the Agriculture Department and related agencies by $7.4 billion from fiscal 1986, although hardly any individual programs were targeted for cutbacks. *(Funding chart, p. 202; continuing resolution, p. 219)*

The House July 24 had passed a $45.3 billion spending bill (HR 5177) for agriculture and later included a slightly more expensive ($45.4 billion) but practically identical measure in its version of the continuing resolution. The Senate did not pass a separate appropriations bill for agriculture, but absorbed into its continuing resolution amendments to HR 5177 approved by its Appropriations Committee Sept. 11.

Both House and Senate bills generally rejected Reagan administration proposals to cut or drop several popular farm and nutrition programs.

Thus the final bill maintained or increased funding for the Extension Service, Rural Electrification Administration loans and soil and water conservation programs, among others.

The measure also increased funding for domestic food programs, effectively adding $1.1 billion to nutrition services and food stamps.

Accounting Reductions

The major reductions showed up in spending for child nutrition programs and for the Commodity Credit Corporation (CCC), the Agriculture Department agency that distributes price- and income-support benefits to farmers.

Yet those reductions were the result of accounting techniques used in the bill; existing law assured there would be no reductions in the operations or benefits of those programs.

For example, the bill provided $16.8 billion for the CCC, $8.1 billion less than the $24.9 billion appropriated in fiscal 1986.

Administration officials had estimated the CCC would need $16.8 billion in fiscal 1987 when it requested a permanent, indefinite appropriation — in effect, open-ended spending authority that would not require annual congressional approval through the regular appropriations process.

The Senate approved a slightly different concept called an annual, indefinite appropriation — open-ended spending authority that must be renewed by Congress each fiscal year.

But the House-Senate conference instead accepted the House-passed version, providing a definite appropriation based on the original administration spending estimates.

However, on top of the $16.8 billion appropriated, the conference agreement made an additional $3 billion available "subject to a request" by the administration. The $3 billion was based on revised administration estimates of CCC expenditures.

Farm Entitlements

The CCC worked like an "entitlement" program, in which the government must pay guaranteed benefits to qualified farmers, and the agency in recent years had required more money at the year's end than administration officials predicted.

The discrepancy occurred primarily because farmers' benefits mainly were based on the difference between commodity prices and "target" prices set by Congress. That gap had been widening, and more farmers had signed up for federal benefits.

In fiscal 1986, the administration estimated the CCC would need only $9.4 billion. Congress appropriated that amount in the fiscal 1986 continuing resolution (PL 99-190) but at the same time made an additional $4 billion available, subject to a request by the administration.

Later, another $12.3 billion was provided in supplemental appropriations bills (PL 99-243, PL 99-263, PL 99-349).

So when the administration officially submitted a request for the additional $3 billion later in the fiscal year, spending authority for agriculture would rise automatically from $45.2 billion to $48.2 billion. If further supplemental appropriations were required, the total would increase beyond that.

Food Programs

A similar accounting technique was used for child nutrition programs. The bill provided $162 million in new spending authority for child nutrition and earmarked another $3.3 billion in transfers from customs receipts.

The Senate had approved $937.6 million in new budget authority for child nutrition. However, the conference adopted the House provision for $162.4 million, making the $775.3 million difference subject to an administration request.

The administration had to submit that request to meet the obligations of the program under existing law. President Reagan's proposals for cuts in child nutrition programs would have effectively reduced the cost of the program to the amount appropriated in the bill, but Congress had consistently rejected those changes.

When the administration submitted its budget request for child nutrition, the amount authorized for the agriculture section of the spending bill then would total about $49 billion.

Other Costs Delayed

The spending bill masked or delayed other costs associated with agriculture programs.

It failed to account for another $1.2 billion in expenditures that would be required to cover the full amount of losses previously incurred by the government's various farm and rural development loan programs.

The Agriculture Department made direct loans and guaranteed private loans through various revolving loan funds, which borrowed money from the Treasury and repaid it from the loan proceeds. The revolving funds incurred shortfalls when the department subsidized interest rates or when borrowers failed to repay loans.

To cover those loan and interest losses, Congress reimbursed the revolving funds through annual appropriations. The reimbursements were made in two-year cycles — the 1987 spending bill made reimbursements for losses incurred in fiscal 1985; the fiscal 1986 spending bill reim-

Fiscal 1987 Appropriations Approved . . .

Following is the budget authority requested by President Reagan, the amounts approved by the House and by the Senate Appropriations Committee and provided under H J Res 738 (PL 99-591) *(in thousands of dollars):*

	Budget Request	House-Passed	Senate-Passed	Final Amount
Agriculture Programs				
Office of the Secretary	$1,790	$1,648	$1,598	$1,623
Assistant Secretary for Administration	495	455	455	455
Rental Payments	57,380	48,728	48,728	48,728
Building Operations and Maintenance	18,800	18,039	18,039	18,039
Advisory Committees	1,323	1,358	1,308	1,308
Departmental Administration	21,920	21,180	21,227	21,227
Working Capital Fund	6,000	5,708	5,708	5,708
Assistant Secretary for Governmental, Public Affairs	345	318	318	318
Office of Governmental and Public Affairs	8,570	8,198	8,280	8,198
Inspector General	46,321	44,461	44,461	44,461
General Counsel	17,430	16,832	17,430	17,131
Assistant Secretary for Economics	485	448	448	448
Economic Research Service	45,475	43,982	43,982	43,982
National Agricultural Statistics Service	59,712	56,787	56,787	56,787
World Agricultural Outlook Board	1,680	1,608	1,608	1,608
Assistant Secretary for Science, Education	380	350	350	350
Agricultural Research Service	513,053	534,248	511,075	537,064
Cooperative State Research Service	246,356	269,092	295,877	300,573
Extension Service	140,000	289,317	328,341	293,545
National Agricultural Library	11,421	10,936	10,936	10,936
Assistant Secretary for Marketing, Inspection	355	327	327	327
Animal Plant and Health Inspection Service	255,503	298,475	304,653	303,213
Food Safety and Inspection Service	365,841	361,400	361,400	361,400
Federal Grain Inspection Service	6,979	6,697	6,697	6,697
Agricultural Cooperative Service	3,698	4,469	4,469	4,469
Agricultural Marketing Service	32,286	34,227	33,120	34,227
Packers and Stockyards Administration	9,093	8,945	8,945	8,945
Under Secretary for International Affairs and Commodity Programs	513	473	473	473
Agricultural Stabilization and Conservation Service (Transfer from Commodity Credit Corporation)	(463,696)	(449,403)	(521,138)	(491,856)
Dairy Indemnity	—	95	95	95
Federal Crop Insurance Corporation	375,628	345,311	409,568	345,311
Commodity Credit Corporation Reimbursement *	—	16,808,806	—	16,808,806
(Amount available subject to budget request)	—	—	—	(3,000,000)
Subtotal	$2,248,832	$19,242,918	$2,546,703	$19,286,452
Rural Development Assistance				
Under Secretary for Small Community and Rural Development	422	394	394	394
Farmers Home Administration	6,425,895	5,371,419	6,601,083	5,225,550
Rural Electrification Administration	27,946	31,038	31,038	31,038
Assistant Secretary for Natural Resources	395	363	363	363

bursed losses of fiscal 1984, and so on.

In the fiscal 1986 spending bill, however, Congress failed to reimburse three of the revolving funds in the Farmers Home Administration for the full amount of losses incurred in 1984. As a result, about $750,000 of the department's $4.2 billion in loan losses were unpaid and were carried over to the fiscal 1987 bill.

But in fiscal 1987, Congress again failed to cover the remaining losses from fiscal 1984 and also appropriated less than requested to cover new losses from fiscal 1985.

The spending bill took the lower House figures for reimbursing the three revolving funds: the Agricultural Credit Insurance Fund, which made production, real estate, conservation and emergency disaster loans; the Rural Housing Insurance Fund, which made loans for rural housing, rental housing and farm laborers' living-quarters; and the Rural Development Insurance Fund, which made loans for water, sewer and community facilities, and rural industrialization.

The new reimbursements covered only $4.7 billion of the $5.2 billion in loan losses for the three funds in fiscal 1985. A $462,000 shortfall for fiscal 1985 left a total of $1.2 billion in unpaid loan losses for the two years combined.

According to budget officials in the Agriculture Department, the shortfall could be made up only in two ways.

One way would be to reduce the amount of new loans issued or guaranteed, thus freeing the funds' remaining capital to cover the previous years' unfunded losses.

But in passing the 1987 spending bill, Congress also required the department to continue making most of its direct and guaranteed loans at 1986 levels.

That meant most of the $1.2 billion shortfall in the revolving funds would have to be made up in the second way: through future appropriations.

. . . For Farm, Food and Nutrition Programs

	Budget Request	House-Passed	Senate-Passed	Final Amount
Soil Conservation Service	457,126	604,545	592,897	608,721
Agricultural Stabilization and Conservation Service	—	201,434	201,001	211,001
Subtotal	$6,911,784	$6,209,193	$7,426,776	$6,077,067
Domestic Food Programs				
Assistant Secretary for Food, Consumer Services	358	330	330	330
Child Nutrition	230,413	162,399	937,680	162,399
(Amount available subject to budget request)	—	(775,281)	—	(775,281)
Special Milk Program	—	14,869	14,869	14,869
Women, Infants and Children (WIC) Program	1,617,000	1,671,500	1,655,494	1,663,497
Commodity Supplemental Food Program	38,605	41,497	41,497	41,497
Food Stamps	12,343,579	12,684,665	12,684,665	12,684,665
Food Donations Programs	187,300	193,589	193,589	193,589
Temporary Emergency Food Assistance Program	—	50,000	50,000	50,000
Food Program Administration	86,100	82,578	83,563	82,578
Nutrition Information	6,876	8,976	6,876	6,876
Subtotal	$14,510,231	$14,910,403	$15,688,563	$14,900,300
International Programs				
Foreign Agricultural Service	71,882	81,109	81,109	81,109
Food for Peace (PL 480)	1,164,400	1,182,718	983,424	1,083,071
Office of International Cooperation	—	6,013	7,631	7,535
Subtotal	$1,239,333	$1,269,840	$1,072,164	$1,171,715
Agencies				
Food and Drug Administration	429,225	437,046	438,309	438,309
Commodity Futures Trading Commission	30,418	29,161	30,418	29,761
Subtotal	$459,643	$466,207	$468,727	$468,070
Total Budget Authority	**$25,369,823**	**$42,098,561**	**$27,182,933**	**$41,903,604**
Section 32 Transfers (Customs Receipts)	$3,234,196	$3,302,710	$3,303,084	$3,303,084
Total Obligational Authority	**$28,604,019**	**$45,401,271**	**$30,486,017**	**$45,206,688**
Direct and Insured Loans	$2,774,000	$5,711,674	$5,720,654	$5,320,654
Guaranteed Loans	$2,725,000	$3,523,775	$3,528,775	$3,523,775
Commodity Credit Corporation Transfers	$463,696	$449,403	$521,138	$491,856

** The administration sought a permanent indefinite appropriation, which the Senate Appropriations Committee incorporated into its bill as an annual, indefinite appropriation. The House rejected the proposal.*

SOURCE: House and Senate Appropriations committees

House Committee Action

The House Appropriations Committee July 15 approved a fiscal 1987 spending bill for agriculture that achieved the overall cuts proposed by the Reagan administration but rejected its proposals to eliminate a number of popular farm programs.

By voice vote, the committee approved HR 5177 (H Rept 99-686), providing $41.95 billion in new spending authority for the Agriculture Department and related agencies, about $2 billion less than fiscal 1986 funding. *(1985 Almanac p. 395)*

The panel's ceiling on budget authority was $74.7 million less than requested by the administration. But the bill's total was $6.2 million less than the request primarily because of increased U.S. Customs revenues, which were used for child nutrition programs.

Including customs receipts, HR 5177 would provide $45.25 billion, the same as the president's budget request. That was $4.3 billion less than the $49.55 billion ceiling for agriculture set by the 1987 budget resolution (S Con Res 120).

The president proposed savings by phasing out programs for rural housing and community development, the Rural Electrification Administration (REA), soil conservation and the Extension Service.

The panel, however, restored funding for those programs to current levels, cutting back instead on the Agriculture Department's authority to reimburse the Treasury for losses in the revolving loan funds of the Farmers Home Administration (FmHA).

The committee approved only $4 billion in spending authority to cover losses from the FmHA's rural housing and farm ownership and operating loan programs. That was $1.15 billion less than the $5.15 billion the administration estimated would be required to cover FmHA loan losses.

The committee also approved $9.23 billion in new borrowing authority for farm loan programs, $1.53 billion less than in fiscal 1986, but $3.74 billion more than requested.

It approved $2 billion in new borrowing authority for direct loans for rural housing and community development projects, for which the president requested nothing. The panel also approved $933.1 million in borrowing authority for the REA's electric and telephone loan programs for rural cooperatives, $708.1 million more than requested.

In direct spending authority, the panel approved a total of $327.9 million for the Extension Service, including $38.6 million in transfers from the food stamp program. The president had requested only $140 million under a proposal to turn most of the county-by-county consultation services for farmers over to state governments.

For the department's various soil conservation programs, the committee approved $806.3 million in spending authority, which was $348.8 million more than requested. The administration proposed to eliminate the Agricultural Stabilization and Conservation Service because the 1985 farm bill (PL 99-198) included a new "conservation reserve" program to pay farmers to retire fragile land.

The cost of the conservation reserve in fiscal 1986 and 1987 was covered by the CCC. The CCC must repay the Treasury each year for losses incurred in the previous year.

For fiscal 1987, the administration proposed to grant the CCC permanent authority to reimburse its net losses directly from the Treasury Department, as needed, rather than through the appropriations process. The president's budget projected the CCC would need $16.8 billion in fiscal 1987, but under this proposal, the CCC could exceed that amount without returning to Congress for supplemental spending authority.

The Appropriations Committee denied the request and instead limited the CCC's spending authority in fiscal 1987 to the budget estimate of $16.8 billion.

House Floor Action

After rejecting an across-the-board cut in farm and food nutrition programs, the House July 24 ratified the Appropriations Committee's recommendations for $45.25 billion in fiscal 1987 spending authority under HR 5177.

The bill, passed on a 329-49 vote, came in about $4 billion below the $49.55 billion ceiling for new budget authority set by the budget resolution. *(Vote 230, p. 68-H)*

However, the Congressional Budget Office (CBO) estimated that budget outlays in fiscal 1987 — the actual rate of spending during the fiscal year for programs authorized in this and previous agriculture appropriations bills — would exceed the budget resolution's spending targets. Fiscal 1987 outlays were expected to total $19.3 billion, $173 million more than the target for outlays in the budget resolution, according to the CBO.

The House was bound by the budget authority ceilings but not by the outlay targets. Senate rules, on the other hand, required spending bills to conform to both budget authority and outlay restrictions, and a spillover in either category was subject to a point of order on the Senate floor.

Bruce A. Morrison, D-Conn., and a group of urban Democrats tried to force an across-the-board cut in budget authority to bring fiscal 1987 outlays in line with the budget resolution.

Morrison's amendment would have reduced all discretionary spending by 0.896 percent, saving a total of $374 million in budget authority. Morrison said that would achieve a $173 million savings in fiscal 1987 outlays, enough to meet the budget resolution target.

But Jamie L. Whitten, D-Miss., chairman of the Appropriations Committee, said he would rather leave the discrepancy in outlays so he would have some bargaining leverage in a House-Senate conference on the bill. Morrison's amendment was rejected, 175-205. *(Vote 229, p. 66-H)*

Senate Committee Action

As approved by the Senate Appropriations Committee Sept. 11, HR 5177 (S Rept 99-438) provided $27.18 billion in new spending authority for the Agriculture Department and related agencies.

Including customs receipts, the bill would provide $30.49 billion in total spending authority, $1.88 billion more than requested by the administration.

The committee accepted nearly all the recommendations approved two days earlier by its Agriculture Subcommittee. The bill would maintain funding for the Extension Service, Rural Electrification Administration loans, soil and water conservation and other farm programs that were scheduled for sharp reductions in the president's fiscal 1987 budget.

The measure also would increase spending for nutrition programs, appropriating $775 million more than the president's request for child nutrition and $341 million more for food stamps.

A proposed reduction in the bill from fiscal 1986 spending levels was a 15 percent cut in the foreign assistance food donation program called Food for Peace (PL 480), which would be scaled back $260 million in fiscal 1987, from $1.24 billion to $983 million.

The Senate bill would provide $14.76 billion less than the House version. However, when the Senate's proposed method of funding farm price-support programs was taken into account, the Senate bill actually provided $2.05 billion more than the version passed by the House.

Under the Senate's annual, open-ended funding method, the CCC would not have to return to Congress for year-end supplemental appropriations if expenditures exceeded beginning-year estimates.

The administration had estimated that the CCC would need $16.81 billion in fiscal 1987, $8.1 billion less than the $24.91 billion appropriated for the CCC in the fiscal year ending Sept. 30, 1986.

Adding the administration's estimate for the CCC to the $30.49 billion provided by the Senate committee's bill would bring the spending total to $47.3 billion.

In comparison, the $45.25 billion total in the House bill included $16.81 billion in direct appropriations for the CCC. House Appropriations Chairman Whitten steadfastly had rejected previous Senate and administration proposals for indefinite appropriations for the agency.

The Senate bill also differed from the House version mainly in the way it reimbursed the revolving loan funds of the Farmers Home Administration (FmHA).

The Senate panel provided all of the $5.15 billion the administration estimated would be required to reimburse the Treasury for prior-year loan losses in the FmHA's rural housing, and farm ownership and operating loan programs. The House provided $1.15 billion less than the estimate.

Before approving the bill, the committee narrowly rejected, 11-12, an effort by Midwestern senators to limit individual farmers to $500,000 a year in total crop subsidy payments. There currently was a $50,000 cap on income subsidies, but there was no limit on other price-support payments.

The amendment's sponsors, Mark Andrews, R-N.D., and Tom Harkin, D-Iowa, said the system let some farmers get multimillion-dollar payments. ∎

D.C. Appropriations

Congress appropriated $560.4 million in federal funds for the District of Columbia for fiscal 1987 and approved another $3.06 billion in District funds for the city.

The funding, contained in the fiscal 1987 continuing appropriations resolution (H J Res 738 — PL 99-591), mirrored President Reagan's request for federal funds and exceeded it for District moneys. Reagan had asked for $2.99 billion in District funds.

The House July 24 had passed a separate D.C. appropriations bill (HR 5175 — H Rept 99-675) containing $530 million in federal funds, the same as had been provided in fiscal 1986. The Senate version (S Rept 99-367), passed Sept. 16, had granted the full amount sought by Reagan. Final funding levels were set in the conference report (H Rept 99-1005) on the continuing resolution, cleared Oct. 17. *(Story, p. 219)*

Federal Funding

Federal funds provided for the District in the continuing resolution included:

- $444.5 million for the federal payment to compensate the District for revenues lost due to the presence of the U.S. government. (Federal property in the city was exempt from local taxes.)
- $28.81 million for water and sewer services furnished to federal government facilities.
- $52.07 million for the federal contribution to retirement funds for police officers, firefighters, teachers and judges.
- $35 million for St. Elizabeths Hospital.

In addition, the House and Senate conferees provided an advance appropriation for fiscal 1988 of $20 million for construction of a new prison in the District, bringing total appropriations for the project to $50 million. In its fiscal 1986 D.C. appropriations bill, Congress allocated $10 million for 1986 and $20 million in advance 1987 appropriations for the prison. *(1985 Almanac p. 359)*

Reagan's approval of the prison funding ended a dispute that had pitted the administration against Congress and the District over the proper origin of the $20 million. The administration contended that the $20 million that had been advanced for the prison was included within the $444.5 million 1987 federal payment. Congress and the District objected to what effectively was a $20 million cut in the federal payment, the House concluding that the money would have to come from elsewhere, and the Senate tacking on the $20 million for 1988.

The conference agreement stipulated that the District would lose all $50 million promised for the project if it had not signed a design and construction contract by Oct. 15, 1986; the Senate limited the proviso to moneys provided for 1987 and 1988 — a total of $40 million. District Mayor Marion S. Barry Jr. Oct. 15 announced the awarding of a $49.8 million contract.

D.C. Appropriations

Following are the budget authority totals in the fiscal 1987 continuing appropriations resolution (H J Res 738 — PL 99-591) for federal funds for the District of Columbia, and the amount approved for District funds. Also included were advance 1988 funds for a new prison in the District and supplemental fiscal 1986 District funds. *(Figures in thousands of dollars)*:

	Budget Request	Final Amount
Federal Funds		
Federal payment	$ 444,500	$ 444,500
Federal reimbursement for water and sewer services	28,810	28,810
Contributions to retirement funds	52,070	52,070
St. Elizabeths Hospital	35,000	35,000
Total, 1987 federal funds	**$ 560,380**	**$ 560,380**
(Advance 1988 federal funds)	—	**($ 20,000)**
Total, federal funds	**$ 560,380**	**$ 580,380**
District of Columbia Funds		
Total, District funds	**$ 2,989,598**	**$ 3,060,407**
(1986 supplemental funds)	—	**($ 31,567)**

Abortion Language

For the second year in a row, conferees on the continuing resolution were the final arbiters of a House-Senate battle over language restricting abortions in the District. And as in 1985, the conferees agreed to the same restrictions that D.C. appropriations bills had carried since 1980.

The language, identical to that approved by the Senate, prohibited the District from using federal funds in the bill to pay for abortions, except when the mother's life would be endangered if the fetus were carried to term, or in cases of rape or incest. The Senate language, approved by a 48-42 vote Sept. 16, replaced a House provision that would have prohibited any funds in the bill — federal or District — from being used for abortions, except in cases endangering the mother's life. *(Vote 263, 45-S)*

Other Provisions

The conferees included Senate-passed language requiring the placement of signs around the Soviet Embassy in downtown Washington identifying the area as "Sakharov Plaza," and added language designating the embassy's proper address as "1 Andrei Sakharov Plaza," after the dissident Soviet physicist.

The 1987 bill also killed a longstanding prohibition against installing meters in District taxis.

The conference agreement included a section providing appropriations and rescissions totaling $31.6 million in additional fiscal 1986 District funds.

The supplemental, which had been approved by the Senate but had never been considered by the House, involved no new federal funds, and was funded entirely with increases in local revenue collections above previously projected levels. ∎

Pentagon Buying Power Falls for Second Year

The main Pentagon appropriations bill for fiscal 1987 — a part of the omnibus continuing appropriations resolution (H J Res 738 — PL 99-591) — sliced $25 billion from the amount requested by President Reagan.

As cleared by Congress Oct. 17, the measure appropriated $274 billion for Department of Defense personnel and operating costs, equipment purchases and military research. That was $3.5 billion more than the Pentagon had to spend on these programs in fiscal 1986, but too small an increase to cover inflation. So for the second year in a row, the Pentagon's purchasing power would decline after rising steadily since the late 1970s. *(Chart, p. 207)*

Combined with congressional cuts in Reagan's funding requests for defense-related programs in other legislation, the reduction in the main defense money bill brought overall defense funding for the year to just under $290 billion, some $32 billion less than Reagan's initial request.

The main defense appropriations bill mirrored budget cuts that were fashioned in the companion defense authorization measure (S 2638) to meet Congress' self-imposed budget ceilings. The fiscal 1987 budget resolution (S Con Res 120) limited new defense budget authority to $292 billion — the amount appropriated for defense in fiscal 1986. In previous years, the annual duel over the defense budget had been resolved purely in terms of budget authority. But under the Gramm-Rudman-Hollings anti-deficit act (PL 99-177), Congress in fiscal 1987 also had to meet the budget resolution's $279 billion outlay ceiling for defense programs. *(Authorization bill, p. 464; budget resolution, p. 542)*

Although separate Pentagon appropriations bills (HR 5438, S 2827) were reported in each chamber, neither was considered individually on the floor. Instead, the committee bills were folded into the omnibus continuing resolution, and differences between the Senate and House versions were resolved as part of the conference on that measure. The conference report on H J Res 738 was filed Oct. 15 (H Rept 99-1005), one day after the conference report on the defense authorization bill. *(Continuing resolution, p. 219)*

Conference Report

As cleared by Congress, the defense appropriations provisions of H J Res 738 reflected the following conference decisions:

Personnel Issues

The conferees approved a ceiling on active-duty military personnel of 2,173,870, a reduction of just over 7,000 men from the budget request that trimmed the bill by $107 million. Another cutback of $77 million resulted from a provision of the authorization bill reducing the ratio of officers to enlisted men.

The conferees approved $1.9 billion to fund a 3 percent pay hike for all military personnel and civilian Pentagon employees, effective Jan. 1, 1987. But they trimmed $2.9 billion from the bill by deferring paydays from the last day of each month to the first day of the following month, so that what would have been the last paycheck of fiscal 1987 would not be paid until Oct. 1, 1987 — the first day of fiscal 1988.

For recruiting costs, including advertising, the conferees approved $1.7 billion, only $69 million less than requested. By contrast, they cut $239 million from the request for re-enlistment bonuses. More than two-thirds of that cut came from the conferees' demand that no more than half of any bonus be paid at the start of a tour of duty.

To pay the expenses of transferring personnel between posts, the conferees approved $2.46 billion, a reduction of $346 million from the request. Congress had been pressing the Pentagon for years to cut down on the cost of transfers, in part by making transfers less frequently. But Army officials vigorously opposed any change in their policy of assigning new recruits abroad for no more than 18 months. Longer assignments abroad erode young soldiers' morale and discipline, they contended.

Conferees froze the number of civilian Pentagon employees abroad at the number employed at the end of fiscal 1986, a major factor behind their $400 million reduction in the budget for pay to U.S. and foreign civilians.

They approved $15 million — one quarter of the amount requested — for a one-day test mobilization of the "individual ready reserve" (IRR). The IRR consists of persons who have left the service after their first enlistment and are not members of an organized reserve unit, but who could be recalled to active duty to replace combat casualties.

A one-day call-up of selected IRR members was planned to test critics' complaints that they could not be counted on. But the House denied funds for the test, charging that it could not duplicate wartime conditions and therefore would not be realistic.

Operations and Maintenance

The conferees cut the budget request for operations and maintenance by 9 percent ($7.7 billion) to $78 billion.

But the conferees said that almost 60 percent of that cutback merely reflected lower-than-budgeted prices for commodities purchased by the Pentagon. This included reductions of:

- $2.84 billion based on declining fuel prices.
- $621 million based on lower-than-budgeted prices for other items.
- $1.035 billion to reflect lower-than-budgeted costs for major overhauls of ships, planes and ground vehicles.

The conferees trimmed the budget for these industrial activities by an additional $136 million and told the services to make it up by boosting employees' productivity.

The budget request included $256 million to overhaul two 1960s-vintage missile-launching submarines; Reagan subsequently decided to scrap those subs and the money was dropped from the bill.

But the conferees reversed a House decision to drop an additional $250 million in hopes of forcing the administration to scrap two other missile subs also scheduled for overhaul. The Pentagon had announced plans to start modifying a bomber within the next few weeks, an action that would place the U.S. nuclear arsenal over one of the weapons ceilings of the unratified 1979 U.S.-Soviet nuclear arms treaty (SALT II). If the two additional subs were broken up, U.S. forces would remain within the SALT II limits. *(SALT II violation, p. 462)*

The budget request for travel (other than transfers

Fiscal 1987 Congressional Appropriations for Defense

	Budget Request	House Passed	Senate Passed	Final Amount
		(in thousands of dollars *)		
Military Personnel	$74,202,900	$72,404,112	$72,678,798	$72,737,378
Operations and Maintenance	85,773,000	78,109,862	77,923,000	78,050,372
Procurement	95,656,700	79,502,330	84,897,136	84,875,632
(transferred from prior appropriations)		(2,473,227)	(584,500)	
Research and Development	41,929,900	33,956,074	36,391,125	35,804,214
(transferred from prior appropriations)		(144,573)		
Other Programs	1,469,638	1,179,238	2,221,338 †	2,531,410
Total New Budget Authority	299,032,138	265,151,616	274,111,397	273,999,006
(transferred from prior appropriations)		(2,617,800)	(584,500)	
Total Funding Available	**$299,032,138**	**$267,769,416**	**$274,695,897**	**$273,999,006**

** Totals may not add due to rounding.*
† Does not include $2.96 billion for a space shuttle orbiter. The Senate had put the orbiter money in the defense section of H J Res 738. In the final version, it was included in the HUD-Independent Agencies section.

between assignments) was cut by $115 million, just under half the amount cut by the Senate. The conferees ordered the Pentagon to explain why the travel budgets of the four armed services differed so widely. The Air Force travel budget was $653 per capita while the Marine Corps allowed only $337 per capita.

The Senate had added to the bill $100 million to pay for Coast Guard operations that supported defense missions, including $15 million for stationing Coast Guard officers on Navy ships to arrest intercepted drug smugglers. The conferees trimmed that to $75 million, noting that the $15 million related to anti-drug enforcement was appropriated in the omnibus drug bill signed by the president Oct. 27 (PL 99-570). *(Story, p. 92)*

The conferees dropped from the bill $439 million requested in the budget for military use of the space shuttle. This included $269 million to reimburse the shuttle program for military satellite launches that had been scheduled to occur during fiscal 1987, but were deferred after the explosion of the shuttle *Challenger* in January. The remaining $170 million of the reduction had been earmarked for various Pentagon activities in support of the shuttle program, principally for running a newly completed shuttle launch site at Vandenberg Air Force Base in California. The Vandenberg facility was being mothballed until the early 1990s.

The Senate included in its version of the bill $2.96 billion for a new shuttle to replace *Challenger*, but those funds subsequently were included in the appropriation for the National Aeronautics and Space Administration, also enacted as part of the continuing resolution. *(Funds, p. 171; shuttle explosion, p. 326)*

Procurement Financing

Conferees sliced 11 percent ($10.8 billion) from the amount requested for procurement.

The cut included $700 million to be saved by a Senate provision changing the formula by which the Pentagon calculated the amount of profit it would allow a firm to include explicitly in a contract price. The new policy, included in the conference report, required contractors to accept a higher degree of risk (in the form of investing their own capital in a project) in return for a given level of profit. Conversely, it would reduce allowed profits for a given level of contractor investment.

The conferees also approved a modified version of a Senate provision requiring contractors to pay the cost of setting up a production line for a new weapon. The conference report required contractors to pay half the cost of tooling up for production, with the Pentagon paying the other half. The 50 percent requirement could be waived if Congress authorized and appropriated funds for the Pentagon to pay for a larger share of the tooling costs.

The conferees also included a modified version of a Senate provision slowing the rate at which funds were doled out to firms while they were carrying out a contract to build a certain number of weapons. The provision did not reduce the amount appropriated to buy a given number of weapons, but it would reduce defense outlays during fiscal 1987, thus helping meet the outlay ceiling mandated by the congressional budget resolution.

Strategic Weapons

To modernize the U.S. force of intercontinental ballistic missiles (ICBMs), the conferees approved the same amounts in the companion defense authorization bill:

- $1.2 billion for 12 additional MX missiles instead of the $1.4 billion requested for 21.
- $1.2 billion of the $1.4 billion requested to develop a single-warhead ICBM, referred to as Midgetman, much smaller than the 10-warhead MX so it could be carried in a mobile launcher.
- $120 million to develop a new method for basing ICBMs that would be less vulnerable to Soviet attack than the underground silos in which 50 MXs would be based. Congress had barred the deployment of more than 50 MXs in silos, arguing that such weapons were too vulnerable to Soviet ICBMs. All MXs purchased in fiscal 1987 and future years would be used for test and training launches.

The budget request included $389 million for research on a more secure ICBM basing technique. But the defense authorization bill conferees slashed that to $120 million, implying that they deemed the Pentagon unlikely to come up with a new basing method that would warrant deployment of more than 50 MXs.

Despite intense congressional resistance to additional

MX deployments, Air Force Gen. John T. Chain, commander of the Strategic Air Command, proposed Oct. 23 that 50 additional MXs be deployed in trains that would evade enemy attack by moving about the country during crises.

Both the amount requested and the amount appropriated to prepare for production of the "stealth" bomber were secret. The plane was designed to evade enemy detection.

To modernize existing B-52 bombers, the conferees approved $397 million of the $413 million requested, $142 million more than had been approved in the defense authorization bill. But the appropriations conferees complained that in years past, the Air Force had too freely diverted to other projects funds appropriated for B-52 modification. They barred such shifts in the future without prior approval of the two Appropriations committees.

Both houses had approved the 14th in a class of huge Trident missile-launching submarines, and the conferees set the appropriation at $1.3 billion, a reduction of $63 million from the request.

The conferees made minor reductions in the amounts requested for the Trident II submarine-launched missile, approving $1.6 billion to continue developing the weapon and $1.1 billion to buy the first 21 of them.

Both houses had approved the $227 million request for three converted jetliners intended to relay orders to submerged missile subs through a five-mile-long towed radio antenna.

The conferees approved $3.2 billion of the $4.8 billion requested for the Pentagon's share of the strategic defense initiative (SDI) — Reagan's program to develop a nationwide anti-missile defense. This was the same reduction the authorization bill had made in the Defense Department portion of SDI. The authorization bill covered additional funds for SDI research by the Energy Department.

Also approved was part of the anti-satellite (ASAT) missile program: $200 million of $278 million requested for development, but none of the $28 million requested to prepare for production.

Ground Combat

Conferees agreed on a minor reduction in the request for M-1 tanks, approving $1.58 billion for 840 tanks.

They approved $896 million for 720 Bradley armored troop carriers, 150 vehicles and $226 million less than the request.

For 120 Apache anti-tank helicopters, the conferees recommended just over $1 billion, as had each house, with minor funding adjustments. This was a reduction of 24 helicopters and $24 million from the request.

The Army currently planned to buy 675 Apaches, ending the production run in fiscal 1988. This would make up only 55 percent of the anti-tank helicopter fleet; left in service would be some 550 of the less heavily armed, 1970s-vintage Cobra helicopters, most of them assigned to reserve or National Guard units. But the conferees ordered the Army to continue buying Apaches until the entire anti-tank force was equipped with them.

They also trimmed to $128 million the amount to equip smaller "scout" helicopters with electronic gear to guide Apaches' missiles into enemy tanks with laser beams. But, unlike the defense authorization conferees, they denied the $29 million requested to equip the scout helicopters with small Stinger missiles, to shoot at armed enemy helicopters.

Both houses had approved $110 million of the $159 million requested to prepare for production of a miniature, remote-controlled airplane called Aquila, designed to carry television cameras and lasers to carry out missions similar to the scout helicopter's.

To replace some 6,000 small, Vietnam-era helicopters used as scouts and troop carriers, the Army was developing a new helicopter, designated the LHX. The conferees approved $143 million of the $156 million requested to develop electronic detection gear and engines for the new copter.

The conferees approved most of the funds requested to develop a method for attacking enemy tank columns up to 100 miles behind their own lines: For an airborne radar (JSTARS) to detect those targets, they provided $350 million of the $447 million requested. For a missile (JTACMS) that would disgorge dozens of anti-tank warheads over the targets, they provided the entire $88 million requested.

For long-range Patriot anti-aircraft missiles, they agreed on $917 million, $34 million less than the request.

On the other hand, they added $30 million to the request for short-range, portable Stinger anti-aircraft missiles, appropriating $282 million. The added funds were earmarked to pay a second contractor to set up a Stinger production line so that by fiscal 1990, General Dynamics Corp. — the current Stinger manufacturer — would face a competitor in bidding for the annual production contract.

To develop new anti-aircraft defenses for combat units in the field, the conferees agreed on the following amounts:

- $63 million to develop a missile (called FOG-M) intended to hunt down armed helicopters hovering out of sight behind a tree or hill up to five miles away. Controllers steer the missile by means of a small television camera in its nose transmitting through a hair-thin glass thread uncoiling behind the missile.
- $21 million to develop an anti-aircraft vehicle carrying heavy machine guns and short-range missiles to protect tank columns. This would replace the ill-fated Sergeant York anti-aircraft gun that Defense Secretary Caspar W. Weinberger canceled in August 1985 because it repeatedly failed certain tests.
- $10 million to design a mounting to carry several Stinger launchers on the back of a large jeep as the main anti-aircraft weapon for lightweight Army units not equipped with either the FOG-M or the York replacement.
- $43 million for a target detection and communications network to tie together all the front-line anti-aircraft equipment.

The conferees approved $121 million of the $159 million requested to resume production of binary chemical weapons — an aerial bomb called Bigeye and an artillery shell that dispensed nerve gas. Binary weapons production would mark the first U.S. production of lethal chemical weapons since 1969.

Tactical Air Combat

For 321 first-line Air Force and Navy fighter planes, the conferees appropriated nearly $6.6 billion, a reduction from the request of $8 billion for 399 of these planes. The conference report included:

- $520 million for 15 F-14s, the Navy's largest aircraft carrier-borne fighter.
- $2.2 billion for 84 FA-18s, used by the Navy as both fighters and small bombers flying from carriers.
- $1.5 billion for 42 F-15s, the most sophisticated Air Force fighter.

Funding for Major Defense Programs, Fiscal 1987

Following is a comparison of the amounts Congress authorized and appropriated for major defense programs in fiscal 1987. Some amounts for weapons procurement include funds for components of items to be bought in future budgets. *(Amounts listed below are in millions of dollars.)*

	Budget Request		Authorized (S 2638)		Appropriated (H J Res 738)	
	Number	Amount	Number	Amount	Number	Amount
Strategic Weapons						
MX missile	21	$ 1,418	12	$ 1,115	12	$1,115
Midgetman missile R&D	—	1,376	—	1,200	—	1,200
Trident submarine	1	1,363	1	1,300	1	1,300
Trident II missile (including R&D)	21	2,757	21	2,699	21	2,682
Strategic defense initiative ("star wars") [1]	—	4,785	—	3,213	—	3,213
B-52 bomber modernization	—	413	—	255	—	397
Ground Combat						
M-1 tank	840	1,644	840	1,579	840	1,579
Bradley troop carrier	870	1,122	720	896	720	896
Apache anti-tank helicopter	144	1,189	120	1,033	120	1,028
Long-range anti-tank missile/radar R&D (JTACMS and JSTARS)	—	507	—	398	—	410
Anti-aircraft R&D	—	224	—	183	—	142
LHX helicopter R&D	—	156	—	144	—	143
Naval Warfare						
Aegis cruiser	2	1,914	3	2,715	3	2,715
Aegis destroyer	3	2,448	3	2,390	2	1,670
Los Angeles-class sub	4	2,048	4	1,966	4	1,966
Seawolf-class sub (including R&D)	—	711	—	711	—	623
Anti-sub helicopters (LAMPS I and LAMPS III)	30	391	30	370	30	368
P-3C anti-sub plane	9	312	9	312	9	312
Tactical Air Combat						
F-15 fighter	48	1,675	42	1,543	42	1,543
F-16 fighter	216	2,882	180	2,353	180	2,308
F-14 carrier-borne fighter	15	541	15	520	15	520
FA-18 carrier-borne fighter/bomber	120	2,896	84	2,250	84	2,210
A-6E carrier-borne bomber	11	279	11	259	11	255
AV-8B vertical-takeoff bomber	42	623	42	623	42	590
Mid-1990s fighter R&D (ATF)	—	294	—	275	—	260
AMRAAM air-to-air missile	260	657	180	537	180	537
Airlift						
C-5 cargo plane	21	1,937	21	1,919	21	1,919
KC-10 tanker/cargo plane	8	104	8	89	8	89
C-17 cargo plane R&D	—	612	—	547	—	650
C-17 production preparation	—	217	—	180	—	50
Osprey hybrid helicopter/airplane R&D	—	387	—	387	—	423

[1] *Does not include SDI funds in Energy Department budget.*

- $2.3 billion for 180 smaller Air Force F-16s.

The budget requested a hefty increase in the production rates of the FA-18 (to 120 planes) and the F-16 (to 216 planes). But, the conference report included only enough money to continue the current production rate for each plane.

In addition, the conferees approved the Pentagon's $411 million request to begin buying a fleet of nearly 300 stripped-down fighter planes to defend North America against bombers.

The conference report included:

- $50 million to put new radar and larger fuel tanks in certain F-4 Phantom jets. The Senate had added these funds arguing that the planes were needed by Air National Guard squadrons earmarked for anti-bomber defense of North America.
- $35 million to equip A-7 ground attack planes with new engines and target locating equipment. This was a House initiative.

To develop a new, top-of-the-line fighter that would enter service in the late-1990s to replace the F-15, the conferees approved $260 million of the $294 million requested.

The conferees approved $537 million (of $657 million requested) to begin production of a new air-to-air missile called AMRAAM. Production had been delayed by cost increases and test failures, and the conferees ordered the Air Force not to sign any checks for fully assembled missiles until certain tests had been successfully completed.

The conferees had agreed to a House initiative adding to the bill $124 million to continue production of the T-46 trainer plane, which the Air Force had canceled early in 1986.

But during Senate debate on the continuing resolution conference report Oct. 16, retiring Armed Services Committee Chairman Barry Goldwater, R-Ariz., offered an amendment to delete the T-46 money. Backers of the plane filibustered for some 23 hours, but on Oct. 17 they accepted an amendment that appropriated no funds for the plane in fiscal 1987 and directed the Air Force to conduct a competition between the T-46 and other trainer planes.

Naval Warfare

The conferees approved $4.38 billion for three cruisers and two smaller destroyers equipped with the Aegis antiaircraft system — a network of computers, powerful radars and missile launchers designed to shield a fleet against swarms of anti-ship missiles.

The budget requested two cruisers and three destroyers for nearly the same amount. The companion defense authorization bill also had boosted to three the number of Aegis cruisers in the fiscal 1987 budget, arguing that this would allow the Navy to continue the competition between two firms currently building these ships, thus keeping prices down. But unlike the continuing resolution, the authorization bill had retained the three destroyers requested.

The conferees also approved $64 million of the $87 million requested to begin production of a short-range antiaircraft missile being developed jointly for the U.S. and West German navies.

For the four *Los Angeles*-class submarine-hunting submarines requested in the budget, the conferees approved $1.97 billion, a reduction of $82 million from the request.

They also approved $623 million of the $711 million requested to continue development and prepare for construction of the *Seawolf*, first of a new class of sub-hunting submarines. But they endorsed the demand of the House Appropriations Committee that the Pentagon set a cap on the price it would pay for the new subs.

The conferees approved essentially the amounts requested for Navy sub-hunting aircraft:

- $197 million for 17 LAMPS III helicopters carried by most of the Navy's post-1970 surface warships.
- $118 million for seven copies of a version of LAMPS III with different detection gear intended for use on aircraft carriers.
- $53 million for six smaller LAMPS I helicopters, carried by some smaller and older surface ships.
- $312 million for nine P-3C land-based patrol planes, based on the 1950s-vintage Electra airliner.

The conferees adopted a Senate provision adding to the bill $200 million to buy equipment that the Coast Guard would use in its wartime role as part of the Navy. Among the items to be purchased were submarine detection equipment for Coast Guard cutters.

Air Transport

The conferees made minor reductions in the funding requested for two kinds of long-range transport planes: They approved $1.9 billion for 21 huge C-5 cargo haulers and $89 million for 8 KC-10 cargo planes also equipped to refuel other aircraft in midair.

To continue development of a new cargo plane, the C-17, intended to haul tanks and other heavy items into primitive landing strips, the conferees approved $650 million instead of the $613 million requested. But they approved only $50 million of the $217 million requested to prepare for production of the plane.

House Committee Action

The House Appropriations Committee reported HR 5438 (H Rept 99-793) on Aug. 14 after adding the same far-reaching provisions relating to arms control that the House had added to its version of the defense authorization bill (HR 4428), which was then pending on the House floor.

The committee then reported HR 5438, which would bring the fiscal 1987 defense budget to $283.9 billion, $36.1 billion less than President Reagan's request.

Two days later, on Aug. 16, Reagan threatened to veto the authorization bill if it contained the arms control provisions. The measures he objected to were:

- A ban on all but the smallest nuclear test explosions, beginning Jan. 1, 1987, provided the Soviet Union agreed to a similar moratorium and to the placement on its territory of monitoring equipment.
- A ban on the deployment of any nuclear weapons that would violate SALT II.
- A reduction to $3.125 billion of the $5.3 billion Reagan requested for SDI.
- A ban on tests against targets in space of the anti-satellite missile, provided the Soviet Union conducted no ASAT tests.
- A continuation for one year of the existing ban on production of lethal chemical weapons.

Painless Cuts

For programs covered by HR 5438, the Pentagon requested $299 billion. The committee recommended $265.1 billion in new budget authority and told the Pentagon to add to that $2.7 billion left over from earlier defense appropriations.

Not including that money transferred from earlier budgets, the committee reduced Reagan's request by $33.9 billion. Nearly $8 billion of that amount came from sources the committee insisted would have no impact on Pentagon programs:

- $2.5 billion was cut from the procurement accounts to be made up by surplus funds appropriated in earlier years but no longer needed for their original purposes.
- $2.7 billion was cut from the budget for fuel oil, to reflect the continuing decline in oil prices.
- $2.75 billion was cut on the assumption that other prices would increase more slowly than had been anticipated.

But the declining value of the dollar against foreign currencies deprived the committee of another "free" budget cut that Congress had used during the past several years, when the dollar's value was on the rise.

U.S. units deployed abroad use dollars to pay for goods and services they purchase from local economies. When the dollar's value was increasing in the early 1980s, fewer dollars were needed than had been budgeted, enabling Congress to cut several hundred million dollars annually from the defense appropriations bill. But when the dollar's value abroad waned, those units' operating costs might be several hundred million dollars higher than was allowed for in the budget request.

The Appropriations Committee authorized the Defense Department to make up any such shortfall with up to $500 million drawn from any funds appropriated for procurement in earlier years that turned out not to be needed for their original purposes.

Nearly all reductions the committee proposed for major weapons programs mirrored those made in the companion authorization bill.

Personnel Costs

The committee approved an active-duty military force of 2,169,370 members. This was 2,000 more than was approved for fiscal 1986, but 11,730 fewer than the administration requested.

As a result, the committee trimmed $140 million from the personnel budget request. Most of that reduction came from the Navy, which had sought the lion's share of the requested increase.

Like the Senate and House Armed Services committees, House Appropriations complained that the ratio of officers to enlisted personnel was too high. The Appropriations panel cut $150 million from the personnel request to force a gradual decrease in the number of officers through fiscal 1990. The Joint Chiefs of Staff had vigorously protested this congressional move.

The panel commended the Pentagon for increasing the proportion of its recruiting budget that was spent on "joint" or multi-service efforts. But since it denied most of the requested increase in manpower, the committee also denied most of the requested increase in recruiting funds: Of $1.73 billion requested, the panel approved $1.66 billion, an increase of about $14 million over fiscal 1986.

The committee also cut $33.6 million from the request for enlistment bonuses and $223 million from the request for re-enlistment bonuses — the latter by reducing from 75 percent to 50 percent the portion of the bonus paid an enlisted member in a lump sum at the start of the re-enlistment.

It ordered the Pentagon to slow down the rate at which it transferred personnel between posts, and cut $564 million from the amount requested to reimburse personnel for moving expenses resulting from such transfers.

The committee cut by $750 million the payroll request for civilian employees, arguing that most of the cut could be taken from programs for which large increases over the fiscal 1986 budget had been requested. That reduction included $412.2 million to pay foreign nationals employed at U.S. facilities abroad — most of whom are Army employees in Europe.

The committee denied the entire $61 million requested to conduct a one-day muster of all 500,000 members of the individual ready reserve.

In turning down the proposal, the committee cited the Army's assessment of a small-scale IRR muster conducted in fiscal 1986: A peacetime exercise would not measure the proportion of reservists who would show up in case of a real crisis.

Strategic Weapons

The Appropriations Committee approved the amounts in the House-passed authorization bill for the principal ICBM programs:

- $1.1 billion for 12 multiple-warhead MX missiles, reducing the request by $303 million and nine missiles.
- $1.58 billion for work on future ICBMs, $541 million less than was requested. The committee did not comment on the effect of this reduction, but according to the House Armed Services Committee, which recommended it, the amount approved included the entire $1.4 billion requested to develop a smaller, single-warhead ICBM, informally referred to as Midgetman.

However, no funds would be available for Pentagon efforts to develop a new MX basing method to allow the deployment of additional missiles, beyond the 50 Congress had approved for deployment in existing missile launch silos.

Contrary to the House-passed authorization bill, the appropriations measure included $1.4 billion for a large Trident missile-launching submarine. The ship was authorized in the Senate version of the defense authorization bill but not in the House version.

Also included in the appropriations measure was $2.9 billion to continue development and prepare for production of the Trident II (or D-5) submarine-launched missile, $133 million less than the request.

Also approved was the request for three E-6A radio planes ($226.7 million), converted jetliners designed to communicate with submerged missile subs through a five-mile-long radio antenna.

Noting that Air Force and Defense Department officials were insistent that they wanted no additional B-1 bombers, the committee did not add to the appropriations bill $200 million added to the House authorization measure to keep open the possibility of future B-1 production. Funds for the last 48 of a planned fleet of 100 B-1s were appropriated in fiscal 1986.

The amounts requested by the Pentagon and approved by the committee for the stealth bomber were secret.

To modernize the aging fleet of B-52 bombers, the committee recommended $397 million — all but $16 million of the amount requested. Also approved was $797 million of the $826 million requested to replace the jet engines on KC-135 tanker planes, used to refuel bombers in midair.

Ground Combat

For the Army's two premier armored combat vehicles, the Appropriations Committee recommended the amounts authorized by the House:

- $1.6 billion for 840 M-1 tanks, $65 million less than was requested.
- $830 million for 593 Bradley armored troop carriers, a reduction from the request of $292 billion (and 277 Bradleys).

The Appropriations panel recommended funds for 120 Apache anti-tank helicopters ($1 billion), which carry laser-guided Hellfire missiles. This was a reduction of 24 helicopters and $156 million from the request.

Like House Armed Services, it ordered the Army to plan to continue building Apaches after fiscal 1988, which would be the last year of production under current plans. The Army plan was to buy 675 Apaches, leaving older machines with weaker armament to fill out the total anti-tank helicopter force of 1,206 craft (including those earmarked for National Guard and reserve units). "Even in light of current tight budget constraints," the Appropriations Committee said, "it does not make sense to shut down production of one of the Army's highest priority programs with only 55 percent of the procurement requirement fulfilled."

The committee recommended $144.3 million to equip small scout helicopters with lasers to guide Apache missiles to their targets, $66 million less than the request. But the panel turned down the request for $28 million to rig these scouts to carry Stinger missiles to defend themselves against armed Soviet helicopters. The Army had not yet decided which air-to-air missile the scouts should carry, the committee said.

Of $156 million requested to develop a new, small helicopter (called LHX), the committee approved $146 million. The Army planned to buy more than 6,000 LHXs to replace 1960s-vintage helicopters used as scouts and troop carriers.

The committee approved $127.5 million of $209.6 million requested to continue developing and begin production of a small, remote-control airplane called Aquila. The little plane was designed to carry a television camera to spy on enemy forces or a laser to guide bombs and missiles to their targets. The House-passed authorization bill included no funds for Aquila, which had had a long string of testing problems. But the Appropriations panel funded the program anyway, contending that the Army needed the weapon to snoop and shoot deep behind enemy lines.

For TOW anti-tank missiles carried by Army and Marine Corps helicopters and ground troops, the committee recommended $101 million (12,000 missiles), a reduction from the request of $67 million (3,400 missiles). And it approved the $49 million requested to develop a TOW replacement (designated the AAWS-M).

The Army also requested 136,000 Swedish-made portable anti-tank rockets, designed to be carried by infantrymen ($82.5 million). Instead, the committee approved $44.5 million to buy 72,000 of the rockets — called AT-4s — from the Swedish manufacturer and an additional $25 million to start up a U.S. production line, producing 10,000 rockets in fiscal 1987.

The committee added to the bill $20 million to test the French-built Milan II anti-tank missile, about midway in size between the TOW and the portable AT-4. It also approved $82 million of the $100 million requested to develop small anti-tank warheads designed to be scattered out of artillery shells and rockets over enemy columns.

But the panel complained that the Army was dispersing its anti-tank research in too many different directions and it denied $105 million requested for three other projects in that field.

The committee also sliced funds for a system of missiles and airborne radars designed to attack tank columns up to 100 miles behind enemy lines: It approved $88 million to develop a missile, called J-TACMS, intended to scatter dozens of anti-tank warheads over a gaggle of enemy vehicles. But for reasons not explained in its report, the panel recommended only $28 million of the $447 million requested to develop and begin building a radar called Joint STARS intended to guide the missile to such targets.

The request for 700 long-range Patriot anti-aircraft missiles was approved, though the committee trimmed the funding by $49 million to $902 million, noting that the contractor's recent bids were lower than had been projected.

But the request for 456 five-mile-range Chaparral missiles ($104 million) was rejected. The committee argued that it was premature to appropriate procurement funds, since the Army had not yet decided whether to have two firms compete for the contract.

It approved the requested purchase of 4,180 shoulder-fired Stinger anti-aircraft missiles, but provided only $109 million of the $252 million requested. Of the reduction, $43 million was earmarked to mount Stinger launchers on the back of Army trucks. The committee said it was premature to begin modifying trucks since the system still was being tested.

A request for $904 million to buy French-designed mobile telephone networks for Army divisions in the field was approved.

Tactical Air Combat

For most of the Air Force's principal combat aircraft programs, the Appropriations Committee recommended essentially the same funding level as the House authorized:

- $1.39 billion for 36 F-15 fighter planes instead of $1.68 billion for 48.
- $2.26 billion for 180 smaller F-16s instead of $2.88 billion for 216.
- $441 million, the amount requested, to buy the first 20 of a projected fleet of 270 relatively inexpensive fighters to defend North America against bomber attack.
- $450 million to develop future fighter planes. The Air Force had requested $294 million to develop a new plane (the Advanced Tactical Fighter), $209 million to work on an improved version of the F-15 and $160 million to develop improvements in other existing Air Force fighters. The Appropriations Committee did not comment on its action, but the House Armed Services Committee, which took parallel action in drawing up the authorization bill, said it was intended to make the Air Force narrow the scope of its efforts to develop new planes.

Unlike Armed Services, House Appropriations included in its bill $35 million to test an upgraded version of the A-7 light bomber.

For budgetary reasons, the Appropriations panel made similar reductions in the budget requests for Navy combat planes. It recommended:

- $2.05 billion for 84 F/A-18s, used both as fighters and small bombers. The Navy requested $2.9 billion for 120 of the planes.
- $520 million for 15 long-range F-14 fighters, $20.7

million less than the budget request.

- $259 million for 11 A-6E medium bombers, a $20 million reduction.
- $590 million for 42 AV-8Bs — small, vertical-takeoff jets used by the Marine Corps as bombers.

The committee made relatively minor reductions in the amounts requested to develop improved versions of two of the Navy craft. It approved $240 million (of $268 million sought) for work on an F-14D, and it recommended $130 million of the $143 million requested for an A-6F.

The panel recommended $537 million of the $657 million requested to begin production of a new air-to-air missile for U.S. fighter planes, called AMRAAM, which had proven substantially more expensive than had been planned. This would reduce from 260 to 180 the number bought.

The committee approved the request for more than 4,400 Sparrow and Sidewinder air-to-air missiles carried by Air Force and Navy fighters, but trimmed the appropriation to $461 million, $26 million less than requested.

It also approved the request for 205 of the longer-range Phoenix missiles carried only by Navy F-14s. But it recommended only $119 million in new budget authority, compared with the $289 million requested. The committee told the Navy to make up $40 million of the reduction from funds appropriated for Phoenix production in earlier years that turned out to be superfluous. The remaining $130 million cut by the committee had been earmarked to pay a second manufacturer to begin competing with Hughes Aircraft Company to build the Phoenix. The panel barred selection of a second contractor, arguing that too few of the missiles would be produced to justify the cost of starting up a second production line.

Naval Warfare

The committee recommended only minor adjustments in the amounts earmarked for five warships carrying the Aegis anti-aircraft system, designed to protect U.S. fleets against swarms of anti-ship missiles. The panel approved:

- $1.88 billion for two cruisers, trimming $37 million from the request.
- $2.35 billion for three smaller destroyers, a $100 million reduction.

The request for nearly 1,200 Standard ship-launched anti-aircraft missiles ($731 million) was approved without change. But, like both the Senate and House Armed Services committees, House Appropriations denied the $9.2 million requested to develop a nuclear-armed version of the Standard.

The committee also denied the entire $137 million requested to continue development and begin production of a smaller anti-aircraft missile (called RAM) intended as a last-ditch defense against anti-ship missiles. The Appropriations panel did not comment on the reduction, but the House Armed Services Committee, which recommended similar action on the defense authorization bill, complained that RAM was getting too expensive and was becoming outmoded by newer types of Soviet anti-ship missiles.

The Appropriations panel denied all funds requested for two programs intended to provide U.S. fleets with long-range radar warning of approaching air attacks:

- $56 million for movable, land-based radar stations designed to see approaching planes "over the horizon" at a much greater distance than they would be detected by a ship's radar — possibly up to 1,000 miles away. The committee complained that the Navy wanted to spend too much on the program before it had been adequately tested.
- $9 million to develop a radar-carrying blimp.

The committee approved the request for 324 Tomahawk long-range cruise missiles, but said they could be bought for $582 million, $140 million less than the request. Ultimately, the Navy planned to deploy Tomahawks on upwards of 200 surface ships and submarines. The missile was designed to attack ships at a range of 250 miles and land-targets at a range of several hundred miles with conventional warheads. A nuclear-armed version had a range of around 1,500 miles.

The request for four *Los Angeles*-class nuclear-powered submarines, designed to hunt other subs, was approved, but the funding request was trimmed by $263 million to $1.78 billion. The committee took a proportionally larger slice out of the request to continue developing a new hunter sub — the so-called *Seawolf* class — and to prepare for construction of the first of the new type: It recommended $428 million of the $711 million requested. The panel complained that the new ship's nuclear-power plant would be more expensive than that used in the *Los Angeles*. The Navy was designing the new sub to have a higher speed.

The House version of the authorization bill approved none of the nine P-3C land-based anti-submarine planes requested ($312 million). But the Appropriations Committee recommended funding two of the planes ($69 million), which it said were needed to carry out a secret international agreement regarding ocean surveillance.

The committee approved 24 of the 30 anti-submarine helicopters requested by the Navy ($287 million), a reduction of $105 million from the request. These small helicopters of two basic types were carried by most of the Navy's surface warships.

A request for four small mine sweepers ($196 million) was denied. The program was dead in the water in any case, as a result of problems with the design. Reluctantly, the committee agreed with the two Armed Services panels that the Navy could buy one foreign-built mine sweeper to be copied by a U.S. shipyard.

Air Transport

The principal air transport programs were approved with some relatively minor funding reductions. The committee recommended:

- $2.26 billion for 21 large C-5 cargo planes, $18 million less than requested.
- $728 million to continue development and to set up a production line for the smaller C-17 cargo hauler, a reduction from the budget of $102 million.
- $89 million for eight KC-10 tanker planes, $15 million less than the request.
- $340 million to continue development of an airplane/helicopter called the Osprey (formerly the JVX), $47 million less than the request. The Marine Corps planned to use the Osprey to haul troops ashore quickly from amphibious landing ships.

Space Launchers

The committee dropped $462.5 million from the budget request because of the halt in operation of the space shuttle, which the Pentagon planned to use to launch military satellites and to conduct experiments. Among the funds cut by the panel were: $287.5 million in shuttle launch fees earmarked to reimburse the National Aeronautics and Space Administration for use of the shuttle; $100 million that would be saved by mothballing for the time being the not-yet-used shuttle launch site at Vandenberg Air Force Base in California; and $75 million in other shuttle-related costs.

Approved without change was $431 million requested for development and production of satellite launch rockets, which the shuttle had been intended to supplant.

The committee warned the administration it was accelerating too rapidly the funding for a so-called "national aerospace plane" designed to take off and land like a conventional airplane and carry passengers and payloads into orbit.

The committee approved $60 million for the project in fiscal 1987, 33 percent more than was appropriated in fiscal 1986, but $89 million less than the administration requested.

Senate Committee Action

The funding bill reported Sept. 17 by the Senate Appropriations Committee (S 2827 — S Rept 99-446) approved $277.7 billion for the Pentagon, $24.6 billion less than President Reagan had requested. This included $277.1 billion in new money and $584 million in funds transferred from earlier budgets.

Counting funds appropriated separately for military construction and other programs, the Senate bill would bring the total defense budget for fiscal 1987 to $302.3 billion, compared with Reagan's request for $320 billion.

The House Appropriations Committee had sliced the $302 billion request to $267.8 billion, a reduction of $34.5 billion. With the other programs, this would bring total defense funding in fiscal 1987 to $285 billion.

More than one-third of the Senate panel's $24.6 billion cut in Reagan's request was made in forms which, the committee insisted, would force no changes in Pentagon operations but merely reflected reductions in the cost of doing business. A total of $9.6 billion of the reduction was based on assumptions that various goods and services would cost less than the budget assumed, partly because inflation was lower than anticipated.

About 10 percent of the committee's reduction reflected its refusal to support requested expansion of several programs. Cuts totaling $1.4 billion were achieved by holding the production rates for four major weapons at their fiscal 1986 levels: the M-1 tank, the Bradley troop carrier and the F-16 and F/A-18 fighter planes. An additional reduction of $944 million resulted from turning down most of the requested increase in military manpower.

But in addition to those fairly routine kinds of reductions, the Senate committee made three policy decisions that accounted for significant cuts:

- Warning that future defense budgets would expand little if at all for several years, the committee delayed the planned start of production of several costly weapons programs. The largest such reductions came from the Midgetman intercontinental missile ($700 million) and from the C-17 transport plane ($466 million).
- Ordering the Pentagon to make contractors accept a larger share of the cost and risk of weapons production, the panel cut $2.2 billion to reflect the anticipated savings.
- The committee rescinded $4.6 billion appropriated in earlier defense budgets but not needed. This did not reduce the amount that the committee had to appropriate in fiscal 1987 for the program it wanted to fund. But it shrank projected Pentagon outlays by enough to allow new appropriations that would otherwise have been impossible under the defense outlay ceiling imposed by the congressional budget resolution (S Con Res 120).

Manpower

The committee sliced $944 million from the budget by approving only a fraction of the requested increase in Pentagon personnel. This reduction consisted of the following cuts:

- $402 million, giving the Pentagon half its requested increase in active duty military personnel. The approved increase of 6,850 would bring the ceiling on active duty manpower to 2,174,250.
- $226 million, allowing an increase in reserve personnel of 20,000 instead of the requested hike of 51,000 reservists. This would bring the ceiling on reservists to 1,120,077 members.
- $316 million, reducing the number of Pentagon civilians by more than 19,000 — to a total of about 1,101,000. The budget requested an increase to nearly 1,123,500.

The committee included funds to pay for a 3 percent military pay raise and a 2 percent pay hike for Pentagon civilians, both to take effect Jan. 1, 1987. The Senate panel did not concur in the House committee's decision to cut some $2 billion from the fiscal 1987 budget by delaying the payday scheduled for Sept. 30, 1987, until the following day, which was the first day of fiscal 1988.

The panel cut $59 million from the request for recruiting operations, including advertising. That amount included $23.7 million the Pentagon had volunteered to give up in light of its decision to focus more recruiting resources on multi-service activities at the expense of each service's own recruiting efforts.

The panel approved the entire amount requested for enlistment bonuses, rejecting a $33.6 million cut proposed by the House committee. It also recommended $590 million for re-enlistment bonuses, a reduction of $212 million from the Pentagon's request.

For the cost of transferring military personnel from one post to another, the committee recommended $2.47 billion, a $335 million reduction from the request. The cut included $145 million the Pentagon said would be saved by recent policy changes; one of these was a decision to transfer personnel less frequently.

An additional reduction of $45 million was made to force the Pentagon to begin reducing the proportion of officers in its active-duty force. The committee endorsed the policy of trimming the number of officers by 2 percent annually for three years beginning in fiscal 1987, a move that had been incorporated into the defense authorization bill by the Senate Armed Services Committee.

The Appropriations panel also complained that too high a proportion of Air Force enlisted personnel were being promoted into the higher enlisted ranks. To halt this, it sliced $85 million from the Air Force budget.

Reserve Initiatives

The reserve forces, including the National Guard, constituted a powerful grass-roots lobby, and they also had been assigned increasingly significant roles in Pentagon war plans in recent years. The congressional defense funding panels had added several hundred million dollars for reserve forces to the last few defense budgets, complaining that the active-duty personnel who dominated the services systematically shortchanged the reserves.

Senate Appropriations followed the pattern, adding

$453 million to buy additional equipment at the discretion of the reserve component chiefs. Almost one-third of the amount was earmarked to buy eight C-130 transport planes.

In addition to the equipment purchased with these added funds, the reserves also would receive some of the equipment requested by the Pentagon and included elsewhere in the bill. For instance, 18 of the 120 Apache anti-tank helicopters included in the bill would go to reserve forces.

In the past, the panel had called for substituting reserve units for some of the active-duty forces deployed overseas, as a cost-cutting measure. However, in its report on S 2827, the panel concluded that such substitutions would be feasible only on a modest scale, largely because most reserve members would agree to serve abroad for no more than three or four weeks at a time, and not every year.

Nevertheless, the committee insisted that the assignment to Europe for short periods of small units and selected individuals from reserve forces would enhance reservists' morale and training. It requested the Pentagon to consider the idea.

The committee also retained $69 million earmarked for a one-day test mobilization of the individual ready reserve. House Appropriations had dropped the funds.

Operations and Maintenance

The committee cut more than $7.8 billion from the request for operations and maintenance, recommending $77.9 billion. But more than half of the cut came from lower-than-anticipated prices. The committee said these price changes could allow funding cuts with no reductions in military activities. Among these "fact of life" cuts:

- $2.97 billion, reflecting the committee's assumption that the 187 million barrels of oil the Pentagon would buy in fiscal 1987 would cost an average of $21.50 rather than the $31.50 per barrel assumed in the budget.
- $623 million, based on the assumption that prices for supplies other than fuel would rise at a rate of about 3 percent rather than the 4 percent inflation on which the budget was based.
- $824 million, on the assumption that other maintenance activities would cost less than the budget assumed.

The committee also recommended trims in several programs that traditionally were targets for congressional budgeteers. Among these were cuts of $238 million in travel funds and $100 million in the budget for consultants.

The $5.9 billion request for routine maintenance of facilities and small construction projects was cut by $391 million. The panel complained that the funds were being spent on non-essential projects — a sailing marina was cited as one example — and that the services too often diverted funds from this account to other purposes.

The committee cut $270 million from the request for military depots where aircraft and other heavy equipment were overhauled. The panel argued that the Pentagon would not have to cut back on its maintenance schedule if workers at these plants increased their productivity by 2.5 percent. The panel complained that there had been no dramatic productivity increase at these facilities in recent years, despite appropriations totaling more than $3 billion for projects intended to increase productivity.

The request for flight operations was cut by $39 million, less than one-fifth the amount sliced by the House Appropriations Committee.

The Senate panel dropped from the budget $206 million requested for overhaul of two 1960s-vintage missile-launching submarines. Reagan had announced in May that the ships would be retired. But members rejected a House Committee proposal to delete an additional $250 million budgeted to overhaul two other missile subs beginning early in 1987.

The House committee intended thereby to enforce continued compliance with SALT II. When he announced plans to retire the first two subs, Reagan declared that, because of Soviet violations of SALT II provisions, he would stop adjusting U.S. nuclear arms stocks to comply with the unratified pact.

Intercontinental Missiles

The committee approved the Pentagon's request for 21 MX missiles, though it trimmed the appropriation by $50 million to $1.37 billion. Members also approved $321 million of the $352 million requested to continue MX development. The House panel had approved only 12 MXs.

But the Senate committee cut $969 million from the $1.76 billion requested for development of future ICBMs. That included a cut of $700 million from the $1.38 billion requested to develop a much smaller ICBM called Midgetman. This would put off by a year or two the start of test flights and accordingly would delay deployment, currently scheduled to begin in 1992.

The committee said that, because of the budget crunch, it decided to emphasize those strategic weapons that would bolster the U.S. inventory sooner than Midgetman. But it also insisted that the Pentagon try to ratchet down the new missile's cost before making a commitment to build it.

Most proponents envisioned a single-warhead missile, small enough to be launched from an armored truck about the size of the largest cargo trucks currently operating on Interstate highways. Backers of the new missile argued that Soviet ICBMs, which are accurate enough to destroy armored underground missile launchers, could not hit mobile launchers, thus reducing the threat of a surprise attack.

Proponents insisted that the Midgetman carry only one warhead, partly to keep the missile light enough so the launchers could roam across country. Another reason was their belief that missiles with multiple warheads posed a greater threat of a surprise attack than would single-warhead missiles.

The Appropriations panel argued in its report that each facet of that vision could make the new missile much more expensive, warhead for warhead, than the MX. The armored mobile launchers might turn out to be as expensive as the missiles; the crews needed to operate them would be much larger, and therefore more expensive, than the handful of people who sat in the control rooms of underground silos; and each of the very expensive missile guidance systems would guide only one warhead.

The committee also approved only $120 million of the $389 million requested to develop new ICBM basing methods other than mobile launchers. The administration hoped to come up with a new basing method, less vulnerable to attack than existing silos, which would persuade Congress to allow the deployment of 50 more MXs, in addition to the 50 already earmarked for silo deployment.

Other Strategic Arms

The committee made relatively modest trims in the request for the Trident II submarine-launched ballistic missile, approving $2.96 billion of the $3.06 billion requested to continue development of the missile and to build the first 21 copies. The Trident was intended to be the first submarine-launched missile accurate enough to destroy armored military targets.

The committee recommended $1.3 billion for a Trident missile-launching submarine, $63 million less than the request. And it approved without change the request for three modified jetliners intended to relay radio messages to submerged missile subs ($227 million).

Both the budget request and the committee recommendation for the stealth bomber were secret. The committee approved $120 million of the $165 million requested to develop an improved version of the SRAM missile, currently carried by U.S. bombers so they could shoot a nuclear warhead at heavily defended targets while remaining a few hundred miles away.

No funds were requested or recommended by the committee to build more B-1 bombers than the 100 funded through fiscal 1986.

The committee approved only $255 million of the $413 million requested for modifications to existing B-52 bombers. The panel complained that, in past years, the Air Force had diverted large sums appropriated for such modernization to other programs.

Members also recommended $739 million of the $826 million requested to refurbish with new engines some KC-135 tanker planes.

Strategic Defense

The committee cut to $3.4 billion the $4.8 billion requested for the Pentagon's share of research on Reagan's SDI program.

Any further cuts, the panel warned, would force significant delays in important experiments. It cited Pentagon claims that $4.1 billion would be needed in fiscal 1987 simply to follow through with existing SDI contracts. But even the lower amount recommended would allow the Pentagon to continue with key tests of anti-missile detection equipment and weapons.

The panel recommended $203 million of the $278 million requested to develop an ASAT missile and $19 million of the $28 million requested to purchase some components for it.

The committee also strongly opposed the provision included in the House versions of both the defense authorization and appropriations bills that would continue to bar full-scale tests of ASAT provided the Soviet Union continued its current ASAT test moratorium. The test bar was included in the fiscal 1986 continuing appropriations resolution (PL 99-190). *(1985 Almanac p. 162)*

Tanks and Tank Hunters

The committee approved production of 720 M-1 tanks ($1.5 billion) instead of the 840 requested, a reduction of $116 million. Ted Stevens, R-Alaska, chairman of the Subcommittee on Defense, had argued for two years that lower-than-projected defense budgets would force the Army to accept the reduced production rate.

For 720 Bradley armored troop carriers, the committee recommended $896 million, $226 million less than the Pentagon had requested for 870 Bradleys.

It also made reductions in several programs for airborne counterweights to the Soviet Union's vast tank fleet. The panel recommended:

- $1.02 billion for 120 Apache missile-armed, anti-tank helicopters. The Army had requested 144 of the Apaches ($1.19 billion).
- $119 million to equip 36 small scout helicopters with a periscope-like laser so they could hide behind trees and ridges while steering laser-guided missiles and artillery shells into their targets. This was a reduction from the request of $46 million.
- $136 million — $20 million less than was requested — to develop a new small helicopter (designated LHX) to replace some 6,000 Vietnam War-era Army helicopters in a variety of roles, including scouting and tank-hunting.
- $60 million to continue development of the small radio-controlled plane called Aquila. The plane was intended to carry a television camera to find enemy tanks and other targets with a missile-guiding laser like the scout helicopter's. The panel also recommended $50 million for Aquila procurement. These represented reductions of $32 million from the development request and $68 million from the production request. The committee complained that the Army was spending too much money developing a night-viewing television camera for Aquila, and ordered it to find a cheaper approach.

The committee recommended holding the production of the widely used TOW anti-tank missile at the fiscal 1986 production rate of 12,000 copies ($137 million), a reduction of 3,400 missiles ($31 million).

The panel also adjusted the funding requests for several other anti-tank weapons planned for production up through the early 1990s. It recommended:

- $8.7 million to develop a guided missile smaller than TOW to replace the current Dragon missile, widely regarded as too hard for troops to operate. This was a $9.4 million reduction.
- $83 million for 130,000 Swedish-built, one-man anti-tank rockets called AT-4s, a reduction of about 22,000 rockets ($11 million) from the request. Like its House counterpart, the Senate panel insisted that the Army use some of the funds to buy the first 10,000 of the rockets from the U.S. manufacturer that would build the AT-4s bought by the Pentagon in the future.
- $67 million — $40 million less than requested — for an artillery shell designed to scatter several warheads over an enemy tank concentration. Each warhead, about the size of a large soup can, was designed to detect a tank and blast a devastatingly powerful metal slug through its roof, where the armor was relatively thin. The shell, called SADARM, had been tested most recently in an exercise whimsically code-named "Chicken Little."
- $88.2 million for an Army missile called TACMS designed to scatter dozens of anti-tank bomblets over a column up to 100 miles behind an enemy's front lines, a reduction of $36 million from the request.
- $371 million for an airborne radar (called JSTARS) intended to guide TACMS missiles to their targets, a reduction of $90 million from the request.

Other Ground Combat

In general, the Senate committee was more supportive than its House counterpart of Army plans to develop a network of anti-aircraft weapons to protect front-line combat units. The committee recommended:

- $252 million to buy Stinger shoulder-fired anti-aircraft missiles, as requested. This included $43 million to mount Stinger launchers on the back of large jeeps. The House committee had denied funds for the jeep-mounted missiles.
- $15 million to develop a beefed-up version of the jeep-

mounted Stinger — probably including machine guns — as the main anti-aircraft weapon for Army units equipped with relatively few heavy vehicles, such as airborne units. The House had denied the entire request for $22 million.

- $64 million to develop several other anti-aircraft weapons, including a missile, called FOG-M, intended to destroy armed helicopters hovering out of sight, behind trees or hills up to five miles away. The Pentagon wanted $104 million for the package and the House approved $84 million for FOG-M alone.
- $10 million for a detection and communication system to tie the whole anti-aircraft network together, $6 million less than the request. The House approved none of these funds.

To buy a French-designed portable telephone network for Army divisions in the field, the committee approved the $904 million requested. But it also approved only $10 million of the $204 million requested for another Army radio system, called SINCGARS. The Army was unhappy with the reliability of SINCGARS and was considering shifting to another contractor.

The committee approved the entire amount requested to develop and produce new types of lethal chemical weapons, called binary munitions: $117 million to build artillery shells and air-dropped bombs, $41 million to build production facilities, and $42 million for continued binary weapons development. The House committee denied all binary weapons funding.

Tactical Air Combat

The committee rejected proposed increases in the production rates of two fighter planes. It approved:

- $2.3 billion for 180 Air Force F-16s. The budget requested 216 of the small fighters ($2.9 billion).
- $2.4 billion for 84 F/A-18s used by the Navy as both a fighter and a small bomber. The budget requested 120 of the planes ($2.9 billion).

The panel approved with no more than minor cuts the amounts requested for other major combat plane programs:

- $1.6 billion for 48 of the Air Force's larger F-15 fighters.
- $520 million for 15 F-14 long-range fighters flown off aircraft carriers.
- $256 million for 11 A-6Es, Navy carrier-based bombers.
- $623 million for 42 AV-8B Harriers, vertical-takeoff jets used by the Marine Corps as small bombers.

Like Senate Armed Services, the Appropriations panel denied the $295 million requested to buy 20 stripped-down fighters as part of a fleet of about 270 planes to defend North America against bomber attack. But the Appropriations Committee also added to the bill $50 million to begin modernizing existing Phantom jets for the home defense mission.

The committee also approved $582 million of the $620 million requested to develop improved versions of the F-14, F-15 and A-6E.

It recommended $163 million — $44 million less than the request — for programs to improve the reliability of jet engines currently used in combat aircraft.

The committee said that the engine manufacturers should gradually assume responsibility for conducting this research.

To develop a new Air Force fighter plane that would begin replacing the F-15 in 1995, the committee recommended $275 million of the $294 million requested.

Naval Warfare

The committee recommended funds for three cruisers to be paid for by $2.1 billion in new budget authority and $584 million appropriated for warships in earlier years and not spent. The budget requested $1.9 billion for two of the ships, which carried the Aegis anti-aircraft system — a set of missiles, radars and computers intended to protect a fleet against simultaneous attack by dozens of anti-ship cruise missiles.

It approved $2.4 billion for three smaller Aegis-armed destroyers, a minor reduction from the request.

The request for nearly 1,200 Standard ship-launched anti-aircraft missiles was approved, though funding was trimmed by $35 million to $696 million. But the committee dropped the $9.2 million requested to develop a nuclear-armed version of Standard, saying that the Navy had abandoned the program.

For four *Los Angeles*-class submarines designed to hunt other subs, the committee recommended $1.97 billion, a reduction of $81 million from the request. The committee approved $607 million of the $844 million requested to continue development and prepare for production of a new class of hunter subs — the *Seawolf*-class (formerly SSN-21). The panel demanded a written guarantee from the secretary of the Navy that the new ships would cost no more than $1 billion each, once the first five or six had been built.

The largest part of the reduction ($188 million) came from the $454 million requested to buy components that would be used in the first of the new subs, due to be included in the fiscal 1989 budget. Such "long lead-time" funds were an exception to Congress' firm rule that weapons purchases be "fully funded" — that is, that the Pentagon request an appropriation large enough to pay for the entire ship or an entire annual production run of tanks or planes. Congress traditionally had allowed long lead-time funding for warships' nuclear power plants, since they must be essentially completed before construction of the ship got very far along. But the Senate committee complained that the Navy had unnecessarily requested long-lead funding for too much other equipment destined for the *Seawolf*.

The panel recommended $335 million, slightly less than requested, for 24 of the LAMPS III anti-submarine helicopters carried by most warships, including seven for use on aircraft carriers and equipped with a different kind of underwater detection gear.

It denied the $53 million requested for six smaller LAMPS I anti-submarine helicopters, a type carried by some older ships.

The committee recommended buying seven of the nine requested P-3C long-range, land-based anti-submarine planes, approving $223 million of the $312 million requested.

As it had done for several years, the committee added to the bill funds to buy aircraft and other equipment the Coast Guard would use in its wartime role as part of the Navy. The fiscal 1987 add-on was $200 million.

Like the other defense funding committees, Senate Appropriations denied the $196 million requested to build four small mine sweepers. The Navy had canceled the program because of problems with the first ship of the class. The committee approved the Navy's decision to buy a mine sweeper of an existing design; however, it insisted that the ship be built in a U.S. shipyard. The Navy's plan, approved by the other committees, was to buy a production-line mine sweeper from a European shipyard with the

Congress Pares Military Construction Funds

Congress sliced President Reagan's $10.5 billion request for construction of military facilities by almost 20 percent to $8.7 billion in the continuing appropriations resolution (H J Res 738 — PL 99-591). *(Continuing resolution, p. 219)*

This kind of congressional whack out of the military building request had become routine in response to recent budget requests that sought increases on the order of 20 percent in military construction funds. For example, the fiscal 1987 budget request marked an increase of nearly $2.4 billion over the $8.1 billion available for military construction in fiscal 1986.

The most controversial proposal in the construction budget was the Navy's plan to build new facilities at Staten Island, N.Y., ($90.5 million) and at Everett, Wash., ($95.4 million) to provide "homeports" for the newly expanded fleet.

Before passing its $8.4 billion version of the military construction bill (HR 5052 — H Rept 99-648) by a 249-174 vote June 25, the House had voted 241-190 to deny all funds for the two projects. The Senate passed its $8.2 billion version of the bill (S Rept 99-368) Aug. 13, 59-41, after rejecting, 34-65, an amendment to delete funding for the projects. *(House vote 182 p. 56-H; vote 177, p. 54-H; Senate vote 230, p. 40-S; vote 181, p. 33-S; military construction authorization, p. 482)*

Conferees on H J Res 738 (H Rept 99-1005) approved $53 million for the New York site and $44 million for Everett.

In both chambers, the military construction bill became the vehicle for debate on President Reagan's proposal to give $100 million in aid to contra guerrillas fighting Nicaragua's leftist government. *(Contra aid, p. 394)*

Provisions

As cleared by Congress, H J Res 738 appropriated these funds for military construction projects *(amounts are in thousands of dollars)*:

	Budget Request	Final Amount
Army	$1,695,200	$1,260,110
(Advance funding for fiscal 1988-89)	383,000	435,000
Navy	1,814,100	1,376,715
Air Force	1,773,200	1,242,530
Defense Agencies	762,100	543,170
NATO Infrastructure	247,000	232,000
Reserve and National Guard	451,200	479,904
Family Housing	3,417,568	3,140,413
(portion applied to debt reduction)	(23,168)	(23,168)
Total appropriated	$ 10,543,368	$ 8,709,842
(portion applied to debt reduction)	−23,168	−23,168
Total available for new projects	**$ 10,520,200**	**$ 8,686,674**

intention of having a U.S. manufacturer copy it.

The request for a large, high-speed supply ship to replenish the food, fuel and ammunition stocks of a combat fleet ($613 million) was rejected as too expensive.

The committee approved with some reductions requests for two tankers ($259 million) designed to refuel other ships under way and for enlarging an existing tanker ($62 million).

Air and Sea Transport

With relatively small reductions, the committee approved the requests for the two largest cargo planes currently in production for the Pentagon:

- $1.9 billion for the last 21 of a planned fleet of huge C-5Bs.
- $89 million for eight KC-10 tankers.

But the committee argued that the Pentagon budget was too tight to begin the planned production of a new large cargo plane, the C-17, intended to haul tanks and other heavy equipment into primitive airstrips. It approved $363 million of the $612 million requested to continue developing the plane and denied the entire $217 million requested to prepare for production.

On the other hand, the committee increased to $431 million the amount requested for development of the hybrid airplane/helicopter called the Osprey. The budget requested $387 million. The Marine Corps intended to use the craft, beginning in 1991, to replace its fleet of helicopters that hauled assault troops and their vehicles ashore from an amphibious fleet. The committee's increase would accelerate design of another version of the craft that would fly off aircraft carriers to hunt submarines.

The panel also increased the budget request to buy commercial ships for the Navy's cargo reserve fleet. The Navy requested $28 million and the committee recommended $78 million.

Space Launchers

The committee added to the bill $2.96 billion to build a new space shuttle orbiter to replace the *Challenger*, which was destroyed in January.

The panel approved only $43 million of the $600 million included in the budget to reimburse the National Aeronautics and Space Administration (NASA) for Pentagon missions scheduled to fly on shuttle flights that had been canceled in the wake of the *Challenger* disaster. The committee also cut from the bill $170 million reflecting an Air Force decision to put in mothballs until 1992 the newly completed shuttle launch site at Vandenberg Air Force Base in California.

It recommended $130 million of the $208 million recommended to develop a successor to the space shuttle — the national aerospace plane, intended to take off and land like an airplane while being able to fly into orbit around the Earth.

The committee said that the current schedule for developing a test version of the plane was too optimistic. It ordered the administration to revise the schedule and to shift more of the burden of paying for the project from the Pentagon to NASA. ∎

$576 Billion Omnibus Funding Bill Approved

In its final hours, the 99th Congress approved the largest spending bill in the history of the nation.

The fiscal 1987 continuing appropriations measure (H J Res 738 — PL 99-591), which cleared Oct. 17, contained a total of $576 billion in spending authority.

The resolution combined all 13 regular annual appropriations bills into a mammoth single measure extending funding authority for most federal programs through Sept. 30, 1987. It incorporated four bills in versions as agreed to in previously completed conference agreements and the remaining nine as negotiated by conferees on H J Res 738. The four covered the legislative branch and the Departments of Labor, Education, Health and Human Services, Transportation, and Housing and Urban Development.

However, H J Res 738 did not include another $400 billion in fiscal 1987 federal spending — for Social Security, interest payments on the federal debt, most of the Medicare program and certain other federal activities — that was funded on a permanent basis.

President Reagan signed the final version of the measure into law on Oct. 30, replacing a flawed, earlier version. *(Public Law number, box, p. 221)*

Final action on the resolution was delayed for nearly three weeks after the end of fiscal 1986 by a long series of disputes, ranging from the fate of the revenue-sharing program to the manufacturing site for certain military training aircraft. Since existing funding authority for government activities had expired on Sept. 30, Congress was forced to pass a string of emergency, short-term spending bills in order to keep the federal government functioning. *(Stopgap measures, p. 223)*

Fiscal Austerity

Despite its huge size, H J Res 738 was viewed by some budget analysts as reflecting a marked trend to fiscal austerity. According to the Congressional Budget Office (CBO), total federal spending in fiscal year 1987 — including both the funds in H J Res 738 and those provided by permanent appropriations — would be less than 1 percent larger than the total for fiscal year 1986.

A prime reason for the small increase was the congressional clampdown on military spending. For the second year, Congress held growth in defense appropriations to a rate below that of inflation. Funding for military programs was set at $290 billion.

Other signs of budget restraint in the bill were a $1 billion cut in foreign aid programs from the fiscal 1986 level, and the termination of funding for revenue sharing. Although a few programs, such as research on acquired immune deficiency syndrome (AIDS), received increases over the previous year, most categories of non-defense spending were frozen at fiscal 1986 levels or reduced.

According to House Appropriations Committee Chairman Jamie L. Whitten, D-Miss., the spending total of H J Res 738 was $1.6 billion below the total budget authority allotted to the Appropriations Committee under the fiscal 1987 budget resolution (S Con Res 120).

The measure assumed that obligation levels would produce $560 billion in outlays — money actually spent during the year. Whitten said that the bill would be $2.5 billion below the budget resolution limit on total outlays.

The Gramm-Rudman-Hollings anti-deficit law (PL 99-177) required each committee to adhere to its budget resolution limit; subcommittee bills — such as the individual appropriations bills — also could not exceed individual subcommittee limits. Except for the foreign operations section, which appeared to be about $300 million over the individual outlay limit for that bill, other sections were said to meet their limits.

Whitten said the totals cited above did not take into account a $1.7 billion appropriation in the bill for a new anti-drug-abuse initiative. With that money added in, Whitten said, the resolution would exceed the budget authority limit by $38 million, but still come below the outlay limit by $1.5 billion, since only $700 million of the drug initiative budget authority would be spent in fiscal 1987.

Conferees dropped an across-the-board spending reduction, opposed by the Reagan administration, that the House had provided to offset the drug spending.

Supplemental Needed

The continuing resolution paved the way for another, "supplemental" appropriations bill in 1987 by assuming but not appropriating for a 3 percent federal pay raise that was expected to cost as much as $2.5 billion.

Also, the Agriculture Department's Commodity Credit Corporation (CCC) received $16.8 billion to cover past losses associated with farm price-support programs. But the CCC routinely would come back to the till during the year and H J Res 738 assumed but did not appropriate an additional $3 billion, if requested by the president.

Foreign aid programs were also expected to need future injections of cash — perhaps $1 billion to $2 billion — to meet U.S. commitments to international development banks, to restore some of the cuts from Reagan's budget request, and to augment $50 million added at the last minute for aid to earthquake victims in El Salvador. As the House acted on the bill, State Department officials were already meeting to discuss their supplemental request.

Another notable feature of H J Res 738 was that it appropriated some funds immediately but specified that they could not be spent for most or all of fiscal 1987. Such

Individual Appropriations

delayed spending did not count against Gramm-Rudman's binding budget allocation limits for fiscal 1987, although as Rep. David R. Obey, D-Wis., said, "It does add to the deficit."

For replacing the destroyed space shuttle *Challenger* the measure appropriated $2.4 billion in budget authority, about $270 million of which was requested for fiscal 1987 outlays. The conference agreement, however, provided just $100 million in outlays, to be available after Aug. 15, 1987.

House Committee Action

The House Appropriations Committee approved an initial version of the continuing resolution (H J Res 730 — H Rept 99-831) by voice vote Sept. 16.

As presented to the Appropriations Committee by Whitten, the resolution included eight appropriations bills as passed by the House: those for agriculture; commerce; the District of Columbia; energy and water; labor, health and human services; military construction; transportation; and the Treasury and Postal Service.

Three others — for defense, foreign operations, and housing and urban development — were incorporated as previously reported by the Appropriations Committee.

One, for the legislative branch, was included in the form approved by a House-Senate conference.

Whitten's draft also included:

- A $2.1 billion appropriation for the new anti-drug initiative approved the previous week by the House. *(Anti-drug initiative, p. 92)*
- About $9.7 billion in appropriations for programs for which fiscal 1987 reauthorizations had not yet been completed. These were primarily health and education programs, but the total also included $3.4 billion for revenue sharing, to extend that program at about 75 percent of its current level.
- Two across-the-board percentage reductions totaling 1.25 percent in all discretionary programs, one linked specifically to funding the anti-drug initiative, the other devoted to bringing the overall discretionary spending total down to the so-called "302 allocation." The allocation represented the total amount allowed by the budget resolution for programs under the committee's jurisdiction.

Whitten explained to the committee that the draft bill's spending total fell below the committee's $261.2 billion allocation for budget authority in discretionary programs, but was $3.3 billion more than the $264.5 billion allocation for fiscal 1987 discretionary outlays.

In the House, under the Gramm-Rudman-Hollings anti-deficit law, a bill exceeding a committee's budget authority allocation was subject to a point of order, which, if upheld, would prevent the full chamber from acting on the measure. Under stricter Gramm-Rudman rules for the Senate, objections could be raised to a bill exceeding allocations for either budget authority or outlays.

Despite technical difficulties in estimating outlays, Gramm-Rudman authors sought to clamp them down for several reasons. The budget deficit was reckoned in outlays. And appropriated but unused budget authority was occasionally shifted among Appropriations subcommittees, resulting in outlays that were higher than anticipated in budget resolutions.

The House Democratic leadership had already decided that the chamber would observe outlay limits.

The committee's ranking Republican, Silvio O. Conte of Massachusetts, senior Democrat Sidney R. Yates of Illinois, and several others heatedly objected to the idea of indiscriminate cuts and to the precedent of such an action. The committee traditionally had fought across-the-board appropriations cuts on the House floor, arguing that such blanket cuts ride roughshod over legislators' responsibility to set priorities.

Conte angrily warned that if the committee backed the cuts, "You're gonna be like a eunuch" in future appropriations floor fights. As for the outlay problem, he said, "Let the Senate worry about it."

Yates proposed what he called a "pay as you go" amendment, which would make appropriations for the drug program and revenue sharing available only if legislation providing new revenues specifically for these purposes was enacted.

The committee rejected Yates' amendment by a 24-28 vote. It then adopted by voice vote Conte's amendment striking the across-the-board cuts. These two votes amounted to a decision not to neutralize the deficit impact of the two programs.

House GOP leader and committee member Robert H. Michel of Illinois tried later to eliminate the revenue-sharing funds. The panel rejected his amendment by a 15-29 show of hands, as one committee member loudly imitated chicken clucks.

Michel warned that the $3.4 billion added for revenue sharing would increase the deficit and the probability of triggering the Gramm-Rudman across-the-board cutting process.

He urged members to abide by previous congressional decisions to let the program die. Congress repealed the program authorization in the fiscal 1986 budget reconciliation bill (PL 99-272), and although a reauthorization (HR 1400) of the program was approved by the House Government Operations Committee in April, no further action had occurred on it. *(Story, p. 555)*

John P. Murtha, D-Pa., who with Whitten claimed the revenue-sharing amendment, said that the loss of program funds would devastate his district. Whitten said, "This is a small amount — but it is a big amount in the budget of every little community."

More Than 60 Amendments

In all, the committee worked its way through more than 60 amendments, reflecting national concerns of members, and also parochial wants, such as reopening a Department of Housing and Urban Development office in Springfield, Ill., and buying a roof to protect a collection of steam engines in Pennsylvania.

The committee turned down few proposals, although it did balk at an amendment by Rep. Bob Livingston, R-La., to force the granting of a patent for a device claimed to be a perpetual motion machine.

Among the amendments included in the committee bill were those by:

- Conte, to impose a one-year, $250,000 limitation on farm program payments in loan, disaster and subsidy programs for 1986-87 crops not yet under federal contract. The Senate Appropriations Committee rejected a $500,000 payment limitation amendment to the fiscal 1987 agriculture appropriations bill (HR 5177).

Conte argued that the current $50,000 limit was being evaded by corporate farms collecting multibillion-dollar farm payments. Whitten agreed with Conte that the huge payments were politically bad for the farm programs, but said Conte's limit was too low.

Public Law Number Changed

The omnibus funding measure for fiscal 1987, which Congress approved in the closing hours of the session, received two different public law numbers.

After H J Res 738 cleared Congress on Oct. 17, it was rushed to the White House for President Reagan's signature on Oct. 18. However, that version of the resolution was missing two pages that specified funding for certain federal buildings.

After the error was discovered, a correct copy of the funding measure was forwarded for presidential approval. Reagan signed that second version Oct. 30, and officials decided to give it a new public law number.

The earlier, flawed version was designated PL 99-500. In the future, however, the $576 billion money bill was to be known as PL 99-591.

- By Vic Fazio, D-Calif., to impose a one-year moratorium on prepayment of certain federal low-income rural housing loans, to keep property owners from ending commitments for low unit rents.
- By Martin Olav Sabo, D-Minn., to incorporate defense procurement reform provisions from the pending defense authorization bill (HR 4428). *(Procurement, p. 475)*
- By Fazio, to prevent what he called "excessive" charges for cleansing irrigation water in the Westlands Water District in California from being levied on those using project water to generate electricity.
- By William Lehman, D-Fla., to require the Federal Aviation Administration to begin procedures requiring small, private aircraft flying in regulated airspace to carry equipment to register the aircraft's location and altitude on flight control radar.
- By Murtha, to add a House-passed labor bill (HR 281) barring a practice known as "double breasting," in which a construction firm seeks to avoid dealing with unions by creating and shifting work to a non-unionized subsidiary. *(Story, p. 595)*
- By Robert J. Mrazek, D-N.Y., to require imported wine, beer and distilled spirits to comply with U.S. additive standards.
- By Steny H. Hoyer, D-Md., to give federal civilian and military employees a 3 percent pay raise, as in the fiscal 1987 budget resolution.

House Floor Action

The House narrowly approved a revised version of the continuing resolution (H J Res 738) Sept. 25. The 201-200 vote for the measure reflected sharp controversies over a wide array of topics, including spending levels, arms control strictures and a new limit on government payments to farmers. *(Vote 383, p. 108-H)*

The measure would appropriate $561.9 billion in new spending authority for every function of the government that had no permanent appropriation. In outlays the bill would yield an estimated $558 billion.

The legislation combined the 13 regular appropriations bills, mostly in versions passed by the House. The spending levels in those bills and many of their policy provisions, such as a requirement that President Reagan honor those parts of the SALT II treaty he had repudiated, provoked vigorous veto threats, as did the entire package. *(Arms control, p. 462)*

The House Appropriations Committee, citing CBO calculations, said H J Res 738 was within critical budgetary "allocations," and therefore complied with Gramm-Rudman. But administration budget director James C. Miller III, using different calculations, said that it did not.

Funding levels were only one of the measure's many controversies. The hairline House vote, whose outcome was in doubt until a final "aye" cast by Ronald V. Dellums, D-Calif., reflected several major factors. Top leadership aides said the "nays" showed Republican hostility to the arms control language and members' soreness at the loss of the revenue sharing program for cities and towns.

An abrupt attempt by Whitten to fund revenue sharing was thwarted by the House Rules Committee. The Rules panel Sept. 24 refused to let the committee bill (H J Res 730) come to the House floor unless Whitten excised the revenue sharing appropriation. It then took an unusual first step toward introducing its own continuing resolution, omitting revenue sharing. This reflected anger among committee members of both parties who found revenue sharing an unaffordable luxury in a time of deficit spending.

Typical was Butler Derrick, D-S.C., who told the House that the extra $3.4 billion pushed the bill beyond budget limits Congress imposed on itself.

Said Derrick, "It's time to buckle up our britches and understand that we've got to live up to some of the things we've been talking about."

Whitten had sought to offset the revenue sharing spending with an across-the-board cut that was rejected in his committee.

Rules did not act solely because of its own members' views. Vehement public and private objections by Rep. Jack Brooks, D-Texas, chairman of the committee with jurisdiction over revenue sharing, were another important factor.

And, Derrick said, "a howl literally went up" at a party caucus as members insisted that they be spared a public choice on whether to let the popular program die, continue it in violation of budget limits, or continue it by cutting into other programs.

Confronted with an adamant Rules Committee, a displeased Whitten introduced a new version of the continuing resolution, identical to that reported by his Appropriations Committee, except that it excluded the revenue sharing money and included a 0.34 percent across-the-board cut to provide $2.1 billion for the anti-drug-abuse initiative.

It was Whitten's substitute for the committee bill that came before the House under a tight rule (H Res 560) permitting only one amendment, on the farm payment limit.

Whitten himself said he told the bill's many critics, "I was more opposed to it than they were."

Besides strong conflicts generated by revenue sharing and arms control, these factors shaped the House vote:

- Continued objections by a number of Democrats to the $100 million in aid to the "contra" rebels fighting the Nicaraguan government. The funding was part of the military construction appropriations bill that had been folded into the omnibus measure. *(Contra aid details, p. 394)*
- Generic displeasure of fiscal conservatives — "There's

an awful lot of people that just like to vote against big spending," is how Fazio put it.

And Trent Lott, R-Miss., baptized the measure the "bloated omnibus money bill — BOMB for short." But still he advised colleagues against blocking it: "Let's go on and shove it through and get it vetoed and then come back and write a clean bill."

- Uneasiness with procedure: Both the across-the-board cut and the tight rule rankled many members. Conte told the House he would lead a revolution if he were not a member of the Appropriations Committee (and thus able to influence legislation in committee).

"You have nothing to say about what's in the continuing resolution, and that's wrong." he said. Conte, who stripped the across-the-board cut from the bill in committee, was infuriated to see it return in the floor version. "It's a travesty," he fumed.

- Unexpected timing: The vote occurred about 8 p.m., an hour before members expected, and the margin might not have been so narrow had some or all of the 32 members who did not vote done so.

As passed by the House, there were only two changes in the committee bill besides the omission of revenue-sharing money and the addition of the across-the-board cut.

The committee bill included the version of the Housing and Urban Development bill (HR 5313) reported by committee, but the House-passed bill substituted the version as passed by the House. Also, Conte on the floor was permitted to revise his committee amendment establishing a new, $250,000 limit on federal farm payments.

Senate Committee Action

The Senate Appropriations Committee reported its version of the continuing resolution by voice vote Sept. 26 (S Rept 99-500). The administration was far happier with the measure, which appropriated $556.1 billion in new budget authority, than it was with the House bill. Budget director Miller wrote committee chairman Mark O. Hatfield, R-Ore., that if certain policy differences were resolved and if a satisfactory separate budget "reconciliation" bill passed, the Senate version's funding levels would be acceptable to the president.

Though apparently smaller than the House bill, the Senate version omitted a $17 billion House appropriation for farm program expenditures of the CCC.

Hatfield brought before his committee a draft comprising the 13 regular appropriations bills reflecting their current status — as passed by the Senate or as reported by committee in that chamber.

In the two areas of foremost concern to the administration, the Senate measure provided $277 billion in budget authority for defense programs, compared with $265.2 billion in the House version. For foreign aid, the Senate provided $13.1 billion in budget authority, the House, $13.0 billion.

The $17 billion omission of CCC funds was explained by a Senate aide as a "scoring convention," reflecting the views of the White House and the Senate committee that the corporation should have an indefinite appropriation, providing money as required without the need for a discrete dollar appropriation, either in a regular money bill or in a supplemental appropriation.

The CCC funds did not count against the Senate committee's budget "allocation" limit, according to this aide.

Citing time pressures, Hatfield successfully urged committee members to withhold both amendments and the directions to specific agencies or programs that some members liked to write into committee reports.

"I reject the prevailing view that this [bill] is going to be vetoed anyway so why show any restraint," Hatfield said. He predicted that the Senate action would take "maybe two days and two nights."

The Senate bill included the policy changes in Senate appropriations bills, some of which the administration found objectionable. But there was nothing of the magnitude of certain House policy changes, such as nuclear testing restrictions, the SALT language and a major labor law revision.

Senate Floor Action

The Senate passed H J Res 738 by an 82-13 vote Oct. 3. *(Vote 330, p. 54-S)*

Action on the measure stretched over five days and one long night, as senators loaded on dozens of amendments. Most of the amendments to the bill, which appropriated $558 billion, involved parochial issues with neither budgetary nor national policy impact. Exceptions were $200 million in additional aid for the Philippines and $1.5 billion for the new anti-drug-abuse initiative. Both amendments were subject to lengthy negotiations and were adopted just before final passage.

For the most part, senators rejected controversial amendments on the grounds that they were unrelated to the bill or that they breached budget limits. Issues ranging from abortion to an alleged Soviet "spy nest" at the United Nations to farmers' woes were paraded through the chamber, only to be turned aside after time-consuming debate and recorded votes.

The Senate bill did not contain a series of House provisions, strenuously opposed by the White House, that banned most nuclear tests, required compliance with portions of the SALT II arms control treaty and barred anti-satellite tests and chemical weapons procurement.

The only time the arms control issue was raised directly in Senate debate on H J Res 738 was when Appropriations Chairman Mark O. Hatfield, R-Ore., passionately urged Democrats to insist on the House provisions.

Hatfield vehemently denounced Reagan's advisers: "They dream of the heavens littered with weapons of war." Their goal, according to Hatfield, was "wreckage of fragile international institutions and agreements, which however imperfect, are all that stand between us and the law of the jungle."

As for Democrats, Hatfield charged them to "face up to the facts. There are only a handful of Republicans ... who will challenge this madness. You are the loyal opposition. Take a stand. The real issue is whether we are going to turn this nuclear juggernaut back.

"I get the impression that you don't know what you're against — let alone what you are for. Those people downtown really have you baffled."

When Hatfield concluded, Ernest F. Hollings, D-S.C., was on his feet to offer an amendment naming a federal courthouse in Aiken, South Carolina.

Preventing Amendments

The Senate voting showed some moderation in senatorial habits of loading many unrelated amendments onto omnibus money bills. Hatfield announced as debate began

Sept. 29 that he would object to any amendment with broad, national policy implications, or that caused the bill to exceed its budget limits.

Amendments that changed authorizing statutes or otherwise constituted unrelated legislation were also unacceptable, he said.

The omnibus measure was governed by separate dollar limits for each of the separate appropriations bills it contained. Hatfield said each bill was already at its so-called section 302(b) allocation limit, which meant proposals to increase spending were subject to a new objection, authorized by Gramm-Rudman. To overturn such an objection required 60 votes — 9 more than the maximum needed to adopt a Senate floor amendment.

On a daily basis Hatfield, who had been hostile to other aspects of Gramm-Rudman, successfully defeated spending amendments using this device. Other amendments fell to objections that they were not germane.

The budget and germaneness objections were deployed by Republican leaders to discourage amendments, and also to defuse difficult issues by casting them as procedural votes. It was clear from the first that the GOP leaders controlled enough votes to enforce their objections. But that did not quell the desire to present amendments, complete with time-consuming speeches and recorded votes.

As the week wore on, the discipline grated upon senators who said only more fortunate colleagues on the Appropriations panel were able to leave an imprint on the legislation — in committee.

The individual bills making up the omnibus measure in fact included a number of provisions that were neither germane nor free from the taint of changes in authorizations — thus violating Hatfield's criteria for floor amendments. Several times, the Senate agreed to extract such provisions from H J Res 738.

One such provision would have revised antitrust law affecting beer distributors. Howard M. Metzenbaum, D-Ohio, and several colleagues, objecting that the changes would foster regional distribution monopolies, blocked Senate action on the bill on Sept. 29 and 30.

Sponsor Dennis DeConcini, D-Ariz., disputed Metzenbaum's interpretation, but by mid-afternoon Sept. 30, Hatfield ascertained with a 56-41 procedural vote that DeConcini was four votes short of the 60 needed to end a filibuster. Hours later, the Senate agreed by voice vote to delete the antitrust provision. *(Vote 303, p. 50-S)*

Philippine Aid, Other Issues

The only other issue debated in the first two days was $200 million in extra economic aid for the Philippines; in the first of three votes on the issue, the Senate on Sept. 29 refused by a 43-51 vote to accept an amendment by Robert C. Byrd, D-W.Va., earmarking the Philippines aid within a larger economic support fund. *(Vote 301, p. 50-S)*

On Oct. 1, the Senate spent much of the day on a multi-part farm aid amendment by David L. Boren, D-Okla.; it then refused on a 45-53 vote to support Boren's motion to waive a budget objection to his amendment. *(Vote 304, p. 51-S)*

Ted Stevens, R-Alaska, objected that the amendment would put the agriculture section of H J Res 738 over its spending limit by $2.9 billion and that a key provision, authorizing early repayment of Rural Electrification Administration loans, would yield short-term gains but multi-billion-dollar long-term losses.

Boren responded that by another measure of spending his proposal actually saved more than $4 billion.

On Oct. 2, the Senate slogged through a marathon session on the bill, setting it aside for several hours to debate and vote on the president's veto of a bill (HR 4868) imposing sanctions on South Africa, and recessing at 5:28 the following morning.

Temporary Extensions OK'd

Delays in enactment of the omnibus fiscal 1987 spending bill forced Congress to rely on a series of short-term emergency funding measures to keep the federal government operating.

Despite their efforts, however, members of Congress were unable to prevent a temporary shutdown of non-essential federal operations on Oct. 17, when authority for the government to spend money lapsed. According to the House Civil Service Subcommittee, the cost of a government shutdown was about $62 million a day.

The first stopgap measure was H J Res 743 (PL 99-434), which cleared on Sept. 30, the last day of fiscal year 1986. The House passed the measure, which ran through Oct. 8, by a 315-101 vote. The Senate promptly cleared it by voice vote. Under the resolution, funding levels were set at the following levels, depending on the status of individual appropriations bills: the lower of appropriations for fiscal 1986 or of amounts in House-passed bills; the lower of amounts in House- or Senate-passed bills; or the amounts in conference agreements. *(Vote 391, p. 110-H)*

On the day that measure expired, the House passed a new resolution (H J Res 748) by a 264-151 vote. The measure, which contained the funding formula in H J Res 743, extended through Oct. 10. *(Vote 407, p. 116-H)*

The Senate passed H J Res 748 by voice vote later on Oct. 8. However, President Reagan vetoed the resolution, objecting to language repealing a prohibition on rehiring air traffic controllers fired in a 1981 labor dispute. *(Veto message, p. 34-D)*

The House then passed a new resolution (H J Res 750 — PL 99-464), dropping the disputed language but otherwise the same as H J Res 748, by a 255-150 vote. The Senate approved it by voice vote, and the president signed it. *(Vote 409, p. 116-H)*

On Oct. 10, the House passed H J Res 751 (PL 99-465), which continued government funding through Oct. 15. The measure was approved 235-143, after which the Senate gave its approval by voice vote. *(Vote 424, p. 120-H)*

Finally, the House passed a one-day extension in the early morning hours of Oct. 16. The vote on the resolution (H J Res 753 — PL 99-491) was 260-97; the Senate gave its assent by voice vote a few hours later. *(Vote 441, p 124-H)*

The expiration of H J Res 753 at midnight, Oct. 16, left the government without funding authority on Oct. 17. With Congress still arguing over provisions of H J Res 738, the Office of Management and Budget sent many government workers home at noon. The full-year funding measure was not cleared until later that evening.

Accepted by voice vote during this period was an amendment increasing by $24 million funding for Fulbright scholarships to be unavailable until the first day of fiscal 1988. And the Senate agreed to eliminate language transferring supervision of airline mergers from the Department of Transportation to the Justice Department.

Other successful amendments during the all-night session included a transfer of $132 million for disaster relief from the Agricultural Credit Insurance fund, and a change relating to life insurance provisions in the just-passed tax overhaul bill (HR 3838), described as "technical" by sponsor J. Bennett Johnston, D-La.

Metzenbaum won an amendment transferring $500,000 from the Commodity Futures Trading Commission to development of "orphan drugs" for rare diseases.

In other action, the Senate refused by a 46-53 vote to accept a proposal by John Heinz, R-Pa. to withhold all U.S. contributions to the United Nations until the president certified that steps were being taken to combat alleged Soviet employees' kickbacks and spying there. It later rejected by a 32-60 vote a second amendment cutting U.N. funding. *(Vote 315, p. 52-S; vote 322, p. 53-S)*

Senators also turned back, by a 57-41 vote, a second Byrd attempt to provide $200 million more in aid to the Philippines, by earmarking it from a special fund for Central American nations. *(Vote 309, p. 52-S)*

Other rejected amendments included one by Jeff Bingaman, D-N.M., to strike language permitting arms export loans to be converted to grants. Supporters of the amendment said it would eventually cost the government $6.9 billion in forgone interest. The amendment was tabled by a 55-43 vote. *(Vote 310, p. 52-S)*

By 5 a.m. the Senate had adopted 28 amendments, largely local interest matters. Hatfield, hoarse by now, vowed to press on, but Byrd angrily objected that colleagues were both tired and sick.

When debate resumed in mid-morning, the Senate rejected by a 34-64 vote an amendment by Gordon J. Humphrey, R-N.H., revoking the tax-exempt status of institutions providing abortions. *(Vote 323, p. 53-S)*

More local interest provisions were approved, as was an amendment by Nancy Landon Kassebaum, R-Kan., striking a restructuring of aid to Africa. Boren won a speedup of "deficiency" payments made to farmers when crop prices were low. John Melcher, D-Mont., succeeded with an amendment urging more use of U.S. farm surpluses for domestic poverty programs and for the Philippines and several other nations.

Finally, the Senate by an 82-14 vote approved a Robert Dole, R-Kan., motion providing that $200 million in extra Philippines aid be taken from other foreign assistance programs, none of which was to be cut by more than 3 percent. *(Vote 328, p. 54-S)*

The anti-drug money, approved by voice vote, was not offset by other cuts, and thus pushed the bill over budget.

Major Issues Resolved

Some of the conspicuous controversies associated with H J Res 738 were resolved in the final version as follows:

- For programs of the Department of Defense and military programs in the Department of Energy and elsewhere, H J Res 738 provided total obligational authority of $290 billion, of which $284.8 billion was new budget authority, and the remainder was previously appropriated budget authority that was reassigned to certain programs.

  The outlay figure for defense was $278 billion.

  President Reagan had requested $320 billion in budget authority; the budget resolution provided $292 billion.

- For foreign operations, the measure appropriated $13.37 billion, $2.1 billion less than Reagan requested. A House-passed outlay cap that the administration strongly opposed was dropped, as was a Senate-passed provision converting past U.S. loans for weapons purchases by foreign nations to grants.

  The much-disputed $100 million in aid for "contra" rebels fighting the Nicaragua government was included in the bill, as was a $200 million increase in Philippines aid voted at the end of the session.

- A Jamie L. Whitten, D-Miss., amendment added in conference requiring the Agriculture Department to refinance loans for farmers was softened to non-binding report language.
- A reauthorization (HR 7) of child nutrition programs, added during Senate debate, was retained by conferees; another Senate amendment, striking down a District of Columbia law barring insurance discrimination against persons testing positive for the acquired immune deficiency syndrome (AIDS) virus, was dropped.

Conference Action

Conference action on H J Res 738 extended for more than a week, with conferees working in small groups to hammer out compromises.

The most contentious issues dividing the House and Senate were a series of defense-related House provisions. House language on nuclear testing, arms control, anti-satellite tests and chemical weapons — as well as related positions on aggregate military spending levels and funding for the strategic defense initiative — was unacceptable to the administration. House-passed funding levels for defense were markedly lower than those of the Senate.

The primary battleground over the House provisions was not the conference on H J Res 738, however, but separate negotiations on the defense authorization bill. The fight took place just as Reagan was preparing to leave for Reykjavik, Iceland, for a summit meeting with Soviet leader Mikhail S. Gorbachev on Oct. 11-12. *(Summit meeting, p. 459)*

Reluctant to appear to be undercutting the president as he headed for summit talks, House leaders agreed Oct. 10 to drop their provisions.

The second most difficult fight concerned foreign aid. Rep. Obey was bitterly resisting a Senate plan to convert arms purchase loans to grants, saying the U.S. government must not give away money to foreign nations when it was charging American students and veterans more for government-backed loans and refusing to forgive or restructure the agonizing debts of American farmers.

Obey was also embroiled in a fight over the technical but critically important matter of how foreign aid funding was counted for purposes of compliance with Gramm-Rudman budget limits.

Agriculture spending presented a third difficult cluster

of issues, as conferees fought over funding levels, the payment limitation, and an administration-backed Senate plan to eliminate a specific, dollar appropriation for the CCC.

The House had included nearly $17 billion for the corporation, which managed farm price-support programs and which was reimbursed after the fact for its losses of earlier years.

It was common for the CCC to need extra money once or several times during a given year; its needs were invariably urgent and gave rise to supplemental appropriations bills that became high-priority legislative vehicles for other amendments.

The administration wanted badly to rid itself of this phenomenon, by simply specifying that the CCC would be reimbursed as needed without a specific appropriation. But Whitten, citing the need for accountability and other factors, objected strongly.

Agriculture conferees decided Oct. 10 to include $16.8 billion for the CCC, with an additional $3 billion available if requested by the president. And Whitten created a new difficulty by adding a new requirement for the refinancing of loans held by farmers suffering disaster losses.

Conferees approved their version of H J Res 738 Oct. 15 (H Rept 99-1005). However, they did not resolve differences on six items, which they returned to the two chambers for final decisions.

Final Action

The House approved the agreement later Oct. 15, by a 235-172 vote. *(Vote 436, p. 122-H)*

Then the House conducted a series of separate votes on the items that conferees had been unable to compromise. Having acceded to the Senate position on two, the House reasserted its stand on the others and sent these items together with the conference agreement on to the Senate.

On Oct. 16 the Senate by voice vote adopted the conference agreement and then, like the House, had to deal separately with the unresolved items. This situation opened the way procedurally for last-ditch attempts by senators to reopen other questions, including a dispute over funding for military training aircraft, which was to delay final Senate action for nearly a day.

The vehicle for the aircraft amendment was one of the items in disagreement, funding for 25 to 30 federal buildings and similar projects.

Barry Goldwater, R-Ariz., proposed to amend this with language virtually eliminating from H J Res 738 $151 million in fiscal 1987 for the T-46 trainer aircraft, which was manufactured primarily in Long Island, New York. If Goldwater succeeded, a rival trainer aircraft, the T-37, manufactured in Kansas, would benefit and New York would lose about 3,500 jobs.

Goldwater's move reflected a bitter struggle between defense authorizing and Appropriations committees and it brought sharp protests from New York Republican Alfonse M. D'Amato.

D'Amato vowed to hold up a vote on Goldwater's amendment indefinitely, saying the T-46 had been slandered with "propaganda." An adamant Goldwater replied that he had no quarrel with the plane itself but that "the Air Force doesn't *want* it."

Appropriations Chairman Hatfield tried twice without success to break the deadlock, which was not resolved until late in the afternoon of Oct. 17.

At that time the principals announced a compromise, accepted by voice vote, that looked more like capitulation to Goldwater.

His amendment was modified to reflect restrictive language already in the defense authorization bill, that neither fiscal 1986 nor fiscal 1987 funds could be spent until "fly-off" competition of the T-46 and other aircraft was completed, by January 1988.

The night before, Hatfield had sought to kill Goldwater's amendment, but the Senate voted 69-21, on Hatfield's motion, that Goldwater's amendment was germane. *(Vote 345, p. 56-S)*

Again, after midnight, Hatfield said efforts to negotiate a solution with high-ranking military officials, including the secretary of the Air Force, had failed, and he tried to kill both the federal building amendment and the proposed Goldwater rider. That Hatfield motion lost on a 29-62 vote and the Senate recessed until later that morning, Oct. 17. *(Vote 349, 57-S)*

Finally, the airplane compromise was announced and accepted; then the Senate agreed by voice vote to accept the House version of the federal buildings amendment, which included money for several projects that had not been authorized.

Earlier, in the Oct. 16 session, the Senate dispatched the other items in disagreement that came from the House. It decided to reject two House-passed provisions. One barred construction firms from evading union strictures by shifting work to non-union subsidiaries; the other, a "Buy-America" rule, required that half the materials and labor used in offshore oil-drilling rigs be of U.S. origin. Both provisions were opposed by the administration.

Senators agreed by voice vote to accept a House-passed $250,000 limit on federal payments to farmers after hearing from Thad Cochran, R-Miss., that the limit was ineffective.

The Senate also accepted House revisions in a Senate amendment transferring operation of Dulles and National airports in Washington, D.C., from the federal government to a regional authority.

Senators' rejection of the labor and "Buy America" provisions meant that H J Res 738 returned once more to the House. That chamber quickly acceded to the Senate decisions on these two items and the public buildings and airplane language, thus completing congressional action on the measure. ∎

HEALTH
EDUCATION
WELFARE

CQ

Health/Education/Welfare

After five years of spending cuts and partisan bickering, Congress in 1986 finally settled some major social policy questions and set the stage for addressing others.

Years of negotiation culminated in successful efforts to reauthorize federal aid to higher education and to provide a variety of services for low-income individuals. Congress also made the first major adjustments in three years in Medicare, the federal health insurance program for the elderly, and broadened eligibility for Medicaid, the federal-state health program for the poor.

In nearly all cases, Congress defied the wishes of the Reagan administration and voted to restore or increase funding for social programs that had suffered cutbacks during President Reagan's first term.

Health

There was new leadership within the Reagan administration on health and welfare policy. Otis R. Bowen took over in December 1985 as secretary of the embattled Department of Health and Human Services (HHS). He succeeded Margaret M. Heckler, a former Republican member of the House from Massachusetts (1967-83), who had been criticized as a weak administrator. Heckler became ambassador to Ireland after leaving HHS.

A retired family physician and former two-term Republican governor of Indiana, "Doc" Bowen proceeded to reorganize the department in short order, filling long-vacant policy positions and generally restoring HHS to its role as a player in the policy process.

Although Congress continued to spurn administration cost-cutting proposals in the health realm, Bowen himself enjoyed considerable respect, and in many cases downright affection, from Republican and Democratic members alike. His late 1986 proposal — ultimately accepted by Reagan — to expand the federal Medicare program to cover the acute-care costs of catastrophic illness won him few friends in the conservative White House, but it brought accolades from lawmakers. The Bowen plan was expected to be the starting point for one of the major health policy debates of 1987.

Medicare Changes

Congress made substantial changes in Medicare in back-to-back fiscal 1986 and fiscal 1987 budget reconciliation bills. The changes were the first of any magnitude since 1983, when lawmakers overhauled the way Medicare paid hospitals, shifting from a cost-based reimbursement system to a "prospective payment system" (PPS) that set fixed fees for treating patients with particular types of illness or injury.

In 1986, lawmakers concerned with health policy sought to ensure that the PPS system did not compromise the quality of care for the 33 million beneficiaries of Medicare. Complaints abounded that hospitals, spurred by financial incentives to reduce the number of days patients spent in their care, were releasing Medicare patients "sicker and quicker." Congress moved to discourage such premature discharges by forcing hospitals to notify patients of their rights to appeal, without loss of coverage, if they felt they were being sent home too soon.

And while initial data showed that the PPS system was helping to curb medical costs, medical inflation continued at a rate well above that for the rest of the economy, rising 7.7 percent in the 12-month period ending Nov. 30, 1986, while the overall Consumer Price Index climbed only 1.3 percent.

In an effort to hold down the out-of-pocket expense borne by Medicare patients, Congress capped the hospital "deductible," the amount beneficiaries were required to pay before Medicare began to cover the cost of a hospital stay. The rising deductible was an unintended byproduct of the PPS system. It served to focus attention on the fact that for the first time since Medicare was created in 1965, the elderly were spending more than 15 percent of their income for health care costs.

Medicaid

Congress repeatedly defied the Reagan administration over Medicaid, the federal-state health insurance program for the poor. It not only rejected administration requests for program cuts, but acted twice to expand eligibility for the progam in an effort to lower what child advocacy groups called the nation's embarrassing infant mortality rate. In two bills advertised as deficit-reduction packages, Congress required states to extend Medicaid coverage for pre- and post-natal care to poor women pregnant with their first child, then later allowed states to offer Medicaid coverage to pregnant women and to children up to age 1 in families with incomes below the poverty line, but too high to qualify for Medicaid automatically.

Mandated Benefits, Vaccine Compensation

Congress in 1986 also fired what many predicted would be the opening shot in a battle with business over mandating benefits. Over the business community's heated objections, Congress required employers of 20 or more people who offer health insurance to allow employees who are laid off to continue to receive insurance coverage at the group rate. The law also required employers to offer continued insurance to dependents of deceased workers.

In an 11th hour compromise, lawmakers dispatched several controversial proposals by rolling them into a massive omnibus health package. One section created a no-fault compensation system for the families of children injured or killed as a result of side effects of vaccines to prevent common childhood diseases. The bill also allowed, in limited situations, the export of drugs not yet approved for use in the United States. Both measures had been hotly debated since the beginning of the Congress. In order to garner support, members also included in the package bills to repeal the nation's basic health planning law and to set up a nationwide computer network to maintain and disseminate information about physicians who had been disciplined or on whose behalf a malpractice settlement had been made.

Education

Education remained a spending priority in 1986, as lawmakers struggled to address charges that the nation was losing its ability to compete with other industrialized countries. Congress boosted funding for a program that provided grants to schools to help provide remedial education for disadvantaged students by nearly half a billion dollars, and added another $400 million to programs to aid education for the handicapped.

Congress compromised on legislation reauthorizing programs that provided aid for education of the handicapped, bolstering incentives for states to begin education efforts at age 3, instead of age 5 as required by federal law. A Senate version of the bill would have required states to begin schooling for the handicapped at age 3.

But the poor and handicapped were not the only beneficiaries of the somewhat more open congressional pocketbook. Spurning Reagan administration proposals to cut back significantly on the amount of aid available to middle-class college students, Congress approved a five-year extension of the law authorizing most of the higher education loan programs, including more than $10 billion for fiscal 1987 alone. The bill tightened eligibility standards for federal aid only slightly, while raising loan limits and vastly expanding aid eligibility to students enrolled less than half time.

Welfare

Poverty continued to decline in 1985, the Census Bureau reported, but with 14.4 percent of the population living below the poverty line, the rate still remained higher than it was in 1980. The poverty rate for children also remained alarmingly high, according to most experts, and actually went up for Hispanic children. Overall in 1985, more than one out of every five children in the United States lived in a family whose income was below the poverty line.

Congress responded in 1986 by beefing up programs to help needy Americans, amidst complaints by some Democrats that the requirements of the Gramm-Rudman-Hollings anti-deficit law prevented them from restoring programs to their pre-Reagan levels, and by Republicans charging that the Democrats were busting the budget.

With only minimal disagreement, Congress passed a bill authorizing a total of $15.79 billion over four years for a raft of non-entitlement programs for the poor, including Head Start and the Low Income Home Energy Assistance Program. Although administration officials complained that the authorized levels were too high, congressional negotiators were so close to agreement on funding levels that the biggest fight in conference was whether Sen. Dan Quayle, R-Ind., should be allowed to keep an amendment that would permit bat boys and bat girls for one of his state's minor-league baseball teams to work past 11 p.m. on school nights. Quayle's amendment was altered to order a study into the matter.

The House and Senate were more deeply divided over proposals to extend welfare benefits to two-parent families in which the principal wage earner was unemployed. This fight over the Aid to Families with Dependent Children (AFDC) program was expected to be revisited in 1987 in a new round of congressional debate over welfare reform.

—By Julie Rovner

Five-Year Higher Education Bill Cleared

Congress Sept. 25 cleared legislation (S 1965 — PL 99-498) that renewed for five years, through fiscal 1991, popular aid programs for colleges and their students under the Higher Education Act.

The conference report on the bill (H Rept 99-861) was adopted by the House on a 385-25 vote Sept. 24. It was adopted by the Senate by voice vote the next day. *(House vote 376, p. 106-H)*

The Senate originally passed S 1965 June 3. The House had passed its version of the bill (HR 3700) in 1985. *(Background, House action, 1985 Almanac p. 294)*

The final measure set stricter eligibility rules for student loans and made other changes designed to target aid to the neediest students. The bill also raised loan limits and for the first time made aid available to students enrolled less than half time.

Most of the bill's funding was to pay for the two largest student aid programs, Pell Grants and Guaranteed Student Loans (GSLs), which according to revised projections were expected to cost $3.9 billion and $3.1 billion, respectively, in fiscal 1987. That left a total of $3.2 billion for all other programs — a ceiling that was to be increased to compensate for inflation in 1988-91. *(Funding chart, p. 233)*

The bill cut student-loan subsidies paid to banks and made other changes in GSLs designed to reduce projected outlays by $445 million over three years — more than the $395 million cut mandated by the fiscal 1987 budget resolution (S Con Res 120).

S 1965 represented a bipartisan rejection of President Reagan's proposals for deep cuts in higher education. But the bill did draw on some proposals backed by the administration, such as tightened financial needs requirements for students seeking guaranteed loans.

Education Secretary William J. Bennett also had backed a proposal to allow students to repay loans in installments geared to their income after graduation. The bill included a pilot project to test such "income-contingent" loan repayments.

However, the measure imposed new restrictions on the education secretary's discretion in writing the crucial "needs analysis" rules that were used to assess the financial resources of aid applicants. The final compromise did not go as far as the House-passed measure, which essentially would have written the rules into law.

Borrowing Limits

While the final version of S 1965 generally drew praise, some educators expressed concern that it did too little to reverse a trend away from outright grants to needy students and toward more loans. "It is the prime irony," said Charles B. Saunders Jr., vice president for governmental relations for the American Council on Education. "The overwhelming weight of testimony [during hearings on the bill] was that the top priority was to shift the balance. But nothing has been done. In fact, the opposite might happen because of the higher loan limits."

Faced with rising college costs, conferees were under pressure to permit students to borrow more per year. Since 1976, the per-student limit had been $2,500 a year for undergraduates and $5,000 for graduate students. Conferees allowed only a small increase, to $2,625 per year, for freshmen and sophomores, but juniors and seniors were allowed to borrow $4,000 annually and graduate students $7,500. The total students could borrow through college and graduate school was more than doubled, from $25,000 to $54,750.

Architects of the bill said they did what they could to discourage unnecessary borrowing and authorized more generous grants to the poorest students. However, there was no assurance Congress would appropriate enough money to finance the larger grants.

Part-Time Students

Another major issue was how Congress should respond to a shift in the demographics of higher education. Federal programs generally were geared to the needs of students 18-to-21 years old who were attending college full time. But an increasing proportion of students did not fit that mold. More people were going to college later in life, usually on a part-time basis while they held down jobs or raised families.

The bill for the first time made eligible for Pell Grants students who were enrolled less than half time. It also expanded their access to other forms of federal aid. The measure included a revised program of support for continuing education, new grants for campus child-care programs and provisions allowing students to postpone repayment of past college loans if they returned to school part time.

Combating Abuse

The bill included several important provisions designed to prevent abuses of financial aid programs by schools and students.

It made it harder for undergraduates under age 24 to declare financial independence of their parents simply to improve their chances of getting financial aid.

The bill required students to maintain a "C" average, or grades consistent with graduation requirements, to keep getting aid after their sophomore year.

S 1965 included measures designed to crack down on schools that had taken advantage of the availability of federal aid to recruit students for shoddy programs or courses for which they were unprepared. For example, it imposed new restrictions on the use of student loans at foreign medical schools, under provisions intended to cut off funds to schools of questionable quality catering to Americans who could not secure admission to a U.S. medical school.

Aid to Colleges

Although most of the money under S 1965 was to go directly to needy students, the bill also reauthorized a wide array of smaller programs aiding colleges.

The Senate tried to resist pressure to create new college aid programs or to maintain existing ones that had not received appropriations in recent years. However, Senate negotiators did accept numerous House proposals to provide new aid in such areas as graduate education and teacher training. And both chambers supported proposals to expand aid to historically black colleges and other institutions serving minority students.

Education Research Programs

In addition to renewing higher education programs, S

1965 incorporated a five-year renewal of the Education Department's research and statistics programs. The House had renewed those programs for three years in separate legislation (HR 2246 — H Rept 99-589), passed May 13, while the Senate had linked it to the higher education bill.

Major Provisions

As signed into law Oct. 17, S 1965 (PL 99-498) contained the following major provisions:

Authorization Levels

• Authorized $10.2 billion for higher education programs in fiscal 1987. That figure included enough to accommodate projected costs for Pell Grants and GSLs and the specific ceilings set for other programs that totaled $2.4 billion. The limits on programs other than Pell Grants and GSLs were to be adjusted for inflation in fiscal 1988-91. Although that was expected to constrain total costs, no fixed ceilings were set for individual programs after fiscal 1987.

Guaranteed Student Loans

• Required all students to pass a financial needs test to qualify for loans, and forbade them to borrow more than they needed; under existing law those requirements applied only to students from families with more than $30,000 annual income. Family assets had to be considered in the needs assessment, not just income as was currently the case.

• Increased the $2,500 annual limit on the amount undergraduates could borrow to $2,625 for freshmen and sophomores, and $4,000 for upperclassmen. Graduate students were allowed to borrow $7,500 a year. The aggregate limits on borrowing were raised from $12,500 to $17,250 for undergraduates, and from $25,000 to $54,750 for those who went on to graduate school.

• Increased the interest rate from 8 percent to 10 percent beginning in the fifth year of repayment.

• Reduced the special allowance paid to banks that made GSLs by 0.25 percentage point. Under existing law the allowance was pegged quarterly to a rate equal to 3.5 percentage points above the rate paid on Treasury bills.

• Required state loan guarantee agencies that helped administer the GSL program to pay a new reinsurance fee to the federal government, with higher fees charged to agencies whose borrowers had high default rates.

• Allowed borrowers to defer repaying GSLs for up to two years if they were unemployed — an extension of the one-year deferment previously allowed.

• Allowed borrowers to defer repaying GSLs if they became teachers in regions or of academic subjects suffering teacher shortages.

• Allowed borrowers to defer repaying past student loans if they returned to school part time and had to borrow again. Existing law allowed such deferments only if borrowers returned to school full time.

• Required banks to inform borrowers of their projected levels of indebtedness on graduation and their estimated monthly repayments.

• Imposed new restrictions on loans to students attending foreign medical schools, allowing GSLs to be used at such schools only if at least 60 percent of the students there were citizens of the country in which the school was located, or if at least 45 percent of its students passed a standardized test of medical knowledge that was administered to foreign students before they could practice in the United States. That minimum pass rate was to rise to 50 percent in fiscal 1989.

• Barred state guarantee agencies from offering inducements to employees and schools to recruit loan applicants.

• Allowed students with more than $5,000 in federal loans to consolidate their debts and take longer to repay them. The repayment period could be extended from 10 years to as much as 25 years, depending on how much students had borrowed.

• Raised the limit on borrowing under a separate program of higher interest "auxiliary loans" currently available to parents of college students as well as to self-supporting and graduate students. The cap was raised from $3,000 to $4,000 a year.

• Lowered the interest on auxiliary loans from the existing level of 12 percent to a rate tied to Treasury bill rates, but no more than 12 percent. Borrowers currently holding 12 percent auxiliary loans could refinance them at the lower rate.

Pell Grants

• Increased the existing $2,100 per-student annual limit on Pell Grants to $2,300 in fiscal 1987. The maximum was increased in $200 annual increments thereafter. Grants continued to be limited to no more than 60 percent of a student's college costs.

• Allowed some students enrolled in college less than half time to receive Pell Grants beginning in fiscal 1989. Initially, eligibility was extended only to the poorest students, whose families could not afford to contribute at all toward college costs. In fiscal 1991, eligibility was to be expanded to include students whose expected family contribution to college costs was up to $200, as determined by a federal formula for assessing financial need.

• Barred students from receiving Pell Grants for more than five years. The limit could be waived for students in five-year degree programs and for other special cases.

Campus-Based Financial Aid

• For students who attended less than half time, expanded access to aid under the three "campus-based" aid programs administered by college officials: Supplemental Educational Opportunity Grants (SEOG), College Work-Study (CWS) and National Direct Student Loans (NDSL). Colleges were required to award such students a "reasonable proportion" of their campus-based funds.

• Revised the formula for distributing campus-based aid, specifying that each school receive no less than it did in fiscal 1985. For appropriations beyond that level, 75 percent of the money was to be distributed by a new formula that based allocations on the financial need of each college's students.

• Raised the annual limit on supplemental grants from $2,000 to $4,000.

• Required colleges, in distributing supplemental grants and direct loans, to give priority to students with exceptional financial need.

• Increased the existing limits on direct loans by 50 percent, allowing students to borrow up to $4,500 over their first two years and $9,000 over all their undergraduate years. Those who went on to graduate school could accumulate up to $18,000 in debt.

• Barred schools from receiving additional direct loan funds if their alumni default rate exceeded 20 percent. The existing cutoff was 25 percent.

Higher Education Authorizations

(in millions of dollars)

	Fiscal 1986 Appropriations	Fiscal 1987 Authorization
Pell Grants	$ 3,578	$ 3,900 *
Guaranteed Student Loans	3,259	3,100 *
Supplemental Educational Opportunity Grants	395	490
National Direct Student Loans	209	275
Income-contingent loan demonstration project	0	5
College Work-Study	567	656
TRIO (special services for the disadvantaged)	169	205
State Student Incentive Grants	73	85
Programs for migrant farm workers	7	9
Commission on college financing	0	2
Merit scholarships	0	8
Child care grants	0	10
Veterans' services	3	5
Continuing education	0	10
College libraries	7	30
Developing institutions	135	245
Teacher training	20	60
International education	27	55
Facilities construction	50	100
Cooperative education	14	17
Graduate education	19	90
Postsecondary improvement	17	25
Urban universities	0	17
TOTAL	**$ 8,549**	**$ 10,199**

** No authorization ceiling is set for Pell Grants and Guaranteed Student Loans. Fiscal 1987 figures represent projected costs.*

- Extended from six months to nine months the period allowed borrowers after leaving school before they had to begin repaying their direct loans.
- Allowed students at proprietary schools to participate in the College Work-Study program.
- Raised from $2,000 to $2,500 the annual limit on awards under the State Student Incentive Grants, a program that provided federal matching funds to states to encourage them to set up and expand their own scholarship programs.

Other Student Aid Provisions

- Required aid recipients, in order to remain eligible, to achieve by the end of their second year a C average or academic standing consistent with their college's graduation requirements.
- Required colleges, in order to participate in student aid programs, to certify that they had a drug-abuse prevention program.
- Authorized $5 million a year for a pilot project making student loans that were to be repaid in installments geared to the borrowers' income after they left school.
- Allowed students who had not earned a high school diploma or its equivalent to qualify for financial aid only if they received counseling and remedial instruction or passed a nationally recognized test assessing their ability to benefit from the postsecondary program they wanted to enter.
- Specified key elements of two formulas for assessing applicants' financial need, with separate needs analysis systems for Pell Grants and for other financial aid programs. The new systems would take effect in fiscal 1988.
- Took account of child care costs in assessing a student's need for aid.
- Specified that home equity not be considered in assessing the financial need of workers seeking mid-career retraining or homemakers preparing to enter the work force.
- Authorized the secretary of education annually to propose changes in the needs analysis formulas, subject to congressional approval by a joint resolution. If the proposal was not approved, the formulas would be automatically updated and adjusted to reflect inflation.
- Established an Advisory Committee on Student Financial Assistance to advise Congress and the education secretary on annual modifications of the needs analysis system.
- Established a simplified needs analysis system, subject to congressional approval by joint resolution, for very-low-income students.
- Barred aid applicants under the age of 24 from qualifying as financially independent of their parents unless they met specified standards — such as being an orphan, veteran or ward of a court; having legal dependents; or demonstrating other unusual circumstances. Graduate and professional students and married students under 24 could qualify as independent if their independence was affirmatively demonstrated to campus officials. Older students would automatically qualify as financially independent.

Institutional Aid

- Overhauled aid to "developing institutions" into a three-part program under Title III of the Higher Education Act:

1) Under Part A, authorized $120 million for aid to financially struggling colleges to improve their management and academic quality, with $51.4 million earmarked for community colleges. In addition, 25 percent of appropriations for Title III above the fiscal 1986 levels was earmarked for institutions serving the highest percentages of minority students.

2) Under Part B, authorized $100 million for 1987 for a new program for historically black colleges to improve their academic programs and facilities, and $5 million for black graduate and professional schools.

3) Under Part C, renewed existing challenge grants to help build the endowments of struggling colleges, which were required to put up matching funds.

Other College Aid Programs

- Overhauled federal aid for continuing education to improve programs for such "non-traditional" students as adults seeking mid-career retraining and homemakers preparing to enter the work force.
- Reauthorized grants to college libraries, with a new stipulation that institutions must demonstrate their need for such aid in order to qualify.
- Renewed the "TRIO" program, which encouraged students from disadvantaged backgrounds to enroll in college.

- Authorized $60 million for new and revised programs to train and recruit schoolteachers, including grants for teacher training centers and joint school-college projects.
- Reauthorized grants for international education and foreign language studies, and set up a new program to help colleges buy foreign periodicals.
- Reauthorized loans to colleges for student housing construction, and expanded their use to include renovation of academic facilities.
- Required the education secretary to sell $579 million worth of loan assets in fiscal 1987 and $314 million in fiscal 1988 under programs that provided loans for construction of college housing and other academic facilities.
- Set up a government-sponsored private corporation to increase the availability of private capital for campus construction and renovation projects by insuring and reinsuring bonds and loans. In the first three years of the corporation's operation, an increasing proportion of its support was to go to schools that might not otherwise be able to obtain such financing.
- Reauthorized grants for cooperative education, which supported programs that allowed students to link off-campus work experience with their classroom studies.
- Established a new graduate education program to recruit more minority students and another to provide fellowships for graduate students in areas of national need, such as engineering and computer science.
- Reauthorized existing graduate and professional fellowships for women and minority groups, raising the stipend from $4,500 to $10,000. Appropriations for these fellowships had to reach at least $18 million before new graduate programs could be funded.
- Reauthorized without major change the Fund for the Improvement of Postsecondary Education and a program to help colleges serving large numbers of minority students to improve their science programs.
- Renewed grants to urban universities and authorized new ones to other colleges to work with local governments, unions and business groups to promote economic development.
- Renewed aid to colleges for programs to encourage the children of migrant farm workers to finish high school and enroll in college.
- Authorized a new program of grants to institutions for child care services for disadvantaged students.

Educational Research

- Renewed programs supporting educational research and statistics-gathering through fiscal 1991, specifying that funding be maintained at no less than fiscal 1985 levels for certain activities, including the National Center for Educational Statistics, the Educational Resources Information Center and a federally supported network of education research centers and laboratories.

Miscellaneous Provisions

- Required universities to report to the Education Department certain information about donations from foreign sources that exceeded $250,000.
- Set up a National Commission on Responsibility for Financing the Cost of Postsecondary Education.
- Reauthorized through fiscal 1988 the U.S. Institute of Peace. Established as part of 1984 defense authorization legislation (PL 98-525), the institute was dedicated to the study of peace and conflict resolution. *(Background, 1984 Almanac p. 498)*

Senate Committee Action

S 1965 was unanimously ordered reported March 19 by the Senate Labor and Human Resources Committee. The bill was formally reported May 13 (S Rept 99-296).

The Senate measure was more austere than the bill passed by the House in 1985. Sensitive to the severe budget climate on Capitol Hill, the Senate panel deflected pressure to create new programs in such areas as graduate education and campus construction. It backed more stringent income limits for students who qualified for Pell Grants and GSLs.

But the committee paid little heed to the Reagan administration's longstanding efforts to make deep cuts in student aid spending. Reagan's fiscal 1987 budget called for reducing the $8 billion student aid budget by $2 billion. Committee Chairman Orrin G. Hatch, R-Utah, said the administration's proposals were "too late and too Draconian" to be reflected in the Senate's higher education bill.

The Senate committee bill authorized about $9.7 billion in fiscal 1987, a $2 billion drop from existing authorization levels but about $1 billion more than the $8.6 billion appropriated in fiscal 1986. The House bill authorized $10.7 billion in fiscal 1987.

Most of the additional funding authorized by S 1965 would be channeled to student aid rather than grants to colleges.

S 1965 repealed several programs — such as aid for urban universities and continuing education — that had not been funded in recent years. And Education Subcommittee Chairman Robert T. Stafford, R-Vt., urged his committee colleagues to refrain from proposing new programs.

Efforts to set up new aid programs had found a more receptive audience in the House. HR 3700 included initiatives in graduate education, teacher education, worker retraining and day care for the children of adult students.

Pell Grants: More for the Poor

Central to S 1965 were its provisions for Pell Grants, a $3.6 billion program in fiscal 1986, and GSLs, a $3.3 billion program. Those two programs accounted for $7.8 billion of the $9.7 billion that would be authorized for fiscal 1987.

In allocating those dollars, the bill generally made it harder for middle-income students to qualify for assistance. But for those students who did qualify, the bill made more aid available by raising the ceilings on grants and loans.

S 1965 increased the existing $2,100 annual limit on Pell Grants to $2,400 in fiscal 1987. In fiscal 1991, a $3,200 maximum grant would be authorized. The House bill raised the maximum to $2,300 in fiscal 1987 and by $200 annually after that.

In a significant change not included in the House bill, S 1965 for the first time barred students from getting Pell Grants if they had more than $30,000 annual family income.

Under existing law, eligibility was determined by rules that took account of a variety of factors in addition to family income, such as the size of the family and the number of dependents in college.

In academic 1983-84, about 1.2 percent of grant recipients — some 35,000 students — had familiy incomes of more than $30,000 a year.

President Reagan drew fire in 1985 when he proposed a $25,000 income cutoff in determining Pell Grant eligibility.

Academic Standards Set

In another departure from the House bill, S 1965 set new academic standards students would have to meet to remain eligible for Pell Grants and other federal aid. S 1965 required aid recipients, by the end of their second year in college, to achieve a C average. But in a concession to college groups that saw the rule as too inflexible, the bill also let students with lower grades remain eligible if their academic standing was deemed "consistent with the requirements for graduation."

As approved by the panel, the bill barred undergraduates from receiving Pell Grants for more than five years. The committee rejected, 5-11, an amendment by Paul Simon, D-Ill., to allow students to receive a Pell Grant for a year of graduate education if they did not exhaust all five years of eligibility as an undergraduate.

The amendment was opposed by Stafford, who said that Congress already found it difficult to provide enough money for needy undergraduates. He said the program was suffering from a funding shortfall that could result in almost 200,000 fewer students receiving grants in 1986-87.

Loan Income Test

For the guaranteed loans, S 1965 raised the $2,500 annual limit on the amount undergraduates could borrow to $3,000 in the first two years of college and $4,000 a year thereafter.

S 1965, like the House measure, required all GSL applicants to undergo a financial needs test to establish eligibility.

The panel adopted, 12-4, a Stafford amendment that required state student loan agencies to bear a greater share of the cost of defaults. State agencies acted as intermediaries between the federal government and banks that made guaranteed loans.

Under existing law, the federal government reimbursed state agencies for all defaults if the states' default rate was less than 5 percent. States with higher default rates had to pay as much as 20 percent of default costs. Under the Stafford amendment, states with default rates above 5 percent would pay as much as 30 percent of default costs.

Senators from states with default rates above 5 percent objected. Simon said the change could cost Illinois up to $10 million.

The committee sidestepped another controversial issue raised by Stafford, who proposed requiring all banks to have a personal or telephone interview with guaranteed loan applicants to ensure students understand the terms of the loan program.

His amendment reflected fears that too many students were taking out loans by mail. He voiced particular concern about aggressive marketing of loans that had resulted in students receiving loans without understanding the repayment obligations.

Hatch objected, saying the requirement would be particularly burdensome in relatively isolated large rural states. He charged that the amendment was being pushed by financial institutions opposed to interstate banking.

The amendment was withdrawn.

Aid for Black Colleges

In other areas, the committee adopted a compromise for restructuring aid to financially struggling colleges — a politically sensitive program that had been a major but dwindling source of aid to historically black colleges. The program, authorized by Title III of the Higher Education Act, was one of the few that provided aid directly to colleges with few strings attached.

The bill set up a separate program within Title III for historically black colleges, authorized at $55 million in 1987.

Other financially struggling colleges would compete for aid under another section of Title III, for which $85 million was authorized for fiscal 1987. However, the committee dropped controversial subcommittee provisions that would have earmarked some $12 million for institutions with large enrollments of Hispanics, Native Americans and other minorities.

Critics said the set-asides would have limited funding for other needy colleges. Also, aides said that some administration officials had questioned whether the provisions amounted to setting quotas for certain minority groups.

Under the compromise that was accepted by the committee, however, minority colleges would be given priority if Title III appropriations were increased.

Other Amendments

In other action, the committee by voice vote adopted:

- A Stafford amendment that incorporated into S 1965 a five-year reauthorization of the Education Department's education research and statistics programs, leaving in place a reorganization of the programs carried out in 1985 by Education Secretary Bennett. That plan abolished the National Institute of Education, the department's research arm, and brought the institute's functions directly under a new assistant secretary of education.
- A Simon amendment to require universities to disclose certain information about large donations by foreign countries. The amendment, similar to a House provision, reflected concern about incidents in which universities had accepted money from foreign sources with restrictions on how the money could be used and what could be taught.
- An amendment offered by Dan Quayle, R-Ind., to allow students at proprietary schools to participate in the College Work-Study program, which provided subsidies for campus employment for needy students.

Senate Floor Action

The Senate June 3 passed S 1965 by a 93-1 vote. Only Jesse Helms, R-N.C., voted against the bill, the first to be approved after the Senate began televising its floor proceedings. *(Vote 110, p. 21-S; TV, p. 43)*

Helms created an unexpected stir on an otherwise uncontroversial bill by pushing for a vote on an amendment to restrict the power of federal courts to order school busing.

An effort to table, and thus kill, the anti-busing amendment failed on a 45-50 vote. However, Helms withdrew the amendment after getting assurances that the issue would be brought back to the floor later in the year. *(Vote 108, p. 21-S)*

Before approving S 1965, the Senate adopted, 60-34, an amendment to scale back proposed increases in grants to poor students and make other cost-saving changes in an effort to accommodate Reagan administration complaints about the bill's price tag. *(Vote 109, p. 21-S)*

But even with those cuts, the bill's fiscal 1987 authorization of $9.5 billion far exceeded the $6.2 billion higher education budget proposed by President Reagan. The House bill had authorized $10.7 billion for fiscal 1987.

Senate, House Bills Compared

Key features of the Higher Education Act reauthorization bills approved by the House (HR 3700) on Dec. 4, 1985, and by the Senate (S 1965) on June 3, 1986, included:

Funding

Existing authorization: $11.7 billion.
Senate: $9.5 billion in fiscal 1987.
House: $10.7 billion in fiscal 1987.

Pell Grants

Maximum award. Existing law: $2,100.
Senate: $2,300 in fiscal 1987, rising to $3,100 in 1991.
House: $2,300 in fiscal 1987, rising to $3,100.
Eligibility. Existing law: No income cap.
Senate: Barred grants to students with more than $30,000 annual family income, after taxes.
House: No income cap.

Guaranteed Student Loans

Undergraduate loan limits. Existing law: $2,500 a year.
Senate: $3,000 a year for the first two years of college, $4,000 thereafter.
House: $2,500 a year for first two years, $5,000 thereafter.
Financial need. Existing law: Students with family income above $30,000 must pass needs test.
Senate: All must pass needs test.
House: All must pass needs test.

(House, Senate bills compared, box, above)

Existing authorizations for higher education programs totaled $11.7 billion, but only about $8.6 billion was actually appropriated for fiscal 1986.

Authorization Cuts

Faced with administration complaints, Education Subcommittee Chairman Stafford, ranking subcommittee Democrat Claiborne Pell, R.I., and Majority Leader Robert Dole, R-Kan., agreed to a package of amendments that reduced the bill's cost by $226 million in fiscal 1987 and by $1.5 billion over five years.

The package, introduced by Dole, trimmed proposed increases in the maximum Pell Grant by $100 a year. Even with that reduction, the bill allowed the grant cap to rise from $2,100 to $2,300 in 1987 and to $3,100 in 1991 — the same grant levels included in the House bill.

The Dole package also made cuts in the special allowance for banks beyond the reduction recommended by the committee. Dole said the additional cut would leave "plenty of room for compromise" in conference with the House, which maintained existing allowance levels.

Dole's amendment also gave the education secretary additional authority to crack down on students who claimed they were financially independent of their parents simply to qualify for more financial aid.

Dole said the amendments were intended to win the administration's support for the bill, but Bennett said S 1965 was still "too expensive," although he termed it "more responsible in terms of cost than the House bill."

The Dole amendment was opposed by Simon, who warned that the cut in bank subsidies went too far. "I think we are jeopardizing this student program, and I think we are fooling ourselves if we do not recognize that," said Simon.

However, critics of that proposal acknowledged that it was politically difficult to oppose trimming subsidies to lenders while urging cuts in benefits to students.

Simon and others warned against reducing the number of Pell Grants while allowing higher ceilings on student loans, saying it would fuel a trend toward increasing student indebtedness to finance college.

Labor Committee Chairman Hatch said he would have preferred reducing loan limits. "If we are to cut the Pell program for our neediest students, we should be trimming this middle-class entitlement as well," he said.

But Stafford said he would resist any effort to scale back loan increases, especially as part of an effort to restore banks' subsidies. "Why should the so-called needs of banks be put ahead once again of the needs of middle-income and low-middle-income families?" he asked.

Busing Flap

Before agreeing to withdraw his anti-busing amendment, Helms won a commitment from Judiciary Committee Chairman Strom Thurmond, R-S.C., that he would try to bring to the floor a similar bill (S 37) that had been bottled up in committee. However, the Senate never acted on S 37.

Helms' amendment would have banned federal courts from ordering busing of schoolchildren more than 10 miles, or a 30-minute ride, round trip. A related measure was approved by the Senate in 1982, but it died in the House. *(1982 Almanac p. 385)*

Arguing that the effort to curb the power of federal courts violated the independence of the judiciary, Lowell P. Weicker Jr., R-Conn., threatened to filibuster the Helms amendment. Weicker charged that Helms proposed the amendment simply to force an election-year roll-call vote on the sensitive busing issue.

"This is a vacuous exercise, never meant to become law, but to put the screws to people on a very passionate issue," Weicker said.

In withdrawing the amendment despite the Senate's failure to kill it, Helms acknowledged that the move was intended "to get a vote so that it could be there for all to see how the Senate feels about forced busing."

Other Amendments

In other action, the Senate by voice vote adopted amendments:

- By Stafford and Pell, authorizing $5 million a year for a pilot project making student loans that would be repaid in installments geared to the borrowers' income after they left school. That concept of "income-contingent" loan repayments was proposed by the administration as part of its fiscal 1987 budget.
- By Phil Gramm, R-Texas, cracking down on student loan defaulters by garnisheeing the wages of federal workers who were in default and by making defaulters ineligible for other forms of federal assistance, such as research grants.
- By Christopher J. Dodd, D-Conn., to set up a private corporation, with initial federal funding, to back bonds and loans for financing construction and renovation of campus facilities.

Major Provisions

As passed by the Senate, S 1965 included major provisions to:

Pell Grants

• Deny Pell Grants to students whose annual family income was more than $30,000 after deductions for federal and state income taxes. The Labor and Human Resources Committee said in its report on S 1965 that it did not expect the income cap to have much effect, citing estimates that less than 3.5 percent of current recipients would have been affected if the cap were already in place.

• Increase the existing $2,100 annual limit on Pell Grants to $2,300 in fiscal 1987. The maximum would increase in $200 annual increments thereafter. Grants would continue to be limited to no more than 60 percent of a student's college costs.

Guaranteed Student Loans

• Require all students to pass a financial needs test to qualify for loans, and allow applicants to borrow no more than they could demonstrate a need for — a requirement that applied under existing law only to students from families with more than $30,000 annual income. Families' assets would have to be considered in the financial needs assessment, not just their income as was currently the case.

• Increase the $2,500 annual limit on the amount undergraduates could borrow to $3,000 in the first two years of college and $4,000 a year thereafter. The existing $5,000 annual limit on graduate student borrowing would be raised to $7,500. The aggregate limits on borrowing would be raised from $12,500 to $18,000 for undergraduates, and from $25,500 to $55,500 for graduate students.

• Increase from 8 percent to 10 percent the interest borrowers must pay on guaranteed loans.

• Reduce the special allowance to banks that made loans by 0.5 percentage point. The allowance currently was pegged quarterly to a rate equal to 3.5 percentage points above the rate paid on Treasury bills.

• Raise the cap on borrowing under a separate program of higher-interest "auxiliary loans" currently available to parents of college students as well as to self-supporting and graduate students. The annual limit for parents would be raised from $3,000 to $4,000; for students, from $2,500 to $4,500.

• Institute a number of measures to improve collections of defaulted loans, including the provision requiring state student loan agencies to bear a greater share of the cost of defaults. The federal government would continue to reimburse state agencies for all default costs if the default rate on loans they guaranteed was less than 5 percent. But states with higher default rates would pay as much as 30 percent of defaults; under existing law, states with high defaults paid no more than 20 percent.

Other Student Aid Provisions

• Establish a simplified financial-aid application for students with family incomes of less than $15,000 a year.

• Set a stiffer standard for determining if aid applicants were financially independent of their parents. Unmarried students under the age of 23 without dependents would have to prove they had been financially independent of their parents for two years before applying, not just one year as was currently the case. The bill also gave the secretary of education authority to require applicants to provide additional information to demonstrate that they had been supporting themselves.

• Include child care expenses as part of applicants' educational costs in assessing their need for federal aid.

• Require each student to contribute $800 of his or her own resources toward education costs before qualifying for federal aid.

• Require student-aid recipients, in order to remain eligible, to achieve by the end of their second year in college a C average or academic standing consistent with their college's graduation requirements.

• Renew three campus-based student-aid programs, which were administered by college officials, setting fiscal 1987 authorizations of $433 million for Supplemental Educational Opportunity Grants, $622 million for College Work-Study and $228 million for National Direct Student Loans. Authorizations would increase about 5 percent a year through fiscal 1991.

• Raise the annual limit on supplemental grants from $2,000 to $3,000 a year, and on direct student loans from $1,500 to $2,000.

• Require colleges, in distributing supplemental grants, to give priority to students who received Pell Grants and others with exceptional financial need.

• Specify that each college receive at least as much in campus-based aid allotments as in fiscal 1985; any increases in appropriations over 1985 levels would be allocated to colleges based on the number of eligible students they enrolled.

• Authorize $76 million a year for State Student Incentive Grants, which provided matching funds for states with their own scholarship programs.

• Authorize $188 million in fiscal 1987 for the so-called "TRIO" programs, which provided special services to encourage disadvantaged students to enroll and remain in college. The spending limit would rise 5 percent a year through 1991.

Institutional Aid

• Overhaul aid to "developing institutions" into a three-part program, including fiscal 1987 authorizations of:

1) $85 million to help financially struggling colleges improve their management and academic quality. Some $51.4 million would be earmarked for junior and community colleges, and institutions with high minority enrollments would be given priority if Congress increased funding over fiscal 1986 levels.

2) $55 million for grants to historically black colleges and universities.

3) $20 million to continue awarding challenge grants to help struggling institutions build their endowments.

Other College Aid Programs

• Repeal several college aid programs for which no money had been appropriated in recent years, including support for adult and continuing education, funding for a national periodical system, aid to urban universities and most teacher training programs.

• Extend and authorize 5 percent annual increases in spending ceilings for other college aid programs including international education, graduate fellowships and the Fund for the Improvement of Postsecondary Education.

• Reauthorize loans to colleges for student housing construction, and expand their use to include renovation of academic facilities.

• Require universities to report to the Education Department certain information about large gifts or donations that they received from foreign countries.

- Renew programs supporting educational research and statistics gathering, authorizing $45 million in fiscal 1987.

Conference

House and Senate conferees Sept. 12 approved a compromise version of S 1965. The House had cleared the way for the conference June 17, when it passed S 1965 after substituting the text of HR 3700, its own reauthorization measure.

The conference agreement (H Rept 99-861) was approved after negotiators agreed to curb student loan spending in line with congressional budget targets and to make more aid available to poor students attending college less than half time.

The final bill authorized $10.2 billion in fiscal 1987, compared with current authorizations of roughly $12 billion and fiscal 1986 appropriations of about $8.5 billion.

Rep. William D. Ford, D-Mich., chief House negotiator, voiced frustration at budget constraints conferees faced. "My hope is that the next time we'll be able to consider what's a rational education policy and then find the dollars to pay for it," said Ford.

Before conferees approved the compromise, Rep. E. Thomas Coleman, R-Mo., won approval of a new provision barring colleges from participating in student aid programs if they had no drug-abuse prevention program. *(Drug bill, p. 92)*

A key element of the compromise fell into place Sept. 10, when conferees adopted student loan proposals designed to comply with the 1987 budget resolution, which called for changes that would reduce projected GSL outlays by $395 million over three years.

The compromise cut the subsidies paid to banks to make up the difference between the low interest paid by borrowers and market rates.

In addition, a new fee would be levied on state agencies that helped administer the GSL program, with higher fees charged to agencies whose borrowers had high default rates.

The compromise also allowed borrowers to defer repayment of GSLs for up to two years if they were unemployed — a deferment limited to one year under existing law. Backers of the change claimed it would save money by avoiding the default costs likely to arise if the unemployed had to repay loans.

Other GSL provisions:

- Allowed some borrowers to defer repayments on past student loans if they returned to school part time and had to borrow again.
- Allowed students to defer repayments of GSLs if they became teachers in regions or in academic subjects where there was a teacher shortage.
- Raised the interest on student loans from 8 percent to 10 percent when borrowers began their fifth year of repayment, which typically lasted 10 years. Conferees dropped a Senate proposal to raise the rate to 10 percent throughout repayment.

Reaching a compromise on one of the most controversial issues before the conference, negotiators agreed to ease existing requirements that students enroll at least half time to qualify for Pell Grants.

The Senate argued that Congress could not afford to expand eligibility to all part-time students, as the House proposed. The compromise allowed only the poorest students to qualify for grants to attend less than half time — and they would not qualify until fiscal 1988. A somewhat larger pool of part-time students would qualify after fiscal 1991.

A last-minute obstacle to agreement arose when Senate negotiators initially refused to accept House provisions for funding projects at colleges in the districts of several House conferees and other key members. The projects were included after conferees agreed to provide an equal sum for projects sought by senators.

House conferees agreed to the deal, 16-4, despite the objections of Rep. Steve Gunderson, R-Wis., to what he called educational "pork barrel." ▮

Congress Clears Omnibus Health Legislation

President Reagan Nov. 14 signed into law a major package of health bills, but he made it clear he did not like key provisions that set up a no-fault compensation system for the families of children injured by vaccines.

The president said he signed the bill (S 1744 — PL 99-660) "with mixed feelings," explaining that he had "serious reservations" about the vaccine provisions.

Congress cleared the bill, which included the texts of nine separate measures, as one of its last actions before adjourning Oct. 18.

The House approved the bill by voice vote late Oct. 17. After heated negotiations that consumed most of the next day, the Senate cleared the package by voice vote just before adjourning.

The final package was put together by Rep. Henry A. Waxman, D-Calif., chairman of the Energy and Commerce Subcommittee on Health and the Environment, and Orrin G. Hatch, R-Utah, chairman of the Senate Labor and Human Resources Committee, along with Rep. Edward R. Madigan, R-Ill., and Sen. Edward M. Kennedy, D-Mass., the ranking minority members of their respective panels.

The president praised the other major bill in the package, which allowed the export of drugs not yet approved for use in the United States. He said this "will increase the competitiveness of the American pharmaceutical industry abroad, create jobs, foster biotechnology and aid other nations."

Another bill in the package sought to cut down on medical malpractice by creating a computerized national data system on doctors with malpractice records and by shielding from private damage suits doctors who "blow the whistle" on colleagues they suspect of malpractice.

Still other included measures required states to create plans to meet the needs of the mentally ill, expanded funding for research into Alzheimer's disease and created a national commission on infant mortality.

The vaccine compensation provisions could not take effect until Congress approved a funding mechanism. Waxman had proposed an excise tax on vaccine manufacturers to finance the compensation fund, but he eventually stripped the tax from the bill because the House Ways and Means Committee did not have time to consider it.

There was also a possibility that Congress would have to reconsider a part of the legislation dealing with the appointment of special masters to decide on the amount of compensation. Federal judiciary and House Judiciary Committee sources said the bill as cleared did not explain how the special masters were to be appointed or what standards they should use for their decisions. The sources said there could be an effort to enact clarifying legislation in 1987.

Provisions

As signed into law by President Reagan, S 1744 included the following major provisions:

Vaccine Compensation

- Directed the secretary of Health and Human Services (HHS) to create a National Vaccine Program and to appoint a director to coordinate federal research, licensing and distribution of vaccines. The director also was to coordinate federal and non-governmental vaccine activities.
- Created a national advisory committee to help the program director ensure a continued supply of safe and effective vaccines and to establish research priorities for enhancing safety and efficacy.
- Authorized a total of $140 million for fiscal years 1987-91 to run the vaccine program and to provide additional funding for other vaccine programs under the national program's jurisdiction.
- Created a National Vaccine Injury Compensation Program, to be administered by HHS, under which payments were to be made to the families of persons who suffered vaccine-related injuries or death as a result of receiving vaccines generally required by state law. These were listed in the bill and included vaccines to prevent diphtheria, polio, tetanus, whooping cough, measles, mumps and rubella (German measles). Individuals did not need to prove negligence to qualify for payments under this compensation program, subsequently referred to here as a "no-fault" program.
- Required those seeking compensation under the program to file a petition in U.S. district court for the district in which the injury or death occurred or in which they resided, and with HHS.
- Required a petitioner, in order to qualify for an award under the system, to demonstrate that the person injured received a vaccine covered by the bill, that as a result of the vaccine the recipient was injured or had a previous injury aggravated, that the injury's effects caused death or lasted more than one year or prompted unreimbursed expenses of more than $1,000 and that the person injured had not collected any other compensation for the injury.
- Provided for court-appointed special masters who were to determine whether a particular injury qualified for compensation and how much the award should be. Awards might be for medical expenses, death benefits, lost earnings and pain and suffering, but no punitive damages would be allowed. Portions of the award intended to cover medical and rehabilitative expenses were to be paid annually and could be revised upwards or downwards according to court determinations and changed circumstances. Awards for attorneys' fees also could be made.
- Provided that persons injured before the effective date of the bill could choose to go through the no-fault system before going to court, but could receive compensation only for ongoing and otherwise unreimbursable medical and remedial expenses.
- Stipulated that in case of death, compensation should be a lump-sum award of $250,000.
- Stipulated that awards for pain and suffering could not exceed $250,000.
- Provided that petitioners could reject an offered award under the program within 90 days and pursue a court case according to applicable state law. Acceptance of the award, however, would preclude bringing civil damage action against a vaccine manufacturer for that injury.
- Provided that in civil court actions, vaccine manufacturers could not be held liable for damages for an injury resulting from an unavoidable side effect if the vaccine was properly prepared and was accompanied by proper directions and warnings.
- Directions and warnings approved by the federal Food and Drug Administration (FDA) were to be presumed sufficient to meet this test, unless the plaintiff could show fraudulent conduct or intentional and unlawful withholding of information from the FDA or could show "clear and convincing evidence" that the manufacturer failed to exercise due care.
- Provided that manufacturers not be held liable as a result of failure to provide warnings directly to the recipient, rather than to the administrator of the vaccine.
- Provided that manufacturers not be held liable for punitive damages unless the plaintiff could show wrongful or illegal acts by the manufacturer that were related to the injury in question.
- Stipulated that civil actions concerning vaccine deaths or injuries be conducted in three separate stages to determine liability, general damages and punitive damages.
- Required health care providers who administer vaccines to keep permanent medical records on all vaccines given, and to notify HHS within seven days of adverse vaccine reactions.
- Required HHS to develop and disseminate materials explaining the diseases that the vaccines were designed to prevent, potential adverse reactions, groups at high risk to suffer such reactions and procedures for reporting adverse reactions. These materials had to be distributed to health care providers, who were then to distribute them to parents before vaccines were administered to their children.
- Imposed record-keeping requirements on vaccine manufacturers and required notification of HHS within 24 hours if a test of a batch of vaccine indicated a potential imminent or substantial public health hazard.
- Authorized civil and criminal penalties of up to $100,000 and one year in prison for intentional destruction, alteration or falsification of required records.
- Required HHS to conduct a study of vaccine risks and the effect of S 1744 on the nation's vaccine supply, and to review vaccine warnings, instructions and precautionary information.
- Authorized HHS to recall vaccine batches determined to present an imminent or substantial hazard to public health, and provided civil penalties for non-compliance with a recall.

Drug Exports

- Permitted U.S. pharmaceutical manufacturers to export drugs and other biological products not yet approved for use in the United States to countries with drug regulatory systems that had approved their use.
- Named the following as countries that could receive unapproved drugs: Australia, Austria, Belgium, Canada,

Denmark, Federal Republic of Germany, Finland, France, Iceland, Ireland, Italy, Japan, Luxembourg, the Netherlands, New Zealand, Norway, Portugal, Spain, Sweden, Switzerland and the United Kingdom.

- Set criteria for adding new countries to the list, including statutory or regulatory requirements regarding the review of drugs for safety and effectiveness.
- Stipulated that drugs could not be exported unless the manufacturer was actively pursuing approval from the FDA, and that no drugs could be exported that had been denied approval for use in the United States.
- Required that manufacturers place a label on the outside of shipping packages listing the countries in which the drug could be offered for sale.
- Required manufacturers to file an application with the FDA at least 90 days before the first export. The application had to identify the drug, name the destination country, certify that all export requirements had been satisfied and include a written agreement from each importer not to ship the drug to third countries not authorized to receive it.
- Permitted the export of drugs deemed by the secretary of HHS to be "safe and effective in the prevention or treatment" of tropical diseases to countries not on the approved list if the country in question had tropical disease problems.
- Authorized HHS to conduct biomedical research directly or through grants for the identification, control, treatment and prevention of diseases not occurring "to a significant extent" in the United States.
- Authorized HHS to seize drugs shipped in violation of the act, to prohibit shipment of drugs even to authorized countries if the secretary found the drug posed "an imminent hazard" in that country and to seek an injunction and criminal penalties against U.S. exporters.

Physician Peer Review

- Required HHS to establish a system to collect information on physicians who had been disciplined or on whose behalf a malpractice settlement had been paid, and to make the information available to hospitals and other entities that might hire or grant practice privileges to physicians.
- Required any entity making a payment as a result of a malpractice action against a physician to report that payment and the circumstances surrounding it to HHS.
- Allowed HHS to seek civil penalties of up to $10,000 for each malpractice payment not reported.
- Stipulated that reporting a payment in settlement of a malpractice claim shall not create a presumption that medical malpractice has occurred.
- Required state boards of medical examiners to report to HHS revocations or suspensions of a physician's license, reprimands, censures or probation periods imposed on a physician.
- Required health care entities to report to state boards of medical examiners (which must in turn report to HHS) actions that adversely affected the clinical privileges of a physician for more than 30 days, as well as actions that resulted in a physician surrendering clinical privileges in return for a waiver of an investigation or proceeding.
- Required professional societies with HHS-approved peer review systems to report to the state board of medical examiners actions that adversely affected the membership of a physician in the society.
- Authorized HHS to bar immunity for health care entities that failed to report information as required.
- Required hospitals to request information from the system before hiring or granting privileges to a physician, and at least every two years thereafter. Hospitals that failed to request information from the system would be presumed to have that information. Conversely, hospitals might not be held liable for relying on information from the system unless the hospital had knowledge that the information provided was false.
- Required that information in the system be kept confidential and disclosed (other than to the physician in question) only for professional review activity, medical malpractice actions or other purposes set forth by regulation, and authorized civil penalties of up to $10,000 for wrongful use of such information.
- Required the HHS secretary to recommend to Congress whether to continue to require reporting of small malpractice payments and whether reports should be filed at the time a claim was made rather than when the case was settled.
- Shielded from liability in private damage suits members and staff of review boards or other bodies that took actions against a physician based on competence or professional conduct if taken "in the reasonable belief that the action was in the furtherance of quality health care." However, the board must make a reasonable effort to obtain the facts and provide adequate notice and the opportunity for a hearing to the physician involved.
- Shielded from personal liability in private damage suits any individual providing information to a review board with regard to a physician's competence or professional conduct, unless that person knowingly provided false information.

Community Mental Health Grants

- Authorized $10 million annually for fiscal 1988-89 for grants to states for the development of comprehensive mental health service plans.
- Required states, beginning in 1988, to submit to HHS a comprehensive mental health service plan to provide for the establishment and implementation of an organized community-based system of care for individuals who had a chronic mental illness. The plan was to include quantitative targets, describe services to be provided and require case management services for each mentally ill individual in the state who received "substantial amounts of public funds or services." Plans also had to provide for the establishment and implementation of an outreach program for mentally ill individuals who were homeless.
- Required HHS to provide technical assistance to help states develop their plans.
- Required HHS to withhold sums equal to the amounts spent by states for fiscal 1986 administrative expenses of the Alcohol, Drug Abuse and Mental Health Services (ADM) block grant from states that failed to develop plans by fiscal 1989 and implement them by fiscal 1991.
- Required HHS, within one year, to develop a model plan for community-based care of the chronically mentally ill. The bill required that the model be developed in consultation with state mental health directors, providers of mental health services, mentally ill individuals and advocates for the mentally ill.
- Required states to establish state mental health service planning councils and authorized the use of ADM block grant funds for this purpose.

• Made homeless mentally ill individuals eligible for services under the community support programs for the mentally ill and increased the authorization for community support programs to $24 million for fiscal 1988 (from $20 million for fiscal 1986).

Training for Geriatric Care

• Authorized $4 million in fiscal 1988 for HHS grants to medical and osteopathic schools, teaching hospitals and graduate medical education programs to train physicians and dentists who planned to teach geriatric medicine or geriatric dentistry.

Repeal of Health Planning

• Effective Jan. 1, 1987, repealed section XV of the Public Health Service Act, which authorized the nation's basic health planning program. (That program sought to control rising medical costs by requiring states to set up approval systems before hospitals could add new beds or make major equipment purchases.)

Alzheimer's Disease Research

• Established within HHS the Council on Alzheimer's Disease, to be composed of a number of HHS officials, including the assistant secretary for health, the surgeon general and the director of the National Institute on Aging. The council was to coordinate research, establish a mechanism for sharing information, and identify the most promising areas of research.

• Established within HHS the Advisory Panel on Alzheimer's Disease, to be composed of researchers, service providers, experts in the financing of long-term care and representatives of organizations concerned with the problems of victims and their families. The panel was to assist in identifying priorities and emerging issues.

• Authorized $100,000 annually for the panel's expenses for fiscal 1988-91.

• Authorized $5 million annually for fiscal 1988-91 for the National Institute on Aging to make research awards to those who made distinguished achievements in biomedical research in areas relating to Alzheimer's disease.

• Authorized $2 million annually for fiscal 1988-91 for grants from the National Institute on Aging for research on the epidemiology of Alzheimer's disease, identification of risk factors and the study of methods to diagnose the disease.

• Authorized $2 million annually for fiscal 1988-91 for grants from the National Institute of Mental Health for research concerning treatment of Alzheimer's disease, ways to obtain information on care of its victims, cost-effectiveness of community and institutional services for victims, ways to combine formal and informal support services for those who care for victims and improved methods to deliver services to victims and their families.

• Authorized $2 million annually for fiscal 1988-91 for grants from the National Center for Health Services Research and Health Care Technology Assessment for research on the costs to Alzheimer's victims and their families of obtaining services.

• Authorized $2 million annually for fiscal 1988-91 for grants from the Health Care Financing Administration for research concerning: the types of services required by Alzheimer's victims and their families to allow the victims to live outside institutions; the costs of providing services, including expenditures for institutional, home and community-based services; an assessment of the benefits provided through the Medicare and Medicaid programs for Alzheimer's victims and a determination of the costs to the Medicare and Medicaid programs of providing covered benefits to Alzheimer's victims.

• Directed the National Institute on Aging to establish a Clearinghouse on Alzheimer's Disease to compile, archive and disseminate information concerning research, demonstration, evaluation and training programs and projects concerning Alzheimer's disease and related dementias.

• Directed that findings of research conducted as required above be made available to the clearinghouse.

• Authorized $300,000 annually for fiscal 1988-91 for the National Institute on Aging to contract with a national organization representing victims of Alzheimer's disease to establish a central computerized information system. The purpose was to compile and disseminate information concerning state and local government and private initiatives to provide programs and services to Alzheimer's victims; to translate scientific and technical information into "readily understandable" language; and to establish a national toll-free telephone line to make such information available, as well as information concerning federal programs, benefits and services.

• Authorized $1 million annually for fiscal 1988-91 for educational programs for personnel of the Social Security Administration, for personnel involved in ensuring public safety and providing public transportation and for providers of care for Alzheimer's victims.

National Commission on Infant Mortality

• Established a National Commission on Infant Mortality to identify and examine federal, state, local and private resources with an impact on infant mortality and authorized "such sums as necessary" for the commission's work.

• Stipulated that areas of study include, but not be limited to: the effectiveness of federal programs that increased access to prenatal and postnatal education, care and nutrition; the effectiveness of federal and state Medicaid policies that sought to ensure access to prenatal and postnatal care for low-income pregnant women, mothers and infants up to age 1; and the adequacy of private health care financing to enable pregnant women and infants to receive comprehensive health care.

• Directed the commission to recommend within one year of enactment a national policy designed to reduce and prevent infant mortality.

Health Maintenance Organizations

• Repealed portions of the Public Health Service Act authorizing federal grants and loans for feasibility surveys, planning and initial development costs for health maintenance organizations (HMOs).

• Provided for a phase-out of federal loans and loan guarantees for the initial cost of HMO operations.

Background

The final version of S 1744 represented a compromise that met key objectives of Rep. Waxman, who had been pressing for a comprehensive vaccine compensation bill, and Sen. Hatch, chairman of the Labor and Human Resources Committee and chief advocate of the drug export measure. Neither bill had been able to clear on its own; together they formed the core of an undefeatable package.

Vaccine Shortages, Compensation

The vaccine legislation was prompted by intermittent shortages in 1984-85 of certain childhood vaccines, most notably the diphtheria-pertussis-tetanus (DPT) vaccine. Worried about the possibility of costly liability suits, drug manufacturers were increasingly reluctant to manufacture and distribute DPT vaccine. In rare instances, the pertussis ("whooping cough") vaccine produced severe adverse effects, including brain damage and death.

All 50 states required children, as a condition of entering school, to be vaccinated against the DPT diseases, polio, mumps, measles and rubella ("German measles").

Immunizations against these childhood diseases have been one of the great public health success stories: In 1934, for example, 7,518 children died from pertussis alone; in 1982-83, the CDC reported just 15 deaths from the disease.

But some vaccines, notably the pertussis vaccine, carried a small but real risk of adverse reactions. And those reactions had provoked lawsuits drug manufacturers described as intolerable.

In 1984, Robert B. Johnson, president of Lederle Laboratories, by then the sole remaining supplier of DPT vaccine, said that the "present dollar demand of the DPT lawsuits against Lederle is 200 times greater than our total sales of DPT vaccine in 1983."

Such increases in legal costs contributed to soaring prices for vaccines; between 1980 and 1985, the price of a single dose of DPT vaccine skyrocketed from 11 cents to more than $11.

In December 1984, with vaccine supplies dwindling, the federal Centers for Disease Control (CDC) requested doctors to delay "booster" shots for older children to ensure that adequate supplies of DPT vaccine would be available for infants.

The shortages continued until April 1985, when Connaught Laboratories — which had dropped out of the field because of liability concerns — said it would resume distributing DPT vaccine.

Manufacturers, fearing huge jury awards, wanted Congress to limit their liability. Parents' groups, while seeking swift compensation for vaccine-caused reactions, wanted to preserve their right to sue vaccine manufacturers — in part to prod them into pursuing safer vaccines. Key members of Congress, led by Waxman and Sen. Paula Hawkins, R-Fla., wanted to ensure that adequate supplies of vaccines would be available and that families would receive fair compensation for vaccine-related injuries.

Drug Exports

Pharmaceutical companies had long sought repeal of the ban against exports of drugs that had not received Food and Drug Administration (FDA) certification as safe and effective. Such drugs could not be sold in the United States, but other nations had approved some of them for sale elsewhere. Only antibiotics were exempt from the export ban.

The pharmaceutical and biotechnology industries argued that the time-consuming FDA drug-approval process put U.S. manufacturers at a competitive disadvantage in the international market. Supporters cited numerous instances in which U.S. firms had decided to locate new facilities overseas in order to make and sell drugs not yet approved in this country.

The push for an end to the export ban was led by smaller firms, including biotechnology companies involved in developing pharmaceutical applications of genetic engineering. Representatives of these companies said the export ban was an obstacle to commercialization of their products. Unlike the big companies, the small biotech firms could not afford to set up manufacturing operations overseas, they testified.

Sponsors argued that many nations with sophisticated drug-screening agencies approved new drugs faster than the FDA, which took seven to 13 years to evaluate the safety and efficacy of a new drug. They cited a 1980 General Accounting Office study that found that 13 of 14 new drugs examined were approved in at least one of five foreign countries before they received FDA approval.

"This legislation," said Hatch, "will save American jobs, prevent the export of American biotechnology, and decrease our balance-of-payments deficit, without increasing the health risk to foreign consumers, without erecting trade barriers that invite retaliation, and without costing the taxpayer money."

The Senate Labor Committee report cited widely varying estimates of the bill's economic impact, from a potential high of $1.76 billion in added exports and 40,000 new jobs annually to a low of $217 million in increased exports and 2,482 new jobs.

Sen. Hatch had introduced a drug export bill in 1984, but the measure died amid complaints by critics that it would promote "dumping" of dubious drugs abroad, particularly in Third World countries that lacked sophisticated testing and monitoring procedures to ensure safe and proper use of the drugs. *(1984 Almanac p. 475)*

Opponents of both the 1984 bill and the 1986 version charged that safeguards designed to prevent unapproved drugs from reaching nations without sophisticated drug regulatory systems were not strong enough.

A leading critic was Sen. Howard M. Metzenbaum, D-Ohio, who said the proposal to ease the ban on exports of unapproved drugs sent a "clear and unambiguous message" to the rest of the world: " 'These drugs aren't good enough for us, but they're good enough for you.' "

Metzenbaum also questioned the adequacy of the drug-regulation systems in the nations to which unapproved drugs could be exported. He cited a 1985 FDA study showing that only 7 percent of drugs first approved in Japan, 12 percent of drugs first approved in France, and 20 percent of drugs first approved in West Germany were ultimately approved by the FDA. "To throw them into a bill and say they have adequate FDAs is legislation by fantasy, not reality," he said.

Legislative History

Vaccine Bills

Although vaccine bills (HR 1780, S 827) were introduced early in the 99th Congress by Waxman and Hawkins, they did not begin moving until August 1986. And when they did finally start to advance, they initially did so only after being stripped of their compensation provisions.

On Aug. 5, 1986, Waxman's Health Subcommittee approved a bare-bones version (HR 5230) of his vaccine legislation. It increased the authorization for a federal program that helped states purchase vaccines, and required HHS to maintain a six-month stockpile of vaccines to forestall future shortfalls.

A day later, the full Senate Labor and Human Resources Committee approved a stripped-down version of Hawkins' bill, S 827. Like the Waxman measure, the version approved by the committee (S Rept 99-483) required HHS stockpiling of vaccines, increased authorizations for the federal vaccine program and required physicians and other providers to report all major adverse vaccine reactions to the CDC.

The full House Energy and Commerce Committee approved HR 5230 on Aug. 13, and it was formally reported two days later (H Rept 99-801). The House passed HR 5230 by voice vote Sept. 16.

On Sept. 18, the House Energy and Commerce Committee approved Waxman's comprehensive vaccine legislation (HR 5546 — H Rept 99-908, Part 1), which included the special compensation system.

The House passed HR 5546 by voice vote Oct. 14 after Waxman had stricken from the bill provisions to create a trust fund to pay victims of adverse vaccine reactions and their families. Those provisions would have required the approval of the Ways and Means Committee, which had no time to consider them.

Although HR 5546 went nowhere in the Senate, its provisions became a part of the final compromise version of S 1744.

That bill, which began as a measure requiring states to develop and implement programs to meet the needs of the chronically mentally ill in the community, had been reported Aug. 6 by the Senate Labor and Human Resources Committee (S Rept 99-380) and passed Aug. 12 by voice vote. As the 99th Congress drew to a close, it became the vehicle to which the vaccine, drug export and other health measures were attached in the House.

The House approved the amended version of S 1744 by voice vote late Oct. 17. After heated negotiations that consumed most of the following day, the Senate cleared the package by voice vote late Oct. 18, just before adjourning.

Drug Export Bill

The drug export bill (S 1848) was reported by the Labor and Human Resources Committee Dec. 18, 1985 (S Rept 99-225). *(1985 Almanac p. 302)*

The Senate passed the legislation by 91-7 on May 14, 1986, after rejecting several amendments by Metzenbaum that sought to tighten controls over the drug exports authorized by the bill. *(Vote 99, p. 19-S)*

While most of Metzenbaum's amendments were rejected, several were adopted. One of these, to strengthen the Infant Formula Act of 1980, had nothing to do with drug exports. That proposal ultimately was enacted as part of omnibus anti-drug legislation (HR 5484). *(Story, p. 92)*

Another amendment not wholly related to the drug export issue was offered by Ohio Democrat John Glenn. By voice vote, the Senate required uniform procedures for notifying foreign governments if substances that were banned or severely restricted in the United States were to be exported to their countries. Such substances included medical devices, food, cosmetics, color additives, pesticides and fabrics. Current notification procedures varied widely and were carried out by three federal agencies under at least six different acts.

The Glenn amendment also required that foreign governments be told why a product was banned or restricted.

A spokesman for the Pharmaceutical Manufacturers Association said the organization was unhappy with the amendment, as well as with the infant formula provisions.

Also by voice vote, the chamber accepted amendments to establish the FDA in statute and make its commissioner subject to Senate confirmation, and to ensure that foreign governments could find out the legal status in the United States of a drug exported to their country.

The Senate tabled four other Metzenbaum amendments:

- By 76-18, to bring antibiotics under the purview of S 1848. *(Vote 95, p. 19-S)*
- By 83-10, to bar export of drugs unless an application for FDA approval had been filed. *(Vote 96, p. 19-S)*
- By 83-8, to prohibit further shipments of any drug found in an unauthorized country. *(Vote 97, p. 19-S)*
- By 62-29, to require the Office of Technology Assessment to study the labeling of drugs sold in foreign countries. *(Vote 98, p. 19-S)*

As passed by the Senate, S 1848 permitted the export of unapproved drugs to developed countries with "an adequate governmental health authority to approve drugs." Such an authority had to include regulatory procedures to ensure adequate scientific review of safety and efficacy studies; to ensure accurate labeling that conformed to local law; to detect and record adverse drug reactions; and to remove from the market drugs shown to present a serious safety problem.

The final version of the bill, as contained in S 1744, was substantially revised from S 1848.

For example, the Senate-passed version set up two "tiers" of countries that could receive unapproved drugs. Tier One countries, those with advanced drug-approval systems, could receive unapproved drugs directly, while Tier Two countries could receive a drug only if it had been approved by a Tier One country. The final version eliminated the second tier, permitting exports only to countries with their own approval systems.

Unlike the bill that passed the Senate, the new version also required manufacturers who wanted to export drugs to be actively pursuing approval in the United States.

Other Proposals

In an effort to garner Republican support in the House and to encourage the president not to veto S 1744, Waxman and Hatch included as part of the package a measure to repeal the authorization for the federal health planning program — a step advocated by the administration. The planning program sought to slow rising health care costs by requiring states to set up approval systems before hospitals could add new beds or make major equipment purchases.

The planning program, unauthorized since 1981, continued to receive funding each year, but officially died at the beginning of fiscal 1987 when appropriators finally gave up on it. The administration had been seeking repeal of the authorizing language since 1981. The House Feb. 4 passed a bill (HR 3010) to continue it only through fiscal 1986, while the Senate Labor and Human Resources Committee Dec. 18, 1985, had approved a measure (S 1855) to reauthorize it through fiscal 1988. *(1985 Almanac p. 299)*

And to keep Metzenbaum, a vehement opponent of the drug export measure, from seeking to block the entire package, Waxman and Hatch included a bill (S 1835) sponsored by Metzenbaum and Sen. Charles E. Grassley, R-Iowa, to expand research into Alzheimer's disease and efforts to help victims and their families.

The package also contained the texts of:

• HR 5540, designed to reduce medical malpractice by facilitating the identification of incompetent physicians.

The bill was reported Sept. 26 by the House Energy and Commerce Committee (H Rept 99-903, Part I), and was passed by the House by voice vote Oct. 14. It required the creation of a nationwide data-collection system to give hospitals access to physicians' malpractice records. It also shielded from liability physicians who turn in colleagues they suspect of malpractice.

• S 1762, reauthorizing a loan fund within HHS to cover defaults of federal loan guarantees for health maintenance organizations (HMOs). The bill repealed language authorizing federal grants and loans to HMOs, whose creation the government encouraged in the 1970s because they tended to be successful at holding down medical costs. The Reagan administration had argued that the financial incentives were no longer needed because HMOs were well-established in most parts of the country. No new financial aid had been provided under the act since 1981. The bill was reported Jan. 22 by the Labor and Human Resources Committee (S Rept 99-229), but it never passed the Senate.

In the House, the Energy and Commerce Committee reported a similar measure (HR 2417 — H Rept 99-154) June 3, and it was passed June 18, 1985. *(Background, 1985 Almanac p. 291)*

• S 1209, to create a national commission on the prevention of infant mortality. The commission was to review federal, state and local government efforts as well as the private sector's role in preventing and reducing infant mortality and to recommend a national action plan.

S 1209 was reported Sept. 30 by the Governmental Affairs Committee (S Rept 99-506), and passed by the full Senate on Oct. 9.

• S 2489, to encourage the training of health professionals specializing in problems of the elderly. The bill authorized grants for the training of such health professionals. ▮

Human Services Funds

President Reagan Sept. 30 signed an omnibus human services bill (HR 4421 — PL 99-425) authorizing $15.79 billion through fiscal 1990 for programs that offered child care, education, nutritional services, energy aid and other community assistance to the poor.

The House Sept. 16 approved the conference report on the bill by voice vote. The Senate followed suit Sept. 18, clearing the bill.

The legislation reauthorized for four years Head Start, Dependent Care, Community Services Block Grant (CSBG), Community Food and Nutrition, and the Low Income Home Energy Assistance Program (LIHEAP).

In its fiscal 1987 budget, the administration had called for outright termination of the Dependent Care and Follow Through programs, and zero funding for CSBG. The programs were last reauthorized in 1984. *(1984 Almanac p. 485)*

Background

CSBG, originally a key element of the "war on poverty" in the 1960s, provided seed money to community agencies seeking to promote economic self-sufficiency.

Head Start, the largest program in the legislation with a $1.09 billion fiscal 1986 appropriation, provided educational, social, nutritional and health services to nearly 500,000 preschool children from low-income families. Studies showed that "graduates" of the 20-year-old program were less likely than other low-income children to need remedial or special education, drop out of school, become involved in crime or go on welfare.

Follow Through was a demonstration program designed to meet the continuing needs of Head Start graduates. Although funds went to only 58 of the nation's more than 14,000 school districts, directly serving just 13,500 children, the techniques and models developed under the program were widely disseminated.

Dependent Care, created in 1984, provided 75 percent matching grants to states to set up child care programs for so-called "latchkey children," youngsters of school age who have no one at home to care for them before or after school. The program also funded efforts to disseminate information on the availability of day care for younger children, the elderly and handicapped individuals.

The Community Food and Nutrition Program, moribund for many years, was revived in 1984. It provided grants to public and private non-profit agencies to plan and implement strategies to meet the nutritional needs of low-income families and individuals.

Provisions

As signed into law Sept. 30, HR 4421 (PL 99-425):

• Authorized a total of $5.2 billion for the Head Start program — $1.2 billion for fiscal 1987, $1.3 billion for fiscal 1988, $1.3 billion for fiscal 1989 and $1.4 billion for fiscal 1990.

• Required that Head Start programs for Indians and migrant workers be funded for 1987-90 at no less than fiscal 1985 levels.

• Authorized $31.85 million for the Follow Through program, with $7.5 million for fiscal 1987, $7.8 million for fiscal 1988, $8.1 million for fiscal 1989 and $8.4 million for fiscal 1990.

• Renamed Dependent Care the State Dependent Care Development Grants, and authorized a total of $80 million for the program — $20 million annually for fiscal 1987-90.

• Eliminated a provision in existing law that permitted before- and after-school child care programs to be provided at community centers only when school facilities were not available.

• Changed the definition of school-age children to include those under age 5 in states that provided younger children free public education.

• Authorized a total of $1.68 billion for the CSBG program — $390 million for fiscal 1987, $409.5 million for fiscal 1988, $430 million for fiscal 1989 and $451.5 million for fiscal 1990.

• Permitted CSBG training funds to be used for national conferences, newsletters and the collection and dissemination of data about CSBG programs and projects.

• Extended eligibility for CSBG funds to organizations created in fiscal 1982 as direct successors to a Community Action Agency.

• Required the secretary of the Department of Health and Human Services (HHS) to report annually to the chairmen of the House Education and Labor and the Senate Labor and Human Resources committees on programs and projects funded under the secretary's discretionary authority, and to make publicly available a catalog of such programs.

• Authorized a total of $12 million for the Community

Food and Nutrition program, with $3 million for each of fiscal 1987-90.

- Authorized $15 million, or $5 million for each of fiscal 1987-89, for grants for a new CSBG demonstration program. These grants were to help fund new approaches to meeting critical needs of the poor. Grants were to be made only for activities not previously funded by the federal government and could not finance more than 50 percent of the costs of any program. In addition, no single grant could exceed $250,000.
- Authorized a total of $8.71 billion for LIHEAP — $2.05 billion for fiscal 1987, $2.13 billion for fiscal 1988, $2.22 billion for fiscal 1989 and $2.31 billion for fiscal 1990.
- Permitted certain community-based organizations to be designated to provide LIHEAP payments for energy crisis intervention, including providing space heaters, blankets, payments and alternative shelter arrangements.
- Stipulated that LIHEAP payments could not be considered as income for the purpose of determining a recipient's eligibility to receive food stamps.
- Authorized the HHS secretary to make grants to states receiving funds under Title XX of the Social Security Act (PL 93-647) to fund scholarships for those working toward a Child Development Associate (CDA) credential, required by many states as a condition for licensing.
- Authorized a total of $6 million for the grants — $1.5 million for each of fiscal 1987-90.
- Defined as eligible to receive scholarship assistance a candidate for a CDA credential whose income did not exceed the federal poverty line by more than 50 percent.
- Required each state receiving grants under the program to provide annually information on the number of eligible individuals assisted under the program, their positions and their salaries before and after receiving their CDA credentials.
- Directed the secretary of labor to study and inform the president and Congress whether changing the permissible hours of employment for bat boys and bat girls would be detrimental to their well-being.
- Required the secretary of education to compile a complete list, by name, of beginning reading instruction programs and methods, including phonics. The listing must be publicized and disseminated nationally on an annual basis.

House Action

The House Education and Labor Committee April 10 unanimously approved HR 4421 (H Rept 99-545). The panel rejected, 7-22, an amendment that would have denied CSBG funds to organizations that provided abortion counseling or referrals.

The LIHEAP reauthorization was reported in a separate bill (HR 4422 — H Rept 99-556, Part I).

The House approved the legislation April 29 by a vote of 377-33. The bill, which made no major alterations in the programs, authorized $390 million for CSBG in fiscal 1987, down from a fiscal 1986 authorization of $415 million. It authorized "such sums as necessary" for CSBG in later years and annually for the rest of the programs. *(Vote 94, p. 30-H)*

Before passage, the House rejected, 161-245, an amendment by Tom Tauke, R-Iowa, to kill the Follow Through program. *(Vote 92, p. 30-H)*

Members also rejected, 140-267, an amendment by Robert S. Walker, R-Pa., to freeze fiscal 1987 funding for CSBG at its fiscal 1986 outlay level of $370.3 million. *(Vote 93, p. 30-H)*

Senate Action

The Senate Labor and Human Resources Committee May 20 unanimously approved S 2444 (S Rept 99-327). After substituting the text of S 2444 for the House bill, the Senate passed HR 4421 by voice vote July 14.

The Senate version authorized a total of $4.8 billion for Head Start over four years; a total of $1.56 billion over four years for CSBG; a total of $9.05 billion for LIHEAP over four years; and a total of $60 million over three years for the Dependent Care program.

The Senate bill also called for the establishment of a $6 million scholarship program for low-income candidates pursuing a Child Development Associate (CDA) credential. The CDA credential was a prerequisite for licensing day care providers in 31 states and the District of Columbia.

By voice vote, the chamber agreed to a number of amendments to HR 4421, one of which consisted of a modified version of a bill (S 140) that sought to improve the treatment of victims of child abuse. The Senate passed S 140 in 1985, but the House version (HR 2999) was tied up in three different committees.

Other amendments approved were:

- By Dan Quayle, R-Ind., to amend the Fair Labor Standards Act to allow 14- and 15-year-olds to serve as bat/ball boys or girls for professional baseball teams. The Labor Department ruled that the use of children under age 16 by the minor-league Indianapolis Indians violated child labor standards under the act.
- By Alfonse M. D'Amato, R-N.Y., to designate New York's Laboratory for Experimental Medicine and Surgery in Primates a regional primate research center, thus making it eligible for additional federal grants.
- By Edward Zorinsky, D-Neb., to require the secretary of education to conduct a study of reading programs.

Conference

A House-Senate conference committee Aug. 13 by voice vote approved HR 4421. The conference report (H Rept 99-815) was filed Sept. 12.

Most of the debate in the conference was devoted to the provision by Quayle that sought an exemption from the Fair Labor Standards Act to allow 14- and 15-year-olds to be bat boys and bat girls for professional baseball teams.

House conferees, led by Education and Labor Chairman Augustus F. Hawkins, D-Calif., and Austin J. Murphy, D-Pa., chairman of the Labor Standards Subcommittee, criticized the measure, objecting that it removed the bat boys/girls from minimum wage requirements. In the conference's final order of business, the Senate conferees agreed to remove the exemption from the bill and instead to request the secretary of labor to study the issue for a year.

The conferees also killed two plans — contained in the Senate bill — to hold a national conference on poverty and to make a New York primate research laboratory eligible for federal grants. ▮

Volunteer Programs Funding

Congress Oct. 8 cleared for the president a bill (HR 4116 — PL 99-551) reauthorizing major domestic volunteer programs for three years, through fiscal 1989.

Final action came when the Senate adopted a conference report on the bill by voice vote. The House approved the report by a 366-33 vote Oct. 2. *(Vote 397, p. 112-H)*

HR 4116 authorized a total of $555.36 million for the Volunteers in Service to America (VISTA) program, the Older American Volunteer Programs and administrative costs for ACTION, the agency that administered them.

The legislation also created a new "literacy corps" within VISTA to help existing public and private efforts aimed at resolving problems of illiteracy. *(Previous reauthorization, 1984 Almanac p. 459)*

Background

Reauthorized under the bill were the nation's major domestic volunteer programs administered by ACTION.

VISTA, a remnant of the 1960s war on poverty that President Reagan had repeatedly sought to abolish, was the domestic federal program providing stipends to full-time volunteers to assist low-income Americans increase their self-reliance. VISTA volunteers were assigned to low-income areas to address such problems as hunger, homelessness, joblessness and illiteracy.

VISTA was sharply cut under Reagan administration budgets. In 1981, $34 million was appropriated for the program. By 1983, that funding had dropped to $11.8 million. The fiscal 1985 appropriation was $19 million.

The Older American Volunteer Programs were designed to promote voluntarism among citizens 60 and over. In 1985 nearly 390,000 volunteers provided more than $350 million worth of services, according to the House Select Committee on Aging.

The largest of these programs was the Retired Senior Volunteer Program (RSVP), in which volunteers worked in programs to deal with such issues as hunger, housing, health, nutrition, education and energy conservation. RSVP volunteers received no stipend, but were reimbursed for meals, transportation and out-of-pocket expenses.

The Foster Grandparents program provided low-income, senior volunteers to help children with physical, emotional and mental handicaps in schools, hospitals, day-care centers and group homes. The Senior Companions program enlisted low-income individuals over age 60 to assist frail, homebound elderly citizens who, without such help, would likely need institutionalization.

Both Foster Grandparents and Senior Companions worked 20 hours a week and received a stipend in addition to transportation, on-the-job meals, annual physical exams and accident and personal liability insurance.

A smaller volunteer anti-poverty effort, the Service Learning Programs, used high school and college student volunteers in projects designed to help the indigent. No stipends were paid, but college students could earn academic credit.

Provisions

As cleared by Congress, HR 4116:

- Authorized a total of $78.04 million in stipends for VISTA volunteers: $25 million for fiscal 1987, $26 million for 1988 and $27.04 million for 1989.
- Authorized an additional $10 million for a new VISTA Literacy Corps: $2 million for fiscal 1987, $3 million for 1988 and $5 million for 1989.
- Authorized a total of $5.4 million for the Service Learning Programs: $1.8 million for each of fiscal 1987, 1988 and 1989.
- Authorized a total of $5.952 million for Special Volunteer Programs: $1.984 million for each of fiscal 1987, 1988 and 1989.
- Authorized a total of $75.94 million for administrative costs for ACTION: $25.31 million for each of fiscal 1987, 1988 and 1989.
- Authorized a total of $99.89 million for the Retired Senior Volunteer Program: $32 million for fiscal 1987, $33.28 million for fiscal 1988 and $34.61 million for fiscal 1989.
- Authorized a total of $187.3 million for the Foster Grandparents program: $60 million for fiscal 1987, $62.4 million for fiscal 1988 and $64.9 million for fiscal 1989.
- Authorized a total of $92.84 million for the Senior Companions Program: $29.74 million for fiscal 1987, $30.93 million for fiscal 1988 and $32.17 million for fiscal 1989.
- Authorized non-needy persons to serve without pay as senior companions and foster grandparents, provided no appropriated funds were used for their expenses.
- Directed ACTION to spend up to $250,000 to recruit individuals to serve as VISTA volunteers.
- Established a VISTA Literacy Corps to develop, strengthen, supplement and expand efforts of local, state and federal public and private, non-profit organizations working to address the problem of illiteracy.
- Stipulated that funds made available for the literacy corps be used to supplement and not supplant other VISTA services, and directed that volunteers be assigned with priority going to programs or projects assisting illiterate individuals in unserved or under-served areas with the highest concentrations of illiteracy and of low-income individuals and families.
- Directed ACTION to conduct an evaluation of the impact of senior volunteer programs that assist families caring for frail and disabled adults.

House Action

The House Education and Labor Committee by voice vote April 23 approved the reauthorization of VISTA and five other programs first established under the Domestic Volunteer Service Act of 1973 (PL 93-113). The committee added to the bill the language of HR 4607, reauthorizing for three years the Older American Volunteer Programs. *(Domestic Volunteer Service Act, 1973 Almanac p. 564)*

As reported by the committee (H Rept 99-588) May 7, the bill authorized $78.8 million in volunteer stipends through fiscal 1989 for VISTA volunteers, and a total of $10 million for a new VISTA literacy corps. The bill authorized $1.8 million annually for the Service Learning Program, almost $2 million per year for the Special Volunteer Program, and $386.02 million over three years for Older American Volunteer Programs. It also authorized $75 million over three years for ACTION, which administered and coordinates all of the programs.

After heated debate, the House June 17 passed HR 4116 by a vote of 360-52. *(Vote 156, p. 48-H)*

Debate on the bill grew partisan over an amendment offered by Tom Tauke, R-Iowa, to lower the bill's authorization levels. Tauke's amendment, which failed 189-221, would have reduced the 1987 authorization to the amount approved in the 1986 appropriation. *(Vote 154, p. 48-H)*

The chamber also defeated, by a vote of 204-208, an amendment offered by Lynn Martin, R-Ill., to freeze the funding floor levels for VISTA at fiscal 1986 levels. The floor levels mandated the number of VISTA volunteer hours funded before money could be spent on the Service Learning and Special Volunteer Programs. The bill increased the funding floor from 2,400 service years in fiscal 1986 to 2,600 in fiscal 1987, 2,730 in fiscal 1988, and 2,865 in fiscal 1989. *(Vote 155, p. 48-H)*

By voice vote, the House also adopted an amendment offered by Al McCandless, R-Calif., to permit Foster Grandparent services to be provided to mentally retarded individuals over age 21.

Senate Action

By voice vote, the Senate Labor and Human Resources Committee June 25 approved S 2324 (S Rept 99-332), legislation reauthorizing domestic anti-poverty volunteer programs for three years.

The bill authorized a total of $77.27 million in stipends for participants in VISTA, and an additional $10 million for a new VISTA literacy corps.

The bill also authorized a total of just under $366 million for the Older American Volunteer programs. Just over $76 million in administrative costs was authorized for ACTION.

S 2324 included a controversial provision requested by the Reagan administration that allowed volunteers to participate in the Senior Companions and Foster Grandparents programs without receiving stipends. Those programs were open only to low-income senior citizens.

After substituting the text of S 2324, the Senate by voice vote July 14 passed HR 4116.

Conference

The conference report on the bill (H Rept 99-954) was filed Oct. 2.

Conferees agreed to authorization levels that were slightly higher than those approved by the Senate and slightly lower than those approved by the House. Overall authorization levels represented a small increase over previous years.

House and Senate conferees agreed on "funding floors" for VISTA of 2,400 full-time volunteers for 1987, 2,500 for 1988 and 2,600 for 1989.

The main sticking point in the conference involved the Senate provision permitting non-needy senior citizens to participate in two senior volunteer programs.

The final version permitted non-needy individuals to serve in the programs without receiving stipends, provided that the costs associated with their efforts came from outside gifts or the volunteers themselves, not from appropriated funds.

Senate conferees, however, insisted on striking the House provision allowing Foster Grandparents to serve mentally retarded adults, as well as children. ▮

Welfare Program Changes

Significant changes in federal welfare laws were included in the omnibus deficit-reduction bill cleared by Congress March 20.

The bill (HR 3128 — PL 99-272) was intended to make spending cuts required by the fiscal 1986 budget resolution. A conference report was filed at the end of the 1985 session, but it took another three months to develop a compromise version acceptable to both chambers.

Although both the House and Senate versions of HR 3128 included changes to the nation's welfare laws that would have resulted in increased federal spending, most so-called "add-on" programs were dropped either in the December 1985 conference report or during the negotiations that followed.

Among the last add-ons dropped was a provision mandating that Aid to Families with Dependent Children (AFDC) benefits be paid to two-parent households in which the primary wage earner was unemployed. Under existing law, states had the option of offering such benefits under AFDC, the principal federal-state welfare program. The Reagan administration strongly opposed the proposal, which later was dropped from the fiscal 1987 reconciliation bill (HR 5300 — PL 99-509) as well.

Post-conference negotiations also resulted in the demise of a proposal to give states a reprieve from sanctions for failure to comply with federally set administrative error rates in Medicaid, the federal-state health insurance program for the poor. But similar sanctions were delayed for AFDC, which, like Medicaid, was jointly funded by the federal and state governments and administered by the states.

On March 28, 26 states, the District of Columbia and three California counties filed suit to void both the AFDC and Medicaid penalties. A federal trial court dismissed the case in November, saying it was brought prematurely.

One add-on program that emerged intact authorized $45 million for both fiscal 1987 and 1988 to help children aged 16 and over in the AFDC foster-care program prepare for independent living.

The proposal was championed by Sen. Daniel Patrick Moynihan, D-N.Y., who cited studies showing that former AFDC foster children in New York City were twice as likely to end up on public assistance as other young people aged 18-21, and that half of all youths in the city's shelters for the homeless were formerly in foster care.

Under the program, states could use the funds to provide services to help former foster children finish high school or obtain vocational training, as well as to provide training in daily living skills such as budgeting.

Provisions. As signed into law April 7, the welfare provisions of HR 3128:

- Altered the way in which a state could satisfy the federal requirement that it "pass through" increases in Supplemental Security Income (SSI) payments, which provided assistance to needy aged, blind or disabled individuals. The change was sought by members from Oklahoma, because that state stood to lose its federal funding due to non-compliance.
- Provided that the federal government, through the Social Security Administration, administer state supplementary payments to institutionalized persons eligible for the $25 per month federal SSI personal needs allowance, if the state requested it. A number of states currently supplemented the personal-needs allowance, which allowed institutionalized Medicaid patients to purchase toiletries and other personal goods not covered by Medicaid.
- Provided that disabled widows and widowers between the ages of 50 and 59 who became ineligible for SSI and Medicaid because of a 1984 increase in their Social Security benefits have their eligibility reinstated. These individuals were given an additional 15 months to file for Medicaid benefits.
- Imposed a two-year moratorium on the collection of sanction payments from states not in compliance with federally set error rates for AFDC.

Under existing law, states that did not keep error rates below federal targets could be required to pay back to the federal government the federal share of the cost of improperly issued benefits.

During the moratorium, HHS and the National Academy of Sciences were to conduct quality control studies.

Based on the results of the studies, the existing quality control system was to be restructured and criteria established for recalculating the amount owed by states currently liable for sanctions. The AFDC sanctions assessed but not yet collected amounted to more than $155 million for 1981 and 1982.

- Directed the secretary of HHS to take action to recover 40 percent of the amounts spent on automated AFDC claims-processing and information-retrieval systems from any state that failed to implement those systems in a timely manner.

The federal government currently paid 90 percent of the cost of development and installation of automated systems if the plans were approved in advance. States would be liable if their systems were not operational on the date specified in the approved planning document; however, the bill also expanded the secretary's authority to extend the deadline if delays resulted from circumstances beyond the state's control.

- Directed the General Accounting Office to conduct a one-year study of per capita payments to American Indians from various funds based on their status as members of an Indian tribe or organization. The study would also document how those payments were treated for purposes of eligibility for means-tested federal programs, and justifications for exemptions.

Under existing law, many per capita payments to Indians were exempt from being counted as income for the purpose of determining eligibility for federally funded benefit programs.

- Required, as a condition of eligibility for AFDC, that recipients cooperate in identifying third parties who might be liable for their health coverage. Such a requirement was already in place for Medicaid eligibility.
- Added a number of provisions to make it easier for adopted and foster children to receive Medicaid benefits. The provisions removed the need for actual adoption assistance payments to be made before an adopted child could be deemed eligible for Medicaid; provided that, should the child move to another state, the new state would provide the child's Medicaid benefits; and established Medicaid eligibility at the time a child was placed for adoption, as long as an adoption assistance agreement was in effect.

Previously, Medicaid eligibility did not begin until the issuance of an interlocutory or judicial decree of adoption.

- Extended through 1987 the ceiling on AFDC foster care funds below which states could transfer unused funds to other child welfare services.
- Extended through 1987 AFDC foster care payments for children removed from their home under a voluntary placement agreement.
- Authorized a new program funded at $45 million in each of fiscal 1987 and 1988, to help AFDC foster care children prepare for independent living, by providing career counseling and other services. Money would be distributed to states by their percentage of AFDC foster children. States would not have to match the federal assistance. ▮

Child Nutrition Programs

One of the 99th Congress' last acts was to approve a three-year reauthorization of five child nutrition programs that had been stalled in a House-Senate conference since early 1986. But the pursuit of a viable vehicle to carry the bill produced a legal headache of some magnitude.

Just before adjournment, Congress attached nearly identical versions of the nutrition legislation to two bills — the fiscal 1987 defense authorization bill (S 2638 — PL 99-661) and the $576 billion continuing appropriations resolution (H J Res 738 — PL 99-591).

The two bills included slightly different language for three provisions, raising questions about which should prevail. The sole discrepancy for two provisions lay in the date that they were to take effect. There was a substantive difference between the two versions of the other provision.

The matter pitted congressional intent against the normal legal precedent of enforcing the last version to be signed by the president. Lawyers at the Department of Agriculture finally decided that the defense bill, the last version to become law, must prevail.

Overdue Reauthorization

Both bills extended authorization through fiscal 1989 for five child nutrition programs: the supplemental feeding program for needy pregnant women, infants and children (WIC); the summer food service program for children; a surplus commodity distribution program; payments to states for administrative expenses; and the nutrition and education training program. In addition, the bills made some changes to the school lunch and breakfast programs and to WIC.

Authorization for the programs expired at the end of fiscal 1984. They were extended under appropriations measures in fiscal 1985 and 1986.

The House passed a new authorization (HR 7 — H Rept 99-96) Sept. 18, 1985, providing a $121 million increase overall in child nutrition programs over three years. The Senate Nov. 22, 1985, bypassed the Agriculture, Nutrition and Forestry Committee and passed a bare-bones, four-year reauthorization containing no increase in funding. President Reagan had requested an $800 million cut. *(1985 Almanac p. 309)*

On Feb. 5, 1986, House-Senate conferees reached a tentative compromise on funding levels, paring the bill's total increase to $46 million. House conferees signed a conference agreement, but Senate Agriculture Chairman Jesse Helms, R-N.C., objected to any increase, and did not circulate the agreement to Senate conferees.

The bill languished until Sen. Paula Hawkins, R-Fla., a chief proponent of the child nutrition programs reauthorization, offered the conference agreement as an amendment to the defense authorization bill. The Senate adopted Hawkins' amendment Aug. 9 by voice vote, then passed the bill later that day.

On Oct. 2, Hawkins again offered the nutrition conference agreement as a floor amendment — this time, to the measure providing continuing appropriations for the government.

Hawkins said it was unclear whether Congress would complete action on the defense authorization bill and added, "I feel it is important to include this amendment in the continuing resolution to ensure that the president will have the opportunity to sign" it into law. Her amendment was adopted by voice vote after the Senate voted 78-17 that the amendment was germane. *(Vote 319, p. 53-S)*

An earlier attempt to attach the child nutrition provisions to the continuing resolution failed as part of a farm-aid amendment by David L. Boren, D-Okla. By a vote of 45-53, the Senate rejected a motion to waive a budget act limitation with respect to that amendment. *(Vote 304, p. 51-S)*

The Provisions in Dispute

The version of HR 7 that had been appended to the defense authorization bill was the same as the conference agreement reached earlier in the year. In that proposal, three provisions were scheduled to take effect Oct. 1, 1986.

One of the provisions allowed partial-day (or "split-session") kindergartens to participate in a program that offered free or subsidized milk, at an estimated cost in fiscal 1987 of $10 million. Another provision provided an additional 6 cents per breakfast to supplement the school breakfast program — 3 cents in cash and 3 cents in commodities. That change was estimated to cost $24 million in 1987. The third provision raised from $1,500 to $2,000 the maximum tuition a private school could charge and remain in the school lunch and breakfast programs — at an approximate cost in 1987 of $2 million.

Oct. 1 had already passed, however, by the time the continuing resolution was being debated. In order to stave off bookkeeping nightmares by changing the law in the midst of the school year, and to keep the bill as close to revenue neutrality as possible, conferees on H J Res 738 decided to advance the effective dates of the three provisions to July 1, 1987.

In addition, House Appropriations Committee member Richard J. Durbin, D-Ill., persuaded conferees to drop the tuition cap altogether, reasoning that the overriding factor in determining eligibility for federal assistance should be the parents' income, not the school's tuition. The fiscal 1987 cost of eliminating the tuition cap — since it would not be removed until July — was estimated at $2 million; it was expected to have an annual cost of $6 million.

As a further measure to balance the bill's funding, the conferees added a three-year sale of agricultural notes and other obligations held in the rural development insurance fund, designed to raise $25 million in fiscal 1987, $36 million in 1988 and $37 million in 1989.

The Timing Problem

The conference report on S 2638 (H Rept 99-1001) was filed Oct. 14; the report on H J Res 738 (H Rept 99-1005) was filed the next day.

The defense authorization bill was cleared for Reagan Oct. 15; the continuing resolution was cleared Oct. 17. Because the spending bill had to be enacted to keep the government running, Reagan signed it Oct. 18. On Oct. 30 he signed a second version (PL 99-591) that contained two pages inadvertently omitted from the earlier bill. *(Continuing resolution, p. 219; defense authorization, p. 464)*

Reagan did not sign the defense authorization bill until Nov. 14.

As a general rule, according to Steven Ross, general counsel to the clerk of the House, when conflicting versions of legislation are passed, the last version enacted prevails. In this case, that was the defense bill.

Congressional intent, however, also plays a key role in disputes of this type. House staffers on the Appropriations and the Education and Labor committees argued that since the last nutrition bill to have been worked on — and, indeed, the last version to be cleared by Congress — was the one on the continuing resolution, that version, with its effective date of July 1, 1987, and removal of the tuition cap, should prevail.

The decision to enforce the defense bill provisions meant that school districts around the country had to implement the disputed provisions immediately, in the middle of a school year. The Senate tuition cap increase also was adopted.

Major Provisions

Funding levels for WIC were set at $1.58 billion in 1986; "such sums as may be necessary" for 1987 and 1988; and $1.78 billion in 1989. The other programs were extended at their existing levels.

The Congressional Research Service had estimated fiscal 1986 spending for those programs at $511.8 million for the commodity distribution program; $121.9 million for the summer food service; $48.9 million for state administrative expenses; and $5 million for the nutrition education and training program.

WIC was aimed at improving the health of low-income pregnant women, infants and children who were determined by medical authorities to be at nutritional risk.

The summer food service program for children provided food for children in low-income areas during the summer months — in essence, a school lunch program for poor children while school was not in session.

The commodity distribution program made surplus agricultural commodities from the stocks of the Commodity Credit Corporation available to low-income pregnant and needy women, infants and children who were at nutritional risk, as well as to eligible elderly participants. The nutrition and education training program provided grants to instruct students on the nutritional value of food.

The remaining program provided for payments to states to assist in meeting the administrative costs of operating the federal child nutrition programs.

WIC Provisions

As enacted, the legislation included the following provisions for WIC:

- Made a state ineligible to participate in the WIC program if it collected state or local taxes on food purchased with WIC funds.
- Allowed a state to carry up to 1 percent of a year's grant for supplemental foods into the next fiscal year without affecting the amount of funds allocated to that state in that year. In addition, a state was allowed to use up to 1 percent of a fiscal year's grant in the preceding fiscal year. This provision was designed to improve program management by reducing states' fears of having to forfeit unused funds at the end of a year.
- Required that nine-tenths of 1 percent of WIC appropriations be available first for providing WIC services to migrants.

Growth in migrant participation in the WIC program lagged far behind the growth in total WIC program participation. National data also indicated that the health and nutrition status of migrants was much worse than the national average.

- Required that if a state determined that benefits had been overissued to participants, the state must recover the cash value of the benefits overissued, unless it determined that it would not be cost-effective to pursue the matter.
- Required the agriculture secretary to report to Congress on March 1, 1987, and every two years thereafter, on the income, nutritional risk and other characteristics of WIC participants.

School Lunch, Breakfast

- Provided automatic eligibility for free meals for children who were members of households receiving food stamps or Aid to Families with Dependent Children (AFDC), in states where the standard for AFDC eligibility did not exceed 130 percent of poverty-level income.
- Required schools to offer whole milk as part of the lunch program.
- Permitted schools to allow students to refuse up to one item in each school breakfast, without having that refusal affect the charge to students or the amount of federal reimbursement for the breakfast. A similar provision was contained in the school lunch program.
- Clarified that it was legal to offer federally assisted school cafeterias and food service equipment or personnel to nutrition programs for the elderly.
- Changed the dates by which the secretary must make an estimate of the value of agricultural commodities to be delivered to schools, and by which the secretary must provide cash payments for any difference between the estimates of available commodities and the amount of commodity support mandated by law. The date for the estimate was changed from May 15 to June 1 of each year; the date to make cash compensation was changed from June 15 to July 1.
- Raised from $1,500 to $1,000 the maximum tuition a private school could charge and remain in the school lunch and breakfast programs.

Other Programs

- Reduced from $75,000 to $50,000 a year the minimum amount of funds a state could receive in any fiscal year for conducting nutrition education and training.
- Allowed local school districts that had been participating in a pilot project studying alternatives to the traditional commodity distribution program to continue their participation, and authorized $50,000 for any expenses related to carrying out the project. ▮

Community Health Centers

After several false starts, Congress April 11 cleared legislation (S 1282 — PL 99-280) to continue direct federal funding for health centers that provided primary health care services to medically underserved areas.

S 1282, the Health Services Amendments Act of 1986, reauthorized through fiscal 1988 programs under the Public Health Service Act that funded health care for nearly 6 million Americans at community health centers and health centers for migrant and seasonal workers.

The grants were the principal federal programs designed to assure availability of health care to medically underserved populations. In 1984, 5.2 million people received care at public and private non-profit community health centers, while migrant centers served half a million persons.

Although the number of persons seeking care had continued to increase, sponsors bowed to fiscal pressures and agreed to freeze authorizations for fiscal 1987 and 1988 at the 1986 appropriation levels of $400 million for community health centers and $45 million for migrant centers.

The legislation also revoked an optional block grant program the administration wanted to keep.

Background. The Reagan administration each year since 1981 had sought to replace the direct funding program with a mandatory block grant, but Congress had rebuffed those efforts. The optional block grant program was created in 1981, but only one state — West Virginia — took advantage of the program, and it gave the money back within the first year. *(1981 Almanac p. 485)*

Authorization for the health programs technically expired Sept. 30, 1984, but they continued to receive funding while both houses haggled over reauthorization attempts. Congress approved reauthorization of the programs as part of an omnibus health professions bill in 1984, but President Reagan vetoed the measure. *(1984 Almanac p. 475)*

Legislative History. The Senate passed S 1282 (S Rept 99-104) on July 19, 1985. *(1985 Almanac p. 290)*

The House version of the bill (HR 2418 — H Rept 99-157) first came to the floor Feb. 18, 1986, under suspension of the rules, a shortcut procedure requiring a two-thirds vote for passage. On Feb. 19, the bill drew a majority in a largely party-line vote of 254-151, but fell 16 short of the necessary two-thirds. *(Vote 22, p. 10-H)*

HR 2418 returned to the floor under regular procedures March 5. Before passing the bill on a 403-6 vote, the House approved the funding freeze, 400-9, and rejected, 94-319, a move to keep the optional block grant program. It dropped provisions that would have established federal grants for plague control as well as new grants to states for planning and development of primary care services. Following passage of HR 2418, the House substituted its text for that of the Senate bill. *(Votes 33-35, p. 12-H)*

The Senate April 11 approved the House version of S 1282 by voice vote, clearing the bill for the president's signature.

Provisions

As signed into law April 24, S 1282 (PL 99-280):

- Authorized $400 million in each of fiscal 1987 and 1988 for grants to community health centers, and $45.4 million each year for grants to migrant health centers.
- Repealed the optional Primary Care Block Grant enacted in 1981.
- Required the secretary of health and human services to establish criteria for deciding if an area or population group was medically underserved. The criteria must take into account comments from state and local officials as well as data on the population's current health status, access to and affordability of primary health care.
- Prohibited the secretary from designating a medically underserved population or terminating such a designation without prior notice to and opportunity for comment from state and local officials and the state's existing community health centers.
- Allowed the secretary to designate as medically underserved areas that did not meet the criteria if state and local officials recommended such a designation because of a particular barrier to access or lack of availability of health care services.
- Permitted the secretary to enter into agreements that would allow states to take a more active role in analyzing the need for primary health services for medically underserved populations, helping oversee the operation of existing centers and assisting in the planning and development of new ones.
- Allowed migrant health grant funds to be used to repay loans made by the Farmers Home Administration for

buildings. (This technical change had been made previously for community health centers.) ∎

Protections for Mentally Ill

Congress May 14 completed action on legislation (S 974 — PL 99-319) to create new legal protection and advocacy services for the institutionalized and recently discharged mentally ill.

S 974 extended to the mentally ill protection and advocacy services already available to the "developmentally disabled" under a 1975 law that was last reauthorized in 1984 (PL 98-527). Developmentally disabled persons included most of the institutionalized mentally retarded and individuals with physical handicaps, such as cerebral palsy, that affect mental function. *(1984 Almanac p. 481)*

The new legislation was developed in response to continuing reports of abuse and neglect of patients in state mental institutions.

The bill authorized the Department of Health and Human Services (HHS) to provide funds to independent statewide agencies with access to facilities and records and authority to investigate alleged instances of abuse and neglect. Eligible agencies must be able to pursue administrative, legal and other remedies on behalf of mental patients. Agencies must also have an advisory board to recommend policies and priorities in protecting and advocating for the mentally ill.

Final Provisions

As signed into law May 23, S 974 (PL 99-319):

- Defined abuse as "any act or failure to act by an employee of a facility rendering care or treatment . . . performed knowingly, recklessly or intentionally, and which caused or may have caused injury to a mentally ill individual." Abuse could include rape or sexual assault, striking an individual, use of excessive force or use of bodily or chemical restraints not in compliance with federal or state laws or regulations.
- Defined neglect as a "negligent act or omission" by anyone responsible for providing care to the mentally ill that caused or might have caused injury, or that placed a mentally ill individual at risk of injury. Neglect could include failure to establish or carry out a treatment plan; failure to provide adequate food, clothing or health care; or failure to provide a safe environment for a mentally ill individual.
- Specified that to be eligible for grants, advocacy agencies — whether public or private — must be independent of any agency providing treatment or services. Agencies must also have access to facilities providing treatment and their records, and authority to investigate allegations of abuse and neglect. They must have authority to pursue administrative, legal and other appropriate remedies on behalf of institutionalized individuals and patients discharged within the preceding 90 days.
- Required that advocacy agencies set up boards to advise them on policies and priorities. Board members must include attorneys, mental health professionals, members of the public knowledgeable about mental illness, and a provider of mental health services. At least half the board members must be individuals who had received or were receiving mental health services, or family members of such individuals.
- Required agencies to exhaust all administrative remedies before instituting legal action on behalf of a patient or former patient.
- Authorized $10 million for fiscal 1986, $10.5 million for fiscal 1987 and $11.025 million for fiscal 1988.
- Restated the "bill of rights for mental health patients" included in Title V of the Mental Health Systems Act of 1980 (PL 96-398) and encouraged states to review and, if necessary, revise laws to conform to that bill of rights. *(1980 Almanac p. 430)*
- Stipulated that such restatement should not be construed as establishing any new rights for mentally ill individuals.
- Directed the secretary of HHS, using available appropriations, to promote the establishment of family support groups for victims of Alzheimer's disease or related memory disorders, and for their families. Such groups would provide educational, emotional and practical support. The secretary also was to promote a national network to coordinate the activities of the family support groups.

Legislative History

Senate, House Action. S 974 was originally passed by the Senate, by voice vote, on July 31, 1985. The Senate bill (S Rept 99-109) stemmed from a six-month staff investigation into the treatment of residents of state mental institutions. *(1985 action, 1985 Almanac p. 291)*

The House passed its version (HR 4055) on Jan. 30, 1986. The bill had been reported as HR 3492 (H Rept 99-401) by the Energy and Commerce Committee in 1985. It passed on a 290-84 vote, despite conservatives' complaints that the action contradicted lawmakers' avowed determination to eliminate the federal budget deficit. *(Vote 10, p. 4-H)*

Conference, Final Action. Conferees filed their report May 5 (H Rept 99-576). The conference agreement authorized a total of $31.53 million for the program over three years: $10 million for fiscal 1986, $10.5 million for fiscal 1987 and $11.025 million for fiscal 1988. These were the figures contained in the Senate version of the bill; House-approved authorization levels were $1.5 million higher.

The $10 million for fiscal 1986 had already been appropriated, on a conditional basis, in the funding bill for HHS (PL 99-178) that was cleared in December 1985. Those funds became available when President Reagan signed S 974 into law May 23.

Conferees agreed to delete a controversial Senate provision that would have limited fees for publicly funded attorneys who prevailed in legal actions on behalf of a mentally ill individual.

House conferees agreed to accept Senate language requiring agencies to exhaust all administrative remedies before going to court.

They also agreed to drop a provision that would have precluded states from receiving funds under the federal alcohol, drug abuse and mental health block grant unless the states agreed to establish the advocacy agencies.

Conferees retained a House provision to promote the creation of a national network of support groups for victims of Alzheimer's disease and related memory disorders and their families. No new funds were authorized for the program.

The House approved the conference report May 13, by a 383-21 vote, and the Senate followed suit by voice vote May 14. *(Vote 111, p. 34-H)* ∎

Major Medicare, Medicaid Changes Enacted

As it had through much of the Reagan era, Congress in 1986 used the annual budget reconciliation process to make major changes in the Medicare and Medicaid programs.

In back-to-back reconciliation bills for fiscal 1986 and 1987, lawmakers sought to trim federal payments to physicians and hospitals while limiting the financial squeeze on patients.

Medicare was the federal health insurance program for the elderly, while Medicaid was a joint federal-state health care program for the poor.

With price tags of $74.3 billion and $42 billion, respectively, for fiscal 1986, Medicare and Medicaid were the nation's largest and most expensive health programs.

Overview: Fiscal 1986 Reconciliation

The fiscal 1986 reconciliation measure (HR 3128 — PL 99-272), cleared March 20, sought to trim Medicare spending by extending through Dec. 31, 1986, a freeze on physicians' fees, and by limiting to 0.5 percent increases in payments to hospitals. *(Background, 1985 Almanac p. 302)*

The freeze on doctors' fees had been in place since July 1, 1984, although total Medicare payments to physicians continued to climb sharply nonetheless — 11 percent in fiscal 1985, more than triple the increase in the Consumer Price Index in that period.

The bill also made Medicare coverage mandatory for all state and local government employees hired after April 1, 1986, and voluntary for previously hired workers. Covered employees and their employers had to pay the Medicare portion of the Social Security payroll tax.

HR 3128 included an array of initiatives unrelated to deficit reduction. Among them were provisions to penalize hospitals that refused to provide emergency care for the poor and to require states to extend Medicaid coverage to pregnant women in two-parent families in which the principal wage-earner was unemployed.

Also included were provisions requiring employers to extend health insurance coverage to laid-off workers and widowed spouses of employees who had been covered by group health plans.

Overview: Fiscal 1987 Reconciliation

The fiscal 1987 reconciliation bill (HR 5300 — PL 99-509), cleared Oct. 17, allowed a 3.2 percent increase in physicians' fees beginning Jan. 1, 1987, and a 1.15 percent increase in Medicare payments to hospitals. *(Full provisions, p. 559)*

The measure also put the brakes on annual increases in the "deductible" that Medicare patients had to pay for each hospital stay. The deductible, which had been based on the cost of one day in the hospital, rose from $400 in 1985 to $492 in 1986. Without congressional action, it would have reached $572 in 1987. Instead, Congress capped the deductible at $520 and based future increases on the percentage payment change that hospitals received each year.

HR 5300 provided one year of Medicare coverage for immunosuppressive drugs needed by organ transplant patients, primarily the recipients of kidney transplants. *(Story, p. 265)*

And it imposed a number of safeguards to ensure that the quality of care received by Medicare patients did not suffer because of cost-cutting incentives created by the 1983 law (PL 98-21) overhauling the Medicare payment system.

Finally, the measure permitted states to extend Medicaid coverage to the disabled, pregnant women and children up to age 5 who did not qualify for welfare but had incomes below the poverty line.

Two important provisions were dropped from the bill at the last minute during House-Senate negotiations.

The first was a Senate provision to extend Medicare coverage to all state and local government employees. House negotiators had offered to phase in the coverage over five years.

The other was a House provision to encourage establishment of risk pools to make health insurance available to people who were otherwise unable to obtain it. *(Access to health care, p. 260)*

Background

Medicare, one of the capstone's of President Lyndon B. Johnson's Great Society, was the most important social welfare program of the post-World War II era. Its enactment in 1965 (PL 89-97) marked the end of a 20-year battle between organized labor and liberals on the one hand, and the American Medical Association on the other. For the first time, the federal government accepted a measure of responsibility for insuring the health care of millions of Americans. *(Congress and the Nation Vol. I, p. 751)*

Before Medicare, about half of those aged 65 and older had no health insurance. Many faced great difficulty obtaining affordable, adequate care. By 1985, virtually all older Americans — some 27 million people — were covered by Medicare, as were 3 million disabled individuals.

While Medicare eased the burden of health costs for many, gaps and restrictions in the program meant that beneficiaries wound up paying far more out-of-pocket than originally anticipated.

According to the House Select Committee on Aging, out-of-pocket expenses for health care represented 15 percent of the mean income of older Americans in 1984 — up from 12 percent in 1977, and about the same as in 1966, the year Medicare went into operation.

Medicare in 1984 paid about 45 percent of the elderly's medical bills. Many beneficiaries bought private insurance policies to guard against some of the costs Medicare would not cover.

If the elderly in the 1980s were paying more than they expected to for medical care, so was the federal government.

When it was enacted, Medicare was expected to cost $8.8 billion in 1990, according to the Office of Management and Budget. By 1985, it actually cost more than $70 billion.

The 1983 Law: A Major Shift

In an effort to curb soaring Medicare costs, Congress in 1983 enacted legislation (PL 98-21) overhauling the way the program paid for hospital costs. *(1983 Almanac p. 391)*

The law set in motion a three-year transition from a cost-based reimbursement system to a "prospective payment system" (PPS). That transition was lengthened by one year under HR 3128, the fiscal 1986 reconciliation bill.

At the heart of the new system were preset flat fees for inpatient treatment of particular illnesses or conditions, from broken bones to brain tumors. Fees varied according to the complexity and length of treatment involved for specific categories of cases, known as diagnosis-related groups (DRGs). Hospitals that could treat a patient with a particular condition for less than the preset fee for that DRG could pocket the difference; those that spent more had to swallow the extra cost themselves.

Proponents of the DRG system credited it with significant reductions in the rate of increase in hospital costs, mostly because of drops in the average length of stay.

According to the Department of Health and Human Services (HHS), the average hospital stay for Medicare patients under the new system dropped from 9.3 days in fiscal 1983 to 7.7 days for the first two-thirds of fiscal 1985. The growth in hospital expenses slowed from 15.8 percent in fiscal 1982 to 5.5 percent in fiscal 1985. Some of that drop was due to a general ebbing of inflation, but the DRG system was given much of the credit.

Quality of Care Concerns

The new system was not an unqualified success. Critics charged that hospitals were responding to the DRG system's incentives to cut costs not simply by operating more efficiently, but also by scrimping on services and discharging patients "quicker and sicker."

A four-month 1985 investigation by the staff of the Senate Aging Committeee found evidence that "seriously ill Medicare patients are inappropriately and prematurely discharged from hospitals."

The study found that some patients had been incorrectly told that they were being discharged because Medicare did not allow longer stays — that their "DRG had run out."

However, the Reagan administration and hospital officials insisted there was no proof of a widespread decline in quality of care for the elderly.

In a letter to Sen. John Heinz, R-Pa., chairman of the Aging Committee, a spokesman for the American Hospital Association said, "A single instance, or even a handful of instances, of poor quality care does not prove that the prospective pricing system is fatally flawed or that the entire industry is adopting practices that jeopardize the quality of care available to Medicare beneficiaries."

HHS officials said an important check on substandard care was the federally designated system of peer review organizations (PROs) — groups of health professionals that monitored the quality of services, appropriateness of admissions and other factors affecting the treatment of Medicare patients within a locality or region.

Agency officials vowed to strengthen existing HHS requirements that hospitals notify Medicare patients that they had a right to appeal to the local PRO if they felt they were being discharged too soon.

'Disproportionate Share' Hospitals

While the DRG system was intended to discourage wasteful practices, critics said some hospitals were losing money through no fault of their own.

Particularly worrisome to key members of Congress was the claim that hospitals serving large numbers of low-income patients were getting short shrift under the new system. Hospitals said that it cost more to treat the poor because they were often sicker than other patients and also often required supplemental services such as translators and social workers.

Responding to that concern, Congress included provisions in HR 3128 to boost payments to hospitals serving a "disproportionate share" of poor people.

Members also were concerned that the DRG system indirectly contributed to an apparent decline in hospitals' willingness to provide charity care to patients who lacked health insurance or the resources to pay their own bills. The DRG system made it harder for hospitals to absorb the cost of providing free care by increasing charges to Medicare patients.

HR 3128 included stiff new penalties for hospitals that refused to provide appropriate emergency room treatment because a patient lacked the ability to pay.

HR 3128: Fiscal 1986 Bill

The fiscal 1986 reconciliation bill did not clear Congress until almost six months after the fiscal year had begun.

In 1985, the measure made it as far as a Senate-House conference committee, but it stalled there over a number of issues — including a few involving Medicare. *(Reconciliation bill, 1985 Almanac p. 498)*

Conference Action

A key issue dividing House and Senate negotiators in conference was a House proposal to extend for one year the three-year transition period for implementing the new DRG system. The Senate wanted to stick to the original schedule and have the new system in place by Oct. 1, 1986.

A December 1985 conference report on HR 3128 included a compromise scheme for delaying the transition for one year, but the issue was reopened when negotiations over HR 3128 resumed in 1986.

As cleared, the measure included the one-year extension of the phase-in period. But an exception was made to allow the original transition schedule to proceed in Oregon, home state of Finance Chairman Bob Packwood, R, where hospitals generally were faring better under the new system than under the old one.

In other provisions affecting Medicare, the legislation provided for increased payments to hospitals serving large numbers of poor people on one hand, and, on the other, reduced Medicare supplements currently paid to teaching hospitals.

For most doctors, the bill extended until Dec. 31, 1986, the existing freeze on what Medicare paid for physician services. As the chambers batted proposals back and forth, the freeze on Medicare payments to physicians temporarily lapsed March 15, as it had for a few hours Dec. 20, 1985, before it was retroactively extended. But the final version of the bill continued the freeze until Dec. 31.

Cost-cutting under the federal-state Medicaid program for the poor came primarily from administrative savings, including improved collections from private insurers who covered low-income patients.

In negotiations in 1986 to make HR 3128 more acceptable to the White House, some changes were made in the health provisions of the original conference report.

A key point of contention was administration objections to proposals that would have increased spending in certain areas.

Before clearing the bill, Congress agreed to drop proposals that expanded certain Medicare benefits and to scale back from 1 percent to 0.5 percent the proposed increase in hospital payment rates for the latter part of fiscal 1986.

The major Medicare proposals that were dropped would have expanded coverage for occupational therapy and optometry, revised the Medicare appeals process, and modified regulations issued by the Department of Health and Human Services (HHS) restricting payments for home health care and medical equipment.

Under Medicaid, negotiators agreed to drop a proposal to give states the option of providing coverage for respiratory services for individuals dependent on ventilators.

However, the cleared bill retained provisions expanding Medicaid coverage for low-income pregnant women.

Lawmakers dropped proposals requiring HHS to support pilot projects in home- and community-based health services as an alternative to institutional long-term care. However, the bill retained provisions designed to make it easier for states to win HHS approval for experimenting with home- and community-based services under Medicaid.

Provisions

As signed into law April 7, HR 3128 (PL 99-272) included health provisions that:

- **Medicare.** Postponed for one year, until Oct. 1, 1987, full implementation of the prospective payment system and delayed an increase in the proportion of hospital costs covered by the new DRG system, which had been scheduled to increase from 50 percent in fiscal 1985 to 75 percent in 1986.

The bill increased the share of hospital costs under the new system to 55 percent in the eighth month of hospitals' fiscal 1986 cost-reporting period.

An exception was made for Oregon, where 75 percent of hospital costs would be paid under the DRG system.

- Delayed for one year a separate transition in which regional DRG rates were to be replaced with uniform national rates by Oct. 1, 1986. Under the bill, DRG rates remained 75 percent regional and 25 percent national in fiscal 1986, as they were in 1985. Existing law would have required a 50-50 split for 1986.
- Provided a 0.5 percent increase in hospital payment rates, effective May 1. Because hospital reimbursement rates were cut 1 percent below fiscal 1985 levels on March 1 under the Gramm-Rudman-Hollings anti-deficit law (PL 99-177), this provision in effect would reduce payments to 0.5 percent below fiscal 1985 rates. Existing law would have permitted an increase of more than 5 percent to compensate for medical inflation.
- Required HHS to implement, as of May 1, a new index of hospital wages and salaries designed to reflect regional payroll differences when computing prospective payments under Medicare. Existing law called for the new index to be applied retroactively to payments made since Oct. 1, 1983.
- Reduced supplemental payments to teaching hospitals for fiscal years 1986-88. The provision revised the formula for calculating special payments, which were supposed to reimburse hospitals for the indirect costs of training medical graduates, such as expenses for extra diagnostic tests that less-experienced interns or resident doctors might order.
- Required HHS to make extra payments to hospitals that served a disproportionate share of poor people, in an effort to compensate for the higher costs of caring for low-income patients.

The bill provided a formula for determining eligible hospitals, and authorized supplements of up to 15 percent of the regular DRG rates for urban hospitals with more than 100 beds, 5 percent for smaller urban hospitals and 4 percent for rural hospitals.

Also eligible for the supplements would be hospitals that received more than 30 percent of their revenues from state and local government payments for indigent care. The provision was to expire at the end of fiscal 1988.

- Permitted certain rural osteopathic hospitals to qualify as rural referral centers under the prospective payments system if they had at least 3,000 patients a year. Existing regulations set 6,000 discharged patients as the criterion.

Rural referral centers received higher Medicare payments than smaller rural hospitals. Their reimbursements were comparable to payments for urban hospitals, reflecting the greater variety and number of cases at such centers.

- Provided for the gradual elimination of special payments to for-profit, investor-owned hospitals, specifying that after fiscal 1989 return on equity no longer would be an allowable capital cost reimbursable by Medicare.
- Provided a special rule for calculating certain capital-related Medicare costs when a state donated a hospital to a non-profit corporation.
- Required HHS to report to Congress with recommendations for addressing problems small rural hospitals faced with regard to Medicare policies on certain patient transfers. Existing law required extra payments for unusually long or costly hospital stays; HHS prescribed the payments in cases where patients were transferred between hospitals.
- Required HHS to provide the Prospective Payment Assessment Commission, Congressional Budget Office, Congressional Research Service and General Accounting Office with up-to-date data on Medicare reimbursements being made to specific hospitals under the prospective payment system. The information would be confidential.
- Required HHS to increase Medicare reimbursements for certain rural hospitals that were the sole source of inpatient care in their communities if they had to add facilities or services that increased costs significantly.
- Expanded the Prospective Payment Assessment Commission by two members, who were to represent nurses and rural hospitals.
- Made permanent a provision in existing law, due to expire Oct. 1, 1986, allowing Medicare reimbursement for hospice care of the terminally ill. Payments to hospices would increase $10 a day, effective April 1.
- Reduced the late enrollment penalty for joining the Medicare "Part A" hospital insurance program. Most Americans were automatically eligible for Part A, but those who were not had to pay a premium for coverage that reflected full actuarial costs. The bill set new limits on the penalty charged those who purchased coverage more than three months after becoming eligible at 65.
- Made Medicare coverage mandatory for all state and local government employees hired after April 1, 1986, and voluntary for previously hired workers. Covered employees and their employers had to pay the Medicare portion of the Social Security payroll tax.
- Required hospitals that participated in Medicare to provide emergency services for people with an urgent need for care, including women in labor, regardless of their ability to pay. The provision prohibited transfers of such patients unless their condition had been stabilized or a doctor certified that the move would be beneficial. Hospitals that violated the "anti-dumping" requirements could be barred from participating in Medicare. Both the hospital and the responsible physician could face civil penalties of up to $25,000 per violation.

• Gave skilled nursing facilities that provided fewer than 1,500 days of Medicare services a year the option of being paid under a new prospective payment system. Payment rates would be set in advance at 105 percent of the mean for nursing facilities in the area. Facilities choosing to participate could file a less-detailed report of their costs than was required under existing law.

• Restructured the way Medicare paid teaching hospitals for the direct costs of graduate medical education, such as residents' salaries. Rather than reimbursing these costs on an open-ended basis, the bill provided for per-resident payments. A 1 percent increase was allowed for fiscal 1986, and hikes in fiscal 1987 and 1988 were limited to the rate of inflation.

• Reduced future Medicare payments for the graduate medical education of residents after they had trained the number of years needed to obtain certification in their chosen medical specialty, plus one year, up to a maximum of five years of training. Payments for training in excess of those limits would be reduced by 25 percent beginning July 1, 1986, and by 50 percent beginning July 1, 1987.

• Cut off reimbursement for residency training of graduates of foreign medical schools unless they had passed a standardized test such as the Foreign Medical Graduate Examination in Medical Sciences.

• Required employers of 20 or more people to offer employees and their spouses aged 70 or over the same health insurance coverage provided to other, younger workers. Existing age-discrimination law protected workers aged 40 through 69. If an aged worker chose the employer's private plan, Medicare covered health care costs only if the private plan did not.

• Authorized an additional $60 million a year in fiscal 1986-88 for cost audits and medical reviews by intermediaries that carried out day-to-day administrative and operational tasks for Medicare.

• Extended through Dec. 31, 1986, a freeze on Medicare payments for physicians who did not agree to accept all Medicare patients on an "assigned" basis — that is, to accept Medicare reimbursement as payment in full without extra charges to patients except required deductibles and co-payments.

However, the freeze on Medicare reimbursements was to be lifted May 1 for doctors who had signed up for a program that committed them to accept all Medicare patients on assignment. What Medicare paid these doctors would be increased for inflation plus 1 percentage point.

Doctors would be able to sign up for or drop out of the assignment program during April.

• Established an 11-member commission to study ways to improve the system for reimbursing physicians under Medicare.

• Extended for one year, through 1988, an existing requirement that premiums charged to participants in Part B of Medicare cover 25 percent of the program's costs. Annual appropriations paid for the remaining costs of Part B, which covered non-hospital expenses.

• Denied Medicare reimbursement for assistant surgeons in routine cataract operations, unless prior approval was obtained from companies that handled Medicare claims or peer review organizations, regional medical groups that monitored services provided to Medicare patients.

• Imposed new limits on Medicare reimbursement for replacement of prosthetic lenses in cataract eyeglasses and contact lenses.

• Authorized HHS to establish demonstration projects in at least five states to determine cost-effectiveness of providing Medicare coverage for services, such as immunizations and drug-abuse prevention, designed to prevent illnesses. Medicare did not cover preventive health services under existing law.

• Imposed ceilings on Medicare fees for clinical laboratory services, setting the limits at 115 percent of the median fee for particular tests beginning July 1 and 110 percent of the median beginning Jan. 1, 1988.

• Required Medicare patients to get a second medical opinion before certain elective surgery, denying Medicare reimbursement to those who failed to do so. Peer review organizations were required to mandate a second opinion for at least 10 surgical procedures, chosen from a list to be prepared by HHS.

• Authorized peer review organizations to deny payment for substandard medical care and monitor care provided by health maintenance organizations (HMOs) for Medicare beneficiaries.

• **Medicaid.** Required states to provide Medicaid coverage for prenatal and postpartum care of low-income women in two-parent families where the chief wage earner was unemployed. Such coverage previously was provided at states' option.

• Allowed states to provide poor pregnant women with a broader range of services than they provided for other beneficiaries under Medicaid. Existing law generally required states to finance the same services for all categories of individuals who were automatically eligible for Medicaid.

• Limited the authority of HHS to disapprove state requests to provide Medicaid coverage for home- and community-based care for patients who otherwise would be institutionalized. States were authorized to pay for such services only if HHS approved a waiver of Medicaid rules.

The bill required HHS to extend for one to five years any waiver that expired in fiscal 1986, if the state requested an extension, and barred HHS from denying federal matching funds on the grounds that a state's actual expenditures for home- and community-based services exceeded approved cost estimates.

• Gave states the option of extending Medicaid coverage to hospice care for the terminally ill.

• Limited individuals' ability to meet Medicaid income and assets tests by putting their assets in a trust. However, states could waive the provision in cases where its application would cause undue hardship.

• Required states to formulate policies for Medicaid coverage of organ transplants.

• Shored up the existing requirement that Medicaid be the payer of last resort for poor patients by requiring states to improve collections from private insurance companies that covered low-income people.

• Eased the existing ban against states increasing Medicaid payments to nursing homes to reflect higher capital costs that resulted solely from the sale of the facility. The provision allowed states' aggregate payments to nursing homes for capital costs to reflect, within specified limits, increases in value resulting from changes in ownership.

• Gave states more leeway to postpone making federally required repairs in facilities for the mentally retarded if a state had an approved plan for deinstitutionalizing patients. Such plans could be approved only in cases where a delay in facility repairs would not pose an immediate threat to the health or safety of residents. HHS could approve only 15 plans a year, although there would be no limit on the number of plans that could be approved in cases where it would cost $2 million or more to make repairs needed to come into compliance with federal standards under Medicaid.

- Allowed adopted or foster children with Medicaid coverage to receive reimbursement for care in the state in which they were placed even if their eligibility was from another state.
- **Other Health Provisions.** Required HHS to establish a task force to develop recommendations for insurance policies to cover long-term health care.
- Required employers of at least 20 people that offered group health insurance plans to offer continued coverage for up to three years for workers' spouses and dependents who otherwise would lose coverage after a death or divorce or because the worker became eligible for Medicare. Continued coverage for up to 18 months would have to be provided for laid-off workers. Qualified beneficiaries could be charged premiums up to 102 percent of the group rate. Employers who did not comply would face penalties including loss of the business tax deduction for their contributions to health plans.
- Established a Council on Graduate Medical Education to assess long-term physician training issues, including the current and future demand for doctors in medical and surgical specialties and issues related to the training of graduates of foreign medical schools.

HR 5300: Fiscal 1987 Bill

The fiscal 1987 reconciliation package began to take shape in late July, as authorizing committees made their recommendations to the House and Senate Budget committees.

The three committees that dealt with most of the nation's health policy approved separate, and in some cases conflicting, recommendations July 23 to reduce Medicare spending by approximately $3 billion over the next three years while expanding eligibility for the Medicaid program.

For the third consecutive year, the committees with jurisdiction over the programs — House Energy and Commerce, House Ways and Means, and Senate Finance — used deficit-reduction bills to make significant cuts and increases in them.

The changes proposed for fiscal 1987 were less extensive than in years past, in part because the programs had been pared extensively over the preceding five years.

The fiscal 1987 budget resolution assumed that each committee would find ways to reduce outlays for Medicare, the federal health insurance program for the elderly, by $550 million in fiscal 1987 and by $3.25 billion over the next three years. In the House, the Energy and Commerce and Ways and Means committees shared jurisdiction over a portion of the Medicare program, but both were given the entire assumed savings for the program as their recommended target.

The budget also assumed that Medicaid would continue at levels provided by current law, and that the committees would authorize an optional program to permit states to extend Medicaid services to low-income elderly and disabled individuals, pregnant women and infants who were not currently eligible.

Medicare Recommendations

The Finance Committee recommended net Medicare savings of approximately $3 billion for fiscal 1987, and $4.7 billion over three years. Ways and Means proposed savings of $1.7 billion for fiscal 1987 and $4.6 billion over three years, according to preliminary estimates. Energy and Commerce, which shared jurisdiction with Ways and Means for Medicare's physician-repayment program, recommended savings of $203 million for 1987, and $1.126 billion for the three years.

While actual proposed spending cuts for all three committees were higher, all offset at least a portion of those savings by authorizing new spending on a variety of initiatives ranging from holding down a projected rise in the first-day hospital deductible beneficiaries must pay to demonstration projects for victims of Alzheimer's disease.

Finance recommended a total of $3.3 billion over three years in new spending, Ways and Means a total of $1.56 billion, and Energy and Commerce a total of $1.37 billion.

House Republicans on both the Ways and Means and Energy and Commerce panels vociferously objected to adding the new spending provisions. Still, an amendment offered by William E. Dannemeyer, R-Calif., to strike from the Energy and Commerce recommendations all new spending provisions failed on a vote of 8-32. All those voting in favor were Republicans.

Highlights of the committee recommendations included:

Physician Payments. Both Ways and Means and Energy and Commerce sought to limit the amount by which Medicare increased payments to physicians when a fee freeze imposed in 1984 expired at the end of 1986.

Without congressional action, the fees would have been allowed to rise by the amount of the medical economic index (MEI), calculated by the government to reflect inflation and increased operating costs. Projections put the MEI for 1987 at 3.2 percent; the Reagan administration proposed an increase of 0.8 percent.

Energy and Commerce approved a provision to allow Medicare to grant the full MEI increase to so-called participating doctors, who had signed up for a program under which they agreed to accept Medicare rates as full payment for all claims for all patients. Non-participating physicians would receive the full increase for assigned claims (those for which they agreed to accept what they got from Medicare as payment in full).

Non-participating doctors would receive only a 1 percent increase on unassigned claims, for which the beneficiary was expected to make up the difference between what the doctor charged and what Medicare paid.

The committee estimated that the provision would save $180 million over three years.

The Ways and Means panel agreed 18-16 to allow all physicians to raise their fees by the full 3.2 percent. However, participating physicians would receive an extra 1 percentage point bonus. Non-participating doctors could also raise their fees by an additional 1 percentage point, but that cost would be borne by beneficiaries, not the government.

Capital-Related Costs. Finance and Ways and Means both delayed acting on a way to include equipment and building costs in Medicare's prospective payment system, which reimbursed hospitals based on average rather than actual costs.

Under provisions of the 1983 Medicare overhaul law (PL 98-21), such a plan was to be devised by Oct. 1, 1986. An amendment to the fiscal 1986 supplemental appropriations bill (PL 99-349), however, effectively postponed the deadlines until Oct. 1, 1987. *(Supplemental, p. 153)*

In the meantime, however, both committees acted to limit capital-cost reimbursement.

The Finance proposal would save $615 million over three years from an across-the-board cut in projected capital outlays of 3 percent in fiscal 1987, 5 percent in fiscal 1988, and 6 percent in fiscal 1989.

The Ways and Means proposal would save $1.12 billion over three years by limiting payments to 10 percent per year over fiscal 1986 actual costs.

Hospital Payments. Under current projections, hospitals covered by PPS would receive a 2 percent rate increase for fiscal 1987. Both Finance and Ways and Means recommended a smaller increase, but both were higher than the administration-recommended hike of 0.5 percent.

The Finance provision would save $670 million over three years by holding the increase to 1.5 percent.

The Ways and Means proposal would save $2.67 billion by granting PPS hospitals a 1.3 percent increase in fiscal 1987, and the full projected increase, less 1.5 percentage points, in fiscal 1988. Hospitals exempt from the PPS system would receive a 1.5 percent increase in fiscal 1987, and the projected increase less 2 percentage points in fiscal 1988.

Prompt Claims Payment. The recommendations of both Finance and Ways and Means achieved large savings by eliminating a program under which hospitals received periodic advance payments from Medicare.

The Finance proposal sought to save $3.4 billion over three years by eliminating the Periodic Interim Payment (PIP) program, and requiring instead that Medicare pay all "clean" claims (those properly submitted and not requiring medical review) both to hospitals and physicians within 24 days of submission.

Ways and Means claimed $1.39 billion in savings over three years by eliminating PIP for most hospitals, and requiring clean claims to be paid within 22 days. Beginning in fiscal 1988, Medicare would have to pay clean claims from participating doctors within 11 days.

Hospital Deductible. One expensive provision included in both the Finance and Ways and Means packages sought to cap the increase in the deductible Medicare beneficiaries must pay for each hospital stay. Without congressional action, the deductible, which rose from $400 to $492 on Jan. 1, 1986, would have risen to $572 on Jan. 1, 1987.

The Finance provision capped the 1987 deductible at $520 and pegged future increases to the average cost per hospital admission rather than the average cost per day by which it was currently calculated. The cost was estimated at $1.79 billion over three years.

The Ways and Means provision simply capped the 1987 payment at $500, without changing the formula, at a cost of $850 million.

Quality. Finance and Ways and Means included provisions based on bills introduced by Fortney H. "Pete" Stark, D-Calif., and Sen. John Heinz, R-Pa., to ensure that the quality of care received by Medicare beneficiaries was not compromised by cost-cutting incentives under the PPS system.

The Finance provisions were estimated to cost $78 million over three years; the Ways and Means provisions $360 million.

Reduced Payments. Senate Finance and House Energy approved provisions designed to fence the authority of the secretary of HHS to reduce Medicare payments for certain services and procedures in light of new technologies or practice patterns.

Ways and Means, on the other hand, sought to bar the secretary from exercising that authority.

The secretary's power to reduce Medicare reimbursements for overpriced procedures and services was expressly recognized by Congress for the first time in the fiscal 1986 budget reconcilation law (PL 99-272). Regulations governing exercise of that authority had not yet been implemented.

The Finance provision sought to modify proposed HHS regulations by requiring the HHS secretary to explain the factors and data used in deciding to reduce Medicare payment for a particular service or procedure. The provision also required a period of public comment before such a reduction could become effective. The committee estimated savings of $325 million over three years from exercise of the secretary's authority.

Energy and Commerce permitted the HHS secretary to reduce Medicare reimbursements only after a public comment period and only with the assurance that patients would not have to pick up the difference in cost.

Kidney Dialysis. All three committees took action to alter administration plans to reduce Medicare payments to doctors and facilities in the End Stage Renal Disease (ESRD) program, which covered kidney dialysis and transplants.

Administration regulations scheduled to take effect Aug. 1 would have cut by $14 per month the reimbursement to doctors who treat dialysis patients at home. The administration had also proposed slashing payments to facilities by $11 per treatment.

The Finance proposal went along with the physician fee reduction, but reduced the facility payment by only $1 per month and required the General Accounting Office to conduct a study of the appropriateness of the rate. The committee estimated savings of $90 million over three years.

Ways and Means reduced payments to kidney dialysis facilities by $5.50 per treatment and to physicians by $14 per month. At the same time, the HHS secretary would have been required to establish networks for patients in the ESRD program. The networks were to collect and validate data, conduct on-site review of care provided, and implement a patient grievance procedure.

The committee estimated that even with expenditures for the networks, the payment reductions would save $297 million over three years.

Energy and Commerce's proposal reduced the payment for doctors who treated home dialysis patients by only $7 per month instead of the $14 recommended by the administration and the other two committees. It also required patient networks. The panel estimated that its ESRD provisions would produce savings of $200 million over three years.

Organ Transplants, Drugs. Energy and Commerce, for the first time, decided to authorize Medicare payments for anti-rejection drugs needed by Medicare recipients who had received organ transplants.

Energy and Commerce also included a proposal to require that hospitals, as a condition of participation in Medicare and Medicaid, develop procedures for routinely seeking organ donations from the next of kin of potential donors.

Outpatient Surgery. The Finance Committee proposed an extension of the Medicare prospective payment system to outpatient surgery performed in hospitals. The committee estimated this would lead to savings of $250 million over three years.

Coverage for Therapists. Senate Finance decided to extend Medicare coverage to occupational therapy provided in a nursing home, clinic, rehabilitation agency or public health agency. The committee estimated the cost at $60 million over three years.

House Energy and Commerce voted to authorize Medicare payment under certain circumstances for services provided by optometrists, occupational therapists, physician assistants and nurse anesthetists.

The committee estimated added costs to the program of $215 million over three years for the vision and physical therapy services, but no costs from authorizing payments to physician assistants and nurse anesthetists, because those payments generally would replace more expensive ones to physicians.

Alzheimer's Projects. House Energy and Commerce approved a provision requiring the HHS secretary to conduct five one-year demonstration projects to assess the feasibility of providing Medicare assistance to victims of Alzheimer's disease and their families.

Taxes. The Senate Finance Committee put itself at odds with its House counterpart by voting to extend the Medicare payroll tax to state and local government workers not already covered.

The Finance Committee proposal was designed to increase revenues by about $5.1 billion over three years.

The fiscal 1986 reconciliation act mandated Medicare enrollment of all newly hired state and local employees, but kept coverage optional for public employees already hired as of April 1, 1986. Before that law was enacted, public employees' participation in Medicare was optional, although most were covered.

The Senate committee voted 12-4 to extend mandatory coverage to include all workers hired prior to April 1, 1986. House Ways and Means tabled a similar proposal by voice vote.

Medicaid Recommendations

As assumed in the budget resolution, both the Finance and Energy and Commerce committees as part of their reconciliation packages authorized states to extend Medicaid coverage to pregnant women, and children under age 1, whose incomes were below the poverty line but not low enough to qualify for Aid to Families with Dependent Children (AFDC). Finance estimated the cost to the government at $220 million over three years; Energy and Commerce at $175 million.

Both committees also included provisions to allow states to extend Medicaid to elderly and disabled individuals with incomes below the poverty line, but too high to qualify for Supplemental Security Income (SSI), the federal welfare program for the blind, elderly and disabled. Under the Finance provision, states could not extend coverage to the elderly and disabled unless they also extended it to pregnant women and children. Both committees estimated the three-year cost at $455 million.

Energy and Commerce's Medicaid provisions also required states to continue providing Medicaid to certain disabled individuals who chose to work and whose income might otherwise make them ineligible.

Both committees proposed spending $50 million to protect Florida, Minnesota, Ohio, and Virginia from losing Medicaid matching funds as a result of a formula change enacted in the 1986 reconciliation law.

Ventilator-Dependent. The Finance Committee also decided to require Medicaid coverage of home care for certain ventilator-dependent individuals following a hospitalization of at least 30 days.

The Homeless. The provisions also clarified that otherwise-eligible homeless individuals could not be denied Medicaid simply because they had no permanent residence or fixed address.

AIDS Victims. Energy and Commerce authorized the HHS secretary to grant waivers to permit Medicaid payments for home and community-based care as alternatives to hospitalization for Medicaid beneficiaries who had acquired immune deficiency syndrome (AIDS), AIDS-related complex, or were chronically mentally ill.

Second Opinion. Energy and Commerce members voted to allow, but not require, states to demand a second opinion on the need for surgery for Medicaid patients. States were also authorized to require hospital pre-admission reviews.

Illegal Aliens. And finally, the committee included provisions to make clear that illegal aliens were not eligible for Medicaid. A recent federal court decision in New York said that in the absence of such a statutory bar, those aliens could not be denied Medicaid.

Budget Committee, Floor Action

The Budget committees in both chambers approved reconciliation packages (HR 5300, S 2706) the week of July 28, rolling in — without change — the recommendations of their authorizing committees.

The Senate passed its version Sept. 20 by 88-7. The bill promised an estimated $12.6 billion in deficit reduction. *(Vote 277, p. 47-S)*

The House passed HR 5300 on Sept. 24 by 309-106. It called for $15.2 billion in total deficit reductions. *(Vote 375, p. 106-H)*

The two contained the following major Medicare and Medicaid provisions:

Hospital Payments. The Senate bill increased Medicare payment rates for hospital services by 1.3 percent; the House bill raised the rates by 1 percent. The Department of Health and Human Services had proposed an increase of 0.5 percent.

Hospital Deductible. The amount Medicare beneficiaries must pay for the first day of a hospital stay was set at $500 in fiscal 1987 by the House, and at $520 by the Senate. Without action, it would have risen from the current $492 to $572.

Expanded Services. Both bills expanded Medicare coverage for home health care and occupational therapy. The House bill also expanded benefits for vision care, health maintenance organizations and other services.

Periodic Hospital Payments. The administration proposed eliminating a system of periodic interim payments (PIP) to most hospitals. Both bills required continuation of these payments to some hospitals.

Medicaid Expansions. Both bills permitted states to expand Medicaid coverage to pregnant women, infants, elderly and disabled people whose incomes were above current entry standards but below the poverty standard.

Medicare Coverage for State and Local Employees. The Senate bill required Medicare coverage of all state and local employees; previously only new employees had to be covered. The House version of the legislation had no similar provision.

Conference Negotiations

House and Senate negotiators began meeting Sept. 26. and vowed to resolve differences on a deficit-cutting measure (HR 5300) in time for it to be counted in an Oct. 6 report on the projected deficit for fiscal 1987. But that goal proved elusive.

While the bills were similar in most areas, there were some sharp differences in several areas, including health.

House negotiators, for example, balked at a Senate proposal to extend Medicare coverage to all state and local government employees.

House Ways and Means Committee Chairman Dan Rostenkowski, D-Ill., said Senate insistence on extending Medicare coverage to all state and local workers "could very well be the vote that sinks this bill."

House conferees offered to phase in such coverage over five years in return for other concessions, but some members objected strongly to that.

Offers and counteroffers whizzed from one side of the Capitol to the other the week of Oct. 6 as the two chambers struggled to clear the reconciliation bill.

Except for the Ways and Means and Finance provisions, most others were settled by compromises.

The Senate agreed to drop altogether its provision requiring Medicare coverage for all state and local government employees. House negotiators had offered to phase in the coverage.

The fiscal 1986 reconciliation bill made such coverage mandatory only for new employees, at a cost of a 1.45 percent tax on wages to be paid by both employers and employees. The Senate version of HR 5300 extended coverage and taxes to current workers, to raise $789 million in fiscal 1987 and $5 billion over three years. The proposal was opposed by states with few recently hired workers.

The five-year compromise would have raised $299 million in fiscal 1987.

And conferees finally agreed to cap the Medicare deductible at $520 per year.

A broad range of other health-related provisions could not be finally settled until conferees agreed on the steps to raise revenues to pay for them, members said.

A breakthrough finally came Oct. 17, when conferees reached agreement and filed their report (H Rept 99-1012). Both chambers approved the conference agreement the same day. ▮

Combating Medical Abuses

The full House passed and the Senate Finance Committee approved legislation (HR 1868) aimed at combating fraud and abuse in the Medicare and Medicaid programs. The measure, however, died in the adjournment rush.

As the law currently stood, the Department of Health and Human Services (HHS) could exclude practitioners from Medicare and Medicaid if they committed fraudulent acts against those programs and their beneficiaries. It could also exclude them from the programs in any state that had revoked or suspended their licenses. HHS was powerless, however, against doctors who moved to another state to evade one state's sanctions. It also lacked authority to exclude those who defrauded private health insurers or federal, state or local government programs other than Medicare and Medicaid.

The bill would have given the HHS secretary and state Medicaid directors broader discretion and wider criteria by which they could bar doctors or health care organizations from participating in Medicare, the federal health insurance program for the elderly and disabled, and Medicaid, the federal-state health care program for low-income people. The Congressional Budget Office estimated that the anti-fraud provisions of HR 1868 would have increased Medicare and Medicaid administrative costs by $16 million over a three-year period.

The House passed HR 1868 June 4, 1985, after the Ways and Means and the Energy and Commerce committees reported the bill (H Rept 99-80, Parts 1 and 2). John Heinz, R-Pa., chairman of the Senate Special Committee on Aging, introduced S 837, the Senate version of the bill, in April 1985. *(1985 Almanac p. 292)*

The Senate committee approved HR 1868 Sept. 10. It was substantially similar to the House version.

Exclusion Powers

Current law required exclusion from Medicaid and Medicare participation of anyone convicted of program-related crimes. HR 1868 also mandated exclusion of those convicted of neglect or abuse of patients.

The bill spelled out 14 new reasons to remove medical practitioners from eligibility. These "permissive exclusions" could be exercised against any doctor or health care organization:

- Convicted of defrauding any federal, state or locally financed health care program.
- Determined by the HHS secretary to have committed fraud, kickbacks or other prohibited acts.
- Convicted of unlawfully manufacturing, distributing, prescribing or dispensing a controlled substance. The Finance Committee modified that exclusion to limit it to those convicted of a felony.
- Whose health care license had been suspended or revoked because of incompetence, unprofessional conduct or lack of financial integrity.
- Suspended or excluded from participation in a federal or state health care program for reasons related to questionable professional competence, conduct or financial integrity.
- Convicted of interfering with the investigation of health-care fraud.
- Determined by the HHS secretary to have claimed excessive charges or unnecessary services under Medicare, or failed to meet professionally recognized standards. The committee narrowed the definition of such charges to "higher than usual" charges for physicians.

The Finance Committee added a provision allowing the HHS secretary to exclude a doctor or health care organization for defaulting on repayment of scholarships or health professions education loans. The HHS secretary could not, however, exclude the only doctor or hospital in a community.

The minimum period of exclusion was five years for persons convicted of program-related crimes or others requiring mandatory exclusion.

Other Provisions

The bill also sought to close loopholes that permitted payment of improper claims (such as double-billing) and clarified penalties for claims submitted by unlicensed physicians.

The Finance Committee added several sections to the bill, fine-tuning the HHS secretary's authority in combating medical fraud and abuse, and agreed to a number of amendments related to the Medicare and Medicaid programs. Chief among these were changes to:

- Increase the authorization level for the Maternal and Child Health Care Services Block Grant in each of fiscal 1987-89 by $75 million, from $478 million to $553 million. Of this, $50 million would be allocated to states' general block grant activities, and $25 million would be set aside to develop primary health services demonstration programs and projects that promoted the development of community-based service networks and case management for children with special health-care needs.
- Revise the conditions that nursing homes must maintain for their patients in order to qualify for Medicaid reimbursement. The amendment consisted of portions of S 2604, a bill introduced by Heinz dealing with nursing home quality reform.
- Include hospitals in Puerto Rico in Medicare's "prospective payment system," a system of preset, flat fees mandated under a 1983 law (PL 98-21) in an effort to curb soaring hospital costs. *(1983 Almanac p. 391)*
- Add diagnostic or therapeutic services provided by a psychologist to inpatient hospital services that would be paid by Medicare.
- Require the HHS secretary to conduct studies on a myriad of subjects, including refinement of the prospective payment system, review of Medicare hospital quality standards, and the quality of care under the prospective payment system. ▮

Access to Health Insurance

Congress in 1986 took the first steps toward helping the estimated 35 million to 37 million Americans who did not have either private or public health insurance.

Fiscal 1986 reconciliation legislation (HR 3128 — PL 99-272) required employers of 20 or more who offered group health insurance plans to allow laid-off workers to continue their coverage at the group rate, as well as spouses, widows and other dependents who would lose coverage due to death or divorce. *(1986 reconciliation bill, p. 555)*

The fiscal 1987 reconciliation bill (HR 5300 — PL 99-509) broadened these access provisions slightly to require that any retiree or dependent who lost employer-based health insurance coverage because the employer filed for Chapter 11 bankruptcy be entitled to remain in the employer's health insurance plan by paying up to 102 percent of the applicable premium. The retiree, his or her spouse, and dependent children could remain in the plan until the retiree's death, with the spouse and children allowed to continue for three years following such death. *(1987 reconciliation bill, p. 559)*

Sweeping Risk Pool Plan Dropped

The House, as part of its version of HR 5300, had tried to go further, but the Senate refused to go along. As a result, House-Senate conferees ultimately dropped House-passed provisions requiring states to set up "risk pools" to offer insurance to the chronically ill and other citizens who were traditionally uninsurable.

Six states already had such pools; four others had passed legislation to create them.

Under the plan, premiums could not exceed 150 percent of the average group premium for the state, and shortfalls in the pool would have to be made up by private employers of 20 or more people.

Employers who refused to participate would have faced an excise tax of 5 percent of their gross payroll.

Fortney H. "Pete" Stark, D-Calif., chairman of the Ways and Means Subcommittee on Health, led the push for the access provisions.

Stark had hoped to include in the reconciliation package a four-part program (HR 4742) to help people without health insurance obtain coverage.

But with time running out and the proposals facing stiff opposition from the business community, he settled for the one provision creating risk pools. In the end, even that was dropped in conference. ▮

Catastrophic Illness

Secretary of Health and Human Services (HHS) Otis R. Bowen Nov. 20 officially kicked off debate on what was expected to be one of Congress' top health issues for 1987 — catastrophic health care costs.

Bowen released a report suggesting ways of dealing with the problem, but stressed that it had not been endorsed by anyone else in the administration.

The report, ordered by President Reagan in his Feb. 4 State of the Union message, made recommendations for financing catastrophic costs for three groups: elderly who need lengthy hospitalizations; elderly who require long-term, non-hospital care; and the under-65 population at financial risk when catastrophic illness strikes. *(State of the Union, p. 3-D)*

In his most controversial proposal, Bowen suggested expanding Medicare, the federal health insurance program for the elderly, to cover the cost of long hospital stays. Medicare at the time paid a declining share of hospital bills for stays longer than 60 days, and it paid nothing after 150 days in the hospital.

Adding $4.92 per month to the premium Medicare beneficiaries paid for non-hospital health insurance could pay for the extended hospital coverage and limit beneficiaries' out-of-pocket costs to $2,000 per year, the report said. Bowen called the added cost "a very modest price to pay for increasing the elderly's peace of mind."

But the proposal upset administration conservatives who saw extended coverage as unnecessary government intrusion into the private "Medigap" insurance market. Two-thirds of all Medicare beneficiaries had Medigap policies, which supplemented Medicare payments.

Modest Plan on Long-term Care

Bowen's other proposals, on long-term, non-hospital care and on how to protect the under-65 population from financial ruin, were considerably more modest.

The report proposed undertaking a major public education campaign to warn the elderly that Medicare — and most Medigap policies — did not cover the cost of long-term care in nursing homes and elsewhere.

A 1984 Gallup Poll, conducted for the American Association of Retired Persons, found that 79 percent of respondents believed — mistakenly — that Medicare paid the bill for nursing home care. Medicare actually covered only 1.8 percent of the nation's $32 billion nursing home bill for 1984, according to the Health Care Financing Administration, the HHS agency responsible for Medicare.

Bowen's report suggested encouraging individuals to open tax-preferred savings accounts for potential long-term care expenses and encouraging the development of private long-term care insurance policies by offering favorable tax treatment for insurers.

For the under-65 population, the report encouraged "state innovation and initiative in the management of health programs." Such initiatives, the report said, might include mandating that employers provide catastrophic coverage as part of any health benefits offered, and the formation of so-called "risk pools" to make insurance affordable for those with health problems that made them otherwise medically uninsurable.

The report was greeted warmly on Capitol Hill. "The acute-care part is something I think we could agree on if the president would buy into it," said Rep. Fortney H. "Pete" Stark, D-Calif., chairman of the Ways and Means Subcommittee on Health. And Sen. Edward M. Kennedy, D-Mass., incoming chairman of the Labor and Human Resources Committee, called Bowen's proposals "a major step in a new direction for the administration." ∎

Help for AIDS Victims

Less than two weeks after a government report predicted geometric increases in the number of people who would be diagnosed with acquired immune deficiency syndrome (AIDS) over the next five years, the Senate Labor and Human Resources Committee on June 25 approved legislation to improve services to AIDS victims. But the measure went no further.

The bill (S 2345 — S Rept 99-337) described AIDS, a fatal disease with no known cure, as the nation's "No. 1 public health priority." It authorized the Public Health Service (PHS) to make $40 million in grants to public and private organizations for the development, establishment or expansion of support systems for AIDS patients.

Under the bill, approved by voice vote, grants could be made to groups that coordinate outpatient or home health care services, counseling and mental health services, case management, and education for health workers about AIDS and how it is spread.

Sponsor Edward M. Kennedy, D-Mass, said the measure would help "develop alternatives to long-term hospital inpatient services, which are proving inefficient and cost-ineffective as an approach to providing medical services for AIDS patients."

The committee action came as the PHS predicted that AIDS cases in the United States would total more than 270,000 by 1991, compared with 21,726 as of June 1986.

Quarrel Over Legal Rights

The administration, meanwhile, seemed divided over the job rights of AIDS victims. A Justice Department memorandum made public June 23 said employers could dismiss workers with AIDS without violating a law barring discrimination against the handicapped, provided the firing was based on fear of contagion and not on the disabling effects of the disease.

In a subtle but pointed rebuttal of that view, Dr. Robert E. Windom, assistant secretary for health of the Department of Health and Human Services (HHS), issued a June 24 press release stressing the department's longstanding assessment that "there is no medical or scientific evidence that the AIDS virus is spread through casual contacts occurring in the workplace, schools or similar settings."

Windom said the Justice opinion "was concerned primarily with the technical legal interpretation of statutory language related to discrimination against the handicapped, and does not reflect any new scientific or medical information in AIDS transmission."

The Court Case

On Dec. 3, the Supreme Court heard arguments in a case that was viewed as a test of the job rights of individuals with contagious diseases such as AIDS.

At issue was whether such persons were protected from dismissal by Section 504 of the Rehabilitation Act of 1973, which barred discrimination against the handicapped. *(1973 Almanac p. 557)*

The case before the court, *School Board of Nassau County, Fla., v. Arline,* involved a teacher who was fired because she had tuberculosis. But its outcome was expected to affect AIDS victims, as well.

Backed by the Reagan administration, the school board argued that "a contagious, infectious disease is not a handicap within the meaning" of Section 504. The teacher's attorneys disagreed, saying it was not possible to separate contagion — "a health condition" — from the underlying disease or handicap. ∎

Plague Control

Legislation aimed at increasing funds for research into control of the deadly bubonic plague was approved by the House Energy and Commerce Committee in 1986, but never made it through the full House.

The bill (HR 4392 — H Rept 99-972), which would have authorized $1 million per year for three years, was originally part of another bill (HR 2418) to reauthorize expenditures for migrant and community health centers. But when that measure on Feb. 19 failed to pass the House under a fast-track procedure requiring a two-thirds vote, the plague provisions were stripped from it.

On April 22, the plague control provisions, by then reintroduced as HR 4392, failed by 22 votes to receive the required two-thirds necessary for passage under suspension of the rules. Although the provisions of HR 4392 had been approved by the full Energy and Commerce Committee during consideration of HR 2418, committee Republicans complained in floor debate that they never had a chance to vote on HR 4392. Republican members of the committee charged that the program would be redundant, because funds for plague research were already available under other programs.

The committee tried again, reporting HR 4392 to the House on Oct. 7. But by then, it was too late to act on the bill during the 99th Congress. ∎

Health Promotion Veto

President Reagan Nov. 5 pocket-vetoed legislation that would have created a national advisory council on health promotion and disease prevention.

The bill (S 2057 — S Rept 99-308) was vetoed automatically because Reagan did not sign it within 10 days of receiving it.

The measure was reported May 21 by the Senate Labor and Human Resources Committee. It was passed by the Senate June 16.

In the House, the legislation was referred to the Energy and Commerce Committee, which was discharged after failing to act.

The bill was passed by the House Oct. 16, and the Senate agreed to House amendments Oct. 18, clearing the measure. All action came by voice votes.

S 2057 would have created a 15-member commission to evaluate federal, state and local health promotion and disease prevention programs. Reagan said the bill would duplicate existing efforts.

Funding of $50,000 for the council was included in the fiscal 1987 continuing appropriations resolution (H J Res 738 — PL 99-591). *(Story, p. 219)*

Indian Health Care

Legislation (HR 1426) to reauthorize Indian health care programs for four years died in the waning hours of the 99th Congress as the House and Senate remained hopelessly divided over a provision involving Indians in Montana.

The bill would have authorized about $200 million through fiscal 1990 for programs run by the Indian Health Service (IHS), part of the Department of Health and Human Services (HHS).

The measure was passed by the House Sept. 18, 308-70. *(Vote 364, p. 104-H)*

The Senate passed HR 1426 on Oct. 8 after adopting a substitute by Mark Andrews, R-N.D., which embodied several provisions from other Indian bills and from the Senate companion to HR 1426 (S 277 — S Rept 99-62), which had been reported May 16, 1985, by the Select Indian Affairs Committee.

The substitute also included a provision offered by John Melcher, D-Mont., that the administration said would guarantee a veto if retained.

HR 1426 was similar to an Indian health care package that President Reagan pocket-vetoed in 1984, but it was stripped of several provisions opposed by the administration.

Still, the president had never signed a separate authorization for the Indian health programs. Since 1983, when their last authorization lapsed, they had been preserved through continuing appropriations resolutions. *(1984 Almanac p. 188)*

Melcher Provision

Melcher's section made the federal government the primary, not residual, provider of medical care to Indians who lived on non-taxable trust lands in Montana. It would have implemented a Jan. 27 ruling by the U.S. District Court in Montana that was being appealed by the government in the case of *McNabb v. Heckler*.

Under the bill, the government would have remained responsible for such care until six months after the decision was finally modified or reversed. Reagan's 1984 Indian health care veto was prompted in part by a similar mandate.

House Action

As passed by the House Sept. 18, HR 1426 represented a compromise worked out between the Interior and Insular Affairs Committee and the Energy and Commerce Committee. The original version was reported by Interior May 14, 1985, and by Energy and Commerce May 23, 1985 (H Rept 99-94, Parts 1 and 2).

On April 29, 1986, a similar Interior-Energy compromise (HR 4600) fell seven votes short of receiving the necessary two-thirds majority to pass under suspension of the rules. The vote was 263-141. *(Vote 90, p. 30-H)*

During debate on HR 1426, the House approved a floor amendment offered by John McCain, R-Ariz., deleting another section opposed by the administration that would have specified certain California Indians as eligible for Indian health services. The vote was 206-180. *(Vote 362, p. 104-H)*

The section would have designated as eligible for aid members of tribes recognized as Indian tribes by the state of California, but not by the federal government. The effect of the amendment was to allow only federally recognized Indian tribes to receive federal aid.

McCain's amendment was vehemently opposed by Henry A. Waxman, D-Calif., chairman of the Energy Subcommittee on Health, who argued that it would terminate IHS coverage for about 53,000 California Indians currently eligible. Howard C. Nielson, R-Utah, called the amendment unfair and inequitable. The amendment's backers, however, emphasized that the change was needed to avert another veto.

Senate Action

In the Senate, HR 1426 was referred to Indian Affairs, which reported it Sept. 25 without a written report.

As passed by both chambers, HR 1426 authorized $56 million in fiscal 1988-90 for programs to enhance Indians' health status.

In addition, the measure authorized $48.76 million in fiscal 1987-90 for scholarships and continuing education programs to help Indians become doctors and to recruit health professionals to serve Indians. And it called for $11.55 million in fiscal 1988-90 to help Indians repair and maintain sanitation facilities.

The Senate reduced from $10.5 million to $3 million the funding approved by the House to improve Indians' access to Medicare and Medicaid in fiscal 1988-90. It increased the House's authorization for a new fund to pay for treating victims of disasters or catastrophic illnesses, from $8 million in each of fiscal 1988-90 to a maximum of $10 million each year.

The Senate added $3 million in fiscal 1988-91 for a new Native Hawaiian health promotion program and $500,000 for a demonstration project for Indian health promotion and disease prevention. Also added was a new program to establish centers to combat diabetes among Indians.

The Senate again approved language deleted by the House that would have made eligible for IHS coverage members of certain tribes recognized as Indian tribes by the state of California but not by the federal government.

The House on Oct. 10 acceded to the Senate on all but the Melcher provision involving Montana's Indians. It returned the bill to the Senate, which on Oct. 18, adjournment day, again added that provision.

The legislation died when the House did not take further action.

Nutrition Monitoring

The House June 26 passed legislation (HR 2436) designed to coordinate government efforts to monitor the nutritional status of the U.S. population and the nation's food supply.

The bill was reported Oct. 3 from the Senate Governmental Affairs Committee (S Rept 99-521), but it died in the final weeks of the 99th Congress.

In the House, the legislation was reported March 4 by the Science and Technology Committee and June 19 by the Agriculture Committee (H Rept 99-481, Parts 1 and 2).

The legislation, the result of an eight-year effort by the two committees, would have made the secretaries of agriculture and health and human services jointly responsible for the development and implementation of a 10-year nutrition-monitoring and research project. It would have created a nutrition-monitoring advisory council and required publication of basic dietary guidelines for the public. The bill authorized no new funds. ▮

Infant Formula Regulation

In a rebuke to the Reagan administration, Congress Oct. 17 cleared legislation strengthening federal standards for the testing and monitoring of infant formula.

The measure was attached to omnibus drug legislation (HR 5484 — PL 99-570) signed into law Oct. 27. *(Story and provisions, p. 92)*

The action was taken in response to charges that a 1980 law designed to ensure the safety of infant formula had been crippled by weak regulations dictated by the formula manufacturers.

A Rider on Other Bills

The infant formula amendment was added to the drug bill Sept. 27 by Sen. Howard M. Metzenbaum, D-Ohio, who earlier had successfully offered a somewhat tougher version as an amendment to separate legislation (S 1848) permitting export to other countries of pharmaceuticals not yet approved for sale in the United States. A modified version of that drug export bill was ultimately cleared as part of an omnibus health bill (S 1744 — PL 99-660). *(Drug exports, p. 238)*

Although boths versions of the infant formula proposal were adopted by the Senate by voice vote, the first Metzenbaum amendment was approved May 13 only after a motion to table it failed by a 29-66 margin. *(Vote 94, p. 19-S)*

Both versions toughened standards created by the 1980 Infant Formula Act (PL 96-359). That law, which set minimum nutritional requirements for infant formulas, came in response to a 1979 incident in which more than 100 infants became ill as a result of consuming formula manufactured by the Syntex Corp. that lacked chloride, a critical nutrient. *(1980 Almanac p. 418)*

Proponents of the measure argued that despite the 1980 law, babies still faced substantial health risks from inadequately tested formula. Sen. Albert Gore Jr., D-Tenn., who as a House member was a sponsor of the original act, said the regulations promulgated under the law by the Food and Drug Administration (FDA) "changed the intent and thrust of the law very significantly and deprived the law of its intended impact."

"It is time to end FDA's policy of 'let the baby beware' and instead to institute the safeguards our children deserve," said Metzenbaum.

Opponents of the measure, led by Orrin G. Hatch, R-Utah, sponsor of the drug export measure to which the infant formula amendment was added, charged that the new regulatory burdens were unnecessary and would drive up the cost of formula. Hatch said support for the amendment was "typical of zero-risk advocates who don't care about the cost," but he admitted that it was "pretty hard not to vote for something that looks like motherhood and apple pie." ▮

Court Rules on Abortion, 'Baby Doe' Rules

Declaring that there is "a certain private sphere of individual liberty" that should "be kept largely beyond the reach of government," the Supreme Court June 11 once again upheld a woman's right to have an abortion.

By 5-4, the court in *Thornburgh v. American College of Obstetricians and Gynecologists* reaffirmed its 1973 decision legalizing abortions and strictly limiting state power to regulate them. *(Decision, p. 8-A)*

Two days earlier, on June 9, the court put another highly personal decision out of the reach of federal interference, ruling that Congress had not authorized the Department of Health and Human Services (HHS) to force hospitals to provide aggressive treatment for severely handicapped infants over parental objections.

By a 5-3 vote, the court invalidated federal regulations designed for that purpose. Parents and their physicians, or in rare instances, state officials, were the appropriate persons to decide the medical treatment of babies born with severe handicaps, the court said in *Bowen v. American Hospital Association. (Decision, p. 10-A)*

Both decisions were major policy defeats for the Reagan administration. Solicitor General Charles Fried had urged the court to overrule its landmark *Roe v. Wade* decision permitting abortions and to approve federal regulations requiring treatment of handicapped newborns.

"It's true we did not win, but I'm not embarrassed by what we did," said Fried of the abortion ruling. He said the administration "did a useful thing" in provoking "a very restrained and a very probing constitutional inquiry which I believe is far from over."

'Roe' Ruling Reaffirmed

Justice Harry A. Blackmun, author of *Roe v. Wade,* was emphatic in announcing its reaffirmation from the bench.

"The states are not free, under the guise of protecting maternal health or potential life, to intimidate women into continuing pregnancies," he declared.

"The constitutional principles that led this court to its decisions in 1973 still provide the compelling reason for recognizing the constitutional dimensions of a woman's right to decide whether to end her pregnancy," Blackmun wrote. "It should go without saying," he added, "that the vitality of these constitutional principles cannot be allowed to yield simply because of disagreement with them."

A Narrowing Margin

But that disagreement was quite evident in the widening gap between the majority and the dissenters in this latest case. The dissenters charged that the majority had gone beyond a mere reaffirmation of *Roe v. Wade* to endorse a policy of "abortion on demand."

And the June 11 decision came by the narrowest vote to date. *Roe v. Wade* was decided by 7-2; Justices William H. Rehnquist and Byron R. White dissented.

In 1983, the court reaffirmed its 1973 ruling, 6-3. Reagan appointee Sandra Day O'Connor joined White and Rehnquist in dissent. *(Akron (Ohio) v. Akron Center for Reproductive Health, 1983 Almanac p. 306)*

In 1986, Chief Justice Warren E. Burger switched sides. A member of the majority in *Roe v. Wade,* he became a dissenter in the *Thornburgh* case.

Background

The June 11 ruling focused on key provisions of a 1982 Pennsylvania law, which the sponsors admitted was designed to discourage women from choosing abortions. The law was challenged by the American College of Obstetricians and Gynecologists as out of line with *Roe v. Wade.* The 3rd U.S. Circuit Court of Appeals agreed, declaring the contested provisions unconstitutional.

The first set of challenged provisions set out specific methods to be used to ensure that a woman seeking an abortion gave her "informed consent" to the procedure.

They required that the woman be informed of the risks of the abortion and of carrying her child to term, of the medical assistance benefits available if she chose to bear the child, and of the father's legally enforceable obligation to assist in supporting the child. In addition, she was to be given materials describing the characteristics of the fetus at two-week intervals throughout gestation.

Other provisions required the physician to report certain information to the state concerning the woman, the abortion and the doctor's determination that the fetus was not viable, that is, that it could not survive outside the womb.

The law also required that when a physician performed an abortion after the point in pregnancy at which the fetus could be viable, he take care to preserve the life of the fetus and that a second physician be present.

The state appealed the ruling that these provisions were in conflict with *Roe v. Wade* and won Supreme Court review, which was surprising in light of the fact that the law at issue was quite similar to the Akron ordinance struck down by the court in 1983.

The Reagan administration urged the court to take this opportunity to overrule *Roe v. Wade.* In unusually blunt language, Solicitor General Fried told the court in a written brief that "the textual, historical and doctrinal basis of that decision is so far flawed that this court should overrule it and return the law to the condition in which it was before the case was decided."

The case was argued in November 1985, along with a case from Illinois, *Diamond v. Charles,* which the court dismissed April 30, finding that since the state had not appealed a ruling that its law was unconstitutional, the individual who had brought that case to the court had no legal standing to do so.

The Right to Choose

The majority found that each of the challenged provisions unconstitutionally operated to "chill" a woman's exercise of her right to choose to have an abortion.

"Our cases have long recognized that the Constitution embodies a promise that a certain private sphere of individual liberty will be kept largely beyond the reach of government," Blackmun concluded. "That promise extends to women as well as to men.

"Few decisions are more personal and intimate, more properly private, or more basic to individual dignity and autonomy, than a woman's decision — with the guidance of her physician and within the limits specified in *Roe* — whether to end her pregnancy. A woman's right to make that choice freely is fundamental. Any other result, in our view, would protect inadequately a central part of the sphere of liberty that our law guarantees equally to all."

The Dissent

Chief Justice Burger stopped short of urging an outright reversal of *Roe v. Wade,* although he said the majority's newest interpretation of that ruling led him to believe that "we should re-examine" it.

"Every member of the *Roe* court rejected the idea of abortion on demand," he said. "The court's opinion today, however, plainly undermines that important principle."

The new ruling, he added, "goes so far as to say that the state may not even require that a woman contemplating an abortion be provided with accurate medical information concerning the risks ... and the availability of state-funded alternatives."

Justice White, writing for himself and Justice Rehnquist, reiterated his long-held opposition to *Roe v. Wade.*

"Abortion is a hotly contested moral and political issue. Such issues, in our society, are to be resolved by the will of the people.... I would return the issue to the people by overruling *Roe v. Wade,*" White said.

White and Rehnquist agreed that "a woman's ability to choose an abortion is a species of 'liberty' that is subject to the general protections of the due process clause," but they disagreed with the strict test that the majority applied to any laws restricting that liberty. White and Rehnquist would give those restrictions only "the most minimal judicial scrutiny."

O'Connor and Rehnquist assailed the majority for resolving the constitutional questions in this case.

Both said they thought that only the procedural questions it presented — having nothing to do with the issue of abortion — should have been addressed.

Reiterating views she first set out in a lengthy concurring opinion in the 1983 *Akron* case, O'Connor wrote that most laws regulating abortion should be upheld if they had a "rational relationship to legitimate purposes," such as ensuring maternal health and protecting potential human life.

Only if the law imposed an "undue burden" on a woman's choice should it be tested against a stricter standard, she wrote, making clear that an undue burden would have to be an absolute ban or a severe limitation on the right to abortion — not just a requirement that discouraged abortions.

'Baby Doe' Case

In the week's other major ruling, the justices rejected the Reagan administration's argument that Section 504 of the 1973 Rehabilitation Act (PL 93-112) provided a sufficient statutory basis for federal intervention in decisions about the treatment of severely handicapped infants. Section 504 stated that "no otherwise qualified handicapped individual" may be denied benefits or subjected to discrimination under any federally assisted program "solely by reason of his handicap." *(1973 Almanac p. 557)*

That law, wrote Justice Stevens, does not authorize the HHS secretary "to give unsolicited advice either to parents, to hospitals or to state officials who are faced with difficult treatment decisions concerning handicapped children."

In the absence of evidence that any hospitals have refused parentally requested treatment for handicapped infants, the court found no reason to approve wholesale federal intervention in such medical decisions, which traditionally have been regulated — if at all — by the states.

The Regulations

The 1984 regulations at issue were formulated by HHS at the direction of the president, who was distressed by a 1982 Indiana case in which "Baby Doe," a newborn with Down's syndrome and other handicaps, died after its parents refused to consent to surgery to open a blocked esophagus.

Under the regulations, hospitals were required to post notices that handicapped infants should not be denied treatment. State child protective services agencies were required to set up procedures to prevent medical neglect of such infants. Hospitals were required to provide immediate access for federal investigators to the records of such patients and to expedite compliance actions.

The regulations were challenged by the American Medical Association and the American Hospital Association, both of which argued that Congress had not given the executive the authority to intervene in such matters.

In 1984, both a federal judge in New York and the 2nd U.S. Circuit Court of Appeals agreed with this view.

No Discrimination Found

The regulations, Stevens wrote in *Bowen v. American Hospital Association,* were issued without evidence that any hospital had discriminated against handicapped infants. Furthermore, he wrote, they were clearly not designed to bar discrimination, but rather to ensure treatment.

"Nothing in the statute authorizes the secretary to dispense with the law's focus on discrimination and instead to employ federal resources to save the lives of handicapped newborns, whether they are victims of discrimination ... or not," he said.

The invalidated regulations, he continued, were based on the "manifestly incorrect perception that withholding of treatment in accordance with parental instructions necessitates federal regulation."

On the contrary, Stevens said, "it would almost certainly be a tort as a matter of state law to operate on an infant without parental consent."

State agencies appeared to be doing a satisfactory job of defending the interests of the child in the rare case in which parental objections to treatment should be overridden, Stevens wrote. "State child protective services agencies are not field offices of the HHS bureaucracy, and they may not be conscripted against their will as the foot soldiers in a federal crusade."

Indeed, although the court did not mention it, Congress, in passing the Child Abuse Amendments of 1984 (PL 98-457), underscored the primacy of state agencies in handling such problems. That law required states to maintain programs to respond to reports of medical neglect of handicapped infants. *(1984 Almanac p. 482)*

Stevens was joined in his opinion by Justices Marshall, Blackmun and Powell. Chief Justice Burger concurred in the judgment but did not join Stevens' opinion.

Dissenting were Justices Brennan, White and O'Connor. They took issue with what they saw as the broad sweep of the ruling — denying the government the power ever to invoke Section 504 in a case involving the medical treatment of handicapped infants.

Justice Rehnquist did not participate in the court's decision. ∎

Food and Drug Administration

Legislation to enhance the status of the Food and Drug Administration (FDA) and require Senate confirmation of its commissioner passed both chambers in 1986, but died in the adjournment rush Oct. 18.

The House passed its version of the bill (HR 4754) Sept. 16 under suspension of the rules. The measure had been approved July 29 by the Energy and Commerce Committee and reported Aug. 12 (H Rept 99-785).

In the Senate, the FDA measure was pushed by Albert Gore Jr., D-Tenn., who succeeded in having it attached as an amendment to unrelated legislation (S 1848) authorizing exports of drugs not yet approved for use in the United States. But it was omitted from the final, compromise version of that bill (S 1744). *(Drug exports, p. 238)*

Instead, Sen. Orrin G. Hatch, R-Utah, on Oct. 18 offered the FDA bill on Gore's behalf as a substitute for the House version (HR 5230) of vaccine legislation. The amendment was adopted, but time ran out before the House could act on the legislation.

The FDA was an agency of the Department of Health and Human Services. Its commissioner was the only head of a major health and safety regulatory agency not already appointed by the president and confirmed by the Senate. ∎

Organ Transplants, Drugs

In fiscal 1987 budget reconciliation legislation (HR 5300 — PL 99-509), Congress provided one year of Medicare coverage for the cost of immunosuppressive drugs needed by organ transplant patients.

It was the first action Congress had taken to help patients pay for such drugs. The drugs, which help prevent rejection of transplated organs, cost between $5,000 and $7,000 per year and must be taken indefinitely. *(Fiscal 1987 reconciliation, p. 559; Medicare, p. 252)*

The principal beneficiaries of the new coverage were likely to be patients suffering from end-stage renal disease. These patients in many instances could be treated more economically through kidney transplants and immunosuppressive drugs than by costly kidney dialysis. Medicare already paid for either approach, although it did not previously cover the costs of drugs associated with transplants.

HR 5300 also contained provisions requiring hospitals, as a condition of participation in Medicare and Medicaid, to establish procedures for encouraging the donation of organs and tissues. Such procedures were to include "routine requests" for donations from a deceased person's next of kin, and notifying the local organ procurement agency when a potential donor was identified.

The bill also required hospitals performing organ transplants to belong to the national network established under the National Organ Transplant Act of 1984 (PL 98-507). *(1984 Almanac p. 476)*

Block Grant Legislation

The Senate Oct. 8 passed, but the House failed to act on, separate legislation to provide block grants to the states to help underwrite the cost of anti-rejection drugs for organ transplant patients.

The bill (S 2536 — S Rept 99-389) authorized $15 million annually for three years for states to purchase immunosuppressive drugs. Under the bill, states could make the drugs available to those who could not otherwise afford them and who were not eligible for full reimbursement by private insurance, Medicare or Medicaid.

An estimated 25 percent of those needing organ transplants fell into one of those categories, according to the bill's supporters, who said many patients were denied transplants because of their inability to pay for the drugs.

The Senate Labor and Human Resources Committee approved S 2536 on June 25, and it was formally reported Aug. 11. ∎

Generic Animal Drugs

Legislation to bring drugs for animals under a 1984 law designed to encourage the development of cheaper, generic copies of brand-name drugs was reported in the Senate, but it did not get beyond the subcommittee stage in the House.

The measure (S 2407, HR 5069) was approved Aug. 6 by the Senate Labor and Human Resources Committee and formally reported Sept. 17 (S Rept 99-448).

It would have brought drugs for animals under the provisions of PL 98-417, a 1984 law that created an expedited drug-approval system for generic drugs, which were exact copies of brand-name medications. That law also gave manufacturers extended patent protections by allowing them to add up to five years to their patents, during which they would maintain exclusive marketing rights. *(1984 Almanac p. 451)*

The House Energy and Commerce Subcommittee on Health and the Environment approved HR 5069 on Aug. 5, but the measure went no further. ∎

ADAMHA Reauthorization

The House Sept. 16 by voice vote approved a three-year reauthorization (HR 5259) of alcohol and drug abuse research programs in the Alcohol, Drug Abuse and Mental Health Administration (ADAMHA) of the National Institutes of Health.

The Senate did not act on the bill, but fiscal 1987 funding was authorized in omnibus anti-drug legislation. *(Story, p. 92)*.

HR 5259 authorized "such sums as may be necessary" in fiscal 1987-89 for programs administered by the National Institute on Alcohol Abuse and Alcoholism (NIAAA) and the National Institute of Drug Abuse (NIDA). Those institutes, along with the National Institute of Mental Health, comprised ADAMHA.

HR 5259 was approved July 29 by the House Energy and Commerce Committee and reported Aug. 15 (H Rept 99-802). ∎

Health Warnings on Alcohol

Reopening a long-running debate, the Senate Labor and Human Resources Committee May 20 approved legislation requiring health warning labels on all alcoholic beverages. But the measure, which drew intense opposition from the liquor industry, went no further in the 99th Congress.

By voice vote, the committee accepted a warning-label amendment to S 2443, a five-year reauthorization of the National Institute on Alcohol Abuse and Alcoholism (NIAAA) and the National Institute on Drug Abuse (NIDA). The amendment, offered by Strom Thurmond, R-S.C., originally required the labels only for hard liquor, but it was changed at the request of Christopher J. Dodd, D-Conn., to include beer and wine.

Earlier in 1986, Congress required smokeless tobacco to carry warning labels, adding it to a product list that also included cigarettes and saccharin. *(Story, p. 267)*

The Proposed Labels

As approved by the committee, S 2443 would have required manufacturers to place "in a conspicuous and prominent place on the container" a label bearing one of five warning statements, to be rotated annually:

- "Warning: The Surgeon General has determined that the consumption of this product, which contains alcohol, during pregnancy can cause birth defects.
- "Warning: Drinking this product, which contains alcohol, can impair your ability to drive a car or operate machinery.
- "Warning: This product contains alcohol and is particularly hazardous in combination with some drugs.
- "Warning: The consumption of this product, which contains alcohol, can increase the risk of developing hypertension, liver disease and cancer.
- "Warning: Rapid consumption of excessive amounts of this product, which contains alcohol, can cause immediate death." (A month later, on June 27, the committee voted to delete this warning label.)

Changing Climate

"We're excited to see this, after so many years, get someplace," said George Hacker, director for alcohol policies for the Center for Science in the Public Interest.

Hacker said the political climate had changed since 1979, when Thurmond got a similar amendment to the same reauthorization measure adopted on the Senate floor, only to see it stripped in conference. "Alcohol has really taken a front seat on the political agenda in the past six years," he said, citing a 1984 law (PL 98-363) to promote a minimum drinking age of 21 and recent initiatives to bar television advertising of beer and wine.

As added proof of the changing times, Thurmond cited the support of the committee's ranking Democrat, Edward M. Kennedy, Mass., who, as chairman of the committee, had voted against the 1979 amendment.

Thurmond paraphrased a Kennedy statement about an unrelated bill the two introduced in April: "Whenever Strom and I introduce a bill together, it is either an idea whose time has come, or one of us has not read the bill."

The 1979 amendment would have affected only hard liquor, and would have imposed only a general warning that "Consumption of alcoholic beverages may be hazardous to your health."

Many public health advocates, including Henry A. Waxman, D-Calif., chairman of the House Energy and Commerce Subcommittee on Health and the Environment, opposed the 1979 amendment on those grounds. Exempting beer and wine from the requirement, said Waxman in a September 1980 interview in the *Journal of Studies on Alcohol,* "could have conveyed a dangerous and erroneous impression to young people that one form of alcoholic beverage was less prone to abuse than another."

Other Amendments

The warning-label amendment was not the only marginally related initiative in the bill, which authorized $83 million for NIDA and $69 million for NIAAA for fiscal 1987 and "such sums as necessary thereafter." The legislation also:

- Required the Department of Health and Human Services to prepare a series of public service announcements for television on the danger to women of cigarette smoking. The legislation authorized $250,000 a year for three years for the program.
- Required that beer and other malt beverages be labeled as to their alcohol content. Hard liquor and most wines were already subject to the requirement. ▮

Smokeless Tobacco Warnings

President Reagan Feb. 27 signed a bill (S 1574 — PL 99-252) requiring manufacturers of "smokeless tobacco" products such as chewing tobacco and snuff to print health warning labels on their packages. Warning labels had been required for cigarettes since 1966.

The bill also prohibited radio and television advertising of such products. A similar ban on broadcast advertising of cigarettes was imposed in 1970.

Congress completed action on S 1574 Feb. 6 when the Senate accepted by voice vote the House-passed version of the bill. The House had passed its version by voice vote Feb. 3. The Senate bill, passed Dec. 16, 1985, did not include the broadcast advertising ban. *(1985 Almanac p. 301)*

As cleared, the labeling provisions S 1574 represented a compromise between the Senate measure and a bill (HR 3510) with stiffer labeling requirements that was pending in the House Energy and Commerce Committee. Rep. Henry A. Waxman, D-Calif., chairman of the Energy and Commerce Subcommittee on Health, brought the compromise straight to the floor without committee approval and offered it as a substitute for the Senate-passed bill.

The final version was the result of extensive negotiations between the smokeless tobacco industry and the Coalition on Smoking or Health, whose member organizations included the American Heart Association, the American Lung Association and the American Cancer Society.

Health advocates pushed for the federal labeling requirements in light of studies linking smokeless tobacco with gum disease, oral cancer and tooth loss. Proponents of the bill feared a growing number of people, especially teenagers, believed smokeless tobacco was a safe alternative to cigarettes.

The smokeless tobacco industry maintained that labeling requirements were unjustified. The industry argued that the link between its products and human disease had not been conclusively established. However, the Smokeless Tobacco Council dropped its opposition to a federal labeling law after several states moved to impose their own requirements.

Major Provisions

As signed into law Feb. 27, S 1574 (PL 99-252) required manufacturers of smokeless tobacco to use one of three labels warning of health hazards. The labels, to be used in rotation on product packages and all print advertising except billboards, read as follows:

- "Warning: This product may cause mouth cancer."
- "Warning: This product may cause gum disease and tooth loss."
- "Warning: This product is not a safe alternative to cigarettes."

The compromise did not include provisions of HR 3510 that also would have required labels to disclose ingredients and to warn that nicotine contained in the product was addictive.

But it did include a requirement, not part of the original Senate-passed bill, that manufacturers use a label design including circles and arrows to draw attention to the warnings. There was no such federally mandated design to highlight the health warnings required on cigarette packages.

Other provisions of the bill:

- Banned smokeless tobacco advertisements from radio and television.
- Required manufacturers to report annually to the secretary of health and human services on the ingredients of smokeless tobacco products, particularly chemical additives. The information, to be used in research on the health effects of such ingredients, would be treated as confidential but could not be withheld from congressional committees.
- Directed the secretary to establish a public education program on the dangers to human health of smokeless tobacco products. ▮

Science Authorization

President Reagan Aug. 21 signed a bill (HR 4184 — PL 99-383) authorizing $1.7 billion in fiscal 1987 funding for the National Science Foundation (NSF), which financed scientific and engineering research and education at universities.

The bill cleared Aug. 6 when the House agreed to the version (S 2184 — S Repts 99-325, 99-338) passed by the Senate Aug. 2. The House originally passed its bill (H Rept 99-619) by a 405-2 vote June 26. *(Vote 185, p. 56-H)*

Both versions of the bill authorized $1.7 billion, the level requested by Reagan. That was a 13 percent increase from the agency's fiscal 1986 funding of $1.45 billion, as reduced by the automatic budget cut imposed in March by the Gramm-Rudman-Hollings deficit-control law (PL 99-177). ▮

Student Loan Changes

Cost-cutting provisions in the Guaranteed Student Loan (GSL) program, which subsidized borrowing by poor and middle-income college students, were included in the fiscal 1986 deficit-reduction bill cleared March 20 (HR 3128 — PL 99-272).

The bill aimed to cut costs primarily through administrative changes, including a variety of measures to improve collections of defaulted student loans and a new requirement that banks disburse loans in at least two installments a year rather than in one lump sum.

House and Senate differences were resolved relatively easily in conference, and student loan provisions were not affected by subsequent changes made in HR 3128 to accommodate White House objections.

Conferees had dropped two of the most controversial proposals in the original House and Senate versions of HR 3128. They dropped a Senate provision to trim the subsidies paid to banks that made the low-interest guaranteed loans — a cut in the so-called "special allowance" that some feared would discourage banks from participating in the program.

And the House agreed to back down from a proposal to require all students to undergo a financial needs test to qualify for loans. Under existing law, only students from families with more than $30,000 annual income had to demonstrate financial need. Senate negotiators had argued that such a change should be addressed as part of a pending full-scale reauthorization of higher education programs, and the extension of the financial-need requirement was included in both the House and Senate reauthorization bills (HR 3700, S 1965). *(Higher education bill, p. 231)*

Provisions

As signed into law April 7, HR 3128 included student-loan provisions that:

- Provided for recalling, in fiscal 1988, $75 million in advances made to encourage states to set up student loan agencies, which helped administer the GSL program. About $120 million in advances were outstanding at the start of 1985.

  Exempted were states with agencies set up less than five years earlier and those that would be unable to meet state reserve-fund requirements if the advance funds were withdrawn. The education secretary was directed to take account of the solvency of agencies' reserve and insurance funds in deciding how much of their advances to recall.
- Required lenders to disburse guaranteed loan payments to students in installments if the student was enrolled in an education program lasting longer than six months. Subsidies would be paid to lenders only for the disbursed amounts, allowing the government to use the balance and earn interest until the remaining funds were disbursed.
- Provided that guaranteed loan checks be sent directly to the school a borrower was attending, but payable to the student.
- Lengthened by 150 days, to 270 days, the period during which banks and state agencies must try to collect defaulted loans before the agencies could seek federal reimbursement.
- Permitted state agencies to be repaid for employing a third party to collect defaulted loans. Payments would be capped at the lesser of 2 percent of a loan or $100.
- Required the secretary of education to reimburse state agencies for administrative costs of the student loan program, in amounts limited to 1 percent of the value of loans made. The provision was made retroactive to Oct. 1, 1984, because the Education Department had refused to make payments for 1985.
- Required states to establish a "lender of last resort" to provide guaranteed loans to eligible students who were otherwise unable to find a willing lender.
- Set up a new program to allow borrowers with more than $5,000 in federal student loans to consolidate their debts and take longer to repay them. The interest charged on consolidated loans generally would be 10 percent, and the special allowance interest subsidy to banks would be reduced.
- Reauthorized the GSL program through fiscal 1988 and extended existing rules for determining how much a loan applicant's family could afford to contribute toward college costs.
- Required the Student Loan Marketing Association to begin repaying $5 billion it owed to the Federal Financing Bank in 1986, one year ahead of schedule.
- Required application of the six-year federal statute of limitations for collecting defaulted loans if a state law had a shorter period of liability.
- Allowed the Education Department to hold borrowers liable for some of the costs of collecting defaulted loans.
- Required reporting of defaulted guaranteed loans to consumer credit bureaus, which in turn must share with government agencies and lenders any information on borrowers that would assist in recovering loans.
- Permitted civil penalties of up to $15,000 on lenders and state agencies for willful or negligent violations of the Higher Education Act.
- Dropped the requirement that National Direct Student Loans (NDSLs), which were financed by federal appropriations rather than commercial lenders, must be in default two years before a school could turn them over to the government for collection.
- Authorized the secretary of education to take responsibility for collecting defaulted NDSLs when a school handling them had not maintained an adequate collection record.
- Required educational institutions to provide borrowers with information on penalties for default.
- Required educational institutions to undergo independent audits at least once every two years.
- Required the Education Department to omit, when calculating family income for purposes of student loans, proceeds from sales of farms or businesses sold as a result of foreclosure, forfeiture or bankruptcy.
- Required students to see whether they were eligible for Pell Grants, the principal federal college aid program, before seeking student loans. The provision was intended to prevent unnecessary borrowing by low-income students who could receive federal grants. ∎

Youth Problems

The Senate did not act on three House-passed bills addressing various young people's problems, and the measures died when the 99th Congress adjourned.

Dropout Rates. The House Aug. 7 by voice vote approved a bill (HR 3042 — H Rept 99-706) aimed at curbing high dropout rates and encouraging children to return to school.

The bill would have set up a three-year program, with a $50 million authorization in fiscal 1987, to aid local dropout prevention projects. Funding would have been allotted by a formula that considered the size of a school district, with 20 percent of the money going to districts with enrollments of more than 250,000.

Gifted Children. Also Aug. 7, the House by voice vote passed a measure (HR 3263 — H Rept 99-705) to resurrect federal aid for the education of gifted and talented children.

The bill would have authorized $10 million in fiscal 1987, rising to $13 million by 1991. Congress in 1981 abolished a similar program and other small education initiatives, replacing them with an education block grant to states. *(1981 Almanac p. 499)*

Suicide Prevention. The House July 14 approved a bill (HR 4650 — H Rept 99-667) aimed at reducing suicide rates among young people.

The bill, approved by voice vote, would have channeled $1 million in fiscal 1987 Education Department funds to support projects that demonstrated methods for preventing youth suicides.

The bill had been approved by the House Education and Labor Committee June 25.

According to Committee Chairman Augustus F. Hawkins, D-Calif., the suicide rate among people aged 15 to 24 had tripled since 1960. In 1985, approximately 6,000 young people killed themselves. ▮

'Effective Schools' Bill

The Senate did not act on House-passed legislation that would have required states to use some of their federal education block grants for a new school improvement program.

The bill (HR 4463), which the House approved by voice vote June 17, also would have set aside some $3 million a year from existing programs for an adult literacy initiative.

The House approved without change the two-pronged education bill that was reported June 16 by the Education and Labor Committee (H Rept 99-640).

The bill would have attached new strings to the use of education block grants, a $478.5 million program in fiscal 1986. Under existing law, states were required to allocate 80 percent of their block grant funds to local school districts and could keep the rest for state activities and their administrative expenses.

HR 4463 would have required half of the state-activities funding, equal to 10 percent of the block grant, to be used for "effective schools" programs. These school improvement programs drew on a body of research that had identified characteristics of effective schools, such as strong administrative leadership and an orderly environment. The funding requirement for effective schools would have been reduced for states already supporting such programs.

The second part of the bill would have earmarked $2 million a year in education block grant appropriations and $1 million in adult education funding for the literacy program. Known as "Even Start," the program would have supported pilot projects to educate illiterate parents to help them prepare their children for school. ▮

School Asbestos Cleanup

President Reagan Oct. 22 signed legislation (HR 5073 — PL 99-519) mandating that the nation's schools clean up hazardous asbestos and requiring the Environmental Protection Agency (EPA) to issue standards for school inspection, cleanup and disposal of the insulating material.

The legislation arose from congressional dissatisfaction with existing EPA efforts to regulate asbestos, a once-common building material that can cause cancer and other diseases. Under regulations issued in 1982, schools were required to inspect for asbestos and to notify parents and employees of the results. However, the agency rules did not require schools to take remedial action if asbestos hazards were found, nor did they set standards for determining when the presence of asbestos posed a health hazard. *(Background, 1984 Almanac p. 492; 1980 Almanac p. 416)*

EPA officials argued that such assessments and decisions were best made at the local level. They said on-site observers were best able to decide whether, as was often the case, it was more dangerous to remove asbestos and risk releasing fibers into the air than to seal it off or take other, less drastic actions.

But critics complained that school officials needed more guidance because, lacking clear federal standards, many schools had undertaken unnecessary removal work or hired incompetent contractors who made the problem worse. Rep. James J. Florio, D-N.J., a leading sponsor of HR 5073, cited EPA estimates that 75 percent of all school cleanup work had been done improperly.

Provisions

As signed into law, HR 5073:

- Required EPA, within one year of enactment, to issue regulations prescribing procedures for mandatory school inspections and reinspections, and to set standards for the safe disposal of asbestos. The agency also would be required to set standards spelling out what steps should be taken to protect "human health and the environment" in different circumstances when asbestos was found.
- Required EPA to develop a model program for states to certify contractors hired to remove asbestos, conduct inspections and help schools develop plans for handling asbestos. States would be required to adopt a program at least as stringent as the EPA model, and schools would have to use accredited contractors.
- Required the National Bureau of Standards to develop a program for accrediting laboratories that did asbestos-related work.
- Spelled out backup standards that would take effect if EPA failed to issue the required regulations by the deadlines set by the bill. The backup provisions would require schools, following a specified timetable, to inspect and clean up asbestos in keeping with an existing EPA guidance document.
- Required school districts, after conducting building inspections, to submit to their state governors for approval plans for cleaning up asbestos in their schools.
- Provided for civil penalties of up to $5,000 a day per violation to be levied against school districts that violated the law, although courts could return funds to schools with an order that they be used to pay the costs of complying with the law.
- Authorized citizens to bring suit against EPA if the agency did not comply with the statutory deadlines.

• Required EPA to study asbestos problems in commercial and public buildings other than schools, and recommend whether they should also be subject to removal requirements.

• Increased by $25 million a year the authorization for aid to schools for abating asbestos hazards by recapturing repayment money from loans made under the 1984 Asbestos School Hazard Abatement Act (PL 98-377).

Legislative Action

The House Energy and Commerce Committee July 29 approved HR 5073 (H Rept 99-763). By voice vote, the House passed the bill Aug. 12 without amendment.

As passed by the House, HR 5073 included a provision prohibiting litigants in damage suits involving asbestos manufacturers from introducing as evidence any requirements of the asbestos law or regulations issued under it. The bill also would have exempted asbestos-removal contractors and school districts from liability for actions taken to comply with the law, unless they were found to be negligent.

The Senate Environment and Public Works Committee approved a similar bill (S 2083 — S Rept 99-427) Aug. 12. The Senate Sept. 10 passed HR 5073 after substituting the text of S 2083. The Senate bill did not include provisions addressing liability or the introduction of evidence in asbestos damage suits.

The Senate, backed by the National Education Association and other critics, said the House bill's limitation on the introduction of evidence would put schools at a heavy disadvantage when they went to court to seek compensation for asbestos removal costs. However, supporters of the House provision said that it was designed to make the legislation "litigation neutral."

A compromise, worked out through staff negotiations, specified that Congress did not intend the bill to influence asbestos-related suits in favor of either plaintiffs or defendants. But it dropped the House ban against using the law as evidence in court, and said that the courts could decide whether and how to weigh such evidence.

Supporters of the limit on damage suits — the second sticking point between the two chambers — said it was needed to alleviate problems contractors and schools had had in obtaining liability insurance. But Senate negotiators opposed the provision, because it would have interfered with state liability laws.

The compromise dropped the provision, but called for a study of the availability and cost of insurance for contractors and school districts.

The House by voice vote approved the compromise version of HR 5073 Oct. 1. The Senate followed suit Oct. 3, thus clearing the measure for the president. ▮

Handicapped Education Programs Renewed

Congress Sept. 24 cleared legislation (S 2294 — PL 99-457) reauthorizing handicapped education programs for three years, with increased emphasis on helping preschool children.

The bill bolstered incentive grants to states that began special education for handicapped children at age 3, and authorized new grants for serving even younger children.

The final version of the measure was a compromise drafted by the House Education and Labor Committee as a substitute for a far more sweeping Senate-passed bill.

In a key change, the compromise dropped provisions of the earlier Senate bill that would have expanded existing handicapped education mandates by requiring states to provide services for all handicapped children beginning at age 3.

Even the incentive-based final version was opposed by the Reagan administration, which objected to its cost and its "hasty enactment."

Incentives vs. Mandates

The legislation amended the Education for All Handicapped Children Act (PL 94-142), which provided grants to states and required them to provide a "free, appropriate public education" for all handicapped children beginning no later than age 5. *(1975 Almanac p. 651)*

Those state grants were permanently authorized, but an array of smaller handicapped education programs were due to expire Sept. 30. S 2294 reauthorized those programs, involving such activities as research and teacher training, through fiscal 1989.

Under PL 94-142, many states already began special education at age 3, but an estimated 70,000 handicapped children between the ages of 3 and 5 were not being served.

S 2294 did not require states to cover those preschool students, but it authorized significant increases in grants to states that did.

Sponsors of the original Senate bill predicted the compromise's financial incentives would have the same practical effect as mandating services for preschool children, but they vowed to monitor the bill's implementation to make sure that was the case.

Major Provisions

As cleared by Congress, S 2294 contained the following major provisions:

• Revised and increased incentive grants to states for serving handicapped children aged 3 to 5. In the fourth year of the program, states would have to serve all handicapped children from age 3 to 5 or lose federal funds for that age group.

That mandate would be postponed until the fifth year of the program if funding for the grants had not totaled $656 million in fiscal 1987-89 and $306 million in 1990.

• Authorized $50 million in fiscal 1987, $75 million in 1988 and "such sums" as Congress considered necessary in 1989-91 for new grants to help states provide services to handicapped children from birth to age 2.

After the fourth year of the program, any state that chose to participate must serve all eligible children in the age group.

• Authorized $184 million in fiscal 1987, $195 million in 1988 and $206 million in 1989 for several existing handicapped programs, including teacher training, research, postsecondary programs and centers for the deaf and blind.

• Authorized $10 million in fiscal 1987, $10.5 million in 1988 and $11.25 million in 1989 for a new program of grants to promote the use of new technologies in handicapped education.

Legislative History

Senate Action

The Senate Labor and Human Resources Committee May 20 approved S 2294 (S Rept 99-315), and the Senate passed the bill without change June 6.

The Senate version of the bill, approved by voice vote, would have required states to provide special education services for handicapped children beginning at age 3. It also would have set up a new $100 million-a-year program of grants to states that began services for handicapped infants at birth.

"The earlier handicapped infants receive intensive intervention services, the greater the educational, emotional and intellectual benefits that child will reap as he or she grows up," said Lowell P. Weicker Jr., R-Conn., principal sponsor of the bill and a leading congressional advocate for the handicapped.

The bill also reauthorized through fiscal 1989 an array of special-purpose handicapped education programs in such areas as teacher training and research.

S 2294 was passed over the objection of Education Secretary William J. Bennett, who said in a letter to Weicker that the bill was "unduly prescriptive, burdensome and costly." He singled out the new $100 million program for serving infants as "clearly excessive."

Weicker took issue, saying that "it is far more expensive in the long run to not provide early educational services for handicapped children."

"The savings to be derived from providing such services are far greater than the actual costs of this program," he said.

House Action

The House Education and Labor Committee Sept. 17 approved its less extensive version of the legislation (HR 5520 — H Rept 99-860).

As approved 33-0, the bill boosted incentive grants to states that served disabled children aged 3 to 5, and it authorized a new $50 million program to help states develop services for infants up to age 2. The measure also reauthorized a number of small education programs for the handicapped.

HR 5520 was a compromise put together in staff negotiations that included Senate aides, to ensure that the end result would be supported by Weicker.

"We wanted a bill very badly this year," said a Weicker aide. "That's why we were willing to negotiate."

The House passed its version Sept. 22, and the Senate agreed to the House changes two days later, completing congressional action on the bill. ▮

Legal Fees for Handicapped

Breaking a prolonged deadlock, Congress July 24 cleared compromise legislation (S 415 — PL 99-372) to allow parents to recover the legal cost of defending the education rights of handicapped children.

A conference report on the measure (H Rept 99-687), which authorized courts to award attorneys' fees to parents who prevailed in special-education legal disputes, was adopted by the Senate by voice vote July 17. It was cleared by the House a week later, also by voice vote.

The compromise was reported by a conference committee after Senate negotiators agreed to drop a controversial proposal to impose new limits on fee awards to publicly funded legal aid lawyers in handicapped education cases. That provision was one of the principal stumbling blocks to an agreement on the bill, which had been in conference since late 1985. *(1985 Almanac p. 297)*

Overturning the Court

The legislation was drafted in response to a 1984 Supreme Court ruling. In the case of *Smith v. Robinson*, the court held that nothing in existing law allowed parents to recover their attorneys' fees when they prevailed in court cases brought under the Education for all Handicapped Children Act (PL 94-142).

That law guaranteed handicapped children a free, appropriate public education. It set up special administrative procedures for resolving disagreements between schools and parents about what special services and education programs were appropriate for a disabled child. When differences could not be resolved in those proceedings, parents could take school officials to court. *(Background, 1975 Almanac p. 651)*

Congress did not authorize the award of attorneys' fees in the handicapped education law, but before *Smith v. Robinson*, some courts had allowed parents to recover legal costs under related anti-bias statutes.

The Supreme Court foreclosed that possibility by ruling that Congress intended the handicapped education law to be the exclusive legal avenue for enforcing the rights of disabled school children. Sponsors of S 415 said the ruling misread congressional intent and denied court access to families that could not afford hefty legal expenses.

S 415 authorized the award of reasonable attorneys' fees under the handicapped education law.

"Without this remedy, many of our civil rights would be hollow pronouncements available only to those who could afford to sue for enforcement of their rights," said Sen. Lowell P. Weicker Jr., R-Conn., a leading sponsor of the bill.

Resolving Differences

While similar in their basic thrust, House and Senate versions of S 415 differed on several controversial points. The provision imposing stricter limits on fee awards to lawyers who worked for publicly funded legal aid groups had been pushed by Sen. Orrin G. Hatch, R-Utah, chairman of the Labor and Human Resources Committee, which handled S 415.

The Senate bill would have allowed such lawyers to receive only their actual litigation costs. By contrast, most awards of attorneys' fees were based on prevailing market rates, which generally were higher than litigation costs.

The restrictive provision was opposed not only by House conferees, but also by Senate Democrats such as John Kerry, D-Mass., who hailed the conference for dropping what he called a "blatant double standard."

Conferees agreed to include other provisions that Hatch said would "protect against excessive reimbursement" of lawyers, such as fee reductions if attorneys unreasonably prolonged disputes.

The conference bill allowed awards to cover attorneys' fees incurred in administrative proceedings as well as in court disputes. Some House Republicans complained that this provision could encourage parents to retain lawyers for administrative negotiations with the schools, making those sessions unduly litigious and adversarial.

Conferees dropped a House provision to cut off after four years the authority for courts to award attorneys' fees incurred at the administrative level.

Provisions

As signed into law Aug. 5, major provisions of S 415 (PL 99-372):

- Authorized courts to award reasonable attorneys' fees to parents who prevailed in legal disputes brought under the Education for All Handicapped Children Act.
- Specified that awards should not be calculated by using "bonuses and multipliers," applied in rare instances by courts to increase fee awards to lawyers in exceedingly complicated cases.
- Stipulated that no fees could be awarded for legal services provided after a school district made a written offer of a settlement if the offer was rejected but proved to be at least as favorable as the relief parents eventually won. An exception was provided to allow reimbursement if the parent was "substantially justified" in rejecting the settlement offer.
- Provided for the reduction of fee awards if a parent unreasonably delayed resolution of a dispute or if the time spent and fees charged by an attorney were excessive. Reductions would not be made in such cases if school officials delayed resolution of the controversy unreasonably or otherwise violated the handicapped education law.
- Required parents to exhaust administrative remedies under the handicapped education law before filing suits under other anti-bias statutes.
- Specified that the bill applied to all cases initiated after July 3, 1984, and to cases pending on July 4, 1984 — the day before the *Smith* decision.
- Required the General Accounting Office to study the effect of the bill. ∎

Vocational Rehabilitation

A five-year reauthorization of popular vocational training programs for the handicapped was cleared by Congress Oct. 3. The legislation (HR 4021 — PL 99-506) extended through fiscal 1991 programs created under the Rehabilitation Act of 1973 (PL 93-112). The programs, which assisted more than 900,000 people a year, were designed to help the handicapped become self-sufficient through employment. *(Background, 1983 Almanac p. 402)*

The bill authorized $1.28 billion in fiscal 1987 for state rehabilitation grants, the principal source of job-related aid to the handicapped, plus $200 million for a variety of smaller programs.

Congress appropriated $1.1 billion for state grants in fiscal 1986 and some $167 million for other programs authorized by the act, such as research and special aid for disabled Indians and migrant workers.

Provisions

As cleared by Congress, HR 4021:

- Authorized $1.28 billion in fiscal 1987 in basic grants to the states for rehabilitation programs. In the succeeding four years, the grants would total at least that much — plus an increase pegged to inflation. Grants would be capped at $1.41 billion in fiscal 1988, $1.55 billion in 1989, $1.71 billion in 1990 and $1.875 billion in 1991.
- Authorized $200 million in fiscal 1987 for an array of smaller related programs, such as joint training projects with industry, allowing 5 percent increases annually in 1988-91. Of the total, $25 million was earmarked in fiscal 1987 for new supported-employment grants.
- Gradually increased, beginning in fiscal 1989, the existing requirement that states put up at least 20 percent of rehabilitation program costs to qualify for federal funds. By fiscal 1993, the bill would increase the matching requirement to 25 percent, but only on sums states received in excess of their fiscal 1988 allotments.
- Required states to spend no less on rehabilitation programs than the average of the amounts they spent in the previous three years.
- Authorized states to use funds from their basic rehabilitation grants for supported employment programs.
- Authorized demonstration projects and a new program of grants to help states provide training and on-the-job services of limited duration for severely handicapped individuals capable of supported employment.
- Required states to include in their rehabilitation plans, which were required in order to receive federal rehabilitation grants, assurances that they had acceptable proposals for using funds made available under the new supported-employment program.
- Required the involvement of an impartial hearing officer in the process for resolving disputes over the provision of rehabilitation services, although that officer's decisions would be subject to final review by a state rehabilitation director.
- Authorized demonstration projects to provide incentives for the development and manufacture of devices to assist individuals with handicaps so rare that firms were not otherwise likely to market such devices.
- Authorized grants to help severely handicapped youths make the transition from school to work.
- Specified that states were not immune from lawsuits if they violated anti-bias laws, including Section 504 of the Rehabilitation Act, which barred discrimination against the disabled by recipients of federal funds.

The provision overturned a 1985 Supreme Court decision in *Atascadero State Hospital v. Scanlon,* which held that the 11th Amendment gave states immunity from such suits unless the state or Congress explicitly waived or overrode the immunity. *(1985 Almanac p. 16-A)*

House Action

Despite sharp divisions among Democrats, the House Education and Labor Committee March 11 approved HR 4021 (H Rept 99-571). As reported from committee, the bill called on the states to pay 25 percent of the cost of their vocational rehabilitation programs after fiscal 1988. Existing law required states to supply 20 percent of the cost.

Bill sponsor Pat Williams, D-Mont., said the increased matching requirement was designed to prod states into spending more on a program that served only a small fraction of those eligible. "In my judgment, states have not done enough," said Williams, chairman of the Education and Labor Subcommittee on Select Education. "It is time that states begin to take a greater role in this partnership."

But the proposal met with opposition from William D. Ford, D-Mich., and several other Democratic panel members who were worried that states would not be able to afford more money for rehabilitation training when they were facing federal budget cuts in other social services.

The House May 7 by a 401-0 vote passed HR 4021. To avoid a floor fight over the increased matching requirement, Williams offered a compromise backed by Ford that would phase in the 25 percent match over five years, beginning in 1989. But even when fully effective, the match would apply only to sums that states received in excess of their 1988 allotment. *(Vote 101, p. 32-H)*

Senate Action

The Senate Labor and Human Resources Committee Aug. 6 approved a four-year reauthorization of vocational rehabilitation programs.

The bill (S 2515 — S Rept 99-388), approved by voice vote, authorized nearly $1.3 billion in fiscal 1987 for state grants.

S 2515 provided $25 million in fiscal 1987 for grants to states to train the severely handicapped for "supported employment" — jobs in which people with severe handicaps receive close supervision and special support services.

On Sept. 8, The Senate approved HR 4021 by voice vote after substituting the text of S 2515.

Conference, Final Action

Senate-House differences were reconciled in staff negotiations without convening a formal conference.

The Senate accepted the House provision calling for a 5 percent increase in states' share of the cost of rehabilitation programs.

The House accepted a Senate proposal to set up a separate $25 million grant program to foster "supported employment" programs.

The House also accepted a Senate provision countering a 1985 Supreme Court decision limiting the application of federal anti-bias laws to state governments.

The House accepted, over the protest of Steve Bartlett, R-Texas, Senate provisions awarding grants to various agencies and institutions in the home states of key members of the Senate Labor and Human Resources Committee. Augustus F. Hawkins, D-Calif., chairman of the House Education and Labor Committee, said he had asked Senate negotiators to meet in conference to discuss the issue, but they had refused. The House had to accept the projects to ensure enactment of the bill before adjournment, he said.

The House adopted the conference report (H Rept 99-955) on the bill Oct. 2 by a 408-0 vote. The Senate approved it by voice vote Oct. 3. *(Vote 398, p. 112-H)* ▮

SSI Work Program Renewal

President Reagan Nov. 10 signed into law a bill (HR 5595 — PL 99-643) making permanent a program that encouraged disabled individuals receiving Supplemental Security Income (SSI) benefits to work if they were able.

SSI was the federal-state welfare program for the needy blind, elderly and disabled. The work program allowed disabled individuals who worked to retain a portion of their SSI benefits as well as eligibility for Medicaid, the state-federal health care program. The program, created in 1980 and extended in 1984, was scheduled to expire June 30, 1987. *(Background, 1980 Almanac p. 434; 1984 Almanac p. 160)*

The House originally passed the bill, which included a number of other minor changes to SSI, on Sept. 30 (H Rept 99-893). On Oct. 8, the Senate approved a version of the bill extending the work program but eliminating the House's other changes.

The House Oct. 15 added back one of the changes, allowing payment of retroactive SSI benefits to the spouse or parents of a deceased individual who was eligible for SSI. The Senate accepted the change Oct. 18, clearing the bill. All votes were by voice. ▮

Senior Citizens' Meals

Congress March 18 cleared for the president legislation (HR 2453 — PL 99-269) to continue a popular federal program that helped provide 225 million meals for senior citizens in 1985.

The Senate adopted the conference report on the bill (H Rept 99-487) by voice vote March 13, and the House approved the report, 344-0, on March 18. *(Vote 55, p. 18-H)*

The bill raised authorization levels through fiscal 1987 for commodity and cash distributions under the Older Americans Act of 1965. *(Previous authorization, 1984 Almanac p. 460)*

Background

Under the Older Americans Act, some 9,000 nutrition projects around the United States provided meals to elderly persons, in both congregate and home settings, through state and area agencies on aging. Several factors, including an increased emphasis on senior citizen nutrition programs at the state and local levels and voluntary contributions from program recipients, helped the programs increase the number of meals served by an additional 12.5 million annually for the preceding five years.

The federal government reimbursed states for the total number of meals served under an approved plan. Reimbursements could be in cash or surplus commodities, or a combination of the two.

Before 1981, there was no ceiling on reimbursements. Congress that year imposed a ceiling based on Agriculture Department estimates of the amount needed to maintain the level of reimbursement for the number of meals served in fiscal 1981. Additional meals would be reimbursed at a lower rate. When the program was reauthorized again in 1984, Congress approved funding levels that were projected to maintain 1983 reimbursement rates plus cost-of-living increases. *(1984 Almanac p. 460)*

HR 2453 was introduced in May 1985, after the Agriculture Department announced that the 1985 authorization level would not only preclude its granting a 4 percent cost-of-living increase, but would force a reduction of 2 cents to 4 cents in the 56.5-cents-per-meal reimbursement rate. The House Select Aging Subcommittee on Human Services estimated that a 3-cent drop in reimbursements would mean a daily reduction of 2 million meals.

In late 1985, Congress appropriated an additional $11 million for the program for fiscal 1986, but some $4 million of that was eliminated in the first round of cuts under the Gramm-Rudman-Hollings anti-deficit law. Much of the remaining $7 million would be used to pay outstanding reimbursements from 1985. *(Gramm-Rudman-Hollings, 1985 Almanac p. 459)*

Legislative Action

The House Education and Labor Committee reported HR 2453 Sept. 23, 1985 (H Rept 99-286), and the House passed it the next day by voice vote. The bill would have raised the authorized levels by "such sums as necessary" to provide reimbursement rates of 56.76 cents per meal for fiscal 1985 and 1986, and an inflation-adjusted rate for fiscal 1987.

The Senate passed HR 2453 by voice vote Feb. 5 after substituting the language of a bill reported by the Labor and Human Resources Committee Jan. 31 (S 1858 — S Rept 99-232). It called for the same 56.76-cent reimbursement rate and authorized $127.8 million for 1985 and $144 million each for 1986 and 1987 to achieve that rate.

Conferees accepted the Senate bill's authorization levels. Those levels were expected to be sufficient to reimburse states at the 56.76-cents-per-meal rate through 1987. ■

TRANSPORTATION
COMMERCE
CONSUMERS

CQ

Transportation/Commerce/Consumers

Despite intense public pressure in 1986 for action to stem soaring prices for liability insurance, Congress backed away from various measures advanced by groups to relieve the problem.

Business interests, including the insurance industry, argued that "tort" laws governing civil injuries needed to be overhauled to prevent outrageous court awards that officials said were raising insurance costs.

Consumers and trial lawyers contended that the real problem was anti-competitive behavior by the insurance industry. They called for elimination of the industry's 40-year exemption from antitrust laws and federal regulation.

But neither side was able to persuade Congress to adopt strong measures. Congress did pass a risk-retention bill — favored by consumer and business interests — to make it easier for various private groups and municipalities to form self-insurance groups.

The main arena of action turned out to be the states, many of which passed laws embracing, in varying proportions, tort law changes and additional industry regulation. Florida, for example, called for premium rollbacks while also putting limits on the damages for which a defendant could be held responsible.

In Congress, much of the debate swirled around a bill, which died in the Senate after a brief filibuster, that would have established federal standards governing compensation to victims of unsafe products. Opponents attacked as unfair a key provision that would have set limits on court awards for pain and suffering. They also said state law should determine the outcome of product liability lawsuits.

Proponents of a product liability measure, including the Reagan administration and manufacturers, said federal intervention was justified because sharp differences between state laws constituted a threat to interstate commerce.

Narrowly cast measures to overhaul liability laws for the fishing industry and the general aviation industry also failed to clear Congress, largely because of objections from trial lawyers and consumer groups.

Backers of greater federal supervision of the insurance industry fared no better in Congress. Insurance officials said the antitrust exemption was needed to allow companies to pool data on risks, and that without access to such information many small firms would go out of business. Officials feared that removal of the exemption would spur lawsuits by disgruntled consumers and state attorneys general.

State insurance commissioners vigorously protested charges of lax regulation. Many state regulators — along with some in the industry — attributed the crunch not to a lack of competition but to volatile swings in interest rates.

Double-digit interest rates of the late 1970s, according to this point of view, led many companies to slash premiums to attract funds for investments. Premium prices shot up when interest rates fell in the early 1980s. But profits dropped as companies were forced to make good on discounted policies and were unable to compensate for losses with investment gains. As reserves to cover losses shrank, new policies were curtailed.

As the 99th Congress wound down, a financial recovery was under way in the property-casualty industry, and a number of congressional offices reported a drop-off in complaints from constituents about high-priced insurance.

Corporate Takeovers

A sensational stock-trading scandal on Wall Street renewed calls by corporate managers and others for legislation to inhibit corporate takeover attempts.

Following an investigation by the Securities and Exchange Commission (SEC), Ivan F. Boesky, a prominent Wall Street investor, admitted to profiting from inside tips about takeovers. Boesky agreed Nov. 14 to pay a $50 million fine and return $50 million in illegal profits in a case that shook the entire investment community.

Boesky also agreed to cooperate with federal investigators, who appeared to be extending the probe to well-known corporate raiders and investment banking firms active in financing takeovers.

Leaders of the Business Roundtable, which represented 200 of the nation's largest corporations, said takeover attempts had created a seamy climate in which abuses by stock market professionals were flourishing. Roundtable leaders called for legislation to erect barriers to hostile takeovers.

Sen. William Proxmire, D-Wis., said he would make passage of anti-takeover legislation a major priority of his chairmanship of the Banking, Housing and Urban Affairs Committee in the 100th Congress. Rep. John D. Dingell, D-Mich., chairman of the Energy and Commerce Committee, also vowed to pursue a legislative remedy.

But others in Congress reacted more cautiously, saying that takeovers were one of the few ways of removing managers of poorly run companies. In 1985, a wave of corporate mergers prompted widespread concern in Congress, but no major bills were moved.

T. Boone Pickens Jr., who had mounted raids on oil companies, said that if there was no check on poor management performance, then stock values would decline, investors would lose confidence in financial markets, capital would continue to be misallocated and America's competitiveness in world markets would further erode.

Railroads

Congress cleared legislation requiring a public stock offering in 1987 of the federal government's 85 percent share of Conrail. Lawmakers rejected the administration's proposal to sell Conrail to another railroad, the Norfolk Southern Corp. Opponents of the merger said it would reduce competition, service and jobs in Conrail's base of operations in the Northeast and Midwest.

The House version of Conrail legislation included a provision — backed by rail labor but opposed by the industry — mandating protection for rail workers in sales of branch lines by major rail carriers to new carriers. But the plan drew stiff opposition from the Senate and was dropped from final legislation.

A coalition of shippers, including many coal producers and electrical utilities, also failed in an effort to link the Conrail legislation to a plan that would have made it easier for them to obtain rate reductions from the Interstate Commerce Commission (ICC). The shippers said they were the victims of price gouging by monopoly railroads. Railroads denied the charges, as did the administration, and the proposal was narrowly defeated in the House Energy and Commerce Committee.

Also on the rail front, the administration once again failed in its push for the elimination of federal subsidies to the Amtrak national passenger railroad. Congress kept funding roughly at fiscal 1986 levels.

Highways, Mass Transit

The 99th Congress failed to pass legislation reauthorizing funding for highway and mass transit programs, threatening cancellation by states of scores of high-priority road projects and the loss of thousands of construction industry jobs.

Authorizations for virtually all road programs expired when the fiscal year ended Sept. 30. While road-user taxes continued to build in the Highway Trust Fund, they could not be spent.

House and Senate members of a conference committee could not resolve disputes on a handful of controversial items, including relaxation of the 55 mph speed limit and federal funding of special "demonstration" projects for particular states and congressional districts.

Negotiators also disagreed on a Senate provision calling for an end to mandatory federal and state compensation of billboard owners for the removal of certain signs along federal highways.

Highway groups said that if the 100th Congress failed to pass a bill by the end of March, much of the construction season would be lost in the cold-weather states of the Northeast, Midwest and West.

Separately, Congress rejected an administration request for elimination of mass transit formula grants funded by general appropriations. Funding was kept roughly at fiscal 1986 levels, although lawmakers did cut by 2.5 percent, or $21 million, subsidies for mass transit operating expenses for cities with more than 1 million people.

—By Paul Starobin

Congress Votes to Sell Conrail Stock to Public

Five years after the Reagan administration proposed returning Conrail to the private sector, Congress agreed to sell the government's 85 percent share of the freight railroad.

However, instead of the direct sale to another railroad that the administration had sought, the legislation enacted in 1986 mandated a public stock offering.

The administration reluctantly embraced the public offering after key House members refused to consider a Senate-passed bill (S 638 — S Rept 99-98) that called for Conrail to be sold for $1.2 billion to the administration's selected buyer, the Norfolk Southern Corp.

A key to passage of the final stock-sale legislation was the desperate search of members to find ways to raise revenue to avoid the spending cuts that might have been required under the Gramm-Rudman-Hollings anti-deficit law (PL 99-177). The sale provisions were included in deficit-reduction "reconciliation" legislation (HR 5300 — PL 99-509) cleared by Congress Oct. 17, with an estimated $2.2 billion in revenues from the sale to be included in the budgetary savings of the bill. *(Gramm-Rudman-Hollings, p. 579; deficit-reduction bill, p. 559)*

The administration first had proposed selling the railroad in 1981 on the grounds that federal subsidies were not justified and that Conrail should be operated by the private sector. However, the system, created by Congress in 1975 from the ashes of the Penn Central railroad and six other failing railroads, became profitable in 1982 and remained so. Administration officials then argued that Conrail needed a partner, such as Norfolk Southern, to stay off federal subsidies.

But the problems that the plan faced after Transportation Secretary Elizabeth Hanford Dole Feb. 8, 1985, recommended the sale to Norfolk Southern, showed that even a money-making Conrail could be hard to sell.

Strong opposition to the plan came from members from the Northeast and Midwest, where Conrail operated. They said the merger, creating the nation's largest railroad with about 33,000 miles of track, would reduce competition, service and employment. Other critics raised antitrust concerns and contended that at the proposed sales price of $1.2 billion, the government was giving away valuable taxpayer property.

Senate supporters got a Conrail-Norfolk Southern merger bill through the Commerce, Science and Transportation Committee in 1985, but foes kept the measure from the floor. *(1985 Almanac p. 272)*

After key opponents agreed to drop their threatened filibuster, the Senate Feb. 4 passed the bill to implement the sale to Norfolk Southern. However, a firestorm of criticism continued in the House.

Rep. John D. Dingell, D-Mich., chairman of the Energy and Commerce Committee, said April 29 that a Norfolk-Southern merger would harm jobs and competition in the rail industry. He questioned the adequacy of the $1.2 billion bid and complained of a potential drain on the Treasury due to tax benefits accruing to the buyer of Conrail.

Dingell refused to consider Norfolk Southern's request even though the railroad at the urging of Secretary Dole raised its offer to $1.9 billion. Dingell called for a sale to the public of stock in an independent Conrail.

Confronted by that formidable opposition and the probability that pending tax-overhaul legislation could make the merger less attractive, Norfolk Southern withdrew its bid Aug. 22. The administration then endorsed the stock offering plan the same day. *(Tax overhaul measure, p. 491)*

Dingell's committee Sept. 17 approved a $2 billion stock offering and sent it to the Budget Committee to be included in the reconciliation legislation. The Senate, before passing its reconciliation measure Sept. 20, adopted a revenue-raising amendment calling for a public offering.

There were sharp differences between the chambers, however. Senators adamantly opposed a House provision mandating protection for certain railroad workers, a provision backed by labor but opposed by the industry.

House and Senate conferees reached agreement Oct. 9 only after House negotiators dropped the proposal, which would have required $25,000 to be paid to a rail worker adversely affected by the sale of branch lines by major rail carriers to new carriers. No compensation was currently required.

Summary: Limiting Future Mergers

The compromise banned any Conrail merger with another line for one year, after which the Interstate Commerce Commission (ICC) could approve a consolidation with another railroad.

The House-passed version of the reconciliation legislation had imposed a three-year ban on ICC consideration of a merger application by Norfolk Southern or its Virginia-based competitor, CSX Corp.

Defenders of the pact said that Conrail executives were against a merger and that no outside railroad could secure a majority of Conrail's voting stock to force management to accept a buy-out.

The House had set a minimum price of $1.7 billion below which Conrail stock could not be sold. Conferees set a non-binding goal of $2 billion to be paid to the government, with an additional mandatory $200 million in cash from Conrail.

The accord retained a House requirement that agricultural shippers disclose the terms of their contracts with railroads. Small shippers hoped disclosure would help them force the ICC to erase advantages railroads might give to large shippers.

The package also included:

- **Cash Payments.** In addition to the mandatory $200 million cash payment from Conrail, the transportation secretary could demand another $100 million.

The House bill called for a $300 million mandatory payment.

- **Investment Banking Firms.** Four to six investment banking firms would manage the sale, with fees shared equally. The transportation secretary would designate one of the "co-lead managers" to coordinate and administer the offering.
- **Ownership Limitations.** For three years after the sale, no person or group could own more than 10 percent of the stock, except a railroad, which could not own more than 10 percent for a year after the sale.

The conference agreement (H Rept 99-1012) was reached and approved by both chambers Oct. 17.

Provisions

As signed into law, HR 5300 contained the following provisions on Conrail:

- **Conrail Tax Treatment.** Stipulated that Conrail be treated as a new corporation that purchased its assets the day after the public sale. No carry-over of net operating losses or other benefits, such as unused investment tax credits, would be allowed for tax purposes.

With one major exception, the public sales price would be allocated among all of Conrail's assets, both depreciable assets, such as equipment and buildings, and non-depreciable assets, such as land. After the sale, Conrail's depreciable assets were expected to be worth considerably less than before the sale. As a result, Conrail likely would suffer a loss in its tax deductions for depreciation.

The sales price would not be allocated among Conrail's existing assets — its inventory and accounts receivable. Without this exemption, Conrail conceivably would have to pay taxes on the difference between the existing value of its accounts receivable — the money owed to it for transportation services — and its reduced value after the sale.

- Required the transportation secretary, in consultation with the Treasury secretary and chairman of the board of Conrail, within 30 days after enactment, to retain the services of investment bankers to manage the sale to the public.
- Directed the transportation secretary to choose four to six investment banking firms as "co-lead managers" of the public offering. One must be designated to coordinate and administer the offering, but all must be compensated equally. Selection criteria must include a firm's financial strength, knowledge of the railroad industry and past contributions in promoting the long-term viability of Conrail. Firms not in existence before Sept. 1, 1986, would be ineligible, and fees must be paid from the proceeds of the stock sale.
- Required an opportunity for minority-owned or controlled firms to participate in the stock sale.
- Permitted the General Accounting Office to audit the accounts of Conrail and the co-lead managers.
- Required Conrail to make a $200 million cash payment to the federal government, within 30 days after enactment. An additional $100 million payment could be required by the transportation secretary, taking into account Conrail's long-term viability.
- Canceled, in consideration for the $200 million cash payment, Conrail's debts to the federal government.
- Directed Conrail to file with the Securities and Exchange Commission a registration statement with respect to the securities to be offered. The transportation secretary could require Conrail to declare a stock split before the filing.
- Directed the transportation secretary to schedule a public offering after the registration statement was declared effective. The transportation secretary, in consultation with the Treasury secretary, Conrail's chairman of the board and the investment bankers, could decide to conduct the sale in stages.
- Required a finding by the transportation secretary, before proceeding with the sale, that the gross proceeds would be "an adequate amount." A $2 billion non-binding goal was set. The secretary's finding was not subject to judicial or administrative review.
- Required Conrail to make minimum capital expenditures of the greater of its financial depreciation or $500 million in each fiscal year over a five-year period following enactment. However, expenditures could be reduced to an average of $350 million per year by Conrail's board of directors.
- Barred dividend payments if Conrail failed to comply with the capital expenditure requirement. After such payments Conrail must have on hand $400 million in cash. Subject to certain restrictions, Conrail could borrow to meet the minimum cash-balance requirement. Common stock dividends could not exceed 45 percent of cumulative net income less the cumulative amount of any preferred stock dividends.
- Required Conrail over the five-year period following enactment to continue its existing affirmative action and minority vendor programs; to continue to offer to sell lines that the ICC approved for abandonment for 75 percent of net liquidation value; not to permit deferral of normal and prudent maintenance on its properties; and not to permit a takeover of all or any substantial part of its assets.
- Required annual certification by Conrail of compliance with all five-year covenants, except for the dividend covenant, for which certification must be provided to the transportation secretary after the declaration of any payments.
- Authorized the transportation secretary to bring legal actions against Conrail or others to require compliance with the five-year covenants and ownership limitations.
- Prohibited ownership of more than 10 percent of Conrail's voting stock over a three-year period beginning on the sale date by anyone, except for the employee stock ownership plan, the transportation secretary, a railroad or certain others.
- Limited major railroads to ownership of 10 percent of voting stock for one year beginning on the sale date. No merger applications could be filed with the ICC during this period. If a merger application was approved, railroad stock must be voted during the three years after a sale in the same proportion as all other common stock was voted.
- Provided for the transition from Conrail's existing board of directors to a board elected by Conrail's public shareholders. After the initial sale date, one director would be elected by shareholders for each 12.5 percent increment of the government's share of Conrail that had been sold. Interim arrangements were provided for in the event that less than 50 percent of the corporation had been sold by June 1, 1987.
- Required Conrail to assume financial liability for the existing supplemental unemployment benefits plan, which had been federally funded, until the sale date.
- Required Conrail to provide labor protection to its employees after the sale, pursuant to a previous agreement with unions representing the workers. The federal government would have no liability for benefits due workers.
- Directed Conrail to pay $200 million to present and former workers in compensation for deferred wages.
- Provided for the distribution of the 15 percent of Conrail stock vested in the employee stock ownership plan to participants and beneficiaries. Individual shares in the plan could not be sold for at least 180 days from the date on which 100 percent of the federal government's shares had been sold.
- Abolished the United States Railway Association, effective April 1, 1987. Congress created the association in 1973 to monitor Conrail.
- Provided that the Regional Rail Reorganization Act of 1973 — the so-called 3R act — should not apply to Conrail after the sale date, with certain exceptions. For example, existing law was retained requiring Conrail to keep its

headquarters in Philadelphia.

• Exempted Conrail's directors and others from lawsuits by stockholders, employees and others, with certain exceptions. For example, a director would not be exempted if he or she made a false statement on the registration form filed with the Securities and Exchange Commission.

• Protected the federal government from any and all liabilities resulting from the implementation of Conrail sale legislation, except for actions brought to require the transportation secretary to proceed with a public offering.

• **Rail Competition.** Required greater public disclosure of the terms of rail contracts between shippers of agricultural goods and rail carriers. The provision was intended to make it easier for small shippers to receive the same favorable contract terms as large shippers.

• Confirmed the legal authority of the ICC to issue a rule to require compensation by major railroads to small railroads for the use of the latter's boxcars.

Senate Action

When Majority Leader Robert Dole, R-Kan., tried to bring the Norfolk Southern sale measure to the floor Jan. 21, several senators objected, and Dole filed a cloture petition to limit debate. Critics included Howard M. Metzenbaum, D-Ohio; Arlen Specter, R-Pa.; John Heinz, R-Pa.; and Larry Pressler, R-S.D.

Although opponents conceded that they did not have the votes to prevail, they continued their delaying tactics. After a Jan. 23 vote of 90-7 to limit debate on a motion to proceed with the bill, some key critics agreed to drop their filibuster. On Jan. 30, senators voted 70-27 to shut off discussion on the measure itself. *(Vote 1, p. 2-S; vote 7, p. 2-S)*

The Senate rejected efforts to alter Norfok Southern's bid or to allow new bids to be considered and on Feb. 4 approved the Norfolk Southern sale, voting 54-39 to allow the railroad to buy the system for $1.2 billion. *(Vote 12, p. 3-S)*

The critics of the sale took some comfort in the vote, interpreting the 39 nay votes as a sign of significant congressional opposition to Norfolk Southern's offer.

The Senate considered the measure Jan. 23, 27, 28, 29, 30 and Feb. 4.

Specter and Metzenbaum had tried to keep the bill off the floor by filibustering the motion to consider it. But minutes before the vote Jan. 23 to impose cloture and limit debate, they announced they would vote to stop their own filibuster.

"I want to make it eminently clear that my going along with it does not indicate in any way that I have slackened my opposition," Metzenbaum said.

Voting not to invoke cloture were Bill Bradley, D-N.J.; Quentin N. Burdick, D-N.D.; Wendell H. Ford, D-Ky.; Pressler; William Proxmire, D-Wis.; William V. Roth Jr., R-Del.; and John C. Stennis, D-Miss.

Specter explained the decision to drop the procedural filibuster, saying it was difficult to mount a filibuster early in the session on a procedural motion, such as one to consider a bill, "because the sense in the Senate is not to have delay." Senators were afraid, he said, that such tactics would lead to legislative gridlock when they faced requirements of the Gramm-Rudman-Hollings budget-cutting law.

The final straw came Jan. 30 when the Senate voted 70-27 to invoke cloture, and thus limit extended debate, on the bill. Majority Leader Dole had hoped for final action shortly after cloture was approved, but a series of post-cloture amendments blocked that from happening.

Also, he was under pressure to recess the Senate so that members could attend a Jan. 31 memorial service in Houston for the lost crew of the *Challenger* space shuttle. *(Challenger, p. 326)*

Metzenbaum made a last-ditch effort to stall the bill by objecting that it would raise revenue for the government and thus, under the Constitution, must originate in the House.

But a motion Feb. 4 by John C. Danforth, R-Mo., to table (kill) Metzenbaum's point of order carried on a 70-17 vote. Danforth was chairman of the Commerce, Science and Transportation Committee and was floor manager of the Conrail bill. *(Vote 11, p. 3-S)*

Debate centered on charges that Norfolk Southern was getting a "sweetheart deal" because its $1.2 billion offer appeared lower than some others and because of significant tax advantages a buyer would gain by acquiring Conrail.

A group of investors organized by Morgan Stanley and Co., a New York investment banking firm, had offered $1.4 billion for Conrail. A third bid — for $1.65 billion — was made Dec. 17, 1985, by Allen & Co. Inc. and First Boston Corp.

Reagan: 'Now Is the Time'

Reagan's active role in lobbying for the bill was a new development that appeared to be linked to his fiscal 1987 budget, scheduled to be released the week of Feb. 3. It was expected to propose selling other government assets, such as federal dams, government loans and perhaps even the U.S. Postal Service, to reduce deficits.

"After nearly 10 years of federal ownership and the provision of subsidies to Conrail, now is the time to get the government out of the railroad business," Reagan said in a Jan. 21 letter to Secretary Dole.

"The sale also will stand as a very visible example to the American people that this administration is committed to privatizing functions which can be handled more efficiently by business than by government."

Efforts to Alter Bid Fail

Both before and after cloture was invoked, the Senate dispensed with a number of amendments aimed at significantly altering the terms of Norfolk Southern's bid or, in some cases, allowing other bids to be considered.

On a 53-39 vote, the Senate Jan. 29 tabled (killed) an amendment by Specter to accept a $1.4 billion offer from the Morgan Stanley group. *(Vote 3, p. 2-S)*

Also, the Senate Jan. 30:

• Agreed by 68-31 to waive the budget act. *(Vote 2, p. 2-S)*

• Tabled 56-37 an amendment by Alan J. Dixon, D-Ill., to subject the proposed Conrail sale to antitrust laws. Dixon said the amendment was needed to ensure the rights of smaller railroads and other parties to challenge anti-competitive aspects of the sale. *(Vote 4, p. 2-S)*

• Tabled 51-45 an amendment by Frank R. Lautenberg, D-N.J., to allow government jurisdictions to go to court seeking traffic rights for non-Conrail lines. The amendment was designed to protect the ports of New York and New Jersey, which currently relied heavily on Conrail. *(Vote 5, p. 2-S)*

• Tabled 64-32 an amendment by Metzenbaum that would have directed the Department of Transportation to solicit new purchase bids. *(Vote 6, p. 2-S)*

- Tabled 69-27 a Metzenbaum amendment that would have repealed legal immunity for fiduciaries charged with protecting the interests of Conrail's workers. Metzenbaum charged that Norfolk Southern's bid would shortchange the employees, who owned 15 percent of Conrail, and that the fiduciaries should be legally responsible for their actions. *(Vote 8, p. 2-S)*
- Tabled 63-33 an amendment by Heinz that would have limited tax deductions and other benefits that would flow to Norfolk Southern after purchasing Conrail. *(Vote 10, p. 3-S)*
- Accepted by voice vote an amendment by Pressler designed to protect regional railroads in the Midwest and elsewhere that were likely to be affected by Conrail's sale.

House Action

The administration plan immediately ran into trouble in the House.

Dingell's announcement of his opposition to selling Conrail to Norfolk Southern inflicted what proved to be a fatal blow to the proposal.

Dingell declared that the idea was "mired in a hopeless swamp of confusion and controversy." He called for a new plan to keep Conrail independent and to give the public "a fair opportunity" to participate in the ownership by buying stock.

Dan Coats, R-Ind., a Commerce panel member, said, "I think the chairman's statement kind of put the last nail in the coffin for Norfolk Southern."

Metzenbaum said, "The Conrail sale appears dead for '86."

Dingell said that DOT had failed to produce "persuasive evidence" that an independent Conrail was "doomed to fail" and had not proven that the Norfolk Southern offer was in the public interest.

Dingell's principal concerns focused on the impact of a Conrail-Norfolk Southern merger on the quality and price of rail service in the Northeast and Midwest, on competition between rail carriers in those regions and on the jobs of Conrail employees.

He also questioned the adequacy of Norfolk's $1.2 billion offer and raised the possibility of a drain on the Treasury due to tax benefits accruing to Norfolk Southern as a result of its acquisition of Conrail.

Many shippers and labor groups echoed those concerns. Shippers were worried about the monopoly that an expanded Norfolk Southern might gain over their businesses, and labor unions representing railroad workers feared that the sale would eliminate jobs on Conrail lines.

However, Secretary Dole said she was confident Dingell's concerns could be addressed. At her request, Dingell and she met the day after his announcement.

Dole in a letter May 6 to Dingell called on Norfolk Southern to raise its offer from $1.2 billion to $1.9 billion and proposed giving the ICC a veto over the transaction.

But Dingell said May 7, "I can only repeat that the proposed sale of Conrail to Norfolk Southern remains unacceptable and that my position is final."

Norfolk Southern raised its bid to $1.9 billion, but the proposed merger did not advance in Dingell's committee. On Aug. 22, Norfolk Southern withdrew its offer, saying there was "no end in sight to the legislative impassee" and indicated pending tax overhaul legislation could make the merger less attractive.

New Controversies Emerge

Despite the endorsement, new controversies threatened to block the return of the railroad to the private sector.

Chief among them were efforts by shippers and rail labor groups to turn a Conrail bill into an omnibus measure to address their complaints of unfair treatment under the partial deregulation of the rail industry and the ICC.

Shippers charged, among other things, that the ICC allowed monopoly railroads to overcharge them, and railroad labor groups wanted to tighten certain job protection rules.

They calculated that the determination of members and the administration to act on Conrail before adjournment would make a Conrail bill an attractive vehicle to accomplish their legislative aims.

But their efforts drew strong opposition from the administration, the Senate and rail carriers. Opponents contended that the shippers' complaints were largely unjustified and departures from current laws and ICC practices would damage the industry's economic recovery that was fostered by deregulation.

House Committee Action

The Energy and Commerce Committee Sept. 17 approved a $2 billion Conrail sale package after narrowly squashing a plea by Dingell to make the revision to rail deregulation laws sought by some shippers.

The unnumbered bill, approved by voice vote, was sent to the Budget Committee for inclusion in pending budget reconciliation legislation.

The bill called for a stock offering, but the sale would be barred if it would not bring in at least $1.7 billion, and Conrail must give the government another $300 million in cash.

The committee action was a reversal for Dingell, who the day before had persuaded the Subcommittee on Commerce, Transportation and Tourism to approve amendments to a Conrail sale bill that included the changes sought by shippers.

The White House threatened to veto legislation that contained "special interest" provisions, and committee members backing a "clean" Conrail bill also argued that attaching unrelated provisions could jeopardize the sale of the railroad.

The next day the full committee by 22-20 adopted an amendment by ranking minority member Norman F. Lent, R-N.Y., that stripped the major deregulation measures from the package. The proposal was backed by James J. Florio, D-N.J., subcommittee chairman, and six other Democrats. *(Vote box, next page)*

Rail Labor Controversy

The bill proposed closing an exemption from job protection requirements that the ICC had given to sales of branch lines by major railroads to new carriers. Some industry analysts said the provision could be devastating to growth of the "short-line," or branch-line, railroad sector.

But rail labor spokesmen said workers needed protection from railroads that were accelerating layoffs, reducing severance pay and denying the rights of unions to bargain collectively on the deployment of workers.

The provision would close an exemption from job protection requirements that the ICC had provided since 1980 to sales of branch lines by major railroads to new carriers. The exemption allowed the new carrier wide latitude in

Committee Vote

Following is how House Energy and Commerce Committee members voted Sept. 17 on an amendment stripping most railroad deregulation changes from the Conrail sale bill. The amendment was adopted 22-20.

For the Amendment:

Republicans (15): Lent, N.Y.; Madigan, Ill.; Moorhead, Calif.; Rinaldo, N.J.; Dannemeyer, Calif.; Whittaker, Kan.; Ritter, Pa.; Bliley, Va.; Fields, Texas; Oxley, Ohio; Nielson, Utah; Bilirakis, Fla.; Schaefer, Colo.; Eckert, N.Y.; and Lott, Miss.

Democrats (7): Scheuer, N.Y.; Waxman, Calif.; Wirth, Colo.; Florio, N.J.; Mikulski, Md.; Collins, Ill.; and Bryant, Texas.

Against the Amendment:

Republicans (2): Tauke, Iowa, and Coats, Ind.

Democrats (18): Dingell, Mich.; Sharp, Ind.; Markey, Mass.; Luken, Ohio; Walgren, Pa.; Swift, Wash.; Leland, Texas; Shelby, Ala.; Synar, Okla.; Tauzin, La.; Wyden, Ore.; Hall, Texas; Eckart, Ohio; Dowdy, Miss.; Richardson, N.M.; Slattery, Kan.; Sikorski, Minn; and Bates, Calif.

making assignments, and severance pay was not required.

The ICC argued that many sales would not take place without the exemption, resulting in the abandonment of low-density branch lines and the loss of service and jobs. The administration endorsed the exemption.

However, barring the exemption did not bring workers affected by short-line transactions under an existing ICC rule that required that workers affected by mergers or abandonments receive six years' pay and benefits, which averaged about $250,000 each. The committee bill set a cap of $25,000 to be paid by the seller for each short-line worker affected.

The bill also required the acquiring company to reach an agreement with workers on "selection of forces" on the new railroad.

The administration opposed the labor provision.

Subcommittee Action

In the Sept. 16 subcommittee markup, Florio offered a package embracing a public offering for Conrail, labor protection provisions covering short-line transactions and limited changes to the 1980 railroad deregulation law known as the Staggers Act (PL 96-448). *(Staggers Act, 1980 Almanac p. 248)*

Florio's proposal addressed complaints made by the shippers' coalition.

Norman F. Lent, R-N.Y., raised the administration's concern that the Conrail bill should not be linked to "extraneous" issues. But his amendment to drop everything except the Conrail sale provisions failed by a 9-9 vote.

W. J. "Billy" Tauzin, D-La., offered a substitute amendment that embraced Florio's Conrail and labor provisions but gave shippers more leverage in establishing before the ICC that rates should be reduced. It also would have required the ICC to order rate reductions proportionate to declines in inflation.

Dingell backed Tauzin's move, blasting the ICC as a "brain-dead" agency that had failed to protect captive shippers.

Over the protests of Florio, who said sweeping Staggers changes could cripple the rail industry, Tauzin's substitute was adopted 10-8.

Full Committee Reversal

At full committee markup Sept. 17, Coats proposed striking the Staggers and labor provisions. Supporters cited a letter from Conrail's chairman, L. Stanley Crane, calling the deregulation law vital to the health of Conrail and the rail industry.

Proponents also maintained that Conrail sale legislation that reimposed new federal regulations on the rail industry would be frowned on by Wall Street and reduce the proceeds of a public stock offering. And they pointed out that a broad range of shippers — including some food, chemical, steel and timber companies — were against any Staggers revisions.

Senior DOT officials were on hand lobbying committee members, and Secretary Dole wrote Dingell that the deregulation reforms "will make Conrail unsalable if enacted into law."

But opponents said that shippers not subject to monopoly pricing paid lower prices because captive shippers were being overcharged and that the Conrail bill was virtually the only legislative vehicle left in the 99th Congress to address those concerns.

"This is the only train that's going all the way to the president's desk for signature," Tauzin declared.

The Coats amendment failed 18-23. Lent, saying that it was "very clear that a clean bill cannot win today," then offered what he called a "compromise cleanup amendment," which was adopted 22-20. While keeping the labor protection provision, the amendment dropped most Staggers changes.

The committee also adopted 32-9 an amendment by Dennis E. Eckart, D-Ohio, that called for at least two investment banking firms to lead the management of the public sale. The subcommittee would not have required more than one lead bank.

The amendment appeared to secure a lead role not only for Goldman Sachs & Co., which under contract advised DOT on a Conrail sale, but for Morgan Stanley Group Inc., which had attempted to organize a public stock offering.

Provisions

Major provisions of the committee bill:

- **Public Offering.** Required the DOT secretary, in consultation with the Treasury secretary, Conrail's chairman and the investment bankers, to determine that the proceeds of a stock sale would yield at least $1.7 billion. After the first stage of the sale, the 15 percent share of Conrail vested in the employee stock ownership plan would revert to the employees, who could sell or retain their shares.
- **Board of Directors.** Provided for a transition from Conrail's current board, which included some members appointed by DOT, to a board elected by public shareholders.
- **Protective Covenants.** For five years after enactment, Conrail must make capital expenditures averaging at least $350 million per year.

Dividend payments would be allowed only if Conrail met its capital expenditure requirement and even then, common stock dividends would be subject to limitations.

For the first three years, no takeover or breakup of

Conrail would be allowed, and Conrail must maintain a cash balance of at least $250 million at the end of each fiscal year.

• **Ownership Limitations.** With a few exceptions, including one for the transportation secretary, no person could own more than 7.5 percent of Conrail for five years after enactment. Total foreign ownership would be limited to 20 percent, and no major railroad would be allowed to own more than 7.5 percent.

Conference

A House-Senate conference on the Conrail sale provisions of the reconciliation bill stalled soon after it began Sept. 29 because of the House labor protection provisions.

Conferees Sept. 29-30 discussed several issues, including whether to set a minimum price for the sale of Conrail's stock and how many investment banking firms should manage the sale, but they came to no agreement.

Some senators, including Pressler, said the labor provisions were potentially devastating to the short-line industry because they might raise the cost of an acquisition. Pressler was not a Conrail conferee but threatened to filibuster the labor protection language.

Danforth argued Sept. 29 that the labor item and other House provisions not directly related to the railroad's sale should be dropped because they would subject the bill to a point of order on the Senate floor because of "extraneous matter" not linked to the budget. He said that it would be very difficult to find the 60 votes required to overturn a parliamentary ruling that the bill was out of order.

There were two other non-Conrail House provisions that were not particularly controversial. One would require agricultural shippers to disclose the terms of their contracts with railroads, and the other ratified an ICC ruling requiring that large railroads adequately pay small railroads for the use of the latter's boxcars.

Pricing Conrail Stock

Danforth also objected to setting a minimum price below which Conrail could not be sold. The House set a $1.7 billion minimum for the sale of stock and required that Conrail pay another $300 million to the government. The Senate set no minimum.

Danforth said the minimum might become a ceiling, with the public deciding that Conrail was worth no more than $1.7 billion. He suggested also that the $300 million cash payment was excessive.

House members proposed dropping the minimum and lowering the cash payment to $200 million. The transportation secretary would have the discretion of requiring an additional $100 million payment. ▮

Highway Reauthorization Dies Amid Disputes

Because House and Senate lawmakers failed to resolve disputes over a handful of controversies, legislation (HR 3129) to reauthorize virtually all major highway and mass transit programs died in the closing hours of the 99th Congress.

Congress adjourned Oct. 18 without finishing a conference on the bill. The programs expired when the fiscal year ended Sept. 30.

Although $6.5 billion in previously allocated funds would be available to states in fiscal 1987, anticipated new funding of $14 billion accumulating in the Highway Trust Fund could not be spent.

The House passed the bill Aug. 15 authorizing a total of about $90 billion through fiscal 1991, including about $68 billion for highway construction programs, $1.5 billion for highway safety and $21 billion for mass transit. The Senate version approved Sept. 24 authorized about $52 billion for highway programs through fiscal 1990 and more than $12 billion for transit through fiscal 1990.

In addition to differences in funding, there were sharp splits over a number of issues.

House leaders strongly objected to a Senate plan to allow states to raise the speed limit to 65 mph on rural Interstate highways.

Senate negotiators were angered by the House's refusal to modify substantially a provision calling for full federal funding of demonstration highway projects that ostensibly were to demonstrate design, engineering or safety improvements. The House had included some 100 projects in its bill.

There also was disagreement over requiring cash payments to billboard owners for their removal. The House provided a cap on the total number of billboards permitted along federal highways but maintained the required cash compensation by the federal government and states. The more restrictive Senate bill knocked out required compensation and established a moratorium on the erection of new billboards.

The House measure extended the Interstate construction program through fiscal 1993 and retained its status as a separate funding category. In a major policy departure proposed by the administration, the Senate wrapped Interstate construction into a new program that included funding for other types of construction and for the Interstate repair program.

Despite a flurry of meetings in the final hours of the session, lawmakers could not resolve their differences on the omnibus bill. They also failed to pass an alternative one-year bill (S 2951) backed by the Reagan administration to give states more flexibility in spending the unallocated $6.3 billion.

In the fiscal 1987 omnibus appropriations bill (H J Res 738 — PL 99-591), Congress provided transit systems with $2 billion in grants. *(Appropriations, p. 176)*

House Action

As reported (H Rept 99-665) July 2 by the House Public Works and Transportation Committee, HR 3129 authorized approximately $13.9 billion annually for highways through fiscal 1991. It also set an annual ceiling on spending from the Highway Trust Fund of $12.6 billion.

The bill made no major changes in existing programs and authorized funds through fiscal 1993 to complete the Interstate Highway System. The measure did alter the formula by which highway repair funds were distributed to states. The proposed formula placed more emphasis on highway usage rather than on the number of miles of highway in each state, as the current formula did.

The measure cut funding for Interstate highways to $3.3 billion annually — a reduction of about $750 million from current levels. In addition, the bill set aside $5 billion in fiscal 1992 and 1993 to pay for the completion of the Interstate Highway System.

The committee approved almost 100 special "demonstration" projects at a five-year cost of more than $1 billion.

While authorizations for programs supported by the Highway Trust Fund totaled about $14.1 billion annually, the measure limited the actual obligation of funds to $12.6 billion annually.

Floor Action

The House Aug. 15 passed the bill by a vote of 345-34. *(Vote 331, p. 92-H)*

The House began debate Aug. 6, but the leadership pulled the bill from the floor Aug. 7 to make way for other legislation.

On Aug. 6, the House narrowly defeated an effort to raise the 55 mph speed limit. The amendment, by Dave McCurdy, D-Okla., would have established a five-year test program permitting states to raise the speed limit to 65 mph on rural, remote sections of the Interstate system. Federal penalties enforcing the 55 mph speed limit would have been suspended.

Proponents argued that few motorists actually complied with the 55 mph limit and that states — rather than the federal government — should be responsible for setting speed limits. They also contended that a decline in recent years in traffic fatalities was due not merely to the 55 mph limit but to improvements in roads and safety features of automobiles.

Opponents, however, said there was "overwhelming" evidence that the 55 mph speed limit had saved thousands of lives since it was enacted in 1974 at the height of the energy crisis.

The House voted 198-218 to reject the McCurdy amendment. *(Vote 273, p. 78-H)*

On billboards, the House Aug. 7 by 251-159 adopted an amendment by Bud Shuster, R-Pa., as a substitute for a more restrictive proposal advanced by E. Clay Shaw Jr., R-Fla. *(Vote 275, p. 78-H)*

The Shuster proposal, which was endorsed by the leadership of the Public Works panel, froze the number of billboards on federal highways while continuing the policy of reimbursing the billboard industry with federal funds for signs that were taken down. The Shaw proposal would not have required cash compensation for billboards that were removed. *(1978 Almanac p. 536)*

On final passage Aug. 15, leaders of the Public Works Committee lost 171-214 in a bruising fight over their motion to recommit the legislation to the committee with instructions to add a provision that would have exempted the Highway Trust Fund from cuts mandated by the Gramm-Rudman-Hollings anti-deficit law (PL 99-177). *(Vote 330, p. 92-H; Gramm-Rudman-Hollings, p. 579)*

They argued that the trust fund was self-financed by road-related user fees and had never contributed to the federal deficit. But Appropriations and Budget Committee leaders successfully countered that if trust fund programs were exempt from Gramm-Rudman cuts, a deeper slash would have to be made in the rest of the budget to reach the cuts required.

"A vote for this motion is the same as a vote to cut education, to cut health care, to cut the whole range of general fund programs," declared Silvio O. Conte, R-Mass., ranking minority member on the Appropriations panel.

Also Aug. 15, the House reversed itself on funding for a controversial Los Angeles mass transit project. On Aug. 7 an amendment by Henry A. Waxman, D-Calif., to strike the funds was adopted 210-201. But in a second vote Aug. 15, the House rejected the Waxman proposal 153-231. *(Vote 277, p. 78-H; vote 329, p. 92-H)*

Senate Action

Trying to clear the way for quick floor action, the Senate Environment and Public Works Committee July 23 deferred several controversies before approving its highway bill (S 2405). The measure was reported (S Rept 99-369) Aug. 5.

Postponed items included changes in the 55 mph speed limit and funding authorizations for mass transit programs, which were under the jurisdiction of the Senate Banking, Housing and Urban Affairs Committee.

Citing budget concerns, the committee set the obligation ceiling governing spending for most federal highway programs at $12.35 billion annually for the next four fiscal years. In addition, about $800 million was authorized for emergency aid and to ensure that each state received at least a certain amount of funds.

The committee rejected, 5-8, an amendment by Steven D. Symms, R-Idaho, to raise the obligation ceiling to $13.125 billion, the current level. Symms argued that cash should not be kept in the Highway Trust Fund to reduce the federal deficit.

But Budget Committee Chairman Pete V. Domenici, R-N.M., a member of Environment and Public Works, insisted that it was not realistic to expect the Senate to increase the deficit or cut other programs in order to raise highway spending.

By 9-4, the panel adopted an amendment to speed up removal of billboards from the nation's highways. The amendment, offered by Chairman Robert T. Stafford, R-Vt., relieved states of their obligation to compensate sign owners in cash for removal of billboards, as required in 1978 (PL 95-599). *(1978 Almanac p. 536)*

It allowed states to use other forms of compensation, such as giving sign owners a limited lease for signs that otherwise would have to be torn down.

James Abdnor, R-S.D., argued that the amendment would devastate the tourism industry, particularly in rural states. But Stafford said that there were no funds for the federal government to help states pay for removal and that some method needed to be found to speed up sign removal, which was originally required by the 1965 Highway Beautification Act (PL 89-285). *(Congress and the Nation Vol. II, p. 476)*

There was little dispute over an amendment to control special highway projects. The House included nearly 100 "demonstration projects," which were intended to exemplify new technology or design and which would be financed entirely by federal funds, above a state's regular allotment of highway money.

The Senate committee by voice vote approved a Symms amendment to give state officials control over the projects and to include the projects in the state's allocation. The net effect of the change would be to give state officials greater ability to shift funds between categories of federal aid for some projects.

To avoid referral of the bill to the Banking, Housing and Urban Affairs Committee, the panel approved by voice vote an amendment by Frank R. Lautenberg, D-N.J., to strike a provision that would have shifted some mass-transit funds from urban states to rural ones.

The panel rejected, on a 7-7 tie vote, a Symms amendment to relax a 1982 requirement (PL 97-424) that 10 percent of federal highway contracts go to minority enterprises. A Symms amendment to eliminate the program was rejected by voice vote.

Symms also proposed that the minimum value of contracts governed by the 1931 Davis-Bacon Act, requiring federal contractors to pay prevailing wages, be raised from $2,000 to $500,000. The amendment was rejected 6-7.

An amendment to exempt a Hawaii road project from environmental laws, hotly opposed by environmentalists, failed to materialize. Stafford said it would be offered on the floor.

Floor Action

The Senate passed the bill Sept. 24 by a vote of 99-0, after substituting the text of its bill for the House-passed measure. *(Vote 288, p. 48-S)*

The Senate authorized $52 billion for highways and more than $12 billion for mass transit through fiscal 1990. It set an annual ceiling of $12.3 billion on money from the Highway Trust Fund that may be obligated for highways.

Transit authorizations were added when the Senate adopted by voice vote an amendment by the leadership of the Banking, Finance and Urban Affairs Committee. The amendment, which was not acted on formally by the panel, froze annual funding roughly at $2 billion for formula grants and $1 billion for discretionary grants.

An amendment by leaders of the Finance Committee, also adopted by voice vote, authorized taxes for the trust fund through fiscal 1992.

On Sept. 23, the first of two days of debate on the measure, the Senate by 56-36 adopted an amendment by Symms to permit states to raise the speed limit to 65 mph on rural Interstate highways. *(Vote 282, p. 47-S)*

Opponents of the Symms amendment, most of whom represented Eastern states, argued that the 55 mph speed limit saved lives as well as fuel.

John C. Danforth, R-Mo., cited a National Safety Council study estimating that 600 to 1,000 lives would be lost annually if the speed limit were raised to 65 mph on rural roads. His effort to table the amendment failed 40-57. *(Vote 280, p. 47-S)*

Proponents said the 55 mph speed limit might make sense in the East but was inappropriate for the lightly traveled highways of the West. They also stressed that the Symms proposal applied only to rural Interstate roads — not to rural sections of other federal highways. The Senate defeated, 36-60, an amendment by Chic Hecht, R-Nev., that would have allowed a speed limit of 65 mph on rural portions of all federal highways. *(Vote 281, p. 47-S)*

President Reagan had endorsed efforts, including the Symms amendment, to "restore greater authority to the states" to raise the speed limit.

Other Proposals

Other key proposals adopted by the Senate included those by:

- Symms, by 49-46, to increase from $2,000 to $250,000 the minimum value of contracts covered by the 1931 Davis-Bacon Act, which required contractors to pay the locally prevailing wage. *(Vote 283, p. 47-S)*

The House kept the threshold at $2,000. An increase in the threshold was favored by highway contractors but opposed by labor groups.

- Lawton Chiles, D-Fla., by voice vote, to relax the ban that had existed for more than seven decades on using federal funds to build toll roads, although not as much as sought by the Reagan administration. The House retained the prohibition.

Under the amendment, tolls would not be allowed on Interstate roads, and states must bear 65 percent of the cost of toll projects. The state share on non-Interstate roads was currently 25 percent.

- Symms, by voice vote, to add 50 "priority" highway projects to the 20 special projects already contained in the bill.
- Symms motion, by 56-41, to table (kill) an amendment by Thad Cochran, R-Miss., to ban the use of imported cement and cement products in federal highway construction projects. The House bill contained a ban. *(Vote 285, p. 48-S)*
- Symms, 65-32, to drop a provision allowing state and local governments to limit highway contracts awarded to firms doing business in South Africa. The House bill had a similar provision. *(Vote 287, p. 48-S; South Africa, p. 359)*

The Senate rejected 16-78 a motion to table (kill) an amendment by Daniel K. Inouye, D-Hawaii, to exempt a Hawaii Interstate project from a 1984 court injunction issued on environmental grounds. The plan was adopted by voice vote. The House exempted the project. *(Vote 284, p. 48-S)*

Conference

Strong, divergent views over the two measures surfaced immediately, with key House members refusing to go to conference unless the Senate agreed to drop its speed-limit provision.

Leaders of the House Public Works Committee Sept. 26 offerred to allow a state to raise the limit to 65 mph on rural Interstate highways if the state demonstrated a 65 percent compliance rate for seat-belt use and banned the use by motorists of radar detectors.

"This proposal would give the Senate what it wants," said James J. Howard, D-N.J., chairman of the committee. "It must be emphasized that the House conferees will not proceed to conference on the highway-transit bill until this issue is settled."

Sen. Stafford said the House "precondition" to a conference threatened to kill the legislation.

Some Progress

House-Senate conferees did meet after House members withdrew their demands, however, and tentatively agreed Oct. 3 to drop a Senate plan to end separate funding for Interstate highway construction.

Senators also indicated they might reject the administration-backed plan ending a ban on using federal funds to construct toll roads.

House conferees accepted a Senate proposal not to shift Interstate repair money from more rural states to more densely populated states.

Despite progress on some key issues, House and Senate conferees failed to resolve the larger disputes over such items as relaxing the 55 mph speed limit and federal funding for special "demonstration" projects. ∎

Product Liability Bill Dies After Filibuster

Legislation that would have set federal standards governing product liability lawsuits died in the Senate in late September after a brief filibuster.

Prospects for the bill faded June 26 after a sharply divided Senate Commerce, Science and Transportation Committee narrowly approved legislation (S 2760 — S Rept 99-422) that imposed limits on certain court awards to alleged victims of unsafe products. Critics said there should not be monetary restrictions on recovery for damages for "pain and suffering."

Despite the bill's poor chances for success, proponents, including Bob Kasten, R-Wis., took their fight to the floor, contending that would increase their chances of enacting legislation in 1987.

But with Ernest F. Hollings, D-S.C., prepared to filibuster the bill, the measure got only as far as approval of a motion to consider before Majority Leader Robert Dole, R-Kan., pulled it from the floor. Hollings, a former trial lawyer, blamed rising insurance costs on the industry, not on any problems with the system of federal and state tort laws. He also contended that common law tradition and state law should govern lawsuits, rather than a federal standard.

Kasten said that the vote of 84-13 in favor of a motion to proceed with floor consideration showed "tremendous support" for new legislation. *(Vote 295, p. 49-S)*

There was no action in the House on product liability legislation, other than hearings.

The only major insurance legislation cleared by Congress was a bill (S 2129) making it easier for businesses, cities and professional groups to band together to insure themselves. *(Story, p. 289)*

Background

Revision of product liability laws was fiercely contested in the 97th and 98th Congresses by manufacturers who sought a federal law, and trial lawyers, unions, consumer groups, state judges and attorneys general who opposed most changes. *(1984 Almanac p. 296; 1982 Almanac p. 330)*

During the 99th Congress, members continued to hear complaints from manufacturers, doctors, municipal governments, hazardous-waste disposers, truckers, tavern owners, day-care providers, pharmaceutical companies and other businesses that faced huge premium increases for liability insurance.

For the property-casualty industry as a whole, premiums went up 21 percent in 1985, compared with 9 percent in 1984. Industry economists predicted another 20 percent jump in 1986.

Insurance companies said the price increases were necessary because premiums and investment income fell far short of meeting claims and other expenses. They charged that costs were high because of excessive litigation and outrageous settlements.

Consumer groups replied that insurance companies distorted their finances to pressure legislators to limit victims' rights to recover damages.

"Complaints are coming in to the members of Congress at a level that is unprecedented," said Rep. James L. Oberstar, D-Minn., chairman of the Public Works and Transportation Subcommittee on Investigations and Oversight, at a Jan. 21 hearing. "There is wholesale confusion, bewilderment and sometimes outrage" among insurance purchasers, he said.

But while the rhetoric heated up and hearings were held, it was not clear what Congress could do to alleviate the problems of either the insurance industry or its customers.

Insurance was unfamiliar territory for Congress. The industry long had been exempted from federal regulation. And the McCarran-Ferguson Act of 1945 (PL 79-15) exempted it from antitrust laws.

Declining Profits

The squeeze on insurance availability and affordability was concentrated in property-casualty insurance, which covered about a third of the insurance market. Within that area, it focused on commercial lines of insurance, where companies said their losses had occurred.

Industry spokesmen said that 1984 was the worst year on record for property-casualty insurance companies and that preliminary figures showed 1985 was just as bad.

The industry's first response to the situation was to raise prices, which the industry contended had been cut during the late 1970s to attract funds to invest while interest rates were high.

While 1985 premiums increased an average of 21 percent overall for property-casualty insurance, price hikes in certain industries were far greater. Bus owners, for example, paid 1985 premiums that averaged 700 percent more than 1984's, according to Wayne Smith, executive director of the United Bus Owners of America, a trade association. Other groups, such as day-care centers, nurse-midwives and hazardous-waste disposers went through periods when no insurance was available.

Insurers were particularly wary of businesses with a "long tail of liability" — those in which an injury or illness could be discovered years after the event. Even though the policy had lapsed, the insurer was responsible for paying damages.

Insurers said that a more fundamental cause of their problems than falling interest rates that made their investments less profitable was the tort-law system. They said that court judgments dramatically increased their costs by making it too easy for injured parties to win large damage awards.

Industry leaders said that judges made insurers responsible for incidents that should not have been covered, that juries awarded outrageous sums to victims and that attorneys fueled the situation with their demands for large fees.

An underlying problem, they said, was a growing tendency in society to insist that someone — particularly someone with "deep pockets," such as an insurance company or a city — must pay whenever a person suffered a loss.

Insurers proposed a number of reforms. They wanted to limit awards for "pain and suffering," a subjective loss going beyond medical bills and lost wages; to hold down the percentages of awards that go to attorneys; and to make each party in a multi-party lawsuit responsible only for its share of fault.

Those legal questions were the purview primarily of states, and insurance companies pressured state courts and legislatures to make changes. Impatient with the slow pace of reform on a state-by-state basis, however, insurance companies pressed the federal government to take over in certain areas. That was notably true for product liability, where insurance represented up to 30 percent of the purchase price of some products.

Federal Role

Since the late 1970s, manufacturers and insurers had pushed to establish federal standards that would override state tort laws in lawsuits seeking damages caused by commercial products. They said that was necessary because products were distributed nationally, and the inconsistency of state laws made it impossible to predict losses. But legislation had been blocked by trial lawyers, consumer groups, and states' rights advocates.

One idea that surfaced on the federal level was to set up alternative systems to compensate victims without the expense and delay of lawsuits. Under those systems, injured people could claim compensation for losses, but they could not receive payments for pain and suffering or punitive damages. Disputes would be settled by binding arbitration.

Many industry critics supported the idea, but one objection was that people using the alternative system would be required to give up their right to sue. Yet they might still need attorneys — paid from their own funds — to bargain effectively with large companies during settlement negotiations.

Insurance companies made little effort to obtain any sweeping federal changes in all tort laws or in federal laws that govern claims against the government.

Critics of the industry were extremely skeptical of the claim that rising court judgments were responsible for the insurance industry's problems. While insurers frequently pointed to a few instances of court judgments that seemed exceptional, critics said the companies produced no evidence to demonstrate that that was common.

Despite the insurance industry's massive ability to collect statistics, it did not publish data on the number of claims, the number going to trial, the average amount of punitive damages and the average settlement.

Administration Calls for Changes

President Reagan in the spring of 1986 endorsed the recommendations of a Domestic Policy Council task force headed by Richard K. Willard, assistant attorney general of the civil division of the Justice Department. Its recommendations were:

- **Strengthen the legal concept of "fault."** The report criticized moves toward "no-fault" concepts in liability cases, including judicial rulings that held manufacturers liable for defects they could not have foreseen.
- **Control expert testimony.** It recommended reducing the impact of unusual testimony by expert witnesses, suggesting, for instance, that expert testimony be accepted only if it had been reviewed by scientific or medical peers.
- **Eliminate "joint and several liability."** The legal concept of "joint and several liability" could be used to hold a party to an injury responsible for the entire amount of damages regardless of how much of the blame he or she bore. The report recommended eliminating the concept unless it was proven that several defendants acted in concert.
- **Limit non-economic damages.** While plaintiffs should be able to recover all medical expenses, property damage and lost wages, the report suggested a limit of $100,000 on awards for pain and punitive damages.
- **Pay large awards for future damages in installments.** When a plaintiff won a claim for future damages, such as lost wages, it should be paid in installments rather than in a lump sum, the report said.
- **Eliminate double recovery.** Some court rules prohibited judges and juries from being told that a plaintiff had another way to recover payment for damages. The task force recommended that awards be reduced by the amount of damages paid by another source, such as another insurance policy.
- **Limit attorneys' fees.** Plaintiffs' attorneys often were paid 30 percent to 50 percent of an award. The task force recommended a sliding scale for fees, from 25 percent for awards under $100,000 to 10 percent for amounts over $300,000.
- **Encourage alternatives to lawsuits.** The report promoted alternatives to traditional litigation, such as binding arbitration and mediation.

Senate Action

The administration April 30 sent to Congress three legislative proposals to revise personal injury laws, which Kasten introduced as amendments to S 100, his bill that was stalled in 1985.

John C. Danforth, R-Mo., chairman of the Commerce Committee, introduced a product liability bill (S 1999) late in 1985, which he continually revised in an effort to reach consensus and unveiled May 12.

At a June 3 committee session, members explored alternatives but took no action until June 12, when they voted 16-1 to endorse a package backed by Danforth, Kasten and Slade Gorton, R-Wash. The negative vote was cast by Hollings.

On June 19, the panel voted 5-12 against the administration proposal offered by Kasten and by 6-10, defeated a second Kasten amendment to establish a federal standard of liability that would require a plaintiff to prove the manufacturer was negligent. Most states maintained a standard of strict liability, which required the plaintiff to show only that a product was defective and was responsible for an injury.

Gorton listed three objections to the liability standard. It would, he said, fail to promote predictability in the legal system, since states would interpret the standard in varying ways; it would stir opposition from state legal officials; and it would make passage of legislation more difficult.

The apparent consensus of the 16-1 vote eroded in subsequent days, however, with several members sharply critical of a provision crafted by Danforth setting a $250,000 limit on court awards for pain and suffering. On June 26, the panel ordered the measure reported by a 10-7 vote.

The cap, contained in an expedited settlement system that Danforth labeled the heart of the Commerce package, would apply if a plaintiff rejected a pretrial settlement offer from a defendant. The Danforth plan also called for penalties against defendants who turned down offers from plaintiffs.

"There's going to be a war on this issue," warned Donald W. Riegle Jr., D-Mich. Citing the $250,000 cap as their principal objection, Riegle, Gorton, Ted Stevens, R-

Alaska, and Daniel K. Inouye, D-Hawaii, voted against the bill.

"This proposal is so deficient and inequitable, in my view," Gorton told committee members in a June 24 letter, "that I — and I am certain many of my colleagues — will feel constrained to object to any motion to proceed to its consideration on the floor."

In a speech widely cited by members for its eloquence and persuasiveness, Inouye, who lost an arm in World War II, said, "It is easy for those who have not been the victims to be setting caps. It is difficult to put yourself in the position of the woman [who has lost fertility]. She may not get married because of that disability. I do not know how much that is worth.

"The guy who loses his arm, because he is not as strong as the rest of us, may become gun-shy and not date women, so he is a bachelor for the rest of his life.

"What do you do? What price tag do you put on that? This much I know: [the cap] is not enough.

"Pain and suffering, I suppose I can stand it, so we can make it zilch," he said. "But I cannot speak for the rest of those who have lost their limbs."

Also voting against the bill were Albert Gore Jr., D-Tenn.; Hollings; and Bob Packwood, R-Ore.

Although a delegation of manufacturers June 25 had urged Danforth to report legislation without the $250,000 cap and to aim for a compromise on settlement incentives that would be offered on the floor, Danforth told his colleagues that he was reluctant to eliminate the cap without substituting an equally powerful settlement incentive. No one on the committee, Danforth said, had presented an alternative that would do as much to resolve disputes in advance of a costly and time-consuming trial.

Consumer, Business Reaction

Consumer groups blasted the Commerce Committee product.

"After spending a full year with this committee trying to devise a way to help people settle product liability cases in an equitable way, we are bitterly disappointed," said Joseph Goffman, an attorney for Public Citizen, a group founded by Ralph Nader. "Supporters of this legislation have to know that we are going to fight their unjust and unworkable proposal every step of the way."

The Product Liability Alliance, an association of more than 200 businesses, expressed support for the package, saying, "This bill has a greater chance of enactment than past efforts."

Consumer groups were opposed not just to the caps but to a provision sponsored by Larry Pressler, R-S.D., that restricted joint and several liability to economic losses.

The package approved by the committee:

- Required that state regulators share with the secretary of commerce data reported to them by insurance companies. Companies would be required to indicate whether compensation to claimants represented economic or non-economic losses. Reporting also would be required from risk-retention groups and self-insured manufacturers.
- Allowed punitive damages only if the plaintiff established by clear and convincing evidence the defendant's "conscious, flagrant indifference" to the safety of those who might be harmed by a product. Mere negligence, or imprudence, would not be sufficient justification for punitive damages.
- Established a "government standards" defense against punitive damages that barred award of punitive damages for injuries caused by a drug that received pre-marketing approval from the Food and Drug Administration or by an aircraft-related product certified by the Federal Aviation Administration.
- Permitted a defendant to escape liability if the plaintiff was under the influence of drugs or alcohol and was more than 50 percent responsible for the injury.
- Set a "statute of repose" that limited the length of time for which a manufacturer could be held liable.
- Established sanctions for attorneys who made frivolous claims or prolonged a trial.
- Set an expedited settlement procedure that allowed either the defendant or the plaintiff to make a settlement offer. The offer would be limited to the plaintiff's net economic loss, plus a $100,000 "dignitary" payment if the plaintiff had experienced particularly severe pain and suffering.

Net economic losses included out-of-pocket expenses, such as medical bills, less non-court benefits, such as workers' compensation. Dignitary losses represented pain and suffering arising from the death of a parent, spouse or child; serious and permanent disfigurement; loss of a limb or organ; or serious and permanent impairment of a bodily function.

If a plaintiff rejected an offer, the plaintiff's recovery would be limited to net economic loss plus $250,000 when the court found that a dignitary loss had occurred. In cases in which there was no dignitary loss, transitory pain and suffering would be capped at twice the plaintiff's recovery for economic loss or $50,000, whichever was less. Punitive damages would not be included in either cap.

If a defendant rejected a plaintiff's offer, and the court award at least equaled the rejected offer, the defendant would be liable for up to $100,000 of the plaintiff's attorneys' fees and costs from the time the offer was rejected.

Floor Action

The bill, however, got only as far as the adoption Sept. 25, by a vote of 84-13, of a motion to proceed with floor consideration. *(Vote 295, p. 49-S)*

After the vote, Majority Leader Dole yanked the measure from the floor because Hollings was prepared to filibuster. "It is not going to happen this year," said Dole, who supported the measure and pushed for a floor vote.

Earlier in the day, a Hollings filibuster on the motion to take up the bill was cut off by a 97-1 vote to invoke cloture and limit debate. The filibuster began Sept. 17 when Kasten first tried to bring up the bill, and action was postponed until Sept. 23, when a cloture petition was filed. *(Vote 291, p. 49-S)*

Risk Retention Bill

Legislation (S 2129 — PL 99-563) that would make it easier for businesses, professionals and other groups to form cooperatives to purchase liability insurance was cleared by Congress Oct. 9.

Final action came when the House by voice vote accepted minor amendments the Senate had approved Oct. 6.

The bill incorporated a House provision permitting states to require "risk retention groups" to show they were financially sound. Concern had been expressed by some members that groups in a hazardous financial condition might escape notice of state regulators.

Under the bill, a risk group chartered to operate in at least one state would not have to obtain a charter to operate in any other states. The bill would allow cooperatives to purchase most types of liability insurance, except for personal insurance such as homeowner's or auto.

The legislation broadened a 1981 law (PL 97-45) that allowed the formation of risk groups to provide product liability insurance only. *(1981 Almanac p. 573)*

A number of groups that had difficulty obtaining liability insurance, such as medical personnel, campaigned for the bill. With the failure of product liability legislation to be enacted by Congress, the measure was one of the few bills addressing the liability crunch that Congress was able to enact in 1986. *(Story, p. 287)*

Although some insurance companies did not welcome competition from risk groups, few actively opposed the legislation.

Legislative History. The Senate July 17 voted 96-1 in favor of a new version of a bill approved March 27 by the Commerce, Science and Transportation Committee (S Rept 99-294). The new version was a compromise between state insurance regulators and potential insurance purchasers that would strengthen the powers of the regulators over risk groups. *(Vote 159, p. 29-S)*

The Senate voted 69-27 to table an amendment by Frank R. Lautenberg, D-N.J., that would have required certain qualifying states to establish guaranty funds to pay claims in the event a risk group became insolvent. The amendment was backed by the National Insurance Consumer Organization, a consumer interest group. *(Vote 158, p. 29-S)*

The House by voice vote passed the bill Sept. 23, amending it to include its state regulators' provision. The Energy and Commerce Committee had reported a bill (HR 5225 — H Rept 99-865) Sept. 23. The House substituted the text of HR 5225 for the Senate-passed legislation.

The Senate Oct. 6 accepted a compromise version of the House changes that had been worked out by House and Senate staff. ∎

FCC Terms

President Reagan June 6 signed a bill (S 2179 — PL 99-334) that reduced the terms of Federal Communications Commission (FCC) members to five years from seven years and altered existing terms to assure that one would expire each year. Absent congressional action, no terms would have expired in 1989 or 1990.

Congress in 1982 had reduced the size of the FCC to five members from seven but had not adjusted members' staggered terms of office to maintain an annual rotation system. *(1982 Almanac p. 204)*

The Senate passed S 2179 (S Rept 99-263) March 27 and the House passed the bill May 22, clearing the bill for the president's signature. ∎

Small-Business Pilot Programs

President Reagan Oct. 27 signed into law a bill (S 2914 — PL 99-567) that extended through Sept. 30, 1988, two small-business pilot programs aimed at assisting minority-owned firms.

One of the pilot programs enhanced the ability of the Small Business Administration (SBA) to direct federal contracts to minority firms. The other allowed the agency to waive bonding requirements for start-up minority firms receiving contracts. The authority for both programs had expired Sept. 30, 1985. *(Background, Congress and the Nation Vol. VI, p. 276)*

Congress completed action on the bill Oct. 14 when the House passed by voice vote a measure approved by the Senate Oct. 9.

The president had vetoed an earlier extension bill (HR 2787) that also included a research project in the home state of Connecticut Republican Lowell P. Weicker Jr., chairman of the Senate Small Business Committee. The revised bill left out the Connecticut project, to which Reagan had objected. Weicker was a strident critic of Reagan's campaign to kill the SBA.

Action on HR 2787

The House Small Business Committee reported HR 2787 (H Rept 99-438) Dec. 12, 1985, and the House approved it by voice vote Dec. 16, 1985. It was reported (S Rept 99-316) by the Senate Small Business panel June 5, 1986.

The Senate passed the bill by voice vote June 25, after adding Weicker's amendment to authorize up to $10 million to pay 50 percent of the cost of establishing a research institute at the University of Bridgeport in Connecticut. The House accepted the Senate change Sept. 19, clearing the bill.

In his Oct. 7 veto message, the president called the project "inappropriate and unwarranted" at a time of budget constraints. Reagan also said extension of the two pilot programs was unnecessary. *(Text of veto message, p. 33-D)* ∎

Daylight-Saving Time

Congress June 24 approved legislation (S 2180 — PL 99-359) to expand daylight-saving time permanently by starting it on the first Sunday in April instead of the last Sunday in April. Daylight saving would continue to end on the last Sunday in October, as provided under existing law.

The three-week extension of daylight time was attached to an unrelated measure authorizing $18.3 million in fiscal 1987 for U.S. fire prevention and control programs under the Federal Emergency Management Agency.

Extension of daylight-saving time culminated a 10-year drive in both chambers. Congress had switched to the existing system in 1976 after experiments with yearlong and eight-month daylight-saving plans prompted by the Arab oil embargo. Extension bills stalled in 1976, 1981 and 1983. *(1983 Almanac p. 551)*

The House in 1985 passed a bill (HR 2095) that would have extended daylight-saving time from the first Sunday in April to the first Sunday in November, adding an extra week in the fall to make sunset occur later on Halloween. *(1985 Almanac p. 271)*

Senate Action on S 2180

The Senate passed S 2180 May 20, 1986, after rejecting on a 36-58 vote a motion to kill the daylight-saving amendment. It then adopted the amendment, offered by Slade Gorton, R-Wash., and passed the bill by voice votes. *(Vote 104, p. 20-S)*

Gorton attached the daylight-saving extension to the non-controversial fire prevention bill to bypass the Commerce, Science and Transportation Committee, where Wendell H. Ford, D-Ky., and other rural- and Midwestern-state senators had bottled up a daylight-saving bill (S 1433) that Gorton had introduced in July 1985. Gorton's amendment to the fire program bill, by dropping the extra week in the fall, was an effort to convert foes such as Ford and J. James Exon, D-Neb.

But when Gorton offered the amendment May 19, Ford painted the extension as "a regional issue," pitting people in the cities on the East and West coasts against rural and agricultural areas. The amendment, he said, "sends a message to Middle America, particularly rural areas, that we have given up on rural America."

Proponents argued that extending daylight saving would conserve energy, reduce traffic fatalities and crime, and have broad economic benefits for industries dependent upon retail sales and recreation. A 1975 study by the Department of Transportation (DOT) documented savings of as much as 2 million barrels of oil a year by expanding daylight-saving time.

In a May 7 letter to Majority Leader Robert Dole, R-Kan., Transportation Secretary Elizabeth Hanford Dole elaborated on the benefits of a daylight-saving time extension. She cited 1983 studies by DOT and other government agencies showing that the extension "would reduce traffic deaths nationwide by a minimum of 22, injuries by a minimum of 1,525, and societal costs from auto accidents by a minimum of $28 million [annually] ... with possible savings being as much as twice as large." Ford blasted the DOT studies as distorted and biased.

Opposition

Much of the opposition to the daylight-saving time extension came from states that either had two time zones or were at the westernmost edge of a time zone.

Because half of Kentucky was on the western fringe of the Eastern time zone, Ford said, sunrises in eastern Kentucky could occur as much as an hour and 15 minutes later than in cities on the East Coast.

Ford expressed concern that rural children would have to go to school in the dark for three extra weeks. While proponents cited studies by DOT and the National Safety Council dismissing the claim that the darkness significantly increased the risk to children, Ford appealed to senators to consider the emotional side of the argument instead of its economic aspect.

"Any Kentucky mother who has sent a first-grader out to catch a bus on a dark, misty April morning takes a dim view about ... electricity that might be saved on the East and West coasts and the number of afternoon tennis games that might be played here in Washington, D.C.," he said.

The National Association of Broadcasters objected to the bill's potential effect on AM stations that operated only during the day. Many of the approximately 2,450 such stations held a "pre-sunrise authorization" (PSA) from the Federal Communications Commission (FCC) allowing them to begin operating at 6 a.m. at reduced power. However, about 450 stations did not have PSAs. The amendment allowed the FCC to make adjustments to remedy any disputes raised through the extension.

Final House Action

The House June 24 passed S 2180 by voice vote, clearing the bill for the president's signature.

Before approving the bill, the House passed its own $18.3 million fire program authorization (HR 4252 — H Rept 99-623) by a 386-28 vote. Members agreed by unanimous consent to drop the additional week of daylight time in the fall. *(Vote 173, p. 52-H)* ▮

Discrimination Loophole

Addressing complaints of groups representing handicapped individuals about a recent Supreme Court decision, Congress Sept. 18 cleared legislation (S 2703 — PL 99-435) that prohibited airlines from discriminating against the handicapped.

The Supreme Court June 27 ruled that section 504 of the Rehabilitation Act of 1973, which banned discrimination against the handicapped in "any program or activity" receiving federal funds, did not apply to commercial airlines because they did not receive such funds directly.

The decision in *U.S. Department of Transportation v. Paralyzed Veterans of America* touched off a storm of protest from groups claiming that the ruling would sanction widespread discrimination by airlines against handicapped people solely on the basis of their ability.

S 2703 amended the Federal Aviation Act to state that no air carrier could discriminate against individuals because they were handicapped.

Legislative History

The bill had been reported (S Rept 99-400) Aug. 13 by the Senate Commerce, Science and Transportation Committee and passed by voice vote Aug. 15. The House Public Works and Transportation Committee was discharged Sept. 8, and the House cleared the Senate measure by voice vote Sept. 18. It was signed by the president Oct. 2. ▮

Pipeline Safety

The Senate Oct. 8 by voice vote cleared a $9.2 million fiscal 1987 authorization (HR 2092 — PL 99-516) for pipeline safety programs that for the first time would require operators to report unsafe conditions that could cause an accident.

Under existing law, operators of pipelines carrying natural gas or hazardous liquids had to report only accidents. The measure, passed by voice vote by the House Sept. 16, mandated that operators report to federal and state authorities conditions that were hazardous to life or property or that could affect the safe operation of the pipelines.

The bill authorized $3.2 million to carry out the Natural Gas Pipeline Safety Act of 1968 (PL 90-481), $800,000 for the Hazardous Liquid Pipeline Safety Act of 1979 (PL 96-129) and $5.2 million in grants for states, which inspect and monitor pipeline operators. Funding would come from user fees imposed by the deficit-reduction reconciliation bill enacted in April (HR 3128 — PL 99-272). *(Story, p. 555)*

The bill was reported May 15, 1985, by the House Public Works and Transportation Committee (H Rept 99-121, Part I), on May 21 by the Energy and Commerce Committee (Part II) and July 8 by the Judiciary Committee (Part III). There was no Senate committee action. ▮

Safety Board Veto

President Reagan Nov. 4 pocket-vetoed a bill (HR 4961) that would have authorized a total of $76.4 million in fiscal 1987-89 for the National Transportation Safety Board (NTSB). A pocket veto occurs when the president withholds his approval of a bill after Congress has adjourned.

The president called the authorizations "excessive" and objected to a requirement that the Federal Aviation Administration establish a clearinghouse to provide information on liability insurance to public airports. *(Text of statement, p. 35-D)*

Funding of $22.2 million was provided for NTSB by the omnibus spending bill (H J Res 738 — PL 99-591). *(Appropriations, p. 176)*

Saying he was not "unsympathetic" to the problems of rising premiums, Reagan argued that it would be "inequitable and unwise" for the government to address the issue on an industry-by-industry basis. Proponents argued that smaller airports did not have the staff to stay on top of the insurance market.

The bill, reported Sept. 18 (H Rept 99-835, Part I), was passed Sept. 30 by the House by voice vote. The Senate, whose Commerce, Science and Transportation Committee had reported a similar bill Sept. 10 (S 2807 — S Rept 99-437), added the liability insurance provisions and passed HR 4961 by voice vote Oct. 10. The House accepted the Senate change Oct. 16, clearing the measure for the president. ▮

Coast Guard Bill Veto

Citing excessive costs and unwarranted special-interest provisions, President Reagan Feb. 14 vetoed a bill (HR 2466) that would have made various revisions in laws affecting the U.S. Coast Guard and incorporated a number of private relief provisions. Congress made no attempt to override the veto.

When the bill was introduced in May 1985, it was designed primarily to correct several omissions and errors in a 1983 reorganization of maritime safety laws (PL 98-89). But by the time it cleared Congress Jan. 29, 1986, it had picked up a broad array of exemptions and amendments objectionable to the administration. *(Veto text, p. 33-D)*

One of the changes in HR 2466 was to extend for five years an exemption from certain fire-safety requirements that had been granted to a paddle-wheel riverboat operating on the Mississippi and Ohio rivers. The boat, the *Delta Queen*, was built in 1926, and was one of two authentic paddle-wheel passenger steamboats in existence in the country, according to the House committee's July 18, 1985, report on the bill (H Rept 99-207).

The *Delta Queen's* wooden superstructure, however, put it at odds with international boating-safety law and Coast Guard safety standards; to continue operating, it required a congressional exemption. The existing exemption was due to expire Nov. 1, 1988; the provision in HR 2466 would have pushed the date to Nov. 1, 1993, and required the *Delta Queen* to notify potential passengers that the boat did not meet fire-safety standards.

When the House passed HR 2466 by voice vote on July 29, the administration objected to three sections of the bill: the *Delta Queen* exemption; a waiver of personnel ceilings at two Coast Guard repair facilities; and a prohibition on "contracting out" for the positioning of navigational aids in the New Jersey Intracoastal Waterway. The last provision contradicted the administration's desire to "privatize" such functions.

The Senate roughly doubled the number of provisions in the bill, passed it by voice vote on Dec. 19, 1985, and returned it to the House, where it was cleared by voice vote.

In his veto message, Reagan objected to two of the sections previously singled out, as well as others that would have:

- Waived restrictions in maritime laws for several vessels. Those provisions were also contained in a private relief bill (HR 739) passed by the House Dec. 3, 1985.
- Required that any funds spent by the Coast Guard to alter a railroad bridge in Portland, Ore., be subject to Davis-Bacon Act prevailing-wage provisions, a change that Reagan said would add about $1.5 million to the cost of the project.
- Established two Coast Guard advisory committees, one to address safety matters with respect to oil and gas development on the Outer Continental Shelf, the other regarding the safety of and insurance for fishing industry vessels. ▮

Maritime Veto

President Reagan Oct. 28 pocket-vetoed legislation (HR 4175) that would have authorized $400 million in fiscal 1987 for maritime programs.

However, separate legislation already signed by the president (H J Res 738 — PL 99-591), the fiscal 1987 continuing appropriations resolution, provided funding for maritime programs at virtually the same level proposed by the authorization. *(Appropriations, p. 189)*

The president said he based his decision chiefly on the refusal of Congress to repeal the authority in existing law for federal loan guarantees to shipbuilders for the construction of commercial vessels.

Concerned about defaults that required the government to pay off some of the guaranteed loans, the Reagan administration in its fiscal 1987 budget request asked to drop the program.

In his memorandum of disapproval of HR 4175, the president said, "The maritime industry must be encouraged to rely on the private credit market, without federal intervention, as its source of capital if we are to continue our progress toward restoring that industry to full health." *(Memorandum text, p. 34-D)*

Congress disputed the president's rationale for phasing out the program. Supporters said the guarantees were necessary to bolster the financially troubled industry.

In House floor debate June 17 on the bill, Norman F. Lent, R-N.Y., declared: "The [House] Merchant Marine and Fisheries Committee — along with every knowledgeable person in the maritime industry — believes that the problem is not the loan guarantee program but the economic conditions facing the U.S. merchant marine."

Reagan also said he objected to authorization of $9 million in financial assistance for six state-run merchant marine training schools.

"Such an authorization ... is entirely inappropriate

during this time of necessary fiscal restraint," Reagan declared.

Lent, however, said in House debate that the schools played a valuable role in training personnel to be available as reserve forces in case of military emergency.

The omnibus spending bill continued the loan program and the funding for the state schools.

Pocket vetoes occur after congressional adjournment. When Congress is in session, a bill becomes law without the president's signature if he does not act upon it within 10 days, excluding Sundays, from the time he gets it. But if Congress adjourns and the president does not sign the legislation within 10 days, the bill dies without a formal veto.

Congress cleared the bill Oct. 14 and adjourned Oct. 18.

Legislative History. The House Merchant Marine and Fisheries Committee reported (H Rept 99-551) the bill April 22, and the House passed it June 17 by a vote of 367-29. *(Vote 158, p. 50-H)*

The only change from the committee bill was an amendment by Mario Biaggi, D-N.Y., that dropped a provision asserting the primary role of the Maritime Administration, rather than the Navy, in the management of the National Defense Reserve Fleet. The provision had met with objections from Charles E. Bennett, D-Fla., chairman of the Armed Services Subcommittee on Seapower.

The total funding level was the same as the administration request. However, the bill decreased the administration's request for research and development and increased its request for training at state maritime academies. The measure authorized $388.2 million for the Maritime Administration and $11.9 million for the Federal Maritime Commission.

The Senate Commerce, Science and Transportation Committee reported (S Rept 99-407) a similar version Aug. 14. The Senate passed it by voice vote Oct. 8, and the House cleared it by accepting the Senate version.

The bulk of the funding in the final bill, $320 million, was for "operating differential" subsidies to U.S. shippers to make up the difference between their operating costs and the lower operating costs of foreign competitors. Labor costs typically are much higher for U.S. shippers.

The omnibus spending bill also provided $320 million for fiscal 1987 operating subsidies. ▮

Airport Transfer Agreement

In the final days of the session, Congress approved legislation backed by the Reagan administration to ease federal control of two metropolitan Washington, D.C., airports.

By a 250-135 vote, the House early Oct. 16 adopted an amendment to the continuing appropriations resolution (H J Res 738 — PL 99-591) that modified a Senate plan to lease Washington-Dulles International Airport and National Airport to a regional authority. The Senate agreed to the changes later that day. *(Continuing resolution, p. 219)*

The Senate-passed version of H J Res 738 had called for a regional authority to lease the airports for $150 million over 50 years. The House amendment adjusted the payments to inflation. Assuming a 4 percent annual inflation rate, the lease would cost $460 million.

The House also attached a provision that extended the legal range of non-stop flights out of National Airport from 1,000 miles to 1,250 miles. The extension would permit non-stop flights to Dallas and Houston, a change sought by House Majority Leader Jim Wright, D-Texas.

The leasing plan also called for a congressional review panel that could veto the decisions of the regional authority. The regional group could issue bonds to raise funds for improvements.

Previous Action

The Senate had added the airport-lease proposal to the continuing resolution, basing it on a bill (HR 5398) approved Aug. 11 by the House Public Works and Transportation Subcommittee on Aviation.

On April 11, the Senate had passed by a 62-28 vote its own measure (S 1017 — S Rept 99-193) to shift management of the two airports to a regional authority. The Senate formally took up the bill March 25 after voting 66-32 to cut off a five-day filibuster on a motion to consider it. Passage came after eight days of debate in which critics unsuccessfully tried to increase the $47 million price of the transaction, and Maryland senators tried with only modest success to change the membership and powers of the authority to protect the interests of Baltimore-Washington International Airport. *(Vote 44, p. 9-S; vote 65, p. 13-S)* ▮

Odometer Tampering

Moving to crack down on illegal tampering with automobile odometers, Congress in 1986 approved legislation (S 475 — PL 99-579) aimed at making it easier for law enforcement officials to detect fraud.

The bill cleared Oct. 8 when the Senate approved the version of the measure that the House passed by voice vote Oct. 6. The Senate had passed a slightly different version of S 475 Dec. 13, 1985. *(1985 Almanac p. 271)*

The bill barred state licensing of a vehicle unless the seller disclosed on the title the odometer reading at the time of the sale.

The maximum penalties for tampering would be increased from one year in prison to three years, and civil fines would be raised from $1,000 per violation to $2,000.

House sponsors said consumers paid dearly for odometer rollbacks. They cited estimates by the National Automobile Dealers Association that more than 3 million vehicles annually were subject to rollbacks that averaged 30,000 miles at a cost to consumers in excess of $2 billion. ▮

Air Safety Violations

The Senate May 6 passed by voice vote a bill (S 1750) that would have allowed the Federal Aviation Administration (FAA) to levy stiffer civil penalties against commercial airlines for safety violations.

The House did not act on a similar bill (HR 4403 — H Rept 99-796, Part I), reported by the Judiciary Committee Aug. 15, and the legislation died at adjournment.

As passed by the Senate, the administration-backed measure would have raised the maximum penalty per violation to $10,000 from the $1,000 limit established in 1938. The bill also would have created a civil penalty of $1,000 for failing to notify the FAA of proposed construction that could pose a hazard to the airways.

In its April 24 report on the bill (S Rept 99-286), the Commerce, Science and Transportation Committee noted that in 1985 only 7 percent of FAA enforcement actions resulted in civil penalties and warned that "without an FAA willingness to impose severe civil penalties where warranted, the authority to assess larger fines does little to deter safety violations."

The FAA levied fines of $1.2 million in 1984 and $2.9 million in 1985, including a $1.5 million penalty against American Airlines, according to the Congressional Budget Office.

Airline Worker Protection

The Senate did not act on a House-passed bill (HR 4838 — H Rept 99-822) that would have required the transportation secretary to require labor protection in airline merger cases to ensure that a merger was fair to employees.

As approved by the House on a 329-72 vote Sept. 16, the bill directed the secretary to investigate merger applications to determine if the merger would reduce jobs, or adversely affect wages or working conditions, including the seniority of employees. *(Vote 355, p. 100-H)*

The bill required the secretary to take whatever steps deemed appropriate "to mitigate such adverse consequences," unless the secretary found that the projected costs of protection would exceed the "anticipated financial benefits of the transaction."

It also put the burden of proof on the proponents of the merger to show that there would no adverse employment consequences or that the projected costs of protection would be excessive.

"The need for this legislation has increased greatly in recent months with a series of airline mergers involving a substantial portion of the industry's employees," declared Norman Y. Mineta, D-Calif., chairman of the Public Works and Transportation Subcommittee on Aviation.

The Civil Aeronautics Board, which was terminated in 1984, routinely required labor protection in airline merger cases, but the Department of Transportation had ignored congressional direction to continue this practice, Mineta charged.

Transportation Authorizations

Several fiscal 1986 funding authorizations for transportation programs were included in deficit-reduction legislation cleared by Congress March 20.

The bill (HR 3128 — PL 99-272) was intended to cut existing programs to meet targets set in the fiscal 1986 budget resolution. It had emerged from conference in December 1985, but further Senate-House negotiations delayed final action for another three months. *(Legislative history, p. 555)*

HR 3128 maintained a provision, opposed by members from Vermont and Wisconsin, that stiffened penalties for states that did not set 21 as the minimum drinking age.

The measure slowed down spending from the Highway Trust Fund, which was supported by gasoline taxes and other road-related fees. But while spending from the trust fund counted in deficit calculations, money not spent remained in the fund and could not be used for other purposes.

Provisions

As signed into law April 7, the transportation provisions of HR 3128:

- **Amtrak.** Reauthorized the federally subsidized national passenger railroad (Amtrak) at $600 million in fiscal 1986, $606.1 million in 1987 and $630.3 million in 1988. *(Background, 1984 Almanac p. 294)*
- Required Amtrak to use capital funds to make up any shortfall rather than reduce service or maintenance.
- Prohibited Amtrak from saving expenses by reducing service on trains that operated three times a week or less.
- Allowed Amtrak to compete for government-paid travel by federal employees.
- Raised from 50 percent to 61 percent the proportion of operating costs Amtrak was expected to pay out of revenues.
- Required Amtrak and rail labor groups to report to Congress on negotiations to change labor agreements in order to reduce Amtrak expenses.
- Allowed Amtrak to transport cars on its "Autotrain" between Virginia and Florida when the cars' drivers did not ride the train. Existing law required drivers to accompany their vehicles.
- Eliminated minimum standards on the number of passengers per mile Amtrak trains must carry, while preserving standards on minimum cost efficiency per passenger mile.
- Allowed Amtrak to discontinue or adjust service on commuter trains if they exceeded cost standards, unless states agreed to subsidize the service.
- Modified the criteria under which the Interstate Commerce Commission allocated costs between Amtrak and freight railroads for use of tracks in the Northeast corridor.
- **Local Rail Service Assistance.** Reauthorized the program of federal-state matching grants for planning and rehabilitation of rail facilities at $12 million in fiscal 1986, $10 million in 1987 and $8 million in 1988.
- **Highways.** Set a ceiling on obligations from the Highway Trust Fund at $13.125 billion in fiscal 1986, $13.525 billion in 1987 and $14.1 billion in 1988. The obligation ceiling had been set in 1982 (PL 97-424) at $14.45 billion for 1986, with no ceilings set for future years. *(1982 Almanac p. 317)*
- Reduced fiscal 1986 authorizations for repair and replacement of Interstate highways by $175 million, for bridge replacement and repairs by $150 million, and for primary federal highways by $75 million.
- Increased the maximum amount of emergency highway aid for natural disasters or failures in calendar 1985 from $30 million to $55 million.
- Reprogrammed existing spending authority to allow up to $65 million to be spent for construction of three bridges over the Ohio River.
- **Minimum Drinking Age.** Provided that fiscal 1986 federal highway funds withheld from states for failure to enact a minimum drinking age of 21 could not be recovered by passage of such a law after Sept. 30, 1988. Funds would be permanently withheld for fiscal years 1989 and beyond for states that did not enact such a law. *(Background, 1984 Almanac p. 283)*
- Allowed states to raise their minimum drinking age to 21 with "grandfather" clauses that would not take away the right to drink from those who currently had it.

Commerce Authorizations

Congress reauthorized an array of commerce-related programs, including a three-year reauthorization for the Corporation for Public Broadcasting, as part of its fiscal 1986 deficit-reduction bill (HR 3128 — PL 99-272). Citing excessive spending, President Reagan in 1984 had vetoed two authorization bills for the corporation, which funneled federal funds to public television and radio stations and to independent producers. *(1984 Almanac p. 288)*

The deficit-reduction bill also reauthorized several ocean and maritime programs and instituted or raised charges for services such as nautical charts, broadcast licenses and foreign fishing permits provided by federal agencies.

Congress completed action on the bill March 20. HR 3128 aimed to cut existing programs to meet requirements set in the fiscal 1986 budget resolution. *(Details, p. 555)*

Provisions

As signed into law April 7, HR 3128 contained the following commerce-related provisions:

• **Public Broadcasting.** Authorized appropriations for fiscal 1987-90 for the Corporation for Public Broadcasting, which received funding authorizations several years in advance to shield it from political interference in programming decisions. The bill authorized $200 million in fiscal 1987, $214 million in 1988, $238 million in 1989 and $254 million in 1990.

• Authorized $24 million in fiscal 1986, $28 million in 1987 and $32 million in 1988 for the Public Telecommunications Facility Program, which provided aid for construction of public radio and TV outlets in unserved areas. Reagan had tried to eliminate the program.

• Eliminated a requirement under existing law that at least 75 percent of capital funds be devoted to new facilities that would reach areas not receiving public television signals. This allowed more funds to be used for replacement or repair of existing facilities.

• **FCC.** Authorized appropriations for the Federal Communications Commission (FCC) of $98.1 million in fiscal 1986 and $97.6 million in 1987.

• Required the FCC to charge fees for regulatory services, such as license approvals, certification of equipment and construction permits. Fees were not to be charged to non-commercial radio and television stations. They were to be based on the cost of providing services and were to be reviewed by the FCC every two years. *(FCC, p. 290)*

• **Boating Safety.** Transferred any unappropriated funds from the boat-safety account of the Aquatic Resources Trust Fund to the general Treasury.

• **NOAA.** Imposed higher charges for nautical and aeronautical charts produced by the National Oceanic and Atmospheric Administration (NOAA). Existing fees covered only printing costs.

• Authorized NOAA programs at $225 million in fiscal 1986 and $235 million in 1987.

• **Foreign Fishing Permit Fees.** Allowed the secretary of commerce to raise fees for fishing permits for foreign ships fishing in U.S. waters three to 200 miles from shore.

• **Coastal Zone Management.** Authorized $41.8 million in fiscal 1986, $45.2 million in 1987, $47.2 million in 1988, $49.3 million in 1989 and $51.6 million in 1990 for coastal zone management programs. *(1985 Almanac p. 202)*

• Reduced the federal share of state management grants, currently set at 80 percent federal funds and 20 percent state funds. The new formula would phase down the federal share from 4-to-1 in 1986 to 2.3-to-1 in 1987, 1.5-to-1 in 1988 and 1-to-1 in 1989.

• **Marine Sanctuaries.** Authorized $10.6 million in fiscal 1986 and $11.1 million in 1987 for marine sanctuaries programs. *(Congress and the Nation Vol. III, p. 799)*

• **Ocean Pollution Research.** Authorized $3.6 million in fiscal 1986 and $3.7 million in fiscal 1987 for ocean pollution research programs. *(1978 Almanac p. 715)*

• **Maritime Programs.** Authorized $93.8 million in fiscal 1986 for maritime programs, including $81.9 million for the Maritime Administration and $11.9 million for the Federal Maritime Commission. *(1984 Almanac p. 292)*

Of the Maritime Administration's budget, $19.6 million was earmarked for training at the Merchant Marine Academy at Kings Point, N.Y., and $15.2 million for state maritime academies.

A fiscal 1987 authorization bill (HR 4175) was vetoed by President Reagan Oct. 23. *(Story, p. 292)* ▮

Coast Guard Authorization

Congress Oct. 16 cleared a bill (HR 4208 — PL 99-640) authorizing $2.15 billion in fiscal 1987 funding for the U.S. Coast Guard, plus $364 million in retirement pay. The $2.51 billion bill, signed Nov. 10 by President Reagan, increased Coast Guard spending authority by $190 million over the president's request of $1.96 billion, while rejecting the administration's perennial call for user fees to help finance certain Coast Guard activities. The administration had requested $354 million for retirement pay.

The House May 6 unanimously passed HR 4208 (H Rept 99-547), authorizing $2.2 billion for Coast Guard expenses and $354 million in retirement pay. The vote was 374-0. *(Vote 100, p. 32-H)*

The bill reported Oct. 6 by the Senate Commerce, Science and Transportation Committee (S Rept 99-530) diminished the funding levels, deleted a section the administration opposed that restricted the Coast Guard's ability to "contract out" — contract with private firms to provide services the Coast Guard had performed itself — and included an amendment revising the Coast Guard's principal maritime drug enforcement law. The last item was added to the 1986 omnibus drug bill (HR 5484 — PL 99-570) as well. *(Story, p. 92)*

The Senate Oct. 16 passed its version of HR 4208 by voice vote; later that day, the House agreed to the revisions and by voice vote sent the bill to the president.

As signed by the president, HR 4208 authorized $1.86 billion — the same as in the administration's request and the original House-passed bill — for Coast Guard operating expenses, including law enforcement, such as stopping drug smuggling and illegal immigration, and search-and-rescue missions.

The bill provided $267 million for procurement, construction and maintenance of vessels, aircraft, shore units and navigation aids. The administration had requested $77 million; the House bill authorized $300 million. In addition, the bill approved $20 million for research and development, $500,000 less than the administration had requested and $15 million less than the $35 million provided in the May 6 House-passed version. ▮

AGRICULTURE

CQ

Agriculture

Even with the hype and political hoopla normally given to agriculture in an election year, Congress hardly tampered in 1986 with the basic tenets of federal farm policy.

Continued hard times on the farm had been expected to spur a raft of legislative efforts to reshape, reshuffle and redesign price- and income-supports. If nothing else, the mere threat of a Democratic takeover of Republican Senate seats in the Farm Belt was supposed to drive the revolt.

But the 99th Congress adjourned in mid-October with barely a bow to farm groups and legislators who, from all points of the political spectrum, had complained about the alleged inequities of the most-recent farm bill, a five-year measure for most of the government's farm and nutrition programs that Congress had struggled for months to pass in 1985.

Farm exports — the lifeblood of the agricultural economy for the 1970s — failed to pick up measurably from the sharp declines recorded since 1981. Congress tried to rectify the foreign trade problem in the 1985 farm bill by allowing the Reagan administration to drive down the price supports for wheat and corn in an effort to bring them more in line with world market prices.

But even with sudden, 40 to 50 percent drops in farm prices in the ensuing year, export sales remained sluggish. Other grain-producing nations, including Argentina, Canada, Australia and the European Community, continued to undersell U.S. exporters.

'No Rebellion'

In the meantime, however, the Reagan administration managed to silence much of the anticipated outcry for change from farmers. The administration's unbridled use of discretionary spending powers granted by the farm bill sent price- and income-support outlays to an unprecedented $26 billion in fiscal 1986, including nearly $13 billion in direct cash payments.

What is more, farmers participated heavily in a new program involving more than $5 billion in government-issued certificates that were being dispersed throughout the country in partial payment of 1986 and early 1987 cash benefits. Farmers could redeem the payment-in-kind (PIK) certificates for the government's massive stocks of surplus food and fiber products, but for a variety of reasons, the "new currency" also took on value as a tradable, money-making commodity.

According to many on Capitol Hill, the novelty of the PIK program succeeded in distracting farmers from the problems of the agricultural economy as a whole and from the election-year efforts to remedy the farm bill's perceived shortcomings.

"There was no rebellion on the farm this year," said Dan Pearson, an aide to Sen. Rudy Boschwitz, R-Minn. "There was no rebellion."

Congress did pass significant legislation by imposing a new $250,000 limit on subsidy payments to farmers and creating a $400 million PIK program for drought and flood relief. Both measures were wrapped into a fiscal 1987 governmentwide spending bill.

But a loophole in the new payment limit was certain to render it ineffectual and actually made it more expensive than the policy it replaced. And the drought and flood relief package showered farmers with little more cash than what the administration had vowed to give them anyway.

Considering the sweeping nature of other remedies for the farm economy that lawmakers promoted agressively in 1986, the palpable results were meager.

Spending Constraints

A major barrier to nearly every new piece of farm spending legislation was the Gramm-Rudman-Hollings anti-deficit law (PL 99-177), which effectively required new spending to be neutralized by revenue increases or program cuts elsewhere.

The tone of the debate was set early in March when the Republican-controlled Senate soundly rejected a Democratic proposal to increase springtime planting loans to farmers by $1 billion.

The farm loan measure, tacked onto a supplemental fiscal 1986 spending bill by the House, was billed as the first real test of Gramm-Rudman. And, at first, it looked like the intensifying, election-year pressure on farm-state Republicans would tip the balance of power in the Senate in favor of anti-Gramm-Rudman Democrats. Indeed, 10 Republicans from rural states voted for the $1 billion addition in farm loans.

But urban Democrats — many of whom had supported Gramm-Rudman to establish their reputations as fiscal conservatives — turned the tables on the farm bloc. Twenty-one Democrats joined conservative Republicans to vote against the plan, leading to a surprisingly lopsided, 61-33 vote.

Robert Dole, R-Kan., whose role as majority leader included being protector to the 1980 class of farm-state Republicans, voted against that bill. But he later found himself one of the victims of the outcome.

Dole, keeping one eye on the Republicans' 53-47 majority in the Senate and another on his own 1988 presidential ambitions, spent the summer trying to persuade the administration to use even more of its discretionary powers to boost farm benefits.

He wanted the president and the new secretary of agriculture, Richard E. Lyng, to do one of two things — expand U.S. export subsidies to all nations, but especially the Soviet Union, or institute a new export-oriented price-support program for wheat and corn that already seemed to be working for cotton and rice farmers.

"If nothing is done to increase agricultural exports within the next two to three months," Dole warned in a June 27 letter to President Reagan, "I expect pressure could build to such a level in Congress that some legislative action will have to be taken."

Over the fierce objections of the president's national security advisers, Dole eventually persuaded Reagan to offer a limited, one-time grain export subsidy to the Soviet Union.

But the Kremlin, given to the end of September to make a deal, never bought a bushel of U.S. grain.

Reviving Mandatory Controls

In the meantime, Democrats were regaining steam after getting the results of a government-sponsored poll of wheat farmers. The Agriculture Department revealed in August that 54 percent of the nation's wheat producers favored a program of strict controls on how much farmers could plant and market, an old but radical method of driving up farm prices through intensive government intervention.

The referendum was not binding but seemed to confirm that farmers wanted a direct say in farm price-support policy. Sens. Edward Zorinsky, D-Neb., and Tom Harkin, D-Iowa, introduced new versions of mandatory controls legislation they had promoted unsuccessfully in 1985. Rep. Richard A. Gephardt, D-Mo., introduced Harkin's bill in the House.

But while many farm-state Democrats lined up as cosponsors with Harkin, Zorinsky and Gephardt, they did not press for floor action.

For one thing, the results of the non-binding poll were not clear-cut. Only 22 percent of the 1.5 million ballots mailed to wheat farmers were returned, giving Lyng and other staunch opponents of mandatory controls reason to label the poll "inconclusive."

In addition, only the more "populist" farm groups of the Midwest strongly supported mandatory controls. The major commodity groups and farm lobbies either remained neutral or actively opposed the referendum. Cotton, rice and dairy interests, for example, had little desire for mandatory controls and did not want to disrupt their own programs by reopening the farm bill debate over wheat and feed grain policies.

Still, the results of the non-binding poll could not be ignored by Midwestern Republicans, and they began scrambling to come up with wheat and feed grain program alternatives to call their own.

Dole began actively promoting a package designed to boost grain exports and pump more money into farmers' pockets. It was the same "marketing loan" scheme that was already in place for cotton and rice, and had been credited widely with breathing life into moribund foreign markets for those U.S. commodities.

The marketing loan worked to drive commodity prices down to world levels by giving farmers added incentive to go ahead and sell their crops at depressed market prices rather than forfeit them to the government at artificially high support rates. The government made up the shortfall with added subsidies.

The effect was to win back some foreign customers for cotton and rice, but it also was to cause problems for U.S. allies, such as Thailand, which depended heavily on income from its own rice exports. Canadian and Australian officials mounted an intensive lobbying campaign with the Reagan administration against implementing a marketing loan for wheat, the primary farm export product of those countries.

Pressing the White House

Dole, undeterred by the foreign policy implications of the marketing loan, continued to press the White House on behalf of farm-state Republicans. The president's chief foreign affairs, trade and finance advisers remained firmly opposed to the idea of undercutting staunch international allies, among them struggling holders of U.S. bank loans. So Dole began drafting marketing loan legislation to force Reagan's hand.

What stifled his bill, however, was not the foreign policy and international banking community. It was a Congressional Budget Office estimate that a marketing loan for wheat and feed grains would cost an additional $5 billion in subsidies over the next three years.

The facts of political life under Gramm-Rudman, as established by the Senate earlier in the year, meant Dole had to look for offsetting reductions for his costly bill within the agriculture budget itself. Even commodity groups pushing hardest for marketing loans were unwilling to go along with that notion, afraid to sacrifice the certainty of direct government subsidies for the less predictable benefits of a new export-incentive program.

The issue ground down amid back-and-forth negotiations between Dole, farm group lobbyists and the administration. In the final two months of the session, it became a running joke on Capitol Hill as Dole announced daily that he was about to introduce his marketing loan measure — as soon, that is, as he could come up with a "deficit-neutral" package.

Dole never introduced a bill.

His difficulty in coming up with a farm policy and spending package acceptable to the administration or a majority of senators presaged the problems other legislators had in passing major changes in farm law.

In October, Sen. David L. Boren, D-Okla., offered a package of amendments to the omnibus fiscal 1987 spending bill, targeted at nearly every special interest in the Senate. His package had provisions for cattlemen, sugar beet growers, wheat farmers, soybean farmers and sunflower producers. Even child nutrition programs were included to curry favor with urban liberals.

"We're engaging in the annual farmfest," griped a coopted Dole.

But Boren's package, in spite of its wide political appeal, would have pushed the cost of agricultural programs over budget by $2.6 billion in fiscal 1987. In the end, Boren faced the same problem a month before Election Day that Democrats had experienced in March.

When Boren asked the Senate to waive the restrictions of Gramm-Rudman, he lost 45-53. Again, although 11 farm-state Republicans voted for the increases in farm spending, the Boren package failed to get the votes of 12 urban Democrats.

"No matter how much we tried, we couldn't keep the Democrats together," said a minority staff aide on the Agriculture Committee. "It was our problem all year."

—*By David Rapp*

Farm Bank Rules Eased to Avoid Cash Bailout

The deficit-reduction bill (HR 5300 — PL 99-509) cleared by Congress Oct. 17 contained provisions easing the accounting requirements for Farm Credit System banks as an alternative to a direct federal cash bailout.

Although Congress in 1985 passed legislation (PL 99-205) specifically authorizing an infusion of funds to keep the Farm Credit System afloat, the political difficulty of bringing tax dollars to the rescue led system officials to come up with a new accounting scheme. It essentially allowed banks to defer losses in anticipation that they could pay off the losses in a healthy agricultural economy in the future. *(1985 Almanac p. 543)*

The House Oct. 6 passed a separate farm credit bill (HR 5635) embracing that principle, and identical legislation was added by conferees to the deficit-reduction measure, known as a reconciliation bill. *(Reconciliation, p. 559)*

The new accounting procedures would let the credit system stretch out over the next two decades the heavy losses system banks expected to incur over two and one-half years.

The Farm Credit System — a nationwide network of borrower-owned cooperatives organized to provide real estate and operating loans to farmers and their cooperatives — raised money by selling bonds. Many of the outstanding bonds carried interest rates far above current market levels.

System officials said the continued high cost of those bonds restricted system banks from lowering their interest rates to farmers when rates of private banks and other commercial lenders began declining rapidly in 1985. Buying back the old bonds with high interest rates would cost $2.8 billion, at least, officials estimated.

Another key change would allow banks to set their own interest rates on loans to farmers without having to get the prior approval of their regulator, the Farm Credit Administration. That was designed to win the support of key lawmakers from Texas and New England, whose farm banks were healthy. They feared that the credit system might tap into their banks' profits to cover losses in weaker districts, a key provision of the rescue legislation passed in 1985.

Agriculture Committee members in both the House and Senate agreed to the new plan after they became convinced it was the only alternative to a cash infusion, a prospect that House Agriculture Chairman E. "Kika" de la Garza, D-Texas, called "physically impossible" in an era of rising budget deficits.

"Faced with this or spending real money, it was a real easy choice for them," a House committee aide said.

Provisions

As signed into law, HR 5300:

- Allowed the system's federal land banks, federal intermediate credit banks and banks for cooperatives to set loan interest rates for farmers without those rates being subject to Farm Credit Administration (FCA) approval.
- Authorized each bank in the system, upon receiving approval and conditions from the Farm Credit Administration, to take certain measures through Dec. 31, 1988, to reduce the costs of its outstanding bonds, many of which carried interest much higher than the market rate on new bond issues.

Those measures included contracting with a third party or a system service organization to pay the interest on bonds issued before Jan. 1, 1985.

Banks also could write off their interest costs for those bonds to the extent those costs exceeded market rates on new bond issues of similar maturities. Unspecified "similar actions" also would be allowed.

Each bank then could amortize over 20 years the cost of the premiums paid to third parties, the interest expense of new bonds or like costs associated with those expense-cutting measures.

- Revised the requirements of the 1985 farm law (PL 99-205) that financial statements of system institutions be prepared in accordance with generally accepted accounting principles (GAAP), allowing exceptions from GAAP for any actions taken to reduce the cost of obligations. This would permit banks to follow more lenient "regulatory accounting practices" to allow some losses and interest costs to be spread over a longer period of time than GAAP permitted.
- Allowed banks, subject to FCA approval, to write off losses that exceeded one-half of 1 percent of the loans outstanding and permitted banks to amortize that amount over 20 years.

Those losses would be repaid from earnings in future years.

- Included a non-binding "policy and objectives" statement that farmers and ranchers were best served by system banks offering competitive interest rates and that system banks should give farmer-borrowers the greatest benefit practicable from savings derived through the new accounting procedures.

Background

New reports issued in September confirmed that the massive Farm Credit System was still losing money at a suicidal rate, despite the comprehensive reorganization and rescue package enacted in 1985.

Different sources placed the system's 1986 losses at from $1.7 billion to $2.9 billion.

The 1985 law authorized a government rescue for the diffuse network of 37 banks and their farmer-owned cooperatives, but the legislation made federal assistance subject to a separate appropriation by Congress. House and Senate Agriculture leaders were under pressure from some members of the system to come up with the actual cash for a bailout by Jan. 1, 1987.

That deadline, which members contended was made more urgent by their intent to adjourn by the target date of Oct. 3, was hotly disputed by the Reagan administration, which maintained that the system could weather its financial difficulties until at least 1988.

The possibility of the Farm Credit System asking for financial aid drew mixed responses from farm lobbyists. They were divided sharply over spending tax dollars on a system that was created by Congress before the Depression but had been making it on its own since then.

Commercial banks and other independent lending institutions, also suffering from the depressed agricultural economy, objected to federal aid going to the Farm Credit System without private lenders getting something of equal value.

And at a time when farm price- and income-support payments already were tearing the agriculture budget at its seams, commodity groups were wary of any new spending proposal that might rip it wide open. Administration officials flatly told the groups that their subsidies would have to be cut to get the money for a system bailout without driving up the deficit.

On the other hand, cattlemen, pork producers and other farm groups that did not have such subsidy programs saw a bailout of the Farm Credit System as a worthy priority for federal largess. They would benefit more by a lending system that could afford to offer lower interest rates.

The concept of lower interest rates had enough political appeal in an election year to generate wide support in both chambers, despite the administration's objections.

Higher Losses Predicted

The nation's largest single agricultural lender with 30 percent of farm loans, the Farm Credit System banks had $61.5 billion in net loan volume. That was down from a peak of more than $85 billion in 1983 and was expected to fall to less than $50 billion by the end of 1988.

A report by the General Accounting Office (GAO) said that operating losses of the system could go as high as $2.9 billion in 1986, far more than the $1.7 billion loss projected by system officials and the Farm Credit Administration.

The GAO, an investigative agency of Congress, said the 1986 losses would practically wipe out the system's remaining capital surplus, already severely depleted by a record $2.7 billion in losses recorded in 1985.

The system's surpluses, estimated at $3.2 billion to $3.4 billion, came from the profits of the healthier districts. These were used to cover the losses of the weaker districts, a contentious issue among the more prosperous members of the system.

If the GAO projections were true, even healthy districts would not have enough capital to make up the shortfall. An infusion of new capital — most likely from the U.S. Treasury — would be necessary to stave off a systemwide equivalent of a "run on the bank."

"The uncertainty about federal involvement and the way it will work could create a crisis of confidence among the system's borrowers ... and among the system's investors," said William J. Anderson, assistant comptroller general of the GAO.

Differing Estimates

Anderson acknowledged Sept. 18 in testimony before the House Agriculture Committee that the GAO projections differed markedly from "equally legitimate" estimates made by the system banks and by the FCA.

The GAO used different assumptions about how many farmers' loans listed as "high risk" actually would have to be written off as losses. System analysts and FCA officials believed the surplus would not be exhausted that quickly and might be sufficient to carry the system until 1988.

But Anderson said the discrepancy was one of timing, not magnitude.

"The exact time at which the system's surplus will be exhausted is not so important as the inevitability of the event," Anderson said.

"The whole operation could start to fall apart if investors stopped buying securities and farmers started to go elsewhere to borrow operating funds.... The system is losing its competitive edge."

House Action

A bill (HR 5635) was rushed through the House to allow system banks to use two sets of books to report their financial condition — one set showing actual earnings and losses, another taking current losses and spreading them over 20 years.

Given that leeway, system officials contended, the banks would not require the multibillion-dollar infusion of federal funds that some experts feared would be necessary by early 1987.

But some members were skeptical. "Aren't we kind of juggling the books so as not to require an immediate Treasury payment?" asked Dan Glickman, D-Kan., at an Oct. 2 meeting of the Agriculture Committee called hastily to consider the bill.

"That's exactly what we're trying to do," said Ed Jones, D-Tenn., chairman of the Credit Subcommittee and sponsor of the bill.

The committee approved the bill by voice vote, and it was reported (H Rept 99-967) the next day. It was passed by the House by voice vote Oct. 6.

Senate Action

Although companion legislation (S 2770) had been introduced in the Senate, its sponsor, Thad Cochran, R-Miss., planned to attach language identical to the House measure to the deficit-reduction reconciliation bill pending in a House-Senate conference.

Sen. Pete V. Domenici, R-N.M., Budget Committee chairman, had been trying to keep unrelated amendments off the reconciliation bill, but an aide said Domenici would not stand in the way of the farm credit measure. Under Senate rules governing reconciliation, an "extraneous" amendment such as farm credit would be subject to a point of order that would require 60 votes to overrule.

"If the Farm Credit System can't find 60 votes for a bipartisan, bicameral bill, then they're really in trouble," an Agriculture Committee aide said.

The reconciliation bill appeared to be the only viable vehicle left, Senate sources agreed, because a separate bill for farm credit would become a magnet for other, more controversial farm relief measures that Senate Republican leaders had been trying to fend off.

"This is the political silly season," Cochran said. "A lot of people don't want to be satisfied right now. They want the issue, not the bill." ▮

1985 Farm Bill Changes

Spurred by relentless dairy interests — and by the election-year anxiety of key Republican senators — Congress early in 1986 rushed through legislation (HR 1614 — PL 99-260) to amend portions of the newly enacted 1985 farm law (PL 99-198) and spare some milk producers the most severe effects of budget cuts required by the Gramm-Rudman-Hollings anti-deficit act.

HR 1614 cleared March 6 when the House accepted by a 283-97 vote the package of so-called technical changes that the Senate had passed the previous day. *(Vote 39, p. 14-H)*

President Reagan had been expected to sign the measure. But on March 7 administration officials raised the threat of a veto, objecting to a purported "non-binding" section of the bill dealing with farm credit relief. White House officials believed the language, offered as a compromise between Sen. Tom Harkin, D-Iowa, and Senate Majority Leader Robert Dole, R-Kan., could require the administration to carry out discretionary provisions of the 1985 farm law that it had strenuously opposed. After Congress revised the bill's language to meet the White House objections, Reagan signed HR 1614 March 20.

The administration did not object to other provisions of the bill, including a key section requiring the Agriculture Department to raise dairy farmer assessments rather than lower price support rates to cover about $80 million in fiscal 1986 spending cuts for federal dairy programs. The dairy industry argued that assessments were a more equitable way of apportioning the cuts among all milk producers.

Pressure for the legislation began when the Agriculture Department announced it would implement budget cuts required by Gramm-Rudman-Hollings through across-the-board reductions in all direct payments to farmers in price support programs, for a total of $1.3 billion. Dairy-state legislators maintained that approach violated an agreement by 1985 farm bill conferees. *(Farm bill, 1985 Almanac p. 517; Gramm-Rudman, p. 579)*

Major Provisions

As signed into law March 20, HR 1614 (PL 99-260):

- Required the agriculture secretary to meet the 4.3 percent outlay reduction in the dairy program in fiscal 1986 mandated by the Gramm-Rudman-Hollings law by increasing the scheduled 40-cents-per-hundredweight assessment on all dairy producers by up to 12 cents per hundredweight. The Agriculture Department had proposed to reduce the dairy support price by 55 cents per hundredweight instead.
- Required the distribution to farmers of government-owned surplus commodities to compensate them in part for reductions in income subsidies caused by changing the formula by which subsidies were determined.

The 1985 farm law based subsidies to wheat, feed grain, cotton and rice farmers on the average yields per acre of 1981 through 1985 crops, excluding the high and low years. Under HR 1614, producers would be compensated for reductions in 1986 crop payments of more than 3 percent from the payment yield calculated for the 1985 crop. For 1987 crops, they would be compensated for reductions of more than 5 percent of the 1985 payment yield. For 1988 and beyond, the program payment yield would be limited to 10 percent below the 1985 figure.

- Revised the so-called underplanting provision of the 1985 farm law by restricting the kinds of unsubsidized crops farmers could grow on acres normally devoted to subsidized crops and still receive full benefits. The bill allowed only conserving crops to be seeded on underplanted acres. Haying and grazing of underplanted acres would be allowed, if a state so requested.

Under the 1985 law, a producer who planted at least 50 percent of his permitted program acres, and who devoted more acres than required under the acreage-reduction program to either conservation uses or non-program crops, would have been eligible to receive deficiency payments on 92 percent of the permitted acres.

HR 1614 allowed the agriculture secretary to make exceptions to the new restriction on non-program crops if he determined that production of such crops was not likely to increase the cost of price support programs and would not adversely affect the farm income of other producers of non-program crops.

- Lowered the salary level of a new White House position of special assistant for agricultural trade and food assistance from Level I ($86,200) to Level III ($73,600).
- Reduced spending requirements from $325 million to $110 million a year in fiscal 1986-88 for the targeted export assistance program, which subsidized U.S. commodity exports. The program used CCC funds or commodities to counter the effects of price or credit subsidies or unfair marketing arrangements used by other countries. (The $325 million funding requirement was retained for 1989 and 1990.)
- Reduced to $1 billion, from $2 billion, the amount of CCC commodities required to be used to enhance and encourage export sales of U.S. agricultural commodities in fiscal 1986-88. The secretary would have discretion to use up to $1.5 billion worth of commodities over the three years.
- Stated the sense of Congress that the secretary should use existing authority to distribute up to 50 percent of farmers' price support loans at the time farmers signed up for federal programs and began planting their crops. Loans normally were issued at harvest.

Legislative History

Senate. The Senate passed its version of the bill (S 2143) March 5 by voice vote after untangling a thicket of objections that had bogged down action in the chamber for a week.

Among other obstacles, Harkin and John Melcher, D-Mont., blocked action on the bill in an attempt to win a concession from the administration to provide immediate credit relief to farmers for spring planting. Harkin threatened to hold up the bill indefinitely unless the administration agreed to use its authority to make crop loans at planting time, rather than at harvest, so credit-pressed farmers would have low-interest money to help them stay afloat another year. Reagan had vetoed similar legislation in 1985, and the administration continued to oppose the idea as a bad precedent. *(1985 Almanac p. 542))*

Harkin finally gave in on his objections when Republican leaders offered to support a "sense-of-Congress" resolution urging the administration to issue advance crop loans. Harkin's resolution was added to the bill by a vote of 65-18, with Dole and several farm-state Republicans voting in favor. *(Vote 25, p. 6-S)*

Following passage of S 2143, the Senate March 6 substituted its text for that of a minor House-passed bill (HR 1614) and returned the measure to the House for final action.

House. The House March 6 approved the Senate-passed version of HR 1614, 283-97, after rejecting, 120-267, an effort by Barney Frank, D-Mass., to strike the provision increasing assessments on dairy farmers to meet deficit-reduction requirements. *(Votes 38, 39, p. 14-H)*

To get the bill to the House floor, the Democratic leadership first had to assure urban liberals that they, too, could look for alternatives to the automatic 4.3 percent cuts in fiscal 1986 programs demanded by the new Gramm-Rudman-Hollings law. Liberals Feb. 27 had blocked consideration of House legislation (HR 4188 — H Rept 99-475) because of what they termed preferential treatment for the dairy industry.

"The next opportunity we get, we're going to try to help the highest priority low-income programs," said Mike Lowry, D-Wash., who led the short-lived revolt against the powerful dairy interests in Congress.

Final Revision. Before HR 1614 was formally enrolled and sent to the president, Congress March 11 adopted a concurrent resolution (S Con Res 114) modifying the bill's farm credit language to ensure against a presidential veto.

Other Farm Bill Changes

HR 1614 was the second measure enacted in 1986 to clarify sections of the 1985 farm law. In previous action, President Reagan Feb. 28 signed another bill (S 2036 — PL 99-253) that revised the way federal benefits were computed for wheat and corn growers and clarified so-called "cross-compliance" requirements for farmers of major crops.

The Senate originally passed S 2036 Jan. 30. The House passed it by a 319-64 vote Feb. 4, with an amendment to free wheat and feed grain farmers from a restrictive formula used to compute base acreage on cotton and rice farms. The Senate accepted the House amendment Feb. 7 by voice vote.

Base histories were used to calculate benefits to farmers. Agriculture Department officials estimated that the new base acreage formula would increase the cost of the five-year, $169.2 billion farm bill by $100 million. Although that violated the new Gramm-Rudman-Hollings spending constraints, no one made a point of order to block passage. *(Vote 11, p. 6-H)*

The bill's cross-compliance provision gave the agriculture secretary authority to allow farmers who received federal benefits on their primary crops to avoid planting restrictions on secondary crops. ∎

Tobacco Price Supports

Congress revamped the tobacco price-support program in 1986, as part of an omnibus deficit-reduction bill cleared March 20 (HR 3128 — PL 99-272).

Conferees had filed their report on the bill in December 1985, but further Senate-House negotiations stalled final action for another three months. *(Details, p. 555)*

A product of yearlong negotiations between cigarette manufacturers and tobacco growers, the tobacco provisions in HR 3128 were designed to salvage a controversial price-support program that tobacco-state legislators had believed was about to collapse. *(Background, 1985 Almanac p. 539)*

The bill lowered the federal price-support levels for various kinds of tobacco while providing for discounted sales of the huge surpluses the government had been forced to take over in recent years.

Since 1982, those surpluses had been financed through assessments on tobacco growers. The increasing burden of those assessments, however, had led many tobacco-state legislators to fear that growers would vote to do away with the price-support system altogether at scheduled referendums in early 1986.

Senate Agriculture Committee Chairman Jesse Helms, R-N.C., along with other legislators from tobacco-growing states, such as North Carolina and Kentucky, organized the negotiations partly to solidify these competing tobacco interests.

Growers were at first noncommittal about the package that emerged from the Helms negotiations, criticizing provisions they said allowed cigarette companies to continue buying cheaper imported tobacco. Such grower complaints prompted Rep. Charlie Rose, D-N.C., a political rival of Helms, to work out his own deal in the House version of HR 3128 to earmark 1 cent of the 16-cents-per-pack tax on cigarettes to finance the existing price-support system.

Rose lost his battle with Helms in conference, however, and ultimately supported the Senate plan.

Along with reducing price-support rates, the package called for cigarette companies to buy up existing surpluses, in many cases at 90 percent discounts, and to share half the cost of the price-support program with growers. The package gave manufacturers a direct role in setting quotas for how much growers could grow and sell each year.

Critics called the measure a bailout that provided more help for cigarette companies than tobacco farmers. Government losses from discounting the price of surplus stocks were estimated by the Office of Management and Budget to be $1.1 billion.

But supporters of the package claimed it would reduce federal outlays for the tobacco program by more than $500 million over the next five years. They said the government would have been financially liable for much of the surplus stocks anyway, had growers voted to do away with the program.

Indeed, before HR 3128 was cleared, growers of three lesser kinds of tobacco rejected government controls and price supports. Nevertheless, farmers of the major crop of "flue-cured" tobacco, grown mainly in North Carolina, voted to continue the system by a 93.7 percent margin. A referendum for burley tobacco, the other major crop grown mainly in Kentucky, was delayed until after the bill was passed; it also was approved.

Under the terms of HR 3128 the tobacco program became permanent law. Supporters said that would free it from the regular attacks of anti-smoking groups that occurred whenever the price-support system previously came up for reauthorization.

Provisions

As signed into law April 7, HR 3128 provided a new permanent tobacco price-support program that:

- Maintained the existing method of price support by offering loans, with tobacco held as collateral, through producers' associations (cooperatives) that contracted with the Commodity Credit Corporation (CCC).

  The cooperatives handled all operations connected with making loan advances to producers, and arranged for receiving, redrying, packing, storing and eventually selling the tobacco under loan. Tobacco not sold at the support rate was consigned to the cooperative, which paid producers with money borrowed from the CCC. The cooperative reimbursed the CCC, with interest, for the loan advances upon sale of the tobacco.
- Set the price-support level for the 1986 crop of flue-cured tobacco at $1.438 per pound; the price-support level for the 1985 and 1986 crops of burley tobacco was set at $1.488 a pound.
- Set the price-support level for the 1987 and subsequent crops of flue-cured and burley tobacco by (1) giving two-thirds weight to the difference between the immediately preceding year's support level and the average market price of three of the five preceding years, with the high and low years excluded; (2) giving one-third weight to an index of production costs incurred by tobacco farmers; and (3) allowing the agriculture secretary to adjust the support price from 65 to 100 percent of the annual increase or decrease resulting from the formula, based on supply-demand considerations.

• Repealed the secretary's authority to reduce price supports on certain low-quality grades of flue-cured tobacco.

• Maintained the existing method of supply control through mandatory marketing quotas on growers of each kind of tobacco, if such quotas were approved in a referendum vote by a two-thirds majority of all producers. The marketing quota translated into a national allotment, and each tobacco farm, based on its historical production, got a pro rata share of the national allotment.

• Required the secretary to set a national marketing quota for flue-cured and burley tobacco within 3 percent of the combined total of (1) a confidential estimate by cigarette manufacturers of the amount of flue-cured or burley tobacco they intended to purchase at auction during the next marketing year; (2) the average annual exports for the three preceding years; and (3) the amount needed to maintain a reserve stock level. From 1986 through 1989, the secretary could not reduce the quota levels more than 6 percent a year. From 1990 through 1993, quotas could not be reduced more than 10 percent a year.

• Established reserve stock levels at the greater of (1) 100 million pounds for flue-cured and 50 million pounds for burley tobacco, or (2) 15 percent of the effective national marketing quotas.

• Reduced the amount of flue-cured and burley tobacco that could be marketed without penalty from 110 to 103 percent of the farm marketing quota.

• Required each cigarette manufacturer to purchase at least 90 percent of flue-cured and burley tobacco a manufacturer intended to buy when quotas were determined. Failure would subject a manufacturer to a double assessment for each pound below 90 percent of intended purchases.

• Revised the current system of requiring producers to pay an assessment into a capital fund (called a "no net cost" account) from which CCC losses on loans were repaid. Assessments would be collected from both producers and purchasers in a way that ensured that both shared equally in maintaining the account. However, future assessments on burley tobacco would be determined without regard to any losses of the CCC from the 1983 crop of burley tobacco.

• Authorized cigarette manufacturers to purchase existing surplus inventories of flue-cured tobacco over an eight-year period and burley tobacco over a five-year period, with each manufacturer purchasing a percentage of the stocks at least equal to the respective percentage of the total number of cigarettes manufactured during the previous 12 months.

• Required the flue-cured association to offer surplus inventories from the 1976 through 1981 crop years at a 90 percent discount from their current base prices, and the 1982 through 1984 crops at a 10 percent discount. The bill also required the burley association to offer surplus inventories from the 1982 crop at the base price in effect on July 1, 1985, and the surplus from the 1984 crop at the association's costs on the date of enactment of the bill.

• Required the CCC to take title to remaining surpluses from the 1983 burley crop and offer the stocks for sale on terms and conditions as the CCC deemed appropriate. Any stocks not sold within two years could be offered for sale at a 90 percent discount. ∎

Drought Aid Approved

A summer-long drought in the Southeast, followed by autumn floods in the Midwest, prompted efforts to beef up relief programs for farmers whose crops were destroyed by natural disasters.

After repeated attempts to pass a separate relief measure bogged down, Congress attached a $400 million package to the fiscal 1987 omnibus spending bill (H J Res 738) to fund government operations. *(Continuing resolution, p. 219)*

The measure required the administration to issue payment-in-kind (PIK) certificates, redeemable for government-owned grain, to farmers in counties where crops had been destroyed by drought, floods or hailstorms.

The House Aug. 6 unanimously passed a $530 million authorization bill (HR 5288 — H Rept 99-737) for relief to drought-stricken Southeastern farmers.

The bill, approved 418-0, would require the use of government-owned surplus grain as payments to farmers in areas where a summer-long heat wave devastated an estimated $2 billion in crops and range land. *(Vote 264, p. 76-H)*

The Senate Aug. 1 attached a similar measure to a bill to raise the ceiling on the national debt (H J Res 668). That measure, however, died over House disagreements on unrelated issues. *(Debt, p. 562)*

The Reagan administration had discretionary power under the 1985 farm bill (PL 99-198) to carry out most of the provisions of the proposals, and Agriculture Secretary Richard E. Lyng announced Aug. 1 that he would permit PIK assistance to farmers and ranchers adversely affected by drought.

The Congressional Budget Office estimated the administration's relief measures would cost about $300 million. HR 5288 would have added another $230 million by allowing farmers of peanuts and soybeans to get disaster payments, in addition to farmers of wheat, feed grains, cotton and rice.

The House-passed bill proposed to offset the $230 million by requiring the Agriculture Department in fiscal 1987 to sell part of its portfolio of rural development loans to private investors. Similar loan sales in 1988 and 1989 also were included in a deficit-reduction measure (HR 5300). *(Deficit reduction, p. 559)*

The bill, reported by the House Agriculture Committee Aug. 2, also would have limited the combined disaster and crop insurance payments a farmer could receive to no more than the actual losses incurred by the drought.

The House debated the bill Aug. 5. ∎

CFTC Bill Clears

The Senate Oct. 17 cleared a three-year funding authorization (HR 4613 — PL 99-641) for the Commodity Futures Trading Commission (CFTC) after acceding to House demands to continue to permit so-called "leverage" contracts in precious metals.

Leverage contracts are long-term installment contracts for the purchase of silver, gold and other non-agricultural commodities. They are not like futures contracts, which are commitments to buy and sell a commodity on a set date at a price determined by auction in exchange markets. Instead, leverage contracts are traded privately by only two authorized dealers: Monex of Newport Beach, Calif., and International Precious Metals of Fort Lauderdale, Fla.

Buyers of the contracts seldom accept delivery of the commodity but make installment payments in the hope that the commodity's value will increase over time.

The bill, passed by the House July 16 by a 401-7 vote, limited leveraged contracts to gold, silver and platinum. However, the bill allowed other companies to enter the business after a two-year period. *(Vote 199, p. 60-H)*

The Senate began debate Sept. 30 on its reauthorization measure, but final action was blocked by Pete Wilson, R-Calif., who objected to the bill's banning all leveraged transactions in two years. However, Wilson agreed to let the measure proceed after he was assured a seat on the conference committee. The Senate Oct. 6 by a vote of 83-1 approved HR 4613 after substituting the text of its bill (S 2045). *(Vote 331, p. 54-S)*

In conference, Wilson joined House members in sucessfully insisting on the House language to protect the practice of leverage.

Proponents of leverage were aided by an unusual shift of position by the administration. Although the CFTC board, comprised of presidential appointees, first proposed that leveraged transactions be abolished, officials in the Justice Department later countermanded that position and lobbied in favor of retaining the House language to preserve the special form of commodities trading.

The bill as agreed to by conferees in sessions Oct. 8-9 combined a Senate floor amendment on grain quality and a similar House-passed bill (HR 5407), agreeing to prohibit exporters from adding dust and foreign material to grain at points of export.

Conferees also rejected a Senate amendment, sponsored by Agriculture Committee Chairman Jesse Helms, R-N.C., to eliminate U.S. sugar quotas for countries that imported sugar from Cuba or failed to cooperate with U.S. anti-drug efforts. *(Drugs, p. 92)*

The House by a vote of 274-130 deleted a Senate provision from the conference report (H Rept 99-995), which had the effect of rejecting the conference agreement. That provision would have transferred certain National Forest System lands to the state of Nebraska. When that language had been deleted, members approved the agreement by voice vote. *(Vote 429, p. 120-H)*

The Senate agreed to the change by voice vote Oct. 17, clearing the measure for the president, who signed it Nov. 10.

Provisions

Major provisions of HR 4613:

- Authorized fiscal 1987-89 appropriations for the CFTC at whatever level Congress determined necessary.
- Restricted leverage contracts to precious metals (gold, silver and platinum), effectively prohibiting future leverage transactions on foreign currencies and copper.
- Removed a CFTC moratorium on allowing new firms to enter the leverage business, effective in two years. The CFTC must survey firms interested in entering the business and report to Congress within two years, offering proposals for regulations to govern leverage dealing and a finding on whether such trading served an "economic purpose."
- Repealed the limitations on options trading, currently allowed on a trial basis, and required the CFTC to establish a permanent program for commodity options trading on contract markets.
- Clarified that fraud was prohibited in both off-exchange and on-exchange trading activities, giving the CFTC express authority, along with individual states, to prosecute fraud committed by off-exchange operators.
- Allowed the National Futures Association, an industry self-regulatory group, to impose disciplinary action against members while those actions were being appealed to the CFTC. The bill also required an expedited appeals process.
- Authorized the commission, on a majority vote, to serve investigatory subpoenas on persons outside the United States.
- Permitted CFTC employees and commissioners to invest in commodities as long as no non-public information was used and the transactions did not involve futures, options or leverage. The commission could develop appropriate exceptions to the restrictions, such as permitting modest holdings in large mutual funds that hedged their portfolios in the futures market.
- Authorized the CFTC to seek appointment of a temporary receiver to protect and manage the property of persons while the commission sought a restraining order to freeze assets or records to prevent suspected law violators from destroying records or removing funds or property.

House Action

The House Agriculture Committee May 7 approved a three-year authorization (HR 4613) for the CFTC after compromising on efforts to restrict leverage contracts.

The panel rejected 12-30 an amendment by Dan Glickman, D-Kan., to remove the special regulatory treatment of leverage contracts and to effectively ban their use.

The committee then approved by voice vote a compromise offered by James M. Jeffords, R-Vt., to restrict leveraged contracts to gold, silver and platinum, removing the authority for contracts on copper and foreign currencies. In addition, the CFTC in two years would have to permit a gradual expansion of the number of firms dealing in leveraged transactions.

The report (H Rept 99-624) was filed June 6.

Before approving the bill by 401-7 July 16, the House at first accepted and then rejected Glickman's amendment to end separate regulatory treatment of leverage transactions. The resounding vote masked sharply divided opinions on the subject of leverage. *(Vote 199, p. 60-H)*

Glickman at first prevailed on a 219-193 vote. *(Vote 195, p. 58-H)*

But supporters of leverage claimed that many members did not understand the subject of the amendment, much less the esoteric arguments for and against the practice of leverage.

E. Thomas Coleman, R-Mo., said many members were confused about what amendment was pending; other expected floor amendments to HR 4613 dealt with the effect of cattle futures on beef markets.

"There are a lot of people who came into this chamber who thought that the Glickman amendment had something to do with the cattle industry, that this had something to do with agricultural products," Coleman said.

Coleman demanded another vote on the amendment, and on the second roll call, 33 members who previously voted for the Glickman proposal switched sides and the House voted 192-218 to reject the plan. *(Vote 198, p. 60-H)*

Other amendments included those by:

- James R. Jones, D-Okla., directing the Agriculture Committee to study the economic purpose of trading in cattle futures, whether the trading was being manipulated and what the economic effects were. Adopted, 406-1. *(Vote 197, p. 58-H)*
- Wes Watkins, D-Okla., to end authority for futures

trading in live cattle by December 1987 unless a majority of cattlemen approved such markets in a referendum. Rejected, 142-265. *(Vote 196, p. 58-H)*

Summary: As passed by the House, HR 4613:

- Reauthorized appropriations for the Commodity Futures Trading Commission for fiscal 1987-89.
- Restricted leverage contracts to precious metals (gold, silver and platinum), thereby prohibiting future leveraged transactions on foreign currencies and copper.
- Removed a moratorium on allowing new firms to enter the leverage business, effective in two years. The CFTC must survey firms interested in entering the leverage business and report the results to Congress within two years, along with proposals for regulations to govern leverage dealing and the commission's finding on whether such trading served an "economic purpose." The regulations would take effect 45 days after being submitted to Congress, although the commission could provide for gradual entry of new firms.
- Repealed the limitations on options trading, currently allowed on a trial basis, and required the commission to establish a permanent program for commodity-options trading on contract markets.
- Permitted commission employees and commissioners to invest in commodities as long as no non-public information was used and the transactions did not involve futures, options or leverage. The commission could develop appropriate exceptions to the restrictions, such as to permit modest holdings in large mutual funds that hedged their portfolios in the futures market.
- Required the Agriculture Committee to study the impact of cattle futures trading on the beef industry, and to report legislation to the House if the study determined that manipulation of cattle futures trading adversely affected cattle producers or the beef industry.

Senate Action

The Senate Agriculture Committee March 25 approved a measure (S 2045) that would have put leveraged transactions for precious metals under the same federal trading rules as commodity futures contracts.

Because leveraged contracts were not sold on exchange markets, the CFTC was required to regulate them separately from other transactions.

The CFTC argued that the separate regulation was neither logical nor necessary. S 2045 eliminated the requirement for the special treatment for leveraged transactions, thereby barring leveraged transactions unless they were conducted on an exchange and supervised by self-regulatory organizations.

But the panel adopted by voice vote an amendment by Richard G. Lugar, R-Ind., that delayed the repeal of the separate regulations for leveraged contracts for two years after enactment.

Wilson, a junior member of the committee, argued that a sudden repeal could put the two companies dealing in leveraged contracts out of business.

The report (S Rept 99-291) was filed April 29.

The bill was considered Sept. 24, and after substituting the text for that of the House-passed bill, HR 4613, the Senate passed HR 4613 by a vote of 83-1 Oct. 6. *(Vote 331, p. 54-S)*

On Sept. 24, members by a vote of 71-26 tabled an amendment by James Abdnor, R-S.D., and others that would have eliminated cattle as a subject for trading on the commodity market. Abdnor argued that the speculation in cattle futures had created price instability that damaged the industry. *(Vote 290, p. 48-S)*

Helms urged members to vote against the proposal because the impact of such trading on the cattle market was under study by the comptroller general.

The Senate adopted by voice vote a catchall amendment by Rudy Boschwitz, R-Minn., which gave the agriculture secretary discretionary authority to vary the frequency of on-site inspection of processed meat products; sped up the income-subsidy payments scheduled to be made to wheat producers for the 1986 crop; exempted the producers of extra-long staple cotton from requirements that they comply with acreage controls on other government-subsidized crops; and allowed highly erodible land previously planted to alfalfa and other grass crops to enter the conservation reserve program.

Also by voice vote, the Senate agreed to an amendment by Charles E. Grassley, R-Iowa, tightening the guidelines on the quality of grain shipped for export.

The Senate also passed by voice votes two amendments that would later prove to be major roadblocks to reaching a final compromise with the House.

One amendment, offered by Agriculture Chairman Helms, would cut off sugar quotas to nations, notably Canada, that imported sugar from Cuba, would eliminate quotas for countries involved in the drug trade that failed to cooperate with U.S. anti-drug efforts, and would guarantee Caribbean Basin nations, Ecuador and the Philippines 1987 sugar quotas at or above 1986 levels, even though quotas were expected to drop for other countries.

The committee's ranking Democrat, Edward Zorinsky, Neb., also won quick floor approval for an amendment requiring the U.S. Forest Service to cede over 173 acres of land to the state of Nebraska for use as park land.

Summary: As approved by the Senate, the bill:

- Clarified and strengthened the enforcement capabilities of the CFTC.
- Made explicit that the anti-fraud provision of the Commodities Exchange Act applied to off-exchange transactions and that the CFTC could serve administrative subpoenas outside the United States.
- Allowed the CFTC, when seeking a restraining order against an alleged violator to freeze assets, to name a receiver to administer the assets.
- Lifted a provision of current law that permitted an automatic stay of disciplinary action against a member of the National Futures Association while that action was being appealed.
- Extended funding authorization through fiscal 1992 at whatever sums Congress considered appropriate.
- Eased some restrictions that had barred a CFTC commissioner or employee from participating in certain transactions.

Conference

The dispute over leverage contracts dominated the conference to resolve differences.

Ultimately, divided Senate negotiators gave in to the unified House contingent, which had denied Glickman a seat on the committee.

In sessions Oct. 8-9, House conferees held fast to their provision to permit the continued trading of precious metals by certain businesses operating outside certified futures exchange markets.

Senior members of the Senate Agriculture Committee supported their chamber's view, but Wilson's presence gave the Senate a divided front in the conference.

"On our side, we have two sides," Helms admitted at the outset.

Lugar made only a token effort at a compromise before caving in to Wilson and the House negotiators.

Lugar cited Wilson's ability to prevent the conference report from returning to the Senate floor for final approval in the waning days of the session. He said CFTC officials, who first pushed for the ban on leverage, finally told him they would rather get reauthorization for the commission than lose the entire bill over the leverage controversy.

"It was a question of debating the issue for two hours or two minutes," said Lugar, who opted for the latter "in the interests of time."

Sugar Amendment Dropped

Helms had no better fortune with his amendment dealing with sugar quotas.

Helms had put an identical amendment on the Senate's version of an omnibus drug bill (HR 5484), but the House stripped it from a revised version of that bill Oct. 8.

Although Helms had no problem attaching the amendment to the CFTC bill Oct. 6, in conference he ran into one of the House's peculiar "turf" battles. Sugar quotas were in the domain of the Ways and Means Subcommittee on Trade, and eight members from that panel were conferees on the CFTC bill, along with members of the Agriculture Committee.

Rep. Sam Gibbons, D-Fla., Trade Subcommittee chairman, insisted that the amendment would damage U.S. relations with Canada and violate international trade agreements.

Gibbons promised a hearing and "possibly a marked up bill" in 1987 but rejected all of Helms' attempts at compromise.

"This is something I care about very, very much," Helms insisted, although he winced when Gibbons suggested that "the best thing we could do for Caribbean Basin countries is to remove some of the textile tariffs" — an issue that hit even closer to home for the North Carolina senator.

Senate conferees prevailed on the Senate floor amendment to allow wheat farmers to receive all of their income-support payments in November, rather than partial payments in November and June. They combined a Senate floor amendment on grain quality and a similar House-passed bill (HR 5407), agreeing to prohibit exporters from adding dust and foreign material to grain at points of export.

Bill Bogs Down

After wending its way through the political controversies associated with leverage trading and sugar quotas, the CFTC bill almost bogged down entirely over a seemingly innocuous Senate provision to turn U.S. forest land over to the Nebraska Game and Parks Commission.

Zorinsky's park land amendment drew strong objections from Rep. Charles Whitley, D-N.C., chairman of the Agriculture Subcommittee on Forests. Whitley said Zorinsky's insistence that the federal land be given away would set a dangerous precedent.

When the conference report went to the House on Oct. 15, Whitley led a successful fight to reject Zorinsky's provision to give the land to his home state. The vote was 274-130. *(Vote 429, p. 120-H)*

Zorinsky, however, threatened to filibuster the conference report when it came up for a vote in the Senate Oct. 17. Only the intervention of Agriculture Secretary Richard E. Lyng enabled the Senate to take final action on the CFTC bill before adjourning for the year.

Lyng gave Zorinsky written assurance that the forest land would be turned over to the state of Nebraska in a bargain-rate, 30-year lease arrangement. The deal meant the state could lease the 173-acre tract for 3 percent of fair market value, rather than the usual 5 percent rate.

The Senate then cleared HR 4613 by voice vote. ▮

Farm Payments Capped

Congress enacted a new cap on farmers' price-support payments that even supporters conceded would produce negligible savings and would serve only as a symbolic gesture against the ballooning costs of agriculture programs.

Southern senators representing powerful cotton and rice interests, the main beneficiaries of the largest government farm subsidies, finally capitulated Oct. 16 and by voice vote accepted a House limit of $250,000 on the amount of federal subsidies a farmer could receive each year. The new ceiling was included in a half-trillion-dollar continuing resolution (H J Res 738 — PL 99-591) to fund government programs. *(Continuing resolution, p. 219)*

The new cap was aimed at restraining farmers who legally escaped the existing $50,000 limit on farm program payments. But a major loophole would allow some farmers to continue to receive multimillion-dollar payments on their crops.

That was because many farmers were expected to forfeit their crops to the government rather than sell them on the open market, further increasing the bulging surpluses under federal control.

According to the Agriculture Department, the $250,000 cap would save little more than $25 million over four years, a pittance in comparison with overall crop subsidy payments, which totaled $12.9 billion in fiscal 1986.

"I think they got off pretty damn easy," said Rep. Silvio O. Conte, R-Mass., who attached the new $250,000 cap to the House version of the appropriations measure.

Background

Although existing law maintained a ceiling of $50,000 per farmer, it exempted from that limit about 40 percent of the price- and income-support payments for wheat, feed grains, cotton and rice. The exceptions were included in a deal in 1985 between farm-state lawmakers and the Reagan administration, which wanted to lower price-support levels for the major crops of wheat, feed grains, cotton and rice. *(1985 Almanac p. 517)*

The 1985 farm law (PL 99-198), for example, maintained a $50,000 cap on direct income-subsidy payments for wheat and feed grains farmers, but exempted from that cap other payments due them as a result of reductions made by the agriculture secretary in the price-support rate.

Other exemptions particularly favored cotton and rice producers, who operated under a different price-support system called the "marketing loan." That system allowed farmers to repay a crop loan at a level below the rate at which it was made, and any gains they realized from those transactions were not covered by the $50,000 cap.

The Agriculture Department estimated that individual payments ranging as high as $5 million to $12.7 million would be made to several large cotton and rice farmers in the West and South. One cotton giant, J. G. Boswell Co., in California's San Joaquin Valley, would qualify for a $20 million payment.

The large payments to big agricultural enterprises exacerbated tension between rural and urban lawmakers who were struggling with the enormous federal deficit.

"It's a scandal," complained Massachusetts' Conte. "The whole [1985] farm bill was sold on the floor as something to save the family farmer. Yet now we're seeing million-dollar payments, and the family farmer is still in trouble."

House Action

The House Sept. 25 avoided a bitter public showdown on the payment-cap issue between farm-state members and their disgruntled urban counterparts. But after passing the amendment on a voice vote, the House narrowly passed H J Res 738 by 201-200, with opposition stemming in part from dissatisfaction over a compromise setting new limits on farm payments. *(Vote 383, p. 108-H)*

The House Appropriations Committee had accepted an amendment by Conte to the continuing appropriations resolution to impose a one-year, $250,000 limit on all loans, payments, purchases and crop-related subsidies that any agricultural entity could receive in 1987. That plan, however, ran into opposition from House Agriculture Committee leaders, who objected to placing a cap on payments that were caused largely by the administration's "free-market" policy of trying to drive down commodity prices to world levels.

Conte argued that farmers should be prevented from receiving multimillion-dollar price-support payments for their crops.

"I want to plug some of the goddamn big loopholes," Conte said. "This Congress can't go home leaving this farm bill unattended."

E. "Kika" de la Garza, D-Texas, Agriculture Committee chairman, was aware of the growing resentment over farm program spending among urban liberals and fiscal conservatives. He accepted Conte's new cap with reluctance but continued to press for concessions.

After two days of bargaining with de la Garza and Edward R. Madigan, R-Ill., ranking minority member of the Agriculture Committee, Conte won agreement on a new compromise that he offered as a floor amendment Sept. 25 during floor debate on the continuing resolution.

The compromise would retain the $50,000 limit and put another $200,000 cap on some of the payments that had been escaping coverage, although there still would be exceptions. The new cap, for instance, did not cover wool, sugar, peanut and dairy programs.

The $250,000 limit would apply to most payments to wheat and feed grains farmers, but only about 2 percent of those farmers combined qualified for more than that anyway.

On the other hand, cotton and rice farmers, who operated larger farms by comparison, received much of their subsidies in payment-in-kind certificates, which were exempt from the new limit.

As a result, the measure was expected to save only $15 million to $100 million out of the $15 billion that went to farmers in direct farm subsidies.

"They've got me over a barrel," Conte said. "But at least I'm getting people from the Farm Belt who are talking to me now and want to negotiate."

Similar Senate Effort

In the Senate, Midwestern farm-state members tried to push proposals similar to Conte's.

Mark Andrews, R-N.D., and Tom Harkin, D-Iowa, nearly succeeded Sept. 11 in including a $500,000 limit in the Senate Appropriations Committee's fiscal 1987 agriculture appropriations bill (HR 5177). *(Appropriations, p. 201)*

They lost on an 11-12 vote, but only after Thad Cochran, R-Miss., chairman of the Agriculture subcommittee and a strong voice in the Senate for cotton and rice interests, produced seven proxy votes against the amendment. Andrews and Harkin promised to try again when the continuing resolution reached the floor.

"I'm getting tired of reading about multimillion-dollar payments," Andrews said. "They're now being used to discredit the whole idea of farm programs."

Harkin teamed up with Charles E. Grassley, R-Iowa, to reoffer the plan as an amendment to the continuing appropriations measure Oct. 1. Their proposal would have applied to wheat, feed grains, cotton, rice and honey through the 1990 crop year.

In addition to capping payments, the proposal would have required the secretary to review regulations defining "person." That was aimed at eventually preventing farmers from subdividing their farms to bring each section under the $50,000 limit.

The Harkin-Grassley amendment was blocked, however, when the Senate voted 47-52 against a motion to rule it germane to the bill. *(Vote 308, p. 51-S)*

Conference Stalemate

Cochran then brought a House-Senate conference on the continuing resolution to a stalemate on the issue. That forced Conte to send the payment limit issue back to each chamber for a second vote.

The House reaffirmed its position Oct. 15 by voice vote, sending the politically volatile issue back to the Senate, where even farm-state senators were sharply divided on the issue.

Senators from wheat- and corn-growing states supported a payment cap to fend off criticism of farm program spending. By pushing for a $250,000 cap, however, they were safely protecting their constituents because only a handful of wheat and corn farmers would be affected. Only 1 percent of wheat farmers and 6 percent of corn farmers would exceed the current limit of $50,000 a year in crop subsidy payments, according to the Agriculture Department.

The Senate by voice vote Oct. 16 agreed to accept the House-passed limit on payments to farmers after Cochran argued that the limits were ineffective.

The Loophole

Although Conte's amendment seemingly covered many of the ways farmers could get around the existing $50,000 cap, it retained one glaring loophole that had to do with the way the price-support program worked.

Farmers of the major crops of wheat, feed grains, cotton, rice and soybeans, plus honey marketers and wool producers, could get a loan from the government in return for cutting back production and then temporarily holding their crops off the market at harvest. The crop became collateral for the loan.

Farmers could ultimately sell their crops, repay the loans and receive subsidies to make up for any losses caused by depressed market prices. Or, they could default on the loan, turn their crops over to the government and keep the loan principal.

In either event, the government made a deficiency payment to cover the difference between the loan rate and a higher "target" price established by Congress.

Cotton and rice producers, however, operated under the marketing loan program that allowed them to repay their crop loans at the prevailing market price, even if that price was lower than the original loan rate.

In that event, they not only got up to $50,000 in normal deficiency payments for the difference between the loan rate and the higher target price, but they also qualified for separate payments to cover the difference between the loan rate and the lower market price.

The second "loan payments" were exempt from the $50,000 cap.

One Last Option

However, in placing a $250,000 cap on all payments along with the existing $50,000 cap on deficiency payments, the Conte amendment failed to cover the farmer's last payment option: loan default.

Farmers of large operations could still take out a loan with no limit on the total.

Those who might be limited to $250,000 in subsidy payments if they had repaid their loans, could simply forfeit the entire crop and keep the original loan amount.

The federal government, in effect, would lose the entire loan, in addition to being saddled with the added expense involved in storing the forfeited crop.

"There's not going to be much restriction on payments," Cochran said as he gave up his fight against the $250,000 cap.

Complained John H. Chafee, R-R.I.: "It's a pretty loose net." ∎

Farm Bankruptcy Bill

As part of a bill (HR 5316 — PL 99-554) to improve the efficiency of bankruptcy courts, a House-Senate conference committee included an amendment to permit small farmers to file for bankruptcy while decreasing the danger of their losing their farms.

The conference report (H Rept 99-958), adopted by the House Oct. 2 and cleared by the Senate Oct. 3, created a Chapter 12 of the U.S. Bankruptcy Code to be used only by persons whose debts were at least 80 percent farm-connected but did not exceed $1.5 million. The new chapter allowed farmers to reorganize their debts without having to sell their farms.

The House had passed a farm bankruptcy bill (HR 2211) June 24, 1985. The Senate passed it May 8, 1986. The House Aug. 12 passed HR 5316, which authorized new bankruptcy judges, and before approving the measure Aug. 16, the Senate added farm bankruptcy provisions. A conference was held on both bills. *(Bankruptcy judges, p. 90; 1985 Almanac p. 545)*

The final measure, signed into law Oct. 27, amended the bankruptcy laws to permit small farmers to reorganize without the consent of their creditors, as required under current law. Rep. Mike Synar, D-Okla., said the effect of the change would be to grant family farmers the same rights already enjoyed by small-business men.

HR 5316 was reported (H Rept 99-764) by the Judiciary Committee Aug. 7. The version approved by the Senate would have established a five-year period in which to use the new provisions. The conference report, which was filed Oct. 2, set a seven-year period.

Provisions

As enacted, the farm bankruptcy section of HR 5316:

- Shifted much of the Chapter 13 bankruptcy laws, which allowed small businesses to restructure their debts, into a new Chapter 12 providing for adjustment of debts of a family farmer with regular annual income.
- Raised the maximum debt limit to qualify for bankruptcy from $450,000 to $1.5 million.
- Limited debt relief to family farms, or those who derived more than 50 percent of their gross income from farming and for whom 80 percent of debt arose out of farming.
- Allowed a farmer 90 days to file a plan, compared with 15 days under Chapter 13. Eliminated the "absolute priority" rule so that a reorganization plan could be confirmed over the objection of creditors if the plan met certain tests to provide equitable treatment of creditors.
- Allowed farmers to sell land or equipment free of any lien attached to it.
- Denied a creditor "lost opportunity costs" which, under previous bankrupcty law, often required a farmer to make a periodic payment to a creditor to cover a drop in the value of the land used as collateral for a loan.
- Provided for the repeal of the new Chapter 12 on Oct. 1, 1993. ∎

GENERAL GOVERNMENT

CQ

General Government

Ending a prolonged deadlock, Congress and the White House in 1986 reached agreement on a new retirement system for federal employees.

The new plan covered all federal civilian and postal employees hired after Jan. 1, 1984. Those workers had to pay Social Security taxes and would draw Social Security benefits when they retired. The pensions provided by the new retirement plan would supplement their Social Security benefits, just as private-sector pensions did. Workers hired before 1984 could either continue under the existing system or transfer into the new one. The new system also included an optional tax-deferred savings plan similar to the private sector's 401(k) plan.

Employee unions strongly supported the plan, which was expected to cost the government about 23 percent of payroll, more than President Reagan wanted but less than the cost of the existing system.

Space Program

The Jan. 28 destruction of the space shuttle *Challenger* triggered a yearlong debate over the future of the nation's space exploration program. The shuttle disintegrated moments after takeoff, killing all seven crew members.

A presidential commission headed by William P. Rogers attributed the accident to a "faulty design unacceptably sensitive to a number of factors." In its June 9 report, the commission cited lack of attention to safety by the National Aeronautics and Space Administration (NASA) as a contributing cause of the accident.

Moving to shore up the troubled agency, the Senate May 6 confirmed James C. Fletcher to serve a second tour of duty as administrator of NASA. Fletcher previously had headed NASA in 1971-77.

Shortly before adjourning Oct. 18, Congress cleared a bill authorizing $7.8 billion for space programs in fiscal 1987. President Reagan pocket-vetoed the measure, however, objecting to provisions that would have created a National Aeronautics and Space Council to be the major policy-making body within the executive branch for civilian space issues.

Reagan noted that funding for civilian space activities, including replacement of the *Challenger*, was provided in the omnibus fiscal 1987 appropriations resolution. That measure transferred $2.4 billion from the Defense Department to NASA to pay for a new orbiter to replace the *Challenger*.

Regulatory Curbs

The regulatory activities of the Office of Management and Budget (OMB) came under attack in 1986, but Congress rejected proposals to cut off funding for OMB's regulatory arm, the Office of Information and Regulatory Affairs (OIRA).

Critics contended that OIRA had overstepped its authority in reviewing and revising regulatory actions by other federal agencies. Some charged that OIRA frequently overruled decisions by federal agencies in order to please business interests. OMB Director James C. Miller III insisted, however, that the agency's regulatory role was purely "advisory and consultative."

Congress ultimately reauthorized OIRA through fiscal 1989, but lawmakers restricted the agency's oversight functions and made future administrators of the office subject to confirmation by the Senate.

Deaver Lobbying

A House subcommittee investigated the lobbying activities of former White House aide Michael K. Deaver and turned evidence of Deaver's "possible perjury" over to a court-appointed independent counsel. Six Republicans joined subcommittee Democrats in censuring Deaver.

Deaver resigned as Reagan's deputy chief of staff in May 1985 and immediately opened a lucrative public relations firm in Washington, with clients ranging from defense contractors to the governments of Canada, South Korea and Saudi Arabia. Questions about his lobbying contacts with former colleagues still in the White House led to the appointment of an independent counsel to determine whether Deaver violated existing conflict-of-interest laws.

Deaver's activities spurred new conflict-of-interest bills in both the House and Senate, but no legislation reached the floor.

Nominations

The Senate confirmed 411 civilian nominations in 1986. Eight nominations were withdrawn and another 69 remained unconfirmed when the 99th Congress adjourned.

Two members of the Supreme Court — Chief Justice William H. Rehnquist and Associate Justice Antonin Scalia — topped the list of nominees confirmed by the Senate in 1986. The Senate also acted on several controversial nominations to lower courts.

As in previous years, ideological or partisan disputes delayed action on a number of foreign policy nominations. Most of the delays were caused by Sen. Jesse Helms, R-N.C., who had objected to several Reagan nominees and demanded that the administration give appointments to some of his allies instead.

Significant changes in the membership of major regulatory agencies during 1986 included three new members of the Federal Reserve Board. The new members and their previous positions: Manuel H. Johnson, assistant secretary of the Treasury; Wayne D. Angell, Kansas farmer and banker; and H. Robert Heller, senior vice president of the Bank of America. One other Reagan appointee was already sitting on the seven-member board. *(Regulatory agency members, next page)*

Membership of Federal Regulatory Agencies, 1986

Commodity Futures Trading Commission

(Five members appointed for five-year terms; not more than three members from one political party.)

Member	Party	Term Expires	Confirmed by Senate
Susan M. Philips (C)	R	4/13/90	10/16/85
Kalo A. Hineman	R	6/19/91	7/24/86
Fowler C. West	D	4/13/87	10/1/82
William E. Seale	D	4/13/88	11/15/83
Robert R. Davis	R	4/13/89	9/28/84

Consumer Product Safety Commission

(Three members appointed for seven-year terms; not more than two members from one political party.)

Member	Party	Term Expires	Confirmed by Senate
Terrence M. Scanlon (C)	D	10/26/89	7/15/86
Carol G. Dawson	R	10/26/92	11/21/85
Anne Graham	R	10/26/91	12/17/85

Equal Employment Opportunity Commission

(Five members appointed for five-year terms; not more than three members from one political party.)

Member	Party	Term Expires	Confirmed by Senate
Clarence Thomas (C)	R	7/1/91	8/12/86
Rosalie Gaull Silberman	R	7/1/90	5/23/85
Fred W. Alvarez	D	7/1/88	5/11/84
Tony E. Gallegos	D	7/1/89	9/26/84
Vacancy			

Federal Communications Commission

(Five members appointed for five-year terms; not more than three members from one political party.)

Member	Party	Term Expires	Confirmed by Senate
Mark S. Fowler (C)	R	6/30/86†	5/14/81
James H. Quello	D	6/30/91	6/15/84
Mimi Weyforth Dawson	D	6/30/88	6/4/81
Dennis R. Patrick	R	6/30/92	7/19/85
Patricia Diaz Dennis	D	6/30/89	6/13/86

† Member sitting on commission pending presidential action.

Federal Election Commission

(Six members appointed for six-year terms; not more than three members from one political party.)

Member	Party	Term Expires	Confirmed by Senate
Scott E. Thomas (C)	D	4/30/91	10/3/86
Thomas J. Josefiak	R	4/30/91	10/3/86
Joan D. Aikens	R	4/30/89	7/29/83
John W. McGarry	D	4/30/89	7/29/83
Danny Lee McDonald	D	4/30/87	7/1/82
Lee Ann Elliott	R	4/30/87	7/1/82

Federal Energy Regulatory Commission

(Five members appointed for four-year terms; not more than three members from one political party.)

Member	Party	Term Expires	Confirmed by Senate
Martha O. Hesse (C)	R	10/20/87	10/6/86
Anthony G. Sousa	R	10/20/88	10/18/85
Charles G. Stalon	D	10/20/87	6/21/84
Charles A. Trabandt	R	10/20/88	11/1/85
C. M. Naeve	D	10/20/89	11/1/85

Federal Reserve System Governors

(Seven members appointed for 14-year terms; no statutory limitation on political party membership.)

Member	Party	Term Expires	Confirmed by Senate
Paul A. Volcker (C)	D	1/31/92	8/2/79
Manuel H. Johnson	R	1/31/2000	2/5/86
Wayne D. Angell	R	1/31/94	2/5/86
Martha Seger	R	1/31/98	6/13/85
H. Robert Heller	R	1/31/96	8/15/86
2 Vacancies			

Federal Trade Commission

(Five members appointed for seven-year terms; not more than three members from one political party.)

Member	Party	Term Expires	Confirmed by Senate
Daniel Oliver (C)	R	9/25/88	4/16/86
Terry Calvani	R	9/25/90	11/16/83
Patricia P. Bailey	R	9/25/87	6/26/80
Mary L. Azcuenaga	I	9/25/91	3/18/85
Andrew J. Strenio Jr.	D	9/25/89	3/14/86

Interstate Commerce Commission

(Five members appointed for five-year terms; not more than three members from one political party.)

Member	Party	Term Expires	Confirmed by Senate
Heather J. Gradison (C)	R	12/31/88	6/16/82
Paul H. Lamboley	D	12/31/89	3/14/86
Frederic N. Andre	R	12/31/87	3/16/82
Malcolm M. B. Sterrett	R	12/31/87	2/9/82
J. J. Simmons III	D	12/31/90	3/14/86

Nuclear Regulatory Commission

(Five members appointed for five-year terms; not more than three members from one political party.)

Member	Party	Term Expires	Confirmed by Senate
Lando W. Zech Jr. (C)	I	6/30/89	3/5/85
Thomas M. Roberts	R	6/30/90	7/8/85
James K. Asselstine	I	6/30/87	5/13/82
Frederick M. Bernthal	R	6/30/88	8/4/83
Kenneth M. Carr	D	6/30/91	8/9/86

Securities and Exchange Commission

(Five members appointed for five-year terms; not more than three members from one political party.)

Member	Party	Term Expires	Confirmed by Senate
John S. R. Shad (C)	R	6/5/86†	4/8/81
Edward H. Fleischman	R	6/5/87	12/16/85
Charles C. Cox	R	6/5/88	11/18/83
Aulana L. Peters	D	6/5/89	5/22/84
Joseph A. Grundfest	D	6/5/90	10/25/85

† Member sitting on commission pending presidential action.

New Federal Retirement Plan Approved

After almost three years of work and six months of House-Senate conference negotiations, Congress May 22 completed action on legislation (HR 2672 — PL 99-335) to create a new federal retirement system.

A prolonged deadlock between Congress and the White House over the scope and cost of the new system had ended May 14 when administration officials accepted a compromise close to what lawmakers had previously proposed.

The three-tiered plan provided retirement benefits for all civilian employees and postal workers hired after Dec. 31, 1983. More senior workers could either join the new plan or remain under the existing retirement system.

The final version was expected to cost the government about 23 percent of payroll — more than the 20 percent President Reagan wanted, but less than the current 25 percent.

Both Senate and House leaders expressed satisfaction with the new system, which also received strong support from federal employee unions.

"Why should the civil servant be locked into an archaic retirement plan while his counterpart in the private sector or state government participates in plans that provide both retirement security and career flexibility?" asked Sen. William V. Roth Jr., R-Del., chairman of the Governmental Affairs Committee.

A new retirement system became necessary after Congress passed legislation in 1983 (PL 98-21) to bring federal workers hired starting Jan. 1, 1984, into the Social Security system. *(1983 Almanac p. 573)*

To prevent those workers from having to pay Social Security taxes plus 7 percent of their pay for the Civil Service Retirement System (CSRS), Congress temporarily limited their CSRS contribution to 1.3 percent. That temporary measure was extended once but expired April 30. Under HR 2672, it was revived until the new plan took effect Jan. 1, 1987. Both employees and the government could obtain refunds of their added contributions to the CSRS.

Legislative History

Action on the new plan began in October 1985, when the Senate Governmental Affairs Committee approved a version (S 1527 — S Rept 99-166) that would have cut the government's total pension costs from 25 percent of payroll to about 21.9 percent. Instead of passing that bill, the Senate on Nov. 7 attached its provisions to HR 2672, a minor, House-passed bill renaming a mail center in Jersey City, N.J., and honoring Michael McDermott, a postal worker killed in a freak accident at the facility.

The House Post Office and Civil Service Committee approved its own, more costly, proposal (HR 3660) on Nov. 14, but decided to skip floor action and go straight to conference with the Senate over HR 2672. *(1985 Almanac p. 410)*

Conferees began meeting in December and reached agreement on a compromise in May 1986 (H Rept 99-606), but the administration — displeased with the plan's cost — threatened a presidential veto. Administration officials finally agreed to the plan, with only minor changes, on May 14. By that time the government and its workers were each contributing 14 percent of pay to Social Security and CSRS combined because the temporary plan had lapsed.

The Senate approved the compromise bill by voice vote May 20, and the House followed suit May 22, completing congressional action.

Private-Sector Model

The new plan consisted of three major parts: Social Security, a required basic plan to supplement Social Security and an optional tax-deferred savings plan similar to private 401(k) plans.

"Through the three-tier system, we can offer federal employees an opportunity to build an annuity that is specifically suited to them," said Mary Rose Oakar, D-Ohio, chairman of the House Post Office Subcommittee on Compensation and Employee Benefits.

The bill established parallel new systems for members of the Foreign Service and employees of the CIA covered by Social Security. It brought those employees into the new system in a manner consistent with those agencies' own retirement systems.

"We had here a rare opportunity to create a new pension system with the best features found in the private sector," said House Post Office Committee Chairman William D. Ford, D-Mich. Ford also noted that the Congressional Budget Office estimated the new plan would reduce the federal budget deficit by $8.3 billion between 1987, when it took effect, and 1991.

Final Provisions

As signed into law June 6, HR 2672 (PL 99-335) created a new Federal Employees' Retirement System (FERS) and specified that benefits payable under the new plan were in addition to Social Security benefits.

Other major provisions:

Basic Plan Eligibility

- Made eligible for the FERS all federal employees (including congressional staff and employees of Gallaudet College, a federally supported college for the deaf in Washington, D.C.) hired, or rehired after a break in service of more than one year, after Dec. 31, 1983.
- Allowed employees covered by CSRS to join the new system between July 1, 1987, and Dec. 31, 1987.
- Excluded from FERS coverage employees of the Defense Department not paid from appropriated funds, such as clerks in post exchanges, and District of Columbia employees hired after Oct. 1, 1987.
- Made special provisions for members of the Foreign Service, certain employees of the CIA, and members of Congress and congressional staff covered by both Social Security and CSRS.

Vesting, Benefits, Service

- Defined "creditable service" to include civilian service subject to Social Security, military service, service covered by the Federal Employees' Retirement Contribution Temporary Adjustment Act of 1983 (PL 98-168), leaves of absence without pay while serving in the military or receiving worker's compensation, and other leaves of absence of six months or less.

• Provided that post-1956 military service was creditable only if the employee contributed to the retirement fund a sum equal to 3 percent of the employee's military base pay for the period claimed.

• Required that workers complete at least five years of service to receive benefits under the basic plan. However, service for which a refund of contributions had been made was irrevocably forfeited as creditable service.

• Required that benefits under the basic plan be based on the average of an employee's three highest consecutive years of salary. Benefits amounted to 1 percent of salary for each year of service if the employee retired before age 62, or 1.1 percent if the employee had reached age 62 before retiring.

• For the basic plan, required employee contributions of 1.3 percent of pay for 1987, 0.94 percent of pay from 1988 to 1990, and 0.8 percent of pay in 1990 and thereafter. Employees also were required to pay Social Security taxes.

• Allowed employees to retire with unreduced benefits at age 60 with 20 or more years of service, and at age 62 with five or more years of service.

• Allowed employees with 30 or more years of service to retire at age 55 until the year 2003, when the minimum would begin to rise, reaching age 57 in the year 2027.

• Allowed employees with at least 10 years of service to retire at age 55 with reduced benefits.

• Provided that former employees with sufficient service should be entitled to benefits when the employee attained the requisite minimum age to be eligible for immediate retirement.

• Made eligible for immediate, full retirement benefits all employees who were at least age 50 with 20 years or more service, or any age with at least 25 years of service, who were removed from government involuntarily.

• Provided that employees who retired at the minimum age with 30 years' service, at age 60 with 20 years' service, or were involuntarily separated when they attained the minimum retirement age could receive an annuity supplement equal to the Social Security benefit until they became eligible for Social Security on their 62nd birthday. The annuity was subject to the same earnings test as Social Security: It would be reduced by $1 for every $2 earned in excess of a set amount ($5,760 for 1986).

• Provided that except for special cases (including firefighters, law enforcement personnel and air traffic controllers), no cost-of-living adjustment (COLA) would be added to the annuity for retirees under age 62. For retirees aged 62 and over, and for those receiving disability or survivor benefits regardless of age, the COLA would be equal to 1 percentage point less than the rise in the Consumer Price Index (CPI) in years when that rise exceeded 3 percent. In years when the CPI rose by less than 3 percent, the COLA would be the lesser of 2 percent or the actual increase in the CPI.

• Allowed firefighters, air traffic controllers and members of Congress to retire at age 50 with 20 years' service or at any age with 25 years' service. Those individuals, along with congressional staff, were required to contribute an additional 0.5 percent of pay, but would receive benefits equal to 1.7 percent of average pay for the first 20 years of service and 1 percent for additional years.

Optional Thrift Plan

• Allowed employees to contribute as much as 10 percent of annual salary to a tax-deferred thrift plan.

• Allowed employees to join or leave the plan, or modify their participation, during a special open season every six months. Newly hired employees must wait until the second open season to enter the plan.

Legislation cleared Oct. 17 (PL 99-509) delayed availability of the plan until April 1, 1987. *(Details, p. 559)*

• Required each employing agency to contribute 1 percent of salary annually for each worker, regardless of whether the worker chose to make any contributions to the plan.

• In addition, required the government to match the first 3 percent of employee contributions dollar for dollar, and the next 2 percent at the rate of 50 cents on the dollar, for a total of 4 percent. Thus, the government's total contribution could amount to 5 percent of annual pay.

• Allowed employees who elected to remain in the CSRS to contribute 5 percent of pay to the thrift plan, tax-deferred, but they would receive no government matching contribution.

• Provided that employee contributions, employer matching funds and any earnings in the thrift account vest immediately. The automatic 1 percent government contribution would vest after three years of service for career employees or two years for political appointees.

• Allowed employees eligible for benefits under the basic plan to withdraw all funds in their thrift account, or receive an annuity, defer an annuity, or transfer the funds into an Individual Retirement Account (IRA) or any other qualified pension plan.

• Allowed employees who were vested in the basic plan but not yet eligible to retire to exercise the same options, except that no withdrawals could be made until the employee was eligible to receive the deferred annuity under the basic plan.

• Required employees leaving the government who were not vested in the basic plan to transfer thrift-account funds into an IRA or any qualified pension plan.

• Provided that after Jan. 1, 1988, employees could borrow from their own contributions to the thrift account. Loans, subject to approval, could be used for such purposes as purchase of a home, educational expenses, medical expenses or financial hardship.

• Allowed employees to have their thrift-account funds invested in a government securities fund, a fixed-income investment fund or a common stock index investment fund. Twice a year, employees could alter how the funds were distributed.

• Required that for the first five years of the plan, all government contributions — and a declining share of worker contributions — be invested in the government securities fund. Beginning in 1988, workers could shift some of their contributions to the fixed-income fund or a stock-index fund. Starting in 1996, they could put all of their own and the government's contributions into any of the funds.

• Required that contributions made by those covered under CSRS remain in the government securities fund.

• Provided for management of the thrift plan by the Federal Retirement Thrift Investment Board, an off-budget agency with five members to be appointed by the president and confirmed by the Senate for four-year terms. The first board would be appointed by the president for one-year terms not subject to confirmation. After that, one appointment was to be made on the recommendation of the Speaker of the House, one on the recommendation of the Senate majority leader and one on the recommendation of the other four board members.

Survivor Benefits

• Entitled a surviving spouse to a lump sum equal to $15,000 (indexed to CPI) plus the higher of one-half the employee's annual pay or one-half of his or her high-three-year average pay.

• Permitted the lump sum to be collected either as an annuity or over a shorter period.

• Guaranteed the surviving spouse an annuity equal to 50 percent of the employee's accrued unreduced annuity if the deceased employee had 10 years of service.

• Provided that unmarried children up to age 18 (or 22 if still in school, or any age if disabled before age 18) receive an annually adjusted amount, offset by Social Security children's benefits. The amount varied depending on the number of children and whether they were orphaned.

• Provided that survivor benefits vest after 18 months of service.

• Created an optional plan under which, after retirement, an employee could forfeit 10 percent of his or her annuity in order to provide a post-death benefit to a surviving spouse. The post-retirement survivor benefit was 50 percent of the employee's unreduced annuity and a supplement payable to age 60 if the surviving spouse was not eligible for Social Security. If the spouse died first, the employee's full annuity would be restored.

Disability Benefits

• Provided that disability benefits vest after 18 months' service.

• Defined disabled employees as unable, because of disease or injury, to render useful and efficient service in the employee's position. Such "occupationally disabled" employees did not meet the Social Security definition of disabled and were thus not entitled to Social Security benefits.

• Barred from receiving disability benefits any occupationally disabled employee who refused reasonable job offers in the same agency and commuting area, at the same pay grade.

• Set the first-year benefit at 60 percent of average pay, minus any Social Security benefits paid, and set the benefit after the first year at 40 percent of average pay.

• For the totally disabled, offset the disability benefit (40 percent of average pay) by 60 percent of the Social Security benefit payable, resulting in a total income ranging from about 58 percent of average pay for lower-income individuals down to 46 percent for those with higher incomes.

• Required that total income from work performed during the disability period not exceed 80 percent of the former job's current pay level.

• Allowed employees on disability to be required to take physical exams.

• Provided that when the worker reached age 62, his or her annuity be recomputed and the annuitant receive the lesser of the total disability benefit or a recomputed retirement benefit. Years on disability would be counted as years of service in computing the retirement benefit.

Transfers From CSRS

• Allowed employees covered by both Social Security and CSRS to transfer into the new plan between July 1, 1987, and Dec. 31, 1987.

• Counted service both before and after the transfer toward eligibility to retire.

• Counted service before the transfer toward vesting in the government's share of contributions to the thrift plan.

• Provided that rehired individuals vested under CSRS (with five years of service) could transfer into the new plan during the 1987 open season or the first six months following rehire, whichever was later. If separated for more than one year, they could also elect to remain in CSRS.

• Provided that unused sick leave credited as service for benefit computation purposes under CSRS would be the number of days credited at the time of transfer or the date of retirement, whichever was less.

• Provided that unused sick leave would not count as service under FERS.

• Made transfers between plans effective with the first pay period beginning after the date of transfer. Transfers would then be irrevocable.

Effective Dates

• Retroactively extended the interim retirement plan created in 1983 through Dec. 31, 1986.

• Authorized refunds of excess retirement contributions required because of the expiration of the temporary plan on April 30, 1986.

• Authorized "such sums as are necessary" for fiscal 1986 and 1987 to pay the expenses of the Federal Retirement Thrift Investment Board. ▮

Standards Bureau Pay, Funds

Congress Oct. 10 cleared legislation (HR 4354 — PL 99-574) reauthorizing programs in the National Bureau of Standards (NBS) and authorizing a five-year experimental overhaul of that agency's pay system.

The bill authorized $124 million for NBS programs and $2.75 million for the Office of Productivity, Technology and Innovation in fiscal 1987. NBS, part of the Commerce Department, conducted research providing the basis for the nation's measurement systems and offered scientific and technical services to government and private industry.

Background

For over a decade, Congress had been seeking a way to pay federal workers enough to compete with the private sector in attracting and retaining talented personnel. The inflexibility of the federal "general schedule" pay categories, used for the majority of the federal government's workers, restricted efforts to keep federal pay comparable with private-sector levels and reward workers for good performance.

Proponents of changing the system, including Rep. Mary Rose Oakar, D-Ohio, chairman of the Post Office and Civil Service Subcommittee on Compensation and Employee Benefits, cited statistics showing federal pay rates trailing those in the private sector by 20 percent; the rates of mid-level managers and senior executives in the federal government lagged by more than 50 percent. Although a law signed in 1971 (PL 91-656) authorized the president to set federal employees' pay rates based on private industry pay surveys, proponents said the goals were largely unfulfilled. *(Congress and the Nation Vol. III, p. 454)*

The five-year NBS pay reform project combined provisions of a bill (HR 4738) sponsored by Oakar, and a proposal by the Reagan administration based on a pay-for-performance experiment at the China Lake Naval Weapons Center in California.

Pay Experiment

Under the pay-for-performance project cleared by Congress, NBS employees then covered by the 18 General Schedule (GS) pay levels and the five Senior Executive Service pay levels would be covered instead by broad "pay bands," each of which would comprise two or more GS grades. The NBS director would be authorized to make an annual percentage increase of all the pay bands based on surveys of the compensation in the private sector for comparable work.

The director would decide whether to increase an employee's basic pay based on an appraisal of his performance that compared and ranked him and his peers. If the employee received a "fully successful" performance rating, he would receive the full annual percentage increase and maintain his relative position in the pay band. If he did not receive such an evaluation, he could be demoted. In addition, the director would be allowed to grant bonuses to recognize exceptional performance and to aid in recruiting and retaining employees.

NBS Authorizations

The authorization levels in HR 4354 represented a compromise among the House and Senate authorizing committees and Office of Management and Budget (OMB). While the funding levels were below those agreed to in both the House and the Senate, the bill authorized programs that the administration had wanted eliminated or greatly cut.

HR 4354 authorized:

- $36.6 million for measurement research and standards programs.
- $35.9 million for engineering measurement and standards programs, of which $3.47 million was for the Center for Building Technology and $5.4 million for the Center for Fire Research. The administration had proposed eliminating those two programs. OMB agreed not to propose further cuts in the centers in fiscal 1988 or 1989 if Congress approved the lower budget levels.
- $22.8 million for research support activities, of which $6.76 million was for the Technical Competence Fund and $6.5 million was for the design, construction and equipment of a proposed cold neutron research facility.
- $21.2 million for materials science and engineering programs.
- $7.5 million for computer science and technology programs, of which $1 million was for computer security activities.

Legislative Action

The House Science and Technology Committee reported HR 4354 (H Rept 99-617) June 4. The House Post Office and Civil Service Committee reported the bill July 25 (H Rept 99-617, Part II). By voice vote the House Aug. 12 passed HR 4354.

The Senate passed the bill, amended, Oct. 3. The House cleared the bill for the president's signature by agreeing to the Senate's amendment Oct. 10. ▮

Federal Health Benefits

President Reagan Feb. 27 signed legislation (HR 4061 — PL 99-251) revising health insurance benefits for federal employees.

The measure was a stripped-down version of a bill (HR 3384) that Reagan had vetoed on Jan. 17. *(Veto, 1985 Almanac p. 422)*

The House passed the revised bill by voice vote Feb. 3; the Senate followed suit two days later, completing congressional action.

The measure authorized federal retirees still enrolled in the federal health insurance program to receive refunds from excess reserves that insurance companies had built up in the Federal Employees Health Benefits Program. Current employees were already authorized to receive the rebate, which 11 insurance firms were to offer in 1986.

Reagan did not object to this section of the earlier version of the bill. However, the president opposed another provision that would have eliminated the 75 percent cap on the government's share of federal workers' health premiums. The president also objected to a provision requiring employees' health insurance to reimburse nurses and nurse-midwives directly without requiring supervision or referral by a physician. Those two provisions were not included in the new bill.

Insurance rebate provisions substantially similar to those in HR 4061 were also included in budget reconciliation legislation cleared March 20 (HR 3128 — PL 99-272). Language eliminating the 75 percent cap was deleted from that bill as well. *(Reconciliation, p. 555)* ▮

Anti-Kickback Bill Cleared

The Senate Oct. 15 cleared legislation (S 2250 — PL 99-634) tightening prohibitions against kickbacks by subcontractors seeking government work.

S 2250 was aimed at eliminating kickbacks — illicit payments made in return for favored treatment — by subcontractors who pay off prime contractors doing business with the federal government in return for sending business or information their way.

Investigations conducted in 1985 and 1986 by the Senate Governmental Affairs Oversight Subcommittee revealed rampant bribery and kickbacks by defense subcontractors.

Although payoffs to induce a prime contractor to grant a subcontract, or to reward him for doing so, were illegal under existing law, payoffs for other improper purposes — such as for information about a competitor's bid — were not addressed.

The Senate panel found that subcontractors were undeterred by relatively toothless penalties in the 1946 law then governing contractor fraud. The bill's supporters complained that the law, which had not been amended in 25 years, was antiquated and riddled with loopholes.

In hearings on the legislation in the House and Senate, representatives from the Defense and Justice departments and the U.S. Chamber of Commerce backed the efforts to reform the anti-kickback law.

Provisions

As cleared by Congress, S 2250 expanded the number of actions that constituted misconduct under the 1946 anti-kickback law in order to close that and other loopholes.

The bill increased criminal penalties for those who knowingly and willfully participated in kickbacks from a maximum of two years' imprisonment and a $10,000 fine to a maximum of 10 years' imprisonment and a $250,000 fine for individuals and a $500,000 fine for corporations.

In addition, S 2250:

- Broadened the definition of a kickback to include the payment, acceptance and inclusion of a kickback in the costs of the contract.
- Imposed civil penalties for those who knowingly engaged in kickbacks of twice the amount of the violation and a fine of up to $10,000 for each kickback. Under existing law, the civil penalties called merely for recovery of the cost of the kickback.
- Set the statute of limitations for civil actions under the law at six years.
- Prohibited attempted as well as actual kickbacks, and covered kickbacks in all contracts. Existing law covered only negotiated contracts.
- Allowed the government to withhold the amount of the kickback from money it owed to the contractor on a contract if a kickback occurred on that contract.
- Required prime government contractors to devise procedures to prevent and detect kickbacks, and required prime contractors and subcontractors to report any suspected kickbacks.

Legislative Action

The Senate Governmental Affairs Committee reported S 2250 (S Rept 99-435) Sept. 9. The Senate passed the bill by voice vote Sept. 12.

The House Government Operations Committee Sept. 23 by voice vote approved a similar bill (HR 4783 — H Rept 99-964, Part I). The full House passed it by voice vote Oct. 7, first as HR 4783, then as S 2250. The Senate cleared the bill Oct. 15 by accepting House amendments. ▮

Curbs on Chauffeured Cars

The House Oct. 15 cleared a bill (HR 3614 — PL 99-550) that would sharply restrict the number of federal employees entitled to what one senator called "the ultimate status symbol for a federal bureaucrat" — home-to-office use of government vehicles.

The bill spelled out a limited number of top-level federal employees eligible for home-to-work transportation. It governed the executive branch as well as the judicial branch and legislative support agencies, such as the Government Accounting Office (GAO), the Congressional Budget Office and the Government Printing Office.

Background

Since 1946, federal law had ostensibly prohibited use of government-owned or leased vehicles to travel from home to work and back, with limited exceptions. But each agency had interpreted the law for itself, and, according to Sen. William Proxmire, D-Wis., most routinely ignored its limits.

A June 1985 GAO study found that of the 128 employees then enjoying government transportation to and from work, nearly two-thirds (79) were not entitled to it.

"While the law has always been quite clear to Chairman [Jack] Brooks [D-Texas] of the House Government Operations Committee and myself, apparently there is not a bureaucrat in town who finds the statute clear," Proxmire told the Senate Oct. 10.

"They have been particularly adept at finding, or creating, loopholes large enough to accommodate a federal car."

Provisions

As cleared, HR 3614 authorized home-to-work transportation for the following federal employees:

- The president and vice president.
- The 13 Cabinet secretaries and the U.S. trade representative, and one principal deputy for each of those officials.
- Up to 10 other federal agency employees.
- The deputy secretary and under secretaries of defense.
- The secretaries of each military branch and the commandant of the Coast Guard.
- The Joint Chiefs of Staff.
- Up to six White House employees.
- The directors of the CIA and the FBI.
- Principal diplomatic and consular officials abroad.
- The U.S. representative to the United Nations.
- The Federal Reserve Board chairman.
- The comptroller general, who was the head of the GAO, and the postmaster general.

The bill also:

- Required the head of the General Services Administration to consult with representatives from the three branches of government and then to write binding, governmentwide rules on special circumstances when a federal employee other than those enumerated could use government vehicles for home-to-work transportation.
- In cases of "a clear or present danger," an emergency or other compelling conditions, permitted agency heads to authorize home-to-work transportation for up to 90 days to employees other than those enumerated in the bill. The bill stressed that comfort and convenience were not sufficiently compelling conditions.
- Required each federal agency to keep logs of its vehicles' use.

Legislative History

The House Government Operations Committee reported HR 3614 (H Rept 99-451) Dec. 19, 1985. The House passed the bill by voice vote March 4, 1986.

The House version of the bill covered only executive agencies. However, Proxmire and Senate Governmental Affairs Chairman William V. Roth Jr., R-Del., worked with Brooks and representatives from GAO and the executive branch to produce a revised version of HR 3614 that also applied to the judicial branch and legislative support offices.

The Senate passed the amended version of HR 3614 by voice vote Oct. 10. By voice vote the House agreed to the Senate's amendments Oct. 15, thus clearing the measure for the president. ▮

Veterans Memorial, Charter

Legislation to establish a Korean War veterans memorial (HR 2205 — PL 99-499) and to approve the charter of the Vietnam Veterans of America (S 8 — PL 99-318) was approved during the second session of the 99th Congress.

Congress Oct. 14 cleared HR 2205 authorizing construction of a memorial in Washington, D.C., or its suburbs in honor of members of the U.S. armed forces who served in the Korean War in 1950-53.

The bill authorized the American Battle Monuments Commission to spend up to $1 million in planning and construction funds for the memorial, which was expected to cost $4 million to $4.5 million. It specified that the construction funding could not be allocated until sufficient private funds had been collected to complete the memorial and provide for its maintenance.

The House Administration Committee reported HR 2205 Oct. 29, 1985 (H Rept 99-341). The House passed the bill Nov. 4, 1985. The Senate Energy and Natural Resources Committee reported the bill Sept. 19, 1986 (S Rept 99-459). The Senate passed HR 2205, amended, Oct. 9. The House agreed to Senate amendments Oct. 14.

During House debate, Bill Frenzel, R-Minn., a Korean War veteran, objected to the Senate amendment authorizing $1 million in federal funds for the memorial, noting that the Vietnam War Memorial was constructed entirely from privately raised funds. *(1985 Almanac p. 408)*

In a related action, the House June 11 rejected a bill (HR 2591) to award gold medals to three Vietnam veterans who led efforts to build the Vietnam Memorial: Jan Scruggs, Robert Doubek and John Wheeler. Considered under suspension of the rules, the bill failed on a 224-186 vote, 50 short of the two-thirds majority required. *(Vote 139, p. 44-H; background 1985 Almanac p. 271)*

Vietnam Veterans Charter

By voice vote the House May 12 cleared for the president a bill (S 8 — PL 99-318) to grant a federal charter to the Vietnam Veterans of America Inc. (VVA), despite objections of conservative Republicans who claimed the organization's leadership had interfered in U.S. foreign policy initiatives in Southeast Asia.

The bill had been held up for more than a year by a handful of senators who charged that VVA activities, including the laying of a wreath at the grave of North Vietnamese leader Ho Chi Minh by VVA President Robert E. Muller, should preclude it from receiving official congressional recognition. The logjam was broken when Jeremiah Denton, R-Ala., a former prisoner of war in Vietnam, withdrew his objections after meetings with Muller. Denton said Muller and other VVA leaders had "realized the past errors."

The Senate Judiciary Committee reported the bill March 26 (S Rept 99-268). The Senate by a vote of 94-3 April 9 passed the measure. Voting against the measure were North Carolina Republicans Jesse Helms and John P. East, and Wyoming Republican Malcolm Wallop. *(Vote 52, p. 11-S)*

The House Judiciary Committee discharged the bill and the full House passed it, clearing it for the president, May 12.

A similar bill had been introduced in the 98th Congress but failed to gain Senate approval. *(1984 Almanac p. 504)* ∎

Former Presidents

Congress May 13 cleared a bill (HR 1349 — PL 99-323) to defray the cost to the government of future presidential libraries. But it failed to complete action on a second measure (S 1047 — S Rept 99-349) that would have limited Secret Service protection and office and staff allowances for former chief executives.

Under HR 1349, private foundations that raised funds for construction of presidential libraries must have established an endowment equal to 20 percent of building costs to help cover operational expenses, which currently were paid entirely by the federal government. Operating costs for the seven existing presidential libraries totaled about $14.6 million in fiscal 1986. The measure also limited the size of libraries to 70,000 square feet, with costs for additional space to be picked up by private funding.

At President Reagan's insistence, the cost-sharing and size limits did not apply to his library, planned for Stanford University.

The bill to limit major perquisites for former presidents, S 1047, would have ended the existing guarantee of lifelong Secret Service protection, limiting it to five years in most cases, and would have placed a ceiling on former presidents' office and staff allowances. The cost to taxpayers of maintaining protection and offices for former presidents mounted steadily in the years since such benefits began, from $160,000 in fiscal year 1959 to $12.56 million in fiscal 1985.

Background

The first presidential library was devised by President Franklin D. Roosevelt to deal with the neglect and loss of presidential papers and records. The Roosevelt library was created through special legislation enacted in 1939. The Presidential Libraries Act of 1955 provided the statutory basis for all subsequent presidential libraries.

Federal compensation for former presidents dated from 1958, when Congress passed a law establishing a pension for former presidents, a pension for their surviving spouses, free mailing privileges for non-political mail, and an allowance for office and staff. In 1965, in the wake of the assassination of President John F. Kennedy, Congress added Secret Service protection to the list of benefits provided to former presidents; in 1968, Secret Service protection was extended to include their spouses, surviving spouses and minor children.

Supporters of S 1047 stressed the absence of threats to former presidents or their families, and cited examples of excessive and unnecessary service. They noted that in March 1985, former President Richard M. Nixon dropped his detail of Secret Service protection to save the government money.

Library Cost Curbs

The House passed HR 1349 in 1985. The Senate Governmental Affairs Committee amendments included a limitation on library size to 70,000 square feet. The committee reported its version March 7, 1986 (S Rept 99-257). The Senate passed the bill March 21. The House by voice vote accepted Senate amendments May 13. *(House action, 1985 Almanac p. 414)*

Presidential Perks Limit

The Senate Governmental Affairs Committee reported S 1047 July 31 (S Rept 99-349). The Senate passed the bill Aug. 15. Passage of S 1047 marked the first time the Senate successfully acted to limit allowances and protection for ex-presidents.

Companion legislation in the House (HR 1236, HR 2113) was bogged down by a multiple referral to four committees that shared jurisdiction over limiting presidential perks.

The House in 1985 voted 199-162 to tack on a Nelson,

D-Fla., amendment to the Treasury Department appropriations bill, to limit office and staff allowances to former presidents. The amendment, which contained the same formula as the one in S 1047, was dropped in conference. *(1985 Almanac p. 331)*

Constitution Bicentennial

Congress Oct. 10 cleared for the president a bill (HR 3559 — PL 99-549) to make some changes in the law that established the Commission on the Bicentennial of the Constitution. The commission was authorized in 1983 (PL 98-101) to organize the commemoration of the 200th anniversary of the Constitution. *(1983 Almanac p. 324)*

The House Post Office and Civil Service Committee reported HR 3559 April 14 (H Rept 99-530, Part I). The House passed the legislation June 24 by a 409-7 vote. By voice vote the Senate passed an amended version Oct. 6, and the House agreed to the Senate amendment Oct. 10. *(House vote 172, p. 52-H)*

The bill raised the ceiling on annual contributions to the 23-member commission from $25,000 to $250,000 for private donors and from $100,000 to $1,000,000 for corporate donors. It also authorized the commission to adopt a seal and a logo, and gave it permission to market the logo as it saw fit. It exempted the commission from federal hiring laws in its hiring of support staff.

HR 3559 also extended the life of the commission by two years, from 1989 to 1991, and extended authorizations for appropriations until 1991.

Congressional approval of HR 3559 came at a time when the Bicentennial Commission had attracted unaccustomed public attention. Chief Justice Warren E. Burger June 17 announced his retirement from the Supreme Court, saying he wanted to devote his full time and attention to his role as the commission's chairman. *(Burger retirement, p. 70)*

One of the goals of the commission was to declare Sept. 17, 1987, as "Constitution Day," a legal public holiday. Legislation (S 2216) to establish the holiday passed the Senate Oct. 8 but failed in the House. *(1984 Almanac p. 422)*

Rose: National Floral Emblem

The House Sept. 23 tackled a thorny issue when it cleared a resolution (S J Res 159 — PL 99-449) declaring the rose the "national floral emblem." The measure was reported Sept. 18 by the House Post Office and Civil Service Committee (H Rept 99-836).

Approval of the resolution, which was passed by the Senate in 1985, brought to a close decades of debate over whether a national flower should be named — and if so, which one. *(1985 Almanac p. 422)*

In the previous 20 years alone, more than 70 resolutions were introduced to designate a national flower, naming such candidates as the mountain laurel, dogwood and corn tassel. The most determined campaign was waged by Everett McKinley Dirksen, R-Ill. (House 1933-49; Senate 1951-69), who fought in vain for the marigold.

Rep. Lindy (Mrs. Hale) Boggs, D-La., leading House backer of the rose resolution, said the flower was worthy of national status because "it is grown in every state of the union, including Alaska, and the rose has become a part of many of our country's official ceremonies."

Backers of the resolution also cited opinion polls showing public support for the rose and noted that fossil evidence indicated that the flower had been native to America for over 35 million years.

Indian Bill Veto

President Reagan Sept. 26 vetoed a bill, HR 3247, that would have reauthorized for fiscal 1987-90 programs that provided grants and contracts to promote economic and social self-sufficiency among American Indians, Alaskan Natives and Native Hawaiians. The programs, created by the 1974 Native American Programs Act, were run by the Administration for Native Americans (ANA), an agency within the Department of Health and Human Services.

The president's reasons for vetoing the bill were unrelated to the substance of the programs, whose objectives and funding he supported. Rather, Reagan objected to new provisions added to the 1974 act that would have revised the process for applying for program grants, and would have imposed new requirements for ANA to receive public comment in its rulemaking procedures.

In his message, Reagan called the new procedural requirements "wasteful and unnecessary," saying, "They would inevitably involve both the Congress and members of the public in second-guessing the ANA on details related to administration of Native American programs." *(Text of veto message, p. 27-D)*

Congress made no effort to override Reagan's veto. Instead, the programs were reauthorized and funded for fiscal 1987 by the continuing appropriations resolution (H J Res 738 — PL 99-591). Reagan suggested such a move in his veto message. *(Continuing resolution, p. 219)*

The House passed HR 3247 (H Rept 99-539) by voice vote April 21, authorizing "such sums as may be necessary" to carry out the programs over the four fiscal years; the Congressional Budget Office estimated a four-year total of $132.7 million. Congress cleared the bill Sept. 11 when the Senate, also by voice vote, passed it unchanged.

Gay Head Indian Land Claim

The House Oct. 7 passed a controversial bill (HR 2868 — H Rept 99-918) authorizing $1.5 million toward a settlement of land claims by a tribe of Massachusetts Indians on the island of Martha's Vineyard.

The bill, passed 217-172, would have resolved several lawsuits over the status of some 240 acres of land currently held by the town of Gay Head, and another 185 acres, held by private parties, that had been claimed by the Wampanoag Indians as historically theirs. The Reagan administration opposed the bill, calling the land claim invalid. *(Vote 402, p. 114-H)*

The Senate passed HR 2868 Oct. 18 after substituting the text of a measure reported by its Select Indian Affairs Committee (S 1452 — S Rept 99-528) Oct. 3. But the Senate and House failed to resolve differences between the two versions, and the legislation died at adjournment.

As passed by the House, HR 2868 would have established a $3 million fund within the U.S. Treasury to permit the Indians to implement a settlement reached among the parties involved in the claims. Under the agreement, the money — $1.5 million provided by the United States and $1.5 million matched by the commonwealth of Massachusetts — would be used to finance the purchase of the privately held property and return it to the Indians. The House Interior Committee added an amendment, designed to placate administration objections, providing that the settlement would become effective only if the Interior secretary granted federal recognition to the Wampanoag Indian Tribe.

The bill included the provisions of two other measures previously passed by the House, which were added on the floor as an amendment by John McCain, R-Ariz. The bills, whose inclusion was agreed to by adopting McCain's amendment by voice vote, would have streamlined the procedures for Indian tribes and groups to be contractors under the 1974 Indian Self-Determination Act (HR 4174 — H Rept 99-761, passed Aug. 11 by voice vote), and provided the Interior secretary with guidelines on the approval or disapproval of tribal constitutions or amendments to such constitutions (HR 1915 — H Rept 99-866, passed Sept. 23 by voice vote).

'Whistleblower' Protection

The House Sept. 22 by voice vote passed legislation reaffirming congressional support for federal employees who reveal waste, fraud and abuse in government. The Senate did not act on the bill, however, and the measure died when Congress adjourned.

The bill (HR 4033, H Rept 99-859) was aimed at reversing a perceived hostility toward whistleblowers on the part of the very office responsible for protecting them. The Office of Special Counsel of the Merit Systems Protection Board (MSPB) was created by the 1978 civil service reorganization law (PL 95-454) to receive and investigate employees' allegations of mismanagement, illegality and waste in the government. *(1978 Almanac p. 818)*

HR 4033 would have amended the 1978 law to establish the Office of Special Counsel as an entity outside the MSPB. The office's primary role would be "to protect employees, especially whistleblowers."

K. William O'Connor, the head of the special counsel's office from 1982 to June 1986, had been blamed by federal workers and committee members for intimidating potential whistleblowers and doing little to assist actual ones.

HR 4033 would have circumvented the problem of intractable appointees to that office by permitting employees to petition the MSPB directly — instead of going through the special counsel — to seek corrective action.

Freedom of Information

The Senate did not act on a House-passed bill (HR 4862 — H Rept 99-832) that would have made it easier for businesses to block the release of trade secrets under the Freedom of Information Act (FOIA).

As passed by voice vote of the House Sept. 22, HR 4862 added a procedure for businesses to request that information they filed with the government be exempted from FOIA disclosure rules. Firms would be required to claim an exemption from FOIA disclosure when they supplied the sensitive information to the government. If someone later requested the information, the government agency would have five working days to notify the organization, after which the company would have 10 days to object.

The agency would have another 10 days to decide whether to release the information and to notify the firm of its decision. The time limits would be shortened if the organization or person requesting the information met certain qualifications for expedited consideration.

Under existing law, government agencies decided for themselves what constituted trade secrets or confidential material, and whether that material should be exempted from FOIA's disclosure requirements. Agencies were not required to notify a company when a request for information was made. *(Previous FOIA revision bill, 1984 Almanac p. 181)*

Small Business Programs

A three-year reauthorization of the Small Business Administration (SBA) was included in the fiscal 1986 deficit-reduction bill cleared March 20 (HR 3128 — PL 99-272).

HR 3128, known as a "reconciliation" bill, was intended to cut existing programs to achieve fiscal 1986 budget targets. The bill had emerged from conference in December 1985 but did not clear until 1986. *(Legislative history, p. 555)*

Conferees on the bill rejected the Reagan administration's efforts to kill the SBA, but they eliminated some programs and sharply trimmed funding for others. *(Background, 1985 Almanac p. 412)*

HR 3128 abolished general direct loans to small businesses, retaining only those targeted to the handicapped, disabled and Vietnam War veterans, and minorities. In addition, the bill barred farmers from receiving disaster loans beginning in fiscal 1986 and dropped a non-physical disaster loan program that had been used to assist firms along the Mexican border that suffered financial loss because of the devaluation of the peso.

Provisions. As signed into law April 7, the small business provisions of HR 3128:

- Reauthorized the SBA through fiscal 1988 and set spending authority at $515 million in 1986, $605 million in 1987 and $634 million in 1988. The fiscal 1985 authorization was $700.3 million.
- Authorized such sums as necessary for disaster loans for the three fiscal years, eliminating the $500 million annual ceiling.
- Abolished general direct loans that had been available to any small business and eliminated direct loans for solar and energy conservation.
- Reduced direct loans for the remaining special small business programs from $257 million authorized in fiscal 1985 to $101 million in fiscal 1986, rising to $111 million in 1987 and $116 million in 1988.

The bill earmarked $15 million each year for firms owned by the handicapped, $20 million each year for those owned by Vietnam and disabled veterans, and $41 million for minority enterprises.

In addition, for firms located in areas of high unemployment or low income, direct loans were set at $25 million, $35 million and $40 million in fiscal 1986-88, respectively.

- Established total loan guarantees at $3.221 million in fiscal 1986, $3.395 million in 1987 and $3.517 million in 1988. That included guarantees for debentures issued by Small Business Investment Corporations (SBICs) of $250 million in fiscal 1986, $261 million in 1987 and $272 million in 1988.
- Authorized loan guarantees of $1.05 million in fiscal 1986, $1.096 million in 1987 and $1.142 million in 1988 for the surety bonds of small business contractors and subcontractors.
- Set guarantees for pollution-control bonds at $75 million each year.
- Required the SBA to utilize all available loan guarantee authority.
- Reduced the maximum guarantee on loans of $155,000 or more from 90 percent to 85 percent and left the maximum guarantee of loans for less at 90 percent.
- Increased the fee that borrowers paid for loan guarantees from 1 percent of the loan to 2 percent.
- Prohibited the Federal Financing Bank from purchasing securities issued by SBICs, in effect requiring SBICs to sell securities on the private market.
- Barred farmers from getting disaster loans, with the exception of applicants qualified during fiscal 1985.
- Eliminated non-physical disaster loans, which in the past had provided compensation for border businesses hurt by devaluation of the peso.
- Established criminal penalties of a $50,000 fine and up to five years' imprisonment for misrepresentation made in writing.
- Authorized a pilot program of selling debentures issued by capital development companies to the private market in fiscal 1986 and 1987. ▮

Debt Collection

President Reagan Oct. 28 signed a bill (S 209 — PL 99-578) allowing the federal government to use private law firms to help it collect its debts.

Congress completed action on S 209 Oct. 8 when the Senate accepted the version of the bill passed by the House Sept. 29. The House had passed S 209 by voice vote after substituting the text of its own measure (HR 5541 — H Rept 99-909). The Senate originally passed its version (S Rept 99-256) March 19 on a 95-1 vote. *(Vote 42, p. 8-S)*

The bill authorized a three-year pilot program in which the Justice Department could hire private attorneys to bring legal action to recover overdue student loans and other debts owed the government.

A 1982 law (PL 97-365) permitted federal agencies to contract with private firms to collect overdue loans, but private collectors could not bring legal action against those who refused to pay. *(Background, 1982 Almanac p. 520; 1984 Almanac p. 187)*

The program was designed to chip away at Justice's enormous backlog of cases — estimated at 95,000 and growing. The backlog had cost taxpayers up to $15.3 million a day because Justice had been unable to sue for recovery of debts before the statute of limitations ran out. According to the Office of Management and Budget, the government was owed about $23.6 billion in non-tax delinquent debt at the end of fiscal 1985. ▮

FY '86 Deficit Bill Changes

The fiscal 1986 deficit-reduction bill cleared March 20 (HR 3128 — PL 99-272) made several changes in programs involving federal employees, mail subsidies and other general government programs.

HR 3128, known as a "reconciliation" bill, aimed to cut existing programs to meet targets set in the fiscal 1986 budget resolution. The bill had emerged from conference in December 1985 but cleared only after three months of further Senate-House negotiations in 1986. *(Details, p. 555; fiscal 1987 reconciliation changes, p. 559)*

Federal Employees

Some important issues affecting federal workers, most notably pay raises and refunds to federal employees and the government of excess health insurance premiums, were dealt with in other measures when it seemed that HR 3128 might never be enacted.

A provision included in the conference report to eliminate the 75 percent cap on the share of federal employee health insurance premiums paid by the government was dropped during negotiations on the bill in early 1986, when a similar provision in HR 3384, a bill making changes in federal employee health programs, prompted a presidential veto.

As signed into law April 7, HR 3128 retained provisions that:

- Froze the pay of civilian federal employees in fiscal 1986, and assumed pay increases in fiscal 1987 and 1988 of up to 5 percent. Pay increases would be determined by a recommendation of the president, as under existing law, but future raises would be delayed until after Jan. 1 of each year.
- Required the Office of Personnel Management to determine the minimum level of necessary reserves for the Federal Employees Health Benefits Program (FEHBP), the health insurance system for civilian federal workers, and required private insurers to refund excess premiums to the FEHBP fund. Refunds would be passed on to employees and the government; the government was authorized to use its portion of the refunds to fund its share of premiums.

The provisions were substantially the same as ones included in HR 4061 (PL 99-251), signed by Reagan Feb. 27. *(Story, p. 318)*

- Permanently changed the annual hours on which federal pay was determined to 2,087 from 2,080. A two-year pilot program showed that the 2,087-hour basis allowed wage rates to be calculated more precisely.
- Prevented part-time employees from switching to full-time work for their last few years of service and thereby qualifying for full-time pension benefits.
- Prohibited any pay rate reduction for certain federal employees in Tucson, Ariz., during fiscal 1986. This amendment was included at the request of Sen. Dennis DeConcini, D-Ariz., to cushion the blow for a group of federal employees who faced a 10 percent wage cut because the area's sagging copper industry skewed downward a prevailing-wage survey conducted in 1985.

Postal Service

HR 3128 limited the fiscal 1986 postal subsidy for non-profit and other "preferred rate" mailers to $749 million and delayed until Jan. 1, 1986, any increase in postage rates for non-profit organizations. Both of these provisions were independently enacted in the fiscal 1986 continuing appropriations resolution (H J Res 465 — PL 99-190). *(1985 Almanac p. 360)*

The bill also:

- Eliminated the second-class "limited circulation" rate that allowed publications with circulations of less than 5,000 that mailed outside their county of origin to obtain a reduced rate. This was expected primarily to affect resort-area newspapers and very small special-interest publications.
- Eliminated the use of the subsidized in-county rate for publications whose circulation within the county of origin was less than half their total circulation, unless the publication's total circulation was under 10,000.

Under existing law, major national magazines were able to obtain the subsidized rate for the county with their highest circulation by declaring it their county of origin.

- Limited to 10 percent of the annual number of copies mailed to subscribers the number of ad-oriented publications sent to non-subscribers at the subsidized in-county rate.
- Directed the Postal Rate Commission to study the amount of subsidized second-, third- and fourth-class mail that consisted primarily of advertising of merchandise or services. The study also was to examine the use of subsidized rates in general and the method by which postal subsidies were calculated. The commission had agreed to conduct the study earlier in 1986 and it was already under way.

Motor Vehicle Fleet

HR 3128 required the General Services Administration and the Office of Management and Budget to improve government motor vehicle fleet management with the goal of reducing the cost by $150 million by fiscal 1988 from their fiscal 1986 budget request. Postal Service, Postal Rate Commission and Tennessee Valley Authority vehicles and other government special purpose vehicles would be exempt. ∎

Means Test on Vets' Care

In clearing omnibus fiscal 1986 deficit-reduction legislation March 20 (HR 3128 — PL 99-272), Congress mandated for the first time a means test for free medical care under programs of the Veterans Administration (VA). The new means test did not apply to veterans with service-connected disabilities or to certain other veterans, who were entitled to free hospital care without regard to income.

Conferees on HR 3128 dropped a House provision that would have required a Medicare-participating hospital to accept the beneficiaries of VA hospital care programs.

As reported by the conferees, the bill had included a 3.1 percent increase in payments to disabled veterans and their dependents. This provision was dropped after it was enacted separately in HR 1538 (PL 99-238). *(1985 Almanac p. 408)*

HR 3128 was designed to change various laws to meet requirements of the fiscal 1986 budget resolution. Although conferees filed their report in December 1985, additional Senate-House negotiations were needed to determine the final shape of the bill. *(Legislative history, p. 555)*

Provisions. As signed into law April 7, HR 3128 made the following changes in veterans' programs:

- Entitled free VA hospital care to veterans with incomes of less than $15,000 and with no dependents. For veterans with one dependent, the income threshold would be $18,000.
- Provided that veterans with incomes between $15,000 and $20,000 (or between $18,000 and $25,000, if they had dependents) would be eligible for VA hospital care if facilities were available. Though the bill said that the VA administrator "may" provide free care to veterans in this category, conferees emphasized that the VA had no discretion to withhold free medical care for these veterans if facilities were available.
- Provided that veterans with incomes of more than $20,000 ($25,000 if they had dependents), would be entitled to VA hospital care if they agreed to make certain payments. For the first 90 days of a hospital stay, the payment would be the lower of the cost of care or the deductible amount that would have to be paid by a Medicare beneficiary — currently $492.

Veterans with incomes above the $20,000 limit also were required to make some payments for nursing home care and for outpatient treatment and home health care that previously was paid for entirely by the VA.

For nursing home care, the veteran would have to pay, in any one-year period, the lower of the cost of care or the Medicare deductible.

For outpatient care, the veteran would have to pay 20 percent of the average cost of an outpatient visit, provided that those payments did not exceed the Medicare deductible in any 90-day period.

- Provided that the various income thresholds would increase annually by the percentage by which VA pensions were increased.
- Increased from $600 to $2,500 the amount that could be spent on structural modifications to the home of any veteran rated as more than 50 percent disabled.
- Entitled the VA to recover the cost of medical care for a veteran from any private insurance plan under which the veteran was covered, up to the level of the "prevailing rate." ∎

Veterans' Benefit Programs

Congress Oct. 8 cleared a catchall bill (HR 5299 — PL 99-576) increasing veterans' disability compensation by 1.5 percent and making other changes in veterans' programs.

The House Aug. 4 passed HR 5299 (H Rept 99-730) with a 2 percent cost-of-living adjustment (COLA) for veterans disabled by service-connected causes. The bill also exempted certain veterans' benefits and programs from automatic across-the-board cuts, or "sequestrations," triggered by the Gramm-Rudman-Hollings anti-deficit law (PL 99-177).

Because the Senate Budget Committee objected to some of the exemptions, the House agreed to drop permanent sequestration exemptions for the Veterans Administration (VA) home loan program and for certain educational assistance programs. As cleared, HR 5299 exempted the education aid program for one year only.

The Senate Sept. 30 passed the bill after amending it

to incorporate the text of S 2422 (S Rept 99-444), which included a COLA equal to that received by Social Security beneficiaries. Senators also tacked on several other bills that the House had passed.

The House changed the COLA to 1.5 percent, made minor revisions in the omnibus bill and passed it Oct. 7. The Senate agreed to the changes, and cleared HR 5299 Oct. 8. All action was by voice vote.

Major Provisions

As cleared by Congress, HR 5299:

- Provided a 1.5 percent COLA in VA disability and survivors' benefits, effective Dec. 1, 1986, to veterans disabled due to service-connected causes, their widows and children.
- Exempted permanently from Gramm-Rudman sequestrations VA life insurance accounts; two revolving funds (for rehabilitation activities and the canteen service); and benefits for housing adapted for disabled veterans, burial of a veteran who died from a service-connected disability, and automobile and adaptive equipment for severely disabled veterans.
- Exempted for one year from Gramm-Rudman sequestrations educational aid programs for disabled veterans, their survivors and dependents.
- Prohibited hiring discrimination against a member of the National Guard or the reserves. The House had passed the provision as a separate bill (HR 2798 — H Rept 99-626) June 17, 409-0. *(Vote 151, p. 48-H)*
- Extended the federal "veterans' readjustment appointment" (VRA) authority from Sept. 30, 1986, to Dec. 31, 1989. The VRA was a hiring preference that permitted Vietnam-era veterans to win federal jobs without taking competitive exams.

The House June 17 passed a VRA extension (HR 4384 — H Rept 99-627) that would have extended the authority through Dec. 31, 1991, and eliminated the 14-year limitation on how much education non-disabled veterans could have and still remain exempt from competitive exams. HR 5299 contained a simple extension, making no change in the 14-year limit. *(Background, 1974 Almanac p. 592)*

- Added frostbite and trauma-induced arthritis to the list of medical conditions which, if they proved to be debilitating, could be presumed to be service-connected if contracted by veterans who were prisoners of war for at least 30 days. Such veterans thus would be eligible for VA treatment. This provision was drawn from a somewhat broader bill (HR 4333 — H Rept 99-728) that was passed by the House on Aug. 6.
- Allowed the secretary of the Army to set aside an area in Arlington National Cemetery and erect memorials or markers to honor members of the armed forces and veterans who were missing in action or whose remains had not been recovered or identified, were buried at sea, were donated to science or were cremated.
- Reauthorized for three years programs for state veterans' home construction, and for contracts and grants for medical care for U.S. veterans in the Philippines.
- Granted authority for three years for the VA to furnish respite care in VA health facilities to chronically ill veterans.
- Authorized the VA administrator, without consulting the attorney general, to engage private attorneys to foreclose on VA home loans and to recover property acquired by the VA.
- Eliminated "gender-based" language distinctions in laws providing veterans' benefits. The House passed this section Aug. 4 as HR 5047 (H Rept 99-735).

Other Veterans' Measures

The fiscal 1986 budget reconciliation bill (HR 3128 — PL 99-272) cleared March 20, for the first time mandated a means test for free medical care under VA programs. The test did not apply to veterans with service-connected disabilities. *(Details, p. 324)*

The House Veterans' Affairs Committee on July 16 killed a bill (HR 585) that would have allowed veterans to go into federal court to appeal adverse claims rulings by the VA. The vote was 20-12.

The Senate had passed companion legislation (S 367) in 1985, but the House committee refused to go along. *(1985 Almanac p. 409)* ▮

OMB Regulatory Review

Reacting to charges that the Office of Management and Budget (OMB) was wrongfully interfering in the federal regulatory process, Congress in 1986 imposed new curbs on OMB's authority to review and revise other agencies' regulatory activities.

The focus of criticism was the Office of Information and Regulatory Affairs (OIRA), a unit of OMB established by the Paperwork Reduction Act of 1980 (PL 96-511). Under executive orders issued by President Reagan in 1981 (No. 12291) and 1985 (No. 12498), OIRA had been reviewing all major regulatory actions of other federal agencies to ensure that they met administration guidelines for cost effectiveness. *(Congress and the Nation Vol. V, p. 849)*

OMB Director James C. Miller III maintained that OMB's regulatory role was purely "advisory and consultative." But others said that because of OMB's power over agency budgets and personnel, its recommendations took on the air of requirements.

Critics charged that OIRA had become a regulatory czar, frequently overruling decisions by federal agencies. Some suggested that OMB, eager to pursue Reagan's oft-stated goal of reducing the burden of regulation on industry, gave business lobbyists an exclusive, off-the-record chance to reargue battles lost at the agency level.

The House, where OIRA had come under increasingly heavy attack, voted to deny $5.4 million in fiscal 1987 appropriations for the regulatory unit. The Senate refused to go along, however, and funding was included in the final version of the omnibus continuing appropriations resolution (H J Res 738 — PL 99-591).

The final version of the continuing resolution reauthorized OIRA through fiscal 1989 at a funding level of $5.5 million annually. But it made future heads of OIRA subject to confirmation by the Senate. And it restricted OIRA's oversight functions to the "sole purpose" of reviewing information-collection requests contained in another agency's proposed rule or regulation. *(Story, p. 193)*

Broader legislation (S 2230 — S Rept 99-347) to restructure OMB was reported by the Senate Governmental Affairs Committee July 31. The full Senate never considered the measure, which also would have required confirmation of OIRA administrators. Senate complaints about OIRA eased after OIRA Administrator Wendy Lee Gramm in June announced new policies to increase public disclosure of the office's rulemaking activities. ▮

Shuttle Disaster Spurs Space Program Review

The Jan. 28 explosion of the space shuttle *Challenger* touched off the most searching review of the U.S. space program since its inception almost 30 years earlier.

President Reagan Feb. 3 appointed a special commission to investigate the loss of the *Challenger*, which disintegrated during launch Jan. 28, killing all seven crew members. *(Astronaut deaths, p. 327)*

He also brought back James C. Fletcher, 66, to head the National Aeronautics and Space Administration (NASA). Fletcher had served as NASA's administrator from 1971 to 1977, as the agency was winding down its Apollo program and initiating the space shuttle program.

Congressional committees, meanwhile, began examining the scope, direction and conduct of the entire space program.

Although NASA had many strong defenders on Capitol Hill, the spectacular and deadly failure of the *Challenger* mission revived old complaints by critics in Congress and the scientific community and brought new charges that NASA had been cavalier about safety problems.

The accident forced a postponement of the next shuttle launch until at least 1988, jeopardizing both military and civilian space projects, while NASA engineers struggled to overcome the problems that caused the accident.

It also cost the U.S. program many of its commercial customers, who shifted to the competing Ariane launch system of the European Space Agency.

And it wreaked special havoc on U.S. scientific missions in space, which had already been losing ground to military missions. *(Militarization of space, p. 331)*

By year's end, Congress had voted to transfer $2.4 billion from the Defense Department to NASA to pay for a new orbiter and related equipment to replace the shuttle *Challenger*. The funds were provided in the fiscal 1987 continuing appropriations resolution (H J Res 738 — PL 99-591).

However, Reagan vetoed a fiscal 1987 reauthorization bill for NASA (HR 5495) because he objected to policy changes Congress sought to implement through the measure, including the creation of a National Aeronautics and Space Council to serve as the principal policy-making body within the executive branch for civilian space issues.

Such a move, Reagan said, "would constitute unacceptable interference with my discretion and flexibility in organizing and managing the Executive Office as I consider appropriate." *(Veto message text, p. 35-D)*

Background

The space shuttle program began in 1972, when President Richard M. Nixon formally requested funds to develop a reusable two-stage spacecraft consisting of a booster and an orbiter, leading ultimately to a permanent orbiting space station.

As described by then-NASA chief Fletcher, the shuttle program was to cost between $7 billion and $8 billion for four orbiters that would each carry a cargo weighing up to 65,000 pounds, have a life of 100 flights and return on a conventional runway. The launch rate would be as high as 60 flights a year, with the first flight projected for early 1978.

Things did not turn out that way. The shuttle's first flight was on April 12, 1981, three years late. By 1986, $14.2 billion had been spent on the shuttle program, according to NASA; the nonpartisan Congressional Budget Office (CBO) put the total cost at $18.3 billion (both in 1982 dollars).

Because of persistent problems with the shuttle's engines and unexpected launch stresses, the orbiters could carry only 47,000 pounds each and were expected to last 50 missions at most. Fourteen launches were scheduled for 1986, which was to have been the shuttle's busiest year. Only one was completed — a Jan. 12-18 flight of the *Columbia* that included Rep. Bill Nelson, D-Fla., among its crew of seven. (Nelson chaired the House Science and Technology Subcommittee on Space and represented Florida's 11th District, which included the Kennedy Space Center at Cape Canaveral.)

To amortize burgeoning costs, NASA won a policy commitment to require all U.S. space ventures — military, scientific or commercial — to use the shuttle. Shuttle customers were charged $71 million for a full shuttle cargo bay and the rate was to have been raised to $74 million in 1988.

NASA's Troubles

To supporters and opponents alike, it was evident in the months following the *Challenger* accident that the U.S. space program was in disarray. The destruction of one of the four space shuttles and the accompanying loss of life gave force to longtime critics who questioned the expenses and benefits of manned space flight.

The grounding of the three remaining shuttles meant that payloads scheduled by Defense Department and commercial users were also grounded. Pentagon officials said they needed both a full fleet of four shuttles and extra "expendable launch vehicles" (ELVs) to meet "national security" requirements, including the launch of new satellites for spying, military communications and navigation, and secret tests of Reagan's strategic defense initiative (SDI).

Only two of the remaining three orbiters — *Atlantis* and *Discovery* — had the capacity to handle the heaviest military payloads. To keep SDI on schedule, Defense Secretary Caspar W. Weinberger told Congress Feb. 19, "we have to get another shuttle."

The space shuttle also remained vital to U.S. plans for putting a space station into orbit by 1994. Reagan in 1984 endorsed the development of a manned space station, estimated to cost about $8 billion by 1992. Congress had approved research funds for it.

"The space station isn't worth a damn unless you have a vehicle to service it with," said Sen. Jake Garn, R-Utah, chairman of the Appropriations subcommittee with jurisdiction over space issues. "That vehicle is the shuttle."

Congress, however, was beginning to move away from total dependency on the shuttle even before *Challenger* exploded. After years of effort, the Air Force finally persuaded members to add about $2 billion to the fiscal 1986 NASA budget for 10 new ELVs. In addition, the Air Force decided to modify 13 old Titan II rockets to launch satellites.

None of those rockets, however, was expected to be ready until 1989 at the earliest. Edward C. Aldridge Jr., under secretary of the Air Force, told Congress in March that the Pentagon wanted 10 more ELVs over the next five years, at an added cost of $2.5 billion.

"Unfortunately, recent events have made the need for ELVs and the need for a mixed fleet of launch vehicles mandatory," he testified March 26. "The issue of whether or not we need ELVs now no longer exists."

Fletcher Nomination

At the time of the *Challenger* disaster, NASA was headed by an acting administrator, William R. Graham. James M. Beggs, the agency's chief since 1981, had begun an indefinite leave of absence Dec. 4, 1985, after being indicted on fraud charges stemming from his duties as an executive of General Dynamics Corp.

Beggs resigned as NASA administrator on Feb. 25, and on March 6, Reagan announced he had persuaded Fletcher to return to NASA for a second tour as administrator. Fletcher had resisted initial White House overtures, saying he did not want to interrupt his consulting and corporate work. But he acceded to Reagan's urgent plea.

One complication Fletcher faced was the need to sever his various business ties to companies dealing with NASA. Fletcher promised to sell his stock and remove himself from any decisions made by the agency relating to those businesses.

According to his financial disclosure statements, Fletcher received more than $45,000 in 1985 as a director of Astrotech International Corp., an aerospace firm.

Fletcher listed himself as vice chairman of General Space Corp., an Astrotech subsidiary, which had proposed a controversial plan for private financing of a new $2 billion shuttle orbiter, which would be leased back to the government.

Senate Hearings

Fletcher breezed through a confirmation hearing April 23 before the Senate Commerce, Science and Transportation Committee, despite questions raised by some senators about his earlier tenure at the embattled agency.

Slade Gorton, R-Wash., chairman of the Subcommittee on Science, Technology and Space, said Fletcher's nomination was "long-awaited and sorely needed."

John Glenn, D-Ohio, a former astronaut, also strongly endorsed Fletcher. "NASA is facing the worst crisis in its 28-year history," he said. "It is vitally important we get leadership over there.... You can't go along with an agency in limbo."

Although Fletcher was widely respected in Congress and NASA for his track record with the agency, two lengthy reports published April 23-24 in *The New York Times* detailed past problems of apparent mismanagement, waste and fraud within the space program, including when Fletcher was NASA administrator.

The sharpest questions directed at Fletcher came from Albert Gore Jr., D-Tenn., who focused on several issues raised by the Times.

Based on a review of more than 500 audits by agency inspectors and the General Accounting Office (GAO), the Times reported that NASA and its contractors wasted at least $3.5 billion on the space shuttle and other programs over the past 15 years.

Specific cases of mismanagement and apparent fraud were cited, including overpricing of parts and falsification of test results. NASA officials, in response, insisted that any flaws that might have existed did not jeopardize the safety of the space shuttle.

Gore keyed on audits that cited Fletcher for misleading Congress and the public in the 1970s about the costs of the shuttle program.

For instance, Gore said, Fletcher projected the cost of each shuttle launch at $10.45 million, when the actual cost turned out to be about $279 million.

Fletcher said some of the higher cost was a result of inflation, but acknowledged that "something happened on the way to the bank." He denied intentionally misleading Congress, and said, "We're still on the learning curve."

Spaceflight-Related Deaths

The Jan. 28 explosion of the space shuttle *Challenger* brought to 14 the number of U.S. astronauts and Soviet cosmonauts killed in spaceflight-related accidents.

There also were numerous close calls, including a perilous return from the moon in April 1970 for the three Apollo 13 astronauts, who spent more than three days huddled in their darkened, cold capsule after a fuel cell that provided oxygen, electricity and water exploded.

The following space travelers were killed:

Francis R. Scobee, Michael J. Smith, Judith A. Resnik, Ronald E. McNair, Ellison S. Onizuka, Gregory B. Jarvis and Christa McAuliffe. An explosion 73 seconds after launch Jan. 28, 1986, destroyed the space shuttle *Challenger* in the worst disaster of the U.S. space program. A special presidential commission found that the accident was caused by failure of two synthetic rubber O-ring pressure seals in one of four joints between segments of the right, solid-fuel booster rocket. The fault allowed white-hot combustion gases to burn through the booster's side, and ultimately, the huge liquid-fuel external tank, and the orbiter disintegrated in a mass of burning hydrogen fuel. The commission recommended design changes and an overhaul of the space program's management.

Roger B. Chaffee, Virgil I. Grissom and Edward H. White. A flash fire raced through their Apollo 1 capsule as it sat on a Cape Kennedy, Fla., launch pad Jan. 27, 1967, undergoing tests with the three men aboard. The incident led to a change in the Apollo hatch design, and elimination of the 100 percent oxygen atmosphere.

Vladimir M. Komarov. He was killed on reentry April 23, 1967, when his Soyuz 1 capsule smashed into the ground. Soviet space capsules were designed to land on the earth, not splash down in the ocean.

Georgi T. Dobrovolsky, Viktor I. Patsayev and Vladislav N. Volkov. After successfully docking with the Salyut space station and remaining aboard for 23 days, the crew of Soyuz 11 died of asphyxiation when their capsule lost pressure during re-entry June 30, 1971. It later became standard procedure for astronauts (and probably cosmonauts) to wear pressurized flight suits for re-entry.

Fletcher defended NASA as "perhaps the best-run agency in the federal government." But Gore said, "The cumulative impression is not a good one.... A lot of this occurred during your tenure."

Easy Confirmation

The Commerce Committee endorsed Fletcher's nomination by 15-1 on April 30, with Gore casting the lone dissenting vote.

The Tennessee Democrat said he did not question Fletcher's integrity, but added, "I do not have confidence in Fletcher's judgment."

The Senate May 6 overwhelmingly confirmed Fletcher's nomination. The vote was 89-9, with all of the "nays" cast by Democrats. *(Vote 90, p. 18-S)*

Three days before the vote, NASA suffered yet another setback, when an unmanned Delta rocket exploded May 3, leaving the nation virtually without a launch capacity for military or commercial payloads.

Gorton said Fletcher's previous NASA experience meant that he could "hit the ground running, which, for NASA, is critical at this point in time."

Gorton said, "Our national prestige is on the line, as is the future of the space program." He urged approval of Fletcher's nomination "so we can restore our civil space program to its previous position of unchallenged superiority."

Gore, one of the nine Democrats to oppose the nomination, said he had "very serious doubts about Dr. Fletcher's ability to provide the kind of leadership that NASA so desperately needs right now."

"The drift, the loss of focus, the mismanagement, the waste — it all began in the period immediately after the Apollo program, during the transition from Apollo to the shuttle," said Gore. "Now we are asked to go back and put him in charge of NASA again. It is a mistake."

The Rogers Commission

The 13-member Presidential Commission on the Space Shuttle *Challenger* Accident was headed by William P. Rogers, who had served as secretary of state in 1969-73 and as attorney general in 1957-61. At the time of his appointment, he was a partner in the law firm of Rogers & Wells in New York City.

The commission's vice chairman was Neil A. Armstrong, a former astronaut and commander of Apollo 11, the first manned lunar landing mission, in July 1969. At the time of his appointment, he was chairman of the board of Computing Technologies for Aviation Inc., of Charlottesville, Va.

Other members included David C. Acheson, former senior vice president and general counsel of Communications Satellite Corp.; Eugene E. Covert, a professor of aeronautics at Massachusetts Institute of Technology; Richard P. Feynman, a Nobel Prize-winning (1965) theoretical physicist at the California Institute of Technology; Robert B. Hotz, a former editor of *Aviation Week & Space Technology* magazine; Air Force Maj. Gen. Donald J. Kutyna, director of Space Systems and Command, Control, Communications; Sally K. Ride, an astronaut and the first American woman in space (1983); Robert W. Rummel, an aerospace engineer and former vice president of TWA Inc.; Joseph F. Sutter, an aeronautical engineer and executive vice president of Boeing Commercial Airplane Co.; Dr. Arthur B. C. Walker Jr., an astronomer and professor of applied physics at Stanford University; physicist Albert D. "Bud" Wheelon, executive vice president of Hughes Aircraft Co.; and former test pilot and retired Air Force Brig. Gen. Charles "Chuck" Yeager.

All 13 commission members signed the report, although Yeager reportedly did not participate in drafting the document.

The commission was asked "to take a hard look at the accident, to make a calm, deliberate assessment of the facts and ways to avoid repetition."

The panel of experts convened Feb. 6, and issued its report on the causes of the shuttle disaster June 9. It recommended a number of major changes in NASA's policies and management.

Reagan June 13 formally endorsed the commission's recommendations and gave NASA 30 days to come up with a plan to implement them. A White House statement said Reagan believed the changes "are essential" to resuming shuttle flights.

NASA Administrator Fletcher said the space agency "welcomes the report," adding: "Where management is weak, we will strengthen it. Where engineering or design or process need improving, we will improve them. Where our internal communications are poor, we will see that they get better."

Commission Findings

The commission found that the loss of *Challenger* was caused by the failure of two synthetic rubber O-ring pressure seals in one of four joints between segments of the right, solid-fuel booster rocket, a cause suspected from the beginning. The fault allowed white-hot combustion gases to burn through the booster's side.

Ultimately, the failing booster broke free from the rest of the shuttle assembly, and the huge liquid-fuel external tank and the orbiter disintegrated in a mass of burning hydrogen fuel, 73 seconds after liftoff.

"No other element of the space shuttle system contributed to this failure," the report said. "There is no evidence of sabotage, either at the launch pad or during other processes prior to or during launch." The commission said it ruled out every other possible cause, such as failure of the external fuel tank, main engines, orbiter or payload, and methodically analyzed each item in detail.

The rocket failed, according to the commission, because of "a faulty design unacceptably sensitive to a number of factors." Those included:

- Extremely cold temperatures, which caused the O-rings to lose resiliency and not seal properly. When *Challenger* was launched, the air temperature around the launch pad was 36 degrees Fahrenheit, 15 degrees lower than any other shuttle launch. The temperature of the right booster joint in the area that failed was estimated to be about 28 degrees — the coldest point on the entire joint.
- Physical dimensions/reusability. The shuttle's solid rocket boosters normally were recovered and reused after launch, and they were sometimes bent slightly out-of-round during shipment back for reassembly. The commission found that while proper procedures were followed in "re-stacking" the rockets, the two segments that later failed had grown in diameter as a result of prior use. Their imperfect shape may have compressed the O-rings and damaged their ability to seal.
- Effects of launch pressures on material. The shuttle's O-ring seals were designed to be pushed into place by internal pressure from rocket ignition. But because of the

tremendous forces at launch, rocket joints were measurably bent and twisted. This distortion, lasting milliseconds, apparently prevented the O-rings from sealing fast enough to stop the leak of hot exhaust gases.

Contributing to the shuttle explosion, the commission found, was a "silent safety" program within NASA that hid problems from launch managers. The report spelled out how top managers of the shuttle program were unaware of a substantial history of problems with the O-rings or failed to comprehend warnings from managers.

Managers at the Marshall Space Flight Center came in for particular criticism for being isolated, territorial and unhelpful to other parts of the space agency.

The commission also criticized the management of booster manufacturer Morton Thiokol Inc. for overruling the vehement warnings of their own engineers not to launch because of the cold weather.

At a press conference after the report's release, Rogers pointed out that his commission was careful not to venture beyond its limited mandate to investigate only the causes of the accident.

For those reasons, he said, the report avoided such controversial issues as overhauling NASA, setting a date for resuming shuttle launches, or allowing civilians on future shuttle flights. Among the *Challenger's* victims was Christa McAuliffe, a Concord, N.H., schoolteacher who was to be the first participant in NASA's civilian-in-space program.

The others killed were mission commander Francis R. Scobee, Navy Cmdr. Michael J. Smith, mission specialist Judith A. Resnik, mission specialist Ronald E. McNair, Air Force Lt. Col. Ellison S. Onizuka, and payload specialist Gregory B. Jarvis.

Commission Recommendations

The commission recommended:

- A design change for the faulty joint and seal in the solid-fuel rocket motor.
- Establishment of a shuttle safety advisory panel, which would include astronauts, to review criteria for launch commitments, flight rules and readiness, and risk management.
- A review of NASA's management structure of the shuttle program.
- A review by NASA and its primary contractors for the shuttle program of all so-called Criticality 1 and 2 items on the shuttle (components that would or could cause loss of mission if they failed).
- Improved communications at Marshall Space Flight Center to eliminate the problem of "management isolation" and establishment of a clear policy about circumstances under which launch constraints were to be imposed or removed.
- Improvement of tire, brake and nose-wheel steering systems on the shuttle. Prohibition of future landings at Kennedy Space Center in Florida until those systems were improved and reliable.
- Crew escape systems for use during controlled gliding flight, and design of more emergency landing options in case of major engine failure during launch.
- Diversification of launch capabilities with unmanned, throwaway rockets, and tightly controlled cargo schedules to limit the pressure to launch.
- A better system for analyzing and reporting performance trends in the most critical components of the shuttle, particularly the liquid-fuel main engines. NASA also was urged to improve its spare parts inventory and "stop the practice of removing parts from one orbiter to supply another."

Congressional Reaction

Members of Congress strongly praised the work of the Rogers commission. Senate Commerce Committee Chairman John C. Danforth, R-Mo., called the commission "a model for what a presidential commission should be."

But lawmakers from both chambers launched a bipartisan attack on NASA, some of its key officials and the maker of the shuttle's failed booster rocket. They also acknowledged their own failure to oversee the civilian space agency vigorously enough.

In June, both the House Science and Technology Committee and the Senate Commerce, Science and Transportation Subcommittee on Space held hearings with members of the Rogers commission.

House members questioned whether NASA and Morton Thiokol Inc. properly had tested the boosters as required by the contract. Several, including Manuel Lujan Jr., N.M., ranking Republican on the House Science and Technology Committee, said that Congress "may have been too trusting of NASA."

Several lawmakers also said the Rogers commission was not tough enough on NASA, Morton Thiokol Inc., maker of the solid-fuel boosters, or the individuals who decided to launch.

Sen. Ernest F. Hollings, D-S.C., faulted the commission for not assigning individual blame. Hollings and several other members, including Reps. F. James Sensenbrenner Jr., R-Wis., and Robert G. Torricelli, D-N.J., strongly suggested that criminal negligence charges should be filed in some cases.

Rogers said such prosecutions probably would not succeed: "I don't think it would be in the national interest, and I hope it doesn't happen. . . . It was a systems failure. There wasn't any one person responsible."

Although the commission said the Marshall Space Flight Center failed to inform higher-level managers at NASA of the extent of the booster problem, the commission noted that the issue was presented to NASA headquarters in August 1985, in a form "sufficiently detailed to require corrective action prior to the next flight."

Other members, among them Reps. Sherwood Boehlert, R-N.Y., and Claudine Schneider, R-R.I., focused on alleged sharp reductions in NASA safety and quality assurance staff. They argued that Congress had provided adequate money over the years, but NASA misplaced its budget priorities, increasing expenditures for public relations while cutting safety staff.

And Rep. James H. Scheuer, D-N.Y., said NASA had grossly underestimated its assessment of possible flight failure to one chance in 100,000 launches, despite studies showing the potential for such failure at one chance in 35.

Costs of Moving Forward

Many members supported construction of a fourth orbiter to replace *Challenger.*

Reagan, in his June 11 news conference, said he supported building a replacement shuttle, but offered no detail of how to pay for it. Internal administration disagreements delayed a decision on building a new orbiter.

Several lawmakers said implementing the commission recommendations would be very expensive. According to CBO estimates, redesigning the boosters, replacing the orbiter, and constructing a fleet of unmanned expendable rockets as an alternative launch system to the shuttle would cost at least $1 billion a year over the next five years.

NASA Authorization

President Reagan Nov. 14 pocket-vetoed a $7.8 billion fiscal 1987 authorization (HR 5495 — H Rept 99-829) for the National Aeronautics and Space Administration (NASA).

The measure included an authorization for construction of a new orbiter to replace the space shuttle *Challenger*, which exploded during launch Jan. 28, killing all seven crew members. *(Story, p. 326)*

Eventually, $2.4 billion for a new orbiter was included in the fiscal 1987 omnibus appropriations bill (H J Res 738 — PL 99-591) enacted shortly before Congress adjourned in October. That legislation transferred $2.4 billion in new budget authority from the Defense Department to NASA. Only $100 million was to be spent in fiscal 1987. *(Appropriations, p. 171)*

Thus, Reagan's veto did not affect replacement of the *Challenger*; it merely blocked various policy changes Congress sought to dictate.

The president objected to three provisions in the bill: the establishment of a National Space Council, which the president's veto message said would "constitute unacceptable interference" in his authority over the executive branch; certain space shuttle launch priorities, which included launches for commercial customers; and a "buy America" restriction on certain NASA procurement activities. *(Veto message, p. 35-D)*

The House had cleared HR 5495 in the final hours of the 99th Congress. The bill sought to address and rectify the problems that faced NASA during 1986.

The Decision to Replace Lost Orbiter

Because of accidents in NASA's manned and unmanned programs, congressional budget reductions required by the Gramm-Rudman-Hollings anti-deficit law (PL 99-177), accusations of long-term mismanagement within the agency and the need to confirm a permanent administrator of NASA, Congress was forced to scrutinize NASA's mission and management closely in the second session of the 99th Congress.

Both Congress and the White House had agreed that funds to replace the lost shuttle should be authorized. In August, after months of delay caused by disputes within a White House interagency group reviewing U.S. space policy, the president submitted a plan to build a fourth orbiter. The administration's scheme called for $272 million for start-up costs in fiscal 1987 and would have diverted funding from other NASA programs for the shuttle.

The House and Senate rejected the White House plan. "Building a new shuttle will cost us new money. We cannot cannibalize NASA for funds, weakening an already distressed agency," said Sens. John C. Danforth, R-Mo., Slade Gorton, R-Wash., and Jake Garn, R-Utah, in a jointly issued statement.

But the chambers wrangled over whether the amount for initial construction costs should be specified. In the end, they agreed to an open-ended authorization. The bill also authorized unspecified amounts to cover Defense Department reimbursements to NASA lost while shuttle flights were postponed.

Dispute Over Space Council

The most controversial item in the NASA bill — and the major cause of the Reagan veto — was a Senate provision creating a National Aeronautics and Space Council "to advise and assist the president" on space issues.

As originally proposed by the Senate, it would have had jurisdiction over both civilian and national security space issues. Its members would have included the vice president, the directors of NASA and the CIA, and the secretaries of defense, state, commerce and transportation.

A space council existed once before, from 1958 to 1973, when it was abolished. According to Rep. Bill Nelson, D-Fla., that early council had proved to be "an effective and efficient policy-making body for the president."

The renewed popularity of the council concept, according to sponsor Sen. Donald W. Riegle Jr., D-Mich., was due to congressional dissatisfaction with the Senior Interagency Group on Space appointed by Reagan. Riegle charged that the interagency group was paralyzed by "bureaucratic infighting" in the wake of the *Challenger* accident.

As the chambers sent the bill back and forth in mid-October, trying to reach agreement without convening a conference, the issue of the space council proved to be the hardest to resolve. The White House voiced its opposition to the council, objecting to its proposed jurisdiction over military and intelligence space projects within NASA. Agreement was finally reached for a council with jurisdiction only over civilian space issues.

Reagan also objected to other provisions of the bill that would have protected the ability of foreign and commercial customers to use the space shuttle, and would have imposed buy America rules on NASA to restrict the purchase of imported goods or materials.

That provision was ultimately watered down to require approval by the U.S. trade representative and the secretaries of commerce and state that NASA consider the public interest and U.S. international trade obligations before "buying American."

After the *Challenger* explosion Jan. 28, the administration decided to prohibit NASA from launching most foreign or commercial payloads, in part to encourage development of a commercial launch industry. But many in Congress believed that policy would force paying customers into the arms of U.S. competitors, and language was added to HR 5495 to keep NASA in the commercial launch business.

Other Provisions

Within NASA's budget, the bill authorized:

- $783.8 million for space shuttle production and operations capabilities, exclusive of procuring a fourth orbiter to replace *Challenger*.
- $1.4 billion for shuttle operations.
- $860.9 million for space tracking.
- $100.6 million for repairs to the shuttle fleet to return to flight status.
- $410 million for design of a permanently manned space station.
- $40 million for development of the "Orient Express" transatmospheric space plane.
- $161.3 million for construction of facilities and $1.4 billion for research and program management.

The bill also contained provisions designed to spur

competition in the development of unmanned expendable rockets for satellite launches, and in the production of solid-fuel rocket boosters used in the space shuttle. A faulty booster was blamed for the destruction of *Challenger.*

As part of the anti-drug campaign by Congress, the bill also called for a mandatory drug-testing program for NASA employees.

House Action

Two House Science and Technology subcommittees approved the fiscal 1987 authorization bill for NASA in April.

The bill (HR 4691) matched President Reagan's $7.69 billion budget request for the agency. The Subcommittee on Space approved HR 4691 on Aug. 14. The three subcommittees refused to specify an amount or source of funding for replacing the space shuttle but did authorize its construction.

House Science and Technology by voice vote reported the bill (which had become HR 5495 — H Rept 99-829) Sept. 11.

The House Sept. 25 voted 407-8 to pass HR 5495. As passed, the bill directed the space agency to build a new orbiter to replace the space shuttle *Challenger*. No specific funding was included in the bill for a new orbiter; that was left to the House and Senate Appropriations committees to determine. *(Vote 380, p. 108-H)*

HR 5495 also included new provisions designed to spur competition in the development of unmanned expendable rockets for satellite launches. During floor debate, the House agreed by voice vote to an amendment requiring NASA to develop a second source for the shuttle's solid-fuel booster rockets. Only one company — Morton Thiokol Inc. — then made the boosters. A faulty booster seal was blamed for the Jan. 28 explosion that destroyed *Challenger.*

Other amendments adopted by voice vote of the House included a "buy American" provision requiring NASA to buy U.S.-made components for the shuttle in most cases, and a mandatory drug-testing program for NASA employees.

Senate Action

Like its House counterpart, the Senate Commerce, Science, and Transportation Committee Aug. 14 reported an incomplete fiscal 1987 NASA authorization bill (S 2714 — S Rept 99-501). The bill called for $7.76 billion for the space agency and authorized replacement of the space shuttle. However, the committee refused to specify the amount or source of funding for the orbiter, signifying, panel members said, their frustration over Reagan administration delays with space policy in the post-*Challenger* era.

NASA supporters on the Commerce Committee attempted, without success, to include in the bill a transfer to NASA of $460 million in excess funds from the federally subsidized Conrail freight system.

The Senate by voice vote Oct. 10 passed HR 5495 with amendments that raised the bill's cost to $8.6 billion, including $272 million for a new orbiter and $531 million to cover lost reimbursements from the Defense Department while shuttle flights were postponed. The Senate also included a provision to create a National Aeronautics and Space Council "to advise and assist the president" on space issues.

Resolving Disagreements

The House by voice vote Oct. 15 passed the bill again, after eliminating the specified amount for a new orbiter and dropping the Senate's space council provision. Total cost of this version of the bill was $7.8 billion.

Shortly before Congress adjourned Oct. 18, the Senate once again amended HR 5495, restoring the space council but modifying its structure. This version also dropped the fixed orbiter funding amounts, but kept the bill at $7.8 billion.

The Senate also added a fiscal 1987 authorization for weather satellite programs in the National Oceanic and Atmospheric Administration (NOAA). The $662 million for NOAA, an arm of the Commerce Department, was not counted against NASA's total.

The House concurred in the Senate amendments just before it adjourned, clearing the bill. ∎

Militarization of Space

The stated goal of the 1958 law launching the U.S. space effort was that space should be used for peaceful purposes. Despite that, by 1986 both the National Aeronautics and Space Administration (NASA) and the space program as a whole were increasingly being put to military purposes. One year after the Jan. 28, 1986, explosion of the *Challenger* space shuttle, the worst disaster in the history of the space program, NASA's scientific missions were gutted, its commercial launch role was targeted for extinction by President Reagan, and the government's civilian projects, such as NASA's own space tracking and relay satellites, were suffering from long delays. *(Space policy, p. 326)*

The Pentagon's space budget in fiscal 1987 surpassed NASA's by at least 2-to-1.

Pentagon Breaks NASA's Monopoly

Another sign of NASA's weakened status was the loss of its virtual monopoly over all U.S. launches, a policy that was designed to defray the massive cost of the shuttle system. After *Challenger*, the Pentagon began building its own fleet of unmanned rockets to get military payloads into orbit without the shuttle.

It also was developing a new unmanned "medium launch vehicle" to launch a military navigational satellite system, and even had its own $3 billion shuttle launch pad at Vandenberg Air Force Base in California, currently mothballed because of the two-year hiatus in shuttle flights.

All this was not cheap. Congress approved $2.1 billion to build 10 new Titan IV rockets in fiscal 1986 shortly before *Challenger* exploded, and also permitted the modification of 13 existing Air Force intercontinental ballistic missiles to launch satellites.

After *Challenger*, Congress gave its blessing to an Air Force "space recovery package" that was ultimately expected to cost an additional $2.5 billion and give the Pentagon 25 more unmanned rockets. Over five years, the Defense Department expected to spend an estimated $4.6 billion for 48 unmanned launchers.

Given NASA's historic dominance in space and its spectacular record of putting men on the moon, exploring the solar system and helping revolutionize telecommunications and other technologies here on Earth, the new military order in space troubled many members of Congress — especially leaders of the space committees.

"There has been a change in policy thinking within this administration, and there is a tilt now toward the defense space program and against NASA," warned Sen. Donald W. Riegle Jr., D-Mich. "The Defense Department is winning, and NASA is losing."

Rep. George E. Brown Jr., D-Calif., said that the growing budgetary inequality between military and civilian space programs was strangling peaceful space science and threatening NASA's role as an independent agency.

"That's about all NASA is at the present time — an appendage to the Pentagon," Brown said.

Riegle in 1985 had asked the General Accounting Office (GAO), the investigative arm of Congress, to look at just how much the United States was spending on military and civilian projects in space and what the implications were. The study was due out early in 1987.

Who Sets Policy?

Not only were battles in store over space policy in general, but a fight was also building over how space issues should be decided.

Reagan Nov. 14 vetoed the fiscal 1987 NASA authorization bill (HR 5495), largely because it would have created a National Space Council mandated by Congress to give a stronger voice in the White House to civilian space activities. *(Story, p. 330)*

The space council was backed by lawmakers frustrated with the bureaucratic infighting within the existing White House policy-making panel, the Senior Interagency Group on Space. That group took eight months after the *Challenger* accident to recommend a replacement orbiter, and was unable to agree on a way to pay for it.

Congress ultimately decided on its own to build a new orbiter, and to use Defense Department money to pay for it.

The Space Budgets

An analysis of budget figures illustrated the trend in U.S. space spending. NASA dominated space spending from 1961, at the advent of President John F. Kennedy's program to put a man on the moon, until Reagan made a national priority of his strategic defense initiative antimissile plan (SDI), popularly called "star wars."

In 1982, the Pentagon's space budget surpassed NASA's for the first time since 1960, consuming 53 percent of total federal spending on space. The gap widened thereafter, largely due to the space-related aspects of SDI; in fiscal 1986, the Pentagon controlled 66 percent of the federal space budget.

As noted in the 1985-86 yearbook published by the Aerospace Industries Association of America, the trade group for contractors that constituted the U.S. space industry, "space sales growth [in the 1980s] was due almost entirely to the rapidly expanding military space program."

Within the Defense Department, the overwhelming portion of the space budget (73 percent in fiscal 1986) was spent by the Air Force on SDI research and development, and on satellites for military communications, surveillance, worldwide weather monitoring and forecasting, mapping, navigation and early attack warning.

Because most SDI research was classified, it was impossible to determine how much was spent on space-related testing. But figures published by the Pentagon clearly indicated SDI's slice of the budget pie was getting bigger: About $1.4 billion was spent on SDI in fiscal 1985, $3 billion in fiscal 1986 and $3.5 billion in fiscal 1987.

According to a July 17 study by the Congressional Research Service, most of the SDI tests in space were to have been conducted on the shuttle, but many were being redesigned to fly on unmanned rockets because of launch delays caused by the *Challenger* disaster.

This shift "could be very costly and perhaps prohibitive," the study noted, depending on how far along the experiments were.

The Militarization of NASA

Another fear of some in Congress was that NASA itself was being increasingly militarized. A 1982 analysis by GAO, requested by Sen. William Proxmire, D-Wis., found that 25 percent of NASA's research and development budget was being spent on military programs.

Critics also pointed to several later developments that suggested a growing military influence over NASA, particularly the decision to use defense funds to pay for a replacement for the *Challenger*. As part of the fiscal 1987 continuing appropriations bill (H J Res 738 — PL 99-591), Congress transferred $2.4 billion in budget authority from the Defense Department to NASA. *(Appropriations bill, p. 171)*

Another example was research funding for the "national aerospace plane," designated by Reagan as the next-generation space vehicle for reaching orbit. The reusable craft would take off and land much like a regular airplane, and be capable of reaching low-Earth orbit (about 160 to 200 miles up).

Although one of NASA's main roles was to function as the leading research and development agency for aeronautics and space technology, the Pentagon had dominated funding for the project so far and seemed likely to control its future development and use.

Research spending on the plane was expected to total about $150 million in fiscal 1987, of which only $40 million (about a fourth) would come from NASA.

The rest — $110 million — was to be provided primarily through the Pentagon's Defense Advanced Research Projects Agency.

The most dramatic evidence of Pentagon influence over NASA was the launch schedule for the space shuttle. When flights resumed in 1988, NASA officials said, priority would be given to working off the backlog of military and national security payloads; secondary attention would go to major scientific projects and key data relay and communications satellites.

With certain exceptions, Reagan ordered NASA to stop providing launch services for commercial or international payloads, which had been seen as a prime role for the shuttle in the past. Those would have to fly on unmanned rockets operated by private industry or foreign governments, such as the European Space Agency's Ariane rocket system.

NASA Administrator James C. Fletcher said Oct. 3 that the Pentagon would claim 11 of the 26 flights planned in the first three years of renewed shuttle operations.

Over the seven-year period from 1988 through 1994, 41 percent of the shuttle flights would be defense-related, 47 percent would be for NASA's own operational and science missions, and 12 percent would be reserved for commercial and foreign customers.

Before *Challenger*, each of those categories took about a third of all shuttle flights.

Scientific Missions

If the entire U.S. space program was in a slump after *Challenger*, its space science projects were almost in a deep-freeze.

Despite the fact that space science had given NASA some of its greatest accomplishments, such as the spectacular pictures of the rings of Uranus sent back by Voyager 2 in January 1986, few purely scientific missions were likely to get off the launch pad for five or six years after the shuttle disaster.

"The space science program has been devastated," said Burton I. Edelson, associate administrator of NASA's Office of Space Science and Applications.

Before the *Challenger* disaster, the equivalent of 50 shuttle missions had been planned for science and applications between 1986 and 1992, according to Edelson. After *Challenger*, two-thirds of the scientific missions — 33 — were dropped. "As of now, 17 are on the manifest, and the average launch has been delayed three years," Edelson said. "That's a measure of how bad the situation is — we'll get 17 out of 50."

One of the immediate casualties was the Spacelab project, a system of pressurized modules that turned the space shuttle into an orbiting laboratory for a variety of experiments. NASA canceled more than half the planned Spacelab missions, and was to fly only three by the end of the decade.

Another victim was NASA's $8 billion space station, which the United States was designing in conjunction with several other nations. As planned, the station was to be devoted almost entirely to space science.

Although NASA was requesting proposals to build the station, rising costs and scheduling uncertainties threatened to reduce its size and push back the projected 1993 launch date.

According to Edelson, the centerpiece of NASA's space science efforts was the $1 billion Hubble space telescope, a state-of-the-art orbiting observatory that was expected to revolutionize scientific knowledge of astronomy. It had been scheduled to be launched on the shuttle in 1986, but could not go up before 1988 when shuttle flights were to resume.

Edelson noted that NASA had a strong incentive to get the telescope in orbit as soon as possible: It cost the government about $7 million a month to store, test and maintain the extremely sensitive and sophisticated device.

Although Edelson acknowledged the priority being given to national security missions once the shuttle started flying again, he chafed at the fact that the Hubble mission would have to wait for the fifth shuttle launch.

"I don't mean to discredit the military importance of it, but we're not fighting a war," he said. "It seems to me the Hubble space telescope is as important to true national security as is a military mission. It represents scientific and technological leadership in the world."

Reports in 1986 by the nation's primary space science advisory groups — the National Academy of Sciences' Space Science Board and NASA's own Space and Earth Sciences Advisory Committee — concluded that the United States had lost pre-eminence in the field to the Soviet Union and the Europeans.

The reports blamed this on the failure of the Reagan administration to provide leadership and set policy goals for U.S. space science programs.

They urged the White House to make space science a formal national policy goal.

Congressional Concern

During NASA hearings held in 1986 by the Senate Commerce Subcommittee on Space, Riegle repeatedly focused on budgetary differences between the military and civilian space programs, and the effects of a shift in space funding away from NASA and toward the Pentagon.

Riegle, at an Aug. 5 hearing with Fletcher, questioned NASA's prospects for the future.

"I do not want to see NASA bled to death by a sort of thousand nicks in this bureaucratic infighting," Riegle said. "I think we stand at a point here where NASA is in jeopardy of beginning an irreversible decline. I think that has to be prevented."

Fletcher, who headed NASA from 1971-77 and was brought back by Reagan to help rebuild the agency after the *Challenger* accident, responded, "We are still fighting the battle. We have not lost yet."

But even some NASA boosters who accepted the agency's defense activities were worried about the trends, including Rep. Bill Nelson, D-Fla., chairman of the House Science and Technology Subcommittee on Space and a crew member on the last successful shuttle flight Jan. 12-18, 1986.

Nelson expressed concern about a "brain drain" of NASA's best engineers and scientists, who were being lured by the higher pay, better resources and more attractive projects in the military's space research program.

"The difference in pay scales, the attrition, raises the possibility of less technical expertise [at NASA] than is needed," Nelson said in an interview. "We're going to have to look at higher remuneration to keep them."

According to Brown, the danger in having the military dominate space science research was that the results were usually classified and rarely saw the light of day. He disputed the argument of some proponents that SDI research would trickle down to benefit all science — such as happened with NASA's development of satellite communications.

"The problem with the military side of it is that there's very poor technology transfer," Brown said. "It's eroding our scientific base, our scientific leadership in space." In the long run, he warned, "that makes us a second-rate nation in a field that's going to be the most important scientific and technological field in the world."

Military Control Disputed

But not everyone in Congress or NASA agreed that the agency was being dominated by the military.

The 1958 National Aeronautics and Space Act (PL 85-568) called for separate civilian and military space programs, and directed that there be "cooperation" between the two bureaucracies. So, there was little dispute that backlogged military missions should get the first crack when shuttle flights resumed.

"Everybody understands the priority is for national security missions," said Nelson. Despite his concerns about NASA's loss of expertise to the Pentagon, Nelson said, "I just don't see the goblins of military control that people keep bringing up."

Slade Gorton, R-Wash., chairman of the Senate Commerce Subcommittee on Space who lost his bid for re-election Nov. 4, 1986, said that simply finding the money to replace *Challenger* was the major space issue in 1986, given the government's budget limitations under the Gramm-Rudman-Hollings anti-deficit law.

"As long as we can get the funding, that's the important thing. I'm less concerned about the source of it," Gorton said. "Getting the orbiter paid for by [the Pentagon] is a much better choice than abandoning the program altogether."

Fletcher, in testimony Sept. 16 before the Senate Appropriations subcommittee that oversaw his agency, said the Defense Department would be using "a significant part" of the shuttle fleet, "so it's appropriate they should pay for it."

Even though most of the early payloads carried by the new orbiter would be military, Fletcher stressed the significance of having the shuttle flown by a civilian agency.

"There was a question about what color we paint it — Air Force blue or NASA white," he said. "We'll both use that shuttle. NASA will continue to operate it no matter who owns it."

Ted Stevens, R-Alaska, outgoing chairman of the Senate Appropriations Subcommittee on Defense, came up with the specific proposal for financing the new orbiter from the Pentagon's budget. He dismissed the issue of military domination of NASA as mere "political rhetoric."

Future Developments

Even though the United States temporarily had no way to put heavy payloads into space, a Congressional Budget Office (CBO) study released in October suggested that actions already being taken might reverse that deficiency in about five years.

According to CBO, building a separate military fleet of rockets, replacing the orbiter and removing commercial payloads from the shuttle could have a combined effect of leaving the United States with twice the launch capacity it needed by the early 1990s.

That excess capacity would be compounded by growing competition for customers from foreign launch operations, at a time when demand for launch services might be falling off because of the longer-lived satellites.

While NASA's space science projects could use the extra launch capacity, funding for those missions would have to be sharply increased — an option not planned.

As a result, CBO warned that administration plans to commercialize the U.S. launch industry "may be a short-sighted option" that would not work. Keeping commercial flights on the shuttle or creating a quasi-public company to market the shuttle's commercial services might be far more cost-effective, the study said.

The CBO analysis was likely to be used as ammunition by congressional Democrats in both the House and Senate who opposed Reagan's plan to "privatize" NASA's launch services.

Riegle said Oct. 10 that keeping commercial flights on the shuttle is "an insurance policy to retain [U.S.] leadership," and is "an important tool of U.S. foreign policy."▮

Indian Gambling

With high-stakes bingo drawing thousands of people — and millions of dollars — onto Indian reservations across the nation, Congress began moving to gain some control over Indian gambling.

By voice vote, the House April 21 approved legislation (HR 1920) to give the federal government a measure of regulatory authority over Indian bingo while barring other types of gambling, such as horse racing and lotteries, for at least four years.

The measure had been approved Dec. 11, 1985, by the House Interior Committee and formally reported March 10, 1986 (H Rept 99-488).

The Senate Indian Affairs Committee approved its version of the bill by 6-3 on Sept. 17, and formally reported it (S Rept 99-493) on Sept. 26. But the measure did not reach the full Senate before Congress adjourned Oct. 18.

The Supreme Court on Feb. 25, 1987, held by 6-3 that states could not regulate high-stakes bingo on Indian lands — a ruling that was likely to renew interest in the federal legislation in the 100th Congress.

About 110 tribes currently sponsored some sort of gambling — usually high-stakes bingo — on their reservations, up from approximately 80 in 1985, according to the Interior Department's Bureau of Indian Affairs. Offering jackpots of $100,000 or more, the bingo games brought in some $100 million a year.

Morris K. Udall, D-Ariz., chairman of the House Interior and Insular Affairs Committee, said it was not surprising that Indians were looking to gambling for revenue in light of severe cuts since 1981 in federal funding for Indian programs.

"Just as there are many states turning to lotteries and other gaming activity to fill the gap left by federal cutbacks, so, too, are the Indian tribes," he said.

Critics said regulation was needed to prevent organized crime from gaining a foothold on the reservations and to protect the tribes from predatory outside interests.

The House bill was spurred in part by the discovery that some tribes were seeking to purchase land far from their current reservations, with the intention of creating new enclaves exempt from local gambling regulations. This could allow Indian gaming operations in most of the 50 states, warned Rep. John F. Seiberling, D-Ohio.

States Lack Authority

Lobbyists for the Indians said the tribes were quite capable of regulating their own activities and suggested that if the federal government wanted to keep organized crime out of gambling, it should start by regulating casino gambling in Nevada and New Jersey.

Such talk upset legislators from those states, who said that the federal government had no business regulating gambling. They wanted Congress to let states regulate gambling on Indian reservations — a repugnant prospect to the tribes that had relied on the federal government and the courts to protect them from what were usually hostile local governments.

The controversy had been raging since 1982, when the Supreme Court let stand a 1981 ruling by a lower court that Florida — and by implication other states — could not regulate bingo on Indian reservations if such games were legal elsewhere in the state.

The Supreme Court's 1987 ruling, in *California v. Cabazon Band of Mission Indians,* expressly stated the same thing.

Games on the reservations still had to abide by federal law and by state criminal laws. If a particular form of gambling, such as roulette, was prohibited altogether under state law, it was also illegal on Indian reservations.

But 45 states permitted bingo, while regulating where the games could be played and what prizes could be offered. On a reservation, those restrictions did not apply. The state could ban bingo outright, but then other groups that used the games for fund raising would be shut out as well.

House Bill vs. Senate Bill

Both the House and Senate versions of HR 1920 would have created a federal commission to supervise Indian bingo and approve contracts with outsiders hired to run such games. Traditional forms of Indian gambling would not be regulated.

Both versions also prohibited new gambling operations on any land outside the tribe's reservation acquired after Dec. 4, 1985, (House) or date of enactment (Senate) unless such activity was approved by the state government.

The House version, but not the Senate's, imposed a four-year ban on any other gambling on reservations not in existence prior to Jan. 1, 1986, while the General Accounting Office completed a study of the issue.

The Reagan administration strongly opposed both versions of the legislation, calling it "an anti-law enforcement measure which fails to accomplish the needed regulation of high-stakes gambling on Indian land." ▮

TRADE POLICY

Trade Policy

The United States' trade problems with other nations around the world persisted in 1986, driving the U.S. trade deficit to a record $169.8 billion and prompting members of Congress to search for legislative remedies aimed at sharpening the country's ability to compete in the international marketplace.

But the trade debate quickly became enmeshed in partisan politics on Capitol Hill and touched off a war of words between members of Congress and the Reagan administration over the appropriate course for U.S. trade policy. Congressional advocates of a toughened trade stance bitterly accused the White House of stonewalling on the trade issue, while President Reagan and other administration officials criticized lawmakers for staking out positions that smacked of protectionism.

In any event, the trade debate remained just that for much of the year — a debate that ended without Congress passing a comprehensive trade bill that many had expected at the outset of the 99th Congress' second session.

Nonetheless, the groundwork was laid for members to return to the trade issue in the 100th Congress. Democrats in particular were emboldened by their success in the 1986 elections, capturing the Senate for the first time in six years and claiming that the trade issue added to their victory margins in some of the races. Even before the year was out, leaders of the incoming Congress proclaimed that trade would be high atop the legislative agenda in the new session.

Fueling the drive for action on trade legislation were cries for help from some of the leading industrial and manufacturing sectors, along with allied labor unions, in the United States. From steel makers and auto workers to high-technology entrepreneurs and telecommunications firms, complaints about the United States' ability to compete against foreign companies continued to echo on Capitol Hill.

The administration responded to some of these complaints by focusing on trade negotiations with other countries and conducting its own investigations into charges of unfair trading practices abroad. At the same time, the administration's ability to block congressional action on a comprehensive trade bill in 1986 demonstrated that Reagan for the most part maintained the upper hand when it came to shaping U.S. trade policy.

Legislative Attempts

The Democratic-controlled House passed an omnibus trade bill in May that would have forced the president in certain situations to retaliate against other countries engaged in unfair trading practices or harming U.S. companies by shipping too much to the United States.

Proponents of the House measure said it was aimed primarily at opening up foreign markets to American goods. Folded into the measure was a panoply of provisions that ranged from negotiation authority for a new round of international trade talks to efforts to boost U.S. agricultural exports.

The Senate never acted on the bill. For much of the year, the Senate Finance Committee was preoccupied with the tax overhaul legislation; when it finally turned its attention to the trade issue in September, time was quickly running out. The committee held a handful of desultory markup sessions, but nothing came of the exercise.

The White House also avoided a major trade defeat when the House in August sustained Reagan's veto the previous December of a bill that would have placed sharp import restrictions on textile and apparel goods coming to the United States.

For months the domestic textile industry and powerful labor unions representing textile and clothing workers had geared up for the vote, depicting it as a jobs issue and key pre-election test of where members of Congress stood on the trade question. But Reagan denounced the legislation as blatantly protectionist and the kind that would have triggered a trade war with some of the United States' major trading partners. House Speaker Thomas P. O'Neill Jr., D-Mass., conceded that the textile bill was basically protectionist. But he decried the administration's trade policies, saying they had contributed to the need for measures like the textile bill.

In one of the few trade-related items completed by Congress, legislators renewed for six years the authorization for the Export-Import Bank. The bank offered financing to overseas buyers of U.S. goods such as planes and other big-ticket items.

The legislation included a $300 million trade "war chest" sought by the administration. The war chest would be used to offer attractive financing to prospective buyers in the form of a combination of grants and loans. But Congress, in its fiscal 1987 catchall spending bill, provided that no more than $100 million in bank funds could be used for the war chest program. Congress also rejected again a longstanding White House proposal to replace the Ex-Im Bank's direct loan program with another system of subsidized loans offered by private lenders.

Analyzing the Problem

Amidst the tug of war between Congress and the administration over trade legislation, economists and others argued over the root causes of the declining U.S. trade posture. The trade deficit had steadily worsened for more than a decade, and more than quadrupled since Reagan entered the White House in 1981.

The large federal deficit took much of the blame since it required huge infusions of foreign capital to help the U.S. government meet its obligations. Foreign investors were attracted by relatively high U.S. interest rates, driving up the value of the dollar compared with other major currencies. The overvalued dollar in turn hobbled American exports by making it more expensive for foreign buyers to purchase U.S. products.

As a rather ominous signal about the extent of the nation's trade problems, the United States in May posted a monthly deficit in agricultural trade amounting to $348.7 million, the first time that farm exports trailed imports on a monthly basis since 1959. U.S. agriculture ended the year with a slight surplus, but it was a far cry from the $26.6 billion surplus in 1981.

And while the strong dollar curtailed U.S. exports, it also lowered the cost of imports to the United States, thereby boosting America's already healthy appetite for goods from countries such as Japan and West Germany.

The dollar began falling after hitting record highs in early 1985, and continued to drop in 1986, particularly against key currencies such as the Japanese yen and West German mark. But promised improvements in the United States' trade balance failed to materialize, touching off debates over whether or not the dollar had fallen enough or if other factors contributed more heavily to the trade deficit.

In particular, many members of Congress — along with Reagan officials — began stressing the need for U.S. industries to concentrate on becoming more competitive in world markets. The emerging "competitiveness" debate, though consisting largely of vague goals rather than specific steps to achieve them, was shaping up by the end of the year to dominate Congress' attention to the trade issue in 1987. And with the administration preparing its own legislative package on competitiveness, there were signs of more cooperation between the White House and Congress on structuring trade policy.

—By Steven Pressman

House Democratic Leaders Push Trade Bill

Alarmed by mounting U.S. trade deficits, Democratic leaders won House approval May 22 of a measure (HR 4800) that threatened import restrictions if foreign markets remained closed to U.S. exports.

The comprehensive bill, passed on a 295-115 vote, was more than a year in the making. Originally reflecting the work of a Democratic task force, it eventually was stitched together from individual bills drafted by six committees. *(Vote 128, p. 40-H)*

The Democrats hoped their tough stand on trade would help the party's congressional candidates in the Nov. 4 elections. The issue did figure in some of the races, and, in the wake of their recapture of the Senate, Democrats served notice that trade would be a top legislative priority in 1987.

HR 4800 addressed issues ranging from international exchange rates to Third World debt. But the primary focus was on stiffer responses to countries accused of keeping out American goods at a time when imports had helped push U.S. trade deficits to record levels, $148.5 billion in 1985. The trade deficit swelled to $169.8 billion in 1986, according to figures released by the Commerce Department on Jan. 30, 1987.

In many areas, the bill would have forced the president to retaliate against countries that discriminated against U.S. exports, unless he decided that taking action would harm American economic interests. Existing law gave the president much wider discretion. *(Background, 1984 Trade Act, 1984 Almanac p. 171)*

President Reagan denounced the measure as "kamikaze" legislation that would spark foreign retaliation against U.S. exports because of what he considered its protectionist stance.

The Republican-controlled Senate, caught in a squeeze between the Democratic-held House and the Reagan administration, never voted on a trade bill. The Senate Finance Committee began markups in mid-September, but took no further action on the issue.

Following the Nov. 4 elections, in which the Democrats won a 10-vote Senate majority, party leaders announced that the Senate would join the House in making trade legislation a top priority in 1987.

House Committee Action

The Democratic-controlled House Ways and Means Committee May 1 approved a comprehensive trade bill over the opposition of Republican members and an administration veto threat.

Committee approval came on a party-line voice vote. Minutes earlier, the committee had rejected a GOP substitute on a 13-23 partisan vote.

Major elements of the bill called for:

- Mandatory retaliation against certain foreign trading practices.
- Tighter limits on the president's discretion in carrying out trade policy.
- Expanded avenues for American firms and workers to obtain relief from import competition.

The committee's action came as President Reagan was heading to Tokyo for the May 4-6 economic summit with heads of state from Japan, West Germany, France, Great Britain, Canada and Italy, some of the United States' leading trading partners. Also attending was a representative of the 12-nation European Economic Community, which was embroiled in an agricultural trade dispute with the United States.

Making of the Omnibus Bill

Six committees contributed portions of the omnibus House trade legislation (HR 4800). They were:

- Ways and Means (HR 4750 — H Rept 99-581, Part I), reported May 6.
- Foreign Affairs (HR 4708 — H Rept 99-580, Part I), reported May 6.
- Banking, Finance and Urban Affairs (HR 4574 — H Rept 99-577, Part I; HR 2373 — H Rept 99-579), reported May 6.
- Energy and Commerce (HR 3131 — H Rept 99-471, Part I; HR 3777 — H Rept 99-468, Part I), reported Feb. 6 and Jan. 30, respectively.
- Education and Labor (HR 4728 — H Rept 99-597), reported May 12.
- Agriculture (no separate bill or report was filed).

Democratic Initiative

The Ways and Means bill (HR 4750 — H Rept 99-581, Part I), reported May 6, contained the heart of the trade initiative that House Democratic leaders identified as a major legislative priority in 1985. The Ways and Means bill was combined with trade-related measures drafted in other House committees and reintroduced as HR 4800 for House floor consideration. *(Bills, box, this page)*

Reagan officials, in opposing the House bill, said it would place rigid restrictions on the president's ability to handle trade matters. They also contended that the bill could lead to retaliation against export-oriented industries in the United States.

"I can't conceive of a circumstance under which the president would sign this bill," said Alan F. Holmer, general counsel in the Office of the U.S. Trade Representative, after the committee's April 29-May 1 deliberations.

Bill supporters, however, counted on nationwide concerns about foreign competition to generate enough political pressure to make it difficult for Reagan to block a trade bill from becoming law.

"If the president wants to tell the American people there is something wrong with cracking down on unfair trade, let him tell them that," said Don J. Pease, D-Ohio, a Ways and Means member. "If he wants to veto this bill, let him veto it."

Sponsors said the measure was intended to help U.S. companies sell more goods abroad by breaking down trading barriers in foreign countries. For example, one section of the bill singled out the U.S. telecommunications industry for assistance by requiring accords with other countries to allow more American products into their markets. Imports from such countries would face U.S. retaliation if such agreements were not reached. A similar, though less comprehensive, plan for U.S. "intellectual property" such as movies and computer software also was included in the bill.

Though the bill by and large took a generic approach, parts of the measure aimed to protect U.S. products ranging from cement and steel to hogs and kiwi fruit. The legislation also contained dozens of "miscellaneous" provisions, most of which would provide U.S. firms with special tariff favors.

Import Practices Attacked

The bill strengthened protections for industries and workers beset by competition from foreign goods coming into the United States. For example, the bill would for the first time require mandatory presidential action against foreign countries that violated trade agreements or engaged in other "unjustifiable" trade practices. The president could avoid retaliation if he determined it was not in the "national economic interest."

Included under the bill's scope of unfair trading violations were export targeting schemes in which a government assisted a domestic industry in expanding its exports through subsidies or other benefits. Japan had frequently been accused of relying on export targeting to build up its semiconductor, machine tool and other export-intensive industries.

Another part of the bill authorized punitive actions against foreign governments that subsidized the cost of their natural resources, such as timber and natural gas, that companies used to make export goods. Canada, Mexico and other countries had been accused of giving their industries such subsidies.

Other provisions in the bill shifted the authority to provide import relief in the United States from the president to the U.S. trade representative. Trade Subcommittee Chairman Sam Gibbons, D-Fla., said the purpose of the shift was to force the president to pay closer attention to his top trade advisers.

Republican Criticism

Even before the committee concluded its markup, GOP Minority Leader Robert H. Michel, Ill., accused Democrats of "crafting a bill they know will never become law" and swatting down Republican amendments to ease some of its provisions.

Hal Daub, R-Neb., warned that U.S. farmers would suffer under the bill if other countries, angered by the legislation, reacted by limiting their purchases of U.S. agricultural exports.

To soften the potential effect on farm exports, the committee agreed to a Daub amendment that would require consultations with the secretary of agriculture before imposing import relief affecting other U.S. industries.

Though some Republicans seemed sympathetic to portions of the bill, the turning point came April 30 when the committee approved 24-11 an amendment by Richard A. Gephardt, D-Mo., that would single out countries maintaining large trade surpluses with the United States and other nations.

Under Gephardt's proposal — dubbed the "Gramm-Rudman of the trade deficit" by one panel member for its mandatory cutbacks — the president would have to negotiate swift trade agreements with such countries, aiming for annual 10 percent reductions in their trade surplus with the United States. Failure to achieve the reductions would force the president to take actions, such as higher tariffs, to bring down offending countries' surpluses.

If the surpluses still did not come down, the president would be required to impose import quotas in order to reach the trade reduction goals. He could avoid the quotas by deciding such action would cause "substantial harm" to the U.S. economy.

Gephardt, who had stressed trade as an attractive political issue for congressional Democrats, described his amendment as "promotionism" for world trade rather than protectionism. His proposal was a watered-down version of a plan he and other Democrats sponsored in 1985 that would have imposed 25 percent surcharges on imports from a wider range of countries that maintained big trade surpluses.

Gephardt said his new plan would affect Japan, Taiwan and West Germany. In 1985, Japan posted a $51.5 billion trade surplus with the United States. The figures for Taiwan and West Germany were $13.4 billion and $12.6 billion, respectively.

Only one Republican, Richard T. Schulze of Pennsylvania, voted with committee Democrats for Gephardt's proposal. Other GOP members complained that it would violate rules established by the multi-nation General Agreement on Tariffs and Trade (GATT).

Daub later said that four or five Republicans might have voted for the trade bill before Gephardt's amendment was attached.

Sparring Over Textiles

There also were signs of Democratic disunity during the committee sessions. At one point, Gibbons admonished a fellow Democrat to back away from an amendment that he said went too far.

Ed Jenkins, D-Ga., wanted to prevent Reagan from agreeing in international trade negotiations to reduce U.S. tariffs on imports that posed a particular threat to domestic textiles, footwear and other products. Jenkins was a leading advocate for the textile industry on the committee.

Gibbons warned that Jenkins' amendment would doom the trade bill because of the rigid restriction it would place on the president. That prompted Bill Frenzel, R-Minn., to note that "there are at least 15 other items that are going to make the president's day already" by inviting a veto.

Textile-state members were angry at Reagan for vetoing a bill in 1985 that would have placed limits on textile imports coming into the United States. The House sustained Reagan's veto on Aug. 6, 1986. *(Story, p. 347)*

A compromise on Jenkins' amendment was reached when the committee voted 25-11 to allow Reagan to negotiate tariff reductions, but permit Congress to disapprove of the lowered duties on "import sensitive" items under expedited procedures.

Other Panels, Other Proposals

Another part of the omnibus trade package — legislation to ease export controls and help U.S. firms sell more products abroad — was approved April 30 by the House Foreign Affairs Committee.

A key section of the bill (HR 4708 — H Rept 99-580, Part I), drafted by Don Bonker, D-Wash., would require the Commerce Department to trim by 40 percent over three years the list of U.S. goods and technology that were subject to export restrictions. The list of deleted goods would then be submitted to Congress, where a decision on actual removal of restrictions would be made.

Some GOP committee members argued that a forced reduction would harm national security; the list was designed to limit the sale of goods with a potential military use, such as electronic gear, to communist countries. The restrictions were imposed under the 1979 Export Administration Act, which was last extended in 1985 (PL 99-180). *(1985 Almanac p. 259)*

Another major item in the bill would establish a special $300 million "war chest" to help underwrite sales of U.S. goods abroad. The money would be used for "mixed credits" that combined loans and grants to finance foreign purchases of U.S. products. The administration had attempted to eliminate mixed credit programs in other countries as an unfair trading practice, but now wanted to use them as a negotiating tool to get others to stop the device. The war chest proposal was approved in separate legislation reauthorizing the Export-Import Bank. *(Story, p. 348)*

The House Banking Committee, meanwhile, approved other measures that were wrapped into the comprehensive trade package.

One of the bills, HR 4574 (H Rept 99-577, Part I), would link increased bank lending to debt-plagued Latin American countries with a greater willingness on their part to dismantle import barriers that kept out U.S. goods.

Other sections of the bill, authored by Stan Lundine, D-N.Y., were designed to bolster the Reagan administration's plan to increase World Bank and private bank lending to debtor nations by $29 billion over the next three years.

House Floor Action

The House May 22 passed HR 4800 by a 295-115 vote. *(Vote 128, p. 40-H)*

The bill attracted nearly unanimous Democratic support, with only four dissenting votes. More surprisingly, the measure also garnered 59 Republican votes — nearly one-third of House GOP membership — even though the White House had threatened to veto it.

The lopsided margin seemed to reflect the election-year zeal of many members to stake out a get-tough attitude toward the nation's trade problems.

A Republican substitute for the 458-page bill was defeated on a largely party-line vote of 145-265. *(Vote 127, p. 40-H)*

Offered by Minority Leader Robert H. Michel, R-Ill., the GOP alternative shared many themes with the Democratic measure, though it did not go nearly as far.

President Reagan criticized the House bill as a protectionist package that would "plunge the world into a trade war, eroding our relations with our allies and free-world trading partners."

But Democratic sponsors accused Reagan of forcing the House to pass a stringent bill by doing little himself to solve the nation's trade problems.

"We don't believe we are protectionists. We believe we are patsies for the rest of the world, and we want to be fair-traders," said Speaker Thomas P. O'Neill Jr., D-Mass.

Hours before the House started debate on the trade bill May 20, Reagan announced that he would ask four foreign nations — Japan, West Germany, Taiwan and Switzerland — to cut voluntarily their exports of machine tools to the United States. A request by the U.S. machine tool industry for import relief had been pending before the administration since March 1983.

The House bill represented an "all-out congressional offensive to modernize and restructure American trade policy," said Ways and Means Committee Chairman Dan Rostenkowski, D-Ill., at the outset of the debate.

Because of the bill's stated emphasis on opening up foreign markets to U.S. goods, sponsors denied they had drafted protectionist legislation. Critics, however, said it deserved that label largely because of the provisions forcing Reagan to retaliate against other countries.

Hitting 'Unfair' Practices

The bill also expanded the definition of unfair foreign trading practices that might trigger retaliation.

The broader scope, for example, would include "export targeting," in which a foreign government subsidized or otherwise supported an industry in order to help it capture a large share of the U.S. market.

Another crucial provision — one that provoked particular White House ire — would force 10 percent annual cuts in the trade surpluses that some countries had with the United States. This section would affect Japan, West Germany and Taiwan.

Sponsored by Gephardt, the provision would force the president to negotiate swift trade agreements with big-surplus countries. If the 10 percent annual reductions were not achieved, the president would have to take actions, such as higher tariffs, to reduce the offending surpluses. If the surpluses still did not come down, the president would be required to impose import quotas, unless he determined that such action would cause "substantial harm" to the U.S. economy.

Other key parts of the bill would:

- Make it easier for U.S. companies to obtain relief when foreign industries used natural resources at subsidized rates in products they sold to the United States. This section, aimed in part against Mexican and Saudi Arabian oil and Canadian timber, would pave the way for countervailing duties — increased tariffs — assessed against imported products in which subsidized natural resources were used.
- Shift authority from the president to the U.S. trade representative in a variety of matters, such as deciding unfair trade cases and authorizing import relief to trade-affected industries and workers.
- Establish a 16-member "industrial competitiveness council" to develop strategies to boost productivity and performance of U.S. businesses.

The council, proposed as an independent agency within the executive branch, had been sharply criticized by some as an ill-advised effort to develop an industrial policy, of the sort Congress had resisted in the past. *(1984 Almanac p. 169)*

White House Wish List

Although the bill attracted strong White House opposition, it included some items Reagan sought.

The bill would strengthen legal protections under U.S. trade laws for intellectual property essential to companies whose products involved trademarks, patents and copyrights. Administration officials and others said U.S. companies were losing their competitive edge in computer software, pharmaceutical and other industries because of infringements on intellectual property rights abroad.

The administration also needed renewed authority from Congress, contained in the House bill, to embark on a new round of multilateral trade negotiations under the auspices of GATT.

Not included in the House-passed bill was the administration's request for a $300 million "war chest" to combat other countries' practices of financing export sales.

Nor did the bill contain changes in antitrust laws, sought by Commerce Secretary Malcolm Baldrige, that would make it easier for companies to merge in order to enhance their international competitiveness.

Amendments

During the May 20-22 floor debate, it was clear that the bill had bipartisan support despite efforts to cast it as a Democratic tarnishing of Republican policies.

Three amendments aimed at eliminating various components of the bill attracted 44, 65 and 98 opposing votes from Republicans, with only a handful of Democrats voting in favor.

The first amendment, by Philip M. Crane, R-Ill., would have eliminated portions of HR 4800 outlining U.S. responses against unfair foreign trading practices under Section 301 of the trade laws.

The amendment, rejected by 137-276, would have struck the export targeting section, the mandatory reductions in other countries' trade surpluses, and a third provision that defined denial of labor rights in foreign countries as an unfair trading practice. *(Vote 120, p. 38-H)*

A second amendment, by Bill Frenzel, R-Minn., would have deleted sections that liberalized relief to U.S. companies and workers harmed by imports. This amendment, involving Section 201 of the trade laws, was rejected 109-306. *(Vote 121, p. 38-H)*

The third amendment, also by Frenzel, sought to scale back a part of the bill dealing with "anti-dumping" enforcement and countervailing duties. Dumping is the practice of selling imported goods in the United States at below-market prices in an effort to force out domestic competitors.

This amendment was defeated 79-338. *(Vote 122, p. 38-H)*

Regional Interests

Votes on these amendments and final passage showed that support for the overall trade initiative was particularly high among members from regions with industries — such as textiles, heavy manufacturing and timber — that were battered by imports.

For example, all but two House members from New England voted for the bill, reflecting the protests of shoemakers, potato farmers and fishermen against Canadian and other imports.

Similarly, the measure attracted widespread support among members from the South, where textile and timber firms were suffering. Even Minority Whip Trent Lott, R-Miss., voted for the bill after first supporting the Republican substitute.

A coalition of labor unions and some manufacturing companies lobbied heavily for the bill, with union lobbyists crowding the corridors outside the House chamber as members prepared to vote on the legislation.

Some of the trade measure's Republican opponents said they were not very surprised with the way many of their party colleagues voted. "Republicans are displaying the same kind of protectionist urges that Democrats are showing because their constituents are showing it," said Frenzel. "They are reflecting what their constituents feel." Frenzel, a leading free-trade advocate in Congress, served as the administration's chief supporter during House consideration of the trade bill.

He and others warned that enactment of the measure would invite massive retaliation against U.S. exports by foreign countries, further exacerbating the trade deficit and costing jobs in export-sensitive industries.

A Trade Chill?

That point of view was shared by several business lobbyists, who put together a last-minute coalition, called the Pro-Trade Group, to fight the bill.

"There's not much in this bill for U.S. companies engaged in international trade that want an expanded market. There's a lot in it that would just chill trade," said Paul T. Murphy of the National Foreign Trade Council, which represented large U.S. firms.

Several farm-state legislators, in particular, worried that agricultural products would be the first to suffer if a protectionist trade war erupted. Echoing that opinion in lobbying against the bill were groups representing soybean growers, wheat producers and other farm interests.

Traditionally, U.S. agricultural exports had far surpassed food imports, but the gap had narrowed.

Edward R. Madigan of Illinois, the senior Republican on the House Agriculture Committee, scored the bill as a "witch's brew of protectionism that is certain to ignite a trade war. And the first victim of that trade war is going to be the American farmer."

To soften the potential trade fallout against agriculture, the bill included a section that, among other things, called for an increased role for the Agriculture Department in handling trade matters that might affect U.S. farm commodities.

Easing Technology Restrictions

While much of the House bill dealt with laws regulating foreign imports, another major section would speed the decontrol of restrictions on the sale overseas of high-technology and other sensitive items. Such sales were subject to control under the Export Administration Act.

For example, the Commerce Department would be required to remove over a three-year period 40 percent of the 200,000 items on a list of restricted goods that required export licenses because they could potentially add to the military capability of the Soviet Union and other adversaries.

This provision was opposed by Defense Secretary Caspar W. Weinberger, who argued that automatic reductions could give the Soviets a windfall of technological know-how.

But Don Bonker, D-Wash., argued that U.S. high-technology exports were hampered by burdensome licensing requirements. Bonker was chairman of the Foreign Affairs Subcommittee on International Economic Policy and Trade.

An amendment by Toby Roth, R-Wis., to remove the control list reduction requirement was rejected 181-238. *(Vote 124, p. 38-H)*

The trade bill also revised the Foreign Corrupt Practices Act, a law that made it illegal for U.S. companies to offer bribes to foreign officials. In clarifying some of the legal standards used in the anti-bribery law, the bill established different tests for determining civil and criminal violations. Sponsors of these changes said U.S. business officials in the past had had a difficult time understanding their legal liabilities. *(Corrupt practices, p. 350)*

In the course of the debate, the House:

- Accepted 408-5 an amendment by Les AuCoin, D-Ore., expressing the sense of Congress that Japan should open up its market to U.S. semiconductor products. AuCoin represented a district that had been hit by layoffs in the semiconductor industry, which had long charged the Japanese with unfair trading practices. *(Vote 123, p. 38-H)*
- Accepted 248-166 an amendment by Bonker striking the bill's creation of Reagan's $300 million war chest to help finance overseas purchases of U.S. exports. *(Vote 125, p. 38-H)*

Instead, Bonker's amendment would allow the Export-Import Bank and Agency for International Development to use existing resources to offer export-financing schemes known as tied aid or mixed credits of loans and grants.

The original provision in the bill, favored by the administration, would have placed tied aid in the hands of the Treasury secretary. Bonker's amendment would require a majority vote of an existing multi-agency council to decide on the funds.

- Rejected 188-221 an amendment by Chalmers P. Wylie, R-Ohio, that would have removed several provisions relating to international exchange rates, Third World debt and creation of the industrial competitiveness council. *(Vote 126, p. 40-H)*

Other Major Provisions

The House-passed bill also contained provisions to:

- Expand the factors used by the U.S. International Trade Commission (ITC) in determining "material injury" to a domestic industry when considering import relief actions.

The bill allowed for "industry adjustment plans" that sought to identify ways to make import-affected industries more competitive. Such plans would be worked out by representatives of labor, management, government and consumers.

- Make it easier for U.S. companies to obtain temporary relief, in the form of tariffs or quotas, from imports coming from communist countries. Among other changes, the provision required that affected industries show that imports were an "important" cause of injury rather than the more stringent existing test of a "significant" cause.
- Broaden the scope of existing laws against foreign companies that "dumped" products at below-market prices in the United States, by including "diversionary" dumping. This provision was aimed against imported goods that included component parts dumped into a country that then used them in finished products brought into the United States.
- Remove a requirement that a U.S. company prove injury in cases that alleged violations of intellectual property rights by other countries. The new standard would require the company to show only that an intellectual property right had been abridged.
- Threaten trade retaliation against foreign countries that imposed barriers to U.S. telecommunications goods and services. This section set out a formula for negotiating better telecommunications trade with other countries, with the prospect for import restrictions if negotiations failed.
- Provide U.S. companies and workers with the right to sue to collect damages against importers found guilty of dumping products into the United States.
- Set harsher civil and criminal penalties for importers in the United States who repeatedly violated anti-dumping laws and other restrictions.
- Give the president five-year authority to negotiate trade agreements with Canada that would reduce or eliminate duties. The United States and Canada already were preparing to negotiate a comprehensive free-trade agreement between the two nations.
- Establish a Fair Trade Advocates Branch in the Office of the U.S. Trade Representative. The office would assist companies potentially harmed by foreign reprisals prompted by U.S. actions taken under unfair trading laws.
- Establish a new trust fund to pay for trade adjustment assistance for workers displaced by foreign competition. The money would come from tariffs or other revenue-producing actions generated by import relief measures ordered by the president. *(Trade adjustment assistance, p. 351)*
- Require the U.S. trade representative to submit annual reports to Congress describing overall trade policy objectives and priorities.
- Set a 30-day time limit in which the president must decide whether to restrict imports affecting national security, after receiving a recommendation from the Commerce Department. The bill also would require the Commerce Department to recommend action within 90 days of such cases being filed, rather than the one-year limit under existing law.
- Further liberalize trade benefits to debt-plagued countries in Latin America participating in the Generalized System of Preferences (GSP). The increased benefits under GSP, which allowed duty-free exports of certain items to the United States, would be transferred from other developing countries that "graduated" out of the program.
- Subject the chairman and vice chairman of the ITC to Senate confirmation. Under existing law, ITC commissioners had to be confirmed, but the chairman and vice chairman were designated by the president. The provision also removed the existing restriction against appointing the two most recently appointed commissioners as chairman or vice chairman.
- Apply existing steel import limits to countries that exported unfinished steel products to other countries, which then exported finished products to the United States. The provision would apply to countries covered then under steel import agreements with the United States.
- Provide statutory authority for a U.S. and Foreign Commercial Service originally created by executive order in 1980. Housed within the Commerce Department, the service was responsible for promoting U.S. exports, with offices located in the United States and foreign countries.
- Create within the Commerce Department a new Market Development Coordinator Program, which would assist U.S. businesses in expanding their export opportunities. The program was modeled after the Foreign Agriculture Service, which sought to increase U.S. agricultural exports.
- Authorize $40.9 million for each of fiscal years 1987 and 1988 to carry out export control activities on technology sales and other items covered in the Export Administration Act.
- Eliminate licensing requirements for U.S. goods that were exported to another country that, in turn, exported them elsewhere. This re-exporting provision applied to countries that already maintained export controls comparable to those in the United States.
- Authorize $123.9 million for each of fiscal years 1987 and 1988 to pay for export promotion activities carried out by the Commerce Department.

• Require the secretary of state to submit to Congress annual reports on the economic and trade policies of U.S. trading partners.

• Call for the creation of a new World Bank affiliate to boost lending and investment capital in developing countries. The proposed affiliate, starting with $1 billion from World Bank resources, would have to be agreed upon by the bank's member countries. Bank officials in the past had expressed reservations about such a plan, which would allow the bank to lend more money than it had in its loan reserves.

• Require U.S. directors of multilateral development banks to vote against proposed loans to countries that restricted imports from the United States and other countries.

• Instruct the U.S. executive director of the World Bank to propose an increase in what was called structural adjustment lending to developing countries. The purpose was to stimulate social and economic reforms in these countries rather than lend money for specific physical projects.

• Set the achievement of a "competitive" currency exchange rate as an explicit U.S. economic policy goal. Exchange rate targets would be used by the Treasury Department in carrying out policies to keep the dollar in line with other major currencies.

The overvalued dollar had been labeled a leading contributor to U.S. trade deficits, although the dollar had fallen sharply against other currencies in recent months.

The bill also would require the president to convene an international conference on exchange rates with other industrialized countries to determine whether reforms were needed. In February, Reagan ordered Treasury Secretary James A. Baker III to look into the possibility of such a conference.

• Require the Treasury secretary to continue negotiations with major industrialized countries to coordinate international economic policy. In particular, this provision encouraged the United States and other industrialized countries to step up their purchases of oil from developing countries as a way to spur those nations' economies.

Administration officials said this provision was unnecessary since the United States already consulted regularly with other leading industrialized nations, such as Japan, West Germany, France and Great Britain.

• Authorize U.S. participation in the Multilateral Investment Guarantee Agency (MIGA), an affiliate of the World Bank. MIGA was aimed at boosting investment in developing countries by insuring against political risks such as war and political disturbances. The administration favored U.S. participation in MIGA.

• Designate the Agriculture Department as the lead federal agency in handling agricultural trade matters. The existing position of under secretary for international affairs and commodity programs would be split into two new positions — one for trade and international affairs and another for commodity programs. While not conferring any additional power on the agency, this provision would emphasize the department's role in trade issues involving farmers.

• Establish a new office within the Agriculture Department to help individuals and groups harmed by unfair agriculture policies abroad. Specifically, the office would assist those pressing trade cases before the Commerce Department, ITC, U.S. Trade Representative and other forums.

• Require the agriculture secretary to prepare annual reports outlining policy on agricultural trade. The reports would be included with the president's annual budgets to Congress.

• Establish a U.S.-Mexico Bilateral Commission to focus on issues affecting the two countries. This provision also called for a bilateral economic summit.

• Require a speedier process for the Commerce Department to seek negotiations with other countries on agreements to limit textile imports under the Multifiber Arrangement, an international textile trade accord.

• Take action against foreign-owned dairies in the United States that were financed through industrial revenue bonds. This provision would declare milk products produced by such dairies ineligible for participation in milk marketing orders, which set minimum milk prices in different regions of the country.

The provision was added by dairy-state lawmakers in response to media reports about an Irish company planning to operate dairies in Georgia, with much of the seed money coming from industrial development bonds.

• Order the Agriculture Department to study whether imported honey and roses were hurting domestic producers.

• Authorize $500 million in fiscal 1987 for programs aimed at improving trade competitiveness by boosting educational and job skills. This provision emphasized aid to the unemployed and adults who did not have high school diplomas. The money would be funneled through state educational agencies.

In addition, $50 million would be earmarked for colleges and universities to upgrade research facilities.

• Authorize $500 million in fiscal 1987 for job training programs aimed at workers whose jobs were harmed by foreign competition. Some 60 percent of the money would be provided under the Job Training Partnership Act, a federal program providing training assistance to the unemployed. The remainder would be allocated to job banks and other worker aid programs. *(Job training act, 1982 Almanac p. 39)* ▮

Export Program Funding

Congress Oct. 18 approved a measure (S 2245 — PL 99-633) authorizing fiscal 1987-88 funding for export promotion programs and export control activities under the Export Administration Act.

The bill authorized President Reagan's full request of $123.9 million to carry out the Commerce Department's export promotion activities in each of those fiscal years. It also authorized $35.9 million in each year for the department's export control functions. The Export Administration Act authorized curbs on trade to block exports of potential military value, to protest other nations' foreign policies or to safeguard domestic supplies. *(Export Administration Act extension, 1985 Almanac p. 259)*

The Senate originally passed S 2245 (S Rept 99-271) by voice vote July 21. The House passed a somewhat different version Oct. 14, 366-0. The bill cleared in the closing hours of the session when the House accepted a Senate amendment striking a $14 million annual ceiling on export enforcement activities. *(House vote 425, p. 120-H)*

Actual funding for the export programs was provided in the omnibus continuing appropriations resolution for fiscal 1987 (H J Res 738). *(Story, p. 219)* ▮

House Sustains Veto of Textile Import Curbs

The House Aug. 6 sustained President Reagan's veto of legislation (HR 1562) to restrict textile imports into the United States. The vote was 276-149, eight shy of the two-thirds needed to override the veto. *(Vote 265, p. 76-H)*

U.S. Trade Representative Clayton K. Yeutter called the House vote a "very gratifying victory" for the administration, which had lobbied vigorously to kill the bill. He said enactment of the textile bill would have been "devastating" to U.S. exports by inviting "massive retaliation" from foreign countries.

The House vote ruled out the need for any Senate action on the issue.

The vetoed legislation would have placed tougher import restrictions on countries shipping textile and apparel goods into the United States. The stiffest limits — requiring about a 30 percent reduction in imports — would have been imposed against South Korea, Taiwan and Hong Kong. Also included in the legislation were Senate-added sections offering import relief to the domestic shoe and copper industries.

Background

Congressional efforts to curb textile imports were prompted by the deepening economic problems of the domestic textile industry. Industry officials said 300,000 U.S. jobs had been lost due to textile and clothing imports since 1980. Hundreds of thousands of additional jobs were imperiled if textile imports continued to rise in the future, they said.

Congress cleared HR 1562 Dec. 3, 1985. Reagan vetoed it two weeks later. The bill originally passed both chambers by substantially less than the two-thirds margin required to override his veto, and bill backers did not seek an override vote in the closing days of the 1985 session.

Instead the House postponed the vote until Aug. 6, 1986, to coincide with the expiration of an international agreement on textile trade, known as the Multifiber Arrangement (MFA). Lawmakers from textile states also figured that scheduling the override attempt closer to the November 1986 elections would give them a greater chance of obtaining enough votes to win. *(Previous action, 1985 Almanac p. 255)*

Reagan Strategy

Reagan won the veto fight Aug. 6 after an intensive lobbying campaign that included dozens of presidential phone calls to wavering Republican House members, accompanied by calls and visits from other high-ranking administration officials. "The president has a lot of power, a lot of bargaining chips," said Ed Jenkins, D-Ga., leader of the override campaign in the House. "He had to play them all to win this vote."

A series of textile trade agreements, all reached within weeks before the vote, helped the White House stave off the threatened override. U.S. trade negotiators concluded pacts with Hong Kong, South Korea and Taiwan, the three primary targets in the textile bill.

Meanwhile, trade officials from 54 countries, meeting in Geneva, agreed Aug. 1 on a five-year extension of the MFA that called for tighter limits on some textile imports. The accord was hailed by the administration, but quickly dismissed by U.S. textile industry officials as offering inadequate protection to domestic producers.

House members who led the fight to override the veto said recent White House trade actions in favor of U.S. wheat farmers and semiconductor manufacturers helped to shore up support for Reagan's position in Farm Belt areas and high-technology states, notably California.

Over the objections of Secretary of State George P. Shultz, Reagan decided Aug. 1 to sell subsidized wheat to the Soviet Union under an export program for surplus U.S. commodities. The administration also reached an agreement July 31 with Japan to boost U.S. semiconductor sales in that country.

Working against the White House, however, was the

South African Textile Pact

Reagan administration efforts to head off a veto override on the textile import bill (HR 1562) were made more difficult by the disclosure July 29 of a new textile trade agreement between the United States and South Africa.

White House aides said that imports of textiles from South Africa had jumped dramatically in the past couple of years and that the new agreement would place tighter restrictions on them. The five-year agreement, which went into effect Sept. 1, called for a 4 percent annual increase in the level of South African textile goods that could be imported into the United States.

By contrast, textile and apparel imports in 1985 rose 139 percent from the previous year, with an 80 percent increase in the 12-month period that ended in May, the U.S. Trade Representative's office noted.

Administration officials also said that an existing trade agreement restricted imports of five categories of textile and apparel products that accounted for only 12 percent of all textile imports from South Africa.

The new agreement covered 13 categories and set import caps on products that accounted for about 38 percent of all textile and apparel imports from South Africa, according to the Trade Representative's office.

As a result, Reagan aides said, the new agreement would make it more difficult for South Africa to penetrate the U.S. market in textile goods.

Several other textile-exporting countries were limited in the amount of goods they could ship into the United States under guidelines contained in an international accord known as the Multifiber Arrangement (MFA). But South Africa was not a signatory to the MFA.

Congressional critics of the administration's South Africa policy pointed to the textile agreement as a sign of Reagan's continued willingness to maintain U.S. economic ties with South Africa.

Alan Cranston, D-Calif., pressed the Senate Foreign Relations Committee to ban all South African textile imports as part of legislation to impose sanctions on the Pretoria government. He lost on an 8-8 vote. *(Sanctions bill, p. 359)*

July 29 disclosure of a controversial textile trade agreement between the United States and South Africa. *(Box, p. 347)*

House Override Vote

Reagan's strong appeals to GOP lawmakers made the difference in the override vote. While 205 Democrats — 82 percent of those who voted — went against Reagan, only 71 Republicans did so, 40 percent of those who voted.

Voting to sustain the veto were 43 Democrats and 106 Republicans.

Reagan managed to win a large majority of Republicans despite energetic lobbying by key GOP lawmakers to override the president's veto. That effort was led by Minority Whip Trent Lott, R-Miss., whose district included several textile plants.

On the morning of the override vote, Lott was counting on 79 Republican votes, precisely the number he needed when combined with the votes from the Democratic side of the aisle.

But 11th-hour lobbying by Reagan stripped away four GOP votes, leaving Lott and others nowhere to turn to make them up. By the time of the vote, Lott told four other Republicans who had committed to the override that they were free to vote with Reagan in order to avoid political embarrassment with the White House.

Textile union lobbyists crowded the corridors leading to the House chamber, corralling members as they walked in and out. Veteran lobbyist Evelyn Dubrow, who represented the International Ladies' Garment Workers' Union, perched herself in one of the brown leather chairs normally occupied by House employees who guard the chamber's entrances.

The House debate on the override underscored the odd political alliances that often form on congressional trade issues. Leading off the argument to sustain the veto was Ways and Means Committee Chairman Dan Rostenkowski, D-Ill., who had been a sharp critic of Reagan's trade policies.

Rostenkowski, however, warned that passing the textile bill would harm the United States' credibility on trade matters with other countries. Instead, he called for enactment of a comprehensive trade bill (HR 4800) passed by the House in May. *(Story, p. 341)*

Backing for the override came from a mixture of Democratic liberals looking to score points against Reagan's trade policies and more conservative Democrats and Republicans from the South and Northeast, where textile and other import-affected industries were concentrated.

"This is protectionist, no question about it," House Speaker Thomas P. O'Neill Jr., D-Mass., told reporters. "On an issue like this, you're voting your locale, you're voting your home."

Bill Goodling, R-Pa., described the textile bill as a "wake-up call to the White House" on trade. And Carroll A. Campbell Jr., R-S.C., urged his colleagues to come to the aid of a domestic industry suffering under a flood of imports. "For God's sake," said Campbell, "try to vote for America one time." ∎

Export-Import Bank Reauthorization Cleared

President Reagan Oct. 15 signed legislation (HR 5548 — PL 99-472) extending the charter of the Export-Import Bank for six years, through Sept. 30, 1992.

The Ex-Im Bank promoted foreign purchases of U.S. goods, primarily big-ticket items such as airplanes and power plants, by providing direct loans and loan guarantees to buyers overseas. The administration had tried for several years to end the bank's most popular program, which directly lent money to foreign purchasers of American goods.

Congress completed action on HR 5548 Oct. 7 when the Senate adopted the conference report (H Rept 99-956) on the bill. The House had adopted the report Oct. 2. The bank's charter had lapsed on Sept. 30, temporarily halting some Ex-Im operations. *(Background, previous extension, 1983 Almanac p. 241)*

A key feature of the bill was an administration-backed, $300 million "war chest" that would combine grants and direct loans to make U.S. exports more attractive to foreign customers. Also known as "tied aid" or "mixed credits," the program was designed to offset similar subsidies provided by other trading nations, particularly Japan and France. The Ex-Im Bank had been giving highly subsidized loans in recent years but had been unable to offer outright grants.

Although HR 5548 authorized the $300 million war chest, conferees on the foreign aid portion of the fiscal 1987 continuing appropriations resolution (H J Res 738) provided that no more than $100 million of the bank's $900 million appropriation could be used for a tied-aid program — and then only if the chairman of the bank certified to Congress that the money was not needed for direct loans. *(Appropriations, p. 162)*

HR 5548 also authorized a controversial new interest-subsidy program known as "I-Match," designed by the White House to replace the Ex-Im Bank's direct lending program. But the bill permitted an I-Match program to proceed only if the bank retained its direct loans and if the subsidies paid under the program were not counted as a direct budget expenditure.

Major Provisions

As cleared by Congress Oct. 7, HR 5548 (PL 99-472):

- Extended the charter of the Export-Import Bank for six years, through Sept. 30, 1992.
- Authorized a new $300 million trade "war chest" to subsidize U.S. exports by offering cut-rate financing to foreign buyers.
- Strengthened existing restrictions on loans to "Marxist-Leninist" countries, listing 30 nations as ineligible. The president would be allowed to remove any countries from the list if he decided they no longer fit the definition. Included in the definition were countries that were "economically and militarily dependent" on the Soviet Union or other communist countries.
- Specifically prohibited Ex-Im loans to Angola until the president certified that troops and military advisers from Cuba and other communist countries had departed. Angola had received Ex-Im loans in the past.
- Allowed the Ex-Im Bank to begin an experimental loan subsidy program known as I-Match. The new program, a combination of loan guarantees and interest subsidies, could be set in place only if Congress appropriated money for interest subsidy payments; if the loan guaran-

tees covered by the payments were considered off-budget; and if the bank maintained a direct loan program that totaled at least $700 million.

- Required the Ex-Im Bank to allow the transfer of bank-provided loan guarantees and insurance from an original lender to other lenders. The purpose was to permit private banks or other kinds of financial institutions that made export loans using Ex-Im guarantees to sell or transfer those loans to others without risking the loss of the guarantees.

House Action

The House July 15 passed a bill (HR 4510) reauthorizing the bank for two years, fiscal 1987-88. The bill, passed by voice vote, set an overall $1.8 billion limit in 1987 for direct loans and for the new loan interest subsidy program sought by the Reagan administration.

In theory, the House bill would give the go-ahead for the administration to implement its new I-Match program, which would replace the bank's principal lending device — direct loans to overseas purchasers of American goods — with a combination of loan guarantees and loan interest subsidies. A main advantage of the new program, according to the administration, was that it would be "off-budget," and so would not count against the federal deficit.

The bill would allow implementation of the new program only if both the House and Senate Budget committees agreed with the administration's contention that I-Match guarantees and subsidies were off-budget and did not require budget authority or constitute outlays from the Treasury. The Congressional Budget Office already had rejected the administration contention, and congressional sources said it was unlikely that both Budget panels would agree with the administration.

Even if the administration was able to start its new I-Match program, the House Banking, Finance and Urban Affairs Committee said in its May 6 report on the bill (H Rept 99-578) that the bank should use both I-Match subsidies and the traditional direct loans in a way "to serve most efficiently the interests of U.S. exporters as a whole."

The bill also included a provision allowing the Ex-Im Bank to sell its loan guarantees to private sources, such as insurance companies or pension funds, that might want the guarantees as investments. Doing so would make the guarantee program more attractive to U.S. businesses, the committee said.

The House bill did not include authorization for the $300 million trade war chest sought by the administration. The Banking Committee had reported that proposal separately in 1985. *(1985 Almanac p. 263)*

Loans to 'Marxist-Leninists'

By voice votes, the House accepted two amendments offered by conservatives to curtail new Ex-Im loans to communist countries:

- By Bill McCollum, R-Fla., barring loans to Angola unless the president certified to Congress that all Cuban troops had left that country. The bank had authorized about $230 million worth of loans for Angola since 1980, primarily to support that country's oil industry. About $153 million of the authorization had been spent so far.

The Reagan administration early in 1986 approved "covert" aid to a guerrilla group that was seeking to overthrow the leftist government of Angola. The government had hired some 25,000-40,000 Cuban troops for protection.

McCollum argued that the United States should not be "supporting a communist dictatorship which has clearly seized power illegally, especially not when there is an ongoing civil war with forces that appear to be pro-Western and democratic in their leanings." The provision was largely symbolic, since the administration appeared unlikely to allow new Ex-Im loans to Angola. *(Angola, p. 387)*

- By Philip M. Crane, R-Ill., broadening a longstanding list of communist countries barred from receiving Ex-Im loans. Under existing law, the bank could not lend to "communist" countries, unless the president notified Congress that such loans were in the U.S. interest.

Crane's amendment would prohibit loans to "Marxist-Leninist" countries, defined as those with centrally planned economies and dependent on the Soviet Union or other communist countries. The amendment listed 30 countries, 12 more than were barred from getting Ex-Im loans under existing law. Of the 12, eight had gotten Ex-Im loans in the past: Angola, Benin, Congo, Ethiopia, Guyana, Mozambique, South Yemen and Surinam.

House managers of the Ex-Im bill accepted Crane's amendment after he agreed not to press for action on another amendment that would have eliminated the president's authority to waive the loan prohibition.

Curtailing Competition

Supporters of the Ex-Im Bank succeeded in watering down an amendment, offered by Nick J. Rahall II, D-W.Va., intended to bar loans that would increase foreign competition to U.S. products and commodities.

By a 307-87 vote, the House amended Rahall's provision to allow Ex-Im loans for foreign competitive items if they would be produced anyway. *(Vote 191, p. 58-H)*

Stephen L. Neal, D-N.C., sponsor of the gutting amendment, charged that Rahall was seeking to protect West Virginia coal producers from foreign competition. The Rahall effort would "backfire," Neal said, because it would merely exclude U.S. firms from competing to win foreign contracts.

Rahall defended his original proposal, saying the United States should not "finance foreign projects that then put our workers out of jobs."

Senate Action

The Senate passed HR 4510 July 22 by voice vote after substituting the provisions of its own 10-year reauthorization bill (S 2247 — S Rept 99-273).

The Senate measure provided the $300 million war chest authorization sought by the administration, but ignored a White House request to drop Ex-Im's direct loans in favor of the I-Match program.

During floor action on the bill, the Senate attached an amendment barring Ex-Im loans that would be used to produce foreign commodities that competed with similar U.S. products. The amendment, by Minority Leader Robert C. Byrd, D-W.Va., was prompted by a $200 million Ex-Im loan to buy U.S. mining equipment for a coal mine in Colombia operated jointly by Exxon Corp. and the Colombian government. Byrd argued that the loan would hamper efforts by U.S. coal producers to sell more coal abroad.

Also approved was an amendment by Don Nickles, R-Okla., that would prevent the United States from supporting similar loans offered by the World Bank and other international lending institutions. Steven D. Symms, R-Idaho, said it was "trade suicide" for the United States to help finance exports from other countries.

The Senate also adopted an amendment by J. Bennett Johnston, D-La., to authorize benefits under the trade adjustment assistance program for workers and firms in the oil and gas industry. The trade adjustment program was designed to help those injured by import competition.

Following the House's lead, the Senate attached provisions aimed against the leftist regime in Angola and other communist countries. An amendment by William Proxmire, D-Wis., would prevent Ex-Im loans to Angola until Cuban and other communist troops left that country. Proxmire's amendment defined other "Marxist-Leninist" countries also ineligible to receive Ex-Im loans. Also adopted was an amendment by Dennis DeConcini, D-Ariz., calling on President Reagan to impose a trade embargo against Angola.

The Senate rejected 47-53 an amendment by Wendell H. Ford, D-Ky., that would have cut nearly $13 million from the Ex-Im war chest and diverted it to farm price-support programs. Ford argued that hard-pressed U.S. farmers were more in need of aid than foreign buyers of U.S. goods. *(Vote 161, p. 30-S)*

New Bill Approved

Further action on the Ex-Im reauthorization was delayed for weeks.

Initially, the bill was delayed by a turf fight between the House Banking and Foreign Affairs committees over who would serve on a conference to iron out House-Senate differences in HR 4510. The tiff stemmed from differences between the two panels over the shape of the war chest program.

That dispute was resolved in September with the passage of HR 5548, a new bill containing, for the most part, language acceptable to both houses. The House passed HR 5548 Sept. 22, and the Senate passed an amended version Sept. 26.

But after conferees on HR 5548 reached agreement Sept. 30, the bill bogged down anew over a plan to sell off some of the bank's loans as a deficit-cutting device. The matter was resolved by an agreement to drop the plan.

Conference Report

The conference report on HR 5548 was filed Oct. 2 (H Rept 99-956). As expected, conferees eliminated or modified a handful of Senate provisions that had raised complaints in the House.

Dropped from the bill was a provision that would have provided cash benefits under the trade adjustment assistance program to unemployed oil and gas workers.

The Senate also agreed to strike a requirement that the United States reduce its contributions to the World Bank and other international banks in response to multilateral loans used by recipient countries to produce agricultural and other commodities already in oversupply around the world. The bill retained language that reiterated existing law urging U.S. officials at the international banks to vote against loans that supported products in oversupply.

Conferees approved a modified version of a Senate amendment urging President Reagan to use the Export Administration Act (PL 99-64) to restrict trade with Angola.

The House approved the conference report by voice vote Oct. 2 and the Senate followed suit Oct. 7, completing congressional action on the bill. ∎

Foreign Bribery Penalties

The Senate Banking Committee approved legislation Sept. 17 to relax a 1977 law against bribery of foreign officials by U.S. companies. The bill (S 430 — S Rept 99-486) was reported Sept. 24, but the full Senate never considered the measure.

Backers of the bill, which the committee approved on a 10-3 vote, said it was needed to clarify portions of the 1977 law that they said had led to confusion in business circles. But William Proxmire, D-Wis., author of the original measure, scorned the bill as a measure to "bring back bribery" by taking the teeth out of the law.

Similar changes in the anti-bribery law were included in an omnibus trade bill (HR 4800) passed by the House in May. The Senate never acted on a comprehensive trade measure. *(House trade bill, p. 341)*

Background

Congress enacted the Foreign Corrupt Practices Act of 1977 (PL 95-213) in the wake of scandals involving large-scale foreign bribery by U.S. firms during the mid-1970s. The law prohibited American firms from making payments to foreign officials or politicians in an attempt to win business contracts from other governments or to influence legislation or regulations of other governments. *(1977 Almanac p. 413)*

Efforts by business and trade groups to ease some of the law's provisions resulted in Senate passage in 1981 of a bill essentially identical to S 430. The House did not act on the measure. The Senate Banking Committee approved the bill again in 1983, but that bill also died. *(1981 action, 1981 Almanac p. 421)*

Proposed Changes

As reported by the Banking Committee, S 430 continued to outlaw bribery, but permitted "facilitating payments" to foreign officials for the purpose of expediting "routine" governmental actions. Critics claimed that routine actions, which were not defined in the bill, could include the awarding of contracts and other substantive decisions.

The bill also allowed payments or gifts offered as a "token of regard or esteem," which Proxmire described as a huge loophole in the law.

Another section of the bill eased a part of the anti-bribery law that pertained to illegal payments made by third-party intermediaries, such as someone acting on a corporation's behalf to secure business in a foreign country. S 430 changed the standard of proof under which corporate officials could be found to violate the anti-bribery law when it came to payments made by intermediaries. Under existing law, such officials who had "reason to know" that bribes had been paid by intermediaries could be prosecuted. Under the measure, those officials would have to authorize a payment directly in order to run afoul of the law, probably a more difficult thing to prove. ∎

Romania Trade Privileges

House conservatives failed in an attempt July 29 to reverse President Reagan's decision to continue special trade privileges for Romania.

Lawmakers upset with Reagan's June 3 action tried to

discharge from the Ways and Means Committee a measure (H Res 475) introduced by Philip M. Crane, R-Ill., opposing extension of most-favored-nation (MFN) status to Romania for one more year.

But a motion by Sam Gibbons, D-Fla., to table Crane's discharge effort passed on a 216-190 vote, scuttling his legislative maneuvering to overturn Reagan's decision. *(Vote 232, p. 68-H)*

Countries accorded MFN status were allowed to ship goods into the United States at the same lower tariff rates that were applied to goods coming in from other U.S. trading partners.

The controversy over Romania was sparked by Reagan's June decision to waive, in that country's case, MFN prohibitions against communist countries unless they had adequate emigration policies. Romania was first granted MFN status by the United States in 1975.

Crane and others argued that Romania was guilty of human rights violations, including restrictive emigration practices, and did not deserve the continued trade benefits provided by MFN status. *(Background, 1983 Almanac p. 264)*

But those defending Reagan's action said providing trade privileges to Romania had succeeded in stimulating emigration and improving overall human rights conditions in that country.

That position was underscored by a letter from Secretary of State George P. Shultz, in which he said that revoking Romania's MFN status would worsen, rather than improve, human rights conditions there. ▮

Trade Adjustment Aid

Congress reauthorized the Trade Adjustment Assistance program as part of deficit-reduction legislation cleared March 20 (HR 3128 — PL 99-272).

Trade adjustment benefits went to workers who had been laid off from industries harmed by import competition. A small portion of the benefits also went to small and medium-sized firms suffering from imports. The Reagan administration opposed the program, which had last been extended in 1983. *(1983 Almanac p. 251)*

While voting a six-year extension of the program, Congress dropped from the final version of the bill a new tax on imports to pay for it. The fee provision had been one of the administration's chief objections to the bill as reported by Senate-House conferees in December 1985. *(Deficit-reduction action, p. 555)*

Also deleted from the final bill were a system of paying workers up to $4,000 for job training costs and a provision that would have required workers to be in training programs in order to receive cash benefits. Instead, these benefits were linked to participation in job search programs.

Other trade-related provisions of HR 3128 established a set of fees to be charged by the U.S. Customs Service to cover inspection costs of passengers and goods arriving in the United States. The fees, however, would not apply to passengers coming from Canada, Mexico, U.S. territories and adjacent islands.

Provisions

As signed into law April 7, the trade provisions of HR 3128:

- **Trade Adjustment Assistance.** Reauthorized for six years, through fiscal 1991, the Trade Adjustment Assistance program that aided workers and firms hurt by import competition. Under the bill, the program would continue providing cash benefits to displaced workers after their unemployment insurance ran out.

The bill provided retroactive benefits to workers who were receiving aid when the program lapsed Dec. 19, 1985.

- Required that workers participate in job search programs in order to receive cash benefits. In addition, the bill required the Labor Department to reimburse workers' expenses for job search workshops and job-finding clubs. An exception to the job search requirement was made in cases where no such program was available.
- Eliminated loans or loan guarantees to firms adversely affected by foreign competition. Instead, firms would be eligible to receive only technical assistance, as previously provided in the program.
- Specifically emphasized that workers in agricultural firms could apply for Trade Adjustment Assistance, as provided under existing law.
- **Customs Service.** Authorized $772.1 million in fiscal 1986 for the Customs Service, of which $53.5 million would go for the agency's air interdiction program. The funding amount for Customs specifically restored the administration's proposed cut of 887 positions in fiscal 1986 and added $27.9 million to hire 800 new employees in fiscal 1986-88.
- Imposed user fees on passengers, vehicles and vessels arriving in the United States to cover the Customs Service's inspection costs. Charges would include $397 for commercial vessels of 100 net tons or more; $25 per year for private aircraft and boats; $5 for each commercial truck and railroad car (not to exceed $100 per year); $5 for each vessel or aircraft passenger arriving from outside Canada, Mexico, U.S. territories and adjacent islands. The fees would go into effect 90 days after enactment. ▮

FOREIGN POLICY

CQ

Foreign Policy

Foreign policy issues dominated the Washington agenda for much of 1986, with President Reagan seeming to fall behind Congress in the endless struggle for political dominance on those kinds of questions.

Reagan gained one major victory, cajoling Congress into restoring military aid to the "contra" guerrillas in Nicaragua. But Congress seized the initiative on other important matters, and the president was critically wounded at year's end by the emergence of a national scandal over the sale of U.S. arms to Iran and the possibly illegal diversion of money from those sales to the contras.

The relationship between Reagan and Congress on foreign affairs issues had never been comfortable. The president had a much more aggressive, militaristic approach to foreign policy than many members of Congress were willing to accept. Reagan also chafed at congressional assertiveness; for example, he seemed to view legislative restrictions on his actions in Central America as unwarranted intrusions into his constitutional powers rather than as legitimate disagreements on policy.

By 1986, Reagan was less able or willing than before to avoid impending legislative defeats by making sudden 11th-hour compromises. Over the years, one of Reagan's remarkable characteristics had been his ability to fashion victories from almost certain defeats. But in the middle of his second term, Reagan often seemed reluctant to make the necessary compromises, so he was left behind as Congress established policy on its own.

The most dramatic instance of congressional lead-taking was Capitol Hill's imposition of economic sanctions against South Africa. Not since 1973, during the reaction against U.S. intervention in Vietnam, had Congress overridden a president so decisively on foreign policy. Congress set the terms on other issues, including the Philippines, arms sales to the Middle East and priorities in foreign aid spending.

Iran-Contra Affair

The first week of November brought a double dose of bad news for Reagan: the Democratic takeover of the Senate in the midterm elections, and the revelation in a Beirut magazine that the United States had been secretly selling arms to Iran.

After first denying reports about the arms sales, Reagan finally acknowledged Nov. 13 that he had allowed shipments to Iran of a "small quantity" of "defensive" weapons.

For weeks on end, Reagan was battered with press reports dredging up details of secret deals in which Reagan had used Israel and shady financiers to sell weapons to Iran in exchange for the freedom of American hostages held by pro-Iranian factions in Beirut. The news was all the more startling because Reagan was shown as having succumbed to the wiles of the Ayatollah Ruhollah Khomeini, the man who taunted America as "the Great Satan" during President Carter's Iranian hostage crisis.

Before the Iran arms furor could die down, Reagan himself acknowledged Nov. 25 that his aides might have diverted profits from those arms sales to benefit the contras. A foreign policy blunder suddenly became a scandal, with possibly illegal acts having been planned inside the White House.

Both chambers of Congress appointed Watergate-style special committees to investigate all aspects of the Iran-contra affair, and Reagan named a three-member commission headed by former Sen. John Tower, R-Texas, to probe the activities of the National Security Council staff. At the administration's request, a three-judge panel also selected noted Oklahoma attorney Lawrence E. Walsh as independent counsel to probe for possible violations of law.

Besides causing enormous political damage to the president, the Iran-contra affair undermined U.S. positions overseas, especially in the Middle East.

The biggest casualty was Reagan's cherished anti-terrorism policy, which stated that the United States would make no deals with terrorists and would use military might to strike against them whenever possible. Reagan had bombed Libya in April to demonstrate his eagerness to attack terrorism at the source. But with each unfolding revelation, Reagan's toughness appeared more superficial than real. The president had been so anguished by the fate of five American hostages, his aides said, that he was willing to offer weapons to a country he had called "Murder Inc."

Contra Aid

In addition to undermining Reagan's credibility, the Iran-contra affair threatened to undo one of the president's most important accomplishments of 1986: getting Congress to restore direct U.S. military aid to the contras. Although the scandal did not change the underlying issues in Central America, it did suggest that the administration was willing to use any means to reach its goal of ousting the leftist Sandinista government in Managua.

Reagan for the third year in a row had to fight every step of the way on the contra issue, losing at first, then scrambling back to wear down the opposition.

In February Reagan asked for $100 million in military and non-military aid for the guerrillas — along with permission to spend the money as he saw fit, with no strings attached. Congress had barred military aid since 1984, although in 1985 it allowed $27 million in non-military supplies for the contras.

The House rejected the $100 million request on a narrow vote in March, but the president and his allies lobbied hard and managed to reverse the vote in June. The

Senate, which for years had narrowly supported Reagan's Nicaragua policies, followed suit in August.

Although Democratic leaders managed to delay final appropriation of the money until October, the nine-vote margin of the crucial House vote in June appeared at the time to break the back of congressional resistance to supporting the contras. Administration officials compared the House action to a watershed May 1984 vote by which that chamber grudgingly accepted Reagan's policy of aiding the embattled government of El Salvador.

Critics acknowledged that Reagan's persistence had paid off and that their own efforts to fashion alternatives had run out of steam. Weeks before the House voted, leaders of the five Central American countries failed in a last-ditch effort to negotiate a peace agreement. Contra aid opponents had held out the prospect of an agreement as a major reason for opposing aid to the contras, so the collapse of peace talks meant that members faced a stark choice of supporting Reagan or opposing him.

At year's end, it was uncertain just how much damage the Iran-contra affair had done to political prospects for the underlying contra aid program. Perhaps as harmful as the scandal was the developing impression in Washington that five years of U.S. support had failed to turn the contras into an effective and unified fighting force.

South Africa Sanctions

Rarely has a president suffered such a crushing defeat on a foreign issue as did Reagan on South Africa. Responding to domestic political concerns and to growing violence and repression in South Africa, Congress in October brushed aside Reagan's objections and imposed economic sanctions on the white minority government in Pretoria. The sanctions fell far short of a complete economic break between the two countries but did repudiate the Reagan policy of coaxing change in South Africa through a friendly process of "constructive engagement."

South Africa was barely an issue during most of Reagan's first term. Outside the State Department's Africa bureau, few administration officials gave much thought to that troubled country. Congress was preoccupied with the budget, Central America and other issues.

But racial violence mounted in South Africa early in 1984, and later that year the world's attention was captured by the eloquence of black Anglican Bishop Desmond Tutu, awarded the Nobel Peace Prize for his non-violent opposition to apartheid. During an extended visit to the United States, Tutu asked Congress to support sanctions against South Africa as a way of pressuring the government into negotiations with black leaders.

Both houses of Congress in 1985 passed bills imposing a limited range of economic sanctions. Reagan at the last minute headed off Senate action on a conference version by signing an executive order imposing his own milder sanctions.

With midterm elections approaching, Congress took up the issue again in 1986. But as the year wore on, it became clear that key Republican leaders had decided that Reagan was out of step with the American public, which was repulsed by Pretoria's brutal tactics in enforcing racial laws, particularly the imposition of strict press censorship and a state of emergency.

Richard G. Lugar, R-Ind., chairman of the Senate Foreign Relations Committee, emerged as the central figure on South Africa. Buoyed by his role earlier in the year in promoting a democratic revolution in the Philippines, Lugar urged Reagan to take a tough stand on South Africa.

Reagan's response — a nationally televised daytime speech that chastised black radicals and barely mentioned the white government — dismayed Lugar and other Republicans who had hoped for presidential leadership.

By an overwhelming margin, the Senate in August passed a bill imposing a wide range of economic and political sanctions on South Africa and threatening more in the future. Lugar then used political muscle and deft parliamentary maneuvering to force the House into accepting the Senate bill.

Once again turning a deaf ear to Lugar's pleas, Reagan vetoed the measure, saying it went too far and would eliminate whatever influence the United States had in South Africa.

But on a dramatic October afternoon, Lugar led the Senate in overriding the veto. The 78-21 vote, following an equally wide margin in the House, formally enacted the sanctions into law and established a new era for U.S. policy toward Africa.

The veto override was the first on a foreign policy issue since 1973, when Congress enacted the War Powers Resolution into law over President Nixon's objections.

Some, including Senate Majority Leader Robert Dole, R-Kan., complained that Congress was reacting more to American political considerations than to the realities of South Africa.

While substantially true, that charge ignored the fact that all U.S. actions overseas had roots in domestic politics. In the aftermath of the Vietnam War, every president had encountered trouble in carrying out unpopular foreign policies. By his seeming defense of a dictatorial regime, Reagan lagged well behind an aroused public, and so Congress was bound to respond.

New Era in Manila

South Africa was an extreme case of a recurrent problem for the United States: what to do, if anything, about friendly countries that happened to have undemocratic governments. The Philippines raised the same question, coupled with a unique set of political problems.

Ever since President Carter made promoting respect for human rights a fundamental goal of U.S. foreign policy, Washington sought with little success to goad or even force its friends into matching its ideals. The Reagan administration, while proclaiming its interest in human rights and democracy overseas, preferred quiet diplomacy in asking allies to adopt those virtues.

A former colony and the home to two important U.S. military bases, the Philippines long had enjoyed a special relationship with the United States. But the dictatorial and corrupt style of Manila's president, Ferdinand E. Marcos, also presented a special dilemma for the Reagan administration. Although a faithful ally, Marcos refused to make meaningful political and economic reforms, fueling a growing communist insurgency that worried U.S. policy makers.

In contrast to U.S. policy toward South Africa, the Reagan administration and Congress worked closely together on the Philippines. Key officials in the State and Defense departments, along with a handful of interested congressional leaders, early in the Reagan years adopted a united strategy of firm, increasingly public pressure on Marcos to reform.

Marcos threw all his critics off balance late in 1985, announcing "snap" presidential elections. Although it appeared at the time to be a brilliant political maneuver, that action ultimately was Marcos' undoing. It provided the needed incentive for the non-communist opposition to unite behind Corazon C. Aquino, the widow of assassinated opposition leader Benigno S. Aquino Jr., and it forced Washington to take a clear stand in favor of clean elections in the Philippines.

By Philippine standards, the election campaign was fair. But on election day, Feb. 7, 1986, Marcos used every tool at his disposal in a successful drive to rig the outcome in his behalf. Led by Lugar, a delegation of U.S. observers witnessed cases of vote fraud, and most came away convinced that Marcos had stolen the election.

Reagan at first wavered in his response, saying in a news conference after the election that "both sides" had committed irregularities. As protests mounted against Marcos in the Philippines and against Reagan on Capitol Hill, the administration finally responded with new demands for an honest vote count.

Then, in a dramatic February weekend, top Philippine military leaders seized an army installation in Manila and declared their loyalty to Aquino. As thousands of civilians surrounded the base to protect it from Marcos loyalists, Reagan sent private and public messages urging the dictator to step down.

The beleaguered Marcos responded just as many critics had predicted: Late on Feb. 25, after having himself sworn in for a new term as president, Marcos climbed aboard a U.S. helicopter and took off for exile in Hawaii.

Marcos left behind a host of troubles, and Washington took only limited steps to help out. Reagan asked for a $100 million extra foreign aid boost for Manila in fiscal 1986; Congress responded with $150 million. Congress promised another $200 million bonus, but the windfall after Aquino made a compelling personal appeal to a joint session, did not last long. Along with all other countries, the Philippines suffered from sharp congressional cutbacks in foreign aid for fiscal 1987.

Less than a year after Marcos' departure, Philippine voters on Feb. 3, 1987, gave Aquino a vote of confidence, ratifying a new constitution allowing her to stay in office until 1992.

The 'Reagan Doctrine'

Early in 1986 the administration put into place the latest major piece of a policy that had come to be known as the "Reagan doctrine."

The White House denied that such a doctrine existed, and so a strict definition was hard to come by, but it was clear that Reagan had initiated a general policy of aiding anti-communist insurgencies around the world. On a practical basis, the Reagan doctrine appeared to provide a broad justification for covert operations by the CIA, especially those targeting leftist regimes.

Early in his presidency, Reagan boosted an ongoing program of U.S. aid to Moslem guerrillas battling the Soviet occupation of Afghanistan, and he opened the new channel of aid to the Nicaraguan contras. Congress in 1985 also initiated a small non-military aid program for anti-Vietnamese forces in Cambodia.

That left Angola. For more than a decade, Reagan and other conservatives had cited Angola as a pre-eminent case of congressional interference in foreign affairs. Congress in 1975-76 ended CIA aid to one of three factions battling for control of Angola. An opposing leftist faction later won, leading American conservatives to complain that Congress had consigned Angola to a communist future.

In 1985, Reagan succeeded in getting Congress to lift all legal restrictions on CIA activities in Angola. Early in 1986 Angolan rebel leader Jonas Savimbi visited Washington — escorted by a public relations firm working on a $600,000 contract — and won Reagan's personal approval of an official U.S. aid program.

The administration in February notified Congress of its plan to ship about $14 million worth of weapons and other supplies to Savimbi's troops. Democrats on the House Intelligence Committee tried to block the aid but were rebuffed overwhelmingly on the House floor.

Reagan's success on Angola raised the question of how far he was prepared to go in bolstering anti-leftist forces. Administration officials insisted that they were seeking negotiated solutions in each case, not outright military victories by the U.S.-supported guerrillas.

But critics charged that the rebel forces did not have the necessary military and political clout to force the negotiations that Washington said it wanted. Another uncertainty was whether Reagan would extend his policy to other leftist countries with potentially vulnerable governments, such as Mozambique and Ethiopia.

Middle East: No Peace

Prospects for an Arab-Israeli peace — never good to begin with — dribbled away in 1986 as political leaders once again failed to take the necessary steps to break real and artificial deadlocks.

U.S. officials had hoped that 1985 would be the year for peace between Israel and Jordan, leading to a resolution of the decades-old dispute over the fate of Palestinian Arabs living on the Israeli-occupied West Bank of the Jordan River. When 1985 came and went, new hope surfaced for 1986, based on the assumption that peace-oriented Prime Minister Shimon Peres would work for an agreement to cap his two years in office, which expired in October.

But both Israel and Jordan continued to pose barriers to an agreement, in many cases procedural obstacles that had more to do with indecision than with the fundamental issues between the two countries. And for all practical purposes, the United States gave up its efforts to act as a middleman. Reagan had never demonstrated much interest in the Middle East peace process, and Secretary of State George P. Shultz was preoccupied with arms control, Central America and other matters.

The administration succeeded in winning congressional approval for a major arms sale to Saudi Arabia a year after being forced to withdraw a similar sale to Jordan. By a one-vote margin, the Senate on June 5 sustained Reagan's veto of a bill that would have blocked the sale of $265 million worth of missiles to Saudi Arabia.

The victory was not a ringing endorsement by Congress, however. Reagan succeeded only after withdrawing from the arms package $89 million worth of Stinger anti-aircraft missiles. Pro-Israel members of Congress, who routinely object to arms sales to Arab countries, claimed that the portable missiles could fall into the hands of terrorists.

Foreign Aid: Cutting Back

Election years are never good times for presidents to ask Congress for substantial increases in foreign aid. Election years in which Congress faces huge cutbacks in popular domestic spending programs are even worse. As a result, no one was surprised when Congress in 1986 slashed more than $2 billion from Reagan's request for foreign assistance

— forcing the State Department to retract promises it had made to dozens of countries for aid programs.

Reagan and Congress had been at odds over foreign aid for years. Early in his presidency, Reagan demanded, and got, huge increases in military aid for friendly countries, making those aid programs the fastest growing part of the federal budget. At the same time, Reagan pared spending on long-term economic development programs for poor countries.

Just as with defense spending, Congress eventually reacted against Reagan's persistent demands for increases in military aid. In both 1985 and 1986, Congress slashed overall totals for foreign aid but mandated minimum spending levels for specific items that were politically popular, such as aid to Israel and Egypt. The net result was that unprotected programs were subjected to extraordinary cuts, reaching 50 percent in some parts of the 1987 appropriations.

Shultz complained that Congress was irresponsibly shirking U.S. duties around the world. But administration critics — particularly David R. Obey, D-Wis., chairman of the House Appropriations Subcommittee on Foreign Operations — insisted that Congress was merely trying to cut the budget deficit and that Reagan was to blame for refusing to raise taxes to pay for the programs he wanted.

GOP Feuding in Senate

Although the most conservative president in decades, Reagan found his administration constantly subjected to ideological purity tests.

A handful of Senate Republicans and their supporters in far-right lobbying organizations repeatedly took the administration to task for falling short at critical junctures. Led by Jesse Helms, R-N.C., the conservatives were especially fond of tackling the State Department, which they said was dominated by career bureaucrats who did not support the Reagan agenda on arms control, Central America and other issues.

Helms shrewdly practiced political guerrilla warfare against an administration of his own party: delaying Senate action on nominees for top State Department positions, making speeches denouncing administration policies with which he disagreed, and having aides selectively leak information that might damage those policies.

In sharp contrast to Helms was Lugar, another conservative who was willing to put practical political considerations above ideological ones. During his two years as Foreign Relations chairman, Lugar skillfully patched together compromises and coalitions that saved Reagan from several potentially embarrassing defeats.

After the November elections, when Democrats took control of the Senate, Helms decided to challenge Lugar for the senior Republican position on Foreign Relations. Lugar had the backing of his fellow committee Republicans — except Helms — who appreciated his leadership skills.

But in a secret-ballot election in January 1987, Senate Republicans accepted Helms' claims that he deserved the top minority slot on the committee by virtue of seniority. Although they joined the committee on the same day in 1979, Helms had seniority over Lugar because he had served longer in the Senate.

The surprise Republican action put the two committee leadership positions in the hands of men often at odds with Reagan administration foreign policy: Chairman Claiborne Pell, D-R.I., a soft-spoken liberal, and Helms, the fire-breathing conservative.

—By John Felton

Hill Overrides Veto of South Africa Sanctions

Elbowing aside a president uncharacteristically resistant to compromise, the Senate on Oct. 2 overrode Ronald Reagan's veto of a measure (HR 4868) imposing economic sanctions against South Africa.

The 78-21 vote enacting the bill into law (PL 99-440) marked the most serious defeat Reagan had suffered on a foreign issue and one of the most stunning blows of his presidency. *(Vote 311, p. 52-S)*

The House had acted on Sept. 29, voting to override Reagan's veto 313-83. Reagan had vetoed the bill Sept. 26, but his aides did not lobby House members on the issue and made only limited efforts to block action in the Republican-controlled Senate. *(Vote 390, p. 110-H)*

As enacted, HR 4868 imposed a series of sanctions, such as barring importation of South African coal, steel and agricultural products and ending landing rights in the United States for the government-owned South African Airways. The measure also threatened future sanctions if the Pretoria government failed to move to end the "apartheid" system of racial segregation.

The final version of the bill was identical to the measure passed by the Senate Aug. 15. The House June 18 had passed a much stronger version that would have forced all U.S. companies to leave South Africa and ended virtually all trade between the two countries. House leaders agreed Sept. 12 to accept the milder Senate bill.

Although fundamentally altering a major U.S. policy, the veto override was not expected to have a long-term effect on Reagan's ability to handle foreign affairs. There was widespread agreement on Capitol Hill that South Africa represented a special case in which Reagan was so out of step with the American public that Congress had no choice but to intervene.

"We believe the president was not being heard loud and clear" in his opposition to South Africa's apartheid system of racial discrimination, said Richard G. Lugar, R-Ind., chairman of the Senate Foreign Relations Committee. With passage of the bill, he said, "We're going to make sure we are all heard with one voice."

Reagan readily accepted the congressional action and promised to implement the law. In a statement issued by the White House after the vote, Reagan said the debate between himself and Congress "was not whether to oppose apartheid but, instead, how best to oppose it and how best to bring freedom to that troubled country."

Nevertheless, Reagan insisted he had been correct in opposing sanctions because "they hurt the very people they are intended to help."

Not surprisingly, the white-minority government of South Africa was not so receptive to the message from Capitol Hill. Foreign Minister Pik Botha said the United States and other countries should "leave us alone." Congress acted "regardless of our reform program, and no reason or argument could stop this emotional wave," he said.

A Historic Vote

The congressional action was the first override of a presidential veto on a major foreign policy issue since 1973, when Congress enacted into law the War Powers Resolution (PL 93-148), giving it the right to withdraw troops from combat situations. *(1973 Almanac p. 905)*

Congress in the mid-1970s forced President Ford to accept modified versions of two major foreign policy bills after he exercised vetoes: an embargo on arms sales to Turkey in 1974 (PL 93-448) and a bill (PL 94-329) in 1976 giving Congress the right to veto foreign arms sales. *(1974 Almanac p. 547; 1976 Almanac p. 213)*

Congress had modified or stalled Reagan's policies on several foreign issues, most often involving Central America. In 1984 and 1985, Congress refused Reagan's requests for military aid to the Nicaraguan "contra" rebels. Political pressure also had forced Reagan to abandon seemingly fixed positions, as in 1984 when he responded to congressional demands and withdrew U.S. Marines from Lebanon.

But until the sanctions veto override, Congress had never repudiated Reagan so decisively. The rebuke was so complete, in fact, that Senate Majority Leader Robert Dole, R-Kan., suggested Congress had taken control of the South Africa issue. "It's going to be our policy; it's going to be the policy the Congress establishes, and then we'll be responsible," Dole told his colleagues minutes before the vote. "Who's going to direct that policy from the Congress of the United States?"

The common theme binding all of Congress' foreign policy battles with Reagan was public sentiment. Although an enormously popular president, Reagan had implemented a number of policies that appeared to have little backing among the voters. In those cases, Congress responded by devising alternatives and then seeking to negotiate with Reagan.

The difference in the South Africa case was that Reagan refused to budge. In 1985 he reluctantly imposed his own sanctions in response to congressional demands. But in 1986 Reagan stood fast in the face of mounting pressure. *(Previous action, 1985 Almanac p. 83; Reagan role, box, next page)*

Final Provisions

As enacted into law Oct. 2 over President Reagan's veto, HR 4868 (PL 99-440) contained the following major provisions:

Policy Goals

The bill set two kinds of policy goals for South Africa: immediate objectives, such as the lifting of the existing state of emergency, and long-term, broader objectives, including the creation of a "non-racial democratic form of government."

The immediate goals of the bill were to encourage the South African government to:

- Suspend the state of emergency imposed in mid-June and respect the principle of equal justice under law for citizens of all races.
- Release from prison African National Congress (ANC) leader Nelson Mandela and his colleagues, black trade union leaders and all political prisoners. While outlawed, the ANC was one of the most prominent black opposition groups in South Africa.
- Allow all South African citizens to form political parties, freely express political opinions and participate in the political process.
- Establish a timetable for eliminating apartheid.

'Less Than Brilliant' Administration Role . . .

Throughout his presidency, Ronald Reagan's successes in Congress had come in large part because of his ability and willingness to strike a deal at the right moment, even on issues that involved his fundamental principles.

But on South Africa, Reagan staked out a position early in his presidency and steadfastly refused to make anything other than minor changes in it.

He ignored or missed several opportunities to shape the course of political sentiment in the United States toward South Africa.

"To put it in the mildest terms," Robert H. Michel, R-Ill., the House minority leader, said Sept. 29, "the administration has been less than brilliant in handling this issue."

In the early years of his presidency, Reagan himself seemed to ignore South Africa, leaving policy making to the State Department's Africa bureau, headed by Assistant Secretary Chester Crocker. Reagan devoted no speeches to and made no comments about South Africa until late 1984, when the movement toward sanctions was beginning to build.

Crocker in 1981 drafted and got Reagan's approval for a policy described as "constructive engagement." As envisioned by Crocker, the policy was to apply to all of southern Africa, and was to include friendly persuasion not only toward racial reform in South Africa but also toward settlement of longstanding disputes involving South Africa and the neighboring countries of Angola, Mozambique and Namibia.

In spite of Crocker's diplomatic success in negotiating limited agreements, the phrase "constructive engagement" was widely interpreted both in the United States and in South Africa as a policy of sympathy for the government in Pretoria. That interpretation was reinforced by some of Reagan's earliest actions toward South Africa — the easing of embargoes that President Carter had imposed on sales of computers and other items to security forces in Pretoria.

Liberals and blacks in the United States condemned constructive engagement from the start, but it took several years for South Africa and Reagan's policy to become a major issue in the United States.

The key event was a demonstration at the South African Embassy in Washington on Thanksgiving Day, 1984. Del. Walter E. Fauntroy, D-D.C., TransAfrica director Randall Robinson and other civil rights leaders demonstrated at the embassy, deliberately getting themselves arrested.

In the following weeks, more than 20 members of Congress — including one senator, Lowell P. Weicker Jr., R-Conn. — joined the hundreds stepping from the embassy picket line into police patrol wagons. Charges were not pressed against any of those arrested, but the demonstrations helped make South Africa a public issue.

Americans also were impressed by the eloquence of Anglican Bishop Desmond Tutu, a black South African awarded the Nobel Peace Prize in December 1984.

Anti-apartheid groups in South Africa stepped up demonstrations early in 1985, provoking a cycle of crackdowns by security forces and more protests. Unrest in South Africa became daily news in the United States, forcing politicians to focus on the substance and results of Reagan's policy toward that country.

Sensing growing concern, many Republicans in Congress — especially those who had been involved in the civil rights struggles of the 1960s — urged Reagan to step up his pressure on South Africa. In December 1984, 35 House conservatives wrote the South African ambassador, Bernardus G. Fourie, threatening to support some economic sanctions unless Pretoria moved to dismantle apartheid.

The House in June 1985 overwhelmingly passed a bill (HR 1460) imposing modest sanctions on South Africa, such as banning bank loans to the government and businesses, barring new business investment there and prohibiting importation of South African gold coins called Krugerrands. The Senate followed suit in July with an even more limited version (S 995) banning bank loans to the Pretoria government and prohibiting most nuclear and computer sales to South Africa, among other things.

A House-Senate conference on July 31, 1985, focused on the Krugerrand issue. Foreign Relations Committee Chairman Richard G. Lugar, Ind., pressed by the House and facing defections by other Senate Republicans, reluctantly agreed to the import ban on those coins.

The August recess interrupted congressional action on the conference bill and gave Reagan time to act on his own. On Sept. 9, 1985, Reagan issued an executive order

- Negotiate with representatives of all races for a new political system.
- End military and paramilitary actions aimed at neighboring countries.

The bill also called on the ANC, the Pan African Congress and their affiliates to: suspend "terrorist activities" so that negotiations would be possible with the government and other black groups, commit to a "free and democratic post-apartheid South Africa" and agree to enter into negotiations for the "peaceful solution" of that country's problems.

The bill supported the right of the ANC and other groups to negotiate with the government, but said the United States would withdraw that support if the South African government took certain steps and the ANC did not. The United States would back negotiations excluding the ANC and related groups, the bill said, if Pretoria agreed to negotiations without preconditions, abandoned "unprovoked violence" against its opponents and committed itself to a free and democratic post-apartheid South Africa — and if the black groups refused to abandon unprovoked violence during negotiations and refused to commit themselves to a free and democratic post-apartheid South Africa.

The bill also called on the ANC to "strongly condemn and take effective action" against "necklacing," a practice in which black militants placed burning, gasoline-filled tires around the necks and legs of blacks suspected of

. . . Contributed to Momentum for Sanctions

imposing many of the sanctions in the bill, including the Krugerrand ban.

Giving Reagan credit for acting, Lugar and Majority Leader Robert Dole, R-Kan., supported a Senate filibuster of the conference bill. Several attempts to stop the filibuster failed; to ensure the bill's death Dole and Lugar took the official copy from the Senate chamber and locked it in the Foreign Relations Committee safe. *(1985 Almanac p. 83)*

Lugar and other Republicans said they hoped Reagan would follow up his executive order with new diplomatic pressure on South Africa for real changes in apartheid. Those hopes were dashed, however, by Reagan's willingness to accept assertions by South Africa's president, P. W. Botha, that his government was moving as quickly as possible.

Sanctions Drive Gathers Speed

Racial violence continued in South Africa in 1986, adding fuel to the pro-sanctions movement in the United States. In June, anticipating demonstrations marking the 10th anniversary of the 1976 black riots in Soweto, Pretoria imposed strict press censorship and a sweeping state of emergency. The press rules — effectively banning any reporting not sanctioned by the government — got Washington's attention as had few other events in South Africa, causing members of Congress to question why Reagan appeared blind to that dictatorship while he was willing to castigate others.

The House in June took up a bill (HR 4868) strengthening the sanctions Reagan had ordered and adding new ones, such as a ban on new business investment in South Africa.

In a calculated gamble, Republicans stepped aside and allowed the House to pass an amendment sponsored by Ronald V. Dellums, D-Calif., suspending virtually all trade with South Africa and forcing U.S. businesses to leave that country within six months.

The Republicans thought the Dellums measure was so extreme that its passage by the House would kill any chance for sanctions legislation in the Senate. They were wrong. Instead, the House action shifted the entire political balance on South Africa, establishing a new set of limits for what Congress could consider and making any other set of sanctions seem moderate by comparison. As Dellums said later, the House had moved back the political "fear barrier" for members.

Reagan apparently failed to recognize the changed circumstances. The turning point came on July 22, when Reagan made a nationally televised speech from the Oval Office intended to quell sanctions fervor in the Senate. The speech was timed specifically to affect action by the Foreign Relations Committee, which had scheduled hearings on South Africa to start on July 23.

The day before the speech, Lugar and Sen. Nancy Landon Kassebaum, R-Kan., went to the White House and asked Reagan to make a strong anti-apartheid speech.

Reagan did come out against apartheid, but that message was lost in his condemnation of sanctions and his sharp attack on the African National Congress. The speech was a political and public relations disaster; rather than calming the furor in Congress, it generated more controversy by seeming to show that the president was unyielding on his policy and more sympathetic toward the Botha government than toward South African blacks.

Dismayed, Lugar immediately set about to forge a consensus for a "moderate" bill. He introduced his own proposal, including several export bans and a prohibition on new business investment in South Africa. In committee, and again on the floor, Lugar accepted strengthening amendments by Democrats as the price for getting a bill passed with broad bipartisan support. But he fought off amendments that might have jeopardized GOP votes.

Hours before leaving for its recess on Aug. 15, the Senate passed the sanctions bill 84-14. Lugar immediately began putting pressure on the House to bypass a conference committee and accept the Senate bill, saying only such a course would prevent a filibuster from killing the bill. In private talks with House leaders, Lugar offered another incentive: If the House accepted the Senate bill, Lugar promised to stand by it, even in the face of an almost certain veto by the president.

The House reluctantly gave in to Lugar's pressure, and on Sept. 12 sent the Senate bill to Reagan by a 308-77 vote. *(Vote 351, p. 100-H)*

Lugar, Kassebaum and others tried but failed to persuade the president to accept it. Reagan vetoed the bill on Sept. 26 — the last of 10 days he had to consider it, saying it would impose "sweeping punitive sanctions that would injure most the very people we seek to help. . . ."

---

cooperating with the government.

For the long term, the bill called for the establishment of a full-fledged democracy and the dismantling of apartheid, but it did not establish specific criteria for judging implementation of those goals. For example, it did not call for any particular political system, such as one-man, one-vote representation.

Sanctions

The bill imposed several new sanctions and directed the president to take other steps. It:

- Required the president, within 10 days of enactment, to direct the Transportation Department to prohibit any South African-owned airline (South African Airways) from operating in the United States, and required the secretary of state to terminate a 1947 air travel agreement between the two countries. It also prohibited U.S. airliners from taking off and landing in South Africa.
- Prohibited importation into the United States of articles produced by South African government-owned or controlled organizations, called "parastatals." Strategic minerals were exempt from the import ban, however, if the president certified to Congress that the amounts of those minerals produced in the United States were inadequate for military needs.
- Banned the importation of these specific items from South Africa: textiles, uranium and uranium ore, iron and steel, coal and agricultural products.

• Barred new U.S. loans to South African businesses, the Pretoria government or any entity it controlled, and forbade U.S. firms to make any new investments in South Africa. The ban on new investments, however, did not apply to firms owned by black South Africans. The ban also did not apply to renewals of existing loans, to short-term financings such as letters of credit, or to reinvestments by U.S. firms of profits earned in South Africa on their existing investments.

• Prohibited U.S. banks from accepting deposits by any South African government agency, except for one account maintained in the United States for diplomatic and consular purposes.

• Prohibited exports to South Africa of crude oil and petroleum products.

• Barred the export to South Africa of any items on the official U.S. list of munitions (primarily weapons and military items), except for items that the president certified would be used solely for commercial purposes and not for use by the South African armed forces, police or other security forces. The president was required to notify Congress 30 days before allowing such sales, giving Congress time to pass a joint resolution rejecting them.

• Prohibited U.S. government agencies from engaging in any form of cooperation, directly or indirectly, with the South African armed forces. The only exception was for activities "reasonably designed to facilitate the necessary collection of intelligence" — and those activities had to be reported in advance to Congress, which had no formal power to stop them.

• Prohibited importation of sugar and sugar-related products from South Africa, and transferred South Africa's portion of the U.S. sugar import quota to the Philippines.

• Terminated immediately a 1946 U.S.-South African treaty intended to prevent businesses from paying taxes on the same income to both countries. Other U.S. laws, however, would continue tax deductions or credits to American individuals or companies in South Africa.

• Prohibited U.S. government agencies from contracting with or buying items from South African government-owned firms, except for those necessary for diplomatic purposes. U.S. agencies were urged to buy from black-owned businesses in South Africa instead.

• Prohibited use of U.S. government funds to promote tourism in South Africa or to promote or subsidize trade with that country. However, another provision authorized the secretary of agriculture to use U.S. subsidy and loan programs to encourage agricultural exports to South Africa.

• Stated that U.S. policy would be to impose more sanctions if South Africa did not make "substantial progress" toward ending apartheid in a year.

If the president determined, after a year, that substantial progress had not been made, he was required to recommend additional sanctions, such as: barring all South Africans from holding U.S. bank accounts, banning importation of South African diamonds and strategic minerals and halting military aid to any country that supplied arms to South Africa. The last provision could affect Israel, which reportedly had sold weapons to Pretoria in the past. Israel had denied selling arms to South Africa in recent years, but to determine the facts, the bill required the president to report to Congress within 180 days on which countries were violating a U.N. arms embargo against South Africa.

• Established the following penalties for violations of the sanctions: a fine of up to $1 million for businesses and a fine of up to $50,000 and/or imprisonment of up to five years for individuals. Anyone guilty of importing the South African gold coins called Krugerrands could be fined up to five times the value of the coins involved.

The bill also declared that any action by foreign companies to take advantage of the U.S. sanctions would be considered an "unfair trade practice," potentially triggering retaliation by the administration.

The bill included two provisions encouraging other nations to act against South Africa. The most important required the president to begin negotiations with other countries toward an international agreement on sanctions and to report to Congress within 180 days on the results of his efforts. If the president reached such an agreement, he could modify the sanctions imposed by the bill to reflect the agreement — but only if he reported the agreement to Congress and Congress within 30 days passed a joint resolution approving his action.

Many of the sanctions in the bill were similar to those adopted by the British Commonwealth in early August. *(Sanctions roundup, box, p. 368)*

The bill stated the sense of Congress that the U.N. Security Council should impose the same sanctions as the United States.

The bill also might have the effect of overturning state and local anti-apartheid laws, such as those barring contracts to companies doing business in South Africa.

Lifting Sanctions

All sanctions imposed by the bill would be ended if the president reported to Congress that the South African government had done five things: freed ANC chief Mandela and all persons persecuted for their political beliefs or detained without trial; repealed the state of emergency and released all persons detained under it; legalized democratic political parties and permitted all South Africans to join political parties, to express political opinions and to participate in the political process; repealed the Group Areas Act and the Population Registration Act, which restricted where non-whites lived and worked, and did not institute other measures with the same purposes; and agreed to enter into good-faith negotiations with "truly representative" black leaders without preconditions.

The president also could suspend or modify any of the sanctions in the bill 30 days after reporting to Congress that Pretoria had released Mandela and the political prisoners, had taken three of the other four actions and had made "substantial progress" toward dismantling apartheid and establishing a non-racial democracy. Congress could overturn the president's decision by passing a joint resolution — over his likely veto — within the 30 days.

Another provision allowed the president, acting on his own, to lift any of the sanctions against South Africa after six months if he reported to Congress that the sanctions would increase U.S. dependence for coal and strategic minerals on communist countries belonging to the Council for Mutual Economic Assistance, which included the Soviet Union, its Eastern European allies and Cuba. The president could act if he found that U.S. dependence on communist countries for any of those materials would increase over the average annual imports during 1981-85.

Reagan's Executive Order

The bill put into permanent law all of the sanctions that President Reagan imposed on South Africa in his Sept. 9, 1985, executive order. Those were bans on:

• The importation of Krugerrands.

- The importation into the United States of arms, ammunition or military vehicles made in South Africa.
- The export of computers, computer software and related items to South Africa for use by government agencies, such as the police, and the government's weapons industries.
- Loans by U.S. banks or companies to the government of South Africa or any organization it controlled. Exempted were loans for educational, housing or health facilities that were accessible to persons of all races.
- The export to South Africa of nuclear-power equipment and supplies, except those needed for "humanitarian" purposes or, if South Africa committed itself to international standards, to reduce the spread of nuclear arms.

Aid to Blacks

The bill reaffirmed the U.S. commitment to help "the victims of apartheid" through direct financial aid and other efforts.

It authorized $40 million annually, beginning in fiscal 1987, for economic aid to disadvantaged South Africans, regardless of race. Of that amount, up to $3 million each year would be provided for training of trade unionists in organizing and other union-related skills. None of the funds could be provided to organizations financed or controlled by the South African government.

Another section of the bill authorized $4 million annually for scholarships for victims of apartheid. The bill also authorized $10 million for the purchase of housing for black South African employees of the U.S. government.

An additional $1.5 million annually was allocated for the State Department's human rights fund, which supported activities by rights groups in South Africa. Individuals or groups involved in necklacing could not receive aid.

U.S. firms employing more than 25 persons in South Africa would be required to adhere to the labor code formulated by the Rev. Leon Sullivan of Philadelphia. Under the code, companies were obliged to practice non-discrimination and to provide housing, education and other benefits for disadvantaged workers.

Other Provisions

In other provisions, the bill:

- Banned the importation of Soviet gold coins.
- Required the attorney general to report to Congress, within 180 days, on actual and alleged violations of the Foreign Agents Registration Act by representatives of governments or opposition groups in southern Africa, including the African National Congress. The foreign agents act required those lobbying in Washington on behalf of foreign governments or groups to register with the Justice Department. The attorney general also was to report on the status of any investigations into such violations.

House Committee Action

Against the backdrop of a renewed government crackdown in South Africa, sanctions legislation moved through two House committees June 10-11.

The Foreign Affairs Committee approved HR 4868 June 10 on a 27-14 vote. Three Republicans on the panel — Jim Leach of Iowa, Olympia J. Snowe of Maine and Christopher H. Smith of New Jersey — joined 24 Democrats in voting for the bill. HR 4868, formally reported June 13 (H Rept 99-638, Part I), had been approved by the Africa Subcommittee on a 6-4 vote June 4.

As reported, the measure contained provisions to bar new U.S. investments and loans in South Africa and cut off imports of South African coal, uranium and steel. In addition, it would stop U.S. participation in South African energy development and threaten to halt American computer company sales to South African government agencies and private firms unless the Pretoria government began "good faith" negotiations with black leaders and freed political prisoners.

One of the bill's advocates, Stephen J. Solarz, D-N.Y., said the administration's constructive engagement policy, begun in 1981, had created an impression of U.S. friendliness toward Pretoria. "Five years later I think the verdict is in," he said. "Despite what may have been the best of intentions, the policy has failed."

Noting that the White House had imposed economic sanctions against countries such as Nicaragua and Libya, Solarz and others said Reagan was being inconsistent by rejecting that tactic against South Africa. "If we are going to stand up against repression in Central America and terrorism in the Middle East, then I think it is time to stand up against racism in South Africa," said Solarz.

The committee brushed aside last-minute pleas against the bill by Secretary of State George P. Shultz and Secretary of Commerce Malcolm Baldrige, both of whom sent letters to committee members.

Shultz called apartheid a "doomed system" that had "simply become unacceptable to the majority of the South African people." But he also said the sanctions in the House measure would undermine administration efforts to seek changes in South Africa's racial policies. "We do not believe it should be our purpose to harm the South African economy; nor do we believe that such action will hasten the end of apartheid," he said.

Joining in criticism of the bill was Foreign Affairs member Henry J. Hyde, R-Ill., who described it as a "Democratic policy of scorched earth for South Africa."

Other Committees

A day after the Foreign Affairs action, the Ways and Means Committee approved the bill (H Rept 99-638, Part 2) on a voice vote. Ways and Means, which had jurisdiction over trade matters, acted on the bill because of the sections banning imports of various South African products.

The bill also banned the mining of natural resources by U.S. firms in Namibia, a territory controlled by South Africa.

Richard T. Schulze, R-Pa., tried to include diamonds on the list of products that would no longer be imported from South Africa. But that was swiftly rejected after supporters said the other products — coal, uranium and steel — were readily available in the United States, and that banning them would not harm the U.S. economy.

Two other House committees — Banking, Finance and Urban Affairs and Public Works and Transportation — had jurisdiction over different parts of the bill but decided against separate markups.

Banking's authority extended to provisions cutting off new bank loans to South African businesses. Public Works' jurisdiction covered a section that would deny U.S. landing rights for South African Airways.

House Floor Action

The House passed HR 4868 June 18 after voting to clamp a comprehensive trade embargo on South Africa and require all U.S. companies there to leave within 180 days of enactment.

The unexpected approval of such far-reaching sanctions occurred when the House on a voice vote approved a substitute offered by Ronald V. Dellums, D-Calif., for the milder sanctions bill pushed by Democratic leaders. Final passage also came on a voice vote.

Although Dellums' legislation was given little chance of passing the Senate, its unanticipated approval in the House came as a jolting message of congressional opposition to the South African white-minority government's policy of apartheid.

Lawmakers said support for the measure was fueled by the South African government's June 12 state of emergency aimed at stifling anti-apartheid protests and international media coverage of the racial tension and violence in that country.

The House "looked at the carnage, the violation of human rights that occurred in the last few days and said, 'That's it,' " said William H. Gray III, D-Pa. Gray was the author of the bill superseded by Dellums' substitute.

Gray and other supporters of his bill said they were delighted with the tougher sanctions bill, predicting that it would pressure both the Senate and the Reagan administration to consider strong steps against South Africa.

The White House responded to the House action by repeating its opposition to economic sanctions against Pretoria. "We believe that legislation of this type would erode our capacity to promote negotiations in South Africa and would likely further separate an already divided society," said White House spokesman Larry Speakes. He said the administration would continue "active diplomacy" to achieve changes.

The House bill prompted a sharp denunciation from Pretoria. "It is clear that the American House of Representatives do not give a fig for the black communities of South Africa," said Foreign Minister Botha.

GOP Strategy: 'Kiss of Death'

Conservative House Republicans who opposed sanctions insisted that approval of the Dellums package could doom approval of any bill. They reasoned that passage of the milder Gray bill would have put more pressure on the Senate to follow suit. "Dellums' bill is a lemon. Frankly, it's the kiss of death," said Mark D. Siljander, R-Mich., a leading opponent of South Africa sanctions.

As part of their strategy, Republican House members did not request a recorded vote on the Dellums substitute, paving the way for its uncontested approval. That decision was made after opponents of sanctions realized that the Gray bill would likely have passed by an overwhelming margin. None of the Republican leaders was on the floor, leaving the last-minute quarterbacking to Siljander and a few other sanctions opponents.

Dellums' victory was in marked contrast to the fate of a similar amendment he offered in June 1985, when the House passed a milder sanctions bill. The House then rejected Dellums' stronger substitute on a 77-345 vote. *(Vote 128, 1985 Almanac p. 42-H)*

During the June 18 debate, Dellums said Gray's legislation was an "inadequate response to what is evolving in South Africa at this very moment." He also rebuffed arguments that sanctions would harm South African blacks by threatening their jobs. Dellums said the same logic could have been used during pre-Civil War days to defend slavery in the United States.

Dellums Substitute

Under Dellums' legislation, the 284 U.S. firms operating in South Africa would be required to leave within six months of the bill's enactment.

Direct investments in South Africa by those companies totaled $1.8 billion in 1984, with another $6.4 billion worth of indirect investments.

The Dellums bill also would cut off all trade between the United States and South Africa. An exception would be made for strategic minerals from South Africa, such as chromium, when the president certified to Congress that quantities needed for U.S. military purposes exceeded domestic supplies.

In 1985, U.S. companies exported $1.2 billion worth of goods to South Africa, with the United States importing South African products valued at more than $2 billion, according to the Commerce Department.

Other Dellums provisions would permanently ban the sale of South African Krugerrand gold coins in the United States and deny U.S. landing rights for South African Airways.

Corporations that violated the House-passed sanctions measure would face fines of up to $500,000. Individuals would be subject to fines of up to $250,000 and up to five years in prison.

Other Amendments

On a 365-49 vote, the House approved an amendment by Dan Burton, R-Ind., that would have prohibited U.S. foreign aid funds to the ANC if any members of that group's governing body were members of the South African Communist Party. *(Vote 160, p. 50-H)*

Opponents said the amendment was irrelevant since no money was earmarked for the ANC, but few members were willing to cast what might be interpreted as a procommunist vote. As it turned out, Burton's amendment was overtaken by Dellums' substitute, which did not include a specific authorization for any foreign aid.

The House also rejected, 150-268, a second Burton amendment that would have exempted from sanctions any companies in South Africa that complied with the Sullivan Principles that sought anti-discrimination policies in the work place. *(Vote 161, p. 50-H)*

Senate Committee Action

The Senate Foreign Relations Committee on Aug. 1 approved strict sanctions against the white minority government in Pretoria. The report on the bill (S 2701 — S Rept 99-370) was filed Aug. 6.

The committee approved S 2701 by a 15-2 vote, with Republicans Jesse Helms of North Carolina and Larry Pressler of South Dakota in opposition. Two other Republicans — Rudy Boschwitz of Minnesota and Frank H. Murkowski of Alaska — had opposed many provisions during the two days of action on the bill, but supported the overall measure on the committee's final vote.

Committee action came little more than a week after President Reagan, in a major policy address on South Africa July 22, called on Congress "to resist this emotional clamor for punitive sanctions." *(Text, p. 25-D)*

Based largely on a proposal by committee Chairman Lugar, the Foreign Relations bill imposed several sanctions targeted at the white government in South Africa and demanded steps toward dismantling the apartheid system. The bill also suggested stronger sanctions in one year if

South Africa did not take significant actions to eliminate apartheid.

Lugar, who gradually had abandoned his own reluctance to impose sanctions on South Africa, skillfully used the power of his chairmanship and sheer political muscle to get the bill through committee.

Because of Reagan's opposition to sanctions, Lugar and other committee leaders stressed the need for a bill that could pass the Senate with at least a two-thirds vote — the margin necessary to override a presidential veto. "If we are serious about legislation, we will look for what will have the most support," Lugar told his colleagues as they started work.

Committee Votes

Endorsing the essential thrust of Lugar's sanction proposal, the committee rejected all major amendments offered by members on the opposite extremes of the issue: Helms, who opposed any sanctions bill, and liberal Democrats, who wanted the much tougher House version cutting off all trade with South Africa.

Helms argued that the committee was voting to undermine an ally — the South African government — setting in motion a process that would lead to communist control of all of Africa. "Here we go again, kicking a friend in the teeth because they don't do what we want them to do," Helms said.

On the other side, committee liberals said Lugar's sanctions were too modest to force the South African government to pay attention. "In confronting an evil as clear as apartheid, we should not take halfway measures," said Alan Cranston, D-Calif.

With neither of those sides able to command a majority, Lugar held his position with a shifting coalition based on his vote and those of four other Republicans: Nancy Landon Kassebaum, Kan.; Charles McC. Mathias Jr., Md.; Daniel J. Evans, Wash.; and Paul S. Trible Jr., Va. They were joined by the Democrats in defeating Helms' weakening amendments, and by other Republicans in defeating the Democrats' strengthening amendments.

The committee's major votes were on these amendments:

- By Cranston, to substitute for the Lugar bill the text of the House-passed measure imposing a total trade embargo on South Africa and requiring U.S. companies to suspend operations there. Rejected 7-9, with Edward Zorinsky, D-Neb., joining eight Republicans in opposition. Murkowski did not vote.
- By Cranston, to substitute for Lugar's bill a series of tougher steps, such as banning all computer sales and barring all South African citizens from holding bank accounts in the United States. Rejected 7-10, with Zorinsky joining all Republicans in opposition.
- By Helms, to "take note" of recent reforms in South Africa. Helms originally had proposed congratulating the government for making "substantial progress" toward eliminating apartheid. Rejected 4-13.
- By Helms, prohibiting any of the sanctions from taking effect until the ANC repudiated the practice of necklacing. On a 13-4 vote, the committee approved a substitute by Christopher J. Dodd, D-Conn., calling on the ANC to denounce such killings.
- A broad amendment by Mathias and Evans toughening several specific provisions of Lugar's original sanctions bill. The most important changes were the addition of a ban on new U.S. business investments in South Africa, and the addition of several goals that would have to be met before the sanctions would be lifted. Adopted 13-4, with Lugar's active support.
- By Pressler, to strike a section authorizing the president to sell U.S. gold stocks to drive down the world price of gold, South Africa's most important export. Rejected 4-13.
- By Kassebaum, to delete a provision authorizing the exclusion of South African government officials from the United States on a case-by-case basis. Rejected 4-10.
- By Murkowski, adding to a list of possible future sanctions a ban on the importation into the United States of "strategic minerals," such as chromium and rhodium, from South Africa. Adopted 10-4.
- By Cranston, to bar imports of South African textiles. Cranston offered his amendment in response to the Reagan administration's recent agreement to expand South Africa's textile import quota. Rejected 8-8. *(Story, p. 347)*

Israel Amendment

In political and theatrical terms, the highlight of the Foreign Relations action was a flip-flop series of votes Aug. 1 on a provision that could target Israel as well as South Africa for a major U.S. sanction.

Acting in what some members said was a state of confusion, the committee at first approved the provision, then deleted it, then approved it again.

Offered by Mathias and Evans as part of their broad amendment, the provision required the president to tell Congress in six months what countries were violating a United Nations-imposed embargo on arms sales to South Africa. Six months later, the president could then choose to recommend that Congress bar all military aid to countries found to be violating the embargo.

Committee sources said the provision could affect several countries, notably Israel, which reportedly had supplied military gear and technical help to South Africa in recent years. Lobbyists from pro-Israel groups and the Israeli Embassy monitored the committee action, but no member publicly mentioned Israel.

Mathias and Evans both argued strongly for the provision, saying it was needed to bolster the U.N. arms embargo. "I cannot understand how we can condone anyone, anyone, shipping bullets to South Africa to maintain the system of apartheid," Evans said.

The committee took three votes on the provision:

- By 5-11, it rejected a motion by Murkowski to delete the provision.
- Less than an hour later, by a 9-8 vote, the committee agreed to delete the provision.
- Later, the committee reinserted the provision by a 10-7 vote. That happened after Dodd, who had voted previously to kill the provision, said he had cast a "bad vote" and asked for a reconsideration.

Cranston, a prominent supporter of Israel who voted consistently against the provision, later said several members had been confused on the first vote, thinking it was on an unrelated Murkowski amendment dealing with strategic minerals.

Botha Stands Fast

Congressional action on sanctions came in the midst of fast-moving diplomacy by Western nations, intended to quell an upsurge of violence in South Africa.

In the eyes of some senators, the South African government threw away its last chance to avoid sanctions on

July 29, when State President P. W. Botha rejected a plea by the European Community for changes.

After meeting with British Foreign Secretary Sir Geoffrey Howe, Botha assailed outside pressure on his country. Howe, representing the European Community, had asked Botha to release ANC leader Nelson Mandela and to begin negotiations with that group.

"I can never commit suicide by accepting threats and prescriptions from outside forces and hand South Africa over to communist forces in disguise," Botha said.

Howe's mission was widely seen as a last-ditch effort by leading European nations to coax positive action out of South Africa and thereby avoid having to impose sanctions.

Senate Floor Action

Breaking with President Reagan, the Senate on Aug. 15 passed HR 4868 by an 84-14 vote after substituting the text of its own measure for that of the House-passed bill. All "no" votes were by Republicans. *(Vote 252, p. 43-S)*

Senators loaded the measure with single-issue provisions but retained a core of sanctions ranging from a ban on new U.S. business investment in South Africa to prohibitions on trade in agricultural products, steel and nuclear supplies. The bill also threatened additional sanctions in a year if South Africa failed to make "substantial progress" toward eliminating apartheid.

In several votes, the Senate rejected conservatives' efforts to add the Soviet Union as a target for sanctions. It also turned back an attempt by liberals to sever nearly all economic ties between the United States and South Africa.

Lugar and other Senate leaders said their overriding goal was a bill that would pass by a wide enough margin to persuade Reagan to sign it, or to override a veto if he did not. In effect, that meant the bill needed about 80 votes — 67 for an override plus a margin to protect against Reagan's vaunted ability to sway wavering Republicans.

Seeking to head off amendments to toughen the bill, Lugar said on Aug. 15: "I still have the hope that the president will support what we are doing." But Lugar said Reagan definitely would not accept the bill if it "goes too far" beyond his own policy of quiet diplomacy.

Lugar also warned Democrats that their effort to add amendments imposing tough sanctions would reduce support for the overall bill.

The House-passed version of the bill called for a near-total trade embargo and disinvestment by U.S. firms. The Senate rejected that approach by a 2-to-1 margin.

Sending Signals

The South Africa bill — like many pieces of foreign policy legislation handled by Congress — primarily was an exercise in what the diplomats call "signal sending."

There were three intended recipients: the South African government, Reagan and the American electorate. Pretoria did everything possible to demonstrate its disregard for Congress' actions; Reagan long had repeated his opposition to sanctions; and it was unclear whether the voters would be impressed.

Covering all three bases, several senators described the bill as largely a moral statement to put the United States on the right side of history.

Lowell P. Weicker Jr., R-Conn., a principal leader of the sanctions movement, noted that he had been in the Senate for 16 years, and "for 16 years nothing was done, as much by this senator as by anybody else." Now, he said, Congress was speaking out against "the greatest moral wrong of our time."

Such statements brought charges of hypocrisy from conservative opponents. Saying that sanctions supporters were ignoring "the far greater evil" of Soviet communism, Malcolm Wallop, R-Wyo., charged: "What we are looking at is middle-class, comfortable white senators playing up to the black population of America and the liberal public of America."

In an ironic reflection of domestic politics, the Senate at the last minute approved an amendment by Don Nickles, R-Okla., opening the potential for subsidies of U.S. farm exports to South Africa. Another provision in the bill barred South African agricultural exports to the United States.

Helms Amendment

In a move to avert delaying tactics by conservatives who opposed any sanctions, the Senate on Aug. 14 accepted a modified amendment by Helms, calling on both the South African government and the African National Congress to renounce violence.

The vote was 67-31, and with it, Helms said he would refrain from offering any of the remaining 14 amendments he had prepared. Other conservatives closely aligned with Helms also withheld most of their amendments. *(Vote 235, p. 40-S)*

Helms' original amendment, supported by Lugar and Majority Leader Dole, set conditions for the ANC and related groups to meet before the United States would demand that they be included in negotiations with the Pretoria government. The most important were that the groups abandon violence and commit themselves to a free and democratic post-apartheid South Africa.

Helms complained that the bill was "one-sided" in attacking the Pretoria government and not demanding more responsible behavior by radical black groups. "Neither side is wholly right and neither side is wholly wrong," he said. Congress' bill "must be evenhanded."

Dole and Lugar supported the amendment, which was substantially watered down from an anti-ANC proposal Helms had floated several days prior to Senate action. Lugar made clear he was doing so for political reasons. The amendment, he said, "is an instrumental factor in bringing about a large majority" for the bill.

Edward M. Kennedy, D-Mass., said Helms was offering a "killer amendment" that would alter fundamentally the bill's original purpose.

Helms responded by noting that 242 blacks had died in South Africa in the past month, most of them the victims of necklacing. "If you want that to continue, vote against this amendment, Mr. Kennedy," Helms said.

Dole also rejected Kennedy's contention, saying: "I don't believe those of us who offered the amendment are any less concerned about apartheid."

Weicker harshly attacked the amendment as a perversion of the bill's intent. The goal of U.S. policy, he said, should be to change the actions of "the government in Pretoria and not those on whose neck they have their foot."

Helms and Weicker, who stood at opposite ends of the Republican Party in the Senate, then negotiated privately on the amendment and produced a compromise that significantly changed its focus. The compromise called on the Pretoria government — as well as the radical black groups — to "abandon unprovoked violence" and to commit to democracy.

Kennedy Amendment

The Senate first rejected, then accepted, an amendment by Kennedy to add to the bill several sanctions that had been adopted by the British Commonwealth. Opposed by Lugar on the grounds that it might endanger overall support for the bill, the amendment barred imports of South African agricultural products, iron and steel, and prohibited exports to that country of U.S. crude oil and petroleum products.

Debate on the amendment provoked charges that senators were practicing trade "protectionism" under the guise of concern about apartheid.

The Senate at first tabled the amendment, by a 51-48 vote on Aug. 14. *(Vote 234, p. 40-S)*

At that point, the amendment contained a provision extending the bill's ban on bank loans to South Africa by prohibiting renewals of current loans and short-term credits. Kennedy said that provision was needed to close a major loophole in the bill.

The next day, Kennedy deleted the provision on renewal of existing loans, eliminating several senators' objections. A second Lugar effort to table it failed 44-55; the amendment then was adopted by voice vote. *(Vote 240, p. 41-S)*

Most of the Aug. 14 debate on the amendment centered on Kennedy's insistence that the bill contained loopholes that undermined its stated purpose. The most important one, he said, allowed U.S. banks to renew past loans — even though the bill was advertised as banning all new loans to South Africa. "Let's not pretend that we're doing something which we're not doing," he said.

Lugar attacked the intent of Kennedy's amendment, which he said was to cut off as many U.S.-South African ties as possible. "The United States in this particular instance is eager to maintain a strong relationship with South Africa," Lugar said. "We do not seek a destruction of that economy. We do not seek a termination of all ties."

Paul Simon, D-Ill., endorsed the amendment as a "meaningful squeeze" on South Africa, citing in particular the ban on steel imports from that country. Simon noted that a new state of Illinois office building in downtown Chicago was constructed with South African steel, even as a steel mill in nearby Gary, Ind., was closing.

That brought a vigorous protest from Lugar, who represented Gary. "The moral basis [of the bill] really falls out if we are engaging in protectionism by another name," he said.

The next day, Lugar himself appeared to invoke a protectionist argument. Referring to the ban on agricultural imports, he noted that the United States in 1985 had a surplus in farm trade with South Africa. If the ban were enacted, he said, "I suspect South Africa would retaliate."

But that argument apparently failed to sway a majority, which promptly voted against Lugar's attempt to kill the amendment.

Toughening Amendments

The Senate rejected other attempts to toughen the bill:

By a 65-33 tabling vote on Aug. 15, the Senate rejected an effort by liberals to attach to the bill the text of the House measure imposing a near-total trade embargo on South Africa. The House measure also would require U.S. businesses to leave South Africa within six months. Offering that proposal, Cranston said: "In confronting apartheid, halfway measures are not satisfactory." Severing all trade, he added, "is the best way to send a strong message" to the government in Pretoria. *(Vote 244, p. 42-S)*

Lugar condemned the proposed embargo as an extreme approach that would eliminate all U.S. influence over South Africa.

The Senate rejected two amendments, to reduce Reagan's power to modify the sanctions in response to developments in South Africa, by:

- Joseph R. Biden Jr., D-Del., that would have made additional sanctions, such as banning importation into the United States of South African diamonds, mandatory in one year if there had been no substantial progress toward dismantling apartheid. The bill left imposition of additional sanctions to the president's discretion.

  It was rejected on a 55-44 tabling vote, Aug. 15. *(Vote 238, p. 41-S)*

- William Proxmire, D-Wis., that would have given Congress a stronger veto power over the president's decision to lift sanctions once events in South Africa warranted. The committee-approved bill allowed Congress to veto such a decision only by passing a joint resolution — over the president's likely veto. Proxmire wanted to require active congressional approval before the sanctions would be lifted. His amendment was tabled 51-46 on Aug. 14. *(Vote 236, p. 40-S)*

New Sanctions

The Senate adopted three major amendments to add new sanctions or toughen existing ones in the bill.

One, by Cranston, added an immediate ban on importation of textiles from South Africa. It was adopted 67-29. *(Vote 231, p. 40-S)*

The amendment was prompted by the administration's decision to sign a new five-year agreement, effective Sept. 1, allowing a 4.4 percent annual increase in South African textile exports to the United States. Calling the pact an "outrage," Cranston said "there is no reason for allowing this surge in textile imports at this time." Lugar argued that the ban would harm black textile workers in South Africa.

Weicker and Kennedy sponsored another successful amendment to tighten several sanctions in the bill, such as ending a U.S.-South Africa treaty on double taxation, barring U.S. government agencies from buying goods or services from South Africa except for diplomatic purposes, and barring U.S. government promotion of tourism and trade to South Africa. Their amendment was adopted by voice vote after little debate.

The Senate also gave voice vote approval to an amendment by Thomas F. Eagleton, D-Mo., to toughen the list of actions the South African government must take before the U.S. sanctions would be lifted. After little debate, Eagleton's amendment was adopted by voice vote.

A third amendment, by Paul S. Sarbanes, D-Md., would make immediate a ban on air travel to and from South Africa by U.S.-owned airlines. The committee-reported bill would have terminated a U.S.-South African agreement within a year — an action that would have had the effect of preventing U.S. airlines from servicing South Africa.

No U.S. airlines currently flew there, but Sarbanes argued that the bill should lock in a ban so that no one would take advantage of another provision barring landing rights in the United States by South African Airways.

The amendment was adopted by voice vote after the Senate refused to table it 42-56. *(Vote 237, p. 40-S)*

Sanctions Levied Against South Africa . . .

	Divestment	Bank Loans
HR 4868 (cleared by Congress Sept. 12, 1986)	Bans new corporate investment in South Africa and any new loans to government agencies ($1.3 billion in remaining U.S. investments in 1985).	Prohibits U.S. banks from accepting deposits from any South African government agency ($329 million held by U.S. banks for South African banks and government agencies in March 1986). Bans loans to South African government agencies ($148 million outstanding in 1985).
Reagan Order No. 12532 (extended Sept. 4, 1986)		Bans new loans by U.S. banks or other agencies to any "apartheid-enforcing agency" in South Africa.
Great Britain (announced or renewed Aug. 5, 1986)	Calls for voluntary end to new investment in South Africa ($418 million in 1983).	
European Economic Community (announced or renewed Sept. 16, 1986)	Bans new investment ($380 million net investment by the community, excluding Britain, in 1984; $418 million investment by Britain in 1983).	
Commonwealth of Nations (endorsed Aug. 5, 1986, by Canada, Australia, the Bahamas, India, Zimbabwe and Zambia)	Bans new investment or reinvestment of profits earned in South Africa (no new investments except by Britain in 1986; British investments were $418 million in 1983). Bans government contracts with majority-owned South African companies.	Bans new bank loans (outstanding South African debts to Britain were $7.1 billion in 1985; few new loans approved in 1986). Ends double taxation agreements.
Japan (announced or renewed Sept. 19, 1986)		

Note: Listed loan and trade figures are approximations.

Sources: South African Embassy, British Embassy, Japanese Embassy, European Community Information Service, Investor Responsibility Research Center, *The New York Times*, Aug. 16, 1986.

. . . By Nations and Economic Communities

Import Restrictions	Export Restrictions	Landing Rights/Tourism
Bans import of steel and iron ($293.6 million in 1985). Bans import of uranium and coal ($140 million, uranium; $43.4 million, coal, in 1985). Bans import of Krugerrand gold coins (1984: $486 million; 1985: $101 million before ban took place). Bans textile imports ($55.1 million in 1985). Bans import of agricultural products ($52 million in fruits and vegetables and $129 million in other products in 1985).	Bars export of computers to South African agencies enforcing apartheid. Prohibits petroleum or crude oil exports to South Africa.	Ends landing rights in United States for South African Airways (95,000 passengers in 1985).
Bans import of Krugerrands with option of waiving the order should South Africa begin implementing reforms.	Bars export of computers to South African agencies enforcing apartheid. Bars export of nuclear technology intended for nuclear production facilities.	
Bans import of steel and iron ($45 million in 1985). Bans import of Krugerrands ($7 million in 1985). Monitoring of an embargo on trade in arms and paramilitary gear.	Halts oil exports to South Africa. Halts export of "sensitive" equipment destined for use by South African police and armed forces.	Calls for a voluntary end to promotion of tourism. Recalls military attachés accredited to South Africa and refuses to accredit their counterparts in European Community.
Bans import of iron and steel effective Sept. 27 ($424 million to 12 community nations in 1985). Monitoring of an embargo on exports and imports of arms and paramilitary gear.	Halts oil exports to South Africa. Halts export of "sensitive" equipment destined for use by South African police and armed forces.	Recalls military attachés accredited to Pretoria and refuses to accredit their counterparts in European Community. Refrains from cultural and scientific agreements and freezes sports and security agreements.
Bans import of agricultural products ($1.1 billion in 1983). Bans government procurement of items contracted for production in South Africa. Bans import of uranium. Bans import of coal ($49 million in 1983). Bans import of iron and steel ($115 million in 1983). Bans Krugerrand imports, as of Sept. 10.	Ends government assistance to, investment in, and trade with South Africa ($2.6 billion in export credits guaranteed by Britain in 1985).	Bans air links with South Africa. Bars South Africans from obtaining visas at Commonwealth consulates in South Africa. Bans promotion of tourism (366,000 tourists from Commonwealth visited, 46 percent of all tourists in South Africa in 1984). Bars government funding for trade missions to South Africa.
Calls for Japanese to refrain from purchase and import of Krugerrands, effective October 1985). Bans import of iron and steel ($200 million in 1985).	Bans export of computers to South African agencies that enforce apartheid, effective October 1985.	Suspends air links with South Africa. Prohibits use of South African Airways by Japanese government officials. Suspends issuing of tourist visas for South Africans. Requests Japanese citizens to refrain from traveling to South Africa.

Deleting Sanctions

Almost as if in compensation for the new sanctions, the Senate deleted two provisions that had been voted by the Foreign Relations panel. Both amendments to kill the provisions were offered by committee members who had failed in those efforts in committee.

Kassebaum apparently provoked widespread second thoughts in the Senate on a provision in the bill that would have allowed South African government officials and representatives to enter the United States only on a case-by-case basis. Her amendment to kill the provision was approved 99-0, gaining the votes even of Lugar and other committee members who had initiated the visa restriction. *(Vote 233, p. 40-S)*

Kassebaum said the United States would "invite retaliation" by restricting visas for foreign officials.

Pressler sponsored another successful amendment to delete from the bill a proviso giving the president the authority to sell gold from U.S. stocks to lower the world price of gold, which was South Africa's principal export. The president already had that authority, and Pressler argued that selling gold to protest apartheid would disrupt world monetary markets. The amendment was adopted 58-41. *(Vote 232, p. 40-S)*

Other Amendments

The Senate also dealt with amendments by:

- Dodd, to expand the bill's ban on imports into the United States of manufactured products from "parastatals," businesses owned or controlled by the South African government. Dodd wanted to bar imports from companies involved in marketing as well as manufacturing.

Dole objected that the amendment would bar imports of agricultural goods produced by state-owned companies, likely prompting South Africa to retaliate by refusing to buy U.S. farm products such as grain. The United States had recently won a major grain contract after South Africa retaliated against Australia for a similar sanction.

The Senate adopted the amendment by voice vote after Dodd modified it to eliminate an immediate ban on U.S. imports of agricultural products from South African parastatals. Instead, the agricultural ban was put on a list of sanctions to be considered by the president in a year.

- Alfonse M. D'Amato, R-N.Y., to prevent the federal government from withholding funds for contracts to which localities had applied such laws. The amendment would have had the effect of allowing state and local governments to retain laws restricting contracts for anti-apartheid purposes. The Department of Transportation had tried earlier in 1986 to withhold highway funds from New York — a move that D'Amato blocked with a similar, short-term amendment to a fiscal 1986 supplemental appropriations bill (PL 99-349).

The Senate tabled the D'Amato amendment, 64-35. But then it adopted, by voice vote, a much narrower amendment that had the effect of giving state and local governments 90 days to bring their laws into conformity with whatever the federal government did, or face the possible loss of federal funds. By implication, the amendment made federal policy pre-eminent, putting into question the validity of state and local anti-apartheid laws. *(Vote 241, p. 41-S)*

- Jeremiah Denton, R-Ala., to prohibit U.S. assistance to groups or individuals in South Africa that supported the practice of necklacing. The amendment was directed at the ANC, which the Pretoria government had accused of promoting necklacing. Adopted by voice vote.
- Carl Levin, D-Mich., to express the sense of the Senate that the administration should ask the Pretoria government for permission for the U.S. ambassador to meet with Mandela. Adopted by voice vote.
- Wallop, to apply the same sanctions to the Soviet Union as were applied in the bill to South Africa, as a protest against Soviet human rights abuses. Rejected 41-57. *(Vote 239, p. 41-S)*
- Boschwitz, to allow the president to waive the entire bill if 40,000 South African blacks were thrown out of work by U.S. sanctions. The amendment also would have provided $1-per-day payments to blacks who lost their jobs. Tabled 81-18. *(Vote 245, p. 42-S)*

Senate Bill Cleared

The House on Sept. 12 overwhelmingly accepted the Senate version of HR 4868, thereby eliminating the need for a Senate-House conference on the issue.

The 308-77 vote was more than enough to override a threatened White House veto. Backing the measure were 218 Democrats and 90 Republicans, while four Democrats and 73 Republicans opposed it. *(Vote 351, p. 100-H)*

Lugar had played a high-stakes game of hardball to force the House to accept the Senate's sanctions bill. First, he warned that there was not enough time in the short September session for a conference committee to meet and resolve the Senate- and House-passed measures, and then for Congress to thwart a presidential veto. If Congress failed to act before the very end of its session, Reagan could kill the bill by a pocket veto.

When House leaders — especially leaders of the Congressional Black Caucus — continued to resist, Lugar played his ace, appointing only two senators other than himself to serve on a potential conference committee: Helms and Claiborne Pell, D-R.I. Lugar and Helms said they would refuse to accept any changes in the Senate bill, thus making a conference useless.

House leaders, including the Black Caucus, gave in to Lugar's pressure on Sept. 10.

Black leaders expressed disappointment that they were unable to press for a somewhat tougher measure. Nevertheless, they hailed passage of the bill as a victory for the anti-apartheid movement and as an important moral statement.

Acknowledging that the bill by itself would not guarantee an end to apartheid, Gray said: "It does guarantee that the rest of the world, including blacks in South Africa, will know that this Congress has witnessed the evil and did not turn away."

Another black House member who pushed hard for a sanctions bill, Mickey Leland, D-Texas, noted that the bill had support from a wide spectrum: "Everybody from Bob Walker to Ron Dellums." Robert S. Walker, R-Pa., was a leading House conservative who specialized in baiting liberal Democrats, and Dellums, the sponsor of the original bill to pull the United States out of South Africa, was one of the most liberal members of the House.

Dellums said he argued with House leaders for a conference but was overridden by those who argued that "Pretoria should not be able to celebrate because of no bill" emerging from Congress. Nevertheless, Dellums said he was proud that his original bill "moved back the fear barrier" for members on the South Africa issue. Advocates of stronger sanctions "will be back" next year, he said.

Lugar lobbied fellow Republicans in the House on behalf of the bill, pointing out its "positive" features such as increased financial aid to black South Africa and playing down the sanctions. In a letter sent to House GOP leaders the morning of the vote, Lugar said the bill "is not so much a radical break with the president's policy as it is a further step in the evolution of U.S. policy toward South Africa."

Lugar's plea was to little avail as four of the seven House Republican leaders to whom he addressed it voted against the bill.

State and Local Conflicts

As House leaders debated whether to accept the Senate bill or to insist on a conference, the issue of preemption of state and local laws arose as the surprise stumbling block. Most members of Congress had paid little attention to the question until press reports suggested that the Senate bill would wipe out scores of anti-apartheid laws, possibly including a newly passed California measure forcing the sale of all state-owned investments in businesses working in South Africa.

During Senate action on the bill, Lugar had insisted that the measure would pre-empt state and local laws. The bill did so, he said, by "occupying the field," of U.S. policy toward South Africa. That interpretation was reinforced by the Senate's rejection of an amendment allowing state and local governments to maintain their anti-apartheid laws. The Senate included a provision barring the federal government, for 90 days after enactment of the bill, from withholding funds for contracts to which any state or local government had applied an anti-apartheid law.

House Democrats strongly rejected that interpretation, saying they did not want passage of a federal anti-apartheid law to bar state and local governments from taking their own actions. Members of the Black Caucus said they would refuse to go along with adoption of the Senate bill if Lugar's pre-emption interpretation held.

As a compromise, leaders of the House Foreign Affairs Committee drafted a procedure under which the House would accompany passage of the Senate bill with a statement rejecting Lugar's interpretation of the issue. In a highly unusual move, that statement was included in the rule (H Res 548) governing House consideration of the bill. The House adopted the rule, and thus the pre-emption statement, 292-92. *(Vote 350, p. 98-H)*

The statement said that "it is not the intent of the House of Representatives that the bill limit, pre-empt or affect, in any fashion, the authority" of state and local governments "to restrict or otherwise regulate any financial or commercial activity respecting South Africa."

The net effect, according to House and Senate sources, was to create confusion about the intent of Congress on the pre-emption, leaving a resolution to the courts.

Ted Weiss, D-N.Y., said that by speaking out on the issue, the House was taking a firm position "even though one member of the other body [Lugar] has seen fit to make a statement that would make it seem otherwise."

House Foreign Affairs Committee Chairman Dante B. Fascell, D-Fla., said adoption of the statement was unnecessary because "there's nothing in the Senate bill" that directly pre-empted state and local laws.

But several Republicans — including some who voted for the bill — objected to the House's attempt to undo the Senate action on pre-emption. Walker said he was voting for the bill with the understanding that it did pre-empt other laws: "We are saying we are pre-empting the ability of others to set foreign policy."

Lugar acknowledged that the conflicting claims would create confusion. Even so, he said, the bill "will put a damper on further foreign policy excursions [by state and local governments] and that was my intent."

Loopholes

Another last-minute issue between the House and Senate was whether the bill's ban on new bank loans and investments in South Africa contained major loopholes.

One important provision of the Senate-passed bill was a ban on new bank loans to South Africa and on new investments by Americans in businesses there. Although that ban largely reaffirmed what already was happening in the marketplace because of instability in South Africa, the ban was seen as significant because it could help deprive Pretoria for years of much-needed foreign exchange.

The Senate bill contained three exemptions to the ban, however: It permitted continued short-term trade credits for South African purchases of American goods, it permitted U.S. firms to reinvest in South Africa profits earned there, and it allowed American firms to make new investments if needed to allow their South African branches to operate in an "economically sound manner."

House leaders insisted those exemptions undermined the thrust of the bans on new investments and loans, and they argued that a conference meeting was necessary to narrow those exceptions. But Lugar insisted that the three exceptions were narrowly drawn and would permit only limited amounts of new U.S. capital to enter South Africa.

As part of an agreement under which the House accepted the Senate bill, Lugar inserted an explanation in the Sept. 11 *Congressional Record* aimed at limiting the impact of the exemptions.

Veto Overridden

President Reagan vetoed HR 4868 on Sept. 26. Reagan said sanctions would be counterproductive, hurting the black majority in South Africa rather than the white-minority government.

Reagan decided not to accompany his veto with an executive order imposing his own sanctions. Such a course had been under consideration to help swing votes in the Senate to sustain a veto. But the president's veto message instead contained veiled "hints" that Reagan might be willing to issue such an executive order if Congress sustained his veto. *(Veto message, p. 28-D)*

The White House delayed announcement of the veto until Sept. 26 — the last of 10 days Reagan had to act — to give Reagan and his lobbyists time to work on wavering senators.

Reagan's veto had been expected ever since the House approved the Senate's sanctions bill on Sept. 12. White House officials had said the president would attempt to kill the bill because of his longstanding opposition to sanctions against friendly governments. Officials also said Reagan saw the legislation as an unwarranted congressional intrusion into his foreign-policy-making powers.

What was unexpected was Reagan's decision not to accompany his veto with an executive order incorporating many of the sanctions originally reported by the Senate Foreign Relations Committee on Aug. 6. White House lobbyists carried a draft executive order to Capitol Hill on Sept. 25 and told Senate leaders Reagan likely would sign it. Later that day, White House Communications Director

Patrick Buchanan said Reagan would not issue an order — indicating a split among the president's top aides.

House, Senate Override Votes

The House voted to override the president's veto Sept. 29, and the Senate followed suit Oct. 2, thus enacting the bill into law.

In the House, where the outcome was never in doubt, the final tally was 313-83 — 49 more than the two-thirds majority required to pass the bill over the president's veto; 81 Republicans joined 232 Democrats in voting to override. *(Vote 390, p. 110-H)*

In the Senate, which originally had passed the sanctions bill by an 84-14 vote, Reagan needed to pick up 20 votes to prevent an override by the required two-thirds majority. On the day of the vote, one senator who said he supported Reagan — Jake Garn, R-Utah — was at home recuperating from surgery; even so, Reagan still needed 34 votes to sustain the veto.

The Senate debated the issue for four hours on Oct. 1, and again for about two hours just before the vote the next day.

As the roll call began, the Senate chamber was extraordinarily quiet, as if to signify the import of the event. In the gallery were several civil rights leaders who had backed the bill, including Coretta Scott King, comedian Dick Gregory and Randall Robinson, head of the TransAfrica lobby group.

Adhering to a normally ignored rule, most senators voted from their seats. When his turn came to vote, Lugar rose to his feet and quietly said "aye," formally breaking with the president he had unswervingly supported on other foreign policy issues.

Democrats voted unanimously to support the veto override — including Southerners who usually supported the president on crucial votes. As Republican after Republican voted "aye" for the override, it became clear the outcome would not even be close.

The final margin was 78-21 — 12 more than the required two-thirds. *(Vote 311, p. 52-S)*

Only six of the Republicans who originally had voted for the bill switched and supported the veto: Thad Cochran, Miss.; Majority Leader Dole; Orrin G. Hatch, Utah; Nickles; Alan K. Simpson, Wyo., the assistant majority leader; and Ted Stevens, Alaska. Barry Goldwater, R-Ariz., who had been absent on the first vote, also backed Reagan on the veto, raising the total to 21.

Thirty-one Republicans supported the override. Among them were six senators who had agreed to support the veto if the vote was close, a White House lobbyist said. When it became clear that Reagan would lose, the White House decided not to press any of those senators for their votes.

In spite of the seriousness of the issue, the administration never pulled out all the stops to support the veto in the Senate. Reagan telephoned and met with several senators, and the State Department dispatched its senior black official — Alan L. Keyes, assistant secretary of state for international organizations — to the Capitol.

Reagan also took two steps to demonstrate his concern about South Africa: On Sept. 29 he sent congressional leaders a letter promising to sign an executive order with limited sanctions if the veto was sustained, and the next day he named Edward Perkins, a senior black Foreign Service officer, as the new U.S. ambassador to Pretoria. Perkins replaced Herman W. Nickel, who had served in South Africa since 1982. *(Text, p. 29-D)*

In spite of those symbolic steps, one lobbyist said the vote was "never winnable" for the president, and so the administration decided not to use up valuable political capital on it.

The administration also made only feeble efforts to link the vote to Reagan's October "pre-summit" meeting in Iceland with Soviet leader Mikhail S. Gorbachev. Talking to undecided Republicans on Sept. 30, Secretary of State George P. Shultz noted that Reagan would need congressional support for his sessions in Iceland. But most senators said the surprise announcement of the Iceland meeting had little effect on the vote because South Africa would not be on the superpower agenda.

Perhaps the most telling indication of the administration's willingness to accept the veto override was the proffered executive order. Its suggested sanctions were substantially weaker than draft proposals that White House lobbyists had floated on Capitol Hill in advance of the veto.

Reagan also got little productive help from his allies on Capitol Hill. While supporting the veto, Dole made only a faint stab at winning the vote. And Lugar, the man to whom most senators would turn for advice on foreign affairs, actively opposed Reagan.

The two senators who spent the most time supporting the veto carried little political clout with their colleagues: Helms and Pressler.

In repeated speeches, they warned that sanctions would not force change in South Africa's racial policies and would instead strengthen the hand of radical black groups.

"The thrust of this legislation is to bring about violence and revolutionary change and, after that, everlasting tyranny," Helms said.

Pressler had supported sanctions in 1985 but changed his mind after traveling to South Africa in 1986. He said Congress was ignoring "fundamental reforms" the Pretoria government had made in apartheid.

Domestic Politics

Some senators and White House officials said the Senate's vote was determined by the calendar: It came just a month before the Nov. 4 elections that would decide which party controlled the Senate in the 100th Congress.

Democrats were eager to exploit Reagan's political weakness on the issue, and some attempted to portray his attitude toward South Africa as a Republican policy.

Nervous Republicans did not want to risk antagonizing black voters for whom South Africa was especially important.

Dole for months had contended that South Africa was a "domestic civil rights issue" as much as a foreign policy matter. Concluding Senate debate, Dole derisively said his colleagues were about to cast a "feel-good vote" for a "feel-good foreign policy."

Several Republican senators who had voted for the bill in August also feared the repercussions of changing their minds on such a highly publicized matter.

Some sanctions supporters readily acknowledged the domestic implications, but insisted they were positive ones arising out of the civil rights struggles of the 1960s. South Africa, they said, was important for the United States precisely because of the recent history of racism here.

"The vote matters not because of what it says about South Africa," said Rep. Lynn Martin, R-Ill., when the House acted. "It matters more because of what it says about America."

Lugar's Role

The key actor in the Senate was Lugar, normally one of Reagan's most loyal and effective supporters. Lugar was the main architect of the Senate bill, and in early September he promised House leaders that he would stand by it — even in the face of a veto — if they would adopt it.

Lugar was joined by Kassebaum, chairman of the African Affairs Subcommittee, who long had questioned whether sanctions would lead to changes the United States sought in South Africa. But in recent months she had supported the sanctions bill as a way of demonstrating U.S. leadership on the issue.

Together, they appealed to Reagan to sign the bill. When he refused, they said Congress should move ahead on its own because Reagan had missed his chance to demonstrate leadership.

Lugar lamented that Reagan "didn't take my advice the first, second, third or even fourth time."

For his stand, Lugar came under harsh attack from some fellow conservatives, including White House Communications Director Buchanan. At a rally on Sept. 29, Buchanan said Lugar held his chairmanship only because of Reagan's popularity. Quoting from Shakespeare's "King Lear," Buchanan said of Lugar: "How sharper than a serpent's tooth, to have a thankless child."

Helms, the second-ranking Republican on Foreign Relations, got in his own jabs. "Dick Lugar and Ted Kennedy" would be responsible for turning South Africa over to "militant blacks" and ultimately the Soviet Union, he told reporters.

Lugar brushed aside such criticism but clearly was concerned about it. Asked about his desertion of Reagan, Lugar repeatedly referred to his record of voting on the president's behalf and pointed to his work for Reagan on Nicaragua and other issues.

As the Senate's debate got under way, Lugar aides sent to the press gallery a list based on Congressional Quarterly figures showing that, from 1981-85, he had voted with Reagan more than any other senator.

Botha's Lobbying

The night before the Senate vote, Lugar and Helms exchanged charges about Helms' involvement in the lobbying of two farm-state senators by South African Foreign Minister Botha.

Lugar learned the afternoon of Oct. 1 that Botha had told Sens. Zorinsky and Charles E. Grassley, R-Iowa, that South Africa would retaliate against sanctions by refusing to buy U.S. farm goods and by barring shipment of those products to neighboring black states whose transportation links were controlled by Pretoria. Lugar also said Botha had promised increased South African grain purchases from the United States if Reagan's veto was sustained.

Botha had telephoned Helms at the Senate Republican Cloakroom; Helms then invited Zorinsky and Grassley to the telephone.

One provision of the sanctions bill barred U.S. imports of agricultural products from South Africa. Lugar and other senators long had warned that the provision likely would provoke retaliation by South Africa.

Lugar angrily charged that Botha's calls were "despicable" and amounted to "foreign bribery and intimidation to change the votes of members of the United States Senate. It is an affront to the decency of the American people." Further, Lugar said, Helms' involvement in the Botha lobbying effort was "inappropriate."

Helms immediately defended his actions and those of Botha, who he said had been a friend for 10 years.

"Methinks Mr. Lugar doth protest too much," Helms said. "I think Ed Zorinsky was entitled to know that the farmers of America will be shot in the foot by Dick Lugar and Ted Kennedy and the others."

Helms later suggested that he might consider challenging Lugar for the Foreign Relations Committee chairmanship "if there are any more outbursts" such as Lugar's charges against him. Questioned about the seriousness of that comment, Helms then contended his suggestion was "flip." Helms in 1984 gave up his claim to the committee chairmanship so he could take the leadership of the Agriculture Committee instead.

Botha defended his lobbying and called "absolutely laughable" Lugar's complaints. He told reporters in Johannesburg: "If you rob us of our markets, we have to look out after the interests of our farmers."

After the Senate voted, Dole and others discounted the effect of Botha's lobbying, noting that Zorinsky and Grassley supported the veto override. "I don't think it made much of a difference," Dole said. "It's no big deal." ▮

Saudi Arms Sale: Senate Upholds Reagan Plan

President Reagan barely averted a major foreign policy defeat June 5, when the Senate upheld a White House plan to sell $265 million worth of weapons to Saudi Arabia.

On a 66-34 vote, the Senate sustained Reagan's May 21 veto of a measure (S J Res 316) that would have blocked the sale. *(Vote 111, p. 21-S)*

A two-thirds majority of those present and voting was required to pass the bill over the president's veto. With all members voting, the 34 "nay" votes — one-third plus one of the Senate's 100 members — were the absolute minimum Reagan needed to prevent a Senate override. Since action by a single chamber was sufficient to sustain the veto, no override vote occurred in the House.

A vigorous White House lobbying effort had succeeded in winning enough votes to turn around the Senate's 73-22 approval May 6 of the measure blocking the Saudi sale. The House had adopted its disapproval resolution (H J Res 589) May 7, 356-62.

Major Jewish organizations, led by the American Israel Public Affairs Committee (AIPAC) opposed selling arms to the Saudis, though most agreed not to lobby actively against the sale.

Weapons Package

By upholding the president's veto, the Senate cleared the way for the administration to sell nearly 1,700 Sidewinder air-to-air missiles and 100 Harpoon air-to-sea missiles. Reagan aides said the Saudis needed the weapons package to bolster their defensive forces, particularly to fend off possible Iranian advances stemming from the Persian Gulf war between Iran and Iraq.

Stripped from the final package, however, were contro-

Arms Sale Veto Procedures

The House Feb. 3 passed and cleared for the president a bill (S 1831 — PL 99-247) to revise procedures used by Congress to block major arms sales to foreign countries.

The Senate passed the measure on Dec. 19, 1985. Both chambers acted by voice vote, with little debate.

The main purpose of the bill was to make existing law on congressional review of arms sales conform to the Supreme Court's 1983 *Chadha* decision, which ruled "legislative vetoes" unconstitutional unless the president had a chance to participate in them. Under existing law, Congress could block a major foreign arms sale by passing a concurrent resolution, which did not have to be signed by the president. *(1983 Almanac p. 565)*

S 1831 required Congress to pass a joint resolution if it wanted to block an arms sale. Such a resolution must be presented to the president for his signature or veto.

Aside from bringing arms sale law into conformity with the court decision, the major effect of S 1831 would be to restore a system of expedited consideration in both the House and Senate of any resolution to block an arms sale. Those procedures included time limits for committee action on the resolutions and made it difficult for opponents to filibuster them in the Senate.

versial Stinger missiles requested by the Saudis. The Stinger, a shoulder-fired, anti-aircraft weapon, had been singled out for criticism by foes of the arms deal on the grounds that it might fall into the hands of terrorists. Elimination of the Stingers, which cut $89 million from the $354 million package, had been suggested by the Saudis to blunt congressional opposition to the weapons sale.

The Saudis originally also had asked to buy F-15 fighter jets, M-1 tanks and other equipment. But the administration had scaled down the proposal in an effort to mollify members of Congress who opposed sales to Arab countries that had not come to peace terms with Israel.

Technically, 200 Stinger launchers and 600 missile reloads remained a part of the final package. But Reagan, in a May 21 letter to Senate Majority Leader Robert Dole, R-Kan., promised not to include the Stingers in the sale. Instead, he said that if the Saudis renewed their request for Stingers in the future, he would respond with a new notification to Congress. *(Veto, Dole letter texts, p. 18-D)*

Arms Sale Record

Reagan had formally submitted his arms sale proposal to Congress on April 8, and by law the Senate and House had 30 calendar days in which to pass legislation blocking it. *(Arms sales procedures, box, this page)*

By voting to sustain the president's veto of S J Res 316, the Senate maintained Congress' record of never having formally blocked a president from selling arms to a foreign country. The Saudi case, however, marked the first time that both chambers had passed resolutions to disapprove an arms sale. Congress in 1985 forced Reagan to delay indefinitely an arms sale to Jordan, but neither chamber reached the point of passing legislation rejecting it outright. *(Jordan sale, box, next page)*

Less than two weeks after the final Senate vote on the Saudi weapons package, Reagan announced June 18 that the United States was about to start delivering five Airborne Warning and Control System (AWACS) radar planes to Saudi Arabia. Congress had cleared the AWACS sale in 1981 following a bruising struggle. *(AWACS, box, p. 376)*

Senate, House Action

In a dramatic blow to the administration, the Senate and House on May 6-7 approved measures to block the Saudi arms sale package by votes well above the two-thirds needed to override Reagan's anticipated veto.

The Senate, acting May 6, approved S J Res 316 (S Rept 99-288) by a 73-22 vote. That was six votes more than the 67 needed to override a presidential veto if all senators voted. Twenty-nine Republicans broke ranks with the White House in voting against the arms sale. Only two Democrats — John C. Stennis of Mississippi and Edward Zorinsky of Nebraska — supported the sale. *(Vote 91, p.18-S)*

A day later, the House approved H J Res 589 (H Rept 99-569) on a 356-62 vote. If all House members voted on the override, 289 would be needed to overcome a veto. *(Vote 102, p. 32-H)*

In both chambers, the roll calls provided the drama on the Saudi issue. Floor debate featured little more than a rehash of earlier arguments.

Only by agreeing to sell a fresh supply of missiles to the Saudis, supporters contended, could the United States demonstrate its commitment to "moderate" Arab states and continue to exercise influence in the region.

"We cannot expect [the Saudis] to respond to our requests if they believe we have disengaged from their security concerns," said Richard G. Lugar, R-Ind., chairman of the Senate Foreign Relations Committee, which had approved the resolution April 23.

Opponents claimed that Saudi Arabia, despite its moderate image, had continued to provide financial support to the radical Syrian government and the Palestine Liberation Organization.

Also frequently mentioned was the Saudis' condemnation of the United States' April 14 attack against Libya. "We want to make clear that it is no longer in the national security interests of the United States to sell advanced weapons to a nation which consistently scorns American interests," said Alan Cranston, D-Calif., who led the Senate fight against the Saudi weapons deal. *(Libya attack, p. 389)*

In the House, opponents of the weapons sale voiced surprise at the size of the vote against it.

Mel Levine, D-Calif., who led the anti-Saudi effort, said his count on the morning of the vote was just shy of 289, the critical two-thirds. He speculated that concerns about terrorism, the Saudi response to the Libyan raid and the inclusion of Stinger missiles added to the margin.

Another weapons foe, Barney Frank, D-Mass., said Reagan unwittingly contributed to the outcome by whipping up anti-Libyan sentiment.

A State Department official said some legislators mistakenly equated the Saudis' criticism of the United States' attack on Libya with support for Libyan leader Muammar el-Qaddafi. He said the administration interpreted the Saudi statements as support for the Libyan people rather than an endorsement of Qaddafi.

Jordan Arms Sale Put Off

Secretary of State George P. Shultz on Feb. 3 formally notified Congress that the Reagan administration was postponing indefinitely a planned arms sale to Jordan.

The administration shelved the controversial $1.5 billion-$2 billion sale as part of an agreement with congressional leaders to head off a legislative defeat.

In a letter to the chairmen of the House Foreign Affairs and Senate Foreign Relations committees, Shultz said the administration would proceed with the sale "after affording Congress adequate time to further review and debate fully the issues involved." In practical terms, he added, that meant Congress would get at least 30 days' advance notice — a period that would run only while Congress was in session.

President Reagan in 1985 proposed a major sale to Jordan of advanced warplanes, anti-aircraft missiles and other weapons. Congress in October delayed the sale until March 1, 1986, unless Jordan and Israel had begun "direct and meaningful" negotiations. *(1985 Almanac p. 93)*

Pro-Israel members of Congress had been maneuvering to block the sale even further — and it was to avert that action that Shultz agreed to the indefinite delay.

The letter had the intended effect: With it in hand, the Foreign Affairs Committee Feb. 4 dropped plans to act on a widely supported resolution (H J Res 428) that would have prevented the sale.

Shultz noted in his letter that the United States was continuing to promote peace negotiations between Israel and Jordan. Any congressional action on the Jordan arms issue at this point "would severely damage the ongoing process," he said.

At a House hearing on Feb. 5, Shultz went further, charging that past congressional opposition to the sale already had been "a major detriment to our ability to move the peace process along."

China Arms Deal Goes Through

The Senate Foreign Relations Committee on May 1 rejected a resolution (S J Res 331) that sought to block a sale of $550 million worth of electronic gear for China's F-8 warplanes — Chinese-built versions of the Soviet MiG-23.

The resolution, sponsored by Jesse Helms, R-N.C., was rejected on a 1-14 vote. Helms cast the only "yes" vote; Frank H. Murkowski, R-Alaska, voted present. At Helms' request, the committee then unanimously reported the resolution to the Senate floor with an unfavorable recommendation (S Rept 99-293). There was no further action before the May 7 deadline for Congress to act on the deal.

The sale was the largest ever to the People's Republic of China, and Helms argued that it would upset the balance of power in the region, posing a particular threat to Taiwan.

Congress in 1985 raised no objection to the first major arms sale to China: $98 million worth of equipment and designs for plants to produce ammunition and explosives.

As in the Senate, debate in the House focused on the United States' strategic concerns in the Mideast and the implications of approving or denying the weapons sale to Saudi Arabia.

"Friends are awfully hard to come by in that part of the world," said Henry J. Hyde, R-Ill., a supporter of the sale. "Passage of this resolution is no way to treat a friend, and it is no contribution to peace."

Levine, however, said Reagan had not succeeded in getting the Saudis to further U.S. security interests. "In fact, selling arms seems to be our only policy with respect to Saudi Arabia."

After the votes, some questioned the vigor with which Reagan officials — preoccupied with budget, tax and other issues — tried to rally support for the arms sale. "I would not say that the president put on a full-court press or a half-court press or even a quarter-court press," said Hyde.

A large part of the reason was that Reagan aides were planning a lobbying strategy focused on sustaining a veto rather than concentrating on the initial round of voting. "It's safe to say we anticipated a loss in terms of the vote," said a State Department official. "We were of course not pleased with the votes in the House and Senate, but we knew we would have to go to sustain a veto."

Reagan Veto

In his May 21 veto message, Reagan said that withholding the Saudi arms would "damage our vital strategic, political and economic interests in the Middle East and undermine our balanced policy in that region." It would, he said, "send the worst possible message as to America's dependability and courage."

Reagan waited to send his veto message to Capitol Hill until Congress was about to start its Memorial Day recess because he had been unable to secure enough votes in the Republican-controlled Senate to sustain the veto.

In a turn that illustrated the cat-and-mouse maneuvering over the issue, a White House messenger bearing Reagan's veto message waited on the Senate floor somewhat sheepishly for about three hours May 21 before he was allowed to present the document.

The delay occurred because Senate GOP leaders at first were uncertain about precisely how many votes they could count on. Once the messenger was recognized, the veto vote would be the first order of business.

The White House courier finally was able to hand over the veto message at 6:45 p.m., after which Majority Leader Dole agreed with Democrats to schedule the vote in early June soon after the Senate returned to Washington.

The momentum appeared to have shifted to Reagan on the Saudi arms issue after he agreed May 20 to remove the controversial Stinger missiles from the weapons package.

Reagan's deal on the Stingers came during a week of hard lobbying, nose-counting and strategic timing by White House officials determined to prevail on the weapons sale. Reagan aides did not want to deliver his veto to Congress until they were confident they had the votes in the Senate to sustain. A fallback position was to send the veto message late enough during the day of May 21 to put off a vote until after the Memorial Day recess.

Final Senate Vote

Offering Reagan the narrowest possible victory, the Senate June 5 voted 66-34 to sustain his veto of the Saudi

AWACS Planes Transferred to Saudi Arabia

President Reagan on June 18 notified Congress that the United States would transfer to Saudi Arabia by late June or early July the first of five AWACS radar planes the Saudis bought in 1981. Reagan's notice prompted objections from some members of Congress, but there was no serious effort to block the transfer of the planes.

Officially known as the Airborne Warning and Control System, the AWACS planes were modified Boeing 707s that were capable of detecting and tracking hundreds of airplanes simultaneously. Israel and its supporters in Congress objected to the sale of the planes to the Saudis, saying they could be used to thwart Israeli air superiority in time of war.

The United States had stationed a fleet of AWACS planes in Saudi Arabia for nearly five years, primarily to help protect Saudi oil fields from spillover effects of the Iran-Iraq war. The new Saudi-owned planes were to replace the U.S. planes.

White House spokesman Larry Speakes put the total value of the AWACS sale at $3.5 billion, which included $1.2 billion for the AWACS planes themselves and the rest for KC-135 refueling tankers, spare parts, training, facilities to handle the planes and maintenance by U.S. contract employees. Speakes said transfer of the planes would be completed about March 31, 1987.

Congress allowed the AWACS sale in October 1981, after Reagan gave assurances that several conditions would be met, including continued Saudi support for Middle East peace negotiations and Saudi agreement to protect sensitive technology in the planes. *(1981 Almanac p. 129)*

In 1985 Congress put those assurances into the law by requiring the president to certify that several conditions had been met before the planes were transferred to Saudi Arabia. The latter requirement was included in the fiscal 1986-87 foreign aid authorizations bill (PL 99-83). *(1985 Almanac p. 55)*

Reagan Letter

In a letter to Congress on June 18, Reagan said that the conditions and assurances "have now been met." Most importantly, the president said, the AWACS sale "will contribute directly to the stability and security of the area and enhance the atmosphere and prospects for progress toward peace. "I also believe that significant progress toward peaceful resolution of disputes in the region has been accomplished with the substantial assistance of Saudi Arabia."

Reagan said Saudi diplomatic actions in 1981-82 demonstrated support for the Middle East peace process. In 1981, King Fahd advanced a plan for peace talks with Israel, and in 1982 most Arab countries endorsed the plan at a meeting in Fez, Morocco. The Saudi-sponsored communique issued at the Fez meeting "moved the formal Arab position from rejection of peace to consideration of how to achieve peace with Israel," Reagan said.

The administration cited these additional factors as evidence of Saudi cooperation with U.S. interests:

- "Tacit" Saudi support for Jordanian King Hussein's abortive effort in 1985 to work out an agreement with Palestine Liberation Organization Chairman Yasir Arafat for the start of negotiations with Israel. The Saudis gave that support, Reagan said, by continuing to provide Jordan with "substantial" financial aid at critical points, such as after Hussein re-established relations with Egypt in September 1984 and after Hussein and Arafat made their negotiating agreement in February 1985. The Hussein-Arafat agreement later collapsed.
- Aid to the anti-Soviet guerrillas in Afghanistan. While details never had been released, U.S. officials and other sources had said Saudi Arabia was a major source of weapons and financial aid to Afghan guerrillas.
- Leadership in negotiating at least two cease-fires in 1983 and 1984 among warring factions in Lebanon. Reagan said the Saudis also backed the Lebanese government's 1984 decision to negotiate with Israel on the withdrawal of Israeli forces.
- Leverage in convincing other Arab countries to allow Egypt to regain membership in the Organization of the Islamic Conference. Egypt was expelled in 1979 after signing its peace treaty with Israel.
- Attempts to settle the Iran-Iraq war. Reagan said the Saudis had "firmly supported every significant diplomatic effort" to end the war. The Saudis supported Iraq, and in return Iran had attacked Saudi shipping in the Persian Gulf. In 1984 the Saudis beat back a planned attack on Saudi territory by Iranian warplanes.
- Support for other moderate Arab or Moslem countries with ties to the United States, including Sudan, Pakistan, Morocco and Tunisia.
- Condemnation by the Saudis of terrorism and the taking of "practical action to oppose terrorism regardless of its origins." Reagan gave no specifics, but noted that Saudi Arabia itself had been a victim of terrorism.

In addition to demanding evidence of Saudi cooperation with peace efforts, Congress in 1981 and 1985 required the administration to negotiate agreements with the Saudis to ensure that the advanced technology contained in the AWACS planes would not fall into enemy hands.

Reagan said all agreements asked by Congress had been reached, and Speakes said that a U.S. Air Force security team would verify Saudi implementation of the security agreements "prior to the delivery of the first AWACS aircraft" and that U.S. military and civilian personnel would remain in Saudi Arabia as long as the planes were operating. The United States also had rights to "on-site security inspection" of the planes, and the Saudis had agreed to share with the United States "continuously and completely" the information obtained by the planes, Reagan said in his letter.

The American Israel Public Affairs Committee (AIPAC) on June 18 called on Congress to monitor carefully the Saudis' use of the AWACS to make sure that the conditions the United States had imposed "are strictly carried out." However, AIPAC signaled that it would not actively fight to block the transfer, largely because the United States would have to reimburse the Saudis for the $3 billion they had already paid for the planes.

arms sale. One additional "yea" vote would have sent the measure to the House for a veto override vote there. In a sign of the symbolic importance of the Senate vote to the administration, Vice President George Bush presided, although he could not vote. *(Vote 111, p. 21-S)*

The president relied on his considerable powers of persuasion to convince eight senators — six Republicans and two Democrats — to switch their positions after voting against the sale initially.

Those changing their positions were: William L. Armstrong, R-Colo.; Lloyd Bentsen, D-Texas; Pete V. Domenici, R-N.M.; John P. East, R-N.C.; J. James Exon, D-Neb.; Chic Hecht, R-Nev.; Jesse Helms, R-N.C.; and William V. Roth Jr., R-Del.

In addition, Reagan won the votes of four out of five senators who were absent during the Senate's initial vote on the Saudi arms package. Of the original absentees, only Paula Hawkins, R-Fla., voted to override the veto. Voting to sustain were Gordon J. Humphrey, R-N.H.; Nancy Landon Kassebaum, R-Kan.; Russell B. Long, D-La.; and Ted Stevens, R-Alaska.

Foreign Relations Chairman Lugar said he began the veto debate the morning of June 5 with 33 votes committed to sustaining the veto, one short of the necessary number. Lugar served as the White House's chief Senate advocate for the sale. The crucial 34th vote was supplied by Armstrong, although Lugar said he had a couple of other "standbys" willing to vote for Reagan if needed.

Despite the close White House victory, the vote showed that Reagan "had to go all out and way out" in order to save the weapons deal, said Sen. Alfonse M. D'Amato, R-N.Y., an opponent of the sale.

He said the narrow vote showed that Congress "is tired of broken promises from the Saudis."

Winning Over the Switchers

Some senators who switched their votes said they did so in light of Reagan's persistent argument that his ability to conduct the nation's foreign policy was at stake.

"The security interests of the United States rest with sustaining the veto," said Exon, who began the three-hour Senate debate by announcing his shift. "Today we have the leader of the free world laying his prestige on the line. That makes it a considerably different situation."

Reagan had made three phone calls to Exon during the previous couple of weeks, including one to Lincoln, Neb., during the Memorial Day recess. Exon also received telephone lobbying pitches from former President Jimmy Carter and former Sen. John G. Tower, R-Texas, who chaired the Armed Services Committee before he retired from the Senate in 1985.

Other Senate switchers, including Armstrong and Domenici, said that Reagan's agreement to delete the Stinger missiles made it easier for them to change their minds and vote for the Saudi package.

Among the 18 GOP senators on the ballot in 1986, 14 voted to override Reagan's veto. All of the nine Democratic incumbents seeking re-election also voted to override. None of the 12 new votes Reagan gained came from senators running again in 1986. Such voting patterns were assumed to reflect a desire on the part of many senators not to alienate Jewish voters and campaign contributors, who constitute an active political constituency nationwide. Republicans seeking re-election "had a lot of trouble voting for the president," Lugar acknowledged.

Reagan said the Senate's action upholding his veto "confirms America's commitment to a security relationship" between the United States and Saudi Arabia stretching back 40 years. "We are determined to work with the Saudis and other friendly states to achieve our shared goals of peace and stability in the region," he said.

Cranston said the narrow vote to sustain Reagan's veto, coupled with the House's 356-62 vote against the weapons deal May 7, should be interpreted as a stern warning to Saudi Arabia. "We have sent a strong message to Saudi Arabia that America wants more support for American security interests and peace in the Middle East, and less support for terrorism," he said. ■

$2.4 Billion Embassy Security Plan Approved

Congress gave final approval Aug. 12 to a five-year, $2.4 billion program aimed at strengthening U.S. overseas diplomatic posts against terrorist attacks.

The authorization fell well short of the $4.4 billion, five-year package that the Reagan administration had requested to rebuild or refurbish more than 250 U.S. diplomatic posts.

The final legislation (HR 4151 — PL 99-399) contained an array of terrorism-related initiatives, ranging from anti-terrorist research and development to cash payments to U.S. hostages who had been held in Iran in 1979-81.

But the heart of the measure was an ambitious embassy construction program originally recommended in June 1985 by a special presidential commission formed after the terrorist attacks in 1983 and 1984 on the U.S. Marine headquarters and embassy compound in Lebanon. That commission, headed by former CIA Deputy Director Bobby R. Inman, reported serious security problems at U.S. diplomatic missions. *(1985 Almanac p. 105)*

The White House responded in President Reagan's fiscal 1987 budget with a proposal for a five-year diplomatic security program. *(Budget message, p. 5-D)*

The funds authorized by HR 4151 would allow the State Department to proceed with such high-priority projects as facilities in Cyprus, Jordan and Honduras. Other priority missions were in Moscow, Cairo, London, Athens and Pretoria, South Africa.

In passing its version in March, the House went along with the administration's full-funding request for the embassy program. The Senate, concerned with spending restraints, limited its bill to a two-year program costing $1.1 billion. The final version authorized five-year funding for capital projects, but only two-year funding for salaries and expenses. Conferees said further funding for salaries and expenses should be considered as part of regular State Department authorizations for fiscal 1988-90.

Congress already had provided $702.1 million for the embassy security program in a fiscal 1986 supplemental appropriations bill (HR 4515 — PL 99-349) signed by

Reagan July 2. The State Department also received $343.4 million in fiscal 1985 supplemental funds that were prompted by the Beirut bombings. *(HR 4515, p. 153)*

Major Provisions

As signed into law Aug. 27, major provisions of HR 4151 (PL 99-399):

• **Diplomatic Security.** Consolidated the security functions of the State Department under a Bureau of Diplomatic Security to be headed by a new assistant secretary of state for diplomatic security.

• Established within the bureau a Diplomatic Security Service whose director should be drawn from the Senior Foreign Service or Senior Executive Service and have demonstrated ability in security, law enforcement, management and public administration.

• Authorized fiscal 1986-87 funding for the diplomatic security program as follows: $308.1 million for salaries and expenses; $857.8 million for acquisition, construction and maintenance at U.S. diplomatic missions abroad; and $15 million for anti-terrorism research and development.

• Increased the fiscal 1987 authorization for anti-terrorism training assistance to $14.7 million from $9.8 million. *(Background, 1985 Almanac p. 60)*

• Authorized $418 million annually in fiscal 1988-90 for acquisition and maintenance of buildings abroad.

• Required that, where "adequate competition" existed, only U.S. contractors be allowed to bid on embassy construction or design projects that exceeded $5 million. This section did not apply in countries that had laws prohibiting the use of American contractors.

• Prohibited use of any of the authorized funds for constructing any diplomatic facilities in Israel.

• **Anti-Terrorism Program.** Authorized the secretary of state to offer rewards for information on major narcotics trafficking and narcotics-related terrorist acts committed primarily outside the United States.

• Earmarked $2 million for the awards program from existing funding and authorized an additional $10 million in fiscal 1987.

• Authorized the secretary to impose controls on certain services to military, police or intelligence agencies of countries that supported terrorism, as determined under the Export Administration Act. Five countries were so classified as of 1986: Libya, Iran, South Yemen, Syria and Cuba.

• Amended the Arms Export Control Act to prohibit exports of munitions that were subject to control to any country designated as a supporter of international terrorism under the Export Administration Act.

• **Nuclear Terrorism.** Authorized the president to suspend nuclear cooperation with nations that had not ratified the Convention on the Physical Protection of Nuclear Materials.

• Established a uniform procedure for criminal history checks of certain employees of nuclear power plants. Under the procedure, the Nuclear Regulatory Commission would channel fingerprint cards from power plant owners to the FBI for identification and a criminal history check. The procedure was similar to that provided in a bill (S 274) passed by the Senate in 1985. *(1985 Almanac p. 237)*

• **Victims Compensation.** Provided about $22,200 — $50 per day — for the U.S. hostages held in Iran for 444 days, from November 1979 until January 1981. Subsequent hostages would also receive compensation at a lower amount, along with health and educational benefits provided to them and their families. *(Iran hostages, 1980 Almanac p. 351)*

• **Maritime Security.** Authorized $62.5 million during fiscal years 1987-91 to boost security at U.S. and foreign seaports.

• Authorized the president to suspend passenger services to any foreign port if he determined the country concerned had aided a terrorist organization that illegally seized or threatened to seize passenger vessels.

• **Extraterritorial Criminal Jurisdiction.** Established U.S. legal jurisdiction over crimes involving violent attacks by terrorists against all U.S. nationals abroad. Existing federal law covered murder and assault only against high-ranking U.S. officials. The conference report made clear that "simple barroom brawls or normal street crime" were not covered.

• **Peace Corps.** Authorized $130 million for the Peace Corps in fiscal 1986 and $137.2 million in fiscal 1987.

• **D.C. Demonstrations.** Repealed a District of Columbia law prohibiting demonstrations within 500 feet of an embassy. Henceforth, demonstrations would be prohibited within 100 feet of Washington embassies under a 1972 federal law applicable elsewhere in the country. *(Congress and the Nation Vol. III, p. 286)*

• **Waldheim Allowance.** Called on the administration to propose eliminating an $81,650 annual "retirement allowance" in the United Nations' budget for former U.N. Secretary-General Kurt Waldheim, the new president of Austria. Waldheim had been accused of Nazi activities during World War II.

• **Proceeds From Espionage.** Prohibited convicted spies from collecting writing or other royalties that stemmed from their espionage activities.

• **Fellowship Program.** Created a fellowship program for U.S. citizens to replace foreign nationals employed in American embassies in Moscow and Eastern European countries. The program was to be named after Rep. Dante B. Fascell, D-Fla., chairman of the House Foreign Affairs Committee.

House Action

Prompted by a get-tough attitude against terrorism, the House March 18 passed HR 4151 by a 389-7 vote. *(Vote 54, p. 18-H)*

In addition to authorizing the five-year embassy security program proposed by the administration, the bill included a panoply of other anti-terrorist provisions ranging from financial compensation for U.S. hostages to authorization of a $125 million program aimed at increasing security at ocean ports and on U.S. vessels.

The bill did not contain a specific funding authorization level. However, it assumed the administration's $4.4 billion estimate for an extensive construction program that would involve 254 embassies and consulates.

Although Democratic leaders were anxious to rush the bill through the House, some members were skittish about voting for a costly measure without direct assurances of support from President Reagan. He complied with a March 17 letter to House members that described embassy security as "one of our highest foreign policy priorities."

"This is a year of great budget stringency, but the well-being of our people is of the utmost importance," said Reagan.

During debate on HR 4151, Rep. Daniel A. Mica, D-Fla., chairman of the Foreign Affairs Subcommittee on

International Operations, said there were about 100 diplomatic posts in a "crisis stage" because of security risks.

Much of the embassy security information was classified by the State Department. But the Foreign Affairs Committee, in its March 12 report on the anti-terrorism legislation (H Rept 99-494), listed some of State's priority building projects for the next five years.

Among the most immediate were U.S. posts in Cyprus, Jordan and Honduras, which borders Nicaragua. Other priority projects, recommended by the committee for funding in fiscal 1987, included missions in Moscow, Cairo, Jerusalem, Paris and Brussels.

Cash for Hostages

A section of the bill dealing with cash payments to U.S. hostages grew out of unsuccessful efforts over the past few years to compensate the group of Americans held for 444 days after the U.S. Embassy in Tehran was seized by Iranians in November 1979.

Under the bill, U.S. government employees and contractors would receive about $66 for each day they were held in captivity. The figure was based on the average travel per diem currently given to government workers.

Since the bill would apply retroactively to the seizure of the embassy in Iran, U.S. hostages held there would receive about $29,300 if the measure was enacted.

The House rejected an amendment by John McCain, R-Ariz., to reduce a hostage's daily cash compensation to $20. McCain said the lower figure, after adjustment for inflation, was closer to the amount given to U.S. soldiers held as prisoners of war in Vietnam. McCain spent nearly six years as a POW in Vietnam.

The House also defeated, 144-252, an amendment by Robert S. Walker, R-Pa., that would have required Congress to authorize and appropriate annually the funds for hostages' compensation. *(Vote 53, p. 18-H)*

The bill made such compensation an entitlement program that did not require ongoing congressional approval.

HR 4151 also contained provisions intended to demonstrate the United States' efforts to combat terrorism.

Senate Action

Rebuffing the administration's request for a five-year $4.4 billion package, the Senate June 25 approved a $1.1 billion version of the bill.

The Senate Foreign Relations Committee, in reporting HR 4151 May 20 (S Rept 99-304), limited the authorization to two fiscal years, 1986 and 1987.

Foreign Relations Chairman Richard G. Lugar, R-Ind., led the Senate effort to reduce the cost of the embassy program, citing budget constraints and staff findings that some of the proposed building projects were unnecessary and too expensive.

The Senate measure, passed on a voice vote, called for $857.8 million for constructing and renovating embassies, with another $245.3 million for salaries and expenses. The money would be used to begin building 75 new embassies, consulates and other diplomatic structures and renovating another 170 missions.

"American diplomatic missions, the people who work in them and their families are the clearest symbols of American interests overseas and are, therefore, prime targets for international terrorists," said Lugar.

Paul S. Sarbanes, D-Md., argued during the June 25 floor debate that the Senate bill should have included more money and called on conferees to increase the funding levels. He had unsuccessfully tried to add $250 million to the program when the Foreign Relations Committee considered the measure in May. The committee rejected his proposal on a 7-10 vote.

During floor debate, the Senate adopted several amendments, including proposals to:

- Make it a crime under U.S. law to commit terrorist assaults on U.S. citizens anywhere in the world. This provision tracked a separate Senate bill (S 1429) that passed the chamber Feb. 19.
- Call for the elimination of the U.N. retirement allowance to Waldheim.
- Prohibit the State Department from using construction funds in the bill to build a new U.S. Embassy in Tel Aviv. The aim of the amendment, offered by Jesse Helms, R-N.C., was to force relocation of the U.S. Embassy from Tel Aviv to Jerusalem. While Israel claimed Jerusalem as its capital, the United States and other countries had refused to relocate their embassies there because of Arab disputes over Jerusalem's status. *(1984 Almanac p. 115)*

Final Action

House and Senate members, along with staff aides, worked out dozens of differences between conflicting versions of the embassy security legislation without formally convening a conference committee.

The resulting "paper conference" paved the way for the compromise measure (H Rept 99-783) to be approved in both chambers Aug. 12 by voice votes. President Reagan signed the bill Aug. 27. ▮

British Extradition Treaty, Irish Aid Approved

The Senate on July 17 approved a long-stalled treaty setting new standards for extraditions between the United States and the United Kingdom.

The impasse on the treaty was broken after it became linked with legislation (HR 4329 — PL 99-415), cleared by Congress Aug. 14, that authorized $120 million in economic aid to Northern Ireland in fiscal 1986-88. Sponsors said the aid would demonstrate U.S. support for a controversial 1985 accord over the future of Northern Ireland.

The main purpose of the treaty (Treaty Doc 99-8) was to make it easier for Great Britain to extradite from the United States members of the outlawed Irish Republican Army (IRA), which sought to end British rule in Northern Ireland. The Senate Foreign Relations Committee approved amendments to the treaty that would narrow the right of persons to escape extradition by claiming that their offenses were "political" in nature. The Senate amendments were subject to approval by the British Parliament.

President Reagan had asked for quick Senate approval of the treaty as a sign of gratitude to Prime Minister Margaret Thatcher for her support of the April 14 U.S. bombing raid against Libya. Thatcher had allowed U.S.

planes to take off from British bases on their way to bomb alleged terrorist sites in Libya. *(Libya attack, p. 389)*

Senate action on the treaty was thwarted by a variety of factors. These included vigorous lobbying against the pact by Irish-American groups and charges that Britain's courts were prejudiced against those accused of anti-British acts in the longstanding conflict in Northern Ireland.

Foreign Relations Committee Chairman Richard G. Lugar, R-Ind., finally was able to press action on the treaty by tying it to the Irish aid issue. Although the House approved an Irish aid measure in March, Lugar delayed action on a Senate aid bill until a deal was struck with Democratic opponents of the treaty.

Background

Signed by U.S. and British officials on June 25, 1985, the treaty was sought by the British government, which had been unable to extradite members of the IRA. Some had been accused of violent crimes, including murder, only to seek refuge in the United States.

Under an existing treaty between the two countries, such persons could avoid extradition by claiming that their crimes were political in nature. That determination was left to U.S. courts to decide. Known as the political offense exception, this provision was included in U.S. extradition agreements with a number of countries.

As sent to the Senate, the treaty removed violent crimes, such as murder, kidnapping and bombing, from the list of offenses that could be claimed as politically protected. That would have taken away the authority of U.S. judges to refuse extradition of persons accused of such crimes.

The Irish aid package was designed to bolster a landmark accord on the future of Northern Ireland that was reached in November 1985 between Great Britain and the Republic of Ireland. That accord gave Ireland a say in governing Northern Ireland, which had been under British rule for 64 years. Ulster, the traditional name for Northern Ireland, had been caught for many years in a cycle of violence between the pro-British Protestant majority and the region's Irish Catholic minority, which wanted to end British rule.

Senate Committee Action

The Senate Foreign Relations Committee approved the extradition treaty June 12 by a 15-2 vote after delicate negotiations removed key Democratic opposition.

The panel then went on to approve a $20 million economic aid package for Northern Ireland.

Extradition Treaty

The committee's approval of the treaty — officially called the Supplementary Extradition Treaty between the United States and the United Kingdom — capped weeks of bitter debate and intense negotiations aimed at resolving critical differences between the pact's supporters and opponents.

A lengthy impasse was broken the previous week when Lugar met for several hours with Thomas F. Eagleton, D-Mo., to hammer out a compromise aimed at resolving major Democratic objections while preserving the thrust of the treaty.

At the insistence of some Democrats, the panel included a section that would allow U.S. courts to guard against political or religious persecution in extradition cases brought by British authorities.

Key language in Article 8 would permit a judge to deny extradition if the accused would "be prejudiced at his trial or punished, detained or restricted in his personal liberty by reason of his race, religion, nationality or political opinions."

As sent to the Senate, the treaty gave the president the authority to deny extradition on such grounds. Critics insisted that U.S. courts retain a role in handling extradition cases.

Democratic opponents also succeeded in inserting language in an accompanying report (Exec Rept 99-17) that would allow U.S. judges to examine the fairness of the British court system when deciding extradition cases. "We have every right to question the court system that exists in Northern Ireland," said Joseph R. Biden Jr., D-Del.

But report language also approved by the committee said it would be a "perversion" of the panel's intent if Article 8 were "used to impede or delay the extradition of those sought for acts of terrorism."

One of the dissenting votes was cast by Jesse Helms, R-N.C., who said the treaty threatened the U.S. tradition of allowing a political test in extradition cases. "We might as well abolish the Fourth of July while we're at it," he said.

One of Helms' objections was that non-democratic countries, such as Nicaragua or Afghanistan, might seek similar treaties in order to try political rebels who flee to the United States. The committee added language that said the Senate would not approve such treaties with "totalitarian" regimes, but Helms said that provision did not satisfy him.

Helms also tried to alter the treaty with amendments that would have removed a retroactivity clause and allowed a political defense in acts against the military but not civilians. The panel rejected both.

The committee approved another Helms amendment to remove a section of the treaty that gave preference to British statutes of limitation applying to fugitives sought in the United States. Treaty supporters said this would have little, if any, practical effect in most extradition cases.

Also voting against the treaty was Edward Zorinsky, D-Neb.

Others, meanwhile, said they were pleased with the outcome. "The vote demonstrates successfully the importance of close bilateral and international cooperation against terrorism," said Nigel Sheinwald, a British Embassy official. "Those accused or convicted of a wide range of offenses will no longer be able to avoid extradition by claiming their crimes were politically motivated."

Some of the treaty's original detractors also voiced satisfaction with the panel's final version. Foreign Relations member John Kerry, D-Mass., said the approved treaty was "night and day different" from the version first submitted to the Senate in June 1985. "The political exception is acknowledged in the treaty. It is alive," he said. "I think we rewrote the treaty."

British and Reagan administration officials had approved the outlines of the compromise worked out by Lugar and Eagleton. A British diplomatic source, while saying his government did not object to the new language added by the Democrats, claimed it was unnecessary. "We don't try people for their thoughts. We try people for their acts in both countries," he said.

Irish Aid

The committee's Irish aid bill (S 2572 — S Rept 99-

326) authorized $20 million over two years, fiscal 1986 and 1987. The Senate package, proposed by Lugar, was substantially smaller than a $250 million, five-year version (HR 4329) that the House approved in March. Lugar said the House figure was too expensive and not likely to be appropriated in the current budget-cutting atmosphere. *(House action, below)*

The administration had proposed $20 million annually for five years, with other aid in the form of loan guarantees for housing and business programs. The Senate bill also allowed loan guarantees.

Lugar agreed to attach various House-approved conditions to the aid package, aimed at ensuring that the money would not be used for military or security purposes in Northern Ireland.

Senate Floor Action

The Senate on July 17 approved the extradition treaty by a 87-10 margin, far above the two-thirds majority required for consent to ratification of a treaty. *(Vote 160, p. 29-S)*

Immediately afterward, as part of a deal among leaders of the Foreign Relations Committee, the Senate passed the Irish aid bill by voice vote.

The Senate tabled two amendments offered by critics of the treaty:

- By Alfonse M. D'Amato, R-N.Y., providing that the treaty would not apply to any individual whose extradition was sought prior to the entry into force of the treaty, or to any offense committed before that time, if the offense was not in violation of the laws of both countries. Tabled 65-33. *(Vote 156, p. 29-S)*
- By Helms, providing that U.S. courts must consider as a defense against extradition a showing that the person sought to be extradited had committed his alleged offense as part of an armed uprising against military authorities, without committing wanton crimes of violence against civilians. Helms called his provision the "Reagan-Shultz-Meese Defense" against extradition, citing support by high administration officials for "freedom fighters." Tabled 87-9. *(Vote 157, p. 29-S)*

House Action on Aid Bill

The House had passed its five-year, $250 million Irish aid bill (HR 4329) on March 11 by voice vote.

"I believe we have an obligation to help promote peace and reconciliation in Northern Ireland in a practical and measurable way," said key supporter Speaker Thomas P. O'Neill Jr., D-Mass., in a rare floor speech.

Another supporter, Mario Biaggi, D-N.Y., described the aid package as a "mini-Marshall plan" to help economically depressed Ulster get on its feet while the accord took effect.

No one spoke against the House bill, which provided $50 million annually in direct financial aid and also allowed Ulster to participate in U.S. loan guarantee programs, which could result in additional indirect U.S. assistance.

The direct cash contributions in fiscal 1986 and 1987 would come from unspent foreign aid already authorized; money for fiscal 1988-90 would require new appropriations.

The bill also prohibited the money from being used for military or security purposes and contained conditions aimed at ensuring that the program did not discriminate on the basis of religion. The president would be required to certify to Congress that the conditions were being met before the money was sent, and to submit annual reports afterward.

The anti-discrimination language was sought by Irish-American groups who feared that financial assistance to Ulster without any limitations could strengthen British rule at the expense of the Catholic minority.

Biaggi said the legislation "recognizes the fact that a root cause of the problem in Northern Ireland is raw, sectarian-based discrimination ... tolerated, if not sanctioned, by the British government." Biaggi was chairman of the Ad Hoc Congressional Committee for Irish Affairs.

Compromise Aid Bill Cleared

The Senate passed a compromise version of HR 4329 by voice vote Aug. 13. The House accepted the Senate version Aug. 14, completing congressional action on the bill.

The compromise, which had been developed without a formal Senate-House conference, authorized $50 million for fiscal 1986 and $35 million annually for fiscal 1987-88. The higher authorization for fiscal 1986 reflected the fact that Congress already had appropriated that amount in a supplemental appropriations bill (HR 4515 — PL 99-349) signed July 2.

Final Provisions

As signed into law Sept. 19, HR 4329 (PL 99-415):

- Authorized $50 million in fiscal 1986 and $35 million in each of fiscal 1987 and 1988 for U.S. contributions to an International Fund established to support the 1985 Anglo-Irish agreement. The contributions were to come out of Economic Support Fund resources.
- Authorized additional aid under four loan and loan guarantee programs carried out under the Foreign Assistance Act: the Housing Guarantee Program and Private Sector Revolving Fund of the Agency for International Development, the Trade and Development Program, and the investment guarantee program of the Overseas Private Investment Corporation.
- Directed the president to make every effort to ensure U.S. representation on the International Fund.
- Required the president to make annual reports to Congress on the progress of the International Fund. ∎

Genocide Treaty Approved

After almost 37 years of intermittent debate, the Senate Feb. 19 overcame opposition by conservatives and approved a treaty declaring genocide to be a crime.

But the Senate's action was largely symbolic, because "reservations" limiting the treaty's application had been attached in 1985 to defuse the conservatives' opposition.

Majority Leader Robert Dole, R-Kan., who played a pivotal role in floor strategy on the treaty, contended that the Senate's action was nonetheless important. He called the treaty a "worldwide statement of outrage and condemnation over very real horrors.

"We have waited long enough," Dole added. "As a nation which enshrines human dignity and freedom as a God-given right in its Constitution, we must correct our anomalous position on this basic rights issue."

The vote to approve the pact was 83-11, and came

after the treaty's principal active opponent, Steven D. Symms, R-Idaho, dropped a filibuster threat. Dole had let Symms know unequivocally that he would press for final action on the issue. *(Vote 15, p. 4-S)*

Also opposing the treaty, which had been ratified by 96 other countries, were Republicans Jeremiah Denton, Ala.; John P. East, N.C.; Jake Garn, Utah; Barry Goldwater, Ariz.; Charles E. Grassley, Iowa; Jesse Helms, N.C.; James A. McClure, Idaho; William V. Roth Jr., Del.; Strom Thurmond, S.C.; and Malcolm Wallop, Wyo.

Helms had voted for the treaty in 1985 when it was reported by the Foreign Relations Committee. But he voted against final approval, he said, as a tribute to the late Sen. Sam J. Ervin Jr., D-N.C., (1954-74), who had voiced strong concerns about the pact.

Helms had blocked action in the past, complaining that the treaty could threaten the Constitution and subject the United States to spurious lawsuits by other countries. *(1985 Almanac p. 98; 1984 Almanac p. 123)*

Senators refused 31-62 to accept a Symms amendment they said would have all but killed the treaty. The Symms proposal would have protected "political" groups from annihilation as well as "national, ethnic, racial or religious" groups, which already were protected in the treaty. *(Vote 14, p. 4-S)*

The Senate, however, agreed 93-1 to a resolution (S Res 347) urging the president to seek inclusion of "political" groups in the treaty, and President Reagan indicated in a letter to Symms he would do so. Goldwater cast the only "nay" vote. *(Vote 16, p. 4-S)*

Despite the Senate-added limits, treaty supporters outside of Congress hailed the pact as significant. Jess Hordes, associate director of the Anti-Defamation League of B'nai B'rith, which had lobbied hard for the treaty, said its approval was "a symbolic affirmation of America's commitment" to human rights.

The Senate's action was particularly satisfying for William Proxmire, D-Wis. He had made a speech urging support for the treaty every day the Senate had been in session — excluding brief "pro forma" meetings — since Jan. 11, 1967. He estimated that he gave about 3,000 genocide speeches. "I felt that by hammering away, it would keep the Senate from forgetting it," Proxmire said after the vote.

Technically, the Senate voted Feb. 19 to approve a resolution of ratification. Actual ratification of the treaty, formally the Convention on the Prevention and Punishment of the Crime of Genocide (Exec O, 81st Cong, 1st Sess), did not occur until President Reagan submitted it to the United Nations.

Congress still had to pass legislation to implement the treaty. The chief provision of that measure would be to make genocide a federal crime. Genocide was not covered under existing federal laws, although someone accused of a mass killing could be prosecuted under murder statutes.

Provisions

As approved by the Senate Feb. 19, major provisions of the genocide treaty:

- Declared genocide to be a crime under international law and instructed treaty signers to prevent and punish the crime.
- Defined genocide as the intentional destruction of national, ethnic, racial or religious groups and covered attempts to kill members of these groups, cause serious bodily or mental harm to members of the groups, deliberately inflict conditions upon these groups designed to physically destroy them, impose measures intended to prevent births within the groups, and forcibly transfer children of a protected group to another group.
- Specified that the crimes covered included genocide, conspiracy to commit genocide, direct and public incitement to commit genocide, attempt to commit genocide and complicity in genocide.
- Provided that persons who committed genocide should be punished, whether they were "constitutionally responsible rulers, public officials or private individuals."
- Specified that genocide would not be considered a "political" crime for purposes of extradition, and provided that parties to the treaty would "pledge" to grant extradition to the requesting country in accordance with existing extradition treaties.

The Senate added a "proviso" making clear that extradition would be granted only in cases in which the activity was a crime in the United States as well as in the requesting country.

- Provided for trial within the territory in which the act was committed or by an international tribunal with jurisdiction over the person charged.
- Provided that disputes between parties to the treaty be submitted to the world court, formally known as the International Court of Justice. The Senate reservation declared that the United States had the right to refuse jurisdiction when it determined that going before the international tribunal would not be in the national interest.

Background

Drafted in response to the Nazi Holocaust, the genocide pact was approved by the United Nations Dec. 9, 1948, and signed by the United States. On June 16, 1949, President Truman first submitted it to the Senate for approval. The Senate failed to approve it, but all subsequent presidents except Dwight D. Eisenhower urged its adoption. Reagan, however, did not signal his support until shortly before the 1984 elections. After that, the Justice and State departments lobbied in a low-key way for its approval.

The treaty had always been opposed by conservatives who saw it as a threat to American sovereignty and who worried that the Soviet Union — already a signatory — could use it against the United States. For several years conservatives had an influential ally in the American Bar Association. But in 1976, after a reappraisal, the lawyers' group supported the treaty.

Proxmire said Feb. 19 that over the last decade the treaty's opponents were always more vocal than its supporters. While presidents wanted the treaty approved, he added, it often got shoved aside for other issues on the executive agenda. The same thing happened in the Senate, where the pact's fate was complicated by the necessity to win a two-thirds majority.

Controversial Reservations

By most accounts, a confluence of events led to final approval: Reagan's support and the effort by Senate Foreign Relations Chairman Richard G. Lugar, R-Ind., to assuage conservatives' concerns through reservations within the treaty.

These reservations were unilateral declarations that excluded or modified the terms of the treaty and affected only the party entering the reservation. However, other signers must acquiesce in the U.S. actions. According to the 1985 Foreign Relations Committee report on the treaty

(Exec Rept 99-2), the practice of reservations was widespread, and the document noted that a number of signatories had entered reservations to the genocide pact.

The most important reservation was one giving the United States the right to exempt itself from compulsory jurisdiction in genocide treaty cases before the world court.

The administration opposed such a reservation in 1984, but it changed course in 1985, apparently because the world court asserted jurisdiction in a suit filed by Nicaragua against the United States over the CIA's mining of Nicaraguan harbors.

The Foreign Relations Committee said the reservation would allow the United States to protect itself if world court jurisdiction were sought for a case that was "brought solely for the propaganda value that might result." A Lugar aide said Feb. 19 that an example would be a suit against the United States for wiping out Indian tribes during the 19th century.

Supporters of the treaty had strenuously opposed this provision, contending that it would weaken U.S. efforts to bring genocide charges before the court. They said another nation could resist the world court's jurisdiction by noting that the United States, itself, was not compelled to come before the court.

The other controversial reservation attached by the committee stated that nothing in the treaty required the United States to take any action that might be prohibited by the U.S. Constitution.

The committee majority said the language was intended to "avoid placing the United States in a position of having to choose between its obligations under the Constitution and those under the [treaty]."

Opponents said the reservation was not needed because the genocide treaty did not conflict with the Constitution.

Despite supporters' concerns about the additional language, they conceded that the reservations were necessary to get final action on the treaty. And it was Lugar's willingness to deal with Helms in 1985 that broke the committee logjam. ▮

Intelligence Authorization: Small Increase

Congress completed action Oct. 6 on a fiscal 1987 authorization bill (HR 4759 — PL 99-569) for the CIA and other intelligence agencies.

As in the past, most of the bill was kept secret. The most important non-secret provision barred the CIA from using its contingency fund to give aid to the "contra" guerrillas who were battling to overthrow the leftist government of Nicaragua. *(Contra aid, p. 394)*

The House had defeated a similar ban on aid to a guerrilla group that was battling the Marxist government of Angola. *(Angola aid, p. 387)*

Although funding amounts in the intelligence bill were classified, Lee H. Hamilton, D-Ind., chairman of the House Select Intelligence Committee, said the measure provided "a small amount of real growth" in spending. Intelligence spending had increased steadily since the late 1970s, with the exception of fiscal 1986, when there was a sharp cut.

The increase authorized in the bill was made possible, Hamilton said, by exempting the intelligence agencies from some of the budget cuts that were imposed on overall Defense Department spending. Actual appropriations for the intelligence agencies were hidden within the Pentagon budget.

Even with the increase, the National Foreign Intelligence Program was "stretched to its utmost in covering the growing demands of intelligence consumers today," said Senate Intelligence Committee Chairman Dave Durenberger, R-Minn.

Constituting about half of all intelligence spending, the National Foreign Intelligence Program included the CIA, the Defense Intelligence Agency and other agencies that collected and analyzed intelligence for the use of policy makers. The other half of intelligence spending came under the heading of Tactical Intelligence and Related Activities, which included the intelligence branches of the military services.

Many of the issues dealt with by the bill were submerged in what Durenberger called the "murky depths" of spies and counterspies. In 1986, the bill itself became the focus of an obscure and confusing tug of war between the CIA and Sen. Jesse Helms, R-N.C.

Helms was a longtime critic of the CIA, which he had accused of having a "pro-Soviet bias" — a bias that he said was demonstrated by the agency's underestimation of Soviet military capabilities. Relations between Helms and the U.S. intelligence community reached a new low in August, when Helms said he suspected that U.S. agencies had spied on him during his trip to Chile the previous month.

During floor consideration of the bill Sept. 24, Helms won Senate approval of two amendments directed at the CIA. One required the agency to report to Congress on human rights violations, government involvement in drug trafficking and other matters in Panama. The other called for reports to Congress by the CIA and other agencies on a variety of subjects, most dealing with alleged CIA failures to analyze Soviet military capabilities.

During conference action, leaders of the House and Senate committees deleted both of Helms' amendments from the bill.

Provisions

In provisions that were made public, the final version of the intelligence bill:

- Put into permanent law a requirement that intelligence agencies notify Congress in advance of "covert" arms transfers to foreign governments or groups valued at $1 million or more.
- Barred the CIA from using its secret contingency fund to aid the contras. The agency could provide contra aid only if Congress specifically authorized it or if money was "reprogrammed" or diverted from other CIA programs.
- Barred U.S. intelligence agencies from cooperating "in any fashion" with the government of South Africa, except for activities "reasonably designed to facilitate the collection of necessary intelligence." Neither the public portion of the bill nor the conference report gave a definition of the exception.

The bill also stated U.S. policy that no intelligence agency could provide information to the South African government that pertained to a South African internal opposition group or individual. In their report, conferees said intelligence agencies could provide information to

Panel Warns of Serious Espionage Threat

The espionage threat to the United States "is more serious than anyone in the government has yet acknowledged publicly," the Senate Intelligence Committee said in a report released Oct. 7. The committee made 95 findings and recommendations, ranging from streamlining the classification of government documents to new means of protecting satellite communication links.

Committee Chairman Dave Durenberger, R-Minn., summarized the report's themes as: "too many secrets, too much access to secrets, too many spies, too little accountability for securing the national secrets and too little effort given to combating the very real threat which spies represent to our national security."

Even so, the report said, "the nation's counterintelligence structure is fundamentally sound."

Without giving specifics, the committee said counterintelligence efforts had been beefed up substantially in recent years. However, the report said many past recommendations for improvements were not carried out.

Committee leaders said they were counting on publicity surrounding recent arrests of foreign spies to serve as an incentive for action. Since 1984, 25 persons had been convicted or had pleaded guilty to spying on the United States for the Soviet Union, China, Poland, Israel and other countries.

New Policies Required

The report called for changes in three broad areas:

- **Personnel Policies.** Various government agencies had conflicting and confusing standards for giving security clearances and for checking up on employees once they had clearances. Rather than setting high standards for granting clearances, the committee said, agencies gave most sensitive clearances to "virtually anyone whose record does not contain clear disqualifying factors."

The committee pointed in particular to the military services, which it said "have been permitted to establish far too many special access programs" with lower security standards than regular ones.

- **Information Security.** Saying the existing system of classifying documents was "unduly complicated" and "breeds cynicism and confusion," the committee recommended changes such as abolition of the "confidential" category of information. That was the lowest category, involving the greatest number of documents, many of which did not need to be classified, the report said.

The committee said all sensitive information should be classified either as "secret" or what was called "sensitive compartmented information," meaning that it was available only to those with a need to know about it.

The committee complained about "leaks" of information, pointing particularly to the executive branch. It said damage to U.S. national security had resulted both from "authorized" leaks (such as when White House officials selectively released classified information to bolster administration policy) and "unauthorized" leaks (when government aides released information, frequently to undermine established policy). The administration should keep records of authorized leaks, the panel said, if only to keep the FBI from spending time investigating cases "that are not real leaks."

The committee also pointed at two other sources of leaks: government contractors and Congress.

Durenberger said there was "an almost total lack of security" in the Senate's handling of secrets. To remedy that, his panel recommended creation of a security office to determine how many Senate employees had access to secret information and to set standards for granting clearances and safeguarding that information.

- **Communications and Computer Security.** Technological advances were making existing satellites, computers and other equipment more vulnerable to espionage activities, the committee said. It noted that an interception station in Lourdes, Cuba, enabled the Soviet Union to monitor most satellite and many telephone communications in the United States. The military had taken steps to protect its communications, the committee said, but businesses — including those that did secret work for the government — remained "highly vulnerable" to electronic interceptions.

Among its recommendations, the committee endorsed a plan by the National Security Agency for development of low-cost telephone equipment that would be "secure" against unauthorized interceptions. It also noted the fiscal 1987 intelligence authorization bill (HR 4759) included funding to begin encrypting, or scrambling, domestic commercial satellite links, which carried many government, as well as private, communications. *(Intelligence bill, p. 383)*

The committee said it had proposed spending about $500 million more each year on security measures than was available in fiscal 1985. But those added costs would have a "significant payoff" in enhanced national security in future years, the panel said.

In a passing reference to civil liberties, the committee acknowleged that enhanced security also could cost the United States some of its freedoms. But the panel said its recommendations were designed to improve protection of secrets "without violating constitutional rights or upsetting the delicate balance between security and freedom."

Soviet U.N. Personnel

As it had for years, the committee demanded reductions in the number of Soviet-bloc personnel allowed into the United States for diplomatic and commercial work. Durenberger said there were some 4,200 Soviet-bloc officials working in the United States — about half from the Soviet Union — and that one-third were known to be intelligence agents.

Under pressure from Congress, the administration had ordered the expulsion of 25 personnel from the Soviet mission to the United Nations. The State Department also had said the mission must be reduced from 275 to 170 diplomatic personnel by April 1988.

The committee opposed a State Department plan to allow 30 new Soviet diplomats to staff a new consulate in New York in return for the opening of a new U.S. consulate in Kiev.

South Africa only if the information "credibly indicates the imminent likelihood of violent action calculated to threaten human life" and providing that information to South Africa "could be expected to contribute to avoidance of that violent action."

- Stated the policy of Congress that the number of personnel permitted at the Soviet Union's mission to the United Nations in New York City could not "substantially exceed" the number of personnel at the U.S. mission. The bill also required reports to Congress on the number of Soviet personnel admitted to the United States for service at the United Nations.
- Authorized $22 million and a personnel limit of 237 for the Intelligence Community Staff, which served the CIA director in his capacity as coordinator of the intelligence agencies.
- Authorized $125.8 million for the CIA retirement and disability fund.
- Gave the FBI mandatory access to state and local criminal records as part of its background investigations for security clearances for government personnel and contract employees. The Defense Department, the CIA and the Office of Personnel Management already had this authority.
- Amended 1978 banking privacy legislation (PL 95-630) to give the FBI, in counterintelligence investigations, authority to subpoena bank records of individuals, companies or other entities suspected of being a foreign power or an agent of a foreign power. The provision pre-empted state and local laws and state constitutional provisions that set stricter privacy protection standards than did the 1978 federal law. Conferees said they expected the FBI to develop guidelines for the use and dissemination of information obtained from the subpoenas. *(Banking law, 1978 Almanac p. 300)*
- Exempted civilian intelligence employees of the military services from many provisions of the civil service laws, thus putting them under the same personnel management system as employees of other intelligence agencies. The provision was designed to allow the military services to promote civilian intelligence specialists without having to make them supervisors.
- Allowed the CIA and the National Security Agency to pay for undergraduate educations of employees, especially in computer sciences, mathematics, and engineering.

Committee Action

The Senate Intelligence Committee reported its version of the intelligence bill (S 2477 — S Rept 99-307) on May 21, and the House panel reported HR 4759 (H Rept 99-690, Part I) on July 17. Supplemental reports (Parts II and III) were filed July 28 by the House Post Office and Civil Service and Armed Services committees.

As in the past, both Intelligence committees refused to make public any significant information about the budgets or operations of U.S. intelligence agencies. Nearly all budget details were included in a classified "annex" to the bill. *(Previous authorization, 1985 Almanac p. 96)*

According to published reports, Reagan requested about $24 billion for all intelligence programs in fiscal 1987. About half of that was broadly defined as the National Foreign Intelligence Program.

The other half was spent on military intelligence programs, technically called Tactical Intelligence and Related Activities. Those programs collected information of value primarily to the armed forces, such as the location of Soviet ships and ground forces.

Both committees noted that intelligence programs would face pressure for budget cuts because of the Gramm-Rudman deficit-control law (PL 99-177). But they came to the opposite conclusion about whether such cuts should be made.

The Senate committee said intelligence programs "must be protected from arbitrary limits" on spending. Because of overall cuts in defense spending — where the intelligence budget was hidden — those programs faced real, after-inflation reductions in fiscal 1986, the committee said.

While saying it supported improved programs, the House committee said intelligence agencies must share in the government's budget pain. The committee said it was recommending a "significant reduction" from Reagan's request. While refusing to provide any direct information on the size of the cut, the committee said the reduction was "commensurate" with that applied to overall defense spending. The cuts would be achieved by deferring some programs, deleting others and increasing some others, the committee said, producing "a reasonable balance between needed capabilities and prudent cost."

The bills gave budget information for only two items:

- The Intelligence Community staff, which served the director of central intelligence in his capacity as coordinator of all intelligence agencies. The House bill provided $21.7 million, for 235 full-time staff members, and the Senate bill $22.3 million, for 239 full-time staffers, in fiscal 1987. Reagan had requested $22.9 million for 246 employees. The 1986 authorized amount was $21 million.
- The CIA's retirement and disability fund, set at $125.8 million.

Major Differences

As part of its long crusade to curtail espionage by Soviet officials, especially those at the United Nations in New York, the Senate committee included provisions aimed at reducing the number of Soviet officials in the United States on diplomatic or trade business. The House bill had no comparable provisions.

The administration had long contended that Soviet officials, particularly those stationed at the U.N. in New York, were spies. The State Department Sept. 17 ordered 25 members of the Soviet mission to the United Nations to leave by Oct. 1 because of alleged espionage.

Other major differences between the two bills included the following:

- The House bill barred aid to the Angolan guerrillas unless it had been publicly debated and approved in advance by Congress. It also sharply restricted the types of aid the CIA could provide to the Nicaraguan contras. The Senate bill did not bar contra funding, but the committee report included a warning to the administration on the subject.
- While both bills expanded FBI access to confidential data, including secret examination of bank records, the Senate bill gave the FBI the authority to subpoena telephone company records of individuals or groups suspected of representing foreign agents, for the purposes of conducting counterintelligence. However, the House committee did not include this provision, which had been requested by FBI Director William H. Webster.
- The House bill exempted civilian intelligence employees of the military from many provisions of the civil service

laws, thus putting them under the same personnel management system as employees of other intelligence agencies. The committee said the main effect of this provision would be to allow the military services to promote civilian intelligence specialists without having to make them supervisors. The services were losing intelligence specialists to the CIA and other civilian services, which could pay more money because of their exemptions from civil service regulations. The provision also authorized the secretary of defense to fire civilian intelligence personnel, with his decision not subject to review or appeal. These provisions would apply to: 2,692 persons in the Army, 1,377 in the Navy and 1,671 in the Air Force, the panel said.

- The House bill allowed the CIA and the National Security Agency to pay for undergraduate college educations of employees in computer sciences, mathematics, engineering, foreign languages and other skills. The committee said the agencies had had difficulty competing with private companies for skilled technicians, especially minorities, and a scholarship program might improve their ability to attract employees.
- The House bill would put into permanent law a requirement enacted in 1985 that the congressional Intelligence committees must be notified of all "covert" or secret arms transfers valued at $1 million or more. Under the provision, those arms transfers — such as the CIA's provision of weapons to anti-communist guerrilla groups in Afghanistan, Angola and elsewhere — would be considered a "significant anticipated intelligence activity." That was the technical term for covert actions that must be reported to Congress, although the Intelligence committees had no automatic power to block them.

House Floor Action

The House Sept. 17 passed HR 4759 by voice vote after rejecting an effort to limit President Reagan's program of covert aid to Angolan guerrillas.

Voting 229-186, House members stripped from the bill a provision that would have barred assistance to the Angolan rebels unless it had been publicly debated and approved by Congress. *(Vote 356, p. 100-H; Angola aid, p. 387)*

Intelligence Committee Chairman Hamilton argued that the secret aid amounted to a major foreign policy shift that should be publicly discussed. Covert aid did not require formal approval by Congress, although the House and Senate Intelligence panels had to be notified in advance.

As reported, the bill prohibited U.S. aid for military or paramilitary operations in Angola unless the president publicly requested the assistance and Congress formally approved it by joint resolution.

But that section was knocked out of the bill by the amendment, offered by Bob Stump, R-Ariz., and Claude Pepper, D-Fla. A coalition of Republicans and mostly Southern Democrats provided the 229 votes to allow the covert aid to continue.

"It's a tough world, and some things must be done in secret to be successful," Stump said. "Congress should not destroy the covert action option for Angola."

Before adopting the Stump-Pepper amendment and passing the bill, the House adopted by voice vote an amendment by Louis Stokes, D-Ohio, to prohibit the sharing of most intelligence information with South Africa. *(South Africa sanctions, p. 359)*

Senate Floor Action

The Senate passed HR 4759 Sept. 24 by voice vote, after substituting the provisions of its version for those of the House-passed bill.

While acting on the intelligence bill, the Senate approved two amendments by Helms demanding reports from the CIA. Both were opposed by CIA Director William J. Casey, who "doesn't want to be told to do anything," said Intelligence Committee Chairman Durenberger.

The more controversial of Helms' amendments, adopted 53-46, would require the CIA to report to Congress by March, 1, 1987, on the extent to which the Panamanian armed forces "violated the human rights of the Panamanian people, are involved in international drug trafficking, arms trafficking or money laundering, or were involved in the death of Dr. Hugo Spadafora." Spadafora was an opposition political leader killed in 1985, allegedly by Panamanian military personnel. *(Vote 289, p. 48-S)*

Helms portrayed his amendment as a simple request "for the truth about Panama, whatever it is." Helms said the Senate needed access to information about government misdeeds in Panama — information he charged had been covered up by the CIA. "Are we going to be namby-pamby about drug trafficking when Panama is up to its armpits in it?" he asked.

Durenberger opposed the amendment on the grounds that it violated the Intelligence Committee's prerogative to order reports from the intelligence agencies. Passage of such an amendment could set a precedent for senators to demand reports on pet subjects, he said.

Helms' other amendment requested information from the CIA and other intelligence agencies on a wide variety of subjects, most of which had been of special concern to conservatives in recent years. Helms listed 32 issues on which he wanted secret information, ranging from CIA assessments of Soviet defense spending and capabilities to "possibilities" such as Soviet sabotage of the space shuttle *Challenger*, which exploded after takeoff in January, and penetration of the CIA and the State Department by the KGB, the Soviet secret police.

Conference

The conference report on the bill was filed Oct. 1 (H Rept 99-952). The House approved the report Oct. 2 and the Senate gave its approval Oct. 6, completing congressional action.

Contingency Funds for Contras

Aside from spending differences, the major conflict between the House and Senate bills concerned the CIA's right to dip into its secret contingency fund to aid the Nicaraguan contras.

Siding with the House, conferees agreed to bar the CIA from using the contingency fund for that purpose. The issue was important because a limitation on the contingency fund would be the only major congressional stricture on contra aid once Congress approved President Reagan's pending request for $100 million in military and non-military support for the Nicaraguan guerrillas. The money was included in an omnibus appropriations bill cleared Oct. 17. *(Story, p. 219)*

Under the intelligence bill's provision, Reagan could use CIA money to aid the contras only if Congress passed another bill allowing him to do so, or if he reprogrammed money to the contras from other programs.

Under normal circumstances, the contingency fund was used to begin "covert action" programs such as aiding anti-communist guerrillas and supporting pro-Western political movements abroad. Reagan used the fund in 1981 and 1982 to launch CIA backing of the contras and again early in 1986 to supply arms and equipment to anti-government guerrillas in Angola.

The amount of money in the fund was one of the government's best-kept secrets, but there had been reports that it was between $50 million and $500 million at any given time. Since 1983, the House Intelligence Committee had tried to bar use of the contingency fund for aid to the contras, and the annual intelligence bills had included such a provision since fiscal 1984.

South Africa

Conferees approved a provision, originated by the House, that barred cooperation by U.S. intelligence agencies with the South African government, except for activities "reasonably designed to facilitate the collection of necessary intelligence." The bill said U.S. agencies could not provide information to the South African government involving internal opposition groups.

Conferees said U.S. agencies could give South Africa intelligence information about the imminent likelihood of violent action threatening human life, if sharing that information could avert the violence.

The South Africa provision was a response to reports early in 1986 that U.S. agencies had shared information with South Africa on the African National Congress and other black opposition groups.

CIA Reports

Conferees deleted two Senate-passed provisions that were part of Helms' campaign of criticism of the CIA. Instead of putting Helms' reporting requirements in the bill, the conferees stated in the conference report that Casey was being asked to provide the information Helms had sought. House conferees refused to have anything to do with the amendment asking reports on the 32 subjects Helms wanted covered, so conferees said the request for that information was coming only from the Senate.

When the conference report reached the Senate floor on Oct. 6, Helms and Durenberger engaged in a prearranged "colloquy" designed to show that the CIA was obliged by law to respond to congressional requests for information. ▮

Angola Aid

Congress in 1986 cleared the way for President Reagan's policy of giving "covert" aid to anti-government guerrillas in Angola.

An effort to block the aid failed Sept. 17, when the House stripped from intelligence authorization legislation (HR 4759) a provision that would have barred assistance to the Angolan rebels unless it had been publicly debated and approved by Congress. The vote was 229-186. *(Vote 356, p. 100-H; intelligence bill action, p. 383)*

The provision was sponsored by Democratic leaders of the House Intelligence Committee, who were angered by Reagan's decision to aid the rebels over their objections.

Reagan in February ordered the CIA to provide up to $15 million worth of arms, ammunition and supplies to an anti-Soviet guerrilla faction known as UNITA, headed by Jonas Savimbi. Although the aid was supposed to be secret, administration officials, members of Congress and UNITA representatives in Washington discussed it publicly.

Background

Savimbi headed the National Union for Total Independence of Angola (UNITA, in the Portuguese acronym), one of three groups that fought for dominance in Angola after Portugal granted independence in 1975. UNITA lost that battle to the leftist Popular Movement for the Liberation of Angola (MPLA), but continued to use its base in southern Angola to fight the victorious Marxist faction.

UNITA for years had relied on arms and financing from South Africa — a fact that made many members of Congress reluctant to support it. The Ford administration aided Savimbi briefly in 1975, until Congress barred all U.S. involvement in the Angolan civil war.

Congress modified that prohibition in 1980 and repealed it in 1985. The landmark vote on the issue came in July 1985, when the House adopted an amendment to a foreign aid bill (PL 99-83) repealing the Angola restriction. The vote was 236-185. *(1985 Almanac p. 51)*

1986 Action

Savimbi appealed for U.S. assistance during a trip to Washington early in 1986. With the aid of a slick public relations campaign and the enthusiastic support of conservative groups, Savimbi carried his message to the White House, to executive agencies and to the halls of Congress for nearly two weeks. Reagan pledged his "moral support" Jan. 30.

Officially informed of the aid proposal in February, the House Intelligence Committee objected, saying the goals were unclear and that U.S. involvement would jeopardize prospects for a negotiated settlement of the war.

Committee Chairman Lee H. Hamilton, D-Ind., and his fellow Democrats then introduced legislation (HR 4276) barring aid to any Angolan military factions unless the president publicly requested the aid and Congress agreed.

The Intelligence panel approved Hamilton's bill in March and the Foreign Affairs Committee approved it in May (H Repts 99-508, Parts I and II). However, the bill never reached the floor, largely because of opposition from Foreign Affairs Chairman Dante B. Fascell, D-Fla., and Rules Committee Chairman Claude Pepper, D-Fla. The strongest supporters of aid to UNITA were Cuban-Americans in Florida who objected to the presence of some 30,000 Cuban troops in Angola. Both Fascell and Pepper represented districts with heavy concentrations of Cuban immigrants.

With action on HR 4276 stalled, Hamilton included that measure in the intelligence authorization bill approved by his committee on July 17.

As approved by the committee over Republican objections, HR 4759 prohibited U.S. aid for military or paramilitary operations in Angola unless the president publicly requested the assistance and Congress formally approved it by joint resolution.

Hamilton inserted language in the committee report (H Rept 99-690, Part I) saying that the president "cannot expect sustained support for foreign policy initiatives, including covert action operations, that are generally unpopular or where a covert action mechanism can be viewed as having been chosen to avoid public debate or a congressional vote on the matter."

Committee Republicans objected to the Hamilton provision, saying it reduced the president's flexibility. The provision, they said, "reflects a naive assumption that the United States can conduct all aspects of its foreign policy in public. . . ."

When the bill reached the House floor, the provision was knocked out on an amendment offered by Bob Stump, R-Ariz., and Pepper. A coalition of Republicans and mostly Southern Democrats provided the 229 votes to allow the covert aid to continue.

In other 1986 action, Congress went on record as opposing continued U.S. business dealings with the Angolan government. The Export-Import Bank reauthorization bill (HR 5548 — PL 99-472) included a provision deploring business support for the Angolan government and requesting the president to use his power under the Export Administration Act to restrict business dealings that were in conflict with U.S. security interests. *(Story, p. 348)* ▮

Helms vs. State on Chile

Sen. Jesse Helms, R-N.C., in 1986 engaged in a full-scale war with high-level State Department officials over department policy toward Chile. The confrontation was sparked by charges that a senior aide to the senator, Christopher Manion, leaked U.S. intelligence information to the government of Chile.

The incident stemmed from Helms' disagreement with the State Department's increased willingness to speak out forcefully against the dictatorial style of Chilean President Augusto Pinochet. The department and the U.S. ambassador to Chile, Harry G. Barnes Jr., in 1986 stepped up their calls for Pinochet to halt human rights abuses and to negotiate with government opponents as a first step toward democratic elections.

While insisting he was "neither pro-Pinochet nor anti-Pinochet," Helms complained bitterly about the department's new policy. During a trip to Chile in July, Helms called on Reagan to fire Barnes, and he later endorsed statements by U.S. citizens living in Chile that Barnes and the department were "cozying up to the communists."

On Aug. 3, *The New York Times* reported that the Senate Intelligence Committee had asked the FBI to investigate charges that Helms or an aide had leaked U.S. intelligence information to the government of Chile.

Government sources later said they were probing evidence that Manion told a Chilean official that the United States had obtained a copy of a secret Chilean report on the July 2 death in Santiago of Rodrigo Rojas, a 19-year-old Chilean exile who had lived in Washington. Rojas' mother and others charged that government security forces killed him, and the Chilean report allegedly confirmed those charges.

Manion, Helms' designated staff member on the Senate Foreign Relations Subcommittee on Western Hemisphere Affairs, chaired by Helms, allegedly gave the Chilean official information he had obtained in a confidential briefing by U.S. intelligence authorities. The Chilean government later identified the informant who passed the report on the Rojas death to U.S. intelligence agents, a congressional source said.

Elliott Abrams, the assistant secretary of state for inter-American affairs, told Senate Intelligence Committee Chairman Dave Durenberger, R-Minn., about the alleged leak. Durenberger and Vice Chairman Patrick J. Leahy, D-Vt., then wrote to the FBI asking for a probe of a "possible violation" of laws and Senate rules against the disclosure of secret information.

Helms heatedly denied as "false and outrageous" any charge that either he or his aides had leaked information. Manion, brother of controversial new federal Judge Daniel A. Manion, also denied the charges. *(Manion judgeship dispute, p. 72)*

During his trip to Chile, Helms criticized Barnes for attending Rojas' funeral. He had given support to a theory that Rojas might have been responsible for his own death, possibly by carrying an incendiary device.

Helms used the furor stemming from the leak charges to attack the State Department and others who had criticized his positions. Helms complained in particular about Abrams, a presidential appointee who had tirelessly advocated Reagan's controversial Central America policies. But he also criticized "a whole under-layer of people" at the State Department who "don't care who the president is."

Helms on Aug. 7 released a 20-page speech attacking State Department policies toward Chile, saying officials were aiding socialist and Marxist groups. "A coalition of the media, the Marxists, and the State Department is seeking to destabilize the transition to a full-fledged democracy in Chile," he said.

Helms accused the CIA of retaliating for his revealing in 1984 that it had financed the presidential campaign of José Napoleón Duarte in El Salvador. "I caught the CIA's hands in the cookie jar," Helms said.

Charges on Mexico

Helms was also at the center of another inter-American controversy, this one involving U.S. relations with Mexico.

In testimony that triggered anti-U.S. demonstrations in Mexico, U.S. Customs Commissioner William von Raab told Helms' subcommittee that Mexico was the largest single source of marijuana and heroin in the United States and charged that attempts to curb the drug trade were hindered by "massive" official corruption.

Helms fueled the controversy a month later, during a June 17 hearing, by accusing the Mexican government of election fraud. The Mexican government immediately denied Helms' charges of election fraud in 1982 and 1986. The State Department and the White House said U.S. officials had not seen any evidence to support the allegations and had no reason to believe them.

Mexican President Miguel de la Madrid attempted to ease tensions during a three-day visit to Washington in August. In bidding de la Madrid goodbye Aug. 13, President Reagan diplomatically referred to corruption on both sides of the border. Reagan said the two leaders had pledged to bolster drug eradication programs and "efforts to bring to justice vicious drug traffickers who have been such a corrupting influence in both our countries." ▮

U.S.-Iceland Treaty

Acting with unaccustomed speed, the Senate Oct. 8 approved a treaty (Treaty Doc 99-31) between the United States and Iceland. The Senate acted just eight days after getting the measure from the White House so that President Reagan could carry it with him to a "pre-summit" meeting in Iceland with Soviet leader Mikhail S. Gorbachev. *(Story, p. 459)*

Approved by voice vote with no debate, the treaty allowed both U.S. and Icelandic shipping firms to compete for the business of carrying huge quantities of U.S. military cargo to a major NATO air base at Keflavik.

Under U.S. cargo preference laws, an American company had gotten most of the shipping business since 1984, angering Iceland. In a Sept. 30 letter to the Senate, Reagan said the dispute "could impair the critical U.S.-Icelandic defense relationship." The treaty resolved the dispute, he said, by ensuring that shippers from both countries would get a share of the business.

Reagan sent the treaty to the Senate on the day of the public announcement of his meeting with Gorbachev. Acting on a White House request for fast action, the Senate Foreign Relations Committee approved the treaty on Oct. 8, and the full Senate acted less than two hours later. Committee aides said the action was the speediest in recent memory.

Nominations Logjam

As in previous years, ideological or partisan disputes delayed Senate action on a number of foreign affairs nominations in 1986. Most of the delays were caused by Jesse Helms, R-N.C., who had objected to some nominations and demanded that the administration give appointments to some of his allies instead. *(Background, 1985 Almanac p. 419)*

During the year, Helms also jousted with State Department officials over department policies toward Chile. *(Story, p. 388)*

The 1986 nominations struggle centered on James L. Malone, a Helms ally named by President Reagan to be ambassador to Belize, a tiny Central American country.

Malone had served as assistant secretary of state for oceans, international environmental and scientific affairs. In 1982, Reagan chose Malone to be chief U.S. negotiator at the Law of the Sea conference, but withdrew the nomination in the face of opposition in the Senate. Malone left his State Department post in July 1985 and sought a new one. To pressure the administration into giving Malone another appointment, Helms delayed Senate action on several other nominations.

Reagan nominated Malone to the Belize post in December 1985. On April 10, 1986, the Foreign Relations Committee rejected Malone — its first disapproval of an overseas ambassadorial nomination in this century. Republican Charles McC. Mathias Jr., Md., joined the committee's eight Democrats on the 9-7 vote against the nomination. Opponents said Malone had mismanaged his State Department bureau, had paid insufficient attention to ethics and had been "less than candid" in testimony before the committee. Malone and Helms rejected those charges.

In August, Mathias agreed to switch his vote if Helms would lift a "hold" he had put on the nomination of Morton I. Abramowitz, a career Foreign Service officer, to be assistant secretary of state for intelligence and research. Helms charged that Abramowitz in past writings had been hostile toward Taiwan and too friendly to the People's Republic of China.

Helms released his hold after Democrats threatened to block all other presidential nominations in retaliation. On Aug. 15, the Senate by voice vote approved Abramowitz; it also confirmed Frank Wisner, another Helms-opposed nominee, as ambassador to Egypt.

On Oct. 2, the Foreign Relations Committee reconsidered the Malone nomination and approved it 9-0, with Democrats boycotting the session and Mathias ensuring a majority.

Democrats then placed a hold on full Senate approval of Malone, prompting Helms to block action on nearly all other diplomatic nominations. After Senate leaders sought in vain to negotiate a deal, Majority Leader Robert Dole, R-Kan., on Oct. 14 broke with tradition and tried to force a floor vote by a motion for the Senate to go into executive session to consider Malone. The Senate agreed to Dole's motion by a party-line 47-42 vote. *(Vote 340, p. 56-S)*

Edward Zorinsky, D-Neb., Malone's sharpest critic, immediately mounted a filibuster against the nomination. Within hours, Malone sent Dole a letter asking for his nomination to be "temporarily laid aside." Dole agreed.

Helms then lifted his hold on 18 other nominations, and the Senate approved them on Oct. 15. The most prominent was that of Edward J. Perkins to be the first black U.S. ambassador to South Africa. Helms also allowed approval of a promotion to Senior Foreign Service status for Edwin G. Corr, the envoy to El Salvador. Helms had blocked the promotion since Oct. 28, 1985.

As part of the last-minute burst of activity, Democrats also allowed the Senate to bypass Foreign Relations and approve Helen Marie Taylor to be a representative to the United Nations General Assembly. Other committees had rejected Taylor for appointments to the National Endowment for the Humanities and the Corporation for Public Broadcasting. She was a prominent donor to conservative causes.

Clashes With Libya Renew War Powers Debate

Frustrated by his inability to punish terrorists who had stalked the Middle East and Europe, President Reagan in 1986 lashed out at Libya, the country he charged with giving the greatest aid and support to terrorists.

The president's military actions against Libya renewed debate about the role of Congress in initiating armed conflict. However, lawmakers took no action on legislation to alter existing war powers restrictions.

Reagan began the year by tightening economic sanctions against Libya in retaliation for terrorist attacks at the Rome and Vienna airports. Making good on his threat to back up the economic sanctions with further action, the president subsequently employed military force against Libya twice in less than a month.

In late March, the president sent massive air and naval forces to challenge Libya's claim to sovereignty over the Gulf of Sidra, provoking a shooting match during which U.S. planes destroyed several Libyan missile sites and ships.

And on April 14, Reagan launched a bombardment of

Libyan military targets in retaliation for that country's alleged backing of terrorism. Announcing the April 14 raid, Reagan said he would "do it again" if necessary.

Later in the year, it was reported that the administration had conducted a "disinformation" campaign aimed at destabilizing the Qaddafi regime by feeding false information to the press.

Economic Sanctions

The president Jan. 7 ordered a total ban on U.S. trade with Libya and directed all Americans there to leave — tightening several sanctions that he and President Carter had imposed since 1978.

The following day, in an effort to protect U.S. corporations in Libya against retaliation, Reagan ordered a freeze on all Libyan government assets located in the United States or held by U.S. banks. Officials said that the freeze affected several hundred million dollars, primarily in cash and other "liquid" assets; it did not affect Libyan assets held by foreign subsidiaries of U.S. banks or other companies. *(Texts of Reagan executive orders, p. 12-D)*

The president said he was holding Libya, especially its leader Muammar el-Qaddafi, responsible for simultaneous attacks Dec. 27 at check-in counters of the El Al Israeli airline at the Rome and Vienna airports. Nineteen persons, including five Americans, were killed and more than 100 persons were wounded in those incidents. Italian and Austrian officials traced the attacks to a renegade Palestinian faction headed by Abu Nidal, and U.S. officials charged that Nidal operated out of Libya with Qaddafi's backing and encouragement.

"Qaddafi deserves to be treated as a pariah in the world community," Reagan said at a Jan. 7 news conference, during which he announced the new sanctions. The president called Qaddafi a "barbarian" and "flaky."

To bolster the U.S. case against Qaddafi, the State Department on Jan. 8 released a "white paper" that traced the history of his alleged involvement with terrorism throughout the world, especially in the Middle East and Western Europe.

"Qaddafi has used terrorism as one of the primary instruments of his foreign policy and supports radical groups which use terrorist tactics," the report said. The primary targets of Libyan attacks, it added, had been Libyan dissidents and officials of moderate Arab and African countries.

Qaddafi at first praised those responsible for the attacks but later said Libya did not harbor Nidal's training camps and had nothing to do with the airport attacks.

Congress had signaled in July 1985 that it was ready for full-scale sanctions against Libya. In the fiscal 1986-87 foreign aid authorizations bill (PL 99-83), Congress authorized the president to ban all trade with Libya or any other country that supported terrorism. Reagan cited that provision as one legal justification for his action. *(1985 Almanac p. 41)*

Reagan also acted under a 1977 law (PL 95-223) allowing him to bar economic activity with other countries by declaring a national emergency. President Carter had used the 1977 law to impose sanctions on Iran, and Reagan had used it previously against Libya, Nicaragua and South Africa. In declaring an emergency Jan. 7, Reagan said Libya's actions "constitute an unusual and extraordinary threat to the national security and foreign policy of the United States." *(1977 Almanac p. 412)*

Reagan's sanctions were the latest in a long series of actions the United States had taken against Qaddafi. Previous major steps included:

- In May 1978, Carter banned exports to Libya of military aircraft and tractors capable of hauling tanks.
- In September 1979, Carter designated Libya as a country that repeatedly supported terrorist acts. That action had the effect of banning exports of equipment with military uses.
- In October 1981, Reagan barred exports of aviation parts and equipment to Libya.
- In December 1981, during a scare about potential attacks on U.S. officials by Libyan "hit squads," Reagan invalidated the use of U.S. passports for travel to, in or through Libya, except for journalistic purposes. As a result, most of the several thousand Americans then in Libya left. By early 1985, some 1,000 to 1,500 Americans remained, most working for foreign firms, the Libyan national oil company or the Libyan government.
- In March 1982, Reagan barred imports of crude oil from Libya and restricted exports of oil and gas technology to that country. Importation of refined petroleum products from Libya was banned in November 1985.

In addition to those public sanctions, Reagan in 1985 reportedly signed an authorization for the CIA to conduct a covert operation to undermine the Qaddafi regime.

Gulf of Sidra Clash

Libyan attacks on U.S. naval forces in the Gulf of Sidra prompted U.S. military actions against that nation on March 24-25. The military clashes were triggered by U.S. naval exercises in the area, which Libya claimed as its own but nearly all other nations regarded as international waters.

After several anti-aircraft missiles were fired from near the Libyan town of Sirte, U.S. ships and planes in the Gulf of Sidra attacked the missile battery and several missile-armed Libyan patrol boats. U.S. officials reported no American casualties.

According to the Defense Department, the 6th Fleet task force participating in the March exercise numbered 30 ships carrying nearly 26,000 men.

Despite administration insistence to the contrary, observers widely speculated — and critics heatedly charged — that the naval maneuvers were intended to provoke Libyan attacks and thus justify U.S. counterstrikes.

'Line of Death'

In 1973, Libya claimed as territorial waters the 150,000 square miles of the Gulf of Sidra south of 32 degrees 30 minutes north latitude. Measured across that line, the gulf was about 275 miles wide. The declared boundary was roughly 90-150 miles north of the Libyan coast.

The United States and most other Western countries generally did not recognize claims of territorial waters running more than 12 miles from land.

In 1981, while a U.S. fleet was exercising north of Libya, two Libyan fighter planes fired missiles at two U.S. F-14s about 60 miles north of the Libyan coast — well inside the boundary claimed by Qaddafi. The U.S. fighters shot down the two Libyan SU-22s.

All told, from 1981 through January 1986, U.S. naval forces conducted exercises near Libya on 18 occasions, seven of which included operations inside what Qaddafi called the "line of death."

Major U.S. Military Interventions, 1946-86

Following are major instances of U.S. military intervention between the end of World War II and the April 14, 1986, bombardment of Libya, not including most involvement in multinational peacekeeping forces:

JULY - AUGUST 1946. President Truman sends U.S. naval units to Trieste, Italy, anticipating a Yugoslav-Soviet attack. After U.S. Army transport planes are shot down, reinforcements arrive in Italy.

AUGUST 1946. To counter Soviet threat to Turkish control of Bosporus Straits, Truman dispatches powerful carrier force as display of resolve.

SEPTEMBER 1946. One U.S. carrier is stationed off Greece during attempted communist takeover.

JANUARY 1948. Marine reinforcements sent to the Mediterranean are seen as a warning to Yugoslavia to stay away from 5,000 U.S. Army troops in Trieste.

JULY 1948. During the Arab-Israeli War, a consular guard is detached from the USS *Kearsarge* and sent to Jerusalem to protect the U.S. consular general. Two Marines are later wounded.

APRIL 1948 - NOVEMBER 1949. U.S. Marines are sent to Nanking and Shanghai to protect the U.S. Embassy and to aid evacuation of American nationals in wake of communist takeover of China.

JUNE 1950 - JULY 1953. Korean War.

JULY 1954 - FEBRUARY 1955. Five U.S. carriers arrive at the Tachen Islands to evacuate Americans and Taiwanese threatened by communist Chinese bombing.

NOVEMBER 1956. During the Suez crisis, one Marine battalion evacuates 1,500 persons, most of them Americans, from Alexandria, Egypt.

FEBRUARY 1957. Marines stationed 550 miles northeast of Sumatra are poised to intervene for protection of Americans during revolt in Indonesia.

JULY 1957. Four U.S. carriers are sent to defend Taiwan during Chinese communist shelling of Quemoy.

JANUARY 1958. When mob violence breaks out in Caracas, Venezuela, the USS *Des Moines*, with one company of U.S. Marines on board, is stationed nearby.

MARCH 1958. A Marine company, attack squadron and helicopter squadron are deployed with the 7th Fleet off Indonesia to protect U.S. citizens.

JULY - OCTOBER 1958. Following civil unrest, President Eisenhower sends 5,000 Marines to Lebanon to "protect American lives" and to "assist Lebanon in preserving its political independence." Eventually 14,000 U.S. soldiers and Marines occupy areas in Lebanon.

JULY 1959 - MAY 1975. Vietnam era. Sent as troop trainers, the first U.S. military are killed in South Vietnam in July 1959. In October 1961, President Kennedy decides to send Green Beret "military advisers." In August 1964, Congress passes Gulf of Tonkin Resolution. In March 1973, last U.S. troops withdraw. At the end of April 1975, last Americans are evacuated.

NOVEMBER 1959 - FEBRUARY 1960. A Marine Ground Task Force is deployed to protect U.S. nationals in Cuba during the revolution.

NOVEMBER 1961. U.S. Navy planes and ships arrive off the Dominican Republic as a show of force to discourage members of Trujillo family from attempting to retake the government they lost when dictator Rafael Trujillo was assassinated the previous May.

MAY - JULY 1962. 5,000 Marines land in Thailand to support the government against communist threat; Marines leave nine weeks later.

OCTOBER - DECEMBER 1962. Challenging a Soviet introduction of missiles into Cuba, Kennedy orders 180 U.S. Navy ships and a B-52 bomber force carrying A-bombs into the Caribbean to effect a quarantine. Troop carrier squadrons of the U.S. Air Force Reserve are being recalled to active duty when Soviet Premier Khrushchev agrees to withdraw the missiles.

MAY 1963. U.S. Marines positioned off Haiti in the wake of domestic protest against the Duvalier regime and a threat of Dominican Republic intervention.

NOVEMBER 1964. U.S. transport aircraft in the Congo carry Belgian paratroopers to rescue Americans and other civilians held hostage by rebels near Stanleyville.

MAY 1964 - JANUARY 1973. Retaliating for the downing of U.S. reconnaissance planes over Laos, U.S. Navy jets attack Pathet Lao communist strongholds.

APRIL 1965. After communist-leaning revolt in the Dominican Republic, President Johnson sends 21,500 U.S. troops to protect Americans and offers military aid to locals. By fall, constitutional government is restored.

JUNE 1967. During the Arab-Israeli War, Johnson sends the U.S. 6th Fleet within 50 miles of Syria as a warning to the Soviets against entering the conflict.

JULY - DECEMBER 1967. Johnson sends C-130 transport planes with crews to help Congolese President Mobutu fight mercenaries and Katangese rebels.

APRIL - JUNE 1970. U.S. ground troops attack communist sanctuaries in Cambodia.

MAY 1975. President Ford sends combined force of Navy, Marine and Air Force to rescue crew of 39 from U.S. merchant ship *Mayaguez*, which had been captured by Cambodian communists.

APRIL 1980. U.S. commando team in Iran aborts effort to rescue American hostages from U.S. Embassy in Tehran. Eight die in plane-helicopter collision.

AUGUST 19, 1981. Navy F-14 fighters shoot down two Libyan SU-22 jets over the Gulf of Sidra, 60 miles off Libya. U.S. officials claim that U.S. jets were practicing military maneuvers in international waters and responded only after the Libyan jets fired.

OCTOBER 1983. U.S. Marines and troops from eastern Caribbean nations invade island of Grenada.

DECEMBER 1983. U.S. planes attack Syrian positions in Lebanon. Two of 28 planes are shot down; one pilot is dead, the other captured. The Rev. Jesse Jackson wins release of captured U.S. Navy Lt. Robert Goodman Jr., Jan. 3, 1984.

MARCH 24, 1986. The U.S. 6th Fleet ventures across the "line of death" over the Gulf of Sidra. Libyans fire SA-5 missiles at U.S. planes. The USS *America* fires A-6 harpoon missiles and sinks Libyan patrol boat. U.S. military operations lead to a temporary shutdown of the Sirte radar station, the sinking of two Libyan patrol boats and the disabling of three others.

April Air Strikes

The United States launched massive air strikes against Libya on April 14.

The U.S. attack, in which two American fliers were lost, was in response to the April 5 bombing of a discothèque in West Berlin frequented by U.S. military personnel. One U.S. soldier and a Turkish woman were killed and more than 200 persons, including some 60 Americans, were injured.

President Reagan later claimed that unequivocal evidence demonstrated that Qaddafi had sponsored the bombing, evidently in retaliation for the U.S. Navy attacks on Libyan forces March 24-25.

The attack was set in motion the evening of April 14 when F-111 bombers, radar-jamming planes and refueling tankers took off from four bases in Great Britain. The planes detoured around Spain, adding 2,400 miles to the round trip. France refused to allow the U.S. planes to fly over its territory.

In the Mediterranean north of Libya, A-6E Navy bombers left the carriers *America* and *Coral Sea* at around 1 a.m., Libyan time, April 15.

The main attacks began about an hour later, with 13 F-111s striking three targets in and around Tripoli:

- Aziziyah barracks, which the administration described as the command and control headquarters for Libyan terrorism. It also was one of several sites used as a residence by Qaddafi. *The Washington Post* quoted unnamed administration officials on April 18 as saying this part of the attack was intended to kill Qaddafi. However, Reagan and other officials denied this was a goal.
- Military facilities at Tripoli's main airport, where three to five Soviet-built Ilyushin-76 jet transport planes were destroyed.
- The Sidi Bilal base, which the administration said was used to train terrorists in underwater sabotage.

A dozen A-6Es attacked two sites in the northeastern part of Libya:

- Jamahiriyah military barracks in Benghazi, described by the administration as another terrorist command post.
- Benina air base, southeast of Benghazi, where "at least" four Soviet-built MiG-23 fighter planes and some helicopters were destroyed, according to the Pentagon.

The French Embassy in Tripoli and several neighboring residential buildings also were hit. U.S. officials acknowledged that the damage might have been caused by bombs that went astray or, perhaps, by the bomb-load of one F-111 that did not return from the attack. Officials speculated that the plane had been shot down by antiaircraft guns.

War Powers Debate

Both military actions against Libya generated strong support in Congress. But some members, especially Democrats, said Reagan failed to meet War Powers act requirements for consulting with Congress in advance.

By declaring that he had the exclusive power to act in "self-defense" against terrorism, Reagan prompted two contradictory responses in Congress: Some members wanted him to consult more extensively with them before sending U.S. troops into combat, while others wanted to give him even more flexibility to act against terrorism without interference from Capitol Hill.

The Reagan administration had fueled questions about its actions by telling Congress that some forms of military response to terrorism were exempt from the consultations requirements of the War Powers Resolution (PL 93-148).

The law required the president to "consult" with Congress before sending troops into hostilities and to report to Congress immediately after military engagements. Enacted in the aftermath of the Vietnam War, the law also required the withdrawal of troops from hostile action after 60 days unless Congress authorized their presence. *(1973 Almanac p. 95)*

By saying he was acting in self-defense against terrorism, Reagan was developing "a new way of going to war which totally bypasses the Constitution" and its requirement that only Congress could declare war, said Dante B. Fascell, D-Fla., chairman of the House Foreign Affairs Committee.

Although Reagan sent reports to Congress after both incidents, in neither report did he say he was acting in accordance with the War Powers Resolution.

The president did not consult with Congress before the Gulf of Sidra operation, and he called in top congressional leaders only three hours before the April 14 bombing got under way.

The Libyan incidents gave "new impetus" to the War Powers debate, Fascell said, with most of the discussion centering on how to improve the consultation process.

Congressional leaders and administration officials approached the matter with some hesitation, apparently fearing the consequences of reopening sensitive political and legal issues that Congress carefully skirted when it wrote the law in 1973 and enacted it over President Ford's veto.

Some congressional leaders long had considered amending the law to toughen it — for example by eliminating loopholes in the consultation requirement.

The Reagan administration had called portions of the act unconstitutional and had avoided taking actions that could be seen as accepting the validity of its provisions.

Nevertheless, the administration insisted it had complied with the law, and Reagan was the first president to invoke officially the law's key section requiring congressional approval for a long-term military action; in 1983 he signed into law a resolution (PL 98-119) authorizing the presence of Marines in a Beirut "peacekeeping" force. *(1983 Almanac p. 113)*

Justifying Reagan's use of force against Libya, the administration contended that the War Powers act did not apply to some military steps directed against terrorists. Under that view, the president also was not required to keep Congress informed about military exercises. ∎

Philippine Aid

Members of Congress applauded the February ouster of Philippine President Ferdinand E. Marcos and gave vigorous support to the government of his successor, Corazon Aquino.

For two decades Washington had overlooked Marcos' many failings because he was a friendly and strategically placed ally. But U.S. officials had been increasingly troubled by a growing communist insurgency in the islands and feared the potential loss of two crucial military bases located in the Philippines. To encourage the new government and to bolster an economy that had suffered under years of

Marcos-inspired "crony capitalism," Congress twice during 1986 voted aid increases for the Philippines.

Acceding to a request by President Reagan, lawmakers voted a $150 million aid package in June. The second increase, totaling $200 million, was approved after Aquino visited Washington Sept. 15-19 to press for help in easing her country's financial problems.

Marcos Ouster

Marcos fled the Philippines Feb. 25, ending a desperate effort to seize victory in elections held two weeks earlier. Aquino, widow of assassinated Marcos foe Benigno S. Aquino Jr., immediately proclaimed herself the winner of the disputed Feb. 7 elections. *(Background, 1985 Almanac p. 113)*

The Reagan administration moved quickly to establish friendly relations with the new government. Secretary of State George P. Shultz announced U.S. recognition of the Aquino government less than an hour after Marcos boarded an American helicopter at the presidential palace. After spending a night at Clark Air Base north of Manila, Marcos flew to Hawaii, where he remained at year's end.

President Reagan, who had been reluctant until the last minute to nudge Marcos to resign, sent Aquino a congratulatory message on Feb. 26 and praised her coming to power as a "triumph of democracy." Reagan had avoided playing a personal role in the Marcos ouster; instead, he sent a series of messages through intermediaries, including Sen. Paul Laxalt, R-Nev., who told the Philippine dictator to "cut and cut cleanly."

In the weeks before and after the election, members of Congress had watched with growing anger as Marcos rigged the voting, the counting of the ballots and then the proclamation of his victory by the National Assembly. Congress had been moving to suspend aid to the Marcos government — an action made unnecessary by events in the Philippines.

Reagan in January had offered a substantial aid increase for the Philippines if the election was fair and if the government carried out necessary economic and military reforms. That offer was shelved immediately after the election but was renewed once Marcos fled.

In October 1985, responding in part to congressional pressures, Reagan had sent Laxalt to Manila with warnings to Marcos that the United States was serious about the need for reform. Laxalt's warnings apparently helped convince Marcos to call the "snap" elections.

At Marcos' request, Reagan sent a delegation of official U.S. observers to the elections, headed by Sen. Richard G. Lugar, R-Ind., and Rep. John P. Murtha, D-Pa. In addition to revealing the electoral fraud to the American public, the Lugar-Murtha observer group apparently helped convince top Reagan administration officials that Aquino had really won the election and that Marcos had stolen it.

Aid Increase Request

President Reagan on April 23 proposed a new $150 million aid program to help the Philippines respond to "new opportunities. It was to be combined with a speeding up of $405 million in previously approved aid. Officials said the aid was part of a plan to provide about $1 billion to the Philippines in the next 18 months; the rest was to come from other nations and international development banks.

Two-thirds of the new aid — $100 million — would go directly to support the Philippine economy. The remaining $50 million would buy equipment, training and services for the armed forces. As part of its speeding up of already-approved aid, the United States would convert $100 million worth of economic aid loans into grants.

The aid was in addition to $236 million Congress had already approved for fiscal 1986. Reagan previously had requested $228 million in aid to the Philippines for fiscal 1987.

Congressional Action

Congress readily approved the $150 million aid package sought by Reagan. The money was provided in a fiscal 1986 supplemental appropriations bill (HR 4515 — PL 99-349) cleared June 26. *(Supplemental, p. 153)*

The second aid increase came harder.

On June 26, the Senate Foreign Relations Committee by a 14-3 vote approved a bill (S 2610 — S Rept 99-330) authorizing an additional $100 million in economic aid advocated by Lugar as a demonstration of "political support" for Aquino.

The full Senate never acted on the bill, which bogged down because of efforts by Sen. John Melcher, D-Mont., to attach farm provisions.

On July 23, the House Foreign Affairs Committee approved, by a 26-2 vote, legislation authorizing $400 million (HR 5081 — H Rept 99-722).

Rep. Stephen J. Solarz, D-N.Y., said the extra money approved by the House panel was needed to ease financial problems facing the Aquino government. Some committee members said the United States was in no fiscal position to afford the aid money. But an amendment by Jim Leach, R-Iowa, to reduce the additional aid to $200 million was defeated on a 7-13 vote.

The House passed HR 5081 Aug. 7, 219-178. *(Vote 281, p. 80-H)*

Debate on the bill reflected the concern over spending limits. An amendment by Gerald B. H. Solomon, R-N.Y., to eliminate the entire authorization, was rejected by a slim 195-203 margin. By a lopsided margin of 320-76, the chamber then approved an amendment by Leach to cut the authorization level to $200 million. *(Votes 279, 280, p. 80-H)*

The Senate did not act on the bill, which also included money for Haiti, international narcotics control and other programs.

The House tried again Sept. 18. Hours after Aquino addressed a joint session of Congress, the House passed a joint resolution (H J Res 732) to appropriate an additional $200 million in fiscal 1986.

House passage of H J Res 732 came on a 203-197 vote. The slim, six-vote margin on the measure demonstrated members' unease over appropriating more for foreign aid at a time of budget austerity.

"President Aquino gave a good speech today, but is that worth a $200 million honorarium?" wondered Toby Roth, R-Wis. *(Vote 360, p. 102-H)*

Again the Senate did not act on the House measure.

Finally, both chambers agreed to include $200 million in additional economic aid for the Philippines in the omnibus appropriations bill for fiscal 1987 (H J Res 738 — PL 99-591), cleared Oct. 17.

Because of overall foreign aid cutbacks, it was uncertain what the final fiscal 1987 amount actually would be. *(Foreign aid funding, p. 162)*

H J Res 738 also repealed an existing $50 million annual limitation on military aid to the Philippines. ∎

Congress Agrees to Renew Contra Arms Aid

After a battle of more than two years, President Reagan in 1986 persuaded Congress to renew military aid to the "contra" guerrillas who were seeking to overthrow the leftist government of Nicaragua.

The fiscal 1987 appropriation marked the first time since mid-1984 that the United States would be legally allowed to give weapons, ammunition and other military supplies to the 10,000-15,000 contras, who were in camps along the Nicaraguan-Honduran border. *(Background, 1985 Almanac pp. 61, 70, 76)*

However, the future of the program was put in doubt late in 1986 by the administration's disclosure that weapons had been sold secretly to Iran, with part of the profits from those sales skimmed for the purpose of arming the contras. *(Iran scandal, p. 415)*

The fiscal 1987 omnibus spending bill (H J Res 738 — PL 99-591) included $70 million in military aid and $30 million in non-military aid for the rebels. It also included $300 million in economic aid for Central American nations other than Nicaragua. Of the $100 million in contra aid, $60 million could be spent at any time in fiscal 1987 and the remaining $40 million was to be spent only after Feb. 15, 1987.

The money resumed the flow of U.S. assistance to the contras. The previous dose, $27 million in non-military aid voted by Congress after a bruising battle in 1985, ran out March 31, 1986.

The deadlock over contra aid was broken June 25, when the House voted for the $100 million by 221-209.

Perhaps more important than providing the money, Congress agreed to lift most of the restrictions that it had imposed in 1984-85 on direct U.S. involvement with the contras. Among other things, the bill allowed the CIA to resume management of the contra aid program. However, the separate fiscal 1987 intelligence authorization bill (HR 4759 — PL 99-569) barred the CIA from tapping into its multimillion-dollar contingency fund to give aid to the contras above $100 million. *(Continuing resolution, p. 219; intelligence bill, p. 383)*

Fallout From Iran Arms Dealings

In the wake of the Nov. 25 announcement of the Iran arms-contra connection, congressional opponents of the Nicaraguan rebels geared up to rein in the aid program.

In the first week of the 100th Congress, opponents introduced legislation to block the final $40 million in 1987 aid. They said they wanted to focus new attention on Reagan's Central America policies before Congress agreed to give even more aid to the contras.

Chief sponsors of these bills (S 184, HR 360, HR 574) were Sens. Christopher J. Dodd, D-Conn., and Lowell P. Weicker Jr., R-Conn.; and Reps. Joe Kolter, D-Pa.; Mel Levine, D-Calif.; and Jim Leach, R-Iowa.

The House bills would withhold the $40 million until after Congress had completed its investigation into the Iran arms sales and the alleged diversion of money from those sales to the contras.

The Senate bill would go further, barring all future aid to the contras. It would reauthorize $300 million in economic aid to Central American countries that Congress intended to approve in 1986. Although the $300 million was included in the omnibus appropriations bill, little of the money was expected to reach Central America because of overall cutbacks in foreign aid.

Apparently conceding to political realities, Reagan scaled back his request for contra assistance for the following fiscal year, 1988. He asked for $105 million, far less than the $300 million to $400 million that contra leaders and some administration officials had wanted.

Reopening the Pipeline

Reagan on Oct. 24 signed legal papers to resume the flow of military aid. In addition to military hardware such as rifles and anti-aircraft and anti-tank weapons, the United States would give the contras military training and guidance. The administration originally planned to have 40 to 50 U.S. Army "Green Beret" trainers work with the contras at camps in Central America. When those countries objected, the Pentagon began drafting new plans to train top contra leaders in the United States.

Administration officials reportedly differed over key elements of the contra program, particularly the strategy for ousting the Sandinista regime in Managua without involving U.S. troops. Some officials advocated high-visibility tactics by the contras such as capturing selected towns; others promoted highly mobile guerrilla operations modeled after the successful Sandinista-led revolution of 1979.

In an Oct. 3 letter to Rep. Lee H. Hamilton, D-Ind., the State Department said it could make no predictions or promises for the aid program, aside from overall improvements in the contras' military and political operations.

Reporting to Congress on Oct. 24, Reagan said the contras had taken several reform steps required by the $100 million aid legislation. Without giving specifics, Reagan said the contras "have agreed to and are beginning to implement" such steps as: broadening their leadership base, coordinating their efforts, eliminating human rights abuses, pursuing a coordinated program for achieving democracy in Nicaragua, subordinating military forces to civilian leadership, and applying rigorous accounting standards to their use of the aid.

Also on Oct. 24, Reagan signed an executive order putting Secretary of State George P. Shultz in overall charge of the contra aid. Most day-to-day details of military operations, however, were to be handled by the CIA and the Pentagon. To get the CIA involved, Reagan also sent Congress a required secret report called a "finding."

Restrictions, 'Contingency Fund' Ban

Of the $100 million in aid, $60 million could be spent at any time and the remaining $40 million could be spent only after Feb. 15, 1987. Until Feb. 15, military aid was restricted to small arms, such as rifles, and "air-defense" equipment, presumably anti-aircraft missiles. After Feb. 15, the United States could provide the contras artillery and other "heavy" weapons.

Of the $30 million in non-military aid, $27 million was for "humanitarian" supplies such as food and clothing; the remaining $3 million would have to be used to monitor the contras' observance of human rights standards.

Other major restrictions were that U.S. government personnel could not help the contras within 20 miles of the Nicaraguan border, and the CIA could not use its "contingency fund" to provide more aid than the $100 million.

The prohibition on using the contingency fund to aid the contras was contained in the fiscal 1987 authorization bill (HR 4759 — PL 99-569) for the CIA and other intelligence agencies.

The Reagan administration denied any intentions of using the multimillion-dollar CIA contingency fund to help the contras. Under normal circumstances, the contingency fund was used to begin "covert action" programs such as aiding anti-communist guerrillas and supporting pro-Western political movements abroad. Reagan used the fund in 1981 and 1982 to launch CIA backing of the contras and again early in 1986 to supply arms and equipment to anti-government guerrillas in Angola. The amount of money in the fund was secret, but there were reports that it was between $50 million and $500 million at any given time.

Under PL 99-569, Reagan could use CIA money to aid the contras only if Congress passed another bill allowing him to do so, or if he "reprogrammed" or diverted money to the contras from other ongoing CIA programs.

To reprogram money, the president first would have to notify the House and Senate Intelligence and Appropriations committees. Technically, the committees could not block reprogrammings, but in reality the administration would have to defer to a "no" from any of the four panels.

Special Congressional Commission

A special congressional commission was to monitor the aid program during the first four months. As mandated by the continuing resolution, the commission was to issue its report in connection with a presidential certification due Feb. 15. After then, Reagan would be able to continue aiding the contras only if he certified to Congress that no Central American peace agreement had been reached and that the Nicaraguan government had not begun "serious dialogue" with its opposition.

Congress could block expenditure of the final $40 million in fiscal 1987 money by passing a joint resolution of disapproval. Such a resolution would be vetoed. A two-thirds vote in both chambers would be needed to override the veto and thus block the aid.

Four of the members of the commission were to be appointed by congressional leaders; they would then select a fifth member as chairman. Under the law, the commission would expire 90 days after issuing its February report.

Three commission members were chosen by the end of October 1986: Edward J. King, a former Army colonel and specialist in guerrilla warfare, named by Senate Minority Leader Robert C. Byrd, D-W.Va.; Kirk O'Donnell, former general counsel to House Speaker Thomas P. O'Neill Jr., D-Mass., named by O'Neill; and the Rev. Ira Gallaway, directing minister of the First United Methodist Church in Peoria, Ill., named by House Minority Leader Robert H. Michel, R-Ill. Gallaway was a founder of the Institute on Religion and Democracy, which promotes democratic reforms overseas.

In December, Senate Majority Leader Robert Dole, R-Kan., appointed Jeane J. Kirkpatrick, former U.S. representative to the United Nations, to the special commission. As of early March 1987, commission members had not selected a chairman.

Legislative History

Contra aid took a tortuous path through Congress in 1986. Reagan unveiled his $100 million aid plan in February, and Congress took it up as a pair of resolutions (H J Res 540, S J Res 283). The House voted the bill down on March 20. The Senate passed its resolution March 27.

The next legislative vehicle in the House was a supplemental appropriations measure for fiscal 1986 (HR 4515). In a complicated legislative ploy, Republicans on April 16 scuttled the contra program rather than see it married to the omnibus spending measure.

House members then tried to get enough signatures — 218 — on a discharge petition to bring up S J Res 283. But by the April 30 deadline, they had garnered only 159 signatures. A factor was the House leadership's agreement to allow a vote on contra aid on a new bill, one appropriating funds for military construction in fiscal 1987 (HR 5052).

The military construction bill was reported by the House Appropriations panel on June 19 (H Rept 99-648); it was passed, along with the contra aid, on June 25.

In the Senate, HR 5052 was reported from Appropriations on July 14 (S Rept 99-368), and passed in floor action on Aug. 13. Although both houses had agreed on the same contra provisions, the underlying bill was one of many to be folded into the continuing appropriations resolution (H J Res 738). That measure was passed by the House on Sept. 25 and the Senate on Oct. 3. Conference on the catchall legislation was concluded and both houses approved the report Oct. 17 (PL 99-591).

Reagan's Request

Reagan submitted his request on Feb. 25 under the provisions of two 1985 laws (PL 99-83 and PL 99-88) that contained the $27 million in non-military aid for the contras. The laws authorized him to make a follow-up request for more aid and established procedures for Congress to consider it. The request was the most far-reaching Reagan had made in public support for the Nicaraguan rebels. He asked Congress to approve:

$100 Million in Aid. The money would be transferred from fiscal 1986 Pentagon funds and would be available for expenditure through fiscal 1987, ending Sept. 30, 1987. Of that amount, $30 million would be used for non-military aid, administered by the State Department's Nicaraguan Humanitarian Assistance Office. Responding to congressional concerns about reported human rights violations by the contras, Reagan proposed setting aside $3 million of the $30 million for training and other efforts to curtail those violations. Reagan would be free to use the remaining $70 million as he saw fit; officials said that money would be used to give the contras ammunition, weapons, helicopters, trucks and other supplies to fight the Nicaraguan government.

One-fourth of the total aid would be available immediately upon congressional approval; additional chunks of 15 percent would be available at 90-day intervals as Reagan sent reports to Congress on developments in Central America.

A major purpose of the fund transfer was to avoid the charge that aiding the contras would add to the federal budget deficit. Reagan acknowledged that a request for an outright supplemental "would have diverted attention" from the issues he wanted discussed. However, Reagan said that he would ask Congress in the future to reimburse the Pentagon for the $100 million, because diverting that money would "inevitably impair ongoing efforts to restore and maintain the readiness of the armed forces."

Lifting Controls. Restrictions previously imposed by Congress on contra aid — primarily on direct involvement by the Pentagon, the CIA and other intelligence

Handling of Non-Military Contra Aid . . .

While Congress debated whether to continue aiding the Nicaraguan contras, investigations were conducted into charges of wrongdoing by some of the rebels and their American supporters.

At issue was the $27 million in "humanitarian" aid that Congress had approved for the rebels in fiscal 1986 (PL 99-83). The House Foreign Affairs Committee on May 8 subpoenaed bank records to determine what happened to $13 million-$15 million of the aid. That panel's Subcommittee on Western Hemisphere Affairs held hearings in June on allegations of corruption, drug-smuggling, gun-running, assassination plots and other misdeeds. And on Dec. 5, the General Accounting Office (GAO) issued a final report on its probe into how the money was spent; it found that some funds were diverted to buy military items and noted discrepancies in record-keeping.

The United States had backed the contras since late 1981, and throughout that period there had been charges that individuals or groups of the rebels had engaged in questionable practices. Most allegations had involved human rights abuses, such as attacks on innocent civilians.

But in late 1985, a handful of former contras and Americans who once worked with them began airing charges involving corruption, drug-smuggling and other activities. Sen. John Kerry, D-Mass., a member of the Foreign Relations Committee, began investigating those charges in December 1985, and other members and congressional panels followed suit.

One prominent supporter of the contras, Rep. Charles W. Stenholm, D-Texas, in April asked President Reagan to look into the matter. Reagan in turn asked for evidence of wrongdoing by the contras, and so Stenholm began his own investigation.

Several news organizations also pursued the charges, raising questions about the activities of contra groups, particularly the Nicaraguan Democratic Force, the largest unit supported officially by the United States.

Contra spokesmen and Reagan administration officials denied most of the charges, saying they were inspired to sway Congress against Reagan's request.

Bosco Matamoras, spokesman for the Nicaraguan Democratic Force, said the charges were "lies and speculation." Nevertheless, Matamoras said the contras would cooperate in any probe.

Spending the $27 Million

The Reagan administration itself generated questions about the contras by its inability to give a full accounting of how the $27 million was spent.

As a result, two kinds of allegations were made: that some of the aid was diverted into private hands or spent on supplies that never reached the contras; and that contra leaders and Honduran officials might have made enormous profits by exchanging U.S. aid dollars for local currencies on the black market. Reagan officials rejected the first kind of allegations but reportedly raised their own concerns about the second.

The Subcommittee on Western Hemisphere Affairs in the fall of 1985 asked GAO to monitor the $27 million. Reporting to the panel in March and May, GAO said the State Department did not have complete records on money spent outside the United States. As of late April, $13.3 million could not be fully documented. The money was deposited in bank accounts of brokers, most located in Miami, who were to buy uniforms, food and other items from suppliers in Central America.

The remaining money was spent in the United States and was accounted for, GAO said.

According to GAO, the State Department's Nicaraguan Humanitarian Assistance Office (NHAO) made the bank deposits on the basis of invoices from suppliers in the region but could not prove that the purchased items actually were delivered to the contras.

Testifying before the Western Hemisphere Affairs Subcommittee on May 8, Frank Conahan of GAO said the State Department "could not assess the validity of the regional receipts, was unable to check out many suppliers, had difficulty establishing reasonableness of prices, and could not verify actual delivery or receipt of items."

The main reason, according to GAO and the State Department, was that the Honduran government would not allow the United States to monitor shipments to the contras, most of which were made through Honduras.

Apparently fearing retaliation from Nicaragua, Honduras refused to acknowledge that the contras operated from its territory or that it supported them.

State Department officials said they did the best they could under difficult circumstances. "Our primary objective has been to get the assistance through" to the contras, said Robert W. Duemling, NHAO director.

The administration was reluctant to give Congress information about expenditure of the $27 million. Officials gave documents to the House Western Hemisphere Affairs Subcommittee in April only after Rep. Leon E. Panetta, D-Calif., filed a resolution of inquiry (H Res 395) demanding information. The State Department classified the documents as "confidential," even though Congress had designed the aid program to be public.

GAO officials also said the State Department prevented them from traveling to Honduras to interview suppliers, contra leaders and others.

To obtain more information, the Foreign Affairs Committee on May 8 voted to subpoena records of accounts in 13 banks through which the $13.3 million was funneled. All but two of the banks were in Miami; the others were in Chicago and Washington, D.C.

The most specific charges about possible misuse of aid involved the State Department's purchase of supplies for the contras through a trading company associated with a neighborhood grocery store in Tegucigalpa, Honduras, called "Supermercado Hermano Pedro."

According to U.S. documents, the State Department paid the trading company nearly $4 million for uniforms, food, medical supplies and other items. Honduran military officers established the company in 1985 specifically to supply the contras and may have made substantial profits on its operations, Capitol Hill sources said.

Administration and congressional investigators said they were convinced that some contra officials had made substantial profits by converting U.S. dollars into Central

. . . Is Questioned by GAO, Hill Members

American currencies on local black markets. Much of the $13.3 million in unaccounted-for money reportedly was changed into Honduran and Costa Rican currencies. If done on the black market, where a premium was paid for dollars, that practice could yield hefty profits.

Some of the $27 million also was used for administration and other purposes that Congress did not spell out in its original legislation on the aid.

Private Aid, Guns, Drugs

Sen. Kerry and Rep. Stenholm focused their investigations on allegations of misuse of private aid, gun-running and drug-smuggling by some contra leaders and supporters in the United States. Several allegations involved the misuse of about $30 million the contras received from private sources, mostly in 1984-85, when Congress barred direct U.S. aid. Most of the private money bought food, medicine and other non-military supplies.

Congressional investigators also probed allegations:

- That supporters in the United States shipped guns and ammunition to the contras without required export licenses. In one case, Cubans in Florida allegedly flew weapons to the contras via El Salvador and Costa Rica.
- That some contras smuggled drugs into the United States, apparently as a way of earning cash to support military operations. Federal officials in Miami probed one alleged drug-smuggling ring among contras but reportedly found insufficient evidence to pursue the case. In its April report to Stenholm, the State Department acknowledged that there was "evidence of a limited number of incidents in which known drug traffickers have tried to establish connections with Nicaraguan resistance groups."

GAO Reports

In reviewing bank records, GAO found that millions of dollars had been transferred to other banks, companies and individuals with no apparent contra connection. In addition, about $1.4 million was paid from two accounts to the armed forces of Honduras, including a $450,000 check in January to the "commander-in-chief."

In an interim report June 11 to the Western Hemisphere Subcommittee, GAO did not identify the country whose armed forces received the contra money. Subcommittee Chairman Michael D. Barnes, D-Md., named Honduras as the "obvious" country. In Tegucigalpa, Honduras' armed forces chief, Gen. Humberto Regalado Hernandez, denied aid diversion charges and called them "a political game by some members of Congress."

Conahan testified before Barnes' subcommittee that "there is enough evidence to be concerned that humanitarian assistance [to the contras] may not be reaching the intended beneficiaries."

He gave examples from bank records:

- As of May 10, the U.S. Treasury had paid $3.3 million into one bank account belonging to an unnamed "broker," who was acting as agent for several suppliers of goods and services to the contras. The U.S. payments were based on the broker's invoices and receipts from 22 firms and people in Central America.

  But none of the checks that the broker wrote on the account went to any of those firms and individuals, Conahan said. Instead, the broker wrote checks totaling nearly $3.8 million to companies and persons in the United States and to bank accounts in the Cayman Islands and the Bahamas.

  Some of the checks might have been drawn from some $730,000 deposited into the broker's account from sources other than the U.S. Treasury, but GAO noted that nearly 80 percent of the money in the account came from the contra aid program.
- The account of another unnamed broker showed two checks totaling $243,750 written to the armed forces of a Central American country — named by Barnes as Honduras. That amount was identical to the totals of invoices and receipts for uniforms that the broker supposedly purchased from commercial suppliers.
- The U.S. Treasury paid $6.6 million into the account of one supplier, and checks were written on that account to the armed forces of the country where the supplier was located ($742,949) and to the commander in chief of the armed forces ($450,000). The endorsement signature on the latter check was illegible, sources said. Gen. Walter Lopez Reyes was the chief military commander in Honduras when the check was written Jan. 10.

  Again, Barnes named the country as Honduras, and other sources said the supplier was a trading firm connected to the Supermercado Hermano Pedro.

Secretary of State George P. Shultz said on June 12 that Democrats had "concocted" the GAO findings to discredit the contra aid program.

GAO's final report on the Nicaragua aid program was issued Dec. 5. The agency found that as of Sept. 4, the State Department had paid $26.8 million to suppliers or their agents. After the press and intelligence reports of diversions, NHAO investigated some transactions:

- $25,870 presumably paid for food, clothes and other items, instead went to buy "uniforms, ammunition and grenades." Duemling acknowledged that $15,000 had been mistakenly used for "bullets and hand grenades." But he said the department got restitution.
- $56,745 went to a rebel official as "advance funds." NHAO investigated and said that in due course all the money was spent for clothing.

GAO said it was satisfied with the controls that NHAO exercised over some $9.8 million paid to suppliers in the United States. The rest of the aid, about $17 million, was spent on goods and services in Central America. It was paid either to suppliers or to their agents.

According to GAO, NHAO provided statements to verify how only $8.4 million of that money was spent. NHAO said, however, that it had no authority to trace payments after they had been made into the suppliers' U.S. bank accounts.

But there were about $707,000 in discrepancies, GAO said. NHAO re-examined the statements and said most of the differences had resulted from "poor bookkeeping" by agents, time lags between suppliers' statements and NHAO payment records, and misinterpretations of what the statements were intended to include, the agency said.

agencies — would be eliminated. Under several existing laws, the Pentagon and the intelligence agencies were allowed to give the contras only aid that had been authorized explicitly by Congress. For example, in the fiscal 1986 intelligence authorization law (PL 99-169), Congress authorized the CIA to give the contras radios, intelligence information and advice but barred training and direct involvement in combat activities. Reagan sought, in effect, to repeal the curb on training and combat involvement.

In return for congressional approval of his request, Reagan pledged five sets of "undertakings," three of which were lengthy restatements of the administration case against Nicaragua and one of which was a promise to send Congress reports on Central America every 90 days.

The only new pledge, which reflected a change in Reagan's policy, was that the United States would begin direct "discussions" (not negotiations) with the Nicaraguan government — if Managua simultaneously agreed to church-mediated negotiations with the contras. The Sandinista regime had asked for direct talks with the United States but had resisted Reagan's demands that they negotiate with the contras.

Reagan said he would continue any discussions with Nicaragua only so long as the Sandinistas took actions he wanted, such as respecting freedom of the press and agreeing not to accept foreign arms and military advisers. Reagan also promised unspecified "other positive actions" to respond to any steps the Nicaraguan government took to address U.S. concerns. Shultz told the Foreign Relations Committee that one action could be the full or partial lifting of the U.S. economic embargo on Nicaragua. *(1985 Almanac p. 68)*

Along with his request, Reagan certified to Congress that previous U.S. efforts to resolve its disputes with Nicaragua had failed. He said those efforts included negotiations with Nicaragua, both directly and through the region-wide "Contadora" process, and the imposition of economic sanctions on Managua.

Expedited Legislative Procedures

Reagan's request triggered a series of procedures that guaranteed expedited votes in both houses of Congress on his full proposal. Unless both chambers approved identical versions, the request would be defeated.

Resolutions to approve the request were referred on Feb. 27 to several committees: in the Senate, the Foreign Relations and Appropriations committees, and in the House, the Appropriations, Armed Services, Foreign Affairs and Intelligence committees.

Under terms of the 1985 contra aid law, the House committees had 15 legislative days to act, after which time the issue went to the floor. After five more days, any member could demand action on the resolution, which was a privileged matter and could not be delayed or amended.

The procedures in the Senate were similar, except that the approval resolution had to be reported by the committees between the eighth and 15th days after introduction. Once reported by committee, the resolution could be raised on the floor at any time; once on the Senate floor it could be amended, but it could not be blocked by filibuster.

Battling Uphill

Reagan's request encountered serious political trouble, primarily because a strong majority in the House opposed direct military aid to the contras.

Four House committees on March 5-6 considered a resolution (H J Res 540) to approve the request, and three voted against it: Appropriations, Foreign Affairs and Intelligence. Only the Armed Services Committee voted in favor. Appropriations and Armed Services acted on voice votes; Foreign Affairs and Intelligence rejected the request on votes of 23-18 and 9-7, respectively. The votes were largely along partisan lines, with most Democrats opposed and most Republicans in favor of the request.

In the early weeks of March, moderates tried to convince the administration to accept a scaled-down contra aid program to avoid a defeat on Capitol Hill.

House Democrats who generally supported Reagan's Nicaragua policy tried to forge a compromise. Major features were:

- Approval of continued non-military aid to the contras, probably in the range of Reagan's $30 million request.
- A demand by Congress that the United States become more actively involved in "Contadora" regional peace negotiations.
- Withholding for several months release of any military aid for the contras, to give the Managua government time to meet U.S. insistence that it negotiate with its opponents.
- Strict limits on CIA support for the contras.

Administration officials resisted a compromise, telling members that nothing less than Reagan's original request was needed to prevent the Sandinistas from consolidating their control.

'A Sea of Red . . . Lapping at Our Borders'

Meanwhile, partisan politics heated up March 5 with statements by Reagan that Democrats saw as red-baiting and even some Republicans called extreme. In two separate statements, he seemed to imply that his critics on Capitol Hill were doing a favor for Sandinista leaders in Nicaragua.

First, in a meeting with reporters, Reagan was asked whether he would equate opposition to his Nicaragua policy with support for the Sandinistas. "It's hard not to," he said.

Later, speaking to Jewish leaders, Reagan said his opponents in Congress "are courting disaster, and history will hold them accountable." He added: "If we don't want to see the map of Central America covered in a sea of red, eventually lapping at our own borders, we must act now."

Reagan's statements came on the heels of a March 5 column in *The Washington Post* by his communications director, Patrick J. Buchanan. "With the contra vote, the Democratic Party will reveal whether it stands with Ronald Reagan and the resistance or [Nicaraguan President] Daniel Ortega and the communists," he wrote.

As could be expected, Democrats responded angrily. Rep. Michael D. Barnes, Md., said: "I don't believe we have heard such offensive nonsense from our top political leaders since the 1950s. These statements are the moral equivalent of McCarthyism."

Patrick J. Leahy, D-Vt., vice chairman of the Senate Intelligence Committee, said Reagan officials were "looking around for scapegoats because their policies have failed."

Some Democrats who generally supported Reagan's policies said the White House rhetoric was backfiring. Rep. Dave McCurdy, D-Okla., a compromise advocate, complained that "the rhetoric is losing votes."

A few Republicans rushed to Reagan's defense. Noting that House Speaker O'Neill once accused Reagan of wanting to send U.S. troops to Nicaragua, Rep. Henry J. Hyde, R-Ill., said "the rhetoric has been harsh on both sides."

But several moderate Republicans said they shared the Democrats' unhappiness with administration rhetoric.

In a March 6 speech in the Senate, Sen. Nancy Landon Kassebaum, R-Kan., complained about administration "distortions": that the contra issue was "a disagreement between Republicans in white hats and Democrats wrapped in red banners" and that "this is a matter of patriotism — those who love America will support the president and those who oppose [him] want to abandon San Diego to the Sandinistas."

Substantive Differences

Aside from political issues, Reagan's request encountered opposition on several grounds:

Money. The $100 million seemed excessive to many members on both sides of the issue. It was nearly four times the $27 million that Congress approved for the contras in 1985, and it stood in sharp contrast to the budget-cutting that many domestic programs faced.

In that context, a March 5 report by the General Accounting Office (GAO) on the use of the previous $27 million had special impact. The GAO said the State Department was unable to prove that clothing, medicine and other supplies bought with the $27 million actually reached the contras. *(Box, p. 396)*

As they read the fine print of Reagan's request, members also found he was asking not just for $100 million, but for authority to tap CIA and Pentagon contingency accounts to aid the contras. Jamie L. Whitten, D-Miss., chairman of the House Appropriations Committee, noted that Reagan wanted money "without any restrictions whatever."

Military Aid. Since mid-1985, a broad majority in Congress had been willing to support non-military aid to the contras, apparently on the theory that giving them boots and medicine meant less U.S. involvement than giving them bullets and guns. But in asking for $70 million in military aid, Rep. Barnes said, "they went too far."

What Next? Administration officials were unable to offer satisfactory answers to members' questions about what would happen when the $100 million ran out. Defense Secretary Caspar W. Weinberger told the House Armed Services Committee that "we think that [amount] will do the job." But other officials said privately the contras were so weak militarily that it might take them years to gain enough strength to force the Sandinistas into making concessions.

Policy. As in the past, Reagan aides and contra leaders gave Congress contradictory and confusing statements about their goals. Shultz, Weinberger and some contra leaders repeated the official policy that the United States was seeking only to pressure the Sandinistas into negotiating with their opponents and calling free elections.

"We don't think it's possible; we don't want a total military defeat," contra political leader Alfonso Robelo said on March 5. The same day, contra military leader Enrique Bermudez said that "with $100 million we are sure we are going to defeat the Sandinistas very fast."

Latin Support. Perhaps the most damaging argument against Reagan's request was that most Latin American leaders in February had asked him to withhold it until they made another effort at negotiating a regional peace treaty for Central America. That gave fresh ammunition to the charge by Democrats that Reagan was ignoring chances for a negotiated settlement. A House Democratic Caucus task force on March 5 released an alternative program for U.S. policy emphasizing the Contadora talks.

Two days later, Reagan said he was sending veteran diplomat Philip C. Habib to Central America "to achieve a diplomatic solution" to the region's troubles.

FIRST HOUSE VOTE: 'NO' TO AID

Reagan's request for $100 million in contra aid (H J Res 540) was firmly rejected by the House on March 20. But the 210-222 vote against the president did not settle the issue; it merely marked the first round in a parliamentary struggle that ended with the president getting most of what he wanted, with some strings. *(Vote 58, p. 20-H)*

Trying to win a handful of votes in the House, Reagan on March 19 offered cosmetic changes in the request. But he balked at substantial policy changes, such as agreeing to unconditional negotiations with the Sandinistas, that might have guaranteed him an immediate legislative victory.

Reagan also may have lost swing votes because of the bitterly partisan tactics employed by some of his aides and conservative members and groups that lobbied on his behalf. "Buchanan was our secret weapon," said Rep. Barnes, a leading Reagan opponent.

In a statement issued shortly after the House vote, Reagan called the action "a dark day for freedom" and expressed his "solemn determination to come back again and again until this battle is won."

Reagan Speech

In a televised speech March 16, four days before the House vote, Reagan blasted the leftist Sandinista regime and the dangers that it posed to its neighbors and the United States. *(Text, p. 11-D)*

The government in Managua was an "outlaw regime" that had attacked ethnic and religious groups, established blacklistings and secret prisons and generally practiced "brutality" against the citizenry, Reagan said.

Reagan portrayed the Sandinistas as surrogates for the Soviet Union and Cuba. With a foothold on the North American continent, he said, the Soviets and their allies "will be in a position to threaten the Panama Canal, interdict our vital Caribbean sea lanes and, ultimately, move against Mexico." The result would be Latin people fleeing to the United States "by the millions."

The Nicaraguans also were attempting to subvert their neighbors by arming leftist guerrilla groups, Reagan said. Showing a map of the region, Reagan charged that weapons supplied by Nicaragua had been found in Costa Rica, El Salvador, Guatemala and Honduras. Further to the south, the Sandinistas had supplied weapons, training, safe haven and other help to subversives throughout South America, he said. The apparent implication that South American countries faced an imminent takeover by communism differed from the impression that administration officials had been trying to give about trends there.

In addition to posing overt and covert military threats to the rest of the hemisphere, Reagan said, Soviet-backed Nicaragua was a source of terrorism and drug trafficking.

Reagan said the Sandinistas sponsored terror that "led" to the mid-1985 murder in El Salvador of four U.S. Marines and several others. An aide said earlier the United States had no evidence that Nicaragua advised the guerrillas to launch that attack or played any other direct role; the link, the aide said, was that the guerrillas got their supplies from Nicaragua and maintained their headquarters there.

Reagan insisted that the United States was seeking a "negotiated peace" in Nicaragua. His administration had met with the Sandinistas 10 times, each time to be "rebuffed." He did not mention that it was the United States that ended direct talks between the two countries in January 1985.

Democratic Response

Speaking for congressional Democrats, Sen. Jim Sasser of Tennessee said they shared Reagan's goals for Central America but disputed his portrayal of the current situation in the region and his prescription for U.S. action to meet it. Sasser gave the Democratic response in a seven-minute speech shortly after Reagan's live address on March 16.

Sasser sought to identify the Democrats with the same concerns that Reagan expressed about the Sandinista government and the potential for Soviet-supported subversion in the Western Hemisphere. But Sasser seemed to portray the Nicaraguan threat as less imminent than did Reagan. The president left no doubt that he considered Nicaragua an active Soviet military base. Sasser seemed to put the danger more in the future, saying that Democrats "agree that Nicaragua must never become a base for Soviet military adventurism in this hemisphere."

Lobbying Blitz

The dramatic March 20 vote capped several weeks of intensive lobbying by Reagan, his aides and outside groups.

Reagan telephoned several dozen members targeted as "swing votes" — spending as much as a half-hour with some — and dispatched top aides to Capitol Hill for intensive lobbying sessions, including Secretary of State Shultz and Central America envoy Habib.

The president had counted heavily on moderate Republicans, including Tom Ridge, Pa.; John G. Rowland, Conn.; Olympia J. Snowe, Maine; Larry J. Hopkins, Ky.; Frank Horton, N.Y.; and Chalmers P. Wylie, Ohio.

All of them eventually voted against him, many citing his administration's uncompromising stance against the Sandinistas and its insistence that military support for the contras was the only way to prevent the spread of communism in Central America.

The president also sought but did not get the support of several undecided Democrats, including Richard H. Stallings, Idaho; Jim Chapman, Texas; Marilyn Lloyd, Tenn.; and Buddy MacKay, Fla. These members in particular recoiled at Buchanan's line that the vote came down to a choice between "Ronald Reagan and the resistance or Daniel Ortega and the communists."

In the weeks leading up to the vote, they were also singled out by conservative organizations that orchestrated telephone and telegram campaigns and bought local radio and newspaper advertisements to champion the contra cause.

Citizens for Reagan, for example, took out newspaper ads in MacKay's 6th District with the headline, "Whose Buddy Is He? . . . Your Congressman & Communist Nicaragua." The ad instructed readers how to send MacKay a telegram at special reduced rates.

MacKay blamed the campaign on the White House. "I don't know about the other congressmen involved, but they [the White House] can take their out-of-state ad campaign and shove it," MacKay told *The Boston Globe.*

Daniel A. Mica, D-Fla., a longtime supporter of Reagan's Nicaraguan policy, voted with the president but nevertheless commiserated with MacKay. "He was subject to some of the most vicious attacks I've ever seen," Mica said. "Had I been subject to those same kind of attacks, I might have felt tempted to vote no myself."

Publicly, the administration and its conservative supporters never backed off from Buchanan's statements. Even moderate Republicans who ended up supporting the president blamed such White House lobbying tactics for the bill's defeat.

"There's no question the debate on the floor is on Pat Buchanan's remarks," said Steve Gunderson, R-Wis., who voted in favor of contra aid after the administration made some last-minute concessions. "It's Pat Buchanan's comment that every Democrat tells me about. If we lose today, it will be his fault."

But Dick Cheney, R-Wyo., chairman of the Republican Policy Committee, denied that assertion after the vote. "I cannot find a vote that Buchanan cost us," he said.

Cheney said the margin of defeat for the president was measured in the number of Democrats who returned to the party fold when Speaker O'Neill March 18 promised them a vote in April on a compromise aid package.

O'Neill, who lobbied hard against the president's request, essentially won the head-to-head battle with Reagan by being the first to offer a compromise.

Looking for Votes: A Compromise

In the days before the vote, both sides claimed imminent victory, apparently in an attempt to demoralize the opposition. But when the House debate began on March 19, White House officials acknowledged they were behind by a handful of votes.

Desperately seeking to swing undecided members, the White House March 19 agreed to a proposal by Rod Chandler, R-Wash., that would delay some of the $70 million in military aid requested by Reagan for 90 days. During that time, Reagan would press for negotiations in Central America, both among countries in the region and between the Nicaraguan government and its internal opposition.

To assure members that he would carry out the talks, Reagan sent Congress a formal message promising to issue an executive order delaying the aid and naming a five-member bipartisan commission to monitor progress on the talks. *(Reagan message, p. 14-D)*

The Chandler plan would not directly change Reagan's basic request. Although its key element was a 90-day delay in military aid, the plan would allow the administration to give the contras "defensive" weapons, such as anti-aircraft missiles, that were their highest priority anyway.

Chandler, however, said the plan enabled him to swallow his doubts about the direction of Reagan's policy. "I like to think this places an emphasis on negotiations that wasn't there before," he said.

The Chandler plan won a handful of votes for Reagan's request, but more significant were the votes it did not attract. Key among them was the vote of McCurdy, who had been negotiating with the White House on a similar plan. McCurdy said he and Reagan aides had gotten "very close" to an agreement during a meeting at the Capitol on March 18 but were unable to resolve key issues involving the conditions under which military aid to the contras would be released.

The Reagan negotiating efforts were too little, too late, McCurdy complained. "I wish the administration had been as eager to work with us over the past 24 weeks as they have been over the past 24 hours," he told the House.

Some House Republican leaders discerned the opposite reason for the failure of administration lobbying efforts. Michel, in particular, expressed frustration that the White House was willing to make too many compromises without getting guarantees of the needed votes in return.

Michel vented his unhappiness in several ways, first by calling White House Chief of Staff Donald T. Regan on March 11 to denounce the talk of compromise. Then, on March 19, as Shultz and Habib were conferring in his office with wavering Republicans, Michel called a press conference to complain about the failures of administration lobbying. "I've just got to the point where I've had it," he said.

House Debate

With Reagan's vote-gathering effort stalled, House Democratic leaders seized the chance to hold on to the votes of McCurdy and others who supported contra aid but wanted more emphasis than Reagan would accept on negotiations in Central America.

O'Neill on March 18 made an offer McCurdy could not resist: a chance to offer any Nicaragua proposal he wanted on April 15, when the House considered a "must-pass" supplemental appropriations bill. McCurdy accepted the proposal and, along with about 20 colleagues, held fast in opposing Reagan's request as it stood.

Reflecting the intense pressure generated by the White House and outside lobbying groups, the debate on March 19-20 was unusually acrimonious and partisan.

Republicans were on the offensive, especially on the first day of debate. They interrupted virtually every Democrat who opposed Reagan's request and jeered and stamped their feet when the Democrats refused to yield the floor.

Several Republicans directly attacked both the Democratic Party and individual members in the House. Among them, Dan Burton, R-Ind., accused Democrats of using "communist disinformation" in their arguments.

When Democrats called for a halt in the partisan attacks, Republicans responded with even more. Answering the Democrats' complaints about Buchanan, Hyde stared straight at the majority side of the aisle and said: "History, not Pat Buchanan, is going to assign to you Democrats the role of pallbearers at the funeral of Democracy in Central America. That is not McCarthyism; that is called accountability."

But at the end of debate, O'Neill took the House floor to denounce the "drumbeat" of attacks on members who opposed Reagan's request. "Today's vote," O'Neill said, "is a matter of conscience, not of politics."

For many members on both sides, the issues were clear and the right choice before the House was obvious. But a handful of members acknowledged that they agonized over their votes.

"This is not an easy decision to make," Marge Roukema, R-N.J., told the House in announcing her vote for Reagan's request. "The so-called facts as claimed by the strong partisans on both sides of the issue are not hard facts at all," Roukema said. It was no surprise, she added, that the "uncommitted majority of Americans remain confused and unconvinced."

E. "Kika" de la Garza, D-Texas, noted that the issue had divided the country's leadership, his constituents and those from whom he had sought counsel and advice. "I have prayed for divine guidance," de la Garza said, in explanation of his decision to vote "no."

Democrats Hold Fast

By the time the vote came in mid-afternoon March 20, the Democratic leaders were confident of victory because Reagan was failing to sway undecided members. Shortly after the 15-minute vote began, it was clear that Reagan would lose, as one by one the red "no" lights were displayed next to the names of key swing members.

A last-minute surprise was the opposition to Reagan's request by Republicans Bill Frenzel of Minnesota and Hopkins of Kentucky. Both had voiced doubts about using the contras to oust the Nicaraguan government but neither had been willing to make a firm commitment until the two-day debate in the House ended.

Only 46 Democrats supported the president — four fewer than GOP leaders had said they needed. Sixteen Republicans opposed Reagan, about twice as many as had voted consistently in the past against contra aid.

Both sides offered partisan explanations for the outcome. Republican leaders charged that House Democrats merely wanted to defeat Reagan out of spite, or, conversely, win a victory for O'Neill. "They want to stick it to the president just one more time," Michel said.

The Democratic leaders rejected that charge, saying most members were making their voting decisions on the merits of Reagan's request, not on party loyalty. "This is not a party-line issue," Majority Leader Jim Wright, D-Texas, said.

The attempt by Democrats to be conciliatory left some Republicans cold. Following the vote, Minority Whip Trent Lott, R-Miss., one of the most vocal denouncers of the Democratic leadership, pointed to the "no" column on his tally sheet and said: "I'll frame this as the day they voted for communism in Nicaragua."

FIRST SENATE VOTE: A NARROW WIN

The Senate on March 27 approved the $100 million in aid for the contras but deprived Reagan of the sweeping bipartisan majority he wanted for the rebel assistance.

By voting for the request 53-47, the Senate helped ensure that Reagan would get most of what he wanted, including military aid. However, Congress moved to attach conditions aimed at slowing down, if not stopping, deepening U.S. involvement in the Nicaraguan war.

The key vote on the Senate resolution (S J Res 283) fell along predictable lines, with 11 Democrats supporting the president and 11 Republicans opposing him. The tally nearly matched the 53-46 margin by which the Senate had approved $14 million in military aid on April 23, 1985. *(Vote 51, p. 10-S; 1985 Almanac p. 66)*

The only surprise on March 27 was the "yes" vote cast by Bill Bradley, D-N.J., who in the past had opposed contra aid. Bradley said he voted for the aid "with misgivings and reservations," and that Reagan had "left us with little choice but to back the contras."

In contrast to previous years, the issue among most senators was not whether to give the contras any help; all but about two dozen senators were willing to support some form of aid. The 1986 dispute was over what conditions Congress should impose on the president's use of the aid — especially whether Congress should try to force Reagan to negotiate with Nicaragua.

Nicaraguans' Honduras Incursion

A complicating factor in the contra program's political outlook was Nicaragua's March 22 invasion of neighboring Honduras in pursuit of camps that the contras had there with the tacit approval of the Honduran government.

The incursion itself was nothing new. Nicaraguan and contra forces had battled along the border hundreds of times, and a large Nicaraguan force had crossed into Honduras to battle the guerrillas in May 1985.

But the timing of the incursion was unusual: just two days after the House voted against contra aid and a few days before the Senate was scheduled to take up the issue. The White House moved to capitalize on the situation, announcing March 24 that some 1,500 Nicaraguan troops had participated in the invasion and declaring it to be a graphic demonstration of the evils of the Managua regime.

In Congress, Reagan's GOP supporters gloated at the news and predicted it would force many Democrats to abandon their opposition to contra aid. Rep. Jack F. Kemp, R-N.Y., suggested that Reagan dramatize the situation by calling the House back to Washington from its Easter recess.

For many Democrats, the invasion revived memories of April 1985, when Nicaraguan President Ortega flew to Moscow a few days after the House had rejected a contra military aid request. Democrats called the Ortega trip a slap in the face, and the 1986 invasion stung just as much.

O'Neill angrily described Ortega as a "bumbling, incompetent, Marxist-Leninist communist." Majority Whip Thomas S. Foley, D-Wash., called the invasion "unjustified and stupid."

But other Reagan critics doubted that the invasion had taken place or was as large as the White House contended. Their skepticism was reinforced by the administration's inability for several days to provide hard evidence of the invasion, by the Honduran government's initial reluctance to confirm it, and by the fact that Washington's early statements were based largely on reports from the contras, who had an obvious reason to play up the Nicaraguan attack.

Three days after the White House announcement, Senate critics such as Dodd and Sasser were referring to the "alleged" invasion. Rep. Barnes, chairman of the House Foreign Affairs Subcommittee on Western Hemisphere Affairs, called a hearing to investigate.

Although Reagan, in a March 27 speech, continued to claim that 1,500 Nicaraguans had entered Honduras, other U.S. officials were quoted as saying the force was closer to 800.

Aside from any embarrassment to Democrats, the invasion seemed to have little immediate effect on the Senate's contra deliberations. Both Sasser, the leading Democratic advocate of a compromise, and Foreign Relations Committee Chairman Richard G. Lugar, R-Ind., said they were unable to name senators who changed their minds because of the invasion. "As far as I can see, votes are based on what it is in the bill, rather than what is happening in Honduras," Lugar said.

Reagan's immediate reaction was to invoke, on March 24, his emergency powers to speed up $20 million in military aid to Honduras, even though the government there apparently had to be persuaded to request the money. Some of the money paid for U.S. helicopters and pilots to ferry some 600 Honduran troops to within a few miles of the battle zone. The Hondurans did no fighting but established a symbolic presence and collected bodies and weapons as evidence of the invasion.

Seeking a Consensus

In private negotiations leading up to the Senate vote, the White House and its GOP allies had hoped to fashion a bipartisan compromise that would capture the votes of an overwhelming majority and put to rest charges that Reagan did not have broad support on Capitol Hill for his policy toward Nicaragua. Majority Leader Dole set a goal of 70-80 votes, which he said would be "more important than 51," a simple majority of the Senate.

Sasser and several other Democrats, including Minority Leader Byrd also sought a compromise to show that they shared Reagan's distaste for the Sandinistas.

Negotiations among Senate and White House staffers began on March 24, and were based on the Reagan request for $70 million in military aid and $30 million in non-military aid for the contras, all to be transferred from existing Defense Department funds.

The goal of the negotiations was to put into law a series of minor changes in the request that Reagan had accepted on March 19, in an unsuccessful effort to win the vote in the House. White House officials believed that Reagan might have prevailed in the House if the changes had been incorporated in law, rather than in a letter he sent Congress and an executive order he promised to issue.

In essence, the March 19 changes would have delayed $75 million of the aid — including all military aid except training and "defensive" weaponry such as anti-aircraft missiles — for 90 days while Reagan pursued regional negotiations. Reagan offered to have "discussions" with the Sandinistas — if they simultaneously negotiated with the contras and other political rivals.

The compromise-drafting talks on Capitol Hill immediately met a major obstacle: Sasser's demand, shared by many Democrats, that Reagan resume direct talks with Nicaragua, regardless of whether the Sandinistas had agreed to the simultaneous negotiations with the contras. White House aides refused to put such a demand into law. Reagan's aides also rebuffed a compromise attempt March 25, leading Sasser to charge that they really did not want an agreement with Democrats.

For all practical purposes, the effort to gain a bipartisan compromise failed on March 26, when Adm. John M. Poindexter, national security adviser, joined the sessions in Dole's office.

As described later by Sasser, Poindexter "steamed into the majority leader's office at flank speed and torpedoed the negotiations without even firing a warning shot across the bow." Poindexter did so, Sasser said, by refusing to discuss language mandating Reagan to hold talks with the Nicaraguans under conditions that he did not like.

Also at issue was a separate proposal by Byrd that Reagan be required to return to Congress at the end of the 90-day waiting period if he wanted to give the contras the remaining $75 million in aid. Byrd's plan for a "second vote" after 90 days would have enabled either chamber to block release of the $75 million.

The White House and Republican leaders rejected the Byrd proposal, countering with a plan allowing Reagan to use the money unless both houses blocked it — a virtual impossibility since Congress would have to override the president's certain veto.

Each side described its position on the second-vote issue as non-negotiable on March 26, and so further attempts to craft a compromise on it were dropped.

With the collapse of the compromise negotiations, Sasser tried to get fellow Democrats to support his alternative for $100 million in aid, on the condition that Reagan negotiate with the Sandinistas. Encountering resistance from liberals who opposed giving the contras any military aid, Sasser quickly pared back his proposal to $30 million in non-military aid.

The White House, meanwhile, focused on swinging a handful of moderates who had specific concerns about Reagan's proposal. Chief among them were Kassebaum, William S. Cohen, R-Maine, and Sam Nunn, D-Ga. — all of whom wanted assurances that Reagan would press for reforms in and unity among the several contra organizations.

The three agreed to back the request once the administration included a provision barring aid after July 1 unless the president reported that the contras "have agreed to and are beginning to implement" reforms such as curtailing human rights abuses and ensuring civilian leaders' control.

Reagan gave further assurances in a March 27 letter to Nunn, saying he would use the $100 million "in a manner which gives primacy to civilian leadership and democratic development within the Nicaraguan opposition."

Amendments Rejected

By the time the Senate began debate on March 27, Republican leaders were confident that Reagan's request would be approved, if only by a narrow margin. Nevertheless, Dole and Lugar continued meeting with individual Democrats in a last-gasp attempt to reach a compromise on the negotiating-with-Nicaragua language.

As debate proceeded, the Senate defeated a series of amendments that offered stark choices on the contra aid issues. The amendments were:

- By Edward M. Kennedy, D-Mass., to prohibit all U.S. aid, in any form, to the contras. Kennedy would have done that by reinstating in law the 1984 "Boland amendment" by which Congress temporarily suspended covert aid to the contras by the CIA. The amendment was rejected, 24-74, attracting votes from the dwindling number of senators who opposed all U.S. involvement with the contras. *(Vote 46, p. 10-S)*
- By Jesse Helms, R-N.C., allowing the president to aid the contras after May 15 if he determined that the Nicaraguan government had not taken steps such as ending "aggression" against other countries, ending importation of military supplies and personnel, expelling Soviet and Cuban military advisers and allowing political parties to organize for future elections. Rejected 39-60. *(Vote 47, p. 10-S)*
- Sasser's omnibus substitute, allowing $30 million in non-military aid to the contras if the United States resumed direct talks with Nicaragua. That failed 33-67, with Mark O. Hatfield, Ore., the only Republican voting for it. Sasser charged that Dole made the amendment a "party-line" issue by demanding that Republicans oppose it. Dole countered that Sasser had provoked partisanship by offering a "Democratic substitute." *(Vote 48, p. 10-S)*
- By Alan Cranston, D-Calif., to allow only "non-lethal" aid to the contras if the Sandinistas took steps such as agreeing to a cease-fire, and if the United States failed to engage in direct bilateral negotiations with the Sandinistas without preconditions other than a cease-fire. Cranston said his amendment was aimed at stopping military aid to the contras "if the president continues to reject direct, meaningful bilateral negotiations." In a March 27 letter to Lugar, Reagan condemned the amendment as "giving the Sandinistas what they want — direct bilateral talks" with the United States. Tabled 66-34. *(Vote 49, p. 10-S)*
- By Kennedy, barring the introduction of U.S. combat forces into Nicaragua unless Congress approved in advance or the president reported that it was needed to evacuate U.S. citizens or to respond to a "clear and present danger" of military attack on the United States. Arguing against this amendment, Dole made an unusually direct political attack on Kennedy, saying: "I would suggest to my friend from Massachusetts that he recently has withdrawn from the '88 race, and I suggest we let the president proceed." Tabled 68-32. *(Vote 50, p. 10-S)*

The key 53-47 vote was on adoption of the White House-approved plan for the $100 million, sponsored by Dole and Lugar. The Senate then adopted, by voice vote, the underlying resolution approving the aid.

A provision of central importance was the delay until July 1 in release of most military aid. At that point, the remaining $75 million was to be released according to a schedule if the president reported to Congress that a comprehensive peace agreement had not been reached in Central America and that the Nicaraguan government had not taken several steps, including engaging in a "serious dialogue with representatives of all elements of the Nicaraguan democratic opposition."

The bill also barred U.S. personnel who trained or advised the contras from entering into Nicaragua, and it explicitly did not authorize armed combat against Nicaragua by U.S. forces.

Reforming the Contras

The delay until July 1 for release of the $75 million in aid also was tied to reforms by the contras. The rebels' behavior had been an important issue since 1983, when significant opposition emerged in Congress to aiding the guerrillas.

Nearly all U.S. aid had gone to the Nicaraguan Democratic Force, organized in 1981 with the help of the CIA. Critics repeatedly hurled two charges at the Force: that most of its military leaders were officers of the Nicaraguan National Guard, which brutally repressed dissent under dictator Anastasio Somoza, who preceded the Sandinista regime; and that some units had committed human rights abuses against civilians.

Contra leaders and U.S. officials denied both charges, but the criticism persisted. In March, the congressional Arms Control and Foreign Policy Caucus charged that 12 of the 13 members of the Force's "high command" were former National Guard officers.

When Reagan asked Congress in February for more aid to the contras, several senators said they would base their decision on whether he was willing to pressure the contras into making reforms. Key among that group were Cohen, Kassebaum and Nunn.

At the insistence of those senators, the White House in late March accepted the conditions that were written into S J Res 283. The three senators voted for the bill, providing the margin that enabled it to pass 53-47.

Under the Senate bill, the remaining $75 million in delayed assistance would be spent after July 1 if Reagan reported to Congress that the contras had "agreed to and are beginning to implement" reforms.

Congress would get a separate report by June 30 from a five-member commission appointed by House and Senate leaders. At that point, Congress could reject Reagan's report and block further aid only by passing a joint resolution — over the president's certain veto.

The major reforms advocated by the Senate bill, and agreed to by Reagan, were aimed at:

- Establishing civilian control of the military. Critics, and even some contra leaders, said military officers were holding the real power in the contra organization. Reagan, in a March 27 letter to Nunn, said he would seek to change this by getting the contras to establish a council, similar to his National Security Council, to ensure "that military activities are conducted under the guidance of responsible civilian leaders." Reagan said U.S. aid would be funneled through civilians, but did not say how the military officers would be forced to accept orders from the civilians.
- Curbing human rights abuses. The Senate bill included $3 million to promote the "observance and advancement of human rights." Administration officials gave Con-

gress little information on how the money would be spent, saying only that it would pay the salaries of some contra leaders and would provide human rights training for contra soldiers. The bill also barred the president from aiding any group that retained in its ranks "any individual who has been found to engage in" human-rights abuses, drug smuggling or misuse of funds.

- Improving contra unity. Under pressure from Kassebaum and others, the administration in March agreed to aid some of the five contra groups other than the Nicaraguan Democratic Force, and to pressure those groups to coordinate their military and political activities.

Kassebaum said the Senate bill "does begin to address the problem of unification and reform of the contras."

But critics said Reagan accepted the conditions only to get contra aid through Congress, and would forget them.

SECOND HOUSE ROUND: 'NO' AGAIN

The second phase of the contra battle in the House also produced a defeat for Reagan, but with a curious procedural twist. In a complicated legislative scenario, Reagan's aid request was attached to a bill (HR 4515) to make supplemental appropriations for fiscal 1986. *(Supplemental, p. 153)*

The linking of assistance for the rebels to the $1.7 billion supplemental, which was considered veto bait because of unrelated spending items that Reagan did not want, prompted House Republicans on April 16 to scuttle the contra aid. That surprise move set off more than two months of jockeying to revive the package.

Rules Committee Action

On April 10, the Rules Committee approved a procedure that would make contra aid part of the supplemental if the House passed that bill. If the supplemental was rejected, aid for the rebels automatically would be attached to the Senate's separate contra bill, S J Res 283.

When the House rejected Reagan's first request on March 20, O'Neill promised another vote on April 15 as part of action on the supplemental. O'Neill, the leading opponent of contra aid, said his promise would guarantee Reagan another chance, since supplementals always pass.

But with HR 4515 in political trouble, the administration and House Republicans asked O'Neill not to attach contra aid to it. O'Neill seemed willing to consider that request until two things happened: White House officials implied that Nicaragua invaded Honduras because the House had rejected aid to the contras, and administration officials on April 9 leaked to *The Washington Post* a cable by Frank V. Ortiz Jr., the U.S. ambassador to Argentina, complaining about the behavior of O'Neill and other Democrats during a trip to Buenos Aires. Ortiz charged that the Democrats sought to elicit opposition to Reagan policies by Argentine leaders. The Democrats countered by showing reporters a videotape of a meeting during which Argentine President Raul Alfonsín needed no prodding to state his opposition to Reagan's policies.

Saying the administration was resuming its attack on Democrats, O'Neill hardened his position on linking contra aid to the supplemental. Nevertheless, he agreed to the complex procedure by which contra aid would remain on the supplemental if the supplemental passed but would be severed and returned to the Senate if the House rejected the supplemental.

The Rules Committee approved that procedure late April 10 by voice vote, with the two GOP members present voting no. One, Minority Whip Lott, complained that the supplemental was "fast becoming a total farce" because of the political maneuvering.

Reagan called leading Democrats to the White House on April 10 in an attempt to get them to support his request without conditions or parliamentary delays. But the president swayed few members, and some walked out of the meeting saying Reagan did not grasp the basic issues under dispute on Capitol Hill.

According to several members, Reagan seemed to express approval when McCurdy explained his proposal for several conditions on the $100 million in contra aid. "Aides had to signify the differences" to Reagan between his request and the McCurdy plan, one Democrat said.

Republicans' Surprise

When the issue came to a vote on April 16, Republicans aborted House consideration of contra aid, because the Democratic leadership had tried to use its power to ensure that the House would impose substantial conditions on Reagan's $100 million request.

Taking Democrats by complete surprise, the Republicans voted for a Democrat-proposed amendment to the supplemental, withholding aid for the contras. That enabled the amendment, which everyone had expected to lose, to pass handily, 361-66. *(Vote 74, p. 24-H)*

With the GOP parliamentary tactic taking the House to the brink of anarchy, Democrats abruptly halted action on the bill, effectively killing the just-passed amendment.

The immediate purpose of the GOP strategy was to prevent the House from considering yet another Democrat-sponsored amendment that Republicans feared might pass. Offered by McCurdy and other conservative and moderate Democrats, that amendment would have required a second vote by Congress in the summer of 1986 to release most of the contra aid.

The Republican maneuver succeeded in the goal of separating the contra issue from the administration-opposed supplemental. Republicans said they feared contra aid would be delayed for months if tied to the supplemental, and they insisted that the contras urgently needed weapons and other supplies.

House Majority Whip Foley said the Republicans had committed "parliamentary suicide" in a fit of pique. But Republicans said they acted carefully and out of frustration that the Democrats had created a legislative situation they could not accept.

Pulling a Surprise

The Republicans succeeded April 16 by employing the element of surprise — rarely used on Capitol Hill because keeping secrets among legislators is nearly impossible.

Michel and other top Republicans decided on their strategy on April 11. They informed two White House aides, but otherwise kept their colleagues in the dark.

On April 15, the House adopted the Democratic rule for action on the supplemental on two close votes: 221-202 and 212-208. The Republicans made those votes party-line issues: Only one Republican voted with the Democrats each time, first John Edward Porter, Ill., and then Bill Green, N.Y. *(Votes 71, 72, p. 24-H)*

As House debate on the issue was moving into high gear on April 16, the Republican leaders called a caucus meeting and told their colleagues about their strategy for scuttling action on the bill.

Under the plan, Republicans were to vote for the first amendment before the House. Offered by Hamilton, chairman of the Intelligence Committee, it contained no military aid for the contras and instead provided $27 million for humanitarian aid to Nicaraguan refugees, whether or not they were contras. The Hamilton amendment also included provisions to prompt Reagan to negotiate directly with Nicaragua and to give more support to Central American peace-making efforts.

Republicans and the White House strongly opposed the Hamilton amendment and would never have supported it under normal circumstances. Democrats expected that only about 170-180 die-hard opponents of contra aid would vote for Hamilton. But the procedure decreed that the McCurdy amendment could not be offered if the Hamilton amendment passed. The Republicans used that procedure to block McCurdy.

As the voting began on the Hamilton amendment, most Republicans withheld their votes. But about halfway into the 15-minute period, Michel pulled a voting card from his wallet and punched the "yea" button in front of his seat. With that signal, dozens of Republicans did the same and the Hamilton amendment surged ahead.

Stunned Democratic leaders huddled together, apparently trying to decide what to do.

Later, the Democrats said they were taken completely by surprise. "We never figure legislative suicide as one of the options," Foley said.

But the Democrats said they did not consider taking the most direct response: switching their votes against the Hamilton amendment to thwart the Republicans.

When the votes for the Hamilton amendment hit the magic 218 majority mark, gleeful Republicans let out a cheer, and a few Democrats joined in. The Hamilton amendment eventually was adopted, 361-66.

Michel immediately sought recognition and launched into a heated explanation of what he called an "unconventional" action by his party.

Waving his fist, his face red and his voice breaking, Michel shouted at the Democrats: "I just happen to feel that my position is one that is shared by a majority of this House, and given a clean shot at it, will win notwithstanding your two efforts to try and beat us down. Just give us that chance."

Michel brought his GOP colleagues to their feet by adding: "I think the president deserves better treatment than what we would propose to be giving him here today by this sham charade."

In response, Foley said it was the Republicans' tactic that had thwarted a House vote on what he called the McCurdy "compromise."

The Democratic leaders later acknowledged that they were taken aback by the vociferous nature of Michel's attack. When the House considered contra aid in 1985, Michel clearly seemed uncomfortable defending the president's policy. But in 1986 Michel threw himself into the debate and led the partisan crusade against the Democrats.

Wright said he felt "sorry for" Michel because he was under pressure from the "young firebrands" in the party. "When he was bellowing like a bull, he was playing to the right wing," Wright said.

If the Republican maneuver surprised the Democratic leadership, it was a particularly rude shock to the Democrats who developed the McCurdy amendment. Early in the afternoon, they anticipated a victory for their proposal mandating a major change in Reagan's policy toward Nicaragua. The amendment would have used the lever of a second vote by Congress on contra aid to force Reagan to resume direct talks with the government in Managua.

Once the Republicans acted, McCurdy was prevented from offering his amendment to the supplemental.

The alternative voting procedure offered by the Republicans was no more attractive to McCurdy. It placed his amendment between two other proposals — making it "the ham in the sandwich," according to Foley, and all but eliminating its chance of adoption.

Liberals Support McCurdy

One outgrowth of the April 16 chaos in the House was the reprieve granted to many liberals who were prepared to support the McCurdy amendment, if with great reluctance.

The language of the McCurdy proposal was carefully crafted to attract votes from both factions of the Democratic Party: McCurdy and others who supported aid to the contras, but were uncomfortable with Reagan's partisan rhetoric or feared that his actions would lead to a war with Nicaragua; and liberals who opposed any aid to the contras and wanted to use diplomatic means to pressure Nicaragua.

The amendment would have imposed conditions on the $100 million in contra aid, such as demanding renewed negotiations and making it easy for Congress later to block the release of $70 million in military aid.

Because the McCurdy language was drafted as an amendment to Reagan's underlying request, supporters of contra aid could vote for it as a way of approving that aid with conditions, while aid opponents could vote for it as a way of restricting Reagan.

Liberal and church groups opposed to contra aid threw their support behind the McCurdy amendment and lobbied House Democrats on its behalf. In a letter to all House members, a coalition of those groups said a vote for McCurdy should be seen as a vote against contra aid — so long as it was followed by a vote against the underlying aid bill.

Even so, many Democrats were hesitant to commit themselves to the McCurdy amendment. At the opening of debate on April 16, leadership vote counts listed nearly 70 Democrats as undecided, many of whom said they did not understand the amendment. But leadership aides said most of the questions and doubts were cleared up by the time the House started voting on the Hamilton amendment. McCurdy's amendment would have passed by a decisive margin, the Democrats insisted.

While cheering McCurdy, liberal support for the amendment galled the Republicans. They faced a situation in which Reagan's request would have been amended by a coalition of Democrats, some of whom would turn around and vote against the underlying aid bill, even with the amendment. "Rather than play that game, we said, 'Screw it,' " explained Cheney, chairman of the Republican Policy Committee.

The Discharge-Petition Ploy

In snarling action on the contra aid bill, Republicans resorted to a high-risk tactic. They opted to pursue a complicated and extremely difficult course in which they sought signatures from a majority of the House — 218 members — to "discharge" or force action on contra aid under terms of debate they had written.

Those terms, included in a proposed rule for action (H Res 419) introduced by Republicans on April 14, were aimed at increasing the likelihood that the House would adopt the contra aid proposal (S J Res 283) passed in March by the

Senate and favored by the White House. That proposal approved the $100 million with few conditions.

The maneuver meant that contra aid would be delayed at least until May 12, the first day the GOP plan could be considered under House rules. Gaining the 218 signatures would be an uphill fight in the Democratic-controlled House. And if the discharge effort were to fall short, Reagan's request would face an even greater delay.

The Republicans said they were willing to run that risk rather than allow the Democrats to tie contra aid to the supplemental.

In a fiery speech to the House immediately after the surprise vote, Michel said: "We refuse to play the role assigned to us by the directors of this farce." The Republican plan, he said, "will eventually give the House a real chance to debate and vote on this very important issue standing alone without being married up to a proposition that is going nowhere."

Responding to such charges of unfairness, Democrats said the real issue was who controlled the House.

Democrats insisted that, as the majority party, they had the right and responsibility to set the terms of debate. Majority Leader Wright on April 15 said the rule proposed by the Democrats was fair, by definition, because it "allows the will of the majority of the members to prevail." The purpose of rules in the House, he said, was to "guarantee that a majority will not be tyrannized by a minority and that a minority will not be taken advantage of by a majority."

But on April 30, O'Neill sidetracked the Republicans' discharge petition by scheduling action on contra aid as part of another piece of legislation.

O'Neill agreed to allow consideration of the rebel assistance the week of June 9 on the fiscal 1987 military construction appropriations bill. O'Neill chose that legislation because it was relatively non-controversial, and contra aid would be "germane" or relevant because the bill dealt with foreign and defense matters. *(Military construction appropriations, p. 218)*

With O'Neill's promise in hand, a group of conservative and moderate Democrats did not sign a petition to force action on Reagan's request, and Republicans garnered only 159 of the 218 signatures they needed by the April 30 deadline. Only seven Democrats defied their leaders and signed; 30 Republicans failed to follow their leaders.

THIRD HOUSE ROUND: REAGAN WINS

The House on June 25 approved Reagan's contra aid proposal, giving the president a key foreign policy victory.

On a landmark 221-209 vote, the House agreed to a Republican-sponsored proposal allowing Reagan to provide $100 million to the contras, including up to $70 million in guns, ammunition and other military supplies. Fifty-one Democrats and all but 11 Republicans joined in supporting the aid. The margin was an almost identical reversal of the 210-222 vote by which the House in March rejected Reagan's request for aid to the contras. *(Vote 178, p. 54-H)*

Reagan prevailed over the Democratic leadership, which since 1983 had opposed direct military aid to the contras. In personal meetings at the White House, in telephone calls and in an unusually conciliatory television speech, Reagan successfully lobbied about two dozen undecided members of both parties.

The president was working from a strong position, since a clear majority of House members supported aid to the contras and the only issue was whether that aid would include military hardware. Leaders of both parties said Reagan convinced enough members that giving military assistance to the contras offered the best hope of convincing the Nicaraguan regime to negotiate seriously with its non-communist opposition and with other countries in the region.

The House attached contra aid to an otherwise unrelated fiscal 1987 military construction appropriations bill (HR 5052), which was passed by a 249-174 vote. *(Vote 182, p. 56-H)*

In addition to military aid, the bill provided $30 million for non-military aid to the contras. It also allowed the CIA to administer the aid and to help the contras militarily, a provision that caused surprisingly little controversy. Earlier CIA backing of the contras, especially the mining of Nicaraguan harbors, led to the cutoff of aid in 1984 and to a June 27 decision by the World Court that the United States violated international law in seeking to oust the Sandinistas.

The bill also provided $300 million in economic aid to Costa Rica, El Salvador, Guatemala and Honduras, on top of about $900 million already allocated for fiscal 1986. The money would be shifted from existing accounts: the contra aid from the Pentagon budget and the economic aid from other foreign assistance.

Emotionally drained after the House vote, Michel said: "I just think we did the right thing for the long haul."

But Democratic leaders warned that approval of the aid could be the first step toward direct U.S. military involvement in Nicaragua. A "proxy war" against the Managua regime had no chance of succeeding, said Foley, and so the United States was launching "a policy in Central America that could become irreversible and irrevocable."

A Trio of Options

When it took up the contra issue on June 25, the House faced three alternatives, only two of which had a real chance of winning a majority.

The first option, the one ultimately approved, was the Reagan-backed plan for contra aid and the $300 million in economic aid to other Central American countries. Its sponsors were Mickey Edwards, R-Okla., and Ike Skelton, D-Mo.

The second plan, sponsored by moderate and conservative Democrats led by McCurdy, would have provided the contra aid and $350 million in economic support for Central American nations. However, it would have barred military aid for the contras at least until Oct. 1, requiring votes in both the House and Senate to release the money. The House never voted on the McCurdy plan.

Option three, sponsored by Hamilton, would have provided $27 million in aid for Nicaraguan refugees and $5 million to promote peace talks, while barring direct aid to the contras. The House eventually rejected the Hamilton plan 183-245. *(Vote 179, p. 54-H)*

All three plans differed in major respects from Reagan's original February request for contra aid, with few strings attached.

While they opposed any aid for the contras, Speaker O'Neill and other Democratic leaders put their parliamentary power behind the McCurdy proposal as the only chance for curbing Reagan's use of the money. The leaders did so by drafting an unusual procedure incorporating the McCurdy plan into the military bill at the outset of House debate, thus eliminating the need for a direct vote on it.

Nevertheless, the McCurdy proposal faced severe political handicaps. Most important, it was nearly everyone's second choice. A majority of Democrats opposed any contra aid, which the plan contained, while a majority of Republicans balked at the conditions McCurdy placed on the aid.

Another fatal flaw was that the McCurdy plan offered only one major alternative to the Reagan-backed proposal: further delay on the overriding military aid question.

By requiring yet another vote for release of that aid in October, the McCurdy plan threatened to prolong an already lengthy process of congressional action, and many members were weary of voting on the issue. Republicans thus were able to portray the proposal as weak and indecisive. "The McCurdy language reaffirms to the world that we just don't know where we stand," Edwards said.

The Republicans took advantage of the situation, building an amendment that borrowed heavily from the most popular parts of the McCurdy plan and that compromised on other issues. For example, the Republicans adopted McCurdy's proposal for economic aid to the four pro-United States countries in Central America; that idea took hold in the House as a positive step to counterbalance military support of the contras.

The Republicans also included several mild conditions in their proposal that gave reluctant members enough reason to support the president. One condition cited by several members was a requirement for accounting standards on the contra money; it was drafted by Richard Ray, D-Ga., who had opposed contra aid earlier in the year.

Reagan Lobbying

The two days preceding House action on the issue were filled with anything but bipartisan spirit.

Shortly after noon on June 23, White House Chief of Staff Regan made a surprise telephone call to O'Neill, asking permission for Reagan to address the House the following day on contra aid. Startled by the request, O'Neill refused, but offered to host a joint session of the House and Senate to hear Reagan. Regan declined the counteroffer.

The White House and O'Neill then traded accusations. White House spokesman Larry Speakes said Reagan was "deeply disappointed" by O'Neill's refusal to allow the speech. O'Neill said Reagan was demanding an "unprecedented" chance to lobby the House, and he later said the request was a "cheap political trick" to embarrass him.

Unable to make his case in person, Reagan made his speech on June 24 from the Oval Office. The address plowed no new ground but was notable for its restrained rhetoric and its concession that many in Congress had "honest questions" about U.S. policy toward Nicaragua. *(Text, p. 22-D)*

However, Reagan's speech was undercut by two factors: only one television network, Cable News Network, carried it live; and a House Republican, Al McCandless, Calif., had demanded an inconsequential procedural vote just as Reagan was reading the opening paragraphs, so most members were rushing to the floor and missed the bulk of Reagan's remarks.

Reagan followed his speech with an intense lobbying campaign. O'Neill said on June 25 that Reagan had converted one Democrat who had never before spoken to a president. "He said, 'I thought I was talking to the pope. I'm so thrilled,' " O'Neill quoted the Democrat, whom he refused to name.

Getting a Majority

Because the House for years had been closely divided on the contra issue, attention focused on about two dozen members who had not staked out firm positions. Some were among the 16 Republicans who had voted against Reagan's aid request in March, and the rest were Democrats who admitted to having mixed feelings.

Reagan and Republican leaders leaned heavily on their colleagues, making the issue one of party unity.

Wylie, who opposed contra aid in March, said Reagan telephoned with assurances that the aid was necessary and would be well spent. Acknowledging that he had trouble naming the countries of Central America, Wylie said he deferred to Reagan's judgment: "He's a very persuasive fellow."

The White House effort paid off, with five Republicans switching to "yes" votes: Wylie, Frenzel, Hopkins, Rowland and Snowe.

The Republican campaign also produced new support among Democrats, including three — Ray, Lloyd and Albert G. Bustamante, Texas — who at one time had worked with McCurdy. Others were: Les Aspin, Wis.; Mario Biaggi, N.Y.; and Carroll Hubbard Jr., Ky.

Michel and the administration also headed off defections by several Democrats who had voted for contra aid in March but had expressed willingness to support McCurdy's proposal instead. Among them were three of McCurdy's Oklahoma colleagues: Glenn English, James R. Jones and Wes Watkins. During action on the Edwards amendment, all three withheld their votes until the outcome was clear, then voted with Reagan.

The most visible convert among the Democrats was Aspin, chairman of the Armed Services Committee. Aspin visited Central America in April and returned advocating at least some aid to the rebels. As the House debate began, Aspin said he opposed further delay.

Aspin's vote caused grumbling among liberals who had backed him for the Armed Services Committee post in a contested election in January 1985. O'Neill said the vote "will give him a hard time the next time he runs for chairman." O'Neill's prediction turned out to be true, as Aspin barely survived a challenge to his chairmanship in the 100th Congress.

Perhaps nothing better demonstrated the Republican determination to win on the issue than Michel's decision to call on George M. O'Brien, R-Ill., who until recently was hospitalized with a severe case of cancer and had been at home recuperating.

Shortly before the key vote, O'Brien, in a wheelchair, was pushed into the chamber, where he was greeted by a long, standing ovation. Struggling to a microphone, O'Brien thanked his colleagues for the "sense of fraternity" but said nothing about contras. Several members later said the incident broke the partisan tension — if only long enough for the vote.

In the end, O'Brien's vote was not needed, but Michel said he had wanted "every possible vote" on hand.

Left Out: The Liberals

For liberal Democrats, the latest round of action on contra aid was frustrating. Long accustomed to playing a major and sometimes decisive role on the issue, the liberals found themselves in a minority, forced to work with a small group of moderates and conservatives who held the balance of power. For some liberals, this frustration was made all the more intense by the Democratic leadership's decision to choose practical politics over ideology and lend its muscle to McCurdy.

Among those most vexed were Democrats on the Rules

$100 Million in Aid for the Contras . . .

The Senate and House, in voting to provide $100 million in military and non-military aid to the Nicaraguan contras, imposed different conditions. Following is an explanation of the major contra aid provisions approved by the Senate in S J Res 283 on March 27 and by the House in HR 5052 on June 25.

Money, Timing

Both measures gave congressional approval to President Reagan's request to provide $100 million for the contras by transferring it from Defense Department accounts. The money was to be available through Sept. 30, 1987. Of that amount, $30 million was earmarked for "humanitarian" or non-military aid; use of the remaining $70 million was left to the president's discretion, presumably for military aid. The aid could be administered by any U.S. agency, including the CIA.

The Senate bill would release $25 million of the aid immediately upon enactment; the remaining $75 million would be released in increments, beginning after the president reported to Congress in July on the status of negotiations and other issues in Central America.

The House bill divided the $100 million into three segments: $40 million to be provided immediately upon enactment, $20 million to be released after Oct. 15, and $40 million to be released after Feb. 15, 1987. In the latter two cases, the money was to be released after Reagan submitted reports on Central America.

In both bills, the initial aid dose could be used for: "humanitarian" or non-military supplies such as food and clothing; logistics advice and assistance; administrative expenses of the contras (under the label of "democratic political and diplomatic activities"); "air defense" equipment such as anti-aircraft missiles; and training in radio communications, collection and use of intelligence, logistics, and small-unit skills and tactics.

The House bill delayed actual delivery of weapons and ammunition until after Sept. 1. The type of weapons would be limited to a secret list that Reagan sent Congress on June 24. Sponsors of the bill said Reagan had agreed not to send "heavy" arms, which they would not define, until February 1987.

In the Senate bill, a presidential report to Congress after July 1 was to trigger the release of aid for military purposes. In that report — and in reports required by the House bill — the president would have to state that Central American countries had not concluded a comprehensive peace treaty, that the Nicaraguan government was not engaged in a "serious dialogue" with its internal opposition and had not lifted curbs on political activity and other freedoms, and that there was "no reasonable prospect" for reaching peace agreements.

Both bills gave Congress 15 days to review each presidential report and to block the use of remaining aid for military purposes by enacting a joint resolution of disapproval. The resolution would get priority action in both chambers, but it would be subject to an almost certain presidential veto, so a two-thirds majority in both houses would be needed to enact it into law. Even if Congress blocked use of the aid for military items, the president still would be free to use it for non-military aid.

The two bills contained similar or identical provisions on four other issues:

- The president had to report to Congress periodically on his actions to advance peace in Central America. Under the Senate bill, the reports were to be issued on a 90-day schedule, with each report freeing up $15 million for the contras. Under the House bill, the first report in October would free up $20 million and a second report in February 1987 would release the final $40 million.
- Before he could spend any money after the initial dose, the president would have to report to Congress on reform steps taken by the contras. *(Details, below)*
- Both bills barred military aid to the contras if the president reported to Congress that regional and internal Nicaraguan peace agreements had been reached, or if Congress enacted into law legislation blocking further aid.
- The president could request more aid beyond the $100 million at any time and Congress would be forced to act on the request using special expedited procedures.

Economic Aid

The House bill provided $300 million for economic aid to Costa Rica, El Salvador, Guatemala and Honduras. The money would be transferred from unspent foreign aid accounts; the accounts were not specified in the bill, but the administration had said about $200 million would come from unused aid for African famine relief. Of that amount, $100 million would have to be obligated by Sept. 30, but the rest would be available through fiscal 1987, ending Sept. 30, 1987.

The bill did not set specific amounts for each country. However, State Department officials told members of Congress that Guatemala and Costa Rica had the most urgent need for infusions of new U.S. economic aid.

The House bill also directed the administration to prepare a plan to "fully fund" the recommendations of a presidential commission, which called in 1984 for a massive, long-term aid program for Central America. Also in keeping with the commission's recommendations, the bill set aside $750,000 for establishment of a Central American Development Organization, which the commission proposed as a regional body to coordinate aid to the region. *(Commission, 1984 Almanac p. 93)*

The Senate bill contained no provisions on economic aid to Central America.

Negotiations

In addition to affirming U.S. support for the regional Contadora negotiations, both measures committed the United States to conducting direct "discussions" — not "negotiations" — with the Sandinista government of Nicaragua.

But both bills affirmed support for Reagan's position that the United States should resume talks with Nicaragua only if the government there "simultaneously engages in a serious dialogue with representatives of all elements of the Nicaraguan democratic opposition." The Sandinistas had refused to negotiate with the contras, and so the administration since 1985 had refused to talk with the Sandinistas.

. . . The House, Senate Bills Compared

Both bills allocated up to $2 million to help Costa Rica, El Salvador, Guatemala and Honduras participate in regional peace talks.

Monitoring Commission

Under both bills, Congress would monitor the president's actions during the early stages of the contra aid program by establishing a five-member commission. The Speaker and minority leader of the House and the majority and minority leaders of the Senate each would appoint one member; those four commission members by unanimous vote would select a fifth member as chairman.

The commission would report on peace talks and other activities in Nicaragua, and on reform steps taken by the contras. The deadline for the report was June 30 in the Senate bill and Jan. 31, 1987, in the House bill.

The Senate bill required the commission to disband 30 days after issuing its report, while the House bill provided an indefinite charter for the commission. The Senate bill also provided $400,000 from the Senate's contingency fund for commission expenses, and the House bill required the State Department to pay the expenses.

CIA, Military Involvement

Both measures allowed expanded involvement with the contras by U.S. intelligence agencies, especially the CIA.

Under several existing laws, the CIA could give the contras intelligence information and advice — but it could not get involved in military operations or provide the contras with training in military tactics. The House and Senate bills lifted the prohibitions, essentially by allowing the CIA to work with the contras in planning military strategy and by administering the U.S. aid program.

Each bill carefully skirted the issue of opening up the CIA contingency fund for aid to the contras. Reagan began aiding the contras in 1981-82 by tapping the CIA's "covert" fund, but Congress had prohibited nearly all direct CIA financing of the contras since 1984. Secret portions of the existing intelligence authorizations law (PL 99-169), which expired on Sept. 30, continued that ban on CIA funding.

The House and Senate contra aid bills stated that they did not authorize the president to give any aid to the contras other than the $100 million transferred from the Pentagon. By itself, that provision did not prohibit such aid; it merely stated that Congress was not lifting the existing restraints.

The State Department in March issued a statement saying that Reagan would not give the contras any aid except for whatever Congress authorized. However, that statement left open the possibility that Reagan could ask Congress to authorize more than the $100 million, either through the CIA or through an openly acknowledged program.

Congress addressed the issue of CIA covert aid in its intelligence agency funding bill for fiscal year 1987. *(Story, p. 383)*

Both bills limited involvement with the contras by U.S. military personnel. The most important limit was that U.S. military and civilian employees were barred from providing advice, training or logistical support to the contras inside Nicaragua. The House bill also barred all U.S. government personnel from providing any training or other services for the contras within 20 miles of the Nicaraguan border in either Honduras or Costa Rica.

Both bills contained a disclaimer stating that they were not to be construed as authorizing U.S. armed forces to engage in combat against Nicaragua. However, neither bill directly banned U.S. combat against Nicaragua.

Contra Reform

Concern about disunity among and reported human rights abuses by the contras prompted both houses to demand reforms as a condition of U.S. aid.

The two bills contained identical provisions barring aid to any group that "retains in its ranks any individual who has been found to engage in" gross human rights abuses, drug smuggling or significant misuse of public or private funds.

Enforcement of that ban on aid was left up to the administration.

The bills also required the president to report to Congress on the status of reforms in the principal contra organization, the United Nicaraguan Opposition. Among those reforms were: broadening and coordinating the leadership, eliminating human rights abuses, and putting military forces under civilian control.

Both bills earmarked $3 million for training and other programs to promote respect for human rights by the contras. Officials said some of that money would subsidize a human rights commission created by the United Nicaraguan Opposition.

The legislation from both houses included several provisions designed to encourage unity among the contras and to broaden the number of contra groups aided by the United States. Most of the earlier U.S. aid had gone to the Nicaraguan Democratic Force, the largest of six major contra groups. Under both bills, however, $5 million each was set aside for two other groups: an army of Indians in northern Nicaragua called the Misurasata, and a small coalition operating out of Costa Rica called the Southern Opposition Bloc.

Both bills declared that it was U.S. policy to aid "all" Nicaraguan opposition groups that were committed to democracy and that respected human rights.

In addition to encouraging unity among the contras, the House bill contained one provision to promote unity in the Reagan administration: It decreed that the secretary of state or his designee "shall be responsible for policy guidance, coordination and supervision" of U.S. actions toward Nicaragua and the contras. House members included that provision in response to complaints that too many U.S. agencies were involved with Nicaragua policy but no one was in charge.

The House bill also required the agency administering the contra aid program to establish standards to ensure that the funds were "fully accounted for and used exclusively for the purposes" intended. The standards were to include: segregation of accounts, monitoring of deliveries, and keeping of complete records to be available to U.S. agencies for auditing.

Committee, who normally could be counted on to support the leadership. During an all-day session June 24 on the floor procedures for debating the issue, several Democrats openly challenged the leadership's backing of McCurdy. One, Tony P. Hall, D-Ohio, said the McCurdy plan "goes so far over that the other side can win, even if they lose."

Foley privately quieted the objections of some committee members, and the panel approved the leadership game plan by voice vote.

Economic Aid

The one new element in the June 25 debate over contra aid was the apparent widespread support for a dose of economic aid to bolster the four pro-U.S. governments in Central America.

McCurdy forged that support almost single-handedly. For months he talked about the need for more U.S. backing of Costa Rica, El Salvador, Guatemala and Honduras — all of which had elected presidents since 1984. In late May, McCurdy led a group of 13 House members on a quick trip to Central America, and nearly all members returned committed to McCurdy's idea for more aid.

In negotiations on contra aid proposals, McCurdy suggested a $500 million aid boost — on top of about $900 mllion in military and economic aid already budgeted for fiscal 1986. Republican leaders responded by agreeing to a $100 million increase.

The two sides eventually ended up at about the same point: $350 million for McCurdy and other Democrats and $300 million for the GOP-sponsored proposal. McCurdy called the aid a "bargain" because it would promote countries that supported the thrust of U.S. policy against Nicaragua.

The proposal was not entirely without controversy. David R. Obey, D-Wis., chairman of the Appropriations Subcommittee on Foreign Operations, said the plan called for "money which is wasted, which is poured down the rathole."

Amendments

After adopting the Republican contra aid proposal, the House acted on two amendments.

The House adopted, 215-212, an amendment by Robert J. Mrazek, D-N.Y., that would bar U.S. personnel from providing training or other services to the contras in Honduras or Costa Rica within 20 miles of the border with Nicaragua. *(Vote 181, p. 54-H)*

Mrazek said he worried that stationing U.S. personnel near the border might provoke attacks, thus giving Reagan a "Gulf of Tonkin pretext" to send troops into Nicaragua.

By a surprisingly wide margin of 198-225, the House rejected an amendment by Barnes that would have barred distribution of aid to the contras until Reagan fully accounted for the $27 million in non-military aid appropriated in 1985. *(Vote 180, p. 54-H)*

Barnes, chairman of the Foreign Affairs Subcommittee on Western Hemisphere Affairs, charged that bank records subpoenaed by his panel showed that some of the $27 million may have been diverted to improper uses.

But Republicans brandished a State Department report that denied some allegations of misused aid. *(Box, p. 396)*

In related action June 25, the Senate Foreign Relations Committee rejected an effort by John Kerry, D-Mass., to obtain subpoena power for an investigation into alleged abuses by the contras. Instead, the panel agreed to an informal staff "inquiry."

BACK TO THE SENATE

The House's June 25 acceptance of the modified contra aid package sent the issue back to the Senate, which had approved Reagan's original proposal on March 27. Because it was part of a new bill, military construction appropriations, contra aid became fair game for senators' efforts to kill it by delay or filibuster.

Ultimately, the Senate approved the $100 million contra package by a narrow margin and after an intensely partisan debate. The Aug. 12-13 action came as part of an elaborate arrangement by which the Senate also dealt with another highly controversial foreign policy issue: South Africa sanctions. *(South Africa, p. 359)*

After voting to shut off filibusters on both issues Aug. 13, the Senate passed the military construction bill, to which contra aid had been attached. The aid included $70 million for military aid and $30 million for non-military supplies. The bill also included a provision originated by moderate House Democrats: $300 million in additional economic assistance for Costa Rica, El Salvador, Guatemala and Honduras.

Early Maneuvering

To speed action on the bill, Senate Republican leaders decided in July to accept nearly all the contra aid provisions voted by the House and backed by the administration. One exception, according to Dole, was the House amendment barring U.S. government personnel from aiding the contras in Honduras or Costa Rica within 20 miles of the Nicaraguan border. "That's unacceptable," Dole said.

Meanwhile, a group of 15 senators — all Democrats except Weicker — met privately on July 14 and agreed to plan a filibuster against contra aid. A key aide later said the senators were not committed to a full-scale filibuster aimed at stopping the bill, but rather to conducting an "educational" campaign on the perils of Reagan's policy toward Nicaragua.

As the strategy sessions and negotiations continued in ensuing weeks, the contra and South Africa issues became intertwined. Further complicating the scenario was an effort by David L. Boren, D-Okla., to get action on a bill limiting campaign donations by political action committees. *(South Africa sanctions, p. 359; PAC bill, p. 42)*

The deadlock over the controversial bills was broken in August, when Senate leaders agreed to a complicated strategy on consideration of both contra aid and South Africa sanctions. Under the plan, the Senate had to invoke cloture on both issues; if cloture had failed on either one, the Senate would have had to devote as much of its August recess as necessary to resolving those matters. *(Box, p. 412)*

Two Key Votes

The Senate approved contra aid on two key votes: on Aug. 12, a 54-46 tabling of an amendment by Sasser, that would have killed the entire aid program; and on Aug. 13, approval by 62-37 of a motion to invoke cloture, or limit debate, on the bill. *(Votes 211, 220, pp. 37-S, 38-S)*

Those votes were ratified Aug. 13 with formal approval of the contra aid and economic aid titles of the military construction bill by a 53-47 vote, and final passage of the entire bill, 59-41. The 53-47 vote differed from the previous day's 54-46 vote on the same issue because of a switch by James Abdnor, R-S.D. *(Votes 229, 230, pp. 39-S, 40-S)*

As expected, the motion to invoke cloture on the contra issue failed on its first attempt on Aug. 13, 59-40. The missing senator was Claiborne Pell, D-R.I., who routinely voted to invoke cloture as a matter of principle. However, Pell was one of the most avid opponents of contra aid, so he sat out the vote rather than give a go-ahead for the bill. *(Vote 218, p. 38-S)*

An hour and a half later, switches by a handful of senators brought a reversal and new life for the contra program. By its 62-37 vote, the Senate invoked cloture, killing any chance for an extended filibuster and guaranteeing passage of the bill.

Pell supported cloture on the second vote, as did three senators who had opposed it the first time around: Mark Andrews, R-N.D.; Robert T. Stafford, R-Vt.; and Edward Zorinsky, D-Neb. Strom Thurmond, R-S.C., did not vote the second time.

Andrews and Stafford were among several liberal Republicans who long had opposed contra aid, but who agreed to support the cloture petition to speed the bill and to guarantee action on South Africa.

On the critical 54-46 vote Aug. 12, the Democrats lost their best shot at killing the entire contra package. The Senate, by that vote, tabled the Sasser amendment that would have stricken all contra aid provisions from the military construction bill.

The vote was identical to the March 27 margin by which the Senate first approved Reagan's request for $100 million — with the exception of a switch by Daniel J. Evans, R-Wash. Evans said he still opposed contra aid, but supported the companion provision to give $300 million in economic aid to other countries in the region.

A 'Clean' Bill

Because they feared reopening the contra issue in conference committee with the House, Senate Republican leaders pulled out all the stops to ensure that the bill passed with no amendments.

Democrats tried 15 times to amend the contra aid provisions — first with major changes such as putting strict limits on CIA involvement in the program, then with relatively minor proposals that under other circumstances would have provoked little controversy. Each time, a nearly united Republican Party staved off the Democrats.

The Democrats sought to amend the contra aid section of the bill so it would be subject to negotiations by a House-Senate conference — and thus possibly to a watering down or further delay of Reagan's request.

As reported by the Appropriations Committee, the bill contained the identical text of the House-passed contra aid plan. If approved by the Senate with no changes, that part of the bill would be immune from conference action. However, the rest of the Senate military construction bill had to go to conference committee because it differed from the House measure.

Republicans openly challenged the Democrats for offering "killer amendments" solely for the purpose of forcing the contra aid provisions into conference. "They are seeking to do by indirection what they could not do by direction," said Lugar, chairman of the Foreign Relations Committee.

Lugar and Majority Leader Dole used the killer amendment argument to beat back all the Democrats' amendments.

CIA Involvement

Senate Democrats raised one issue that their House counterparts seemingly had abandoned: CIA involvement in the contra war.

Administration officials had made clear for months that Reagan would turn most operational aspects of the contra aid program over to the CIA. The agency was responsible for U.S. funding of the guerrillas from late 1981 until Congress suspended military aid in 1984 following revelations that CIA agents had supervised the mining of Nicaraguan harbors.

The House-passed contra aid bill allowed Reagan to reinstate CIA involvement with the rebels. It also opened the possibility that the agency could tap its contingency fund to give the contras arms and other supplies beyond the $100 million.

In spite of past controversy about the CIA's role in the Nicaraguan war, House members did not raise the issue when their chamber supported contra aid in June.

But in the Senate, Democrats jumped on the question of putting the CIA back into Nicaragua.

Saying he was seeking to prevent the administration from using "backdoor" means, such as the CIA, to finance the contras, Minority Leader Byrd on Aug. 12 offered an amendment requiring that any aid be specifically authorized by Congress. In particular, it barred use of the CIA contingency fund unless Congress passed legislation approving it.

The Senate tabled Byrd's amendment on a largely party-line vote of 51-47. *(Vote 213, p. 37-S)*

Byrd failed again in a second attempt on his amendment the next day: The Senate tabled it 52-48. *(Vote 228, p. 39-S)*

Byrd cited a report in the July 7 issue of *Newsweek* magazine that the CIA secretly was preparing to back the contras with an additional $400 million worth of logistical, intelligence and other aid.

"If the administration has a secret plan, let them come in the front door here," Byrd said, pointing to the main door at the rear of the Senate chamber. If the administration did not have a "hidden program," Byrd said, the amendment would not cause it any harm.

Lugar insisted that the intent of Byrd's amendment was "identical" to language already in the bill. That language said the president was not authorized to provide additional assistance without congressional approval.

But Byrd noted that the bill's language was "a long way" from actually barring covert CIA aid.

The votes on Byrd's amendment were the closest the Democrats came to forcing a major change in the bill. It was close because many Democrats who had voted with the Republicans on the underlying proposal stuck by Byrd, while most Republicans who opposed contra aid voted with their party's leadership. One Republican, John H. Chafee, R.I., waited until the last moment to vote with the Democrats.

The Senate on Aug. 13 rejected yet another effort to restrain CIA involvement: an amendment sponsored by Leahy of the Intelligence panel. Tabled 57-42, the amendment would have barred CIA participation in the contra war. *(Vote 221, p. 38-S)*

Leahy said the administration should be focusing the CIA's attention on arms control, terrorism and other issues, "and not sending them down to some sordid little war."

It took years to rebuild the agency's reputation from the scandals of the mid-1970s, Leahy said, but renewed CIA management of the contra war would come at a "very high" price.

Senate's Climate of Partisanship Yields . . .

It took more than two weeks to negotiate, sometimes in closed-door meetings among senators and staff, other times on the floor of the Senate, with tempers flaring and the traditional senatorial courtesy frayed almost to the breaking point. When completed, it took nearly an hour for the majority leader to read aloud to his colleagues, and when printed in the *Congressional Record* it consumed three pages.

It was so complicated that many senators admitted they could not understand it even after two or three readings.

It was not a piece of legislation, and it will never enter the law books. It was merely a "unanimous consent agreement," in most cases a routine procedure by which the Senate agrees without objection on a schedule for conducting its business.

But when the Senate prepared to take up the issues of sanctions against South Africa and military aid to the "contra" guerrillas in Nicaragua, there was no unanimous consent for anything. The two questions, tinged with partisanship, were among the most emotional and vexing facing Congress, so no one was surprised when the Senate tied itself in knots just trying to figure out how to deal with them.

The root of the Senate's problem: An overwhelming majority of senators in both parties, certainly more than the 60 needed to shut off a filibuster, wanted to pass legislation imposing sanctions against the white-minority government of South Africa. However, only a bare majority, nearly all of them Republicans, wanted to give President Reagan $100 million to aid the Nicaraguan contras.

Dole vs. Byrd

Enter Majority Leader Robert Dole, R-Kan., acting on behalf of the contra assistance, and Minority Leader Robert C. Byrd, D-W.Va., acting against the contra aid and on behalf of South Africa sanctions. Never on the best of terms, the two men on July 24 began a series of direct and indirect negotiations that were aimed at producing an agreement for the Senate to consider both issues.

Each leader had leverage. Dole's advantages were his prerogative as majority leader to schedule legislation and his willingness to threaten the cherished mid-August recess if the Senate did not complete action on the contras. Byrd's bargaining chip was the knowledge that he had the votes to shut off a filibuster against the South Africa bill and that Dole was uncertain whether he had the votes to stop one on the contras.

In the middle of negotiations, a third actor and issue entered the scene: David L. Boren, D-Okla., who reminded Dole that he had promised action in 1986 on a proposal to curtail contributions to congressional campaigns by political action committees.

Legislative Skirmishing

Meanwhile, the Senate debated two major pieces of legislation — an extension of the federal debt limit and a 1987 defense authorization bill — both of which were candidates for amendments on the South Africa and contra issues. Sen. Edward M. Kennedy, D-Mass., a prime sponsor of South Africa sanctions, repeatedly threatened to raise the issue on those bills, angering Dole.

The negotiations among Dole, Byrd and other senators proceeded slowly during the week of July 28, as the Senate worked on the debt bill. By Aug. 1, Dole and Byrd had reached a partial agreement to finish work on the debt bill but to stop short of final passage so it could be held in reserve for amendments on the contras and South Africa.

The next week, the Senate turned to the defense bill. On Aug. 4, Dole surprised Democrats by introducing a

Dave Durenberger, R-Minn., the Intelligence Committee chairman, opposed the amendment even though he had criticized CIA involvement in the contra war. Unless the agency managed the program, he said, Congress would not get reliable intelligence information about the conflict.

U.S. Troops

The Senate retained one House-passed provision that had been strongly opposed by the administration. It banned any U.S. agency from providing aid, directly or indirectly, to the contras in Honduras or Costa Rica within 20 miles of the border with Nicaragua.

However, the Senate defeated efforts by Democrats to bar introduction of U.S. combat troops into Nicaragua, or to prohibit U.S. personnel anywhere in Honduras or Costa Rica.

Originally sponsored by Rep. Mrazek, the 20-mile limit provision was adopted by the House 215-212.

Mrazek said his amendment was not intended to bar intelligence-gathering, and he portrayed it as merely an extension of the administration's own rules that prohibited U.S. military personnel in Honduras from operating within seven miles of the Nicaraguan border.

But administration officials complained that the provision was an unconstitutional restriction on the president, and they insisted it would damage the U.S. ability to give effective aid to the contras. Lugar said the amendment was "not wise," but admitted that the Senate leadership had no choice but to accept it as part of the strategy to duplicate the House bill.

The bill contained another House-originated provision barring U.S. military or other personnel from entering Nicaragua to provide training, advice or logistical support to the contras.

The Senate rejected two amendments to place further restrictions on U.S. troops. They were by:

- Kennedy to prohibit introduction of U.S. troops into Nicaragua unless Congress had approved in advance or the president had reported to Congress that doing so was necessary to protect the lives or property of U.S. citizens. Tabled 60-40. *(Vote 212, p. 37-S)*
- Tom Harkin, D-Iowa, to bar U.S. military and government personnel from aiding the contras anywhere in Honduras or Costa Rica. Rejected 32-67. *(Vote 215, p. 38-S)*

. . . An Agreement of Unusual Complexity

petition to invoke cloture (shut off debate) on that measure. If successful, it would have precluded senators from offering other amendments, such as South Africa and contras, to that bill.

In response, Byrd on Aug. 5 offered a South Africa amendment to the defense bill, including with it a cloture petition that, if passed, would have blocked a contra amendment. Furious, Dole countered with his own amendment coupling South Africa and contra aid, also along with a cloture petition. Although Dole claimed that Byrd sprang his amendment with no warning, Dole clearly was prepared with his own amendment and cloture petition signed by 17 senators.

The two leaders then engaged in an acrimonious finger-pointing contest over who had violated the spirit of the negotiations. Others said they feared that the dispute damaged the possibility of getting an agreement, but staffers and senators continued work.

Byrd took an unusual step on Aug. 6, releasing to reporters a description of his latest proposal for an agreement; that prompted a flurry of leaks, with each side attempting to portray its position in the best light.

As negotiations proceeded, the Senate repeatedly established times for, then postponed, votes on cloture. The Senate took only one such vote, on Aug. 6, with Dole's original cloture petition falling seven votes short of the 60 needed to end debate.

The Senate was facing an "invisible filibuster," said Alan Cranston, D-Calif. Nobody was actually filibustering either South Africa or contra aid, but opponents on each side stood ready to do so, jeopardizing the recess.

Something for Everyone

By Saturday, Aug. 9, with the defense bill still on the floor, Dole, Byrd, and a half-dozen other senators directly involved reached an agreement. Dole read it to the Senate shortly after 1 p.m., admitting at the end that it "may be somewhat confusing." Senators laughed, but some also had last-minute qualms, and so Dole and Byrd again tinkered with the text in hopes of satisfying everyone.

In essence, the agreement provided that the Senate would: debate the Boren campaign finance proposal and the contra aid on Aug. 11; vote on the Boren proposal and amendments to contra aid on Aug. 12; vote on cloture petitions on both South Africa and the contras on Aug. 13; and finish both issues during the rest of the week if cloture was invoked on both, or use as much of the recess as necessary if cloture was not invoked on both. Somehow along with those votes, the Senate was to consider up to 93 amendments on South Africa (most offered by Republicans) and 31 amendments on contra aid (most offered by Democrats).

Senators on all sides said the agreement was fair, and praised both Dole and Byrd for leading the negotiations producing it. Ted Stevens, R-Alaska, who had fought Dole for the majority leadership, called it "a monumental agreement, the best one I have ever seen in my 18 years here."

Both Dole and Byrd got what they wanted. But Dole, by virtue of his leadership clout, may have gotten the most. The key clause of the agreement — inserted at Dole's insistence — provided that the Senate had to invoke cloture on both South Africa and the contras before it could pass either bill. That meant Democrats who opposed contra aid would have to give up a filibuster against it if they wanted to pass the South Africa sanctions.

The strategy worked, and on Aug. 13 the Senate invoked cloture on both bills. But while a substantial accomplishment, the unanimous consent agreement was not the finished product. The product was to be the legislation that, for a while, had become secondary to the Senate's need to straitjacket itself.

Charges of Abuses

In its debate and votes, the Senate dealt with another perennial issue: charges that the contras had committed human rights abuses and other crimes, especially against civilians in Nicaragua. The Reagan administration and contra spokesmen had rejected most of the charges, but reports of abuses persisted.

The Senate rejected two amendments:

- By Dodd to bar use of funds in the bill for planning, directing, executing or supporting military actions in, over or off the shore of Nicaragua that were directed against civilians or that would likely result in the loss of civilian lives. Tabled 51-47. *(Vote 214, p. 38-S)*
- By Pell, establishing a $10 million fund to compensate civilian victims of contra abuses. The amendment would have established a bipartisan commission to investigate allegations of contra abuses and to make awards to victims. Rejected 17-82. *(Vote 216, p. 38-S)*

Senate action on those amendments took place amidst a continuing effort by Kerry to get the Foreign Relations Committee to investigate contra abuses.

A member of the panel, Kerry had tried to get Lugar to issue subpoenas to obtain administration documents on the matter and to compel testimony by reluctant witnesses. Lugar in the past refused, saying the committee should conduct only an informal "review" of charges and should confine its focus to foreign policy issues.

But Lugar said on Aug. 12 that the Justice Department had not been "forthcoming" in providing information requested by the committee, and he said he would consider subpoenaing information if necessary.

Economic Aid

Virtually ignored in the debate was the one major provision originated by House Democrats: the $300 million economic aid fund for Costa Rica, El Salvador, Guatemala and Honduras.

The fund had been advocated by McCurdy and other moderate Democrats in the House, and adopted by the House Republican leadership.

The administration also had embraced the fund, while saying that overall budget constraints would make it difficult to pay the money. Most of the money was to come from an unspent $225 million fiscal 1986 appropriation for

African famine relief, officials said.

To prevent total depletion of the famine fund, the Senate Appropriations Committee added a provision to the bill that appeared to restore the entire $300 million in famine and other funds. However, the net effect of the amendment was to provide only $75 million in restored money for famine relief.

Complaining about the raid on the famine relief account, John Melcher, D-Mont., on Aug. 13 offered an amendment that would have stricken a provision in the bill authorizing the administration to use that account for the economic aid. His amendment was tabled 51-49. *(Vote 217, p. 38-S)*

Other Amendments

The Senate on Aug. 13 also considered amendments:

- By Byrd, to earmark $450,000 of the aid funds to assist the Nicaraguan opposition newspaper *La Prensa*. The Managua government closed the paper shortly after the June 25 House vote to aid the contras. Tabled 57-43. *(Vote 223, p. 39-S)*

Republicans said that amendment — like others — was a "killer" one because it would force a conference on contra aid.

But Byrd said: "Let's don't let freedom of the press perish because we don't want to go to conference."

- By Kerry, to terminate the contra aid program if the countries of Central America — including Nicaragua — signed a "Contadora" peace treaty including provisions outlined in April by Costa Rica, El Salvador, Guatemala and Honduras.

Kerry sought to attach his amendment to the title of the bill dealing with economic aid to those countries, thus avoiding the "killer amendment" charge by Republicans. GOP leaders nevertheless complained that the amendment would restrict unduly Reagan's diplomatic leverage. Rejected 46-54. *(Vote 224, p. 39-S)*

- By Joseph R. Biden Jr., D-Del., barring transfer of the contra aid until the United States proposed to hold direct bilateral talks with Nicaragua's Sandinista government aimed at promoting a Contadora peace pact. The Reagan administration wanted the Sandinistas to negotiate with the contras. Tabled 54-45. *(Vote 222, p. 39-S)*
- By Paul Simon, D-Ill., to require the president to give the comptroller general a full accounting each month of the funds provided to the contras, and to require the comptroller general to analyze for Congress each presidential report. Tabled 57-43. *(Vote 225, p. 39-S)*
- By Simon, to provide $50 million for drought relief and agricultural development in Africa. The money was to be taken from the $300 million earmarked in the bill for economic aid to Central American countries. Tabled 64-36. *(Vote 226, p. 39-S)*
- By Harkin, to transfer half of the $100 million in contra aid to drought relief for American farmers. Tabled 58-41. *(Vote 227, p. 39-S)*

Slippery Slope

Senators on both sides said the $100 million probably would be just the latest installment in a long-term U.S. effort to oust the Nicaraguan government.

Democrats argued that the eventual cost of the war could be billions of dollars and thousands of men. The bill before the Senate was putting the United States on a "slippery slope" to direct military involvement, just as in Vietnam, they said.

But Republicans insisted that funding the contras in 1986 would be cheaper than fighting a direct war later with U.S. troops.

Invoking words and symbols of the Vietnam War, Democrats compared the contra aid legislation to the 1964 Gulf of Tonkin resolution, by which Congress gave its blanket assent to the escalation of U.S. involvement in Southeast Asia.

"We're going precisely down the path that this country traveled in Vietnam," Sasser said. During a trip to Honduras — where the United States managed the contra war — Sasser said he encountered Pentagon and State Department personnel who had served in Vietnam.

They acknowledged the similarities between the two wars, he noted.

And Harkin pointed to the administration's use of military advisers and trainers for the contras as an indication of its intention to fight a full-scale war against Nicaragua.

Leahy said he believed Reagan's protestations that he did not want to send U.S. troops into Central America. But, he said, "events have their own way of building their own momentum and making decisions for us."

Republicans acknowledged a superficial parallel between Vietnam and Nicaragua, but insisted that Reagan and Congress both had carefully imposed limits on direct U.S. involvement in Nicaragua to prevent an escalation there.

Lugar, for example, noted that Reagan had not allowed U.S. troops to engage in combat with Nicaraguans, and the bill itself was drawn to avoid repeating the congressional blank check of the Tonkin Gulf resolution.

The first step on the slippery slope to war was not support of the contras, Lugar said, but "ineffective support" of them. Abandoning them, he said, would lead to a "one-party Marxist Nicaragua, a Nicaragua that subverts its neighbors, that makes developing possibilities around Nicaragua virtually impossible," and eventually to Soviet bases there.

"What are the stoppers then?" he asked.

Lugar conceded the Democrats' point that the $100 million was not enough to oust the Nicaraguan government. That money would make "a substantial impact" on Nicaragua, he said, but it would "not be enough to complete the task." Lugar refused, however, to speculate on the ultimate cost to American taxpayers of the war against Nicaragua. ∎

Special Report: The Iran-Contra Affair

In a foreign policy blunder that turned into a scandal, the Reagan administration late in 1986 made the startling revelation that it had been secretly selling arms to Iran, with some of the profits possibly diverted to the U.S.-backed "contra" guerrillas in Nicaragua.

Disclosing the Iran-contra link Nov. 25, President Reagan said he had not been "fully informed" of it at the time. Two key figures in the affair were immediate staff casualties: Lt. Col. Oliver L. North, a National Security Council (NSC) aide, was fired for his role in the arms dealings, and his boss, national security adviser Vice Adm. John M. Poindexter, resigned. Three months later, Reagan replaced his chief of staff.

A week later, Reagan named Frank C. Carlucci, a Washington insider, to succeed Poindexter. Carlucci became Reagan's fifth national security adviser in six years.

The two controversial policies — selling arms to Iran, apparently in exchange for American hostages, and arming the contras, possibly illegally — triggered multiple investigations.

To conduct "a comprehensive review" of the NSC's operations, Reagan on Nov. 26 named a three-man committee, headed by former Sen. John Tower, R-Texas. Other committee members were former senator and secretary of state Edmund S. Muskie, and President Ford's national security adviser, Brent Scowcroft.

On Capitol Hill, the Senate and House set up special committees to investigate all aspects of the Iran arms sale and the reported diversion of profits from those sales to the contras. Members of the two panels were appointed Dec. 16-17; the panels were constituted officially at the beginning of the 100th Congress in January 1987. Daniel K. Inouye, D-Hawaii, was named to chair the Senate committee and Lee H. Hamilton, D-Ind., was selected to chair its House counterpart. *(Box, p. 423)*

But before those panels could get under way, the Senate and House Intelligence committees and the House Foreign Affairs Committee held hearings into the Iran-contra arms dealings. The Senate Intelligence panel, after news leaks and under administration pressure to make its findings public, released a report Jan. 29, 1987. The report chronicled the administration's arms-for-hostages dealings but drew no conclusions. *(Details, p. 436; chronology of events, p. 448)*

Meanwhile, a three-judge panel Dec. 19 appointed Lawrence E. Walsh as independent counsel to investigate possible illegalities. Walsh was a former federal judge and president of the American Bar Association. His investigative charter was much broader than the Reagan administration had sought; under it, he was looking into possible irregularities in support for the contras dating from 1984. *(Box, p. 426)*

And at the White House, Reagan appointed David Abshire, the U.S. ambassador to NATO, to coordinate the administration's responses to all probes in the arms affair. Abshire was given Cabinet rank and was serving as a special counselor to the president.

Fallout on Capitol Hill

The Iran-contra scandal sent Reagan into the final two years of his presidency with his credibility damaged and the competence of his administration questioned. Although supporters rallied to him, and critics said they did not want to see a crippled presidency, many in Washington agreed that Reagan's ability to govern had been severely damaged.

"There's something wrong if the president doesn't know what is going on in the basement of the White House," said Senate Democratic leader Robert C. Byrd, W.Va.

The diversion of the Iranian arms money also was likely to make it more difficult for Reagan to continue arming the contras. Reagan had planned to ask Congress in 1987 for several hundred million dollars for the guerrillas, who were battling the Managua regime, but scaled back his request in the wake of the scandal. *(Contra aid, p. 394)*

The administration's actions toward Iran and the contras prompted a wholesale review of laws on the conduct of foreign policy, with the prospect that Congress would move in 1987 to strengthen some of those laws.

The most likely prospect for congressional action seemed to be a toughening of requirements that the president consult with Capitol Hill before, and even after, authorizing secret operations such as the sale of arms to Iran. Members of both parties were outraged that Reagan refused for more than 10 months to tell anyone in Congress — even his closest allies — about the dealings with Iran.

Reagan had approved covert arms sales on Jan. 17, 1986, but ordered CIA Director William J. Casey not to tell Congress about them. He later rescinded that secrecy order, officials said. *(Text, p. 418)*

For Congress, the notification issue was uppermost because it involved ancient disputes running to the very heart of the executive-legislative relationship. Members of Congress said they needed information to do their jobs and, just as important, they insisted that Hill involvement beforehand could lead to better presidential decision making.

In the Iran case, congressional leaders said that Reagan's refusal to notify them violated the spirit, and possibly the letter, of several laws. *(Details, p. 421)*

Tower Board Reports, Regan Resigns

The Tower commission issued a report of its investigation of the Iran-contra affair and the NSC's role on Feb. 26, 1987. The board said Reagan had lost control of his staff, which had mismanaged the Iran-contra policies.

"I believe that the president was poorly advised and

poorly served," Tower said. "I think that he should have followed up more and monitored this operation more closely. I think he was not aware of a lot of the things that were going on and the way the operation was structured and who was involved in it. He very clearly didn't understand all that."

Following up on Feb. 27, Reagan selected former Senate Majority Leader Howard H. Baker Jr., R-Tenn., as his new chief of staff, replacing Donald T. Regan, who had been sharply criticized by the Tower panel.

The Tower panel was harshly critical of Regan, who was said to have "asserted personal control over the White House staff" in his two years as chief. Regan should have "insisted that an orderly process be observed" in carrying out policy, the panel said, and he should have laid plans for handling the inevitable public disclosure of the arms sale. "He must bear primary responsibility for the chaos that descended upon the White House when such disclosure did occur," the panel's report said.

Baker, who gave up a 1988 presidential bid to take the post, became Reagan's third chief of staff: Treasury Secretary James A. Baker III served in that post during the president's first term.

Among the Tower commission's major findings:

- The Iran-contra arms dealings represented a failure of people to use the foreign policy-making system properly, not a failure of the system itself.
- Although intended to improve political and diplomatic relations with Tehran, the Iran initiative almost from the beginning became an arms-for-hostages deal.
- Reagan did not seem to know that money from the Iran arms sales was secretly being diverted to the Nicaraguan contras.
- Chief of Staff Donald T. Regan and former national security adviser John M. Poindexter shared in blame for policy failures.
- Secretary of State George P. Shultz and Defense Secretary Caspar W. Weinberger, who opposed the Iran arms deals, should have done more than distance themselves from decisions.
- The Iran and contra operations were handled unprofessionally and never rigorously reviewed. Reagan knew little of his aides' actions and did almost nothing to find out.

Among the Tower commission's key recommendations:

- So the National Security Council would continue to have flexibility to provide each president with independent advice, Congress should not mandate changes in the NSC's structure and operation.
- In particular, the national security adviser should not be made subject to Senate confirmation.
- Every administration should carefully follow existing procedures for making, implementing and reviewing foreign policy, especially for covert actions.
- Congress should consider merging the House and Senate Intelligence committees into a joint panel with a small staff. *(More details of Tower report, p. 439)*

Arms for Hostages

The Iran issue exploded on the public scene shortly after the Nov. 4 midterm elections with media reports that the United States had directly shipped weapons and other military equipment in an attempt to gain freedom for American hostages held by pro-Iranian factions in Lebanon. The first account appeared in a Syrian-backed magazine in Lebanon; U.S. officials publicly refused comment but provided details and speculation that kept the issue on the front pages.

Congressional leaders — all of whom had been kept in the dark about U.S. ties to Iran — demanded explanations, forcing the administration to abandon its official news blackout. Reagan briefed top House and Senate leaders on Nov. 12, and White House aides later consulted with several others.

The next day, in a nationally televised White House speech, Reagan made the first official acknowledgment that the United States had directly shipped weapons and other military equipment to Iran's revolutionary government. However, he labeled as "wildly speculative and false" the reports that he had supplied the arms in direct exchange for Tehran's cooperation since September 1985 in releasing the three American hostages.

"We did not — repeat — did not trade weapons or anything else for hostages — nor will we," he said.

While refusing to give more than sketchy details, Reagan and his aides insisted the arms transfers did not violate a U.S. policy of refusing to negotiate with terrorists for the release of hostages. The shipments also did not violate a U.S. arms embargo in effect against Iran since 1979, White House officials said, because Reagan had secretly authorized exemptions in January 1986. *(Text, p. 37-D)*

The issue was especially threatening to Reagan because of the stormy history of U.S.-Iranian relations. Of all world leaders, perhaps none was more despised by the American public and politicians than Ayatollah Ruhollah Khomeini, Iran's de facto leader. Khomeini, who had called the United States "the great Satan," symbolized Iran when American diplomats were held hostage in Tehran.

Reagan had sought over the years to keep alive Khomeini's negative image as a terrorist. Reagan also had sought to establish the United States as the foremost proponent of the principle of not making concessions to terrorists, saying he would not negotiate with or pay ransom to hostage-takers.

In that context, news that Reagan had authorized direct and indirect arms shipments to Iran in hopes of winning freedom for hostages in Lebanon was especially shocking.

"We have been saying for years that we wouldn't deal with these people, and now it seems we're sending them weapons. What's going on here?" asked one frustrated Reagan backer, William S. Broomfield, Mich., ranking Republican on the House Foreign Affairs Committee.

Broomfield's comments were echoed by many others in Congress, with the harshest criticism coming from Democrats. "It's one of the dumbest things I've ever heard of," said Rep. Dave McCurdy, D-Okla., a member of the House Armed Services and Intelligence committees. "If Jimmy Carter pulled that stunt, he would have been hung from the rafters."

Reagan Explanation

In his speech, Reagan offered no apologies; instead, he attacked the news media for revealing and speculating about the arms deals.

The president set his policy in the context of seeking to foster better ties with a former ally that "encompasses some of the most critical geography in the world." The United States had three related goals, Reagan said: to seek an "honorable end" to the Iran-Iraq War, which had dragged on since September 1980; to eliminate state-sponsored terrorism and subversion; and to achieve the safe return of all hostages.

By making "overtures" to Iran, Reagan said, the United States was not damaging any of its goals or policies.

Reagan said he had authorized the transfer to Iran of only "small amounts of defensive weapons and spare parts" — several shipments that, in total, would fit into one cargo plane and could not affect the outcome of the Iran-Iraq War.

A White House official told reporters that the amount of arms was greater than what could be carried by a Boeing 747 jumbo jet but less than the payload of a giant C-5 transport. The official defined "defensive" arms broadly to include such items as anti-aircraft and anti-tank missiles. However, he excluded from the definition spare parts of U.S.-supplied F-4 warplanes — a major component of reported Israeli arms shipments to Iran made with U.S. concurrence.

Influencing Iran

The purpose of the arms shipments, Reagan said, was not to buy freedom for hostages but to send Tehran "a signal that the United States was prepared to replace the animosity between us with a new relationship."

One specific purpose, the senior White House official said, was to bolster "moderate elements" in Iran. "The people that we're dealing with have got to have some credibility within the country," he said.

The official acknowledged that arms shipments to Iran from Israel and the United States occurred about the same time as the three U.S. hostages were released by pro-Iranian factions in Lebanon. But he insisted that the shipments were not direct payments.

The hostages were: the Rev. Benjamin Weir, released in September 1985, about the same time as an Israeli arms shipment to Iran; the Rev. Lawrence Jenco, released in July 1986; and David P. Jacobsen, released on Nov. 2, 1986. The Jenco and Jacobsen releases occurred at about the same time the United States directly sent arms supplies to Iran.

Reagan gave only the barest details about one peculiar incident: the visit to Tehran in May 1986 by former national security adviser Robert C. McFarlane and four U.S. officials. Ali Akbar Hashemi Rafsanjani, Speaker of the Iranian Parliament, had said the Americans were carrying false Irish passports and bearing several gifts, including a key-shaped cake and a Bible signed by Reagan.

Many congressional leaders were upset that Reagan refused for more than a year to tell them anything about his dealings with Iran. At the least, members saw this as a breach of trust between the two branches of government; at worst, some said, the administration might have violated or skirted the laws requiring notification to Congress of overseas arms shipments.

"The White House has been more willing to trust some of the factions in Iran than they were to trust the Republican and Democratic leadership of the House and the Senate," said Patrick J. Leahy, D-Vt., vice chairman of the Senate Intelligence Committee.

In his speech, Reagan insisted that his actions were "in full compliance with federal law." An administration official said that statement was based, in part, on Reagan's having secretly signed his executive order in January authorizing the arms transfers to Iran. In effect, that order created exemptions to President Carter's 1979 arms embargo on Iran.

Reagan skirted the issue of whether members of Congress had been notified in the past about his actions toward Iran. Instead, he put administration actions in the present and future tenses, saying "the relevant committees of Congress are being and will be fully informed."

A senior administration official said on Nov. 13 that the House and Senate Intelligence committees had been notified about the operation before the recent public disclosures. However, leaders and senior staffers of both panels disputed that statement.

Reagan on the Defensive

As the Iran issue continued to dominate the front pages, Reagan defended his actions during a nationally televised news conference Nov. 19. But he provoked as many questions as he answered.

Reagan rejected contentions that the secret arms shipments to Iran had been wrong. "I don't think a mistake was made," he said. "It was a high-risk gamble, and it was a gamble that, as I've said, I believe the circumstances warranted. And I don't see that it has been a fiasco or a great failure of any kind."

Reagan insisted — as he had in his Nov. 13 speech — that the arms shipments were intended to signal his good faith to moderates in Iran who might succeed the Khomeini regime.

The shipments were not, he said, ransom payments for U.S. hostages held by pro-Iranian factions in Lebanon. Reagan played down the shipments as "minuscule" ones that did nothing to alter the military balance in the six-year-old Iran-Iraq War.

Although promising that he would not authorize any further arms shipments to Iran, Reagan rejected suggestions that he revoke his Jan. 17 secret executive order authorizing the past shipments.

Reagan repeatedly justified on secrecy grounds his decision not to tell Congress about the dealings with Iran. Further, he said he had the right to "defer" legally required notifications to Congress on such matters.

During the half-hour of questions, Reagan seemed unusually nervous and confused. The president stumbled on sensitive issues, and he displayed little of the humor that had gotten him through tough spots in the past. Reagan, however, said he was disappointed at a reporter's question that included a statement that he was beleaguered and defensive. "I've just been trying to answer your questions as well as I can," he said. "And I don't feel that I have anything to defend about at all."

Congressional leaders said the next day that Reagan's convoluted answers to some questions indicated that he was ignorant about significant details of the Iran operation. "He's not a liar. He's not deceitful," said Dave Durenberger, R-Minn., outgoing chairman of the Senate Intelligence Committee. "He's just not fully informed."

Democrats on the Offensive

Democrats sought to take the offensive, saying Reagan had damaged U.S. credibility by secretly buying freedom for American hostages while he was publicly maintaining a tough policy of no negotiations with terrorists.

"The point is, we were exchanging arms for hostages," said Senate Democratic leader Byrd.

Democrats also insisted that Reagan become more willing to compromise with Congress to reach a bipartisan consensus for his policies. "Bipartisanship requires a two-way street," said David L. Boren, D-Okla., the incoming

Texts of Administration Documents . . .

On Jan. 9, the White House released the text of the secret intelligence "finding" that allowed the sale of weapons to Iran. The finding, dated Jan. 17, 1986, and signed by President Reagan, linked the arms sales to attempts to gain the release of American hostages held by pro-Iranian groups in Lebanon.

Accompanying the finding was a background paper from Vice Adm. John M. Poindexter, then the national security adviser. This document was prepared by Lt. Col. Oliver L. North, then on the National Security Council staff. The notation at the bottom says that the "president was briefed verbally from this paper" with Vice President George Bush, Chief of Staff Donald T. Regan and Donald R. Fortier, the late deputy national security adviser, present. Following are texts:

Jan. 17 Intelligence Finding

Finding Pursuant to Section 662 of The Foreign Assistance Act of 1961 As Amended, Concerning Operations Undertaken by the Central Intelligence Agency in Foreign Countries, Other Than Those Intended Solely for the Purpose of Intelligence Collection.

I hereby find that the following operation in a foreign country (including all support necessary to such operation) is important to the national security of the United States, and due to its extreme sensitivity and security risks, I determine it is essential to limit prior notice, and direct the Director of Central Intelligence to refrain from reporting this Finding to the Congress as provided in Section 501 of the National Security Act of 1947, as amended, until I otherwise direct.

Scope: Iran

Description: Assist selected friendly foreign liaison services, third countries and third parties which have established relationships with Iranian elements, groups, and individuals sympathetic to U.S. Government interests and which do not conduct or support terrorist actions directed against U.S. persons, property or interests, for the purpose of: (1) establishing a more moderate government in Iran, (2) obtaining from them significant intelligence not otherwise obtainable, to determine the current Iranian Government's intentions with respect to its neighbors and with respect to terrorist acts, and (3) furthering the release of the American hostages held in Beirut and preventing additional terrorist acts by these groups. Provide funds, intelligence, counter-intelligence, training, guidance and communications and other necessary assistance to these elements, groups, individuals, liaison services and third countries in support of these activities.

The USG will act to facilitate efforts by third parties and third countries to establish contact with moderate elements within and outside the Government of Iran by providing these elements with arms, equipment and related materiel in order to enhance the credibility of these elements in their effort to achieve a more pro-U.S. government in Iran by demonstrating their ability to obtain requisite resources to defend their country against Iraq and intervention by the Soviet Union. This support will be discontinued if the U.S. Government learns that these elements have abandoned their goals of moderating their government and appropriated the materiel for purposes other than that provided by this Finding.

Ronald Reagan

The White House,
Washington, D.C.
January 17, 1986

Poindexter Memorandum

Memorandum for the President

From: John M. Poindexter
Subject: Covert Action Finding Regarding Iran

Prime Minister Peres of Israel secretly dispatched his special advisor on terrorism with instructions to propose a plan by which Israel, with limited assistance from the U.S., can create conditions to help bring about a more moderate government in Iran. The Israelis are very concerned that Iran's deteriorating position in the war with Iraq, the potential for further radicalization in Iran, and the possibility of enhanced Soviet influence in the Gulf all pose significant threats to the security of Israel. They believe it is essential that they act to at least preserve a balance of power in the region.

The Israeli plan is premised on the assumption that moderate elements in Iran can come to power if these factions demonstrate their credibility in defend-

chairman of the Senate Intelligence Committee.

Many Republicans moved to shield the president from direct responsibility by blaming key White House advisers, especially Poindexter and Chief of Staff Donald T. Regan.

However, some Republicans said Reagan could soothe some of the anger in Congress by admitting his arms dealings with Iran had been wrong. "The president ought to admit that a mistake was made and move on to something else," said Senate Republican leader Robert Dole, Kan.

There was a consensus that Reagan needed to reassess his policy-making apparatus, especially the role of the NSC staff, which directed most of the arms dealings with Iran in conjunction with the CIA.

Leaders of both parties suggested that Reagan seek help from senior foreign policy advisers — including those who served in previous administrations — to revamp his administration.

Key Democrats said Reagan's explanations of his dealings with Iran were incoherent and contradictory — signs that he had not clearly thought through the policy. Incoming House Speaker Jim Wright, D-Texas, said the president's handling of questions was characteristic: Reagan, Wright said, "is not careful with factual accuracy."

The most damning critique came from Sam Nunn, D-Ga., the incoming chairman of the Senate Armed Services Committee. A respected expert on military affairs, Nunn was a major Democratic spokesman on foreign policy. In a news conference Nov. 20, Nunn listed seven "contradictions" or misstatements by Reagan on Iran. Nunn said other administration officials had given Congress evidence contradicting Reagan's statements that:

- The United States provided only "defensive" arms to Iran. That description was "erroneous," Nunn said, given Iran's stated goal of settling its war with Iraq by toppling the government in Baghdad. "If you give them any weapons in that context, in my view, they are offensive weapons," he said. Nunn cited in particular TOW anti-tank missiles provided by the United States. Those missiles gave Iran a "very significant offensive capability," Nunn said, because Iraq depended on tanks to defend its territory.
- The arms shipments were "minuscule." Nunn said that description was "not in accord with all the information

. . . Justifying Arms-for-Hostages Deal

ing Iran against Iraq and in deterring Soviet intervention. To achieve the strategic goal of a more moderate Iranian government, the Israelis are prepared to unilaterally commence selling military materiel to Western-oriented Iranian factions. It is their belief that by so doing they can achieve a heretofore unobtainable penetration of the Iranian governing hierarchy. The Israelis are convinced that the Iranians are so desperate for military materiel, expertise and intelligence that the provision of these resources will result in favorable long-term changes in personnel and attitudes within the Iranian government. Further, once the exchange relationship has commenced, a dependency would be established on those who are providing the requisite resources, thus allowing the provider(s) to coercively influence near-term events. Such an outcome is consistent with our policy objectives and would present significant advantages for U.S. national interests. As described by the Prime Minister's emissary, the only requirement the Israelis have is an assurance that they will be allowed to purchase U.S. replenishments for the stocks that they sell to Iran. We have researched the legal problems of Israel's selling U.S. manufactured arms to Iran. Because of the requirement in U.S. law for recipients of U.S. arms to notify the U.S. government of transfers to third countries, I do not recommend that you agree with the specific details of the Israeli plan. However, there is another possibility. Some time ago Attorney General William French Smith determined that under an appropriate finding you could authorize the CIA to sell arms to countries outside of the provisions of the laws and reporting requirements for foreign military sales. The objectives of the Israeli plan could be met if the CIA, using an authorized agent as necessary, purchased arms from the Department of Defense under the Economy Act and then transferred them to Iran directly after receiving appropriate payment from Iran.

The Covert Action Finding attached at Tab A provides the latitude for the transactions indicated above to proceed. The Iranians have indicated an immediate requirement for 4,000 basic TOW weapons for use in the launchers they already hold.

The Israelis are also sensitive to a strong U.S. desire to free our Beirut hostages and have insisted that the Iranians demonstrate both influence and good intent by an early release of the five Americans. Both sides have agreed that the hostages will be immediately released upon commencement of this action. Prime Minister Peres had his emissary pointedly note that they well understand our position on not making concessions to terrorists. They also point out, however, that terrorist groups, movements, and organizations are significantly easier to influence through governments than they are by direct approach. In that we have been unable to exercise any suasion over Hizballah during the course of nearly two years of kidnappings, this approach through the government of Iran may well be our *only* way to achieve the release of the Americans held in Beirut. It must again be noted that since this dialogue with the Iranians began in September, Reverend Weir has been released and there have been no Shia terrorist attacks against American or Israeli persons, property, or interests.

Therefore it is proposed that Israel make the necessary arrangements for the sale of 4000 TOW weapons to Iran. Sufficient funds to cover the sale would be transferred to an agent of the CIA. The CIA would then purchase the weapons from the Department of Defense and deliver the weapons to Iran through the agent. If all of the hostages are not released after the first shipment of 1000 weapons, further transfers would cease.

On the other hand, since hostage release is in some respects a byproduct of a larger effort to develop ties to potentially moderate forces in Iran, you may wish to redirect such transfers to other groups within the government at a later time.

The Israelis have asked for our urgent response to this proposal so that they can plan accordingly. They note that conditions inside both Iran and Lebanon are highly volatile. The Israelis are cognizant that this entire operation will be terminated if the Iranians abandon their goal of moderating their government or allow further acts of terrorism. You have discussed the general outlines of the Israeli plan with Secretaries Shultz and Weinberger, Attorney General Meese and Director Casey. The Secretaries do not recommend you proceed with this plan. Attorney General Meese and Director Casey believe the short-term and long-term objectives of the plan warrant the policy risks involved and recommend you approve the attached Finding. Because of the extreme sensitivity of this project, it is recommended that you exercise your statutory prerogative to withhold notification of the Finding to the Congressional oversight committees until such time that you deem it to be appropriate.

I have received" from other administration aides. Those officials, in private briefings, had acknowledged that the amount of arms was "very substantial," he said. Reagan and his aides said all U.S.-sponsored arms shipments could fit into one cargo plane; the aides, however, described such a plane as being about the size of a giant C-5 cargo transport, which carries more than 100 tons.

Wright said officials told him the United States had sold Iran 2,008 TOW missiles, which he valued at more than $12 million. Iran also received parts for 235 Hawk anti-aircraft batteries, Wright said.

- The arms shipments did not shift the balance between Iran and Iraq. U.S. intervention could alter, in Iran's favor, the "psychological balance," which Nunn said was a major factor in the stalemated war. Reagan also ignored the likelihood that other nations would see the U.S. arms shipments as "the green light" to resume their own profit-making sales to Iran, Nunn said.
- The United States did not swap arms for Iran's pressure on terrorist groups in Lebanon to release the three American hostages. That statement was "contrary to information I have received," Nunn said, citing Reagan's statements that the release of hostages was a sign of "good faith" by Iran, and that the United States reciprocated with the arms.
- That the United States did not condone arms shipments to Iran by other countries, especially Israel. In his news conference, Reagan repeatedly denied that the United States was involved with or approved shipments to Iran by Israel. Minutes after the news conference, Reagan issued a statement correcting himself by saying "there was a third country involved in our secret project with Iran." Top White House aides also have said the United States gave official approval for at least one Israeli shipment to Iran in September 1985.
- That Congress did not have to be notified about the arms shipments to Iran. "The president seems to think that he can notify Congress any time he chooses to," Nunn said. "That is simply contrary to the letter and spirit of the law." Nunn noted that existing law called for prior notification to Congress of all but the most "extraordinary" covert operations.

• That the United States was providing arms to "moderates" in Iran, who were responsible for a "lessening" of terrorist activities by their country.

"When we use the word 'lessening,' it means it is still there; it is simply less than it was," Nunn said. And Wright said Reagan erred in implying that none of the arms went to the Khomeini regime. "Whose army benefited from the arms?" he asked.

Intelligence Committees' Probes

The first congressional investigations into the matter began on Nov. 21, when the House and Senate Intelligence committees heard from CIA Director Casey and top State and Defense Department aides.

Members said the officials had been forthcoming but had not been able to answer all questions, particularly about the involvement of Israel in the arms deals. Senate Intelligence Committee leaders Durenberger and Leahy immediately sent Reagan a letter saying they were "deeply disturbed" by his refusal to inform Congress.

Durenberger said that, in the past, administration officials "deliberately went out of their way to keep the Congress in the dark, and they still apparently believe that was the right course of action." That, he added, "is going to be incredibly deleterious to the course of American foreign policy."

Some Intelligence members also met privately with Poindexter at the White House. Those sessions were intended to head off a confrontation over whether Poindexter would be called to testify on Capitol Hill. White House officials earlier had said Reagan would cite "executive privilege" to keep Poindexter from giving formal testimony.

Iran Sales: Legal Questions

Reagan's policy of supplying weapons and other military goods to Iran raised two kinds of legal questions, in addition to underlying policy issues: Did the president illegally or improperly fail to tell Congress about what he was doing, and did he violate or skirt laws limiting arms aid to terrorist countries?

The White House said that Attorney General Edwin Meese III certified all of Reagan's actions as legal and proper. Reagan himself, in his Nov. 19 news conference, insisted that he had the right, in the interest of keeping secrets, to "defer" telling Congress about such matters.

But many members of Congress and their legal experts insisted that Reagan violated at least the spirit, and possibly the letter, of several U.S. laws. "It appears that laws have been broken," said Wright. He said Reagan withheld "vital information from the Congress for 18 months in contravention of the law." And Wright charged that Reagan skirted a ban on arms sales to terrorist countries.

Some of the president's supporters on Capitol Hill were slightly more charitable. After listening to Reagan's Nov. 19 explanation, Richard G. Lugar, R-Ind., outgoing chairman of the Senate Foreign Relations Committee, said: "I suspect the president does not understand the law on informing Congress on these things."

Informing Congress

Responding to the Vietnam War and the revelations in the mid-1970s of various CIA misdeeds, Congress had enacted several laws requiring the administration to report on covert operations and other diplomatic and military actions overseas.

The laws were based on the Washington axiom that information is power: The administration generated and possessed most information about policy, and it could shut members of Congress out of the policy-making process merely by keeping them in the dark.

Members of Congress also insisted that keeping them informed was good for the president; by consulting congressional leaders in advance, he usually could gain their support and benefit from their experience in foreign affairs.

The information-sharing laws most relevant to the Iran dealings concerned covert operations and arms sales.

Covert Operations. Legislation (PL 93-559) passed in 1974 required the president to tell Congress "in a timely fashion" about covert operations by the CIA and other intelligence agencies. It also required the president to give personal approval to each covert operation by signing a "finding" stating its justification and general goals.

Complaining that it was having to report covert actions to seven congressional committees — with the resulting danger of leaks — the Carter administration in 1980 sought and won a revised law (PL 96-450) requiring that notices be given only to the House and Senate Intelligence committees. *(1980 Almanac p. 66; text, p. 421)*

That law, inserted into the 1947 National Security Act as section 501, required the administration to tell the Intelligence panels in advance about most proposed intelligence operations, including covert actions; under undefined "extraordinary circumstances," that notice could be limited to the eight senior congressional leaders, four of whom were on the Intelligence panels.

If the administration did not notify the committees before an operation began, the president himself would have to do so afterward "in a timely fashion" and explain why the advance notice was not given.

The Senate Intelligence Committee, which drafted the 1980 law, said in a report (S Rept 96-730) that it was "intended to mean that the committees shall be informed at the time of the presidential finding that authorizes" each covert operation. "Arrangements for notice are to be made forthwith, without delay."

Wright told reporters on Nov. 20 that the law was "not ambiguous" on the issue of timing. "It does not suggest you can do it and then tell the Congress 18 months later."

However, House Intelligence Committee member Henry J. Hyde, R-Ill., insisted that the law was "deliberately vague" to give presidents flexibility. Hyde said, though, that Reagan had made a political mistake in not informing Congress months ago.

The law contained one clause that both the Carter and Reagan administrations viewed as a possible loophole. In its preamble, the law stated that the requirements were imposed "to the extent consistent with all applicable authorities and duties, including those conferred by the Constitution upon the executive and legislative branches of the government. . . ."

Administration officials said that clause meant the president could cite his constitutional role as commander in chief as allowing him to withhold information from Congress.

White House spokesman Larry Speakes said on Nov. 14 that "the judgment was made that it was not necessary under the law" to inform Congress.

Most members of Congress rejected the administration's explanations, noting that the Constitution said nothing about intelligence activities and that it did not excuse

1980 Intelligence Reporting Law: A Text

Following are the provisions of Section 413 of the Intelligence Oversight Act of 1980 (PL 96-450) dealing with intelligence agencies' responsibility to report to Congress:

SEC. 501. [50 U.S.C. 413] (a) To the extent consistent with all applicable authorities and duties, including those conferred by the Constitution upon the executive and legislative branches of the Government, and to the extent consistent with due regard for the protection from unauthorized disclosure of classified information and information relating to intelligence sources and methods, the Director of Central Intelligence and the heads of all departments, agencies, and other entities of the United States involved in intelligence activities shall —

(1) keep the Select Committee on Intelligence of the Senate and the Permanent Select Committee on Intelligence of the House of Representatives (hereinafter in this section referred to as the "intelligence committees") fully and currently informed of all intelligence activities which are the responsibility of, are engaged in by, or are carried out for or on behalf of, any department, agency, or entity of the United States, including any significant anticipated intelligence activity, except that (A) the foregoing provisions shall not require approval of the intelligence committees as a condition precedent to the initiation of any such anticipated intelligence activity, and (B) if the President determines it is essential to limit prior notice to meet extraordinary circumstances affecting vital interests of the United States, such notice shall be limited to the chairman and ranking minority members of the intelligence committees, the Speaker and minority leader of the House of Representatives, and the majority and minority leaders of the Senate;

(2) furnish any information or material concerning intelligence activities which is in the possession, custody, or control of any department, agency, or entity of the United States and which is requested by either of the intelligence committees in order to carry out its authorized responsibilities; and

(3) report in a timely fashion to the intelligence committees any illegal intelligence activity or significant intelligence failure and any corrective action that has been taken or is planned to be taken in connection with such illegal activity or failure.

(b) The President shall fully inform the intelligence committees in a timely fashion of intelligence operations in foreign countries, other than activities intended solely for obtaining necessary intelligence, for which prior notice was not given under subsection (a) and shall provide a statement of the reasons for not giving prior notice.

(c) The President and the intelligence committees shall each establish such procedures as may be necessary to carry out the provisions of subsections (a) and (b).

(d) The House of Representatives and the Senate, in consultation with the Director of Central Intelligence, shall each establish, by rule or resolution of such House, procedures to protect from unauthorized disclosure all classified information and all information relating to intelligence sources and methods furnished to the intelligence committees or to Members of the Congress under this section. In accordance with such procedures, each of the intelligence committees shall promptly call to the attention of its respective House, or to any appropriate committee or committees of its respective House, any matter relating to intelligence activities requiring the attention of such House or such committee or committees.

(e) Nothing in this Act shall be construed as authority to withhold information from the intelligence committees on the grounds that providing the information to the intelligence committees would constitute the unauthorized disclosure of classified information or information relating to intelligence sources and methods.

the president from obeying the law.

"In that we are a government of laws and not a government of men, even the president of the United States is compelled to respect and obey the law," Wright said.

The Senate Intelligence Committee acknowledged in its 1980 report that there was a "gray area resulting from the overlap between the Constitutional authorities and duties of the [executive and legislative] branches."

In his news conference, Reagan gave another reason for not notifying Congress. If he had told Congress about the secret dealings with Iran, he said, "I would not have been able to keep them as secret as they were."

However, congressional sources noted the law specifically rejected such an argument by the president. Section 501(e) stated that the president could not use the possibility of "unauthorized disclosure" as a reason for withholding information from Congress.

Casey Agreement. In July 1984, after a blowup over the CIA's failure to tell Congress about the mining of Nicaraguan harbors, CIA Director Casey agreed in writing to tell the Senate Intelligence Committee in advance about all "significant" covert actions. The agreement later was strengthened, committee sources said. *(Background, 1984 Almanac p. 88)*

Casey Nov. 21 showed the House Intelligence panel Reagan's Jan. 17 authorization for the Iran operation, which directed Casey not to tell Congress about it. There were reports that Reagan did so to protect Casey from congressional complaints if the operation became public.

That tactic appeared to work: After listening to Casey, Senate committee members said he had clearly violated the agreement, but they blamed the president for forcing him to do so.

Daniel Finn, minority counsel to the Senate committee, said the laws and the agreement with Casey "were not intended to deal with a case under which notification was not allowed" by the president.

Covert Arms Shipments. In 1985, Congress further amended the covert-action-notification law to require the Intelligence committees to be told whenever an intelligence agency provided weapons or defense services (such as training) to any entity outside the U.S. government. That provision, made permanent in the fiscal 1987 intelligence authorization law (PL 99-569), contained a major loophole: The notice was required only if each weapon or defense service was worth $1 million or more. *(Intelligence law, box, this page)*

Congressional sources said it was possible that Reagan's shipments to Iran were exempt from this law because of the loophole. None of the items reportedly sold to Iran — such as spare parts for anti-aircraft missile batteries — cost more than $1 million apiece.

Regular Arms Sales. The Arms Export Control Act (PL 90-629), enacted in 1968 and amended frequently since then, required the administration to tell Congress about all major arms sales to foreign countries made through regular channels. That included direct sales by the U.S. government to foreign governments and "commercial" sales over-

Fresh Questions Are Raised on the Role . . .

The Iran-contra affair touched off another round in a perennial debate over who has the power to do what, specifically, the role of the staff of the National Security Council (NSC) in foreign policy.

On Nov. 25, Vice Adm. John M. Poindexter resigned as national security adviser, and one of his aides, Marine Corps Lt. Col. Oliver L. North, was fired in connection with the scandal.

The next day, President Reagan named a three-member panel to study the NSC staff's role. They were:

- Former Sen. John Tower, R-Texas (1961-85), former chairman of the Armed Services Committee, chairman.
- Former Sen. Edmund S. Muskie, D-Maine (1959-80), who was the first chairman of the Senate Budget Committee and secretary of state under President Carter.
- Lt. Gen. Brent Scowcroft, an Air Force officer who had run Henry A. Kissinger's NSC staff.

On Dec. 2, Reagan picked Frank C. Carlucci, a veteran Washington insider, to succeed Poindexter at the NSC, effective Jan. 2, 1987. Carlucci and his advisers decided on the main lines of the organization, removing the NSC staff from an operational role in covert activities and disbanding North's politico-military section.

Tower Report

In a Feb. 26, 1987, report, the Tower group found that White House aides had "largely ignored" established channels, depriving Reagan of advice from his political appointees and career specialists. "Using the process will not always produce brilliant ideas. But history suggests it can at least help prevent bad ideas from becoming presidential policy," the Tower board said.

The panel blamed Reagan for not involving himself in the details of policy and not pressing his staff to evaluate the arms sales. His aides were faulted for not impressing on Reagan the policy's risks.

But the review panel opposed any changes in the 39-year-old law (PL 253) governing the national security adviser, the NSC or its staff. "The problem at heart was one of people, not process," Scowcroft said.

The Tower group described the NSC as a marketplace of ideas, the principal forum in which the president hears advisers debate policy options.

The council's members were the president, vice president, and secretaries of state and defense. The directors of central intelligence and of the Arms Control and Disarmament Agency were designated by law as "advisers" to the NSC, while most presidents routinely also included the White House chief of staff and the chairman of the Joint Chiefs of Staff in NSC meetings.

Under the Tower group's "marketplace" theory of NSC operations, a heavy burden fell on the president's assistant for national security affairs — the job held by Robert C. McFarlane and Poindexter.

The Tower group called the Iran-contra arms dealings a case study of the risks a president runs if he carries out policy without the systematic consultation of his principal national security aides.

The president and his aide should have foreseen that the Iran arms transfer and contra funding issues would arouse vehement public opposition. However, neither policy was subjected to the administration's routine procedures for interagency review, nor to the special procedures the president had set up in January 1985 for reviewing proposed covert operations.

According to the review group:

- The president did not get to hear a thorough debate over the two policies. "Two or three Cabinet-level reviews in a period of 17 months was not enough."
- Because of a concern for secrecy, the proposals were not thoroughly scrutinized by professionals in executive branch agencies. "This deprived those responsible for the [Iran] initiative of considerable expertise."

The Tower group also complained that the president received no analysis by U.S. intelligence agencies of key aspects of the Iran dealings: Israel's initial proposal to transfer the arms, Israel's motivation in making the proposal, credibility questions about Iranian arms dealer Manucher Ghorbanifar or other Iranian middlemen.

Because the Iran and contra policies were conducted

---

seas by private U.S. companies. It also included so-called "third-party transfers": shipments of U.S.-originated arms from the country that first bought them to another country.

That law required the president to report to Congress at the end of each quarter every "letter of offer" by the United States to sell any major military equipment valued at $1 million or more. The president also had to report to Congress 30 days in advance each proposed sale in which any item was valued at $14 million or more, or in which the total amount of weapons was $50 million or more.

The purpose of the advance notice was to give Congress the chance to block controversial arms sales. Congress had come close to blocking several sales to Arab countries, but it stopped short each time. Earlier in 1986, for example, Congress failed to override Reagan's veto of a resolution (S J Res 316) stopping the sale of missiles to Saudi Arabia. *(Saudi arms, p. 373)*

The president could waive all legal restrictions on his ability to make foreign arms sales by invoking "special authorities" included in section 614 of the permanent foreign aid laws. If he did this, however, he had to notify Congress that doing so was "vital" to the U.S. national security interests.

Congressional sources said Reagan gave no arms sales notices about Iran and that it was uncertain whether he was required to have done so.

Several committees sent their legal experts scurrying to law books to resolve questions about Reagan's compliance with the law. But one senior Senate aide said the arms sale law, in particular, was "so byzantine that it could take months" for answers.

Anti-Terrorism Laws

The Export Administration Act of 1979 (PL 96-72) required the secretary of state to send Congress an annual report listing countries that had "repeatedly provided support for acts of international terrorism." Iran had been on

. . . Of the National Security Adviser, Staff

by McFarlane, Poindexter, North and other NSC staff members in isolation from the rest of the national security bureaucracy, the execution was "unprofessional," the Tower group concluded.

The Tower group held Reagan responsible: "The NSC system will not work unless the president makes it work."

All three panel members said that Reagan should take a more active role in managing his administration's national security policy. But they also reiterated the contention in their report that Reagan's aides should have compensated for his laid-back management style by taking pains to keep him informed of risks and alternatives.

Ducking Responsibility

The Tower panel faulted all Reagan's national security advisers for allowing the Iran arms transfer program to become settled policy after such casual review.

The report singled out for blame:

- Donald T. Regan, White House chief of staff: "He must bear primary responsibility for the chaos that descended upon the White House when such disclosure did occur."
- Presidential assistant Poindexter "failed grievously" by either ignoring or not understanding the legal and political risks posed by the contra diversion.
- CIA Director William J. Casey also did not act on information about the contra diversion, which he received a month before the activity became public.
- Defense Secretary Caspar W. Weinberger and Casey should have demanded a formal assessment of the arms deal on the Iran/Iraq military balance.
- Secretary of State George P. Shultz and Weinberger abdicated their responsibility to keep advising Reagan on the Iranian arms deal — which they opposed.

Doing It Right

The Tower panel recommended that Reagan and future presidents accept an orderly policy-making process that entails review of presidential initiatives by the government's career national security specialists.

Both the assistant and the other NSC principals should have direct access to the president, the group recommended, but none of them should use these private meetings to circumvent the system of consultation.

Like the NSC staff, the assistant generally should not conduct policy, the panel recommended.

The NSC staff should be drawn from across the agencies dealing with national security issues, with no one agency having a preponderant influence, the report said. As a rule, members should not remain on the staff for more than four years, according to the recommendation.

The panel also opposed three proposed changes in the NSC's charter:

- A ban on policy implementation by the NSC staff, partly because of the difficulty of defining "implementation."
- A cap on the size of the NSC staff. The panel opposed legislation in this area that might be too rigid.
- A requirement that the Senate confirm the president's assistant for national security affairs.

The panel also recommended that:

- The assistant to the president chair interdepartmental committees to review issues within the NSC system.
- Presidents make and adhere to rules "for restricted consideration of covert action."
- Intelligence agencies and administration officials take care not to let officials' support for a policy bias intelligence estimates.
- The position of legal adviser to the NSC be upgraded. Carlucci said Feb. 26 that he had named Paul S. Stevens as general counsel to the NSC with wide-ranging authority to attend any meetings and examine any issues.
- Congress consolidate the Senate and House Select Intelligence committees into a joint intelligence oversight committee. If administrations had to inform fewer members and staff aides of covert operations, they would have a harder time citing leaks as a reason to keep Congress in the dark, the Tower panel said.
- Use of private individuals as diplomatic intermediaries be strictly limited and supervised.

---

that list each year since 1980.

The 1979 export law also required the secretaries of state and the Treasury to report to Congress 30 days before approving exports to those terrorist-supporting countries of goods or technology valued at $7 million or more. However, that notice was necessary only if the administration determined that an export would "make significant contributions to the military potential" of the country involved or would enhance its ability to support international terrorism.

Congressional sources said the Carter and Reagan administrations sent few reports to Congress in compliance with this requirement. In the Iran case, they said, the administration could have argued that reports were unnecessary on the grounds that the arms sales did not make "significant contributions" to Iran's military potential. Administration officials insisted that the United States shipped only small quantities of "defensive" arms that improved Iran's military capabilities only marginally.

Congress in 1986 toughened the restriction on arms sales to terrorist countries. A bill (PL 99-399) boosting funding for the security of U.S. embassies overseas included a flat ban on military exports to countries on the terrorism-supporting list. The president could waive the prohibition only by determining that such an export was "important to the national interests of the United States." If he did so, however, he had to report to Congress within 90 days justifying his decision. *(Embassy security bill, p. 377)*

Reagan signed that prohibition into law on Aug. 27 — months after at least two of the arms shipments to Iran. The administration did not acknowledge making any shipments after that date.

Arms Embargo. Reagan's approval of arms shipments to Iran clearly violated an embargo on all military exports to Iran imposed by President Carter in November 1979 following the taking of American hostages at the U.S. Embassy. Carter barred the exports in an executive order

(No. 12170), which White House officials said remained in effect.

Speakes said Reagan created exceptions to the embargo on Jan. 17, 1986, when he signed his secret executive order authorizing the Iran operation.

The Contra Bombshell

Reagan had made little progress in recovering from two solid weeks of controversy over his policy of secretly selling weapons to Iran when, on Nov. 24, Meese gave him evidence that $10 million-$30 million in profits from the Iranian arms deals had been diverted to the Nicaraguan contras.

The next day, Reagan informed congressional leaders and announced that he had fired the NSC staffer who had helped manage the Iran operation, Marine Corps Lt. Col. North. National security adviser Poindexter, who Meese said knew about the diversion of money to the contras, resigned and asked to be returned to the Navy.

Officials later barred North from the White House grounds; it was alleged that he had shredded some documents possibly connected to the case.

At a hastily called Nov. 25 news conference, a grim and shaken Reagan read a statement acknowledging that he had not been "fully informed" about the Iran arms deals. "This action raises serious question of propriety," he said. However, he continued to insist that his Iran policy was "well founded." He conceded only that "in one aspect, implementation of that policy was seriously flawed." *(Text, p. 38-D)*

Meese said at the news conference that no other top U.S. officials, including Reagan and Cabinet members, knew about the transfer of Iranian money to the contras. Meese later amended his statement to say some persons with "tangential" ties to the government might have known about or been involved in the money transfers.

Asked why administration statements should be believed, Meese said Reagan had established credibility "by the full disclosure of the facts." He pledged that the Justice Department would continue to investigate the matter and that further information would be made public. Meese later ordered the FBI to launch a full-scale probe into possible criminal violations.

Many congressional leaders and others in Washington expressed skepticism that the diversion of arms profits to the contras was carried out with the assent or knowledge of only two White House officials.

"It defies credulity" that a middle-level official such as North could be making foreign policy, said Wright. If that was the truth, he added, "if nobody knew of it, that in itself is a confession of a great void in the execution of our foreign policy."

Durenberger said: "Ollie North is not a Lone Ranger. ... There are some undisclosed sources that gave him at least an amber light."

Within hours of Reagan's press conference, the most widely quoted statement on Capitol Hill was the famous question that then-Sen. Howard H. Baker Jr., R-Tenn., repeated during the Watergate hearings of 1973: "What did the president know and when did he know it?"

Only sketchy details were disclosed about how the Iranian arms payments found their way to the contras. Meese said that Iran paid money for the arms into one or more Swiss bank accounts and that some of that money went to the contras.

Wright said congressional leaders were told that, in one transaction, Iran paid $19 million for anti-tank missiles and other items from Defense Department stockpiles. The CIA reimbursed $3 million to the Pentagon for the cost of the weapons, and about $12 million remained in a Swiss bank account, supposedly for use by the contras. That left about $4 million that might have gone to arms dealers as a commission or finder's fee, Wright said.

Congressional Response

The Iran-contra connection stunned members of Congress, many of whom were still flabbergasted by the underlying controversy over Reagan's arms sales to Tehran.

Most Republicans rallied behind the president personally but criticized White House aides for misleading him and carrying out policies of their own.

Some GOP leaders called for understanding of the president's dilemma, while insisting that Reagan remain firmly in control. "This nation is not rudderless," said Sen. John W. Warner, R-Va., a former secretary of the Navy. "The president is at the helm, and it's steady as she goes."

Members on both sides of the aisle called on Reagan to provide full information to Congress as quickly as possible. Although the demands for a special prosecutor came mainly from Democrats, Republican leaders joined in saying Congress should conduct its own investigations.

Probes of the Iranian arms sales already were under way in both houses, and leaders expanded those inquiries to cover the connection with the contras.

While claiming they sought no partisan advantage, Democrats clearly were trying to exploit the political opportunity created by Reagan's sudden weakness. Some also appeared to be settling scores with a president who for years had mocked them as weak on national security issues: For the first time, Democrats were able to portray themselves as tougher than Reagan, saying they would not have armed Iran.

"We now discover that the emperor has no clothes," said Rep. Robert G. Torricelli, D-N.J., at a Foreign Affairs Committee hearing Nov. 25.

Nevertheless, most Democrats seemed to recognize the risks in appearing to be jackals attacking an injured but still popular president. While rushing to the television studios to demand full investigations, Democratic leaders insisted they were not seeking to destroy yet another presidency.

"We all want to see a strong president," Byrd said. "We don't want to see a fatally damaged presidency."

Nevertheless, Democrats described the Iran case as merely the latest in a series of Reagan foreign policy fiascoes. They pointed to revelations in September 1986 that the administration had planned a "disinformation" campaign to mislead Libyan leader Muammar el-Qaddafi, Reagan's handling of the arrest in the Soviet Union of American journalist Nicholas Daniloff, and the president's sudden lurch toward nuclear disarmament during his October summit meeting with Soviet leader Mikhail S. Gorbachev. *(Summit, p. 459)*

"These guys [in the administration] were living on borrowed time, and time ran out," said Rep. Les Aspin, D-Wis., chairman of the House Armed Services Committee.

Boren, often a Reagan backer on foreign policy issues, said the White House was playing "Amateur Hour" and needed a new chief of staff, plus greater involvement by Secretary of State George P. Shultz and others with "the greatest expertise."

North and the Contras

Contra officials denied receiving any of the money from the Iranian arms sales, although they said it was possible someone might have used the money to buy supplies for them without their knowledge.

However, Wright quoted Meese as saying Adolfo Calero, one of three top contra leaders, drew $12 million in Iranian funds from a Swiss bank account.

The new controversy had deep roots in the history of the contra assistance: After Congress cut off U.S. military backing of the rebels in 1984, the administration turned to private anti-communist groups to keep weapons, uniforms and other supplies flowing.

Coordinating that private aid program was North, a covert action specialist working out of the Executive Office Building next to the White House. North's activities reportedly had the blessing of two consecutive national security advisers, both of whom also were involved in the Iran operation: McFarlane and Poindexter.

In 1985, when investigative reporters uncovered some of North's mysterious work on behalf of the contras, congressional critics demanded to know what the White House was doing. McFarlane told investigators that North was acting properly.

Although reports of North's involvement in aiding the contras continued to surface in 1986, the administration brushed aside congressional efforts to investigate the matter. White House officials told Congress in the summer of 1986 that North was no longer involved with the contras and that private aid would not be necessary once the United States resumed official backing.

But congressional interest was renewed in October when a private plane carrying supplies to the contras was downed in Nicaragua and the sole surviving crewman, Eugene Hasenfus, claimed to be working for the CIA.

In that context, word of North's involvement in skimming Iranian arms profits provoked special interest on the Hill and revived old issues the administration had hoped would die.

Launching Investigations

Under heavy pressure from Capitol Hill, Reagan on Dec. 2 supported a probe by an independent counsel, quelling some of the concern that his administration would cover up wrongdoing or be less than eager to ferret it out. "If illegal acts were undertaken, those who did so will be brought to justice," Reagan said in a nationally televised speech.

Reagan also named Carlucci as national security adviser. That choice met with the approval of many critics who had worried about the quality of foreign policy advice the president was getting.

However, Reagan stood by his refusal to fire Chief of Staff Regan or admit that he had made a mistake in selling arms to Iran.

Both houses of Congress moved to set up select committees to investigate. Incoming House Speaker Wright on Dec. 4 announced plans for a 15-member special committee, to consolidate hearings and investigations planned by several committees. Senate leaders agreed on an 11-member panel the same day.

The agreement by top leaders of both parties to appoint special committees killed the prospect of a special session of Congress for that purpose. Senate Republican leader Dole had campaigned for a special session so a panel selected by his chamber could begin work as soon as possible. But key Democrats opposed the idea: Their Senate leader, Byrd, said it would heighten "an atmosphere of hysteria and crisis."

In the meantime, the Senate Intelligence Committee began closed hearings on Dec. 1, and the House Foreign Affairs and Intelligence committees opened their own sessions the week of Dec. 8.

The Senate Intelligence panel was hampered by the refusal of two key witnesses to talk. Poindexter and North both declined to answer questions on grounds that doing so might incriminate them.

Committee members informally discussed granting immunity to compel testimony. But the panel was reluctant to take such a step, largely because doing so might complicate the work of the independent counsel.

Reagan's Steps

By calling for an independent counsel, Reagan calmed some of the criticism that he had failed to realize the extent of the crisis and was unwilling to deal with it.

"I certainly think the president went a long way, in getting back on track," said Sen. Nancy Landon Kassebaum, R-Kan. "Up to that time, he had appeared to be very uncertain, not clear about what was going on."

And administration officials insisted that Reagan was moving quickly to handle the situation.

Defending the president whose administration he had been investigating, Attorney General Meese said ultimately "it will be shown that this president acted promptly, acted properly. . . ."

But on Capitol Hill, some Democrats worried that the independent counsel would not have a broad enough charter. Sen. John Kerry, D-Mass., wanted the counsel to probe the White House-inspired network of private groups aiding the contras. If the counsel did not do so, he said, Congress would have to.

Earlier in 1986, Kerry had tried, with only limited success, to get the GOP-led Foreign Relations Committee to look into the private contra-aid network.

Some Democrats also questioned Reagan's statement that he and his administration would "cooperate fully" with Congress. After North and Poindexter refused to answer questions before the Senate Intelligence panel on Dec. 2-3, Vice Chairman Leahy said Reagan should "rewrite the script" in his speeches to indicate that there were major exceptions to the promised cooperation.

Reagan took steps to gain control over the NSC staff, which was responsible for the Iran-contra operations. The choice of Carlucci had the most immediate impact. A former deputy director of the CIA and deputy secretary of defense, Carlucci was known as a hard-driving official who brooked no independent operations. He said that he would have direct access to Reagan, something Poindexter lacked.

Reagan also said Dec. 1 that he had directed the NSC staff not to engage in covert operations.

The special House and Senate committees consolidated hearings and investigations under way by about a half-dozen panels. However, three panels continued their investigations through December.

The Senate Intelligence panel began its closed-door hearings with testimony from current and former officials. The committee issued subpoenas for documents and witnesses. *(Major witnesses, box, p. 429)*

The House Foreign Affairs and Intelligence committees also held hearings.

Independent Counsel Gets a Broad Mandate

Lawrence E. Walsh, a former federal district judge, diplomat and deputy attorney general, was named Dec. 19 to be the independent counsel to investigate the Iranian arms deal and the diversion of funds to Nicaraguan contras.

The special three-judge court that named Walsh, 74, also instructed him to look into the "provision or coordination of support" for the contras since 1984.

That directive was particularly important because of allegations that Marine Lt. Col. Oliver L. North, who was fired in November as a National Security Council official, coordinated a network of private organizations to provide aid to the contras.

The permission to probe the contras followed requests from members of Congress, who wrote the three judges asking them to permit an investigation into covert funding for the Nicaraguan rebels.

The jurisdiction set by the court was broader than that requested by Attorney General Edwin Meese III. Meese did not seek a probe generally into the "provision or coordination of support" for the contras.

Futhermore, the three-judge court appeared to have enlarged the time span that would be covered by the investigation. Meese's proposal referred to events "in or around January 1985," whereas the court's mandate to Walsh covered events "in or about 1984" to the present.

North was the only official named in the court's order. However, the judges directed Walsh to investigate other government officials or other individuals or organizations "acting in concert" with North or other aides.

Questions of Immunity

At a brief news conference Dec. 19 after he was sworn in at the federal courthouse in Washington, D.C., Walsh said he wanted to coordinate with members of Congress investigating the Iran-contra affair. In response to a question, he said he did not believe that the congressional investigations would hurt his own probe.

North and his former boss, Vice Adm. John M. Poindexter, had been called to testify earlier in December before House and Senate committees, but they exercised their Fifth Amendment right to remain silent.

President Reagan Dec. 16 asked Congress to grant the two men immunity so they would testify, but the Intelligence commitees refused to do so.

Some members and legal experts said that such a move could hamper an independent counsel's investigation, because North and Poindexter could not be prosecuted for any criminal law violations that might come to light as a result of their testimony.

While a prosecutor could seek charges on information gathered independently, legal experts pointed out that Walsh had not had time to do his own probe.

On Jan. 13, 1987, Walsh sent a letter and 13-page legal memorandum to the House and Senate Iran investigating panels, asking them not to grant immunity to any witnesses before he had completed his inquiry.

Two weeks later, on Jan. 28, Walsh empaneled a grand jury.

Judge, Prosecutor, Diplomat

The Dec. 19 selection of Walsh came after a two-week search by the three judges. His name, however, had surfaced days before the official announcement, and it was not a surprise when word finally came.

Walsh had had a multifaceted career, holding important jobs in the public and private sectors.

A lifelong Republican, he had served several administrations. President Dwight D. Eisenhower appointed him to the federal bench in New York in 1954, and 3½ years later made him deputy attorney general.

In 1969, President Richard M. Nixon tapped him to become an ambassador with the U.S. delegation to the Vietnam peace conference in Paris.

Rep. Dan Glickman, D-Kan., whose Judiciary subcommittee had jurisdiction over the special prosecutor law (PL 97-409), said he was not disturbed by Walsh's Republican affiliation.

"I think it's probably even better," Glickman said. "He probably will do his best to be independent."

Walsh was born in Port Maitland, Nova Scotia, in 1912. He earned a bachelor's degree and law degree at Columbia University, the latter in 1935. He was admitted to the New York bar in 1936.

For the next two years he served as a special assistant attorney general in New York, investigating murder and racketeering. From 1938-41 he worked as a deputy assistant district attorney under Thomas E. Dewey. After Dewey was elected governor, Walsh served as the governor's counsel.

Walsh also served as counsel to the New York Public Service Commission and as general counsel and executive director of the Waterfront Commission of New York.

In 1961, Walsh became a partner in the New York law firm of Davis, Polk and Wardwell, where he worked until 1981. During that time he served a year — 1975-76 — as president of the American Bar Association. In 1981, Walsh went to Oklahoma, where he became a member of its bar and worked with the firm of Crowe and Dunlevy.

Taking Aim at Regan, Casey

In the midst of Washington's furor, there seemed to be near-unanimous agreement on only one thing: Regan had to go. Republicans, Democrats, virtually everybody argued that Regan had not served his boss well and should resign or be fired.

But those in disagreement were the most important ones: Regan and Reagan. Both appeared to be hoping that the controversy would die down.

The most important calls for Regan's firing came from congressional leaders who said he had no defense on the question of whether he knew about the diversion of Iranian arms sales funds to the contras: If he did know, he should have stopped it; if he did not know what his subordinates were doing, he should have.

Lugar, outgoing chairman of the Senate Foreign Relations Committee, was among the first calling on Regan and Casey to leave. "It appears to me that both Mr. Regan and Mr. Casey are going to be heavily involved in the investigations," he said on Dec. 2. "They ought to spend their time preparing for that."

In addition, Lugar said: "I just think the president has not been as well served as he needs to be by his staff, by the intelligence apparatus and the National Security Council."

House Minority Leader Robert H. Michel, R-Ill., normally one of the most cautious Republican leaders, on Dec. 3 joined the call for Regan's departure, saying: "There have been enough inferences and enough statements made that when one does not pull his share of the load, I guess maybe he ought to think in terms of leaving."

Few congressional leaders disagreed with that advice, and those who did offered only ambiguous reasons in doing so. Alan K. Simpson, Wyo., the Senate Republican whip, noted that the president faced decisions on the budget and other matters. "You can't leave him alone to do that," he said.

Although some Republicans expressed hope that Regan's departure would go a long way toward calming the controversy, Michel quoted Reagan as saying that probably would not happen. "What good does it do to fire, have a wholesale firing, if that does not solve the problem?" Michel asked in relating the president's views to reporters. "It doesn't kill the issue by firing this person or that person."

The calls for Regan's ouster came so quickly, and with such force, largely because the chief of staff had alienated many public officials in Washington with his boasts of personal power. "Always wrong, and with a loud voice," was the description of Regan by one prominent House Republican.

Bush to the Defense

In a Dec. 3 speech, Vice President George Bush offered the administration's most candid explanation at that point of why the Iranian initiative was taken and what the consequences had been.

Bush's speech was an effort to restore public confidence in Reagan and to minimize damage to his hopes for the presidency in 1988. Until his speech, Bush had been conspicuously silent on the Iran-contra matter, leading to speculation that he had gone into hiding.

Unlike Reagan, Bush admitted: "Clearly, mistakes were made." He did not specify them, but he seemed to be referring to the funneling of Iranian arms profits to the contras — something in which he said he had not been involved.

However, Bush defended the underlying policy toward Iran — a country toward which he acknowledged sharing the "hatred" of the American people. While the means of selling arms was "arguable," he said, the goal of improving relations with Iran had merit. "We may not like the current Iranian regime, and I've said we don't. But it would be irresponsible to ignore its geopolitical and strategic importance," he said.

Even so, Bush acknowledged, "the question remains of how the administration could violate its own policy of not selling arms to Iran. Simple human hope explains it perhaps better than anything else," he said.

"The president hoped that we could open a channel that would serve the interests of the United States and of our allies in a variety of ways. Call it leadership. Given 20-20 hindsight, call it a mistaken tactic if you want to. It was risky but potentially of long-term value." Now that investigations are under way, Bush said: "Let the chips fall where they may. We want the truth."

Shultz, McFarlane Testify

The Senate and House Intelligence committees and the House Foreign Affairs Committee made progress in December in their investigations.

Testifying before Foreign Affairs on Dec. 8, Secretary of State Shultz and former national security adviser McFarlane gave their reports on how the administration conceived and conducted its policy toward Iran. Both painted a picture of an administration making important decisions on an ad hoc basis without the involvement of major policy makers. *(Texts, pp. 40-D, 43-D)*

Members of both parties said they were especially unhappy to hear senior officials describe how decisions on such a sensitive issue as arms sales to Iran could be made with little or no involvement by the secretary of state.

"Every normal process and procedure that we've understood, and every agency, it seems, has been bypassed" in the Iran case, House Foreign Affairs Chairman Dante B. Fascell, D-Fla., said Dec. 8. "It certainly doesn't appear to be a good process that we want to support."

William S. Cohen, R-Maine, a member of the Senate Intelligence panel, said administration policy was conducted "by a few individuals short-circuiting the secretary of state, perhaps the secretary of defense, perhaps the CIA." It was "an operation run out of an office in the White House without full accountability."

Testimony produced these major examples of departures from standard procedures:

- The use of what McFarlane called an "oral finding" by Reagan in August 1985 to authorize secret talks with Iranians and to approve Israel's sale of U.S.-made weapons to Iran. McFarlane said Reagan's oral approval was equivalent to a regular, written "finding" — the legal term for a presidential authorization for a covert operation by the CIA. Meese had determined, McFarlane said, that the authority "need not be a written finding" but merely had to involve a decision by the president.

Congressional legal experts disputed the validity of an oral finding, saying that only a written authorization, reported to Congress, would have met the requirements of 1974 and 1980 laws (PL 93-559, PL 96-450) on covert action. Among other things, the August 1985 decision apparently had the effect of waiving the law (PL 90-629) that barred other countries from transferring U.S.-made arms to countries, such as Iran, that supported terrorism. Normally, the president had to report to Congress, in writing, whenever he gave permission for purchasers of U.S. weapons to transfer them to third countries. "That's a new concept," House Intelligence Chairman Hamilton said of the oral finding. "There is no such thing."

Hamilton appeared to get some support for that contention from unexpected quarters: the White House. Speakes and other officials repeatedly rejected McFarlane's assertion that Reagan had given any advance approval — oral or otherwise — to the Israeli arms deals. The administration approved the Israeli shipments after the fact, officials said, but that was not done in any form of presidential finding.

- Shultz' statement that he had not been told about Reagan's Jan. 17 finding that authorized direct U.S. arms shipments to Iran. The finding also was kept secret from other key officials, including those in anti-terrorism units in the White House and at the State Department.

Asked about the finding, Shultz told the committee: "I was notified of it at about the same time you were notified of it" — in November, when White House officials said Reagan secretly had approved the finding as a means of waiving the U.S. arms embargo on Iran.

Shultz said he had participated in a Jan. 7, 1986, White House meeting on the issue and came away with the impression that Reagan was about to side with those advocating the arms sales to Iran.

After that meeting, Shultz said he had only "sporadic and fragmentary" knowledge of the arms sales and was unaware that Reagan had signed a finding. He also hinted that he did not even want to know about White House dealings with Iran. Because of the danger of leaks, he said he had decided that "I didn't need to know things that were not in my sphere to do something about."

Shultz also said he knew nothing about the diversion of Iranian arms sales money to the contras.

Nevertheless, Shultz said he was aware of the U.S.-approved Israeli arms shipments in 1985.

- The use of private arms dealers and another country — Israel — to funnel weapons to Iran.

Normally, when the United States wanted to sell arms to another country, it would do so directly, with the State and Defense departments making all the arrangements. U.S. law (PL 90-629) also provided for "commercial" or private sales, but they were strictly regulated and had to be reported to Congress.

In the Iran case, however, the White House and the CIA arranged for weapons to be taken from Pentagon stocks, shipped to Israel and then transferred through private arms dealers to Iran — all without notification to Congress. Arms dealers then put the money that Iran paid for the weapons into secret Swiss bank accounts, and the CIA reimbursed the Pentagon for its expenses.

Initial financing for at least some of the deals was handled by a syndicate led by Saudi arms merchant Adnan Khashoggi. One of the investors who expected to get substantial profits from the deals, based on inflated prices paid by Iran, was Roy M. Furmark, a New York businessman.

Fascell complained that the procedure amounted to the "privatizing of foreign policy."

- Shultz' surprise revelation to the committee that the U.S. ambassador to Lebanon, John H. Kelly, from Oct. 30-Nov. 4 had made secret "back-channel" communications with Poindexter, North, retired Air Force Maj. Gen. Richard V. Secord and other officials in Washington without telling his boss — Shultz.

The secretary said he had been "shocked" to learn about the communications, which dealt with the release during that time of American hostage Jacobsen. In response to a general request to all U.S. diplomats for information on the Iran-contra affair, Kelly on Dec. 6 sent Shultz a cable describing his communications with the White House.

Shultz ordered Kelly back to Washington; the ambassador arrived on Dec. 9 and was immediately interviewed by State Department officials. Shultz said Kelly's dealings with the White House had violated the normal chain of command, something that would be justified only by a "good reason."

- The mission to Tehran, late in May 1985, by McFarlane, North, another NSC staffer, Howard J. Teicher, and others aboard a plane carrying U.S.-made parts for Iranian anti-aircraft missiles. The Americans met for four days with mid-level Iranians but reached no agreements, according to McFarlane. The unusual mission apparently was undertaken without the knowledge of State Department experts on Iran and the Middle East.

- The State Department's request that the sultan of Brunei make a donation to the contras.

Elliott Abrams, the assistant secretary of state for inter-American affairs, reportedly asked the sultan of the oil-rich nation on the South China Sea to donate several million dollars to the contras, which he did.

Shultz defended the action as legal, noting that the 1985 law (PL 99-83) authorizing U.S. non-military aid to the contras had specifically said the State Department could seek similar aid from other countries.

- A request by North to Texas millionaire H. Ross Perot to make $2 million available as a ransom payment for American hostages in Lebanon. Perot confirmed that he shipped $2 million to a Swiss bank at North's request, but the money was never used.

Shultz told the committee he had been unaware of North's request to Perot and called it "outrageous."

Hostage Releases as a Goal

In all his public statements, Reagan insisted that he did not swap the arms for hostages, and that the United States provided the small amounts of military hardware to Iran mainly as a way of boosting the standing of reformist elements there.

However, the evidence compiled by the congressional committees appeared to indicate that securing release of U.S. hostages played a greater role in the Iranian arms sales than the president was admitting.

The issue was central to the entire debate over the Iranian arms sales, which appeared, on the surface, to contradict the stated U.S. policy of not providing weapons to countries, such as Iran, that supported the taking of hostages and other terrorist acts.

In his testimony before Foreign Affairs, McFarlane said the United States sanctioned the Israelis' arms shipments to Iran in August 1985, as a way of boosting the standing of moderates there who were opposed to terrorism and to the continuation of the Iran-Iraq War. The United States was not seeking to buy freedom for American hostages, he said.

But McFarlane said he became convinced by late November 1985 that the Iranians viewed their dealings with the United States as centering on the hostages. All dealings "were being skewed toward the hostages alone," he said in a prepared statement to the committee.

For that reason, McFarlane said, he recommended in December 1985 that U.S. approval for Israeli arms shipments to Iran be ended. Reagan accepted that recommendation, but a month later formally approved direct U.S. arms shipments to Iran.

While insisting that U.S. officials never saw the issue as a direct arms-for-hostages swap, McFarlane acknowledged that Reagan agreed to the sales in part because he was "terribly, terribly concerned" about the fate of the hostages. That concern, McFarlane said, was "a very leading underpinning of the whole initiative" toward Iran.

Shultz also acknowledged that freeing the hostages was one goal of the U.S. arms sales, and that "when you have something that has a variety of objectives to it, these things can get mixed up."

The widely held impression that the administration was hypocritical in its denunciations of other countries for

A Parade of Witnesses to Capitol Hill

Witness	Committee	Hearing Date
Lt. Col. Oliver L. North, former NSC deputy director of political-military affairs; cited the Fifth Amendment each time	S Intelligence H Intelligence H Foreign Affairs	Dec. 1 (c) Dec. 9 (c) Dec. 9 (o)
Vice Adm. John M. Poindexter, former national security adviser; testified Nov. 21; cited the Fifth Amendment thereafter	S Intelligence S Intelligence H Foreign Affairs H Intelligence	Nov. 21 (c) Dec. 3 (c) Dec 9. (o) Dec. 10 (c)
William J. Casey, director of Central Intelligence	H Intelligence S Intelligence H Foreign Affairs H Intelligence	Nov. 21 (c) Nov. 21 (c) Dec. 10 (c) Dec. 11 (c)
Robert M. Gates, CIA deputy director	S Intelligence H Intelligence	Dec. 4 (c) Dec. 10 (c)
Michael H. Armacost, under secretary of state	S Intelligence	Nov. 21 (c)
George P. Shultz, secretary of state	H Foreign Affairs S Intelligence	Dec.8 (o) Dec. 16 (c)
Robert C. McFarlane, former national security adviser	S Intelligence H Foreign Affairs H Foreign Affairs H Intelligence S Intelligence	Dec. 1 (c) Dec. 8 (o) Dec. 8 (c) Dec. 10 (c) Dec 18 (c)
John C. Whitehead, deputy secretary of state	H Foreign Affairs	Nov. 24 (o)
Richard W. Murphy, assistant secretary of state for Near Eastern affairs	H Foreign Affairs S Intelligence	Nov. 24 (o) Nov. 21 (c)
John N. McMahon, former deputy director of CIA	S Intelligence	Dec. 1 (c)
Adm. William J. Crowe, chairman, Joint Chiefs of Staff	H Armed Services	Nov. 25 (o)
Maj. Gen. (Ret.) Richard V. Secord, executive director of Stanford Technology Trading Inc. of Vienna, Va.; cited the Fifth Amendment	S Intelligence H Intelligence	Dec. 9 (c) Dec. 23 (c)
Col. (Ret.) Robert C. Dutton, assistant to Secord and employee of Stanford Technology Inc.; cited the Fifth Amendment	S Intelligence	Dec. 10 (c)
Richard L. Armitage, assistant secretary of defense	S Intelligence S Intelligence	Nov. 21 (c) Dec. 11 (c)
Robert Owen, former contra-aid consultant; cited the Fifth Amendment	S Intelligence	Dec. 8 (c)
Roy M. Furmark, New York businessman	S Intelligence H Intelligence	Dec. 11 (c) Dec. 18 (c)
Howard J. Teicher,* NSC staff	S Intelligence S Intelligence	Dec. 12 (c) Dec. 16 (c)
Col. Robert L. Earl, NSC staff; refused to testify	S Intelligence	Dec. 12 (c)
Michael Ledeen, Former NSC consultant	S Intelligence	Dec. 9 (c)
Donald T. Regan, White House chief of staff	S Intelligence H Intelligence	Dec. 16 (c) Dec. 18 (c)
Casper W. Weinberger, secretary of defense	S Intelligence H Intelligence	Dec. 17 (c) Dec. 18 (c)
Edwin Meese III, attorney general	S Intelligence H Intelligence	Dec. 17 (c) Dec. 18 (c)

** Teicher refused to testify Dec. 12; testified Dec. 16. S Senate H House (c) closed (o) open*

dealing with terrorists was a prominent issue in the congressional hearings.

Bob Dornan, R-Calif., a staunch Reagan backer, said he was among the members who had urged the families of hostages to be patient and had pointed to Reagan's statements that the United States would never pay ransom for hostages.

"I thought we had such a clear policy that I'm confused and hurt" by the arms sales revelations, he told McFarlane.

Shultz also appeared to take issue with Reagan's statements that Iran had reduced its support for terrorism in the last year. White House officials had justified those statements, made on Nov. 19 and 25, on the grounds that no Americans had been taken hostage by pro-Iranian groups in Lebanon for about a year.

Shultz said the lapse in hostage-taking "conceivably shows the beginnings of the modification of Iranian behavior." But, he added, Iran was involved in the taking of three American hostages during the fall of 1986 and in other recent hostage cases.

"If we're going to have an impact internationally in the fight against terrorism, we've got to view it internationally and we've got to be as concerned about terrorist acts against others as we are against ourselves," Shultz said.

Poindexter, North Take the Fifth

A major cause of important gaps in the Iran-contra chronology was the refusal of North and Poindexter to testify.

Both invoked their Fifth Amendment right to refuse to testify, on grounds that doing so might incriminate them, in closed sessions of the Intelligence committees and in an open Foreign Affairs Committee hearing Dec. 9 that was broadcast live nationwide.

Capitol Hill investigators said Poindexter and North

seemed to be the only U.S. officials who knew most, or all, details about the arms sales and the diversion of funds to the contras.

Referring to Reagan's description of North as a "national hero," Senate Intelligence panel leader Durenberger said: "Somebody is going to have to define for them what 'national hero' means. It doesn't mean you come in here and stiff the whole country."

Senate Democratic leader Byrd was even more blunt, saying it was "a mockery for individuals to wear the uniform of our country and take the Fifth Amendment."

Although their reported actions had deeply embarrassed their president and both men faced criminal investigations, Poindexter and North were greeted with praise when they came before the Foreign Affairs panel Dec. 9.

Ranking Republican Broomfield told Poindexter he had "a great deal of respect for you," and Dornan said the committee could benefit greatly from the admiral's expertise on "geopolitical" matters.

It was the lower-ranking North, however, who generated the greatest adulation from committee members. Outfitted in his Marine uniform with ribbons and decorations on the left and a Purple Heart on the right, North appeared the very image of a dashing military officer.

Gerald B. H. Solomon, R-N.Y., who represented North's home district, said: "You are truly a great American, Colonel, and we back home deeply admire and respect your past history and what you've done for your country."

Dornan recited part of a Rudyard Kipling poem, with North's name inserted, paying tribute to soldiers who fight for their countries.

And Tom Lantos, D-Calif., announced to North that "it would be my privilege" to contribute to a legal defense fund that conservative groups had established for him.

In spite of the praise, Poindexter and North were of little help to the committee; each invoked the Fifth Amendment twice.

Hamilton, the committee's second-ranking Democrat, praised Poindexter as an "exceedingly honorable man." But Hamilton said he was distressed that a military officer would not answer the committee's questions "at a time when the Congress is seeking, in the only way it knows how, to get the full disclosure about events that we consider to be enormously important to the national interest of the United States."

Research by the Library of Congress had produced no evidence of any other admiral in the nation's history refusing to testify before a committee by invoking his Fifth Amendment rights, Hamilton said.

Michael D. Barnes, D-Md., provoked a sharp response from Poindexter's lawyer by suggesting that the admiral risk going to jail for the greater "responsibility to the nation" of helping unravel the mystery of what had happened in the Iran-contra affair.

Barnes told Poindexter that "the worst thing that can happen" would be for the admiral to receive a suspended sentence for whatever crimes he might have committed.

Richard Beckler, Poindexter's attorney, denounced that statement as "nothing less than outrageous," prompting applause from Republicans and producing an apology from Barnes.

Both Poindexter and North seemed ill at ease in their unusual roles. Puffing on a pipe, Poindexter said his "sincere desire" was to help the committee in its inquiry.

And North, refusing to respond to a query by Hamilton, appeared to be fighting back tears as he said: "I don't think there is another person in America who wants to tell his story as much as I do."

That prompted Daniel A. Mica, D-Fla., to say that "I don't think I've ever seen more anguish or distress on the face" of a witness before the committee. While "laws may have been broken," said Mica, "I think Col. North has acted in what he thought was the best interest of the country."

Poindexter's and North's silence prompted some of Reagan's GOP allies to urge the president to get his ex-aides to reveal what they knew. Sen. Paul Laxalt, R-Nev., Reagan's closest friend on Capitol Hill, said it would be "just absolutely fantastic" if the president would call in both former aides and say: " 'Now, tell me, gentlemen, what in the world happened?' "

In a letter published Dec. 12 in *The Washington Post,* Dole called on Poindexter and North to talk voluntarily because "they are in the position to do something decisive to help the country out of the current predicament."

Others Refuse to Testify

In addition to North and Poindexter, several private individuals involved in the Iran-contra affair came into public view. Three invoked the Fifth Amendment in refusing to testify in closed sessions of the Senate Intelligence Committee: retired Air Force Maj. Gen. Secord, who ran a Virginia company called Stanford Technology Trading Inc., and his aide, retired Col. Robert C. Dutton, and Robert Owen, a former consultant to the State Department's non-military aid program for the contras.

Two other NSC staff members appeared before Senate Intelligence Dec. 12 but refused to testify: NSC staffer Howard J. Teicher, who did not have an attorney and who was refused the services of the White House legal office; and Col. Robert L. Earl, an NSC staffer who pleaded inadequate time to prepare.

On Dec. 11, the committee heard from Furmark, the New York businessman who reportedly was one of several private investors who helped finance some of the shipments of U.S. arms to Iran through Israel. Casey said it was Furmark who tipped him off in early October to the possible diversion of Iranian funds to the contras.

Fixing Responsibility

New attention was focused on the question of whether Reagan — in spite of his statements — knew about the alleged diversion of Iranian arms sales profits to the contras.

Reagan said Nov. 25 that he had not been "fully informed" about that aspect of the Iran sales; in succeeding weeks he and Regan said he knew nothing about it.

Any official U.S. participation in diverting money to the contras in late 1984 through Sept. 30, 1986, could have been illegal under several versions of the "Boland amendment." That law barred direct or indirect U.S. military aid to the contras. *(1985 Almanac p. 76)*

Most members of Congress said they were willing to believe Reagan's statements — although some questioned similar denials by Regan, who was Poindexter's immediate supervisor.

"I'm working on the assumption that people are telling the truth, including the president, certainly the president," Rep. Hamilton said.

But a handful of Democrats said they believed Reagan either was lying or had forgotten his role in the decision to divert funds to the contras. One of the most prominent was

Stephen J. Solarz, N.Y., fourth-ranking Democrat on the Foreign Affairs Committee.

Solarz said Dec. 10 that "circumstances and logic" led him to the conclusion that Reagan "must have known about the decision" to divert money to the contras.

In his testimony before Foreign Affairs, McFarlane helped promote speculation about Reagan's role. Noting that the national security adviser was not supposed to make decisions himself "on matters of policy change or initiative," McFarlane said of the decision to allow fund diversions to the contras: "I find it hard to imagine that it was undertaken without higher authority." *(Excerpts of text, p. 43-D)*

Aside from saying that Cabinet members normally would be involved in such matters, McFarlane did not define what he meant by higher authority.

Some congressional leaders said the issue of Reagan's knowledge was important not so much for fixing blame as for demonstrating why his administration got into trouble.

"If the president did not know what was going on here, and did not know of the diversion [of funds], then I think he should have known," Hamilton said Dec. 9. "The fact that he did not know would suggest that he does not have close control of his policy."

'Full' Cooperation?

In his Dec. 2 televised address from the Oval Office, Reagan promised that his administration would "cooperate fully" with congressional inquiries. He cited as an example his "unprecedented step" of allowing McFarlane and Poindexter to testify before Congress on what they had done while serving as national security adviser.

But within days, there were sharply conflicting reports from Capitol Hill about the real extent of cooperation by the administration.

"There obviously has not been a decision at the White House to make available the information that we need," Hamilton said Dec. 9.

But Bernard F. McMahon, staff director of the Senate Intelligence Committee, said the next day: "We have no indication in any way whatsoever that they [the administration] are stonewalling us or [are] not willing to cooperate."

The most obvious limit on administration cooperation was the refusal of Poindexter and North to testify. Foreign Affairs Chairman Fascell said the result was a "mixed signal" of cooperation.

Present administration officials and their agencies were cooperating to various degrees, said congressional sources. In spite of CIA Director Casey's legendary reluctance to hand over information to Capitol Hill, lower-level officials in that agency were among the most cooperative, the sources said, and representatives of the White House were the least forthcoming.

"The CIA has been very helpful," one senior House aide said. "They're worried about this thing damaging them, so they seem to want to get on our good side."

However, Foreign Affairs Committee members complained about Casey's own professed lack of knowledge. At several points in his sworn testimony Dec. 10, Casey turned to aides for answers, prompting Fascell to swear them in as well.

Solarz said Casey's own knowledge appeared so thin that he would be "better informed" if he spent more time reading the daily newspapers.

Hamilton expressed frustration at the refusal of several agencies, especially the White House, to provide his committee with documents. "I don't think we have any documentation," he said, noting that "there must be all kinds of" memorandums, legal opinions and correspondence bearing on the affair.

An Intelligence Committee aide said the administration had provided some documents "that shed some light." But he said several committee requests had gone unanswered.

Senate Intelligence was having better luck getting documents, after delays, and committee members were not raising much of a fuss.

"There is a tendency to accept the president at his word at this point that they are fully cooperating," Cohen said.

Chairman Durenberger was among those saying that it was in the administration's best interest to get information to Congress. "I think it is one of the scandals that gets larger by our inability to get the facts," he told reporters.

Durenberger on Dec. 5 asked the White House for a long list of documents. By Dec. 8, he demanded the documents within 24 hours — a demand that was not met.

Reagan spokesman Speakes said Dec. 10 that the White House had given Senate Intelligence "all of the documents they have requested, which we could identify based on what they have asked for."

That statement was somewhat premature; about a half-dozen documents — less than half that the committee had requested — arrived on Capitol Hill on Dec. 11. Senate committee spokesman David Holliday said the documents were helpful and that the White House was expected to provide further documents as soon as they could be found.

The White House refused to provide copies of documents to the Foreign Affairs Committee, saying that panel did not have adequate facilities to store highly classified material. Speakes said two committee staff members were allowed on Dec. 9 to read and make notes on documents at the White House but were not permitted to make copies or verbatim records of them.

One Foreign Affairs member, Toby Roth, R-Wis., said Congress brought on itself whatever reluctance the administration had to share information.

Roth said members "rushed to the cameras" to disclose what was said at private meetings. That "makes a mockery of congressional investigations and shows why the president cannot come to Congress with delicate information," he said.

What Did Contras Get?

One of the most perplexing questions facing congressional investigators was this: What happened to the money that supposedly was diverted to the contras from the Iranian arms sales?

Meese said on Nov. 25 that $10 million-$30 million in profits from the Iranian arms sales was put in a Swiss bank account controlled by the contras.

But officials from the CIA, the State Department and other agencies said there was little evidence that the contras in 1986 got anything near that amount of money from sources other than readily identifiable ones such as the U.S. government. Contra leaders also denied having a Swiss bank account or getting large sums of money from such an account.

Ironically, evidence that the money did not reach the contras would get the Reagan administration off the hook of one charge: that, by funneling the Iranian money to arm

Two Watergate-Style Panels Set Up . . .

Congress' dual-track approach toward investigating the Reagan administration's Iranian arms dealings got under way in December with the selection of special House and Senate committees.

Both chambers passed legislation (S Res 23, H Res 12) officially authorizing two Watergate-style panels immediately after the 100th Congress convened. The Senate on Jan. 6, 1987, voted to establish its special panel, formally named the Select Committee on Secret Military Assistance to Iran and the Nicaraguan Opposition. The next day, the House created its 15-member Select Committee to Investigate Covert Arms Transactions with Iran on a 416-2 vote.

In the Senate, incoming Majority Leader Robert C. Byrd, D-W.Va., worked with outside legislative experts in mid-December 1986 to draft a committee charter.

"I think it's very evenhanded. It treats everyone fairly. It's a very broad charter that will get at the facts," said Rufus L. Edmisten, who helped in the drafting. Edmisten was deputy chief counsel to the Senate Watergate committee and later attorney general of North Carolina.

The Senate's 11-member select committee was chaired by Daniel K. Inouye, D-Hawaii, a former Intelligence Committee chairman and member of the Senate Watergate panel that in 1973-74 investigated the activities of the Nixon White House.

In the House, Lee H. Hamilton, D-Ind., headed the 15-member special investigating committee. Hamilton was the outgoing chairman of the Intelligence Committee.

The senior Republicans on the two panels were Sen. Warren B. Rudman of New Hampshire and Rep. Dick Cheney of Wyoming, who served as chief of staff under President Ford.

Announcing the Senate membership on Dec. 16, Byrd said he picked six Democrats "who will be fair, who will be tough, who will not be out to get anybody, and who will not be out to protect anybody." Besides Inouye, the Democrats were George J. Mitchell of Maine, Sam Nunn of Georgia, Paul S. Sarbanes of Maryland, Howell Heflin of Alabama and David L. Boren of Oklahoma.

The GOP members named by Senate Republican leader Robert Dole of Kansas were Rudman, James A. McClure of Idaho, Orrin G. Hatch of Utah, William S. Cohen of Maine and Paul S. Trible Jr. of Virginia.

Dole, who had been lobbied heavily by several GOP senators wanting to be on the panel, said he picked members who had been "fairly quiet" about the Iranian arms scandal, "not suggesting anybody be fired or prosecuted or anything else."

House Committee Members

In the House, incoming Speaker Jim Wright, D-Texas, and Minority Leader Robert H. Michel, R-Ill., named their special committee members Dec. 17. Wright said the nine Democratic members "represent our highest level of experience, knowledge, judgment and wisdom" and described Hamilton, the chairman, as "impartial, judicious and fair."

Five of the Democrats were guaranteed a seat because they chaired committees with jurisdiction over various aspects of the Iran arms deal. These were: Dante B. Fascell of Florida, Foreign Affairs; Peter W. Rodino Jr. of New Jersey, Judiciary; Jack Brooks of Texas, Government Operations; Les Aspin of Wisconsin, Armed Services; and Louis Stokes of Ohio, new chairman of Intelligence.

The remaining four positions went to Hamilton, newly elected Majority Leader Thomas S. Foley of Washington, Edward P. Boland of Massachusetts and Ed Jenkins of Georgia.

In choosing his six members, Michel decided against naming all of the senior Republicans on the five committees. He appointed William S. Broomfield of Michigan, the senior Republican on Foreign Affairs, and Henry J. Hyde of Illinois, who was the ranking Republican on Intelligence.

Besides designating Cheney as the senior Republican on the panel, Michel dipped into the ranks of more junior House members for the remaining slots. They were filled by Michael DeWine of Ohio, Bill McCollum of Florida and Jim Courter of New Jersey.

Michel said he looked for Republicans with experience in foreign and intelligence matters, as well as those who had focused on legal issues on the Judiciary panel.

Cheney, explaining the selection of some junior lawmakers, noted that members of Congress had no "necessary wisdom" simply because of their seniority.

Ideological Splits

Ideologically, the House panel appeared more sharply divided than its Senate counterpart, with striking contrasts between ardent Democratic opponents and Republican supporters of Reagan's foreign policy, particularly on aid to the Nicaraguan contras.

Differences were a little softer on the Senate panel, where a more moderate to conservative tinge cut across party lines. For example, eight of the 11 Senate panel members — three Democrats and all five Republicans — voted to provide $100 million in military and other aid to the contras in a key vote in March. *(Vote 51, p. 10-S)*

In contrast, six of the nine Democrats on the House panel voted against contra aid in a similar vote in June, while three of them joined with all six Republicans in supporting Reagan. *(Vote 178, p. 54-H)*

Leaders of the two committees said they would try to cooperate with each other by exchanging information and trying to avoid competition.

"Many of us are headline seekers, and we may find one committee trying to outdo the other one in scoops and headlines," said Inouye.

Watergate Threads

Although virtually everyone on Capitol Hill had been playing down comparisons between Iran and Watergate, the selection of the two special panels included several threads linking them to the Watergate period. Foremost was Inouye's selection, since he also served on the Watergate panel.

In addition, the Senate committee included two members — Cohen and Sarbanes — who were members of the House Judiciary Committee that voted articles of

. . . To Investigate Iran-Contra Affair

impeachment against Richard M. Nixon in 1974, shortly before he resigned the presidency. *(1974 Almanac p. 867)*

Rodino and Brooks, on the House committee, also served on the Judiciary Committee that voted to impeach Nixon.

At his Dec. 17 press conference, Inouye dropped several references to Watergate, at one point recalling that Nixon's status as a "wounded president" invited "mischief" by foreign adversaries such as the Soviet Union.

"I'm not suggesting that our president [Reagan] is wounded badly, but there is no question that he has been injured," said Inouye.

Congressional leaders in both chambers, meanwhile, vowed that the panels would dig to the bottom of the administration's clandestine arms deals with Iran and the question of where the proceeds ended up.

Scope of Panels

As approved the week of Jan. 5, 1987, the charters set dates for both investigations. The Senate panel was scheduled to conclude its work by Aug. 1, 1987, although its charter allowed the Senate to vote to continue through October. The House panel had until Oct. 30, 1987, to wrap up unless the House extended the deadline.

The charters also gave both panels broad mandates, allowing them to go far beyond the Iran-contra connection. For example, the charters were written broadly enough to cover inquiries into efforts to channel private funds to the contras in 1984-86, when Congress had prohibited the U.S. government from arming the rebels.

The House's charter contained virtually no limits. Besides the Iran sales and diversion to the contras, the resolution empowered the committee to look into the "operational activities and the conduct of foreign and national security policy" by National Security Council and other White House staff members.

Another provision allowed the committee to look into "authorization and supervision or lack thereof" by the president and other officials over Iran-contra dealings and related matters.

The Senate resolution also authorized an inquiry into "the generation and use of any other money, item of value or service" to aid the contras.

Leaders of the House and Senate panels, however, said they would likely restrict their investigations, at least initially, to the Iran weapons sales and the diversion of profits. "It is not the intention of the committee to conduct an investigation into any private funding of the contras in which there is no direct or indirect government involvement," said Inouye.

Hamilton said the principal purpose of his investigation would be the Iran sales and money connection to the contras. But he added that the eventual scope of the committee's investigation would depend on "where the trail of evidence is going to lead."

In the House, several Republicans, including members of the Iran committee, criticized the breadth and duration of the investigation. Broomfield said, "This is not an investigation of the past six years of the Reagan administration. We should finish by April, not drag on until October."

But Cheney, the Iran panel's ranking Republican, reminded his colleagues: "We are not here today because of a plot by anybody in the Congress to create problems for the administration or for our party.... We are here today because problems developed in the administration."

House Staff Members

After an organizational meeting Jan. 8, Hamilton and Cheney announced their top staffers on the panel:

- John P. O'Hara, executive director. A former FBI agent and past staff director of the House Public Works Subcommittee on Investigations and Oversight, O'Hara was vice president for corporate security at Flying Tiger Line Inc., a Los Angeles-based air charter company. That post subsequently posed a conflict, and O'Hara left the committee job within two weeks. He was replaced by his personal executive assistant, Casey Miller.
- John W. Nields Jr., chief counsel. A Washington lawyer, Nields was chief counsel for the House ethics committee during its probe of the Korean bribery scandal in 1977-79.
- Tom R. Smeeton, minority counsel. He was a former CIA official who worked for years on the Republican staff of the House Foreign Affairs Committee. Since November 1986, he had been the minority counsel for the House Intelligence Committee.
- George Van Cleve, deputy minority counsel. At the time he was appointed, he was minority counsel for the House Interior Subcommittee on Water and Power Resources, of which Cheney was senior Republican. Van Cleve also worked for Cheney during his tenure as chief of staff for President Ford.

Senate Staff Members

Inouye and Rudman announced their top staff appointments on Jan. 22. They were:

- Arthur L. Liman, chief counsel. Known as a tough litigator, he was a member of Paul, Weiss, Rifkind, Wharton & Garrison, a blue-chip New York law firm. He specialized in complicated white-collar cases such as securities fraud, had been an assistant U.S. attorney in New York, and had been chief counsel to a special state commission set up in the early 1970s to investigate the uprising at Attica state prison.
- Paul Barbadoro, deputy chief counsel. A lawyer in Concord, N.H., Barbadoro was a former counsel for Rudman and was involved in the Senate impeachment proceedings against convicted U.S. District Judge Harry E. Claiborne. *(Story, p. 75)*
- Mary Jane Checchi, executive director. A Washington political consultant, Checchi was the staff director for the Senate Democratic Policy Committee from 1975-80.
- Lance Morgan, press secretary. A former press aide to Sen. Daniel Patrick Moynihan, D-N.Y., Morgan left that position in 1986 for a job at Burston-Marsteller, a public relations firm.
- Mark A. Belnick, one of Liman's partners at the Paul, Weiss firm, executive assistant to Liman.

the contras, it had violated the Boland amendment.

A senior State Department official who closely monitored the situation in Central America told reporters on Dec. 3 that there were no sudden surges of money or weapons reaching the contras in 1986.

The official acknowledged that the contras did receive military supplies "that were not provided by the United States government." But the amounts were small and apparently came from private sources, he said.

"It was clear to me that there was not much money coming in" to the contras, he said. "They were chronically under-supported and broke."

Durenberger said CIA officials who testified before his committee "came to the conclusion that they couldn't see the evidence of any substantial sums of money" going to the contras.

Congressional sources offered two possible explanations for the lack of information about money and weapons reaching the contras:

- North and others responsible for the diversion of aid to the contras somehow managed to mislead the State Department and the CIA, which supposedly were monitoring all of the contras' supply routes. Under this theory — for which there apparently was little hard evidence — weapons and other supplies bought with Iranian funds were delivered to the contras through circuitous routes to allay the suspicions even of sympathetic U.S. officials, who would be required to report any findings through official channels in Washington.
- Much of the money wound up in the pockets of arms dealers, who charged what Durenberger called a "markup for their services." That markup, he said, could have consumed most or all of the profits on the Iranian deals.

Two of the middlemen in the arms deal — Khashoggi of Saudi Arabia and Manucher Ghorbanifar of Iran — told ABC News Dec. 11 that they did not know what happened to profits from the sales.

Whatever amount of money ended up in the contras' hands, the alleged involvement of North revived questions on Capitol Hill about his role in directing a network of private aid to them.

Several congressional committees had looked into reports since 1984 that North was responsible for arranging financing of the contras by conservative groups. But the Reagan administration flatly denied each such report. For example, in September 1985, the Senate Intelligence Committee quoted McFarlane as saying that "no NSC staff member either personally assisted the resistance [contras] or solicited outside assistance on their behalf. At no time did anyone act as a go-between or focal point for such aid."

Reagan Seeks Immunity for Ex-Aides

Reagan Dec. 16 asked the Senate Intelligence Committee to short-cut investigations by granting limited "use" immunity to Poindexter and North. But committee members refused.

White House spokesman Speakes said Reagan was making that request because of "an urgent need for full disclosure of all facts," and that granting immunity to the two former aides was the fastest way of getting the information.

Meeting in closed session the following day, the committee rejected Reagan's request by "consensus," Durenberger said. Committee members, along with most other congressional leaders, called the request "premature."

Rather than taking such an action to hasten the inquiry, both chambers of Congress proceeded with their plan to appoint special Iran-contra committees.

Byrd and Dole on Dec. 16 appointed their committee of six Democrats and five Republicans, reflecting the party ratio of the Democratic-controlled Senate in the 100th Congress.

In the House, Speaker-designate Wright and Minority Leader Michel named a committee of nine Democrats and six Republicans.

Reagan's request for congressional immunity for Poindexter and North was widely viewed on Capitol Hill as a sign of the president's anxiety at the lingering public perception — evidenced in opinion polls — that he had something to hide.

The special Senate committee's vice chairman, Warren B. Rudman, R-N.H., said the president acted "out of frustration and anguish" that his two former aides had not told their stories. Along with most leaders of both parties, Rudman said immunity grants might be appropriate at some time — but not until the special committees and the independent counsel had been able to start their work.

Some members suggested that the president, in his request, was attempting to divert attention away from the troubles of his administration by creating a situation that would lead to squabbling in Congress. Leahy, for one, called the request "grandstanding."

A senior White House aide lent some credence to the latter interpretation, acknowledging that the president succeeded, if only temporarily, in putting his critics in Congress on the defensive. By rejecting the request, the official said, Congress rather than Reagan appeared to be blocking the pursuit of information.

This official said Reagan was aware when he made the request that the Senate committee would not approve it, having been warned as much by Dole. But the request "did demonstrate that the president wants the facts out and that it is up to Congress to act under the [immunity] procedures it established," the official said.

Although the reaction against Reagan's request came from members of both parties, some Republicans charged that the uniformly negative response of Democrats demonstrated their partisan interest in keeping the Iran-contra issue alive.

Orrin G. Hatch, R-Utah, said that with testimony by Poindexter and North, "we could resolve this in a matter of days, if not a couple weeks." But Democrats have decided that it is "politically astute" to "drag out this thing," charged Hatch, a member of the special investigating committee.

Byrd and other Democrats heatedly denied that charge and said they, too, wanted to settle the controversy as quickly as possible.

Aside from the political issues, there also were disputes on the Hill about the practicality of Reagan's request. The 1970 law (PL 91-452) allowing for limited, or "use" immunity, provided for built-in delays before it could be granted by a congressional committee. First, a committee had to approve the grant of immunity by a two-thirds vote. The attorney general or the independent counsel (if appointed) would have to have 10 days to review the committee decision, and he could ask for an additional 20-day delay.

Even if it had approved Reagan's request, the current Intelligence Committee probably would not have had time to obtain the testimony from Poindexter and North before the 99th Congress ended on Jan. 3, 1987. At that point, the two special committees and the independent counsel were starting their work — and they would oppose any apparent interference by the Intelligence Committee.

Some members used timing as the principal argument to go along with the president's request. Sen. Arlen Specter, R-Pa., said the committee "ought to take steps down the immunity path," if only to save the 10 days' notice time. The panel could later decide not to go through with immunity, Specter said, "but we can't recapture those 10 days."

Who Was in Charge?

In an unusual development, White House Chief of Staff Regan testified under oath before both Intelligence committees Dec. 16-18. Afterward, he told reporters that "I have done nothing wrong." Chiefs of staff rarely testify before Congress, and Regan did so after the president waived the traditional claim of executive privilege.

The testimony of Regan and other high government officials seemed to confirm that key White House decisions were made on a surprisingly informal basis and that Reagan allowed even mid-level aides such as North wide latitude.

The committees focused many of their questions on how, and by whom, two important decisions were made: the approval in 1985 of Israeli shipments to Iran of U.S.-made weapons and military supplies, and the authorization for funds from the Iranian arms sales to be diverted to the contras. Senior aides to Reagan provided sharply conflicting testimony on the first matter, and they all denied knowing anything at all about the second one.

Administration officials had given confusing and contradictory explanations of the U.S. decision to approve Israel's shipments of some 500 TOW anti-tank missiles to Iran in August and September 1985.

Briefing reporters Nov. 14 under the cloak of anonymity, Poindexter said the United States approved the Israeli shipments in advance — as part of an evolving White House policy of opening ties to "moderates" in Iran.

But in later statements, Poindexter and other officials said the United States did not approve those Israeli shipments until after they were made — probably in November, when Israel was preparing to send Iran parts for U.S.-made Hawk anti-aircraft missiles.

Regan and Meese both gave that version in their testimony on Capitol Hill. Regan told reporters Dec. 18 that the president was informed of the proposed Israeli shipments in August 1985, but opposed them. After learning that the shipments had been made, Regan said, the United States decided to "put up with it. It had happened. It was water over the dam."

However, McFarlane, who was Reagan's national security adviser at the time, repeatedly insisted that the president approved of, rather than opposed, the Israeli shipments before the fact.

Testifying in private to the two Intelligence committees and in public on Dec. 8 to the House Foreign Affairs Committee, McFarlane said Reagan did so by issuing an oral version of a "finding" — the legal term for presidential approval of an official covert operation by the U.S. government.

At the center of the disagreement was what happened at an Aug. 6 White House meeting during which the issue was discussed.

After listening to Regan, Meese and McFarlane, Senate Intelligence members seemed to give credence to McFarlane's assertion that the president had approved the Israeli shipments. "I would characterize McFarlane's testimony as much more explicit, much more definitive" than that of other officials, Durenberger said. "I think that with a little bit of reminding, the president would admit he gave some authorization" for the sale.

In addition to bearing on the truthfulness of key officials, the issue was important because the Israeli shipments were of questionable legality unless the United States gave advance approval.

Under PL 90-629, countries that bought American weapons could not turn around and sell them to other countries without first getting Washington's approval. Failure to get such approval could be punished by a cutoff of U.S. aid. Because of its closeness to Washington, Israel did not need to fear a suspension of aid. However, any public allegation that Israel violated U.S. law would embarrass both countries.

Israeli officials insisted that they got prior U.S. approval for the 1985 sales.

The separate question of who authorized the diversion of Iranian arms sales funds to the contras proved equally troubling to the administration and congressional investigators.

Regan told both Intelligence panels that the diversion was not an officially approved policy.

"I can tell you that Col. North or nobody else was ever authorized to divert funds from the proceeds of sales of arms to Iranians to the contras or anyone else," Regan said Dec. 16. "I had no idea the funds were diverted," he said.

Regan also said he believed the president was unaware that the Iranian funds were being diverted.

Meese Dec. 19 said North had told him that only he, Poindexter and McFarlane knew about the diversion.

Those statements prompted conflicting reactions from committee members. An example was the disagreement between Durenberger and Leahy.

Durenberger said he believed that North "was not operating under anybody's authority" when he established Swiss bank accounts that were used to funnel money from the Iranian sales to arms dealers and, reportedly, to the contras. "There is no evidence that anyone else gave him the blessing, or gave the wink or gave the authority at all. It's Ollie North and that's it."

Acknowledging that he had no hard evidence, Leahy said he had concluded that North acted in cooperation with other officials, possibly including superiors at the White House. "If he set up a Swiss bank account and moved money to the contras, I think someone else was involved," he said.

Tracing the Money

Without testimony by North, congressional investigators were unable to get precise answers about what happened to the money from the Iranian arms sales. One conclusion some drew, however, was that the amount that reached the contras probably was at the low end of the $10 million-$30 million range that Meese gave on Nov. 25. The actual diversion to the contras might have been as little as $5 million, sources said.

Meese said his figure was a "rough estimate" and that "we don't know exactly how much money was involved."

Iranian arms dealer Ghorbanifar said that he deposited $35 million into Swiss bank accounts as payment for U.S. arms sales, and administration officials said the CIA reimbursed the Defense Department about $12 million for those weapons.

The direct U.S. arms shipments to Iran reportedly were made in February, May, August and October of 1986. In all, according to administration and congressional officials, the United States sold Iran 2,008 TOW anti-tank missiles, parts for Hawk anti-aircraft missiles and supplies for several other pieces of military equipment that Iran had bought in the 1970s.

Although Reagan and his aides said in November that the total amount of arms could fit into one large cargo plane, officials subsequently said that claim vastly understated the extent of the arms shipments.

CIA and State Department officials insisted that the contras did not receive large, unaccounted-for infusions of aid during the period when profits from the Iranian sales supposedly were diverted.

Hamilton summarized the lack of hard evidence this way on Dec. 17: "The Iranians got the arms. They paid money to somebody. It probably initially went to some of the arms dealers. Eventually, part of that money, we've been told, ended up in a CIA account. Where the diversion occurred, I don't know. How much of a diversion, I don't know. How much of a profit was made by the arms dealers, I don't know."

Another issue was whether the administration deliberately discounted the value of the weapons sold to Iran so that profits would be made. Sen. Cohen said the Intelligence Committee had received evidence that the Pentagon provided the weapons at "at least wholesale" prices. In some cases, the arms were then sold to Iran at a markup of 400 percent, he said.

The pricing issue was important for two reasons: a deliberate under-pricing of U.S. equipment might be illegal, and it might show that diversion of money was an intended side-benefit of the Iranian sales.

Specter said he had seen "ample evidence to prosecute" someone, whom he would not name. The most likely crime that anybody could be charged with is "fraudulent conversion" of federal property, he said.

The congressional committees did not have access to one source of information: the Swiss bank accounts. Responding to the Justice Department, the Swiss government froze four accounts that North and others reportedly used to handle money from the Iranian deals.

Pardons Rejected

Incoming House Speaker Wright suggested Dec. 21 that Reagan pardon two key figures in the scandal in exchange for their testimony on Capitol Hill. But White House spokesman Speakes said Reagan did not intend to take that step.

Wright, in a television interview with John McLaughlin, said a pardon would provide the "ultimate immunity" to Poindexter and North, who had invoked their Fifth Amendment rights against self-incrimination.

But Speakes told reporters Dec. 22 that Reagan had ruled out a pardon of North and Poindexter. The spokesman said such an action "would not allow the punishment of any wrongdoing, if there were wrongdoing in this matter."

Senate Intelligence Report

After working nearly full time for two weeks, the Senate Intelligence Committee wrapped up its probe on Dec. 18. Its House counterpart called Secord to testify in its final session Dec. 23; the retired Air Force general invoked the Fifth Amendment. *(Major witnesses, box, p. 429)*

Leaders of the Intelligence panels said their probes uncovered substantial amounts of information, but failed to answer some of the most important questions, especially those involving the proceeds from the Iran arms sales.

The most important questions were: Who authorized the reported diversion of funds to the contras from the Iran arms sales; what happened to the diverted money; and did Reagan give advance approval in 1985 to Israel's shipments of U.S. arms to Iran?

Because key figures, notably Poindexter and North, refused to testify, the committees were stymied in their efforts to answer the first two questions. The Intelligence hearings produced conflicting testimony from senior Reagan aides on the last question.

Nevertheless, Reagan pressed the Senate Intelligence Committee on Dec. 23 to provide him with a report on its investigation so that he could present a declassified version

Casey Replaced at CIA

William J. Casey, the Central Intelligence Agency's (CIA) combative and controversial director since 1981, resigned Feb. 2, 1987, in the wake of surgery to remove a brain tumor.

To succeed Casey, President Reagan named Robert M. Gates, a career intelligence and national security official who had been the CIA's deputy director since April 1986. But Gates' nomination ran into trouble in early March 1987, after the Tower review board raised questions about his role in the Iran-contra affair.

Casey was hospitalized Dec. 15, one day before he had been scheduled to testify for the second time before the Senate Intelligence Committee. He first testified before the committee Nov. 21, and also appeared before the House Intelligence and Foreign Affairs committees.

In a five-hour operation Dec. 18, doctors removed the tumor from the left side of Casey's brain. Preliminary examinations indicated it was a lymphoma, a form of cancer.

Although it was clear for weeks that Casey would be unable to return to work, Reagan ordered White House officials not to speculate on a possible successor — apparently fearing that press reports might endanger the recovery of his longtime friend.

In spite of Reagan's orders, there was considerable behind-the-scenes maneuvering, with various political factions in Washington promoting their own candidates. White House Chief of Staff Donald T. Regan approached former Sen. Howard H. Baker Jr., R-Tenn. (1967-85), who said he did not want the job.

The appointment of Gates surprised most Washington observers, who had expected Reagan to choose either a well-known political figure or another high-level intelligence official with political connections, such as Lt. Gen. William Odom, director of the National Security Agency.

Gates' ties to Casey apparently were enough; intelligence officials said Reagan almost certainly appointed the new director on Casey's recommendation.

to the public. The panel voted Jan. 5, 1987, not to release the staff report, but much of the information in it subsequently was leaked to the news media.

Staff's Findings Leaked

One version, obtained Jan. 8 by NBC News, noted that freeing the American hostages was a primary goal of the secret Iran arms deals. Durenberger said it was a "rough, earlier draft" that did not include a full summary of testimony before the committee.

The urgency of getting the hostages released was underscored by Reagan's Jan. 17, 1986, intelligence "finding" and the companion memorandum that authorized the Iran arms sales. Those two documents were released by the White House in the wake of the NBC report.

Among other things, the leaked Senate Intelligence staff report stated:

- No evidence could be found that Reagan knew about the diversion of Iranian arms money to the contras. The White House used this part of the report to bolster its contention that North had acted on his own in arranging the diversion.

Poindexter also knew of the diversion, the report said. It said Regan testified that Poindexter had allowed the diversion because he "felt sorry for the contras once Congress cut off their aid."

- If any Iranian arms sale money actually reached the contras, the amount probably was less than $10 million. But Durenberger said evidence showed that only about $8.5 million probably was diverted in mid-1986 — most of it money owed a consortium of businessmen who financed the arms sales.
- Israel played a major role in the arms sales to Iran. Acting on behalf of the United States, Israel made at least three shipments to Iran in 1985. In December of that year, after Reagan decided to suspend U.S. involvement in the shipments, a senior Israeli official — counterterrorism expert Amiram Nir — helped persuade the White House to reconsider.

Ten days later, the Senate Intelligence panel's staff conclusions were published in *The New York Times.* Among those conclusions were that top Reagan officials ignored or did not receive repeated warnings in 1986 that the U.S. initiative toward Iran had "gone wrong."

Administration officials were particularly reluctant to heed CIA misgivings about the key Iranian intermediary, Ghorbanifar. CIA analysts concluded that Ghorbanifar could not be trusted, the report said, but higher-level policy makers continued to do business with him. It was Ghorbanifar who ultimately leaked to a Middle East magazine the news that Reagan was selling arms to Iran in exchange for the release of hostages.

The staff conclusions condemned the administration's handling of the Iran episode. The only officials escaping criticism were unnamed middle-level CIA aides who, the report said, issued unheeded warnings. Other warnings came from McFarlane and former CIA official George Cave.

The CIA did come in for criticism in the report. Because the CIA saw the Iran program as the NSC's responsibility, the report said, the agency "appears to have allowed itself to participate in actions it may have rejected if they had been proposed for CIA implementation."

The report also faulted Casey for his Nov. 21 testimony; the staff concluded that it "contained several misleading statements and omitted certain significant points."

The staff also concluded that the administration violated or skirted several laws and its own foreign policy guidelines.

Among these:

- The failure to give Congress "timely" notice about the arms sales, which Reagan had authorized as a CIA covert action. The administration insisted that the president could defer indefinitely its notice to Congress of especially sensitive CIA operations. But the staff said the legislative history of PL 96-450 showed that the president could defer notice to Congress only because of "rapidly changing events," and not because he feared disclosure. The staff also concluded that the administration "never seriously considered" invoking a procedure under which eight senior Hill leaders could be notified.
- Reagan's retroactive authorization in January 1986 of the CIA's 1985 role in aiding at least one Israeli arms shipment to Iran. Such after-the-fact approval, the report said, damaged both congressional oversight of the CIA and the president's own ability to control covert actions.
- The "possible" violation of the Boland amendment (PL 99-169), the legal ban on direct or indirect U.S. military aid to the contras in fiscal 1985-86. The alleged contra aid diversion needed further investigation, the Senate committee staff found, but evidence suggested the administration at least "failed to take the steps necessary to ensure compliance" with the law.
- The skirting of several of Reagan's own guidelines for handling covert actions. The report said the administration failed to follow three 1981 guidelines — that all approvals for covert actions be given in writing; that all covert actions be reviewed periodically by senior national security officials; and that the CIA be responsible for carrying out all covert actions unless the president specifically ruled otherwise.

Committee spokesman Holliday branded the Times' action in publishing the staff's conclusions as "irresponsible" and said some information in the report was incorrect. Other sources said the document reproduced by the newspaper was genuine.

Releasing the Report

With the Democrats taking control of the committee in the 100th Congress, the panel's new chairman, Sen. Boren, took charge of rewriting the report.

The panel voted 14-1 on Jan. 29, 1987, to send the revised report to the Senate's select committee investigating the Iran-contra affair. In a game of pingpong, the select committee then voted unanimously to send the document back to the Intelligence panel with a recommendation that it be released.

The Intelligence panel then released the 65-page report, which provided details of White House involvement in the arms-for-hostages deals and the alleged diversion of funds to the contras.

Unlike the previously leaked staff report, however, the new Intelligence Committee document did not draw conclusions. Instead, it recited the history of U.S. dealings with Iran and aid to the contras, based on the testimony of 36 witnesses and thousands of pages of documents.

Boren said the report generally showed "serious problems" in the administration's policy-making apparatus. In some cases, policy was made by "amateurs," he said, and the White House relied too heavily on private individuals, including foreign arms dealers, to carry out policy.

The panel listed in its report 14 "unresolved issues"

for the select panel to investigate. Several of these centered on the role played by White House aides, other U.S. officials and private individuals in the affair. The panel also appeared to suggest a broader inquiry into support for the contras by the government and private sources.

Iranian Arms Sales

U.S. dealings with Iran resulted from a convergence of four developments in late 1984 and early 1985, according to the report:

- Suggestions by mid-level U.S. officials that it was time to review policy toward Iran, in part to thwart possible Soviet designs on that country.
- A campaign by private Middle Eastern arms dealers to promote weapons trade between the United States and Iran.
- Israel's interest in improving ties with Iran, which was engaged in a fierce war with Iraq, one of Israel's most feared enemies.
- Washington's desire to gain freedom for American hostages in Lebanon.

The report emphasized the connection between the arms sales and the freeing of the hostages. Testimony showed that Reagan had a "deep personal concern" for the welfare of the hostages, the report said, and the possibility that they could be released "was brought up repeatedly in conjunction" with the arms sales.

In all of his public statements on the matter, Reagan had said getting freedom for hostages was only one of many reasons for dealing with Iran.

The committee also confirmed reports that, three times in 1986, the United States gave Iran intelligence information on Iraqi military positions. There had been reports that the CIA deliberately supplied inaccurate information; the agency denied those accounts and the Intelligence panel did not address the issue.

The report cited several cases in which the White House bypassed regular channels — especially the State Department — in dealing with Iran. That started early in 1985 when then national security adviser McFarlane asked a White House consultant, Michael Ledeen, to discuss Iran with Shimon Peres, Israel's prime minister at the time. Shultz later protested, but the White House continued its own dealings in the Middle East. Eventually, the report said, Shultz wrote himself out of the Iran operation by allowing the White House to run it.

The United States was involved in the following arms shipments to Iran, according to the report:

- 508 U.S.-made TOW anti-tank missiles sent from Israel to Iran via a third country. The missiles left Israel Aug. 30 and arrived in Iran Sept. 13, 1985. The panel cited conflicting testimony from White House officials about whether Reagan knew about and authorized this shipment in advance or months later. The report quoted Shultz, who opposed the deal, as saying that four American hostages were supposed to be released in Lebanon in exchange for the arms. But on Sept. 15, only one hostage was freed — the Rev. Weir. McFarlane said Reagan was "elated."

Washington later provided Israel with replacement missiles.

- 18 Hawk anti-aircraft missiles, shipped by a CIA-owned airline from Israel to Iran in late November 1985. Two key actors became involved in the Iran operation at this point, making arrangements for this shipment: National Security Council staff member North and retired Air Force Maj. Gen. Secord.

Iran rejected the missiles, saying they wanted more sophisticated Improved-Hawk missiles instead.

After temporarily suspending U.S. involvement with Iran, Reagan on Jan. 17, 1986, signed the formal authorization for CIA covert arms dealings with Tehran; Reagan ordered the CIA not to tell Congress.

- 1,000 TOW missiles, shipped by the CIA to Israel on Feb. 15-16, 1986, and then transferred in two deliveries to Iran. One plane picked up and returned to Israel the 18 Hawk missiles that Iran had rejected earlier. No American hostages were released.
- A small quantity of spare parts for Hawk missiles, delivered to Tehran on a plane carrying a diplomatic delegation headed by McFarlane. The May 25-28, 1986, mission was to establish high-level U.S.-Iran contacts and to lead to the release of all American hostages in Lebanon. McFarlane was able to meet only with mid-level officials, however, and no hostages were freed. Reagan had approved the trip and the arms delivery on May 15.
- Additional Hawk spare parts, delivered to Iran Aug. 3, 1986. One hostage, the Rev. Jenco, had been released in Lebanon on July 29 — possibly as an Iranian signal of renewed interest in continuing the relationship with the United States.
- 500 TOW missiles, shipped from Israel to Iran Oct. 29, 1986. The United States reimbursed Israel for the missiles Nov. 6. David Jacobsen, an American hostage, was released from Lebanon Nov. 2, and the next day a Lebanese magazine broke the news that the United States had been shipping weapons to Iran.

U.S. officials continued clandestine meetings with Iranians even after the arms dealings were made public. In November 1986, a U.S. team led by North met with Iranian sources; it was for those meetings that Reagan inscribed in a Bible his hope for improved relations with Iran.

Representatives of the State Department and the CIA also met with Iranian contacts on Dec. 13, 1986; the State Department official left the meeting when the Iranians called for additional arms sales.

Contra Aid, Israeli Connection

The Senate report, in a 22-page section dealing with the alleged diversion of funds to the Nicaraguan rebels, did not include any direct evidence that Reagan was aware of the plan.

When Attorney General Meese informed Reagan and Chief of Staff Regan on Nov. 24, 1986, that he had discovered the diversion program, according to the report, "Meese said the president looked shocked and very surprised, as did Regan, who uttered an expletive."

While it did not resolve several outstanding questions about the contra funding, the report outlined in considerable detail the chain of events that surrounded the apparent origins of the diversion, some of the key officials involved and how it was carried out.

The committee traced a "direct connection" between the Iran weapons sales and contra funding to discussions in January 1986 between North and Nir, Peres' anti-terrorism adviser.

According to the report, notes from a November meeting between North and Meese indicated that Nir proposed using profits from the Iran deals to aid the contras. But Meese also testified that he was uncertain whether it was North or Nir who brought up the contras.

The report quoted North telling Meese that shortly after his meeting with Nir, he contacted contra leader

Adolfo Calero, after which three bank accounts were opened in Switzerland.

North gave the account numbers to the Israelis, who then deposited money from the arms sales, according to the report's account of Meese's interview with North. "North guessed the money got to the contras; they knew money came and were appreciative," said the report.

Israeli officials had denied suggesting the contra diversion, insisting instead they only passed the money from the weapons sales into bank accounts at the request of U.S. officials.

Another suggestion to funnel money to the contras, according to the report, came from Albert Hakim, an Iranian-American associated with North and in business with Secord. Hakim proposed that the Iranians contribute to the contras while acting as an interpreter between the Americans and Iranians at a meeting on arms sales that took place in Europe in early 1986.

The account of Hakim's activities came from notes of a November meeting between Assistant Attorney General Charles Cooper and Tom Green, a lawyer representing North and Secord. The notes were described in the Senate report.

Green, according to Cooper's notes, said money from arms shipments in February and May 1986 was routed to the contras through the Israelis and Hakim's financial network.

According to Cooper's notes, Green also said Hakim and Secord "felt like they were doing the Lord's work. They believed they were not violating any laws."

A White House memorandum drafted on or shortly after April 4, 1986, outlined the Iran arms program and its link to funding the contras. According to the report, a section of the memo said $12 million from the weapons sales would be used to buy for the contras "critically needed supplies."

At the bottom of one of the memo's pages was a recommendation that presidential approval be obtained for portions of the plan dealing with Iran that did not include diverting money to the contras.

The memo was not signed "and it is not clear to the committee who, if anyone, saw it," said the Senate report.

Meese confronted North about the memo after Justice Department officials discovered it in NSC files in November 1986. Meese told the committee that North confirmed the memo's contents and was "surprised and visibly shaken."

According to notes from Meese's inquiry, North said he had not discussed the matter with Reagan. North also told Meese that he would have had a record showing the president's approval if one were given.

The report said that North told Meese he had informed McFarlane about the contra diversion in April or May 1986 "and that the only three people who could know in the U.S. were McFarlane, Poindexter and North."

McFarlane told the Intelligence Committee that he learned about the contra diversion when he and North were returning from a secret mission to Tehran in May 1986.

When McFarlane asked North in November who had approved the contra program, the report said, "North responded that he would never do anything without it being approved by higher authority and that he could not account for who was involved beyond Poindexter." It was not precisely clear from the report when North told Poindexter about the contra program. Meese said Poindexter told him on Nov. 24 that North had given Poindexter "enough hints" to let him know about the diversion, but that he "didn't inquire further" into the matter.

Other details about the contra connection in the Senate report included:

- Evidence that a Swiss bank account suspected of being used by North, Hakim and Secord to funnel Iranian funds to the contras was also used for U.S.-solicited contributions to the contras from other countries. The nation of Brunei had been identified elsewhere as having agreed to contribute $10 million to the contras, but whether or not the money was ever received remained in dispute.
- Details about an offer in September 1986 by Israel to ship captured Soviet weapons to the contras. Poindexter briefed Reagan on the offer before the president met at the White House on Sept. 15 with Peres. Regan said Reagan never told him what was discussed in a private 15-minute conversation with Peres, and that the Soviet arms shipment did not come up in an open White House meeting.
- Suspicions by CIA officials in September 1986 about the possible diversion of Iranian funds to the contras. There was evidence that the matter was brought to the attention of Casey in early October. The report also recounted an Oct. 9 meeting involving Casey, North and CIA Deputy Director Robert M. Gates at which North "made very cryptic references" to Swiss bank accounts and money for the contras, according to Gates' committee testimony.

When Casey and Gates pressed North on CIA involvement in the diversion, North assured them that the agency was "completely clean," said Gates.

- Unconfirmed information showing Iranian funds intended for the contras deposited into accounts in Crédit Fiducière Services, a Swiss bank. The bank then allegedly transferred money to its subsidiaries in Grand Cayman which disbursed it to the contras.

Tower Report

In its Feb. 26, 1987, report, the Tower commission described three foundations for the Iran-contra policy disaster: Reagan's hands-off management style; the failure of his aides to compensate for the president's lack of attention to detail; and the eagerness of White House staffers to brush aside the institutional process for making and carrying out decisions.

The panel squarely placed much of the blame on Reagan, saying he made little effort to find out what his staff was doing and allowed his compassion for the American hostages in Lebanon to override his stated policies of not dealing with terrorists.

During most of the Iranian arms operation, the board said, Reagan knew few details and expressed little interest in actions taken in his name. "The president simply was not told the details of what was going on, and did not ask the kinds of forcing questions which would have brought many of these issues to the surface," board member Brent Scowcroft said.

Reagan's principal failure, the board said, was that he did not demand that his staff — especially aides to the NSC — follow normal procedures. Reagan "should have ensured that the NSC system did not fail him," the report said. Instead, "he did not force his policy to undergo the most critical review of which the NSC participants and the process were capable. At no time did he insist upon accountability and performance review." *(NSC, p. 422)*

With a string of institutional failures, the board said, "it is the president who must take responsibility for the

NSC system and deal with the consequences."

Given what it called Reagan's "management style," the panel said the White House staff had a special obligation to keep him informed. "It was incumbent upon the other participants in the system to ensure that the president was absolutely clear about what was going on," Scowcroft said. "There should have been bells ringing, lights flashing and so on. . . ."

Instead, administration aides were obsessed with secrecy, running their own operations and often hiding their doings from one another as well as from the president. The board criticized Reagan's two national security advisers during the Iran operation — first McFarlane, then Poindexter — for failing to keep Reagan and fellow officials, including Cabinet members, informed. Poindexter also was singled out for not exercising control over North.

Secretary of State Shultz and Defense Secretary Weinberger "distanced themselves from the march of events," the panel said, and "were not energetic in attempting to protect the president from the consequences" of his obsession with freeing the hostages.

The Tower panel also produced evidence that White House officials attempted to cover up Reagan's role once the Iranian arms deals became public knowledge in November 1986. It cited, in particular, testimony by McFarlane that he helped draft a chronology of events that tried to "blur" the president's approval of the arms sales.

Administration officials highlighted two findings that they said bolstered Reagan's previous statements. The board said it found no evidence that the president knew about or approved the alleged diversion of Iranian arms money to the contras, or that he participated in any cover-up of wrongdoing.

Describing himself as a strong supporter of the president, Tower insisted to reporters that the Iran-contra affair was an "aberration" in an otherwise "pretty satisfactory" performance by the Reagan administration.

Reagan critics, however, said the failures of the administration were more fundamental than a temporary mishap. They pointed to other blunders, notably the October 1986 summit meeting in Iceland during which Reagan suddenly agreed to a drastic proposal of nuclear disarmament, apparently with little consideration of the consequences and without consulting allies and key military aides.

"I do not think it was an aberration. I think it goes deeper than that," said Sen. Nunn. "You can't have all these people running around town making foreign policy decisions on their own."

THE ARMS-FOR-HOSTAGES DEALINGS

The Tower panel traced the origin of U.S. arms sales to Iran to a White House effort late in 1984 to reassess overall policy toward Tehran. But, it said, intervention by Israel resulted in the policy developing faster than Washington had planned, and the initiative became inextricably linked with hostages rather than broader foreign policy objectives.

Laying fact upon fact, citing one internal White House memo after another, the commission report demolished Reagan's claims that he had not traded arms for hostages. The entire arrangement of U.S. and Israeli arms sales during a period of more than a year "was premised on Iran's ability to secure [the hostages'] release," the commission said.

Tower, Muskie and Scowcroft agreed in their report that the stated goal of improving relations with Iran "may have been in the national interest."

But, they said, the United States "should never have been a party to the arms transfers. As arms-for-hostages trades, they could not help but create an incentive for further hostage-taking."

The report detailed the development of U.S. arms sales to Iran, beginning with the policy reviews in 1984 and continuing through the final shipment of missiles in late October 1986 — just a few days before the secret dealings became public knowledge.

Roots of the Policy

The State Department in October 1984 produced an inter-agency study suggesting that there was little the United States could do to influence events in Iran. This study was requested by national security adviser McFarlane, who was concerned that the United States had no plan for dealing with possible turmoil in Iran once the leader there, the Ayatollah Ruhollah Khomeini, died.

Concerns about Iran continued, however, and on May 20, 1985, the White House and CIA produced a special intelligence estimate raising the prospect of Soviet gains if Iran were to descend into chaos. On June 11, McFarlane's aides drafted a National Security Decision Directive outlining U.S. goals toward Iran. One was to encourage allies "to help Iran meet its important requirements," including "selected military equipment."

Secretary of State Shultz and Defense Secretary Weinberger vigorously objected to the proposal; Weinberger, according to previous reports, called it "absurd." CIA Director Casey, however, was said to "strongly endorse" the thrust of the document, although he did not address the arms sale issue.

Apparently because of the objections by Shultz and Weinberger, the proposal was scrapped and never submitted to Reagan.

While this debate was under way in Washington, two other sets of discussions were taking place.

Israeli officials and arms dealers were talking about using arms sales to Iran to obtain the release of American hostages in Lebanon and to open talks with Tehran, and Israeli and U.S. officials were conducting their own talks on Iran. Involved at that point were the men who later emerged as main characters in the arms sales saga: McFarlane, NSC consultant Michael Ledeen, exiled Iranian businessman Manucher Ghorbanifar, Israeli arms dealers Adolph Schwimmer and Jacob Nimrodi, Saudi Arabian businessman Adnan Khashoggi, and Israeli officials David Kimche and Amiram Nir.

On May 4 or 5, 1985, Ledeen met in Jerusalem with Prime Minister Shimon Peres and asked if Israel would share with the United States its intelligence information on Iran.

The Israeli response apparently came on July 3, when Kimche — director general of the Foreign Ministry — met with McFarlane in Washington. McFarlane testified that Kimche asked whether the United States was interested in talking to Iranians. To demonstrate their "bona fides," Kimche told McFarlane, the Iranians would try to win freedom for American hostages; the Iranians would need something in return, probably arms.

McFarlane said Reagan agreed to explore the proposal. The president's reaction, McFarlane testified Feb. 21, was "quite enthusiastic and perhaps excessively enthusiastic, given the many uncertainties involved."

McFarlane noted that Reagan's approval came shortly

after the conclusion of a Middle East hostage crisis. Two Lebanese men on June 14 had hijacked a TWA airliner, killed an American sailor on board, and held 39 passengers hostage in Beirut. The hostages were released June 30 — possibly after the intervention of Iranian officials. Reagan, according to Muskie, became emotionally involved in that hostage crisis, especially on July 2, when he welcomed the hostages back to the United States and placed flowers on the grave of Robert D. Stethem, the Navy diver who had been shot.

On July 13, Ledeen passed to McFarlane a message from Schwimmer, the Israeli arms dealer, saying the Iranians believed they could win freedom for the seven Americans then held hostage in Lebanon in return for 100 TOW anti-tank missiles to be provided by Israel. McFarlane said he understood the deal was to be only part of a broader "private dialogue" with Iran.

Shultz, then traveling in Australia, agreed to opening talks with the Iranians but said in a cable to McFarlane that McFarlane should "handle this probe personally." Shultz also raised a caution about the Israeli proposal, noting that "Israel's interest and ours are not necessarily the same."

Reagan, recovering in Bethesda Naval Hospital from a cancer operation, approved the talks, according to testimony by McFarlane and White House Chief of Staff Regan.

August: The Disputed Decision

Exactly what happened in the next sequence of events was disputed by the participants, the Tower commission found. This sequence started with an Aug. 2 White House meeting between McFarlane and Kimche, who asked for the U.S. position on arms sales to Iran. McFarlane said Washington would not sell arms directly to Tehran, but he promised an answer on whether the United States would approve of Israeli sales. How he got that answer was "murky," the report said.

The panel got these versions of the events of early August 1985:

- McFarlane said he had numerous discussions with Reagan and other U.S. officials. Early in August, McFarlane said, Reagan told him in a telephone conversation that the United States should not sell its arms to Iran, but Israel could sell U.S.-made weapons, and could buy replacements from the United States, if the result did not upset the military balance in the region and if no major weapons systems were involved. McFarlane said he passed Reagan's approval on to Kimche and to top U.S. officials, including Shultz and Weinberger. McFarlane's version of events generally had been consistent in all of his public and private statements.
- Shultz and Weinberger both recalled meetings at which they expressed opposition to Israeli arms sales to Iran. Shultz cited Aug. 6 as the date of a key meeting, but others could not pinpoint an exact date.
- Regan told the board that in an early August meeting, the president expressed concern about swapping arms for hostages but supported developing contacts with Iran. Regan said the president was surprised and "upset" in September when McFarlane told him Israel had sold arms to Iran in hopes of freeing hostages. Regan told reporters Dec. 18 that "to the best of my recollection the president was against the shipment."
- Reagan gave the Tower board three versions. On Jan. 26, 1987, he supported McFarlane's story, saying that he had approved the Israeli shipment sometime in August but could not recall the exact date. Reagan gave the board a marked copy of McFarlane's Jan. 16, 1986, testimony to the Senate Foreign Relations Committee, apparently indicating his agreement with what McFarlane had said.

Two weeks later, on Feb. 11, Reagan told the board that, after discussing the matter repeatedly with Regan, he could not recall giving advance approval in August for an Israeli arms shipment.

Told by aides that his testimony was inconsistent, Reagan wrote a letter to the Tower panel Feb. 20 saying that "I'm afraid that I let myself be influenced by others' recollections, not my own." Admitting he had no records, Reagan said: "The only honest answer is to state that try as I might, I cannot recall anything whatsoever about whether I approved an Israeli sale in advance or whether I approved replenishment of Israeli stocks around August of 1985. My answer therefore and the simple truth is, 'I don't remember — period.' "

Confronted with those conflicting recollections, the Tower commission appeared to believe McFarlane.

"Absent any evidence to the contrary, we have to conclude that the president's recollection of when the first shipment was approved is faulty," Tower said. The board made a "plausible judgment," he added, that Reagan approved the shipment before it was made on Aug. 30, as McFarlane said.

In addition to bearing on the credibility of the individuals involved, the issue of whether Reagan gave advance approval for Israeli shipments of U.S. arms was important from a legal standpoint. Under U.S. law, any country buying American weapons cannot transfer them to another nation without getting Washington's approval in advance. Failure to do so could result in a loss of foreign aid.

Israel relied heavily on U.S. aid totaling $3 billion a year, and Israeli officials had said they would not have sold arms to Iran without approval.

The First Shipments

Israel's first supply of arms to Iran was in two parts: 100 TOW missiles on Aug. 30 and 408 missiles on Sept. 14. The board quoted Ghorbanifar as saying the second shipment was supposed to contain 400 missiles, but eight extras were on the Israeli plane when it landed in Tabriz, Iran.

The number of missiles also may have startled the White House. McFarlane testified that he was "surprised by the move from 100 to at least 400" missiles.

Kimche called McFarlane early in September, saying that all U.S. hostages in Lebanon would be released, and McFarlane said he passed that word on to Reagan and other officials.

At about this time, NSC aide North entered the Iran arms picture. North in late August obtained a passport from the State Department bearing the name "William P. Goode"; the Tower panel quoted a North computer memo saying he was to use the passport on a "sensitive operation to Europe" in connection with the hostages. However, the board quoted one official as saying North stayed in Washington at the time.

Ledeen testified that North told him in September 1985 that he was handling "all the operational aspects" of the Iran deals.

The arms deal bore fruit Sept. 15, but not to the extent that Israel and the United States had hoped. A pro-Iranian group released only one hostage, the Rev. Weir.

The deals were financed in a peculiar manner that was

to become the model for arms shipments to Iran.

To guarantee payment on the 100 TOWs, Ghorbanifar gave Khashoggi a $1 million postdated check. Khashoggi deposited $1 million in a Swiss bank account controlled by Nimrodi (the Israeli arms dealer), Iran put $1.2 million into a Swiss account to pay for the shipment, Israel delivered the missiles, and Ghorbanifar gave Khashoggi the go-ahead to cash his check.

Financing of the second shipment worked the same way. Khashoggi provided $4 million in up-front money for 400 missiles, and Iran paid $5 million once they were delivered, plus $250,000 for the extra eight missiles.

Sending Hawks to Iran

In spite of the disappointing results of the first shipments, Israel and the United States continued the contacts with Iran during the fall of 1985, and Israel launched plans for a more important shipment in November.

This planning occurred during a rush of world events in October and November, especially the hijacking of the *Achille Lauro* cruise ship and the first summit meeting in Geneva between Reagan and Soviet leader Mikhail S. Gorbachev. The Tower panel said U.S. officials were preoccupied with those events, not Iran.

Apparently assuming that the United States had provided open-ended approval for arms shipments to Iran, Israel drafted plans to ship Hawk anti-aircraft missiles in exchange for the release of four or five American hostages in Lebanon. Early plans called for delivery of 80 or 120 missiles, according to documents cited by the board, but in the end only 18 were delivered. Direct U.S. involvement in this shipment also was much greater than in the earlier shipments.

As before, the financing was circuitous. Ghorbanifar paid Israel $24 million in advance for 120 missiles, but Iran canceled the deal and demanded its money back. Nimrodi returned $19 million, deducting $5 million for the 18 missiles that were delivered. After Israel retrieved the missiles in February 1986, Iran apparently deducted about $4 million from a later payment to get its money back.

The November shipment was bungled at several points, resulting in a three-day delay. Iran ultimately returned 17 of the missiles to Israel, saying they were out of date; the 18th missile was test-fired, possibly at an Iraqi target, according to the report.

Most importantly, the shipment failed to meet its major goal: Not a single hostage was released.

Preparing for the shipment, North in mid-November brought into the operation retired Air Force Major Gen. Richard V. Secord, asking him to help arrange for planes carrying the arms to pass through Portugal. At North's request, the CIA also became involved in the operation, approving the use of its own airline (reportedly St. Lucia Airways) to fly cargo to Iran disguised as "oil drilling equipment."

Reagan gave the Tower board conflicting testimony about the November shipment, first saying that he had objected to it, leading to the return of the missiles to Israel. At his second appearance, Reagan told the board that neither he nor Regan could remember discussions about the shipment.

Discovering later that an agency-owned airline had been involved in an arms shipment to Iran, CIA Deputy Director John McMahon ordered preparation of a legal authorization — called a "finding" — to be signed by the president. Drafted by CIA General Counsel Stanley Sporkin in December, the finding would have retroactively approved CIA participation in the shipment and given blanket approval for future shipments designed to win release of hostages. The proposed finding also contained an unusual provision directing the CIA not to inform Congress about the operation.

The Tower board said it could not locate evidence that Reagan signed the draft finding. However, Reagan did sign two later findings in January 1986 that could be interpreted as giving retroactive approval to CIA actions in November.

Reagan Approves U.S. Role

The failure of the November arms-for-hostages swap resulted in a temporary suspension of U.S. dealings with Iran — but not before North proposed yet another trade.

On Dec. 4 — the day McFarlane announced his resignation and Reagan named Vice Adm. John M. Poindexter as his successor — North produced a plan for an even more ambitious arms deal. According to the report, North proposed that Israel sell Iran 3,300 TOW missiles and 50 Hawk missiles in exchange for one French and five American hostages in Beirut. The arms were to be delivered in five stages over a 24-hour period, coinciding with the release of hostages.

North's plan prompted one of the rare discussions on Iran involving all senior U.S. officials. At the White House on Dec. 7, Shultz and Weinberger argued against North's arms deals; Regan told the Tower board he argued for it, but Reagan and Shultz both took notes indicating that Regan opposed the plan. The board said it found no records of what was decided.

The next day — saying he was acting on Reagan's orders — McFarlane flew to London and told Ghorbanifar that the United States would engage in no more arms deals with Iran. At a White House meeting Dec. 10, McFarlane reported on his trip. The Tower report cited conflicting evidence on whether anything was decided then. One odd memo by CIA Director Casey said Reagan had "argued mildly" for allowing Israel to sell arms to Iran because of a concern that ending the deals would lead to retaliation against the hostages.

McFarlane officially left government service Dec. 11, and later said he believed at that time that the arms-for-hostages dealing had ended.

During this time, Ghorbanifar traveled to Washington to meet with U.S. officials. During one trip, on Jan. 11, 1986, the CIA gave him a lie detector test and Ghorbanifar was found to have lied on nearly every question. The Tower board quoted one top CIA official describing Ghorbanifar as "a guy who lies with zest." The White House nonetheless continued to use Ghorbanifar as its contact with Iran.

North sent Poindexter another arms deal plan on Dec. 9. North also continued meeting with Secord, Ghorbanifar and Israeli officials.

On Jan. 2, 1986, Nir gave Poindexter a proposal that appeared to revive the Iran initiative. Its greatest importance may have been its timing — Nir appeared in Washington "just when the initiative seemed to be dying," the Tower report said.

Under Nir's plan, Israel would exchange several pro-Iranian prisoners it held in Beirut, along with 3,000 TOW missiles, for the U.S. hostages. Reagan and his top aides discussed the plan Jan. 7; as in previous meetings, Shultz and Weinberger were opposed and the others, especially Casey, were in favor.

The Jan. 7 meeting may have been superfluous. A day earlier, Reagan had signed a draft version of a finding authorizing arms sales to Iran. Regan told the Tower board that the president may have signed the document "in error." Reagan himself told the board that he did not recall signing it.

Reagan signed a final version of the finding Jan. 17 after Poindexter briefed him again on the arms plan Nir and North had produced.

The plan outlined in Poindexter's memo had one major difference from what Nir had proposed: Rather than authorizing Israeli sales to Iran, Reagan for the first time approved direct sales by the United States. The plan called for shipping 1,000 TOW missiles to Iran; if the hostages were released, another 3,000 missiles would follow. Reagan's finding also directed that Congress not be told about it.

Reagan told the board that he did not read the three-page memo from Poindexter describing the arms plan. Reagan also said he did not understand, or had not been told about, several aspects of the operation: the specifics of how it would be implemented, that Iran would be given intelligence information along with weapons, and that there were "downside risks" in having the NSC staff run the operation. Casey, Reagan said, never suggested that the CIA should run it.

Shultz said he was unaware of the finding until Nov. 10, 1986, when Poindexter told him about it.

North put the operation into effect almost immediately, ordering the Pentagon to get ready to transfer 4,000 TOW missiles to the CIA, and ordering the CIA to prepare intelligence information to be turned over to Iran. The latter happened first: on June 25 or 26, CIA official Charles Allen met Ghorbanifar in London and gave him information about Iraqi military positions. In exchange, Ghorbanifar handed over information about Iranian terrorism, the Tower report said.

North also drafted what he called a "notional timeline" for the Iran operation covering Jan. 24-Feb. 25. It called for the delivery of 1,000 TOW missiles to Iran on Feb. 8, to be followed Feb. 9 by the release of American hostages and pro-Iranian prisoners in Lebanon. Another 3,000 TOW missiles were then to be sent to Iran over the next two weeks, along with intelligence information. The plan called for Secord, rather than the CIA, to handle details of the arms shipments.

On Feb. 11, according to North's timeline, "Khomeini steps down." That did not happen, and North gave no indication where he got the idea.

In any case, a U.S.-leased plane delivered 500 TOW missiles to Iran Feb. 18 and returned to Israel the old Hawk missiles that Iran did not want.

North met in Frankfurt, West Germany, on Feb. 24 with Ghorbanifar and an official from the Iranian prime minister's office — the first official contact in the arms deals between the two countries. The two sides agreed that U.S. hostages would be released, to be followed by a higher-level meeting between the United States and Iran. Poindexter around that time asked McFarlane if he would be willing to head a U.S. delegation, and McFarlane agreed. Three days after the Frankfurt meeting, another 500 TOWs were shipped to Iran.

Iran was charged $12 million for 1,000 missiles that the CIA had bought from the Pentagon for only $3.7 million, leaving about $6.7 unaccounted for. As with previous deals, Khashoggi advanced money to finance the sale and Ghorbanifar offered postdated checks as a guarantee of payment by Iran. This transaction was complicated by Iran's apparent decision to deduct $4 million from its payment as a refund for the Hawk missiles it rejected.

Shultz told the board that Poindexter said Feb. 28 that the American hostages would be released in a few days. They weren't.

McFarlane's Trip to Tehran

U.S. officials were disappointed that the shipments of missiles did not produce hostages, the Tower board said. But, the report added, "disappointment was gilded in hope, and the effort was pursued."

In preparation for McFarlane's trip, North and other officials held several meetings with Ghorbanifar, including one in Washington early in April. After one false start, it was agreed that a delegation led by McFarlane would travel to Tehran in late May, coinciding with the release of all American hostages in Lebanon.

During this period — when top U.S. officials were at an economic summit meeting of industrialized nations in Tokyo — Shultz received evidence that U.S. arms dealings with Iran were continuing. He told the Tower board that Poindexter and Casey both assured him the Iran operation had been ended.

Reagan on May 15 approved the McFarlane trip, along with a North-drafted statement of the "pillars" of U.S. foreign policy generally and the "principles" of U.S. policy toward Iran in particular. Among the principles, North stated: "We view the Iranian revolution as a fact. The U.S. is not trying to turn the clock back."

Reagan's approval triggered two major financial transactions: as an advance on the weapons delivery, Khashoggi deposited $15 million into a Swiss bank account controlled by North under the name "Lake Resources Inc.," and North shifted $6.5 million into a CIA Swiss account to cover the cost of the Hawk parts.

Although Iran had demanded 240 different parts for Hawk missiles, it is not clear whether Reagan knew in mid-May just what arms were to be shipped to Tehran. In any event, McFarlane's plane carried only one pallet of Hawk parts, and a second plane carrying other parts was never sent to Tehran once McFarlane realized that hostages would not be released.

The McFarlane delegation arrived in Tehran on May 25; its members included North, Cave, Nir and a CIA official. North carried a chocolate cake, baked in Israel, apparently symbolizing the opening of relations between Iran and the United States.

McFarlane and his crew stayed nearly four days, meeting with mid-level officials but none of the senior leaders promised by Ghorbanifar. In one cable to Poindexter in Washington on May 26, McFarlane said:

"The incompetence of the Iranian government to do business requires a rethinking on our part of why there have been so many frustrating failures to deliver on their part."

Disappointed by the lack of substance, the delegation left Tehran on May 28, and the next day McFarlane reported to Reagan on the trip. McFarlane told the board that he recommended ending the initiative to Iran.

The Tower board pinpointed one apparent source of trouble that should have been apparent at this point: repeated misunderstandings between the Iranians and some Americans about what the dealings would produce. For example, the board said it compiled evidence that North and CIA officials knew that only one hostage would be released even if all the Hawk parts were delivered to Iran. McFarlane and Poindexter probably thought all hostages were to be released; as a result, McFarlane rejected any lesser deal with Iran.

On June 20, according to the report, Reagan decided not to allow any further official meetings with the Iranians until the hostages were released. But North met again with Ghorbanifar in London on July 21, discussing the release of hostages in return for the remaining Hawk parts.

On July 26, a Lebanese group released one U.S. hostage, the Rev. Lawrence Jenco. North claimed in a memo that the release "undoubtedly" was a result of McFarlane's trip, and he later recommended that Reagan approve shipping the Hawk parts to Iran. Reagan did so July 30.

A New 'Channel'

The release of Jenco sparked new U.S. interest in the Iranian operation but did nothing to ease Washington's frustrations about the demonstrated unreliability of Ghorbanifar.

A full year of dealings between the United States and Iran "had been marked by great confusion, broken promises and increasing frustration on the U.S. side," the Tower report said. North and others in Washington "apparently blamed these problems more on Mr. Ghorbanifar than on Iran."

In July 1986, the report said, an Iranian living in London suggested that the United States could deal with a second "channel" to Iran: the relative of someone the report called "a powerful Iranian official."

After introductory meetings in Europe, the new Iranian came to Washington Sept. 19, 1986, and met with North, Cave and a CIA official. Reagan was told about the new Iranian twice in September, the report said.

From Oct. 5-7, North, Cave and Secord met with the Iranian in Frankfurt. It was to that meeting that North carried a Bible signed by Reagan.

The Tower board reported that North, during the Frankfurt meetings, "misrepresented his access to the president and attributed to the president things the president never said."

Among the latter, the board said, was a statement by North that the United States recognized that Saddam Hussein "must go" — a reference to the Iranian demand for the ouster of the Iraqi president.

Reagan told the Tower board that North's reported statements were an "absolute fiction."

During the meeting in early October, North agreed to sell Iran 500 TOW missiles in exchange for the release of two hostages.

Plans for the exchange were completed at meetings Oct. 26-28, during which North discussed a nine-point agenda — including arms sales — for future meetings.

Israel delivered 500 TOWS to Iran on Oct. 29. Regan told the Tower board that the president gave his approval that same day.

A week later, on Nov. 7, the United States sent Israel replacements for the missiles.

The CIA said Iran paid $4 million for these missiles, and North in a memo said Iran paid $7 million. The Pentagon charged the CIA slightly over $2 million, leaving $2 million to $5 million unaccounted for.

American hostage David Jacobsen was released in Lebanon on Nov. 2, and the next day a Beirut magazine published an account of the McFarlane trip to Tehran in May.

THE CONTRA CONNECTION

The Tower commission, in probing the effort to divert profits from the Iran arms sales to the contras, announced what White House officials undoubtedly wanted to hear — that Reagan apparently did not know of the skimming.

"We are satisfied that the president had no knowledge of any diversionary effort," said commission Chairman Tower on Feb. 26, 1987.

The report also said it was "extremely difficult" to prove that funds had actually gone to the contras, noting that large sums from the Iran sales had not been accounted for.

Efforts by the commission to learn more about the contra diversion were hampered by the lack of testimony from central figures such as Poindexter and North. The panel also was unable to examine records of Swiss bank accounts where arms sale proceeds apparently were deposited.

Nevertheless, the report found "considerable evidence" of a contra diversion program and included a series of complex charts tracking the money flow. "But the board has no hard proof," said the report.

Beyond the contra diversion, however, the Tower board devoted much of its report to a highly secretive — and potentially illegal — White House effort to assist the contras in their attempts to topple the Sandinista regime in Nicaragua. That effort, spearheaded by North, also involved former national security advisers McFarlane and Poindexter.

The report contained evidence that all three misled Congress by denying their involvement in a concerted campaign to aid the contras during a time when Congress prohibited U.S. military assistance to the Nicaraguan rebels.

According to the commission's document and other reports, North was the central figure in the contra supply network, a shadowy web of private individuals and secret bank accounts.

Although it was unable to trace the excess profits from the Iran weapons sales, the commission found that nearly $23 million was available based on inflated prices charged to the Iranians for five arms shipments sold to them in 1985 and 1986.

Of that amount, about $19.8 million represented the excess amounts resulting from four direct arms deliveries between the United States and Iran in 1986. The remaining $3 million in extra funds came from an Israeli shipment in August-September 1985.

Who Suggested Diversion?

Like the Senate Intelligence Committee before it, the Tower commission was unable to conclude who first suggested the contra diversion idea.

Instead, the report recounted that the subject apparently came up during a January 1986 meeting between North and Nir, the anti-terrorism adviser to Israeli Prime Minister Peres.

When Meese interviewed North about the Iran arms deals in November 1986, North told him that Nir proposed the diversion. Israeli officials have denied bringing up the idea or having any role in the diversion.

According to the report, the contra diversion came up again in February 1986 when Iranian arms dealer Ghorbanifar discussed the first direct U.S. sale of TOW missiles to Iran that month with North and Secord.

Ghorbanifar told the Tower board that North and Secord were worried about keeping aid flowing to the contras and that North asked him if the Iranians would pay $10,000 for each TOW missile instead of $6,500.

"When told that Iran would pay that price, Mr. Ghorbanifar said Lt. Col. North was greatly relieved — 'he was a changed man,'" said the report.

The following month, retired CIA officer George Cave met with Ghorbanifar in Paris. Cave later wrote in a memorandum describing the March 7-8 meeting that Ghorbanifar "proposed that we use profits from these deals and others to fund support to the rebels in Afghanistan. We could do the same with Nicaragua."

But Cave, testifying before the Tower panel, said that neither he nor Ghorbanifar ever mentioned the diversion during the Paris meeting.

Testifying before the Tower board, Meese said North told him in November 1986 that $3 million to $4 million was diverted to the contras after the February shipment of TOW missiles to Iran. According to Meese, North said that more money had been diverted after the May arms shipment; North did not remember how much.

Justice Department notes from Meese's interview with North indicated that North said Israeli officials handled the money and that he gave them the numbers of Swiss bank accounts opened by contra leader Adolfo Calero.

Linked to White House Memo

One piece of evidence directly linking the Iran arms operation with the contra diversion was a White House memo prepared by North in early April 1986, entitled "Release of American Hostages in Beirut." The memo was written as a background to Reagan's approval of a secret mission to Tehran, headed, the following month, by McFarlane.

The memo, included in the report, said that $12 million "will be used to purchase critically needed supplies for the Nicaraguan Democratic Resistance Forces." The money, North said, was needed to cover shortages in contra inventories "and to 'bridge' the period between now and when congressionally-approved lethal assistance ... can be delivered."

At the time, Congress had prohibited U.S. military aid to the contras, though it later approved $100 million in military and humanitarian assistance.

The Tower panel, like the Senate Intelligence Committee, found no evidence that North's memo, written for Poindexter, was seen by Reagan.

Another part of North's memo said that Iranian contacts had previously been told by U.S. officials that their aiding of Nicaragua's Sandinista regime "is unacceptable to us and they have agreed to discuss this matter in Tehran" during McFarlane's trip.

North's preoccupation with the contras surfaced in other discussions. A few weeks after his April memo was drafted, he sent a note to the late Donald Fortier, an NSC official at the time. In it, he warned about the future of U.S. support for the contras.

The "picture is dismal unless a new source of 'bridge' funding can be identified.... We need to explore this problem urgently or there won't be a force to help when the Congress finally acts," said North.

Because North and Poindexter declined to talk about their role in the Iran-contra scandal, neither the Tower board nor congressional investigators had determined whether other White House officials knew of the diversion plan.

Poindexter's Role

The Tower report said that North kept Poindexter "exhaustively informed" about his Iran-related activities, but he apparently never communicated to him directly about the diversion.

Nonetheless, White House Chief of Staff Regan told the board that Poindexter told him in November that he had strong hints.

"I had a feeling that something bad was going on, but I didn't investigate it and I didn't do a thing about it," Regan quoted Poindexter as saying. "I really didn't want to know. I was so damned mad at Tip O'Neill for the way he was dragging the contras around I didn't want to know what, if anything, was going on. I should have, but I didn't."

Meese told the board that Poindexter informed him about his knowledge of the diversion after Meese interviewed North in November. "Ollie North had given him enough hints that he knew what was going on, but he didn't want to look further into it," Meese told the commission. "But that he in fact did generally know that money had gone to the contras as a result of the Iran shipment."

In concluding what went wrong in the Iran-contra affair, the Tower board charged that Poindexter "failed grievously" by not looking into the diversion program after he learned of it.

Also singled out for criticism was former CIA Director Casey, who apparently learned about the diversion at least several weeks before it was publicly revealed in November. "He, too, did not move promptly to raise the matter with the president. Yet his responsibility to do so was clear," said the Tower report.

The only other person known for sure to be aware of the contra diversion before it was brought to light was McFarlane. He told the Tower board that North informed him of the diversion while standing on the tarmac at the Tel Aviv airport after the May 1986 mission to Iran.

McFarlane was dejected after the failed four-day effort in Tehran to win release of the remaining U.S. hostages. According to McFarlane's testimony, "North said well, don't be too downhearted, that the one bright spot is that the government is availing itself of part of the money for application to Central America, as I recall, although I took it to be Nicaragua."

North apparently remained sanguine about the diversion nearly up to the day it was made public.

Assistant Secretary of Defense Richard L. Armitage told the Tower commission that North told him sometime in November, "It's going to be just fine ... as soon as everyone knows that ... the ayatollah is helping us with the contras."

Contra Supply Network

The Tower report painted a picture of the Reagan administration wrapped up in a determined effort to keep the contras financed during a time when Congress had cut off military aid.

In December 1982, Congress passed its first version of the "Boland amendment," prohibiting the United States from trying to overthrow the Nicaraguan government.

Nearly two years later, in October 1984, Congress went one step further by cutting off all funds to the contras and preventing the Pentagon, CIA and any other agency "involved in intelligence activities" from supporting military operations in Nicaragua.

Members of Congress argued that the Boland amendment proscriptions applied to the NSC staff on the grounds that the agency is involved in intelligence activities. That position was backed up in Reagan's Executive Order 12333, issued in December 1981, dealing with intelligence agencies and covert activities. It described the NSC as the "highest executive branch entity" that reviews and directs intelligence activities.

However, Reagan's Intelligence Oversight Board apparently provided the NSC with a legal justification for involvement in the contra supply network without violating the Boland amendment, according to the Tower report.

A classified legal memo found in North's White House safe, apparently prepared by the intelligence board, said the NSC "is not covered by the prohibition" against aiding the contras for a variety of reasons, among them being that the NSC's role was to coordinate rather than implement covert action. "None of Lt. Col. North's activities during the past year constitutes a violation of the Boland amendment," said the memo.

In its report, the Tower commission said it found no evidence that Reagan knew of the potentially illegal efforts to aid the contras along with the Iran diversion scheme. The president, in his Jan. 26, 1987, appearance before the commission, said he did not know that NSC staff members were trying to help the contras.

But North seemed to suggest at one point that Reagan knew of the NSC aide's "private U.S. operation" to funnel assistance to the contras.

He discussed Reagan's possible knowledge in a computer message to Poindexter dated May 16, 1986, that discussed a potential effort to reprogram $15 million to the CIA for authorized aid to the contras.

"I have no idea what Don Regan does or does not know re my private U.S. operation but the president obviously knows why he has been meeting with several select people to thank them for their 'support for Democracy' " in Central America, North told Poindexter.

Poindexter in turn showed signs of keeping things quiet on the contra supply effort. When North suggested a meeting on the reprogramming with the president and others, Poindexter replied, "I don't want a meeting with RR, Shultz and Weinberger." Because both Shultz and Weinberger opposed the arms-for-hostages deals, Poindexter apparently believed that they would be skeptical of North's contra activities.

Whatever Reagan knew, the Tower report was emphatic in depicting North as the linchpin in the effort to keep supplies and other aid flowing to the contras. "Between 1984 and 1986, Lt. Col. North, with the acquiescence of the national security adviser, performed activities the CIA was unable to undertake itself, including the facilitation of outside fund-raising efforts and oversight of a private network to supply lethal equipment to the contras," said the report.

The commission did not uncover any record of North receiving authorization to carry out the program. But he did keep McFarlane and later Poindexter informed, the report said.

Keeping Quiet

Poindexter worried about North's contra activities becoming public, as well as news of his own knowledge seeping out. "From now on, I don't want you to talk to anybody else, including [CIA Director] Casey, except me about any of your operational roles. In fact, you need to quietly generate a cover story that I have insisted that you stop," Poindexter told North in a message on May 15, 1986.

Three months later, North was interviewed by the House Intelligence Committee. According to an internal NSC staff account described by the Tower report, North denied any contra connections involving military operations or fund raising.

Poindexter shortly afterward sent North a message: "Well done."

Private Fund Raising

With congressionally approved money for the contras running out, North suggested to McFarlane in April 1985 that $20 million to $20 million be raised from private sources.

The precise purpose of the money was not clear, according to the Tower report, but memos written by North at the time indicated that the funds were for arms and lethal aid.

"Evidence suggests that at least by November 1985, Lt. Col. North had assumed a direct operational role, coordinating logistical arrangements to ship privately purchased arms to the contras," said the Tower report.

McFarlane, in written statements to the Tower board, said that a foreign official, acting "without solicitation" from U.S. officials, offered $1 million a month from "personal funds" to aid the contras. Sometime in 1985, McFarlane told the commission, the official doubled his gift to $2 million each month.

The foreign official, reportedly a member of Saudi Arabia's royal family, may have contributed up to $30 million. The only other known source of voluntary contributions to the contras was the sultan of Brunei, who gave $10 million in 1986 after he was solicited by the State Department. What happened to the money is not known.

Other private contributions to the contras, meanwhile, were funneled through a network of private individuals and secret bank accounts that North dubbed "Project Democracy."

The Tower commission said there did not appear to be a link between North's Project Democracy and the National Endowment for Democracy, created by Congress in 1983 to support democratic institutions around the world. The congressional action grew out of an earlier similar administration initiative, also known as Project Democracy.

By July 1986, North told Poindexter in a computer message that his Project Democracy assets were worth over $4.5 million and included six aircraft, warehouses, ships, leased houses, munitions, communications equipment and a 6,520-foot runway in Costa Rica used as a secret airfield for contra supplies.

When Costa Rica decided to disclose the airfield's existence and close it down, North and other U.S. officials discussed a plan to have North call Costa Rican President Oscar Arias and threaten to cancel $80 million in U.S. foreign aid along with Arias' upcoming meeting with Reagan.

Assistant Secretary of State Elliott Abrams and Lewis Tambs, the U.S. ambassador to Costa Rica, confirmed the discussion with North but said that Tambs called Arias and did not threaten the aid cutoff.

Later, Costa Rica announced the discovery and closure of the airstrip.

North's Secret Network

By 1986, North had established a secret communications network, with 15 encryption devices provided by the National Security Agency ostensibly to support his official counterterrorist activities as part of his NSC duties.

According to the Tower report, one of the devices, which allowed for secure communications, was given to Secord and another to a CIA field officer posted in Costa Rica.

"Through this mechanism, North coordinated the resupply of the contras with military equipment apparently purchased with funds provided by the network of private benefactors," said the Tower board.

Messages to North from Secord and the CIA officer asked him to spell out the logistics for arms deliveries to the contras, informed him of arms requirements and kept him informed of how much money was involved, according to the report.

At least nine arms shipments were delivered to the contras through North's private network between March and June 1986, the report said. "This was all lethal. Benefactors only sent lethal stuff," said the CIA field officer in Costa Rica.

The CIA officer, known by the code name "Tomas Castillo," was disciplined by the agency in January after an investigation turned up evidence that he had helped coordinate the airlift of military supplies to the contras during a time when such activities were illegal.

Clash With Customs

North on at least two occasions contacted U.S. Customs Service officials to complain about their investigations into clandestine airline operations supplying the contras.

North contacted Assistant Customs Commissioner William Rosenblatt after a C-123 cargo plane crashed in Nicaragua during a supply flight to the contras. The sole survivor, American Eugene Hasenfus, was captured and convicted on terrorism charges but later released.

Rosenblatt told the Tower panel that North told him the Customs probe had focused on "good guys" who had not committed any crimes.

Customs investigators then limited their inquiry into the individual aircraft that crashed rather than on the activities of Corporate Air Services Inc., an air freight company linked to the Hasenfus flight.

North earlier had complained to Customs Commissioner William von Raab about an inquiry into another aircraft suspected of supporting the contras. But Rosenblatt and von Raab said North never asked them to close out their investigations.

In the Hasenfus case, North suggested to McFarlane that they find a "high-powered lawyer and benefactor" to provide a legal defense for the captured American in Managua.

North also told McFarlane in the Oct. 12, 1986, message that Reagan was briefed on the plan to assist Hasenfus before he left for the U.S.-Soviet summit in Iceland. North said he was concerned that "when people begin to think of things other than meetings in cold places, he [Reagan] will remember this and nothing will have been done."

In describing North's seemingly endless quest to help the contras, the Tower report also portrayed him as straining from his activities. At one point, North referred to himself in a message to Poindexter as "one slightly confused Marine LtCol" trying to manage the contra operation.

On that same day, June 10, 1986, McFarlane sent a note to Poindexter expressing concern about the pressures on North. He said that the "Democratic left" was after North because of speculation about his contra activities "and that eventually they will get him."

McFarlane suggested that North be sent to Bethesda Naval Hospital to appear before a disability review board. That would "represent a major loss to the staff and contra effort but I think we can probably find a way to continue to do those things. In the end it may be better anyway," said McFarlane.

EFFORT TO 'BLUR' REAGAN ROLE

Almost from the moment the Iranian arms deals became public, White House officials took steps to hide or obscure major facts, the Tower commission found.

In a 14-page section of its report, the board discussed a White House effort in mid-November 1986 to "blur" Reagan's role in the Iran arms deals, apparently to protect the president politically.

McFarlane told the board of the frantic preparation at the White House on Nov. 18 of a chronology of the Iranian arms deals. The main objective of those writing the chronology, McFarlane said, "was to describe a sequence of events that would distance the president from the initial approval of the Iran arms sale, distance him from it to blur his association with it."

A more serious cover-up attempt may have taken place in North's office later in November, when Attorney General Meese was beginning his investigations into the possible diversion of Iranian arms money to the contras.

North's secretary at the time, Fawn Hall, reportedly told the independent counsel's office that early in November 1986 she altered several key documents to obscure the role of North's superiors. FBI agents reportedly located copies of the originals, however.

Hall also was quoted as telling Walsh's investigators that she helped North destroy some documents and internal computer messages on Nov. 21, shortly before Justice Department officials were scheduled to begin reviewing National Security Council files.

Aside from quoting McFarlane, the Tower board report did not discuss the cover-up issue. However, Chairman Tower said that "there was a deliberate effort to mislead by those who prepared" the information that Reagan used in his early statements on the Iran arms sales. "I don't believe that the president wittingly misled the American people," Tower said. ∎

Chronology of Events in the Iran-Contra Affair

The following chronology traces the key events that occurred in conjunction with the Reagan administration's secret arms deals with Iran and the diversion of funds from the sales to the Nicaraguan contras. Much of the information comes from the Senate Intelligence Committee's Jan. 29, 1987, report, which was based on the panel's three-week inquiry in December 1986 into the Iran-contra affair.

1984

Late 1984 — The United States begins a formal reappraisal of its policy toward Iran when the National Security Council (NSC) issues a National Security Study Directive for the CIA, State Department and Department of Defense to look into ways of improving U.S.-Iran relations.

1985

May 1985 — The CIA's intelligence officer for the Middle East submits a five-page memo to the NSC and the State Department on ways to improve relations with Iran. In part, the memo suggests that the United States permit its allies to sell arms to Iran as a way to increase Western influence there. In response, NSC staff members prepare a draft National Security Decision Directive to implement CIA proposals.

May 4-5, 1985 — Michael Ledeen, an NSC consultant, meets in Israel with then-Prime Minister Shimon Peres to discuss Iran.

June 5-7, 1985 — Secretary of State George P. Shultz complains to national security adviser Robert C. McFarlane that the State Department was bypassed in Ledeen's May trip to Israel. He also warns that Israel has different interests with respect to Iran from those of the United States. McFarlane writes to Shultz two days later that Ledeen acted "on his own hook" and "I am turning it [the Iran initiative] off entirely."

June 14, 1985 — TWA flight 847 is hijacked to Beirut by Lebanese Shiite Moslems. According to White House Chief of Staff Donald T. Regan, McFarlane discussed the possibility of using Israeli contacts with Iran to end the crisis.

June 29, 1985 — Shultz tells McFarlane in a memo that the NSC's proposal to sell arms to Iran is "perverse" and "contrary to our own interests." Defense Secretary Caspar W. Weinberger writes in the margin, "This is almost too absurd to comment on."

July 3, 1985 — David Kimche, then director general of Israel's foreign ministry, tells McFarlane that Israel has succeeded in establishing contact with Iran and that the Iranians expressed interest in talking to U.S. officials. According to McFarlane, there was no Iranian request for arms but Kimche raised the possibility that Iran might seek arms in the future.

July 13 or 14, 1985 — McFarlane visits President Reagan, who is in the hospital recovering from colon cancer surgery. McFarlane requests Reagan's authority to use an Israeli contact as a channel to the Iranians and says arms might enter into the picture. According to McFarlane, the president approved the plan and hoped that it might lead to the release of U.S. hostages held by pro-Iranian groups in Beirut. A conflict exists between McFarlane and Regan over whether Iranian arms merchant Manucher Ghorbanifar was discussed at the hospital meeting. Regan told the Senate Intelligence Committee that McFarlane defended Ghorbanifar's reputation. McFarlane told the committee that Ghorbanifar was not discussed, and that he did not learn of his identity until December.

Early August 1985 — At a meeting between McFarlane and Kimche, the Israeli official says the Iranians seek a "dialogue with America" and that they will obtain the release of U.S. hostages in exchange for arms.

Aug. 8, 1985 — Members of the National Security Council, including Reagan and Vice President George Bush, are briefed on Kimche's plan by McFarlane at a White House meeting. Later testimony revealed conflicts over whether Reagan subsequently approved Israel's shipment of TOW anti-tank missiles to Iran. Regan said the president declined to authorize the sale because of misgivings about Ghorbanifar. McFarlane testified that Reagan approved the Israeli shipment sometime after the meeting, and that the president told Shultz, Weinberger and CIA Director William J. Casey of his decision.

August 1985 — McFarlane tells Ledeen that the United States is going ahead with the Iran initiative, including the arms sale. McFarlane, believing that the sale of TOWs would lead to freedom for the hostages, instructs Ledeen to work out arrangements with Kimche for their release.

August-September 1985 — A shipment of 508 TOWs leaves Israel on Aug. 30 and arrives in Iran, via a third country, on Sept. 13. According to McFarlane, there was no official contact between the U.S. and Israeli governments regarding the shipment. Regan said the shipment was not sanctioned by Washington.

Sept. 15, 1985 — The Rev. Benjamin F. Weir is released after 16 months in captivity in Lebanon. The announcement of his release is delayed until Sept. 18 in the hope that other hostages also will be freed.

Nov. 19-21, 1985 — During the U.S.-Soviet summit in Geneva, McFarlane tells Reagan that the Israelis are considering another arms shipment to Iran. According to Regan, McFarlane told the president that hostages might be released if the operation was a success. Shultz testified that McFarlane told him he had cleared the shipment with Reagan.

Late November 1985 — A CIA-supplied aircraft flies 18 Hawk missiles, claimed by U.S. officials to be oil drilling parts, from Israel to Iran. In order to satisfy countries where flight clearances are needed, U.S. officials in some cases inform foreign officials that the purpose of the flight involves the American hostages.

Nov. 25, 1985 — John McMahon, CIA deputy director, learns that the aircraft has flown arms to Iran without his knowledge or approval. He instructs that no further CIA activity in support of an NSC operation be undertaken without a presidential "finding" to authorize covert action. Stanley Sporkin, CIA general counsel, the next day drafts such a finding that provides retroactive approval of all previous covert missions involving the Iran initiative. The Senate Intelligence Committee found no evidence that the finding was signed by the president.

Dec. 4, 1985 — McFarlane announces his resignation

as national security adviser effective Dec. 11. Reagan replaces him with Vice Adm. John M. Poindexter, McFarlane's deputy.

Dec. 7, 1985 — Reagan meets with Shultz, Weinberger, McFarlane, Poindexter and McMahon to discuss the Iran program. Later testimony by participants suggested that a consensus formed at the meeting to end arms shipments to Iran. But McMahon testified that no such decision or consensus was reached.

Dec. 8, 1985 — McFarlane and Lt. Col. Oliver L. North, an NSC aide, meet in London with Kimche, Ghorbanifar and Jacob Nimrodi, an arms dealer and former Israeli Embassy official in Iran. McFarlane said he told the others that the United States would no longer sell arms to Iran. Ghorbanifar argued for continued U.S. arms transfers.

Dec. 23, 1985 — Casey writes a memo to Reagan advising caution on U.S. dealings with Ghorbanifar, who traveled to Washington that month to meet for the first time with CIA officials who were aware of the Iran arms program.

1986

Early January 1986 — Amiram Nir, an anti-terrorism adviser to Israeli Prime Minister Peres, travels to Washington where he urges Reagan and Poindexter to consider the resumption of arms sales to Iran in exchange for release of the hostages. According to evidence obtained by the Senate Intelligence Committee, a proposal that profits from the Iran arms sales be diverted to the Nicaraguan contras was made at this time in a meeting between Nir and North. North later told Attorney General Edwin Meese III that Nir suggested the contra diversion, but Israeli officials have denied that they were behind the idea.

Jan. 7, 1986 — Reagan meets in the Oval Office with Bush, Shultz, Weinberger, Casey, Meese and Poindexter to discuss the Iran program. Shultz and Weinberger argue against further arms shipments. According to participants, Reagan decided to keep the Iranian channel open, but left the issue of additional weapons sales unresolved.

Jan. 17, 1986 — Reagan signs a secret intelligence finding to authorize direct U.S. arms shipments to Iran through the CIA and to instruct the CIA not to inform Congress of the covert action. Poindexter had orally briefed Reagan, along with Bush and Regan, on the finding.

Jan. 21, 1986 — North requests the CIA to open a Swiss bank account for proceeds of the arms sales to Iran.

Jan. 25, 1986 — CIA and NSC officials meet to discuss turning over intelligence information to Iran. According to then-CIA Deputy Director Robert M. Gates, who had replaced McMahon, he objected to providing Iran with information related to Iraq but was overruled by NSC officials. A CIA official was then instructed to turn the information over to Ghorbanifar, the Iranian arms merchant.

Feb. 15-18, 1986 — 1,000 TOW missiles are flown from the United States to Israel, after which half of them are delivered to Iran. The 18 Hawk missiles delivered to Iran in November are returned to Israel after Iranian officials complain they are obsolete.

Late February 1986 — The remaining 500 TOW missiles are delivered to Iran.

April 4 or 5, 1986 — An unsigned White House memo, apparently drafted by North, summarizes plans for a visit by U.S. officials to Iran originally scheduled later in the month. The memo said that the hostages would be released several hours after the Americans arrived in Tehran and detailed how much money Iran would pay for Hawk missile parts, to be shipped separately. The memo also said that $12 million from the sale would be used to buy "critically needed supplies for the Nicaraguan Democratic Resistance Forces."

May 2-3, 1986 — Shultz, attending the economic summit in Tokyo, learns from the U.S. Embassy in London that Ghorbanifar and Adnan Khashoggi, a Saudi Arabian arms merchant, are trying to arrange a line of credit in Britain for U.S.-approved arms sales. Shultz testified that he asked Regan in Tokyo to talk to the president and end the Iran program. According to Shultz, Poindexter and Casey later told him the operation had ended.

May 15, 1986 — Reagan approves McFarlane's secret trip to Tehran.

May 23-25, 1986 — McFarlane and other officials travel to Iran via Europe and Israel. The delegation includes North, NSC aide Howard J. Teicher, retired CIA officer and interpreter George Cave and Nir, the Israeli anti-terrorism adviser. Also on the plane are some Hawk missile parts.

May 25-28, 1986 — McFarlane and the others spend four days in Iran, meeting on and off with Iranian officials. But the talks do not lead to the release of any hostages. According to McFarlane, North told him on the return trip that funds from the arms sales were being diverted to the contras.

June 26, 1986 — The House, for the first time in three years, approves Reagan's request for military aid to the contras.

Mid-July 1986 — The Iranians are told through various sources that the United States will not make further moves unless a hostage is released. Iran agrees to do so and also agrees to pay $4 million for the Hawk parts delivered on McFarlane's plane in May.

July 29, 1986 — The Rev. Lawrence Jenco is released from Lebanon after nearly 17 months in captivity. On the same day, Vice President Bush meets with Nir at the King David Hotel in Jerusalem for a briefing on the Iran program. According to a memo written a week later by Bush aide Craig Fuller, who attended the meeting, Nir told Bush that the United States and Israel were dealing with Iranian radicals who were trying to "squeeze" as much as they could from the Americans in exchange for the hostages.

Aug. 3, 1986 — The remaining portion of the Hawk missile parts, undelivered during McFarlane's May trip to Iran, arrive in Tehran.

Aug. 8, 1986 — Assistant Secretary of State Elliott Abrams meets with a representative from a country, which has been identified as Brunei, and asks for a $10 million "humanitarian" contribution to the contras. After Brunei agrees to the gift, a bank account is set up in the Bahamas for the contras to receive the money.

Aug. 13, 1986 — The Senate approves legislation providing $70 million in military aid and $30 million in humanitarian assistance to the contras.

Oct. 7, 1986 — New York businessman Roy M. Furmark tells Casey that two Canadians who helped finance the arms sales have not been repaid and are threatening to reveal the operation. On the same day, CIA national intelligence officer Charles Allen briefs Casey about the possibility that funds from the Iran arms sales were diverted to the contras.

Oct. 9, 1986 — North meets with Casey and Gates at CIA headquarters after meeting with a new Iranian contact in Europe. Gates said North assured them that the CIA was not involved in diverting funds to the contras.

Oct. 29, 1986 — Israel ships 500 U.S. TOW missiles to Iran after the Iranians pay $4 million. On the same day, North sends a message to Poindexter that says the United States is assured of getting two hostages released "in the next few days."

Nov. 2, 1986 — David P. Jacobsen is released from Lebanon after 17 months in captivity.

Nov. 3, 1986 — A weekly magazine in Beirut, *Al Shiraa*, publishes a story disclosing McFarlane's May trip to Tehran. The visit is confirmed by Ali Akbar Hashemi Rafsanjani, Speaker of Iran's Parliament.

Nov. 6, 1986 — Reagan declines to comment on U.S. arms sales to Iran, telling reporters that speculation could harm efforts to free the hostages. On the same day, Israel is reimbursed by the U.S. government for the 500 TOW missiles delivered to Iran on Oct. 29.

Nov. 13, 1986 — In a nationally televised speech, Reagan describes arms shipments to Iran as good-faith gestures to establish contact with Iranian moderates. Reagan denies that he has engaged in an arms-for-hostages trade.

Nov. 19, 1986 — Reagan says at a news conference that he has ruled out any future arms deliveries to Iran. He also denies that he has condoned Israeli arms shipments to Iran. Following the press conference, the White House acknowledges that a third country — Israel — sent arms to Iran with U.S. approval.

Nov. 21, 1986 — Congress begins investigations into the Iran arms program with closed hearings by the House and Senate Intelligence committees. In testimony before the Senate panel, Casey does not mention the possibility of a diversion of funds to the contras.

Nov. 25, 1986 — Reagan announces the resignation of Poindexter and North's dismissal because of evidence discovered by Meese that funds from the Iran arms sales had been diverted to the contras. Reagan denies knowledge of the contra diversion, saying he had not been "fully informed" about the Iran arms deals.

Nov. 26, 1986 — Reagan names a three-member commission, headed by former Sen. John Tower, R-Texas, to review the operations of the National Security Council.

Dec. 4, 1986 — Meese petitions a three-judge court to appoint an independent counsel to investigate allegations of misconduct in connection with the arms sales.

Early December 1986 — Following disclosure of the contra diversion, the House and Senate Intelligence committees resume their inquiries.

Dec. 16, 1986 — Reagan urges congressional committees to grant limited immunity to Poindexter and North in exchange for their testimony. The initial response from Congress is that granting such immunity would be premature.

Dec. 19, 1986 — Lawrence E. Walsh is named by the panel of federal judges to be the independent counsel in the Iran-contra affair, with the task of probing for criminal violations.

1987

Jan. 6-7, 1987 — The Senate and House vote to establish select committees to investigate the Iran-contra affair.

Jan. 29, 1987 — The Senate Intelligence Committee releases a 65-page report detailing what it learned about the Iran-contra operation during a three-week investigation in December. ∎

DEFENSE

CQ

Defense

In 1986, as it had done in the two previous years, Congress sent President Reagan the message that it would not tolerate continued expansion of the defense budget at the expense of further reductions in domestic discretionary programs.

Once again, Congress sliced a hefty amount from Reagan's annual defense budget request, without changing the program's fundamental shape. It approved an overall defense program of just under $290 billion, cutting Reagan's request by more than $30 billion.

Given Reagan's adamant opposition to a tax increase, the trade-off of defense hikes for domestic cuts had been implicit in Reagan's budget for years. But in 1986, the rigid deficit ceilings set by the Gramm-Rudman-Hollings deficit-reduction law highlighted the linkage.

At no point during the year was there any realistic prospect that Congress would approve Reagan's request to increase the defense budget to $320 billion in fiscal 1987, some 12 percent above the $284 billion defense budget for fiscal 1986.

Of the amount requested, $311.6 billion was for the Defense Department with the remainder earmarked for defense-related programs in the Energy Department and other agencies.

From the moment Reagan's fiscal 1987 budget request arrived on Capitol Hill, the defense budget debate focused on a range between "real zero growth" and "zero real growth" — that is, between the amount Congress had approved for defense in fiscal 1986 ($287 billion) and that amount plus an increase to cover the cost of inflation ($301 billion).

Aside from Congress' continuing insistence on large cuts at the margin of Reagan's request for defense funds, there were several other indications during the year that, despite Reagan's extraordinary personal popularity, support for his national security policies on Capitol Hill stood at a low ebb.

Most dramatically, the House adopted early in August a raft of amendments to the annual defense authorization bill repudiating several key facets of administration policy on nuclear arms and arms control. The most radical of these measures — an amendment that would have banned all but the smallest test explosions of nuclear weapons — was approved by a ratio of 3-to-2. Despite strong White House opposition to this amendment, 34 Republicans voted "aye."

The most onerous of the amendments — including the nuclear test moratorium — were dropped in conference on the eve of Reagan's meeting with Soviet leader Mikhail S. Gorbachev. But the scope of Reagan's political defeat in the House was significant.

Congress also continued its running criticism of the way the Pentagon bought things, adding a few more provisions to the large stack of so-called "procurement reform" legislation enacted since 1983. Taken at face value, most of these measures dealt with intricate details of contract negotiation, weapons testing, the proprieties of job hunting by executive branch officials and the like. And each of the reform proposals was rooted in some specific "horror story" that critics thought would have been forestalled by the procedures enacted.

But the passion with which the reform effort was prosecuted, and the overwhelming margins by which House members across a wide sweep of the political spectrum embraced them despite fervent objections by the Pentagon, demonstrated a more fundamental drive behind the legislation: It was a vote of no confidence in Defense Secretary Caspar W. Weinberger's stewardship of the budgets which Congress had increased so rapidly in the early years of Reagan's administration.

Congress also repudiated the views of Weinberger and his aides, notably Navy Secretary John F. Lehman Jr., by enacting two bills substantially changing the organization of the military high command. The bills gave more bureaucratic clout to the chairman of the Joint Chiefs of Staff and to the commanders responsible for military operations in various parts of the world at the expense of the separate armed services.

Significantly, some of the most hard-nosed Pentagon backers on Capitol Hill were among the reorganization bills' leading proponents. Their avowed purpose was to weaken the parochial perspectives of the separate services, thus giving more weight to professional military advice framed in a multi-service, or "joint" perspective. Weinberger and his aides had vigorously opposed the reorganization efforts when they began in 1985. Officially, Weinberger and most of the others supported the bills after certain compromises were agreed to.

Defense Budget

Because of the Gramm-Rudman act, the annual defense budget debate got off to an unusual start: The Pentagon reduced by $13.8 billion the amount Congress had appropriated for defense budget authority in fiscal 1986. This left a total of $286 billion in new budget authority in fiscal 1985, of which $278.4 billion was for the Defense Department with the remainder going to defense-related programs in the Energy Department and other agencies.

The reduction was required to meet an overall deficit ceiling for fiscal 1986 set by the Gramm-Rudman act. President Reagan exempted from the reduction a handful of programs, including the military payroll and the strategic defense initiative (SDI) — his program to develop anti-missile defenses. All other defense programs were cut by an average of 4.9 percent.

Defense Secretary Weinberger insisted that Reagan's fiscal 1987 Pentagon request of $311.6 billion amounted to an inflation-adjusted increase of only 3 percent over the amount Congress had agreed to approve for fiscal 1986 in a deal struck with the White House in August 1985.

But Weinberger's mathematics was widely discounted by other participants in the defense budget debate who argued that the fiscal 1987 request amounted to an increase of 11 percent in absolute terms and an increase of 8 percent adjusting for the cost of inflation.

Two factors accounted for the disagreement:

• In the August 1985 agreement, Congress had promised to appropriate $294.5 billion for the Department of Defense in fiscal 1986, but it subsequently approved only $289.5 billion.

• The Gramm-Rudman reductions in January 1986 further reduced the fiscal 1986 total for the Defense Department to $278.4 billion.

Weinberger insisted that the proper baseline for measuring the increase in fiscal 1987 was the amount Congress had promised to provide in fiscal 1986, regardless of the fact that the actual fiscal 1986 amount was lower.

The congressional budget resolution set the overall ceiling on defense budget authority at $292 billion. Congress authorized approximately the full amount permitted under the budget resolution, but defense-related appropriations dipped a few billion dollars below the ceiling.

Most of the reduction came from the usual kind of congressional cheese-paring — though this time on a larger scale than ususal. Some production lines were slowed down, and the congressional defense committees made reductions that reflected changes in the economic facts of life facing the Pentagon — for instance, slicing nearly $3 billion to take advantage of lower-than-anticipated fuel prices.

But Congress also had to make some unusual reductions to cut not only budget authority, the amount appropriated in fiscal 1987, but also outlays, the amount actually spent. The two figures differ substantially for the defense budget because amounts appropriated for major weapons are spent in installments over several years.

In addition to limiting defense budget authority to $292 billion, the congressional budget resolution limited defense outlays to about $279 billion, thus confronting Congress with a dilemma. For most major weapons, relatively small amounts of an appropriation are spent in the year for which Congress provides the funds; so to trim outlays by a given amount takes a much larger cut in budget authority.

On the other hand, appropriations for personnel costs and for operations and maintenance are spent mostly in the year for which they are appropriated. This makes those parts of the budget an easier place to find outlay reductions than the weapons production accounts.

But personnel and operating costs are more closely related than procurement accounts to the combat-readiness of forces in the field. So in recent years, most members had been loath to cut personnel and operating costs.

To meet the defense outlay ceiling on the fiscal 1987 budget, Congress resorted to what members frankly acknowledged were "gimmicks." The most notable example was its requirement of a 24-hour delay, from Sept. 30 to Oct. 1, 1987, for the last military payday of fiscal 1987. By the new timetable, the payday would occur in fiscal 1988, so the $2.9 billion cost of that payroll would count against the fiscal 1988 budget and fiscal 1987 outlays would be correspondingly reduced.

Arms Control

In a series of votes beginning Aug. 8, the House adopted five amendments to the fiscal 1987 defense authorization bill that would have:

• Halted tests of all nuclear warheads with an explosive force of more than 1 kiloton, provided the Soviet Union continued its existing moratorium on nuclear tests and agreed to the placement on its territory of U.S. measurement equipment.

• Continued the existing moratorium on full-scale tests of the anti-satellite (ASAT) missile, provided that the Soviet Union conducted no ASAT tests.

• Blocked production of new types of lethal chemical weapons — so-called "binary munitions."

• Forced continued U.S. observance of limits on certain kinds of nuclear weapons that were contained in the unratified 1979 U.S.-Soviet strategic arms limitation treaty (SALT II).

• Sliced by more than 40 percent, from $5.3 billion to $3.12 billion, the fiscal 1987 authorization for SDI.

In part, the House actions reflected widespread public frustration with Reagan's approach to arms control, which had run five years without producing an agreement with Moscow. But good organization and political hardball also played a role in the critics' ability to round up nearly 200 Democrats and around 30 Republicans for all but one of the five amendments.

Several factors contributed to the House arms control outcomes:

• Liberal arms control activists compromised on some of their highest-priority goals to make alliances with Democratic and Republican centrists.

• Some leading centrists had powerful political incentives to deal with the liberals, who had a strong hand in the Democratic Caucus: Armed Services Committee Chairman Les Aspin, D-Wis., already was under fire from some liberals for having supported Reagan on some politically sensitive issues, and Majority Leader Jim Wright, D-Texas, needed to head off any possible liberal challenge to his run for the speakership that would be vacated in January 1987 by Thomas P. O'Neill Jr., D-Mass.

• Once deals were cut on the specific amendments to be pushed, the liberal-centrist coalition squeezed the maximum tactical advantage from the Democratic leadership's control over the timetable and procedure for floor debates. For example, votes on the major arms control amendments were spread out over several days. This allowed members who voted against Reagan on those amendments to follow with "pro-Reagan" votes on other amendments in order to assuage conservative sentiment in their districts.

House conferees on the authorization bill hung tough on the nuclear test moratorium and the SALT II compliance provisions until Oct. 10, the day before Reagan's meeting in Iceland with Gorbachev. Then, under a barrage of demands by Reagan that Congress not undermine his bargaining position, the House leadership dropped the two issues until 1987.

—By Pat Towell

Major Pentagon Reorganization Bill Approved

President Reagan signed into law Oct. 1 a measure embodying the most sweeping reorganization of the U.S. military establishment since Congress created the Department of Defense in 1947.

The bill (HR 3622 — PL 99-433) was designed to shift power from the separate military services to those officials and Pentagon agencies intended to coordinate them.

Under the existing organization, proponents of the changes insisted, the services' parochial viewpoints impeded interservice coordination and deprived the president of coherent military advice. The new arrangement, by contrast, was intended to strengthen the bureaucratic clout of military officers with multi-service, or "joint," points of view. For instance, under HR 3622:

- The chairman of the Joint Chiefs of Staff, at the time Adm. William J. Crowe Jr., was to be designated the president's principal military adviser and given control over the Joint Staff to assist him in developing his advice to the president. Under the existing system, the title of principal military adviser was held collectively by the Joint Chiefs, a committee consisting of the uniformed chief of each service plus the chairman. Critics charged that as a practical matter the members of the committee deferred to the special interests of each service, with the collective recommendations often a muddy compromise.
- The seven commanders in chief (CINCs) who were responsible for unified command of multi-service operations in specified geographic areas were to be given much more authority over their units. Under the existing system, according to its critics, the four services retained undue control over units nominally under a CINC's command.

Enactment of the bill represented a political defeat for Defense Secretary Caspar W. Weinberger, who had complained that major changes might undermine civilian control of the military by confronting a president with only a single military option in times of crisis.

That view was decisively repudiated by the House and Senate Armed Services committees, Capitol Hill's two strongest bastions of sympathy for the military viewpoint.

The House originally passed HR 3622, strengthening the Joint Chiefs chairman, in November 1985. A separate bill dealing with other facets of Pentagon reorganization was attached to the House version of the fiscal 1987 defense authorization bill (HR 4428), passed Aug. 15, 1986. *(1985 House action, 1985 Almanac p. 172)*

The Senate version of HR 3622, passed May 7, 1986, dealt with the entire range of reorganization issues.

Congress completed action on HR 3622 Sept. 17 when the House approved by voice vote a conference report on the measure that had been reported by Senate-House conferees Sept. 12 (H Rept 99-824). The Senate had adopted the conference report by voice vote Sept. 16.

Major Provisions

As signed into law Oct. 1, HR 3622 (PL 99-433) was entitled the Goldwater-Nichols Reorganization Act.

Joint Chiefs Chairman

While the bill designated the Joint Chiefs chairman as the principal military adviser to the president and secretary of defense, it also required him to inform them, as he considered it appropriate, of the range of military opinion on any matter for which advice had been requested.

The chairman was required to transmit to the president and secretary the dissenting views of other Joint Chiefs members who requested him to do so, provided that preparation of the dissenting view did not delay the chairman's advice.

Orders from the president or secretary of defense to the CINCs could be transmitted by the Joint Chiefs chairman, but to underscore the primacy of civilian control over the military, the bill expressly barred the chairman from having command authority over the combat forces.

Senate-House conferees also made the chairman responsible for preparing:

- Overall strategic plans that were consistent with the budget forecasts of the secretary of defense.
- Plans for specific military contingencies, including the associated supply and transportation requirements.
- Estimates of the extent to which the budgets of the armed services met the priorities set by the CINCs. The chairman also was charged with proposing changes in the services' budgets that would better serve the needs of the CINCs.

Chairman's Resources

To give the Joint Chiefs chairman the wherewithal to exercise his newly mandated independence, the bill gave him two important resources:

- A vice chairman, from a service other than the chairman's, to carry out whatever duties the chairman assigned. Like the chairman, the vice chairman would be appointed by the president, subject to Senate confirmation, for up to three terms of two years each. He would be the nation's second-ranking military officer — junior only to the chairman — and would serve as acting chairman in the chairman's absence. He could participate in Joint Chiefs deliberations, but would not have a vote, unless acting as chairman.
- Control over the Joint Staff, which under the existing system worked for the Joint Chiefs as a body. The final bill provided that the Joint Staff was to assist the chairman, vice chairman and other members of the Joint Chiefs, while operating under the chairman.

Unified Commanders

The conferees skirted an emotionally charged philosophical debate over how to define the relationship between the CINCs of unified commands and their subordinate forces.

Under existing law, the CINCs were accorded "operational command" of the units assigned to them. Arguing that this had allowed the services to retain undue control over units nominally assigned to the CINCs, critics insisted that the CINCs be given total, unmodified "command" over the forces assigned to them.

The House-passed legislation would have given the CINCs "command" over their subordinates. As initially drafted, the Senate version had done so, too. But in a compromise aimed at winning a broad consensus of support for their bill, Armed Services Committee leaders agreed to revise it to give the CINCs "operational command" plus a range of other specified powers.

The conferees decided to use neither "command" nor "operational command" to define the CINCs' authority. Instead, they stipulated a range of subjects on which the CINCs had control over units assigned to them, including:

- All aspects of military operations, interservice training and supplies.
- The chain of command within the CINC's sphere of operations. Under existing procedures, as a general rule the unified commands were organized as a federation of self-contained components from each service, so that a CINC dealt with any unit only through the so-called "component commander" in charge of all the units of that service assigned to the CINC.
- Assigning command authority within his sphere of operations.
- Coordinating administrative, supply, organizational and disciplinary policy among assigned units to the degree necessary to carry out missions assigned to the CINC.

Officers could be assigned to any CINC's staff only with his concurrence and he could suspend any officer assigned to his command.

The conference bill also required that any combat forces operating in a CINC's sphere of responsibility be assigned to his command. Also, a CINC would be allowed to monitor communications between units assigned to him and other Pentagon entities, for instance between a Navy fleet and the Navy Department.

The House measures had included provisions that would have required each CINC to draw up a budget covering joint training exercises by units under his command. The conferees dropped that specific procedure from the bill, saying it was too detailed to be included in legislation. But the conference report required the secretary of defense to submit to Congress a separate budget covering the joint training exercises and other activities of each CINC.

'Joint' Specialists

Along the general lines approved by the House, the compromise bill required the secretary of defense to establish an occupational category for officers in joint operations.

Critics had charged that officers in joint assignments who did not support their services' points of view were punished by being denied promotion. Partly for that reason, they argued, the most talented officers eschew interservice duty.

To break that cycle, the House measure had required that joint specialists and officers on the Joint Staff be promoted at the same rate as officers assigned to the headquarters staff of each service.

The conference report dropped the mandatory promotion rate but required the secretary of defense to ensure that the officers assigned to joint duty were talented enough that they would be promoted in due course at the rate the House would have mandated. And it required the secretary of defense to establish guidelines for each service's personnel system to prevent discrimination against officers on joint assignments.

The conference report also required that at least one officer with joint experience serve on the board of officers reviewing for promotion any officer in a joint assignment. It also allowed the Joint Chiefs chairman to review the results of each promotion board for compliance with the secretary's guidelines for non-discrimination against officers in joint duty assignments. Promotion disputes between the chairman and the service would have to be resolved by the defense secretary.

Headquarters Consolidation

The conference report accepted in part House-passed provisions to consolidate the two parallel hierarchies at the top of the Army, Navy and Air Force departments.

Each of those three agencies was headed by a civilian secretary who had a staff of civilian subordinates in charge of the service's facets. But there was in addition a military headquarters for each service, headed by a chief of staff assisted by military officers whose division of labor was very similar to those of the secretary's civilian aides.

The Navy Department, with one civilian secretariat, had two service headquarters: the Navy's and the Marine Corps'.

The conference report required the civilian staff to take over certain functions, including purchasing, auditing, congressional relations and public affairs.

Partly on grounds that these provisions reduced unnecessary duplication of effort, the conference report required the Pentagon to transfer 16,513 military and civilian personnel from headquarters jobs to other positions by the end of fiscal 1988. This amounted to a reduction of 10.3 percent in the Defense Department's total headquarters staff.

Background

Under existing law, the president was commander in chief of the armed forces and the secretary of defense was his civilian deputy. The Army, Navy and Air Force each was headed by a civilian secretary and each had a uniformed service chief (in the Navy's case, two chiefs — one each for the Navy and the Marine Corps).

The Joint Chiefs of Staff, consisting of those four officers plus a fifth acting as chairman, collectively were the president's official source of military advice under existing law.

But neither the separate services nor the Joint Chiefs actually commanded forces in the field. That job was vested in 10 CINCs, seven of whom headed so-called unified commands including forces from more than one service. Each of the unified commands was responsible for military action in a specified region, such as Europe or the Pacific Ocean.

The services were responsible only for training, equipping and manning the forces assigned to the CINCs.

Proponents of more "jointness" contended that each of the services, concentrating on its warfare specialty, had only a limited perspective on overall defense needs. But those parochial views had undue influence on the advice provided to the president by the Joint Chiefs and on the combat resources provided to the CINCs, the critics charged.

The Joint Chiefs system fostered compromises in which each service respected the fundamental interests of the others, according to this view. As a result, advice to the president avoided considering options that undermined service viewpoints and budgets were constructed with too little concern for meeting the CINCs' war-fighting needs at a politically feasible funding level.

A Longtime Crusade

President Eisenhower had recommended shifting additional power from the services to joint Pentagon institutions in 1958, as had numerous study groups since that time. But such proposals had been squelched in the past by a coalition of the services — particularly the Navy — and leading congressional defense experts. *(Reorganization background, Congress and the Nation Vol. I, p. 256)*

The stalemate began to break early in 1982 when then-Joint Chiefs of Staff Chairman David C. Jones, an Air Force general, and Army Chief of Staff Gen. E. C. Meyer both called for sweeping organizational changes along the lines ultimately taken in HR 3622. That initiative, supported by some other senior retired officers, gradually won over some of Capitol Hill's most prominent Pentagon allies.

By 1985, the staunchly pro-defense House Armed Services Committee, following the lead of Reps. Bill Nichols, D-Ala., Ike Skelton, D-Mo., and Larry J. Hopkins, R-Ky., was overwhelmingly committed to bolstering the joint side of the Pentagon. So were both the chairman and the senior Democrat on the Senate Armed Services Committee, Barry Goldwater, Ariz., and Sam Nunn, Ga., respectively.

The call for reorganization by pro-military wheelhorses like Goldwater attracted to the cause other members who were unhappy with the defense establishment. In part, that unhappiness was rooted in the sheer size of Reagan's defense budgets and the concomitant efforts to slash popular domestic programs. Another factor was an apparently widespread belief among congressional defense specialists that Weinberger — like Reagan — displayed only a sketchy grasp of many defense issues.

Weinberger's Limited Support

Weinberger's limited political support was manifest in congressional attacks triggered by a series of "horror stories" that were widely publicized beginning in late 1982. These were cases of costly weapons that failed critical tests or of mundane items for which the Pentagon was billed a seemingly outrageous amount.

The phenomenon was summed up in the "$640 toilet seat" added to Weinberger's attire in the work of *Washington Post* cartoonist Herblock.

The drive for stronger joint voices in the Pentagon gathered momentum when critics of the status quo cited the failure of the 1980 effort to rescue U.S. hostages in Iran and glitches in the generally successful October 1983 attack on Grenada as evidence that combat units were not cooperating efficiently across service lines.

Strong congressional support for centralizing authority over defense policy might not have sufficed, had Reagan — invoking his authority as commander in chief and his formidable political assets — challenged the advocates of change. But though Reagan repeatedly lauded Weinberger's management of the Pentagon, the administration invested no political capital in the secretary's battle against his congressional critics.

To the contrary, Reagan in 1985 overrode Weinberger's strong objections to create a blue-ribbon commission to investigate defense organization. Critics of the existing system on Capitol Hill and within the administration predicted, accurately, that the panel — chaired by defense industrialist and former Deputy Secretary of Defense David Packard — would support their agenda for strengthening the Pentagon's joint institutions.

On Feb. 28, 1986, the Packard commission issued an interim report that, as had been expected, called in general terms for the kinds of changes gaining steam in the House and Senate. President Reagan implemented some of the recommendations administratively April 2.

Senate Committee Action

The Senate Armed Services Committee approved its version of the reorganization measure March 6 by a 19-0 vote. The bill was reported April 14 as S 2295 (S Rept 99-280).

In hopes of allaying fears that the Joint Chiefs chairman might shut out some options, the committee made more explicit his responsibility to convey to the president the entire range of military options. And it underscored in the bill the right of the other Joint Chiefs to insist on conveying their individual views to the president.

The committee also gave the president and defense secretary authority to waive some of the bill's provisions.

But despite energetic efforts by John W. Warner, R-Va., and some other skeptics, a majority of the panel dug in on the fundamental principles that the chairman should be the president's regular source of military advice, and that the CINCs should have greater control over their subordinates.

Two issues in particular were debated at great length:

In the first place, while agreeing that the chairman should become principal military adviser, Pentagon critics of the bill wanted it to recognize the "corporate" character of the Joint Chiefs of Staff. They seized on the fact that the Packard panel applied this term to the Joint Chiefs at one point in its interim report.

But to the reorganization proponents, the word smacked of the old system, which, they argued, had a very strong — albeit unofficial — bias toward compromise positions.

Most of the current Joint Chiefs had opposed the addition of a vice chairman to the committee from the outset. Though yielding on that point, they strongly opposed vesting in him the role of acting chairman when the chairman was away from Washington. Under the existing system, each service chief in turn served as acting chairman for three months at a time. That experience broadened their viewpoint, they argued, making them more effective.

But the reorganization proponents insisted that a permanent stand-in was needed to ensure continuity of a genuinely joint point of view at the top of the military hierarchy. The existing "rotation" system was rejected 8-11, in one of the few roll-call votes taken during the markup. But the provision designating the vice chairman as acting chairman was amended to allow the secretary of defense to waive the requirement.

Senate Floor Action

The Senate May 7 passed HR 3622 after substituting the text of S 2295 for that of the House-passed bill. The vote was 95-0. *(Vote 93, p. 18-S)*

Nunn, one of the measure's architects, said it was intended "to emphasize and give authority to those elements of the Department of Defense responsible for thinking beyond one service."

Goldwater, the bill's other chief sponsor, framed the debate in similar terms: "The battle lines are drawn between those who seek a truly unified defense effort and those who would cling to traditional service prerogatives."

As passed, the bill was essentially unchanged from the form in which it was approved early in March by the Senate Armed Services Committee.

Senate passage of HR 3622 represented a clear political defeat for Weinberger and some of his aides.

"Elements of the Pentagon have fought us every inch of the way," Goldwater said May 7, although by the time the bill reached the Senate floor, the Defense Department officially opposed only a few provisions.

The Barry Goldwater Bill

In part, the overwhelming congressional support for Pentagon reorganization reflected the backing of some of Capitol Hill's most prominent defense specialists — including members with impeccably "hawkish" political pedigrees like Goldwater, Nunn and House Armed Services member Nichols.

In the past decade, Nunn's meticulous scrutiny of defense issues had earned him a reputation as one of the country's premier defense thinkers.

But in the Senate battle over HR 3622, Goldwater's role may have been even more important. A retired major general in the Air Force Reserve, and the elder statesman of modern conservatism, Goldwater's commitment to the reorganization drive carried tremendous political weight. He led not so much by the force of his technical arguments as by the intensity of his conviction that the existing system needed reform.

"Everybody knew where Chairman Goldwater stood on the defense issue," said GOP conservative Phil Gramm, Texas. "There were few who were going to challenge him in the area of defense efficiency."

In a rare gesture, the Senate adopted an amendment offered by Nunn to name the bill after the Arizonan, who was retiring at the end of the year. (Conferees later named the final bill the Goldwater-Nichols Reorganization Act.)

Much of the seven-hour-long Senate debate on the bill was a paean to Goldwater for his crusty integrity and his determination to press the issue.

Responding to one of Nunn's many commendations, the 77-year-old Goldwater's voice faltered momentarily. "The hell with it," he growled. "You get to the point when you get old that you can't say thank you."

Senate Floor Issues

By the time the bill came to the Senate floor, the Pentagon opposed only four substantive provisions:

- Designating the vice chairman as the second-ranking military officer, senior to the service chiefs.

Once Goldwater and Nunn had won the battle over the Joint Chiefs "corporate" status, the vice chairman's status vis-à-vis the service chiefs became the last line of resistance for supporters of a stronger service role. But here, too, Goldwater and Nunn were adamant: If the vice chairman were not senior to the service chiefs, Nunn argued, "we will be continuing a disproportionate authority for the service officers at the expense of the very jointness that the committee is trying to achieve."

- Providing that a chairman's term of office would automatically end six months after a new president took office, thus making it easier for a newly elected commander in chief to select his own principal military adviser. The provision, sponsored by Carl Levin, D-Mich., was the only one in which the White House appeared to give more than nominal support to the Pentagon's objections. One proponent of the bill warned that the provision might be "veto bait" if it remained in the measure's final version.
- Reducing the number of deputy chiefs of staff and assistant chiefs of staff in the Navy and the Air Force.
- Slicing Pentagon manpower by nearly 17,700 by the end of fiscal 1988.

But the committee refused to yield and no amendments were offered regarding these issues.

The Senate agreed to only a handful of significant amendments to the bill, all by voice vote:

- By Ted Stevens, R-Alaska, dropping a provision that would allow the Pentagon to reshuffle current military command arrangements in Alaska. Stevens, who chaired the Appropriations Subcommittee on Defense, had added a rider to the fiscal 1986 defense appropriations measure that would bar any change in the existing Alaskan command arrangements.
- By Alan J. Dixon, D-Ill., stipulating that one of the two under secretaries of defense would be in charge of all defense purchases. This proposal sparked a brief but heated sparring match between Dixon and Dan Quayle, R-Ind., who chaired the Armed Services subcommittee on defense procurement policy.

Dixon, a member of Quayle's panel, had a longstanding claim on the idea of a Pentagon "procurement czar" as a way of forestalling future procurement horror stories.

But Quayle had staked out his own claim to the lead in committee action on procurement. His subcommittee was nearing completion of a bill dealing with several aspects of the politically explosive issue of procurement reform. By far the most politically visible element of Quayle's package was the creation of a procurement czar. Stripped of that symbol, Quayle's bill might drift off into limbo. *(Procurement, p. 475)*

A Nunn compromise was quickly agreed to: The bill established the office of under secretary of defense for acquisition but did not define it, thus leaving unchanged the status of the testing office.

The Senate also tabled, 63-34, an amendment by Dennis DeConcini, D-Ariz., that would have barred transfer of Stinger missiles to Afghan and Angolan rebels unless the president certified certain conditions had been met. *(Vote 92, p. 18-S)*

House Action on CINCs

As passed by the House in 1985, HR 3622 strengthened the role of the Joint Chiefs chairman but did not enhance the role of the CINCs. Before going to conference with the Senate in 1986, however, the House addressed that issue in other legislation.

On July 21, 1986, the Armed Services Committee reported a separate reorganization bill (HR 4370 — H Rept 99-700) designed to shift power within the Pentagon from the separate services to the CINCs, who would be responsible for all combat operations in time of war. The House Aug. 5 attached that measure to the fiscal 1987 defense authorization bill (HR 4428) by a 406-4 vote. The House passed the authorization bill Aug. 15. *(Vote 257, p. 74-H; details, defense authorization, p. 464)*

Though a few members criticized the CINC measure's three chief provisions, no amendments were offered to those parts of the measure. Offered by Nichols, chairman of the Armed Services Subcommittee on Investigations, the committee proposal:

- Gave the CINCs full command of the forces operating under them, including increased authority over their supply plans and a small budget to conduct joint training exercises. The Senate bill retained the language in existing law under which the CINCs had "full operational command" over their subordinates. According to some proponents of change, the services used the latter formula to restrict CINCs' authority over their operations.

Critics warned that the added responsibilities would distract the CINCs from planning for their wartime missions.

- Created a career specialty for officers in joint operations. These officers would remain members of their respective services, and would alternate between joint assignments and other posts. Unlike the Senate bill, the House amendment would allow only joint specialists to become CINCs. Moreover, to ensure that joint specialists were not penalized for dissenting from their respective services' prevailing points of view, the amendment prescribed that, as a group, they be promoted at least as fast as officers assigned to the headquarters staffs of the services.

According to critics, this part of the amendment created an elite corps of officers who risked losing touch with the realities of field service while they honed their skills as Washington paper-shufflers.

- Combined the military and civilian headquarters staffs within each of the services, and reduced the total number of staff members by 15 percent.

By thus depriving a service secretary of a totally civilian staff to check the advice given him by the service military leaders, critics contended, this provision might erode civilian control of the armed forces.

Conference Agreement

House-Senate conferees reached agreement Sept. 11 on a compromise version of HR 3622. Their report (H Rept 99-824) was filed the following day. *(Details, final provisions, p. 455)*

The Senate adopted the conference report by voice vote Sept. 16.

The House adopted it Sept. 17, also by voice vote, clearing the bill for the president's signature. ∎

Reagan, Gorbachev Meet in Iceland Summit

President Reagan and Soviet leader Mikhail S. Gorbachev met in a surprise summit Oct. 11-12 in Reykjavik, Iceland, and discussed making sweeping reductions in their countries' nuclear arsenals.

The talks broke down, however, over Gorbachev's demand for a 10-year moratorium on field tests of components of Reagan's strategic defense initiative (SDI), also known as "star wars." Reagan adamantly refused to agree to limit efforts on development of his proposed anti-missile defense system, even in return for major cuts in Soviet weapons levels.

The meeting, which followed up on the Geneva summit held in November 1985, was billed officially as "presummit" talks preparatory to a formal summit to be held in the United States. However, the breakdown of the Iceland negotiations left prospects for future meetings — and, indeed, for the course of arms-control efforts in general — in doubt. *(Geneva summit, arms control issues, 1985 Almanac pp. 109, 175)*

After the meeting, spokesmen for both countries said that all proposals made during the two-day meeting remained on the table, to be pursued in ongoing negotiations in Geneva or in other forums. But the Soviets soon made it clear that they regarded the various offers as valid only as components of a comprehensive package that included stringent limits on SDI testing.

The meeting also produced uncertain political effects, both on the outlook for SDI and on Reagan's domestic political strength. Immediately after the collapse of the talks, Secretary of State George P. Shultz and other weary U.S. officials described the outcome as a bitterly disappointing failure. Critics quickly predicted that Reagan's intransigence on SDI would undermine public support for the project.

Upon returning to Washington, however, administration officials shifted to a more positive tone, touting both the progress made on many arms issues and Reagan's fortitude in refusing to give in to Gorbachev's demands. It soon became clear that the American public had responded to their arguments; polls showed that a solid majority opposed trading SDI for arms reductions. Even so, Reagan's attempts to make support for SDI into a major issue in the November elections were unsuccessful, with Republicans losing control of the Senate.

In the weeks that followed the summit, other voices questioned whether the talks — announced Sept. 30, with less than two weeks' notice — had not revealed basic weaknesses in the administration's foreign-policy decision-making process. Critics said that Reagan and his aides went to Reykjavik with inadequate preparation, allowing themselves to be drawn into discussions of a radical reshaping of world strategic power without months of planning and consultations.

Sam Nunn, D-Ga., who was to become chairman of the Senate Armed Services Committee in the 100th Congress, was especially critical of Reagan's apparent willingness to consider abolition of all nuclear weapons within 10 years. Nunn warned that that idea would leave U.S. allies with little protection against the Soviet Union's stronger conventional forces. Administration officials insisted that they had only discussed doing away with nuclear missiles.

The Road to Reykjavik

At their Geneva summit, Reagan and Gorbachev had promised to meet again in 1986, with the meeting to be held in the United States. Setting a specific date for that summit proved extremely difficult, however, with scheduling affected both by the general tenor of U.S.-Soviet relations and the state of progress on arms-control talks.

The Soviets protested the U.S. bombing of Libya in April, for example, by delaying negotiations for a time. Soviet officials consistently refused to schedule a meeting until there was evidence that the two heads of government would be able to nail down some significant arms control accord.

While diplomats argued over when to hold the meeting, arms-control negotiations made uneven progress. Although Reagan and Gorbachev had agreed in Geneva to negotiate a 50-percent reduction in long-range nuclear missiles aimed at each other's territory, that accord papered over vast differences regarding precisely what should be reduced by 50 percent.

More fundamentally, the two governments were divided by Soviet insistence that reductions in offensive weapons be linked to restrictions on development of SDI.

On "intermediate-range nuclear forces" (INF) — missiles based in or aimed at Europe or Soviet Asia — however, there were signs of progress. The two leaders had agreed in Geneva to try to work out an interim INF agreement independently of other strategic issues. On Jan. 15, Gorbachev included a possible INF compromise as part of a three-stage plan for the abolition of nuclear weapons by the end of the century. His proposal called for destruction of U.S. medium-range missiles in Europe, and similar Soviet missiles within range of Europe. In response, Reagan on Feb. 24 proposed that the two countries abandon their medium-range missiles "by the end of the decade."

By the end of the summer, negotiators appeared to have made significant progress toward an INF agreement. The U.S. position called for elimination of INF forces by the end of 1989, with an interim limit of 100 INF missiles able to reach targets in Europe and 100 missiles able to reach targets in Asia. The Soviets favored unspecified "deep" reductions in INF forces based in or targeted at Europe, and "token" cuts in Soviet missiles aimed at Asia.

Daniloff Affair

Prospects for improvement of U.S.-Soviet relations ran into a serious obstacle in late August, however, after the Soviets arrested Nicholas S. Daniloff, a correspondent for *U.S. News & World Report*, on espionage charges. Daniloff had been arrested on Aug. 30, a week after the arrest on espionage charges in New York of Gennadi F. Zakharov, a Soviet employee of the United Nations. Despite Soviet denials, U.S. observers generally agreed that the American journalist's arrest was intended to give the Russians bargaining leverage with which to secure Zakharov's release.

The Reagan administration's initial reaction to Daniloff's arrest was mixed, but the case quickly seized center stage in the arena of U.S.-Soviet relations. The administration insisted that there could be no progress toward the INF reduction agreement nor towards scheduling the summit until Daniloff was freed.

The administration from the first refused a trade of Daniloff for Zakharov, rejecting on principle any action that equated the two cases. Nevertheless, on Sept. 12, by agreement of the two governments, Daniloff was released into the custody of the U.S. ambassador in Moscow while Zakharov was turned over to the Soviet envoy to the United Nations, though the spy charges remained pending in each case. The ensuing negotiations included more than 20 hours of meetings between Shultz and Soviet Foreign Minister Eduard A. Shevardnadze, and a Sept. 19 meeting between Shevardnadze and Reagan.

During that session, the Soviet official handed Reagan a letter from Gorbachev proposing a brief pre-summit meeting in Iceland or Britain. The next day, Reagan agreed to the meeting, contingent on Daniloff's release.

On Sept. 29, the two governments agreed to a settlement:

- The charges against Daniloff were dropped and he and his wife left the Soviet Union.
- On Sept. 30, Zakharov pleaded no-contest to his spy charges in a federal court in New York and was convicted of three counts of espionage. He was sentenced to five years' probation, on the condition that he leave the country and not come back.
- The United States dropped its Sept. 17 demand that 25 specific Soviet nationals on the U.N. payroll leave the country by Oct. 1.
- Yuri F. Orlov, a Soviet human rights activist, was allowed to leave the Soviet Union.

Reagan administration officials insisted that the arrangement did not represent a trade of Daniloff for Zakharov. But the deal was widely viewed as a straightforward swap, and some congressional hard-liners protested that Reagan had set a precedent that would lead to the arrest of a U.S. citizen in the Soviet Union every time a Soviet spy was arrested in the United States.

At the Summit

The first effect of the Reykjavik summit occurred before Reagan and Gorbachev even began their meetings. Anxious to show support for the president — and to avoid blame in case the talks were a failure — House Democrats announced Oct. 10 that they were putting off until 1987 their legislative efforts to mandate certain arms control policies.

The Democrats agreed to drop amendments to the defense authorization bill (S 2638 — PL 99-661) barring all but the smallest nuclear weapons tests and requiring compliance with certain provisions of the unratified 1979 U.S.-Soviet treaty limiting strategic weapons (SALT II). *(Stories, pp. 462, 464)*

In the days before Reagan's departure for Iceland, administration officials stressed that they did not expect any substantive agreement from the sessions. What was hoped for, they said, was an "impulse" from the two leaders that would accelerate the conclusion of formal agreements in the ongoing Geneva arms reduction talks.

Instead, the two leaders and a handful of their top national security aides apparently agreed on major elements of a comprehensive arms-reduction package. According to Reagan's national security adviser, Vice Admiral John M. Poindexter, discussions between U.S. and Soviet aides on the night of Oct. 11 and morning of Oct. 12 came to the following tentative conclusions:

- The total number of intercontinental ballistic missiles and bombers would be cut to 1,600 for each country. The total number of missile warheads and bomber-dropped nuclear bombs carried by this fleet would be reduced to 6,000.

But an important dispute remained over how large a reduction was required in each type of weapon. U.S. officials insisted that intercontinental ballistic missiles (ICBMs), which accounted for the bulk of Soviet nuclear firepower, be reduced in proportion to other kinds of strategic launchers. The Soviets rejected that idea, but said they would consider "significant" reductions in their force of very large ICBMs.

- The total number of INF warheads would be cut to 100 for each country: 100 U.S. Pershing IIs and cruise missiles, each of which carried one warhead, and 33 of the triple-warheaded Soviet SS-20 missiles. None of the allowed U.S. missiles would be stationed in Western Europe and none of the allowed Soviet missiles would be based within striking distance of Western Europe.
- Talks would begin toward the eventual banning of nuclear weapons tests. Initially, the two sides would negotiate improved verification techniques for two treaties negotiated in the 1970s but never ratified. After that, the negotiators would seek further limitations on nuclear testing. Soviet officials wanted those talks to be characterized as comprehensive test ban talks, while the U.S. side said that an absolute end to nuclear testing would have to coincide with the abolition of nuclear weapons.

Anti-Missile Treaty

Gorbachev was adamant that all those tentative agreements could be made only if Reagan took two steps with regard to the 1972 U.S.-Soviet treaty limiting anti-ballistic missile (ABM) weapons:

- A pledge not to exercise for 10 years the provision of the 1972 treaty that allowed either party to withdraw from the pact on six months' notice. No militarily significant anti-missile system could be deployed without withdrawing from the pact.
- An amendment to the 1972 treaty that would restrict SDI research to work conducted in the laboratory.

With the SDI issue blocking the package of agreements, the U.S. side offered a second proposal on Oct. 12:

- Neither side would withdraw from the ABM treaty for five years.
- ICBMs, submarine-launched missiles and long-range bombers would be reduced by 50 percent.
- At the end of that five-year period, both sides would renew the five-year pledge not to withdraw from the ABM treaty. Concurrently, they would begin a five-year process of dismantling all remaining offensive ballistic missiles, including ICBMs, INF ballistic missiles and shorter-range nuclear missiles.
- During the entire 10-year period, both sides would be free to conduct ABM research, development and testing as currently permitted by the 1972 treaty. At the end of that period, both sides would be free to deploy anti-missile weapons.

Gorbachev quickly rejected the second U.S. package unless it incorporated a ban on SDI testing outside the laboratory. Reagan refused, and the talks ended. ▮

Nuclear Testing Foes Show Strength in House

House arms-control advocates showed unexpected strength during 1986 on the issue of nuclear weapons testing. House members voted twice by comfortable margins during the year in favor of bringing to an end the Reagan administration's program of underground nuclear tests.

The votes did not lead to any changes in law. One was on adoption of a non-binding resolution (H J Res 3) calling for negotiations with the Soviet Union on a comprehensive test ban. The other was on approval of an amendment to the defense authorization bill (HR 4428) calling for a moratorium on all but the smallest nuclear tests. The amendment was dropped in conference with the Senate. *(Defense authorization, p. 464)*

Nevertheless, the House actions were seen as a significant rebuke to the testing policies of the administration, the first administration in three decades not to seek a comprehensive test ban treaty with the Soviets. Administration officials argued that a test ban would be unverifiable and would be dangerous until after deep reductions in nuclear arsenals were agreed to.

The Soviet Union called for a joint test moratorium on Aug. 6, 1985 — the 40th anniversary of the atomic bomb attack on Hiroshima — and announced a temporary unilateral moratorium of its own. Moscow subsequently extended its moratorium several times during 1986. The Reagan administration continued to conduct underground tests, arguing that testing was needed to ensure that existing nuclear weapons did not lose their explosive power through aging of the nuclear materials or mechanical parts.

Test-Ban Negotiations

H J Res 3 was cosponsored by Iowa representatives Berkley Bedell, D, and Jim Leach, R. In addition to urging test-ban negotiations, it also called on the president to seek Senate approval of two treaties signed in the mid-1970s but never ratified. The pacts would limit underground nuclear explosions to a force of 150 kilotons — that is, the explosive power of 150,000 tons of TNT. Existing treaties banned all but underground nuclear tests.

In 1984, the Senate had adopted the language of H J Res 3 as an amendment to the fiscal 1985 defense authorization bill by a vote of 77-22. *(1984 Almanac p. 51)*

H J Res 3 originally had been scheduled for floor action in October 1985. House Speaker Thomas P. O'Neill Jr., D-Mass., deferred action on the resolution at the request of Secretary of State George P. Shultz, who cited President Reagan's impending Geneva summit meeting with Soviet leader Mikhail S. Gorbachev. *(1985 Almanac p. 177)*

The House considered H J Res 3 on Feb. 26, under a rule that provided for a vote on only one amendment: an administration-backed substitute offered by Reps. Henry J. Hyde, R-Ill., and Beverly B. Byron, D-Md. That proposal endorsed the administration contentions that a comprehensive test ban should await deep reductions in nuclear stockpiles, and that the two unratified treaties should be amended to provide improved systems for verifying compliance.

Liberal arms-control groups mounted a strong grassroots lobbying campaign in support of the resolution. Administration officials were sharply critical of the proposal, but did not mount an all-out effort to block it.

The key vote on H J Res 3 came when the House rejected the Hyde-Byron amendment by a 158-258 margin. Members then approved the resolution on a 268-148 vote. *(Votes 27, 29, p. 10-H)*

During debate, opponents of the resolution argued that continued nuclear testing was needed for new weapons, such as the Midgetman single-warhead intercontinental missile. Supporters countered that an already tested warhead was planned for the Midgetman.

But a more fundamental theme in the supporters' argument was that even some improvements that would be desirable in theory were worth giving up for the sake of cutting off the qualitative race in weapons improvements. Members also disagreed over whether a comprehensive treaty could be verified, and whether the reliabilty of existing U.S. weapons could be tested without full-scale underground nuclear blasts.

Reagan denounced H J Res 3 in a March 11 letter to Senate Majority Leader Robert Dole, R-Kan.

The Senate adopted the language of H J Res 3 as an amendment to its version of the defense authorization bill (S 2638) Aug. 7. The amendment, offered by Charles McC. Mathias Jr., R-Md., was approved by a comfortable 64-35 margin. *(Vote 189, p. 34-S)*

Test Moratorium

After approval of the non-binding resolution, the efforts of arms-control forces focused on a tougher provision, sponsored by Democratic Reps. Patricia Schroeder, Colo., and Thomas J. Downey, N.Y., to impose a testing moratorium, provided the Soviets continued to refrain from testing.

As the spring wore on, sponsors began to think that they had a realistic chance of succeeding with their proposal. One sign was a House Appropriations Committee action on the funding bill for the Energy Department, which conducted weapons tests for the Pentagon. An amendment, offered by Bill Green, R-N.Y., to cut off funds for testing was rejected by only a three-vote margin, 29-26.

So Schroeder, Downey and Edward J. Markey, D-Mass., began negotiating with a group of moderate Democrats led by Armed Services Committee Chairman Les Aspin, Wis., and Richard A. Gephardt, Mo., chairman of the Democratic Caucus, to come up with a version that might win a majority in the House.

A key change in the amendment aimed at accommodating the widespread concern over whether Soviet compliance with a test moratorium would be verified: The amendment would bar only tests of more than 1 kiloton, on the grounds that smaller tests could not be reliably detected. Subsequently, sponsors agreed to another change, delaying the ban's effective date until 1987, in order to give the administration time to conduct any last-minute tests it deemed essential.

The final version of the measure was offered as an amendment to HR 4428, the defense authorization bill, by Aspin and Gephardt. It was adopted by a 234-155 vote Aug. 8. *(Vote 287, p. 82-H)*

As approved, the provision allowed only U.S. nuclear blasts with an explosive power of 1 kiloton or less, and only at the Energy Department's Nevada test site. The amendment enforced the ban only if the Soviet Union conducted no nuclear tests of greater than 1 kiloton, or conducted a test anywhere than at its Semiplatinsk testing site in Siberia.

In addition, the amendment was contingent on each of the two governments agreeing to let the other place monitoring equipment on its soil to verify compliance.

The ban was to be effective between Jan. 1 and Sept. 30, 1987.

The test ban amendment subsequently became a major bone of contention in the prolonged House-Senate conference on the defense authorization bill (S 2638), as Senate Republicans, backed by Reagan, strenuously objected to the provision.

Fearful of seeming to undermine Reagan on the eve of his Reykjavik summit with Gorbachev, House Democrats agreed Oct. 10 to drop the amendment. However, they did secure a promise from Reagan to seek Senate ratification in 1987 of the two test-ban treaties. ∎

Reagan Steps Away From SALT Treaty

President Reagan announced May 27 that the United States would no longer observe the terms of the strategic arms limitation treaty (SALT II) with the Soviet Union. The decision ended a six-year policy of informal compliance with the agreement, which was signed by President Carter in 1979 but never ratified.

Reagan said that he was taking the step because the Soviets had repeatedly violated the terms of the treaty.

The United States formally exceeded the numerical weapons limits in the treaty on Nov. 28, when it put into service the 131st B-52 bomber equipped to carry long-range cruise missiles. That gave the United States one weapon more than the SALT II limit of 1,320 ballistic missiles with multiple-warheads (MIRVs) and missile-armed bombers.

Reagan's May 27 announcement was the target of strong congressional criticism from arms-control advocates. In reaction, the House passed an amendment to the defense authorization bill (HR 4428) mandating continued U.S. observation of three of the numerical limits on weapons in the treaty.

There was no comparable provision in the Senate version of the bill, and the Reagan administration and the Republican majority in the Senate vigorously opposed the amendment in conference. After an extended deadlock, House Democrats finally agreed to drop the amendment from the bill. But the final version of the defense measure included non-binding language urging the president to continue to observe the limits. *(Defense bill, p. 464)*

Background

Carter brought the SALT II agreement to the Senate in 1979, but later asked that it be set aside in the wake of the Soviet invasion of Afghanistan. However, both he and Reagan as his successor declared that they would take no action that would undercut the treaty, provided the Soviets did the same.

The first test of Reagan's continued observance of the treaty came in June 1985, when construction of the Trident submarine *Alaska* threatened to push the number of U.S. weapons over the limit set by the accord. Under strong pressure from American allies, Reagan ordered the dismantling of the existing sub *Sam Rayburn* in order to keep the United States under the limit.

In doing so, however, Reagan stressed that his future policy would be dependent on Soviet compliance with existing arms treaties, and progress in seeking new treaties. Administration officials and many defense experts pointed to three developments that they said represented significant Soviet violations of SALT II. They were:

- Deploying two new types of land-based intercontinental missiles (ICBMs), contrary to the SALT II provision allowing each country only one new type.
- Exceeding the treaty's limit on the total number of "strategic nuclear delivery vehicles" — long-range bombers, ICBM launchers and launchers on nuclear-missile submarines.
- Putting in code missile data radioed to Earth from test missiles. SALT II barred such encryption when it impeded verification of compliance with the treaty.

Reagan Announcement

In his May 27 statement announcing the end of his policy of informal SALT II compliance, Reagan said he would continue modifying B-52 bombers to carry long-range cruise missiles, breaching the treaty's limits by year's end.

Along with his decision about the ultimate U.S. stance

on SALT II, however, Reagan announced that the United States was remaining temporarily in compliance with the treaty by breaking up two Poseidon missile-launching submarines. Had the 20-year-old ships not been earmarked for dismantling, the United States would have broken one of the SALT II ceilings on May 28, when the new Trident missile-launching submarine *Nevada* went to sea.

Reagan emphasized that the two older ships, *Nathanael Greene* and *Nathan Hale*, were being dismantled because of the cost of overhauling them and refueling their nuclear reactors — estimated at more than $100 million per ship. Had he been convinced that the ships' military effectiveness was worth the cost, he said, he would have kept them in service.

Two SALT II ceilings were involved in the U.S. deliberations over submarines and bombers:

- A limit of 1,200 on the number of long-range land-launched and submarine-launched ballistic missiles with multiple warheads (MIRVs).
- The limit of 1,320 on the number of such MIRVed missiles and long-range bombers equipped with cruise missiles.

The *Nevada*, carrying 24 MIRVed Trident I missiles, would have violated the 1,200 MIRV limit, had Reagan not retired two ships each carrying 16 MIRVed Poseidons.

That transaction put the U.S. MIRVed missile total at 1,190. Therefore, 130 bombers could be equipped with cruise missiles under the combined ceiling of 1,320. Under the treaty, any additional cruise missile-armed bombers would have to be compensated for by the retirement of additional MIRVed missiles.

In his statement, Reagan presented the upcoming decision on the bomber as a proportionate response to Soviet treaty violations. The Senate had endorsed a "proportionate response" policy in a 1985 resolution that called for continued U.S. observance of the treaty. *(1985 Almanac p. 176)*

Reagan emphasized that he anticipated no large increase in the number of U.S. bombers and that the total number of nuclear warheads would not be increased above the Soviet level.

Congressional Response

Congressional critics reacted to Reagan's announcement by arguing that it was not a sensible response to Soviet treaty violations. Instead, they said, the United States should react in kind — by accelerating development of the Minuteman missile, for example, in reaction to Soviet deployment of a forbidden "second new type" of ICBM.

Critics also warned that abrogation of the treaty limits would allow Moscow to expand its nuclear force far more rapidly than the United States.

The first congressional move against the new administration policy came June 12, when the House Foreign Affairs Committee approved a non-binding resolution (H Con Res 350) calling on Reagan to continue observing certain of the treaty's numerical limitations, so long as the Soviets did likewise. The resolution was approved on a 29-11 vote.

The resolution urged compliance with three "sublimits" set by the treaty. They were:

- 820 ICBMs with multiple warheads (MIRVs).
- 1,200 MIRVed ICBMs and similarly equipped submarine-launched missiles.
- 1,320 MIRVed missiles of any type and bombers equipped with long-range cruise missiles.

The House then approved H Con Res 350 by a 256-145 vote June 19. Before approving the resolution, the House rejected on a 187-222 vote a Republican substitute amendment. *(Vote 166, p. 52-H; vote 164, p. 50-H)*

Arguing for the resolution on the floor, Foreign Affairs Committee Chairman Dante B. Fascell, D-Fla., said that preservation of the three-tiered sublimits was "really a question of common sense."

"Why should we give away something which, imperfect as it is ... in some way restricts hardware?" he asked.

Fascell and several other proponents warned that the Soviets could boost their arsenal quickly by adding warheads to the large ICBMs already in their force and by speeding up several missile and bomber production lines already in operation.

Moreover, they said, the tight budgets in prospect for years would not accommodate post-SALT acceleration of Reagan's arms buildup.

"Congress ... is loath to start a new and ever more costly round in the leapfrogging race of nuclear weapons," said Majority Leader Jim Wright, D-Texas.

The predominantly Republican opponents objected that the resolution singled out only the numerical subceilings the Russians were not violating, while ignoring administration charges that the Soviets violated the ban on a second new type of missile and on data encryption. "Aren't qualitative restrictions important?" demanded Henry J. Hyde, R-Ill.

"This resolution does everything it can to excuse the [Soviet] violations," Dan Lungren, R-Calif., charged.

The rejected GOP amendment, offered by William S. Broomfield, Mich., would have urged the president to observe all SALT II provisions so long as the Russians observed the entire treaty.

Hyde sneered at SALT proponents' arguments that Congress would not provide enough funds to match the Soviets in a post-SALT arms race. "You cut defense and then say, 'My God, we've got to appease the Russians. We can't keep up.' "

The opponents also charged that adoption of the resolution would undermine U.S. efforts to negotiate an arms reduction agreement. "It is a sign of weakness that our negotiators in Geneva will not be able to overcome," declared William Carney, R-N.Y.

Defense Authorization

The next step for SALT II proponents was an amendment to the defense authorization bill mandating what H Con Res 350 had urged. Offered by Norman D. Dicks, D-Wash., the amendment was adopted on a 225-186 vote. *(Vote 302, p. 86-H)*

In a replay of action on H Con Res 350, Broomfield offered a substitute amendment waiving the limits if the Soviets violated any portion of the treaty. It was rejected 199-214. *(Vote 301, p. 84-H)*

In the Senate, SALT II proponents had mustered some strength in April, when they rounded up 52 signatures on a letter urging Reagan to continue complying with the three sublimits. However, plans to offer such an amendment to the defense authorization bill were dropped when administration allies threatened to force a Senate vote on the entire treaty — a vote which most observers thought would go against the pact. The failure of the amendment set the stage for the conference confrontation with the House over the provision, and the language was watered down. ∎

Congress Authorizes $217.4 Billion for Defense

Winding up a session-long debate on the defense budget, Congress Oct. 15 approved legislation (S 2638 — PL 99-661) authorizing $217.4 billion for military programs in fiscal 1987.

The annual authorization bill set a ceiling on the amount that could be appropriated for Defense Department programs, excluding military payroll costs, as well as military-related programs of the Energy Department.

It had become customary to discuss the authorization measure in terms of the total defense budget that would result from its enactment. As enacted, S 2638 would bring total appropriations for military programs for fiscal 1987 to $291.8 billion — $28.5 billion less than the administration had requested.

In the fiscal 1987 budget resolution (S Con Res 120), Congress had committed itself to hold new defense budget authority — the amount actually appropriated — to $292.2 billion, the amount appropriated for defense in fiscal 1986. The budget resolution also set a $279.2 billion cap on defense outlays, the amount of money actually disbursed by the government. While not binding on the authorization bill, the outlay ceiling was binding on the companion defense appropriations bill under terms of the Gramm-Rudman-Hollings deficit-reduction act (PL 99-177). *(Budget resolution, p. 542)*

Armed Services Committee leaders in both chambers contended that it was technically impossible to produce a sensible defense budget that provided $292 billion in new budget authority but no more than $279 billion in outlays. So the panels resorted to what they frankly called "gimmicks" to work out a compromise version of the defense authorization bill that used nearly all the allowed budget authority while remaining under the outlay cap.

The actual defense appropriations for fiscal 1987, embedded in an omnibus continuing resolution (H J Res 738 — PL 99-591), provided $274 billion for Pentagon personnel and operating costs, equipment purchases and military research. *(Spending bill, p. 219)*

Major Policy Issues

The conference report on the authorization bill (H Rept 99-1001) was agreed to by the House Oct. 15 by a vote of 283-128. The Senate agreed to it by voice vote later the same day. *(House vote 431, p. 122-H)*

Final action on S 2638 came more than two weeks after Senate-House conferees hammered out agreements on nearly all of more than 1,500 spending disputes. *(Conference action, p. 481)*

Conferees on S 2638 then were deadlocked over several issues of policy. The most widely publicized of these involved House-passed provisions challenging Reagan's arms control policies.

Arms Control Maneuvers

On Oct. 10, the day before President Reagan began "pre-summit" discussions with Soviet leader Mikhail S. Gorbachev in Iceland, House Democratic leaders dropped their immediate challenges to Reagan on arms control. *(Iceland meeting, p. 459; nuclear testing, p. 461)*

At issue were nuclear testing, continued U.S. observance of certain provisions of the unratified 1979 U.S.-Soviet strategic arms limitation treaty (SALT II), and production of lethal chemical weapons.

The conferees agreed to drop a House-passed provision banning all but the smallest nuclear tests. In return, Reagan promised in a letter to seek Senate approval in 1987 of two treaties limiting the size of nuclear tests. The treaties were negotiated in the 1970s but never ratified.

And conferees accepted the House position retaining an existing ban on tests of the anti-satellite (ASAT) missile against a target in space.

But on two other points, general agreements reached Oct. 10 turned out to be the subject of further dickering on Oct. 14-15.

- The House had included a provision requiring continued U.S. compliance with certain SALT II provisions that Pentagon plans might have violated within the next several weeks. The conferees agreed in principle on Oct. 10 to include in the bill "tough, non-binding language," expressing the sense of Congress that the United States should continue observing those SALT II provisions.

House sources later claimed that they understood that the Senate would allow them to draft the compromise language. But Senate conferees subsequently insisted that the compromise language include a provision asserting the right of the United States to disregard any treaty the Soviet Union was violating.

House conferees, led by Armed Services Committee Chairman Les Aspin, D-Wis., balked. They had given up their demand for binding law on the issue, Aspin later told reporters. The Senate's proposed language would have allowed Reagan to claim that Congress was sending mixed signals on the SALT II question. "The least we could accept was unambiguous non-binding language," Aspin said. The proposed Senate revision was dropped.

The administration did exceed SALT II limits Nov. 28 by deploying a B-52 bomber armed with cruise missiles without dismantling existing weapons.

- The details of the chemical weapons agreement also resisted settlement until the last minute. Finally, the conferees agreed to allow purchase of a nerve gas artillery shell, though production actually would not begin before late 1987. They approved $35 million for a nerve gas-carrying aerial bomb called Bigeye, but barred production of that weapon before Oct. 1, 1987.

Strategic Arms Issues

The conferees split the difference on funding for Reagan's strategic defense initiative (SDI). They approved $3.53 billion for the anti-missile defense program, about two-thirds the amount the president had requested. The Senate had included $3.96 billion for the project, the House $3.125 billion.

For production of 12 additional MX intercontinental ballistic missiles (ICBMs), the conferees approved $1.1 billion, as passed by the House. Reagan had requested and the Senate approved 21 missiles ($1.4 billion).

Reagan also had requested $389 million to develop a new basing method, better able to survive a nuclear attack than the existing missile silos in which the Pentagon would emplace 50 MXs already approved for deployment. The House intended to prevent additional MX deployments and conferees cut basing research funding to $120 million.

Defense Authorizations for Fiscal 1987

The conference report on the fiscal 1987 defense authorization bill (S 2638 — H Rept 99-1001) authorized $217.4 billion for defense programs, out of an overall defense budget of $291.8 billion. The bill included Defense Department programs as well as nuclear weapons programs conducted by the Energy Department.

Totals reflect final adjustments; they may not add because of rounding *(in millions of dollars).*

	Reagan Request	House Amount	Senate Amount	Conference Agreement
Procurement	$ 95,746.8	$ 78,657.8	$ 85,592.6	$ 85,065.1
Research and Development	41,929.9	33,801.3	36,358.1	36,215.6
Operation and Maintenance	85,875.6	81,351.6	80,707.3	78,597.3
Working Capital Funds	1,179.3	1,155.8	1,097.3	908.3
Other	738.5	1,091.5	692.5	582.5
Military Construction	6,569.6	5,062.7	5,310.3	5,226.2
Family Housing	3,417.6	3,284.8	3,201.1	3,183.1
Total, Milcon/Housing	9,987.1	8.347.6	8,512.4	8,409.3
Total, Department of Defense Military	235,475.2	204,405.5	212,960.2	209,878.0
Total, Department of Energy National Security Programs	8,098.4	7,451.0	7,425.2	7,451.0
Total, Other Defense-Related Activities	126.6	126.6	231.6	120.6
GRAND TOTAL	**$ 243,700.2**	**$ 211,983.1**	**$ 220,617.0**	**$ 217,449.6**

SOURCE: Conference report on S 2638

To continue development of the Midgetman missile — a much smaller ICBM carrying a single nuclear warhead instead of the 10 carried by MX — the conferees approved $1.2 billion of the $1.4 billion Reagan wanted. The Senate had halved that request.

They approved the entire secret amount requested to prepare for production of the "stealth" bomber, designed to evade enemy detection. Like the amount requested, the amounts authorized in the two versions of the bill were secret. However, according to some sources, the House had made a reduction.

Also authorized was a secret amount requested to prepare for production of a stealth cruise missile to be launched by bombers.

The conferees dropped $100 million the House had added to keep alive the production line for components of the B-1 bomber. The last of a planned fleet of 100 B-1s were funded in fiscal 1986.

For a giant Trident missile-launching submarine, the conferees included $1.5 billion. The House had rejected the request on budgetary concerns. Both houses had approved the $1.4 billion request for 21 Trident II nuclear missiles to equip these subs.

Conventional Forces

Conferees approved the 840 M-1 tanks requested by the administration, but trimmed the funding to $2.05 billion, from the $2.12 billion requested.

Both houses had approved only 120 of 144 requested Apache anti-tank helicopters. The conferees recommended $1.17 billion for the purchase.

The budget requested two cruisers and three smaller destroyers, all equipped with Aegis, a network of computers, radars and missiles designed to protect U.S. fleets from swarms of anti-ship missiles. The conferees approved six Aegis ships, three of each type. They said the larger cruiser purchase would allow the Navy to continue its highly successful policy of keeping down the price of those ships by having two shipyards compete for the contract.

Both houses authorized four *Los Angeles*-class nuclear submarines ($2.3 billion) designed to hunt Soviet subs.

The conferees agreed to $8.53 billion for 321 front-line fighter planes for the Air Force and Navy, compared with the requested 399 planes ($9.97 billion).

They also approved $296 million to buy less complex fighter planes that would be used to defend North America against bomber attack. The Senate had denied the funds.

For two controversial programs, the conferees approved substantial funding, but with strings attached. They recommended purchase of:

- 720 Bradley armored troop carriers, but also approved language generally similar to that adopted by the House requiring very specific tests of the vehicle, some of them to be observed by non-Army personnel.
- 180 AMRAAM missiles to be fired by fighter planes at aerial targets. The purchase would be barred until the missile successfully completed certain additional flight tests.

The conferees also approved $728 million of the $830 million requested to prepare for production of a new large cargo plane, the C-17. These funds could not be spent until April 15, 1987, thus allowing time for a General Accounting Office study of whether the new plane was needed.

Senate Committee Action

The Senate Armed Services Committee reported S 2638 July 8 (S Rept 99-331).

As reported, the bill was consistent with an overall defense budget for fiscal 1987 of $301 billion, $19.2 billion less than Reagan requested.

Primarily because the annual authorization bill did not specifically cover the budget for military personnel costs, the amount explicitly authorized by S 2638 was $225.7 billion. The largest components of that figure were earmarked for procurement, research, operations, construction of facilities, and research and production involving nuclear energy conducted on behalf of the Pentagon by the Department of Energy.

The bill also dealt with some military personnel policy issues that accounted for an estimated $2 billion of the committee's $19.2 billion reduction.

But the panel's cuts fell short of the fiscal 1987 budget resolution adopted June 26, days after the Armed Services panel had finished work on its bill. On July 23, the committee agreed to offer a floor amendment reducing defense budget authority to $295 billion, $3 billion over the budget resolution ceiling. The $6.8 billion cut involved no reduction in specific programs. Lower-than-planned inflation accounted for $5.97 billion; the remaining $640 million trim came from a reduced estimate of the price of oil. Outlays still would be $7 billion above the limit set by the budget resolution.

Apportioning Cuts

To cut Reagan's overall budget by 6 percent, the Senate panel trimmed the operations and maintenance request by 5.3 percent and the procurement request by 6.2 percent. By contrast, the request for research and development was reduced 11.2 percent and the facilities request by 11.9 percent.

The lion's share of the committee reduction came from:

- Cuts in the operations and maintenance budget that reflected changing economic circumstances and accordingly should have no impact on Pentagon operations.
- Across-the-board reductions levied for purely budgetary reasons against broad categories of programs, leaving it to the military services to decide how to apportion the reductions among specific programs.
- Relatively hefty cuts in 17 major weapons programs for policy reasons (as in the case of SDI) or because of overall budgetary limits.

The committee recommended a $4.5 billion reduction (to $81.2 billion) in Reagan's request for operations and maintenance. The committee justified nearly half the reduction ($2.2 billion) on grounds that fuel prices were lower than was anticipated when the budget was drawn up in mid-1985.

By the same token, the panel reduced the account by an additional $975 million on grounds that prices for commodities purchased with these funds would be lower than anticipated.

The remaining one-third of the overall reduction in operations and maintenance funding came from across-the-board cuts in broad categories of activities (for instance, base operations and supply operations), leaving the Pentagon discretion to apply the reductions within those categories.

The committee cut the Pentagon's procurement request by $5.9 billion (to $89.8 billion). Of that reduction, nearly $1.7 billion was in across-the-board cuts assigned to categories such as Navy aircraft or Air Force missiles, leaving the Pentagon to decide how much of the cutback should be taken from any program.

The committee, driven by its desire to boost ammunition stockpiles, imposed one general restriction on the Pentagon's discretion. Both the Navy and Air Force budgets lumped requests for bombs and ammunition into catchall accounts labeled "Other Procurement." The Senate panel insisted, in allocating among specific programs the reductions in those accounts, that the Navy and Air Force not reduce munitions funding.

For the same reason, the committee increased by 3.9 percent (to $2.3 billion) the Army's account for ammunition procurement.

The panel cut an additional $786 million from the procurement accounts on the grounds that a like amount left over from earlier years could be transferred to the fiscal 1987 budget.

The bulk of the remainder the committee cut from the procurement request was made up of relatively large slices taken from 14 programs.

The committee's $4.7 billion reduction in the amount requested for research and development (to $37.2 billion) had an even simpler composition, with four factors accounting for nearly 90 percent of the cut:

- $2.77 billion was in the form of across-the-board cuts to be applied according to the services' judgment.
- $1.19 billion came from SDI.
- $700 million from Midgetman.
- $188 million from efforts to develop future MX basing methods.

SDI Funds Cut

By a one-vote margin, the committee turned the bill into a fundamental challenge to President Reagan's crusade to develop a nationwide anti-missile shield.

The committee's nine Democrats and Republican William S. Cohen, Maine, overrode the strong objections of the panel's other nine Republicans to slice by more than 25 percent Reagan's $5.32 billion request for SDI. The panel approved a total of $3.96 billion.

But even more significant than the committee's SDI budget cut was its call for a fundamental shift in the program's emphasis. In contrast to Reagan's repeated call for a shield that would make nuclear ballistic missiles "impotent and obsolete," the committee recommended a more technically modest — though still very expensive — emphasis on defending U.S. nuclear forces.

The panel's slim, 10-member majority also warned that Reagan was under-funding conventional weapons development to pay for SDI.

Strategic offensive weapons — long-range, land-based nuclear missiles, or ICBMs — accounted for two other contentious issues in S 2638:

- Though the Senate panel approved the entire $1.4 billion requested for 21 MX multiple-warhead ICBMs, it approved only $200 million of the $389 million Reagan had requested to develop a basing method that potentially would pave the way for deployment of the administration's planned total of 100 of the missiles. Congress had limited deployment of the MX to 50 in existing silos, citing their vulnerability to Soviet attack. Reagan had sought the $389 million to develop a less vulnerable basing method for 50 additional missiles.

Because of pressure for budget reductions, the committee had adopted a general rule of cutting funding requests for strategic programs that would not bear fruit until 1990 or later. Accordingly, it sliced the request for future MX basing methods.

- The panel also cited its rule favoring pre-1990 strategic

improvements in trimming to $676 million the $1.38 billion requested to develop a small Midgetman ICBM.

Strategic Warfare

Other than slicing the SDI request by a quarter and approving half the amount sought for Midgetman, the committee's recommendations for strategic arms were relatively non-controversial.

The panel approved the administration's $1.6 billion request for development of the Trident II (or D-5) submarine-launched missile and the $1.1 billion requested for purchase of the first 21 production-line versions of that weapon. The D-5 was designed to be the first submarine-launched missile accurate enough to destroy an armored underground missile launcher.

The committee also recommended authorization of the $1.4 billion requested for the 14th in a class of huge missile-launching submarines, designed to carry Trident missiles.

Also approved was $227 million requested for three E-6As — modified jetliners equipped to radio orders to submerged missile subs through trailing antennas some five miles long.

The Air Force sought a secret amount to continue development of the stealth bomber. The committee report suggested that the request was approved.

The last of the planned 100 B-1 bombers had been funded in the fiscal 1986 budget. John Glenn, D-Ohio, had urged his colleagues to add to the bill $200 million to preserve the option of buying additional B-1s if the stealth became too expensive or experienced technical problems. However, the committee rejected Glenn's proposal.

The committee trimmed to $120 million the $165 million requested to develop a new version of the short-range attack missile (SRAM) carried by existing bombers to attack targets 100 miles distant.

It also reduced to $255 million the request for $413 million to modernize existing B-52 bombers, most of which were 25-30 years old. The panel approved funds to equip the planes with long-range cruise missiles, but denied funds earmarked to update some radar and other electronic gear.

The committee approved $782 million to put new, much more powerful engines on 50 existing KC-135 tanker planes, used to refuel long-range bombers in midair. According to the panel, the job could be done for $80 million less than the Air Force requested because of lower than anticipated prices and because some money left over from earlier years could be used.

The committee approved $216 million of the $278 million requested for ASAT development and repealed a provision of the fiscal 1986 law that barred U.S. ASAT tests against a target in space as long as the Soviet Union continued its current ASAT test moratorium. The panel also recommended the $28 million requested to improve the ASAT production line, though no funds were sought to build more missiles.

Ground Combat Forces

The committee approved the Pentagon's request for 840 M-1 tanks ($1.6 billion).

It recommended purchase of 720 Bradley armored troop carriers ($927 million), a reduction of 150 vehicles (and $195 million) from the administration request. But the panel emphasized that the reduction was due to budgetary limits alone, and that it rejected widely publicized charges that the Army had not adequately tested the Bradley's performance.

Budgetary limits also were cited for approving 120 Apache anti-tank helicopters ($1.06 billion) instead of the 144 requested (for $1.19 billion).

The committee approved $155 million requested to develop a small helicopter dubbed LHX. The Army planned to buy some 6,000 of these planes beginning in the mid-1990s to replace Vietnam War-vintage helicopters currently used to haul troops and attack ground targets. The panel warned that the plan's projected $40 billion price tag might require the Army to settle for a less sophisticated future helicopter.

The request was approved for $56 million to buy laser-guided anti-tank artillery shells that could home in on a tank. But the committee recommended only $50 million of the $118 million requested to begin buying small robot airplanes (called Aquila), which carried lasers to spotlight targets for Copperhead shells. The panel endorsed the need for a program like Aquila, but it ordered the Army to negotiate with the manufacturer a substantial reduction in the program's estimated $1.1 billion cost.

The committee strongly endorsed continuing development of an airborne radar called JSTARS to locate enemy tank columns tens of miles behind their own lines and a ground-launched missile called JTACMS that would blanket them with dozens of anti-tank warheads. It approved the $535 million requested for the two programs and told the Pentagon not to reduce that amount in the course of parceling out the panel's across-the-board cuts.

The committee approved 700 Patriot long-range anti-aircraft missiles ($920 million). It also approved the request for more than 4,000 Stinger short-range, one-man anti-aircraft missiles ($252 million).

The panel also strongly endorsed the request for $186 million to build controversial "binary munitions" — artillery shells and aerial bombs (called Bigeye) that dispensed lethal nerve gas.

Approved without change was $904 million for French-designed cellular telephone systems for use as a mobile communications network by Army combat units in the field.

The committee was sharply critical of the Army's plans for major weapons purchases in the next several years warning that, for example:

- It was planning to phase out production of M-1 tanks even though half the tank fleet consisted of older vehicles and there was no firm plan to begin building a more modern version.
- The planned end to production of Apache helicopters came as older and less powerful aircraft still would make up 60 percent of the attack helicopter force. Some LHXs were earmarked to replace those older planes, but that program might not survive tight future budgets.

The panel told the Army to draw up by March 1, 1987, a long-term weapons modernization plan that would include modified versions of weapons currently in production.

Tactical Air Combat

The request for 48 F-15 fighter planes ($1.7 billion) was approved. But because of budget limits, the committee recommended purchase of 192 of the smaller F-16 fighters ($2.64 billion), a reduction of 20 planes (and $296 million).

The panel recommended denial of the entire $296 million requested to buy 20 relatively inexpensive fighter planes intended to defend North America against bombers. The Air Force at the time was conducting a competition between the Northrop F-20 and a stripped-down version of the General Dynamics F-16 for this mission. But the committee argued that the projected $3 billion price tag for nearly 300 home-defense planes was too high given current budget limits.

The full $294 million requested for development of a new, first-line fighter plane that would replace the F-15 in the mid-1990s was approved. And the committee added to the bill $35 million to test whether the A-7 — a 1960s-vintage light bomber — could be updated relatively inexpensively to attack enemy tank units.

Similarly, the committee made few changes in the request for Navy combat planes. Because of budgetary limits, it recommended 96 F/A-18s — jets used both as fighter planes and as small bombers — instead of the 120 requested, a reduction from $2.9 billion to $2.5 billion. But funding requests for the Navy's other principal combat planes were approved:

- $541 million for 14 F-14 fighter planes.
- $268 million to develop an improved version of the F-14.
- $279 million for A-6E medium bombers.
- $146 million for an improved version of the A-6E, labeled the A-6F.
- $623 million for 42 Harrier vertical-takeoff jets, used by the Marine Corps as small bombers.

The committee approved the request for 260 AMRAAM air-to-air missiles ($657 million), although the missile had come under heavy fire for rising costs and test failures. The panel insisted that AMRAAM was needed because, with its sophisticated guidance system, one U.S. fighter could shoot at several targets simultaneously.

Also approved without change was $776 million requested for nearly 5,000 copies of three other kinds of air-to-air missiles.

Nearly the same amount — $750 million — was approved for 3,240 HARM missiles, designed to be fired at enemy radar sets by small U.S. bombers. For nearly 6,000 Maverick air-to-ground missiles, equipped with various kinds of target-finding equipment, the committee recommended $732 million. For budgetary reasons, it reduced the request by 1,100 missiles ($100 million).

Also approved as requested was $166 million for nearly 750 copies of a 2,000-pound "smart bomb" designed to be dropped by a plane and home in on a target miles distant.

And the committee approved the request for nearly 30,000 cluster bombs ($567 million), each of which carried hundreds of small grenades designed to destroy lightly armored vehicles with a warhead and kill people with a shower of shrapnel.

Naval Forces

The committee approved the five large surface warships requested by the Navy: two cruisers ($1.9 billion) and three destroyers ($2.5 billion), all equipped with the Aegis defense system. Aegis was a combination of long-range radars, powerful computers and anti-aircraft missiles designed to protect a U.S. fleet against swarms of high-speed anti-ship missiles.

The $9.8 million requested to test radar-carrying blimps as long-range naval sentries also was recommended.

The panel also approved nearly 1,200 Standard long-range, ship-launched anti-aircraft missiles ($731 million). However, it denied the $13 million requested to develop a nuclear-armed version of the Standard.

The committee denied the entire amount requested for a short-range anti-aircraft rocket, called RAM, and it told the Navy to kill off the program. The Navy had requested $24 million for development of RAM, which was being carried on in collaboration with West Germany, and $63 million to buy the first 50 missiles. The panel complained that the project was behind schedule and over budget and that its guidance system would be ineffective against many new types of Soviet anti-ship missiles.

Four *Los Angeles*-class nuclear-powered submarines, designed chiefly to hunt other subs, were approved as requested ($2 billion). The committee also backed the $257 million request to develop a new type of sub-hunting submarine, the so-called *Seawolf* class (formerly the SSN-21).

The request for $118 million to develop the Sea Lance missile, designed to be fired by U.S. subs at enemy submarines tens of miles away, was approved. But the panel blocked development of a nuclear-armed version of the missile. It deleted from the bill $4.6 million requested to develop that version of the missile and $47 million requested to set up production facilities for its nuclear warhead.

The panel approved the request for $312 million to buy nine long-range, land-based P-3C anti-submarine patrol planes built by Lockheed Corp. But in hopes of encouraging the manufacturer to keep down the price of the new planes, it added to the bill a provision allowing the Navy to use up to $120 million of that amount to modernize existing planes.

It recommended authorization of the requested 24 SH-60 ship-based helicopters designed to hunt submarines. But it barred the use of funds to equip any SH-60s with the Norwegian-designed Penguin anti-ship missile. The ships earmarked to carry the missile-armed helicopters already were equipped with Harpoon anti-ship missiles having a much longer range than the Penguin, the committee said.

The committee also opposed authorization of $53 million for six smaller SH-2F anti-sub helicopters.

The committee denied funds for two kinds of naval vessels:

- $613 million for a high-speed supply ship designed to carry fuel, food and ammunition for an entire fleet.
- $196 million for four small coastal mine sweepers. Congress previously had approved funds for five of these fiberglass ships, designed with a novel hull shape, but tests had shown design flaws. The panel ordered the Navy to use up to $100 million of the previously appropriated money to buy a European mine sweeper that could be duplicated by a U.S. shipyard.

Air Transports

Some observers had speculated that budgetary pressures would discourage funding of major new production programs. But the committee recommended one of the largest prospective new programs with only a minor reduction: the C-17 long-range transport plane, designed to haul tanks and other heavy equipment into primitive airstrips. The panel approved $547 million of the $612 million requested for development of the plane and the entire $182 million requested to gear up for C-17 production beginning in fiscal 1988.

The committee also approved without change four other large programs for transport aircraft, including:

- $1.9 billion for 21 huge C-5B cargo jets.
- $104 million for eight copies of a DC-10 jetliner (called KC-10s) modified both to haul military cargo and to refuel other planes in midair.

• $387 million to develop a hybrid airplane/helicopter, called the V-22 Osprey (formerly the JVX), designed to carry Marine Corps infantry from ship to shore.

Personnel Issues

The committee set the fiscal 1987 ceiling for active-duty military personnel at 2,174,250. This was 6,880 persons more than the fiscal 1986 ceiling, slightly more than half the increase the administration requested.

But the panel also complained that the officer corps had been growing nearly twice as fast as the entire active-duty force. Between fiscal 1980 and fiscal 1985, the total number of active-duty personnel grew by 4.9 percent but the number of officers grew by 11.3 percent. So the committee added to the bill a provision requiring that the number of officers be trimmed by 2 percent in fiscal 1987 and by the same percentage in each of the two following fiscal years.

The committee froze the number of reservists paid to participate in regular drills at the level set for fiscal 1986: 1,103,576.

However, the panel approved an administration request to give the president a freer hand in calling up reserve units for temporary duty without declaring war or a state of national emergency. Under existing law, the president could order to active duty up to 100,000 drilling reservists for up to 90 days. Under the committee's provision, the president could order to active duty up to 250,000 reservists and could extend their service beyond 90 days, but Congress could dismiss them from active duty by concurrent resolution.

Procurement

The committee incorporated into the bill several provisions revising the way the Pentagon bought weapons:

• Establishing the position of civilian procurement "czar" in charge of the entire weapons purchasing system, including the office of independent operational testing, created by Congress in 1983. *(Procurement changes, box, p. 475)*

• Allowing the Pentagon to designate some weapons programs as "enterprise programs" and thus exempting them from certain procedural requirements to give their managers more flexibility.

• Directing the Pentagon to put more emphasis on purchasing commercially available items, so that fewer items needed to be custom-designed.

• Repealing a requirement for the Pentagon to keep certain data about contractors' labor and material costs.

House Committee Action

The House Armed Services Committee reported its version of the bill July 25 (HR 4428 — H Rept 99-718). As reported, the bill authorized $217.8 billion, compared with Reagan's request for $243.7 billion.

In addition to the direct reduction of $25.9 billion in budget authority, the committee bill included other provisions that would produce an additional $2.2 billion savings in the companion defense appropriations bill. These cuts included giving the president less of an increase than he wanted in military personnel and reducing his request for military pay and benefits.

The largest part of HR 4428 dealt with the authorizations for operations and maintenance costs, procurement and military research and development. But the bill also included authorizations for two other parts of the defense budget that had been separately authorized in previous years:

• $8.64 billion of the $9.99 billion requested for construction of military facilities, including family housing.

• $7.56 billion of the $8.10 billion sought for defense-related programs conducted by the Energy Department, including the development and manufacture of all nuclear explosives.

The committee completed marking up its bill July 24, one day after voting to boost overall defense budget authority from $285 billion, the figure it originally approved, to the $292 billion level allowed in the budget resolution. With that increase in budget authority, the outlays associated with the bill increased from $282 billion to $285 billion, $6 billion more than the defense outlay ceiling.

Members and aides on both Armed Services panels insisted there was no practical way to meet the two defense ceilings set by the budget resolution: Any feasible defense budget that used $292 billion in budget authority would produce outlays well over $279 billion.

The reason, they said, was that conferees on the budget resolution arrived at the two numbers by political compromise rather than budgetary analysis. "It's something for everyone," said House Armed Services Chairman Les Aspin, D-Wis. "They compromise by giving the conservatives a high budget authority number and the liberals a low outlay number."

Military Personnel Issues

The committee recommended holding the number of military personnel on active duty at about 2.17 million, approving an increase of only 2,000 over the personnel ceiling in fiscal 1986. Reagan had requested an increase of more than 13,700.

In conformity with the congressional budget resolution, the panel authorized a 3 percent military pay raise effective Jan. 1, 1987.

The committee also added to the bill several changes in personnel policy designed to reduce the manpower costs. Among the reductions were:

• $594 million resulting from various changes intended to reduce the frequency with which service members were transferred between posts at government expense.

• $100 million resulting from an order to reduce slightly the ratio of officers to enlisted personnel on active duty.

• $112 million, from putting a ceiling of $5.08 billion on the amount that could be spent for reserve training.

The committee also added to the bill a provision requiring an inspection by Defense Department technicians of any commercial airliner chartered to carry military personnel. This was in response to the death of 248 soldiers in a charter-plane crash in Newfoundland in 1985.

Operations and Maintenance

Because of concerns about the "combat readiness" of units in the field, the committee made a relatively small trim in the Pentagon's request for operations and maintenance funds: a 5 percent cut compared with an overall average of 14 percent chopped from the other major parts of Reagan's defense budget.

Moreover, a large part of the committee's reduction in the operations account reflected anticipated decreases in the cost of doing business since the time the budget was drawn up. These savings, such as lower-than-anticipated prices for fuel oil and other consumable items, amounted to

$2.89 billion of the operations reduction, which were expected to have no impact on Pentagon programs.

The committee added $495 million to the operations budget to cover the higher cost of units stationed abroad because of the decline in the dollar's strength against foreign currencies.

It also added $37 million to pay for anti-drug-smuggling operations by reserve and National Guard units and to modify some aircraft that would be used in such missions.

Strategic Offensive Weapons

The committee approved production of 12 MX missiles ($1.1 billion) instead of the 21 requested.

Like Senate Armed Services, the House panel opposed further efforts to develop another basing method for MX — beyond the current plan to put the controversial new missiles in existing missile silos. Accordingly, the panel sliced the amount for continued MX development to $200 million, $152 million less than the request, and it denied the entire request of $389 million to develop new MX basing methods.

But the House committee approved the entire $1.4 billion request to continue development of a Midgetman single-warhead intercontinental missile. Complaining that some administration officials were trying to delay the project, the committee added to the bill a provision barring deployment of more than 10 MXs until Midgetman development passed certain key thresholds.

Both the amount requested and the committee's recommendation for the stealth bomber were secret. But the panel added to the bill $200 million to continue buying components of the B-1 bomber. The last of a planned 100 B-1s was funded in the fiscal 1986 budget, but the committee insisted that the added money provided a hedge against technical problems with the new plane and an incentive for the stealth manufacturer to keep down the plane's price tag.

The committee also sliced $712 million from the secret amount requested for development and production of a long-range stealth cruise missile to be carried by the B-1. The panel also denied $165 million requested to develop a shorter-range SRAM II bomber missile and barred use of any of the money recommended for the stealth cruise missile until the Air Force decided whether it wanted to buy that weapon or SRAM II.

The entire amount requested to modernize existing B-52 bombers ($413 million) was approved. And the panel trimmed to $1.5 billion the $1.8 billion requested to put new engines on 50 KC-135 tanker planes used to refuel bombers in midair.

Citing budgetary limits, the committee denied the $1.36 billion requested for the 14th of a class of large submarines designed to carry the Trident nuclear missile. But it approved the entire $1.1 billion requested for 21 long-range Trident II missiles to be carried by that class of ship. And it proposed only a minor reduction in the authorization for Trident II development, approving $1.5 billion, $133 million less than the request.

The panel approved $83 million for an E-6A radio plane: a converted jetliner that would relay commands to submerged missile submarines through a five-mile-long radio antenna. The Navy had sought $227 million for three of the planes. The panel cited budgetary limits as the reason for the cut and ordered the Navy to consider replacing the E-6A program with alternative communication systems, such as space satellites that would use a laser to flash coded messages to the ocean region where a sub was known to be lurking.

Strategic Defensive Weapons

The committee recommended a reduction of $1.54 billion in Reagan's $5.3 billion request for SDI development.

The amount recommended included $3.4 billion (of $4.8 billion requested) for programs conducted by the Pentagon, and an additional $371 million (of $508 million requested) for SDI-related research conducted by the Energy Department.

The committee ordered the Pentagon to earmark $50 million of the total for development of an anti-missile defense that would be effective against short-range nuclear missiles fired at Western Europe from Soviet-bloc territory.

The committee recommended lifting the current congressional ban on testing the ASAT missile against a target in space, and added to the bill a provision that would reinstate the ban only if the Soviet Union dismantled its existing ASAT missiles.

However, the panel appeared to place little confidence in the U.S. weapon. It approved only $140 million of the $278 million requested for ASAT development and denied the $28 million requested to organize a production line for the missiles. None of the funds approved could be used to prepare for production of the ASAT.

Ground Combat

The committee approved the request for 840 M-1 tanks ($1.98 billion). But it objected to the Army's current plan to end M-1 purchases in fiscal 1989, leaving about half the Army's tank fleet equipped with older vehicles and no new tank ready for production until the late 1990s. The panel ordered the Army to recommend to Congress a plan for continued M-1 production.

Like the Senate panel, the House committee reduced the authorization request for Bradley armored troop carriers, but emphasized that this was because of budgetary limits and not because the committee endorsed any of the widely publicized critiques of the Bradley. The committee recommended production of 593 Bradleys ($830 million) of 870 requested ($1.12 billion).

Also because of the budget crunch, the committee recommended 120 Apache anti-tank helicopters ($1.05 billion) instead of the 144 requested ($1.19 billion). But the committee criticized the current plan to purchase no more Apaches after fiscal 1988, noting that nearly half of the Army's attack helicopters would be older models and that no new attack helicopter would be built before the mid-1990s at the earliest. It ordered the Army to recommend a plan to continue Apache production and to consider the feasibility of having two contractors build the helicopter.

The panel recommended a slowdown in the conversion of existing "scout" helicopters to carry lasers used to guide Hellfire anti-tank missiles launched from Apaches. Because this so-called AHIP scout had failed certain tests, the committee approved $144 million of the $210 million requested for the program.

But the committee approved the $29 million requested to equip AHIPs with Stinger missiles for use against enemy helicopters.

The panel approved $146 million of the $156 million requested to develop a new helicopter (LHX) that would enter production in the mid-1990s to replace thousands of small, 1960s-vintage helicopters the Army used to haul troops and attack ground targets.

The committee approved the request for 15,400 copies of the TOW anti-tank missile used by the Army and Marine Corps but noted that they could be bought for $146 million, slightly less than the budget assumed. But the panel denied the $49 million requested to develop a new missile to replace the TOW (called AAWS-M), complaining that the planned program would take too long.

Also approved was the $82 million requested for 136,000 copies of a small Swedish-designed rocket launcher (the AT-4) to be issued to individual soldiers, though the committee questioned the weapon's adequacy.

The panel added to the bill $157 million to test certain anti-tank missiles — including the European-built Milan — and one type of anti-tank cannon, as potential replacements for TOW and the AT-4.

The request for 220 laser-guided Copperhead artillery shells, designed to home in on enemy tanks, was approved ($8.2 million), although the committee complained that the Army was planning to buy too few of the weapons. But citing testing problems and cost increases, it denied the $118 million requested to begin production of a miniature remote-controlled airplane called Aquila, intended to beam a laser at Copperhead targets.

The committee approved $88 million requested to develop a missile, called J-TACMS, intended to scatter a cloud of anti-tank warheads over enemy columns up to 100 miles away. But for reasons not explained in its report, it approved only $28 million of the $447 million requested to develop and begin building an airborne radar called Joint STARS intended to guide J-TACMS to such targets.

The Army's requests for anti-aircraft missiles were approved by the panel: 700 long-range Patriots ($952 million), 456 10-mile-range Chaparrals and nearly 4,200 short-range, shoulder-fired Stingers ($252 million). But without explaining its actions in the report, the committee denied most of the funds the Army requested to develop a replacement for the canceled Sergeant York (or DIVAD) anti-aircraft gun, approving only $30 million of $224 million requested for four major Army anti-aircraft research programs.

Of $158 million requested for production of binary munitions, the committee approved $90 million.

Citing budget limits, the committee approved $854 million of the $904 million requested to buy French-designed cellular telephone systems for use by Army divisions in the field. And it denied the entire $204 million requested for 16,000 combat radios (called SINCGARS) that had had testing problems.

Tactical Air Combat

Driven by budget limits, the committee trimmed the requests for production of the Air Force's two front-line fighter planes. It recommended 36 F-15s ($1.6 billion) instead of the 48 requested ($1.68 billion) and 180 of the smaller F-16s ($2.4 billion) instead of the 216 requested ($2.8 billion).

It approved the entire amount requested ($411 million) to begin buying stripped-down fighter planes for anti-bomber defense of North America, beginning with 20 planes in fiscal 1987.

But the panel complained that Air Force plans for future combat planes were too diffuse: The Air Force requested $294 million for a new fighter plane (called the ATF) and $369 million for five other programs, each aimed at modernizing an existing Air Force combat plane. The committee recommended a lump sum of $450 million for development of future Air Force combat planes (compared with a total of $663 million requested for the six programs) and told the Air Force to cancel three of the six.

The panel commented specifically that improved F-16s carrying new weapons might obviate the need for the new ATF, and it restricted the purchase of additional F-15s until the Air Force decided whether to continue F-15 production or begin building the new plane.

By contrast, the Navy's plans for buying new combat aircraft fared somewhat better with the panel. Because of budget limits, it approved 96 F/A-18s used as both fighter planes and small bombers ($2.47 billion) instead of the 120 requested ($2.9 billion). But it approved the amounts requested for three other combat planes: 15 F-14 fighters ($541 million), 11 A-6E mid-size bombers ($279 million) and 42 Harrier vertical-takeoff bombers used by the Marine Corps ($706 million).

The committee also recommended only minor reductions in the amounts requested to develop improved models of two of the planes: an A-6F ($130 million) and an F-14D ($240 million).

The committee approved the request for more than 4,400 Sparrow and Sidewinder missiles, designed to be fired from fighter planes at airborne targets. But citing lower-than-anticipated contract prices, it authorized $463 million for the purchase, $24 million less than the budget request.

The market was even more favorable for the larger Phoenix, carried only by the Navy's F-14s and able to reach targets more than 50 miles distant: The committee authorized purchase of 300 Phoenixes for $276 million, which was $14 million less than the Pentagon requested for only 205 of the missiles.

But the committee insisted on maintaining tight limits imposed by Congress the previous year on the cost and performance standards of a new air-to-air missile called AMRAAM. And it recommended a sharp reduction in the requested production rate: 135 missiles in fiscal 1987 ($388 million) instead of the 260 requested ($657 million).

The committee also cut significantly from the amount requested for several kinds of guided missiles designed to be launched from planes at ground targets. It approved the request for 1,800 laser-guided Maverick missiles, but recommended only 780 of the Maverick version guided by an infrared television camera designed to see targets at night ($100 million). The Pentagon had requested more than 5,100 copies of the night-viewing Maverick ($634 million).

The panel complained that a much larger missile — the AGM-130, carrying a 2,000-pound warhead — was taking too long to be put into production and it denied the entire request for 51 of the missiles ($27 million). The committee added to the bill $5 million to test cheaper foreign-built weapons that could be used instead.

The request for 3,240 HARM missiles, to be fired by U.S. planes at enemy radar sites ($750 million), was trimmed to 2,570 missiles ($619 million).

Naval Warfare

The committee recommended three cruisers equipped with the Aegis anti-aircraft system ($2.72 billion) instead of the two requested ($1.91 billion). Three ships would be needed to continue the evidently successful practice of keeping the ships' cost down by having two firms compete for the building contracts, the committee said.

To make up the cost of the additional cruiser, the committee approved only two smaller Aegis-equipped destroyers ($1.75 billion) instead of the three requested ($2.45 billion).

The committee approved the request for nearly 1,200 long-range, ship-launched anti-aircraft missiles called Standards ($731 million). But it denied $9.2 million requested to develop a nuclear-armed Standard.

It also refused all funding requested for a small, shorter-range missile (called RAM) designed as a last-ditch defense against anti-ship cruise missiles. The Navy requested $63 million to begin buying RAMs and $24 million to continue developing the weapon. Instead, the committee added to the bill $90 million to test various kinds of detection devices, decoys and short-range missiles to defend ships.

As requested, the panel recommended four *Los Angeles*-class nuclear submarines ($2.05 billion). To continue development of a new *Seawolf* class of hunter subs and to prepare for building the first one in fiscal 1989, the committee approved $704 million, $6 million less than the amount requested.

It approved as requested 200 ASROC missiles, designed to throw an anti-submarine torpedo tens of miles from a surface ship ($74 million), and it recommended $115 million of the $118 million requested to develop a similar missile (called Sea Lance) that would be fired from a submerged submarine at a distant sub.

The panel slowed production of the Navy's two newest anti-submarine torpedoes, partly so that both production lines would remain open longer, thus being available for a future production surge. The committee recommended 50 long-range Mark 48s, designed to be fired from submarines ($215 million), instead of the 227 requested ($508 million). And it approved 67 smaller Mark 50s, designed to be carried by planes and helicopters ($95 million), instead of the 84 requested ($110 million).

Insisting that the Navy come up with a better plan for modernizing its fleet of large, land-based anti-submarine patrol planes, the committee denied the request for nine additional P-3Cs ($312 million). But it added to the bill $93 million to prepare for production of an improved version of the plane (called the P-3G). The bill also required that the new type be purchased by competitive procedures.

Because of budgetary limits, the committee recommended 11 LAMPS III (or SH-60B) helicopters carried by cruisers and destroyers to hunt subs ($129 million), instead of the 17 LAMPS IIIs requested ($200 million). But it approved the request for seven modified versions of the helicopter (the SH-60F) equipped with different submarine detection gear for $118 million, $21 million less than the Navy had requested for those helicopters.

The committee approved without change the $53 million requested for six smaller LAMPS I anti-sub helicopters, a type carried by some older ships. And it approved the $36 million requested to begin modernizing existing LAMPS Is.

Citing problems in building copies of the type previously funded, the committee denied the request for four small mine sweepers ($196 million).

It approved as requested $613 million for a large fuel and ammunition supply ship, designed to cruise with a combat fleet, and two tankers of the *Henry J. Kaiser* class designed to refuel ships while steaming in mid-ocean ($276 million). But it turned down a request for $62 million to enlarge (or "jumboize") an existing refueling ship, arguing that it would be cheaper to build additional *Kaiser*-class ships.

Air Transport

The panel recommended $1.9 billion for 21 large C-5B cargo planes, a minor reduction from the request; and $78 million for eight KC-10 tanker planes, designed to refuel other planes in midair, a reduction of $26 million from the amount requested for eight planes.

It also recommended $768 million of the $830 million requested to continue development of a new cargo plane, the C-17, and to gear up for its production.

Approved without change was the $150 million requested to develop a hybrid spaceship/airplane designed to travel at many times the speed of sound.

At the other end of the air travel spectrum, the committee approved the request for 14 of the large CH-53E helicopters used by the Marine Corps to haul troops and cargo from ship to shore. It recommended only $170 million of the $387 million requested to develop a hybrid airplane/helicopter (called Osprey, formerly JVX) intended to replace existing Marine helicopters. The panel complained that the Osprey would be too expensive if used for only one mission. But it agreed that the Navy could add to the program an additional $170 million from its budget if it agreed to use the craft for anti-submarine patrol.

Senate Floor Action

In a rare Saturday session, the Senate Aug. 9 passed S 2638 by an 86-3 vote. *(Vote 207, p. 37-S)*

S 2638 authorized a total of $219.8 billion for the Defense Department and for military-related programs of the Energy Department, $23.1 billion less than Reagan's request. That total included $8.5 billion for construction of military facilities and $7.4 billion for Energy Department activities, including the development and manufacture of nuclear warheads. As passed, the bill would bring total military spending to $296 billion in fiscal 1987.

During five days of debate on the measure, administration allies staved off several efforts to repudiate President Reagan's arms policies, even as the House was approving several such moves during debate on a counterpart bill. *(House floor action, below)*

But Reagan barely averted some important Senate defeats:

- By a 50-49 tabling vote, the Senate killed an amendment that would have reduced to $3.24 billion the authorization for SDI research.
- An effort to kill production of the Bigeye nerve-gas bomb failed on a 50-50 tie vote, after which Vice President George Bush cast a symbolic tie-breaking vote. The House voted to defer production of any lethal chemical weapons until after fiscal 1987.

SDI: Settling for Half

By a razor-thin margin, the Senate on Aug. 5 rebuffed extra-deep cuts in Reagan's SDI program. But it adopted an already substantial cut that had been voted by the Armed Services Committee in hopes of protecting the program from a political savaging.

At the initiative of Sam Nunn, D-Ga., and William S. Cohen, R-Maine, the panel had cut the $5.3 billion request for SDI research and development to $3.9 billion. Sustaining that amount, the Senate narrowly rejected two amendments to cut SDI further.

Republican supporters of Reagan's full request made no attempt to restore the money cut by the Armed Services panel, tacitly acknowledging that they lacked the votes. And Nunn said the $3.9 billion annual authorization would be the SDI's "high-water mark."

Reagan was under pressure from three sides on the issue: liberals who wanted to slow or stop the program, moderates who wanted him to scale back his promises that it might make nuclear war obsolete, and hard-line conservatives who were worried that he ultimately might bargain away the program in arms control negotiations with the Soviet Union.

The day after the Senate acted, some of the conservatives took their concerns directly to Reagan at the White House. One, Gordon J. Humphrey, R-N.H., said he had withheld his vote on the Senate amendments as a "signal" to Reagan of the worries among staunch pro-SDI members.

Reagan responded immediately to the conservatives, saying in an Aug. 6 speech to SDI backers that the program "is no bargaining chip" and that the United States would deploy the space weapons once they were developed.

The Senate's two votes on SDI produced identical margins, but with a slight shift of players:

- First, by a 50-49 vote, the Senate tabled an amendment by J. Bennett Johnston, D-La., that would have cut Reagan's request to $3.24 billion, $712 million less than the committee-approved amount. Johnston said that would represent a 3 percent increase over the 1986 level, after inflation. *(Vote 176, p. 33-S)*

Of 49 senators who had signed a letter in May calling for a cut to that amount, only Orrin G. Hatch, R-Utah, voted for the motion to kill Johnston's amendment.

- Next, by a 49-50 vote, the Senate defeated outright an amendment by J. James Exon, D-Neb., cutting Reagan's request to $3.56 billion, an amount Exon said would represent a 15 percent "real" increase over 1986. *(Vote 177, p. 33-S)*

Exon had voted against the Johnston amendment, saying its 3 percent figure was too low. But his vote for his own amendment was offset by another switch: Bob Packwood, R-Ore., had supported the Johnston amendment, but after conferring with GOP leaders he voted against the Exon amendment.

In spite of the defeats, Johnston and other SDI critics declared victory, claiming that the narrow votes — coupled with the Armed Services panel's cut — demonstrated congressional unhappiness about the rapid spending increases Reagan sought.

Nunn said the more important Senate message was that Reagan must "refocus" the mission of SDI.

Citing language in the committee report that cast doubt on Reagan's professed dream of a space-based, missile-proof defense, Nunn said the committee had launched "a very considerable change in the goals of the program." Nunn labeled as "grandiose and unrealistic" Reagan's insistence that SDI eventually could protect the entire United States from Soviet nuclear missile attacks. Nunn noted that the committee shifted about $500 million into research on conventional warfare technology such as tank-killing devices.

The Senate dealt by voice vote with additional SDI amendments:

- By Kerry, barring any nuclear weapons tests associated with SDI. Though administration officials frequently claimed the system was intended to be a non-nuclear defense, one potential SDI component was an X-ray laser that would be triggered by exploding a nuclear bomb in outer space. Rejected Aug. 8.
- By Carl Levin, D-Mich., declaring the sense of Congress that the 1972 U.S.-Soviet treaty limiting anti-ballistic missile (ABM) systems should be preserved and that funding SDI was not intended to indicate support for abrogation of that pact. Supporters and critics of SDI differed over how far SDI research could go without violating the ABM treaty. However, to accommodate administration supporters, the amendment was silent on this question. Adopted Aug. 9.
- By Levin and Warner, temporarily stopping the Pentagon from chartering a quasi-independent think tank to work on questions related to SDI. Critics had complained that such an institute might be used by the Pentagon as a public relations device to counter vociferous opposition to SDI in the academic science community.

The amendment would require reports from the Pentagon and the General Accounting Office justifying the creation of an SDI institute and would bar any action on the project for 30 legislative days after the report was received. Since the 99th Congress likely would adjourn in less than 30 legislative days, this would delay the matter until 1987. Adopted Aug. 6.

The Senate also agreed Aug. 9 to an amendment by Glenn barring the Pentagon from awarding SDI research contracts to foreign governments or firms if U.S. firms could "reasonably" carry out the contracts. It first rejected 33-64 a motion to table the amendment. *(Vote 199, p. 36-S)*

Chemical Weapons

With Vice President Bush casting a "no" vote, the Senate Aug. 7 defeated, 50-51, an amendment barring production of the Bigeye bomb, intended to be lofted from airplanes on enemy troops. *(Vote 184, p. 34-S)*

Bush's vote broke a 50-50 tie, but was unnecessary, since the amendment would have failed on the tie. However, the vote showed the administration's determination to win on the issue, which it had portrayed as a key element of the U.S. defense buildup.

The Senate earlier had defeated, 43-57, an amendment by Mark O. Hatfield, R-Ore., restating a provision of current law barring production of 155mm binary artillery shells until Congress ratified a presidential report that the North Atlantic Council had "formally approved" incorporating the weapon into NATO plans. *(Vote 182, p. 34-S)*

The amendment was meant to overturn the administration's July 30 certification that NATO had approved the weapon. Hatfield said the administration ignored the intent of Congress by getting approval only of the lower-level NATO Defense Planning Committee, composed of military officials.

Chemical weapons had been a major issue in Congress since 1981, when Reagan first sought money to research and develop replacements for the aging munitions stored at bases in the United States and Europe. The administration contended that the existing weapons were obsolete and dangerous to store, and that new ones were needed to counter a Soviet buildup of chemical arms. Opponents said the administration should put more effort into negotiating a treaty banning the weapons.

Congress had put strings on every step of both the artillery and Bigeye programs, but Reagan gradually had won permission to proceed with actual production. *(1985 Almanac p. 15)*

Both sides treated the amendment to delay Bigeye

production as the year's major challenge to chemical weapons. Sponsored by David Pryor, D-Ark., it would have deleted all funds for initial production: $104 million in unspent fiscal 1986 money and $56.8 million from the pending 1987 bill. However, the amendment would have allowed continued research and development on the weapon.

Pryor argued that the Army had failed to prove that the Bigeye was safe and workable. After years of research and development, "the Bigeye bomb has not met the test," he said.

Even supporters acknowledged that the Bigeye was not yet a proven weapon. Reagan was asking Congress "to take a chance" on the bomb, Nunn said. "It might end up not being a bomb. It might be a bum."

But Cohen insisted that the Army had corrected many of the problems uncovered in initial tests. He compared the Bigeye to weapons such as the M-1 tank and the Harpoon anti-ship missile, both of which encountered serious troubles early in their development that later were fixed.

After Cohen's motion to table the Pryor amendment failed, 49-50, administration supporters quickly moved for a turnaround on the vote on actual adoption. *(Vote 183, p. 34-S)*

They took two steps: They arranged for John C. Stennis, D-Miss., a Bigeye supporter who had missed the vote, to come to the Senate chamber, and they called on Bush.

As the follow-up vote was proceeding, two senators vacillated: David L. Boren, D-Okla., and William V. Roth Jr., R-Del. Both had opposed chemical weapons in recent years, but had voted to table Pyror's amendment. They voted for the amendment during the early minutes of the second vote, but both later switched and voted against Pryor.

Boren was the center of attention during the vote, with senators on both sides of the issue making their pitches.

Although insisting he had studied the question and had decided weeks earlier to abandon his longtime opposition to chemical weapons, Boren later admitted he had voted in confusion. When the second vote came up, he said, "I didn't even know what it was."

After Pryor explained the amendment as a temporary delay in deployment of the Bigeye, Boren voted for it. But then Nunn told him the delay could be as long as two years if the amendment passed, and so Boren switched his vote to "no."

"I was prepared to support a short-term suspension, but not a long one," he said. Boren's vote put the tally at 50-50, and Bush then voted "no" to confirm the amendment's defeat.

Nevertheless, nerve gas opponents said they would continue their battle. "There will never be a Bigeye," said John Isaacs, lobbyist for the Natural Resources Defense Council. "It just won't work."

Navy Homeporting

The Senate endorsed the Navy's controversial plan to build 12 new "homeports" to house 60 ships. The House had rejected the plan, while acting June 25 on a military construction appropriations bill (HR 5052).

By a 34-65 vote, the Senate on Aug. 6 rejected an amendment by Jeff Bingaman, D-N.M., that would have deleted from the bill $141.6 million for the first two new homeports: $56.2 million for a new port on Staten Island, N.Y., and $85.4 million for a new port in Everett, Wash. The amendment would have shifted the money to procurement of naval ammunition. *(Vote 181, p. 33-S)*

Senators on both sides insisted their positions were based on the substance of the issue, not on politics. Those statements came from senators representing states where homeports would be located, as well as from senators representing states with existing ports that stood to lose business. *(Homeports, box, p. 482)*

But in a brief, prickly speech near the end of the five-hour debate on the issue, Armed Services Chairman Barry Goldwater, R-Ariz., punctured that posturing. Noting that 26 senators could benefit from the new ports, he said: "It was a brilliant political idea" on the Navy's part. "I thought of having one in Arizona." The plan was "a terrific waste of money," he said, predicting it "is going to cost over $10 billion before you're through fooling around."

Advocates insisted the homeporting plan was an efficient way to disperse ships. Recalling the attack on Pearl Harbor, which caused extensive damage because most of the U.S. Pacific fleet was concentrated in one port, Howell Heflin, D-Ala., said: "Don't put all your eggs in one basket."

But John Glenn, D-Ohio, used that argument to attack the plan, saying that ships in seven new ports in the Gulf of Mexico could be bottled up in wartime by enemy ships patrolling the narrow sea lanes.

Although the vote dealt only with two of the bases, members treated it as a referendum on the entire five-year, $799 million homeporting plan. That was demonstrated by Glenn, who voted against the plan because of his opposition to the new Gulf of Mexico ports, even though he supported the bases at Staten Island and Everett.

Supporters of the homeporting plan were confident from the outset that they had the votes; one, Daniel Patrick Moynihan, D-N.Y., issued a press release proclaiming victory hours before the Senate voted.

Immediately after the vote, in a small sign of homeporting costs to come, the Senate adopted an amendment by Lloyd Bentsen, D-Texas, earmarking $200,000 for community planning for the gulf homeport cities.

Nuclear Test Ban

By surprisingly wide margins Aug. 7, the Senate took two votes rebuffing Reagan policy on a nuclear test ban treaty with the Soviets and rejecting a Republican effort to endorse administration policy on the issue.

First, by a 64-35 vote, the Senate adopted an amendment by Charles McC. Mathias Jr., R-Md., calling on the president to propose immediate negotiations with the Soviets on a comprehensive test ban treaty.

The amendment also asked the president to submit to the Senate two limited test ban treaties signed in the 1970s but never ratified: the 1974 Threshold Test Ban Treaty and the 1976 Peaceful Nuclear Explosion Treaty. The administration had questioned whether Soviet compliance with those treaties could be verified, so the amendment suggested that Reagan suggest changes on that score.

The amendment's language was identical to a provision the Senate adopted in 1984. *(Vote 189, p. 34-S; 1984 action, 1984 Almanac p. 51)*

Then, the Senate rejected, 42-57, an effort by Richard G. Lugar, R-Ind., chairman of the Foreign Relations Committee, to overturn the thrust of Mathias' amendment. Lugar insisted that voting for both Mathias' amendment and his would be consistent, but a large majority disagreed. *(Vote 190, p. 35-S)*

Lugar offered a substitute generally endorsing the ad-

Pentagon Gets a New Procurement 'Czar'

In approving the fiscal 1987 defense bill, Congress created a new position in the Pentagon's hierarchy: a "czar" responsible for all procurement and — proponents of the move hoped — able to cut defense costs by making Pentagon purchasers drive harder bargains.

The new official, with the title of under secretary for defense acquisition, outranked all other Pentagon officials except the secretary of defense and his deputy.

Even before conferees on the defense bill agreed on the fine points of his job, however, the Senate on Sept. 25 had confirmed Richard P. Godwin, a former official of the Bechtel Corp., for the new post. Godwin was sworn in Oct. 1.

The conferees on the defense bill (S 2638) had battled for days over two facets of the czar's authority:

- Under the House bill, the new official would "supervise" the weapons procurement process, currently in the hands of the separate armed services. The Senate bill provided that the under secretary would "direct" the services' purchases. The services strongly opposed the more intrusive role the czar would have in their affairs under the Senate language, but the conferees accepted the House position.
- The House also prevailed in exempting from the new procurement director's authority the director of operational testing, a job created by Congress in 1983 to ensure that the services subject new weapons to realistic tests under battlefield conditions. The Senate bill had placed the test director under authority of the new procurement czar. House conferees objected that this might compromise the test director's independence.

The conferees also smoothed out relatively minor differences in a provision allowing the secretary of defense to streamline the management and funding of some major weapons programs, designated as "enterprise programs."

The officers managing these programs would be exempted from supervision by all but a few layers of bureaucracy and from all procedural regulations except the basic federal purchasing rules.

The secretary of defense could request congressional authorization of funds for a program to cover periods of up to five years for either full-scale prototype development and testing or full-scale production. He would agree to a so-called "baseline" — a cost limit, performance specifications and timetable for the program.

Once granted a multi-year authorization, a program would not be dealt with in the annual defense authorization bill unless it fell short of the stipulated cost, performance or schedule limits. In that case, Congress would have to reauthorize the program after the defense secretary informed Congress of a revised baseline.

Regardless, enterprise programs would continue to require annual appropriations from Congress.

The conferees also agreed to require the Pentagon to have at least two competing contractors build prototypes of any major proposed weapon and to require realistic combat testing of any new major weapon. Either requirement could be waived by the secretary of defense if he deemed it impractical and explained the decision to Congress.

'Revolving Door'

The conferees expanded the scope of a provision enacted as part of the fiscal 1986 defense authorization bill barring certain Pentagon officials from going to work for certain defense contractors for two years after they left the government. The provision covered presidential appointees who acted as the government's principal negotiator in any dealings with a contractor. *(Background, 1985 Almanac p. 164)*

The conferees on the fiscal 1987 bill banned any Pentagon official for two years after leaving the government from going to work for a contractor if he had:

- Served as a government representative at that contractor's plant, or
- Participated "personally and substantially" and in a decision-making capacity in negotiations with that contractor during more than half the time in the official's last two years in the government.

A senior official who supervised a large number of contracts with different companies would not be barred from working for any contractor immediately after leaving the government except that if he had personally negotiated a dispute with a firm, he would be barred for two years only from going to work for that firm.

On another hotly contested procurement policy issue, the conferees dropped a Senate provision that would have repealed a provision adopted in 1985 requiring contractors to make available to the Pentagon certain data about their material and labor costs. Many major defense firms had made repeal of this so-called "should-cost" provision a top lobbying priority in 1986, complaining that it required a sweeping revision of their existing records.

The conferees amended the fiscal 1986 provision to stipulate that no firm would be required to keep new data not currently collected or to organize the data in any new way because of the "should-cost" provision.

The conferees dropped a House-passed provision requiring that any contract be awarded to a U.S. firm if the company's bid exceeded by no more than 5 percent the lowest bid of a non-U.S. firm.

---

ministration's arms control policy, which emphasized joint Soviet-U.S. nuclear reductions.

It praised recent efforts by both countries to resolve verification issues on the two limited test ban treaties, and it called on Reagan to report to Congress by February 1987, on whether a comprehensive test ban treaty would be in U.S. interests.

Anti-Satellite Weapons

Holding its position of previous years, the Senate tabled an amendment by John Kerry, D-Mass., putting into permanent law a ban on U.S. testing of an ASAT missile — so long as the Soviet Union continued its moratorium on such tests. The vote was 55-43. *(Vote 192, p. 35-S)*

Congress in 1985 had imposed a U.S. moratorium, as

part of its fiscal 1986 omnibus continuing appropriations resolution (PL 99-190). But that ban would expire on Sept. 30, the end of the fiscal year, and the Air Force was anxious to resume testing.

Midgetman Missile

In debate on the bill, the Senate's first contested vote on the Midgetman program came on a complicated amendment by Midgetman critic Pete Wilson, R-Calif., that was killed on a 64-30 tabling vote. *(Vote 198, p. 36-S)*

Wilson's amendment would have barred use of funds to begin work on a prototype Midgetman unless the Pentagon certified that the weapon could be cost-effective and able to survive a Soviet attack. Deployment of more than 50 of the much larger, multi-warhead MX missiles also would face the same prohibition.

Arms control advocates, including Albert Gore Jr., D-Tenn., and Cohen, had argued that the small missile, carrying only a single warhead, would promote stability in the U.S.-Soviet nuclear balance. They claimed that if the two countries deployed roughly equal numbers of missiles, neither could gain a military advantage by attacking first, since it would have to use up as many missiles as it destroyed.

Wilson rejected that argument and emphasized that single-warhead missiles were more expensive per warhead than multi-warhead weapons like MX.

B-1 and Stealth

As it had done for years, the Senate took steps to ensure that no more than 100 B-1 bombers would be built and that development of the stealth bomber would not be delayed.

By voice vote, the Senate agreed to an amendment by Robert C. Byrd, D-W.Va., specifying that none of the funds for the stealth bomber be used for any other purpose and that no funds be used for any purpose related to deployment of more than 100 B-1s.

By a vote of 50-43, the Senate tabled an amendment by Glenn to Byrd's amendment that would have barred the assembly of a 101st B-1 but held open the possibility of building more B-1 components. *(Vote 206, p. 37-S)*

Glenn argued that the B-1 production line should be kept "warm" as a hedge against technical problems or price hikes in the stealth program.

Managing People and Land

The Senate adopted on Aug. 8 two amendments by Ted Stevens, R-Alaska; each deleted from the bill a provision that would have changed administrative procedures for the Pentagon. Stevens insisted the changes should be handled on a governmentwide basis. The amendments:

- Deleted a provision establishing a personnel system outside the regular Civil Service system for Pentagon engineers, scientists and specialists in the management of weapons procurement programs. The provision, sponsored by the Senate Armed Services Committee, was modeled on an experimental program conducted at two Navy installations in California. It would allow local managers much more discretion over employees' pay raises and promotions than the Civil Service system.

The amendment was agreed to by voice vote after the Senate rejected 44-52 a motion to table it. *(Vote 195, p. 35-S)*

- Deleted a provision that would have allowed the Pentagon to sell land it deemed surplus and use the proceeds to build new facilities. Under existing law, all federal agencies turned over their excess property to the General Services Administration, which sold it if no other agency needed it.

Committee members argued that their revision would have given the Pentagon an incentive currently lacking to dispose of surplus property. But Stevens and other critics countered that, while the Pentagon's costs might decline, the cost to the government as a whole would increase, since other agencies that currently got surplus military land would have to pay more for comparable facilities. The amendment was agreed to by voice vote.

Procurement Reform

The Armed Services Committee narrowly won the only fight over weapons procurement policy that was fought out on the Senate floor.

At issue was a provision of the bill that created an under secretary of defense in charge of all facets of procurement, including the office of operational weapons testing.

The provision reflected the committee's basic judgment that the way to clean up weapons procurement was to give this one senior official the authority and responsibility for managing the process.

But Roth, Pryor, and Nancy Landon Kassebaum, R-Kan., who had led the 1983 fight to establish the independent testing office over fierce Pentagon opposition, offered an amendment that would have left the operational testing office independent of the acquisition chief and reporting directly to the secretary.

They argued that the 1983 change had been driven by a determination to insulate operational testing from the agencies that developed the weapons in the first place and, they charged, inevitably became blind to the weapons' flaws.

The committee approach would "once again make testing subordinate to procurement," Pryor predicted. Moreover, he warned, the proposed shift would be interpreted as a signal of flagging congressional interest in independent testing.

But Nunn insisted to the contrary that the real independence of the tester would depend on that official's fortitude and the vigor of congressional oversight.

The amendment by Roth, Pryor and Kassebaum was tabled 51-48. The 16 Democrats who voted to table were almost all conservatives or members of the Armed Services Committee. *(Vote 191, p. 35-S)*

Labor Issues

The Senate treated separately two parts of an amendment by Edward M. Kennedy, D-Mass., to delete provisions of the bill that would boost the number of Pentagon contracts exempted from certain labor laws.

The laws were designed to require certain types of federal contractors to pay locally prevailing wages. However, for decades critics of organized labor had contended that the laws inflated wages, partly because of anomalies in the procedure for computing "locally prevailing wages."

The two parts of Kennedy's amendment, voted on Aug. 8, aimed to:

- Delete the provision increasing from $2,500 to $1 million the threshold below which Pentagon contracts with commercial firms for housekeeping services, such as janitorial work and kitchen service, would be exempt from the Service Contracts Act.

Kennedy's proposal to reject this change and retain

the existing threshold was agreed to 62-34. *(Vote 193, p. 35-S)*

- Delete the committee provision increasing from $2,000 to $250,000 the threshold below which construction contracts were exempt from the Davis-Bacon Act that applied the "locally prevailing wages" standard to federal construction projects. This change in the committee bill was rejected 44-51. *(Vote 194, p. 35-S)*

Salvaging Programs

By voice vote, the Senate approved Aug. 9 two amendments aimed at partially salvaging programs the committee had judged wanting. The amendments were offered:

- By Wilson, authorizing $64.2 million to begin production of the Navy's RAM short-range, anti-aircraft missile, but only if the funds could be squeezed out of other programs authorized by the bill.

The committee had denied all funds for the program, complaining that the RAM was costing too much and taking too long to develop and that it could not successfully attack some new types of Soviet anti-ship missiles. But the missile was being developed jointly with West Germany, which lobbied strongly to continue the program.

- By Bob Kasten, R-Wis., to provide that a small mine sweeper could be purchased from a foreign shipyard, as the committee's bill directed, only after the secretary of the Navy certified to Congress that no U.S. shipyard could demonstrate an ability to build such a ship in a timely fashion.

The committee denied the $196 million requested for four small mine sweepers (called MSHs). Funds had been appropriated in earlier budgets to buy five of the ships, built to a novel design. But a test indicated that the chosen design was not resilient enough to survive nearby explosions.

In addition to denying the funds sought for more MSHs, the committee ordered the Navy to use $100 million of the money previously appropriated for the program to buy a European-built mine sweeper that could be adapted for U.S. manufacture.

Kasten, whose state contained two shipyards that built ships of mine-sweeper size for the Navy, conceded that no U.S. shipbuilder could build the vessel the Navy wanted right away, but he objected to U.S. firms being shut out of the bidding. His amendment would allow U.S. firms to buy the rights to build an existing, foreign-designed ship and offer to build it for the Navy.

Tobacco and Alcohol

On Aug. 9, the Senate adopted what some members referred to as the "fuel for freedom" amendment by Mark Andrews, R-N.D. The effect of this would be to retain a provision of the fiscal 1986 defense appropriations bill that required that alcoholic beverages purchased for sale on any military base be bought from a wholesaler within the state where the base was located.

The Pentagon had established a centralized purchasing system for the alcoholic beverages sold in on-base clubs, but that was superseded by the 1986 act, which Senate Armed Services would have repealed. Andrews' amendment, which deleted the committee provision from the bill, was adopted by voice vote after a motion to table was rejected 41-56. *(Vote 202, p. 36-S)*

On the other hand, on Aug. 6 the Senate rejected an amendment by Boren and Jeff Bingaman, D-N.M., that would have increased the price of tobacco products in commissaries and post exchanges on bases by requiring that they be sold for the locally prevailing price including state and local taxes.

Currently, such taxes were excluded from calculation of commissary and exchange prices. Since facilities on military bases did not pay state and local taxes, some of the increased revenues could be funneled into health and fitness promotion campaigns.

The amendment was tabled 57-43. *(Vote 179, p. 33-S)*

Other Amendments

Other amendments considered by the Senate included those by:

- John C. Danforth, R-Mo., restoring a $556.3 million Pentagon payment to NASA for military uses of past space shuttle flights. A motion to table the amendment failed 37-61, then Danforth's amendment passed 58-40. *(Votes 187, 188, p. 34-S)*

The Armed Services panel had deleted the money on budgetary grounds. The payment was an "absolute impossibility," Goldwater said, insisting that making it would cut into funds for equipment and troop levels.

But Danforth said the Pentagon's failure to pay the money would cripple the shuttle program, delaying the already-delayed flight schedule by a half-year or more.

- Dennis DeConcini, D-Ariz., barring the sale or transfer of Stinger anti-aircraft missiles to foreign guerrillas — such as the Nicaraguan contras or the UNITA rebels in Angola — unless they adhered to the same strict security standards for guarding the missiles as foreign governments. DeConcini said his amendment was needed to prevent the portable missile from falling into terrorist hands. But opponents said DeConcini was addressing CIA "covert" actions, and the amendment belonged on bills dealing with that agency. Rejected 37-63. *(Vote 185, p. 34-S)*
- Byrd, to require the Joint Chiefs of Staff to report to Congress by Nov. 1, 1986, on the military impact of Reagan's decision to no longer comply with provisions of SALT II. Byrd said the Joint Chiefs had refused to take a position on the issue. Adopted 97-1, with Lugar voting "no." *(Vote 178, p. 33-S)*
- Cohen, creating a joint military command for special forces and a position of assistant secretary of defense for special operations. The amendment was in response to the reported lack of coordination in military engagements involving special forces, such as the failed Iranian hostage rescue mission in 1980 and the invasion of Grenada in 1983. Adopted by voice vote.
- Roth, providing that the office of independent operational testing would continue to report to the secretary of defense, instead of the new weapons procurement czar. Tabled, 51-48. *(Vote 191, p. 35-S)*
- Frank R. Lautenberg, D-N.J., allowing uniformed military personnel to wear items of religious apparel that were "neat and conservative." Tabled 51-49. *(Vote 186, p. 34-S)*

The Supreme Court ruled in March that the military had the authority to prohibit an Orthodox Jew from wearing a yarmulke, or skullcap. *(Court ruling, p. 11-A)*

Carl Levin, D-Mich., a supporter of the amendment, said: "This is one of the rights we're fighting to protect: the right of religious pluralism."

But Goldwater gruffly countered: "If you're not happy in the uniform, get out of the uniform."

Among other amendments to S 2638 adopted by voice vote by the Senate were the following:

- By Cohen, adding to the bill $212 million to pay for

military activities intended to cooperate with the Customs Service and other police agencies to intercept drug smugglers and to buy some aircraft and equipment for the Customs Service. Well over half the amount ($138 million) was to give the Customs Service four Hawkeye radar observation planes, a type used by the Navy. The amendment was adopted by voice vote.

- By Pennsylvania Republicans Arlen Specter and John Heinz, requiring the Pentagon to buy at least 300,000 tons of anthracite coal in fiscal 1987 for steam generating plants at military bases in the United States. For years, Congress had required the Pentagon to use U.S.-mined coal at bases in Europe, creating mining jobs in Pennsylvania's anthracite belt, but creating pollution that had aroused political objections in West Germany.

To deal with this problem and with the political clout of the coal states, the Pentagon had produced a plan to convert bases in the U.S. to coal power, with a target of buying 1.6 million tons of coal annually (including 300,000 tons of anthracite) by fiscal 1994.

The Armed Services Committee included in the bill a provision repealing existing law that barred the Pentagon from converting any coal-fired facility to another power source. Conversion of some bases in West Germany to local power sources would save $20 million to $40 million in annual costs, the panel said, in addition to heading off the need to spend $385 million to install pollution-control devices needed to bring coal-fired plants into compliance with German law. Specter's amendment, adopted by voice vote, put into law the Pentagon's goals for domestic coal consumption.

- By Roth, requiring that diplomats from Cuba and Soviet-bloc Eastern Europe be subject to the same travel restrictions as Soviet diplomats. The amendment was adopted by voice vote.

House Floor Action

Despite administration threats of a presidential veto, the House approved HR 4428 Aug. 15 by 255-152. Of 168 Republicans who voted, all but 23 voted "nay." As passed, the bill authorized $212 billion. *(Vote 328, p. 92-H)*

In a series of votes beginning Aug. 8, the House adopted amendments that would thwart key elements of Reagan's defense program by:

- Halting tests of all but the smallest nuclear weapons.
- Continuing the current moratorium on full-scale tests of the ASAT missile.
- Blocking production of new types of lethal chemical weapons.
- Forcing continued U.S. observance of certain limits set by SALT II.
- Slicing by more than 40 percent, from $5.3 billion to $3.125 billion, the fiscal 1987 authorization for SDI.

The bill also would slice Reagan's overall fiscal 1987 defense spending request by 11 percent ($35 billion) to $285 billion.

On Aug. 14, the day before the final vote, the administration and its allies mounted a counterattack. Several House Republicans denounced the bill and vowed to work for its defeat.

White House spokesman Larry Speakes charged that the House bill would undercut the U.S. position in arms reduction talks with the Russians. In its existing form, he said, "I am confident that the president's advisers would unanimously recommend the president veto the bill."

Before voting on final passage, House members rejected 163-247 a motion to strip the bill of several of the administration-opposed amendments. The motion was made by William L. Dickinson, Ala., the House Armed Services Committee's senior Republican. *(Vote 327, p. 92-H)*

Proponents of the five controversial amendments claimed that the House action reflected widespread public frustration with Reagan's approach to arms control, which had run five years without producing an agreement with Moscow.

But good organization and hard politicking also played a major role in the Reagan critics' domination of the debate on HR 4428. Several liberal and moderate groups collaborated to round up nearly 200 Democrats and nearly 30 Republicans for all but one of the five amendments.

Nuclear Test Ban

In the most sweeping congressional assault on Reagan's arms control policies since 1983, the House Aug. 8 adopted a moratorium on all but the smallest nuclear tests. The vote was 234-155. *(Vote 287, p. 82-H)*

The proposal, cosponsored by Armed Services Committee Chairman Les Aspin, D-Wis., and Democratic Caucus Chairman Richard A. Gephardt of Missouri, was pushed by a coalition of liberals and moderates.

The administration, which flatly opposed the amendment, had not been so strongly challenged on arms control since the nuclear weapons freeze campaign, which peaked on Capitol Hill in 1982-83. *(1983 Almanac p. 205)*

The partial nuclear test moratorium approved by the House would allow only U.S. nuclear blasts with an explosive power no greater than 1 kiloton (1,000 tons of TNT) and only at the Energy Department's Nevada test site, provided:

- The Soviet Union conducted no nuclear tests larger than 1 kiloton at its Semiplatinsk testing site in Siberia and no tests at any other site.
- Each of the two governments agreed to let the other place monitoring equipment on its soil to verify compliance with the 1-kiloton limit.

The ban would take effect Jan. 1, 1987, and would continue for the remaining nine months of fiscal 1987, until Sept. 30, 1987.

However, if the two countries negotiated some other limitation on nuclear testing in the meantime, the new agreement would supplant the legislatively imposed moratorium.

In the past three years, predominantly liberal backers of an overall nuclear weapons freeze had focused increasingly on a nuclear test moratorium as a first step toward their ultimate goal. But it was not until the weeks immediately before the House took up HR 4428 that a partial test moratorium emerged as the common legislative goal of freeze backers and a group of politically influential moderates, including Aspin, Gephardt, Majority Leader Jim Wright, D-Texas, and Majority Whip Thomas S. Foley, D-Wash.

SDI Funding

On Aug. 12, the House voted 239-176 for an amendment by Charles E. Bennett, D-Fla., authorizing $2.85 billion in Defense Department funds for SDI, bringing the overall total for SDI to $3.125 billion. The Armed Services panel had recommended authorization of $3.7 billion. *(Vote 300, p. 84-H)*

Earlier the same day, the House rejected three other SDI funding amendments:

- By Bob Dornan, R-Calif., to bring total SDI funding to $5.1 billion, nearly the amount requested. Rejected 94-324. *(Vote 297, p. 84-H)*
- By Ronald V. Dellums, D-Calif., to bring total SDI funding to $1.3 billion. Rejected 114-302. *(Vote 298, p. 84-H)*
- By Robert E. Badham, R-Calif., to bring total SDI funding to $3.56 billion. This amendment was drafted by SDI supporters to head off Bennett's by making a smaller reduction from the committee recommendation. Rejected 196-218. *(Vote 299, p. 84-H)*

Many of the Bennett amendment's leading proponents hoped the cut would be deep enough to delay until after Reagan left office SDI-related tests that they claimed would violate the 1972 U.S.-Soviet treaty limiting anti-missile defenses. However, during debate on the SDI amendments, many members cited budgetary limits as the reason they would vote for the lowest authorization proposed.

SALT II Compliance

Also on Aug. 12, the House adopted an amendment by Norman D. Dicks, D-Wash., barring the deployment of any long-range nuclear weapons that would exceed three limits set by SALT II: no more than 820 multiple-warhead (or MIRVed) ICBMs; no more than 1,200 MIRVed missiles of any kind, either land-based ICBMs or sea-launched missiles; and no more than 1,320 MIRVed missiles and cruise-missile-armed long-range bombers.

The vote on the Dicks amendment was 225-186. *(Vote 302, p. 86-H)*

A substitute by William S. Broomfield, R-Mich., that would have waived the limitation if the Soviets violated any SALT II provision, was rejected 199-214. *(Vote 301, p. 84-H)*

It was widely believed that the Russians had violated other SALT II provisions and that, accordingly, the Broomfield amendment would have nullified Dicks' intent. Perhaps because criticism of SALT II had been a keystone of GOP policy, Dicks' drew the least Republican support of any of the five amendments; only 19 voted "aye."

ASAT Test Ban

On Aug. 13, the House approved 222-197 the ASAT test moratorium amendment offered by George E. Brown Jr., D-Calif. *(Vote 309, p. 86-H)*

Brown's amendment would continue the test moratorium — contingent on Soviet abstention from ASAT tests — which Congress imposed over administration objections as part of the fiscal 1986 continuing appropriations resolution (PL 99-190).

Chemical Weapons Ban

An amendment by John Edward Porter, R-Ill., Dante B. Fascell, D-Fla., and Marge Roukema, R-N.J., barring through Sept. 30, 1987, production of lethal chemical weapons called binary munitions, was adopted, 210-209. *(Vote 311, p. 88-H)*

The final vote on this amendment fluctuated for several minutes while protagonists rounded up missing allies, and there were several vote switches in both directions.

However, in the words of John Isaacs of the Council for a Liveable World, a leader of the fight against binary munitions, presiding officer Marty Russo, D-Ill., "was there with the gavel at the right time," to close the vote while amendment supporters were on top.

Of the five amendments, this had the fewest Democratic backers — 172 — evidently because of strong opposition by Aspin, John M. Spratt Jr., D-S.C., and other moderates. But it also garnered the most Republican supporters of the five: 38 votes.

Republicans like Porter, Roukema and former Rep. Ed Bethune, R-Ark. (1979-85), traditionally had taken the lead in the five-year-long fight against binary weapons.

Procurement Reform

The House on Aug. 5 adopted a far-ranging package of provisions changing the Pentagon's weapons procurement procedures after handily rejecting alternatives that would have softened some of the new rules.

For months, an Armed Services Committee task force chaired by Nicholas Mavroules, D-Mass., had studied proposed changes in the purchasing and budgeting system, in hopes of developing a consensus.

As a result, the Armed Services panel included in HR 4428 one set of proposals, several of which had been recommended by a White House advisory commission chaired by former Deputy Defense Secretary David Packard. These included provisions:

- Creating the position of under secretary of defense in charge of all acquisition, to supervise all facets of the weapons procurement system.
- Streamlining the Pentagon's management of weapons development programs. The bill would reduce the number of administrative supervisors within each service to whom a program manager would have to answer.
- Creating incentives for the Pentagon to buy more equipment "off the shelf," instead of insisting on development of new items from scratch to meet unnecessary specifications.

Other proposed procurement changes were more controversial, so the committee agreed to battle them out on the House floor. Mavroules assembled one package incorporating 10 separate changes. Jim Courter, R-N.J., put together a rival amendment that was identical to Mavroules' in several respects but was less restrictive on a few points.

The House rejected Courter's alternative 164-245 and then adopted the Mavroules package 347-60. *(Votes 260, 261, p. 74-H)*

Among the components of Mavroules' amendment were provisions:

- Barring any Pentagon procurement official who had had personal and substantial responsibility for a defense contract, for two years after he left the government, from going to work for a firm awarded that contract.
- Retaining a provision enacted as part of the fiscal 1986 defense authorization bill requiring defense contractors to provide the Pentagon with certain data on production costs. House Armed Services had added to HR 4428 a provision repealing that so-called "work measurement" or "should cost" law.
- Limiting to 10 percent of the amount spent by a service in each quarter the amount that could be allocated to open-ended contracts for which no total price has been negotiated.
- Creating a corps of acquisition specialists in the Pentagon.
- Requiring the Pentagon to identify the portion of the budget request for each major part of the defense budget

that was earmarked to cover the cost of inflation. Funds appropriated to cover inflation would go into a Treasury fund and would be allocated for Pentagon expenditures only after measurable inflation occurred.

- Requiring the Pentagon to test competing prototypes of any new weapon, unless the secretary of defense certified that it was impractical and justified that judgment with a comparison of the estimated total cost of building the weapon with and without competitively tested prototypes.
- Making corporation officials criminally liable if their firm sought Pentagon reimbursement for any costs that were not allowable. Under existing law, company officials had to certify that cost claims were accurate to the best of their knowledge and belief.

Courter offered an amendment that would have retained that existing standard, but it was rejected 157-251. *(Vote 258, p. 74-H)*

The House also adopted 241-163 an amendment to the Mavroules package by James A. Traficant Jr., D-Ohio, requiring the Pentagon to purchase U.S.-built goods rather than competing foreign-built goods if the price of the U.S. items was not more than 5 percent higher than the foreign items. *(Vote 259, p. 74-H)*

Pentagon Reorganization

By a vote of 406-4, the House on Aug. 5 added to the bill a package of provisions designed to shift power within the Pentagon from the separate services to the commanders in chief (or CINCs) who would be responsible for all combat operations in time of war. *(Vote 257, p. 74-H)*

Separate Pentagon reorganization legislation was enacted later in the year. *(Story, p. 455)*

Davis-Bacon Modification

By a vote of 406-5, the House adopted an amendment by Augustus F. Hawkins, D-Calif., raising from $2,000 to $25,000 the value below which military construction contracts would be exempt from the Davis-Bacon Act. *(Vote 325, p. 92-H)*

Earlier, the House rejected 167-244 a Dickinson amendment that would have raised the exemption threshold to $250,000. *(Vote 324, p. 92-H)*

Spending Ceilings

On Aug. 8, the House adopted an amendment placing a cap on the bill's total spending.

On a vote of 245-156, the House approved an amendment by Spratt to reduce from $292 billion to $285 billion the overall defense budget authority associated with the bill. *(Vote 285, p. 80-H)*

His amendment dropped from the bill several weapons the committee added late in July after it had finished an earlier version of the bill.

The amendment was intended to reduce fiscal 1987 defense outlays to $279.2 billion, the limit set by the budget resolution Congress adopted June 27. As reported by the Armed Services Committee, the bill was expected to result in defense outlays of $285 billion.

The House then defeated, 181-224, an amendment by Dickinson that would have reduced fiscal 1987 defense outlays to $279 billion by ordering the Pentagon to reduce the rate at which it paid contractors for work in progress.

But the amendment would not have reduced the $292 billion in defense budget authority, the amount of money that could be appropriated in a fiscal year. *(Vote 286, p. 82-H)*

Major Cutbacks

As it had done routinely in recent years, the House rejected two attempts to make substantial reductions in the size of the U.S. military. These were amendments:

- By Dellums, to reduce to $255.4 billion the overall defense budget resulting from the bill. This was $65 billion less than Reagan's request and $30 billion less than the amount resulting from the bill as passed.

The amendment would have canceled several strategic weapons programs, including the MX and Trident II missiles and SDI, which Dellums said were aimed at achieving the ability to launch a surprise attack on the Soviet Union. It also would have sliced out funds for several other weapons that he said either did not work right or were intended for military intervention in developing nations.

The amendment was rejected 56-365. *(Vote 310, p. 88-H)*

- By Patricia Schroeder, D-Colo., who had cosponsored Dellums' amendment, to require that half the U.S. ground troops currently stationed in Europe and one-third of the U.S. ground troops stationed elsewhere abroad be returned to the United States over a five-year period. Half those brought home would be demobilized.

Schroeder insisted that the reduction would not necessarily reduce the military strength of U.S. alliances if Japan and the principal European allies picked up the slack by expanding their own defense efforts. In contrast to the period after World War II when the current U.S. overseas deployments were made, Schroeder argued, the allies now could easily afford to contribute more to the cost of their own defense.

But Stephen J. Solarz, D-N.Y., and others warned that a troop cut would be seen by the Soviets as well as U.S. allies as a weakening of American commitment, thus increasing the risk of war. Moreover, they warned, if war came, U.S. forces would be forced more quickly to use nuclear weapons for self-defense, in light of the increased Soviet advantage in conventional forces. Rejected 90-322. *(Vote 315, p. 88-H)*

Weapons Under Fire

The House rejected amendments aimed at three weapons that, for various reasons, had become politically controversial:

- By Bennett, to drop from the bill the $1.1 billion authorized for 12 MX missiles. Under a provision of the fiscal 1986 defense authorization bill, these and all future MXs purchased could be used only as test missiles, unless Congress approved the deployment of more than the 50 funded in prior years. *(1985 Almanac p. 138)*

Bennett offered two amendments to delete MX production funds. One that would have added $250 million to various conventional weapons programs was rejected 178-210. The other, which would have added $550 million to conventional programs, was rejected 179-217. *(Votes 288, 289, p. 82-H)*

Several observers speculated that members were tired of the MX fight, which had wracked the House from 1982 to 1985. Then, MX opponents and some supporters agreed to a compromise that would allow the deployment of only 50 of the missiles in existing launch silos. Reagan had planned to deploy 100.

Mavroules, who had led the battle against MX, and played a key role in the 50-missile compromise, voted for both Bennett amendments. He complained that the Pentagon was responsible for the issue having been raised at all in 1986. No amendment would have been offered had the Pentagon not provoked members by calling for deployment of "a second 50" MXs, Mavroules declared.

- By Ted Weiss, D-N.Y., blocking production of the D-5 or Trident II submarine-launched missile. The $1.43 billion included in the bill for Trident II procurement would be used instead to buy additional Trident I missiles, under the amendment.

Many liberal arms control advocates long had warned that the D-5 would be an especially dangerous weapon since it was designed to be sufficiently accurate to destroy Soviet missiles in their underground silos, as was the MX. But MX became vulnerable to political attack, not because of its alleged impact on the U.S.-Soviet nuclear balance but because of a belief that it would be vulnerable to Soviet attack if deployed, as Reagan wished, in existing U.S. missile silos.

But missile-launching submarines were generally deemed invulnerable to surprise attack. Moreover, many MX critics covered their political flanks by committing themselves fervently to supporting the Trident II. So Weiss and his allies had fought a long and losing battle to block the missile; 1986 was no exception as the House rejected his amendment 94-306. *(Vote 296, p. 84-H)*

- By Mel Levine, D-Calif., and Beverly B. Byron, D-Md., to limit the number of Bradley armored troop carriers that could be built until the Army conducted certain tests of the Bradley's ability to survive enemy fire. The bill authorized 593 of the vehicles in fiscal 1987. Critics had charged that the Army cooked its testing of the Bradley to conceal the vehicle's vulnerability. The Army denied this.

Levine's amendment would have barred any Bradley purchases in fiscal 1987 until stipulated tests were conducted. Byron's amendment, allowing production of about half the authorized Bradleys before the testing was completed, was expected by many observers to pass since it represented a compromise between Levine and several members of the Armed Services Committee. But first Byron's amendment was rejected 179-223 and then Levine's 123-277. *(Votes 292, 293, p. 82-H)*

Adding Weapons

The House rejected an effort by Sam Gejdenson, D-Conn., to add to the bill $1.5 billion for a Trident missile sub, which likely would be built in his district at Groton. The administration had requested the huge ship — which would be the 14th of its class — but the committee had dropped it from the bill, partly for budgetary reasons.

Submarine-launched missiles typically were the least politically controversial of U.S. nuclear arms. Gejdenson modified his amendment to accept Spratt's stipulation that the ship would be authorized only if at least $1.5 billion was cut from other programs in the bill, thus guaranteeing that the ship would not increase the amount authorized by the bill. Nevertheless, Gejdenson's effort was rejected 188-211. *(Vote 294, p. 84-H)*

On the other hand, the House upheld the decision of the Armed Services Committee to add to the bill $151 million to continue production of the T-46 trainer plane that the Air Force canceled earlier in the year, largely for budgetary reasons.

The plane, which was built on Long Island by Fairchild Industries, was strongly championed by the New York congressional delegation, while the Air Force decision to cancel it was backed just as ardently by members of Congress from Kansas, home of Cessna Aircraft, builder of the T-37 trainer that the new plane was designed to replace. If the T-46 was canceled, Cessna likely would receive a contract to refurbish the T-37s.

The House Armed Services Subcommittee on Procurement, chaired by Democrat Samuel S. Stratton, dean of the New York House delegation, recommended — and the full committee agreed — that $151 million should be cut from the amount requested for F-15 and F-16 fighters and used to fund continued T-46 production.

Two amendments were rejected that would have blocked T-46 production and earmarked the $151 million for additional F-15s and F-16s. An effort by Dickinson was rejected 125-277; one by Spratt was defeated 190-213. *(Votes 290, 291, p. 82-H)*

Other Amendments

On Aug. 14, the House also considered the following amendments:

- By Tommy F. Robinson, D-Ark., requiring that alcoholic beverages sold on military bases be purchased from wholesalers located in the same state, thus ensuring that service members' clubs would pay state and local liquor taxes. That restriction, already enacted into existing law as part of the fiscal 1986 continuing appropriations resolution, would be repealed by HR 4428. Robinson's amendment was rejected 149-265. *(Vote 316, p. 90-H)*
- By G. V. "Sonny" Montgomery, D-Miss., barring any governor from blocking the participation of his state's National Guard units in a Pentagon-sponsored training exercise because of the location or purpose of the exercise. Several governors had refused to allow their National Guard units to go on training exercises in Central America. Adopted 261-159. *(Vote 318, p. 90-H)*
- By Duncan L. Hunter, R-Calif., requiring that each of the Navy's aircraft carriers, which were getting top-to-bottom overhauls called SLEPs, be serviced in a shipyard on whichever U.S. coast the ship currently was stationed. Currently, all such overhauls were being performed in the Philadelphia Navy Yard and the amendment was designed to shift some of the work to the West Coast. Rejected 69-350. *(Vote 319, p. 90-H)*
- By Thomas S. Foley, D-Wash., barring the deployment of U.S. ground combat troops in Nicaragua. This was agreed to by voice vote as was an amendment by Hunter waiving the Foley prohibition in case of a Nicaraguan attack on U.S. allies or if MiG combat jets or nuclear weapons were deployed in Nicaragua.
- By Gerald B. H. Solomon, R-N.Y., providing that no person who was required by law to register with the Selective Service and had not done so could hold a job under any contract with the Pentagon. Similar provisions of law sponsored by Solomon since 1982 barred non-registrants from federal employment, federally funded job training and federally assisted higher education. Approved 284-120. *(Vote 322, p. 90-H)*

Conference

The conferees' compromise bill, cleared for President Reagan Oct. 15, reduced overall defense budget authority for the year to $292 billion, compared with Reagan's request for $320 billion.

Most of the $29.4 billion reduction in defense budget authority associated with the bill came from routine kinds of congressional cuts — albeit on nearly twice the usual scale. These included such moves as slowing some produc-

$8.4 Billion for Military Construction

Conferees on the defense authorization bill (S 2638 — H Rept 99-1001) approved $8.4 billion for military construction projects in fiscal 1987, compared with the Pentagon's request for $9.99 billion.

They basically split the difference between the House-passed authorization of $8.35 billion and the Senate-passed amount of $8.51 billion. *(Appropriations, p. 218; fiscal 1986 authorization, 1985 Almanac p. 182)*

'Homeporting'

The conferees approved a controversial plan to station Navy flotillas at several newly constructed "homeports." The fiscal 1987 budget requested funds for two of the planned sites: New York City and Everett, Wash.

The Navy said the new sites were closer to critical sea lanes, but critics said the project was too expensive and was intended partly to give the Navy more pork-barrel support on Capitol Hill.

The administration said the new basing facilities — also proposed in Texas, Louisiana, Mississippi, Alabama and Florida — were needed to accommodate ships Congress already had funded to meet the administration's goal of a "600-ship Navy." Since new piers and repair shops would have to be built in any case, officials argued, building new ports would cost $799 million — only about $200 million more than expanding the existing homeports.

In approving funds for New York and Everett, conferees told the Navy that they expected it to follow through in fiscal 1988-89 by requesting funds for several facilities in Gulf Coast states that were heavily represented in the conference on S 2638.

For construction at Everett, the conferees approved $43.6 million, almost exactly half the $85 million authorized by the Senate. The request was for $95 million and the House approved no funds.

But the conferees stipulated that the funds could not be spent until all necessary federal, state and local permits were obtained for the planned dredging and the state of Washington appropriated its agreed on share of certain roads and other facilities needed by the new base.

They agreed to provide $54 million, the House-passed amount, for construction at the New York site, on Staten Island. The Pentagon requested $92 million for New York and the Senate approved $58 million.

Other Issues

For improvements at Clark Air Base, Subic Bay Naval Base and other facilities in the Philippines, the conferees approved $45 million of the $73 million requested. The Senate had approved most of the request, but the House authorized no funds because the question of continued U.S. access to the bases would be up for renegotiation with the Philippine government in 1988.

The House had denied all of the $127 million requested for construction to house a new Army division in Alaska, but the Senate approved $97 million. Conferees settled on $72 million for the project.

tion lines and taking advantage of lower-than-budgeted prices for fuel and other commodities.

But leaders described as "gimmicks" some of the steps they took to rein in defense spending. The special gimmicks were aimed mostly at reducing outlays rather than budget authority. The $279 billion cap on outlays contained in the congressional budget resolution was a far more difficult requirement to meet than the resolution's budget authority cap of $292 billion.

For example, the conferees retroactively reduced by $3.8 billion the amounts appropriated for various programs in fiscal years 1985-86, thus reducing outlays in fiscal 1987.

However, in their report on the compromise bill (H Rept 99-1001), filed Oct. 14, the conferees conceded that one of the actions they took to meet the outlay ceiling was a serious departure from a fundamental congressional priority. The conferees reduced by $7.3 billion (about 8.5 percent) Reagan's $85.9 billion request for military operations and maintenance funds.

Protection of the budgets for operations and maintenance had been a byword among congressional defense specialists since the late 1970s, when the Senate and House Armed Services committees warned that low funding for those accounts was reducing the combat readiness of forces in the field.

The conferees on S 2638 acknowledged the risk of cutting back on readiness-related funds.

As justification for reducing the operations and maintenance authorization to a lower level than either house had passed, the conferees said they had anticipated cuts that were in prospect in the companion defense appropriations.

Almost all operating funds were spent in the year they were appropriated, while money to buy weapons dribbled out over several years, with less than 20 percent becoming outlays in the year in which they were appropriated. Therefore, to realize a given reduction in outlays required a much deeper cut in budget authority earmarked to buy weapons than in budget authority allocated to operations.

The conferees on S 2638 strongly recommended one outlay-oriented ploy to the conferees on the companion defense appropriations measure, but did not enact it in the authorization bill: a 24-hour delay in Pentagon paydays. This would defer one payday from Sept. 30, 1987 — the last day of fiscal 1987 — to Oct. 1, 1987 — the first day of fiscal 1988. The effect would be to reduce fiscal 1987 outlays artificially by some $2.9 billion. The appropriations conferees agreed.

Of the $26.3 billion directly trimmed from the amount for which Reagan requested authorization in S 2638 — not counting the reductions in the military payroll — almost $8 billion came from cuts the conferees said would require no changes in Pentagon programs. These reductions included:

- $3.8 billion on the assumption that inflation would be lower than had been planned for in the fiscal 1987 budget request.
- $2.7 billion on the assumption that fuel prices also would be lower.

• $662 million on the assumption that various other commodity prices would rise more slowly than assumed.

• $539 million to be made up for by the same amount left over from the fiscal 1986 budget because of lower-than-planned costs.

The Senate-House conference on S 2638 dragged through more than three weeks, from late September until mid-October. One obstacle was a series of arms control-related provisions in the House version of the bill.

Offensive Nuclear Weapons

The conferees approved $1.1 billion for 12 MX missiles, nine missiles and $303 million less than the request. They also approved $290 million of the $352 million requested to continue development of the missile.

Congress had approved deployment of 50 MXs, all of which would be deployed in existing underground silos, which were vulnerable to Soviet nuclear missiles. The conferees approved only $120 million of the $389 million requested for development of a more secure basing method that could be used for additional MX deployments. Moreover, they declared it unlikely that they would accept a proposal to deploy additional MXs in new launch silos that were "superhardened" with thick layers of steel and concrete.

To develop a much smaller single-warhead ICBM — informally dubbed the Midgetman — conferees approved $1.2 billion of the $1.4 billion requested. The House had approved the entire request but the Senate had cut it by more than half.

The amounts requested and approved to prepare for production of the stealth bomber both were secret. The conferees dropped a House initiative that would have added $200 million to the budget to protect the option of buying B-1 bombers beyond the 100 funded through fiscal 1986.

To equip existing B-52 bombers with new electronic gear, the conferees agreed with the Senate to approve $255 million of the $413 million requested. Because of funds left over from earlier budgets, they said, this amount would cover most of the planned modifications.

They approved the amount requested for a long-range, bomber-launched stealth cruise missile. The House had cut that secret amount by $712 million.

The conferees approved the $1.4 billion requested for a huge Trident missile-launching submarine, which the House had dropped from the bill because of budgetary limits. They also approved with only a minor reduction the request for continued development of the long-range Trident II missile ($1.6 billion) and to build the first 21 of the missiles ($1.1 billion).

They approved the $227 million requested to build three E-6A radio relay planes designed to send messages to submerged missile subs through a five-mile-long trailing antenna. The House had cut two planes ($144 million).

Strategic Defense

Splitting the difference between the House and Senate, the conferees authorized $3.53 billion for SDI. In other provisions related to the anti-missile defense program, the conferees:

• Barred establishment of a Pentagon-funded SDI "think tank" unless it was authorized in subsequent legislation. Opponents worried that the proposed SDI "institute" would provide fervent political support for the program rather than dispassionate analysis of its merits.

• Dropped a Senate provision barring the award of any SDI contract to a non-U.S. firm unless no domestic firm could carry out the contract.

• Endorsed the Senate Armed Services Committee's recommendation that SDI be refocused to put less emphasis on trying to provide a nationwide defense of the population and more emphasis on defending selected military targets, such as U.S. missile launchers.

The conferees also retained a House provision barring through fiscal 1987 tests against a target in space of the ASAT missile, provided the Soviet Union conducted no further ASAT tests. They approved $200 million of the $278 million requested for ASAT development and denied the $28 million requested to buy components for the missiles.

To continue building very-long-range radars intended to detect enemy bombers approaching North America, the conferees approved $110 million of the $188 million requested. They also approved $41 million requested to replace existing long-range missile detection radars with vastly improved equipment. The House had dropped all funds for both radar projects.

Ground Combat

The Pentagon's request for 840 M-1 tanks was approved ($1.6 billion) with only a minor funding reduction. And the conferees agreed to 720 of the requested 870 Bradley armored troop carriers ($896 million). The Senate had approved 720 of the vehicles, but the House had approved only 593, citing critics' charges that the Bradley was unduly vulnerable to anti-tank missiles. The conferees agreed that various proposed modifications to the Bradley should be tested under combatlike conditions.

Both houses had approved 120 of the requested 144 Apache anti-tank helicopters. The conferees authorized $1.05 billion for the purchase.

They also approved $145 million of the $210 million requested to equip small "scout" helicopters with electronic gear to locate enemy tanks and guide anti-tank missiles to them. An additional $29 million was approved, as requested, to equip the scouts with small Stinger anti-aircraft missiles for use against armed Soviet helicopters.

The Army had cut back its plan to modernize the scouts to help pay for development of a new small helicopter, designated LHX. The service planned to buy these helicopters in the 1990s to replace its fleet of some 6,000 Vietnam War-era attack helicopters and troop carriers. Conferees approved $148 million of the $157 million requested for LHX development.

They approved $110 million of the $210 million requested for Aquila — a small, remotely controlled airplane that could carry a television camera and other equipment to duplicate some of the scout helicopter's work. The House had denied all funds, citing continued test problems and increasing costs. The compromise funding was contingent on certification by the Army that the Aquila was performing up to its contract specifications.

Also approved was the lion's share of the money requested to develop an airborne radar that would steer missiles carrying swarms of anti-tank bombs at troop columns up to 100 miles behind enemy lines. For the radar, called JSTARS, conferees approved $300 million of the $355 million requested for development but only $10 million of the $63 million requested to begin production. For the missiles, called JTACMS, they approved the requested $88 million for development.

The request for 700 Patriot long-range anti-aircraft missiles was approved with a slight reduction in funding to $920 million.

Approved without change was the request for nearly 4,200 Stinger short-range, shoulder-launched anti-aircraft missiles. The conferees also added to the bill $1 million to develop an electronically coded lock that would render a Stinger inoperable if an unauthorized person tried to fire it. Proposed transfers of Stingers to U.S.-allied governments and guerrilla groups had been opposed by some members of Congress who warned that if the portable weapons fell into the hands of terrorists, they could be used against civilian jetliners.

Air Combat

The conferees approved $6.7 billion for 321 front-line fighter planes of various sorts, a reduction of about 20 percent from the administration request. Most of the reduction came from turning down requests for large increases in the Air Force F-16 and the Navy FA-18 production rates.

Amounts authorized were:

- $520 million for 15 Navy F-14s, the number of planes requested. The House had authorized 10 planes.
- $1.54 billion for 42 Air Force F-15s, six fewer than the number requested. The Senate had approved all 48 planes requested; the House authorized only 24.
- $2.25 billion for 84 FA-18s. The Navy had requested $2.9 billion for 120 of the planes.
- $2.35 billion for 180 F-16s, a reduction of 36 planes ($529 million) from the request. The Senate had authorized 192 planes, the House 150.

The conferees also approved the $296 million requested to buy the first 20 of a projected fleet of some 270 stripped-down fighter planes to defend North America against bomber attack. The Senate had denied all funds for the project.

Conferees added to the measure $35 million to begin modernizing more than 300 existing A-7 small bombers, dating from the late 1960s, for use through the turn of the century.

For development of a new fighter plane, intended to enter service in the late 1990s, the conferees approved $275 million, a reduction of $19 million from the request.

For four types of missiles used by fighter planes to shoot down other aircraft, the conferees approved nearly $1.3 billion. This included nearly 2,100 radar-guided Sparrow missiles ($331 million) and more than 2,300 shorter-range, heat-seeking Sidewinder missiles ($140 million). The conferees approved the number of each type requested and made only small reductions in the funding for each.

They authorized $267 million — $22 million less than requested — for the Navy's very-long-range Phoenix missiles, but insisted that this could buy 300 missiles rather than the 205 the Pentagon had budgeted for.

For the first 180 copies of a new, radar-guided missile — designated AMRAAM — the conferees authorized $537 million. This was 80 missiles and $119 million less than the request. The Senate had approved the request but the House allowed only 135 missiles ($388 million).

The conferees authorized $631 million for nearly 2,800 HARM missiles, designed to be fired by planes at anti-aircraft radars. This was 475 missiles and $119 million less than the request, roughly half the cut recommended by the House.

For nearly 5,600 Maverick missiles, designed to be fired by planes at ground targets, the conferees approved $626 million. The $191 million approved for 1,800 laser-guided versions of Maverick was only $8 million less than requested. For nearly 3,800 copies of another version, guided by an infrared television camera able to see targets in the dark, the conferees approved $431 million. This was 1,300 missiles and $198 million below the request.

Naval Warfare

The Senate had approved the budget request for five ships equipped with the Aegis system of computer-driven radars and missile launchers intended to protect U.S. fleets from swarms of anti-ship missiles: two cruisers ($1.9 billion) and three smaller destroyers ($2.45 billion).

The House had dropped two of the destroyers to pay for a third cruiser, so the Navy could continue its program of keeping the price of those ships down by having two shipyards compete for each year's group. Three ships would allow the Navy to award two contracts to the lower-bidding yard while giving the other yard one contract to keep it in business so it could compete again the following year.

The conferees agreed with the logic of the House position but decided not to reduce the number of destroyers: They approved three cruisers ($2.7 billion) and three destroyers ($2.4 billion).

They also approved the request for nearly 1,200 Standard long-range, ship-launched, anti-aircraft missiles ($731 million).

But they approved only $64 million of the $87 million requested to begin production of a small, short-range missile — called RAM — intended as a last-ditch defense against anti-ship missiles. Citing the program's rising cost and continued test problems, the conferees said that they would have canceled the program were it not conducted jointly with West Germany. They approved funds to begin RAM production, provided the secretary of defense certified that the Navy would spend no more than $220 million to develop the weapon and that the missiles would cost no more than $100,000 apiece.

For four *Los Angeles*-class submarines, designed to hunt other subs, the conferees approved $1.97 billion, essentially the amount requested. Also approved was the entire $711 million requested to continue designing and preparing to build the *Seawolf* — the first of a new class of anti-sub submarines.

The conferees authorized $200 million for 17 of the LAMPS III anti-submarine helicopters carried by most of the Navy's large warships and an additional $118 million for seven modified versions that would be carried by aircraft carriers, basically the amounts requested.

The conferees also approved the request for six smaller LAMPS I anti-sub helicopters ($53 million) used on some older ships. But citing overall budget limits, they told the Navy to buy no more LAMPS Is, even though this would mean that some anti-submarine ships with reserve crews would be assigned only one helicopter instead of the two they could carry.

As requested, they authorized $312 million for nine P-3C, long-range, land-based, anti-submarine planes based on the 1950s-vintage Electra airliner. The House had denied the funds.

Citing production delays in building the Mark 48 torpedoes carried by U.S. subs, the conferees approved only $255 million of the $509 million, providing for purchase of 50 torpedoes rather than the 227 requested.

The conferees also authorized $95 million for the first 67 of a new, smaller torpedo, the Mark 50, designed to be launched from surface ships and aircraft.

The Navy had dropped its request for four small mine sweepers ($196 million) because of severe problems building the first ship of that type, which had been funded in an earlier budget. The conferees approved the Navy's new plan to use $115 million appropriated in an earlier budget to build a mine sweeper in a U.S. shipyard to a different design, purchased from an Italian firm.

They authorized $499 million — $114 million less than requested — to build a high-speed ship intended to keep a small fleet supplied with fuel and ammunition. The Senate had denied the entire request.

The conferees made a minor reduction to $259 million in the amount authorized for two tankers designed to refuel combat ships under way. And they approved $32 million of the $62 million requested to enlarge an existing refueling tanker.

Air Transport

Only minor reductions were made in the funding requests for two kinds of large transport planes. The conferees authorized 21 C-5B cargo planes ($1.92 billion) and 8 KC-10s, versions of the DC-10 jetliner designed to haul cargo and to refuel other planes in midair ($89 million).

The conferees authorized $728 million, $102 million less than the request, to prepare for production of the C-17 cargo plane. Smaller than the C-5B, the new plane was intended to carry equally bulky cargo — such as tanks — into primitive landing strips near combat zones.

They approved the entire $387 million requested to continue development of the Osprey, a hybrid airplane/helicopter being developed primarily as a troop carrier for the Marine Corps.

Personnel Issues

Following the Senate's lead, the conferees approved an active-duty manpower ceiling of 2,174,250, an increase of about 4,900 over the current ceiling. The administration had requested an increase of 11,800 and the House had approved no expansion.

The two houses had agreed to different formulas for cutting back on the number of officers, which, they argued, had expanded disproportionately in recent years. The compromise formula required a reduction of 1 percent by the end of fiscal 1987, and additional reductions of 2 percent and 3 percent by the end of the two following fiscal years, respectively.

Both houses adopted provisions that would increase the number of reservists the president could order to active duty for 90 days without a formal declaration of war or national emergency. The Senate had increased the current limit of 100,000 to 250,000, but the conferees accepted the House-passed increase to 200,000. The compromise also would let the president extend the reservists' 90-day period of active duty for an additional 90 days, provided he notified Congress.

The House had added to the bill $509.1 million for equipment earmarked for National Guard and reserve units. The Senate added $454.3 million for the same purpose. The conferees upped the ante to $563.5 million.

The conferees dropped a House provision stipulating that service members could wear religious apparel so long as it was "neat and conservative" and did not interfere with a member's military duties. The provision grew out of a court decision upholding the right of Air Force officials to bar an orthodox Jew from wearing a yarmulke, or skullcap. The military services strongly opposed the House provision.

Other Provisions

Military Construction. Splitting the difference between the House and Senate, conferees agreed on an $8.4 billion authorization for military construction projects in fiscal 1987. And they backed the Navy's controversial homeport plan. *(Box, p. 482)*

Procurement. Conferees approved significant changes in Defense Department procurement practices, including creation of a new official to direct the weapons procurement process. *(Box, p. 475)*

Minority Contracts. The House bill required the Pentagon to reserve for minority-owned firms 10 percent of the value of contracts awarded under the bill. Conferees agreed to a non-binding goal of 5 percent for three years.

Davis-Bacon. The Senate increased from $2,500 to $250,000 the threshold above which military construction contracts would be governed by the Davis-Bacon Act, which set wage rates on federal construction projects. The House raised the threshold to $25,000 and made other changes in existing law. Conferees dropped both provisions, leaving the Davis-Bacon law unchanged.

Planes for Turkey. A Senate provision allowing the Pentagon to give obsolescent weapons — including Phantom jets and A-7 small bombers — to Turkey, Greece and Portugal was viewed by many observers as an effort to modernize Turkey's aging arsenal in spite of the longstanding policy of keeping military aid to Greece and Turkey in a ratio of 7-to-10. The conferees accepted the Senate language with the proviso that any weapons transfers be guided by existing arms transfer policy, including the 7-to-10 ratio.

'Special Operations.' The conferees also melded provisions passed by both houses to set up a top-level office within the Pentagon to promote the interests of "special operations forces" — units trained for guerrilla warfare, anti-terrorist operations and other combat situations that were not large-scale wars. Critics charged that the armed services routinely shortchanged special operations units when it came to budgets, training and promotions.

The compromise provision established an assistant secretary of defense in charge of special operations and created a military commander in chief in charge of all such units, whether from the Army, Navy or Air Force. Like the 10 other commanders in chief who, among them, command all U.S. combat units, the special operations commander would report directly to the secretary of defense.

Angolan Oil. The conferees modified a House-passed provision that would have barred the Pentagon from doing business with any firm producing oil in or buying oil from Angola. The House provision embodied an effort by conservative activists to impose an economic boycott on Angola's Marxist government.

But the conferees warned that so sweeping a bar might make it hard to buy fuel for U.S. units stationed in the Middle East and Africa. So they agreed to bar only the purchase of Angolan oil from firms producing oil in Angola and they authorized the secretary of defense to waive the ban on a case-by-case basis.

Sales of Alcohol. Conferees retained a House-passed provision requiring that any alcoholic beverages sold on a military base be purchased within the same state. ■

Military Health Programs

Congress in 1986 authorized the government to seek private health insurance payments for some military hospital services provided to non-active-duty beneficiaries, and extended the reach of the Pentagon's medical program for dependents and retirees, called CHAMPUS, the Civilian Health and Medical Plan of the Uniformed Services.

The provisions were included in an $18.2 billion fiscal 1986 deficit-reduction bill (HR 3128 — PL 99-272) cleared March 20. HR 3128 aimed to cut existing programs to meet requirements of the fiscal 1986 budget resolution. *(Details, p. 555)*

Conferees on HR 3128 dropped Senate provisions concerning the military retirement system that had already been approved in the fiscal 1986 defense authorization bill (S 1160 — PL 99-145). *(1985 Almanac p. 138)*

Provisions. As signed into law April 7, the military health provisions of HR 3128:

- Provided that the government could bill outside insurers for inpatient medical care to non-active-duty military personnel, but not for more than the rate the companies typically would pay for the services in question — the so-called "prevailing rate."
- Required hospitals that participated in Medicare to accept patients under CHAMPUS and to accept CHAMPUS payments as full payment for those patients. A small program under which CHAMPUS paid for hospital care of certain veterans also would be covered by this provision. ▮

Military Retirement Cuts

Congress June 26 completed action on a measure (HR 4420 — PL 99-348) that was expected to trim the cost of the military retirement system by about $3.2 billion annually.

The bill reduced annuities to personnel who left active duty after less than 30 years of service. The change did not affect anyone already in the service or receiving a pension.

The House originally passed HR 4420 (H Rept 99-513) April 22 by a 399-7 vote. The Senate passed HR 4420 by a 92-1 vote May 15 after substituting the text of its own version (S 2395 — S Rept 99-292). *(House vote 85, p. 26-H; Senate vote 103, p. 20-S)*

Conferees from the Senate and House Armed Services committees reported the compromise bill June 25 (H Rept 99-659). The Senate approved it by voice vote the same day. The House followed suit, also by voice vote, the next day.

Changes in Law

Under existing law, military personnel could retire after 20 years of service with an annuity equal to 50 percent of their basic pay (which excluded certain special bonuses and fringe benefits). The proportion of basic pay (or "multiplier") increased with each additional year of active duty until the 30th year, after which service members could retire with an annuity of 75 percent of their basic pay. In each case, the multiplier was applied to the person's average basic pay in his three highest-paid years of service.

Under HR 4420, the annuity for a 20-year retiree was reduced to 40 percent of a person's basic pay, averaged over his three highest-paid years. The House version had applied the 40 percent multiplier to basic pay averaged over the highest five years for a 20-year retiree. Under the Senate version, the same individual's annuity would have been 44 percent of the basic pay averaged over the highest three years.

The formula for retirement after 30 years of active duty remained unchanged: 75 percent of basic pay averaged over the highest three years.

The final bill adopted the Senate's provision for cost-of-living adjustments: Annuities would be increased annually by a percentage equal to the annual increase in the consumer price index (CPI) minus 1 percentage point.

When the retiree reached age 62, his annuity would be increased to the level it would have reached if all of his cost-of-living adjustments had equaled the increase in the CPI. But subsequent increases would be the CPI percentage minus 1 percentage point.

Background

The existing military pension system, which allowed service members to retire after 20 years with a pension of 50 percent of their basic pay, long had been under attack on two fronts. It was widely criticized as unduly generous and thus too costly. Moreover, some defense analysts objected that it provided a strong incentive for specialists to leave after 20 years, even though their experience still made them useful to the service.

Defense officials made the case that some service members should retire in their early 40s, to make room for younger men able to handle the physical rigors of combat. But, they said, the military must offer these members the incentive of a considerable pension while they began a new career.

Proponents of the status quo also insisted that the government had a moral commitment to keep the option of a 20-year/half-pay retirement for persons already in the service or retired.

In the past 15 years, there had been nine major proposals for cost-cutting changes in the pension system. But the Pentagon repeatedly had staved off any fundamental changes.

Earlier efforts to change the retirement system failed partly because they promised budget savings too remote to induce members of Congress to override the potent opposition of the Pentagon and military retirees.

In 1985, Les Aspin, D-Wis., newly elected chairman of the House Armed Services Committee, called for a $4 billion reduction in the $18 billion request for military pensions. Thanks to a new bookkeeping system adopted in 1984, Aspin argued, the cut could be absorbed by reducing future pensions, while protecting current retirees and yielding immediate budget savings.

With political pressure mounting on Capitol Hill to restrain President Reagan's Pentagon buildup, Congress concurred in the basic approach. The fiscal 1986 defense authorization bill (PL 99-145) mandated a $2.9 billion reduction in funds appropriated for military retirement. The fiscal 1986 continuing appropriations resolution (PL 99-190) set a May 1, 1986, deadline for enacting the required changes, but the deadline subsequently was extended until June 30 (PL 99-331). *(Fiscal 1986 authorization, 1985 Almanac p. 138; appropriations, p. 377)*

Had Congress failed to act, the Pentagon would have been forced to lay off some 330,000 active-duty personnel — roughly one service member in seven. ▮

ECONOMIC POLICY

CQ

Economic Policy

With the pace of a glacier, the federal government's fiscal troubles began showing signs of improvement in 1986.

After vowing in late 1985 to make real strides toward deficit reduction, Congress, in fact, moved in halting half-steps. At year's end the nation was left with its largest-ever budget and trade deficits and a much-slowed economy, although *de minimis* inflation, falling interest rates and a steady flow of foreign investment kept the four-year expansion alive.

The promise of Gramm-Rudman-Hollings — the anti-deficit law that was supposed to force Congress and the administration to agree on spending cuts and revenue increases to reduce the budget deficit by $36 billion annually — was far from realized.

There was no grand budget compromise; in fact, the Reagan administration stayed farther away from budget negotiations than it had in any of the previous five years. Perhaps it was afraid of being drawn into endorsement of a tax hike, but the White House largely allowed Congress to go its own way on the budget. The timetable for action — accelerated by Gramm-Rudman — was not met, however. And key spending and deficit-reduction bills did not clear by the start of the fiscal year, much less in accordance with deadlines.

The $221 billion deficit in fiscal 1986 was nearly $50 billion greater than the Gramm-Rudman target. Congress, relying on sales of loans and other assets, said it would meet the $144 billion deficit target for fiscal 1987, but before 1986 was over more current estimates put the real deficit in the vicinity of $175 billion. And the Supreme Court struck down the automatic-spending-cut mechanism of Gramm-Rudman, leaving as its only enforcement tool the political will of Congress.

Nevertheless, the budget deficit was showing a downward trend, primarily because the brakes had been thrown a year earlier on a five-year run-up of defense spending. The rate of growth of all federal government outlays was expected to be less than 1 percent in 1987.

If the targets for declining deficits looked overly optimistic, their rate of descent was about what the law expected. Moreover, there seemed to be a broad consensus on Capitol Hill that spending decisions must be closely scrutinized; increases would have to be offset by new revenues or cuts elsewhere. Nowhere was that better seen than in the committee, floor and conference deliberations on a sweeping overhaul of the federal income tax code.

Tax Reform: A Two-Year Success Story

It had been President Reagan's No. 1 domestic priority of his second term: An overhaul of the federal tax code, the likes of which had not been seen in 40 years or more, was accomplished against exceedingly heavy odds.

The year before, the House had done its part, but that chamber was more closely controlled. Still, it took Reagan's personal appeal to keep the bill alive in 1985. In 1986 in the Senate, it took — to use Finance Committee Chairman Bob Packwood's phrase — "a miracle."

Ironically, it was the budget deficit that nearly derailed the tax bill, and it was the deficit, and the understanding that the tax bill must not contribute to it, that kept the bill on track.

Early in 1986, a majority of the Senate said it wanted deficit reduction to take precedence over tax reform. Packwood persevered, however, and the demand was forgotten. But between Reagan's absolute aversion to a tax increase, and the understanding that the deficit must not grow, Packwood and his allies kept the bill free of amendments restoring major tax breaks for businesses and individuals that had been curtailed or eliminated in the name of reform.

Yet it took Packwood's "miracle" bill, which cut rates far below what anyone dreamed possible and put an end to favorable treatment of capital gains and most tax shelters, to carry the day.

There was general agreement that the tax code was made more fair, if not more simple: Six million of the working poor were freed from the burden of paying taxes, for example. But there was also concern that not every effort to close off avenues of tax avoidance was successful, and that the "level playing field" sought by heavily taxed industries had not been achieved.

As they did during Congress' deliberations on the bill, after it was law, economists disagreed over the new law's ultimate impact. Some objected that it would serve as a disincentive to individual savings, and others complained that sharp reductions in tax rates denied Congress the opportunity for gaining revenue that could be applied to the budget deficit.

Undisputed, however, was that the year-to-year revenue fluctuations caused by the phasing in of the law's provisions could spell trouble for continued attempts to ratchet down the deficit. The magnitude of those fluctuations remained unclear, however.

State of the Economy

It was hard to imagine a year with such bad and good economic portents scattered throughout.

The bad news was everywhere: a record budget deficit of $220.7 billion for fiscal 1986; a record trade deficit of $169.8 billion for calendar 1986; inflation-adjusted economic growth of only 2.7 percent over the previous year (compared with the administration's February 1986 forecast of 4.0 percent).

Yet, by one measure inflation was only 1.1 percent, the lowest since 1961; interest rates, though high in real terms, continued to fall to their lowest level since 1978; and the value of the dollar overseas — seen as one crucial measure of bringing exports and imports into balance — plummeted under direct intervention by the Treasury, the Federal Reserve Board and some U.S. trading partners.

Nevertheless, foreign investors kept their eyes on the declining, but still high, budget deficit and the year's big gains on Wall Street, and found that dollar-based investments remained valuable.

The dollar's fall, particularly compared with the Japanese yen and West German mark, was steady for the second year, and helped to yield a sharp one-month drop in the trade deficit in December. But many economists were reluctant to say that the adjustment necessarily meant significant long-term improvement.

Trade continued to be a concern, but White House opposition to "protectionism" prevented enactment of a restrictive textile trade bill. Loss of exports and competition from imports so upset the farm and textile economies, however, that Democrats capitalized in states dominated by those industries, and won back control of the Senate.

The administration turned from being Congress' adversary on trade matters to being more of a partner as the year ended, and Reagan began talking of improving the nation's "competitiveness." Protectionism remained out of bounds, but trade had moved to the fore.

And there was talk from private economists, as well as those for the executive and legislative branches, that, assuming improvement in both the trade and budget deficits, economic growth would rebound in 1987. By October 1987 the nation would have experienced the longest peacetime expansion since World War II, if growth continued unabated.

—John R. Cranford

Congress Enacts Sweeping Overhaul of Tax Law

The Tax Reform Act of 1986, praised by its supporters as good medicine for the economy — and for the nation's spirits, as well — was signed into law by President Reagan Oct. 22.

The signing of the measure (HR 3838 — PL 99-514), with its large reductions in tax rates and its elimination or curtailment of many special tax breaks for both individuals and corporations, climaxed years of work by both the administration and Congress. *(Evolution of tax bill, p. 492; chronology, p. 505; House bill, 1985 Almanac p. 480; president's proposal, 1985 Almanac p. 20-D)*

The final version, as written in the House-Senate conference committee, had been passed by the House Sept. 25, by a 292-136 vote, and cleared by the Senate 74-23, on Sept. 27. *(Vote 379, p. 108-H; vote 296, p. 50-S)*

Reagan called the measure "the best anti-poverty bill, the best pro-family measure and the best job-creation program ever to come out of the Congress of the United States."

He hailed the ending of "the steeply progressive income tax," which was reduced to a two-rate tax under the new law, and said the previous 14-rate tax that "our Founding Fathers ... never imagined ... struck at the heart of the economic life of the individual, punishing that special effort and extra hard work that has always been the driving force of our economy."

But the benefits went beyond the economic, Reagan said.

"I believe that history will record this moment as something more, as the return to the first principles this country was founded on: faith in the individual, not groups or classes but faith in the resources and bounty of each and every separate human soul."

Key Tax Changes

The new law reduced the top individual tax rate from 50 to 28 percent and taxed 85 percent of all individuals at the bottom rate of 15 percent. Its dual origins were a Democratic tax "reform" proposal first advanced in August 1982 by Sen. Bill Bradley, D-N.J., and Rep. Richard A. Gephardt, D-Mo., and Reagan's call, in his January 1984 State of the Union message, for a "historic reform" of the tax laws, aimed at "fairness, simplicity and incentives for growth."

As enacted, the legislation cut individual tax rates more than either the Reagan plan or the Bradley-Gephardt bill envisioned. The president proposed a top individual rate of 35 percent and Bradley-Gephardt put it at 30 percent.

On the other hand, corporate taxes were cut slightly less than either proposal envisioned. The new law reduced the top corporate rate from 46 percent to 34 percent. The president proposed 33 percent and Bradley-Gephardt 30 percent.

Nevertheless, the law was expected to shift more than $120 billion in tax liability from individuals to corporations over its first five years, reversing a long trend of corporate taxes supplying a decreasing share of federal revenues. *(Change in corporate share, p. 499; percentage change in individual tax liability, by income class, p. 495; number of taxpayers with increases and decreases, by income class, p. 497)*

The law eliminated some tax breaks that the president did not ask to have ended — the crackdown on real estate tax shelters was an example, as was elimination of the traditional lower tax rate on capital gains. The law also failed to eliminate some tax breaks the president wanted killed: deductions for state and local income and property taxes, for example.

The same was true of Bradley-Gephardt. The new law failed to make some changes the two Democrats proposed, such as basing depreciation deductions on the actual loss of economic value of business plants and equipment, and it also included some changes they did not recommend, such as restrictions on tax avoidance by multinational corporations.

Many provisions of the law were in both Reagan's proposal and Bradley-Gephardt, among them repeal of the 10 percent investment tax credit, which many firms protested.

Impact on the Deficit

Enactment of the measure was accomplished through the perseverance of its chief backers in Congress and over the objections of many special interests who stood to lose their favored status under the tax code.

And despite Reagan's having made tax reform his No. 1 domestic priority for his second term, there was never a groundswell of support from the public at large. Public opinion surveys reflected widespread doubt that whatever Congress did with the tax laws would not be real reform.

If anything, the public perception was that record-high federal budget deficits were a more critical concern for Congress than tax reform. But in no small part, enactment of the bill resulted from enforcement of a stern prohibition against raising taxes through overhaul of the code, and a conscious ignoring of the deficit problem.

Reagan stood fast against a tax increase, and the result was adherence in the House, in the Senate and in conference to the principle of revenue-neutrality — defined for this purpose as neither raising nor reducing total federal tax collections over a five-year period after enactment.

Ultimately, that principle allowed the bill's adherents to turn back costly amendments to restore tax breaks because their sponsors could not produce offsetting revenues.

Had even one such change — restoration of full deductibility for Individual Retirement Account contributions, for example — been adopted on the Senate floor, it was feared the foundation of the bill would collapse like a house of cards.

Nevertheless, the perceived need to reduce the budget deficit collided with Reagan's insistence that the tax bill be revenue-neutral.

The bill was nearly derailed in the Senate early in 1986 by forces seeking to force a showdown on the deficit before acting on tax overhaul. And in the end, the bill's year-to-year fluctuations in tax collections — including an estimated $11 billion revenue gain for fiscal 1987 — further complicated the deficit picture. Only by counting the 1987 revenue gain was Congress able to meet, however tenuously, the requirements of the Gramm-Rudman-Hollings anti-deficit law (PL 99-177). *(Gramm-Rudman developments, p. 579; fiscal 1987 budget, p. 542; deficit-reduction action, p. 559)*

Evolution of Proposals to Overhaul the Tax Code . . .

	Existing Law	Reagan Plan [1]
Individual tax rates	11-50 percent (14 brackets)	15, 25 and 35 percent
Corporate tax rates	15-40 percent on first $100,000 of income; 46 percent thereafter	15-25 percent up to $75,000; 33 percent above $75,000
Capital gains	60 percent exclusion; top effective rate of 20 percent	50 percent exclusion; top effective rate of 17.5 percent, but limits on eligible assets
Minimum tax	20 percent "alternative" minimum tax imposed on individuals who greatly limit their tax liability through tax breaks; 15 percent "add-on" minimum tax for corporations that use tax breaks to reduce their liability greatly	Revise the way of computing the individual minimum tax to include more taxpayers; redesign the corporate minimum tax as an "alternative" to tax the value of some so-called preferences, but not depreciation
Personal exemption	$1,080 (1986)	$2,000
State and local taxes	Deductible	Deduction eliminated
Charitable donations	Deductible	Full deductions for itemizers; none for non-itemizers
Interest deductions	Deductions for home mortgage and non-business interest	Unlimited deduction for mortgages on primary residences; additional interest deductions capped at $5,000
Retirement benefits	Tax-deductible Individual Retirement Account (IRA) contributions of $2,000 for each worker and $200 for each non-working spouse; employer-sponsored 401(k) tax-exempt savings plans with maximum contributions of $30,000 annually	Allow non-working spouse IRA contributions of $2,000; limit 401(k) contributions to $8,000 annually, less amounts contributed to IRAs
Investment tax credit	6-10 percent	Repealed
Depreciation	Recovery periods of 3-19 years with accelerated write-off	More generous write-off over 4-28 years; value adjusted for inflation
Business expenses	Deductible	Deduction for entertainment repealed; limit on meals
Tax-exempt bonds	Bonds earning tax-free interest allowed for governmental and many non-governmental purposes, such as sports arenas and mortgages	Effectively eliminate use of bonds for non-governmental purposes

SOURCES: Treasury Department, House Ways and Means Committee, Senate Finance Committee, Joint Committee on Taxation

. . . From Existing Law Through HR 3838 as Cleared

House Bill [2]	Senate Bill [3]	HR 3838 [4]
15, 25, 35 and 38 percent	15 and 27 percent (lower rate phased out for high-income taxpayers)	15 and 28 percent (lower rate phased out for high-income taxpayers)
15-30 percent up to $75,000; 36 percent above $75,000	15-30 percent up to $75,000; 33 percent above $75,000	15-30 percent up to $75,000; 34 percent above $75,000
42 percent exclusion; top effective rate of 22 percent	Special exclusion repealed; taxed at same rates as regular income	Special exclusion repealed; taxed at same rates as regular income
Increase the rate on the individual and corporate minimum tax to 25 percent and revise it to tax more so-called preferences	Retain the individual minimum tax rate of 20 percent but revise it to tax more so-called preferences; retain the 20 percent corporate minimum tax but redesign it to include more preferences, basing the tax on "book income" in order to include many corporations that escape taxation	Increase the rate on the individual minimum tax to 21 percent and revise it to tax more so-called preferences; retain the 20 percent corporate minimum tax and redesign it to include more preferences, basing the tax on "book income" to include many firms that escape taxation
$2,000 for non-itemizers; $1,500 for itemizers	$2,000 for low- and middle-income taxpayers (exemption phased out for high-income taxpayers)	$2,000 by 1989 for most taxpayers (exemption phased out for high-income taxpayers)
No change from existing law	Income, real estate and personal property taxes deductible; sales tax deduction limited to 60 percent of the amount in excess of state income taxes	Income, real estate and personal property taxes deductible; sales taxes not deductible
Full deduction for itemizers; non-itemizers could deduct amount above $100; appreciated value of charitable gifts subject to minimum tax	Full deductions for itemizers; none for non-itemizers	Full deductions for itemizers; none for non-itemizers; appreciated value of charitable gifts subject to minimum tax
Unlimited deduction for mortgages on first and second residences; additional deduction of $10,000 ($20,000 for joint returns) plus the value of a taxpayer's investment income	Unlimited deduction for mortgages on first and second residences; no consumer interest deduction; interest paid on borrowing to produce investment income deductible equal to the value of the investment earnings	Unlimited deduction for mortgages on first and second residences; limits on mortgage borrowing for unrelated purposes; no consumer interest deduction; interest paid on borrowing to produce investment income deductible equal to the value of the earnings
Continue existing law on tax-exempt IRA contributions; restrict 401(k) contributions to $7,000 annually; limit to $2,000 the total exemption for contributions by an individual to both an IRA and a 401(k) plan, to encourage 401(k) and discourage IRA contributions	Limit tax-exempt IRA contributions to persons not covered by pension plans; restrict 401(k) contributions to $7,000 annually; make sweeping changes in private pension plans to improve coverage and restrict benefits for high-income persons	Limit tax-exempt IRA contributions to persons not covered by pension plans or those below specified income levels; restrict 401(k) contributions to $7,000 annually; make sweeping changes in private pensions to improve coverage and restrict benefits for high-income persons
Repealed	Repealed retroactively to Jan. 1, 1986	Repealed retroactively to Jan. 1, 1986
Recovery periods of 3-30 years; partially indexed for inflation	Retain existing system of rapid write-offs, permitting larger write-offs for most property over longer periods	Retain system of rapid write-offs similar to existing law; permit larger write-offs for most property, but over longer periods
Deduction of 80 percent of business meals and 80 percent of entertainment costs	Similar to House for meals and entertainment; most miscellaneous deductions eliminated	Deduction of 80 percent of business meals and entertainment costs; miscellaneous employee business expenses limited
Cap use of non-governmental bonds; reserve a portion for charitable organizations; some interest subject to minimum tax	Cap use of non-governmental bonds, exclude multifamily rental housing and charitable organizations from the cap	Cap use of non-governmental bonds, exclude charitable organizations from the cap; some interest subject to minimum tax

[1] *Proposed May 28, 1985* [2] *Passed Dec. 17, 1985* [3] *Passed June 24, 1986* [4] *Cleared Sept. 27, 1986*

With the tax bill's enactment came an end to the political usefulness of revenue-neutrality and an end to the extraordinary bipartisan cooperation that characterized much of its passage through Congress. Attention was turned once more to the basic fiscal policy divisions between Reagan and Congress.

The president told the hundreds of spectators on the South Lawn of the White House as he signed the bill, "Now that we've come this far, we cannot, and we will not, allow tax reform to be undone with rate hikes. . . . I'll oppose with all my might any attempt to raise tax rates on the American people." That line got the loudest, longest applause of the day.

House Ways and Means Committee Chairman Dan Rostenkowski, D-Ill., was asked after the ceremony, whether he thought the president's remarks violated the bipartisan spirit of the occasion. He indicated that the implicit partisanship in what Reagan had said was all right with him.

"The tax bill is completed and I'm going to start talking about the president," he said. "He ought to start thinking about the deficit. This is Reagan's deficit — and what is he going to do about it?"

Technical Corrections Die

The measure Reagan signed included many acknowledged errors that members said would have to be corrected in the next Congress. The mistakes remained in the bill because the House and Senate proved unable, in the final days before their Oct. 18 *sine die* adjournment, to agree on the contents of a resolution (H Con Res 395) that would have made the necessary corrections. *(Box, p. 523)*

The measure died not because the House and Senate could not agree to fix recognized errors, but rather because members of both chambers tried to add substantive provisions to which their colleagues across the Capitol objected.

Major Provisions

As adopted by the House Sept. 25 and cleared for the president's signature by the Senate Sept. 27, the conference agreement on the Tax Reform Act of 1986 (HR 3838) was expected to reduce the taxes paid by individuals by $121.9 billion over the five years 1987-91 while increasing the taxes of corporations by $120.3 billion and miscellaneous taxes by $1.4 billion.

The full tax-rate reduction for individuals was to take effect for tax year 1988, but even in 1987, four out of five individual taxpayers were expected to receive tax cuts, despite the curtailment or elimination of many existing deductions, exclusions and credits.

The compromise measure, which had been agreed to Aug. 16 by a House-Senate conference committee, essentially followed the Senate version of the bill, passed June 24, in its adherence to two, dramatically reduced tax rates for individuals. The conference bill eliminated more business tax breaks than did the Senate bill and more individual tax breaks than did the House bill.

At least 682 so-called "transition rules," which would reduce the taxes of a great variety of businesses and institutions by about $10.6 billion over the five years 1987-91, were included in the bill. Most were written to benefit a single taxpaying entity, although some were designed to aid broader groups of taxpayers. Most were aimed at easing the transition from old law to new for those unfairly affected by the change, but not all met this test.

Most provisions in the conference committee bill were to take effect Jan. 1, 1987; provisions with different effective dates are indicated below, as are provisions that were to be phased in.

As cleared, HR 3838 included provisions to:

Individuals

• **Rates.** Replace the existing 14 tax brackets (15 for single taxpayers), which ranged from 11 to 50 percent, with a temporary five-bracket system for 1987 only, and a two-bracket system, with rates of 15 and 28 percent, for 1988 and later years.

Under the two-bracket system, the use of the 15 percent rate would be phased out — that is, gradually eliminated — for taxpayers with relatively high incomes. For those with the highest incomes, it would be completely eliminated.

Within the range of incomes affected by the phase-out, the benefits of the 15 percent bottom rate would be eliminated by imposing a 5 percent surtax on income above the starting point for the phase-out. Taxpayers in this phase-out range would thus be subject to a marginal tax rate (on their top dollars of income) of 33 percent, though their overall tax rate would never quite reach 28 percent. For those with the highest incomes, beyond the phase-out range, all taxable income would be subject to the 28 percent top rate.

To eliminate the possibility that high-income married couples would try to avoid the phase-out of the 15 percent rate, couples filing separate returns would be required to calculate the phase-out based on their joint income.

For joint returns, taxable income up to $29,750 (the "break-point") would be taxed at 15 percent, and income above that at 28 percent. The 15 percent bracket would be phased out on taxable incomes of between $71,900 and $149,250; couples with income above that would pay 28 percent on all taxable income.

For single individuals, the break-point at which the 28 percent rate would start to apply would be $17,850 of taxable income and use of the 15 percent rate would be phased out between $43,150 and $89,560 of taxable income.

For single heads of households, the 28 percent rate would begin to apply at $23,900 of taxable income and use of the 15 percent rate would be phased out between $61,650 and $123,790 of taxable income.

The 15 and 28 percent rates would go into effect Jan. 1, 1988, and the various break-points would be indexed annually thereafter to reflect inflation.

• Establish, for calendar 1987 only, a five-rate structure.

For taxable income on joint returns between zero and $3,000 — 11 percent; between $3,000 and $28,000 — 15 percent; $28,000 and $45,000 — 28 percent; $45,000 and $90,000 — 35 percent; and above $90,000 — 38.5 percent.

For taxable income on returns of single persons between zero and $1,800 — 11 percent; between $1,800 and $16,800 — 15 percent; $16,800 and $27,000 — 28 percent; $27,000 and $54,000 — 35 percent; and above $54,000 — 38.5 percent.

For taxable income on returns of single heads of households between zero and $2,500 — 11 percent; between $2,500 and $23,000 — 15 percent; $23,000 and $38,000 — 28 percent; $38,000 and $80,000 — 35 percent; and above $80,000 — 38.5 percent.

There would be no phase-out of the lower rates in 1987.

• **Personal Exemption.** Increase the personal exemp-

Who Pays What Share of Income Tax and How Much They Pay

Income Class	Percentage of Total Tax Collections, 1988 — Current Law	Percentage of Total Tax Collections, 1988 — HR 3838	Average Income Tax Payment by Taxpayer, 1988 — Current Law	Average Income Tax Payment by Taxpayer, 1988 — HR 3838	Average Income Tax Payment by Taxpayer, 1988 — Tax Cut
Less than $10,000	0.6 %	0.2 %	$ 60	$ 21	$ 39
$10,000 - $20,000	6.4	5.3	895	695	200
$20,000 - $30,000	11.8	11.3	2,238	2,018	220
$30,000 - $40,000	12.0	11.8	3,527	3,254	273
$40,000 - $50,000	10.9	10.6	5,335	4,849	486
$50,000 - $75,000	16.2	16.9	8,538	8,388	150
$75,000 - $100,000	6.7	7.1	14,469	14,293	176
$100,000 - $200,000	11.9	12.4	27,965	27,353	612
$200,000 and above	23.4	24.3	138,463	135,101	3,362
Total / **Average**	100 %	100 %	$ 3,176	$ 2,982	$ 194

NOTE: Totals may not add due to rounding.

SOURCE: Joint Committee on Taxation (as of Oct. 1, 1986)

tion for taxpayers and their dependents from the existing $1,080 to $1,900 in 1987, $1,950 in 1988 and $2,000 in 1989. The exemption would be indexed to reflect inflation beginning in 1990.

Use of the personal exemption would be phased out, through use of a 5 percent surtax, on taxable income above the level at which the phase-out of the 15 percent tax bracket is completed. The start of the phase-out of the personal exemption would thus be $149,250 for married couples, $89,560 for single individuals and $123,790 for single heads of households. The end of the phase-out range would depend on the number of exemptions. For a couple with no children it would be $171,090; for a couple with two children, it would be $192,930.

The phase-out of the personal exemption would begin in 1988; there would be no phase-out in 1987.

- Eliminate the use of the personal exemption by any individual (usually a child) who must file a tax return but would also be eligible to be claimed as a dependent on another person's tax return.
- Repeal the additional personal exemption for elderly and blind persons and replace it with an extra standard deduction, intended to ensure that elderly or blind non-itemizers pay no more tax than under existing law. *(See below)*
- **Standard Deduction.** Reinstate for those who do not itemize deductions, the majority of taxpayers, the standard deduction in place of the existing zero bracket amount in the tax tables. The new standard deduction, effective in 1988 and thereafter, would be $5,000 on joint returns, $3,000 for single individuals and $4,400 for single heads of households.

The standard deduction would be indexed for inflation beginning in 1989.

For 1987 only, the standard deduction would be $3,760 on joint returns, $1,880 for single individuals and $2,540 for single heads of households.

- Provide an additional standard deduction for elderly or blind persons of $750 for single taxpayers and $600 for each partner on a joint return. A person who is both elderly and blind would be allowed both additional deductions.

These additional standard deductions would be indexed for inflation beginning in 1989.

- Permit an individual who is claimed as a dependent on another person's tax return to use only $500 of the standard deduction to offset unearned income. The deduction may be used in full against earned income.
- **State and Local Taxes.** Retain the deduction for state and local property and income taxes but eliminate it for sales taxes, effective Jan. 1, 1987.
- **Charitable Contributions.** Allow the deduction permitted those who do not itemize deductions to expire at the end of 1986. Itemizers would continue to be allowed to deduct all charitable contributions.
- **Medical Costs.** Require medical expenses to exceed 7.5 percent of a taxpayer's adjusted gross income, instead of 5 percent as under existing law, before such expenses may be deducted. As under existing law, capital expenditures incurred to accommodate a residence to the needs of a physically handicapped person would be deductible as a medical expense.
- **Business and Investment Expenses and Miscellaneous Deductions.** Allow deductions only to the extent they exceed 2 percent of a taxpayer's adjusted gross income. Among the deductions subject to this "floor" are business expenses borne by employees, such as union dues and safety equipment; expenses for producing income, such as commissions on stock purchases and investment advice; and miscellaneous deductions, such as subscriptions to professional publications. Expenses of moving, for employment purposes, would continue to be subject to all existing limitations but would not be subject to the 2 percent floor. Gambling losses, deductible to the extent that they do not exceed gambling winnings, would also be exempt from the floor. An exception to the floor for performing artists would cover such expenses as fees paid to agents.
- **Unemployment Compensation.** Tax all unemployment benefits as income.
- **Dividends.** Repeal the existing exclusion from income of up to $100 in dividends received by an individual ($200 for a married couple).
- **Marriage Penalty.** Repeal the deduction for two-

earner couples. Changes in the rates, personal exemption and standard deduction were designed to ensure a tax cut for most married taxpayers, but their taxes would be higher than those of two single individuals with the same total income as theirs.

• **Mortgage and Consumer Interest.** Allow taxpayers to take an unlimited mortgage interest deduction for first and second residences.

Phase out, over five years, deductions for interest on consumer purchases, credit cards, charge accounts and other forms of consumer interest. Among existing interest deductions that would be disallowed in the future are interest payments on delinquent taxes.

The potential loophole that would be opened by the combination of the continuing deductibility of mortgage interest combined with the ban on deductions for consumer interest would be partially closed by a complex provision limiting the deductibility of interest on new loans secured by a taxpayer's first or second residence. Loans for any purpose other than educational or medical expenses could not exceed the cost of the residence, plus improvements. That limitation would not apply to borrowings against a residence for certain educational or medical purposes.

Loans using a first or second residence as security that were made on or before Aug. 16, 1986, would be exempt from the new restrictions.

• **Investment Interest.** Allow taxpayers with investment income to deduct interest paid on borrowings used to make the investments, but limit such deductions to the amount of net investment income. Interest deductions disallowed in one year could be carried forward and deducted in subsequent years against net investment income.

• **Meals, Travel and Entertainment.** Limit deductions for business meals and entertainment to 80 percent of the amount spent, except that when an employer bears the cost (and is, thereby, subject to the 80 percent limit) the employee may be reimbursed for the full cost of meals and entertainment.

A few types of entertainment, such as employer-provided holiday parties and tickets for charitable sporting events would remain fully deductible.

Most hotel and transportation costs would remain deductible, but no deduction would be allowed for attending investment seminars or conventions. Deductions for business travel on cruise ships or other luxury liners would be limited. Deductions for travel taken for educational purposes would be disallowed, as would travel to engage in charitable activities, unless there is no significant element of recreation or vacation.

Deductions for rentals of "skyboxes" at sports arenas would be disallowed, after a three-year phase-out.

• **Income Averaging.** Repeal income averaging, which allowed taxpayers with dramatic fluctuations in income to reduce their tax liabilities. Such fluctuations would have much less impact under the new two-bracket tax system than under existing law.

• **Earned Income Credit.** Increase the existing earned income tax credit for working poor families to 14 percent of the first $5,714 of income, to a maximum of $800. The credit would be phased out between $9,000 and $17,000. The change would be effective Jan. 1, 1988, and the credit would be indexed to reflect all inflation since August 1984.

Employers would be required to notify persons whose incomes are so low that they have had no tax withheld that they may be eligible for the credit. Such persons would be informed that they must file a tax return to claim the credit, which is paid in cash to some persons who owe no tax against which to deduct it. The timing and form of the notices would be spelled out in Treasury regulations.

• **Rounding.** Adjust downward to the nearest $50 the standard deduction, personal exemption and rate brackets, when indexed for inflation in future years. The earned income tax credit would be rounded down to the nearest $10, making that adjustment relatively more generous.

• **Adoption Expense.** Abolish the existing deduction for up to $1,500 in expenses related to adoption of hard-to-place children and expand a direct spending program to compensate for the change.

• **Scholarships and Fellowships.** Tax as income scholarships and fellowships that are not used for tuition or equipment required for courses, or are received by students who are not degree candidates. Scholarships and fellowships granted before Aug. 17, 1986, would be exempt from this provision.

• **Prizes and Awards.** Repeal the existing exemption from taxable income for awards won for charitable, educational, religious and similar achievements, unless the award is transferred by a taxpayer to a charitable or governmental organization. Certain employee achievement awards for length of service or safety achievements would continue to be tax-exempt, providing they meet certain limitations, but must be in the form of property, not cash.

• **Handicapped.** Permit a severely handicapped employee to deduct the cost of attendant care and other services necessary to enable the employee to work.

• **Ministers and Military Personnel.** Allow ministers and military personnel receiving tax-free housing allowances to deduct mortgage interest or real property tax payments.

• **Home Offices.** Limit deductions for home offices to a taxpayer's net income from the business, except that excess deductions may be carried forward and taken against income in future years. Under existing law, the deduction could not exceed gross income. The limitations would also apply in cases where a taxpayer leases a home office to his employer.

• **Hobbies.** Expand the definition of "hobbies" for which expense deductions are more limited than for regular businesses. A business activity would be a hobby if it is not profitable in at least three out of five consecutive years, instead of two out of five years as under existing law. Horse breeding or racing would be exempt from the tightened restrictions.

• **Political Contributions.** Repeal the existing $50 credit ($100 for joint returns) for contributions to political campaigns and certain political campaign organizations. The existing presidential campaign "checkoff" of $1 for individuals and $2 for joint returns would be retained.

Corporate Taxes

• **Corporate Tax Rate.** Reduce the top corporate rate from 46 percent on taxable income over $75,000 to 34 percent.

The four lower corporate tax brackets under existing law would be collapsed into two: Income up to $50,000 would be taxed at a rate of 15 percent and income from $50,000 to $75,000 would be taxed at 25 percent. The graduated rates would be phased out on taxable incomes between $100,000 and $335,000 so that corporations with taxable income above $335,000 would pay a flat rate of 34 percent on all income.

These rates would be effective for taxable years begin-

Winners and Losers: How Many Pay More, How Many Less

Income Class	Computed for 1987 (Thousands of Tax Returns)		Computed for 1988 (Thousands of Tax Returns)	
	Returns Showing a Tax Increase	Returns Showing a Tax Decrease	Returns Showing a Tax Increase	Returns Showing a Tax Decrease
Less than $10,000	1,666	11,997	1,692	12,315
$10,000 - $20,000	3,368	22,072	4,198	22,463
$20,000 - $30,000	3,095	16,982	4,677	16,547
$30,000 - $40,000	2,580	11,334	3,519	10,537
$40,000 - $50,000	1,445	7,078	1,697	6,797
$50,000 - $75,000	3,100	4,817	2,947	4,927
$75,000 - $100,000	989	854	722	1,186
$100,000 - $200,000	791	880	655	1,126
$200,000 and above	319	326	311	393
Total	17,353	76,338	20,419	76,291
Percent of Total	18.5 %	81.5 %	21.1 %	78.9 %

NOTE: Totals may not add due to rounding.

SOURCE: Joint Committee on Taxation (as of Sept. 25, 1986)

ning on or after July 1, 1987. Corporations with taxable years beginning earlier than July 1, 1987, would be subject to a blended rate for 1987, reflecting the portion of the taxable year that falls before July 1, 1987. Calendar year corporations, for example, would have a top rate of 40 percent for 1987.

• **Dividends.** Reduce from 85 percent to 80 percent the percentage of dividends received that could be deducted by a corporation.

• **Business Tax Credits.** Reduce from 85 percent to 75 percent the amount by which businesses could use business tax credits to reduce the amount of their tax liability in excess of $25,000. Firms would still be allowed to use business tax credits to reduce all of their regular tax liability up to $25,000.

• **Targeted Jobs Credit.** Extend for three years the credit now available for those who hire economically disadvantaged youths, welfare recipients and other hard-to-place workers.

The so-called targeted jobs tax credit would be reduced from the existing level of 50 percent of the first $6,000 of wages in the first year and 25 percent in the second year to 40 percent in the first year only. The first-year credit could not be taken unless the worker is employed for at least 90 days.

• **Corporate Liquidations.** Repeal what is known as the General Utilities doctrine, thus taxing corporations on the gains from liquidation of their assets, which under existing law were taxed only when distributed as dividends to shareholders. Existing law provided an incentive for corporate mergers and acquisitions, in the view of many who opposed it.

The change would not apply to small, closely held corporations.

• **Corporate Takeovers.** Deny deductions for expenses relating to repurchase of a corporation's own stock, whether to fend off a hostile takeover, or for any other reason. The denial was made effective for repurchases on or after March 1, 1986.

• **Net Operating Losses.** Impose a variety of restrictions on the use of net operating loss carry-overs following a change in ownership of a corporation, in an effort to remove a tax incentive for corporate acquisitions.

• **REMICs.** Create a new entity, known as a real estate mortgage investment company (REMIC), which, like mutual funds, would be allowed to pass along taxable gains to its investors. It would not, itself, be taxable.

Capital Gains

• **Individuals.** Tax capital gains at the same rates as ordinary income: 15 percent and 28 percent, beginning in 1987. The higher rates in effect on ordinary income for 1987 would not apply to capital gains. Under existing law, capital gains were taxed at 40 percent of the ordinary income rate, which put the top effective rate at 20 percent.

• **Corporations.** Tax capital gains at the same rates as ordinary income, or 34 percent for the top bracket, beginning in 1987.

For both individuals and corporations, the existing, separate statutory structure setting capital gains rates would be retained to facilitate reinstatement of a reduced capital gains rate if there is a future increase in tax rates on ordinary income.

Minimum Tax

• Revise the minimum tax to make it more difficult for high-income individuals and corporations with substantial profits to combine various tax benefits — known as preferences — elsewhere in the tax code in ways that would permit them to escape all, or nearly all, tax.

• **Individuals.** Retain the basic structure of the tax, by which certain preference items are added back into taxable income. The rate of the tax would be raised from the existing 20 percent to 21 percent. Some new preferences would be added to the list that goes into the calculation of the tax and others eliminated.

The amount of tax-exempt income that could be earned by Americans who work abroad (cut to $70,000 by the bill) would no longer be a preference subject to the minimum tax.

The interest on newly issued, tax-exempt industrial development bonds, except for those issued by charitable, or 501(c)(3), organizations, would become a preference, subject to the tax. This marked the first time that interest on any form of tax-exempt bonds was made subject to the individual income tax.

Other additions to the list of preferences subject to the tax include the benefits of investing in most tax shelters, which would be eliminated entirely over five years by other sections of the bill, but would become fully subject to the minimum tax in 1987, without any phase-in; deductions for the appreciated value of property donated to charitable organizations; and most of the preferences contained in the corporate minimum tax, such as those for excess depreciation, when used by owners of unincorporated businesses filing as individuals.

• **Corporations.** Redesign the corporate minimum tax with the objective of making it close to airtight. The heart of the new tax is its use of reported "book income" as a separate new test of taxability, in addition to a list of "preference" items given favorable treatment under regular provisions of the tax law that would be subject to the minimum tax.

• Interest on all tax-exempt securities, outstanding and new, public or private purpose, would be included in "book income" for corporations subject to that test of taxability. Interest on non-governmental purpose bonds issued on or after Aug. 8, 1986 (except for those issued by 501(c)(3) organizations), would become a tax preference for corporations.

Other major new preferences include: accelerated depreciation, insofar as it exceeds what could be deducted using what is called Asset Depreciation Range (ADR) depreciable lives and the 150 percent declining balance method; the so-called completed contract method of tax payment for government and construction contractors; the installment method used by retailers and other sellers; and intangible drilling costs for oil and gas wells.

• A two-level method of figuring the tax would be used. A company would, first, calculate its taxable income under existing law, including all the various deductions, exemptions and exclusions. Then, starting with taxable income, it would add these preferences back and make other adjustments, and from this calculate minimum taxable income. Next it would compare this minimum taxable income total with book income, as reported to shareholders or a regulatory agency or a bank for purposes of obtaining a loan. If book income is more than the minimum taxable income, one-half of the difference would be added to the minimum taxable income and the tax would be calculated on this total amount at a 20 percent rate. A few existing preferences would remain untouched, even with the use of the book-income concept. One of the largest is the expensing, or writing off in one year, of research and development costs.

• The book income basis for calculating the corporate minimum tax would remain in effect for three years, starting in 1987, after which the basis would shift to the "earnings and profits" concept.

Tax Shelters

• **Real Estate.** Eliminate, over a five-year phase-out period, provisions allowing so-called passive losses generated by investments in limited partnerships in real estate and most other types of tax shelters, in which the investor takes no active management role. Such losses could, under existing law, be used to reduce wage or portfolio income for tax purposes.

Passive losses arise principally from depreciation deductions, and investment tax and other credits, which are large in the early years of investments. A typical shelter investor sells out of the partnership when income from the real estate starts to exceed the deductions. Depreciation deductions then start all over again for the new buyer.

An exception to the ban on deducting passive losses would be provided individuals who have at least a 10 percent interest in rental property and actively participate in its management. Such persons may deduct up to $25,000 in passive losses annually.

• Apply to some real estate transactions existing, so-called "at risk" rules preventing investors from deducting losses greater than the amount actually invested.

• **Oil Shelters.** Create a new class of passive losses in cases in which an investor in an oil or gas drilling enterprise has a working interest in the partnership, defined as some liability beyond his original investment. Passive losses created by such deductions as the expensing of intangible drilling costs would still be permitted for working-interest partners.

• **Effective Date.** As for most provisions of the bill, the effective date for the passive loss sections would be Jan. 1, 1987. However, in order to take advantage of the five-year phase-out, rather than losing passive-loss deductions immediately, investments in these tax shelters must be made no later than the date of enactment of the bill.

Tax-Exempt Bonds

• **Public Use.** Continue to exempt from regular federal income taxes the interest earned on bonds issued by state and local governments for public purposes, such as the construction of schools or roads.

• **Industrial Development Bonds.** Define as non-public-purpose bonds those in which more than 10 percent of the money raised (or $15 million, for some public utilities) is used for other than a public purpose. The existing maximum was 25 percent. Bonds that exceeded this limit would be designated industrial development bonds (IDBs) and subject to various limitations.

The bill imposed a new and generally lower ceiling on the volume of IDBs that could be issued annually in each state, and placed more types of non-government-purpose bonds under the caps. Under existing law, the cap was $150 per resident, or $200 million, whichever was greater. For 1987, the cap would be set at $75 per person or $250 million; and for 1988 and thereafter, the cap would be $50 per person or $150 million. Bonds issued to fund multifamily housing and single-family mortgage revenue bonds would come under the cap for the first time.

• **Section 501(c)(3) Organizations.** Bonds issued by charitable, educational and other organizations whose own operations are tax-exempt under section 501(c)(3) of the Internal Revenue Code would not come under the cap. However, private universities could have no more than $150 million in tax-exempt bonds outstanding at one time, a cap that would keep 20 or 30 large private universities from issuing any new tax-exempt bonds for the foreseeable future.

• **Minimum Tax.** For corporations subject to the minimum tax, the interest on both outstanding and new tax-exempt bonds, including those issued by governmental en-

New Law Halts Shrinkage of Corporate Tax Share

A key, intended result of the tax bill (PL 99-514) was to reverse the decline in the corporate share of total tax payments, which had persisted almost without interruption throughout the post-World War II period.

Many economists and business executives expressed fears that the additional corporate tax burden would prove harmful to economic growth. The law was projected to shift about $120 billion in taxes from individuals to corporations over the five years 1987-91.

But despite the increased importance of corporate taxes, their share of federal tax collections was still expected to be lower than it was at any time between the end of World War II and 1979.

From Some Paying Nothing . . .

From the tax debate's beginnings, attention was repeatedly focused on the corporate sector's tax burden. Two separate and somewhat different studies, published the week of July 15 — in the midst of the tax bill conference — showed that one out of six of the largest, profitable corporations paid no federal income tax in 1985.

The surveys, updates of earlier work in both cases, were aimed at influencing conferees who were considering which of a large number of existing corporate tax breaks to repeal or restrict.

In one analysis, Citizens for Tax Justice, largely funded by organized labor, found that 42 of 250 corporations paid no federal income tax in 1985, and 130 — more than half — paid none in at least one of the five years, 1981-85, surveyed. The group was responsible for a widely publicized 1984 study of no-tax and low-tax companies that helped create public pressure for reform.

Tax Analysts, an organization supported solely by income from sales of its publications to corporations, tax lawyers and accountants, found that 95 of the 604 corporations it studied paid no tax in 1985.

Citizens for Tax Justice based its study on data from corporate annual reports and filings with the Securities and Exchange Commission (SEC). Tax Analysts used the SEC filings but also attempted to get additional information from the companies themselves to make more detailed analyses.

"For most of America's largest corporations, no-tax years are now commonplace," said Robert S. McIntyre, head of Citizens for Tax Justice. Thomas F. Field, executive director of Tax Analysts, said, "It is fair to conclude on the basis of our figures that the U.S. corporate income tax is seriously flawed. In particular, the finding that effective corporate tax rates continue to vary widely from industry to industry means that our tax system promotes misallocation of capital and losses of economic efficiency."

Tax Analysts identified apparel, newspaper, tobacco and non-durable goods wholesalers as the highest tax industries, with rates of tax paid ranging from 34 to 46 percent. Construction, railroad, motion picture and large oil companies had the lowest tax rates, ranging from net tax rebates to 8 percent.

Overall, Tax Analysts found that in 1985, the Treasury was collecting an average tax of 18.7 percent on the income earned in this country by large corporations, compared with 23.2 percent in 1984. CTJ found that its 250 corporations had paid average taxes of 14.9 percent over the past four years. The statutory tax rate on large corporations was 46 percent those years.

Share of Income Tax Payments

Fiscal Years	Individuals	Corporations
1957	62.7 %	37.3 %
1967	64.4	35.6
1977	74.2	25.8
1978	75.2	24.8
1979	76.8	23.2
1980	79.1	20.9
1981	82.4	17.6
1982	85.8	14.2
1983	88.6	11.4
1984	84.0	16.0
1985	84.5	15.5
1986	83.3	16.7
1987 (est) *	76.9	23.1
1988 (est) *	75.5	24.5

* *For 1987 and 1988, Office of Management and Budget estimates adjusted to show effects of Tax Reform Act of 1986, as estimated by Joint Committee on Taxation.*

SOURCES: Office of Management and Budget, Joint Tax Committee

. . . To Paying More

Treasury Secretary James A. Baker III, in response to complaints from the business community, repeatedly argued during the yearlong tax debate that the corporate share had greatly declined. He noted that in 1967 corporate taxes represented 22.8 percent of total federal receipts, whereas they had been estimated to equal only 10.2 percent in 1987, under existing law.

Under the new law, the figure was expected to rise to 13.2 percent for 1987, when changes were to be only partly in effect, and to 13.4 percent in 1988.

Baker also cited the proportion of all income taxes represented by corporate income taxes, which many analysts considered more valid because it left out of the calculation taxes whose rise in recent decades had dwarfed the changes in all others. These fund "social insurance" programs, principally Social Security.

Counting only income taxes, and leaving out social insurance, excise, estate and miscellaneous taxes, corporate taxes showed the same declining pattern displayed when their share of all tax payments was calculated. Under the new law, the corporate share of income taxes would revert to where it was in 1979. *(Table, this page)*

tities, would be included in the book income calculation of the tax. For both individuals and corporations, interest on IDBs issued after Aug. 8, 1986, except for those issued by 501(c)(3) organizations, would become a preference under the minimum tax.

• **Prohibited Uses.** Tax-exempt financing could no longer be used for privately owned air or water pollution control facilities; sports, convention or trade show facilities; parking garages; industrial parks, or facilities such as restaurants and office buildings adjacent to an airport that are in excess of the size needed to serve airport passengers and employees. This would be effective Aug. 15, 1986.

• **Bank Interest Deductions.** Repeal the existing provision that permitted banks, unlike other investors in tax-exempt bonds, to deduct some of the interest on loans used to purchase the bonds. The existing 80 percent deduction would be continued only for public purpose bonds or those issued by 501(c)(3) organizations that do not issue more than $10 million of such bonds a year.

• **Arbitrage and Advance Refunding.** Permit the Treasury to recapture the excessive profits from, and thus discourage, the practice known as arbitrage, which involves using funds raised from the sale of tax-exempt securities to buy taxable securities carrying a higher interest rate. Advance refundings, use of which can raise tax-exempt money several times for the same purpose, without repayment of the old indebtedness, would be limited to government-purpose bonds and those issued by 501(c)(3) organizations.

• **Costs of Issuance.** Payments for services of architects, engineers, lawyers and underwriters, and other costs of issuing IDBs, may not exceed 2 percent of the amount being raised by the bond issue.

Depreciation

• **Investment Tax Credit.** Repeal, effective Jan. 1, 1986, the existing 10 percent tax credit (6 percent for certain short-lived assets) allowed for a taxpayer's investment in machinery and equipment.

Permit businesses with investment tax credits they could not use in the past — because their profits were too small — to use up to 82.5 percent of their unused investment tax credits to offset taxes owed in 1987, and up to 65 percent in later years. Currently, firms could carry the full amount of unused credits forward 15 years or back three.

A variety of both generic and special transitional rules were provided to determine whether a specific piece of property was eligible for the investment tax credit despite not having been acquired by a binding, written contract by the cutoff date of Dec. 31, 1985.

• **Accelerated Depreciation.** Lengthen the periods of time over which many categories of business equipment and machinery would be depreciated, but permit these assets to be written off under a 200 percent declining balance system, rather than the existing 150 percent, in most cases. The net result would be somewhat smaller depreciation deductions for most businesses.

Automobiles and light trucks would be depreciated over five years, instead of three years, as under existing law, as would equipment used in research and development. Users of these assets would, however, gain the benefit of 200 percent declining balance depreciation. Other assets whose costs could, under existing law, be recovered over three years would remain in the three-year class. Some assets with an existing five-year cost-recovery period would remain in the five-year class, but others would be shifted to a seven-year class, with 200 percent declining balance depreciation. Assets in the 15- and 20-year classes would be depreciated at a 150 percent declining balance rate.

The shifts in and out of various cost-recovery classes were based on type of asset, rather than the industry that uses them, for the most part. However, there are some specific industry provisions, essentially favorable to the industries involved. Among them are telephone central office switching equipment, which would be given a depreciable life of 5 years, as other computers; railroad tracks, given a depreciable life of 7 years; and single-purpose agricultural structures, such as henhouses, given a life of 15 years.

Real estate would be among the hardest-hit areas. Residential rental property would be depreciated, using the straight-line system, over 27.5 years and non-residential over 31.5 years. Under existing law, both were depreciated over 19 years.

• **Effective Date.** Businesses for which the new depreciation rules would be advantageous may elect to use them for any equipment put into service on or after Aug. 1, 1986. Use of the new rules would be required of all businesses as of Jan. 1, 1987, covering property constructed or acquired under a binding, written contract by March 1, 1986. A number of exceptions to this date were provided.

• **Expensing for Small Businesses.** Allow taxpayers to write off in one year, or expense, up to $10,000 in personal property used in a trade or business, providing their total investment in such property does not exceed $200,000. The existing expensing limit was $5,000.

• **Handicapped Barriers.** Extend permanently a deduction for up to $35,000 in expenses for removing architectural and transportation barriers for the handicapped and elderly, instead of writing them off over a long period.

Financial Institutions

• **Bad-Debt Reserves.** Limit the deduction commercial banks with assets of $500 million or more — about 450 of the nation's largest banks — could take to cover bad loans, allowing deductions only when actual losses are incurred.

Banks with assets of less than $500 million would be able to take the more generous deduction allowed under existing law, which was based on a percentage of the bank's outstanding loans or on its past record of bad debts.

The balance of existing reserves would be recaptured through taxation over five years: 10 percent in 1987; 20 percent in 1988; 30 percent in 1989; and 40 percent in 1990. There would be an exemption from the recapture provision for a bank in years when it is "troubled," defined as having non-performing loans exceeding 75 percent of its capital.

• Allow some thrift institutions to take bad-debt deductions equal to 8 percent of their taxable income or an amount based on their past experience with bad loans, in contrast with the more generous 40 percent deduction allowed under existing law.

• **Investment Interest Deduction.** Eliminate a deduction financial institutions could take under existing law for 80 percent of the interest payments they made on debt used to invest in tax-exempt obligations.

Banks that invested in tax-exempt bonds issued by small jurisdictions for governmental purposes or by charitable organizations could continue to deduct the interest they paid on money used to purchase the bonds, so long as the jurisdiction limited its qualified bond issues to $10 million in a calendar year. The provision would apply to interest earned after Dec. 31, 1986, on bonds purchased after Aug. 7, 1986.

• **Thrift Reorganization.** Repeal special tax advantages for the reorganization of troubled "thrift" institutions, including a provision that allowed troubled savings and loans to be acquired tax-free. This provision would be effective for reorganizations after Dec. 31, 1988.

• **Bankruptcy.** Make it easier for individuals to claim losses when their financial institution becomes bankrupt or insolvent.

• **Net Operating Losses.** Change special rules allowing commercial banks and thrift institutions to deduct their net operating losses against income from the preceding 10 taxable years or the succeeding five taxable years. The 10-year carry-back deduction for commercial banks would be retained for bad-debt losses incurred before 1994; otherwise, the 10-year carry-back would be repealed. Thrift institutions would be allowed to carry forward for eight years losses incurred after 1981 and before 1986.

Accounting

• **Installment Sales.** Eliminate for some taxpayers and restrict for others the tax benefits realized by so-called installment sale contracts, which under existing law allowed deferral of taxes on the proceeds from such sales spread over two or more years.

Deferral of taxes under the installment method would be disallowed for sales pursuant to revolving credit accounts, and for sales of certain publicly traded property, such as stocks and bonds, effective for sales after Dec. 31, 1986.

For other installment sales, including those involving real estate, deferral of taxes would be limited by use of new accounting methods that measure the ratio of a taxpayer's total debts to assets. Sales of crops, livestock for slaughter and certain farm property would not be subject to this limit, and sales of certain residential lots and timeshares (such as those commonly used by vacation resort developers) could be counted as installment sales, except the taxpayer would have to pay interest on the tax deferred. The new limitations on installment sales would be effective for tax years after Dec. 31, 1986, and for sales effective after Feb. 28, 1986.

• **Long-Term Contracts.** Restrict a special accounting method that allows defense and construction contractors to delay tax payments until work on a project has been completed, thus often dramatically reducing or permanently postponing their tax liabilities. The ability of some defense contractors, in particular, to avoid all taxes, despite large profits, through use of the "completed contract method" of accounting was one of the major sources of public complaint about the tax law.

Basically, the provision would require contractors to calculate each year what proportion of the contract they had completed and pay taxes on an amount equal to 40 percent of that proportion of the total payments expected from the contract. Taxes on the other 60 percent would be deferred until the contract was completed, as under existing law. Some stricter capitalization requirements were also imposed.

• **Cash Method.** Prevent the use of the so-called "cash method" of accounting for businesses with gross receipts exceeding $5 million a year. But professionals, such as lawyers and accountants, farm and timber businesses, partnerships and certain personal service companies, would be exempt. Tax shelters would also be prohibited from using the cash method.

Critics charged that cash accounting — where income is declared at the time cash is received and deductions are taken when an expense is actually paid — does not accurately reflect a company's economic circumstances and allowed some firms to delay tax payments unduly.

Instead, companies exceeding the $5 million limit would be required to use accrual accounting, where income and expenses are reported at the time they are earned or incurred, but not necessarily paid.

• **Bad-Debt Reserves.** Prevent businesses and large banks from taking deductions for reserves held to cover bad debts. Instead, deductions would be allowed when specific loans become partially or wholly worthless.

Smaller financial institutions and finance companies would retain a partial benefit from the bad-debt reserve deduction, but it would be severely limited for thrifts.

• **Capitalization.** Adopt a uniform set of rules for most costs incurred in manufacturing or construction of property, or in purchase and holding of property for resale. The rules would also apply to some interest costs, but not to research expenses, oil, gas and mineral properties, or some farming operations.

Wholesalers and retailers with sales of $10 million or more a year would have to capitalize over a period of time certain inventory costs rather than deduct the costs in one year.

• **Small Businesses.** Allow certain firms with incomes of less than $5 million to use an inventory accounting practice known as simplified LIFO (for last in, first out). The practice benefits businesses at times of rising costs because it effectively raises the value of older, less-expensive inventory when it is sold.

• **Utilities.** Require utilities using the accrual method of accounting to report income as of the time utility services are provided to customers, rather than when billed.

• **Taxable Years.** Require all partnerships, so-called "subchapter S" corporations and "personal service" corporations to conform their taxable years to the taxable years of their owners. The provision was intended to prevent deferral of taxes.

Low-Income Housing

• **Tax Credit.** Provide a new tax credit to owners of low-income rental housing projects, which would apply only to units occupied by low-income persons. At least 20 percent of the units and space in a project would have to be occupied by persons whose incomes are below 50 percent of the median income for the area or 40 percent would have to be occupied by persons whose incomes are below 60 percent of the area median. Both income figures would be adjusted to take family size into account for the first time under any of the various tax-incentive programs for low-income housing.

The credit would be 9 percent a year of the value of the units occupied by the low-income tenants, and not otherwise benefited by federal subsidies. It would be used over a period of 10 years, and adjusted for inflation. For buildings receiving other federal subsidies, the credit would be 4 percent. The credit would be subject to recapture, with penalties, if the units were converted to any other use for a period of 15 years.

Newly constructed, acquired or rehabilitated buildings would be eligible.

There would be exceptions to the restrictions on deductions of "passive losses," contained in the tax shelter section of the bill, for low-income housing.

The low-income housing credit would, with some exceptions, apply only to buildings placed in service before Jan. 1, 1990.

Historic Rehabilitation

• **Tax Credit.** Replace existing-law credits of 15 percent for the rehabilitation of buildings at least 30 years old and 20 percent for buildings at least 40 years old with a 10 percent credit that could be used only for buildings constructed before 1936.

• Reduce from 25 percent to 20 percent the tax credit allowed for rehabilitation of certified historic buildings.

• **"Passive Losses."** Permit limited exceptions to the general ban on deduction of tax-shelter "passive losses" for investments in historic rehabilitation.

Agriculture, Timber, Energy and Minerals

• **Agriculture.** Allow farmers to continue writing off in one year the cost of soil and water conservation measures, instead of depreciating the costs over several years, provided the improvements are consistent with Agriculture Department-approved plans. The deduction would be limited to 25 percent of gross farm income.

• Retain one-year write-offs for certain fertilizer and soil conditioning costs, but repeal retroactively to Jan. 1, 1986, the write-off for land-clearing expenses.

• Exempt certain farmers from accounting rules to which they would otherwise be subject, as under existing law. Generally, farmers using the cash method of accounting could not deduct the prepaid costs of seed, fertilizer or other expenses, if they were used in the year following prepayment, and if more than 50 percent of the farmer's costs were prepaid.

• Exclude from taxable income a discharge of indebtedness granted farmers. The provision was designed to permit marginally solvent farmers to take advantage of federal farm credit programs guaranteeing loans in exchange for debt forgiveness.

• **Timber.** Repeal special capital gains treatment for corporations and individuals on the proceeds from timber sales; capital gains would be taxed at the same rates as regular income.

• Allow taxpayers a 10 percent tax credit for reforestation costs, and allow up to $10,000 annually of such costs to be written off over seven years, as under existing law.

• Allow most costs for timber production to be written off in the year paid or incurred, as under existing law.

• **Oil and Gas.** Retain nearly all existing-law provisions granting favorable tax treatment for exploration and development of oil and gas property by domestic producers.

Upon sale of oil, gas or geothermal property, expensed intangible drilling costs and percentage depletion deductions that reduced a taxpayer's basis in the property would be recaptured as ordinary income for tax purposes. The provision would apply to property acquired after Dec. 31, 1986, unless acquired pursuant to a contract binding on Sept. 25, 1985.

Intangible drilling expenses and exploration and development costs incurred outside the United States would have to be written off over 10 years or under a cost-depletion system; 30 percent of domestic intangible drilling costs incurred by some producers would be written off over five years.

• **Coal, Iron and Hard Minerals.** Retain nearly all existing-law provisions granting favorable tax treatment for exploration and development of mineral property by domestic producers.

Upon sale of mineral property, expensed exploration and development costs and percentage depletion deductions that reduced a taxpayer's basis in the property would be recaptured as ordinary income for tax purposes. The provision would apply to property acquired after Dec. 31, 1986, unless acquired pursuant to a contract binding on Sept. 25, 1985.

Intangible drilling expenses and exploration and development costs incurred outside the United States would have to be written off over 10 years or under a cost-depletion system; 30 percent of domestic corporate exploration and development costs would have to be written off over five years.

• **Energy Credits.** Allow all residential credits to expire, as under existing law.

• Extend business credits for innovative energy sources: for solar energy at 15 percent in 1986, 12 percent in 1987 and 10 percent in 1988; for geothermal energy at 15 percent in 1986, and 10 percent in 1987 and 1988; for ocean thermal energy at 15 percent through 1988; and for other new energy sources at lower rates for shorter periods of time.

• **Alcohol Fuels.** Retain the 6-cents-per-gallon exemption from federal fuel excise taxes for fuels containing 10 percent alcohol. The existing 9-cents-per-gallon excise tax exemption for fuels that are at least 85 percent alcohol would be reduced to 6 cents.

Research and Development

• **Existing Tax Credit.** Extend through 1988, but reduce from 25 percent to 20 percent, the tax credit for new research and development expenses. The bill would tighten the definition of research and development to focus it exclusively on "research that is technological in nature." Research in economics or marketing, for example, would not qualify.

The bill would apply the general limitation on use of business credits to offset tax liability to the research and development credit.

• **University and Non-Profit Research.** Allow a new 20 percent tax credit for three years for corporate contributions to or contracts with universities or non-profit organizations to conduct new research and development. The provision would take effect Jan. 1, 1987.

• **Charitable Deduction.** Expand an existing charitable deduction allowed businesses for donations of newly manufactured scientific equipment to colleges and universities for physical or biological science research. The bill would allow deductions for donations to organizations primarily involved in research that qualifies as charitable under section 501(c)(3) of the Internal Revenue Code. Private foundations would not qualify.

• **Orphan Drugs.** Extend through 1990 a 50 percent tax credit now available for clinical testing of certain drugs, called "orphan" drugs, for rare diseases and conditions. The credit was due to expire at the end of 1987.

Insurance

• **Life.** Repeal an existing-law percentage deduction that life insurance firms used to cap their top tax rate at 36.8 percent, instead of the 46 percent top rate paid by other corporations under existing law. The deduction, 20 percent of certain income, would be eliminated because the bill would reduce tax rates substantially. But the effect for 1987, because of the higher blended top corporate tax rate of 40 percent for that year, would be a one-year tax rate increase for some life insurance firms.

• Continue the existing tax-exempt treatment of the increased value of life insurance policies, called "inside buildup."

• Eliminate business deductions for interest on large life insurance policy loans that, in effect, provided tax-deferred retirement savings.

• Repeal a $1,000 exclusion survivors claimed under existing law for interest they receive on the unpaid proceeds of their spouses' life insurance policies. The provision would be effective for deaths after the date of enactment and tax years beginning after Dec. 31, 1986.

• **Property and Casualty.** Restrict deductions for loss reserves, by requiring a discount for part of the financial advantage to the company of retaining the money for other uses until claims are actually paid.

• Require property and casualty firms to count as income 20 percent of any increases in the value of special reserves used for soliciting premium income in advance of providing insurance coverage.

• **Blue Cross.** Repeal an existing tax exemption for Blue Cross and Blue Shield insurers, which critics argued gave them an unfair advantage over competitors. Blue Cross and Blue Shield insurers would be treated as stock property and casualty firms, with certain exceptions, including a "fresh start" for accounting purposes and loss reserves. Some YMCA, church-sponsored and other similar insurers would retain their tax-free status.

Foreign

• **Income Exclusion.** Reduce the existing $80,000 exclusion of income earned by U.S. citizens working abroad to $70,000. The bill also would add Libya to the list of countries to which the exclusion does not apply.

• **Foreign Tax Credits.** Revise a complex system of tax credits allowed U.S. corporations, which reduce their U.S. tax liability by the amount of foreign taxes they pay on income earned overseas. The provisions would alter the existing overall limitation on the extent to which taxes on foreign income may be used as credits against U.S. taxes, replacing the overall limit with a variety of separate limitations, which would restrict their usefulness in reducing U.S. tax liabilities.

• **Sourcing.** Impose new sourcing rules for interest expenses and research and development costs with the aim of restricting the ability of multinational companies to claim that expenditures were made in the United States and thus were deductible against U.S.-source income.

The conferees eliminated a major restriction contained in the House bill, however, that would have stopped U.S. firms from claiming that income had a foreign source if the title to a product or other property had merely changed hands in a foreign country.

• **Financial Services.** Terminate the ability of multinational companies to defer U.S. tax on income from overseas banking operations, unless the interest is earned in connection with export activities. Impose a separate limit on foreign tax credits against income from overseas financial services so that credits arising from other types of foreign activities cannot be used to offset income from financial services.

• **Space and the High Seas.** Discard the general rule that the United States asserts primary tax jurisdiction only over income generated within its borders and territorial waters. Most income derived from space or ocean activities would be treated as if produced in the country of residence of the person generating the income.

• **Foreign Taxpayers.** Enact a number of new provisions taxing more of the income earned in the United States by foreign individuals and businesses, including earnings by foreign government corporations.

• **Tax-Haven Income.** Make extensive revisions in subpart F of the Internal Revenue Code to limit tax avoidance through investments in "tax-haven" countries.

• **U.S. Possessions.** Impose a variety of new restrictions on the use of tax credits to eliminate virtually all U.S. tax on income earned by corporations in Puerto Rico, the Virgin Islands and other possessions.

• **Copyrights and Patents.** Require adequate royalty payments back to the United States, where they would be taxable, for patents and copyrights transferred to subsidiaries operating overseas, including those in U.S. possessions.

• **Transportation Income.** Eliminate the deferral of U.S. tax on reinvested income from foreign-flag shipping.

• **Foreign Investment Companies.** Restrict deferrals of tax and conversion of ordinary income into capital gains by U.S. shareholders in foreign investment companies.

Trusts and Estates

• **Child's Income.** Tax the unearned income in excess of $1,000 of a child under 14 years of age at the parent's tax rate, instead of at the child's rate, regardless of the source of the assets from which the income is derived. The first $500 of a child's unearned income would be offset by the standard deduction and the second $500 taxed at the child's rate. The $500 figures would be indexed to increase with inflation after 1988.

Use of so-called Clifford Trusts, another method used by parents to transfer income to their children to avoid taxes, would be effectively repealed for transfers of income-producing assets after March 1, 1986.

• **Estimated Tax.** Require both new and existing trusts and estates to pay estimated tax in the same manner as individuals, except that new estates would be exempted for their first two years.

• **Taxable Years.** Require all trusts, except charitable trusts, to adopt calendar years as taxable years to prohibit unwarranted deferral of tax.

• **Generation-Skipping Tax.** Revise the so-called "generation-skipping tax" imposed on those who try to avoid paying estate taxes by passing wealth on to their grandchildren, instead of to their children. The changes would allow a couple to pass on $4 million to a grandchild without paying the generation-skipping tax.

The existing-law tax was more stringent, but also considered so complex that few taxpayers complied and the Internal Revenue Service never enforced it. It would be repealed retroactively to June 11, 1976, but earlier transfers would still be subject to estate taxes.

Pensions

• **Individual Retirement Accounts.** Continue the existing tax-deductible contribution to Individual Retirement Accounts (IRAs) for individuals with incomes up to $25,000 and married couples up to $40,000 or those at any income level not covered by employer-provided pension plans, including 401(k) plans. If one spouse is covered by a pension plan, both would be considered covered. Persons not yet vested in a pension plan would be considered covered. Those with incomes between $25,000 and $35,000, if single, or $40,000 and $50,000, if married, would be subject to a phase-down of the amount of the tax-free contribution they would be allowed.

Taxpayers ineligible to make tax-deductible contributions could continue to add to IRAs, although the contributions would be taxable. The interest earned by IRAs held by taxpayers ineligible for tax-deductible contributions would continue to be tax-deferred, however.

The basic deduction limits, without reference to the phase-down, would remain unchanged at $2,000 (or total earned income, whichever is lower) per employed person and $2,250 for joint returns where one spouse has no earned income.

Taxpayers would have until April 15, 1987, to make their 1986 tax-free contributions to IRAs under the old rules.

• **401(k) Plans.** Reduce the maximum tax-exempt employee contribution to a 401(k) savings plan from $30,000 a year to $7,000 annually, a figure that would be indexed for inflation beginning in 1988.

Tighten the non-discrimination rules governing employer contributions to these plans, which may still be as much as $30,000 annually per employee.

• **Government Retirees.** Eliminate a provision in existing law allowing public employees to receive tax-free pension benefits until the benefit payments exceed the total contributions made by the individual to his pension plan. Instead, the tax-free portion of the benefits would be spread out over the retiree's life expectancy. The new rule would apply to pensions received beginning July 1, 1986.

• **Other Pension Changes.** Make sweeping changes in tax laws governing private pension plans in an attempt to encourage firms to provide greater coverage for their lower- and middle-income employees, to shut off a variety of avenues for favoring highly compensated employees and to discourage employers from shifting a greater share of the cost of retirement savings to employees. Generally, the changes would be effective for pension plan years beginning after Dec. 31, 1988.

• Require that for an employer's pension plan to qualify for special tax treatment, the plan must cover 70 percent of the firm's employees. Under existing law, employers were required to cover only 56 percent or "a fair cross-section" of workers as the test of whether a pension plan treated employees fairly. Employers could still use the "fair cross-section" standard, but would then be required to provide all employees with at least 70 percent of the benefits received by those fully covered by the pension plan.

• Provide full vesting of employees in pension plans after five years on the job, instead of the existing 10 years. Alternatively, employees could be vested 20 percent after three years and 20 percent each year thereafter until 100 percent vested after seven years. The 10-year rule would be retained for multi-employer plans.

• Prohibit an employer from limiting an employee's retirement benefits by more than 50 percent, if the employer takes Social Security benefits into account when calculating the employee's benefits. Under existing law, some workers had their pension benefits entirely eliminated because anticipated Social Security benefits exceeded the anticipated pension amount.

• Impose a 10 percent tax on pension payments to an individual in excess of $112,500 a year.

• Encourage employers with 25 or fewer employees to set up Simplified Employee Pension plans, by permitting greater flexibility in how employer contributions are made and reducing administrative requirements.

• **Employee Stock Ownership Plans.** The 10 percent tax on assets returning to an owner upon termination of an ESOP would be eliminated. The penalties for withdrawals from ESOPs before age 59½ would be eliminated. Both of these exceptions to rules applied to other pension plans would expire in 1990.

Fringe Benefits

• **Overall.** Establish comprehensive non-discrimination rules for coverage of employee benefit plans, including health and life insurance coverage, and dependent care.

• **Health Insurance.** Allow self-employed individuals to deduct 25 percent of their health insurance premiums when calculating their tax liability. This provision would expire Jan. 1, 1990.

• **Prepaid Legal Assistance.** Extend for two years the exclusion from taxable income of employer-prepaid legal services.

• **Education Assistance.** Extend for two years the exclusion from taxable income of $5,250 in employer-paid education aid.

• **Child Care.** Limit to $5,000 a year the exclusion allowed for employer-provided child care assistance.

Compliance

• **Penalties.** Increase assorted penalties for failure to pay taxes or to file required information with the Internal Revenue Service (IRS). Penalties for tax underpayments due to negligence would be increased from 10 percent to 20 percent of the underpayment. Penalties for tax underpayments due to fraud would increase from 50 percent to 75 percent of the underpayment.

Interest rates on underpaid taxes would be adjusted to reflect changes in market rates more promptly, and interest owed would not be deductible, as it was under existing law.

Information reporting requirements to the IRS would also be expanded. For example, oil and gas royalties in excess of $100 would have to be reported to the IRS; existing law required reporting of royalties in excess of $600. Real estate brokers would be required for the first time to report transactions to the IRS. Tax-exempt interest would have to be reported after Dec. 31, 1987.

• **Estimated Tax Payments.** Increase estimated tax payments for individuals who do not have enough taxes withheld.

• **Revised Withholding Allowances.** Require the IRS to modify withholding schedules to reflect changes made by the bill, and to require all workers to file new withholding certificates (so-called W-4 forms) by Oct. 1, 1987, to prevent insufficient withholding as a result of changes in the withholding schedules.

• **Return-Free System.** Require a report from the IRS within six months of enactment on how it would implement a return-free tax system.

Background

Despite sporadic congressional interest in overhauling the federal income tax code, dating to early versions of the so-called Kemp-Roth tax cut proposal of 1981 (named for its authors, Rep. Jack F. Kemp, R-N.Y., and Sen. William V. Roth Jr., R-Del.) the task truly got under way following the president's call for reform in January 1984. *(Kemp-Roth tax cut, 1981 Almanac p. 91)*

The Treasury Department produced its version of an

Chronology of Congressional Tax Overhaul Efforts

- **August 1982.** Sen. Bill Bradley, D-N.J., and Rep. Richard A. Gephardt, D-Mo., introduce their "Fair Tax" plan (S 409, HR 800) to set individual tax rates at 14, 26 and 30 percent.
- **January 1984.** President Reagan calls in his State of the Union address for simplification of the federal tax system. He directs Treasury Secretary Donald T. Regan to draw up a plan by December 1984, one month following the next presidential election. *(1984 Almanac p. 6-E)*
- **April 1984.** Rep. Jack F. Kemp, R-N.Y., and Sen. Bob Kasten, R-Wis., introduce the "Fair and Simple Tax" (HR 2222, S 1006) to impose a flat 24 percent tax rate.
- **Fall 1984.** Democratic presidential candidate Walter F. Mondale accuses Reagan of having a "secret plan" to raise taxes after the election, and releases his own proposal to raise taxes to reduce the federal deficit.
- **November 1984.** The Treasury Department releases its blueprint for overhauling the federal tax system. Reagan's reaction is lukewarm and he says he is open to suggestions before submitting his own plan.
- **May 1985.** Reagan announces his tax-overhaul plan, which lowers individual and corporate tax rates, limits numerous special tax breaks and raises the same amount of revenue as the current tax system. House Ways and Means Committee Chairman Dan Rostenkowski, D-Ill., says Democrats will work with the president to draw up a bill. A summer of hearings begins in both the Ways and Means and Senate Finance committees. *(1985 Almanac p. 20-D)*
- **September 1985.** Ways and Means Committee staff draws up a draft tax plan, similar to Reagan's proposal, and the committee begins to mark up a bill.
- **October 1985.** Markup bogs down when Ways and Means Committee members vote to give banks a costly new tax advantage. Rostenkowski breaks the deadlock with backroom negotiations, including informal agreement that the state and local tax deduction will be retained.
- **Nov. 23, 1985.** Committee completes its markup amid growing partisanship. Republicans complain they were shut out of decision making in final hours, and talk of offering a substitute plan.
- **Dec. 4, 1985.** Reagan expresses lukewarm support for the Ways and Means bill and asks Congress to vote for either it or GOP plan to keep the tax-rewrite effort alive.
- **Dec. 11, 1985.** Tax bill is dealt a severe blow when the House votes 202-223 to reject the rule allowing the measure to come to the floor. Of 178 Republicans voting, only 14 voted for the rule.
- **Dec. 17, 1985.** After intense lobbying by the White House, the House reverses its vote on the rule and the Ways and Means tax bill is approved by voice vote. *(1985 Almanac p. 480)*
- **March 13, 1986.** His committee having rejected using the Ways and Means bill as its markup document, Finance Chairman Bob Packwood, R-Ore., puts his own plan on the table. Full of wish-list items, the bill uses controversial revenue-raisers, including restriction or elimination of individual deductions for most state and local taxes.
- **March 19, 1986.** The municipal bond market shuts down over a provision in Packwood's plan to subject all previously tax-free municipal bond income to the minimum tax. Some Finance members immediately object to the bond provision.
- **March 24, 1986.** Finance begins markup and in a 19-0 vote limits application of minimum tax to municipal bond interest to newly issued bonds.
- **April 18, 1986.** During three weeks of work, Finance members endorse additional tax breaks for Packwood's draft that would cost $29 billion in lost revenue over five years. Packwood suspends the markup, and over lunch with committee staff chief Bill Diefenderfer decides to offer a radical bill with a top individual rate of 25 percent and virtually no deductions.
- **May 7, 1986.** Committee votes 20-0 in favor of a bill with top rates of 27 percent for individuals and 33 percent for corporations after a day of open markup and a week of closed-door sessions.
- **June 24, 1986.** Senate votes 97-3 in favor of a bill largely unchanged from that reported by Finance. The key vote comes June 11, when proponents of a provision severely limiting Individual Retirement Accounts (IRAs) beat back 51-48 an effort to restore the tax break.
- **July 17, 1986.** Conferees begin work, but the conference bogs down over individual rates and the tax "hit" on corporations. Most of the work is done in one-house conferences, with offers passed back and forth. As negotiations drag into the second week of August, Rostenkowski and Packwood negotiate privately, taking agreements back to their colleagues for ratification.
- **Aug. 16, 1986.** Conference, by voice vote, endorses a bill that strongly resembles the Senate version. Of the 22 conferees, every Democrat is in favor and only five Republicans are opposed.
- **Sept. 25, 1986.** House votes 292-136 in favor of the conference agreement. It adopts at the same time a resolution making "technical corrections" in the conference bill, and sends both measures to the Senate.
- **Sept. 27, 1986.** Senate clears conference report by a vote of 74-23. Disagreements over provisions in the corrections resolution prevent its adoption, however, and the cleared tax bill is kept from the White House.
- **Oct. 22, 1986.** Reagan signs tax bill into law, and the technical corrections measure dies.

overhaul bill in November 1984, and in May 1985 Reagan offered up his own, somewhat different, proposal. It was only then that the Ways and Means and Finance committees settled into months of hearings on the idea.

Work began in the House, since the Constitution requires that chamber to generate revenue bills. In September, Ways and Means began a two-month period of closed, contentious markups, finally reporting HR 3838 on Dec. 7 (H Rept 99-426).

More than once during the markup it appeared that the votes were not there for the bill, and in the early morning hours of Nov. 23, it required Chairman Rostenkowski to engage in a spate of deal-cutting on rates, taxation of fringe benefits and other issues to win final support for the bill.

A formal vote was delayed for more than a week so that the complex legislation, previously agreed to in sketchy, outline form, could be drafted by staffers of the Ways and Means Committee and Joint Committee on Taxation.

Ways and Means members approved the bill Dec. 3 by a vote of 28-8. All 23 of the committee's Democrats and five Republicans voted for it. Of the five Republicans, only two — Raymond J. McGrath, N.Y., and Bill Gradison, Ohio — said they would definitely vote for the bill on the House floor, a signal of difficulties to come. The others said they were undecided, but voted for the bill in committee to move the debate to the full House.

Before the final vote, Republicans offered an alternative package, nearly identical to one offered later on the House floor. The proposal was defeated by an almost straight party-line vote of 12-24. The only Republican to vote against the alternative was McGrath, who opposed limits it would have placed on deducting state and local tax payments.

Trouble on the House Floor

Republican opposition to the measure was strong, and Democratic support weak. Rostenkowski, who many thought would never be able to get the bill through committee, began working feverishly behind the scenes to line up Democratic votes.

He was helped by many outside interest groups, including labor unions, small-business organizations and high-tech industries that favored the measure. However, their impact was muted by the strong opposition of other business groups, including the U.S. Chamber of Commerce and the National Association of Manufacturers.

And when the measure got to the floor Dec. 11, the House almost killed it, voting 202-223 against a rule to allow floor debate and keeping the bill off the floor for another week.

Democrats were not going to pass the bill without GOP help, but only 14 of 182 House Republicans voted for the rule. This was despite a plea from Reagan to pass the legislation — however flawed it may have been — so it could be improved in the Senate. Many GOP opponents were upset at the last-minute deals, charging that the measure fell short of Reagan's reform goals and would hurt the economy.

Unnerved by the devastating blow, Reagan and his lieutenants stepped up their campaign to pass the bill. Their tactics included a spate of phone calls and visits with wavering Republicans and an unusual trip by Reagan to Capitol Hill on Dec. 16.

Reagan reportedly told House Republicans, assembled in the Rayburn House Office Building, that "if tax reform is killed, if it doesn't pass the House in any form, then there will be no tax reform. I just can't accept we would let this historic initiative slip through our fingers."

But the president's personal appeal appeared to have less influence than assurances that he would send a letter to members vowing to veto any tax bill that reached his desk without a number of changes.

The letter, which members received the next day, set what Reagan called the "minimum requirements" for a bill that he would sign: lower rates, a higher personal exemption and more incentives for U.S. industries than were called for in the Ways and Means bill.

In addition, House Republican leaders won concessions from Democratic leaders the evening of Reagan's visit to make what amounted to little more than face-saving changes to the rule, which allowed them to offer a substitute, and a non-binding resolution regarding the measure's effective dates, but no amendments to the Ways and Means bill.

Many Republicans had complained that the Jan. 1, 1986, effective dates of many provisions in the bill were unfair in light of Senate inaction in 1985. The uncertainty, they argued, could hurt the economy.

With the agreement, House Speaker Thomas P. O'Neill Jr., D-Mass., received a phone call from Reagan telling him that he had rounded up at least 50 Republican votes for both the rule and final passage of the bill. The switches included some GOP leaders who had been united in opposition a week earlier. The Speaker had set the 50-vote requirement for bringing the bill back to the House floor.

On to the Senate

With 70 Republicans joining 188 Democrats, the rule was adopted Dec. 17 by a vote of 258-168. With that, the tide began to change.

The House then agreed to two Democratic amendments, including one restoring a form of the political contributions credit.

In debate on the overall bill, Republicans and some Democrats charged that HR 3838 would hurt the economy by eliminating tax incentives for new business investment. And they complained that the 1,000-page-plus bill did little to simplify existing tax law and was rife with the kinds of special-interest provisions that "tax reform" was intended to repeal.

But in the end, GOP Policy Committee Chairman Dick Cheney, Wyo., later acknowledged, the "powerful alliance" of the White House and the House majority could not be beaten.

In an impassioned speech before a full chamber, O'Neill asked members of both parties to vote for the rule to keep the bill alive. "It is a vote for the working people of America over the special interests. It is a vote for the individual taxpayer over the well-financed corporations," he said. "It is a vote to restore the confidence of our neighbor in the tax code."

As anticipated, the GOP alternative was turned down, by a nearly party-line vote of 133-294. And by a vote of 171-256, the House rejected a motion by Philip M. Crane, R-Ill., to recommit the bill to committee, a move that effectively would have killed the measure.

Then, in an anticlimactic finale to the emotional and lengthy fight, the House approved the Ways and Means bill without a recorded vote; it was apparently an oversight by

GOP leaders, who failed to ask for a roll call.

Afterwards, toasting his hard-won victory, Rostenkowski smiled and raised a glass of champagne not only to the accomplishment of the House, but "to a bumpy ride in the Senate."

Senate Committee Action

Just as the House eased slowly into the treacherous waters of the tax code, so, too, did the Senate. With HR 3838 in its hands at the start of 1986 and a clear mandate to make significant changes in it, the Finance Committee was far from united in the view that wholesale revision of the tax laws was necessary.

Finance Committee Chairman Bob Packwood, R-Ore., led his 19 colleagues on a private retreat Jan. 24 and 25 to begin assessing the House bill and their options, particularly how to pay for the changes Reagan had insisted upon, such as dropping the House bill's top individual tax rate of 38 percent to at least 35 percent.

Sufficient revenues — not particular tax code provisions — were clearly the biggest trouble to getting a bill that would pass, and the president would sign.

During the retreat, for example, Packwood floated the idea of ending or limiting individual deductions for state and local tax payments, a proposal that had been strongly opposed in the House. Some Finance members played down the early significance of the discussion, saying that the subject merely had not been "taken off the table," as Rostenkowski had done to gain votes during the House markup.

And the issue, in fact, was far from decided during the retreat. But the revenue gain proved too valuable, and eight months later the proposal had survived in the final bill, in the form of elimination of deductions for sales taxes.

But revenues also posed a different problem. Congress was quite sensitive to budget deficits in the aftermath of Gramm-Rudman. And as Packwood worked with Finance Committee staff members to prepare for markup, other senators pressed first for an agreement between Congress and the White House to reduce the deficit — using taxes, if necessary.

Finding the Money

Finance members rejected the idea of working from the House version of HR 3838, which was opposed by almost every member of the panel. Instead, they asked Packwood to produce a revenue-neutral markup draft of his own.

In the meantime, pressure continued to grow to reduce the deficit first, and to find sources of revenue to pay for retaining tax benefits lost in the House bill.

Senate Democrats by a vote of 31-3 Feb. 25 adopted a set of "tax policy principles" that rejected the use of any new taxes "to protect tax loopholes for the privileged few." Instead, the Democrats said, any new revenues should be used to help reduce the deficit.

And Reagan effectively cut off any consideration of an oil import fee, when he told reporters March 5 that he would oppose such a fee to keep the tax bill from increasing the deficit.

Packwood was not fazed by a letter sent by 50 senators March 4 to Reagan asking that action be delayed on the tax bill until agreement was reached between Congress and the White House on a budget. Seven of the signers were members of the Finance Committee, but the chairman released his draft bill March 13, and the panel went to work March 19.

The First Attempt

Many of the committee's 20 members gave tacit approval to the chairman's plan as a "starting point," but none embraced the package as a whole. He got a strong endorsement from ranking committee Democrat Russell B. Long of Louisiana, and Reagan reviewed the Packwood plan in a private meeting March 11 and reportedly gave his go-ahead.

The draft bill called for a top individual income tax rate of 35 percent and a personal exemption of $2,000 for taxpayers and their dependents in the lower- and middle-income tax brackets. It would have dramatically shifted the tax burden from individuals to corporations, but not by as much as the House-passed bill. And, as under the House bill, more than 6 million low-income taxpayers would have been dropped from the rolls. At the same time, Packwood would have kept the existing rapid depreciation system for business investments, although the investment tax credit would have been repealed.

The chairman proposed to pay for these expensive concessions with some controversial changes. He would have restricted or eliminated deductions for state and local sales, personal property and income taxes — leaving only real estate taxes fully deductible — and would have abolished business deductions for excise tax payments and tariffs. Packwood also would have allowed excise taxes on liquor, cigarettes and gasoline to rise with increases in product prices.

Eliminating the business excise-tax deduction would have raised $62 billion over five years, and the increase in excise taxes would have added another $13 billion. In the committee's first meeting on the bill March 19, however, several senators strongly criticized eliminating the tax deduction as an indirect tax increase on consumers that was being used to finance tax breaks for the wealthy.

Eleven committee members signed a letter to Packwood March 21 asking that hearings be held on the proposal, which was not considered by the House. Packwood responded that the panel would have to find alternatives: "Without that revenue, or a net equivalent source of revenue, then the things I tried to do in the draft cannot be done," he said.

In constructing his package, Packwood had made no secret that he acceded to what he called "the parochial interests" of committee members.

For example, he left existing tax breaks for the oil and gas industry intact for oil-state members Lloyd Bentsen, D-Texas; David L. Boren, D-Okla.; and Long. He protected timber industry tax breaks for himself, Long and George J. Mitchell, D-Maine. And he eliminated a proposal to restrict severely tax advantages for defense contractors at the request of John C. Danforth, R-Mo. Missouri's largest employer is McDonnell Douglas, one of the Pentagon's main aircraft and missile contractors.

In fact, just about every member of the panel had one or two provisions put in the package at the member's request.

The Bond Market Collapses

Provisions of the House-passed bill and Packwood's draft sent the municipal bond market into a state of panic as the markup began.

Trading in tax-exempt bonds already had slowed because of House provisions that would have — effective in 1986 — sharply curtailed their use for some purposes.

So, Packwood, Long, Rostenkowski, Ways and Means ranking Republican John J. Duncan of Tennessee and Treasury Secretary James A. Baker III agreed March 14 that no restrictions on the issuance of any bonds used for strictly governmental purposes would go into effect before Sept. 1, 1986, or the date of enactment of a tax-overhaul bill, whichever came first.

Left uncovered by the agreement were industrial development and other tax-exempt bonds issued by state and local governments for private purposes.

The announcement eased the market's tensions for several days. Then, as details of Packwood's plan became clear March 19, the market shut down.

Packwood had crafted a minimum tax proposal that, he said, was designed to be escape proof. To do so, he had proposed taxing the proceeds of otherwise tax-free municipal bonds. Only those wealthy individuals whose ordinary income tax liability was very low, triggering minimum tax provisions, would have been affected. Nevertheless, they were a substantial part of the municipal bond market.

Municipal bond interest had never before been subject to even the minimum tax, and Packwood's draft bill would have taxed all such previously tax-exempt holdings, including those issued before enactment of the bill.

The House bill would have applied the minimum tax only to newly issued tax-exempt bonds, leaving alone bonds already owned or up for resale in the market. It also would not have applied to bonds issued to finance essential government services.

The result was an immediate drop in the market value of existing bonds and the inability of state and local governments to issue bonds at low interest rates. New York state, for example, postponed a planned sale of $450 million in general obligation bonds because of the confusion.

An administration official denied claims by Packwood that the Treasury Department had requested he make the change, but said instead that officials suggested the chairman phase in the proposal, as he did, or apply it only to newly acquired bonds, "if he meant to go that far."

The day the bond market collapsed, 10 Finance members wrote Packwood that the provision was "not warranted and should be immediately reversed." But the chairman defended it March 21 as the only way to construct an "inescapable" minimum tax, ensuring that all wealthy individuals and profit-making corporations pay some tax.

Despite his concerns, the committee agreed 19-0 March 24, in its first markup vote, to limit the municipal tax provision to bonds issued after Jan. 1, 1987. It left uncertain the status of bonds issued after that date.

The issue continued to be debated all year, but momentum favored those who would tax some municipal bond interest.

Alfonse M. D'Amato, R-N.Y., and Long succeeded in killing a similar proposal to include tax-exempt interest in the minimum tax during Senate floor consideration of the Tax Equity and Fiscal Responsibility Act of 1982 (PL 97-248). *(1982 Almanac pp. 35, 44-S)*

"To some, the issue of taxing individual income from municipal bonds may sound like an esoteric subject for financiers only," said D'Amato. "But what we are really talking about is the ability of local government to repair roads, build hospitals, and collect the garbage without the necessity of raising taxes."

But they had less success in 1986. As enacted, the bill included a provision subjecting interest on most private-purpose municipal bonds issued after Aug. 8, 1986, to the minimum tax.

More Trouble Ahead

The bond crisis was not the only sign that markup would be difficult.

Committee members made little secret the first few days that they would try to retain special tax advantages that Packwood proposed to eliminate. For example, a majority of the panel appeared inclined to approve a business depreciation system more generous than current law.

In fact, the only Packwood proposals debated during the first week that received little criticism were those to retain or expand existing tax breaks for agriculture, energy, timber and other natural resources, such as oil, gas and coal.

The initial sessions March 24-26 were also marked by confusion and some criticism from members about markup procedures and the lack of information about the economic impact of proposed tax changes, a complaint heard throughout the two years of debate on the bill.

"It seems to me like we're taking a huge gamble with our economy," said Steve Symms, R-Idaho, an outspoken opponent of the bill. "I think we'd be a heck of a lot better off just to adjourn."

But for those on the committee who wanted the tax code overhauled, the initial sessions were not totally disheartening.

Some Finance members had been outspoken for months about their reluctance to eliminate existing tax breaks. And the meetings gave members a chance to feel each other out on their positions and to engage in some of the posturing that often was necessary before difficult decisions could be made.

"I think they were three good days," said Bradley. "You begin to see where the threats are.... You begin to get a sense of what you need to do to get a bill through."

Digging a Hole

The committee's willingness to restore or retain tax breaks began to cost. After three more days of voting, April 8-10, the committee found itself more than $10 billion in the hole in its effort to keep revenues at their existing level over five years.

Meanwhile, the full Senate reiterated earlier warnings that Reagan's cherished tax effort could be derailed unless the White House moved to negotiate on a deficit-reduction package.

By a vote of 72-24, the Senate agreed April 10 to a non-binding resolution that the tax bill should not be considered or debated on the floor "until a firm, definite budget agreement has been reached" between Reagan and Congress. *(Vote 60, p. 12-S)*

Although some members voted "aye" to force action on the budget, Packwood charged that an ulterior motive for many was to kill the tax bill. Opponents "are willing to use every dilatory tactic they can to avoid considering a tax bill," he told colleagues on the floor.

Thirteen of the 20 Finance members voted for the resolution, and Packwood insisted the Senate vote would have no impact on the committee's work. Yet there were signs of deterioration in the committee. "None of us are committed to tax reform," Malcolm Wallop, R-Wyo., observed during the markup.

The biggest blight on the overhaul efforts was the panel's 12-8 vote April 10 in favor of a new depreciation system for business investments that would cost about $14.3 billion more than existing law over five years, and about $10 billion more than Packwood's draft.

Charging that the House-passed tax bill would hurt U.S. international competitiveness, members agreed to create a new category of what they labeled "productive" investments that would qualify for generous depreciation benefits.

Covered by the change would have been an array of investments, including those in equipment for manufacturing, mining, construction, agriculture, land improvements, transportation and telephone communications.

The panel agreed, however, not to include an administration-backed proposal to index the value of investments to reflect increases in inflation, a proposal that would have cost an additional $7 billion over five years.

Earlier that week, the committee had rejected attempts to limit existing tax advantages for the oil, gas, timber, mineral and other "natural resource" industries, and to eliminate a number of energy-related tax credits.

Packwood would have retained or expanded tax advantages enjoyed by these industries at a cost of about $1 billion over five years. And Bradley made a futile attempt to delete the tax breaks with a series of amendments; he was never able to get more than three votes of support.

Bradley noted that a number of the tax advantages the committee wanted to retain primarily benefited the wealthy. For example, he said, half of the benefits of a one-year write-off for "intangible" oil and gas drilling costs, such as labor and fuel, go to 31,000 taxpayers with adjusted gross incomes over $100,000.

But oil-state members on the panel complained that with oil prices dropping rapidly, the industry could ill afford to have drilling incentives reduced. "I couldn't think of a worse time to do this," said Bentsen.

But the committee did turn down one request for special treatment.

It narrowly rejected an amendment by John Heinz, R-Pa., to allow firms that rent tuxedos and other formal wear to write off their investments over a three-year period, instead of five years as in the draft bill.

Heinz, whose state was home to two large formal-wear manufacturers, argued that most rental tuxedos do not last for five years. But the estimated $100 million, five-year cost for the change was too much for other panel members.

"There are some things that make us look foolish and there are some things that make us look really foolish.... This is outrageous," said Packwood.

The amendment was rejected 5-6.

Markup Suspended

The week of April 14 nearly broke the committee's back. Five more days of dealing like the previous seven culminated April 18 in Packwood's decision to suspend the markup.

With the panel already $10 billion in the hole, it approved a series of changes affecting private pensions, tax-exempt bonds, foreign taxation and other issues that left it a total of $29 billion short of producing a revenue-neutral bill.

One of the most significant changes, at a five-year cost to the Treasury of $4.7 billion, was designed to encourage firms to provide more retirement coverage for their lower- and middle-income employees. By a vote of 18-2, the panel April 16 adopted a package of changes proposed by Heinz to limit so-called "top-heavy" plans, which primarily benefited the highest-paid workers.

In addition, the panel agreed by voice vote to a costly amendment by John H. Chafee, R-R.I., that would have allowed public employees to continue paying no taxes on their pension benefits until the benefit payments exceeded the amount the individual contributed to the pension plan.

Packwood's proposal, as well as the House bill, would have required these beneficiaries to pay taxes on at least some portion of their benefits as soon as they retired.

Although the total amount of taxes on the benefits would not change, more would have to be paid in the earlier years of retirement, raising an estimated $7.4 billion over five years.

Chafee and others argued that many federal, state and local workers had based their retirement plans on the assumption they would have up to three years of tax-free benefits. The provision, strenuously opposed by federal employee groups, proved extremely controversial in the House and almost prevented House floor consideration of the tax bill.

Ironically, Chafee was one of the few Finance members who had spoken strongly in favor of limiting special tax breaks so that overall rates could be reduced. He repeatedly had criticized colleagues for proposing costly amendments that could jeopardize the bill.

When reminded of this by Packwood as he proposed a revenue-losing amendment, Chafee replied that cost "hasn't seemed to slow anybody else down. I'm at the point where if you can't beat 'em, join 'em.... And it's a large crowd to join."

Markup was suspended late the morning of April 18, surprising both members and observers, as the panel was preparing to address a series of Packwood proposals to limit deductions for individual taxpayers, including those taken for state and local tax payments and for business meal and entertainment expenses.

Packwood said it was clear from a number of private conversations with committee members that he would lose on several votes to limit the deductions and the costs could prove disastrous.

Moreover, Packwood's proposal to raise $75 billion through a package of excise tax increases and elimination of business deductions for excise payments seemed in certain trouble.

"I don't want to give any impression that we have any idea of quitting," Packwood said, but it was clear he was uncertain how to proceed. "I think the time has come to simply reflect on the way we are going," Packwood said. He added later that he "did not want to run the risk of killing this bill by going ahead."

Committee members had acknowledged for several days that the panel was fast approaching a crisis point that made Packwood's decision inevitable.

The Ways and Means Committee hit a similar turning point in its markup, when panel members did the most politically attractive thing and voted to retain special-interest tax breaks. It was only after tough behind-the-scenes negotiating by Rostenkowski that a bill began to emerge.

"I think we're at a predictable point in these deliberations," said Bradley. "I think we are going to be in the back room making some trades. It won't be as pure as I would like, but I think we can come out with something that reduces rates for the majority, gets low-income people off the rolls and improves the economy."

Lunch and a Beer

The afternoon of April 18, over lunch and a couple of pitchers of beer, Packwood and his staff director, William Diefenderfer, devised the strategy that would ultimately bring a bill to the Senate floor. Their concept — it was hardly more — was to chop tax rates far more dramatically than had previously been discussed, and at the same time eliminate virtually all deductions.

It took two weeks of private negotiations, and another major revision, but their simple plan was forged into a bill that survived the committee, the Senate floor and, in its essence, the conference.

Though it was unknown until the committee finished its work, the successful strategy for reviving the bill was hung on what Packwood described as a "core group of Democrats and Republicans, liberals and conservatives, rural and urban" senators. The six other members were Democrats Bradley, Mitchell and Daniel Patrick Moynihan of New York, and Republicans Chafee, Wallop and Danforth.

They met privately every day with staff and sometimes also with Deputy Treasury Secretary Richard G. Darman, beginning April 18.

The key was for these senators to stop trying to preserve or expand tax benefits enjoyed by their own constituents and supporters in exchange for the prospect of a major reduction in tax rates and simplification of the tax law.

"It was like a poker game. Everyone anted up to make the pot worthwhile," Packwood said.

On April 24, the committee got its first glimpse of Packwood's radical plan, but opposition developed to some of its key elements.

Members were shown a three-page document prepared for Packwood by the staff of the Joint Committee on Taxation, outlining one option for achieving two individual income tax rates — 15 percent and 25 percent. All deductions, including those for home mortgage interest, state and local tax payments, charitable donations and Individual Retirement Accounts, were slated for elimination.

The proposal also called for a drop in the top corporate tax rate from the current 46 percent to 33 percent. It assumed continuation of some corporate tax advantages already approved by the committee, including those for rapid depreciation of business investments.

Corporate taxes would have been increased $70 billion over five years and individual tax collections would have been cut $95 billion. To keep the bill revenue-neutral, excise taxes would have been increased by $25 billion.

The proposal was publicly released the following day, the second consecutive Friday for a surprising tax announcement. Packwood, however, backed away from its details, which he credited to David H. Brockway, staff director of the Joint Taxation Committee.

Packwood said he wanted to keep some individual deductions, and was looking for ways to do so, but not lose revenue.

In hopes of finding common ground, the core group and the full committee met again behind closed doors for most of the week of April 28, reviewing additional options from Joint Taxation that pushed rates a percentage point or two higher, while altering the mix of preserved tax breaks.

Then, in yet another Friday surprise, Packwood announced May 2 that panel members had reached a consensus on a proposal to cut the top individual income tax rate to 27 percent and to curtail a number of special tax breaks, especially those used for tax shelter investments.

Making a Miracle

The committee sat down May 5 to work on this final option in open session, and in a turnabout of such swiftness and scope that it astounded the very men who brought it off, the committee unanimously approved the outlines of the bill barely a day later. Only 28 hours elapsed from the time the committee took its first formal votes on amendments to the time it voted final approval.

Ultimately, the bill was not reported until May 29 (S Rept 99-313); it took the Finance and Joint Taxation staffs that long to translate the general principles agreed to by committee members into legislative language. Perhaps more surprising, the bill as reported survived almost intact on the Senate floor, and became the basis for the bill drafted in conference.

The proposed changes in the individual income tax were the most fundamental since 1943, when tax withholding and a steeply progressive tax-rate structure first became law. And, while the changes in corporate taxation were less basic, they were major and were expected to have diverse effects on different types of businesses.

The bill was expected to cut individual income taxes (and a few minor taxes) by an estimated $105 billion and increase the total tax load on corporations by the same amount.

Because the panel moved with such swiftness, and there was so little detail available — to senators or to the public — the usual coterie of tax lobbyists was able to do little more than watch and wince as cherished provisions were eliminated. Since the House markup began in September 1985, lobbyists had lined the halls outside meeting rooms, buttonholing members and sending in messages with staff.

Despite concern from some sectors, however, the bill quickly earned considerable business support, particularly from those who preferred much lower tax rates and creation of a "level playing field," without special provisions that favored investment in some industries over others.

Key Provisions

Major provisions of the Finance Committee bill as it directly affected individuals would have:

- Reduced the existing individual tax rate structure of 14 brackets, ranging from 11 to 50 percent, to two brackets, 15 and 27 percent, with 80 percent of all taxpayers taxed solely at the 15 percent rate.
- Removed more than 6 million of the working poor, all those with incomes at or slightly above the officially defined poverty level, from the tax rolls.
- Taxed capital gains at the same rates as ordinary income.
- Abolished a long list of deductions and exemptions, some used by middle-income families and others almost entirely by the well-to-do. Among those tax breaks to be eliminated were: interest on consumer purchases and loans, the $2,000 annual tax-exempt investment in Individual Retirement Accounts, which would have been restricted to those not covered by any pension plan except Social Security, the use of tax shelter investments to offset income with paper losses, except for certain investments in exploration for oil.

Despite the limitations and terminations of these and other tax breaks, most individuals were expected to wind up paying lower taxes, and the average cut was projected to be about 6 percent.

The abolition of most tax shelters was estimated to

bring in $48.5 billion in revenue over five years, which, along with elimination of the special capital gains rate, was the key to the sharply reduced rates in the bill.

Major provisions as they affected corporate taxation would have:

- Reduced the top corporate tax rate from 46 to 33 percent.
- Repealed the 10 percent investment tax credit, retroactive to Jan. 1, 1986 — the only major retroactive provision anywhere in the bill. Loss of the tax credit would have been somewhat offset by more generous deductions for depreciation.
- Tightened the corporate minimum tax.
- Maintained existing tax breaks for the oil and gas industry, and other mining and natural resources businesses.

The Finance bill also would have left excise taxes unchanged.

As reported, the measure contained at least one group of provisions that would have had little effect on tax revenues but that are of widespread importance: those dealing with qualified pension plans.

The bill would have increased the number of persons who must be covered under such plans, shortened the time periods for vesting and limited the extent to which employers were allowed to offset the benefits paid retired workers by the amount of their income from Social Security.

The chief beneficiaries of these changes were expected to be women, who tended to remain in jobs for shorter periods of time than men, and blue-collar and other less highly paid employees.

The Last Battle

During the measure's consideration by the full Finance Committee May 5 and 6 and until 12:19 a.m. May 7, dozens of amendments were added.

Most were small in their revenue impact. More importantly, under an agreement Packwood successfully pressed on the committee early in its deliberations (over the objections of former Chairman Long and a few others) all amendments were required to be revenue-neutral. One big package of more than three dozen amendments, $14 billion-plus worth of revenue-losers and an equal dollar value in gainers, was hammered out in a five-hour, closed-door meeting late May 6.

It was this session that later produced the final public dispute in the committee's remarkable two days of work, and almost the only issue that was argued in public with any obvious anger.

That was the decision essentially to exempt oil investments from the crackdown on tax shelters.

Advocates of this change said investors in these shelters were taking real economic risks, and thus entitled to deduct their losses, whereas opponents claimed the decision to continue deductibility of losses from oil shelter investments rested on nothing except the political power of the oil industry in the committee.

Bradley made two attempts to undo the oil shelter provision — first all of it and then part of it — but lost both times.

When it was all over, and the unexpected 20-0 vote to report the bill had been recorded, Packwood said that some people who had come by to shake his hand after the session had told him that approval of such a bill was "a miracle."

"If you don't believe in miracles, you're just not a realist," he said.

Senate Floor Action

Senate floor debate on the tax bill (HR 3838) opened June 4 with bipartisan praise and surprisingly, for legislation that admittedly would have adverse effects on an unknown number of individuals and businesses, with only one senator even raising the possibility that he might vote against it.

That was John Melcher, D-Mont., who expressed concern about the bill's consequences for Montana's three largest industries — agriculture, mining and timber, all of which were depressed.

Three weeks later, after 13 days and not a few nights of debate and amendment, the Senate June 24 passed the bill that nearly everyone agreed was worthy of its name: the Tax Reform Act of 1986.

The vote was 97-3. The lone dissenters, all Democrats, were Carl Levin of Michigan, Paul Simon of Illinois and Melcher. *(Vote 148, p. 27-S)*

The non-partisanship that characterized most of the bill's time on the floor was at least as extraordinary as the contents of the measure itself. But the opening debate nonetheless featured numerous complaints about specific provisions of the bill, and the intention of the bill's backers to push it through the Senate quickly, with no amendments.

Democrats, in particular, protested that they had not had time to study the 1,489-page bill, which had reached their desks only two days before.

Mostly, however, there was praise for the committee and the bill.

Packwood, setting the rhetorical tone at the beginning of debate, said: "Somehow this country was founded, settled, explored, mined, timbered, farmed and finally moved west without any tax code. Babies were born even when there was no personal exemption. Companies were founded when there was no special capital gains treatment."

He begged the Senate to "seize an opportunity that probably will not come again in a generation" to break "that ever-increasing cycle of raise the rates and raise the deductions and raise the rates and raise the deductions."

Anti-Amendment Rule

Despite the rhetoric, floor action got off to a slow start, with nearly four days of delays and posturing before the first votes.

Some of the posturing — particularly a series of speeches attacking the bill's limits on Individual Retirement Accounts, was credited to the Senate's first experience with broadcast television coverage of its proceedings. The chamber was opened to cameras June 2, and the tax bill was the first major item on the agenda in the new era. *(Senate TV, p. 43)*

An additional problem was the requirement that amendments be revenue-neutral; this restriction was enforced by Packwood in the committee, and he insisted on adhering to it on the floor.

But the chief reason for the delay was that no one wanted to be the first to offer an amendment to the bill before the waters had been tested by someone else. As Packwood put it June 11: "No one wants to go first and get beaten 55-45 or 60-40 or worse."

Once the Senate began debating amendments, however, many fell by the wayside, usually because of the demand for revenue-neutrality. Sponsors of amendments that would have reduced taxes in some way were unable to attract majority support for any method of raising the counterbalancing tax increases.

Some amendments failed, however, simply because of the consensus that there should be none, for fear that approval of even one would open the floodgates to many others.

Among these was a proposal by Gordon J. Humphrey, R-N.H., Jesse Helms, R-N.C., and William L. Armstrong, R-Colo., to terminate the tax-exempt status of any organization that performed or financed abortions or permitted its facilities to be used for them. The provision would have hit non-profit hospitals and abortion clinics and tax-exempt organizations, such as foundations, that fund these institutions.

The three senators dropped their plans for the amendment without formally introducing it after a meeting with the president at the White House. Humphrey said the president wanted no amendments to the bill but also promised he would support their amendment if they offered it later to some other essential piece of legislation.

Other amendments that were dropped without formal action under the no-amendment principle included two that would have denied tax benefits to personal income and corporate profits earned in countries that support terrorism.

Fighting Off IRAs

The real test of the Senate's determination to fend off amendments came, however, over Individual Retirement Accounts (IRAs).

It was the subject on which senators received by far the most mail — Symms said he had gotten more than 900 pieces a week. Senators said the letters were handwritten for the most part, demonstrating their grass-roots origins, not the preprinted post cards that interest groups sometimes distributed for signature and mailing.

The key IRA amendment, sponsored by D'Amato, was killed June 11, by a 51-48 vote, on a motion to table it. Senators of both parties who faced re-election in 1986 disproportionally voted to keep tax breaks for IRAs; all nine Democrats who were running voted that way, as did half of the 18 Republicans. *(Vote 125, p. 23-S)*

D'Amato's amendment would have replaced the existing law $2,000 tax-deductible IRA contribution for all wage earners with a tax credit of 15 percent of $2,000, or $300. The change would have resulted in a somewhat smaller revenue loss over five years than the existing deduction. D'Amato would have covered the revenue loss with an increase in the minimum tax rate.

Packwood concentrated his attack on both the concentration of IRAs among those taxpayers with incomes above $40,000 and the increase in the minimum tax, which the Finance bill already would have raised dramatically.

His success in killing D'Amato's amendment, and two others restoring IRAs that fell immediately afterwards by large margins, set the stage for turning back other amendments that had strong backing, including one restoring deductions for state and local sales taxes.

As part of their strategy to defeat D'Amato's amendment, Packwood earlier the same day made sure every senator had a chance to tell his constituents that he had really tried to protect their IRA deductions, by voting for a sense-of-the-Senate amendment affirming the Senate's commitment to restoring IRA benefits in conference with the House.

The amendment called for Senate conferees to assign "highest priority to maintaining maximum possible tax benefits for IRAs." But it also required conferees to do this "in a manner which does not adversely affect the tax rates or distribution by income class" of the tax cuts voted by the Finance Committee. It passed 96-4, just before D'Amato's amendment was killed. *(Vote 124, p. 23-S)*

The point that this language had no binding effect was made repeatedly and angrily by advocates of a substantive amendment restoring IRA benefits. Senate Minority Leader Robert C. Byrd, D-W.Va., protested that "the sense-of-the-Senate resolution does not accomplish anything. [It is] an effort to make people believe that something has been done."

But Roth, the resolution's sponsor, said the amendment, if adopted by an overwhelming vote — as it was — "will preserve the IRA." Roth's promise, however, went only partially fulfilled.

Sales Tax Deduction

The next major fight on the floor erupted the next day, June 12, over the bill's elimination of the sales tax deduction.

Senators from states that relied heavily on sales taxes objected that the provision was unfair, and that the bill would pressure states to adopt other revenue sources. The assumption was that if state income or property taxes were deductible on federal returns and sales taxes were not, there would be demands for greater use of the other taxes, since they would cost a citizen less after the federal deduction.

Long, whose home state of Louisiana collected 68 percent of its revenue from a sales tax, noted that, if states did adopt property or income taxes in lieu of sales taxes, over time the U.S. Treasury would suffer because the amount of income or property tax deductions would rise.

An amendment by Alan J. Dixon, D-Ill., restoring full deductibility for sales taxes, balanced by a partial disallowance of all types of itemized deductions, was defeated by voice vote after lengthy debate.

Then a second amendment, sponsored by Daniel J. Evans, R-Wash., and Phil Gramm, R-Texas, was withdrawn. Neither Washington state nor Texas had an income tax. And Evans and Gramm would have permitted individuals to deduct either the sales tax or the income tax on their federal returns. "The fact that citizens in other states can deduct their income taxes is just fine. We ought to have that same privilege in Washington," Evans said.

They withdrew the amendment after Bradley pointed out that its adoption would have put the issue of deductibility of state income taxes on the conference table. Senators from the 42 states that had income taxes did not want to risk that.

After turning aside the substantive sales tax amendments, senators borrowed from the book on IRAs and voted in vain 76-21 to tell conferees to keep all deductions for state and local taxes. *(Vote 129, p. 24-S)*

Key Packwood Victory

The commitment to defeating all major changes in the tax rates and basic reform elements of the bill as written in committee was most strikingly demonstrated with the defeat June 18, by a lopsided 71-29 vote, of what ordinarily might have been considered a politically irresistible amendment. *(Vote 137, p. 25-S)*

That was a proposal by Mitchell to provide a bigger tax reduction for middle-income taxpayers by taxing the well-to-do somewhat more, and other taxpayers somewhat less. His amendment would have changed the two rates of 15 and 27 percent in the committee's bill to a three-rate system of 14, 27 and 35 percent.

"My amendment has one purpose and one purpose only," Mitchell said, "to provide meaningful tax relief to the millions of Americans in the middle class.... It will fulfill the missing promise of the Finance Committee bill by extending to middle-income taxpayers the real tax relief that the bill promises to all but delivers only to the rich and the poor."

Packwood led the fight against the amendment.

"I fear this Trojan Horse amendment is going to be the front for every interest group to say, 'Please give us now our special exemption because you've raised the rates too high for us to invest in low-income housing or venture capital or contribute to charity, or whatever.' "

Mitchell emphasized, in particular, the bill's relatively small tax cut for individuals and families with incomes of $30,000 to $40,000 — $129 a year, on the average, or less than $2.50 a week — compared with larger figures for every other income group, except those with incomes of $10,000 or less, who paid little income tax under existing law.

He argued that his proposal would have given a big tax cut to many wealthy persons, though it would not have been as large as under the committee bill.

Persons with incomes of $200,000 a year or more who had not been "extensively sheltering" their income with various legal tax-saving devices would have received an annual tax cut of about $35,000 a year under his proposal, he said, compared with $53,000 under the committee bill.

He said he had been surprised by figures from the Joint Committee on Taxation, which showed that only one-third to one-half of those in this upper-income group did make extensive use of tax shelters.

Upper-income persons who had been avoiding most or all income tax would have seen their taxes increased substantially, however, so that the entire group with more than $200,000 in income would have paid an average of $3,050 a year more under the Mitchell amendment. Under the committee bill, despite the termination of most tax-shelter opportunities, this group would have received an average tax cut of $5,892.

When the roll was finally called, June 18, after five hours' debate, scarcely more than half the Democrats voted for the amendment, and only four Republicans, including three who faced tough re-election races in 1986: Mark Andrews, N.D.; Slade Gorton, Wash.; and Arlen Specter, Pa.

A second attempt to give the middle class a bigger tax cut than under the committee bill, sponsored by Dennis DeConcini, D-Ariz., went down by a much larger margin the next day: 92-7. DeConcini would have increased the income levels at which the 27 percent tax rate was to take effect. *(Vote 141, p. 26-S)*

After that, the Senate passed, 94-1, yet another sense-of-the-Senate amendment, offered by Donald W. Riegle Jr., D-Mich., this time instructing Senate conferees to give "highest priority" to increasing the tax cut for all middle-income persons. *(Vote 143, p. 26-S)*

Granting Members' Wishes

As debate wound down in the third week, senators stood firm against major amendments, but they also began the traditional Senate process of loading up the bill with many small "presents" for specific interests.

The sudden approval of numerous amendments, benefiting such narrow interests as a physicians' self-insurance company in Omaha and such broad ones as farmers trying to renegotiate their debts, appeared partly a matter of deliberate strategy on the part of their sponsors.

The "Christmas tree" tradition called for sponsors to wait before submitting amendments until the Senate was too tired, and too impatient to pass the bill, to give them much scrutiny. Many who offered amendments said, however, that they had been delayed by the necessity of obtaining estimates of the revenue effects of their proposals from the overworked staff of the Joint Committee on Taxation.

In either event, the fact was that Senate Majority Leader Robert Dole, R-Kan., had repeatedly, through days of listless debate and no action, begged senators to bring up their amendments for consideration. But almost none did until Dole began talking about bringing about a final vote on the bill within 48 hours or so.

Many of the special interest amendments that were finally proffered were defeated, more often than not because of objections to the way that the necessary offsetting revenues were to be raised.

A Break in the Dam?

The vote that first demonstrated that significant amendments could be added to the bill came June 17 on an amendment sponsored by Howard M. Metzenbaum, D-Ohio. The amendment reversed the Finance Committee's decision to repeal a law enacted in 1980, the Foreign Investors Real Property Tax Act (FIRPTA), which imposed taxes on capital gains made by foreign investors on real estate in the United States.

The motion to kill this amendment failed, 18-80, and even Packwood and Bradley, the two staunchest advocates of keeping all amendments off the bill, voted with Metzenbaum. *(Vote 134, p. 25-S)*

There were several obvious reasons why Metzenbaum succeeded. First, many senators were clearly embarrassed at the idea of making it more attractive for rich foreigners to buy land from distressed American farmers, though Wallop, who made the motion to table the amendment, argued that near-bankrupt farmers would be glad to see any purchaser who came along.

Perhaps even more important politically, however, were the uses to which the Metzenbaum amendment would put the $1.2 billion the amendment was expected to raise.

Of the total, $1 billion was to be used to permit deductions of medical expenses that exceeded 9 percent of adjusted gross income, instead of the 10 percent in the committee bill. The "floor" was 5 percent under existing law.

The other $200 million was to be used to permit farmers to continue income averaging, a special calculation that reduced the taxes of persons whose income varies significantly from year to year. The Finance Committee bill would have eliminated averaging.

Mounting pressure from the elderly to reduce the floor under medical deductions, and from farmers to permit them to continue income averaging, had made it likely that amendments to deal with both of these issues might have to be added to the bill in any event. The Metzenbaum amendment presented an easy opportunity to accomplish both objectives.

Sales Taxes Win Temporary Reprieve

After the amendment dam broke, broad-based public concern about the loss of sales tax deductions finally led to adoption of a second Evans and Gramm amendment to restore part of the deduction.

Packwood accepted the Evans-Gramm amendment June 19, without a fight.

The amendment, adopted by voice vote, would have permitted deductions for 60 percent of the amount of state and local sales taxes paid that exceeded the amount of state and local income tax paid. In states with no income tax, that would have meant that 60 percent of the sales tax could be deducted.

The relatively minor revenue loss of $2 billion was to be recouped by requiring all who claimed a dependent over the age of four to get and report a Social Security number for the dependent. Claims of dependents by more than one person were thought to be a major method of illegal tax evasion by middle-income persons. The Evans-Gramm amendment would also have tightened the tax rules surrounding the complicated transactions known as commodity "straddles."

Although it was expected that the Senate would yield in conference on the sales tax question — the House bill retained the full deduction — even the modest Evans-Gramm compromise did not make it into the final bill.

Transition Rule Imbroglio

Before the Senate could finish action on the bill, it had to deal with Metzenbaum, who single-mindedly fought many provisions, usually called "transition rules," that granted special tax treatment to individual firms.

He had a raft of amendments to eliminate some of the bill's 174 such provisions, and his first effort to strike one, aiding Union Oil Co. of California (Unocal), was successful.

The committee bill would have saved Unocal an estimated $50 million in taxes, but Metzenbaum argued that a Unocal transaction granted a tax credit in the committee bill was not eligible for such treatment either under existing law or under the other language of the bill.

Thus, he said, the provision was improper under the principle that was supposed to govern transition rules; namely, that they were to help those unfairly treated by changes from existing law to new.

His view prevailed, as the Senate voted down, 33-60, a motion by Pete Wilson, R-Calif., to kill the amendment. Among those voting with Metzenbaum were Packwood and Dole. *(Vote 131, p. 25-S)*

In part because Metzenbaum complained so loudly about existing transition rules in the bill, Packwood was able to fight off a host of amendments granting similar rules.

More than 200 were said to have been proposed in the last few days the bill was on the floor.

Packwood said it would be impossible to scrutinize them in less than a matter of weeks and promised they would get full consideration in the conference committee. He also openly criticized their sponsors for offering them so late in the game.

That drew a furious response from Ted Stevens, R-Alaska, who voiced the frustrations of many others.

Stevens said it was not until he saw the transition rules permitted for other senators' constituents that he recognized that he had constituents with the same problems. But his proposed amendments were required to be "revenue neutral," whereas those that went into the committee bill were not.

"All I'm asking is fairness," he said. "The Senate should demand no less."

Other Amendments Defeated, Adopted

As for broader amendments, interest groups and lawmakers who backed them were largely forced to abandon hope.

Groups of senators who had wanted to ease the committee's restrictions on real estate tax shelters, and to keep the capital gains tax at its existing 20 percent top rate instead of the 27 percent in the committee bill, made no formal fight for amendments. Instead, they contented themselves with "colloquies," choreographed discussions among senators on the floor, to make a record of the arguments that they hoped would influence the conference.

The Senate did act on a large number of amendments, including the following:

- By Bob Kasten, R-Wis., and Daniel K. Inouye, D-Hawaii, that would have retained the existing law right of persons who did not itemize deductions to take a deduction for charitable contributions. Its revenue loss would have been counterbalanced by reducing the personal exemption for additional upper-income taxpayers. It lost, 51-44, June 13. *(Vote 130, p. 25-S)*
- By Lowell P. Weicker Jr., R-Conn., to put the same restrictions on oil and gas industry tax shelters as on other types of shelters, instead of providing a special exception for persons defined as having some liability, beyond their original investment, in oil and gas drilling.

The Weicker amendment provoked a sarcastic outburst from Dole, whose home state produced some oil, mostly from relatively small wells.

"This is an exception," he said. "But there are other exceptions. I hope that if we are going to start down that track we are going to go all the way ... [and] also exclude employer-paid group health and life insurance. These are big incentives to a lot of insurance companies, maybe even some in Connecticut. We knew we were not going to produce a perfect bill. We did the very best we could." Weicker's amendment was tabled, 77-20, June 12. *(Vote 128, p. 24-S)*

- By David Pryor, D-Ark., to eliminate a section of the committee bill that would have given the steel industry the right to carry back unused investment tax credits for 15 years, instead of the existing law three years, and thus receive refunds of taxes they paid earlier, in profitable years.

The provision was estimated to cost $500 million, or one-tenth of the total for all transition rules in the bill.

Heinz June 17 succeeded in killing Pryor's attempt to strike this provision, by a vote of 65-29, on a motion to table. Heinz' success was attributed in part to the perceived national security need to maintain a domestic steel industry. But also important was the fact that he was the first Republican, apart from the original bipartisan "core group" of seven senators, publicly to announce his support for Packwood's low-tax and few-special-benefits bill. *(Vote 136, p. 25-S)*

By voice vote, the Senate later adopted a related amendment by Paul Simon, D-Ill., requiring all the refunds to be invested in the steel industry.

- By Metzenbaum, to strike a provision granting exemptions to eight limited partners in Cimmaron Coal Co. from capital gains taxes on sales of royalty rights. Killed June 17, 68-31, on a motion to table. *(Vote 133, p. 25-S)*
- By Paul S. Trible Jr., R-Va., to retain tax benefits for federal retirees and some state and local government and private industry retirees, who received tax-exempt returns of their own pension contributions for up to three years

under existing law. Killed June 17, 57-42, on a motion to table. *(Vote 135, p. 25-S)*

- By Moynihan, to permit the Associated Press, a taxable non-profit cooperative, to offset losses from its sales to members against its profits from sales to non-members. Moynihan said other non-profit organizations, such as the American Automobile Association, operated under a similar rule. Adopted by voice vote June 18.
- By Armstrong, to permit ministers who had made what was supposed to be an irrevocable decision to withdraw from the Social Security system to come back in. The decision to come back was to be irrevocable. Adopted by voice vote June 18.
- By Nancy Landon Kassebaum, R-Kan., to extend to all farmers the ability to renegotiate their debts without having taxed as income any portion of the debt that is forgiven by a bank or other lender. The committee bill applied this provision only to farmers with a debt-to-asset ratio of at least 7-3. Adopted by voice vote June 18.
- By Melcher, to keep the top capital gains tax at 20 percent on sales of farm land or timber from wood lots owned by active farmers with incomes of $100,000 or less.

The amendment was tabled, 63-32, June 18 primarily because of the proposed means of making up the lost revenue: inclusion in the minimum tax on corporations of profits that they have earned overseas but not yet brought back to the United States.

Packwood objected vehemently to this, on the ground that it would be a major change in the law on which no hearings had been held in recent years. *(Vote 139, p. 26-S)*

- By Metzenbaum, expressing the sense of the Senate that the conference report on the bill should contain the name of every business or group receiving special treatment under the bill. Adopted by voice vote June 19.
- By James A. McClure, R-Idaho, a mining state, allowing individuals to invest in gold or silver coins for their Individual Retirement Accounts. Adopted by voice vote June 19.
- An amendment by Max Baucus, D-Mont., permitting farmers to carry unused investment tax credits forward 15 years, and apply them against future taxes owed. Adopted by voice vote June 19.
- By Stevens, to exempt from tax the sale of reindeer or reindeer products from herds that are held in trust. Adopted by voice vote June 20.
- By Dale Bumpers, D-Ark., to eliminate a provision that would immunize from criminal prosecution persons who had not paid, or had underpaid, their taxes, and who were not otherwise engaged in criminal activity, who confessed to the Internal Revenue Service (IRS) and paid up before IRS came after them. Adopted by voice vote June 20.

The $200 million that was expected to be lost as a result of the amendment was to be counterbalanced by a limitation on future loss carry-backs by corporations. An attempt by Baucus to tighten eligibility for the so-called "amnesty" provisions lost earlier June 20 on a 40-43 roll-call vote. *(Vote 145, p. 27-S)*

Fluctuating Revenues

On the next to last day of debate, June 23, the Senate dealt with the problem the bill's uneven year-to-year revenue effects would have created under the Gramm-Rudman anti-deficit law.

It adopted by voice vote an amendment by Pete V. Domenici, R-N.M., chairman of the Senate Budget Committee, which said, in effect, that Congress and the administration would simply pretend that the revenues gained in some years and lost in others did not exist.

The bill was expected to be revenue-neutral over five years, but it would have raised tax receipts in the first two years, lost them in the next two, and increased them slightly in the fifth year.

Domenici's amendment said that the fluctuations would just not be taken into account in congressional budgeting, in the formulation of budgets the president would submit to Congress until 1991, and in calculating compliance with Gramm-Rudman deficit targets.

Adoption of the amendment was a defeat for Dole, who had repeatedly said he would like to spend the extra $11 billion in revenues that the tax bill was expected to raise in fiscal 1987. Dole never said how he would deal with the decline in revenues that would occur in later years.

He was conspicuously absent from the floor during debate on the Domenici amendment, and it was obvious that he had agreed, behind the scenes, to let it pass without his support. Ultimately, the revenue effects did play a part in budget negotiations in 1986, and the provision artificially restricting their use in budget calculations was dropped in conference.

After adopting Domenici's amendment, the Senate adopted by voice vote a sense-of-the-Senate amendment offered by Chiles, ranking Democrat on the Budget Committee, telling the tax conferees to write a bill that "produces a revenue path with minimum revenue fluctuations."

Congratulatory Mood

The mood on the Senate floor as the bill came to its final vote was one of joyful self-congratulation.

Compliments flowed freely across party lines. Dole and Packwood even praised Metzenbaum, who had blocked dozens of one-company amendments that other senators wanted. Packwood thanked him for sharing the role of "hair shirt."

The votes of the three senators who opposed the bill came as no surprise. All had announced in advance their decisions to vote "no" and each had a long list of criticisms of the bill.

Melcher, who was the first to declare himself, worried from the start about the bill's impact on the three main industries of his state: agriculture, mining and timber, all of which were depressed. With some tenacious fighting, he won reinstatement of income averaging for farmers, but it was not enough to make him a supporter.

In the end, he condemned the bill this way:

"Remember Rube Goldberg, the fellow who built contraptions? Well, the Senate Finance Committee found him and they hired him. This bill is full of whistles and bells and pulleys, like a Rube Goldberg contraption, but it doesn't work."

Simon and Levin criticized the failure of the measure to deal with the deficit, the relatively small tax cuts for middle-income persons and a number of specific provisions, such as the elimination of deductions for interest paid on consumer purchases.

Revenue-Neutrality Upheld

Near the end of debate June 24, the Senate upheld, by a vote of 54-39, a motion to prohibit consideration of an amendment by Melcher, on the ground that it reduced revenues in violation of the 1974 Congressional Budget and Impoundment Control Act (PL 93-344).

Differences in Two Tax Measures Ranged . . .

There were countless differences between the 1,379-page House version and the 1,489-page Senate version of the officially titled Tax Reform Act of 1986 (HR 3838). What follows is a summary of the more significant ones: *(House bill, 1985 Almanac p. 480)*

Impact by Income Group

The combination of all House bill provisions affecting individuals would have given larger average tax cuts to middle-income taxpayers — those in the $20,000-$40,000 income group — than the Senate bill.

Shift of Tax Burden to Corporations

The House bill shifted approximately $140 billion of taxes over the next five years from individuals to corporations; the Senate bill, about $105 billion.

Rates

The House bill would have preserved more of the traditional, progressive income tax with a four-step individual rate structure: 15, 25, 33 and 38 percent. The Senate bill had only two rates: 15 and 27 percent, although provisions phasing out the personal exemption and standard deduction for upper-income taxpayers created a marginal rate of 32 percent during the phase-out. The top corporate tax rate was lower in the Senate bill, 33 percent, compared with 36 percent in the House bill.

Personal Deductions

The Senate bill would have restricted or repealed deductions for medical expenses, interest payments, charitable contributions, personal business expenses and political contributions, whereas the House largely would have expanded them or continued them unchanged.

Pensions

The House bill contained a number of important changes, most of them aimed at limiting the generosity of pensions paid to highly compensated employees, but the Senate's changes were more sweeping and fundamental.

The Senate bill required full vesting of workers after five years, instead of 10, as under existing law; it required coverage of 80 percent of employees, instead of the 56 percent or a "fair cross-section," as under existing law; and it prohibited the reduction of pension benefits by more than 50 percent through the use of assumed, offsetting Social Security benefits.

Capital Gains

The House bill increased the maximum tax rate on capital gains income from 20 percent, as under existing law, to 22 percent. The Senate bill, however, abandoned the 65-year tradition of favored tax treatment for capital gains realized by individuals by imposing the same rates as on ordinary income.

Corporate capital gains taxes would have been kept at 28 percent in the Senate bill but increased to 36 percent by the House.

Minimum Tax

This tax, aimed at preventing wealthy individuals and highly profitable corporations from legally escaping all or nearly all federal income tax, would have raised much more tax from individuals under the House bill and much more from corporations under the Senate bill.

The House bill, but not the Senate bill, included in the minimum tax interest earned on otherwise tax-exempt, non-governmental bonds (known as industrial development bonds). The House minimum tax would have raised $19.1 billion from individuals over five years, compared with the Senate's $6.5 billion.

On the corporate side, the Senate, in a new approach, based its minimum tax on the generally larger "book income" that corporations reported to shareholders or regulatory agencies, rather than what they reported to the Internal Revenue Service. The Senate's minimum tax on corporations would have raised $33.3 billion over five years, compared with $5.8 billion in the House bill.

The budget act prohibited floor consideration of measures increasing or decreasing revenues for a given year, if a budget resolution for the year in question had not been adopted. Budget conferees continued to work on the fiscal 1987 budget resolution (S Con Res 120) throughout the period the tax bill was on the Senate floor. *(Vote 146, p. 27-S; budget resolution, p. 542; budget act, 1974 Almanac p. 145)*

The requirement that amendments be revenue-neutral had previously been followed without a test; Melcher was the only senator to challenge it. The budget act rule could have been overturned by a majority vote waiving a point of order made against an unbalanced amendment.

Final Amendments, Minor and Major

Many minor amendments were adopted in the final days — amendments that were said to be genuine "transition rules." That is, the changes were aimed at helping those who would be injured by provisions of the new law that were not in effect when certain business and financial commitments were made.

The beneficiaries included the following: a truck-leasing company in Des Moines, Iowa; corporations created under the Alaska Native Claims Settlement Act; and a housing project in Massachusetts.

In addition, it appeared that the final version of the bill might contain a host of similar amendments that never came before the Senate. In the final hours of debate, many senators announced that they would not be offering planned amendments because "we have worked it out."

In some cases, that meant agreement had been reached to consider an amendment on some other bill, or at least to have hearings. In many other cases, it meant that Packwood had pledged to try to get the amendment accepted in conference, though this was not always publicly stated.

Metzenbaum had succeeded in having an amendment adopted by voice vote that expressed the sense of the Senate that the names of all the beneficiaries of transition

. . . From Deductions to Pensions to Timber

Individual Retirement Accounts (IRAs)

The Senate would have no longer permitted individuals to contribute up to $2,000 tax-free to an IRA, if they had an employer-maintained pension plan. Taxable contributions would have still been allowed, however, and the buildup of interest and dividends would have remained tax-exempt until withdrawn.

The House would have continued tax-free IRA contributions, but imposed some restrictions on workers also covered by 401(k) tax-deferred savings plans.

State and Local Taxes

The House bill continued the full deductibility of all state and local income, property and sales taxes. The Senate would have limited the deduction of sales taxes to 60 percent of the amount by which they exceeded the state and local income tax also paid by the same taxpayer.

Tax-Exempt Bonds

The House bill would have cut back more on tax-exempt financing.

The House bill's single, annual cap on the volume of tax-exempt, non-governmental industrial development bonds allowed to be sold was lower than the multiple caps in the Senate bill. The House bill had a lower limit on the portion of a government facility built with tax-exempt bonds allowed to be used for non-governmental purposes. Its list of projects that would not be allowed at all under tax-exempt financing was longer. And, unlike the Senate, it added no new projects eligible for such financing.

Tax Shelters

The Senate bill would have eliminated the benefit of paper losses created by investments in real estate, farm and most other tax shelters. Losses from some oil shelters were still eligible to reduce taxes on other income, but only if the investor had a financial stake beyond his initial investment. The House bill, which preserved tax shelters, included paper losses in its minimum tax.

Low-Income Housing

In an effort to blunt one of the main criticisms of its crackdown on tax shelters — namely, that it would have discouraged investment in low-cost rental housing — the Senate approved an entirely new tax credit for building, rehabilitating or buying and maintaining rental housing for low-income families.

The House bill expanded a variety of existing incentives for low-income housing.

Oil and Gas Drilling

The House bill would have cut back on both of the two main remaining tax preferences of the oil and gas industry, the depletion allowance and the immediate deductions for so-called "intangible drilling costs." The Senate bill would have left the preferences intact.

Timber

The House bill would have ended the treatment of sales of timber as a capital gain, and would have taxed it as ordinary income. The Senate bill would have retained preferential capital gains treatment for timber.

Foreign Income and Foreign Taxpayers

In the lengthiest and most complex section of the two bills, that affecting foreign taxpayers and U.S. firms doing business overseas, the House would have raised $11.5 billion, mostly from foreign branches of U.S. corporations; the Senate would have raised $4.3 billion.

Depreciation

Both bills made extensive changes in depreciation allowances, partly to compensate for the repeal of the investment tax credit. The Senate's were more generous.

Bad-Debt Reserves

The House bill would have restricted deductions for bad-debt reserves for most corporations, including large banks. The Senate bill would not have hit the banks.

---

rules be included in the conference report, but there was little expectation that it would be carefully followed.

Another amendment adopted the final day would have expressed the sense of Congress, not just the Senate, that once enacted, the bill's provisions should remain unchanged for five years. It was sponsored by Mack Mattingly, R-Ga., and adopted 50-47. *(Vote 147, p. 27-S)*

Both of these two provisions were lost in conference, however.

Only two amendments with broad impact were adopted in the last two days of debate, both by voice votes.

The first, offered by George J. Mitchell, D-Maine, would have created a new tax credit as an incentive for the construction, rehabilitation and maintenance of multifamily, low-income housing.

Its provisions required the percentage of units occupied by low- and very-low-income tenants to be higher, the maximum rent levels lower, and the length of time the buildings must be dedicated to housing low-income families longer than under existing tax incentives for low-income housing.

Mitchell's amendment raised the necessary offsetting revenue by providing that the five-year phase-in of the new restrictions on tax shelters be permitted to be used only by those who made tax shelter investments before enactment of the bill. And a second balancing revenue-raiser dealt with conforming the taxable years of partnerships to those of the partners, to reduce opportunities for unwarranted postponements of tax payments.

The other broad amendment, sponsored by William L. Armstrong, R-Colo., would have permitted mutual funds, which were at the time required to get 90 percent of their income from dividends and interest, to include profits from stock options, futures contracts, options on stock indexes and foreign currency transactions in that 90 percent.

The amendment also gave mutual funds 60 days, instead of the existing 45, to send year-end financial information to shareholders, and it loosened restrictions on the way some funds with multiple portfolios had to report their taxes.

Armstrong took exactly 120 seconds to explain the provision and no one else spoke on it; it was the last amendment before the Senate voted final passage.

Conference Action

As Congress prepared to return from its Fourth of July recess and write the final version of the bill, there was still much pulling and hauling over the mechanics of the House-Senate conference: who would serve on it, who would chair it and whether it would be held in a room big enough to let all the lobbyists in.

Yet, in the face of all those questions, the basic outlines of the bill seemed clearer and clearer.

Packwood and Rostenkowski publicly staked out surprisingly similar positions: The top individual tax rate of 27 percent in the Senate bill was so attractive that everything possible must be done to keep it, even if a larger share of the tax burden had to be shifted from individuals to businesses than the president, many Republicans and even quite a few Democrats would like — well, so be it.

Reagan let it be known that, in broad outline, he agreed.

Points of Contention, and Similarities

At the start it was not clear what the hardest issues facing the conference would be. There were some key points of disagreement. *(Box, p. 516)*

But concentration on the differences obscured the point that a significant number of issues were already decided, because the House and Senate versions were identical, or nearly so.

Among the settled points:

- The principle was set that the working poor should pay no federal income tax. Some 6 million of them who paid taxes under existing law would come off the tax rolls, and stay off, because the threshold of taxation was to be indexed for inflation.
- Provisions designed to offset the "marriage penalty" would be repealed. Most working couples were expected to get a tax cut, compared with existing law, but many would be more seriously disadvantaged, compared with two single people with a total income equal to theirs.
- Unemployment compensation was to be taxed in full, like other income.
- The exclusion of the first $100 of dividend income from tax, $200 for a married couple, was to disappear.
- Only 80 percent of the cost of business meals and entertainment would be deductible.
- Some widely used avenues for saving taxes by transferring wealth to children would be closed.
- The investment tax credit on business purchases of machinery and equipment was to be repealed, retroactive to Jan. 1, 1986.
- Construction of privately owned convention centers, sports arenas and pollution control facilities, among other things, could no longer be funded with tax-exempt bonds.

An issue on which differences were emerging was the size of the tax cut that middle-income individuals and families would get.

It was generally assumed that this concern applied to the $20,000 to $50,000 income bracket.

Rostenkowski said that "if the House conferees have one mission, it's to guarantee fairness for middle-income families." He had promised them a tax cut of at least the size contained in the House bill and saw the issue as the only one that might yield some real political benefits for the Democratic Party.

Packwood said he, too, wanted more relief for middle-income taxpayers, even though that would mean accepting some of the revenue-raising provisions that were in the House bill, in order to balance off the revenue loss from bigger middle-income cuts.

Down to Business

After convening July 17, the conference did little in two days of work, except for naming Rostenkowski as chairman. He had prevailed in his assertion that it was his turn, even though Packwood had refused to accept chairmanship of their last conference, on a minor bill, because he was hoping to chair the tax conference.

It did quickly become clear, however, that finishing by Aug. 15, the start of Congress' Labor Day recess, would be difficult, and that Rostenkowski, unlike Packwood, was in complete control of the conferees from his chamber.

The Democratic conferees he picked, in violation of House tradition and over the furious objections of Majority Leader Jim Wright, D-Texas, were tested allies who were expected to vote as he wished when told it was important.

Packwood, on the other hand, was expected to have problems holding a majority of the Senate conferees, particularly on issues involving business taxation. Republicans Wallop, Danforth and Roth seemed almost certain to desert. Dole was a possible defector; so, too, were Democrats Bentsen, Long and Spark M. Matsunaga of Hawaii.

The choice of Senate conferees also somewhat violated seniority rules but there was no big flap about it. Almost everyone seemed to want Bradley, who was very junior, on the conference. Junior member Wallop was added to balance Bradley's vote, on oil issues in particular.

Slow Going

Despite early agreement to work on the bill's broad outlines, particularly provisions affecting individuals, progress was slow. A second week of meetings of the entire conference committee, separate caucuses of Senate and House conferees, and even caucuses of the House Democratic conferees — all of them behind closed doors except for a June 21 session — yielded no agreements.

The conference got good news and bad July 24 as the Joint Committee on Taxation presented updated estimates of the revenue effects of the Senate and House bills.

The first piece of good news was that the Senate bill would give bigger tax cuts than originally thought to individuals in the $10,000 to $50,000 income group.

The second good news was that it would cost less than previously thought to retain deductibility of contributions to IRAs for middle-income taxpayers. The Senate bill would have eliminated these deductions for persons covered by other pension plans.

The bad news was that the Senate bill was no longer revenue-neutral. It would lose the government $21.2 billion in revenues over the five years 1987-91, and that revenue would have to be made up by increasing the taxes paid by somebody. The Joint Taxation Committee staff provided a partial re-estimate for the House bill, showing that it would increase government revenues by $38.3 billion over the five years. But the staff cautioned that its figures "significantly overstate" the increase, because of a variety of technical factors.

The most significant result of the re-estimates, however, was to make it easier for the conferees to hold the top individual income tax rate at or close to the 27 percent contained in the Senate bill, while reducing the actual taxes paid by those with incomes of $50,000 or less as much as the House bill did.

Despite these changes, there was still a problem under the Senate bill with the $30,000-$40,000 income group, who were still expected to get a smaller tax cut than the income groups on either side of them, and one a good bit smaller than the House bill would have provided — 7.2 percent, compared with 9.2 percent.

An Offer, and a Counteroffer

As the desultory conference continued the week of July 28 in mostly separate meetings of House and Senate conferees, issues other than business taxes, which had once loomed as large for Republican senators as for House Democrats, slipped to a lower priority.

Among these were: a bigger tax cut for those in the $20,000-$50,000 income bracket, some kind of reasonably generous deduction for money put into Individual Retirement Accounts, and fixing "the stagger."

The so-called stagger was the prospect of widespread individual income tax increases in 1987 because the tax rate cuts, under both the House and Senate bills, were not to go into effect until six months after the elimination of various deductions, exemptions and credits.

But the issue of the tax burden on businesses — always foreseeable as crucial in the conference — became important as each chamber's conferees made package offers to the other to resolve their differences.

The question was: How large an increase in the taxes on business the senators would accept in order to keep the individual income tax rates at 15 and 27 percent and the top corporate rate at 33 percent — and still restore some tax breaks for individuals? In particular, for Republican senators, some Democrats and the Reagan administration as well, the issue was how large a cutback in business deductions for depreciation they were willing to agree to in order to hold those tax rates.

As Danforth described it, "The question is how hard we can hit business without causing very serious effects on the economy."

Early in the week of July 28, Danforth had described his reaction to a compromise the Senate conferees had offered the House, which would have cut depreciation deductions (increasing taxes by $7 billion), and yielded to the House on a number of other points of business taxation.

"I choked and gulped and gasped and gagged — and swallowed it," he said, adding that he thought this proposal was as far as the Senate could, or should, go on business taxation.

Even Packwood said of the Senate proposal, "There is a strong feeling that this is as far as we're going. It's all we want to spend to take care of all the differences we have."

The House Democratic conferees, in a counterproposal that covered all the major issues in dispute between the two chambers, asked for restrictions on depreciation that would add some $23 billion to business taxes over the five years 1987-91 and bring about an overall shift of taxes from individuals to businesses of $142 billion.

They argued that their offer was reasonable, not only because they had come down considerably from the $39 billion cutback in depreciation deductions the House originally approved, but also because they had abandoned their earlier attempt to impose a whole new system of depreciation, which business and the administration intensely disliked.

Senate reaction, from Republicans and some Democrats, was very unfavorable to the House offer.

How Tax Conferees Voted

House Democrats	
Dan Rostenkowski, Ill.	Yes
J. J. Pickle, Texas	Yes
Charles B. Rangel, N.Y.	Yes
Fortney H. "Pete" Stark, Calif.	Yes *
Richard A. Gephardt, Mo.	Yes
Marty Russo, Ill.	Yes
Don J. Pease, Ohio	Yes
House Republicans	
John J. Duncan, Tenn.	Yes
Bill Archer, Texas	No
Guy Vander Jagt, Mich.	Yes
Philip M. Crane, Ill.	No *
Senate Republicans	
Bob Packwood, Ore.	Yes
Robert Dole, Kan.	Yes *
William V. Roth Jr., Del.	No *
John C. Danforth, Mo.	No
John H. Chafee, R.I.	Yes
Malcolm Wallop, Wyo.	No *
Senate Democrats	
Russell B. Long, La.	Yes
Lloyd Bentsen, Texas	Yes *
Spark M. Matsunaga, Hawaii	Yes
Daniel Patrick Moynihan, N.Y.	Yes
Bill Bradley, N.J.	Yes

* *Announced position; absent for the vote.*

Finding Middle Ground

By Aug. 8, as the conferees continued to work mostly in one-house caucuses and always behind closed doors, each proposal and counterproposal brought the sides closer together.

Business taxes continued to be a point of enormous controversy, particularly such major issues as depreciation, the taxation of foreign-source income, the treatment of oil and gas and mining industries, and the corporate minimum tax. But there was considerable movement toward agreement, and conferees had reached all but final agreement on an impressive list of issues, including nearly every one affecting individuals.

On business taxes, however, the gross numbers got somewhat closer. The figures showed this. The most recent proposal by Packwood, which was not formally accepted by his fellow senators, would have shifted $121 billion in tax payments from individuals to businesses. The latest House offer, just over $141 billion.

Thus, conferees were about $20 billion apart on this most basic issue, compared with something on the order of $60 billion when they started. Interestingly, House Republican conferees also suggested a $121 billion shift, but in ways that were somewhat different from Packwood's. The number began to look not only like the seed of a compromise, but perhaps the upper limit for many conferees.

The Senate had yielded heavily to the House on big-ticket items, but mostly in ways that hit businesses across the board. The Senate conferees agreed to reduce depreciation deductions, to eliminate special tax rates for capital gains realized by corporations, raising $4 billion, and to accept some House provisions on pension plans, raising $3.6 billion.

Differences remained on depreciation and taxation of foreign income.

Originally, the House wanted to pick up an additional $39 billion in business taxes from reducing depreciation deductions. Its offer dropped the tax increase to $23 billion. The Senate, in two steps, raised its offer to $7.4 billion.

Through foreign tax changes, the House bill would have raised $13.6 billion; the Senate bill, $4 billion. The Senate had offered one change, totaling $1.3 billion.

Fixing IRAs

IRAs, sales tax deductions and the stagger were subject, also, to negotiation.

There was movement on IRAs; House and Senate conferees decided that only those they defined as lower- and middle-income taxpayers should be allowed to continue to save $2,000 a year, tax-free, in IRAs.

The remaining argument, a big one, was whether those not allowed to make tax-free contributions should enjoy the interest buildup in their IRA accounts, tax-free, until it was withdrawn. The Senate wanted to do this; the House did not.

As for sales tax deductions, money was the only issue. The Senate fought for a partial disallowance, because it did not want to lose the revenue.

On the stagger, there was also progress of a sort. House conferees proposed to move the effective dates of the tax cut back from July 1 to Jan. 1, 1987, but to offset the lost revenue by imposing higher rates, for 1987 only, on those above what it considered middle income.

The Senate had a different solution. It would have put the rate cuts into effect March 15 and offset the $23 billion of revenue lost by eliminating the 1989 inflation adjustments — called indexing — on individual income tax brackets, the personal exemption and the standard deduction.

That proposal brought an immediate howl of protest from House conferees, who noted that the personal exemption and standard deduction were particularly important to lower-income individuals and the stagger chiefly would have hurt those above middle income.

More Roadblocks

After a week of negotiations that were as unusual as they were intense, conferees came up to the evening of Aug. 15 facing a huge new barrier to agreement.

The latest official forecast for the national economy showed that the tax bill would have to raise $17 billion more than previously thought in order to remain revenue-neutral.

Rostenkowski and Packwood had spent the day, as they had spent most of the week, in a series of lengthy, closed-door negotiations between just the two of them. They had been assigned by their fellow conferees to try to work things out, after the full conference of 11 senators and 11 representatives found that little except increased acrimony came out of their first meeting together in more than a week, Aug. 12.

Packwood claimed the two "would have reached an agreement in two more hours" but for the sudden, unpleasant discovery that the latest version of the bill, after a good bit of yielding and compromising on both sides, did not raise enough revenue. Of the shortfall, $7 billion resulted from larger than expected individual tax reductions, and $10 billion from smaller than estimated yields from corporate provisions of the bill.

Both men seemed determined to reach agreement in principle on a conference bill — and get it approved by the full conference committee before Congress recessed. Packwood explained why. "It is critical," he said, that everything that has been agreed to be locked in, "so the special interests and lobbyists don't have three weeks to hit on our members to change what is in this most remarkable tax package."

Pressure for Resolution

The general view was that almost no one wanted the bill dead. The reduction of the top individual tax rate finally began to catch the imagination of millions of ordinary people. Reducing the top corporate tax rate was regarded as the No. 1 objective by many large, influential corporations.

In addition, there was strong support for the bill from those who thought curtailment or outright elimination of many tax preferences would improve the performance of the economy, and the spirits of the electorate, as well.

They pointed to provisions that had been fully, or mostly, agreed to, including the virtual outlawing of many types of tax shelter investments and changing the corporate and individual minimum tax to catch many more high-income, low-tax-paying individuals and corporations than before. And, it appeared that the final version of the bill would contain some curtailment of tax breaks for banks, government contractors, and the insurance, timber, and oil and gas industries.

With Rostenkowski and Packwood again delegated to figure out a compromise, the pieces fell into place. The top individual rate went to 28 percent, and the top corporate rate to 34 percent, each 1 percentage point above the rates in the Senate bill, and well below what many had believed possible. The sales tax deduction was lost, but the partial IRA deduction was retained. And special, higher rates for 1987 were substituted for the stagger.

The shift in taxes from individuals to businesses wound up just short of $122 billion. And the private, chairman-to-chairman negotiations allowed individual conferees to tell angry constituents and contributors that they had little or no control over the decisions.

The one thing conferees were never quite able to achieve for individuals was a steady downward-sloping line of tax cuts, with the biggest percentage cuts at the bottom and the smallest at the top.

And those who had supported simplification of the tax code and an end to special tax breaks were disappointed.

Despite the widespread claims of wholesale elimination or curtailment of special tax breaks, many tax preferences were kept and many new ones were added, even though most new ones were rather narrow.

Most were added at the insistence of some particular senator or representative, most of them members of Finance or Ways and Means, who had a constituent with a problem. Moynihan, for example, won special treatment for

Deficit Cut Bill: $6 Billion in Revenues

Congress March 20 approved a fiscal 1986 deficit-reduction bill that was expected to raise about $6 billion in revenues over a three-year period.

One of the central, controversial provisions of the bill (HR 3128 — PL 99-272) made permanent the 16-cent-per-pack cigarette tax, which had been scheduled to drop to 8 cents in March. The measure also contained several other provisions to raise revenues.

Known as a "reconciliation" bill, HR 3128 was intended to cut existing programs to meet targets set in the fiscal 1986 budget resolution. The bill had emerged from conference in December 1985 but cleared only after three months of further Senate-House negotiations in 1986.

HR 3128, which also served as a major vehicle for revisions in tobacco subsidies and the Medicare and Medicaid programs, was approved after an unprecedented round of legislative pingpong between the House and Senate. Many legislators from coastal states supported the measure because it divided approximately $6.4 billion from offshore drilling revenues between the states and the federal government. *(Legislative history of HR 3128, p. 555)*

Fiscal 1987 Reconciliation

Some additional revenue changes were included in a fiscal 1987 reconciliation bill (HR 5300 — PL 99-509) approved Oct. 17. Revenue provisions of that measure included several changes in the sweeping Tax Reform Act of 1986 (HR 3838 — PL 99-514), which cleared Sept. 27. *(Provisions of fiscal 1987 reconciliation bill, p. 559; provisions of Tax Reform Act, p. 494)*

Revenue Provisions of HR 3128

As signed into law April 7, the revenue provisions of HR 3128:

- **Tobacco.** Extended permanently the 16-cents-a-pack excise tax on cigarettes, which was imposed in 1982. The tax temporarily dropped March 16 to the pre-1982 level of 8 cents a pack, but the bill made the increase retroactive. *(Previous extensions, 1985 Almanac p. 502)*

- Established an excise tax of 8 cents a pound on chewing tobacco and 24 cents a pound on snuff.

- **Black Lung Trust Fund.** Increased the excise tax on coal manufacturers that supported the Black Lung Disability Trust Fund, effective Jan. 1, 1986, through Dec. 31, 1995. The tax would be the lesser of $1.10 per ton for coal from underground mines and 55 cents per ton from surface mines, or 4.4 percent of the sales price.

  The trust fund, which paid benefits to lung-diseased coal miners or their survivors when no mine operator was held responsible, had a deficit of about $2.5 billion at the end of fiscal 1984. That amount was advanced from general Treasury revenues, to be repaid with interest. But the bill provided a one-time, five-year forgiveness of interest payments on the trust fund's borrowings from the general fund. *(Background, 1981 Almanac p. 114)*

- **Unemployment Compensation.** Made permanent existing federal unemployment tax exemptions for wages paid to certain fishing-boat crew members and to summer camp counselors who were full-time students.

  The bill also extended an exemption for certain non-resident farm workers for wages paid through 1987.

- **Railroad Retirement Benefits.** Required that all railroad retirement benefits in excess of those that would have been received under Social Security be fully taxable to the extent that they exceeded previously taxed contributions.

- **Full-Time Students.** Barred a taxpayer who was a full-time student during any of the three previous years from averaging income for those years to compute income-tax liability. Income averaging was intended to benefit taxpayers whose incomes fluctuated greatly from year to year. It was repealed by the tax reform bill cleared Sept. 27.

- **Airline Employees.** Excluded from an airline employee's income the value of free or discounted airline tickets used by his or her parents. The value of such tickets was previously taxed as income.

  The value of airline passes used by employees of certain airline affiliates would also be excluded from taxable income.

- **Insolvent Individuals.** Provided that insolvent individuals such as farmers who sold property used for business to satisfy a debt or to avoid foreclosure did not have to count any capital gains from the sale for purposes of computing their minimum income tax.

- **Tax-Exempt Bonds.** Permitted the Gulf Coast Waste Disposal Authority to issue tax-exempt industrial development bonds for acquisition of existing air and water pollution control facilities.

- **Multinational Firms.** Extended for one year a law allowing large multinational firms to deduct research expenses from income subject to U.S. taxes, even if the research related to the firm's foreign operations.

- **Treasury Borrowing Authority.** Increased the Treasury Department's authority to issue bonds at rates above a 4¼ percent ceiling, from $200 billion to $250 billion. That would allow Treasury to continue operating in the long-term bond market through 1986.

- **Farmers' Cooperatives.** Allowed a farmers' cooperative to retain its tax-exempt status if it offset certain earnings and losses in determining amounts for distribution to patrons.

- **Internal Revenue Service.** Authorized the appropriation of an additional $46.5 million in each of fiscal years 1986, 1987 and 1988 for the Internal Revenue Service. The sum would permit the hiring of 1,550 additional agents and examination employees, which would allow increased tax collections estimated at $2 billion over three years.

the personal business expenses of performing artists, many of whom lived and worked in his state.

And many of the new provisions were expected to complicate, not simplify, the preparation of tax returns, even for individuals with fairly uncomplicated financial lives. For example, there were separate sets of basic tax rates for 1987 and 1988. And many new limitations and restrictions were to be phased in over a period of three to five years, so that each year's calculation would be somewhat different from the one before.

In the end all 12 Democrats and five of the 10 Republicans supported the conference agreement. *(Conference vote, p. 519)*

Final Action

Although the conferees finished their work Aug. 16, it was more than a month before the formal conference report on HR 3838 was filed. Much of the time was devoted to drafting detailed legislative language, but some provisions had to be resolved by Rostenkowski and Packwood, particularly decisions concerning transition rules.

The last major issue was settled at about 4 a.m. Sept. 18, involving the deferral of taxes on long-term contract payments. The 2,000-page conference report (H Rept 99-841), including the bill text and accompanying narrative, was filed later that same day.

During the interval, members returned home for their Labor Day recess. Upon returning to Washington, legislators of both political parties and both houses reported that they had heard from constituents who knew or believed that their taxes would be increased by the bill. Members also reported an almost complete absence of active support for the bill.

Many of the business organizations that supported the Senate version of the bill said they continued to favor the conference version and were working for it — but they were not much in evidence around the Capitol.

Two weeks before the House finally took up the conference agreement, the chamber agreed to a procedure for floor debate that helped to smoothe the way. On Sept. 9, in an action that was not exactly rare but not routine either, the House agreed to waive all points of order — objections to floor consideration — that might have arisen because the conference had gone beyond its charter to change provisions not contained in either the House or Senate bills.

The Final House Debate

Although there was anxious speculation that it might do otherwise, the House Sept. 25 passed the Tax Reform Act of 1986, and the vote was not even close. The size of the House vote for the bill surprised its strongest backers, who had worried because there was no active grass-roots support for the measure and a good bit of active opposition from a variety of sources.

The vote on final passage, however, was 292-136. On what was the real key vote, the motion of Rep. Bill Archer, R-Texas, to send the bill back to the conference committee, and thus probably kill it, was defeated 160-268. That 108-vote margin compared with the "30, 40 or 50 votes" that had been predicted earlier that same day by Rostenkowski. *(Votes 379, 378, p. 108-H)*

At least a dozen alleged virtues and defects of the bill were cited during the House debate, but the prime issue for advocates was the degree of fairness the bill was said to achieve.

For opponents of the bill, the focal argument was the risks to which they believed it would expose the economy by going too far in reducing the tax breaks now accorded business investment and personal savings.

Rostenkowski, in opening the nearly four hours of debate — extraordinarily lengthy for a conference bill that could not be amended — said the "opponents are those who are determined to protect the status quo and all the abuses and tax dodges that go with it."

Others echoed the theme.

Lynn Martin, R-Ill., said she was worried about some aspects of the bill, "but I am more worried about the present [tax] code." Passage, she said, will prove "a final and permanent victory over the special interests."

Hal Daub, R-Neb., said the bill "strikes at the heart of the pin-stripe brigade that stood outside the door" while Ways and Means worked on it.

Protests From Left and Right

Opponents of the bill answered these charges, in particular challenging the assertion of improved fairness.

Mike Lowry, D-Wash., protested the termination of the deduction for state and local sales taxes, which he called "a serious inequity" and one that would hurt school systems, in particular. And Archer asked rhetorically, "What's fair about a tax bill that will allow deductions for interest on a second home but not on a first car?" He also criticized the elimination of the special deduction for two-earner families and other elements of the bill he considered unfair.

As leader of the opposition forces in the House — a role he took on because Duncan, the ranking Republican on Ways and Means, supported the bill — Archer principally addressed the economic impact of the measure.

"Why should we gamble [with the economy] when we don't have to?" he asked. He noted that most of a group of economists who recently testified before the Joint Economic Committee had said the bill would restrict economic growth in the short run, though some said "it might be OK" in the long run.

Bill Frenzel, R-Minn., also dealt at length with economic issues. He expressed fears that the cutback on tax-exempt contributions to Individual Retirement Accounts and 401(k) retirement plans would reduce the savings of individuals and that the repeal of the investment tax credit and stretching out of depreciation deductions would hurt business investment.

Playing Politics

The bipartisanship of the support for the bill masked the role politics had played in the tax debate for more than two years. Kemp, who opposed the House bill — though he voted for it — and who in the final days announced his support for the conference bill, asked rhetorically, "Who will get the credit for this bill? Democrats or Republicans? Reagan or the Congress? I think I know who will get the credit: the folks who vote for it."

Guy Vander Jagt, R-Mich., who chaired the National Republican Congressional Committee, was even more baldly political: "I personally would give my right arm to run against an incumbent who voted against this bill," he said.

It remained for Speaker O'Neill to make the closing speech. He set the tone that Reagan would echo in signing the bill. Referring to the fact that the bill was expected to take 6 million employed poor people off the tax rolls, O'Neill called HR 3838 "the best anti-poverty bill in this

Measure to 'Correct' Tax Bill 'Errors' Dies

In the days after the massive tax overhaul bill (HR 3838) was cleared, the irritation and tension that built up for months between the House and Senate focused anew on a separate resolution to correct the tax bill's hundreds of "technical" errors.

The corrections resolution (H Con Res 395) was passed twice by each chamber in differing versions. But, though seen as urgent by some, it died when House and Senate negotiators could not agree on what was supposed to be included in the measure.

The corrections resolution was designed to make changes in the copy of the bill that was to be sent to the White House. It was a vain hope that the version signed into law might be devoid of most, if not all, of the errors that got into the 925-page bill during its drafting.

So, while negotiations dragged on for nearly three weeks from the date the tax bill cleared Sept. 27 until Congress adjourned Oct. 18, the tax bill was kept off the president's desk.

Source of the Argument

H Con Res 395 would have done more than fix obvious typographical or drafting errors in HR 3838 — the usual function of such resolutions. It would also have enacted a large number of substantive changes. Ultimately the resolution was hung up not over the recognized errors — even though new ones were being found right up until adjournment — but over a few differing substantive provisions the House and Senate wanted to add.

It became a matter of increasingly heated argument whether many of the substantive changes were in fact corrections of errors or, conversely, an attempt to wedge something into the tax bill that was not supposed to be in it.

One reason for the uncertainty was that almost no one, including the two principals, knew everything that House Ways and Means Committee Chairman Dan Rostenkowski, D-Ill., and Senate Finance Committee Chairman Bob Packwood, R-Ore., decided in mid-September, when the two negotiated the conference agreement on the tax bill in meetings that often ran until dawn.

Only a few staff members were present. No one had notes on the whole thing. Many details were left up to the staffs of Ways and Means, Finance and the Joint Committee on Taxation, to draft in accord with the basic concepts that Rostenkowski and Packwood had agreed upon.

Thus, some of the changes contained in H Con Res 395 represented items that the two chairmen did intend to put into the tax bill, but that somehow got left out of the measure. Some other changes, though not originally intended by the two chairmen, were not a matter of controversy between them.

In many cases, these additional provisions merely applied some special, advantageous rule — often a later effective date for some restrictive change — to additional taxpayers who were in the same circumstances as the original beneficiaries.

But there were provisions that the two could not agree on, some of which were fought over to the end. A central example of a provision in disagreement was an item granting continued capital gains treatment to a particular type of bond called a "deep discount bond" owned by insurance companies.

At issue was how many insurance companies would be allowed to retain a special benefit, enacted in 1984, which taxed them at the advantageous capital gains rate on the difference between the purchase price and the redemption value of some of these bonds. Under normal tax rules, this increase in value of a discounted bond was considered interest, and taxed at higher rates.

HR 3838 limited the special treatment to 15 large insurance companies, but Packwood tried in the Senate version of H Con Res 395 to extend the rule to all insurance firms. Rostenkowski was adamantly opposed.

Other items in dispute would have extended the length of time for tax-free financing of a new Madison Square Garden, expanded to all states where airplanes used in general aviation were manufactured, instead of just four, the continued availability of the investment tax credit on purchases of such planes, and granted special tax advantages to a sale-leaseback by the Los Angeles Library.

Legislative History

H Con Res 395 was born in the week after the conference report on HR 3838 was filed Sept. 18. It passed the House by voice vote Sept. 25, immediately after the tax bill conference report was adopted.

It was passed in a somewhat different form by the Senate Oct. 16.

The final stalemate arose after the resolution had passed the House and then the Senate again on Oct. 17. The second time around, each chamber yielded to the other on some provisions — deleting some it had proposed; accepting some proposed by the other.

When the bill came back to the House for the third time Oct. 18, it contained two provisions in particular that Rostenkowski and his fellow House members were determined not to accept.

One would have given Phillips Petroleum Co. and Texaco Inc. an additional exception, on top of one already in the bill, to what were called "interest allocation provisions." The restrictive provisions were intended to limit a tax-avoidance device used by multinational corporations.

The other dispute involved what were known as "key man" insurance policies, which companies bought for their most valued executives and against which these executives could borrow money. The issue was deductibility of the interest, which the tax bill had outlawed, effective June 20, 1986. The Senate, under pressure from insurance agents who sold such policies after the cutoff date, wanted to move the ban on deductions to the date the president signed the bill.

In the final half-hour before the 99th Congress came to a close, the House disagreed to the Senate's most recent amendments, and returned the resolution to the Senate, where it died.

House for at least half a dozen years."

Overall, he said, the bill "is the most sweeping tax reform legislation in the history of this nation. If we approve it, the 99th Congress will assume a special place in history."

After that came the votes.

The Final Senate Debate

The Senate began its final debate on the bill the day after the House voted. At 4 p.m. Saturday, Sept. 27, after two days of debate, a large portion of which was taken up with angry exchanges between Packwood and Metzenbaum over transition rules, the Senate adopted the conference report, 74-23.

On the broader provisions of the bill, the chief opponent was Danforth, who had been a part of the core group of seven Finance Committee members who wrote the original Senate bill.

But the conference committee, Danforth said, in its determination to keep the tax rates in the final version as close as possible to those in the Senate bill, "was willing to dump more and more taxes on our industrial sector, on research and development, on education, in order to placate this god of low rates."

As a result, he said, although the conferees increased the top tax rates only 1 percentage point from those in the Senate bill — to 28 percent for individuals and 34 percent for corporations — "I defected."

Danforth said he knew he could not defeat the bill but was making his lengthy speech so that senators would know the dangers he saw in it.

The wide margin in the Senate vote on the bill displayed a curious collection of Democrats and Republicans, liberals, moderates and conservatives, on both sides.

Despite the bad-tempered exchanges over transition rules, debate in the Senate was considerably less emotional than the House debate earlier in the week, presumably because there was never any question that the Senate would approve the bill by a big margin.

More Transition Rules

There were at least 682 transition rules in the conference report, about twice as many as had been presumed. Many were presumed to be political favors granted to gain votes for the bill.

The extent of the rules was brought to light Sept. 25, when Metzenbaum forced the release of a compilation provided by the staffs of the congressional tax-writing committees. Such information had apparently never before been made public.

Most of the transition rules granted a special tax break to just one corporation, university, stadium authority or other category of beneficiary. A few applied to a fairly large number of taxpayers, such as businesses that needed to replace equipment lost due to floods in West Virginia in November 1985, after one of the eligibility cutoff dates for the investment tax credit, which was repealed retroactively by the bill.

In between were what congressional tax technicians called the semi-generics — provisions that benefited small groups of businesses that were all in the same position: steel companies that had not had enough profits to use up all their tax credits or firms whose activities were disrupted by the suspension of the space shuttle program.

Metzenbaum's list showed 287 transition rules that had been in either the House or Senate bill, or both, of which 47 provided tax benefits of $20 million or more. The largest beneficiary was identified as United Telcom of Kansas City, Mo., which was granted an exception to the depreciation or investment tax credit rules expected to save it $234 million in taxes.

Other recipients of benefits in excess of $100 million were identified as follows: John Deere of Moline, Ill., $212 million; Pacific-Texas Pipeline, from Los Angeles to Midland, Texas, $187 million; New York Solid Waste, $140 million; Kern River Pipeline of California, $129 million; Dineh Power of New Mexico, $119 million.

Another 395 transition rules were added in conference — or in the period after the conference concluded its business and before the report was filed — by the two committee chairmen. They were reported to have picked from among an estimated 1,000 transition rule requests from other members. Of them, 46 provided tax savings of $20 million or more. The largest in this group was a saving of $78 million on two Chrysler Corp. plants, one near St. Louis, Mo., and the other in Belvidere, Ill.

There were 102 provisions listed for which no tax-benefit figure was given. In all, the transition rules were said to save their beneficiaries a total of $10.6 billion over five years, 1987-91. The list, and the estimates of tax savings, were prepared by the staffs of the Joint Committee on Taxation, Ways and Means and Finance.

Worry About the Economy

As in the House, there were many expressions of doubt about the impact on the economy of such a wide-ranging and complicated piece of legislation.

Typical of liberal critics was Christopher J. Dodd, D-Conn., who said there was no economist or member of the Senate who could say where the bill would lead the economy.

Dodd added that his own view was that the bill "has the real potential to push this nation into a recession."

Dodd also denounced the bill as "less tax reform and more a continuation of the philosophy of Ronald Reagan that government has no role to play in meeting the needs of the American people."

Among the many supporters who confessed uncertainties was Budget Committee Chairman Domenici, who noted that he had long been concerned, and remained so, over the budget implications of the bill. He warned his colleagues that the revenue losses resulting from the bill for fiscal 1988, estimated at $16.7 billion, "will come back to haunt us....

"I used to wonder," he continued, "if this was the right time to pass this bill. I have concluded there will never be a right time if we wait around for economists to say we are ready.... I conclude it is absolutely the right time because we are ready and the people are ready."

Questions about the impact on the economy were mentioned again and again, by both opponents and supporters.

Packwood, himself, in his final speech just before the vote, admitted that "the basic decisions on this bill have to be subjective decisions. Will this bill help the economy or hurt the economy? There is not a person in this room" — he paused to name half a dozen who had been prominent in the debate — "who can tell you for sure.

"But taxes are about more than money, they are about more than economics. They are about fairness — and this bill is fair."

The vote made plain that a 3-1 majority of the Senate agreed with the Finance chairman. ▮

Reagan Budget Projected $143.6 Billion Deficit

President Reagan sent Congress Feb. 5 a fiscal 1987 budget that provided a blueprint for his vision of a "streamlined federal government — stripped of marginal, nonessential and inappropriate functions and activities."

It would have been a government that pulled out of areas such as public housing, mass transit construction and crop insurance, while increasing spending on defense and foreign military assistance.

But as in prior years, Reagan's budget was met with little enthusiasm on Capitol Hill. His blueprint for change was largely ignored in the budget resolution (S Con Res 120) adopted June 27, and the administration ultimately sat out most of Congress' budget debate in 1986. *(Budget resolution, p. 542)*

Moreover, two days after the president's budget was released, the lever expected to force Congress and the president to make the tough choices needed for a budget compromise was lost when a federal district court struck down the chief enforcement mechanism of the Balanced Budget and Emergency Deficit Control Act of 1985 (PL 99-177), also known as Gramm-Rudman-Hollings. The Supreme Court July 7 upheld the lower court's ruling, which declared a system of automatic, across-the-board spending cuts to be unconstitutional. *(Gramm-Rudman developments, p. 579)*

Near Trillion-Dollar Budget

The president's budget called for $1.1 trillion in new budget authority, which would have yielded $994 billion in outlays (actual spending) during fiscal 1987 against a revenue base of $850.4 billion.

The resulting deficit would have been $143.6 billion, slightly below the 1987 Gramm-Rudman deficit target of $144 billion. A deficit of $202.8 billion was forecast for fiscal 1986, but that figure ultimately rose to $230 billion, a record. *(Fiscal 1986 deficit, p. 551)*

As expected, Reagan proposed no new taxes, but asked for $6.3 billion in new user fees and other receipts; he vowed to veto any tax increase that Congress might send him. The budget proposed an additional $34.2 billion for defense over fiscal 1986 appropriations, a 12 percent increase, and requested more money for foreign aid.

Program changes, including a few increases, were to yield a $38.2 billion cut in the "baseline" fiscal 1987 deficit. *(Major initiatives, p. 528; Reagan budget message, p. 5-D)*

Deficit-reduction efforts focused on the 8.5 percent of the budget composed of "discretionary domestic spending" — federal programs that are "relatively controllable." Savings are difficult or impossible to achieve from "uncontrollable" expenditures such as interest payments and pensions. *(Chart, p. 531)*

Social Security, approximately 20 percent of the budget, remained untouched, in keeping with compromises Reagan made with Congress in 1985. The president said he had protected the "safety net" of programs that help the poor, but he proposed changes that would cut Medicare, Medicaid, food stamps and Aid to Families with Dependent Children.

Most of the cuts in domestic programs had been proposed in prior budgets, including the termination of dozens of small federal agencies. The major new initiatives involved selling off federal assets such as oil fields, portfolios of government loans and agencies that market electricity from dams. *(Terminations and privatizations, p. 536)*

Congress Reacts

On Capitol Hill, increased pressure to reduce deficits led members to concede that some of the proposed cutbacks would be more palatable in 1986, even though Congress had rejected most of them in previous years. Members said they were more likely to slash defense spending, and many said some type of tax increase would be inevitable, regardless of the president's opposition.

But talk of a House-Senate-White House compromise to reduce deficits by a combination of defense and domestic cuts and some type of tax increase led Treasury Secretary James A. Baker III to object Feb. 5, "We ought not to be talking about grand compromises."

Administration officials and members agreed that it would be a crucial year for deficit reduction, primarily because of Gramm-Rudman-Hollings procedures. Some relatively small automatic cuts were scheduled to take ef-

President's Projected Budget and Deficit Targets

(in billions of dollars) †

	1985	1986*	1987*	1988*	1989*	1990*	1991*
Total Budget Authority	1,074.1	1,058.7	1,102.0	1,165.9	1,218.0	1,261.3	1,310.1
Total Outlays	946.3	979.9	994.0	1,026.8	1,063.6	1,093.8	1,122.7
Total Receipts	734.1	777.1	850.4	933.2	996.1	1,058.1	1,124.0
Budget Deficit/(Surplus)	−212.3	−202.8	−143.6	−93.6	−67.5	−35.8	(1.3)
Gramm-Rudman-Hollings Deficit Targets		−171.9	−144.0	−108.0	−72.0	−36.0	0.0
Difference		30.9	−0.4	−14.4	−4.5	−0.2	−1.3

† Totals include Social Security, which is off-budget; totals may not add due to rounding.
** Estimates*

SOURCE: Fiscal 1987 Budget

fect March 1 for fiscal 1986 — 4.3 percent for domestic programs and 4.9 percent for defense — and the president's budget presumed they would take effect.

The judicial rejection of Gramm-Rudman's automatic cuts, notwithstanding, the law still contained procedural tools to hold spending in line with the budget resolution and deficits in line with Gramm-Rudman targets.

Budget Totals

The president's plan would have led to total government outlays of $994 billion in fiscal 1987, $1.03 trillion in 1988 and $1.06 trillion in 1989.

Fiscal 1986 spending was estimated at $979.9 billion. *(Table, p. 525)*

Outlays represented the amount of funds disbursed from the Treasury during the fiscal year. Some expenditures would come from budget authority granted in previous years, and some new budget authority granted in fiscal 1987 would not be actually spent until future years. *(Chart, p. 538)*

Outlays are the basis against which deficits are calculated.

Deficits would have fallen from $143.6 billion in 1987 to $93.6 billion in 1988 and $67.5 billion in 1989, on the way to a balanced budget by 1991. This was slightly faster than the Gramm-Rudman schedule of $144 billion in 1987, $108 billion in 1988, $72 billion in 1989, and $36 billion in 1990.

The deficit represented 5 percent of the gross national product (GNP) — the measure of the nation's total output of goods and services — in 1985. Administration economists said reducing that percentage would boost the economy by making credit available for purchases of houses and factories. Reagan said deficit reductions over the next three years would represent $1,900 for every American household.

There was some question whether the president's fiscal 1987 budget would indeed meet the $144 billion deficit target. Analysts questioned the administration's estimates of how quickly defense funds would be spent, saying the estimates were too low.

If the military disbursed its funds at a rate closer to historical averages, they said that would add almost $15 billion to fiscal 1987 outlay projections and push deficits over the target.

The president proposed new budget authority for defense programs of $320.3 billion in 1987, $341.6 billion in 1988, and $363.2 billion in 1989. The administration argued that the 1987 level represented an increase of 3 percent over the rate of inflation, and was essential for national security.

Members challenged this calculation, saying the actual increase was 8 percent over inflation, or 12 percent total.

The difference came from the "baselines" used for comparison.

The administration based its defense figures on 1987 estimates worked out in negotiations between Congress and the White House in July 1985 for the fiscal 1986 budget resolution (S Con Res 32), when the president reluctantly agreed to accept some defense cuts. *(1985 Almanac p. 441)*

Congress never provided that much money, however, and members said the correct baseline was the amount actually appropriated, which was more than 10 percent lower.

Domestic programs were calculated against actual appropriations, less the 4.3 percent Gramm-Rudman-Hollings cuts for 1986.

Winners and Losers

The different methods of calculating defense and domestic spending reflected a two-track approach in the budget, with programs the president favored being protected and those he disliked being served up as sacrifices to deficit reduction.

In the budget message to Congress that accompanied the budget documents, Reagan outlined his views of budget priorities in this way:

- **"High priority programs should be adequately funded."** Chief among these was defense, which the president said had to be increased to reverse past decreases "and enable us to move forward with meaningful arms reduction negotiations with the Soviet Union."

Also falling into this category, with spending increased or protected, were foreign aid, protection of U.S. embassies and efforts to thwart drug smugglers.

- **"Unnecessary programs are no longer affordable."** As examples of outmoded or ill-conceived government programs, the president cited the Interstate Commerce Commission, federal aid to keep alive Amtrak, the national passenger railroad, the Small Business Administration, grants for urban redevelopment and Appalachian development, and loan guarantees for ship construction.

All of these would have been eliminated in his budget.

- **"Many other programs should be reduced to a more appropriate scale."** Medicare, Medicaid, Civil Service pensions, subsidies to the U.S. Postal Service and subsidized housing had grown too fast and must be cut back substantially, the president said.
- **"The government should not compete with the private sector."** Reagan proposed selling government assets and turning over to the private sector such activities as power production from federal dams and oil reserves originally acquired for the Navy. He also suggested contracting more federal activities to private firms.

Rather than aid school districts directly for assistance to educationally disadvantaged students, Reagan proposed to convert aid to vouchers that parents could spend for public or private services. Similarly, housing aid would have been converted from direct loans and subsidies into vouchers for families to give to private landlords.

- **"Many services can be provided better by state and local governments."** The budget proposed abandoning federal assistance for local sewage treatment systems, airports, law enforcement and coastal protection programs. Some federal assistance for highways and mass transit, funded by federal gasoline taxes, would have been converted into block grants for local governments. The agricultural extension service, which provided research information for farmers through thousands of field offices, would have been cut.
- **"User fees should be charged for services where appropriate."** Federal services were still to be provided for activities such as loan guarantees, national parks and recreation facilities, Coast Guard and Customs inspections, and meat and poultry inspection, but fees would have been charged to pay for the programs.

'Government Is the Problem'

If the budget had been implemented, it would have created a federal government with a far different profile from the one Reagan inherited. Several agencies would have been shrunk to shadows of their former selves. The Department of Housing and Urban Development, for instance, was to get only $5.5 billion in new budget authority in 1987, vs. $33.4 billion appropriated for fiscal 1981. The Agriculture and Transportation departments also would have been hard hit.

As an example of his zeal to reduce the regulatory burden on U.S. business, the president would have eliminated the ICC, the nation's oldest regulatory agency.

The change was in keeping with the conservative philosophy the president had outlined in virtually every speech — from his inaugural address in 1981, when he said, "Government is not the solution to our problem. Government is the problem" — to the State of the Union address given Feb. 4. *(State of the Union text, p. 3-D)*

Meanwhile, spending for the Defense Department was to rise from 22.5 percent of federal outlays in 1981 to 27.5 percent in 1987.

In defending the special treatment accorded to military spending in the budget, Miller told reporters: "Go back and read Adam Smith [author of "The Wealth of Nations," 1776]. Defense is sort of the first-line function of government."

To cement his reshaped government into place for the future, the president renewed his calls for budget reforms, including a line-item veto, a balanced-budget constitutional amendment, and asked that the congressional budget resolution require his signature. He also called for study of multi-year appropriations and a separate capital budget for the federal government.

"The congressional budget process is foundering; last year it fell apart time and time again," he said.

But Congress was not receptive to proposals that would give the president more control over the budget process than he already had. Democrats were incensed by the president's analysis of the problem. They said his 1981 tax cuts and steady increases in military funding, rather than congressional spending for domestic programs, had sent deficits soaring.

Spending Increases

In keeping with the theme of slowing federal spending, the president proposed few new programs. The largest was a five-year, $4.4 billion program to increase security at American embassies abroad.

Reagan also sought a $300 million war chest to reduce the international trade imbalance by subsidizing foreign purchases of U.S. exports. The program was announced by the president in a speech in September 1985 to head off protectionist legislation in Congress. *(Trade action, p. 341)*

The budget asked for $43 million in 1986 and $75 million in later years to expand teacher training programs. And an increase of $181 million for drug enforcement efforts was shared by the FBI, Drug Enforcement Administration, Coast Guard, Defense Department, and Border Patrol.

Administration officials labeled as "high-priority programs" air safety activities of the Federal Aviation Administration and research into acquired immune deficiency syndrome (AIDS). But the budgets for these programs were proposed at or below 1986 levels.

Economic Prognosis

Meeting the president's deficit targets depended in large measure on the economic assumptions on which much of the budget was based, such as projections of economic growth and revenues. These were seen as optimistic and challenged by some economists. *(Chart, p. 541)*

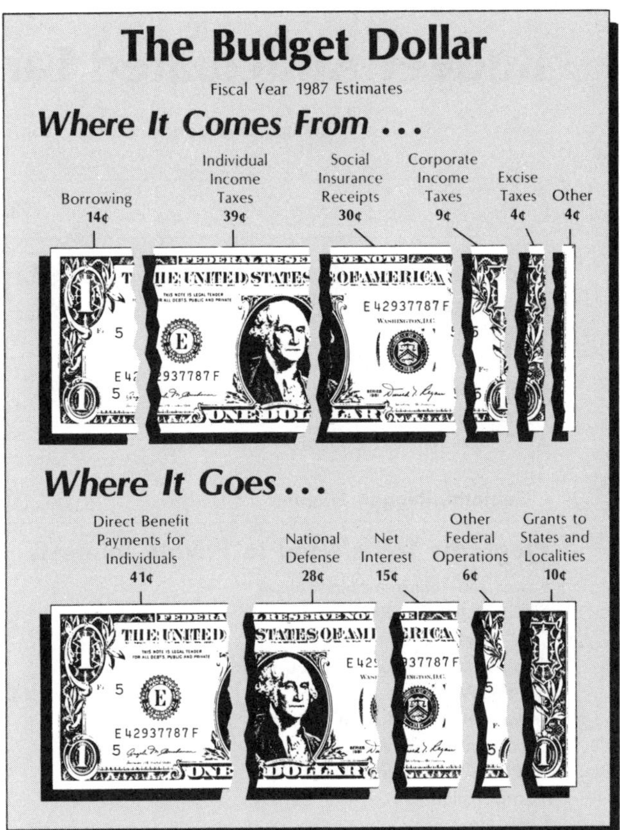

In his State of the Union address and his message to Congress on the budget, the president boasted of economic gains during his administration, and predicted they would continue. "The economic expansion we are now enjoying is one of the most vigorous in 35 years," he said.

The budget forecast 4 percent GNP growth after inflation for 1986 and 1987. It predicted inflation of 3.5 percent in 1986 and 4.1 percent in 1987, as measured by the Consumer Price Index.

Unemployment was expected to drop from 7.1 percent in 1985 to 6.7 percent in 1986 and 6.5 percent in 1987. Long-term interest rates were predicted to decline in both years from 10.6 percent in 1985 to 8.9 percent in 1986 and 8.5 percent in 1987. Short-term interest rates, it was assumed, would be 7.3 percent in 1986 and 6.5 percent in 1987.

The budget also predicted a gradual lessening of the trade imbalance, which put the United States into the status of a debtor nation for the first time in 1985.

Skeptics noted that small changes in the figures, such as a 1 percent increase in unemployment, could increase deficits substantially. But Beryl W. Sprinkel, chairman of the president's Council of Economic Advisers, said Feb. 5 that private forecasters were revising their projections to be closer to the administration's figures. "We expect to be in the middle of the herd when it finally settles," he said.

Three weeks after the president's budget went to Congress, the Congressional Budget Office (CBO) threw a damper on the administration's projections, forecasting significantly higher deficits in the near- and long-term, based on different expectations.

CBO projected economic growth at 3.2 percent in 1986,

Budget Anticipated Large Cuts, Some Increases . . .

This chart displays outlay savings from the major policy initiatives of the fiscal 1987 budget.

	1986	1987	1988	1989	1990	1991
Reagan Priority Programs — Spending Changes						
National Security Programs	$	2,453	4,252	5,987	8,488	12,400
Diplomatic Security	(87)	(628)	(731)	(1,013)	(1,061)	(844)
U.S. Space Programs	23	4	(55)	(42)	25	(339)
Enforcement of Drug Laws		(146)	(181)	(186)	(188)	(190)
Aviation Safety	(1)	(17)	233	357	427	610
AIDS Research and Control	15	15	9	13	17	20
Subtotal, Reagan Priorities	**$ (50)**	**1,681**	**3,527**	**5,116**	**7,708**	**11,657**
Programs Transferred to Private Interests						
Power Marketing Administrations	$	162	1,597	1,151	5,430	4,392
Naval Petroleum Reserves		1,018	1,859	(494)	(454)	(428)
GSA Asset Sales		462	568	178	178	178
Compensatory Education Vouchers		(3)	(49)	1	100	189
Housing Vouchers	1,140	3,818	5,108	5,839	6,386	6,858
Federal Housing Administration		146	(93)	(42)	23	66
Export-Import Bank Direct Loans		183	329	451	525	384
Overseas Private Investment Corporation		4	6	8	4	5
Crop Insurance		338	447	544	589	645
Amtrak		617	644	668	689	706
LANDSAT		54	60	41	13	2
Subtotal, Privatization	**$1,140**	**6,799**	**10,476**	**8,345**	**13,483**	**12,997**
Programs With Diminished Federal Role						
Ground Transportation Block Grant	$ 26	82	666	1,394	1,454	2,205
Federal-Aid Highways		446	675	1,249	1,943	2,520
Pollution Control Block Grant		12	26	37	48	58
Waste Treatment Construction Grants		25	128	374	742	1,281
Primary Care Block Grant	11	42	68	91	112	129
Justice State Grants	41	122	193	194	198	199
Cooperative Extension Service Grants		160	185	227	239	248
Community Development Block Grant		20	390	738	557	530
Community Services Block Grant	124	306	383	397	410	420
Subtotal, Federalism	**$ 202**	**1,215**	**2,714**	**4,701**	**5,703**	**7,590**
Charges for Government Services						
Park and Forest Recreation	$	70	71	75	77	78
Meat and Poultry Inspection		350	353	356	359	361
Coast Guard		238	476	476	476	476
Navigation		203	223	240	255	270
IRS and Customs	60	913	910	924	937	950
Ocean Sportfishing License		20	30	50	50	50
Pension Guaranty Premium	200	199	214	227	235	241
Uranium Enrichment		235	270	270	270	270
Federal Timber and Minerals		308	267	268	270	271
Subtotal, Charges for Services	**$ 260**	**2,536**	**2,814**	**2,886**	**2,929**	**2,967**

. . . To Reduce Deficit by $38.2 Billion in Fiscal 1987

(Figures in outlay savings, in millions of dollars; parentheses indicate spending increases.)

	1986	1987	1988	1989	1990	1991
Program Eliminations						
Interstate Commerce Commission	$	36	49	50	51	51
Urban Development Action Grants	11	61	148	188	273	323
Economic Development Administration and Appalachian Regional Commission	18	74	164	240	304	346
Small Business Credit Programs		1,445	1,961	1,822	1,244	948
Legal Services Corporation		266	315	328	340	353
Conservation Financial Assistance Programs	62	243	479	512	534	549
Selected Maritime Subsidies	48	131	160	168	170	170
Sea Grants and Coastal Zone Management State Grants	39	65	77	81	83	86
The New GI Bill		9	(28)	9	96	144
Subtotal, Eliminations	**$ 178**	**2,330**	**3,325**	**3,398**	**3,095**	**2,970**
Social Service Program Changes						
Medicare	$ 17	4,681	7,738	10,632	13,693	17,039
Assistance for Dislocated Workers	(2)	(29)	(7)	17	32	36
Job Corps	17	197	279	297	302	305
Summer Youth Employment Program		176	133	208	208	208
Vocational Education	4	152	359	447	486	510
Student Aid	124	1,315	2,406	2,582	3,080	3,474
Health Professions Training Subsidies	78	147	229	237	244	249
Child Nutrition Subsidies		697	826	918	1,001	1,091
Medicaid		1,280	2,622	3,463	4,345	5,347
Food Stamp Administration	69	313	403	506	572	572
Aid to Families with Dependent Children		238	233	231	239	231
Food Program for Women, Infants, Children		14	69	77	81	83
Veterans Medical Care	10	579	983	1,285	1,307	1,329
Work Incentive Program	38	191	222	235	243	249
Refugee and Entrant Assistance	21	104	89	91	99	83
Biomedical Research	42	353	493	816	974	1,106
Indian Health Service	28	111	148	183	209	238
Railroad Retirement	3	161	179	182	181	178
Subtotal, Social Service Revisions	**$ 449**	**10,680**	**17,404**	**22,407**	**27,296**	**32,328**
Changes in Management of Government Programs						
Credit Program Phaseouts and Reductions	$ 240	1,006	586	558	1,476	1,509
Credit User Fees		206	121	310	368	367
Federal and Federally Sponsored Credit Agencies		60	289	589	900	1,251
Loan Asset Sales		1,726	747	(30)	(687)	(1,094)
Civil Service Retirement		1,604	2,571	3,179	3,842	4,411
Federal Employee Health Benefits	(11)	1,186	677	790	1,043	1,278
Strategic Petroleum Reserve		399	374	368	373	371
National Defense Stockpile		250	500	500	500	500
Subtotal, Government Management	**$ 229**	**6,437**	**5,865**	**6,264**	**7,815**	**8,593**
TOTAL, MAJOR POLICY INITIATIVES	**$2,408**	**31,678**	**46,124**	**53,117**	**68,029**	**79,102**
Net Effect of Other Actions	**386**	**6,509**	**10,275**	**18,323**	**22,501**	**26,102**
TOTAL DEFICIT REDUCTION	**$2,794**	**38,187**	**56,399**	**71,440**	**90,530**	**105,204**

SOURCE: Fiscal 1987 Budget

for example, but it also calculated, as some complained at the time the budget was released, that outlays for defense would be significantly higher than OMB anticipated.

For fiscal 1987, CBO said the deficit would be $15.7 billion higher than the administration's estimate. For fiscal 1991, however, the administration forecast a budget surplus of $1.3 billion, while CBO projected a $40.1 billion deficit. The latter discrepancy was mostly due to differing economic assumptions.

Revenues

"A tax increase would jeopardize our economic expansion and might well prove counterproductive in terms of its effect on the deficit," Reagan wrote in his message to Congress, reflecting his bedrock political position.

Revenues, however, were projected to rise by 9.4 percent to $850.4 billion in his fiscal 1987 budget.

Some $6.3 billion of the revenue increase was to come from taxes and fees proposed by the administration, although they did not fall into the category of a tax increase that would arouse the president's wrath. About $1.7 billion was expected from extension of the 16-cents-per-pack federal tax on cigarettes, which at the time was scheduled to fall to 8 cents in March 1986 (the then-pending and ultimately enacted fiscal 1986 deficit-reduction bill, however, extended the cigarette tax permanently at 16 cents per pack). *(Deficit reduction, p. 555; 1985 Almanac p. 498)*

Increases in fees that funded black-lung payments to coal miners, changes in the unemployment program for rail workers, and speeded up deposits by state and local governments of Social Security payroll taxes were expected to raise other revenues.

New or higher user fees for services of agencies such as the Internal Revenue Service and the Nuclear Regulatory Commission were to provide an estimated $2.4 billion, Miller said.

The budget calculated that the various tax cuts enacted at Reagan's urging in 1981 (PL 97-34) reduced receipts by $244.8 billion in fiscal 1987, more than the projected deficit. *(1981 Almanac p. 91)*

Some of these revenues were made up by other legislative changes in subsequent years, but revenues were still $150.6 billion less than they would have been had tax rates remained unchanged.

Baker said, however, that these lost receipts had led to economic expansion that increased revenues in other areas. "The Ronald Reagan tax cuts are not responsible for our current fiscal difficulties," he said.

Baker reiterated the administration's adamant opposition to using the tax-reform measure under consideration in the Senate to become a vehicle for reducing the deficit. "The president will not compromise on his principles," he said Feb. 5. "He will not permit tax reform to degenerate into a tax increase in disguise."

Reagan said that in view of reductions in the international price of oil, he might accept some type of oil import fee — but only if it was part of a revenue-neutral tax-reform package, not to reduce the deficit. *(Tax overhaul, p. 491)*

The administration pointed out that while tax receipts had not risen as fast as they would have without the tax cuts, they remained a fairly constant percentage when measured against the gross national product — increasing slightly from 19 percent in fiscal 1986 to 19.4 percent in fiscal 1989, primarily because many taxpayers moved into higher tax brackets and because increases in Social Security taxes were scheduled to go into effect in 1988.

Supplementals and Rescissions

The budget proposed relatively little in additional funding to supplement fiscal 1986 appropriations, and suggested rescinding some of the money Congress provided for fiscal 1986.

Supplemental requests totaled $1.9 billion, compared with $8.3 billion for additional funding and pay increases sought in the previous year's budget.

The largest request was $707 million for additional security at overseas embassies. The budget also sought $340 million for the Internal Revenue Service, which it said would increase the collection of taxes.

Rescissions, which only took effect if approved by Congress, totaled $10 billion, compared with $1.7 billion sought for fiscal 1986.

The administration had sought to reclaim $4.4 billion from HUD in line with its proposal to replace housing subsidies with less-expensive vouchers. It also proposed rescinding $760 million for the fourth-quarter payment in fiscal 1986 for state and local government revenue sharing and $456 million from student aid.

Under Gramm-Rudman-Hollings, supplemental appropriations had to be offset by action to raise or save an equivalent amount of money. While the administration's rescission proposals far exceeded its supplemental requests, key committee chairmen were skeptical of the chances for any supplemental appropriations for fiscal 1986. *(Supplementals, p. 153)*

Credit Budget

In addition to proposing spending reductions, the president's budget suggested a major overhaul of government lending programs. While these were not counted as direct federal spending in budget calculations, they did compete with private funds for credit. According to OMB figures, federal loans accounted for one-seventh of the nation's $7 trillion in total outstanding debt.

Government credit programs were mainly of two types: direct loans, which a government agency made to a lender, and loan guarantees, which consisted of the government's promise to repay a private lender if the borrower defaulted. In recent years, agricultural programs such as the Farmers Home Administration and the Commodity Credit Corporation accounted for the largest share of direct loans, while loan guarantees were dominated by housing loans through the Federal Housing Administration and the Veterans Administration.

Both types of loans, the administration argued, represented a subsidy to beneficiaries that soaked up credit that would otherwise be available. The budget would have scaled direct loans back from $41.6 billion in fiscal 1986 to $30.6 billion in fiscal 1987. The value of guaranteed loans would have dropped from $93.9 billion in fiscal 1986 to $79.8 billion in fiscal 1987.

The administration proposed to phase out loans under the Small Business Administration, Community Development Block Grants, the Rural Electrification Administration, the Maritime Administration and college housing programs.

Housing loans from the Farmers Home Administration would have been converted into a voucher program.

Assistance from the Export-Import Bank would have been shifted from direct loans to interest subsidies.

The administration proposed raising fees and interest

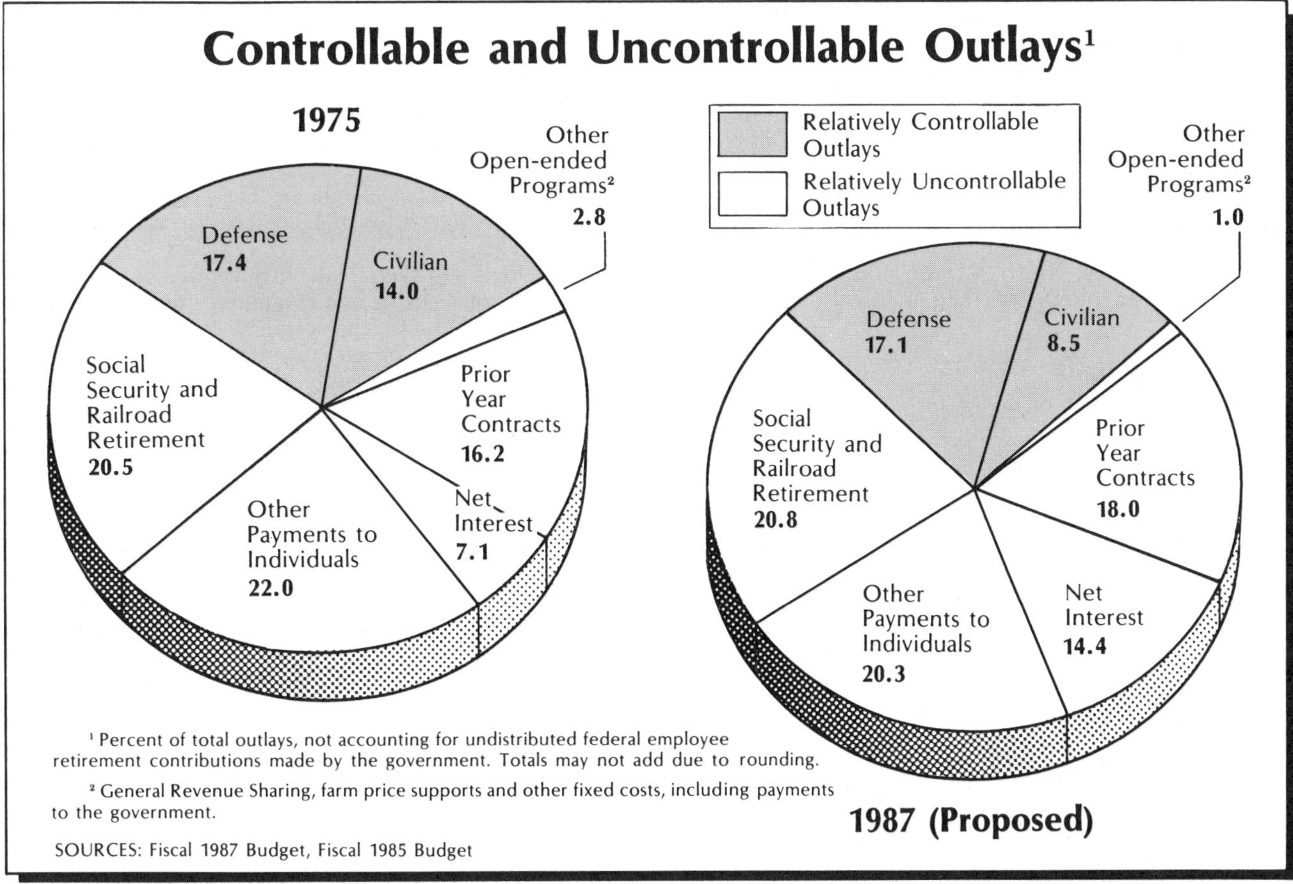

[1] Percent of total outlays, not accounting for undistributed federal employee retirement contributions made by the government. Totals may not add due to rounding.

[2] General Revenue Sharing, farm price supports and other fixed costs, including payments to the government.

SOURCES: Fiscal 1987 Budget, Fiscal 1985 Budget

rates it charged for lending money, particularly for mortgage and student loans.

Perhaps the most radical suggestion, however, was that the government sell off some of its loans, beginning with a portfolio with a face value of $4.4 billion in fiscal 1987. These were to come from 13 programs, including $2.3 billion in SBA loans, $1.1 billion in college housing loans and $400 million in agriculture loans.

Selling the loans was expected to bring in an estimated $1.7 billion for fiscal 1987, although receipts in future years would have been reduced because the government no longer would have been collecting payments on the loans it had sold.

Management Reforms

In 1986, for the first time, Reagan added a separate volume on management reform to the series of budget documents.

In 1982, the president began a program called "Reform '88" to streamline federal procedures. The volume cited progress on a number of fronts, such as increasing the percentage of government payments made on time from 25 percent to 99 percent, and reducing federal publications by 25 percent.

The budget proposed a 3 percent pay increase for civilian employees in January 1987, and a 4 percent increase for military personnel in October 1986.

An increase in retirement pay for civilian and military retirees, scheduled to take effect January 1987, would have been eliminated.

Major Proposals

The following is a summary of categorical proposals in the president's fiscal 1987 budget:

National Defense

Reagan requested an 8 percent inflation-adjusted increase in budget authority for national defense over the amount that was available in fiscal 1986 after Gramm-Rudman-Hollings reductions took effect March 1. *(Defense appropriations, p. 206)*

Citing the congressional budget resolution (S Con Res 32) adopted in August 1985, administration officials insisted that the $320.3 billion request was only 3 percent higher than Congress had agreed to approve for fiscal 1986 — an amount it subsequently had not approved.

For the Defense Department, $311.6 billion in new budget authority was requested. Other defense programs, chiefly in the Energy Department, which developed and manufactured nuclear weapons for the Pentagon, brought the total defense request to $320.3 billion in budget authority. The actual fiscal 1986 budgets were $278.4 billion for the Defense Department, and $286.1 billion for the broader category of national defense.

According to the administration, its request would have resulted in outlays of $274.3 billion for the Defense Department and $282.2 billion for the broader category. But some private and congressional budget analysts insisted that outlays would run up to $15 billion higher than those estimates.

The request would have continued Reagan's program of an across-the-board modernization of the U.S. arsenal, with few concessions to budgetary stringency. It would have continued the purchase of MX intercontinental missiles and the development of a smaller Midgetman missile and "stealth" bomber while beginning production of the Trident II submarine-launched missile. It would have increased from $2.75 billion to $4.8 billion the budget for research on a nationwide anti-missile defense. It would have continued the procurement of most major conventional weapons on schedule, including 840 M-1 tanks and nine major warships. Nearly a third more combat planes would have been purchased than in fiscal 1986 — 485 planes.

International Affairs

Reagan proposed increases for most foreign affairs programs, especially for military and economic aid to friendly countries and to boost security at U.S. diplomatic posts overseas. *(Foreign aid appropriations, p. 162)*

Foreign aid programs were budgeted at $16.2 billion for fiscal 1987 — an 8.4 percent increase over the fiscal 1986 amount, after Gramm-Rudman cuts. As with defense, the administration essentially asked for funding levels it had wanted but Congress did not approve in fiscal 1986.

Reagan's major new foreign initiative was a $4.4 billion, five-year program to beef up security at embassies and other diplomatic posts. That included a $707 million supplemental for fiscal 1986 and $1.4 billion for fiscal 1987.

Foreign aid traditionally was an unpopular spending issue in Congress, and members were particularly unhappy that Reagan would again promote such programs at a time of budget austerity. David R. Obey, D-Wis., chairman of the House Appropriations Subcommittee on Foreign Operations, said immediately after the budget was released that he was ready to cut foreign aid by up to 50 percent, perhaps with an exemption for congressionally popular aid to Israel and Egypt.

As in past years, Reagan boosted "security assistance" — economic and military aid. For fiscal 1987, Reagan sought $11.3 billion for these, a 10 percent increase over the post-Gramm-Rudman level for fiscal 1986. The biggest chunk — some $5.3 billion — was for Israel and Egypt.

Spending for development and health programs, however, would have been frozen or cut; the administration's proposal to cut $46 million from two United Nations programs prompted complaints from House members.

The budget request included proposed budget authority of about $1.4 billion for various multilateral development banks. About half of this amount — $750 million — was proposed for the International Development Association, an arm of the World Bank.

The administration renewed a proposal to eliminate a direct lending program run by the Export-Import Bank that provided loans to foreign buyers of U.S. exports. The lending program, in fiscal 1986 funded at $1.1 billion, was to be replaced by an interest-subsidy plan that would have relied on loans from private banks.

The budget included a request for a new $300 million program to counter what U.S. trade officials considered unfair government export subsidies offered by other countries. The money was to be used to provide loans and grants to potential foreign purchasers of U.S. products.

Agriculture

The Reagan administration banked on the quick success of revised price-support programs in the 1985 farm law (PL 99-198) to compensate for sweeping reductions proposed for other agriculture programs in fiscal 1987. *(Agriculture appropriations, p. 201; farm program changes, p. 302)*

The president's budget limited spending for all farm and nutrition programs to $44.6 billion in fiscal 1987, a $9.5 billion cut from the Agriculture Department's fiscal 1986 spending limit of $54.2 billion. That represented a 17.7 percent reduction on top of 4.3 percent fiscal 1986 Gramm-Rudman cuts.

The most substantial cuts involved the eventual elimination of rural housing and community development programs, crop insurance, the Rural Electrification Administration (REA) and the agriculture extension service.

The administration proposed to continue its policy of reducing direct operating loans to farmers through the Farmers Home Administration (FmHA), and to encourage private lenders to make those loans with repayment guarantees from the government. The use of guaranteed loans, combined with the elimination of farm ownership and emergency disaster loans, was expected to save $3.3 billion in fiscal 1987, according to department estimates.

The budget also called for farmers and ranchers to begin paying user fees for many of the government's marketing and inspection programs now provided free of charge. That was expected to save $475 million in fiscal 1987.

Generally left untouched, however, were the basic price- and income-support devices that Congress had just reauthorized for the next five years. Those devices were designed to reduce the market prices for major commodities and, it was hoped, expand the demand for U.S. farm products overseas.

With that ideal in mind, the administration said it would propose legislation to reduce some of the export incentive programs traditionally used to spur foreign sales. The administration wanted to cut the required level of government export credit guarantees for agriculture products from $5.2 billion to $3 billion, with the added proviso that a 5 percent origination fee be placed on each loan guarantee.

The administration also sought to reduce outlays for Food for Peace (PL 480) shipments on the assumption that food aid needs in sub-Saharan Africa would decline, and that lower commodity prices would soon prevail.

The budget assumed that partial income-support payments would be made to farmers in the spring, rather than after harvest. Due to overlapping calendars of fiscal years and crop years, these advance payments were expected to raise fiscal 1986 spending for price-support programs by $2.2 billion, to $20.3 billion, an all-time record. But making those payments up front would relieve some fiscal 1987 spending obligations, reducing outlays to $16.2 billion and actually creating a one-year budget "savings" of $4.2 billion.

To pay for the added, year-end expenses in fiscal 1986, however, the administration said it would ask for nearly $8 billion in supplemental spending authority for the Commodity Credit Corporation, the agency that disbursed price-support loans and income subsidies.

Department officials said such a supplemental appropriation, since it would be a reimbursement for realized losses, would be exempt from Gramm-Rudman-Hollings spending restraints. *(CCC supplemental appropriations for fiscal 1986, p. 161)*

A Glossary of Budget Terminology

The federal budget is the president's financial plan for the federal government. It accounts for how government funds have been raised and spent, and it proposes financial policies for the coming **fiscal year** and beyond. Fiscal year 1987 began Oct. 1, 1986, and ended Sept. 30, 1987.

The budget discusses **receipts**, amounts the government expects to raise in taxes and other fees; **budget authority**, amounts federal agencies are allowed to obligate or lend; and **outlays**, amounts actually paid out by the government during the year. Examples of outlays are funds spent to buy equipment or property to meet the government's liability under a contract or to pay employees' salaries. Outlays also include net lending — the difference between amounts the government loans out and repayments.

The budget earmarks funds to cover two kinds of spending. **Mandatory** spending covers **entitlement** programs, such as food stamps, Social Security and farm subsidies, that may be used by anyone who meets eligibility criteria. Mandatory spending may not be limited in the annual appropriations process. **Discretionary** spending is set annually through appropriations.

The budget has a twofold purpose: to establish priorities among federal programs and to chart U.S. **fiscal policy**, which is the coordinated use of taxes and expenditures to affect the economy.

Congress adopts its version of the budget in the form of a **budget resolution**, which is supposed to be adopted by April 15, setting binding figures for taxes and spending, broken down among major budget categories, called **functions**. It also includes **reconciliation** instructions directing committees to recommend changes in laws governing programs under their jurisdictions to meet revenue and spending targets.

If Congress fails to meet deficit targets set by the Gramm-Rudman-Hollings law (PL 99-177), it is supposed to vote on a **sequester order** making across-the-board cuts, half from defense and half from domestic programs, to achieve the required deficit reduction.

An **authorization** is an act of Congress that establishes government programs. It defines the scope of programs and sets a ceiling for how much can be spent on them. Authorizations do not actually spend money. In the case of authority to enter contractual obligations, though, Congress authorizes the administration to make firm commitments for which funds must later be provided. Congress also occasionally includes mandatory spending requirements in an authorization to ensure spending at a certain level.

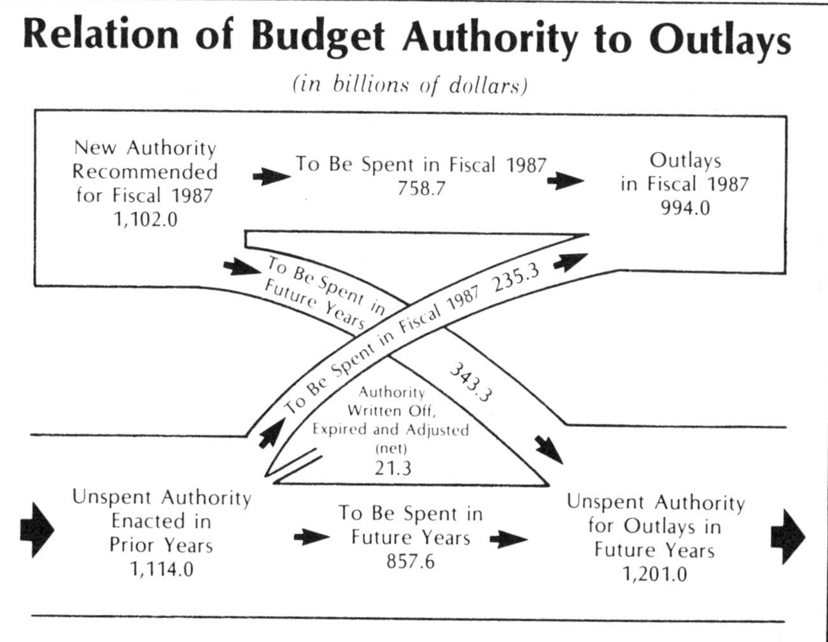

An **appropriation** provides money for programs within the limits established in authorizations. An appropriation may be for a single year, a specified number of years or an indefinite period.

Appropriations generally take the form of budget authority, which may differ from actual outlays. That is because, in practice, funds actually spent or obligated during a year may be drawn partly from budget authority conferred in the year in question and partly from budget authority conferred in previous years.

Education

The administration proposed a $15.2 billion budget for the Department of Education that called for substantial cuts in college student assistance and vocational education grants, while maintaining current spending levels for major elementary and secondary education programs. *(Education appropriations, p. 196)*

The department also proposed rescinding $1 billion of the $17.8 billion provided for fiscal 1986.

The fiscal 1987 budget would have reduced the number of college students receiving federal financial aid by about 1.3 million, to 4.3 million. The biggest cuts would have come in Guaranteed Student Loans, a popular source of aid for middle-class as well as low-income students. The administration proposed tighter eligibility rules to curb loans to middle-income students, sharply cutting interest subsidies for those who do qualify and reducing payments made to banks to encourage them to make student loans. *(Student loan program changes, p. 268)*

The administration also proposed revamping a smaller

program, National Direct Student Loans, into a system of unsubsidized loans. The new program was to link loan repayments to borrowers' income after they left school and allow people to take longer to repay.

Vocational education aid would have been cut almost in half, with the remaining funds targeted for helping the handicapped and disadvantaged. The budget proposed to keep funding at roughly this year's levels for the department's major programs supporting bilingual education and elementary and secondary education for the poor and the handicapped. But a wide range of smaller programs, including $122 million in aid to libraries, would have been eliminated.

Undaunted by past congressional inaction on controversial education proposals, the administration again called for providing education vouchers for disadvantaged schoolchildren and tax credits for private school tuition.

Energy

The president's fiscal 1987 budget for the Energy Department reflected continuing efforts to dismantle some of its functions — years after Congress discouraged his efforts to eliminate the entire agency.

One Energy Department function the president proposed to build up rather than dismantle was nuclear weapons and defense activities. Dramatic increases in defense would have offset massive cuts in other energy programs, with the net result being a slight increase in the overall Energy Department budget. *(Energy appropriations, p. 183)*

Reagan asked for $12.1 billion in 1987 as compared with $11.97 billion in 1986 spending.

His proposal for defense production and support was $4.8 billion, an increase of $498 million. That money would have gone for things such as nuclear missile warheads and submarine fuel.

Funds for research and development, another major departmental mission, would have been cut to $4.5 billion in 1987, about $330 million less than 1986 levels. Although research cuts would have been spread among most types of energy, cuts would have been most drastic for fossil, solar and renewable energy and conservation.

The president proposed to end other Energy Department functions altogether, either in 1987 or within several years. For example, he proposed no further filling of the Strategic Petroleum Reserve, the underground oil supply meant to cushion the nation in the event of another oil embargo. Reagan's budget also proposed selling off the Naval Petroleum and Oil Shale reserves and federal power marketing agencies such as the Bonneville Power Administration. In addition, the budget proposed easing the federal government out of the business of enriching uranium for private utilities and letting private companies do the job.

Environment

Reagan would cut the Environmental Protection Agency's (EPA) operating budget only slightly in fiscal 1987, but he proposed eliminating altogether grants to help cities and counties build sewage treatment plants.

The result was that Reagan's 1987 request of $2.4 billion for EPA was scarcely over half of the $4.7 billion he requested for the agency in fiscal 1986. The sewer program, funded at about $2.4 billion annually in recent years, accounted for most of the drop. *(EPA appropriations, p. 179)*

At the time of the budget request, however, Congress had not passed legislation reauthorizing either sewer grants or the "superfund" hazardous-waste cleanup program, the other major item in EPA's budget. Because both 1986 and 1987 spending were contingent on enactment of that legislation, the spending situation was confused.

The 1987 budget request was almost constant for the half of EPA's budget that went to operate its regulatory programs for pollution control — $1.38 billion in 1987 compared with $1.43 billion for 1986. Although Reagan proposed no funds for the sewer grant program, he said he would propose $1.8 billion once a Clean Water Act reauthorization was enacted. *(Clean Water Act, p. 136)*

He proposed $1.05 billion for the superfund program to clean up abandoned toxic-waste dumps in 1987. That is higher than annual spending in any year since the program began in 1981 — but lower than the $1.5 billion annual level approved by the Senate and the $2 billion level approved by the House. *(Superfund, p. 111)*

Health

In another effort to put the brakes on the growth of Medicare, the budget called for changes in the massive federal health insurance program for the elderly that would save a projected $4.7 billion in fiscal 1987.

The administration budget proposed new limits on what the program paid for hospitals' capital expenses, sharp cuts in subsidies for graduate medical education and increases in the premiums and deductibles that elderly paid out-of-pocket.

The administration did not propose, as it did for fiscal 1986, to continue the existing freeze on physicians' fees under the program. But the fiscal 1987 budget proposed to save $432 million by making other changes in the physicians' fee structures, including cuts in what Medicare paid for certain services the administration considered "overpriced." *(Medicare/Medicaid, p. 252)*

For Medicaid, the health-insurance program for the poor, the administration recycled a proposal to cap federal matching payments to states under the jointly financed program. The proposed $23.6 billion cap was $1.3 billion below projections for fiscal 1986.

The administration said it considered research on acquired immune deficiency syndrome (AIDS) a priority, but the $213 million it requested for the enterprise was less than the $224 million appropriated for fiscal 1986. Spending for other biomedical research conducted by the National Institutes of Health would have totaled $4.9 billion, down from $5.3 billion in fiscal 1986. *(Health appropriations, p. 196)*

The president requested $1.6 billion for the department's four major health block grants — enough to restore the programs to fiscal 1986 levels before Gramm-Rudman automatic cuts. The administration also proposed eliminating programs, already deeply cut in recent years, to support the training of doctors, nurses and other health professionals.

Housing and Economic Development

Subsidized housing for the poor would have been cut 65 percent this fiscal year and another 39 percent in fiscal 1987, under Reagan's proposed budget.

Existing funds available for subsidized housing totaled $10.88 billion, according to the Department of Housing and Urban Development (HUD). The budget would have chopped out $7 billion through rescissions, deferrals or cuts mandated by Gramm-Rudman, leaving $3.74 billion in budget authority for fiscal 1986.

That would have supported 67,064 units of housing, compared with the 111,500 approved by Congress. HUD proposed providing 50,000 new units each year from 1987 through 1991.

In fiscal 1987, budget authority for assisted housing would have been cut to $2.3 billion.

The budget proposed to cut 1986 budget authority of about $17 billion for all HUD activities by more than a third, to $10.7 billion. In fiscal 1987, budget authority would have been cut again almost by half, down to $5.54 billion. *(HUD appropriations, p. 171)*

To make those cuts, Reagan proposed to eliminate construction programs for housing owned and operated by local public housing authorities, and rental housing for the elderly and handicapped. Construction for those programs virtually ended when Reagan took office. In addition, the administration would have ended rental housing development grants, rental rehabilitation grants and rehabilitation loans and loan guarantees. *(Housing program changes, p. 585)*

New subsidized housing would have been available only through vouchers provided by the government, which low-income renters would use like cash to rent private housing they found on their own. Federal housing subsidies traditionally had been in the form of a contract between the government and a landlord. Congress in the past approved 87,000 vouchers.

Because the administration again proposed eliminating rural housing and rural development programs in the Agriculture Department's FmHA, HUD would have been expected to divide its housing funds evenly between rural and urban areas.

In addition, HUD proposed changes in Federal Housing Administration (FHA) mortgage insurance that would have added about $3,000 to $4,000 to the average cost of FHA-backed mortgages, while targeting aid to families with incomes less than $40,000 a year. Borrowers' premiums would have been raised from 3.8 percent of a loan to 5 percent and would have been paid in a lump sum.

FHA would have no longer insured loans for investors and second homes. A limit of $50.9 billion in FHA mortgage insurance commitments would have been imposed, $9.1 billion less than the fiscal 1986 level.

The only area in HUD proposed to receive a budget increase was Fair Housing and Equal Opportunity, which would have gone from $6.3 million in fiscal 1986 to $12 million in fiscal 1987 to combat housing discrimination. The funds would have paid for special teams to improve fair-housing enforcement, investigate complaints and prepare cases for court action.

Several popular community and economic development programs would have been eliminated.

They included the Small Business Administration, the Economic Development Administration, the Appalachian Regional Commission and Urban Development Action Grants.

The budget also proposed a $500 million deferral of fiscal 1986 Community Development Block Grant funds into fiscal 1987, and funding CDBG at $2.12 billion next fiscal year. With the $500 million deferred from fiscal 1986, CDBG funding in fiscal 1987 would have dropped 16 percent from the level authorized by Congress.

Human Services

True to his presidential campaign promise, Reagan proposed no cuts in Social Security benefits for the elderly — one of the few major elements of the domestic budget to escape the ax entirely. Although the president's State of the Union message called for a study of the entire welfare system, his budget called only for limited changes that had previously been proposed and rejected by Congress.

As in the past, Reagan called for stiffer work requirements for recipients of food stamps and Aid to Families with Dependent Children, the principal federal-state welfare program.

In a new attempt to extend the block-grant concept of funding social services, the administration proposed consolidating several existing child abuse and family violence programs into a state block grant for family crisis and protective services.

Among the panoply of domestic programs the administration proposed eliminating were the Community Services Block Grant and the Work Incentive program, which helped welfare recipients find jobs. The administration also proposed savings in the food stamp program by repealing changes made in the 1985 farm bill that expanded eligibility. The administration also proposed eliminating the 25-cents-per-meal subsidy on school lunches for middle-income children.

Law Enforcement

The president proposed $7.12 billion in budget authority for the administration of justice, an increase of $490 million over fiscal 1986.

Funding in this area involved law enforcement and civil legal programs, with more than half of the money — $3.94 billion — earmarked for law enforcement activity. Spending would have been spread out primarily in four areas: the Justice Department, the Treasury Department's Bureau of Alcohol, Tobacco and Firearms, the U.S. Customs Service, which helps police the nation's borders, and the U.S. Secret Service. *(Treasury appropriations, p. 193; Justice appropriations, p. 189)*

The largest segment of funding in this area would have gone to the Justice Department — $4.18 billion for fiscal 1987. This would have been an increase of $342 million over fiscal 1986. Another $1.25 billion was proposed for the federal judiciary; this amount is submitted directly to Congress by the courts.

As in the previous five years, Reagan proposed no money for the Legal Services Corporation, which provided legal assistance to the nation's poor. Congress continued to fund the corporation, however, but at reduced rates.

In the law enforcement area, which the budget described as a major initiative, new resources were targeted at drug enforcement. The Drug Enforcement Administration (DEA), for example, would have received an additional $8.6 million and 112 positions to strengthen heroin, cocaine and "dangerous" drugs investigations. The FBI budget, proposed at $1.2 billion, would have increased by 738 positions and $69.4 million.

The administration also proposed $133.8 million in the federal prison budget of $767.5 million for construction of three new medium-security prisons. When completed, these facilities would have added 2,250 beds to the prison system.

Although the administration wanted to beef up drug enforcement, the U.S. Customs Service faced some cuts for work in this area. Budget authority for the agency's air interdiction program, designed to help prevent illegal drugs from entering the country, would have increased slightly

Program Termination and 'Privatization' Proposals

The Reagan administration wanted to end, phase out or sell to private investors — "privatize" — the following major programs or agencies. Many of the program terminations had been suggested in previous years: *(Estimated deficit reductions, chart, p. 528)*

Terminations

- Air service subsidies to communities for service lost through deregulation
- Agency for International Development housing guarantees — phase out beginning in 1987
- Agricultural Stabilization and Conservation Service cost-sharing
- Amtrak — end in 1987
- Appalachian Regional Commission
- Carl Perkins Scholarships for high school graduates interested in teaching
- Categorical aid to migrant health centers, black-lung clinics and family-planning clinics, to be wrapped into a block grant program
- Coastal zone management state grant program
- College housing loans — phase out beginning in 1987
- Commercial fishing industry assistance
- Community Services Block Grant
- Crop insurance subsidies — phase out by 1991
- Economic Development Administration
- Energy conservation grants and state energy-planning and extension programs
- Environmental Protection Agency loans for asbestos removal
- Federal Housing Administration — develop proposals in 1987 to turn agency over to private sector
- Farmers Home Administration housing and rural aid programs, wrapped into the Department of Housing and Urban Development (HUD)
- GI enhanced recruitment bill (PL 98-525)
- Graduate education programs, including fellowships for women and minorities and for law and public service students
- HUD grants for rental housing development and rehabilitation; rental rehabilitation loans; and new subsidized housing construction
- Immigrant education
- Impact Aid Part B for schools serving U.S. employees' children
- Interstate Commerce Commission
- Legal Services Corporation
- Library aid, for public library research and librarian training
- Justice Department grants for juvenile justice, state and local aid
- Mariel Cubans and regional information sharing system programs — turned over to states to run with no federal funding.
- Maritime subsidies — ship construction loan guarantees, aid to six state maritime schools, research and development (after 1987), and the cargo preference requirement included in the 1985 farm bill (PL 99-198).
- National Sea Grant college program
- Postal Service subsidy
- Public Health Service training grants
- Railroad rehabilitation loans — phase out beginning in 1987
- Rail service assistance to states
- Revenue sharing — end in 1987
- Rural Electrification Administration
- Soil Conservation Service programs on private lands, including the small watershed program.
- Small Business Administration credit assistance programs
- State Student Incentive Grants
- Tennessee Valley Authority regional economic aid
- Urban Development Action Grants
- U.S. Travel and Tourism Administration
- Waste treatment construction grants — phase out by 1990
- Work Incentive Program (WIN) for adults receiving benefits under Aid to Families with Dependent Children

Privatization

Power Marketing Administrations. Sell the power-generating and transmission facilities (but not the dams) of the five federal PMAs (Bonneville, Western Area, Southeastern, Southwestern, Alaska).

Naval Petroleum Reserves. Sell the oil fields at Elk Hills, Calif., and Teapot Dome, Wyo.

Surplus Government Property. Step up sales of federal property to private buyers. Sales have averaged $100 million to $150 million a year since 1981, could rise to $2 billion over the next five years.

Federal Loans. Sell off $4.4 billion worth of loans over five years, as a start toward a larger-scale disposition of the federal loan portfolio.

Compensatory Education. Provide vouchers to parents of disadvantaged children, to be spent on private schooling, if desired, instead of public school compensatory education programs.

Housing Vouchers. Provide housing vouchers to 50,000 additional poor households per year, to be used to buy or rent housing privately. Federally supported housing assistance would be terminated.

Federal Housing Administration. Develop a plan for turning the FHA, which provides mortgage insurance, over to the private sector.

Export-Import Bank Loans. Substitute interest-rate subsidies for direct loans to U.S. exporters.

Overseas Private Investment Corporation. Study ways to privatize OPIC, which insures U.S. investments in developing countries.

Crop Insurance. Phase out federal subsidies over five years, letting the private sector provide crop insurance without federal reinsurance.

Amtrak. End federal subsidies to the passenger service railroad and let private business, states or localities buy and run it if they wish.

LANDSAT. End subsidies and let private users buy the government's five land remote sensing satellites.

from $52.5 million in 1986 to $54.7 million in fiscal 1987, but outlays would have declined from $89.96 million to $74.2 million.

Labor

The Labor Department proposed $23.24 billion in outlays, a program reduction of $420 million from the existing level. A key element within the budget was $4.2 billion proposed for employment and training programs, about $600 million less than fiscal 1986 outlays. More than half of the money — $3.1 billion — would have been for the Training and Employment Service, which provided funds for programs authorized by the Job Training Partnership Act (PL 97-300). This program was created in 1982 to give the private sector a greater role in providing job training and as an alternative to the Comprehensive Employment Training Act. *(1982 Almanac p. 39)*

Within this employment category, the administration proposed phasing down the Jobs Corps, a program of residential centers that provide basic skills and vocational training for severely disadvantaged youths. The administration in the past had proposed killing this program, but this year Labor officials said they wanted to redirect its resources and make it more efficient.

The proposed fiscal 1987 outlay was $397.6 million, about 65 percent of the fiscal 1986 outlay of $633.4 million. *(Labor appropriations, p. 196)*

The department estimated that average weekly unemployment benefits would rise from $126.10 per week in 1986 to $131.50 per week in fiscal 1987. The budget estimated the total amount to be paid in fiscal 1987 at $15.1 billion.

The administration also proposed scaling back the Summer Youth Employment and Training program, which provided summer employment to those 14-21 years of age. The proposal called for a rescission of $208 million for fiscal 1987, putting the total budget authority at $428 million and outlays at $495.7 million.

Natural Resources and Water Projects

The president's proposal of $6.2 billion in budget authority for the Interior Department in fiscal 1987 would have taken savings out of construction and land-acquisition programs, while leaving funds for operating and maintaining federal lands fairly constant.

That budget took a bite out of the $6.4 billion spending level for 1986 and $7 billion for 1985. Few major programs would have been eliminated. But many of the president's 1987 cuts were ones Congress had repeatedly rejected in previous years. *(Interior funds, p. 179)*

The president's budget proposed to eliminate grants to the states for trout and salmon, endangered species, historic preservation, recreation and Alaskan native subsistence. Funding for 31 mineral institutes also would have been zeroed out.

Typical was the budget for the 80-million-acre National Park System. Under the department's assumptions, the Park Service's budget would have dropped from $794 million in 1986 to $734 million in 1987. The biggest cuts were to come from a near halt in spending to purchase new park land and build new facilities in parks. But the budget for daily operation of the park system would actually have increased from $624 million to $656 million — but only if Congress enacted proposed new or increased fees on national park users; otherwise park operations were to get $596 million.

Reagan's 1987 budget would have increased spending for hydroelectric dams, irrigation canals, port construction and other water projects — traditionally among the first targets of administration budget-cutters. The spending came in budgets for the Army Corps of Engineers and the Interior Department's Bureau of Reclamation. For the corps, Reagan proposed about $3.1 billion in spending, although if Congress enacted new user fees, net spending would have amounted to only $2.9 billion. The Bureau of Reclamation's budget would have been $853 million — a significant increase from the 1986 level of $744 million. *(Water projects, p. 127)*

Research and Development

Federal funding for research and development (R&D) would have grown by almost $9 billion, or 16 percent, above the fiscal 1986 level of $54 billion, under Reagan's proposed fiscal 1987 budget. Military R&D in the Defense Department was slated to receive the largest increase — 25 percent — while several civilian research programs would be cut. Research on the anti-missile strategic defense initiative accounted for much of that increase. *(Defense appropriations, p. 206)*

Two major research projects that would have received funding increases were the National Aeronautics and Space Administration's (NASA) orbiting space station, and development of a hypersonic airplane that could fly at 25 times the speed of sound.

NASA's budget, drafted before the Jan. 28 explosion of the space shuttle *Challenger*, called for an increase of less than 1 percent. The administration ultimately proposed to replace the shuttle, but proposed to find the money within existing NASA programs. *(NASA authorization, p. 330; appropriations, p. 171)*

Transportation

Reagan proposed significant cuts in federal highway and mass transit programs, and elimination of all federal funds for Amtrak, as part of his fiscal 1987 budget for the Department of Transportation (DOT). The 1987 DOT request was $21.7 billion, well below the 1986 level of $26.8 billion. Most of the reduction would have been in the budgets for the Federal Highway Administration, the Urban Mass Transit Administration and the Federal Railroad Administration.

The administration proposed to eliminate funds for most new mass transit projects. It would have created a new block grant to provide $3.3 billion for states to use as they wished for capital projects for transit or for major urban roads and bridges. There would have been sharp limits on the use of the funds for operating subsidies. The budget proposed that 84 percent of the department's budget be financed by various user fees. *(Transportation appropriations, p. 176)*

Reagan proposed capping spending from the Highway Trust Fund at $12.8 billion in fiscal 1987, compared with a 1986 level of $14.7 billion. For the Urban Mass Transit Administration, budget authority would have been reduced from $3.3 billion in 1986 to $1.2 billion in 1987, with $1.1 billion coming from 1 cent of the federal gasoline tax.

Transit spending would have been merged with highway aid under a new system of transportation block grants to give local and state governments flexibility in spending. The budget would have eliminated entirely the federal subsidy for Amtrak, the passenger rail service, which amounted to $562 million in 1986. ∎

Fiscal 1987 Budget by Function: $994 Billion in . . .

(in millions of dollars†)

	BUDGET AUTHORITY‡			OUTLAYS		
	1985	1986 est.	1987 est.	1985	1986 est.	1987 est.
NATIONAL DEFENSE						
Military Defense	$286,802	$278,412	$311,600	$245,371	$258,425	$274,265
Atomic Energy Defense Activities	7,325	7,232	8,230	7,098	7,152	7,708
Defense-related Activities	528	471	510	279	250	265
TOTAL	294,656	286,115	320,340	252,748	265,827	282,238
INTERNATIONAL AFFAIRS						
International Security Assistance	13,730	10,241	11,272	9,391	9,695	10,939
International Development and Humanitarian Assistance	6,496	4,672	4,893	5,409	4,902	4,978
Conduct of Foreign Affairs	2,510	2,996	3,830	2,054	2,364	3,055
Foreign Information and Exchange Activities	940	970	1,129	793	931	1,043
International Financial Programs	2,776	1,913	1,511	−1,471	−751	−1,395
TOTAL	26,453	20,792	22,636	16,176	17,141	18,619
GENERAL SCIENCE, SPACE AND TECHNOLOGY						
General Science and Basic Research	2,227	2,119	2,464	2,019	2,167	2,362
Space Research and Technology	6,925	6,701	6,988	6,607	6,732	6,826
TOTAL	9,152	8,820	9,452	8,627	8,899	9,188
ENERGY						
Energy Supply	5,511	4,577	3,651	2,615	2,745	2,858
Energy Conservation	472	428	39	491	470	265
Emergency Energy Preparedness	2,056	113	6	1,838	516	240
Energy Information, Policy and Regulation	719	673	658	740	702	654
TOTAL	8,758	5,791	4,355	5,685	4,433	4,017
NATURAL RESOURCES AND ENVIRONMENT						
Pollution Control and Abatement	4,303	4,578	4,099	4,465	4,588	4,466
Water Resources	4,087	3,540	3,711	4,122	3,977	3,847
Conservation and Land Management	1,446	783	457	1,481	1,051	600
Recreational Resources	1,574	1,376	1,147	1,621	1,547	1,365
Other Natural Resources	1,934	1,686	1,523	1,668	1,742	1,680
TOTAL	13,344	11,963	10,937	13,357	12,905	11,958
AGRICULTURE						
Farm Income Stabilization	25,569	26,232	18,057	23,751	24,017	17,938
Agricultural Research and Services	1,911	1,830	1,526	1,813	1,854	1,603
TOTAL	27,480	28,062	19,583	25,565	25,871	19,541
COMMERCE AND HOUSING CREDIT						
Mortgage Credit and Deposit Insurance	7,081	2,778	2,944	871	179	−3,067
Postal Service	2,639	3,974	3,515	1,351	1,345	2,683
Other Advancement of Commerce	2,389	1,975	3,736	2,007	2,279	1,743
TOTAL	12,109	8,727	10,195	4,229	3,802	1,359
TRANSPORTATION						
Ground Transportation	20,318	18,963	14,350	17,606	18,615	17,251
Air Transportation	6,011	5,360	5,460	4,895	4,954	5,184
Water Transportation	3,105	3,115	2,630	3,201	3,397	2,905
Other Transportation	126	119	126	137	140	163
TOTAL	29,559	27,556	22,565	25,838	27,106	25,503
COMMUNITY AND REGIONAL DEVELOPMENT						
Community Development	4,262	3,476	2,462	4,598	4,602	3,918
Area and Regional Development	3,664	2,798	2,027	3,117	2,956	2,768
Disaster Relief and Insurance	239	548	−715	—35	364	−161
TOTAL	8,166	6,823	3,775	7,680	7,922	6,525
EDUCATION, TRAINING, EMPLOYMENT, SOCIAL SERVICES						
Elementary, Secondary and Vocational Education	7,963	7,331	7,242	7,633	7,350	7,361
Higher Education	9,763	8,083	6,746	8,211	8,955	6,792
Research and General Education Aids	1,223	1,123	1,118	1,121	1,245	1,219
Training and Employment	5,422	4,487	4,250	4,972	5,221	4,467
Other Labor Services	716	680	715	678	694	714
Social Services	7,285	6,914	6,895	6,728	7,206	6,896
TOTAL	32,372	28,617	26,965	29,342	30,671	27,447

. . . Expenditures, $1.1 Trillion in Budget Authority

(in millions of dollars†)

	BUDGET AUTHORITY‡			OUTLAYS		
	1985	1986 est.	1987 est.	1985	1986 est.	1987 est.
HEALTH						
Health Care Services	$ 26,454	$ 28,425	$ 28,857	$ 26,984	$ 28,565	$ 28,354
Health Research	5,402	5,447	5,360	4,908	5,487	5,435
Education and Training of Health Care Work Force	549	349	279	468	455	360
Consumer and Occupational Health and Safety	1,196	1,148	849	1,182	1,162	848
TOTAL	33,601	35,368	35,344	33,542	35,669	34,997
MEDICARE	71,701	86,664	82,265	65,822	68,661	70,234
INCOME SECURITY						
General Retirement and Disability Insurance	6,564	7,382	6,526	5,617	5,344	5,442
Federal Employee Retirement and Disability	68,506	73,790	80,014	38,591	41,412	42,444
Unemployment Compensation	21,001	21,083	22,324	17,475	16,482	16,885
Housing Assistance	26,879	7,175	2,986	25,263	12,358	12,230
Food and Nutrition Assistance	18,655	18,769	18,151	18,540	18,732	18,094
Other Income Security	22,499	23,230	23,313	22,715	23,765	23,280
TOTAL	164,103	151,430	153,315	128,200	118,093	118,374
SOCIAL SECURITY	199,501	199,415	227,871	188,623	200,053	212,213
On-Budget	8,527	4,830	5,702	5,189	8,050	5,702
Off-Budget	190,973	194,586	222,168	183,434	192,004	206,510
VETERANS' BENEFITS AND SERVICES						
Income Security	15,089	15,378	15,616	14,714	15,110	15,366
Education, Training and Rehabilitation	1,180	1,015	665	1,120	633	553
Housing	306	200	—	214	219	−50
Hospital and Medical Care	10,005	9,990	9,581	9,547	9,872	9,720
Other Benefits and Services	828	796	839	758	785	831
TOTAL	27,408	27,379	26,702	26,352	26,619	26,420
ADMINISTRATION OF JUSTICE						
Federal Law Enforcement Activities	3,709	3,657	3,943	3,526	3,721	3,857
Federal Litigative and Judicial Activities	2,204	2,205	2,234	2,064	2,208	2,199
Federal Correctional Activities	599	588	758	537	646	681
Criminal Justice Assistance	220	179	184	150	213	211
TOTAL	6,733	6,629	7,119	6,277	6,788	6,948
GENERAL GOVERNMENT						
Legislative Functions	1,358	1,474	1,616	1,355	1,522	1,633
Executive Direction and Management	118	110	117	113	113	116
Central Fiscal Operations	3,875	4,007	3,943	3,485	3,819	3,831
General Property and Records Management	407	299	314	96	384	251
Central Personnel Management	149	136	142	164	127	140
Other General Government	565	858	609	521	816	645
Deductions for Offsetting Receipts	−506	−510	−555	−506	−510	−555
TOTAL	5,967	6,373	6,186	5,228	6,270	6,060
GENERAL PURPOSE FISCAL ASSISTANCE	6,322	5,248	1,742	6,353	6,236	1,739
NET INTEREST						
Interest on the Public Debt	179,063	196,095	206,855	179,063	196,095	206,855
Interest Received by On-Budget Trust Funds	−22,071	−26,654	−29,631	−22,071	−26,654	−29,631
Interest Received by Off-Budget Trust Funds	−4,118	−4,418	−4,716	−4,118	−4,418	−4,716
Other Interest	−23,437	−22,283	−24,511	−23,437	−22,283	−24,511
TOTAL	129,437	142,740	147,996	129,437	142,740	147,996
On-Budget	133,555	147,158	152,713	133,555	147,158	152,713
Off-Budget	−4,118	−4,418	−4,716	−4,118	−4,418	−4,716
ALLOWANCES	—	—	770	—	—	754
UNDISTRIBUTED OFFSETTING RECEIPTS	−32,759	−35,776	−38,128	−32,759	−35,776	−38,128
On-Budget	−30,250	−32,933	−34,951	−30,250	−32,933	−34,951
Off-Budget	−2,509	−2,843	−3,177	−2,509	−2,843	−3,177
GRAND TOTAL	**$1,074,063**	**$1,058,736**	**$1,101,985**	**$946,323**	**$979,928**	**$994,002**
On-Budget	889,716	871,411	887,709	769,515	795,185	795,386
Off-Budget	184,346	187,324	214,275	176,807	184,743	198,617

† Figures may not add to totals due to rounding. *‡ Primarily appropriations.*

SOURCE: Fiscal 1987 Budget

Budget Authority and Outlays by Agency

(Fiscal years; dollar amounts in billions†)

	BUDGET AUTHORITY			OUTLAYS		
AGENCY	1985 actual	1986 estimate	1987 estimate	1985 actual	1986 estimate	1987 estimate
Legislative branch	$ 1.7	$ 1.8	$ 2.0	$ 1.6	$ 1.9	$ 2.0
The Judiciary	1.1	1.0	1.2	1.0	1.1	1.2
Executive Office of the President	0.1	0.1	0.1	0.1	0.1	0.1
Funds appropriated to the president	20.5	15.3	15.6	12.0	12.5	13.8
Agriculture	61.9	56.7	45.8	55.5	54.2	44.6
Commerce	2.3	1.9	1.8	2.1	2.0	2.1
Defense — Military [1]	286.8	278.4	311.6	245.4	258.4	274.3
Defense — Civil	30.4	34.0	36.6	18.8	20.6	20.9
Education	19.1	16.7	15.2	16.7	17.8	15.4
Energy	12.6	9.9	10.3	10.6	10.1	10.2
Health and Human Services, except Social Security	141.1	154.5	151.0	132.1	140.9	139.1
Health and Human Services, Social Security	191.0	194.6	222.2	183.4	192.0	206.5
Housing and Urban Development	31.4	10.7	5.5	28.7	15.2	13.9
Interior	5.0	4.3	3.9	4.8	4.6	4.3
Justice	3.8	3.8	4.3	3.6	3.8	4.1
Labor	27.7	27.2	28.5	23.9	23.1	23.2
State	3.6	4.1	4.9	2.6	2.9	3.6
Transportation	28.8	26.8	21.7	25.0	26.3	24.7
Treasury	166.3	184.0	190.3	165.1	184.7	188.3
Environmental Protection Agency	4.3	4.6	4.2	4.5	4.6	4.5
General Services Administration	0.3	0.2	0.2	−0.2	*	−*
National Aeronautics and Space Administration	7.6	7.3	7.7	7.3	7.3	7.5
Office of Personnel Management	41.6	42.9	46.6	23.7	24.1	24.7
Small Business Administration	1.3	0.9	0.1	0.7	0.9	0.1
Veterans Administration	27.3	27.0	26.6	26.3	26.5	26.4
Other Agencies	15.5	17.0	15.7	9.8	10.9	10.1
Allowances [2]	—	—	0.8	—	—	0.8
Undistributed Offsetting Receipts:						
Interest received by on-budget trust funds	−22.1	−26.7	−29.6	−22.1	−26.7	−29.6
Interest received by off-budget trust funds	−4.1	−4.4	−4.7	−4.1	−4.4	−4.7
Interest received from Outer Continental Shelf escrow account	−*	−0.3	—	−*	−0.3	—
Employer share, employee retirement (on-budget)	−24.7	−26.3	−28.5	−24.7	−26.3	−28.5
Employer share, employee retirement (off-budget)	−2.5	−2.8	−3.2	−2.5	−2.8	−3.2
Rents and royalties on the Outer Continental Shelf	−5.5	−5.5	−5.3	−5.5	−5.5	−5.3
Sale of major physical assets (proposed)	—	−1.2	−1.2	—	−1.2	−1.2
Total undistributed offsetting receipts	−59.0	−67.1	−72.5	−59.0	−67.1	−72.5
On-budget	(−52.3)	(−59.9)	(−64.6)	(−52.3)	(−59.9)	(−64.6)
Off-budget	(−6.6)	(−7.3)	(−7.9)	(−6.6)	(−7.3)	(−7.9)
TOTAL	**1,074.1**	**1,058.7**	**1,102.0**	**946.3**	**979.9**	**994.0**
On-budget	(889.7)	(871.4)	(887.7)	(769.5)	(795.2)	(795.4)
Off-budget	(184.3)	(187.3)	(214.3)	(176.8)	(184.7)	(198.6)

† Figures may not add to totals due to rounding.
** Less than $50 million.*
[1] Includes allowances for civilian and military pay raises for Department of Defense.
[2] Includes allowances for civilian agency pay raises, military pay raises for the Coast Guard, and contingencies.

SOURCE: Fiscal 1987 Budget

Reagan Administration Economic Assumptions

(Calendar years; dollar amounts in billions)

	Actual 1984	FORECAST 1985	1986	1987	ASSUMPTIONS 1988	1989	1990	1991
Major Economic Indicators:								
Gross national product (percent change, fourth quarter over fourth quarter):								
Current dollars	9.0	5.8	8.0	8.3	7.7	7.0	6.2	5.6
Constant (1982) dollars	4.7	2.5	4.0	4.0	4.0	3.7	3.6	3.5
GNP deflator (percent change, fourth quarter over fourth quarter)	4.1	3.2	3.8	4.1	3.6	3.2	2.5	2.0
Consumer Price Index (percent change, fourth quarter over fourth quarter) [1]	3.6	3.3	3.7	4.1	3.5	3.2	2.5	2.0
Unemployment rate (percent, fourth quarter) [2]	7.1	6.9	6.7	6.5	6.2	6.0	5.7	5.5
Annual Economic Assumptions:								
Gross national product:								
Current dollars:								
Amount	3,775	3,992	4,274	4,629	4,995	5,359	5,709	6,036
Percent change, year over year	11.0	5.8	7.0	8.3	7.9	7.3	6.5	5.7
Constant (1982) dollars:								
Amount	3,492	3,574	3,695	3,842	3,996	4,151	4,301	4,454
Percent change, year over year	6.6	2.3	3.4	4.0	4.0	3.9	3.6	3.5
Incomes:								
Personal income	3,112	3,294	3,486	3,756	4,012	4,266	4,506	4,748
Wages and salaries	1,835	1,961	2,078	2,247	2,418	2,587	2,743	2,901
Corporate profits before tax	238	228	281	330	366	394	424	430
Price level:								
GNP deflator:								
Level (1982 = 100), annual average	108.1	111.7	115.7	120.5	125.0	129.1	132.7	135.5
Percent change, year over year	4.1	3.3	3.5	4.2	3.7	3.3	2.8	2.1
Consumer Price Index: [1]								
Level (1967 = 100), annual average	307.6	318.5	329.5	343.1	356.0	367.7	378.0	386.0
Percent change, year over year	3.4	3.5	3.5	4.1	3.7	3.3	2.8	2.1
Unemployment rates:								
Total, annual average [2]	7.4	7.1	6.7	6.5	6.3	6.1	5.8	5.6
Insured, annual average [3]	2.8	2.8	2.7	2.6	2.5	2.3	2.2	2.0
Federal pay raise (percent):								
Military (October) [4]	4.0	7.0	4.0	4.8	5.1	4.9	4.5	NA
Civilian (January)	4.0	3.5	—	3.0	3.0	3.0	3.0	3.0
Interest rate, 91-day Treasury bills (percent) [5]	9.6	7.5	7.3	6.5	5.6	4.8	4.3	4.0
Interest rate, 10-year Treasury notes (percent)	12.4	10.6	8.9	8.5	7.3	5.5	4.8	4.5

[1] *CPI for urban wage earners and clerical workers. Two versions of the CPI are now published. The index shown here is that currently used, as required by law, in calculating automatic cost-of-living increases for indexed federal programs. The manner in which this index measures housing costs changed significantly in January 1985.*

[2] *Percent of total labor force, including armed forces residing in the United States.*

[3] *This indicator measures unemployment under state regular unemployment insurance as a percentage of covered employment under that program. It does not include recipients of extended benefits under that program.*

[4] *The 1984 pay raise occurred in January. There were 2 military pay raises in calendar year 1985: 4% in January and 3% in October.*

[5] *Average rate on new issues within period, on a bank discount basis. These projections assume, by convention, that interest rates decline with the rate of inflation.*

SOURCE: Fiscal 1987 Budget

Congress OKs Nation's First $1 Trillion Budget

The government's first trillion-dollar budget, adopted a minute after midnight June 26, denied President Reagan his desired growth in defense spending and generally ignored his demands for heavy pruning of domestic programs. It did, however, hew to the president's opposition to new taxes: There were none, except for negligible revenue increases proposed by Reagan himself.

The concurrent resolution on the budget for fiscal 1987 (S Con Res 120) set the following targets: budget authority, $1.094 trillion; outlays, $995 billion; revenues, $852.4 billion; deficit, $142.6 billion. The Gramm-Rudman-Hollings balanced-budget law (PL 99-177) set a deficit target for the year of $144 billion. *(Table, this page; president's budget request, p. 525; Gramm-Rudman, 1985 Almanac p. 459)*

In addition, S Con Res 120 assumed the following:

- **New Revenues.** Limited to those requested by President Reagan: $3.5 billion in fiscal 1987, $8.5 billion over three years.
- **Defense.** Fiscal 1987 budget authority, $292.2 billion; outlays, $279.2 billion. Budget authority figure was $28 billion less than Reagan requested, and future growth was assumed at a rate less than anticipated inflation.
- **Domestic.** Frozen or reduced spending, except for selected priority programs (primarily health and education), which were to receive increases. No program was to be terminated.
- **Contingency Fund.** Allowed additional spending ($4.8 billion in fiscal 1987 outlays) for critical unmet needs, if Reagan requested it, and if he proposed new revenues or spending cuts to pay for it. Defense could receive $3 billion in additional outlays; the rest could go to domestic programs or deficit reduction.

The budget resolution also assumed an increase in the ceiling on the federal debt, from $2.079 trillion to $2.323 trillion. Under a special rule, the House, in approving the conference agreement, was deemed to have passed the debt ceiling increase (H J Res 668), which was sent to the Senate for further consideration. *(Debt limit, p. 562; automatic House procedure, 1985 Almanac p. 458)*

The spending and revenue targets were based on the following economic assumptions, provided by the Congressional Budget Office (CBO) in mid-February: economic growth of 3.3 percent in fiscal 1986 and 3.1 percent in fiscal 1987; inflation of 3.6 percent in fiscal 1986 and 4.1 percent in fiscal 1987; unemployment of 6.7 percent in both years. At the time of its adoption, these assumptions were presumed to be overly optimistic.

Under terms of the 1974 Congressional Budget and Impoundment Control Act (PL 93-344), budget resolutions were congressional documents, and not signed into law by the president. The budget did bind Congress to revenue and spending totals in some 22 broad categories, ranging from national defense and agriculture to interest on the federal debt (at $143.5 billion, the third-largest item in the budget in terms of actual spending). *(Budget totals by function, p. 545; budget terms, p. 533)*

Budget act procedures, which had been stiffened by Gramm-Rudman a year earlier, existed to force adherence to the resolution's spending totals. A single member could object to floor consideration of a bill breaching the limits, unless Congress specifically voted to waive them, often by three-fifths majority votes. *(1974 Almanac p. 145)*

For fiscal year 1987 the resolution assumed actions to reduce the deficit totaling $40.2 billion, most of which were to come from cuts in appropriations or already anticipated changes in programs.

The measure included specific instructions for deficit-reducing "reconciliation" legislation worth $9.2 billion in fiscal 1987 and $24.2 billion in fiscal years 1987-89. Reconciliation was the process by which specific committees were required by the budget resolution to make changes in laws under their jurisdiction to produce the required deficit reduction. *(Reconciliation, p. 559; instructions to committees, p. 570)*

Of these savings, $3.5 billion in 1987 and $8.5 billion over three years were to be achieved through new revenues, the rest from legislated spending cuts. The revenue totals were equal to the president's revenue request.

Savings were calculated against a CBO baseline level of spending, showing what expenditures would be under existing law, with some allowances for inflation.

Hitting the Deficit Target

It was not a budget that elicited praise. House Budget Committee Chairman William H. Gray III, D-Pa., called it "credible," while Senate Majority Leader Robert Dole, R-Kan., admitted to "mild" support.

Rep. Silvio O. Conte, R-Mass., who voted for the measure, summed up the feelings of its harshest critics: that the enforced spending cuts in the budget were "as phony as a $3 bill."

The White House sourly declared that the budget "cut too much from defense ... and is way too limiting" in future years. But administration officials said they were pleased that the resolution called for no additional taxes.

And many members were disturbed by the prospect that the deficit target ultimately would not be met. "What's been produced here is a sorry child, whose future we can only hope for," said one budget conferee, Sen. Slade Gorton, R-Wash.

Although the projected deficit met the Gramm-Rudman target for fiscal 1987 (but not 1988 or 1989), the measure's sponsors conceded that the deficit estimate

Budget Resolution Totals

(In billions; totals may not add due to rounding.)

	Fiscal 1987	Fiscal 1988	Fiscal 1989
Budget Authority	$1,093.4	$1,166.5	$1,215.9
Outlays	995.0	1,045.4	1,079.0
Revenues	852.4	929.8	1,001.1
Deficit	−142.6	−115.7	−77.9
Gramm-Rudman Deficit Targets	−144.0	−108.0	−72.0

SOURCE: S Con Res 120

would increase significantly as the year went on, threatening the possibility of a "sequester" — Gramm-Rudman's uniform across-the-board spending cuts.

The threat came from changing economic conditions, which were expected to reduce revenues, and from accelerating rates of spending in certain programs, notably defense and agriculture. In fact, by the Oct. 1 start of fiscal 1987, the deficit estimate, as calculated for Gramm-Rudman purposes, was $163.4 billion, and budget experts predicted in early 1987 that the year's actual deficit might exceed $175 billion.

In the end, however, by enacting a reconciliation bill saving $11.7 billion and through other actions, Congress managed to dodge the Gramm-Rudman sequester bullet. *(Gramm-Rudman developments, p. 579)*

11th-Hour Success

Before leaving on a scheduled two-week vacation, the House adopted the conference report on the budget (H Rept 99-664), on a 333-43 vote, at 11:16 p.m. June 26. *(Vote 189, p. 56-H)*

The Senate gave final approval by voice vote 45 minutes later, with only four senators in the chamber. Present were Senate Budget Committee Chairman Pete V. Domenici, R-N.M.; ranking committee Democrat Lawton Chiles of Florida; Assistant Majority Leader Alan K. Simpson, R-Wyo.; and Dole.

John Glenn, D-Ohio, complained about the Senate's voting "in the middle of the night in the interest of getting out of here for the Fourth of July." But, at the request of Senate leaders, Glenn dropped his threat to force a roll-call vote, and left the chamber before the budget was adopted.

What passed was a compromise worked out in by-then-routine marathon private sessions by Domenici, Gray, Chiles and ranking House Budget Committee Republican Delbert L. Latta of Ohio. Their negotiations, lasting into the early morning hours of several days, began after the formal conference had stalled.

Unlike previous years, the administration stayed out of the bargaining, ignoring strenuous congressional efforts to engage the president's attention and cooperation.

The optional contingency fund was the last remnant of $10.7 billion in tax increases included in both the House and Senate resolutions in a frustrated effort to prod Reagan into changing his mind on taxes.

Although the effort appeared blunted, Domenici said the fight over taxes was far from over, and that mounting pressures could call the contingency fund into play in coming months. In fact, the administration never made a request to use the fund. And one program the contingency fund was expected to cover — replacement of the space shuttle *Challenger* — managed to be funded within the spending limits set by S Con Res 120. *(Challenger, p. 326; HUD/Independent Agencies appropriations, p. 171)*

Domenici and Chiles, close allies in the year's budget debates, argued that only a modest increase in the absolute size of the tax base could bring a lasting deficit cure, since so much of the budget was immune from major cuts, either for political reasons or, in the case of interest on the federal debt, legal barriers.

The two senators believed that if both chambers voted for a tax increase, Reagan would be pressured into accepting it. But two factors prevented it. First, the major tax overhaul bill survived its tortuous trip though Congress due in no small part to the promise that it would neither increase, nor reduce revenues. Second, the House would not commit itself to a tax increase without a change first in Reagan's stance. Chiles said House Democrats did not want to "have the president be able to say that we are the tax and spend guys."

Domenici told the Senate he was not proud of the budget compromise, and could not promise that it would be "sequester-proof." Nonetheless, he said he was satisfied that if Congress actually carried out all the savings mandates of the spending plan, it might hold off a sequester or at least greatly soften its impact.

Referring to the difficult negotiations leading to the compromise, Domenici said flatly, "We just can't do any more than the United States Congress lets us do, and the president will support. That's it."

Major Assumptions

Following is a summary of major policy assumptions underlying the spending and revenue targets of S Con Res 120.

The assumptions, not formally part of the budget resolution, were developed by the staffs and members of the Budget committees as suggested methods of achieving the savings or, in a few cases, increases in spending incorporated into the resolution's numerical targets.

Savings and revenue increases required by reconciliation were binding on committees but the policy assumptions underlying those numbers were not.

The overall targets of the resolution and the functional spending totals were not technically binding, except that budget law as amended by Gramm-Rudman authorized objections ("points of order") against legislation breaching both overall targets and exceeding spending totals allocated to individual committees under the budget resolution. In the House, most such objections could be waived by a simple majority; in the Senate, a "super-majority" of 60 members was generally required for a waiver.

The assumptions listed below were compiled from separate summaries of the House and Senate Budget committees. Some applied only to the House or Senate; others to both chambers. In some instances, the assumptions specified cuts in budget authority, money that could be obligated in a given period of time, and in outlays, money actually disbursed in a given year.

Revenue Increases

- A revenue increase was assumed of $6 billion above the fiscal 1987 baseline, with $700 million coming from additional revenues for the "superfund" toxic-waste cleanup program, $1.8 billion from improved collection efforts by the Internal Revenue Service and $3.5 billion in unspecified revenue increases. The $3.5 billion figure (or $8.5 billion for fiscal years 1987-89), was reconciled and was the amount requested by Reagan.

The total fiscal 1987 revenue base was assumed to be $852.4 billion, which was $4.8 billion less than the House- and Senate-passed resolutions.

Domestic Spending Freeze

- The conference agreement broadly assumed a freeze in federal spending, holding expenditures in fiscal 1987 at fiscal 1986 levels, as revised downward by the March 1 automatic spending cut order ("sequester") mandated by Gramm-Rudman. However, numerous exceptions put anticipated spending above or below the freeze level for specified purposes.

Contingency Funding

• The conference agreement assumed a special contingency fund of $9.95 billion in fiscal 1987 budget authority ($4.8 billion in outlays), to be devoted to "unmet national needs," primarily defense growth and replacement of the space shuttle.

Over three years, the fund was to total $38.3 billion in budget authority and $27.1 billion in outlays. Of that, $6.9 billion in fiscal 1987 budget authority and $3 billion in outlays ($25.5 billion and $16.7 billion, respectively, over three years) was to be dedicated to defense.

The fund was to be used only if the president requested extra money for specific purposes. He also would have to specify spending cuts, revenue increases or other means of offsetting the additional spending, in new or existing legislation. The fund was not reconciled.

In a separate contingency arrangement, the conference agreement assumed continuation of the general revenue sharing program only if offsetting revenues were provided. The program was scheduled to expire at the end of fiscal 1986.

Defense

• Budget authority was to be $292.2 billion in fiscal 1987, $304.1 billion in fiscal 1988 and $316.7 billion in fiscal 1989. These figures reflected, for fiscal 1987, a 2 percent increase above the fiscal 1986, post-sequester level. The 1988 and 1989 figures assumed 1 percent increases above inflation, as in the Senate-passed resolution. The House had assumed a freeze in defense spending for the two-year period. Reagan requested fiscal 1987 budget authority of $320.3 billion, reflecting an estimated 8 percent growth above inflation.

Fiscal 1987 outlays were assumed to be $279.2 billion, compared with $282 billion assumed by the administration and the Senate, and $276.2 billion assumed by the House. *(Defense authorization, p. 464; appropriations, p. 206)*

• Military and civilian defense employee pay increases of 3 percent, provided in January of each year, 1987-89, were assumed. The president and the House had assumed 3 percent, the Senate 2 percent.

• An additional $6.9 billion in fiscal 1987 budget authority, $3 billion in outlays (for fiscal 1987 totals of $299 billion and $282.2 billion, respectively) was to be available if the contingency fund described above was used.

• House and Senate Armed Services committees were to consider barring the Defense Department from estimating inflation costs in major weapons systems on "arbitrary" factors, that is, factors other than historical or factual data. The House resolution had required the committees to report such legislation.

International Affairs

• To enhance security of U.S. embassies, funding of $1.1 billion in fiscal years 1986-87 was assumed, the full amount requested by the administration. *(Embassy security, p. 377)*

• Foreign aid appropriations were assumed to be 10 percent less than the fiscal 1986 level. *(Foreign aid appropriations, p. 162)*

Science and Technology

• NASA funding was to be frozen at the fiscal 1986 level, but with some increases for basic research. Overall increases were also assumed for Department of Energy general science programs. The House summary of the agreement also assumed a 2.5 percent across-the-board reduction in Science and Technology spending.

• Replacement of the space shuttle was assumed only as part of the contingency fund described above.

Energy

• For the Strategic Petroleum Reserve, the House summary of the agreement assumed $500 million in fiscal 1987 for oil purchases and $150 million for construction costs. The House had assumed $300 million in additional 1987 funding for purchases, while the Senate resolution assumed $75 million less.

• For basic energy research, the House resolution assumed a $50 million increase in fiscal 1987 budget authority.

• New Nuclear Regulatory Commission user fees were to yield $100 million (compared with $300 million assumed in the House-passed resolution). The Senate resolution did not assume the new fees, which were to be in addition to those in the fiscal 1986 budget reconciliation law (PL 99-272).

• New Federal Energy Regulatory Commission user fees, as required by the fiscal 1986 reconciliation law, were to yield $50 million, as in the House-passed resolution.

• Rural Electrification Administration loan asset sales, as provided in the fiscal 1986 supplemental appropriations bill (HR 4515 — PL 99-349), were to yield $1.4 billion in outlay reductions in fiscal 1987. (Before a compromise on the appropriations measure gave the administration authority to veto individual loan sales, the estimated long-term interest losses resulting from these sales was put at $20 billion.) *(Supplemental appropriations, p. 153)*

• The Naval Petroleum Reserve was to be sold, to produce a one-time savings of $2.4 billion in fiscal 1988. The sale was not reconciled.

Natural Resources and Environment

• Funding for the Bureau of Reclamation was to be at the fiscal 1986 level, as in the Senate resolution. The House resolution would have cut bureau programs by 20 percent.

• Construction of roads by the U.S. Forest Service was funded at $40 million in fiscal 1987 budget authority, $20 million in outlays. The House resolution had not funded the road construction, for an annual savings of $100 million in budget authority.

• Navigation user fees, based on enactment of a port tax, were assumed as in the House-passed resolution.

• A 4 percent across-the-board reduction in natural resources and environment programs was assumed. The agreement omitted the user fees for grazing, mineral leasing, recreation, sport fishing and U.S. Geological Survey materials that had been included in the House or Senate resolutions.

Agriculture

• Existing policy funding of $18 billion in fiscal 1987 for farm price-support programs of the Commodity Credit Corporation and for other farm income stabilization programs was assumed.

• Increased budget authority of $150 million a year was assumed for farm credit programs, as in both House and Senate resolutions.

• The agreement omitted the House resolution's user fees for Agriculture Department grain inspections, market news services, egg processing, plant inspections and veterinary services.

Commerce and Housing Credit

• The Postal Service was to be funded at the fiscal 1986 level of $716 million, as in the Senate resolution. The House had assumed a $100 million reduction.

• Rural housing and Small Business Administration (SBA) business programs were to be continued at fiscal 1986 levels, as in the House-passed resolution.

• An additional $750 million in premium income for the Federal Housing Administration mortgage insurance program was assumed for fiscal 1987, based on an assumed increase in the program's commitment ceiling, to $120 billion in 1986 and $80 billion in 1987.

• Sale of rural housing loan assets, yielding proceeds of $1.2 billion in fiscal 1987, as in the House-passed resolution, was assumed and was to be part of the reconciliation process. The Senate had assumed more modest sales, yielding $100 million annually in fiscal years 1987-89.

• A 2.5 percent across-the-board reduction in this function, as in the House-passed resolution, was assumed.

Transportation

• A 7.5 percent reduction in the federal highway program was assumed, resulting in an annual authority level of $13.5 million, an obligation ceiling of $12.5 million each year, and total fiscal 1987 obligations of $13.1 million. The reduced highway program obligations were reconciled. *(Highway programs, p. 284)*

• The sale of Conrail was assumed, yielding receipts of $1.9 billion, about $700 million more than offered by Norfolk Southern Corp., in the bid favored by the administration. The sale of the government-owned freight railroad had been assumed in previous budget resolutions, but delayed because Rep. John D. Dingell, D-Mich., objected to the administration's recommendation. The Conrail sale was not reconciled. *(Conrail sale, p. 279)*

• Operating assistance for local mass transit systems and "Section 3" grants for construction of new mass transit systems each were to be reduced by 10 percent, with remaining transit programs continued at existing levels. Total fiscal 1987 transit budget authority was to be $3.4 billion. The cut in the Section 3 grants was not reconciled.

• Federal Aviation Administration (FAA) funding was to increase by $200 million in fiscal 1987 to $2.9 billion, the House total. This total assumed $280 million for research and engineering, $1.2 billion for facilities and equipment, and an obligation ceiling of $955 million for airport improvement grants. The Senate total for the FAA had assumed a $500 million increase.

• Coast Guard funding of $1.7 billion for operations and $263 million for acquisition represented a split between House and Senate numbers. The agreement also assumed new user fees for Coast Guard services, yielding $50 million annually (not $150 million as in the House-passed resolution). The $50 million figure was reconciled but the savings could be achieved by means other than the new fees.

Community, Regional Development

• Reductions of 10 percent below a freeze in fiscal 1987 were assumed for the Economic Development Administration, Urban Development Action Grants (UDAG), the Appalachian Regional Commission and rental housing subsidies.

• Disapproval of the fiscal 1986 deferrals proposed by Reagan in the community development block grant program, the Economic Development Administration and the rehabilitation loan fund were assumed. Disapproval meant

FY 1987 Budget by Function

(In billions; totals may not add due to rounding.)

Category	President's Request	Budget Resolution
National Defense		
Budget Authority	$320.3	$292.2
Outlays	282.2	279.2
International Affairs		
Budget Authority	22.6	17.5
Outlays	18.6	14.0
Science and Space		
Budget Authority	9.5	9.1
Outlays	9.2	8.9
Energy		
Budget Authority	4.4	4.9
Outlays	4.0	3.5
Natural Resources		
Budget Authority	10.9	12.4
Outlays	12.0	12.6
Agriculture		
Budget Authority	19.6	23.8
Outlays	19.5	23.5
Commerce and Housing		
Budget Authority	10.2	10.3
Outlays	1.4	2.1
Transportation		
Budget Authority	22.6	25.4
Outlays	25.5	25.9
Community Development		
Budget Authority	3.8	6.2
Outlays	6.5	7.0
Education and Social Services		
Budget Authority	27.0	33.5
Outlays	27.4	30.6
Health		
Budget Authority	35.3	38.6
Outlays	35.0	38.3
Medicare		
Budget Authority	82.3	83.0
Outlays	70.2	73.3
Income Security		
Budget Authority	153.3	163.5
Outlays	118.4	121.8
Social Security		
Budget Authority	222.2	227.1
Outlays	206.5	209.4
Veterans' Benefits		
Budget Authority	26.7	27.0
Outlays	26.4	26.6
Justice		
Budget Authority	7.1	7.2
Outlays	6.9	7.2
General Government		
Budget Authority	6.2	5.5
Outlays	6.1	5.5
General Fiscal Assistance		
Budget Authority	1.7	2.0
Outlays	1.7	2.8
Net Interest		
Budget Authority	148.0	143.7
Outlays	148.0	143.7
Allowances		
Budget Authority	0.8	0.9
Outlays	0.8	−0.1
Offsetting Receipts		
Budget Authority	−38.1	−40.1
Outlays	−38.1	−40.3
TOTALS		
Budget Authority	$1,102.0	$1,093.4
Outlays	994.0	995.0
Revenues	850.4	852.4
Deficit	−143.6	−142.6

SOURCES: President's budget request, Senate Budget Committee

that the money would have to be spent.

• The sales of $1 billion in Small Business Administration Disaster Loan assets and of $500 million in Rural Development Insurance Fund assets were assumed and reconciled.

• A fiscal 1986 supplemental appropriation ($250 million in direct appropriation and a $2.9 billion transfer from emergency planning) for the Federal Emergency Management Agency's disaster relief programs was assumed.

• The House summary of the agreement assumed Indian child welfare services would be increased above inflation in fiscal 1987 by $4 million, as in the House-passed resolution's children's initiative.

Education, Training, Employment, Social Services

• For all education programs except guaranteed student loans, funding at the full fiscal 1986 level (before the March 1 Gramm-Rudman sequester order) plus inflation was assumed, with $400 million additional funding for increases in math and science education. There also was to be $200 million in additional funding for a new training and education program to improve U.S. trade competitiveness. The House resolution had assumed a $500 million program in fiscal 1987 for this initiative.

• Guaranteed student loan savings of $390 million over fiscal years 1987-89 were assumed through administrative changes and were reconciled. The savings, which compared with the $1.3 billion assumed in the Senate resolution, were to come from restricting eligibility, increasing student interest payments and reducing yields to lenders and subsidies to state agencies guaranteeing the loans.

• A $50 million fiscal 1987 increase in child nutrition programs, as provided in the proposed conference agreement on HR 7, was assumed, as in the House resolution.

• A $75 million budget authority increase, above inflation, in fiscal 1987 for the Women, Infants and Children feeding program (WIC) was assumed, as in the House resolution.

• The House summary of the agreement assumed additional funding for high-priority education, training, social service and low-income programs.

• Increased funding of $265 million, for education of the handicapped, was assumed.

• Sales of education loan assets to the private sector were assumed and reconciled.

• An increase in funding for the Job Training Partnership Act, of $344 million over the fiscal 1986 level, was assumed, including $64 million for the Job Corps.

Health

• Medicaid, the federal-state medical program for the poor, was assumed to continue at levels provided by existing law, without the $260 million fiscal 1987 reduction in funds for state administrative expenses that was assumed in the Senate resolution. The baseline (existing law) level of Medicaid funding was to increase by $100 million in fiscal 1987 and $700 million over three years, to give states the option of providing coverage to elderly citizens whose income was below the poverty line. The agreement also assumed states would be given the option of expanding coverage for low-income pregnant women and infants under age 1.

• Unspecified savings of $100 million in fiscal 1987 and $300 million over three years was assumed as part of the reconciliation process. The savings were to come from the federal employee health benefit program or from other programs under the jurisdiction of appropriate committees.

• Funding levels for discretionary health programs were assumed to be $600 million in budget authority above a freeze level for fiscal 1987.

Medicare

• The resolution assumed $600 billion in fiscal 1987, or $3.3 billion over three years, would be saved through limits on payments to doctors, hospitals and other health-care providers, with no increased costs to beneficiaries. The Senate resolution had assumed $800 million in fiscal 1987 savings or $5.8 billion over three years. Reagan had requested a fiscal 1987 Medicare reduction of $4.7 billion. The Medicare savings were reconciled.

• The resolution assumed $250 million additional funding in fiscal 1987, or $1 billion over three years, to limit future increases in the Medicare hospital deductible. The Senate resolution had assumed the costs of the limit would be offset by equivalent new revenues or spending cuts elsewhere; the final version dropped this requirement, instead assuming the extra money to be included in total program funding of $83 billion in fiscal 1987 budget authority, $73.3 billion in outlays.

Income Security

• The agreement assumed a baseline funding level of $8.1 billion in fiscal 1987 budget authority for subsidized housing to support 95,000 new units. The agreement also assumed a financing charge to capital grants. The Senate resolution had assumed a 25 percent reduction, to 71,000 new units.

• A cost-of-living adjustment (COLA) at the actual rate of inflation, estimated to be 2 percent, was assumed for civilian and military retirees' pensions. Existing law did not require an adjustment in a year when inflation dropped below 3 percent, but both chambers assumed enactment of legislation providing an inflation adjustment anyway.

• A freeze at the fiscal 1986 level for unemployment insurance administrative costs was assumed.

• The conference agreement (PL 99-335) on the supplemental retirement plan for federal employees was assumed. *(Federal employee retirement, p. 315)*

• Additional funding for WIC and child nutrition, as above, and also for nutrition assistance for Puerto Rico, and aid to the homeless, was assumed.

Social Security

• Social Security administrative expenses were to be allowed to rise for inflation, as in the House resolution. The Senate version froze these costs.

• A COLA adjustment at the actual rate of inflation, estimated to be 2 percent, was assumed for Social Security benefits. Existing law did not require an adjustment in a year when inflation dropped below 3 percent, but both chambers assumed enactment of legislation providing an inflation adjustment anyway.

Veterans

• A COLA at the actual rate of inflation, estimated to be 2 percent, was assumed for veterans' compensation and pension benefits.

• A freeze in most discretionary programs, except for veterans' medical care, was assumed for fiscal 1987-89.

• For health care programs, a full inflation allowance was assumed, plus additional funds for certain high-priority activities.

• The agreement assumed spending of $400 million above the baseline, to allow for inflation and certain high-priority veterans' medical care programs.

Administration of Justice

• All administration of justice programs were to be funded at rates allowing for inflation; the agreement also assumed $200 million in funding above this level for the Customs Service, and $50 million more for the Drug Enforcement Administration, to fund drug interdiction activities.

General Government

• Full funding of $4.1 billion for the administration's request for the Internal Revenue Service, to improve taxpayer compliance, was assumed.

• For the legislative branch, a $100 million increase above the fiscal 1986 level was assumed.

• Unspecified cuts of $200 million in fiscal 1987 budget authority and outlays were assumed.

• Additional user fees for Customs Service activities were reconciled and were assumed to yield $300 million in fiscal 1987, $295 million in fiscal 1988 and $290 million in fiscal 1989.

General Purpose Fiscal Assistance

• The general revenue sharing program was assumed to continue into fiscal 1987, providing a new authorization was enacted for the program and providing additional revenues were found to cover the cost. *(Revenue sharing, p. 585)*

Net Interest

• The resolution assumed net interest on the federal debt to be $143.7 billion. The calculation was based on a higher gross interest payment, offset by the receipt of interest paid by the Treasury to government trust funds whose balances were invested in U.S. government securities.

Allowances

• The agreement assumed 3 percent pay raises for federal civilian employees, Coast Guard personnel and Defense Department civilian and military personnel for fiscal 1987-89, with the raise delayed until Jan. 1 of each year. The cost of the raises was to be partially absorbed by offsetting cuts in individual agency budgets.

• The budget resolution assumed federal pay would be calculated on the basis of a 2,087-hour work year. This saving was reconciled.

• Sale of U.S. government loan assets was assumed, to yield $1 billion in net savings in fiscal 1987-89, with savings reconciled.

Offsetting Receipts

• Legislation recovering $2.5 billion in oil overcharges, in fiscal years 1987-89, was assumed. (The recovery was to be $1.3 billion in fiscal 1987.) This item was reconciled, but there was language excusing committees from reconciliation if outside circumstances, such as a pending legal settlement, made the savings unachievable.

Senate Committee Action

The Senate Budget Committee, in open revolt against the president, agreed March 19 to a budget that called for $18.7 billion in new taxes and slashed $25 billion from the president's defense request for fiscal 1987. The committee budget also called for reductions in non-military spending totaling $14.4 billion — about half the cutbacks in these accounts that the president had wanted.

In a 13-9 vote, six committee Democrats joined with seven Republicans in agreeing to report S Con Res 120 (S Rept 99-264) as proposed by Domenici and Chiles. It was the first bipartisan resolution to come out of the Senate committee since the late 1970s.

Domenici said the plan was "pretty close to a consensus budget" and "what will ultimately have to be done" by Congress given the imperatives of politics and Gramm-Rudman.

Votes against the resolution came from both the right and left: conservative Republicans who shared Reagan's abhorrence of new taxes and his desire for higher defense spending, and Democrats who wanted higher spending levels for such programs as education and research.

But support was broad enough to suggest that Domenici and Chiles had tapped a strong consensus in the Senate.

Liberal Democrat Howard M. Metzenbaum of Ohio, whose "aye" vote was unexpected, said he was pleased with the amount allotted to defense, as well as some domestic initiatives. And, he said, "The majority of Republicans saw fit to stand up and be counted for tax revenues. That showed me they were willing to stand up to their president, and I felt they were entitled to some support."

Asked his opinion of the resolution, Dole replied coolly, "I think it keeps the process alive — barely."

Reaction from the administration was prompt and hostile. Even before the committee acted, one White House budget official said, "Speaking for myself, I hope whatever they pass will fail completely, and the administration can wash its hands of it." This official declared himself "profoundly bored by the Budget Committee. What they do doesn't make a bit of difference."

Office of Management and Budget Director James C. Miller III criticized the measure's revenue increases and defense cuts as "too much" and its reductions in non-defense accounts as "timid and minimal." Presidential spokesman Larry Speakes said that the Domenici-Chiles plan "achieves a desirable goal by means of totally unacceptable methods."

Meanwhile, House Budget Committee Chairman Gray had not even scheduled formal budget action, but he called the Senate committee plan "a good start."

A Freeze With Exceptions

The Domenici-Chiles resolution assumed total fiscal 1987 budget authority of $1.097 trillion, and fiscal 1987 outlays of $1.007 trillion. It estimated revenues at $863 billion, leaving a deficit of $143.9 billion. Deficit-reducing measures to reach that level — a spending freeze, cuts below the freeze and new revenues — totaled $38.8 billion for fiscal 1987.

For defense, the resolution called for budget authority of $295 billion, which sponsors said would allow for inflation in fiscal 1987, while others disputed that claim. The resolution assumed somewhat lower inflation than CBO projected and a 3 percent military pay raise — instead of the 4 percent assumed by CBO. It cut $4 billion from CBO's baseline for defense, which was supposed to allow only enough of an increase in 1987 to cover inflation.

The resolution assumed that budget authority for defense would grow by 1 percent above inflation in fiscal 1988 and 1989.

Defense was the major exception to an overall freeze of budget authority at fiscal 1986 levels, with no inflation allowance. Other exceptions would have taken certain programs, including foreign aid, mass transit subsidies and subsidized housing, well below the freeze level.

A few high-priority items were allowed modest growth. The increases were worth $2.3 billion altogether, according to Domenici. Like the military, federal civilian employees would have received 3 percent pay raises; federal retirees were to get full cost-of-living adjustments.

Other high-priority items included:

- A $100 million Medicaid initiative to combat infant mortality.
- $350 million for the Federal Aviation Administration to improve aviation safety.
- $400 million for certain high-priority education programs including Head Start.
- $500 million for the Internal Revenue Service.
- $1 billion to begin replacing the destroyed space shuttle *Challenger*, if the replacement were authorized (the resolution assumed a total of $2.7 billion over three years for the shuttle replacement).
- $200 million for a new farm credit initiative ($600 million over three years).
- $1.8 billion for an extra half-year of revenue sharing, scheduled to expire at the end of fiscal 1986, if Congress voted to continue it.

For the most part the budget resolution omitted the president's proposed sales of federal assets, such as regional electric power generating plants, and program terminations, such as the Rural Electrification Administration (REA). Sales to private investors of some federally owned loans were assumed, however.

Of the new revenues assumed in the committee's budget, about $5.9 billion was proposed by the president's budget. To that, Domenici and Chiles added $12.6 billion in unspecified new taxes.

Other major departures from Reagan's budget included:

- Continuation of the $1.1 billion Export-Import Bank direct loan program, which Reagan had wanted to replace with a privately financed loan program backed by an interest rate subsidy.
- Medicare cuts totaling $5.8 billion over three years, not the $22.7 billion in the Reagan budget.
- Continued filling, but at a slower rate, of the Strategic Petroleum Reserve. Reagan's budgets for fiscal 1985 and 1986 proposed to halt construction and filling of the oil stockpile.

Markup Gets Under Way

For Reagan, the 1986 budget fight began on several inauspicious notes.

On March 4, the day before markup began, panel member Rudy Boschwitz, R-Minn., released a letter to Reagan, signed by 50 senators, declaring deficit-reduction as their top priority. The president's favored tax "reform" initiative had to wait, the letter said, until there was agreement on deficit reduction.

Then, in its March 5 markup meeting, the committee began considering not a specific budget resolution but a staff-prepared "markup book" that, among other things, listed as options about $69 billion worth of tax increases and other revenue-raisers, including amnesty for delinquent taxpayers.

At that meeting, the panel also made the important technical decision to calculate its decisions from the CBO baseline, which, unlike the previous year assumed no growth in defense beyond an allowance for inflation. The CBO baseline set a starting point for committee negotiations on defense of $301 billion, compared with the president's request of $320.2 billion, which assumed an 8 percent growth beyond inflation.

Then on March 6 the committee rejected Reagan's fiscal 1987 budget request by a 6-16 vote. Siding with committee Democrats against the president were Republicans Mark Andrews, N.D.; John C. Danforth, Mo.; Gorton; Charles E. Grassley, Iowa; Nancy Landon Kassebaum, Kan.; and Bob Kasten, Wis. Voting for the president's budget were Republicans William L. Armstrong, Colo.; Boschwitz; Domenici; Orrin G. Hatch, Utah; Dan Quayle, Ind.; and Steve Symms, Idaho.

The March 5 session was awash in warm expressions of bipartisan resolve. Sen. J. Bennett Johnston, D-La., told Domenici, "I, for one, will follow your lead.... I don't think [a budget] can be done in a partisan manner."

The next day the mood turned testy as Armstrong and Quayle accused colleagues of "president-bashing." Johnston smoothly replied, "I like the president ... even though I find his budget to be unworkable, mean-spirited and wrongheaded."

Domenici said he had scheduled the early vote on the president's budget because Democrats would have insisted on it anyway.

Negotiations Bog Down

In seeking a bipartisan budget, Domenici began negotiations with Chiles, but disagreements, including an apparent $10 billion misunderstanding over what the two thought they had agreed to for defense, led to an impasse.

On March 13 Domenici surprised observers by laying before the panel his own alternative budget. Domenici said he did so, instead of waiting for agreement with Chiles, to hasten committee decisions.

Domenici's budget called for $16.2 billion in fiscal 1987 revenue increases and slashed Reagan's defense request to $299 billion, which he said would allow for an inflation increase above fiscal 1986, but no more. For the following two years, Domenici assumed defense growth beyond inflation of 1 percent; the president wanted 3 percent beyond a much higher base.

The proposal generally assumed that program spending would be frozen at fiscal 1986 levels, with increases only for a few high-priority programs.

For many of the program terminations urged by Reagan, Domenici substituted spending cuts of 10 to 15 percent. He mitigated large Reagan cuts in such sensitive programs as Medicare and Medicaid, but still would have sliced $7.3 billion from Medicare over three years.

The plan also called for revenue increases totaling $70.3 billion over three years, including $21.6 billion from Reagan's budget, some reconciliation-mandated revenues and $48 billion in unspecified taxes.

Seeking Bipartisanship

Election-year pressures on some GOP senators and the White House's refusal to negotiate on the budget were primary reasons Domenici sought to work with Chiles and the Democrats. The Republicans had pushed their own budget in 1985, but frankly acknowledged in 1986 that they would need Democratic votes.

At the same time, Senate Democrats were internally divided by the powerful temptation to let GOP rivals fail on the high-visibility budget issue and the desire to make the best use of their new bargaining position. But it was clear that Domenici would have to deliver a sizable number of Republican votes to guarantee Democratic support.

Eventually, he and Chiles reached agreement on the budget that the committee accepted, and the White House blasted. Though public defiance of the White House had not been Domenici's style, the administration left him little choice, he said March 19.

"They almost acted as if they didn't care. We got no input. We got no alternatives. We didn't even get any real meetings," Domenici said.

Domenici told the committee he would consider alternatives, but said, "I'm not going off with anyone and make a one-sided compromise." Any compromises with Republican or Democratic leaders or the White House "will be made with Sen. Chiles and Sen. Domenici working together," Domenici vowed.

Turning Back Amendments

In its March 19 session, the committee approved the Domenici-Chiles plan after a day of speeches and votes against an alternative sponsored by Frank R. Lautenberg, D-N.J., and against four amendments to increase education, health and revenue sharing funds.

Chiles and some other Democrats sided with Domenici against the amendments, although Chiles indicated that they might have brought the budget closer to what he thought the nation's priorities should be.

The amendments were:

- A proposal by Andrews to add $500 million in outlays above the freeze level for education programs. It was rejected 9-11.
- A proposal by Andrews to add $700 million in outlays above the freeze level for certain health programs. It was rejected 7-13.
- A proposal by Daniel Patrick Moynihan, D-N.Y., to assume an additional full year of spending for revenue sharing, if reauthorized and funded with new revenues. It was rejected 9-12.
- A proposal by Metzenbaum to add $197 million to childhood health, immunization and food programs, with the additional spending to be offset by increasing the estimated proceeds from the sale of Conrail. It was rejected 6-15.
- A substitute budget by Lautenberg to reduce defense spending by about $20 billion below the Domenici-Chiles plan, to increase revenues by about $1 billion and to distribute the extra funding among education, health, environmental and other non-defense accounts. It was rejected 5-16.

Reaching a Consensus

The final Domenici-Chiles compromise dropped Domenici's earlier proposal of $299 billion in defense budget authority down to $295 billion. It added back funds for health, education and the "superfund" hazardous-waste cleanup program. And it rescued rural housing programs, rent subsidies and certain job training programs targeted for extinction by Domenici.

As the final committee session began, Domenici was still one vote short of the needed Republican seven.

Andrews, counted as a "nay," launched an extensive public complaint about the compromise's treatment of agriculture, education, health and REA programs. Hours later, Domenici abruptly offered to eliminate about $200 million worth of REA spending reductions, substituting a $200 million increase on the tax side of the ledger.

Said a grumpy Metzenbaum, whose amendment had just lost, "I guess that's called buying votes." Domenici replied, "I don't think so." Andrews later voted for the resolution.

Senate Floor Action

Although it took more than a month of delays, floor battles and another round of bartering, a strong bipartisan majority of the Senate at about 1 a.m. May 2 approved a $1 trillion version of the budget that was much more like the committee bill than it was different.

In an obvious victory for Domenici, the Republican-controlled chamber, by a 70-25 vote, approved a compromise budget that — like the committee version — defied Reagan in calling for $10.7 billion in new taxes, sliced $19 billion from his defense request, and ignored many of the sharp reductions in non-defense spending he wanted. *(Vote 89, p. 17-S)*

Presidential spokesman Larry Speakes said the Senate had "struggled to meet its obligations," but that the president had "serious reservations" about the product.

In the final vote, 32 Republicans and 38 Democrats voted "aye." The bulk of the "nays" were from outspoken GOP conservatives including Armstrong and Phil Gramm of Texas. Before adopting the resolution, the Senate had accepted the compromise by a 66-29 vote, as a partial substitute for the committee bill. *(Vote 88, p. 17-S)*

The compromise cut about $5.5 billion from the recommended new taxes of the committee version. It increased defense budget authority by nearly $6 billion, and outlays by about $2 billion. Democratic supporters said the compromise also added an equivalent amount of outlays for non-defense programs in science and technology, education, job training, trade promotion and child health and immunization.

The committee measure had generally frozen non-defense spending, but for selective cuts and increases.

To make up the money lost from the reduction in revenues and additions to spending, the compromise assumed further cuts in the rate of growth of selected non-defense programs, and lower costs for several large budget items, including federal retirees' cost-of-living adjustments (COLAs).

Some reduced costs reflected anticipated lower inflation rates.

The Senate budget assumed $1.101 trillion in new budget authority, $1.001 trillion in outlays, $857 billion in revenues, and a $144 billion deficit.

Floor Action Delayed

Despite a Gramm-Rudman deadline to adopt the budget by April 15, Senate GOP leader Dole kept S Con Res 120 off the floor for three weeks in hope of finding an alternative that would appeal to the White House and conservative Senate Republicans.

Gramm circulated a "conservative alternative" budget but, apparently lacking enough votes, told reporters he would not offer it on the Senate floor. And, though Dole spoke of working with the administration on some sort of Republican alternative, White House officials continued to reject compromise, insisting that only the president's budget or something very close to it was acceptable. The administration did not even back Gramm's alternative.

On April 8 Dole told the Senate that if the White House was not interested in compromise, "then Congress will have to go it alone." And Domenici, who was pushing for action, had his hand strengthened April 10 when the Senate by an impressive 72-24 vote approved a non-binding resolution, offered by Symms, to take no action on the tax overhaul bill until there was agreement with the White House on a budget. *(Vote 60, p. 12-S)*

Although the vote on Symms' resolution was as much a statement of Senate displeasure with the progress of the tax bill as it was a signal of concern about the deficit, it kept up the heat. *(Tax bill, p. 491)*

Finally to the Floor

Debate on the resolution began April 21, as White House and GOP conservatives continued to snipe at its tax hikes and cuts in Reagan's defense request. And early votes suggested that many members, though unhappy with S Con Res 120, would not be able to muster enough votes for more than marginal changes in it.

Gramm, for instance, had insisted on deeper domestic cuts. But his colleagues' reluctance to hack away at these programs was apparent April 23 when, by a lopsided 14-83 vote, the Senate rejected an amendment terminating some 43 programs, as proposed by Reagan in February. *(Vote 76, p. 15-S)*

Domenici, who offered the amendment with Chiles, invited "those who think it is the domestic, discretionary component of this budget that has run wild" to vote "aye." Gramm and a handful of other conservatives did so, but Quayle, who collected 24 signatures on a letter opposing S Con Res 120, voted against the amendment. So did 10 others who signed his letter. Quayle characterized the vote as "crap."

Also on April 23, the Senate upped the tax and spending totals of the budget resolution by approving 60-38 an Andrews amendment to increase education outlays by $300 million and the revenue total by the same amount. *(Vote 77, p. 15-S)*

The next day, April 24, however, the tide turned as the Senate rejected by bipartisan majorities three more spending amendments.

Making Changes

As the Senate entered its second week of floor debate on the budget, Dole continued to seek a compromise that would win a majority on his side of the aisle. At the same time, votes continued on amendments, some of which were accepted, including proposals:

- By Bill Bradley, D-N.J., a non-binding resolution disapproving about $600 million in deferred spending for the Strategic Petroleum Reserve, accepted by voice vote April 28.
- By Dennis DeConcini, D-Ariz., to transfer $200 million in budget authority for fiscal 1987 from the international affairs and general government functions to the law enforcement function, accepted April 29 by voice vote after the Senate refused 42-55 to kill it. DeConcini said the money was to stop the influx of drugs from abroad. *(Vote 81, p. 16-S)*
- By Pete Wilson, R-Calif., transferring to health $280.5 million over three years from the account that included congressional newsletters. Wilson said the money should go for research on acquired immune deficiency syndrome (AIDS) and Alzheimer's disease. Accepted April 30 by a 95-2 vote. *(Vote 84, p. 16-S)*
- By Moynihan, to restore the Work Incentive (WIN) program at a cost of $211 million per year and to finance the program with new revenues. The committee resolution assumed the program would be terminated. Accepted April 30 by a 55-40 vote. *(Vote 86, p. 16-S)*
- By Alfonse M. D'Amato, R-N.Y., to transfer $100 million for drug addiction treatment from government furnishings. Accepted May 1 by a 82-12 vote. *(Vote 87, p. 17-S)*

Rejected 32-65 was a "growth through investment" amendment by Chiles and Gary Hart, D-Colo., that would have added $3 billion in fiscal 1987 budget authority for science, education, and resource development, and financed the programs with additional revenues. *(Vote 83, p. 16-S)*

11th-Hour Compromise

The compromise agreed to by the Senate was devised late May 1, shortly before the final vote. Dole had consulted with Domenici and Chiles, and also checked with White House Chief of Staff Donald T. Regan, who was in Indonesia with the president en route to the economic summit in Japan.

By law, the budget resolution could be debated for no more than 50 hours, and time was running out that evening. As time expired, Dole asked Regan if the administration wanted S Con Res 120 killed, and when Regan said to keep the budget moving, Dole launched into the final stage of negotiation.

His overriding interest was a budget that would garner a majority of Republican votes. And his own objections to the measure were considered an obstacle to getting that Republican majority. GOP votes were, in turn, considered necessary to winning many Democratic votes.

The compromise, in addition to paring back the new taxes to about $10.7 billion, and increasing defense budget authority by $6 billion to $301 billion, cut an additional $7.5 billion from non-defense spending, Domenici said.

The estimated costs of certain programs were cut by $5 billion to $6 billion to reflect revised inflation estimates and other factors. The resolution assumed that cost-of-living increases, including those for Social Security benefits, would be 2 percent, not the 3.4 percent assumed by the committee. And civilian and military pay raises were chopped from the committee's 3 percent to 2 percent.

In addition, although defense budget authority was increased by the compromise, supporters said the budget would still just cover inflation, based on somewhat different assumptions than had been used in the committee bill.

The compromise also included all amendments to the committee resolution adopted earlier by the Senate, including retention of the WIN program that the committee plan assumed would end.

House Committee Action

House Democrats did not settle down to public work on the budget until May, preferring to caucus quietly and to let the Senate finish before committing themselves. But, like the Senate, the House gave an early public thrashing to Reagan's budget request.

The president's budget (H Con Res 296) was defeated 12-312 on March 13. Republican members charged the vote was a waste of time and an exercise in "president-bashing." No Democrat voted in favor of the bill, although one (Earl Hutto of Florida) joined 77 Republicans in voting

1986 Deficit $220.7 Billion

The Treasury Department and Office of Management and Budget (OMB) jointly determined that the federal budget deficit was a record $220.7 billion in fiscal 1986, which ended Sept. 30. Previously, the largest annual deficit was in fiscal 1985: $211.9 billion. *(1985 Almanac p. 439)*

The fiscal 1986 figure was well above the $202.8 billion that was projected in February 1986 as part of President Reagan's fiscal 1987 budget request, and higher still than the $180 billion projected in his fiscal 1986 budget request in February 1985. *(1985 Almanac p. 427)*

In August, the fiscal 1986 deficit was estimated at $230.2 billion by OMB and at $224 billion by the Congressional Budget Office (CBO). The final figures were lower because tax collections were higher than had been anticipated, and there was less than expected spending for interest on the public debt, agriculture and other federal programs.

Treasury's final figures for revenues, outlays and deficits for fiscal years 1985 and 1986 *(in billions of dollars)*:

	Actual FY 1985	Budget FY 1986	Actual FY 1986
Outlays	$946.0	$973.7	$989.8
Receipts	734.1	793.7	769.1
Deficit	$211.9	$180.0	$220.7

SOURCES: Treasury Department, OMB

"present." *(Vote 48, p. 16-H)*

As soon as the Senate voted on its budget, however, the House Budget Committee got busy. Trying to outdo the Senate in deficit reduction, it approved a budget resolution May 8 (H Con Res 337 — H Rept 99-598) that would have produced a fiscal 1987 deficit of $137 billion — $7 billion less than the Senate's measure.

Within an overall limit of $1.086 trillion in budget authority, Democrats on the committee voted to spend $285 billion on defense, $35 billion less than the president's request, $16 billion below the Senate total and $1.8 billion less than the fiscal 1986 level. Like the Senate, the committee voted to increase tax revenues by $10.7 billion. But the House budget earmarked the extra $4.7 billion over the president's request for deficit reduction.

The budget would have cut most domestic programs below their fiscal 1986 level, although programs for children and low-income persons were exempted.

Looking for a Fight

Working from a draft proposal offered by Gray, the committee made a few changes, then approved the budget on a mostly party-line vote of 21-11, in sharp contrast to the Senate. Vin Weber, R-Minn., was the lone Republican to vote for it. W. Henson Moore, R-La., who bucked his party to vote for the budget resolution in the committee in 1985, voted "present."

Latta, the committee's ranking Republican, vowed to fight the tax increase on the House floor.

Defense Secretary Caspar W. Weinberger said the House budget "would destroy the recent and impressive momentum we have made in rearming America." And Domenici complained, "I thought they were going to be responsible and realistic, and they're neither."

"Many think the Senate went too far when it reduced defense spending budget authority to $301 billion, but the House's $285 billion level is irresponsible and totally unrealistic," said Dole.

Dole promised White House officials that he would break up the conference rather than agree to defense numbers the administration could not accept, staff aides said. Replied Gray: "It disturbs me to see the leader of the Senate announcing that he is prepared to break up the budget process because he expects the House to totally move to the Senate figure."

Administration budget director Miller said the House proposal "adds insult to the injury already occurring in the budget process." He criticized the defense cuts, revenue increases, and level of domestic spending.

Weber's vote for the budget led Gray to proclaim a bipartisan victory, but committee Republicans complained they had been frozen out of the process.

Weber, a member of the Conservative Opportunity Society, said he had broken ranks with his party colleagues because "this is a budget I can live with. It's not my first choice, however, and I may support an alternative on the floor."

Republicans were not shown the proposals until the night before the markup, and they did not get to see the complete set of papers until after they were given to reporters at the beginning of the markup.

Even at that late hour, there was still some hope for a compromise — based on higher defense spending — that would produce a bipartisan resolution. But after opening discussions and a lunch break, it was clear that Republicans were not being offered a package they could accept.

"We know you have the votes and you can do whatever you want," Latta lamented.

Skittish About Taxes

The markup took only a single day, but it culminated weeks of closed-door meetings among committee Democrats and delicate negotiations with the party leadership focusing on the politically sensitive issue of taxes.

House Speaker Thomas P. O'Neill Jr., D-Mass., had repeatedly vowed that Democrats would not consider tax revenues over the $5.9 billion in the president's budget unless he was sure they would not become a partisan issue.

For months O'Neill had said the House would not include new revenues unless Reagan promised to support them, but in recent weeks he softened, saying it would be enough to get the support of House Minority Leader Robert H. Michel, R-Ill., Dole, and a majority of Senate Republicans.

Though the House revenue figures were identical to those in the Senate budget, leaders hoped the hedge of the special deficit-reduction account would protect them from being accused of voting for higher taxes to preserve federal spending.

Outlays Under $1 Trillion

The hallmark of the budget was that it would have brought the deficit down to $141.8 billion without using more revenues than called for in the president's budget. With another $4.7 billion in revenue, the deficit would have declined to $137.1 billion in fiscal 1987, $105.9 billion in 1988, and $64.3 billion in 1989.

Overall, the $1.086 trillion in fiscal 1987 budget authority called for by the House plan was $14.9 billion less than the Senate resolution. The budget called for $994.3 billion in outlays and $857.2 billion in revenues, including the deficit-reduction reserve.

The House committee achieved its totals by slicing defense and foreign affairs $17 billion below Senate levels, and providing $2 billion more for domestic programs.

In many domestic categories, however, the House panel cut even deeper than the Senate. The only budget categories to receive significant increases were Social Security and income programs, which were allowed to keep up with inflation.

The philosophy behind the House budget was to ensure that defense and domestic programs shared the pain of budget cuts equally, the same formula used to calculate across-the-board cuts under Gramm-Rudman.

Like the Senate, the House budget was calculated against the CBO baseline, but Senate and House baselines for spending and revenues were not directly comparable, since the House committee included spending changes and tax increases under the 1986 deficit-reduction bill (PL 99-272), while the Senate did not. The measure cleared after the Senate committee began its work. *(Fiscal 1986 deficit reduction, p. 555)*

The House budget took away CBO's 3.4 percent inflation adjustment from most domestic programs, and then sliced an additional 2.5 percent from them. Low-income programs were allowed to grow with inflation. These included food stamps, subsidized housing, Aid to Families with Dependent Children, Supplemental Security Income, student aid, legal services, and vocational rehabilitation.

Programs that won increases over inflation included Medicaid, child nutrition, Head Start, maternal and child health, Indian education, and special health programs. An additional $1.5 billion was earmarked for "high priority" programs such as Job Corps, summer youth, older Americans and handicapped education.

The budget did not terminate any federal programs, and rejected the president's proposal to sell federal assets such as regional electric power systems. It did allow the sale of some federal loans, however.

It assumed a 2 percent cost-of-living allowance (COLA) for military and civilian retirees, the same level included in the Senate budget. Civilian and military personnel were presumed to receive 3 percent pay raises, effective in January 1987. The Senate provided 2 percent. The president had requested 4 percent for military personnel and 3 percent for civilians.

Adjustments to Win Votes

The defense totals represented an area where Democrats were vulnerable to defections within their party. In the days before the markup, Democrats added approximately $9 billion in budget authority and $5 billion in outlays to satisfy defense-oriented members.

Republicans argued that the cut, coupled with expected inflation, would impose serious restrictions on military preparedness. But Democrats countered that the new spending authority was $14 billion more than defense would get if across-the-board Gramm-Rudman cuts went into effect.

Denny Smith, R-Ore., offered an amendment during markup to raise defense spending to $293 billion by cutting other programs, but it was defeated by a party-line vote of 12-20. Seven Republicans deserted Latta when he proposed cutting other programs to raise defense spending to the Senate level of $301 billion; he lost 6-27.

House Armed Services Committee Chairman Les Aspin, D-Wis., said he would withhold comment on the budget until he had conferred with members of his committee, several of whom were unhappy with the totals.

On the domestic side, there were relatively few amendments to Gray's markup proposal.

By voice vote on an amendment by George Miller, D-Calif., the committee added $250 million in fiscal 1987 to keep the Medicare hospital deductible at $540, instead of letting it rise to $572, as scheduled under existing law.

On a 13-11 vote that crossed party lines, the committee added $300 million in fiscal 1987 budget authority, and $200 million in outlays, for the National Aeronautics and Space Administration, on an amendment offered by Buddy MacKay, D-Fla.

In a reversal that embarrassed some members, Democrats at first accepted by voice vote an amendment by Hank Brown, R-Colo., to eliminate $111 million for an agricultural program to support honey producers, and then, a few hours later, put the money back in on a 17-10 vote.

Democrats said that while they did not like the honey program, they were convinced that the Agriculture and Appropriations committees would preserve it.

"I am ashamed to say this, but the honey program is stronger [than we are]," said Miller.

Democrats made a symbolic gesture by approving, on a 20-11 party-line vote, a continuation of revenue sharing provided that it was reauthorized. Lynn Martin, R-Ill., criticized Democrats for failing to stand up to pressure from mayors to revive the program. "Maybe girls learn to say no easier than boys," she chided her male colleagues.

Connie Mack, R-Fla., offered an amendment to eliminate the $4.7 billion in new revenues reserved for deficit reduction. It was rejected on a 13-20 party-line vote. An amendment by Bill Goodling, R-Pa., to eliminate $2.3 billion in new revenues not reserved for deficit reduction was rejected 3-25.

The committee rejected proposals by Republicans to eliminate the Legal Services Corporation, the Appalachian Regional Commission, the Small Business Administration loan program, and to reduce Amtrak subsidies.

House Floor Action

With surprisingly little difficulty, the House May 15 adopted the committee budget resolution intact.

The House voted 245-179 in favor of the measure with only 17 Republican "yea" votes and 19 Democratic defections. Republicans staged a fight, but debate went quickly and there was little suspense about the outcome. *(Vote 117, p. 36-H)*

Reagan immediately denounced the resolution's "radical anti-defense budget," and military spending levels were obviously to be the main issue in conference.

"It's quite obvious that the Democratic strategy was to beat the hell out of the defense budget in order to placate all the social welfare pleaders," Michel complained.

But Democrats said they had cut equally from defense and domestic programs, and noted that a Republican alternative defeated on the floor had allowed only 3 percent more for defense.

"This is a new day for the Democratic Party," said

Charles E. Schumer, D-N.Y., one of several Budget panel members who voted against Gramm-Rudman in 1985 but worked to surpass its goals for 1987. "Balancing the budget is more important than just about any other priority."

Democrats on the Foreign Affairs and Armed Services committees were particularly unhappy with the bill's provisions for their areas, but most ended up voting for it, especially when it became clear that in conference the defense spending figure would be increased.

The House approved the rule to govern debate on the issue by voice vote May 14. It allowed consideration of three substitutes for the committee resolution, but no other amendments. Debate on the resolution centered on defense and taxes, with little discussion of the tight domestic spending limits the bill would impose on many federal agencies.

Agencies and many domestic programs had suffered a 4.3 percent reduction from fiscal 1986 appropriation levels in March, when the first automatic cuts required by Gramm-Rudman took effect. The House budget would have reduced most domestic programs another 2.5 percent below that level. Adding the effects of inflation, that would have left affected agencies with almost 10 percent less purchasing power in fiscal 1987 than at the start of 1986.

Republicans, who faced significant divisions within their own party, did not decide to offer a substitute until a few hours before debate began.

The substitute that was finally proposed by Latta was designed partly to keep moderates from voting for the Democratic budget, and some conservatives voted against it. His amendment allowed $293 billion for defense budget authority, cut deeply into some domestic programs, and held revenues below the amount requested by the president.

The amendment attracted only 145 of the 182 Republicans and no Democrats. It was defeated 145-280. *(Vote 116, p. 36-H)*

Another alternative budget offered by Mickey Leland, D-Texas, and supported by the Congressional Black Caucus, was defeated 61-359, while William E. Dannemeyer, R-Calif., offered a substitute that would have used low-interest bonds based on the gold standard to reduce deficits; it lost 73-338. *(Votes 115, 114, p. 36-H)*

Support Built Slowly

House leaders had feared that the tax, defense and domestic spending provisions could alienate some members. But an unusual coalition of liberals and conservatives created the plan and enthusiastically sold it to the party.

The keys to the budget were that it would split budget cuts equally between defense and domestic programs, and would increase taxes above the president's request only to cut the deficit more than required by Gramm-Rudman, not to protect federal spending.

It had something for everyone: Liberals would get defense spending down, while conservatives believed it would put the party on record as taking the initiative on deficit reduction. Social programs dear to the hearts of Democrats were to be protected from cuts.

Budget Committee members credited a relative newcomer to the panel, Democrat Marvin Leath of Texas, as the driving force behind the decision to use new revenues to push the projected deficit significantly below $144 billion. Leath, put on the committee at the beginning of the 99th Congress to satisfy conservatives, had been a hawk on defense. But he was convinced that deficits were the nation's No. 1 problem, and was willing to sacrifice some defense dollars to get deficits down, so long as domestic programs felt the pain as well.

In 1985, Leath had joined with two other moderate-to-conservative Democrats who had been appointed with him to the Budget panel, MacKay and Jim Slattery of Kansas, in trying to raise taxes and cut Social Security to reduce deficits. They won only 56 votes with a floor amendment, but thought that if they dropped the COLA issue, they could form a centrist bloc to reduce deficits.

The three united in 1986 to support revenues dedicated solely to deficit reduction. And at the other end of the political spectrum, a small group of liberal Democrats — including Miller, Schumer, Mike Lowry of Washington and Vic Fazio of California — saw an enticing possibility: If they supported Leath on revenues, they might be able to cut defense spending, which they thought was bloated.

Leath convinced Armed Services members that the only alternative to the budget was Gramm-Rudman cuts that would be worse. Fazio, chairman of the Appropriations Legislative Branch Subcommittee, took the same tack with his fellow subcommittee chairmen, nearly all of whom eventually supported the measure.

At the end of the drafting process, a few concessions were made to other committees, such as adding back money for transportation at the insistence of Public Works and Transportation Committee Chairman James J. Howard, D-N.J.

And on the sensitive tax issue, Ways and Means Chairman Dan Rostenkowski, D-Ill., demanded and got a promise that he would not have to recommend legislation calling for additional tax revenues, unless the president also specifically embraced them.

Conference Action

House and Senate conferees on S Con Res 120 met May 20, agreeing that defense and taxes were the most divisive issues under consideration. They talked of problems with possible compromises on those issues, directed staff to develop compromises in less contentious areas, and adjourned until after the Memorial Day recess, which ended the first week in June.

Some conferees stressed the unusual closeness between House and Senate resolutions and the possibility for early compromise. Both cut sharply into defense, both generally froze domestic spending and both called for $10.7 billion in new revenues.

But others, notably Domenici, emphasized the two chambers' different defense spending levels and their different approaches to new taxes.

Despite the fact that both chambers would increase revenues by the same amount, differences between the two reflected the overriding political problem of the increase: Reagan's familiar veto threats.

Domenici complained about the deal with Rostenkowski over not requiring that $4.7 billion in revenues be "reconciled," meaning that the House budget did not require the Ways and Means Committee to produce legislation raising the revenues.

House leaders said the absence of reconciliation instructions reflected Democrats' determination to pressure Republicans into bringing the president to the budget bargaining table.

Dole suggested that an expected first-year surplus of revenues from the pending tax bill (HR 3838) could be devoted to deficit reduction. Gray and Domenici both criticized this "one-shot" approach and said what was needed was separate revenue legislation, apart from HR 3838, to produce a lasting revenue increase.

Chiles noted that although HR 3838 might generate money at first, projections showed it losing revenues in the second and third years. Then, Chiles continued, "we'll be back here trying to decide what programs to cut" to keep the deficit from growing.

Building to a Stall

In sessions June 3-6, conferees settled minor differences in a few programs, but postponed debate on defense, taxes and foreign aid, as well as secondary disputes such as Medicare.

Conferees agreed to split their non-controversial differences in agriculture, justice and general fiscal assistance accounts. They settled technical differences between the resolutions on cost-of-living adjustments for Social Security and other federal retirement benefits, affirming that these would match the Consumer Price Index. They argued over funds for a future space station, sought by the Senate, a House-passed trade and education initiative, and House cuts in subsidies for Western timber and energy industries.

The next session was set for the following week and conference chairman Gray said he hoped to finish work then. Domenici predicted that compromise could be reached by then on all but the three central issues, which, he said, would be resolved only if the White House dropped objections to tax increases, to which defense and foreign aid were tightly linked.

Domenici turned out to be correct, and negotiations stalled. At a June 6 meeting Domenici warned White House Chief of Staff Regan, national security adviser John M. Poindexter and budget director Miller that "defense will get clobbered," as he put it, unless the president relented on taxes. But there was no movement from Reagan.

Looking for Agreement

In an effort to keep the talks moving, Senate conferees June 13 proposed to freeze all federal spending in 1987 at 1986 levels, unless Reagan went along with $45 billion in new taxes over three years, most of it in a special reserve to fund growth in defense and certain domestic programs.

The Senate compromise was a clear statement to Reagan that defense growth would have to be paid for with new taxes, and to congressional advocates of non-defense programs that they, too, would have to pay for their priorities.

What Senate conferees proposed was a "bare-bones" budget — in Chiles' phrase — which assumed spending would continue at rates required by existing law, with increases for inflation or for growing caseloads in certain programs, as required by law.

It included a few reductions below this baseline, such as for Medicare, and it also incorporated the few compromises, in agriculture, energy and federal pay, that conferees had informally agreed upon.

It assumed enactment of modest revenue increases, as requested by Reagan.

For the key defense account, the compromise split the difference between House and Senate figures. The compromise called for fiscal 1987 defense budget authority of $293 billion, and outlays in that year of $279 billion.

The reserve was to be divided roughly equally between defense and non-defense programs only if Reagan signed legislation providing a tax increase.

Defense would receive an additional $3 billion in fiscal 1987 outlays and about $6 billion in budget authority. Some $3.4 billion in outlays would go to special initiatives bringing spending above the baseline in education, child health, basic research, law enforcement, transportation and farm credit.

The rest of the reserve would be dedicated to embassy security, replacement of the destroyed space shuttle and deficit reduction.

The Senate offer was a frank bid to House conferees to join in forcing an aloof president to compromise, but House conferees, and the House leadership, remained fearful that they would be left out on a limb.

Gray called the Senate offer "encouraging," but said it did not provide enough protection for domestic programs valued by Democrats, nor from Gramm-Rudman cuts. In conference sessions Gray repeatedly asked Domenici if the Senate would override a veto of a tax increase. Domenici demurred, saying it would not come to that if the two chambers united on the issue.

Gray also asked Domenici the opinion of Dole, the pivotal Senate majority leader. Domenici said Dole had not objected to the general concept of the Senate plan.

But away from the conference, Gray said, "Even if the Senate can come up with a two-thirds majority to override a veto, I don't know where *I'm* going to get it." In the unlikely event that all 252 House Democrats agreed, that was not enough to sustain a veto override without Republican votes. But Republican leaders said they, like the president, would not budge on new taxes.

Meanwhile, at a June 11 press conference, Reagan reiterated in the strongest terms his objections to any new taxes. He also chastised Congress for cutting his defense spending request, and for generally ignoring his call for steep reductions in domestic spending.

Reaching a Compromise

House conferees June 16 rejected the Senate offer, and a House counteroffer, omitting both the Senate tax reserve and a special tax "account" dedicated to deficit reduction that was in the House budget, drew cool reactions from the Senate.

The four Budget Committee leaders — Chiles, Domenici, Gray and Latta — then began closed-door discussions to reach an agreement. The picture brightened after a meeting between Gray and O'Neill, in which Gray said a budget without some extra revenues did not appear feasible, and O'Neill told Gray to negotiate on the reserve concept.

Meanwhile, the House openly — but quietly — acknowledged the difficulties imposed by Gramm-Rudman's deficit targets as well as its stiff budget timetable. On June 19 the chamber waived a Gramm-Rudman rule that was meant to block the upcoming July 4 recess if Congress had failed by June 30 to pass all regular appropriations bills and any required reconciliation measure to implement an adopted budget resolution.

No appropriations bills had come to the House floor, and there could be no reconciliation absent a budget, which under Gramm-Rudman was to be completed by April 15.

The private talks finally led to a compromise on defense and agreement over a $4.8 billion contingency fund, part of which could be used for defense and part for domestic spending, but none at all without a presidential request for the money and a means — new revenues or spending cuts — to pay for it.

Though defense and taxes had tied up the conference, another hard-fought issue had been Medicare. A bitter, $1 billion dispute between House and Senate principals on this program delayed the scheduled last conference session all day June 26.

Both the House and Senate budgets had assumed a new, lower limit on the rapidly rising Medicare deductible, a payment by beneficiaries covering the first day of hospitalization. But the Senate had specified that the limit must be financed by new revenues or some other unspecified offset, while the House had included $1 billion for fiscal years 1987-89 to defray the cost. The House finally won.

Overall, the budget's $83 billion Medicare total for fiscal 1987 assumed savings of $600 million, with three-year savings of $3.3 billion. The Senate resolution had sought $800 million first-year savings and $5.8 billion over the three years; House savings had been about half that.

Other major agreements in the conference compromise were:

- Defense spending of $292.2 billion in fiscal 1987 budget authority and $279.2 billion in outlays. The budget authority total, though higher than that for fiscal 1986, was estimated by CBO to fall below an inflation-adjusted increase.

And the ratio between budget authority and outlays was of critical concern; for technical reasons, an improper ratio meant that defense personnel and other readiness programs would be most harshly cut, sparing major weapons systems that had been the targets of substantial criticism.

Glenn told the Senate just before the final vote that the outlay-budget authority ratio was badly skewed. Domenici, who had fought for higher defense numbers, did not disagree and suggested that the problem would increase pressure to use the contingency fund.

Including the fund, the fiscal 1987 defense level was $299.1 billion in budget authority and $282.2 billion in outlays.

For fiscal years 1988 and 1989, the budget assumed defense growth of 1 percent above inflation, as in the Senate budget resolution. The House had frozen spending for these two years.

- Three percent pay raises for civilian and military employees, as in the House resolution. The Senate had provided 2 percent.
- Cost-of-living adjustments (COLAs) for Social Security and other federal civilian and military retirees that were to be the same as Consumer Price Index increases.
- A 10 percent reduction below fiscal 1986 levels for foreign aid, but $1.1 billion in fiscal 1987 budget authority for enhanced embassy security, as the president had requested. The Senate had cut the security figure sharply.
- Increased funding in selected domestic programs, including: education, health care, biomedical research, reduction of infant mortality, science and technology, a supplemental food program for impoverished women, infants and children (WIC), assistance to the homeless, the Coast Guard and law enforcement.
- Rejection of a Senate and administration proposal to cut administrative costs for Medicaid.
- Revenue sharing, scheduled to expire at the end of fiscal 1986, was to be continued only if reauthorized and only if offsetting receipts or spending cuts were enacted. ∎

Holdover Deficit-Reduction Bill Approved

Congress in March completed action on a fiscal 1986 deficit-reduction bill that had appeared doomed when the 1985 session adjourned three months earlier. The final version of the bill (HR 3128 — PL 99-272) was expected to reduce federal deficits $18 billion over three years.

The official text of HR 3128, sent to the president April 1, took 310 pages of printed parchment to describe hundreds of changes in federal programs to reduce the deficit in accordance with budget decisions made eight months earlier.

The bill's complexity matched its tortuous journey through Congress, which was unprecedented. "I know the reading clerks were awfully glad to see the last of it," said one clerk, noting the two-foot-high stack of documents that had to be lugged through the Capitol corridors every time one chamber acted on it.

From the time conferees supposedly settled their differences Dec. 19, 1985, until the House cleared the bill March 20, 1986, the measure was lobbed back and forth from chamber to chamber nine times.

A titter went up on the House floor the evening of March 20 when House Budget Committee Chairman William H. Gray III, D-Pa., read the parliamentary boilerplate to describe the action on HR 3128.

Officially, the House was considering "the Senate amendment to the House amendment to the Senate amendment to the House amendment to the Senate amendment."

And Gray had a motion to amend it yet another time.

An objection blocked Gray's motion. The House then voted 230-154 to end the jousting between the chambers by accepting the latest Senate amendment, which dropped several provisions to gain the administration's promise to sign the bill. *(Vote 60, p. 20-H)*

Along the way, the measure had been given up for dead several times, particularly when Congress ended the first session of the 99th Congress without completing action on it.

It was exhumed largely by the eagerness of members from tobacco-producing and coastal states, who wanted provisions that would benefit their constituents by revamping tobacco programs and giving states more than $1.4 billion from disputed revenues from offshore oil drilling. *(Political football, box, p. 557)*

The final form of the bill marked something of a triumph for James C. Miller III, director of the Office of Management and Budget (OMB), who took an unyielding stance in negotiating with Congress and won most of what he asked for by threatening a presidential veto unless several key provisions were dropped. The Senate amended the bill to meet Miller's objections, and the House finally yielded.

Some Programs Expanded

Almost lost at the end was the bill's impact on the deficit, which was its original reason for being. The measure was the product of a complicated budget process in

1985 Reconciliation Provisions

As signed into law April 7, 1986, the Consolidated Omnibus Budget Reconciliation Act of 1985 (HR 3128 — PL 99-272) in most respects followed the conference report filed Dec. 19, 1985; some provisions changed in the course of negotiations during the first three months of 1986.

Major provisions of the final bill are described elsewhere in this volume, as follows:

- **Commerce, Merchant Marine**, p. 295
- **Military Health,** p. 486
- **Student Loans**, p. 268
- **Environment, Energy**, p. 147
- **Federal Employees, Postal Service**, p. 323
- **Medicare, Medicaid**, p. 252
- **Housing**, p. 586
- **Pensions, Unemployment**, p. 592
- **Revenue Measures**, p. 521
- **Small Business Administration**, p. 322
- **Social Security**, p. 594
- **Tobacco Price Supports**, p. 304
- **Trade Adjustment Aid**, p. 351
- **Transportation**, p. 294
- **Veterans' Care,** p. 324
- **Welfare Benefits**, p. 247

which committees proposed spending cuts and revenue increases to "reconcile" programs with deficit targets set in the fiscal 1986 budget resolution. Hence, it was known as a "reconciliation" bill.

The Congressional Budget Office (CBO) estimated that it would reduce expenditures $12.1 billion for fiscal years 1986, 1987 and 1988, and raise revenues $6.1 billion, for a total deficit reduction of $18.2 billion. Over four years, the bill was estimated to cut $24.9 billion from the deficit.

These estimates were far below the initial figures that showed three-year savings of $74 billion. The long delay in passing the bill reduced its impact somewhat, but most of the other savings were accomplished in the interim through action on appropriations bills and other measures.

The bill cut spending for areas such as student loans, highways, veterans, small businesses, housing, and Medicare payments to hospitals and doctors, and added revenues from cigarette taxes, customs fees and federal pension insurance premiums.

But HR 3128 also expanded federal programs in some areas, such as Medicare and Medicaid, tobacco price supports, and Trade Adjustment Assistance.

These expansions were the focus of initial White House objections to the measure.

The bill's major provisions included:

- **Tobacco.** The 16-cents-a-pack cigarette tax would be extended permanently, rather than revert to 8 cents. New taxes would be imposed on chewing tobacco and snuff.

A new tobacco price-support program would allow cigarette manufacturers to help set quotas for growers and to buy surplus tobacco at sharp discounts, while half the cost of the program would be shifted from farmers to manufacturers.

- **Offshore Drilling Revenues.** Approximately $6.4 billion in revenues from offshore drilling activities that crossed federal-state boundaries was to be divided between state and federal governments. The action would settle a longstanding dispute between coastal states and the federal government that had tied up funds since 1978 in an escrow account.

The federal government would receive approximately $4.9 billion for deficit reduction, while Louisiana, Texas, California, Alabama, Alaska, Mississippi and Florida would divide approximately $1.4 billion immediately and a share of future revenues.

- **Health.** The bill made significant changes in the Medicare and Medicaid programs. In addition to provisions designed to save money, it included steps to penalize hospitals that refused emergency care to the poor, improve private health insurance for some workers and their spouses, and modify a new system of repaying hospitals for treatment under Medicare. It also extended until Dec. 31, 1986, the existing freeze on Medicare payments for doctors' services.
- **Trade.** The bill reauthorized the Trade Adjustment Assistance program, designed to help workers hurt by foreign imports.
- **Pensions.** The bill made changes to shore up the financially troubled Pension Benefit Guaranty Corporation, which guaranteed pension plans for workers.
- **Veterans.** The bill required for the first time a means test for free medical care under programs of the Veterans Administration.

Tucked away in the bill were dozens of little-noticed provisions that benefited various groups. For instance, the bill exempted airline employees from paying federal income taxes on the value of free air tickets used by employees' parents. Those fringe benefits had been made taxable by 1984 legislation (PL 98-369) to raise revenues.

Key Changes Dropped

Some equally significant provisions were dropped from the bill in the course of its passage. They included:

- A broad-based excise tax on manufacturers to pay for an expanded "superfund" toxic-waste cleanup program.

This provision was dropped because of intense opposition by the White House, which feared it would open the door to a value-added tax, and by the House, which preferred a tax on petrochemical manufacturers.

- An omnibus bill reauthorizing housing programs that would extend various housing and community programs and create several new programs, including one for the homeless.
- Provisions to limit textile, apparel and shoe imports to reduce the U.S. trade deficit. These were added to the bill on the Senate floor, but then dropped when Senate leaders allowed the import measure to be passed separately.
- Proposals to trim subsidies to banks for student loans and to require all students to meet a financial needs test.
- A fee on imports to pay for the Trade Adjustment Assistance program.
- Provisions to remove trust funds for highway and airport improvements from the federal budget.
- A provision requiring the interior secretary to give equal weight to environmental impacts and economic benefits when considering offshore oil drilling leases.
- A requirement that offshore drilling rigs be made in America with American steel.
- A block grant program that would share federal reve-

Playing Political Football With Reconciliation

At various points in its life span, the reconciliation bill was an important political vehicle.

The bill was held up on the Senate floor for almost three weeks in the fall of 1985 after senators from textile- and shoe-manufacturing states succeeded in attaching a major amendment to limit imports.

The bill moved forward only after Senate leaders agreed to allow a separate import-limiting bill to move forward. That measure, HR 1562, was vetoed by President Reagan Dec. 17, 1985.

Tobacco politics, which are sometimes a world unto themselves, also played an important role. Sen. Jesse Helms, R-N.C., chairman of the Agriculture Committee, succeeded in forcing onto the bill a major revamping of the tobacco price-support program as the price for allowing the cigarette tax to be extended.

Helms' new program appealed to cigarette manufacturers, but tobacco growers were not so happy with it and only reluctantly supported the bill. There were also several unsuccessful moves by anti-smoking advocates to raise the cigarette tax even higher.

In the end, the tobacco provisions became a major force in the revival of the bill, as tobacco-state members realized that it would be difficult to enact the changes through separate legislation. In the House, Democrats from tobacco-growing regions joined Republicans to help get the Senate version passed. By that point, there was no difference between Senate and House versions of the bill on the tobacco program.

The desire of coastal states to get money from settlement of the dispute over offshore drilling was another important factor. With states such as Louisiana and Texas suffering from the decline in oil prices, the prospect of a $635 million windfall for Louisiana or $424 million for Texas was tempting. Settlement of the dispute would also free almost $5 billion from an escrow account for the federal Treasury, which appealed to members from other states anxious to save domestic programs from cutbacks.

Senate Candidates Clash

The chief rivals for the Louisiana Senate seat being vacated by Democrat Russell B. Long — Democratic Rep. John B. Breaux and Republican Rep. W. Henson Moore — jockeyed for position to get credit for the offshore drilling revenues.

Breaux, chairman of a Merchant Marine subcommittee, claimed credit for initiating the move to include funds from the settlement in the original House budget resolution (H Con Res 152), during committee consideration in 1985. *(1985 Almanac p. 441)*

Moore, a member of the Budget Committee, then tried to negotiate the issue with David A. Stockman, at the time director of the Office of Management and Budget (OMB), to try to get his approval.

In most negotiations over the issue between the House and Senate, Breaux took the lead role on the issue.

As the bill neared completion, however, the White House and Senate Republicans found ways to bypass Breaux and bring Moore into the picture.

When Miller, Stockman's successor at OMB, finally agreed to guarantee OMB support as part of a deal that included a reduction in the amount of offshore revenues going to the states, Moore was invited to the White House for a March 13 meeting to win Reagan's final approval. Moore emerged from his meeting to announce to television cameras that he had "saved" the settlement money for Louisiana.

Moore's late-hour involvement irritated Sen. J. Bennett Johnston, D-La., a Breaux supporter who had been a midwife for the deal in the Senate. Before the Senate committee passed its final amendments March 14, Johnston read a poem poking fun at Moore and Miller.

"...So back to the drawing board Miller did go,
But this time with only Moore and Republicans in tow.
He said, 'Cut back the amount, restructure the deal.
Make it look different and the credit we'll steal.'
Off to the White House they eagerly did go —
For a picture with the Great Communicator the press to show....
There's a moral to this game of political chess:
With Breaux you get more, but with Moore you get less."

Reagan appeared at a March 27, 1986, fund-raiser for Moore in New Orleans, at which he gave Moore credit for the settlement. "He was in the Oval Office presenting Louisiana's case and, let's just say, Henson knows how to get your attention," Reagan said.

nues from undisputed offshore leases with coastal states.

- A change in Aid to Families with Dependent Children (AFDC) that would prevent states from denying aid to two-parent households if they met other criteria.
- A provision removing a cap on the government's share of federal employee health plan costs.

The last five deletions, along with a reduction in the state share of disputed oil revenues, were demanded by Miller as the price of OMB's support for the bill. The Senate adopted the administration proposal as an amendment March 14, and it was that amendment that the House — against the wishes of its Democratic leaders — adopted to clear the bill.

Legislative History

1985: Stalemate

The complex legislation began life in the House as two bills: HR 3128 (H Rept 99-241, Part I), from the Ways and Means Committee, and HR 3500 (H Rept 99-300), from the Budget Committee. *(Details of 1985 action, 1985 Almanac p. 498)*

Ways and Means approved its package of spending cuts and revenue increases July 24, 1985 — a week before the fiscal 1986 budget resolution (S Con Res 32) cleared Congress — partly because the panel wanted to clear the decks for the markup of its tax reform measure.

The largest elements of the Ways and Means bill were extension of the 16-cents-per-pack cigarette tax and a series of changes that would save money in Medicare but liberalize some welfare provisions.

Three other committees then added their own medical, pension and Medicare provisions.

The bill was delayed on its way to the floor when the Rules Committee refused to grant a rule to guide floor debate, on the grounds that the three-year estimate of $19.5 billion in savings was $2.1 billion short of the target the committee needed to meet the budget resolution.

The obstacle was overcome Oct. 29 when the committee added $3.1 billion in estimated revenues from the superfund program.

Despite objections by Republicans to tobacco and new spending provisions, the bill was approved Oct. 31, 245-174.

HR 3500, meanwhile, was moving on a parallel track. Authorizing committees made their recommendations throughout the summer, and they were rolled together Oct. 3 by the Budget Committee on a party-line 18-10 vote, with Republicans complaining that the bill expanded too many programs and that they had been excluded from writing it.

There was controversy over the inclusion of provisions for a comprehensive reauthorization of housing programs, suggested by the Banking, Finance and Urban Affairs Committee, and a move by Public Works and Transportation to take highway and airport trust funds off the budget.

But even though Budget Committee leaders criticized some of the program expansions, they argued that the 1974 Congressional Budget and Impoundment Control Act (PL 93-344) gave them no authority to change the recommendations of the committees.

Many members of the Budget and Appropriations committees did support a successful move on the House floor Oct. 24 to strike the trust fund provisions.

The House passed HR 3500 Oct. 24, 228-199.

In the Senate, the recommendations of the authorizing committees were reported Oct. 2 as S 1730 (S Rept 99-146).

The only Senate committee that did not achieve its reconciliation target was Armed Services, which fell $186 million short of its three-year totals and did not approve a long-term restructuring of military retirement programs assumed by the budget resolution.

The Finance Committee recommended adding a manufacturers' tax to pay for the superfund program and a revised tobacco price-support program, as part of the agreement with tobacco interests to extend the cigarette tax.

The Senate considered the bill sporadically on the floor from Oct. 15 to Nov. 14, when it was approved 93-6.

Much of the delay was because the bill became a vehicle for legislation to correct the U.S. trade deficit, but once Senate leaders agreed to consider that separately, the bill moved quickly and was approved Nov. 14.

A conference on the measure was slow to get off the ground because of Thanksgiving and the focus on the Gramm-Rudman-Hollings anti-deficit measure.

When the conference began Dec. 6, it was a massive affair, with more than 240 House and Senate conferees meeting in 31 subgroups — believed to be exceeded only by the 1981 reconciliation conference. *(1981 Almanac p. 257)*

Most issues were settled fairly quickly, but the superfund tax issue was difficult to solve. And work was slowed by periodic veto threats from OMB.

Sen. Bob Packwood, R-Ore., chairman of the Finance Committee, insisted on the broad manufacturers' tax to pay for the superfund cleanup program, and asserted that without it "there will be no reconciliation." Even though the tax was opposed by House Ways and Means Chairman Dan Rostenkowski, D-Ill., Packwood had the upper hand among conferees, and finally won a 9-4 vote to report the manufacturers' tax as part of the conference report.

Shortly after the conference concluded Dec. 19, the Senate voted 78-1 to approve it, with only Barry Goldwater, R-Ariz., opposing it.

But in the House, opposition to the manufacturers' tax was so strong that the Rules Committee reported a rule that would strip out the superfund tax. The House Dec. 19 approved the rule 205-151 and sent the bill back to the Senate.

From there, action proceeded as follows in the waning days of the first session:

- Dec. 19: The Senate rejected the House proposal, and insisted on the superfund tax.
- Dec. 20: The House rebuffed the Senate move, and returned the conference report to the Senate. The House then adjourned, putting the Senate in a take-it-or-leave-it situation.
- Dec. 20: As the first session wound down to its final hours, Packwood indicated that he was willing to let the superfund issue be removed from the bill and settled in a separate conference on the superfund reauthorization bill (HR 2005). But he insisted that the House give on some issues in return, and Senate leaders were reluctant to push the bill without assurances that the president would sign it. So the Senate insisted on its agreement and asked for a new conference on the bill.

1986: Reviving the Bill

Many members gave up the reconciliation bill for dead when Congress went home without taking action. But the bill was revived in 1986, largely by the keen interest of members who wanted the tobacco program revisions and the oil-revenue settlement.

With the agreement to consider the superfund tax issue separately, the differences between the House and Senate narrowed. But White House opposition to the bill took on heightened importance, as members were unwilling to devote time to the bill only to have it vetoed.

The administration complained about the offshore oil settlement, AFDC, "Buy American" requirements for drilling rigs, and the block grant proposal for federal offshore drilling revenues.

Senate negotiators began dealing directly with Miller, and Senate leaders began to carry the administration's position as their own.

Senate negotiators made an offer to their House counterparts March 3 that tried to meet administration objections concerning Medicare and Medicaid, offshore leasing and AFDC. The House responded March 6 by agreeing, 314-86, to scale back some of the expansions of Medicare and Medicaid programs, and to drop the states' claim to some offshore oil revenues. But the House insisted on keeping the AFDC provisions. *(Vote 36, p. 12-H)*

The administration said the House offer did not go far enough. Senate negotiators worked out a package of amendments with Miller that guaranteed, for the first time, that the president would sign the bill. But, the administration said, even the slightest change would lead to a veto recommendation.

The amendments — which were the ones finally cleared by Congress — were adopted by the Senate March

14 by voice vote. Two minor changes were made on the floor. One withheld Louisiana's share of offshore oil revenues until Oct. 1 in order to allow time for a referendum in that state on what to do with them. The other, offered by Packwood, allowed Oregon hospitals to benefit from a change in Medicare repayment schedules a year earlier than the rest of the country.

Members had said that the deadline for enactment of the package was March 15, the date the cigarette tax extension and the Medicare freeze on physicians' fees expired. But the deadline passed without final action, since the House had already adjourned for the weekend by the time the Senate acted. Members said, however, that the freeze and the tax could be extended retroactively.

House leaders said the Senate amendments were unacceptable, and argued that in trying to accommodate the White House, the Senate was reopening issues that had been settled in the conference and that had majority support in both chambers.

But the House's position began to erode March 18, when House Republicans moved to accept the Senate amendments. Democratic leaders were hard-pressed to keep members who wanted the tobacco, offshore oil and trade adjustment provisions from supporting the GOP. The Republican-sponsored motion was tabled, or killed, by a slender 25-vote margin, and some members said they would have voted the other way if that would have passed the bill. *(Vote 50, p. 18-H)*

The Senate wasted no time in insisting on its amendments that same day, and negotiations over the next two days between Senate Majority Leader Robert Dole, R-Kan., and House Speaker Thomas P. O'Neill Jr., D-Mass., failed to produce a compromise.

With the House eager to leave town for the Easter recess, the Democratic leadership could not hold up the bill any longer. Under House rules, a motion to accept the Senate position had precedence on the floor, meaning that Democrats could not keep Republicans from making the motion and forcing a vote.

When Republicans made their move the evening of March 20, they were joined by Democrats from tobacco-producing and offshore-oil-drilling states, and the Democratic leadership put up only token opposition. The vote to accept the Senate amendments was 230-154. *(Vote 60, p. 20-H)*

The bill had one last twitch of controversy after it was cleared. A normally routine resolution (H Con Res 305) making technical corrections to the Pension Benefit Guaranty Corporation provisions of the bill was approved by the House March 20. But it was held up in the Senate by disputes over how the corrections would affect the attempt of the Wheeling-Pittsburgh Steel Corp. to terminate an old pension plan and create a new one.

An agreement between the government, Wheeling-Pitt and the United Steelworkers Union cleared the way after several days of negotiations, and the Senate approved the technical corrections March 26.

In its final form, the bill contained five degrees of amendments, as a product of the long exchange between the two bodies. Parliamentary rules normally prohibit amendments beyond the second degree (for example, a House amendment to a Senate amendment), but procedural rules were used, particularly on the House floor, to protect the bill from objections.

Parliamentarians said they knew of no bill that had been amended so many times. ∎

$11.7 Billion Deficit-Reduction Bill Cleared

With enactment of an $11.7 billion deficit-reduction bill (HR 5300 — PL 99-509), which cleared Oct. 17, Congress finished its fiscal 1987 budget work the day before it adjourned for the year and more than two weeks after the fiscal year began Oct. 1.

At the time Congress acted, it was assumed that the fiscal 1987 deficit, for purposes of calculations under the 1985 Gramm-Rudman-Hollings anti-deficit act (PL 99-177), would be about $151 billion. The law set a deficit target of $144 billion, but allowed a $10 billion margin of error before requiring Congress to vote on uniform, across-the-board cuts to achieve the target. *(Gramm-Rudman developments, p. 579; 1985 Almanac p. 459)*

The deficit projection came from the Congressional Budget Office (CBO), and was based on all legislation cleared in the final days of the 99th Congress. Even so, because of the way estimates of spending and revenues were calculated under Gramm-Rudman, it was assumed that the deficit in fact would be much higher. In January 1987, administration budget experts were predicting that the actual fiscal 1986 deficit would come in at about $175 billion, still substantially below the record $220.7 billion deficit for fiscal 1986. *(Fiscal 1986 deficit, p. 551)*

The measure was called a "reconciliation" bill because it was designed to reconcile existing laws with specific instructions in the fiscal 1987 budget resolution (S Con Res 120) adopted June 27. *(Budget resolution, p. 542; reconciliation instructions, p. 570)*

HR 5300 depended heavily on a package of one-shot asset sales and accounting gimmicks to reach its deficit-reduction goals, rather than more direct cuts in spending or increases in revenues. But it also included enough changes in Medicare and Medicaid programs — many of which were designed to increase spending — to make it one of the major health bills of the 99th Congress.

Because reconciliation bills tended to be "must" legislation, comprising the deficit-cutting recommendations of most congressional committees, they were attractive vehicles for provisions to increase spending as well. The fiscal 1986 reconciliation bill (PL 99-272) likewise contained major changes in health law. *(Fiscal 1986 reconciliation bill, p. 555)*

Included in the $11.7 billion deficit-reduction estimate for HR 5300 were $644 million in savings from loan sales and Guaranteed Student Loan program changes authorized by the higher education bill (S 1965 — PL 99-498) and $2.4 billion in increased tax collections from additional spending for the Internal Revenue Service contained in the omnibus appropriations bill (H J Res 738 — PL 99-591). *(Higher education reauthorization, p. 231; Treasury-Postal Service appropriations, p. 193)*

In addition to HR 5300, other actions that helped to push down the fiscal 1987 deficit projection were an estimated first-year windfall of $11 billion from the massive tax overhaul bill (HR 3838 — PL 99-514) and $2.9 billion gained in the defense authorization bill (S 2638 — PL 99-661) by delaying by one day the date on which military personnel were paid, so that the last paycheck of September would be pushed into the following fiscal year. *(Defense authorization, p. 464; tax bill, p. 491)*

Final Passage

The final compromise on the bill was reached Oct. 17, and the conference report (H Rept 99-1012) was filed that afternoon. An hour after the report was filed, the House passed the measure 305-70; before midnight the Senate voted 61-25 to approve it. *(Vote 450, p. 126-H; vote 353, p. 57-S)*

There was virtually no opposition uttered against the conference report on either floor, in part because of the late date, and in part because the measure allowed nearly everyone to declare victory and go home.

Early versions of reconciliation legislation (S 2706 — S Rept 99-348; HR 5300 — H Rept 99-727) had been approved by the Senate and House Budget committees July 31.

Those bills never reached the floor after it became clear that administrative actions and accounting procedures had sharply reduced their savings potential. Negotiators from the House, Senate and administration then came up with additional deficit-reduction provisions to add to the omnibus bills. The Senate passed its revamped bill Sept. 20; the House passed its version Sept. 24.

A conference to settle differences on the bill fought over provisions concerning welfare, revenues, Medicare coverage of state employees, and health programs. But those issues were resolved, in some cases through agreements to put off the fights until 1987.

One possible, last-minute objection arose over the inclusion of a provision raising the ceiling on the federal debt by $189 billion, to $2.3 trillion. A separate debt-ceiling measure had been held hostage for months over amendments added in the Senate to resurrect the automatic-spending-cut mechanism of Gramm-Rudman.

Advocates of the Gramm-Rudman amendment agreed not to hold up proceedings further, because the debt-limit provision was written to expire May 15, 1987, thereby guaranteeing them another shot at the issue. *(Debt limit, p. 562)*

Major Provisions

As signed into law, HR 5300 contained major provisions that:

Agriculture

- **Income Support Payments.** Required the secretary of agriculture to make part of the 1987 season's estimated income-support payments for wheat, feed grains, upland cotton and rice farmers on an advance basis after the producer signed up for a crop-reduction program. Wheat and feed grains producers had to receive a minimum of 40 percent of projected income-supports in advance, cotton and rice producers a minimum of 30 percent. The measure authorized up to half of the advance payments to be made in government-owned commodities or negotiable certificates, which could be redeemed for commodities.
- **REA Loan Prepayment.** Required the Federal Financing Bank (FFB) to waive prepayment penalties on a minimum of $2,017,500 of rural cooperatives' loans issued by the FFB and guaranteed by the Rural Electrification Administration (REA). That amount of prepayments was estimated to save $800,000 in fiscal 1987 outlays. The sale or discounted prepayment of REA direct loans was prohibited after fiscal 1987.
- **Farm Credit System.** Allowed the Farm Credit System to change its accounting practices. Each bank in the system was allowed to write off over 20 years certain debts and excessive interest expense incurred between July 1, 1986, and Dec. 31, 1988. Specifically, each bank, upon receiving approval and conditions from the Farm Credit Administration, was authorized to take certain measures through Dec. 31, 1988, to reduce the costs of its outstanding bonds, many of which carried interest rates much higher than the market rates on new bond issues.

  Those measures included contracting with a third party or a system service organization to pay the interest on bonds issued before Jan. 1, 1985.

  Banks also were authorized to write off their interest costs for those bonds to the extent those costs exceeded market rates on new bond issues of similar maturities. Unspecified "similar actions" also were allowed.

  Each bank then could amortize over 20 years the cost of the premiums paid to third parties, the interest expense of new bonds or like costs associated with those cost-cutting measures.
- Revised the requirements of the 1985 farm law (PL 99-205) that financial statements of Farm Credit System institutions be prepared in accordance with generally accepted accounting principles (GAAP), allowing exceptions from GAAP for any actions taken to reduce the cost of obligations. This permitted banks to follow so-called "regulatory accounting principles" to allow some losses and interest costs to be spread out over a longer period of time than GAAP permitted.
- Allowed Farm Credit System banks, subject to Farm Credit Administration approval, to write off their losses that exceeded 0.5 percent of the loans outstanding and permitted banks to amortize that amount over 20 years.

  Those losses would be repaid from earnings in future years.
- Allowed the Farm Credit System's federal land banks, federal intermediate credit banks and banks for cooperatives to set loan interest rates for farmers without those rates being subject to Farm Credit Administration approval. *(Additional details, p. 301)*
- Included a non-binding "policy and objectives" statement that farmers and ranchers were best served by Farm Credit System banks offering competitive interest rates and that system banks should give farmer-borrowers the greatest benefit practicable from savings derived through the new accounting procedures.

Asset Sales

- **Agricultural Loans.** Required the secretary of agriculture to sell enough notes or other obligations in the Rural Development Insurance Fund (RDIF) to generate at least $1 billion in revenues in fiscal 1987, $552 million in fiscal 1988 and $547 million in fiscal 1989. The RDIF fund provided loans to private and public institutions to build water and sewer projects and community facilities in rural areas. Purchasers of the notes had to show the ability and resources to service the loans. Banks in the Farm Credit System were made eligible to purchase, service, collect and dispose of the notes.
- Prohibited the sale of notes from the Agricultural

Credit Insurance Fund (ACIF) during fiscal years 1987 through 1989 without prior approval by Congress. The ACIF provided production and real estate loans to farmers and rural citizens.

• **Conrail.** Required a public stock offering of the government's share of the Conrail freight railroad. *(Conrail sale, p. 279)*

• **Economic Development Administration Loans.** Directed the commerce secretary to raise $50 million in fiscal 1987 through the sale of defaulted notes held by the Economic Development Administration (EDA).

The notes represented loans made by private lenders for which EDA had guaranteed payment upon default by the borrower. Loans typically were made to businesses in high-unemployment areas. Loans delinquent by at least 180 days would be considered in default and eligible for sale.

• **Export-Import Bank Loans.** The Export-Import Bank was directed to raise $1.5 billion in fiscal 1987 through the sale of loans it had made to foreign governments or companies purchasing American-made goods.

The sales were expected to be made at substantial discounts — perhaps as large as 20 percent, according to the conference report — in order to raise the money quickly. The Ex-Im Bank was required to report to Congress on the amount of the discount before the sale, and the comptroller general was required to audit the sales.

The conference report said that the loan sales would reduce the Ex-Im Bank's capital by more than $400 million, potentially affecting its ability to make additional loans to encourage the export of expensive U.S.-made goods, such as airplanes and telecommunications equipment. *(Ex-Im Bank reauthorization, p. 348)*

• **Rural Housing Loans.** The secretary of agriculture was directed to raise $1.7 billion in fiscal 1987 through the sale of rural housing loans the Farmers Home Administration (FmHA) had made to families.

The sales were expected to be made at substantial discounts — perhaps as large as 20 percent, according to the conference report — in order to raise the money quickly. The agriculture secretary was required to report to Congress on the amount of the discount before the sale, and the comptroller general was required to audit the sales.

Budget Procedures

• **Gramm-Rudman Exemptions.** Exempted from uniform percentage budget cuts that might be imposed in the future under the Gramm-Rudman-Hollings anti-deficit law scheduled cost-of-living adjustments for civilian and military retirement and disability programs.

• Exempted from uniform percentage cuts that might be imposed under Gramm-Rudman the retirement benefits of railroad workers that were paid by the federal government.

• **Revenue Sharing.** Authorized early disbursement of the fiscal 1986 fourth-quarter payment of general revenue sharing funds to local governments, so that the $680 million expenditure would appear in fiscal 1986 rather than fiscal 1987.

• **Extraneous Amendments.** Extended through 1987 a Senate rule prohibiting the inclusion of extraneous material in a reconciliation bill.

Debt Limit

• Increased the statutory limit on the public debt to $2.3 trillion, but only until May 15, 1987, at which time it was to revert to $2.111 trillion.

Energy and Environment

• **Oil Price Overcharge Penalties.** Specified procedures for distribution of penalties assessed against businesses for violations of price controls on oil during the 1970s. The provision exempted funds governed by an Energy Department administrative order or by a July 7 settlement of a federal court case in Kansas that split some penalties equally between the states and the federal government.

The provision required that attempts be made to provide direct restitution to individuals and businesses that were overcharged. The rest of the federal share of the funds was to supplement appropriations for federal conservation programs up to a maximum of $200 million in total spending per fiscal year.

• Required that actions against companies for violating oil pricing guidelines be brought within six years of the date of violation, or by Sept. 30, 1988, whichever occurred later.

• Directed the energy secretary to study domestic oil production and refining capacity.

• **Strategic Petroleum Reserve.** Authorized appropriations for buying oil for the Strategic Petroleum Reserve of $200 million in fiscal 1987, $291 million in fiscal 1988, and $479 million in fiscal 1989.

• Required the Energy Department to fill the Strategic Petroleum Reserve at a minimum rate of 75,000 barrels of oil per day, rather than the existing 35,000 barrels per day, until the reserve held 750 million barrels.

• Forbade the sale of oil from the Naval Petroleum Reserve near Elk Hills, Calif., if the Strategic Petroleum Reserve was not filled at 75,000 barrels per day.

• **User Fees.** Required the Federal Energy Regulatory Commission to charge fees to cover the cost of its operations.

• **Mine Research.** Within the Interior Department, transferred research and demonstration activities on abandoned mines from the Office of Surface Mining, Reclamation and Enforcement to the Bureau of Mines.

• **Swamp Cleanup.** Required the Environmental Protection Agency (EPA) to report on the cleanup of asbestos and other contaminants from the Great Swamp National Wildlife Refuge in New Jersey.

General Government

• **Civil Service Pensions.** Altered a key provision of the Federal Employees Retirement System Act of 1986 (PL 99-335), concerning federal worker contributions to newly created tax-deferred savings plans, similar to so-called 401(k) savings plans available to private-sector employees.

Under PL 99-335, the new savings plans were to be available Jan. 1, 1987, for workers covered by the new Federal Employment Retirement System (FERS). Delays in creating an investment board to manage the savings plans caused conferees on HR 5300 to delay the availability of the savings plans until April 1, 1987. Under PL 99-335, workers covered by the existing Civil Service Retirement System (CSRS), were eligible to begin contributing to savings plans July 1, but conferees on HR 5300 agreed to make them eligible April 1 also. *(Story, p. 315)*

Workers covered by both FERS and CSRS were authorized to increase their contributions during part of 1987 to make up for lost contributions from Jan. 1 through April 1. Matching government contributions for workers covered by FERS were to be correspondingly increased.

• **Trust Fund Investment and Disinvestment.** Au-

Temporary $2.3 Trillion Debt Ceiling Voted . . .

Legislation to raise the ceiling on total borrowing by the federal government was tucked at the last minute into a deficit-reducing "reconciliation" bill (HR 5300 — PL 99-509), in order to win votes for the unpopular provision and to protect it from amendments and filibusters. The bill cleared Oct. 17, as Congress rushed to adjourn for the year.

A free-standing measure (H J Res 668) to increase the debt limit had been ensnared in a fight over resurrecting the automatic-spending-cut provisions of the Gramm-Rudman-Hollings anti-deficit act (PL 99-177); it never cleared. The automatic procedure was struck down by the Supreme Court July 7. *(Gramm-Rudman developments, p. 579; 1985 Almanac p. 459)*

As enacted in PL 99-509, the debt ceiling was allowed to rise to $2.3 trillion, but the provision was to expire May 15, 1987, at which time the limit was to revert to $2.111 trillion. That figure was set in a short-term debt-ceiling increase (HR 5395 — PL 99-384) enacted Aug. 16, as the Treasury bumped against a $2.079 trillion debt limit enacted in 1985, and the government was threatened with default.

Sen. Phil Gramm, R-Texas, author of the anti-deficit law, had vowed to block any debt extension that did not "fix" the law. He succeeded in attaching such amendments to both H J Res 668 and HR 5395. The House never considered the long-term bill after the Senate amended it, and it struck the Gramm-Rudman fix from HR 5395 before it cleared.

Gramm and ally William L. Armstrong, R-Colo., had threatened the conference agreement on the deficit-reduction bill, with its temporary debt-ceiling provision. But they backed off because the temporary extension was designed to allow an opportunity to fight the issue again in May 1987.

Permanent Increase

When the House gave final approval to the fiscal 1987 budget resolution (S Con Res 120) in late June, it was deemed, under a special rule, to have also approved an increase in the size of the federal debt, to $2.323 trillion from $2.079 trillion. *(Budget resolution, p. 542; automatic debt-limit increase, 1985 Almanac p. 458)*

The debt measure (H J Res 668) was automatically sent to the Senate, where it was reported (S Rept 99-335) July 18 from the Finance Committee with an amendment limiting the circumstances under which the Social Security trust funds could be tapped to cover shortfalls under the debt limit.

In prior years the Treasury had sold government securities, in which the trust fund balances had been invested, in order to borrow more from the public to pay bills. *(Social Security disinvestment, p. 594)*

Once on the Senate floor, H J Res 668 acquired a load of controversial amendments, including the Gramm-Rudman fix, aid to drought-stricken farmers and new criminal penalties for money laundering. Floor action stalled when the bill became hostage to a Senate fight over South Africa sanctions and U.S. aid to "contra" rebels fighting the Nicaraguan government. A break in that conflict permitted the Senate Aug. 9 to pass H J Res 668 by a 47-40 vote. *(Vote 208, p. 37-S)*

House leaders of both parties intensely disliked the Gramm-Rudman amendment, however, and refused to go to conference with the Senate, letting the measure die. Like the debt-limit provision itself, however, many of the amendments to the measure migrated to other bills that became law.

Gramm-Rudman Fix

The defunct section of Gramm-Rudman that had provided for automatic cuts had involved deficit calculations by the Congressional Budget Office (CBO) and the Office of Management and Budget (OMB). Those calculations were to be reviewed and changed, as necessary, by the General Accounting Office (GAO).

It was the GAO's role that the court found unconstitutionally intrusive on the executive branch, so efforts to fix the law involved vesting full power to OMB to determine the magnitude and distribution of cuts.

The debt measure came to the Senate floor July 23, but deliberations on an early version of the Gramm-Rudman amendment were stopped a day later by Dole. There was enough distrust of OMB, sparked by its controversial former director, David A. Stockman, that the amendment apparently faced defeat without curbs on OMB. *(Stockman, 1985 Almanac p. 448)*

After days of private negotiations among the three sponsors, Gramm, Warren B. Rudman, R-N.H., and Ernest F. Hollings, D-S.C., and Budget chiefs Pete V. Domenici, R-N.M., and Lawton Chiles, D-Fla., debate resumed on the amendment and a package of modifications. Domenici chaired the Senate Budget Committee and Chiles was its senior Democrat.

The modified amendment, which put severe restrictions on OMB's latitude was adopted July 30 by a 63-36 vote. *(Vote 167, p. 31-S; details, p. 325)*

Before adopting the amendment the Senate agreed by a 66-33 vote to kill a motion by J. James Exon, D-Neb., to insist that Congress use the Gramm-Rudman "fall-back" procedure, which required congressional and presidential approval of the cuts, instead of restoring the automatic process. *(Vote 166, p. 31-S)*

The day after adopting the modified Gramm-Rudman amendment, the Senate rejected on a 30-69 vote an amendment by Gary Hart, D-Colo., and Daniel Patrick Moynihan, D-N.Y., that would have repealed the entire Gramm-Rudman-Hollings law. *(Vote 168, p. 32-S)*

Farm Payments, Windfall Profits Repeal

The next vote was a 91-7 approval of an Exon amendment requiring the federal government to make so-called advance deficiency payments to farmers in fall 1986. *(Vote 169, p. 32-S)*

The payments, based on the difference between market prices and statutory target prices, could not be calculated until the following year's crops were grown and sold; nevertheless, it had become customary to advance farmers part of these payments even before the crops on which

. . . After Amendment Stalls Yearlong Increase

they were to be based were in the ground. OMB had announced that it would not make the payments in advance, which, under existing law, was optional. This provision was eventually incorporated in an omnibus fiscal 1987 appropriations bill (H J Res 738). *(Continuing resolution, p. 219)*

Next was an amendment by Don Nickles, R-Okla., to repeal the so-called windfall profits tax on petroleum. Only Howard M. Metzenbaum, D-Ohio, objected strongly, scorning the amendment as "another runaway grab by the oil industry and its friends in the U.S. Senate."

Advocates, including Domenici, argued that repeal was a critical incentive for an industry rocked by plunging global oil prices. Supporters also said that oil prices had fallen so low that the government would not lose money, because the fees were inoperative. But Metzenbaum snapped, "Oil prices *will* go back up."

When enacted in 1980, the fee had been expected to generate $227.3 billion in federal revenues by January, 1988. As of August 1986, however, the cumulative yield of the tax had been about $80 billion. *(1980 Almanac p. 473)*

The Senate first refused 47-51 to kill the amendment and later adopted it by voice vote. *(Vote 170, p. 32-S)*

Money Laundering, Drought Aid

There were no objections to adoption July 31, 98-0, of a "money laundering" amendment offered by Alfonse M. D'Amato, R-N.Y., which was reported from the Senate Judiciary Committee as a separate bill (S 2683) earlier the same day. This provision ultimately was added to an omnibus anti-drug bill (HR 5484). *(Vote 171, p. 32-S; drug bill, p. 92)*

By now the July 31 session, which began at 9 a.m., had moved into the evening hours, and tempers heated up during debate on an unsuccessful Hart amendment to impose a $10-per-barrel oil import fee, which Hart said would cut the deficit by $18 billion. The amendment was killed on an 82-15 vote. *(Vote 172, p. 32-S)*

After Hart's proposal died, senators happily accepted by voice vote a Social Security COLA amendment by Paula Hawkins, R-Fla. Existing law did not require COLAs to be paid when inflation dropped below 3 percent, as was then the case.

Hawkins' amendment would have eliminated the trigger, setting COLAs at the inflation rate. Advocates said it would save money because existing law required "catch-up" spending in a year following one in which the COLA was not paid. This provision, like the debt-limit increase, was added to the reconciliation bill.

The Senate then began debating an amendment by Jim Sasser, D-Tenn., providing payments in the form of surplus, government-owned grain, and other forms of aid to farmers suffering losses from the extended drought in Southeastern states.

There was an unusually sharp debate for several hours as senators wrangled over which party could claim credit for the idea. The session recessed at 1:20 a.m. Aug. 1, with Sasser's amendment pending. It was adopted later in the day Aug. 1, and when the debt-limit bill faltered was added to the omnibus fiscal 1987 spending bill.

A handful of other amendments adopted would have barred disinvestment of Civil Service retirement funds, exempted federal civilian and military pension benefits from Gramm-Rudman automatic cuts, and selectively enhanced disaster aid.

Before the measure was passed, one last controversy erupted over an amendment by Jesse Helms, R-N.C., adopted by voice vote, that would have overturned a District of Columbia City Council measure barring discrimination by insurance companies against persons exposed to the AIDS virus. The Senate earlier voted 41-53 not to table the amendment. *(Vote 174, p. 32-S)*

Helms said the amendment had been requested by 600 black ministers in D.C., who were concerned that "the D.C. law discriminates in favor of a special class of people whose lifestyle places them at risk for AIDS . . . and then everybody else has got to pick up the tab."

This amendment also gravitated to the omnibus appropriations bill, but was dropped in conference. *(Issues resolved, box, p. 224)*

Short-Term Increase

The existing debt ceiling, adopted in 1985, was expected to carry the government until September, but the House's objections to the Gramm-Rudman fix made it clear that H J Res 668 would not clear before Congress adjourned for a Labor Day recess expected to last until Sept. 8.

So, on Aug. 13, the House Ways and Means Committee agreed by a 22-10 vote to report an emergency measure (HR 5395 — H Rept 99-789), raising the debt ceiling from $2.079 trillion to $2.152 trillion, which was presumed to be enough to last through September.

The House passed the bill Aug. 14 by a vote of 216-199. First, however, in a parliamentary move to prevent a GOP amendment incorporating deficit-reduction provisions, the House voted 244-178 to cut off debate. *(Votes 320, 321, p. 90-H)*

When HR 5395 moved to the Senate Aug. 15, hopes of early resolution evaporated because of demands by Gramm and Rudman that a version of the Gramm-Rudman fix be added to it. The amendment was adopted by voice vote after the Senate rejected, 29-63, a motion to kill it. *(Vote 253, p. 43-S)*

The Senate also changed the debt ceiling to $2.111 trillion, a smaller amount than in the House version.

When it came time to pass the bill, however, the Senate initially rejected it, 34-47. A few minutes later, the Senate agreed to reconsider its vote and passed the measure, 36-35, after an agreement that the House's vote on the automatic mechanism would settle the matter. *(Votes 254, 255, p. 43-S)*

With virtually no debate, the House accepted the lower debt ceiling and voted 175-133 to strip off the Gramm-Rudman amendment, sending the bill back to the Senate. *(Vote 332, p. 94-H)*

The Senate then receded from its amendment and cleared the measure by voice vote, shortly before Congress departed for its Labor Day recess early in the morning hours of Aug. 16.

thorized the secretary of the Treasury to withhold investment of excess receipts of the Civil Service Retirement and Disability Fund, if such investment would cause the government to exceed the legal debt limit.

If necessary to prevent total federal borrowing from exceeding the debt limit, the Treasury secretary was also authorized to sell prematurely federal securities held by the trust fund, but only to the extent necessary to cover obligations of the trust fund.

Any amounts not invested in a timely manner were to be made up once the government had sufficient borrowing authority to do so, and any lost interest due to failure to invest had to be restored.

• **Reduced-Rate Mail Subsidies.** Revised the method of computing the federal appropriation that covered the cost of reduced-rate postage. The provision was to take effect after the next adjustment in postal rates, but no later than Jan. 1, 1989. It was expected to result in increased costs for certain types of mail. The intent was to reduce the cost to the government by $200 million in fiscal 1989. The total appropriation to the U.S. Postal Service in fiscal 1987 was $650 million.

• **Civil Fraud Penalties.** Established a new administrative procedure to penalize persons who recklessly or knowingly misrepresented facts to a federal agency, and was especially aimed at contractor fraud. The provisions were adopted from a bill (S 1134 — S Rept 99-212) reported Dec. 10, 1985, by the Senate Governmental Affairs Committee.

The procedure could be used for any false claim, or identifiable false portion of a claim, up to $150,000. The penalty for each false claim would be limited to $5,000 plus double the amount of the claim.

If an agency determined that a fraudulent claim had been filed, it was to submit the case to the Justice Department, which had to approve or disapprove of further administrative action. If approved by the Justice Department, the matter was to be referred to an administrative law judge, who would hear evidence and determine if a fraud had been committed and, if so, set an appropriate penalty.

The decision of an administrative law judge could be appealed to the head of the applicable agency, who could affirm, reduce or settle the judgment. The decision of an agency head could be appealed to U.S. district court.

Maternal and Child Health

• **Authorization.** Increased the authorization level for the Maternal and Child Health block grant program to $553 million for fiscal 1987, $557 million for fiscal 1988 and $561 million for fiscal 1989.

• **Genetic Screening.** Required a specific amount (7 percent in fiscal 1987, 8 percent in fiscal 1988 and 9 percent in fiscal 1989) of authorized and appropriated new funds to be allocated to the secretary of health and human services (HHS) for projects to screen newborn infants for sickle-cell anemia and other genetic disorders.

• **Adoption Information.** Established a National Adoption Information Clearinghouse within HHS to collect, compile, maintain and disseminate available material on all aspects of adoption of infants and children with special needs.

The HHS secretary was also required to create an advisory committee to identify the national needs for data relating to adoption and foster care and to evaluate alternative ways of collecting such data on a comprehensive basis. Such a data collection system was to be implemented no later than Oct. 1, 1991, with information to be disseminated through the National Adoption Information Clearinghouse.

Maritime Programs

• **Ship Financing.** Changed federal bankruptcy laws to permit the Departments of Transportation and Commerce to foreclose on bankrupt fishing and cargo ships that were built with federal loan guarantees. Existing law prohibited the government from seizing ships that had received such guarantees while owners were undergoing reorganization under federal bankruptcy law.

• Reduced the overall limit on federal financing for fishing vessels or fishing facilities from 87.5 percent to a maximum of 80 percent of the project cost.

• Prohibited financing for federal loan guarantees for the construction of fishing and cargo ships to be made through the Federal Financing Bank.

• **Ship Capacity Standards.** Provided for the application of international conventions on load lines and tonnage measurements to U.S. vessels engaged in international commerce. With certain exceptions, such as for towing vessels, the load-line convention was also applied to vessels engaged in domestic trade.

The load-line convention contained safety rules on permissible below-water depths for vessels. The tonnage convention provided for a standardized means of measuring the capacities of vessels.

• Permitted the Coast Guard to charge fees for load-line and tonnage measurement of cargo ships. Annual revenues of $2 million were projected.

• **Drilling Rig Evacuation.** Directed the transportation secretary to study the feasibility of using standby vessels for evacuation of personnel from offshore drilling rigs. The Coast Guard was preparing a broad set of regulations covering safety requirements for drilling rigs, including evacuation procedures. There was disagreement among members of Congress on the necessity of requiring standby vessels owned and operated by the rig owner; the provision for a study represented a compromise.

Medicaid

• **Eligibility.** Allowed states to offer Medicaid coverage to all pregnant women, infants up to age 1, and, on an incremental basis, children up to age 5, whose income placed them below the federal poverty line, but above the cutoff needed to qualify for Aid to Families with Dependent Children (AFDC). (AFDC recipients qualified for Medicaid automatically.) *(Medicaid, p. 252)*

Coverage for pregnant women was to be limited to pregnancy-related services and was to extend through the 60 days following pregnancy. Coverage of children aged 1 through 5 was to be phased in beginning Oct. 1, 1987, one year at a time. States were not permitted to reduce AFDC payment levels to pay for the new Medicaid coverage.

• Allowed states that chose to extend Medicaid coverage to pregnant women, infants, and children also to extend Medicaid coverage to elderly and disabled individuals with incomes below the poverty line, but too high to qualify for Supplemental Security Income (SSI), the federal-state welfare program for the needy elderly, blind and disabled.

Alternatively, states were allowed to pay just the cost-sharing obligations under Medicare for Medicare-eligible elderly and disabled individuals with incomes below the poverty line but too high to qualify for SSI. Cost-sharing obligations included premiums, deductibles, and co-insurance Medicare required beneficiaries to pay.

• Required states to continue to provide Medicaid coverage for severely disabled individuals who lost SSI eligibility because of income from work. Such individuals had to continue to be disabled, to meet all except income eligibility requirements for SSI, to be seriously inhibited from working by a loss of Medicaid coverage, and to be unable to obtain similar benefits.

• Clarified that states and localities could not deny Medicaid to an individual simply because of a lack of a fixed address. As part of the omnibus drug bill (HR 5484 — PL 99-570), signed by the president Oct. 27, states had to devise a method of making Medicaid cards available to eligible homeless individuals. *(Drug bill, p. 92)*

• Stipulated that states could not use federal funds to extend Medicaid services to an alien who was illegally in the United States, unless the individual was otherwise eligible and had a medical condition requiring emergency care, including impending childbirth. S 1200 (PL 99-603), the immigration bill cleared by Congress Oct. 17, barred from Medicaid eligibility for five years most illegal aliens who acquired legal status as a result of the legislation. *(Immigration bill, p. 61)*

• **Home- and Community-Based Care.** Allowed states to extend home- and community-based services authorized under Medicaid to individuals who, except for those services, would have required Medicaid-covered hospital or nursing home care.

• **Mental Health Care.** Authorized the HHS secretary to waive certain Medicare and Medicaid requirements to allow states to implement demonstration programs aimed at improving the continuity, quality, and cost-effectiveness of mental health services available to chronically mentally ill Medicaid beneficiaries. Also directed the HHS secretary to waive Medicare and Medicaid requirements for up to 10 demonstration projects that provided comprehensive health services to the frail elderly at risk of institutionalization.

• **State Matching Funds.** Held states harmless from loss of Medicaid matching funds due to a change from biennial to annual calculation mandated as part of the fiscal 1986 reconciliation law (PL 99-272).

• **HMO Review.** Extended to Medicaid, a Medicare requirement that states provide for an annual, independent, external review of services provided to beneficiaries by health maintenance organizations (HMOs) and other prepaid medical plans.

• **Second Surgical Opinions.** Prohibited the HHS secretary from requiring states to establish and operate mandatory second surgical opinion programs or hospital pre-admission review programs for Medicaid beneficiaries until 180 days after submitting a report to Congress on the effectiveness of existing programs.

• **Special Needs.** Prohibited the HHS secretary from limiting Medicaid payment adjustments to hospitals that served a disproportionate number of low-income patients with special needs.

• **HMOs.** Required HMOs that contracted with states to provide Medicaid services to report certain financial transactions, and required prior review and approval by the HHS secretary of all such contracts in excess of $100,000. The measure also provided for civil damages of up to $10,000 for failure of an HMO or other entity to provide medically necessary items and services to Medicaid beneficiaries.

• **Long-Term Care.** Permitted New York state to pay for certain long-term care services for Medicaid beneficiaries at a higher rate than otherwise authorized.

• **Respirators.** Allowed states to cover under Medicaid the cost of home respiratory care services for individuals who were medically dependent on a ventilator at least six hours per day, and who, but for the home services, would otherwise have needed inpatient services covered by Medicaid.

• **Respite Care.** Required the HHS secretary to allow New Jersey to conduct a pilot program to provide respite care services to Medicaid-eligible and other elderly and disabled persons.

Respite care services, which included companion and sitter services, homemaker and personal care services, and adult day care, gave family care-givers time off from the constant attention many elderly and disabled individuals required, and in some cases, meant the difference between an individual being cared for at home and requiring institutionalization. Such services were to be provided without regard to income (with cost-sharing required for those who could afford it), but with priority going to those who would have been eligible for Medicaid benefits upon institutionalization.

Medicare

• **Hospital Deductible.** Capped at $520 the 1987 deductible that Medicare beneficiaries had to pay before the program picked up the cost of a hospital stay. The measure based future increases on the same factors that determined the increase in Medicare payments to hospitals, rounded to the nearest $4.

Previously, the increase in the deductible was based on the cost of a day's stay in the hospital. Because hospital stays had shortened considerably in recent years due to Medicare cost-cutting reforms, the cost of a single day had risen correspondingly. Without congressional action, the 1987 deductible would have risen to $572. *(Medicare, p. 252)*

• **Hospital Payment Increase.** Granted an increase for fiscal 1987 of 1.15 percent in payments to hospitals under the Medicare prospective payment system (PPS), as well as to PPS-exempt hospitals. PPS, under which Medicare made payments on the basis of a patient's diagnosis rather than on what the hospital actually spent to treat that patient, was instituted as a cost-cutting measure in 1983 under PL 98-21. The administration proposed granting only a 0.5 percent increase. *(1983 Almanac p. 391)*

• Required the HHS secretary to set the fiscal 1988 increase at the medical inflation rate less 2 percent. It also required the HHS secretary to adjust annually the diagnosis-related group (DRG) rates to reflect the use of new technologies and other practice-pattern changes.

• Required the secretary to establish separate methods for making payments to urban and rural hospitals for so-called "outliers"; cases that were far more expensive to treat than most others within that DRG.

• Changed the formula by which hospital payments were calculated to reflect the average cost per patient, rather than the average cost per hospital.

• Extended a program that paid certain rural and suburban "regional referral centers" at (higher) urban rates for three years, and stipulated that existing regional referral centers continue receiving the urban rate. The bill also created new criteria for hospitals to qualify as regional referral centers.

• Reduced payments for capital-related costs (construction and equipment, for example) by 3.5 percent for fiscal 1987, by 7 percent for fiscal 1988 and by 10 percent for fiscal 1989. Hospitals that were the sole providers for their communities were exempted from the reductions. The HHS secretary was authorized, in the absence of further congressional action, to incorporate capital costs into the prospective payment system beginning Oct. 1, 1987, but only if the total capital payments would have been the same as under the existing system.

• Required that hospitals in Puerto Rico be included in the prospective payment system beginning Oct. 1, 1987.

• Required the HHS secretary, within two years, to submit to Congress proposed legislation to refine the prospective payment system to take into account severity of illness and case complexity.

• Required hospitals serving Medicare patients, as a condition of eligibility, to provide patients with a written notice of their right to appeal what they considered a premature discharge from the hospital. Hospitals were also required to have in place a discharge planning program to help ensure that Medicare patients received appropriate and needed care after leaving the hospital.

• Extended the so-called "waiver of liability" under Medicare to hospices and home health services providing homebound and intermittent care. The waiver allowed non-hospital health agencies to be reimbursed by Medicare for non-covered services if the providers reasonably thought they were providing covered services.

• Established a new category for rural hospitals to qualify for increased PPS payments if they served a "disproportionate share" of low-income patients and extended for one year, until Oct. 1, 1989, disproportionate-share payments to qualifying hospitals. The payments were to end Oct. 1, 1988.

• Changed the method of payments for hospital outpatient departments for ambulatory surgical procedures.

• **Periodic Payments.** Discontinued the Periodic Interim Payment (PIP) system for PPS hospitals, except those serving rural areas or a high proportion of low-income patients. PIP allowed hospitals to receive biweekly payments based not on actual claims submitted, but on the average of all claims over a full year. At the end of the year, payments and claims were reconciled.

The measure also required that hospitals and physicians receive payment on 95 percent of their "clean" claims (those requiring no further information or documentation) within 30 calendar days in fiscal 1988, 25 days in fiscal 1989 and 24 days in fiscal 1990 and thereafter.

HHS was also required to pay so-called "participating physicians" (those who accepted Medicare payments as full fees for services) on 95 percent of their clean claims within 19 days in fiscal 1988, 18 days in fiscal 1989 and 17 days in fiscal 1990 and thereafter.

• **HMOs and CMPs.** Required health maintenance organizations (HMOs) and competitive medical plans (CMPs) to provide their Medicare beneficiaries with an annual explanation of their rights to services under the plan.

HMOs and CMPs provided all medical services for a single monthly fee, instead of charging for each service provided. Medicare beneficiaries were allowed to disenroll from an HMO or CMP at any local Social Security office, and civil penalties of up to $10,000 were imposed for HMOs that "fail substantially" to provide necessary services to Medicare patients.

• **Hospital Stay Incentives.** Prohibited hospitals from making incentive payments to physicians for shortening hospital stays or otherwise reducing services to Medicare (or Medicaid) beneficiaries. HMOs and CMPs were also prohibited from making such payments beginning April 1, 1989.

• **Graduate Medical Training.** Clarified circumstances under which hospitals could be reimbursed under Medicare for the costs of graduate medical training when medical residents performed duties outside a hospital setting.

• **Home Health Providers.** Required that Medicare calculate what it would pay providers of home health services on an aggregate basis for all services rather than on a discipline-specific (skilled nurse or physical therapist, for example) basis.

• **Effectiveness Study.** Required the HHS secretary to provide for a research program on patient outcomes of selected medical treatments and surgical procedures, in order to assess their appropriateness, necessity, and effectiveness, and authorized $21 million for the study for fiscal 1987-89.

• **Organ Donation.** Required hospitals, as a condition for participation in the Medicare and Medicaid programs, to establish procedures for encouraging the donation of organs and tissue. Such procedures had to include "routine requests" for donations from a deceased person's next of kin, and notifying the local organ procurement agency when a potential organ donor was identified.

Hospitals performing organ transplants were required to be members of the national organ transplant network established under the National Organ Transplant Act of 1984 (PL 98-507). Organ procurement agencies were required to meet certain criteria in order to be eligible to receive Medicare or Medicaid reimbursement for the costs of organ procurement. *(Organ transplants, p. 265)*

• **Disabled Persons.** Made Medicare the secondary payer for disabled persons who elected to be covered by employer-based health insurance of an employer with 100 or more employees. This provision was scheduled to terminate in 1991.

• **Nurse-Anesthetists.** Extended through Oct. 1, 1988, procedures by which hospitals were reimbursed for the costs of nurse-anesthetists on staff, and authorized direct reimbursement for anesthesia services and related care furnished by a nurse-anesthetist who was legally authorized to perform such services. Required nurse-anesthetists to accept Medicare reimbursement as payment in full and provided civil penalties for violations.

• **Physician Payments.** Granted to all physicians a 3.2 percent increase in prevailing charges effective Jan. 1, 1987. The amount equaled the medical inflation rate for physician services as determined by the Medicare Economic Index (MEI).

The measure stipulated that in future years all physicians were to receive increases equal to the percentage increase in the MEI, and made permanent the existing 4.15 percent differential between payments participating physicians received over non-participating physicians.

The HHS secretary was prohibited from changing the way the MEI was calculated until completion of a study to ensure that the index reflected medical economic changes in a fair and equitable way.

• **Cataract Surgery.** Required participating and non-participating cataract surgeons to reduce their charges by 10 percent, effective Jan. 1, 1987, and by an additional 2 percent, effective Jan. 1, 1988. Non-participating physicians were not permitted to make up the reduction by charging patients more, with civil penalties for violators. The HHS secretary was required to reduce payments for cataract surgery anesthesia.

• **Kidney Dialysis.** Required the HHS secretary to reduce the per-treatment rate for facilities providing kidney dialysis services to Medicare patients in the End Stage Renal Disease (ESRD) program by $2, effective Oct. 1, 1986. The rate could not be altered for two years.

Medicare was authorized to pay for up to one year of immunosuppressive drugs, which helped prevent rejection of transplanted organs. The HHS secretary was required to impose standards and conditions under which Medicare would make payments to ESRD facilities that reused dialysis filters. *(Immunosuppressive drugs, p. 265)*

• Required the HHS secretary to consolidate the existing 32 ESRD networks, charged with ensuring quality of care for ESRD patients, into 17 networks. Increased the role and responsibilities of the networks, including requiring that networks set up grievance procedures for ESRD patients, conduct on-site review of ESRD facilities, and gather and analyze data. Stipulated that the networks' activities be funded by reducing the per-treatment payment to facilities by 50 cents.

• **Vision Care.** Authorized Medicare to pay for optometrist services if the services were among those for which Medicare would pay if performed by a physician and if the optometrist was licensed to provide such services.

• **Occupational Therapy.** Extended Medicare Part B coverage of occupational therapy services to include those provided in nursing homes (when Part A Medicare coverage had lapsed), clinics, rehabilitation agencies and other locations. The measure extended coverage, on a different reimbursement basis, to services performed in a therapist's office or the patient's home, if a physician had certified the need for such services.

• **Physician Assistants.** Authorized Medicare coverage of services performed by physician assistants under the supervision of a physician in hospitals, nursing homes or as an assistant at surgery.

• **Claim Appeals.** Permitted Medicare beneficiaries who were dissatisfied with reimbursement of claims submitted under Part B of Medicare to obtain a hearing by an administrative law judge if the amount in controversy was $500 or more, and judicial review if the amount was over $1,000. Stipulated that national coverage determinations could not be overturned solely on the basis of not having met the notice and comment requirements under the Administrative Procedures Act.

• **Alzheimer's Disease.** Required the HHS secretary to conduct up to 10 demonstration projects to determine the effectiveness, cost and impact of providing comprehensive services to Medicare beneficiaries with Alzheimer's disease. Services could include home- and community-based services, outpatient drug therapy, respite care, mental health services and supportive services and counseling for family members. The measure limited spending for the projects to $40 million over three years.

• **PROs.** Expanded the role of peer review organizations (PROs) in ensuring that Medicare beneficiaries received quality medical care and required a consumer representative to be placed on each PRO governing board. PROs were required to share certain confidential information with state licensing boards and national accreditation organizations.

• **Continued Health Insurance.** Amended the continuing access to health insurance provisions instituted in fiscal 1986 reconcilation law (PL 99-272) to require that any retiree or dependent who lost employer-based health insurance coverage because the employer filed for Chapter 11 bankruptcy would be entitled to remain in the employer's health insurance plan by paying up to 102 percent of the applicable premium. The retiree, his or her spouse, and dependent children were allowed to remain in the plan until the retiree's death, with the spouse and children allowed to continue for three years following such death.

Pensions

• **Retirement Age Limits.** Prevented employers from cutting off an employee's right to continue accruing pension rights simply because he had reached the normal retirement age under his pension plan, usually age 65. Under the new law, if an employee needed to work 30 years before getting a full pension but reached the age of 65 after only 27 years of work, his pension rights could continue to accrue so long as he continued to work after age 65.

Under existing law, an employer could cut off the worker's pension rights simply because he reached retirement age, even though he was still working.

Anticipated savings to the government of at least $1 million would result because employees remaining in the work force after age 65 would be less likely to draw Social Security benefits, and would continue to pay income tax on earnings.

Revenues

• **Conrail Tax Treatment.** Stipulated the tax treatment of the sale of the government's 85 percent share of Conrail. Conrail was to be treated as a new corporation that purchased its assets the day after the public sale. No carryover of net operating losses or other benefits, such as unused investment tax credits, was to be allowed for tax purposes. *(Conrail sale, p. 279)*

With one major exception, the public sales price was to be allocated among all of Conrail's assets, both depreciable assets, such as equipment and buildings, and non-depreciable assets, such as land. After the sale, Conrail's depreciable assets were expected to be worth considerably less than before the sale. As a result, Conrail was likely to suffer a loss in its tax deductions for depreciation.

The sales price was not to be allocated among Conrail's existing assets — its inventory and accounts receivable. Without this exemption, Conrail conceivably would have had to pay taxes on the difference between the existing value of its accounts receivable — the money owed to it for transportation services — and its reduced value after the sale.

• **Customs Fee.** Imposed a fee on the value of commercial merchandise imports of 0.22 percent, beginning Dec. 1, 1986. The fee was to go into a fund to pay for the costs of U.S. Customs Service commercial activities.

The fee was to decrease to 0.17 percent in fiscal 1988, and expire after fiscal 1989. The fee could be reduced below 0.17 percent if it would otherwise raise more than needed to pay for the commercial activities of the U.S. Customs Service.

Exempted from the fee were Schedule 8 imports (those not otherwise subject to duty) and products of least-developed countries, U.S. insular possessions, and countries included in the Caribbean Basin Initiative.

Fees could be lowered for small airports where existing

user fees already supported the entire cost of customs activities.

• Authorized fiscal 1987 appropriations for the U.S. Customs Service of $1.0 billion.

• **Tax Collections.** Increased the penalty for employers and other taxpayers who failed to make timely deposits of withheld Social Security, income or other taxes from the existing 5 percent of the amount of under-deposit to 10 percent. The provision applied to penalties assessed after the date of enactment.

• Increased the penalty for substantial understatement of income tax liability on tax returns from the existing 10 percent of the amount understated to 25 percent. The provision applied to penalties assessed after the date of enactment. (The 1986 tax overhaul bill had increased the penalty to 20 percent, but the need for revenue prompted Congress to increase it even further.)

• Increased the frequency with which state and local governments had to make deposits of Social Security tax contributions by putting them on the same footing as private businesses.

• Relieved state governments from responsibility for collecting Social Security contributions from local governments.

• Speeded up collection of excise taxes on beer, wine, distilled spirits and tobacco.

• **Foreign Tax Credits.** Denied tax credits usually given to companies for taxes paid to foreign governments if the other country was designated by the secretary of state as one that supported terrorism, or was one with which the United States did not have diplomatic relations. Such taxes could be counted as deductions, however.

• **Oil-Spill Liability.** Established procedures to collect funds for a new oil-spill liability trust fund, to pay for the costs of cleaning up offshore oil spills. The fund was to be financed by a tax of 1.3 cents per barrel on domestic crude oil and imported petroleum products. It was not to become effective, however, unless separate authorizing legislation was enacted by Sept. 1, 1987.

Both chambers passed enacting legislation (S 2799, HR 2005), the House as part of its "superfund" toxic-waste cleanup bill. But differences centering on whether federal law on oil-spill liability should pre-empt state laws could not be resolved before adjournment, and the provisions died. *(Oil-spill liability, p. 146)*

The fund provisionally established in the reconciliation bill was to have a limit of $300 million. No more than $500 million could be paid for any single incident; if more than $300 million had to be paid, the fund could borrow from the general Treasury.

• **Tax Bill Changes.** Provided a "transition rule" for a Des Moines, Iowa, trucking company permitting it to take a 10 percent investment tax credit on purchases of new equipment, even though the company did not meet the requirement of the new tax law (PL 99-514) of having had a binding contract to make such purchases as of Jan. 1, 1986. The provision was similar to those given to scores of other companies in the tax bill. *(Tax bill, p. 491)*

• Expanded, for rural low-income housing, protection from the full effects of the new tax law on real estate tax shelters for those who had multi-year commitments to invest in such shelters in rural areas.

Under the new tax law, investors were still permitted to take deductions for their paper losses in such shelters provided they had made the investment commitment before Aug. 16, 1986, the date of the conference agreement on the tax bill, and providing they still owed 50 percent or more of the total they had agreed to invest. Under the reconciliation bill provision, the 50 percent requirement was reduced to 35 percent for some rural housing funded in part by the Farmers Home Administration.

• Liberalized the rule in the new tax law under which investors in low-income housing projects could claim credit for investing in such projects even if they were using borrowed funds. Under the provision, if the loan was made by a disinterested third party, such as a bank, rather than by the developer of the housing project, it would qualify as money the investor had "at risk" and thus would become part of the basis for the credit.

Social Security

• **Cost-of-Living Increases.** Eliminated the 3 percent trigger for Social Security cost-of-living increases (COLAs). Previously, COLAs were not provided in years following one in which the Consumer Price Index (CPI) rose by less than 3 percent. Under the new law, COLAs would be provided in any year in which inflation was greater than zero.

Eliminating the trigger for Social Security COLAs also eliminated it for several programs tied by law to the Social Security increase, including insurance premiums under Part B of Medicare, railroad retirement, Supplemental Security Income, and veterans' pension benefits, and eligibility standards for Medicaid, food stamps, housing assistance and Aid to Families with Dependent Children.

Transportation

• **Conrail.** Required the transportation secretary, in consultation with the Treasury secretary and chairman of the board of Conrail, within 30 days after enactment, to retain the services of investment bankers to manage the sale to the public of the federal government's 85 percent share of the Conrail freight railroad.

• Directed the transportation secretary to choose four to six investment banking firms as "co-lead managers" of the public offering. One was to be designated to coordinate and administer the offering, but all had to be compensated equally. Selection criteria had to include a firm's financial strength, knowledge of the railroad industry and past contributions in promoting the long-term viability of Conrail. Firms not in existence before Sept. 1, 1986, were ineligible, and fees were to be paid from the proceeds of the stock sale.

• Required an opportunity for minority-owned or controlled firms to participate in the stock sale.

• Permitted the General Accounting Office to audit the accounts of Conrail and the co-lead managers.

• Required Conrail to make a $200 million cash payment to the federal government, within 30 days after enactment. An additional $100 million payment could be required by the transportation secretary, taking into account Conrail's long-term viability.

• Canceled, in consideration for the $200 million cash payment, Conrail's debts to the federal government.

• Directed Conrail to file with the Securities and Exchange Commission a registration statement with respect to the securities to be offered. The transportation secretary could require Conrail to declare a stock split before the filing.

• Directed the transportation secretary to schedule a public offering after the registration statement was declared effective. The transportation secretary, in consultation with the Treasury secretary, Conrail's chairman of the board, and the investment bankers, could decide to conduct the sale in stages.

- Required a finding by the transportation secretary, before proceeding with the sale, that the gross proceeds would be "an adequate amount." A $2 billion non-binding goal was set. The secretary's finding was not subject to judicial or administrative review.
- Required Conrail to make minimum capital expenditures of the greater of its financial depreciation or $500 million in each fiscal year over a five-year period following enactment. However, expenditures could be reduced to an average of $350 million per year by Conrail's board of directors.
- Barred dividend payments if Conrail was out of compliance with the capital expenditure requirement. After such payments Conrail also had to have on hand $400 million in cash. Subject to certain restrictions, Conrail could borrow to meet the minimum cash-balance requirement. Common stock dividends could not exceed 45 percent of cumulative net income less the cumulative amount of any preferred stock dividends.
- Required Conrail over the five-year period following enactment to continue its existing affirmative action and minority vendor programs; to continue to offer to sell lines that the Interstate Commerce Commission (ICC) had approved for abandonment for 75 percent of net liquidation value; not to permit deferral of normal and prudent maintenance on its properties; and not to permit a takeover of all or any substantial part of its assets.
- Required annual certification by Conrail of compliance with all five-year covenants, except for the dividend covenant, for which certification had to be provided to the transportation secretary after the declaration of any payments.
- Provided the transportation secretary with the authority to bring legal actions against Conrail or others to require compliance with the five-year covenants and ownership limitations.
- Prohibited ownership of more than 10 percent of Conrail's voting stock over a three-year period beginning on the sale date by anyone except for the employee stock ownership plan, the transportation secretary, a railroad, or certain others.
- Limited major railroads to ownership of 10 percent of voting stock for 1 year beginning on the sale date. No merger applications could be filed with the ICC during this period. Except if a merger application was approved, railroad stock had to be voted during the three years after a sale in the same proportion as all other common stock.
- Provided for the transition from Conrail's existing board of directors to a board elected by Conrail's public shareholders. After the initial sale date, one director was to be elected by shareholders for each 12.5 percent increment of the government's share of Conrail that had been sold. Interim arrangements were provided for in the event that less than 50 percent of the corporation had been sold by June 1, 1987.
- Required Conrail to assume financial liability for the existing supplemental unemployment benefits plan, which had been federally funded, until the sale date.
- Required Conrail to provide labor protection to its employees after the sale date, pursuant to a previous agreement with union representatives of the workers. The federal government would have no liability for benefits due workers.
- Directed Conrail to pay $200 million to present and former workers in compensation for deferred wages.
- Provided for the distribution of the 15 percent of Conrail stock vested in the employee stock ownership plan to participants and beneficiaries. Individual shares in the plan could not be sold for at least 180 days from the date on which 100 percent of the federal government's shares were sold.
- Abolished the United States Railway Association, effective April 1, 1987. Congress created the association, a government corporation, in 1973 to finance and monitor Conrail.
- Provided that the Regional Rail Reorganization Act of 1973 — the so-called 3R act — should not apply to Conrail after the sale date, with certain exceptions. For example, existing law was retained requiring Conrail to keep its headquarters in Philadelphia.
- Exempted Conrail's directors and others from lawsuits by stockholders, employees and others, with certain exceptions. For example, a director would not be exempted if he or she made a false statement on the registration form filed with the Securities and Exchange Commission.
- Protected the federal government from any and all liabilities resulting from the implementation of Conrail sale legislation, except for actions brought to require the transportation secretary to proceed with a public offering.
- **Rail Competition.** Required greater public disclosure of the terms of rail contracts between shippers of agricultural goods and rail carriers. The provision was intended to make it easier for small shippers to receive the same favorable contract terms as large shippers.
- Confirmed the legal authority of the ICC to issue a rule to require compensation by major railroads to small railroads for the use of the latter's boxcars.

Welfare

- **Eligibility.** Eliminated the requirement that states use income and eligibility verification systems to check the eligibility of all recipients of public assistance in an effort to make better use of limited resources and make the system more productive.
- **AFDC.** Restored, for fiscal 1987 only, the biennial calculation of the federal share of Aid to Families with Dependent Children benefits for the 13 states that lost funds as a result of a shift to an annual calculation mandated by fiscal 1986 reconciliation law (PL 99-272).
- **Child Support.** Required states that participated in the federal child support enforcement program to change their laws to bar retroactive changes in child support court orders and provide that child support payments be modified only from the date that notice was given by the parent desiring the change to the other parent.

Committee Markup

Most authorizing committees made their recommendations the week of July 21 to reconcile existing law with spending targets set by the budget resolution (S Con Res 120) adopted June 27.

As required by the 1974 Congressional Budget and Impoundment Control Act (PL 93-344), the House and Senate Budget committees made no changes in the recommendations, but simply rolled them together into omnibus bills (HR 5300; S 2706) and sent them on to the floor July 31. *(Budget act, 1974 Almanac p. 145)*

Reconciliation by Senate Committees

The conference agreement on the fiscal 1987 budget resolution (S Con Res 120 — H Rept 99-664) directed nine Senate committees to draft legislation altering programs or raising revenues to achieve the reductions in budget authority (BA) and outlays (O) listed below.

The committees were to report their "reconciliation" recommendations to the Budget Committee for inclusion in the fiscal 1987 deficit-reduction bill (S 2706) that was sent to the floor July 31. The budget made assumptions about how savings were to be achieved, but committees were not bound to follow them to reach the targets. *(Figures in millions of dollars):*

Senate Committees	FY 1987		FY 1988		FY 1989		Three-Year	
	BA	O	BA	O	BA	O	BA	O
Agriculture, Nutrition and Forestry								
Rural Development Insurance Fund								
Loan Asset Sales	$ −55	$ −55	$ −49	$ −49	$ −43	$ −43	$ −147	$ −147
Loan Asset Sales	0	−500	0	−500	0	−500	0	−1,500
Total Agriculture	−55	−555	−49	−549	−43	−543	−147	−1,647
Banking, Housing and Urban Affairs								
Rural Housing Loans	642	−1158	0	−23	164	−46	806	−1,227
Loan Asset Sales	0	−500	0	−500	0	−500	0	−1,500
Total Banking	642	−1,658	0	−523	164	−546	806	−2,727
Commerce, Science and Transportation								
Coast Guard User Fees	−50	−50	−50	−50	−50	−50	−150	−150
Total Commerce	−50	−50	−50	−50	−50	−50	−150	−150
Energy & Natural Resources								
FERC User Fees	−31	−31	−56	−56	−56	−56	−143	−143
Oil Overcharge Funds	−994	−1,186	−344	−365	−344	−356	−1,682	−1,907
Total Energy	−1,024	−1,217	−400	−421	−400	−412	−1,825	−2,050
Environment & Public Works								
User Fees	−100	−100	−100	−100	−100	−100	−300	−300
Highways	−1,783	−191	−2,243	−1,023	−2,723	−1,574	−6,749	−2,788
Total Environment	−1,883	−291	−2,343	−1,123	−2,823	−1,674	−7,049	−3,088
Finance								
Medicare Provider Payment Reforms		−550		−1,200		−1,500		−3,250
Customs User Fees		−300		−295		−290		−885
Total Finance (Spending)		−850		−1,495		−1,790		−4,135
Revenues		3,500		2,600		2,400		8,500
Governmental Affairs								
Unspecified	−100	−100	−100	−100	−100	−100	−300	−300
Total Governmental	−100	−100	−100	−100	−100	−100	−300	−300
Labor & Human Resources								
Guaranteed Student Loans	−25	−25	−150	−135	−250	−235	−425	−395
Education Loan Asset Sales	0	−579	0	−314	0	94	0	−799
Total Labor & Human Resources	−25	−604	−150	−449	−250	−141	−425	−1,194
Small Business								
SBA Disaster Loan Asset Sales	−438	−343	−399	−55	−223	−14	−1,060	−412
Total Small Business	−438	−343	−399	−55	−223	−14	−1,060	−412
Total, Spending	−$2,934	−$5,668	−$3,491	−$4,765	−$3,725	−$5,270	−$10,150	−$15,703
Total, Revenues		$3,500		$2,600		$2,400		$8,500
Total, Deficit Reduction		−$9,168		−$7,365		−$7,670		−$24,203

SOURCE: S Con Res 120 — H Rept 99-664

Reconciliation by House Committees

The conference agreement on the fiscal 1987 budget resolution (S Con Res 120 — H Rept 99-664) directed 10 House committees to draft legislation altering programs or raising revenues to achieve the reductions in budget authority (BA) and outlays (O) listed below.

The committees were to report their "reconciliation" recommendations to the Budget Committee for inclusion in the fiscal 1987 deficit-reduction bill (HR 5300) that was sent to the floor July 31. The budget made assumptions about how savings were to be achieved, but committees were not bound to follow them to reach the targets. *(Figures in millions of dollars):*

House Committees	FY 1987		FY 1988		FY 1989		Three-Year	
	BA	O	BA	O	BA	O	BA	O
Agriculture								
Rural Development Insurance Fund								
Loan Asset Sales	$ −55	$ −55	$ −49	$ −49	$ −43	$ −43	$ −147	$ −147
Loan Asset Sales	0	−500	0	−500	0	−500	0	−1,500
Total Agriculture	−55	−555	−49	−549	−43	−543	−147	−1,647
Banking, Finance and Urban Affairs								
Rural Housing Loans	642	−1158	0	−23	164	−46	806	−1,227
Loan Asset Sales	0	−500	0	−500	0	−500	0	−1,500
Total Banking	642	−1,658	0	−523	164	−546	806	−2,727
Education and Labor								
Guaranteed Student Loans	−25	−25	−150	−135	−250	−235	−425	−395
Education Loan Asset Sales	0	−579	0	−314	0	94	0	−799
Total Education and Labor	−25	−604	−150	−449	−250	−141	−425	−1,194
Energy and Commerce								
User Fees	−100	−100	−100	−100	−100	−100	−300	−300
FERC User Fees	−31	−31	−56	−56	−56	−56	−143	−143
Medicare Provider Payment Reforms	0	−550	0	−1,200	0	−1,500	0	−3,250
Oil Overcharge Funds	−994	−1,186	−344	−365	−344	−356	−1,682	−1,907
Total Energy and Commerce	−1,125	−1,867	−500	−1,721	−500	−2,012	−2,125	−5,600
Interior and Insular Affairs								
User Fees	−100	−100	−100	−100	−100	−100	−300	−300
Total Interior	−100	−100	−100	−100	−100	−100	−300	−300
Merchant Marine and Fisheries								
Coast Guard User Fees	−50	−50	−50	−50	−50	−50	−150	−150
Total Merchant Marine	−50	−50	−50	−50	−50	−50	−150	−150
Post Office and Civil Service								
Unspecified	−100	−100	−100	−100	−100	−100	−300	−300
Total Post Office	−100	−100	−100	−100	−100	−100	−300	−300
Public Works and Transportation								
Highways	−1,783	−191	−2,243	−1,023	−2,723	−1,574	−6,749	−2,788
Total Public Works	−1,783	−191	−2,243	−1,023	−2,723	−1,574	−6,749	−2,788
Small Business								
SBA Disaster Loan Asset Sales	−438	−343	−399	−55	−223	−14	−1,060	−412
Total Small Business	−438	−343	−399	−55	−223	−14	−1,060	−412
Ways and Means								
Total Ways and Means Deficit Reduction		−4,350		−4,095		−4,190		−12,635
TOTAL, Deficit Reduction *	−$2,934	−$9,168	−$3,491	−$7,365	−$3,725	−$7,670	−$10,150	−$24,203

** Totals do not add because in two instances, where two committees shared jurisdiction over a program, the full amount to be reconciled was listed for each committee.*

SOURCE: S Con Res 120 — H Rept 99-664

But, while the bills were less broad than the fiscal 1986 reconciliation bill, which was tied up for months over controversial provisions and only cleared in April 1986, there were again proposals expected to cause trouble either on the floor, in conference or with the administration. Possible difficulties included:

- A proposal by the House Public Works and Transportation Committee to take four transportation trust funds off the budget to protect them from deficit-reduction cuts.
- A proposal by the Senate Finance Committee to raise the tax on cigarettes from 16 cents to 24 cents per pack.
- A House Ways and Means Committee recommendation to require states to allow two-parent households to qualify for Aid to Families with Dependent Children (AFDC), the chief federal welfare program.
- Changes in the Medicare and Medicaid health programs for the elderly and poor made by committees in both chambers.

Some of the proposals, such as those on AFDC and the trust funds, revisited controversies that were dropped from the fiscal 1986 bill.

And some major assumptions of the budget resolution, such as sale of $412 million in Small Business Administration loans and receipts of $2.5 billion over three years from settling oil overcharge lawsuits, were ignored by authorizing committees.

Within each chamber, committees sometimes conflicted on the same subject. House Ways and Means had health proposals that clashed with those of Energy and Commerce, for instance.

And, although the budget resolution gave each committee a target to meet, the panels had discretion over how to do so. Committees were allowed to expand programs in some areas as long as they made cuts in other areas to offset the costs.

Missing the Targets

As reported July 31, however, both S 2706 and HR 5300 fell short of their savings targets, by sizable amounts, and changing economic conditions already made it appear that the required savings of $9.2 billion would leave Congress as much as $10 billion shy of the Gramm-Rudman deficit target, with signs that the situation would only get worse as the year progressed.

By early analysis, the Senate bill was expected to reduce the deficit by $8.1 billion; the House measure claimed savings of $7.6 billion.

Both bills used a combination of revenue increases and spending cuts in an effort to reach their targets, and both depended heavily on asset sales to reach their goals. More than $3 billion of the assumed fiscal 1987 savings in the House measure and $2.8 billion in the Senate bill would have been raised by the sale of government-sponsored loans.

Both measures came closer to meeting the three-year goal of $24.2 billion. The House bill would have saved $463 million more than required, while the Senate bill fell short by $2.4 billion.

The chairmen of the Budget committees — Sen. Pete V. Domenici, R-N.M., and Rep. William H. Gray III, D-Pa. — said they hoped to boost the first-year savings when they got to the floor.

But heavy opposition to some existing provisions was expected from the White House, which also rejected the two committees' deficit-reduction claims. A July 30 letter from Office of Management and Budget Director James C. Miller III said an initial look at the Senate package showed it would reduce the deficit by a maximum of $2.4 billion. Most of that reduction would come from the cigarette tax increase, which the administration opposed.

Some of the asset sales included in the bill also could have been made without action by Congress, Miller said, making passage of the bill less compelling. And the letter complained that Senate Finance Committee provisions would increase Medicare and Medicaid spending by $1.7 billion in 1987.

House Committee Action

The House bill, approved by voice vote, missed its deficit-reduction target chiefly because the proposals from the Ways and Means Committee, while meeting three-year goals, fell $1.9 billion short in the first year.

Gray said that Ways and Means Chairman Dan Rostenkowski, D-Ill., had promised him that he would meet the target with subsequent action.

Ed Jenkins, D-Ga., who served on both panels, said that if members "engaged in harassment that we didn't meet our targets," Rostenkowski would offer a floor amendment to raise cigarette taxes and perhaps wine taxes as well. Rostenkowski's committee July 23 rejected a cigarette tax increase 4-28, however, with the chairman opposed.

Republicans were skeptical even of the advertised savings in the House package. They said CBO would not count some of the loan asset sales as savings because, under the terms set by the committees, the government would have still been responsible for the loans. CBO also would not give the bill credit for receipts from oil-company payments for overcharges during the 1970s, they said, because the funds were still tied up in court.

Senate Committee Action

The Senate package was approved 18-1, with Ernest F. Hollings, D-S.C., voting against it, and the bill had problems similar to the House bill. It missed the savings target because the Energy Committee did not get $1 billion in credit for the disputed oil overcharge funds and because the Small Business Committee's $343 million in loan sales were not really savings, since the government would retain responsibility for defaults.

Budget Committee members said because they could only roll together the proposals of the authorizing committees without change, they expected moves on the floor to boost savings, as well as to replace the cigarette tax.

And Domenici noted that there was "a noticeable absence of extraneous amendments" in the recommendations. A Senate rule adopted as part of the 1986 reconciliation bill was designed to keep extraneous amendments off reconciliation bills in that chamber, and it was expected to hold down the number of floor amendments.

A similar prohibition also applied to conference reports, which was expected to give senators some leverage with House members in fighting attempts to make policy changes that did not save money.

Politicking Over Tobacco

The Senate Finance Committee's 11-8 vote to raise the cigarette tax from 16 cents a pack to 24 cents caused a brief political firestorm the week of July 28, involving the North Carolina Senate race, the White House and an aborted attempt to get the Finance panel to rescind its recommendation.

Sen. James T. Broyhill, R-N.C., lost little time in visiting the White House and calling a press conference to announce that he had persuaded Reagan to fight the tax hike — even though the administration had previously announced its opposition.

But Broyhill's opponent in the tight Senate race, former Gov. Terry Sanford, got in the act, claiming that he had won the battle for North Carolina tobacco farmers by persuading David L. Boren, D-Okla., to change his vote.

Majority Leader Robert Dole, R-Kan., had already begun a campaign to reverse the committee action, and Boren's switch made the vote 11-9 against the tax.

But the action fizzled when tax opponent Russell B. Long, D-La., refused to sign a letter from the new majority officially reversing the committee's action. "I just didn't like the procedure," Long said.

That did not end the war, however, only the momentary battle.

Floor Action

The failure of both panels to successfully engineer deficit reductions in compliance with budget resolution requirements was bad enough. But anticipated deficit calculations due the middle of August were expected to make congressional efforts to avoid votes on automatic Gramm-Rudman cuts even more difficult.

(Gramm-Rudman had included a procedure of making automatic, across-the-board cuts if Congress failed to meet its deficit targets. That procedure was struck down by the Supreme Court in July as unconstitutional, leaving intact a requirement that Congress vote on such cuts if triggered by a failure to meet the targets.)

The Senate, meanwhile, was tied up with fights over economic sanctions on South Africa and aid to the contra rebels fighting the leftist Nicaraguan government, so the reconciliation bills were laid off to the side for about six weeks. *(South Africa sanctions, p. 359; contra aid, p. 394)*

Budget leaders, however, continued discussions of how to enact greater savings than those assumed in the two bills. Congress departed Aug. 16 for a three-week, Labor Day recess.

On Aug. 20, CBO and OMB released their joint estimate that the fiscal 1987 deficit — as calculated for Gramm-Rudman purposes — would be $163.4 billion without further action by Congress. That estimate was $19.4 billion above the Gramm-Rudman target of $144 billion, but a $10 billion margin of error allowed by the anti-deficit law theoretically meant deficit-reducing actions totaling about $9.4 billion would stave off the need to vote on across-the-board cuts.

Staving Off Uniform Cuts

Upon returning from vacation, budget leaders went back to work, as mild pressure continued that there might be votes on uniform cuts as required by Gramm-Rudman.

House Speaker Thomas P. O'Neill Jr., D-Mass., ordered renewed efforts to find savings, as congressional and administration experts announced that the existing reconciliation bills saved even less than previously assumed.

CBO said that under Gramm-Rudman rules, the House bill would have saved only $900 million and the Senate bill $3.7 billion. OMB put the numbers even lower: $300 million for the House bill and $3.2 billion for the Senate version.

The shortfall came from several sources. Both bills lost more than $4 billion in estimated savings because the administration had imposed new Medicare regulations in August that pre-empted legislative moves to achieve similar cuts. And a provision in the House bill to allow cost-of-living allowances for Social Security recipients despite low inflation was expected to cost $800 million.

A special joint House-Senate committee, as required by Gramm-Rudman, agreed by voice vote Sept. 11 to report resolutions (H J Res 723, S J Res 412) affirming the Aug. 20 CBO-OMB report, which said domestic spending would have to be cut by 7.6 percent and defense by 5.6 percent to meet the deficit target.

The pressure was on because, under Gramm-Rudman, any member could have forced a vote on the cuts as early as Sept. 19.

And Domenici told the special joint panel, "I believe we ought to vote it out and send it to the president, and let it get signed." Enacting the resolution would on Oct. 1 have temporarily put the cuts in effect, pending a revised Oct. 6 report, perhaps forcing action to make more selective cuts in spending. If Congress acted before the revised report to meet the $154 billion target (allowing for the margin of error), the uniform cuts would have been canceled.

Finding Common Ground

The pressure worked. In a rare show of cooperation, negotiators from the House, Senate and administration agreed the week of Sept. 15 on a package of cuts to meet the deficit target. In slightly different House and Senate versions, the package would have pared $13 billion to $15 billion from the fiscal 1987 deficit. But the way the proposal achieved its savings found few friends.

"It isn't even close to a good solution," said Domenici. Dole called the package "a very sensible approach." And Lawton Chiles of Florida, ranking Democrat on the Senate Budget Committee, said, "It's midway between the best we could do and the worst that could happen."

The Senate and House packages, which were to be floor amendments to the original bills, had some differences, but members said they were confident they could be settled quickly in a way that would ensure the president's signature. Fear of the political ramifications of votes to impose Gramm-Rudman cuts had impelled leaders of both parties and both chambers to try to bypass usual controversies. And they met several times in the Capitol with administration budget director Miller to iron out differences with the administration.

Neither package contained any significant increases in taxes or cuts in federal spending, although the House plan included a $1 billion across-the-board cut. The administration opposed such a move because it would have reduced defense spending, and members of the Appropriations committees were expected to fight it as well.

Attempts to raise revenues through higher excise taxes or to cut spending through large across-the-board cuts fizzled during the week, largely because of opposition from the administration.

The package would have increased revenues by selling assets such as loan portfolios and Conrail, the government-owned freight railroad, and by trying to increase compliance with existing tax laws.

Some members scoffed at the new package, saying it contained almost no real savings or revenues. "We're about to pull the ultimate scam," said a winking Rep. Marvin Leath, D-Texas, as he emerged from a House Budget Committee meeting. "Everybody's in on it — CBO, OMB, the media."

One-Shot Savings

Criticisms centered on the fact that the savings in the new plan failed to address the long-term deficit problem either by permanently reducing expenditures or increasing revenues.

The package, for instance, promised to increase tax revenues by $4.1 billion by taking steps to make sure more Americans paid income taxes they already owed, and by speeding up some excise and payroll tax collections.

More than $7 billion was to come from sales of government assets, which would not recur and could even lose revenue in future years since the government would not be receiving payments on loans it no longer owned.

The package also would have pared $680 million from the fiscal 1987 deficit by speeding up revenue-sharing payments to state and local governments — shifting the amount into the fiscal 1986 deficit.

William L. Armstrong, R-Colo., a member of the Senate Budget Committee, called it "a travesty of responsible budgeting. It is a package of golden gimmicks. It is a package of smoke and mirrors."

But, Armstrong said, he would vote for it because it would sell Conrail.

And, while the final touches were being applied to the House package, Rep. George Miller, D-Calif., said derisively, "We're fine-tuning the smoke and mirror proportions — too much of one blinds you, too much of the other burns you."

House Majority Leader Jim Wright, D-Texas — a member of the Budget Committee — was irritated by the failure to deal with long-term revenue and spending problems, and by the sale of government assets.

"Selling off your assets is what bankrupt companies do," Wright said. Assets such as Conrail and loan portfolios would be bought for less than full value by speculators, he said, and the government would lose revenues from the assets in future years.

"I'm not enthusiastic about any additional tax, but I am less enthusiastic about piling up more debt for the next generation," Wright said.

Gas Tax Fizzles

The package came together after an initial flurry of activity to raise excise taxes subsided.

O'Neill first said Sept. 12 that the House would support increases in taxes on cigarettes and wine. Then, when it became apparent that only about $2 billion could be raised this way, the Ways and Means Committee turned to an increase in the federal tax on gasoline.

But when Ways and Means met to consider raising gasoline taxes by as much as 13 cents per gallon, its members rebelled.

"Why are we doing this six weeks before the election?" one committee member asked.

The administration reiterated its opposition to tax hikes, and the next day, Sept. 17, O'Neill declared flatly, "I am opposed to a gas tax." Talk of new taxes faded quickly after that.

The Senate had flirted with its own tax controversy when Finance voted to raise the cigarette tax as part of its original reconciliation recommendations.

Not unexpectedly, the revised Senate package dropped the cigarette tax.

Senate Floor Action

The Senate took up its version of the proposal Sept. 19, and promptly adopted the amendment by voice vote. Then, after staving off most amendments, the Senate in the early morning of Sept. 20 passed S 2706 by a vote of 88-7. Revised estimates put its savings at $12.6 billion. *(Vote 277, p. 47-S)*

Budget leaders successfully used new procedural prohibitions against unrelated material against an amendment by Dan Quayle, R-Ind., and J. James Exon, D-Neb., to give the president a modified form of line-item veto by allowing him to rescind individual appropriations unless Congress specifically reapproved the spending.

The proposal was rejected when the Senate voted 34-62 not to waive a prohibition against non-germane amendments. *(Vote 270, p. 46-S)*

The Senate also struck from the bill a section of the bill that would have earmarked for state energy conservation programs $256 million from fines paid by oil companies for overcharges during the 1970s. By a 32-61 vote, the Senate failed to waive the germaneness requirement. *(Vote 276, p. 47-S)*

The Senate accepted, by voice vote, an amendment by Charles E. Grassley, R-Iowa, to deny foreign tax credits to companies operating in countries that the United States did not recognize or that supported terrorist activities.

Amendments rejected by the Senate would have:

- Struck a provision raising from 10 percent to 25 percent the penalty for avoidance of income taxes.
- Leased Washington-Dulles International Airport and National Airport to a regional authority.
- Preserved the seniority rights of employees of TWA and Ozark airlines, which had recently merged.

House Floor Action

The House, with surprisingly little dissension in comparison with previous reconciliation bills, passed HR 5300 Sept. 24, with an estimated $15.2 billion in savings, by a vote of 309-106. The compromise package to increase the bill's savings was added to the bill as part of the rule governing debate, which was adopted 255-177. *(Votes 374, 375, p. 106-H)*

Two amendments were expected, but neither was offered. One would have removed a provision allowing the government to repossess vessels when shipowners defaulted on government-backed bonds. The other would have removed provisions incorporated from an omnibus housing bill (HR 1) from the package. The housing provisions had been added to HR 5300 in its original incarnation, after it appeared the Senate would not take action on HR 1. That bill had passed the House June 12. *(Housing bill, p. 585)*

An expected fight involving the sale of Conrail failed to materialize. Energy and Commerce Committee Chairman John D. Dingell, D-Mich., had been expected to press for stronger provisions to protect shippers who had no alternative to using railroads, but he spoke in support of the bill. Dingell's attempt to add such provisions had been narrowly defeated in his committee Sept. 17.

Some elements in the bipartisan package announced Sept. 19 had disappeared by the time the package got to the House floor. The House Banking, Finance and Urban Affairs Committee, for instance, refused to raise $310 million by charging fees for insurance coverage by the Federal Deposit Insurance Corporation (FDIC) on deposits by U.S. banks held overseas.

The most important changes to the package were

made by the Ways and Means Committee. At a markup Sept. 22, the panel failed to go along with some elements of the bipartisan agreement, including raising $789 million by extending Medicare coverage and taxes to all state and local government workers and $150 million by speeding up collection of taxes on distilled spirits as well as beer, wine and tobacco.

Instead, the committee recommended raising $1.8 billion through the customs fee on commercial merchandise imports, which would have started at 0.5 percent for fiscal 1987 and fallen to 0.2 percent thereafter.

The administration objected to the proposal, saying it would violate the General Agreement on Tariffs and Trade and would inspire retaliation by other countries. Opponents such as Bill Frenzel, R-Minn., objected to calling the customs charge a "user fee," since it would have raised twice the amount expended by the Customs Service.

But Ways and Means Chairman Rostenkowski said that other countries such as France, Spain and Sweden imposed similar fees.

A provision in the original version of HR 5300 that would have allowed the Agriculture Department to reduce the frequency of federal meat inspections in processing plants was deleted.

Also taken out by the Rules Committee before forwarding the bill to the floor was a provision to remove transportation trust funds from the overall federal budget.

Stay of Execution

Passage of the reconciliation bills granted members a stay of political execution, as the need for across-the-board Gramm-Rudman spending cuts was at least temporarily avoided.

Immediately after passing its reconciliation bill, the Senate defeated, 15-80, S J Res 412, which would have mandated $19.4 billion in uniform reductions to meet the deficit target. To preserve the threat of the cuts in case the reconciliation bill stalled, however, Dole left pending a motion to reconsider that vote. *(Vote 278, p. 47-S)*

The House avoided a vote on its identical resolution (H J Res 723) under a Sept. 19 agreement among leaders of both parties.

Conference Action

Budget leaders hoped to resolve their differences in conference before the Gramm-Rudman re-estimate that was due Oct. 6. But sharper than expected disagreements and the complexities of coordinating more than 200 conferees in 25 subconferences on the multiple sections of the bill proved formidable.

While the bills were similar in most areas, they had divisive differences, principally the customs fee and across-the-board reduction in most appropriations accounts, both in the House bill, but also provisions involving the sale of Conrail and health care, and the Senate's insistence on extending Medicare coverage to all state and local government employees.

One controversy that did not develop involved the housing bill, which conferees agreed to drop in the face of Senate and administration opposition.

OMB Director Miller said the administration objected to the appropriations cut, the customs fee, labor protection provisions of the Conrail sale, a delay in new Medicare regulations, limits on reimbursement to hospitals for capital costs, and a provision to raise the minimum rate at which oil was put into the Strategic Petroleum Reserve. All were in the House bill, but not the Senate's.

A principal objection, which had tied the fiscal 1986 reconciliation bill in knots, was a House provision requiring states to allow two-parent households to get AFDC benefits when one parent was unemployed.

"We'll veto a reconciliation bill if it's larded up," Miller said. "I'm not out to pick a fight; I'm just saying what the situation is."

Another Missed Deadline

The Oct. 6 Gramm-Rudman deficit re-estimate came without further resolution in the reconciliation conference. And because nothing more had happened in Congress to reduce the anticipated deficit, the report was identical to that issued in August.

But the report did not set in motion the law's uniform cuts, because congressional leaders were confident of eventually meeting the deficit target.

Not only was the reconciliation bill expected to yield sizable savings, but the tax bill, which cleared Sept. 27, was calculated to produce an $11 billion revenue increase in fiscal 1987 (and shortfalls in future years). And an omnibus appropriations bill (H J Res 738), was expected to provide further savings. *(Continuing appropriations, p. 219)*

"It's not terribly harmful that we missed the deadline," said Domenici. "Nobody can say we failed, or that somebody's cheating." And even Sen. Phil Gramm, R-Texas, a principal author of the law, agreed that it did not matter much when Congress hit the deficit target, so long as it did so.

Negotiations continued, as House conferees offered to phase in Medicare coverage for all state and local workers over four years in return for other concessions, and senators said they were willing to accept some form of import fee to pay for customs services. But neither was resolved right away.

Some issues were tentatively settled by conferees, including a limit on sales of loans by the Export-Import Bank to $1.5 billion, and sale of $1.7 billion in rural housing loans.

But other agreements fell apart when the administration objected. Miller complained in an Oct. 1 letter that some subconferences were settling issues in a way "most disturbing" to the administration, and again said the bill could be vetoed.

A Welfare Snag

As more issues settled out, confrontation escalated over extending welfare benefits to two-parent families. The administration had threatened to veto the bill if the AFDC provision was retained. Reagan Oct. 9 sent a telegram reiterating the veto threat to Dole from Iceland, where the president was to meet with Soviet leader Mikhail S. Gorbachev.

The AFDC controversy was longstanding. Under existing law, it was optional for states to allow AFDC benefits for two-parent families in which the principal wage-earner was unemployed. The House provision would have made the program mandatory as of Jan. 1, 1988. Although it would have had no impact on the fiscal 1987 budget, it would have cost the federal government an estimated $370 million over the following two years, and cost states up to $250 million over two years.

Wright said the House dropped the provision from the 1986 bill in return for a promise from Dole and Senate

Finance Committee Chairman Bob Packwood, R-Ore., that they would support the change in the 1987 bill.

But Dole and Packwood said they did not remember such an agreement. They allowed Long, a Democratic opponent of the provision, to fight it in conference. Long said the requirement would cost his home state of Louisiana $12 million to $15 million a year, and would not succeed in keeping families intact.

Gray said the existing system "encourages the father to leave the family, just so the mother can get full benefits. [But] all the statistics show that when both parents are together, the chances are much greater for the family to get out of poverty."

Most of the 24 states that did not allow such eligibility were in the South and West.

If the program were not made mandatory, "some of the Southern states will never adopt it," said Rep. Harold E. Ford, D-Tenn., chairman of the Ways and Means Subcommittee on Public Assistance and Unemployment Compensation.

Other Agreements

Among the issues that began to be resolved was Medicare coverage of state and local workers; House conferees offered to phase it in over five years.

Another major controversy had involved a House proposal to raise $1.8 billion from a new fee on commercial imports. The administration opposed the fee, saying it would violate international trade agreements because it would raise more than twice the cost of U.S. Customs Service activities. Conferees agreed on a reduced fee to raise about $790 million for fiscal 1987.

Other conference agreements:

- Dropped a House provision calling for an across-the-board cut to save $1 billion in fiscal 1987 outlays.
- Dropped labor-protection provisions from the Conrail sale.
- Imposed a tax of 1.3 cents per barrel on domestic crude oil and imported petroleum products to pay for cleaning up oil spills from tankers or offshore oil facilities.
- Dropped the sale of Small Business Administration loans.
- Dropped new fees to support the Nuclear Regulatory Commission and the Environmental Protection Agency.

And the House and Senate versions agreed on allowing automatic cost-of-living adjustments for Social Security recipients even if the inflation rate were below 3 percent, the existing trigger level. And negotiators agreed to cap the Medicare deductible at $520. The deductible, which beneficiaries paid for a hospital stay, was $492 and scheduled to rise to $572.

A Final Compromise

Congress was finally able to declare victory in its year-long struggle to reduce the deficit when negotiators agreed Oct. 17 on a final package of reconciliation provisions, with savings worth about $11.7 billion, pared down from as much as $15 billion in the House-passed version.

The way was cleared when House negotiators agreed to drop the AFDC provision. In return, the Senate backed off from requiring Medicare coverage for all state and local government employees, and agreed to reduce the future tax basis for Conrail, the government-owned railroad, once it was sold. The Conrail provision was expected to increase the taxes owed by the railroad after it was sold, which had led to fears that the sales price would be reduced.

The actions of the administration and Long in opposing the AFDC provision angered some House members. "We're very upset about it," said Rep. Mickey Leland, D-Texas, chairman of the Congressional Black Caucus. "It's obscene what Sen. Long did." In return for the House dropping the provision, Dole and other Senate leaders signed a letter promising to reconsider the issue in 1987.

Other items dropped from the reconciliation bill would have:

- Increased coverage and fees for the Federal Deposit Insurance Corporation.
- Required that equipment used for oil drilling in coastal waters be at least half American-made.
- Created a new offshore pollution compensation program, and changed criteria for ocean-dumping permits.
- Established a new system of voluntary fees for Coast Guard services to boaters.
- Changed the date on which the president was to submit his budget from the first Monday after Jan. 3 to the first Tuesday in February.
- Extended the 3 percent federal telephone excise tax, due to expire at the end of 1987, through 1989.
- Extended the 0.8 percent tax on wages to pay for extended unemployment compensation benefits; it was scheduled to decline to 0.6 percent at the end of 1987.
- Provided incentives and penalties to encourage establishment of risk pools to make health insurance available to people who were otherwise unable to obtain it. ∎

President's Deferral Authority

A dispute between the Reagan administration and Capitol Hill over a White House decision to defer the spending of some $5 billion in appropriated fiscal 1986 funds was only partially resolved at year's end.

The disputed funds had been released, and the U.S. Court of Appeals of the District of Columbia ruled Jan. 20, 1987, to uphold a lower court ruling that the administration could not resort to such deferrals to implement its policies. It was not clear if the administration would pursue the case further. At the same time, new administration deferrals in early 1987 continued to be challenged in court.

The deferrals, or spending delays, became controversial because they imposed funding freezes or cuts that President Reagan had proposed a year earlier and that Congress had rejected.

Reagan included in his Feb. 5, 1986, budget request about $23 billion in deferrals, affecting several dozen programs. But the controversy centered principally on cuts in a handful of housing and community development programs and the strategic petroleum reserve (SPR), a crude oil stockpile meant to cushion the nation against disruptions in energy supplies.

Most of the remaining delays were uncontested because they postponed spending for such management reasons as construction holdups.

On May 16, a federal district court in Washington, D.C. overturned $5.1 billion of the deferrals affecting housing and related programs for the poor, elderly and handicapped. The court stayed release of the money pending appeal, but Congress in June disapproved the deferrals — forcing the administration to spend the money — with passage of the fiscal 1986 supplemental appropriations bill (PL 99-349).

A unanimous, three-judge panel of the appeals court upheld the district court in early 1987, ruling that the president could not halt spending of appropriated funds for policy reasons, although he could still delay such spending for routine management reasons, such as unanticipated delays in federal construction projects.

The suit challenging the administration's proposals was brought by the National League of Cities, a number of individual cities and four members of the House: Bruce A. Morrison, D-Conn.; Mike Lowry, D-Wash.; Charles E. Schumer, D-N.Y.; and Barbara Boxer, D-Calif.

They argued that Reagan had illegally used deferral authority to try to kill or shrink programs Congress wanted maintained.

Court Rulings

Like the district court, the appeals court stated emphatically, and repeatedly, that the president had no legal authority to make policy deferrals. On every point raised by Justice Department attorneys in defense of the deferrals, both courts disagreed.

In the new ruling, written by Judge Harry T. Edwards, the appeals court found that Congress would not have granted deferral authority in 1974 without giving itself the check contained in the now-defunct legislative veto. The two were inseparable, Edwards wrote, concluding that the 1974 policy deferral authority was thus also invalid.

Joining Edwards in the ruling were Judges Robert H. Bork and Luther M. Swygert. Bork's position was of interest because, as a Justice Department official in the Nixon administration, he had argued the opposite view, that a president could unilaterally withhold appropriated funds.

But courts, for the most part, disagreed with that argument in a lengthy series of impoundment cases in the early 1970s, after which Congress passed the 1974 act.

The latest opinion had important implications not only for budget policy but also for a wide range of other federal statutes that included so-called "legislative vetoes." In a landmark 1983 decision, the Supreme Court invalidated such vetoes of executive branch actions but left open the fate of specific laws that included legislative vetoes. *(1983 Almanac p. 565)*

The heart of the ruling was that Congress, in enacting the 1974 Congressional Budget and Impoundment Control Act (PL 93-344), viewed the legislative veto as an inseparable part of a provision defining the president's authority to defer spending. Under the law, either house acting alone could overturn — or "veto" — a proposed deferral. *(1974 Almanac p. 145)*

Absent the now-defunct veto, the court found, the administration had no authority to defer for policy reasons the spending of appropriated money.

The deferral case was thus an important test of whether authority granted the executive branch by Congress could stand apart — be "severable" — from the legislative veto with which it had been coupled.

The Supreme Court heard arguments Dec. 1 in an unrelated case that sought to clarify when provisions in various laws should remain in effect and when they should be invalidated because they were inextricably tied to the legislative veto. A decision was expected in 1987. *(Story, p. 49)*

The appeals court also turned down an administration argument that might have reopened the policy deferral fight on a different front.

The 1950 Anti-Deficiency Act provided general deferral authority, empowering a president to withhold appropriated funds because of changing requirements, improved efficiency or for "other developments." Nixon had used the last phrase to justify his disputed impoundments.

In the 1974 act, Congress struck the words "other developments." Justice Department attorneys asked, in effect, that the language be restored, but Edwards wrote that there was no reason to take this step. The 1974 act's elimination of the phrase "is fully consistent with the expressed intent of Congress to control presidential impoundments."

The opinions of both courts echoed the vehement complaints of Reagan's congressional critics, including Sen. Mark O. Hatfield, R-Ore., chairman of the Senate Appropriations Committee. Hatfield contended the disputed deferrals were, in effect, potent, selective line-item vetoes, and that neither the Constitution nor Congress gave a president such finely tuned power to change congressional spending decisions.

Challenged Delays

Among the challenged spending delays was a $500 million deferral of community development block grant (CDBG) funds. Reagan's budget proposed to reduce and narrowly target CDBG spending, used for housing rehabilitation, community development, public works and a variety of other purposes.

Reagan also proposed a $251 million deferral of funds for Urban Development Action Grants (UDAGs), which the administration proposed to end in 1985 and 1986. The grants were intended to stimulate new investment and promote economic development in depressed areas.

Sen. James A. McClure, R-Idaho, said a new $187.9 million SPR deferral, which assumed a moratorium on program spending, struck "many of us as more of a stalling action than a good-faith effort to come to terms with Congress."

McClure said he and his colleagues thought they had reached agreement with the administration on a slower rate of SPR spending in 1985, a decision ratified in a 1985 supplemental appropriations bill that disapproved a deferral proposed by Reagan that year (PL 99-88).

The General Accounting Office (GAO), in a Feb. 25 letter, informed the Senate and the House that the bulk of the SPR deferral was "not in accordance with existing statutory authority."

Under the 1974 act, the GAO's finding reclassified the SPR deferral as a rescission, or cancellation of enacted spending, which had to be approved by Congress within 45 days in order to go into effect. The administration subsequently released a portion of the money and Congress, in the fiscal 1986 supplemental appropriations bill, insisted that the remainder also be made available.

Congressional Action

While the fiscal 1986 supplemental appropriations bill overturned the contested deferrals, a House-passed amendment that would have sharply restricted presidential deferral authority was dropped in conference after veto threats from Reagan.

As approved by the House May 8, the supplemental spending bill (HR 4515) would have repealed the section of the 1974 law that required the president to report deferrals to Congress and allowed one chamber of Congress to veto a deferral by passing a resolution of disapproval.

However, Dick Armey, R-Texas, claimed the bill language would repeal only the reporting requirement, not the deferral power itself, a position backed by the Congressional Research Service, but disputed by other legal experts. Armey offered an amendment to retain current law, but it lost, 163-224. The 1974 law had not created presidential deferral authority, but instead placed limits on pre-existing authority. *(Vote 105, p. 34-H)*

A second amendment, by Minority Whip Trent Lott, R-Miss., would have blocked deferral of spending included in HR 4515 but left the authority itself untouched for the future. His proposal also lost, 179-203. *(Vote 106, p. 34-H)*

Jack Brooks, D-Texas, urged the House to pass the deferral section to "send a message to the White House" that Congress was serious on the issue, despite Reagan's threat to veto the supplemental if the deferral provisions remained in it.

The bill passed the House, 242-132. However, the Senate Appropriations Committee deleted the deferral language when it marked up the measure May 15. *(Vote 108, p. 34-H)* ∎

Balanced-Budget Amendment

By one vote March 25, the Senate defeated a proposed constitutional amendment to require a balanced federal budget, effectively killing the issue for the 99th Congress.

The final tally on the measure (S J Res 225) was 66-34, one short of the two-thirds majority — 67 in this case — required for passage of a proposed constitutional amendment. *(Vote 45, p. 9-S)*

The vote was a turnaround from the Senate's last consideration of the proposal, in 1982. Then the amendment passed 69-31, only to fail in the House. A similar amendment was reported in the Senate in 1984 but did not reach the floor. *(Background, 1982 Almanac p. 391; 1984 Almanac p. 261)*

Senators attributed the apparent switch in sentiment from 1982 to a change in Senate membership and to the enactment in 1985 of the Gramm-Rudman-Hollings anti-deficit act. That law (PL 99-177) set strict deficit targets over the next five years, leading to a balanced budget by 1991. *(1985 Almanac p. 459)*

"This amendment picks up where Gramm-Rudman-Hollings leaves off," said amendment supporter Paul Simon, D-Ill. But Daniel J. Evans, R-Wash., who led the opposition to the proposal, said it was "completely unworkable." "We should at least allow the Gramm-Rudman-Hollings plan a chance to work before we seek a constitutional amendment," he added.

Another ingredient in the debate was the continuing threat of a constitutional convention to consider a budget amendment. By 1985, 32 states had called on Congress to assemble a convention on the budget proposal. Under Article V of the Constitution, Congress must call a convention if two-thirds of the states (34) request one. Because no procedures existed for such a convention, some members feared a "runaway" session that would open up the entire Constitution for amendment. Any amendment adopted by a convention would have to be ratified by three-fourths of the states. *(Background, 1985 Almanac p. 233)*

The lineup of interest groups lobbying on the budget amendment was virtually identical to the 1982 fight. Organized labor, led by the AFL-CIO and the American Federation of State, County and Municipal Employees (AFSCME), along with senior citizens' groups, opposed the amendment. A coalition lobbying for the proposal was spearheaded by two groups that had worked for years for a balanced-budget amendment, the National Taxpayers Union (NTU) and the National Tax Limitation Committee.

Compromise Measure

The resolution the Senate rejected March 25 was a compromise between two measures reported by the Judiciary Committee in October 1985 (S J Res 225 — S Rept 99-163, S J Res 13 — S Rept 99-162). *(Committee action, 1985 Almanac p. 233)*

The compromise measure would have required a balanced federal budget unless three-fifths of the House and Senate agreed to deficit spending or in case of a declared war. A tax hike would have been allowed to balance the budget if a majority of the whole House and Senate — 218 representatives and 51 senators — agreed to the increase.

And the national debt ceiling, which limited the government's borrowing authority, could not have been increased except by a three-fifths vote of Congress. The debt-ceiling provision was added on the floor March 13, 57-40. *(Vote 35, p. 7-S)*

Finally, the president would have been required to submit a balanced budget to Congress each year. That provision was first tabled, 54-44, on March 11, but sponsors subsequently accepted it in an effort to pick up support for the resolution. *(Vote 29, p. 7-S)*

Reagan supported S J Res 225 even though it differed in key respects from the type of amendment he had wanted. The proposal he supported, S J Res 13, would have limited most tax increases to the rate of growth in the economy in the previous year.

In addition, S J Res 13 would not have required the president to submit a balanced budget, nor did it include the debt-ceiling provision.

Senate Floor Action

Twenty-three Democrats joined 43 Republicans in supporting the amendment on the 66-34 vote March 25, but it was the loss of 10 GOP votes that sealed the amendment's fate.

Six senators switched their votes from 1982. Four who had voted "aye" changed to "nay" March 25: Quentin N. Burdick, D-N.D.; Robert C. Byrd, D-W.Va.; Mark O. Hatfield, R-Ore.; and Robert T. Stafford, R-Vt. Two who voted "nay" in 1982, Wendell H. Ford, D-Ky., and Claiborne Pell, D-R.I., changed their votes to "aye."

In addition, opponents picked up another vote because of a change in membership. Frank R. Lautenberg, D-N.J., who voted "nay," replaced Nicholas Brady, R-N.J. (April 20-Dec. 27, 1982), who had voted for the amendment in 1982.

Two of the new opponents, Stafford and Burdick, said they wanted to give the new Gramm-Rudman-Hollings deficit-reduction law a chance to work before enacting a constitutional amendment.

Byrd, who had offered his own alternative, said he did not believe S J Res 225 would be "effective or workable." Hatfield said that while he supported a constitutional amendment in principle, he was opposed to this one because of the ongoing budget fight with the administration.

The vote on S J Res 225 wound up a generally low-key, drawn-out debate. Most discussion had ended March 13, but senators agreed to put off a vote until March 25. *(Amendments, votes 29-35, p. 7-S)* ∎

Gramm-Rudman: A Year of Mixed Success

The law that was supposed to balance the federal budget in five years, by forcing Congress and the president to agree on spending cuts and revenue increases or else face the consequences of harsh, automatic, across-the-board cuts, saw some — but not all — of its promise unfulfilled in 1986.

The Gramm-Rudman-Hollings anti-deficit act (PL 99-177) was enacted in 1985 to prevent the continued growth of multibillion-dollar deficits. Its methods were conceded to be extreme, but so was the problem. And its results were, from the beginning, mixed. *(Gramm-Rudman, 1985 Almanac p. 459)*

For example:

- The first round of automatic cuts, which had been effectively mandated by the law, took effect permanently as planned March 1. But the Supreme Court later in the year eviscerated the law, striking down the method for automatic cuts as unconstitutional.
- The law managed to keep a tight rein on spending. Its deficit targets and new procedures for floor action, particularly in the Senate, enabled deficit-minded members to fight off legislation that was considered too costly. The threat of Gramm-Rudman (if not the fact) helped keep on track the year's most significant legislative achievement — overhaul of the tax code (HR 3838 — PL 99-514). No amendment, either in committee or on the floor, was in order unless it was "revenue-neutral," that is, unless it would have paid for itself, thereby not adding to the deficit. *(Tax bill, p. 491)*

Yet fiscal 1986 ended with a record deficit of $220.7 billion. *(Story, p. 551)*

- Congress and the president followed the letter of the law: President Reagan submitted a fiscal 1987 budget that met the $144 billion Gramm-Rudman deficit target, but the Congressional Budget Office (CBO) pronounced it $16 billion over the limit, chiefly because of differences in the ways the administration's Office of Management and Budget (OMB) and CBO calculated rates of defense spending. *(President's budget, p. 525)*

Congress adopted a budget (S Con Res 120) that purported to meet the deficit target, even though many members knew the promise could not be fulfilled. And, after waiting until the last minute to do so, Congress enacted the largest-ever single spending bill (H J Res 738 — PL 99-591), which still kept the growth in spending down, and an $11.7 billion deficit-reducing "reconciliation" bill (HR 5300 — PL 99-509), which relied heavily on sales of government loans and other assets for its "savings." *(Budget resolution, p. 542; continuing appropriations resolution, p. 219; reconciliation, p. 559)*

Together with an $11 billion one-year uptick in tax receipts expected from the tax bill, Congress came within $10 billion of the deficit target, close enough for Gramm-Rudman not to require floor votes on across-the-board cuts.

Fiscal 1986 Sequester

The law's first direct effect was felt Jan. 15, when CBO and OMB issued a report calling for $11.7 billion in outlay cuts from fiscal 1986 appropriations. The date of the report, and even that precise number, had been specified in the law.

Based on anticipated levels of defense and non-defense spending (outlays in each broad category, minus exempted programs, were to be reduced by $5.85 billion), the report required a uniform 4.9 percent reduction in defense budget authority and a uniform 4.3 percent cut in non-defense budget authority to yield sufficient outlay cuts.

As part of the calculation, the two agencies jointly predicted that the fiscal 1986 deficit would come in at $220.5 billion (only $200 million shy of the actual number, as calculated by the Treasury Department at the end of the year).

Although Gramm-Rudman specified a 1986 deficit no larger than $171.9 billion, the first round of automatic cuts was limited to $11.7 billion, to prevent disastrously large cuts in the middle of a fiscal year.

The cuts were ratified by the General Accounting Office (GAO) Jan. 21. Although the GAO could have made major adjustments, the agency let stand the earlier report (after resolving a very minor dispute between CBO and OMB that had no real bearing on the cuts).

The cuts took effect temporarily Feb. 1, when, as required by Gramm-Rudman, President Reagan issued an order requiring them, and they became permanent March 1, after Congress did not vote an alternative method of cutting $11.7 billion from the deficit.

There was an attempt by Republicans Feb. 5 to force House committees to report such alternative cuts. But a motion to amend a resolution allocating money for House committee studies and investigations (H Res 368) failed on a mostly party-line 146-255 vote. *(Vote 14, p. 6-H)*

Court Decisions

A special three-judge panel of the federal district court in Washington dealt Gramm-Rudman its first blow Feb. 7. It was the same week that Reagan's budget, with its contested deficit estimate was released.

The court held that the GAO's role in ratifying the amount and scope of automatic, across-the-board cuts — which would have to be followed explicitly by the president in ordering the cuts — was constitutionally impermissible under the doctrine of separation of powers. *(Legal challenge to Gramm-Rudman, 1985 Almanac p. 461)*

The GAO, though it had some minimal executive functions, was deemed to be essentially a legislative branch agency. As such, it could not bind the president, head of the executive branch. The crucial point for the court was the fact that Congress, not the president, had the authority to remove the comptroller general, head of the GAO.

The likelihood of a legal challenge was anticipated even before Gramm-Rudman was enacted, and a special, expedited procedure was written into the law to govern its challenge.

The Supreme Court agreed two weeks after the lower court ruling to hear the case April 23. And on July 7, the high court upheld the district court's ruling, using the same grounds. *(Decision, p. 18-A)*

In striking down the portion of the law providing for automatic cuts, the lower court held — and the Supreme Court affirmed — that the first round of cuts already in effect were invalid. There was never any doubt, however, that Congress would preserve the cuts.

On July 17 first the House, and then the Senate,

adopted a pair of resolutions restoring the cuts. The first, H J Res 672 (PL 99-366), was a resolution to enact as law the initial CBO-OMB report specifying the cuts. The second, H Con Res 368, was a technical measure authorizing changes in H J Res 672 to conform it to the slightly different version of the cuts specified in the GAO report.

Both were approved in one vote by the House, 339-72. The Senate followed suit, adopting both by voice votes. *(Vote 202, p. 60-H)*

In the view of Senate Majority Leader Robert Dole, R-Kan., the cuts were approved by Congress because they were "history. What's done is done."

A more prosaic reason was that the year's budget deliberations were by then months old, and nearing completion. The "baseline" from which the fiscal 1987 budget was calculated assumed the fiscal 1986 budget had been cut $11.7 billion. Had the cuts not been reinstated, the baseline, and the deficit for fiscal 1987, would have grown by $11.7 billion overnight.

Procedural Benefits and Drawbacks

Even with the procedure for automatic cuts gone from the law, Gramm-Rudman altered significantly the way Congress did its business of raising and spending the taxpayers' money in 1986.

During Senate floor debate on the tax overhaul bill, amendments were successfully opposed unless they were "revenue-neutral," that is, they would neither have increased nor decreased revenues over five years. The tactic, an outgrowth of the Gramm-Rudman requirement that bills or amendments on the Senate floor be "deficit-neutral," was successful even though for technical reasons the requirement probably did not apply to most tax bill amendments.

That was but one example of how congressional processes and attitudes adjusted in the wake of Gramm-Rudman.

More directly, a $1 billion spring drive to boost aid for the economically depressed farm sector was scotched by a Gramm-Rudman-based objection to floor consideration in the Senate, upheld on a 61-33 vote. *(Vote 38, p. 8-S; farm aid, p. 161)*

And Jamie L. Whitten, D-Miss., chairman of the House Appropriations Committee, failed to resurrect one of his favorite spending programs, general revenue sharing, which was targeted for expiration. Continuing the program would have cost $3.4 billion, and members simply did not want to cut other spending, or raise taxes, to pay for it. Unless they did so, however, under Gramm-Rudman the money for revenue sharing was not there. *(Revenue sharing, p. 585)*

But, if Gramm-Rudman was seen as beneficial for focusing Congress' attention on the deficit throughout the year, it also was seen as contributing a greater than usual reason for delay to the process.

When the courts deleted the automatic cut process, they left in place a "fallback" procedure, whereby CBO and OMB would still file a report Aug. 20, anticipating the upcoming year's deficit, and the size of across-the-board cuts required to meet the deficit target.

A special congressional committee was to meet to report those cuts to the floor of each chamber, where, after only a short delay, votes could be forced on them.

After adopting the budget resolution in late June, little was done on legislation that actually would have served to reduce the deficit until the fiscal year was near its end.

Gramm-Rudman's scheme of mid-August deficit estimates, followed by a period during which alternatives to voting for across-the-board cuts were to be considered, created a powerful incentive not to do anything.

Fiscal 1987 Sequester

In fact, perhaps the biggest disappointment for those members who hoped Gramm-Rudman would serve to reduce the deficit by sizable, predictable amounts each year was the outcome of deficit-reduction efforts in 1986.

Not only did the process delay action on the deficit-reduction bill until after fiscal 1987 began, but the final deficit estimate was in the range of $151 billion, not $144 billion as specified in the law. A $10 billion "margin of error" built in for purposes of deficit calculations that were to trigger automatic cuts provided, in the end, a de facto substitute deficit target of $154 billion.

And Congress brushed aside the requirement for a vote on across-the-board cuts. Following the August CBO-OMB report, the special congressional committee did report a pair of resolutions (H J Res 723, S J Res 412) embodying 5.6 percent cuts in defense spending and 7.6 percent cuts in non-defense spending to reduce a projected $163.4 billion deficit to $144 billion.

The House never brought its resolution up for a vote; members argued that progress was being made on the deficit-reducing reconciliation bill. In the Senate, S J Res 412 was defeated on a 15-80 vote Sept. 19. But Majority Leader Dole reserved a motion to reconsider, by which he hoped to keep up pressure to enact the deficit-reduction bill. *(Vote 278, p. 47-S)*

The reconciliation measure finally cleared Oct. 17, after a second required CBO-OMB report on Oct. 6 reaffirmed the original requirement for across-the-board cuts. No action was taken on this second report at all.

Gramm-Rudman 'Fix'

One of Gramm-Rudman's more enduring legacies was the attention it drew in 1985 and 1986 to essential measures to raise the ceiling on the federal debt. Because federal borrowing could not exceed a statutory ceiling, bills to raise the ceiling were seen as among the most urgent.

If the ceiling were not raised, the government would either shut down — forcing it into the awkward position of failing to make good on contract payments and other legally required disbursements — or it would go into default.

It was just such a measure in 1985 that became host to the amendment known as Gramm-Rudman. And it was the 1986 debt-limit bill (H J Res 668) that in the Senate acquired an amendment crafted to restore the automatic cuts, by giving OMB final authority to determine the size and scope of the cuts, not GAO. *(Debt limit, p. 562)*

In giving such authority to OMB, the amendment was similar to the original 1985 version of Gramm-Rudman. Democrats, particularly, opposed vesting that much authority in an agency controlled by the White House.

Opposition to the so-called Gramm-Rudman "fix," crafted by original Gramm-Rudman sponsor Sen. Phil Gramm, R-Texas, tied the debt-limit increase in knots. The measure never cleared, and a short-term increase in the debt ceiling was added to the reconciliation bill.

A similar fix amendment was added by the Senate to a short-term debt-limit bill (HR 5395 — PL 99-384) that became necessary when H J Res 668 bogged down. That amendment, too, was unacceptable to House Democrats, who stripped it off. The Senate acquiesced in that action. ▮

Reagan Nominees Rejected

The Reagan administration lost two nomination fights in the Senate Labor and Human Resources Committee in 1986. On May 20, the committee rejected the nomination of Jeffrey Zuckerman to be general counsel of the Equal Employment Opportunity Commission (EEOC). On June 18, the committee rejected the nomination of Texas lawyer Robert E. Rader Jr. to a review panel within the Occupational Safety and Health Administration (OSHA).

The vote to reject Zuckerman was 5-10, with three Republicans — Charles E. Grassley, Iowa; Robert T. Stafford, Vt.; and Lowell P. Weicker Jr., Conn. — joining the committee's seven Democrats to kill the nomination.

Paula Hawkins, R-Fla., abstained.

Zuckerman was chief of staff for Clarence Thomas, chairman of the EEOC, an independent agency that examines employment discrimination complaints, attempts to mediate disputes and has the authority to bring court actions to enforce anti-bias laws.

Zuckerman was nominated in the fall of 1985 to be the agency's general counsel, but from the start civil rights advocates maintained he lacked commitment to the enforcement of civil rights laws.

He came under particular scrutiny for challenging court rulings on age discrimination and for what he described as a "fundamental disagreement" with civil rights groups over the use of hiring goals and timetables — so-called affirmative action plans — to increase the number of women and blacks who are working.

During the May 20 debate, Howard M. Metzenbaum, D-Ohio, criticized Zuckerman's lack of civil rights enforcement experience. "I find it astounding that the administration would nominate for this position a man . . . who has never dealt with the reality of how civil rights statutes are applied or enforced in the courtroom," he said.

Committee Chairman Orrin G. Hatch, R-Utah, sought to defend Zuckerman, saying he had shown his commitment to civil rights and was an able lawyer.

After the vote, Zuckerman issued a statement saying, "I am deeply disappointed, but take solace from the fact that when Justice [John Marshall] Harlan said in 1896 that the Constitution of the United States was colorblind, he was voted down 8-1."

Rader Nomination

Rader's nomination was rejected when the committee split 8-8 on a motion to send his name to the floor with a favorable recommendation. A second vote to send his name to the Senate without a recommendation also failed on an 8-8 tie. Under Senate rules, a tie vote is not sufficient to carry a motion.

On both votes, Weicker sided with the committee's seven Democrats to block the nomination.

President Reagan had selected Rader, 41, more than a year earlier for a six-year term on the OSHA Health and Review Commission, a three-member body that hears appeals of OSHA citations involving alleged violations of health and safety laws.

Reagan had put Rader on the commission as a recess appointment in the fall of 1985, but without Senate approval his term ran out in late 1986.

Organized labor was against Rader's nomination, contending that as a practicing attorney, he opposed OSHA's efforts to inspect the work place. Rader denied the charges.

There was only brief debate in the committee June 18, all of it coming from Democrats. Metzenbaum, who led the fight against Rader with Edward M. Kennedy, D-Mass., asserted that Rader's record "demonstrated that he cannot be a fair-minded and unbiased member of the OSHA review commission." He cited one statement made by Rader that "employers should realize there is very little information that they must furnish OSHA."

Kennedy charged that Rader has "made a career of undermining activities of OSHA," and said his nomination "added insult to injury."

In a prepared statement that he did not read, Hatch refuted charges that Rader was biased against OSHA. He said Rader's view that OSHA inspectors needed search warrants to inspect businesses has been upheld by the Supreme Court.

After the markup, Hatch complained that Rader's "qualifications were not judged today. His politics were."

President Reagan did win one labor nomination fight in 1986, when the Senate confirmed the nomination of Thomas to a second term as a member of the EEOC. The Aug. 12 confirmation meant Thomas could continue as chairman of the commission, a post he assumed in 1982.

During confirmation hearings, Thomas was criticized for ordering EEOC atttorneys to stop seeking minority hiring goals and timetables in job discrimination cases, but after he promised the Labor Committee he would resume efforts to enforce goals and timetables, the panel recommended his confirmation on a 14-2 vote Aug. 6. ■

Mandatory Retirement Ban

Congress cleared legislation Oct. 17 barring most employers from setting mandatory retirement ages. A seven-year exemption was included for firefighters and law enforcement officers and for colleges and universities.

The bill (HR 4154 — PL 99-592) amended the 1967 Age Discrimination Act, which had been amended in 1978 to raise the mandatory retirement age from 65 to 70. The law protected employees after they had reached the age of 40 and covered those businesses with 20 or more workers. Mandatory retirement for most federal employees was abolished in 1978. *(1978 Almanac p. 265)*

Final action came when the House, by voice vote, accepted the Senate version of the bill. The Senate had passed the measure a day earlier, also by voice vote.

Passage of HR 4154 was of special importance to Rep. Claude Pepper, D-Fla., the oldest member of Congress at 86, who lobbied long and hard for the measure. When it finally cleared, Pepper told colleagues: "This legislation is an important step in guaranteeing the elderly of this nation a fundamental civil right — the right to work as long as they are willing and able."

While the legislation was hailed by groups representing senior citizens, it was opposed by business groups like the U.S. Chamber of Commerce and the National Association of Manufacturers (NAM), who said it would mean a disruption in turnover cycles, slower advancement for qualified workers and fewer jobs for young people.

NAM's Jim Conway said eliminating the mandatory retirement age also would lead to a sharp increase in the cost of benefits, because more elderly workers would be covered by health care plans.

Fred Krebs of the Chamber of Commerce warned that

the bill could mean the dismissal of more older employees for incompetency. He said companies may no longer be willing to make allowances for older workers if they cannot count on their retirement at a certain age.

According to John Heinz, R-Pa., the chief Senate sponsor of the bill, there were 1.1 million Americans aged 70 and over in the work force in 1986.

A Department of Labor study projected that some 200,000 workers who would otherwise have retired would remain in the work force because of the legislation.

Additionally, the Congressional Budget Office estimated that lifting the ban would save the federal government $25 million annually by 1991 in reduced Social Security and Medicare payments.

Exemptions

The biggest fight on HR 4154 was over the exemptions for law enforcement groups, which in large part mirrored the controversy over the 1978 amendments.

The push for the exemption was motivated by a 1985 Supreme Court decision in which the justices ruled that the city of Baltimore could not require that all firefighters retire at the age of 55.

The age discrimination law included a general exemption allowing employers to set maximum ages when "age is a bona fide occupational qualification reasonably necessary to the normal operation of the particular business."

But the court said Baltimore could not justify its policy under this language. *(1985 Almanac p. 8-A)*

The original House bill, which passed Sept. 23, simply exempted law enforcement and firefighters. But the Senate modified that by limiting the exemption to seven years and adding a similar exception for colleges and universities. The Senate also required the Labor Department and the Equal Employment Opportunity Commission (EEOC) to make studies during this period. The studies were to evaluate and propose physical and mental fitness tests for police and firefighters and to study the effect eliminating mandatory retirement would have on higher education. The House accepted that change.

House Action

The House Education and Labor Committee July 24 approved HR 4154 (H Rept 99-756) by voice vote, after the committee turned back efforts to exempt firefighters, law enforcement officers and tenured university professors. Pepper had warned the committee that any exemptions would start a stampede of similar requests and have the practical effect of killing the legislation.

The crucial fight came on an amendment by Austin J. Murphy, D-Pa., allowing state and local governments to set mandatory retirement ages for firefighters and law enforcement officers.

Murphy's amendment was replaced by a substitute offered by Matthew G. Martinez, D-Calif. The Martinez substitute, approved 22-8, called for a study by the EEOC on exactly what physical requirements were necessary to carry out firefighting and law enforcement duties.

By voice vote, the committee defeated an amendment by E. Thomas Coleman, R-Mo., that would have provided an exemption for tenured university professors. Coleman argued that without mandatory retirement, tenured faculty would, in effect, be guaranteed jobs for life, depriving universities of regular turnover.

Some college and university officials lobbied heavily against HR 4154, as did faculty members. Alfred D. Sumberg of the American Association of University Professors said that without a mandatory retirement age, faculty members would have to wait longer for tenure. This would make it much harder to interest young people in the profession, he warned.

Floor Passage

When HR 4154 reached the floor Sept. 23, Murphy offered his amendment again and this time he won. The House voted 291-103 to allow an exemption for state and local public safety officers. *(Vote 371, p. 106-H)*

HR 4154 was then passed by the House, 394-0. *(Vote 372, p. 106-H)*

Murphy argued that Congress needed to make an explicit exemption so that state and local governments could decide for themselves whether to set a mandatory retirement age for those responsible for public safety.

"I submit that we should not replace our opinion" for the opinion of local jurisdictions, he said, "in saying that people who are 87 years of age or 90 years of age should be chasing drug smugglers down the street."

Pepper and Augustus F. Hawkins, D-Calif., chairman of the Education and Labor Committee, argued that police and firefighters who were too old to do the job could still be forced to retire on grounds of incompetency.

Pepper also urged defeat of the Murphy amendment for tactical reasons, saying he feared that one exception would open the bill up to a slew of amendments when it reached the Senate floor.

Other Amendments Blocked

Pepper's defeat on the Murphy amendment came after he successfully blocked other floor amendments to the bill.

Coleman had prepared an amendment exempting tenured faculty members who turned 70 before July 1, 2000. Coleman argued that tenure was an agreement to trade job security for retirement at a certain age.

He said prohibiting mandatory retirement without a transition period would mean no regular turnover of teachers and would make colleges reluctant to grant tenure.

"The loss or curtailment of tenure," he added, "would jeopardize academic freedom."

At Pepper's request, Coleman agreed not to introduce his amendment. In return, he extracted a promise from Pepper that if the Senate adopted a similar provision, Pepper would support it in conference.

Another amendment — this one by James M. Jeffords, R-Vt. — would have applied HR 4154 to congressional employees. Jeffords argued that it was hypocritical to leave Congress out.

Again, Pepper said he agreed in principle but was opposed on tactical grounds.

Leon E. Panetta, D-Calif., chairman of the House Administration Subcommittee on Personnel and Police, tried to talk Jeffords out of his amendment by promising action in the 100th Congress on a House rule prohibiting age discrimination in Congress. Panetta argued that because of the need to maintain a constitutional separation of powers, provisions applying to congressional employees should not be written into the law.

But Jeffords would not be swayed and he led an unsuccessful fight against the rule governing consideration of HR 4154, which did not allow for his amendment. The rule was adopted 335-66. *(Vote 370, p. 106-H)* ∎

Polygraph Examinations

The House March 12 passed legislation (HR 1524) barring most private employers from requiring employees to take lie detector tests in order to get or keep a job. However, members added a number of exemptions to the bill, with the effect of permitting polygraph tests in selected industries.

The Senate Labor and Human Resources Committee approved a similar bill (S 1815) June 25, but the full Senate failed to act on it.

The House vote on HR 1524 was 236-173, and represented a significant victory for organized labor, which had lobbied heavily for the measure. *(Vote 42, p. 14-H)*

Union leaders said they were generally satisfied with the legislation except for one exemption that would allow nursing homes and day-care centers to give lie detector tests to employees who had "direct contact" with children or with the elderly.

In addition to that exemption, which was offered by C. W. Bill Young, R-Fla., and a general exemption for all state, local and federal government employers, the House approved these other exemptions by voice vote:

- By Marge Roukema, R-N.J., to allow polygraph tests for employees who work as security guards in a variety of places, including nuclear power facilities, financial institutions and toxic-waste sites, and for any guard whose job has "a significant impact" on the health or safety of state or local governments or on national security.
- By William S. Broomfield, R-Mich., allowing lie detector tests for workers, job applicants and contractors who work in public utilities.

The House rejected two amendments that sought to exempt financial institutions and gambling casinos from coverage. By a vote of 194-217, it rejected a proposal by Bill McCollum, R-Fla., to cover financial institutions. McCollum said it was illogical to allow lie detector tests for security guards who carry money and other financial instruments from one place to another but to bar testing of employees who actually handle the money and the financial documents. *(Vote 41, p. 14-H)*

By voice vote, the House also rejected an amendment by William J. Hughes, D-N.J., to allow polygraph testing of gambling casino employees.

Prior to final passage, the House rejected, 173-241, a substitute proposal offered by Young and George "Buddy" Darden, D-Ga., that would have allowed private-sector polygraph testing as long as the employer followed certain standards and told employees the test was voluntary. *(Vote 40, p. 14-H)*

Pat Williams, D-Mont., chief sponsor of HR 1524, said that even with the exemptions in the bill, it still would protect about 80 percent of employees in the private sector from having to take lie detector tests. The bill would halt "the epidemic growth" in the use of the tests, he said.

HR 1524 gave the secretary of labor the authority to assess civil fines against employers who violated the law and to seek court orders barring employers from violating the law.

Committee Approval

HR 1524 was approved by the Education and Labor Committee by voice vote Oct. 23, 1985. *(1985 Almanac p. 475)*

The committee report (H Rept 99-416), issued Dec. 5, said about 2 million polygraph tests were being administered each year, about 98 percent of them in private industry. Nearly 75 percent of the tests were given prior to employment, the rest during investigations.

The report said lie detector tests, which assume that "there is a direct correlation between deception and physiological responses," were not reliable. "In fact, a lie detector does not register deception," the report said. "It registers stress through physiological responses — whether out of fear, anger or nervousness."

While 31 states and the District of Columbia had laws regulating the use of lie detectors in the work place, the report said they had not been effective and that a national law was needed to give workers uniform protections.

Several committee members, led by Republicans Roukema and Bill Goodling, Pa., filed opposing views, contending that the majority report relied in its arguments on "a selective and arguably inaccurate recitation of federal studies" while ignoring private studies showing a "relatively high degree of accuracy" for lie detector tests.

The tests might not be perfect, the dissenters said, but they saw "no reason why polygraphs should not continue to be available to employers and employees to supplement other means to verify employee honesty."

Senate Action

The Senate Labor and Human Resources Committee June 25 approved S 1815, which barred employers from requiring, requesting or suggesting that employees or prospective employees take lie detector tests for any purpose.

The bill made an exception only for federal, state and local government employees and for personnel of Defense Department contractors with access to classified information.

The measure was approved 11-5 without amendment, after Chairman Orrin G. Hatch, R-Utah, the sponsor of the bill, pleaded with the committee not to make changes. Hatch acknowledged that some amendments might be warranted — and that without them the bill surely would be vetoed by the president — but said he wanted to wait until he had time to work out differences between organized labor, which supported the bill, and business groups that opposed some provisions.

At two previous committee meetings, action on S 1815 was blocked by two of Hatch's Republican colleagues: Strom Thurmond, S.C., and Malcolm Wallop, Wyo. Both had threatened to offer dozens of amendments to delay action. ■

Job Training Expanded

Legislation to expand coverage of a job training program was signed by President Reagan Oct. 16.

The measure (S 2069 — PL 99-496) was cleared by the House Oct. 1. The Senate had given final approval Sept. 29.

S 2069 amended the 1982 Job Training Partnership Act (PL 97-300), which was passed to help youths and unskilled adults find work and to aid displaced workers. Under the law, money was sent to states to set up job training programs, with an emphasis on involving the private sector.

The 1986 amendment allowed unemployed farmers to participate in the job training partnership programs. It also added new training programs for older individuals and authorized summer youth employment programs to make educational projects part of the job training.

A summary of the legislation prepared by the Senate Labor and Human Resources and House Education and Labor committees said the educational project provision was included because the "deficit of basic education skills among the targeted population of youth is so acute."

The legislation also established presidential awards to acknowledge outstanding private sector involvement in operating job training programs.

Dangerous Substance Notice

The House Education and Labor Committee June 25 approved a bill that would establish a national system for identifying and notifying employees exposed to dangerous substances in the work place.

The sponsor of the bill (HR 1309 — H Rept 99-691), Joseph M. Gaydos, D-Pa., called it "a giant step toward eliminating cancer." But Rod Chandler, R-Wash., said it was "hardly feasible and incredibly expensive."

The measure never reached the House floor, but supporters said they would make it a priority in the 100th Congress.

HR 1309 was approved on an almost straight party-line vote of 20-8. The only Republican to vote in favor of the measure was Marge Roukema, N.J. No Democrats voted against it.

As approved, HR 1309 created a Risk Assessment Board of public health professionals who would evaluate medical and scientific data to identify groups of workers who were "at risk." Under the bill, a group of workers exposed to a hazardous substance would be "at risk" if the group had a 30 percent higher incidence of disease than unexposed workers.

Once the board identified such a group, it would recommend that the secretary of the Department of Health and Human Services (HHS) notify individual workers. The secretary would be bound to follow the board's recommendation as long as prescribed procedures had been followed by the board.

The notification, which would also go to former workers, would include identification of the hazardous substance and associated diseases, known latency periods and the type of testing and subsequent monitoring recommended.

The bill did not include any provision for the treatment of occupational disease.

Employers would be required to pay for the testing and monitoring of current workers, but former employees would have to pay for their own.

HR 1309 authorized $25 million annually for fiscal years 1987 and 1988 to pay the expenses of the Risk Assessment Board, the notification process and 10 regional health centers that would be established to provide additional information and services to notified workers.

HR 1309 prohibited discrimination against employees notified that they are at risk. If health concerns required their transfer to another assignment, employers would be forced to provide a job equal in pay, benefits and seniority.

The bill was opposed by the Reagan administration. Secretary of Labor William E. Brock III, in a June 24 letter to Education and Labor Committee Chairman Augustus F. Hawkins, D-Calif., said a mechanism for warning workers already existed within the Occupational Safety and Health Administration. He said HR 1309 created a new, unnecessary government bureaucracy.

Chandler, who led the opposition in the committee, noted that several business groups were opposed to the bill and warned that the costs imposed on employers would make American industry less competitive.

Chandler offered amendments giving the secretary of HHS more discretion, deleting the requirement that former workers be notified and providing a more flexible definition of an "at risk" group. But all were defeated.

Parental Leave Bill

Over the protests of Republican members, the House Education and Labor Committee June 24 approved legislation to require most public and private employers to grant their workers unpaid family and disability leave under certain conditions.

The Family and Medical Leave Act of 1986 (HR 4300 — H Rept 99-699, Part II) was approved by the panel on a voice vote, but it never reached the House floor.

Although the bill was supported by labor, women's rights and health groups, spokesmen for the business community vehemently opposed it, saying it would impose unreasonable burdens on many businesses.

As approved, the bill required public and private employers with 15 or more workers to grant up to 18 weeks of unpaid family leave to employees to care for newborn, newly adopted or seriously ill children or parents. The legislation also required employers to grant up to 26 weeks of unpaid disability leave to employees with serious medical conditions.

In both cases, employers would be required to continue health insurance benefits while the employee was on leave, and the employee upon return to work would have a right to reclaim his or her old job, or a comparable one, with full benefits and seniority.

Compromise Adopted

The voice vote ordering the bill reported masked deep differences among committee members over the wisdom of guaranteed-leave legislation in general and the scope of HR 4300 in particular.

Before approving the bill, the committee adopted, 22-10, a substitute offered by William L. Clay, D-Mo., chairman of the Subcommittee on Labor-Management Relations. The substitute was the result of negotiations between Clay and Republican members of the committee, including James M. Jeffords of Vermont, the full committee's ranking Republican. Joining the committee's Democrats in voting for the substitute were Republicans Jeffords, Tom Tauke of Iowa, and E. Thomas Coleman of Missouri.

After the parental leave legislation was approved by the subcommittee June 12, Jeffords and others had expressed concerns that some of the bill's provisions could place an intolerable burden on small businesses. The substitute adopted by the full committee increased the small-business exemption from five to 15 workers, instituted a vesting period of three months before workers could become eligible for leave, limited the combined leave an employee could take to 36 weeks per year, and required certification of medical conditions before leave could be taken. The substitute also contained a new provision requiring employees to give prior notice and to schedule leave to accommodate the employer, when possible.

Before adopting the Clay substitute, the committee rejected, 13-19, a substitute by Marge Roukema, R-N.J.

Roukema's substitute, similar to one rejected earlier in subcommittee, would have increased the small-business exemption to 50 employees, decreased maximum family leave from 18 to eight weeks, and disability leave from 26 to 13 weeks. It also would have required employees to work for a year before becoming eligible for leave, and would have created a "business necessity" exemption allowing employers to deny leave to workers whose salaries placed them in the top 20 percent of a firm's wage earners.

Republican members, including some who voted for the Clay substitute on grounds that it was an improvement over the original version, expressed deep reservations about the legislation. "This bill clearly establishes a new precedent for federal involvement in employer-employee relations," said Tauke. "This is a very serious issue that has not been handled today in a very serious manner."

Congressional Coverage?

Work on the bill nearly reached an impasse over the issue of whether congressional employers would be subject to the mandate.

Democratic sponsors said they agreed that Congress ought to be covered by the bill, like any other federal employer, and vowed to support an amendment to that effect on the House floor. Nevertheless, committee Chairman Augustus F. Hawkins, D-Calif., ruled out of order an amendment by Steve Bartlett, R-Texas, to extend the leave guarantee to congressional employees.

Hawkins said the section of the bill mandating leave for other federal employees did not fall under the Labor Committee's jurisdiction. An amendment to that section would delay the bill by requiring a referral to the Post Office and Civil Service Committee and to the House Administration Committee, he said.

The Post Office Committee had approved the provisions concerning federal employees (H Rept 99-699, Part I) June 11.

Bartlett appealed, but Hawkins' ruling was upheld on a 25-4 vote. ▮

Revenue Sharing Dies

The general revenue sharing program died when Congress adjourned Oct. 18, despite repeated efforts to keep the program alive.

Early in the year, local governments opened a major lobbying campaign to save revenue sharing. In response, the House Government Operations Committee April 22 voted 28-10 to renew the program for three more years, despite strong objections from Chairman Jack Brooks, D-Texas. The committee measure (HR 1400 — H Rept 99-610) was reported May 21, but went no further.

The fiscal 1987 budget resolution (S Con Res 120), approved June 27, allowed revenue sharing to continue only if Congress reauthorized it and offsetting budget cuts were made in other programs. Congress already had decided not to include a program reauthorization in its fiscal 1986 budget reconciliation bill (HR 3128), cleared March 20. But that bill delayed the scheduled Sept. 30 expiration date of the program until Dec. 31 or the date of adjournment. *(Budget resolution, p. 542; fiscal 1986 reconciliation, p. 555)*

In a last-ditch effort to keep the program from dying, House Appropriations Committee Chairman Jamie L. Whitten, D-Miss., tried in the final weeks of the session to add $3.4 billion for revenue sharing to the continuing appropriations resolution for fiscal 1987 (H J Res 738). But the Rules Committee refused to move the bill with revenue sharing included, and Whitten was forced to yield. *(Continuing resolution, p. 219)*

General revenue sharing was born in 1972 as a product of the Nixon administration's efforts to return power to state and local governments. In its 14 years, revenue sharing had distributed an estimated $83 billion to state and local governments with virtually no strings attached. State governments were weaned from the program starting in fiscal 1981. *(Congress and the Nation Vol. III, p. 97; 1983 Almanac p. 226)* ▮

Housing Reauthorization Fails Despite Pact

Bills to reauthorize and revamp federal housing programs died when Congress adjourned, despite an earlier agreement among key lawmakers on the general scope of the legislation and last-ditch efforts to attach the provisions to widely supported measures.

Housing programs had not been routinely reauthorized since 1980 and had continued under appropriations measures or temporary extension bills. *(1985 Almanac p. 303)*

The agreement called for House Democrats to accept a spending freeze for housing programs, many of which President Reagan wanted to slash or eliminate. They also agreed to an expansion of the Urban Development Action Grant (UDAG) economic development program in Republican areas of the South and West.

Major parties to the pact included Rep. Henry B. Gonzalez, D-Texas, chairman of the Banking Subcommittee on Housing and Urban Development; Rep. Stewart B. McKinney, Conn., the subcommittee's ranking Republican; and Sen. Jake Garn, R-Utah, chairman of the Banking, Housing and Urban Affairs Committee.

Garn's committee May 21 approved a bill (S 2507 — S Rept 99-314) encompassing the main points of the agreement, but it never reached the floor because of filibuster threats by Phil Gramm, R-Texas, and William L. Armstrong, R-Colo., and the crowded agenda as Congress neared adjournment.

The House passed its bill (HR 1) June 12, including a major policy shift toward renovation of existing public housing instead of new construction.

As efforts in the Senate bogged down, the House tried to force action by including the text of HR 1 in a fiscal 1987 budget reconciliation measure (HR 5300 — PL 99-509). The provisions, however, were dropped by conferees. *(Reconciliation, p. 559)*

The House also attached HR 1 to an omnibus bank regulatory bill (HR 5576) that it passed Oct. 7. While Reagan wanted the bank regulatory changes, he threatened to veto HR 5576 if it retained the housing provisions.

The Senate refused to accept the linkage, and the bill died. *(Banking, p. 588)*

House Committee Action

The House Banking, Finance and Urban Affairs Committee in June 1985 approved HR 1, an omnibus $16.3 billion fiscal 1986 housing authorization. When the Senate

Deficit Reduction Bill Provisions

Several housing and community development provisions were included in a fiscal 1986 deficit-reduction bill that Congress approved March 20 (HR 3128 — PL 99-272).

HR 3128, known as a "reconciliation" bill, aimed to cut existing programs to meet targets set in the fiscal 1986 budget resolution. The bill had emerged from conference in December 1985 but cleared only after three months of further Senate-House negotiations in 1986. *(Details, p. 555)*

When conferees could not agree on the scope of the housing provisions contained in HR 3128, they dropped most of them, pending enactment of a separate authorization that would revise housing and community development programs. Most programs had been extended temporarily in a series of separate bills. *(Housing authorization, p. 585)*

Provisions

As signed into law April 7, HR 3128 (PL 99-272) retained housing and community development provisions that:

- Prohibited the Federal Financing Bank (FFB) from purchasing Community Development Block Grant loans guaranteed by the Department of Housing and Urban Development (HUD) after June 30, 1986, thereby requiring the loans to be financed by the private sector.

This would produce estimated savings to the government of $165 million over fiscal years 1986-88.

- Authorized $2.15 billion in loan guarantees provided by the Farmers Home Administration (FmHA) in fiscal 1986, including $1.2 billion for home ownership; $900 million for rental units; $19 million for farm worker housing; $1 million for site-acquisition loans to developers; and $17 million for repair loans.
- Prohibited the FFB from financing FmHA rural housing loan guarantees, pushing the cost into the private sector. Borrowers who defaulted on their loans would be assured a reasonable period of time to meet their payments before foreclosure proceedings began.
- Authorized $1.28 billion in fiscal 1986 for operating subsidies for public housing, a reduction from the previously authorized level of $1.4 billion. This amount was equal to that in the fiscal 1986 HUD appropriations bill (HR 3038 — PL 99-160). *(Appropriations, 1985 Almanac p. 317)*
- Authorized HUD to forgive previous loans made to build or modernize public housing and to replace the existing long-term financing method with one-time capital grants.
- Authorized a total of 7,000 new public and Indian housing units for fiscal 1986.
- Delayed the Sept. 30, 1986, expiration date of the general revenue sharing program until Dec. 31 or adjournment of the 99th Congress, and required local governments to use or obligate funds by Oct. 1, 1987, allowing six more months than the Senate originally would have permitted. The effect of the changes was to give local governments more time to use fiscal 1986 revenue sharing funds already appropriated.

Banking Committee failed to mark up its own bill, House Democrats cut HR 1's cost to $14.3 billion and added its provisions to their version of the fiscal 1986 budget reconciliation measure (HR 3128). *(Box, this page)*

But Senate Republicans balked at what they viewed as an abuse of the reconciliation process, and the housing sections were stripped from the conference agreement.

Democrats could not revive the housing measure when the second session started because of bipartisan objections that the bill continued some expensive subsidized programs the administration wanted to cut and established new programs. HR 1 had not been cleared by the Rules Committee.

Critics singled out in particular three new programs that would be created by HR 1: a child care program for public housing tenants, a proposal to provide funds to help middle- and low-income families buy homes and a "fair housing initiative" sought by Reagan to prevent racial discrimination in housing.

Key House members agreed on a new bill that they intended to offer as a substitute if Rules would release HR 1.

The new bill kept some new proposals, such as the so-called "Nehemiah" grants to help low-income first-time home buyers, the fair housing initiative sought by the administration, and aid for shelters for the homeless.

It also blocked a number of user fees proposed by the administration and limited efforts by the Department of Housing and Urban Development (HUD) to reduce its total stock of subsidized multifamily housing units.

It continued the popular UDAG and Community Development Block Grants (CDBGs). The administration had proposed abolishing UDAG and cutting CDBGs.

House Floor Action

The House June 12 overwhelmingly passed a revised HR 1 that made several major changes in federal housing policy. After five days of debate over several weeks and dozens of amendments, the House passed the bill by a vote of 340-36. *(Vote 149, p. 46-H)*

Major changes in housing policy:

- A shift from past emphasis on construction of new public housing, with priority instead placed on the modernization, repair and rehabilitation of existing units.
- New programs promoting home ownership by low-income families. One of the very few initiatives in the bill, the Nehemiah program, named after the prophet who rebuilt Jerusalem, would help finance construction of houses in distressed areas for first-time home buyers. An effort by Bill McCollum, R-Fla., to kill the Nehemiah program failed June 11 by 123-300. *(Vote 141, p. 44-H)*

Another provision allowed certain public housing tenants to buy their dwellings at 25 percent of the prevailing market value, with low-interest loans from the government. This amendment, offered the same day by Jack F. Kemp, R-N.Y., was adopted 238-176. *(Vote 143, p. 44-H)*

- The fair housing initiative.

• Incentives for public housing tenants to manage and rehabilitate their projects.

• Greater autonomy for well-run local public housing authorities to raise rents and operate without control by HUD.

• Endorsement of the enterprise zone concept advocated by Kemp and Reagan. An amendment by Robert Garcia, D-N.Y., adopted 366-32 June 12, would help establish 100 zones around the country designed to entice businesses to blighted areas. One-third of the zones would have to be in rural areas. Unlike earlier proposals, the amendment provided no federal tax breaks for businesses in zones and relied instead on state and local tax incentives. *(Vote 146, p. 46-H; 1985 Almanac p. 304)*

• Expansion of UDAG to include more rural areas in the South and West.

• New requirements that public housing tenants report their Social Security and employee identification numbers, to help prevent fraud or abuse.

During debate, the House replaced the original and far more expensive provisions of HR 1 with the text of HR 4746, a scaled-down compromise worked out by Gonzalez and McKinney.

Before passing the measure, the House rejected, 131-262, an even smaller housing authorization offered by Chalmers P. Wylie of Ohio, ranking Republican on the full committee. *(Vote 147, p. 46-H)*

The House also rejected, 160-224, an attempt by Wylie to send the bill back to committee with instructions to freeze federal spending on housing programs at fiscal 1986 levels. *(Vote 148, p. 46-H)*

Public Housing, UDAG

The key vote on public housing construction came on an amendment by Steve Bartlett, R-Texas, to redirect $860 million in unobligated fiscal 1986 appropriations for construction of public housing projects, which were built and operated by public housing authorities to house low-income persons.

Bartlett wanted to allow new construction only to complete projects under way or in other specific, limited cases. In fiscal 1987, new construction would be allowed only if the local housing authority had brought 90 percent of its dwellings up to housing code standards.

His amendment was adopted by a vote of 223-180. *(Vote 134, p. 42-H)*

Edward P. Boland, D-Mass., chairman of the Appropriations Subcommittee on HUD-Independent Agencies, warned that the amendment "would kill the construction of new public housing." He said the public housing program, which provided an estimated 1.3 million units sheltering some 4 million people, was the only housing program for "the desperately poor."

According to Bartlett, the $860 million earmarked for fiscal 1986 public housing construction would build only 4,600 new units. But that same money, he said, would renovate 27,700 units in severe need of repair, many of which were vacant, and 64,300 units in need of moderate repair.

During debate June 4-5, 19 amendments were approved, all by voice vote, including those by:

• Tom Tauke, R-Iowa, prohibiting UDAG or CDBG grants for projects that helped foreign businesses at the expense of domestic U.S. firms.

• Thomas J. Manton, D-N.Y., permitting greater use of housing vouchers in low-income cooperatives and allowing them to be used to prevent the displacement of tenants of dwellings renovated under the federal rental rehabilitation program. Vouchers were certificates that tenants might use like cash for rental housing.

• Toby Roth, R-Wis., establishing a demonstration program in which vouchers could be used for any private rental housing. The current program generally restricted vouchers to rehabilitated rental housing.

• Sala Burton, D-Calif., allowing health, religious and financial exemptions from mandatory meal programs at elderly housing projects. An amendment by Bruce A. Morrison, D-Conn., adding enforcement provisions, also was adopted by voice vote.

Senate Committee Action

The Senate Banking Committee by voice vote May 21 approved S 2507, its omnibus housing reauthorization bill. The Senate committee bill largely would have frozen housing programs at their current funding levels.

Also like the House compromise, the Senate committee bill did not include specific funding authorization levels for most programs. It also included the fair housing initiative proposed by the administration to fight housing discrimination and Nehemiah housing grants.

Amendments adopted by the banking panel included those by:

• Alan J. Dixon, D-Ill., 11-4, to promote tenant management at public housing projects.

• Dixon, by voice vote, delaying until the end of 1986 the implementation of new regulations dealing with home improvement loans.

• Dixon, 9-5, reauthorizing an Emergency Food and Shelter program for the homeless for two years, through fiscal 1988, instead of one year.

Amendments defeated included those by:

• Armstrong, 6-9, to eliminate the UDAG program.

• Gramm, 6-9, exempting housing projects under $1 million from the Davis-Bacon law that controlled wages at government construction sites.

• Gramm, 6-9, to eliminate the Solar Energy Bank and the Neighborhood Development Demonstration programs.

• Gramm, 7-9, to reduce the income level for families participating in the Nehemiah home ownership program. ▮

FHA Extension

A one-year extension of the popular Federal Housing Administration (FHA) home mortgage guarantee program was cleared by the House by voice vote Sept. 30 and signed into law the same day by President Reagan (S J Res 353 — PL 99-430).

FHA had limped through a series of short-term extensions and was to expire Oct. 1. The Senate passed the measure by voice vote Sept. 27.

Final action in the House was delayed for a day by Fernand J. St Germain, D-R.I., chairman of the House Banking, Finance and Urban Affairs Committee, who blocked an attempt Sept. 29 to pass the non-controversial bill.

Henry B. Gonzalez, D-Texas, Housing Subcommittee chairman, sought to bring the bill to the floor by unanimous consent, but St Germain rushed to the chamber and blocked the request, complaining that he had not been consulted about the move in advance. Because of the impending expiration of FHA programs, the bill had not been referred to the Banking Committee.

Gonzalez later attributed the incident to "a communications breakdown" between committee staffs. He called up S J Res 353 again Sept. 30 when St Germain was not on the floor, and the bill passed without debate.

"It took exactly 29 seconds," Gonzalez said.

Tie to Housing Measure

FHA helped raise private mortgage capital by insuring single-family home mortgages. It had become a pawn in a larger battle between the House and Senate over a controversial fiscal 1987 reauthorization bill (HR 1) for federal housing programs, which passed the House June 12 and had been blocked in the Senate. *(Housing, p. 585)*

Liberal House Democrats had tried to use the FHA extension as leverage to prompt action on the housing bill by conservative Senate Republicans, who supported FHA but objected to various provisions in HR 1.

S J Res 353 was the eighth continuation of FHA voted by Congress in fiscal 1986. Temporary lapses in FHA's insurance authority forced the agency to suspend approval of applications earlier in the year.

Indian Housing Insurance

Before adjourning Oct. 18, Congress approved a bill (HR 5564 — PL 99-601) to ensure continued availability of FHA mortgage insurance for properties within the Seneca Indian Reservation in Salamanca, N.Y.

Some homeowners in Salamanca had been unable to sell their houses because 99-year federal leases on the land were to expire in 1991 and local lenders would not offer mortgages on the properties beyond that date. Rep. Stan Lundine, D-N.Y., whose district included Salamanca, said the bill was designed to restore local financing by guaranteeing that FHA mortgage insurance would be available for the properties even after the federal leases ran out.

The House passed the bill Sept. 29 on a 277-112 vote, and the Senate approved it without change Oct. 18. *(Vote 388, p. 110-H)*

Major Banking Legislation Stalls in Last Hours

Congress was unable to clear major banking legislation before adjournment Oct. 18, partly because of time pressures and partly because of serious disagreement among members and between the chambers over the scope of the measures.

The disputes involved longstanding differences between the chairmen of the two Banking committees over deregulation of the banking industry to allow banks to offer new commercial services.

The Reagan administration and Sen. Jake Garn, R-Utah, chairman of the Senate Banking, Housing and Urban Affairs Committee, pushed for omnibus deregulation of the industry. Rep. Fernand J. St Germain, D-R.I., chairman of the House Banking, Finance and Urban Affairs Committee, generally leaned toward individual bills targeted on specific issues.

Garn, for example, included in an omnibus bill (S 2592) a ban on "non-bank banks" — businesses that escaped the federal prohibition of interstate banking by limiting the financial services they offered. St Germain opposed deregulation and addressed the non-bank bank issue in one bill (HR 20).

Adding to those divisions were disagreements within the House over St Germain's controversial non-bank bank measure, and also among the House, administration and Senate over housing and consumer issues.

In the closing weeks of the session, St Germain tried to force action on his non-bank bank bill, which had been blocked in the Rules Committee for more than a year. He threatened to withhold Banking Committee approval of widely backed legislation to help regulators deal with failing banks. The proposals (HR 4701, HR 4709) would expand the authority of bank regulators to shore up ailing institutions and refinance the Federal Savings and Loan Insurance Corporation (FSLIC) insurance fund, which was strained by the numbers of failing S&Ls. *(1985 Almanac p. 276)*

When it became clear that Banking Committee members refused to accept his strategy, St Germain agreed to abandon the non-bank bank issue and move the bank regulatory measures.

However, he wrapped the legislation into one bill (HR 5576) and added a housing authorization (HR 1) and a consumer protection measure opposed by the White House and some senators. The committee approved the package Sept. 23 by a vote of 47-1, and the House passed it by voice vote Oct. 7. *(Housing, p. 585)*

In the Senate, Garn tried, in the waning days of the session, to develop compromise legislation on the bank regulatory powers and FSLIC bailout. But he was unable to persuade William Proxmire, D-Wis., to drop his amendment to ban non-bank banks until Oct. 17, the day before Congress adjourned.

The last day of the session, Oct. 18, the Senate by voice vote passed a scaled-down banking bill (S 2747) addressing the bank regulatory and FSLIC issues. However, the House was operating under restrictions that prohibited amendments, roll-call votes or controversial legislation, and St Germain refused to consider the measure.

The Senate then attached a revised bill to a separate House-passed measure (HR 2443), but St Germain also rejected that. The banking legislation died as Congress adjourned.

"The Senate waited until the final hours to move anything and then ignored and/or emasculated key consumer, housing and regulatory measures, to the detriment of the public interest," St Germain said. "Clearly, the Senate hoped to force the House into a take-it-or-leave-it position."

Garn blamed the death of the banking bills on "the unyielding attitude of some members on both sides of the aisle."

Remaining Issues

The failure to enact legislation left these key issues unresolved:

- **FSLIC.** The fund that guarantees deposits at federally insured S&Ls was expected to dwindle to $1 billion by the end of 1986 and needed an infusion of cash. By some estimates, FSLIC might need as much as $29 billion over two years to close or merge about 250 troubled S&Ls.

- **Regulatory Powers.** Banking agencies sought greater power to arrange the sale of insolvent banks to healthy out-of-state buyers that wanted to expand into new territory. They expected about 160 commercial banks to fail in 1986, up from 1985's record of 120.
- **Non-Bank Banks.** The non-bank banks used a loophole in federal law: Because they offered either checking accounts or commercial loans, but not both, they did not fit the legal definition of a bank and could cross state lines. Members feared that their proliferation would endanger local institutions and undercut traditional regulated banks.
- **Check Holds.** Consumer groups sought, and banks opposed, legislation to limit the amount of time a financial institution could hold a check before giving a depositor access to his funds.

Check Holds

The House passed a check-hold bill (HR 2443) Jan. 23 by 282-11. The measure had been reported (H Rept 99-404) in 1985. *(Vote 6, p. 2-H; 1985 Almanac p. 278)*

Long a priority of consumer groups, the bill would require financial institutions to credit local checks to customers' accounts in one to three business days and within six days for out-of-state checks. S&Ls and credit unions would be entitled to an extra day's hold.

After three years, the hold limit would shrink to one day for local and interstate checks and three days for all other checks. Limits would not apply to new accounts or checks for more than $5,000.

The measure aimed to restrict what critics called the "float game." While banks contended that they must hold checks to be sure they did not bounce, consumer advocates said the banks made millions of dollars by lending the money before depositors could draw on it. The banking industry strongly opposed the measure.

The House by 156-146 adopted an amendment by Norman D. Shumway, R-Calif., permitting longer holds if banks had a "reasonable belief" a check might be bad. By 80-211, it rejected his amendment to leave the issue up to the Federal Reserve Board. *(Votes 4, 5, p. 2-H)*

The House later included the provisions of HR 2443 in its omnibus banking bill (HR 5576), but neither was acted on by the Senate.

Just before it adjourned, the Senate passed a bill (S 2747) that included a check-hold provision merely requiring disclosure of banks' policies. The measure died in the House.

Non-Bank Banks

The House Banking Committee's approval Sept. 23 of an omnibus banking package heralded the formal end of St Germain's attempts to close two controversial holes in banking law.

One was the non-bank bank loophole. The second, called the South Dakota loophole, allowed South Dakota banks to sell insurance across state lines despite federal prohibitions. Both would have been closed by HR 20.

The Rules Committee refused to act on HR 20, at first because St Germain insisted that it be linked to a companion measure (HR 2707) that would have legalized nationwide branch banking by 1990. The second measure was strongly opposed by lawmakers from states with regional banking laws, including Rules Committee Chairman Claude Pepper, D-Fla.

St Germain eventually gave up the linkage, but heavy lobbying by financial firms against the non-bank bank bill continued.

In an effort to pry HR 20 from the committee, St Germain blocked action on the administration's bank regulatory power (HR 4701) and FSLIC bills (HR 4709). St Germain argued that non-bank banks threatened the government's most valuable tool for handling insolvent banks and S&Ls: Selling them to healthy out-of-state financial institutions that wanted to expand into new territory.

That would not work if potential buyers found it easier and cheaper to open their own non-bank banks instead, he said.

Confronted by strong opposition, St Germain Sept. 18 announced he would drop his fight against non-bank banks and would move the other banking legislation as an omnibus bill. The committee approved HR 5565, which was reintroduced as HR 5576 and was passed by the House.

In the Senate, Proxmire continued to threaten to filibuster the bills unless language was added to prohibit new non-bank banks for at least a year. Garn argued that adding the provision would make the regulatory bill much too controversial to pass.

Banking Deregulation

Garn introduced an omnibus banking bill (S 2592) June 24 that would have made major changes in how U.S. financial institutions do business, including closing the non-bank bank loophole. But he was forced to abandon it Aug. 7.

Besides time constraints, the bill faced opposition from St Germain, who wanted to deal with banking issues in separate bills. In addition, Garn's foes included non-bank financial service companies, which objected to the bill's closing the non-bank bank loophole.

S 2592 also would have expanded the power of federal regulators to handle problem banks and S&Ls and allowed commercial banks to expand into the securities business.

In addition, it would have required banks to disclose credit card interest rates more fully and limited the time banks could hold customers' checks before giving them access to their money.

Major elements of S 2592 would have:

- Closed the non-bank loophole by defining a bank as any institution insured by the Federal Deposit Insurance Corporation (FDIC).
- Allowed bank and thrift holding companies to underwrite municipal bonds, mutual funds and mortgage-backed securities by creating affiliates regulated by the Securities and Exchange Commission.
- Permitted FSLIC to charge higher premiums of S&Ls that engage in shaky investment practices. Existing premiums were not "risk based."

In abandoning the bill, Garn said he would concentrate on separate legislation (S 2752) containing only the FSLIC and regulators' provisions to ensure the "safety and soundness" of the nation's financial system.

FSLIC, Regulators' Bills

Federal bank officials said new legislation was needed to help deal with the growing number of problem banks and to maintain the "safety and soundness" of the nation's banking system.

According to the FDIC, about 160 federally insured banks were expected to fail in 1986 — well beyond the 120 banks that failed in 1985 and the most since federal deposit insurance was created in 1930.

"Failure to act now could only increase the risks," Federal Reserve Board Chairman Paul A. Volcker said in congressional testimony in support of the regulatory legislation. "We want to forestall a crisis, not to pick up the pieces after the damage has been done."

In addition, FSLIC would need about $16 billion in new funding over the next three to five years to cover anticipated S&L failures, according to Edwin J. Gray, chairman of the Federal Home Loan Bank Board.

"We must address soon — this year — the absolutely critical need for adequate long-term recapitalization of FSLIC," Gray told the House Banking Subcommittee on Financial Institutions.

The regulators' proposal would beef up federal banking resources in two ways.

First, it would pump about $15 billion into FSLIC through a complicated series of transactions, using a $3 billion loan from the Federal Home Loan Bank system to raise the money on the bond market.

Second, it would give federal bank regulatory agencies greater powers to sell, merge and manage problem banks and S&Ls. Regulators would be allowed to take over institutions before they actually failed and to temporarily manage and operate a bank until a new owner was found, something they could not do under current law.

The administration pointed out that keeping a government-insured bank open avoided draining federal insurance funds that otherwise would have to be spent to close down an institution and pay off depositors.

Senate Action

The Senate Banking Committee Aug. 13 approved S 2752, which embraced the FSLIC and bank regulators' proposals.

The committee by 7-8 rejected an amendment by Proxmire to cancel the regulators' emergency interstate acquisition powers after 18 months. Proxmire said the additional powers violated states rights.

The most serious challenge to the measure came from Proxmire, the committee's ranking Democrat, who offered another amendment to close the "nonbank-bank loophole."

It would have imposed a one-year moratorium on new non-bank bank charters and restricted existing non-bank banks from "cross marketing" — advertising one service such as mortgage loans in another wholly owned subsidiary such as a real estate sales office.

Proxmire withdrew the amendment, admitting, "I don't have the votes." But he threatened to filibuster the bill on the floor unless a similar non-bank bank amendment was added.

House Action

Although the House Banking Subcommittee on Financial Institutions approved HR 4701 and HR 4709 in June and July, respectively, St Germain refused to take further action unless his non-bank bank bill was moved by the Rules Committee.

Because of his refusal to act, impatient Republicans on the Banking Committee made a brief but unsuccessful attempt during the summer to force action.

In a July 30 letter to St Germain, 16 of the 19 GOP members of the 49-member committee requested that the full committee vote on several major banking bills, including the FSLIC and bank regulators' bill. The move was a parliamentary maneuver designed to override St Germain's power as chairman to control the committee's agenda.

However, such a "discharge petition" required the signatures of a majority of the committee, which the GOP minority could not muster. As a result, the petition failed.

St Germain responded to the GOP petition with a letter expressing disappointment that the authors did not also ask for action on non-bank banks and consumer protection legislation.

On Sept. 18, St Germain announced he would abandon his non-bank bank demand and would offer a bill that included the FSLIC and regulators' bills, check holds and a House-passed bill (HR 1) reauthorizing federal housing programs due to expire Sept. 30, when the fiscal year ended.

The housing provisions had also been included in a budget reconciliation measure (HR 5300) passed by the House Sept. 24. *(Reconciliation, p. 559)*

HR 5576 was approved by the committee Sept. 23 but Majority Leader Jim Wright, D-Texas, blocked efforts to bring it to the floor Sept. 29. Wright said he was concerned that the Federal Home Loan Bank Board, which regulated S&Ls, would use the new powers unfairly against Texas lenders. He said he feared overly aggressive regulation of S&Ls would cause needless bankruptcies.

After Wright won assurance from regulators that they would cooperate with Texas S&Ls seeking to restructure loans, the bill was passed Oct. 7 by voice vote.

Major Issues

As passed by the House, HR 5576 addressed the following major issues:

- **FSLIC Recapitalization.** The 12 regional Federal Home Loan Banks would invest $3 billion in a new financing corporation, which in turn would use the money to raise an additional $12 billion to $15 billion by selling bonds to investors over the next three years.

The money raised would be injected into FSLIC to handle S&L liquidations and mergers.

Of the original $3 billion, $2.2 billion would be invested in long-term zero-coupon bonds, which at maturity would assure repayment of the debt. Zero-coupon bonds were long-term investments, similar to savings bonds, that were purchased at a deep discount and deferred interest until maturity.

The remaining $800 million, plus insurance assessments from FSLIC-member banks, would be used to repay interest on the bonds raised on the private market.

By creating a new financing corporation, the borrowings were considered by the Congressional Budget Office to be "off-budget," and would not be counted as federal debt.

- **Emergency Acquisition Powers.** The bill would override state and federal laws barring interstate banking, and allow regulators to sell troubled institutions to a healthy out-of-state bank.

It would permit federal regulators to merge banks in the process of failing; current law allowed them to sell only failed institutions. Regulators also would be given expanded powers to operate and manage insolvent institutions, and arrange short-term management (so-called "bridge banks") until permanent new owners could be found.

Also, the legislation would lower from $500 million to $250 million the asset threshold required of a troubled bank to be taken over by an out-of-state buyer, thereby allowing regulators to avoid liquidation of smaller banks.

- **Check Holds.** This section was identical to HR 2443, which passed the House Jan. 23.
- **Housing.** The bill reauthorized federal housing programs for fiscal 1987. It did not include a specific authorization level for housing programs, leaving it to the House and Senate Appropriations committees to set spending.

As incorporated in HR 5576, HR 1 made a major policy shift from construction of new public housing to rehabilitation of existing housing stock. It also provided incentives for public housing tenants to buy their units.

The White House disliked HR 1 because it preserved programs the administration wanted to kill and even created some new ones.

- **Garn-St Germain.** The bill also included an extension to July 15, 1989, of the net worth certificate provisions of the Garn-St Germain Act of 1982 (PL 97-320), which provided for a series of paper transactions to help ailing institutions. *(Garn-St Germain, 1982 Almanac p. 45)*

The bill also clarified the use of S&L "secondary reserves" for the recapitalization of FSLIC. Secondary reserves were established by S&Ls in the early 1960s to cover special losses by the FSLIC insurance fund.

The measure also provided for phasing out by 1991 the special assessment on deposits that S&Ls pay to FSLIC. The special assessment, begun in 1984, amounted to one-eighth of 1 percent of S&L deposits. It was in addition to the permanent assessment of one-twelfth of 1 percent of S&L deposits.

Problems in the Senate

In the Senate, the legislation faced major problems over housing programs, which William L. Armstrong, R-Colo., and Phil Gramm, R-Texas, wanted to cut. In addition, it faced Proxmire's filibuster threat if a non-bank bank ban was not included.

According to Senate staff, it was not until Oct. 17 that Garn finally was able to persuade Proxmire to drop his non-bank bank amendment and fashion a compromise bill. Just hours before Congress adjourned Oct. 18, the Senate passed the only major banking bills (S 2747, HR 2443) it had passed in two years. Both departed substantially from the House-passed versions.

S 2747 did not include the FSLIC recapitalization or expanded bank regulatory powers wanted by the Reagan administration and the House. But it did contain the following items:

- A nine-month extension, through June 30, 1987, of the 1982 Garn-St Germain emergency acquisition powers, providing for interstate sales of insolvent banks. The so-called net worth certificate provisions of Garn-St Germain were dropped.
- A check-hold provision that merely required banks to disclose check-hold policies.
- Bridge bank authority for the FDIC to allow regulators to temporarily take over a failing bank and keep it alive until a permanent out-of-state buyer was found.

Because of unrelated delays in other legislative business, the Senate did not pass S 2747 until about 4 p.m. Oct. 18 — less than six hours before Congress adjourned. According to staff, senators expected the House to amend the measure to include the FSLIC and bank regulatory provisions, and send it back.

Restrictions in the House

But that turned out to be impossible because the House was operating under parliamentary restrictions that prohibited amendments, roll-call votes or controversial legislation. Congress had finished its major budgetary work the day before, and many members already had left town.

When senators discovered the House could not amend S 2747, they amended and quickly passed another measure — HR 2443, the check-hold bill passed by the House Jan. 23. The Senate passed this amended version of HR 2443 about 7:30 p.m. Oct. 18.

It contained the following provisions:

- Recapitalization of FSLIC, but limited only to $3 billion instead of $15 billion.
- A moderate expansion of the emergency interstate acquisition powers of the 1982 Garn-St Germain Act. However, this would last only 11 months, until Aug. 1, 1987. The net-worth certificate provisions of Garn-St Germain were dropped.
- Creation of bridge bank powers for the FDIC.
- Expansion of conservatorship powers for the National Credit Union Administration, which regulates federally insured credit unions.

But St Germain already had rejected considering the measure; Banking Committee Democrats, at two caucuses earlier that week, had refused to separate housing and check-hold issues from the FSLIC and bank regulatory legislation.

"We are not going to accept or have shoved down our throats at the last minute of this session anything that we do not agree to," St Germain said. "Nothing is going to be railroaded through this House."

At 9:34 p.m., the House adjourned for the year. All remaining legislation — including the banking bills — expired when the 99th Congress ended. ∎

'Truth in Savings'

A bill that would have required uniform disclosure of interest rates and conditions imposed on most bank accounts and all credit cards died when Congress adjourned Oct. 18.

The House Oct. 7 by voice vote passed the "Truth in Savings and Credit Cards" bill (HR 5613), but the Senate did not consider the measure.

Of the Senate's inaction on the bill, staff director of the Senate Banking, Housing and Urban Afairs Committee M. Danny Wall claimed, "No one has even introduced a bill like that over here, and we haven't even considered it. Institutionally, we've got some problems with that over here."

HR 5613 would have forced federally insured banks and Savings and Loans (S&Ls) to disclose more about interest-bearing accounts in their ads. Required information would have included the annual percentage yield and duration on accounts, minimum balance and time requirements, early withdrawal penalties and special conditions. Also, all applications for bank, S&L and retail credit cards would have had to list annual percentage rates, fees, interest-free grace periods and transaction charges.

The legislation faced opposition from the banking industry, which complained that it was unnecessary and that it would be expensive and burdensome to comply with its regulations. ∎

Securities Dealer Regulations

Congress Oct. 9 cleared legislation (HR 2032 — PL 99-571) to tighten federal regulation of government securities.

Prompted by the collapse of eight unregulated securities firms between 1975 and 1986, the measure put previously unregulated securities dealers under the regulatory thumbs of the Treasury Department and the Securities and Exchange Commission (SEC). Specifically, legislators pointed to the 1985 collapse of E.S.M. Government Securities Inc., of Fort Lauderdale, Fla., which caused more than $300 million in losses to local governments and savings and loan institutions (S&Ls) and triggered a depositors' run in Ohio.

Before final passage of the bill, Congress had to overcome a substantial hurdle. The House bill (H Rept 99-258), originally passed Sept. 17, 1985, favored control of the government-securities industry by the Federal Reserve Board of Governors. A similar bill in the Senate (S 1416 — S Rept 99-426) favored control by the Treasury Department.

The Senate Sept. 16, 1986, passed HR 2032 after substituting the text of S 1416. The House then amended the bill, vesting the Treasury Department with regulatory power as proposed by the Senate but terminating those powers after five years (Oct. 1, 1991) unless they were renewed by Congress. In addition, the legislation required reports in 1990 from the Comptroller General, Treasury Department and the SEC on how the rules had worked and what changes should be made. The House Oct. 6 by voice vote approved the Senate version of HR 2032 with an amendment. The Senate accepted the House amendment to the bill Oct. 9, also by voice vote.

Provisions

HR 2032 applied only to dealers in U.S. Treasury securities and federally guaranteed securities and mortgage pools, such as those guaranteed by the Federal Housing Administration and the Government National Mortgage Association. Dealers in municipal- and state-issued securities were governed by separate "self-regulatory organizations"and were not covered by the bill.

"Secondary dealers," those that sold government securities to smaller institutional investors, including S&Ls and state and municipal governments, were the main target of the legislation.

("Primary dealers" bought directly from the government: about two-thirds were brokers or banks that made financial reports voluntarily to the Federal Reserve or various bank regulatory agencies, and the rest were unregulated firms that specialized in securities.)

The bill required, but did not specify the detail of, new regulations "designed to prevent fraudulent and manipulative acts and practices, and to protect the integrity, liquidity and efficiency of the market for government securities."

In addition, as signed into law, HR 2032 required:

- Brokerage firms, banks and S&Ls currently regulated as government-securities dealers to file with the SEC or the appropriate federal bank regulatory agency, giving notice that they were already regulated.
- Unregulated dealers, for the first time, to register with the SEC. Independently audited and certified balance sheets and income statements had to be filed once a year or more often.
- Dealers to meet minimum financial standards, showing they had adequate cash reserves and were properly managing customers' accounts and securities.
- Newly registered dealers that were not previously regulated to join a stock exchange or the National Association of Securities Dealers, which governed the over-the-counter securities market and regulated advertising by security dealers.
- The Federal Reserve Bank of New York to continue its brokerage relationship with the primary dealer firms that bought directly from the government. However, those dealers would be treated the same for reporting purposes as secondary dealers.
- Federal regulators to publish the new regulations within four months after enactment of the law to receive public comment, and publish them in final form not more than three months later. The rules took effect as temporary regulations seven months after enactment and became final after nine months. ∎

Pension Safeguards Added to Deficit-Cut Bill

Deficit-reduction legislation cleared by Congress March 20 (HR 3128 — PL 99-272) included stronger measures to safeguard workers' pensions and other labor-related provisions.

HR 3128, known as a "reconciliation" bill, aimed to cut existing programs to meet requirements of the fiscal 1986 budget resolution. The bill had emerged from conference in December 1985 but underwent three months of further Senate-House negotiations in 1986. *(Details, p. 555)*

Pension Benefit Guaranty Corporation

The deficit reduction bill included a package of changes in the financially troubled Pension Benefit Guaranty Corporation (PBGC), a self-financing government entity set up to protect workers against loss of retirement benefits if employers canceled their pension plans. The PBGC provisions amended the Employee Retirement Income Security Act (PL 93-406). *(1985 Almanac p. 475)*

The main thrust of the changes was to shore up the PBGC single-employer insurance fund that covered individual firms and to prevent companies from terminating their pension plans arbitrarily, thus leaving the PBGC with considerable liability for retirees.

A separate fund insured multi-employer pension programs that applied to an entire industry.

When the House Ways and Means Committee reported HR 3128 July 31, 1985, the only provision related to the PBGC was one to raise employers' premiums for the single-employer insurance fund. However, on Oct. 15 Ways and Means agreed to add a new section making other changes in the program. That action was in response to a contrary package of changes from the Education and Labor Committee that was included in a separate deficit-reduction measure reported by the Budget Committee (HR 3500).

The final version of HR 3128 was an amalgam of these

two measures and recommendations made by the Senate Labor and Human Resources Committee in S 1730.

Provisions. As signed into law April 7, HR 3128 (PL 99-272):

- Raised from $2.60 to $8.50 the premium that employers paid for each employee to the PBGC single-employer insurance fund. The premium increase was retroactive to Jan. 1.

Congress also agreed to require the PBGC to study the insurance premium structure and make recommendations for change. The study would be analyzed by an advisory group appointed by the chairmen of the House Education and Labor and Ways and Means committees, and the chairmen of the Senate Labor and Human Resources and Finance committees.

The study was due within a year of enactment of HR 3128 and the advisory group's report was due within six months of that.

- Clarified an employer's authority to freeze future benefits by requiring at least 15 days' notice to each participant in the plan and to each beneficiary. Existing law included no advance notice requirement.
- Clarified the circumstances under which an employer could terminate a pension plan, distinguishing between "standard terminations" in which there were sufficient assets to pay all benefits and "distress terminations."

Distress terminations involved employers who had petitioned bankruptcy court seeking liquidation of assets or reorganization, or cases where pension costs had become unreasonably burdensome because of a declining work force.

- Established a formula for an employer's liability to the PBGC under a distress termination. Under existing law, an employer was liable to the PBGC for 30 percent of his net worth payable at the date of termination of the plan.

Under HR 3128, an employer was still liable for 30 percent of his net worth upon termination of a pension plan. In addition, an employer was liable for 75 percent of unfunded guaranteed benefits, less the 30 percent already paid.

- Established a general framework for repayment to the PBGC when liability for unfunded guaranteed benefits exceeded 30 percent of net worth. The bill specified that payment of the excess was to be made at "commercially reasonable" terms under a repayment schedule worked out between the PBGC and an employer. The agreement provided further for a one-year deferral of 50 percent of the amount owed in any year in which the PBGC determined an employer had no pre-tax profits.
- Set up new procedures within the PBGC for distributing benefits under a distress termination to active employees and retirees who had suffered benefit losses. An employer would be liable to a "termination trust" for the lesser of two amounts: 75 percent of the difference between all non-forfeitable, or vested, benefits under the terminated plan, and benefits guaranteed by the PBGC, or 15 percent of total non-forfeitable benefits.

The bill specified that a payment schedule would be negotiated between the employer and the termination trust administrator at "commercially reasonable terms."

If the amount owed was less than $100,000, payment could be made in equal annual installments along with interest, and the PBGC was given the authority to increase the $100,000 ceiling by regulation.

The bill also provided for deferral of 75 percent of the amount owed to the trust in any year in which the employer had no pre-tax profits.

- Required 60 days' notice of intent to terminate a plan to participants, beneficiaries and unions.
- Required the PBGC to conduct annual audits of selected terminated plans to determine if participants and beneficiaries had received the benefits to which they were entitled.
- Barred the PBGC from proceeding with the voluntary termination of a plan if the termination would violate a collective bargaining agreement.
- Required the PBGC to begin proceedings to terminate a pension plan if the PBGC determined that the plan did not have assets available to pay benefits currently due under the terms of the plan.
- Authorized the Internal Revenue Service (IRS) to require security before waiving the requirement of minimum funding for a pension plan. The IRS would have to notify the PBGC of a waiver application, and interested parties, including the PBGC, could send comments to the IRS.
- Gave virtually all parties involved in a pension plan, including the employer, the employee and those individuals handling benefit trusts, the right to sue in federal district court to stop acts or practices of any other party that violated the employer liability provisions. The PBGC's right to sue under existing law was retained.
- Established detailed procedures governing pension plan terminations pending prior to or at the time of enactment. These requirements were designed to make sure that the PBGC could determine if sufficient assets existed to pay employees and to give employees time to file complaints concerning plan terminations.

Exceptions could be made allowing a speedy plan termination if an employer could demonstrate to the PBGC that he was "experiencing substantial business hardship." This was defined to mean operating at an economic loss.

- Established Jan. 1, 1986, as the effective date for all provisions except those covering specified studies to be delivered to Congress. Some provisions, however, were subject to transitional rules that would give affected parties more options in handling their pension programs.

Railroad Unemployment

HR 3128 made several changes in the relationship between unemployment and retirement accounts that benefited railroad workers. The bill:

- Made permanent the authority of the railroad unemployment insurance program to borrow from the railroad retirement program. Under previous law, the borrowing authority had been permanent, but in 1983 Congress set an expiration date of Sept. 30, 1985. HR 3128 once again made the borrowing authority permanent.
- Established an automatic surcharge of 3.5 percent for any loan from the retirement program to the unemployment insurance program. This surcharge applied only to new loans made after Sept. 30, 1985.
- Increased the tax levied on the unemployment system for repayment of loans from the retirement account.

Under existing law, the tax was to begin July 1, 1986, at 2 percent of the first $7,000 in wages paid to a rail employee; it would rise steadily to 3.2 percent in 1990. Under HR 3128 the tax was set at 4.3 percent in 1986, 4.7 percent in 1987 and 6 percent in 1988, after which the tax would drop to the same levels it would be under existing law — 2.9 percent in 1989 and 3.2 percent in 1990.

The higher tax would raise a total of $199 million through fiscal 1988. Slightly more than half, $101 million, would come in 1987, and the rest, $98 million, would come in 1988.

Unemployment Compensation

Other provisions of HR 3128 restored federal unemployment benefits to jobless Pennsylvanians who lost coverage due to National Guard service in a June 1985 flood.

At issue were payments from the Federal Supplemental Compensation program, which formerly provided added compensation after individuals' regular state benefits were exhausted.

The program expired in April 1985, but benefits continued for those receiving them at the time it ended. However, some jobless Guard members forfeited benefits when they were unable to collect payment in consecutive weeks, as required by law. *(1985 Almanac p. 472)*

To address this problem, HR 3128:

- Allowed states to enter into agreements with one another and with the federal government to recoup unemployment benefits that were overpaid to an individual. For example, if a state were to make an overpayment of benefits to an individual who later moved to another state, the second state could withhold the individual's unemployment benefits and reimburse the first state for its overpayment.

Under existing law, when a state found that it had overpaid an individual, it could withhold a future unemployment benefit due the same individual. But there was no provision for one state to withhold a payment on behalf of another state. ▮

Social Security Adjustments

Minor adjustments to the Social Security program were included in the omnibus deficit-reduction bill cleared March 20 (HR 3128 — PL 99-272). *(Story, p. 555)*

As signed into law April 7, the bill:

- Exempted from Social Security payroll taxes the wages of federal judges who reached retirement age but continued working. Their pay also could not be used in calculating earnings to see if benefits should be reduced under the Social Security retirement earnings test.
- Extended for five years the HHS secretary's authority to waive legal requirements that otherwise would prevent recipients of Social Security disability payments from participating in demonstration projects to ease their return to work.

A 1980 law authorized HHS to develop the projects, but the department has not done so.

- Required the appointment of an ad hoc Disability Advisory Council to make recommendations to Congress by Dec. 31, 1986, on policies and procedures for the disability program.
- Eliminated U.S. tax withholding on Social Security payments to American Samoans, consistent with tax treatment of citizens of other U.S. possessions.
- Allowed great-grandchildren who were dependent on a Social Security recipient and under age 18 to receive benefits. Children and grandchildren could get benefits under existing law.
- Clarified that an individual's Social Security disability payments were to be reduced by the amount of all disability benefits paid under a federal or state worker-compensation program.

Social Security Disinvestment

After the Treasury Department revealed in 1985 that it had redeemed long-term Social Security investments to keep the government operating when Congress failed in a timely manner to raise the ceiling on total federal borrowing, members demanded quick action to prevent a repeat. But despite House and Senate efforts to pass a legislative remedy, the issue was left unresolved at the end of 1986.

On July 22 the House unanimously approved legislation (HR 5050) prohibiting any future "disinvestment" of Social Security trust funds to circumvent the statutory debt ceiling. The legislation would have allowed the managers of the funds to redeem long-term assets only if needed to handle an internal Social Security funding crisis. *(Vote 213, p. 62-H)*

Disinvestment of Social Security trust funds occurred in September and October 1984, and September, October and November 1985, when the government's debt was about to exceed the ceiling. Redeeming the securities reduced the government's indebtedness and allowed the Treasury to sell new securities to stay in operation. *(1985 Alamanac p. 465)*

The bill also would have made the Social Security Administration (SSA), at the time a part of the Department of Health and Human Services, an independent agency as it had been from its creation in 1935 until 1939.

In addition, the legislation attempted to resolve a long-standing controversy over the administration of the Social Security disability program by providing that claimants whose cases received a favorable ruling by an administrative law judge would receive payments if a subsequent review of the claim by the agency's Appeals Council took more than 90 days. If the decision was ultimately adverse to the claimant, he or she would not have to repay benefits already received.

The measure was approved by the House Ways and Means Committee June 25 by voice vote.

Senate Version

The Senate did not take up an independent agency bill, but approved, as part of its version of a bill (H J Res 668 — S Rept 99-335) to increase the debt limit, provisions that would have allowed the Treasury secretary to disinvest the Social Security trust funds under certain limited conditions. *(Debt limit, p. 562)*

But the House refused to accept — or to go to conference on — the Senate's version of H J Res 668, which had been amended to restore automatic cut procedures of the Gramm-Rudman-Hollings anti-deficit act (PL 99-177), and the measure died.

As approved by the Senate Aug. 9, the bill would have:

- Permitted disinvestment during debt-limit crises only to provide enough money to pay Social Security benefits and administrative expenses, not to pay other government costs.
- Authorized appropriations as needed, once the debt ceiling was increased, to restore to the trust funds the full amount of interest lost as a result of disinvestment.
- Required investment of Social Security payroll tax receipts in Treasury securities as soon as was permissible under the debt ceiling, thereby barring delays that would have allowed receipts to be used for other purposes.
- Increased the number of Social Security trustee meetings and required special trustee reports in the event of a

fund disinvestment.

- Repealed in 1990 the "normalized tax transfer," an accounting mechanism that credited Social Security trust funds with anticipated revenues at the beginning of each month. This would have resulted in the funds being credited daily as receipts came in.
- Exempted the costs of printing and mailing Social Security benefit checks from any across-the-board spending cuts required by the Gramm-Rudman-Hollings anti-deficit law.

The provisions were identical to those adopted by the Senate Finance Committee July 22 as a modification to its original amendment to the debt-limit bill. An earlier version, reported by the committee July 18, would not have allowed disinvestment of the trust funds to pay Social Security benefits.

During floor debate of the measure Aug. 1, the Senate by voice vote adopted an amendment to bar disinvestment of the Civil Service Retirement and Disability Fund by imposing on it the same rules and restrictions as adopted for the Social Security trust funds. ▮

Construction Labor Practices

The House April 17 passed a union-backed measure (HR 281) designed to bar companies from circumventing labor laws to hire non-union workers for construction projects. However, the Senate did not act on the measure and the bill died at adjournment.

The House passed HR 281 on a 229-173 vote. The bill, reported by the Education and Labor Committee in 1985 (H Rept 99-311, Parts I and II), was aimed at stopping the practice known as "double breasting." *(House vote 80, p. 26-H; background, 1985 Almanac p. 474)*

This practice occurred when a unionized company set up a non-union subsidiary to do the same work as the original firm to avoid dealing with unions or to shift work from a union shop. In some cases, bill sponsors said, the unionized company went out of business while the owners continued to do the same work through the non-union company.

To prevent this, HR 281 specified that multiple construction firms should be considered a single employer if there was "directly or indirectly substantial common ownership, common management or common control" among the nominally separated firms that did the same or similar work. The employer would have to apply the terms of a collective-bargaining agreement to all of his related entities within the geographical area covered by the agreement.

The bill also would protect "pre-hire" agreements common to the construction industry. These were arrangements made between a company and a union prior to the start of a project that had the same binding status as a collective-bargaining agreement.

This practice resulted from a 1959 labor law that gave special consideration to the construction industry in establishing working conditions for building projects. However, the National Labor Relations Board and the Supreme Court had ruled that employers could repudiate pre-hire agreements unless a union could demonstrate that a majority of workers on a job site were represented by that union.

HR 281 would have required an employer to abide by the pre-hire agreement unless the workers sought and supported decertification of the union involved in the project.

Opponents of HR 281, led by Marge Roukema, R-N.J., and Steve Bartlett, R-Texas, said the bill was far too broad. They said any abuses could be covered under existing law.

Bartlett offered an amendment to narrow the definition of a "single employer," but his proposal was rejected 165-247. *(Vote 77, p. 24-H)*

Another Bartlett amendment to let construction workers vote by secret ballot on whether they wanted to be covered by a union contract also was rejected, 123-286. *(Vote 78, p. 26-H)*

The House rejected, 121-283, an amendment by Dick Armey, R-Texas, to limit the compulsory payment of union dues to those workers who were a formal party to a pre-hire agreement and not to employees who worked for related companies. *(Vote 79, p. 26-H)*

Senate Bars Labor-Violence Bill

The Senate April 16 handily rejected an effort by Republican members to bring a labor-violence measure to the floor. The bill (S 1774) would amend the Hobbs Act, the federal anti-extortion law, to cover violence that occurs during strikes. By a 44-54 vote — 16 short of the required 60 — the Senate refused to cut off a filibuster on a motion to take up the bill. Fifteen Republicans joined 39 Democrats in voting against the move. *(Vote 67, p. 13-S)* ▮

SUPREME COURT

CQ

Reagan's Arguments Rebuffed by High Court

It will take more than the appointment of conservative Judge Antonin Scalia to win the Supreme Court over to President Reagan's point of view.

That much was clear after a 1985-86 term in which a fragmented but tenacious majority of the court consistently rebuffed the administration on virtually every social policy argument it raised.

Coupled with a similar record in the preceding term, the court's chilly reception for Reagan's initiatives demonstrated that the 1983-84 term, in which the court seemed to turn sharply to the right, was an aberration, not the beginning of a new conservative era at the court. *(1984 Almanac p. 3-A)*

Indeed, during the term that began Oct. 7, 1985, and ended July 7, 1986, the court emphatically reaffirmed two "liberal" tenets that the White House, with equal consistency, had rejected.

First, the court declared — in decisions about jury selection, voting rights and affirmative action — that the nation must continue to work actively toward the goal of equality for all of its citizens.

Reagan, while espousing a "colorblind" society, had argued that sufficient progress had been made toward that goal to permit an end to some of the more aggressive civil rights measures, such as affirmative action.

Second, the court continued to claim a major role for the federal courts in preserving and protecting individual rights. Not only did the justices reaffirm a woman's right to have an abortion, but they also refused to curtail access to the courts or curb judges' power to order the losing side in a civil rights case to pay the winners' lawyers.

This, too, ran directly counter to the Reagan administration's argument that judges should do less and elected officials more.

"This term witnessed the most significant defeats for the policy objectives of a chief executive in half a century," said Bruce Fein, an adjunct scholar at the American Enterprise Institute who had written extensively on the contemporary court.

"Not since the Supreme Court scuttled President Franklin D. Roosevelt's efforts to fashion a domestic New Deal program in a flurry of 1935 rulings has a president's policy agenda fared so poorly before the high court," he added.

Swapping One Vote for Another

The only two justices who consistently supported the administration's position were Chief Justice Warren E. Burger, who announced his retirement June 17, and Justice William H. Rehnquist, who was confirmed Sept. 17 as his successor. Scalia, a conservative member of the U.S. Court of Appeals for the District of Columbia, took over the seat Rehnquist vacated.

Because Scalia's appointment simply replaced one conservative vote — Burger — with another, it was unlikely to have any immediate impact on the court's responsiveness to Reagan's social agenda.

What might prove more significant for the near term was the movement of Reagan's first Supreme Court appointee, Justice Sandra Day O'Connor, away from the consistently conservative stands of Burger and Rehnquist, which she had generally supported in the past, toward a more centrist position on the court. That shift, which began last year, became more pronounced during this term.

Reagan's Crusade

Despite major setbacks in the 1984-85 term, especially in its drive to lower the wall between church and state, the administration intensified its campaign to swing the court to a more conservative stance. *(1985 Almanac p. 3-A)*

Attorney General Edwin Meese III criticized the court for opinions that were "on the whole, more policy choices than articulations of constitutional principle." He urged the court to abandon this "jurisprudence of idiosyncrasy" and adopt a jurisprudence of original intent, relying upon the views of the men who wrote the Constitution as the standard for interpretation.

As part of the administration's stepped-up crusade, Solicitor General Charles Fried filed briefs arguing that the court should overturn the 1973 *Roe v. Wade* ruling legalizing abortion and that it should proclaim most affirmative action plans unconstitutional. In the past, the administration had stopped short of asking the court to reverse itself on these issues.

The new, harder line did not play well at the court. First the justices denied Fried's request that he be permitted to make his arguments in person. Then they rejected the arguments.

As in previous terms, many of the administration's most controversial positions were outlined in advisory *amicus curiae* ("friend-of-the-court") briefs in cases in which the government was not directly involved.

The Reagan administration filed a record number of these briefs. Almost half the briefs filed by the solicitor general this term fell in that category. But Fried said in March that "the really important part of the story is whether we got it right" — whether the court agreed with the points made in the government's briefs.

Evaluating that record at the end of the term, Fried said he felt "pretty good" about the court's response.

Of the 39 *amicus* briefs filed in cases resolved on the merits by the court, only nine were clear losses for the administration. Twenty-six were victories. In four cases, the outcome was in line with what the administration sought, but the court did not adopt the policy stance Fried had suggested.

Although Fried objected strenuously to any characterization of certain *amicus* cases as more important than others, it was difficult to overlook the fact that the administration's losses included major rulings on abortion, affirmative action, voting rights, attorneys' fees and racial bias in jury selection.

Fried listed as significant victories decisions upholding the disciplinary authority of school officials, curtailing inmate suits against prison officials, refusing to expand existing protection for suspects' rights, and recognizing First Amendment concerns in cable television franchise disputes.

A Divided Court

There was far more discord among the justices this term than in the preceding several years. Two out of three cases in each of the last two terms were decided with little or no dissent. But this term, the level of agreement within the court dropped precipitously. Almost half of the 158 decisions came by margins of 6-3 and 5-4. The number of cases closely dividing the court jumped from 48 last term to 72 this term.

Justice Lewis F. Powell Jr., a centrist, once again played a critical role on a number of split decisions, voting with the majority on 28 of the 36 cases decided by 5-4 votes.

Among the cases in which he cast the decisive vote were those involving abortion, affirmative action and the Reagan administration's "Baby Doe" regulations, which required aggressive treatment of all newborns with birth defects, regardless of parental wishes. With Powell casting the fifth vote, the court invalidated those regulations, 5-3. Rehnquist did not take part in that decision.

Powell typically dissented less than any of his colleagues, but this term, he dissented in almost twice as many cases as last term — 15 vs. eight.

While O'Connor's dissent rate dropped almost as low as his, there was a dramatic increase in dissents by Justice Harry A. Blackmun, from 19 last term to 41 this term.

Fallout to Come

Some of the court's decisions this term were certain to have major political reverberations.

Congress, for example, wrestled inconclusively for months to deal with the July 7 decision striking down the key provisions of the Gramm-Rudman-Hollings budget-balancing law.

And in a June 30 decision, *Davis v. Bandemer,* the justices opened the doors of federal courthouses around the country to suits challenging political gerrymanders — the rigging of electoral district lines to benefit one party.

First Amendment Issues

In contrast to last year, when the administration lost arguments over silent prayer and aid to parochial schools, the court issued no major church-state decisions this term.

The cases it did resolve in this area involved narrower questions — whether a rabbi in the Air Force could wear his yarmulke in violation of uniform regulations (no), whether a blind ministry student could receive state vocational rehabilitation aid (yes), and whether an Indian family could claim a religious exemption from a requirement that they list their child's Social Security number on a food stamp application (no).

Other First Amendment rights, notably those of free press and free speech, were at stake in some important rulings this term.

The news media won two major libel decisions. The court made it easier to win dismissal of such charges before trial, and more difficult for private figures to recover damages. In addition, the justices reaffirmed the right of press and public to attend pretrial hearings in criminal cases.

On the last day of the term, the court upheld, 7-2, the power of school officials to discipline students for using vulgar language, and endorsed, 6-3, the use of public nuisance statutes to close an "adult" bookstore where prostitution and other lewd activities occurred.

Earlier in the term, the court had approved a city's use of its zoning power to keep "adult" theaters and bookstores out of residential neighborhoods.

And in a different kind of free-speech case, the justices ruled that states could not require corporations to enclose messages with which they disagreed in bills to their customers. However, the court allowed governments to ban advertising for certain legal but "harmful" products and services — in this case, casino gambling in Puerto Rico.

Individual Rights

The court's decisions endorsing the continued use of affirmative action were not its last words on that issue. On July 7, the justices accepted two more affirmative action cases for review in the term that began Oct. 6, 1986.

One of them, *Johnson v. Transportation Agency, Santa Clara County, Calif.,* was the first test of alleged "reverse discrimination" based on sex, rather than race. The other, *United States v. Paradise,* involved the court-ordered use of racial quotas for promotions.

On questions of personal privacy, the court struck down a Pennsylvania law regulating abortion but upheld a Georgia law making sodomy a crime.

The justices rejected the administration's "Baby Doe" regulations, but accepted its view that the federal ban on discrimination against the handicapped did not apply to commercial airlines, even though they benefited from the federally funded air traffic control system.

The court for the first time defined sexual harassment as unlawful sex discrimination, and the justices made it easier for blacks to win voting rights challenges against multi-member electoral districts and other practices that dilute their political influence.

Crime and Punishment

A decade after reinstating capital punishment in the United States, the court was still facing a variety of questions about the death penalty.

In the most significant of its eight capital punishment cases this term, the court ruled 6-3 that opponents of the death penalty could be excluded from juries in capital cases, even if that increased the likelihood that the jury would convict the defendant. Virtually all of the 1,714 people on death row in May 1986 were convicted by such juries; the ruling was expected to expedite the pace of executions.

But on July 7, the court accepted for review in its next term what could be the last major challenge to use of the death penalty. In *McCleskey v. Kemp,* a black man sentenced to die for killing a white police officer argued that someone who killed a white person was far more likely to be executed than someone who killed a black person.

Death row inmates won three of this term's capital cases. Among their victories were rulings that it is unconstitutional to execute someone who has lost the mental ability to understand what is happening and why, and that a defendant in a capital case, whose victim was of a different race, has a right to have prospective jurors asked about their racial biases.

In other decisions, the court made clear that racial bias has no place in the nation's courtrooms, holding that blacks may not be excluded from juries and guaranteeing a new trial for anyone indicted by a grand jury from which blacks had been shut out.

—By Elder Witt

Supreme Court Decisions, 1985-86 Term

CRIMINAL LAW

Search and Seizure

New York v. Class, decided by a 5-4 vote, Feb. 25, 1986. O'Connor wrote the opinion; Brennan, Marshall, Stevens and White dissented.

A police officer conducted a reasonable search when he reached into a car to move papers on the dashboard covering the vehicle identification number — normally visible through the windshield — and saw a gun protruding from under the driver's seat. The gun can properly be used as evidence against the driver, who was charged with illegal possession of firearms.

United States v. Quinn, dismissed as improvidently granted by a 7-2 vote, April 21, 1986. Burger and Blackmun dissented.

The court, after hearing oral arguments, declined to decide whether a boat owner who had never used the vessel but had loaned it to others could challenge the legality of a search of the boat by Coast Guard agents, who suspected it was being used to smuggle drugs.

New York v. P.J. Video, Inc., decided by a 6-3 vote, April 22, 1986. Rehnquist wrote the opinion; Brennan, Marshall and Stevens dissented.

Police seeking a warrant authorizing seizure of allegedly obscene movies do not have to meet a "higher" standard of probable cause than if they were seeking a warrant to seize some other type of evidence not arguably protected under the First Amendment.

California v. Ciraolo, decided by a 5-4 vote, May 19, 1986. Burger wrote the opinion; Powell, Brennan, Marshall and Blackmun dissented.

The warrantless observation by police of an enclosed back yard, from an aircraft lawfully in public airspace, is not a search within the meaning of the Fourth Amendment, and thus any evidence obtained as a result may be used against the owner of the yard.

Dow Chemical Company v. United States, decided by a 5-4 vote, May 19, 1986. Burger wrote the opinion; Powell, Brennan, Marshall and Blackmun dissented.

The Environmental Protection Agency did not violate the Fourth Amendment by using aerial photography of an enclosed industrial plant for the purpose of monitoring the plant's compliance with Clean Air Act standards. That photography, from an aircraft lawfully in public airspace, is not a search that requires a warrant.

Self-Incrimination

Miller v. Fenton, decided by an 8-1 vote, Dec. 3, 1985. O'Connor wrote the opinion; Rehnquist dissented.

When a prisoner seeks a writ of *habeas corpus* from a federal court, claiming that a confession was obtained in violation of his Fifth Amendment right not to be compelled to incriminate himself, the federal judge hearing that petition is not bound by a state court's decision that the confession was voluntary.

"The ultimate question of whether, under the totality of the circumstances, the challenged confession was obtained" in a constitutional fashion "is a matter for independent federal determination," O'Connor wrote.

Wainwright v. Greenfield, decided by a 9-0 vote, Jan. 14, 1986. Stevens wrote the opinion.

Prosecutors violate a defendant's right to remain silent after his arrest when they use that silence to challenge his defense that he was insane at the time of the crime with which he is charged. The right to remain silent contains within it a promise that a defendant's silence will not be used against him. "It is fundamentally unfair to promise an arrested person that his silence will not be used against him and thereafter to breach that promise by using the silence to impeach his trial testimony . . . [or] to overcome a defendant's plea of insanity."

Moran v. Burbine, decided by a 6-3 vote, March 10, 1986. O'Connor wrote the opinion; Brennan, Marshall and Stevens dissented.

Confessions made by a suspect after he was warned of his right to remain silent and to have the aid of an attorney, and after he waived those rights, need not be excluded from evidence — even if police failed to inform the suspect that a public defender contacted by his family had called to offer her services.

Allen v. Illinois, decided by a 5-4 vote, July 1, 1986. Rehnquist wrote the opinion; Brennan, Stevens, Blackmun and Marshall dissented.

The Fifth Amendment privilege against compelled self-incrimination does not apply to civil-type proceedings so long as an individual's answers to questions in those proceedings may not be used against him in a subsequent criminal proceeding. The court upheld a state court's finding that the privilege did not apply in proceedings under the state law providing for institutionalization of persons charged with certain sex offenses.

Double Jeopardy

Heath v. Alabama, decided by a 7-2 vote, Dec. 3, 1985. O'Connor wrote the opinion; Brennan and Marshall dissented.

The double jeopardy guarantee does not prevent two states from each trying a defendant for the same crime — the murder of his wife in one state and dumping the body in another state.

Morris v. Mathews, decided by a 7-2 vote, Feb. 26, 1986. White wrote the opinion; Brennan and Marshall dissented.

A violation of the double jeopardy clause can be remedied by modifying the defendant's conviction on the lesser included charge; a new trial is not required.

Smalis v. Pennsylvania, decided by a 9-0 vote, May 5, 1986. White wrote the opinion.

Once a trial judge finds that the state does not have enough evidence to support a conviction of a particular defendant on a particular charge, the guarantee against double jeopardy forbids the government from appealing that decision.

Fair, Speedy Trial

United States v. Rojas-Contreras, decided by a 9-0 vote, Dec. 16, 1986. Burger wrote the opinion.

The Speedy Trial Act does not require that the 30-day period to prepare for trial be started over again for a defendant when he is indicted for a second time on the same charge.

United States v. Loud Hawk, decided by a 5-4 vote, Jan. 21, 1986. Powell wrote the opinion; Brennan, Marshall, Blackmun and Stevens dissented.

An 11-year delay between arrest and trial does not deny a defendant his right to a speedy trial (and require dismissal of the charges) if the defendant for much of that time was not under indictment or in custody, and if some of the delay is attributable to the defendant's frivolous appeals and motions.

This decision cleared the way for the government to prosecute former Indian leader Dennis Banks and three other Indian activists on 1975 charges that they illegally transported guns and dynamite.

Holbrook v. Flynn, decided by a 9-0 vote, Jan. 14, 1986. Marshall wrote the opinion.

A defendant is not denied his right to a fair trial, specifically his right to be presumed innocent, by the presence of four uniformed and armed state troopers behind him in the courtroom during his trial.

Henderson v. United States, decided by a 5-4 vote, May 19, 1986. Powell wrote the opinion; White, Brennan, Marshall and Blackmun dissented.

Under the Speedy Trial Act, time that elapses between the filing of a pretrial motion and the conclusion of a hearing on the motion is excluded from the 70-day maximum period allowed between charge and trial. This time is excluded whether or not it includes delays that appear unreasonable.

Crane v. Kentucky, decided by a 9-0 vote, June 9, 1986. O'Connor wrote the opinion.

A defendant has a constitutional right to present evidence at his trial about the way in which his confession was obtained so that the jury may decide whether his confession was voluntary, even if the judge has already found that it was.

Rose v. Clark, decided by a 6-3 vote, July 2, 1986. Powell wrote the opinion; Brennan, Marshall and Blackmun dissented.

Jury instructions that shift the burden of proof to the defendant, in violation of the due process guarantee, may be found to be harmless error when the reviewing court finds the verdict otherwise valid.

Right to Counsel

Hill v. Lockhart, decided by a 9-0 vote, Nov. 18, 1985. Rehnquist wrote the opinion.

A defendant who seeks release through a federal writ of *habeas corpus*, arguing that his guilty plea was involuntary because his attorney advised him incorrectly of the date at which he would be eligible for parole, is not entitled to a full hearing on that claim in federal court.

Maine v. Moulton, decided by 5-4 vote, Dec. 10, 1985. Brennan wrote the opinion; Burger, Rehnquist, White and O'Connor dissented.

Once a suspect invokes his right to legal counsel, police must not question him without his counsel present — and "questioning" includes use of an undercover informant to solicit information, as well as direct interrogation by police. The fact that the undercover agent may be trying to solicit information about other crimes than the one for which the suspect has been indicted is irrelevant; any evidence obtained by that agent concerning that crime must be suppressed.

Nix v. Whiteside, decided by a 9-0 vote, Feb. 26, 1986. Burger wrote an opinion joined by four justices; Blackmun wrote for the other four members of the court.

An attorney does not violate his client's rights to the aid of counsel and to a fair trial when he insists that the client testify truthfully and not commit perjury.

Michigan v. Jackson, Michigan v. Bladel, decided by a 6-3 vote, April 1, 1986. Stevens wrote the opinion; Rehnquist, Powell and O'Connor dissented.

Once a defendant is charged and invokes his right to legal counsel, police must not try to obtain a confession from him until after his attorney arrives and is present. If police question the suspect during this interim and obtain a confession, it is not admissible. Any waiver of the right to an attorney during that period is invalid.

Murray v. Carrier, decided by a 7-2 vote, June 26, 1986. O'Connor wrote the opinion; Brennan and Marshall dissented.

A lawyer's inadvertent failure to make a particular claim on appeal is not sufficient cause to excuse that default and permit the claim to serve as part of the basis for a petition for *habeas corpus.*

Kimmelman v. Morrison, decided by a 9-0 vote, June 26, 1986. Brennan wrote the opinion.

A prisoner who did not make a claim about an unreasonable search to state courts and therefore cannot raise that claim in seeking a writ of *habeas corpus* can argue that his failure to raise the search issue earlier was the result of ineffective assistance of his lawyer at trial.

Kuhlmann v. Wilson, decided by a 6-3 vote, June 26, 1986. Powell wrote the opinion; Brennan, Marshall and Stevens dissented.

The Constitution is not violated when a police informant, placed in a suspect's cell, tells police about the suspect's unsolicited remarks.

Confrontation

United States v. Inadi, decided by a 7-2 vote, March 10, 1986. Powell wrote the opinion; Marshall and Brennan dissented.

The general rule that statements made out of court may not be used as evidence without proof that the persons making them are unavailable to testify does not apply when those persons are alleged co-conspirators with the person on trial.

Delaware v. Van Arsdall, decided by a 7-2 vote, April 7, 1986. Rehnquist wrote the opinion; Marshall and Stevens dissented.

Denying a defendant his constitutional right to cross-examine the witnesses that testify against him does not necessarily require reversal of the resulting conviction. Such a denial may in some circumstances be harmless error, depending upon a number of factors, including the importance of the witnesses' testimony and the strength of the prosecution's case.

Lee v. Illinois, decided by a 5-4 vote, June 3, 1986. Brennan wrote the opinion; Blackmun, Burger, Powell and Rehnquist dissented.

Prosecutors may not, as a general rule, use the confession of a co-defendant against a person charged with the same crime unless that co-defendant testifies at the trial. Because the co-defendant stands to gain by implicating another person in the crime, that statement is presumed suspect and must be subjected to cross-examination, the court held.

New Mexico v. Earnest, decided by a 9-0 vote, June 27, 1987. *Per curiam* (unsigned) opinion.

The court sent back to state courts a ruling that a non-testifying co-defendant's out-of-court statement involving defendant in a crime could not be admitted as evidence. The court suggested that the lower court reconsider that ruling in light of *Lee v. Illinois (above).*

Cruel and Unusual Punishment

Whitley v. Albers, decided by a 5-4 vote, March 4, 1986. O'Connor wrote the opinion; Marshall, Brennan, Blackmun and Stevens dissented.

The use of deadly force in halting a prison riot, even if it results in the unreasonable or unnecessary shooting of a prison inmate, does not constitute cruel and unusual punishment prohibited by the Constitution.

"To be cruel and unusual punishment, conduct that does not purport to be punishment at all must involve more than ordinary lack of due care for the prisoner's interests or safety.... It is obduracy and wantonness, not inadvertence or error in good faith, that characterize the conduct prohibited by the Cruel and Unusual Punishments Clause."

Capital Punishment

Cabana v. Bullock, decided by a 5-4 vote, Jan. 22, 1986. White wrote the opinion; Brennan, Marshall, Blackmun and Stevens dissented.

A person cannot be convicted of murder without a finding that he intended the death of his victim, but that determination may be made by a judge as well as by a jury.

Skipper v. South Carolina, decided by a 9-0 vote, April 29, 1986. White wrote the opinion.

A defendant found guilty of a capital offense must be permitted during the sentencing process to introduce evidence of his good behavior during his pretrial incarceration. Any relevant mitigating factor should be admitted at this proceeding.

Turner v. Murray, decided by a 7-2 vote, April 30, 1986. White wrote the opinion; Brennan and Marshall dissented in part; Powell and Rehnquist dissented in part.

A capital defendant accused of an interracial crime is entitled to have the prospective jurors informed of the race of his victim and questioned to ascertain their own racial bias or lack thereof.

Declaring that "the risk of racial prejudice infecting a capital sentencing proceeding is especially serious in light of the complete finality of the death sentence," the court vacated a death sentence imposed upon a black man convicted of killing a white man. The defendant's request that jurors be questioned concerning their racial bias had been rejected by the judge. The court did not vacate his conviction, only his sentence. On this point, Justices Brennan and Marshall dissented.

Lockhart v. McCree, decided by a 6-3 vote, May 5, 1986. Rehnquist wrote the opinion; Marshall, Brennan and Stevens dissented.

Opponents of the death penalty may be excluded from juries in capital cases if their opposition is sufficiently strong to impede their objective assessment of the evidence in the case, even if their exclusion increases the likelihood that the jury will convict the defendant.

Neither the requirement that the jury be drawn from a fair cross-section of the community nor one that the jury be impartial is offended by the exclusion of these opponents of capital punishment from the jury. An impartial jury is simply one composed of jurors who will conscientiously apply the law and find the facts.

With this ruling, the court rejected one of the last broad legal challenges to the way that the death penalty is imposed in the United States. This ruling was expected to expedite executions of some of the 1,714 persons on death row in the United States at the time this decision was announced.

Poland v. Arizona, decided by a 6-3 vote, May 5, 1986. White wrote the opinion; Marshall, Brennan and Blackmun dissented.

The constitutional guarantee against double jeopardy does not prevent the imposition of a second death sentence on a defendant whose initial death sentence was vacated because the reviewing court found insufficient evidence to support the single aggravating circumstance cited by the sentencing judge, but did find sufficient evidence to support another aggravating circumstance.

Darden v. Wainwright, decided by a 5-4 vote, June 23, 1986. Powell wrote the opinion; Brennan, Blackmun, Marshall and Stevens dissented.

A prosecutor's remarks, while offensive and improper, did not so prejudice the trial and the jury in a 1974 murder case as to require a retrial.

Ford v. Wainwright, decided by votes of 7-2 and 5-4, June 26, 1986. Marshall wrote the opinion; Rehnquist and Burger dissented; White and O'Connor dissented in part.

The Constitution forbids the execution of an insane prisoner, the court ruled 5-4. By 7-2, it also held inadequate Florida's procedures for deciding whether a death row inmate had lost his capacity to understand why he was being executed. The major defect in the state's procedures, the court said, was the fact that it permitted the decision on the inmate's sanity to be made entirely within the executive branch, without any participation by the courts.

Smith v. Murray, decided by a 5-4 vote, June 26, 1986.

O'Connor wrote the opinion; Brennan, Marshall, Stevens and Blackmun dissented.

The court refused to nullify a death sentence imposed upon a man convicted of rape and murder, even though the sentencing proceedings included the prosecution's use of the testimony of a psychiatrist based upon the defendant's unwarned remarks to him. This potential constitutional error had not been reviewed in the courts because the defendant's attorneys did not raise the issue in state courts. The Supreme Court refused to nullify the sentence because the issue did not call into question the guilt or innocence of the individual.

Sentencing

Texas v. McCullough, decided by a 6-3 vote, Feb. 26, 1986. Burger wrote the opinion; Marshall, Blackmun and Stevens dissented.

It is not necessary to presume judicial vindictiveness when, after a retrial, a judge imposes a sentence harsher than that imposed by a jury at the original trial. That presumption, first employed in *North Carolina v. Pearce* (1969), does not apply when the sentencing body differs and when the new trial is the result of the judge's finding of prosecutorial misconduct at the first trial.

Grand Jury Procedures

United States v. Mechanik, decided by an 8-1 vote, Feb. 25, 1986. Rehnquist wrote the opinion; Marshall dissented.

Violations of the federal rules governing the conduct of grand jury proceedings may always be considered harmless if the person indicted as a result of the flawed proceedings is eventually convicted on the charges brought by the grand jury.

Husband-Wife Testimony

United States v. Koecher, dismissed as moot, Feb. 25, 1986.

After the man and wife involved in this case — which tested the scope of the privilege protecting one spouse from being forced to testify against the other — were returned to Czechoslovakia as part of a "spy swap" in early 1986, the court dismissed this case as moot — at the government's request.

Misjoinder

United States v. Lane, Lane v. United States, decided by votes of 9-0 and 7-2, Jan. 27, 1986. Burger wrote the opinion; Stevens and Marshall dissented.

Misjoinder of criminal defendants, the holding of one trial on two sets of charges that should have been tried separately, does not always require a new trial. A new trial is required when the misjoinder actually prejudiced the defendants' case.

Guns

McLaughlin v. United States, decided by a 9-0 vote, April 29, 1986. Stevens wrote the opinion.

An unloaded gun is a "dangerous weapon" within the meaning of the federal law providing a more severe penalty for a person who uses a dangerous weapon to threaten or attack another person during a bank robbery.

McMillan v. Pennsylvania, decided by a 5-4 vote, June 19, 1986. Rehnquist wrote the opinion; Marshall, Brennan, Blackmun and Stevens dissented.

A state may provide mandatory sentences for persons convicted of committing a crime while carrying a gun — without requiring that possession of the gun be proved beyond a reasonable doubt.

Department of the Treasury v. Galioto, decided by a 9-0 vote, June 27, 1986. Burger wrote the opinion.

The court held moot a constitutional challenge to portions of federal firearms statutes that provided a way for certain felons, but not former mental patients, to win exemption from the ban on ownership of firearms. New regulations afforded both groups the same opportunity to win exemption.

Equal Protection

Vasquez v. Hillery, decided by a 6-3 vote, Jan. 14, 1986. Marshall wrote the opinion; Powell, Burger and Rehnquist dissented.

Anyone indicted by a grand jury selected in racially discriminatory fashion has the right to a new trial, regardless of how long ago the indictment occurred. "Intentional discrimination in the selection of grand jurors is a grave constitutional trespass ... wholly within the power of the state to prevent." Such discrimination "undermines the structural integrity of the criminal tribunal itself."

Batson v. Kentucky, decided by a 7-2 vote, April 30, 1986. Powell wrote the opinion; Burger and Rehnquist dissented.

It is unconstitutional for prosecutors or other attorneys to use peremptory challenges to exclude black citizens from serving on a jury because they assume that black jurors will not fairly consider the state's case against a black defendant.

Swain v. Alabama (1965) is overruled to the extent that it required evidence of a pattern or practice of excluding blacks from jury service through the use of peremptory challenges before that particular practice in a single case could successfully be challenged. "To dictate that 'several must suffer discrimination' before one could object ... would be inconsistent with the promise of equal protection to all," the court said.

INDIVIDUAL, CIVIL RIGHTS

Abortion

Diamond v. Charles, dismissed by a 9-0 vote, April 30, 1986. Blackmun wrote the opinion.

Six months after hearing arguments on this case involving an Illinois law regulating abortion, the court dismissed it, holding that the individual physician/parent asking the court to reinstate the law lacked standing to make such a request since the state itself had not appealed a lower court ruling invalidating the statute.

Thornburgh v. American College of Obstetricians and Gynecologists, decided by a 5-4 vote, June 11, 1986. Blackmun wrote the opinion; White, Rehnquist, O'Connor and Burger dissented.

The court reaffirmed its landmark 1973 ruling legalizing abortion as it struck down a Pennsylvania law which, sponsors admitted, was designed to discourage women from choosing abortions.

Among the challenged provisions invalidated by the court were those setting out specific methods to be used to ensure that a woman gave her "informed consent" to an abortion, requiring physicians to report certain information to the state concerning the abortion, and requiring a physician who performed an abortion after the point at which the fetus might survive outside the womb to take special care to preserve the life of the fetus and to have a second physician present.

Affirmative Action

Wygant v. Jackson Board of Education, decided by a 5-4 vote, May 19, 1986. Powell announced the court's decision in an opinion joined by three other justices, Burger, Rehnquist and O'Connor; O'Connor and White concurred; Brennan, Marshall, Stevens and Blackmun dissented.

An affirmative action plan adopted voluntarily by the school board of Jackson, Mich., under which white teachers with greater seniority were laid off when necessary to preserve the jobs of newly hired black teachers, is unconstitutional. This plan denies white teachers their right to equal protection of the law.

The primary flaw that the court found was that the affirmative action plan had been adopted without any showing that the school board had previously discriminated against black teachers. Justice O'Connor wrote separately to emphasize that the court agreed that affirmative action, carefully used, was an appropriate remedy for past or present discrimination by a public employer.

Local #28 of the Sheet Metal Workers' International v. Equal Employment Opportunity Commission, decided by a 5-4 vote, July 2, 1986. Brennan wrote the opinion; White, Burger, Rehnquist and O'Connor dissented.

Court-ordered minority quotas for union admission do not violate Title VII of the 1964 Civil Rights Act, which bans discrimination in employment based on race, sex, religion or national origin. The court upheld a federal court order requiring a union that had persistently refused to admit blacks to increase its non-white membership to 29.23 percent by August 1987.

Local #93, International Association of Firefighters v. City of Cleveland and Cleveland Vanguards, decided by a 6-3 vote, July 2, 1986. Brennan wrote the opinion; White, Burger and Rehnquist dissented.

Race-based job promotions do not violate Title VII of the 1964 Civil Rights Act when they are part of a consent decree settling a job bias case against a city, and when the promotion plan is for a limited period of time.

Attorneys' Fees

Evans v. Jeff D., decided by a 6-3 vote, April 21, 1986. Stevens wrote the opinion; Brennan, Marshall and Blackmun dissented.

The Civil Rights Attorney's Fee Act of 1976 does not prohibit plaintiffs in a civil rights case from waiving their right to a court order directing the defendants to pay their attorney's fees, when that waiver is part of a settlement ending the case.

City of Riverside v. Rivera, decided by a 5-4 vote, June 27, 1986. Brennan wrote the opinion; Rehnquist, Burger, White and O'Connor dissented.

Court-awarded attorneys' fees may be reasonable even if they exceed the damages won by the attorneys for their clients. To rule that such awards can never exceed damages won would "seriously undermine" the purpose of the Civil Rights Attorney's Fee Act of 1976, the court held.

Library of Congress v. Shaw, decided by a 6-3 vote, July 1, 1986. Blackmun wrote the opinion; Brennan, Marshall and Stevens dissented.

Sovereign immunity bars an award of interest to an attorney who wins a fee award against the federal government under the 1964 Civil Rights Act — even if the interest is intended to compensate him for the delay in payment.

Damage Suits

Cleavinger v. Saxner, decided by a 6-3 vote, Dec. 10, 1985. Blackmun wrote the opinion; Rehnquist, Burger and White dissented.

Members of a federal prison disciplinary committee are not entitled to absolute immunity from civil rights damage suits by prisoners who argue that their rights were violated by unjustified prison discipline.

Davidson v. Cannon, decided by a 6-3 vote, Jan. 21, 1986. Rehnquist wrote the opinion; Brennan, Marshall and Blackmun dissented.

Daniels v. Williams, decided by a 9-0 vote, Jan. 21, 1986. Rehnquist wrote the opinion.

Negligence by prison officials, even if it results in injury to inmates, does not provide a basis for a constitutional claim upon which inmates can build a civil rights damage suit against the officials. "Lack of due care simply does not approach the sort of abusive government conduct that the due process clause was designed to prevent," the court said, partly overturning its 1981 decision in *Parratt v. Taylor,* which had been interpreted by some to permit such suits.

Malley v. Briggs, decided by a 9-0 vote, March 5, 1986. White wrote the opinion.

Police officers can be sued for damages by persons they arrest with a warrant if the warrant was issued without probable cause.

The police officer cannot shield himself by arguing that the magistrate who issued the warrant is absolutely immune from such a suit.

Pembaur v. City of Cincinnati, decided by a 6-3 vote, March 25, 1986. Brennan wrote the opinion; Powell, Burger and Rehnquist dissented.

A municipal government may be held liable for decisions that a policy-making government official made concerning conduct of city employees in a single incident.

Memphis Community School District v. Stachura, decided by a 9-0 vote, June 25, 1986. Powell wrote the opinion.

Damages awarded in a civil rights damage suit cannot include compensatory damages based on the abstract value or importance of the constitutional or civil rights violated; such awards should be based primarily on the actual injury suffered as a result of the rights violation.

Due Process

United States v. Von Neumann, decided by a 9-0 vote, Jan. 14, 1986. Brennan wrote the opinion.

There is no constitutional right to speedy disposition of petitions by persons who seek to regain property seized by customs agents.

Paulussen v. Herion, dismissed March 25, 1986.

The court dismissed this case concerning Pennsylvania's six-year statute of limitations on paternity actions, noting that the contested law had been repealed.

Aetna Life Insurance Co. v. Lavoie, decided by an 8-0 vote, April 22, 1986. Burger wrote the opinion; Stevens did not participate.

The insurance company's right to due process was denied by the participation, in a case charging it with bad-faith refusal to pay a claim, of a judge who had himself filed similar charges against other insurance companies — cases that could be affected by his decision in this case.

Bowen v. Owens, decided by a 6-3 vote, May 19, 1986. Powell wrote the opinion; Brennan, Marshall and Blackmun dissented.

Divorced, widowed spouses of wage earners were not denied their rights to equal protection and due process by a provision of the Social Security Act in effect from 1979 until 1983 that permitted payment of survivor's benefits to widowed spouses of wage earners who remarried after the age of 60, but not to divorced widowed spouses who remarried after that age. It was rational for Congress to conclude that widows and widowers were more likely to have been dependent upon their spouses for support than divorced widowed spouses.

Lyng v. Payne, decided by an 8-1 vote, June 17, 1986. O'Connor wrote the opinion; Stevens dissented.

The Farmers Home Administration need not reopen a disaster loan program to aid farmers in Florida whose crops were lost as a result of torrential rains in 1973, even though lower courts found that the agency failed to comply with its own rules by not publicizing the fact that Congress had extended the deadline for applications.

Lyng v. Castillo, decided by a 6-3 vote, June 27, 1986. Stevens wrote the opinion; Brennan, White and Marshall dissented.

Congress did not violate the equal protection guarantee when it wrote into the Food Stamp Act a requirement that all groups of related persons living in a single dwelling be treated as a single "household" for purposes of determining their allotment of food stamps.

Discrimination Against Handicapped

Bowen v. American Hospital Association, decided by a 5-3 vote, June 9, 1986. Stevens wrote the opinion; Brennan, O'Connor and White dissented. Rehnquist did not take part in the decision.

The federal ban on discrimination against handicapped persons by programs receiving federal aid does not authorize the Department of Health and Human Services to force hospitals to provide aggressive medical treatment for severely handicapped infants over their parents' objections. This ruling struck down "Baby Doe" regulations requiring such treatment. The regulations had been promulgated under Section 504 of the Rehabilitation Act of 1973.

Department of Transportation v. Paralyzed Veterans of America, decided by a 6-3 vote, June 27, 1986. Powell wrote the opinion; Brennan, Marshall and Blackmun dissented.

Section 504 of the Rehabilitation Act of 1973, which bans discrimination against the handicapped in "any program or activity" receiving federal funds, generally does not apply to commercial airlines.

Federal aid to airports and to the air traffic control system does not bring commercial airlines within the reach of Section 504.

Other regulations require air carriers to provide safe and adequate service to all passengers and prohibit unjust discrimination.

Illegitimate Children

Reed v. Campbell, decided by a 9-0 vote, June 11, 1986. Stevens wrote the opinion.

The court's 1977 decision in *Trimble v. Gordon* that states may not by law deny illegitimate children the right to inherit from their fathers applies to an illegitimate child whose father died before that decision but whose claim was filed after that ruling.

Employment Discrimination

Bazemore v. Friday, United States v. Friday, decided by votes of 9-0 and 5-4, July 1, 1986. *Per curiam* (unsigned) opinion; Burger, Powell, Rehnquist and O'Connor dissented in part.

Employers must eliminate any disparity in wage scales between black and white workers holding similar jobs, even if the difference stems from a system in place before federal laws barring job bias took effect.

"Each week's paycheck that delivers less to a black than to a similarly situated white is a wrong actionable under Title VII, regardless of the fact that this pattern was begun prior to the effective date of Title VII," declared the court in a case involving the North Carolina Agricultural Extension Service.

The court was divided over a challenge of continuing discrimination in the operation of 4-H and Homemaker clubs, ruling that the state had no further duty to try to integrate those formerly segregated clubs.

Privacy and Sodomy Laws

Bowers v. Hardwick, decided by a 5-4 vote, June 30, 1986. White wrote the opinion; Blackmun, Brennan, Marshall and Stevens dissented.

The constitutional guarantee of personal liberty and privacy does not protect private homosexual conduct between consenting adults.

The court upheld against constitutional challenge Georgia's anti-sodomy law, which banned oral or anal sex.

Residency Requirements

Attorney General of New York v. Soto-Lopez, decided by a 6-3 vote, June 17, 1986. Brennan wrote the opinion; Stevens, O'Connor and Rehnquist dissented.

New York violates the constitutional guarantee of equal protection by giving bonus points to civil service exam scores of war veterans who lived in the state at the time they entered the military.

By denying bonus points to veterans who moved to New York after their military service, the law discriminated against newer residents, denying them equal protection.

Sex Discrimination

Meritor Savings Bank v. Vinson, decided by a 9-0 vote, June 19, 1986. Rehnquist wrote the opinion.

In its first ruling on the issue, the court held that sexual harassment in the work place is sex discrimination barred by Title VII of the 1964 Civil Rights Act. Such harassment is illegal not only when it results in the loss of a job or a promotion, but also when it creates an offensive or hostile working environment.

State Suits

University of Tennessee v. Elliott, decided by votes of 8-0 and 5-3. White wrote the opinion; Stevens, Brennan and Blackmun dissented; Marshall did not participate in the case.

Federal courts must defer to state agency decisions on disputed issues of fact in federal court cases brought under century-old civil rights laws, but not in cases brought under Title VII of the 1964 Civil Rights Act.

Voting Rights

Davis v. Bandemer, decided by votes of 6-3 and 7-2, June 30, 1986. White wrote the opinion; O'Connor, Burger and Rehnquist dissented in part; Powell and Stevens dissented in part.

Political gerrymanders are subject to constitutional challenge and review by federal courts, even if the disputed districts meet the "one person, one vote" test, the court held 6-3.

By 7-2, however, the justices upheld a 1981 Indiana reapportionment plan that heavily favored the Republican Party — saying that more than one election's results are necessary to prove a gerrymander unconstitutional.

Thornburg v. Gingles, decided by votes of 9-0 and 6-3, June 30, 1986. Brennan wrote the opinion; Stevens, Blackmun and Marshall dissented in part.

The court agreed with a lower court that six of North Carolina's multi-member legislative districts impermissibly diluted the strength of black votes in violation of the Voting Rights Act.

This was the first time that the court applied 1982 amendments to the Voting Rights Act (PL 97-205) that required courts to look at the results of a challenged practice, not just its intent, in deciding whether it was discriminatory. *(1982 Almanac p. 373)*

Those amendments were adopted to reverse a 1980 Supreme Court decision, *Mobile v. Bolden,* that required proof of discriminatory intent before a violation of the Voting Rights Act could be found. *(1980 Almanac p. 9-A)*

The court rejected the argument that once one or more black candidates have been elected from a challenged district, the district is immune from challenge under the Voting Rights Act.

FIRST AMENDMENT

Church and State

Witters v. Washington Department of Services for the Blind, decided by a 9-0 vote, Jan. 27, 1986. Marshall wrote the opinion.

It does not violate the First Amendment's ban on government establishment of religion for a state to grant vocational rehabilitation aid to a blind man studying to become a minister. "The Establishment Clause is not violated every time money previously in the possession of a state is conveyed to a religious institution," the court held, particularly since this aid would be paid directly to the student and would then flow to a religious college "only as a result of the genuinely independent and private choice of [the] aid recipient."

Bender v. Williamsport Area School District, decided by a 5-4 vote, March 25, 1986. Stevens wrote the opinion; Burger, Rehnquist, White and Powell dissented.

An individual school board member and parent lacks standing to pursue an appeal that the full board has declined to pursue. In this case, the appeal was from a court decision permitting a high school student religious group to meet during the school day on school grounds. The school officials denied the group permission to meet because they were concerned that such a meeting would violate the Establishment Clause; the district court reversed the officials' decision.

Goldman v. Weinberger, decided by a 5-4 vote, March 25, 1986. Rehnquist wrote the opinion; Brennan, Marshall, Blackmun and O'Connor dissented.

The First Amendment guarantee of freedom of religion does not require the Air Force to permit an officer who is also an Orthodox Jewish rabbi to wear his yarmulke, or skullcap, indoors while in uniform and on duty.

Bowen v. Roy, decided by an 8-1 vote, June 11, 1986. Burger wrote the opinion; White dissented.

Freedom of religion is not violated by a requirement that citizens applying for food stamps report Social Security numbers for all members of their family, even if obtaining and using a Social Security number for a child is against the religious beliefs of the parents.

Freedom of Speech

Pacific Gas & Electric Co. v. Public Utilities Commission, decided by a 5-3 vote, Feb. 25, 1986. Powell wrote the opinion; Rehnquist, White and Stevens dissented; Blackmun did not participate in the decision.

Corporations may not be forced to spread the message of groups with which they disagree. The court nullified an order of the California Public Utilities Commission requiring Pacific Gas & Electric Co., a privately owned utility, to include printed inserts from a consumer group in its billing envelopes four times a year.

"For corporations as for individuals, the choice to speak includes within it the choice of what not to say," the court declared.

City of Los Angeles v. Preferred Communications Inc., decided by a 9-0 vote, June 2, 1986. Rehnquist wrote the opinion.

Cable television operators have some First Amendment rights that are implicated in a city's decision to limit cable franchises.

The court left for another case a decision defining the extent to which a city might limit the access of cable operators.

Posadas de Puerto Rico Associates v. Tourism Council of Puerto Rico, decided by a 5-4 vote, July 1, 1986. Rehnquist wrote the opinion; Brennan, Stevens, Blackmun and Marshall dissented.

The First Amendment does not preclude a state from prohibiting advertising of some activities, such as gambling, even though they are legal in that state.

Bethel School District No. 403 v. Fraser, decided by a 7-2 vote, July 7, 1986. Burger wrote the opinion; Marshall and Stevens dissented.

High school officials do not violate the First Amendment by suspending a student for a lewd speech at a school assembly.

"It is a highly appropriate function of public school education to prohibit the use of vulgar and offensive terms in public discourse," the court declared.

Arcara v. Cloud Books, decided by a 6-3 vote, July 7, 1986. Burger wrote the opinion; Brennan, Marshall and Blackmun dissented.

The First Amendment does not prohibit a state from closing a bookstore as a public nuisance after an investigation reveals that the bookstore is being used as a place of prostitution and other lewd conduct.

Freedom of Press

Philadelphia Newspapers, Inc. v. Hepps, decided by a 5-4 vote, April 21, 1986. O'Connor wrote the opinion; Stevens, Burger, Rehnquist and White dissented.

Private persons who sue for libel must prove the falsity of the challenged report as well as fault on the part of the media before they can recover damages. The court applied this standard to cases in which the alleged libel involves some issue of public concern.

The court held invalid a Pennysylvania law that required the media defendant in such a case to prove the truth of the contested report in order to avoid a damage award.

At least eight other states had such laws.

Anderson v. Liberty Lobby Inc., decided by a 6-3 vote, June 25, 1986. White wrote the opinion; Brennan, Rehnquist and Burger dissented.

Judges should summarily dismiss libel charges brought by a public figure unless they find "clear and convincing evidence" of actual malice in the challenged report, the same standard of proof that a plaintiff must meet to prevail at trial.

Press-Enterprise Co. v. Superior Court, decided by a 7-2 vote, June 30, 1986. Burger wrote the opinion; Rehnquist and Stevens dissented.

The First Amendment guarantees that pretrial criminal proceedings be open to the public unless they must be closed to preserve some higher value, and unless closure is narrowly tailored to serve that interest.

BUSINESS LAW

Antitrust

Fisher v. City of Berkeley, Calif., decided by an 8-1 vote, Feb. 26, 1986. Marshall wrote the opinion; Brennan dissented.

Federal antitrust law forbidding price-fixing conspiracies does not prevent cities from adopting and enforcing rent-control ordinances. Such laws are unilaterally imposed by the city and thus do not represent the sort of concerted action that the antitrust laws were written to prevent.

Matsushita Electric Industrial Co. Ltd. v. Zenith Radio Corp., decided by a 5-4 vote, March 26, 1986. Powell wrote the opinion; White, Brennan, Blackmun and Stevens dissented.

Zenith Radio failed to present sufficient evidence to justify a trial on its claim that Japanese television manufacturers conspired to sell television sets at particularly low prices in order to push U.S. manufacturers out of the market. Therefore, the federal district court was correct in dismissing the suit, a decision the appeals court was wrong to overturn.

This decision moved this long-running antitrust case, first filed in 1970, closer to a conclusion. The court sent the case back to the appeals court, pointing out that it was free to consider whether Zenith had any additional evidence to present.

Square D Co. v. Niagara Frontier Tariff Bureau, decided by an 8-1 vote, May 27, 1986. Stevens wrote the opinion; Marshall dissented.

Under *Keogh v. Chicago & Northwestern Railway Co.* (1922), private parties may not sue regulated truckers for treble damages, arguing that the truckers' rates, filed with the Interstate Commerce Commission, are in fact illegal price fixing in violation of antitrust laws. By virtue of ICC approval, these rates are legal and cannot be used as the basis for such a suit.

Federal Trade Commission v. Indiana Federation of Dentists, decided by a 9-0 vote, June 2, 1986. White wrote the opinion.

Dentists may not escape the reach of federal antitrust laws by arguing that their coordinated decision to refuse to supply insurance companies with patients' X-rays was necessary to preserve the moral and ethical standards of their profession.

Banking

Board of Governors of the Federal Reserve System v. Dimension Financial Corp., decided by a 9-0 vote, Jan. 22, 1986. Burger wrote the opinion.

The Board of Governors exceeded its authority to administer the Bank Holding Company Act of 1956 when it redefined key terms in that law — "demand deposits" and "commercial loans" — in an effort to bring limited-service banks within the scope of federal regulation. These "nonbank banks" either make commercial loans *or* accept demand deposits, but not both.

Federal Deposit Insurance Corp. v. Philadelphia Gear Corp., decided by a 6-3 vote, May 27, 1986. O'Connor wrote the opinion; Blackmun, Marshall and Rehnquist dissented.

Standby letters of credit are not federally insured bank deposits. Such letters of credit are simply not the sort of assets that Congress intended to protect by setting up a federal deposit insurance plan.

Liability

Eastern Air Lines Inc. v. Mahfoud, affirmed by an equally divided court, 4-4, Dec. 10, 1985. Brennan did not participate in the case.

After two rounds of argument, the court left intact a lower court ruling permitting awards of both pre- and post-judgment interest in wrongful-death lawsuits brought under the Warsaw Treaty, which governs suits growing out of international airplane crashes.

East River Steamship Corp. v. Transamerica Delaval Inc., decided by a 9-0 vote, June 16, 1986. Blackmun wrote the opinion.

Product liability claims based on negligence and theories of strict liability may be decided under general maritime law. But in a case that causes injury only to the product, not to any other property or individual, the manufacturer is not liable; economic losses by a commercial product user can only be recovered under contract law.

Property Rights

MacDonald, Sommer & Frates v. Yolo County, decided by a 5-4 vote, June 25, 1986. Stevens wrote the opinion; White, Powell, Rehnquist and Burger dissented.

For the fourth time in five years, the court sidestepped a decision on whether property owners may win compensation when local governments diminish the potential value of their property by restricting the uses to which it may be devoted. In a case from California, the court upheld a state court ruling denying developers such compensation.

Regulation

Louisiana Public Service Commission v. Federal Communications Commission, decided by a 5-2 vote, May 27, 1986. Brennan wrote the opinion; Burger and Blackmun dissented; Powell and O'Connor did not participate.

Congress, in passing the Communications Act of 1934, specifically forbade the FCC to interfere in setting intrastate telephone rates. The FCC's 1983 order requiring local telephone companies to accelerate their depreciation of plant equipment is therefore invalid, pre-empting a decision that Congress intended to be left to the states.

Public Service Commission of Maryland v. Chesapeake and Potomac Telephone Company of Maryland, vacated by a 7-0 vote, May 27, 1986. *Per curiam* (unsigned) opinion; Powell and O'Connor did not take part in the decision.

The court sent back to the U.S. Court of Appeals for the 4th Circuit a related case in which that court had required Maryland utility regulators to use the FCC's new depreciation method. The court directed the appeals court to take a second look at this case in light of the ruling in *Louisiana Public Service Commission v. FCC* (above).

Young v. Community Nutrition Institute, decided by an 8-1 vote, June 17, 1986. O'Connor wrote the opinion; Stevens dissented.

The Food and Drug Administration is within its authority in using informal, rather than formal, methods to regulate the level in foods of aflatoxin, a cancer-causing mold that grows naturally on crops such as corn.

Securities

Randall v. Loftsgaarden, decided by an 8-1 vote, July 2, 1986. O'Connor wrote the opinion; Brennan dissented.

An investor who sues for damages after he has been defrauded by a tax shelter promotion does not face having his damages reduced by the amount of tax-shelter benefits he enjoyed.

Commodity Futures Trading Commission v. Schor, decided by a 7-2 vote, July 7, 1986. O'Connor wrote the opinion; Brennan and Marshall dissented.

The Commodity Futures Trading Commission has the authority to decide counterclaims based on state law when those counterclaims arise in the course of resolving complaints based on charges that federal commodities trading laws have been violated.

Taxation

United States v. American College of Physicians, decided by a 9-0 vote, April 22, 1986. Marshall wrote the opinion.

A tax-exempt organization that realizes a profit on the advertising it sells in its journal must pay federal income tax on that profit unless it can show that its solicitation and coordination of the advertising is substantially related to the organization's primary reason for being.

Sorenson v. Secretary of the Treasury, decided by an 8-1 vote, April 22, 1986. Blackmun wrote the opinion; Stevens dissented.

Congress intended, under a provision included in the Omnibus Budget Reconciliation Act of 1981 (PL 97-35), to permit the Treasury to intercept tax refunds owed to persons who have failed to meet their child-support obligations, including refunds resulting from excess earned-income credits.

United States v. Hughes Properties, decided by 7-2 vote, June 3, 1986. Blackmun wrote the opinion; Stevens and Burger dissented.

A gambling casino using the accrual method of tax accounting may deduct the amount shown on its progressive slot machines jackpot indicators at the close of a taxable year as an ordinary business expense incurred during that taxable year.

United States v. Hemme, decided by a 9-0 vote, June 3, 1986. Marshall wrote the opinion.

Changes in federal estate taxes enacted in October 1978 apply retroactively to transactions during the previous month.

United States v. American Bar Endowment, decided by a 6-1 vote, June 23, 1986. Marshall wrote the opinion; Stevens dissented; Powell and O'Connor did not participate.

Tax-exempt organizations must pay federal taxes on the profits earned from selling group insurance to their members; no portion of the premium paid for such insurance may be claimed as a charitable contribution.

LABOR LAW

National Labor Relations Board v. Financial Institution Employees of America, Local 1182, decided by a 9-0 vote, Feb. 26, 1986. Brennan wrote the opinion.

An NLRB rule requiring non-union employees to be permitted to take part in elections to decide whether a local union would affiliate with an international union is irrational. Unless the board has reason to believe that the affiliation would change the union into a different entity, the NLRB should not interfere in this matter, but should consider it an internal union affair.

Chicago Teachers Union Local #1 v. Hudson, decided by a 9-0 vote, March 4, 1986. Stevens wrote the opinion.

Public employee unions must take special care and set up clear procedures to ensure that non-members who pay representation fees are not being forced to contribute to support "ideological" activities of the union with which they disagree.

The First Amendment protects non-union members from being forced to fund such activities.

Unions that collect representation fees from non-members must provide an adequate explanation of the size of the fee, a "reasonably prompt opportunity" to challenge the amount before a neutral decision-maker, and must see that the disputed amount is placed in escrow pending a decision.

AT&T Technologies v. Communication Workers of America, decided by a 9-0 vote, April 7, 1986. White wrote the opinion.

Whether a contractual arbitration agreement obligates parties to arbitrate a particular dispute is an issue for courts to decide, not to pass on to the arbitrator.

Equal Employment Opportunity Commission v. Federal Labor Relations Authority, dismissed by a vote of 7-2, April 29, 1986. *Per curiam* (unsigned) opinion; White and Stevens dissented.

The court dismissed, after argument, a case concerning the negotiability of a union proposal requiring a federal agency to comply with federal guidelines for contracting-out work.

Brock v. Pierce County, decided by a 9-0 vote, May 19, 1986. Marshall wrote the opinion.

Under the Comprehensive Employment and Training Act, the secretary of labor could move to recover misspent funds from grant recipients — even if he did not meet the law's 120-day deadline for resolving charges that funds had been misused.

Connolly v. Pension Benefit Guaranty Corp., decided by a 9-0 vote, May 26, 1986. White wrote the opinion.

Provisions of the Multi-employer Pension Plan Amendments of 1980 (PL 96-364) that require employers who withdraw from such plans to pay a share of the cost of future benefits to be paid under the plan do not violate the Constitution's ban on the taking of private property for public use without just compensation.

"In the course of regulating commercial and other human affairs, Congress routinely creates burdens for some that directly benefit others," the court observed. "Given the propriety of the governmental power to regulate, it cannot be said that the Taking Clause is violated whenever legislation requires one person to use his or her assets for the benefit of another."

International Longshoremen's Association, AFL-CIO v. Davis, decided by votes of 8-1 and 5-4, May 27, 1986. White wrote the opinion; Rehnquist, Powell, Stevens and O'Connor dissented in part; Blackmun dissented in part.

The court with only one dissenting vote upheld a jury award against the International Longshoremen's Association to a man who lost his job because he tried to organize an affiliate of the union. He sued the union for failing to make good on its pledge to get his job back. The National Labor Relations Board's regional office rejected his unfair labor practice claim, holding that he was a supervisor, not an employee; at that point he successfully sued the union in state court for misrepresentation. The court upheld the award because the union had failed to show that this case was subject to federal labor law.

The court also held, 5-4, that the union was entitled to resolution of its belated claim that state court jurisdiction over this case was pre-empted by federal labor law.
Feb. 26, 1986. Brennan wrote the opinion.

Offshore Logistics Inc. v. Tallentire, decided by votes of 9-0 and 5-4, June 23, 1986. O'Connor wrote the opinion; Powell, Brennan, Marshall and Stevens dissented in part.

A state tort law may not be applied to an accident that occurs on the high seas. The federal Death on the High Seas Act pre-empts application of state tort law beyond the state's territorial waters.

International Union, United Automobile, Aerospace and Agricultural Implement Workers of America v. Brock, decided by a 5-4 vote, June 25, 1986. Marshall wrote the opinion; White, Burger, Powell and Rehnquist dissented.

A labor union has standing to sue the government in a dispute over trade readjustment benefits allegedly due some of its members. Associations are permitted to bring such cases on behalf of aggrieved members, as an alternative to class action suits.

ENVIRONMENT

United States v. Riverside Bayview Homes, Inc., decided by a 9-0 vote, Dec. 4, 1985. White wrote the opinion.

The court approved the government's broad definition of "wetlands" protected by the Clean Water Act against development without the approval of the Army Corps of Engineers. Under the approved definition, "wetlands" need not be frequently flooded but need only be sufficiently saturated by surface or groundwater to support vegetation typical of swamps, marshes and bogs.

Midlantic National Bank v. New Jersey Department of Environmental Protection, O'Neill v. City of New York, decided by a 5-4 vote, Jan. 27, 1986. Powell wrote the opinion; Rehnquist, Burger, White and O'Connor dissented.

The trustee of a bankrupt company whose property includes sites contaminated with toxic waste may not simply abandon those sites, forcing the state to clean them up.

The fact that federal bankruptcy law permits a trustee to abandon burdensome property does not permit abandonment of sites that create a major threat to public health. This provision of federal law does not pre-empt state environmental laws.

Exxon Corp. v. Hunt, decided by a 7-1 vote, March 10, 1986. Marshall wrote the opinion; Stevens dissented; Powell did not participate.

The federal "superfund" law, the Comprehensive Environmental Response, Compensation and Liability Act (PL 96-510), pre-empts states' power to levy their own taxes against oil and chemical companies to fund cleanups of abandoned hazardous-waste dumps. States are free under the law to impose such taxes for other purposes, such as victim compensation and other costs not covered by the federal law.

Japan Whaling Association v. American Cetacean Society, Baldrige v. American Cetacean Society, decided by a 5-4 vote, June 30, 1986. White wrote the opinion; Marshall, Brennan, Blackmun and Rehnquist dissented.

Neither the Pelly Amendment to the 1967 Fisherman's Protective Act, nor the Packwood Amendment to the Magnuson Fishery Conservation and Management Act requires the secretary of commerce to certify Japan for refusing to abide by whale harvest quotas established by international commission — and thereby to impose economic sanctions on Japan — so long as Japan complies with an executive agreement providing for an end of all commercial whaling by 1988.

Pennsylvania v. Delaware Valley Citizens' Council, decided by votes of 6-3 and 9-0, July 2, 1986. White wrote the opinion; Brennan, Marshall and Blackmun dissented in part.

The Clean Air Act authorizes awards of attorneys' fees for work before administrative agencies as well as before courts. It is not appropriate for courts to award higher-than-usual fees based on the court's view of the quality of the legal work involved.

The court agreed to hear reargument in the October 1986 term on a related question — whether a higher-than-usual fee can be awarded because of the risk of losing in the particular case.

ENERGY

Transcontinental Gas Pipe Line Corp. v. State Oil and Gas Board of Mississippi, decided by a 5-4 vote, Jan. 22, 1986. Blackmun wrote the opinion; Rehnquist, Powell, Stevens and O'Connor dissented.

In deregulating the price of natural gas through the Natural Gas Policy Act of 1978, Congress did not intend to allow states to require interstate gas pipeline companies to buy gas from all owners of a common gas pool. Such "ratable taking" laws are still pre-empted by federal law.

United States v. City of Fulton, decided by a 9-0 vote, April 7, 1986. Marshall wrote the opinion.

The secretary of energy has the power to impose interim rate increases for electricity generated by federal hydroelectric projects, subject to eventual approval by the Federal Energy Regulatory Commission.

Nantahala Power & Light Co. v. Thornburg, decided by a 7-0 vote, June 17, 1986. O'Connor wrote the opinion; Powell and Stevens did not participate.

North Carolina lacks authority to order a utility to sell power to in-state customers at rates lower than recommended by the Federal Energy Regulatory Commission.

SOCIAL SECURITY

Bowen v. City of New York, decided by a 9-0 vote, June 2, 1986. Powell wrote the opinion.

A class of persons with severe mental disabilities challenging the now-discarded policy of the Department of Health and Human Services under which they were denied Social Security disability benefits may pursue their case in federal court despite the fact that they have not exhausted all the other avenues of protest available to them.

Bowen v. Michigan Academy of Family Physicians, decided by an 8-0 vote, June 9, 1986. Stevens wrote the opinion; Rehnquist did not participate in the decision.

Congress did not intend to bar judicial review of regulations under the Medicare program authorizing differing payment levels for similar physicians' services.

Bowen v. Public Agencies Opposed to Social Security Entrapment, decided by a 9-0 vote, June 19, 1986. Powell wrote the opinion.

Congress acted within its constitutional powers when it told state and local governments they could no longer withdraw their employees from the Social Security System. Congress terminated this withdrawal option as part of its 1983 overhaul (PL 98-21) of Social Security. That termination had been challenged as an unconstitutional taking of a state's property — its right to withdraw — without just compensation. *(1983 Almanac p. 219)*

Atkins v. Rivera, decided by a 9-0 vote, June 23, 1986. Blackmun wrote the opinion.

Under federal Medicaid regulations, states may use a six-month, rather than one-month, base period for determining the Medicaid eligibility of persons who may qualify not because of low income but because of high medical bills.

STATE POWERS

Pre-emption

Wisconsin Department of Industry v. Gould, Inc., decided by a 9-0 vote, Feb. 26, 1986. Blackmun wrote the opinion.

Enforcing the National Labor Relations Act (NLRA) is a federal responsibility that states may not share. A Wisconsin law barring the state from purchasing products from persons and firms found to have violated that federal law at least three times in five years is invalid, pre-empted by the NLRA.

Golden State Transit Corp. v. City of Los Angeles, decided by an 8-1 vote, April 1, 1986. Blackmun wrote the opinion; Rehnquist dissented.

The National Labor Relations Act forbids states and cities to intervene in private labor disputes. Los Angeles acted improperly when it conditioned renewal of a taxicab company's franchise upon its settlement of a drivers' strike.

Baker v. General Motors Corp., decided by a 6-3 vote,

July 2, 1986. Stevens wrote the opinion; Brennan, Marshall and Blackmun dissented.

National Labor Relations Act does not pre-empt state laws denying unemployment compensation to striking workers who contribute to a strike fund that finances their unemployment.

11th Amendment

Papasan v. Mississippi, decided by votes of 6-3 and 5-4, July 1, 1986. White wrote the opinion; Burger, Powell and Rehnquist dissented in part, Brennan, Marshall, Blackmun and Stevens dissented in part.

The 11th Amendment, which protects states from being sued without their consent in federal court, bars a federal court from hearing a suit by Mississippi counties charging the state with mismanaging federal land grant funds earmarked for aid to public schools. The court's vote on this point was 5-4.

But the 11th Amendment does not bar a federal court suit by those counties when they charge that the mismanagement of funds resulted in a denial of equal protection. The vote on this point was 6-3.

Regulation

Brown-Forman Distillers Corp. v. New York State Liquor Authority, decided by a 5-3 vote, June 3, 1986. Marshall wrote the opinion; Stevens, White and Rehnquist dissented. Brennan did not participate in the decision.

A state may not require distillers to give in-state wholesalers the same discounts given in any other state during a particular month, because that requirement effectively creates a national uniform pricing law and unconstitutionally restricts interstate commerce.

A state may seek lower prices for its residents, but it cannot insist that residents of other states surrender any competitive advantages they might have, the court held.

Maine v. Taylor, decided by an 8-1 vote, June 23, 1986. Blackmun wrote the opinion; Stevens dissented.

Maine law prohibiting importation of live baitfish discriminates on its face against interstate commerce. It is nevertheless permissible, because it serves the legitimate purpose of protecting local fish from parasites prevalent in out-of-state fish, and no less discriminatory means of protection are available.

Taxation

Wardair Canada Inc. v. Florida Department of Revenue, decided by an 8-1 vote, June 18, 1986. Brennan wrote the opinion; Blackmun dissented.

States do not violate federal law nor international agreements by requiring foreign airlines to pay state tax on all fuels purchased within those states. The court upheld a Florida law challenged by 23 foreign nations and an airline that operates charter flights between Canada and the United States.

Zoning Powers

City of Renton v. Playtime Theatres Inc., decided by a 7-2 vote, Feb. 25, 1986. Rehnquist wrote the opinion; Brennan and Marshall dissented.

A city may use its zoning power to forbid adult theaters from locating in or near residential neighborhoods. "Cities may regulate adult theaters by dispersing them ... or by effectively concentrating them," the court held. "The First Amendment requires only that Renton refrain from effectively denying respondents a reasonable opportunity to open and operate an adult theater within the city, and the ordinance before us easily meets that requirement."

Miscellaneous

Regents of the University of Michigan v. Ewing, decided by a 9-0 vote, Dec. 12, 1985. Stevens wrote the opinion.

When federal judges review a decision by college officials to expel a student from a university or medical school, they should place great weight on the academic judgment of the school officials. Judges should not override such a decision "unless it is such a substantial departure from accepted academic norms" that it calls into question the professional judgment of the person making the decision.

United States v. Maine, exception to the report of the special master overruled by an 8-0 vote, Feb. 25, 1986. Stevens wrote the opinion; Marshall did not participate.

Nantucket Sound does not constitute "internal waters" of Massachusetts; its seabeds belong to the United States. A state must establish its claim to coastline jurisdiction by evidence "clear beyond doubt."

United States v. James, decided by a 6-3 vote, July 2, 1986. Powell wrote the opinion; Stevens, Marshall and O'Connor dissented.

The Flood Control Act precludes an award of damages against the federal government for death or personal injuries resulting from the government's negligence in warning of dangers related to the release of water from dams or other flood control sites.

FEDERAL COURTS

Pennsylvania Bureau of Correction v. U.S. Marshals Service, decided by an 8-1 vote, Nov. 18, 1985. Powell wrote the opinion; Stevens dissented.

Congress has not authorized federal judges to order U.S. marshals to bring state prisoners to federal courthouses to testify.

Green v. Mansour, decided by a 5-4 vote, Dec. 3, 1985. Rehnquist wrote the opinion; Brennan, Marshall, Blackmun and Stevens dissented.

The 11th Amendment, which limits federal jurisdiction over lawsuits filed by citizens against a state, denies a federal judge the power to order a state to notify welfare recipients that they can sue the state in state court because of past mistakes in benefit calculations.

Lake Coal Co. Inc. v. Roberts & Schaefer Co., dismissed as moot, Dec. 3, 1985.

The court dismissed as moot a case concerning the proper course of action for a federal court asked to act in a case similar to one pending in state court.

Thomas v. Arn, decided by a 6-3 vote, Dec. 4, 1985. Marshall wrote the opinion; Brennan, Stevens and Blackmun dissented.

A federal appeals court acted within its power in denying defendants who failed to file timely objections to a magistrate's report on a *habeas corpus* petition the right to appeal a district judge's adoption of that report.

Parsons Steel, Inc. v. First Alabama Bank of Montgomery, N.A., decided by a 9-0 vote, Jan. 27, 1986. Rehnquist wrote the opinion.

A federal court may not enjoin a state court proceeding because it finds that the state court has incorrectly interpreted the effect of a federal court ruling.

Icicle Seafoods, Inc. v. Worthington, decided by an 8-1 vote, April 21, 1986. Rehnquist wrote the opinion; Stevens dissented.

When a federal court of appeals reviews a lower court's decision that certain workmen were "seamen" excluded from the overtime benefits provisions of the Fair Labor Standards Act, it should not engage in fact-finding on its own but should uphold the lower court's decision unless it appeared "clearly erroneous."

Schiavone v. Fortune, decided by a 6-3 vote, June 18, 1986. Blackmun wrote the opinion; Stevens, Burger and White dissented.

Federal rules of civil procedure do not allow a complaint that is filed too late, according to a statute of limitations, to be maintained anyway by relating the complaint to one filed earlier, within the time limits.

Celotex Corp. v. Catrett, decided by a 5-4 vote, June 25, 1986. Rehnquist wrote the opinion; Blackmun, Brennan, Burger and Stevens dissented.

Under federal rules of civil procedure, a defendant moving for summary judgment is not required to support that motion with evidence negating the complaint if a showing can be made that there is an absence of evidence supporting the plaintiff's complaint.

Ohio Civil Rights Commission v. Dayton Christian Schools, decided by a 9-0 vote, June 27, 1986. Rehnquist wrote the opinion.

The "abstention doctrine" set out in *Younger v. Harris* (1971) requiring federal courts to avoid intervening in state criminal proceedings except when necessary to prevent great and immediate irreparable injury applies to limit federal court intervention in state administrative proceedings under state job bias laws. A federal district judge should have abstained from ruling upon a request by a Christian school for an order halting a state proceeding on a claim of sex bias against the school, even though the request was couched in terms of injury to the school's First Amendment rights.

Merrell Dow Pharmaceuticals Inc. v. Thompson, decided by a 5-4 vote, July 7, 1986. Stevens wrote the opinion; Brennan, White, Marshall and Blackmun dissented.

A case may not be removed from state to federal court just because one element of the state court charge is that there has been a violation of a federal law for which no private right of action is provided.

INDIANS

South Carolina v. Catawba Indian Tribe of South Carolina, decided by a 6-3 vote, June 2, 1986. Stevens wrote the opinion; Blackmun, Marshall and O'Connor dissented.

State statutes of limitations limit the time within which a tribe can bring federal court action against a state seeking possession of former tribal lands and trespass damages.

United States v. Mottaz, decided by a 9-0 vote, June 11, 1986. Blackmun wrote the opinion.

The 12-year statute of limitations contained in the Quiet Title Act bars a 1981 lawsuit by an Indian, claiming that the government's 1954 sale of allotment land was void, because she knew by at least 1967 that the government did not consider her to have title to that allotment land.

United States v. Dion, decided by a 9-0 vote, June 11, 1986. Marshall wrote the opinion.

The Eagle Protection Act, which bars hunting of bald or golden eagles in the United States, divested Sioux Indians of the right to hunt those eagles, terminating rights reserved to them by an 1858 treaty.

Three Affiliated Tribes of the Fort Berthold Reservation v. Wold Engineering P.C., decided by a 6-3 vote, June 16, 1986. O'Connor wrote the opinion; Rehnquist, Burger and Stevens dissented.

Indian tribes do not have to agree to be sued in state courts in order for them to sue a non-Indian in a state court.

SEPARATION OF POWERS

Bowsher v. Synar, Senate v. Synar, O'Neill v. Synar, decided by a 7-2 vote, July 7, 1986. Burger wrote the opinion; White and Blackmun dissented.

Congress violated the constitutional separation of powers among the judicial, executive and legislative branches when it included in the 1985 Gramm-Rudman-Hollings anti-deficit law (PL 99-177) a provision granting the comptroller general the power to tell the president what fixed-percentage cuts he must make in federal spending in order to meet the deficit-reduction targets set by the bill.

The comptroller general is removable from office only at the initiative of Congress, through a joint resolution. This, the court reasoned, placed him under congressional control.

"By placing the responsibility for execution of the Balanced Budget and Emergency Deficit Control Act in the hands of an officer who is subject to removal only by itself, Congress in effect has retained control over the execution of the act and has intruded into the executive function," wrote Chief Justice Burger. *(Excerpts from majority, concurring and dissenting opinions, p. 18-A)*

Supreme Court's Gramm-Rudman Opinions

Following are excerpts from the Supreme Court's July 7 majority, concurring and dissenting opinions in the case of Bowsher v. Synar, *which tested the constitutionality of the 1985 Gramm-Rudman-Hollings anti-deficit law (PL 99-177).*

The majority opinion was written by Chief Justice Warren E. Burger on behalf of himself and Justices William J. Brennan Jr., Lewis F. Powell Jr., William H. Rehnquist and Sandra Day O'Connor. The concurring opinion was written by Justice John Paul Stevens, joined by Justice Thurgood Marshall. Justices Byron R. White and Harry A. Blackmun wrote separate dissents.

Majority Opinion

The question presented by these appeals is whether the assignment by Congress to the Comptroller General of the United States of certain functions under the Balanced Budget and Emergency Deficit Control Act of 1985 violates the doctrine of separation of powers.

* * * *

Even a cursory examination of the Constitution reveals the influence of Montesquieu's thesis that checks and balances were the foundation of a structure of government that would protect liberty. The Framers provided a vigorous legislative branch and a separate and wholly independent executive branch, with each branch responsible ultimately to the people. The Framers also provided for a judicial branch equally independent with "[t]he judicial Power ... extend[ing] to all Cases, in Law and Equity, arising under this Constitution, and the Laws of the United States." Article III, § 2.

Other, more subtle, examples of separated powers are evident as well. Unlike parliamentary systems such as that of Great Britain, no person who is an officer of the United States may serve as a Member of the Congress. Article I, § 6. Moreover, unlike parliamentary systems, the President, under Article II, is responsible not to the Congress but to the people, subject only to impeachment proceedings which are exercised by the two Houses as representatives of the people. Article II, § 4. And even in the impeachment of a President the presiding officer of the ultimate tribunal is not a member of the legislative branch, but the Chief Justice of the United States. Article I, § 3.

That this system of division and separation of powers produces conflicts, confusion, and discordance at times is inherent, but it was deliberately so structured to assure full, vigorous and open debate on the great issues affecting the people and to provide avenues for the operation of checks on the exercise of governmental power.

The Constitution does not contemplate an active role for Congress in the supervision of officers charged with the execution of the laws it enacts. The President appoints "Officers of the United States" with the "Advice and Consent of the Senate...." Article II, § 2. Once the appointment has been made and confirmed, however, the Constitution explicitly provides for removal of Officers of the United States by Congress only upon impeachment by the House of Representatives and conviction by the Senate. An impeachment by the House and trial by the Senate can rest only on "Treason, Bribery or other high Crimes and Misdemeanors." Article II, § 4. A direct congressional role in the removal of officers charged with the execution of the laws beyond this limited one is inconsistent with separation of powers.

* * * *

... [W]e conclude that Congress cannot reserve for itself the power of removal of an officer charged with the execution of the laws except by impeachment. To permit the execution of the laws to be vested in an officer answerable only to Congress would, in practical terms, reserve in Congress control over the execution of the laws. As the District Court observed, "Once an officer is appointed, it is only the authority that can remove him, and not the authority that appointed him, that he must fear and, in the performance of his functions, obey." ... The structure of the Constitution does not permit Congress to execute the laws; it follows that Congress cannot grant to an officer under its control what it does not possess.

Our decision in *Immigration and Naturalization Service v. Chadha* ... supports this conclusion. In *Chadha,* we struck down a one house "legislative veto" provision by which each House of Congress retained the power to reverse a decision Congress had expressly authorized the Attorney General to make:

> "Disagreement with the Attorney General's decision on Chadha's deportation — that is, Congress' decision to deport Chadha — no less than Congress' original choice to delegate to the Attorney General the authority to make that decision, involves determinations of policy that Congress can implement in only one way; bicameral passage followed by presentment to the President. Congress must abide by its delegation of authority until that delegation is legislatively altered or revoked."

To permit an officer controlled by Congress to execute the laws would be, in essence, to permit a congressional veto. Congress could simply remove, or threaten to remove, an officer for executing the laws in any fashion found to be unsatisfactory to Congress. This kind of congressional control over the execution of the laws, *Chadha* makes clear, is constitutionally impermissible.

* * * *

Appellants urge that the Comptroller General performs his duties independently and is not subservient to Congress. We agree with the District Court that this contention does not bear close scrutiny.

The critical factor lies in the provisions of the statute defining the Comptroller General's office relating to removability.... Although the Comptroller General is nominated by the President from a list of three individuals recommended by the Speaker of the House of Representatives and the President pro tempore of the Senate ... and confirmed by the Senate, he is removable only at the initiative of Congress. He may be removed not only by impeachment but also by Joint Resolution of Congress "at any time" resting on any one of the following bases:

> "(i) permanent disability;
> "(ii) inefficiency;
> "(iii) neglect of duty;
> "(iv) malfeasance; or
> "(v) a felony or conduct involving moral turpitude."

* * * *

... The Comptroller General heads the General Accounting Office, "an instrumentality of the United States Government independent of the executive departments" ... which was created by Congress in 1921 as part of the Budget and Accounting Act of 1921.... Congress created the office because it believed that it "needed an officer, responsible to it alone, to check upon the application of public funds in accordance with appropriations." ...

It is clear that Congress has consistently viewed the Comptroller General as an officer of the Legislative Branch. The Reorganization Acts of 1945 and 1949, for example, both stated that the Comptroller General and the GAO are "a part of the legislative branch of the Government." ... Similarly, in the Accounting and Auditing Act of 1950, Congress required the Comptroller General to conduct audits "as an agent of the Congress." ...

Over the years, the Comptrollers General have also viewed themselves as part of the Legislative Branch. In one of the early Annual Reports of Comptroller General, the official seal of his office was described as reflecting:

"the independence of judgment to be exercised by the General Accounting Office, subject to the control of the legislative branch.... The combination represents an agency of the Congress independent of other authority auditing and checking the expenditures of the Government as required by law and subjecting any questions arising in that connection to quasi-judicial determination."

* * * *

The primary responsibility of the Comptroller General under the instant Act is the preparation of a "report." This report must contain detailed estimates of projected federal revenues and expenditures. The report must also specify the reductions, if any, necessary to reduce the deficit to the target for the appropriate fiscal year. The reductions must be set forth on a program-by-program basis.

In preparing the report, the Comptroller General is to have "due regard" for the estimates and reductions set forth in a joint report submitted to him by the Director of CBO and the Director of OMB, the President's fiscal and budgetary advisor. However, the Act plainly contemplates that the Comptroller General will exercise his independent judgment and evaluation with respect to those estimates. The Act also provides that the Comptroller General's report "shall explain fully any differences between the contents of such report and the report of the Directors." ...

Appellants suggest that the duties assigned to the Comptroller General in the Act are essentially ministerial and mechanical so that their performance does not constitute "execution of the law" in a meaningful sense. On the contrary, we view these functions as plainly entailing execution of the law in constitutional terms. Interpreting a law enacted by Congress to implement the legislative mandate is the very essence of "execution" of the law. Under § 251, the Comptroller General must exercise judgment concerning facts that affect the application of the Act. He must also interpret the provisions of the Act to determine precisely what budgetary calculations are required. Decisions of that kind are typically made by officers charged with executing a statute.

The executive nature of the Comptroller General's functions under the Act is revealed in § 252(a)(3) which gives the Comptroller General the ultimate authority to determine the budget cuts to be made. Indeed, the Comptroller General commands the President himself to carry out, without the slightest variation (with exceptions not relevant to the constitutional issues presented), the directive of the Comptroller General as to the budget reductions.

* * * *

...By placing the responsibility for execution of the Balanced Budget and Emergency Deficit Control Act in the hands of an officer who is subject to removal only by itself, Congress in effect has retained control over the execution of the Act and has intruded into the executive function. The Constitution does not permit such intrusion.

* * * *

Severance at this late date of the removal provisions enacted 65 years ago would significantly alter the Comptroller General's office, possibly by making him subservient to the Executive Branch. Recasting the Comptroller General as an officer of the Executive Branch would accordingly alter the balance that Congress had in mind in drafting the Budget and Accounting Act of 1921 and the Balanced Budget and Emergency Deficit Control Act, to say nothing of the wide array of other tasks and duties Congress has assigned the Comptroller General in other statutes.... Thus appellant's argument would require this Court to undertake a weighing of the importance Congress attached to the removal provisions in the Budget and Accounting Act of 1921 as well as in other subsequent enactments against the importance it placed on the Balanced Budget and Emergency Deficit Control Act of 1985.

Fortunately this is a thicket we need not enter. The language of the Balanced Budget and Emergency Deficit Control Act itself settles the issue. In § 274(f), Congress has explicitly provided "fallback" provisions in the Act that take effect "[i]n the event ... *any* of the reporting procedures described in section 251 are invalidated." ... Assuming that appellants are correct in urging that this matter must be resolved on the basis of congressional intent, the intent appears to have been for § 274(f) to be given effect in this situation. Indeed, striking the removal provisions would lead to a statute that Congress would probably have refused to adopt. As the District Court concluded,

> "the grant of authority to the Comptroller General was a carefully considered protection against what the House conceived to be the pro-executive bias of the OMB. It is doubtful that the automatic deficit reduction process would have passed without such protection, and doubtful that the protection would have been considered present if the Comptroller General were not removable by Congress itself...."

Accordingly, rather than perform the type of creative and imaginative statutory surgery urged by appellants, our holding simply permits the fallback provisions to come into play....

No one can doubt that Congress and the President are confronted with fiscal and economic problems of unprecedented magnitude, but "the fact that a given law or procedure is efficient, convenient, and useful in facilitating functions of government, standing alone, will not save it if it is contrary to the Constitution. Convenience and efficiency are not the primary objectives — or the hallmarks — of democratic government...."

We conclude the District Court correctly held that the powers vested in the Comptroller General under § 251 violate the command of the Constitution that the Congress play no direct role in the execution of the laws. Accordingly, the judgment and order of the District Court are affirmed.

Our judgment is stayed for a period not to exceed 60 days to permit Congress to implement the fallback provisions.

Concurring Opinion

...I agree with the Court that the "Gramm-Rudman-Hollings" Act contains a constitutional infirmity so severe that the flawed provision may not stand. I disagree with the Court, however, on the reasons why the Constitution prohibits the Comptroller General from exercising the powers assigned to him by § 251(b) and § 251(c)(2) of the Act. It is not the dormant, carefully circumscribed congressional removal power that represents the primary constitutional evil. Nor do I agree with the conclusion of both the majority and the dissent that the analysis depends on a labeling of the functions assigned to the Comptroller General as "executive powers." ... Rather, I am convinced that the Comptroller General must be characterized as an agent of Congress because of his longstanding statutory responsibilities; that the powers assigned to him under the Gramm-Rudman-Hollings Act require him to make policy that will bind the Nation; and that, when Congress, or a component or an agent of Congress, seeks to make policy that will bind the Nation, it must follow the procedures mandated by Article I of the Constitution — through passage by both Houses and presentment to the President. In short, Congress may not exercise its fundamental power to formulate national policy by delegating that power to one of its two Houses, to a legislative committee, or to an individual agent of the Congress such as the Speaker of the House of Representatives, the Sergeant at Arms of the Senate, or the Director of the Congressional Budget Office.... That principle, I believe, is applicable to the Comptroller General.

* * * *

Thus, the critical inquiry in this case concerns not the manner in which Executive officials or agencies may act, but the manner in which Congress and its agents may act. As we emphasized in *Chadha,* when Congress legislates, when it makes binding policy, it must follow the procedures prescribed in Article I. Neither the unquestioned urgency of the national budget crisis nor the Comptroller General's proud record of professionalism and dedication provides a justification for allowing a congressional agent to set policy that binds the Nation. Rather than turning the task over to its agent, if the Legislative Branch decides to act with conclusive effect, it must do so through a process akin to that specified in the fallback provision — through enactment by both Houses and presentment to the President.

I concur in the judgment.

Justice White's Dissent

The Court, acting in the name of separation of powers, takes upon itself to strike down the Gramm-Rudman-Hollings Act, one of the most novel and far-reaching legislative responses to a national crisis since the New Deal. The basis of the Court's action is a solitary provision of another statute that was passed over sixty years ago and has lain dormant since that time. I cannot concur in the Court's action. Like the Court, I will not purport to speak to the wisdom of the policies incorporated in the legislation the Court invalidates; that is a matter for the Congress and the Executive, *both* of which expressed their assent to the statute barely half a year ago. I will, however, address the wisdom of the Court's willingness to interpose its distressingly formalistic view of separation of powers as a bar to the attainment of governmental objectives through the means chosen by the Congress and the President in the legislative process established by the Constitution. Twice in the past four years I have expressed my view that the Court's recent efforts to police the separation of powers have rested on untenable constitutional propositions leading to regrettable results. See *Northern Pipeline Construction Co. v. Marathon Pipe Line Co.,* 458 U.S. 50, 92-118 (1982) (White, J., dissenting); *INS v. Chadha,* 462 U.S. 919, 967-1003 (White, J., dissenting). Today's result is even more misguided. As I will explain, the Court's decision rests on a feature of the legislative scheme that is of minimal practical significance and that presents no substantial threat to the basic scheme of separation of powers.

* * * *

... The question to be answered is whether the threat of removal of the Comptroller General for cause through joint resolution as authorized by the Budget and Accounting Act renders the Comptroller sufficiently subservient to Congress that investing him with "executive" power can be realistically equated with the unlawful retention of such power by Congress itself; more generally, the question is whether there is a genuine threat of "encroachment or aggrandizement of one branch at the expense of the other." ... Common sense indicates that the existence of the removal provision poses no such threat to the principle of separation of powers.

* * * *

The practical result of the removal provision is not to render the Comptroller unduly dependent upon or subservient to Congress, but to render him one of the most independent officers in the entire federal establishment. Those who have studied the office agree that the procedural and substantive limits on the power of Congress and the President to remove the Comptroller make dislodging him against his will practically impossible.

* * * *

... The wisdom of vesting "executive" powers in an officer removable by joint resolution may indeed be debatable — as may be the wisdom of the entire scheme of permitting an unelected official to revise the budget enacted by Congress — but such matters are for the most part to be worked out between the Congress and the President through the legislative process, which affords each branch ample opportunity to defend its interests. The Act vesting budget-cutting authority in the Comptroller General represents Congress' judgment that the delegation of such authority to counteract ever-mounting deficits is "necessary and proper" to the exercise of the powers granted the Federal Government by the Constitution; and the President's approval of the statute signifies his unwillingness to reject the choice made by Congress.... Under such circumstances, the role of this Court should be limited to determining whether the Act so alters the balance of authority among the branches of government as to pose a genuine threat to the basic division between the lawmaking power and the power to execute the law. Because I see no such threat, I cannot join the Court in striking down the Act.

I dissent.

Justice Blackmun's Dissent

Assuming that the Comptroller General's functions under § 251 of the Deficit Control Act cannot be exercised by an official removable by joint resolution of Congress, we must determine whether legislative goals would be frustrated more by striking down § 251 or by invalidating the 1921 removal provision. That question is not answered by the "fallback" provisions of the 1985 Act, which takes effect "[i]n the event that any of the reporting procedures described in section 251 [of the Act] are invalidated." The question is whether the reporting procedures should be invalidated in the first place. The fallback provisions simply make clear that Congress would prefer a watered-down version of the Deficit Control Act to none at all; they provide no evidence that Congress would rather settle for the watered-down version than surrender its statutory authority to remove the Comptroller General. The legislative history of the Deficit Control Act contains no mention of the 1921 statute, and both Houses of Congress have argued in this Court that, if necessary, the removal provision should be invalidated rather than § 251.... To the extent that the absence of express fallback provisions in the 1921 statute signifies anything, it appear [*sic*] to signify only that, if the removal provision were invalidated, Congress preferred simply that the remainder of the statute should remain in effect without alteration....

In the absence of express statutory direction, I think it is plain that, as both Houses urge, invalidating the Comptroller General's functions under the Deficit Control Act would frustrate congressional objectives far more seriously than would refusing to allow Congress to exercise its removal authority under the 1921 law.

* * * *

I do not claim that the 1921 removal provision is a piece of statutory deadwood utterly without contemporary significance. But it comes close. Rarely if ever invoked even for symbolic purposes, the removal provision certainly pales in importance beside the legislative scheme the Court strikes down today — an extraordinarily far-reaching response to a deficit problem of unprecedented proportions. Because I believe that the constitutional defect found by the Court cannot justify the remedy it has imposed, I respectfully dissent. ∎

POLITICAL REPORT

CQ

Failed Campaign Cost Republicans the Senate

The 1986 Senate elections were a Republican disaster that need not have happened.

It is always possible in the aftermath of a result such as the one that cost the GOP eight seats and a majority to argue that it carried a silver lining, or that it was a statistical fluke, or that it was inevitable, or some combination of the three.

After all, Republicans point out, they gained eight governorships and avoided serious erosion in the House.

Even on the Senate side, they can argue, Republicans would have preserved their majority if they picked up no more than 55,000 votes in five states. And in any case, they were struggling against history — they had to keep their losses to three seats to maintain control, and no party holding the White House has ever lost that few at its six-year point in power.

Those defenses are easy to erect; they are even easier to knock down.

Any set of competitive Senate contests produces quite a few that turn on a small number of votes. An additional 42,000 would have kept the Senate Democratic in the Reagan landslide of 1980. If another 55,000 votes would have saved the Republican majority this year, 150,000 in the other direction would have given Democrats a majority of 58-42.

The argument from history presents similar problems. All of the other midterm Senate debacles of modern times occurred against the backdrop of serious problems in the country — a national recession in 1958, the Vietnam War in 1966, the Watergate scandal in 1974. No such problem existed for the Republicans in 1986.

And while the GOP can draw legitimate consolation from their gubernatorial showing and their single-digit losses in the House, those successes simply underscore the only lesson one can fairly draw from the day's voting. There was no landslide, no "six-year itch," not even a discernible national trend against voting Republican.

The only valid explanation for the Republicans' poor electoral performance was a failed Republican Senate campaign.

Senate		House	
99th Congress:		*99th Congress:*	
Democrats	47	Democrats	253
Republicans	53	Republicans	182 *
100th Congress:		*100th Congress:*	
Democrats	55	Democrats	258
Republicans	45	Republicans	177

Based on apparent winners as of Nov. 7.

**** Including two vacancies.***

It is possible to glean some of the reasons for that failure in the transcripts of the speeches President Reagan gave as he barnstormed the country in an effort to boost his party's candidates the week before the election.

His speech for Sen. James T. Broyhill in North Carolina on Oct. 28 is a fairly typical example.

"It's wonderful to be here in North Carolina," the president began. "You probably know I couldn't do this much traveling when Congress was in session.... That's because some of those folks need watching."

He went on to describe himself and Broyhill as part of the "1980 cleanup crew."

Ever since Reagan took office, his critics have marveled at his ability, as head of the national government, to ridicule that government, hold himself apart from it and ask the electorate to help him protect them from the absurdities of the political system he has been chosen to lead.

On Nov. 4, Reagan and the Republican Senate paid the price for their ability to distance themselves from government. After six years in power, they appealed to the country one more time as the opposition, and it was one time too many.

When a house is messy, its residents welcome a cleanup crew. When the place is clean again, they thank the crew, pay them, and let them leave. If the crew wants to stay, it has to offer reasons why it is still needed.

Republicans campaigned for the Senate in 1986 somewhat in the manner that former Minnesota Sen. Eugene J. McCarthy campaigned for the White House in 1968. Asked if he really wanted to be president, Democrat McCarthy took a moment to consider the question and then said simply he was "willing to be president."

By and large, this year's Republicans offered themselves as the party willing to perform the unpleasant chore of governing the country in order to prevent the Democratic villains of the 1970s from returning to power and making a mess again.

To be fair, the president and his allies did spend some time talking about the economic successes of the past few years and the importance of the Reagan military buildup. But these issues were not offered consistently or clearly enough to drown out the trivia that dominated the campaign on both sides.

The absence of a national theme in the 1986 Senate election has been cited all year as a curiosity of modern campaign strategy or a function of ideological lethargy in the closing years of the Reagan era. With the benefit of hindsight, it is possible to see this themelessness for what it was — an important Republican miscalculation.

It is perfectly true that the Democrats offered no theme either, but they did not need one. The theme of any opposition party is opposition. It is the vehicle for whatever protests voters may choose to make against the party perceived as holding power. It is the job of those representing the party in power to offer a coherent rationale for their re-election. Few Republicans did that.

In Georgia in 1986, after Democrat Wyche Fowler Jr. won his party's Senate nomination, Republican incumbent Mack Mattingly launched his own campaign with a blistering attack on Fowler's attendance as a member of the House. It seemed to work: Fowler's poll numbers plummeted.

But after the initial impact wore off, the tactic allowed Fowler to suggest to voters that after six years in office, the incumbent could think of nothing better to run on than his challenger's attendance record.

With the benefit of hindsight, it is possible to see the lack of a national campaign theme for what it was — an important Republican miscalculation.

Meanwhile, in South Dakota, Republican Sen. James Abdnor was fighting to hold off Democrat Thomas A. Daschle with commercials charging that Daschle was friendly with Jane Fonda, the liberal actress. Again, Daschle sustained some damage. After a few weeks, though, it began to seem that Abdnor was running a challenger-style campaign.

For an incumbent senator, and an incumbent party, to run full blast against the people trying to unseat them, is indeed a novel tactic. Perhaps it worked in 1986 in some places. In general, though, it is not what voters expect, and it is not what they reward.

Penalizing the Leaders

The irony of the Republican failure to campaign forthrightly as the governing party was that it most penalizes those who tried hardest to govern — the party's leaders in the Senate.

The split Congress established by the 1980 election generated one set of legislators — Senate Republicans — who had every reason to govern responsibly and a special reason to fear failure. As the majority in their chamber, they were the president's agents in Congress, and also the spokesmen for Congress in negotiating with the president.

If voters became dissatisfied, these Republicans would be the obvious scapegoats no matter which institution seemed to be at fault.

Republican leader Robert Dole of Kansas and such chairmen as Bob Packwood of Oregon at Finance, Pete V. Domenici of New Mexico at Budget, and Richard G. Lugar of Indiana at Foreign Relations proved they were more than competent as the governing party, and they showed no signs of embarrassment at having to govern.

Theirs was a case that Republican senators might have made all over the country in 1986, and if they had, the result might have been different. ▮

Voters Restore Democrats to Senate Control

Boosted by farm-state turmoil and a partial resurgence of traditional voting habits in the South, Democrats Nov. 4, 1986, laid to rest the specter of the GOP's stunning 1980 Senate sweep.

Six Republicans who won their seats that year were defeated in their bids for re-election, as Democrats captured a total of nine GOP seats and lost only one of their own to take a 55-45 Senate majority. Their net pickup of eight seats was the party's largest since 1958. In all, Democrats won 20 of the 34 Senate contests at stake.

The results also gave them their largest class of freshman senators since 1958; of the 13 new senators elected, 11 were Democrats. *(State-by-state returns, p. 24-B; membership, p. 9-B; switched seats, p. 7-B)*

U.S. Senate

99th Congress		100th Congress	
Democrats	47	Democrats	55
Republicans	53	Republicans	45

Democrats

Freshmen	11
Incumbents re-elected	9
Incumbents defeated	0

Republicans

Freshmen	2
Incumbents re-elected	12
Incumbents defeated	7

(Jeremiah Denton, Ala.; Paula Hawkins, Fla.; Mack Mattingly, Ga.; James T. Broyhill, N.C.; Mark Andrews, N.D.; James Abdnor, S.D.; Slade Gorton, Wash.)

The party's most significant set of victories came in the South, where Democrats won every Senate contest but one. Republican freshmen Paula Hawkins of Florida, Mack Mattingly of Georgia and Jeremiah Denton of Alabama all lost. In North Carolina, Republican James T. Broyhill, who was appointed to the Senate earlier in 1986 after fellow Republican John P. East's suicide, was also defeated.

In addition, Democratic Rep. John B. Breaux overcame an early lead by GOP Rep. W. Henson Moore to hold onto the Louisiana seat of retiring Democratic Sen. Russell B. Long. Only Oklahoma Sen. Don Nickles managed to stave off the Democratic tide in the region.

Democrats' gains elsewhere were sprinkled across the map. In the Midwest, farm unrest cost two GOP members of the class of 1980 their seats: Mark Andrews of North Dakota lost to state Tax Commissioner Kent Conrad, and James Abdnor of South Dakota fell to Rep. Thomas A. Daschle.

In Washington state, controversy over the possible siting of a high-level nuclear-waste site in Hanford helped unseat Republican Slade Gorton.

The Democrats' other gains came in Maryland, where Rep. Barbara A. Mikulski easily won the seat of retiring GOP Sen. Charles McC. Mathias Jr., and in Nevada, where Rep. Harry Reid defeated former Rep. Jim Santini for the right to succeed retiring GOP Sen. Paul Laxalt.

The sole Republican pickup was in Missouri. There, former Gov. Christopher S. "Kit" Bond defeated Lt. Gov. Harriett Woods to win the seat held by retiring Democratic veteran Thomas F. Eagleton.

Using the Democrats' overpowering Senate performance to draw conclusions about the two parties' relative standing is chancy, given the GOP's strong showing in governors' races and the virtual standoff in House elections. But the Senate campaign does deserve special notice for what it says about the state of electioneering in the latter half of the 1980s.

Most spectacularly, it laid to rest a theory that took hold in 1980 — that the GOP's superior financial resources give it an infallible ability to win close contests. The notion gained widespread currency in 1982, when the GOP's high-tech campaign techniques and last-minute infusions of money saved several endangered Republican candidates. That year, the GOP won five of the six contests in which the winner took 52 percent or less.

But in 1986, of the 11 races won by 52 percent or less, nine went to Democrats. That achievement came in spite of daunting obstacles: the National Republican Senatorial Committee's nearly 8-to-1 funding advantage over its Democratic counterpart, a $10 million nationwide GOP get-out-the-vote effort, and an army of consultants, pollsters, media advisers and GOP field staff at the disposal of Republican candidates.

The difference lay in what each side did with the resources at its disposal. In many contests, Democrats latched onto issues — of substance

Democrat Wyche Fowler Jr. celebrates his Senate victory in Georgia.

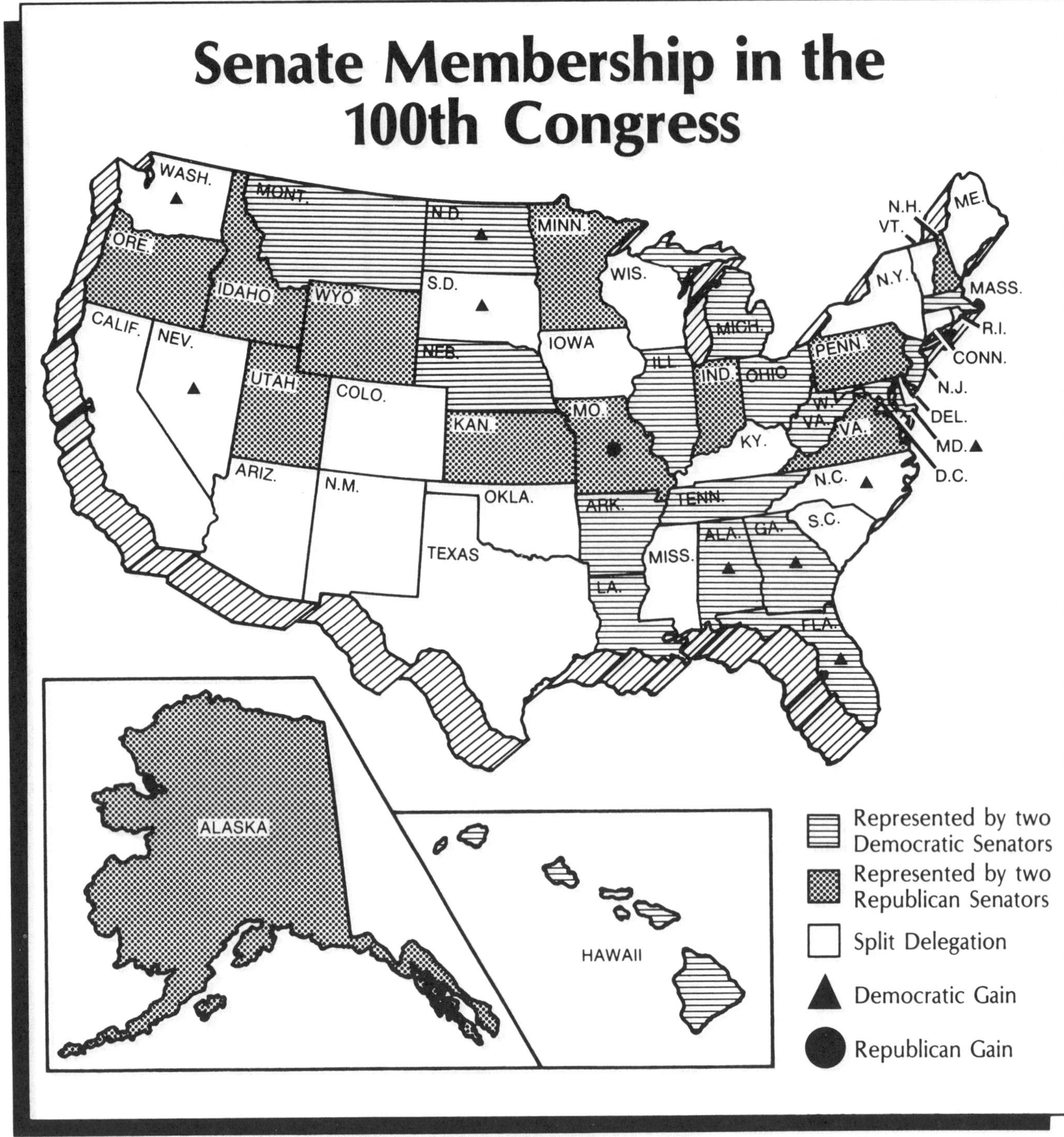

and of personality — that by Election Day were helping them frame the terms of the debate.

Even more important, while the GOP was spending much of its money on TV advertising and on a technology-driven voter mobilization effort, Democrats built on their strength at the grass roots. They developed extensive local organizations and — especially in the South — reawakened old party apparatuses and alliances.

Not every potentially close election broke the Democrats' way. In Oklahoma and Pennsylvania, Democratic Reps. James R. Jones and Bob Edgar tried to turn local economic troubles to their advantage. Neither, however, could arouse the core Democratic constituency in the western half of their states. Nickles and Pennsylvania Republican Arlen Specter both won handily. And in Idaho, Democratic Gov. John V. Evans failed to capitalize on the state's "triple recession" in mining, timber and farming; he lost to conservative Republican Steven D. Symms.

But in a year when there were so many close contests, the Republicans' lack of organizational depth hurt them, particularly in states where Democrats latched onto local issues that seemed more compelling to voters than national Republican pleas to keep the Senate in GOP hands.

Not even President Reagan's help could overcome the Democrats' advantages — of the 16 states to which Reagan traveled after Labor Day, Republican Senate candidates won only four; and only in Idaho could Reagan's presence be said to have boosted his candidate over the top.

'The North Carolina Way'

The most striking examples of the Democrats' ability to out-campaign their opponents came in the South. Each Democrat there used a variation on a single theme — that he was a home-grown state patriot, while his opponent was a national Republican with little interest in local affairs. And each used his state's traditional Democratic base to surmount better-financed Republican efforts.

In North Carolina, for example, Democrat Terry Sanford stressed his longstanding ties to the state, as governor from 1961-65, and later as president of Duke University, while painting Broyhill as a captive of the Washington establishment.

He spent much of the campaign traveling the state, touching base with local Democratic leaders and getting acquainted with the generation of reporters and editors that had come into their jobs since he last held office. When he came under fire for spending his time in such low-profile work while Broyhill was constantly on TV, Sanford responded that he was running the "North Carolina way."

His efforts paid off. Where former Democratic Gov. James Hunt relied extensively on his personal organization in his unsuccessful 1984 Senate bid, Sanford tied in with conservative Democratic officials. They gave his campaign vital credibility, especially in the eastern part of the state, where conservative Democrats form a base of support for GOP Sen. Jesse Helms. Sanford ran far ahead of Broyhill in the east, and he also cut deeply into Broyhill's strength in the moderately Republican counties of central North Carolina's Piedmont region.

In Alabama, Rep. Richard C. Shelby lashed out at Denton as more interested in his personal agenda of "family" and social issues than in helping Alabama's economy. Late in the campaign, he issued a series of hard-hitting attacks that accused Denton of voting to cut Social Security benefits. The approach enabled the conservative Shelby to develop links to his state's well-organized labor and black communities — groups he had largely avoided during his House career.

Moore Blunders, Breaux Wins

The most persuasive examples of the power of the Democrats' localized approach came in Louisiana and Georgia, where both Breaux and Democratic Rep. Wyche Fowler Jr. used it to overcome strong Republican leads.

From the start, Breaux hammered away at Moore as a representative of Republican policies that were hurting Louisiana's farmers and its oil and gas industry. Moore, Breaux said over and over, owed his allegiance to the national GOP and not to Louisiana — a point the Democrat summed up in his slogan, "Louisiana First."

With Louisiana's economy in a deep slump, and the state ranking first in the nation in unemployment, Breaux's message was bound to get a sympathetic hearing. But several miscalculations by the Republicans also helped Breaux score his victory.

Moore initially had pegged his campaign to a parochial appeal. He maintained that the state's scandal-ridden Democratic administration and faltering economy called out for new leadership. The Republicans, Moore contended, were the only ones capable of getting the state back to work.

As long as he stuck with that approach, Moore remained in front. But as the nonpartisan September primary approached and the GOP mounted an all-out push to win more than 50 percent of the vote — and so avoid a runoff — he faltered. His campaign shifted its emphasis towards attacking Breaux, while the national GOP launched a program to purge ineligible voters from the rolls in black precincts, which angered black voters.

The result was that Moore ran worse than expected in the primary, while Breaux did better. Though Moore tried to recoup by shifting back to his original tack, the damage had been done. Many voters had been turned off by his attacks on Breaux, and Democrats who had ignored the campaign or sided with Moore began to shift to Breaux. Working hard to mobilize both the Democratic base in New Orleans and white Democratic parish officials in southern Louisiana, Breaux overtook Moore.

Fowler's Flair Prevails

In Georgia, Fowler ran an almost picture-perfect campaign. Mattingly won in 1980 largely because Democratic Sen. Herman E. Talmadge had

Senate Switched Seats, Newcomers, Losers

State	99th	100th	Winner	Loser	Incumbent
Alabama	R	D	Richard C. Shelby (D)	Jeremiah Denton (R)	Denton
Arizona	R	R	John McCain (R)	Richard Kimball (D)	Barry Goldwater (R) *
Colorado	D	D	Timothy E. Wirth (D)	Ken Kramer (R)	Gary Hart (D) *
Florida	R	D	Bob Graham (D)	Paula Hawkins (R)	Hawkins
Georgia	R	D	Wyche Fowler Jr. (D)	Mack Mattingly (R)	Mattingly
Louisiana	D	D	John B. Breaux (D)	W. Henson Moore (R)	Russell B. Long (D) *
Maryland	R	D	Barbara A. Mikulski (D)	Linda Chavez (R)	Charles McC. Mathias Jr. (R) *
Missouri	D	R	Christopher S. "Kit" Bond (R)	Harriett Woods (D)	Thomas F. Eagleton (D) *
Nevada	R	D	Harry Reid (D)	Jim Santini (R)	Paul Laxalt (R) *
North Carolina	R	D	Terry Sanford (D)	James T. Broyhill (R)	Broyhill
North Dakota	R	D	Kent Conrad (D)	Mark Andrews (R)	Andrews
South Dakota	R	D	Thomas A. Daschle (D)	James Abdnor (R)	Abdnor
Washington	R	D	Brock Adams (D)	Slade Gorton (R)	Gorton

** Retired*

been badly tarnished by misconduct charges. In 1986, Mattingly's greatest strength was his conservatism; Fowler, who has represented Atlanta since 1977, was the Georgia delegation's most liberal member.

But Mattingly had a serious weakness — he had not built a political base. Without it, he had to rely heavily on media advertising.

Fowler, on the other hand, is an accomplished stump campaigner who — despite his urban base — showed an actor's deft touch at setting conservative rural Georgians at ease. While Mattingly based his campaign on television attacks that accused Fowler of being too liberal and missing votes in the House, Fowler traveled the state, lining up "courthouse crowds."

The thrust of Fowler's campaign was to paint Mattingly as a captive of GOP policies that were doing harm to his state. "Republican policies are threatening family farms, small business and the rural way of life," ran one Fowler ad. "What has Republican Mack Mattingly done to help?" He coupled that approach with a series of populist attacks on the GOP as the party of the affluent. Mattingly, he said, "votes to protect the wealthy and powerful."

Despite Georgia's huge size, which makes a media-dominated campaign almost a necessity, Fowler's travels paid off. Like Sanford, he brought local Democratic officials to his side, and they helped him undercut rural voters' suspicion of his Atlanta background. His attacks on Mattingly mobilized his Atlanta base and voters in the state's smaller, less cosmopolitan areas. Fowler carried just under two-thirds of the state's 159 counties.

The Dakotas Revolt

Other Democrats elsewhere in the country also proved adept at finding issues that helped them cut into Republican strength. Both Conrad and Daschle, for example, jumped on the farm crisis at the start of their campaigns and never let go.

In South Dakota's cold economic climate, with farmers worrying about bankruptcy and normally Republican small businessmen feeling the pinch of hard times on the farm, Daschle's vigorous attacks on Republican farm policies put Abdnor on the defensive. Abdnor also had to deal with widespread sentiment that Daschle would be a more aggressive and eloquent spokesman for the state in Washington. Toward the end of the campaign, the avuncular Abdnor tried to make the most of his rather ineloquent manner, airing an enormously successful ad playing on his likability. "So I'm not a great speaker," he told viewers. "Heck, I'm not a great dancer, either."

The ad helped Abdnor make up ground, but not enough. Helped by a massive effort to get farmers to the polls, Daschle turned out a strong vote in the state's rural counties.

Conrad Paints a Bleak Picture

In North Dakota, Conrad carefully crafted a campaign to take advantage both of the state's farm problems and of Andrews' personal difficulties. Although Andrews had stood up against the administration's farm policies — especially its effort to cut wheat target prices — Conrad questioned the Republican's ability to deliver for his state.

He painted a bleak picture of the economic prosperity enjoyed by the East and West coasts while North Dakota suffered. "We need someone who will fight for us, for our way of life," one of his ads commented.

The issue was enough to bring Conrad within striking distance, but several other factors helped him. A longstanding legal battle between Andrews and his family physicians grated on some voters, and the senator also was dogged by a feeling among some voters that he had lost touch with North Dakota as his stature had grown in Washington.

Moreover, as Conrad continued to hammer at Andrews and began to draw almost even in the polls, Andrews was mired in Washington as the congressional session dragged on into mid-October. When Congress finally adjourned and Andrews started campaigning full time, he tried to arouse suspicion of Conrad by calling him "a favorite of the East Coast limousine liberals." The tack did not succeed. With help from the political network of Democratic Rep. Byron L. Dorgan, Conrad won by about 2,000 votes.

Paths to Power

Though the Democrats' ability to blend grass-roots organizing with innovative campaign tactics was crucial to their success, it was not a prerequisite everywhere. In some states, one or the other sufficed on its own.

In Colorado, for example, Democratic Rep. Timothy E. Wirth was never able to gain the upper hand against GOP Rep. Ken Kramer on the issues alone. Kramer's support for the strategic defense initiative and his dedication to a balanced budget proved popular in Colorado, and his ad declaring, "I'm not slick, just good," helped him stay even with Wirth in the public relations battle.

The difference was provided by the two candidates' organizations. Wirth's was extensive, sophisticated and smoothly run, while Kramer's was inefficient and limited. On Election Day, Wirth's was able to deliver its vote. Kramer, who relied extensively on help from the state GOP and from the national party's computerized get-out-the-vote program, fell short.

In Washington state, former Transportation Secretary Brock Adams rode into office on the strength of the Hanford issue. He ran ads pledging to "stop this nuclear garbage dead in its tracks," and repeatedly questioned Gorton's ability to stop the administration from choosing the site.

Gorton, who never managed to build much of a personal following as senator, could not dodge the issue. He tried to deflect it by following the national GOP script and challenging Adams' attendance record as a House member from 1965-77. He also tried to convince voters he was working hard to see that Hanford would not be chosen. But the president undercut Gorton by traveling to the state on his behalf and not giving any indication he would rule out a waste facility at Hanford.

Democrats also dominated the two states where media ads played a crucial role, California and Florida. In Florida, Democratic Gov. Bob Graham, a popular moderate, put Hawkins on the defensive by portraying her as a Senate lightweight with a narrow focus. Hawkins sought to turn her emphasis on anti-drug legislation and children's issues into an advantage, but wound up with only 45 percent — the worst showing of any Senate incumbent.

In California, Democratic Sen. Alan Cranston ran a masterly campaign that for much of its length kept Rep. Ed Zschau's legislative record in the spotlight and prevented the Republican from focusing on Cranston's performance. Zschau's hard-hitting effort to label Cranston as soft on drugs and terrorism helped him gain considerable ground late in the campaign, but he fell short of his goal.

Senate Membership in the 100th Congress

Democrats - 55 Republicans - 45

Freshman senators - 13

Seats switched D to R - 1 Seats switched R to D - 9

Senators elected in 1986 are *italicized*

 # Freshman senators

✓ Seat switched parties

ALABAMA
Howell Heflin (D)
✓ *Richard C. Shelby (D)#*

ALASKA
Frank H. Murkowski (R)
Ted Stevens (R)

ARIZONA
Dennis DeConcini (D)
John McCain (R)#

ARKANSAS
Dale Bumpers (D)
David Pryor (D)

CALIFORNIA
Alan Cranston (D)
Pete Wilson (R)

COLORADO
William L. Armstrong (R)
Timothy E. Wirth (D)#

CONNECTICUT
Christopher J. Dodd (D)
Lowell P. Weicker Jr. (R)

DELAWARE
Joseph R. Biden Jr. (D)
William V. Roth Jr. (R)

FLORIDA
Lawton Chiles (D)
✓ *Bob Graham (D)#*

GEORGIA
✓ *Wyche Fowler Jr. (D)#*
Sam Nunn (D)

HAWAII
Daniel K. Inouye (D)
Spark M. Matsunaga (D)

IDAHO
James A. McClure (R)
Steven D. Symms (R)

ILLINOIS
Alan J. Dixon (D)
Paul Simon (D)

INDIANA
Richard G. Lugar (R)
Dan Quayle (R)

IOWA
Charles E. Grassley (R)
Tom Harkin (D)

KANSAS
Robert Dole (R)
Nancy Landon Kassebaum (R)

KENTUCKY
Wendell H. Ford (D)
Mitch McConnell (R)

LOUISIANA
John B. Breaux (D)#
J. Bennett Johnston (D)

MAINE
George J. Mitchell (D)
William S. Cohen (R)

MARYLAND
✓ *Barbara A. Mikulski (D)#*
Paul S. Sarbanes (D)

MASSACHUSETTS
Edward M. Kennedy (D)
John Kerry (D)

MICHIGAN
Carl Levin (D)
Donald W. Riegle Jr. (D)

MINNESOTA
Rudy Boschwitz (R)
Dave Durenberger (R)

MISSISSIPPI
John C. Stennis (D)
Thad Cochran (R)

MISSOURI
✓ *Christopher S. "Kit" Bond (R)#*
John C. Danforth (R)

MONTANA
Max Baucus (D)
John Melcher (D)

NEBRASKA
J. James Exon (D)
Edward Zorinsky (D)

NEVADA
✓ *Harry Reid (D)#*
Chic Hecht (R)

NEW HAMPSHIRE
Gordon J. Humphrey (R)
Warren B. Rudman (R)

NEW JERSEY
Bill Bradley (D)
Frank R. Lautenberg (D)

NEW MEXICO
Jeff Bingaman (D)
Pete V. Domenici (R)

NEW YORK
Alfonse M. D'Amato (R)
Daniel Patrick Moynihan (D)

NORTH CAROLINA
Jesse Helms (R)
✓ *Terry Sanford (D)#*

NORTH DAKOTA
Quentin N. Burdick (D)
✓ *Kent Conrad (D)#*

OHIO
John Glenn (D)
Howard M. Metzenbaum (D)

OKLAHOMA
David L. Boren (D)
Don Nickles (R)

OREGON
Mark O. Hatfield (R)
Bob Packwood (R)

PENNSYLVANIA
John Heinz (R)
Arlen Specter (R)

RHODE ISLAND
John H. Chafee (R)
Claiborne Pell (D)

SOUTH CAROLINA
Ernest F. Hollings (D)
Strom Thurmond (R)

SOUTH DAKOTA
✓ *Thomas A. Daschle (D)#*
Larry Pressler (R)

TENNESSEE
Albert Gore Jr. (D)
Jim Sasser (D)

TEXAS
Lloyd Bentsen (D)
Phil Gramm (R)

UTAH
Jake Garn (R)
Orrin G. Hatch (R)

VERMONT
Patrick J. Leahy (D)
Robert T. Stafford (R)

VIRGINIA
Paul S. Trible Jr. (R)
John W. Warner (R)

WASHINGTON
✓ *Brock Adams (D)#*
Daniel J. Evans (R)

WEST VIRGINIA
Robert C. Byrd (D)
John D. Rockefeller IV (D)

WISCONSIN
Bob Kasten (R)
William Proxmire (D)

WYOMING
Alan K. Simpson (R)
Malcolm Wallop (R)

Years of Expiration of Senate Terms

— 1988 —

(33 Senators: 19 Democrats, 14 Republicans)

Bentsen, Lloyd, D-Texas
Bingaman, Jeff, D-N.M.
Burdick, Quentin N., D-N.D.
Byrd, Robert C., D-W.Va.
Chafee, John H., R-R.I.
Chiles, Lawton, D-Fla.
Danforth, John C., R-Mo.
DeConcini, Dennis, D-Ariz.
Durenberger, Dave, R-Minn.
Evans, Daniel J., R-Wash.
Hatch, Orrin G., R-Utah
Hecht, Chic, R-Nev.
Heinz, John, R-Pa.
Kennedy, Edward M., D-Mass.
Lautenberg, Frank R., D-N.J.
Lugar, Richard G., R-Ind.
Matsunaga, Spark M., D-Hawaii
Melcher, John, D-Mont.
Metzenbaum, Howard M., D-Ohio
Mitchell, George J., D-Maine
Moynihan, Daniel Patrick, D-N.Y.
Proxmire, William, D-Wis.
Riegle, Donald W. Jr., D-Mich.
Roth, William V. Jr., R-Del.
Sarbanes, Paul S., D-Md.
Sasser, Jim, D-Tenn.
Stafford, Robert T., R-Vt.
Stennis, John C., D-Miss.
Trible, Paul S. Jr., R-Va.
Wallop, Malcolm, R-Wyo.
Weicker, Lowell P. Jr., R-Conn.
Wilson, Pete, R-Calif.
Zorinsky, Edward, D-Neb.

— 1990 —

(33 Senators: 16 Democrats, 17 Republicans)

Armstrong, William L., R-Colo.
Baucus, Max, D-Mont.
Biden, Joseph R. Jr., D-Del.
Boren, David L., D-Okla.
Boschwitz, Rudy, R-Minn.
Bradley, Bill, D-N.J.
Cochran, Thad, R-Miss.
Cohen, William S., R-Maine
Domenici, Pete V., R-N.M.
Exon, J. James, D-Neb.
Gore, Albert Jr., D-Tenn.
Gramm, Phil, R-Texas
Harkin, Tom, D-Iowa
Hatfield, Mark O., R-Ore.
Heflin, Howell, D-Ala.
Helms, Jesse, R-N.C.
Humphrey, Gordon J., R-N.H.
Johnston, J. Bennett, D-La.
Kassebaum, Nancy Landon, R-Kan.
Kerry, John, D-Mass.
Levin, Carl, D-Mich.
McClure, James A., R-Idaho
McConnell, Mitch, R-Ky.
Nunn, Sam, D-Ga.
Pell, Claiborne, D-R.I.
Pressler, Larry, R-S.D.
Pryor, David, D-Ark.
Rockefeller, John D. IV, D-W.Va.
Simon, Paul, D-Ill.
Simpson, Alan K., R-Wyo.
Stevens, Ted, R-Alaska
Thurmond, Strom, R-S.C.
Warner, John W., R-Va.

— 1992 —

(34 Senators: 20 Democrats, 14 Republicans)

Adams, Brock, D-Wash.
Bond, Christopher S. "Kit," R-Mo.
Breaux, John B., D-La.
Bumpers, Dale, D-Ark.
Conrad, Kent, D-N.D.
Cranston, Alan, D-Calif.
D'Amato, Alfonse M., R-N.Y.
Daschle, Thomas A., D-S.D.
Dixon, Alan J., D-Ill.
Dodd, Christopher J., D-Conn.
Dole, Robert, R-Kan.
Ford, Wendell H., D-Ky.
Fowler, Wyche Jr., D-Ga.
Garn, Jake, R-Utah
Glenn, John, D-Ohio
Graham, Bob, D-Fla.
Grassley, Charles E., R-Iowa
Hollings, Ernest F., D-S.C.
Inouye, Daniel K., D-Hawaii
Kasten, Bob, R-Wis.
Leahy, Patrick J., D-Vt.
McCain, John, R-Ariz.
Mikulski, Barbara A., D-Md.
Murkowski, Frank H., R-Alaska
Nickles, Don, R-Okla.
Packwood, Bob, R-Ore.
Quayle, Dan, R-Ind.
Reid, Harry, D-Nev.
Rudman, Warren B., R-N.H.
Sanford, Terry, D-N.C.
Shelby, Richard C., D-Ala.
Specter, Arlen, R-Pa.
Symms, Steven D., R-Idaho
Wirth, Timothy E., D-Colo.

A Year of Little Turmoil in House Elections

Voters in the Nov. 4, 1986, House elections flouted the widely heralded "six-year-itch" theory by not scratching.

Any frustration they felt with the Republicans' six-year reign in the White House was vented in Senate contests. House GOP incumbents had remarkably little trouble on Election Day.

Democrats registered a net gain of five seats in the House, giving the party a 258-177 edge over the GOP for the 100th Congress.

While celebrating their 81-seat advantage, House Democratic leaders cannot claim to have kept pace with the rhythms of recent House election history.

In the last four elections held during a party's second term in control of the White House — 1938, 1958, 1966 and 1974 — the party in power has lost an average of 52 House seats. Given that track record, the GOP's five-seat setback in 1986 hardly qualifies as a resounding repudiation. One has to go back to 1902 to find a sixth-year midterm election in which the party in power fared better.

The 'Ins' Stay In

Actually, it was an extraordinarily good election for incumbents of both parties. Only five Republican House members went down to defeat: Reps. Mike Strang of Colorado; Webb Franklin of Mississippi; Fred J. Eckert of New York; and Bill Cobey and Bill Hendon, both of North Carolina. The Democrats, meanwhile, suffered only one incumbent casualty: Rep. Robert A. Young of Missouri *(State-by-state returns, p. 24-B; membership, p. 16-B; switched seats, newcomers and losers, p. 14-B)*

The number of incumbents defeated in the 1986 House elections was the lowest in postwar history. In addition to the six November losers, two more incumbents lost primaries during 1986.

The previous low for incumbents defeated was 13, in 1968, when nine lost in the general election and four lost in primaries.

The small number of House incumbents defeated is particularly remarkable when compared with the outcome in the Senate elections; six Senate incumbents were defeated in this year's balloting.

Most GOP Incumbents Avoid the 'Itch'

The small number of House incumbents defeated is particularly remarkable when compared with the outcome in the Senate elections; six Senate incumbents were defeated in this year's balloting.

Open Seats a Wash

There was little partisan turbulence in the 44 districts left open by House incumbents who died, retired, lost in primaries or ran for other offices. Democrats picked up eight seats previously occupied by Republicans, but the GOP responded by wrenching away seven seats that had been in the Democratic column. The result — a net Democratic gain of one open seat — was essentially a partisan wash.

The combination of open-seat outcomes and challenger victories yielded a freshman House class of 1986 of 50 members, which included 23 Republicans and 27 Democrats. That was larger than the 43-member freshman class of 1984, but was much smaller than the 74-member GOP-dominated class of 1980 and the Democrat-heavy, 80-member contingent elected in 1982.

What the 1986 freshman House class lacks in numbers, however, it makes up for in sheer diversity. Its membership ranges from Republican Fred Grandy of Iowa's 6th District — an actor best-known for his portrayal of the hapless "Gopher" on the television sitcom "The Love Boat" — to Democrat Floyd H. Flake of New York's 6th District, an African Methodist Episcopal minister given to sharp, tailored suits and the captivating, oratorical cadences of the black church.

Competing Theories

There is no shortage of theories to explain the limited turnover in the 1986 House elections.

Republicans like to argue that they were able to thwart the six-year itch theory in 1986 because of the presence of a popular president, relative economic prosperity and the absence of any major political blunders

Democrat Mike Espy is Mississippi's first black U.S. House member since 1883.

Actor-turned-politician Fred Grandy won Iowa's 6th District for the Republicans.

— such as Watergate, which dragged House Republicans down in the six-year midterm election of 1974.

Democrats, for their part, cite their ability to play good defense during Reagan's 1984 presidential landslide. By limiting their losses in that election to 14 seats, they argue, the party did not have to go back in 1986 and recover a great deal of lost ground.

As Tony Coelho, the Democrat from California who chaired the Democratic Congressional Campaign Committee, never tired of saying in 1986, "We can't win back seats we didn't lose."

There is truth to both those arguments. But there is also another, institutional factor that has helped shrink the window of vulnerability for incumbents of both parties.

Crafty cartographers, through the redistricting process, have significantly reduced the number of competitive House districts by increasing the number of safe constituencies that are enjoyed by Democrats and Republicans alike.

Challengers must necessarily temper their expectations in an era in which roughly two-thirds of all House members routinely win re-election with 60 percent of the vote or more.

Revisiting North Carolina

Of the five victories Democrats registered by defeating GOP incumbents, perhaps none were sweeter for the party's national leadership than the two seats won in North Carolina.

Coelho and other national strategists resented Republican advances made in 1984 in the traditionally Democratic Tarheel State; buoyed by the top-of-the-ticket presence of Reagan and Sen. Jesse Helms, the Republicans gained three House seats that year. National Democrats regarded 1986 as an important opportunity for revenge.

They got it in the central North Carolina-based 4th District by capitalizing on a GOP-created opening. Republican Cobey had an aura of vulnerability entering the 1986 election, stemming from two factors: his mixed record of political success (Cobey lost a 1980 bid for lieutenant governor and a 1982 bid for the 4th before finally winning election in 1984), and the Democratic nature of the district, which is anchored by college communities and a pool of state government employees in Raleigh.

But if those factors placed Cobey in tight competition with Democratic challenger David E. Price, it was a Cobey blunder that helped put Price over the edge. In mid-September, Cobey created a controversy by mailing out a campaign letter — under the heading, "Dear Christian Friend" — that urged fundamentalists to support him "so that our voice will not be silenced and then replaced by someone who is not willing to take a strong stance for the principles outlined in the word of God."

Price, a political science professor with a Yale divinity school degree, complained that the letter impugned his piety. With other Democrats and the news media loath to let voters forget the letter's remarks, Price was able to win easily. He posted a 56-44 percentage-point victory.

The other measure of Democratic revenge came in North Carolina's 11th District, where James McClure Clarke has been engaged in a political pas de deux with Republican Hendon for the last three House elections.

Bolstered by protest over the recession-racked economy, Clarke turned Hendon out of office in 1982, only to return the district to the Republican amidst the GOP tide that washed over mountainous western North Carolina two years later.

In 1986, Clarke came back, defying predictions that at 69, he was too old to make an effective challenger. He took advantage of concern about the possibility of a nuclear-waste dump site being located in the 11th to establish a 51 to 49 percent edge.

Landmark Win in the Delta

Another Democratic triumph in the South came in Mississippi's 2nd District, where two-term Republican Franklin was defeated by Mike Espy, a former assistant state attorney general. Espy's victory makes him the first black person Mississippi voters have sent to the House since Republican John R. Lynch left the chamber in 1883.

Members of the Delta-based 2nd District's black community had dreams of making that breakthrough in both 1982 and 1984, when Franklin faced off against a veteran civil rights leader, state Rep. Robert G. Clark. But Franklin managed to carve out narrow victories by capitalizing on a slight turnout advantage among white voters.

Espy managed to overcome Franklin by developing a sophisticated grass-roots organization that targeted previously untapped black voters, and by making a bolder bid

U.S. House Members Defeated

	Terms
Mike Strang, R-Colo.	1
Webb Franklin, R-Miss.	2
Robert A. Young, D-Mo.	5
Fred J. Eckert, R-N.Y.	1
Bill Cobey, R-N.C.	1
Bill Hendon, R-N.C.	2

1987 House Makeup, Party Gains and Losses

		99th Congress		100th Congress		
	Seats	Dem.	Rep.	Dem.	Rep.	Gain/ Loss
Ala.	7	5	2	5	2	
Alaska	1	0	1	0	1	
Ariz.	5	1	4	1	4	
Ark.	4	3	1	3	1	
Calif.	45	27	18	27	18	
Colo.	6	2	4	3	3	+1D/-1R
Conn.	6	3	3	3	3	
Del.	1	1	0	1	0	
Fla.	19	12	7	12	7	
Ga.	10	8	2	8	2	
Hawaii	2	2	0	1	1	-1D/+1R
Idaho	2	1	1	1	1	
Ill.	22	13	9	13	9	
Ind.	10	5	5	6	4	+1D/-1R
Iowa	6	2	4	2	4	
Kan.	5	2	3	2	3	
Ky.	7	4	3	4	3	
La.	8	6	2	5	3	-1D/+1R
Maine	2	0	2	1	1	+1D/-1R
Md.	8	6	2	6	2	
Mass.	11	10	1	10	1	
Mich.	18	11	7	11	7	
Minn.	8	5	3	5	3	
Miss.	5	3	2	4	1	+1D/-1R
Mo.	9	6	3	5	4	-1D/+1R
Mont.	2	1	1	1	1	
Neb.	3	0	3	0	3	
Nev.	2	1	1	1	1	
N.H.	2	0	2	0	2	
N.J.	14	8	6	8	6	
N.M.	3	1	2	1	2	
N.Y.	34	19	15	20	14	+1D/-1R
N.C.	11	6	5	8	3	+2D/-2R
N.D.	1	1	0	1	0	
Ohio	21	11	10	11	10	
Okla.	6	5	1	4	2	-1D/+1R
Ore.	5	3	2	3	2	
Pa.	23	13	10	12	11	-1D/+1R
R.I.	2	1	1	1	1	
S.C.	6	3	3	4	2	+1D/-1R
S.D.	1	1	0	1	0	
Tenn.	9	6	3	6	3	
Texas	27	17	10	17	10	
Utah	3	0	3	1	2	+1D/-1R
Vt.	1	0	1	0	1	
Va.	10	4	6	5	5	+1D/-1R
Wash.	8	5	3	5	3	
W.Va.	4	4	0	4	0	
Wis.	9	5	4	5	4	
Wyo.	1	0	1	0	1	
TOTALS	435	253	182	258	177	+5D/-5R

than Clark had made for white votes. The Democrat benefited further from feelings that Republican policies were not reviving the wilting agricultural economy.

GOP Breakthrough

In Louisiana's 8th District, the site of another contest between a black Democrat and a conservative white Republican, fortune smiled on the GOP.

Nursery owner Clyde Holloway, who had fallen short in two previous bids for this central Louisiana-based House seat, edged out black teacher and attorney Faye Williams. The contest — held to replace retiring Democratic Rep. Cathy (Mrs. Gillis) Long — forced many of the district's white Democrats to choose between race and party.

There are a total of 23 black members of the House in the 100th Congress, including Walter E. Fauntroy, the non-voting delegate from the District of Columbia.

Beating the Odds

In Colorado's 3rd District, GOP freshman Strang's re-election race had been billed as a cowboys-and-Indians contest, a reference to Strang's white Stetson hat and the North Cheyenne ancestry of Ben Nighthorse Campbell, his Democratic opponent.

For once, the Indian won. By emphasizing issues such as local water rights and farmers' needs, Campbell was able to hold down Strang's margin among voters along the conservative Western Slope and to emerge with an upset victory.

New York 30th

In New York's 30th District, the central issue was freshman Republican Eckert's personality. An aggressive, sometimes abrasive conservative Eckert had trouble shoring up support even among some members of his own party, who were more accustomed to the gentler style and moderate Republicanism practiced by former GOP Rep. Barber B. Conable Jr., Eckert's predecessor in the 30th.

Democrat Louise Slaughter, a two-term state assemblywoman who was born in Kentucky and projects a soft-spoken Southern charm, was well-positioned to take advantage of voter dissatisfaction with Eckert's manner. She picked up substantial crossover support and won by 12,000 votes.

Time Ran Out on Young

The surprising thing about the Democrats' lone incumbent casualty — Young of suburban St. Louis, Missouri — was the timing.

National Republican strategists have long been predicting that demographics would eventually catch up to the craggy, five-term incumbent. The GOP maintained that changes in the 2nd District's composition had cut into Young's blue-collar base and enhanced the political power of more affluent GOP suburbanites.

But Young's ability to fend off former state Rep. Jack Buechner in 1984 — despite the top-of-the-ticket presence of President Reagan — left doubts in the minds of even some Missouri Republicans about Buechner's chances in the 1986 rematch.

Buechner organized and raised money earlier than he had in his 1984 campaign, but ultimately, the amiable Republican may have Democratic Senate nominee Harriett Woods to thank for his victory.

Buechner had never been on the best terms with hard-core conservatives in St. Louis County, largely because of the moderate-to-liberal reputation he had built during his tenure

House Switched Seats, Newcomers and Losers

State	District	Old	New	Winner	Loser	Incumbent
Alabama	7	D	D	Claude Harris (D)	Bill McFarland (R)	Richard C. Shelby (D) [1]
Arizona	1	R	R	John J. Rhodes III (R)	Harry Braun III (D)	John McCain (R) [1]
	4	R	R	Jon Kyl (R)	Philip R. Davis (D)	Eldon Rudd (R) [2]
California	2	R	R	Wally Herger (R)	Stephen C. Swendiman (D)	Gene Chappie (R) [2]
	12	R	R	Ernest L. Konnyu (R)	Lance T. Weil (D)	Ed Zschau (R) [1]
	21	R	R	Elton Gallegly (R)	Gilbert R. Saldana (D)	Bobbi Fiedler (R) [3]
Colorado	2	D	D	David Skaggs (D)	Michael J. Norton (R)	Timothy E. Wirth (D) [1]
	3	R	D	Ben Nighthorse Campbell (D)	Mike Strang (R)	Strang
	5	R	R	Joel Hefley (R)	Bill Story (D)	Ken Kramer (R) [1]
Florida	2	D	D	Bill Grant (D)	unopposed	Don Fuqua (D) [2]
Georgia	5	D	D	John Lewis (D)	Portia A. Scott (R)	Wyche Fowler Jr. (D) [1]
Hawaii	1	D	R	Patricia Saiki (R)	Mufi Hannemann (D)	Neil Abercrombie (D) [4]
Illinois	4	R	R	Jack Davis (R)	Shawn Collins (D)	George M. O'Brien (R) [5]
	14	R	R	J. Dennis Hastert (R)	Mary Lou Kearns (D)	John E. Grotberg (R) [2, 9]
Indiana	5	R	D	Jim Jontz (D)	James R. Butcher (R)	Elwood Hillis (R) [2]
Iowa	3	R	D	David R. Nagle (D)	John McIntee (R)	Cooper Evans (R) [2]
	6	D	R	Fred Grandy (R)	Clayton Hodgson (D)	Berkley Bedell (D) [2]
Kentucky	4	R	R	Jim Bunning (R)	Terry L. Mann (D)	Gene Snyder (R) [2]
Louisiana	6	R	R	Richard Baker (R)	unopposed	W. Henson Moore (R) [1]
	7	D	D	Jimmy Hayes (D)	Margaret Lowenthal (D)	John B. Breaux (D) [1]
	8	D	R	Clyde Holloway (R)	Faye Williams (D)	Cathy (Mrs. Gillis) Long (D) [2]
Maine	1	R	D	Joseph E. Brennan (D)	H. Rollin Ives (R)	John R. McKernan Jr. (R) [6]
Maryland	3	D	D	Benjamin L. Cardin (D)	Ross Z. Pierpont (R)	Barbara A. Mikulski (D) [1]
	4	R	D	Thomas McMillen (D)	Robert R. Neall (R)	Marjorie S. Holt (R) [2]
	7	D	D	Kweisi Mfume (D)	Saint George I. B. Crosse III (R)	Parren J. Mitchell (D) [7]
	8	D	R	Constance A. Morella (R)	Stewart Bainum Jr. (D)	Michael D. Barnes (D) [3]
Massachusetts	8	D	D	Joseph P. Kennedy II (D)	Clark C. Abt (R)	Thomas P. O'Neill Jr. (D) [2]
Michigan	4	R	R	Fred Upton (R)	Dan Roche (D)	Mark D. Siljander (R) [4]
Mississippi	2	R	D	Mike Espy (D)	Webb Franklin (R)	Franklin
Missouri	2	D	R	Jack Buechner (R)	Robert A. Young (D)	Young
Nevada	1	D	D	James H. Bilbray (D)	Bob Ryan (R)	Harry Reid (D) [1]
New York	1	R	D	George J. Hochbrueckner (D)	Gregory J. Blass (R)	William Carney (R) [2]
	6	D	D	Floyd H. Flake (D)	Richard Dietl (R)	Alton R. Waldon Jr. (D) [4]
	30	R	D	Louise Slaughter (D)	Fred J. Eckert (R)	Eckert
	34	D	R	Amory Houghton Jr. (R)	Larry M. Himelein (D)	Stan Lundine (D) [7]
North Carolina	3	D	D	Martin Lancaster (D)	Gerald B. Hurst (R)	Charles Whitley (D) [2]
	4	R	D	David E. Price (D)	Bill Cobey (R)	Cobey
	10	R	R	Cass Ballenger (R)	Lester D. Roark (D)	James T. Broyhill (R) [1]
	11	R	D	James McClure Clarke (D)	Bill Hendon (R)	Hendon
Ohio	8	R	R	Donald E. "Buz" Lukens (R)	John W. Griffin (D)	Thomas N. Kindness (R) [1]
	14	D	D	Thomas C. Sawyer (D)	Lynn Slaby (R)	John F. Seiberling (D) [2]
Oklahoma	1	D	R	James M. Inhofe (R)	Gary D. Allison (D)	James R. Jones (D) [1]
Oregon	4	D	D	Peter A. DeFazio (D)	Bruce Long (R)	James Weaver (D) [2]
Pennsylvania	7	D	R	Curt Weldon (R)	Bill Spingler (D)	Bob Edgar (D) [1]
South Carolina	1	R	R	Arthur Ravenel Jr. (R)	Jimmy Stuckey (D)	Thomas F. Hartnett (R) [7]
	4	R	D	Elizabeth Patterson (D)	William D. Workman III (R)	Carroll A. Campbell Jr. (R) [6]
South Dakota	AL	D	D	Tim Johnson (D)	Dale Bell (R)	Thomas A. Daschle (D) [1]
Texas	21	R	R	Lamar Smith (R)	Pete Snelson (D)	Tom Loeffler (R) [8]
Utah	2	R	D	Wayne Owens (D)	Tom Shimizu (R)	David S. Monson (R) [2]
Virginia	2	R	D	Owen B. Pickett (D)	A. J. "Joe" Canada Jr. (R)	G. William Whitehurst (R) [2]

[1] Ran for Senate.
[2] Retired.
[3] Defeated in Senate primary.
[4] Defeated in primary.
[5] Died July 17, 1986.
[6] Ran for governor.
[7] Ran for lieutenant governor.
[8] Defeated in gubernatorial primary.
[9] Died November 15, 1986.

in the Missouri Legislature. But local conservatives were eager for the opportunity to come out to vote against Woods — whom they deride as an unabashed liberal. Having cast that vote, many conservatives in the 2nd District stayed on the GOP ballot and chose Buechner.

Farm Belt Vote a Mixed Bag

Anyone searching for signs of a significant rural revolt in the 1986 House contests will find mixed results. Democrats had hoped that farmers throughout the Midwest would blame the Republican Party for their economic woes. Some didn't; some did.

Democrat Tim Johnson capitalized on farm discontent to register a stronger-than-expected victory in the race for South Dakota's at-large House seat, left vacant due to Democrat Thomas A. Daschle's successful Senate candidacy. And in Iowa, farm fury contributed at least in part to Democrat Dave Nagle's triumph in the 3rd District, vacant because of GOP Rep. Cooper Evans' retirement.

But elsewhere in Iowa, there were no signs of the storm. Republican Reps. Tom Tauke and Jim Lightfoot both held off farm protest candidates; in the open 6th District, vacated by retiring Democratic Rep. Berkley Bedell, corn and soybean grower Clayton Hodgson lost out to television actor — and Republican — Fred Grandy. Similarly, Republican Reps. E. Thomas Coleman and Bill Emerson of Missouri turned back challenges from farmers.

U.S. House

99th Congress		100th Congress	
Democrats	253	Democrats	258
Republicans	182	Republicans	177

Democrats

Net Gain	5
Freshmen	27
Incumbents re-elected	231
Incumbents defeated	1

Republicans

Net Loss	5
Freshmen	23
Incumbents re-elected	154
Incumbents defeated	5

The Unexpected

Nonetheless, Democrats did enjoy some surprises. In South Carolina, state Sen. Elizabeth Patterson took the 4th District seat vacated by GOP Rep. Carroll A. Campbell Jr., who was elected governor. Patterson had been considered an underdog against Greenville Mayor William D. Workman.

In Indiana, Democrats took advantage of the retirement of 5th District Republican Rep. Elwood Hillis to steal away a traditionally GOP seat. State Sen. Jim Jontz, an astute politician whose career reflects his ability to buck the electoral odds, won the seat for the Democrats.

GOP Surprises

The GOP was not without its own surprises, however. Republican Pat Saiki became the first person of her party ever to win a House seat in Hawaii. She defeated Democrat Mufi Hannemann for the right to represent the Honolulu-based 1st District.

Republicans also derived satisfaction from capturing two districts vacated by Democrats who ran unsuccessfully for the Senate. Even as Pennsylvania's Bob Edgar and Oklahoma's James R. Jones were losing, Republicans Curt Weldon and James M. Inhofe were winning House seats.

House Membership in 100th Congress . . .

House Lineup

Democrats 258	**Republicans 177**
Freshman Democrats - 27	Freshman Republicans - 23
# Freshman Representative	† Former Representative

ALABAMA
1. Sonny Callahan (R)
2. William L. Dickinson (R)
3. Bill Nichols (D)
4. Tom Bevill (D)
5. Ronnie G. Flippo (D)
6. Ben Erdreich (D)
7. Claude Harris (D) #

ALASKA
AL Don Young (R)

ARIZONA
1. John J. Rhodes III (R) #
2. Morris K. Udall (D)
3. Bob Stump (R)
4. Jon Kyl (R) #
5. Jim Kolbe (R)

ARKANSAS
1. Bill Alexander (D)
2. Tommy F. Robinson (D)
3. John Paul Hammerschmidt (R)
4. Beryl Anthony Jr. (D)

CALIFORNIA
1. Douglas H. Bosco (D)
2. Wally Herger (R) #
3. Robert T. Matsui (D)
4. Vic Fazio (D)
5. Sala Burton (D)
6. Barbara Boxer (D)
7. George Miller (D)
8. Ronald V. Dellums (D)
9. Fortney H. "Pete" Stark (D)
10. Don Edwards (D)
11. Tom Lantos (D)
12. Ernest L. Konnyu (R) #
13. Norman Y. Mineta (D)
14. Norman D. Shumway (R)
15. Tony Coelho (D)
16. Leon E. Panetta (D)
17. Charles Pashayan Jr. (R)
18. Richard H. Lehman (D)
19. Robert J. Lagomarsino (R)
20. William M. Thomas (R)
21. Elton Gallegly (R) #
22. Carlos J. Moorhead (R)
23. Anthony C. Beilenson (D)
24. Henry A. Waxman (D)
25. Edward R. Roybal (D)
26. Howard L. Berman (D)
27. Mel Levine (D)
28. Julian C. Dixon (D)
29. Augustus F. Hawkins (D)
30. Matthew G. Martinez (D)
31. Mervyn M. Dymally (D)
32. Glenn M. Anderson (D)
33. David Dreier (R)
34. Esteban Edward Torres (D)
35. Jerry Lewis (R)
36. George E. Brown Jr. (D)
37. Al McCandless (R)
38. Bob Dornan (R)
39. William E. Dannemeyer (R)
40. Robert E. Badham (R)
41. Bill Lowery (R)
42. Dan Lungren (R)
43. Ron Packard (R)
44. Jim Bates (D)
45. Duncan L. Hunter (R)

COLORADO
1. Patricia Schroeder (D)
2. David Skaggs (D) #
3. Ben Nighthorse Campbell (D) #
4. Hank Brown (R)
5. Joel Hefley (R) #
6. Daniel L. Schaefer (R)

CONNECTICUT
1. Barbara B. Kennelly (D)
2. Sam Gejdenson (D)
3. Bruce A. Morrison (D)
4. Stewart B. McKinney (R)
5. John G. Rowland (R)
6. Nancy L. Johnson (R)

DELAWARE
AL Thomas R. Carper (D)

FLORIDA
1. Earl Hutto (D)
2. Bill Grant (D) #
3. Charles E. Bennett (D)
4. Bill Chappell Jr. (D)
5. Bill McCollum (R)
6. Buddy MacKay (D)
7. Sam Gibbons (D)
8. C.W. Bill Young (R)
9. Michael Bilirakis (R)
10. Andy Ireland (R)
11. Bill Nelson (D)
12. Tom Lewis (R)
13. Connie Mack (R)
14. Daniel A. Mica (D)
15. E. Clay Shaw Jr. (R)
16. Larry Smith (D)
17. William Lehman (D)
18. Claude Pepper (D)
19. Dante B. Fascell (D)

GEORGIA
1. Robert Lindsay Thomas (D)
2. Charles Hatcher (D)
3. Richard Ray (D)
4. Pat Swindall (R)
5. John Lewis (D) #
6. Newt Gingrich (R)
7. George "Buddy" Darden (D)
8. J. Roy Rowland (D)
9. Ed Jenkins (D)
10. Doug Barnard Jr. (D)

HAWAII
1. Patricia Saiki (R) #
2. Daniel K. Akaka (D)

IDAHO
1. Larry E. Craig (R)
2. Richard H. Stallings (D)

ILLINOIS
1. Charles A. Hayes (D)
2. Gus Savage (D)
3. Marty Russo (D)
4. Jack Davis (R) #
5. William O. Lipinski (D)
6. Henry J. Hyde (R)
7. Cardiss Collins (D)
8. Dan Rostenkowski (D)
9. Sidney R. Yates (D)
10. John Edward Porter (R)
11. Frank Annunzio (D)
12. Philip M. Crane (R)
13. Harris W. Fawell (R)
14. J. Dennis Hastert (R) #
15. Edward R. Madigan (R)
16. Lynn Martin (R)
17. Lane Evans (D)
18. Robert H. Michel (R)
19. Terry L. Bruce (D)
20. Richard J. Durbin (D)
21. Melvin Price (D)
22. Kenneth J. Gray (D)

INDIANA
1. Peter J. Visclosky (D)
2. Philip R. Sharp (D)
3. John Hiler (R)
4. Dan Coats (R)
5. Jim Jontz (D) #
6. Dan Burton (R)
7. John T. Myers (R)
8. Frank McCloskey (D)
9. Lee H. Hamilton (D)
10. Andrew Jacobs Jr. (D)

IOWA
1. Jim Leach (R)
2. Tom Tauke (R)
3. Dave R. Nagle (D) #
4. Neal Smith (D)
5. Jim Lightfoot (R)
6. Fred Grandy (R) #

KANSAS
1. Pat Roberts (R)
2. Jim Slattery (D)
3. Jan Meyers (R)
4. Dan Glickman (D)
5. Bob Whittaker (R)

KENTUCKY
1. Carroll Hubbard Jr. (D)
2. William H. Natcher (D)
3. Romano L. Mazzoli (D)
4. Jim Bunning (R) #
5. Harold Rogers (R)
6. Larry J. Hopkins (R)
7. Carl C. Perkins (D)

LOUISIANA
1. Bob Livingston (R)
2. Lindy (Mrs. Hale) Boggs (D)
3. W. J. "Billy" Tauzin (D)
4. Buddy Roemer (D)
5. Jerry Huckaby (D)
6. Richard Baker (R) #
7. Jimmy Hayes (D) #
8. Clyde Holloway (R) #

MAINE
1. Joseph E. Brennan (D) #
2. Olympia J. Snowe (R)

MARYLAND
1. Roy Dyson (D)
2. Helen Delich Bentley (R)
3. Benjamin L. Cardin (D) #
4. Thomas McMillen (D) #
5. Steny H. Hoyer (D)
6. Beverly B. Byron (D)
7. Kweisi Mfume (D) #
8. Constance A. Morella (R) #

MASSACHUSETTS
1. Silvio O. Conte (R)
2. Edward P. Boland (D)
3. Joseph D. Early (D)
4. Barney Frank (D)
5. Chester G. Atkins (D)
6. Nicholas Mavroules (D)
7. Edward J. Markey (D)
8. Joseph P. Kennedy II (D) #
9. Joe Moakley (D)
10. Gerry E. Studds (D)
11. Brian J. Donnelly (D)

MICHIGAN
1. John Conyers Jr. (D)
2. Carl D. Pursell (R)
3. Howard Wolpe (D)
4. Fred Upton (R) #
5. Paul B. Henry (R)
6. Bob Carr (D)
7. Dale E. Kildee (D)
8. Bob Traxler (D)
9. Guy Vander Jagt (R)
10. Bill Schuette (R)
11. Robert W. Davis (R)
12. David E. Bonior (D)
13. George W. Crockett Jr. (D)
14. Dennis M. Hertel (D)
15. William D. Ford (D)
16. John D. Dingell (D)
17. Sander M. Levin (D)
18. William S. Broomfield (R)

MINNESOTA
1. Timothy J. Penny (D)
2. Vin Weber (R)
3. Bill Frenzel (R)
4. Bruce F. Vento (D)
5. Martin Olav Sabo (D)
6. Gerry Sikorski (D)

. . . Reflects Strong Showing by Incumbents

7. Arlan Stangeland (R)
8. James L. Oberstar (D)

MISSISSIPPI
1. Jamie L. Whitten (D)
2. Mike Espy (D) #
3. G. V. "Sonny" Montgomery (D)
4. Wayne Dowdy (D)
5. Trent Lott (R)

MISSOURI
1. William L. Clay (D)
2. Jack Buechner (R) #
3. Richard A. Gephardt (D)
4. Ike Skelton (D)
5. Alan Wheat (D)
6. E. Thomas Coleman (R)
7. Gene Taylor (R)
8. Bill Emerson (R)
9. Harold L. Volkmer (D)

MONTANA
1. Pat Williams (D)
2. Ron Marlenee (R)

NEBRASKA
1. Doug Bereuter (R)
2. Hal Daub (R)
3. Virginia Smith (R)

NEVADA
1. James H. Bilbray (D) #
2. Barbara F. Vucanovich (R)

NEW HAMPSHIRE
1. Robert C. Smith (R)
2. Judd Gregg (R)

NEW JERSEY
1. James J. Florio (D)
2. William J. Hughes (D)
3. James J. Howard (D)
4. Christopher H. Smith (R)
5. Marge Roukema (R)
6. Bernard J. Dwyer (D)
7. Matthew J. Rinaldo (R)
8. Robert A. Roe (D)
9. Robert G. Torricelli (D)
10. Peter W. Rodino Jr. (D)
11. Dean A. Gallo (R)
12. Jim Courter (R)
13. H. James Saxton (R)
14. Frank J. Guarini (D)

NEW MEXICO
1. Manuel Lujan Jr. (R)
2. Joe Skeen (R)
3. Bill Richardson (D)

NEW YORK
1. George J. Hochbrueckner (D) #
2. Thomas J. Downey (D)
3. Robert J. Mrazek (D)
4. Norman F. Lent (R)
5. Raymond J. McGrath (R)
6. Floyd H. Flake (D) #
7. Gary L. Ackerman (D)
8. James H. Scheuer (D)
9. Thomas J. Manton (D)
10. Charles E. Schumer (D)
11. Edolphus Towns (D)
12. Major R. Owens (D)
13. Stephen J. Solarz (D)
14. Guy V. Molinari (R)
15. Bill Green (R)
16. Charles B. Rangel (D)
17. Ted Weiss (D)
18. Robert Garcia (D)
19. Mario Biaggi (D)
20. Joseph J. DioGuardi (R)
21. Hamilton Fish Jr. (R)
22. Benjamin A. Gilman (R)
23. Samuel S. Stratton (D)
24. Gerald B. H. Solomon (R)
25. Sherwood L. Boehlert (R)
26. David O'B. Martin (R)
27. George C. Wortley (R)
28. Matthew F. McHugh (D)
29. Frank Horton (R)
30. Louise M. Slaughter (D) #
31. Jack F. Kemp (R)
32. John J. LaFalce (D)
33. Henry J. Nowak (D)
34. Amory Houghton Jr. (R) #

NORTH CAROLINA
1. Walter B. Jones (D)
2. Tim Valentine (D)
3. Martin Lancaster (D) #
4. David E. Price (D) #
5. Stephen L. Neal (D)
6. Howard Coble (R)
7. Charlie Rose (D)
8. W. G. "Bill" Hefner (D)
9. J. Alex McMillan (R)
10. Cass Ballenger (R) #
11. James McClure Clarke (D)† #

NORTH DAKOTA
AL Byron L. Dorgan (D)

OHIO
1. Thomas A. Luken (D)
2. Bill Gradison (R)
3. Tony P. Hall (D)
4. Michael G. Oxley (R)
5. Delbert L. Latta (R)
6. Bob McEwen (R)
7. Michael DeWine (R)
8. Donald E. "Buz" Lukens (R)† #
9. Marcy Kaptur (D)
10. Clarence E. Miller (R)
11. Dennis E. Eckart (D)
12. John R. Kasich (R)
13. Don J. Pease (D)
14. Tom Sawyer (D) #
15. Chalmers P. Wylie (R)
16. Ralph Regula (R)
17. James A. Traficant Jr. (D)
18. Douglas Applegate (D)
19. Edward F. Feighan (D)
20. Mary Rose Oakar (D)
21. Louis Stokes (D)

OKLAHOMA
1. James M. Inhofe (R) #
2. Mike Synar (D)
3. Wes Watkins (D)
4. Dave McCurdy (D)
5. Mickey Edwards (R)
6. Glenn English (D)

OREGON
1. Les AuCoin (D)
2. Robert F. Smith (R)
3. Ron Wyden (D)
4. Peter A. DeFazio (D) #
5. Denny Smith (R)

PENNSYLVANIA
1. Thomas M. Foglietta (D)
2. William H. Gray III (D)
3. Robert A. Borski (D)
4. Joe Kolter (D)
5. Richard T. Schulze (R)
6. Gus Yatron (D)
7. Curt Weldon (R) #
8. Peter H. Kostmayer (D)
9. Bud Shuster (R)
10. Joseph M. McDade (R)
11. Paul E. Kanjorski (D)
12. John P. Murtha (D)
13. Lawrence Coughlin (R)
14. William J. Coyne (D)
15. Don Ritter (R)
16. Robert S. Walker (R)
17. George W. Gekas (R)
18. Doug Walgren (D)
19. Bill Goodling (R)
20. Joseph M. Gaydos (D)
21. Tom Ridge (R)
22. Austin J. Murphy (D)
23. William F. Clinger Jr. (R)

RHODE ISLAND
1. Fernand J. St Germain (D)
2. Claudine Schneider (R)

SOUTH CAROLINA
1. Arthur Ravenel Jr. (R) #
2. Floyd Spence (R)
3. Butler Derrick (D)
4. Elizabeth J. Patterson (D) #
5. John M. Spratt Jr. (D)
6. Robin Tallon (D)

SOUTH DAKOTA
AL Tim Johnson (D) #

TENNESSEE
1. James H. Quillen (R)
2. John J. Duncan (R)
3. Marilyn Lloyd (D)
4. Jim Cooper (D)
5. Bill Boner (D)
6. Bart Gordon (D)
7. Don Sundquist (R)
8. Ed Jones (D)
9. Harold E. Ford (D)

TEXAS
1. Jim Chapman (D)
2. Charles Wilson (D)
3. Steve Bartlett (R)
4. Ralph M. Hall (D)
5. John Bryant (D)
6. Joe L. Barton (R)
7. Bill Archer (R)
8. Jack Fields (R)
9. Jack Brooks (D)
10. J. J. Pickle (D)
11. Marvin Leath (D)
12. Jim Wright (D)
13. Beau Boulter (R)
14. Mac Sweeney (R)
15. E. "Kika" de la Garza (D)
16. Ronald D. Coleman (D)
17. Charles W. Stenholm (D)
18. Mickey Leland (D)
19. Larry Combest (R)
20. Henry B. Gonzalez (D)
21. Lamar Smith (R) #
22. Thomas D. DeLay (R)
23. Albert G. Bustamante (D)
24. Martin Frost (D)
25. Michael A. Andrews (D)
26. Dick Armey (R)
27. Solomon P. Ortiz (D)

UTAH
1. James V. Hansen (R)
2. Wayne Owens (D)† #
3. Howard C. Nielson (R)

VERMONT
AL James M. Jeffords (R)

VIRGINIA
1. Herbert H. Bateman (R)
2. Owen B. Pickett (D) #
3. Thomas J. Bliley Jr. (R)
4. Norman Sisisky (D)
5. Dan Daniel (D)
6. James R. Olin (D)
7. D. French Slaughter Jr. (R)
8. Stan Parris (R)
9. Frederick C. Boucher (D)
10. Frank R. Wolf (R)

WASHINGTON
1. John R. Miller (R)
2. Al Swift (D)
3. Don Bonker (D)
4. Sid Morrison (R)
5. Thomas S. Foley (D)
6. Norman D. Dicks (D)
7. Mike Lowry (D)
8. Rod Chandler (R)

WEST VIRGINIA
1. Alan B. Mollohan (D)
2. Harley O. Staggers Jr. (D)
3. Bob Wise (D)
4. Nick J. Rahall II (D)

WISCONSIN
1. Les Aspin (D)
2. Robert W. Kastenmeier (D)
3. Steve Gunderson (R)
4. Gerald D. Kleczka (D)
5. Jim Moody (D)
6. Thomas E. Petri (R)
7. David R. Obey (D)
8. Toby Roth (R)
9. F. James Sensenbrenner Jr. (R)

WYOMING
AL Dick Cheney (R)

Republicans Take Solace in Governors' Races

Wins in South Include Texas and Florida

Democratic efforts to portray the 1986 elections as a repudiation of the Republican Party were mitigated by the strong GOP showing in gubernatorial contests. Republicans made a net gain of eight governorships.

The Democrats, who entered the election holding 34 of the 50 governorships, saw their advantage drop to 26-24. The GOP count is the largest since 1970, when the party last held a majority of the governorships. *(State-by-state returns, p. 24-B; governors in 1987, p. 20-B)*

Despite the overall Republican success in the gubernatorial elections, the party lost three of its open seats: Oregon, Pennsylvania and Tennessee. But these defeats were offset by the unseating of Democratic incumbents in Texas and Wisconsin, and by GOP victories in nine Democratic open seats — including upset wins in Alabama and Arizona and a solid victory in megastate Florida.

Republicans benefited from Democratic self-destruction in several states, particularly Alabama and Illinois. Democrats also suffered from the problem of "exposure." They defended 27 governorships, the GOP only 9. Democrats won a majority of the 36 seats at stake, but that was not enough to avoid losing ground to the GOP.

An Eye on the Future

The Republican success could put the party in a more favorable position to influence congressional redistricting in the early 1990s. If, for instance, GOP governors in fast-growing Texas and Florida seek and win re-election in 1990, they may be able to see that the GOP reaps some of the new seats those states are sure to gain. Similarly, if GOP Gov. James R. Thompson wins another term in 1990, he could work to protect his party's interests in Illinois, which is likely to lose seats.

But there was also disappointment for Republicans seeking more influence in redistricting: The GOP failed to dent Democratic domination of the state legislatures. Democrats claimed to have picked up at least 150 legislative seats and to have gained control of four more state chambers.

A more immediate result of the GOP gubernatorial gains is that the party's 1988 presidential nominee will find more helping hands in state capitals across the country.

GOP Incumbents Thrive

The base of the Republican success on Nov. 4 was a small core of popular incumbents. California's George Deukmejian defeated Los Angeles Mayor Tom Bradley by less than 1 percentage point in 1982, but as the state deficit he inherited turned into a surplus, his political stock rose. Bradley campaigned aggressively in 1986, accusing the incumbent of failing to deal with toxic wastes. But Deukmejian maintained his image as a competent fiscal manager and won easily.

GOP incumbents in New England won re-election: Rhode Island Gov. Edward DiPrete swamped Democratic businessman Bruce G. Sundlun by 2-to-1, while New Hampshire's John H. Sununu won more modestly, with 54 percent, over Democrat Paul McEachern. Also in New England, the GOP picked up Maine, where Democratic Gov. Joseph E. Brennan ran successfully for the House seat of GOP Rep. John R. McKernan Jr. McKernan won the governorship, taking 40 percent in a four-candidate race.

Unpopularity of Democratic incumbents helped produce GOP victories in Wisconsin and Texas. Democratic Gov. Anthony S. Earl never lived down the "Tony the Taxer" label he received after pushing through Wisconsin tax increases in 1983, and he lost to state House Minority Leader Tommy G. Thompson.

In Texas, a budget shortfall resulting from the state's energy and farm recessions forced Democratic Gov. Mark White to propose a tax increase during the 1986 campaign. He also had antagonized several key groups, including teachers, who opposed his push for competency testing. White lost to the man he had ousted from office in 1982, Republican William Clements.

GOP Progress in the South

Despite the GOP's poor showing in Senate elections in the South, Republicans looking for evidence of realignment can point out that the party made its greatest gubernatorial gains in that region. A big plum was Florida, where Tampa Mayor Bob Martinez, a former Democrat, will succeed Democratic Sen.-elect Bob Graham.

Martinez' pledge to support Reagan administration priorities helped him overcome doubts of conservative Republicans, who were skeptical about his recent party switch and his former support for President Carter.

Martinez also appealed to conservative Democrats who disliked their party's liberal nominee, former state Rep. Steve Pajcic, and he won the backing of many Cuban-Americans, although he is of Spanish, not Cuban, descent.

Oklahoma voters endorsed the political comeback attempt of Henry Bellmon, a former GOP governor and senator. The economic stagnation that made the outgoing Democratic administration unpopular also made Bellmon a strong favorite. But a vigorous

Governorships

Current lineup		1987	
Democrats	34	Democrats	26
Republicans	16	Republicans	24

Democrats

Net loss	8
Incumbents re-elected	10
Incumbents defeated	2

(Anthody S. Earl, Wis: Mark White, Texas)

Republicans

Net Gain	8
Incumbents re-elected	5
Incumbents defeated	0

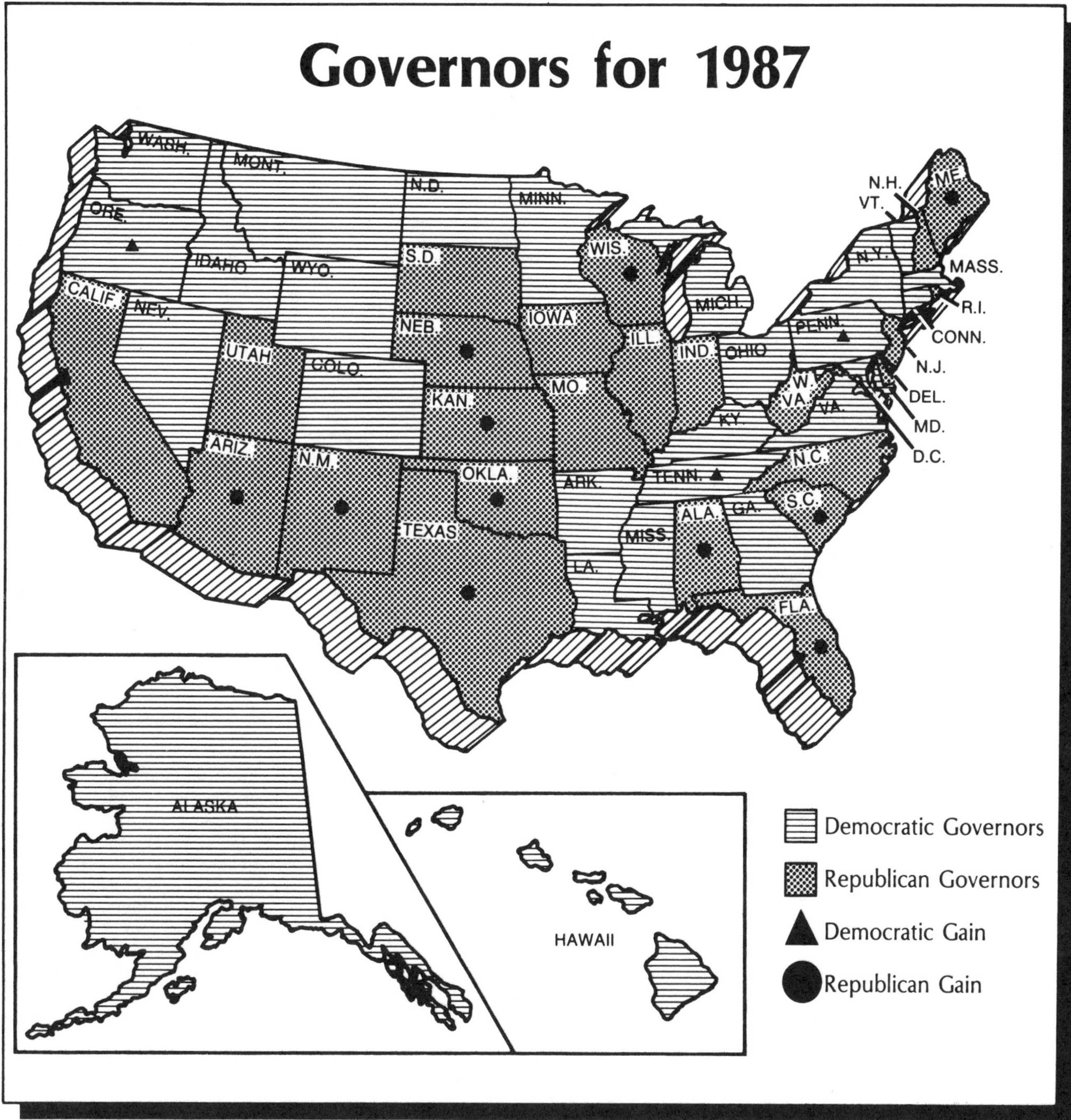

campaign by conservative Democratic businessman David Walters, an upset primary winner, held Bellmon to a slimmer-than-expected victory.

The farm crisis that helped oust at least two Republican senators did not hurt most of the party's gubernatorial nominees. Iowa incumbent Terry E. Branstad won narrowly, as did GOP candidates for open governorships in South Dakota, Nebraska and Kansas. Their victories gave the GOP a strong hold on the breadbasket. Minnesota incumbent Rudy Perpich was the only Democrat to win in a Midwestern state where agriculture was a major issue.

Self-Destruction

In several states, Democrats were their own worst enemies. Alabama Democratic Gov. George C. Wallace's retirement sparked a fierce squabble over the Democratic nomination that helped Guy Hunt become the state's first Republican governor since Reconstruction.

The state Democratic Party's reversal of conservative state Attorney General Charles Graddick's apparent runoff win over Lt. Gov. William J. Baxley (because of illegal Republican crossover votes for Graddick) led to court challenges that lasted long into the campaign. Graddick dropped a threatened write-in campaign just before the election, but blasted Baxley, a moderate with support from blacks and labor, as the candidate of "special interests."

Baxley did not offset conservative animosity by portraying Hunt, a for-

1987 Occupants of the Nation's Statehouses

Here is a list of the governors and governors-elect of the 50 states, and the years in which each office is next up for election. The names of governors elected on Nov. 4 are *italicized.* Asterisks (*) denote incumbents re-elected.

Alabama — *Guy Hunt (R) 1990*
Alaska — *Steve Cowper (D) 1990*
Arizona — *Evan Mecham (R) 1990*
Arkansas — *Bill Clinton (D) 1990**
California — *George Deukmejian (R) 1990**
Colorado — *Roy Romer (D) 1990*
Connecticut — *William A. O'Neill (D) 1990**
Delaware — Michael N. Castle (R) 1988
Florida — *Bob Martinez (R) 1990*
Georgia — *Joe Frank Harris (D) 1990**
Hawaii — *John Waihee (D) 1990*
Idaho — *Cecil D. Andrus (D) 1990*
Illinois — *James R. Thompson (R) 1990**
Indiana — Robert D. Orr (R) 1988
Iowa — *Terry E. Branstad (R) 1990**
Kansas — *Mike Hayden (R) 1990*
Kentucky — Martha Layne Collins (D) 1987
Louisiana — Edwin W. Edwards (D) 1987
Maine — *John R. McKernan Jr. (R) 1990*
Maryland — *William Donald Schaefer (D) 1990*
Massachusetts — *Michael S. Dukakis (D) 1990**
Michigan — *James J. Blanchard (D) 1990**
Minnesota — *Rudy Perpich (D) 1990**
Mississippi — Bill Allain (D) 1987
Missouri — John Ashcroft (R) 1988
Montana — Ted Schwinden (D) 1988
Nebraska — *Kay A. Orr (R) 1990*
Nevada — *Richard H. Bryan (D) 1990**
New Hampshire — *John H. Sununu (R) 1988**
New Jersey — Thomas H. Kean (R) 1989
New Mexico — *Garrey E. Carruthers (R) 1990*
New York — *Mario M. Cuomo (D) 1990**
North Carolina — James G. Martin (R) 1988
North Dakota — George Sinner (D) 1988
Ohio — *Richard F. Celeste (D) 1990**
Oklahoma — *Henry Bellmon (R) 1990*
Oregon — *Neil Goldschmidt (D) 1990*
Pennsylvania — *Bob Casey (D) 1990*
Rhode Island — *Edward DiPrete (R) 1988**
South Carolina — *Carroll A. Campbell Jr. (R) 1990*
South Dakota — *George S. Mickelson (R) 1990*
Tennessee — *Ned McWherter (D) 1990*
Texas — *Bill Clements (R) 1990*
Utah — Norman H. Bangerter (R) 1988
Vermont — *Madeleine M. Kunin (D) 1988**
Virginia — Gerald L. Baliles (D) 1989
Washington — Booth Gardner (D) 1988
West Virginia — Arch A. Moore Jr. (R) 1988
Wisconsin — *Tommy G. Thompson (R) 1990*
Wyoming — *Mike Sullivan (D) 1990*

mer county probate judge and Amway distributor, as unqualified. A huge Democratic crossover vote boosted Hunt to his surprise victory. As the 1978 GOP gubernatorial nominee, he lost by 3-to-1.

In Arizona, Republican Evan Mecham's victory to succeed Democratic Gov. Bruce Babbitt was even more surprising. Mecham, a conservative perennial candidate, was an underdog against the Democratic state school Superintendent Carolyn Warner. But businessman Bill Schulz jumped in as an independent and split the Democratic vote, enabling Mecham to win a plurality.

At one time, Illinois' Thompson was viewed as vulnerable to Democrat Adlai E. Stevenson III, whom he narrowly beat in 1982. But Stevenson's challenge fizzled when two associates of Lyndon H. LaRouche Jr. won Democratic primaries for state office. Stevenson disowned the pair and renounced his Democratic nomination, but his independent bid fell far short.

Democrats Pick Off GOP Seats

The biggest accomplishment for Democrats was their success at taking over seats being given up by Republican incumbents. The Democrats took three of four seats in that category. Their largest catch was Pennsylvania, where former state Auditor Bob Casey beat Lt. Gov. William W. Scranton III to succeed Republican Gov. Dick Thornburgh.

In Tennessee, state House Speaker Ned Ray McWherter, a populist-style Democrat, thwarted the comeback of former GOP Gov. Winfield Dunn. And in Oregon, former Portland Mayor Neil Goldschmidt held off former Oregon Secretary of State Norma Paulus.

Other Democratic bright spots were the landslide victories of two incumbents often mentioned as possible Democratic presidential contenders — New York's Mario M. Cuomo and Massachusetts' Michael S. Dukakis. Economic comebacks in the "Rust Belt" helped Democrats James J. Blanchard of Michigan and Richard F. Celeste of Ohio score easy wins.

As expected, Baltimore Mayor William Donald Schaefer took Maryland's open seat by a huge margin. Democrats maintained control in tighter open-seat races in Alaska, Colorado, Hawaii, Idaho and Wyoming.

Democratic Gov. Madeleine M. Kunin won re-election in Vermont, though she failed to take the majority necessary to keep the contest from being settled by the Legislature in January, 1987. Bernard Sanders, Burlington's socialist mayor, took 15 percent of the vote, helping hold Kunin to 47 percent. Democrats control the state Senate, and they gained a tie in the state House, so she had no trouble winning the Legislature's support.

Kunin's victory and the win in Nebraska of GOP state Treasurer Kay A. Orr over former Lincoln Mayor Helen Boosalis increase the number of women governors to three (Kentucky Democrat Martha Layne Collins is the third). But other women running as major-party nominees lost in Arizona, Connecticut, Oregon and Nevada.

Two major-party black candidates also fell short — Bradley in California, and Wayne County Executive William Lucas in Michigan. The landslide loss of Lucas, who switched from the Democratic Party to the GOP in 1985, underlined the difficulty of persuading Republican voters to support black candidates. ∎

Democrats Extend Dominance in States

While Republicans took comfort in the eight gubernatorial gains that accompanied their loss of Senate control, they did not score so well in other contests at the state level. In legislative contests it was the Democrats who came out on top, further underscoring the lack of a clear partisan trend in the 1986 elections.

Nationwide, Democrats improved their lead in the number of legislative seats they controlled by 179, yielding modest gains in the number of states where they controlled both chambers. In 1987 Democrats would control legislatures in 28 states, compared with 26 states before the election. *(Chart, next page)*

The true balance of power was shown in the fact that Republicans in 1986 would control both chambers in only 10 states, down from 11 in 1986. The number of states where legislative control would be split between the two parties would decrease from 12 to 11.

In all, Democrats gained four legislative majorities, bringing the number of chambers under their control to 66 out of 98. Republicans took over two chambers, bringing their total to 29. Three chambers were tied.

Redistricting Role

Control of state legislatures had become a particular focus of both national parties, with more at stake than the issues to be legislated in 1987. The parties were looking to 1991, when legislatures would redraw congressional districts, potentially altering the partisan lineup in the U.S. House.

Both parties invested at least $1 million in legislative contests in 1986. The Democrats did so through Project 500, a coalition of party, labor and liberal groups, while the Republican National Committee had the 1991 Plan. Republicans had also given heavily through GOPAC, an independent political action committee set up to boost candidates at the state level.

Legislative losses in 1986 would make it more difficult for the GOP to achieve an ambitious goal of controlling half of the country's legislatures by the time redistricting occurred. In 1987, the states where Republicans would control accounted for only 36 U.S. House seats. The states where Democrats would control accounted for 276.

One of the most significant Democratic victories in 1986 came in Connecticut, a state that provided one of the party's most striking setbacks in 1984. With President Reagan at the top of the ticket in 1984, Republicans made great gains and won control of both chambers. In 1986, a strong showing by Democratic Gov. William A. O'Neill helped Democrats regain control, taking 14 seats in the state Senate and 27 in the state House.

But gubernatorial politics did not appear to have much impact on legislative contests in several other states.

In Wisconsin, where the GOP was three seats short of a majority in the Assembly, it lost two seats while winning an upset in the gubernatorial contest. In Oregon, where Democrats had narrow majorities in both chambers, Republicans made small gains while losing the governorship.

Democrats also took control of the Minnesota Legislature and the Nevada Assembly. They gained a tie in the Vermont House and made large gains in three states where they were in the minority: New Hampshire, Indiana and Utah.

Republicans took over the Montana House, gained a tie in the state Senate, and won a slim majority in Nevada's Senate. And they protected recent gains in Southern legislatures long dominated by Democrats. Republicans picked up seats in Florida, South Carolina and Texas, and in North Carolina lost a fraction of what they picked up two years earlier.

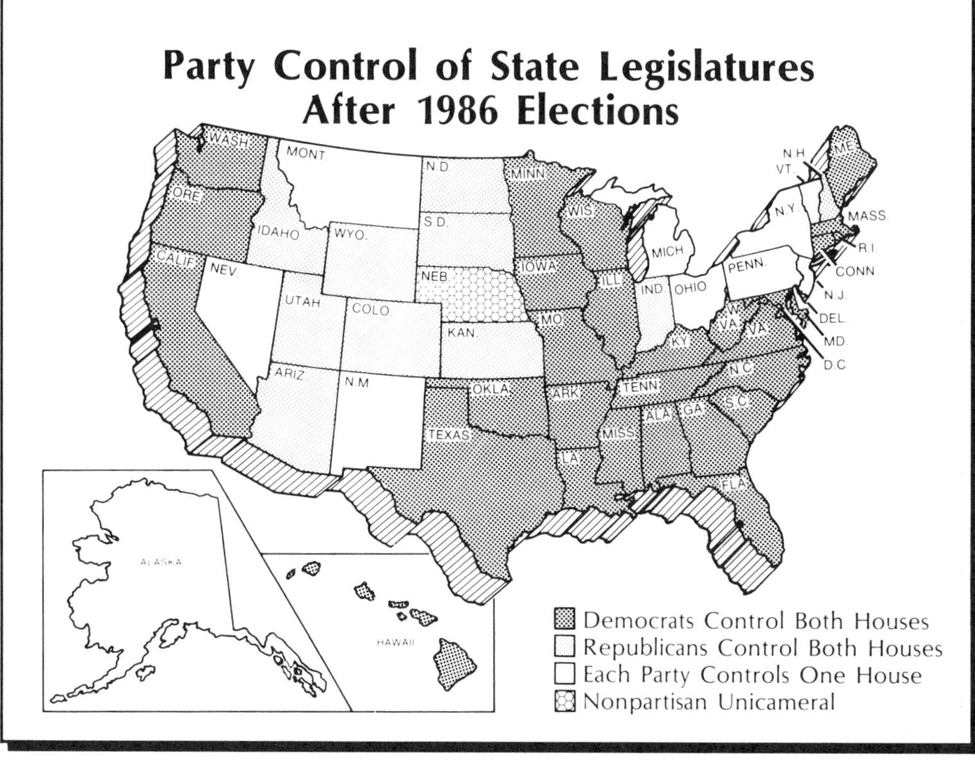

Partisan Lineups of State Legislatures . . .

State	Governor	1987 Legislature	October 1986 Upper House			January 1987 Upper House		
Alabama	•R	D	31D	4R		30D	5R	
Alaska	D	X	9D	11R		8D	11R	1U
Arizona	•R	R	12D	18R		11D	19R	
Arkansas	D	D	31D	4R		31D	4R	
California	R	D	26D	14R		24D	15R	1I
Colorado	D	R	11D	24R		10D	25R	
Connecticut	D	•D	12D	24R		26D	10R	
Delaware	R	X	13D	8R		13D	8R	
Florida	•R	D	30D	10R		25D	15R	
Georgia	D	D	47D	9R		45D	11R	
Hawaii	D	D	21D	4R		20D	5R	
Idaho	D	R	14D	28R		16D	26R	
Illinois	R	D	31D	28R		31D	28R	
Indiana	R	R	20D	30R		20D	30R	
Iowa	R	D	29D	21R		30D	20R	
Kansas	•R	R	16D	24R		16D	24R	
Kentucky	D	D	28D	10R		28D	10R	
Louisiana	D	D	38D	1R		38D	1R	
Maine	•R	D	23D	11R	1V	20D	15R	
Maryland	D	D	41D	6R		40D	7R	
Massachusetts	D	D	32D	8R		32D	8R	
Michigan	D	X	18D	20R		18D	20R	
Minnesota	D	•D	41D	26R		47D	20R	
Mississippi	D	D	49D	3R		49D	3R	
Missouri	R	D	21D	13R		21D	13R	
Montana	D	X	28D	22R		25D	25R	
Nebraska	•R		49-seat nonpartisan unicameral legislature					
Nevada	D	X	10D	10R	1V	9D	12R	
New Hampshire	R	R	6D	18R		8D	16R	
New Jersey	R	X	23D	17R		23D	17R	
New Mexico	•R	X	21D	21R		21D	21R	
New York	D	X	26D	35R		26D	35R	
North Carolina	R	D	38D	12R		40D	10R	
North Dakota	D	R	24D	28R	1V	26D	27R	
Ohio	D	X	15D	18R		15D	18R	
Oklahoma	•R	D	34D	14R		30D	17R	1V
Oregon	•D	D	18D	12R		17D	13R	
Pennsylvania	•D	X	23D	27R		24D	26R	
Rhode Island	R	D	38D	12R		38D	12R	
South Carolina	•R	D	36D	10R		34D	9R	3V
South Dakota	R	R	10D	25R		11D	24R	
Tennessee	•D	D	23D	10R		23D	10R	
Texas	•R	D	25D	6R		25D	6R	
Utah	R	R	6D	23R		8D	21R	
Vermont	D	X	18D	12R		19D	11R	
Virginia	D	D	31D	9R		31D	9R	
Washington	D	D	27D	22R		25D	23R	1U
West Virginia	R	D	30D	4R		27D	7R	
Wisconsin	•R	D	19D	14R		20D	13R	
Wyoming	D	R	11D	19R		11D	19R	

TOTAL PARTY CONTROL:
Democrats: 28
Republicans: 10
Split: 11
(Nebraska's Legislature is nonpartisan)

October 1986 Upper House:
Democrats: 1,184
Republicans: 759
Vacancies: 3

January 1987 Upper House:
Democrats: 1,185
Republicans: 754
Independents: 1
Undecided: 2
Vacancies: 4

SOURCE: National Conference of State Legislatures

. . . And Governorships for 1987 Sessions

October 1986 Lower House			January 1987 Lower House			Upper House Gains †	Lower House Gains †	State
87D	14R	4I	88D	17R		+1 R	+1 D, +3R	Alabama
21D	18R	1L	24D	16R		Undecided	+3 D	Alaska
22D	38R		24D	36R		+1 R	+2 D	Arizona
91D	8R	1V	91D	9R		No change	+1 R	Arkansas
47D	33R		44D	36R		+1 R	+3 R	California
18D	47R		25D	40R		+1 R	+7 D	Colorado
66D	85R		93D	58R		+14 D	+27 D	Connecticut
19D	22R		19D	22R		No change	No change	Delaware
76D	44R		75D	45R		+5 R	+1 R	Florida
153D	27R		153D	27R		+2 R	No change	Georgia
40D	11R		40D	11R		+1 R	No change	Hawaii
17D	67R		20D	64R		+2 D	+3 D	Idaho
67D	51R		67D	51R		No change	No change	Illinois
39D	61R		48D	52R		No change	+9 D	Indiana
60D	40R		58D	42R		+1 D	+2 R	Iowa
49D	76R		51D	74R		No change	+2 D	Kansas
74D	26R		73D	27R		No change	+1 R	Kentucky
82D	22R	1V	82D	22R	1V	No change	No change	Louisiana
84D	66R	1V	86D	65R		+4 R	+2 D	Maine
124D	17R		125D	16R		+1 R	+1 D	Maryland
126D	34R		129D	30R	1I	No change	+3 D	Massachusetts
57D	53R		63D	47R		No change	+6 D	Michigan
65D	69R		83D	51R		+6 D	+18 D	Minnesota
114D	7R	1V	114D	7R	1V	No change	No change	Mississippi
108D	55R		111D	52R		No change	+3 D	Missouri
50D	50R		48D	52R		+3 R	+2 R	Montana
								Nebraska
15D	27R		29D	13R		+2 R	+14 D	Nevada
99D	284R	17V	133D	267R		+2 D	+34 D	New Hampshire
30D	50R		30D	50R		No change	No change	New Jersey
43D	27R		47D	23R		No change	+4 D	New Mexico
94D	56R		94D	56R		No change	No change	New York
82D	38R		85D	35R		+2 D	+3 D	North Carolina
40D	63R	3V	45D	61R		+2 D	+5 D	North Dakota
59D	40R		60D	39R		No change	+1 D	Ohio
70D	31R		70D	31R		+3 R	No change	Oklahoma
34D	26R		31D	29R		+1 R	+3 R	Oregon
103D	100R		104D	99R		+1 D	+1 D	Pennsylvania
77D	22R	1I	80D	20R		No change	+3 D	Rhode Island
92D	29R	3V	91D	32R	1V	−2D, −1R	+3 R	South Carolina
13D	57R		21D	49R		+1 D	+8 D	South Dakota
62D	37R		61D	38R		No change	+1 R	Tennessee
95D	55R		94D	56R		No change	+1 R	Texas
14D	61R		27D	48R		+2 D	+13 D	Utah
72D	78R		75D	75R		+1 D	+3 D	Vermont
65D	33R	2I	65D	33R	2I	No change	No change	Virginia
53D	45R		61D	36R	1U	+1 R	+8 D	Washington
73D	27R		78D	22R		+3 R	+5 D	West Virginia
52D	47R		54D	45R		+1 D	+2 D	Wisconsin
18D	46R		20D	44R		No change	+2 D	Wyoming

October 1986 Lower House:
Democrats: 3,111
Republicans: 2,320
Independents: 7
Libertarian: 1
Vacancies: 27

January 1987 Lower House:
Democrats: 3,289
Republicans: 2,170
Independents: 3
Undecided: 1
Vacancies: 3

SYMBOLS
D = Democrat
R = Republican
L = Libertarian
I = Independent
V = Vacancy
U = Undecided contests as of Nov. 15, 1986
● = Change in party control
X = Party control split

† Due to the addition of seats through redistricting, one party's gains may not equal the other's losses.

Returns for Governor, Senate and House

Here are nearly complete unofficial 1986 vote returns compiled by Congressional Quarterly from various sources, including the News Election Service, as of Nov. 8, 1986. In some cases, there will be significant changes in final, official returns.

The box below shows party designation symbols. Because percentages are rounded, they do not all equal 100.

* indicates incumbents.

x denotes candidates without major-party opposition.

— denotes minor parties for which the vote was not available.

ALABAMA

	Vote Total	Per-cent
Governor		
Bill Baxley (D)	530,051	44
Guy Hunt (R)	687,832	56
Senate		
Jeremiah Denton (R) *	593,153	49
Richard C. Shelby (D)	606,568	51
House		
1 Sonny Callahan (R) *	x	x
(No Democratic candidate)		
2 William L. Dickinson (R) *	105,910	66
Mercer Stone (D)	53,543	34
3 Bill Nichols (D) *	114,862	81
Whit Guerin (R)	27,567	19
4 Tom Bevill (D) *	130,832	77
Al DeShazo (R)	38,174	23
5 Ronnie G. Flippo (D) *	123,513	79
Herb McCarley (R)	33,078	21
6 Ben Erdreich (D) *	139,590	73
L. Morgan Williams (R)	51,916	27
Martin J. Boyers (SOC WORK)	—	—
7 Claude Harris (D)	101,974	59
Bill McFarland (R)	71,413	41

ALASKA

	Vote Total	Per-cent
Governor		
Steve Cowper (D)	74,405	52
Arliss Sturgulewski (R)	68,203	48
Mary O'Brannon (LIBERT)	—	—
Joe Vogler (AMI)	—	—
Senate		
Frank H. Murkowski (R) *	81,855	55
Glenn Olds (D)	67,259	45
Chuck House (LIBERT)	—	—
House		
AL Don Young (R) *	85,593	58
Pegge Begich (D)	61,236	42
Betty "Belle Blue" Breck (LIBERT)	—	—

ARIZONA

	Vote Total	Per-cent
Governor		
Carolyn Warner (D)	293,944	34
Evan Mecham (R)	339,773	40
Bill Schulz (I)	221,633	26
Senate		
Richard Kimball (D)	335,509	39
John McCain (R)	515,554	61
Paul C. Rodriguez (write-in)	—	—
House		
1 Harry Braun III (D)	50,780	29
John J. Rhodes III (R)	126,439	71
2 Morris K. Udall (D) *	76,425	76
Sheldon Clark (R)	24,202	24
Lorrenzo Torrez (I)	—	—
3 Bob Stump (R) *	x	x
(No Democratic candidate)		
4 Philip R. Davis (D)	63,940	35
Jon Kyl (R)	119,939	65
5 Jim Kolbe (R) *	117,617	65
Joel Ireland (D)	63,853	35

ARKANSAS

	Vote Total	Per-cent
Governor		
Bill Clinton (D) *	425,372	64
Frank White (R)	240,464	36
Senate		
Dale Bumpers (D) *	423,800	63
Asa Hutchinson (R)	250,183	37
House		
1 Bill Alexander (D) *	104,480	64
Rick H. Albin (R)	58,430	36
2 Tommy F. Robinson (D) *	126,718	75
Keith Hamaker (R)	41,425	25
3 John Paul Hammerschmidt (R) *	140,590	81
Su Sargent (D)	32,140	19
4 Beryl Anthony Jr. (D) *	110,042	82
Lamar Keels (R)	24,332	18
Stephen A. Bitely (I)	—	—

CALIFORNIA

	Vote Total	Per-cent
Governor		
George Deukmejian (R) *	4,365,336	62
Tom Bradley (D)	2,704,404	38
Joseph Fuhrig (LIBERT)	—	—
Gary V. Miller (AMI)	—	—
Maria Elizabeth Munoz (PFP)	—	—
Senate		
Alan Cranston (D) *	3,545,860	51
Ed Zschau (R)	3,427,698	49
Paul Kangas (PFP)	—	—
Breck McKinley (LIBERT)	—	—
Edward B. Vallen (AMI)	—	—
House		
1 Douglas H. Bosco (D) *	135,161	72
Floyd G. Sampson (R)	53,098	28
Elden McFarland (PFP)	—	—
2 Stephen C. Swendiman (D)	73,817	41
Wally Herger (R)	107,920	59
Harry Hugh Pendery (LIBERT)	—	—
3 Robert T. Matsui (D) *	156,667	76
Lowell Landowski (R)	49,524	24

ABBREVIATIONS FOR PARTY DESIGNATIONS

AM	— American	*LIBERT*	— Libertarian
AMI	— American Independent	*LAB F*	— Labor and Farm
C	— Conservative	*NA*	— New Alliance
CIT	— Citizens	*PFP*	— Peace and Freedom
CON	— Consumer	*POP*	— Populist
D	— Democratic	*PRG SC*	— Progressive Social
DFL	— Democratic Farmer-Labor	*R*	— Republican
I	— Independent	*RTL*	— Right to Life
IL SOL	— Illinois Solidarity	*SOC WORK*	— Socialist Workers
I-R	— Independent-Republican	*WL*	— Workers League
L	— Liberal		

		Vote Total	Per-cent
4	Vic Fazio (D) *	105,605	69
	Jack D. Hite (R)	46,770	31
5	Sala Burton (D) *	122,140	77
	Mike Garza (R)	35,877	23
	Samuel K. Grove (LIBERT)	—	—
	Theodore Zuur (PFP)	—	—
6	Barbara Boxer (D) *	140,699	74
	Franklin "Harry" Ernst III (R)	49,671	26
7	George Miller (D) *	122,918	67
	Rosemary Thakar (R)	61,546	33
8	Ronald V. Dellums (D) *	120,369	61
	Steven Eigenberg (R)	75,754	39
	Lawrence R. Manuel (PFP)	—	—
9	Fortney H. "Pete" Stark (D) *	112,592	70
	David M. Williams (R)	48,695	30
10	Don Edwards (D) *	83,039	73
	Michael R. La Crone (R)	31,137	27
	Perr Cardestam (LIBERT)	—	—
	Bradley L. Mayer (PFP)	—	—
11	Tom Lantos (D) *	110,245	74
	G. M. "Bill" Quraishi (R)	38,617	26
12	Lance T. Weil (D)	68,386	39
	Ernest L. Konnyu (R)	108,860	61
	Bill White (LIBERT)	—	—
13	Norman Y. Mineta (D) *	106,064	70
	Bob Nash (R)	45,755	30
14	Norman D. Shumway (R) *	144,063	73
	Bill Steele (D)	52,640	27
	Bruce A. Daniel (LIBERT)	—	—
15	Tony Coelho (D) *	91,364	72
	Carol Harner (R)	34,872	28
	Richard M. Harris (LIBERT)	—	—
16	Leon E. Panetta (D) *	126,133	80
	Louis Darrigo (R)	30,801	20
	Bill Anderson (LIBERT)	—	—
	Ron Wright (PFP)	—	—
17	Charles Pashayan Jr. (R) *	86,736	60
	John Hartnett (D)	57,452	40
18	Richard H. Lehman (D) *	99,556	71
	David C. Crevelt (R)	40,096	29
19	Robert J. Lagomarsino (R) *	117,320	73
	Wayne B. Norris (D)	44,101	27
	George Hasara (LIBERT)	—	—
20	William M. Thomas (R) *	120,660	72
	Jules H. Moquin (D)	46,188	28
21	Gilbert R. Saldana (D)	53,028	30
	Elton Gallegly (R)	126,721	70
	Daniel Wiener (LIBERT)	—	—
22	Carlos J. Moorhead (R) *	136,315	76
	John G. Simmons (D)	42,839	24
	Jona Joy Bergland (LIBERT)	—	—
	Joel Lorimer (PFP)	—	—
23	Anthony C. Beilenson (D) *	117,849	68
	George Woolverton (R)	56,537	32
	Tom Hopke (PFP)	—	—
	Taylor Rhodes (LIBERT)	—	—
24	Henry A. Waxman (D) *	x	x
	George Abrahams (LIBERT)	—	—
	James Green (PFP)	—	—
25	Edward R. Roybal (D) *	60,959	78
	Gregory L. Hardy (R)	16,763	22
	Ted Brown (LIBERT)	—	—
26	Howard L. Berman (D) *	95,582	65
	Robert M. Kerns (R)	51,155	35
27	Mel Levine (D) *	107,672	65
	Rob Scribner (R)	57,386	35
	Larry Leathers (LIBERT)	—	—
	Thomas L. O'Connor Jr. (PFP)	—	—
28	Julian C. Dixon (D) *	90,630	78
	George Adams (R)	25,003	22
	Howard Johnson (LIBERT)	—	—
29	Augustus F. Hawkins (D) *	76,398	85
	John Van de Brooke (R)	13,089	15

		Vote Total	Per-cent
	Waheed Boctor (LIBERT)	—	—
30	Matthew G. Martinez (D) *	57,911	64
	John W. Almquist (R)	32,664	36
	Kim J. Goldsworthy (LIBERT)	—	—
31	Mervyn M. Dymally (D) *	76,209	72
	Jack McMurray (R)	29,603	28
	B. Kwaku Duren (PFP)	—	—
32	Glenn M. Anderson (D) *	89,047	70
	Joyce M. Robertson (R)	37,954	30
	John S. Donohue (PFP)	—	—
33	David Dreier (R) *	115,648	73
	Monty Hempel (D)	43,510	27
	Mike Noonan (PFP)	—	—
34	Esteban Edward Torres (D) *	65,307	60
	Charles M. House (R)	42,717	40
35	Jerry Lewis (R) *	124,953	77
	R. "Sarge" Hall (D)	37,742	23
36	George E. Brown Jr. (D) *	77,242	57
	Bob Henley (R)	57,804	43
37	Al McCandless (R) *	120,437	64
	David E. Skinner (D)	68,905	36
38	Bob Dornan (R) *	64,843	57
	Richard Robinson (D)	49,744	43
	Lee Connelly (LIBERT)	—	—
39	William E. Dannemeyer (R) *	129,210	76
	David D. Vest (D)	41,806	24
	Frank Boeheim (PFP)	—	—
40	Robert E. Badham (R) *	116,556	61
	Bruce W. Sumner (D)	73,964	39
	Steve Sears (PFP)	—	—
41	Bill Lowery (R) *	131,323	69
	Dan Kripke (D)	58,986	31
	Dick Rider (LIBERT)	—	—
42	Dan Lungren (R) *	136,242	75
	Michael P. Blackburn (D)	46,556	25
	Kate McClatchy (PFP)	—	—
43	Ron Packard (R) *	132,935	75
	Joseph Chirra (D)	43,926	25
	Phyllis Avery (LIBERT)	—	—
44	Jim Bates (D) *	63,800	65
	Bill Mitchell (R)	34,084	35
	Shirley Isaacson (PFP)	—	—
	Dennis Thompson (LIBERT)	—	—
45	Duncan L. Hunter (R) *	115,638	78
	Hewitt Fitts Ryan (D)	31,978	22
	Lee Schwartz (LIBERT)	—	—

COLORADO

		Vote Total	Per-cent
Governor			
	Roy Romer (D)	615,653	59
	Ted Strickland (R)	433,938	41
	Earl F. Dodge (I)	—	—
Senate			
	Timothy E. Wirth (D)	528,925	51
	Ken Kramer (R)	512,695	49
	Michael Martin Bush (I)	—	—
	Michael R. Chamberlain (SOC WORK)	—	—
	Calvin G. Dodge (I)	—	—
	Henry John Olshaw (I)	—	—
House			
1	Patricia Schroeder (D) *	105,891	68
	Joy Wood (R)	49,115	32
2	David Skaggs (D)	91,123	51
	Michael J. Norton (R)	85,895	49
3	Mike Strang (R) *	88,509	48
	Ben Nighthorse Campbell (D)	95,352	52
4	Hank Brown (R) *	118,182	70
	David Sprague (D)	50,310	30
5	Bill Story (D)	52,485	30
	Joel Hefley (R)	120,789	70

		Vote Total	Per-cent
6	Dan L. Schaefer (R) *	104,359	66
	Chuck Norris (D)	53,834	34
	John Heckman (I)	—	—

CONNECTICUT

		Vote Total	Per-cent
Governor			
	William A. O'Neill (D) *	571,946	58
	Julie D. Belaga (R)	413,677	42
	Frank Longo (I)	—	—
Senate			
	Christopher J. Dodd (D) *	621,631	65
	Roger W. Eddy (R)	337,792	35
House			
1	Barbara B. Kennelly (D) *	128,929	74
	Herschel A. Klein (R)	44,210	26
2	Sam Gejdenson (D) *	108,459	67
	Francis M. "Bud" Mullen (R)	52,275	33
3	Bruce A. Morrison (D) *	112,667	70
	Ernest J. Diette Jr. (R)	49,111	30
4	Stewart B. McKinney (R) *	77,210	53
	Christine M. Niedermeier (D)	67,236	47
5	John G. Rowland (R) *	98,356	61
	Jim Cohen (D)	63,304	39
6	Nancy L. Johnson (R) *	107,528	65
	Paul S. Amenta (D)	59,118	35

DELAWARE

		Vote Total	Per-cent
House			
AL	Thomas R. Carper (D) *	106,351	66
	Thomas Stephen Neuberger (R)	54,569	34
	Patrick F. Harrison (AM)	—	—

FLORIDA

		Vote Total	Per-cent
Governor			
	Steve Pajcic (D)	1,489,272	46
	Bob Martinez (R)	1,767,971	54
Senate			
	Paula Hawkins (R) *	1,482,311	45
	Bob Graham (D)	1,812,353	55
House			
1	Earl Hutto (D) *	90,624	65
	Greg Neubeck (R)	48,502	35
2	Bill Grant (D)	x	x
	(No Republican candidate)		
3	Charles E. Bennett (D) *	x	x
	(No Republican candidate)		
4	Bill Chappell Jr. (D) *	x	x
	(No Republican candidate)		
5	Bill McCollum (R) *	x	x
	(No Democratic candidate)		
6	Buddy MacKay (D) *	142,494	69
	Larry Gallagher (R)	63,280	31
7	Sam Gibbons (D) *	x	x
	(No Republican candidate)		
8	C. W. Bill Young (R) *	x	x
	(No Democratic candidate)		
9	Michael Bilirakis (R) *	162,627	71
	Gabe Cazares (D)	67,316	29
10	Andy Ireland (R) *	117,858	72
	David B. Higginbottom (D)	46,933	28
11	Bill Nelson (D) *	142,912	73
	Scott Ellis (R)	52,595	27
12	Tom Lewis (R) *	x	x
	(No Democratic candidate)		
13	Connie Mack (R) *	180,078	75
	Addison S. Gilbert III (D)	60,673	25
14	Daniel A. Mica (D) *	169,870	74
	Rick Martin (R)	60,469	26
15	E. Clay Shaw Jr. (R) *	x	x
	(No Democratic candidate)		
16	Larry Smith (D) *	116,427	70
	Mary Collins (R)	50,939	30

	Vote Total	Per-cent
17 William Lehman (D) *	x	x
(No Republican candidate)		
18 Claude Pepper (D) *	77,156	74
Tom Brodie (R)	27,359	26
19 Dante B. Fascell (D) *	95,035	69
Bill Flanagan (R)	42,047	31

GEORGIA

	Vote Total	Per-cent
Governor		
Joe Frank Harris (D) *	821,957	70
Guy Davis (R)	347,556	30
Senate		
Mack Mattingly (R) *	598,340	49
Wyche Fowler Jr. (D)	621,295	51
House		
1 Robert Lindsay Thomas (D) *	x	x
(No Republican candidate)		
2 Charles Hatcher (D) *	x	x
(No Republican candidate)		
3 Richard Ray (D) *	x	x
(No Republican candidate)		
4 Pat Swindall (R) *	86,331	53
Ben Jones (D)	75,857	47
5 John Lewis (D)	93,033	75
Portia A. Scott (R)	30,477	25
6 Newt Gingrich (R) *	75,472	60
Crandle Bray (D)	51,336	40
7 George "Buddy" Darden (D) *	89,133	67
Joe Morecraft (R)	43,523	33
8 J. Roy Rowland (D) *	82,064	86
Eddie McDowell (R)	12,879	14
9 Ed Jenkins (D) *	x	x
(No Republican candidate)		
10 Doug Barnard Jr. (D) *	78,407	67
Jim Hill (R)	37,797	33

HAWAII

	Vote Total	Per-cent
Governor		
John Waihee (D)	165,081	52
D. G. "Andy" Anderson (R)	151,929	48
Senate		
Daniel K. Inouye (D) *	229,629	74
Frank Hutchinson (R)	82,309	26
House		
1 Mufi Hannemann (D)	58,786	39
Patricia Saiki (R)	92,795	61
Blase Harris (LIBERT)	—	—
2 Daniel K. Akaka (D) *	119,732	78
Maria M. Hustace (R)	34,087	22
Ken Schoolland (LIBERT)	—	—

IDAHO

	Vote Total	Per-cent
Governor		
Cecil D. Andrus (D)	193,367	50
David H. Leroy (R)	190,011	50
James A. Miller (I)	—	—
Senate		
Steven D. Symms (R) *	196,908	52
John V. Evans (D)	185,094	48
House		
1 Larry E. Craig (R) *	120,200	67
Bill Currie (D)	58,726	33
David W. Shepherd (I)	—	—
2 Richard H. Stallings (D) *	102,637	54
Mel Richardson (R)	86,244	46

ILLINOIS

	Vote Total	Per-cent
Governor		
James R. Thompson (R) *	1,600,605	57
(No Democratic candidate)		
Diane Roling (SOC WORK)	—	—
Gary L. Shilts (LIBERT)	—	—
Adlai E. Stevenson (IL SOL)	1,203,426	43
Senate		
Alan J. Dixon (D) *	1,954,255	65
Judy Koehler (R)	1,018,489	34
Einar V. Dyhrkopp (IL SOL)	15,211	1
Omari Musa (SOC WORK)	—	—
Donald M. Parrish Jr. (LIBERT)	—	—
House		
1 Charles A. Hayes (D) *	112,961	96
Joseph C. Faulkner (R)	4,260	4
2 Gus Savage (D) *	90,337	83
Ron Taylor (R)	18,391	17
3 Marty Russo (D) *	101,196	66
James J. Tierney (R)	51,900	34
4 Shawn Collins (D)	57,650	48
Jack Davis (R)	61,517	52
5 William O. Lipinski (D) *	81,333	70
Daniel John Sobieski (R)	34,535	30
6 Henry J. Hyde (R) *	97,621	75
Robert H. Renshaw (D)	31,876	25
7 Cardiss Collins (D) *	82,450	81
Caroline K. Kallas (R)	19,582	19
Jerald Wilson (I)	—	—
8 Dan Rostenkowski (D) *	79,263	79
Thomas J. DeFazio (R)	21,578	21
9 Sidney R. Yates (D) *	89,674	72
Herbert Sohn (R)	35,564	28
10 John Edward Porter (R) *	87,530	75
Robert A. Cleland (D)	28,990	25
11 Frank Annunzio (D) *	102,847	71
George S. Gottlieb (R)	42,815	29
12 Philip M. Crane (R) *	88,481	78
John A. Leonardi (D)	25,354	22
13 Harris W. Fawell (R) *	106,881	73
Dominick J. Jeffrey (D)	38,752	27
14 Mary Lou Kearns (D)	70,230	48
J. Dennis Hastert (R)	77,208	52
15 Edward R. Madigan (R) *	x	x
(No Democratic candidate)		
16 Lynn Martin (R) *	92,982	67
Kenneth F. Bohnsack (D)	46,087	33
17 Lane Evans (D) *	85,254	56
Sam McHard (R)	67,993	44
18 Robert H. Michel (R) *	93,033	62
Jim Dawson (D)	57,094	38
19 Terry L. Bruce (D) *	109,492	66
Al Salvi (R)	55,535	34
20 Richard J. Durbin (D) *	126,556	68
Kevin B. McCarthy (R)	59,391	32
21 Melvin Price (D) * ●	65,965	50
Robert H. Gaffner (R)	64,803	50
22 Kenneth J. Gray (D) *	94,978	53
Randy Patchett (R)	83,223	47

INDIANA

	Vote Total	Per-cent
Senate		
Dan Quayle (R) *	927,676	61
Jill Lynette Long (D)	590,433	39
Rockland R. Snyder (AM)	—	—
Bradford L. Warren (LIBERT)	—	—
House		
1 Peter J. Visclosky (D) *	86,093	74
William Costas (R)	29,853	26
Tracy E. Kyle (WL)	—	—
James E. Willis (LIBERT)	—	—
2 Philip R. Sharp (D) *	102,430	62
Donald J. Lynch (R)	61,747	38
3 John Hiler (R) *	75,952	50
Thomas W. Ward (D)	75,786	50
Kenneth K. Donnelly (LIBERT)	—	—
4 Dan Coats (R) *	98,190	70
Gregory Alan Scher (D)	42,294	30
Stephen L. Dasbach (LIBERT)	—	—
5 James Jontz (D)	80,292	52
James R. Butcher (R)	75,305	48
6 Dan Burton (R) *	117,011	69
Thomas F. McKenna (D)	53,068	31
7 John T. Myers (R) *	104,541	68
L. Eugene Smith (D)	49,330	32
Barbara J. Bourland (LIBERT)	—	—
8 Frank McCloskey (D) *	106,709	53
Richard D. McIntyre (R)	93,413	47
9 Lee H. Hamilton (D) *	120,028	73
Robert Walter Kilroy (R)	45,381	27
10 Andrew Jacobs Jr. (D) *	66,506	58
Jim Eynon (R)	47,565	42

IOWA

	Vote Total	Per-cent
Governor		
Terry E. Branstad (R) *	463,635	52
Lowell L. Junkins (D)	430,922	48
Senate		
Charles E. Grassley (R) *	575,365	66
John P. Roehrick (D)	296,467	34
John Masters (I)	—	—
House		
1 Jim Leach (R) *	86,071	66
John R. Whitaker (D)	43,678	34
2 Tom Tauke (R) *	87,085	61
Eric Tabor (D)	55,058	39
3 John McIntee (R)	67,115	45
David R. Nagle (D)	80,397	55
4 Neal Smith (D) *	105,983	68
Bob Lockard (R)	48,912	32
5 Jim Lightfoot (R) *	84,546	59
Scott Hughes (D)	58,063	41
6 Clayton Hodgson (D)	78,272	49
Fred Grandy (R)	81,173	51

KANSAS

	Vote Total	Per-cent
Governor		
Tom Docking (D)	400,313	48
Mike Hayden (R)	431,627	52
Senate		
Robert Dole (R) *	570,511	70
Guy MacDonald (D)	243,232	30
House		
1 Pat Roberts (R) *	140,383	76
Dale Lyon (D)	43,321	24
2 Jim Slattery (D) *	108,744	71
Phill Kline (R)	45,041	29
3 Jan Meyers (R) *	x	x
(No Democratic candidate)		
4 Dan Glickman (D) *	108,315	64
Bob Knight (R)	59,618	36
5 Bob Whittaker (R) *	115,697	71
Kym E. Myers (D)	47,400	29

KENTUCKY

	Vote Total	Per-cent
Senate		
Wendell H. Ford (D) *	499,162	74
Jackson M. Andrews (R)	172,763	26
House		
1 Carroll Hubbard Jr. (D) *	x	x
(No Republican candidate)		
2 William H. Natcher (D) *	x	x
(No Republican candidate)		
3 Romano L. Mazzoli (D) *	81,943	74
Lee Holmes (R)	29,348	26
Estelle DeBates (SOC WORK)	—	—

	Vote Total	Per-cent
4 Terry L. Mann (D)	53,270	44
Jim Bunning (R)	66,909	56
Walter T. Marksberry (I)	—	—
W. Ed Parker (AM)	—	—
5 Harold Rogers (R) *	x	x
(No Democratic candidate)		
6 Larry J. Hopkins (R) *	75,290	74
Jerry W. Hammond (D)	26,088	26
7 Carl C. Perkins (D) *	90,225	79
James T. Polley (R)	23,289	21

LOUISIANA

Senate

	Vote Total	Per-cent
John B. Breaux (D)	722,847	53
W. Henson Moore (R)	645,176	47

House

	Vote Total	Per-cent
1 Bob Livingston (R) *	x	x
2 Lindy (Mrs. Hale) Boggs (D) *	x	x
3 W. J. "Billy" Tauzin (D) *	x	x
4 Buddy Roemer (D) *	x	x
5 Jerry Huckaby (D) *	x	x
6 Richard Baker (R)	x	x
7 Jimmy Hayes (D)	108,550	57
Margaret Lowenthal (D)	81,924	43
8 Faye Williams (D)	96,783	49
Clyde Holloway (R)	102,022	51

MAINE

Governor

	Vote Total	Per-cent
James Tierney (D)	127,896	30
John R. McKernan Jr. (R)	167,583	40
Sherry E. Huber (I)	63,358	15
John E. Menario (I)	63,063	15

House

	Vote Total	Per-cent
1 Joseph E. Brennan (D)	120,740	54
H. Rollin Ives (R)	97,984	43
Plato Truman (I)	7,179	3
2 Olympia J. Snowe (R) *	148,599	77
Richard R. Charette (D)	43,608	23

MARYLAND

Governor

	Vote Total	Per-cent
William Donald Schaefer (D)	876,577	82
Thomas J. Mooney (R)	189,284	18

Senate

	Vote Total	Per-cent
Barbara A. Mikulski (D)	657,449	61
Linda Chavez (R)	424,293	39

House

	Vote Total	Per-cent
1 Roy Dyson (D) *	85,184	67
Harlan C. Williams (R)	41,874	33
2 Helen Delich Bentley (R) *	94,404	59
Kathleen Kennedy Townsend (D)	66,943	41
3 Benjamin L. Cardin (D)	96,843	79
Ross Z. Pierpont (R)	26,180	21
4 Thomas McMillen (D)	64,799	50
Robert R. Neall (R)	64,289	50
5 Steny H. Hoyer (D) *	80,614	82
John Eugene Sellner (R)	17,612	18
6 Beverly B. Byron (D) *	98,193	72
John Vandenberge (R)	38,136	28
7 Kweisi Mfume (D)	77,938	87
Saint George I. B. Crosse III (R)	11,679	13
8 Stewart Bainum Jr. (D)	79,908	47
Constance A. Morella (R)	90,147	53

MASSACHUSETTS

Governor

	Vote Total	Per-cent
Michael S. Dukakis (D) *	1,052,900	69
George Kariotis (R)	478,742	31

House

	Vote Total	Per-cent
1 Silvio O. Conte (R) *	111,124	78
Robert S. Weiner (D)	31,567	22
2 Edward P. Boland (D) *	88,443	66
Brian P. Lees (R)	45,767	34
3 Joseph D. Early (D) *	x	x
(No Republican candidate)		
4 Barney Frank (D) *	x	x
(No Republican candidate)		
Thomas D. DeVisscher (write-in)	—	—
5 Chester G. Atkins (D) *	x	x
(No Republican candidate)		
6 Nicholas Mavroules (D) *	x	x
(No Republican candidate)		
7 Edward J. Markey (D) *	x	x
(No Republican candidate)		
8 Joseph P. Kennedy II (D)	104,397	73
Clark C. Abt (R)	39,402	27
9 Joe Moakley (D) *	x	x
(No Republican candidate)		
Robert W. Horan (write-in)	—	—
10 Gerry E. Studds (D) *	120,441	65
Ricardo M. Barros (R)	49,388	27
Alexander Byron (write-in)	15,674	8
11 Brian J. Donnelly (D) *	x	x
(No Republican candidate)		

MICHIGAN

Governor

	Vote Total	Per-cent
James J. Blanchard (D) *	1,611,242	69
William Lucas (R)	740,501	31
Martin McLaughlin (WL)	—	—

House

	Vote Total	Per-cent
1 John Conyers Jr. (D) *	94,615	90
Bill Ashe (R)	10,429	10
Peter Banta Bowen (I)	—	—
Andrew Pulley (I)	—	—
2 Carl D. Pursell (R) *	78,735	59
Dean Baker (D)	54,531	41
3 Howard Wolpe (D) *	78,720	60
Jackie McGregor (R)	51,677	40
4 Dan Roche (D)	41,739	37
Fred Upton (R)	69,724	63
Richard H. Gillmor (I)	—	—
5 Paul B. Henry (R) *	100,187	71
Teresa S. Decker (D)	40,607	29
6 Bob Carr (D) *	74,653	57
Jim Dunn (R)	57,048	43
7 Dale E. Kildee (D) *	101,185	80
Trudie Callihan (R)	24,844	20
Gene Schenk (I)	—	—
8 Bob Traxler (D) *	97,328	73
John A. Levi (R)	36,313	27
9 Guy Vander Jagt (R) *	87,091	64
Richard J. Anderson (D)	48,645	36
10 Bill Schuette (R) *	78,316	51
Donald J. Albosta (D)	74,488	49
11 Robert W. Davis (R) *	90,355	64
Robert C. Anderson (D)	51,454	36
Phil Bellfy (I)	—	—
12 David E. Bonior (D) *	84,764	66
Candice S. Miller (R)	43,507	34
13 George W. Crockett Jr. (D) *	76,623	86
Mary Griffin (R)	12,455	14
Barbara L. Putnam (I)	—	—
Lucy Bell Randolph (I)	—	—
14 Dennis M. Hertel (D) *	89,834	73
Stanley T. Grot (R)	33,187	27
William Osipoff (I)	—	—
15 William D. Ford (D) *	77,339	76
Glen Kassel (R)	24,956	24
James H. Stamps (I)	—	—
16 John D. Dingell (D) *	101,606	78
Frank W. Grzywacki (R)	28,973	22
17 Sander M. Levin (D) *	105,028	77
Calvin Williams (R)	30,876	23
Charles E. Martell (I)	—	—
18 William S. Broomfield (R) *	109,999	74
Gary L. Kohut (D)	39,132	26

MINNESOTA

Governor

	Vote Total	Per-cent
Rudy Perpich (DFL) *	787,307	57
Cal R. Ludeman (I-R)	605,334	43
W.Z. "Bill" Brust (WL)	—	—
Tom Jaax (SOC WORK)	—	—
Joseph A. Rohner III (LIBERT)	—	—

House

	Vote Total	Per-cent
1 Timothy J. Penny (DFL) *	123,640	72
Paul H. Grawe (I-R)	46,918	28
2 Vin Weber (I-R) *	100,243	52
Dave Johnson (DFL)	93,973	48
3 Bill Frenzel (I-R) *	127,388	70
Ray Stock (DFL)	54,263	30
4 Bruce F. Vento (DFL) *	112,664	73
Harold Stassen (I-R)	41,994	27
5 Martin Olav Sabo (DFL) *	104,947	74
Rick Serra (I-R)	37,687	26
Clifford Mark Greene (I)	—	—
6 Gerry Sikorski (DFL) *	110,430	64
Barbara Zwach Sykora (I-R)	57,135	36
7 Arlan Stangeland (I-R) *	94,100	50
Collin C. Peterson (DFL)	93,889	50
Jon Hall (CIT)	—	—
8 James L. Oberstar (DFL) *	112,093	72
Dave Rued (I-R)	43,887	28

MISSISSIPPI

House

	Vote Total	Per-cent
1 Jamie L. Whitten (D) *	59,695	66
Larry Cobb (R)	30,224	34
2 Webb Franklin (R) *	67,771	48
Mike Espy (D)	72,443	52
3 G. V. "Sonny" Montgomery (D) *	x	x
(No Republican candidate)		
4 Wayne Dowdy (D) *	81,575	71
Gail Healy (R)	33,149	29
5 Trent Lott (R) *	75,043	82
Larry L. Albritton (D)	16,219	18

MISSOURI

Senate

	Vote Total	Per-cent
Harriett Woods (D)	693,904	47
Christopher S. "Kit" Bond (R)	771,168	53

House

	Vote Total	Per-cent
1 William L. Clay (D) *	91,218	66
Robert J. Wittmann (R)	46,619	34
2 Robert A. Young (D) *	93,661	48
Jack Buechner (R)	101,171	52
3 Richard A. Gephardt (D) *	116,645	69
Roy Amelung (R)	52,445	31
4 Ike Skelton (D) *	x	x
(No Republican candidate)		
5 Alan Wheat (D) *	101,030	72
Greg Fisher (R)	39,340	28
Jay Manifold (LIBERT)	—	—
6 E. Thomas Coleman (R) *	94,319	57
Doug R. Hughes (D)	71,724	43
7 Gene Taylor (R) *	114,175	67
Ken Young (D)	56,242	33
8 Bill Emerson (R) *	78,848	53
Wayne Cryts (D)	71,172	47
9 Harold L. Volkmer (D) *	95,951	57
Ralph Uthlaut Jr. (R)	70,930	43

MONTANA

House

Candidate	Vote Total	Percent
1 Pat Williams (D) *	98,472	62
Don Allen (R)	61,219	38
2 Ron Marlenee (R) *	83,329	53
Richard "Buck" O'Brien (D)	72,872	47

NEBRASKA

Governor

Candidate	Vote Total	Percent
Helen Boosalis (D)	260,638	47
Kay A. Orr (R)	290,883	53

House

Candidate	Vote Total	Percent
1 Doug Bereuter (R) *	121,042	64
Steve Burns (D)	66,999	36
2 Hal Daub (R) *	97,867	59
Walter M. Calinger (D)	69,381	41
3 Virginia Smith (R) *	132,460	70
Scott E. Sidwell (D)	57,832	30

NEVADA

Governor

Candidate	Vote Total	Percent
Richard H. Bryan (D) *	187,264	73
Patty Cafferata (R)	65,081	25
Louis R. Tomburello (LIBERT)	—	—

Senate

Candidate	Vote Total	Percent
Harry Reid (D)	130,952	51
Jim Santini (R)	116,606	45
Kent Cromwell (LIBERT)	—	—

House

Candidate	Vote Total	Percent
1 James H. Bilbray (D)	61,827	55
Bob Ryan (R)	50,340	45
Gordon Michael Morris (LIBERT)	—	—
2 Barbara F. Vucanovich (R) *	83,479	58
Pete Sferrazza (D)	59,444	42

NEW HAMPSHIRE

Governor

Candidate	Vote Total	Percent
John H. Sununu (R) *	134,674	54
Paul McEachern (D)	116,154	46

Senate

Candidate	Vote Total	Percent
Warren B. Rudman (R) *	153,707	66
Endicott Peabody (D)	79,037	34
Bruce Valley (I)	—	—

House

Candidate	Vote Total	Percent
1 Robert C. Smith (R) *	70,738	56
James M. Demers (D)	54,934	44
2 Judd Gregg (R) *	84,618	74
Laurence Craig-Green (D)	29,723	26

NEW JERSEY

House

Candidate	Vote Total	Percent
1 James J. Florio (D) *	92,599	76
Fred A. Busch (R)	28,904	24
Jerry Zeldin (LIBERT)	—	—
2 William J. Hughes (D) *	82,883	71
Alfred J. Bennington Jr. (R)	34,646	29
Len Smith (I)	—	—
3 James J. Howard (D) *	73,684	59
Brian T. Kennedy (R)	51,558	41
4 Christopher H. Smith (R) *	79,691	62
Jeffrey Laurenti (D)	48,938	38
Earl G. Dickey (I)	—	—
5 Marge Roukema (R) *	97,454	75
H. Vernon Jolley (D)	31,758	25
6 Bernard J. Dwyer (D) *	67,365	70
John D. Scalamonti (R)	28,258	30
Rose (Zeidwerg) Monyek (I)	—	—
7 Matthew J. Rinaldo (R) *	96,701	80
June S. Fischer (D)	24,581	20
8 Robert A. Roe (D) *	57,293	63
Thomas P. Zampino (R)	33,730	37
9 Robert G. Torricelli (D) *	87,680	69
Arthur F. Jones (R)	39,231	31
10 Peter W. Rodino Jr. (D) *	x	x
Chris Brandlon (SOC WORK)	—	—
William D. Payne (I)	—	—
11 Dean A. Gallo (R) *	75,336	68
Frank Askin (D)	34,951	32
12 Jim Courter (R) *	72,729	64
David B. Crabiel (D)	41,593	36
13 H. James Saxton (R) *	81,351	65
John Wydra (D)	43,120	35
14 Frank J. Guarini (D) *	62,754	73
Albio Sires (R)	23,667	27
Austin L. Harrold (I)	—	—
William Link (I)	—	—
Herbert H. Shaw (I)	—	—

NEW MEXICO

Governor

Candidate	Vote Total	Percent
Ray B. Powell (D)	179,748	47
Garrey E. Carruthers (R)	203,640	53

House

Candidate	Vote Total	Percent
1 Manuel Lujan Jr. (R) *	83,762	71
Manny Garcia (D)	34,529	29
2 Joe Skeen (R) *	77,755	63
Mike Runnels (D)	45,992	37
3 Bill Richardson (D) *	94,308	71
David F. Cargo (R)	37,853	29

NEW YORK

Governor

Candidate	Vote Total	Percent
Mario M. Cuomo (D, L) *	2,683,678	65
Andrew P. O'Rourke (R, C)	1,335,598	32
Denis E. Dillon (RTL)	132,509	3
Lenora B. Fulani (NA)	—	—

Senate

Candidate	Vote Total	Percent
Alfonse M. D'Amato (R, C, RTL) *	2,363,270	57
Mark Green (D)	1,673,488	41
John Dyson (L)	59,429	2
Frederick D. Newman (NA)	—	—
Michael Shur (SOC WORK)	—	—

House

Candidate	Vote Total	Percent
1 George J. Hochbrueckner (D)	64,865	51
Gregory J. Blass (R)	54,247	43
Dominic J. Santoro (C)	4,360	3
William J. Doyle (RTL)	4,101	3
2 Thomas J. Downey (D) *	66,214	63
Jeffrey A. Butzke (R, C)	35,882	34
Veronica Windishman (RTL)	3,545	3
3 Robert J. Mrazek (D) *	82,812	56
Joseph A. Guarino (R, C)	60,066	41
Charles W. Welch (RTL)	4,317	3
4 Norman F. Lent (R, C) *	92,169	65
Patricia Sullivan (D, L)	43,279	31
George E. Patterson (RTL)	6,511	4
5 Raymond J. McGrath (R,C) *	93,133	65
Michael T. Sullivan (D, L, RTL)	49,707	35
6 Floyd H. Flake (D)	57,668	68
Richard Dietl (R, C)	27,477	32
7 Gary L. Ackerman (D) *	59,197	76
Edward Nelson Rodriguez (R, C)	18,392	24
8 James H. Scheuer (D, L) *	68,528	90
(No Republican candidate)		
Gustave Reifenkugel (C)	7,614	10
9 Thomas J. Manton (D) *	49,771	69
Salvatore J. Calise (R)	17,729	25
Thomas V. Ognibene (C)	4,723	6
10 Charles E. Schumer (D, L) *	74,505	93
(No Republican candidate)		
Alice Gaffney (C)	5,481	7
11 Edolphus Towns (D, L) *	40,295	88
Nathaniel Hendricks (R)	4,414	10
Alfred J. Hamel (C)	867	2
12 Major R. Owens (D, L) *	40,666	91
Owen Augustin (R)	2,833	6
Joseph N. O. Caesar (C, RTL)	1,160	3
13 Stephen J. Solarz (D, L) *	59,275	82
Leon Nadrowski (R)	10,654	15
Samuel Roth (C)	2,104	3
14 Guy V. Molinari (R, C) *	63,698	68
Barbara Walla (D)	27,335	29
Joseph F. Sulley (L)	2,424	3
15 Bill Green (R) *	55,454	58
George A. Hirsch (D, L)	40,136	42
16 Charles B. Rangel (D, R, L) *	59,894	98
Michael R. Berns (C)	1,341	2
17 Ted Weiss (D, L) *	89,751	86
Thomas A. Chorba (R, C)	15,153	14
18 Robert Garcia (D, L) *	42,511	94
Melanie Chase (R)	2,380	5
Lorraine Verhoff (C)	512	1
19 Mario Biaggi (D, R, L) *	86,326	90
John J. Barry (RTL)	2,987	3
Alice Farrell (C)	6,820	7
20 Joseph J. DioGuardi (R, C) *	78,169	54
Bella S. Abzug (D)	64,430	44
Florence T. O'Grady (RTL)	2,669	2
21 Hamilton Fish Jr. (R, C) *	97,306	76
Lawrence W. Grunberger (D)	27,672	22
Karen A. Gormley-Vitale (RTL)	3,069	2
22 Benjamin A. Gilman (R) *	88,236	69
Eleanor F. Burlingham (D)	34,512	27
Richard Bruno (RTL)	4,440	4
23 Samuel S. Stratton (D) *	x	x
James Joseph Callahan (SOC WORK)	—	—
24 Gerald B. H. Solomon (R, C, RTL) *	111,883	71
Ed Bloch (D)	46,769	29
25 Sherwood L. Boehlert (R) *	98,401	69
Kevin J. Conway (D)	32,257	22
Robert S. Barstow (C, RTL)	12,416	9
26 David O'B. Martin (R, C) *	x	x
(No Democratic candidate)		
27 George C. Wortley (R, C) *	82,865	50
Rosemary S. Pooler (D)	82,354	49
Dennis R. Burns (RTL)	2,137	1
28 Matthew F. McHugh (D) *	96,680	67
Mark R. Masterson (R, C, RTL)	46,740	33
29 Frank Horton (R) *	97,220	70
James R. Vogel (D)	33,433	24
Robert C. Byrnes Jr. (C)	6,013	4
Donald M. Peters (RTL)	2,337	2
30 Fred J. Eckert (R, C) *	81,719	49
Louise M. Slaughter (D)	84,639	51
31 Jack F. Kemp (R, C, RTL) *	85,351	57
James P. Keane (D)	63,983	42
Gerald R. Morgan (L)	882	1
32 John J. LaFalce (D, L) *	90,422	91
(No Republican candidate)		
Anthony J. Murty (RTL)	3,605	3
Dean L. Walker (C)	5,879	6
33 Henry J. Nowak (D, L) *	100,804	85
Charles A. Walker (R, C)	17,817	15
34 Larry M. Himelein (D)	58,222	41
Amory Houghton Jr. (R, C)	84,751	59

NORTH CAROLINA

	Vote Total	Percent
Senate		
James T. Broyhill (R) *	758,239	48
Terry Sanford (D)	818,457	52
Rich Stuart (write-in)	—	—
House		
1 Walter B. Jones (D) *	90,715	70
Howard Moye (R)	39,752	30
2 Tim Valentine (D) *	91,724	74
Bud McElhaney (R)	31,675	26
3 Martin Lancaster (D)	71,186	64
Gerald B. Hurst (R)	39,374	36
4 Bill Cobey (R) *	73,332	44
David E. Price (D)	91,545	56
5 Stephen L. Neal (D) *	85,977	54
Stuart Epperson (R)	73,353	46
6 Howard Coble (R) *	72,408	50
Robin Britt (D)	72,327	50
7 Charlie Rose (D) *	76,877	66
Thomas J. Harrelson (R)	40,388	34
8 W. G. "Bill" Hefner (D) *	78,859	58
William G. Hamby Jr. (R)	57,715	42
9 J. Alex McMillan (R) *	79,644	51
D. G. Martin (D)	76,063	49
10 Lester D. Roark (D)	61,829	43
Cass Ballenger (R)	83,240	57
11 Bill Hendon (R) *	89,100	49
James McClure Clarke (D)	91,780	51

NORTH DAKOTA

	Vote Total	Percent
Senate		
Mark Andrews (R) *	141,489	49
Kent Conrad (D)	143,764	50
Anna Belle Bourgois (I)	3,203	1
House		
AL Byron L. Dorgan (D) *	215,428	76
Syver Vinje (R)	66,712	24
Gerald W. Kopp (I)	—	—

OHIO

	Vote Total	Percent
Governor		
Richard F. Celeste (D) *	1,856,305	61
James A. Rhodes (R)	1,207,048	39
Senate		
John Glenn (D) *	1,946,639	62
Thomas N. Kindness (R)	1,173,360	38
House		
1 Thomas A. Luken (D) *	90,305	62
Fred E. Morr (R)	56,015	38
2 Bill Gradison (R) *	104,818	71
William F. Stineman (D)	43,469	29
3 Tony P. Hall (D) *	98,238	74
Ron Crutcher (R)	35,130	26
4 Michael G. Oxley (R) *	115,667	81
Clem T. Cratty (D)	26,371	19
Raven L. Workman (I)	—	—
5 Delbert L. Latta (R) *	104,977	64
Tom Murray (D)	57,906	36
6 Bob McEwen (R) *	109,247	72
Gordon Roberts (D)	42,104	28
Amos Seeley (I)	—	—
7 Michael DeWine (R) *	x	x
(No Democratic candidate)		
8 John W. Griffin (D)	46,151	32
Donald E. Lukens (R)	98,395	68
9 Marcy Kaptur (D) *	105,248	77
Mike Shufeldt (R)	30,688	23
10 Clarence E. Miller (R) *	106,257	70
John M. Buchanan (D)	44,856	30
11 Dennis E. Eckart (D) *	104,641	74
Margaret R. Mueller (R)	35,831	26
Werner J. Lange (I)	—	—
12 John R. Kasich (R) *	117,323	73
Timothy C. Jochim (D)	42,826	27
13 Don J. Pease (D) *	87,107	63
William D. Nielsen Jr. (R)	51,811	37
14 Thomas C. Sawyer (D)	82,979	54
Lynn Slaby (R)	71,517	46
15 Chalmers P. Wylie (R) *	99,423	64
David L. Jackson (D)	55,379	36
16 Ralph Regula (R) *	118,111	76
William J. Kennick (D)	36,619	24
17 James A. Traficant Jr. (D) *	112,837	72
James H. Fulks (R)	43,329	28
John F. Geletka (I)	—	—
18 Douglas Applegate (D) *	x	x
(No Republican candidate)		
19 Edward F. Feighan (D) *	97,371	55
Gary C. Suhadolnik (R)	81,246	45
20 Mary Rose Oakar (D) *	110,665	85
Bill Smith (R)	19,746	15
21 Louis Stokes (D) *	99,569	82
Franklin H. Roski (R)	22,521	18

OKLAHOMA

	Vote Total	Percent
Governor		
David Walters (D)	363,971	49
Henry Bellmon (R)	384,701	51
Jerry Brown (I)	—	—
Nelson Freckles Little (I)	—	—
Senate		
Don Nickles (R) *	457,330	54
James R. Jones (D)	382,112	46
House		
1 Gary D. Allison (D)	59,660	44
James M. Inhofe (R)	77,415	56
Carl E. McCullough Jr. (I)	—	—
2 Mike Synar (D) *	114,544	73
Gary K. Rice (R)	41,796	27
3 Wes Watkins (D) *	108,753	78
Patrick K. Miller (R)	29,944	22
4 Dave McCurdy (D) *	88,149	76
Larry Humphreys (R)	27,484	24
5 Mickey Edwards (R) *	86,249	70
Donna Compton (D)	36,501	30
6 Glenn English (D) *	x	x
(No Republican candidate)		

OREGON

	Vote Total	Percent
Governor		
Neil Goldschmidt (D)	518,490	52
Norma Paulus (R)	472,954	48
Senate		
Bob Packwood (R) *	615,198	64
Rick Bauman (D)	353,168	36
House		
1 Les AuCoin (D) *	132,620	62
Anthony "Tony" Meeker (R)	80,297	38
2 Robert F. Smith (R) *	107,190	60
Larry Tuttle (D)	71,666	40
3 Ron Wyden (D) *	160,053	86
Thomas H. Phelan (R)	25,758	14
4 Peter A. DeFazio (D)	105,069	54
Bruce Long (R)	87,879	46
5 Denny Smith (R) *	117,783	60
Barbara Ross (D)	77,966	40

PENNSYLVANIA

	Vote Total	Percent
Governor		
Bob Casey (D)	1,704,845	51
William W. Scranton (R)	1,632,365	49
Heidi J. Hoover (I)	—	—
Senate		
Arlen Specter (R) *	1,902,083	57
Bob Edgar (D)	1,438,369	43
Lance S. Haver (CON)	—	—
House		
1 Thomas M. Foglietta (D) *	83,028	75
Anthony J. Mucciolo (R)	28,148	25
2 William H. Gray III (D) *	x	x
(No Republican candidate)		
Linda R. Ragin (NA)	—	—
3 Robert A. Borski (D) *	102,227	61
Robert A. Rovner (R)	64,976	39
4 Joe Kolter (D) *	86,097	61
Al Lindsay (R)	55,123	39
Emily C. Fair (POP)	—	—
5 Richard T. Schulze (R) *	86,836	66
Tim Ringgold (D)	45,514	34
6 Gus Yatron (D) *	98,196	69
Norm Bertasavage (R)	43,968	31
7 Bill Spingler (D)	68,920	39
Curt Weldon (R)	109,647	61
8 Peter H. Kostmayer (D) *	85,561	55
David A. Christian (R)	69,965	45
9 Bud Shuster (R) *	x	x
(No Democratic candidate)		
10 Joseph M. McDade (R) *	117,343	75
Robert C. Bolus (D)	39,801	25
11 Paul E. Kanjorski (D) *	111,670	71
Marc Holtzman (R)	46,639	29
12 John P. Murtha (D) *	95,220	67
Kathy Holtzman (R)	46,266	33
13 Lawrence Coughlin (R) *	99,774	58
Joseph M. Hoeffel (D)	71,836	42
14 William J. Coyne (D) *	103,357	95
(No Republican candidate)		
Richard Edward Caligiuri (LIBERT)	5,909	5
Phyllis Gray (WL)	—	—
Thomas R. McIntyre (POP)	—	—
Mark Weddleton (SOC WORK)	—	—
15 Don Ritter (R) *	74,668	57
Joe Simonetta (D)	56,947	43
16 Robert S. Walker (R) *	100,514	75
James D. Hagelgans (D)	34,304	25
17 George W. Gekas (R) *	99,174	74
Michael S. Ogden (D)	35,492	26
18 Doug Walgren (D) *	104,001	63
Ernie Buckman (R)	61,202	37
19 Bill Goodling (R) *	100,128	73
Richard F. Thornton (D)	37,265	27
20 Joseph M. Gaydos (D) *	x	x
(No Republican candidate)		
Alden W. Vedder (WL)	—	—
21 Tom Ridge (R) *	110,699	81
Joylyn Blackwell (D)	26,293	19
22 Austin J. Murphy (D) *	x	x
(No Republican candidate)		
23 William F. Clinger Jr. (R) *	79,378	55
Bill Wachob (D)	63,756	45

RHODE ISLAND

	Vote Total	Percent
Governor		
Edward D. DiPrete (R) *	203,500	67
Bruce G. Sundlun (D)	101,024	33
Anthony D. Affigne (CIT)	—	—
Robert J. Healey Jr. (I)	—	—
House		
1 Fernand J. St Germain (D) *	82,828	58
John A. Holmes Jr. (R)	60,727	42
2 Claudine Schneider (R) *	110,517	72
Donald J. Ferry (D)	42,473	28

SOUTH CAROLINA

	Vote Total	Percent
Governor		
Mike Daniel (D)	358,153	48
Carroll A. Campbell Jr. (R)	381,484	52
William Griffin (LIBERT)	—	—
Millard Smith (AM)	—	—

	Vote Total	Percent
Senate		
Ernest F. Hollings (D) *	449,221	64
Henry D. McMaster (R)	253,519	36
Ray Hillyard (AM)	—	—
Steve Vandervelde (LIBERT)	—	—
House		
1 Jimmy Stuckey (D)	55,139	48
Arthur Ravenel Jr. (R)	60,710	52
2 Floyd Spence (R) *	73,220	54
Fred Zeigler (D)	63,093	46
3 Butler Derrick (D) *	79,077	68
Richard Dickison (R)	36,487	32
4 Liz J. Patterson (D)	66,488	52
Bill Workman (R)	61,360	48
Bob Wilson (AM)	—	—
5 John M. Spratt Jr. (D) *	x	x
(No Republican candidate)		
6 Robin Tallon (D) *	91,222	75
Robbie Cunningham (R)	29,658	25

SOUTH DAKOTA

	Vote Total	Percent
Governor		
R. Lars Herseth (D)	140,566	48
George S. Mickelson (R)	150,416	52
Senate		
James Abdnor (R) *	141,428	48
Thomas A. Daschle (D)	151,610	52
House		
AL Tim Johnson (D)	170,152	59
Dale Bell (R)	116,652	41

TENNESSEE

	Vote Total	Percent
Governor		
Ned McWherter (D)	657,426	54
Winfield Dunn (R)	552,900	46
House		
1 James H. Quillen (R) *	82,330	70
John B. Russell (D)	36,053	30
2 John J. Duncan (R) *	96,322	76
John F. Bowen (D)	30,174	24
3 Marilyn Lloyd (D) *	74,946	54
Jim Golden (R)	64,004	46
4 Jim Cooper (D) *	x	x
(No Republican candidate)		
5 Bill Boner (D) *	84,864	59
Terry Holcomb (R)	58,363	41
Kenneth Wayne Bloodworth (I)	—	—
Charlie Daniels (I)	—	—
Russell Hancock (I)	—	—
6 Bart Gordon (D) *	101,871	77
Fred Vail (R)	30,757	23
7 Don Sundquist (R) *	93,962	72
M. Lloyd Hiler (D)	35,681	28
8 Ed Jones (D) *	101,523	81
Dan H. Campbell (R)	24,571	19
9 Harold E. Ford (D) *	x	x
(No Republican candidate)		
Issac Richmond (I)	—	—

TEXAS

	Vote Total	Percent
Governor		
Mark White (D) *	1,567,150	47
Bill Clements (R)	1,791,212	53
Theresa Doyle (LIBERT)	—	—
Charles Lee (write-in)	—	—
J. Muriel (write-in)	—	—
House		
1 Jim Chapman (D) *	x	x
(No Republican candidate)		
2 Charles Wilson (D) *	77,761	67
Julian Gordon (R)	38,826	33
Sam I. Paradice (I)	—	—
3 Steve Bartlett (R) *	x	x
(No Democratic candidate)		
Brent Barnes (I)	—	—
Don Gough (LIBERT)	—	—
4 Ralph M. Hall (D) *	96,126	72
Thomas Blow (R)	37,895	28
5 John Bryant (D) *	57,410	59
Tom Carter (R)	39,945	41
Bob Brewer (LIBERT)	—	—
6 Joe L. Barton (R) *	83,432	56
Pete Geren (D)	66,642	44
7 Bill Archer (R) *	129,583	88
Harry Kniffen (D)	17,627	12
Roger Plail (LIBERT)	—	—
8 Jack Fields (R) *	65,897	68
Blaine Mann (D)	30,506	32
Wesley J. Moshay (write-in)	—	—
9 Jack Brooks (D) *	73,278	62
Lisa D. Duperier (R)	45,737	38
10 J. J. Pickle (D) *	136,046	72
Carole Keeton Rylander (R)	51,987	28
11 Marvin Leath (D) *	x	x
(No Republican candidate)		
12 Jim Wright (D) *	84,611	69
Don McNeil (R)	38,491	31
13 Beau Boulter (R) *	85,018	65
Doug Seal (D)	45,812	35
14 Mac Sweeney (R) *	74,199	52
Greg Laughlin (D)	67,495	48
15 E. "Kika" de la Garza (D) *	x	x
(No Republican candidate)		
16 Ronald D. Coleman (D) *	50,590	66
Roy Gillia (R)	26,411	34
17 Charles W. Stenholm (D) *	x	x
(No Republican candidate)		
18 Mickey Leland (D) *	x	x
(No Republican candidate)		
Joanne Kuniansky (I)	—	—
19 Larry Combest (R) *	67,276	62
Gerald McCathern (D)	41,085	38
20 Henry B. Gonzalez (D) *	x	x
(No Republican candidate)		
21 Pete Snelson (D)	63,362	39
Lamar Smith (R)	100,099	61
Bob Campbell (write-in)	—	—
Jim Robinson (LIBERT)	—	—
22 Thomas D. DeLay (R) *	73,628	72
Susan Director (D)	28,733	28
23 Albert G. Bustamante (D) *	x	x
(No Republican candidate)		
Ken Hendrix (LIBERT)	—	—
24 Martin Frost (D) *	69,368	67
Bob Burk (R)	33,819	33
Patricia Smith (write-in)	—	—
25 Michael A. Andrews (D) *	x	x
(No Republican candidate)		
26 Dick Armey (R) *	101,542	68
George Richardson (D)	47,587	32
27 Solomon P. Ortiz (D) *	x	x
(No Republican candidate)		

UTAH

	Vote Total	Percent
Senate		
Jake Garn (R) *	313,736	73
Craig Oliver (D)	115,887	27
Hugh A. Butler (LIBERT)	—	—
Mary C. Zins (I)	—	—
House		
1 James V. Hansen (R) *	82,146	52
Gunn McKay (D)	77,109	48
2 Wayne Owens (D)	76,513	56
Tom Shimizu (R)	60,665	44
Scott Alan Breen (I)	—	—
Stephen Carmichael Carr (LIBERT)	—	—
3 Howard C. Nielson (R) *	86,449	67
Dale F. Gardiner (D)	42,389	33
David P. Hurst (I)	—	—

VERMONT

	Vote Total	Percent
Governor		
Madeleine M. Kunin (D) *	92,178	47
Peter Smith (R)	74,678	38
Bernard Sanders (I)	28,451	15
Richard F. Gottlieb (LIBERT)	494	—
Senate		
Patrick J. Leahy (D) *	123,462	64
Richard A. Snelling (R)	67,263	34
Anthony N. Doria (C)	3,086	2
Jerry Levy (LIBERT)	—	—
House		
AL James M. Jeffords (R) *	154,588	96
(No Democratic candidate)		
Peter Diamondstone (LIBERT)	6,749	4
Morris Earle (I)	—	—
John T. McNulty (I)	—	—

VIRGINIA

	Vote Total	Percent
House		
1 Herbert H. Bateman (R) *	80,708	56
Robert C. Scott (D)	63,453	44
2 Owen B. Pickett (D)	54,490	54
A. J. "Joe" Canada Jr. (R)	46,133	46
Stephen P. Shao (I)	—	—
3 Thomas J. Bliley Jr. (R) *	74,423	69
Kenneth E. Powell (D)	32,867	31
J. Stephen Hodges (I)	—	—
4 Norman Sisisky (D) *	x	x
(No Republican candidate)		
5 Dan Daniel (D) *	x	x
(No Republican candidate)		
J.F. "Frank" Cole (I)	—	—
6 James R. Olin (D) *	87,032	70
Flo Neher Traywick (R)	37,380	30
7 D. French Slaughter Jr. (R) *	x	x
(No Democratic candidate)		
8 Stan Parris (R) *	71,335	62
James H. Boren (D)	43,742	38
9 Frederick C. Boucher (D) *	x	x
(No Republican candidate)		
10 Frank R. Wolf (R) *	94,069	60
John G. Milliken (D)	62,534	40

WASHINGTON

	Vote Total	Percent
Senate		
Slade Gorton (R) *	582,839	49
Brock Adams (D)	611,378	51
Jill Fein (SOC WORK)	—	—
House		
1 John R. Miller (R) *	87,950	51
Reese Lindquist (D)	84,852	49
2 Al Swift (D) *	113,698	73
Thomas S. Talman (R)	43,119	27
3 Don Bonker (D) *	106,997	74
Joe Illing (R)	37,747	26
4 Sid Morrison (R) *	94,969	72
Robert Goedecke (D)	36,806	28
5 Thomas S. Foley (D) *	115,084	75
Floyd L. Wakefield (R)	38,756	25
6 Norman D. Dicks (D) *	73,881	72
Kenneth W. Braaten (R)	29,188	28
7 Mike Lowry (D) *	112,294	73
Don McDonald (R)	40,906	27
8 Rod Chandler (R) *	94,756	65
David E. Giles (D)	50,902	35

WEST VIRGINIA

	Vote Total	Percent
House		
1 Alan B. Mollohan (D) *	x	x
(No Republican candidate)		
2 Harley O. Staggers Jr. (D) *	76,074	70
Michele Golden (R)	33,368	30
3 Bob Wise (D) *	72,878	65
Tim Sharp (R)	39,246	35
4 Nick J. Rahall II (D) *	57,653	71
Martin Miller (R)	23,484	29

WISCONSIN

	Vote Total	Percent
Governor		
Anthony S. Earl (D) *	701,261	47
Tommy G. Thompson (R)	800,200	53
Kathryn A. Christensen (LAB F)	—	—
Darold E. Wall (I)	—	—
Sanford Knapp (I)	—	—
Senate		
Bob Kasten (R) *	753,302	52
Ed Garvey (D)	701,861	48
Eugene A. Hem (I)	—	—
Margo Storsteen (SOC WORK)	—	—
Peter Y. Taylor Sr. (I)	—	—
House		
1 Les Aspin (D) *	106,166	75
Iris Peterson (R)	34,577	25
John Graf (LAB F)	—	—
2 Robert W. Kastenmeier (D) *	105,606	56
Ann J. Haney (R)	84,061	44
Syed Ameen (PRG SC)	—	—
3 Steve Gunderson (R) *	103,985	64
Leland E. Mulder (D)	58,312	36
4 Gerald D. Kleczka (D) *	x	x
(No Republican candidate)		
5 Jim Moody (D) *	x	x
(No Republican candidate)		
6 Thomas E. Petri (R) *	x	x
(No Democratic candidate)		
John Richard Daggett (I)	—	—
7 David R. Obey (D) *	106,641	63
Kevin J. Hermening (R)	63,445	37
Joseph D. Damrell (LAB F)	—	—
8 Toby Roth (R) *	116,315	67
Paul F. Willems (D)	56,574	33
9 F. James Sensenbrenner Jr. (R) *	138,014	78
Thomas G. Popp (D)	38,590	22

WYOMING

	Vote Total	Percent
Governor		
Mike Sullivan (D)	88,827	54
Pete Simpson (R)	75,775	46
House		
AL Dick Cheney (R) *	110,612	69
Rick Gilmore (D)	49,083	31

Three States Hold Special House Elections

Special elections were held in three states in 1986 to replace House members who died or resigned from office during the year.

New York

In the Queens-based 6th District of New York, the April death of veteran Democratic Rep. Joseph P. Addabbo touched off a summer-long succession battle in which the winner of the special election to fill out Addabbo's term subsequently lost his party's nomination to seek a full term.

Ever since redistricting in 1983 made the 6th a black-majority district, it had been expected that a black would win the district when it eventually became open. Addabbo's death left the 6th open sooner than anyone expected, and disagreement over who should succeed him divided the Queens Democratic organization, traditionally the most potent center of power in both the white and black communities of the 6th. When Democratic leaders met in May to decide on a designee for the June 10 special election to replace Addabbo, it took them three ballots to coalesce behind two-term state Assemblyman Alton R. Waldon Jr., a former official with the state Division of Human Rights.

Three other men who had been in contention for the Democratic designation decided to challenge Waldon by running in the special election on different party lines — a display of independence that signaled the weakening of the Democratic machine. The district's vastly outnumbered GOP organization also sponsored a candidate, rounding out the special election field at five.

The strongest of Waldon's challengers was the Rev. Floyd H. Flake, who began with a sizable base of support in the 4,000-member Allen African Methodist Episcopal Church. He built on that base with the help of other religious organizations and an endorsement from *The New York Times.*

When the polls closed June 10th, first place belonged to Flake, but by a slim 208-vote plurality over Waldon. After absentee ballots were counted, Waldon emerged with a 278-vote lead. Official special election results:

Alton R. Waldon Jr. (Democrat)	12,654	32.8%
Floyd R. Flake (Unity)	12,376	32.1
Richard Dietl (Republican)	6,502	16.8
Kevin McCabe (Good Government)	3,738	9.7
Andrew Jenkins (Liberal)	3,233	8.6

A protracted court fight ensued, with Flake claiming that the absence of his name from absentee ballots deprived him of the opportunity to win. Flake's candidacy initially had been rejected by the New York City Board of Elections on a technicality. He was reinstated by court order, and his name appeared on the ballot in voting machines. However, absentee and military ballots had been printed before Flake's reinstatement, so they did not include his name. Flake ultimately lost his lawsuit, and Waldon was sworn into Congress July 29.

But when Waldon sought nomination to a full term in the Sept. 9 primary, Flake broadened his base by fusing his support in the black church with elements of black organized labor, and he also won an endorsement from New York City Mayor Edward I. Koch. Flake won the primary by taking almost a majority of the vote against Waldon and two other candidates, and he easily prevailed in the general election.

Hawaii

Voters in Hawaii's vacant 1st District bestowed a rare and undesired distinction on candidate Neil Abercrombie: He won and lost the Honolulu-based 1st on the same day.

Abercrombie, a Democratic state senator, won a Sept. 20 special election to complete the unexpired term of Democratic Rep. Cecil Heftel, who resigned his seat in July for what turned out to be an unsuccessful run for governor. But in the Democratic primary that coincided with the special election, Abercrombie lost to corporate lobbyist Mufi Hannemann. In their primary, GOP voters nominated Patricia Saiki.

It was an unconventional result for a politician whose trademark had been nonconformity. Abercrombie, a New York transplant who broke into politics as an anti-war U.S. Senate candidate in 1970, sported long hair and a beard in his House contest. He maintained a liberal core constituency after entering the state Legislature in 1975, and, thanks to strong constituent service, broadened his following to include some more-moderate voters.

Abercrombie edged Saiki by less than 1,000 votes in the special election, in which all candidates ran on a single ballot, regardless of party. Saiki also had strong name identification as a former state legislator, a former chairman of the state Republican Party, and an unsuccessful 1982 candidate for lieutenant governor. Hannemann, making his first run for political office, finished a close third. Complete, official special election results:

Neil Abercrombie (D)	42,031	29.9%
Patricia Saiki (R)	41,067	29.2
Mufi Hannemann (D)	39,800	28.3
Steve Cobb (D)	16,721	11.9
Louis Agard (D)	566	0.4
Blase Harris (Nonpartisan)	460	0.3

But the primary for a full term in the 100th Congress yielded a different result. Saiki was alone on the ballot for the GOP nomination, and several thousand people who had voted for her in the special election cast their primary vote on the Democratic side, most of them for Hannemann. That lifted him to a narrow victory for the nomination.

Abercrombie blamed his failure to win the primary on a Hannemann ad that cited a 16-year-old newspaper story about Abercrombie's alleged favorable attitude toward marijuana. Before leaving Hawaii for his Sept. 23 swearing-in, Abercrombie said he would not endorse Hannemann. In the November general election, Democratic disunity helped

Saiki defeat Hannemann, an outcome that made her the first Hawaii Republican House member since statehood in 1959.

North Carolina

Republican Rep. James T. Broyhill's departure did not threaten Republican hegemony in North Carolina's 10th District, which encompasses some of the state's most heavily Republican territory. Voters in the district chose GOP state Sen. Cass Ballenger to succeed Broyhill, who was appointed in July to complete the term of GOP Sen. John P. East. East committed suicide June 29.

In 1985, East had announced plans to leave the Senate. Broyhill declared plans to retire from the House and seek East's Senate seat; in North Carolina's May primary, Broyhill won the GOP Senate nomination. Also in the May primary, voters in the 10th nominated Republican Ballenger and Democrat Lester D. Roark to compete for the district in November. When Broyhill was appointed to the Senate, the special election to fill out the remainder of his House term was set to coincide with the November general election.

Although Democrats had a credible candidate in Roark, a former state deputy attorney general, he could not overcome the Republican tilt of the 10th. Ballenger won both the special election and the general election for a full term by the same percentage. Complete, official special election results:

Cass Ballenger (R)	82,973	57.5%
Lester D. Roark (D)	61,205	42.5

Because Broyhill's appointment to the Senate ran only to the general election, a special Senate election also was held Nov. 4 to fill out the last weeks of the Senate term. The winner in the special election, just as in the vote for a full six-year term, was Democrat Terry Sanford. Complete, official special election results:

Terry Sanford (D)	780,967	50.9%
James T. Broyhill (R)	753-881	49.1

VOTING STUDIES

CQ

Hard-Fought Battles Mark Key Votes in 1986

Key House and Senate votes in 1986 showed that President Reagan could still have his way on Capitol Hill, but he had to work harder to get it.

Reagan won important victories on Central American policy, trade issues and judicial nominations. But his wins often came only after close votes, veto fights and other confrontations with an increasingly independent Congress.

Election-year resistance to Reagan policies came not only from House Democrats eager to stake out their party's alternatives but also from Senate Republicans seeking to distance themselves from administration positions that were unpopular with their constituents.

Among the most forthright bipartisan challenges to the president were the decisive votes, in the Senate as well as the House, to override Reagan's veto of legislation (HR 4868 — PL 99-440) imposing stiff sanctions against the white-minority government in South Africa.

Reagan did prevail in two other veto confrontations, when Congress failed to override his veto of a bill (HR 1562) limiting textile imports and of another (S J Res 316) blocking a proposed arms sale to Saudi Arabia.

In another area where Reagan faced increased resistance, the Senate approved the nominations of William H. Rehnquist to be chief justice of the United States and Daniel A. Manion to be a federal appeals court judge — but only after Democrats mounted protracted confirmation fights.

In the ongoing defense debate between the president and Congress, the Senate by a one-vote margin saved an administration plan to begin producing chemical weapons known as "binary" munitions.

Congressional dissatisfaction with Reagan's arms control policies was in evidence in both chambers, but it was the House that mounted the most dramatic challenge to them.

The House approved a proposal, eventually dropped under pressure from the administration, to ban all but the smallest nuclear tests.

But the House handed Reagan his major foreign policy victory of the year when it abandoned three years of opposition and approved his request to renew military aid to rebels fighting Nicaragua's government.

Backing another element of Reagan's policy of support for guerrillas opposing leftist regimes, the House also rejected a ban on covert U.S. aid to anti-government guerrillas in Angola.

How Votes Were Selected

Congressional Quarterly each year selects a series of key votes on major issues.

Selection of Issues. An issue is judged by the extent it represents one or more of the following:

- A matter of major controversy.
- A matter of presidential or political power.
- A decision of potentially great impact on the nation and lives of Americans.

Selection of Votes. For each group of related votes on an issue, one key vote usually is chosen. This is the vote that, in the opinion of Congressional Quarterly editors, was important in determining the outcome.

In the description of the key votes, the designation "ND" denotes Northern Democrats and "SD" denotes Southern Democrats.

Partisanship Waxes and Wanes

Election-year partisanship came into play on such issues as trade and farm policy, where Democrats tried to saddle their Republican colleagues with responsibility for unpopular Reagan policies.

But there was an extraordinary display of bipartisanship in congressional action on Reagan's No. 1 domestic priority for his second term — legislation (HR 3838 — PL 99-514) overhauling the tax code.

In crafting the tax overhaul bill and its fiscal 1987 budget (S Con Res 120), Congress bowed to Reagan's adamant opposition to tax hikes, despite some lawmakers' hopes that he could be convinced that increased taxes should be part of the federal strategy for reducing the deficit.

In a reversal of its 1982 stance, the Senate rejected Reagan's favored deficit-reduction tool — a constitutional amendment requiring a balanced budget (S J Res 225).

But other important votes reflected Congress' preoccupation with fiscal matters during its first year of operating under the constraints of the 1985 Gramm-Rudman-Hollings anti-deficit law (PL 99-177).

Early in the year, the drive to reduce the deficit was strong enough in the Senate to help derail a $1 billion add-on for the farm loan program, at a time when members were under heavy pressure to help the ailing agriculture economy.

The Gramm-Rudman law also bolstered those seeking to rein in the president's defense budget, including his funding request for the anti-missile system known as the strategic defense initiative. Pressure for the Pentagon to share the burden of reducing the federal deficit was greatest in the House, which initially voted to cut the fiscal 1987 defense budget below fiscal 1986 appropriations levels.

After the Supreme Court in July struck down the key Gramm-Rudman enforcement mechanism, the House and Senate divided over what to do in response. The House refused to accept a Senate proposal to correct the law's constitutional flaws, although the issue was likely to be revisited in 1987.

Despite Congress' penchant for procrastination, more conclusive action was taken in 1986 on some issues that had languished for years. Most notably, an overhaul of the nation's immigration laws (S 1200) was enacted at the end of the session after five years of struggle.

Senate Key Votes

1. Senate TV Coverage

The Senate finally joined the House in permitting television and radio broadcasts of its floor proceedings. A resolution (S Res 28) allowing TV cameras and audio microphones was approved Feb. 27, 67-21: R 35-14; D 32-7 (ND 24-2, SD 8-5).

The action came nearly 40 years after Sen. Claude Pepper, D-Fla., now a House member, first proposed that the infant invention of television be welcomed into the Senate. The House, meanwhile, began in 1979 to provide gavel-to-gavel coverage of its floor action to commercial and public broadcasting networks.

The Senate had remained camera-shy for several reasons. A brief experience, the televised swearing-in of Nelson A. Rockefeller as vice president in 1974, left some members complaining about the heat and brightness of camera lights. After 1979, members chose to wait and watch the House experience; they were not encouraged when the House initially seemed to suffer an upsurge in partisanship, with junior Republicans using the floor as a national stage to confront the majority Democrats.

After 1984, the Senate TV effort lost its chief proponent when Majority Leader Howard H. Baker Jr., R-Tenn., retired. But the biggest impediment to Senate broadcasts was a fear among an influential minority that TV would doom what they saw as the Senate's valuable and traditional role as the more deliberative of the two chambers. The leading opponents were Louisiana's Democratic senators, Russell B. Long and J. Bennett Johnston.

In 1986, neither man made an all-out effort to kill the broadcasting resolution. Also, Majority Leader Robert Dole, R-Kan., dropped his earlier opposition and joined Minority Leader Robert C. Byrd, D-W.Va., in lobbying for the change.

Finally, the resolution picked up some support when it became a vehicle for unrelated proposals to change Senate rules to restrict obstructionist tactics.

The final version of the TV-radio resolution included several rules changes, the most significant of which reduced from 100 hours to 30 hours the time allowed for additional debate after the Senate votes to invoke cloture.

The Senate, by an unexpectedly large margin, refused to add a budget-busting $1 billion to farm loan programs.

2. Farm Program Supplemental

Less than three months after President Reagan signed the landmark 1985 farm bill (PL 99-198) on Dec. 23, 1985, Congress and the White House renewed their political battle over agriculture. Mixed into the fray this time around, however, was a new element — the anti-deficit requirements of the Gramm-Rudman-Hollings law (PL 99-177) enacted at the end of 1985.

When it came to farm programs, the Gramm-Rudman strictures seemed particularly distasteful to Republicans holding a slim 53-47 majority in the Senate. Conservative demands for fiscal restraint did not take into account the election-year pressures on nearly a dozen GOP incumbents from mainly rural states.

A pivotal showdown materialized quickly over an emergency fiscal 1986 supplemental appropriations bill (H J Res 534 — PL 99-263) for agriculture programs. House Democrats opened the assault by insisting that spending for farm operating and real estate loans should be kept at a level previously appropriated for fiscal 1986, even though the 1985 farm bill had subsequently cut 1986 farm loans by nearly $1 billion. By putting $1 billion back into the farm loan program, the supplemental would push federal spending over the new Gramm-Rudman spending limits.

In a Senate showdown late March 13, election-year pressures were clearly evident. "I think we're down to the first real vote on Gramm-Rudman-Hollings," said that law's co-author, Phil Gramm, R-Texas. "I wish we had a test case that did not involve such a popular program."

As expected, 10 farm-state Republicans voted in favor of the $1 billion in added farm spending. But 21 urban Democrats broke ranks with their party leadership and joined conservative Republicans to vote against it. In a surprisingly lopsided vote, the Senate killed the new spending plan, 61-33: R 40-10; D 21-23 (ND 17-14, SD 4-9).

In rather convincing fashion, the Senate thus demonstrated that even in an election year, the strictures of Gramm-Rudman-Hollings could be used against politically popular funding proposals. The showdown established the political as well as fiscal ground rules for spending proposals for the rest of the year.

3. Balanced-Budget Amendment

Despite pressures to reduce the federal deficit and balance the budget, the Senate March 25 rejected a constitutional amendment to require a balanced budget.

The vote was 66-34, one short of the required two-thirds majority of those present and voting (67 in this case). The major reason for the defeat was the defection of key Republicans, including John H. Chafee, R.I., chairman of the Republican Conference, the caucus of all Senate Republicans, and John Heinz, Pa., chairman of the National Republican Senatorial Campaign Committee, which raises money to help elect Republican senators. They were among 10 Republicans who voted against the proposal, despite President Reagan's strong support for it: R 43-10; D 23-24 (ND 10-23, SD 13-1).

The vote came only about three months after Congress enacted the Gramm-Rudman-Hollings anti-deficit law (PL 99-177) and suggested that members' fervor for extraordinary methods of fiscal restraint was waning.

The amendment would have allowed deficit spending only with approval of a three-fifths majority of the total of both chambers, or during time of war.

While supporters said the constitutional proposal was necessary to force Congress to balance the budget, opponents said it would not work. Appropriations Chairman Mark O. Hatfield, R-Ore, called it "subterfuge."

The vote was a turnaround from 1982, when the Senate passed a similar amendment 69-31, only to see it killed in the House.

4. 'Contra' Aid

The Senate long had supported, by narrow margins, President Reagan's policy of giving military aid to the "contra" guerrillas in Nicaragua, who were battling to oust the leftist government in Managua. So there was little surprise on March 27, when the Senate voted 53-47: R 42-11; D 11-36 (ND 2-31, SD 9-5), to approve Reagan's latest request for $70 million in military aid and $30 million in non-military aid to the contras. The vote nearly matched the 53-46 margin by which the Senate had approved $14 million in aid to the contras in April 1985.

Reversing its position, the House approved the aid in June. The Senate took another series of votes on the issue in August and approved the aid by the same margin as on March 27.

Two senators switched their votes: James Abdnor, R-S.D., voted for the contra aid on March 27 and against it on Aug. 13; Daniel J. Evans, R-Wash., shifted the opposite way.

The $100 million was included in the military construction section of the fiscal 1987 omnibus appropriations bill (H J Res 738 — PL 99-500).

5. Fiscal 1987 Budget Resolution

A strong, bipartisan majority in the Senate May 2 approved a fiscal 1987 budget resolution (S Con Res 120) that defied President Reagan in calling for $10.7 billion in new taxes, slicing $19 billion from his defense request, and ignoring many of the sharp reductions in domestic programs he had wanted. The resolution was adopted 70-25: R 32-19; D 38-6 (ND 26-4, SD 12-2).

The Senate vote was the high-water mark in a drive led by Republican Pete V. Domenici of New Mexico, chairman of the Budget Committee, and the panel's ranking Democrat, Lawton Chiles of Florida.

The two hoped that both parties, in both chambers, would join to force Reagan to accept a tax increase as part of a budget compromise. But this plan was frustrated by a skittish House. The final budget resolution did cut Reagan's defense request markedly and bolstered domestic programs he wanted to cut, but it included only the $5.9 billion in new revenues that Reagan himself had sought.

House leaders refused to join with the Senate in supporting the $10.7 billion tax increase unless Reagan reversed his oft-stated objections to such a hike. The House version of the resolution did include a $10.7 billion tax increase for fiscal 1987. But of that, $4.7 billion — the amount Democrats said exceeded Reagan's own revenue request in his budget — was put in a special account earmarked for deficit reduction. When Congress finally adopted S Con Res 120 in late June, this account was gone, supplanted by a "contingency reserve," authorizing spending on defense or other high-priority programs if requested by the president, and if the president's request included offsetting tax increases or spending cuts. Reagan did not request the fund's use before Congress adjourned.

The Senate once again narrowly approved U.S. military aid to "contra" rebels fighting the government in Nicaragua.

The Senate vote came only after Majority Leader Robert Dole, R-Kan., and GOP conservatives had pressed for changes in the Budget Committee version of S Con Res 120. Dole's overriding interest was in a budget that would garner a majority of Republican votes. The GOP votes were, in turn, considered necessary to winning Democratic votes for the measure. Conservative Republicans had kept up a barrage of complaints about the committee's higher tax figure and lower defense spending. And Dole's refusal to endorse the committee version was considered a major obstacle to getting the Republican majority he wanted.

In lengthy private negotiations, Domenici and Chiles finally agreed to trim by nearly $6 billion the amount in new taxes recommended by the committee, and to raise the committee's defense figure by about the same amount. To keep Democratic votes, an equivalent amount of extra funding was provided for selected science, education, job training, trade and child health programs. This compromise, adopted 66-29 before the Senate vote on passage, showed the pervasive influence of the Gramm-Rudman-Hollings anti-deficit law (PL 99-177), under which automatic spending cuts were to be divided equally among defense and non-defense programs.

6. Daylight-Saving Time

Over the protests of rural- and Midwestern-state senators, the Senate May 20 voted to begin daylight-saving time three weeks earlier in the spring. The move culminated a 10-year campaign to approve a permanent expansion of daylight-saving time.

Opponents, led by Wendell H. Ford, D-Ky., and J. James Exon, D-Neb., had bottled up similar House legislation in the Commerce Committee for nearly a year, contending that any extension would hurt farmers and endanger schoolchildren in rural areas at the western edge of time zones. Bypassing the committee, Slade Gorton, R-Wash., attached the daylight-saving extension to a routine bill (S 2180) to authorize fire prevention programs.

Without a vote to spare, the Senate sustained President Reagan's veto of a measure to block a long-delayed sale of Harpoon missiles and other weapons to Saudi Arabia.

The vote came on a motion by Majority Leader Robert Dole, R-Kan., to table, or kill, Gorton's daylight-saving time amendment. That motion was rejected by a vote of 36-58: R 16-33; D 20-25 (ND 10-21, SD 10-4). Following that vote, the Senate by voice vote adopted the amendment and then passed the bill.

The bill moved the start of daylight-saving time from the last Sunday in April to the first Sunday in April. The House-passed version had included an additional week in the fall, to include Halloween.

But Gorton agreed to drop that extra week in an attempt to appease his foes.

7. Saudi Arms

Major arms sales to Arab countries regularly provoke fierce battles in Congress, largely because of behind-the-scenes opposition to them by Israel and active opposition by the influential pro-Israel lobby. President Reagan's decision early in 1986 to approve a long-delayed sale of missiles and other equipment to Saudi Arabia generated the expected battle in Congress, but with a twist: both Israel and the American Israel Public Affairs Committee took public stands of neutrality.

Nevertheless, opposition to the $354 million sale mounted in both houses, and Congress on May 7 sent Reagan a bill (S J Res 316) blocking it. As expected, Reagan vetoed the measure, saying it would damage U.S. relations with a key moderate Arab country.

But to bolster the chances of sustaining his veto, Reagan deleted from the arms package the single most controversial item: $89 million worth of Stinger missiles, a hand-held, anti-aircraft weapon that some members feared could fall into the hands of Middle East terrorists.

The Senate on May 21 sustained Reagan's veto by the barest of margins, 66-34: R 24-29; D 42-5 (ND 31-2, SD 11-3). Thirty-four votes (one-third plus one) were needed to uphold the veto. Reagan claimed that he had other "stand-bys" willing to vote his way, and there never was much doubt that he would prevail on the final vote in the Senate. Even so, the vote demonstrated the continuing difficulty that presidents faced in forging military ties to Arab countries that technically remained at war with Israel.

8. Tax Overhaul

Among the hundreds of provisions of the big tax overhaul bill (HR 3838) of 1986 there was only one that produced a grass-roots reaction from every corner of the nation. That was the proposal, which originated in the Senate Finance Committee, to eliminate the $2,000 annual deduction for contributions to an Individual Retirement Account (IRA) for anyone who was covered by another pension plan.

Despite thousands of letters of protest, the Senate, by a three-vote margin June 11, defeated the effort to preserve at least part of the tax break. The vote came on a motion by Finance Chairman Bob Packwood, R-Ore., to table, and thus kill, a pro-IRA amendment sponsored by Alfonse M. D'Amato, R-N.Y.

D'Amato would have converted the $2,000 IRA deduction to a credit of 15 percent of the amount contributed to an IRA, to a maximum of $300.

The IRA vote provided a crucial test of the Senate's willingness to approve the Finance Committee's version of the bill without major change. That version, which laid the groundwork for the law eventually enacted, greatly reduced tax rates for both individuals and corporations, but made up the lost revenue by eliminating or curtailing scores of special tax breaks.

Packwood and the other key backers of the Finance Committee bill warned the Senate repeatedly that a vote to restore even one major tax break could open the floodgates to countless other changes and ultimately cause the whole bill to go down. The widespread public support for keeping IRAs the way they were thus made the IRA vote the best possible issue for those who advocated other amendments, or even sought to defeat the entire bill.

The strength of the public pressure on senators was demonstrated by the votes in favor of continuing the IRA tax break, unchanged, that were cast by all nine Democrats and half of the 18 Republicans who were running for re-election.

Those who wanted to keep the massive tax overhaul intact prevailed. The Senate vote to table the D'Amato amendment was 51-48: R 35-17; D 16-31 (ND 10-23, SD 6-8).

The Senate passed its version of the tax bill 97-3 on June 24, with only three Democrats opposing it. And the final conference committee version of the bill passed the Senate 74-23. It retained the full $2,000 IRA deduction for single persons with incomes up to $25,000 and married couples up to $40,000, with a phase-out of the deduction for those above these income levels. *(House key vote 13)*

9. Manion Nomination

In one of the most dramatic judicial nomination fights in years, Senate Democrats forced a vote June 26 on the controversial appointment of Daniel A. Manion to be a federal appeals court judge.

They thought they had the votes to defeat Manion, who critics said was not qualified for the bench. But their plan went awry when Republican Slade Gorton, Wash., voted for Manion — a move that shocked Democrats who thought Gorton opposed the nomination.

On the tally, Manion was confirmed 48-46: R 45-4; D 3-42 (ND 1-30, SD 2-12). That vote did not represent a true test of Manion's strength, however. Minority Leader Robert C. Byrd, D-W.Va., who had voted against Manion, abruptly switched his vote to "aye" and then moved to reconsider the vote. This blocked the tally from becoming final. (Only senators voting on the prevailing side can move for reconsideration.)

Gorton said later he decided to vote for Manion after White House officials told him they would move on a district court nomination he had pressed for. (William Dwyer eventually was nominated by President Reagan, but the Senate Judiciary Committee failed to act on his nomination before Congress adjourned.)

The Gorton vote was not the only unusual one. Because two Republicans were absent June 26 — Paula Hawkins, Fla., and Bob Packwood, Ore. — Majority Leader Robert Dole, R-Kan., was reluctant to proceed with a vote. He said these were two votes for Manion. But Joseph R. Biden Jr., Del., the ranking Judiciary Democrat, told Dole he wanted a vote right away. Although he said he doubted Packwood supported Manion, Biden agreed to give up, or "pair," his vote with Hawkins, and Democrat Daniel K. Inouye, Hawaii, paired his vote with Packwood.

A third glitch developed over the absent Barry Goldwater, R-Ariz. Dan Quayle, R-Ind., Manion's chief supporter, persuaded Nancy Landon Kassebaum, R-Kan., to withdraw her "nay" vote and pair it with Goldwater, who Quayle said was a Manion supporter. Later, Kassebaum said she had been misled by Quayle because Goldwater had not made up his mind.

Almost a month after this confusion, Manion's confirmation became official when the Senate refused 49-50 to reconsider the June 26 vote. Goldwater voted against reconsideration — essentially a vote for Manion, while Packwood voted for reconsideration.

10. Gramm-Rudman-Hollings 'Fix'

The Senate moved swiftly to repair the Gramm-Rudman-Hollings anti-deficit law (PL 99-177) after the Supreme Court July 7 found the measure's automatic spending-cut process to be unconstitutional. On July 30 the Senate approved a different version of the automatic procedure, giving the Office of Management and Budget (OMB) final authority to determine the magnitude of cuts required to meet the deficit targets set by the statute. The revision was adopted as an amendment to legislation (H J Res 668) raising the ceiling on the federal debt. The vote for the so-called Gramm-Rudman "fix" amendment was 63-36: R 42-10; D 21-26 (ND 10-23, SD 11-3).

The Senate, which had produced Gramm-Rudman the previous year, was determined to show its devotion to deficit reduction by resuscitating the enforcement mechanism of the statute. But the large winning margin masked considerable unease with the enhanced powers assigned OMB by the amendment. In part, this reflected institutional resistance to encroachments by the executive branch agency. A second factor was distrust generated by OMB's controversial former director, David A. Stockman.

In the House, suspicion of OMB and animosity to the fix was so great that the legislation was ignored and died at the end of the session. Nor would the House accept a one-year version of the Gramm-Rudman language, rejecting that by a 175-133 vote when it arrived from the Senate as part of a short-term debt-ceiling increase (HR 5395).

In its July 7 decision the high court had faulted the role of the General Accounting Office (GAO) in Gramm-Rudman's automatic process. The justices found that GAO was a legislative agency and as such, improperly involved in a procedure that compelled the executive branch to promulgate spending cuts. After the court acted, Senate sponsors of the antideficit law devised a new version of the automatic procedure giving OMB the final say on the cuts. But the amendment faced defeat in the Senate until sponsors agreed to restrictions specifying, among other things, what economic assumptions and spending rates would be used in determining the deficit and any required cuts.

The Senate, facing pressure to clear HR 5395, the short-term debt-limit increase, before the Labor Day recess, did not insist on its one-year Gramm-Rudman fix. But, just prior to adjournment in October, Senate and House leaders agreed to a debt-limit increase lasting only until May 15, 1987, at which time the Gramm-Rudman amendment could be revived. *(House key vote 10)*

11. Strategic Defense Initiative

The Senate Aug. 5 came within one vote of slashing by 40 percent, to $3.24 billion, President Reagan's $5.3 billion request to continue the strategic defense initiative (SDI), or "star wars" program, intended to develop a nationwide shield against nuclear missiles. Instead, it approved an already substantial cut, to $3.9 billion, approved by the Armed Services Committee.

Reagan announced the SDI program early in 1983 with the goal of rendering nuclear missiles "impotent and obsolete." Arms control activists strongly opposed the effort from the outset, arguing that it could not produce an effective missile defense, but would trigger a new round of the arms race in outer space.

In 1985, SDI critics unsuccessfully made several efforts in both the Senate and House to block specific parts of the SDI program they deemed inconsistent with the 1972 U.S.-Soviet treaty limiting anti-missile weapons. For 1986, leading SDI opponents decided to try instead to curb SDI funding increases so that it would be politically easier to kill off the program after Reagan left office.

The arms control activists focused their attention on efforts to "freeze" SDI funding in the House, where the preponderance of liberal Democrats gave them an advantage. But in the Senate, two centrist Democrats, J. Bennett Johnston, La., and Lawton Chiles, Fla., and liberal William Proxmire, D-Wis., decided early in the year to try to allow only a small increase in SDI funding above the cost of inflation. In a lengthy report to the three senators, aides had argued that there was widespread skepticism in the scientific community that SDI was technically sound.

Beginning in mid-May, the three plus Republican Daniel J. Evans, Wash., quickly rounded up the signatures of 48 senators on a letter to Reagan calling on him to allow SDI funding for fiscal 1987 to increase by only 3 percent above the cost of inflation. The letter cited many arguments in support of that view, including the contention that SDI funding should not be boosted by 77 percent above the fiscal 1986 appropriation, as Reagan urged, when Congress was trying to hold down the defense budget overall.

On Aug. 5, during the Senate debate on the fiscal 1987 defense authorization bill (S 2638), a Johnston amendment that would have trimmed SDI funding to $3.24 billion was tabled (thus killed) 50-49: R 41-11; D 9-38 (ND 5-28, SD 4-10). *(House key vote 8)*

12. Chemical Weapons

As it had done several times since 1982, the Senate narrowly approved President Reagan's request to resume production of lethal chemical weapons for the first time since 1969. At issue was a request to begin manufacturing so-called binary munitions — artillery shells and "Bigeye" air-dropped bombs that would dispense nerve gas.

The Pentagon argued that existing chemical weapons stocks needed replacement because they were deteriorating, and that the proposed new weapons would be safer for U.S. military personnel to store and transport. But opponents contended that existing nerve gas weapons were adequate to deter the Soviet Union from using their own chemical weapons stockpile. And resistance to the new weapons was swelled by a revulsion against chemical weapons among some centrist and conservative members of Congress.

Staunch opposition in the House to the new weapons had staved off procurement. But in 1985, members gave the go-ahead for procurement to begin in fiscal 1987, subject to numerous conditions.

In 1986, Senate opponents of chemical weapons concentrated on blocking production of the Bigeye, citing a long string of technical problems revealed by testing. An amendment to block Bigeye production was rejected 50-51: R 14-39; D 36-11 (ND 29-4, SD 7-7).

Vice President George Bush, in his constitutional role as the Senate's presiding officer, voted against the amendment. However, the amendment would have failed on a 50-50 tie, even if Bush had not voted.

In 1983, Bush twice saved binary weapons from defeat with tie-breaking votes. *(House key vote 9)*

President Reagan named William H. Rehnquist as the 16th chief justice of the United States, to succeed Warren E. Burger.
AP/Wide World Photos

13. Rehnquist Nomination

The Senate Sept. 17 confirmed William H. Rehnquist to be the 16th chief justice of the United States, but only after a six-week confirmation fight centering on Rehnquist's conservative ideology and his candor in testifying before the Judiciary Committee.

The vote was 65-33: R 49-2; D 16-31 (ND 4-29, SD 12-2). The 33 "nay" votes against Rehnquist were the largest number ever cast against a Supreme Court nominee who won confirmation. Rehnquist also tied the record for the second-highest number of "nay" votes received by a 20th century Supreme Court nominee — the 26 cast against him when he was first named to the court in 1971.

Critics, led by Democrats Edward M. Kennedy, Mass., Howard M. Metzenbaum, Ohio, and Joseph R. Biden Jr., Del., said Rehnquist had shown an insensitivity to minority and individual rights and had failed to testify fully before the committee about alleged voter harassment in Phoenix, Ariz., in the 1960s and about his failure to step down during court consideration of a 1972 case challenging the Army's domestic surveillance program. Rehnquist had participated in discussions about the program while he was an assistant attorney general.

14. South Africa Sanctions

Congress in 1986 dismantled one of President Reagan's most controversial foreign policies: the use of "constructive engagement" to encourage internal reforms in South Africa and peace between Pretoria and its neighbors.

In spite of administration claims of success, the policy was widely seen both in the United States and in South Africa as tacit U.S. blessing for the white-minority government in Pretoria. Both houses of Congress passed legislation in 1985 imposing economic sanctions against South Africa. Reagan headed off final action by signing an executive order imposing mild sanctions on his own, including a ban on imports of South African gold coins.

Spurred on in part by election-year pressures, the pro-sanctions drive picked up steam in 1986. Surprising everyone, the House in June passed a sanctions bill (HR 4868) cutting off virtually all economic ties between the United States and South Africa.

The Senate in mid-August passed by 84-14 its own version that, while milder than the House bill, included stronger sanctions than Senate leaders had expected. The bill barred imports of South African steel, textiles and agricultural goods, suspended air service between the United States and South Africa, and barred new U.S. business investment there.

When Congress returned from its August recess, Senate Foreign Relations Committee Chairman Richard G. Lugar, R-Ind., pressured the House into accepting the Senate version and sending it to Reagan. Unless the House did so, he said, the bill would fall victim to an end-of-session filibuster in the Senate.

Ignoring pleas by Lugar and other congressional leaders, Reagan on Sept. 26 vetoed the bill, saying it would hurt South African blacks. The House quickly voted to override the veto, on Sept. 29, by a 313-83 vote.

Reagan made a feeble effort to sustain his veto in the Republican-controlled Senate — promising, for example, to sign another executive order containing limited sanctions — but was rebuffed overwhelmingly. The 78-21 vote on Oct. 2 was well above the two-thirds margin needed to override the veto and enact the bill into law: R 31-21; D 47-0 (ND 33-0, SD 14-0).

Democrats voted unanimously to override the veto. Only six of the Republicans who originally had voted for the bill switched to support Reagan: Thad Cochran, Miss.; Robert Dole, Kan., the majority leader; Orrin G. Hatch, Utah; Don Nickles, Okla.; Alan K. Simpson, Wyo., the assistant majority leader; and Ted Stevens, Alaska. Barry Goldwater, R-Ariz., absent on the first vote, also backed the president. *(House key vote 15)*

15. Pesticide Regulation

The Senate Oct. 6 reversed a key House vote and affirmed the right of states to set stricter standards than the federal government for how much pesticide residue should be allowed in food.

The controversy was one that ultimately helped doom a bill designed to break years of legislative deadlock over pesticide law. The bill (HR 2482) would have speeded up testing of pesticides for health hazards, a process that had not been completed for most of the 600 active ingredients then in use. Both chambers passed the bill, but they failed to reconcile the two versions and it died with adjournment.

The amendment in question, offered by Dave Durenberger, R-Minn., deleted language to let the federal government set national standards for allowable pesticide residues (called "tolerances"), while prohibiting states from setting stricter tolerances, except in certain cases.

The Durenberger amendment was approved by voice vote Oct. 6, soon after the Senate rejected a motion to table it, 34-45: R 23-16; D 11-29 (ND 4-24, SD 7-5). The tabling motion was offered by Richard G. Lugar, R-Ind.

Farm and food industry groups supported the uniform tolerance, saying individual state tolerances would make marketing food products too difficult. The National Governors' Association and some environmental groups supported Durenberger, arguing that states have a right to protect their own citizens' health.

The Senate vote broke partly along lines of party and ideology (with Republicans and conservatives tending to support uniform tolerance), as did the vote in the House. Farm-state members also tended to favor the uniform tolerance, but with less cohesion than in the House vote. *(House key vote 12)*

House Key Votes

1. Gun Control

After a seven-year fight, the National Rifle Association (NRA) succeeded in winning passage of legislation that significantly relaxed federal gun control laws.

On April 10, the House passed a bill that made important changes in the 1968 Gun Control Act (PL 90-351), including lifting the ban on interstate sales of rifles and shotguns. The vote was 292-130: R 161-15; D 131-115 (ND 62-103, SD 69-12).

The Senate subsequently approved the House bill, which President Reagan signed (PL 99-308).

An earlier Senate-passed bill also would have lifted the ban on interstate sales of handguns. But that drew the ire of law enforcement groups, and with quiet backing from

A House-Senate deadlock over states' regulatory powers helped doom a rewrite of the nation's basic pesticide law.

Handgun Control Inc., a Washington-based gun control group, the police organizations persuaded Congress that the final bill should not lift the ban on handguns.

The police groups were still unhappy with other sections of the bill, and they won enactment of separate legislation (S 2414 — PL 99-360) that narrowed the circumstances under which weapons could be carried interstate.

While enactment of the new gun law once more demonstrated the NRA's clout, it also mobilized police organizations, which were likely to become more visible players on Capitol Hill in the future.

2. Public Housing

The House endorsed a major change in federal housing policy June 5, voting to shift from the traditional emphasis on the construction of low-income public housing units toward repair and rehabilitation of existing dwellings.

The Reagan administration had supported such a change, arguing that new construction was too costly and that the current supply of housing was adequate. Although the House provision did not become law — because other disputes blocked enactment of a fiscal 1987 housing authorization bill (HR 1) — the vote marked the first time the House had endorsed the proposal.

The key vote came on an amendment offered by Rep. Steve Bartlett, R-Texas, to redirect $860 million in unobligated fiscal 1986 appropriations from construction of public housing projects to repair and modernization of existing units, completion of construction already under way and a few new starts in specific cases.

Critics of the amendment contended that in some parts of the country, housing was scarce, rents were high and new construction was the only source of housing for the poor. They also said it would be cheaper to demolish and replace dilapidated public housing in many cases than to rehabilitate.

But Bartlett maintained that his proposal "creates a new priority that recognizes the reality of modern times," when the government does not have the money for major new projects. Repair and rehabilitation of public housing would be a far more efficient use of federal funds, he said,

The House voted to shift public housing policy away from new construction toward rehabilitation of existing units.

returning more abandoned and unsafe units to productive use than otherwise would be built.

Bartlett's amendment to redirect funding was adopted June 5 by a vote of 223-180: R 148-19; D 75-161 (ND 35-125, SD 40-36).

3. 'Contra' Aid

The House June 25 abandoned three years of opposition to President Reagan's support for anti-government "contra" guerrillas in Nicaragua. By a 221-209 vote: R 170-11; D 51-198 (ND 8-159, SD 43-39), the House agreed to Reagan's request for $70 million in military aid and $30 million in non-military aid for the contras, who were battling to overthrow the leftist government in Managua.

The House had opposed military aid for the contras since 1983 and had rejected Reagan's latest request only three months before, on March 20.

Strong lobbying by the president, as well as disorganization among critics of the contra aid program, helped make the reversal possible.

The aid later was included in the military construction portion of the fiscal 1987 omnibus appropriations bill (H J Res 738 — PL 99-500). *(Senate key vote 4)*

4. Textile Imports

President Reagan narrowly won the major vote of the year on his trade policies, but not because of strong congressional support for those policies. Frustration on Capitol Hill about rising trade deficits was nearly matched by uncertainty about what to do. While legislation retaliating against "unfair" foreign trading practices generated broad support in Congress, many members were concerned about setting off trade wars with unforeseen consequences.

The test case for a tougher trade policy involved textiles, one of the U.S. industries hardest hit by foreign competition. Both chambers in late 1985 passed legislation (HR 1562) restricting textile and apparel imports, forcing a reduction of about 30 percent. The bill also provided import relief to the domestic shoe and copper industries.

Reagan vetoed the bill in December 1985, but House Democratic leaders postponed a veto override attempt until the following August, hoping that the approaching elections and a few more months of bad trade news would bolster support for the bill. In the weeks before the Aug. 6 vote, however, the administration signed new textile agreements with Hong Kong, South Korea and Taiwan, the three primary targets of the bill. The administration also took steps to promote grain sales to the Soviet Union and semiconductor sales to Japan — strengthening its free-trade case among representatives from farm and high-technology states.

The House voted 276-149 to override the veto, eight votes shy of the necessary two-thirds majority: R 71-106; D 205-43 (ND 132-36, SD 73-7).

5. 55 mph Speed Limit

Claiming widespread public support, a group of lawmakers pressed hard in 1986 for relaxation of the 55 mph speed limit. Those urging a change argued the limit was unreasonably low and difficult to enforce; supporters of the limit contended it saved thousands of lives each year.

Sentiment for higher limits was particularly strong among Westerners, who said highways in their region typically were far less congested than those in the East, and that each state should be able to set its own speed limit.

Under a 1974 law (PL 93-643) enacted during the height of the energy crisis, states that did not comply with the 55 mph speed limit lost 10 percent of their federal highway aid. Critics said the measure's original rationale — to save fuel — had largely disappeared.

Matters came to a head during House floor debate Aug. 6 over omnibus highway legislation (HR 3129). Dave McCurdy, D-Okla., offered an amendment to permit states to raise the speed limit to 65 mph on rural sections of Interstate highways.

The amendment was fiercely opposed by James J. Howard, D-N.J., chairman of the Public Works and Transportation Committee, who said highway deaths would mount if it were adopted.

The McCurdy amendment was narrowly rejected, 198-218: R 117-57; D 81-161 (ND 45-120, SD 36-41).

Just over a week later, President Reagan for the first time expressed support for relaxing the speed limit. The Senate Sept. 23 adopted, 56-36, an amendment to highway legislation (S 2405) offered by Steven D. Symms, R-Idaho, to permit states to raise the limit to 65 mph on rural Interstates.

The issue contributed to the ultimate failure of House and Senate conferees to agree on a highway bill.

6. Defense Budget

The Democratic-controlled House underscored its insistence that the Pentagon bear a hefty share of deficit-reduction efforts with a vote Aug. 8 that reduced the fiscal 1987 defense budget authorization to $285 billion in new budget authority, nearly $8 billion less than Congress had appropriated for fiscal 1986.

From 1983 on, it had become evident early each year that Congress would allow the defense budget to increase by no more than 3 percent in addition to the cost of inflation, regardless of Secretary of Defense Caspar W. Weinberger's requests for larger increases.

In 1986, the administration seemed to bow to the inevitable, requesting for fiscal 1987 $320.3 billion — an inflation-adjusted increase of 3 percent above the fiscal 1986 appropriation of $292.6 billion.

But President Reagan and Congress had raised the political stakes in the budget game late in 1985 by enacting the Gramm-Rudman-Hollings deficit reduction act (PL 99-177), mandating across-the-board cuts in all federal programs if the deficit exceeded certain limits. A modest foretaste of the automatic cuts came March 1, when the fiscal 1986 defense budget was sliced from the $292.6 billion appropriated to $283.6 billion.

The only way to avoid much larger, Draconian cuts in the fiscal 1987 budget was to restrain all spending. By late February 1986, both houses were moving rapidly toward a defense "freeze" as part of an overall austerity package.

Conferees on the congressional budget resolution (S Con Res 120) settled on a defense budget ceiling of $292.2 billion in new budget authority — $30 billion less than Reagan's request. The House Armed Services Committee reported a fiscal 1987 defense authorization bill (HR 4428) that would have brought the defense budget to that level.

But in addition to setting limits on budget authority (or appropriations) for defense and other government programs, the congressional budget resolution sets a limit on outlays (the amount actually spent in the same year) for each of those functions. Outlay limits had been ignored routinely in the past, but Gramm-Rudman made them binding. By most estimates, a further cut in defense budget authority to $285 billion was needed to remain under the budget resolution's limit of $279 billion on defense outlays.

Senior members of the Armed Services Committee argued that outlays could be restrained without additional cuts in budget authority. But the House adopted an amendment to the defense authorization bill Aug. 8 making the additional reduction by a vote of 245-156: R 37-130; D 208-26 (ND 152-7, SD 56-19).

7. Nuclear Test Ban

Congressional unease over President Reagan's approach to nuclear arms issues was signified by the large margin by which the House voted Aug. 8 to bar for one year all but the very smallest nuclear test explosions, provided the Soviet Union conducted no test explosions during that period. The ban would have taken effect if the United States and the Soviet Union each agreed to let the other place monitoring equipment on its territory.

In recent years, arms control activists oriented to grass-roots lobbying had embraced a nuclear test ban as a first step toward a freeze on the testing, production and deployment of new nuclear weapons. But many of their colleagues who concentrate on legislative lobbying were reluctant to seek a congressional ban on weapons testing, fearing it was too radical a step.

On Feb. 26, however, the House adopted a non-binding test ban resolution (H J Res 3) over strong administration objections, and did so by a larger margin than many of the measure's backers had anticipated.

In part, support for a test ban reflected widespread public frustration with Reagan's approach to U.S.-Soviet arms control negotiations, which had run five years without producing a single agreement. Moreover, the administration took a particularly tough line on the notion of a comprehensive test ban, refusing even to begin negotiations on the subject.

House backers of a test ban decided that their basic goal enjoyed enough support that it was worth trying to come up with a binding proposal that could win a House majority.

To that end, they agreed to exempt tests with an explosive power of less than one kiloton, which some analysts believd could not be reliably detected.

The proposal was embraced by some leading Democratic centrists looking for common ground with the liberal activists who dominated the House Democratic Caucus. Prominent among them were Majority Leader Jim Wright, Texas, who wanted to be elected Speaker in 1987, and Armed Services Committee Chairman Les Aspin, Wis., who wanted to keep his job despite some liberals' objections to his support for some key Reagan policies.

The White House made no concerted effort to head off the coalition favoring a ban, and on Aug. 8 the House adopted the test ban as an amendment to the fiscal 1987 defense authorization bill (HR 4428) by a vote of 234-155: R 34-124; D 200-31 (ND 152-8, SD 48-23).

8. Strategic Defense Initiative

The House Aug. 12 sliced by more than 40 percent, from $5.3 billion to $3.125 billion, President Reagan's fiscal 1987 request for the so-called strategic defense initiative (SDI), or "star wars" program, intended to develop a nationwide shield against nuclear missiles.

Arms control activists had strongly opposed SDI since Reagan announced the program in 1983, arguing that it could not work but would trigger a new round of the arms

A House-Senate fight over relaxing the 55 mph speed limit helped derail a major highway reauthorization bill this year.

race in outer space. Until 1986, however, they had failed to curb the program significantly.

In 1986, leading opponents first decided to attempt to freeze SDI spending at the fiscal 1986 level. By the time the annual defense authorization bill (HR 4428) came to the House floor in August, they had settled on $3.125 billion: an increase to cover the cost of inflation plus 3 percent. Many SDI critics insisted that they were not necessarily trying to kill off the program but were merely adapting it to fiscal realities. Since the Pentagon budget as a whole clearly was going to be held down, they said it was unthinkable to boost SDI funding by some 77 percent.

On Aug. 12, the House adopted an amendment limiting SDI funds for fiscal 1987 to $3.125 billion by a vote of 239-176: R 33-142; D 206-34 (ND 154-8, SD 52-26). *(Senate key vote 11)*

9. Chemical Weapons

By a margin of one vote, the House voted to block production of lethal chemical weapons until Oct. 1, 1987.

At issue was Reagan's five-year-long effort to begin manufacturing so-called binary munitions — artillery shells and "Bigeye" air-dropped bombs that would dispense nerve gas. The Pentagon argued that existing chemical weapons stocks were deteriorating, and that the proposed new weapons would be safer to store and transport.

But opponents said existing stockpiles were adequate to deter the Soviet Union from using its own chemical weapons. Opposition to new munitions was swelled by a revulsion against chemical weapons among some centrist and conservative members of Congress.

Until 1985, the House had blocked production of binary weapons. Then it approved procurement beginning in fiscal 1987 — subject to numerous conditions.

After taking soundings in the House in the summer of 1986, binary weapons opponents decided it was too risky to try to rescind the fiscal 1986 authorization and to block the funds requested in fiscal 1987. So they offered an amendment to the fiscal 1987 defense authorization bill (HR 4428) that would block production of the new weapons until Oct. 1, 1987. The amendment was agreed to 210-209: R 38-137; D 172-72 (ND 142-23, SD 30-49). *(Senate key vote 12)*

10. Gramm-Rudman-Hollings 'Fix'

The House in mid-August refused to revive the automatic budget-cutting device of the Gramm-Rudman-Hollings anti-deficit law (PL 99-177), which the Supreme Court on July 7 had declared unconstitutional.

The three Senate sponsors of the anti-deficit law devised another version of the automatic procedure, making the Office of Management and Budget (OMB) the final arbiter on the cuts. During consideration of a House-passed measure (H J Res 668) raising the ceiling on the federal debt for the duration of fiscal 1987, the Senate July 30 adopted this Gramm-Rudman "fix." The debt bill, with the Gramm-Rudman change and numerous unrelated amendments, was passed Aug. 9 and returned to the House.

House leaders from both parties objected to the stronger role granted OMB, and interest in the anti-deficit law itself was waning. Moreover, members badly wanted to go home to campaign during the August recess.

The House ignored the amended version of H J Res 668 and instead passed a temporary debt-ceiling increase (HR 5395) Aug. 14 to last until the end of September. To this, the Senate Aug. 15 attached a revised, one-year version of the Gramm-Rudman fix. But senators, also anxious to leave town and weary of the issue, passed HR 5395 by only 36-35, following an initial rejection. The House agreed to a Senate reduction in the debt-limit increase. But with virtually no debate, members voted in the early hours of Aug. 16 to delete the Gramm-Rudman amendment and send the bill back to the Senate, which cleared it.

The House vote was 175-133: R 21-119; D 154-14 (ND 108-6, SD 46-8).

The Gramm-Rudman fix got little attention thereafter, and Congress eventually postponed action until 1987. *(Senate key vote 10)*

11. Covert Aid to Angola

Accepting President Reagan's policy of using proxy guerrilla forces to oust selected leftist regimes in the Third World, the House on Sept. 17 effectively approved U.S. aid to the UNITA rebels in Angola.

The House deleted from the 1987 intelligence authorization bill (HR 4759 — PL 99-569) a provision that would have barred U.S. aid to anti-government guerrillas in Angola unless it was publicly debated and approved by Congress. The provision had been drafted by the House Intelligence Committee, which had opposed Reagan's February decision to give UNITA up to $15 million in CIA "covert" military aid. Covert aid does not require formal approval by Congress, although the House and Senate Intelligence panels must be notified in advance.

The House vote completed a transformation of congressional sentiment on the issue. In 1976, Congress cut off a CIA aid program to UNITA; it weakened the ban in 1980 and repealed it in 1985. The latest vote was 229-186: R 166-7; D 63-179 (ND 16-148, SD 47-31).

12. Pesticide Regulation

The House, after a passionately fought battle, voted to impose uniform federal limits (called "tolerances") on the amount of pesticide residues allowed in food.

Disagreement with the Senate over whether states should be permitted to set stricter tolerances than the federal government helped doom a bill (HR 2482) to renew the nation's pesticide law and force health testing of common pesticide ingredients.

The House showdown came on an amendment offered by Leon E. Panetta, D-Calif., aimed at forestalling a stiffer uniform tolerance amendment proposed by Pat Roberts, R-Kan., and Charles W. Stenholm, D-Texas.

Panetta's amendment specified rulemaking procedures to give states a hearing before the federal government set a uniform national tolerance. It also shifted the burden of proof from the state, as in the Roberts amendment, to the federal government — requiring it to show that uniform standards were needed to protect interstate commerce. Panetta's amendment was rejected on Sept. 19 by 157-183: R 22-118; D 135-65 (ND 111-25, SD 24-40).

The Roberts amendment was then adopted, 214-121.

Absenteeism was a factor in the vote, which came on a Friday afternoon six weeks before the Nov. 4 elections, when many members were impatient to go home. The 91 members who failed to vote constituted more than three times the margin by which the issue was decided. *(Senate key vote 15)*

13. Tax Overhaul

The "remarkable bipartisan achievement" represented by the Tax Reform Act of 1986 — the words were those of Secretary of the Treasury James A. Baker III — faced its last major test Sept. 25, when the House approved the conference committee version of the bill (HR 3838 — PL 99-514).

The vote was 292-136: R 116-62; D 176-74 (ND 132-36, SD 44-38).

Two main threads ran through the unusually long debate that preceded the vote. One was the uncertainty of it all. The big tax bill had so many provisions on so many different subjects that no one could guess what its ultimate consequences would be. Many of the unknowns centered on the impact on the economy, both short term and long term. Furthermore, many representatives wondered if it made sense to go to all this trouble to rewrite the tax laws when the legislation did nothing to reduce the huge budget deficits.

On the other side there were two powerful motives for a "yes" vote. One was the sizable tax rate cuts, from the current top rate of 50 percent to 28 percent for individuals and from 46 percent to 34 percent for large corporations. The other was fairness. The working poor would be taken off the tax rolls entirely. And there would be much less opportunity for wealthy individuals and profitable corporations to avoid all, or nearly all, federal tax.

Despite the uncertainties, a majority of House members of both parties voted for the bill.

Still, there were doubters at the end. The vote that preceded the final vote, on a motion by Bill Archer, R-Texas, to send the bill back to committee, and thus kill it, was closer, 160-268. But even on that one, majorities of Republicans and Democrats voted to keep the bill alive. There were switchers in both directions on the two votes, but most who changed were Republicans who, after going on record with their concerns, voted for final passage. *(Senate key vote 8)*

14. Fiscal 1987 Continuing Appropriations

Few members of Congress liked the huge, comprehensive appropriations bills, known as continuing resolutions, that had become routine at the end of a legislative session. The fiscal 1987 version (H J Res 738) was particularly unpopular, as shown by the narrow 201-200 vote by which it passed the House Sept. 25: R 15-157; D 186-43 (ND 127-25, SD 59-18).

The $562 billion measure was the largest money bill in the nation's history. Many "nay" votes came from members, particularly fiscal conservatives, who habitually voted against continuing resolutions to protest government spending. Some "nays" were protests against the practice of folding unfinished regular appropriations bills — all 13 in this case — into a last-minute omnibus measure. Critics said that only members of Appropriations committees could shoehorn their favored amendments into the mammoth bill, and that nobody else really knew what was in it or could change it.

Still other "nay" votes came from Democrats objecting to $100 million in aid to "contra" rebels fighting the leftist Nicaraguan government, included in the mammoth bill as part of the military construction appropriations bill. And some reflected disapproval of arms control provisions that the Reagan administration strongly opposed.

A final factor was timing. The vote on passage occurred in the early evening, about an hour before members expected, and the margin would probably not have been so close if some or all of the missing 32 representatives had voted.

15. South Africa Sanctions

Spurred on by election-year pressures, Congress overrode President Reagan's veto and ordered economic sanctions against the white racist government of South Africa.

Surprising everyone, the House in June by voice vote passed a sanctions bill (HR 4868) cutting off virtually all economic ties between the United States and South Africa.

The Senate in mid-August passed its own version that, while much milder than the House bill, included stronger sanctions than Senate leaders had expected. The bill barred imports of South African steel, textiles and agricultural goods; suspended air service between the United States and South Africa; and barred new U.S. business investment there.

When Congress returned from its August recess, Senate Foreign Relations Committee Chairman Richard G. Lugar, R-Ind., pressured the House into accepting the Senate version and sending it to Reagan. Unless the House did so, he said, the bill would fall victim to an end-of-session filibuster in the Senate.

Ignoring advice from Lugar and other congressional leaders, Reagan on Sept. 26 vetoed the bill, saying it would hurt South African blacks.

The House quickly voted to override the veto, on Sept. 29. The 313-83 vote was well above the two-thirds margin needed: R 81-79; D 232-4 (ND 163-0, SD 69-4).

The Senate followed suit three days later, enacting the bill into law over President Reagan's opposition. *(Senate key vote 14)*

16. Immigration Reform

For the second Congress in a row, both chambers passed controversial legislation transforming the nation's immigration laws. This time, however, the bill (HR 3810) went to President Reagan, who signed it (PL 99-603).

HR 3810 nearly died when the House Sept. 26 rejected a rule limiting floor amendments, particularly on a disputed farm worker provision. However, sponsors huddled for a week, and on Oct. 9 they brought the bill back to the House with a modified farm labor section.

After spirited debate, the House passed the measure 230-166: R 62-105; D 168-61 (ND 126-29, SD 42-32).

The margin was considerably greater than in 1984, when a similar bill barely passed, 216-211.

Charles E. Schumer, D-N.Y., the architect of the farm worker provisions, said it was this section that helped boost the margin of passage, particularly among Democrats who had been concerned that the 1984 bill would lead to exploitation of migrant laborers. In 1984, 125 Democrats voted for the bill while 138 voted against it, a sharp contrast to this year's 168-61 Democratic split.

The California delegation also reflected changed perceptions about the bill. In 1984 the delegation voted 12-33 against the bill; this year the split was 32-12 in favor.

The Senate had passed an immigration bill in 1985, and after House passage, the two sides went to conference. The House adopted the conference report Oct. 15 and the Senate adopted it Oct. 17.

	1	2	3	4	5	6	7	8
ALABAMA								
Denton	Y	N	Y	Y	N	N	N	N
Heflin	Y	N	Y	Y	N	Y	Y	N
ALASKA								
Murkowski	Y	Y	Y	Y	Y	?	Y	N
Stevens	Y	N	Y	Y	Y	N	N	Y
ARIZONA								
Goldwater	?	?	Y	Y	?	N	N	?
DeConcini	Y	Y	Y	N	Y	Y	Y	N
ARKANSAS								
Bumpers	+	N	N	N	Y	Y	Y	N
Pryor	Y	N	Y	N	N	Y	Y	Y
CALIFORNIA								
Wilson	Y	Y	Y	Y	N	N	Y	N
Cranston	Y	Y	N	N	Y	N	Y	N
COLORADO								
Armstrong	Y	Y	Y	Y	N	N	N	Y
Hart	Y	?	N	N	N	N	Y	Y
CONNECTICUT								
Weicker	Y	Y	N	N	Y	N	Y	N
Dodd	Y	Y	N	N	Y	N	Y	N
DELAWARE								
Roth	Y	Y	Y	Y	N	N	N	Y
Biden	Y	N	N	N	?	N	Y	Y
FLORIDA								
Hawkins	Y	Y	Y	Y	?	?	Y	N
Chiles	Y	Y	Y	Y	Y	N	Y	N
GEORGIA								
Mattingly	N	Y	Y	Y	N	Y	Y	N
Nunn	N	?	Y	Y	Y	Y	Y	N
HAWAII								
Inouye	?	?	N	N	?	Y	Y	N
Matsunaga	Y	N	N	N	Y	Y	Y	N
IDAHO								
McClure	Y	Y	Y	Y	N	N	N	Y
Symms	Y	Y	Y	Y	N	N	Y	Y
ILLINOIS								
Dixon	+	Y	Y	Y	Y	N	Y	N
Simon	Y	Y	Y	N	Y	N	Y	N
INDIANA								
Lugar	Y	Y	Y	Y	Y	N	N	Y
Quayle	N	Y	Y	Y	Y	N	N	Y
IOWA								
Grassley	N	N	Y	Y	N	Y	Y	Y
Harkin	Y	N	Y	N	N	N	Y	N
KANSAS								
Dole	Y	Y	Y	Y	Y	Y	N	Y
Kassebaum	?	Y	N	Y	Y	Y	N	Y
KENTUCKY								
McConnell	N	Y	Y	Y	Y	Y	N	Y
Ford	Y	N	Y	N	Y	Y	Y	N
LOUISIANA								
Johnston	N	N	Y	Y	Y	N	Y	Y
Long	N	Y	Y	Y	Y	Y	N	Y
MAINE								
Cohen	Y	Y	N	Y	Y	N	Y	Y
Mitchell	Y	N	N	N	Y	N	Y	Y
MARYLAND								
Mathias	Y	?	N	N	Y	?	N	Y
Sarbanes	?	N	N	N	Y	N	Y	N
MASSACHUSETTS								
Kennedy	Y	N	N	N	Y	N	Y	Y
Kerry	?	Y	N	N	Y	N	Y	N
MICHIGAN								
Levin	Y	Y	N	N	Y	N	Y	N
Riegle	Y	N	N	N	Y	N	Y	N
MINNESOTA								
Boschwitz	N	Y	Y	Y	Y	N	Y	Y
Durenberger	-	N	Y	N	Y	Y	Y	Y
MISSISSIPPI								
Cochran	Y	N	Y	Y	Y	Y	N	Y
Stennis	N	N	Y	Y	Y	N	N	Y
MISSOURI								
Danforth	N	Y	Y	Y	Y	N	Y	Y
Eagleton	?	N	N	N	+	?	Y	Y
MONTANA								
Baucus	Y	N	N	N	Y	Y	Y	Y
Melcher	Y	N	Y	N	Y	N	Y	N
NEBRASKA								
Exon	+	N	Y	N	Y	Y	N	N
Zorinsky	Y	N	Y	N	N	Y	N	N
NEVADA								
Hecht	N	Y	Y	Y	N	N	N	N
Laxalt	N	?	Y	Y	N	N	N	N
NEW HAMPSHIRE								
Humphrey	Y	Y	Y	Y	N	N	N	N
Rudman	N	Y	Y	Y	Y	N	Y	Y
NEW JERSEY								
Bradley	Y	Y	N	Y	Y	N	Y	Y
Lautenberg	Y	Y	N	N	Y	N	Y	N
NEW MEXICO								
Domenici	Y	Y	Y	Y	Y	N	N	N
Bingaman	Y	Y	Y	N	Y	N	Y	N
NEW YORK								
D'Amato	Y	Y	Y	Y	Y	N	Y	N
Moynihan	Y	Y	N	N	Y	?	Y	Y
NORTH CAROLINA								
Broyhill[1]								
Helms	N	Y	Y	Y	N	Y	N	Y
NORTH DAKOTA								
Andrews	Y	N	Y	N	Y	Y	Y	N
Burdick	N	N	N	N	Y	Y	Y	N
OHIO								
Glenn	Y	N	N	N	N	N	Y	N
Metzenbaum	Y	Y	N	N	Y	N	Y	N
OKLAHOMA								
Nickles	Y	N	Y	Y	Y	Y	Y	Y
Boren	Y	N	Y	Y	Y	Y	Y	Y
OREGON								
Hatfield	N	N	N	N	Y	N	Y	N
Packwood	?	Y	Y	N	Y	?	Y	Y
PENNSYLVANIA								
Heinz	Y	Y	N	Y	Y	N	Y	Y
Specter	Y	Y	Y	N	N	N	Y	N
RHODE ISLAND								
Chafee	Y	Y	N	N	Y	N	N	Y
Pell	Y	Y	Y	N	Y	N	Y	N
SOUTH CAROLINA								
Thurmond	Y	Y	Y	Y	Y	N	N	Y
Hollings	N	Y	Y	Y	Y	Y	Y	N
SOUTH DAKOTA								
Abdnor	Y	N	Y	Y	Y	Y	Y	N
Pressler	Y	N	Y	Y	Y	Y	Y	N
TENNESSEE								
Gore	Y	N	Y	N	Y	Y	Y	N
Sasser	Y	N	Y	N	Y	Y	Y	N
TEXAS								
Gramm	Y	Y	Y	Y	N	Y	N	Y
Bentsen	Y	Y	Y	Y	Y	N	N	Y
UTAH								
Garn	Y	Y	Y	Y	N	N	N	Y
Hatch	Y	Y	Y	Y	N	N	N	Y
VERMONT								
Stafford	N	Y	N	N	Y	N	N	Y
Leahy	Y	Y	N	N	Y	N	Y	N
VIRGINIA								
Trible	Y	Y	Y	Y	Y	N	Y	Y
Warner	Y	Y	Y	Y	Y	N	N	Y
WASHINGTON								
Evans	Y	Y	N	N	Y	N	N	Y
Gorton	Y	Y	N	N	Y	N	Y	Y
WEST VIRGINIA								
Byrd	Y	Y	N	N	Y	Y	Y	N
Rockefeller	?	Y	N	N	Y	Y	Y	Y
WISCONSIN								
Kasten	Y	Y	Y	Y	N	Y	Y	N
Proxmire	N	Y	Y	N	Y	Y	Y	Y
WYOMING								
Simpson	Y	Y	Y	Y	Y	N	N	Y
Wallop	N	Y	Y	Y	N	Y	N	Y

KEY

- Y Voted for (yea).
- # Paired for.
- \+ Announced for.
- N Voted against (nay).
- X Paired against.
- \- Announced against.
- P Voted "present."
- C Voted "present" to avoid possible conflict of interest.
- ? Did not vote or otherwise make a position known.

Democrats ***Republicans***

ND - Northern Democrats SD - Southern Democrats (Southern states - Ala., Ark., Fla., Ga., Ky., La., Miss., N.C., Okla., S.C., Tenn., Texas, Va.)

[1] Sen. James T. Broyhill, R-N.C., was sworn in July 14, 1986, to succeed John P. East, R, who died June 29, 1986.

1. S Res 28. Broadcast Coverage of Senate Proceedings. Adoption of the resolution to allow a test period from at least May 1 through July 15, 1986, during which Senate floor proceedings would be broadcast on radio and television, and to change certain procedural rules of the Senate. Adopted 67-21: R 35-14; D 32-7 (ND 24-2, SD 8-5), Feb. 27, 1986.

2. H J Res 534. Commodity Credit Corporation Supplemental Appropriation, Fiscal 1986. Domenici, R-N.M., motion to table (kill) the Cochran, R-Miss., appeal of the chair's ruling that the House amendment to the Senate amendment violated the spending-limitation requirement contained in the 1985 Balanced Budget and Emergency Deficit Control Act (the Gramm-Rudman-Hollings balanced-budget law, PL 99-177) and thus was not in order. Motion agreed to 61-33: R 40-10; D 21-23 (ND 17-14, SD 4-9), March 13, 1986. A "yea" was a vote supporting the president's position.

3. S J Res 225. Balanced Budget Constitutional Amendment. Passage of the joint resolution to propose a constitutional amendment to require a balanced federal budget every year unless a three-fifths majority of the total membership of both houses of Congress votes for a specific amount of deficit spending; to require that the public debt of the United States may be increased only by a law enacted by a three-fifths majority of the total membership of both houses of Congress; to require that a bill to increase revenue shall become law only if passed by a majority of the total membership of both houses of Congress; to require the president to submit annually a proposed balanced budget to Congress; and to allow Congress to waive the requirement for a balanced budget during a declared war. Rejected 66-34: R 43-10; D 23-24 (ND 10-23, SD 13-1), March 25, 1986. A two-thirds majority of those present and voting (67 in this case) is required for passage of a constitutional amendment. A "yea" was a vote supporting the president's position.

4. S J Res 283. Aid to Nicaraguan Rebels. Lugar, R-Ind., substitute to approve use of $100 million in Defense Department funds to provide aid to the Nicaraguan "contras." Of that amount, $25 million for non-military aid, training and "defensive" weapons would be released immediately upon enactment of the resolution; the remainder would be released at 90-day intervals after July 1, 1986. Adopted 53-47: R 42-11; D 11-36 (ND 2-31, SD 9-5), March 27, 1986. (The joint resolution subsequently was passed by voice vote.) A "yea" was a vote supporting the president's position.

5. S Con Res 120. Budget Resolution, Fiscal 1987. Adoption of the concurrent resolution to set budget targets for the fiscal year ending Sept. 30, 1987, as follows: budget authority, $1,101.3 billion; outlays, $1,001.2 billion; revenues, $857 billion; deficit, $144 billion. Adopted 70-25: R 32-19; D 38-6 (ND 26-4, SD 12-2), in the session that began May 1, 1986.

6. S 2180. Federal Fire Protection/Daylight-Saving Time. Dole, R-Kan., motion to table (kill) the Gorton, R-Wash., amendment to change the start of daylight-saving time from the last Sunday in April to the first Sunday in April. Motion rejected 36-58: R 16-33; D 20-25 (ND 10-21, SD 10-4), May 20, 1986. (The Gorton amendment subsequently was adopted by voice vote, and the bill was passed by voice vote.)

7. S J Res 316. Saudi Arms Sale. Passage, over President Reagan's May 21 veto, of the joint resolution to block the sale of weapons to Saudi Arabia. Rejected (thus sustaining the president's veto) 66-34: R 24-29; D 42-5 (ND 31-2, SD 11-3), June 5, 1986. A two-thirds majority of those present and voting (67 in this case) of both houses is required to override a veto. A "nay" was a vote supporting the president's position.

8. HR 3838. Tax Overhaul. Packwood, R-Ore., motion to table (kill) the D'Amato, R-N.Y., amendment to the Dodd, D-Conn.-D'Amato amendment, to create a 15 percent tax credit on Individual Retirement Account contributions (to a maximum of $300) and to offset the resulting revenue loss with an increase in the corporate and individual minimum tax rate from 20 percent to 22.6 percent. Motion agreed to 51-48: R 35-17; D 16-31 (ND 10-23, SD 6-8), June 11, 1986. (The Dodd-D'Amato amendment subsequently was rejected by voice vote.) A "yea" was a vote supporting the president's position.

	9	10	11	12	13	14	15
ALABAMA							
Denton	Y	N	Y	N	Y	N	?
Heflin	Y	Y	Y	N	Y	Y	Y
ALASKA							
Murkowski	Y	Y	Y	N	Y	Y	?
Stevens	Y	Y	Y	N	Y	N	Y
ARIZONA							
Goldwater	#	?	Y	N	?	N	Y
DeConcini	N	N	N	Y	Y	Y	N
ARKANSAS							
Bumpers	N	Y	N	Y	Y	Y	Y
Pryor	N	Y	N	Y	Y	Y	N
CALIFORNIA							
Wilson	Y	Y	Y	N	Y	Y	Y
Cranston	N	N	N	Y	N	Y	N
COLORADO							
Armstrong	Y	Y	Y	N	Y	N	Y
Hart	N	N	N	Y	N	Y	N
CONNECTICUT							
Weicker	N	N	N	Y	N	Y	?
Dodd	N	Y	N	Y	N	Y	?
DELAWARE							
Roth	Y	N	Y	N	Y	Y	?
Biden	X	Y	N	Y	N	Y	?
FLORIDA							
Hawkins	#	N	+	N	Y	Y	?
Chiles	N	Y	N	N	Y	Y	Y
GEORGIA							
Mattingly	Y	Y	Y	N	Y	Y	Y
Nunn	N	Y	Y	N	Y	Y	N
HAWAII							
Inouye	X	N	N	Y	N	Y	?
Matsunaga	N	N	N	Y	N	Y	N
IDAHO							
McClure	Y	Y	Y	N	Y	N	Y
Symms	Y	Y	Y	N	Y	N	?
ILLINOIS							
Dixon	N	Y	N	Y	Y	Y	Y
Simon	N	Y	N	Y	N	Y	N
INDIANA							
Lugar	Y	Y	Y	N	Y	Y	Y
Quayle	Y	Y	Y	N	Y	Y	Y
IOWA							
Grassley	Y	N	N	Y	Y	Y	Y
Harkin	N	N	N	Y	N	Y	N
KANSAS							
Dole	Y	Y	Y	N	Y	N	?
Kassebaum	X	Y	N	Y	Y	Y	Y
KENTUCKY							
McConnell	Y	Y	Y	N	Y	Y	Y
Ford	N	Y	N	Y	Y	Y	Y
LOUISIANA							
Johnston	N	N	N	Y	Y	Y	#
Long	Y	Y	N	N	Y	Y	Y
MAINE							
Cohen	Y	Y	Y	N	Y	Y	N
Mitchell	N	N	N	Y	N	Y	N
MARYLAND							
Mathias	N	N	N	Y	N	Y	N
Sarbanes	N	N	N	Y	N	Y	N
MASSACHUSETTS							
Kennedy	N	Y	N	Y	N	Y	N
Kerry	N	N	N	Y	N	Y	N
MICHIGAN							
Levin	N	Y	N	Y	N	Y	N
Riegle	N	N	N	Y	N	Y	N
MINNESOTA							
Boschwitz	Y	Y	Y	N	Y	Y	N
Durenberger	Y	Y	Y	Y	Y	Y	N
MISSISSIPPI							
Cochran	Y	Y	Y	N	Y	N	Y
Stennis	N	Y	Y	N	Y	Y	?
MISSOURI							
Danforth	Y	Y	Y	Y	Y	Y	?
Eagleton	N	N	N	Y	N	Y	N
MONTANA							
Baucus	N	Y	N	Y	N	Y	N
Melcher	N	N	N	Y	N	Y	Y
NEBRASKA							
Exon	N	N	Y	N	N	Y	N
Zorinsky	N	Y	Y	N	Y	Y	Y
NEVADA							
Hecht	Y	Y	Y	N	Y	N	Y
Laxalt	Y	Y	Y	N	Y	N	?
NEW HAMPSHIRE							
Humphrey	Y	Y	Y	N	Y	N	N
Rudman	Y	Y	Y	N	Y	N	N
NEW JERSEY							
Bradley	N	N	N	Y	N	Y	N
Lautenberg	N	N	N	Y	N	Y	X
NEW MEXICO							
Domenici	Y	Y	Y	N	Y	Y	Y
Bingaman	N	N	Y	N	N	Y	N
NEW YORK							
D'Amato	Y	Y	Y	N	Y	Y	?
Moynihan	N	N	N	Y	N	Y	?
NORTH CAROLINA							
Broyhill[1]		Y	Y	N	Y	N	+
Helms	Y	Y	Y	N	Y	N	Y
NORTH DAKOTA							
Andrews	Y	N	N	Y	Y	Y	Y
Burdick	N	N	N	Y	N	Y	N
OHIO							
Glenn	N	N	Y	N	N	Y	Y
Metzenbaum	N	N	N	Y	N	Y	N
OKLAHOMA							
Nickles	Y	Y	Y	N	Y	N	Y
Boren	N	Y	N	N	Y	Y	Y
OREGON							
Hatfield	Y	N	N	Y	Y	Y	N
Packwood	#	Y	N	Y	Y	Y	N
PENNSYLVANIA							
Heinz	Y	Y	Y	Y	Y	Y	?
Specter	N	Y	N	Y	Y	Y	N
RHODE ISLAND							
Chafee	Y	Y	N	N	Y	Y	N
Pell	N	N	N	Y	N	Y	N
SOUTH CAROLINA							
Thurmond	Y	Y	Y	N	Y	N	+
Hollings	N	Y	Y	N	Y	Y	N
SOUTH DAKOTA							
Abdnor	Y	Y	Y	N	Y	Y	Y
Pressler	Y	N	Y	N	Y	N	Y
TENNESSEE							
Gore	N	N	N	Y	N	Y	N
Sasser	N	N	N	Y	N	Y	N
TEXAS							
Gramm	Y	Y	Y	N	Y	N	Y
Bentsen	N	Y	N	Y	Y	Y	Y
UTAH							
Garn	Y	Y	Y	N	+	?	?
Hatch	Y	Y	Y	N	Y	N	Y
VERMONT							
Stafford	Y	N	N	Y	Y	Y	N
Leahy	N	Y	N	Y	N	Y	N
VIRGINIA							
Trible	Y	Y	Y	N	Y	Y	N
Warner	Y	Y	Y	N	Y	Y	N
WASHINGTON							
Evans	N	Y	N	Y	Y	Y	N
Gorton	Y	Y	Y	Y	Y	Y	N
WEST VIRGINIA							
Byrd	Y	N	Y	Y	N	Y	N
Rockefeller	N	N	N	Y	N	Y	N
WISCONSIN							
Kasten	Y	Y	Y	N	Y	Y	N
Proxmire	N	Y	N	Y	Y	Y	N
WYOMING							
Simpson	Y	Y	Y	N	Y	N	Y
Wallop	Y	Y	Y	N	Y	N	Y

KEY

- Y Voted for (yea).
- # Paired for.
- + Announced for.
- N Voted against (nay).
- X Paired against.
- \- Announced against.
- P Voted "present."
- C Voted "present" to avoid possible conflict of interest.
- ? Did not vote or otherwise make a position known.

Democrats ***Republicans***

ND - Northern Democrats SD - Southern Democrats (Southern states - Ala., Ark., Fla., Ga., Ky., La., Miss., N.C., Okla., S.C., Tenn., Texas, Va.)

[1] Sen. James T. Broyhill, R-N.C., was sworn in July 14, 1986, to succeed John P. East, R, who died June 29, 1986.

9. Manion Nomination. Confirmation of President Reagan's nomination of Daniel A. Manion of Indiana to be U.S. circuit judge for the 7th Circuit. Confirmed 48-46: R 45-4; D 3-42 (ND 1-30, SD 2-12), June 26, 1986. A "yea" was a vote supporting the president's position.

10. H J Res 668. Public Debt Limit/Anti-Deficit Act. Rudman, R-N.H., amendment to the Finance Committee amendment, to make changes in the Gramm-Rudman-Hollings anti-deficit law (PL 99-177) to reinstate the law's automatic spending cuts procedure (previously voided as a violation of the Constitution's separation-of-powers doctrine) by granting final authority for determining the automatic cuts to the director of the Office of Management and Budget, with certain limitations. The amendment also would change to the first Tuesday in February of each year the date by which the president is required to submit his budget request to Congress. Adopted 63-36: R 42-10; D 21-26 (ND 10-23, SD 11-3), July 30, 1986.

11. S 2638. Department of Defense Authorization, Fiscal 1987. Warner, R-Va., motion to table (kill) the Johnston, D-La., amendment to set a limit of $3.24 billion for research and development on the strategic defense initiative, or "star wars" program. President Reagan had requested $5.3 billion. Motion agreed to 50-49: R 41-11; D 9-38 (ND 5-28, SD 4-10), Aug. 5, 1986. A "yea" was a vote supporting the president's position.

12. S 2638. Department of Defense Authorization, Fiscal 1987. Pryor, D-Ark., amendment to delete funds for production of the "Bigeye" chemical bomb. Rejected 50-51: R 14-39; D 36-11 (ND 29-4, SD 7-7), with Vice President George Bush casting a "nay" vote, Aug. 7, 1986. A "nay" was a vote supporting the president's position.

13. Rehnquist Nomination. Confirmation of President Reagan's nomination of Associate Justice William H. Rehnquist of Virginia to be chief justice of the United States. Confirmed 65-33: R 49-2; D 16-31 (ND 4-29, SD 12-2), Sept. 17, 1986. A "yea" was a vote supporting the president's position.

14. HR 4868. South Africa Sanctions. Passage, over President Reagan's Sept. 26 veto, of the bill to impose sanctions against South Africa. Among the sanctions imposed were bans on imports of South African iron, steel, sugar and other agricultural products. The bill also prohibited exports to South Africa of petroleum products, banned new U.S. investments there and banned imports of South African uranium, coal and textiles. Passed (thus enacted into law) 78-21: R 31-21; D 47-0 (ND 33-0, SD 14-0), Oct. 2, 1986. A two-thirds majority of those present and voting (66 in this case) of both houses is required to override a veto. A "nay" was a vote supporting the president's position.

15. S 2792. Pesticide Control Reauthorization. Lugar, R-Ind., motion to table (kill) the Durenberger, R-Minn., amendment to strike provisions allowing federal regulations to pre-empt stricter, state-set standards (or "tolerances") for the amount of pesticide residues allowable on food products. Motion rejected 34-45: R 23-16; D 11-29 (ND 4-24, SD 7-5), Oct. 6, 1986. (The Durenberger amendment subsequently was adopted by voice vote. Later, the Senate moved to remove the text of HR 2482, the House-passed version of the bill, and insert the provisions of S 2792. Then, the Senate passed HR 2482 by voice vote.)

1. HR 4332. Firearms Law Reform. Passage of the bill to revise the 1968 Gun Control Act to allow the interstate sale of rifles and shotguns and the interstate transportation of all types of firearms, to ease record-keeping requirements for firearms transactions and to limit federal agents to one unannounced inspection per year of a gun dealer's premises. Passed 292-130: R 161-15; D 131-115 (ND 62-103, SD 69-12), April 10, 1986. (The House subsequently moved to strike the language of S 49, the Senate-passed version of the bill, and insert instead the language of HR 4332.) A "yea" was a vote supporting the president's position.

2. HR 1. Housing Act. Bartlett, R-Texas, amendment to limit the obligation of funds for new construction of public housing units to repair and renovation of existing units, except in limited circumstances. Adopted 223-180: R 148-19; D 75-161 (ND 35-125, SD 40-36), June 5, 1986.

3. HR 5052. Military Construction Appropriations, Fiscal 1987/Aid to Nicaraguan Rebels. Edwards, R-Okla., substitute for title II of the bill, to provide $70 million in military aid and $30 million in non-military aid to the "contra" guerrillas in Nicaragua and $300 million in economic aid to Costa Rica, El Salvador, Guatemala and Honduras. Adopted 221-209: R 170-11; D 51-198 (ND 8-159, SD 43-39), June 25, 1986. A "yea" was a vote supporting the president's position.

4. HR 1562. Textile Import Quotas. Passage, over President Reagan's Dec. 17, 1985, veto, of the bill to place import restrictions on textile and apparel goods. Rejected 276-149: R 71-106; D 205-43 (ND 132-36, SD 73-7), Aug. 6, 1986. A two-thirds majority of those present and voting (284 in this case) of both houses is required to override a veto. A "nay" was a vote supporting the president's position.

5. HR 3129. Omnibus Highway Bill. McCurdy, D-Okla., amendment to establish a five-year test program permitting states to raise the speed limit from 55 mph to 65 mph on rural sections of the Interstate system. Rejected 198-218: R 117-57; D 81-161 (ND 45-120, SD 36-41), Aug. 6, 1986.

6. HR 4428. Defense Authorization, Fiscal 1987. Spratt, D-S.C., amendment to reduce the total national defense budget for fiscal 1987 to $285 billion in budget authority and $279 billion in outlays. Adopted 245-156: R 37-130; D 208-26 (ND 152-7, SD 56-19), Aug. 8, 1986.

7. HR 4428. Defense Authorization, Fiscal 1987. Aspin, D-Wis., amendment to bar tests between Jan. 1, 1987, and Sept. 30, 1987, of nuclear weapons with an explosive power greater than 1 kiloton provided the Soviet Union conducts no nuclear tests in the meantime and provided the United States and Soviet Union agree to permit equipment to be placed in their territory to monitor compliance with the ban. Adopted 234-155: R 34-124; D 200-31 (ND 152-8, SD 48-23), Aug. 8, 1986. A "nay" was a vote supporting the president's position.

8. HR 4428. Defense Authorization, Fiscal 1987. Bennett, D-Fla., amendment to decrease from $3.4 billion to $2.85 billion the amount authorized for research on the strategic defense initiative, or "star wars." Adopted 239-176: R 33-142; D 206-34 (ND 154-8, SD 52-26), Aug. 12, 1986. A "nay" was a vote supporting the president's position.

[1] Rep. Neil Abercrombie, D-Hawaii, was sworn in Sept. 23, 1986, to succeed Cecil Heftel, D, who resigned July 11, 1986, to run for governor of Hawaii.
[2] Rep. George M. O'Brien, R-Ill., died July 17, 1986.
[3] Rep. John E. Grotberg, R-Ill., has not participated in House business this session due to a serious illness.
[4] Rep. Thomas P. O'Neill Jr., D-Mass., as Speaker, votes at his own discretion.
[5] Rep. Alton R. Waldon Jr., D-N.Y., was sworn in July 29, 1986, to succeed Joseph P. Addabbo, D, who died April 10, 1986.
[6] James T. Broyhill; R-N.C., resigned July 13, 1986, to fill the vacant seat resulting from the June 29 death of Sen. John P. East.

KEY

- Y Voted for (yea).
- # Paired for.
- + Announced for.
- N Voted against (nay).
- X Paired against.
- \- Announced against.
- P Voted "present."
- C Voted "present" to avoid possible conflict of interest.
- ? Did not vote or otherwise make a position known.

Democrats ***Republicans***

	1	2	3	4	5	6	7	8
ALABAMA								
1 ***Callahan***	Y	Y	Y	Y	N	N	N	N
2 ***Dickinson***	Y	Y	Y	Y	Y	N	N	N
3 Nichols	#	Y	Y	Y	N	N	N	N
4 Bevill	Y	Y	Y	Y	Y	Y	N	N
5 Flippo	Y	N	Y	Y	Y	Y	Y	?
6 Erdreich	Y	N	Y	Y	Y	Y	Y	N
7 Shelby	Y	N	Y	Y	?	N	X	N
ALASKA								
AL ***Young***	Y	Y	Y	N	Y	N	N	N
ARIZONA								
1 ***McCain***	Y	Y	Y	N	+	N	N	N
2 Udall	Y	N	N	Y	Y	?	Y	Y
3 ***Stump***	Y	?	Y	N	Y	N	N	N
4 ***Rudd***	Y	Y	Y	N	Y	N	N	N
5 ***Kolbe***	Y	Y	Y	N	Y	N	N	N
ARKANSAS								
1 Alexander	Y	N	N	Y	N	Y	Y	Y
2 Robinson	Y	Y	Y	Y	N	N	N	N
3 ***Hammerschmidt***	Y	Y	Y	Y	N	N	N	N
4 Anthony	Y	Y	N	Y	N	Y	Y	Y
CALIFORNIA								
1 Bosco	Y	N	N	Y	N	Y	Y	Y
2 ***Chappie***	Y	?	Y	N	Y	N	N	N
3 Matsui	N	N	N	N	N	Y	Y	Y
4 Fazio	N	N	N	Y	Y	Y	Y	Y
5 Burton	N	N	N	Y	N	Y	Y	?
6 Boxer	N	N	N	Y	N	Y	Y	Y
7 Miller	N	?	N	N	Y	Y	Y	Y
8 Dellums	N	X	N	Y	N	Y	Y	Y
9 Stark	N	N	N	N	Y	Y	Y	Y
10 Edwards	N	N	N	Y	N	Y	Y	Y
11 Lantos	Y	N	N	Y	N	Y	Y	Y
12 ***Zschau***	Y	?	Y	N	Y	Y	?	N
13 Mineta	N	N	N	N	N	Y	Y	Y
14 ***Shumway***	Y	Y	Y	N	Y	N	N	N
15 Coelho	Y	?	N	Y	Y	Y	Y	Y
16 Panetta	N	N	N	N	Y	Y	Y	Y
17 ***Pashayan***	Y	Y	Y	Y	N	N	N	N
18 Lehman	Y	N	N	Y	Y	Y	Y	Y
19 ***Lagomarsino***	Y	Y	Y	N	Y	N	N	N
20 ***Thomas***	Y	Y	Y	Y	Y	N	N	N
21 ***Fiedler***	Y	?	Y	N	Y	N	N	N
22 ***Moorhead***	Y	Y	Y	N	Y	N	N	N
23 Beilenson	N	Y	N	N	N	Y	Y	Y
24 Waxman	N	N	N	N	N	Y	Y	Y
25 Roybal	N	N	N	Y	Y	Y	Y	Y
26 Berman	N	N	N	N	N	Y	Y	Y
27 Levine	N	?	N	N	N	Y	Y	Y
28 Dixon	N	N	N	Y	N	Y	Y	?
29 Hawkins	N	?	?	Y	N	Y	Y	Y
30 Martinez	N	N	N	Y	N	Y	Y	Y
31 Dymally	N	N	N	Y	N	Y	Y	Y
32 Anderson	Y	N	N	N	N	N	Y	Y
33 ***Dreier***	Y	Y	Y	N	Y	N	N	N
34 Torres	N	N	N	Y	N	+	Y	Y
35 ***Lewis***	Y	Y	Y	N	Y	?	?	X
36 Brown	N	N	N	Y	N	?	Y	Y
37 ***McCandless***	Y	Y	Y	N	Y	N	N	N
38 ***Dornan***	Y	Y	Y	N	Y	N	N	N
39 ***Dannemeyer***	Y	Y	Y	N	Y	N	N	N
40 ***Badham***	Y	?	Y	N	Y	N	X	N
41 ***Lowery***	Y	Y	Y	N	Y	N	N	N
42 ***Lungren***	Y	Y	Y	N	Y	X	X	N
43 ***Packard***	Y	Y	Y	N	N	N	N	N
44 Bates	N	N	N	Y	N	Y	Y	Y
45 ***Hunter***	Y	Y	Y	Y	N	N	N	N
COLORADO								
1 Schroeder	N	N	N	Y	Y	Y	Y	Y
2 Wirth	Y	N	N	N	Y	Y	Y	Y
3 ***Strang***	Y	Y	Y	N	Y	N	N	N
4 ***Brown***	Y	Y	Y	N	Y	Y	Y	Y
5 ***Kramer***	Y	?	Y	N	Y	N	Y	N
6 ***Schaefer***	Y	Y	Y	N	Y	N	N	N
CONNECTICUT								
1 Kennelly	N	N	N	Y	N	Y	Y	Y
2 Gejdenson	N	N	N	Y	N	Y	Y	Y
3 Morrison	N	N	N	Y	N	Y	Y	#
4 ***McKinney***	N	N	N	Y	Y	Y	Y	Y
5 ***Rowland***	Y	N	Y	N	N	N	Y	N
6 ***Johnson***	Y	N	Y	N	N	N	Y	N
DELAWARE								
AL Carper	N	Y	N	Y	N	Y	Y	Y
FLORIDA								
1 Hutto	Y	Y	Y	Y	N	N	N	N
2 Fuqua	Y	N	Y	Y	Y	Y	Y	N
3 Bennett	N	N	Y	N	N	N	Y	Y
4 Chappell	Y	N	Y	Y	Y	N	N	N
5 ***McCollum***	Y	Y	Y	N	Y	N	N	N
6 MacKay	Y	Y	N	N	N	Y	Y	Y
7 Gibbons	N	Y	Y	N	N	N	Y	Y
8 ***Young***	Y	Y	Y	N	Y	N	N	N
9 ***Bilirakis***	Y	N	Y	Y	Y	N	N	N
10 ***Ireland***	#	Y	Y	N	Y	N	N	N
11 Nelson	Y	Y	Y	N	N	N	N	N
12 ***Lewis***	Y	N	Y	N	Y	N	N	N
13 ***Mack***	Y	Y	Y	N	Y	N	N	N
14 Mica	N	N	Y	N	N	Y	Y	Y
15 ***Shaw***	Y	Y	Y	N	Y	N	X	N
16 Smith	N	N	Y	Y	N	Y	Y	Y
17 Lehman	N	N	N	Y	N	Y	Y	Y
18 Pepper	N	N	Y	#	N	Y	Y	Y
19 Fascell	N	N	Y	Y	N	Y	Y	Y
GEORGIA								
1 Thomas	Y	Y	Y	Y	N	Y	Y	N
2 Hatcher	Y	N	Y	Y	Y	Y	Y	Y
3 Ray	Y	Y	Y	Y	N	Y	N	Y
4 ***Swindall***	Y	Y	Y	Y	Y	N	N	N
5 Fowler	Y	Y	N	Y	?	?	?	?
6 ***Gingrich***	Y	Y	Y	Y	Y	N	N	N
7 Darden	Y	Y	Y	Y	Y	N	N	N
8 Rowland	Y	N	Y	Y	N	Y	Y	Y
9 Jenkins	Y	Y	Y	Y	Y	Y	Y	?
10 Barnard	Y	Y	Y	Y	Y	N	Y	N
HAWAII								
1 Abercrombie [1]								
2 Akaka	N	N	N	N	N	?	Y	Y
IDAHO								
1 ***Craig***	Y	Y	Y	N	Y	N	N	N
2 Stallings	Y	N	N	N	Y	Y	Y	Y
ILLINOIS								
1 Hayes	N	N	N	Y	Y	Y	Y	Y
2 Savage	N	N	N	Y	N	Y	Y	Y
3 Russo	N	Y	N	Y	N	Y	Y	Y
4 Vacancy [2]								
5 Lipinski	N	Y	Y	Y	N	Y	N	N
6 ***Hyde***	Y	Y	Y	N	Y	N	N	N
7 Collins	N	N	N	Y	Y	Y	Y	Y
8 Rostenkowski	N	Y	N	N	N	Y	?	Y
9 Yates	N	N	N	Y	N	Y	Y	Y
10 ***Porter***	N	Y	Y	N	Y	Y	Y	Y
11 Annunzio	N	Y	N	Y	N	Y	Y	Y
12 ***Crane***	Y	Y	Y	N	Y	N	N	N
13 ***Fawell***	N	Y	Y	N	N	Y	Y	Y
14 ***Grotberg*** [3]	?	?	?	?	?	?	?	?
15 ***Madigan***	Y	Y	Y	N	Y	N	?	N
16 ***Martin***	Y	Y	Y	N	N	N	N	N
17 Evans	N	N	N	Y	N	Y	Y	Y
18 ***Michel***	Y	Y	Y	N	Y	N	N	N
19 Bruce	Y	N	N	Y	N	Y	Y	Y
20 Durbin	N	N	N	Y	Y	Y	#	Y
21 Price	Y	N	N	Y	Y	Y	Y	Y
22 Gray	Y	N	N	Y	Y	Y	Y	N
INDIANA								
1 Visclosky	N	N	N	Y	N	Y	Y	Y
2 Sharp	Y	Y	N	Y	Y	Y	Y	Y
3 ***Hiler***	Y	Y	Y	N	Y	N	N	N
4 ***Coats***	Y	Y	Y	N	Y	N	N	N
5 ***Hillis***	Y	Y	Y	Y	?	?	?	?

ND - Northern Democrats SD - Southern Democrats

	1	2	3	4	5	6	7	8
6 ***Burton***	Y	Y	Y	N	Y	N	N	N
7 ***Myers***	Y	Y	Y	N	Y	N	?	N
8 McCloskey	Y	Y	N	Y	Y	Y	Y	Y
9 Hamilton	Y	Y	N	N	Y	Y	Y	Y
10 Jacobs	N	Y	N	Y	N	N	Y	Y
IOWA								
1 ***Leach***	Y	Y	N	N	N	Y	Y	Y
2 ***Tauke***	Y	Y	N	N	Y	Y	Y	Y
3 ***Evans***	Y	Y	Y	N	Y	Y	Y	Y
4 Smith	Y	Y	N	N	Y	Y	Y	Y
5 ***Lightfoot***	Y	Y	N	N	Y	Y	Y	N
6 Bedell	N	Y	N	C	N	Y	Y	Y
KANSAS								
1 ***Roberts***	Y	Y	Y	N	Y	Y	N	Y
2 Slattery	Y	Y	N	N	Y	Y	Y	Y
3 ***Meyers***	Y	Y	Y	N	N	Y	Y	Y
4 Glickman	Y	Y	N	N	Y	Y	Y	Y
5 ***Whittaker***	Y	Y	Y	N	Y	N	N	N
KENTUCKY								
1 Hubbard	Y	N	Y	Y	Y	Y	Y	Y
2 Natcher	Y	Y	N	Y	N	Y	Y	Y
3 Mazzoli	Y	N	N	N	N	Y	?	Y
4 ***Snyder***	Y	Y	Y	N	N	?	?	N
5 ***Rogers***	Y	Y	Y	Y	N	N	N	N
6 ***Hopkins***	Y	Y	Y	Y	Y	N	Y	N
7 Perkins	Y	N	N	Y	N	Y	Y	Y
LOUISIANA								
1 ***Livingston***	Y	Y	Y	N	Y	N	N	N
2 Boggs	Y	N	N	Y	N	Y	Y	Y
3 Tauzin	Y	Y	Y	Y	Y	Y	N	N
4 Roemer	Y	Y	Y	Y	Y	Y	Y	N
5 Huckaby	Y	Y	Y	Y	Y	?	?	N
6 ***Moore***	Y	Y	Y	?	?	?	?	?
7 Breaux	Y	?	Y	Y	?	?	?	?
8 Long	Y	N	N	#	?	?	?	Y
MAINE								
1 ***McKernan***	Y	N	Y	Y	Y	N	Y	Y
2 ***Snowe***	Y	N	Y	Y	N	Y	Y	Y
MARYLAND								
1 Dyson	Y	Y	Y	Y	Y	N	N	Y
2 ***Bentley***	Y	Y	Y	Y	N	N	N	N
3 Mikulski	N	N	N	Y	N	Y	Y	?
4 ***Holt***	Y	Y	Y	N	?	?	?	N
5 Hoyer	N	N	N	Y	N	Y	Y	Y
6 Byron	Y	Y	Y	Y	N	Y	N	Y
7 Mitchell	N	N	N	Y	?	Y	#	?
8 Barnes	N	N	N	Y	N	#	#	#
MASSACHUSETTS								
1 ***Conte***	Y	N	N	Y	N	Y	Y	Y
2 Boland	N	N	N	Y	N	Y	Y	Y
3 Early	N	N	N	Y	N	Y	Y	Y
4 Frank	N	N	N	Y	Y	Y	Y	Y
5 Atkins	N	N	N	Y	N	Y	Y	Y
6 Mavroules	N	N	N	Y	N	Y	Y	Y
7 Markey	N	N	N	Y	N	Y	Y	Y
8 O'Neill [4]				Y				
9 Moakley	N	N	N	Y	N	?	Y	Y
10 Studds	N	N	N	Y	N	Y	Y	Y
11 Donnelly	N	N	N	Y	N	?	#	Y
MICHIGAN								
1 Conyers	N	N	N	Y	N	?	?	Y
2 ***Pursell***	N	Y	Y	N	N	N	Y	Y
3 Wolpe	-	N	N	Y	N	Y	Y	Y
4 ***Siljander***	Y	Y	Y	?	Y	N	N	N
5 ***Henry***	N	Y	Y	Y	Y	N	Y	Y
6 Carr	Y	Y	N	Y	Y	Y	Y	Y
7 Kildee	N	N	N	Y	N	Y	Y	Y
8 Traxler	Y	N	N	Y	Y	Y	Y	Y
9 ***Vander Jagt***	Y	Y	Y	N	Y	N	N	N
10 ***Schuette***	Y	Y	Y	Y	N	N	N	N
11 ***Davis***	Y	?	Y	Y	Y	N	Y	N
12 Bonior	N	N	N	Y	?	Y	Y	Y
13 Crockett	N	N	N	Y	Y	Y	Y	Y
14 Hertel	N	N	N	Y	N	Y	Y	Y
15 Ford	Y	N	N	Y	?	Y	Y	Y
16 Dingell	Y	N	N	Y	N	Y	Y	Y
17 Levin	N	N	N	Y	N	Y	Y	Y
18 ***Broomfield***	N	Y	Y	N	N	N	N	N
MINNESOTA								
1 Penny	Y	Y	N	N	N	Y	Y	Y
2 ***Weber***	Y	Y	Y	N	Y	Y	N	N
3 ***Frenzel***	Y	Y	Y	N	Y	Y	Y	Y
4 Vento	N	N	N	Y	N	Y	Y	Y
5 Sabo	N	N	N	Y	N	Y	Y	Y
6 Sikorski	Y	N	N	Y	N	Y	Y	Y
7 ***Stangeland***	Y	Y	Y	N	N	Y	N	N
8 Oberstar	Y	N	N	Y	N	Y	Y	Y
MISSISSIPPI								
1 Whitten	Y	Y	N	Y	N	Y	N	Y
2 ***Franklin***	Y	Y	Y	Y	Y	Y	X	N
3 Montgomery	Y	Y	Y	Y	N	N	N	N
4 Dowdy	Y	Y	Y	Y	N	N	Y	Y
5 ***Lott***	Y	Y	Y	Y	Y	N	N	N
MISSOURI								
1 Clay	N	N	N	Y	N	Y	Y	?
2 Young	Y	Y	N	Y	N	Y	Y	Y
3 Gephardt	X	N	N	Y	N	Y	Y	Y
4 Skelton	Y	N	Y	Y	Y	N	N	N
5 Wheat	N	Y	N	Y	N	Y	Y	Y
6 ***Coleman***	Y	Y	Y	Y	Y	N	N	N
7 ***Taylor***	Y	Y	Y	Y	N	N	N	N
8 ***Emerson***	Y	Y	Y	Y	Y	N	N	N
9 Volkmer	Y	Y	N	Y	N	Y	Y	Y
MONTANA								
1 Williams	Y	N	N	Y	Y	Y	Y	Y
2 ***Marlenee***	Y	Y	Y	N	Y	N	N	Y
NEBRASKA								
1 ***Bereuter***	Y	Y	Y	N	Y	Y	N	Y
2 ***Daub***	Y	Y	Y	N	Y	N	N	N
3 ***Smith***	Y	Y	Y	N	Y	Y	X	Y
NEVADA								
1 Reid	Y	N	N	Y	Y	Y	N	N
2 ***Vucanovich***	Y	Y	Y	N	Y	N	N	N
NEW HAMPSHIRE								
1 ***Smith***	Y	Y	Y	Y	Y	N	N	N
2 ***Gregg***	Y	Y	Y	Y	Y	N	Y	N
NEW JERSEY								
1 Florio	Y	N	N	Y	N	Y	Y	Y
2 Hughes	N	Y	N	Y	N	Y	Y	Y
3 Howard	N	N	N	Y	N	Y	Y	Y
4 ***Smith***	Y	Y	Y	Y	N	Y	Y	N
5 ***Roukema***	N	Y	Y	Y	N	Y	N	Y
6 Dwyer	N	N	N	Y	N	Y	Y	Y
7 ***Rinaldo***	Y	N	Y	Y	N	Y	N	N
8 Roe	N	N	N	Y	N	Y	Y	Y
9 Torricelli	N	?	N	Y	N	Y	Y	Y
10 Rodino	N	N	N	Y	N	Y	Y	Y
11 ***Gallo***	Y	Y	Y	N	N	N	N	N
12 ***Courter***	Y	Y	Y	N	N	N	N	N
13 ***Saxton***	Y	Y	Y	N	N	N	N	N
14 Guarini	N	N	N	Y	N	Y	Y	Y
NEW MEXICO								
1 ***Lujan***	?	Y	Y	N	Y	Y	N	N
2 ***Skeen***	Y	Y	Y	Y	Y	N	N	N
3 Richardson	Y	N	N	Y	Y	Y	Y	N
NEW YORK								
1 ***Carney***	Y	Y	Y	N	Y	N	N	N
2 Downey	N	N	N	N	N	Y	Y	Y
3 Mrazek	N	Y	N	Y	Y	Y	Y	Y
4 ***Lent***	Y	N	Y	N	N	?	?	N
5 ***McGrath***	Y	N	Y	Y	N	N	N	Y
6 Waldon [5]				Y	N	Y	Y	Y
7 Ackerman	N	N	N	Y	N	Y	Y	Y
8 Scheuer	N	N	N	Y	N	Y	Y	Y
9 Manton	N	N	N	Y	N	Y	Y	Y
10 Schumer	N	N	N	N	N	Y	Y	Y
11 Towns	N	N	N	Y	N	Y	Y	Y
12 Owens	N	N	N	Y	N	Y	Y	Y
13 Solarz	N	N	N	N	N	Y	Y	Y
14 ***Molinari***	Y	Y	Y	Y	N	N	N	N
15 ***Green***	N	N	N	N	N	Y	Y	Y
16 Rangel	N	N	N	Y	N	Y	Y	Y
17 Weiss	N	N	N	Y	N	Y	Y	Y
18 Garcia	N	N	N	Y	?	Y	Y	Y
19 Biaggi	N	N	Y	Y	Y	Y	Y	Y
20 ***DioGuardi***	N	N	Y	Y	N	Y	Y	N
21 ***Fish***	Y	N	Y	Y	N	N	Y	Y
22 ***Gilman***	Y	-	Y	Y	N	N	Y	N
23 Stratton	N	N	Y	Y	Y	N	N	N
24 ***Solomon***	Y	Y	Y	Y	Y	N	N	N
25 ***Boehlert***	Y	N	N	Y	N	N	Y	N
26 ***Martin***	Y	Y	Y	Y	Y	N	N	N
27 ***Wortley***	Y	Y	Y	N	N	N	N	N
28 McHugh	N	N	N	N	N	Y	Y	Y
29 ***Horton***	Y	N	N	Y	Y	N	Y	Y
30 ***Eckert***	Y	Y	Y	N	Y	N	N	N
31 ***Kemp***	Y	Y	Y	N	Y	N	N	N
32 LaFalce	N	N	N	N	N	?	#	Y
33 Nowak	N	N	N	Y	N	Y	Y	Y
34 Lundine	Y	?	N	Y	N	?	?	Y
NORTH CAROLINA								
1 Jones	Y	N	N	Y	N	Y	Y	Y
2 Valentine	Y	Y	N	Y	N	Y	N	Y
3 Whitley	Y	N	N	Y	N	Y	Y	Y
4 ***Cobey***	Y	Y	Y	Y	Y	N	N	N
5 Neal	Y	N	N	Y	Y	Y	Y	Y
6 ***Coble***	Y	Y	Y	Y	Y	N	N	Y
7 Rose	Y	?	N	Y	Y	Y	Y	Y
8 Hefner	Y	N	N	Y	N	Y	Y	Y
9 ***McMillan***	Y	Y	Y	Y	Y	N	N	N
10 ***Broyhill*** [6]	Y	Y	Y					
11 ***Hendon***	Y	Y	Y	Y	Y	N	N	N
NORTH DAKOTA								
AL Dorgan	Y	Y	N	N	Y	Y	Y	Y
OHIO								
1 Luken	Y	N	N	N	Y	Y	Y	Y
2 ***Gradison***	N	Y	Y	N	Y	N	N	N
3 Hall	N	Y	N	Y	Y	Y	Y	Y
4 ***Oxley***	Y	Y	Y	N	Y	N	N	N
5 ***Latta***	Y	Y	Y	N	N	N	N	N
6 ***McEwen***	Y	Y	Y	N	Y	N	?	N
7 ***DeWine***	Y	Y	Y	N	N	?	?	N
8 ***Kindness***	Y	Y	Y	Y	Y	N	?	N
9 Kaptur	N	N	N	Y	N	Y	#	Y
10 ***Miller***	Y	Y	Y	Y	Y	N	N	N
11 Eckart	Y	Y	N	Y	N	Y	Y	Y
12 ***Kasich***	Y	Y	Y	N	Y	N	N	N
13 Pease	Y	Y	N	N	N	Y	Y	Y
14 Seiberling	N	Y	N	N	N	Y	Y	Y
15 ***Wylie***	N	Y	Y	N	N	N	N	N
16 ***Regula***	Y	Y	Y	Y	N	N	N	Y
17 Traficant	N	N	N	Y	N	Y	Y	Y
18 Applegate	Y	Y	N	Y	N	Y	Y	Y
19 Feighan	N	N	N	Y	N	Y	Y	Y
20 Oakar	N	N	N	Y	N	Y	Y	Y
21 Stokes	X	N	N	Y	N	Y	Y	Y
OKLAHOMA								
1 Jones	Y	Y	Y	Y	Y	Y	?	Y
2 Synar	Y	Y	N	Y	N	Y	Y	Y
3 Watkins	Y	Y	Y	Y	Y	Y	?	Y
4 McCurdy	Y	Y	N	Y	Y	Y	N	Y
5 ***Edwards***	Y	Y	Y	N	Y	N	N	N
6 English	Y	Y	Y	Y	Y	Y	N	Y
OREGON								
1 AuCoin	Y	N	N	N	N	Y	Y	Y
2 ***Smith, R.***	Y	Y	Y	N	Y	Y	N	Y
3 Wyden	Y	N	N	N	Y	Y	Y	Y
4 Weaver	Y	N	N	Y	Y	Y	Y	Y
5 ***Smith, D.***	Y	Y	Y	Y	Y	N	N	N
PENNSYLVANIA								
1 Foglietta	N	N	N	Y	N	Y	Y	Y
2 Gray	N	N	N	Y	N	Y	Y	Y
3 Borski	N	N	N	Y	N	Y	Y	Y
4 Kolter	Y	N	N	Y	N	Y	Y	Y
5 ***Schulze***	#	?	Y	Y	N	N	N	N
6 Yatron	Y	N	N	Y	N	Y	Y	Y
7 Edgar	N	N	N	Y	N	Y	Y	Y
8 Kostmayer	Y	N	N	Y	N	Y	Y	Y
9 ***Shuster***	Y	Y	Y	Y	N	N	N	N
10 ***McDade***	Y	N	Y	Y	Y	N	N	N
11 Kanjorski	Y	N	N	Y	Y	Y	Y	Y
12 Murtha	Y	Y	Y	Y	N	N	N	N
13 ***Coughlin***	N	Y	Y	Y	N	Y	Y	Y
14 Coyne	N	N	N	Y	N	Y	Y	Y
15 ***Ritter***	Y	Y	Y	Y	Y	Y	N	N
16 ***Walker***	Y	Y	Y	N	Y	Y	N	N
17 ***Gekas***	Y	N	Y	N	N	N	N	N
18 Walgren	N	Y	N	Y	N	Y	Y	Y
19 ***Goodling***	Y	Y	Y	Y	N	Y	Y	N
20 Gaydos	Y	N	?	Y	N	Y	Y	N
21 ***Ridge***	Y	Y	N	Y	N	N	Y	Y
22 Murphy	Y	Y	N	Y	N	Y	Y	Y
23 ***Clinger***	Y	Y	Y	Y	N	N	N	N
RHODE ISLAND								
1 St Germain	N	N	N	Y	N	Y	Y	Y
2 ***Schneider***	N	N	N	Y	N	?	Y	Y
SOUTH CAROLINA								
1 ***Hartnett***	Y	?	Y	Y	Y	?	?	N
2 ***Spence***	Y	Y	Y	Y	Y	N	N	N
3 Derrick	Y	N	N	Y	N	Y	Y	Y
4 ***Campbell***	Y	?	Y	Y	Y	X	X	X
5 Spratt	Y	N	N	Y	N	Y	Y	Y
6 Tallon	Y	N	Y	Y	Y	Y	Y	Y
SOUTH DAKOTA								
AL Daschle	Y	Y	N	N	Y	Y	Y	Y
TENNESSEE								
1 ***Quillen***	Y	Y	Y	Y	N	N	?	N
2 ***Duncan***	Y	Y	Y	Y	N	N	N	N
3 Lloyd	Y	?	Y	Y	Y	N	N	N
4 Cooper	Y	N	N	Y	Y	Y	Y	Y
5 Boner	Y	N	N	Y	Y	?	?	N
6 Gordon	Y	Y	N	Y	Y	Y	Y	Y
7 ***Sundquist***	Y	Y	Y	Y	N	N	N	N
8 Jones	Y	Y	N	Y	Y	?	?	N
9 Ford	N	N	N	Y	?	#	#	Y
TEXAS								
1 Chapman	Y	Y	N	Y	N	Y	Y	Y
2 Wilson	Y	?	Y	Y	N	N	N	N
3 ***Bartlett***	Y	Y	Y	N	Y	Y	N	N
4 Hall	Y	Y	Y	Y	Y	Y	N	N
5 Bryant	Y	Y	N	Y	N	Y	Y	Y
6 ***Barton***	Y	Y	Y	N	Y	N	N	N
7 ***Archer***	Y	Y	Y	N	Y	N	N	N
8 ***Fields***	Y	Y	Y	N	Y	N	N	N
9 Brooks	Y	?	N	Y	N	Y	Y	Y
10 Pickle	Y	#	N	N	Y	N	Y	N
11 Leath	Y	Y	Y	Y	Y	Y	Y	Y
12 Wright	N	N	N	Y	N	Y	Y	Y
13 ***Boulter***	+	Y	Y	N	Y	N	N	N
14 ***Sweeney***	Y	Y	Y	Y	?	N	N	N
15 de la Garza	Y	N	N	Y	Y	N	N	Y
16 Coleman	Y	N	N	Y	Y	N	Y	N
17 Stenholm	Y	Y	Y	Y	Y	Y	N	Y
18 Leland	N	N	N	Y	Y	Y	Y	Y
19 ***Combest***	Y	Y	Y	Y	Y	N	N	N
20 Gonzalez	N	N	N	Y	N	N	Y	Y
21 ***Loeffler***	Y	Y	Y	Y	Y	N	N	N
22 ***DeLay***	Y	Y	Y	N	Y	N	N	N
23 Bustamante	Y	N	Y	Y	Y	Y	N	Y
24 Frost	N	Y	N	Y	N	Y	Y	Y
25 Andrews	Y	Y	N	Y	N	Y	Y	N
26 ***Armey***	Y	Y	Y	N	Y	Y	N	N
27 Ortiz	Y	N	Y	Y	Y	N	N	Y
UTAH								
1 ***Hansen***	Y	Y	Y	N	Y	N	N	N
2 ***Monson***	Y	Y	Y	N	Y	Y	N	N
3 ***Nielson***	Y	Y	Y	N	Y	N	N	N
VERMONT								
AL ***Jeffords***	Y	Y	N	Y	N	Y	Y	Y
VIRGINIA								
1 ***Bateman***	Y	Y	Y	N	Y	N	N	N
2 ***Whitehurst***	N	?	Y	N	N	N	N	N
3 ***Bliley***	Y	Y	Y	Y	Y	N	N	N
4 Sisisky	Y	Y	Y	Y	Y	Y	N	N
5 Daniel	Y	Y	Y	Y	N	Y	N	N
6 Olin	Y	Y	N	Y	N	Y	Y	Y
7 ***Slaughter***	Y	Y	Y	Y	N	N	N	N
8 ***Parris***	Y	Y	Y	Y	Y	N	N	N
9 Boucher	Y	Y	N	Y	Y	Y	Y	Y
10 ***Wolf***	Y	Y	Y	N	N	N	N	N
WASHINGTON								
1 ***Miller***	N	Y	Y	N	N	+	-	N
2 Swift	Y	N	N	N	N	Y	Y	Y
3 Bonker	Y	N	N	N	Y	Y	Y	Y
4 ***Morrison***	Y	?	Y	N	Y	N	N	N
5 Foley	Y	N	N	X	N	Y	Y	Y
6 Dicks	Y	N	N	N	Y	Y	Y	Y
7 Lowry	N	N	N	N	N	Y	Y	Y
8 ***Chandler***	Y	Y	Y	N	Y	N	N	Y
WEST VIRGINIA								
1 Mollohan	Y	?	N	Y	N	N	N	Y
2 Staggers	Y	N	N	Y	N	Y	Y	Y
3 Wise	Y	N	N	Y	N	Y	Y	Y
4 Rahall	Y	N	N	Y	N	Y	Y	Y
WISCONSIN								
1 Aspin	Y	Y	Y	Y	Y	Y	Y	Y
2 Kastenmeier	N	N	N	Y	Y	Y	Y	Y
3 ***Gunderson***	Y	Y	Y	Y	Y	Y	Y	Y
4 Kleczka	Y	N	N	N	N	Y	Y	Y
5 Moody	Y	Y	N	Y	N	Y	Y	Y
6 ***Petri***	Y	Y	Y	N	Y	Y	N	Y
7 Obey	Y	N	N	Y	N	Y	Y	Y
8 ***Roth***	Y	Y	Y	N	Y	Y	N	N
9 ***Sensenbrenner***	Y	Y	Y	N	Y	N	N	N
WYOMING								
AL ***Cheney***	Y	Y	Y	N	Y	N	N	N

Southern states - Ala., Ark., Fla., Ga., Ky., La., Miss., N.C., Okla., S.C., Tenn., Texas, Va.

9. HR 4428. Defense Authorization, Fiscal 1987. Porter, R-Ill., amendment to prohibit the production of binary chemical weapons before Oct. 1, 1987. Adopted 210-209: R 38-137; D 172-72 (ND 142-23, SD 30-49), Aug. 13, 1986. A "nay" was a vote supporting the president's position.

10. HR 5395. Temporary Debt Limit Increase. Foley, D-Wash., motion to concur in the Senate amendment raising from $2.079 trillion to $2.111 trillion the ceiling on the federal debt and to disagree to the Senate amendment to make changes in the Gramm-Rudman-Hollings anti-deficit law (PL 99-177) to reinstate, for 1987 only, the law's automatic spending cuts procedure (previously voided as a violation of the Constitution's separation-of-powers doctrine) by granting final authority for determining the automatic cuts to the director of the Office of Management and Budget, with certain limitations. The amendment also would change to the first Tuesday in February of each year the date in the Gramm-Rudman law by which the president is required to submit his budget request to Congress. Motion agreed to 175-133: R 21-119; D 154-14 (ND 108-6, SD 46-8), in the session that began Aug. 15, 1986.

11. HR 4759. Intelligence Authorization, Fiscal 1987. Stump, R-Ariz., amendment to strike a section of the bill restricting covert military aid to UNITA rebels in Angola. Adopted 229-186: R 166-7; D 63-179 (ND 16-148, SD 47-31), Sept. 17, 1986. (The bill, to authorize fiscal 1987 funds for the CIA and other federal intelligence agencies, subsequently was passed by voice vote. Most of the authorization levels contained in the bill were classified.) A "yea" was a vote supporting the president's position.

12. HR 2482. Pesticide Control Reauthorization. Panetta, D-Calif., amendment to the Roberts, R-Kan., amendment. The Panetta amendment would have given the Environmental Protection Agency (EPA) more discretion than did the Roberts amendment in setting uniform national standards for pesticide residues on foods, and would have shifted the burden onto EPA to prove the standards necessary to prevent disruption of commerce. It also would have required EPA to respond to comments submitted during rulemaking procedures to set the standards. Rejected 157-183: R 22-118; D 135-65 (ND 111-25, SD 24-40), Sept. 19, 1986. (The Roberts amendment subsequently was adopted, by a vote of 214-121.)

13. HR 3838. Tax Overhaul. Adoption of the conference report on the bill to revise the federal income tax system by reducing individual and corporate tax rates, eliminating or curtailing many deductions, credits and exclusions, repealing the investment tax credit, taxing capital gains as regular income and making other changes. Adopted 292-136: R 116-62; D 176-74 (ND 132-36, SD 44-38), Sept. 25, 1986. A "yea" was a vote supporting the president's position.

14. H J Res 738. Continuing Appropriations, Fiscal 1987. Passage of the joint resolution to appropriate $561.9 billion in budget authority for all government programs funded by regular fiscal 1987 appropriations bills, with the funds to be available through Sept. 30, 1987. The measure included several policy changes, including bans on nuclear testing and nerve gas production, a requirement that President Reagan observe portions of the SALT II arms control agreement he has repudiated, and a new $250,000 limit on farm program payments. Passed 201-200: R 15-157; D 186-43 (ND 127-25, SD 59-18), Sept. 25, 1986. A "nay" was a vote supporting the president's position.

15. HR 4868. South African Sanctions. Passage, over President Reagan's Sept. 26 veto, of the bill to impose economic sanctions against South Africa. Passed 313-83: R 81-79; D 232-4 (ND 163-0, SD 69-4), Sept. 29, 1986. A two-thirds majority of those present and voting (264 in this case) of both houses is required to override a veto. A "nay" was a vote supporting the president's position.

16. HR 3810. Immigration Reform. Passage of the bill to overhaul the nation's immigration laws by creating a new system of penalties against employers who knowingly hire illegal aliens, providing legal status to millions of illegal aliens already in the United States, and creating a special program for foreigners to gain legal status if they have a history of working in U.S. agriculture. Passed 230-166: R 62-105; D 168-61 (ND 126-29, SD 42-32), Oct. 9, 1986. (The House subsequently moved to strike the provisions of S 1200, the Senate-passed version of the bill, and insert the provisions of HR 3810. The House then passed S 1200 by voice vote.)

[1] *Rep. Neil Abercrombie, D-Hawaii, was sworn in Sept. 23, 1986, to succeed Cecil Heftel, D, who resigned July 11, 1986, to run for governor of Hawaii.*

[2] *Rep. George M. O'Brien, R-Ill., died July 17, 1986.*

[3] *Rep. John E. Grotberg, R-Ill., has not participated in House business this session due to a serious illness.*

[4] *Rep. Thomas P. O'Neill Jr., D-Mass., as Speaker, votes at his own discretion.*

[5] *James T. Broyhill, R-N.C., resigned July 13, 1986, to fill the vacant seat resulting from the June 29 death of Sen. John P. East.*

KEY

- Y Voted for (yea).
- # Paired for.
- \+ Announced for.
- N Voted against (nay).
- X Paired against.
- \- Announced against.
- P Voted "present."
- C Voted "present" to avoid possible conflict of interest.
- ? Did not vote or otherwise make a position known.

Democrats *Republicans*

	9	10	11	12	13	14	15	16
ALABAMA								
1 *Callahan*	N	N	Y	N	Y	N	N	N
2 *Dickinson*	N	?	Y	?	Y	N	N	N
3 Nichols	N	?	Y	N	Y	Y	Y	X
4 Bevill	N	?	N	N	Y	Y	Y	N
5 Flippo	?	?	?	N	Y	Y	Y	N
6 Erdreich	Y	?	Y	N	Y	N	Y	N
7 Shelby	N	N	Y	N	Y	N	Y	N
ALASKA								
AL *Young*	N	N	Y	N	N	N	Y	N
ARIZONA								
1 *McCain*	N	Y	Y	Y	Y	N	Y	N
2 Udall	Y	?	N	?	Y	?	Y	Y
3 *Stump*	N	N	Y	N	Y	N	N	N
4 *Rudd*	N	?	Y	?	Y	N	N	?
5 *Kolbe*	Y	N	Y	?	Y	N	Y	N
ARKANSAS								
1 Alexander	N	?	N	N	Y	#	Y	Y
2 Robinson	N	N	Y	N	N	N	Y	N
3 *Hammerschmidt*	N	N	Y	N	N	N	N	N
4 Anthony	N	?	Y	N	Y	Y	#	Y
CALIFORNIA								
1 Bosco	N	?	N	Y	N	Y	Y	Y
2 *Chappie*	N	?	Y	N	N	N	N	N
3 Matsui	Y	Y	N	Y	Y	Y	Y	Y
4 Fazio	N	Y	N	?	N	Y	Y	Y
5 Burton	?	?	?	?	?	?	?	?
6 Boxer	Y	Y	N	Y	Y	Y	Y	Y
7 Miller	Y	Y	N	Y	Y	Y	?	Y
8 Dellums	Y	Y	N	Y	Y	Y	Y	N
9 Stark	Y	Y	N	Y	Y	Y	Y	Y
10 Edwards	Y	?	N	Y	Y	Y	Y	N
11 Lantos	Y	?	Y	Y	Y	Y	Y	Y
12 *Zschau*	N	?	?	?	Y	N	?	Y
13 Mineta	Y	Y	N	Y	Y	Y	Y	Y
14 *Shumway*	N	Y	Y	N	N	N	N	N
15 Coelho	Y	Y	N	N	Y	Y	Y	Y
16 Panetta	Y	Y	N	Y	Y	Y	#	Y
17 *Pashayan*	N	N	Y	N	Y	N	Y	Y
18 Lehman	Y	Y	N	N	N	Y	Y	Y
19 *Lagomarsino*	N	N	Y	N	Y	N	Y	Y
20 *Thomas*	N	?	Y	?	N	N	?	N
21 *Fiedler*	N	?	Y	N	Y	N	?	N
22 *Moorhead*	N	N	Y	N	N	N	N	Y
23 Beilenson	Y	?	N	Y	Y	Y	Y	Y
24 Waxman	Y	?	N	Y	Y	Y	Y	Y
25 Roybal	Y	Y	N	Y	Y	Y	Y	N
26 Berman	Y	Y	N	Y	Y	Y	Y	Y
27 Levine	Y	?	N	Y	Y	Y	Y	Y
28 Dixon	Y	?	N	?	N	Y	Y	Y
29 Hawkins	Y	?	N	?	Y	Y	Y	N
30 Martinez	Y	#	N	Y	Y	X	Y	N
31 Dymally	Y	?	N	?	N	Y	Y	N
32 Anderson	Y	Y	N	Y	Y	Y	Y	Y
33 *Dreier*	N	N	Y	N	N	N	N	N
34 Torres	Y	Y	N	Y	Y	Y	Y	Y
35 *Lewis*	N	?	Y	?	Y	N	N	Y
36 Brown	Y	?	N	?	Y	Y	Y	Y
37 *McCandless*	N	X	Y	N	N	N	N	Y
38 *Dornan*	N	N	Y	N	Y	N	N	Y
39 *Dannemeyer*	N	-	Y	-	N	N	N	Y
40 *Badham*	N	?	Y	?	N	-	-	Y
41 *Lowery*	N	N	Y	N	Y	N	Y	Y
42 *Lungren*	N	N	Y	N	Y	N	N	Y
43 *Packard*	N	N	Y	?	Y	N	N	Y
44 Bates	Y	Y	N	Y	Y	N	Y	Y
45 *Hunter*	N	N	Y	N	Y	N	N	N
COLORADO								
1 Schroeder	Y	?	N	Y	N	Y	Y	N
2 Wirth	Y	N	N	?	Y	Y	Y	N
3 *Strang*	N	N	Y	N	Y	N	N	Y
4 *Brown*	Y	N	Y	N	Y	N	Y	N
5 *Kramer*	N	N	Y	N	Y	N	?	N
6 *Schaefer*	N	N	Y	?	N	N	N	Y
CONNECTICUT								
1 Kennelly	Y	Y	N	Y	Y	Y	Y	Y
2 Gejdenson	Y	Y	N	Y	N	Y	Y	Y
3 Morrison	?	?	N	Y	Y	Y	Y	Y
4 *McKinney*	Y	Y	N	N	N	Y	Y	Y
5 *Rowland*	N	N	Y	N	Y	N	Y	Y
6 *Johnson*	N	N	Y	N	Y	N	Y	Y
DELAWARE								
AL Carper	N	N	Y	Y	Y	Y	Y	Y
FLORIDA								
1 Hutto	N	Y	Y	Y	N	Y	N	Y
2 Fuqua	N	?	Y	?	Y	Y	Y	Y
3 Bennett	Y	Y	N	N	Y	Y	Y	Y
4 Chappell	N	?	Y	?	N	Y	Y	Y
5 *McCollum*	N	?	Y	N	Y	N	N	N
6 MacKay	Y	Y	Y	N	Y	Y	Y	Y
7 Gibbons	N	?	N	?	Y	Y	Y	Y
8 *Young*	N	?	Y	N	Y	N	N	N
9 *Bilirakis*	N	Y	Y	N	Y	N	N	N
10 *Ireland*	N	N	Y	?	Y	N	Y	N
11 Nelson	N	Y	Y	N	Y	Y	Y	Y
12 *Lewis*	Y	N	#	-	N	N	Y	N
13 *Mack*	N	N	Y	N	Y	N	N	N
14 Mica	Y	?	Y	Y	N	Y	Y	Y
15 *Shaw*	N	N	Y	N	Y	N	N	Y
16 Smith	Y	Y	Y	Y	Y	Y	Y	Y
17 Lehman	Y	?	N	?	Y	Y	Y	Y
18 Pepper	Y	Y	Y	Y	Y	+	Y	Y
19 Fascell	Y	?	Y	Y	Y	Y	Y	Y
GEORGIA								
1 Thomas	N	Y	Y	N	N	Y	Y	Y
2 Hatcher	N	?	Y	N	Y	Y	?	Y
3 Ray	N	N	Y	N	N	Y	Y	N
4 *Swindall*	N	N	Y	N	N	N	N	N
5 Fowler	?	?	?	?	Y	Y	?	?
6 *Gingrich*	N	N	Y	?	Y	N	Y	Y
7 Darden	N	Y	Y	N	N	N	Y	Y
8 Rowland	N	Y	Y	N	N	Y	Y	Y
9 Jenkins	Y	Y	Y	N	Y	Y	Y	Y
10 Barnard	N	Y	Y	X	Y	N	Y	X
HAWAII								
1 Abercrombie [1]					Y	Y	Y	Y
2 Akaka	Y	Y	N	?	N	Y	Y	N
IDAHO								
1 *Craig*	N	?	Y	N	N	N	N	N
2 Stallings	Y	?	Y	N	Y	N	Y	Y
ILLINOIS								
1 Hayes	Y	Y	N	Y	Y	Y	Y	N
2 Savage	Y	?	N	Y	Y	Y	Y	N
3 Russo	Y	Y	N	#	Y	N	Y	?
4 Vacancy [2]								
5 Lipinski	N	Y	Y	Y	Y	Y	Y	Y
6 *Hyde*	N	?	Y	N	Y	N	N	N
7 Collins	Y	Y	N	Y	Y	Y	Y	Y
8 Rostenkowski	Y	Y	N	?	Y	?	?	Y
9 Yates	Y	?	N	Y	Y	Y	Y	?
10 *Porter*	Y	?	Y	N	Y	N	N	Y
11 Annunzio	Y	Y	N	Y	Y	Y	Y	Y
12 *Crane*	N	N	Y	N	N	N	N	N
13 *Fawell*	N	N	Y	N	Y	N	Y	N
14 *Grotberg* [3]	?	?	?	?	?	?	?	?
15 *Madigan*	N	N	Y	?	N	?	Y	N
16 *Martin*	Y	N	Y	N	Y	N	Y	Y
17 Evans	Y	Y	N	Y	Y	Y	Y	N
18 *Michel*	N	N	Y	N	Y	N	N	Y
19 Bruce	Y	Y	N	Y	N	N	Y	Y
20 Durbin	Y	Y	N	Y	Y	Y	Y	Y
21 Price	N	?	N	Y	Y	Y	Y	Y
22 Gray	N	Y	N	Y	Y	Y	Y	Y
INDIANA								
1 Visclosky	Y	Y	N	N	Y	Y	Y	Y
2 Sharp	?	Y	N	Y	Y	Y	Y	Y
3 *Hiler*	N	N	Y	?	Y	N	Y	N
4 *Coats*	Y	N	Y	N	Y	N	Y	N
5 *Hillis*	?	?	Y	?	Y	N	Y	?

ND - Northern Democrats SD - Southern Democrats

	9	10	11	12	13	14	15	16
6 ***Burton***	N	N	Y	N	N	N	N	N
7 ***Myers***	N	Y	Y	N	N	Y	N	N
8 McCloskey	N	Y	N	N	Y	Y	Y	Y
9 Hamilton	N	Y	N	N	Y	N	Y	Y
10 Jacobs	Y	N	N	Y	N	?	Y	N
IOWA								
1 ***Leach***	Y	Y	N	N	Y	N	Y	Y
2 ***Tauke***	Y	N	Y	N	Y	N	Y	?
3 ***Evans***	N	?	Y	N	Y	N	Y	Y
4 Smith	Y	Y	N	N	Y	Y	Y	Y
5 ***Lightfoot***	N	N	Y	N	Y	N	Y	Y
6 Bedell	Y	?	N	Y	Y	Y	Y	Y
KANSAS								
1 ***Roberts***	N	Y	Y	N	N	N	Y	N
2 Slattery	N	Y	N	N	Y	N	Y	Y
3 ***Meyers***	Y	N	Y	Y	Y	N	Y	N
4 Glickman	N	Y	Y	N	Y	N	Y	Y
5 ***Whittaker***	N	N	Y	N	N	N	N	N
KENTUCKY								
1 Hubbard	N	N	Y	N	N	N	Y	N
2 Natcher	Y	Y	Y	N	Y	Y	Y	Y
3 Mazzoli	Y	?	N	N	Y	N	Y	Y
4 ***Snyder***	N	?	Y	N	Y	N	N	N
5 ***Rogers***	N	N	Y	N	Y	Y	N	Y
6 ***Hopkins***	N	N	Y	N	Y	N	Y	N
7 Perkins	Y	Y	N	N	N	Y	Y	Y
LOUISIANA								
1 ***Livingston***	N	N	Y	N	Y	N	N	Y
2 Boggs	Y	Y	Y	Y	Y	Y	Y	Y
3 Tauzin	N	Y	Y	N	Y	Y	Y	N
4 Roemer	N	Y	N	Y	Y	N	Y	N
5 Huckaby	Y	N	Y	Y	Y	N	?	Y
6 ***Moore***	?	?	?	?	Y	?	?	?
7 Breaux	?	?	?	?	Y	X	?	?
8 Long	Y	?	N	Y	Y	Y	Y	Y
MAINE								
1 ***McKernan***	Y	N	Y	Y	Y	N	Y	Y
2 ***Snowe***	Y	N	Y	Y	Y	N	Y	Y
MARYLAND								
1 Dyson	N	Y	Y	N	N	N	Y	Y
2 ***Bentley***	N	Y	Y	N	N	N	Y	N
3 Mikulski	Y	?	N	?	Y	Y	Y	Y
4 ***Holt***	N	Y	Y	N	N	N	N	N
5 Hoyer	Y	Y	N	Y	N	Y	Y	Y
6 Byron	N	N	Y	N	Y	N	Y	Y
7 Mitchell	Y	?	N	Y	N	Y	Y	X
8 Barnes	Y	?	N	Y	N	N	Y	Y
MASSACHUSETTS								
1 ***Conte***	Y	Y	N	Y	Y	Y	Y	Y
2 Boland	Y	Y	X	?	Y	Y	Y	#
3 Early	Y	?	N	?	Y	Y	Y	Y
4 Frank	Y	Y	N	Y	Y	Y	Y	Y
5 Atkins	Y	?	N	Y	Y	Y	Y	Y
6 Mavroules	Y	?	N	Y	Y	Y	Y	Y
7 Markey	Y	?	N	Y	Y	Y	Y	Y
8 O'Neill [4]							Y	
9 Moakley	Y	?	N	Y	Y	Y	Y	Y
10 Studds	Y	?	N	?	Y	Y	Y	Y
11 Donnelly	Y	?	N	Y	Y	Y	Y	Y
MICHIGAN								
1 Conyers	Y	?	N	?	N	N	Y	X
2 ***Pursell***	Y	N	Y	N	Y	?	Y	N
3 Wolpe	Y	Y	N	Y	Y	Y	Y	Y
4 ***Siljander***	N	?	Y	?	Y	N	?	N
5 ***Henry***	Y	N	Y	N	Y	N	Y	Y
6 Carr	Y	Y	N	N	N	Y	Y	N
7 Kildee	Y	Y	N	Y	Y	Y	Y	Y
8 Traxler	Y	?	N	?	Y	Y	Y	?
9 ***Vander Jagt***	N	N	Y	N	Y	N	?	N
10 ***Schuette***	N	N	Y	?	Y	N	Y	N
11 ***Davis***	N	?	Y	N	Y	Y	Y	Y
12 Bonior	Y	Y	N	Y	Y	N	Y	Y
13 Crockett	Y	?	N	?	Y	X	Y	?
14 Hertel	Y	?	N	Y	N	N	Y	Y
15 Ford	?	?	N	Y	N	Y	Y	Y
16 Dingell	N	Y	N	Y	N	Y	Y	Y
17 Levin	Y	Y	N	Y	Y	Y	Y	Y
18 ***Broomfield***	N	?	Y	N	Y	N	N	N
MINNESOTA								
1 Penny	Y	Y	N	N	Y	Y	Y	Y
2 ***Weber***	Y	N	Y	N	Y	N	Y	Y
3 ***Frenzel***	N	N	Y	N	N	N	Y	Y
4 Vento	Y	Y	N	Y	Y	Y	Y	Y
5 Sabo	Y	Y	N	Y	Y	Y	Y	Y
6 Sikorski	Y	Y	N	Y	Y	Y	Y	N
7 ***Stangeland***	N	N	Y	?	Y	N	?	Y
8 Oberstar	Y	Y	N	Y	Y	Y	Y	Y
MISSISSIPPI								
1 Whitten	Y	Y	Y	N	Y	Y	Y	N
2 ***Franklin***	N	?	Y	?	Y	N	Y	N
3 Montgomery	N	?	Y	N	N	Y	N	N
4 Dowdy	N	?	N	?	N	Y	Y	N
5 ***Lott***	N	?	Y	?	Y	N	N	Y
MISSOURI								
1 Clay	Y	Y	X	?	N	Y	Y	Y
2 Young	N	Y	N	N	Y	Y	Y	Y
3 Gephardt	Y	Y	N	?	Y	?	Y	#
4 Skelton	N	Y	Y	N	Y	?	?	N
5 Wheat	Y	Y	N	Y	Y	Y	Y	Y
6 ***Coleman***	N	?	Y	N	N	N	?	Y
·7 ***Taylor***	N	N	Y	N	N	N	N	N
8 ***Emerson***	N	N	Y	N	Y	N	N	N
9 Volkmer	N	Y	Y	N	Y	N	Y	N
MONTANA								
1 Williams	Y	Y	N	N	N	Y	Y	Y
2 ***Marlenee***	N	Y	Y	N	N	N	N	N
NEBRASKA								
1 ***Bereuter***	N	N	Y	N	Y	N	Y	N
2 ***Daub***	N	N	Y	N	Y	N	Y	N
3 ***Smith***	N	N	Y	N	Y	Y	Y	Y
NEVADA								
1 Reid	Y	Y	N	Y	Y	N	Y	N
2 ***Vucanovich***	N	N	Y	N	N	N	N	Y
NEW HAMPSHIRE								
1 ***Smith***	N	N	Y	Y	Y	N	N	N
2 ***Gregg***	Y	N	Y	?	Y	N	?	N
NEW JERSEY								
1 Florio	Y	?	N	Y	Y	Y	Y	Y
2 Hughes	Y	Y	N	Y	Y	N	Y	N
3 Howard	Y	Y	N	Y	Y	Y	Y	Y
4 ***Smith***	Y	Y	Y	Y	Y	Y	Y	Y
5 ***Roukema***	Y	N	Y	Y	Y	N	Y	N
6 Dwyer	Y	Y	N	Y	Y	Y	Y	Y
7 ***Rinaldo***	Y	Y	Y	Y	?	Y	Y	N
8 Roe	Y	Y	?	Y	Y	Y	Y	Y
9 Torricelli	Y	Y	N	Y	Y	Y	Y	Y
10 Rodino	Y	?	N	Y	Y	Y	Y	Y
11 ***Gallo***	N	N	Y	Y	Y	N	Y	N
12 ***Courter***	N	N	Y	Y	Y	N	Y	N
13 ***Saxton***	N	N	Y	Y	Y	N	Y	N
14 Guarini	Y	Y	N	Y	Y	#	Y	N
NEW MEXICO								
1 ***Lujan***	N	?	Y	N	Y	N	Y	N
2 ***Skeen***	N	N	Y	N	Y	N	N	N
3 Richardson	Y	Y	N	?	Y	Y	Y	Y
NEW YORK								
1 ***Carney***	N	N	Y	Y	N	N	Y	N
2 Downey	Y	Y	N	Y	Y	Y	Y	Y
3 Mrazek	Y	?	N	?	N	Y	Y	Y
4 ***Lent***	N	?	Y	?	N	N	Y	N
5 ***McGrath***	Y	Y	Y	N	Y	N	Y	N
6 Waldon	Y	Y	N	?	N	Y	Y	Y
7 Ackerman	Y	?	N	Y	N	Y	Y	Y
8 Scheuer	Y	Y	N	Y	Y	Y	Y	Y
9 Manton	Y	Y	N	N	N	Y	Y	Y
10 Schumer	Y	Y	N	Y	Y	Y	Y	Y
11 Towns	Y	?	N	Y	Y	Y	Y	N
12 Owens	Y	?	N	Y	Y	Y	Y	Y
13 Solarz	Y	?	N	Y	Y	Y	Y	#
14 ***Molinari***	Y	N	Y	Y	N	N	Y	N
15 ***Green***	Y	N	Y	Y	N	Y	Y	Y
16 Rangel	Y	Y	N	Y	Y	Y	Y	Y
17 Weiss	Y	Y	N	+	N	Y	Y	?
18 Garcia	Y	?	N	?	Y	?	Y	N
19 Biaggi	Y	?	Y	?	Y	?	Y	Y
20 ***DioGuardi***	N	N	Y	N	Y	N	Y	Y
21 ***Fish***	Y	?	N	Y	Y	Y	Y	Y
22 ***Gilman***	N	Y	Y	N	N	Y	Y	Y
23 Stratton	N	Y	Y	?	Y	Y	Y	Y
24 ***Solomon***	N	N	Y	N	Y	N	N	-
25 ***Boehlert***	N	N	Y	Y	Y	N	Y	Y
26 ***Martin***	N	?	Y	N	N	N	?	N
27 ***Wortley***	Y	N	Y	N	Y	N	Y	Y
28 McHugh	Y	Y	N	Y	Y	Y	Y	Y
29 ***Horton***	Y	?	N	N	N	N	Y	N
30 ***Eckert***	N	Y	Y	N	Y	N	N	N
31 ***Kemp***	N	?	Y	?	Y	N	N	N
32 LaFalce	Y	Y	N	Y	Y	Y	Y	Y
33 Nowak	Y	Y	N	Y	Y	Y	Y	Y
34 Lundine	Y	Y	N	Y	Y	Y	Y	Y
NORTH CAROLINA								
1 Jones	N	?	N	N	Y	N	?	N
2 Valentine	N	?	Y	N	Y	Y	Y	N
3 Whitley	N	Y	N	?	N	Y	Y	N
4 ***Cobey***	N	N	Y	?	Y	N	N	N
5 Neal	N	Y	N	Y	Y	N	Y	Y
6 ***Coble***	Y	N	Y	Y	Y	N	N	N
7 Rose	N	?	N	Y	Y	Y	?	Y
8 Hefner	N	?	Y	?	Y	Y	Y	?
9 ***McMillan***	N	N	Y	N	Y	N	N	Y
10 Vacancy [5]								
11 ***Hendon***	N	N	Y	N	Y	N	N	N
NORTH DAKOTA								
AL Dorgan	Y	?	N	Y	Y	N	Y	Y
OHIO								
1 Luken	Y	?	N	N	Y	Y	Y	Y
2 ***Gradison***	Y	?	Y	?	Y	N	Y	N
3 Hall	Y	?	N	Y	N	Y	Y	?
4 ***Oxley***	N	N	Y	N	Y	N	X	N
5 ***Latta***	N	N	Y	?	Y	N	N	N
6 ***McEwen***	N	N	Y	N	Y	N	N	#
7 ***DeWine***	N	Y	Y	N	Y	N	N	Y
8 ***Kindness***	N	N	#	?	N	N	?	?
9 Kaptur	Y	?	N	N	N	Y	Y	?
10 ***Miller***	N	N	Y	N	N	N	N	N
11 Eckart	Y	Y	N	Y	Y	N	Y	Y
12 ***Kasich***	N	N	Y	N	Y	N	Y	N
13 Pease	Y	Y	N	Y	Y	Y	Y	Y
14 Seiberling	Y	Y	N	Y	Y	Y	Y	Y
15 ***Wylie***	N	N	Y	N	Y	N	Y	N
16 ***Regula***	Y	N	Y	N	N	N	Y	N
17 Traficant	Y	Y	N	Y	Y	Y	Y	N
18 Applegate	Y	?	N	N	N	?	Y	N
19 Feighan	Y	Y	N	Y	Y	?	Y	Y
20 Oakar	Y	Y	N	?	Y	Y	Y	Y
21 Stokes	Y	Y	N	?	?	#	Y	Y
OKLAHOMA								
1 Jones	N	?	Y	?	N	N	Y	Y
2 Synar	Y	Y	N	Y	N	N	Y	Y
3 Watkins	N	Y	Y	N	N	Y	Y	N
4 McCurdy	N	?	Y	N	N	Y	Y	?
5 ***Edwards***	N	N	Y	N	N	N	?	?
6 English	N	N	Y	N	N	N	Y	N
OREGON								
1 AuCoin	Y	N	N	Y	Y	Y	Y	Y
2 ***Smith, R.***	Y	N	Y	N	Y	N	N	N
3 Wyden	Y	Y	N	Y	Y	N	Y	Y
4 Weaver	Y	?	N	Y	N	?	?	?
5 ***Smith, D.***	N	N	Y	N	N	N	N	N
PENNSYLVANIA								
1 Foglietta	Y	?	N	Y	Y	Y	Y	Y
2 Gray	Y	Y	N	Y	Y	Y	Y	Y
3 Borski	Y	Y	N	Y	Y	Y	Y	Y
4 Kolter	Y	Y	N	N	N	N	Y	N
5 ***Schulze***	N	N	Y	?	Y	N	Y	?
6 Yatron	Y	?	Y	?	Y	Y	Y	N
7 Edgar	Y	Y	N	?	Y	Y	Y	?
8 Kostmayer	Y	Y	N	Y	Y	Y	Y	Y
9 ***Shuster***	N	?	Y	N	N	N	N	N
10 ***McDade***	N	?	Y	N	Y	Y	?	Y
11 Kanjorski	Y	Y	N	Y	Y	Y	Y	Y
12 Murtha	N	Y	Y	Y	Y	Y	Y	Y
13 ***Coughlin***	Y	N	Y	Y	Y	N	Y	Y
14 Coyne	Y	Y	N	Y	Y	Y	Y	Y
15 ***Ritter***	N	N	Y	N	Y	N	N	N
16 ***Walker***	N	N	Y	N	Y	N	Y	N
17 ***Gekas***	N	N	Y	N	N	N	Y	N
18 Walgren	Y	N	N	Y	Y	?	Y	Y
19 ***Goodling***	Y	N	Y	N	Y	N	Y	Y
20 Gaydos	N	?	Y	Y	Y	Y	?	N
21 ***Ridge***	N	N	Y	N	Y	N	Y	Y
22 Murphy	N	Y	N	N	N	N	Y	N
23 ***Clinger***	Y	N	Y	N	Y	N	Y	Y
RHODE ISLAND								
1 St Germain	Y	Y	N	Y	Y	N	Y	Y
2 ***Schneider***	Y	N	N	Y	Y	Y	+	?
SOUTH CAROLINA								
1 ***Hartnett***	?	?	#	?	N	?	?	?
2 ***Spence***	N	N	Y	N	N	N	N	N
3 Derrick	Y	Y	N	Y	Y	Y	?	Y
4 ***Campbell***	?	?	#	?	Y	?	?	?
5 Spratt	N	Y	N	Y	Y	Y	Y	Y
6 Tallon	N	Y	Y	?	N	Y	Y	N
SOUTH DAKOTA								
AL Daschle	Y	Y	N	Y	N	N	Y	Y
TENNESSEE								
1 ***Quillen***	N	N	Y	?	Y	N	N	Y
2 ***Duncan***	N	N	Y	N	Y	N	Y	N
3 Lloyd	N	Y	Y	N	Y	N	Y	N
4 Cooper	Y	Y	N	?	Y	Y	Y	Y
5 Boner	N	?	N	Y	Y	Y	Y	N
6 Gordon	Y	Y	N	N	N	?	Y	N
7 ***Sundquist***	N	N	Y	N	N	N	N	N
8 Jones	N	Y	N	N	Y	Y	Y	N
9 Ford	Y	Y	X	?	Y	?	Y	Y
TEXAS								
1 Chapman	N	Y	Y	Y	N	Y	Y	N
2 Wilson	N	Y	Y	?	Y	Y	Y	Y
3 ***Bartlett***	N	N	Y	N	N	N	N	N
4 Hall	N	Y	Y	N	N	N	?	N
5 Bryant	Y	Y	Y	Y	N	Y	Y	Y
6 ***Barton***	N	N	Y	?	Y	N	N	N
7 ***Archer***	N	N	Y	N	N	N	N	N
8 ***Fields***	N	N	Y	N	N	N	N	N
9 Brooks	Y	Y	N	Y	N	Y	Y	?
10 Pickle	Y	N	Y	Y	Y	Y	Y	Y
11 Leath	N	?	N	N	N	Y	Y	N
12 Wright	Y	Y	N	N	N	Y	Y	Y
13 ***Boulter***	N	N	Y	N	Y	N	N	N
14 ***Sweeney***	N	N	Y	N	N	N	N	N
15 de la Garza	N	Y	N	N	N	Y	Y	N
16 Coleman	N	Y	N	Y	N	Y	Y	N
17 Stenholm	N	Y	Y	N	N	N	N	N
18 Leland	Y	Y	N	Y	N	Y	Y	N
19 ***Combest***	N	N	Y	N	N	N	N	N
20 Gonzalez	Y	Y	N	Y	N	Y	Y	N
21 ***Loeffler***	N	?	Y	?	N	N	N	N
22 ***DeLay***	N	N	Y	N	N	N	N	N
23 Bustamante	N	Y	Y	?	N	Y	Y	Y
24 Frost	Y	Y	Y	Y	N	Y	Y	Y
25 Andrews	N	Y	Y	N	Y	Y	Y	N
26 ***Armey***	N	N	Y	N	Y	N	N	N
27 Ortiz	N	Y	Y	?	N	Y	Y	Y
UTAH								
1 ***Hansen***	N	?	Y	?	N	N	N	N
2 ***Monson***	N	N	Y	?	N	N	N	Y
3 ***Nielson***	N	N	Y	N	N	N	N	Y
VERMONT								
AL ***Jeffords***	Y	Y	N	Y	Y	Y	Y	Y
VIRGINIA								
1 ***Bateman***	N	Y	Y	N	N	N	Y	N
2 ***Whitehurst***	N	?	Y	?	N	?	Y	N
3 ***Bliley***	N	N	Y	N	Y	N	Y	N
4 Sisisky	N	Y	N	N	N	Y	Y	Y
5 Daniel	N	N	Y	N	N	N	N	?
6 Olin	Y	Y	N	Y	N	Y	Y	N
7 ***Slaughter***	N	N	Y	N	Y	N	N	N
8 ***Parris***	N	Y	Y	N	N	N	N	N
9 Boucher	Y	?	N	?	N	Y	Y	Y
10 ***Wolf***	N	Y	Y	N	N	N	Y	N
WASHINGTON								
1 ***Miller***	Y	N	Y	Y	Y	N	Y	Y
2 Swift	Y	Y	N	Y	N	?	Y	Y
3 Bonker	Y	?	X	Y	N	Y	?	Y
4 ***Morrison***	N	N	Y	N	Y	Y	Y	Y
5 Foley	Y	Y	N	Y	Y	Y	Y	Y
6 Dicks	N	Y	N	Y	Y	Y	Y	Y
7 Lowry	Y	Y	N	Y	N	N	Y	Y
8 ***Chandler***	N	N	Y	N	N	N	Y	Y
WEST VIRGINIA								
1 Mollohan	N	Y	Y	N	Y	Y	Y	Y
2 Staggers	Y	Y	N	Y	Y	Y	Y	Y
3 Wise	Y	Y	N	Y	Y	Y	Y	Y
4 Rahall	Y	Y	N	Y	Y	Y	Y	Y
WISCONSIN								
1 Aspin	N	?	N	?	Y	Y	Y	Y
2 Kastenmeier	Y	Y	N	Y	Y	+	Y	Y
3 ***Gunderson***	Y	N	Y	N	Y	N	Y	Y
4 Kleczka	Y	Y	N	Y	Y	Y	Y	N
5 Moody	Y	Y	N	?	Y	N	Y	Y
6 ***Petri***	N	N	Y	N	Y	N	Y	N
7 Obey	Y	Y	N	Y	Y	Y	Y	Y
8 ***Roth***	N	N	Y	N	Y	N	N	N
9 ***Sensenbrenner***	Y	N	Y	N	N	N	Y	N
WYOMING								
AL ***Cheney***	N	N	Y	?	N	N	N	Y

Southern states - Ala., Ark., Fla., Ga., Ky., La., Miss., N.C., Okla., S.C., Tenn., Texas, Va.

Hill Support for President Drops to 10-Year Low

Ronald Reagan's success in Congress dipped for the fifth consecutive year, illustrating that for legislators as well as their constituents, the president's policies were less popular than he was.

Reagan won 56.1 percent of the roll-call votes on issues for which he clearly had staked a position, according to Congressional Quarterly's annual analysis.

That was the lowest success rate in a decade, since Republican Gerald R. Ford in 1976 prevailed on 53.8 percent of such votes in a Congress totally dominated by Democrats. Reagan's 1986 score was the fourth lowest in the 34 years that CQ had compiled the analysis.

Reagan's decline, however, was wholly due to losses in the Democratic-controlled House. There was a notable increase over the previous year in the percentage of victories Reagan won in the Republican-controlled Senate.

The drop in the president's overall success rating from 1985 was small, 3.8 percentage points. But it brought to just over 26 points the slippage Reagan suffered since 1981, his first year in office, when Congress bowed to his election mandate and all but rubber-stamped his program of budget and tax cuts. For that honeymoon year, his scorecard in Congress showed an 82.4 percent success rate. The grades since had declined each year.

Separate scores for Reagan's success in the House and Senate followed the expected pattern, with victories common in the Senate and defeats a fact of political life in the House.

Of the Senate roll-call votes analyzed, Reagan was on the winning side 81 percent of the time. That was an increase of more than 9 percentage points from the year before. It partly reversed the 14-point decline that Reagan suffered in 1985, a time when members of both parties opposed him on numerous trade and farm-policy votes.

Reagan's success in the Senate in part contradicted signs of growing restiveness, not only among Democrats in the minority but also among some Republicans facing reelection in 1986 who had divorced themselves from administration policies on trade, agriculture, foreign policy and the environment.

In the House, in contrast, only one of three roll-call votes, 33 percent, went Reagan's way. The 1986 score was 12 percentage points lower than in 1985, and less than half of Reagan's stunning 72 percent success rate in 1981. This was the third year of Reagan's six years in office that he won House votes less than half the time.

Three-fourths of the House roll-call votes that Reagan lost were on budget and domestic-spending questions, arms control, trade restrictions or South Africa sanctions.

The tracking of Reagan's dwindling success in the House in part offered rough evidence that members were taking advantage of a consistent finding of public opinion polls: That while Reagan had strong personal support nationwide, many of his proposals did not.

Rep. William H. Gray III, D-Pa., said Congress would buck the president on issues "where he has clearly gotten out of step with the American people." In 1986, Gray added, that translated into opposition to Reagan's proposed domestic program cuts and defense spending hikes, and rejection of his foreign policy toward the government in South Africa.

That was true as well in the Senate. The finding that Reagan's percentage of victories was up appreciably in that chamber masked several significant defeats for the president, including initial approval of South Africa sanctions, a subsequent 78-21 override of his veto on sanctions and the 88-8 passage of an expanded "superfund" toxic-waste cleanup program.

"Congress is asserting itself, and has been ever since Reagan's first two years in office," said Rep. Anthony C. Beilenson, D-Calif.

Walter Kravitz, an adjunct professor at the Catholic University of America in Washington, agreed. "Congress clearly acted more independently this year than in the previous Reagan years," he said. "I wouldn't go so far as to say the president is a lame duck; that's absurd. His strength is still based on enormous public popularity. And that can't help but influence Congress."

Some Caveats

This analysis is based on 173 votes, 90 in the House

Success Rate

Following are the annual percentages of presidential victories since 1953 on congressional votes where the presidents took a clear-cut position:

Eisenhower	
1953	89.0%
1954	82.8
1955	75.0
1956	70.0
1957	68.0
1958	76.0
1959	52.0
1960	65.0

Kennedy	
1961	81.0%
1962	85.4
1963	87.1

Johnson	
1964	88.0%
1965	93.0
1966	79.0
1967	79.0
1968	75.0

Nixon	
1969	74.0%
1970	77.0
1971	75.0
1972	66.0
1973	50.6
1974	59.6

Ford	
1974	58.2%
1975	61.0
1976	53.8

Carter	
1977	75.4%
1978	78.3
1979	76.8
1980	75.1

Reagan	
1981	82.4%
1982	72.4
1983	67.1
1984	65.8
1985	59.9
1986	56.1

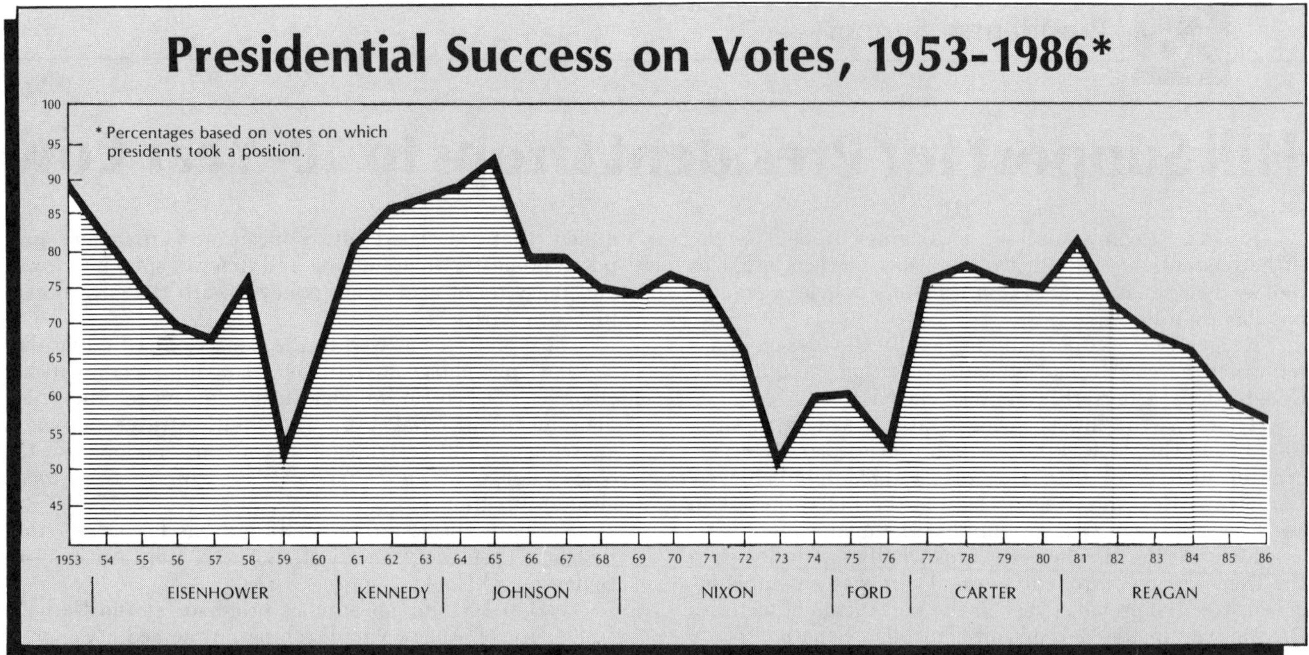

and 83 in the Senate, for which the president had a well-known position. *(Ground rules, box, p. 23-C)*

The study is two-pronged. First, it measures the president's *success* — that is, his percentage of victories on roll-call votes. And second, it separately assesses members' *support* or *opposition* to the president's positions, regardless of whether those positions were the winning ones. Support and opposition are measured for each chamber, both parties and individual members.

Since President Eisenhower's first year in office in 1953, these CQ studies have been a gauge of relations between Congress and seven presidents. For Reagan, like his predecessors, the results show that a chief executive's legislative wishes traditionally get a cooler reception in Congress the longer the president is in office.

Despite the study's value as a yardstick measuring the political distance between the White House and Capitol Hill, readers and researchers should be aware of several limitations.

First, the analysis does not show how much of the president's program was enacted. Victories in the Senate, for instance, are meaningless if Reagan then loses in the House. Also, the CQ study considers only issues that were put to roll-call votes on the House or Senate floors; Reagan's initiatives that never made it to the floor, or those that won or lost on unrecorded voice votes, are not included.

For example, because the House June 18 called for a near-total break in trade relations with South Africa by voice vote, the CQ study does not reflect that blow to Reagan's policy of maintaining economic ties with that country's white-minority government. (However, the study does include three later votes on South Africa sanctions, two when the House acted Sept. 12 to accept the Senate version of the bill (HR 4868) and the Sept. 29 vote to override Reagan's veto.)

A second cautionary note is that the study takes account only of those votes for which the president had a clear and unmistakable opinion.

Third, all votes have equal weight, regardless of an issue's importance or the closeness of the vote. In addition, the study does not take into account whether Congress or the president initiated the proposal. Thus, a measure embraced by the administration late in the legislative process is given equal weight with a proposal that originated in the White House.

For example, in gauging House support for Reagan, a minor bill adding land to the Gettysburg National Military Park (HR 4259), which passed 408-1 on July 16 with administration support, carries the same weight as the narrow June 25 vote approving the president's request for $100 million in aid to Nicaraguan rebels, a major triumph for his foreign policy.

Finally, issues that are the subject of numerous roll-call votes can have disproportionate impact on study results. Of the 83 Senate roll-call votes studied, 24 — or 29 percent — were on Reagan's policy of support for rebels trying to overthrow Nicaragua's government, a policy that has the Republican Senate's support. All but one of the 24 votes went in the president's favor, contributing heavily to his success rating for the Senate.

A reporter or researcher interested in how a member voted on specific aspects of Reagan's program should look at that legislator's record. One gauge is CQ's annual selection and analysis of the year's key votes.

Support: Party, Regional Patterns

As usual, support for Reagan was far greater in the Senate than in the House, and much higher among his fellow Republicans than among Democrats.

Overall, senators supported Reagan's stance on 58 percent of the roll-call votes — roughly the same percentage he has received from the start of his administration.

(The support rate is different from the success rate. The support score is based on all votes cast by individual members, and is not affected by whether the president wins or loses the vote. Success scores, on the other hand, compare the outcome of votes with the president's position.)

House support for the president was 42 percent, the

Ground Rules for CQ Presidential Support-Opposition

Presidential Issues — CQ tries to determine what the president personally, as distinct from other administration officials, does and does not want in the way of legislative action by analyzing his messages to Congress, press conference remarks and other public statements and documents. Members must be aware of the position when the vote is taken.

Borderline Cases — By the time an issue reaches a vote, it may differ from the original form in which the president expressed himself. In such cases, CQ analyzes the measure to determine whether, on balance, the features favored by the president outweigh those he opposed or vice versa. Only then is the vote classified.

Some Votes Excluded — Occasionally, important measures are so extensively amended on the floor that it is impossible to characterize final passage as a victory or defeat for the president.

Procedural Votes — Votes on motions to recommit, to reconsider or to table often are key tests that govern the legislative outcome. Such votes are necessarily included in the presidential support tabulations.

Appropriations — Generally, votes on passage of appropriations bills are not included in the tabulations, since it is rarely possible to determine the president's position on the revisions Congress almost invariably makes in the sums allowed. However, votes on amendments to cut or increase specific amounts requested in the president's budget are included.

Failure to Vote — In tabulating the support or opposition scores of members on the selected presidential-issue votes, CQ counts only "yea" and "nay" votes on the ground that only these affect the outcome. Most failures to vote reflect absences because of illness or official business. Failures to vote lower both support and opposition scores equally.

Weighting — All presidential-issue votes have equal statistical weight in the analysis.

Changed Positions — Presidential support is determined by the position of the president at the time of a vote, even though that position may be different from an earlier position, or may have been reversed after the vote was taken.

lowest of the Reagan years. House support for Reagan was greatest — 54 percent — in 1981.

Among Republicans, support for the president stayed fairly constant. Republican senators cast 78 percent of their votes in support of Reagan's position, up 3 points from 1985. The House Republican support score was 65 percent, down 2 points from 1985.

Among Democrats, senators supported him 37 percent of the time in 1986, 2 percentage points higher than their 1985 low of 35 percent.

House Democrats set a new low for support — 25 percent, down 5 points from 1985.

A breakdown by party and region (East, West, South and Midwest) shows little change from 1985, except that Reagan regained support he had lost among Southern senators from both parties.

Senate Allies, Foes

One Southern Republican, Sen. Phil Gramm of Texas, gave Reagan 99 percent support — the only member of Congress to do so in 1986.

The Senate Republican who opposed Reagan most in 1986, with an unusually high opposition score of 65 percent, was Arlen Specter of Pennsylvania. Specter was typically among the president's more reliable backers; in the previous five years, his opposition scores ranged from 22 percent to 44 percent. But he faced re-election, and Reagan's policies, particularly on trade, were odious to many Pennsylvanians. Twenty-two of the Senate's 47 Democrats supported Reagan more often than Republican Specter.

Republican Bob Packwood of Oregon, who was also up for re-election, but was no longer considered in danger of defeat, opposed Reagan on 45 percent of the votes. That score was up markedly from 25 percent in 1985.

Reagan's top 10 supporters among Senate Democrats were mostly Southerners and Nebraska's Edward Zorinsky, a former Republican. Russell B. Long of Louisiana, retiring after 38 years, was Reagan's most frequent Democratic ally, with 77 percent support. The Democrat most likely to oppose Reagan in 1986, Donald W. Riegle Jr. of Michigan, did so 82 percent of the time.

Senate Minority Leader Robert C. Byrd of West Virginia supported Reagan 36 percent of the time, about the average for his fellow Senate Democrats.

In contrast, Byrd's only declared challenger for the Democratic leadership post, J. Bennett Johnston of Louisiana, had the eighth highest score among Democrats in support of Reagan, 58 percent.

The comparison illustrated Senate Democrats' dilemma: While some wanted a more forceful and articulate leader, especially if their party regained control of the Senate, they were wary of turning to a conservative who supported the Republican president more often than not.

Loyal Support and Opposition in the House

In the previous year, Texas Republicans dominated the list of Reagan's top House supporters. In 1986, the distinction belonged to Republicans from California; half of the top 10 Reagan loyalists were from that state. But the highest score, 88 percent, belonged to Arizona Republican Bob Stump.

Republicans most often opposed to Reagan continued to be members from Northeastern states. Of those, most often at odds with the president was Silvio O. Conte of Massachusetts, with an opposition score of 72 percent.

All of Reagan's top Democratic supporters in the House were Southerners. No. 1, with 66 percent, was Charles W. Stenholm of Texas.

Majority Leader Jim Wright of Texas, who was considered likely to be elected House Speaker in the 100th Congress, backed Reagan 19 percent of the time in 1986.

Freshman Democrat James A. Traficant Jr. of Ohio opposed Reagan more often than any member, 90 percent of the time.

Average Scores

Following are composites of Democratic and Republican scores for 1986 and 1985:

	1986		1985	
	Dem.	**Rep.**	**Dem.**	**Rep.**
		SUPPORT		
Senate	37%	78%	35%	75%
House	25	65	30	67
		OPPOSITION		
Senate	61%	19%	61%	19%
House	70	29	66	30

Regional Averages

SUPPORT

Regional presidential support scores for 1986; scores for 1985 are in parentheses:

	East		West		South		Midwest	
DEMOCRATS								
Senate	30%	(31)	28%	(27)	53%	(44)	31%	(34)
House	20	(26)	19	(23)	35	(41)	20	(25)
REPUBLICANS								
Senate	66%	(67)	80%	(77)	86%	(78)	77%	(78)
House	56	(58)	71	(72)	70	(72)	64	(66)

OPPOSITION

Regional presidential opposition scores for 1986; scores for 1985 are in parentheses:

	East		West		South		Midwest	
DEMOCRATS								
Senate	67%	(66)	69%	(69)	44%	(52)	67%	(62)
House	74	(70)	76	(72)	59	(55)	76	(72)
REPUBLICANS								
Senate	31%	(29)	15%	(16)	12%	(16)	22%	(20)
House	41	(39)	22	(24)	24	(26)	29	(31)

(CQ defines regions of the United States as follows: ***East:*** *Conn., Del., Maine, Md., Mass., N.H., N.J., N.Y., Pa., R.I., Vt., W.Va.* ***West:*** *Alaska, Ariz., Calif., Colo., Hawaii, Idaho, Mont., Nev., N.M., Ore., Utah, Wash., Wyo.* ***South:*** *Ala., Ark., Fla., Ga., Ky., La., Miss., N.C., Okla., S.C., Tenn., Texas, Va.* ***Midwest:*** *Ill., Ind., Iowa, Kan., Mich., Minn., Mo., Neb., N.D., Ohio, S.D., Wis.)*

Highest Scorers — Support

Highest individual scorers in presidential support — those who voted most often for Reagan's position in 1986.

SENATE

Democrats		Republicans	
Long, La.	77%	Gramm, Texas	99%
Heflin, Ala.	76	Armstrong, Colo.	94
Hollings, S.C.	70	Wallop, Wyo.	93
Boren, Okla.	67	Simpson, Wyo.	92
Zorinsky, Neb.	64	Dole, Kan.	92
Stennis, Miss.	63	Hatch, Utah	92
Bentsen, Texas	60	Humphrey, N.H.	92
Johnston, La.	58	McClure, Idaho	92
Nunn, Ga.	58		

HOUSE

Democrats		Republicans	
Stenholm, Texas	66%	Stump, Ariz.	88%
Daniel, Va.	61	Mack, Fla.	86
Montgomery, Miss.	58	Shumway, Calif.	86
Hutto, Fla.	57	Lungren, Calif.	86
Ray, Ga.	56	McCollum, Fla.	84
Hall, Texas	56	Packard, Calif.	83
Barnard, Ga.	54	DeLay, Texas	83
Lloyd, Tenn.	53	Dreier, Calif.	83
Leath, Texas	53		
Dyson, Md.	53		

1986 Presidential Position Votes

Following is a list of all Senate and House recorded votes in 1986 on which President Reagan took a position. The votes, listed by CQ vote number, appear in the vote charts in the 1986 Weekly Reports.

Senate Votes (83)

Presidential Victories (67) — 1, 2, 3, 10, 12, 15, 16, 26, 39, 40, 41, 42, 46, 48, 49, 50, 51, 90, 92, 99, 101, 111, 125, 126, 127, 148, 152, 155, 160, 162, 163, 164, 167, 176, 177, 181, 182, 184, 192, 196, 211, 212, 213, 214, 215, 216, 217, 220, 221, 222, 223, 224, 225, 226, 227, 228, 229, 230, 234, 265, 266, 267, 296, 299, 339, 340, 346.

Presidential Defeats (16) — 45, 56, 76, 91, 94, 112, 113, 183, 189, 190, 218, 231, 264, 311, 329, 342.

House Votes (90)

Presidential Victories (30) — 22, 40, 54, 60, 68, 69, 81, 90, 178, 179, 180, 193, 198, 202, 215, 217, 221, 232, 264, 265, 293, 296, 298, 310, 315, 356, 362, 372, 378, 379.

Presidential Defeats (60) — 18, 27, 28, 33, 35, 36, 42, 44, 45, 48, 50, 58, 71, 72, 80, 85, 92, 94, 97, 102, 108, 117, 120, 121, 122, 124, 125, 126, 128, 130, 154, 155, 156, 164, 166, 177, 181, 195, 246, 250, 252, 287, 299, 300, 301, 309, 311, 327, 337, 338, 350, 351, 369, 383, 390, 407, 408, 416, 417, 434.

High Scorers — Opposition

Highest individual scorers in presidential opposition — those who voted most often against Reagan's position in 1986.

SENATE

Democrats		Republicans	
Riegle, Mich.	82%	Specter, Pa.	65%
Sarbanes, Md.	81	Hatfield, Ore.	57
Burdick, N.D.	81	Mathias, Md.	52
Melcher, Mont.	80	Weicker, Conn.	52
Harkin, Iowa	78	Packwood, Ore.	45
Cranston, Calif.	78	Andrews, N.D.	42
Simon, Ill.	78	Stafford, Vt.	40
Levin, Mich.	77		

HOUSE

Democrats		Republicans	
Traficant, Ohio	90%	Conte, Mass.	72%
Kildee, Mich.	87	Horton, N.Y.	67
Gejdenson, Conn.	87	Schneider, R.I.	66
Waxman, Calif.	86	McKinney, Conn.	64
Wheat, Mo.	86	Green, N.Y.	62
Dellums, Calif.	86	Jeffords, Vt.	58
Evans, Ill.	86	Rinaldo, N.J.	58
Hayes, Ill.	84	Henry, Mich.	57
Studds, Mass.	84	Fish, N.Y.	56
Edwards, Calif.	84		

	1	2
ALABAMA		
Denton	84	14
Heflin	76	24
ALASKA		
Murkowski	80	17
Stevens	83	11
ARIZONA		
Goldwater	70	8
DeConcini	43	53
ARKANSAS		
Bumpers	39	59
Pryor	35	60
CALIFORNIA		
Wilson	82	18
Cranston	20	78
COLORADO		
Armstrong	94	5
Hart	23	73
CONNECTICUT		
Weicker	45	52
Dodd	25	73
DELAWARE		
Roth	83	16
Biden	27	67
FLORIDA		
Hawkins	66	12
Chiles	57	39
GEORGIA		
Mattingly	82	17
Nunn	58	39
HAWAII		
Inouye	17	70
Matsunaga	25	71
IDAHO		
McClure	92	6
Symms	86	6
ILLINOIS		
Dixon	51	46
Simon	19	78
INDIANA		
Lugar	88	11
Quayle	90	8
IOWA		
Grassley	67	31
Harkin	19	78
KANSAS		
Dole	92	8
Kassebaum	70	24
KENTUCKY		
McConnell	87	13
Ford	34	66
LOUISIANA		
Johnston	58	42
Long	77	19
MAINE		
Cohen	78	22
Mitchell	31	66
MARYLAND		
Mathias	36	52
Sarbanes	18	81
MASSACHUSETTS		
Kennedy	28	69
Kerry	22	75
MICHIGAN		
Levin	23	77
Riegle	18	82
MINNESOTA		
Boschwitz	84	16
Durenberger	64	33
MISSISSIPPI		
Cochran	88	10
Stennis	63	23
MISSOURI		
Danforth	80	20
Eagleton	29	65
MONTANA		
Baucus	30	66
Melcher	20	80
NEBRASKA		
Exon	34	64
Zorinsky	64	36
NEVADA		
Hecht	89	10
Laxalt	86	7
NEW HAMPSHIRE		
Humphrey	92	5
Rudman	90	8
NEW JERSEY		•
Bradley	51	48
Lautenberg	30	69
NEW MEXICO		
Domenici	88	12
Bingaman	41	58
NEW YORK		
D'Amato	77	23
Moynihan	40	59
NORTH CAROLINA		
Broyhill † [1]	86	8
Helms	90	10
NORTH DAKOTA		
Andrews	57	42
Burdick	18	81
OHIO		
Glenn	42	52
Metzenbaum	24	76
OKLAHOMA		
Nickles	86	14
Boren	67	30
OREGON		
Hatfield	42	57
Packwood	49	45
PENNSYLVANIA		
Heinz	69	31
Specter	31	65
RHODE ISLAND		
Chafee	67	31
Pell	30	67
SOUTH CAROLINA		
Thurmond	89	10
Hollings	70	30
SOUTH DAKOTA		
Abdnor	73	27
Pressler	77	20
TENNESSEE		
Gore	29	71
Sasser	24	76
TEXAS		
Gramm	99	1
Bentsen	60	37
UTAH		
Garn	80	5
Hatch	92	8
VERMONT		
Stafford	55	40
Leahy	24	70
VIRGINIA		
Trible	83	16
Warner	87	13
WASHINGTON		
Evans	76	23
Gorton	73	25
WEST VIRGINIA		
Byrd	36	64
Rockefeller	31	69
WISCONSIN		
Kasten	81	19
Proxmire	28	72
WYOMING		
Simpson	92	8
Wallop	93	5

KEY

† Not eligible for all recorded votes in 1986 (sworn in after Jan. 21) or voted "present" to avoid possible conflict of interest.

Democrats ***Republicans***

Presidential Support and Opposition: Senate

1. Reagan Support Score, 1986. Percentage of 83 Reagan-issue recorded votes in 1986 on which senator voted "yea" or "nay" *in agreement* with the president's position. Failures to vote lower both Support and Opposition scores.

2. Reagan Opposition Score, 1986. Percentage of 83 Reagan-issue recorded votes in 1986 on which representative voted "yea" or "nay" *in disagreement* with the president's position. Failures to vote lower both Support and Opposition scores.

[1] *Sen. James T. Broyhill, R-N.C., was sworn in July 14, 1986, to succeed John P. East, R, who died June 29, 1986. East's 1986 presidential support score was 86 percent; opposition was 8 percent.*

Presidential Support and Opposition: House

1. Reagan Support Score, 1986. Percentage of 90 Reagan-issue recorded votes in 1986 on which representative voted "yea" or "nay" *in agreement* with the president's position. Failures to vote lower both Support and Opposition scores.

2. Reagan Opposition Score, 1986. Percentage of 90 Reagan-issue recorded votes in 1986 on which representative voted "yea" or "nay" *in disagreement* with the president's position. Failures to vote lower both Support and Opposition scores.

** Rep. John E. Grotberg, R-Ill., has not participated in House business this year due to a serious illness.*

[1] Rep. Neil Abercrombie, D-Hawaii, was sworn in Sept. 23, 1986, to succeed Cecil Heftel, D, who resigned July 11, 1986, to run for governor of Hawaii. Heftel's 1986 presidential support score was 6 percent; opposition was 63 percent.

[2] Rep. George M. O'Brien, R-Ill., died July 17, 1986. O'Brien's 1986 presidential support score was 17 percent; opposition was 27 percent.

[3] Rep. Thomas P. O'Neill Jr., D-Mass., as Speaker votes at his own discretion.

[4] Rep. Alton R. Waldon Jr., D-N.Y., was sworn in July 29, 1986, to succeed Joseph P. Addabbo, D, who died April 10, 1986. Addabbo's 1986 presidential support score was 0 percent; opposition was 33 percent.

[5] James T. Broyhill, R-N.C., resigned on July 13, 1986, to fill the vacant seat resulting from the June 29 death of Sen. John P. East. Broyhill's 1986 House presidential support score was 63 percent; opposition was 29 percent.

KEY

† Not eligible for all recorded votes in 1986 (sworn in after Jan. 21) or voted "present" to avoid possible conflict of interest.

Democrats ***Republicans***

	1	2
ALABAMA		
1 ***Callahan***	73	21
2 ***Dickinson***	71	22
3 Nichols	49	36
4 Bevill	40	58
5 Flippo	33	53
6 Erdreich	40	59
7 Shelby	44	49
ALASKA		
AL ***Young***	61	33
ARIZONA		
1 ***McCain***	68	29
2 Udall	19	77
3 ***Stump***	88	11
4 ***Rudd***	64	8
5 ***Kolbe***	69	29
ARKANSAS		
1 Alexander	22	67
2 Robinson	46	50
3 ***Hammerschmidt***	69	31
4 Anthony	27	64
CALIFORNIA		
1 Bosco	21	72
2 ***Chappie***	63	19
3 Matsui	20	80
4 Fazio	20	80
5 Burton	11	54
6 Boxer	13	78
7 Miller	14	80
8 Dellums	12	86
9 Stark	18	77
10 Edwards	16	84
11 Lantos	23	76
12 ***Zschau***	52	19
13 Mineta	22	76
14 ***Shumway***	86	14
15 Coelho	21	71
16 Panetta	20	77
17 ***Pashayan***	58	40
18 Lehman	20	76
19 ***Lagomarsino***	80	19
20 ***Thomas***	76	19
21 ***Fiedler***	66	17
22 ***Moorhead***	82	17
23 Beilenson	18	81
24 Waxman	12	86
25 Roybal	16	80
26 Berman	18	80
27 Levine	16	81
28 Dixon	13	74
29 Hawkins	19	73
30 Martinez	18	76
31 Dymally	13	83
32 Anderson	22	78
33 ***Dreier***	83	16
34 Torres	18	80
35 ***Lewis***	63	21
36 Brown	18	71
37 ***McCandless***	77	18
38 ***Dornan***	80	13
39 ***Dannemeyer***	81	17
40 ***Badham***	64	12
41 ***Lowery***	76	21
42 ***Lungren***	86	12
43 ***Packard***	83	16
44 Bates	19	81
45 ***Hunter***	78	20
COLORADO		
1 Schroeder	19	78
2 Wirth	27	72
3 ***Strang***	76	22
4 ***Brown***	67	32
5 ***Kramer***	64	27
6 ***Schaefer***	76	21
CONNECTICUT		
1 Kennelly	20	78
2 Gejdenson	13	87
3 Morrison	16	68
4 ***McKinney***	31	64
5 ***Rowland***	61	39
6 ***Johnson***	52	43
DELAWARE		
AL Carper	30	69
FLORIDA		
1 Hutto	57	40
2 Fuqua	40	51
3 Bennett	33	67
4 Chappell	43	50
5 ***McCollum***	84	14
6 MacKay	29	70
7 Gibbons	33	62
8 ***Young***	72	26
9 ***Bilirakis***	77	21
10 ***Ireland***	74	18
11 Nelson	43	56
12 ***Lewis***	71	26
13 ***Mack***	86	12
14 Mica	26	72
15 ***Shaw***	79	19
16 Smith	27	73
17 Lehman	20	78
18 Pepper	30	59
19 Fascell	28	70
GEORGIA		
1 Thomas	47	53
2 Hatcher	34	54
3 Ray	56	43
4 ***Swindall***	82	18
5 Fowler	17	42
6 ***Gingrich***	72	23
7 Darden	49	48
8 Rowland	44	56
9 Jenkins	41	52
10 Barnard	54	32
HAWAII		
1 Abercrombie [1] †	27	64
2 Akaka	18	79
IDAHO		
1 ***Craig***	79	21
2 Stallings	42	58
ILLINOIS		
1 Hayes	13	84
2 Savage	14	80
3 Russo	18	79
4 Vacancy [2]		
5 Lipinski	42	54
6 ***Hyde***	76	21
7 Collins	12	71
8 Rostenkowski	19	66
9 Yates	18	77
10 ***Porter***	59	39
11 Annunzio	23	73
12 ***Crane***	82	16
13 ***Fawell***	69	30
14 ***Grotberg*** *	0	0
15 ***Madigan***	67	23
16 ***Martin***	74	24
17 Evans	13	86
18 ***Michel***	74	18
19 Bruce	20	80
20 Durbin	17	82
21 Price	27	73
22 Gray	28	71
INDIANA		
1 Visclosky	19	81
2 Sharp	24	73
3 ***Hiler***	78	21
4 ***Coats***	70	29
5 ***Hillis***	44	29

	1	2
6 ***Burton***	81	18
7 ***Myers***	67	31
8 McCloskey	24	76
9 Hamilton	33	67
10 Jacobs	17	80
IOWA		
1 ***Leach***	47	52
2 ***Tauke***	53	43
3 ***Evans***	54	32
4 Smith	22	70
5 ***Lightfoot***	70	30
6 Bedell	16	80
KANSAS		
1 ***Roberts***	69	31
2 Slattery	34	66
3 ***Meyers***	59	39
4 Glickman	28	70
5 ***Whittaker***	67	31
KENTUCKY		
1 Hubbard	52	48
2 Natcher	29	71
3 Mazzoli	40	58
4 ***Snyder***	73	22
5 ***Rogers***	70	29
6 ***Hopkins***	72	27
7 Perkins	22	78
LOUISIANA		
1 ***Livingston***	76	19
2 Boggs	22	72
3 Tauzin	49	51
4 Roemer	50	48
5 Huckaby	41	49
6 ***Moore***	33	21
7 Breaux	21	28
8 Long	20	73
MAINE		
1 ***McKernan***	43	53
2 ***Snowe***	44	54
MARYLAND		
1 Dyson	53	47
2 ***Bentley***	57	38
3 Mikulski	11	80
4 ***Holt***	63	21
5 Hoyer	21	79
6 Byron	50	50
7 Mitchell	11	69
8 Barnes	11	68
MASSACHUSETTS		
1 ***Conte***	27	72
2 Boland	20	71
3 Early	13	80
4 Frank	18	81
5 Atkins	18	77
6 Mavroules	19	80
7 Markey	11	80
8 O'Neill [3]		
9 Moakley	16	79
10 Studds	16	84
11 Donnelly	18	79
MICHIGAN		
1 Conyers	11	73
2 ***Pursell***	51	46
3 Wolpe	16	82
4 ***Siljander***	73	20
5 ***Henry***	43	57
6 Carr	21	74
7 Kildee	13	87
8 Traxler	19	73
9 ***Vander Jagt***	62	23
10 ***Schuette***	60	39
11 ***Davis***	39	43
12 Bonior	16	79
13 Crockett	12	76
14 Hertel	14	83
15 Ford	18	79
16 Dingell	24	70
17 Levin	19	81
18 ***Broomfield***	70	29
MINNESOTA		
1 Penny	34	66
2 ***Weber***	69	31
3 ***Frenzel***	66	32
4 Vento	19	81
5 Sabo	20	80
6 Sikorski	17	81

	1	2
7 ***Stangeland***	68	29
8 Oberstar	18	79
MISSISSIPPI		
1 Whitten	30	64
2 ***Franklin***	56	30
3 Montgomery	58	42
4 Dowdy	29	66
5 ***Lott***	78	18
MISSOURI		
1 Clay	8	78
2 Young	26	74
3 Gephardt	16	53
4 Skelton	48	47
5 Wheat	14	86
6 ***Coleman***	67	28
7 ***Taylor***	68	23
8 ***Emerson***	69	31
9 Volkmer	33	67
MONTANA		
1 Williams	12	82
2 ***Marlenee***	74	22
NEBRASKA		
1 ***Bereuter***	58	42
2 ***Daub***	78	22
3 ***Smith***	64	32
NEVADA		
1 Reid	26	74
2 ***Vucanovich***	69	24
NEW HAMPSHIRE		
1 ***Smith***	82	18
2 ***Gregg***	74	24
NEW JERSEY		
1 Florio	19	80
2 Hughes	28	72
3 Howard	21	78
4 ***Smith***	46	54
5 ***Roukema***	56	43
6 Dwyer	19	80
7 ***Rinaldo***	40	58
8 Roe	22	77
9 Torricelli	19	74
10 Rodino	16	72
11 ***Gallo***	70	29
12 ***Courter***	69	29
13 ***Saxton***	64	34
14 Guarini	22	76
NEW MEXICO		
1 ***Lujan***	57	20
2 ***Skeen***	68	30
3 Richardson	24	76
NEW YORK		
1 ***Carney***	66	18
2 Downey	18	81
3 Mrazek	17	77
4 ***Lent***	61	33
5 ***McGrath***	60	37
6 Waldon [4] †	14	80
7 Ackerman	12	79
8 Scheuer	18	79
9 Manton	18	77
10 Schumer	17	78
11 Towns	14	77
12 Owens	11	83
13 Solarz	18	76
14 ***Molinari***	69	29
15 ***Green***	38	62
16 Rangel	17	73
17 Weiss	12	79
18 Garcia	13	81
19 Biaggi	27	70
20 ***DioGuardi***	57	43
21 ***Fish***	40	56
22 ***Gilman***	43	53
23 Stratton	50	43
24 ***Solomon***	79	16
25 ***Boehlert***	46	54
26 ***Martin***	53	41
27 ***Wortley***	63	37
28 McHugh	23	76
29 ***Horton***	27	67
30 ***Eckert***	81	17
31 ***Kemp***	69	26
32 LaFalce	19	76
33 Nowak	18	82
34 Lundine	14	60

	1	2
NORTH CAROLINA		
1 Jones	27	62
2 Valentine	41	57
3 Whitley	31	68
4 ***Cobey***	70	28
5 Neal	28	71
6 ***Coble***	68	31
7 Rose	29	64
8 Hefner	30	67
9 ***McMillan***	66	32
10 Vacancy [5]		
11 ***Hendon***	62	36
NORTH DAKOTA		
AL Dorgan	26	73
OHIO		
1 Luken	21	77
2 ***Gradison***	61	34
3 Hall	14	83
4 ***Oxley***	80	16
5 ***Latta***	63	18
6 ***McEwen***	67	22
7 ***DeWine***	78	20
8 ***Kindness***	58	22
9 Kaptur	17	77
10 ***Miller***	77	22
11 Eckart	21	78
12 ***Kasich***	70	29
13 Pease	26	74
14 Seiberling	16	81
15 ***Wylie***	63	31
16 ***Regula***	56	44
17 Traficant	10	90
18 Applegate	24	74
19 Feighan	17	81
20 Oakar	16	80
21 Stokes	11	82
OKLAHOMA		
1 Jones	33	56
2 Synar	24	71
3 Watkins	32	67
4 McCurdy	31	62
5 ***Edwards***	71	23
6 English	43	51
OREGON		
1 AuCoin	29	67
2 ***Smith, R.***	66	31
3 Wyden	23	76
4 Weaver	7	71
5 ***Smith, D.***	74	21
PENNSYLVANIA		
1 Foglietta	16	68
2 Gray	13	77
3 Borski	20	77
4 Kolter	26	72
5 ***Schulze***	58	37
6 Yatron	22	76
7 Edgar	14	51
8 Kostmayer	17	81
9 ***Shuster***	77	22
10 ***McDade***	49	42
11 Kanjorski	22	78
12 Murtha	42	56
13 ***Coughlin***	48	49
14 Coyne	17	81
15 ***Ritter***	70	29
16 ***Walker***	82	17
17 ***Gekas***	76	23
18 Walgren	13	81
19 ***Goodling***	60	37
20 Gaydos	33	59
21 ***Ridge***	47	53
22 Murphy	21	77
23 ***Clinger***	52	47
RHODE ISLAND		
1 St Germain	21	74
2 ***Schneider***	31	66
SOUTH CAROLINA		
1 ***Hartnett***	51	10
2 ***Spence***	69	30
3 Derrick	28	68
4 ***Campbell***	32	14
5 Spratt	28	71
6 Tallon	40	56
SOUTH DAKOTA		
AL Daschle	20	80

	1	2
TENNESSEE		
1 ***Quillen***	62	33
2 ***Duncan***	69	29
3 Lloyd	53	44
4 Cooper	31	68
5 Boner	30	61
6 Gordon	27	72
7 ***Sundquist***	74	24
8 Jones	29	63
9 Ford	16	73
TEXAS		
1 Chapman	37	61
2 Wilson	38	50
3 ***Bartlett***	77	23
4 Hall	56	40
5 Bryant	18	80
6 ***Barton***	76	22
7 ***Archer***	82	17
8 ***Fields***	79	20
9 Brooks	21	69
10 Pickle	39	57
11 Leath	53	43
12 Wright	19	73
13 ***Boulter***	66	32
14 ***Sweeney***	67	28
15 de la Garza	27	64
16 Coleman	29	69
17 Stenholm	66	34
18 Leland	9	83
19 ***Combest***	78	22
20 Gonzalez	17	82
21 ***Loeffler***	51	21
22 ***DeLay***	83	14
23 Bustamante	32	63
24 Frost	23	66
25 Andrews	37	61
26 ***Armey***	82	17
27 Ortiz	36	59
UTAH		
1 ***Hansen***	79	16
2 ***Monson***	73	19
3 ***Nielson***	74	23
VERMONT		
AL ***Jeffords***	41	58
VIRGINIA		
1 ***Bateman***	69	29
2 ***Whitehurst***	61	24
3 ***Bliley***	69	30
4 Sisisky	39	60
5 Daniel	61	36
6 Olin	36	64
7 ***Slaughter***	80	17
8 ***Parris***	70	27
9 Boucher	23	72
10 ***Wolf***	67	33
WASHINGTON		
1 ***Miller***	56	43
2 Swift	19	78
3 Bonker	23	70
4 ***Morrison***	59	41
5 Foley	23	73
6 Dicks	27	73
7 Lowry	17	83
8 ***Chandler***	56	37
WEST VIRGINIA		
1 Mollohan	36	61
2 Staggers	18	82
3 Wise	23	72
4 Rahall	21	76
WISCONSIN		
1 Aspin	28	64
2 Kastenmeier	16	81
3 ***Gunderson***	52	44
4 Kleczka	24	76
5 Moody	18	82
6 ***Petri***	73	27
7 Obey	19	79
8 ***Roth***	68	27
9 ***Sensenbrenner***	73	27
WYOMING		
AL ***Cheney***	81	11

Partisanship Hit New High in 99th Congress

Staking out their positions for the Election Day battle for control of the Senate, Democrats and Republicans divided sharply on most votes in 1986, making the 99th Congress the most partisan in at least three decades.

According to a Congressional Quarterly analysis, a majority of voting Democrats opposed a majority of voting Republicans on 55 percent of all recorded votes in 1986, with party-line divisions showing up on most of the major issues.

That gave the 99th Congress the highest score since 1954, when CQ first started measuring partisanship in this way. In 1985, Congress divided along party lines on 56 percent of its votes, up sharply from 44 percent in 1984. No other Congress exceeded 50 percent in the CQ series.

As a party, Democrats in Congress hung together on 78 percent of all votes in 1986. That is only 1 percentage point lower than 1985, which saw the highest party unity scores ever recorded by CQ. Republicans voted together on 71 percent of all votes in 1986, a 4-point decline from 1985.

Norman J. Ornstein, resident scholar at the American Enterprise Institute, attributed the rise in partisanship in both 1985 and 1986 in the Senate to the question of who would control that chamber. "As soon as the dust had settled from the 1984 election, everyone knew that the Democrats had come within striking distance in the Senate, and they began looking toward 1986," he said.

Majority Leader Robert Dole, R-Kan., designed votes to try to improve Republican prospects, Ornstein said, and that meant drawing distinctions between the parties.

In the House, Ornstein said, a trend toward partisanship had stemmed from growing GOP dissatisfaction with its minority role and an attempt among Democrats to pull their party together.

Party-Line Issues

The House continued to be the more partisan body, as it had been since 1982. Of 451 recorded votes, 57 percent divided along party lines. That was 4 percentage points less than 1985, but far higher than the first two years of the Reagan administration, when the two parties were pitted against each other on roughly one-third of all votes.

In the Senate in 1986, a majority of Republicans voted against a majority of Democrats on 52 percent of roll calls — 2 percentage points higher than 1985, 12 points higher than 1984, and the highest since the 62 percent recorded in 1961, the first year of the Kennedy administration.

Both parties were successful at controlling the outcome of most votes in the chambers they dominated. House Democrats won 84 percent of the partisan votes in their chamber, a 4-point increase from 1985. Republicans won 75 percent of the partisan votes in the Senate, up from 66 percent in 1985.

The Senate's partisan gulf was largely due to votes on economic issues such as budget, appropriations, the debt limit and the tax bill — even though the budget resolution itself (S Con Res 120) was approved 70-25 with bipartisan support. But there were also numerous divisive votes on issues such as aid to Nicaraguan rebels, South Africa sanctions and defense.

A seemingly nonpartisan issue, the transfer of two airports near Washington, D.C., to a regional authority, produced 13 of the 185 partisan votes.

In the House, 63 divided votes came on appropriations bills. Partisanship scores were also boosted by 34 votes to approve the *Journal* of the previous day's proceedings, a procedural motion that Republicans had opposed to express their resentment over the outcome of the 1984 election in Indiana's 8th Congressional District, in which Democrats seated Frank McCloskey, D, over GOP candidate Richard D. McIntyre.

But even if the *Journal* votes were removed from the study, the House score would have been 52 percent — exceeded only twice (1983 and 1985) in the past 20 years.

House Democrats kept closed ranks most often, voting with their party 79 percent of the time. Republican senators stuck together 76 percent of the time. Senate Democrats had a 72 percent score; House Republicans had 70 percent.

Party Dissenters

In both chambers Southern Democrats continued to show the least party unity, voting against their party 39 percent of the time in the Senate and 22 percent of the time in the House. Northern Republicans were the mavericks within their party, voting in opposition on 22 percent of Senate partisan votes and 25 percent of such votes in the House. Both of these findings continued long-established patterns.

In the Senate, Arlen Specter, a Republican facing a close election contest in nominally Democratic Pennsylvania, voted against his party 68 percent of the time — more than twice as often as he did in 1984.

Other Senate Republicans up for re-election also deserted their party on votes fairly often: North Dakota's

Definitions

Party Unity Votes. Recorded votes in the Senate or House that split the parties, with a majority of voting Democrats opposing a majority of voting Republicans.

Party Unity Scores. Percentage of Party Unity votes on which a member votes "yea" or "nay" *in agreement* with a majority of his party. Failure to vote, even if a member announced his stand, lowers his score.

Opposition-to-Party Scores. Percentage of Party Unity votes on which a member votes "yea" or "nay" *in disagreement* with a majority of his party. A member's Party Unity and Opposition-to-Party scores add up to 100 percent only if he voted on all Party Unity votes.

Mark Andrews (50 percent), Oregon's Bob Packwood (36 percent) and New York's Alfonse M. D'Amato (32 percent).

Two retiring senators posted high opposition scores: Russell B. Long, D-La., with 64 percent, and Charles McC. Mathias Jr., R-Md., with 55 percent. Long's score was the highest among Senate Democrats; he was followed by Howell Heflin, D-Ala., with 57 percent.

Rep. Stewart B. McKinney, R-Conn., had the highest opposition score in Congress, 75 percent. This was a significant shift from 1985, when he posted a 49 percent score.

In the House, McKinney was joined by other Republicans from the Northeast in voting against their party most often, as had been the case in recent years. Frank Horton, N.Y., posted a 74 percent opposition score, followed by Bill Green, N.Y., and Silvio O. Conte, Mass., with 73 percent.

Among House Democrats, Charles W. Stenholm of Texas voted against his party 67 percent of the time. The 1985 opposition leader, Buddy Roemer of Louisiana, dropped his opposition score from 72 percent to 55 percent.

Party Loyalists

In the Senate, Republicans with the highest party unity scores were 1985 party unity leader, Chic Hecht of Nevada, plus Phil Gramm of Texas and Jesse Helms of North Carolina. All scored 95 percent. Among Republicans up for re-election, Dan Quayle, Ind., scored 94 percent, and Majority Leader Dole, 92 percent.

Donald W. Riegle Jr. of Michigan and Paul S. Sarbanes of Maryland voted most often with their Democratic colleagues in the Senate with scores of 96 percent.

Among House Democrats, Sander M. Levin, Mich., and Dale E. Kildee, Mich., voted with their party 97 percent of the time. They were followed by Alan Wheat, D-Mo., and Sam Gejdenson, D-Conn., with 96 percent scores.

Dick Armey of Texas led House Republicans with a 97 percent party unity score, followed by Robert C. Smith, N.H., and Robert S. Walker, Pa., at 96 percent.

House Majority Leader Jim Wright, D-Texas, the heir apparent to Speaker Thomas P. O'Neill Jr., D-Mass., voted with his party 83 percent of the time and against it 5 percent. Majority Whip Thomas S. Foley, D-Wash., who was running for majority leader, voted with his party 91 percent of the time and against it 4 percent.

Party Unity Scoreboard

The following table shows the proportion of Party Unity recorded votes in recent years:

	Total Recorded Votes	Party Unity Recorded Votes	Percentage of Total
1986			
Both Chambers	805	440	55%
Senate	354	185	52
House	451	255	57
1985			
Both Chambers	820	457	56
Senate	381	189	50
House	439	268	61
1984			
Both Chambers	683	302	44
Senate	275	110	40
House	408	192	47
1983			
Both Chambers	869	439	51
Senate	371	162	44
House	498	277	56
1982			
Both Chambers	924	369	40
Senate	465	202	43
House	459	167	36
1981			
Both Chambers	836	363	43
Senate	483	231	48
House	353	132	37
1980			
Both Chambers	1,135	470	41
Senate	531	243	46
House	604	227	38
1979			
Both Chambers	1,169	550	47
Senate	497	232	47
House	672	318	47
1978			
Both Chambers	1,350	510	38
Senate	516	233	45
House	834	277	33
1977			
Both Chambers	1,341	567	42
Senate	635	269	42
House	706	298	42
1976			
Both Chambers	1,349	493	37
Senate	688	256	37
House	661	237	36
1975			
Both Chambers	1,214	584	48
Senate	602	288	48
House	612	296	48
1974			
Both Chambers	1,081	399	37
Senate	544	241	44
House	537	158	29
1973			
Both Chambers	1,135	463	41
Senate	594	237	40
House	541	226	42
1972			
Both Chambers	861	283	33
Senate	532	194	36
House	329	89	27
1971			
Both Chambers	743	297	40
Senate	423	176	42
House	320	121	38
1970			
Both Chambers	684	219	32
Senate	418	147	35
House	266	72	27

1986 Victories, Defeats

	Senate	House	Total
Democrats won, Republicans lost	47	215	262
Republicans won, Democrats lost	138	40	178
Democrats voted unanimously	4	3	7
Republicans voted unanimously	4	2	6

Party Scores

Party Unity and Opposition-to-Party scores below are composites of individual scores and show the percentage of time the average Democrat and Republican voted with or against his party majority in disagreement with the other party's majority. Failures to vote lower both Party Unity and Opposition-to-Party scores. Averages are closer to House figures because the House has more members.

	1986		1985	
	Dem.	Rep.	Dem.	Rep.
Party Unity	78%	71%	79%	75%
Senate	72	76	75	76
House	79	70	80	75
Opposition	14%	22%	14%	19%
Senate	25	19	20	18
House	13	22	13	19

Sectional Support, Opposition

SENATE	Support	Opposition
Northern Democrats	78%	19%
Southern Democrats	57	39
Northern Republicans	74	22
Southern Republicans	85	12

HOUSE	Support	Opposition
Northern Democrats	84%	9%
Southern Democrats	68	22
Northern Republicans	68	25
Southern Republicans	75	16

Party Unity History

Composite Party Unity scores showing the percentage of time the average Democrat and Republican voted with his party majority in partisan votes in recent years:

Year	Democrats	Republicans
1986	78%	71%
1985	79	75
1984	74	72
1983	76	74
1982	72	71
1981	69	76
1980	68	70
1979	69	72
1978	64	67
1977	67	70

Individual Scores

Highest Party Unity Scores. Those who in 1986 most consistently voted with their party majority against the majority of the other party:

SENATE

Democrats		Republicans	
Riegle, Mich.	96%	Hecht, Nev.	95%
Sarbanes, Md.	96	Gramm, Texas	95
Levin, Mich.	91	Helms, N.C.	95
Harkin, Iowa	91	Quayle, Ind.	94
Simon, Ill.	89	Wallop, Wyo.	94
Sasser, Tenn.	87	Dole, Kan.	92
Burdick, N.D.	87	Hatch, Utah	92

HOUSE

Democrats		Republicans	
Levin, Mich.	97%	Armey, Texas	97%
Kildee, Mich.	97	Smith, N.H.	96
Wheat, Mo.	96	Walker, Pa.	96
Gejdenson, Conn.	96	Fields, Texas	95
Sabo, Minn.	95	Dreier, Calif.	95
Edwards, Calif.	95	Mack, Fla.	94
Hoyer, Md.	95	Swindall, Ga.	94
Evans, Ill.	95	Burton, Ind.	94
Coyne, Pa.	95	Barton, Texas	93
Mineta, Calif.	95		
Dwyer, N.J.	95		

Highest Opposition-to-Party Scores. Those who in 1986 most consistently voted against their party majority:

SENATE

Democrats		Republicans	
Long, La.	64%	Specter, Pa.	68%
Heflin, Ala.	57	Mathias, Md.	55
Zorinsky, Neb.	55	Andrews, N.D.	50
Boren, Okla.	54	Weicker, Conn.	44
Stennis, Miss.	52	Hatfield, Ore.	43
Bentsen, Texas	50	Heinz, Pa.	41
Hollings, S.C.	46	Packwood, Ore.	36

HOUSE

Democrats		Republicans	
Stenholm, Texas	67%	McKinney, Conn.	75%
Hall, Texas	59	Horton, N.Y.	74
Lloyd, Tenn.	55	Green, N.Y.	73
Roemer, La.	55	Conte, Mass.	73
Daniel, Va.	52	Jeffords, Vt.	69
Hubbard, Ky.	49	Gilman, N.Y.	67
Ray, Ga.	48	Smith, N.J.	66
Hutto, Fla.	45	Rinaldo, N.J.	63
Montgomery, Miss.	45	Schneider, R.I.	60
Tauzin, La.	44	Fish, N.Y.	60
Robinson, Ark.	41	Johnson, Conn.	58
Penny, Minn.	39	McDade, Pa.	58
Dyson, Md.	39		

Party Unity and Party Opposition: House

1. Party Unity, 1986. Percentage of 255 House Party Unity recorded votes in 1986 on which representative voted "yea" or "nay" *in agreement* with a majority of his party. (Party Unity roll calls are those on which a majority of voting Democrats opposed a majority of voting Republicans. Failures to vote lower both Party Unity and Party Opposition scores.)

2. Party Opposition, 1986. Percentage of 255 House Party Unity recorded votes in 1986 in which representative voted "yea" or "nay" *in disagreement* with a majority of his party.

** Rep. John E. Grotberg, R-Ill., did not participate in House business this year due to a serious illness.*

[1] Rep. Neil Abercrombie, D-Hawaii, was sworn in Sept. 23, 1986, to succeed Cecil Heftel, D-Hawaii, who resigned July 11, 1986, to run for governor of Hawaii. Heftel's 1986 Party Unity support score was 55 percent; opposition was 4 percent.

[2] Rep. George M. O'Brien, R-Ill., died July 17, 1986. O'Brien's 1986 Party Unity support score was 12 percent; opposition was 18 percent.

[3] Rep. Thomas P. O'Neill Jr., D-Mass., as Speaker, voted at his discretion.

[4] Rep. Alton R. Waldon Jr., D-N.Y., was sworn in July 29, 1986, to succeed Joseph P. Addabbo, D, who died April 10, 1986. Addabbo's 1986 Party Unity support score was 30 percent; opposition was 0 percent.

[5] Rep. James T. Broyhill, R-N.C., resigned July 13, 1986, after he was named to the Senate to fill the vacancy resulting from the June 29 death of Sen. John P. East. Broyhill's 1986 House Party Unity support score was 68 percent; opposition was 24 percent.

KEY

† Not eligible for all recorded votes in 1986 (sworn in after Jan. 21) or voted "present" to avoid possible conflict of interest.

Democrats ***Republicans***

	1	2
ALABAMA		
1 ***Callahan***	75	21
2 ***Dickinson***	78	14
3 Nichols	36	35
4 Bevill	67	26
5 Flippo	64	19
6 Erdreich	67	29
7 Shelby	58	33
ALASKA		
AL ***Young***	63	31
ARIZONA		
1 ***McCain***	67	25
2 Udall	89	4
3 ***Stump***	92	6
4 ***Rudd***	48	22
5 ***Kolbe***	84	13
ARKANSAS		
1 Alexander	80	8
2 Robinson	54	41
3 ***Hammerschmidt***	69	29
4 Anthony	78	11
CALIFORNIA		
1 Bosco	78	7
2 ***Chappie***	73	5
3 Matsui	94	3
4 Fazio	93	5
5 Burton	63	1
6 Boxer	84	4
7 Miller	84	4
8 Dellums	89	4
9 Stark	86	4
10 Edwards	95	3
11 Lantos	89	5
12 ***Zschau***	59	16
13 Mineta	95	5
14 ***Shumway***	82	16
15 Coelho	87	4
16 Panetta	87	9
17 ***Pashayan***	62	33
18 Lehman	87	4
19 ***Lagomarsino***	92	7
20 ***Thomas***	82	10
21 ***Fiedler***	73	5
22 ***Moorhead***	92	7
23 Beilenson	89	7
24 Waxman	87	4
25 Roybal	88	5
26 Berman	89	5
27 Levine	92	3
28 Dixon	80	2
29 Hawkins	77	9
30 Martinez	82	5
31 Dymally	92	2
32 Anderson	84	14
33 ***Dreier***	95	4
34 Torres	91	2
35 ***Lewis***	63	14
36 Brown	82	3
37 ***McCandless***	84	11
38 ***Dornan***	82	10
39 ***Dannemeyer***	90	5
40 ***Badham***	73	7
41 ***Lowery***	68	22
42 ***Lungren***	87	9
43 ***Packard***	79	18
44 Bates	83	15
45 ***Hunter***	85	11
COLORADO		
1 Schroeder	66	28
2 Wirth	76	15
3 ***Strang***	86	12
4 ***Brown***	92	7
5 ***Kramer***	80	10
6 ***Schaefer***	84	11
CONNECTICUT		
1 Kennelly	91	4
2 Gejdenson	96	3
3 Morrison	81	4
4 ***McKinney***	19	75
5 ***Rowland***	59	40
6 ***Johnson***	38	58
DELAWARE		
AL Carper	78	21
FLORIDA		
1 Hutto	51	45
2 Fuqua	64	16
3 Bennett	82	18
4 Chappell	65	24
5 ***McCollum***	81	16
6 MacKay	72	19
7 Gibbons	71	19
8 ***Young***	75	18
9 ***Bilirakis***	88	9
10 ***Ireland***	87	7
11 Nelson	69	30
12 ***Lewis***	82	14
13 ***Mack***	94	4
14 Mica	82	13
15 ***Shaw***	86	10
16 Smith	88	9
17 Lehman	92	4
18 Pepper	80	7
19 Fascell	88	7
GEORGIA		
1 Thomas	72	28
2 Hatcher	67	18
3 Ray	50	48
4 ***Swindall***	94	4
5 Fowler	30	8
6 ***Gingrich***	85	8
7 Darden	60	37
8 Rowland	73	27
9 Jenkins	65	28
10 Barnard	52	33
HAWAII		
1 Abercrombie [1] †	93	5
2 Akaka	89	6
IDAHO		
1 ***Craig***	85	9
2 Stallings	62	34
ILLINOIS		
1 Hayes	89	5
2 Savage	79	4
3 Russo	81	13
4 Vacancy [2]		
5 Lipinski	74	18
6 ***Hyde***	75	18
7 Collins	78	3
8 Rostenkowski	84	5
9 Yates	88	3
10 ***Porter***	68	28
11 Annunzio	90	5
12 ***Crane***	87	4
13 ***Fawell***	83	17
14 ***Grotberg****	0	0
15 ***Madigan***	70	18
16 ***Martin***	81	16
17 Evans	95	4
18 ***Michel***	73	20
19 Bruce	88	12
20 Durbin	90	9
21 Price	91	6
22 Gray	84	8
INDIANA		
1 Visclosky	93	7
2 Sharp	81	16
3 ***Hiler***	89	9
4 ***Coats***	84	15
5 ***Hillis***	38	27

	1	2
6 ***Burton***	94	4
7 ***Myers***	54	45
8 McCloskey	84	13
9 Hamilton	83	17
10 Jacobs	61	38
IOWA		
1 ***Leach***	58	39
2 ***Tauke***	71	25
3 ***Evans***	64	18
4 Smith	80	13
5 ***Lightfoot***	83	16
6 Bedell	80	11
KANSAS		
1 ***Roberts***	87	11
2 Slattery	68	30
3 ***Meyers***	73	27
4 Glickman	76	21
5 ***Whittaker***	83	15
KENTUCKY		
1 Hubbard	49	49
2 Natcher	89	11
3 Mazzoli	78	20
4 ***Snyder***	59	25
5 ***Rogers***	76	23
6 ***Hopkins***	82	16
7 Perkins	89	10
LOUISIANA		
1 ***Livingston***	71	21
2 Boggs	85	10
3 Tauzin	56	44
4 Roemer	40	55
5 Huckaby	53	31
6 ***Moore***	27	11
7 Breaux	24	11
8 Long	75	6
MAINE		
1 ***McKernan***	58	37
2 ***Snowe***	53	47
MARYLAND		
1 Dyson	57	39
2 ***Bentley***	60	30
3 Mikulski	75	4
4 ***Holt***	58	22
5 Hoyer	95	3
6 Byron	55	37
7 Mitchell	67	8
8 Barnes	70	3
MASSACHUSETTS		
1 ***Conte***	25	73
2 Boland	82	2
3 Early	80	6
4 Frank	91	8
5 Atkins	86	6
6 Mavroules	87	5
7 Markey	86	5
8 O'Neill [3]		
9 Moakley	87	3
10 Studds	93	3
11 Donnelly	86	4
MICHIGAN		
1 Conyers	71	4
2 ***Pursell***	50	46
3 Wolpe	91	7
4 ***Siljander***	77	11
5 ***Henry***	67	31
6 Carr	75	21
7 Kildee	97	2
8 Traxler	79	7
9 ***Vander Jagt***	76	15
10 ***Schuette***	76	20
11 ***Davis***	36	42
12 Bonior	90	1
13 Crockett	77	5
14 Hertel	90	8
15 Ford	84	4
16 Dingell	80	5
17 Levin	97	2
18 ***Broomfield***	69	23
MINNESOTA		
1 Penny	61	39
2 ***Weber***	80	17
3 ***Frenzel***	74	22
4 Vento	94	5
5 Sabo	95	3
6 Sikorski	79	20

	1	2
7 ***Stangeland***	71	22
8 Oberstar	92	4
MISSISSIPPI		
1 Whitten	76	16
2 ***Franklin***	62	24
3 Montgomery	53	45
4 Dowdy	68	15
5 ***Lott***	79	14
MISSOURI		
1 Clay	71	11
2 Young	85	9
3 Gephardt	69	1
4 Skelton	66	26
5 Wheat	96	3
6 ***Coleman***	76	20
7 ***Taylor***	65	29
8 ***Emerson***	82	18
9 Volkmer	79	20
MONTANA		
1 Williams	76	8
2 ***Marlenee***	80	9
NEBRASKA		
1 ***Bereuter***	73	26
2 ***Daub***	89	9
3 ***Smith***	62	33
NEVADA		
1 Reid	84	16
2 ***Vucanovich***	84	12
NEW HAMPSHIRE		
1 ***Smith***	96	4
2 ***Gregg***	85	9
NEW JERSEY		
1 Florio	87	6
2 Hughes	78	20
3 Howard	93	4
4 ***Smith***	32	66
5 ***Roukema***	62	26
6 Dwyer	95	3
7 ***Rinaldo***	34	63
8 Roe	89	6
9 Torricelli	85	7
10 Rodino	84	2
11 ***Gallo***	71	27
12 ***Courter***	75	24
12 ***Saxton***	67	33
14 Guarini	89	8
NEW MEXICO		
1 ***Lujan***	60	22
2 ***Skeen***	79	20
3 Richardson	90	9
NEW YORK		
1 ***Carney***	67	11
2 Downey	91	4
3 Mrazek	86	8
4 ***Lent***	65	27
5 ***McGrath***	61	31
6 Waldon [4]	86	2
7 Ackerman	91	0
8 Scheuer	88	5
9 Manton	88	3
10 Schumer	88	5
11 Towns	81	4
12 Owens	89	2
13 Solarz	89	5
14 ***Molinari***	75	24
15 ***Green***	26	73
16 Rangel	89	2
17 Weiss	81	4
18 Garcia	83	2
19 Biaggi	82	7
20 ***DioGuardi***	55	43
21 ***Fish***	33	60
22 ***Gilman***	31	67
23 Stratton	60	31
24 ***Solomon***	84	10
25 ***Boehlert***	53	45
26 ***Martin*** †	56	34
27 ***Wortley***	53	42
28 McHugh	91	6
29 ***Horton***	18	74
30 ***Eckert***	75	21
31 ***Kemp***	52	29
32 LaFalce	80	11
33 Nowak	92	5
34 Lundine	56	4

	1	2
NORTH CAROLINA		
1 Jones	76	11
2 Valentine	67	31
3 Whitley	78	17
4 ***Cobey***	91	7
5 Neal	75	18
6 ***Coble***	84	14
7 Rose	78	12
8 Hefner	80	13
9 ***McMillan***	69	28
10 Vacancy [5]		
11 ***Hendon***	76	22
NORTH DAKOTA		
AL Dorgan	82	15
OHIO		
1 Luken	84	9
2 ***Gradison***	59	38
3 Hall	78	13
4 ***Oxley***	85	8
5 ***Latta***	71	13
6 ***McEwen***	63	26
7 ***DeWine***	85	13
8 ***Kindness***	66	11
9 Kaptur	84	4
10 ***Miller***	83	14
11 Eckart	87	13
12 ***Kasich***	75	22
13 Pease	92	8
14 Seiberling	87	4
15 ***Wylie***	58	36
16 ***Regula***	56	43
17 Traficant	87	13
18 Applegate	75	20
19 Feighan	90	5
20 Oakar	92	2
21 Stokes	87	2
OKLAHOMA		
1 Jones	51	29
2 Synar	83	11
3 Watkins	75	22
4 McCurdy	70	21
5 ***Edwards***	72	20
6 English	63	34
OREGON		
1 AuCoin	82	11
2 ***Smith, R.***	82	13
3 Wyden	89	11
4 Weaver	73	8
5 ***Smith, D.***	86	7
PENNSYLVANIA		
1 Foglietta	79	5
2 Gray	88	1
3 Borski	93	6
4 Kolter	83	15
5 ***Schulze***	60	29
6 Yatron	80	15
7 Edgar	58	3
8 Kostmayer	87	9
9 ***Shuster***	85	11
10 ***McDade***	31	58
11 Kanjorski	83	14
12 Murtha	76	15
13 ***Coughlin***	51	46
14 Coyne	95	3
15 ***Ritter***	65	29
16 ***Walker***	96	4
17 ***Gekas***	83	16
18 Walgren	83	10
19 ***Goodling***	69	28
20 Gaydos	73	17
21 ***Ridge***	59	37
22 Murphy	75	19
23 ***Clinger***	48	49
RHODE ISLAND		
1 St Germain	87	6
2 ***Schneider***	29	60
SOUTH CAROLINA		
1 ***Hartnett***	37	6
2 ***Spence***	75	23
3 Derrick	81	13
4 ***Campbell***	23	5
5 Spratt	84	13
6 Tallon	59	31
SOUTH DAKOTA		
AL Daschle	84	15

	1	2
TENNESSEE		
1 ***Quillen***	49	40
2 ***Duncan***	62	36
3 Lloyd	39	55
4 Cooper	80	14
5 Boner	70	15
6 Gordon	83	12
7 ***Sundquist***	86	13
8 Jones	69	16
9 Ford	71	4
TEXAS		
1 Chapman	69	24
2 Wilson	61	18
3 ***Bartlett***	91	7
4 Hall	38	59
5 Bryant	84	12
6 ***Barton***	93	4
7 ***Archer***	81	15
8 ***Fields***	95	4
9 Brooks	76	7
10 Pickle	63	25
11 Leath	55	33
12 Wright	83	5
13 ***Boulter***	85	13
14 ***Sweeney***	70	18
15 de la Garza	72	16
16 Coleman	81	16
17 Stenholm	32	67
18 Leland	88	2
19 ***Combest***	82	18
20 Gonzalez	90	7
21 ***Loeffler***	62	12
22 ***DeLay***	91	4
23 Bustamante	82	9
24 Frost	74	11
25 Andrews	72	24
26 ***Armey***	97	2
27 Ortiz	78	14
UTAH		
1 ***Hansen***	80	8
2 ***Monson***	82	8
3 ***Nielson***	84	15
VERMONT		
AL ***Jeffords***	29	69
VIRGINIA		
1 ***Bateman***	64	35
2 ***Whitehurst***	61	21
3 ***Bliley***	82	16
4 Sisisky	75	21
5 Daniel	44	52
6 Olin	71	25
7 ***Slaughter***	86	11
8 ***Parris***	71	22
9 Boucher	83	6
10 ***Wolf***	74	25
WASHINGTON		
1 ***Miller***	60	36
2 Swift	93	4
3 Bonker	80	7
4 ***Morrison***	56	42
5 Foley	91	4
6 Dicks	90	7
7 Lowry	88	12
8 ***Chandler***	66	25
WEST VIRGINIA		
1 Mollohan	79	15
2 Staggers	89	8
3 Wise	88	8
4 Rahall	90	6
WISCONSIN		
1 Aspin	83	8
2 Kastenmeier	92	5
3 ***Gunderson***	66	29
4 Kleczka	85	9
5 Moody	87	7
6 ***Petri***	74	25
7 Obey	92	5
8 ***Roth***	79	17
9 ***Sensenbrenner***	89	11
WYOMING		
AL ***Cheney***	81	9

	1	2
ALABAMA		
Denton	82	16
Heflin	42	57
ALASKA		
Murkowski	81	15
Stevens †	83	15
ARIZONA		
Goldwater	59	9
DeConcini	62	35
ARKANSAS		
Bumpers	77	20
Pryor	70	24
CALIFORNIA		
Wilson †	88	12
Cranston	85	9
COLORADO		
Armstrong †	89	5
Hart	81	14
CONNECTICUT		
Weicker	47	44
Dodd	71	28
DELAWARE		
Roth	83	13
Biden	83	12
FLORIDA		
Hawkins	64	14
Chiles	56	43
GEORGIA		
Mattingly	81	19
Nunn	50	43
HAWAII		
Inouye	72	16
Matsunaga	77	19
IDAHO		
McClure	87	9
Symms	84	6
ILLINOIS		
Dixon	62	36
Simon	89	11
INDIANA		
Lugar	89	10
Quayle	94	5
IOWA		
Grassley	72	28
Harkin	91	5
KANSAS		
Dole	92	7
Kassebaum	77	21
KENTUCKY		
McConnell	90	10
Ford	74	25
LOUISIANA		
Johnston	61	37
Long	32	64
MAINE		
Cohen	63	33
Mitchell	84	14
MARYLAND		
Mathias	31	55
Sarbanes	96	3
MASSACHUSETTS		
Kennedy	79	16
Kerry	85	12
MICHIGAN		
Levin	91	9
Riegle	96	4
MINNESOTA		
Boschwitz	84	16
Durenberger	65	32
MISSISSIPPI		
Cochran	88	10
Stennis	29	52
MISSOURI		
Danforth	77	21
Eagleton	71	15
MONTANA		
Baucus	74	22
Melcher	86	14
NEBRASKA		
Exon	66	31
Zorinsky	44	55
NEVADA		
Hecht	95	4
Laxalt	81	8
NEW HAMPSHIRE		
Humphrey	83	14
Rudman	89	10
NEW JERSEY		
Bradley	66	24
Lautenberg	79	15
NEW MEXICO		
Domenici	89	10
Bingaman	70	29
NEW YORK		
D'Amato	66	32
Moynihan	72	25
NORTH CAROLINA		
Broyhill [1] †	82	12
Helms	95	5
NORTH DAKOTA		
Andrews	46	50
Burdick	87	13
OHIO		
Glenn	74	23
Metzenbaum	86	13
OKLAHOMA		
Nickles	82	18
Boren	42	54
OREGON		
Hatfield	54	43
Packwood	58	36
PENNSYLVANIA		
Heinz	56	41
Specter	27	68
RHODE ISLAND		
Chafee	64	34
Pell	75	20
SOUTH CAROLINA		
Thurmond	91	8
Hollings	54	46
SOUTH DAKOTA		
Abdnor	72	26
Pressler	72	25
TENNESSEE		
Gore	83	17
Sasser	87	13
TEXAS		
Gramm	95	4
Bentsen	46	50
UTAH		
Garn	73	4
Hatch	92	8
VERMONT		
Stafford	53	33
Leahy	83	11
VIRGINIA		
Trible	85	14
Warner	86	13
WASHINGTON		
Evans	72	23
Gorton	74	25
WEST VIRGINIA		
Byrd	84	16
Rockefeller	79	19
WISCONSIN		
Kasten	74	26
Proxmire	76	24
WYOMING		
Simpson	90	8
Wallop	94	3

KEY

† Not eligible for all recorded votes in 1986 (sworn in after Jan. 21) or voted "present" to avoid possible conflict of interest.

Democrats *Republicans*

Party Unity and Party Opposition: Senate

1. Party Unity, 1986. Percentage of 185 Senate Party Unity votes in 1986 on which senator voted "yea" or "nay" *in agreement* with a majority of his party. (Party Unity roll calls are those on which a majority of voting Democrats opposed a majority of voting Republicans. Failures to vote lower both Party Unity and Party Opposition scores.)

2. Party Opposition, 1986. Percentage of 185 Senate Party Unity votes in 1986 on which senator voted "yea" or "nay" *in disagreement* with a majority of his party.

[1] *Sen. James T. Broyhill, R-N.C., was sworn in July 14, 1986, to succeed John P. East, R, who died June 29, 1986. East's 1986 Party Unity support score was 94 percent; opposition was 6 percent.*

Voting Participation Approaches Record High

Despite election-year pressures to return home to campaign, members of Congress maintained a high rate of voting participation in 1986.

Members on average voted on 93 percent of the roll-call votes, 2 percentage points more than in 1984, the last year in which a general election was held. Participation scores generally are higher in non-election years.

In 1985, when the participation score averaged 94 percent, members missed fewer roll-call votes than at any time since Congressional Quarterly began keeping tabs on the subject 34 years earlier.

The high participation might reflect the growing fear of incumbents that they would suffer at the polls if they missed roll-call votes. Negative political advertising — including assaults on members' attendance records — had dominated the 1986 congressional election campaigns.

The voting participation study is the closest approach to an attendance record for Congress, but it is only an approximation. *(Definition, next page)*

The voting average for the Senate was 95 percent, matching the 1985 score. The House score was 92 percent, down 2 percentage points from 1985.

Senate Democrats answered roll calls slightly more often than Republicans, 96 percent vs. 95 percent. House Democrats and Republicans each recorded scores of 92 percent. For both chambers combined, Republicans and Democrats each recorded positions 93 percent of the time. In 1985, Republicans in Congress outscored Democrats 94 percent to 93 percent.

There were 805 recorded votes in Congress in 1986, 15 fewer than in 1985 but 122 above the number in 1984. There were 354 Senate roll calls, compared with 381 in 1985, and 451 House roll calls, compared with 439 in 1985.

Ten House members had scores of 100 percent and another 48 scored 99 percent. In 1985 four representatives had scores of 100 percent, while 43 achieved a 99 percent score.

For the 33rd consecutive year, William H. Natcher, D-Ky., scored 100 percent. Natcher had answered 10,807 consecutive roll calls since he came to Congress in 1953. Charles E. Bennett, D-Fla., scored 100 percent for the seventh year in a row; and Timothy J. Penny, D-Minn., did not miss a roll call for the third year in a row.

In the Senate, William Proxmire, D-Wis., scored 100 percent for the 20th consecutive year. Ernest F. Hollings, D-S.C., and Jim Sasser, D-Tenn., scored 100 percent for the second year in a row.

Some low scores in both chambers were due to the member's prolonged illness; Rep. John E. Grotberg, R-Ill., for example, was hospitalized much of the year, missing all recorded votes. In the Senate, Paula Hawkins, R-Fla., underwent surgery in April and missed a number of votes as a consequence.

Some of the lowest House scores were recorded by members seeking to move up to the Senate. In most cases, the challengers — unlike the incumbents — faced stiff primary competition that forced them to campaign hard just to win their party nominations.

Democratic Rep. Wyche Fowler Jr., who was vying for the Georgia Senate seat held by Republican Mack Mattingly, scored 36 percent. Mattingly answered the roll call 99 percent of the time.

Democratic Rep. Bob Edgar of Pennsylvania, who was seeking the Senate seat held by Republican Arlen Specter, scored 64 percent, against 95 percent for Specter.

Republican Rep. Ed Zschau of California, who hoped to capture the Senate seat held by Democrat Alan Cranston, scored 75 percent, against 94 percent for Cranston.

Republican Rep. Thomas N. Kindness, who was trying to unseat Democratic Sen. John Glenn of Ohio, also scored 75 percent, against 95 percent for Glenn.

In a Senate race involving two House members, Democrat John B. Breaux, running for the Louisiana seat being vacated by Democrat Russell B. Long, scored 31 percent. Breaux's opponent, Republican W. Henson Moore, scored 37 percent.

Winners of the Senate races were Fowler, Specter, Cranston, Glenn and Breaux.

Absences

Among members of Congress absent for a day or more in 1986 because they were sick or because of illness or death in their families were:

Senate Democrats: Bumpers, Ark.; Exon, Neb.; Inouye, Hawaii; Leahy, Vt.; Melcher, Mont.; Metzenbaum, Ohio; Pryor, Ark.; Riegle, Mich.

Senate Republicans: Garn, Utah; Goldwater, Ariz.; Hawkins, Fla.

House Democrats: Ackerman, N.Y.; Alexander, Ark.; Boland, Mass.; Byron, Md.; Burton, Calif.; Collins, Ill.; English, Okla.; Erdreich, Ala.; Flippo, Ala.; Ford, Tenn.; Jones, N.C.; Markey, Mass.; Obey, Wis.; Stokes, Ohio; Torres, Calif.; Traxler, Mich.; Weiss, N.Y.; Wright, Texas; Yates, Ill.

House Republicans: Bentley, Md.; Boulter, Texas; Chandler, Wash.; Davis, Mich.; Eckert, N.Y.; Franklin, Miss.; Grotberg, Ill.; Gunderson, Wis.; Ireland, Fla.; Kindness, Ohio; Latta, Ohio; Lujan, N.M.; Miller, Ohio; Packard, Calif.; Rinaldo, N.J.; Rudd, Ariz.; Sensenbrenner, Wis.; Stangeland, Minn.

Failure to vote often is due to conflicting duties. Members frequently have to be away from Washington on official business. Leaves of absence, not listed here, are granted members for these purposes.

Party Scores

Composites of Democratic and Republican voting participation scores for 1986 and 1985:

	1986		1985	
	Dem.	Rep.	Dem.	Rep.
Senate	96%	95%	95%	94%
House	92	92	93	94

Regional Scores

Regional voting participation breakdowns for 1986 with 1985 scores in parentheses:

	East		West		South		Midwest	
DEMOCRATS								
Senate	96%	(96)	95%	(95)	96%	(94)	97%	(96)
House	91	(93)	92	(91)	91	(93)	94	(94)
REPUBLICANS								
Senate	94%	(94)	92%	(92)	96%	(93)	98%	(97)
House	95	(94)	92	(94)	91	(95)	91	(94)

(CQ defines regions of the United States as follows: ***East:*** *Conn., Del., Maine, Md., Mass., N.H., N.J., N.Y., Pa., R.I., Vt., W.Va.* ***West:*** *Alaska, Ariz., Calif., Colo., Hawaii, Idaho, Mont., Nev., N.M., Ore., Utah, Wash., Wyo.* ***South:*** *Ala., Ark., Fla., Ga., Ky., La., Miss., N.C., Okla., S.C., Tenn., Texas, Va.* ***Midwest:*** *Ill., Ind., Iowa, Kan., Mich., Minn., Mo., Neb., N.D., Ohio, S.D., Wis.)*

Highest Scorers

SENATE

Democrats		Republicans	
Sasser, Tenn.	100%	Hatch, Utah	100%
Hollings, S.C.	100	East, N.C. [1]	100
Proxmire, Wis.	100	Helms, N.C.	100
Byrd, W.Va.	99	Nickles, Okla.	100
Simon, Ill.	99	Wilson, Calif.†	100
Levin, Mich.	99	Kasten, Wis.	100
Heflin, Ala.	99	Boschwitz, Minn.	100
Melcher, Mont. #	99	Grassley, Iowa	99
Bingaman, N.M.	99	McConnell, Ky.	99
Ford, Ky.	99	Mattingly, Ga.	99
Riegle, Mich. #	99	Dole, Kan.	99
Dodd, Conn.	99	Hecht, Nev.	99
Metzenbaum, Ohio #	99	Warner, Va.	99
Zorinsky, Neb.	99	Lugar, Ind.	99
Gore, Tenn.	99	Domenici, N.M.	99
Burdick, N.D.	99	Thurmond, S.C.	99
		Rudman, N.H.	99

HOUSE

Democrats		Republicans	
Bruce, Ill.	100%	Emerson, Mo.	100%
Rowland, Ga.	100	Combest, Texas	100
Tauzin, La.	100	Smith, N.H.	100
Bennett, Fla.	100	Fawell, Ill.	99
Natcher, Ky.	100	Walker, Pa.	99
Visclosky, Ind.	100	Lightfoot, Iowa	99
Penny, Minn.	100	Brown, Colo.	99
Lowry, Wash.	99	Rowland, Conn.	99
Reid, Nev.	99	Petri, Wis.	99
Wyden, Ore.	99	Moorhead, Calif.	99
Wheat, Mo.	99	Conte, Mass.	99
Durbin, Ill.	99	Lagomarsino, Calif.	99
Thomas, Ga.	99	Meyers, Kan.	99
Daschle, S.D.	99	Molinari, N.Y.	99
Perkins, Ky.	99	Wolf, Va.	99
Hamilton, Ind.	99	Gekas, Pa.	99
Pease, Ohio	99	Skeen, N.M.	99
Anderson, Calif.	99	Snowe, Maine	99
Edwards, Calif.†	99	Sensenbrenner, Wis. #	99
Hughes, N.J.	99	Saxton, N.J.	99
Levin, Mich.	99	Nielson, Utah	99
Traficant, Ohio	99	Armey, Texas	99
Abercrombie, Hawaii [2] †	99	Bartlett, Texas	99
Evans, Ill.	99	Smith, N.J.	99
Carper, Del.	99	Green, N.Y.	99
Gejdenson, Conn.	99	Rogers, Ky.	99
Vento, Minn.	99		
Stenholm, Texas	99		
Kildee, Mich.	99		
Hubbard, Ky.	99		
Nelson, Fla.	99		
Eckart, Ohio	99		

Definition

Voting Participation. Percentage of recorded votes on which a member voted "yea" or "nay." Failures to vote "yea" or "nay" lower scores — even if the member votes "present," enters a live pair or announces his stand in the *Congressional Record.* Only votes of "yea" or "nay" directly affect the outcome of a vote. Voting participation is the closest approach to an attendance record, but it is only an approximation. A member may be present and nevertheless decline to vote "yea" or "nay" — usually because he has entered a live pair with an absent member.

Lowest Scorers

SENATE

Democrats		Republicans	
Stennis, Miss.	83%	Goldwater, Ariz. #	67%
Eagleton, Mo.	86	Garn, Utah #	72
Inouye, Hawaii #	86	Hawkins, Fla. #	72
Bradley, N.J.	92	Mathias, Md.	83
Leahy, Vt. #	93	Symms, Idaho	85
Pryor, Ark. #	93	Stafford, Vt.	85

HOUSE

Democrats		Republicans	
Breaux, La.	31%	Grotberg, Ill. [6] #	0%
Addabbo, N.Y. [4]	35	O'Brien, Ill. [3]	26
Fowler, Ga.	36	Campbell, S.C.	31
Burton, Calif. #	61	Moore, La.	37
Edgar, Pa.	64	Hartnett, S.C.	45
Lundine, N.Y.	64	Hillis, Ind.	68
Heftel, Hawaii [5]	65	Rudd, Ariz. #	71
Gephardt, Mo.	70	Kindness, Ohio #	75
Nichols, Ala.	74	Zschau, Calif.	75
Barnes, Md.	75	Loeffler, Texas	75
Conyers, Mich.	75		

[1] *Sen. John P. East, R-N.C., died June 29, 1986.*

[2] *Rep. Neil Abercrombie, D-Hawaii, was sworn in Sept. 23, 1986.*

[3] *Rep. George M. O'Brien, R-Ill., died July 17, 1986.*

[4] *Rep. Joseph P. Addabbo, D-N.Y., died on April 10, 1986.*

[5] *Rep. Cecil Heftel resigned July 11, 1986, to run for governor of Hawaii.*

[6] *Rep. John E. Grotberg, R-Ill., has not participated in House business this session, due to a serious illness.*

† *Not eligible for all recorded votes in 1986 (sworn in after Jan. 21) or voted "present" to avoid possible conflict of interest.*

Member absent a day or more in 1986 due to illness or to illness or death in family.

ALABAMA	
Denton	97
Heflin	99
ALASKA	
Murkowski	94
Stevens †	95
ARIZONA	
Goldwater #	67
DeConcini	97
ARKANSAS	
Bumpers #	96
Pryor #	93
CALIFORNIA	
Wilson †	100
Cranston	94
COLORADO	
Armstrong †	95
Hart	95
CONNECTICUT	
Weicker	91
Dodd	99
DELAWARE	
Roth	97
Biden	94
FLORIDA	
Hawkins #	72
Chiles	95
GEORGIA	
Mattingly	99
Nunn	95
HAWAII	
Inouye #	86
Matsunaga	95
IDAHO	
McClure	97
Symms	85
ILLINOIS	
Dixon	97
Simon	99
INDIANA	
Lugar	99
Quayle	98
IOWA	
Grassley	99
Harkin	97
KANSAS	
Dole	99
Kassebaum	96
KENTUCKY	
McConnell	99
Ford	99
LOUISIANA	
Johnston	98
Long	97
MAINE	
Cohen	96
Mitchell	98
MARYLAND	
Mathias	83
Sarbanes	98
MASSACHUSETTS	
Kennedy	95
Kerry	95
MICHIGAN	
Levin	99
Riegle #	99
MINNESOTA	
Boschwitz	100
Durenberger	97
MISSISSIPPI	
Cochran	98
Stennis	83
MISSOURI	
Danforth	98
Eagleton	86
MONTANA	
Baucus	97
Melcher #	99
NEBRASKA	
Exon #	96
Zorinsky	99
NEVADA	
Hecht	99
Laxalt	88
NEW HAMPSHIRE	
Humphrey	95
Rudman	99
NEW JERSEY	
Bradley	92
Lautenberg	95
NEW MEXICO	
Domenici	99
Bingaman	99
NEW YORK	
D'Amato	98
Moynihan	96
NORTH CAROLINA	
Broyhill [1] †	93
Helms	100
NORTH DAKOTA	
Andrews	96
Burdick	99
OHIO	
Glenn	95
Metzenbaum #	99
OKLAHOMA	
Nickles	100
Boren	94
OREGON	
Hatfield	96
Packwood	90
PENNSYLVANIA	
Heinz	98
Specter	95
RHODE ISLAND	
Chafee	98
Pell	96
SOUTH CAROLINA	
Thurmond	99
Hollings	100
SOUTH DAKOTA	
Abdnor	98
Pressler	95
TENNESSEE	
Gore	99
Sasser	100
TEXAS	
Gramm	98
Bentsen	96
UTAH	
Garn #	72
Hatch	100
VERMONT	
Stafford	85
Leahy #	93
VIRGINIA	
Trible	98
Warner	99
WASHINGTON	
Evans	96
Gorton	97
WEST VIRGINIA	
Byrd	99
Rockefeller	98
WISCONSIN	
Kasten	100
Proxmire	100
WYOMING	
Simpson	97
Wallop	95

KEY

† Not eligible for all recorded votes in 1986 (sworn in after Jan. 21) or voted "present" to avoid possible conflict of interest.

Members absent a day or more in 1986 due to illness or illness or death in family.

Democrats   ***Republicans***

Voting Participation Scores: Senate

Voting Participation, 1986. Percentage of 354 roll calls in 1986 on which senator votes "yea" or "nay."

[1] *Sen. James T. Broyhill, R-N.C., was sworn in July 14, 1986, to succeed John P. East, R, who died June 29, 1986. East's 1986 voting participation score was 100 percent.*

Voting Participation Scores: House

Voting Participation, 1986. Percentage of 451 recorded votes in 1986 on which representative voted "yea" or "nay."

[1] *Rep. Neil Abercrombie, D-Hawaii, was sworn in Sept. 23, 1986, to succeed Cecil Heftel, D, who resigned July 11, 1986, to run for governor of Hawaii. Heftel's voting participation score was 65 percent.*

[2] *Rep. George M. O'Brien, R-Ill., died July 17, 1986. O'Brien's voting participation score was 26 percent.*

[3] *Rep. John E. Grotberg, R-Ill., has not participated in House business this session due to a serious illness.*

[4] *Rep. Thomas P. O'Neill Jr., D-Mass., as Speaker, votes at his own discretion.*

[5] *Rep. Alton R. Waldon Jr., D-N.Y., was sworn in July 29, 1986, to succeed Joseph P. Addabbo, D, who died April 10, 1986. Addabbo's voting participation score was 35 percent.*

[6] *Rep. James T. Broyhill, R-N.C., resigned on July 13, 1986, to fill the vacant seat resulting from the June 29 death of Sen. John P. East. Broyhill's House voting participation score was 93 percent.*

KEY

† Not eligible for all recorded votes in 1986 (sworn in after Jan. 21) or voted "present" to avoid possible conflict of interest.

Member absent a day or more in 1986 due to illness or illness or death in family.

Democrats ***Republicans***

Member	Score
ALABAMA	
1 ***Callahan***	96
2 ***Dickinson***	92
3 Nichols	74
4 Bevill	94
5 Flippo #	82
6 Erdreich #	97
7 Shelby	92
ALASKA	
AL ***Young***	93
ARIZONA	
1 ***McCain*** †	93
2 Udall	93
3 ***Stump***	98
4 ***Rudd*** #	71
5 ***Kolbe***	96
ARKANSAS	
1 Alexander #	90
2 Robinson	96
3 ***Hammerschmidt***	98
4 Anthony	90
CALIFORNIA	
1 Bosco	86
2 ***Chappie***	77
3 Matsui	97
4 Fazio	98
5 Burton #	61
6 Boxer	88
7 Miller	87
8 Dellums	93
9 Stark	88
10 Edwards †	99
11 Lantos	94
12 ***Zschau***	75
13 Mineta	97
14 ***Shumway***	97
15 Coelho	90
16 Panetta	95
17 ***Pashayan***	95
18 Lehman	91
19 ***Lagomarsino***	99
20 ***Thomas***	91
21 ***Fiedler***	78
22 ***Moorhead***	99
23 Beilenson	97
24 Waxman	92
25 Roybal	94
26 Berman	95
27 Levine	96
28 Dixon	85
29 Hawkins	89
30 Martinez	89
31 Dymally	94
32 Anderson	99
33 ***Dreier***	98
34 Torres #	94
35 ***Lewis***	80
36 Brown	85
37 ***McCandless***	94
38 ***Dornan***	94
39 ***Dannemeyer***	95
40 ***Badham***	83
41 ***Lowery***	92
42 ***Lungren***	96
43 ***Packard*** #	96
44 Bates	98
45 ***Hunter***	96
COLORADO	
1 Schroeder	95
2 Wirth	91
3 ***Strang***	98
4 ***Brown***	99
5 ***Kramer***	91
6 ***Schaefer***	95
CONNECTICUT	
1 Kennelly	96
2 Gejdenson	99
3 Morrison	86
4 ***McKinney***	92
5 ***Rowland***	99
6 ***Johnson***	97
DELAWARE	
AL Carper	99
FLORIDA	
1 Hutto	96
2 Fuqua	83
3 Bennett	100
4 Chappell	90
5 ***McCollum***	97
6 MacKay	91
7 Gibbons	92
8 ***Young***	94
9 ***Bilirakis***	97
10 ***Ireland*** #	92
11 Nelson	99
12 ***Lewis***	96
13 ***Mack***	98
14 Mica	94
15 ***Shaw***	96
16 Smith	96
17 Lehman †	96
18 Pepper	89
19 Fascell	96
GEORGIA	
1 Thomas	99
2 Hatcher	86
3 Ray	98
4 ***Swindall***	98
5 Fowler	36
6 ***Gingrich***	92
7 Darden	97
8 Rowland	100
9 Jenkins	94
10 Barnard	81
HAWAII	
1 Abercrombie [1] †	99
2 Akaka	94
IDAHO	
1 ***Craig***	95
2 Stallings	96
ILLINOIS	
1 Hayes	94
2 Savage	84
3 Russo	93
4 Vacancy [2]	
5 Lipinski	93
6 ***Hyde***	94
7 Collins #	81
8 Rostenkowski	85
9 Yates #	92
10 ***Porter***	96
11 Annunzio	96
12 ***Crane, P.***	92
13 ***Fawell***	99
14 ***Grotberg*** [3] #	0
15 ***Madigan***	90
16 ***Martin***	98
17 Evans	99
18 ***Michel***	92
19 Bruce	100
20 Durbin	99
21 Price	97
22 Gray	93
INDIANA	
1 Visclosky	100
2 Sharp	96
3 ***Hiler***	98
4 ***Coats***	98
5 ***Hillis***	68

6 ***Burton*** 97
7 ***Myers*** 98
8 McCloskey 97
9 Hamilton 99
10 Jacobs 98

IOWA
1 ***Leach*** † 98
2 ***Tauke*** 96
3 ***Evans*** 84
4 Smith 94
5 ***Lightfoot*** 99
6 Bedell † 92

KANSAS
1 ***Roberts*** 98
2 Slattery 98
3 ***Meyers*** 99
4 Glickman 98
5 ***Whittaker*** 97

KENTUCKY
1 Hubbard 99
2 Natcher 100
3 Mazzoli 98
4 ***Snyder*** 87
5 ***Rogers*** 99
6 ***Hopkins*** 98
7 Perkins 99

LOUISIANA
1 ***Livingston*** 92
2 Boggs 95
3 Tauzin 100
4 Roemer † 95
5 Huckaby 86
6 ***Moore*** 37
7 Breaux 31
8 Long 82

MAINE
1 ***McKernan*** 95
2 ***Snowe*** 99

MARYLAND
1 Dyson 97
2 ***Bentley*** # 91
3 Mikulski 82
4 ***Holt*** 83
5 Hoyer 98
6 Byron # 94
7 Mitchell 77
8 Barnes 75

MASSACHUSETTS
1 ***Conte*** 99
2 Boland # 83
3 Early 87
4 Frank 98
5 Atkins 92
6 Mavroules 92
7 Markey # 90
8 O'Neill [4]
9 Moakley 91
10 Studds 96
11 Donnelly 92

MICHIGAN
1 Conyers 75
2 ***Pursell*** 96
3 Wolpe 97
4 ***Siljander*** 88
5 ***Henry*** 98
6 Carr 97
7 Kildee 99
8 Traxler # 89
9 ***Vander Jagt*** 88
10 ***Schuette*** 95
11 ***Davis*** # 82
12 Bonior 92
13 Crockett 84
14 Hertel 97
15 Ford 91
16 Dingell 88
17 Levin 99
18 ***Broomfield*** 92

MINNESOTA
1 Penny 100
2 ***Weber*** 97
3 ***Frenzel*** 95
4 Vento 99
5 Sabo 98
6 Sikorski 97
7 ***Stangeland*** # 92
8 Oberstar 96

MISSISSIPPI
1 Whitten 92
2 ***Franklin*** # 85
3 Montgomery 98
4 Dowdy 84
5 ***Lott*** 93

MISSOURI
1 Clay 83
2 Young 96
3 Gephardt 70
4 Skelton 93
5 Wheat 99
6 ***Coleman*** 94
7 ***Taylor*** 95
8 ***Emerson*** 100
9 Volkmer 98

MONTANA
1 Williams 88
2 ***Marlenee*** 91

NEBRASKA
1 ***Bereuter*** 98
2 ***Daub*** 98
3 ***Smith*** 94

NEVADA
1 Reid 99
2 ***Vucanovich*** 96

NEW HAMPSHIRE
1 ***Smith*** 100
2 ***Gregg*** 94

NEW JERSEY
1 Florio 94
2 Hughes 99
3 Howard 97
4 ***Smith*** 99
5 ***Roukema*** 96
6 Dwyer 97
7 ***Rinaldo*** # 96
8 Roe 95
9 Torricelli 92
10 Rodino 87
11 ***Gallo*** 98
12 ***Courter*** 97
12 ***Saxton*** 99
14 Guarini 97

NEW MEXICO
1 ***Lujan*** # 82
2 ***Skeen*** 99
3 Richardson 97

NEW YORK
1 ***Carney*** 78
2 Downey 95
3 Mrazek 94
4 ***Lent*** 93
5 ***McGrath*** 91
6 Waldon [5] † 86
7 Ackerman # 88
8 Scheuer 94
9 Manton 92
10 Schumer 94
11 Towns 89
12 Owens 91
13 Solarz 93
14 ***Molinari*** 99
15 ***Green*** 99
16 Rangel 91
17 Weiss # 85
18 Garcia 85
19 Biaggi 90
20 ***DioGuardi*** 98
21 ***Fish*** 92
22 ***Gilman*** 98
23 Stratton 90
24 ***Solomon*** 93
25 ***Boehlert*** 98
26 ***Martin*** † 89
27 ***Wortley*** 96
28 McHugh 98
29 ***Horton*** 92
30 ***Eckert*** # 94
31 ***Kemp*** 81
32 LaFalce 93
33 Nowak 98
34 Lundine 64

NORTH CAROLINA
1 Jones # 87
2 Valentine 98
3 Whitley 95
4 ***Cobey*** 98
5 Neal 94
6 ***Coble*** 98
7 Rose 88
8 Hefner 92
9 ***McMillan*** 97
10 Vacancy [6]
11 ***Hendon*** 97

NORTH DAKOTA
AL Dorgan 96

OHIO
1 Luken 93
2 ***Gradison*** 96
3 Hall 92
4 ***Oxley*** 93
5 ***Latta*** # 84
6 ***McEwen*** 88
7 ***DeWine*** 97
8 ***Kindness*** # 75
9 Kaptur 88
10 ***Miller*** # 97
11 Eckart 99
12 ***Kasich*** 98
13 Pease 99
14 Seiberling 93
15 ***Wylie*** 95
16 ***Regula*** 98
17 Traficant 99
18 Applegate 96
19 Feighan 97
20 Oakar 93
21 Stokes # 90

OKLAHOMA
1 Jones 80
2 Synar 94
3 Watkins 96
4 McCurdy 92
5 ***Edwards*** 90
6 English # 96

OREGON
1 AuCoin 94
2 ***Smith, B.*** 95
3 Wyden 99
4 Weaver 77
5 ***Smith, D.*** 94

PENNSYLVANIA
1 Foglietta 83
2 Gray 90
3 Borski 98
4 Kolter 97
5 ***Schulze*** 88
6 Yatron 97
7 Edgar 64
8 Kostmayer 97
9 ***Shuster*** 96
10 ***McDade*** 88
11 Kanjorski 98
12 Murtha 91
13 ***Coughlin*** 97
14 Coyne 98
15 ***Ritter*** 94
16 ***Walker*** 99
17 ***Gekas*** 99
18 Walgren 94
19 ***Goodling*** 96
20 Gaydos 92
21 ***Ridge*** 97
22 Murphy 95
23 ***Clinger*** 95

RHODE ISLAND
1 St Germain 92
2 ***Schneider*** 90

SOUTH CAROLINA
1 ***Hartnett*** 45
2 ***Spence*** 98
3 Derrick 94
4 ***Campbell*** 31
5 Spratt 97
6 Tallon 93

SOUTH DAKOTA
AL Daschle 99

TENNESSEE
1 ***Quillen*** 90
2 ***Duncan*** 98
3 Lloyd 95
4 Cooper 95
5 Boner 84
6 Gordon 96
7 ***Sundquist*** 98
8 Jones 88
9 Ford # 78

TEXAS
1 Chapman 94
2 Wilson 81
3 ***Bartlett*** 99
4 Hall 98
5 Bryant 96
6 ***Barton*** 97
7 ***Archer*** 96
8 ***Fields*** † 98
9 Brooks 83
10 Pickle 89
11 Leath 90
12 Wright # 89
13 ***Boulter*** # 97
14 ***Sweeney*** 88
15 de la Garza 85
16 Coleman 98
17 Stenholm 99
18 Leland 89
19 ***Combest*** 100
20 Gonzalez 98
21 ***Loeffler*** 75
22 ***DeLay*** 95
23 Bustamante 92
24 Frost 86
25 Andrews 97
26 ***Armey*** 99
27 Ortiz 92

UTAH
1 ***Hansen*** 88
2 ***Monson*** 90
3 ***Nielson*** 99

VERMONT
AL ***Jeffords*** 98

VIRGINIA
1 ***Bateman*** 97
2 ***Whitehurst*** 82
3 ***Bliley*** 97
4 Sisisky † 97
5 Daniel 96
6 Olin 97
7 ***Slaughter*** 97
8 ***Parris*** 93
9 Boucher 90
10 ***Wolf*** 99

WASHINGTON
1 ***Miller*** 98
2 Swift 97
3 Bonker 87
4 ***Morrison*** 98
5 Foley 95
6 Dicks 97
7 Lowry 99
8 ***Chandler*** # 91

WEST VIRGINIA
1 Mollohan 94
2 Staggers 97
3 Wise 96
4 Rahall 96

WISCONSIN
1 Aspin 91
2 Kastenmeier 98
3 ***Gunderson*** # 96
4 Kleczka 95
5 Moody 94
6 ***Petri*** 99
7 Obey # 97
8 ***Roth*** 94
9 ***Sensenbrenner*** # 99

WYOMING
AL ***Cheney*** 91

Conservatives: A Rise in Unity but Not Victories

The "conservative coalition" voting bloc of Republicans and Southern Democrats appeared more often in 1986 than the year before, but with somewhat less success.

A Congressional Quarterly vote analysis shows the conservative coalition emerged in 16 percent of all recorded votes in 1986, an increase of 2 percentage points from 1985 and the same level that was registered in 1984.

However, its rate of victory in outvoting Northern Democrats dropped 2 percentage points, to 87 percent. But the coalition maintained the relatively high level of success it had achieved throughout President Reagan's tenure in the White House.

In the Republican-controlled Senate, the coalition was as effective as it was in 1985, prevailing on 93 percent of the votes on which it appeared. But in the Democratic-controlled House, the coalition won only 78 percent of the votes on which it showed up — a drop of 6 percentage points from 1985 and the lowest rate of success since 1983.

For the purposes of CQ's annual study, the conservative coalition does not refer to any organized group or to an ideological definition of conservatism. Instead, it refers to a voting alliance that occurs when a majority of Republicans and Southern Democrats vote against a majority of Northern Democrats in the House or Senate. *(Box, this page)*

CQ had been studying the voting patterns of the conservative coalition since 1957. Since Reagan took office, Republicans and Southern Democrats had joined forces in opposition to Northern Democrats less often than they did during the 1970s. Their highest rate since the survey began was in 1971, when the coalition formed in 30 percent of all recorded votes.

But when it had appeared during the Reagan era, the coalition had been far more effective than it was in the 1970s. Its greatest performance was in 1981, when Republicans and Southern Democrats united to enact Reagan's tax and spending cuts and won 92 percent of the votes on which the coalition appeared. From 1970 to 1979, the coalition's average rate of victory was 64 percent.

Definitions

Conservative Coalition. As used in this study, the term "conservative coalition" means a voting alliance of Republicans and Southern Democrats against the Northern Democrats in Congress. This meaning, rather than any philosophic definition of the "conservative coalition" position, provides the basis for CQ's selection of coalition votes.

Conservative Coalition Vote. Any vote in the Senate or the House on which a majority of voting Southern Democrats and a majority of voting Republicans opposed the stand taken by a majority of voting Northern Democrats. Votes on which there is an even division within the ranks of voting Northern Democrats, Southern Democrats or Republicans are not included.

Southern States. The Southern states are Alabama, Arkansas, Florida, Georgia, Kentucky, Louisiana, Mississippi, North Carolina, Oklahoma, South Carolina, Tennessee, Texas and Virginia. The other 37 states are grouped as the North in this study.

Conservative Coalition Support Score. Percentage of conservative coalition votes on which members votes "yea" or "nay" *in agreement* with the position of the conservative coalition. Failures to vote, even if a member announces a stand, lower the score.

Conservative Coalition Opposition Score. Percentage of conservative coalition votes on which a member votes "yea" or "nay" *in disagreement* with the position of the conservative coalition.

Foreign Policy, Defense

As in previous years, the conservative coalition emerged most often in votes on foreign policy and defense issues.

In the Senate, approving funds for the anti-communist "contra" rebels in Nicaragua was the predominant issue, accounting for 16 of the coalition's 76 votes, or 21 percent; it prevailed on all but one of the contra votes. Other major issues were approving the sale of the government-owned Conrail freight railroad system (nine votes) and protecting the Pentagon from budget cuts or restrictions (seven votes).

In the House, supporting the defense budget was the coalition's major issue in 1986, accounting for 12 of its 50 votes, or 24 percent; it won all but two of those defense votes. Relaxing federal gun control laws and approving aid to the contras were the next most important issues for the coalition, accounting for six votes each.

However, there also were some notable votes in the House on which the conservative coalition did not appear: a ban on underground nuclear tests greater than one kiloton; a ban on funds to deploy any weapons that would violate the SALT II arms control treaty; and a ban on tests of anti-satellite missiles.

All three issues were based on reciprocal action by the Soviet Union, and all three were approved despite strong opposition from Reagan, who had indicated he would ignore future SALT II limitations.

While the conservative coalition normally might be expected to vote against those proposals, its absence was interpreted by some observers as a sign of the strong political appeal that arms control had for many voters and lawmakers.

Party and Regional Support

In the Senate, Republican support for the coalition increased 3 percentage points over 1985 to 80 percent, which was countered by a drop of 3 percentage points, to 37 percent, among Democrats.

In the House, Democrats increased their support for the coalition by 2 percentage points, to 38 percent. But Republicans showed a 2-point percentage point drop in support, to 79 percent.

The largest regional changes in conservative coalition voting patterns were among lawmakers from the West and Midwest, where the hard-hit farming economy had caused political repercussions. Senate Democrats from the Midwest voted against the coalition 72 percent of the time in 1986 — an increase of 9 percentage points from 1985; Senate Democrats from the West posted a 67 percent opposition score, up 5 percentage points. Among House Republicans from the Midwest, support for the coalition dropped 5 percentage points from 1985.

Individual Scores

In the House, the conservative coalition's most loyal allies were three Republican freshmen from Texas — Dick Armey, Thomas D. DeLay and Larry Combest. Each voted with the coalition 100 percent of the time.

Among Southern Democrats, top supporters were W. J. "Billy" Tauzin, La., who scored 98 percent; and Michael A. Andrews, Texas, and Robert Lindsay Thomas, Ga., who each scored 96 percent.

Among Northern Democrats, the coalition's top supporters both came from Maryland: Roy Dyson, at 88 percent, followed by Beverly B. Byron at 78 percent.

In the Senate, Republicans Don Nickles, Okla., and Chic Hecht, Nev., both voted with the coalition 99 percent of the time, followed by Strom Thurmond, S.C., and Phil Gramm, Texas, at 97 percent. Among Southern Democrats, David L. Boren, Okla., voted with the coalition 92 percent of the time. Next was Lloyd Bentsen, Texas, at 87 percent.

In the House, Democrats increased their coalition support by 2 percentage points to 38 percent. But Republicans showed a 2-point drop in support, to 79 percent.

For the sixth year in a row, Edward Zorinsky, Neb., led all Northern Democrats in backing the coalition by voting with it 71 percent of the time — 4 percentage points more than in 1985. He was followed by Dennis DeConcini, Ariz., at 61 percent, and Alan J. Dixon, Ill., 59 percent.

Opponents of the coalition in the House were led by five Northern Democrats, all of whom voted against the alliance 94 percent of the time: Bruce F. Vento, Minn.; William J. Coyne, Pa.; Don Edwards, Calif.; Dale E. Kildee, Mich.; and Mike Lowry, Wash. Technically, House Speaker Thomas P. O'Neill Jr., D-Mass., and Neil Abercrombie, D-Hawaii, opposed the coalition 100 percent of the time. But those scores were meaningless. O'Neill, who as Speaker generally did not vote, participated in only two of the 50 conservative-coalition votes, and Abercrombie, who won a special election Sept. 20, participated in just four.

Among Southern Democrats, two liberal Texans voted against the coalition most often: Mickey Leland opposed it 90 percent of the time, and Henry B. Gonzalez, 88 percent. Top Republican opponents were Silvio O. Conte, Mass., who voted against the coalition 76 percent of the time, and Bill Green, N.Y., who opposed it on 64 percent of the votes.

In the Senate, Paul S. Sarbanes, Md., and Donald W. Riegle Jr., Mich., posted the highest opposition scores among Northern Democrats: 95 percent for both. Albert Gore Jr., Tenn., led the Southern Democratic opposition, voting against the coalition 67 percent of the time. Among Republicans, Arlen Specter, Pa., had the highest opposition score with 64 percent. He was followed by Charles McC. Mathias Jr., Md., with 62 percent.

Coalition Appearances

Following is the percentage of the recorded votes for both houses of Congress on which the coalition appeared:

1969	27%	1978	21%
1970	22	1979	20
1971	30	1980	18
1972	27	1981	21
1973	23	1982	18
1974	24	1983	15
1975	28	1984	16
1976	24	1985	14
1977	26	1986	16

Coalition Victories

Year	Total	Senate	House
1969	68%	67%	71%
1970	66	64	70
1971	83	86	79
1972	69	63	79
1973	61	54	67
1974	59	54	67
1975	50	48	52
1976	58	58	59
1977	68	74	60
1978	52	46	57
1979	70	65	73
1980	72	75	67
1981	92	95	88
1982	85	90	78
1983	77	89	71
1984	83	94	75
1985	89	93	84
1986	87	93	78

Average Scores

Following are the composite conservative coalition support and opposition scores for 1986 (scores for 1985 are in parentheses):

	Southern Democrats		Republicans		Northern Democrats	
Coalition Support						
Senate	67%	(68)	80%	(77)	25%	(29)
House	64	(64)	79	(81)	25	(22)
Coalition Opposition						
Senate	30%	(26)	16%	(17)	72%	(67)
House	28	(31)	15	(15)	69	(73)

Regional Scores

Following are the parties' coalition support and opposition scores by region for 1986 (scores for 1985 are in parentheses):

REGIONAL SUPPORT

	East		West		South		Midwest	
Democrats								
Senate	22%	(23)	27%	(32)	67%	(68)	26%	(33)
House	24	(22)	22	(20)	64	(64)	27	(23)
Republicans								
Senate	60%	(60)	84%	(80)	91%	(86)	82%	(80)
House	70	(68)	84	(86)	87	(90)	76	(81)

REGIONAL OPPOSITION

	East		West		South		Midwest	
Democrats								
Senate	75%	(73)	67%	(62)	30%	(26)	72%	(63)
House	68	(73)	71	(74)	28	(31)	69	(72)
Republicans								
Senate	34%	(33)	10%	(13)	6%	(7)	17%	(17)
House	26	(28)	10	(10)	6	(8)	17	(16)

(CQ defines regions of the United States as follows: **East:** *Conn., Del., Maine, Md., Mass., N.H., N.J., N.Y., Pa., R.I., Vt., W.Va.* **West:** *Alaska, Ariz., Calif., Colo., Hawaii, Idaho, Mont., Nev., N.M., Ore., Utah, Wash., Wyo.* **South:** *Ala., Ark., Fla., Ga., Ky., La., Miss., N.C., Okla., S.C., Tenn., Texas, Va.* **Midwest:** *Ill., Ind., Iowa, Kan., Mich., Minn., Mo., Neb., N.D., Ohio, S.D., Wis.)*

Individual Support Scores

Highest Coalition Support Scores. Those who voted with the conservative coalition most consistently in 1986:

SENATE

Southern Democrats

Boren, Okla.	92%
Bentsen, Texas	87
Long, La.	86
Heflin, Ala.	84
Chiles, Fla.	76
Stennis, Miss.	75
Nunn, Ga.	75
Hollings, S.C.	74
Johnston, La.	67
Pryor, Ark.	55

Republicans

Nickles, Okla.	99%
Hecht, Nev.	99
Thurmond, S.C.	97
Gramm, Texas	97
Wallop, Wyo.	95
Quayle, Ind.	95
Hatch, Utah	95
Domenici, N.M.	95
Helms, N.C.	95
Dole, Kan.	95

Northern Democrats

Zorinsky, Neb.	71%
DeConcini, Ariz.	61
Dixon, Ill.	59
Exon, Neb.	45
Bingaman, N.M.	41

HOUSE

Southern Democrats

Tauzin, La.	98%
Andrews, Texas	96
Thomas, Ga.	96
Nelson, Fla.	94
Hubbard, Ky.	94
Robinson, Ark.	94
Montgomery, Miss.	92
Lloyd, Tenn.	92
Hutto, Fla.	92

Republicans

Armey, Texas	100%
DeLay, Texas	100
Combest, Texas	100
Fields, Texas	98
Archer, Texas	98
Swindall, Ga.	98
Mack, Fla.	98
Callahan, Ala.	98

Northern Democrats

Dyson, Md.	88%
Byron, Md.	78
Skelton, Mo.	76
Stallings, Idaho	72
Mollohan, W.Va.	70
Murtha, Pa.	68
Slattery, Kan.	62
Stratton, N.Y.	62
Gaydos, Pa.	62

1986 Coalition Votes

Following is a list of all 1986 votes on which the conservative coalition appeared. The votes are listed by CQ vote number and may be found in the vote charts appearing in the 1986 Weekly Reports.

SENATE VOTES (76)

Coalition Victories (71) — 2, 3, 4, 6, 7, 8, 10, 11, 12, 32, 35, 39, 40, 46, 48, 49, 50, 51, 53, 79, 85, 92, 95, 98, 108, 115, 133, 137, 144, 156, 158, 166, 167, 168, 170, 174, 179, 181, 182, 185, 194, 196, 208, 211, 212, 215, 220, 221, 222, 226, 227, 229, 230, 235, 241, 244, 253, 265, 266, 274, 276, 280, 282, 283, 287, 298, 308, 309, 324, 326, 346.

Coalition Defeats (5) — 22, 45, 218, 315, 332.

HOUSE VOTES (50)

Coalition Victories (39) — 60, 64, 65, 67, 68, 69, 134, 170, 176, 178, 179, 180, 182, 196, 198, 208, 209, 218, 220, 225, 243, 268, 288, 289, 292, 293, 295, 296, 298, 317, 318, 322, 343, 344, 356, 365, 366, 426, 440.

Coalition Defeats (11) — 66, 177, 181, 195, 279, 281, 311, 345, 360, 419, 420.

Individual Opposition Scores

Highest Coalition Opposition Scores. Those who voted against the conservative coalition most consistently in 1986:

SENATE

Southern Democrats

Gore, Tenn.	67%
Sasser, Tenn.	63
Ford, Ky.	53
Bumpers, Ark.	47

Republicans

Specter, Pa.	64
Mathias, Md.	62
Hatfield, Ore.	47
Stafford, Vt.	45
Weicker, Conn.	43

Northern Democrats

Sarbanes, Md.	95%
Riegle, Mich.	95
Metzenbaum, Ohio	93
Harkin, Iowa	91
Levin, Mich.	88
Hart, Colo.	87

HOUSE

Southern Democrats

Leland, Texas	90%
Gonzalez, Texas	88
Lehman, Fla.	76
Synar, Okla.	70
Ford, Tenn.	70
Fascell, Fla.	60
Perkins, Ky.	60

Republicans

Conte, Mass.	76%
Green, N.Y.	64
Leach, Iowa	63
McKinney, Conn.	62
Schneider, R.I.	58
Jeffords, Vt.	56

Northern Democrats

Abercrombie, Hawaii	100% [1]
O'Neill, Mass.	100 [2]
Vento, Minn.	94
Coyne, Pa.	94
Edwards, Calif.	94
Kildee, Mich.	94
Lowry, Wash.	94

[1] *Sworn in Sept. 23; only four votes were counted.*
[2] *Traditionally, House Speaker does not vote; only two votes counted.*

Conservative Coalition Support and Opposition: House

1. Conservative Coalition Support, 1986. Percentage of 50 conservative coalition recorded votes in 1986 on which representative voted "yea" or "nay" *in agreement* with the position of the conservative coalition. Failures to vote lower both support and opposition scores.

2. Conservative Coalition Opposition, 1986. Percentage of 50 conservative coalition recorded votes in 1986 on which representative voted "yea" or "nay" *in disagreement* with the position of the conservative coalition. Failures to vote lower both support and opposition scores.

** Rep. John E. Grotberg, R-Ill., did not participate in House business this year due to a serious illness.*

[1] Rep. Neil Abercrombie, D-Hawaii, was sworn in Sept. 23, 1986, to succeed Cecil Heftel, D-Hawaii, who resigned July 11, 1986, to run for governor of Hawaii. Heftel's 1986 conservative coalition support score was 19 percent; opposition was 31 percent.

[2] Rep. George M. O'Brien, R-Ill., died July 17, 1986. O'Brien's 1986 conservative coalition support score was 11 percent; opposition was 0 percent.

[3] Rep. Thomas P. O'Neill Jr., D-Mass., as Speaker, voted at his discretion.

[4] Rep. Alton R. Waldon Jr., D-N.Y., was sworn in July 29, 1986, to succeed Joseph P. Addabbo, D, who died April 10, 1986. Addabbo's 1986 conservative coalition support score was 0 percent; opposition was 0 percent.

[5] Rep. James T. Broyhill, R-N.C., resigned on July 13, 1986, to fill the vacant seat resulting from the June 29 death of Sen. John P. East. Broyhill's 1986 House conservative coalition support score was 94 percent; opposition was 6 percent.

KEY

† Not eligible for all recorded votes in 1986 (sworn in after Jan. 21) or voted "present" to avoid possible conflict of interest.

Democrats ***Republicans***

	1	2
ALABAMA		
1 ***Callahan***	98	0
2 ***Dickinson***	88	2
3 Nichols	80	0
4 Bevill	82	18
5 Flippo	60	16
6 Erdreich	82	16
7 Shelby	84	8
ALASKA		
AL ***Young***	90	4
ARIZONA		
1 ***McCain***	76	18
2 Udall	18	76
3 ***Stump***	92	6
4 ***Rudd***	70	4
5 ***Kolbe***	88	8
ARKANSAS		
1 Alexander	58	40
2 Robinson	94	6
3 ***Hammerschmidt***	90	10
4 Anthony	62	36
CALIFORNIA		
1 Bosco	36	50
2 ***Chappie***	74	4
3 Matsui	18	82
4 Fazio	30	64
5 Burton	2	54
6 Boxer	12	82
7 Miller	8	80
8 Dellums	2	92
9 Stark	4	92
10 Edwards †	4	94
11 Lantos	40	60
12 ***Zschau***	52	24
13 Mineta	20	80
14 ***Shumway***	90	8
15 Coelho	40	46
16 Panetta	30	66
17 ***Pashayan***	84	12
18 Lehman	26	68
19 ***Lagomarsino***	88	12
20 ***Thomas***	84	12
21 ***Fiedler***	82	2
22 ***Moorhead***	96	4
23 Beilenson	20	80
24 Waxman	2	92
25 Roybal	16	74
26 Berman	12	82
27 Levine	6	86
28 Dixon	12	70
29 Hawkins	6	80
30 Martinez	16	70
31 Dymally	8	86
32 Anderson	32	68
33 ***Dreier***	94	2
34 Torres	10	84
35 ***Lewis***	56	16
36 Brown	16	76
37 ***McCandless***	94	6
38 ***Dornan***	88	12
39 ***Dannemeyer***	88	8
40 ***Badham***	86	6
41 ***Lowery***	80	18
42 ***Lungren***	80	16
43 ***Packard***	88	8
44 Bates	24	76
45 ***Hunter***	90	8
COLORADO		
1 Schroeder	14	82
2 Wirth	24	66
3 ***Strang***	94	6
4 ***Brown***	84	16
5 ***Kramer***	82	10
6 ***Schaefer***	90	4
CONNECTICUT		
1 Kennelly	20	74
2 Gejdenson	12	88
3 Morrison	8	68
4 ***McKinney***	36	62
5 ***Rowland***	82	18
6 ***Johnson***	68	32
DELAWARE		
AL Carper	54	46
FLORIDA		
1 Hutto	92	8
2 Fuqua	76	18
3 Bennett	50	50
4 Chappell	72	20
5 ***McCollum***	96	4
6 MacKay	60	38
7 Gibbons	56	34
8 ***Young***	84	14
9 ***Bilirakis***	96	4
10 ***Ireland***	86	0
11 Nelson	94	6
12 ***Lewis***	86	8
13 ***Mack***	98	0
14 Mica	60	40
15 ***Shaw***	90	6
16 Smith	38	56
17 Lehman	18	76
18 Pepper	46	48
19 Fascell	36	60
GEORGIA		
1 Thomas	96	4
2 Hatcher	78	16
3 Ray	82	16
4 ***Swindall***	98	2
5 Fowler	24	16
6 ***Gingrich***	80	14
7 Darden	80	8
8 Rowland	88	12
9 Jenkins	70	16
10 Barnard	70	4
HAWAII		
1 Abercrombie [1] †	0	100
2 Akaka	28	68
IDAHO		
1 ***Craig***	92	6
2 Stallings	72	26
ILLINOIS		
1 Hayes	4	92
2 Savage	2	90
3 Russo	26	64
4 Vacancy [2]		
5 Lipinski	52	42
6 ***Hyde***	80	20
7 Collins	6	84
8 Rostenkowski	36	58
9 Yates	2	86
10 ***Porter***	68	32
11 Annunzio	32	66
12 ***Crane***	90	4
13 ***Fawell***	78	22
14 ***Grotberg*** *	0	0
15 ***Madigan***	82	10
16 ***Martin***	80	18
17 Evans	6	92
18 ***Michel***	76	18
19 Bruce	34	66
20 Durbin	22	78
21 Price	44	56
22 Gray	48	50
INDIANA		
1 Visclosky	20	80
2 Sharp	42	56
3 ***Hiler***	88	8
4 ***Coats***	84	16
5 ***Hillis***	48	16

	1	2
6 ***Burton***	96	4
7 ***Myers***	82	18
8 McCloskey	52	48
9 Hamilton	48	52
10 Jacobs	26	74
IOWA		
1 ***Leach*** †	37	63
2 ***Tauke***	58	38
3 ***Evans***	68	14
4 Smith	44	52
5 ***Lightfoot***	84	16
6 Bedell	24	74
KANSAS		
1 ***Roberts***	90	8
2 Slattery	62	38
3 ***Meyers***	70	30
4 Glickman	60	40
5 ***Whittaker***	90	10
KENTUCKY		
1 Hubbard	94	6
2 Natcher	58	42
3 Mazzoli	62	38
4 ***Snyder***	78	10
5 ***Rogers***	92	8
6 ***Hopkins***	96	4
7 Perkins	40	60
LOUISIANA		
1 ***Livingston***	92	6
2 Boggs	48	44
3 Tauzin	98	2
4 Roemer	82	18
5 Huckaby	80	4
6 ***Moore***	38	2
7 Breaux	32	0
8 Long	36	52
MAINE		
1 ***McKernan***	60	38
2 ***Snowe***	64	36
MARYLAND		
1 Dyson	88	12
2 ***Bentley***	80	14
3 Mikulski	10	64
4 ***Holt***	70	10
5 Hoyer	26	72
6 Byron	78	18
7 Mitchell	6	70
8 Barnes	6	74
MASSACHUSETTS		
1 ***Conte***	22	76
2 Boland	22	62
3 Early	16	78
4 Frank	12	88
5 Atkins	10	88
6 Mavroules	18	80
7 Markey	8	84
8 O'Neill [3]		
9 Moakley	16	84
10 Studds	6	88
11 Donnelly	18	82
MICHIGAN		
1 Conyers	4	78
2 ***Pursell***	74	22
3 Wolpe	10	88
4 ***Siljander***	78	12
5 ***Henry***	66	34
6 Carr	56	44
7 Kildee	6	94
8 Traxler	34	54
9 ***Vander Jagt***	76	10
10 ***Schuette***	82	8
11 ***Davis***	76	14
12 Bonior	6	84
13 Crockett	2	80
14 Hertel	10	90
15 Ford	12	78
16 Dingell	32	58
17 Levin	12	86
18 ***Broomfield***	72	26
MINNESOTA		
1 Penny	48	52
2 ***Weber***	80	20
3 ***Frenzel***	76	24
4 Vento	6	94
5 Sabo	12	88
6 Sikorski	22	76

	1	2
7 ***Stangeland***	84	10
8 Oberstar	18	82
MISSISSIPPI		
1 Whitten	60	34
2 ***Franklin***	90	4
3 Montgomery	92	8
4 Dowdy	74	14
5 ***Lott***	84	4
MISSOURI		
1 Clay	2	74
2 Young	48	48
3 Gephardt	18	54
4 Skelton	76	20
5 Wheat	12	88
6 ***Coleman***	82	16
7 ***Taylor***	82	14
8 ***Emerson***	92	8
9 Volkmer	60	40
MONTANA		
1 Williams	18	74
2 ***Marlenee***	82	12
NEBRASKA		
1 ***Bereuter***	78	22
2 ***Daub***	90	10
3 ***Smith***	78	16
NEVADA		
1 Reid	48	52
2 ***Vucanovich***	90	10
NEW HAMPSHIRE		
1 ***Smith***	94	6
2 ***Gregg***	84	10
NEW JERSEY		
1 Florio	28	66
2 Hughes	32	68
3 Howard	20	78
4 ***Smith***	60	40
5 ***Roukema***	64	36
6 Dwyer	22	78
7 ***Rinaldo***	60	40
8 Roe	28	68
9 Torricelli	20	68
10 Rodino	10	88
11 ***Gallo***	86	14
12 ***Courter***	84	14
12 ***Saxton***	78	22
14 Guarini	28	70
NEW MEXICO		
1 ***Lujan***	82	6
2 ***Skeen***	94	6
3 Richardson	52	44
NEW YORK		
1 ***Carney***	78	16
2 Downey	16	80
3 Mrazek	16	80
4 ***Lent***	72	18
5 ***McGrath***	70	26
6 Waldon [4] †	19	65
7 Ackerman	4	82
8 Scheuer	8	92
9 Manton	30	60
10 Schumer	14	82
11 Towns	8	86
12 Owens	6	90
13 Solarz	16	80
14 ***Molinari***	76	24
15 ***Green***	36	64
16 Rangel	4	92
17 Weiss	4	76
18 Garcia	2	84
19 Biaggi	36	54
20 ***DioGuardi***	74	24
21 ***Fish***	56	38
22 ***Gilman***	66	30
23 Stratton	62	26
24 ***Solomon***	92	4
25 ***Boehlert***	66	32
26 ***Martin***	86	8
27 ***Wortley***	82	14
28 McHugh	18	82
29 ***Horton***	48	40
30 ***Eckert***	88	10
31 ***Kemp***	72	10
32 LaFalce	20	64
33 Nowak	16	82
34 Lundine	14	40

	1	2
NORTH CAROLINA		
1 Jones	56	30
2 Valentine	90	8
3 Whitley	64	30
4 ***Cobey***	90	6
5 Neal	54	40
6 ***Coble***	92	8
7 Rose	54	42
8 Hefner	64	26
9 ***McMillan***	94	6
10 Vacancy [5]		
11 ***Hendon***	86	14
NORTH DAKOTA		
AL Dorgan	44	56
OHIO		
1 Luken	34	50
2 ***Gradison***	60	34
3 Hall	20	74
4 ***Oxley***	86	14
5 ***Latta***	88	8
6 ***McEwen***	84	4
7 ***DeWine***	82	18
8 ***Kindness***	68	8
9 Kaptur	24	68
10 ***Miller***	86	14
11 Eckart	40	60
12 ***Kasich***	88	12
13 Pease	32	68
14 Seiberling	6	92
15 ***Wylie***	76	22
16 ***Regula***	80	20
17 Traficant	24	76
18 Applegate	50	50
19 Feighan	14	86
20 Oakar	8	88
21 Stokes	2	80
OKLAHOMA		
1 Jones	72	20
2 Synar	24	70
3 Watkins	66	32
4 McCurdy	72	24
5 ***Edwards***	82	10
6 English	82	18
OREGON		
1 AuCoin	36	64
2 ***Smith, R.***	86	12
3 Wyden	38	62
4 Weaver	20	62
5 ***Smith, D.***	90	10
PENNSYLVANIA		
1 Foglietta	10	82
2 Gray	8	82
3 Borski	24	76
4 Kolter	54	44
5 ***Schulze***	60	14
6 Yatron	48	44
7 Edgar	6	62
8 Kostmayer	24	74
9 ***Shuster***	90	8
10 ***McDade***	66	24
11 Kanjorski	54	46
12 Murtha	68	28
13 ***Coughlin***	58	40
14 Coyne	6	94
15 ***Ritter***	88	10
16 ***Walker***	94	6
17 ***Gekas***	92	8
18 Walgren	24	74
19 ***Goodling***	76	24
20 Gaydos	62	26
21 ***Ridge***	68	32
22 Murphy	50	42
23 ***Clinger***	84	14
RHODE ISLAND		
1 St Germain	20	78
2 ***Schneider***	34	58
SOUTH CAROLINA		
1 ***Hartnett***	38	2
2 ***Spence***	94	2
3 Derrick	52	48
4 ***Campbell***	44	0
5 Spratt	54	46
6 Tallon	86	8
SOUTH DAKOTA		
AL Daschle	44	56

	1	2
TENNESSEE		
1 ***Quillen***	82	8
2 ***Duncan***	94	6
3 Lloyd	92	6
4 Cooper	52	40
5 Boner	60	26
6 Gordon	56	40
7 ***Sundquist***	92	6
8 Jones	68	22
9 Ford	12	70
TEXAS		
1 Chapman	86	10
2 Wilson	72	12
3 ***Bartlett***	94	6
4 Hall	88	10
5 Bryant	54	46
6 ***Barton***	92	4
7 ***Archer***	98	2
8 ***Fields***	98	2
9 Brooks	50	34
10 Pickle	80	18
11 Leath	82	16
12 Wright	40	46
13 ***Boulter***	86	6
14 ***Sweeney***	94	0
15 de la Garza	64	32
16 Coleman	64	36
17 Stenholm	88	12
18 Leland	2	90
19 ***Combest***	100	0
20 Gonzalez	10	88
21 ***Loeffler***	86	2
22 ***DeLay***	100	0
23 Bustamante	58	30
24 Frost	52	38
25 Andrews	96	4
26 ***Armey***	100	0
27 Ortiz	70	22
UTAH		
1 ***Hansen***	84	8
2 ***Monson***	82	8
3 ***Nielson***	84	14
VERMONT		
AL ***Jeffords***	44	56
VIRGINIA		
1 ***Bateman***	88	12
2 ***Whitehurst***	64	16
3 ***Bliley***	94	6
4 Sisisky	70	30
5 Daniel	80	14
6 Olin	66	30
7 ***Slaughter***	86	12
8 ***Parris***	76	20
9 Boucher	36	50
10 ***Wolf***	78	22
WASHINGTON		
1 ***Miller***	58	40
2 Swift	22	76
3 Bonker	34	58
4 ***Morrison***	80	18
5 Foley	40	54
6 Dicks	46	54
7 Lowry	6	94
8 ***Chandler***	74	26
WEST VIRGINIA		
1 Mollohan	70	28
2 Staggers	32	68
3 Wise	40	60
4 Rahall	34	66
WISCONSIN		
1 Aspin	42	48
2 Kastenmeier	4	92
3 ***Gunderson***	78	20
4 Kleczka	28	70
5 Moody	16	80
6 ***Petri***	76	24
7 Obey	20	76
8 ***Roth***	88	8
9 ***Sensenbrenner***	80	20
WYOMING		
AL ***Cheney***	92	0

	1	2
ALABAMA		
Denton	91	8
Heflin	84	16
ALASKA		
Murkowski	88	5
Stevens	88	9
ARIZONA		
Goldwater	68	4
DeConcini	61	37
ARKANSAS		
Bumpers	49	47
Pryor	55	38
CALIFORNIA		
Wilson	93	7
Cranston	9	86
COLORADO		
Armstrong	91	5
Hart	9	87
CONNECTICUT		
Weicker	46	43
Dodd	29	70
DELAWARE		
Roth	80	17
Biden	25	71
FLORIDA		
Hawkins	74	14
Chiles	76	22
GEORGIA		
Mattingly	92	8
Nunn	75	16
HAWAII		
Inouye	18	66
Matsunaga	28	66
IDAHO		
McClure	93	4
Symms	88	1
ILLINOIS		
Dixon	59	38
Simon	13	86
INDIANA		
Lugar	88	9
Quayle	95	3

	1	2
IOWA		
Grassley	82	18
Harkin	5	91
KANSAS		
Dole	95	4
Kassebaum	80	13
KENTUCKY		
McConnell	92	8
Ford	47	53
LOUISIANA		
Johnston	67	30
Long	86	12
MAINE		
Cohen	74	25
Mitchell	25	74
MARYLAND		
Mathias	26	62
Sarbanes	3	95
MASSACHUSETTS		
Kennedy	24	70
Kerry	16	79
MICHIGAN		
Levin	11	88
Riegle	5	95
MINNESOTA		
Boschwitz	84	16
Durenberger	66	34
MISSISSIPPI		
Cochran	91	4
Stennis	75	12
MISSOURI		
Danforth	82	17
Eagleton	22	67
MONTANA		
Baucus	37	54
Melcher	14	86
NEBRASKA		
Exon	45	53
Zorinsky	71	28
NEVADA		
Hecht	99	0
Laxalt	87	5

	1	2
NEW HAMPSHIRE		
Humphrey	86	9
Rudman	91	8
NEW JERSEY		
Bradley	36	61
Lautenberg	12	86
NEW MEXICO		
Domenici	95	5
Bingaman	41	59
NEW YORK		
D'Amato	66	30
Moynihan	36	63
NORTH CAROLINA		
Broyhill[1] †	89	7
Helms	95	5
NORTH DAKOTA		
Andrews	61	39
Burdick	20	80
OHIO		
Glenn	29	70
Metzenbaum	5	93
OKLAHOMA		
Nickles	99	1
Boren	92	4
OREGON		
Hatfield	50	47
Packwood	63	30
PENNSYLVANIA		
Heinz	59	38
Specter	29	64
RHODE ISLAND		
Chafee	62	37
Pell	16	80
SOUTH CAROLINA		
Thurmond	97	0
Hollings	74	26
SOUTH DAKOTA		
Abdnor	83	16
Pressler	82	16
TENNESSEE		
Gore	33	67
Sasser	37	63

KEY

† Not eligible for all recorded votes in 1986 (sworn in after Jan. 21) or voted "present" to avoid possible conflict of interest.

Democrats ***Republicans***

	1	2
TEXAS		
Gramm	97	1
Bentsen	87	9
UTAH		
Garn	75	3
Hatch	95	5
VERMONT		
Stafford	43	45
Leahy	21	75
VIRGINIA		
Trible	91	8
Warner	87	12
WASHINGTON		
Evans	76	22
Gorton	72	26
WEST VIRGINIA		
Byrd	30	70
Rockefeller	18	80
WISCONSIN		
Kasten	87	13
Proxmire	22	78
WYOMING		
Simpson	92	4
Wallop	95	1

Conservative Coalition Support and Opposition: Senate

1. Conservative Coalition Support, 1986. Percentage of 76 conservative coalition votes in 1986 on which senator voted "yea" or "nay" *in agreement* with the position of the conservative coalition. Failures to vote lower both support and opposition scores.

2. Conservative Coalition Opposition, 1986. Percentage of 76 conservative coalition votes in 1986 on which senator voted "yea" or "nay" *in disagreement* with the position of the conservative coalition. Failures to vote lower both support and opposition scores.

[1] Sen. James T. Broyhill, R-N.C., was sworn in July 14, 1986, to succeed John P. East, R, who died June 29, 1986. East's 1986 conservative coalition support score was 94 percent; opposition was 6 percent.

PRESIDENTIAL MESSAGES

CQ

Reagan's State of the Union Address

Following is the White House text of President Reagan's State of the Union address, as delivered Feb. 4 before a joint session of Congress.

Mr. Speaker, Mr. President, distinguished members of the Congress, honored guests and fellow citizens, thank you for allowing me to delay my address until this evening. We paused together to mourn and honor the valor of our seven *Challenger* heroes. And I hope that we are now ready to do what they would want us to do — go forward America and reach for the stars. (Applause.) We will never forget those brave seven, but we shall go forward.

Salute to O'Neill

Mr. Speaker, before I begin my prepared remarks, may I point out that tonight marks the 10th and last State of the Union message that you've presided over. And on behalf of the American people, I want to salute you for your service to Congress and the country. (Applause.)

On the Move

I have come to review with you the progress of our nation, to speak of unfinished work, and to set our sights on the future. I am pleased to report the state of our Union is stronger than a year ago, and growing stronger each day. (Applause.) Tonight, we look out on a rising America — firm of heart, united in spirit, powerful in pride and patriotism — America is on the move!

'The Great American Comeback'

But, it wasn't long ago that we looked out on a different land — locked factory gates, long gasoline lines, intolerable prices and interest rates turning the greatest country on Earth into a land of broken dreams. Government growing beyond our consent had become a lumbering giant, slamming shut the gates of opportunity, threatening to crush the very roots of our freedom.

What brought America back? The American people brought us back — with quiet courage and common sense; (applause) with undying faith that in this nation under God the future will be ours, for the future belongs to the free.

Tonight the American people deserve our thanks — for 37 straight months of economic growth; for sunrise firms and modernized industries creating 9 million new jobs in three years; interest rates cut in half, inflation falling over from 12 percent in 1980 to under 4 today; and a mighty river of good works, a record $74 billion in voluntary giving just last year alone.

And despite the pressures of our modern world, family and community remain the moral core of our society, guardians of our values and hopes for the future. Family and community are the costars of this Great American Comeback. They are why we say tonight: Private values must be at the heart of public policies.

What is true for families in America is true for America in the family of free nations. History is no captive of some inevitable force. History is made by men and women of vision and courage. Tonight, freedom is on the march. The United States is the economic miracle, the model to which the world once again turns. We stand for an idea whose time is now: Only by lifting the weights from the shoulders of all can people truly prosper and can peace among all nations be secure.

An 'Agenda for the Future'

Teddy Roosevelt said that a nation that does great work lives forever. We have done well, but we cannot stop at the foothills when Everest beckons. It's time for America to be all that we can be.

We speak tonight of an "Agenda for the Future," an agenda for a safer, more secure world. And we speak about the necessities for actions to steel us for the challenges of growth, trade and security in the next decade and the year 2000. And we will do it — not by breaking faith with bedrock principles, but by breaking free from failed policies. (Applause.)

Let us begin where storm clouds loom darkest — right here in Washington, D.C. This week I will send you our detailed proposals; tonight, let us speak of our responsibility to redefine government's role: Not to control, not to demand or command, not to contain us; but to help in times of need, and above all, to create a ladder of opportunity to full employment so that all Americans can climb toward economic power and justice on their own.

Broken Budget Process

But we cannot win the race to the future shackled to a system that can't even pass a federal budget. We cannot win that race held back by horse-and-buggy programs that waste tax dollars and squander human potential. We cannot win that race if we're swamped in a sea of red ink.

Now, Mr. Speaker, you know, I know, and the American people know the federal budget system is broken. It doesn't work. Before we leave this city, let's you and I work together to fix it. (Applause.) And then we can finally give the American people a balanced budget. (Applause.)

Promise of Gramm-Rudman-Hollings

Members of Congress, passage of Gramm-Rudman-Hollings gives us an historic opportunity to achieve what has eluded our national leadership for decades, forcing federal government to live within its means.

Your schedule now requires that the budget resolution be passed by April 15th, the very day America's families have to foot the bill for the budgets that you produce.

How often we read of a husband and wife both working, struggling from paycheck to paycheck to raise a family, meet a mortgage, pay their taxes and bills. And yet, some in Congress say taxes must be raised. Well, I'm sorry — they're asking the wrong people to tighten their belts. (Applause.) It's time we reduce the federal budget and left the family budget alone. (Applause.) We do not face large deficits because American families are undertaxed; we face those deficits because the federal government overspends.

The detailed budget that we will submit will meet the Gramm-Rudman-Hollings target for deficit reductions, meet our commitment to ensure a strong national defense, meet our commitment to protect Social Security and the truly less fortunate, and, yes, meet our commitment to not raise taxes. (Applause.)

How should we accomplish this? Well, not by taking from those in need. As families take care of their own, government must provide shelter and nourishment for those who cannot provide for themselves. But we must revise or replace programs enacted in the name of compassion that degrade the moral worth of work, encourage family breakups, and drive entire communities into a bleak and heartless dependency.

Call for Line-Item Veto

Gramm-Rudman-Hollings can mark a dramatic improvement. But experience shows that simply setting deficit targets does not assure they'll be met. We must proceed with Grace Commission reforms against waste. And tonight, I ask you to give me what 43 Governors have — give me a line-item veto this year. (Applause.) Give me the authority to veto waste, and I'll take the responsibility, I'll make the cuts, I'll take the heat.

This authority would not give me any monopoly power, but simply prevent spending measures from sneaking through that could not pass on their own merit. And you can sustain or override my veto — that's the way the system should work. Once we've made the hard choices, we should lock in our gains with a balanced budget amendment to the Constitution. (Applause.)

Commitment to Defense

I mentioned that we will meet our commitment to national defense. We must meet it. Defense is not just another budget expense. Keeping America strong, free, and at peace is solely the responsibility of the Federal Government; it is Government's prime responsibility. We have devoted five years trying to narrow a dangerous gap born of illusion and neglect. And we've made important gains. Yet the threat from Soviet forces, conventional and strategic, from the Soviet drive for domination, from the increase in espionage and state terror remains great. This is reality. Closing our eyes will not make reality disappear.

We pledge together to hold real growth in defense spending to the bare minimum. My budget honors that pledge. And I'm now asking you, the Congress, to keep its end of the bargain. The Soviets must know that if America reduces her defenses, it will be because of a reduced threat, not a reduced resolve. (Applause.)

Keeping America strong is as vital to the national security as controlling Federal spending is to our economic security. But, as I have said before, the most powerful force we can enlist against the Federal deficit is an ever-expanding American economy, unfettered and free.

Push for Tax Overhaul

The magic of opportunity — unreserved, unfailing, unrestrained — isn't this the calling that unites us? I believe our tax rate cuts for the people have done more to spur a spirit of risk-taking and help America's economy break free than any program since John Kennedy's tax cut almost a quarter century ago.

Now history calls us to press on, to complete efforts for an historic tax reform providing new opportunity for all and ensuring that all pay their fair share — but no more. We've come this far. Will you join me now and we'll walk this last mile together? (Applause.)

You know my views on this. We cannot and we will not accept tax reform that is a tax increase in disguise. True reform must be an engine of productivity and growth, and that means a top personal rate no higher than 35 percent. True reform must be truly fair and that means raising personal exemptions to $2,000. True reform means a tax system that at long last is pro-family, pro-jobs, pro-future, and pro-America. (Applause.)

Efforts for Freer Trade

As we knock down the barriers to growth, we must redouble our efforts for freer and fairer trade. We have already taken actions to counter unfair trading practices to pry open closed foreign markets. We will continue to do so. We will also oppose legislation touted as providing protection that in reality pits one American worker against another, one industry against another, one community against another, and that raises prices for us all. If the United States can trade with other nations on a level playing field, we can out-produce, out-compete, and out-sell anybody, anywhere in the world. (Applause.)

International Currencies

The constant expansion of our economy and exports requires a sound and stable dollar at home and reliable exchange rates around the world. We must never again permit wild currency swings to cripple our farmers and other exporters. Farmers, in particular, have suffered from past unwise government policies. They must not be abandoned with problems they did not create and cannot control. We've begun coordinating economic and monetary policy among our major trading partners. But there's more to do, and tonight I am directing Treasury Secretary Jim Baker to determine if the nations of the world should convene to discuss the role and relationship of our currencies. (Applause.)

Social Agenda

Confident in our future, and secure in our values, Americans are striving forward to embrace the future. We see it not only in our recovery, but in three straight years of falling crime rates, as families and communities band together to fight pornography, drugs, and lawlessness, and to give back to their children the safe and, yes, innocent childhood they deserve.

We see it in the renaissance in education, the rising SAT scores for three years — last year's increase the greatest since 1963. It wasn't government and Washington lobbies that turned education around, it was the American people who, in reaching for excellence, knew to reach back to basics. We must continue the advance by supporting discipline in our schools; vouchers that give parents freedom of choice; and we must give back to our children their lost right to acknowledge God in their classrooms. (Applause.)

We are a nation of idealists, yet today there is a wound in our national conscience; America will never be whole as long as the right to life granted by our Creator is denied to the unborn. For the rest of my time, I shall do what I can to see that this wound is one day healed. (Applause.)

Re-evaluating Welfare Programs

As we work to make the American Dream real for all, we must also look to the condition of America's families. Struggling parents today worry how they will provide their children the advantages that their parents gave them. In the welfare culture, the breakdown of the family, the most basic support system, has reached crisis proportions — in female and child poverty, child abandonment, horrible crimes and deteriorating schools. After hundreds of billions of dollars in poverty programs, the plight of the poor grows more painful. But the waste in dollars and cents pales before the most tragic loss — the sinful waste of human spirit and potential.

We can ignore this terrible truth no longer. As Franklin Roosevelt warned 51 years ago, standing before this chamber, he said, "Welfare is a narcotic, a subtle destroyer of the human spirit." And we must now escape the spider's web of dependency. Tonight I am charging the White House Domestic Council to present me by December 1, 1986, an evaluation of programs and a strategy for immediate action to meet the financial, educational, social, and safety concerns of poor families. I am talking about real and lasting emancipation, because the success of welfare should be judged by how many of its recipients become independent of welfare. (Applause.)

Affordable Health Insurance

Further, after seeing how devastating illness can destroy the financial security of the family, I am directing the Secretary of Health and Human Services, Dr. Otis Bowen, to report to me by year end with recommendations on how the private sector and government can work together to address the problems of affordable insurance for those whose life savings would otherwise be threatened when catastrophic illness strikes.

Message to Young People

And tonight I want to speak directly to America's younger generation, because you hold the destiny of our nation in your hands. With all the temptations young people face it sometimes seems the allure of the permissive society requires superhuman feats of self-control. But the call of the future is too strong, the challenge too great to get lost in the blind alleyways of dissolution, drugs, and despair.

Wonder and Achievement

Never has there been a more exciting time to be alive — a time of rousing wonder and heroic achievement. As they said in the film "Back to the Future": "Where we are going, we don't need roads." Well, today physicists peering into the infinitely small realms of subatomic particles find reaffirmations of religious faith. Astronomers build a space telescope that can see to the edge of the universe and possibly back to the moment of creation.

Continuing the Space Program

So, yes, this nation remains fully committed to America's space program. We're going forward with our shuttle flights, we're going forward to build our space station, and we are going forward with research on a new Orient Express that could, by the end of the next decade, take off from Dulles Airport, accelerate up to 25 times the speed of sound, attaining low Earth orbit or flying to Tokyo within two hours. (Applause.)

Anti-Missile Defense

And the same technology transforming our lives can solve the greatest problem of the 20th century. A security shield can one day render nuclear weapons obsolete and free mankind from the prison of nuclear terror. (Applause.) America met one historic challenge and went to the moon. Now America must meet another — to make our strategic defense real for all the citizens of planet Earth.

U.S.-Soviet Relations

Let us speak of our deepest longing for the future — to leave our children a land that is free and just and a world at peace. It is my hope that our fireside summit in Geneva and Mr. Gorbachev's upcoming visit to America can lead to a more stable relationship. Surely no people on Earth hate war more or love peace more than we Americans. (Applause.)

But we cannot stroll into the future with childlike faith. Our differences with a system that openly proclaims and practices an alleged right to command people's lives and to export its ideology by force are deep and abiding.

Logic and history compel us to accept that our relationship be guided by realism — rock-hard, cleareyed, steady, and sure. Our negotiators in Geneva have proposed a radical cut in offensive forces by each side, with no cheating. They have made clear that Soviet compliance with the letter and spirit of agreements is essential. If the Soviet government wants an agreement that truly reduces nuclear arms, there will be an agreement. (Applause.)

But arms control is no substitute for peace. We know that peace follows in freedom's path and conflicts erupt when the will of the people is denied. So we must prepare for peace not only by reducing weapons but by bolstering prosperity, liberty, and democracy however and wherever we can. (Applause.)

Advancing Opportunity

We advance the promise of opportunity every time we speak out on behalf of lower tax rates, freer markets, sound currencies around the world. We strengthen the family of freedom every time we work with allies and come to the aid of friends under siege. And we can enlarge the family of free nations if we will defend the unalienable rights of all God's children to follow their dreams.

Support for 'Freedom Fighters'

To those imprisoned in regimes held captive, to those beaten for daring to fight for freedom and democracy — for their right to worship, to speak, to live and to prosper in the family of free nations — we say to you tonight: You are not alone, Freedom Fighters. America will support you with moral and material assistance your right not just to fight and die for freedom, but to fight and win freedom — (applause) — to win freedom in Afghanistan; in Angola; in Cambodia; and in Nicaragua. (Applause.)

This is a great moral challenge for the entire world. Surely, no issue is more important for peace in our own hemisphere, for the security of our frontiers, for the protection of our vital interests — than to achieve democracy in Nicaragua and to protect Nicaragua's democratic neighbors.

This year I will be asking Congress for the means to do what must be done for the great and good cause. As "Scoop" Jackson, the inspiration for our Bipartisan Commission on Central America, once said, "In matters of national security, the best politics is no politics." (Applause.)

The Race to the Future

What we accomplish this year, in each challenge we face, will set our course for the balance of the decade, indeed for the remainder of the century. After all we've done so far, let no one say that this nation cannot reach the destiny of our dreams. America believes, America is ready, America can win the race to the future — and we shall.

The American Dream is a song of hope that rings through night winter air. Vivid, tender music that warms our hearts when the least among us aspire to the greatest things — to venture a daring enterprise; to unearth new beauty in music, literature, and art; to discover a new universe inside a tiny silicon chip or a single human cell.

'Heroes of Our Hearts'

We see the dream coming true in the spirit of discovery of Richard Cavoli — all his life he's been enthralled by the mysteries of medicine. And Richard, we know that the experiment that you began in high school was launched and lost last week, yet your dream lives. And as long as it's real, work of noble note will yet be done — work that could reduce the harmful effects of X-rays on patients and enable astronomers to view the golden gateways of the farthest stars.

We see the dream glow in the towering talent of a 12-year-old, Tyrone Ford — a child prodigy of gospel music, he has surmounted personal adversity to become an accomplished pianist and singer. He also directs the choirs of three churches and has performed at the Kennedy Center.

With God as your composer, Tyrone, your music will be the music of angels.

We see the dream being saved by the courage of the 13-year-old, Shelby Butler — honor student and member of her school's safety patrol. Seeing another girl freeze in terror before an out-of-control school bus, she risked her life and pulled her to safety.

With bravery like yours, Shelby, America need never fear for our future.

And we see the dream born again in the joyful compassion of a 13-year-old, Trevor Ferrell. Two years ago, age 11, watching men and women bedding down in abandoned doorways — on television he was watching — Trevor left his suburban Philadelphia home to bring blankets and food to the helpless and homeless. And now, 250 people help him fulfill his nightly vigil.

Trevor, yours is the living spirit of brotherly love. Would you four stand up for a moment? (Applause.)

Thank you, thank you. You are heroes of our hearts. We look at you and know it's true — in this land of dreams fulfilled, where greater dreams may be imagined, nothing is impossible, no victory is beyond our reach, no glory will ever be too great.

So now, it's up to us, all of us, to prepare America for that day when our work will pale before the greatness of America's champions in the 21st century. The world's hopes rest with America's future; America's hopes rest with us. So let us go forward to create our world of tomorrow in faith, in unity, and in love.

God bless you and God bless America. (Applause.) ■

For Fiscal Year 1987:

President's Budget Message

Following is the text of President Reagan's budget message to Congress for fiscal year 1987, dated Feb. 5.

To the Congress of the United States:

The economic expansion we are now enjoying is one of the most vigorous in 35 years. Family income is at an all-time high; production and productivity are increasing; employment gains have been extraordinary; and inflation, which raged at double-digit rates when I took office, has been reduced dramatically. Defense capabilities, which had been dangerously weakened during the 1970s, are being rebuilt, restoring an adequate level of national security and deterrence to war. Moreover, an insupportable growth in tax burdens and Federal regulations has been halted.

Let me give you a few highlights:

- Employment has grown by 9.2 million in the past three years, while the unemployment rate has fallen by 3.8 percentage points; during the three years preceding my administration, employment grew by only 5.5 million and the unemployment rate rose 0.8 percentage points.
- The highest proportion of our adult population (60%) is now at work, with more blacks and other minorities employed (14 million) than ever before.
- Inflation, which averaged 11.6% a year during the three years before I took office, has averaged only a third of that — 3.8% — during the last three years.
- Real GNP has grown at a 4.5% annual rate during the past three years, compared with only a 2.2% annual rate during the last three years of the previous administration.
- The prime rate of interest and other key interest rates are less than half what they were when I took office.
- Some 11,000 new business incorporations are generated every week, and since early 1983, investment in plant and equipment has risen 44% in real terms.
- During the past three years, industrial

production has risen by 25%.

- During the same period, corporate profits increased 117% and stocks nearly doubled in value.
- Federal tax revenues have returned to historic levels of approximately 18½% of GNP, as tax rates have been cut across-the-board and indexed for inflation.
- As a result of all of the above, real after-tax personal income has risen 10.6% during the last three years — an average increase of $2,500 for each American household.

This dramatic improvement in the performance of our economy was no accident. We have put in place policies that reflect our commitment to reduce Federal Government intrusion in the private sector and have eliminated many barriers to the process of capital formation and growth. We continue to maintain a steadfast adherence to the four fundamental principles of the economic program I presented in February 1981:

- Reducing the growth of Federal spending;
- Limiting tax burdens;
- Relieving the economy of excessive regulation; and
- Supporting a sound and stable monetary policy.

Conditions are now in place for a sustained era of national prosperity. But, there is a major threat looming on the horizon; the Federal deficit. If this deficit is not brought under control, we risk losing all we've achieved — and more.

We cannot let this happen. Therefore, the budget I am presenting has as its major objective setting the deficit on a downward path to a balanced budget by 1991. In so doing, my budget meets or exceeds the deficit reduction targets set out in the Balanced Budget and Emergency Deficit Control Act, commonly known for its principal sponsors as Gramm-Rudman-Hollings.

At the end of the last session of Congress there emerged a bipartisan consensus that something had to be done about the deficit. The result — Gramm-Rudman-Hollings — committed both the President and the Congress to a fixed schedule of progress. By submitting this budget, I am abiding by the law and keeping my part of the bargain.

This budget shows, moreover, that eliminating the deficit is possible *without* raising taxes, *without* sacrificing our defense preparedness, and *without* cutting into legitimate programs for the poor and the elderly. A tax increase would jeopardize our economic expansion and might well prove counterproductive in terms of its effect on the deficit. We can hardly back away from our defense build-up without creating confusion among friends and adversaries alike about our determination to maintain our commitments and without jeopardizing our prospects for meaningful arms control talks. And frankly we must not break faith with those poor and elderly who depend on Federal programs for their security.

THE DEFICIT AND ECONOMIC GROWTH

Until the Second World War, the Federal budget was kept in balance or ran a surplus during peacetime as a matter of course. But in the early 1960s this traditional fiscal discipline and political rectitude began to break down. We have run deficits during 24 of the last 25 years. In the past ten years, they have averaged 2.5% of GNP. But last year the deficit was over 5% of GNP. This trend is clearly in the wrong direction and must be reversed.

Last year's deficit amounted to nearly $1,000 for every man, woman, and child in the United States. To eliminate the deficit solely by increasing taxes would mean imposing an extra $2,400 burden on each American household. But taxes are already higher relative to GNP than they were during the 1960s and early 1970s — before inflation pushed them to levels that proved insupportable. The American people have made it clear they will not tolerate a higher tax burden. Spending is the problem — not taxes — and spending must be cut.

The program of spending cuts and other reforms contained in my budget will lead to a balanced budget at the end of five years and will thus remove a serious impediment to the continuation of our economic expansion. As this budget shows, such reforms can be accomplished in an orderly manner, without resorting to desperate measures.

Inappropriate and outmoded programs, and activities that cannot be made cost effective, must be ended. Activities that are essential, but that need not be carried out by the Federal Government, can be placed in the private sector or, if they are properly public in nature, turned over to State and local governments. As explained in the Management Report I am also submitting today, efficiencies can be realized through improved management techniques, increased productivity, and program consolidations.

The need to cut unnecessary Federal spending and improve management of necessary programs must be made a compelling guide to our policy choices. The result will be a leaner, better integrated, more streamlined Federal Government — stripped of marginal, nonessential and inappropriate functions and activities, and focusing its energies and resources entirely on its proper tasks and constitutional responsibilities. That way, resources will be allocated more efficiently — those things best done by government will be done by government; those things best done by the private sector will be directed by the marketplace.

The Balanced Budget and Emergency Deficit Control Act (Gramm-Rudman-Hollings) requires that spending be reduced in accord with a prescribed formula if projected deficits exceed the predetermined targets. This mechanism will operate in a limited fashion during the current fiscal year. However, we should avoid such across-the-board cuts in the future, and they will not be necessary if Congress adopts this budget. Achieving budget savings by taking into account relative priorities among programs is a much better way than resorting to an arbitrary formula. The latter could dangerously weaken vital programs involving the national security or public health and safety, while leaving marginal programs substantially intact.

If the spending cuts and other reforms proposed in this budget are approved, the Federal deficit will be reduced by $166 billion over the next three years. This represents about $700 for every individual American and about $1,900 for every household. I believe this is the appropriate way to deal with the deficit: cut excessive Federal spending rather than attack the family budget by increasing taxes, or risk a deterioration in our national security posture, or break faith with the dependent poor and elderly.

RESTRUCTURING AND RETURNING THE FEDERAL GOVERNMENT TO ITS PROPER ROLE

The task of reducing the deficit must be pursued with an eye toward narrowing the current wide scope of Government activities to the provision of those, but only those, necessary and essential services toward which all taxpayers should be contributing — and providing them as efficiently as possible. This is the underlying philosophy that I have used in shaping this year's budget. Let me explain:

High priority programs should be adequately funded. — Despite the very tight fiscal environment, this budget provides funds for maintaining — and in some cases expanding — high priority programs in crucial areas of national interest. Necessary services and income support for the dependent poor and the elderly receive significant funding in this budget. So do other programs of national interest, including drug enforcement, AIDS research, the space program, nonmilitary research, and national security.

While national security programs continue to be one of my highest priorities, they have not been exempt from general budgetary stringency. Last summer I reluctantly agreed with Congress to scale back the planned growth of defense appropriations to a zero real increase for 1986 and only a 3% real increase each year thereafter. Congressional action on 1986 appropriations and the subsequent sequestration for 1986 under Gramm-Rudman-Hollings have cut defense budget authority well below last year's level. The budget I am submitting would return defense funding to a steady, well-managed growth pattern consistent with the program levels agreed to in last year's budget resolution and consistent with what the country needs in order to provide for our national security.

During the past five years, we have reversed the decline in defense spending and have made significant progress in restoring our military capabilities. The moderate increases that are now requested are necessary to maintain this progress and enable us to move forward with meaningful arms reduction negotiations with the Soviet Union.

Unnecessary programs are no longer affordable. — Some government programs have become outmoded, have accomplished their original purpose, represent an inappropriate area for Federal involvement in the first place, or are marginal in the current tight budgetary environment. If it would not be appropriate or feasible for the private sector or for State or local governments to assume such functions, this budget proposes that programs of this variety be terminated immediately, phased out in an orderly manner, or eliminated when their legal authority expires. Examples include Small Business Administration credit programs, Amtrak grants, Urban Development Action Grants, the Appalachian Regional Commission, the Economic Development Administration, the Interstate Commerce Commission, Maritime Administration loan guarantees, education subsidies for health professionals, the work incentives program, and subsidies for air carriers.

Many other programs should be reduced to a more appropriate scale. — Some Federal programs have become overextended, misdirected, or operate on too expansive a scale given the current tight budgetary environment. This budget proposes reforms to limit the costs and future growth of medicare and medicaid, subsidized housing, Civil Service pensions and health benefits, postal subsidies, interstate highway grants, the Forest Service, and many other programs.

The Government should not compete with the private sector. — Traditionally, governments supply the type of needed services that would not be provided by the private marketplace. Over the years, however, the Federal Government has acquired many commercial-type operations. In most cases, it would be better for the Government to get out of the business and stop competing with the private sector, and in this budget I propose that we begin that process. Examples of such "privatization" initiatives in this budget include sale of the power marketing administrations and the naval petroleum reserves; and implementation of housing and education voucher programs. I am also proposing the sale of unneeded assets, such as loan portfolios and surplus real estate, and contracting out appropriate Federal services.

Many services can be provided better by State and local governments. — Over the years, the Federal Government has preempted many functions that properly ought to be operated at the State or local level. This budget contemplates an end to unwarranted Federal intrusion into the State and local sphere and restoration of a more balanced, constitutionally appropriate, federalism with more clearly delineated roles for the various levels of government. Examples include new consolidations of restrictive small categorical grant programs into block grants for transportation and environmental protection, at reduced Federal costs. Continued funding is maintained for existing block grants for social services, health, education, job training, and community development.

Administration of the agricultural extension service should be turned over to State and local governments. Also, the Federal Government should get out of the business of paying for local sewage treatment systems, local airports, local law enforcement, subsidies to State maritime schools, and local coastal management.

Remaining Federal activities should be better managed. — As we proceed with the deficit reduction process over the next several years, it is important that all remaining Federal operations be well managed and coordinated to avoid duplication, reduce costs, and minimize regulatory burdens imposed on the private sector. Management efficiencies must accompany the process of developing a leaner, more carefully focused Federal role. We can no longer afford unnecessary overhead and inefficiencies when we are scaling back the role and cost of the Federal Government.

Substantial savings in overhead costs have been achieved under provisions of the Deficit Reduction Act of 1984. As described in my Management Report, more savings are possible, and these effects are incorporated in this budget. Outmoded, inefficient systems of agency cash and credit management are being replaced; administrative policies and procedures, approaches to automatic data processing, and agency field structures will be streamlined and upgraded; and waste, fraud, and abuse will be further reduced. All these initiatives, part of our Reform '88 program, will take advantage of efficiencies made possible by modern management techniques, improved communications, and new information technology. We shall run the Federal Government on a business-like basis — improving service delivery and reducing taxpayer costs.

Administration of Federal agencies will be made more efficient through the adoption of staffing standards, automation of manual processes, consolidation of similar functions, and reduction of administrative overhead costs. A program to increase productivity by 20% by 1992 in all appropriate Government functions is being instituted, and a major effort is proposed to revamp our outmoded management of a $250 billion Federal credit portfolio. This effort will include establishing prescreening, origination fees, administration and penalty charges, use of collection agencies, charging appropriate interest rates, and the sale of loan portfolios.

Our management improvement program will result in a leaner and more efficient Federal structure and is described in greater detail in my separate Management Report. Improving the management of the Government must be accorded a crucial role and the priority it deserves.

We must also reduce unnecessary costs and burdens on the nonfederal sector and have already made considerable progress in reducing the costs imposed on businesses and State and local governments by Federal regulations. These savings are estimated to total $150 billion over a 10-year period. We have reduced the number of new regulations in every year I have been in office and have eliminated or reduced paperwork requirements by over 500 million hours. In addition, regulations are now more carefully crafted to achieve the greatest public protection for the least cost, and wherever possible to use market forces instead of working against them.

Finally, user fees should be charged for services where appropriate. — Those who receive special benefits and services from the Federal Government should be the ones to bear the costs of those services, not the general taxpayer. Accordingly, this budget imposes fees and premiums for Federal guarantees of loans, and imposes user fees and charges for Federal cost recovery for meat and poultry inspection, National park and forest facilities, harbor and inland waterway use, Coast Guard and Customs inspections, and for many other services.

REFORM OF THE BUDGET PROCESS

Over the years, Federal spending constituencies have become increasingly powerful. In part because of their strong and effective advocacy, Congress has become less and less able to face up to its budgetary responsibilities. The Congressional budget process is foundering; last year it fell apart time and time again. The budget resolution and appropriations bills were months late in passing, and few real deficit reductions were achieved.

Gramm-Rudman-Hollings offers a significant opportunity to avoid many of these problems in the future. That act not only sets deficit targets leading to a balanced budget by 1991, it provides a mechanism for automatic spending cuts and incorporates certain reforms in the budget process itself. But Gramm-Rudman-Hollings does not go far enough in this regard. To meet the clear need for a greatly strengthened budget process, I propose a number of additional reform measures.

As before, I ask Congress to pass a balanced budget amendment to the Constitution. In addition, I continue to seek passage of a line item veto — authority now possessed by 43 of the Nation's governors. I also urge, for 1988 and beyond, changing the budget resolution to a joint resolution subject to Presidential signature and establishing binding expenditure subcategories within the resolution budget totals. Moreover, I urge that serious study be given to proposals for multiyear appropriations and to the development of a capital budget.

As I have pointed out time and again, there's not a State in the Union that doesn't have a better budget process than the Federal Government. We can — and we must — do better.

CONCLUSION

As I said in my address to Congress yesterday, the State of the Union is strong and growing stronger. We've had some extraordinarily good years, and our economy is performing well, with inflation coming under control. Economic growth and investment are up, while interest rates, tax rates, and unemployment have all come down substantially. Our national security is being restored. The proliferation of unnecessary and burdensome Federal regulations has been halted. A significant beginning has been made toward curbing the excessive and unsustainable growth of domestic spending. Improving the management of the Government has been given priority and is achieving results. I think most Americans would agree that America is truly on the move!

The large and stubbornly persistent budget deficit remains as a dark and threatening cloud on the horizon. It threatens our prosperity and our hopes for continued healthy economic growth.

Congress has recognized this threat. It has mandated a gradual, orderly movement to a balanced budget over the next five years. The proposals in this budget are a blueprint for achieving those targets while preserving legitimate programs for the aged and needy, providing for our national security, and doing this without raising taxes.

I realize it will be difficult for elected officials to make the hard choices envisioned in this budget. But we must find the political will to face up to our responsibilities and resist the pleadings of special interests whose "era of power" in Washington must be brought to an end — for taxpayers as a whole can no longer be expected to carry them on their backs. All this will call for statesmanship of a high order. We must all realize that the deficit problem is also an opportunity — an opportunity to construct a new, leaner, better focused, and better managed Federal structure. Let's do it.

I look forward to working with Congress on meeting these formidable challenges. It is our job. Let's get on with it.

RONALD REAGAN

February 5, 1986 ∎

Transmitted to Congress on Feb. 6:

Reagan's Economic Report

Following is the White House text of President Reagan's Economic Report, sent to Congress Feb. 6.

TO THE CONGRESS
OF THE UNITED STATES:

The major economic objectives of my Administration from its beginning have been strong, sustainable, noninflationary economic growth and expanding economic opportunities for all Americans. To achieve these goals, we have pursued policies that are in the long-term best interest of the Nation.

The benefits of this approach are now clear. The economy has entered the fourth year of a robust expansion that has dramatically increased opportunities for all Americans. Millions of new jobs have been created. Investment opportunities have increased. Standards of living have risen. Moreover, this success has been accomplished without rekindling inflation.

We are committed to continuing and extending policies that encourage the private investment and innovation that are the foundation of this expansion. We continue to resist unnecessary increases in government spending and unwarranted interference in private markets. Sustained, strong economic growth depends critically on allowing the market system to function as freely as possible. Free markets provide proper incentives to work, save, and invest, and they ensure that the interests of consumers are served.

These basic principles were embodied in our 1981 Program for Economic Recovery and reaffirmed in the second-term Program for Growth and Opportunity. These programs do not offer "quick fixes" but rely on the inherent ability of the free market system to allocate resources efficiently and to generate economic prosperity. The fundamental responsibility of the Federal Government should be to provide a stable environment within which people can make economic decisions, not to make those decisions for them. To this end, our initial program involved four essential elements:

- Restrain the growth of Federal spending,
- Reduce personal and business taxes,
- Reduce regulatory excesses, and
- Encourage stable and moderate monetary growth.

THE CURRENT EXPANSION

The success of our policies is now apparent. Even though economic growth slowed a bit in 1985 compared with its strong performance in 1983 and 1984, the expansion has nonetheless proceeded at an encouraging pace. It is already 4 months longer in duration than the average peacetime expansion since World War II. If the expansion continues as expected throughout 1986, it will be the third longest in the postwar period.

This expansion has been characterized by unusually strong real business investment in plant and equipment due to our successful attack on inflation and to our tax policy, which stimulated investment. Real business investment has contributed nearly twice as much to real gross national product (GNP) growth in this expansion as it typically has in previous postwar expansions; as a share of real GNP, it is higher than at any other time in the postwar period. Stronger U.S. investment means not only a stronger economy today, but also higher productivity and the potential for faster growth in the future.

Strong employment growth is another outstanding feature of this recovery. Since the end of the last recession in November 1982, the U.S. economy has employed more than 9 million new workers. Furthermore, the unemployment rate fell from 10.6 percent in November 1982 to 6.9 percent in December 1985. Despite this dramatic improvement, however, we will not be satisfied until all American workers can find jobs at wages commensurate with their skills.

When we initiated our Program for Economic Recovery, we were confident that a resourceful, flexible economy, unencumbered by excessive governmental intervention, would create jobs. At the same time, we believed that restrained monetary growth would reduce inflation. Our optimism was justified. The rate of inflation is now less than one-third of the rate in 1980. During this expansion, inflation has maintained its lowest level in more than a decade despite the tremendous employment growth that the economy has generated. Reflecting in part the reduction in inflation, interest rates — especially long-term rates — have declined throughout 1985 and by the end of the year were at their lowest levels in 6 years.

Our success in reducing inflation came as a surprise to some. As inflation rose in the 1970s, some businesses and individuals incurred debt in order to purchase assets, expecting the income generated by these assets to rise with inflation while the real burden of servicing the debt decreased. With the decline in inflation, the real burden of debt servicing rose and the income generated by many assets fell. This combination of events has strained some U.S. financial institutions. Falling farm incomes have hampered the ability of some farmers to pay interest on their debt. Similarly, many less developed countries have had difficulty repaying loans from U.S. financial institutions. The stress that the undesirable rise in inflation and its desirable but unexpectedly rapid decline have imposed on the U.S. financial system emphasizes the importance of achieving and maintaining long-term price stability.

America's optimism concerning continued growth in economic opportunities is shared by businesses and individuals throughout the world. The United States has been and remains one of the few major immigrant-receiving countries, reflecting in part the economy's ability to generate economic opportunities. During the current expansion, profitable investment opportunities in the United States have also attracted foreign capital, helping to finance the rapid growth in investment. The inflow of foreign capital indicates a strong economy. As other nations continue to move toward market-oriented policies and reduce excessive government spending, taxation, and structural rigidities, they too will generate increased investment opportunities, resulting in increased growth and stronger currencies as more capital flows into their economies.

THE ECONOMIC OUTLOOK

Many factors point to continuation of the current expansion. Economic conditions at the end of 1985 were more favorable than they were at the beginning of the year and are expected to improve further. Monetary growth during the past year has been sufficient to accommodate growth in the economy. The leading economic indicators have risen in 11 of the past 12 months. Inventories are relatively low, and as sales continue to expand, production should increase to replenish depleted inventories. Interest rates have continued their decline, promising to spur additional capital spending. Furthermore, the warning signals that typically precede the end of expansions have not been observed. Thus, we feel confident that the current expansion will continue through 1986.

We expect increased growth in real GNP of 4 percent in 1986, continuing throughout 1987 and 1988 and declining gradually in 1989-91 as the economy approaches its long-run real growth trend. Given the monetary and exchange rate developments during the past year, we anticipate a slight rise in inflation in 1986-87. However, if the Federal Reserve reaffirms its resolve to achieve price stability, a goal that I support without reservation, the downturn in inflation should resume in later years.

Changing events, including erratic monetary and fiscal policies, can bring any expansion to an abrupt and unexpected halt. Our projections for the longer term are premised on the assumption that stable economic policies will foster continued economic growth and will also provide the needed flexibility for the economy to respond to external disturbances. Our policy goals reflect this commitment to economic stability as the key contribution to sustained growth, stable prices, declining interest rates, and falling unemployment. The American people have a right to expect such results and, with the cooperation of the Congress and the Federal Reserve, we expect to continue to deliver them.

THE ECONOMIC ROLE OF GOVERNMENT

In formulating our program for healthy and continued economic expansion, we recognized the limited role that government properly plays. The Federal Government cannot provide prosperity or generate economic growth; it can only encourage private initiative, innovation, and entrepreneurial activity that produce economic opportunities. An overly active government actually hinders economic progress. Federal spending absorbs resources, many of which could be better used by the private sector. Excessive taxation distorts relative prices and relative rates of return. By arbitrarily reallocating resources, it inhibits the economy's ability to grow. Thus, the best way for government to promote economic growth is to provide a foundation of stable, predictable economic policies, and then to stand back and let the creative potential of the American people flourish.

The Federal Government has several definite responsibilities that my Administration continues to uphold. The first is to provide an adequate national defense. World peace and security require the United States, as the leader of the free world, to demonstrate its willingness and ability to defend its own national security and to contribute to the defense of its allies.

Furthermore, we will not ignore the less fortunate in this society. My Administration continues to provide an appropriate safety net to aid those individuals who need help. At the same time, we have worked to develop a strong, vibrant, opportunity-generating economy that can offer meaningful jobs to all who are able to work. The economic expansion has done much more to reduce poverty than any government transfer program. The significant decline in the percentage of the population in poverty in 1984 reflects both the success of our programs and the strength of the economy. Moreover, tax reform will benefit the working poor. My proposed tax reforms eliminate the Federal income tax burden of most working poor.

Finally, even though we believe that markets generally allocate resources most efficiently, there are a few special cases, such as air and water pollution, in which the market mechanism alone may be inadequate. In these instances, government intervention is necessary, but even here, it should be based on market principles. For example, the Environmental Protection Agency has approved arrangements that enable firms to earn credits for reducing emissions below the required limits, which they can sell to other firms facing higher costs of emission control. In this way, environmental quality is maintained and improved while the costs of compliance decline.

Control Federal Spending

Fulfillment of these limited responsibilities, however, does not require the level or the rate of growth of Federal spending that the Nation has been experiencing. In spite of our efforts, spending remains excessive and has been the primary cause of the large budget deficit. Tax rate cuts did not generate this deficit; in fact, current tax receipts are as large a share of GNP as they were in the late 1970s, even after the reduction in tax rates that we initiated in 1981. The key to resolving the Federal budget deficit is to restrain unneeded spending. Spending, not the deficit, is the true indicator of the cost of government, because it measures the total economic resources diverted from the private sector. Excessive spending affects the economy in deleterious ways regardless of whether it is financed through taxations, borrowing, or even inflation. Private capital formation is reduced, resources are inefficiently allocated, and economic growth is slowed.

I applaud and support the newly enacted Balanced Budget and Emergency Deficit Control Act of 1985, known commonly as Gramm-Rudman-Hollings, as a way to work with the Congress to reduce Federal spending and the deficit. I intend to submit budgets in each of the coming years that satisfy the act's deficit targets, not by sacrificing the programs essential to the Nation, but by reforming or eliminating those programs that are ineffective or nonessential. I reject the notion of increased taxes. Higher taxes would only encourage more Federal spending and limit the economy's ability to grow.

Gramm-Rudman-Hollings accomplishes only part of our long-term objective of Federal fiscal responsibility. Properly applied, it will produce a balanced budget by 1991, but it does not guarantee a continued balanced budget thereafter. We must now direct our attention to a constitutional amendment providing for a permanently balanced budget. Together, these two measures will provide an orderly transition to a balanced budget, restrain future spending, and ensure that future fiscal decisions are prudent and responsive to the national interests. Accordingly, I continue to support strongly and to urge the adoption of a balanced-budget constitutional amendment. I also seek legislation that would authorize the President to veto individual line items in appropriations measures. Such authority is essential to ensure that only effective and essential government programs are funded.

Reform Taxes

Over the years, successive modifications of the Federal tax code have resulted in a complex tax system that contains many loopholes and artificially encourages some types of activities at the expense of others. Furthermore, the inflation of the 1970s distorted the overall pattern of capital taxation and pushed personal incomes into ever-higher tax brackets, discouraging saving and investment. Our actions to reduce tax rates have corrected many of these distortions and inequities. Individual income tax rates have been reduced and indexed to the inflation rate; effective tax rates on new investment have been lowered substantially. Still, more must be done.

In May 1985, I submitted to the Congress a comprehensive reform of the tax code to make it simpler, fairer, and more conducive to economic growth. I proposed reducing marginal tax rates for individuals and businesses, broadening the tax base by eliminating the majority of existing loopholes, taxing different activities consistently so that resources are allocated on the basis of economic merit and not tax considerations, and compensating for or eliminating much of the remaining influence of inflation on effective tax rates on capital. Just before it recessed, the House of Representatives passed a tax reform bill that incorporated some of these principles. Despite substantive differences between my proposal and the House bill, I urged its passage to move the legislative process forward. We will now work with the Senate to generate a fair and simple tax code that is truly pro-family, pro-jobs, and pro-growth.

Eliminate Counterproductive Regulation

Tax reform is only one part of our goal to enable markets to function more efficiently in allocating resources. We have also worked hard to identify and remove government regulations that impede the operation of markets, inhibit competition, or impose unnecessary costs on firms and unnecessarily high prices on consumers. The regulation of domestic oil prices provides a good example of the deleterious economic effects that regulation can have as it distorts relative prices and prevents necessary adjustments. The results of my accelerating the deregulation of oil prices in January 1981 are now apparent. Oil imports have declined, and the Organization of Petroleum Exporting Countries has found it impossible to sustain its previous levels of high prices. In contrast, the natural gas market is still plagued by distortions induced by price controls. In 1983, we unsuccessfully urged the Congress to deregulate natural gas prices. We will again pursue legislation that would completely deregulate natural gas prices. In addition, we are proposing further deregulation of the trucking industry.

We will continue efforts to reduce government involvement in two particular sectors of the economy. First, the banking and credit system remains rife with regulations and loan guarantees that arbitrarily allocate credit and hamper the system's ability to adapt to changing economic conditions. While we must continue to protect the public against severe economic disturbances, we should allow financial institutions greater freedom in determining the composition of their assets and liabilities so that they can respond more flexibly to the changes they encounter.

Second, heavy government involvement also persists in many agricultural markets. Government policies, intended as solutions, have so distorted incentives that they have actually caused some of agriculture's current problems. The legislation that I proposed in 1985 was designed to return American agriculture gradually to a free market. The bill passed by the Congress in late 1985 contained some of my proposed reforms, but preserved some of the policies that now hamper agriculture. In particular, it maintained counterproductive government intervention in the dairy industry, mandated export subsidies, and continued costly distortions of the sugar market. We will continue to pursue further agricultural reform that lessens government involvement in these areas and increases opportunities for farmers to compete successfully in world markets.

Transfer Some Services To the Private Sector

The Federal Government has increasingly sought to provide services that can be more efficiently provided by the private sector. To address this problem, I have established a working group to investigate which government functions could be effectively returned to the private sector. I have also included several initiatives in this area in the recently released budget. This strategy does not necessarily require eliminating services now provided by the government. Rather, it would make private alternatives available. Such a strategy ensures production of services that are demanded by consumers, not those chosen by government bureaucrats. It also leads to more efficient and lower cost production of those services, and often removes government-imposed restraints on competition.

Maintain Free and Fair Trade

Our pursuit of unencumbered markets is not confined to the domestic economy. Our international trade policy rests firmly on the foundation of free and open markets. The benefits of free trade are well known: it generates more jobs, a more productive use of a nation's resources, more rapid innovation, and higher standards of living both for this Nation and its trading partners. While a unilateral commitment to free trade benefits the Nation, Americans gain even more when U.S. trading partners also open their markets. My Administration will actively pursue this goal. An important part of our trade program is to begin a new round of multilateral trade negotiations. Under the auspices of the General Agreement on Tariffs and Trade, we are seeking to engage U.S. trading partners in comprehensive negotiations that will generate freer trade, increased access for U.S. exports, and a stronger international trading system. To complement this initiative, we are continuing to explore the possibility of establishing bilateral free trade zones with some U.S. trading partners.

We do not blindly pursue free trade. We also strive to ensure that trade is fair by vigilantly enforcing current trade laws. Unfair trade practices abroad harm U.S. exporters as well as reduce standards of living worldwide; this is unacceptable. In an unprecedented move, I have asked the U.S. Trade Representative to initiate unfair trade practice investigations under Section 301 of the Trade Act of 1974. Such investigations are not intended to produce retaliatory action by the United States, but rather to achieve more open markets internationally. In this way, we hope to convey the message that a commitment to free and fair trade is a reciprocal obligation in this increasingly interrelated world trading community.

The large trade deficit that has evolved during the current expansion has subjected our free and fair trade policy to much criticism, especially from the Congress. During the past year, more than 300 pieces of protectionist legislation have been considered or proposed. While the conditions that have led to the trade deficit have adversely affected some U.S. industries, increased protectionism is not the solution. Protectionist measures will have little effect on the trade balance and will only decrease standards of living and inefficiently redistribute resources within the economy.

Our agreement with four other major industrialized nations in September 1985 was an important recognition that economic policy changes across countries (not only in the United States) are essential to correct trade imbalances worldwide and to realign currency values. To this end, we reaffirmed our commitment to continue efforts to reduce the Federal Government deficit by lowering spending as a share of GNP. We urged the Congress to enact Gramm-Rudman-Hollings to achieve that goal. America's trading partners, in turn, committed themselves to policies designed to foster increased internally generated economic growth and, hence, increased demand for U.S. exports. These policy objectives are important for less developed countries as well. Indeed, a central facet of the Secretary of the Treasury's recent initiatives to assist in resolving the debt-servicing problems of these countries is that they pursue policies to promote growth, reduce inflation, and secure balance of payments adjustment.

CONCLUSION

My Administration recognizes the responsibility of the Federal Government to promote economic growth and individual opportunity through policies that lead to maximum employment, production, and purchasing power. We intend to maintain this course with policies that continue to promote strong, sustainable, noninflationary growth and provide expanding economic opportunities for all. We shall continue to resist additional government involvement as a solution to short-term problems. Such involvement has been unsuccessful in the past and ultimately becomes part of the problem rather than part of the solution. With the cooperation and support of the Congress and the independent agencies, we will pursue the appropriate policies necessary to sustain the current expansion and to stabilize prices.

RONALD REAGAN

February 6, 1986

Reagan's Speech on Aid to Nicaraguan Rebels

Following is the White House text of President Reagan's televised address, as delivered March 16, on his request for $100 million in aid to the Nicaraguan "contras."

My fellow Americans, I must speak to you tonight about a mounting danger in Central America that threatens the security of the United States. This danger will not go away; it will grow worse, much worse, if we fail to take action now. I am speaking of Nicaragua, a Soviet ally on the American mainland only two hours' flying time from our own borders. With over a billion dollars in Soviet-bloc aid, the communist government of Nicaragua has launched a campaign to subvert and topple its democratic neighbors.

Using Nicaragua as a base, the Soviets and Cubans can become the dominant power in the crucial corridor between North and South America. Established there, they will be in a position to threaten the Panama Canal, interdict our vital Caribbean sea lanes, and, ultimately, move against Mexico. Should that happen, desperate Latin peoples by the millions would begin fleeing north into the cities of the southern United States, or to wherever some hope of freedom remained.

The United States Congress has before it a proposal to help stop this threat. The legislation is an aid package of $100 million for the more than 20,000 freedom fighters struggling to bring democracy to their country and eliminate this communist menace at its source. But this $100 million is not an additional $100 million. We are not asking for a single dime in new money. We are asking only to be permitted to switch a small part of our present defense budget — to the defense of our own southern frontier.

Gathered in Nicaragua already are thousands of Cuban military advisers, contingents of Soviets and East Germans and all the elements of international terror — from the PLO to Italy's Red Brigades. Why are they there? Because, as Colonel Qaddafi has publicly exulted: "Nicaragua means a great thing; it means fighting America near its borders — fighting America at its doorstep."

For our own security the United States must deny the Soviet Union a beachhead in North America. But let me make one thing plain. I am not talking about American troops. They are not needed; they have not been requested. The democratic resistance fighting in Nicaragua is only asking America for the supplies and support to save their own country from communism.

The question the Congress of the United States will now answer is a simple one: Will we give the Nicaraguan democratic resistance the means to recapture their betrayed revolution, or will we turn our backs and ignore the malignancy in Managua until it spreads and becomes a mortal threat to the entire New World?

Will we permit the Soviet Union to put a second Cuba, a second Libya, right on the doorstep of the United States?

How can such a small country pose such a great threat? Well, it is not Nicaragua alone that threatens us, but those using Nicaragua as a privileged sanctuary for their struggle against the United States.

Their first target is Nicaragua's neighbors. With an army and militia of 120,000 men, backed by more than 3,000 Cuban military advisers, Nicaragua's armed forces are the largest Central America has ever seen. The Nicaraguan military machine is more powerful than all its neighbors combined.

This map represents much of the Western Hemisphere. Now let me show you the countries in Central America where weapons supplied by Nicaraguan communists have been found: Honduras, Costa Rica, El Salvador, Guatemala. Radicals from Panama to the south have been trained in Nicaragua. But the Sandinista revolutionary reach extends well beyond their immediate neighbors. In South America and the Caribbean, the Nicaraguan communists have provided support in the form of military training, safe haven, communications, false documents, safe transit and sometimes weapons to radicals from the following countries: Colombia, Ecuador, Brazil, Chile, Argentina, Uruguay, and the Dominican Republic. Even that is not all, for there was an old communist slogan that the Sandinistas have made clear they honor: The road to victory goes through Mexico.

If maps, statistics and facts aren't persuasive enough, we have the words of the Sandinistas and Soviets themselves. One of the highest-level Sandinista leaders was asked by an American magazine whether their communist revolution will — and I quote — "be exported to El Salvador, then Guatemala, then Honduras, and then Mexico?" He responded, "That is one historical prophecy of Ronald Reagan that is absolutely true."

Well, the Soviets have been no less candid. A few years ago, then Soviet Foreign Minister Gromyko noted that Central America was, quote, "boiling like a cauldron" and ripe for revolution. In a Moscow meeting in 1983, Soviet Chief of Staff Marshal Ogarkov declared: "Over two decades — there are Nicaragua" — I should say, "there was only Cuba in Latin America. Today there are Nicaragua, Grenada, and a serious battle is going on in El Salvador."

But we don't need their quotes; the American forces who liberated Grenada captured thousands of documents that demonstrated Soviet intent to bring communist revolution home to the Western Hemisphere.

So, we're clear on the intentions of the Sandinistas and those who back them. Let us be equally clear about the nature of their regime. To begin with, the Sandinistas have revoked the civil liberties of the Nicaraguan people, depriving them of any legal right to speak, to publish, to assemble or to worship freely. Independent newspapers have been shut down. There is no longer any independent labor movement in Nicaragua nor any right to strike. As AFL-CIO leader Lane Kirkland has said, "Nicaragua's headlong rush into the totalitarian camp cannot be denied but — by anyone who has eyes to see."

Well, like communist governments everywhere, the Sandinistas have launched assaults against ethnic and religious groups. The capital's only synagogue was desecrated and firebombed — the entire Jewish community forced to flee Nicaragua. Protestant Bible meetings have been broken up by raids, by mob violence, by machine guns. The Catholic Church has been singled out — priests have been expelled from the country, Catholics beaten in the streets after attending Mass. The Catholic primate of Nicaragua, Cardinal Obando y Bravo, has put the matter forthrightly. "We want to state clearly," he says, "that this government is totalitarian. We are dealing with an enemy of the Church."

Evangelical pastor Prudencio Baltodano found out he was on a Sandinista hit list when an army patrol asked his name: "You don't know what we do to the evangelical pastors. We don't believe in God," they told him. Pastor Baltodano was tied to a tree, struck in the forehead with a rifle butt, stabbed in the neck with a bayonet — finally his ears were cut off, and he was left for dead. "See if your God will save you," they mocked. Well, God did have other plans for Pastor Baltodano. He lived to tell the world his story — to tell it, among other places, right here in the White House.

I could go on about this nightmare — the blacklists, the secret prisons, the Sandinista-directed mob violence. But, as if all this brutality at home were not enough, the Sandinistas are transforming their nation into a safe house, a command post for international terror.

The Sandinistas not only sponsor terror in El Salvador, Costa Rica, Guatemala and Honduras — terror that led last summer to the murder of four U.S. Marines in a cafe in San Salvador — they provide a sanctuary for terror. Italy has charged Nicaragua with harboring their worst terrorists, the Red Brigades.

The Sandinistas have even involved themselves in the international drug trade. I know every American parent concerned about the drug problem will be outraged to learn that top Nicaraguan government officials are deeply involved in drug trafficking. This picture, secretly taken at a mili-

Texts of Executive Orders on Libya

Following are the White House texts of President Reagan's Jan. 7 executive order (No. 12543) prohibiting trade and certain transactions involving Libya, and of his Jan. 8 executive order (No. 12544) blocking Libyan government property in the United States or held by U.S. persons.

Executive Order 12543

By the authority vested in me as President by the Constitution and laws of the United States of America, including the International Emergency Economic Powers Act (50 U.S.C. 1701 *et seq.*), the National Emergencies Act (50 U.S.C. 1601 *et seq.*), sections 504 and 505 of the International Security and Development Cooperation Act of 1985 (PL 99-83), section 1114 of the Federal Aviation Act of 1958, as amended (49 U.S.C. 1514), and section 301 of title 3 of the United States Code,

I, RONALD REAGAN, President of the United States of America, find that the policies and actions of the Government of Libya constitute an unusual and extraordinary threat to the national security and foreign policy of the United States and hereby declare a national emergency to deal with that threat.

I hereby order:

Section 1. The following are prohibited, except to the extent provided in regulations which may hereafter be issued pursuant to this Order:

(a) The import into the United States of any goods or services of Libyan origin, other than publications and materials imported for news publications or news broadcast dissemination;

(b) The export to Libya of any goods, technology (including technical data or other information) or services from the United States, except publications and donations of articles intended to relieve human suffering, such as food, clothing, medicine and medical supplies intended strictly for medical purposes;

(c) Any transaction by a United States person relating to transportation to or from Libya; the provision of transportation to or from the United States by any Libyan person or any vessel or aircraft of Libyan registration; or the sale in the United States by any person holding authority under the Federal Aviation Act of any transportation by air which includes any stop in Libya;

(d) The purchase by any United States person of goods for export from Libya to any country;

(e) The performance by any United States person of any contract in support of an industrial or other commercial or governmental project in Libya;

(f) The grant or extension of credits or loans by any United States person to the Government of Libya, its instrumentalities and controlled entities;

(g) Any transaction by a United States person relating to travel by any United States citizen or permanent resident alien to Libya, or to activities by any such person within Libya, after the date of this Order, other than transactions necessary to effect such person's departure from Libya, to perform acts permitted until February 1, 1986, by Section 3 of this Order, or travel for journalistic activity by persons regularly employed in such capacity by a newsgathering organization; and

(h) Any transaction by any United States person which evades or avoids, or has the purpose of evading or avoiding, any of the prohibitions set forth in this Order.

For purposes of this Order, the term "United States person" means any United States citizen, permanent resident alien, juridical person organized under the laws of the United States or any person in the United States.

Section 2. In light of the prohibition in Section 1(a) of this Order, section 251 of the Trade Expansion Act of 1962, as amended (19 U.S.C. 1881), and section 126 of the Trade Act of 1974, as amended (19 U.S.C. 2136) will have no effect with respect to Libya.

Section 3. This Order is effective immediately, except that the prohibitions set forth in Section 1(a), (b), (c), (d) and (e) shall apply as of 12:01 a.m. Eastern Standard Time, February 1, 1986.

Section 4. The Secretary of the Treasury, in consultation with the Secretary of State, is hereby authorized to take such actions, including the promulgation of rules and regulations, as may be necessary to carry out the purposes of this Order. Such actions may include prohibiting or regulating payments or transfers of any property or any transactions involving the transfer of anything of economic value by any United States person to the Government of Libya, its instrumentalities and controlled entities, or to any Libyan national or entity owned or controlled, directly or indirectly, by Libya or Libyan nationals. The Secretary may redelegate any of these functions to other officers and agencies of the Federal government. All agencies of the United States government are directed to take all appropriate measures within their authority to carry out the provisions of this Order, including the suspension or termination of licenses or other authorizations in effect as of the date of this Order.

This Order shall be transmitted to the Congress and published in the *Federal Register.*

RONALD REAGAN

The White House,
January 7, 1986.

Executive Order 12544

By the authority vested in me as President by the Constitution and laws of the United States, including the International Emergency Economic Powers Act (50 U.S.C. 1701 *et seq.*), the National Emergencies Act (50 U.S.C. 1601 *et seq.*) and section 301 of title 3 of the United States Code, in order to take steps with respect to Libya additional to those set forth in Executive Order No. 12543 of January 7, 1986, to deal with the threat to the national security and foreign policy of the United States referred to in that Order,

I, RONALD REAGAN, President of the United States, hereby order blocked all property and interests in property of the Government of Libya, its agencies, instrumentalities and controlled entities and the Central Bank of Libya that are in the United States, that hereafter come within the United States or that are or hereafter come within the possession or control of U.S. persons, including overseas branches of U.S. persons.

The Secretary of the Treasury, in consultation with the Secretary of State, is authorized to employ all powers granted to me by the International Emergency Economic Powers Act, 50 U.S.C. 1701 *et seq.*, to carry out the provisions of this Order.

This Order is effective immediately and shall be transmitted to the Congress and published in the *Federal Register.*

RONALD REAGAN

The White House,
January 8, 1986.

tary airfield outside Managua, shows Federico Vaughn, a top aide to one of the nine Commandantes who rule Nicaragua, loading an aircraft with illegal narcotics, bound for the United States.

No, there seems to be no crime to which the Sandinistas will not stoop — this is an outlaw regime.

If we return for a moment to our map, it becomes clear why having this regime in Central America imperils our vital security interests.

Through this crucial part of the Western Hemisphere passes almost half our foreign trade, more than half our imports of crude oil, and a significant portion of the military supplies we would have to send to the NATO Alliance in the event of a crisis. These are the choke points where the sea lanes could be closed.

Central America is strategic to our Western alliance, a fact always understood by foreign enemies. In World War II, only a few German U-boats, operating from bases 4,000 miles away in Germany and occupied Europe, inflicted crippling losses on U.S. shipping right off our southern coast.

Today, Warsaw Pact engineers are building a deep water port on Nicaragua's Caribbean coast, similar to the naval base in Cuba for Soviet-built submarines. They are also constructing, outside Managua, the largest military airfield in Central America — similar to those in Cuba, from which Russian Bear Bombers patrol the U.S. East Coast from Maine to Florida.

How did this menace to the peace and security of our Latin neighbors, and ultimately ourselves, suddenly emerge? Let me give you a brief history.

In 1979, the people of Nicaragua rose up and overthrew a corrupt dictatorship. At first the revolutionary leaders promised free elections and respect for human rights. But among them was an organization called the Sandinistas. Theirs was a communist organization and their support of the revolutionary goals was sheer deceit. Quickly and ruthlessly they took complete control.

Two months after the revolution, the Sandinista leadership met in secret, and, in what came to be known as the "72-hour Document," described themselves as the "vanguard" of a revolution that would sweep Central America, Latin America and finally the world. Their true enemy, they declared: the United States.

Rather than make this document public, they followed the advice of Fidel Castro, who told them to put on a façade of democracy. While Castro viewed the democratic elements in Nicaragua with contempt, he urged his Nicaraguan friends to keep some of them in their coalition, in minor posts, as window dressing to deceive the West. And that way, Castro said, you can have your revolution and the Americans will pay for it.

And we did pay for it. More aid flowed to Nicaragua from the United States in the first 18 months under the Sandinistas than from any other country. Only when the mask fell, and the face of totalitarianism became visible to the world, did the aid stop.

Confronted with this emerging threat, early in our administration I went to Congress and, with bipartisan support, managed to get help for the nations surrounding Nicaragua. Some of you may remember the inspiring scene when the people of El Salvador braved the threats and gunfire of communist guerrillas, guerrillas directed and supplied from Nicaragua, and went to the polls to vote decisively for democracy. For the communists in El Salvador it was a humiliating defeat.

But there was another factor the communists never counted on, a factor that now promises to give freedom a second chance — the freedom fighters of Nicaragua.

You see, when the Sandinistas betrayed the revolution, many who had fought the old Somoza dictatorship literally took to the hills, and like the French Resistance that fought the Nazis, began fighting the Soviet-bloc communists and their Nicaraguan collaborators. These few have now been joined by thousands.

With their blood and courage, the freedom fighters of Nicaragua have pinned down the Sandinista army and bought the people of Central America precious time. We Americans owe them a debt of gratitude. In helping to thwart the Sandinistas and their Soviet mentors, the resistance has contributed directly to the security of the United States.

Since its inception in 1982, the Democratic Resistance has grown dramatically in strength. Today it numbers more than 20,000 volunteers and more come every day. But now the freedom fighters' supplies are running short, and they are virtually defenseless against the helicopter gunships Moscow has sent to Managua.

Now comes the crucial test for the Congress of the United States. Will they provide the assistance the freedom fighters need to deal with Russian tanks and gunships, or will they abandon the Democratic Resistance to its communist enemy?

In answering that question, I hope Congress will reflect deeply upon what it is the resistance is fighting against in Nicaragua. Ask yourselves, what in the world are Soviets, East Germans, Bulgarians, North Koreans, Cubans and terrorists from the PLO and the Red Brigades doing in our hemisphere, camped on our own doorstep? Is that for peace?

Why have the Soviets invested $600 million to build Nicaragua into an armed force almost the size of Mexico's, a country 15 times as large, and 25 times as populous. Is that for peace?

Why did Nicaragua's dictator, Daniel Ortega, go to the Communist Party Congress in Havana and endorse Castro's call for the worldwide triumph of communism? Was that for peace?

Some members of Congress ask me, why not negotiate? That's a good question, and let me answer it directly. We have sought, and still seek, a negotiated peace and a democratic future in a free Nicaragua. Ten times we have met and tried to reason with the Sandinistas. Ten times we were rebuffed. Last year, we endorsed church-mediated negotiations between the regime and the resistance. The Soviets and the Sandinistas responded with a rapid arms buildup of mortars, tanks, artillery and helicopter gunships.

Clearly, the Soviet Union and the Warsaw Pact have grasped the great stakes involved, the strategic importance of Nicaragua. The Soviets have made their decision — to support the communists. Fidel Castro has made his decision — to support the communists. Arafat, Qaddafi and the Ayatollah Khomeini have made their decision — to support the communists. Now, we must make our decision. With Congress' help, we can prevent an outcome deeply injurious to the national security of the United States. If we fail, there will be no evading responsibility — history will hold us accountable. This is not some narrow partisan issue; it is a national security issue, an issue on which we must act not as Republicans, not as Democrats, but as Americans.

Forty years ago Republicans and Democrats joined together behind the Truman Doctrine. It must be our policy, Harry Truman declared, to support peoples struggling to preserve their freedom. Under that doctrine, Congress sent aid to Greece just in time to save that country from the closing grip of a communist tyranny. We saved freedom in Greece then — and with that same bipartisan spirit we can save freedom in Nicaragua today.

Over the coming days I will continue the dialogue with members of Congress, talking to them, listening to them, hearing out their concerns. Senator "Scoop" Jackson, who led the fight on Capitol Hill for an awareness of the danger in Central America, said it best: On matters of national security, the best politics is no politics.

You know, recently one of our most distinguished Americans, Clare Boothe Luce, had this to say about the coming vote. "In considering this crisis," Mrs. Luce said, "my mind goes back to a similar moment in our history — back to the first years after Cuba had fallen to Fidel. One day during those years, I had lunch at the White House with a man I had known since he was a boy — John F. Kennedy. 'Mr. President,' I said, 'no matter how exalted or great a man may be, history will have time to give him no more than one sentence. George Washington — he founded our country. Abraham Lincoln — he freed the slaves and preserved the Union. Winston Churchill — he saved Europe.' 'And what, Clare,' John Kennedy said, 'did you believe — or do you believe my sentence will be?' 'Mr. President,' " she answered, " 'your sentence will be that you stopped the communists — or that you did not.' "

Well, tragically, John Kennedy never had the chance to decide which that would be. Now, leaders of our own time must do so. My fellow Americans, you know where I stand. The Soviets and the Sandinistas must not be permitted to crush freedom in Central America and threaten our own security on our own doorstep.

Now the Congress must decide where it stands. Mrs. Luce ended by saying, "Only this is certain. Through all time to come, this, the 99th Congress of the United States, will be remembered as that body of men and women that either stopped the communists before it was too late — or did not."

So tonight I ask you to do what you've done so often in the past. Get in touch with your Representative and Senators and urge them to vote yes; tell them to help the freedom fighters — help us prevent a communist takeover of Central America.

I have only three years left to serve my country, three years to carry out the responsibilities you entrusted to me, three years to work for peace. Could there be any greater tragedy than for us to sit back and permit this cancer to spread, leaving my successor to face far more agonizing decisions in the years ahead? The freedom fighters seek a political solution. They are willing to lay down their arms and negotiate to restore the original goals of the revolution, a democracy in which the people of Nicaragua choose their own government. That is our goal also but it can only come about if the democratic resistance is able to bring pressure to bear on those who have seized power.

We still have time to do what must be done so history will say of us, we had the vision, the courage and good sense to come together and act — Republicans and Democrats — when the price was not high and the risks were not great. We left America safe; we left America secure; we left America free — still a beacon of hope to mankind, still a light unto the nations.

Thank you and God bless you. ∎

On March 19:

Reagan's Message to Congress On Aid to Nicaraguan 'Contras'

Following are excerpts from the White House text of President Reagan's March 19 message to Congress on aid to the Nicaraguan "contras."

TO THE CONGRESS OF
THE UNITED STATES:

Since I transmitted my message to the Congress on February 25 requesting additional assistance for the Nicaraguan democratic resistance, I have heard from many thoughtful Members of Congress, as well as from Latin American leaders and the leaders of the Nicaraguan democratic resistance. Many have raised the question of how the additional authority I have requested could be implemented so as to help persuade the Government of Nicaragua to engage in a serious effort to resolve the conflict in Central America through peaceful means....

If the Congress approves my request I will send my special envoy on an urgent mission to the capitals of the Contadora and Support Group nations. He will ask them to join with us in urging the Government of Nicaragua to initiate a national dialogue with representatives of all elements of the democratic opposition, designed to achieve the goals set out in the widely heralded proposal announced by six opposition Nicaraguan political parties on February 7, 1986. Their proposal, which has been endorsed by the Nicaraguan democratic resistance, calls for an immediate cease-fire, an effective general amnesty, abolition of the state of emergency, agreement on a new electoral process and general elections, effective fulfillment of international commitments for democratization, and observance of implementation by relevant international groups and bodies.

President Duarte's additional proposal for simultaneous dialogue with the Salvadoran guerrillas, a proposal endorsed by the democratic Presidents of Costa Rica, Honduras, and Guatemala, reinforces the importance of an internal dialogue in Nicaragua to address the objectives of the six-party proposal of February 7.

In order to give the Government of Nicaragua every reasonable opportunity to respond favorably, and to provide an incentive for a positive response, I will limit the assistance to be provided to the Nicaraguan democratic resistance for 90 days following approval of my request to the following:

(1) humanitarian assistance, as defined in section 722(g) of PL 99-83, including support for programs and activities to strengthen respect for human rights;

(2) logistics advice and assistance;

(3) equipment and supplies necessary for defense against air attack;

(4) support for democratic political and diplomatic activities; and

(5) training in radio communications, collection and utilization of intelligence, logistics, and small-unit skills and tactics.

Following this 90-day period, additional types of assistance will be provided to the Nicaraguan democratic resistance only if —

(1) I have determined, after consultation with the Congress,

(a) that the Central American countries have not concluded a comprehensive agreement based on the Contadora Document of Objectives;

(b) the Government of Nicaragua is not engaged in a serious dialogue with representatives of all elements of the democratic opposition, accompanied by a cease-fire and an effective end to the existing constraints on freedom of speech, assembly, and religion; and

(c) there is no reasonable prospect of achieving these developments through further diplomatic measures, multilateral or bilateral, without additional assistance to the Nicaraguan democratic resistance;

(2) I have reported my determination to the Congress; and

(3) Fifteen days have elapsed following my report to the Congress, during which the Congress may take such legislative or other action as it deems appropriate.

Should the conditions described in subparagraph (a) or (b) of paragraph (1) later be achieved, assistance to the Nicaraguan democratic resistance will again be limited to the categories, described above, available during the initial 90 days following approval of my request, for so long as the Government of Nicaragua acts in good faith to maintain those conditions.

In order to keep the Congress fully and currently informed of developments relating to diplomatic efforts to achieve a peaceful resolution of the conflict during the 90 days following approval of my request, I will appoint a special bipartisan commission to report on negotiations, whose reports will be made available to the Congress. This commission shall be composed of individuals, none of whom shall be a Member or employee of the Congress or an officer or employee of the United States, recommended by the Speaker and Minority Leader of the House of Representatives and the Majority and Minority Leaders of the Senate, with a fifth member of the commission to be recommended by the four other commissioners.

This approach represents a sincere effort to achieve peace through negotiations. In order to further this effort, I will make $2,000,000 of the funds I have requested for assistance to the Nicaraguan democratic resistance available to the Central American democracies (Costa Rica, El Salvador, Guatemala, and Honduras) to facilitate their participation in regional meetings and negotiations. In addition, I will encourage those countries and the Contadora and Support Group nations to make regular and public reports on the status of negotiations, the likelihood of achieving a comprehensive agreement, progress toward national reconciliation, and the obstacles thereto.

Moreover, the United States will assist all indigenous groups which are committed to work together for democratic national reconciliation in Nicaragua based on the six-party proposal. We will require only that they respect international standards of conduct, refraining from violations of human rights or other criminal acts, and that they work together toward this common goal.

In this regard, the democratic resistance has been broadening its representative base.... Toward this end, I will reserve not less than $10,000,000 of the funds I have requested for assistance to resistance forces otherwise eligible and not currently included within UNO [the United Nicaraguan Opposition], one-half of which shall be for BOS [the Southern Opposition Bloc] and one-half shall be for the Indian resistance force Misurasata.

However, no group shall receive assistance from the United States if it retains in its ranks any individual who engages in —

(1) gross violations of human rights (including summary executions, torture, kidnapping, forced recruitment, or other such violations of the integrity of the person); or

(2) drug smuggling, or significant misuse of public or private funds.

There are two other issues, relating to funding, that I ask you to consider.

First, there has been inaccurate public speculation about what additional funds for assistance to the Nicaraguan democratic resistance might be available beyond the $100 million for fiscal years 1986 and 1987 that I have requested be transferred from amounts already appropriated to the Department of Defense. I want to state unequivocally that I will not augment this $100 million through the use of CIA or any other funds that have not been approved by the Congress for this purpose.

Second, when I proposed to the Congress a Central America Democracy, Peace, and Development Initiative to implement the recommendations of the National Bipartisan Commission on Central America, I included Nicaragua among the countries that could benefit from this initiative. The Congress accepted my recommendation in enacting a new chapter of the Foreign Assistance Act of 1961. The Congress also authorized in that Act, as the Bipartisan Commission recommended and I requested, the appropriation of the full $1,200,000,000 in nonmilitary assistance for Central America for fiscal years 1988 and 1989. However, the current authorization for fiscal year 1987 falls short of this goal. This, combined with appropriations shortfalls from previous years, is an obstacle to timely progress. I will ask the Secretary of State, the Administrator of the Agency for International Development, and the Director of the Office of Management and Budget to develop a plan to overcome the funding shortfalls that have occurred. In addition, I urge the Congress to provide the full amounts of economic assistance I have requested in my budget for fiscal year 1987 so that the necessary long-term commitment urged by the Bipartisan Commission will be fulfilled, and so that the promises of peace and freedom will be realized throughout Central America.

Upon the enactment of a joint resolution approving my request, I shall issue an Executive order to provide for the implementation of the undertakings I have expressed in this message and in my message of February 25. The Secretary of State, or his designee, will be responsible, under my direction, for policy guidance and coordination of United States Government activities under that Executive order.

In conclusion, I must stress that our diplomacy cannot succeed without the demonstrated resolve of the United States to protect its own interests and those of the brave men and women who are fighting for democracy in Central America. The time for decision is now. Your vote on my request will be a fateful one. I need and urge your support on this vital issue.

RONALD REAGAN

The White House,
March 19, 1986.

Reagan Remarks on Trade and Foreign Policy

Following is the White House text of President Reagan's April 23 remarks on international trade and foreign policy, as delivered to an international forum of the U.S. Chamber of Commerce, in Washington, D.C.

Thank you very much. Thank you. I appreciate this opportunity to be here with you today. One of America's greatest assets is the skill and professionalism of its men and women of commerce and industry — the peppery, can-do spirit of our business community is in stark contrast to the inefficiency and poor performance often associated with other economic systems. Of course, mistakes do happen. There is the story of the fellow who ordered a bouquet of flowers to be sent to the opening of his friends' new branch office. When he got there he was shocked to see flowers with the inscription: "Rest in Peace." (Laughter.) He was so outraged that on the way home he stopped at the florist to complain. "Don't get so upset," the florist said. "Just think of it this way — today someone in this city was buried beneath a flower arrangement with the inscription: 'Good luck in your new location.'" (Laughter).

I understand we've got some students with us today. One of the joys of my Presidency has been getting to meet and know the young men and women who, in the not-too-distant future, will be America's champions of freedom and enterprise. And I don't have to tell you this new crop of young people filling the ranks of our businesses and corporations are as talented and diligent as any we've ever had. Today's young Americans will come into their own with freedom, know-how and resources far beyond anything the world has ever known. Henry David Thoreau once wrote of free people: "This world is but canvas to our imaginations." Those words were never more true than they are now. We've got every reason to look to the future with unbounding optimism. Today, a refreshing breeze can be felt across the face of mankind — winds of freedom are blowing, clearing the air, opening the view of a new and wondrous horizon.

Worldwide Expansion of Democracy

In a few days, Nancy and I, as you've been told, will be heading west, embarking on a journey which will culminate in Tokyo with a summit of the major democracies. And as we lift off aboard *Air Force One*, circling half the globe, the winds of freedom will be propelling my mission. Those winds are blowing in Latin America where, in recent years, we've witnessed one of the greatest expansions of democracy in history. Today, 90 percent of the population of this hemisphere lives in democratic countries or countries in transition to democracy.

In Europe, the new vigorous democracies in Spain and Portugal and the revitalized democratic process in Turkey have proven the pessimists wrong. The Democratic Workers' Movement in Poland — Solidarity — those suffering repression still persists. In Nicaragua, Angola, Afghanistan and Cambodia, freedom fighters struggling for liberty and independence inspire the West with their courage in the face of a powerful enemy.

As I fly westward over our majestic land, I go knowing that we're witnessing an awakening to those self-evident truths to which our forefathers pledged their lives, their fortunes and their sacred honor.

Government and the Economy

In future years, I think we may look back on the period we're going through as the eternal — the vernal equinox of the human spirit. That moment in history when the light finally exceeded the darkness. In the 1970s, the Western democracies suffered economic and political reversals which sapped their confidence and gutted the resilience of their social systems. The maladies to which I'm referring — with a logical result of wrong ideas and flawed policies. The innovators, entrepreneurs and profit-seeking risk takers who had always been on the cutting edge of change, were gradually being pushed out or phased out. The resources and decision making of the West were being channeled into the hands of central planners, government officials and bureaucratic managers.

In our country, government spending tripled in the 1970s and the federal tax take doubled between 1976 and 1981. By 1980, we suffered double-digit inflation, economic stagnation, sky-high interest rates and unprecedented national uncertainty. Nothing could be done, we were told, to escape this quagmire. Our citizens would have to lower their expectations. The American people never believed that guff and I didn't either.

Looking out over the United States today, I'm confident that our country's best days lie ahead. The winds of freedom are indeed blowing and if America puts its mind to it, there's nothing we can't accomplish.

By bringing the growth of government under control, by easing the regulatory burden, by reducing the tax rates, giving people incentives and rewards to work, invest and build, we've set America on a new upward course. Astounding the so-called experts, our economic engines have powered us forward with 40 straight months of growth — a record 669,000 businesses were incorporated last year alone. Interest rates are down. Inflation has remained low. Over the last three months it has been minus 1.9 percent, the lowest in more than 30 years, and for the last 12 months it has been 2.3 percent. Almost ten million new jobs have been created here in the last three years, while Europe has seen a net loss of jobs in the last decade.

Marxism's Failure

Today the world — especially the developing world — is leaving behind the dismal failures of statism and redistribution. Central planning and government authority did not, as promised, usher in a new era of plenty. Instead, Marxist-Leninist models of development have left a path of poverty and deprivation wherever they have been tried.

The late John Dos Passos put it well. "Marxism," he said, "has not only failed to promote human freedom — it has failed to produce food." The developing world has been told that it is necessary to give up freedom in order to achieve progress. Nothing could be further from the truth. Freedom and economic advance go hand in hand. They are two sides of the same coin. The mainspring of human progress is found not in controlling and harnessing human energy, but in setting it free. The most valuable resource is not oil or precious metals, or even territory — it is the infinite richness of human potential. The creative genius and diligence unleashed when people are free and working to improve their lot and that of their families is the greatest force for good on this planet.

Development of Pacific Rim

The winds of freedom are nowhere more evident than on the Pacific Rim, which of course includes my home state of California. Seriously, though, after the Second World War, Japan was in ruins and devastation was heavy throughout the region. It is becoming difficult to think of the Pacific as being undeveloped, but only a generation ago that was a fair characterization. Pacific nations with almost no territory and few natural resources have become dynamic centers of commerce and production almost beyond imagination.

Over the last 15 years annual growth in the region has averaged about 6 percent. This was accomplished despite rising oil prices and at a time when some countries short on land to begin with were forced to absorb influxes of refugees. The energy and enterprise on the Pacific Rim is changing the economic center of gravity. The United States and our northern neighbor Canada now exchange more goods with Asia and the Pacific than with Europe. Almost one-third of total U.S. trade now flows west. Our trade enriches the quality of life on both sides of the Pacific, and while much attention has been focused on imports from the region, we must not overlook our exports. Today we export $54 billion worth of American products annually to East Asia and the Pacific compared to $20 billion just 10 years ago. Again, the relationship between freedom and prosperity, between democratic government and economic progress, is clear.

New Opportunities in Philippines

We recently witnessed an upheaval in the Philippines. A major cause for discontent in the Philippines was that much of the country's business and trade was not open to all citizens. As a result, the Philippines lagged behind its Pacific neighbors. Today, the Philippine people have new opportunities, economic and political. As their friends, we wish them the very best and will help where we can.

Communist Stagnation

Of course, those countries forced to endure centralized communist planning face the prospects of continued stagnation. This, while much of the Pacific marches into an exciting new age of enterprise and commerce. Vietnam, isolated from the dynamism of its Pacific neighbors by its continued occupation of Cambodia, is perhaps the best example of what I'm talking about.

'The Pacific Century'

On my upcoming trip, I'll stop in Indonesia, and there, I will be discussing Cambodia as well as other economic and security issues with President Soeharto and with representatives of six nations which make up ASEAN, the Association of Southeast Asian Nations. Most important through my trip, I'll be reconfirming that the United States considers itself a Pacific Rim country and we will continue to be an important part of the economic and political forces that shape the future of this vital area of the world.

If the next century is the Pacific century, as some have suggested, America will be leading the way.

Economic Summit - 1

From Indonesia, I will head to Japan, the site of the 12th economic summit. That this meeting is in Tokyo reminds us again of an emerging Japan. Over these last few decades, this former enemy has become a trusted friend, a major political and economic partner, and a strategic ally — the pillar of our Pacific policy.

Japan's Success Story

Prime Minister Nakasone of Japan is moving his country toward a new and expanded international role. Together our countries exercise enormous political and economic influence on the world. I think that all our peoples can be proud that we're using our power for benevolent ends — to secure democracy, to foster economic progress, and to maintain peace in a dangerous world.

Japan's is a dramatic story of democracy's success. That it has been built into the world's second largest market economy and is now taking on greater international responsibilities bodes well for the future. The winds of freedom blow both east and west — man's desire to improve his lot, his longing for freedom and his yearning to live in dignity and peace are never limited by geography. These universals tie all free peoples and those who would be free together.

Economic Summit - 2

Our annual economic summit stands in glorious defiance of the totalitarian theory that sovereign, democratic societies are too independent, too bogged down by short-sighted self-interest to be able to cooperate on matters of significance. Especially matters concerning money and finances. Well, the issues may vary, but if there are two watchwords of our economic summits, those words are "freedom" and "cooperation."

Each year's gathering is an opportunity to renew acquaintances, to take stock of economic prospects and to discuss frankly and openly issues of common interest. And this year, there is much to discuss. The continuing upward momentum of the American economy has been a major impetus to growth in the rest of the world in both summit and non-summit countries. Now, we urge others to join us in tackling those domestic policies and structural problems that inhibit growth and serve only as roadblocks to progress.

High tax rates, over-regulation are like a ball and chain holding too many nations back. The substantial decline in world oil prices offers in the industrial democracies as well as the developing world a dramatic opportunity. We hope our summit partners will translate the benefits of lower oil prices into stronger growth and higher employment. Now is the time to accelerate the pace of structural change and pave the way for higher sustained growth in future years.

Collapse of OPEC

These economic summits, with the denouement of the shock waves that went through the world economy after the oil price hikes of the early 1970s, an oil cartel artificially jacked the price of petroleum far beyond its true market value. Today's implosion of that cartel is evidence that, in the long run, the market works.

Those oil price increases remind me a bit of the businessman who, every day would stop at a pretzel stand just outside his office, and every day he would put 25 cents on the plate, but he'd never take a pretzel. And this went on for quite some time. He'd stop, put the quarter on the plate and walk on into the office, never taking one. Then one day, as he put a quarter on the plate, the woman running the stand grabbed him by the arm. And he said, "You probably want to know why I've been putting 25 cents on your plate every day and never taking a pretzel." And she said, "Well, no. Really I just wanted you to know pretzels have gone up to 35 cents." (Laughter.)

Open Markets to Third World

As the United States has demonstrated, strong, growing economies in the major industrial countries will do much to help those in the developing world. Succinctly put, our policies toward the Third World should be aimed at establishing partners in trade, not recipients of aid. Our approach should be to keep open our markets, not to empty our Treasury.

Last October, Secretary Baker proposed, as I'm sure he will further explain in his remarks, a program for sustained growth intended as a declaration of independence for debtor nations. Its purpose is to move them toward self-sufficiency, to assist them in developing free-market, pro-growth policies and to help them climb out of the pit of indebtedness and up to the level plateau of competitive enterprise and productivity.

And then — well, the debt initiative that's proposed by Secretary Baker, which we'll discuss in Tokyo, is focused not just on postponing a day of reckoning, but on solving a problem. It has the strong support of the international community. Our legacy must not be to engender dependence among debtor countries, but provide the incentives, the tools and the opportunity for them to work, produce and grow their way to self-sufficiency.

Free Trade for All

We want all people in every country to live healthier, more productive, opportunity-filled lives. Free and unfettered trade between nations is a vital part of the formula for achieving this goal. We're ready and willing to work with those with whom we have commerce to maximize the benefits of a worldwide open trading system. Keeping trade fair and open will be a major topic of discussion in Tokyo. Our summit partners have already helped start up the preparatory process for a new round of multilateral trade negotiations. And we hope they'll continue their efforts to ensure that those negotiations are launched this September.

As an economics major, I was taught the law of comparative advantage. And it ought to govern the exchange of goods and services across national boundaries. If our farmers in California can grow larger and cheaper oranges than their counterparts in Japan, a housewife in Osaka ought to be able to buy those oranges without additional cost. At home, our citizens should have the same right. Protectionist moves basically profit special interests at the expense of the consumer and at the risk of retaliation, costing Americans their jobs.

Danger of Protectionism

Now, admittedly, the strong dollar has been a legitimate concern of those of you trying to sell overseas. The value of the dollar is in the process of adjusting as the economies in other nations improve. And now is not the time to surrender to trade-killing protectionism. The trade imbalance should be solved through multilateral negotiation that open markets, not unilateral legislation that closes them. The right answer is not decreasing imports, but increasing our exports. I'll resist any attempt to restrict or close our markets. It would cost Americans jobs. It's bad for the consumer, bad for business and it's bad for America.

I'm old enough to remember the Smoot-Hawley Tariff Act, which helped spread the Depression worldwide. And I'm not about to let that happen. And on the other hand, I can assure you I'm not about to let this good and great country be taken advantage of. Our trading partners have been sent the message, and I'll reinforce it in Tokyo, that the United States is moving forward aggressively and vigorously to keep the markets of the world open and to see to it that American interests are treated fairly.

Economic Progress and World Peace

In Tokyo we'll primarily be discussing issues of economic importance. Yet all of us meeting there are fully aware of how totally dependent economic progress is on maintaining a peaceful and stable world. Those who will gather in Tokyo represent countries which by working together have given the world 41 years of peace — in Europe ushering in the greatest strides in science and industry in the history of mankind.

U.S.-Soviet Relations

The United States, in pursuit of peace, is working in close consultation with its partners, seeking a more stable and constructive relationship with the Soviet Union. In Tokyo we'll discuss arms reduction and other initiatives connected with my meetings with General Secretary Gorbachev last November. During those meetings General Secretary Gorbachev and I talked together about the differences between our systems. I challenged him to compete with us — not in the manufacture of bombs and weapons, but in the arena of ideas. We can and should have peaceful competition between our systems. We should let the world decide, based not on the size of our arsenals, but on the attractiveness of our ways of life. Let us be measured by our results, not our rhetoric; our deeds, not our words.

Now whether the General Secretary takes me up on my challenge remains to be determined. In the meantime, preserving peace is not just the business of the United States or of the United States and the Soviet Union. Our summit partners each share this responsibility.

First Lady's Anti-Drug Crusade

One area of exemplary cooperation has been our mutual efforts to combat international drug trafficking, which undermines the respect for law and attacks the fundamental health of our nations. The threat is particularly grave to our youth. Nancy has taken on the war against drugs as a personal mission and she has made me very proud. While I'm in Tokyo, she will be carrying her message to Malaysia and Thailand, where she will join in a comprehensive review of the anti-drug efforts of those two important nations.

Terrorism - 1

Coming to grips with threats posed by such evils as drugs will require all free people to work together. The democratic nations decided long ago they would stand shoulder-to-shoulder in such fights. Nowhere is this more imperative than in the battle against terrorism. These vicious, cowardly acts will, if we let them, erect a wall of fear around nations and neighborhoods. It will dampen the joy of travel, the flow of trade, the exchange of ideas.

In short, terrorism undeterred will deflect the winds of freedom. And let no one mistake this for a conflict between the Western democracies and the Arab world. Those who condone making war by cowardly attacks on unarmed third parties, including women and children, are but a tiny minority. Arab nations themselves have been force[d] to endure savage terrorist attacks from this minority. We hope and pray the Arab world will join with us to eliminate this scourge on civilization.

Qaddafi's Hypocrisy

I might add that Colonel Qaddafi's expectation of unquestioned support from the Islamic world strikes me as hypocritical. Nowhere is the slaughter of Moslem people greater than in Afghanistan. And, yet, Colonel Qaddafi allies himself with those perpetrating this crime on Islam and all of mankind.

Terrorism - 2

Decent people can no longer tolerate cowardly terrorist attacks. Government-sponsored terrorism, in particular, cannot continue without gravely threatening the social fabric of all free societies. Unilateral response is not enough. It must be dealt with forcefully and collectively. And this, undoubtedly, will be a topic of discussion in Tokyo.

U.S. Attack on Libya

James Russell Lowell, in a poem entitled "The Present Crisis" and later made into a familiar hymn wrote:

> Once to every man and nation
> comes the moment to decide,
> In the strife of Truth with Falsehood, for the good or evil side....

Well, over the past few months we've had to make some tough decisions. But in the end, the decision was made for us, when a despot — despite our political, economic and diplomatic attempts to change his ways — continued his murderous attacks on our fellow citizens.

Well, America will never watch passively as our innocent citizens are murdered by those who would do our country harm.

We are — (applause) — we're slow to wrath and hesitant to use the military power available to us. By nature we prefer to solve problems peacefully. But as we proved last week, no one can kill Americans and brag about it. No one. We bear the people of Libya no ill will, but if their government continues its campaign of terror against Americans, we will act again. (Applause.)

Terrorism - 3

There was a funeral a short time ago in Annapolis. A local family, the kind you can find in any neighborhood across our country, had suffered the horror of a terrorist attack. A young man, Warren Klug, buried his wife, his baby daughter, and his mother-in-law. All were innocent victims of the bombing of a TWA airliner. After the memorial service, his baby daughter lying in the coffin with her mother, Warren Klug told his fellow citizens of the world: "To those responsible for this cowardly act, you've succeeded in devastating our family. But you will never destroy the heart and spirit of America."

Well, all of us stand united, hand-in-hand, with the Klug family and the others who've suffered. We're all part of the same family. As your — President, I promise you that we as a people will have the courage and the honor to do what is right. This is and will remain the land of the free and the home of the brave. The winds of freedom will be preserved, not just for our citizens, but for all mankind.

And in Tokyo, I'll remind our allies of the truth of what Edmund Burke said long ago: "When bad men combine, the good must associate else they will fall one by one." Well, together the free people of this world will ensure that liberty not only survives, but triumphs and that our sons and daughters, too, will know the blessings of the winds of freedom.

Thank you, and God bless you. ▮

Veto Message and Letter on Saudi Arms Sale

Following is the White House text of President Reagan's message accompanying his May 21 veto of S J Res 316, which disapproved the president's proposed sale of missiles to Saudi Arabia, and the White House text of the president's letter to Senate Majority Leader Robert Dole, R-Kan., notifying Dole of his intention to withdraw the request for Stinger anti-aircraft missiles and missile reloads. It was Reagan's eighth veto of a public bill during the 99th Congress.

TO THE SENATE OF
THE UNITED STATES:

I am returning herewith without my approval S J Res 316, a resolution that would halt the proposed sale of defensive missiles to Saudi Arabia.

The U.S. defense relationship with Saudi Arabia was started by President Roosevelt in 1943 and endorsed by every President since. I cannot permit the Congress to dismantle this longstanding policy, damage our vital strategic, political and economic interests in the Middle East and undermine our balanced policy in that region.

The American people and their representatives should understand that this sale is in our interests. It is not just a favor to our friends in Saudi Arabia. Moreover, it is not being done at anyone's expense.

The security of Israel remains a top priority of this Administration. This sale will not endanger Israel's defenses, a fact that is underscored by Israel's decision not to oppose the sale.

Stability of the oil-rich Persian Gulf is another goal of great importance. In a region living in the shadow of the tragic and gruesome Iran-Iraq war, and threatened by religious fanaticism at its worst, we cannot afford to take stability for granted. Saudi willingness to stand up to Iranian threats has been key in preventing the spread of chaos. It has been Saudi Arabia's confidence in our commitment to its security that has allowed it to stand firm.

But Saudi Arabia produces no weapons of its own and we have not sold the Saudis new arms in almost 2 years. If we suddenly shut off that supply, it will weaken our own credibility, as well as the Saudis' ability to defend themselves. It would send the worst possible message as to America's dependability and courage.

Behind the scenes, the Saudis have aided the effort to combat terrorism, which is as much, if not more, of a threat to them as it is to us. Recently, they refused Qaddafi's requests for aid. Several times in recent months, they have been instrumental in offsetting unjust criticism of the United States and preventing radical states from undertaking joint action against our country.

The Saudis have proven their friendship and good will. They have assisted our efforts to support responsible governments in Egypt, Jordan, and Sudan. They have worked quietly in the search for peace in Lebanon, in the Arab-Israeli conflict, and in the Iran-Iraq war. They also provide impressive assistance to the government of Pakistan and to Afghan refugees.

In the long run this sale will be good for America, good for Israel, good for Saudi Arabia, and good for the cause of peace.

I ask members of both parties to sustain this veto and to join me in protecting our country's vital interest.

RONALD REAGAN

The White House,
May 21, 1986. ▮

May 21, 1986

Dear Bob:

For the past two weeks, I have shared your concern for our ability to gain necessary congressional support for the Saudi missile sale in its present configuration. Yesterday I met with the Saudi Ambassador to the United States, His Royal Highness Prince Bandar bin Sultan, to discuss this issue. Prince Bandar informed me that the Saudi Government, recognizing the particular sensitivity of Stingers being transferred to any country and the importance of the sale to the security of the Persian Gulf area, has decided to withdraw its request for Stingers.

Today I am signing a message to the Senate vetoing S J Res 316, which would disapprove the sale of all missiles included in this notification: AIM-9L, AIM-9P, Harpoon, and Stinger. If my veto is sustained, I will proceed with the sale but will not include the 200 Stinger launcher systems and the 600 missile reloads. A subsequent Saudi renewal of their request for Stingers would require the submission of another notification of the sale to the Congress in accordance with Section 36(b) of the Arms Export Control Act.

It is my sincere hope that with this modification of the Saudi request, the Congress will agree to this sale. It remains a vital and timely symbol of U.S. security commitments in the Middle East.

Sincerely,

RONALD REAGAN

Reagan's Statement on Arms Treaty Policy

Following is the White House text of President Reagan's May 27 statement on U.S. policy on compliance with the SALT I and II arms-control agreements.

On the eve of the Strategic Arms Reductions Talks (START) in 1982, I decided that the United States would not undercut the expired SALT I Interim Offensive Agreement or the unratified SALT II agreement as long as the Soviet Union exercised equal restraint. I took this action, despite my concerns about the flaws inherent in those agreements, to foster an atmosphere of mutual restraint conducive to serious negotiations on arms reductions. I made clear that our policy required reciprocity and that it must not adversely affect our national security interests in the face of the continuing Soviet military buildup.

U.S. Observance of Pacts

Last June, I reviewed the status of U.S. interim restraint policy. I found that the United States had fully kept its part of the bargain. As I have documented in three detailed reports to the Congress, most recently in December 1985, the Soviet Union, regrettably, has not. I noted last June that the pattern of Soviet non-compliance with their existing arms control commitments increasingly affected our national security. This pattern also raised fundamental concerns about the integrity of the arms control process itself. A country simply cannot be serious about effective arms control unless it is equally serious about compliance.

Going the Extra Mile

In spite of the regrettable Soviet record, I concluded last June that it remained in the interest of the United States and its allies to try, once more, to establish an interim framework of truly mutual restraint on strategic offensive arms as we pursued, with renewed vigor, our objective of deep reductions in existing U.S. and Soviet nuclear arsenals through the Geneva negotiations. Therefore, I undertook to go the extra mile, dismantling a Poseidon submarine, *U.S.S. Sam Rayburn*, to give the Soviet Union adequate time to take the steps necessary to join us in establishing an interim framework of truly mutual restraint. However, I made it clear that, as subsequent U.S. deployment milestones were reached, I would assess the overall situation and determine future U.S. actions on a case-by-case basis in light of Soviet behavior in exercising restraint comparable to our own, correcting their non-compliance, reversing their unwarranted military buildup, and seriously pursuing equitable and verifiable arms reduction agreements.

Later this month, the 8th Trident submarine, *U.S.S. Nevada*, begins sea trials. In accordance with our announced policy, I have assessed our options with respect to that milestone. I have considered Soviet actions since my June 1985 decision, and U.S. and Allied security interests in light of both those actions and our programmatic options. The situation is not encouraging.

Soviet Pattern of Non-Compliance

While we have seen some modest indications of improvement in one or two areas, there has been no real progress toward meeting U.S. concerns with respect to the general pattern of Soviet non-compliance with major arms control commitments, particularly in those areas of most obvious and direct Soviet non-compliance with the SALT and ABM agreements. The deployment of the SS-25, a forbidden second new Intercontinental Ballistic Missile (ICBM) type, continues apace. The Soviet Union continues to encrypt telemetry associated with its ballistic missile testing in a manner which impedes verification. The Krasnoyarsk radar remains a clear violation. We see no abatement of the Soviet strategic force buildup. Finally, since the November summit, we have yet to see the Soviets follow up constructively on the commitment made by General Secretary Gorbachev and myself to achieve early progress in the Geneva negotiations, in particular in areas where there is common ground, including the principle of 50 percent reductions in the strategic nuclear arms of both countries, appropriately applied, as well as an interim agreement on Intermediate-range Nuclear Forces (INF).

Based on Soviet conduct since my June 1985 decision, I can only conclude that the Soviet Union has not, as yet, taken those actions that would indicate its readiness to join us in an interim framework of truly mutual restraint. At the same time, I have also considered the programmatic options available to the U.S. in terms of their overall net impact on U.S. and Allied security.

When I issued guidance on U.S. policy on June 10, 1985, the military plans and programs for fiscal year 1986 were about to be implemented. The amount of flexibility that any nation has in the near term for altering its planning is modest at best. Our military planning will take more time to move out from under the shadow of previous assumptions, especially in the budgetary conditions which we now face. These budgetary conditions make it essential that we make the very best possible use of our resources.

The United States had long planned to retire and dismantle two of the oldest Poseidon submarines when their reactor cores were exhausted. Had I been persuaded that refueling and retaining these two Poseidon submarines would have contributed significantly and cost-effectively to the national security, I would have directed that these two Poseidon submarines not be dismantled, but be overhauled and retained. However, in view of present circumstances, including current military and economic realities, I have directed their retirement and dismantlement as planned.

As part of the same decision last June, I also announced that we would take appropriate and proportionate responses when needed to protect our own security in the face of continuing Soviet non-compliance. It is my view that certain steps are now required by continued Soviet disregard of their obligations.

Needless to say, the most essential near-term response to Soviet non-compliance remains the implementation of our full strategic modernization program, to underwrite deterrence today, and the continued pursuit of the Strategic Defense Initiative (SDI) research program, to see if it is possible to provide a safer and more stable basis for our future security and that of our Allies. The strategic modernization program, including the deployment of the second 50 Peacekeeper missiles, is the foundation for all future U.S. offensive force options. It provides a solid basis which can and will be adjusted over time to respond most efficiently to continued Soviet non-compliance. The SDI program represents our best hope for a future in which our security can rest on the increasing contribution of defensive systems that threaten no one.

It is absolutely essential that we maintain full support for these programs. To fail to do so would be the worst response to Soviet non-compliance. It would immediately and seriously undercut our negotiators in Geneva by removing the leverage that they must have to negotiate equitable reductions in both U.S. and Soviet forces. It would send precisely the wrong signal to the leadership of the Soviet Union about the seriousness of our resolve concerning their non-compliance. And, it would significantly increase the risk to our security for years to come. Therefore, our highest priority must remain the full implementation of these programs.

Secondly, the development by the Soviet Union of its massive ICBM forces continues to challenge seriously the essential balance which has deterred both conflict and coercion. Last June, I cited the Soviet Union's SS-25 missile, a second new type of ICBM prohibited under SALT II, as a clear and irreversible violation. With the number of deployed SS-25 mobile ICBMs growing, I now call upon the Congress to restore bipartisan support for a balanced, cost-effective, long-term program to restore both the survivability and effectiveness of the U.S. ICBM program. This program should include the full deployment of the 100 Peacekeeper ICBMs. But it must also look beyond the Peacekeeper and toward additional U.S. ICBM requirements in the future, including the Small ICBM to complement Peacekeeper. Therefore, I have directed the Department of Defense to provide to me by November 1986 an assessment of the best options for carrying out such a comprehensive ICBM program. This assessment will address the basing of the second 50 Peacekeeper missiles and specific alternative configurations for the Small ICBM in terms of size, number of warheads, and production rates.

Finally, I have also directed that the Advanced Cruise Missile program be accelerated. This would not direct any increase in the total program procurement at this time, but rather would establish a more efficient program that both saves money and accelerates the availability of additional options for the future.

This brings us to the question of the SALT agreements. SALT II was a fundamentally flawed and unratified treaty. Even if ratified, it would have expired on December 31, 1985. When presented to the U.S. Senate in 1979, it was considered by a broad range of critics, including the Senate Armed Services Committee, to be unequal and unverifiable in important provisions. It was, therefore, judged by many to be inimical to genuine arms control, to the security interests of the United States and its allies, and to global stability. The proposed treaty was clearly headed for defeat before my predecessor asked the Senate not to act on it.

The most basic problem with SALT II was that it codified major arms buildups rather than reductions. For example, even though at the time the Treaty was signed in 1979, the U.S. had, and only planned for, 550 MIRVed ICBM launchers, and the Soviet Union possessed only about 600, SALT II permitted each side to increase the number of such launchers to 820. It also permitted a buildup to 1,200 MIRVed ballistic launchers (both ICBMs and Submarine Launched Ballistic Missiles, SLBMs) even though the U.S. had only about 1,050 and the Soviet Union had only about 750 when the treaty was signed. It permitted the Soviet Union to retain all of its heavy ballistic missiles. Finally, it limited ballistic missile launchers, not the missiles or the warheads carried by the ballistic missiles. Since the signing of SALT II, Soviet ballistic missile forces have grown to within a few launchers of each of the 820 and 1,200 MIRVed limits, and from about 7,000 to over 9,000 warheads today. What is worse, given the failure of SALT II to constrain ballistic missile warheads, the number of warheads on Soviet ballistic missiles will continue to grow very significantly, even under the Treaty's limits, in the continued absence of Soviet restraint.

Call for 'Mutual Restraint'

In 1982, on the eve of the START negotiations, I undertook not to undercut existing arms control agreements to the extent that the Soviet Union demonstrated comparable restraint. Unfortunately, the Soviet Union did not exercise comparable restraint, and uncorrected Soviet violations have seriously undermined the SALT structure. Last June, I once again laid out our legitimate concerns but decided to go the extra mile, dismantling a Poseidon submarine, not to comply with or abide by a flawed and unratified treaty, but rather to give the Soviet Union one more chance and adequate time to take the steps necessary to join us in establishing an interim framework of truly mutual restraint. The Soviet Union has not used the past year for this purpose.

Given this situation, I have determined that, in the future, the United States must base decisions regarding its strategic force structure on the nature and magnitude of the threat posed by Soviet strategic forces, and not on standards contained in the SALT structure which has been undermined by Soviet non-compliance, and especially in a flawed SALT II treaty which was never ratified, would have expired if it had been ratified, and has been violated by the Soviet Union.

Since the United States will retire and dismantle two Poseidon submarines this summer, we will remain technically in observance of the terms of the SALT II Treaty until the U.S. equips its 131st B-52 heavy bomber for cruise missile carriage near the end of this year. However, given the decision that I have been forced to make, I intend at that time to continue deployment of U.S. B-52 heavy bombers with cruise missiles beyond the 131st aircraft as an appropriate response without dismantling additional U.S. systems as compensation under the terms of the SALT II Treaty. Of course, since we will remain in technical compliance with the terms of the expired SALT II Treaty for some months, I continue to hope that the Soviet Union will use this time to take the constructive steps necessary to alter the current situation. Should they do so, we will certainly take this into account.

The United States seeks to meet its strategic needs, given the Soviet buildup, by means that minimize incentives for continuing Soviet offensive force growth. In the longer term, this is one of the major motives in our pursuit of the Strategic Defense Initiative. As we modernize, we will continue to retire older forces as our national security requirements permit. I do not anticipate any appreciable numerical growth in U.S. strategic offensive forces. Assuming no significant change in the threat we face, as we implement the strategic modernization program the United States will not deploy more strategic nuclear delivery vehicles than does the Soviet Union. Furthermore, the United States will not deploy more strategic ballistic missile warheads than does the Soviet Union.

In sum, we will continue to exercise the utmost restraint, while protecting strategic deterrence, in order to help foster the necessary atmosphere for significant reductions in the strategic arsenals of both sides. This is the urgent task which faces us. I call on the Soviet Union to seize the opportunity to join us now in establishing an interim framework of truly *mutual* restraint.

Finally, I want to emphasize that no policy of interim restraint is a substitute for an agreement on deep and equitable reductions in offensive nuclear arms, provided that we can be confident of Soviet compliance with it. Achieving such reductions has received, and continues to receive, my highest priority. I hope the Soviet Union will act to give substance to the agreement I reached with General Secretary Gorbachev in Geneva to achieve early progress, in particular in areas where there is common ground, including the principle of 50 percent reductions in the strategic nuclear arms of both countries, appropriately applied, as well as an interim INF agreement. If the Soviet Union carries out this agreement, we can move now to achieve greater stability and a safer world. ■

Text of Reagan's Letter On AWACS for Saudi Arabia

Following are the White House texts of President Reagan's June 18 letter to the Speaker of the House and president of the Senate regarding the transfer of U.S. airborne warning and control system (AWACS) aircraft to Saudi Arabia, and the president's certifications of the conditions for the transfer.

By letter dated October 28, 1981, I assured then-Senate Majority Leader Baker that the proposed transfer to Saudi

Arabia of AWACS aircraft would not occur until I had certified to the Congress that specified conditions had been met. Subsequently, Section 131 of the International Security and Development Cooperation Act of 1985 ("ISDCA") incorporated the text of that letter, with its conditions for certification, into legislation.

I am pleased to inform you that all conditions set forth in my October 28 letter and repeated in Section 131 of the ISDCA have now been met and that I herewith forward to you my certification to that effect. Through the extensive efforts of the Defense and State Departments, agreements and other actions necessary to fulfill these requirements have been concluded.

I now wish to draw particular attention to the sixth condition that I have certified. I remain convinced that, as I stated in 1981, the sale of these AWACS aircraft to Saudi Arabia will contribute directly to the stability and security of the area and enhance the atmosphere and prospects for progress toward peace. I also believe that significant progress toward peaceful resolution of disputes in the region has been accomplished with the substantial assistance of Saudi Arabia. These perceptions are strengthened by a review of events of the last five years.

The current deployment of U.S. AWACS aircraft to Saudi Arabia has contributed significantly to the stability and security of Saudi Arabia and the region as a whole. The Royal Saudi Air Force's (RSAF) gradual assumption of the role now performed by the U.S. AWACS aircraft will continue this contribution. Over the past five years the U.S. AWACS aircraft have demonstrated their ability to detect approaching Iranian aircraft well before they would be detected by ground-based radar. This early detection, coupled with the demonstrated resolve of the RSAF to deploy its F-15s and engage aggressor aircraft, has deterred Iran from escalating attacks against targets on land and in Gulf waters under the Saudi protective umbrella. The Saudi commitment to a strong defense as evidenced by such measures as the AWACS acquisition, past defensive military action, and efforts to organize collective security among the member states of the Gulf Cooperation Council (GCC), taken together with the Kingdom's obvious lack of aggressive intent, have contributed and will continue to contribute to the stability and security of the area. Our continued success in helping to support regional stability will diminish prospects that U.S. forces might be called upon to protect the governments, shipping lanes, or vital petroleum resources of the region.

Saudi Arabia has firmly supported every significant diplomatic effort to end the Iran-Iraq war. Mediation missions under the auspices of the United Nations, the Organization of the Islamic Conference, and third countries acting independently have received Saudi diplomatic and facilitative assistance. In encouraging a negotiated settlement of the conflict, the Saudis have made clear their preference that the war end without concessions of sovereignty by either side.

Saudi efforts to advance the Arab-Israeli peace process have been substantial. The Fahd Peace Plan and the Arab endorsement of the plan embodied in the 1982 Fez Communiqué significantly and irreversibly modified the Arab consensus of the three "no's" enunciated at the 1968 Khartoum Summit, i.e., no recognition, no negotiation, and no conciliation with Israel. The Fez Communiqué moved the formal Arab position from rejection of peace to consideration of *how* to achieve peace with Israel. The plan's statement that all states in the region should be able to live in peace was an implicit acceptance of the right of Israel to a secure existence. The concept of land for peace was a direct reflection of U.N. Resolution 242. While various elements of the Fez Plan differ from our views, the Plan remains the single largest step toward peace on which the Arab world has been able to agree. The existence of this consensus provided a base from which King Hussein felt he could launch his initiative to bring Israel, Jordan, and the Palestinians to the negotiating table in 1984-85.

Saudi Arabia has signaled its tacit support for King Hussein's moves to lay the foundation for peace negotiations by continuing substantial financial assistance payments to Jordan following critical steps in the process, i.e., after Jordan resumed diplomatic relations with Egypt and again after the February 1985 agreement between Hussein and PLO Chairman Arafat. Despite vocal Syrian opposition, the Saudis sent official observers to the Amman Palestine National Council meeting in late 1984 where moderate Palestinians made a decision to break with the radicals, thereby opening the way for King Hussein to begin his peace initiative.

During the subsequent and continuing debate over how to make peace with Israel, the Saudis have consistently lent support to moderate Arab governments. Egypt's readmission to the Organization of the Islamic Conference was significantly assisted by crucial Saudi support for a procedural motion calling for a secret ballot on the readmission vote. Following the police riots in Cairo in February of this year, the Saudi Council of Ministers issued a statement supporting President Mubarak.

Although its efforts, like our own, met with limited success, Saudi Arabia played a major and highly visible role in attempts to arrange a lasting cease-fire in Lebanon. In the August 1983 efforts of Crown Prince Abdullah and Prince Bandar to bring an end to fighting in the Shuf mountains, and again through observers at the Geneva and Lausanne Lebanese national reconciliation talks, Saudi Arabia sought to bring peace to a moderate Arab nation and establish the framework for stable government. The Saudis also proved supportive of Lebanese efforts to negotiate directly with Israel conditions for Israeli withdrawal from southern Lebanon. In this regard, the Saudis supported Lebanese efforts to win Syrian consent to compromises necessary to reach agreement.

Saudi Arabia has provided crucial support for Sudan during that country's transition to a democratic form of government. Furthermore, it has established a significant record in working for regional stability and settlement of regional disputes in countries beyond its immediate neighborhood. Saudi aid has been crucial to the Afghan cause and significant to Pakistan, Morocco, and Tunisia. Despite limitations imposed by concern for its own security, the depth of regional animosities, and the need to establish and work within an Arab consensus, Saudi Arabia has assisted substantially the significant progress that has been made in the peaceful resolution of disputes in the region.

Saudi Arabia has publicly condemned terrorism and terrorist actions, having itself been a victim of terrorism. More important, it has taken practical actions to oppose terrorism regardless of its origins.

I am convinced that the assurances I made in my letter to Senator Baker have been amply fulfilled. A firm foundation has been laid for close and continued U.S.-Saudi cooperation in operating the Saudi AWACS and in building an air defense system for Saudi Arabia and the GCC. By contributing to the self-defense of these countries, we are diminishing the likelihood of direct intervention by U.S. forces in defense of vital Western interests. At the same time, we are encouraging forces of moderation which, if they prevail, will bring lasting peace to a turbulent region.

Certification of Conditions

In accordance with Section 131 of the International Security and Development Cooperation Act of 1985, PL 99-83, I hereby certify that the conditions set forth in my communication of October 28, 1981, to the Senate with respect to the transfer to Saudi Arabia of five E-3A airborne warning and control system (AWACS) aircraft have been met, specifically:

1. Security of Technology

A. That a detailed plan for the security of equipment, technology, information, and supporting documentation has been agreed to by the United States and Saudi Arabia and is in place; and

B. The security provisions for Saudi AWACS aircraft are no less stringent than measures employed by the United States for protection and control of its equipment of like kind outside the continental United States; and

C. The United States has the right of continual on-site inspection and surveillance by U.S. personnel of security arrangements for all operations during the useful life of the AWACS. It is further provided that security arrangements will be supplemented by additional U.S. personnel if it is deemed necessary by the two parties; and

D. Saudi Arabia will not permit citizens of third nations either to perform maintenance on the AWACS or to modify any such equipment without prior, explicit mutual consent of the two governments; and

E. Computer software, as designated by the United States Government, will remain the property of the United States Government.

2. Access to Information

That Saudi Arabia has agreed to share with the United States continuously and completely the information that it acquires from use of the AWACS.

3. Control Over Third-Country Participation

A. That Saudi Arabia has agreed not to share access to AWACS equipment, technology, documentation, or any information developed from such equipment or technology with any nation other than the United States without the prior, explicit mutual consent of both governments; and

B. There are in place adequate and effective procedures requiring the screening and security clearance of citizens of Saudi Arabia and only cleared Saudi citizens and cleared U.S. nationals will have access to AWACS equipment, technology, or documentation, or information derived therefrom, without the prior, explicit mutual consent of the two governments.

4. AWACS Flight Operations

That the Saudi AWACS will be operated solely within the boundaries of Saudi Arabia, except with the prior, explicit mutual consent of the two governments, and solely for defensive purposes as defined by the United States, in order to maintain security and regional stability.

5. Command Structure

That agreements as they concern organizational command and control structure for the operation of AWACS are of such a nature to guarantee that the commitments above will be honored.

6. Regional Peace and Security

That the sale contributes directly to the stability and security of the area and enhances the atmosphere and prospects for progress toward peace. Significant progress toward the peaceful resolution of disputes in the region has been accomplished with the substantial assistance of Saudi Arabia.

I will provide separately to the Congress, under appropriate procedures, those contracts and agreements pertinent to this sale and certification, including those whose confidentiality must be preserved.∎

Reagan's June 24 Address On Aid to Nicaraguan 'Contras'

Following is the White House text of President Reagan's address, as delivered June 24, on the proposal to send military aid to the anti-government rebels in Nicaragua, called "contras."

My fellow citizens, the matter that brings me before you today is a grave one and concerns my most solemn duty as President. It is the cause of freedom in Central America and the national security of the United States. Tomorrow the House of Representatives will debate and vote on this issue. I had hoped to speak directly and at this very hour to Members of the House of Representatives on this subject, but was unable to do so. Because I feel so strongly about what I have to say, I have asked for this time to share with you — and Members of the House — the message I would have otherwise given.

Nearly 40 years ago a Democratic President, Harry Truman, went before the Congress to warn of another danger to democracy, a civil war in a faraway country in which many Americans could perceive no national security interest.

Some of you can remember the world then. Europe lay devastated. One by one, the nations of Eastern Europe had fallen into Stalin's grip. The democratic government of Czechoslovakia would soon be overthrown. Turkey was threatened, and in Greece, the home of democracy, communist guerrillas, backed by the Soviet Union, battled democratic forces to decide the nation's fate.

Most Americans did not perceive this distant danger, so the opinion polls reflected little of the concern that brought Harry Truman to the well of the House that day. But go he did. And it is worth a moment to reflect on what he said.

In a hushed chamber, Mr. Truman said that we had come to a time in history when every nation would have to choose between two opposing ways of life. One way was based on the will of the majority — on free institutions and human rights. "The second way of life," he said, "is based upon the will of a minority forcibly imposed upon the majority. It relies upon terror and oppression, a controlled press and radio, fixed elections and the suppression of personal freedoms. I believe," President Truman said, "that it must be the policy of the United States to support free peoples who are resisting attempted subjugation by armed minorities or by outside pressures."

When Harry Truman spoke, Congress was controlled by the Republican Party. But that Congress put America's interest first, and supported Truman's request for military aid to Greece and Turkey just as four years ago Congress put America's interest first by supporting my request for military aid to defend democracy in El Salvador.

I speak today in that same spirit of bipartisanship. My fellow Americans and Members of the House, I need your help. I ask first for your help in remembering — remembering our history in Central America so we can learn from the mistakes of the past. Too often in the past the United States failed to identify with the aspirations of the people of Central America for freedom and a better life. Too often our government appeared indifferent when democratic values were at risk. So we took the path of least resistance and did nothing.

Today, however, with American support, the tide is turning in Central America. In El Salvador, Honduras, Costa Rica — and now in Guatemala — freely elected governments offer their people the chance for a better future — a future the United States must support.

But there is one tragic, glaring exception to that democratic tide — the communist Sandinista government in Nicaragua. It is tragic because the United States extended a generous hand of friendship to the new revolutionary government when it came to power in 1979. Congress voted $75 million in economic aid. The United States helped renegotiate Nicaragua's foreign debt. America offered teachers, doctors and Peace Corps volunteers to help rebuild the country. But the Sandinistas had a different agenda.

From the very first day a small clique of communists worked steadily to consolidate power and squeeze out their democratic allies. The democratic trade unionists who had fought Somoza's national guard in the streets were now told by the Sandinistas that the right to strike was illegal and that their revolutionary duty was to produce more for the state.

The newspaper, *La Prensa*, whose courage and determination had inspired so much of the Nicaraguan revolution, found its pages censored and suppressed. Violeta Chamorro, widow of the assassinated editor, soon quit the revolutionary government to take up the struggle for democracy again in the pages of her newspaper.

The leader of the Catholic Church in Nicaragua, Archbishop — now Cardinal — Obando y Bravo, who had negotiated the release of the Sandinista leaders from prison during the revolution, was now vilifed as a traitor by the very men he helped to free.

Soviet arms and bloc personnel began arriving in Nicaragua. With Cuban, East German, and Bulgarian advisers at their side, the Sandinistas began to build the largest standing army in Central American history and to erect all the odious apparatus of the modern police state.

Under the Somoza dictatorship, a single facility held all political prisoners. Today there are eleven. Eleven prisons in place of one.

The Sandinistas claim to defend Nicaraguan independence. But you and I know the truth. The proud people of Nicaragua did not rise up against Somoza and struggle, fight, and die — to have Cubans, Russians, Bulgarians, East Germans, and North Koreans running their prisons, organizing their army, censoring their newspapers, and suppressing their religious faith. One Nicaraguan nationalist, who fought in the revolution, says: "We are an occupied country today."

I could go on, but I know that even the administration's harshest critics in Congress hold no brief for Sandinista repression. Indeed the final verdict has already been written by Cardinal Obando himself in *The Washington Post*. Listen carefully to the Cardinal's words.

He says that the Sandinista regime "is a democratic government, legitimately constituted, which seeks the welfare and peace of the people and enjoys the support of the overwhelming majority" is not true.

To accept this as true, the Cardinal says, "is to ignore the mass exodus of the Miskito Indians, the departure of tens of thousands of Nicaraguan men and women of every age, profession, economic status and political persuasion. It is to ignore the most terrible violation of freedom of the press and of speech in the history of our country, the expulsion of priests and the mass exodus of young people eligible for military service." As for the Catholic Church in Nicaragua, we have been "gagged and bound," the Cardinal says.

Many brave Nicaraguans have stayed in their country despite mounting repression — defying the security police, defying the Sandinista mobs that attack and deface their homes. Thousands — peasants, Indians, devout Christians, draftees from the Sandinista army — have concluded that they must take up arms again to fight for the freedom they thought they had won in 1979.

The young men and women of the democratic resistance fight inside Nicaragua today in grueling mountain and jungle warfare. They confront a Soviet-equipped army, trained and led by Cuban officers. They face murderous helicopter gunships without any means of defense. And still they volunteer. And still their numbers grow.

Who among us would tell these brave young men and women, "Your dream is dead; your democratic revolution is over; you will never live in the free Nicaragua you fought so hard to build"?

The Sandinistas call these freedom fighters "contras" — for "counter-revolutionaries." But the real counter-revolutionaries are the Sandinista commandantes, who betrayed the hopes of the Nicaraguan revolution, and sold out their country to the Soviet empire.

The commandantes even betrayed the memory of the Nicaraguan rebel leader Sandino, whose legacy they falsely claim. For the real Sandino — because he was a genuine nationalist — was opposed to communism. In fact, Sandino broke with the Salvadoran communist leader, Farabundo Marti, over this very issue.

The true Nicaraguan nationalists are the leaders of the United Nicaraguan Opposition: Arturo Cruz — jailed by Somoza, a former member of the Sandinista government; Adolfo Calero — who helped organize a strike of businessmen to bring Somoza down; and Alfonso Robelo — a social democrat, and once a leader of the revolutionary government.

These good men refused to make any accommodation with the Somoza dictatorship. Who among us can doubt their commitment to bring democracy to Nicaragua?

So, the Nicaraguan people have chosen to fight for their freedom. Now we Americans must also choose.

For you and I and every American has a stake in this struggle.

Central America is vital to our own national security — and the Soviet Union knows it. The Soviets take the long view, but their strategy is clear — to dominate the strategic sea lanes and vital chokepoints around the world.

Half of America's imports and exports, including oil, travels through the area today. In a crisis, over half of NATO's supplies woud pass through this region. And Nicaragua, just 277 miles from the Panama Canal, offers the Soviet Union ports on both the Atlantic and Pacific oceans.

The Soviet Union already uses Cuba as an air and submarine base in the Caribbean. It hopes to turn Nicaragua into the first Soviet base on the mainland of North America.

If you doubt it, ask yourself: Why have the last four Soviet leaders — with a mounting economic crisis at home — already invested over a billion dollars and dispatched thousands of Soviet bloc advisers into a tiny country in Central America?

I know that no one in Congress wants to see Nicaragua become a Soviet military base. My friends, I must tell you in all seriousness, Nicaragua is becoming a Soviet base every day that we debate and debate and debate — and do nothing.

In the three months since I last asked the House to aid the democratic resistance, four military cargo ships have arrived at Nicaraguan ports, this time directly from the Soviet Union. Recently we have learned that Russian pilots are flying a Soviet AN-30 reconnaissance plane for the Sandinistas.

Now, the Sandinistas claim this is just for making civilian maps. Well, our intelligence services believe this could be the first time Soviet personnel have taken a direct role in support of military operations on the mainland of North America.

Think again how Cuba became a Soviet air and naval base. You'll see what Nicaragua will look like if we continue to do nothing. Cuba became a Soviet base gradually over many years. There was no single dramatic event — once the missile crisis passed — that captured the nation's attention. And so it will be with Nicaragua.

The Sandinistas will widen and deepen another port while we debate: Is it for commercial vessels or Soviet submarines? The Sandinistas will complete another airstrip while we argue: Is it for 707s or Backfire bombers? A Soviet training brigade will come to Nicaragua. Half will leave and half will stay. And we will debate: Are they soldiers or engineers?

Eventually, we Americans will have to stop arguing among ourselves. We will have to confront the reality of a Soviet military beachhead inside our defense perimeters — about 500 miles from Mexico. A future President and Congress will then face nothing but bad choices, followed by worse choices.

My friends in the House, for over 200 years, the security of the United States has depended on the safety of unthreatened borders, north and south. Do we want to be the first elected leaders in U.S. history to put our borders at risk?

Some of you may say, well, this is fear-mongering. Such a danger to our security will never come to pass. Well, perhaps it won't. But in making our decisions on my request for aid tomorrow, consider this: What are the consequences for our country if you're wrong?

I know some members of Congress who share my concern about Nicaragua have honest questions about my request for aid to the democratic resistance. Let me try to address them. Do the freedom fighters have the support of the Nicaraguan people? I urge members of the House to ask their colleague, the Chairman of the House Armed Services Committee, who recently visited a town in Nicaragua that was a Sandinista stronghold during the revolution. He heard peasants, trade unionists, farmers, workers, students, and shopkeepers all call on the United States to aid the armed resistance.

Or listen to the report from *Time* magazine of Central American scholar Robert Leiken, who once had hopes for the Sandinista revolution. He says, "I have gone to a number of towns in Nicaragua where I have found that the youth are simply not there. I ask the parents where they've gone, and they say they've gone off to join the contras." In Managua, Leiken reports 250 Nicaraguans stood on a bread line for three hours. "Who is responsible for this?" he asked. "The Sandinistas are responsible. The Sandinistas." That's what the people said. "The Sandinistas," Leiken concluded, "have not only lost support. I think they are detested by the population."

Can the democratic forces win? Consider there are 20 times as many Nicaraguans fighting the Sandinista dictatorship today as there were Sandinista fighters a year before Somoza fell. This is the largest peasant army raised in Latin America in more than 50 years. And thousands more are waiting to volunteer if American support comes through.

Some members of Congress — and I know some of you — fear that military aid to the democratic resistance will be only the first step down the slippery slope toward another Vietnam. Now, I know those fears are honest. But think where we heard them before. Just a few years ago, some argued in Congress that U.S. military aid to El Salvador would lead inevitably to the involvement of U.S. combat troops. But the opposite turned out to be true.

Had the United States failed to provide aid then, we might well be facing the final communist takeover of El Salvador and mounting pressures to intervene. Instead, with our aid, the government of El Salvador is winning the war — and there is no prospect whatever of American military involvement.

El Salvador still faces serious problems that require our attention. But democracy there is stronger, and both the communist guerrillas and the right-wing death squads are weaker. And Congress shares credit for that accomplishment. American aid and training is helping the Salvadoran army become a professional fighting force, more respectful of human rights. With our aid, we can help the Nicaraguan resistance accomplish the same goal.

I stress this point because I know many members of Congress and many Americans are deeply troubled by allegations of abuses by elements of the armed resistance. I share your concerns. Even though some of those charges are Sandinista propaganda, I believe such abuses have occurred in the past, and they are intolerable.

As President, I repeat to you the commitments I made to Sen. Sam Nunn. As a condition of our aid, I will insist on civilian control over all military forces; that no human rights abuses are tolerated; that any financial corruption be rooted out; that American aid go only to those committed to democratic principles. The United States will not permit this democratic revolution to be betrayed nor allow a return to the hated repression of the Somoza dictatorship.

The leadership of the United Nicaraguan Opposition shares these commitments and I welcome the appointment of a bipartisan Congressional commission to help us see that they are carried out.

Some ask: What are the goals of our policy toward Nicaragua? They are the goals the Nicaraguan people set for themselves in 1979: democracy, a free economy, and national self-determination. Clearly the best way to achieve these goals is through a negotiated settlement. No humane person wants to see suffering and war.

The leaders of the internal opposition and the Catholic Church have asked for dialogue with the Sandinistas. The leaders of the armed resistance have called for a cease-fire and negotiations at any time, in any place. We urge the Sandinistas to heed the pleas of the Nicaraguan people for a peaceful settlement.

The United States will support any negotiated settlement or Contadora treaty that will bring real democracy to Nicaragua. What we will not support is a paper agreement that sells out the Nicaraguan people's right to be free. That kind of agreement would be unworthy of us as a people. And it would be a false bargain. For internal freedom in Nicaragua and the security of Central America are indivisible. A free and democratic Nicaragua will pose no threat to its neighbors, or to the United States. A communist Nicaragua, allied with the Soviet Union, is a permanent threat to us all.

President Azcona of Honduras emphasized this point in a recent nationwide address: "As long as there is a totalitarian regime in Central America that has expansionist ambitions and is supported by an enormous military apparatus . . . the neighboring countries sharing common borders with the country that is the source of the problem will be under constant threat." If you doubt his warning, consider this: The Sandinistas have already sent two groups of communist guerrillas into Honduras. Costa Rican revolutionaries are already fighting alongside Sandinista troops.

My friends in the Congress, with democracy still a fragile root in Central America — with Mexico undergoing an economic crisis — can we responsibly ignore the long-term danger to American interests posed by a communist Nicaragua, backed by the Soviet Union, and dedicated — in the words of its own leaders — to a "revolution without borders"?

My friends, the only way to bring true peace and security to Central America is to bring democracy to Nicaragua. And the only way to get the Sandinistas to negotiate seriously about democracy is to give them no other alternative. Seven years of broken pledges, betrayals and lies have taught us that.

And that's why the measure the House will consider tomorrow — offered I know in good faith — which prohibits military aid for at least another three months — and perhaps forever — would be a tragic mistake. It would not bring the Sandinistas to the bargaining table. Just the opposite.

The bill, unless amended, would give the Sandinistas and the Soviet Union what they seek most — time. Time to crush the democratic resistance, time to consolidate power. And it would send a demoralizing message to the democratic resistance: that the United States is too divided and paralyzed to come to their aid in time.

Recently, I read the words of a leader of the internal democratic opposition. What he said made me feel ashamed.

This man has been jailed, his property confiscated and his life threatened by the security police. Still he continues to fight. And he said, "You Americans have the strength, the opportunity, but not the will. We want to struggle, but it is dangerous to have friends like you — to be left stranded on the landing beaches of the Bay of Pigs. Either help us or leave us alone."

My friends in the House of Representatives, I urge you to send a message tomorrow to this brave Nicaraguan — and thousands like him. Tell them it is not dangerous to have friends like us. Tell them America stands with those who stand in defense of freedom.

When the Senate voted earlier this year for military aid, Republicans were joined by many Democratic leaders: Bill Bradley of New Jersey, Sam Nunn of Georgia, David Boren of Oklahoma, Howell Heflin of Alabama, Lloyd Bentsen of Texas, Bennett Johnston and Russell Long of Louisiana, Fritz Hollings of South Carolina, John Stennis of Mississippi and Alan Dixon of Illinois.

Today, I ask the House for that kind of bipartisan support for the amendment to be offered tomorrow by Democrats Ike Skelton of Missouri and Richard Ray of Georgia and Republicans Mickey Edwards of Oklahoma and Rod Chandler of Washington. This bipartisan amendment will provide the freedom fighters with what they need — now.

With that amendment, you also send another message to Central America. For democracy there faces many enemies: poverty, illiteracy, hunger and despair. And the United States must also stand with the people of Central America against these enemies of democracy.

And that's why — just as Harry Truman followed his request for military aid to Greece and Turkey with the Marshall Plan — I urge Congress to support $300 million in new economic aid to the Central American democracies.

The question before the House is not only about the freedom of Nicaragua and the security of the United States, but who we are as a people.

President Kennedy wrote on the day of his death that history had called this generation of Americans to be "watchmen on the walls of world freedom." A Republican President, Abraham Lincoln, said much the same thing on the way to his inauguration in 1861.

Stopping in Philadelphia, Lincoln spoke in Independence Hall, where our Declaration of Independence had been signed. He said far more had been achieved in that hall than just American independence from Britain. Something permanent — something unalterable had happened. He called it "hope to the world for all future time."

Hope to the world for all future time. In some way, every man, woman and child in our world is tied to those events at Independence Hall, to the universal claim to dignity, to the belief that all human beings are created equal, that all people have a right to be free.

We Americans have not forgotten our revolutionary heritage. But sometimes it takes others to remind us of what we ourselves believe.

Recently I read the words of a Nicaraguan Bishop, Pablo Vega, who visited

Washington a few weeks ago. Somoza called Pablo Vega the "communist Bishop." Now, the Sandinistas revile him as "the Contra Bishop." But Pablo Vega is really a humble man of God. "I am saddened," the good Bishop said, "that so many North Americans have a vision of democracy that — has only to do with materialism —" The Sandinistas "speak of human rights as if they were talking of the rights of a child — the right to receive from the bountifulness of the state — but even the humblest campesino knows what it means to have the right to act. We are defending," Pablo Vega said, "the right of man to be."

Well, Reverend Father, we hear you. For we Americans believe with you that even the humblest campesino has the right to be free. My fellow citizens, Members of the House, let us not take the path of least resistance in Central America again. Let us keep faith with these brave people struggling for their freedom. Give them, give me, your support; and together, let us send this message to the world: that America is still a beacon of hope, still a light unto the nations.

A light that casts its glow across the land and our continent and even back across the centuries — keeping faith with a dream of long ago.

Thank you and God bless you. ∎

Text of Reagan's July 22 Address on South Africa

Following is the White House text of President Reagan's address on South Africa, as delivered July 22 at the White House to the members of the World Affairs Council and the Foreign Policy Association.

Thank you very much. Mr. Vice President, Secretary Shultz. I would like to express my appreciation to Leonard Marks, the World Affairs Council, and the Foreign Policy Association for helping bring this group together today.

For more than a year now, the world's attention has been focused upon South Africa — the deepening political crisis there, the widening cycle of violence. And today, I'd like to outline American policy toward that troubled republic and toward the region of which it is a part — a region of vital importance to the West.

Apartheid Root of Disorder

The root cause of South Africa's disorder is apartheid — that rigid system of racial segregation, wherein black people have been treated as third-class citizens in a nation they helped to build.

America's view of apartheid has been, and remains, clear. Apartheid is morally wrong and politically unacceptable. The United States cannot maintain cordial relations with a government whose power rests upon the denial of rights to a majority of its people based on race.

If South America [*sic*] wishes to belong to the family of Western nations, an end to apartheid is a precondition. Americans, I believe, are united in this conviction.

Second, apartheid must be dismantled. Time is running out for the moderates of all races in South Africa.

Disagreement on Methods

But if we Americans are agreed upon the goal, a free and multiracial South Africa associated with free nations and the West, there is deep disagreement about how to reach it.

First, a little history. For a quarter century now, the American government has been separating itself from the South African government. In 1962, President Kennedy imposed an embargo on military sales. Last September, I issued an Executive Order further restricting U.S. dealings with the Pretoria government. For the past 18 months, the marketplace has been sending unmistakable signals of its own. U.S. bank lending to South Africa has been virtually halted. No significant new investment has come in. Some Western businessmen have packed up and gone home.

And now, we've reached a critical juncture. Many in Congress and some in Europe are clamoring for sweeping sanctions against South Africa. The Prime Minister of Great Britain has denounced punitive sanctions as "immoral" and "utterly repugnant." Well, let me tell you why we believe Mrs. Thatcher is right.

Problems With Economic Sanctions

The primary victims of an economic boycott of South Africa would be the very people we seek to help. Most of the workers who would lose jobs because of sanctions would be black workers.

We do not believe the way to help the people of South Africa is to cripple the economy upon which they and their families depend for survival.

Alan Paton, South Africa's great writer, for years the conscience of his country, has declared himself emphatically: "I am totally opposed to disinvestment," he says. "It is primarily for a moral reason. Those who will pay most grievously for disinvestment will be the black workers of South Africa. I take very seriously the teachings of the gospels. In particular, the parables about giving drink to the thirsty and food to the hungry. I will not help to cause any such suffering to any black person." Nor will we.

Region's Economic Interdependence

Looking at a map, southern Africa is a single economic unit tied together by rails and roads. Zaire and its southern mining region depends upon South Africa for three-fourths of her food and petroleum. More than half the electric power that drives the capital of Mozambique comes from South Africa. Over one-third of the exports from Zambia and 65 percent of the exports of Zimbabwe leave the continent through South African ports.

The mines of South Africa employ 13,000 workers from Swaziland, 19,000 from Botswana, 50,000 from Mozambique and 110,000 from the tiny, landlocked country of Lesotho. Shut down these productive mines with sanctions and you have forced black mine workers out of their jobs and forced their families back in their home countries into destitution. I don't believe the American people want to do something like that. As one African leader remarked recently, "Southern Africa is like a zebra. If the white parts are injured, the black parts will die too."

Well, Western nations have poured billions in foreign aid and investment loans into southern Africa. Does it make sense to aid these countries with one hand, and with the other to smash the industrial engine upon which their future depends?

Damage to Racial Progress

Wherever blacks seek equal opportunity, higher wages, and better working conditions, their strongest allies are the American, British, French, German, and Dutch businessmen who bring to South Africa ideas of social justice formed in their own countries.

If disinvestment is mandated, these progressive Western forces will depart and South African proprietors will inherit, at fire sale prices, their farms and factories and plants and mines. And how would this end apartheid?

Our own experience teaches us that racial progress comes swiftest and easiest, not during economic depression, but in times of prosperity and growth. Our own history teaches us that capitalism is the natural enemy of such feudal institutions as apartheid.

Sharing the Outrage

Nevertheless, we share the outrage Americans have come to feel.

Night after night, week after week, television has brought us reports of violence by South African security forces bringing injury and death to peaceful demonstrators and innocent bystanders. More recently, we read of violent attacks by blacks against blacks. Then there is the calculated terror by elements of the African National Congress: the mining of roads, the bombings of public places, designed to bring about further repression, the imposition of martial law, eventually creating the conditions for racial war.

The most common method of terror is the so-called "necklace." In this barbaric way of reprisal, a tire is filled with kerosene or gasoline, placed around the neck of an alleged "collaborator," and ignited. The victim may be a black policeman, a teacher, a soldier, a civil servant. It makes no difference. The atrocity is designed to terrorize blacks into ending all racial cooperation — and to polarize South Africa as prelude to a final, climactic struggle for power.

Government's Excessive Actions

In defending their society and people, the South African government has a right and responsibility to maintain order in the face of terrorists. But by its tactics, the government is only accelerating the descent into bloodletting. Moderates are being trapped between the intimidation of radical youths and countergangs of vigilantes.

And the government's state of emergency next went beyond the law of necessity. It, too, went outside the law by sweeping up thousands of students, civic leaders, church leaders and labor leaders, thereby contributing to further radicalization. Such repressive measures will bring South Africa neither peace nor security.

Another 'Truth' of South Africa

It's a tragedy that most Americans only see or read about the dead and injured in South Africa — from terrorism, violence, and repression. For behind the terrible television pictures, lies another truth: South Africa is a complex and diverse society in a state of transition. More and more South Africans have come to recognize that change is essential for survival. The realization has come hard and late; but the realization has finally come to Pretoria that apartheid belongs to the past.

In recent years, there's been a dramatic change. Black workers have been permitted to unionize, bargain collectively, and build the strongest free trade union movement in all of Africa. The infamous pass laws have been ended, as have many of the laws denying blacks the right to live, work, and own property in South Africa's cities. Citizenship, wrongly stripped away, has been restored to nearly six million blacks. Segregation in universities and public facilities is being set aside. Social apartheid laws prohibiting interracial sex and marriage have been struck down. It is because State President Botha has presided over these reforms that extremists have denounced him as a traitor.

We must remember, as the British historian Paul Johnson reminds us, that South Africa is an African country as well as a Western country.

And, reviewing the history of that continent in the quarter century since independence, historian Johnson does not see South Africa as a failure: "... only in South Africa," he writes, "have the real incomes of blacks risen very substantially.... In mining, black wages have tripled in real terms in the last decade.... South Africa is the ... only African country to produce a large black middle class." "Almost certainly," he adds, "there are now more black women professionals in South Africa than in the whole of the rest of Africa put together."

Despite apartheid, tens of thousands of black Africans migrate into South Africa from neighboring countries to escape poverty and take advantage of the opportunities in an economy that produces nearly a third of the income in all of sub-Saharan Africa.

It's tragic that the — in the current crisis social and economic progress has been arrested. And, yet, in contemporary South Africa — before the state of emergency — there was a broad measure of freedom of speech, of the press, and of religion there. Indeed, it's hard to think of a single country in the Soviet bloc — or many in the United Nations — where political critics have the same freedom to be heard as did outspoken critics of the South African government.

Continue Dismantling Apartheid

But, by Western standards, South Africa still falls short, terribly short, on the scales of economic and social justice. South Africa's actions to dismantle apartheid must not end now. The state of emergency must be lifted. There must be an opening of the political process. That the black people of South Africa should have a voice in their own governance is an idea whose time has come. There can be no turning back. In the multiracial society that is South Africa, no single race can monopolize the reins of political power.

No Negotiations With Communists

Black churches, black unions, and indeed, genuine black nationalists have a legitimate role to play in the future of their country. But the South African government is under no obligation to negotiate the future of the country with any organization that proclaims a goal of creating a communist state and uses terrorist tactics and violence to achieve it. (Applause.)

Importance of Southern Africa

Many Americans, understandably, ask: Given the racial violence, the hatred, why not wash our hands and walk away from that tragic continent and bleeding country? Well, the answer is: We cannot.

In southern Africa, our national ideals and strategic interests come together.

South Africa matters because we believe that all men are created equal and are endowed by their Creator with unalienable rights. South Africa matters because of who we are. One of eight Americans can trace his ancestry to Africa.

Strategically, this is one of the most vital regions of the world. Around the Cape of Good Hope passes the oil of the Persian Gulf — which is indispensable to the industrial economies of Western Europe. Southern Africa and South Africa are repository of many of the vital minerals — vanadium, manganese, chromium, platinum — for which the West has no other secure source of supply.

The Soviet Union is not unaware of the stakes. A decade ago, using an army of Cuban mercenaries provided by Fidel Castro, Moscow installed a client regime in Angola. Today, the Soviet Union is providing that regime with the weapons to attack UNITA — a black liberation movement which seeks for Angolans the same right to be represented in their government that black South Africans seek for themselves.

Apartheid Threat to U.S. Interests

Apartheid threatens our vital interests in southern Africa, because it's drawing neighboring states into the vortex of violence. Repeatedly, within the last 18 months, South African forces have struck into neighboring states. I repeat our condemnation of such behavior. Also the Soviet-armed guerrillas of the African National Congress — operating both within South Africa and from some neighboring countries — have embarked upon new acts of terrorism inside South Africa. I also condemn that behavior.

But South Africa cannot shift the blame for these problems onto neighboring states, especially when those neighbors take steps to stop guerrilla actions from being mounted from their own territory.

If this rising hostility in southern Africa — between Pretoria and the frontline states — explodes, the Soviet Union will be the main beneficiary. And the critical ocean corridor of South Africa and the strategic minerals of the region would be at risk.

Thus, it would be an historic act of folly for the United States and the West — out of anguish and frustration and anger — to write off South Africa.

A South African Solution

Ultimately, however, the fate of South Africa will be decided there, not here. We Americans stand ready to help. But whether South Africa emerges democratic and free or takes a course leading to a downward spiral of poverty and repression will finally be their choice, not ours.

The key to the future lies with the South African government. As I urge Western nations to maintain communication and involvement in South Africa, I urged Mr. Botha not to retreat into the "laager," not to cut off contact with the West. Americans and South Africans have never been enemies — and we understand the apprehension and fear and concern of all of your people. But an end to apartheid does not necessarily mean an end to the social, economic, and physical security of the white people in this country they love and have sacrificed so much to build.

Ally to Oppressed South Africans

To the black, "colored," and Asian peoples of South Africa, too long treated as second- and third-class subjects, I can only say: In your hopes for freedom, social justice, and self-determination, you have a friend and ally in the United States. Maintain your hopes for peace and reconciliation; and we will do our part to keep that road open.

We understand that behind the rage and resentment in the townships is the memory of real injustices inflicted upon generations of South Africans. Those to whom evil is done, the poet wrote, often do evil in return.

But if the people of South Africa are to have a future in a free country where the rights of all are respected, the desire for retribution will have to be set aside. Otherwise, the future will be lost in a blood quarrel over the past.

Outline for Peace

It would be an act of arrogance to insist that uniquely American ideas and institutions, rooted in our own history and traditions, be transplanted to South African soil. Solutions to South Africa's political crisis must come from South Africans themselves. Black and white, "colored" and Asian, they have their own traditions. But let me outline what we believe are necessary components of progress toward political peace.

First, a timetable for elimination of apartheid laws should be set.

Second, all political prisoners should be released.

Third, Nelson Mandela should be released — to participate in the country's political process.

Fourth, black political movements should be unbanned.

Fifth, both the government and its opponents should begin a dialogue about constructing a political system that rests upon the consent of the governed — where the rights of majorities and minorities, and individuals, are protected by law. And the dialogue should be initiated by those with power and authority — the South African government itself.

Sixth, if post-apartheid South Africa is to remain the economic locomotive of southern Africa, its strong and developed economy must not be crippled. And, therefore, I urge the Congress — and the countries of Western Europe — to resist this emotional clamor for punitive sanctions.

Work, Not Run

If Congress imposes sanctions, it would destroy America's flexibility, discard our diplomatic leverage and deepen the crisis. To make a difference, Americans — who are a force for decency and progress in the world — must remain involved.

We must stay and work, not cut and run.

It should be our policy to build in South Africa, not to bring down. Too often in the past, we Americans — acting out of anger and frustration and impatience — have turned our backs on flawed regimes, only to see disaster follow.

Those who tell us the moral thing to do is embargo the South African economy and write off South Africa should tell us exactly what they believe will rise in its place. What foreign power would fill the vacuum — if its ties with the West are broken?

Coordination With Allies

To be effective, however, our policy must be coordinated with our key Western allies, and with the frontline states in southern Africa. These countries have the greatest concern and potential leverage on the situation in South Africa. I intend to pursue the following steps:

Secretary Shultz has already begun intensive consultations with our Western allies, whose roots and presence in South Africa are greater than our own, on ways to encourage internal negotiations. We want the process to begin now; and we want open channels to all the principal parties. The key nations of the West must act in concert. And together, we can make the difference.

We fully support the current efforts of the British government to revive hopes for negotiations. Foreign Secretary Howe's visits with South Africa's leaders this week will be of particular significance.

Coordination With Region's Leaders

And second, I urge the leaders of the region to join us in seeking a future South Africa where countries live in peace and cooperation.

South Africa is the nation where the industrial revolution first came to Africa; its economy is a mighty engine that could pull southern Africa into a prosperous future. The other nations of southern Africa — from Kinshasa to the Cape — are rich in natural resources and human resources.

U.S. Aid to Southern Africa

Third, I have directed Secretary Shultz and AID Administrator McPherson to undertake a study of America's assistance role in southern Africa — to determine what needs to be done, and what can be done to expand the trade, private investment and transport prospects of southern Africa's landlocked nations. In the past five years, we have provided almost a billion dollars in assistance to South Africa's neighbors. And this year we hope to provide an additional $45 million to black South Africans.

We're determined to remain involved, diplomatically and economically, with all the states of southern Africa that wish constructive relations with the United States.

For a New South Africa

This administration is not only against broad economic sanctions and against apartheid; we are for a new South Africa, a new nation where all that has been built up over generations is not destroyed, a new society where participation in the social, cultural, and political life is open to all peoples — a new South Africa that comes home to the family of free nations where she belongs.

To achieve that, we need — not a Western withdrawal — but deeper involvement by the Western business community, as agents of change and progress and growth. The international business community needs not only to be supported in South Africa, but energized. We'll be at work on that task. If we wish to foster the process of transformation, one of the best vehicles for change is through the involvement of black South Africans in business, job-related activities and labor unions.

But the vision of a better life cannot be realized so long as apartheid endures and instability reigns in South Africa.

If the peoples of southern Africa are to prosper, leaders and peoples of the region — of all races — will have to elevate their common interests above their ethnic divisions.

We and our allies cannot dictate to the government of a sovereign nation. Nor should we try. But we can offer to help find a solution that is fair to all the people of South Africa. We can volunteer to stand by and help bring about dialogue between leaders of the various factions and groups that make up the population of South Africa. We can counsel and advise and make it plain to all that we are there as friends of all the people of South Africa.

In that tormented land, the window remains open for peaceful change. For how long, we know not. But we in the West, privileged and prosperous and free, must not be the ones to slam it shut. Now is a time for healing. The people of South Africa, of all races, deserve a chance to build a better future. And we must not deny or destroy that chance.

Thank you. (Applause.)

Vetoed on Sept. 26:

Reagan's Veto Message On Indian Programs Bill

Following is the White House text of President Reagan's message accompanying his Sept. 26 veto of HR 3247, a bill reauthorizing certain programs for American Indians. It was Reagan's ninth veto of a public bill during the 99th Congress.

I am returning herewith without my signature HR 3247, which would extend and amend the Native American Programs Act of 1974.

I fully support the objectives of the Native American Programs Act of 1974 to help American Indians, Alaskan Natives, and Native Hawaiians achieve economic and social self-sufficiency. My decision not to approve HR 3247 is based on my belief that this bill would seriously undermine the administrative flexibility needed to ensure responsiveness to individual tribes and Native American organizations — flexibility that is essential to the effectiveness of the Native American programs.

The Executive branch must be allowed to carry out its responsibilities to administer the laws effectively. HR 3247 would cause undue interference with ongoing program management. This legislation, if signed into law, would make effective administration of this important program extremely difficult by creating delays in implementing program policy that can only hurt rather than help the Native Americans it is intended to serve.

If HR 3247 were to become law, it would require diverting scarce resources away from program-related activities to meet wasteful and unnecessary administrative requirements and would involve the Congress inappropriately in ongoing administrative activities that should be left to the Executive branch. Specifically, the bill would:

- Require "notice and comment" rulemaking for rules and policy statements that have been and should continue to be handled informally, without permitting exceptions for good cause or in other circumstances where exceptions generally apply, thereby substantially increasing administrative costs and delays;
- Require the Administration for Native Americans (ANA) to use peer review panels to review and rank all grant applications, even though the use of such panels is not appropriate in all cases; and
- Require the Secretary of Health and Human Services to report and explain to the Congress all decisions on grant applications at variance with recommendations of the peer review panels.

These provisions of HR 3247 would unnecessarily increase administrative requirements and thereby shift resources away from technical assistance and other activities more directly related to helping applicants and grantees. Equally troublesome, they would inevitably involve both the Congress and members of the public in second-guessing the ANA on details related to administration of Native American programs. This would have adverse results for the programs and would potentially set a dangerous precedent for unnecessary restrictions disrupting the operations of other Federal human services programs.

Quite simply, the Executive branch cannot effectively carry out its responsibilities to implement the laws if agencies are required, as a routine procedure, to justify each grant decision to the Congress, or if every general statement of agency policy or procedure must be made through formal notice and comment rulemaking.

The provisions of HR 3247 also raise concerns about confidentiality, in requiring the Commissioner of the ANA to discuss publicly the weaknesses and problems of applications submitted by individual tribal organizations. This could well have a chilling effect on the competitive grant process. New and less experienced organizations could be more hesitant to apply, and established Native American organizations might be disturbed about public distribution of information about their applications.

I reiterate my support for the continuation of the Native American programs. I therefore urge the Congress to provide funding for these programs in the fiscal year 1987 continuing resolution and urge that the 100th Congress promptly consider new legislation to authorize appropriations for these programs. The Administration, through the Department of Health and Human Services, looks forward to working with the Congress to develop legislation that will meet the Congress' legitimate concerns for accountability of the Executive branch, while also meeting our concerns that the law not be burdened with requirements incompatible with our responsibility to achieve the statutory purposes of these programs.

RONALD REAGAN

The White House,
September 26, 1986.

Reagan Message on South Africa Sanctions Veto

Following is the White House text of President Reagan's message accompanying his Sept. 26 veto of HR 4868, the South Africa sanctions bill. It was Reagan's 10th veto of a public bill during the 99th Congress.

TO THE HOUSE OF REPRESENTATIVES:

I am returning herewith without my approval HR 4868, the Comprehensive Anti-Apartheid Act of 1986. Title III of this bill would seriously impede the prospects for a peaceful end to apartheid and the establishment of a free and open society for all in South Africa.

This Administration has no quarrel with the declared purpose of this measure. Indeed, we share that purpose: To send a clear signal to the South African Government that the American people view with abhorrence its codified system of racial segregation. Apartheid is an affront to human rights and human dignity. Normal and friendly relations cannot exist between the United States and South Africa until it becomes a dead policy. Americans are of one mind and one heart on this issue.

But while we vigorously support the purpose of this legislation, declaring economic warfare against the people of South Africa would be destructive not only of their efforts to peacefully end apartheid, but also of the opportunity to replace it with a free society.

The sweeping and punitive sanctions adopted by the Congress are targeted directly at the labor intensive industries upon which the victimized peoples of South Africa depend for their very survival. Black workers — the first victims of apartheid — would become the first victims of American sanctions.

Banning the import of sugar, for example, would threaten the livelihood of 23,000 black farmers. Banning the import of natural resources is a sanction targeted directly at the mining industries of South Africa, upon which more than half a million black laborers depend for their livelihood.

By prohibiting the importation of food and agricultural products, the measure would invite retaliation by South Africa, which since June has purchased over 160,000 tons of wheat from the United States. Denying basic foodstuffs to South Africa — much of which go to feed the black population — will only lead to privation, unrest, and violence. It will not advance the goals of peaceful change.

Are we truly helping the black people of South Africa — the lifelong victims of apartheid — when we throw them out of work and leave them and their families jobless and hungry in those segregated townships? Or are we simply assuming a moral posture at the expense of the people in whose name we presume to act?

This, then, is the first and foremost reason I cannot support this legislation. Punitive economic sanctions would contribute directly and measurably to the misery of people who already have suffered enough. Using America's power to deepen the economic crisis in this tortured country is not the way to reconciliation and peace. Black South Africans recognize that they would pay with their lives for the deprivation, chaos, and violence that would follow an economic collapse. That is why millions of blacks and numerous black leaders in South Africa are as firm in their opposition to sanctions as in their abhorrence of apartheid.

The imposition of punitive sanctions would also deliver a devastating blow to the neighboring states in southern Africa that depend on Pretoria for transportation, energy, markets, and food. An estimated million-and-a-half foreign workers, legal and illegal, now live in South Africa. The number of people, women and children especially, outside South Africa who are dependent upon the remittances of these workers for their survival has been estimated to be over five million. Do we truly wish to be directly responsible for increased suffering, and perhaps starvation, in southern Africa? Do we truly wish our action to be the rationale Pretoria invokes for expelling these workers? Do we truly wish to trigger a cycle of economic sanctions and counter-sanctions that end up crippling the economy of South Africa and devastating the economies of the frontline states? What sense does it make to send aid to those impoverished countries with one hand while squeezing their economies with the other?

Disrupting the South African economy and creating more unemployment will only fuel the tragic cycle of violence and repression that has gripped that troubled country. Black unemployment in South Africa in some areas is over 50 percent — and adding to it will create more anger, more violence, and more competition among blacks struggling to survive. It will not improve prospects for negotiations.

Another feature of the bill would require the Administration to publicly identify within six months any and all nations that have chosen not to join us in observing the U.N. arms embargo against South Africa, "with a view to terminating United States military assistance to those countries." But the United States will not revert to a single-minded policy of isolationism, with its vast and unforeseen effects on our international security relationships, that would be dictated by the unilateral decisions of our allies. No single issue, no matter how important, can be allowed to override in this way all other considerations in our foreign policy. Our military relationships must continue to be based upon a comprehensive assessment of our national defense needs and the security of the West.

Not only does this legislation contain sweeping punitive sanctions that would injure most the very people we seek to help, the legislation discards our economic leverage, constricts our diplomatic freedom, and ties the hands of the President of the United States in dealing with a gathering crisis in a critical subcontinent where the Soviet Bloc — with its mounting investment of men and arms — clearly sees historic opportunity. Therefore, I am also vetoing the bill because it contains provisions that infringe on the President's constitutional prerogative to articulate the foreign policy of the United States.

There are, however, several features of the measure that the Administration supports. Title II of the bill, for example, mandates affirmative measures to eliminate apartheid and provide assistance to its victims, including support for black participation in business enterprises as owners, managers, and professionals. It authorizes the President to take steps for the purpose of assisting firms to fight apartheid and extend equal opportunity to blacks in investment, management, and employment. The bill also contains a number of other useful and realistic provisions, such as those calling upon the African National Congress (ANC) to reexamine its communist ties and mandating a report on the activities of the Communist Party in South Africa and the extent to which it has infiltrated South African political organizations. Still other portions of the bill call upon the ANC to condemn the practice of "necklacing" and terrorism and to state affirmatively that it will support a free and democratic post-apartheid South Africa. These provisions, as well as many others in the bill, reflect the agreement of the Congress and the Administration on important aspects of an overall anti-apartheid policy.

The Administration has been — and remains — prepared to work with the Congress to devise measures that manifest the American people's united opposition to apartheid — without injuring its victims. We remain ready to work with the Congress in framing measures that — like the 1962 U.S. embargo of military sales and the carefully targeted sanctions of my own Executive order of 1985 — keep the United States at arm's distance from the South African regime, while keeping America's beneficent influence at work bringing about constructive change within that troubled society and nation.

It remains my hope that the United States can work with its European allies to fashion a flexible and coordinated policy — consistent with their recent actions — for constructive change inside South Africa. I believe we should support their measures with similar executive actions of our own, and I will work with the Congress toward that goal. It remains my hope that, once again, Republicans and Democrats can come together on the common ground that, after all, we both share: an unyielding opposition both to the unacceptable doctrine of apartheid as well as the unacceptable alternative of Marxist tyranny — backed by the firm determination that the future of South Africa and southern Africa will belong to the free. To achieve that, we must stay and build, not cut and run.

That Americans should recoil at what their television screens bring them from South Africa — the violence, the repression, the terror — speaks well of us as a people. But the historic crisis in South Africa is not one from which the leading nation of the West can turn its back and walk away. For the outcome of that crisis has too great a bearing upon the future of Afriea, the future of NATO, the future of the West.

Throughout the postwar era, we Americans have succeeded when we left our partisan differences at the water's edge — and persevered; as we did in the rebuilding of Europe and Japan, as we are doing today in El Salvador. We have failed when we permitted our exasperation and anger and impatience at present conditions to persuade us to forfeit the future to the enemies of freedom.

Let us not forget our purpose. It is not to damage or destroy any economy, but to help the black majority of South Africa and southern Africa enjoy a greater share of the material blessings and bounties their labor has helped to produce — as they secure as well their legitimate political rights. That is why sweeping punitive sanctions are the wrong course to follow, and increased American and Western investment — by firms that are breaking down apartheid by providing equal opportunity for the victims of official discrimination — is the right course to pursue.

Our goal is a democratic system in which the rights of majorities, minorities, and individuals are protected by a bill of rights and firm constitutional guarantees.

RONALD REAGAN

The White House,
September 26, 1986.

Sent by President Reagan Sept. 29:

President Reagan's Letter on South Africa Executive Order

Following is the White House text of a Sept. 29 letter from President Reagan to Senate Majority Leader Robert Dole, R-Kan., and Speaker of the House Thomas P. O'Neill Jr., D-Mass., outlining Reagan's executive order imposing new sanctions on South Africa.

Dear Mr. Majority Leader (Mr. Speaker):

I understand and share the very strong feelings and sense of frustration in the Congress and in our Nation about apartheid, an unconscionable system that we all reject. The ongoing tragedy in South Africa tests our resolve as well as our patience. None of us wants to aggravate that tragedy.

Move Toward Internal Repression

In the last several months, the South African Government, instead of moving further down the once promising path of reform and dialogue, has turned to internal repression. We all know that South Africa's real problem traces to the perpetuation of apartheid. And we know that the solution to this problem can only be found in lifting the present State of Emergency, repealing all racially discriminatory laws, releasing political prisoners, and unbanning political parties — necessary steps opening the way for negotiations aimed at creating a new, democratic order for all South Africans. The South African Government holds the key to the opening of such negotiations. Emerging from discussion among South Africans, we want to see a democratic system in which the rights of majorities, minorities, and individuals are protected by a bill of rights and firm constitutional guarantees. We will be actively pursuing diplomatic opportunities and approaches in an effort to start a movement toward negotiations in South Africa.

Problems With Sanctions Bill

I outlined in my message to the House of Representatives on Friday my reasons for vetoing the Comprehensive Anti-Apartheid Act of 1986, principally my opposition to punitive sanctions that harm the victims of apartheid and my desire to work in concert with our Allies. I also indicated in that message that I am prepared to sign an expanded Executive order that strongly signals our rejection of apartheid and our desire to actively promote rapid positive change in South Africa. I am prepared to expand the range of restrictions and other measures that will characterize our relations with South Africa. There would be strong sanctions in my new order, sanctions that I earnestly wish were unnecessary. These sanctions, directed at the enforcers not the victims of apartheid, encompass measures recently adopted by many of our allies, as well as many elements of the original Senate committee version of the bill. They are incontestably necessary in today's circumstances. My intention is to make it plain to South Africa's leaders that we cannot conduct business-as-usual with a government that mistakes the silence of racial repression for the consent of the governed.

Executive Order Provisions

My new Executive order will, therefore, reaffirm and incorporate the measures I imposed last year (i.e., bans on loans to the South African Government and its agencies, all exports of computers to apartheid-enforcing entities and the military and police, all nuclear exports except those related to health, safety, and IAEA programs, imports of South African weapons, the import of Krugerrands, and a requirement for all U.S. firms to apply fair labor standards based on the Sullivan principles). The Executive order will also add:

- a ban on new investments other than those in black-owned firms or companies applying the fair labor standards of the Sullivan principles;
- a ban on the import from South Africa of iron and steel;
- a ban on bank accounts for the South African Government and its agencies;
- a requirement to identify countries taking unfair advantage of U.S. measures against South Africa with a view to restricting their exports to the United States by the amount necessary to compensate for the loss to U.S. companies;
- a requirement to report and make recommendations on means of reducing U.S. dependence on strategic minerals from southern Africa;
- a requirement to provide at least $25 million in assistance for scholarships, education, community development, and legal aid to disadvantaged South Africans with a prohibition on such assistance to any group or individual who has been engaged in gross violation of internationally recognized human rights;
- the imposition of severe criminal and civil penalties under several statutes for violation of the provisions of my Executive order;
- a requirement to consult with Allies in order to coordinate policies and programs toward South Africa;
- a requirement to report on whether any of these prohibitions has had the effect of increasing U.S. or allied dependence on the Soviet bloc for strategic or other critical materials, with a view to appropriate modifications of U.S. measures under my Executive order should such dependency have been increased;
- and a clear statement that the Executive order constitutes a complete and comprehensive statement of U.S. policy toward South Africa, with the intent of preempting inconsistent State and local laws which under our Constitution may be preempted.

Importance of Positive Steps

Sanctions, in and of themselves, do not add up to a policy for South Africa and the southern Africa region. Positive steps as well as negative signals are necessary. This unusually complex and interrelated part of the world is one that cries out for better understanding and sympathy on our part. We must consider what we can do to contribute to development of healthy economies and democratic institutions throughout the region and to help those who are the victims of apartheid.

Following the Congress' lead and building on existing programs, I plan to expand our assistance to those suffering the cost of apartheid and to help blacks as they prepare to play their full role in a free South Africa. We spent $20 million in FY 86 and have requested $25 million in FY 87. We will do more, much of it along the lines incorporated in the South Africa bill.

I am also committed to present to the next Congress a comprehensive multi-year program designed to promote economic reform and development in the black-ruled states of southern Africa. We intend to seek the close collaboration of Japan and our European allies in this constructive effort. Our goal is to create a sound basis for a post-apartheid region — a southern Africa where democracy and respect for fundamental human rights can flourish.

I believe the United States can assist responsibly in resolving southern Africa's tragic dilemma. Many observers in and outside South Africa regard present trends with despair, seeing in them a bloody inevitability as positions harden over the central question of political power. This is a grim scenario that allows no free choice and offers a racial civil war as the only solution. It need not be so if wisdom and imagination prevail.

South Africans continue to search for solutions. Their true friends should help in this search. As I have said before, our humanitarian concerns and our other national interests converge in South Africa as in few other countries. With the actions I propose today, I believe it is clear that my Administration's intentions and those of the Congress are identical. May we unite so that U.S. foreign policy can be effective in bringing people of good will and imagination in South Africa together to rebuild a better, just, and democratic tomorrow.

Sincerely,

Ronald Reagan ▮

As Delivered Oct. 13:

Text of Reagan's Speech on U.S.-Soviet Iceland Summit

Following is the White House text of President Reagan's speech, as delivered Oct. 13, on his meetings in Iceland with Soviet leader Mikhail S. Gorbachev.

Good evening. As most of you know, I have just returned from meetings in Iceland with the leader of the Soviet Union, General Secretary Gorbachev. As I did last year when I returned from the summit conference in Geneva, I want to take a few moments tonight to share with you what took place in these discussions.

The implications of these talks are enormous and only just beginning to be understood. We proposed the most sweeping and generous arms control proposal in history. We offered the complete elimination of all ballistic missiles — Soviet and American — from the face of the Earth by 1996. While we parted company with this

American offer still on the table, we are closer than ever before to agreements that could lead to a safer world without nuclear weapons.

But first, let me tell you that, from the start of my meetings with Mr. Gorbachev, I have always regarded you, the American people, as full participants. Believe me, without your support, none of these talks could have been held, nor could the ultimate aims of American foreign policy — world peace and freedom — be pursued. And it is for these aims I went the extra mile to Iceland.

Definition of Terms

Before I report on our talks though, allow me to set the stage by explaining two things that were very much a part of our talks, one a treaty and the other a defense against nuclear missiles which we are trying to develop. Now you've heard their titles a thousand times — the ABM Treaty and SDI. Those letters stand for, ABM, anti-ballistic missile, SDI, strategic defense initiative.

M.A.D. and Anti-Missile Defense

Some years ago, the United States and the Soviet Union agreed to limit any defense against nuclear missile attacks to the emplacement in one location in each country of a small number of missiles capable of intercepting and shooting down incoming nuclear missiles, thus leaving our real defense — a policy called Mutual Assured Destruction, meaning if one side launched a nuclear attack, the other side could retaliate. And this mutual threat of destruction was believed to be a deterrent against either side striking first.

So here we sit with thousands of nuclear warheads targeted on each other and capable of wiping out both our countries. The Soviets deployed the few anti-ballistic missiles around Moscow as the treaty permitted. Our country didn't bother deploying because the threat of nationwide annihilation made such a limited defense seem useless.

Soviet ABM Treaty Violation

For some years now we have been aware that the Soviets may be developing a nationwide defense. They have installed a large modern radar at Krasnoyarsk which we believe is a critical part of a radar system designed to provide radar guidance for anti-ballistic missiles protecting the entire nation. Now this is a violation of the ABM Treaty.

Strategic Defense Initiative - 1

Believing that a policy of mutual destruction and slaughter of their citizens and ours was uncivilized, I asked our military a few years ago to study and see if there was a practical way to destroy nuclear missiles after their launch but before they can reach their targets rather than to just destroy people. Well, this is the goal for what we call SDI and our scientists researching such a system are convinced it is practical and that several years down the road we can have such a system ready to deploy. Now, incidentally, we are not violating the ABM Treaty which permits such research. If and when we deploy, the treaty — also allows withdrawal from the treaty upon six months' notice. SDI, let me make it clear, is a non-nuclear defense.

Iceland Summit Talks

So here we are at Iceland for our second such meeting. In the first and in the months in between, we have discussed ways to reduce and in fact eliminate nuclear weapons entirely. We and the Soviets have had teams of negotiators in Geneva trying to work out a mutual agreement on how we could reduce or eliminate nuclear weapons. And so far, no success.

On Saturday and Sunday, General Secretary Gorbachev and his Foreign Minister Shevardnadze and Secretary of State George Shultz and I met for nearly 10 hours. We didn't limit ourselves to just arms reductions. We discussed what we call violation of human rights on the part of the Soviets, refusal to let people emigrate from Russia so they can practice their religion without being persecuted, letting people go to rejoin their families, husbands and wives separated by national borders being allowed to reunite.

In much of this the Soviet Union is violating another agreement — the Helsinki Accords they had signed in 1975. Yuri Orlov, whose freedom we just obtained, was imprisoned for pointing out to his government its violations of that pact, its refusal to let citizens leave their country or return.

We also discussed regional matters such as Afghanistan, Angola, Nicaragua, and Cambodia. But by their choice the main subject was arms control.

We discussed the emplacement of intermediate-range missiles in Europe and Asia and seemed to be in agreement they could be drastically reduced. Both sides seemed willing to find a way to reduce even to zero the strategic ballistic missiles we have aimed at each other. This then brought up the subject of SDI.

Strategic Defense Initiative - 2

I offered a proposal that we continue our present research and if and when we reached the stage of testing we would sign now a treaty that would permit Soviet observation of such tests. And if the program was practical we would both eliminate our offensive missiles, and then we would share the benefits of advanced defenses. I explained that even though we would have done away with our offensive ballistic missiles, having the defense would protect against cheating or the possibility of a madman sometime deciding to create nuclear missiles. After all, the world now knows how to make them. I likened it to our keeping our gas masks even though the nations of the world had outlawed poison gas after World War I.

We seemed to be making progress on reducing weaponry although the General Secretary was registering opposition to SDI and proposing a pledge to observe ABM for a number of years as the day was ending.

Negotiations Through the Night

Secretary Shultz suggested we turn over the notes our note-takers had been making of everything we'd said to our respective teams and let them work through the night to put them together and find just where we were in agreement and what differences separated us. With respect and gratitude, I can inform you those teams worked through the night till 6:30 a.m.

Yesterday, Sunday morning, Mr. Gorbachev and I, with our foreign ministers, came together again and took up the report of our two teams. It was most promising. The Soviets had asked for a 10-year delay in the deployment of SDI programs.

U.S. Arms Proposal

In an effort to see how we could satisfy their concerns while protecting our principles and security, we proposed a 10-year period in which we began with the reduction of all strategic nuclear arms, bombers, air-launched cruise missiles, intercontinental ballistic missiles, submarine launched ballistic missiles and the weapons they carry. They would be reduced 50 percent in the first five years. During the next five years, we would continue by eliminating all remaining offensive ballistic missiles, of all ranges. And during that time we would proceed with research, development and testing of SDI — all done in conformity with ABM provisions. At the 10-year point, with all ballistic missiles eliminated, we could proceed to deploy advanced defenses, at the same time permitting the Soviets to do likewise.

U.S.-Soviet Debate

And here the debate began. The General Secretary wanted wording that, in effect, would have kept us from developing the SDI for the entire 10 years. In effect, he was killing SDI. And unless I agreed, all that work toward eliminating nuclear weapons would go down the drain — canceled.

I told him I had pledged to the American people that I would not trade away SDI — there was no way I could tell our people their government would not protect them against nuclear destruction. I went to Reykjavik determined that everything was negotiable except two things: our freedom and our future.

I'm still optimistic that a way will be found. The door is open and the opportunity to begin eliminating the nuclear threat is within reach.

Realistic Approach to Soviets

So you can see, we made progress in Iceland. And we will continue to make progress if we pursue a prudent, deliberate, and, above all, realistic approach with the Soviets. From the earliest days of our administration, this has been our policy. We made it clear we had no illusions about the

Soviets or their ultimate intentions. We were publicly candid about the critical moral distinctions betweeen totalitarianism and democracy. We declared the principal objective of American foreign policy to be not just the prevention of war but the extension of freedom. And, we stressed our commitment to the growth of democratic government and democratic institutions around the world. And that's why we assisted freedom fighters who are resisting the imposition of totalitarian rule in Afghanistan, Nicaragua, Angola, Cambodia, and elsewhere. And, finally, we began work on what I believe most spurred the Soviets to negotiate seriously — rebuilding our military strength, reconstructing our strategic deterrence, and, above all, beginning work on the strategic defense initiative.

And yet, at the same time we set out these foreign policy goals and began working toward them, we pursued another of our major objectives: that of seeking means to lessen tensions with the Soviets, and ways to prevent war and keep the peace.

Now, this policy is now paying dividends — one sign of this in Iceland was the progress on the issue of arms control. For the first time in a long while, Soviet-American negotiations in the area of arms reductions are moving, and moving in the right direction — not just toward arms control, but toward arms reduction.

But for all the progress we made on arms reductions, we must remember there were other issues on the table in Iceland, issues that are fundamental.

Human Rights in Soviet Union

As I mentioned, one such issue is human rights. As President Kennedy once said, "And, is not peace, in the last analysis, basically a matter of human rights?"

I made it plain that the United States would not seek to exploit improvement in these matters for purposes of propaganda. But I also made it plain, once again, that an improvement of the human condition within the Soviet Union is indispensable for an improvement in bilateral relations with the United States. For a government that will break faith with its own people cannot be trusted to keep faith with foreign powers. So, I told Mr. Gorbachev — again in Reykjavik as I had in Geneva — we Americans place far less weight upon the words that are spoken at meetings such as these, than upon the deeds that follow. When it comes to human rights and judging Soviet intentions, we're all from Missouri — you got to show us.

Soviet Military Actions

Another subject area we took up in Iceland also lies at the heart of the differences between the Soviet Union and America. This is the issue of regional conflicts. Summit meetings cannot make the American people forget what Soviet actions have meant for the peoples of Afghanistan, Central America, Africa, and Southeast Asia. Until Soviet policies change, we will make sure that our friends in these areas — those who fight for freedom and independence — will have the support they need.

Cultural Exchanges

Finally, there was a fourth item. And this area was that of bilateral relations, people-to-people contacts. In Geneva last year, we welcomed several cultural exchange accords; in Iceland, we saw indications of more movement in these areas. But let me say now the United States remains committed to people-to-people programs that could lead to exchanges between not just a few elite but thousands of everyday citizens from both our countries.

So I think, then, that you can see that we did make progress in Iceland on a broad range of topics. We reaffirmed our four-point agenda; we discovered major new grounds of agreement; we probed again some old areas of disagreement.

Strategic Defense Initiative - 3

And let me return again to the SDI issue. I realize some Americans may be asking tonight: Why not accept Mr. Gorbachev's demand? Why not give up SDI for this agreement?

Well, the answer, my friends, is simple. SDI is America's insurance policy that the Soviet Union would keep the commitments made at Reykjavik. SDI is America's security guarantee — if the Soviets should — as they have done too often in the past — fail to comply with their solemn commitments. SDI is what brought the Soviets back to arms control talks at Geneva and Iceland. SDI is the key to a world without nuclear weapons.

The Soviets understand this. They have devoted far more resources for a lot longer time than we, to their own SDI. The world's only operational missile defense today surrounds Moscow, the capital of the Soviet Union. What Mr. Gorbachev was demanding at Reykjavik was that the United States agree to a new version of a 14-year-old ABM Treaty that the Soviet Union has already violated. I told him we don't make those kinds of deals in the United States.

Why Not Have Missile Defense?

And the American people should reflect on these critical questions.

How does a defense of the United States threaten the Soviet Union or anyone else? Why are the Soviets so adamant that America remain forever vulnerable to Soviet rocket attack? As of today, all free nations are utterly defenseless against Soviet missiles — fired either by accident or design. Why does the Soviet Union insist that we remain so — forever?

So, my fellow Americans, I cannot promise, nor can any President promise, that the talks in Iceland or any future discussions with Mr. Gorbachev will lead inevitably to great breakthroughs or momentous treaty signings.

We will not abandon the guiding principle we took to Reykjavik. We prefer no agreement than to bring home a bad agreement to the United States.

Prospects for Another Summit

And on this point, I know you're also interested in the question of whether there will be another summit. There was no indication by Mr. Gorbachev as to when or whether he plans to travel to the United States, as we agreed he would last year in Geneva. I repeat tonight that our invitation stands and that we continue to believe additional meetings would be useful. But that's a decision the Soviets must make.

Dealing From Strength

But whatever the immediate prospects, I can tell you that I'm ultimately hopeful about the prospects for progress at the summit and for world peace and freedom. You see, the current summit process is very different from that of previous decades; it's different because the world is different; and the world is different because of the hard work and sacrifice of the American people during the past five and a half years. Your energy has restored and expanded our economic might; your support has restored our military strength. Your courage and sense of national unity in times of crisis have given pause to our adversaries, heartened our friends, and inspired the world. The Western democracies and the NATO alliance are revitalized and all across the world nations are turning to democratic ideas and the principles of the free market. So because the American people stood guard at the critical hour, freedom has gathered its forces, regained its strength, and is on the march.

So, if there's one impression I carry away with me from these October talks, it is that, unlike the past, we're dealing now from a position of strength, and for that reason we have it within our grasp to move speedily with the Soviets toward even more breakthroughs.

Our ideas are out there on the table. They won't go away. We're ready to pick up where we left off. Our negotiators are heading back to Geneva, and we're prepared to go forward whenever and wherever the Soviets are ready. So, there's reason — good reason for hope.

I saw evidence of this in the progress we made in the talks with Mr. Gorbachev. And I saw evidence of it when we left Iceland yesterday, and I spoke to our young men and women at our naval installation at Keflavik — a critically important base far closer to Soviet naval bases than to our own coastline.

Committed to Freedom

As always, I was proud to spend a few moments with them and thank them for their sacrifices and devotion to country. They represent America at her finest: committed to defend not only our own freedom but the freedom of others who would be living in a far more frightening world — were it not for the strength and resolve of the United States.

"Whenever the standard of freedom

and independence has been ... unfurled, there will be America's heart, her benedictions, and her prayers," John Quincy Adams once said. He spoke well of our destiny as a nation. My fellow Americans, we're honored by history, entrusted by destiny with the oldest dream of humanity — the dream of lasting peace and human freedom.

Another President, Harry Truman, noted that our century had seen two of the most frightful wars in history. And that "the supreme need of our time is for man to learn to live together in peace and harmony."

Pursuit of an Ideal

It's in pursuit of that ideal I went to Geneva a year ago and to Iceland last week. And it's in pursuit of that ideal that I thank you now for all the support you've given me, and I again ask for your help and your prayers as we continue our journey toward a world where peace reigns and freedom is enshrined.

Thank you and God bless you.

'Private Relief' Provisions Cited:

Veto Message on Coast Guard Law Changes

Following is the White House text of President Reagan's Feb. 14 message accompanying his veto of HR 2466, making various revisions in laws affecting the U.S. Coast Guard. It was his seventh veto of a public bill during the 99th Congress.

TO THE HOUSE OF REPRESENTATIVES:

I am returning herewith without my approval HR 2466, a bill "To make miscellaneous changes in laws affecting the United States Coast Guard, and for other purposes."

This legislation was originally intended to make technical and editorial corrections to subtitle II of title 46 of the United States Code. These corrections were necessitated by errors made in the codification of that title in 1983. This bill contains sections that I do support; however, provisions were added that I simply cannot support.

Improving the management of the Federal government has been, and remains, a fundamental goal of my Administration. But close cooperation between our branches of government is critical if we are to conduct our affairs in a businesslike fashion. Far from giving the Executive branch requisite flexibility to manage efficiently, it creates significant new impediments and contains unwarranted private relief provisions that would set highly undesirable precedents.

For example, the bill would require that any funds expended under the Truman-Hobbs Act by the Coast Guard to alter the Burlington-Northern Railroad bridge be subject to the requirements of the Davis-Bacon Act, adding approximately $1.5 million to the cost of the project. It would prohibit the trial contracting out of certain aids to navigation functions on the Intracoastal Waterway in New Jersey, significantly diminishing the scope of this project. It would establish two unnecessary advisory committees, and exempt certain Coast Guard facilities from personnel ceilings.

It would also reimburse the owners of a bridge in Texas for costs of alterations that under current law are nonreimbursable. Finally, the bill would grant a specific vessel an inappropriate exception to the Merchant Marine Act of 1936, relieving that vessel of its statutory duty to repay a construction differential subsidy. Both of these provisions would discriminate unfairly and inequitably against those similarly situated. At a time when we are taking difficult steps to reduce the budget deficit, this strikes me as especially unwise.

For these reasons I am compelled to return HR 2466 without my approval.

RONALD REAGAN

The White House,
February 14, 1986.

Accompanying Reagan's Oct. 7 Veto:

Reagan's Veto of Bill Extending SBA Pilot Programs

Following is the White House text of the message accompanying President Reagan's Oct. 7 veto of HR 2787, a bill reauthorizing certain Small Business Administration pilot programs. It was the president's 11th veto of a public bill during the 99th Congress.

TO THE HOUSE OF REPRESENTATIVES:

I am returning herewith without my approval HR 2787. Title I of this bill would reauthorize and extend through September 30, 1988, two Small Business Administration (SBA) pilot programs, and Title II would authorize the appropriation of $10 million for the establishment of a new Technology Transfer Institute in Bridgeport, Connecticut.

The appropriation authorization of $10 million for a new Federally assisted project is inappropriate and unwarranted at a time when there is a critical need to operate within severe budgetary constraints and to fund adequately higher priority programs. Although the stated purpose of the proposed Institute would be to "revitalize the competitiveness of small business industry in America, particularly in the international marketplace, and to serve as a regional demonstration center transferring emerging technology . . . ," it is not clear that the Institute would provide the best means to accomplish this goal.

Additionally, in light of current budgetary constraints, it is particularly unfortunate that the bill accords special treatment to a specific institution and does not require selection on a competitive basis. Selecting recipients competitively helps to ensure that the taxpayers' money is spent on projects that address an acknowledged need and demonstrate the greatest promise of success. Legislative provisions that accord special treatment to certain applicants or, as here, identify the sole recipient of assistance are particularly objectionable. I am concerned also that the Institute, proposed as a "regional demonstration center," would set an undesirable precedent for the noncompetitive establishment of additional regional centers, without a demonstrated need for a Federal role in this area.

Finally, I note that Title I of the bill would unnecessarily extend two SBA pilot programs. The goal of the pilot procurement program can be accomplished under existing authorities. The extension of the surety bond waiver program provided in Title I has proved unnecessary, as no waivers have been requested since the program was first authorized in 1978.

The White House, RONALD REAGAN
October 7, 1986.

Text of Veto Message of Two-Day Appropriations Bill

Following is the White House text of the message accompanying President Reagan's Oct. 9 veto of H J Res 748, a two-day continuing appropriations resolution for fiscal 1987. It was Reagan's 12th veto of a public bill during the 99th Congress.

TO THE HOUSE OF REPRESENTATIVES:

I am returning herewith without my approval H J Res 748, continuing appropriations for the fiscal year 1987 for two more days until the Congress can agree on a full-year budget.

The Congress has been informed of the Administration's position on a Continuing Resolution, including provisions that warrant my veto. As I had previously made clear, the provision included in this resolution providing for the rehire of air traffic controllers who engaged in the 1981 strike is totally unacceptable. I cannot accept this and certain other provisions included in this measure.

The Administration will continue to work closely with the Congress to reach agreement on an acceptable full-year Continuing Resolution. The Congress has had over eight months to do its job, and complete action on FY 1987 appropriations. The time for action is long past due.

RONALD REAGAN

The White House,
October 9, 1986.

Memorandums From Oct. 28-Nov. 14:

Texts of Reagan Messages On Six Pocket Vetoes

Following are the White House texts of President Reagan's memorandums of disapproval accompanying his pocket vetoes of six bills: on Oct. 28, HR 4175, the fiscal 1987 maritime authorization bill; on Nov. 1, HR 5465, the National Appliance Energy Conservation Act; on Nov. 4, HR 4961, the 1986 Independent Safety Board Act Amendments; on Nov. 5, S 2057, to establish a presidential council on health promotion; on Nov. 6, S 1128, the Clean Water Act reauthorization; and on Nov. 14, HR 5495, the fiscal 1987 authorization bill for the National Aeronautics and Space Administration. Respectively, they were Reagan's 13th, 14th, 15th, 16th, 17th and 18th vetoes of public bills during the 99th Congress.

Maritime Authorization

I am withholding my approval of HR 4175, a bill "To authorize appropriations for fiscal year 1987 for certain maritime programs of the Department of Transportation and the Federal Maritime Commission."

I am disapproving HR 4175 because it would not repeal the Maritime Administration's Title XI loan program, as I proposed in the 1987 Budget. This program is one of several Federal credit programs that I proposed to reduce or phase out in order to limit the government's intervention in the Nation's lending market.

Achievement of our credit reform goals is important to the maritime industry and the economy as a whole. The maritime industry must be encouraged to rely on the private credit market, without Federal intervention, as its source of capital if we are to continue our progress toward restoring that industry to full health. Borrowers in general must be freed from the government's pre-emptive allocation of credit, which forces unsubsidized borrowers to pay more for credit and may result in some borrowers being "crowded out" entirely.

I am also not approving HR 4175 because it would continue to authorize appropriations for financial assistance to State maritime schools. Such an authorization of appropriations is entirely inappropriate during this time of necessary fiscal restraint.

RONALD REAGAN

The White House,
October 28, 1986.

Appliance Energy Bill

I am withholding my approval of HR 5465, the "National Appliance Energy Conservation Act of 1986."

This legislation would have established specific, minimum energy efficiency standards for home appliances without regard to technological feasibility or the need for economic justification. The bill intrudes unduly on the free market, limits the freedom of choice available to consumers who would be denied the opportunity to purchase lower-cost appliances, and constitutes a substantial intrusion into traditional State responsibilities and prerogatives.

It also mandates a complicated series of 19 rulemakings over the next 20 years for 52 subcategories of appliances, virtually assuring extensive litigation, increasing Federal regulation many years into the future.

Moreover, although I share the interest in the need for conserving energy resources that led the Congress to pass this bill, HR 5465 fails to advance this goal in a manner that takes account of the tremendous cost to consumers, who would have to spend an estimated extra $1.4 billion per year on appliances purchases. Higher prices would force many to buy more expensive appliances than than they would prefer, and make some delay or forgo some appliance purchases altogether. By eliminating the lower-priced models, the bill would hit low-income consumers particularly hard. It could also discourage and slow the introduction of useful product innovations.

Disapproval of this bill does not mean, however, that the energy efficiency of appliances will be wholly without Federal regulation. Under current law, the Department of Energy is required to conduct a rulemaking which may lead to the imposition of Federal standards, and any such standards would preempt existing State law.

Thus, the choice is between Federal regulation of appliance standards under this bill and regulation under current law, which requires the Department of Energy to take account of technological feasibility and economic factors. Under these circumstances, I think current law is preferable.

In addition, I note that the Congress included in HR 5465 amendments requiring the Federal Energy Regulatory Commission to issue a declaratory order in a pending proceeding and setting a deadline for the Commission to resolve a pending rate case. I am in agreement with what the Congress sought to achieve in requiring the Commission to issue a declaratory order and am asking the Secretary of Energy to take appropriate action before the Federal Energy Regulatory Commission so that this matter will be promptly and favorably resolved. I also agree with the Congress that the rate case matter should be resolved swiftly and urge the Commission to exert its best efforts to meet the deadline the Congress has sought to impose.

RONALD REAGAN

The White House,
November 1, 1986.

Independent Safety Board

I am withholding my approval of HR 4961, the "Independent Safety Board Act Amendments of 1986," for reasons unrelated to improving transportation safety — a cause to which I remain firmly committed. My Administration is actively implementing new aviation technology, both on the ground and on-board aircraft. Furthermore, over the last five years, my Administration has increased funding for the Federal Aviation Administration by 50 percent. Our multibillion-dollar safety modernization program for the Nation's air traffic system — already the safest in the world — has contributed to a decline in the accident rate by over 50 percent during the last decade. We have been equally dedicated to improving highway safety. In the past decade, the highway fatality rate has declined by about 25 percent. Still, my 1987 budget request for motor carrier safety exceeded 1982 funding fivefold.

I remain steadfast in my commitment to transportation safety, but HR 4961 would authorize excessive appropriations for the National Transportation Safety Board (NTSB) for fiscal years 1987, 1988, and 1989 and would lead the Federal government to become involved in an industry-by-industry approach to the larger problem of liability insurance.

I find several provisions of this legislation objectionable. First, the bill would authorize appropriations for NTSB in 1988 and 1989 that would be $8.7 million, or 20 percent, more than the projections in my 1987 budget. Specifically, these authorization levels exceed the projections by the following amounts: (1) $3.7 million in 1988 — $25.4 million versus $21.7 million projected and (2) $5 million in 1989 — $27 million versus $22 million projected. Given our current efforts to reduce the size of the Federal deficit, the size of these increases is unacceptable. I point out that the NTSB's budget has already grown 26 percent in the past five years and that my budgets provide sufficient funding for the NTSB to maintain its safety functions. Moreover, since funds have already been appropriated for the NTSB in 1987, NTSB activities will continue uninterrupted even with my disapproval of this bill.

Second, HR 4961 directs the Administrator of the Federal Aviation Administration to establish an airport liability insurance clearinghouse and, with the Secretary of Transportation, to prepare reports on the increasing costs of general liability insurance coverage for airports and the implications of those increasing costs for airports. A final report would include recommendations for actions that the Federal government might undertake to assist in ameliorating the liability insurance difficulties of airports used by the public.

Many Americans are caught by the spiraling costs of liability insurance. While I am not unsympathetic to those who are bearing the cost of rising insurance premiums, I believe it would be inequitable and unwise for the Federal government to address this issue on an industry-by-industry basis.

For these reasons, I am compelled to withhold my approval from the bill. In so doing, I reemphasize that the disapproval will not disrupt the NTSB's activities in 1987 and that my Administration remains firmly committed to ensuring safe transportation.

RONALD REAGAN

The White House,
November 4, 1986.

Health Promotion Council

I am withholding my approval of S 2057, which would establish a President's Council on Health Promotion and Disease Prevention.

Many Federal health promotion and disease prevention activities are under way at the Department of Health and Human Services, which has set an ambitious agenda of health promotion and disease prevention goals to be achieved by 1990. I am encouraged by the progress that is being made toward those objectives and the plans which lie ahead. These plans include a national conference in late 1989 or early 1990, and many individual programs such as the Low Birth Weight Prevention Initiative, the National High Blood Pressure Education Program, and the Healthy Older People Public Education Program. Because our Federal commitment to such activities must, and will, continue, a President's Council on Health Promotion and Disease Prevention is not necessary at this time.

RONALD REAGAN

The White House,
November 5, 1986.

Clean Water Act

I am withholding my approval of S 1128, the "Water Quality Act of 1986."

On March 25, 1985, Lee M. Thomas, Administrator of the Environmental Protection Agency, sent to the Congress a proposal to amend and reauthorize appropriations under the Clean Water Act. As that proposal demonstrated, this Administration remains committed to the Act's objectives, and I am proud that we can report remarkable progress in this massive national cleanup effort.

Unfortunately, this bill so far exceeds acceptable levels of intended budgetary commitments that I must withhold my approval. Central to my proposal of last year was the phasing-out over a period of four years, and the termination by 1990, of the huge sewage treatment grant program. With the backlog of needed treatment plants financed in major part by the Federal government since 1972, it is now necessary for the Federal government to reduce its expenditures and complete the transition from Federal to State and local responsibility. The Environmental Protection Agency has already spent $44 billion to assist municipalities in meeting a need that was estimated to be $18 billion when the program was established in 1972. My proposal would have extended another $6 billion to finish the projects that had been started with Federal funds.

Notwithstanding my recommendations, S 1128 would authorize $18 billion or triple the amount I requested for that grant program, expand the allowable uses of Federal funds, and continue Federal grants for another nine years. By 1993 S 1128 would increase outlays by as much as $10 billion over the projections in my 1987 Budget and would reverse important reforms enacted in 1981 that targeted funds to the completion of construction of sewage treatment plants — the program's original and principal remaining purpose.

S 1128 makes several programmatic changes that would improve the overall Clean Water Act, including expanded Federal enforcement authorities and an easing of the regulatory and financial burden on cities in dealing with stormwater discharges. We will work diligently with the 100th Congress to address these concerns. S 1128 also would authorize some new programs — at a five-year total of $500 million — that my Administration has strongly opposed. Principal among them is the reinstatement of a Federal financial assistance program to pay for local plans to control diffuse sources of pollution. Over $500 million was spent on a similar program between 1973 and 1981 with little or no positive result. Restarting expensive planning grant programs that have failed in the past is not justifiable.

For these reasons, I cannot approve S 1128. I must emphasize, however, that my action will have no impact on the current conduct of water pollution control programs under the Clean Water Act. All regulatory, enforcement, and permit issuance activities will continue under permanent law. Although authorization to appropriate for the sewage treatment grant program and other grant and research programs expired between 1983 and 1985, funds have been appropriated for them annually, and they are funded in the Continuing Resolution for 1987.

My Administration will work closely with the next Congress to pass acceptable legislation. We will continue our commitment to improve and protect our Nation's water quality by working with the Congress to modify current law to help cities handle stormwater discharge permits.

RONALD REAGAN

The White House,
November 6, 1986.

NASA Authorization

I am withholding my approval of HR 5495, the "National Aeronautics and Space Administration Authorization Act, 1987."

This legislation would authorize

appropriations for 1987 for the National Aeronautics and Space Administration (NASA); authorize appropriations for the Office of Commercial Space Transportation in the Department of Transportation; establish a National Space Council in the Executive Office of the President to advise me on space-related matters; make numerous other amendments involving the Space Shuttle; amend the Land Remote-Sensing Commercialization Act in various respects; and authorize appropriations for a variety of programs of the National Oceanic and Atmospheric Administration in the Department of Commerce.

The establishment of a National Space Council in the Executive Office of the President would constitute unacceptable interference with my discretion and flexibility in organizing and managing the Executive Office as I consider appropriate. Besides creating additional and unnecessary bureaucracy, the National Space Council would duplicate the functions of the interagency bodies — the Senior Interagency Group (Space), the Interagency Group (Space), and the Economic Policy Council — that already coordinate the development and implementation of space policy. Because the proposed National Space Council would unnecessarily limit my authority to organize and manage the Executive Office while offering nothing by way of improvement in space policymaking, I am compelled to reject it.

I find two other provisions of HR 5495 troublesome. First, by mandating certain space shuttle launch priorities, the bill does not adequately recognize the importance the Administration places on the development of a commercial space launch industry or my specific decision to allow NASA to launch certain foreign payloads. Second, section 111 of HR 5495 would impose a "buy America" restriction on certain NASA procurement activities, in violation of the General Agreement on Tariffs and Trade Agreement on Government Procurement. Enactment of this proposal could subject the United States to significant retaliation by other countries.

Withholding of my approval of this legislation should not be interpreted as any diminution of my support for our Nation's space program. I strongly support and affirm the goals of that program and of United States space policy to strengthen national security, maintain our leadership in space, and promote international cooperation in space. I also stress that my action on HR 5495 will in no way adversely affect the Federal government's ongoing space programs. Adequate funding for those programs for 1987 has already been appropriated in the recently enacted Continuing Resolution (Public Law 99-500).

RONALD REAGAN

The White House,
November 14, 1986.

The Reagan Administration and the Iran-'Contra' Affair:

Text of Reagan's Address On Arms Shipments to Iran

Following is the White House text of President Reagan's address, as delivered Nov. 13, on U.S. shipments of arms to Iran.

Good evening. I know you have been reading, seeing, and hearing a lot of stories the past several days attributed to Danish sailors, unnamed observers at Italian ports and Spanish harbors, and especially unnamed government officials of my administration. Well, now you are going to hear the facts from a White House source, and you know my name.

Secret Discussions With Iran - 1

I wanted this time to talk with you about an extremely sensitive and profoundly important matter of foreign policy. For 18 months now we have had under way a secret diplomatic initiative to Iran. That initiative was undertaken for the simplest and best of reasons — to renew a relationship with the nation of Iran, to bring an honorable end to the bloody six-year war between Iran and Iraq, to eliminate state-sponsored terrorism and subversion, and to effect the safe return of all hostages.

Without Iran's cooperation, we cannot bring an end to the Persian Gulf war; without Iran's concurrence, there can be no enduring peace in the Middle East.

Getting to the Facts

For 10 days now, the American and world press have been full of reports and rumors about this initiative and these objectives.

Now, my fellow Americans, there is an old saying that nothing spreads so quickly as a rumor. So I thought it was time to speak with you directly — to tell you first-hand about our dealings with Iran. As Will Rogers once said, "Rumor travels faster, but it don't stay put as long as truth." So let's get to the facts.

No Arms-for-Hostages Swap

The charge has been made that the United States has shipped weapons to Iran as ransom payment for the release of American hostages in Lebanon — that the United States undercut its allies and secretly violated American policy against trafficking with terrorists.

Those charges are utterly false.

The United States has not made concessions to those who hold our people captive in Lebanon. And we will not. The United States has not swapped boatloads or planeloads of American weapons for the return of American hostages. And we will not.

Other reports have surfaced alleging U.S. involvement. Reports of a sealift to Iran using Danish ships to carry American arms. Of vessels in Spanish ports being employed in secret U.S. arms shipments. Of Italian ports being used. Of the U.S. sending spare parts and weapons for combat aircraft. All these reports are quite exciting, but as far as we are concerned, not one of them is true.

Arms Shipments to Iran

During the course of our secret discussions, I authorized the transfer of small amounts of defensive weapons and spare parts for defensive systems to Iran. My purpose was to convince Tehran that our negotiators were acting with my authority, to send a signal that the United States was prepared to replace the animosity between us with a new relationship. These modest deliveries, taken together, could easily fit into a single cargo plane. They could not, taken together, affect the outcome of the six-year war between Iran and Iraq — nor could they affect in any way the military balance between the two countries.

Those with whom we were in contact took considerable risks and needed a signal of our serious intent if they were to carry on and broaden the dialogue.

Iran's Influence in Hostages' Release

At the same time we undertook this initiative, we made clear that Iran must oppose all forms of international terrorism as a condition of progress in our relationship. The most significant step which Iran could take, we indicated, would be to use its influence in Lebanon to secure the release of all hostages held there.

Some progress has already been made. Since U.S. government contact began with Iran, there's been no evidence of Iranian government complicity in acts of terrorism against the United States. Hostages have come home — and we welcome the efforts that the government of Iran has taken in the past and is currently undertaking.

Strategic Importance of Iran

But why, you might ask, is any relationship with Iran important to the United States?

Iran encompasses some of the most critical geography in the world. It lies between the Soviet Union and access to the warm waters of the Indian Ocean. Geography explains why the Soviet Union has sent an army into Afghanistan to dominate that country and, if they could, Iran and Pakistan.

Iran's geography gives it a critical position from which adversaries could interfere with oil flows from the Arab states that border the Persian Gulf. Apart from geography, Iran's oil deposits are important to the long-term health of the world economy.

For these reasons, it is in our national interest to watch for changes within Iran that might offer hope for an improved relationship. Until last year, there was little to justify that hope.

No Need for Permanent Conflict

Indeed, we have bitter and enduring disagreements that persist today. At the heart of our quarrel has been Iran's past sponsorship of international terrorism. Iranian policy has been devoted to expelling all Western influence from the Middle East. We cannot abide that, because our interests in the Middle East are vital. At the same time, we seek no territory or special position in Iran. The Iranian revolution is a fact of history, but between American and Iranian basic national interests there need be no permanent conflict.

Since 1983, various countries have made overtures to stimulate direct contact between the United States and Iran. European, Near East, and Far East countries have attempted to serve as intermediaries. Despite a U.S. willingness to proceed, none of these overtures bore fruit.

With this history in mind, we were receptive last year when we were alerted to the possibility of establishing a direct dialogue with Iranian officials.

U.S. Interest in Dialogue - 1

Now, let me repeat. America's long-standing goals in the region have been to help preserve Iran's independence from Soviet domination; to bring an honorable end to the bloody Iran-Iraq war; to halt the export of subversion and terrorism in the region. A major impediment to those goals has been an absence of dialogue, a cutoff in communication between us.

It's because of Iran's strategic importance and its influence in the Islamic world that we chose to probe for a better relationship between our countries.

Secret Discussions With Iran - 2

Our discussions continued into the spring of this year. Based upon the progress we felt we had made, we sought to raise the diplomatic level of contacts. A meeting was arranged in Tehran. I then asked my former national security adviser, Robert McFarlane, to undertake a secret mission and gave him explicit instructions. I asked him to go to Iran to open a dialogue, making stark and clear our basic objectives and disagreements.

The four days of talks were conducted in a civil fashion, and American personnel were not mistreated. Since then, the dialogue has continued and step-by-step progress continues to be made.

U.S. Interest in Dialogue - 2

Let me repeat: Our interests are clearly served by opening a dialogue with

Iran and thereby helping to end the Iran-Iraq war. That war has dragged on for more than six years, with no prospect of a negotiated settlement. The slaughter on both sides has been enormous; and the adverse economic and political consequences for that vital region of the world have been growing. We sought to establish communication with both sides in that senseless struggle, so that we could assist in bringing about a ceasefire and, eventually, a settlement. We have sought to be evenhanded by working with both sides and with other interested nations to prevent a widening of the war.

This sensitive undertaking has entailed great risk for those involved. There is no question but that we could never have begun or continued this dialogue had the initiative been disclosed earlier. Due to the publicity of the past week, the entire initiative is very much at risk today.

Precedent for Secret Diplomacy

There is ample precedent in our history for this kind of secret diplomacy. In 1971, then-President Nixon sent his national security adviser on a secret mission to China. In that case, as today, there was a basic requirement for discretion and for a sensitivity to the situation in the nation we were attempting to engage.

Danger of False Rumors

Since the welcome return of former hostage David Jacobsen, there has been unprecedented speculation and countless reports that have not only been wrong, but have been potentially dangerous to the hostages and destructive of the opportunity before us. The efforts of courageous people like Terry Waite have been jeopardized. So extensive have been the false rumors and erroneous reports that the risks of remaining silent now exceed the risks of speaking out. And that's why I decided to address you tonight.

It's been widely reported, for example, that the Congress, as well as top Executive Branch officials, were circumvented. Although the efforts we undertook were highly sensitive and involvement of government officials was limited to those with a strict need to know, all appropriate Cabinet Officers were fully consulted. The actions I authorized were and continue to be in full compliance with Federal law. And the relevant committees of Congress are being and will be fully informed.

No Tilt Toward Iran

Another charge is that we have tilted toward Iran in the Gulf war. This, too, is unfounded. We have consistently condemned the violence on both sides. We have consistently sought a negotiated settlement that preserves the territorial integrity of both nations. The overtures we've made to the government of Iran have not been a shift to supporting one side over the other. Rather, it has been a diplomatic initiative to gain some degree of access and influence within Iran — as well as Iraq — and to bring about an honorable end to that bloody conflict. It is in the interests of all parties in the Gulf region to end that war as soon as possible.

'No Concessions' Policy Intact

To summarize, our government has a firm policy not to capitulate to terrorist demands. That "no concessions" policy remains in force — in spite of the wildly speculative and false stories about arms for hostages and alleged ransom payments. We did not — repeat — did not trade weapons or anything else for hostages — nor will we. Those who think that we have "gone soft" on terrorism should take up the question with Colonel Gadhafi.

We have not, nor will we, capitulate to terrorists.

We will, however, get on with advancing the vital interests of our great nation — in spite of terrorists and radicals who seek to sabotage our efforts and immobilize the United States.

Our goals have been, and remain:

- to restore a relationship with Iran,
- to bring an honorable end to the war in the Gulf,
- to bring a halt to state-supported terror in the Middle East,
- and finally, to effect the safe return of all hostages from Lebanon.

As President, I've always operated on the belief that, given the facts, the American people will make the right decision. I believe that to be true now.

I cannot guarantee the outcome. But, as in the past, I ask for your support because I believe you share the hope for peace in the Middle East, for freedom for all hostages, and for a world free of terrorism. Certainly there are risks in this pursuit but there are greater risks if we do not persevere.

It will take patience and understanding; it will take continued resistance to those who commit terrorist acts; and it will take cooperation with all who seek to rid the world of this scourge.

Thank you and God bless you. ∎

Reagan, Meese on Iran-Nicaragua Arms Deals

Following is the White House text of the Nov. 25 statements by President Reagan and Attorney General Edwin Meese III regarding the U.S. role in arms shipments to Iran and the transfer of funds to the anti-government Nicaraguan rebels ("contras"). The statements were made before reporters, and a 40-minute question-and-answer session with Meese followed the attorney general's statement.

President Reagan's Statement

PRESIDENT REAGAN: Last Friday, after becoming concerned whether my national security apparatus had provided me with a security, or a complete factual record with respect to the implementation of my policy toward Iran, I directed the Attorney General to undertake a review of this matter over the weekend and report to me on Monday. And yesterday, Secretary Meese provided me and the White House Chief of Staff with a report on his preliminary findings. And this report led me to conclude that I was not fully informed on the nature of one of the activities undertaken in connection with this initiative. This action raises serious questions of propriety.

I've just met with my National Security advisers and Congressional leaders to inform them of the actions that I'm taking today. Determination of the full details of this action will require further review and investigation by the Department of Justice.

Looking to the future, I will appoint a special review board to conduct a comprehensive review of the role and procedures of the National Security Council staff in the conduct of foreign and national security policy.

I anticipate receiving the reports from the Attorney General and the special review board at the earliest possible date. Upon the completion of these reports, I will share their findings and conclusions with the Congress and the American people.

Although not directly involved, Vice Admiral John Poindexter has asked to be relieved of his assignment as Assistant to the President for National Security Affairs and to return to another assignment in the Navy. Lieutenant Colonel Oliver North has been relieved of his duties on the National Security Council staff.

I am deeply troubled that the implementation of a policy aimed at resolving a truly tragic situation in the Middle East has resulted in such controversy. As I've stated previously, I believe our policy goals toward Iran were well-founded. However, the information brought to my attention yesterday convinced me that in one aspect, implementation of that policy was seriously flawed.

While I cannot reverse what has happened, I'm initiating steps, including those I've announced today, to assure that the implementation of all future, foreign, and national security policy initiatives will proceed only in accordance with my authorization.

Over the past six years, we've realized many foreign policy goals. I believe we can yet achieve, and I intend to pursue, the objectives on which we all agree — a safer, more secure and stable world.

And now, I'm going to ask Attorney General Meese to brief you.

Q: What was the flaw?

Q: Do you still maintain you didn't make a mistake, Mr. President?

P: Hold it.

No Mistake Was Made

Q: Did you make a mistake in sending arms to Tehran, sir?

P: No, and I'm not taking any more questions, and — just a second, I'm going to ask Attorney General Meese to brief you on what we presently know of what he has found out.

Q: Is anyone else going to be let go, sir?

Q: Can you tell us — did Secretary Shultz —

Q: Is anyone else going to be let go? There have been calls for —

P: No one was let go; they chose to go.

Q: What about Secretary Shultz, Mr. President?

Q: Is Shultz going to stay, sir?

Q: How about Secretary Shultz and Mr. Regan, sir?

Q: What about Secretary Shultz, sir?

Q: Can you tell us if Secretary Shultz is going to stay?

Q: Can you give Secretary Shultz a vote of confidence if you feel that way?

P: May I give you Attorney General Meese?

Q: And who is going to run National Security?

Q: What about Shultz, sir?

Q: Why won't you say what the flaw is?

ATTORNEY GENERAL MEESE: That's what I'm going to say — what it's all about.

Q: Why can't he?

MEESE: Why don't I tell you what is the situation and then I'll take your questions.

Attorney General Meese's Statement

On Friday afternoon — or Friday at noon, the President asked me to look into and bring together the facts concerning the — particularly the implementation of the strategic initiative in Iran and more precisely, anything pertaining to the transfer of arms. Over the weekend this inquiry was conducted. Yesterday evening I reported to the President. We continued our inquiry and this morning the President directed that we make this information immediately available to the Congress and to the public through this medium this noon.

Let me say that all of the information is not yet in. We are still continuing our inquiry. But he did want me to make available immediately what we know at the present time.

What is involved is that in the course of the arms transfers, which involved the United States providing the arms to Israel and Israel in turn transferring the arms — in effect, selling the arms to representatives of Iran. Certain monies which were received in the transaction between representatives of Israel and representatives of Iran were taken and made available to the forces in Central America which are opposing the Sandinista government there.

In essence, the way in which the transactions occurred was that a certain amount of money was negotiated by representatives outside of the United States with Iran for arms. This amount of money was then transferred to representatives as best we know that can be described as representatives of Israel. They, in turn, transferred to the CIA, which was the agent for the United States government under a finding prepared by the President — signed by the President in January of 1986. And, incidentally, all of these transactions that I am referring to took place between January of 1986 and the present time. They transferred to the CIA the exact amount of the money that was owed to the United States government for the weapons that were involved plus any costs of transportation that might be involved. This money was then repaid by the CIA to the Department of Defense under the normal procedures and all governmental funds and all governmental property was accounted for and statements of that have been verified by us up to the present time.

The money — the difference between the money owed to the United States government and the money received from representatives of Iran was then deposited in bank accounts which were under the control of representatives of the forces in Central America. ∎

Executive Order on Review Board

Following is the White House text of President Reagan's Dec. 1 executive order (No. 12575) establishing a special review board to investigate activities of the National Security Council concerning secret arms sales to Iran, and the transfer of funds to the Nicaraguan anti-government "contra" rebels.

Executive Order 12575

By the authority vested in me as President by the Constitution and laws of the United States of America, and in order to establish, in accordance with the Federal Advisory Committee Act, as amended (5 U.S.C. App. I), a Special Review Board to review activities of the National Security Council, it is hereby ordered as follows:

Section 1. Establishment. (a) There is established the President's Special Review Board on the future role of the National Security Council staff. The Board shall consist of three members appointed by the President from among persons with extensive experience in foreign policy and national security affairs.

(b) The President shall designate a Chairman from among the members of the Board.

Section 2. Functions. (a) The Board shall conduct a comprehensive study of the future role and procedures of the National Security Council (NSC) staff in the development, coordination, oversight, and conduct of foreign and national security policy; review the NSC staff's proper role in operational activities, especially extremely sensitive diplomatic, military, and intelligence missions; and provide recommendations to the President based upon its analysis of the manner in which foreign and national security policies established by the President have been implemented by the NSC staff.

(b) The Board shall submit its findings and recommendations to the President within 60 days of the date of this Order.

Section 3. Administration. (a) The heads of Executive departments, agencies, and independent instrumentalities, to the extent permitted by law, shall provide the Board, upon request, with such information as it may require for purposes of carrying out its functions.

(b) Members of the Board shall receive compensation for their work on the Board at the daily rate specified for GS-18 of the General Schedule. While engaged in the work of the Board, members appointed from among private citizens of the United States may be allowed travel expenses, including per diem in lieu of subsistence, as authorized by law for persons serving intermittently in the government service (5 U.S.C. 5701-5707).

(c) To the extent permitted by law and subject to the availability of appropriations, the Office of Administration, Executive Office of the President, shall provide the Board with such administrative services, funds, facilities, staff, and other support services as may be necessary for the performance of its functions.

Section 4. General Provision. The Board shall terminate 30 days after submitting its report to the President.

RONALD REAGAN

The White House,
December 1, 1986.

At House Foreign Affairs Dec. 8:

Text of Shultz' Testimony On Role in Iran Arms Scandal

Following are excerpts from the New York Times *text of the Dec. 8 testimony of Secretary of State George P. Shultz before the House Foreign Affairs Committee on secret arms sales to Iran and the transfer of funds to Nicaraguan "contra" rebels.*

SECRETARY SHULTZ: . . . You asked in one way or another about my role in the diversion of funds for aid to the Nicaraguan resistance. My role in that was zero. I knew nothing about it, until it came out. So I don't have anything that I can contribute to your deliberations on exactly how that came about. . . .

The hearings you are holding . . . come at a crucial point for the nation. The president has recognized that serious problems have been created on our conduct of foreign affairs by the manner in which some individuals implemented our effort to establish better contacts with Iran, and by the diversion of funds from arms sales to the Nicaraguan democratic resistance.

He has taken the lead in rectifying any problems that may exist. . . .

I want to put to rest now any doubt as to my readiness to respond to questions about my prior knowledge and activity. I have already made all the information at my disposal available to the FBI. I have been interviewed by the Department of Justice. I am ready in this open session to bring forward all the materials I properly can, and at whatever appropriate time you choose I am prepared to make a statement and to answer questions in closed session, giving classified details of my knowledge and activities. . . .

Reagan's Foreign Policy Leadership

Where do we stand after six years of President Reagan's leadership in foreign affairs? Working with Congress and with the broad support of the American people, President Reagan's policies have brought us to a threshold of a new and remarkably different world, a world in which America's interests, America's pride and America's ideals are flourishing. . . .

Only a few years ago, the democracies of the world were believed to be an embattled, shrinking handful of nations. Today, people struggling under oppressive regimes of the right and the left can see democracy as a vital force for the future. Vital but non-violent movements toward more open societies have succeeded. The failure of closed, command economies is more evident every day. A new wind of change is blowing. People who are ready to stand up for freedom and have no choice but to fight for their rights now know that communism's march is not inevitable.

President Reagan is a freedom fighter and the world knows it. And I stand with Ronald Reagan. Strong defenses, sound alliances and support for the free economic and political development of peoples everywhere, that's what President Reagan stands for. His policies are not the policies of a party, they are the policies of all the American people. They are inevitable policies if our country is to remain the best and greatest on Earth, and the hope of humanity everywhere. . . .

Shultz' Opposition

Q: *Now, it has been alleged that you were opposed to this Iranian initiative. . . . If you were, did you convey your concern to the president and, if you did, when did you do it?*

A: I conveyed my concerns on many occasions, in two full meetings, on another occasion, according to my records, and I don't think anyone involved in this is under any illusion whatever about my views. . . .

I supported and continue to support, as my statement indicates, the idea of trying to see if we can't rearrange the furniture a little bit insofar as Iran is concerned. And there are various ways to try to do that which I support, and which is the president's basic intent. So I support his policy. However, when it comes to the use of arms, I have a different view. But I do believe that it's a legitimate subject for debate as a policy matter. The president listened to views, pro and con, and he has said publicly that in the end he decided that he should send a signal — I think that was his word — to Iran to show our serious intent. And so he authorized some arms shipments to Iran for that purpose. . . .

Soliciting Foreign Contributions

Q: *Over the weekend, we read about the Sultan of Brunei contributing large sums of money into a secret Swiss bank account to support the contras. I wonder how many other Third World countries have done the same thing, who has control of this fund and who handles it, basically? What knowledge do you have on that particular fund that circumvents what I believe the spirit of the law in support of the contra effort in Nicaragua?*

A: First of all, it would not be proper for me to talk about any particular third country and so I will not do that. I did see a report in the press that during a visit to Brunei last summer, I raised this issue, or sold the Sultan on transferring funds. That is not correct. I did visit Brunei, it was the only ASEAN country that I had not visited and I wanted to visit each of them, just as I try to stop in the Pacific island states . . . on that same trip. But there were no conversations with any Bruneian during that visit by me of this matter.

'Perfectly Proper Activity'

Having said that, let me go on and say — first reminding you that in August 1985, Congress approved $27 million in humanitarian aid for the Nicaraguan democratic resistance. The funds were appropriated in December for obligation through March 31, 1986. At the time the Congress expressly confirmed that, in addition to expending this $27 million the law did not preclude — I'm quoting from the law that you passed — "activities of the Department of State to solicit such humanitarian assistance for the Nicaraguan democratic resistance." So it was a perfectly proper activity for the Department of State, for me, to do that. There's nothing illegal about it, there's nothing improper about it. . . .

We went about it very carefully and considered it last summer because, with the delays, you remember, in enacting the final appropriations — even though both houses had voted — the resistance was having great trouble. They were incurring debts, they didn't have funds. And so, in discussions with Assistant Secretary [Elliott] Abrams, we tried to think through where we might properly solicit some funds. We wanted to be very careful that we lived completely by the spirit, let alone the letter, of the law and didn't get involved with a country where it might be thought that we had tremendous leverage, say, because of our aid program or something of that kind. So we were very, very careful about that.

And we did successfully persuade one government to make a contribution. So that is what we did. The discussions with the government were conducted by Assistant Secretary Abrams, but with my authority explicitly. . . .

Error of Shipping Arms

Q: *I have two things I'd like you to comment on. Mr. McFarlane has said publicly, "I talked to the secretary of state repeatedly and often of every item in the relationship with Iran."*

And secondly, I'd like you to clarify for me what the administration believes the mistakes to have been. . . . Was the mistake in supplying arms to Iran? Was the mistake in diverting funds to the contras? Was the mistake in not informing the Congress. . . ?

A: Well, very clearly it was a mistake to get involved in the illegal arms transfer — or funds transfer.

Q: *To the contras?*

A: To the extent — I don't know the ins and outs of that, I don't want to act like a judge passing judgment on what happened. I don't have the facts. But from what I have seen and what the attorney general said, some things took place that were illegal. And so that's clearly a mistake. I might say it's not only a mistake because it's illegal but it has — it has confused the situation insofar as our support for the Nicaraguan resistance is concerned. And unfairly to them, because they have no part in that. And so it's a mistake from that standpoint as well.

Shultz' Knowledge of Shipments

I do not know in detail — in fact, I don't know much at all — about the arms transfers that apparently took place in the calendar year 1986. I know more about what took place during 1985, and I'm prepared in a closed session, based on documents that I have, cable traffic and notes that were taken at the time — and I don't claim that my notes encompass everything that I knew, but I've tried to stick in what I've prepared for a closed session to things that I could be pretty confident of. Recognizing that in these things, when you go into them and you are questioned and people remind you of this or that, it jogs your memory.

But at any rate, I knew that arms transfers to Iran were periodically considered after June 1985 as part of an effort to improve relations with Iran and secure the release of our hostages. There was a lot — there was considerable discussion between Mr. McFarlane and I about that, and at least on one occasion that I distinctly recall, with the president.

I learned not as a result of being involved in the development of the plan but, so to speak, as a plan was about to be implemented. I learned in various ways of two proposed transfers during 1985, but I was never informed and had the impression that they were not consummated. I later learned — heard — that one shipment had misfired, that is, it had been delivered but due to Iranian rejection of the arms involved, was not — not consummated.

I knew that in December 1985, following a full-scale discussion of this matter with the president, that we instructed a mission that talked with the Iranians that were being — that were the interlocutors, or representing themselves as the interlocutors — they were told on instructions that we would engage the Iranians in a dialogue if they release our hostages but that we would not sell them arms. That was an explicit part of the instruction that the president had authorized.

So there was, you might say, a period of time from more or less the middle of 1985 until this period following the December meeting in which there was a fair amount of discussion of the subject — and I expressed my views during that period — in which some things were apparently structured. I can't tell you exactly how, but which, so far as I could see, never came off. And at the end of this process, after a full discussion, wanting to see the dialogue with Iran continue but not — but having become convinced that there shouldn't be an arms transfer connected with it, the instructions that I referred to were the instructions of the mission. . . .

The subject was reviewed again by the president in a full-scale meeting in January of 1986. This was not a meeting in which an explicit decision was stated. People made arguments, I made my arguments. However, I could fairly conclude from the meeting that the point of view that I thought had prevailed in December was not — didn't seem to be prevailing. But it wasn't as though there was some sharp decision.

I learned in November that a finding was made authorizing among other things arms sales, but I was not informed of that finding at the time so I can't tell you anything about the thinking that went into the finding as such. That came as a —

Q: *The finding was in January, Mr. Secretary.*

A: The finding was in January, and I was notified of it at about the same time you were notified of it. I did not learn about any transfers of arms during 1986 in a direct way. But, as is always the case, you have bits and pieces of evidence float in and so I weighed in on the basis of that, restating my views. What I heard was conflicting: at times that there was some sort of deal or signal in the works, and at other times that the operation was closed down. And, in fact, the word used at one time with me was that the people involved had been told to stand down.

So, again, there was this ambiguity from my standpoint. I would say to you that I did take the position in part because of all the problems that we have with leaks, and recognizing that if the president's initiative had any chance of success it would have to be a secret initiative for all the reasons that have been developed — perfectly good reasons. That whenever I would be called upon to do something to carry out those policies, I needed to know, but I didn't need to know things that were not in my sphere to do something about.

'Back Channel' Messages

Now this past weekend, our ambassador in Beirut, Mr. John Kelly, responded to an all-posts directive that we put out. We put out a directive from the State Department — I don't have the date of it but shortly after this investigation started — telling our posts to discover anything that they had about this, to secure it and to make it available here in Washington. So I got a response from Mr. John Kelly and I will read his response.

"I met in Washington in July or August 1986 with Robert McFarlane, who briefed me on the hostage negotiations involving arms to Iran as an inducement. Between the dates of Oct. 30 and Nov. 4, 1986, I had numerous conversations with Lt. Col. Oliver North and Richard V. Secord, relating to the hostage negotiations with Iran. During that period, I received and sent numerous 'back channel' messages to and from the White House, Admiral Poindexter, concerning the hostage negotiations. Those messages were transmitted and received in what is referred to as the 'privacy channel,' using CIA communications facilities.

"In accordance with our standard practice at Embassy Beirut" — which they have to do, given the situation there — "all of that message traffic was destroyed thereafter, at my direction." That is a standing order in a post like Beirut; nothing wrong with that. "I would assume that copies may be available at CIA headquarters or at the White House situation room. With regard to my conversations with McFarlane, North and Secord, I stand ready to discuss them with appropriate officials upon the Department's direction."

I have instructed Ambassador Kelly to return to Washington immediately, bringing with him all records of such activities, to be available to the FBI and other appropriate investigative bodies. I am, to put it mildly, shocked to learn this, after the event, from an ambassador, but at any rate, I'm just reading you this report.

Agreed With Reagan's Objective

Throughout the entire period, I opposed the transfer of arms to Iran until Iran stopped the war in the Gulf, ended its support for terrorism and obtained the release of the hostages. Throughout the entire period, I fully agreed with the president's objective of finding a way to modify Iran's behavior in a manner consistent with our strategic interests, and those of our friends in the region and around the world.

The president has confirmed publicly that he believed in principle, in the light of all the circumstances, that we should use a limited amount of arms to send a signal. There are legitimate arguments to be made in favor of this decision and the president has made them. And I fully accept their legitimacy, and the legitimacy and propriety of the president's decision, and right to make that decision, and support that.

It's difficult for me to talk about particular incidents without violating security requirements, to give you a full accounting — which, as I've said, I'm perfectly prepared to do. But it must be done in a way that is proper. But I believe a review of the classified record, if you go through it with me, will support the statements that I have made. And it will also show that my knowledge of what took place was sporadic and fragmentary, and materially incomplete. So I'm not the witness to tell you all of the things that took place because I'm not informed.

Insofar as any question — I'm repeating, but I want to repeat — any question of diversion of funds to support the Nicaraguan democratic resistance, my knowledge was not fragmentary, it was non-existent. . . .

State Department's Involvement

Q: *Did the Inter-American Affairs Bureau at State have any knowledge of, or was it involved in the coordination of, funds for the contras from the Iran arms sales?*

A: No.

Q: *Was the bureau aware of any —*

A: Let me say, not to their knowledge. If there were some funds put somewhere, that were useful, then they were trying to provide, properly, humanitarian aid when that was authorized. And, since the $100 million authorized, they've been involved in that. And there is an explicit congressional mandate for the State Department to play a strong role in that, and we're trying to do that. But nobody in our bureau, that I know of — and I'm certain Elliott Abrams and his group had no knowledge of this Iranian funds transfer question at all. Zero.

Q: *Well, was the bureau aware of the method by which the contras were receiving lethal aid during the period in which the Boland amendment was in effect?*

A: We are — we don't presume to know everything that a person may do somewhere in the government. It was clear that — from private sources, presumably — some aid was flowing to the people fighting for freedom and independence in Nicaragua. And personally, I applaud that. There's a lot of aid flowing from America to the Nicaraguan communists, quite a few Americans down there. That's their right to be. And it shouldn't be surprising that there are Americans who want to help the people fighting for freedom.

Q: *To what extent do intelligence operatives from other agencies apprise the bureau of their activities with respect to coordinating funding for contra operations, and does the assistant secretary for inter-American affairs receive such reports?*

A: He does, and he chairs the interagency group that includes people from all of the agencies involved whose task it is to evaluate what is going on and to make recommendations, if needed, for new legislation or what our policy should be, and to oversee the tactics involved.

Q: *... Are you apprised on a regular basis of the department's involvement in contra operations by Assistant Secretary Abrams, and do these reports include summaries of the intelligence community's operations?*

A: Well, I see reports from time to time. I see Elliott Abrams frequently. And so I try to keep abreast of what is going on, as best I can....

Q: *Can you tell us whether you were under any constraint, or whether the department was under any constraint, not to reveal any of the information with regard to the Iranian arms sales?*

A: No. We were, of course, bound by the decisions that would be made about something that was to be held in confidence. But as far as our measuring up to our responsibilities were concerned, we were engaged, you might say, in an argument about what should be done. And there were these incidents that came along that I have pointed up for you, without being in a position to — for various reasons; partly lack of knowledge, partly because of the nature of the open hearing here — to give you full information about them.

Necessity to Consult Congress

Q: *But once the project was under way, didn't you feel that the department had a necessity of consulting with the Congress with regard to these initiatives?*

A: Well, I don't feel that we should sort of bring all our internal debates to the Congress, particularly on something like this. Of course, policy toward Iran, policy toward terrorism, all of these basic things that have been laid out, we have discussed here in the committee many times.

Q: *... Once that was under way and some of that was brought to the department's attention, wasn't there then a responsibility to the department to consult with Congress?*

A: Well, perhaps so. I don't — I'm not here to claim that my actions in all of this were all that they should be. You'll have to judge that for yourself. And I can tell you what I knew and what I didn't.

Chain of Command

Q: *You mention Ambassador Kelly's report to the CIA but a failure to report to your office. Is that an unusual or a unique situation, or something that's in violation of any of the State Department's regulations?*

A: I hope it's unique. Ambassadors — there is supposed to be, I say supposed to be — a chain of command that goes from the president, to me — not to the NSC, to me — and through the assistant secretary, by and large, to the ambassador. That's the chain of command.

Q: *And was that a violation, sir?*

A: And if something comes up that causes an ambassador to go outside the chain of command, there needs to be a good reason. Now it may be very well that Ambassador Kelly will say that he was told on the authority of the president that he was supposed to do this and that. And I would think that he would have checked with me to see if that were so.

Q: *Who would enable such an ambassador to waive that responsibility?*

A: At this point, all I can tell you is the cable that I got. I don't consider it a satisfactory situation.

I do have to — I think we should recognize, however, what life is like in Washington. Now, come on, here we are. And who was it? The Canadian ambassador coined the phrase, "It's never over." Nothing ever gets settled in this town. It's not like running a company, or even a university. It's — it's a seething debating society in which the debate never stops, in which people never give up, including me. And so that's the atmosphere in which you administer. And what I try to do is stay as close to the president as I can, and I feel very close to him. And I admire and respect him tremendously. I think he has transformed the situation, done a marvelous job. And I try to stay very close to him and I support his policies.

I don't win every argument, by a long shot, but I am in the argument. And when the president decides something, then I do my best to make it work....

Damage to U.S. Credibility

Q: *For six years the administration has said it would never yield to the demands of terrorists, pay ransom for hostages, or sell arms to states that sponsor and support terrorism. It now turns out that we've done all three. How could this have happened? How much damage has it done to our credibility, and what assurance can you give us that it won't happen again?*

A: Well, the president decided to give a signal. I'm just quoting the president here, and he's made a public statement of what he authorized and why. And he has acknowledged that in doing so he recognized that there were risks as well as potential benefits, and he had to weigh that. And right now, because of the way this has blown up, the emphasis is all on the risks. I dare say that if somehow we had our hostages all returned, and we saw a different kind of situation in one way or another emerging in Iran, and this came out, people would say, well, the president showed guts....

Perot Ransom Payment

Q: *Were you consulted or informed about the request of Lt. Col. North to Ross Perot to pay $2 million in ransom money for the release of our hostages? And is it conceivable to you that Lt. Col. North would have made such a request without the approval of the president or some higher authority?*

A: I was not informed. And, so far as I know, the president wasn't informed. But I have no knowledge about Lt. Col. North's activities in this regard. I think the offer of Mr. Perot, if that is what took place — I don't know, I just read about it — I think it's outrageous.

A Constitutional Confrontation?

Q: *... In the past when those of us have differed with you, the issues have entirely been those of judgment and policy. It appears today we have a political crisis that's become a constitutional confrontation.*

A: I don't believe it's a constitutional confrontation at all. What the president has done is — is move out people who seem to be involved, he has put in a new and outstanding National Security Council director, he has appointed — or asked for the appointment of a special prosecutor. He has said that he will make available to the Congress, and instructed me to come here and talk to you. Where is the constitutional crisis? There is no constitutional crisis....

Foreign Policy Duplicity

Q: *... Now as the Cabinet officer who is responsible for the conduct of this nation's foreign policy, if you are telling us* *this morning — and I believe all of us feel you're stating the truth — that your role was zero, or non-existent, then how is it —*

A: My role was non-existent insofar as the apparent reported use of funds generated by sales of arms to Iran and the diversion of those funds to help the Nicaraguan resistance. I knew nothing about that. I did not say that I knew nothing about any of the other things. On the contrary, I tried to tell you what I knew about it.

Q: *I appreciate that clarification. But nonetheless, many of these activities were directly contrary to stated policies of our government. My question is, how is it possible for this duplicitous activity to go on? In other words, how is it possible that another agency, aside from the State Department, is engaged in activity, or operations, that are contrary to the official policy of the United States? Shouldn't the State Department assert its natural, constitutional, proper role over the conduct of the foreign policy so we don't end up with contradictory policies that possibly confuse not only our allies but people here in America?*

A: First of all, the president made a public statement explaining his reasoning for sending a signal. A signal involving arms transfers that you have characterized in various ways and which have been widely characterized as such.

There is a whole other side to that argument which the president presented, explaining to the American people and to you why he decided to send that signal. Knowing full well the risks involved but seeking an objective that, if it could be achieved I'm sure everybody would applaud. So that's the decision that the president made, legitimately.

Now insofar as the State Department is concerned, I believe it is correct to say that we do not have a foreign policy in the State Department. The president has a foreign policy. I work for the president and we are engaged in a process — and I am by directive and by common understanding and, I hope, by my association with the president — principal foreign policy adviser to him. But it is the president's policy.... ∎

Before House Foreign Affairs Dec. 8:

Ex-NSC Adviser McFarlane On Iran-'Contra' Affair

Following are excerpts from the Associated Press text of former national security adviser Robert C. McFarlane's Dec. 8 testimony before the House Foreign Affairs Committee on secret arms sales to Iran and the transfer of funds to Nicaraguan "contra" rebels. The text was printed in The Washington Post.

MR. McFARLANE: It wasn't until the summer of last year that [moderate political] elements surfaced [in Iran] and we became aware that elements that were both in the government and close to it as advisers wanted to know whether the United States had any interest in such a discourse.

The elements making the proposal from within Iran, high officials, made clear that for them to be able to sustain that dialogue and over time exert any influence to change policy within Iran, they would need to strengthen themselves. And in their terms this would require them to reach out to elements within the military, the revolutionary guards, or both and that the currency of that undertaking was arms....

The president acknowledged, faced with this opportunity, that any elements within Iran who truly were committed to change and reform were certainly going to be very vulnerable.

And he acknowledged that the transfer, indirectly, of weapons to support these individuals and allow them to build a constituency would indeed not be a violation of policy but to the extent that it dealt with people who opposed Iranian policy, opposed terrorism, that modest levels which could not affect the balance in the war with Iraq nor could be applied to terrorist undertakings would be sensible....

Q: *Did you ever receive any instructions ... not to inform the House or Senate select committees on intelligence of the Iranian initiative or related activities?*

A: Never in my recollection did I have any explicit proscription of that.... But I understand after I left that there were other decisions taken....

Q: *[McFarlane was asked for comment on a news article stating that President Reagan gave general authorization to proceed with sale or resale of arms as early as fall 1985.]*

A:... In sum, to say that the president authorized the indirect delivery of small levels of arms to Iran for the purpose of strengthening elements that were against terrorism and that that was communicated ultimately to the Iranian authorities and that in the conduct of that, that certain transfers occurred, which were reviewed again in December of last year.

Q: *When did that authorization occur?*

A: In August of 1985....

Q: *Was it your understanding at the time that these weapons, be they offensive or defensive, would be utilized to allow Iran to continue its war with Iraq?*

A: No.

Q: *What was your understanding...?*

A: Well, sir, the value, the utility of these systems, which could not have had a significant effect on the war, was it engendered the political figures involved to be able to consolidate more of a power base within Iran.

Q: *In any of your conversations with the president or any other White House representatives, did you ever discuss the issue of diversion of payments from Iran to the Nicaraguan contras?*

A: No.

Q: *Did you ever discuss with the president the component that hostage negotiations played in this policy?*

A: Yes.... It seemed to me that after two or three months, roughly in November ... there was a skewing of the emphasis toward the hostages and, as important as they are, the more fundamental issue was the political stability of [the] U.S.-Iranian relationship. I recommended that we reorient it as originally planned and start dealing directly with the Iranians and make clear that we could not be party to the transfer of U.S. weapons. The president agreed....

Q: *I'm very curious as to how it's possible ... for a lieutenant colonel on the NSC staff to have the authority by himself to divert millions of dollars in arms sales to aid to the contras....*

A: The events ... occurred after I left the government, and I can't really account for how a diversion such as has been alleged could have occurred.

Q: *Is it possible?*

A: Of course, it's theoretically possible. As to whether it is plausible ... I can only comment on the basis of my knowledge of the individuals concerned.... Lt. Col. [Oliver L.] North is a person of integrity ... and thus would not have acted contrary to U.S. law, nor would he have taken initiatives without higher authority. Similarly, Adm. [John M.] Poindexter is a man of integrity ... and it seems to me very, very unlikely he would have acted in any way contrary to law....

Q: *When did you first learn of this diversion of funds?*

A:... From the Iranian relationship to Central American accounts in May of this year in connection with a mission I was asked to undertake to Iran. Either en route or returning, I was advised in a very summary fashion that the U.S. government had applied certain Iranian funds to Central American programs.... I took it to have been a matter of established approved policy sanctioned by higher authority than the officer who conveyed it, who was Lt. Col. North....

Q: *On that flight back from Tehran, when you learned first of the diversion of funds ... did you ask Lt. Col. North whether he was acting on the authority of the president or a person of higher rank....*

A: No....

Q: *Did you say, "Ollie, you're breaking the law"...?*

A: When you are told in a very brief space of time a finding has been approved which allows the transfer of arms, that some have been transferred, further that no hostages have come out and yet an arrangement is now in place for all of them to come, and the government is applying some of these monies to Central America — the several elements here were all elements with which I had no knowledge prior to the time but were presented as elements within an integral whole which ... did not seem to me to be at the time a matter where the authority did not exist.

Q: *Who ... could have directed Adm. Poindexter to allow Lt. Col. North to take such action?*

A: I firmly believe that the president did not know of and did not approve of such actions. I also ... find it hard to imagine that Adm. Poindexter did....

Q: *I'm a little puzzled about how these weapons got to the military in Iran without the leaders knowing about it.*

A: That is a central question to be answered ... best ... in a closed session.... I think you can be very confident that very high-level officials within the Iranian government were both aware of and supportive of this entire initiative. We certainly would not have undertaken it with people of lesser standing....

Q: *When you had discussions with those moderate elements, did you raise [the] issue of their bringing forward hostages ... to prove their good faith?*

A: Yes.

Q: *What then did you ask them to do other than that? Did you think that by opening the channels and asking them to get out the hostages we were then dealing with moderate elements which would justify a policy exception which would leave in shambles every single policy which we had in place?...*

A: I didn't have any of those thoughts in mind.... I believe it is not in United States' interests to have the eternal enmity of ... Iran. It's plausible to believe that some in Iran ... might also agree....

Q: *Isn't it true that you actually resigned your NSC directorship in order to perpetuate this policy as a private citizen?*

A: That is absolutely false and an outrageous statement....

Q: The Miami Herald *has been carrying a story ... that there had been knowledge prior to the condoning of the transshipment of American arms through Israel to Iran.... Was [there] any discussion of the appropriateness of the transshipment with [knowledge] that Iran had in fact paid for the blowing up of the Marine barracks?*

A: At the time of the attack on the barracks in October of '83, the reports that elements within Lebanon that had links to Iran might well have been responsible....

Q: *On the trip to or from Iran, did Lt. Col. North also tell you he had asked Ross Perot to make a $2 million ransom payment?*

A: ... In the return, when we made an intervening stop in the Middle East ... I was advised on whether or not Lt. Col. North planned to travel to another location at the time. In context, the issue ... was to see whether a separate and entirely distinct effort ... was maturing or working out or not. I was advised at the time that it involved Mr. Perot. The nitty-gritty of it I wasn't advised of.

Q: *Were you told that it involved the payment of ransom?*

A: No, in the way it was portrayed to me, it wasn't a ransom. My impression was that it involved sources and source payments ... but it wasn't a matter of dealing directly with the captors.

Q: *... Would it be fair to say that it was your view at the time that this decision to divert funds from Iran to the contras must have been approved by the president himself?*

A: No ... I have described a model of decision-making that existed when I was in the government, but I don't know how decisions were reached since....

Q: *Would it have been conceivable to you that the policy could have been approved without the approval of the president?*

A: It is conceivable....

Q: *The finding ... in August of last year by the president — you said it was an oral finding. And as I understand it, that was a finding which allowed, which constituted the formal approval in your judgment by this government at the proper level of authority and in the proper manner, to approve the shipment of arms from Israel to Iran in August of 1985. Is that correct?*

A: I'd be glad to deal with the countries involved in a closed session.... The thrust of your point is correct, that the president in August provided the decision basis for events that followed.

Q: *Am I correct in my recollection that you said it was an oral finding by the president...?*

A: That's correct.

Q: *Can you tell us in whose presence...?*

A: The decision followed consultation and advice by the president with his Cabinet officers — the secretary of state, defense, the chief of staff, the director of central intelligence, myself.

Q: *To whom did the president orally convey this finding?*

A: To me and ... his Cabinet officers in separate but related talks ... one-on-one or in groups.

Q: *Can we assume that ... every statutory member at least of the National Security Council was made aware at that time...?*

A: I believe you can....

Q: *This had the effect of authorizing the transfer of U.S.-supplied weapons from a third country to Iran. Is that correct?*

A: That is correct....

Q: *Was there a legal opinion rendered at the time with respect to that authorization?*

A: The legal considerations were discussed, but in terms of something formally in writing, no, sir....

Q: *Was the chief of staff, Mr. [Donald T.] Regan ... [informed] at the same time as you...?*

A: ... There isn't any doubt but that each member of the NSC was involved and conscious of the course of the arguments pro and con, Mr. Regan and all others.... ∎

PUBLIC LAWS

Public Laws, 99th Congress, 2nd Session

PL 99-241 (S 2013) Delay the referendum with respect to the 1986-88 crops of flue-cured tobacco and delay the proclamation of national marketing quotas for the 1986-88 crops of burley tobacco. Introduced by HELMS, R-N.C., Jan. 22, 1986. Senate passed Jan. 22. House passed Jan. 23. President signed Jan. 30, 1986.

PL 99-242 (HR 4027) Extend the waiver authority of the District of Columbia Revenue Bond Act of 1985 to certain revenue bond acts of the District of Columbia. Introduced by FAUNTROY, D-D.C., Jan. 22, 1986. House District of Columbia discharged. House passed Jan. 27. Senate passed Jan. 30. President signed Feb. 7, 1986.

PL 99-243 (H J Res 520) Make an urgent supplemental appropriation for fiscal year 1986 for the Commodity Credit Corporation. Introduced by WHITTEN, D-Miss., Feb. 6, 1986. House passed Feb. 6. Senate passed Feb. 6. President signed Feb. 10, 1986.

PL 99-244 (S J Res 74) Provide for the designation of February 1986 as "National Black (Afro-American) History Month." Introduced by THURMOND, R-S.C., March 6, 1985. Senate Judiciary reported Nov. 14. Senate passed Nov. 18. House Post Office and Civil Service discharged. House passed Feb. 6, 1986. President signed Feb. 11, 1986.

PL 99-245 (S J Res 219) Designate Feb. 9-15, 1986, as "National Humanities Week, 1986." Introduced by HATCH, R-Utah, Oct. 17, 1985. Senate Judiciary reported Oct. 31. Senate passed Nov. 4. House Post Office and Civil Service discharged. House passed Feb. 6, 1986. President signed Feb. 11, 1986.

PL 99-246 (S J Res 234) Designate Feb. 9-15, 1986, as "National Burn Awareness Week." Introduced by WILSON, R-Calif., Nov. 6, 1985. Senate Judiciary reported Jan. 30, 1986. Senate passed Feb. 4. House Post Office and Civil Service discharged. House passed Feb. 6. President signed Feb. 11, 1986.

PL 99-247 (S 1831) Amend the Arms Export Control Act to require that congressional vetoes of certain arms export proposals be enacted into law. Introduced by CRANSTON, D-Calif., Nov. 5, 1985. Senate Foreign Relations reported Dec. 12. Senate passed Dec. 19. House passed, under suspension of the rules, Feb. 3, 1986. President signed Feb. 12, 1986.

PL 99-248 (S J Res 150) Designate March 1986 as "National Hemophilia Month." Introduced by BRADLEY, D-N.J., June 21, 1985. Senate Judiciary reported Oct. 3. Senate passed Oct. 4. House Post Office and Civil Service discharged. House passed Feb. 6, 1986. President signed Feb. 18, 1986.

PL 99-249 (S J Res 231) Designate 1986 as the "Centennial Year of the Gasoline Powered Automobile." Introduced by RIEGLE, D-Mich., Nov. 5, 1985. Senate passed Dec. 18. House Post Office and Civil Service discharged. House passed Feb. 6, 1986. President signed Feb. 18, 1986.

PL 99-250 (HR 1185) Amend the act establishing the Petrified Forest National Park. Introduced by UDALL, D-Ariz., Feb. 20, 1985. House Interior and Insular Affairs reported March 28 (H Rept 99-30). House passed, under suspension of the rules, April 2. Senate Energy and Natural Resources reported Nov. 18 (S Rept 99-184). Senate passed, amended, Dec. 3. House agreed to Senate amendments Feb. 6, 1986. President signed Feb. 27, 1986.

PL 99-251 (HR 4061) Amend title 5, U.S. Code, to expand the class of individuals eligible for funds or other returns of contributions from contingency reserves in the Employees Health Benefits Fund, and make miscellaneous amendments relating to the Civil Service Retirement System and the Federal Employees Health Benefits Program. Introduced by OAKAR, D-Ohio, Jan. 28, 1986. House passed, under suspension of the rules, Feb. 3. Senate passed Feb. 5. President signed Feb. 27, 1986.

PL 99-252 (S 1574) Provide for public education concerning the health consequences of using smokeless tobacco products. Introduced by LUGAR, R-Ind., Aug. 1, 1985. Senate Labor and Human Resources reported Dec. 4 (S Rept 99-209). Senate Commerce, Science and Transportation reported Dec. 16. Senate passed Dec. 16. House passed, amended, under suspension of the rules, Feb. 3, 1986. Senate agreed to House amendment Feb. 6. President signed Feb. 27, 1986.

PL 99-253 (S 2036) Make certain technical corrections to amendments made by the Food Security Act of 1985. Introduced by DOLE, R-Kan., Jan. 30, 1986. Senate passed Jan. 30. House passed, amended, under suspension of the rules, Feb. 4. Senate agreed to House amendment Feb. 7. President signed Feb. 28, 1986.

PL 99-254 (H J Res 499) Designate the week beginning March 2, 1986, as "Women's History Week." Introduced by BOXER, D-Calif., Jan. 22, 1986. House Post Office and Civil Service discharged. House passed Feb. 6. Senate Judiciary reported Feb. 20. Senate passed Feb. 27. President signed March 4, 1986.

PL 99-255 (HR 4130) Establish, for the purpose of implementing any order issued by the president for fiscal 1986 under any law providing for sequestration of new loan guarantee commitments, a guaranteed loan limitation amount applicable to chapter 37 of title 38, U.S. Code, for fiscal 1986. Introduced by SHELBY, D-Ala., Feb. 5, 1986. House Veterans' Affairs reported Feb. 20 (H Rept 99-472). House passed, under suspension of the rules, Feb. 25. Senate passed Feb. 25. President signed March 7, 1986.

PL 99-256 (H J Res 409) Direct the president to issue a proclamation designating Feb. 16, 1986, as "Lithuanian Independence Day." Introduced by RUSSO, D-Ill., Oct. 3, 1985. House Post Office and Civil Service discharged. House passed Dec. 12. Senate Judiciary reported Feb. 20, 1986. Senate passed Feb. 27. President signed March 10, 1986.

PL 99-257 (H J Res 371) Designate March 16, 1986, as "Freedom of Information Day." Introduced by WIRTH, D-Colo., Aug. 1, 1985. House Post Office and Civil Service discharged. House passed Feb. 27, 1986. Senate passed March 4. President signed March 14, 1986.

PL 99-258 (HR 3851) Amend the Alaska National Interest Lands Conservation Act. Introduced by YOUNG, R-Alaska, Dec. 4, 1985. House Interior and Insular Affairs reported Dec. 12 (H Rept 99-437). House passed Dec. 12. Senate Energy and Natural Resources reported Feb. 6, 1986 (S Rept 99-234). Senate passed March 4. President signed March 19, 1986.

PL 99-259 (H J Res 345) Designate March 1986 as "Music in Our Schools Month." Introduced by AKAKA, D-Hawaii, July 23, 1985. House Post Office and Civil Service discharged. House passed Feb. 27, 1986. Senate Judiciary reported March 6. Senate passed March 11. President signed March 19, 1986.

PL 99-260 (HR 1614) Make certain improvements to amendments made by the Food Security Act of 1985. Introduced by FOLEY, D-Wash., March 20, 1985. House Agriculture reported May 23 (H Rept 99-146). House passed, under suspension of the rules, June 4. Senate Agriculture, Nutrition and Forestry discharged. Senate passed, amended, March 6, 1986. House agreed to Senate amendments March 6. President signed March 20, 1986.

PL 99-261 (S J Res 205) Designate March 21, 1986, as "National Energy Education Day." Introduced by McCLURE, R-Idaho, Sept. 20, 1985. Senate Judiciary reported March 6, 1986. Senate passed March 11. House Post Office and Civil Service discharged. House passed March 13. President signed March 21, 1986.

PL 99-262 (S J Res 272) Authorize and request the president to issue a proclamation designating March 21, 1986, as "Afghanistan Day," a day to commemorate the struggle of the people of Afghanistan against the occupation of their country by Soviet forces. Introduced by HUMPHREY, R-N.H., Feb. 7, 1986. Senate Judiciary reported March 6. Senate passed March 19. House Post Office and Civil Service discharged. House passed March 20. President signed March 21, 1986.

PL 99-263 (H J Res 534) Make an urgent supplemental appropriation for the Department of Agriculture for fiscal year 1986. Introduced by WHITTEN, D-Miss., Feb. 26, 1986. House passed Feb. 26. Senate Appropriations reported March 4. Senate passed, amended, March 5. House agreed to Senate amendment with an amendment March 13. Senate agreed to conference report March 13 (H Rept 99-493). Senate agreed to House amendment with an amendment March 18. House disagreed to Senate amendment March 18. Senate insisted on its amendment March 18. Senate agreed to conference report March 19 (H Rept 99-499). House agreed to conference report March 20. President signed March 24, 1986.

PL 99-264 (S 1396) Settle unresolved claims relating to certain allotted Indian lands on the White Earth Indian Reservation, and remove clouds from the titles to certain lands. Introduced by BOSCHWITZ, R-Minn., June 27, 1985. Senate Select Indian Affairs reported Nov. 19 (S Rept 99-192). Senate passed Dec. 13. House Interior and Insular Affairs reported March 10, 1986 (H Rept 99-489). House passed, under suspension of the rules, March 11. President signed March 24, 1986.

PL 99-265 (S J Res 254) Designate 1987 as the "National Year of Thanksgiving." Introduced by DOLE, R-Kan., Dec. 19, 1985. Senate Judiciary reported Jan. 30, 1986. Senate passed Feb. 4. House Post Office and Civil Service discharged. House passed March 13. President signed March 25, 1986.

PL 99-266 (HR 4399) Designate the federal building located in Jamaica, Queens, N.Y., as the "Joseph P. Addabbo Federal Building." Introduced by BIAGGI, D-N.Y., March 13, 1986. House Public Works and Transportation discharged. House passed March 19. Senate passed March 19. President signed March 27, 1986.

PL 99-267 (H J Res 563) Provide for the temporary extension of certain programs relating to housing and community development. Introduced by GONZALEZ, D-Texas, March 12, 1986. House Banking, Finance and Urban Affairs discharged. House passed March 12. Senate passed March 19. President signed March 27, 1986.

PL 99-268 (S J Res 226) Designate April 6-12, 1986, as "World Health Week," and designate April 7, 1986, as "World Health Day." Introduced by RIEGLE, D-Mich., Oct. 23, 1985. Senate Judiciary reported Jan. 30, 1986. Senate passed Feb. 4. House Post Office and Civil Service discharged. House passed March 20. President signed March 27, 1986.

PL 99-269 (HR 2453) Amend the Older Americans Act of 1965, to increase the amounts authorized to be appropriated for fiscal years 1985, 1986 and 1987 for commodity distribution. Introduced by BIAGGI, D-N.Y., May 9, 1985. House Education and Labor reported Sept. 23 (H Rept 99-286). House passed, under suspension of the rules, Sept. 24. Senate Labor and Human Resources discharged. Senate passed, amended, Feb. 5, 1986. Senate agreed to conference report March 13 (H Rept 99-487). House agreed to conference report March 18. President signed April 1, 1986.

PL 99-270 (H J Res 573) Make a repayable advance to the Hazardous Substance Response Trust Fund. Introduced by BOLAND, D-Mass., March 20, 1986. House passed March 20. Senate passed March 21. President signed April 1, 1986.

PL 99-271 (S J Res 262) Authorize and request the president to issue a proclamation designating June 2-8, 1986, as "National Fishing Week." Introduced by WALLOP, R-Wyo., Jan. 30, 1986. Senate Judiciary reported Feb. 27. Senate passed March 4. House Post Office and Civil Service discharged. House passed March 20. President signed April 1, 1986.

PL 99-272 (HR 3128) Make changes in spending and revenue provisions for purposes of deficit reduction and program improvement, consistent with the budget process. Introduced by ROSTENKOWSKI, D-Ill., July 31, 1985. House Ways and Means reported July 31 (H Rept 99-241, Part 1). House Education and Labor reported Sept. 11 (H Rept 99-241, Part 2). House Judiciary reported Sept. 11 (H Rept 99-241, Part 3). House Energy and Commerce discharged. House passed Oct. 31. Senate Finance reported Nov. 14. Senate passed, amended, Nov. 14. House agreed to Senate amendment with an amendment Dec. 5. Senate agreed to conference report Dec. 19 (H Rept 99-453). House rejected conference report Dec. 19. House receded from its amendment and concurred in the Senate amendment with an amendment Dec. 19. Senate agreed to House amendment with an amendment Dec. 19. House disagreed to Senate amendment Dec. 20. Senate insisted on its amendment Dec. 20. House receded from its disagreement to Senate amendment and agreed to Senate amendment with an amendment March 6, 1986. Senate agreed to House amendment with an amendment March 14. House disagreed to Senate amendment March 18. Senate insisted on its amendment March 18. House agreed to Senate amendment March 20. President signed April 7, 1986.

PL 99-273 (S J Res 52) Designate April 1986 as "National School Library Month." Introduced by MOYNIHAN, D-N.Y., Feb. 19, 1985. Senate Judiciary reported April 3. Senate passed April 15. House Post Office and Civil Service discharged. House passed, amended, Feb. 6, 1986. Senate agreed to House amendments March 27. President signed April 9, 1986.

PL 99-274 (S J Res 261) Designate April 14-20, 1986, as "National Mathematics Awareness Week." Introduced by DOMENICI, R-N.M., Jan. 29, 1986. Senate Judiciary reported Feb. 27. Senate passed March 4. House Post Office and Civil Service discharged. House passed April 10. President signed April 17, 1986.

PL 99-275 (S J Res 136) Authorize and request the president to issue a proclamation designating the week beginning April 13, 1986, as "National Garden Week." Introduced by HATFIELD, R-Ore., May 15, 1985. Senate Judiciary reported June 13. Senate passed June 18. House Post Office and Civil Service discharged. House passed April 14, 1986. President signed April 18, 1986.

PL 99-276 (H J Res 582) Designate April 20, 1986, as "Education Day U.S.A." Introduced by MICHEL, R-Ill., March 25, 1986. House Post Office and Civil Service discharged. House passed April 14. Senate passed April 17. President signed April 22, 1986.

PL 99-277 (S J Res 315) Designate May 1986 as "Older Americans Month." Introduced by GRASSLEY, R-Iowa, April 9, 1986. Senate Judiciary reported April 10. Senate passed April 11. House Post Office and Civil Service discharged. House passed April 14. President signed April 23, 1986.

PL 99-278 (HR 4551) Extend for three months the emergency acquisition and net worth guarantee provisions of the Garn-St Germain Depository Institutions Act of 1982. Introduced by St GERMAIN, D-R.I., April 10, 1986. House passed, under suspension of the rules, April 14. Senate passed April 16. President signed April 24, 1986.

PL 99-279 (H J Res 599) Commemorate the 25th anniversary of the Bay of Pigs invasion to liberate Cuba from communist tyranny. Introduced by PEPPER, D-Fla., April 14, 1986. House Post Office and Civil Service discharged. House passed April 17. Senate passed April 17. President signed April 24, 1986.

PL 99-280 (S 1282) Revise and extend provisions of the Public Health Service Act relating to primary care. Introduced by HATCH, R-Utah, June 12, 1985. Senate Labor and Human Resources reported July 8 (S Rept 99-104). Senate passed July 19. House passed, amended, March 5, 1986. Senate agreed to House amendments April 11. President signed April 24, 1986.

PL 99-281 (S J Res 286) Designate April 20-26, 1986, as "National Reading Is Fun Week." Introduced by HATFIELD, R-Ore., March 3, 1986. Senate Judiciary reported March 20. Senate passed March 21. House Post Office and Civil Service discharged. House passed April 22. President signed April 24, 1986.

PL 99-282 (S J Res 303) Designate April 1986 as "Fair Housing Month." Introduced by DOLE, R-Kan., March 20, 1986. Senate Judiciary reported April 10. Senate passed April 11. House Post Office and Civil Service discharged. House passed April 17. President signed April 24, 1986.

PL 99-283 (S 1684) Declare that the United States holds certain Chilocco Indian School lands in trust for the Kaw, Otoe-Missouria, Pawnee, Ponca and Tonkawa Indian Tribes of Oklahoma. Introduced by NICKLES, R-Okla., Sept. 20, 1985. Senate Select Indian Affairs reported Nov. 18 (S Rept 99-188). Senate passed Dec. 3. House Interior and Insular Affairs reported March 20, 1986 (H Rept 99-500). House passed April 21. President signed May 1, 1986.

PL 99-284 (S 2319) Provide for the continuation of the Martin Luther King Jr. Federal Holiday Commission until April 20, 1989. Introduced by DOLE, R-Kan., April 17, 1986. Senate passed April 17. House passed April 22. President signed May 1, 1986.

PL 99-285 (S J Res 214) Provide for the reappointment of Carlisle H. Humelsine as a citizen regent of the Board of Regents of the Smithsonian Institution. Introduced by GOLDWATER, R-Ariz., Oct. 4, 1985. Senate Rules and Administration reported Dec. 11 (S Rept 99-217). Senate passed Dec. 12. House Committee on House Administration discharged. House passed, amended, April 17, 1986. Senate agreed to House amendments April 22. President signed May 1, 1986.

PL 99-286 (S J Res 215) Provide for the reappointment of William G. Bowen as a citizen regent of the Board of Regents of the Smithsonian Institution. Introduced by GOLDWATER, R-Ariz., Oct. 4, 1985. Senate Rules and Administration reported Dec. 11 (S Rept 99-218). Senate passed Dec. 12. House Committee on House Administration discharged. House passed, amended, April 17, 1986. Senate agreed to House amendments April 22. President signed May 1, 1986.

PL 99-287 (S J Res 275) Designate May 11-17, 1986, as "Jewish Heritage Week." Introduced by D'AMATO, R-N.Y., Feb. 19, 1986. Senate Judiciary reported March 6. Senate passed March 11. House Post Office and Civil Service discharged. House passed April 22. President signed May 1, 1986.

PL 99-288 (S J Res 296) Designate Oct. 16, 1986, as "World Food Day." Introduced by DANFORTH, R-Mo., March 13, 1986. Senate Judiciary reported March 20. Senate passed March 21. House Post Office and Civil Service discharged. House passed April 22. President signed May 1, 1986.

PL 99-289 (HR 4602) Authorize the Federal Housing Administration and the Government National Mortgage Association to enter into additional commitments to insure loans and guarantee mortgage-backed securities during fiscal year 1986. Introduced by WYLIE, R-Ohio, April 15, 1986. House passed, under suspension of the rules, April 21. Senate passed, amended, April 29. House agreed to Senate amendment April 30. President signed May 2, 1986.

PL 99-290 (H J Res 220) Reaffirm Congress' recognition of the vital role played by members of the National Guard and Reserve in the national defense. Introduced by MONTGOMERY, D-Miss., March 28, 1985. House Armed Services reported March 20, 1986 (H Rept 99-504). House passed, under suspension of the rules, April 14. Senate passed, amended, April 23. House agreed to Senate amendments April 29. President signed May 2, 1986.

PL 99-291 (H J Res 544) Designate May 7, 1987, as "National Barrier Awareness Day." Introduced by VUCANOVICH, R-Nev., Feb. 27, 1986. House Post Office and Civil Service discharged. House passed April 22. Senate Judiciary discharged. Senate passed May 2. President signed May 7, 1986.

PL 99-292 (H J Res 569) Designate May 8, 1986, as "Naval Aviation Day." Introduced by HUTTO, D-Fla., March 18, 1986. House Post Office and Civil Service discharged. House passed April 30. Senate passed May 2. President signed May 8, 1986.

PL 99-293 (S J Res 264) Designate April 28, 1986, as "National Nursing Home Residents Day." Introduced by PRYOR, D-Ark., Feb. 6, 1986. Senate Judiciary reported March 20. Senate passed March 21. House Post Office and Civil Service discharged. House passed April 28. President signed May 8, 1986.

PL 99-294 (HR 1116) Implement certain recommendations made pursuant to PL 98-360, with respect to the Garrison Diversion project in North Dakota. Introduced by DORGAN, D-N.D., Feb. 19, 1985. House

Interior and Insular Affairs reported April 9, 1986 (H Rept 99-525, Part 1). Supplemental report filed April 22 (H Rept 99-525, Part 2). House passed April 23. Senate passed April 28. President signed May 12, 1986.

PL 99-295 (S 1952) Provide for the striking of medals to commemorate the Young Astronaut Program. Introduced by GARN, R-Utah, Dec. 16, 1985. Senate Banking, Housing and Urban Affairs reported March 26, 1986. Senate passed March 27. House Banking, Finance and Urban Affairs discharged. House passed April 28. President signed May 12, 1986.

PL 99-296 (S J Res 187) Designate Patrick Henry's last home and burial place, known as Red Hill, in Virginia, as a national memorial to Patrick Henry. Introduced by WARNER, R-Va., Aug. 1, 1985. Senate Energy and Natural Resources reported Nov. 18 (S Rept 99-183). Senate passed Dec. 3. House Interior and Insular Affairs reported April 28, 1986 (H Rept 99-557). House passed, under suspension of the rules, April 28. President signed May 12, 1986.

PL 99-297 (S J Res 285) Designate May 11-17, 1986, as "National Osteoporosis Awareness Week of 1986." Introduced by GRASSLEY, R-Iowa, Feb. 28, 1986. Senate Judiciary reported March 6. Senate passed March 11. House Post Office and Civil Service discharged. House passed April 30. President signed May 12, 1986.

PL 99-298 (S 2308) Authorize the president to award congressional gold medals to Anatoly and Avital Shcharansky in recognition of their dedication to human rights, and authorize the secretary of the Treasury to sell bronze duplicates of those medals. Introduced by LAUTENBERG, D-N.J., April 15, 1986. Senate Banking, Housing and Urban Affairs reported May 8. Senate passed May 8. House passed May 12. President signed May 13, 1986.

PL 99-299 (S J Res 293) Designate May 1986 as "National Child Safety Month." Introduced by HAWKINS, R-Fla., March 11, 1986. Senate Judiciary reported April 17. Senate passed April 22. House Post Office and Civil Service discharged. House passed April 30. President signed May 13, 1986.

PL 99-300 (HR 4022) Authorize the secretary of the interior to release restrictions on certain property located in Calcasieu Parish, La. Introduced by BREAUX, D-La., Jan. 21, 1986. House Interior and Insular Affairs reported April 16 (H Rept 99-540). House passed April 21. Senate passed May 2. President signed May 14, 1986.

PL 99-301 (S J Res 281) Designate May 11-17, 1986, as "Senior Center Week." Introduced by NUNN, D-Ga., Feb. 27, 1986. Senate Judiciary reported April 10. Senate passed April 11. House Post Office and Civil Service discharged. House passed May 7. President signed May 14, 1986.

PL 99-302 (S J Res 284) Designate May 1986 as "Better Hearing and Speech Month." Introduced by METZENBAUM, D-Ohio, Feb. 28, 1986. Senate Judiciary reported April 10. Senate passed April 11. House Post Office and Civil Service discharged. House passed April 30. President signed May 14, 1986.

PL 99-303 (S 1818) Prevent the sexual molestation of children in Indian country. Introduced by DENTON, R-Ala., Nov. 1, 1985. Senate Judiciary reported Nov. 26 (S Rept 99-202). Senate passed Dec. 5. House passed, amended, April 28, 1986. Senate agreed to House amendments May 6. President signed May 15, 1986.

PL 99-304 (S J Res 289) Designate 1988 as the "Year of New Sweden" and recognize the New Sweden '88 American Committee. Introduced by ROTH, R-Del., March 6, 1986. Senate Judiciary reported April 17. Senate passed April 22. House Post Office and Civil Service discharged. House passed April 30. President signed May 15, 1986.

PL 99-305 (S J Res 288) Designate May 1986 as "National Birds of Prey Month." Introduced by McCLURE, R-Idaho, March 5, 1986. Senate Judiciary reported April 17. Senate passed April 22. House Post Office and Civil Service discharged. House passed May 7. President signed May 19, 1986.

PL 99-306 (S J Res 324) Designate the week beginning May 18, 1986, as "National Digestive Diseases Awareness Week." Introduced by GORE, D-Tenn., April 15, 1986. Senate Judiciary reported April 17. Senate passed April 22. House Post Office and Civil Service discharged. House passed May 7. President signed May 19, 1986.

PL 99-307 (HR 739) Related to the documentation of the vessel *Marilyn* to be employed in the coastwise trade. Introduced by HOLT, R-Md., Jan. 24, 1985. House Merchant Marine and Fisheries reported Nov. 20 (H Rept 99-389). House passed Dec. 3. Senate Commerce, Science and Transportation reported April 22, 1986 (S Rept 99-284). Senate passed, amended, April 24. House agreed to Senate amendments May 1. President signed May 19, 1986.

PL 99-308 (S 49) Protect firearms owners' constitutional rights, civil liberties and rights to privacy. Introduced by DOLE, R-Kan., Jan. 3, 1985. Senate passed July 9. House Judiciary discharged. House passed, amended, April 10, 1986. Senate agreed to House amendments May 6. President signed May 19, 1986.

PL 99-309 (S J Res 337) Designate May 18-24, 1986, as "Just Say No to Drugs Week." Introduced by DOLE, R-Kan., April 30, 1986. Senate Judiciary reported May 1. Senate passed May 5. House Post Office and Civil Service discharged. House passed May 15. President signed May 20, 1986.

PL 99-310 (H J Res 427) Designate the week beginning May 11, 1986, as "National Asthma and Allergy Awareness Week." Introduced by O'BRIEN, R-Ill., Oct. 23, 1985. House Post Office and Civil Service discharged. House passed April 30, 1986. Senate Judiciary discharged. Senate passed May 15. President signed May 20, 1986.

PL 99-311 (HR 1207) Award a special gold medal to the family of Harry Chapin. Introduced by DORGAN, D-N.D., Feb. 21, 1985. House passed, under suspension of the rules, May 5, 1986. Senate Banking, Housing and Urban Affairs reported May 8. Senate passed May 8. President signed May 20, 1986.

PL 99-312 (S J Res 247) Designate the week of June 1-7, 1986, as "National Theater Week." Introduced by McCLURE, R-Idaho, Dec. 12, 1985. Senate Judiciary reported Jan. 30, 1986. Senate passed Feb. 4. House Post Office and Civil Service discharged. House passed May 7. President signed May 20, 1986.

PL 99-313 (S J Res 251) Designate the week of May 11-17, 1986, as "National Science Week, 1986." Introduced by HATCH, R-Utah, Dec. 16, 1985. Senate Judiciary reported March 20, 1986. Senate passed March 21. House Post Office and Civil Service discharged. House passed May 13. President signed May 20, 1986.

PL 99-314 (S J Res 323) Designate May 21, 1986, as "National Andrei Sakharov Day." Introduced by D'AMATO, R-N.Y., April 15, 1986. Senate Judiciary discharged. Senate passed April 29. House passed May 12. President signed May 20, 1986.

PL 99-315 (HR 4767) Deauthorize the project for improvements at Racine Harbor, Wis. Introduced by HOWARD, D-N.J., May 7, 1986. House Public Works and Transportation discharged. House passed May 8. Senate passed May 13. President signed May 21, 1986.

PL 99-316 (S J Res 267) Designate the week of May 26-June 1, 1986, as "Older Americans Melanoma/Skin Cancer Detection and Prevention Week." Introduced by HEINZ, R-Pa., Feb. 6, 1986. Senate Judiciary reported March 20. Senate passed March 21. House Post Office and Civil Service discharged. House passed May 7. President signed May 21, 1986.

PL 99-317 (H J Res 234) Designate the week of May 18-24, 1986, as "National Food Bank Week." Introduced by HALL, D-Ohio, April 4, 1985. House Post Office and Civil Service discharged. House passed April 14, 1986. Senate Judiciary discharged. Senate passed May 15. President signed May 23, 1986.

PL 99-318 (S 8) Grant a federal charter to the Vietnam Veterans of America Inc. Introduced by BYRD, D-W.Va., Jan. 3, 1985. Senate Judiciary reported March 26, 1986 (S Rept 99-268). Senate passed April 9. House Judiciary discharged. House passed May 12. President signed May 23, 1986.

PL 99-319 (S 974) Provide for protection and advocacy for mentally ill persons. Introduced by WEICKER, R-Conn., April 23, 1985. Senate Labor and Human Resources reported July 25 (S Rept 99-109). Senate passed July 31. House Energy and Commerce discharged. House passed, amended, Jan. 30, 1986. House agreed to conference report May 13 (H Rept 99-576). Senate agreed to conference report May 14. President signed May 23, 1986.

PL 99-320 (S 2329) Make technical corrections in the higher education title of the Consolidated Omnibus Budget Reconciliation Act of 1985. Introduced by QUAYLE, R-Ind., April 17, 1986. Senate Labor and Human Resources discharged. Senate passed April 24. House passed May 13. President signed May 23, 1986.

PL 99-321 (S J Res 246) Designate May 25, 1986, as "Hands Across America Day," for the purpose of helping people to help themselves and commending United Support of Artists for Africa and all participants for their efforts toward combating domestic hunger with a 4,000-mile human chain from coast to coast. Introduced by DIXON, D-Ill., Dec. 12, 1985. Senate Judiciary reported March 3, 1986. Senate passed March 4. House passed May 15. President signed May 23, 1986.

PL 99-322 (S 2416) Revise further the limitation applicable to chapter 37 of title 38, U.S. Code, for fiscal year 1986, for the purpose of implementing any order issued by the president for such fiscal year under any law providing for the sequestration of new loan guarantee commitments. Introduced by SIMPSON, R-Wyo., May 6, 1986. Senate passed May 6. House passed, amended, under suspension of the rules, May 21. Senate agreed to House amendments May 21. President signed May 23, 1986.

PL 99-323 (HR 1349) Reduce the costs of operating presidential libraries. Introduced by ENGLISH, D-Okla., Feb. 28, 1985. House Government Operations reported May 15 (H Rept 99-125). House passed, under suspension of the rules, June 4. Senate Governmental Affairs reported March 7, 1986 (S Rept 99-257). Senate passed, amended, March 21. House agreed to Senate amendment May 13. President signed May 27, 1986.

PL 99-324 (S J Res 266) Authorize and request the president to designate June 1986 as "Youth Suicide Prevention Month." Introduced by DENTON, R-Ala., Feb. 6, 1986. Senate Judiciary reported Feb. 20. Senate passed Feb. 27. House Post Office and Civil Service discharged. House passed May 15. President signed May 27, 1986.

PL 99-325 (HR 4382) Require the Architect of the Capitol to place a plaque at the original site of Providence Hospital. Introduced by BLILEY, R-Va., March 12, 1986. House Public Works and Transportation discharged. House passed May 13. Senate passed May 14. President signed May 28, 1986.

PL 99-326 (H J Res 492) Designate the week beginning June 1, 1986, as "National Neighborhood Housing Services Week." Introduced by MINETA, D-Calif., Dec. 17, 1985. House Post Office and Civil Service discharged. House passed May 7, 1986. Senate Judiciary discharged. Senate passed May 15. President signed May 28, 1986.

PL 99-327 (H J Res 526) Designate the week of May 25-31, 1986, as "Critical Care Week." Introduced by DANNEMEYER, R-Calif., Feb. 19, 1986. House Post Office and Civil Service discharged. House passed May 7. Senate Judiciary discharged. Senate passed May 21. President signed May 28, 1986.

PL 99-328 (H J Res 613) Allow qualified persons representing all the states to be naturalized on Ellis Island on July 3 or 4, 1986. Introduced by RODINO, D-N.J., April 29, 1986. House Judiciary reported May 7 (H Rept 99-587). House passed, under suspension of the rules, May 12. Senate passed May 15. President signed May 28, 1986.

PL 99-329 (S J Res 271) Designate "Baltic Freedom Day." Introduced by RIEGLE, D-Mich., Feb. 6, 1986. Senate Judiciary reported Feb. 20. Senate passed Feb. 27. House Foreign Affairs discharged. House Post Office and Civil Service discharged. House passed May 15. President signed May 28, 1986.

PL 99-330 (S 173) Settle and adjust the claim of the Tehran American School for $13,333.94. Introduced by STAFFORD, R-Vt., Jan. 3, 1985. Senate Judiciary reported Nov. 7 (S Rept 99-177). Senate passed Nov. 21. House Judiciary reported May 7, 1986 (H Rept 99-582). House passed May 20. President signed May 29, 1986.

PL 99-331 (S 2460) Extend until June 30, 1986, the date on which certain limitations become effective with respect to obligations that may be made from the military personnel accounts of the Department of Defense for fiscal year 1986. Introduced by WILSON, R-Calif., May 15, 1986. Senate passed May 15. House passed May 22. President signed May 31, 1986.

PL 99-332 (H J Res 636) Designate June 26, 1986, as "National Interstate Highway Day." Introduced by HOWARD, D-N.J., May 15, 1986. House passed May 15. Senate Judiciary discharged. Senate passed May 21. President signed June 5, 1986.

PL 99-333 (S J Res 344) Designate the week beginning June 8, 1986, as "National Children's Accident Prevention Week." Introduced by THURMOND, R-S.C., May 14, 1986. Senate Judiciary discharged. Senate passed May 15. House passed May 22. President signed June 5, 1986.

PL 99-334 (S 2179) Amend the Communications Act of 1934 to provide for reduction in the term of office of members of the Federal Communications Commission. Introduced by GOLDWATER, R-Ariz., March 11, 1986. Senate Commerce, Science and Transportation reported March 21 (S Rept 99-263). Senate passed March 27. House passed May 22. President signed June 6, 1986.

PL 99-335 (HR 2672) Amend title 5, U.S. Code, to establish a new retirement and disability plan for federal employees, postal employees and members of Congress. Introduced by GUARINI, D-N.J., June 5, 1985. House Post Office and Civil Service discharged. House passed July 8. Senate Governmental Affairs reported Oct. 30. Senate passed, amended, Nov. 7. Senate agreed to conference report May 20, 1986 (S Rept 99-302). House agreed to conference report May 22 (H Rept 99-606). President signed June 6, 1986.

PL 99-336 (HR 3570) Amend title 28, U.S. Code, to reform and improve the federal justice and judges survivors' annuities program. Introduced by KASTENMEIER, D-Wis., Oct. 16, 1985. House Judiciary reported Dec. 6 (H Rept 99-423, Part 1). House passed, under suspension of the rules, Dec. 16. Senate Judiciary reported March 21, 1986. Senate passed, amended, April 11. House agreed to Senate amendments May 22. President signed June 19, 1986.

PL 99-337 (H J Res 131) Designate the week of June 16-22, 1986, as "National Safety in the Work Place Week." Introduced by HYDE, R-Ill., Feb. 6, 1985. House Post Office and Civil Service discharged. House passed June 11, 1986. Senate Judiciary discharged. Senate passed June 13. President signed June 19, 1986.

PL 99-338 (H J Res 382) Authorize the continued use of certain lands within the Sequoia National Park by portions of an existing hydroelectric project. Introduced by PASHAYAN, R-Calif., Sept. 11, 1985. House Interior and Insular Affairs reported Nov. 13 (H Rept 99-370). House passed Nov. 14. Senate Energy and Natural Resources reported Feb. 6, 1986 (S Rept 99-237). Senate passed, amended, May 21. House agreed to Senate amendments June 9. President signed June 19, 1986.

PL 99-339 (S 124) Authorize funds for fiscal years 1986-90 for programs of the Safe Drinking Water Act, including public water systems and protection of underground sources of drinking water. Introduced by DURENBERGER, R-Minn., Jan. 3, 1985. Senate Environment and Public Works reported May 15 (S Rept 99-56). Senate passed May 16. House passed, amended, June 17. House agreed to conference report May 13, 1986 (H Rept 99-575). Senate agreed to conference report May 21. President signed June 19, 1986.

PL 99-340 (S J Res 220) Provide for the designation of Sept. 19, 1986, as "National P.O.W./M.I.A. Recognition Day." Introduced by MATTINGLY, R-Ga., Oct. 21, 1985. Senate Judiciary reported Dec. 5. Senate passed Dec. 6. House Post Office and Civil Service discharged. House passed June 11, 1986. President signed June 19, 1986.

PL 99-341 (S J Res 310) Proclaim the week of June 15-21, 1986, as "National Agricultural Export Week." Introduced by HELMS, R-N.C., March 26, 1986. Senate Judiciary reported April 17. Senate passed April 22. House Post Office and Civil Service discharged. House passed June 11. President signed June 19, 1986.

PL 99-342 (S J Res 347) Designate the week of May 19-24, 1986, as "National Homelessness Awareness Week." Introduced by LEVIN, D-Mich., May 15, 1986. Senate Judiciary discharged. Senate passed May 21. House Post Office and Civil Service discharged. House passed, amended, May 22. Senate agreed to House amendments June 10. President signed June 19, 1986.

PL 99-343 (H J Res 479) Designate Oct. 8, 1986, as "National Firefighters Day." Introduced by ASPIN, D-Wis., Dec. 12, 1985. House Post Office and Civil Service discharged. House passed May 22, 1986. Senate Judiciary reported June 5. Senate passed June 10. President signed June 23, 1986.

PL 99-344 (S J Res 321) Designate October 1986 as "National Down's Syndrome Month." Introduced by LUGAR, R-Ind., April 14, 1986. Senate Judiciary reported April 17. Senate passed April 22. House Post Office and Civil Service discharged. House passed June 11. President signed June 23, 1986.

PL 99-345 (H J Res 652) Provide for the temporary extension of certain programs relating to housing and community development. Introduced by GONZALEZ, D-Texas, June 11, 1986. House Banking, Finance and Urban Affairs discharged. House passed June 12. Senate passed, amended, June 18. House agreed to Senate amendment with an amendment June 19. Senate agreed to House amendment with an amendment June 23. House agreed to Senate amendment June 24. President signed June 24, 1986.

PL 99-346 (S 1106) Provide for the use and distribution of funds appropriated in satisfaction of judgments awarded to the Saginaw Chippewa Tribe of Michigan in dockets numbered 57, 59 and 13E of the Indian Claims Commission and docket numbered 13F of the U.S. Claims Court. Introduced by RIEGLE, D-Mich., May 8, 1985. Senate Select Indian Affairs reported July 30 (S Rept 99-119). Senate passed July 31. House Interior and Insular Affairs reported March 20, 1986 (H Rept 99-502). House passed, amended, under suspension of the rules, June 10. Senate agreed to House amendment June 16. President signed June 30, 1986.

PL 99-347 (S J Res 346) Designate June 21, 1986, as "National Save American Industry and Jobs Day." Introduced by METZENBAUM, D-Ohio, May 15, 1986. Senate Judiciary reported June 5. Senate passed June 10. House Post Office and Civil Service discharged. House passed June 19. President signed June 30, 1986.

PL 99-348 (HR 4420) Establish a revised retirement system for new members of the uniformed services, and revise the method of determining cost-of-living adjustments under the revised retirement system. Introduced by ASPIN, D-Wis., March 17, 1986. House Armed Services reported April 8 (H Rept 99-513). House passed April 22. Senate Armed Services discharged. Senate passed, amended, May 15. Senate agreed to conference report June 25 (H Rept 99-659). House agreed to conference report June 26. President signed July 1, 1986.

PL 99-349 (HR 4515) Make urgent supplemental appropriations for fiscal year 1986. Introduced by WHITTEN, D-Miss., March 25, 1986. House Appropriations reported March 25 (H Rept 99-510). House passed May 8. Senate Appropriations reported May 15 (S Rept 99-301). Senate passed, amended, June 6. House agreed to conference report June 24 (H Rept 99-649). House agreed to certain Senate amendments, insisted on its disagreement to certain Senate amendments, and agreed to certain Senate amendments with amendments, June 24. Senate agreed to conference report June 26. Senate agreed to certain House amendments to Senate amendments, receded from certain amendments, and agreed to a House amendment to a Senate amendment, with an amendment, June 26. House disagreed to Senate amendment to House amendment to Senate amendment June 26. Senate receded from its amendment to House amendment to Senate amendment June 26. President signed July 2, 1986.

PL 99-350 (H J Res 297) Designate the week beginning July 27, 1986, as "National Nuclear Medicine Week." Introduced by SCHEUER, D-N.Y., May 23, 1985. House Post Office and Civil Service discharged.

House passed April 30, 1986. Senate Judiciary reported June 19. Senate passed June 20. President signed July 2, 1986.

PL 99-351 (H J Res 429) Designate July 2, 1986, as "National Literacy Day." Introduced by FLORIO, D-N.J., Oct. 24, 1985. House Post Office and Civil Service discharged. House passed June 19, 1986. Senate passed June 26. President signed July 2, 1986.

PL 99-352 (H J Res 664) Designate July 3, 1986, as "Let Freedom Ring Day," and request the president to issue a proclamation encouraging the people of the United States to ring bells on such day immediately following the relighting of the torch of the Statue of Liberty. Introduced by MARTIN, R-Ill., June 19, 1986. House Post Office and Civil Service discharged. House passed June 26. Senate passed June 26. President signed July 2, 1986.

PL 99-353 (S J Res 290) Designate July 4, 1986, as "National Immigrant Day." Introduced by DeCONCINI, D-Ariz., March 7, 1986. Senate Judiciary reported June 12. Senate passed June 16. House Post Office and Civil Service discharged. House passed June 19. President signed July 2, 1986.

PL 99-354 (S J Res 365) Reaffirm congressional support for the valiant struggle of the Afghan people, and welcome the delegation of the Islamic Unity of Afghan Mujahideen, led by spokesman Burhanuddin Rabbani on the occasion of his first official visit to the United States. Introduced by HUMPHREY, R-N.H., June 18, 1986. Senate passed June 18. House Foreign Affairs discharged. House passed June 24. President signed July 2, 1986.

PL 99-355 (S J Res 188) Designate July 6, 1986, as "National Air Traffic Control Day." Introduced by KASSEBAUM, R-Kan., Aug. 1, 1985. Senate Judiciary reported April 10, 1986. Senate passed April 11. House Post Office and Civil Service discharged. House passed June 19. President signed July 3, 1986.

PL 99-356 (S J Res 350) Designate 1987 as the "National Year of the Americas." Introduced by LUGAR, R-Ind., May 19, 1986. Senate Judiciary reported June 5. Senate passed June 10. House Post Office and Civil Service discharged. House passed June 19. President signed July 3, 1986.

PL 99-357 (HR 4841) Amend the Carl D. Perkins Vocational Education Act with respect to state allotments under the act. Introduced by PERKINS, D-Ky., May 15, 1986. House Education and Labor reported June 16 (H Rept 99-641). House passed, under suspension of the rules, June 17. Senate passed June 25. President signed July 8, 1986.

PL 99-358 (S 1625) Authorize the conveyance of 470 acres in Nevada to the University of Nevada for use as a research and development center. Introduced by LAXALT, R-Nev., Sept. 11, 1985. Senate Energy and Natural Resources reported March 27, 1986 (S Rept 99-277). Senate passed May 2. House Interior and Insular Affairs reported June 25 (H Rept 99-658). House passed June 26. President signed July 8, 1986.

PL 99-359 (S 2180) Authorize funds for activities under the Federal Fire Prevention and Control Act of 1974, and change the annual start of daylight-saving time from the last Sunday in April to the first Sunday in April. Introduced by GORTON, R-Wash., March 11, 1986. Senate Commerce, Science and Transportation reported March 26 (S Rept 99-267). Senate passed May 20. House passed June 24. President signed July 8, 1986.

PL 99-360 (S 2414) Amend title 18, U.S. Code, relating to the interstate transportation of firearms. Introduced by THURMOND, R-S.C., May 6, 1986. Senate passed May 6. House passed June 24. President signed July 8, 1986.

PL 99-361 (HR 237) Amend the Fair Debt Collection Practices Act, to require that any attorney who collects debts on behalf of a client be subject to the provisions of such act. Introduced by ANNUNZIO, D-Ill., Jan. 3, 1985. House Banking, Finance and Urban Affairs reported Nov. 26 (H Rept 99-405). House passed, under suspension of the rules, Dec. 2. Senate Banking, Housing and Urban Affairs reported May 21, 1986. Senate passed June 26. President signed July 9, 1986.

PL 99-362 (HR 5036) Make technical corrections to the National Foundation on the Arts and the Humanities Act of 1965. Introduced by WILLIAMS, D-Mont., June 17, 1986. House Education and Labor discharged. House passed June 17. Senate passed, amended, June 25. House agreed to Senate amendment June 26. President signed July 9, 1986.

PL 99-363 (HR 4801) Amend section 994 of title 28, U.S. Code, to clarify certain duties of the U.S. Sentencing Commission. Introduced by RODINO, D-N.J., May 13, 1986. House Judiciary reported May 28 (H Rept 99-614). House passed, under suspension of the rules, June 3. Senate Judiciary discharged. Senate passed June 26. President signed July 11, 1986.

PL 99-364 (S J Res 274) Designate Aug. 1-3, 1986, as "National Family Reunion Weekend." Introduced by GRASSLEY, R-Iowa, Feb. 19, 1986. Senate Judiciary reported June 19. Senate passed June 20. House Post Office and Civil Service discharged. House passed July 16. President signed July 29, 1986.

PL 99-365 (S J Res 279) Designate October 1986 as "Lupus Awareness Month." Introduced by GORE, D-Tenn., Feb. 24, 1986. Senate Judiciary reported March 20. Senate passed March 21. House Post Office and Civil Service discharged. House passed July 16. President signed July 29, 1986.

PL 99-366 (H J Res 672) Ratify and affirm the president's sequestration order based on the Jan. 15, 1986, report of the director of the Office of Management and Budget and director of the Congressional Budget Office with respect to fiscal year 1986. Introduced by WRIGHT, D-Texas, July 17, 1986. House passed July 17. Senate passed July 17. President signed July 31, 1986.

PL 99-367 (S 1068) Eliminate unnecessary paperwork and reporting requirements contained in section 15(1) of the Outer Continental Shelf Lands Act, and sections 601 and 606 of the Outer Continental Shelf Lands Act Amendments of 1978. Introduced by JOHNSTON, D-La., May 3, 1985. Senate Energy and Natural Resources reported June 14 (S Rept 99-84). Senate passed July 9. House Merchant Marine and Fisheries reported April 29, 1986 (H Rept 99-558, Part 1). House passed, under suspension of the rules, July 21. President signed July 31, 1986.

PL 99-368 (HR 4409) Authorize funds for fiscal 1987 for the operation and maintenance of the Panama Canal. Introduced by LOWRY, D-Wash., March 13, 1986. House Merchant Marine and Fisheries reported April 16 (H Rept 99-536). House passed May 1. Senate Armed Services reported June 25. Senate passed July 17. President signed Aug. 1, 1986.

PL 99-369 (HR 4985) Authorize the distribution within the United States of the U.S. Information Agency film entitled "The March." Introduced by FRANK, D-Mass., June 11, 1986. House passed, under suspension of the rules, July 15. Senate passed July 17. President signed Aug. 1, 1986.

PL 99-370 (HR 3511) Amend title 18, U.S. Code, with respect to certain bribery and related offenses. Introduced by CONYERS, D-Mich., Oct. 7, 1985. House Judiciary reported Oct. 28 (H Rept 99-335). House passed, under suspension of the rules, Oct. 29. Senate Judiciary reported Dec. 13. Senate passed, amended, Feb. 4, 1986. House agreed to Senate amendments with an amendment June 24. Senate agreed to House amendment to Senate amendment with an amendment June 24. House agreed to Senate amendment June 26. President signed Aug. 4, 1986.

PL 99-371 (S 1874) Authorize quality educational programs for deaf individuals, foster improved educational programs for deaf individuals throughout the United States, and re-enact and codify certain provisions of law relating to the education of the deaf. Introduced by WEICKER, R-Conn., Nov. 21, 1985. Senate Labor and Human Resources reported April 29, 1986 (S Rept 99-290). Senate passed May 6. House passed, amended, June 26. Senate agreed to House amendment July 17. President signed Aug. 4, 1986.

PL 99-372 (S 415) Amend the Education of the Handicapped Act, authorize the award of reasonable attorneys' fees to certain prevailing parties, and clarify the effect of the Education of the Handicapped Act on rights, procedures and remedies under other laws relating to the prohibition on discrimination. Introduced by WEICKER, R-Conn., Feb. 6, 1985. Senate Labor and Human Resources reported July 25 (S Rept 99-112). Senate passed July 30. House Education and Labor discharged. House passed, amended, Nov. 12. Senate agreed to conference report July 17, 1986 (H Rept 99-687). House agreed to conference report July 24. President signed Aug. 5, 1986.

PL 99-373 (H J Res 623) Authorize the designation of a calendar week in 1986 and 1987 as "National Infection Control Week." Introduced by WAXMAN, D-Calif., May 5, 1986. House Post Office and Civil Service discharged. House passed July 16. Senate passed July 23. President signed Aug. 6, 1986.

PL 99-374 (S J Res 371) Designate Aug. 1, 1986, as "Helsinki Human Rights Day." Introduced by DeCONCINI, D-Ariz., June 26, 1986. Senate Judiciary reported July 17. Senate passed July 23. House Post Office and Civil Service discharged. House Foreign Affairs discharged. House passed July 31. President signed Aug. 6, 1986.

PL 99-375 (HR 1406) Authorize appropriations for non-game fish and wildlife conservation during fiscal years 1986, 1987 and 1988. Introduced by BREAUX, D-La., March 5, 1985. House Merchant Marine and Fisheries reported May 9 (H Rept 99-75). House passed, under suspension of the rules, July 29. Senate passed July 25, 1986. President signed Aug. 7, 1986.

PL 99-376 (HR 4434) Amend the act entitled "An act granting a charter to the General Federation of Women's Clubs." Introduced by GLICKMAN, D-Kan., March 18, 1986. House Judiciary reported May 12 (H Rept 99-595). House passed, under suspension of the rules, May 19. Senate Judiciary discharged. Senate passed July 25. President signed Aug. 7, 1986.

PL 99-377 (HR 1904) Provide for the use and distribution of funds appropriated in satisfaction of judgments awarded to the Chippewas of the Mississippi in Docket No. 18-S before the Indian Claims Commission. Introduced by OBERSTAR, D-Minn., April 2, 1985. House Interior and Insular Affairs reported Sept. 12 (H Rept 99-269). House passed Oct. 7. Senate Select Indian Affairs reported May 21, 1986 (S Rept 99-309). Senate passed July 25. President signed Aug. 8, 1986.

PL 99-378 (S J Res 356) Recognize and support the efforts of the U.S. Committee for the Battle of Normandy Museum to encourage American awareness and participation in development of a memorial to the Battle of Normandy. Introduced by MATHIAS, R-Md., June 5, 1986. Senate Judiciary reported July 17. Senate passed July 23. House passed July 28. President signed Aug. 8, 1986.

PL 99-379 (S J Res 256) Designate Aug. 12, 1986, as "National Neighborhood Crime Watch Day." Introduced by TRIBLE, R-Va., Jan. 22, 1986. Senate Judiciary reported June 19. Senate passed June 20. House Post Office and Civil Service discharged. House passed Aug. 8. President signed Aug. 12, 1986.

PL 99-380 (HR 1740) Direct the secretary of the interior to release a reversionary interest in certain lands in Orange County, Fla., which were previously conveyed to Orange County, Fla. Introduced by NELSON, D-Fla., March 26, 1985. House Interior and Insular Affairs reported Oct. 30 (H Rept 99-347). House passed Nov. 4. Senate Energy and Natural Resources reported July 25, 1986 (S Rept 99-343). Senate passed Aug. 2. President signed Aug. 14, 1986.

PL 99-381 (HR 1795) Exempt certain lands in Mississippi from a restriction set forth in the act of April 21, 1806. Introduced by DOWDY, D-Miss., March 28, 1985. House Interior and Insular Affairs reported Oct. 30 (H Rept 99-346). House passed Nov. 4. Senate Energy and Natural Resources reported July 25, 1986 (S Rept 99-344). Senate passed Aug. 2. President signed Aug. 14, 1986.

PL 99-382 (S 1073) Amend the Stevenson-Wydler Technology Act of 1980 to improve the availability of Japanese science and engineering literature in the United States. Introduced by BAUCUS, D-Mont., May 6, 1985. Senate Commerce, Science and Transportation reported Nov. 4 (S Rept 99-175). Senate passed Nov. 23. House Science and Technology reported June 4, 1986 (H Rept 99-618). House passed, amended, under suspension of the rules, June 23. Senate agreed to House amendments Aug. 2. President signed Aug. 14, 1986.

PL 99-383 (HR 4184) Authorize funds for the National Science Foundation for fiscal year 1987. Introduced by FUQUA, D-Fla., Feb. 19, 1986. House Science and Technology reported June 4 (H Rept 99-619). House passed June 26. Senate passed, amended, Aug. 2. House agreed to Senate amendment Aug. 6. President signed Aug. 21, 1986.

PL 99-384 (HR 5395) Increase the statutory limit on the public debt. Introduced by ROSTENKOWSKI, D-Ill., Aug. 12, 1986. House Ways and Means reported Aug. 13 (H Rept 99-789). House passed Aug. 14. Senate passed, amended, Aug. 16. House agreed to a Senate amendment and disagreed to a Senate amendment Aug. 16. Senate receded from its amendment Aug. 16. President signed Aug. 21, 1986.

PL 99-385 (H J Res 683) Provide for a temporary prohibition of strikes or lockouts with respect to the Maine Central Railroad Co. and Portland Terminal Co. labor-management dispute. Introduced by FLORIO, D-N.J., July 24, 1986. House Energy and Commerce reported Aug. 12 (H Rept 99-784). House passed, under suspension of the rules, Aug. 12. Senate passed Aug. 12. President signed Aug. 21, 1986.

PL 99-386 (S 992) Discontinue or amend certain requirements for agency reports to Congress. Introduced by COHEN, R-Maine, April 24, 1985. Senate Governmental Affairs reported Dec. 9 (S Rept 99-211). Senate passed March 14, 1986. House Government Operations discharged. House passed, amended, July 28. Senate agreed to House amendment Aug. 9. President signed Aug. 22, 1986.

PL 99-387 (HR 850) Modify the boundary of the Humboldt National Forest in Nevada. Introduced by VUCANOVICH, R-Nev., Jan. 30, 1985. House Interior and Insular Affairs reported Nov. 20 (H Rept 99-384). House passed Dec. 9. Senate Energy and Natural Resources reported Aug. 1, 1986 (S Rept 99-359). Senate passed Aug. 11. President signed Aug. 23, 1986.

PL 99-388 (HR 1963) Increase the development ceiling at Allegheny Portage Railroad National Historic Site and Johnstown Flood National Memorial in Pennsylvania, and for other purposes, and provide for the preservation and interpretation of the Johnstown Flood Museum in the Cambria County Library Building, Pa. Introduced by MURTHA, D-Pa., April 3, 1985. House Interior and Insular Affairs reported Sept. 30 (H Rept 99-291). House passed, under suspension of the rules, Sept. 30. Senate Energy and Natural Resources reported Aug. 1, 1986 (S Rept 99-363). Senate passed Aug. 11. President signed Aug. 23, 1986.

PL 99-389 (HR 3212) Declare that the United States holds certain lands in trust for the Reno Sparks Indian colony. Introduced by VUCANOVICH, R-Nev., Aug. 1, 1985. House Interior and Insular Affairs reported March 20, 1986 (H Rept 99-501). House passed April 21. Senate Energy and Natural Resources reported Aug. 1 (S Rept 99-364). Senate passed Aug. 11. President signed Aug. 23, 1986.

PL 99-390 (HR 3556) Provide for the exchange of land for the Cape Henry Memorial Site in Fort Story, Va. Introduced by WHITEHURST, R-Va., Oct. 10, 1985. House Interior and Insular Affairs reported Dec. 16 (H Rept 99-442, Part 1). House passed, under suspension of the rules, March 11, 1986. Senate Energy and Natural Resources reported Aug. 1 (S Rept 99-365). Senate passed Aug. 11. President signed Aug. 23, 1986.

PL 99-391 (H J Res 377) Designate Dec. 5, 1986, as "Walt Disney Recognition Day." Introduced by DORNAN, R-Calif., Sept. 9, 1985. House Post Office and Civil Service discharged. House passed Dec. 3. Senate passed, amended, Dec. 6. House agreed to Senate amendments Aug. 8, 1986. President signed Aug. 23, 1986.

PL 99-392 (H J Res 529) Designate the week of Sept. 21-27, 1986, as "Emergency Medical Services Week." Introduced by MANTON, D-N.Y., Feb. 19, 1986. House Post Office and Civil Service discharged. House passed July 16. Senate Judiciary reported July 31. Senate passed Aug. 9. President signed Aug. 23, 1986.

PL 99-393 (H J Res 630) Designate the College of William and Mary as the official U.S. representative to the Tercentenary Celebration of the Glorious Revolution, to be celebrated jointly in the United States, the Netherlands and the United Kingdom. Introduced by BATEMAN, R-Va., May 8, 1986. House passed, under suspension of the rules, July 28. Senate passed Aug. 9. President signed Aug. 23, 1986.

PL 99-394 (H J Res 642) Designate the week beginning May 17, 1987, as "National Tourism Week." Introduced by BONER, D-Tenn., May 22, 1986. House Post Office and Civil Service discharged. House passed July 16. Senate Judiciary reported July 31. Senate passed Aug. 9. President signed Aug. 23, 1986.

PL 99-395 (HR 1343) Authorize the use of funds from rental of floating drydock and other marine equipment to support the National Maritime Museum in San Francisco, Calif. Introduced by BURTON, D-Calif., Feb. 28, 1985. House Interior and Insular Affairs reported June 27 (H Rept 99-183). House passed, under suspension of the rules, July 15. Senate Energy and Natural Resources reported Aug. 1, 1986 (S Rept 99-361). Senate passed, amended, Aug. 11. House agreed to Senate amendments Aug. 14. President signed Aug. 27, 1986.

PL 99-396 (HR 2478) Amend the Revised Organic Act of the Virgin Islands, amend the Covenant to Establish a Commonwealth of the Northern Mariana Islands, amend the Organic Act of Guam, and provide for the governance of the insular areas of the United States. Introduced by de LUGO, D-Virgin Islands, May 14, 1985. House Interior and Insular Affairs reported May 15 (H Rept 99-116). Supplemental report filed May 21 (H Rept 99-116, Part 2). House passed Dec. 3. Senate Energy and Natural Resources reported Feb. 6, 1986 (S Rept 99-236). Senate passed, amended, April 24. House agreed to a Senate amendment, disagreed to a Senate amendment, and agreed to certain Senate amendments with amendments Aug. 1. Senate receded from an amendment and agreed to House amendments to certain Senate amendments Aug. 9. President signed Aug. 27, 1986.

PL 99-397 (HR 3108) Amend title 17, U.S. Code, to clarify the definition of the local service area of a primary transmitter in the case of a low-power television station. Introduced by KASTENMEIER, D-Wis., July 30, 1985. House Judiciary reported June 3, 1986 (H Rept 99-615). House passed, under suspension of the rules, July 28. Senate passed, amended, Aug. 9. House agreed to Senate amendment Aug. 15. President signed Aug. 27, 1986.

PL 99-398 (HR 3554) Provide for the restoration of the federal trust relationship with, and federal services and assistance to, the Klamath Tribe of Indians and individual members thereof consisting of the Klamath and Modoc tribes and the Yahooskin Band of Snake Indians. Introduced by ROBERT F. SMITH, R-Ore., Oct. 10, 1985. House Interior and Insular Affairs reported June 11, 1986 (H Rept 99-630). House passed, under suspension of the rules, June 16. Senate Select Indian Affairs discharged. Senate passed Aug. 15. President signed Aug. 27, 1986.

PL 99-399 (HR 4151) Provide enhanced diplomatic security and combat international terrorism. Introduced by MICA, D-Fla., Feb. 6, 1986. House Foreign Affairs reported March 12 (H Rept 99-494). House passed March 18. Senate Foreign Relations reported May 20 (S Rept 99-304). Senate passed, amended, June 25. House agreed to conference report Aug. 12 (H Rept 99-783). Senate agreed to conference report Aug. 12. President signed Aug. 27, 1986.

PL 99-400 (HR 5371) Extend until Sept. 15, 1986, the emergency acquisition and net worth guarantee provisions of the Garn-St Germain Depository Institutions Act of 1982. Introduced by St GERMAIN, D-R.I., Aug. 8, 1986. House Banking, Finance and Urban Affairs discharged. House passed Aug. 13. Senate passed Aug. 15. President signed Aug. 27, 1986.

PL 99-401 (S 140) Amend the Child Abuse Amendments of 1984 to encourage states to enact child protection reforms designed to improve legal and administrative proceedings regarding the investigation and prosecution of sexual child abuse cases. Introduced by HAWKINS, R-Fla., Jan. 3, 1985. Senate Labor and Human Resources reported July 31 (S Rept 99-123). Senate passed Aug. 1. House passed, amended, under suspension of the rules, Aug. 4, 1986. Senate agreed to House amendments Aug. 12. President signed Aug. 27, 1986.

PL 99-402 (S 1888) Provide for a program of cleanup and maintenance on federal lands. Introduced by BUMPERS, D-Ark., Dec. 2, 1985. Senate Energy and Natural Resources reported Aug. 1, 1986 (S Rept 99-355). Senate passed Aug. 11. House Interior and Insular Affairs discharged. House passed Aug. 15. President signed Aug. 27, 1986.

PL 99-403 (S J Res 249) Proclaim Oct. 23, 1986, as "A Time of Remembrance" for all victims of terrorism throughout the world. Introduced by DENTON, R-Ala., Dec. 13, 1985. Senate Judiciary reported Jan. 30, 1986. Senate passed Feb. 4. House Post Office and Civil Service discharged. House passed Aug. 13. President signed Aug. 27, 1986.

PL 99-404 (S J Res 298) Designate the week of Oct. 5-11, 1986, as "Mental Illness Awareness Week." Introduced by QUAYLE, R-Ind., March 18, 1986. Senate Judiciary reported April 17. Senate passed April 22. House Post Office and Civil Service discharged. House passed Aug. 13. President signed Aug. 27, 1986.

PL 99-405 (S J Res 338) Designate Nov. 18, 1986, as "National Community Education Day." Introduced by RIEGLE, D-Mich., May 1, 1986. Senate Judiciary reported July 31. Senate passed Aug. 9. House Post Office and Civil Service discharged. House passed Aug. 13. President signed Aug. 27, 1986.

PL 99-406 (S J Res 358) Designate September 1986 as "Adult Literacy Awareness Month." Introduced by HEINZ, R-Pa., June 10, 1986. Senate Judiciary reported July 31. Senate passed Aug. 9. House Post Office and Civil Service discharged. House passed Aug. 13. President signed Aug. 27, 1986.

PL 99-407 (S J Res 386) Designate Oct. 6, 1986, as "National Drug Abuse Education Day." Introduced by DODD, D-Conn., Aug. 5, 1986. Senate Judiciary reported Aug. 7. Senate passed Aug. 9. House Post Office and Civil Service discharged. House passed Aug. 13. President signed Aug. 27, 1986.

PL 99-408 (HR 3132) Amend chapter 44, title 18, U.S. Code, to regulate the manufacture, importation and sale of armor-piercing ammunition. Introduced by BIAGGI, D-N.Y., July 31, 1985. House Judiciary reported Nov. 6 (H Rept 99-360). House passed, under suspension of the rules, Dec. 17. Senate passed, amended, March 6, 1986. House agreed to Senate amendments with amendments Aug. 11. Senate agreed to House amendments Aug. 13. President signed Aug. 28, 1986.

PL 99-409 (HR 4331) Authorize the secretary of agriculture to make grants for the purpose of establishing institutes of rural technology development. Introduced by WATKINS, D-Okla., March 6, 1986. House passed March 6. Senate Agriculture, Nutrition and Forestry reported Aug. 12. Senate passed Aug. 16. President signed Aug. 28, 1986.

PL 99-410 (HR 4393) Consolidate and improve provisions of law relating to absentee registration and voting in elections for federal office by members of uniformed services and persons who reside overseas. Introduced by SWIFT, D-Wash., March 12, 1986. House Committee on House Administration reported Aug. 7 (H Rept 99-765). House passed Aug. 12. Senate passed Aug. 16. President signed Aug. 28, 1986.

PL 99-411 (H J Res 713) Make a repayable advance to the Hazardous Substance Response Trust Fund. Introduced by BOLAND, D-Mass., Aug. 15, 1986. House passed Aug. 15. Senate passed Aug. 15. President signed Aug. 28, 1986.

PL 99-412 (S 410) Repeal provisions of the National Energy Conservation Policy Act that require electric and gas utilities to offer comprehensive site-specific audit services to those customers who are owners of multifamily dwellings and commercial buildings. Introduced by JOHNSTON, D-La., Feb. 6, 1985. Senate Energy and Natural Resources reported June 27 (S Rept 99-94). Senate passed July 29. House Energy and Commerce discharged. House passed, amended, March 11, 1986. Senate agreed to conference report Aug. 15 (H Rept 99-787). Senate receded from its disagreement to House amendment Aug. 15. House agreed to conference report Aug. 15. President signed Aug. 28, 1986.

PL 99-413 (HR 4843) Provide for a minimum price and an alternative production rate for petroleum produced from the naval petroleum reserves. Introduced by SHARP, D-Ind., May 15, 1986. House Energy and Commerce reported Aug. 8 (H Rept 99-775, Part 1). House Armed Services discharged. House passed Aug. 13. Senate passed Aug. 16. President signed Aug. 29, 1986.

PL 99-414 (H J Res 580) Designate the week beginning Sept. 7, 1986, as "National Freedom of Information Act Awareness Week." Introduced by KLECZKA, D-Wis., March 25, 1986. House Post Office and Civil Service discharged. House passed June 11. Senate Judiciary discharged. Senate passed Sept. 10. President signed Sept. 16, 1986.

PL 99-415 (HR 4329) Authorize U.S. contributions to the international fund established pursuant to the Nov. 15, 1985, agreement between the United Kingdom and Ireland. Introduced by FASCELL, D-Fla., March 6, 1986. House passed, under suspension of the rules, March 11. Senate passed, amended, Aug. 13. House agreed to Senate amendments Aug. 14. President signed Sept. 19, 1986.

PL 99-416 (HR 3443) Designate the Closed Basin Conveyance Channel of the Closed Basin Division, San Luis Valley Project, Colo., as the "Franklin Eddy Canal." Introduced by STRANG, R-Colo., Sept. 26, 1985. House Interior and Insular Affairs reported Oct. 2 (H Rept 99-297). House passed Oct. 9. Senate Energy and Natural Resources reported Feb. 6, 1986 (S Rept 99-233). Senate passed Sept. 10. President signed Sept. 23, 1986.

PL 99-417 (H J Res 60) Designate the week beginning Sept. 15, 1986, as "National School-Age Child Care Awareness Week." Introduced by McKERNAN, R-Maine, Jan. 3, 1985. House Post Office and Civil Service discharged. House passed Aug. 1. Senate Judiciary discharged. Senate passed, amended, Sept. 12, 1986. House agreed to Senate amendments Sept. 18. President signed Sept. 23, 1986.

PL 99-418 (S 2462) Provide for the awarding of a special gold medal to Aaron Copland. Introduced by KENNEDY, D-Mass., May 15, 1986. Senate Banking, Housing and Urban Affairs reported Aug. 13. Senate passed Aug. 15. House Banking, Finance and Urban Affairs discharged. House passed Sept. 9. President signed Sept. 23, 1986.

PL 99-419 (H J Res 692) Designate the week of Oct. 19-26, 1986, as "National Housing Week." Introduced by AuCOIN, D-Ore., Aug. 1, 1986. House Post Office and Civil Service discharged. House passed Aug. 13. Senate Judiciary reported Sept. 11. Senate passed Sept. 12. President signed Sept. 25, 1986.

PL 99-420 (S 720) Establish a permanent boundary for the Acadia National Park, Maine, and provide for the acquisition of lands for that park. Introduced by MITCHELL, D-Maine, March 20, 1985. Senate Energy and Natural Resources reported Nov. 22 (S Rept 99-198). Senate passed Dec. 3. House Interior and Insular Affairs reported May 5, 1986 (H Rept 99-572). House passed, amended, under suspension of the rules, May 5. Senate agreed to House amendment with amendments June 6. House agreed to certain Senate amendments and disagreed to a Senate amendment July 24. Senate receded from its amendment Sept. 11. President signed Sept. 25, 1986.

PL 99-421 (S J Res 196) Designate Sept. 22, 1986, as "American Business Women's Day." Introduced by HAWKINS, R-Fla., Sept. 11, 1985. Senate Judiciary reported June 5, 1986. Senate passed June 10. House Post Office and Civil Service discharged. House passed Sept. 18. President signed Sept. 25, 1986.

PL 99-422 (S J Res 357) Designate the week of Sept. 15-21, 1986, as "National Historically Black Colleges Week." Introduced by THURMOND, R-S.C., June 5, 1986. Senate Judiciary reported June 12. Senate passed June 13. House Post Office and Civil Service discharged. House passed Sept. 18. President signed Sept. 25, 1986.

PL 99-423 (HR 1483) Authorize the Smithsonian Institution to plan and construct facilities for the Smithsonian Astrophysical Observatory and the Smithsonian Tropical Research Institute. Introduced by MINETA, D-Calif., March 7, 1985. House passed, under suspension of the rules, Oct. 7. Senate Rules and Administration reported Nov. 19 (S Rept 99-189). Senate passed, amended, June 24, 1986. House agreed to Senate amendment Sept. 18. President signed Sept. 30, 1986.

PL 99-424 (HR 3002) Provide for the establishment of an experimental program relating to the acceptance of voluntary services from participants in an executive exchange program of the government. Introduced by HORTON, R-N.Y., July 16, 1985. House Post Office and Civil Service reported March 25, 1986 (H Rept 99-505). House passed, under suspension of the rules, April 8. Senate Governmental Affairs reported Aug. 15 (S Rept 99-409). Senate passed, amended, Sept. 11. House agreed to Senate amendments Sept. 16. President signed Sept. 30, 1986.

PL 99-425 (HR 4421) Authorize funds for fiscal years 1987-90 to carry out the Head Start, Follow Through, Dependent Care, Community Services Block Grant and community food and nutrition programs. Introduced by KILDEE, D-Mich., March 17, 1986. House Education and Labor reported April 17 (H Rept 99-545). House passed April 29. Senate Labor and Human Resources discharged. Senate passed, amended, July 14. House agreed to conference report Sept. 16 (H Rept 99-815). Senate agreed to conference report Sept. 18. President signed Sept. 30, 1986.

PL 99-426 (HR 4530) Amend the Department of Defense Authorization Act of 1985 to provide that members of the Commission on Merchant Marine and Defense shall not be considered to be federal employees for certain purposes; extend the deadline for reports of the commission; and extend the availability of funds appropriated to the commission. Introduced by BENNETT, D-Fla., April 9, 1986. House Armed Services reported May 13 (H Rept 99-601). House passed May 19. Senate passed Sept. 12. President signed Sept. 30, 1986.

PL 99-427 (S 1963) Direct the secretary of the interior to convey certain interests in lands in Socorro County, N.M., to the New Mexico Institute of Mining and Technology. Introduced by DOMENICI, R-N.M., Dec. 17, 1985. Senate Energy and Natural Resources reported July 25, 1986 (S Rept 99-341). Senate passed Aug. 2. House Interior and Insular Affairs discharged. House passed, amended, Aug. 11. Senate agreed to House amendment Sept. 17. President signed Sept. 30, 1986.

PL 99-428 (S 2095) Reauthorize the Tribally Controlled Community College Assistance Act of 1978 and the Navajo Community College Act. Introduced by ANDREWS, R-N.D., Feb. 25, 1986. Senate Select Indian Affairs reported June 18 (S Rept 99-324). Senate passed June 25. House Education and Labor discharged. House passed Sept. 16. President signed Sept. 30, 1986.

PL 99-429 (S 2888) Delay temporarily the repeal of the U.S. Trustee System. Introduced by SIMPSON, R-Wyo., Sept. 27, 1986. Senate passed Sept. 28. House passed Sept. 29. President signed Sept. 30, 1986.

PL 99-430 (S J Res 353) Provide for the extension of certain programs relating to housing and community development. Introduced by GARN, R-Utah, May 21, 1986. Senate Banking, Housing and Urban Affairs reported May 21. Senate passed Sept. 27. House passed Sept. 30. President signed Sept. 30, 1986.

PL 99-431 (S J Res 415) Provide for a settlement to the Maine Central Railroad Co. and Portland Terminal Co. labor-management dispute. Introduced by BYRD, D-W.Va., Sept. 16, 1986. Senate passed Sept. 17. House passed, under suspension of the rules, Sept. 23. President signed Sept. 30, 1986.

PL 99-432 (HR 3358) Reauthorize the Atlantic Striped Bass Conservation Act. Introduced by STUDDS, D-Mass., Sept. 18, 1985. House Merchant Marine and Fisheries reported April 16, 1986 (H Rept 99-532). House passed, under suspension of the rules, April 29. Senate passed, amended, June 26. House agreed to Senate amendment, under suspension of the rules, Sept. 16. President signed Oct. 1, 1986.

PL 99-433 (HR 3622) Amend title 10, U.S. Code, to reorganize and strengthen the position of the chairman of the Joint Chiefs of Staff and provide for more efficient and effective operation of the armed forces. Introduced by NICHOLS, D-Ala., Oct. 24, 1985. House Armed Services reported Nov. 14 (H Rept 99-375). House passed Nov. 20. Senate Armed Services discharged. Senate passed, amended, May 7, 1986. Senate agreed to conference report Sept. 16 (H Rept 99-824). House agreed to conference report Sept. 17. President signed Oct. 1, 1986.

PL 99-434 (H J Res 743) Make continuing appropriations for fiscal year 1987 through Oct. 8, 1986. Introduced by WHITTEN, D-Miss., Sept. 30, 1986. House Appropriations discharged. House passed Sept. 30. Senate passed Sept. 30. President signed Oct. 1, 1986.

PL 99-435 (S 2703) Amend the Federal Aviation Act of 1958 to provide that prohibitions of discrimination against handicapped individuals shall apply to air carriers. Introduced by DOLE, R-Kan., July 30, 1986. Senate Commerce, Science and Transportation reported Aug. 13 (S Rept 99-400). Senate passed Aug. 15. House Public Works and Transportation discharged. House passed Sept. 18. President signed Oct. 2, 1986.

PL 99-436 (S J Res 207) Designate Nov. 15, 1986, as "National Philanthropy Day." Introduced by WILSON, R-Calif., Sept. 25, 1985. Senate Judiciary reported Oct. 24. Senate passed Oct. 25. House Post Office and Civil Service discharged. House passed, amended, June 11, 1986. Senate agreed to House amendments Sept. 18. President signed Oct. 2, 1986.

PL 99-437 (S J Res 263) Designate September 1986 as "National Independent Retail Grocer Month." Introduced by BOSCHWITZ, R-Minn., Feb. 4, 1986. Senate Judiciary reported March 20. Senate passed March 21. House Post Office and Civil Service discharged. House passed, amended, Sept. 18. Senate agreed to House amendments Sept. 29. President signed Oct. 2, 1986.

PL 99-438 (S J Res 402) Designate July 2 and 3, 1987, as "The United States-Canada Days of Peace and Friendship." Introduced by LUGAR, R-Ind., Aug. 15, 1986. Senate Judiciary reported Sept. 11. Senate passed Sept. 12. House Post Office and Civil Service discharged. House passed Sept. 18. President signed Oct. 2, 1986.

PL 99-439 (S 2759) Relating to telephone services for senators. Introduced by MATHIAS, R-Md., Aug. 14, 1986. Senate Rules and Administration reported Aug. 14 (S Rept 99-404). Senate passed Aug. 16. House Committee on House Administration discharged. House passed Sept. 18. President signed Oct. 2, 1986.

PL 99-440 (HR 4868) Impose economic and other sanctions against South Africa, including a ban on new U.S. investments in South Africa and prohibitions against importation of South African agricultural products, coal, uranium and steel. Introduced by GRAY, D-Pa., May 21, 1986. House Foreign Affairs reported June 13 (H Rept 99-638, Part 1). House Ways and Means reported June 16 (H Rept 99-638, Part 2). House passed June 18. Senate passed, amended, Aug. 15. House agreed to Senate amendment Sept. 12. President vetoed Sept. 26. House passed over presidential veto Sept. 29. Senate passed over presidential veto Oct. 2. Became public law without presidential approval Oct. 2, 1986.

PL 99-441 (HR 5480) Extend the expiration date of the Defense Production Act of 1950, and authorize funds for the purpose of that act. Introduced by LaFALCE, D-N.Y., Aug. 15, 1986. House passed, under suspension of the rules, Sept. 23. Senate passed, amended, Sept. 25. House agreed to Senate amendment Sept. 29. President signed Oct. 3, 1986.

PL 99-442 (S J Res 317) Designate November 1986 as "National Hospice Month." Introduced by HEINZ, R-Pa., April 9, 1986. Senate Judiciary reported April 17. Senate passed April 22. House Post Office and Civil Service discharged. House passed Sept. 18. President signed Oct. 3, 1986.

PL 99-443 (HR 4260) Provide the Small Business Administration continuing authority to administer a program for small innovative firms for research and development. Introduced by MAVROULES, D-Mass., Feb. 26, 1986. House Small Business reported June 18 (H Rept 99-646, Part 1). House Select Intelligence reported July 17 (H Rept 99-646, Part 2). House Science and Technology reported July 31 (H Rept 99-646, Part 3). House Energy and Commerce reported Aug. 1 (H Rept 99-646, Part 4). House Armed Services discharged. House Foreign Affairs discharged. House Veterans' Affairs discharged. House passed, under suspension of the rules, Aug. 13. Senate passed Sept. 18. President signed Oct. 6, 1986.

PL 99-444 (H J Res 710) Designate the week beginning Oct. 12, 1986, as "National Children's Television Awareness Week." Introduced by WIRTH, D-Colo., Aug. 14, 1986. House Post Office and Civil Service discharged. House passed Sept. 18. Senate passed Sept. 24. President signed Oct. 6, 1986.

PL 99-445 (S 1542) Amend the National Trails System Act by designating the Nez Perce (Nee-Me-Poo) Trail as a component of the National Trails System. Introduced by McCLURE, R-Idaho, July 31, 1985. Senate Energy and Natural Resources reported Aug. 7, 1986 (S Rept 99-382). Senate passed Aug. 11. House Interior and Insular Affairs reported Sept. 24 (H Rept 99-873). House passed Sept. 24. President signed Oct. 6, 1986.

PL 99-446 (S J Res 354) Designate the week of Oct. 5-11, 1986, as "National Drug Abuse Education and Prevention Week." Introduced by CHILES, D-Fla., May 21, 1986. Senate Judiciary reported June 26. Senate passed July 15. House Post Office and Civil Service discharged. House passed Sept. 18. President signed Oct. 6, 1986.

PL 99-447 (S J Res 362) Designate the week of Dec. 14-20, 1986, as "National Drunk and Drugged Driving Awareness Week." Introduced by HUMPHREY, R-N.H., June 16, 1986. Senate Judiciary reported June 19. Senate passed June 20. House Post Office and Civil Service discharged. House passed Sept. 18. President signed Oct. 6, 1986.

PL 99-448 (S J Res 405) Designate Sept. 11, 1986, as "911 Emergency Number Day." Introduced by GLENN, D-Ohio, Aug. 15, 1986. Senate Judiciary discharged. Senate passed Sept. 10. House Post Office and Civil Service discharged. House passed, amended, Sept. 18. Senate agreed to House amendments Sept. 29. President signed Oct. 6, 1986.

PL 99-449 (S J Res 159) Designate the rose as the national floral emblem. Introduced by JOHNSTON, D-La., July 11, 1985. Senate Judiciary reported Sept. 12. Senate passed Sept. 16. House Post Office and Civil Service reported Sept. 18, 1986 (H Rept 99-836). House passed, under suspension of the rules, Sept. 23. President signed Oct. 7, 1986.

PL 99-450 (HR 1246) Establish a federally declared floodway for the Colorado River below Davis Dam. Introduced by CHENEY, R-Wyo., Feb. 25, 1985. House Interior and Insular Affairs reported Sept. 10 (H Rept 99-261). House passed, under suspension of the rules, Sept. 24. Senate Environment and Public Works discharged. Senate passed, amended, Sept. 15, 1986. House agreed to Senate amendment Sept. 23. President signed Oct. 8, 1986.

PL 99-451 (HR 5506) Amend the International Claims Settlement Act of 1949, to provide that the value of claims be based on the fair market value of the property taken. Introduced by BONKER, D-Wash., Sept. 11, 1986. House Foreign Affairs reported Sept. 18 (H Rept 99-837). House passed, under suspension of the rules, Sept. 22. Senate passed Sept. 24. President signed Oct. 8, 1986.

PL 99-452 (HR 5521) Extend until Oct. 13, 1986, the emergency acquisition and net worth guarantee provisions of the Garn-St Germain Depository Institutions Act of 1982. Introduced by St GERMAIN, D-R.I., Sept. 16, 1986. House Banking, Finance and Urban Affairs discharged. House passed Sept. 16. Senate passed Sept. 27. President signed Oct. 8, 1986.

PL 99-453 (H J Res 547) Designate October 1986 as "Polish-American Heritage Month." Introduced by BORSKI, D-Pa., March 5, 1986. House Post Office and Civil Service discharged. House passed July 24. Senate Judiciary reported Sept. 19. Senate passed Sept. 24. President signed Oct. 8, 1986.

PL 99-454 (H J Res 611) Designate the period of Dec. 1-7, 1986, as "National Aplastic Anemia Awareness Week." Introduced by CARPER, D-Del., April 23, 1986. House Post Office and Civil Service discharged. House passed Sept. 18. Senate passed Sept. 24. President signed Oct. 8, 1986.

PL 99-455 (H J Res 721) Designate the week of Oct. 12-18, 1986, as

National Job Skills Week." Introduced by MARTINEZ, D-Calif., Sept. 11, 1986. House Post Office and Civil Service discharged. House passed Sept. 18. Senate passed Sept. 24. President signed Oct. 8, 1986.

PL 99-456 (S 1766) Designate the Cumberland terminus of the Chesapeake and Ohio Canal National Historical Park in honor of J. Glenn Beall Sr. Introduced by MATHIAS, R-Md., Oct. 16, 1985. Senate Energy and Natural Resources reported July 25, 1986 (S Rept 99-340). Senate passed Aug. 2. House Interior and Insular Affairs discharged. House passed Sept. 24. President signed Oct. 8, 1986.

PL 99-457 (S 2294) Reauthorize certain programs under the Education of the Handicapped Act, to authorize an early intervention program for handicapped infants. Introduced by WEICKER, R-Conn., April 14, 1986. Senate Labor and Human Resources reported June 2 (S Rept 99-315). Senate passed June 6. House Education and Labor discharged. House passed, amended, Sept. 22. Senate agreed to House amendments Sept. 24. President signed Oct. 8, 1986.

PL 99-458 (S J Res 202) Designate November 1986 as "American Liver Foundation National Liver Awareness Month." Introduced by HATCH, R-Utah, Sept. 18, 1985. Senate Judiciary reported Nov. 14. Senate passed Nov. 18. House Post Office and Civil Service discharged. House passed, amended, Sept. 18, 1986. Senate agreed to House amendments Sept. 29. President signed Oct. 8, 1986.

PL 99-459 (S J Res 245) Designate the week of Dec. 1-7, 1986, as "National Epidermolysis Bullosa Awareness Week." Introduced by HATFIELD, R-Ore., Dec. 12, 1985. Senate Judiciary reported May 1, 1986. Senate passed May 5. House Post Office and Civil Service discharged. House passed Oct. 1. President signed Oct. 8, 1986.

PL 99-460 (S J Res 318) Designate November 1986 as "National Diabetes Month." Introduced by ABDNOR, R-S.D., April 9, 1986. Senate Judiciary reported April 17. Senate passed April 22. House Post Office and Civil Service discharged. House passed Oct. 1. President signed Oct. 8, 1986.

PL 99-461 (S J Res 368) Designate October 1986 as "National Spina Bifida Month." Introduced by DIXON, D-Ill., June 25, 1986. Senate Judiciary reported Aug. 7. Senate passed Aug. 9. House Post Office and Civil Service discharged. House passed Oct. 1. President signed Oct. 8, 1986.

PL 99-462 (S J Res 406) Designate Oct. 4, 1986, as "National Outreach to the Rural Disabled Day." Introduced by TRIBLE, R-Va., Aug. 15, 1986. Senate Judiciary reported Sept. 11. Senate passed Sept. 12. House Post Office and Civil Service discharged. House passed Oct. 1. President signed Oct. 8, 1986.

PL 99-463 (H J Res 749) Waive the printing on parchment of certain enrolled bills and joint resolutions during the remainder of the second session of the 99th Congress. Introduced by MINETA, D-Calif., Oct. 8, 1986. House passed Oct. 8. Senate passed Oct. 8. President signed Oct. 9, 1986.

PL 99-464 (H J Res 750) Make continuing appropriations for fiscal year 1987 through Oct. 10, 1986. Introduced by WHITTEN, D-Miss., Oct. 8, 1986. House passed Oct. 8. Senate passed Oct. 8. President signed Oct. 9, 1986.

PL 99-465 (H J Res 751) Make continuing appropriations for fiscal year 1987 through Oct. 15, 1986. Introduced by WHITTEN, D-Miss., Oct. 9, 1986. House passed Oct. 10. Senate passed Oct. 10. President signed Oct. 11, 1986.

PL 99-466 (HR 2183) Amend title 28, U.S. Code, to make certain changes with respect to the participation of judges of the Court of International Trade in judicial conferences. Introduced by RODINO, D-N.J., April 23, 1985. House Judiciary reported Nov. 21 (H Rept 99-390). House passed, under suspension of the rules, Dec. 9. Senate Judiciary reported Sept. 24, 1986. Senate passed Sept. 29. President signed Oct. 14, 1986.

PL 99-467 (HR 2721) Amend title 13, U.S. Code, to require the collection of statistics on domestic apparel and textile industries. Introduced by GARCIA, D-N.Y., June 11, 1985. House Post Office and Civil Service reported April 8, 1986 (H Rept 99-511). House passed, under suspension of the rules, April 14. Senate Governmental Affairs reported Sept. 19 (S Rept 99-450). Senate passed Sept. 29. President signed Oct. 14, 1986.

PL 99-468 (HR 2971) Grant the consent of Congress to the amendments to the Susquehanna River Basin Compact. Introduced by GEKAS, R-Pa., July 11, 1985. House Judiciary reported May 12, 1986 (H Rept 99-596). House passed, under suspension of the rules, May 19. Senate Judiciary discharged. Senate passed Sept. 29. President signed Oct. 14, 1986.

PL 99-469 (HR 4217) Provide for the settlement of certain claims of the Papago Tribe of Arizona arising from the construction of Tat Momolik Dam. Introduced by UDALL, D-Ariz., Feb. 24, 1986. House Interior and Insular Affairs reported Sept. 19 (H Rept 99-852). House passed, under suspension of the rules, Sept. 23. Senate passed Oct. 1. President signed Oct. 14, 1986.

PL 99-470 (HR 4588) Authorize funds for and increase authorized membership in the Administrative Conference of the United States. Introduced by GLICKMAN, D-Kan., April 15, 1986. House Judiciary reported May 15 (H Rept 99-603). House passed, under suspension of the rules, May 19. Senate Judiciary discharged. Senate passed Sept. 29. President signed Oct. 14, 1986.

PL 99-471 (S J Res 390) Authorize and request the president to proclaim the week of Nov. 23-30, 1986, as "American Indian Week." Introduced by CRANSTON, D-Calif., Aug. 8, 1986. Senate Judiciary reported Sept. 11. Senate passed Sept. 12. House Post Office and Civil Service discharged. House passed Oct. 1. President signed Oct. 14, 1986.

PL 99-472 (HR 5548) Amend the Export-Import Bank Act of 1945, extend the authority of that act through fiscal year 1997, and change the Export-Import Bank's medium-term direct credit program. Introduced by NEAL, D-N.C., Sept. 18, 1986. House passed, under suspension of the rules, Sept. 22. Senate Banking, Housing and Urban Affairs discharged. Senate passed, amended, Sept. 26. House agreed to conference report Oct. 2 (H Rept 99-956). Senate agreed to conference report Oct. 7. President signed Oct. 15, 1986.

PL 99-473 (HR 4545) Authorize funds for the American Folklife Center for fiscal years 1987-89. Introduced by OAKAR, D-Ohio, April 9, 1986. House Committee on House Administration reported Aug. 15 (H Rept 99-800). House passed, under suspension of the rules, Sept. 16. Senate Rules and Administration reported Oct. 1. Senate passed Oct. 3. President signed Oct. 16, 1986.

PL 99-474 (HR 4718) Amend title 18, U.S. Code, to provide additional penalties for fraud and related activities in connection with access devices and computers. Introduced by HUGHES, D-N.J., April 30, 1986. House Judiciary reported May 22 (H Rept 99-612). House passed, under suspension of the rules, June 3. Senate Judiciary discharged. Senate passed, amended, Oct. 3. House agreed to Senate amendment Oct. 6. President signed Oct. 16, 1986.

PL 99-475 (HR 5522) Authorize the release to museums in the United States of certain objects owned by the U.S. Information Agency. Introduced by MICA, D-Fla., Sept. 16, 1986. House passed, under suspension of the rules, Sept. 22. Senate Foreign Relations reported Sept. 30. Senate passed Oct. 1. President signed Oct. 16, 1986.

PL 99-476 (H J Res 210) Designate the Study Center for Trauma and Emergency Medical Systems at the Maryland Institute for Emergency Medical Systems at the University of Maryland as the "Charles McC. Mathias Jr. National Study Center for Trauma and Emergency Medical Systems." Introduced by MIKULSKI, D-Md., March 26, 1985. House passed, under suspension of the rules, Sept. 29, 1986. Senate passed Oct. 3. President signed Oct. 16, 1986.

PL 99-477 (H J Res 555) Designate the week beginning Nov. 24, 1986, as "National Family Caregivers Week." Introduced by SNOWE, R-Maine, March 6, 1986. House Post Office and Civil Service discharged. House passed Oct. 1. Senate passed Oct. 3. President signed Oct. 16, 1986.

PL 99-478 (H J Res 588) Commemorate Jan. 28, 1987, as a National Day of Excellence in honor of the crew of the space shuttle *Challenger*. Introduced by KOLBE, R-Ariz., April 9, 1986. House Post Office and Civil Service discharged. House passed Sept. 18. Senate Judiciary reported Oct. 2. Senate passed Oct. 3. President signed Oct. 16, 1986.

PL 99-479 (H J Res 617) Designate the week beginning Sept. 21, 1986, as "National Adult Day Care Center Week." Introduced by HERTEL, D-Mich., April 30, 1986. House Post Office and Civil Service discharged. House passed Sept. 18. Senate Judiciary reported Oct. 2. Senate passed Oct. 3. President signed Oct. 16, 1986.

PL 99-480 (H J Res 635) Designate the school year of September 1986 through May 1987 as "National Year of the Teacher," and Jan. 28, 1987, as "National Teacher Appreciation Day." Introduced by SHAW, R-Fla., May 14, 1986. House Post Office and Civil Service discharged. House passed Oct. 1. Senate passed Oct. 3. President signed Oct. 16, 1986.

PL 99-481 (H J Res 678) Designate October 1986 as "Crack/Cocaine Awareness Month." Introduced by GARCIA, D-N.Y., July 22, 1986. House Post Office and Civil Service discharged. House passed Aug. 13. Senate Judiciary reported Oct. 2. Senate passed Oct. 3. President signed Oct. 16, 1986.

PL 99-482 (H J Res 686) Designate Aug. 12, 1986, as "National Civil Rights Day." Introduced by VISCLOSKY, D-Ind., July 24, 1986. House Post Office and Civil Service discharged. House passed Aug. 8. Senate Judiciary reported Sept. 11. Senate passed, amended, Sept. 12. House agreed to Senate amendments Oct. 1. President signed Oct. 16, 1986.

PL 99-483 (H J Res 741) Designate March 1987 as "Developmental Disabilities Awareness Month." Introduced by HANSEN, R-Utah, Sept. 26, 1986. House Post Office and Civil Service discharged. House passed Oct. 1. Senate passed Oct. 3. President signed Oct. 16, 1986.

PL 99-484 (S 2062) Designate the federal building and U.S. Courthouse to be constructed and located in Newark, N.J., as the "Martin Luther

King Jr. Federal Building and United States Courthouse." Introduced by LAUTENBERG, D-N.J., Feb. 6, 1986. Senate Environment and Public Works reported Sept. 23 (S Rept 99-471). Senate passed Sept. 24. House passed Oct. 6. President signed Oct. 16, 1986.

PL 99-485 (S 2788) Designate the federal building located in San Diego, Calif., as the "Jacob Weinberger Federal Building." Introduced by WILSON, R-Calif., Aug. 15, 1986. Senate Environment and Public Works reported Sept. 23 (S Rept 99-472). Senate passed Sept. 24. House passed Oct. 6. President signed Oct. 16, 1986.

PL 99-486 (S 2884) Amend the Fair Labor Standards Act of 1938, to require that wages based on individual productivity be paid to handicapped workers employed under certificates issued by the secretary of labor. Introduced by PACKWOOD, R-Ore., Sept. 26, 1986. Senate passed Sept. 27. House passed Oct. 1. President signed Oct. 16, 1986.

PL 99-487 (S J Res 280) Designate November 1986 as "National Alzheimer's Disease Month." Introduced by HEINZ, R-Pa., Feb. 25, 1986. Senate Judiciary reported April 17. Senate passed April 22. House Post Office and Civil Service discharged. House passed Oct. 1. President signed Oct. 16, 1986.

PL 99-488 (S J Res 385) Designate Oct. 23, 1986, as "National Hungarian Freedom Fighters Day." Introduced by RIEGLE, D-Mich., Aug. 1, 1986. Senate Judiciary reported Sept. 19. Senate passed Sept. 29. House Post Office and Civil Service discharged. House passed Oct. 1. President signed Oct. 16, 1986.

PL 99-489 (S J Res 395) Designate Oct. 1, 1986, through Sept. 30, 1987, as "National Institutes of Health Centennial Year." Introduced by HATCH, R-Utah, Aug. 13, 1986. Senate Judiciary reported Sept. 19. Senate passed Sept. 24. House Post Office and Civil Service discharged. House passed Oct. 10. President signed Oct. 16, 1986.

PL 99-490 (HR 5166) Designate certain lands in the Cherokee National Forest in Tennessee as wilderness areas. Introduced by QUILLEN, R-Tenn., July 15, 1986. House Interior and Insular Affairs reported Sept. 19 (H Rept 99-853, Part 1). House passed, under suspension of the rules, Sept. 22. Senate passed Oct. 3. President signed Oct. 16, 1986.

PL 99-491 (H J Res 753) Make further continuing appropriations for fiscal 1987 through Oct. 16, 1986. Introduced by WHITTEN, D-Miss., Oct. 15, 1986. House Appropriations discharged. House passed Oct. 16. Senate passed Oct. 16. President signed Oct. 16, 1986.

PL 99-492 (HR 5362) Extend the authority of the Supreme Court Police to provide protective services for justices and court personnel. Introduced by GLICKMAN, D-Kan., Aug. 8, 1986. House Judiciary reported Sept. 27 (H Rept 99-912). House passed, under suspension of the rules, Sept. 29. Senate passed, amended, Sept. 30. House agreed to Senate amendment Oct. 7. President signed Oct. 16, 1986.

PL 99-493 (HR 5430) Amend the Gila River Pima-Maricopa Indian Community judgment distribution plan. Introduced by UDALL, D-Ariz., Aug. 14, 1986. House Interior and Insular Affairs reported Sept. 23 (H Rept 99-869). House passed Sept. 23. Senate passed Oct. 3. President signed Oct. 16, 1986.

PL 99-494 (H J Res 671) Designate 1987 as the "Year of the Reader." Introduced by OAKAR, D-Ohio, July 16, 1986. House Post Office and Civil Service discharged. House passed Oct. 1. Senate passed Oct. 3. President signed Oct. 16, 1986.

PL 99-495 (S 426) Amend the Federal Power Act to provide for more protection to electric consumers. Introduced by WALLOP, R-Wyo., Feb. 7, 1985. Senate Energy and Natural Resources reported Oct. 22 (S Rept 99-161). Senate passed April 17, 1986. House passed, amended, April 21. House agreed to conference report Oct. 2 (H Rept 99-934). Senate agreed to conference report Oct. 3. President signed Oct. 16, 1986.

PL 99-496 (S 2069) Make clarifying and technical changes to the Job Training Partnership Act. Introduced by QUAYLE, R-Ind., Feb. 7, 1986. Senate Labor and Human Resources reported June 5 (S Rept 99-317). Senate passed June 13. House Education and Labor discharged. House passed, amended, Aug. 11. Senate agreed to House amendments with an amendment Sept. 29. House agreed to Senate amendment Oct. 1. President signed Oct. 16, 1986.

PL 99-497 (HR 2182) Authorize the inclusion of certain additional lands within the Apostle Islands National Lakeshore. Introduced by OBEY, D-Wis., April 23, 1985. House Interior and Insular Affairs reported Dec. 16 (H Rept 99-441). House passed, under suspension of the rules, Dec. 16. Senate Energy and Natural Resources reported Sept. 27, 1986 (S Rept 99-499). Senate passed Oct. 8. President signed Oct. 17, 1986.

PL 99-498 (S 1965) Reauthorize aid to colleges and needy students through fiscal year 1991, authorizing appropriations of $10.2 billion in fiscal 1987. Introduced by STAFFORD, R-Vt., Dec. 17, 1985. Senate Labor and Human Resources reported May 13, 1986 (S Rept 99-296). Senate passed June 3. House passed, amended, June 17. House agreed to conference report Sept. 24 (H Rept 99-861). Senate agreed to conference report Sept. 25. President signed Oct. 17, 1986.

PL 99-499 (HR 2005) Reauthorize the "superfund" hazardous-waste cleanup program for fiscal years 1987-91 at a funding level of $8.5 billion, and establish a new program for cleanup of leaking underground storage tanks at $500,000. Introduced by JONES, D-Okla., April 4, 1985. House Ways and Means reported May 7 (H Rept 99-69). House passed, under suspension of the rules, May 14. Senate Finance discharged. Senate passed, amended, Sept. 26. House agreed to Senate amendments with amendments Dec. 10. Senate agreed to conference report Oct. 3, 1986 (H Rept 99-962). House agreed to conference report Oct. 8. President signed Oct. 17, 1986.

PL 99-500 (H J Res 738) Make continuing appropriations for fiscal 1987. Introduced by WHITTEN, D-Miss., Sept. 24, 1986. House passed Sept. 25. Senate Appropriations reported Sept. 26 (S Rept 99-500). Senate passed, amended, Oct. 3. House agreed to conference report Oct. 15 (H Rept 99-1005). House agreed to a Senate amendment, agreed to certain Senate amendments with amendments, and insisted on its disagreement to a Senate amendment, Oct. 15. House agreed to certain Senate amendments Oct. 16. Senate agreed to conference report Oct. 16. Senate disagreed to certain House amendments to Senate amendments, agreed to a House amendment to a Senate amendment and receded from an amendment, Oct. 16. Senate agreed to a House amendment to a Senate amendment, with an amendment, Oct. 17. House receded from certain amendments to Senate amendments and agreed to a Senate amendment to a House amendment to a Senate amendment Oct. 17. President signed Oct. 18, 1986.

PL 99-501 (HR 3526) Provide for the settlement of certain claims respecting the San Carlos Apache Tribe of Arizona. Introduced by McCAIN, R-Ariz., Oct. 8, 1985. House Interior and Insular Affairs reported June 11, 1986 (H Rept 99-631). House passed June 26. Senate Select Indian Affairs reported Sept. 23 (S Rept 99-474). Senate passed Oct. 3. President signed Oct. 20, 1986.

PL 99-502 (HR 3773) Amend the Stevenson-Wydler Technology Innovation Act of 1980 to promote technology transfer by authorizing government-operated laboratories to enter into cooperative research agreements and by establishing a Federal Laboratory Consortium for Technology Transfer within the National Science Foundation. Introduced by FUQUA, D-Fla., Nov. 18, 1985. House Science and Technology reported Dec. 5 (H Rept 99-415). House passed, under suspension of the rules, Dec. 9. Senate Commerce, Science and Transportation reported April 21, 1986 (S Rept 99-283). Senate Judiciary discharged. Senate passed, amended, Aug. 9. Senate agreed to conference report Oct. 3 (H Rept 99-953). House agreed to conference report Oct. 7. President signed Oct. 20, 1986.

PL 99-503 (HR 4216) Provide for the settlement of certain claims of the Papago Tribe of Arizona arising from the operation of Painted Rock Dam. Introduced by UDALL, D-Ariz., Feb. 24, 1986. House Interior and Insular Affairs reported Sept. 19 (H Rept 99-851). House passed, under suspension of the rules, Sept. 23. Senate passed Oct. 1. President signed Oct. 20, 1986.

PL 99-504 (S 816) Establish the Pine Ridge Wilderness and Soldier Creek Wilderness in the Nebraska National Forest in Nebraska. Introduced by EXON, D-Neb., March 28, 1985. Senate Energy and Natural Resources reported July 31 (S Rept 99-122). Senate passed Aug. 1. House Interior and Insular Affairs reported Sept. 19, 1986 (H Rept 99-854, Part 1). House passed, amended, under suspension of the rules, Sept. 23. Senate agreed to House amendments Oct. 3. President signed Oct. 20, 1986.

PL 99-505 (HR 2224) Amend the Immigration and Nationality Act to permit non-immigrant alien crewmen on fishing vessels to stop temporarily at ports in Guam. Introduced by BLAZ, R-Guam, April 25, 1985. House Judiciary reported May 8, 1986 (H Rept 99-592). House passed, under suspension of the rules, May 12. Senate Judiciary reported Sept. 9. Senate passed Oct. 3. President signed Oct. 21, 1986.

PL 99-506 (HR 4021) Reauthorize federal aid for vocational rehabilitation of the handicapped through fiscal year 1991 under the Rehabilitation Act Amendments of 1973. Introduced by WILLIAMS, D-Mont., Jan. 21, 1986. House Education and Labor reported May 5 (H Rept 99-571). House passed, under suspension of the rules, May 7. Senate Labor and Human Resources discharged. Senate passed, amended, Sept. 8. House agreed to conference report Oct. 2 (H Rept 99-955). Senate agreed to conference report Oct. 3. President signed Oct. 21, 1986.

PL 99-507 (HR 4212) Provide for the reauthorization of the Deep Seabed Hard Mineral Resources Act and authorize appropriations of $1.5 million in each of fiscal years 1987-89. Introduced by MIKULSKI, D-Md., Feb. 24, 1986. House Interior and Insular Affairs reported May 20 (H Rept 99-609, Part 1). House Merchant Marine and Fisheries reported June 10 (H Rept 99-609, Part 2). House passed, under suspension of the rules, July 21. Senate Energy and Natural Resources reported Sept. 19 (S Rept 99-460). Senate Commerce, Science and Transportation discharged. Senate passed Oct. 8. President signed Oct. 21, 1986.

PL 99-508 (HR 4952) Amend title 18, U.S. Code, to extend privacy guarantees with respect to the interception of communications involving cellular telephones and messages transmitted and stored in computers. Introduced by KASTENMEIER, D-Wis., June 5, 1986. House Judiciary reported June 19 (H Rept 99-647). House passed, under suspension of the rules, June 23. Senate passed, amended, Oct. 1. House agreed to Senate amendment Oct. 2. President signed Oct. 21, 1986.

PL 99-509 (HR 5300) Reduce the projected fiscal year 1987 federal budget deficit by $11.7 billion by reconciling current laws with the fiscal 1987 budget resolution. Introduced by GRAY, D-Pa., July 31, 1986. House Budget reported July 31 (H Rept 99-727). House passed Sept. 24. Senate passed, amended, Sept. 25. House agreed to conference report Oct. 17 (H Rept 99-1012). Senate agreed to conference report Oct. 17. President signed Oct. 21, 1986.

PL 99-510 (H J Res 517) Provide for the reappointment of David C. Acheson as a citizen regent of the Board of Regents of the Smithsonian Institution. Introduced by BOLAND, D-Mass., Feb. 5, 1986. House Committee on House Administration discharged. House passed Sept. 16. Senate passed Oct. 8. President signed Oct. 21, 1986.

PL 99-511 (H J Res 666) Express the sense of Congress in support of a commemorative structure within the National Park System dedicated to the promotion of understanding, knowledge, opportunity and equality for all people. Introduced by LELAND, D-Texas, June 26, 1986. House Interior and Insular Affairs discharged. House passed June 26. Senate Energy and Natural Resources reported Sept. 19 (S Rept 99-463). Senate passed Oct. 8. President signed Oct. 21, 1986.

PL 99-512 (H J Res 735) Designate Dec. 11, 1986, as "National SEEK and College Discovery Day." Introduced by GARCIA, D-N.Y., Sept. 23, 1986. House Post Office and Civil Service discharged. House passed Oct. 1. Senate passed Oct. 9. President signed Oct. 21, 1986.

PL 99-513 (S 2048) Encourage international efforts to designate the shipwreck of the R.M.S. *Titanic* as an international maritime memorial and provide for reasonable research, exploration and, if appropriate, salvage activities with respect to the shipwreck. Introduced by WEICKER, R-Conn., Feb. 5, 1986. Senate Foreign Relations reported Sept. 11. Senate passed Sept. 24. House passed, under suspension of the rules, Oct. 6. President signed Oct. 21, 1986.

PL 99-514 (HR 3838) Revise the federal income tax system by reducing individual and corporate tax rates, eliminating or curtailing many deductions, credits and exclusions, repealing the investment tax credit, taxing capital gains as regular income and making other changes. Introduced by ROSTENKOWSKI, D-Ill., Dec. 3, 1985. House Ways and Means reported Dec. 7 (H Rept 99-426). House passed Dec. 17. Senate Finance reported May 29, 1986 (S Rept 99-313). Senate passed, amended, June 24. House agreed to conference report Sept. 25 (H Rept 99-841). Senate agreed to conference report Sept. 27. President signed Oct. 22, 1986.

PL 99-515 (HR 1593) Direct the secretary of the interior to release on behalf of the United States certain restrictions in a previous conveyance of land to the town of Jerome, Ariz. Introduced by STUMP, R-Ariz., March 19, 1985. House Interior and Insular Affairs reported Oct. 30 (H Rept 99-345). House passed Nov. 4. Senate Energy and Natural Resources reported July 25, 1986 (S Rept 99-342). Senate passed, amended, Oct. 8. House agreed to Senate amendment Oct. 10. President signed Oct. 22, 1986.

PL 99-516 (HR 2092) Amend the Natural Gas Pipeline Safety Act of 1968 and the Hazardous Liquid Pipeline Safety Act of 1979 to authorize appropriations for fiscal year 1987. Introduced by HOWARD, D-N.J., April 17, 1985. House Public Works and Transportation reported May 15 (H Rept 99-121, Part 1). House Energy and Commerce reported May 21 (H Rept 99-121, Part 2). House Judiciary reported July 8 (H Rept 99-121, Part 3). House passed, under suspension of the rules, Sept. 16, 1986. Senate passed Oct. 8. President signed Oct. 22, 1986.

PL 99-517 (HR 3005) Direct the secretary of the interior to convey certain lands, withdrawn by the Bureau of Reclamation for townsite purposes, to the Huntley Project Irrigation District in Ballantine, Mont. Introduced by MARLENEE, R-Mont., July 16, 1985. House Interior and Insular Affairs reported June 25, 1986 (H Rept 99-657). House passed June 26. Senate Energy and Natural Resources reported Aug. 8 (S Rept 99-386). Senate passed Oct. 8. President signed Oct. 22, 1986.

PL 99-518 (HR 4492) Permit the transfer of certain airport property to Algona, Iowa. Introduced by BEDELL, D-Iowa, March 25, 1986. House Public Works and Transportation reported Sept. 12 (H Rept 99-821). House passed, under suspension of the rules, Sept. 16. Senate passed Oct. 8. President signed Oct. 22, 1986.

PL 99-519 (HR 5073) Amend the Toxic Substances Control Act to require the Environmental Protection Agency to promulgate regulations requiring inspection for asbestos-containing material in the nation's schools, development of asbestos management plans for such schools, and response actions with respect to friable asbestos-containing material in such schools. Introduced by FLORIO, D-N.J., June 24, 1986. House Energy and Commerce reported Aug. 7 (H Rept 99-763). House passed, under suspension of the rules, Aug. 12. Senate passed, amended, Sept. 10. House agreed to Senate amendment with an amendment Oct. 1. Senate agreed to House amendment Oct. 3. President signed Oct. 22, 1986.

PL 99-520 (H J Res 438) Designate Oct. 31, 1986, as "National Child Identification and Safety Information Day." Introduced by LUNGREN, R-Calif., Oct. 31, 1985. House Post Office and Civil Service discharged. House passed Oct. 1, 1986. Senate passed Oct. 8. President signed Oct. 22, 1986.

PL 99-521 (S 1124) Amend title 49, U.S. Code, to reduce regulation of surface freight forwarders. Introduced by PACKWOOD, R-Ore., May 14, 1985. Senate Commerce, Science and Transportation reported July 31 (S Rept 99-120). Senate passed Nov. 4. House passed, amended, under suspension of the rules, Sept. 30, 1986. Senate agreed to House amendment Oct. 8. President signed Oct. 22, 1986.

PL 99-522 (S 2266) Establish a ski area permit system on national forest lands. Introduced by WALLOP, R-Wyo., March 27, 1986. Senate Energy and Natural Resources reported Sept. 18 (S Rept 99-449). Senate passed Oct. 9. House passed Oct. 10. President signed Oct. 22, 1986.

PL 99-523 (S J Res 169) Commemorate the bicentennial anniversary of the first patent and the first copyright laws. Introduced by MATHIAS, R-Md., July 23, 1985. Senate Judiciary reported June 5, 1986. Senate passed June 10. House Post Office and Civil Service discharged. House passed Oct. 10. President signed Oct. 22, 1986.

PL 99-524 (S J Res 299) Designate the week of Dec. 7-13, 1986, as "National Alopecia Areata Awareness Week." Introduced by COCHRAN, R-Miss., March 19, 1986. Senate Judiciary reported Sept. 11. Senate passed Sept. 12. House Post Office and Civil Service discharged. House passed Oct. 10. President signed Oct. 22, 1986.

PL 99-525 (S J Res 304) Designate the week of Nov. 16-22, 1986, as "National Arts Week." Introduced by SIMON, D-Ill., March 21, 1986. Senate Judiciary reported June 5. Senate passed June 10. House Post Office and Civil Service discharged. House passed Oct. 10. President signed Oct. 22, 1986.

PL 99-526 (S J Res 306) Designate the week beginning Nov. 23, 1986, as "National Adoption Week." Introduced by HATCH, R-Utah, March 24, 1986. Senate Judiciary reported April 10. Senate passed April 11. House Post Office and Civil Service discharged. House passed Oct. 10. President signed Oct. 22, 1986.

PL 99-527 (S J Res 311) Designate the week beginning Nov. 9, 1986, as "National Women Veterans Recognition Week." Introduced by CRANSTON, D-Calif., March 27, 1986. Senate Judiciary reported June 12. Senate passed June 13. House Post Office and Civil Service discharged. House passed Oct. 10. President signed Oct. 22, 1986.

PL 99-528 (S J Res 396) Designate the week of Oct. 26-Nov. 1, 1986, as "National Adult Immunization Awareness Week." Introduced by HATCH, R-Utah, Aug. 13, 1986. Senate Judiciary reported Sept. 19. Senate passed Sept. 24. House Post Office and Civil Service discharged. House passed Oct. 10. President signed Oct. 22, 1986.

PL 99-529 (S 1917) Amend the Foreign Assistance Act of 1961 to provide assistance to promote immunization and oral rehydration. Introduced by BRADLEY, D-N.J., Dec. 10, 1985. Senate Foreign Relations reported Aug. 8, 1986 (S Rept 99-385). Senate passed Aug. 15. House Foreign Affairs discharged. House passed, amended, Sept. 25. Senate agreed to House amendments with an amendment Oct. 3. House agreed to Senate amendment Oct. 6. President signed Oct. 24, 1986.

PL 99-530 (HR 2826) Amend the Wild and Scenic Rivers Act by designating a segment of the Horsepasture River in North Carolina as a component of the National Wild and Scenic Rivers System. Introduced by HENDON, R-N.C., June 20, 1985. House Interior and Insular Affairs reported July 15, 1986 (H Rept 99-671). House passed, under suspension of the rules, July 28. Senate Energy and Natural Resources discharged. Senate passed Oct. 15. President signed Oct. 27, 1986.

PL 99-531 (S 2370) Authorize the Francis Scott Key Park Foundation Inc. to erect a memorial in the District of Columbia. Introduced by MURKOWSKI, R-Alaska, April 24, 1986. Senate Energy and Natural Resources reported Sept. 19 (S Rept 99-457). Senate passed Oct. 9. House Committee on House Administration discharged. House passed Oct. 14. President signed Oct. 27, 1986.

PL 99-532 (S J Res 308) Designate March 25, 1987, as "Greek Independence Day: A National Day of Celebration of Greek and American Democracy." Introduced by HELMS, R-N.C. (in behalf of SPECTER, R-Pa.), March 25, 1986. Senate passed March 25. House Post Office and Civil Service discharged. House passed, amended, Oct. 1. Senate agreed to House amendments Oct. 8. President signed Oct. 27, 1986.

PL 99-533 (S J Res 232) Designate Oct. 6-10, 1986, as "National Social Studies Week." Introduced by SIMON, D-Ill., Nov. 6, 1985. Senate Judiciary reported Nov. 14. Senate passed Nov. 18. House Post Office and Civil Service discharged. House passed Oct. 10, 1986. President signed Oct. 27, 1986.

PL 99-534 (S J Res 322) Designate Dec. 7, 1986, as "National Pearl Harbor Remembrance Day" on the occasion of the anniversary of the attack on Pearl Harbor. Introduced by LAUTENBERG, D-N.J., April 15, 1986. Senate Judiciary reported Aug. 7. Senate passed Aug. 9. House Post Office and Civil Service discharged. House passed Oct. 10. President signed Oct. 27, 1986.

PL 99-535 (S J Res 339) Designate the week of Nov. 30-Dec. 6, 1986, as "National Home Care Week." Introduced by HATCH, R-Utah, May 6, 1986. Senate Judiciary reported Sept. 19. Senate passed Sept. 24. House Post Office and Civil Service discharged. House passed Oct. 10. President signed Oct. 27, 1986.

PL 99-536 (S J Res 352) Designate the week beginning Oct. 19, 1986, as "Gaucher's Disease Awareness Week." Introduced by METZENBAUM, D-Ohio, May 21, 1986. Senate passed Oct. 3. House Post Office and Civil Service discharged. House passed Oct. 10. President signed Oct. 27, 1986.

PL 99-537 (S J Res 407) Designate Nov. 12, 1986, as "Salute to School Volunteers Day." Introduced by CHILES, D-Fla., Sept. 8, 1986. Senate Judiciary discharged. Senate passed Oct. 9. House Post Office and Civil Service discharged. House passed Oct. 10. President signed Oct. 27, 1986.

PL 99-538 (S J Res 410) Designate the week of Feb. 9-15, 1987, as "National Burn Awareness Week." Introduced by WILSON, R-Calif., Sept. 11, 1986. Senate Judiciary reported Oct. 2. Senate passed Oct. 3. House Post Office and Civil Service discharged. House passed Oct. 10. President signed Oct. 27, 1986.

PL 99-539 (S J Res 414) Designate March 16, 1987, as "Freedom of Information Day." Introduced by PACKWOOD, R-Ore., Sept. 16, 1986. Senate Judiciary reported Oct. 2. Senate passed Oct. 3. House Post Office and Civil Service discharged. House passed Oct. 10. President signed Oct. 27, 1986.

PL 99-540 (S J Res 418) Designate Feb. 4, 1987, as "National Women in Sports Day." Introduced by PACKWOOD, R-Ore., Sept. 23, 1986. Senate Judiciary reported Oct. 2. Senate passed Oct. 3. House Post Office and Civil Service discharged. House passed Oct. 10. President signed Oct. 27, 1986.

PL 99-541 (S J Res 422) Commemorate the 100th anniversary of the birth of the first prime minister of Israel, David Ben-Gurion. Introduced by BOSCHWITZ, R-Minn., Sept. 30, 1986. Senate Foreign Relations reported Sept. 30. Senate passed Oct. 1. House Post Office and Civil Service discharged. House passed Oct. 10. President signed Oct. 27, 1986.

PL 99-542 (HR 1390) Authorize additional long-term leases in the El Portal administrative site adjacent to Yosemite National Park, Calif. Introduced by COELHO, D-Calif., March 4, 1985. House Interior and Insular Affairs reported June 27 (H Rept 99-182). House passed, under suspension of the rules, July 15. Senate Energy and Natural Resources reported Aug. 1, 1986 (S Rept 99-362). Senate passed, amended, Oct. 9. House agreed to Senate amendments, under suspension of the rules, Oct. 14. President signed Oct. 27, 1986.

PL 99-543 (HR 2067) Validate conveyances of certain lands in California that form part of the right-of-way granted by the United States to the Central Pacific Railway Co. Introduced by SHUMWAY, R-Calif., April 16, 1985. House Interior and Insular Affairs reported Nov. 20 (H Rept 99-388). House passed Dec. 3. Senate Energy and Natural Resources reported Sept. 19, 1986 (S Rept 99-455). Senate passed Oct. 9. President signed Oct. 27, 1986.

PL 99-544 (HR 2722) Amend title 13, U.S. Code, to eliminate the requirement relating to decennial censuses of drainage. Introduced by GARCIA, D-N.Y., June 11, 1985. House Post Office and Civil Service reported Sept. 4 (H Rept 99-254). House passed, under suspension of the rules, Nov. 12. Senate Governmental Affairs reported Sept. 19, 1986 (S Rept 99-451). Senate passed, amended, Sept. 29. House agreed to Senate amendments Oct. 10. President signed Oct. 27, 1986.

PL 99-545 (HR 2921) Authorize the secretary of agriculture to issue permanent easements for water conveyance systems in order to resolve title claims arising under acts repealed by the Federal Land Policy and Management Act of 1976. Introduced by STRANG, R-Colo., June 27, 1985. House Interior and Insular Affairs reported April 23, 1986 (H Rept 99-554, Part 1). House Agriculture discharged. House passed May 7. Senate Energy and Natural Resources discharged. Senate passed Oct. 9. President signed Oct. 27, 1986.

PL 99-546 (HR 3113) Implement the Coordinated Operations Agreement, the Suisun Marsh Preservation Agreement, and amend the Small Reclamation Projects Act of 1956, as amended. Introduced by MILLER, D-Calif., July 30, 1985. House Interior and Insular Affairs reported Sept. 9 (H Rept 99-257). House passed, under suspension of the rules, Sept. 9. Senate Energy and Natural Resources reported March 25, 1986 (S Rept 99-265). Senate passed, amended, July 16. House agreed to conference report, under suspension of the rules, Oct. 14 (H Rept 99-991). Senate agreed to conference report Oct. 15. President signed Oct. 27, 1986.

PL 99-547 (HR 3168) Require the director of the Office of Management and Budget to prepare an annual report consolidating the available data on the geographic distribution of federal funds. Introduced by BROOKS, D-Texas, Aug. 1, 1985. House Government Operations reported Dec. 19 (H Rept 99-452). House passed, under suspension of the rules, March 4, 1986. Senate Governmental Affairs reported Sept. 19. Senate passed Oct. 8. President signed Oct. 27, 1986.

PL 99-548 (HR 3352) Transfer certain real property to the city of Mesquite, Nev. Introduced by REID, D-Nev., Sept. 18, 1985. House Interior and Insular Affairs reported Sept. 26, 1986 (H Rept 99-897). House passed, under suspension of the rules, Sept. 30. Senate passed Oct. 9. President signed Oct. 27, 1986.

PL 99-549 (HR 3559) Amend the act establishing a Commission on the Bicentennial of the Constitution of the United States to clarify the status of employees of the commission and raise the limits on private contributions. Introduced by BOGGS, D-La., Oct. 11, 1985. House Post Office and Civil Service reported April 14, 1986 (H Rept 99-530, Part 1). House Judiciary discharged. House passed, under suspension of the rules, June 24. Senate passed, amended, Oct. 3. Passage vitiated Oct. 3. Senate passed, amended, Oct. 6. House agreed to Senate amendment Oct. 10. President signed Oct. 27, 1986.

PL 99-550 (HR 3614) Restrict the use of government vehicles for transportation of officers and employees of the federal government between their residences and places of employment. Introduced by BROOKS, D-Texas, Oct. 24, 1985. House Government Operations reported Dec. 19 (H Rept 99-451). House passed, under suspension of the rules, March 4, 1986. Senate passed, amended, Oct. 10. House agreed to Senate amendment Oct. 15. President signed Oct. 27, 1986.

PL 99-551 (HR 4116) Reauthorize for three years anti-poverty programs administered by the ACTION agency. Introduced by WILLIAMS, D-Mont., Feb. 4, 1986. House Education and Labor reported May 7 (H Rept 99-588). House passed June 17. Senate Labor and Human Resources discharged. Senate passed, amended, July 14. House agreed to conference report Oct. 2 (H Rept 99-954). Senate agreed to conference report Oct. 8. President signed Oct. 27, 1986.

PL 99-552 (HR 4712) Provide for the restoration of the fishery resources in the Klamath River Basin. Introduced by BOSCO, D-Calif., April 30, 1986. House Merchant Marine and Fisheries reported Sept. 25 (H Rept 99-894, Part 1). House Interior and Insular Affairs discharged. House passed, under suspension of the rules, Sept. 30. Senate passed Oct. 3. President signed Oct. 27, 1986.

PL 99-553 (HR 5056) Permit registered public utility holding companies to own certain interests in qualifying cogeneration facilities. Introduced by BRYANT, D-Texas, June 19, 1986. House passed, under suspension of the rules, Sept. 22. Senate passed, amended, Oct. 15. House agreed to Senate amendment Oct. 15. President signed Oct. 27, 1986.

PL 99-554 (HR 5316) Amend title 28, U.S. Code, to provide for the appointment of additional bankruptcy judges and provide for the appointment of U.S. trustees to serve in bankruptcy cases in judicial districts throughout the United States. Introduced by RODINO, D-N.J., Aug. 1, 1986. House Judiciary reported Aug. 7 (H Rept 99-764). House passed, under suspension of the rules, Aug. 12. Senate passed, amended, Aug. 16. House agreed to conference report Oct. 2 (H Rept 99-958). Senate agreed to conference report Oct. 3. President signed Oct. 27, 1986.

PL 99-555 (HR 5496) Designate certain National Forest System lands in Georgia to the National Wilderness Preservation System. Introduced by JENKINS, D-Ga., Sept. 10, 1986. House Interior and Insular Affairs reported Sept. 26 (H Rept 99-898, Part 1). House passed, under suspension of the rules, Sept. 30. Senate Agriculture, Nutrition and Forestry discharged. Senate passed Oct. 9. President signed Oct. 27, 1986.

PL 99-556 (HR 5626) Make technical corrections in the Federal Employees' Retirement Act of 1986. Introduced by FORD, D-Mich., Oct. 1, 1986. House passed, under suspension of the rules, Oct. 6. Senate passed Oct. 8. President signed Oct. 27, 1986.

PL 99-557 (H J Res 17) Consent to an amendment enacted by the Legislature of Hawaii to the Hawaiian Homes Commission Act of 1920. Introduced by AKAKA, D-Hawaii, Jan. 3, 1985. House Interior and Insular Affairs reported Feb. 25, 1986 (H Rept 99-473). House passed, under suspension of the rules, April 8. Senate Energy and Natural Resources reported Sept. 23 (S Rept 99-478). Senate passed Oct. 8. President signed Oct. 27, 1986.

PL 99-558 (H J Res 142) Authorize the erection of a memorial on federal land in the District of Columbia and its environs to honor slaves and free black persons who served as soldiers and sailors or provided civilian assistance during the American Revolution, and to honor the black men, women and children who ran away from slavery or filed petitions with courts and legislatures seeking their freedom. Introduced by JOHNSON, R-Conn., Feb. 7, 1985. House Committee on House Administration reported Oct. 29 (H Rept 99-340). House passed, under suspension of the rules, Nov. 6. Senate Energy and Natural Resources reported Sept. 19, 1986 (S Rept 99-462). Senate passed, amended, Oct. 17. House agreed to Senate amendments Oct. 17. President signed Oct. 27, 1986.

PL 99-559 (H J Res 754) Provide compensation for furloughed employees. Introduced by WHITTEN, D-Miss., Oct. 17, 1986. House passed Oct. 17. Senate passed Oct. 17. President signed Oct. 27, 1986.

PL 99-560 (S 1082) Grant the consent of Congress to the Arkansas-Mississippi Great River Bridge Construction Compact. Introduced by COCHRAN, R-Miss., May 7, 1985. Senate Judiciary reported Nov. 21. Senate passed Dec. 3. House Judiciary discharged. House passed, amended, Sept. 29, 1986. Senate agreed to House amendment Oct. 9. President signed Oct. 27, 1986.

PL 99-561 (S 1352) Enhance the carrying out of fish and wildlife conservation and natural resource management programs on military reservations. Introduced by CHAFEE, R-R.I., June 25, 1985. Senate Environment and Public Works reported June 25. Senate passed Oct. 3, 1986. House passed, under suspension of the rules, Oct. 14. President signed Oct. 27, 1986.

PL 99-562 (S 1562) Amend the False Claims Act and title 18, U.S. Code, regarding penalties for false claims against the federal government. Introduced by GRASSLEY, R-Iowa, Aug. 1, 1985. Senate Judiciary reported July 28, 1986 (S Rept 99-345). Senate passed Aug. 11. House Judiciary discharged. House passed, amended, Sept. 9. Senate agreed to House amendments with an amendment Oct. 3. House agreed to Senate amendment Oct. 7. President signed Oct. 27, 1986.

PL 99-563 (S 2129) Promote the formation of self-insurance groups among businesses, municipalities and professional groups. Introduced by KASTEN, R-Wis., Feb. 28, 1986. Senate Commerce, Science and Transportation reported May 9 (S Rept 99-294). Senate passed July 17. House Energy and Commerce discharged. House passed, amended, Sept. 23. Senate agreed to House amendments with an amendment Oct. 6. House agreed to Senate amendment Oct. 9. President signed Oct. 27, 1986.

PL 99-564 (S 2320) Amend an act to add certain lands on the island of Hawaii to Hawaii Volcanoes National Park. Introduced by INOUYE, D-Hawaii, April 17, 1986. Senate Energy and Natural Resources reported Aug. 15 (S Rept 99-418). Senate passed Sept. 10. House Interior and Insular Affairs reported Oct. 7 (H Rept 99-971). House passed Oct. 10. President signed Oct. 27, 1986.

PL 99-565 (S 2506) Establish the Great Basin National Park in Nevada. Introduced by HECHT, R-Nev., May 21, 1986. Senate Energy and Natural Resources reported Sept. 19 (S Rept 99-458). Senate passed Sept. 30. House passed, amended, under suspension of the rules, Oct. 6. Senate agreed to House amendments Oct. 9. President signed Oct. 27, 1986.

PL 99-566 (S 2750) Establish a property tax fund for the Houlton Band of Maliseet Indians in furtherance of the Maine Indian Claims Settlement Act of 1980. Introduced by COHEN, R-Maine, Aug. 13, 1986. Senate Select Indian Affairs reported Sept. 23 (S Rept 99-469). Senate passed Sept. 24. House Interior and Insular Affairs discharged. House passed Oct. 10. President signed Oct. 27, 1986.

PL 99-567 (S 2914) Extend through fiscal year 1988 Small Business Administration pilot programs under section 8 of the Small Business Act. Introduced by WEICKER, R-Conn., Oct. 9, 1986. Senate passed Oct. 9. House passed, under suspension of the rules, Oct. 14. President signed Oct. 27, 1986.

PL 99-568 (S J Res 392) Designate December 1986 as "Made in America Month." Introduced by THURMOND, R-S.C., Aug. 12, 1986. Senate Judiciary reported Sept. 11. Senate passed Sept. 12. House Post Office and Civil Service discharged. House passed Oct. 10. President signed Oct. 27, 1986.

PL 99-569 (HR 4759) Authorize funds for the CIA and other federal intelligence agencies for fiscal year 1987. Introduced by HAMILTON, D-Ind., May 7, 1986. House Select Intelligence reported July 17 (H Rept 99-690, Part 1). House Post Office and Civil Service reported July 28 (H Rept 99-690, Part 2). House Armed Services reported July 28 (H Rept 99-690, Part 3). House Judiciary discharged. House passed Sept. 17. Senate passed, amended, Sept. 24. House agreed to conference report Oct. 2 (H Rept 99-952). Senate agreed to conference report Oct. 6. President signed Oct. 27, 1986.

PL 99-570 (HR 5484) Authorize $1.7 billion for federal drug interdiction, enforcement, education, treatment and rehabilitation efforts. Introduced by WRIGHT, D-Texas, Sept. 8, 1986. House passed Sept. 11. Senate passed, amended, Sept. 30. House agreed to Senate amendment with an amendment Oct. 8. Senate agreed to House amendment with an amendment Oct. 15. House agreed to Senate amendment to House amendment with an amendment Oct. 17. Senate agreed to House amendment Oct. 17. President signed Oct. 27, 1986.

PL 99-571 (HR 2032) Amend the Securities Exchange Act of 1934 to provide improved protection for investors in government securities. Introduced by DINGELL, D-Mich., April 15, 1985. House Energy and Commerce reported Sept. 9 (H Rept 99-258). House passed, under suspension of the rules, Sept. 17. Senate Banking, Housing and Urban Affairs discharged. Senate passed, amended, Sept. 16, 1986. House agreed to Senate amendments with an amendment Oct. 6. Senate agreed to House amendment Oct. 9. President signed Oct. 28, 1986.

PL 99-572 (HR 2205) Authorize the erection of a memorial on federal land in the District of Columbia and its environs to honor members of the U.S. armed forces who served in the Korean War. Introduced by FLORIO, D-N.J., April 24, 1985. House Committee on House Administration reported Oct. 29 (H Rept 99-341). House passed, under suspension of the rules, Nov. 6. Senate Energy and Natural Resources reported Sept. 19, 1986 (S Rept 99-459). Senate passed, amended, Oct. 9. House agreed to Senate amendment Oct. 14. President signed Oct. 28, 1986.

PL 99-573 (HR 3578) Provide permanent authority for hearing commissioners in the District of Columbia courts, and modify certain procedures of the District of Columbia Judicial Nomination Commission and the District of Columbia Commission on Judicial Disabilities and Tenure. Introduced by DYMALLY, D-Calif., Oct. 17, 1985. House District of Columbia reported Oct. 23 (H Rept 99-326). House passed Oct. 28. Senate Governmental Affairs reported Sept. 23, 1986 (S Rept 99-477). Senate passed, amended, Oct. 3. House agreed to Senate amendment Oct. 10. President signed Oct. 28, 1986.

PL 99-574 (HR 4354) Authorize programs of the National Bureau of Standards for fiscal 1987, and initiate an experimental revision of the federal pay system in that agency. Introduced by FUQUA, D-Fla., March 10, 1986. House Science and Technology reported June 4 (H Rept 99-617). House Post Office and Civil Service reported July 25 (H Rept 99-617, Part 2). House passed, under suspension of the rules, Aug. 12. Senate passed, amended, Oct. 3. House agreed to Senate amendment Oct. 10. President signed Oct. 28, 1986.

PL 99-575 (HR 4873) Authorize certain transfers affecting the Pueblo of Santa Ana in New Mexico. Introduced by RICHARDSON, D-N.M., May 21, 1986. House Interior and Insular Affairs reported Sept. 12 (H Rept 99-818). House passed, under suspension of the rules, Sept. 16. Senate passed, amended, Oct. 6. House agreed to Senate amendments Oct. 15. President signed Oct. 28, 1986.

PL 99-576 (HR 5299) Increase veterans' disability compensation by 1.5 percent and make other changes in veterans' programs. Introduced by MONTGOMERY, D-Miss., July 31, 1986. House Veterans' Affairs reported July 31 (H Rept 99-730). House passed, under suspension of the rules, Aug. 4. Senate passed, amended, Sept. 30. House agreed to Senate amendments with amendments Oct. 7. Senate agreed to House amendments Oct. 8. President signed Oct. 28, 1986.

PL 99-577 (HR 5598) Provide for the transfer of the Coast Guard cutter *Taney* to the city of Baltimore, Md., for use as a maritime museum and display. Introduced by MIKULSKI, D-Md., Sept. 25, 1986. House Merchant Marine and Fisheries reported Oct. 6 (H Rept 99-969). House passed, under suspension of the rules, Oct. 6. Senate passed Oct. 15. President signed Oct. 28, 1986.

PL 99-578 (S 209) Authorize contracts retaining private counsel to furnish legal services in the case of indebtedness owed the United States. Introduced by D'AMATO, R-N.Y., Jan. 21, 1985. Senate Governmental Affairs reported March 7, 1986 (S Rept 99-256). Senate passed March 19. House Judiciary discharged. House passed, amended, Sept. 29. Senate agreed to House amendments Oct. 8. President signed Oct. 28, 1986.

PL 99-579 (S 475) Amend section 408 of the Motor Vehicle Information and Cost Savings Act to strengthen, for the protection of consumers, the provisions respecting disclosure of motor vehicle mileage when motor vehicles are transferred. Introduced by EXON, D-Neb., Feb. 19, 1985. Senate Commerce, Science and Transportation reported May 14 (S Rept 99-47). Senate passed Dec. 13. House Energy and Commerce discharged. House passed, amended, Oct. 6, 1986. Senate agreed to House amendment Oct. 8. President signed Oct. 28, 1986.

PL 99-580 (S J Res 367) Designate Oct. 28, 1986, as "National Kidney Program Day." Introduced by HEINZ, R-Pa., June 23, 1986. Senate Judiciary reported Aug. 7. Senate passed Aug. 9. House Post Office and Civil Service discharged. House passed, amended, Oct. 10. Senate agreed to House amendments Oct. 15. President signed Oct. 28, 1986.

PL 99-581 (HR 2776) Direct the secretary of the interior to convey title to the Robert F. Kennedy Memorial Stadium to the District of Columbia. Introduced by FAUNTROY, D-D.C., June 17, 1985. House District of Columbia reported June 18 (H Rept 99-176, Part 1). House Interior and Insular Affairs discharged. House passed June 24. Senate Energy and Natural Resources reported Nov. 18 (S Rept 99-185). Senate Governmental Affairs discharged. Senate passed, amended, Oct. 16, 1986. House agreed to Senate amendment Oct. 16. President signed Oct. 29, 1986.

PL 99-582 (HR 3415) Authorize the minting of coins in commemoration of the bicentennial of the U.S. Constitution. Introduced by ANNUNZIO, D-Ill., Sept. 23, 1985. House Banking, Finance and Urban Affairs discharged. House passed Oct. 1, 1986. Senate passed, amended, Oct. 16. House agreed to Senate amendments Oct. 16. President signed Oct. 29, 1986.

PL 99-583 (HR 4037) Provide for the establishment of the Indiana Dunes National Lakeshore. Introduced by VISCLOSKY, D-Ind., Jan. 23, 1986. House Interior and Insular Affairs reported Aug. 7 (H Rept 99-762). House passed, under suspension of the rules, Aug. 11. Senate Energy and Natural Resources discharged. Senate passed, amended, Oct. 17. House agreed to Senate amendment Oct. 17. President signed Oct. 29, 1986.

PL 99-584 (HR 4685) Adjust the boundaries of areas of the National Wilderness Preservation System in Texas. Introduced by WILSON, D-Texas, April 23, 1986. House Interior and Insular Affairs reported July 15 (H Rept 99-674, Part 1). House Agriculture discharged. House passed, under suspension of the rules, July 21. Senate Agriculture, Nutrition and Forestry discharged. Senate passed, amended, Oct. 17. House agreed to Senate amendment Oct. 17. President signed Oct. 29, 1986.

PL 99-585 (HR 5181) Designate the U.S. Courthouse at 68 Court St., Buffalo, N.Y., as the "Michael J. Dillon Memorial United States Courthouse." Introduced by NOWAK, D-N.Y., July 16, 1986. House Public Works and Transportation reported Sept. 24 (H Rept 99-880). House passed Oct. 6. Senate Environment and Public Works discharged. Senate passed Oct. 18. President signed Oct. 29, 1986.

PL 99-586 (HR 5218) Provide that certain National Guard technicians who are involuntarily separated from service be accorded competitive status for the purpose of transferring to federal jobs in the competitive service. Introduced by LONG, D-La., July 22, 1986. House passed, under suspension of the rules, Oct. 6. Senate Governmental Affairs discharged. Senate passed Oct. 17. President signed Oct. 29, 1986.

PL 99-587 (HR 5459) Direct the release, on behalf of the United States, of certain conditions and reservations contained in a conveyance of land to the state of Utah. Introduced by HANSEN, R-Utah, Aug. 15, 1986. House Interior and Insular Affairs reported Sept. 29 (H Rept 99-919). House passed, under suspension of the rules, Sept. 30. Senate Energy and Natural Resources discharged. Senate passed Oct. 16. President signed Oct. 29, 1986.

PL 99-588 (HR 5470) Designate the U.S. Courthouse for the Eastern District of Virginia, in Alexandria, Va., as the "Albert V. Bryan United States Courthouse." Introduced by PARRIS, R-Va., Aug. 15, 1986. House Public Works and Transportation reported Sept. 24 (H Rept 99-879). House passed Oct. 6. Senate Environment and Public Works discharged. Senate passed Oct. 18. President signed Oct. 29, 1986.

PL 99-589 (H J Res 620) Designate the week beginning Jan. 4, 1987, as "National Bowling Week." Introduced by HERTEL, D-Mich., May 1, 1986. House Post Office and Civil Service discharged. House passed Oct. 10. Senate Judiciary discharged. Senate passed Oct. 18. President signed Oct. 29, 1986.

PL 99-590 (HR 4350) Amend the Wild and Scenic Rivers Act to protect several rivers by designating them as wild and scenic rivers. Introduced by VENTO, D-Minn., March 6, 1986. House Interior and Insular Affairs reported March 20 (H Rept 99-503). House passed, under suspension of the rules, April 8. Senate Energy and Natural Resources discharged. Senate passed, amended, Sept. 12. House agreed to Senate amendment with amendments Oct. 8. Senate agreed to House amendments with an amendment Oct. 15. House agreed to Senate amendment Oct. 16. President signed Oct. 30, 1986.

PL 99-591 (H J Res 738) Make continuing appropriations for fiscal year 1987. Introduced by WHITTEN, D-Miss., Sept. 24, 1986. House passed Sept. 25. Senate Appropriations reported Sept. 26 (S Rept 99-500). Senate passed, amended, Oct. 3. House agreed to conference report Oct. 15 (H Rept 99-1005). House agreed to a Senate amendment, agreed to certain Senate amendments with amendments, and insisted on its disagreement to a Senate amendment, Oct. 15. House agreed to certain Senate amendments Oct. 16. Senate agreed to conference report Oct. 16. Senate disagreed to certain House amendments to Senate amendments, agreed to a House amendment to a Senate amendment and receded from an amendment, Oct. 16. Senate agreed to a House amendment to a Senate amendment, with an amendment, Oct. 17. House receded from certain amendments to Senate amendments and agreed to a Senate amendment to a House amendment to a Senate amendment Oct. 17. President signed Oct. 18, 1986 (PL 99-500). President signed upon resubmittal Oct. 30, 1986.

PL 99-592 (HR 4154) Amend the Age Discrimination in Employment Act of 1967 to remove the maximum age limitation applicable to employees who are protected under the act. Introduced by PEPPER, D-Fla., Feb. 6, 1986. House Education and Labor reported Aug. 6 (H Rept 99-756). House passed Sept. 23. Senate passed, amended, Oct. 16. House agreed to Senate amendment Oct. 17. President signed Oct. 31, 1986.

PL 99-593 (HR 4576) Designate the U.S. Attorney's Building for the Southern District of New York as the "Silvio James Mollo Federal Building." Introduced by BIAGGI, D-N.Y., April 15, 1986. House Public Works and Transportation reported Sept. 25 (H Rept 99-885). House passed Oct. 6. Senate Environment and Public Works discharged. Senate passed Oct. 18. President signed Oct. 31, 1986.

PL 99-594 (HR 5215) Authorize the construction by the secretary of agriculture of a salinity laboratory at Riverside, Calif. Introduced by BROWN, D-Calif., July 22, 1986. House Agriculture reported Oct. 3 (H Rept 99-966). House passed, under suspension of the rules, Oct. 7. Senate Agriculture, Nutrition and Forestry discharged. Senate passed Oct. 18. President signed Oct. 31, 1986.

PL 99-595 (HR 5679) Extend the exclusion from federal unemployment tax of wages paid to certain alien farm workers. Introduced by ROSTENKOWSKI, D-Ill., Oct. 9, 1986. House passed Oct. 10. Senate Finance discharged. Senate passed Oct. 18. President signed Oct. 31, 1986.

PL 99-596 (HR 5682) Authorize the secretary of the Navy to make a certain conveyance of real property. Introduced by DYSON, D-Md., Oct. 9, 1986. House Armed Services discharged. House passed Oct. 17. Senate passed Oct. 18. President signed Nov. 3, 1986.

PL 99-597 (S 2948) Authorize the president to promote posthumously the late Lt. Col. Ellison S. Onizuka to the grade of colonel. Introduced by MATSUNAGA, D-Hawaii, Oct. 17, 1986. Senate passed Oct. 17. House passed Oct. 18. President signed Nov. 3, 1986.

PL 99-598 (HR 2484) Amend title 28, U.S. Code, to exempt states from the statute of limitations applicable to quiet title actions against the United States. Introduced by BERMAN, D-Calif., May 14, 1985. House Judiciary reported Sept. 29, 1986 (H Rept 99-924). House passed, under suspension of the rules, Sept. 30. Senate passed Oct. 17. President signed Nov. 4, 1986.

PL 99-599 (HR 4118) Designate the building commonly known as the Old Post Office in Worcester, Mass., as the "Harold D. Donohue Federal Building." Introduced by EARLY, D-Mass., Feb. 4, 1986. House Public Works and Transportation reported Sept. 24 (H Rept 99-881). House passed Oct. 6. Senate Environment and Public Works discharged. Senate passed Oct. 18. President signed Nov. 5, 1986.

PL 99-600 (HR 5167) Declare that the United States holds certain public domain lands in trust for the Pueblo of Zia. Introduced by RICHARDSON, D-N.M., July 15, 1986. House Interior and Insular Affairs reported Sept. 12 (H Rept 99-819). House passed, under suspension of the rules, Sept. 16. Senate Energy and Natural Resources discharged. Senate passed, amended, Oct. 16. House agreed to Senate amendments Oct. 16. President signed Nov. 5, 1986.

PL 99-601 (HR 5564) Provide for the eligibility of certain property for single-family mortgage insurance. Introduced by LUNDINE, D-N.Y., Sept. 19, 1986. House passed, under suspension of the rules, Sept. 29. Senate passed Oct. 18. President signed Nov. 5, 1986.

PL 99-602 (H J Res 645) Designate 1988 as the "National Year of Friendship with Finland." Introduced by OBERSTAR, D-Minn., May 22, 1986. House Post Office and Civil Service discharged. House passed Oct. 17. Senate passed Oct. 18. President signed Nov. 5, 1986.

PL 99-603 (S 1200) Overhaul the nation's immigration laws by penalizing employers who knowingly hire illegal aliens, providing legal status to millions of illegal aliens already in the country, and setting up a new program to grant legal status to foreign farm workers with a history of working in American agriculture. Introduced by SIMPSON, R-Wyo., May 23, 1985. Senate Judiciary reported Aug. 28 (S Rept 99-132). Senate Budget reported Sept. 19. Senate passed Sept. 19. House passed, amended, Oct. 9, 1986. House agreed to conference report Oct. 15 (H Rept 99-1000). Senate agreed to conference report Oct. 17. President signed Nov. 6, 1986.

PL 99-604 (HR 897) Recognize the Army and Navy Union of the United States of America. Introduced by SEIBERLING, D-Ohio, Jan. 31, 1985. House Judiciary reported May 6 (H Rept 99-63). House passed, under suspension of the rules, May 13. Senate Judiciary reported Oct. 2, 1986. Senate passed Oct. 18. President signed Nov. 6, 1986.

PL 99-605 (HR 1452) Extend for two years the authorization of appropriations for refugee assistance. Introduced by MAZZOLI, D-Ky., March 7, 1985. House Judiciary reported May 15 (H Rept 99-132, Part 1). House Foreign Affairs discharged. House passed June 13. Senate Judiciary reported June 13 (S Rept 99-154). Senate passed, amended, Oct. 18, 1986. House agreed to Senate amendments Oct. 18. President signed Nov. 6, 1986.

PL 99-606 (HR 1790) Withdraw certain public lands for military purposes. Introduced by BYRON, D-Md., March 28, 1985. House Interior and Insular Affairs discharged. House Armed Services discharged. House passed Oct. 17, 1986. Senate passed Oct. 18. President signed Nov. 6, 1986.

PL 99-607 (HR 2434) Authorize appropriations for the Patent and Trademark Office in the Department of Commerce. Introduced by KASTENMEIER, D-Wis., May 8, 1985. House Judiciary reported May 15 (H Rept 99-104). House passed, under suspension of the rules, June 24. Senate Judiciary reported May 20, 1986 (S Rept 99-305). Senate passed, amended, June 6. House agreed to certain Senate amendments, and agreed to certain Senate amendments with amendments, Oct. 2. Senate agreed to House amendments to Senate amendments Oct. 18. President signed Nov. 6, 1986.

PL 99-608 (HR 4244) Authorize funds to preserve the official papers of former Speaker of the House Joseph W. Martin Jr. (R-Mass., 1925-67; Speaker, 1947-49, 1953-55). Introduced by CONTE, R-Mass., Feb. 26, 1986. House passed, under suspension of the rules, Sept. 16. Senate Labor and Human Resources discharged. Senate passed, amended, Sept. 30. House agreed to Senate amendment Oct. 16. President signed Nov. 6, 1986.

PL 99-609 (HR 5554) Transfer the Community Development Credit Union Revolving Loan Fund to the National Credit Union Administration and authorize the National Credit Union Administration Board to administer the fund. Introduced by GARCIA, D-N.Y., Sept. 18, 1986. House passed, under suspension of the rules, Sept. 29. Senate passed Oct. 18. President signed Nov. 6, 1986.

PL 99-610 (H J Res 36) Authorize the establishment of a memorial on federal land in the District of Columbia and its environs to honor women who have served in the U.S. armed forces. Introduced by OAKAR, D-Ohio, Jan. 3, 1985. House Committee on House Administration reported Oct. 29 (H Rept 99-342). House passed, under suspension of the rules, Nov. 6. Senate Energy and Natural Resources reported Sept. 19, 1986 (S Rept 99-461). Senate passed, amended, Oct. 17. House agreed to Senate amendments Oct. 17. President signed Nov. 6, 1986.

PL 99-611 (H J Res 594) Designate the week beginning May 3, 1987, as "National Correctional Officers Week." Introduced by FAZIO, D-Calif., April 10, 1986. House Post Office and Civil Service discharged. House passed Oct. 10. Senate Judiciary discharged. Senate passed Oct. 18. President signed Nov. 6, 1986.

PL 99-612 (H J Res 684) Call for recognition of United Way's 100th anniversary. Introduced by MICHEL, R-Ill., July 24, 1986. House Post Office and Civil Service discharged. House passed Sept. 18. Senate Judiciary discharged. Senate passed Oct. 17. President signed Nov. 6, 1986.

PL 99-613 (H J Res 755) Provide for the convening of the first session of the 100th Congress. Introduced by FOLEY, D-Wash., Oct. 17, 1986. House passed Oct. 17. Senate passed Oct. 18. President signed Nov. 6, 1986.

PL 99-614 (S 386) Confirm a conveyance of certain real property by the Southern Pacific Transportation Co. to Ernest Pritchett and his wife, Dianna Pritchett. Introduced by PACKWOOD, R-Ore., Feb. 5, 1985. Senate Governmental Affairs reported Nov. 26. Senate passed Feb. 4, 1986. House Interior and Insular Affairs discharged. House passed, amended, Oct. 15. Senate agreed to House amendments Oct. 18. President signed Nov. 6, 1986.

PL 99-615 (S 511) Change the name of the Loxahatchee National Wildlife Refuge in Florida to the Arthur R. Marshall Loxahatchee National Wildlife Refuge. Introduced by CHILES, D-Fla., Feb. 26, 1985. Senate Environment and Public Works reported Oct. 2, 1986. Senate passed Oct. 9. House passed Oct. 16. President signed Nov. 6, 1986.

PL 99-616 (S 1230) Amend the patent laws implementing the Patent Cooperation Treaty. Introduced by MATHIAS, R-Md., June 4, 1985. Senate Judiciary reported Dec. 10 (S Rept 99-275). Senate passed Oct. 17, 1986. House passed Oct. 17. President signed Nov. 6, 1986.

PL 99-617 (S 1311) Designate the U.S. Courthouse and Customhouse in Louisville, Ky., as the "Gene Snyder United States Courthouse and Customhouse," and authorize the Board of Regents of the Smithsonian Institution to construct the Charles McC. Mathias Jr. Laboratory for Environmental Research in Edgewater, Md. Introduced by GOLDWATER, R-Ariz., June 17, 1985. Senate Rules and Administration reported Aug. 15, 1986 (S Rept 99-414). Senate passed Sept. 15. House passed, amended, Oct. 16. Senate agreed to House amendments Oct. 18. President signed Nov. 6, 1986.

PL 99-618 (S 2852) Authorize the secretary of transportation to release restrictions on the use of certain property conveyed to the Peninsula Airport Commission in Virginia for airport purposes. Introduced by TRIBLE, R-Va., Sept. 23, 1986. Senate Commerce, Science and Transportation reported Sept. 26. Senate passed Oct. 9. House passed Oct. 17. President signed Nov. 6, 1986.

PL 99-619 (S 2864) Provide for a deputy secretary of labor, an assistant secretary of labor for administration and management, and three additional assistant secretaries of labor. Introduced by HATCH, R-Utah, Sept. 24, 1986. Senate Labor and Human Resources reported Sept. 24 (S Rept 99-484). Senate passed Oct. 10. House passed Oct. 16. President signed Nov. 6, 1986.

PL 99-620 (S J Res 43) Authorize establishment of a memorial to honor the American Armored Force. Introduced by THURMOND, R-S.C., Feb. 5, 1985. Senate Energy and Natural Resources reported Aug. 1 (S Rept 99-127). Senate passed Sept. 20. House Committee on House Administration discharged. House passed, amended, Oct. 16, 1986. Senate agreed to House amendments Oct. 17. President signed Nov. 6, 1986.

PL 99-621 (S J Res 268) Provide for reappointment of Murray Gell-Mann as a citizen regent of the Board of Regents of the Smithsonian Institution. Introduced by GOLDWATER, R-Ariz., Feb. 6, 1986. Senate Rules and Administration reported Oct. 2 (S Rept 99-517). Senate passed Oct. 3. House Committee on House Administration discharged. House passed, amended, Oct. 14. Senate agreed to House amendments Oct. 18. President signed Nov. 6, 1986.

PL 99-622 (S J Res 336) Express the sense of Congress on recognition of the contributions of the seven *Challenger* astronauts by supporting establishment of a Children's Challenge Center for Space Science. Introduced by GARN, R-Utah, April 29, 1986. Senate Commerce, Science and Transportation reported Sept. 29 (S Rept 99-502). Senate passed Oct. 1. House Science and Technology discharged. House passed, amended, Oct. 17. Senate agreed to House amendment Oct. 18. President signed Nov. 6, 1986.

PL 99-623 (S J Res 427) Reaffirm our friendship and sympathy with the people of El Salvador following the devastating earthquake of Oct. 10, 1986. Introduced by KASSEBAUM, R-Kan., Oct. 15, 1986. Senate passed Oct. 15. House passed Oct. 16. President signed Nov. 6, 1986.

PL 99-624 (HR 4302) Establish a commission for the purpose of encouraging and providing for the commemoration of the centennial of the birth of President Dwight D. Eisenhower. Introduced by ROBERTS, R-Kan., March 4, 1986. House Post Office and Civil Service reported Sept. 18 (H Rept 99-842). House passed, under suspension of the rules, Sept. 23. Senate passed Oct. 18. President signed Nov. 7, 1986.

PL 99-625 (HR 4531) Improve the operation of certain fish and wildlife programs. Introduced by BREAUX, D-La., April 9, 1986. House Merchant Marine and Fisheries reported July 16 (H Rept 99-679). House passed, under suspension of the rules, Sept. 9. Senate Environment and Public Works reported Sept. 23 (S Rept 99-475). Senate passed, amended, Oct. 3. House agreed to Senate amendment with amendments Oct. 14. Senate agreed to House amendments Oct. 18. President signed Nov. 7, 1986.

PL 99-626 (HR 4731) Amend chapter 131 of title 46, U.S. Code, relating to recreational boating safety, and enhance boating safety by requiring a report relating to the display on gasoline pumps of the type of alcohol, the percentage of each type of alcohol, and the percentage of cosolvents, if any, contained in the gasoline. Introduced by DAVIS, R-Mich., May 1, 1986. House Merchant Marine and Fisheries reported Oct. 6 (H Rept 99-968). House passed, under suspension of the rules, Oct. 6. Senate Commerce, Science and Transportation discharged. Senate passed, amended, Oct. 18. House agreed to Senate amendments Oct. 18. President signed Nov. 7, 1986.

PL 99-627 (HR 5420) Amend section 3726 of title 31, U.S. Code, relating to payment for transportation, permit prepayment audits for selected transportation bills, authorize permanently payment of transportation audit contractors from carrier overpayments collected, and authorize net overpayments collected to be transferred to the Treasury. Introduced by COLLINS, D-Ill., Aug. 13, 1986. House Government Operations reported Sept. 30 (H Rept 99-932). House passed, under suspension of the rules, Oct. 6. Senate passed Oct. 18. President signed Nov. 7, 1986.

PL 99-628 (HR 5560) Ban the production and use of advertisements for child pornography or solicitations for child pornography. Introduced by HUGHES, D-N.J., Sept. 19, 1986. House Judiciary reported Sept. 27 (H Rept 99-910). House passed, under suspension of the rules, Sept. 29. Senate passed Oct. 18. President signed Nov. 7, 1986.

PL 99-629 (H J Res 10) Designate the week beginning Jan. 19, 1987, as "Shays' Rebellion Week" and Sunday, Jan. 25, 1987, as "Shays' Rebellion Day." Introduced by CONTE, R-Mass., Jan. 3, 1985. House Post Office and Civil Service discharged. House passed Oct. 10, 1986. Senate Judiciary discharged. Senate passed Oct. 18. President signed Nov. 7, 1986.

PL 99-630 (H J Res 67) Call for a wildlife sanctuary for humpback whales in the West Indies. Introduced by WHITEHURST, R-Va., Jan. 3, 1985. House passed, under suspension of the rules, Sept. 23, 1986. Senate Foreign Relations reported Oct. 9. Senate passed Oct. 17. President signed Nov. 7, 1986.

PL 99-631 (H J Res 756) Make corrections in the Comprehensive Anti-Apartheid Act of 1986. Introduced by WOLPE, D-Mich., Oct. 17, 1986. House Foreign Affairs discharged. House passed Oct. 17. Senate passed Oct. 18. President signed Nov. 7, 1986.

PL 99-632 (S 565) Provide for the transfer of certain lands in the state of Arizona. Introduced by DeCONCINI, D-Ariz., March 5, 1985. Senate Energy and Natural Resources reported July 25, 1986 (S Rept 99-339). Senate passed Aug. 9. House Interior and Insular Affairs reported Sept. 26 (H Rept 99-900). House passed, amended, under suspension of the rules, Sept. 30. Senate agreed to House amendments with an amendment Oct. 9. House agreed to Senate amendment Oct. 10. President signed Nov. 7, 1986.

PL 99-633 (S 2245) Authorize appropriations to carry out the Export Administration Act of 1979 and export promotion activities. Introduced by HEINZ, R-Pa., March 26, 1986. Senate Banking, Housing and Urban Affairs reported March 26 (S Rept 99-271). Senate passed

July 21. House passed, amended, under suspension of the rules, Oct. 14. Senate agreed to House amendment with an amendment Oct. 18. House agreed to Senate amendment Oct. 18. President signed Nov. 7, 1986.

PL 99-634 (S 2250) Strengthen the prohibition of kickbacks relating to subcontracts under federal government contracts. Introduced by LEVIN, D-Mich., March 26, 1986. Senate Governmental Affairs reported Sept. 9 (S Rept 99-435). Senate passed Sept. 12. House Government Operations discharged. House Judiciary discharged. House passed, amended, Oct. 7. Senate agreed to House amendment Oct. 15. President signed Nov. 7, 1986.

PL 99-635 (S 2351) Revise the boundaries of Olympic National Park and Olympic National Forest in the state of Washington. Introduced by EVANS, R-Wash., April 22, 1986. Senate Energy and Natural Resources reported Oct. 1 (S Rept 99-510). Senate passed Oct. 10. House passed Oct. 15. President signed Nov. 7, 1986.

PL 99-636 (S 2452) Provide for the naming or renaming of certain buildings of the U.S. Postal Service. Introduced by HOLLINGS, D-S.C., May 15, 1986. Senate Governmental Affairs reported Sept. 19. Senate passed Sept. 29. House Post Office and Civil Service discharged. House passed, amended, Oct. 15. Senate agreed to House amendments Oct. 18. President signed Nov. 7, 1986.

PL 99-637 (S 2534) Authorize the acquisition and development of a mainland tour boat facility for the Fort Sumter National Monument in South Carolina. Introduced by THURMOND, R-S.C., June 10, 1986. Senate Energy and Natural Resources reported Sept. 23 (S Rept 99-476). Senate passed Oct. 10. House Interior and Insular Affairs discharged. House passed, amended, Oct. 15. Senate agreed to House amendment Oct. 18. President signed Nov. 7, 1986.

PL 99-638 (HR 2663) Credit time spent in the Cadet Nurse Corps during World War II as creditable service for civil service retirement, and provide civil service retirement credit for certain employees and former employees of non-appropriated fund instrumentalities under the jurisdiction of the armed forces. Introduced by SLATTERY, D-Kan., June 4, 1985. House passed, under suspension of the rules, Oct. 6, 1986. Senate passed, amended, Oct. 18. House agreed to Senate amendments Oct. 18. President signed Nov. 10, 1986.

PL 99-639 (HR 3737) Deter immigration-related marriage fraud and other immigration fraud. Introduced by McCOLLUM, R-Fla., Nov. 12, 1985. House Judiciary reported Sept. 26, 1986 (H Rept 99-906). House passed, under suspension of the rules, Sept. 29. Senate passed Oct. 18. President signed Nov. 10, 1986.

PL 99-640 (HR 4208) Authorize appropriations for the Coast Guard for fiscal year 1987. Introduced by STUDDS, D-Mass., Feb. 20, 1986. House Merchant Marine and Fisheries reported April 18 (H Rept 99-547). House passed May 6. Senate Commerce, Science and Transportation reported Oct. 6 (S Rept 99-530). Senate passed, amended, Oct. 16. House agreed to Senate amendment Oct. 16. President signed Nov. 10, 1986.

PL 99-641 (HR 4613) Reauthorize appropriations to carry out the Commodity Exchange Act, and make technical improvements to that act. Introduced by de la GARZA, D-Texas, April 17, 1986. House Agriculture reported June 6 (H Rept 99-624). House passed July 16. Senate passed, amended, Oct. 6. House rejected conference report Oct. 15 (H Rept 99-995). House agreed to Senate amendment with an amendment Oct. 15. Senate agreed to House amendment Oct. 17. President signed Nov. 10, 1986.

PL 99-642 (HR 5180) Designate the federal building at 111 W. Huron St., Buffalo, N.Y., as the "Thaddeus J. Dulski Federal Building." Introduced by NOWAK, D-N.Y., July 16, 1986. House Public Works and Transportation reported Sept. 24 (H Rept 99-876). House passed Oct. 6. Senate Environment and Public Works discharged. Senate passed Oct. 18. President signed Nov. 10, 1986.

PL 99-643 (HR 5595) Make permanent and improve the provisions of section 1619 of the Social Security Act. Introduced by FORD, D-Tenn., Sept. 25, 1986. House Ways and Means reported Sept. 25 (H Rept 99-893). House passed, under suspension of the rules, Sept. 30. Senate passed, amended, Oct. 8. House agreed to Senate amendments with amendments Oct. 15. House agreed to Senate amendment to the title of the bill Oct. 16. House agreed to Senate amendment to the text of the bill with further amendments Oct. 16. Senate agreed to House amendments Oct. 18. President signed Nov. 10, 1986.

PL 99-644 (S 485) Clarify the treatment of submerged lands and ownership by the Alaskan Native Corporation. Introduced by MURKOWSKI, R-Alaska, Feb. 20, 1985. Senate Energy and Natural Resources reported Oct. 1, 1986 (S Rept 99-507). Senate passed Oct. 16. House passed Oct. 16. President signed Nov. 10, 1986.

PL 99-645 (S 740) Promote the conservation of migratory waterfowl, and offset or prevent the serious loss of wetlands by the acquisition of wetlands and other essential habitat. Introduced by CHAFEE, R-R.I., March 26, 1985. Senate Environment and Public Works reported Sept. 16, 1986 (S Rept 99-445). Senate Energy and Natural Resources reported Sept. 25. Senate passed Oct. 3. House passed, under suspension of the rules, Oct. 14. President signed Nov. 10, 1986.

PL 99-646 (S 1236) Make minor or technical amendments to provisions enacted by the Comprehensive Crime Control Act of 1984. Introduced by THURMOND, R-S.C., June 4, 1985. Senate Judiciary reported April 4, 1986 (S Rept 99-278). Senate passed April 17. House Judiciary discharged. House passed, amended, Oct. 17. Senate agreed to House amendment Oct. 18. President signed Nov. 10, 1986.

PL 99-647 (S 1374) Establish the Blackstone River Valley National Heritage Corridor in Massachusetts and Rhode Island. Introduced by CHAFEE, R-R.I., June 27, 1985. Senate Energy and Natural Resources reported Sept. 25, 1986 (S Rept 99-488). Senate passed Oct. 8. House Interior and Insular Affairs discharged. House passed, amended, Oct. 15. Senate agreed to House amendment Oct. 17. President signed Nov. 10, 1986.

PL 99-648 (S 2000) Clarify the exemptive authority of the Securities and Exchange Commission. Introduced by ROCKEFELLER, D-W.Va.-BYRD, D-W.Va., Dec. 20, 1985. Senate Banking, Housing and Urban Affairs reported Aug. 13, 1986. Senate passed Aug. 15. House passed, amended, Sept. 29. Senate agreed to House amendment Oct. 17. President signed Nov. 10, 1986.

PL 99-649 (S 2648) Improve the public health through the prevention of childhood injuries. Introduced by KENNEDY, D-Mass., July 16, 1986. Senate Labor and Human Resources reported Sept. 3 (S Rept 99-434). Senate passed Oct. 3. House passed Oct. 16. President signed Nov. 10, 1986.

PL 99-650 (HR 2946) Establish an independent jury system for the Superior Court of the District of Columbia. Introduced by DYMALLY, D-Calif., July 10, 1985. House District of Columbia reported Oct. 23 (H Rept 99-324). House passed Oct. 28. Senate Governmental Affairs reported Sept. 23, 1986 (S Rept 99-473). Senate passed, amended, Oct. 18. House agreed to Senate amendments Oct. 18. President signed Nov. 14, 1986.

PL 99-651 (HR 3004) Improve the delivery of legal services in the criminal justice system to those persons financially unable to obtain adequate representation. Introduced by KASTENMEIER, D-Wis., July 16, 1985. House Judiciary reported Dec. 5 (H Rept 99-417). House passed, under suspension of the rules, Dec. 9. Senate Judiciary discharged. Senate passed, amended, Oct. 6, 1986. House agreed to Senate amendment with an amendment Oct. 14. Oct. 14 proceedings vacated Oct. 15. House agreed to Senate amendment with an amendment Oct. 15. Senate agreed to House amendment Oct. 17. President signed Nov. 14, 1986.

PL 99-652 (HR 4378) Provide standards for placement of commemorative works on certain federal lands in the District of Columbia and its environs. Introduced by UDALL, D-Ariz., March 11, 1986. House Interior and Insular Affairs reported May 5 (H Rept 99-574). House passed, under suspension of the rules, May 5. Senate Energy and Natural Resources reported Aug. 15 (S Rept 99-421). Senate passed, amended, Sept. 10. House agreed to Senate amendments with amendments Sept. 29. Senate agreed to House amendments Oct. 16. President signed Nov. 14, 1986.

PL 99-653 (HR 4444) Amend the Immigration and Nationality Act to provide for the issuance of certificates of citizenship for children adopted by U.S. citizens. Introduced by RODINO, D-N.J., March 18, 1986. House Judiciary reported Sept. 26 (H Rept 99-916). House passed, under suspension of the rules, Sept. 29. Senate passed, amended, Oct. 18. House agreed to Senate amendment Oct. 18. President signed Nov. 14, 1986.

PL 99-654 (HR 4745) Amend title 18, U.S. Code, to revise and reform federal sexual abuse statutes. Introduced by CONYERS, D-Mich., May 5, 1986. House Judiciary reported May 9 (H Rept 99-594). House passed, under suspension of the rules, May 12. Senate Judiciary reported Oct. 3. Senate passed Oct. 18. President signed Nov. 14, 1986.

PL 99-655 (HR 5028) Authorize the secretary of the interior to construct, operate and maintain the Lower Colorado Water Supply Project, to supply water for domestic, municipal, industrial and recreational purposes. Introduced by LEWIS, R-Calif., June 12, 1986. House Interior and Insular Affairs reported June 23 (H Rept 99-650). House passed, under suspension of the rules, June 24. Senate Energy and Natural Resources reported Sept. 27 (S Rept 99-496). Senate passed, amended, Oct. 9. House agreed to certain amendments and disagreed to an amendment Oct. 15. Senate receded from its amendment Oct. 18. President signed Nov. 14, 1986.

PL 99-656 (HR 5363) Amend the interest provisions of the Declaration of Taking Act. Introduced by GLICKMAN, D-Kan., Aug. 8, 1986. House Judiciary reported Sept. 27 (H Rept 99-914). House passed, under suspension of the rules, Sept. 29. Senate passed, amended, Oct. 17. House agreed to Senate amendment with an amendment Oct. 17. Senate agreed to House amendment Oct. 17. President signed Nov. 14, 1986.

PL 99-657 (HR 5674) Amend title 28, U.S. Code, with respect to the composition of, and places of holding court in, certain judicial districts. Introduced by KASTENMEIER, D-Wis., Oct. 8, 1986. House Judiciary discharged. House passed Oct. 14. Senate passed Oct. 18. President signed Nov. 14, 1986.

PL 99-658 (H J Res 626) Approve the Compact of Free Association between the United States and the government of Palau. Introduced by SEIBERLING, D-Ohio, May 6, 1986. House Foreign Affairs reported June 26 (H Rept 99-663, Part 1). House Interior and Insular Affairs reported July 23 (H Rept 99-663, Part 2). House Appropriations discharged. House Ways and Means reported Sept. 17 (H Rept 99-663, Part 3). House Judiciary discharged. House Armed Services discharged. House Merchant Marine and Fisheries reported Sept. 19 (H Rept 99-663, Part 4). House passed, under suspension of the rules, Sept. 29. Senate passed, amended, Oct. 6. House agreed to Senate amendment Oct. 16. President signed Nov. 14, 1986.

PL 99-659 (S 991) Amend certain provisions of the law regarding the fisheries of the United States. Introduced by DANFORTH, R-Mo., April 24, 1985. Senate Commerce, Science and Transportation reported May 21 (S Rept 99-67). Senate passed Oct. 2. House passed, amended, under suspension of the rules, Aug. 12, 1986. Senate agreed to House amendments with amendments Oct. 15. House agreed to Senate amendments with amendments Oct. 16. Senate agreed to House amendments Oct. 18. President signed Nov. 14, 1986.

PL 99-660 (S 1744) Establish a no-fault compensation system for the families of children who are injured or die from side effects of vaccines against major childhood diseases; permit U.S. pharmaceutical manufacturers to export to certain countries drugs and other biological products not yet approved for use in this country; require states to develop and implement state comprehensive mental health plans; and make several other health program changes. Introduced by KENNEDY, D-Mass., Oct. 8, 1985. Senate Labor and Human Resources reported Aug. 6, 1986 (S Rept 99-380). Senate passed Aug. 12. House Energy and Commerce discharged. House passed, amended, Oct. 17. Senate agreed to House amendment Oct. 18. President signed Nov. 14, 1986.

PL 99-661 (S 2638) Authorize appropriations in fiscal year 1987 for defense programs of the Departments of Defense and Energy. Introduced by GOLDWATER, R-Ariz., July 8, 1986. Senate Armed Services reported July 8 (S Rept 99-331). Senate passed Aug. 9. House passed, amended, Sept. 18. House agreed to conference report Oct. 15 (H Rept 99-1001). Senate agreed to conference report Oct. 15. President signed Nov. 14, 1986.

PL 99-662 (HR 6) Authorize the Army Corps of Engineers to undertake various water resources development projects. Introduced by HOWARD, D-N.J., Jan. 3, 1985. House Public Works and Transportation reported Aug. 1 (H Rept 99-251, Part 1). House Interior and Insular Affairs reported Sept. 16 (H Rept 99-251, Part 2). House Ways and Means reported Sept. 23 (H Rept 99-251, Part 3). House Merchant Marine and Fisheries reported Sept. 23 (H Rept 99-251, Part 4). House passed Nov. 13. Senate passed, amended, March 26, 1986. House agreed to conference report Oct. 17 (H Rept 99-1013). Senate agreed to conference report Oct. 17. President signed Nov. 17, 1986.

PL 99-663 (HR 5705) Protect and provide for the enhancement of the resources of the Columbia River Gorge. Introduced by WEAVER, D-Ore., Oct. 15, 1986. House passed Oct. 16. Senate passed Oct. 17. President signed Nov. 17, 1986.

PL 99-664 (HR 5730) Provide for a land exchange in the state of Alaska. Introduced by YOUNG, R-Alaska, Oct. 17, 1986. House Interior and Insular Affairs discharged. House passed Oct. 17. Senate passed Oct. 17. President signed Nov. 17, 1986. ∎

CONGRESS
and Its MEMBERS

CQ

Glossary of Congressional Terms

Act—The term for legislation once it has passed both houses of Congress and has been signed by the president or passed over his veto, thus becoming law. *(See below.)* Also used in parliamentary terminology for a bill that has been passed by one house and engrossed. *(See Engrossed Bill.)*

Adjournment Sine Die—Adjournment without definitely fixing a day for reconvening; literally "adjournment without a day." Usually used to connote the final adjournment of a session of Congress. A session can continue until noon, Jan. 3, of the following year, when, under the 20th Amendment to the Constitution, it automatically terminates. Both houses must agree to a concurrent resolution for either house to adjourn for more than three days.

Adjournment to a Day Certain—Adjournment under a motion or resolution that fixes the next time of meeting. Under the Constitution, neither house can adjourn for more than three days without the concurrence of the other. A session of Congress is not ended by adjournment to a day certain.

Amendment—A proposal of a member of Congress to alter the language, provisions or stipulations in a bill or in another amendment. An amendment usually is printed, debated and voted upon in the same manner as a bill.

Amendment in the Nature of a Substitute—Usually an amendment that seeks to replace the entire text of a bill. Passage of this type of amendment strikes out everything after the enacting clause and inserts a new version of the bill. An amendment in the nature of a substitute also can refer to an amendment that replaces a large portion of the text of a bill.

Appeal—A member's challenge of a ruling or decision made by the presiding officer of the chamber. In the Senate, the senator appeals to members of the chamber to override the decision. If carried by a majority vote, the appeal nullifies the chair's ruling. In the House, the decision of the Speaker traditionally has been final; seldom are there appeals to the members to reverse the Speaker's stand. To appeal a ruling is considered an attack on the Speaker.

Appropriations Bill—A bill that gives legal authority to spend or obligate money from the Treasury. The Constitution disallows money to be drawn from the Treasury "but in Consequence of Appropriations made by Law."

By congressional custom, an appropriations bill originates in the House, and it is not supposed to be considered by the full House or Senate until a related measure authorizing the funding is enacted; appropriations bills need not provide the full amount permissible under the authorization measures. Under the 1985 Gramm-Rudman-Hollings law, the House Appropriations Committee is supposed to report by June 10 the last regular appropriations bill for the fiscal year starting the following Oct. 1. *(See also Budget Process.)*

In addition to general appropriations bills, there are two specialized types. *(See Continuing Resolution, Supplemental Appropriations Bill.)*

Authorization—Basic, substantive legislation that establishes or continues the legal operation of a federal program or agency, either indefinitely or for a specific period of time, or which sanctions a particular type of obligation or expenditure. An authorization normally is a prerequisite for an appropriation or other kind of budget authority. Under the rules of both houses, the appropriation for a program or agency may not be considered until its authorization has been considered. An authorization also may limit the amount of budget authority to be provided or may authorize the appropriation of "such sums as may be necessary." *(See also Backdoor Spending.)*

Backdoor Spending—Budget authority provided in legislation outside the normal appropriations process. The most common forms of backdoor spending are borrowing authority, contract authority and entitlements. *(See below.)*

In some cases, such as interest on the public debt, a permanent appropriation is provided that becomes available without further action by Congress.

Bills—Most legislative proposals before Congress are in the form of bills and are designated by HR in the House of Representatives or S in the Senate, according to the house in which they originate, and by a number assigned in the order in which they are introduced during the two-year period of a congressional term. "Public bills" deal with general questions and become public laws if approved by Congress and signed by the president. "Private bills" deal with individual matters such as claims against the government, immigration and naturalization cases, land titles, etc., and become private laws if approved and signed. *(See also Concurrent Resolution, Joint Resolution, Resolution.)*

Bills Introduced—In both the House and Senate, any number of members may join in introducing a single bill or resolution. The first member listed is the sponsor of the bill, and all members' names following his are the bill's cosponsors.

Many bills are committee bills and are introduced under the name of the chairman of the committee or subcommittee. All appropriations bills fall into this category. A committee frequently holds hearings on a number of related bills and may agree to one of them or to an entirely new bill. *(See also Report, Clean Bill, By Request.)*

Bills Referred—When introduced, a bill is referred to the committee or committees that have jurisdiction over the subject with which the bill is concerned. Under the standing rules of the House and Senate, bills are referred by the Speaker in the House and by the presiding officer in the Senate. In practice, the House and Senate parliamentarians act for these officials and refer the vast majority of bills.

Borrowing Authority—Statutory authority that permits a federal agency to incur obligations and make payments for specified purposes with borrowed money.

Budget—The document sent to Congress by the president early each year estimating government revenue and expenditures for the ensuing fiscal year.

Budget Authority—Authority to enter into obligations that will result in immediate or future outlays involving federal funds. The basic forms of budget authority are appropriations, contract authority and borrowing authority. Budget authority may be classified by (1) the period of availability (one-year, multiple-year or without a time limitation), (2) the timing of congressional action (current or permanent), or (3) the manner of determining the amount available (definite or indefinite).

Budget Process—Congress in 1985 attempted to strengthen its 11-year-old budget process with the goal of balancing the federal budget by October 1990. The law, known as Gramm-Rudman-Hollings for its congressional sponsors, established annual maximum deficit targets and mandated across-the-board automatic cuts if the deficit goals were not achieved through regular budget and appropriations actions.

The 1985 law also established an accelerated timetable for presidential submission of budgets and for congressional approval of budget resolutions and reconciliation bills, two mechanisms created by the Congressional Budget and Impoundment Control Act of 1974. Budget resolutions, due by April 15 annually, set guidelines for congressional action on spending and tax measures; they are adopted by the House and Senate but are not signed by the president and do not have the force of law. Reconciliation bills, due by June 15, actually make changes in existing law to meet budget resolution goals. *(See Budget Reconciliation.)*

The Supreme Court in 1986 found Gramm-Rudman's automatic spending cut mechanism to be unconstitutional. The mechanism was to be activated in mid-August each year if deficit re-estimates showed Congress and the president had not managed through conventional legislation to hold deficits below targets set by the statute. Absent the automatic device, the cuts necessitated by those estimates would take effect only if approved by Congress and the president. The Supreme Court upheld a lower court ruling that the automatic mechanism violated the separation-of-powers doctrine, because it assigned executive-type responsibilities to the General Accounting Office, which the court found to be a legislative entity. Under the remaining procedure deficit re-estimates would still be made, but Congress and the president must approve any spending cuts.

Budget Reconciliation—The 1974 budget act provided for a "reconciliation" procedure for bringing existing tax and spending laws into conformity with the congressional budget resolutions. Under the procedure, Congress instructs designated legislative committees to approve measures adjusting revenues and expenditures by a certain amount. The committees have a deadline by which they must report the legislation, but they have the discretion of deciding what changes are to be made. The recommendations of the various committees are consolidated without change by the Budget committees into an omnibus reconciliation bill, which then must be considered and approved by both houses of Congress.

By Request—A phrase used when a senator or representative introduces a bill at the request of an executive agency or private organization but does not necessarily endorse the legislation.

Calendar—An agenda or list of business awaiting possible action by each chamber. The House uses five legislative calendars. *(See Consent, Discharge, House, Private and Union Calendar.)*

In the Senate, all legislative matters reported from committee go on one calendar. They are listed there in the order in which committees report them or the Senate places them on the calendar, but may be called up out of order by the majority leader, either by obtaining unanimous consent of the Senate or by a motion to call up a bill. The Senate also uses one non-legislative calendar; this is used for treaties and nominations. *(See Executive Calendar.)*

Calendar Wednesday—In the House, committees, on Wednesdays, may be called in the order in which they appear in Rule X of the House, for the purpose of bringing up any of their bills from either the House or the Union Calendar, except bills that are privileged. General debate is limited to two hours. Bills called up from the Union Calendar are considered in Committee of the Whole. Calendar Wednesday is not observed during the last two weeks of a session and may be dispensed with at other times by a two-thirds vote. This procedure is rarely used and routinely is dispensed with by unanimous consent.

Call of the Calendar—Senate bills that are not brought up for debate by a motion, unanimous consent or a unanimous consent agreement are brought before the Senate for action when the calendar listing them is "called." Bills must be called in the order listed. Measures considered by this method usually are non-controversial, and debate is limited to a total of five minutes for each senator on the bill and any amendments proposed to it.

Chamber—The meeting place for the membership of either the House or the Senate; also the membership of the House or Senate meeting as such.

Clean Bill—Frequently after a committee has finished a major revision of a bill, one of the committee members, usually the chairman, will assemble the changes and what is left of the original bill into a new measure and introduce it as a "clean bill." The revised measure, which is given a new number, then is referred back to the committee, which reports it to the floor for consideration. This often is a timesaver, as committee-recommended changes in a clean bill do not have to be considered and voted on by the chamber. Reporting a clean bill also protects committee amendments that might be subject to points of order concerning germaneness.

Clerk of the House—Chief administrative officer of the House of Representatives, with duties corresponding to those of the secretary of the Senate. *(See also Secretary of the Senate.)*

Cloture—The process by which a filibuster can be ended in the Senate other than by unanimous consent. A motion for cloture can apply to any measure before the Senate, including a proposal to change the chamber's rules. A cloture motion requires the signatures of 16 senators to be introduced, and to end a filibuster the cloture motion must obtain the votes of three-fifths of the entire Senate membership (60 if there are no vacancies), except that to end a filibuster against a proposal to amend the standing rules of the Senate a two-thirds vote of senators present and voting is required. The cloture request is put to a roll-call vote one hour after the Senate meets on the second day following introduction of the motion. The bill or amendment in question comes to a final vote after 30 hours of post-cloture debate. *(See Filibuster.)*

Committee—A division of the House or Senate that prepares legislation for action by the parent chamber or makes investigations as directed by the parent chamber. There are several types of committees. *(See Standing and Select or Special Committees.)* Most standing committees are divided into subcommittees, which study legislation, hold hearings and report bills, with or without amendments, to the full committee. Only the full committee can report legislation for action by the House or Senate.

Committee of the Whole—The working title of what is formally "The Committee of the Whole House (of Representatives) on the State of the Union." The membership is composed of all House members sitting as a committee. Any 100 members who are present on the floor of the chamber to consider legislation constitute a quorum of the committee. Any legislation, however, must first have passed through the regular legislative or Appropriations committee and have been placed on the calendar.

Technically, the Committee of the Whole considers only bills directly or indirectly appropriating money, authorizing appropriations or involving taxes or charges on the public. Because the Committee of the Whole need number only 100 representatives, a quorum is more readily attained, and legislative business is expedited. Before 1971, members' positions were not individually recorded on votes taken in Committee of the Whole. *(See Teller Vote.)*

When the full House resolves itself into the Committee of the Whole, it supplants the Speaker with a "chairman." A measure is debated and amendments may be proposed, with votes on amendments as needed. *(See Five-Minute Rule.)*

When the committee completes its work on the measure, it dissolves itself by "rising." The Speaker returns, and the chairman of the Committee of the Whole reports to the House that the committee's work has been completed. At this time members may demand a roll-call vote on any amendment *adopted* in the Committee of the Whole. The final vote is on passage of the legislation.

Committee Veto—A requirement added to a few statutes directing that certain policy directives by an executive department or agency be reviewed by certain congressional committees before they are implemented. Under common practice, the government department or agency and the committees involved are expected to reach a consensus before the directives are carried out. *(See also Legislative Veto.)*

Concurrent Resolution—A concurrent resolution, designated H Con Res or S Con Res, must be adopted by both houses, but it is not sent to the president for his signature and therefore does not have the force of law. A concurrent resolution, for example, is used to fix the time for adjournment of a Congress. It also is used as the vehicle for expressing the sense of Congress on various foreign policy and domestic issues, and it serves as the vehicle for coordinated decisions on the federal budget under the 1974 Congressional Budget and Impoundment Control Act. *(See also Bills, Joint Resolution, Resolution.)*

Conference—A meeting between the representatives of the House and the Senate to reconcile differences between the two houses on provisions of a bill passed by both chambers. Members of the conference committee are appointed by the Speaker and the presiding officer of the Senate and are called "managers" for their respective chambers. A majority of the managers for each house must reach agreement on the provisions of the bill (often a compromise between the versions of the two chambers) before it can be considered by either chamber in the form of a "conference report." When the conference report goes to the floor, it cannot be amended, and, if it is not approved by both chambers, the bill may go back to conference under certain situations, or a new conference must be convened. Many rules and informal practices govern the conduct of conference committees.

Bills that are passed by both houses with only minor differences need not be sent to conference. Either chamber may "concur" in the other's amendments, completing action on the legislation. Sometimes leaders of the committees of jurisdiction work out an informal compromise instead of having a formal conference. *(See Custody of the Papers.)*

Confirmations—*(See Nominations.)*

Congressional Record—The daily, printed account of proceedings in both the House and Senate chambers, showing substantially verbatim debate, statements and a record of floor action. Highlights of legislative and committee action are embodied in a Daily Digest section of the Record, and members are entitled to have their extraneous remarks printed in an appendix known as "Extension of Remarks." Members may edit and revise remarks made on the floor during debate, and quotations from debate reported by the press are not always found in the Record.

The Record provides a way to distinguish remarks spoken on the floor of the House and Senate from undelivered speeches. In the Senate, all speeches, articles and other matter that members insert in the Record without actually reading them on the floor are set off by large black dots, or bullets. However, a loophole allows a member to avoid the bulleting if he delivers any portion of the speech in person. In the House, undelivered speeches and other material are printed in a distinctive typeface.

Congressional Terms of Office—Normally begin on Jan. 3 of the year following a general election and are two years for representatives and six years for senators. Representatives elected in special elections are sworn in for the remainder of a term. A person may be appointed to fill a Senate vacancy and serves until a successor is elected; the successor serves until the end of the term applying to the vacant seat.

Consent Calendar—Members of the House may place on this calendar most bills on the Union or House Calendar that are considered to be non-controversial. Bills on the Consent Calendar normally are called on the first and third Mondays of each month. On the first occasion that a bill is called in this manner, consideration may be blocked by the objection of any member. The second time, if there are three objections, the bill is stricken from the Consent Calendar. If less than three members object, the bill is given immediate consideration.

A bill on the Consent Calendar may be postponed in another way. A member may ask that the measure be passed over "without prejudice." In that case, no objection is recorded against the bill, and its status on the Consent Calendar remains unchanged. A bill stricken from the Consent Calendar remains on the Union or House Calendar.

Cosponsor—*(See Bills Introduced.)*

Continuing Resolution—A joint resolution drafted by Congress "continuing appropriations" for specific ongoing activities of a government department or departments when a fiscal year begins and Congress has not yet enacted all of the regular appropriations bills for that year. The continuing resolution usually specifies a maximum rate at which the agency may incur obligations. This usually is based on the rate for the previous year, the president's budget request or an appropriation bill for that year passed by either or both houses of Congress, but not cleared.

Contract Authority—Budget authority contained in an authorization bill that permits the federal government to enter into contracts or other obligations for future payments from funds not yet appropriated by Congress. The assumption is that funds will be available for payment in a subsequent appropriation act.

Controllable Budget Items—In federal budgeting this refers to programs for which the budget authority or outlays during a fiscal year can be controlled without changing existing, substantive law. The concept "relatively uncontrollable under current law" includes outlays for open-ended programs and fixed costs such as interest on the public debt, Social Security benefits, veterans' benefits and outlays to liquidate prior-year obligations.

Correcting Recorded Votes—Rules prohibit members from changing their votes after the result has been announced. But occasionally hours, days or months after a vote has been taken, a member may announce that he was "incorrectly recorded." In the Senate, a request to change one's vote almost always receives unanimous consent. In the House, members are prohibited from changing their votes if tallied by the electronic voting system installed in 1973. If taken by roll call, it is permissible if consent is granted.

Current Services Estimates—Estimated budget authority and outlays for federal programs and operations for the forthcoming fiscal year based on continuation of existing levels of service without policy changes. These estimates of budget authority and outlays, accompanied by the underlying economic and policy assumptions upon which they are based, are transmitted by the president to Congress when the budget is submitted.

Custody of the Papers—To reconcile differences between the House and Senate versions of a bill, a conference may be arranged. The chamber with "custody of the papers" — the engrossed bill, engrossed amendments, messages of transmittal — is the only body empowered to request the conference. By custom, the chamber that asks for a conference is the last to act on the conference report once agreement has been reached on the bill by the conferees.

Custody of the papers sometimes is manipulated to ensure that a particular chamber acts either first or last on the conference report.

Deferral—Executive branch action to defer, or delay, the spending of appropriated money. The 1974 Congressional Budget and Impoundment Control Act requires a special message from the president to Congress reporting a proposed deferral of spending. Deferrals may not extend beyond the end of the fiscal year in which the message is transmitted. A federal district court in 1986 struck down the president's authority to defer spending for policy reasons; the ruling was upheld by a federal appeals court in 1987. *(See also Rescission Bill.)*

Dilatory Motion—A motion made for the purpose of killing time and preventing action on a bill or amendment. House rules outlaw dilatory motions, but enforcement is largely within the discretion of the Speaker or chairman of the Committee of the Whole. The Senate does not have a rule banning dilatory motions, except under cloture.

Discharge a Committee—Occasionally, attempts are made to relieve a committee from jurisdiction over a measure before it. This is attempted more often in the House than in the Senate, and the procedure rarely is successful.

In the House, if a committee does not report a bill within 30 days after the measure is referred to it, any member may file a discharge motion. Once offered, the motion is treated as a petition needing the signatures of 218 members (a majority of the House). After the required signatures have been obtained, there is a delay of seven days. Thereafter, on the second and fourth Mondays of each month, except during the last six days of a session, any member who has signed the petition must be recognized, if he so desires, to move that the committee be discharged. Debate on the motion to discharge is limited to 20 minutes, and, if the motion is carried, consideration of the bill becomes a matter of high privilege.

If a resolution to consider a bill is held up in the Rules Committee for more than seven legislative days, any member may enter a motion to discharge the committee. The motion is handled like any other discharge petition in the House.

Occasionally, to expedite non-controversial legislative business, a committee is discharged by unanimous consent of the House, and a petition is not required. *(Senate procedure, see Discharge Resolution.)*

Discharge Calendar—The House calendar to which motions to discharge committees are referred when they have the required number of signatures (218) and are awaiting floor action.

Discharge Petition—*(See Discharge a Committee.)*

Discharge Resolution—In the Senate, a special motion that any senator may introduce to relieve a committee from consideration of a bill before it. The resolution can be called up for Senate approval or disapproval in the same manner as any other Senate business. *(House procedure, see Discharge a Committee.)*

Division of a Question for Voting—A practice that is more common in the Senate but also used in the House; a member may demand a division of an amendment or a motion for purposes of voting. Where an amendment or motion can be divided, the individual parts are voted on separately when a member demands a division. This procedure occurs most often during the consideration of conference reports.

Division Vote—*(See Standing Vote.)*

Enacting Clause—Key phrase in bills beginning, "Be it enacted by the Senate and House of Representatives. . . ." A successful motion to strike it from legislation kills the measure.

Engrossed Bill—The final copy of a bill as passed by one chamber, with the text as amended by floor action and certified by the clerk of the House or the secretary of the Senate.

Enrolled Bill—The final copy of a bill that has been passed in identical form by both chambers. It is certified by an officer of the house of origin (clerk of the House or secretary of the Senate) and then sent on for the signatures of the House Speaker, the Senate president pro tempore and the president of the United States. An enrolled bill is printed on parchment.

Entitlement Program—A federal program that guarantees a certain level of benefits to persons or other entities who meet requirements set by law, such as Social Security or unemployment benefits. It thus leaves no discretion with Congress on how much money to appropriate.

Executive Calendar—This is a non-legislative calendar in the Senate on which presidential documents such as treaties and nominations are listed.

Executive Document—A document, usually a treaty, sent to the Senate by the president for consideration or approval. Executive documents are identified for each session of Congress as Executive A, 97th Congress, 1st Session; Executive B, etc. They are referred to committee in the same manner as other measures. Unlike legislative documents, however, treaties do not die at the end of a Congress but remain "live" proposals until acted on by the Senate or withdrawn by the president.

Executive Session—A meeting of a Senate or House committee (or occasionally of either chamber) that only its members may attend. Witnesses regularly appear at committee meetings in executive session — for example, Defense Department officials during presentations of classified defense information. Other members of Congress may be invited, but the public and press are not allowed to attend.

Expenditures—The actual spending of money as distinguished from the appropriation of funds. Expenditures are made by the disbursing officers of the administration; appropriations are made only by Congress. The two are rarely identical in any fiscal year. In addition to some current budget authority, expenditures may represent budget authority made available one, two or more years earlier.

Filibuster—A time-delaying tactic associated with the Senate and used by a minority in an effort to prevent a vote on a bill or amendment that probably would pass if voted upon directly. The most common method is to take advantage of the Senate's rules permitting unlimited debate, but other forms of parliamentary maneuvering may be used. The stricter rules used by the House make filibusters more difficult, but delaying tactics are employed occasionally through various procedural devices allowed by House rules. *(Senate filibusters, see Cloture.)*

Fiscal Year—Financial operations of the government are carried out in a 12-month fiscal year, beginning on Oct. 1 and ending on Sept. 30. The fiscal year carries the date of the calendar year in which it ends. (From fiscal year 1844 to fiscal year 1976, the fiscal year began July 1 and ended the following June 30.)

Five-Minute Rule—A debate-limiting rule of the House that is invoked when the House sits as the Committee of the Whole. Under the rule, a member offering an amendment is allowed to speak five minutes in its favor, and an opponent of the amendment is allowed to speak five minutes in opposition. Debate is then closed. In practice, amendments regularly are debated more than 10 minutes, with members gaining the floor by offering pro forma amendments or obtaining unanimous consent to speak longer than five minutes. *(See Strike Out the Last Word.)*

Floor Manager—A member who has the task of steering legislation through floor debate and the amendment process to a final vote in the House or the Senate. Floor managers are usually chairmen or ranking members of the committee that reported the bill. Managers are responsible for apportioning the debate time granted supporters of the bill. The ranking minority member of the committee normally apportions time for the minority party's participation in the debate.

Frank—A member's facsimile signature, which is used on envelopes in lieu of stamps, for the member's official outgoing mail. The "franking privilege" is the right to send mail postage-free.

Germane—Pertaining to the subject matter of the measure at hand. All House amendments must be germane to the bill being considered. The Senate requires that amendments be germane when they are proposed to general appropriation bills, bills being considered once cloture has been adopted, or, frequently, when proceeding under a unanimous consent agreement placing a time limit on consideration of a bill. The 1974 budget act also requires that amendments to concurrent budget resolutions be germane. In the House, floor debate must be germane, and the first three hours of debate each day in the Senate must be germane to the pending business.

Grandfather Clause—A provision exempting persons or other entities already engaged in an activity from rules or legislation affecting that activity. Grandfather clauses sometimes are added to legislation in order to avoid antagonizing groups with established interests in the activities affected.

Grants-in-Aid—Payments by the federal government to states, local governments or individuals in support of specified programs, services or activities.

Guaranteed Loans—Loans to third parties for which the federal government in the event of default guarantees, in whole or in part, the repayment of principal or interest to a lender or holder of a security.

Hearings—Committee sessions for taking testimony from witnesses. At hearings on legislation, witnesses usually include specialists, government officials and spokesmen for persons or entities affected by the bill or bills under study. Hearings related to special investigations bring forth a variety of witnesses. Committees sometimes use their subpoena power to summon reluctant witnesses. The public and press may attend open hearings, but are barred from closed, or "executive," hearings. The vast majority of hearings are open to the public. *(See Executive Session.)*

Hold-Harmless Clause—A provision added to legislation to ensure that recipients of federal funds do not receive less in a future year than they did in the current year if a new formula for allocating funds authorized in the legislation would result in a reduction to the recipients. This clause has been used most frequently to soften the impact of sudden reductions in federal grants.

Hopper—Box on House clerk's desk where members deposit bills and resolutions to introduce them. *(See also Bills Introduced.)*

Hour Rule—A provision in the rules of the House that permits one hour of debate time for each member on amendments debated in the House of Representatives sitting as the House. Therefore, the House normally amends bills while sitting as the Committee of the Whole, where the five-minute rule on amendments operates. *(See Committee of the Whole, Five-Minute Rule.)*

House—The House of Representatives, as distinct from the Senate, although each body is a "house" of Congress.

House as in Committee of the Whole—A procedure that can be used to expedite consideration of certain measures such as continuing resolutions and, when there is debate, private bills. The procedure can only be invoked with the unanimous consent of the House or a rule from the Rules Committee and has procedural elements of both the House sitting as the House of Representatives, such as the Speaker presiding and the previous question motion being in order, and the House sitting as the Committee of the Whole, such as the five-minute rule pertaining.

House Calendar—A listing for action by the House of public bills that do not directly or indirectly appropriate money or raise revenue.

Immunity—The constitutional privilege of members of Congress to make verbal statements on the floor and in committee for which they cannot be sued or arrested for slander or libel. Also, freedom from arrest while traveling to or from sessions of Congress or on official business. Members in this status may be arrested only for treason, felonies or a breach of the peace, as defined by congressional manuals.

Impoundments—Any action taken by the executive branch that delays or precludes the obligation or expenditure of budget authority previously approved by Congress. *(See also Deferral, Rescission Bill.)*

Joint Committee—A committee composed of a specified number of members of both the House and Senate. A joint committee may be investigative or research-oriented, an example of the latter being the Joint Economic Committee. Others have housekeeping duties such as the joint committees on Printing and on the Library of Congress.

Joint Resolution—A joint resolution, designated H J Res or S J Res, requires the approval of both houses and the signature of the president, just as a bill does, and has the force of law if approved. There is no practical difference between a bill and a joint resolution. A joint resolution generally is used to deal with a limited matter such as a single appropriation.

Joint resolutions also are used to propose amendments to the Constitution in Congress. They do not require a presidential signature, but become a part of the Constitution when three-fourths of the states have ratified them.

Journal—The official record of the proceedings of the House and Senate. The *Journal* records the actions taken in each chamber, but, unlike the *Congressional Record*, it does not include the substantially verbatim report of speeches, debates, etc.

Law—An act of Congress that has been signed by the president or passed over his veto by Congress. Public bills, when signed, become public laws, and are cited by the letters PL and a hyphenated number. The two digits before the number correspond to the Congress, and the one or more digits after the hyphen refer to the numerical sequence in which the bills were signed by the president during that Congress. Private bills, when signed, become private laws. *(See also Slip Laws, Statutes at Large, U.S. Code.)*

Legislative Day—The "day" extending from the time either house meets after an adjournment until the time it next adjourns. Because the House normally adjourns from day to day, legislative days and calendar days usually coincide. But in the Senate, a legislative day may, and frequently does, extend over several calendar days. *(See Recess.)*

Legislative Veto—A procedure, no longer allowed, permitting either the House or Senate, or both chambers, to review proposed executive branch regulations or actions and to block or modify those with which they disagreed.

The specifics of the procedure varied, but Congress generally provided for a legislative veto by including in a bill a provision that administrative rules or action taken to implement the law were to go into effect at the end of a designated period of time unless blocked by either or both houses of Congress. Another version of the veto provided for congressional reconsideration and rejection of regulations already in effect.

The Supreme Court June 23, 1983, struck down the legislative veto as an unconstitutional violation of the law-making procedure provided in the Constitution.

Lobby—A group seeking to influence the passage or defeat of legislation. Originally the term referred to persons frequenting the lobbies or corridors of legislative chambers in order to speak to lawmakers.

The definition of a lobby and the activity of lobbying is a matter of differing interpretation. By some definitions, lobbying is limited to direct attempts to influence lawmakers through personal interviews and persuasion. Under other definitions, lobbying includes attempts at indirect, or "grass-roots," influence, such as persuading members of a group to write or visit their district's representative and state's senators or attempting to create a climate of opinion favorable to a desired legislative goal.

The right to attempt to influence legislation is based on the First Amendment to the Constitution, which says Congress shall make no law abridging the right of the people "to petition the government for a redress of grievances."

Majority Leader—The majority leader is elected by his party colleagues. In the Senate, in consultation with the minority leader and his colleagues, the majority leader directs the legislative schedule for the chamber. He also is his party's spokesman and chief strategist. In the House, the majority leader is second to the Speaker in the majority party's leadership and serves as his party's legislative strategist.

Majority Whip—In effect, the assistant majority leader, in either the House or Senate. His job is to help marshal majority forces in support of party strategy and legislation.

Manual—The official handbook in each house prescribing in detail its organization, procedures and operations.

Marking Up a Bill—Going through the contents of a piece of legislation in committee or subcommittee, considering its provisions in large and small portions, acting on amendments to provisions and proposed revisions to the language, inserting new sections and phraseology, etc. If the bill is extensively amended, the committee's version may be introduced as a separate bill, with a new number, before being considered by the full House or Senate. *(See Clean Bill.)*

Minority Leader—Floor leader for the minority party in each chamber. *(See also Majority Leader.)*

Minority Whip—Performs duties of whip for the minority party. *(See also Majority Whip.)*

Morning Hour—The time set aside at the beginning of each legislative day for the consideration of regular, routine business. The "hour" is of indefinite duration in the House, where it is rarely used.

In the Senate it is the first two hours of a session following an adjournment, as distinguished from a recess. The morning hour can be terminated earlier if the morning business has been completed. Business includes such matters as messages from the president, communications from the heads of departments, messages from the House, the presentation of petitions, reports of standing and select committees and the introduction of bills and resolutions. During the first hour of the morning hour in the Senate, no motion to proceed to the consideration of any bill on the calendar is in order except by unanimous consent. During the second hour, motions can be made but must be decided without debate. Senate committees may meet while the Senate conducts morning hour.

Motion—In the House or Senate chamber, a request by a member to institute any one of a wide array of parliamentary actions. He "moves" for a certain procedure, the consideration of a measure, etc. The precedence of motions, and whether they are debatable, is set forth in the House and Senate manuals. *(See some specific motions above and below.)*

Nominations—Presidential appointments to office subject to Senate confirmation. Although most nominations win quick Senate approval, some are controversial and become the topic of hearings and debate. Sometimes senators object to appointees for patronage reasons — for example, when a nomination to a local federal job is made without consulting the senators of the state concerned. In some situations a senator may object that the nominee is "personally obnoxious" to him. Usually other senators join in blocking such appointments out of courtesy to their colleagues. *(See Senatorial Courtesy.)*

One-Minute Speeches—Addresses by House members at the beginning of a legislative day. The speeches may cover any subject but are limited to one minute's duration.

Override a Veto—If the president disapproves a bill and sends it back to Congress with his objections, Congress may try to override his veto and enact the bill into law. Neither house is required to attempt to override a veto. The override of a veto requires a recorded vote with a two-thirds majority in each chamber. The question put to each house is: "Shall the bill pass, the objections of the president to the contrary notwithstanding?" *(See also Pocket Veto, Veto.)*

Oversight Committee—A congressional committee, or designated subcommittee of a committee, that is charged with general oversight of one or more federal agencies' programs and activities. Usually, the oversight panel for a particular agency also is the authorizing committee for that agency's programs and operations.

Pair—A voluntary arrangement between two lawmakers, usually on opposite sides of an issue. If passage of the measure requires a two-thirds majority vote, a pair would require two members favoring the action to one opposed to it. Pairs can take one of three forms — specific, general and live. The names of lawmakers pairing on a given vote and their stands, if known, are published in the *Congressional Record.*

The specific pair applies to one or more votes on the same subject. On special pairs, lawmakers usually specify how they would have voted.

A general pair in the Senate, now rarely used, applies to all votes on which the members pairing are on opposite sides. It usually does not specify the positions of the senators pairing. In a general pair in the House, no agreement is involved. A representative expecting to be absent may notify the House clerk he wishes to make a "general" pair. His name then is paired arbitrarily with that of another member desiring a pair, and the list is published in the *Congressional Record.* He may or may not be paired with a member taking the opposite position. General pairs in the House give no indication of how a member would have voted.

A live pair involves two members, one present for the vote, the other absent. The member present casts his vote and then withdraws it and votes "present." He then announces that he has a live pair with a colleague, identifying how each would have voted on the question. A live pair subtracts the vote of the member in attendance from the final vote tabulation.

Petition—A request or plea sent to one or both chambers from an organization or private citizens' group asking support of particular legislation or favorable consideration of a matter not yet receiving congressional attention. Petitions are referred to appropriate committees.

Pocket Veto—The act of the president in withholding his approval of a bill after Congress has adjourned. When Congress is in session, a bill becomes law without the president's signature if he does not act upon it within 10 days, excluding Sundays, from the time he gets it. But if Congress adjourns sine die within that 10-day period, the bill will die even if the president does not formally veto it.

The Supreme Court early in 1987 sidestepped a decision on whether the president may pocket veto a bill during recesses and between sessions of the same Congress, or only between Congresses, as a lower court had ruled. *(See also Veto.)*

Point of Order—An objection raised by a member that the chamber is departing from rules governing its conduct of business. The objector cites the rule violated, the chair sustaining his objection if correctly made. Order is restored by the chair's suspending proceedings of the chamber until it conforms to the prescribed "order of business."

President of the Senate—Under the Constitution, the vice president of the United States presides over the Senate. In his absence, the president pro tempore, or a senator designated by the president pro tempore, presides over the chamber.

President Pro Tempore—The chief officer of the Senate in the absence of the vice president; literally, but loosely, the president for a time. The president pro tempore is elected by his fellow senators, and the recent practice has been to elect the senator of the majority party with the longest period of continuous service.

Previous Question—A motion for the previous question, when carried, has the effect of cutting off all debate, preventing the offering of further amendments, and forcing a vote on the pending matter. In the House, the previous question is not permitted in the Committee of the Whole. The motion for the previous question is a debate-limiting device and is not in order in the Senate.

Printed Amendment—A House rule guarantees five minutes of floor debate in support and five minutes in opposition, and no other debate time, on amendments printed in the *Congressional Record* at least one day prior to the amendment's consideration in the Committee of the Whole.

In the Senate, while amendments may be submitted for printing, they have no parliamentary standing or status. An amendment submitted for printing in the Senate, however, may be called up by any senator.

Private Calendar—In the House, private bills dealing with individual matters such as claims against the government, immigration, land titles, etc., are put on this calendar. The private calendar must be called on the first Tuesday of each month, and the Speaker may call it on the third Tuesday of each month as well.

When a private bill is before the chamber, two members may block its consideration, which recommits the bill to committee. Backers of a recommitted private bill have recourse. The measure can be put into an "omnibus claims bill" — several private bills rolled into one. As with any bill, no part of an omnibus claims bill may be deleted without a vote. When the private bill goes back to the House floor in this form, it can be deleted from the omnibus bill only by majority vote.

Privilege—Privilege relates to the rights of members of Congress and to the relative priority of the motions and actions they may make in their respective chambers. The two are distinct. "Privileged questions" deal with legislative business. "Questions of privilege" concern legislators themselves.

Privileged Questions—The order in which bills, motions and other legislative measures are considered by Congress is governed by strict priorities. A motion to table, for instance, is more privileged than a motion to recommit. Thus, a motion to recommit can be superseded by a motion to table, and a vote would be forced on the latter motion only. A motion to adjourn, however, takes precedence over a tabling motion and thus is considered of the "highest privilege." *(See also Questions of Privilege.)*

Pro Forma Amendment—*(See Strike Out the Last Word.)*

Public Laws—*(See Law.)*

Questions of Privilege—These are matters affecting members of Congress individually or collectively. Matters affecting the rights, safety, dignity and integrity of proceedings of the House or Senate as a whole are questions of privilege in both chambers.

Questions involving individual members are called questions of "personal privilege." A member rising to ask a question of personal privilege is given precedence over almost all other proceedings. An annotation in the House rules points out that the privilege rests primarily on the Constitution, which gives him a conditional immunity from arrest and an unconditional freedom to speak in the House. *(See also Privileged Questions.)*

Quorum—The number of members whose presence is

necessary for the transaction of business. In the Senate and House, it is a majority of the membership. A quorum is 100 in the Committee of the Whole House. If a point of order is made that a quorum is not present, the only business that is in order is either a motion to adjourn or a motion to direct the sergeant-at-arms to request the attendance of absentees.

Readings of Bills—Traditional parliamentary procedure required bills to be read three times before they were passed. This custom is of little modern significance. Normally a bill is considered to have its first reading when it is introduced and printed, by title, in the *Congressional Record*. In the House, its second reading comes when floor consideration begins. (This is the most likely point at which there is an actual reading of the bill, if there is any.) The second reading in the Senate is supposed to occur on the legislative day after the measure is introduced, but before it is referred to committee. The third reading (again, usually by title) takes place when floor action has been completed on amendments.

Recess—Distinguished from adjournment *(see above)* in that a recess does not end a legislative day and therefore does not interrupt unfinished business. The rules in each house set forth certain matters to be taken up and disposed of at the beginning of each legislative day. The House usually adjourns from day to day. The Senate often recesses, thus meeting on the same legislative day for several calendar days or even weeks at a time.

Recognition—The power of recognition of a member is lodged in the Speaker of the House and the presiding officer of the Senate. The presiding officer names the member who will speak first when two or more members simultaneously request recognition.

Recommit to Committee—A motion, made on the floor after a bill has been debated, to return it to the committee that reported it. If approved, recommittal usually is considered a death blow to the bill. In the House, a motion to recommit can be made only by a member opposed to the bill, and, in recognizing a member to make the motion, the Speaker gives preference to members of the minority party over majority party members.

A motion to recommit may include instructions to the committee to report the bill again with specific amendments or by a certain date. Or, the instructions may direct that a particular study be made, with no definite deadline for further action. If the recommittal motion includes instructions to "report the bill back forthwith" and the motion is adopted, floor action on the bill continues; the committee does not actually reconsider the legislation.

Reconciliation—*(See Budget Reconciliation.)*

Reconsider a Vote—A motion to reconsider the vote by which an action was taken has, until it is disposed of, the effect of putting the action in abeyance. In the Senate, the motion can be made only by a member who voted on the prevailing side of the original question or by a member who did not vote at all. In the House, it can be made only by a member on the prevailing side.

A common practice in the Senate after close votes on an issue is a motion to reconsider, followed by a motion to table the motion to reconsider. On this motion to table, senators vote as they voted on the original question, which allows the motion to table to prevail, assuming there are no switches. The matter then is finally closed and further motions to reconsider are not entertained. In the House, as a routine precaution, a motion to reconsider usually is made every time a measure is passed. Such a motion almost always is tabled immediately, thus shutting off the possibility of future reconsideration, except by unanimous consent.

Motions to reconsider must be entered in the Senate within the next two days of actual session after the original vote has been taken. In the House they must be entered either on the same day or on the next succeeding day the House is in session.

Recorded Vote—A vote upon which each member's stand is individually made known. In the Senate, this is accomplished through a roll call of the entire membership, to which each senator on the floor must answer "yea," "nay" or, if he does not wish to vote, "present." Since January 1973, the House has used an electronic voting system for recorded votes, including yea-and-nay votes formerly taken by roll calls.

When not required by the Constitution, a recorded vote can be obtained on questions in the House on the demand of one-fifth (44 members) of a quorum or one-fourth (25) of a quorum in the Committee of the Whole. *(See Yeas and Nays.)*

Report—Both a verb and a noun as a congressional term. A committee that has been examining a bill referred to it by the parent chamber "reports" its findings and recommendations to the chamber when it completes consideration and returns the measure. The process is called "reporting" a bill.

A "report" is the document setting forth the committee's explanation of its action. Senate and House reports are numbered separately and are designated S Rept or H Rept. When a committee report is not unanimous, the dissenting committee members may file a statement of their views, called minority views and referred to as a minority report. Members in disagreement with some provisions of a bill may file additional or supplementary views. Sometimes a bill is reported without a committee recommendation.

Adverse reports occasionally are submitted by legislative committees. However, when a committee is opposed to a bill, it usually fails to report the bill at all. Some laws require that committee reports — favorable or adverse — be made.

Rescission Bill—A bill rescinding or canceling budget authority previously made available by Congress. The president may request a rescission to reduce spending or because the budget authority no longer is needed. Under the 1974 budget act, however, unless Congress approves a rescission bill within 45 days of continuous session after receipt of the proposal, the funds must be made available for obligation. *(See also Deferral.)*

Resolution—A "simple" resolution, designated H Res or S Res, deals with matters entirely within the prerogatives of one house or the other. It requires neither passage by the other chamber nor approval by the president, and it does not have the force of law. Most resolutions deal with the rules or procedures of one house. They also are used to express the sentiments of a single house such as condolences to the family of a deceased member or to comment on foreign policy or executive business. A simple resolution is the vehicle for a "rule" from the House Rules Committee. *(See also Concurrent and Joint Resolutions, Rules.)*

Rider—An amendment, usually not germane, that its sponsor hopes to get through more easily by including it in other legislation. Riders become law if the bills embodying them are enacted. Amendments providing legislative directives in appropriations bills are outstanding examples of riders, though technically legislation is banned from appropriations bills. The House, unlike the Senate, has a strict germaneness rule; thus, riders usually are Senate devices to get legislation enacted quickly or to bypass lengthy House consideration and, possibly, opposition.

Rules—The term has two specific congressional meanings. A rule may be a standing order governing the conduct of House or Senate business and listed among the permanent rules of either chamber. The rules deal with duties of officers, the order of business, admission to the floor, parliamentary procedures on handling amendments and voting, jurisdictions of committees, etc.

In the House, a rule also may be a resolution reported by its Rules Committee to govern the handling of a particular bill on the floor. The committee may report a "rule," also called a "special order," in the form of a simple resolution. If the resolution is adopted by the House, the temporary rule becomes as valid as any standing rule and lapses only after action has been completed on the measure to which it pertains. A rule sets the time limit on general debate. It also may waive points of order against provisions of the bill in question such as non-germane language or against certain amendments intended to be proposed to the bill from the floor. It may even forbid all amendments or all amendments except those proposed by the legislative committee that handled the bill. In this instance, it is known as a "closed" or "gag" rule as opposed to an "open" rule, which puts no limitation on floor amendments, thus leaving the bill completely open to alteration by the adoption of germane amendments.

Secretary of the Senate—Chief administrative officer of the Senate, responsible for overseeing the duties of Senate employees, educating Senate pages, administering oaths, handling the registration of lobbyists, and handling other tasks necessary for the continuing operation of the Senate. *(See also Clerk of the House.)*

Select or Special Committee—A committee set up for a special purpose and, usually, for a limited time by resolution of either the House or Senate. Most special committees are investigative and lack legislative authority — legislation is not referred to them and they cannot report bills to their parent chamber. *(See also Standing Committees.)*

Senatorial Courtesy—Sometimes referred to as "the courtesy of the Senate," it is a general practice — with no written rule — applied to consideration of executive nominations. Generally, it means that nominations from a state are not to be confirmed unless they have been approved by the senators of the president's party of that state, with other senators following their colleagues' lead in the attitude they take toward consideration of such nominations. *(See Nominations.)*

Sequester Order—The Gramm-Rudman-Hollings law of 1985 established an automatic budget-cutting procedure that the Supreme Court declared unconstitutional a year later. Under that procedure, the Congressional Budget Office (CBO) and the Office of Management and Budget (OMB) must separately calculate deficits for an upcoming fiscal year and the across-the-board cuts that would be needed to meet the deficit fixed by the statute. The General Accounting Office (GAO) would review, and could revise, the CBO-OMB numbers. GAO would then submit the final figures to the president, who must issue a "sequester" order making the cuts. Although the Supreme Court invalidated the automatic feature, another section of the law provided that the cuts would take effect if the president and Congress approved them. *(See Budget Process.)*

Sine Die—*(See Adjournment Sine Die.)*

Slip Laws—The first official publication of a bill that has been enacted and signed into law. Each is published separately in unbound single-sheet or pamphlet form. *(See also Law, Statutes at Large, U.S. Code.)*

Speaker—The presiding officer of the House of Representatives, selected by the caucus of the party to which he belongs and formally elected by the whole House.

Special Session—A session of Congress after it has adjourned sine die, completing its regular session. Special sessions are convened by the president.

Spending Authority—The 1974 budget act defines spending authority as borrowing authority, contract authority and entitlement authority *(see above)*, for which budget authority is not provided in advance by appropriation acts.

Sponsor—*(See Bills Introduced.)*

Standing Committees—Committees permanently established by House and Senate rules. The standing committees of the House were last reorganized by the committee reorganization of 1974. The last major realignment of Senate committees was in the committee system reorganization of 1977. The standing committees are legislative committees — legislation may be referred to them and they may report bills and resolutions to their parent chambers. *(See also Select or Special Committees.)*

Standing Vote—A non-recorded vote used in both the House and Senate. (A standing vote also is called a division vote.) Members in favor of a proposal stand and are counted by the presiding officer. Then members opposed stand and are counted. There is no record of how individual members voted.

Statutes at Large—A chronological arrangement of the laws enacted in each session of Congress. Though indexed, the laws are not arranged by subject matter, and there is not an indication of how they changed previously enacted laws. *(See also Law, Slip Laws, U.S. Code.)*

Strike From the Record—Remarks made on the House floor may offend some member, who moves that the offending words be "taken down" for the Speaker's cognizance, and then expunged from the debate as published in the *Congressional Record.*

Strike Out the Last Word—A motion whereby a House member is entitled to speak for five minutes on an amendment then being debated by the chamber. A member gains recognition from the chair by moving to "strike out the last word" of the amendment or section of the bill under consideration. The motion is pro forma, requires no vote and does not change the amendment being debated.

Substitute—A motion, amendment or entire bill introduced in place of the pending legislative business. Passage of a substitute measure kills the original measure by supplanting it. The substitute also may be amended. *(See also Amendment in the Nature of a Substitute.)*

Supplemental Appropriation Bill—Legislation appropriating funds after the regular annual appropriation bill *(see above)* for a federal department or agency has been enacted. A supplemental appropriation provides additional budget authority beyond original estimates for programs or activities, including new programs authorized after the enactment of the regular appropriation act, for which the need for funds is too urgent to be postponed until enactment of the next year's regular appropriation bill.

Suspend the Rules—Often a time-saving procedure for passing bills in the House. The wording of the motion, which may be made by any member recognized by the Speaker, is: "I move to suspend the rules and pass the bill. . . ." A favorable vote by two-thirds of those present is required for passage. Debate is limited to 40 minutes and no amendments from the floor are permitted. If a two-thirds favorable vote is not attained, the bill may be considered later under regular procedures. The suspension procedure is in order every Monday and Tuesday and is intended to be reserved for non-controversial bills.

Table a Bill—A motion to "lay on the table" is not debatable in either house, and usually it is a method of making a final, adverse disposition of a matter. In the Senate, however, different language sometimes is used. The motion may be worded to let a bill "lie on the table," perhaps for subsequent "picking up." This motion is more flexible, keeping the bill pending for later action, if desired. Tabling motions on amendments are effective debate-ending devices in the Senate.

Teller Vote—This is a largely moribund House procedure in the Committee of the Whole. Members file past tellers and are counted as for, or against, a measure, but they are not recorded individually. In the House, tellers are ordered upon demand of one-fifth of a quorum. This is 44 in the House, 20 in the Committee of the Whole.

The House also has a recorded teller vote, now largely supplanted by the electronic voting procedure, under which the votes of each member are made public just as they would be on a recorded vote. *(See above.)*

Treaties—Executive proposals — in the form of resolutions of ratification — which must be submitted to the Senate for approval by two-thirds of the senators present. Treaties today are normally sent to the Foreign Relations Committee for scrutiny before the Senate takes action. Foreign Relations has jurisdiction over all treaties, regardless of the subject matter. Treaties are read three times and debated on the floor in much the same manner as legislative proposals. After approval by the Senate, treaties are formally ratified by the president.

Unanimous Consent—Proceedings of the House or Senate and action on legislation often take place upon the unanimous consent of the chamber, whether or not a rule of the chamber is being violated. Unanimous consent is used to expedite floor action and frequently is used for routine procedural requests.

Unanimous Consent Agreement—A device used in the Senate to expedite legislation. Much of the Senate's legislative business, dealing with both minor and controversial issues, is conducted through unanimous consent or unanimous consent agreements. On major legislation, such agreements usually are printed and transmitted to all senators in advance of floor debate. Once agreed to, they are binding on all members unless the Senate, by unanimous consent, agrees to modify them. An agreement may list the order in which various bills are to be considered, specify the length of time bills and contested amendments are to be debated and when they are to be voted upon and, frequently, require that all amendments introduced be germane to the bill under consideration. In this regard, unanimous consent agreements are similar to the "rules" issued by the House Rules Committee for bills pending in the House. *(See above.)*

Union Calendar—Bills that directly or indirectly appropriate money or raise revenue are placed on this House calendar according to the date they are reported from committee.

U.S. Code—A consolidation and codification of the general and permanent laws of the United States arranged by subject under 50 titles, the first six dealing with general or political subjects, and the other 44 alphabetically arranged from agriculture to war. The code is revised every six years, and a supplement is published after each session of Congress. *(See also Law, Slip Laws, Statutes at Large.)*

Veto—Disapproval by the president of a bill or joint resolution (other than one proposing an amendment to the Constitution). When Congress is in session, the president must veto a bill within 10 days, excluding Sundays, after he has received it; otherwise, it becomes law without his signature. When the president vetoes a bill, he returns it to the house of origin along with a message stating his objections. *(See also Pocket Veto, Override a Veto.)*

Voice Vote—In either the House or Senate, members answer "aye" or "no" in chorus, and the presiding officer decides the result. The term also is used loosely to indicate action by unanimous consent or without objection.

Whip—*(See Majority and Minority Whip.)*

Without Objection—Used in lieu of a vote on non-controversial motions, amendments or bills that may be passed in either the House or Senate if no member voices an objection.

Yeas and Nays—The Constitution requires that yea-and-nay votes be taken and recorded when requested by one-fifth of the members present. In the House, the Speaker determines whether one-fifth of the members present requested a vote. In the Senate, practice requires only 11 members. The Constitution requires the yeas and nays on a veto override attempt. *(See Recorded Vote.)*

How a Bill Becomes Law

This graphic shows the most typical way in which proposed legislation is enacted into law. There are more complicated, as well as simpler, routes, and most bills never become law. The process is illustrated with two hypothetical bills, House bill No. 1 (HR 1) and Senate bill No. 2 (S 2). Bills must be passed by both houses in identical form before they can be sent to the president. The path of HR 1 is traced by a solid line, that of S 2 by a broken line. In practice most bills begins as similar proposals in both houses.

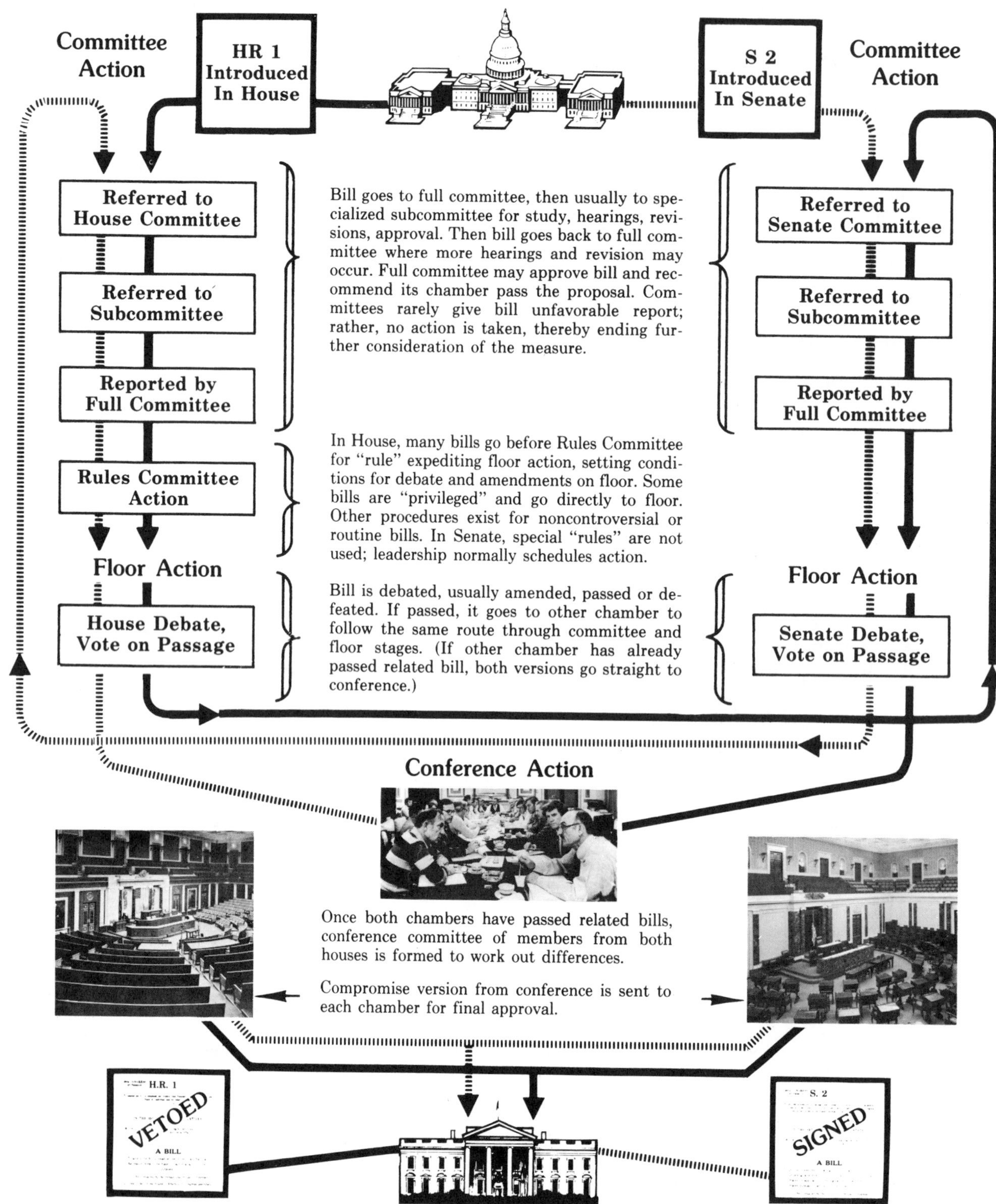

Committee Action
HR 1 Introduced In House
S 2 Introduced In Senate
Committee Action
Referred to House Committee
Referred to Subcommittee
Reported by Full Committee
Rules Committee Action
Floor Action
House Debate, Vote on Passage
Bill goes to full committee, then usually to specialized subcommittee for study, hearings, revisions, approval. Then bill goes back to full committee where more hearings and revision may occur. Full committee may approve bill and recommend its chamber pass the proposal. Committees rarely give bill unfavorable report; rather, no action is taken, thereby ending further consideration of the measure.
In House, many bills go before Rules Committee for "rule" expediting floor action, setting conditions for debate and amendments on floor. Some bills are "privileged" and go directly to floor. Other procedures exist for noncontroversial or routine bills. In Senate, special "rules" are not used; leadership normally schedules action.
Bill is debated, usually amended, passed or defeated. If passed, it goes to other chamber to follow the same route through committee and floor stages. (If other chamber has already passed related bill, both versions go straight to conference.)
Referred to Senate Committee
Referred to Subcommittee
Reported by Full Committee
Floor Action
Senate Debate, Vote on Passage
Conference Action
Once both chambers have passed related bills, conference committee of members from both houses is formed to work out differences.
Compromise version from conference is sent to each chamber for final approval.
H.R. 1
VETOED
A BILL
S. 2
SIGNED
A BILL

Compromise bill approved by both houses is sent to the president, who can sign it into law or veto it and return it to Congress. Congress may override veto by a two-thirds majority vote in both houses; bill then becomes law without president's signature.

The Legislative Process in Brief

Note: Parliamentary terms used below are defined in the glossary.

Introduction of Bills

A House member (including the resident commissioner of Puerto Rico and non-voting delegates of the District of Columbia, Guam, the Virgin Islands and American Samoa) may introduce any one of several types of bills and resolutions by handing it to the clerk of the House or placing it in a box called the hopper. A senator first gains recognition of the presiding officer to announce the introduction of a bill. If objection is offered by any senator, the introduction of the bill is postponed until the following day.

As the next step in either the House or Senate, the bill is numbered, referred to the appropriate committee, labeled with the sponsor's name, and sent to the Government Printing Office so that copies can be made for subsequent study and action. Senate bills may be jointly sponsored and carry several senators' names. Until 1978, the House limited the number of members who could cosponsor any one bill; the ceiling was eliminated at the beginning of the 96th Congress. A bill written in the executive branch and proposed as an administration measure usually is introduced by the chairman of the congressional committee that has jurisdiction.

Bills—Prefixed with "HR" in the House, "S" in the Senate, followed by a number. Used as the form for most legislation, whether general or special, public or private.

Joint Resolutions—Designated H J Res or S J Res. Subject to the same procedure as bills, with the exception of a joint resolution proposing an amendment to the Constitution. The latter must be approved by two-thirds of both houses and is thereupon sent directly to the administrator of general services for submission to the states for ratification rather than being presented to the president for his approval.

Concurrent Resolutions—Designated H Con Res or S Con Res. Used for matters affecting the operations of both houses. These resolutions do not become law.

Resolutions—Designated H Res or S Res. Used for a matter concerning the operation of either house alone and adopted only by the chamber in which it originates.

Committee Action

A bill is referred to the appropriate committee by a House parliamentarian on the Speaker's order, or by the Senate president. Sponsors may indicate their preferences for referral, although custom and chamber rule generally govern. An exception is the referral of private bills, which are sent to whatever group is designated by their sponsors. Bills are technically considered "read for the first time" when referred to House committees.

When a bill reaches a committee it is placed on the group's calendar. At that time it comes under the sharpest congressional focus. Its chances for passage are quickly determined — and the great majority of bills fall by the legislative roadside. Failure of a committee to act on a bill is equivalent to killing it; the measure can be withdrawn from the group's purview only by a discharge petition signed by a majority of the House membership on House bills, or by adoption of a special resolution in the Senate. Discharge attempts rarely succeed.

The first committee action taken on a bill usually is a request for comment on it by interested agencies of the government. The committee chairman may assign the bill to a subcommittee for study and hearings, or it may be considered by the full committee. Hearings may be public, closed (executive session), or both. A subcommittee, after considering a bill, reports to the full committee its recommendations for action and any proposed amendments.

The full committee then votes on its recommendation to the House or Senate. This procedure is called "ordering a bill reported." Occasionally a committee may order a bill reported unfavorably; most of the time a report, submitted by the chairman of the committee to the House or Senate, calls for favorable action on the measure since the committee can effectively "kill" a bill by simply failing to take any action.

When a committee sends a bill to the chamber floor, it explains its reasons in a written statement, called a report, which accompanies the bill. Often committee members opposing a measure issue dissenting minority statements that are included in the report.

Usually, the committee "marks up" or proposes amendments to the bill. If they are substantial and the measure is complicated, the committee may order a "clean bill" introduced, which will embody the proposed amendments. The original bill then is put aside and the "clean bill," with a new number, is reported to the floor.

The chamber must approve, alter or reject the committee amendments before the bill itself can be put to a vote.

Floor Action

After a bill is reported back to the house where it originated, it is placed on the calendar.

There are five legislative calendars in the House, issued in one cumulative calendar titled *Calendars of the United States House of Representatives and History of Legislation*. The House calendars are:

The Union Calendar to which are referred bills raising revenues, general appropriations bills and any measures directly or indirectly appropriating money or property. It is the Calendar of the Committee of the Whole House on the State of the Union.

The House Calendar to which are referred bills of public character not raising revenue or appropriating money or property.

The Consent Calendar to which are referred bills of a non-controversial nature that are passed without debate when the Consent Calendar is called on the first and third Mondays of each month.

The Private Calendar to which are referred bills for relief in the nature of claims against the United States or private immigration bills that are passed without debate when the Private Calendar is called the first and third Tuesdays of each month.

The Discharge Calendar to which are referred motions to discharge committees when the necessary signatures are signed to a discharge petition.

There is only one legislative calendar in the Senate and one "executive calendar" for treaties and nominations submitted to the Senate. When the Senate Calendar is called, each senator is limited to five minutes' debate on each bill.

Debate. A bill is brought to debate by varying procedures. If a routine measure, it may await the call of the calendar. If it is urgent or important, it can be taken up in the Senate either by unanimous consent or by a majority vote. The policy committee of the majority party in the Senate schedules the bills that it wants taken up for debate.

In the House, precedence is granted if a special rule is obtained from the Rules Committee. A request for a special rule is usually made by the chairman of the committee that favorably reported the bill, supported by the bill's sponsor and other committee members. The request, considered by the Rules Committee in the same fashion that other committees consider legislative measures, is in the form of a resolution providing for immediate consideration of the bill. The Rules Committee reports the resolution to the House where it is debated and voted upon in the same fashion as regular bills. If the Rules Committee should fail to report a rule requested by a committee, there are several ways to bring the bill to the House floor — under suspension of the rules, on Calendar Wednesday or by a discharge motion.

The resolutions providing special rules are important because they specify how long the bill may be debated and whether it may be amended from the floor. If floor amendments are banned, the bill is considered under a "closed rule," which permits only members of the committee that first reported the measure to the House to alter its language, subject to chamber acceptance.

When a bill is debated under an "open rule," amendments may be offered from the floor. Committee amendments are always taken up first, but may be changed, as may all amendments up to the second degree; i.e., an amendment to an amendment to an amendment is not in order.

Duration of debate in the House depends on whether the bill is under discussion by the House proper or before the House when it is sitting as the Committee of the Whole House on the State of the Union. In the former, the amount of time for debate is determined either by special rule or is allocated with an hour for each member if the measure is under consideration without a rule. In the Committee of the Whole the amount of time agreed on for general debate is equally divided between proponents and opponents. At the end of general discussion, the bill is read section by section for amendment. Debate on an amendment is limited to five minutes for each side.

Senate debate is usually unlimited. It can be halted only by unanimous consent by "cloture," which requires a three-fifths majority of the entire Senate except for proposed changes in the Senate rules. The latter requires a two-thirds vote.

The House sits as the Committee of the Whole when it considers any tax measure or bill dealing with public appropriations. It can also resolve itself into the Committee of the Whole if a member moves to do so and the motion is carried. The Speaker appoints a member to serve as the chairman. The rules of the House permit the Committee of the Whole to meet with any 100 members on the floor, and to amend and act on bills with a quorum of the 100, within the time limitations mentioned previously. When the Committee of the Whole has acted, it "rises," the Speaker returns as the presiding officer of the House and the member appointed chairman of the Committee of the Whole reports the action of the committee and its recommendations (amendments adopted).

Votes. Voting on bills may occur repeatedly before they are finally approved or rejected. The House votes on the rule for the bill and on various amendments to the bill. Voting on amendments often is a more illuminating test of a bill's support than is the final tally. Sometimes members approve final passage of bills after vigorously supporting amendments that, if adopted, would have scuttled the legislation.

The Senate has three different methods of voting: an untabulated voice, a standing vote (called a division) and a recorded roll call to which members answer "yea" or "nay" when their names are called. The House also employs voice and standing votes, but since January 1973 yeas and nays have been recorded by an electronic voting device, eliminating the need for time-consuming roll calls.

Another method of voting, used in the House only, is the teller vote. Traditionally, members filed up the center aisle past counters; only vote totals were announced. Since 1971, one-fifth of a quorum can demand that the votes of individual members be recorded, thereby forcing them to take a public position on amendments to key bills. Electronic voting now is commonly used for this purpose.

After amendments to a bill have been voted upon, a vote may be taken on a motion to recommit the bill to committee. If carried, this vote removes the bill from the chamber's calendar. If the motion is unsuccessful, the bill then is "read for the third time." An actual reading usually is dispensed with. Until 1965, an opponent of a bill could delay this move by objecting and asking for a full reading of an engrossed (certified in final form) copy of the bill. After the "third reading," the vote on final passage is taken.

The final vote may be followed by a motion to reconsider, and this motion itself may be followed by a move to lay the motion on the table. Usually, those voting for the bill's passage vote for the tabling motion, thus safeguarding the final passage action. With that, the bill has been formally passed by the chamber. While a motion to reconsider a Senate vote is pending on a bill, the measure cannot be sent to the House.

Action in Second House

After a bill is passed it is sent to the other chamber. This body may then take one of several steps. It may pass the bill as is — accepting the other chamber's language. It may send the bill to committee for scrutiny or alteration, or reject the entire bill, advising the other house of its actions. Or it may simply ignore the bill submitted while it continues work on its own version of the proposed legislation. Frequently, one chamber may approve a version of a bill that is greatly at variance with the version already passed by the other house, and then substitute its amendments for the language of the other, retaining only the latter's bill designation.

A provision of the Legislative Reorganization Act of 1970 permits a separate House vote on any non-germane amendment added by the Senate to a House-passed bill and requires a majority vote to retain the amendment. Previously, the House was forced to act on the bill as a whole; the only way to defeat the non-germane amendment was to reject the entire bill.

Often the second chamber makes only minor changes. If these are readily agreed to by the other house, the bill then is routed to the White House for signing. However, if the opposite chamber basically alters the bill submitted to it, the measure usually is "sent to conference." The chamber that has possession of the "papers" (engrossed bill, engrossed amendments, messages of transmittal) requests a conference and the other chamber must agree to it. If the second house does not agree, the bill dies.

Conference, Final Action

Conference. A conference undertakes to harmonize conficting House and Senate versions of a bill. The conference is usually staffed by senior members (conferees), appointed by the presiding officers of the two houses, from the committees that managed the bills. Under this arrangement the conferees of one house have the duty of trying to maintain their chamber's position in the face of amending actions by the conferees (also referred to as "managers") of the other house.

The number of conferees from each chamber may vary, the range usually being from three to nine members in each group, depending upon the length or complexity of the bill involved. There may be five representatives and three senators on the conference committee, or the reverse. But a majority vote controls the action of each group so that a large representation does not give one chamber a voting advantage over the other chamber's conferees.

Theoretically, conferees are not allowed to write new legislation in reconciling the two versions before them, but this curb sometimes is bypassed. Many bills have been put into acceptable compromise form only after new language was provided by the conferees. The 1970 Reorganization Act attempted to tighten restrictions on conferees by forbidding them to introduce any language on a topic that neither chamber sent to conference or to modify any topic beyond the scope of the different House and Senate versions.

Frequently the ironing out of difficulties takes days or even weeks. Conferences on involved appropriations bills sometimes are particularly drawn out.

As a conference proceeds, conferees reconcile differences between the versions, but generally they grant concessions only insofar as they remain sure that the chamber they represent will accept the compromises. Occasionally, uncertainty over how either house will react, or the positive refusal of a chamber to back down on a disputed amendment, results in an impasse, and the bills die in conference even though each was approved by its sponsoring chamber.

Conferees sometimes go back to their respective chambers for further instructions, when they report certain portions in disagreement. Then the chamber concerned can either "recede and concur" in the amendment of the other house, or "insist on its amendment."

When the conferees have reached agreement, they prepare a conference report embodying their recommendations (compromises). The reports, in document form, must be submitted to each house.

The conference report must be approved by each house. Consequently, approval of the report is approval of the compromise bill.

Final Steps. After a bill has been passed by both the House and Senate in identical form, all of the original papers are sent to the enrolling clerk of the chamber in which the bill originated. He then prepares an enrolled bill, which is printed on parchment paper. When this bill has been certified as correct by the secretary of the Senate or the clerk of the House, depending on which chamber originated the bill, it is signed first (no matter whether it originated in the Senate or House) by the Speaker of the House and then by the president of the Senate. It is next sent to the White House to await action.

If the president approves the bill, he signs it, dates it and usually writes the word "approved" on the document. If he does not sign it within 10 days (Sundays excepted) and Congress is in session, the bill becomes law without his signature.

However, should Congress adjourn before the 10 days expire, and the president failed to sign the measure, it does not become law. This procedure is called a pocket veto.

A president vetoes a bill by refusing to sign it and, before the 10-day period expires, returning it to Congress with a message stating his reasons. The message is sent to the chamber that originated the bill. If no action is taken there on the message, the bill dies. Congress, however, can attempt to override the president's veto and enact the bill, "the objections of the president to the contrary notwithstanding." Overriding of a veto requires a two-thirds vote of those present, who must number a quorum and vote by roll call.

Debate can precede this vote, with motions permitted to lay the message on the table, postpone action on it, or refer it to committee. If the president's veto is overridden by a two-thirds vote in both houses, the bill becomes law. Otherwise it is dead.

When bills are passed finally and signed, or passed over a veto, they are given law numbers in numerical order as they become law. There are two series of numbers, one for public and one for private laws, starting at the number "1" for each two-year term of Congress. They are then identified by law number and by Congress — i.e., Private Law 21, 99th Congress; Public Law 183, 99th Congress (or PL 99-183).

SENATE ROLL-CALL VOTES

CQ

CQ Senate Votes 1 - 8

Corresponding to Congressional Record Votes 1, 2, 3, 4, 5, 6, 7, 8

	1	2	3	4	5	6	7	8
ALABAMA								
Denton	Y	Y	Y	Y	Y	Y	Y	Y
Heflin	Y	Y	N	Y	Y	N	N	N
ALASKA								
Murkowski	Y	Y	Y	N	Y	Y	Y	Y
Stevens	Y	Y	?	Y	Y	Y	Y	Y
ARIZONA								
Goldwater	Y	Y	?	Y	Y	Y	Y	Y
DeConcini	Y	Y	Y	Y	N	Y	Y	Y
ARKANSAS								
Bumpers	Y	N	N	Y	N	Y	Y	Y
Pryor	?	Y	Y	Y	Y	Y	Y	Y
CALIFORNIA								
Wilson	Y	Y	N	Y	Y	Y	Y	Y
Cranston	Y	N	N	N	N	N	Y	N
COLORADO								
Armstrong	Y	Y	N	Y	Y	Y	Y	?
Hart	Y	N	?	N	N	N	N	N
CONNECTICUT								
Weicker	Y	Y	Y	Y	Y	Y	Y	Y
Dodd	Y	Y	N	Y	N	Y	N	Y
DELAWARE								
Roth	N	Y	Y	Y	Y	Y	N	Y
Biden	Y	N	Y	N	N	Y	N	N
FLORIDA								
Hawkins	Y	Y	N	N	Y	Y	Y	Y
Chiles	Y	N	?	N	N	Y	Y	Y
GEORGIA								
Mattingly	Y	Y	Y	Y	Y	Y	Y	Y
Nunn	Y	Y	?	?	?	?	?	?
HAWAII								
Inouye	Y	Y	Y	?	?	?	?	?
Matsunaga	Y	N	Y	Y	Y	Y	Y	Y
IDAHO								
McClure	Y	Y	Y	Y	Y	Y	Y	Y
Symms	Y	Y	Y	Y	Y	Y	Y	Y
ILLINOIS								
Dixon	Y	N	N	N	N	N	Y	N
Simon	Y	N	N	N	N	N	N	N
INDIANA								
Lugar	Y	Y	N	Y	Y	Y	Y	Y
Quayle	Y	Y	Y	Y	Y	Y	Y	Y
IOWA								
Grassley	Y	Y	Y	N	Y	Y	Y	Y
Harkin	Y	N	N	N	N	N	N	N
KANSAS								
Dole	Y	Y	Y	Y	Y	Y	Y	Y
Kassebaum	?	Y	?	Y	Y	Y	Y	Y
KENTUCKY								
McConnell	Y	Y	N	N	N	N	Y	Y
Ford	N	N	N	N	N	N	N	N
LOUISIANA								
Johnston	Y	Y	Y	N	N	N	Y	Y
Long	Y	Y	N	?	Y	Y	Y	N
MAINE								
Cohen	Y	Y	Y	Y	Y	Y	Y	Y
Mitchell	Y	Y	Y	Y	N	Y	Y	Y
MARYLAND								
Mathias	Y	N	N	?	N	N	N	Y
Sarbanes	Y	N	N	N	N	N	N	N
MASSACHUSETTS								
Kennedy	Y	Y	Y	Y	N	Y	Y	Y
Kerry	Y	Y	Y	N	N	Y	Y	N
MICHIGAN								
Levin	Y	N	N	N	N	N	N	N
Riegle	Y	N	N	N	N	N	N	N
MINNESOTA								
Boschwitz	Y	Y	N	Y	N	Y	Y	Y
Durenberger	Y	Y	Y	Y	Y	Y	Y	Y
MISSISSIPPI								
Cochran	Y	Y	Y	?	Y	Y	Y	Y
Stennis	N	Y	+	Y	Y	Y	Y	Y
MISSOURI								
Danforth	Y	Y	Y	Y	Y	Y	Y	Y
Eagleton	Y	Y	Y	Y	Y	Y	Y	Y
MONTANA								
Baucus	Y	?	?	?	?	?	+	?
Melcher	Y	N	N	N	N	N	N	N
NEBRASKA								
Exon	Y	N	N	N	N	N	N	N
Zorinsky	Y	N	N	N	N	N	N	Y
NEVADA								
Hecht	Y	Y	Y	Y	Y	Y	Y	Y
Laxalt	Y	Y	Y	Y	Y	Y	Y	Y
NEW HAMPSHIRE								
Humphrey	Y	Y	Y	Y	Y	Y	Y	Y
Rudman	Y	Y	Y	Y	Y	Y	Y	Y
NEW JERSEY								
Bradley	N	N	Y	N	N	N	N	N
Lautenberg	Y	N	N	N	N	N	N	N
NEW MEXICO								
Domenici	Y	Y	Y	Y	Y	Y	Y	Y
Bingaman	Y	Y	Y	Y	Y	Y	Y	Y
NEW YORK								
D'Amato	Y	Y	Y	Y	N	Y	Y	Y
Moynihan	Y	Y	Y	N	N	N	Y	Y
NORTH CAROLINA								
East	Y	Y	Y	Y	Y	Y	Y	Y
Helms	Y	Y	Y	Y	Y	Y	Y	Y
NORTH DAKOTA								
Andrews	Y	N	N	N	N	N	N	Y
Burdick	N	N	Y	N	N	N	N	N
OHIO								
Glenn	Y	N	N	N	N	N	N	N
Metzenbaum	Y	N	N	N	N	N	N	N
OKLAHOMA								
Nickles	Y	Y	Y	Y	Y	Y	Y	Y
Boren	Y	Y	Y	Y	Y	Y	Y	Y
OREGON								
Hatfield	Y	Y	Y	Y	Y	Y	Y	Y
Packwood	Y	Y	Y	Y	Y	Y	Y	Y
PENNSYLVANIA								
Heinz	Y	N	N	N	N	N	N	N
Specter	Y	N	N	N	N	N	N	Y
RHODE ISLAND								
Chafee	Y	Y	Y	Y	Y	Y	Y	Y
Pell	Y	N	N	?	N	N	Y	N
SOUTH CAROLINA								
Thurmond	Y	Y	Y	Y	Y	Y	Y	Y
Hollings	Y	Y	Y	Y	Y	Y	Y	Y
SOUTH DAKOTA								
Abdnor	Y	Y	N	N	N	Y	Y	Y
Pressler	N	Y	N	N	N	N	Y	Y
TENNESSEE								
Gore	Y	Y	Y	N	N	Y	Y	N
Sasser	Y	Y	Y	Y	N	N	Y	N
TEXAS								
Gramm	Y	Y	Y	Y	Y	Y	Y	Y
Bentsen	?	Y	Y	Y	N	Y	Y	Y
UTAH								
Garn	Y	Y	Y	Y	Y	Y	Y	Y
Hatch	Y	Y	Y	Y	Y	Y	Y	Y
VERMONT								
Stafford	Y	N	N	N	N	N	N	Y
Leahy	Y	N	N	Y	N	Y	Y	Y
VIRGINIA								
Trible	Y	Y	Y	Y	Y	Y	Y	Y
Warner	Y	Y	N	Y	Y	Y	Y	Y
WASHINGTON								
Evans	Y	Y	N	Y	Y	Y	Y	Y
Gorton	Y	Y	N	Y	Y	Y	Y	Y
WEST VIRGINIA								
Byrd	Y	N	N	N	N	N	N	N
Rockefeller	Y	N	N	N	N	N	N	N
WISCONSIN								
Kasten	Y	Y	Y	N	Y	Y	Y	Y
Proxmire	N	N	N	N	N	N	N	N
WYOMING								
Simpson	Y	Y	Y	Y	Y	Y	Y	Y
Wallop	Y	Y	Y	Y	?	?	Y	Y

KEY

Y Voted for (yea).
Paired for.
+ Announced for.
N Voted against (nay).
X Paired against.
- Announced against.
P Voted "present."
C Voted "present" to avoid possible conflict of interest.
? Did not vote or otherwise make a position known.

Democrats *Republicans*

ND - Northern Democrats SD - Southern Democrats (Southern states - Ala., Ark., Fla., Ga., Ky., La., Miss., N.C., Okla., S.C., Tenn., Texas, Va.)

1. S 638. Conrail Sale. Dole, R-Kan., motion to invoke cloture (thus limiting debate) on the Dole motion to proceed to the consideration of the bill to implement the sale of Conrail to Norfolk Southern Corp. Motion agreed to 90-7: R 50-2; D 40-5 (ND 30-3, SD 10-2), Jan. 23, 1986. A three-fifths majority vote (60) of the total Senate is required to invoke cloture. A "yea" was a vote supporting the president's position.

2. S 638. Conrail Sale. Danforth, R-Mo., motion to waive provisions contained in the 1974 Congressional Budget and Impoundment Control Act (PL 93-344) that would bar consideration of the bill to implement the sale of Conrail to Norfolk Southern Corp. Motion agreed to 68-31: R 48-5; D 20-26 (ND 9-23, SD 11-3), Jan. 29, 1986. A "yea" was a vote supporting the president's position.

3. S 638. Conrail Sale. Danforth, R-Mo., motion to table (kill) the Specter, R-Pa., substitute for the Danforth substitute, to sell Conrail to an investor group headed by Morgan Stanley and Co. Inc. Motion agreed to 53-39: R 34-16; D 19-23 (ND 12-19, SD 7-4), Jan. 29, 1986. A "yea" was a vote supporting the president's position.

4. S 638. Conrail Sale. Danforth, R-Mo., motion to table (kill) the Dixon, D-Ill., amendment to the Danforth substitute, to subject Norfolk Southern Corp.'s proposed purchase of Conrail to antitrust laws. Motion agreed to 56-37: R 40-11; D 16-26 (ND 8-22, SD 8-4), Jan. 30, 1986.

5. S 638. Conrail Sale. Danforth, R-Mo., motion to table (kill) the Lautenberg, D-N.J., amendment to the Danforth substitute, to permit port authorities and other government jurisdictions to seek court action against monopolistic practices and to ensure railroad traffic following the Conrail sale. Motion agreed to 51-45: R 42-10; D 9-35 (ND 3-28, SD 6-7), Jan. 30, 1986.

6. S 638. Conrail Sale. Danforth, R-Mo., motion to table (kill) the Metzenbaum, D-Ohio, amendment to the Danforth substitute, to direct the Department of Transportation to solicit other bids to purchase Conrail. Motion agreed to 64-32: R 45-7; D 19-25 (ND 10-21, SD 9-4), Jan. 30, 1986.

7. S 638. Conrail Sale. Thurmond, R-S.C., motion to invoke cloture (thus limiting debate) on the Danforth, R-Mo., substitute to implement committee changes. Motion agreed to 70-27: R 47-6; D 23-21 (ND 12-19, SD 11-2), Jan. 30, 1986. A three-fifths majority (60) of the total Senate is required to invoke cloture.

8. S 638. Conrail Sale. Danforth, R-Mo., motion to table (kill) the Metzenbaum, D-Ohio, substitute to repeal legal immunity granted to fiduciaries responsible for protecting rights of Conrail employees. Motion agreed to 69-27: R 51-1; D 18-26 (ND 10-21, SD 8-5), Jan. 30, 1986.

	9	10	11	12
ALABAMA				
Denton	Y	Y	Y	Y
Heflin	Y	Y	Y	N
ALASKA				
Murkowski	Y	Y	?	?
Stevens	Y	Y	Y	Y
ARIZONA				
Goldwater	?	?	Y	Y
DeConcini	Y	Y	Y	Y
ARKANSAS				
Bumpers	Y	N	?	Y
Pryor	Y	Y	Y	Y
CALIFORNIA				
Wilson	Y	Y	Y	Y
Cranston	Y	N	N	N
COLORADO				
Armstrong	Y	Y	Y	Y
Hart	Y	N	N	N
CONNECTICUT				
Weicker	N	Y	Y	Y
Dodd	Y	N	Y	N
DELAWARE				
Roth	Y	Y	Y	N
Biden	Y	Y	Y	N
FLORIDA				
Hawkins	Y	Y	Y	Y
Chiles	Y	Y	Y	N
GEORGIA				
Mattingly	Y	Y	Y	Y
Nunn	?	?	Y	Y
HAWAII				
Inouye	?	?	?	+
Matsunaga	Y	Y	?	Y
IDAHO				
McClure	Y	Y	Y	Y
Symms	Y	Y	Y	Y
ILLINOIS				
Dixon	Y	N	Y	N
Simon	Y	N	N	N
INDIANA				
Lugar	Y	Y	?	+
Quayle	N	Y	Y	Y
IOWA				
Grassley	Y	Y	Y	N
Harkin	Y	N	?	N
KANSAS				
Dole	Y	Y	Y	Y
Kassebaum	Y	Y	?	?
KENTUCKY				
McConnell	Y	Y	Y	N
Ford	Y	N	N	N
LOUISIANA				
Johnston	Y	Y	Y	Y
Long	Y	Y	Y	Y
MAINE				
Cohen	Y	N	Y	Y
Mitchell	Y	N	Y	Y
MARYLAND				
Mathias	Y	Y	Y	N
Sarbanes	Y	N	?	N
MASSACHUSETTS				
Kennedy	Y	Y	?	+
Kerry	Y	N	?	?
MICHIGAN				
Levin	Y	N	N	N
Riegle	Y	N	N	N
MINNESOTA				
Boschwitz	Y	Y	Y	Y
Durenberger	Y	Y	Y	Y
MISSISSIPPI				
Cochran	Y	Y	?	?
Stennis	?	?	?	Y
MISSOURI				
Danforth	Y	Y	Y	Y
Eagleton	Y	Y	Y	Y
MONTANA				
Baucus	Y	N	Y	N
Melcher	Y	N	N	N
NEBRASKA				
Exon	Y	N	N	N
Zorinsky	Y	N	Y	N
NEVADA				
Hecht	Y	Y	Y	Y
Laxalt	Y	Y	Y	Y
NEW HAMPSHIRE				
Humphrey	Y	Y	Y	Y
Rudman	Y	Y	Y	Y
NEW JERSEY				
Bradley	Y	Y	Y	N
Lautenberg	Y	N	N	N
NEW MEXICO				
Domenici	Y	Y	Y	Y
Bingaman	Y	Y	Y	Y
NEW YORK				
D'Amato	Y	Y	?	Y
Moynihan	Y	Y	Y	Y
NORTH CAROLINA				
East	Y	Y	Y	Y
Helms	Y	Y	Y	Y
NORTH DAKOTA				
Andrews	Y	N	Y	N
Burdick	Y	N	N	N
OHIO				
Glenn	Y	N	N	N
Metzenbaum	Y	N	N	N
OKLAHOMA				
Nickles	Y	Y	Y	Y
Boren	N	Y	Y	Y
OREGON				
Hatfield	Y	Y	Y	Y
Packwood	Y	Y	Y	Y
PENNSYLVANIA				
Heinz	Y	N	N	N
Specter	Y	N	N	N
RHODE ISLAND				
Chafee	Y	Y	Y	Y
Pell	Y	N	N	N
SOUTH CAROLINA				
Thurmond	Y	Y	Y	Y
Hollings	Y	Y	Y	Y
SOUTH DAKOTA				
Abdnor	Y	N	Y	N
Pressler	Y	Y	Y	N
TENNESSEE				
Gore	Y	Y	Y	Y
Sasser	Y	N	Y	Y
TEXAS				
Gramm	Y	Y	Y	Y
Bentsen	Y	Y	Y	Y
UTAH				
Garn	Y	Y	Y	Y
Hatch	Y	Y	Y	Y
VERMONT				
Stafford	Y	N	Y	N
Leahy	Y	N	Y	N
VIRGINIA				
Trible	Y	Y	Y	Y
Warner	Y	Y	Y	Y
WASHINGTON				
Evans	Y	Y	Y	N
Gorton	Y	Y	Y	N
WEST VIRGINIA				
Byrd	Y	N	Y	N
Rockefeller	Y	N	N	N
WISCONSIN				
Kasten	Y	Y	Y	Y
Proxmire	N	N	N	N
WYOMING				
Simpson	Y	Y	Y	Y
Wallop	N	Y	Y	Y

KEY

- Y Voted for (yea).
- # Paired for.
- + Announced for.
- N Voted against (nay).
- X Paired against.
- \- Announced against.
- P Voted "present."
- C Voted "present" to avoid possible conflict of interest.
- ? Did not vote or otherwise make a position known.

Democrats ***Republicans***

ND - Northern Democrats SD - Southern Democrats (Southern states - Ala., Ark., Fla., Ga., Ky., La., Miss., N.C., Okla., S.C., Tenn., Texas, Va.)

9. Procedural Motion. Dole, R-Kan., motion to instruct the sergeant-at-arms to request the attendance of absent senators. Motion agreed to 91-5: R 49-3; D 42-2 (ND 31-1, SD 11-1), Jan. 30, 1986.

10. S 638. Conrail Sale. Danforth, R-Mo., motion to table (kill) the Heinz, R-Pa., amendment to prevent the Norfolk Southern Corp. from getting certain tax advantages from the purchase of Conrail. Motion agreed to 63-33: R 46-6; D 17-27 (ND 8-24, SD 9-3), Jan. 30, 1986. A "yea" was a vote supporting the president's position.

11. S 638. Conrail Sale. Danforth, R-Mo., motion to table (kill) the Metzenbaum, D-Ohio, point of order that the Danforth substitute is unconstitutional because it is a revenue measure, which must originate in the House. Motion agreed to 70-17: R 46-2; D 24-15 (ND 13-14, SD 11-1), Feb. 4, 1986. (Under Senate precedents, constitutional points of order are not determined by the chair but are submitted to the Senate for its determination. The Danforth substitute subsequently was adopted by voice vote.)

12. S 638. Conrail Sale. Passage of the bill to approve the sale of the Conrail freight railroad to the Norfolk Southern Corp. Passed 54-39: R 37-12; D 17-27 (ND 6-24, SD 11-3), Feb. 4, 1986. A "yea" was a vote supporting the president's position.

CQ Senate Votes 13 - 18

Corresponding to Congressional Record Votes 13, 14, 15, 16, 17, 18

	13	14	15	16	17	18
ALABAMA						
Denton	N	Y	N	Y	Y	Y
Heflin	P	N	Y	Y	Y	Y
ALASKA						
Murkowski	Y	N	Y	Y	Y	Y
Stevens	Y	N	Y	Y	Y	Y
ARIZONA						
Goldwater	N	Y	N	N	?	Y
DeConcini	Y	N	Y	Y	Y	Y
ARKANSAS						
Bumpers	Y	N	Y	Y	Y	Y
Pryor	Y	N	Y	Y	Y	Y
CALIFORNIA						
Wilson	Y	N	Y	Y	Y	Y
Cranston	Y	N	Y	Y	Y	Y
COLORADO						
Armstrong	Y	Y	Y	Y	Y	Y
Hart	Y	N	Y	Y	Y	Y
CONNECTICUT						
Weicker	Y	N	Y	Y	Y	Y
Dodd	Y	N	Y	Y	Y	Y
DELAWARE						
Roth	Y	Y	N	Y	Y	Y
Biden	Y	N	Y	Y	Y	?
FLORIDA						
Hawkins	Y	Y	Y	Y	Y	Y
Chiles	Y	N	Y	Y	Y	Y
GEORGIA						
Mattingly	Y	Y	Y	Y	Y	Y
Nunn	Y	N	Y	Y	Y	Y
HAWAII						
Inouye	?	?	?	?	?	?
Matsunaga	Y	N	Y	Y	Y	Y
IDAHO						
McClure	Y	Y	N	Y	Y	?
Symms	N	Y	N	Y	Y	?
ILLINOIS						
Dixon	Y	N	Y	Y	Y	Y
Simon	Y	N	Y	Y	Y	Y
INDIANA						
Lugar	Y	N	Y	Y	Y	Y
Quayle	Y	N	Y	Y	Y	Y
IOWA						
Grassley	Y	Y	N	Y	Y	N
Harkin	Y	N	Y	Y	Y	Y
KANSAS						
Dole	Y	N	Y	Y	Y	Y
Kassebaum	Y	N	Y	Y	Y	Y
KENTUCKY						
McConnell	Y	N	Y	Y	Y	Y
Ford	Y	N	Y	Y	Y	Y
LOUISIANA						
Johnston	Y	N	Y	Y	Y	?
Long	Y	Y	Y	Y	Y	Y
MAINE						
Cohen	Y	Y	Y	Y	Y	?
Mitchell	Y	-	+	+	+	Y
MARYLAND						
Mathias	?	?	+	?	?	?
Sarbanes	Y	N	Y	Y	Y	Y
MASSACHUSETTS						
Kennedy	Y	N	Y	Y	Y	Y
Kerry	Y	N	Y	Y	Y	Y
MICHIGAN						
Levin	Y	N	Y	Y	Y	Y
Riegle	Y	N	Y	Y	Y	Y
MINNESOTA						
Boschwitz	Y	N	Y	Y	Y	N
Durenberger	+	-	+	?	+	N
MISSISSIPPI						
Cochran	Y	N	Y	Y	Y	Y
Stennis	Y	?	Y	Y	?	Y
MISSOURI						
Danforth	Y	N	Y	Y	Y	Y
Eagleton	Y	N	Y	Y	Y	N
MONTANA						
Baucus	Y	N	Y	Y	Y	Y
Melcher	N	N	Y	Y	Y	Y
NEBRASKA						
Exon	+	?	?	?	?	?
Zorinsky	Y	Y	Y	Y	Y	Y
NEVADA						
Hecht	N	Y	Y	Y	Y	N
Laxalt	Y	Y	Y	Y	Y	N
NEW HAMPSHIRE						
Humphrey	Y	Y	Y	Y	Y	?
Rudman	Y	Y	Y	Y	Y	Y
NEW JERSEY						
Bradley	Y	N	Y	Y	Y	Y
Lautenberg	Y	N	Y	Y	Y	Y
NEW MEXICO						
Domenici	Y	Y	Y	Y	Y	Y
Bingaman	Y	N	Y	Y	Y	Y
NEW YORK						
D'Amato	Y	N	Y	Y	Y	Y
Moynihan	Y	N	Y	Y	Y	Y
NORTH CAROLINA						
East	N	Y	N	Y	Y	Y
Helms	N	Y	N	Y	Y	N
NORTH DAKOTA						
Andrews	Y	N	Y	Y	Y	Y
Burdick	Y	N	Y	Y	Y	Y
OHIO						
Glenn	+	?	+	?	?	?
Metzenbaum	Y	N	Y	Y	Y	Y
OKLAHOMA						
Nickles	Y	Y	Y	Y	Y	Y
Boren	Y	N	Y	Y	Y	Y
OREGON						
Hatfield	Y	N	Y	Y	Y	Y
Packwood	Y	N	Y	Y	Y	Y
PENNSYLVANIA						
Heinz	Y	N	Y	Y	Y	Y
Specter	Y	N	Y	Y	Y	Y
RHODE ISLAND						
Chafee	Y	N	Y	Y	Y	Y
Pell	Y	N	Y	Y	Y	Y
SOUTH CAROLINA						
Thurmond	N	Y	N	Y	Y	Y
Hollings	Y	Y	Y	Y	Y	Y
SOUTH DAKOTA						
Abdnor	Y	Y	Y	Y	Y	Y
Pressler	Y	Y	Y	Y	Y	Y
TENNESSEE						
Gore	Y	N	Y	Y	Y	Y
Sasser	Y	N	Y	Y	Y	Y
TEXAS						
Gramm	Y	Y	Y	Y	Y	Y
Bentsen	Y	N	Y	Y	Y	Y
UTAH						
Garn	Y	Y	N	Y	Y	Y
Hatch	Y	Y	Y	Y	Y	Y
VERMONT						
Stafford	Y	N	Y	Y	Y	Y
Leahy	Y	N	Y	Y	Y	Y
VIRGINIA						
Trible	Y	Y	Y	Y	Y	Y
Warner	Y	Y	Y	Y	Y	Y
WASHINGTON						
Evans	Y	N	Y	Y	Y	Y
Gorton	Y	N	Y	Y	Y	Y
WEST VIRGINIA						
Byrd	Y	N	Y	Y	Y	Y
Rockefeller	Y	N	Y	Y	Y	Y
WISCONSIN						
Kasten	Y	Y	Y	Y	Y	Y
Proxmire	Y	N	Y	Y	Y	N
WYOMING						
Simpson	Y	N	Y	Y	Y	Y
Wallop	N	Y	N	Y	Y	N

KEY

- Y Voted for (yea).
- # Paired for.
- + Announced for.
- N Voted against (nay).
- X Paired against.
- \- Announced against.
- P Voted "present."
- C Voted "present" to avoid possible conflict of interest.
- ? Did not vote or otherwise make a position known.

Democrats ***Republicans***

ND - Northern Democrats SD - Southern Democrats (Southern states - Ala., Ark., Fla., Ga., Ky., La., Miss., N.C., Okla., S.C., Tenn., Texas, Va.)

13. S Res 345. Philippine Elections. Adoption of the resolution to condemn the Feb. 7 presidential and vice presidential elections in the Philippines as having been "marked by such widespread fraud that they cannot be considered a fair reflection of the will of the people of the Philippines. . . ." Adopted 85-9: R 43-8; D 42-1 (ND 29-1, SD 13-0), Feb. 19, 1986.

14. Exec O, 81st Cong, 1st Sess. Genocide Treaty. Symms, R-Idaho, amendment to include "political" groups among those protected from genocide under the treaty. Rejected 31-62: R 28-23; D 3-39 (ND 1-28, SD 2-11), Feb. 19, 1986.

15. Exec O, 81st Cong, 1st Sess. Genocide Treaty. Adoption of the resolution of ratification of the treaty to make genocide a crime and to require treaty signatories to enact legislation making genocide a crime and providing punishment for violators. Adopted 83-11: R 40-11; D 43-0 (ND 29-0, SD 14-0), Feb. 19, 1986. A two-thirds majority of those present and voting (63 in this case) is required for adoption of resolutions of ratification. A "yea" was a vote supporting the president's position.

16. S Res 347. Amendment of Genocide Treaty. Adoption of the resolution to express the sense of the Senate that the president should seek to amend the genocide treaty to include protection for "political" groups. Adopted 93-1: R 50-1; D 43-0 (ND 29-0, SD 14-0), Feb. 19, 1986. A "yea" was a vote supporting the president's position.

17. S 1429. Terrorist Prosecution. Passage of the bill to authorize federal prosecution of terrorists who attack U.S. citizens abroad. Passed 92-0: R 50-0; D 42-0 (ND 29-0, SD 13-0), Feb. 19, 1986.

18. S Res 28. Broadcast Coverage of Senate Proceedings. Dole, R-Kan., motion to recommit to the Rules and Administration Committee the resolution to authorize radio broadcasts and limited television coverage of Senate proceedings, with instructions to report it back immediately with several changes in Senate rules, including new limits on filibusters and non-germane amendments. Motion agreed to 81-9: R 41-7; D 40-2 (ND 27-2, SD 13-0), Feb. 20, 1986. (The effect of the motion was to put before the Senate a substitute linking a package of rules changes, which had not been included in the version of S Res 28 first reported by the committee, to the radio-TV broadcasting proposal.)

	19	20	21	22	23	24
ALABAMA						
Denton	N	Y	N	Y	N	Y
Heflin	Y	Y	Y	N	N	Y
ALASKA						
Murkowski	Y	Y	N	Y	N	Y
Stevens	Y	Y	N	N	N	Y
ARIZONA						
Goldwater	Y	N	Y	N	Y	?
DeConcini	Y	Y	N	N	N	Y
ARKANSAS						
Bumpers	+	?	?	?	?	+
Pryor	Y	N	N	N	Y	Y
CALIFORNIA						
Wilson	Y	Y	N	N	N	Y
Cranston	Y	N	N	Y	N	Y
COLORADO						
Armstrong	Y	Y	N	N	N	Y
Hart	Y	Y	N	N	N	Y
CONNECTICUT						
Weicker	Y	Y	N	Y	N	Y
Dodd	Y	Y	Y	Y	Y	Y
DELAWARE						
Roth	Y	Y	N	N	N	Y
Biden	Y	N	N	Y	N	Y
FLORIDA						
Hawkins	Y	Y	N	Y	N	Y
Chiles	Y	Y	N	Y	N	Y
GEORGIA						
Mattingly	Y	Y	Y	N	Y	N
Nunn	Y	N	Y	N	?	N
HAWAII						
Inouye	Y	N	N	Y	N	?
Matsunaga	Y	N	N	N	N	Y
IDAHO						
McClure	Y	Y	N	N	N	Y
Symms	Y	Y	N	N	N	Y
ILLINOIS						
Dixon	Y	Y	?	?	?	+
Simon	Y	Y	N	Y	N	Y
INDIANA						
Lugar	Y	Y	N	Y	N	Y
Quayle	Y	N	Y	N	Y	N
IOWA						
Grassley	Y	Y	N	Y	Y	N
Harkin	Y	Y	N	Y	?	Y
KANSAS						
Dole	Y	Y	N	N	N	Y
Kassebaum	Y	N	N	N	N	?
KENTUCKY						
McConnell	Y	Y	Y	Y	Y	N
Ford	Y	N	N	N	N	Y
LOUISIANA						
Johnston	Y	N	Y	Y	Y	N
Long	Y	N	Y	N	Y	N
MAINE						
Cohen	Y	N	N	N	N	Y
Mitchell	Y	Y	N	Y	N	Y
MARYLAND						
Mathias	?	?	N	N	N	Y
Sarbanes	Y	N	?	?	?	?
MASSACHUSETTS						
Kennedy	Y	Y	N	Y	N	Y
Kerry	Y	N	?	?	?	?
MICHIGAN						
Levin	Y	N	Y	Y	Y	Y
Riegle	+	N	N	Y	N	Y
MINNESOTA						
Boschwitz	Y	Y	Y	Y	Y	N
Durenberger	Y	Y	Y	Y	?	-
MISSISSIPPI						
Cochran	Y	Y	N	Y	N	Y
Stennis	Y	N	Y	N	Y	N
MISSOURI						
Danforth	Y	Y	Y	N	Y	N
Eagleton	Y	Y	?	?	?	?
MONTANA						
Baucus	Y	N	N	N	N	Y
Melcher	Y	N	N	Y	N	Y
NEBRASKA						
Exon	?	?	?	?	?	+
Zorinsky	Y	Y	N	N	N	Y
NEVADA						
Hecht	Y	Y	Y	N	Y	N
Laxalt	Y	Y	?	Y	Y	N
NEW HAMPSHIRE						
Humphrey	Y	Y	N	Y	N	Y
Rudman	Y	N	N	Y	Y	N
NEW JERSEY						
Bradley	Y	Y	Y	Y	Y	Y
Lautenberg	Y	Y	N	Y	N	Y
NEW MEXICO						
Domenici	Y	Y	N	Y	N	Y
Bingaman	Y	N	N	Y	N	Y
NEW YORK						
D'Amato	Y	Y	N	Y	N	Y
Moynihan	Y	N	N	Y	N	Y
NORTH CAROLINA						
East	Y	Y	Y	Y	Y	N
Helms	Y	Y	Y	N	Y	N
NORTH DAKOTA						
Andrews	Y	Y	N	Y	N	Y
Burdick	Y	N	Y	N	Y	N
OHIO						
Glenn	Y	N	Y	Y	Y	Y
Metzenbaum	Y	N	N	Y	N	Y
OKLAHOMA						
Nickles	Y	N	N	N	N	Y
Boren	Y	N	Y	N	Y	Y
OREGON						
Hatfield	Y	Y	Y	N	Y	N
Packwood	Y	Y	?	?	?	?
PENNSYLVANIA						
Heinz	Y	Y	N	Y	N	Y
Specter	Y	Y	N	N	N	Y
RHODE ISLAND						
Chafee	Y	Y	N	N	N	Y
Pell	Y	N	Y	Y	N	Y
SOUTH CAROLINA						
Thurmond	Y	Y	N	N	N	Y
Hollings	Y	Y	Y	Y	Y	N
SOUTH DAKOTA						
Abdnor	Y	Y	N	N	N	Y
Pressler	Y	Y	N	Y	N	Y
TENNESSEE						
Gore	Y	N	N	Y	N	Y
Sasser	Y	N	Y	Y	N	Y
TEXAS						
Gramm	Y	Y	N	N	?	Y
Bentsen	Y	N	Y	Y	Y	Y
UTAH						
Garn	Y	Y	N	N	N	Y
Hatch	Y	Y	N	N	N	Y
VERMONT						
Stafford	Y	N	Y	Y	Y	N
Leahy	Y	Y	N	Y	N	Y
VIRGINIA						
Trible	Y	Y	N	N	N	Y
Warner	Y	Y	N	Y	N	Y
WASHINGTON						
Evans	Y	N	N	N	N	Y
Gorton	Y	Y	N	Y	N	Y
WEST VIRGINIA						
Byrd	Y	N	N	N	N	Y
Rockefeller	Y	N	?	?	?	?
WISCONSIN						
Kasten	Y	Y	N	N	N	Y
Proxmire	Y	N	Y	N	Y	N
WYOMING						
Simpson	Y	Y	Y	Y	N	Y
Wallop	Y	Y	Y	Y	Y	N

KEY

- Y Voted for (yea).
- # Paired for.
- + Announced for.
- N Voted against (nay).
- X Paired against.
- - Announced against.
- P Voted "present."
- C Voted "present" to avoid possible conflict of interest.
- ? Did not vote or otherwise make a position known.

Democrats *Republicans*

ND - Northern Democrats SD - Southern Democrats (Southern states - Ala., Ark., Fla., Ga., Ky., La., Miss., N.C., Okla., S.C., Tenn., Texas, Va.)

19. S Res 351. Support for New Philippine Government. Adoption of the resolution to express support for the new government in the Philippines of President Corazon Aquino, and to praise the Philippine people and "the progress toward restoration of democracy in the Philippines." Adopted 95-1: R 51-1; D 44-0 (ND 31-0, SD 13-0), Feb. 26, 1986.

20. S Res 28. Broadcast Coverage of Senate Proceedings. Armstrong, R-Colo., amendment to strike language that would have replaced existing Senate rules allowing non-germane amendments on legislation with a new rule allowing the Senate, by three-fifths vote of those present, to bar non-germane amendments from a bill or resolution. Adopted 60-37: R 44-8; D 16-29 (ND 13-19, SD 3-10), Feb. 26, 1986.

21. S Res 28. Broadcast Coverage of Senate Proceedings. Johnston, D-La., amendment to the Dole, R-Kan., substitute for the Rules and Administration Committee substitute, to restrict television coverage of Senate proceedings to legislative business for which a time agreement limits debate and to matters for which the Senate gives unanimous consent to allow television coverage. Rejected 30-61: R 14-37; D 16-24 (ND 7-20, SD 9-4), Feb. 27, 1986. (Subsequently, the Dole substitute was adopted by voice vote, after which the committee substitute, as amended by the Dole substitute, was adopted by voice vote.)

22. S Res 28. Broadcast Coverage of Senate Proceedings. Bradley, D-N.J., motion to table (kill) the Evans, R-Wash., amendment to impose a Senate rule that senators vote from their assigned desks. Motion agreed to 49-43: R 24-28; D 25-15 (ND 19-8, SD 6-7), Feb. 27, 1986.

23. S Res 28. Broadcast Coverage of Senate Proceedings. Long, D-La., amendment to provide television coverage only for those matters and for an amount of time specified in a motion adopted by a majority vote of the Senate. Rejected 28-60: R 15-35; D 13-25 (ND 6-20, SD 7-5), Feb. 27, 1986.

24. S Res 28. Broadcast Coverage of Senate Proceedings. Adoption of the resolution to allow a test period from at least May 1 through July 15, 1986, during which Senate floor proceedings will be broadcast on radio and television, and to change certain procedural rules of the Senate. Adopted 67-21: R 35-14; D 32-7 (ND 24-2, SD 8-5), Feb. 27, 1986.

CQ Senate Votes 25 - 28

Corresponding to Congressional Record Votes 25, 26, 27, 28

	25	26	27	28
ALABAMA				
Denton	Y	Y	Y	Y
Heflin	Y	Y	Y	Y
ALASKA				
Murkowski	Y	Y	Y	Y
Stevens	?	?	?	?
ARIZONA				
Goldwater	N	?	Y	Y
DeConcini	Y	Y	Y	Y
ARKANSAS				
Bumpers	Y	Y	Y	Y
Pryor	Y	Y	Y	Y
CALIFORNIA				
Wilson	N	Y	Y	Y
Cranston	Y	Y	Y	Y
COLORADO				
Armstrong	?	Y	Y	Y
Hart	Y	Y	Y	Y
CONNECTICUT				
Weicker	Y	Y	Y	Y
Dodd	Y	Y	Y	Y
DELAWARE				
Roth	N	Y	Y	Y
Biden	Y	Y	Y	Y
FLORIDA				
Hawkins	N	Y	Y	Y
Chiles	?	Y	Y	Y
GEORGIA				
Mattingly	Y	Y	Y	Y
Nunn	Y	Y	Y	Y
HAWAII				
Inouye	?	?	?	?
Matsunaga	Y	Y	Y	Y
IDAHO				
McClure	Y	Y	N	Y
Symms	Y	Y	N	N
ILLINOIS				
Dixon	Y	Y	Y	Y
Simon	Y	Y	Y	Y
INDIANA				
Lugar	Y	Y	Y	Y
Quayle	Y	Y	N	Y
IOWA				
Grassley	Y	Y	Y	Y
Harkin	Y	Y	Y	Y
KANSAS				
Dole	Y	Y	Y	Y
Kassebaum	+	Y	Y	Y
KENTUCKY				
McConnell	Y	Y	N	Y
Ford	Y	Y	Y	Y
LOUISIANA				
Johnston	?	Y	Y	Y
Long	+	Y	Y	Y
MAINE				
Cohen	N	Y	Y	Y
Mitchell	Y	Y	Y	Y
MARYLAND				
Mathias	?	Y	Y	Y
Sarbanes	Y	Y	Y	Y
MASSACHUSETTS				
Kennedy	Y	Y	Y	Y
Kerry	Y	Y	Y	Y
MICHIGAN				
Levin	Y	Y	Y	Y
Riegle	?	N	Y	Y
MINNESOTA				
Boschwitz	Y	Y	Y	Y
Durenberger	Y	Y	Y	Y
MISSISSIPPI				
Cochran	Y	Y	Y	Y
Stennis	?	Y	Y	Y
MISSOURI				
Danforth	Y	Y	Y	Y
Eagleton	?	Y	Y	Y
MONTANA				
Baucus	Y	Y	Y	Y
Melcher	Y	Y	Y	Y
NEBRASKA				
Exon	Y	Y	Y	Y
Zorinsky	Y	Y	Y	Y
NEVADA				
Hecht	N	Y	Y	Y
Laxalt	?	Y	Y	Y
NEW HAMPSHIRE				
Humphrey	?	Y	Y	Y
Rudman	N	Y	Y	Y
NEW JERSEY				
Bradley	?	Y	Y	Y
Lautenberg	N	Y	Y	Y
NEW MEXICO				
Domenici	Y	Y	Y	Y
Bingaman	Y	Y	Y	Y
NEW YORK				
D'Amato	Y	Y	Y	Y
Moynihan	Y	Y	Y	Y
NORTH CAROLINA				
East	N	Y	N	Y
Helms	N	Y	N	Y
NORTH DAKOTA				
Andrews	Y	Y	Y	Y
Burdick	+	Y	Y	Y
OHIO				
Glenn	Y	Y	Y	Y
Metzenbaum	Y	Y	Y	Y
OKLAHOMA				
Nickles	Y	Y	Y	Y
Boren	Y	Y	Y	Y
OREGON				
Hatfield	Y	Y	Y	Y
Packwood	Y	Y	Y	Y
PENNSYLVANIA				
Heinz	Y	Y	Y	Y
Specter	?	Y	Y	Y
RHODE ISLAND				
Chafee	N	Y	Y	Y
Pell	N	Y	Y	Y
SOUTH CAROLINA				
Thurmond	Y	Y	Y	Y
Hollings	Y	Y	Y	Y
SOUTH DAKOTA				
Abdnor	Y	Y	Y	Y
Pressler	Y	Y	N	Y
TENNESSEE				
Gore	Y	Y	Y	Y
Sasser	Y	Y	Y	Y
TEXAS				
Gramm	N	Y	Y	Y
Bentsen	Y	Y	Y	Y
UTAH				
Garn	N	Y	N	Y
Hatch	N	Y	N	Y
VERMONT				
Stafford	?	Y	Y	Y
Leahy	Y	Y	Y	Y
VIRGINIA				
Trible	N	Y	Y	Y
Warner	N	Y	Y	Y
WASHINGTON				
Evans	N	Y	Y	Y
Gorton	Y	Y	Y	Y
WEST VIRGINIA				
Byrd	Y	Y	Y	Y
Rockefeller	Y	Y	Y	Y
WISCONSIN				
Kasten	Y	Y	Y	Y
Proxmire	Y	N	Y	Y
WYOMING				
Simpson	Y	Y	N	Y
Wallop	Y	Y	Y	Y

KEY

- Y Voted for (yea).
- # Paired for.
- + Announced for.
- N Voted against (nay).
- X Paired against.
- - Announced against.
- P Voted "present."
- C Voted "present" to avoid possible conflict of interest.
- ? Did not vote or otherwise make a position known.

Democrats *Republicans*

ND - Northern Democrats SD - Southern Democrats (Southern states - Ala., Ark., Fla., Ga., Ky., La., Miss., N.C., Okla., S.C., Tenn., Texas, Va.)

25. S 2143. Corrections to 1985 Farm Bill. Harkin, D-Iowa, amendment to express the sense of Congress that the agriculture secretary shall use authorities provided in the 1985 Food Security Act (PL 99-198) to make advance price-support loans to producers of wheat, feed grains, cotton and rice. Adopted 65-18: R 29-16; D 36-2 (ND 26-2, SD 10-0), March 5, 1986. (The bill subsequently was passed by voice vote, and its text substituted for that of HR 1614.)

26. Lyng Nomination. Confirmation of President Reagan's nomination of Richard E. Lyng of Virginia to be secretary of agriculture. Confirmed 95-2: R 51-0; D 44-2 (ND 30-2, SD 14-0), March 6, 1986. A "yea" was a vote supporting the president's position.

27. S 104. Armor-Piercing Bullets. Thurmond, R-S.C., motion to table (kill) the Symms, R-Idaho, amendment to revise the definition of armor-piercing bullets to cover only those "intended for use in a handgun." Motion agreed to 88-10: R 42-10; D 46-0 (ND 32-0, SD 14-0), March 6, 1986.

28. HR 3132. Armor-Piercing Bullets. Passage of the bill to bar the importation, manufacture and sale of armor-piercing bullets. Passed 97-1: R 51-1; D 46-0 (ND 32-0, SD 14-0), March 6, 1986. (The Senate had previously moved to strike the text of the House-passed bill and insert instead the text of S 104, the Senate version of HR 3132.)

	29	30	31	32	33	34	35	36
ALABAMA								
Denton	Y	N	N	N	Y	Y	Y	Y
Heflin	N	N	N	Y	Y	N	Y	N
ALASKA								
Murkowski	Y	N	Y	Y	N	Y	Y	Y
Stevens	Y	N	N	Y	Y	Y	Y	Y
ARIZONA								
Goldwater	Y	N	N	?	N	N	?	?
DeConcini	Y	N	Y	Y	N	Y	Y	N
ARKANSAS								
Bumpers	N	N	N	N	N	Y	N	N
Pryor	N	N	N	Y	Y	Y	Y	N
CALIFORNIA								
Wilson	Y	N	Y	Y	N	N	Y	N
Cranston	N	Y	N	N	Y	Y	N	N
COLORADO								
Armstrong	N	N	Y	Y	N	N	Y	N
Hart	N	Y	Y	N	N	Y	N	?
CONNECTICUT								
Weicker	N	N	Y	Y	N	Y	N	N
Dodd	N	Y	N	N	N	Y	N	N
DELAWARE								
Roth	Y	N	Y	Y	N	Y	Y	Y
Biden	N	N	N	Y	Y	Y	N	N
FLORIDA								
Hawkins	Y	N	Y	N	N	Y	Y	N
Chiles	N	N	Y	N	N	Y	Y	N
GEORGIA								
Mattingly	Y	N	N	Y	N	N	Y	N
Nunn	N	N	N	Y	Y	Y	Y	Y
HAWAII								
Inouye	N	Y	N	N	Y	Y	N	?
Matsunaga	N	Y	N	N	Y	Y	N	N
IDAHO								
McClure	Y	N	Y	Y	Y	N	Y	Y
Symms	Y	N	Y	Y	N	N	?	N
ILLINOIS								
Dixon	Y	N	Y	Y	N	Y	Y	N
Simon	Y	N	Y	Y	N	Y	Y	N
INDIANA								
Lugar	Y	N	Y	Y	N	Y	N	N
Quayle	Y	N	N	Y	N	Y	Y	Y
IOWA								
Grassley	Y	N	Y	Y	N	Y	Y	N
Harkin	N	Y	N	N	Y	Y	N	N
KANSAS								
Dole	Y	N	Y	Y	N	Y	Y	Y
Kassebaum	Y	N	Y	Y	N	Y	Y	N
KENTUCKY								
McConnell	Y	N	Y	Y	N	Y	Y	Y
Ford	?	?	N	N	Y	Y	N	N
LOUISIANA								
Johnston	N	N	N	N	Y	Y	N	N
Long	Y	?	Y	Y	N	Y	Y	N
MAINE								
Cohen	Y	N	N	N	N	Y	Y	N
Mitchell	N	N	N	N	N	Y	N	N
MARYLAND								
Mathias	N	Y	N	N	Y	Y	?	?
Sarbanes	N	N	N	N	Y	Y	N	N
MASSACHUSETTS								
Kennedy	N	N	N	N	Y	Y	N	N
Kerry	N	Y	N	N	Y	Y	N	N
MICHIGAN								
Levin	N	Y	N	Y	Y	Y	N	N
Riegle	N	N	N	N	N	Y	N	N
MINNESOTA								
Boschwitz	Y	N	Y	Y	N	Y	Y	Y
Durenberger	Y	N	Y	Y	N	Y	N	Y
MISSISSIPPI								
Cochran	Y	N	Y	Y	N	Y	Y	Y
Stennis	N	N	N	Y	N	Y	Y	N
MISSOURI								
Danforth	Y	N	Y	Y	N	Y	Y	Y
Eagleton	N	Y	N	N	Y	Y	N	N
MONTANA								
Baucus	N	N	N	Y	Y	Y	Y	N
Melcher	N	N	N	N	Y	Y	N	N
NEBRASKA								
Exon	-	N	N	Y	Y	Y	N	N
Zorinsky	Y	N	Y	Y	N	N	Y	N
NEVADA								
Hecht	Y	N	Y	Y	N	Y	Y	N
Laxalt	Y	N	Y	Y	?	Y	Y	Y
NEW HAMPSHIRE								
Humphrey	N	N	Y	Y	N	N	Y	N
Rudman	Y	N	Y	Y	N	Y	Y	N
NEW JERSEY								
Bradley	N	N	N	N	N	Y	N	N
Lautenberg	N	Y	N	N	N	Y	N	N
NEW MEXICO								
Domenici	Y	N	Y	Y	N	Y	Y	N
Bingaman	N	Y	N	Y	Y	Y	N	N
NEW YORK								
D'Amato	Y	N	Y	N	N	Y	Y	N
Moynihan	N	N	Y	N	Y	N	N	N
NORTH CAROLINA								
East	Y	N	Y	Y	N	Y	Y	Y
Helms	Y	N	Y	Y	N	N	Y	N
NORTH DAKOTA								
Andrews	N	N	N	N	Y	Y	Y	Y
Burdick	N	N	Y	N	N	Y	Y	N
OHIO								
Glenn	N	Y	N	N	Y	Y	N	N
Metzenbaum	N	Y	Y	N	Y	Y	N	N
OKLAHOMA								
Nickles	N	N	Y	Y	N	Y	Y	N
Boren	N	N	N	Y	Y	Y	Y	N
OREGON								
Hatfield	Y	N	Y	Y	N	Y	N	N
Packwood	Y	N	Y	Y	N	Y	N	Y
PENNSYLVANIA								
Heinz	Y	N	N	N	N	Y	N	N
Specter	Y	N	Y	N	N	Y	Y	N
RHODE ISLAND								
Chafee	Y	N	N	N	N	Y	N	N
Pell	N	N	N	N	Y	Y	N	N
SOUTH CAROLINA								
Thurmond	Y	N	Y	Y	N	Y	Y	Y
Hollings	N	N	Y	Y	N	Y	N	N
SOUTH DAKOTA								
Abdnor	Y	N	Y	Y	N	Y	Y	N
Pressler	Y	N	Y	N	N	Y	Y	Y
TENNESSEE								
Gore	N	N	N	N	Y	Y	N	Y
Sasser	N	N	N	N	Y	Y	N	Y
TEXAS								
Gramm	Y	N	Y	Y	N	Y	Y	N
Bentsen	Y	N	N	Y	Y	Y	Y	N
UTAH								
Garn	Y	N	Y	Y	N	N	Y	N
Hatch	Y	N	Y	Y	N	Y	Y	Y
VERMONT								
Stafford	Y	N	Y	Y	N	Y	Y	N
Leahy	N	N	N	N	Y	Y	Y	N
VIRGINIA								
Trible	Y	N	Y	Y	N	Y	Y	N
Warner	Y	N	Y	Y	Y	Y	Y	Y
WASHINGTON								
Evans	Y	N	N	N	N	Y	N	Y
Gorton	Y	N	N	N	N	Y	N	Y
WEST VIRGINIA								
Byrd	N	N	N	N	Y	Y	N	N
Rockefeller	N	N	N	N	N	Y	N	N
WISCONSIN								
Kasten	Y	N	Y	N	N	Y	Y	N
Proxmire	Y	N	Y	Y	N	Y	Y	N
WYOMING								
Simpson	Y	N	Y	Y	N	Y	Y	Y
Wallop	Y	N	N	Y	N	N	Y	Y

KEY

- Y Voted for (yea).
- # Paired for.
- + Announced for.
- N Voted against (nay).
- X Paired against.
- - Announced against.
- P Voted "present."
- C Voted "present" to avoid possible conflict of interest.
- ? Did not vote or otherwise make a position known.

Democrats ***Republicans***

ND - Northern Democrats SD - Southern Democrats (Southern states - Ala., Ark., Fla., Ga., Ky., La., Miss., N.C., Okla., S.C., Tenn., Texas, Va.)

29. S J Res 225. Balanced Budget Constitutional Amendment. DeConcini, D-Ariz., motion to table (kill) the Metzenbaum, D-Ohio, amendment to the Thurmond, R-S.C., substitute, to require the president to submit a balanced budget to Congress. Motion agreed to 54-44: R 47-6; D 7-38 (ND 5-27, SD 2-11), March 11, 1986. (The Metzenbaum amendment was reintroduced on March 12 and adopted by voice vote. The Thurmond substitute would bar deficit spending except during a declared war or when three-fifths of Congress voted to allow it, and would require that any bill to increase revenues must be approved by an absolute majority vote of each house of Congress.)

30. S J Res 225. Balanced Budget Constitutional Amendment. Metzenbaum, D-Ohio, amendment to the Thurmond, R-S.C., substitute, to allow states to file lawsuits to enforce the requirement of a balanced federal budget. Rejected 14-84: R 1-52; D 13-32 (ND 13-20, SD 0-12), March 11, 1986.

31. S J Res 225. Balanced Budget Constitutional Amendment. Simon, D-Ill., motion to table (kill) the Heflin, D-Ala., amendment to the Thurmond, R-S.C., substitute, to provide that the constitutional requirement for a balanced budget would be automatically waived when the United States was involved in a declared war. Motion agreed to 52-48: R 40-13; D 12-35 (ND 9-24, SD 3-11), March 12, 1986.

32. S J Res 225. Balanced Budget Constitutional Amendment. Thurmond, R-S.C., motion to table (kill) the Metzenbaum, D-Ohio, amendment to the Thurmond substitute, to bar cuts in Social Security benefits for the purpose of balancing the budget. Motion agreed to 57-42: R 39-13; D 18-29 (ND 10-23, SD 8-6), March 12, 1986.

33. S J Res 225. Balanced Budget Constitutional Amendment. Byrd, D-W.Va., substitute for the Thurmond, R-S.C., substitute, to provide that federal expenditures may not exceed receipts in any year, except during a declared war or when three-fifths of the members of Congress vote for deficit spending. Rejected 35-64: R 6-46; D 29-18 (ND 20-13, SD 9-5), March 12, 1986.

34. S J Res 225. Balanced Budget Constitutional Amendment. Thurmond, R-S.C., motion to table (kill) the McClure, R-Idaho, amendment to the Thurmond substitute, to limit outlays in a fiscal year to not more than 20 percent of national income for that fiscal year. Motion agreed to 87-13: R 43-10; D 44-3 (ND 31-2, SD 13-1), March 12, 1986.

35. S J Res 225. Balanced Budget Constitutional Amendment. Hatch, R-Utah, amendment to the Thurmond, R-S.C., substitute, to require a three-fifths vote of both the House and Senate to increase the debt ceiling. Adopted 57-40: R 41-9; D 16-31 (ND 8-25, SD 8-6), March 13, 1986.

36. S Res 353. Committee Funding. Stevens, R-Alaska, amendment to establish a $1.5 million special reserve fund, in addition to regular funding for Senate committee operations, to help committees that have extraordinary and unexpected expenses. Rejected 27-69: R 24-27; D 3-42 (ND 0-31, SD 3-11), March 13, 1986.

CQ Senate Votes 37 - 42

Corresponding to Congressional Record Votes 37, 38, 39, 40, 41, 42

	37	38	39	40	41	42
ALABAMA						
Denton	N	N	Y	Y	Y	Y
Heflin	N	N	Y	N	N	N
ALASKA						
Murkowski	N	Y	Y	Y	Y	Y
Stevens	N	N	Y	Y	Y	Y
ARIZONA						
Goldwater	?	?	?	Y	Y	Y
DeConcini	N	Y	?	Y	#	Y
ARKANSAS						
Bumpers	N	N	Y	?	?	Y
Pryor	N	N	Y	Y	Y	Y
CALIFORNIA						
Wilson	N	Y	N	Y	Y	Y
Cranston	N	Y	N	N	N	Y
COLORADO						
Armstrong	N	Y	Y	Y	Y	Y
Hart	?	?	?	N	N	Y
CONNECTICUT						
Weicker	N	Y	N	Y	Y	Y
Dodd	N	Y	N	N	N	Y
DELAWARE						
Roth	N	Y	N	Y	Y	Y
Biden	N	N	-	N	N	Y
FLORIDA						
Hawkins	N	Y	N	Y	Y	Y
Chiles	N	Y	N	N	N	Y
GEORGIA						
Mattingly	N	Y	Y	Y	Y	Y
Nunn	?	?	?	N	N	Y
HAWAII						
Inouye	?	?	?	?	?	?
Matsunaga	N	N	N	N	N	Y
IDAHO						
McClure	N	Y	Y	Y	?	?
Symms	N	Y	Y	Y	Y	Y
ILLINOIS						
Dixon	N	Y	Y	N	N	Y
Simon	N	Y	N	Y	Y	Y
INDIANA						
Lugar	N	Y	Y	Y	Y	Y
Quayle	N	Y	Y	Y	Y	Y
IOWA						
Grassley	N	N	Y	Y	Y	Y
Harkin	N	N	?	N	N	Y
KANSAS						
Dole	N	Y	Y	Y	Y	Y
Kassebaum	N	Y	Y	Y	Y	Y
KENTUCKY						
McConnell	N	Y	Y	Y	Y	Y
Ford	N	N	Y	N	N	Y
LOUISIANA						
Johnston	N	N	Y	Y	N	Y
Long	N	Y	Y	Y	N	Y
MAINE						
Cohen	N	Y	N	Y	Y	Y
Mitchell	N	N	N	N	N	Y
MARYLAND						
Mathias	?	?	?	?	?	?
Sarbanes	?	N	N	N	N	Y
MASSACHUSETTS						
Kennedy	N	N	?	N	N	Y
Kerry	N	Y	N	N	N	Y
MICHIGAN						
Levin	N	Y	N	N	N	Y
Riegle	N	N	N	N	N	Y
MINNESOTA						
Boschwitz	N	Y	Y	Y	Y	Y
Durenberger	Y	N	N	Y	Y	Y
MISSISSIPPI						
Cochran	N	N	Y	Y	Y	Y
Stennis	N	N	Y	Y	N	Y
MISSOURI						
Danforth	N	Y	Y	Y	Y	Y
Eagleton	N	N	?	N	N	Y
MONTANA						
Baucus	N	N	N	Y	N	Y
Melcher	N	N	N	N	N	Y
NEBRASKA						
Exon	N	N	Y	N	N	Y
Zorinsky	N	N	Y	Y	N	Y
NEVADA						
Hecht	N	Y	Y	Y	Y	Y
Laxalt	?	?	N	Y	Y	Y
NEW HAMPSHIRE						
Humphrey	N	Y	Y	Y	Y	Y
Rudman	N	Y	Y	Y	Y	Y
NEW JERSEY						
Bradley	N	Y	N	N	N	Y
Lautenberg	N	Y	N	N	N	Y
NEW MEXICO						
Domenici	N	Y	Y	Y	Y	Y
Bingaman	N	Y	Y	N	N	Y
NEW YORK						
D'Amato	N	Y	N	Y	Y	Y
Moynihan	N	Y	N	N	N	Y
NORTH CAROLINA						
East	N	Y	Y	Y	Y	Y
Helms	N	Y	Y	Y	Y	Y
NORTH DAKOTA						
Andrews	N	N	Y	Y	Y	Y
Burdick	N	N	Y	N	N	Y
OHIO						
Glenn	N	N	Y	N	N	Y
Metzenbaum	N	Y	N	N	N	Y
OKLAHOMA						
Nickles	N	N	Y	Y	Y	Y
Boren	N	N	Y	Y	N	?
OREGON						
Hatfield	N	N	Y	Y	Y	Y
Packwood	N	Y	N	Y	Y	Y
PENNSYLVANIA						
Heinz	N	Y	N	Y	N	Y
Specter	N	Y	?	Y	N	Y
RHODE ISLAND						
Chafee	N	Y	Y	Y	Y	Y
Pell	N	Y	N	Y	Y	Y
SOUTH CAROLINA						
Thurmond	N	Y	Y	Y	Y	Y
Hollings	N	Y	N	Y	N	Y
SOUTH DAKOTA						
Abdnor	N	N	Y	Y	Y	Y
Pressler	N	N	Y	Y	Y	Y
TENNESSEE						
Gore	N	N	N	N	N	Y
Sasser	N	N	N	N	N	Y
TEXAS						
Gramm	N	Y	Y	Y	Y	Y
Bentsen	N	Y	Y	Y	N	Y
UTAH						
Garn	N	Y	Y	Y	Y	Y
Hatch	N	Y	N	Y	Y	Y
VERMONT						
Stafford	N	Y	N	Y	Y	Y
Leahy	N	Y	N	N	X	Y
VIRGINIA						
Trible	N	Y	?	Y	Y	Y
Warner	N	Y	Y	Y	Y	Y
WASHINGTON						
Evans	N	Y	N	Y	Y	Y
Gorton	N	Y	Y	Y	Y	Y
WEST VIRGINIA						
Byrd	N	Y	Y	N	N	Y
Rockefeller	N	Y	Y	N	N	Y
WISCONSIN						
Kasten	N	Y	Y	Y	Y	Y
Proxmire	N	Y	N	N	N	Y
WYOMING						
Simpson	N	Y	Y	Y	Y	Y
Wallop	N	Y	Y	Y	Y	Y

KEY

- Y Voted for (yea).
- # Paired for.
- \+ Announced for.
- N Voted against (nay).
- X Paired against.
- \- Announced against.
- P Voted "present."
- C Voted "present" to avoid possible conflict of interest.
- ? Did not vote or otherwise make a position known.

Democrats *Republicans*

ND - Northern Democrats SD - Southern Democrats (Southern states - Ala., Ark., Fla., Ga., Ky., La., Miss., N.C., Okla., S.C., Tenn., Texas, Va.)

37. H J Res 534. Commodity Credit Corporation Supplemental Appropriation, Fiscal 1986. Gramm, R-Texas, motion to waive the spending-limitation requirement contained in the 1985 Balanced Budget and Emergency Deficit Control Act (the Gramm-Rudman-Hollings balanced-budget law, PL 99-177) with respect to the House amendment to the Senate amendment. The House amendment would provide funds for the Farmers Home Administration at the level provided in the continuing funding resolution (PL 99-190), instead of the level provided in the 1985 farm bill (PL 99-198). Motion rejected 1-92: R 1-49; D 0-43 (ND 0-30, SD 0-13), March 13, 1986. A three-fifths majority (60) of the total Senate is required to waive the spending-limitation requirement contained in Gramm-Rudman.

38. H J Res 534. Commodity Credit Corporation Supplemental Appropriation, Fiscal 1986. Domenici, R-N.M., motion to table (kill) the Cochran, R-Miss., appeal of the chair's ruling that the House amendment *(see vote 37, above)* to the Senate amendment violated the spending-limitation requirement contained in the 1985 Balanced Budget and Emergency Deficit Control Act (the Gramm-Rudman-Hollings balanced-budget law, PL 99-177) and thus was not in order. Motion agreed to 61-33: R 40-10; D 21-23 (ND 17-14, SD 4-9), March 13, 1986.

39. HR 3128. Omnibus Budget Reconciliation, Fiscal 1986. Domenici, R-N.M., motion to table (kill) the Wilson, R-Calif., amendment to the Simpson, R-Wyo.-Domenici amendment to the House amendment, to require the secretary of the interior to give equal weight to environmental and economic considerations in determining whether to override a state's objections to offshore drilling leases. Motion agreed to 53-35: R 36-13; D 17-22 (ND 8-18, SD 9-4), March 14, 1986. (The Senate subsequently agreed, by voice vote, to the Simpson motion to concur in the House amendment with a further amendment (the Simpson-Domenici amendment). The House amendment was an amendment to the Senate amendment to the House amendment to the Senate amendment to the bill. The original Senate amendment was the conference agreement on the bill.) A "yea" was a vote supporting the president's position.

40. Fitzwater Nomination. Dole, R-Kan., motion to invoke cloture (thus limiting debate) on President Reagan's nomination of Sidney A. Fitzwater of Texas to be U.S. district judge for the northern district of Texas. Motion agreed to 64-33: R 52-0; D 12-33 (ND 5-27, SD 7-6), March 18, 1986. A three-fifths majority (60) of the total Senate is required to invoke cloture. A "yea" was a vote supporting the president's position.

41. Fitzwater Nomination. Confirmation of President Reagan's nomination of Sidney A. Fitzwater of Texas to be U.S. district judge for the northern district of Texas. Confirmed 52-42: R 49-2; D 3-40 (ND 2-28, SD 1-12), March 18, 1986. A "yea" was a vote supporting the president's position.

42. S 209. Federal Debt Recovery Act. Passage of the bill to authorize the hiring of private attorneys to work under the direction of the Department of Justice to pursue, and, if necessary, litigate the collection of delinquent non-tax debts owed the federal government. Passed 95-1: R 51-0; D 44-1 (ND 32-0, SD 12-1), March 19, 1986. A "yea" was a vote supporting the president's position.

	43	44	45
ALABAMA			
Denton	Y	Y	Y
Heflin	N	Y	Y
ALASKA			
Murkowski	Y	Y	Y
Stevens	Y	Y	Y
ARIZONA			
Goldwater	N	N	Y
DeConcini	Y	Y	Y
ARKANSAS			
Bumpers	N	N	N
Pryor	N	Y	Y
CALIFORNIA			
Wilson	Y	Y	Y
Cranston	N	N	N
COLORADO			
Armstrong	Y	Y	Y
Hart	N	Y	N
CONNECTICUT			
Weicker	Y	Y	N
Dodd	?	Y	N
DELAWARE			
Roth	Y	Y	Y
Biden	N	N	N
FLORIDA			
Hawkins	Y	Y	Y
Chiles	N	N	Y
GEORGIA			
Mattingly	Y	Y	Y
Nunn	N	Y	Y
HAWAII			
Inouye	?	Y	N
Matsunaga	Y	Y	N
IDAHO			
McClure	?	N	Y
Symms	Y	Y	Y
ILLINOIS			
Dixon	Y	Y	Y
Simon	N	N	Y
INDIANA			
Lugar	Y	Y	Y
Quayle	Y	Y	Y
IOWA			
Grassley	Y	Y	Y
Harkin	N	N	Y
KANSAS			
Dole	Y	Y	Y
Kassebaum	Y	Y	N
KENTUCKY			
McConnell	Y	Y	Y
Ford	N	N	Y
LOUISIANA			
Johnston	N	N	Y
Long	?	Y	Y
MAINE			
Cohen	?	?	N
Mitchell	N	?	N
MARYLAND			
Mathias	?	N	N
Sarbanes	N	N	N
MASSACHUSETTS			
Kennedy	N	N	N
Kerry	N	Y	N
MICHIGAN			
Levin	N	N	N
Riegle	N	N	N
MINNESOTA			
Boschwitz	Y	Y	Y
Durenberger	Y	Y	Y
MISSISSIPPI			
Cochran	Y	Y	Y
Stennis	N	N	Y
MISSOURI			
Danforth	?	Y	Y
Eagleton	N	N	N
MONTANA			
Baucus	N	N	N
Melcher	N	N	Y
NEBRASKA			
Exon	N	N	Y
Zorinsky	Y	Y	Y
NEVADA			
Hecht	Y	Y	Y
Laxalt	Y	Y	Y
NEW HAMPSHIRE			
Humphrey	N	N	Y
Rudman	Y	Y	Y
NEW JERSEY			
Bradley	?	N	N
Lautenberg	?	Y	N
NEW MEXICO			
Domenici	Y	Y	Y
Bingaman	N	N	Y
NEW YORK			
D'Amato	Y	Y	Y
Moynihan	N	Y	N
NORTH CAROLINA			
East	Y	Y	Y
Helms	Y	Y	Y
NORTH DAKOTA			
Andrews	N	Y	Y
Burdick	N	N	N
OHIO			
Glenn	Y	Y	N
Metzenbaum	N	N	N
OKLAHOMA			
Nickles	Y	Y	Y
Boren	Y	Y	Y
OREGON			
Hatfield	Y	Y	N
Packwood	Y	Y	Y
PENNSYLVANIA			
Heinz	N	N	N
Specter	Y	Y	Y
RHODE ISLAND			
Chafee	Y	Y	N
Pell	Y	Y	Y
SOUTH CAROLINA			
Thurmond	Y	Y	Y
Hollings	N	N	Y
SOUTH DAKOTA			
Abdnor	N	Y	Y
Pressler	N	N	Y
TENNESSEE			
Gore	N	Y	Y
Sasser	N	N	Y
TEXAS			
Gramm	Y	Y	Y
Bentsen	?	Y	Y
UTAH			
Garn	Y	Y	Y
Hatch	Y	Y	Y
VERMONT			
Stafford	Y	Y	N
Leahy	-	N	N
VIRGINIA			
Trible	Y	Y	Y
Warner	Y	Y	Y
WASHINGTON			
Evans	Y	Y	N
Gorton	Y	Y	N
WEST VIRGINIA			
Byrd	N	N	N
Rockefeller	N	Y	N
WISCONSIN			
Kasten	Y	Y	Y
Proxmire	N	N	Y
WYOMING			
Simpson	Y	Y	Y
Wallop	Y	Y	Y

KEY

- Y Voted for (yea).
- # Paired for.
- + Announced for.
- N Voted against (nay).
- X Paired against.
- \- Announced against.
- P Voted "present."
- C Voted "present" to avoid possible conflict of interest.
- ? Did not vote or otherwise make a position known.

Democrats *Republicans*

ND - Northern Democrats SD - Southern Democrats (Southern states - Ala., Ark., Fla., Ga., Ky., La., Miss., N.C., Okla., S.C., Tenn., Texas, Va.)

43. S 1017. Metropolitan Washington Airports Transfer. Dole, R-Kan., motion to invoke cloture (thus limiting debate) on the Dole motion to proceed to the consideration of the bill to transfer two metropolitan Washington, D.C., airports to a regional authority. Motion rejected 50-39: R 43-6; D 7-33 (ND 6-22, SD 1-11), March 21, 1986. A three-fifths majority (60) of the total Senate is required to invoke cloture.

44. S 1017. Metropolitan Washington Airports Transfer. Dole, R-Kan., motion to invoke cloture (thus limiting debate) on the Dole motion to proceed to the consideration of the bill to transfer two metropolitan Washington, D.C., airports to a regional authority. Motion agreed to 66-32: R 46-6; D 20-26 (ND 13-19, SD 7-7), March 25, 1986. A three-fifths majority (60) of the total Senate is required to invoke cloture.

45. S J Res 225. Balanced Budget Constitutional Amendment. Passage of the joint resolution to propose a constitutional amendment to require a balanced federal budget every year unless a three-fifths majority of the total membership of both houses of Congress votes for a specific amount of deficit spending; to require that the public debt of the United States may be increased only by a law enacted by a three-fifths majority of the total membership of both houses of Congress; to require that a bill to increase revenue shall become law only if passed by a majority of the total membership of both houses of Congress; to require the president to submit annually a proposed balanced budget to Congress; and to allow Congress to waive the requirement for a balanced budget during a declared war. Rejected 66-34: R 43-10; D 23-24 (ND 10-23, SD 13-1), March 25, 1986. A two-thirds majority of those present and voting (67 in this case) is required for passage of a constitutional amendment. A "yea" was a vote supporting the president's position.

CQ Senate Votes 46 - 51

Corresponding to Congressional Record Votes 46, 47, 48, 49, 50, 51

	46	47	48	49	50	51
ALABAMA						
Denton	N	Y	N	Y	Y	Y
Heflin	N	Y	N	Y	Y	Y
ALASKA						
Murkowski	N	Y	N	Y	Y	Y
Stevens	N	Y	N	Y	Y	Y
ARIZONA						
Goldwater	N	Y	N	Y	Y	Y
DeConcini	N	N	Y	Y	Y	N
ARKANSAS						
Bumpers	N	N	Y	N	Y	N
Pryor	N	N	Y	N	Y	N
CALIFORNIA						
Wilson	N	Y	N	Y	Y	Y
Cranston	Y	N	Y	N	N	N
COLORADO						
Armstrong	N	Y	N	Y	Y	Y
Hart	Y	N	Y	N	N	N
CONNECTICUT						
Weicker	Y	N	N	Y	N	N
Dodd	Y	N	Y	N	N	N
DELAWARE						
Roth	N	Y	N	Y	Y	Y
Biden	N	N	Y	N	N	N
FLORIDA						
Hawkins	N	Y	N	Y	Y	Y
Chiles	N	N	N	Y	Y	Y
GEORGIA						
Mattingly	N	Y	N	Y	Y	Y
Nunn	N	N	N	Y	Y	Y
HAWAII						
Inouye	Y	N	Y	N	N	N
Matsunaga	?	N	Y	N	N	N
IDAHO						
McClure	N	Y	N	Y	Y	Y
Symms	N	Y	N	Y	Y	Y
ILLINOIS						
Dixon	N	N	N	Y	Y	Y
Simon	Y	N	Y	N	N	N
INDIANA						
Lugar	N	Y	N	Y	Y	Y
Quayle	N	Y	N	Y	Y	Y
IOWA						
Grassley	N	N	N	Y	Y	Y
Harkin	Y	N	Y	N	N	N
KANSAS						
Dole	N	Y	N	Y	Y	Y
Kassebaum	N	N	N	Y	Y	Y
KENTUCKY						
McConnell	N	Y	N	Y	Y	Y
Ford	Y	N	N	Y	Y	N
LOUISIANA						
Johnston	N	N	N	Y	Y	Y
Long	?	N	N	Y	Y	Y
MAINE						
Cohen	N	N	N	N	Y	Y
Mitchell	N	N	Y	N	N	N
MARYLAND						
Mathias	Y	N	N	N	N	N
Sarbanes	Y	N	Y	N	N	N
MASSACHUSETTS						
Kennedy	Y	N	Y	N	N	N
Kerry	Y	N	Y	N	N	N
MICHIGAN						
Levin	Y	N	Y	N	N	N
Riegle	Y	N	Y	N	N	N
MINNESOTA						
Boschwitz	N	N	N	Y	Y	Y
Durenberger	N	N	N	Y	Y	N
MISSISSIPPI						
Cochran	N	Y	N	Y	Y	Y
Stennis	N	N	N	Y	Y	Y
MISSOURI						
Danforth	N	Y	N	Y	Y	Y
Eagleton	N	N	Y	N	N	N
MONTANA						
Baucus	N	N	Y	N	N	N
Melcher	Y	N	Y	N	N	N
NEBRASKA						
Exon	N	N	Y	N	N	N
Zorinsky	N	Y	N	Y	Y	N
NEVADA						
Hecht	N	Y	N	Y	Y	Y
Laxalt	N	Y	N	Y	Y	Y
NEW HAMPSHIRE						
Humphrey	N	Y	N	Y	Y	Y
Rudman	N	N	N	Y	Y	Y
NEW JERSEY						
Bradley	N	N	N	Y	Y	Y
Lautenberg	N	N	Y	N	N	N
NEW MEXICO						
Domenici	N	Y	N	Y	Y	Y
Bingaman	Y	N	N	N	N	N
NEW YORK						
D'Amato	N	Y	N	Y	Y	Y
Moynihan	N	N	Y	Y	Y	N
NORTH CAROLINA						
East	N	Y	N	Y	Y	Y
Helms	N	Y	N	Y	Y	Y
NORTH DAKOTA						
Andrews	N	N	N	Y	Y	N
Burdick	Y	N	Y	N	N	N
OHIO						
Glenn	N	N	Y	N	Y	N
Metzenbaum	Y	N	Y	N	N	N
OKLAHOMA						
Nickles	N	Y	N	Y	Y	Y
Boren	N	Y	N	Y	Y	Y
OREGON						
Hatfield	Y	N	Y	N	N	N
Packwood	N	N	N	Y	Y	N
PENNSYLVANIA						
Heinz	N	N	N	Y	Y	Y
Specter	Y	N	N	Y	N	N
RHODE ISLAND						
Chafee	N	N	N	Y	Y	N
Pell	Y	N	Y	N	N	N
SOUTH CAROLINA						
Thurmond	N	Y	N	Y	Y	Y
Hollings	N	N	N	Y	Y	Y
SOUTH DAKOTA						
Abdnor	N	Y	N	Y	Y	Y
Pressler	N	Y	N	Y	Y	Y
TENNESSEE						
Gore	N	N	Y	N	N	N
Sasser	N	N	Y	N	N	N
TEXAS						
Gramm	N	Y	N	Y	Y	Y
Bentsen	N	N	N	Y	Y	Y
UTAH						
Garn	N	Y	N	Y	Y	Y
Hatch	N	Y	N	Y	Y	Y
VERMONT						
Stafford	Y	N	N	Y	Y	N
Leahy	Y	N	N	Y	N	N
VIRGINIA						
Trible	N	Y	N	Y	Y	Y
Warner	N	Y	N	Y	Y	Y
WASHINGTON						
Evans	N	N	N	Y	Y	N
Gorton	N	N	N	Y	Y	N
WEST VIRGINIA						
Byrd	N	N	Y	N	Y	N
Rockefeller	N	-	Y	N	N	N
WISCONSIN						
Kasten	N	Y	N	Y	Y	Y
Proxmire	Y	N	Y	N	N	N
WYOMING						
Simpson	N	Y	N	Y	Y	Y
Wallop	N	Y	N	Y	Y	Y

KEY

- Y Voted for (yea).
- # Paired for.
- + Announced for.
- N Voted against (nay).
- X Paired against.
- \- Announced against.
- P Voted "present."
- C Voted "present" to avoid possible conflict of interest.
- ? Did not vote or otherwise make a position known.

Democrats ***Republicans***

ND - Northern Democrats SD - Southern Democrats (Southern states - Ala., Ark., Fla., Ga., Ky., La., Miss., N.C., Okla., S.C., Tenn., Texas, Va.)

46. S J Res 283. Aid to Nicaraguan Rebels. Kennedy, D-Mass., substitute to prohibit U.S. aid, in any form, to military or paramilitary organizations in Nicaragua. Rejected 24-74: R 5-48; D 19-26 (ND 18-14, SD 1-12), March 27, 1986. A "nay" was a vote supporting the president's position.

47. S J Res 283. Aid to Nicaraguan Rebels. Helms, R-N.C., substitute to allow aid to the Nicaraguan "contras" after May 15 if the president determined and reported to Congress that the Nicaraguan government had not taken steps such as ending "aggression" against other countries, ending importation of military supplies and personnel, expelling Soviet and Cuban military advisers and allowing political parties to organize for future elections. Rejected 39-60: R 36-17; D 3-43 (ND 1-31, SD 2-12), March 27, 1986.

48. S J Res 283. Aid to Nicaraguan Rebels. Sasser, D-Tenn., substitute to provide $30 million in non-military aid to the Nicaraguan "contras" and to state that the United States would begin serious bilateral negotiations with the government of Nicaragua if a cease-fire was in effect in that country. Rejected 33-67: R 1-52; D 32-15 (ND 28-5, SD 4-10), March 27, 1986. A "nay" was a vote supporting the president's position.

49. S J Res 283. Aid to Nicaraguan Rebels. Lugar, R-Ind., motion to table (kill) the Cranston, D-Calif., amendment to the Lugar substitute, to allow only "non-lethal" aid to the Nicaraguan "contras" if the Nicaraguan government took steps such as agreeing to a cease-fire, and if the president of the United States failed to engage in direct bilateral negotiations with the Nicaraguan government without preconditions other than a cease-fire. Motion agreed to 66-34: R 50-3; D 16-31 (ND 6-27, SD 10-4), March 27, 1986. A "yea" was a vote supporting the president's position.

50. S J Res 283. Aid to Nicaraguan Rebels. Lugar, R-Ind., motion to table (kill) the Kennedy, D-Mass., amendment to the Lugar substitute, to prohibit the introduction of U.S. combat forces into Nicaragua unless Congress approved in advance or the president reported that the action was necessary to evacuate U.S. citizens or to respond to a "clear and present danger" of military attack on the United States. Motion agreed to 68-32: R 49-4; D 19-28 (ND 7-26, SD 12-2), March 27, 1986. A "yea" was a vote supporting the president's position.

51. S J Res 283. Aid to Nicaraguan Rebels. Lugar, R-Ind., substitute to approve use of $100 million in Defense Department funds to provide aid to the Nicaraguan "contras." Of that amount, $25 million for non-military aid and for training and "defensive" weapons would be released immediately upon enactment of the resolution; the remainder would be released at 90-day intervals after July 1, 1986. Adopted 53-47: R 42-11; D 11-36 (ND 2-31, SD 9-5), March 27, 1986. (The joint resolution subsequently was passed by voice vote.) A "yea" was a vote supporting the president's position.

	52	53	54	55	56
ALABAMA					
Denton	Y	Y	Y	Y	Y
Heflin	Y	Y	N	Y	N
ALASKA					
Murkowski	Y	Y	Y	Y	Y
Stevens	Y	Y	Y	Y	Y
ARIZONA					
Goldwater	Y	?	Y	Y	Y
DeConcini	Y	Y	N	Y	Y
ARKANSAS					
Bumpers	Y	Y	N	Y	Y
Pryor	Y	Y	N	Y	Y
CALIFORNIA					
Wilson	Y	Y	Y	N	Y
Cranston	Y	N	N	Y	Y
COLORADO					
Armstrong	Y	Y	Y	N	N
Hart	Y	N	N	N	Y
CONNECTICUT					
Weicker	Y	N	N	Y	Y
Dodd	Y	N	Y	Y	Y
DELAWARE					
Roth	Y	Y	Y	Y	Y
Biden	Y	N	N	Y	Y
FLORIDA					
Hawkins	+	?	?	?	?
Chiles	Y	Y	N	Y	Y
GEORGIA					
Mattingly	Y	Y	Y	Y	Y
Nunn	Y	Y	Y	Y	Y
HAWAII					
Inouye	Y	N	Y	Y	Y
Matsunaga	Y	N	N	Y	Y
IDAHO					
McClure	Y	Y	Y	N	N
Symms	Y	Y	Y	N	N
ILLINOIS					
Dixon	Y	N	N	Y	N
Simon	Y	N	N	Y	Y
INDIANA					
Lugar	Y	Y	Y	Y	Y
Quayle	Y	Y	Y	N	N
IOWA					
Grassley	Y	Y	N	Y	Y
Harkin	Y	N	N	Y	Y
KANSAS					
Dole	Y	Y	Y	Y	Y
Kassebaum	Y	Y	Y	Y	Y
KENTUCKY					
McConnell	Y	Y	Y	Y	Y
Ford	Y	Y	N	Y	Y
LOUISIANA					
Johnston	Y	N	Y	Y	Y
Long	Y	Y	Y	Y	Y
MAINE					
Cohen	Y	Y	Y	Y	Y
Mitchell	Y	N	N	Y	Y
MARYLAND					
Mathias	Y	N	N	Y	Y
Sarbanes	Y	N	N	Y	Y
MASSACHUSETTS					
Kennedy	Y	N	N	Y	Y
Kerry	Y	N	Y	Y	Y
MICHIGAN					
Levin	Y	N	N	Y	Y
Riegle	Y	N	N	Y	Y
MINNESOTA					
Boschwitz	Y	Y	N	Y	Y
Durenberger	Y	Y	Y	N	Y
MISSISSIPPI					
Cochran	Y	Y	Y	Y	Y
Stennis	Y	Y	?	?	?
MISSOURI					
Danforth	Y	Y	Y	Y	Y
Eagleton	?	?	?	?	?
MONTANA					
Baucus	Y	N	N	Y	Y
Melcher	Y	N	N	Y	Y
NEBRASKA					
Exon	Y	Y	N	Y	Y
Zorinsky	Y	Y	N	N	Y
NEVADA					
Hecht	Y	Y	Y	Y	Y
Laxalt	Y	Y	Y	Y	?
NEW HAMPSHIRE					
Humphrey	Y	Y	Y	N	N
Rudman	Y	Y	Y	Y	Y
NEW JERSEY					
Bradley	Y	N	N	Y	Y
Lautenberg	Y	N	Y	Y	Y
NEW MEXICO					
Domenici	Y	Y	Y	Y	Y
Bingaman	Y	N	N	Y	Y
NEW YORK					
D'Amato	Y	N	Y	Y	Y
Moynihan	Y	N	N	Y	Y
NORTH CAROLINA					
East	N	Y	Y	N	Y
Helms	N	Y	Y	N	Y
NORTH DAKOTA					
Andrews	Y	Y	N	Y	Y
Burdick	Y	N	N	Y	Y
OHIO					
Glenn	Y	N	N	Y	Y
Metzenbaum	Y	N	Y	Y	Y
OKLAHOMA					
Nickles	Y	Y	Y	Y	Y
Boren	Y	Y	N	Y	Y
OREGON					
Hatfield	Y	N	Y	Y	Y
Packwood	Y	Y	Y	Y	Y
PENNSYLVANIA					
Heinz	Y	Y	N	Y	Y
Specter	Y	N	N	Y	?
RHODE ISLAND					
Chafee	Y	Y	Y	Y	Y
Pell	Y	N	N	Y	Y
SOUTH CAROLINA					
Thurmond	Y	Y	Y	Y	Y
Hollings	Y	N	N	Y	Y
SOUTH DAKOTA					
Abdnor	Y	Y	N	Y	Y
Pressler	Y	Y	N	Y	Y
TENNESSEE					
Gore	Y	N	Y	Y	Y
Sasser	Y	N	N	Y	Y
TEXAS					
Gramm	Y	Y	Y	N	N
Bentsen	Y	N	Y	Y	Y
UTAH					
Garn	Y	Y	Y	Y	N
Hatch	Y	Y	N	N	N
VERMONT					
Stafford	?	?	?	?	?
Leahy	Y	N	N	Y	Y
VIRGINIA					
Trible	Y	Y	Y	Y	Y
Warner	Y	Y	Y	Y	Y
WASHINGTON					
Evans	Y	Y	Y	Y	Y
Gorton	Y	Y	Y	Y	N
WEST VIRGINIA					
Byrd	Y	N	N	Y	Y
Rockefeller	Y	N	Y	Y	Y
WISCONSIN					
Kasten	Y	Y	Y	Y	Y
Proxmire	Y	N	N	Y	Y
WYOMING					
Simpson	Y	Y	Y	Y	Y
Wallop	N	Y	Y	N	N

KEY

- Y Voted for (yea).
- # Paired for.
- + Announced for.
- N Voted against (nay).
- X Paired against.
- - Announced against.
- P Voted "present."
- C Voted "present" to avoid possible conflict of interest.
- ? Did not vote or otherwise make a position known.

Democrats ***Republicans***

ND - Northern Democrats SD - Southern Democrats (Southern states - Ala., Ark., Fla., Ga., Ky., La., Miss., N.C., Okla., S.C., Tenn., Texas, Va.)

52. S 8. Vietnam Veterans of America Charter. Passage of the bill to grant a federal charter to the Vietnam Veterans of America Inc. Passed 94-3: R 48-3; D 46-0 (ND 32-0, SD 14-0), April 9, 1986.

53. S 1017. Metropolitan Washington Airports Transfer. Trible, R-Va., motion to table (kill) the Lautenberg, D-N.J., amendment to express the sense of the Senate that the Federal Aviation Administration should rehire air traffic controllers fired in 1981 following an illegal strike. Motion agreed to 57-39: R 45-5; D 12-34 (ND 3-29, SD 9-5), April 9, 1986.

54. S 1017. Metropolitan Washington Airports Transfer. Trible, R-Va., motion to table (kill) the Pressler, R-S.D., amendment to the Pressler amendment, to change the representation on the regional airports authority from five members from Virginia, three from the District of Columbia, two from Maryland and one presidential appointee, to two members each from Virginia, the District of Columbia and Maryland and five presidential appointees. Motion agreed to 52-44: R 41-10; D 11-34 (ND 6-26, SD 5-8), April 9, 1986. (The underlying Pressler amendment subsequently was withdrawn.)

55. S 1017. Metropolitan Washington Airports Transfer. Kassebaum, R-Kan., motion to table (kill) the Gramm, R-Texas, substitute for the Kassebaum amendment, to require the transportation secretary and the administrator of the Federal Aviation Administration to reclaim all allocated landing and takeoff slots at National Airport near Washington, D.C., LaGuardia and Kennedy airports in New York City, and O'Hare Airport in Chicago, and sell them back to the highest bidder. Motion agreed to 82-14: R 39-12; D 43-2 (ND 30-2, SD 13-0), April 9, 1986. (The Kassebaum amendment subsequently was adopted *(see vote 56, below).*)

56. S 1017. Metropolitan Washington Airports Transfer. Kassebaum, R-Kan., amendment to repeal a Department of Transportation rule permitting airlines to buy and sell takeoff and landing slots at National Airport near Washington, D.C., LaGuardia and Kennedy airports in New York City, and O'Hare Airport in Chicago, and require the administrator of the Federal Aviation Administration to set up procedures for redistributing unused or underused slots and establish "scheduling committees" to allocate slots at each airport. Adopted 82-12: R 39-10; D 43-2 (ND 31-1, SD 12-1), April 9, 1986. A "nay" was a vote supporting the president's position.

CQ Senate Votes 57 - 61

Corresponding to Congressional Record Votes 57, 58, 59, 60, 61

	57	58	59	60	61
ALABAMA					
Denton	Y	Y	Y	Y	Y
Heflin	Y	N	Y	Y	Y
ALASKA					
Murkowski	Y	Y	Y	Y	Y
Stevens	Y	Y	Y	Y	Y
ARIZONA					
Goldwater	N	N	N	?	N
DeConcini	N	N	Y	Y	N
ARKANSAS					
Bumpers	N	N	Y	N	N
Pryor	Y	N	Y	Y	N
CALIFORNIA					
Wilson	Y	Y	Y	Y	Y
Cranston	N	N	Y	N	N
COLORADO					
Armstrong	Y	Y	Y	Y	Y
Hart	N	?	Y	N	Y
CONNECTICUT					
Weicker	Y	Y	N	Y	N
Dodd	Y	Y	N	Y	N
DELAWARE					
Roth	Y	Y	Y	N	Y
Biden	N	N	Y	N	N
FLORIDA					
Hawkins	?	?	+	?	?
Chiles	Y	N	Y	Y	N
GEORGIA					
Mattingly	Y	N	Y	Y	Y
Nunn	N	N	Y	Y	Y
HAWAII					
Inouye	Y	Y	Y	N	Y
Matsunaga	N	N	N	Y	N
IDAHO					
McClure	Y	Y	Y	Y	Y
Symms	Y	Y	Y	Y	Y
ILLINOIS					
Dixon	N	N	Y	Y	Y
Simon	Y	N	Y	Y	N
INDIANA					
Lugar	Y	Y	Y	Y	Y
Quayle	Y	Y	Y	Y	Y
IOWA					
Grassley	Y	Y	Y	N	Y
Harkin	N	N	Y	Y	N
KANSAS					
Dole	Y	Y	Y	Y	Y
Kassebaum	Y	Y	Y	Y	Y
KENTUCKY					
McConnell	Y	Y	Y	Y	Y
Ford	N	N	Y	Y	N
LOUISIANA					
Johnston	N	Y	Y	Y	Y
Long	N	Y	Y	Y	Y
MAINE					
Cohen	N	Y	Y	Y	N
Mitchell	N	N	Y	N	N
MARYLAND					
Mathias	N	N	Y	Y	N
Sarbanes	N	N	Y	N	N
MASSACHUSETTS					
Kennedy	N	N	Y	N	N
Kerry	N	N	Y	Y	N
MICHIGAN					
Levin	N	N	Y	Y	N
Riegle	Y	N	Y	N	N
MINNESOTA					
Boschwitz	Y	Y	Y	Y	Y
Durenberger	Y	Y	Y	Y	Y
MISSISSIPPI					
Cochran	Y	Y	Y	Y	Y
Stennis	?	N	Y	Y	Y
MISSOURI					
Danforth	Y	Y	Y	Y	Y
Eagleton	N	N	Y	Y	N
MONTANA					
Baucus	N	N	Y	Y	N
Melcher	N	N	Y	Y	N
NEBRASKA					
Exon	Y	N	Y	Y	N
Zorinsky	Y	N	Y	Y	N
NEVADA					
Hecht	Y	Y	Y	Y	Y
Laxalt	Y	Y	Y	Y	Y
NEW HAMPSHIRE					
Humphrey	Y	N	N	N	N
Rudman	Y	Y	N	Y	Y
NEW JERSEY					
Bradley	Y	N	N	N	N
Lautenberg	N	N	N	N	N
NEW MEXICO					
Domenici	Y	?	Y	Y	Y
Bingaman	N	N	Y	N	N
NEW YORK					
D'Amato	Y	Y	N	Y	Y
Moynihan	N	N	N	?	N
NORTH CAROLINA					
East	Y	Y	Y	Y	Y
Helms	Y	Y	Y	Y	Y
NORTH DAKOTA					
Andrews	Y	N	Y	Y	?
Burdick	N	N	Y	Y	N
OHIO					
Glenn	N	N	Y	Y	Y
Metzenbaum	N	N	Y	N	N
OKLAHOMA					
Nickles	Y	Y	Y	Y	Y
Boren	N	N	Y	Y	N
OREGON					
Hatfield	Y	Y	Y	N	Y
Packwood	Y	Y	Y	N	Y
PENNSYLVANIA					
Heinz	N	N	Y	Y	N
Specter	Y	Y	Y	Y	Y
RHODE ISLAND					
Chafee	Y	Y	Y	N	Y
Pell	N	N	N	N	N
SOUTH CAROLINA					
Thurmond	Y	Y	Y	Y	Y
Hollings	N	N	Y	Y	N
SOUTH DAKOTA					
Abdnor	Y	Y	Y	Y	Y
Pressler	Y	Y	Y	Y	Y
TENNESSEE					
Gore	Y	Y	Y	N	N
Sasser	N	N	Y	N	N
TEXAS					
Gramm	Y	N	Y	Y	Y
Bentsen	Y	N	Y	Y	N
UTAH					
Garn	Y	Y	Y	Y	Y
Hatch	Y	Y	Y	Y	Y
VERMONT					
Stafford	?	?	?	?	?
Leahy	N	N	Y	Y	N
VIRGINIA					
Trible	Y	Y	Y	Y	Y
Warner	Y	Y	Y	Y	Y
WASHINGTON					
Evans	Y	Y	Y	Y	Y
Gorton	Y	Y	Y	Y	Y
WEST VIRGINIA					
Byrd	N	N	Y	N	N
Rockefeller	Y	Y	Y	Y	Y
WISCONSIN					
Kasten	Y	Y	Y	N	Y
Proxmire	N	N	N	Y	N
WYOMING					
Simpson	Y	Y	Y	Y	Y
Wallop	Y	Y	Y	Y	Y

KEY

- Y Voted for (yea).
- # Paired for.
- + Announced for.
- N Voted against (nay).
- X Paired against.
- - Announced against.
- P Voted "present."
- C Voted "present" to avoid possible conflict of interest.
- ? Did not vote or otherwise make a position known.

Democrats ***Republicans***

ND - Northern Democrats SD - Southern Democrats (Southern states - Ala., Ark., Fla., Ga., Ky., La., Miss., N.C., Okla., S.C., Tenn., Texas, Va.)

57. S 1017. Metropolitan Washington Airports Transfer. Trible, R-Va., motion to table (kill) the Sarbanes, D-Md., amendment to require nighttime noise limitations at National Airport to remain or be made more restrictive. Motion agreed to 60-37: R 47-4; D 13-33 (ND 8-25, SD 5-8), April 10, 1986.

58. S 1017. Metropolitan Washington Airports Transfer. Trible, R-Va., motion to table (kill) the Hollings, D-S.C., amendment to require the regional airports authority's lease payments be sufficient to repay the federal government the fair market value of Washington-Dulles International Airport and National Airport, with imputed interest, within 35 years of the date of transfer, with the sum to be fixed at not less than $111.4 million. Motion agreed to 49-47: R 43-7; D 6-40 (ND 3-29, SD 3-11), April 10, 1986.

59. S 1017. Metropolitan Washington Airports Transfer. Baucus, D-Mont., amendment to the Symms, R-Idaho, amendment, to express the sense of the Senate that the secretary of agriculture should increase the purchase of red meat for school-lunch and other federal programs to reduce the effect of the slaughter of dairy cows on the price of beef. Adopted 86-12: R 46-5; D 40-7 (ND 26-7, SD 14-0), April 10, 1986. (The Symms amendment subsequently was adopted *(see vote 60, below)*.)

60. S 1017. Metropolitan Washington Airports Transfer. Symms, R-Idaho, amendment, as amended by the Baucus, D-Mont., amendment *(vote 59, above)*, to express the sense of the Senate that tax reform legislation should not be considered until a budget agreement has been reached by Congress and the president. Adopted 72-24: R 43-7; D 29-17 (ND 18-14, SD 11-3), April 10, 1986.

61. S 1017. Metropolitan Washington Airports Transfer. Trible, R-Va., motion to table (kill) the Mathias, R-Md., amendment to bar operating revenues or capital improvement funds generated by one airport from being used at the other airport. Motion agreed to 54-43: R 44-6; D 10-37 (ND 5-28, SD 5-9), April 10, 1986.

	62	63	64	65	66	67	68	69
ALABAMA								
Denton	Y	Y	Y	Y	Y	Y	Y	Y
Heflin	N	N	Y	N	Y	N	Y	Y
ALASKA								
Murkowski	Y	Y	Y	Y	Y	N	Y	Y
Stevens	Y	Y	Y	Y	Y	N	Y	Y
ARIZONA								
Goldwater	N	?	N	N	?	?	?	?
DeConcini	N	N	N	N	Y	Y	Y	Y
ARKANSAS								
Bumpers	N	N	N	N	Y	Y	Y	Y
Pryor	?	N	N	N	N	Y	Y	Y
CALIFORNIA								
Wilson	Y	N	Y	Y	Y	Y	Y	Y
Cranston	N	N	N	Y	Y	N	Y	Y
COLORADO								
Armstrong	?	?	?	?	Y	Y	Y	Y
Hart	?	N	N	Y	N	N	N	N
CONNECTICUT								
Weicker	Y	N	Y	Y	Y	N	Y	Y
Dodd	N	Y	Y	Y	Y	N	N	Y
DELAWARE								
Roth	?	?	?	?	Y	Y	Y	Y
Biden	N	N	N	Y	Y	N	Y	N
FLORIDA								
Hawkins	?	?	?	?	?	?	?	?
Chiles	N	N	N	N	Y	Y	N	Y
GEORGIA								
Mattingly	Y	N	Y	N	Y	Y	Y	Y
Nunn	Y	N	N	Y	Y	N	Y	Y
HAWAII								
Inouye	Y	#	Y	Y	N	N	Y	N
Matsunaga	?	Y	N	Y	Y	N	Y	Y
IDAHO								
McClure	Y	Y	Y	Y	Y	Y	Y	Y
Symms	Y	Y	Y	Y	Y	Y	Y	Y
ILLINOIS								
Dixon	N	Y	N	Y	N	N	Y	Y
Simon	N	N	N	N	N	N	Y	Y
INDIANA								
Lugar	Y	Y	Y	Y	Y	Y	Y	Y
Quayle	Y	Y	Y	Y	Y	Y	Y	Y
IOWA								
Grassley	Y	Y	Y	Y	Y	Y	Y	Y
Harkin	?	?	?	?	N	N	N	N
KANSAS								
Dole	Y	Y	Y	Y	Y	Y	Y	Y
Kassebaum	Y	Y	Y	Y	Y	Y	Y	Y
KENTUCKY								
McConnell	Y	Y	Y	Y	Y	Y	Y	Y
Ford	N	N	N	N	Y	N	Y	Y
LOUISIANA								
Johnston	#	Y	N	Y	Y	N	Y	Y
Long	Y	?	Y	Y	Y	N	Y	Y
MAINE								
Cohen	Y	Y	Y	Y	Y	Y	Y	Y
Mitchell	N	N	N	N	Y	N	Y	Y
MARYLAND								
Mathias	N	N	N	N	Y	N	Y	Y
Sarbanes	N	N	N	N	N	N	N	N
MASSACHUSETTS								
Kennedy	?	?	N	N	N	N	N	N
Kerry	N	N	N	Y	Y	N	Y	N
MICHIGAN								
Levin	N	N	N	N	Y	N	Y	Y
Riegle	N	N	N	N	Y	N	Y	Y
MINNESOTA								
Boschwitz	Y	Y	Y	Y	Y	Y	Y	Y
Durenberger	Y	Y	Y	Y	Y	N	Y	Y
MISSISSIPPI								
Cochran	Y	Y	Y	Y	Y	Y	Y	Y
Stennis	Y	?	Y	N	Y	N	N	N
MISSOURI								
Danforth	Y	Y	Y	Y	Y	N	Y	Y
Eagleton	N	N	N	N	N	N	Y	Y
MONTANA								
Baucus	N	N	N	N	N	N	N	N
Melcher	N	N	N	N	Y	N	N	N
NEBRASKA								
Exon	N	N	N	N	N	N	N	N
Zorinsky	N	N	Y	Y	Y	Y	N	N
NEVADA								
Hecht	Y	Y	Y	Y	Y	Y	Y	Y
Laxalt	Y	Y	Y	Y	Y	Y	Y	Y
NEW HAMPSHIRE								
Humphrey	N	N	Y	N	Y	Y	Y	Y
Rudman	Y	Y	Y	Y	Y	Y	Y	Y
NEW JERSEY								
Bradley	?	?	?	?	Y	N	N	?
Lautenberg	?	?	Y	Y	Y	N	N	N
NEW MEXICO								
Domenici	Y	Y	Y	Y	Y	Y	Y	Y
Bingaman	N	N	N	N	Y	N	Y	Y
NEW YORK								
D'Amato	Y	Y	Y	Y	Y	N	Y	Y
Moynihan	?	?	Y	Y	Y	N	Y	Y
NORTH CAROLINA								
East	Y	Y	Y	Y	Y	Y	Y	Y
Helms	Y	Y	Y	Y	Y	Y	Y	Y
NORTH DAKOTA								
Andrews	?	?	?	?	N	N	N	N
Burdick	N	N	N	N	N	N	N	N
OHIO								
Glenn	N	N	Y	N	Y	N	Y	Y
Metzenbaum	Y	N	Y	Y	N	N	N	N
OKLAHOMA								
Nickles	Y	Y	Y	Y	Y	Y	Y	Y
Boren	Y	Y	#	Y	Y	Y	Y	Y
OREGON								
Hatfield	Y	Y	Y	Y	Y	N	Y	Y
Packwood	Y	Y	Y	Y	Y	N	Y	Y
PENNSYLVANIA								
Heinz	Y	Y	?	-	Y	N	Y	Y
Specter	N	N	?	?	Y	N	Y	Y
RHODE ISLAND								
Chafee	Y	Y	Y	Y	Y	Y	Y	Y
Pell	N	N	N	Y	N	Y	N	N
SOUTH CAROLINA								
Thurmond	Y	Y	Y	Y	Y	Y	Y	Y
Hollings	N	N	N	N	Y	N	Y	Y
SOUTH DAKOTA								
Abdnor	Y	Y	Y	Y	Y	Y	N	N
Pressler	Y	Y	Y	Y	N	Y	N	N
TENNESSEE								
Gore	Y	Y	Y	Y	N	N	N	N
Sasser	N	N	N	Y	N	N	Y	N
TEXAS								
Gramm	Y	N	Y	N	Y	Y	Y	Y
Bentsen	N	N	Y	Y	Y	Y	Y	Y
UTAH								
Garn	Y	Y	Y	Y	Y	Y	Y	Y
Hatch	Y	Y	Y	Y	Y	Y	Y	Y
VERMONT								
Stafford	?	?	?	?	Y	N	Y	Y
Leahy	X	X	X	-	Y	N	Y	Y
VIRGINIA								
Trible	Y	Y	Y	Y	Y	Y	Y	Y
Warner	Y	Y	Y	Y	Y	Y	Y	Y
WASHINGTON								
Evans	Y	N	Y	Y	Y	N	Y	Y
Gorton	Y	Y	Y	Y	Y	N	Y	Y
WEST VIRGINIA								
Byrd	N	N	N	N	Y	N	Y	Y
Rockefeller	Y	Y	Y	Y	Y	N	Y	Y
WISCONSIN								
Kasten	Y	Y	Y	Y	Y	Y	Y	Y
Proxmire	N	N	N	N	Y	N	N	N
WYOMING								
Simpson	Y	Y	Y	Y	Y	Y	Y	Y
Wallop	Y	Y	Y	Y	Y	Y	Y	Y

KEY

- Y Voted for (yea).
- # Paired for.
- + Announced for.
- N Voted against (nay).
- X Paired against.
- \- Announced against.
- P Voted "present."
- C Voted "present" to avoid possible conflict of interest.
- ? Did not vote or otherwise make a position known.

Democrats *Republicans*

ND - Northern Democrats SD - Southern Democrats (Southern states - Ala., Ark., Fla., Ga., Ky., La., Miss., N.C., Okla., S.C., Tenn., Texas, Va.)

62. S 1017. Metropolitan Washington Airports Transfer. Trible, R-Va., motion to table (kill) the Exon, D-Neb., amendment to change the representation on the regional airports authority from five members from Virginia, three from the District of Columbia, two from Maryland and three presidential appointees to three members each from Virginia, the District of Columbia and Maryland and four presidential appointees. Motion agreed to 52-33: R 44-4; D 8-29 (ND 3-22, SD 5-7), April 11, 1986.

63. S 1017. Metropolitan Washington Airports Transfer. Trible, R-Va., motion to table (kill) the Mathias, R-Md., amendment to put a floor of $108.6 million under the price to be paid by the regional airports authority to the federal government for the 50-year lease of two metropolitan Washington, D.C., airports. Motion agreed to 46-39: R 39-8; D 7-31 (ND 4-22, SD 3-9), April 11, 1986.

64. S 1017. Metropolitan Washington Airports Transfer. Trible, R-Va., motion to table (kill) the Sarbanes, D-Md., amendment to tighten restrictions on commercial development at Washington-Dulles International Airport. Motion agreed to 57-32: R 44-2; D 13-30 (ND 8-22, SD 5-8), April 11, 1986.

65. S 1017. Metropolitan Washington Airports Transfer. Passage of the bill to transfer management of Washington-Dulles International Airport and National Airport from the federal government to a regional airports authority under a 50-year lease. Passed 62-28: R 41-5; D 21-23 (ND 14-16, SD 7-7), April 11, 1986.

66. S 426. Hydroelectric Re-licensing. McClure, R-Idaho, motion to table (kill) the Hart, D-Colo., amendment to provide for federal "recapture" of hydroelectric facilities licensed by the federal government to privately owned utilities upon expiration of those licenses. Motion agreed to 80-18: R 49-2; D 31-16 (ND 20-13, SD 11-3), April 15, 1986.

67. S 1774. Hobbs Act Amendments. Dole, R-Kan., motion to invoke cloture (thus limiting debate) on the Dole motion to proceed to consideration of the bill to amend the Hobbs Act, the federal anti-extortion law, to make violence that occurs during a labor dispute punishable under federal law. Motion rejected 44-54: R 36-15; D 8-39 (ND 3-30, SD 5-9), April 16, 1986. A three-fifths majority (60) of the total Senate is required to invoke cloture.

68. S 426. Hydroelectric Re-licensing. McClure, R-Idaho, motion to table (kill) the Melcher, D-Mont., amendment to provide specific authority for the Federal Energy Regulatory Commission to order a utility to "wheel" power (to transfer power across its transmission lines for another utility) when it does not unduly affect the cost of service to its customers. Motion agreed to 77-21: R 48-3; D 29-18 (ND 18-15, SD 11-3), April 16, 1986.

69. S 426. Hydroelectric Re-licensing. McClure, R-Idaho, motion to table (kill) the Melcher, D-Mont., amendment to provide that the Federal Energy Regulatory Commission, in deciding whether to issue an order for the "wheeling" of electric power *(see vote 68, above)*, need consider only the existing customers and level of service of the company potentially subject to the order. Motion agreed to 75-22: R 48-3; D 27-19 (ND 16-16, SD 11-3), April 16, 1986.

CQ Senate Votes 70 - 75

Corresponding to Congressional Record Votes 70, 71, 72, 73, 74, 75

	70	71	72	73	74	75
ALABAMA						
Denton	Y	Y	Y	Y	Y	Y
Heflin	Y	Y	Y	Y	Y	Y
ALASKA						
Murkowski	Y	Y	Y	Y	Y	Y
Stevens	Y	Y	Y	N	Y	Y
ARIZONA						
Goldwater	?	?	?	?	?	?
DeConcini	Y	Y	Y	Y	Y	N
ARKANSAS						
Bumpers	Y	Y	N	Y	Y	Y
Pryor	Y	Y	Y	Y	Y	Y
CALIFORNIA						
Wilson	Y	Y	Y	Y	Y	Y
Cranston	Y	Y	Y	Y	Y	Y
COLORADO						
Armstrong	Y	Y	Y	Y	Y	Y
Hart	Y	Y	N	Y	N	N
CONNECTICUT						
Weicker	?	?	?	Y	Y	Y
Dodd	Y	Y	Y	Y	Y	Y
DELAWARE						
Roth	Y	Y	Y	Y	Y	Y
Biden	Y	N	Y	Y	N	N
FLORIDA						
Hawkins	?	?	?	?	?	#
Chiles	Y	Y	Y	?	Y	Y
GEORGIA						
Mattingly	Y	Y	Y	Y	Y	Y
Nunn	Y	Y	Y	Y	Y	Y
HAWAII						
Inouye	Y	Y	Y	Y	Y	Y
Matsunaga	Y	Y	Y	Y	Y	Y
IDAHO						
McClure	Y	Y	Y	Y	Y	Y
Symms	Y	Y	Y	Y	Y	Y
ILLINOIS						
Dixon	Y	Y	?	Y	Y	Y
Simon	Y	Y	Y	Y	Y	N
INDIANA						
Lugar	Y	Y	Y	Y	Y	Y
Quayle	Y	N	Y	N	Y	Y

	70	71	72	73	74	75
IOWA						
Grassley	Y	Y	Y	Y	Y	Y
Harkin	N	Y	N	Y	N	N
KANSAS						
Dole	Y	Y	Y	Y	Y	Y
Kassebaum	Y	Y	Y	Y	Y	Y
KENTUCKY						
McConnell	Y	Y	Y	Y	Y	Y
Ford	Y	Y	Y	Y	Y	Y
LOUISIANA						
Johnston	Y	Y	Y	Y	Y	Y
Long	Y	Y	Y	Y	Y	Y
MAINE						
Cohen	Y	Y	Y	Y	Y	Y
Mitchell	Y	Y	Y	Y	Y	Y
MARYLAND						
Mathias	Y	Y	Y	Y	Y	Y
Sarbanes	N	Y	N	Y	N	N
MASSACHUSETTS						
Kennedy	N	?	Y	Y	Y	Y
Kerry	Y	Y	?	?	?	Y
MICHIGAN						
Levin	Y	Y	Y	Y	Y	Y
Riegle	Y	Y	Y	Y	Y	Y
MINNESOTA						
Boschwitz	Y	Y	Y	Y	Y	Y
Durenberger	Y	Y	Y	Y	Y	Y
MISSISSIPPI						
Cochran	Y	Y	Y	Y	Y	Y
Stennis	N	?	?	?	?	Y
MISSOURI						
Danforth	Y	Y	Y	Y	Y	Y
Eagleton	Y	Y	Y	Y	Y	Y
MONTANA						
Baucus	N	Y	N	Y	N	Y
Melcher	N	Y	N	Y	N	Y
NEBRASKA						
Exon	N	Y	N	Y	N	N
Zorinsky	N	Y	N	Y	N	N
NEVADA						
Hecht	Y	Y	Y	Y	Y	Y
Laxalt	Y	Y	Y	Y	Y	Y

	70	71	72	73	74	75
NEW HAMPSHIRE						
Humphrey	Y	Y	Y	Y	Y	Y
Rudman	Y	Y	Y	Y	Y	Y
NEW JERSEY						
Bradley	N	Y	N	Y	N	Y
Lautenberg	N	Y	N	Y	N	Y
NEW MEXICO						
Domenici	Y	Y	Y	Y	Y	Y
Bingaman	Y	Y	Y	Y	Y	Y
NEW YORK						
D'Amato	Y	Y	Y	Y	Y	Y
Moynihan	Y	Y	Y	Y	Y	Y
NORTH CAROLINA						
East	Y	Y	Y	Y	Y	Y
Helms	Y	Y	Y	Y	Y	Y
NORTH DAKOTA						
Andrews	Y	Y	Y	Y	Y	Y
Burdick	N	Y	N	Y	N	Y
OHIO						
Glenn	Y	Y	Y	Y	Y	Y
Metzenbaum	Y	Y	N	Y	N	N
OKLAHOMA						
Nickles	Y	Y	Y	Y	Y	Y
Boren	Y	Y	Y	Y	Y	Y
OREGON						
Hatfield	Y	Y	Y	?	?	Y
Packwood	Y	Y	Y	Y	Y	Y
PENNSYLVANIA						
Heinz	Y	Y	Y	Y	Y	Y
Specter	Y	Y	Y	Y	Y	Y
RHODE ISLAND						
Chafee	Y	Y	Y	Y	Y	Y
Pell	Y	Y	N	Y	Y	Y
SOUTH CAROLINA						
Thurmond	Y	Y	Y	Y	Y	Y
Hollings	Y	Y	Y	Y	Y	Y
SOUTH DAKOTA						
Abdnor	N	Y	Y	Y	Y	X
Pressler	Y	Y	Y	Y	Y	N
TENNESSEE						
Gore	N	Y	N	Y	Y	N
Sasser	Y	Y	N	Y	Y	N

KEY

- Y Voted for (yea).
- # Paired for.
- + Announced for.
- N Voted against (nay).
- X Paired against.
- \- Announced against.
- P Voted "present."
- C Voted "present" to avoid possible conflict of interest.
- ? Did not vote or otherwise make a position known.

Democrats ***Republicans***

	70	71	72	73	74	75
TEXAS						
Gramm	Y	Y	Y	Y	Y	Y
Bentsen	Y	Y	Y	Y	Y	Y
UTAH						
Garn	Y	Y	Y	Y	Y	Y
Hatch	Y	Y	Y	Y	Y	Y
VERMONT						
Stafford	Y	Y	Y	Y	Y	N
Leahy	Y	Y	Y	Y	Y	N
VIRGINIA						
Trible	Y	Y	Y	Y	Y	Y
Warner	Y	Y	Y	Y	Y	Y
WASHINGTON						
Evans	Y	Y	Y	Y	Y	Y
Gorton	Y	Y	Y	Y	Y	Y
WEST VIRGINIA						
Byrd	Y	Y	Y	Y	Y	Y
Rockefeller	Y	Y	Y	Y	Y	Y
WISCONSIN						
Kasten	Y	Y	Y	Y	Y	Y
Proxmire	N	N	N	N	N	Y
WYOMING						
Simpson	Y	Y	Y	Y	Y	Y
Wallop	Y	Y	Y	Y	Y	Y

ND - Northern Democrats SD - Southern Democrats (Southern states - Ala., Ark., Fla., Ga., Ky., La., Miss., N.C., Okla., S.C., Tenn., Texas, Va.)

70. S 426. Hydroelectric Re-licensing. Johnston, D-La., motion to table (kill) the Melcher, D-Mont., motion to reconsider the vote by which the McClure, R-Idaho, motion to table the Melcher amendment *(see vote 69, p. 13-S)* was agreed to. Motion agreed to 83-14: R 49-1; D 34-13 (ND 22-11, SD 12-2), April 16, 1986.

71. Procedural Motion. McClure, R-Idaho, motion to instruct the sergeant-at-arms to request the attendance of absent senators. Motion agreed to 92-3: R 49-1; D 43-2 (ND 30-2, SD 13-0), April 16, 1986.

72. S 426. Hydroelectric Re-licensing. McClure, R-Idaho, motion to table (kill) the Melcher, D-Mont., amendment to provide specific authority for the Federal Energy Regulatory Commission to order a utility to "wheel" power (to transfer power across its transmission lines for another utility) when it does not unduly affect the cost of service to its customers. Motion agreed to 78-16: R 50-0; D 28-16 (ND 18-13, SD 10-3), April 16, 1986.

73. Procedural Motion. McClure, R-Idaho, motion to instruct the sergeant-at-arms to request the attendance of absent senators. Motion agreed to 91-3: R 48-2; D 43-1 (ND 31-1, SD 12-0), April 16, 1986.

74. S 426. Hydroelectric Re-licensing. McClure, R-Idaho, motion to table (kill) the Melcher, D-Mont., amendment to provide specific authority for the Federal Energy Regulatory Commission to order a utility to "wheel" electric power *(see vote 72, above)* in cases where it would not significantly alter the competitive relationship between the utility and its retail customers. Motion agreed to 82-13: R 50-0; D 32-13 (ND 19-13, SD 13-0), April 16, 1986.

75. S 426. Hydroelectric Re-licensing. Passage of the bill to give holders of expired hydroelectric power licenses a re-licensing "preference" over competing applications when all other factors are equal. Passed 83-14: R 48-2; D 35-12 (ND 23-10, SD 12-2), April 17, 1986.

	76	77	78	79	80
ALABAMA					
Denton	N	N	Y	Y	Y
Heflin	N	Y	N	Y	N
ALASKA					
Murkowski	N	Y	N	Y	Y
Stevens	N	Y	Y	Y	Y
ARIZONA					
Goldwater	?	?	Y	Y	Y
DeConcini	N	Y	N	N	N
ARKANSAS					
Bumpers	N	Y	N	N	N
Pryor	N	Y	N	N	N
CALIFORNIA					
Wilson	N	N	Y	Y	Y
Cranston	N	Y	Y	N	N
COLORADO					
Armstrong	Y	N	Y	Y	Y
Hart	N	Y	N	N	N
CONNECTICUT					
Weicker	N	Y	Y	N	N
Dodd	N	Y	Y	N	N
DELAWARE					
Roth	N	N	Y	Y	Y
Biden	N	Y	N	N	N
FLORIDA					
Hawkins	?	?	-	-	?
Chiles	N	N	Y	Y	N
GEORGIA					
Mattingly	N	N	Y	Y	Y
Nunn	N	N	Y	Y	N
HAWAII					
Inouye	N	Y	N	N	N
Matsunaga	N	Y	N	N	N
IDAHO					
McClure	Y	N	Y	Y	Y
Symms	Y	N	?	?	?
ILLINOIS					
Dixon	N	Y	N	N	Y
Simon	N	Y	N	N	N
INDIANA					
Lugar	N	N	Y	Y	Y
Quayle	N	N	Y	Y	Y
IOWA					
Grassley	N	Y	Y	Y	Y
Harkin	-	Y	N	N	N
KANSAS					
Dole	N	N	Y	Y	Y
Kassebaum	N	N	Y	Y	Y
KENTUCKY					
McConnell	N	N	Y	Y	Y
Ford	N	Y	N	N	N
LOUISIANA					
Johnston	N	N	N	Y	Y
Long	N	N	N	N	Y
MAINE					
Cohen	N	Y	Y	N	N
Mitchell	N	Y	Y	N	N
MARYLAND					
Mathias	N	Y	?	?	?
Sarbanes	N	Y	N	N	N
MASSACHUSETTS					
Kennedy	N	Y	Y	N	N
Kerry	N	Y	N	N	N
MICHIGAN					
Levin	N	Y	N	N	N
Riegle	N	Y	N	N	N
MINNESOTA					
Boschwitz	N	N	Y	Y	Y
Durenberger	N	Y	N	Y	Y
MISSISSIPPI					
Cochran	N	N	Y	Y	Y
Stennis	N	Y	Y	Y	Y
MISSOURI					
Danforth	N	Y	Y	Y	Y
Eagleton	N	Y	Y	Y	N
MONTANA					
Baucus	N	Y	Y	N	N
Melcher	N	Y	?	N	N
NEBRASKA					
Exon	N	N	Y	Y	N
Zorinsky	N	N	N	Y	N
NEVADA					
Hecht	Y	N	Y	Y	Y
Laxalt	Y	N	Y	Y	Y
NEW HAMPSHIRE					
Humphrey	Y	N	Y	Y	Y
Rudman	Y	N	Y	Y	Y
NEW JERSEY					
Bradley	N	Y	N	N	N
Lautenberg	N	Y	N	N	?
NEW MEXICO					
Domenici	N	N	Y	Y	Y
Bingaman	N	Y	N	Y	N
NEW YORK					
D'Amato	N	Y	N	N	Y
Moynihan	N	Y	N	N	N
NORTH CAROLINA					
East	Y	N	Y	Y	Y
Helms	Y	N	Y	Y	Y
NORTH DAKOTA					
Andrews	N	Y	N	N	N
Burdick	N	Y	N	N	N
OHIO					
Glenn	N	Y	N	N	N
Metzenbaum	N	Y	N	N	N
OKLAHOMA					
Nickles	N	N	Y	Y	N
Boren	N	Y	Y	Y	N
OREGON					
Hatfield	N	Y	Y	Y	Y
Packwood	N	Y	Y	Y	Y
PENNSYLVANIA					
Heinz	N	Y	N	Y	Y
Specter	N	Y	N	N	N
RHODE ISLAND					
Chafee	N	Y	Y	N	Y
Pell	N	Y	Y	N	Y
SOUTH CAROLINA					
Thurmond	N	N	Y	Y	Y
Hollings	N	Y	N	Y	N
SOUTH DAKOTA					
Abdnor	N	Y	N	Y	Y
Pressler	N	Y	Y	Y	Y
TENNESSEE					
Gore	N	Y	N	N	N
Sasser	N	Y	N	N	N
TEXAS					
Gramm	Y	N	Y	Y	Y
Bentsen	N	Y	Y	Y	N
UTAH					
Garn	Y	N	Y	Y	Y
Hatch	Y	N	N	Y	Y
VERMONT					
Stafford	N	Y	Y	Y	Y
Leahy	N	Y	N	N	N
VIRGINIA					
Trible	N	N	Y	Y	Y
Warner	N	N	Y	Y	Y
WASHINGTON					
Evans	N	N	?	?	?
Gorton	N	Y	Y	Y	Y
WEST VIRGINIA					
Byrd	N	Y	N	N	N
Rockefeller	N	Y	N	N	N
WISCONSIN					
Kasten	N	Y	N	Y	Y
Proxmire	Y	N	Y	Y	N
WYOMING					
Simpson	N	N	Y	Y	Y
Wallop	Y	N	Y	Y	Y

KEY

- Y Voted for (yea).
- # Paired for.
- + Announced for.
- N Voted against (nay).
- X Paired against.
- \- Announced against.
- P Voted "present."
- C Voted "present" to avoid possible conflict of interest.
- ? Did not vote or otherwise make a position known.

Democrats *Republicans*

ND - Northern Democrats SD - Southern Democrats (Southern states - Ala., Ark., Fla., Ga., Ky., La., Miss., N.C., Okla., S.C., Tenn., Texas, Va.)

76. S Con Res 120. Budget Resolution, Fiscal 1987. Domenici, R-N.M.-Chiles, D-Fla., amendment to reduce fiscal 1987 budget authority by $4.46 billion and reduce outlays and revenues by $4.06 billion through elimination or substantial reduction in spending for 43 domestic programs, as proposed in the president's fiscal 1987 budget request. Rejected 14-83: R 13-38; D 1-45 (ND 1-31, SD 0-14), April 23, 1986. A "yea" was a vote supporting the president's position.

77. S Con Res 120. Budget Resolution, Fiscal 1987. Andrews, R-N.D., amendment to increase fiscal 1987 budget authority by $1.2 billion and increase outlays and revenues by $300 million to restore current services spending for education programs. Adopted 60-38: R 20-31; D 40-7 (ND 30-3, SD 10-4), April 23, 1986.

78. S Con Res 120. Budget Resolution, Fiscal 1987. Domenici, R-N.M., motion to table (kill) the Moynihan, D-N.Y., amendment to allow for continuation through fiscal 1988 of the general revenue sharing program at an amount up to $4.6 billion annually, provided that separate authorizing and revenue-raising legislation is also enacted. Motion agreed to 54-41: R 40-9; D 14-32 (ND 9-23, SD 5-9), April 24, 1986.

79. S Con Res 120. Budget Resolution, Fiscal 1987. Domenici, R-N.M., motion to table (kill) the Metzenbaum, D-Ohio, amendment to increase fiscal 1987 budget authority by $200 million and increase outlays and revenues by $145 million to increase spending for the supplemental food program for needy women, infants and children (WIC), the maternal and child health block grant program, the childhood immunization program and the community health centers program. Motion agreed to 56-40: R 43-6; D 13-34 (ND 5-28, SD 8-6), April 24, 1986.

80. S Con Res 120. Budget Resolution, Fiscal 1987. Lugar, R-Ind., motion to table (kill) the Bumpers, D-Ark., amendment to increase fiscal 1987 budget authority for the childhood immunization program by $25 million and increase outlays by $17 million, and to decrease fiscal 1987 foreign aid budget authority by $25 million and decrease outlays by $17 million. Motion agreed to 49-46: R 44-5; D 5-41 (ND 2-30, SD 3-11), April 24, 1986.

Corresponding to Congressional Record Votes 81, 82, 83, 84, 85, 86

	81	82	83	84	85	86
ALABAMA						
Denton	N	Y	N	Y	Y	Y
Heflin	N	Y	N	Y	Y	N
ALASKA						
Murkowski	N	Y	N	Y	Y	Y
Stevens	Y	Y	N	Y	Y	N
ARIZONA						
Goldwater	Y	Y	?	Y	Y	?
DeConcini	N	N	Y	Y	N	Y
ARKANSAS						
Bumpers	N	Y	N	Y	N	Y
Pryor	N	Y	Y	Y	Y	Y
CALIFORNIA						
Wilson	N	Y	N	Y	N	N
Cranston	N	Y	N	Y	N	Y
COLORADO						
Armstrong	N	Y	N	Y	Y	N
Hart	Y	Y	Y	?	N	Y
CONNECTICUT						
Weicker	Y	Y	N	Y	Y	Y
Dodd	N	Y	N	Y	N	Y
DELAWARE						
Roth	N	N	N	Y	Y	N
Biden	Y	Y	Y	Y	N	Y
FLORIDA						
Hawkins	-	?	?	?	-	?
Chiles	N	Y	Y	Y	Y	N
GEORGIA						
Mattingly	N	Y	N	Y	Y	N
Nunn	N	Y	N	Y	Y	N
HAWAII						
Inouye	Y	N	Y	Y	N	Y
Matsunaga	N	N	Y	Y	N	Y
IDAHO						
McClure	N	Y	N	Y	Y	N
Symms	N	Y	N	Y	Y	N
ILLINOIS						
Dixon	N	Y	N	Y	Y	Y
Simon	Y	N	Y	Y	N	Y
INDIANA						
Lugar	Y	Y	N	Y	Y	N
Quayle	Y	Y	N	Y	Y	N
IOWA						
Grassley	N	Y	N	Y	Y	Y
Harkin	N	N	Y	Y	N	Y
KANSAS						
Dole	Y	Y	N	Y	Y	N
Kassebaum	Y	Y	N	Y	Y	N
KENTUCKY						
McConnell	Y	Y	N	Y	Y	N
Ford	N	N	Y	Y	Y	Y
LOUISIANA						
Johnston	Y	Y	Y	Y	Y	N
Long	N	Y	Y	Y	Y	Y
MAINE						
Cohen	?	?	N	Y	N	Y
Mitchell	N	Y	Y	Y	N	Y
MARYLAND						
Mathias	?	?	?	?	?	?
Sarbanes	Y	N	Y	Y	N	Y
MASSACHUSETTS						
Kennedy	Y	Y	Y	Y	N	Y
Kerry	N	Y	Y	Y	N	Y
MICHIGAN						
Levin	Y	Y	Y	Y	N	Y
Riegle	N	N	Y	Y	N	Y
MINNESOTA						
Boschwitz	Y	Y	N	Y	N	N
Durenberger	Y	Y	N	N	N	Y
MISSISSIPPI						
Cochran	Y	Y	N	Y	Y	N
Stennis	Y	Y	N	Y	Y	?
MISSOURI						
Danforth	Y	Y	N	Y	N	N
Eagleton	Y	Y	N	Y	N	Y
MONTANA						
Baucus	N	N	Y	Y	N	Y
Melcher	N	N	Y	Y	N	Y
NEBRASKA						
Exon	N	Y	N	Y	Y	N
Zorinsky	N	Y	N	Y	Y	N
NEVADA						
Hecht	Y	Y	N	Y	Y	N
Laxalt	N	Y	N	Y	Y	N
NEW HAMPSHIRE						
Humphrey	Y	Y	N	N	N	N
Rudman	Y	Y	N	Y	N	N
NEW JERSEY						
Bradley	N	Y	Y	Y	N	Y
Lautenberg	N	Y	Y	Y	N	Y
NEW MEXICO						
Domenici	Y	Y	N	Y	Y	?
Bingaman	N	Y	Y	Y	Y	Y
NEW YORK						
D'Amato	N	Y	N	Y	N	Y
Moynihan	Y	Y	N	Y	N	Y
NORTH CAROLINA						
East	N	Y	N	Y	Y	N
Helms	Y	Y	N	Y	Y	N
NORTH DAKOTA						
Andrews	N	Y	N	Y	Y	Y
Burdick	N	N	Y	Y	N	Y
OHIO						
Glenn	N	Y	N	Y	Y	Y
Metzenbaum	Y	Y	Y	Y	Y	Y
OKLAHOMA						
Nickles	N	Y	N	Y	Y	N
Boren	N	Y	Y	Y	Y	Y
OREGON						
Hatfield	Y	Y	N	Y	Y	Y
Packwood	Y	Y	N	Y	N	Y
PENNSYLVANIA						
Heinz	N	Y	N	Y	N	Y
Specter	N	Y	Y	Y	N	Y
RHODE ISLAND						
Chafee	Y	Y	N	Y	N	Y
Pell	Y	N	Y	Y	N	Y
SOUTH CAROLINA						
Thurmond	N	Y	N	Y	Y	Y
Hollings	Y	Y	N	Y	Y	N
SOUTH DAKOTA						
Abdnor	N	Y	N	Y	Y	N
Pressler	N	N	N	Y	Y	N
TENNESSEE						
Gore	N	N	Y	Y	Y	Y
Sasser	N	N	Y	Y	Y	Y
TEXAS						
Gramm	N	Y	N	Y	Y	N
Bentsen	N	Y	N	Y	N	Y
UTAH						
Garn	Y	Y	N	Y	Y	N
Hatch	N	N	N	Y	Y	Y
VERMONT						
Stafford	Y	Y	N	Y	N	Y
Leahy	N	Y	N	Y	N	Y
VIRGINIA						
Trible	Y	Y	N	Y	Y	N
Warner	Y	Y	N	Y	Y	N
WASHINGTON						
Evans	Y	Y	N	Y	Y	N
Gorton	Y	Y	N	Y	N	N
WEST VIRGINIA						
Byrd	N	N	Y	Y	N	Y
Rockefeller	N	Y	Y	Y	N	Y
WISCONSIN						
Kasten	Y	Y	N	Y	N	Y
Proxmire	N	Y	N	Y	N	N
WYOMING						
Simpson	Y	Y	N	Y	Y	N
Wallop	N	Y	N	Y	Y	N

KEY

- Y Voted for (yea).
- # Paired for.
- + Announced for.
- N Voted against (nay).
- X Paired against.
- \- Announced against.
- P Voted "present."
- C Voted "present" to avoid possible conflict of interest.
- ? Did not vote or otherwise make a position known.

Democrats *Republicans*

ND - Northern Democrats SD - Southern Democrats (Southern states - Ala., Ark., Fla., Ga., Ky., La., Miss., N.C., Okla., S.C., Tenn., Texas, Va.)

81. S Con Res 120. Budget Resolution, Fiscal 1987. Domenici, R-N.M., motion to table (kill) the DeConcini, D-Ariz., amendment to reduce total fiscal 1987 budget authority by $63 million; to decrease fiscal 1987 foreign aid budget authority by $163 million and outlays by $84 million; to decrease fiscal 1987 general government budget authority by $100 million and outlays by $84 million; and to increase fiscal 1987 administration of justice budget authority by $200 million and outlays by $168 million to improve federal drug interdiction efforts. Motion rejected 42-55: R 28-22; D 14-33 (ND 11-22, SD 3-11), April 29, 1986. (The DeConcini amendment subsequently was adopted by voice vote.)

82. S Con Res 120. Budget Resolution, Fiscal 1987. Domenici, R-N.M., motion to table (kill) the Melcher, D-Mont., amendment to reduce fiscal 1987 defense budget authority by $21 million and outlays by $21 million, and to increase fiscal 1987 Energy Department budget authority by $21 million and outlays by $21 million to provide money for research into electricity generation through the process of magnetohydrodynamics. Motion agreed to 79-18: R 47-3; D 32-15 (ND 21-12, SD 11-3), April 29, 1986.

83. S Con Res 120. Budget Resolution, Fiscal 1987. Hart, D-Colo., amendment to increase total fiscal 1987 budget authority by $2.8 billion and total fiscal 1987 revenues and outlays by $2.7 billion to provide additional money for science and technology education and research. Rejected 32-65: R 1-49; D 31-16 (ND 23-10, SD 8-6), April 29, 1986.

84. S Con Res 120. Budget Resolution, Fiscal 1987. Wilson, R-Calif., amendment to reduce fiscal 1987 budget authority and outlays for congressional postal subsidies by $73.3 million and to increase fiscal 1987 budget authority and outlays for health programs by $73.3 million to provide increased spending for research into acquired immune deficiency syndrome and Alzheimer's disease; and to reallocate $1 million from congressional postage subsidies to the Office of the U.S. Trade Representative. Adopted 95-2: R 49-2; D 46-0 (ND 32-0, SD 14-0), April 30, 1986.

85. S Con Res 120. Budget Resolution, Fiscal 1987. Domenici, R-N.M., motion to table (kill) the Lautenberg, D-N.J., amendment to increase total fiscal 1987 budget authority by $350 million; to reduce total fiscal 1987 outlays by $70 million; to reduce the fiscal 1987 deficit by $70 million; to reduce fiscal 1987 outlays for uranium enrichment by $108 million; to reduce fiscal 1987 budget authority and outlays for interest payments on the federal debt by $3 million; and to increase fiscal 1987 budget authority for natural resources and environment programs by $353 million and outlays by $41 million to restore funding for the "superfund" hazardous-waste cleanup program to the level contained in S 51, the Senate-passed version of the superfund reauthorization, and to increase the operating budget for the Environmental Protection Agency. Motion agreed to 54-44: R 36-15; D 18-29 (ND 6-27, SD 12-2), April 30, 1986.

86. S Con Res 120. Budget Resolution, Fiscal 1987. Moynihan, D-N.Y., amendment to increase total fiscal 1987 budget authority by $211 million and to increase total fiscal 1987 revenues and outlays by $174 million, and to increase fiscal 1987 budget authority for education and training programs by $211 million and outlays by $174 million to restore funding for the Work Incentive (WIN) program that provides job training and placement assistance to welfare recipients. Adopted 55-40: R 17-32; D 38-8 (ND 30-3, SD 8-5), April 30, 1986.

	87	88	89
ALABAMA			
Denton	Y	Y	N
Heflin	Y	N	N
ALASKA			
Murkowski	Y	Y	Y
Stevens	Y	Y	Y
ARIZONA			
Goldwater	?	?	?
DeConcini	Y	Y	Y
ARKANSAS			
Bumpers	Y	Y	Y
Pryor	Y	N	N
CALIFORNIA			
Wilson	Y	Y	N
Cranston	Y	Y	Y
COLORADO			
Armstrong	Y	Y	N
Hart	Y	N	N
CONNECTICUT			
Weicker	Y	Y	Y
Dodd	Y	Y	Y
DELAWARE			
Roth	Y	N	N
Biden	Y	?	?
FLORIDA			
Hawkins	+	?	?
Chiles	Y	Y	Y
GEORGIA			
Mattingly	Y	Y	N
Nunn	?	Y	Y
HAWAII			
Inouye	?	?	?
Matsunaga	Y	Y	Y
IDAHO			
McClure	Y	N	N
Symms	Y	N	N
ILLINOIS			
Dixon	Y	Y	Y
Simon	Y	Y	Y
INDIANA			
Lugar	N	Y	Y
Quayle	N	Y	Y

	87	88	89
IOWA			
Grassley	Y	N	N
Harkin	Y	N	N
KANSAS			
Dole	Y	Y	Y
Kassebaum	Y	Y	Y
KENTUCKY			
McConnell	Y	Y	Y
Ford	Y	Y	Y
LOUISIANA			
Johnston	N	N	Y
Long	N	Y	Y
MAINE			
Cohen	Y	Y	Y
Mitchell	Y	Y	Y
MARYLAND			
Mathias	?	Y	Y
Sarbanes	Y	N	Y
MASSACHUSETTS			
Kennedy	Y	N	Y
Kerry	Y	N	Y
MICHIGAN			
Levin	N	N	Y
Riegle	Y	Y	Y
MINNESOTA			
Boschwitz	Y	Y	Y
Durenberger	N	Y	Y
MISSISSIPPI			
Cochran	Y	Y	Y
Stennis	?	Y	Y
MISSOURI			
Danforth	Y	Y	Y
Eagleton	Y	+	+
MONTANA			
Baucus	Y	Y	Y
Melcher	Y	N	Y
NEBRASKA			
Exon	N	Y	Y
Zorinsky	Y	Y	N
NEVADA			
Hecht	Y	N	N
Laxalt	Y	N	N

	87	88	89
NEW HAMPSHIRE			
Humphrey	Y	Y	N
Rudman	Y	Y	Y
NEW JERSEY			
Bradley	Y	Y	Y
Lautenberg	Y	Y	Y
NEW MEXICO			
Domenici	Y	Y	Y
Bingaman	Y	Y	Y
NEW YORK			
D'Amato	Y	Y	Y
Moynihan	Y	N	Y
NORTH CAROLINA			
East	Y	N	N
Helms	Y	N	N
NORTH DAKOTA			
Andrews	Y	Y	Y
Burdick	Y	N	Y
OHIO			
Glenn	N	N	N
Metzenbaum	Y	Y	Y
OKLAHOMA			
Nickles	Y	Y	Y
Boren	N	Y	Y
OREGON			
Hatfield	Y	Y	Y
Packwood	Y	Y	Y
PENNSYLVANIA			
Heinz	Y	Y	Y
Specter	Y	N	N
RHODE ISLAND			
Chafee	Y	Y	Y
Pell	Y	N	Y
SOUTH CAROLINA			
Thurmond	Y	Y	Y
Hollings	N	Y	Y
SOUTH DAKOTA			
Abdnor	Y	Y	Y
Pressler	Y	Y	Y
TENNESSEE			
Gore	Y	N	Y
Sasser	Y	N	Y

KEY

- Y Voted for (yea).
- # Paired for.
- + Announced for.
- N Voted against (nay).
- X Paired against.
- - Announced against.
- P Voted "present."
- C Voted "present" to avoid possible conflict of interest.
- ? Did not vote or otherwise make a position known.

Democrats *Republicans*

	87	88	89
TEXAS			
Gramm	Y	Y	N
Bentsen	Y	Y	Y
UTAH			
Garn	Y	N	N
Hatch	Y	N	N
VERMONT			
Stafford	N	Y	Y
Leahy	Y	Y	Y
VIRGINIA			
Trible	Y	Y	Y
Warner	Y	Y	Y
WASHINGTON			
Evans	Y	N	Y
Gorton	Y	Y	Y
WEST VIRGINIA			
Byrd	Y	Y	Y
Rockefeller	Y	Y	Y
WISCONSIN			
Kasten	Y	N	N
Proxmire	N	Y	Y
WYOMING			
Simpson	Y	Y	Y
Wallop	Y	Y	N

ND - Northern Democrats SD - Southern Democrats (Southern states - Ala., Ark., Fla., Ga., Ky., La., Miss., N.C., Okla., S.C., Tenn., Texas, Va.)

87. S Con Res 120. Budget Resolution, Fiscal 1987. D'Amato, R-N.Y., amendment to reduce fiscal 1987 budget authority and outlays for furniture and furnishings of the federal government by $100 million and to increase fiscal 1987 budget authority and outlays for health programs by $100 million to provide increased spending for drug prevention and rehabilitation programs. Adopted 82-12: R 46-4; D 36-8 (ND 28-4, SD 8-4), May 1, 1986.

88. S Con Res 120. Budget Resolution, Fiscal 1987. Domenici, R-N.M.-Chiles, D-Fla., substitute to set budget targets for the fiscal year ending Sept. 30, 1987, as follows: budget authority, $1,101.3 billion; outlays, $1,001.2 billion; revenues, $857 billion; deficit, $144 billion. The amendment reduced estimated outlays in several budget categories by approximately $3 billion to take into account reduced inflation projections; increased outlays for defense by approximately $2 billion; increased outlays for scientific research, education, job training, trade promotion, and child health and immunization by $1.5 billion; and reduced new revenues by approximately $5.5 billion from the $18.7 billion in the committee resolution. Adopted 66-29: R 38-13; D 28-16 (ND 19-11, SD 9-5), in the session that began May 1, 1986.

89. S Con Res 120. Budget Resolution, Fiscal 1987. Adoption of the concurrent resolution to set budget targets for the fiscal year ending Sept. 30, 1987, as follows: budget authority, $1,101.3 billion; outlays, $1,001.2 billion; revenues, $857 billion; deficit, $144 billion. Adopted 70-25: R 32-19; D 38-6 (ND 26-4, SD 12-2), in the session that began May 1, 1986.

CQ Senate Votes 90 - 93

Corresponding to Congressional Record Votes 90, 91, 92, 93

	90	91	92	93
ALABAMA				
Denton	Y	N	Y	Y
Heflin	Y	Y	Y	Y
ALASKA				
Murkowski	Y	Y	Y	Y
Stevens	?	?	Y	Y
ARIZONA				
Goldwater	Y	N	Y	Y
DeConcini	N	Y	N	Y
ARKANSAS				
Bumpers	Y	Y	Y	Y
Pryor	Y	Y	N	Y
CALIFORNIA				
Wilson	Y	Y	Y	Y
Cranston	Y	Y	N	Y
COLORADO				
Armstrong	Y	Y	Y	Y
Hart	N	Y	N	Y
CONNECTICUT				
Weicker	Y	Y	Y	Y
Dodd	Y	Y	Y	Y
DELAWARE				
Roth	Y	Y	Y	Y
Biden	Y	Y	N	Y
FLORIDA				
Hawkins	?	+	?	?
Chiles	Y	Y	Y	Y
GEORGIA				
Mattingly	Y	Y	Y	Y
Nunn	Y	Y	Y	Y
HAWAII				
Inouye	Y	Y	N	Y
Matsunaga	Y	Y	N	Y
IDAHO				
McClure	Y	N	Y	Y
Symms	Y	Y	Y	Y
ILLINOIS				
Dixon	Y	Y	Y	Y
Simon	N	Y	N	Y
INDIANA				
Lugar	Y	N	Y	Y
Quayle	Y	N	Y	Y
IOWA				
Grassley	Y	Y	Y	Y
Harkin	Y	Y	N	Y
KANSAS				
Dole	Y	N	Y	Y
Kassebaum	Y	?	N	Y
KENTUCKY				
McConnell	Y	N	Y	Y
Ford	Y	Y	N	Y
LOUISIANA				
Johnston	Y	Y	N	Y
Long	Y	?	Y	Y
MAINE				
Cohen	Y	Y	Y	Y
Mitchell	Y	Y	Y	Y
MARYLAND				
Mathias	Y	N	N	?
Sarbanes	Y	Y	N	Y
MASSACHUSETTS				
Kennedy	Y	Y	N	Y
Kerry	N	Y	N	Y
MICHIGAN				
Levin	Y	Y	Y	Y
Riegle	Y	Y	N	Y
MINNESOTA				
Boschwitz	Y	Y	N	Y
Durenberger	Y	Y	Y	Y
MISSISSIPPI				
Cochran	Y	N	Y	Y
Stennis	Y	N	Y	Y
MISSOURI				
Danforth	Y	Y	N	Y
Eagleton	N	Y	N	Y
MONTANA				
Baucus	Y	Y	N	Y
Melcher	Y	Y	N	Y
NEBRASKA				
Exon	Y	Y	Y	Y
Zorinsky	Y	N	Y	Y
NEVADA				
Hecht	Y	Y	Y	Y
Laxalt	Y	N	Y	Y
NEW HAMPSHIRE				
Humphrey	Y	?	?	?
Rudman	Y	Y	Y	Y
NEW JERSEY				
Bradley	Y	Y	N	Y
Lautenberg	Y	Y	N	Y
NEW MEXICO				
Domenici	Y	Y	Y	Y
Bingaman	Y	Y	Y	Y
NEW YORK				
D'Amato	Y	Y	Y	Y
Moynihan	Y	Y	Y	?
NORTH CAROLINA				
East	Y	Y	Y	Y
Helms	Y	Y	Y	Y
NORTH DAKOTA				
Andrews	Y	Y	Y	Y
Burdick	Y	Y	N	Y
OHIO				
Glenn	Y	Y	Y	Y
Metzenbaum	Y	Y	N	Y
OKLAHOMA				
Nickles	Y	Y	Y	Y
Boren	Y	Y	Y	Y
OREGON				
Hatfield	Y	Y	Y	Y
Packwood	Y	Y	?	?
PENNSYLVANIA				
Heinz	Y	Y	Y	Y
Specter	Y	Y	N	Y
RHODE ISLAND				
Chafee	Y	N	N	Y
Pell	Y	Y	N	Y
SOUTH CAROLINA				
Thurmond	Y	N	Y	Y
Hollings	Y	Y	N	Y
SOUTH DAKOTA				
Abdnor	Y	Y	Y	Y
Pressler	Y	Y	Y	Y
TENNESSEE				
Gore	N	Y	N	Y
Sasser	N	Y	N	Y
TEXAS				
Gramm	Y	N	Y	Y
Bentsen	Y	Y	Y	Y
UTAH				
Garn	Y	N	Y	Y
Hatch	Y	N	Y	Y
VERMONT				
Stafford	Y	N	Y	Y
Leahy	Y	Y	N	Y
VIRGINIA				
Trible	Y	Y	Y	Y
Warner	Y	N	Y	Y
WASHINGTON				
Evans	Y	N	Y	Y
Gorton	Y	Y	Y	Y
WEST VIRGINIA				
Byrd	N	Y	Y	Y
Rockefeller	Y	Y	Y	Y
WISCONSIN				
Kasten	Y	Y	Y	Y
Proxmire	N	Y	N	Y
WYOMING				
Simpson	Y	N	Y	Y
Wallop	Y	N	Y	Y

KEY

- Y Voted for (yea).
- # Paired for.
- + Announced for.
- N Voted against (nay).
- X Paired against.
- \- Announced against.
- P Voted "present."
- C Voted "present" to avoid possible conflict of interest.
- ? Did not vote or otherwise make a position known.

Democrats ***Republicans***

ND - Northern Democrats SD - Southern Democrats (Southern states - Ala., Ark., Fla., Ga., Ky., La., Miss., N.C., Okla., S.C., Tenn., Texas, Va.)

90. Fletcher Nomination. Confirmation of President Reagan's nomination of James C. Fletcher of Virginia to be administrator of the National Aeronautics and Space Administration. Confirmed 89-9: R 51-0; D 38-9 (ND 26-7, SD 12-2), May 6, 1986. A "yea" was a vote supporting the president's position.

91. S J Res 316. Saudi Arms Sale. Passage of the joint resolution to prohibit the administration's proposed $354 million sale of missiles to Saudi Arabia. Passed 73-22: R 29-20; D 44-2 (ND 32-1, SD 12-1), May 6, 1986. A "nay" was a vote supporting the president's position.

92. S 2295. Joint Chiefs of Staff Reorganization. Goldwater, R-Ariz., motion to table (kill) the DeConcini, D-Ariz., amendment to bar the transfer of Stinger anti-aircraft missiles to anti-government rebels in Afghanistan and Angola unless the president certified that certain conditions had been met. Motion agreed to 63-34: R 44-6; D 19-28 (ND 11-22, SD 8-6), May 7, 1986. A "yea" was a vote supporting the president's position.

93. HR 3622. Joint Chiefs of Staff Reorganization. Passage of the bill to change the system of the Joint Chiefs of Staff by designating the chairman of the Joint Chiefs as principal military adviser to the president, creating the post of vice chairman and otherwise shifting power from the separate military services to the Defense Department agencies intended to coordinate them. Passed 95-0: R 49-0; D 46-0 (ND 32-0, SD 14-0), May 7, 1986. (The Senate previously had moved to strike the House-passed text of the bill and insert instead the text of S 2295, the Senate version of the bill.)

Corresponding to Congressional Record Votes 94, 95, 96, 97, 98, 99, 100, 101

	94	95	96	97	98	99	100	101
ALABAMA								
Denton	N	Y	Y	Y	Y	Y	Y	Y
Heflin	N	Y	Y	Y	Y	Y	Y	N
ALASKA								
Murkowski	N	Y	Y	Y	Y	Y	Y	Y
Stevens	N	Y	Y	Y	Y	Y	Y	N
ARIZONA								
Goldwater	Y	Y	Y	?	Y	Y	Y	Y
DeConcini	N	Y	Y	Y	Y	Y	Y	N
ARKANSAS								
Bumpers	N	N	Y	Y	Y	Y	Y	Y
Pryor	N	Y	Y	Y	N	Y	Y	Y
CALIFORNIA								
Wilson	N	Y	Y	Y	Y	Y	Y	Y
Cranston	N	Y	Y	Y	N	Y	Y	Y
COLORADO								
Armstrong	Y	Y	?	?	?	Y	Y	Y
Hart	N	N	N	N	N	N	Y	Y
CONNECTICUT								
Weicker	Y	Y	Y	Y	?	Y	Y	N
Dodd	N	Y	Y	Y	Y	Y	Y	Y
DELAWARE								
Roth	Y	Y	Y	Y	Y	Y	Y	Y
Biden	N	Y	N	N	N	N	Y	Y
FLORIDA								
Hawkins	?	?	?	?	?	?	+	?
Chiles	N	Y	Y	N	N	Y	?	?
GEORGIA								
Mattingly	N	Y	Y	Y	Y	Y	Y	Y
Nunn	N	Y	Y	Y	Y	Y	Y	Y
HAWAII								
Inouye	N	N	N	N	Y	Y	Y	Y
Matsunaga	N	N	Y	Y	?	Y	Y	Y
IDAHO								
McClure	Y	Y	Y	Y	?	Y	N	N
Symms	Y	Y	?	?	Y	Y	Y	Y
ILLINOIS								
Dixon	N	Y	Y	Y	Y	Y	Y	Y
Simon	N	N	N	Y	N	Y	N	Y
INDIANA								
Lugar	Y	Y	Y	Y	Y	Y	Y	Y
Quayle	Y	Y	Y	Y	Y	Y	Y	Y
IOWA								
Grassley	N	Y	Y	Y	Y	Y	Y	Y
Harkin	N	N	N	N	N	N	Y	Y
KANSAS								
Dole	N	Y	Y	Y	Y	Y	Y	Y
Kassebaum	N	Y	Y	Y	Y	Y	Y	Y
KENTUCKY								
McConnell	Y	Y	Y	Y	Y	Y	Y	Y
Ford	N	Y	Y	Y	Y	Y	Y	Y
LOUISIANA								
Johnston	N	Y	Y	Y	Y	Y	Y	N
Long	Y	Y	Y	Y	Y	Y	N	Y
MAINE								
Cohen	N	Y	Y	Y	Y	Y	Y	Y
Mitchell	N	N	Y	Y	N	Y	Y	Y
MARYLAND								
Mathias	?	?	Y	Y	N	Y	?	?
Sarbanes	N	N	N	N	N	N	Y	N
MASSACHUSETTS								
Kennedy	N	N	Y	Y	N	Y	Y	Y
Kerry	N	N	Y	Y	N	Y	Y	Y
MICHIGAN								
Levin	N	N	Y	Y	N	Y	Y	Y
Riegle	N	Y	Y	Y	N	Y	Y	Y
MINNESOTA								
Boschwitz	N	Y	Y	Y	Y	Y	Y	Y
Durenberger	N	Y	Y	Y	Y	Y	Y	?
MISSISSIPPI								
Cochran	Y	Y	Y	Y	Y	Y	Y	N
Stennis	Y	Y	Y	?	Y	Y	Y	?
MISSOURI								
Danforth	Y	Y	Y	Y	Y	Y	Y	Y
Eagleton	N	Y	#	Y	Y	Y	N	Y
MONTANA								
Baucus	N	Y	Y	Y	N	Y	Y	Y
Melcher	N	N	N	Y	N	Y	?	Y
NEBRASKA								
Exon	N	#	Y	Y	N	Y	Y	Y
Zorinsky	Y	Y	Y	Y	Y	Y	N	Y
NEVADA								
Hecht	Y	Y	Y	Y	Y	Y	Y	Y
Laxalt	Y	Y	Y	Y	Y	Y	Y	N
NEW HAMPSHIRE								
Humphrey	?	?	?	?	?	Y	?	Y
Rudman	N	Y	Y	Y	Y	Y	Y	Y
NEW JERSEY								
Bradley	N	Y	Y	Y	N	Y	Y	Y
Lautenberg	N	Y	Y	Y	Y	Y	Y	Y
NEW MEXICO								
Domenici	Y	Y	Y	Y	Y	Y	Y	Y
Bingaman	N	N	Y	Y	Y	Y	Y	Y
NEW YORK								
D'Amato	N	Y	Y	Y	?	Y	Y	N
Moynihan	N	N	N	Y	N	Y	Y	N
NORTH CAROLINA								
East	Y	Y	Y	Y	Y	Y	Y	Y
Helms	Y	Y	Y	Y	Y	Y	Y	Y
NORTH DAKOTA								
Andrews	N	Y	Y	Y	Y	Y	Y	Y
Burdick	N	N	Y	Y	N	Y	Y	Y
OHIO								
Glenn	N	Y	Y	Y	?	Y	Y	Y
Metzenbaum	N	N	N	N	N	N	N	Y
OKLAHOMA								
Nickles	N	Y	Y	Y	Y	Y	Y	Y
Boren	N	Y	Y	Y	Y	Y	Y	Y
OREGON								
Hatfield	N	Y	Y	Y	Y	Y	Y	Y
Packwood	?	?	?	?	?	?	?	?
PENNSYLVANIA								
Heinz	N	Y	Y	Y	Y	Y	Y	Y
Specter	N	Y	Y	?	N	Y	Y	N
RHODE ISLAND								
Chafee	N	Y	Y	Y	Y	Y	Y	Y
Pell	N	N	Y	Y	Y	Y	Y	Y
SOUTH CAROLINA								
Thurmond	Y	Y	Y	Y	Y	Y	Y	Y
Hollings	N	Y	Y	Y	Y	Y	Y	Y
SOUTH DAKOTA								
Abdnor	N	Y	Y	Y	Y	Y	Y	Y
Pressler	N	Y	Y	Y	Y	Y	Y	Y
TENNESSEE								
Gore	N	Y	Y	Y	N	Y	Y	Y
Sasser	N	Y	Y	Y	N	Y	Y	N
TEXAS								
Gramm	Y	Y	Y	Y	Y	Y	Y	Y
Bentsen	N	Y	Y	Y	N	Y	Y	Y
UTAH								
Garn	Y	Y	Y	Y	Y	Y	Y	Y
Hatch	Y	Y	Y	Y	Y	Y	Y	N
VERMONT								
Stafford	Y	Y	Y	?	Y	Y	Y	Y
Leahy	-	X	X	Y	N	N	Y	Y
VIRGINIA								
Trible	N	Y	Y	Y	Y	Y	Y	Y
Warner	Y	Y	Y	Y	Y	Y	Y	Y
WASHINGTON								
Evans	Y	Y	Y	Y	Y	Y	Y	Y
Gorton	Y	Y	Y	Y	Y	Y	Y	Y
WEST VIRGINIA								
Byrd	N	Y	Y	Y	N	Y	Y	Y
Rockefeller	N	Y	Y	Y	N	Y	Y	Y
WISCONSIN								
Kasten	N	Y	Y	Y	Y	Y	Y	Y
Proxmire	N	N	N	N	N	N	N	Y
WYOMING								
Simpson	Y	Y	Y	Y	Y	Y	Y	Y
Wallop	Y	Y	Y	Y	Y	Y	?	?

KEY

- Y Voted for (yea).
- # Paired for.
- \+ Announced for.
- N Voted against (nay).
- X Paired against.
- \- Announced against.
- P Voted "present."
- C Voted "present" to avoid possible conflict of interest.
- ? Did not vote or otherwise make a position known.

Democrats *Republicans*

ND - Northern Democrats SD - Southern Democrats (Southern states - Ala., Ark., Fla., Ga., Ky., La., Miss., N.C., Okla., S.C., Tenn., Texas, Va.)

94. S 1848. Pharmaceutical Export Amendments. Hatch, R-Utah, motion to table (kill) the Metzenbaum, D-Ohio, amendment to strengthen standards under the 1980 Infant Formula Act (PL 96-359). Motion rejected 29-66: R 26-23; D 3-43 (ND 1-31, SD 2-12), May 13, 1986. (The Metzenbaum amendment subsequently was adopted by voice vote.) A "yea" was a vote supporting the president's position.

95. S 1848. Pharmaceutical Export Amendments. Hatch, R-Utah, motion to table (kill) the Metzenbaum, D-Ohio, amendment to apply the same standards for export of antibiotics as for other drugs. Motion agreed to 76-18: R 49-0; D 27-18 (ND 14-17, SD 13-1), May 13, 1986.

96. S 1848. Pharmaceutical Export Amendments. Hatch, R-Utah, motion to table (kill) the Metzenbaum, D-Ohio, amendment to bar from export drugs for which Food and Drug Administration approval has not been sought. Motion agreed to 83-10: R 48-0; D 35-10 (ND 21-10, SD 14-0), May 13, 1986.

97. S 1848. Pharmaceutical Export Amendments. Hatch, R-Utah, motion to table (kill) the Metzenbaum, D-Ohio, amendment to prohibit future shipments of any drug found in a country not authorized under the bill to receive it. Motion agreed to 83-8: R 45-0; D 38-8 (ND 26-7, SD 12-1), May 13, 1986.

98. S 1848. Pharmaceutical Export Amendments. Hatch, R-Utah, motion to table (kill) the Metzenbaum, D-Ohio, amendment to require the Office of Technology Assessment to conduct a study of labeling of drugs sold in foreign countries. Motion agreed to 62-29: R 44-2; D 18-27 (ND 9-22, SD 9-5), May 14, 1986.

99. S 1848. Pharmaceutical Export Amendments. Passage of the bill to allow for the export to certain countries of drugs not yet approved for sale in the United States. Passed 91-7: R 51-0; D 40-7 (ND 26-7, SD 14-0), May 14, 1986. A "yea" was a vote supporting the president's position.

100. S 2395. Military Retirement Reform. Glenn, D-Ohio, motion to table (kill) the Simon, D-Ill., amendment to provide that cost-of-living adjustments for military retirees be calculated on the basis of the retiree's initial annuity without including previous cost-of-living adjustments. Motion agreed to 86-7: R 47-1; D 39-6 (ND 27-5, SD 12-1), May 15, 1986.

101. S 2395. Military Retirement Reform. Goldwater, R-Ariz., amendment to bar the purchase of T-46 trainer planes with any funds appropriated for fiscal 1986. Adopted 79-14: R 40-8; D 39-6 (ND 30-3, SD 9-3), May 15, 1986. A "yea" was a vote supporting the president's position.

CQ Senate Votes 102 - 106
Corresponding to Congressional Record Votes 102, 103, 104, 105, 106

	102	103	104	105	106
ALABAMA					
Denton	N	Y	N	Y	Y
Heflin	Y	Y	Y	Y	Y
ALASKA					
Murkowski	Y	Y	?	?	?
Stevens	Y	Y	N	Y	Y
ARIZONA					
Goldwater	N	Y	N	?	?
DeConcini	Y	Y	Y	Y	Y
ARKANSAS					
Bumpers	N	Y	Y	Y	Y
Pryor	Y	Y	Y	Y	Y
CALIFORNIA					
Wilson	N	Y	N	Y	Y
Cranston	?	?	N	Y	Y
COLORADO					
Armstrong	N	Y	N	Y	Y
Hart	Y	Y	N	Y	Y
CONNECTICUT					
Weicker	N	Y	N	N	Y
Dodd	Y	Y	N	Y	Y
DELAWARE					
Roth	Y	Y	N	Y	?
Biden	Y	Y	N	Y	Y
FLORIDA					
Hawkins	-	-	?	?	?
Chiles	?	?	N	Y	Y
GEORGIA					
Mattingly	Y	Y	Y	Y	Y
Nunn	Y	Y	Y	Y	Y
HAWAII					
Inouye	N	Y	Y	Y	Y
Matsunaga	Y	Y	Y	Y	Y
IDAHO					
McClure	Y	Y	N	Y	Y
Symms	Y	Y	N	Y	Y
ILLINOIS					
Dixon	Y	Y	N	Y	Y
Simon	Y	Y	N	Y	Y
INDIANA					
Lugar	Y	Y	N	Y	Y
Quayle	N	Y	N	N	Y
IOWA					
Grassley	Y	Y	Y	Y	Y
Harkin	N	Y	N	Y	Y
KANSAS					
Dole	Y	Y	Y	Y	Y
Kassebaum	Y	Y	Y	Y	Y
KENTUCKY					
McConnell	Y	Y	Y	Y	Y
Ford	N	Y	Y	Y	Y
LOUISIANA					
Johnston	Y	Y	N	Y	Y
Long	Y	Y	Y	Y	Y
MAINE					
Cohen	N	Y	N	Y	Y
Mitchell	Y	Y	N	Y	Y
MARYLAND					
Mathias	?	?	?	?	Y
Sarbanes	N	Y	N	Y	Y
MASSACHUSETTS					
Kennedy	N	Y	N	Y	Y
Kerry	Y	Y	N	Y	Y
MICHIGAN					
Levin	Y	Y	N	Y	Y
Riegle	N	Y	N	Y	Y
MINNESOTA					
Boschwitz	Y	Y	N	Y	Y
Durenberger	Y	Y	Y	Y	Y
MISSISSIPPI					
Cochran	Y	Y	Y	Y	Y
Stennis	Y	Y	N	?	Y
MISSOURI					
Danforth	Y	Y	N	Y	Y
Eagleton	Y	Y	?	?	Y
MONTANA					
Baucus	Y	Y	Y	Y	Y
Melcher	Y	Y	N	Y	Y
NEBRASKA					
Exon	Y	Y	Y	Y	Y
Zorinsky	Y	Y	Y	Y	Y
NEVADA					
Hecht	Y	Y	N	Y	Y
Laxalt	N	Y	N	?	Y
NEW HAMPSHIRE					
Humphrey	Y	Y	N	Y	Y
Rudman	Y	Y	N	Y	Y
NEW JERSEY					
Bradley	Y	Y	N	?	Y
Lautenberg	Y	Y	N	Y	Y
NEW MEXICO					
Domenici	Y	Y	N	Y	Y
Bingaman	Y	Y	N	Y	Y
NEW YORK					
D'Amato	N	N	N	Y	Y
Moynihan	Y	Y	?	?	Y
NORTH CAROLINA					
East	N	Y	Y	Y	Y
Helms	N	Y	Y	Y	Y
NORTH DAKOTA					
Andrews	Y	Y	Y	Y	Y
Burdick	Y	Y	Y	Y	Y
OHIO					
Glenn	N	Y	N	Y	Y
Metzenbaum	Y	Y	N	Y	Y
OKLAHOMA					
Nickles	Y	Y	Y	Y	Y
Boren	Y	Y	Y	Y	Y
OREGON					
Hatfield	Y	Y	N	Y	Y
Packwood	?	?	?	?	?
PENNSYLVANIA					
Heinz	Y	Y	N	Y	Y
Specter	N	Y	N	Y	Y
RHODE ISLAND					
Chafee	Y	Y	N	Y	Y
Pell	N	Y	N	Y	Y
SOUTH CAROLINA					
Thurmond	N	Y	N	Y	Y
Hollings	N	Y	Y	Y	Y
SOUTH DAKOTA					
Abdnor	Y	Y	Y	Y	Y
Pressler	?	?	Y	Y	Y
TENNESSEE					
Gore	Y	Y	Y	Y	Y
Sasser	N	Y	Y	Y	Y
TEXAS					
Gramm	Y	Y	Y	Y	Y
Bentsen	Y	Y	N	Y	Y
UTAH					
Garn	N	Y	N	N	Y
Hatch	N	Y	N	Y	Y
VERMONT					
Stafford	Y	Y	N	Y	Y
Leahy	N	Y	N	Y	Y
VIRGINIA					
Trible	Y	Y	N	Y	Y
Warner	N	Y	N	Y	Y
WASHINGTON					
Evans	Y	Y	N	Y	?
Gorton	Y	Y	N	Y	Y
WEST VIRGINIA					
Byrd	Y	Y	Y	Y	Y
Rockefeller	Y	Y	Y	Y	Y
WISCONSIN					
Kasten	N	Y	Y	Y	Y
Proxmire	Y	Y	Y	N	Y
WYOMING					
Simpson	Y	Y	N	Y	Y
Wallop	?	?	Y	Y	Y

KEY

- Y Voted for (yea).
- # Paired for.
- + Announced for.
- N Voted against (nay).
- X Paired against.
- - Announced against.
- P Voted "present."
- C Voted "present" to avoid possible conflict of interest.
- ? Did not vote or otherwise make a position known.

Democrats — ***Republicans***

ND - Northern Democrats SD - Southern Democrats (Southern states - Ala., Ark., Fla., Ga., Ky., La., Miss., N.C., Okla., S.C., Tenn., Texas, Va.)

102. S 2395. Military Retirement Reform. Nunn, D-Ga., motion to table (kill) the Glenn, D-Ohio, amendment to provide that after the 40th anniversary of a retiree's joining the service, future cost-of-living increases in the retirement annuity would equal the rate of increase in the Consumer Price Index. Motion agreed to 64-29: R 31-17; D 33-12 (ND 24-8, SD 9-4), May 15, 1986.

103. HR 4420. Military Retirement Reform. Passage of the bill to reduce the annuity for a person retiring after 20 years of active military service from 50 percent of basic pay to 44 percent. Passed 92-1: R 47-1; D 45-0 (ND 32-0, SD 13-0), May 15, 1986. (The Senate had previously moved to strike the House-passed text of the bill and insert instead the text of S 2395, the Senate version of the bill.)

104. S 2180. Federal Fire Protection/Daylight-Saving Time. Dole, R-Kan., motion to table (kill) the Gorton, R-Wash., amendment to change the start of daylight-saving time from the last Sunday in April to the first Sunday in April. Motion rejected 36-58: R 16-33; D 20-25 (ND 10-21, SD 10-4), May 20, 1986. (The Gorton amendment subsequently was adopted by voice vote, and the bill was passed by voice vote.)

105. Procedural Motion. McClure, R-Idaho, motion to instruct the sergeant-at-arms to request the attendance of absent senators. Motion agreed to 86-4: R 44-3; D 42-1 (ND 29-1, SD 13-0), May 20, 1986.

106. S 124. Safe Drinking Water. Adoption of the conference report on the bill to authorize appropriations to carry out the Safe Drinking Water Act of 1974 (PL 93-523) for fiscal 1987-91 — \$170.15 million for fiscal 1987, \$145.15 million for 1988, and \$169.54 million annually for 1989-91 — and to amend certain provisions regulating drinking-water safety. Adopted (thus cleared for the president) 94-0: R 47-0; D 47-0 (ND 33-0, SD 14-0), May 21, 1986.

Corresponding to Congressional Record Votes 107, 108, 109, 110, 111, 112, 113

	107	108	109	110	111	112	113
ALABAMA							
Denton	?	N	Y	Y	N	Y	Y
Heflin	?	Y	N	Y	Y	Y	Y
ALASKA							
Murkowski	N	N	Y	Y	Y	Y	Y
Stevens	N	N	Y	Y	N	Y	Y
ARIZONA							
Goldwater	N	N	Y	Y	N	N	Y
DeConcini	Y	N	N	Y	Y	Y	Y
ARKANSAS							
Bumpers	N	Y	N	Y	Y	Y	Y
Pryor	?	?	?	?	Y	Y	Y
CALIFORNIA							
Wilson	N	N	Y	Y	Y	N	Y
Cranston	Y	Y	N	Y	Y	Y	Y
COLORADO							
Armstrong	N	N	Y	Y	N	N	N
Hart	Y	Y	N	Y	Y	Y	Y
CONNECTICUT							
Weicker	N	Y	N	Y	Y	N	N
Dodd	Y	Y	N	Y	Y	Y	Y
DELAWARE							
Roth	N	N	Y	Y	N	N	N
Biden	Y	?	?	?	Y	Y	Y
FLORIDA							
Hawkins	Y	N	Y	Y	Y	?	?
Chiles	Y	N	Y	Y	Y	Y	Y
GEORGIA							
Mattingly	N	N	Y	Y	Y	Y	Y
Nunn	Y	N	Y	Y	Y	Y	Y
HAWAII							
Inouye	Y	Y	N	Y	Y	Y	Y
Matsunaga	Y	Y	N	Y	Y	Y	Y
IDAHO							
McClure	N	N	Y	Y	N	Y	Y
Symms	N	N	Y	Y	Y	Y	Y
ILLINOIS							
Dixon	N	Y	N	Y	Y	+	?
Simon	Y	Y	N	Y	Y	Y	Y
INDIANA							
Lugar	N	Y	Y	Y	N	N	N
Quayle	N	N	Y	Y	N	Y	Y
IOWA							
Grassley	N	N	Y	Y	Y	Y	Y
Harkin	?	?	?	?	Y	Y	Y
KANSAS							
Dole	N	N	Y	Y	N	N	Y
Kassebaum	N	N	Y	Y	N	N	Y
KENTUCKY							
McConnell	N	N	Y	Y	N	N	Y
Ford	Y	N	N	Y	Y	Y	Y
LOUISIANA							
Johnston	Y	N	N	Y	Y	Y	Y
Long	N	N	N	Y	N	N	Y
MAINE							
Cohen	N	Y	Y	Y	Y	N	N
Mitchell	Y	Y	Y	Y	Y	Y	N
MARYLAND							
Mathias	N	Y	Y	Y	N	Y	Y
Sarbanes	Y	Y	N	Y	Y	Y	Y
MASSACHUSETTS							
Kennedy	Y	?	?	?	Y	Y	N
Kerry	?	Y	N	Y	Y	Y	Y
MICHIGAN							
Levin	Y	Y	Y	Y	Y	Y	Y
Riegle	Y	Y	N	Y	Y	Y	Y
MINNESOTA							
Boschwitz	N	Y	Y	Y	Y	Y	Y
Durenberger	N	Y	Y	Y	Y	Y	Y
MISSISSIPPI							
Cochran	N	N	Y	Y	N	N	Y
Stennis	Y	Y	N	Y	N	Y	Y
MISSOURI							
Danforth	N	N	Y	Y	Y	N	Y
Eagleton	Y	Y	N	Y	Y	Y	Y
MONTANA							
Baucus	Y	Y	N	Y	Y	Y	Y
Melcher	Y	Y	N	Y	Y	Y	Y
NEBRASKA							
Exon	N	N	N	Y	N	Y	Y
Zorinsky	N	N	Y	Y	N	Y	Y
NEVADA							
Hecht	N	N	Y	Y	N	Y	Y
Laxalt	N	N	Y	Y	N	N	Y
NEW HAMPSHIRE							
Humphrey	N	N	Y	Y	N	N	N
Rudman	N	Y	Y	Y	Y	N	N
NEW JERSEY							
Bradley	Y	Y	?	?	Y	N	N
Lautenberg	N	Y	N	Y	Y	N	N
NEW MEXICO							
Domenici	N	N	Y	Y	N	N	Y
Bingaman	Y	Y	N	Y	Y	N	Y
NEW YORK							
D'Amato	Y	N	Y	Y	Y	N	Y
Moynihan	Y	Y	N	Y	Y	N	Y
NORTH CAROLINA							
East	N	N	Y	Y	N	N	N
Helms	N	N	Y	N	N	N	N
NORTH DAKOTA							
Andrews	N	N	Y	Y	Y	Y	Y
Burdick	Y	Y	N	Y	Y	Y	Y
OHIO							
Glenn	Y	Y	N	Y	Y	Y	N
Metzenbaum	Y	Y	N	Y	Y	N	N
OKLAHOMA							
Nickles	N	N	Y	Y	Y	Y	Y
Boren	Y	N	N	Y	Y	Y	Y
OREGON							
Hatfield	N	Y	Y	Y	Y	N	Y
Packwood	N	Y	Y	Y	Y	Y	Y
PENNSYLVANIA							
Heinz	N	Y	Y	Y	Y	N	N
Specter	Y	Y	N	Y	Y	Y	Y
RHODE ISLAND							
Chafee	N	Y	Y	Y	N	N	N
Pell	N	Y	Y	Y	Y	N	Y
SOUTH CAROLINA							
Thurmond	N	N	Y	Y	N	Y	N
Hollings	Y	N	Y	Y	Y	Y	Y
SOUTH DAKOTA							
Abdnor	-	?	+	+	Y	Y	Y
Pressler	N	N	Y	Y	Y	Y	Y
TENNESSEE							
Gore	Y	Y	N	Y	Y	Y	Y
Sasser	Y	N	N	Y	Y	Y	Y
TEXAS							
Gramm	N	N	Y	Y	N	N	N
Bentsen	Y	N	Y	Y	N	Y	Y
UTAH							
Garn	N	N	Y	Y	N	Y	N
Hatch	N	N	Y	Y	N	N	N
VERMONT							
Stafford	N	Y	Y	Y	N	Y	Y
Leahy	N	Y	Y	Y	Y	Y	Y
VIRGINIA							
Trible	N	N	Y	Y	Y	Y	N
Warner	N	N	Y	Y	N	Y	Y
WASHINGTON							
Evans	N	Y	Y	Y	N	N	Y
Gorton	N	Y	Y	Y	Y	N	Y
WEST VIRGINIA							
Byrd	Y	Y	N	Y	Y	Y	Y
Rockefeller	Y	Y	N	Y	Y	Y	Y
WISCONSIN							
Kasten	N	N	Y	Y	Y	Y	N
Proxmire	N	N	Y	Y	Y	N	N
WYOMING							
Simpson	N	N	Y	Y	N	N	N
Wallop	N	N	Y	Y	N	N	Y

KEY

- Y Voted for (yea).
- # Paired for.
- + Announced for.
- N Voted against (nay).
- X Paired against.
- - Announced against.
- P Voted "present."
- C Voted "present" to avoid possible conflict of interest.
- ? Did not vote or otherwise make a position known.

Democrats *Republicans*

ND - Northern Democrats SD - Southern Democrats (Southern states - Ala., Ark., Fla., Ga., Ky., La., Miss., N.C., Okla., S.C., Tenn., Texas, Va.)

107. S 1965. Higher Education Act Amendments. Bingaman, D-N.M., amendment to authorize a new program of up to 5,000 fellowships a year to attract talented undergraduates and mid-career professionals into teaching. Rejected 37-57: R 3-48; D 34-9 (ND 24-7, SD 10-2), June 3, 1986.

108. S 1965. Higher Education Act Amendments. Helms, R-N.C., motion to table (kill) the Helms amendment to bar federal courts from ordering school busing except in narrowly defined circumstances. Motion rejected 45-50: R 15-37; D 30-13 (ND 26-4, SD 4-9), June 3, 1986. (Helms, who moved to table his own amendment to force a vote on the issue, subsequently withdrew his amendment.)

109. S 1965. Higher Education Act Amendments. Dole, R-Kan., substitute for the Stafford, R-Vt., amendment, to cut the cost of the bill by $1.5 billion over five years by trimming proposed increases in Pell Grants to poor students, and to make other changes in college student aid. Adopted 60-34: R 50-2; D 10-32 (ND 6-23, SD 4-9), June 3, 1986. (The Stafford amendment, as amended by the Dole substitute, subsequently was adopted by voice vote.)

110. S 1965. Higher Education Act Amendments. Passage of the bill to reauthorize aid to colleges and college students under the Higher Education Act through fiscal 1991, authorizing approximately $9.5 billion in fiscal 1987 and more in subsequent years. Passed 93-1: R 51-1; D 42-0 (ND 29-0, SD 13-0), June 3, 1986.

111. S J Res 316. Saudi Arms Sale. Passage, over President Reagan's May 21 veto, of the joint resolution to block the sale of weapons to Saudi Arabia. Rejected (thus sustaining the president's veto) 66-34: R 24-29; D 42-5 (ND 31-2, SD 11-3), June 5, 1986. A two-thirds majority of those present and voting (67 in this case) of both houses is required to override a veto. A "nay" was a vote supporting the president's position.

112. HR 4515. Urgent Supplemental Appropriations, Fiscal 1986. Judgment of the Senate whether the Appropriations Committee amendment was germane. The amendment would allow prepayment of Rural Electrification Administration loans without penalty, and would allow farmers to keep advance crop subsidy payments in the event planting was prevented by bad weather. Ruled germane 62-36: R 24-28; D 38-8 (ND 25-7, SD 13-1), June 5, 1986. (The Appropriations Committee amendment subsequently was adopted by voice vote.) A "nay" was a vote supporting the president's position.

113. HR 4515. Urgent Supplemental Appropriations, Fiscal 1986. Hatfield, R-Ore., motion to table (kill) the Humphrey, R-N.H., amendment to permit studies of the sale of power marketing administrations. Motion agreed to 73-25: R 34-18; D 39-7 (ND 25-7, SD 14-0), June 5, 1986. A "nay" was a vote supporting the president's position.

CQ Senate Votes 114 - 120

Corresponding to Congressional Record Votes 114, 115, 116, 117, 118, 119, 120

	114	115	116	117	118	119	120
ALABAMA							
Denton	Y	Y	Y	N	Y	Y	Y
Heflin	N	Y	Y	Y	Y	N	Y
ALASKA							
Murkowski	Y	Y	Y	Y	Y	N	Y
Stevens	Y	Y	Y	Y	Y	N	Y
ARIZONA							
Goldwater	Y	Y	Y	N	N	?	Y
DeConcini	N	Y	Y	Y	Y	N	N
ARKANSAS							
Bumpers	N	Y	Y	N	Y	N	N
Pryor	N	Y	Y	N	Y	N	N
CALIFORNIA							
Wilson	Y	Y	Y	N	N	Y	Y
Cranston	Y	N	N	N	N	N	N
COLORADO							
Armstrong	Y	Y	Y	N	?	?	?
Hart	Y	N	N	N	Y	N	N
CONNECTICUT							
Weicker	Y	Y	N	Y	N	N	Y
Dodd	Y	Y	Y	N	Y	Y	N
DELAWARE							
Roth	Y	Y	Y	N	N	N	Y
Biden	Y	N	N	Y	Y	N	N
FLORIDA							
Hawkins	?	?	?	?	?	?	?
Chiles	Y	Y	Y	N	Y	N	N
GEORGIA							
Mattingly	N	Y	Y	N	N	Y	Y
Nunn	Y	Y	Y	N	Y	Y	N
HAWAII							
Inouye	Y	N	Y	Y	?	?	?
Matsunaga	Y	N	N	N	Y	N	Y
IDAHO							
McClure	Y	Y	Y	Y	Y	N	Y
Symms	Y	Y	Y	Y	N	N	Y
ILLINOIS							
Dixon	?	N	Y	N	Y	Y	N
Simon	Y	N	Y	N	Y	N	N
INDIANA							
Lugar	Y	Y	Y	N	N	N	Y
Quayle	Y	Y	Y	N	N	N	Y
IOWA							
Grassley	N	Y	Y	Y	N	Y	N
Harkin	N	N	N	Y	Y	N	N
KANSAS							
Dole	Y	Y	Y	Y	N	Y	Y
Kassebaum	N	Y	Y	Y	N	Y	N
KENTUCKY							
McConnell	Y	Y	Y	Y	N	N	Y
Ford	N	Y	Y	Y	Y	N	N
LOUISIANA							
Johnston	Y	N	Y	Y	Y	N	Y
Long	Y	N	Y	Y	Y	N	Y
MAINE							
Cohen	Y	Y	Y	N	N	Y	N
Mitchell	Y	N	N	N	Y	Y	N
MARYLAND							
Mathias	Y	N	N	Y	?	?	N
Sarbanes	N	N	N	N	Y	N	N
MASSACHUSETTS							
Kennedy	Y	N	N	Y	Y	N	N
Kerry	Y	N	Y	Y	Y	N	N
MICHIGAN							
Levin	N	N	Y	N	Y	N	N
Riegle	N	N	Y	N	Y	N	N
MINNESOTA							
Boschwitz	Y	Y	Y	N	N	Y	N
Durenberger	Y	Y	Y	N	N	N	N
MISSISSIPPI							
Cochran	Y	Y	Y	Y	N	N	Y
Stennis	Y	?	?	?	Y	?	Y
MISSOURI							
Danforth	Y	N	Y	N	N	Y	N
Eagleton	Y	N	N	N	?	?	-
MONTANA							
Baucus	Y	Y	Y	N	Y	N	Y
Melcher	Y	Y	Y	N	Y	N	Y
NEBRASKA							
Exon	N	Y	Y	N	N	N	N
Zorinsky	N	Y	Y	N	N	N	N
NEVADA							
Hecht	Y	Y	Y	Y	N	Y	Y
Laxalt	Y	Y	Y	Y	Y	Y	?
NEW HAMPSHIRE							
Humphrey	Y	Y	Y	Y	N	N	Y
Rudman	Y	Y	Y	Y	N	Y	Y
NEW JERSEY							
Bradley	N	N	N	N	Y	N	N
Lautenberg	N	N	N	N	Y	N	N
NEW MEXICO							
Domenici	Y	N	Y	N	Y	N	Y
Bingaman	N	N	Y	N	Y	Y	Y
NEW YORK							
D'Amato	Y	Y	Y	Y	Y	Y	Y
Moynihan	Y	N	N	Y	Y	N	Y
NORTH CAROLINA							
East	N	Y	Y	N	N	Y	Y
Helms	N	N	Y	N	N	Y	Y
NORTH DAKOTA							
Andrews	N	Y	Y	Y	Y	Y	Y
Burdick	N	Y	Y	N	Y	N	Y
OHIO							
Glenn	Y	Y	Y	N	Y	Y	N
Metzenbaum	N	N	N	N	Y	Y	N
OKLAHOMA							
Nickles	N	Y	Y	Y	Y	Y	Y
Boren	N	Y	Y	Y	Y	Y	Y
OREGON							
Hatfield	Y	Y	Y	Y	Y	N	Y
Packwood	Y	Y	Y	Y	N	N	Y
PENNSYLVANIA							
Heinz	Y	Y	Y	N	Y	Y	Y
Specter	N	Y	Y	N	Y	Y	N
RHODE ISLAND							
Chafee	Y	Y	Y	N	N	Y	N
Pell	N	N	N	N	Y	N	N
SOUTH CAROLINA							
Thurmond	Y	Y	Y	Y	Y	Y	Y
Hollings	Y	Y	Y	Y	N	N	N
SOUTH DAKOTA							
Abdnor	Y	Y	Y	Y	Y	Y	N
Pressler	N	Y	Y	N	N	Y	N
TENNESSEE							
Gore	Y	Y	Y	N	Y	N	N
Sasser	Y	Y	Y	N	Y	N	N
TEXAS							
Gramm	Y	N	Y	N	N	?	Y
Bentsen	Y	N	Y	N	Y	N	Y
UTAH							
Garn	Y	Y	Y	Y	N	Y	Y
Hatch	Y	Y	Y	Y	N	Y	Y
VERMONT							
Stafford	Y	N	Y	N	N	N	N
Leahy	N	N	Y	Y	Y	N	N
VIRGINIA							
Trible	Y	Y	Y	N	N	Y	Y
Warner	Y	Y	Y	N	N	Y	Y
WASHINGTON							
Evans	Y	Y	Y	N	N	Y	Y
Gorton	Y	Y	Y	Y	N	N	N
WEST VIRGINIA							
Byrd	Y	Y	Y	Y	Y	N	N
Rockefeller	Y	N	Y	N	Y	N	N
WISCONSIN							
Kasten	N	Y	Y	N	N	Y	N
Proxmire	N	N	N	N	N	Y	N
WYOMING							
Simpson	Y	Y	Y	N	Y	Y	Y
Wallop	Y	Y	Y	N	N	Y	Y

KEY

- Y Voted for (yea).
- # Paired for.
- + Announced for.
- N Voted against (nay).
- X Paired against.
- \- Announced against.
- P Voted "present."
- C Voted "present" to avoid possible conflict of interest.
- ? Did not vote or otherwise make a position known.

Democrats *Republicans*

ND - Northern Democrats SD - Southern Democrats (Southern states - Ala., Ark., Fla., Ga., Ky., La., Miss., N.C., Okla., S.C., Tenn., Texas, Va.)

114. HR 4515. Urgent Supplemental Appropriations, Fiscal 1986. Stevens, R-Alaska, motion to table (kill) the Proxmire, D-Wis., appeal of the chair's ruling that the Proxmire amendment was legislation on an appropriations bill and thus not germane. The Proxmire amendment would have reduced the limit on outside honoraria earnings from 40 percent of a senator's salary to 30 percent. Motion agreed to 68-30: R 42-10; D 26-20 (ND 17-15, SD 9-5), June 5, 1986.

115. HR 4515. Urgent Supplemental Appropriations, Fiscal 1986. Abdnor, R-S.D., motion to waive the spending-limitation requirement contained in the 1985 Balanced Budget and Emergency Deficit Control Act (the Gramm-Rudman-Hollings balanced-budget law, PL 99-177) with respect to the Appropriations Committee amendment. The Appropriations Committee amendment would prohibit the Internal Revenue Service from implementing new vehicle record-keeping requirements. Motion agreed to 65-33: R 46-6; D 19-27 (ND 9-24, SD 10-3), June 5, 1986. A three-fifths majority (60) of the total Senate is required to waive the spending-limitation requirement contained in Gramm-Rudman. (The Appropriations Committee amendment subsequently was adopted *(see vote 116, below)*.)

116. HR 4515. Urgent Supplemental Appropriations, Fiscal 1986. Appropriations Committee amendment to prohibit the Internal Revenue Service from implementing new vehicle record-keeping requirements. Adopted 81-17: R 50-2; D 31-15 (ND 18-15, SD 13-0), June 5, 1986.

117. HR 4515. Urgent Supplemental Appropriations, Fiscal 1986. Weicker, R-Conn., motion to table (kill) the Danforth, R-Mo., amendment to strike $80.6 million for defense research projects at certain universities. Motion rejected 40-58: R 25-27; D 15-31 (ND 9-24, SD 6-7), in the session that began June 5, 1986. (The Danforth amendment subsequently was adopted by voice vote.)

118. HR 4515. Urgent Supplemental Appropriations, Fiscal 1986. Johnston, D-La., motion to waive the new-spending-authority limitation contained in the 1985 Balanced Budget and Emergency Deficit Control Act (the Gramm-Rudman-Hollings balanced-budget law, PL 99-177) with respect to the Johnston amendment. The Johnston amendment would make workers and firms that supply parts and services for the oil and gas industry eligible for trade adjustment assistance. Motion agreed to 55-40: R 15-35; D 40-5 (ND 27-4, SD 13-1), June 6, 1986. (The Johnston amendment subsequently was adopted by voice vote.)

119. HR 4515. Urgent Supplemental Appropriations, Fiscal 1986. Judgment of the Senate whether the Wilson, R-Calif., amendment, to prohibit members of Congress from using franking privileges for mass mailings of unsolicited material, was germane. Ruled non-germane 40-52: R 31-17; D 9-35 (ND 7-24, SD 2-11), June 6, 1986.

120. HR 4515. Urgent Supplemental Appropriations, Fiscal 1986. Hatfield, R-Ore., motion to table (kill) the Exon, D-Neb., amendment to prevent the Federal Energy Regulatory Commission from deregulating the price structure of old natural gas. Motion agreed to 48-47: R 36-14; D 12-33 (ND 6-25, SD 6-8), June 6, 1986.

	121	122	123	124	125	126	127
ALABAMA							
Denton	N	N	N	Y	N	Y	Y
Heflin	N	N	N	Y	N	Y	N
ALASKA							
Murkowski	Y	N	Y	Y	N	Y	Y
Stevens	?	N	Y	Y	Y	Y	Y
ARIZONA							
Goldwater	?	N	N	Y	?	?	?
DeConcini	Y	Y	Y	Y	N	Y	Y
ARKANSAS							
Bumpers	N	Y	Y	Y	N	Y	Y
Pryor	N	Y	Y	Y	Y	N	Y
CALIFORNIA							
Wilson	N	N	Y	N	N	Y	Y
Cranston	N	Y	Y	Y	N	Y	Y
COLORADO							
Armstrong	?	?	?	Y	Y	Y	Y
Hart	N	Y	Y	N	Y	Y	Y
CONNECTICUT							
Weicker	Y	Y	Y	Y	N	Y	?
Dodd	Y	Y	Y	Y	N	Y	Y
DELAWARE							
Roth	Y	N	Y	Y	Y	Y	Y
Biden	N	Y	Y	Y	Y	Y	Y
FLORIDA							
Hawkins	?	?	?	Y	N	-	-
Chiles	N	Y	?	Y	N	?	?
GEORGIA							
Mattingly	N	N	Y	Y	N	Y	Y
Nunn	N	N	Y	Y	N	N	N
HAWAII							
Inouye	?	?	?	Y	N	N	N
Matsunaga	Y	Y	Y	Y	N	Y	Y
IDAHO							
McClure	N	N	Y	Y	Y	Y	Y
Symms	N	N	Y	Y	Y	Y	Y
ILLINOIS							
Dixon	N	Y	Y	Y	N	N	N
Simon	N	Y	Y	Y	N	N	N
INDIANA							
Lugar	Y	N	Y	Y	Y	N	N
Quayle	Y	N	Y	Y	Y	Y	Y
IOWA							
Grassley	N	N	Y	Y	Y	Y	N
Harkin	N	Y	Y	Y	N	N	N
KANSAS							
Dole	Y	N	Y	Y	Y	Y	Y
Kassebaum	Y	N	?	Y	Y	Y	Y
KENTUCKY							
McConnell	N	N	Y	Y	Y	Y	Y
Ford	N	Y	Y	Y	N	N	N
LOUISIANA							
Johnston	Y	Y	Y	Y	Y	Y	Y
Long	Y	Y	Y	Y	Y	Y	Y
MAINE							
Cohen	Y	Y	?	Y	Y	Y	Y
Mitchell	Y	Y	Y	Y	Y	N	Y
MARYLAND							
Mathias	Y	Y	Y	Y	Y	N	Y
Sarbanes	Y	Y	Y	Y	N	N	Y
MASSACHUSETTS							
Kennedy	Y	Y	Y	Y	Y	Y	Y
Kerry	N	Y	Y	Y	N	Y	Y
MICHIGAN							
Levin	Y	Y	Y	Y	N	Y	Y
Riegle	N	Y	Y	Y	N	N	Y
MINNESOTA							
Boschwitz	N	N	Y	Y	Y	Y	Y
Durenberger	N	N	Y	Y	Y	Y	Y
MISSISSIPPI							
Cochran	Y	N	Y	Y	Y	Y	Y
Stennis	Y	N	Y	Y	Y	N	Y
MISSOURI							
Danforth	N	N	Y	Y	Y	Y	Y
Eagleton	?	?	?	Y	Y	Y	Y
MONTANA							
Baucus	N	Y	Y	N	Y	N	N
Melcher	N	Y	Y	Y	N	N	N
NEBRASKA							
Exon	N	Y	Y	Y	N	N	N
Zorinsky	N	Y	Y	Y	N	Y	Y
NEVADA							
Hecht	Y	N	Y	Y	N	Y	Y
Laxalt	?	?	?	Y	N	Y	Y
NEW HAMPSHIRE							
Humphrey	Y	N	N	Y	N	Y	Y
Rudman	Y	N	Y	Y	Y	Y	Y
NEW JERSEY							
Bradley	N	Y	Y	N	Y	Y	Y
Lautenberg	?	?	?	Y	N	Y	Y
NEW MEXICO							
Domenici	Y	N	N	Y	N	Y	Y
Bingaman	Y	N	?	Y	N	Y	Y
NEW YORK							
D'Amato	Y	N	?	Y	N	Y	Y
Moynihan	Y	Y	Y	Y	Y	Y	Y
NORTH CAROLINA							
East	Y	N	Y	Y	Y	Y	Y
Helms	Y	N	N	Y	Y	Y	Y
NORTH DAKOTA							
Andrews	N	Y	?	Y	N	Y	Y
Burdick	N	Y	+	Y	N	N	N
OHIO							
Glenn	N	Y	Y	Y	N	Y	Y
Metzenbaum	Y	Y	Y	Y	N	Y	Y
OKLAHOMA							
Nickles	N	N	Y	Y	Y	Y	Y
Boren	N	Y	Y	Y	Y	Y	Y
OREGON							
Hatfield	Y	Y	Y	Y	N	Y	Y
Packwood	Y	Y	Y	Y	Y	Y	Y
PENNSYLVANIA							
Heinz	Y	N	Y	Y	Y	Y	Y
Specter	N	Y	Y	Y	N	N	N
RHODE ISLAND							
Chafee	?	?	?	Y	Y	Y	Y
Pell	+	+	+	Y	N	Y	N
SOUTH CAROLINA							
Thurmond	N	N	Y	Y	Y	Y	Y
Hollings	N	N	Y	Y	N	Y	Y
SOUTH DAKOTA							
Abdnor	N	N	Y	Y	N	Y	Y
Pressler	N	N	Y	Y	N	Y	Y
TENNESSEE							
Gore	N	Y	?	Y	N	N	N
Sasser	N	Y	Y	Y	N	N	N
TEXAS							
Gramm	Y	N	N	Y	Y	Y	Y
Bentsen	Y	Y	?	Y	Y	N	Y
UTAH							
Garn	Y	N	Y	Y	Y	Y	Y
Hatch	Y	N	Y	Y	Y	Y	Y
VERMONT							
Stafford	Y	N	?	Y	Y	Y	Y
Leahy	N	Y	?	Y	N	Y	Y
VIRGINIA							
Trible	Y	N	?	Y	Y	Y	Y
Warner	Y	N	Y	Y	Y	Y	Y
WASHINGTON							
Evans	Y	N	Y	Y	Y	Y	Y
Gorton	Y	N	Y	Y	Y	Y	Y
WEST VIRGINIA							
Byrd	N	Y	Y	Y	N	Y	Y
Rockefeller	Y	Y	Y	Y	Y	Y	Y
WISCONSIN							
Kasten	N	N	Y	Y	N	Y	N
Proxmire	Y	Y	N	Y	Y	Y	Y
WYOMING							
Simpson	Y	N	Y	Y	Y	Y	Y
Wallop	Y	N	-	Y	Y	Y	Y

KEY

- Y Voted for (yea).
- # Paired for.
- + Announced for.
- N Voted against (nay).
- X Paired against.
- \- Announced against.
- P Voted "present."
- C Voted "present" to avoid possible conflict of interest.
- ? Did not vote or otherwise make a position known.

Democrats *Republicans*

ND - Northern Democrats SD - Southern Democrats (Southern states - Ala., Ark., Fla., Ga., Ky., La., Miss., N.C., Okla., S.C., Tenn., Texas, Va.)

121. HR 4515. Urgent Supplemental Appropriations, Fiscal 1986. Hatfield, R-Ore., motion to table (kill) the Abdnor, R-S.D., appeal of the chair's ruling that the Abdnor amendment was legislation on an appropriations bill and thus not germane. The Abdnor amendment would have allowed debt-stressed farmers to participate in the interest rate reduction program for guaranteed Farmers Home Administration loans, and would have allowed balloon payments on such loans. Motion agreed to 46-44: R 30-17; D 16-27 (ND 12-17, SD 4-10), June 6, 1986.

122. HR 4515. Urgent Supplemental Appropriations, Fiscal 1986. Judgment of the Senate whether the Kennedy, D-Mass., amendment, to transfer $62 million from the Department of Defense budget for President Reagan's strategic defense initiative (or "star wars") to increase funds for certain nutrition programs, was germane. Ruled non-germane 45-47: R 7-42; D 38-5 (ND 28-1, SD 10-4), June 6, 1986.

123. HR 4515. Urgent Supplemental Appropriations, Fiscal 1986. Passage of the bill to provide total supplemental spending authority of $3.9 billion for fiscal year 1986. Passed 71-8: R 36-6; D 35-2 (ND 25-1, SD 10-1), June 6, 1986.

124. HR 3838. Tax Overhaul. Packwood, R-Ore., amendment to the Roth, R-Del., amendment, to instruct Senate conferees to give highest priority to retaining tax deductions for Individual Retirement Accounts but without requiring increased tax rates or changing the distribution of tax cuts by income group. Adopted 96-4: R 52-1; D 44-3 (ND 30-3, SD 14-0), June 11, 1986. (The Roth amendment, as amended by the Packwood amendment, subsequently was adopted by voice vote.)

125. HR 3838. Tax Overhaul. Packwood, R-Ore., motion to table (kill) the D'Amato, R-N.Y., amendment to the Dodd, D-Conn.-D'Amato amendment, to create a 15 percent tax credit on Individual Retirement Account contributions (to a maximum of $300) and to offset the resulting revenue loss with an increase in the corporate and individual minimum tax rate from 20 percent to 22.6 percent. Motion agreed to 51-48: R 35-17; D 16-31 (ND 10-23, SD 6-8), June 11, 1986. (The Dodd-D'Amato amendment subsequently was rejected by voice vote.) A "yea" was a vote supporting the president's position.

126. HR 3838. Tax Overhaul. Packwood, R-Ore., motion to table (kill) the Baucus, D-Mont., amendment to create a 15 percent credit on Individual Retirement Account contributions (to a maximum of $300) and to offset the resulting revenue loss with a $310 decrease in the personal exemption for itemizers. Motion agreed to 76-21: R 48-3; D 28-18 (ND 22-11, SD 6-7), June 11, 1986. A "yea" was a vote supporting the president's position.

127. HR 3838. Tax Overhaul. Packwood, R-Ore., motion to table (kill) the Dixon, D-Ill., amendment to create a 15 percent credit on Individual Retirement Account contributions and to offset the resulting revenue loss with a floor on itemized deductions of 1 percent of adjusted gross income. Motion agreed to 78-18: R 46-4; D 32-14 (ND 24-9, SD 8-5), June 11, 1986. A "yea" was a vote supporting the president's position.

CQ Senate Votes 128 - 129

Corresponding to Congressional Record Votes 128, 129

	128	129
ALABAMA		
Denton	Y	Y
Heflin	Y	Y
ALASKA		
Murkowski	Y	N
Stevens	Y	N
ARIZONA		
Goldwater	Y	Y
DeConcini	N	Y
ARKANSAS		
Bumpers	Y	Y
Pryor	Y	Y
CALIFORNIA		
Wilson	Y	Y
Cranston	Y	Y
COLORADO		
Armstrong	Y	Y
Hart	Y	N
CONNECTICUT		
Weicker	N	Y
Dodd	N	Y
DELAWARE		
Roth	Y	N
Biden	Y	Y
FLORIDA		
Hawkins	?	?
Chiles	Y	Y
GEORGIA		
Mattingly	Y	Y
Nunn	Y	Y
HAWAII		
Inouye	Y	Y
Matsunaga	Y	Y
IDAHO		
McClure	Y	Y
Symms	Y	Y
ILLINOIS		
Dixon	Y	Y
Simon	Y	Y
INDIANA		
Lugar	Y	Y
Quayle	Y	Y
IOWA		
Grassley	Y	Y
Harkin	N	Y
KANSAS		
Dole	Y	Y
Kassebaum	Y	Y
KENTUCKY		
McConnell	Y	Y
Ford	Y	Y
LOUISIANA		
Johnston	Y	Y
Long	Y	Y
MAINE		
Cohen	N	Y
Mitchell	N	Y
MARYLAND		
Mathias	N	N
Sarbanes	N	Y
MASSACHUSETTS		
Kennedy	Y	N
Kerry	Y	Y
MICHIGAN		
Levin	N	Y
Riegle	Y	Y
MINNESOTA		
Boschwitz	Y	Y
Durenberger	Y	Y
MISSISSIPPI		
Cochran	Y	Y
Stennis	Y	Y
MISSOURI		
Danforth	Y	N
Eagleton	Y	N
MONTANA		
Baucus	Y	N
Melcher	Y	N
NEBRASKA		
Exon	Y	Y
Zorinsky	Y	Y
NEVADA		
Hecht	Y	Y
Laxalt	Y	Y
NEW HAMPSHIRE		
Humphrey	Y	N
Rudman	N	N
NEW JERSEY		
Bradley	Y	N
Lautenberg	N	Y
NEW MEXICO		
Domenici	Y	Y
Bingaman	Y	Y
NEW YORK		
D'Amato	N	Y
Moynihan	Y	Y
NORTH CAROLINA		
East	Y	Y
Helms	Y	N
NORTH DAKOTA		
Andrews	Y	Y
Burdick	Y	Y
OHIO		
Glenn	Y	Y
Metzenbaum	N	Y
OKLAHOMA		
Nickles	Y	Y
Boren	Y	Y
OREGON		
Hatfield	N	Y
Packwood	Y	N
PENNSYLVANIA		
Heinz	Y	Y
Specter	Y	Y
RHODE ISLAND		
Chafee	Y	N
Pell	N	N
SOUTH CAROLINA		
Thurmond	Y	Y
Hollings	N	Y
SOUTH DAKOTA		
Abdnor	Y	Y
Pressler	?	?
TENNESSEE		
Gore	Y	Y
Sasser	Y	Y
TEXAS		
Gramm	Y	Y
Bentsen	Y	Y
UTAH		
Garn	?	?
Hatch	Y	Y
VERMONT		
Stafford	N	Y
Leahy	N	Y
VIRGINIA		
Trible	Y	N
Warner	Y	N
WASHINGTON		
Evans	Y	Y
Gorton	Y	Y
WEST VIRGINIA		
Byrd	Y	Y
Rockefeller	Y	Y
WISCONSIN		
Kasten	N	Y
Proxmire	N	Y
WYOMING		
Simpson	Y	N
Wallop	Y	N

KEY

Y Voted for (yea).
\# Paired for.
\+ Announced for.
N Voted against (nay).
X Paired against.
\- Announced against.
P Voted "present."
C Voted "present" to avoid possible conflict of interest.
? Did not vote or otherwise make a position known.

Democrats ***Republicans***

ND - Northern Democrats SD - Southern Democrats (Southern states - Ala., Ark., Fla., Ga., Ky., La., Miss., N.C., Okla., S.C., Tenn., Texas, Va.)

128. HR 3838. Tax Overhaul. Nickles, R-Okla., motion to table (kill) the Weicker, R-Conn., amendment to disallow passive losses from oil and gas investments in the same way passive losses from other types of tax shelters are disallowed in the bill: by eliminating the bill's exception for those who have some liability beyond their initial investment. Motion agreed to 77-20: R 42-8; D 35-12 (ND 22-11, SD 13-1), June 12, 1986.

129. HR 3838. Tax Overhaul. Chiles, D-Fla.-Domenici, R-N.M., amendment to express the sense of the Senate that deductibility of state and local sales, real and personal property and income taxes should be preserved in full. Adopted 76-21: R 36-14; D 40-7 (ND 26-7, SD 14-0), June 12, 1986.

Corresponding to Congressional Record Votes 130, 131, 132, 133, 134, 135, 136, 137

	130	131	132	133	134	135	136	137
ALABAMA								
Denton	N	N	Y	Y	N	N	Y	Y
Heflin	N	Y	Y	Y	N	N	Y	Y
ALASKA								
Murkowski	Y	Y	Y	Y	N	Y	Y	Y
Stevens	Y	Y	Y	Y	Y	N	N	Y
ARIZONA								
Goldwater	Y	Y	?	Y	Y	Y	?	Y
DeConcini	N	N	N	N	N	N	N	Y
ARKANSAS								
Bumpers	N	N	Y	N	N	N	N	N
Pryor	Y	N	Y	Y	N	Y	N	Y
CALIFORNIA								
Wilson	N	Y	Y	Y	N	N	Y	Y
Cranston	N	Y	?	Y	N	Y	Y	N
COLORADO								
Armstrong	N	Y	Y	Y	Y	Y	Y	Y
Hart	Y	Y	Y	Y	Y	Y	Y	Y
CONNECTICUT								
Weicker	N	N	?	N	Y	N	N	Y
Dodd	Y	N	Y	N	N	Y	Y	Y
DELAWARE								
Roth	Y	Y	Y	Y	N	Y	N	Y
Biden	?	?	?	N	N	Y	Y	N
FLORIDA								
Hawkins	-	?	?	Y	N	N	?	Y
Chiles	N	N	Y	N	N	N	?	Y
GEORGIA								
Mattingly	Y	N	Y	Y	N	Y	N	Y
Nunn	N	N	Y	N	N	Y	N	N
HAWAII								
Inouye	N	N	Y	Y	?	N	Y	N
Matsunaga	Y	N	Y	Y	N	Y	Y	Y
IDAHO								
McClure	Y	Y	Y	Y	Y	Y	?	Y
Symms	Y	Y	Y	Y	Y	Y	Y	Y
ILLINOIS								
Dixon	N	N	Y	Y	N	N	Y	Y
Simon	N	N	Y	N	N	N	Y	N
INDIANA								
Lugar	Y	Y	Y	Y	N	Y	Y	Y
Quayle	Y	Y	Y	Y	N	Y	Y	Y
IOWA								
Grassley	Y	N	Y	Y	N	Y	N	Y
Harkin	N	N	N	N	N	N	Y	N
KANSAS								
Dole	Y	N	Y	Y	N	Y	N	Y
Kassebaum	Y	N	Y	Y	?	Y	Y	Y
KENTUCKY								
McConnell	Y	Y	Y	Y	N	Y	Y	Y
Ford	N	N	Y	Y	N	N	Y	Y
LOUISIANA								
Johnston	Y	N	Y	Y	N	N	Y	Y
Long	Y	Y	Y	Y	N	Y	Y	Y
MAINE								
Cohen	Y	N	Y	Y	N	Y	N	Y
Mitchell	N	N	Y	N	N	N	N	N
MARYLAND								
Mathias	N	N	Y	Y	Y	N	Y	N
Sarbanes	N	N	N	N	N	N	Y	N
MASSACHUSETTS								
Kennedy	Y	N	Y	Y	N	?	Y	Y
Kerry	Y	N	?	N	N	Y	Y	N
MICHIGAN								
Levin	N	N	N	N	N	Y	Y	N
Riegle	N	N	Y	N	N	Y	Y	N
MINNESOTA								
Boschwitz	Y	Y	Y	Y	N	Y	Y	Y
Durenberger	Y	N	Y	Y	N	Y	Y	Y
MISSISSIPPI								
Cochran	N	N	Y	Y	Y	Y	Y	Y
Stennis	Y	Y	Y	Y	N	N	?	N
MISSOURI								
Danforth	Y	Y	Y	Y	Y	Y	Y	Y
Eagleton	Y	?	Y	N	N	N	Y	N
MONTANA								
Baucus	Y	N	Y	Y	N	Y	Y	Y
Melcher	N	N	Y	N	N	N	Y	N
NEBRASKA								
Exon	N	N	Y	N	N	Y	N	Y
Zorinsky	N	N	?	N	N	Y	N	Y
NEVADA								
Hecht	N	Y	Y	Y	Y	Y	Y	Y
Laxalt	N	Y	?	Y	Y	Y	?	Y
NEW HAMPSHIRE								
Humphrey	N	N	Y	Y	Y	Y	N	Y
Rudman	Y	N	Y	Y	N	Y	N	Y
NEW JERSEY								
Bradley	Y	N	Y	Y	N	Y	Y	Y
Lautenberg	?	?	?	N	N	N	Y	N
NEW MEXICO								
Domenici	Y	Y	Y	Y	N	N	Y	Y
Bingaman	N	N	Y	N	N	N	N	N
NEW YORK								
D'Amato	N	N	Y	N	N	N	Y	Y
Moynihan	Y	N	Y	Y	N	Y	Y	Y
NORTH CAROLINA								
East	N	Y	Y	Y	N	Y	Y	Y
Helms	Y	Y	Y	Y	N	Y	Y	Y
NORTH DAKOTA								
Andrews	N	N	Y	Y	N	N	N	N
Burdick	N	N	N	N	N	N	N	N
OHIO								
Glenn	N	N	N	N	N	N	Y	Y
Metzenbaum	N	N	N	N	N	Y	N	N
OKLAHOMA								
Nickles	Y	Y	Y	Y	N	Y	N	Y
Boren	Y	Y	Y	Y	N	Y	Y	Y
OREGON								
Hatfield	Y	Y	Y	Y	N	N	Y	Y
Packwood	Y	N	Y	Y	N	Y	Y	Y
PENNSYLVANIA								
Heinz	N	N	Y	Y	N	Y	Y	Y
Specter	N	N	N	?	N	N	Y	N
RHODE ISLAND								
Chafee	Y	N	Y	Y	N	N	N	Y
Pell	N	N	N	N	N	N	N	Y
SOUTH CAROLINA								
Thurmond	Y	N	Y	Y	N	Y	Y	Y
Hollings	N	N	Y	N	N	N	N	N
SOUTH DAKOTA								
Abdnor	N	N	Y	Y	N	N	N	Y
Pressler	?	?	?	Y	N	N	N	Y
TENNESSEE								
Gore	N	N	N	Y	N	N	Y	N
Sasser	N	N	N	Y	N	N	Y	N
TEXAS								
Gramm	Y	Y	?	Y	N	Y	Y	Y
Bentsen	Y	N	Y	Y	Y	Y	Y	Y
UTAH								
Garn	?	?	Y	Y	N	N	Y	Y
Hatch	Y	Y	Y	Y	Y	N	Y	Y
VERMONT								
Stafford	Y	Y	Y	N	Y	Y	Y	Y
Leahy	N	N	N	N	N	Y	N	N
VIRGINIA								
Trible	Y	Y	?	Y	N	N	Y	Y
Warner	Y	Y	Y	Y	N	N	Y	Y
WASHINGTON								
Evans	Y	?	Y	Y	N	Y	Y	Y
Gorton	Y	N	Y	Y	N	Y	Y	N
WEST VIRGINIA								
Byrd	N	N	Y	N	N	N	Y	N
Rockefeller	Y	N	Y	N	N	Y	Y	N
WISCONSIN								
Kasten	N	N	N	Y	N	Y	N	Y
Proxmire	Y	N	N	N	N	Y	N	Y
WYOMING								
Simpson	Y	Y	?	Y	Y	Y	Y	Y
Wallop	Y	Y	Y	Y	Y	Y	Y	Y

KEY

- Y Voted for (yea).
- # Paired for.
- + Announced for.
- N Voted against (nay).
- X Paired against.
- \- Announced against.
- P Voted "present."
- C Voted "present" to avoid possible conflict of interest.
- ? Did not vote or otherwise make a position known.

Democrats *Republicans*

ND - Northern Democrats SD - Southern Democrats (Southern states - Ala., Ark., Fla., Ga., Ky., La., Miss., N.C., Okla., S.C., Tenn., Texas, Va.)

130. HR 3838. Tax Overhaul. Packwood, R-Ore., motion to table (kill) the Kasten, R-Wis., amendment to allow deductions for charitable contributions by taxpayers who do not itemize deductions, and to reduce the committee bill threshold for phasing out the personal exemption. Motion agreed to 51-44: R 34-16; D 17-28 (ND 11-20, SD 6-8), June 13, 1986.

131. HR 3838. Tax Overhaul. Wilson, R-Calif., motion to table (kill) the Metzenbaum, D-Ohio, amendment to eliminate a provision allowing Unocal, the Union Oil Co. of California, to claim foreign tax credits on interest paid on $4.4 billion in debt incurred to fight a takeover attempt. Motion rejected 33-60: R 27-22; D 6-38 (ND 2-28, SD 4-10), June 13, 1986. (The Metzenbaum amendment subsequently was adopted by voice vote.)

132. HR 3838. Tax Overhaul. Boren, D-Okla., motion to table (kill) the Metzenbaum, D-Ohio, amendment to eliminate a transition rule exempting Phillips Petroleum Co. of Oklahoma from a 10 percent tax on funds withdrawn from its pension plan, and to use the $50 million in revenues raised thereby to permit farmers to continue to use income averaging. Motion agreed to 73-14: R 43-2; D 30-12 (ND 18-10, SD 12-2), June 16, 1986.

133. HR 3838. Tax Overhaul. Armstrong, R-Colo., motion to table (kill) the Metzenbaum, D-Ohio, amendment to eliminate from the bill a provision that would permit eight limited partners in the Cimarron Coal Co. of Colorado to continue to pay capital gains tax at the current-law rate of 20 percent on gains from sales of royalties under a 1985 lease. Motion agreed to 68-31: R 49-3; D 19-28 (ND 9-24, SD 10-4), June 17, 1986.

134. HR 3838. Tax Overhaul. Wallop, R-Wyo., motion to table (kill) the Metzenbaum, D-Ohio, amendment to reinstate the capital gains tax on foreign investment in real estate in the United States; to apply $200 million of the revenues raised to allow farmers to use income averaging; and to apply $1 billion to reduce the "floor" on medical deductions, which the committee bill would increase from 5 percent to 10 percent of adjusted gross income. Motion rejected 18-80: R 16-36; D 2-44 (ND 1-31, SD 1-13), June 17, 1986. (The Metzenbaum amendment subsequently was adopted on a division vote.)

135. HR 3838. Tax Overhaul. Packwood, R-Ore., motion to table (kill) the Trible, R-Va., amendment to retain current-law tax treatment of pension plans of federal, and some state, local and private, employees, permitting tax-free return of their own contributions for the first three years of their retirement. Motion agreed to 57-42: R 35-18; D 22-24 (ND 17-15, SD 5-9), June 17, 1986.

136. HR 3838. Tax Overhaul. Heinz, R-Pa., motion to table (kill) the Pryor, D-Ark., amendment to delete the section of the bill permitting steel companies to carry back 50 percent of their unused investment tax credits for 15 years, instead of the present three years, and thus receive refunds of taxes paid in those earlier years when they had taxable profits. Motion agreed to 65-29: R 34-15; D 31-14 (ND 23-10, SD 8-4), in the session that began June 17, 1986.

137. HR 3838. Tax Overhaul. Packwood, R-Ore., motion to table (kill) the Mitchell, D-Maine, amendment to add a third tax rate of 35 percent, reduce the bottom rate from 15 percent to 14 percent and retain the bill's top capital gains rate at 27 percent. Motion agreed to 71-29: R 49-4; D 22-25 (ND 14-19, SD 8-6), June 18, 1986.

CQ Senate Votes 138 - 143

Corresponding to Congressional Record Votes 138, 139, 140, 141, 142, 143

	138	139	140	141	142	143
ALABAMA						
Denton	+	N	Y	Y	Y	Y
Heflin	Y	N	Y	Y	N	Y
ALASKA						
Murkowski	Y	Y	Y	Y	Y	Y
Stevens	Y	Y	Y	Y	Y	Y
ARIZONA						
Goldwater	Y	?	Y	Y	?	N
DeConcini	Y	N	Y	N	Y	Y
ARKANSAS						
Bumpers	Y	N	Y	Y	N	Y
Pryor	Y	N	Y	Y	N	Y
CALIFORNIA						
Wilson	Y	Y	Y	Y	Y	Y
Cranston	Y	N	Y	Y	N	Y
COLORADO						
Armstrong	Y	Y	Y	Y	Y	Y
Hart	Y	Y	Y	Y	Y	Y
CONNECTICUT						
Weicker	Y	Y	Y	Y	Y	Y
Dodd	Y	N	Y	Y	Y	Y
DELAWARE						
Roth	Y	Y	Y	Y	Y	Y
Biden	Y	Y	Y	Y	Y	Y
FLORIDA						
Hawkins	+	?	Y	Y	Y	Y
Chiles	Y	Y	Y	Y	N	Y
GEORGIA						
Mattingly	Y	Y	Y	Y	Y	Y
Nunn	Y	Y	Y	Y	N	Y
HAWAII						
Inouye	Y	N	Y	N	N	Y
Matsunaga	Y	N	Y	Y	Y	Y
IDAHO						
McClure	Y	Y	Y	Y	?	?
Symms	Y	Y	?	?	?	?
ILLINOIS						
Dixon	Y	Y	Y	Y	N	Y
Simon	Y	Y	Y	Y	N	Y
INDIANA						
Lugar	Y	Y	Y	Y	Y	Y
Quayle	Y	Y	Y	Y	Y	Y
IOWA						
Grassley	Y	Y	Y	Y	N	Y
Harkin	Y	N	Y	Y	N	Y
KANSAS						
Dole	Y	Y	Y	Y	Y	Y
Kassebaum	Y	Y	Y	Y	Y	Y
KENTUCKY						
McConnell	Y	Y	Y	Y	Y	Y
Ford	Y	N	Y	Y	N	Y
LOUISIANA						
Johnston	Y	?	Y	Y	N	Y
Long	Y	Y	Y	Y	N	Y
MAINE						
Cohen	Y	N	Y	Y	N	Y
Mitchell	Y	N	Y	Y	N	Y
MARYLAND						
Mathias	Y	Y	Y	Y	Y	Y
Sarbanes	Y	N	Y	Y	N	Y
MASSACHUSETTS						
Kennedy	Y	Y	Y	Y	Y	?
Kerry	Y	Y	Y	Y	Y	Y
MICHIGAN						
Levin	Y	N	Y	Y	N	Y
Riegle	Y	Y	Y	Y	N	Y
MINNESOTA						
Boschwitz	Y	Y	Y	Y	Y	Y
Durenberger	Y	Y	Y	Y	?	?
MISSISSIPPI						
Cochran	Y	Y	Y	Y	Y	Y
Stennis	Y	?	Y	Y	?	?
MISSOURI						
Danforth	Y	Y	Y	Y	Y	Y
Eagleton	Y	Y	Y	Y	Y	Y
MONTANA						
Baucus	Y	N	Y	Y	Y	Y
Melcher	Y	N	Y	N	N	Y
NEBRASKA						
Exon	Y	N	Y	Y	N	Y
Zorinsky	Y	N	Y	Y	N	Y
NEVADA						
Hecht	Y	Y	Y	Y	Y	Y
Laxalt	Y	Y	Y	Y	Y	Y
NEW HAMPSHIRE						
Humphrey	Y	Y	Y	Y	Y	Y
Rudman	Y	Y	Y	Y	Y	Y
NEW JERSEY						
Bradley	Y	Y	Y	Y	Y	Y
Lautenberg	Y	Y	Y	Y	Y	Y
NEW MEXICO						
Domenici	Y	Y	Y	Y	Y	Y
Bingaman	Y	?	Y	Y	Y	Y
NEW YORK						
D'Amato	Y	Y	Y	Y	Y	Y
Moynihan	Y	Y	Y	Y	Y	Y
NORTH CAROLINA						
East	Y	Y	Y	Y	Y	Y
Helms	Y	Y	Y	Y	Y	Y
NORTH DAKOTA						
Andrews	Y	N	Y	Y	N	Y
Burdick	Y	N	Y	N	N	Y
OHIO						
Glenn	Y	Y	Y	Y	Y	Y
Metzenbaum	Y	Y	Y	N	N	Y
OKLAHOMA						
Nickles	Y	N	Y	Y	N	Y
Boren	Y	N	Y	Y	N	Y
OREGON						
Hatfield	Y	Y	Y	Y	Y	Y
Packwood	Y	Y	Y	Y	Y	Y
PENNSYLVANIA						
Heinz	Y	Y	Y	Y	Y	Y
Specter	Y	Y	Y	Y	Y	Y
RHODE ISLAND						
Chafee	Y	Y	Y	Y	Y	Y
Pell	Y	Y	Y	Y	Y	Y
SOUTH CAROLINA						
Thurmond	Y	Y	Y	Y	Y	Y
Hollings	Y	Y	Y	N	N	Y
SOUTH DAKOTA						
Abdnor	Y	N	Y	Y	N	Y
Pressler	Y	N	Y	Y	N	Y
TENNESSEE						
Gore	Y	N	Y	N	Y	Y
Sasser	Y	N	Y	Y	N	Y
TEXAS						
Gramm	Y	Y	Y	Y	Y	Y
Bentsen	Y	Y	Y	Y	N	Y
UTAH						
Garn	Y	Y	Y	Y	Y	Y
Hatch	Y	Y	Y	Y	Y	Y
VERMONT						
Stafford	Y	Y	Y	Y	Y	Y
Leahy	Y	N	Y	Y	N	Y
VIRGINIA						
Trible	Y	Y	Y	Y	Y	Y
Warner	Y	Y	Y	Y	Y	Y
WASHINGTON						
Evans	Y	N	Y	Y	Y	Y
Gorton	Y	N	Y	Y	Y	Y
WEST VIRGINIA						
Byrd	Y	N	Y	Y	N	Y
Rockefeller	Y	Y	Y	Y	Y	Y
WISCONSIN						
Kasten	Y	N	Y	Y	N	Y
Proxmire	Y	Y	Y	Y	Y	Y
WYOMING						
Simpson	Y	Y	Y	Y	Y	Y
Wallop	Y	Y	Y	Y	Y	Y

KEY

- Y Voted for (yea).
- # Paired for.
- + Announced for.
- N Voted against (nay).
- X Paired against.
- \- Announced against.
- P Voted "present."
- C Voted "present" to avoid possible conflict of interest.
- ? Did not vote or otherwise make a position known.

Democrats ***Republicans***

ND - Northern Democrats SD - Southern Democrats (Southern states - Ala., Ark., Fla., Ga., Ky., La., Miss., N.C., Okla., S.C., Tenn., Texas, Va.)

138. S J Res 365. Welcome to Afghan Rebels. Passage of the joint resolution to welcome the delegation of the Islamic Unity of Afghan Mujahideen, the rebels fighting the Soviet-backed government in Afghanistan. Passed 98-0: R 51-0; D 47-0 (ND 33-0, SD 14-0), June 18, 1986.

139. HR 3838. Tax Overhaul. Packwood, R-Ore., motion to table (kill) the Melcher, D-Mont., amendment to retain current-law capital gains treatment for farmers and owners of small wood lots, and to add deferred, foreign-earned income of U.S. firms' foreign subsidiaries as a preference item to the corporate minimum tax. Motion agreed to 63-32: R 42-9; D 21-23 (ND 16-16, SD 5-7), June 18, 1986.

140. HR 3838. Tax Overhaul. Division 1 of the bill to make certain changes in the treatment of Employee Stock Ownership Plans (ESOPs). Adopted 99-0: R 52-0; D 47-0 (ND 33-0, SD 14-0), June 19, 1986. (The effect of the vote was to confirm the Senate's support for the committee amendment dealing with ESOP provisions.)

141. HR 3838. Tax Overhaul. Packwood, R-Ore., motion to table (kill) the DeConcini, D-Ariz., amendment to raise the income level at which the bill's higher individual income tax rate would take effect, reduce the higher individual tax rate to 26 percent, change the foreign tax credit to a deduction and raise the minimum corporate and individual tax rate by 1.25 percentage points. Motion agreed to 92-7: R 52-0; D 40-7 (ND 28-5, SD 12-2), June 19, 1986.

142. HR 3838. Tax Overhaul. Packwood, R-Ore., motion to table (kill) the Harkin, D-Iowa, amendment to adjust, for the purpose of taxation when it is sold, the value of a farm or small business to keep pace with inflation, up to $500,000, and to impose an excise tax on mergers of corporations when the value of the acquired company is $250 million or more. Motion agreed to 60-35: R 42-7; D 18-28 (ND 17-16, SD 1-12), June 19, 1986.

143. HR 3838. Tax Overhaul. Riegle, D-Mich., amendment to express the sense of the Senate that the Senate conferees on HR 3838 give the highest priority to increasing the tax cut for the middle class. Adopted 94-1: R 49-1; D 45-0 (ND 32-0, SD 13-0), June 19, 1986.

Corresponding to Congressional Record Votes 144, 145, 146, 147, 148, 149, 150, 151

	144	145	146	147	148	149	150	151
ALABAMA								
Denton	N	Y	N	Y	Y	Y	Y	Y
Heflin	N	Y	N	N	Y	N	Y	Y
ALASKA								
Murkowski	?	?	Y	Y	Y	Y	Y	Y
Stevens	N	Y	Y	Y	Y	Y	Y	Y
ARIZONA								
Goldwater	?	Y	Y	Y	Y	Y	Y	Y
DeConcini	Y	N	N	Y	Y	Y	Y	Y
ARKANSAS								
Bumpers	Y	N	N	N	Y	Y	Y	Y
Pryor	Y	N	N	N	Y	Y	Y	Y
CALIFORNIA								
Wilson	Y	N	Y	Y	Y	Y	Y	Y
Cranston	?	?	N	Y	Y	Y	Y	Y
COLORADO								
Armstrong	Y	N	Y	N	Y	Y	Y	Y
Hart	Y	N	Y	N	Y	Y	Y	Y
CONNECTICUT								
Weicker	?	?	?	?	Y	Y	Y	Y
Dodd	Y	N	N	N	Y	Y	Y	Y
DELAWARE								
Roth	N	Y	Y	N	Y	Y	Y	Y
Biden	N	Y	Y	N	Y	Y	Y	Y
FLORIDA								
Hawkins	?	?	Y	N	Y	N	Y	+
Chiles	Y	?	N	?	Y	Y	Y	Y
GEORGIA								
Mattingly	Y	N	N	Y	Y	N	Y	Y
Nunn	N	Y	-	?	Y	Y	Y	Y
HAWAII								
Inouye	Y	N	?	N	Y	Y	Y	Y
Matsunaga	N	Y	N	N	Y	Y	Y	Y
IDAHO								
McClure	?	?	?	Y	Y	Y	Y	Y
Symms	?	?	Y	Y	Y	Y	Y	Y
ILLINOIS								
Dixon	-	+	N	N	Y	N	Y	Y
Simon	Y	N	N	N	N	Y	Y	Y
INDIANA								
Lugar	Y	N	N	N	Y	Y	Y	Y
Quayle	Y	N	Y	Y	Y	Y	Y	Y
IOWA								
Grassley	Y	Y	Y	N	Y	N	Y	Y
Harkin	Y	N	N	N	Y	Y	Y	Y
KANSAS								
Dole	Y	N	Y	Y	Y	Y	Y	Y
Kassebaum	N	Y	Y	N	Y	Y	Y	Y
KENTUCKY								
McConnell	Y	N	Y	Y	Y	Y	Y	Y
Ford	Y	N	N	Y	Y	Y	Y	Y
LOUISIANA								
Johnston	N	Y	N	N	Y	Y	Y	Y
Long	N	Y	N	N	Y	Y	Y	Y
MAINE								
Cohen	Y	N	N	N	Y	Y	Y	Y
Mitchell	N	Y	N	N	Y	Y	Y	Y
MARYLAND								
Mathias	N	N	N	Y	Y	Y	Y	Y
Sarbanes	Y	N	N	N	Y	Y	Y	Y
MASSACHUSETTS								
Kennedy	N	Y	Y	N	Y	Y	Y	Y
Kerry	N	Y	?	N	Y	Y	Y	Y
MICHIGAN								
Levin	Y	N	N	N	N	Y	Y	Y
Riegle	N	N	N	N	Y	Y	Y	Y
MINNESOTA								
Boschwitz	N	Y	Y	Y	Y	Y	Y	Y
Durenberger	Y	N	Y	N	Y	Y	Y	Y
MISSISSIPPI								
Cochran	Y	N	Y	Y	Y	Y	Y	Y
Stennis	N	Y	N	N	Y	Y	Y	Y
MISSOURI								
Danforth	Y	N	Y	N	Y	Y	Y	Y
Eagleton	Y	N	Y	N	Y	Y	Y	Y
MONTANA								
Baucus	N	Y	N	N	Y	Y	Y	Y
Melcher	N	Y	N	Y	N	Y	Y	Y
NEBRASKA								
Exon	Y	N	N	Y	Y	N	Y	Y
Zorinsky	Y	N	N	Y	Y	N	Y	Y
NEVADA								
Hecht	?	?	Y	N	Y	Y	Y	?
Laxalt	?	N	Y	Y	Y	Y	Y	?
NEW HAMPSHIRE								
Humphrey	?	?	Y	Y	Y	Y	Y	Y
Rudman	Y	N	Y	Y	Y	Y	Y	Y
NEW JERSEY								
Bradley	N	Y	Y	N	Y	Y	Y	Y
Lautenberg	?	?	Y	N	Y	Y	Y	Y
NEW MEXICO								
Domenici	N	Y	Y	Y	Y	Y	Y	Y
Bingaman	N	Y	Y	N	Y	Y	Y	Y
NEW YORK								
D'Amato	N	Y	Y	N	Y	Y	Y	Y
Moynihan	N	Y	Y	N	Y	Y	Y	Y
NORTH CAROLINA								
East	Y	N	Y	Y	Y	Y	Y	Y
Helms	Y	N	Y	Y	Y	N	Y	Y
NORTH DAKOTA								
Andrews	N	Y	N	Y	Y	Y	Y	Y
Burdick	N	Y	N	N	Y	Y	Y	Y
OHIO								
Glenn	Y	N	Y	N	Y	Y	Y	Y
Metzenbaum	Y	N	Y	Y	Y	Y	Y	Y
OKLAHOMA								
Nickles	N	Y	N	Y	Y	N	Y	Y
Boren	N	Y	Y	Y	Y	Y	Y	Y
OREGON								
Hatfield	N	Y	Y	Y	Y	Y	Y	Y
Packwood	N	Y	Y	Y	Y	Y	?	?
PENNSYLVANIA								
Heinz	Y	N	Y	Y	Y	Y	Y	Y
Specter	Y	N	Y	N	Y	Y	Y	Y
RHODE ISLAND								
Chafee	?	?	Y	Y	Y	Y	Y	?
Pell	N	Y	+	Y	Y	Y	Y	Y
SOUTH CAROLINA								
Thurmond	N	Y	Y	Y	Y	Y	Y	+
Hollings	Y	N	N	N	Y	Y	Y	Y
SOUTH DAKOTA								
Abdnor	Y	N	N	N	Y	Y	Y	Y
Pressler	Y	N	?	Y	Y	Y	Y	Y
TENNESSEE								
Gore	N	Y	N	N	Y	Y	Y	Y
Sasser	Y	N	N	Y	Y	N	Y	Y
TEXAS								
Gramm	?	?	Y	Y	Y	Y	Y	Y
Bentsen	?	?	N	Y	Y	Y	Y	Y
UTAH								
Garn	?	?	Y	Y	Y	Y	Y	Y
Hatch	N	N	Y	Y	Y	Y	Y	Y
VERMONT								
Stafford	N	Y	Y	Y	Y	Y	Y	Y
Leahy	?	?	N	Y	Y	Y	Y	Y
VIRGINIA								
Trible	N	Y	Y	Y	Y	Y	Y	Y
Warner	N	Y	Y	N	Y	Y	Y	Y
WASHINGTON								
Evans	N	Y	N	Y	Y	Y	Y	Y
Gorton	N	Y	Y	Y	Y	Y	Y	Y
WEST VIRGINIA								
Byrd	Y	N	N	N	Y	N	Y	Y
Rockefeller	Y	N	Y	N	Y	Y	Y	Y
WISCONSIN								
Kasten	N	Y	Y	Y	Y	Y	Y	Y
Proxmire	Y	N	Y	N	Y	N	Y	Y
WYOMING								
Simpson	N	Y	Y	Y	Y	Y	Y	Y
Wallop	?	?	Y	Y	Y	N	Y	Y

KEY

Y Voted for (yea).
\# Paired for.
\+ Announced for.
N Voted against (nay).
X Paired against.
\- Announced against.
P Voted "present."
C Voted "present" to avoid possible conflict of interest.
? Did not vote or otherwise make a position known.

Democrats ***Republicans***

ND - Northern Democrats SD - Southern Democrats (Southern states - Ala., Ark., Fla., Ga., Ky., La., Miss., N.C., Okla., S.C., Tenn., Texas, Va.)

144. HR 3838. Tax Overhaul. Bumpers, D-Ark., motion to table (kill) the Baucus, D-Mont., substitute for the Bumpers amendment, to reinstate provisions granting immunity from criminal prosecution, but not civil penalties, to those who confess to unpaid taxes; to make the provisions contingent on a $200 million appropriation to the Internal Revenue Service for enforcement; to make the provisions inapplicable to income from illegal sources; and to limit the immunity from criminal prosecution to two years. Motion rejected 41-41: R 19-21; D 22-20 (ND 16-13, SD 6-7), June 20, 1986. (The Baucus substitute subsequently was rejected *(see vote 145, below)*, after which the Bumpers amendment, to strike the immunity provisions and to offset the $200 million revenue loss by limiting net operating loss carry-backs by corporations, was adopted by voice vote.)

145. HR 3838. Tax Overhaul. Baucus, D-Mont., substitute for the Bumpers, D-Ark., amendment *(see vote 144, above)*, to reinstate provisions granting immunity from criminal prosecution, but not civil penalties, to those who confess to unpaid taxes; to make the provisions contingent on a $200 million appropriation to the Internal Revenue Service for enforcement; to make the provisions inapplicable to income from illegal sources; and to limit the immunity from criminal prosecution to two years. Rejected 40-43: R 21-21; D 19-22 (ND 12-17, SD 7-5), June 20, 1986. (The Bumpers amendment subsequently was adopted by voice vote.)

146. HR 3838. Tax Overhaul. Packwood, R-Ore., motion to table (kill) the Melcher, D-Mont., motion to waive the revenue-neutrality requirement contained in the 1974 Congressional Budget and Impoundment Control Act (PL 93-344) with respect to the Melcher amendment. The Melcher amendment would have restored a 30 percent capital gains exclusion for farmers, ranchers and wood lot owners. Motion agreed to 54-39: R 41-9; D 13-30 (ND 12-18, SD 1-12), June 24, 1986.

147. HR 3838. Tax Overhaul. Mattingly, R-Ga., amendment to express the sense of Congress that once the bill is signed into law there be no changes in the tax code for five years. Adopted 50-47: R 38-14; D 12-33 (ND 8-25, SD 4-8), June 24, 1986.

148. HR 3838. Tax Overhaul. Passage of the bill to revise the federal income tax system by reducing individual and corporate tax rates, eliminating or curtailing many deductions, credits and exclusions, repealing the investment tax credit, taxing capital gains as regular income and making other changes. Passed 97-3: R 53-0; D 44-3 (ND 30-3, SD 14-0), June 24, 1986. A "yea" was a vote supporting the president's position.

149. HR 1483. Smithsonian Institution Science Facilities. Passage of the bill to authorize $11.1 million for the Smithsonian Institution's Tropical Research Institute in Panama and $4.5 million for the Smithsonian's Fred Lawrence Whipple Observatory in Arizona. Passed 87-13: R 47-6; D 40-7 (ND 28-5, SD 12-2), June 24, 1986.

150. HR 4151. Diplomatic Security. Simon, D-Ill., amendment to urge the State Department to strengthen foreign language requirements for foreign service officers. Adopted 99-0: R 52-0; D 47-0 (ND 33-0, SD 14-0), June 25, 1986.

151. HR 4151. Diplomatic Security. Byrd, D-W.Va., amendment to express opposition to the Soviet Union's policies in Afghanistan. Adopted 94-0: R 47-0; D 47-0 (ND 33-0, SD 14-0), June 25, 1986. (The Senate later passed the bill, to authorize $1.1 billion to bolster security at U.S. embassies around the world, by voice vote.)

CQ Senate Votes 152 - 154

Corresponding to Congressional Record Votes 152, 153, 154

	152	153	154
ALABAMA			
Denton	Y	Y	N
Heflin	Y	Y	N
ALASKA			
Murkowski	Y	Y	Y
Stevens	Y	Y	Y
ARIZONA			
Goldwater	#	N	?
DeConcini	N	Y	N
ARKANSAS			
Bumpers	N	N	N
Pryor	N	N	Y
CALIFORNIA			
Wilson	Y	N	Y
Cranston	N	N	Y
COLORADO			
Armstrong	Y	N	N
Hart	N	N	Y
CONNECTICUT			
Weicker	N	Y	Y
Dodd	N	Y	Y
DELAWARE			
Roth	Y	N	Y
Biden	X	Y	Y
FLORIDA			
Hawkins	#	?	?
Chiles	N	N	Y
GEORGIA			
Mattingly	Y	N	N
Nunn	N	N	Y
HAWAII			
Inouye	X	Y	Y
Matsunaga	N	Y	Y
IDAHO			
McClure	Y	Y	N
Symms	Y	Y	N
ILLINOIS			
Dixon	N	N	Y
Simon	N	N	Y
INDIANA			
Lugar	Y	Y	N
Quayle	Y	Y	N
IOWA			
Grassley	Y	Y	N
Harkin	N	Y	Y
KANSAS			
Dole	Y	Y	Y
Kassebaum	X	Y	Y
KENTUCKY			
McConnell	Y	Y	N
Ford	N	Y	Y
LOUISIANA			
Johnston	N	Y	Y
Long	Y	Y	Y
MAINE			
Cohen	Y	N	Y
Mitchell	N	N	Y
MARYLAND			
Mathias	N	N	Y
Sarbanes	N	N	Y
MASSACHUSETTS			
Kennedy	N	Y	Y
Kerry	N	Y	Y
MICHIGAN			
Levin	N	N	Y
Riegle	N	Y	Y
MINNESOTA			
Boschwitz	Y	N	Y
Durenberger	Y	N	Y
MISSISSIPPI			
Cochran	Y	Y	Y
Stennis	N	Y	Y
MISSOURI			
Danforth	Y	N	N
Eagleton	N	N	Y
MONTANA			
Baucus	N	Y	Y
Melcher	N	Y	Y
NEBRASKA			
Exon	N	Y	N
Zorinsky	N	N	N
NEVADA			
Hecht	Y	Y	Y
Laxalt	Y	Y	Y
NEW HAMPSHIRE			
Humphrey	Y	Y	N
Rudman	Y	Y	Y
NEW JERSEY			
Bradley	N	N	Y
Lautenberg	N	N	Y
NEW MEXICO			
Domenici	Y	Y	Y
Bingaman	N	N	Y
NEW YORK			
D'Amato	Y	Y	Y
Moynihan	N	Y	Y
NORTH CAROLINA			
East	Y	Y	N
Helms	Y	N	N
NORTH DAKOTA			
Andrews	Y	Y	?
Burdick	N	Y	N
OHIO			
Glenn	N	N	N
Metzenbaum	N	N	Y
OKLAHOMA			
Nickles	Y	Y	N
Boren	N	Y	Y
OREGON			
Hatfield	Y	Y	Y
Packwood	#	?	?
PENNSYLVANIA			
Heinz	Y	Y	Y
Specter	N	N	Y
RHODE ISLAND			
Chafee	Y	Y	Y
Pell	N	Y	Y
SOUTH CAROLINA			
Thurmond	Y	Y	N
Hollings	N	Y	N
SOUTH DAKOTA			
Abdnor	Y	Y	N
Pressler	Y	Y	N
TENNESSEE			
Gore	N	N	Y
Sasser	N	N	Y

KEY

Y Voted for (yea).
\# Paired for.
\+ Announced for.
N Voted against (nay).
X Paired against.
\- Announced against.
P Voted "present."
C Voted "present" to avoid possible conflict of interest.
? Did not vote or otherwise make a position known.

Democrats ***Republicans***

	152	153	154
TEXAS			
Gramm	Y	N	N
Bentsen	N	N	Y
UTAH			
Garn	Y	Y	Y
Hatch	Y	Y	Y
VERMONT			
Stafford	Y	Y	Y
Leahy	N	Y	Y
VIRGINIA			
Trible	Y	N	N
Warner	Y	N	Y
WASHINGTON			
Evans	N	N	N
Gorton	Y	Y	N
WEST VIRGINIA			
Byrd	Y	Y	Y
Rockefeller	N	N	Y
WISCONSIN			
Kasten	Y	N	Y
Proxmire	N	N	N
WYOMING			
Simpson	Y	N	Y
Wallop	Y	N	N

ND - Northern Democrats SD - Southern Democrats (Southern states - Ala., Ark., Fla., Ga., Ky., La., Miss., N.C., Okla., S.C., Tenn., Texas, Va.)

152. Manion Nomination. Confirmation of President Reagan's nomination of Daniel A. Manion of Indiana to be U.S. circuit judge for the 7th Circuit. Confirmed 48-46: R 45-4; D 3-42 (ND 1-30, SD 2-12), June 26, 1986. (Robert C. Byrd, D-W.Va., subsequently moved to reconsider the vote by which the nomination was confirmed, after which Robert Dole, R-Kan., moved to table (kill) the Byrd motion. Byrd's motion was rejected July 23 *(see vote 162, p. 30-S)*.) A "yea" was a vote supporting the president's position.

153. HR 4515. Urgent Supplemental Appropriations, Fiscal 1986. Hatfield, R-Ore., motion to concur in the House amendment to the Senate amendment, to earmark $55.6 million in previously appropriated defense research funding for nine specific universities and colleges. Motion agreed to 56-42: R 32-19; D 24-23 (ND 17-16, SD 7-7), June 26, 1986. (The conference report on HR 4515 had been adopted by voice vote.)

154. HR 4515. Urgent Supplemental Appropriations, Fiscal 1986. Hatfield, R-Ore., motion to concur in the House amendment to Senate amendment, to provide $50 million in economic aid to the International Fund for Northern Ireland and Ireland. Motion agreed to 65-31: R 27-22; D 38-9 (ND 27-6, SD 11-3), June 26, 1986. (The conference report on HR 4515 had been adopted by voice vote.)

	155	156	157	158	159	160
ALABAMA						
Denton	Y	Y	Y	Y	Y	Y
Heflin	Y	Y	Y	N	Y	Y
ALASKA						
Murkowski	?	Y	Y	Y	Y	Y
Stevens	Y	Y	Y	Y	Y	Y
ARIZONA						
Goldwater	Y	Y	?	Y	Y	Y
DeConcini	Y	N	N	N	Y	N
ARKANSAS						
Bumpers	Y	N	Y	N	Y	Y
Pryor	N	Y	Y	N	Y	Y
CALIFORNIA						
Wilson	Y	Y	Y	Y	Y	Y
Cranston	N	N	Y	Y	Y	Y
COLORADO						
Armstrong	Y	Y	N	Y	Y	Y
Hart	N	N	Y	N	Y	Y
CONNECTICUT						
Weicker	Y	N	Y	Y	Y	N
Dodd	N	N	N	Y	Y	N
DELAWARE						
Roth	Y	Y	Y	Y	Y	Y
Biden	N	N	Y	N	Y	Y
FLORIDA						
Hawkins	Y	Y	Y	Y	Y	Y
Chiles	N	N	Y	Y	Y	Y
GEORGIA						
Mattingly	Y	Y	Y	Y	Y	Y
Nunn	Y	Y	Y	Y	Y	Y
HAWAII						
Inouye	Y	N	Y	Y	Y	Y
Matsunaga	Y	N	Y	N	Y	Y
IDAHO						
McClure	Y	N	Y	Y	Y	Y
Symms	?	?	?	?	?	?
ILLINOIS						
Dixon	Y	Y	Y	Y	Y	Y
Simon	N	Y	Y	N	Y	Y
INDIANA						
Lugar	Y	Y	Y	Y	Y	Y
Quayle	Y	Y	Y	Y	Y	Y
IOWA						
Grassley	Y	Y	Y	Y	Y	Y
Harkin	N	N	Y	Y	Y	Y
KANSAS						
Dole	Y	Y	Y	Y	Y	Y
Kassebaum	Y	Y	Y	Y	Y	Y
KENTUCKY						
McConnell	Y	Y	Y	Y	Y	Y
Ford	N	Y	Y	Y	Y	Y
LOUISIANA						
Johnston	N	Y	Y	N	Y	Y
Long	?	N	Y	Y	Y	Y
MAINE						
Cohen	Y	N	Y	Y	Y	Y
Mitchell	N	N	Y	N	Y	Y
MARYLAND						
Mathias	Y	Y	Y	Y	Y	Y
Sarbanes	N	N	Y	N	Y	Y
MASSACHUSETTS						
Kennedy	N	Y	Y	N	Y	Y
Kerry	N	N	Y	N	Y	Y
MICHIGAN						
Levin	N	N	Y	N	Y	Y
Riegle	N	N	Y	N	Y	Y
MINNESOTA						
Boschwitz	Y	Y	Y	Y	Y	Y
Durenberger	Y	N	Y	Y	Y	N
MISSISSIPPI						
Cochran	Y	Y	Y	Y	Y	Y
Stennis	Y	Y	Y	Y	Y	Y
MISSOURI						
Danforth	Y	Y	Y	Y	Y	Y
Eagleton	Y	Y	Y	N	Y	Y
MONTANA						
Baucus	Y	Y	Y	Y	Y	Y
Melcher	Y	Y	Y	N	Y	Y
NEBRASKA						
Exon	N	Y	Y	Y	Y	Y
Zorinsky	Y	N	N	Y	Y	N
NEVADA						
Hecht	?	Y	Y	Y	Y	Y
Laxalt	Y	Y	Y	Y	Y	Y
NEW HAMPSHIRE						
Humphrey	Y	Y	N	Y	Y	N
Rudman	Y	Y	Y	Y	Y	Y
NEW JERSEY						
Bradley	N	N	Y	N	Y	Y
Lautenberg	N	N	Y	N	N	Y
NEW MEXICO						
Domenici	Y	Y	Y	Y	Y	Y
Bingaman	N	Y	Y	N	Y	Y
NEW YORK						
D'Amato	Y	N	N	N	Y	N
Moynihan	N	N	Y	N	Y	Y
NORTH CAROLINA						
Broyhill*	Y	Y	Y	Y	Y	Y
Helms	Y	N	N	Y	Y	N
NORTH DAKOTA						
Andrews	Y	Y	Y	Y	Y	Y
Burdick	N	Y	Y	Y	Y	Y
OHIO						
Glenn	N	Y	Y	N	Y	Y
Metzenbaum	N	Y	Y	N	Y	Y
OKLAHOMA						
Nickles	Y	Y	Y	Y	Y	Y
Boren	Y	Y	Y	Y	Y	Y
OREGON						
Hatfield	Y	Y	Y	?	+	+
Packwood	N	Y	?	Y	Y	Y
PENNSYLVANIA						
Heinz	Y	N	Y	Y	Y	Y
Specter	Y	N	N	?	Y	N
RHODE ISLAND						
Chafee	Y	Y	Y	Y	Y	Y
Pell	Y	Y	Y	N	Y	Y
SOUTH CAROLINA						
Thurmond	Y	Y	Y	Y	Y	Y
Hollings	N	Y	Y	Y	Y	Y
SOUTH DAKOTA						
Abdnor	Y	Y	Y	Y	Y	Y
Pressler	Y	Y	Y	Y	Y	Y
TENNESSEE						
Gore	N	Y	Y	Y	Y	Y
Sasser	N	N	Y	N	Y	Y
TEXAS						
Gramm	Y	Y	Y	Y	Y	Y
Bentsen	N	Y	Y	Y	Y	Y
UTAH						
Garn	Y	Y	Y	Y	Y	Y
Hatch	Y	N	N	Y	Y	N
VERMONT						
Stafford	Y	?	?	?	?	?
Leahy	N	N	Y	Y	Y	Y
VIRGINIA						
Trible	Y	Y	Y	Y	Y	Y
Warner	Y	Y	Y	Y	Y	Y
WASHINGTON						
Evans	Y	Y	Y	Y	Y	Y
Gorton	Y	Y	Y	Y	Y	Y
WEST VIRGINIA						
Byrd	N	N	Y	Y	Y	Y
Rockefeller	N	N	Y	Y	Y	Y
WISCONSIN						
Kasten	Y	Y	Y	Y	Y	Y
Proxmire	N	Y	Y	N	Y	Y
WYOMING						
Simpson	Y	Y	Y	Y	Y	Y
Wallop	Y	Y	Y	Y	Y	Y

KEY

- Y Voted for (yea).
- # Paired for.
- + Announced for.
- N Voted against (nay).
- X Paired against.
- \- Announced against.
- P Voted "present."
- C Voted "present" to avoid possible conflict of interest.
- ? Did not vote or otherwise make a position known.

Democrats ***Republicans***

ND - Northern Democrats SD - Southern Democrats (Southern states - Ala., Ark., Fla., Ga., Ky., La., Miss., N.C., Okla., S.C., Tenn., Texas, Va.)

155. Scanlon Nomination. Confirmation of President Reagan's nomination of Terrence M. Scanlon of the District of Columbia to be chairman of the Consumer Product Safety Commission. Confirmed 63-33: R 49-1; D 14-32 (ND 9-24, SD 5-8), July 15, 1986. A "yea" was a vote supporting the president's position.

156. Treaty Doc 99-8. United States-United Kingdom Extradition Treaty. Lugar, R-Ind., motion to table (kill) the D'Amato, R-N.Y., amendment to provide that the treaty would not apply to any individual whose extradition was sought prior to the entry into force of the treaty, or to any offense committed before that time, if the offense was not in violation of the laws of both countries. Motion agreed to 65-33: R 42-9; D 23-24 (ND 13-20, SD 10-4), July 16, 1986.

157. Treaty Doc 99-8. United States-United Kingdom Extradition Treaty. Lugar, R-Ind., motion to table (kill) the Helms, R-N.C., amendment to provide that U.S. courts shall consider as a defense against extradition a showing that the person sought to be extradited committed his alleged offense as part of an armed uprising against military authorities, without committing wanton crimes of violence against civilians. Motion agreed to 87-9: R 43-6; D 44-3 (ND 30-3, SD 14-0), July 16, 1986.

158. S 2129. Risk Retention. Kasten, R-Wis., motion to table (kill) the Lautenberg, D-N.J., amendment to require certain qualifying states to establish guaranty funds that would pay claims in the event a risk retention self-insurance group becomes insolvent. Motion agreed to 69-27: R 48-1; D 21-26 (ND 12-21, SD 9-5), July 17, 1986.

159. S 2129. Risk Retention. Passage of the bill to promote the formation of self-insurance groups among businesses, municipalities and professional groups. Passed 96-1: R 50-0; D 46-1 (ND 32-1, SD 14-0), July 17, 1986.

160. Treaty Doc 99-8. United States-United Kingdom Extradition Treaty. Adoption of the resolution of ratification of the supplementary treaty to establish new standards for extraditions between the United States and the United Kingdom. Adopted 87-10: R 43-7; D 44-3 (ND 30-3, SD 14-0), July 17, 1986. A two-thirds majority of those present and voting (65 in this case) is required for adoption of resolutions of ratification. A "yea" was a vote supporting the president's position.

** Sen. John P. East, R-N.C., died on June 29, 1986. The last vote for which he was eligible was CQ vote 154. James T. Broyhill, R-N.C., was sworn in on July 14, 1986. The first vote for which he was eligible was CQ vote 155.*

CQ Senate Votes 161 - 163

Corresponding to Congressional Record Votes 161, 162, 163

	161	162	163
ALABAMA			
Denton	Y	N	Y
Heflin	Y	N	Y
ALASKA			
Murkowski	N	N	Y
Stevens	N	N	Y
ARIZONA			
Goldwater	N	X	?
DeConcini	Y	#	Y
ARKANSAS			
Bumpers	Y	Y	Y
Pryor	Y	Y	Y
CALIFORNIA			
Wilson	N	N	Y
Cranston	N	Y	Y
COLORADO			
Armstrong	N	N	Y
Hart	Y	Y	Y
CONNECTICUT			
Weicker	N	Y	Y
Dodd	Y	Y	Y
DELAWARE			
Roth	N	N	Y
Biden	N	Y	Y
FLORIDA			
Hawkins	N	N	?
Chiles	N	Y	Y
GEORGIA			
Mattingly	Y	N	Y
Nunn	Y	Y	Y
HAWAII			
Inouye	N	Y	Y
Matsunaga	Y	Y	Y
IDAHO			
McClure	Y	N	Y
Symms	Y	N	Y
ILLINOIS			
Dixon	Y	Y	Y
Simon	Y	Y	Y
INDIANA			
Lugar	N	N	Y
Quayle	N	N	Y
IOWA			
Grassley	Y	N	Y
Harkin	Y	Y	Y
KANSAS			
Dole	N	N	Y
Kassebaum	N	Y	Y
KENTUCKY			
McConnell	Y	N	Y
Ford	Y	Y	Y
LOUISIANA			
Johnston	N	Y	Y
Long	N	N	Y
MAINE			
Cohen	N	N	Y
Mitchell	N	Y	Y
MARYLAND			
Mathias	N	Y	Y
Sarbanes	N	Y	Y
MASSACHUSETTS			
Kennedy	Y	Y	Y
Kerry	N	Y	Y
MICHIGAN			
Levin	Y	Y	Y
Riegle	Y	Y	Y
MINNESOTA			
Boschwitz	N	N	Y
Durenberger	N	N	Y
MISSISSIPPI			
Cochran	Y	N	Y
Stennis	Y	Y	Y
MISSOURI			
Danforth	N	N	Y
Eagleton	Y	Y	Y
MONTANA			
Baucus	Y	Y	Y
Melcher	Y	Y	Y
NEBRASKA			
Exon	Y	Y	Y
Zorinsky	Y	Y	Y
NEVADA			
Hecht	N	N	Y
Laxalt	N	N	Y
NEW HAMPSHIRE			
Humphrey	N	N	Y
Rudman	N	N	Y
NEW JERSEY			
Bradley	N	Y	Y
Lautenberg	N	Y	Y
NEW MEXICO			
Domenici	N	N	Y
Bingaman	N	Y	Y
NEW YORK			
D'Amato	N	N	Y
Moynihan	N	Y	Y
NORTH CAROLINA			
Broyhill	Y	N	Y
Helms	Y	N	N
NORTH DAKOTA			
Andrews	Y	N	Y
Burdick	Y	Y	Y
OHIO			
Glenn	Y	Y	Y
Metzenbaum	Y	Y	Y
OKLAHOMA			
Nickles	Y	N	Y
Boren	Y	Y	Y
OREGON			
Hatfield	N	N	Y
Packwood	N	Y	Y
PENNSYLVANIA			
Heinz	N	N	Y
Specter	N	Y	Y
RHODE ISLAND			
Chafee	N	N	Y
Pell	N	Y	Y
SOUTH CAROLINA			
Thurmond	Y	N	Y
Hollings	Y	Y	Y
SOUTH DAKOTA			
Abdnor	Y	N	Y
Pressler	Y	N	Y
TENNESSEE			
Gore	Y	Y	Y
Sasser	Y	Y	Y
TEXAS			
Gramm	N	N	Y
Bentsen	N	Y	Y
UTAH			
Garn	N	N	?
Hatch	N	N	Y
VERMONT			
Stafford	N	N	Y
Leahy	Y	Y	Y
VIRGINIA			
Trible	N	N	Y
Warner	N	N	Y
WASHINGTON			
Evans	N	N	Y
Gorton	N	N	Y
WEST VIRGINIA			
Byrd	Y	Y	Y
Rockefeller	Y	Y	Y
WISCONSIN			
Kasten	Y	N	Y
Proxmire	Y	Y	Y
WYOMING			
Simpson	N	N	Y
Wallop	N	N	Y
VICE PRESIDENT			
Bush		N	

KEY

- Y Voted for (yea).
- # Paired for.
- \+ Announced for.
- N Voted against (nay).
- X Paired against.
- \- Announced against.
- P Voted "present."
- C Voted "present" to avoid possible conflict of interest.
- ? Did not vote or otherwise make a position known.

Democrats *Republicans*

ND - Northern Democrats SD - Southern Democrats (Southern states - Ala., Ark., Fla., Ga., Ky., La., Miss., N.C., Okla., S.C., Tenn., Texas, Va.)

161. HR 4510. Export-Import Bank. Ford, D-Ky., amendment to delete nearly $13 million from the bill's $300 million authorization for an export financing "war chest." The amendment would divert the money to farming price support programs. Rejected 47-53: R 15-38; D 32-15 (ND 22-11, SD 10-4), July 22, 1986.

162. Manion Nomination. Byrd, D-W.Va., motion to reconsider the June 26 vote *(vote 152, p. 28-S)* to confirm Daniel A. Manion of Indiana to be U.S. circuit judge for the 7th Circuit Court of Appeals. Motion rejected 49-50: R 5-47; D 44-2 (ND 32-0, SD 12-2), with Vice President George Bush casting a "nay" vote, July 23, 1986. A "nay" was a vote supporting the president's position.

163. Treaty Doc 98-30. Tax Agreement With China. Adoption of the resolution of ratification to reduce or eliminate the double taxation of income earned by U.S. citizens and residents doing business in the People's Republic of China. The resolution includes language (supplementary protocol Treaty Doc 99-26) designed to prevent third-country residents from obtaining unintended benefits from the treaty. Adopted 96-1: R 49-1; D 47-0 (ND 33-0, SD 14-0), July 24, 1986. A two-thirds majority of those present and voting (65 in this case) is required for adoption of resolutions of ratification. A "yea" was a vote supporting the president's position.

	164	165	166	167
ALABAMA				
Denton	?	Y	Y	N
Heflin	Y	Y	Y	Y
ALASKA				
Murkowski	?	Y	Y	Y
Stevens	Y	Y	Y	Y
ARIZONA				
Goldwater	?	-	?	?
DeConcini	Y	Y	N	N
ARKANSAS				
Bumpers	Y	Y	Y	Y
Pryor	?	Y	Y	Y
CALIFORNIA				
Wilson	Y	Y	Y	Y
Cranston	?	Y	N	N
COLORADO				
Armstrong	?	Y	Y	Y
Hart	Y	Y	N	N
CONNECTICUT				
Weicker	?	Y	Y	N
Dodd	Y	Y	N	Y
DELAWARE				
Roth	Y	Y	Y	N
Biden	?	Y	Y	Y
FLORIDA				
Hawkins	?	Y	Y	N
Chiles	Y	Y	Y	Y
GEORGIA				
Mattingly	?	N	Y	Y
Nunn	Y	N	Y	Y
HAWAII				
Inouye	?	N	N	N
Matsunaga	?	Y	N	N
IDAHO				
McClure	Y	Y	Y	Y
Symms	?	Y	Y	Y
ILLINOIS				
Dixon	?	Y	Y	Y
Simon	Y	Y	Y	Y
INDIANA				
Lugar	Y	Y	Y	Y
Quayle	Y	N	Y	Y
IOWA				
Grassley	?	N	Y	N
Harkin	Y	Y	N	N
KANSAS				
Dole	Y	Y	Y	Y
Kassebaum	Y	N	Y	Y
KENTUCKY				
McConnell	Y	Y	Y	Y
Ford	Y	Y	N	Y
LOUISIANA				
Johnston	Y	N	N	N
Long	Y	N	Y	Y
MAINE				
Cohen	Y	Y	Y	Y
Mitchell	Y	Y	N	N
MARYLAND				
Mathias	Y	Y	N	N
Sarbanes	?	Y	N	N
MASSACHUSETTS				
Kennedy	Y	Y	Y	Y
Kerry	?	Y	N	N
MICHIGAN				
Levin	Y	Y	Y	Y
Riegle	Y	Y	N	N
MINNESOTA				
Boschwitz	Y	Y	Y	Y
Durenberger	Y	Y	Y	Y
MISSISSIPPI				
Cochran	Y	Y	Y	Y
Stennis	Y	N	N	Y
MISSOURI				
Danforth	Y	N	Y	Y
Eagleton	Y	Y	N	N
MONTANA				
Baucus	+	Y	N	Y
Melcher	Y	Y	N	N
NEBRASKA				
Exon	Y	Y	N	N
Zorinsky	Y	Y	Y	Y
NEVADA				
Hecht	Y	N	Y	Y
Laxalt	?	N	Y	Y
NEW HAMPSHIRE				
Humphrey	Y	Y	Y	Y
Rudman	Y	N	Y	Y
NEW JERSEY				
Bradley	Y	Y	N	N
Lautenberg	Y	Y	N	N
NEW MEXICO				
Domenici	Y	Y	Y	Y
Bingaman	?	Y	N	N
NEW YORK				
D'Amato	Y	Y	Y	Y
Moynihan	Y	Y	N	N
NORTH CAROLINA				
Broyhill	?	Y	Y	Y
Helms	N	N	Y	Y
NORTH DAKOTA				
Andrews	Y	Y	Y	N
Burdick	?	N	N	N
OHIO				
Glenn	Y	Y	N	N
Metzenbaum	Y	Y	N	N
OKLAHOMA				
Nickles	Y	Y	Y	Y
Boren	Y	Y	Y	Y
OREGON				
Hatfield	Y	N	N	N
Packwood	Y	Y	Y	Y
PENNSYLVANIA				
Heinz	Y	Y	Y	Y
Specter	Y	Y	Y	Y
RHODE ISLAND				
Chafee	Y	Y	Y	Y
Pell	Y	Y	N	N
SOUTH CAROLINA				
Thurmond	Y	Y	Y	Y
Hollings	N	N	Y	Y
SOUTH DAKOTA				
Abdnor	Y	Y	Y	Y
Pressler	Y	Y	Y	N
TENNESSEE				
Gore	Y	Y	N	N
Sasser	Y	Y	N	N
TEXAS				
Gramm	Y	Y	Y	Y
Bentsen	Y	Y	Y	Y
UTAH				
Garn	?	N	Y	Y
Hatch	Y	Y	Y	Y
VERMONT				
Stafford	Y	Y	Y	N
Leahy	?	Y	N	Y
VIRGINIA				
Trible	Y	Y	Y	Y
Warner	Y	Y	Y	Y
WASHINGTON				
Evans	Y	Y	Y	Y
Gorton	Y	Y	Y	Y
WEST VIRGINIA				
Byrd	Y	Y	N	N
Rockefeller	Y	Y	N	N
WISCONSIN				
Kasten	Y	Y	Y	Y
Proxmire	Y	N	Y	Y
WYOMING				
Simpson	Y	N	Y	Y
Wallop	Y	N	Y	Y

KEY

- Y Voted for (yea).
- # Paired for.
- + Announced for.
- N Voted against (nay).
- X Paired against.
- - Announced against.
- P Voted "present."
- C Voted "present" to avoid possible conflict of interest.
- ? Did not vote or otherwise make a position known.

Democrats ***Republicans***

ND - Northern Democrats SD - Southern Democrats (Southern states - Ala., Ark., Fla., Ga., Ky., La., Miss., N.C., Okla., S.C., Tenn., Texas, Va.)

164. Abramowitz Nomination. Dole, R-Kan., motion to proceed to executive session to consider President Reagan's nomination of Morton L. Abramowitz of Massachusetts to be an assistant secretary of state. Motion agreed to 74-2: R 40-1; D 34-1 (ND 22-0, SD 12-1), July 25, 1986. A "yea" was a vote supporting the president's position.

165. Continuation of Senate Broadcasts. Judgment of the Senate whether radio and television coverage of the Senate should continue permanently, as well as several rules changes that had been included in S Res 28, which was approved Feb. 27 and provided for an experimental period of broadcasting floor proceedings prior to a final vote on the question. Affirmed 78-21: R 39-13; D 39-8 (ND 30-3, SD 9-5), July 29, 1986.

166. H J Res 668. Public Debt Limit/Anti-Deficit Act. Heinz, R-Pa., motion to table (kill) the Exon, D-Neb., motion to commit the joint resolution to the Governmental Affairs Committee with instructions to report the resolution back to the Senate with a sense-of-the-Senate provision that Congress utilize the so-called fallback provisions of the Gramm-Rudman-Hollings anti-deficit law (PL 99-177) to enact across-the-board spending cuts, if necessary to meet the law's deficit targets. Motion agreed to 66-33: R 50-2; D 16-31 (ND 7-26, SD 9-5), July 30, 1986.

167. H J Res 668. Public Debt Limit/Anti-Deficit Act. Rudman, R-N.H., amendment to the Finance Committee amendment, to make changes in the Gramm-Rudman-Hollings anti-deficit law (PL 99-177) to reinstate the law's automatic spending cuts procedure (previously voided as a violation of the Constitution's separation-of-powers doctrine) by granting final authority for determining the automatic cuts to the director of the Office of Management and Budget, with certain limitations. The amendment also would change to the first Tuesday in February of each year the date by which the president is required to submit his budget request to Congress. Adopted 63-36: R 42-10; D 21-26 (ND 10-23, SD 11-3), July 30, 1986. A "yea" was a vote supporting the president's position.

CQ Senate Votes 168 - 175

Corresponding to Congressional Record Votes 168, 169, 170, 171, 172, 173, 174, 175

KEY

- Y Voted for (yea).
- # Paired for.
- + Announced for.
- N Voted against (nay).
- X Paired against.
- \- Announced against.
- P Voted "present."
- C Voted "present" to avoid possible conflict of interest.
- ? Did not vote or otherwise make a position known.

Democrats *Republicans*

	168	169	170	171	172	173	174	175
ALABAMA								
Denton	Y	Y	N	Y	Y	Y	N	N
Heflin	N	Y	N	Y	Y	Y	N	N
ALASKA								
Murkowski	N	Y	N	Y	Y	N	N	Y
Stevens	N	Y	N	Y	Y	N	N	Y
ARIZONA								
Goldwater	N	Y	?	?	?	?	Y	Y
DeConcini	Y	Y	Y	Y	Y	N	N	N
ARKANSAS								
Bumpers	N	Y	N	Y	Y	Y	Y	N
Pryor	N	?	N	Y	Y	Y	N	N
CALIFORNIA								
Wilson	N	Y	N	Y	Y	N	N	N
Cranston	Y	Y	Y	Y	Y	Y	Y	X
COLORADO								
Armstrong	N	Y	N	Y	Y	N	N	Y
Hart	Y	Y	N	Y	N	Y	Y	?
CONNECTICUT								
Weicker	Y	N	Y	Y	Y	N	?	?
Dodd	N	Y	Y	Y	Y	Y	Y	N
DELAWARE								
Roth	Y	Y	Y	Y	Y	N	N	?
Biden	N	Y	Y	Y	Y	Y	Y	N
FLORIDA								
Hawkins	Y	Y	Y	Y	Y	?	N	?
Chiles	N	Y	Y	Y	Y	N	Y	N
GEORGIA								
Mattingly	N	Y	N	Y	Y	Y	N	Y
Nunn	N	Y	N	Y	Y	Y	Y	Y
HAWAII								
Inouye	Y	Y	Y	Y	Y	Y	N	N
Matsunaga	Y	Y	N	Y	Y	Y	N	N
IDAHO								
McClure	N	Y	N	Y	Y	N	N	?
Symms	N	Y	N	Y	Y	N	?	?
ILLINOIS								
Dixon	N	Y	N	Y	Y	Y	N	Y
Simon	N	Y	Y	Y	N	Y	Y	N
INDIANA								
Lugar	N	Y	N	Y	Y	N	N	Y
Quayle	N	Y	N	Y	Y	N	N	Y
IOWA								
Grassley	N	Y	Y	Y	Y	N	N	Y
Harkin	Y	Y	Y	Y	Y	Y	Y	N
KANSAS								
Dole	N	Y	N	Y	Y	N	N	Y
Kassebaum	Y	Y	N	Y	Y	N	N	Y
KENTUCKY								
McConnell	N	Y	N	Y	Y	N	N	Y
Ford	N	Y	N	Y	Y	Y	N	N
LOUISIANA								
Johnston	Y	Y	N	Y	N	Y	Y	N
Long	N	Y	N	Y	N	Y	N	Y
MAINE								
Cohen	N	Y	Y	Y	Y	N	Y	?
Mitchell	N	Y	Y	Y	Y	Y	?	N
MARYLAND								
Mathias	Y	N	Y	Y	N	N	Y	N
Sarbanes	Y	Y	Y	Y	Y	Y	Y	N
MASSACHUSETTS								
Kennedy	N	Y	Y	Y	Y	Y	Y	N
Kerry	N	Y	Y	Y	Y	Y	Y	N
MICHIGAN								
Levin	N	Y	Y	Y	N	Y	Y	N
Riegle	Y	Y	Y	Y	Y	Y	Y	N
MINNESOTA								
Boschwitz	N	Y	N	Y	Y	N	Y	Y
Durenberger	N	Y	Y	Y	Y	N	Y	Y
MISSISSIPPI								
Cochran	N	Y	N	Y	Y	Y	N	Y
Stennis	N	Y	N	Y	?	?	Y	Y
MISSOURI								
Danforth	N	Y	Y	Y	Y	N	N	?
Eagleton	Y	Y	Y	Y	N	Y	Y	N
MONTANA								
Baucus	N	Y	N	Y	Y	Y	Y	N
Melcher	Y	Y	N	Y	N	Y	Y	Y
NEBRASKA								
Exon	Y	Y	N	Y	Y	Y	N	Y
Zorinsky	N	Y	N	Y	Y	Y	N	N
NEVADA								
Hecht	N	Y	N	Y	Y	N	N	Y
Laxalt	N	Y	N	Y	Y	?	N	Y
NEW HAMPSHIRE								
Humphrey	N	N	N	Y	Y	N	N	?
Rudman	N	N	Y	Y	Y	N	N	Y
NEW JERSEY								
Bradley	Y	Y	Y	Y	Y	Y	Y	#
Lautenberg	Y	Y	Y	Y	Y	Y	Y	N
NEW MEXICO								
Domenici	N	Y	N	Y	N	N	N	Y
Bingaman	Y	Y	N	Y	N	Y	N	Y
NEW YORK								
D'Amato	N	Y	Y	Y	Y	N	Y	?
Moynihan	Y	N	Y	Y	Y	Y	Y	?
NORTH CAROLINA								
Broyhill	N	Y	Y	Y	Y	Y	N	Y
Helms	N	Y	N	Y	Y	N	N	Y
NORTH DAKOTA								
Andrews	Y	Y	N	Y	Y	Y	Y	N
Burdick	Y	Y	N	Y	Y	Y	Y	N
OHIO								
Glenn	Y	Y	Y	Y	Y	Y	N	N
Metzenbaum	Y	Y	Y	Y	Y	Y	Y	N
OKLAHOMA								
Nickles	N	Y	N	Y	N	Y	N	Y
Boren	N	Y	N	Y	N	Y	N	Y
OREGON								
Hatfield	Y	N	Y	Y	N	N	Y	Y
Packwood	N	Y	Y	Y	Y	N	?	?
PENNSYLVANIA								
Heinz	N	Y	Y	Y	Y	N	Y	Y
Specter	N	Y	Y	Y	Y	N	Y	N
RHODE ISLAND								
Chafee	N	Y	Y	Y	Y	N	Y	Y
Pell	Y	Y	Y	Y	Y	Y	Y	?
SOUTH CAROLINA								
Thurmond	N	Y	N	Y	Y	Y	N	Y
Hollings	N	Y	N	Y	N	Y	N	Y
SOUTH DAKOTA								
Abdnor	N	Y	Y	Y	Y	Y	N	Y
Pressler	N	Y	Y	Y	Y	Y	N	Y
TENNESSEE								
Gore	N	Y	Y	Y	Y	Y	N	N
Sasser	N	Y	Y	Y	Y	Y	N	N
TEXAS								
Gramm	N	Y	N	Y	Y	N	N	Y
Bentsen	N	Y	N	Y	N	Y	N	Y
UTAH								
Garn	N	Y	N	Y	Y	N	N	?
Hatch	N	Y	N	Y	Y	N	N	Y
VERMONT								
Stafford	Y	Y	Y	Y	Y	N	Y	Y
Leahy	N	Y	Y	Y	Y	Y	Y	N
VIRGINIA								
Trible	N	Y	N	Y	Y	Y	N	?
Warner	N	Y	N	Y	Y	Y	?	Y
WASHINGTON								
Evans	N	Y	N	Y	Y	N	Y	?
Gorton	N	Y	N	Y	Y	N	Y	Y
WEST VIRGINIA								
Byrd	Y	Y	Y	Y	Y	Y	N	N
Rockefeller	N	N	Y	Y	Y	Y	N	N
WISCONSIN								
Kasten	N	Y	Y	Y	Y	Y	N	Y
Proxmire	N	Y	Y	Y	Y	N	Y	Y
WYOMING								
Simpson	?	?	-	?	?	?	?	?
Wallop	N	Y	N	Y	Y	N	N	Y

ND - Northern Democrats SD - Southern Democrats (Southern states - Ala., Ark., Fla., Ga., Ky., La., Miss., N.C., Okla., S.C., Tenn., Texas, Va.)

168. H J Res 668. Public Debt Limit/Anti-Deficit Law. Hart, D-Colo., amendment to the Finance Committee amendment, to repeal the 1985 Balanced Budget and Emergency Deficit Control Act (the Gramm-Rudman-Hollings anti-deficit law, PL 99-177). Rejected 30-69: R 9-43; D 21-26 (ND 20-13, SD 1-13), July 31, 1986. (The Finance Committee amendment would prevent disinvestment of the Social Security trust funds.)

169. H J Res 668. Public Debt Limit/Deficiency Payments to Farmers. Exon, D-Neb., amendment to the Finance Committee amendment *(see vote 168, above)*, to require the Agriculture Department to advance to wheat, corn, cotton and rice farmers a portion of anticipated deficiency payments (the difference between market prices and legislated target prices) on their 1987 crops. Adopted 91-7: R 47-5; D 44-2 (ND 31-2, SD 13-0), July 31, 1986.

170. H J Res 668. Public Debt Limit/Windfall Profits Tax. Heinz, R-Pa., motion to table (kill) the Nickles, R-Okla., amendment to the Finance Committee amendment *(see vote 168, above)*, to repeal the windfall profits tax on domestic crude oil. Motion rejected 47-51: R 20-31; D 27-20 (ND 24-9, SD 3-11), July 31, 1986. (The Nickles amendment later was adopted by voice vote.)

171. H J Res 668. Public Debt Limit/Money Laundering. D'Amato, R-N.Y., amendment to the Finance Committee amendment *(see vote 168, above)*, to increase penalties for and to stiffen rules regarding monetary transactions designed to disguise profits from illegal activities (known as "money laundering"). Adopted 98-0: R 51-0; D 47-0 (ND 33-0, SD 14-0), July 31, 1986.

172. H J Res 668. Public Debt Limit/Oil Import Tariff. Heinz, R-Pa., motion to table (kill) the Hart, D-Colo., amendment to the Finance Committee amendment *(see vote 168, above)*, to increase the existing tariff on crude oil and refined petroleum products by $10 a barrel. Motion agreed to 82-15: R 47-4; D 35-11 (ND 27-6, SD 8-5), July 31, 1986.

173. H J Res 668. Public Debt Limit/Aid to Drought-Stricken Farmers. Sasser, D-Tenn., motion to waive the new-spending-authority limitation contained in the 1985 Balanced Budget and Emergency Deficit Control Act (the Gramm-Rudman-Hollings anti-deficit law, PL 99-177) with respect to the Sasser amendment to the Finance Committee amendment *(see vote 168, above)*. The Sasser amendment would provide emergency aid to drought-stricken farmers in the form of surplus, government-owned commodities; delay scheduled milk price support reductions in drought areas; allow federal cost-sharing of soil-erosion countermeasures in drought areas; and express the sense of Congress that government and private lenders should be lenient in collecting debts from and foreclosing on drought-stricken farmers. Motion agreed to 55-40: R 12-37; D 43-3 (ND 31-2, SD 12-1), in the session that began July 31, 1986. (The Sasser amendment was adopted Aug. 1 by voice vote.)

174. H J Res 668. Public Debt Limit/D.C. AIDS-Insurance Law. Mathias, R-Md., motion to table (kill) the Helms, R-N.C., amendment to the Finance Committee amendment *(see vote 168, above)*, to disapprove the District of Columbia law banning discrimination by insurance companies against persons testing positive for the virus causing acquired immune deficiency syndrome (AIDS). Motion rejected 41-53: R 14-34; D 27-19 (ND 22-10, SD 5-9), Aug. 1, 1986. (The Helms amendment subsequently was adopted by voice vote.)

175. H J Res 668. Public Debt Limit/Social Security. Heinz, R-Pa., motion to table (kill) the Bumpers, D-Ark., amendment to the Finance Committee amendment *(see vote 168, above)*, to exempt administrative expenses of the Social Security system from the across-the-board spending cuts required under the 1985 Balanced Budget and Emergency Deficit Control Act (the Gramm-Rudman-Hollings anti-deficit law, PL 99-177). Motion agreed to 45-36: R 34-5; D 11-31 (ND 5-23, SD 6-8), Aug. 1, 1986.

Corresponding to Congressional Record Votes 176, 177, 178, 179, 180, 181

	176	177	178	179	180	181
ALABAMA						
Denton	Y	N	Y	Y	Y	N
Heflin	Y	N	Y	Y	Y	N
ALASKA						
Murkowski	Y	N	Y	Y	Y	N
Stevens	Y	N	Y	N	?	N
ARIZONA						
Goldwater	Y	N	Y	Y	Y	Y
DeConcini	N	Y	Y	Y	Y	N
ARKANSAS						
Bumpers	N	Y	Y	Y	N	Y
Pryor	N	Y	Y	Y	N	Y
CALIFORNIA						
Wilson	Y	N	Y	Y	Y	N
Cranston	N	Y	Y	Y	N	Y
COLORADO						
Armstrong	Y	N	Y	N	Y	N
Hart	N	Y	Y	N	N	Y
CONNECTICUT						
Weicker	N	Y	Y	Y	Y	N
Dodd	N	Y	Y	Y	N	N
DELAWARE						
Roth	Y	N	Y	N	Y	N
Biden	N	Y	Y	Y	N	N
FLORIDA						
Hawkins	+	-	Y	Y	Y	N
Chiles	N	Y	Y	Y	N	N
GEORGIA						
Mattingly	Y	N	Y	Y	Y	N
Nunn	Y	N	Y	Y	N	Y
HAWAII						
Inouye	N	Y	Y	Y	N	Y
Matsunaga	N	Y	Y	N	N	Y
IDAHO						
McClure	Y	N	Y	Y	Y	N
Symms	Y	N	Y	Y	Y	N
ILLINOIS						
Dixon	N	Y	Y	Y	N	Y
Simon	N	Y	Y	N	N	Y
INDIANA						
Lugar	Y	N	N	N	Y	N
Quayle	Y	N	Y	N	Y	N
IOWA						
Grassley	N	Y	Y	Y	Y	Y
Harkin	N	Y	Y	N	N	Y
KANSAS						
Dole	Y	N	Y	Y	Y	N
Kassebaum	N	Y	Y	N	Y	Y
KENTUCKY						
McConnell	Y	N	Y	Y	Y	N
Ford	N	Y	Y	Y	N	N
LOUISIANA						
Johnston	N	Y	Y	Y	N	N
Long	N	Y	Y	Y	N	N
MAINE						
Cohen	Y	N	Y	Y	Y	N
Mitchell	N	Y	Y	Y	N	N
MARYLAND						
Mathias	N	Y	Y	N	N	N
Sarbanes	N	Y	Y	N	N	N
MASSACHUSETTS						
Kennedy	N	Y	Y	N	N	Y
Kerry	N	Y	Y	Y	N	Y
MICHIGAN						
Levin	N	Y	Y	N	N	Y
Riegle	N	Y	Y	N	N	Y
MINNESOTA						
Boschwitz	Y	N	Y	Y	Y	N
Durenberger	Y	N	Y	N	Y	Y
MISSISSIPPI						
Cochran	Y	N	Y	Y	Y	N
Stennis	Y	N	Y	Y	Y	N
MISSOURI						
Danforth	Y	N	Y	N	Y	N
Eagleton	N	Y	Y	N	N	Y
MONTANA						
Baucus	N	Y	Y	N	N	N
Melcher	N	Y	Y	Y	N	Y
NEBRASKA						
Exon	Y	Y	Y	Y	N	Y
Zorinsky	Y	N	Y	Y	Y	N
NEVADA						
Hecht	Y	N	Y	Y	Y	N
Laxalt	Y	N	?	Y	Y	?
NEW HAMPSHIRE						
Humphrey	Y	N	Y	N	Y	N
Rudman	Y	N	Y	Y	Y	N
NEW JERSEY						
Bradley	N	Y	Y	N	N	N
Lautenberg	N	Y	Y	N	N	N
NEW MEXICO						
Domenici	Y	N	Y	Y	Y	Y
Bingaman	Y	N	Y	N	N	Y
NEW YORK						
D'Amato	Y	N	Y	N	Y	N
Moynihan	N	Y	Y	Y	N	N
NORTH CAROLINA						
Broyhill	Y	N	Y	Y	Y	N
Helms	Y	N	Y	Y	Y	N
NORTH DAKOTA						
Andrews	N	Y	Y	Y	N	Y
Burdick	N	Y	Y	N	N	Y
OHIO						
Glenn	Y	N	Y	N	N	Y
Metzenbaum	N	Y	Y	N	N	Y
OKLAHOMA						
Nickles	Y	N	Y	Y	Y	N
Boren	N	Y	Y	N	N	N
OREGON						
Hatfield	N	Y	Y	N	N	N
Packwood	N	N	Y	N	Y	N
PENNSYLVANIA						
Heinz	Y	N	Y	N	Y	N
Specter	N	Y	Y	Y	N	N
RHODE ISLAND						
Chafee	N	Y	Y	N	Y	N
Pell	N	Y	Y	N	Y	N
SOUTH CAROLINA						
Thurmond	Y	N	Y	Y	Y	N
Hollings	Y	N	Y	Y	N	N
SOUTH DAKOTA						
Abdnor	Y	N	Y	Y	Y	Y
Pressler	Y	N	Y	Y	Y	N
TENNESSEE						
Gore	N	Y	Y	N	N	Y
Sasser	N	Y	Y	Y	N	N
TEXAS						
Gramm	Y	N	Y	Y	Y	N
Bentsen	N	Y	Y	Y	N	N
UTAH						
Garn	Y	N	Y	N	Y	N
Hatch	Y	N	Y	N	Y	N
VERMONT						
Stafford	N	Y	Y	N	Y	N
Leahy	N	Y	Y	N	N	Y
VIRGINIA						
Trible	Y	N	?	Y	Y	Y
Warner	Y	N	Y	Y	Y	N
WASHINGTON						
Evans	N	Y	Y	N	Y	N
Gorton	Y	N	Y	N	Y	N
WEST VIRGINIA						
Byrd	Y	N	Y	Y	N	Y
Rockefeller	N	Y	Y	N	N	Y
WISCONSIN						
Kasten	Y	N	Y	Y	Y	N
Proxmire	N	Y	Y	N	N	Y
WYOMING						
Simpson	Y	N	Y	N	Y	N
Wallop	Y	N	Y	Y	Y	N

KEY

- Y Voted for (yea).
- # Paired for.
- \+ Announced for.
- N Voted against (nay).
- X Paired against.
- \- Announced against.
- P Voted "present."
- C Voted "present" to avoid possible conflict of interest.
- ? Did not vote or otherwise make a position known.

Democrats ***Republicans***

ND - Northern Democrats SD - Southern Democrats (Southern states - Ala., Ark., Fla., Ga., Ky., La., Miss., N.C., Okla., S.C., Tenn., Texas, Va.)

176. S 2638. Defense Authorization, Fiscal 1987. Warner, R-Va., motion to table (kill) the Johnston, D-La., amendment to provide a limit of $3.24 billion for research and development on the strategic defense initiative, or "star wars" program. President Reagan had requested $5.3 billion. Motion agreed to 50-49: R 41-11; D 9-38 (ND 5-28, SD 4-10), Aug. 5, 1986. A "yea" was a vote supporting the president's position.

177. S 2638. Defense Authorization, Fiscal 1987. Exon, D-Neb., amendment to provide a limit of $3.56 billion for research and development on the strategic defense initiative, or "star wars" program. President Reagan had requested $5.3 billion. Rejected 49-50: R 10-42; D 39-8 (ND 29-4, SD 10-4), Aug. 5, 1986. A "nay" was a vote supporting the president's position.

178. S 2638. Defense Authorization, Fiscal 1987. Byrd, D-W.Va., amendment to require the Joint Chiefs of Staff to submit to Congress by Nov. 1, 1986, reports on the possible military impact of Soviet responses to President Reagan's decision to exceed certain limits of the SALT II arms control treaty. Adopted 97-1: R 50-1; D 47-0 (ND 33-0, SD 14-0), Aug. 6, 1986.

179. S 2638. Defense Authorization, Fiscal 1987. Ford, D-Ky., motion to table (kill) the Bingaman, D-N.M., amendment to require that tobacco products at military commissaries, exchanges and ships stores be sold at prevailing market prices. Motion agreed to 57-43: R 32-21; D 25-22 (ND 13-20, SD 12-2), Aug. 6, 1986.

180. S 2638. Defense Authorization, Fiscal 1987. Rudman, R-N.H., motion to invoke cloture (thus limiting debate) on the bill authorizing appropriations in fiscal 1987 for the Defense Department. Motion rejected 53-46: R 48-4; D 5-42 (ND 3-30, SD 2-12), Aug. 6, 1986. A three-fifths majority (60) of the total Senate is required to invoke cloture.

181. S 2638. Defense Authorization, Fiscal 1987. Bingaman, D-N.M., amendment to delete from the bill $141.6 million to build new naval "homeports" at Staten Island, N.Y., and Everett, Wash. Rejected 34-65: R 8-44; D 26-21 (ND 22-11, SD 4-10), Aug. 6, 1986. A "nay" was a vote supporting the president's position.

CQ Senate Votes 182 - 189

Corresponding to Congressional Record Votes 182, 183, 184, 185, 186, 187, 188, 189

KEY

- Y Voted for (yea).
- # Paired for.
- + Announced for.
- N Voted against (nay).
- X Paired against.
- \- Announced against.
- P Voted "present."
- C Voted "present" to avoid possible conflict of interest.
- ? Did not vote or otherwise make a position known.

Democrats *Republicans*

	182	183	184	185	186	187	188	189
ALABAMA								
Denton	N	Y	N	N	Y	N	Y	N
Heflin	N	Y	N	N	N	N	Y	N
ALASKA								
Murkowski	N	Y	N	N	Y	Y	N	Y
Stevens	N	Y	N	N	Y	N	Y	N
ARIZONA								
Goldwater	N	Y	N	N	Y	Y	N	N
DeConcini	N	N	Y	Y	N	Y	N	Y
ARKANSAS								
Bumpers	N	N	Y	N	N	N	Y	Y
Pryor	Y	N	Y	Y	N	N	Y	Y
CALIFORNIA								
Wilson	N	Y	N	N	N	N	Y	N
Cranston	Y	N	Y	Y	N	N	Y	Y
COLORADO								
Armstrong	N	Y	N	N	Y	N	Y	N
Hart	Y	N	Y	Y	N	N	Y	Y
CONNECTICUT								
Weicker	Y	N	Y	Y	Y	N	Y	Y
Dodd	Y	N	Y	N	Y	N	Y	Y
DELAWARE								
Roth	N	Y	N	N	N	Y	N	Y
Biden	Y	N	Y	Y	N	Y	N	Y
FLORIDA								
Hawkins	N	Y	N	N	N	N	Y	N
Chiles	N	Y	N	N	N	?	?	Y
GEORGIA								
Mattingly	N	Y	N	N	Y	N	Y	N
Nunn	N	Y	N	N	Y	Y	N	Y
HAWAII								
Inouye	Y	N	Y	Y	N	N	Y	Y
Matsunaga	Y	N	Y	Y	N	N	Y	Y
IDAHO								
McClure	N	Y	N	N	Y	N	Y	N
Symms	N	Y	N	N	Y	N	Y	N
ILLINOIS								
Dixon	N	N	Y	N	N	N	Y	Y
Simon	Y	N	Y	Y	N	Y	N	Y
INDIANA								
Lugar	N	Y	N	N	Y	Y	N	N
Quayle	N	Y	N	N	Y	Y	N	N
IOWA								
Grassley	Y	N	Y	N	N	N	Y	Y
Harkin	Y	N	Y	Y	Y	N	Y	Y
KANSAS								
Dole	N	Y	N	N	Y	N	Y	N
Kassebaum	Y	N	Y	Y	Y	N	Y	Y
KENTUCKY								
McConnell	N	Y	N	N	N	Y	N	N
Ford	Y	N	Y	Y	N	N	Y	Y
LOUISIANA								
Johnston	N	N	Y	Y	N	N	Y	Y
Long	N	Y	N	N	Y	N	Y	N
MAINE								
Cohen	N	Y	N	N	Y	Y	N	Y
Mitchell	Y	N	Y	Y	N	Y	N	Y
MARYLAND								
Mathias	Y	N	Y	Y	N	N	Y	Y
Sarbanes	Y	N	Y	Y	N	N	Y	Y
MASSACHUSETTS								
Kennedy	Y	N	Y	Y	N	Y	N	Y
Kerry	Y	N	Y	Y	N	N	Y	Y
MICHIGAN								
Levin	Y	N	Y	N	N	Y	N	Y
Riegle	Y	N	Y	Y	N	N	Y	Y
MINNESOTA								
Boschwitz	N	Y	N	N	Y	N	Y	N
Durenberger	Y	N	Y	N	Y	Y	N	Y
MISSISSIPPI								
Cochran	N	Y	N	N	Y	N	N	N
Stennis	N	?	N	N	Y	Y	N	?
MISSOURI								
Danforth	Y	N	Y	N	Y	N	Y	Y
Eagleton	Y	N	Y	Y	Y	N	?	Y
MONTANA								
Baucus	Y	N	Y	N	Y	Y	N	Y
Melcher	Y	N	Y	Y	N	Y	N	Y
NEBRASKA								
Exon	N	Y	N	N	Y	Y	N	Y
Zorinsky	N	Y	N	N	Y	N	Y	N
NEVADA								
Hecht	N	Y	N	N	Y	Y	N	N
Laxalt	N	Y	N	N	Y	N	Y	N
NEW HAMPSHIRE								
Humphrey	N	Y	N	N	N	Y	N	N
Rudman	N	Y	N	N	Y	N	Y	N
NEW JERSEY								
Bradley	Y	N	Y	Y	N	Y	N	Y
Lautenberg	Y	N	Y	Y	N	N	Y	Y
NEW MEXICO								
Domenici	N	Y	N	N	Y	N	Y	N
Bingaman	N	Y	N	Y	N	N	Y	Y
NEW YORK								
D'Amato	N	Y	N	Y	N	N	Y	Y
Moynihan	Y	N	Y	N	N	Y	N	Y
NORTH CAROLINA								
Broyhill	N	Y	N	N	Y	Y	N	N
Helms	N	Y	N	N	Y	N	Y	N
NORTH DAKOTA								
Andrews	Y	N	Y	N	Y	Y	N	Y
Burdick	Y	N	Y	Y	Y	Y	N	Y
OHIO								
Glenn	N	Y	N	N	Y	N	Y	Y
Metzenbaum	Y	N	Y	Y	N	N	Y	Y
OKLAHOMA								
Nickles	N	Y	N	N	N	N	N	N
Boren	N	Y	N	N	N	Y	N	Y
OREGON								
Hatfield	Y	N	Y	Y	Y	N	Y	Y
Packwood	Y	N	Y	Y	N	N	Y	Y
PENNSYLVANIA								
Heinz	Y	N	Y	N	N	N	Y	Y
Specter	Y	N	Y	Y	N	Y	N	Y
RHODE ISLAND								
Chafee	Y	Y	N	Y	Y	N	Y	Y
Pell	Y	N	Y	Y	N	N	Y	Y
SOUTH CAROLINA								
Thurmond	N	Y	N	N	Y	Y	N	N
Hollings	N	Y	N	Y	Y	N	Y	Y
SOUTH DAKOTA								
Abdnor	N	Y	N	N	Y	Y	N	N
Pressler	N	Y	N	N	N	?	Y	N
TENNESSEE								
Gore	N	N	Y	Y	N	Y	N	Y
Sasser	Y	N	Y	Y	N	N	Y	Y
TEXAS								
Gramm	N	Y	N	N	Y	N	Y	N
Bentsen	N	N	Y	N	N	N	Y	Y
UTAH								
Garn	N	Y	N	N	Y	N	Y	N
Hatch	N	Y	N	N	N	N	Y	N
VERMONT								
Stafford	Y	N	Y	N	Y	Y	N	Y
Leahy	Y	N	Y	Y	N	Y	N	Y
VIRGINIA								
Trible	N	Y	N	N	Y	N	Y	Y
Warner	N	Y	N	N	Y	Y	N	N
WASHINGTON								
Evans	Y	N	Y	N	Y	N	Y	N
Gorton	N	N	Y	N	Y	N	Y	Y
WEST VIRGINIA								
Byrd	Y	N	Y	N	N	N	N	Y
Rockefeller	N	N	Y	N	Y	N	Y	Y
WISCONSIN								
Kasten	N	Y	N	N	N	N	Y	Y
Proxmire	Y	N	Y	Y	N	Y	N	Y
WYOMING								
Simpson	N	Y	N	N	Y	Y	N	Y
Wallop	N	Y	N	N	Y	Y	N	N
VICE PRESIDENT								
Bush			N					

ND - Northern Democrats SD - Southern Democrats (Southern states - Ala., Ark., Fla., Ga., Ky., La., Miss., N.C., Okla., S.C., Tenn., Texas, Va.)

182. S 2638. Defense Authorization, Fiscal 1987. Hatfield, R-Ore., amendment to prohibit procurement or assembly of "binary" chemical munitions until Congress gives its approval. Rejected 43-57: R 14-39; D 29-18 (ND 26-7, SD 3-11), Aug. 7, 1986. A "nay" was a vote supporting the president's position.

183. S 2638. Defense Authorization, Fiscal 1987. Cohen, R-Maine, motion to table (kill) the Pryor, D-Ark., amendment to delete funds for production of the "Bigeye" chemical bomb. Motion rejected 49-50: R 39-14; D 10-36 (ND 4-29, SD 6-7), Aug. 7, 1986. (The Pryor amendment subsequently was rejected *(see vote 184, below).*) A "yea" was a vote supporting the president's position.

184. S 2638. Defense Authorization, Fiscal 1987. Pryor, D-Ark., amendment to delete funds for production of the "Bigeye" chemical bomb. Rejected 50-51: R 14-39; D 36-11 (ND 29-4, SD 7-7), with Vice President George Bush casting a "nay" vote, Aug. 7, 1986. A "nay" was a vote supporting the president's position.

185. S 2638. Defense Authorization, Fiscal 1987. DeConcini, D-Ariz., amendment to prohibit the sale or transfer of "Stinger" portable anti-aircraft missiles to U.S.-backed guerrilla movements in foreign countries unless strict security measures were taken to guard the missiles. Rejected 37-63: R 8-45; D 29-18 (ND 23-10, SD 6-8), Aug. 7, 1986.

186. S 2638. Defense Authorization, Fiscal 1987. Warner, R-Va., motion to table (kill) the Lautenberg, D-N.J., amendment to allow military personnel to wear religious apparel under certain conditions. Motion agreed to 51-49: R 38-15; D 13-34 (ND 9-24, SD 4-10), Aug. 7, 1986.

187. S 2638. Defense Authorization, Fiscal 1987. Warner, R-Va., motion to table (kill) the Danforth, R-Mo., amendment to require the Defense Department to pay the National Aeronautics and Space Administration $556.3 million, in accordance with an agreement between the two agencies, for military payloads on space missions. Motion rejected 37-61: R 19-33; D 18-28 (ND 14-19, SD 4-9), Aug. 7, 1986. (The Danforth amendment subsequently was adopted *(see vote 188, below).*)

188. S 2638. Defense Authorization, Fiscal 1987. Danforth, R-Mo., amendment to require the Defense Department to pay the National Aeronautics and Space Administration $556.3 million, in accordance with an agreement between the two agencies, for military payloads on space missions. Adopted 58-40: R 32-21; D 26-19 (ND 17-15, SD 9-4), Aug. 7, 1986.

189. S 2638. Defense Authorization, Fiscal 1987. Mathias, R-Md., perfecting amendment to the Kennedy, D-Mass., amendment, to call on President Reagan to submit to the Senate two nuclear test ban treaties — the Peaceful Nuclear Explosions Treaty and the Threshold Test Ban Treaty — and to propose an immediate resumption of negotiations with the Soviet Union toward a comprehensive nuclear test ban treaty. Adopted 64-35: R 21-32; D 43-3 (ND 32-1, SD 11-2), Aug. 7, 1986. (The Kennedy amendment later was adopted by voice vote. It expressed the sense of Congress that the president should seek Senate approval of those two treaties and resume negotiations with the Soviet Union seeking a ban on all nuclear explosions.) A "nay" was a vote supporting the president's position.

CQ Senate Votes 190 - 197

Corresponding to Congressional Record Votes 190, 191, 192, 193, 194, 195, 196, 197

	190	191	192	193	194	195	196	197
ALABAMA								
Denton	Y	Y	Y	N	N	Y	Y	Y
Heflin	Y	Y	Y	Y	Y	N	Y	Y
ALASKA								
Murkowski	Y	Y	Y	Y	Y	N	Y	N
Stevens	Y	N	Y	Y	Y	N	Y	N
ARIZONA								
Goldwater	Y	Y	Y	N	N	Y	Y	Y
DeConcini	N	Y	Y	Y	X	N	Y	N
ARKANSAS								
Bumpers	N	N	N	Y	N	N	N	N
Pryor	N	N	N	Y	N	Y	N	Y
CALIFORNIA								
Wilson	Y	Y	Y	N	N	Y	Y	Y
Cranston	N	N	N	Y	Y	N	N	Y
COLORADO								
Armstrong	Y	Y	Y	N	N	Y	Y	Y
Hart	N	N	N	Y	Y	Y	N	N
CONNECTICUT								
Weicker	N	N	N	?	?	?	?	?
Dodd	N	Y	N	Y	Y	Y	N	Y
DELAWARE								
Roth	Y	N	Y	N	N	N	Y	Y
Biden	N	N	N	Y	Y	N	N	Y
FLORIDA								
Hawkins	Y	Y	Y	N	N	N	Y	Y
Chiles	N	N	Y	Y	N	Y	Y	Y
GEORGIA								
Mattingly	Y	Y	Y	N	N	Y	Y	Y
Nunn	N	Y	Y	Y	N	Y	Y	Y
HAWAII								
Inouye	N	N	N	Y	Y	N	N	Y
Matsunaga	N	N	N	Y	Y	Y	N	Y
IDAHO								
McClure	Y	Y	Y	N	N	Y	Y	N
Symms	Y	Y	Y	N	N	Y	Y	N
ILLINOIS								
Dixon	N	Y	Y	Y	Y	N	Y	Y
Simon	N	N	N	Y	Y	N	N	Y
INDIANA								
Lugar	Y	Y	Y	N	N	Y	Y	Y
Quayle	Y	Y	Y	N	N	Y	Y	N
IOWA								
Grassley	Y	N	Y	N	N	N	Y	Y
Harkin	N	N	N	Y	Y	N	N	Y
KANSAS								
Dole	Y	N	Y	N	N	Y	Y	Y
Kassebaum	Y	N	N	N	N	N	Y	Y
KENTUCKY								
McConnell	Y	Y	Y	N	N	Y	Y	Y
Ford	N	N	N	Y	Y	N	Y	Y
LOUISIANA								
Johnston	N	Y	N	Y	Y	Y	N	Y
Long	Y	N	Y	Y	Y	Y	Y	Y
MAINE								
Cohen	N	Y	Y	N	N	N	Y	Y
Mitchell	N	N	N	Y	Y	N	N	Y
MARYLAND								
Mathias	N	N	N	Y	Y	N	?	?
Sarbanes	N	N	N	Y	Y	N	N	Y
MASSACHUSETTS								
Kennedy	N	N	N	Y	Y	Y	N	Y
Kerry	N	N	N	Y	Y	Y	N	Y
MICHIGAN								
Levin	N	Y	N	Y	Y	N	N	Y
Riegle	N	N	N	Y	Y	N	N	Y
MINNESOTA								
Boschwitz	Y	Y	Y	Y	N	Y	Y	Y
Durenberger	N	N	Y	Y	Y	N	Y	Y
MISSISSIPPI								
Cochran	Y	Y	Y	N	N	N	Y	Y
Stennis	?	Y	Y	Y	N	Y	Y	Y
MISSOURI								
Danforth	N	Y	Y	Y	Y	Y	Y	Y
Eagleton	N	N	?	?	?	?	?	?
MONTANA								
Baucus	N	Y	N	Y	Y	Y	N	N
Melcher	N	N	N	Y	Y	N	N	N
NEBRASKA								
Exon	N	Y	Y	Y	N	Y	Y	N
Zorinsky	Y	Y	Y	X	N	N	Y	Y
NEVADA								
Hecht	Y	Y	Y	N	N	Y	Y	N
Laxalt	Y	Y	Y	N	N	N	Y	N
NEW HAMPSHIRE								
Humphrey	Y	Y	Y	N	N	Y	Y	Y
Rudman	Y	N	Y	N	N	Y	Y	Y
NEW JERSEY								
Bradley	N	N	N	#	#	?	?	?
Lautenberg	N	N	N	Y	Y	N	N	Y
NEW MEXICO								
Domenici	Y	Y	Y	Y	N	Y	Y	N
Bingaman	N	Y	N	Y	Y	Y	Y	N
NEW YORK								
D'Amato	Y	Y	Y	Y	Y	N	Y	Y
Moynihan	N	Y	N	Y	Y	Y	N	Y
NORTH CAROLINA								
Broyhill	Y	Y	Y	N	N	Y	Y	Y
Helms	Y	N	Y	N	N	Y	Y	N
NORTH DAKOTA								
Andrews	N	N	N	Y	Y	N	Y	N
Burdick	N	Y	N	Y	Y	N	N	N
OHIO								
Glenn	N	N	Y	Y	Y	N	Y	Y
Metzenbaum	N	N	N	Y	Y	N	N	Y
OKLAHOMA								
Nickles	Y	N	Y	N	N	Y	Y	Y
Boren	N	?	Y	Y	N	N	Y	Y
OREGON								
Hatfield	N	N	N	Y	N	N	N	Y
Packwood	N	N	N	Y	Y	N	N	Y
PENNSYLVANIA								
Heinz	N	N	N	Y	Y	Y	Y	Y
Specter	N	Y	N	Y	Y	N	N	Y
RHODE ISLAND								
Chafee	N	Y	N	Y	N	Y	N	Y
Pell	N	N	N	Y	Y	N	N	Y
SOUTH CAROLINA								
Thurmond	Y	Y	Y	N	N	Y	Y	Y
Hollings	N	N	Y	Y	N	N	Y	Y
SOUTH DAKOTA								
Abdnor	Y	Y	Y	N	N	N	Y	N
Pressler	Y	Y	Y	N	N	N	?	?
TENNESSEE								
Gore	N	N	N	Y	Y	N	N	Y
Sasser	N	N	N	Y	Y	N	N	Y
TEXAS								
Gramm	Y	Y	Y	N	N	Y	Y	Y
Bentsen	N	Y	N	Y	N	Y	Y	N
UTAH								
Garn	Y	Y	Y	N	N	N	Y	N
Hatch	Y	Y	Y	N	N	Y	Y	N
VERMONT								
Stafford	N	Y	N	Y	?	?	?	?
Leahy	N	N	N	Y	Y	N	N	Y
VIRGINIA								
Trible	Y	N	Y	N	N	N	Y	Y
Warner	Y	Y	Y	N	N	N	Y	N
WASHINGTON								
Evans	Y	N	?	Y	N	N	Y	Y
Gorton	N	Y	Y	Y	N	Y	Y	Y
WEST VIRGINIA								
Byrd	N	Y	Y	Y	Y	N	Y	N
Rockefeller	N	N	N	Y	Y	N	N	Y
WISCONSIN								
Kasten	N	Y	Y	Y	N	N	Y	Y
Proxmire	N	N	N	Y	Y	N	N	Y
WYOMING								
Simpson	Y	N	Y	N	N	Y	Y	N
Wallop	Y	Y	Y	N	N	Y	Y	Y

KEY

Y Voted for (yea).
\# Paired for.
\+ Announced for.
N Voted against (nay).
X Paired against.
\- Announced against.
P Voted "present."
C Voted "present" to avoid possible conflict of interest.
? Did not vote or otherwise make a position known.

Democrats ***Republicans***

ND - Northern Democrats SD - Southern Democrats (Southern states - Ala., Ark., Fla., Ga., Ky., La., Miss., N.C., Okla., S.C., Tenn., Texas, Va.)

190. S 2638. Defense Authorization, Fiscal 1987. Lugar, R-Ind., substitute for the Kennedy, D-Mass., amendment, to express the sense of Congress that the president should seek Senate approval of the U.S.-Soviet treaties banning both nuclear weapons tests and nuclear explosions for peaceful purposes that are more powerful than 150 kilotons, provided the Soviet Union agrees to improved techniques for verifying compliance with the treaties. Rejected 42-57: R 39-14; D 3-43 (ND 1-32, SD 2-11), Aug. 7, 1986. (The Kennedy amendment subsequently was adopted by voice vote. It expressed the sense of Congress that the president should seek Senate approval of those two treaties and resume negotiations with the Soviet Union seeking a ban on all nuclear explosions.) A "yea" was a vote supporting the president's position.

191. S 2638. Defense Authorization, Fiscal 1987. Quayle, R-Ind., motion to table (kill) the Roth, R-Del., amendment to provide that the Pentagon's director of operational testing report directly to the secretary of defense. Motion agreed to 51-48: R 35-18; D 16-30 (ND 11-22, SD 5-8), Aug. 8, 1986.

192. S 2638. Defense Authorization, Fiscal 1987. Warner, R-Va., motion to table (kill) the Kerry, D-Mass., amendment to bar tests against a target in space of the anti-satellite (ASAT) missile providing the Soviet Union conducts no ASAT tests. Motion agreed to 55-43: R 42-10; D 13-33 (ND 6-26, SD 7-7), Aug. 8, 1986. A "yea" was a vote supporting the president's position.

193. S 2638. Defense Authorization, Fiscal 1987. Division 1 of the Kennedy, D-Mass., amendment, to delete a provision that would raise to $1 million from $2,500 the value of service contracts below which contracting firms are exempt from certain provisions of the Service Contract Act. Adopted 62-34: R 18-34; D 44-0 (ND 30-0, SD 14-0), Aug. 8, 1986.

194. S 2638. Defense Authorization, Fiscal 1987. Division 2 of the Kennedy, D-Mass., amendment, to delete a provision that would raise to $250,000 from $2,000 the value of construction contracts below which contracting firms would be exempt from certain provisions of the Davis-Bacon Act. Rejected 44-51: R 10-41; D 34-10 (ND 28-2, SD 6-8), Aug. 8, 1986.

195. S 2638. Defense Authorization, Fiscal 1987. Quayle, R-Ind., motion to table (kill) the Stevens, R-Alaska, amendment to delete a provision establishing an alternative personnel system for scientists, engineers and acquisition managers in the Defense Department. Motion rejected 44-52: R 28-23; D 16-29 (ND 9-22, SD 7-7), Aug. 8, 1986. (The Stevens amendment subsequently was adopted by voice vote.)

196. S 2638. Defense Authorization, Fiscal 1987. Warner, R-Va., motion to table (kill) the Kerry, D-Mass., amendment to bar tests of any nuclear weapon in connection with the strategic defense initiative, or "star wars." Motion agreed to 61-33: R 45-4; D 16-29 (ND 7-24, SD 9-5), Aug. 8, 1986. A "yea" was a vote supporting the president's position.

197. S 2638. Defense Authorization, Fiscal 1987. Nunn, D-Ga., motion to table (kill) the McClure, R-Idaho, amendment to require that the amount of raw material stored in the strategic material stockpile be established by law. Motion agreed to 69-25: R 34-15; D 35-10 (ND 23-8, SD 12-2), Aug. 8, 1986.

CQ Senate Votes 198 - 205

Corresponding to Congressional Record Votes 198, 199, 200, 201, 202, 203, 204, 205

	198	199	200	201	202	203	204	205
ALABAMA								
Denton	N	N	Y	Y	Y	Y	Y	Y
Heflin	Y	Y	Y	Y	N	Y	Y	Y
ALASKA								
Murkowski	N	N	Y	Y	N	Y	Y	N
Stevens	Y	Y	Y	Y	N	Y	Y	Y
ARIZONA								
Goldwater	N	Y	Y	Y	Y	Y	Y	Y
DeConcini	N	N	Y	Y	N	N	N	Y
ARKANSAS								
Bumpers	Y	N	Y	Y	N	N	Y	Y
Pryor	Y	N	N	Y	N	N	Y	Y
CALIFORNIA								
Wilson	N	Y	Y	Y	Y	Y	N	N
Cranston	Y	N	Y	Y	Y	N	Y	N
COLORADO								
Armstrong	N	Y	Y	Y	N	Y	N	Y
Hart	Y	N	Y	Y	Y	N	Y	Y
CONNECTICUT								
Weicker	?	N	Y	Y	N	Y	Y	N
Dodd	Y	N	Y	Y	N	N	N	Y
DELAWARE								
Roth	N	Y	Y	Y	Y	Y	Y	Y
Biden	Y	N	Y	Y	Y	N	Y	Y
FLORIDA								
Hawkins	N	N	Y	Y	N	Y	Y	Y
Chiles	Y	N	Y	Y	N	N	N	Y
GEORGIA								
Mattingly	N	N	Y	Y	N	Y	Y	Y
Nunn	Y	Y	Y	Y	Y	N	Y	Y
HAWAII								
Inouye	Y	N	N	Y	N	Y	Y	Y
Matsunaga	Y	N	Y	Y	N	N	Y	N
IDAHO								
McClure	N	N	Y	Y	Y	Y	Y	N
Symms	N	N	Y	Y	Y	Y	Y	N
ILLINOIS								
Dixon	Y	N	Y	Y	N	N	Y	N
Simon	Y	N	Y	Y	N	N	Y	Y
INDIANA								
Lugar	N	Y	Y	Y	Y	Y	Y	Y
Quayle	N	Y	Y	Y	Y	Y	N	Y
IOWA								
Grassley	Y	N	Y	Y	Y	Y	Y	Y
Harkin	Y	N	N	Y	Y	N	Y	Y
KANSAS								
Dole	N	Y	Y	Y	Y	Y	Y	N
Kassebaum	Y	Y	Y	Y	N	Y	Y	Y
KENTUCKY								
McConnell	N	Y	Y	Y	N	Y	Y	Y
Ford	Y	N	Y	Y	N	Y	Y	Y
LOUISIANA								
Johnston	Y	N	Y	Y	N	N	Y	Y
Long	Y	N	Y	Y	N	N	Y	Y
MAINE								
Cohen	Y	Y	Y	Y	Y	Y	N	?
Mitchell	Y	N	Y	Y	Y	N	N	Y
MARYLAND								
Mathias	?	Y	Y	Y	N	Y	Y	N
Sarbanes	Y	N	Y	Y	N	N	N	Y
MASSACHUSETTS								
Kennedy	Y	N	Y	Y	Y	N	Y	Y
Kerry	Y	N	Y	Y	Y	N	Y	Y
MICHIGAN								
Levin	Y	N	Y	Y	Y	N	Y	Y
Riegle	Y	N	Y	Y	N	N	N	Y
MINNESOTA								
Boschwitz	Y	Y	Y	Y	N	Y	Y	N
Durenberger	Y	Y	Y	Y	N	N	Y	Y
MISSISSIPPI								
Cochran	Y	Y	Y	Y	N	Y	Y	Y
Stennis	Y	Y	Y	Y	Y	N	Y	Y
MISSOURI								
Danforth	Y	Y	Y	Y	Y	Y	Y	Y
Eagleton	?	?	?	?	?	?	?	?
MONTANA								
Baucus	Y	N	Y	Y	N	N	Y	Y
Melcher	Y	N	N	N	N	Y	Y	Y
NEBRASKA								
Exon	Y	N	Y	Y	Y	Y	Y	Y
Zorinsky	Y	N	Y	Y	N	Y	Y	Y
NEVADA								
Hecht	N	Y	Y	Y	Y	Y	Y	Y
Laxalt	Y	Y	Y	Y	Y	N	Y	?
NEW HAMPSHIRE								
Humphrey	Y	Y	Y	Y	Y	Y	N	Y
Rudman	N	N	Y	Y	Y	Y	N	Y
NEW JERSEY								
Bradley	?	?	?	?	?	?	?	?
Lautenberg	Y	N	Y	Y	Y	Y	Y	Y
NEW MEXICO								
Domenici	N	N	Y	Y	N	N	Y	Y
Bingaman	Y	N	Y	Y	N	N	Y	Y
NEW YORK								
D'Amato	N	N	Y	Y	N	Y	N	Y
Moynihan	Y	N	Y	Y	Y	N	N	Y
NORTH CAROLINA								
Broyhill	Y	N	Y	Y	N	Y	N	Y
Helms	N	N	Y	Y	N	Y	N	Y
NORTH DAKOTA								
Andrews	Y	N	Y	Y	N	Y	Y	Y
Burdick	Y	N	N	N	N	Y	Y	Y
OHIO								
Glenn	Y	N	Y	Y	Y	Y	Y	N
Metzenbaum	Y	N	N	Y	Y	Y	Y	Y
OKLAHOMA								
Nickles	N	N	Y	Y	N	Y	Y	N
Boren	Y	N	Y	Y	N	N	Y	N
OREGON								
Hatfield	Y	N	Y	N	N	?	?	?
Packwood	Y	Y	Y	Y	N	Y	Y	Y
PENNSYLVANIA								
Heinz	Y	N	Y	Y	Y	N	Y	Y
Specter	Y	N	Y	Y	N	Y	N	Y
RHODE ISLAND								
Chafee	Y	Y	Y	Y	N	Y	Y	N
Pell	Y	N	N	Y	N	N	Y	Y
SOUTH CAROLINA								
Thurmond	N	Y	Y	Y	Y	Y	Y	Y
Hollings	Y	N	Y	Y	Y	N	N	Y
SOUTH DAKOTA								
Abdnor	N	N	Y	Y	N	Y	Y	Y
Pressler	?	Y	Y	Y	N	Y	Y	Y
TENNESSEE								
Gore	Y	N	Y	Y	Y	N	N	Y
Sasser	Y	N	Y	Y	Y	N	N	N
TEXAS								
Gramm	N	Y	Y	Y	Y	Y	Y	Y
Bentsen	Y	Y	Y	Y	N	N	Y	N
UTAH								
Garn	Y	N	Y	Y	N	Y	N	Y
Hatch	N	N	Y	Y	N	Y	Y	Y
VERMONT								
Stafford	?	?	?	?	?	?	?	?
Leahy	Y	N	Y	Y	N	N	Y	Y
VIRGINIA								
Trible	N	Y	Y	Y	N	N	Y	Y
Warner	N	Y	Y	Y	N	Y	Y	Y
WASHINGTON								
Evans	Y	Y	Y	Y	N	Y	Y	Y
Gorton	Y	N	Y	Y	Y	Y	Y	N
WEST VIRGINIA								
Byrd	Y	N	Y	Y	Y	N	N	Y
Rockefeller	Y	N	Y	Y	Y	N	Y	Y
WISCONSIN								
Kasten	N	N	Y	Y	N	Y	Y	Y
Proxmire	Y	N	N	N	N	Y	N	Y
WYOMING								
Simpson	N	Y	Y	Y	N	Y	Y	Y
Wallop	N	Y	Y	Y	Y	Y	N	N

KEY

- Y Voted for (yea).
- # Paired for.
- + Announced for.
- N Voted against (nay).
- X Paired against.
- \- Announced against.
- P Voted "present."
- C Voted "present" to avoid possible conflict of interest.
- ? Did not vote or otherwise make a position known.

Democrats ***Republicans***

ND - Northern Democrats SD - Southern Democrats (Southern states - Ala., Ark., Fla., Ga., Ky., La., Miss., N.C., Okla., S.C., Tenn., Texas, Va.)

198. S 2638. Defense Authorization, Fiscal 1987. Cohen, R-Maine, motion to table (kill) the Wilson, R-Calif., amendment to bar the use of funds for full-scale development of a small mobile intercontinental ballistic missile or for deployment of more than 50 MX missiles unless the secretary of defense certifies that that small missile and the MX would be able to survive an enemy attack and that it would cost more for an enemy to nullify them than it would to build them. Motion agreed to 64-30: R 20-29; D 44-1 (ND 30-1, SD 14-0), Aug. 8, 1986.

199. S 2638. Defense Authorization, Fiscal 1987. Warner, R-Va., motion to table (kill) the Glenn, D-Ohio, amendment to bar Defense Department contracts with foreign governments or foreign firms to conduct research associated with the strategic defense initiative, or "star wars," that could be reasonably performed by a U.S. firm. Motion rejected 33-64: R 29-23; D 4-41 (ND 0-31, SD 4-10), Aug. 9, 1986. (The Glenn amendment subsequently was adopted by voice vote.)

200. S 2638. Defense Authorization, Fiscal 1987. Warner, R-Va., motion to table (kill) the Melcher, D-Mont., amendment to reduce the amount authorized by 20 percent of the amount of Pentagon funds from prior appropriations that have not been contractually obligated as of Sept. 30, 1986. Motion agreed to 89-8: R 52-0; D 37-8 (ND 24-7, SD 13-1), Aug. 9, 1986.

201. S 2638. Defense Authorization, Fiscal 1987. Warner, R-Va., motion to table (kill) the Melcher, D-Mont., amendment to reduce the amount authorized for research and development by 15 percent. Motion agreed to 93-4: R 51-1; D 42-3 (ND 28-3, SD 14-0), Aug. 9, 1986.

202. S 2638. Defense Authorization, Fiscal 1987. Goldwater, R-Ariz., motion to table (kill) the Andrews, R-N.D., amendment to delete a provision that would repeal the current law requiring that alcoholic beverages intended for resale on military bases be purchased in the same state. Motion rejected 41-56: R 21-31; D 20-25 (ND 15-16, SD 5-9), Aug. 9, 1986. (The Andrews amendment subsequently was adopted by voice vote.)

203. S 2638. Defense Authorization, Fiscal 1987. Goldwater, R-Ariz., motion to table (kill) the Simon, D-Ill., amendment to increase from $7.3 million to $18.3 million the amount authorized to pay bonuses to military personnel who are proficient in a foreign language. Motion agreed to 57-39: R 46-5; D 11-34 (ND 9-22, SD 2-12), Aug. 9, 1986.

204. S 2638. Defense Authorization, Fiscal 1987. Dole, R-Kan., motion to table (kill) the Moynihan, D-N.Y., amendment to bar the subsidized sale of any goods or services to any communist government. Motion agreed to 72-24: R 39-12; D 33-12 (ND 23-8, SD 10-4), Aug. 9, 1986.

205. S 2638. Defense Authorization, Fiscal 1987. Goldwater, R-Ariz., motion to table (kill) the Glenn, D-Ohio, amendment to the Byrd, D-W.Va., amendment, to bar the use of any funds authorized by the bill to assemble more than 100 B-1 bombers and to require the Defense Science Board to study what types of bombers should be purchased. Motion agreed to 75-19: R 37-12; D 38-7 (ND 27-4, SD 11-3), Aug. 9, 1986. (The Byrd amendment, to bar the use of any funds authorized for expenditures related to any B-1s more than the 100 previously authorized, subsequently was adopted by voice vote.)

	206	207	208	209	210	211	212	213
ALABAMA								
Denton	Y	Y	N	N	Y	Y	Y	Y
Heflin	N	Y	Y	Y	N	Y	Y	Y
ALASKA								
Murkowski	Y	Y	Y	Y	Y	Y	Y	Y
Stevens	Y	Y	Y	N	Y	Y	Y	Y
ARIZONA								
Goldwater	Y	Y	?	Y	Y	Y	Y	Y
DeConcini	N	Y	N	Y	N	N	N	N
ARKANSAS								
Bumpers	N	Y	N	Y	Y	N	Y	N
Pryor	N	?	?	Y	N	N	N	N
CALIFORNIA								
Wilson	Y	Y	Y	Y	Y	Y	Y	Y
Cranston	N	Y	N	N	N	N	N	N
COLORADO								
Armstrong	Y	Y	N	N	Y	Y	Y	Y
Hart	Y	Y	N	Y	Y	N	N	N
CONNECTICUT								
Weicker	Y	?	?	N	Y	N	N	N
Dodd	Y	Y	Y	Y	N	N	N	N
DELAWARE								
Roth	Y	Y	Y	N	N	Y	Y	Y
Biden	N	Y	Y	+	N	N	N	N
FLORIDA								
Hawkins	Y	Y	Y	Y	Y	Y	Y	Y
Chiles	N	Y	Y	Y	N	Y	Y	N
GEORGIA								
Mattingly	Y	Y	N	Y	Y	Y	Y	Y
Nunn	N	Y	N	Y	N	Y	Y	N
HAWAII								
Inouye	N	Y	Y	Y	N	N	N	N
Matsunaga	N	Y	Y	Y	N	N	N	N
IDAHO								
McClure	Y	Y	N	N	Y	Y	Y	Y
Symms	Y	Y	N	N	Y	Y	Y	Y
ILLINOIS								
Dixon	N	Y	N	Y	Y	Y	Y	N
Simon	N	Y	Y	Y	N	N	N	N
INDIANA								
Lugar	Y	Y	Y	N	Y	Y	Y	Y
Quayle	Y	Y	Y	N	Y	Y	Y	Y
IOWA								
Grassley	Y	Y	N	Y	Y	Y	Y	Y
Harkin	N	N	N	Y	N	N	N	N
KANSAS								
Dole	Y	Y	Y	N	Y	Y	Y	Y
Kassebaum	Y	Y	?	Y	Y	Y	Y	Y
KENTUCKY								
McConnell	Y	Y	Y	N	Y	Y	Y	Y
Ford	N	Y	N	Y	N	N	N	N
LOUISIANA								
Johnston	N	?	?	Y	N	Y	Y	Y
Long	N	Y	Y	N	N	Y	Y	Y
MAINE								
Cohen	?	?	?	Y	Y	Y	Y	Y
Mitchell	N	Y	N	Y	N	N	N	N
MARYLAND								
Mathias	Y	Y	Y	Y	Y	N	N	N
Sarbanes	N	Y	N	Y	N	N	N	N
MASSACHUSETTS								
Kennedy	N	Y	Y	Y	N	N	N	N
Kerry	N	Y	N	Y	Y	N	N	N
MICHIGAN								
Levin	N	Y	Y	Y	N	N	N	N
Riegle	N	Y	N	Y	N	N	N	N
MINNESOTA								
Boschwitz	Y	Y	Y	N	Y	Y	Y	Y
Durenberger	Y	Y	Y	N	Y	N	Y	Y
MISSISSIPPI								
Cochran	Y	Y	Y	N	Y	Y	Y	Y
Stennis	N	Y	Y	Y	N	Y	Y	?
MISSOURI								
Danforth	Y	Y	Y	N	N	Y	Y	Y
Eagleton	?	?	?	Y	N	N	N	N
MONTANA								
Baucus	N	?	?	Y	Y	N	Y	N
Melcher	N	N	N	Y	Y	N	N	N
NEBRASKA								
Exon	N	Y	N	Y	N	N	N	N
Zorinsky	N	Y	N	N	Y	N	Y	N
NEVADA								
Hecht	Y	Y	Y	N	Y	Y	Y	Y
Laxalt	?	?	?	N	Y	Y	Y	Y
NEW HAMPSHIRE								
Humphrey	Y	Y	N	N	Y	Y	Y	Y
Rudman	Y	Y	Y	Y	Y	Y	Y	Y
NEW JERSEY								
Bradley	?	?	?	Y	N	Y	Y	N
Lautenberg	N	Y	N	Y	N	N	N	N
NEW MEXICO								
Domenici	Y	Y	Y	N	Y	Y	Y	Y
Bingaman	N	Y	N	Y	N	N	N	N
NEW YORK								
D'Amato	Y	Y	Y	Y	Y	Y	Y	Y
Moynihan	N	Y	Y	Y	N	N	N	N
NORTH CAROLINA								
Broyhill	Y	Y	N	N	Y	Y	Y	Y
Helms	Y	Y	N	N	Y	Y	Y	Y
NORTH DAKOTA								
Andrews	Y	Y	N	Y	Y	N	N	Y
Burdick	N	Y	N	Y	N	N	N	N
OHIO								
Glenn	N	Y	N	Y	N	N	Y	?
Metzenbaum	N	Y	N	Y	N	N	N	N
OKLAHOMA								
Nickles	Y	Y	Y	Y	Y	Y	Y	Y
Boren	N	Y	Y	Y	N	Y	N	N
OREGON								
Hatfield	?	X	?	Y	Y	N	N	N
Packwood	Y	Y	Y	Y	Y	N	Y	N
PENNSYLVANIA								
Heinz	?	#	+	N	Y	Y	Y	Y
Specter	Y	Y	Y	Y	Y	N	N	N
RHODE ISLAND								
Chafee	Y	Y	Y	Y	Y	N	Y	N
Pell	N	Y	Y	Y	N	N	N	N
SOUTH CAROLINA								
Thurmond	Y	Y	Y	Y	Y	Y	Y	Y
Hollings	N	Y	Y	Y	N	Y	Y	Y
SOUTH DAKOTA								
Abdnor	Y	Y	Y	Y	Y	Y	Y	Y
Pressler	Y	Y	N	Y	Y	Y	Y	Y
TENNESSEE								
Gore	N	Y	Y	Y	N	N	N	N
Sasser	N	Y	Y	Y	N	N	N	N
TEXAS								
Gramm	Y	Y	Y	N	Y	Y	Y	Y
Bentsen	N	Y	Y	Y	N	Y	N	N
UTAH								
Garn	Y	Y	N	N	Y	Y	Y	Y
Hatch	Y	Y	N	N	Y	Y	Y	Y
VERMONT								
Stafford	?	?	?	Y	Y	N	N	Y
Leahy	N	Y	N	Y	N	N	N	N
VIRGINIA								
Trible	Y	Y	N	Y	Y	Y	Y	Y
Warner	Y	Y	N	Y	Y	Y	Y	Y
WASHINGTON								
Evans	Y	Y	Y	N	Y	Y	Y	Y
Gorton	Y	Y	Y	Y	Y	N	Y	Y
WEST VIRGINIA								
Byrd	N	Y	N	Y	N	N	N	N
Rockefeller	N	Y	N	Y	N	N	N	N
WISCONSIN								
Kasten	Y	Y	N	Y	Y	Y	Y	Y
Proxmire	N	N	N	Y	N	N	N	N
WYOMING								
Simpson	Y	Y	Y	Y	Y	Y	Y	Y
Wallop	Y	Y	Y	N	Y	Y	Y	Y

KEY

Y Voted for (yea).
\# Paired for.
\+ Announced for.
N Voted against (nay).
X Paired against.
\- Announced against.
P Voted "present."
C Voted "present" to avoid possible conflict of interest.
? Did not vote or otherwise make a position known.

Democrats *Republicans*

ND - Northern Democrats SD - Southern Democrats (Southern states - Ala., Ark., Fla., Ga., Ky., La., Miss., N.C., Okla., S.C., Tenn., Texas, Va.)

206. S 2638. Defense Authorization, Fiscal 1987. Packwood, R-Ore., motion to table (kill) the Byrd, D-W.Va., amendment to reduce the amount of time within which the president would have to act on petitions filed by U.S. firms requesting that limits be placed on competing imports on national security grounds under the Trade Expansion Act of 1962. Motion agreed to 50-43: R 48-0; D 2-43 (ND 2-29, SD 0-14), Aug. 9, 1986.

207. S 2638. Defense Authorization, Fiscal 1987. Passage of the bill to authorize $219.8 billion for military programs of the Departments of Defense and Energy in fiscal 1987. Passed 86-3: R 47-0; D 39-3 (ND 27-3, SD 12-0), Aug. 9, 1986.

208. H J Res 668. Public Debt Limit. Passage of the joint resolution to raise the ceiling on the federal debt from $2.079 trillion to $2.323 trillion; to prevent future disinvestment of the Social Security trust funds; to restore the automatic spending cuts procedure of the Gramm-Rudman-Hollings anti-deficit act (PL 99-177); to provide assistance to drought-stricken farmers; to create a new federal crime of money laundering — engaging in monetary transactions designed to conceal other criminal activity; and for other purposes. Passed 47-40: R 29-16; D 18-24 (ND 9-21, SD 9-3), Aug. 9, 1986.

209. S 655. Campaign Finance/PAC Spending. Boren, D-Okla., amendment to reduce limits on political action committee (PAC) contributions to congressional campaigns, to increase limits on individual contributions, and to require broadcasters to provide equal time to subjects of negative advertising by PACs. Adopted 69-30: R 26-27; D 43-3 (ND 30-2, SD 13-1), Aug. 12, 1986.

210. S 655. Campaign Finance/PAC Spending. Boschwitz, R-Minn., amendment to prohibit political action committee (PAC) contributions to national political parties, to require disclosure of all "soft money" accepted by national party committees, and to remove equal-time requirements on broadcasters for subjects of negative advertising by PACs. Adopted 58-42: R 51-2; D 7-40 (ND 6-27, SD 1-13), Aug. 12, 1986. (S 655 later was set aside without final action.)

211. HR 5052. Military Construction Appropriations, Fiscal 1987/Aid to Nicaraguan Rebels. Mattingly, R-Ga., motion to table (kill) the Sasser, D-Tenn., amendment to strike titles II and III from the bill. Title II would provide $100 million in military and non-military aid to the Nicaraguan "contra" guerrillas, and $300 million in economic aid to Costa Rica, El Salvador, Guatemala and Honduras. Title III would reimburse the PL 480 "Food for Peace" account for up to $300 million diverted to economic aid for the four Central American countries. Motion agreed to 54-46: R 43-10; D 11-36 (ND 2-31, SD 9-5), Aug. 12, 1986. A "yea" was a vote supporting the president's position.

212. HR 5052. Military Construction Appropriations, Fiscal 1987/Aid to Nicaraguan Rebels. Lugar, R-Ind., motion to table (kill) the Kennedy, D-Mass., amendment to bar the introduction of U.S. troops into Nicaragua unless Congress had approved in advance or the president reported to Congress that such an action was necessary for purposes such as protecting the lives of U.S. citizens. Motion agreed to 60-40: R 47-6; D 13-34 (ND 5-28, SD 8-6), Aug. 12, 1986. A "yea" was a vote supporting the president's position.

213. HR 5052. Military Construction Appropriations, Fiscal 1987/Aid to Nicaraguan Rebels. Lugar, R-Ind., motion to table (kill) the Byrd, D-W.Va., amendment to allow the CIA, the Pentagon and other U.S. agencies to give the Nicaraguan "contras" only aid that had been specifically authorized by Congress. The amendment also would have barred the CIA from using its secret contingency fund to aid the contras unless Congress had approved in advance. Motion agreed to 51-47: R 47-6; D 4-41 (ND 0-32, SD 4-9), Aug. 12, 1986. A "yea" was a vote supporting the president's position.

	214	215	216	217	218	219	220	221
ALABAMA								
Denton	Y	N	N	Y	Y	N	Y	Y
Heflin	Y	N	N	Y	Y	Y	Y	Y
ALASKA								
Murkowski	Y	N	N	Y	Y	Y	Y	Y
Stevens	Y	N	N	Y	Y	Y	Y	Y
ARIZONA								
Goldwater	Y	N	N	Y	Y	Y	Y	Y
DeConcini	N	N	N	N	Y	Y	Y	Y
ARKANSAS								
Bumpers	N	Y	N	N	N	Y	N	N
Pryor	N	N	N	N	N	Y	N	N
CALIFORNIA								
Wilson	Y	N	N	Y	Y	Y	Y	Y
Cranston	N	Y	Y	N	N	Y	N	N
COLORADO								
Armstrong	Y	N	N	Y	Y	N	Y	Y
Hart	N	Y	N	N	N	Y	N	N
CONNECTICUT								
Weicker	N	Y	N	N	Y	Y	Y	N
Dodd	N	Y	N	N	N	Y	N	N
DELAWARE								
Roth	Y	N	N	Y	Y	Y	Y	?
Biden	N	Y	Y	N	N	Y	N	N
FLORIDA								
Hawkins	Y	N	N	Y	Y	Y	Y	Y
Chiles	Y	N	N	N	Y	Y	Y	Y
GEORGIA								
Mattingly	Y	N	N	Y	Y	Y	Y	Y
Nunn	N	N	N	N	Y	Y	Y	Y
HAWAII								
Inouye	N	Y	Y	N	N	Y	N	N
Matsunaga	N	Y	Y	N	N	Y	N	N
IDAHO								
McClure	Y	N	N	Y	Y	N	Y	Y
Symms	Y	N	N	Y	Y	N	Y	Y
ILLINOIS								
Dixon	Y	N	N	N	Y	Y	Y	Y
Simon	N	Y	Y	N	N	Y	N	N
INDIANA								
Lugar	Y	N	N	Y	Y	Y	Y	Y
Quayle	Y	N	N	Y	Y	Y	Y	Y
IOWA								
Grassley	Y	N	N	Y	Y	Y	Y	N
Harkin	N	Y	Y	N	N	Y	N	N
KANSAS								
Dole	Y	N	N	Y	Y	Y	Y	Y
Kassebaum	Y	N	N	Y	Y	Y	Y	N
KENTUCKY								
McConnell	Y	N	N	Y	Y	Y	Y	Y
Ford	N	Y	N	N	N	Y	N	N
LOUISIANA								
Johnston	N	N	N	N	Y	Y	Y	Y
Long	Y	N	N	N	Y	Y	Y	Y
MAINE								
Cohen	N	N	N	Y	Y	Y	Y	Y
Mitchell	N	Y	N	N	N	Y	N	N
MARYLAND								
Mathias	N	Y	N	Y	N	Y	N	N
Sarbanes	N	Y	Y	N	N	Y	N	N
MASSACHUSETTS								
Kennedy	N	Y	Y	N	N	Y	N	N
Kerry	N	Y	Y	N	N	Y	N	N
MICHIGAN								
Levin	N	Y	N	N	N	Y	N	N
Riegle	N	Y	Y	N	N	Y	N	N
MINNESOTA								
Boschwitz	Y	N	N	Y	Y	Y	Y	Y
Durenberger	Y	N	N	Y	Y	Y	Y	Y
MISSISSIPPI								
Cochran	Y	N	N	Y	Y	Y	Y	Y
Stennis	?	?	?	N	Y	Y	Y	Y
MISSOURI								
Danforth	Y	N	N	Y	Y	Y	Y	Y
Eagleton	N	Y	Y	N	N	Y	N	N
MONTANA								
Baucus	N	N	N	N	N	Y	N	N
Melcher	N	Y	N	N	N	Y	N	N
NEBRASKA								
Exon	N	N	N	N	N	Y	N	N
Zorinsky	Y	N	N	N	N	Y	Y	N
NEVADA								
Hecht	Y	N	N	Y	Y	N	Y	Y
Laxalt	Y	N	N	Y	Y	Y	Y	Y
NEW HAMPSHIRE								
Humphrey	Y	N	N	Y	Y	N	Y	Y
Rudman	Y	N	N	Y	Y	Y	Y	Y
NEW JERSEY								
Bradley	N	N	N	N	Y	Y	Y	Y
Lautenberg	N	Y	N	N	N	Y	N	N
NEW MEXICO								
Domenici	Y	N	N	Y	Y	Y	Y	Y
Bingaman	N	Y	Y	N	N	Y	N	N
NEW YORK								
D'Amato	Y	N	N	Y	Y	Y	Y	Y
Moynihan	N	N	N	N	N	Y	N	Y
NORTH CAROLINA								
Broyhill	Y	N	N	Y	Y	N	Y	Y
Helms	Y	N	N	Y	Y	N	Y	Y
NORTH DAKOTA								
Andrews	Y	N	N	N	N	N	Y	N
Burdick	N	Y	Y	N	N	Y	N	N
OHIO								
Glenn	?	N	N	Y	N	Y	N	Y
Metzenbaum	N	Y	N	N	N	Y	N	N
OKLAHOMA								
Nickles	Y	N	N	Y	Y	Y	Y	Y
Boren	Y	N	N	N	Y	Y	Y	Y
OREGON								
Hatfield	N	Y	Y	N	N	Y	N	N
Packwood	N	Y	N	Y	N	Y	N	Y
PENNSYLVANIA								
Heinz	N	N	N	Y	Y	Y	Y	Y
Specter	N	Y	N	N	N	Y	N	N
RHODE ISLAND								
Chafee	N	Y	N	Y	Y	Y	Y	N
Pell	N	Y	Y	N	?	Y	Y	N
SOUTH CAROLINA								
Thurmond	Y	N	N	Y	Y	Y	+	Y
Hollings	Y	N	N	Y	Y	Y	Y	Y
SOUTH DAKOTA								
Abdnor	Y	N	N	N	Y	Y	Y	Y
Pressler	Y	N	N	N	Y	Y	Y	Y
TENNESSEE								
Gore	N	N	N	N	N	Y	N	N
Sasser	N	Y	N	N	N	Y	N	N
TEXAS								
Gramm	Y	N	N	Y	Y	N	Y	Y
Bentsen	N	N	N	N	Y	Y	Y	Y
UTAH								
Garn	Y	N	N	Y	Y	Y	Y	Y
Hatch	Y	N	N	Y	Y	Y	Y	Y
VERMONT								
Stafford	N	N	N	Y	N	Y	Y	N
Leahy	N	Y	Y	N	N	Y	N	N
VIRGINIA								
Trible	Y	N	N	Y	Y	Y	Y	Y
Warner	Y	N	N	Y	Y	Y	Y	Y
WASHINGTON								
Evans	Y	N	N	Y	Y	Y	Y	Y
Gorton	Y	N	N	Y	N	Y	N	Y
WEST VIRGINIA								
Byrd	N	N	N	N	Y	Y	Y	N
Rockefeller	N	N	N	Y	N	Y	N	N
WISCONSIN								
Kasten	Y	N	N	Y	Y	Y	Y	Y
Proxmire	N	Y	Y	N	N	Y	N	N
WYOMING								
Simpson	Y	N	N	Y	Y	Y	Y	Y
Wallop	Y	N	N	Y	Y	N	Y	Y

KEY

- Y Voted for (yea).
- # Paired for.
- + Announced for.
- N Voted against (nay).
- X Paired against.
- \- Announced against.
- P Voted "present."
- C Voted "present" to avoid possible conflict of interest.
- ? Did not vote or otherwise make a position known.

Democrats ***Republicans***

ND - Northern Democrats SD - Southern Democrats (Southern states - Ala., Ark., Fla., Ga., Ky., La., Miss., N.C., Okla., S.C., Tenn., Texas, Va.)

214. HR 5052. Military Construction Appropriations, Fiscal 1987/Aid to Nicaraguan Rebels. Lugar, R-Ind., motion to table (kill) the Dodd, D-Conn., amendment to bar use of funds in the bill for planning, directing, executing or supporting military actions in, over or off the shore of Nicaragua that are directed against civilians or that would likely result in the loss of civilian lives. Motion agreed to 51-47: R 44-9; D 7-38 (ND 2-30, SD 5-8), Aug. 12, 1986. A "yea" was a vote supporting the president's position.

215. HR 5052. Military Construction Appropriations, Fiscal 1987/Aid to Nicaraguan Rebels. Harkin, D-Iowa, amendment to prohibit U.S. military personnel or agents from providing training or other aid inside Honduras or Costa Rica to the Nicaraguan "contra" guerrillas. Rejected 32-67: R 6-47; D 26-20 (ND 23-10, SD 3-10), Aug. 13, 1986. A "nay" was a vote supporting the president's position.

216. HR 5052. Military Construction Appropriations, Fiscal 1987/Aid to Nicaraguan Rebels. Pell, D-R.I., amendment to establish a $10 million fund to compensate civilian victims of the Nicaraguan "contra" guerrillas. The amendment would have established a bipartisan commission to investigate allegations of contra abuses and to make awards to victims. Rejected 17-82: R 1-52; D 16-30 (ND 16-17, SD 0-13), Aug. 13, 1986. A "nay" was a vote supporting the president's position.

217. HR 5052. Military Construction Appropriations, Fiscal 1987/Aid to Nicaraguan Rebels. Lugar, R-Ind., motion to table (kill) the Melcher, D-Mont., amendment to strike from the bill an authorization for the administration to use unspent fiscal 1986 African famine relief funds for a new $300 million economic aid program for Central American countries. Motion agreed to 51-49: R 47-6; D 4-43 (ND 2-31, SD 2-12), Aug. 13, 1986. A "yea" was a vote supporting the president's position.

218. HR 5052. Military Construction Appropriations, Fiscal 1987/Aid to Nicaraguan Rebels. Dole, R-Kan., motion to invoke cloture (thus limiting debate) on titles II and III of the bill, which would provide $100 million in aid for the Nicaraguan "contra" guerrillas and $300 million for economic aid to Central American countries. Motion rejected 59-40: R 46-7; D 13-33 (ND 4-28, SD 9-5), Aug. 13, 1986. A three-fifths majority (60) of the total Senate is required to invoke cloture. A "yea" was a vote supporting the president's position.

219. S 2701. South Africa Sanctions. Kennedy, D-Mass., motion to invoke cloture (thus limiting debate) on the bill to impose economic and other sanctions on South Africa. Motion agreed to 89-11: R 42-11; D 47-0 (ND 33-0, SD 14-0), Aug. 13, 1986. A three-fifths majority (60) of the total Senate is required to invoke cloture.

220. HR 5052. Military Construction Appropriations, Fiscal 1987/Aid to Nicaraguan Rebels. Dole, R-Kan., motion to invoke cloture (thus limiting debate) on titles II and III of the bill, which would provide $100 million in aid for the Nicaraguan "contra" guerrillas and $300 million for economic aid to Central American countries. Motion agreed to 62-37: R 47-5; D 15-32 (ND 6-27, SD 9-5), Aug. 13, 1986. A three-fifths majority (60) of the total Senate is required to invoke cloture. A "yea" was a vote supporting the president's position.

221. HR 5052. Military Construction Appropriations, Fiscal 1987/Aid to Nicaraguan Rebels. Mattingly, R-Ga., motion to table (kill) the Leahy, D-Vt., amendment to prohibit expenditure by the CIA or any other intelligence agency of the funds in the bill for aid to the Nicaraguan "contra" guerrillas. Motion agreed to 57-42: R 43-9; D 14-33 (ND 5-28, SD 9-5), Aug. 13, 1986. A "yea" was a vote supporting the president's position.

	222	223	224	225	226	227	228	229
ALABAMA								
Denton	Y	Y	N	Y	Y	Y	Y	Y
Heflin	Y	Y	N	Y	Y	N	Y	Y
ALASKA								
Murkowski	Y	Y	N	Y	Y	Y	Y	Y
Stevens	Y	Y	N	Y	Y	Y	Y	Y
ARIZONA								
Goldwater	Y	Y	N	Y	Y	Y	Y	Y
DeConcini	Y	N	Y	N	N	Y	N	N
ARKANSAS								
Bumpers	N	N	Y	N	Y	N	N	N
Pryor	N	N	Y	N	N	N	N	N
CALIFORNIA								
Wilson	Y	Y	N	Y	Y	Y	Y	Y
Cranston	N	N	Y	N	N	N	N	N
COLORADO								
Armstrong	Y	Y	N	Y	Y	Y	Y	Y
Hart	N	N	Y	N	N	N	N	N
CONNECTICUT								
Weicker	N	Y	N	N	Y	Y	N	N
Dodd	N	N	Y	N	N	N	N	N
DELAWARE								
Roth	Y	Y	N	Y	Y	Y	Y	Y
Biden	N	N	Y	N	N	N	N	N
FLORIDA								
Hawkins	Y	Y	N	Y	Y	Y	Y	Y
Chiles	Y	Y	N	N	Y	Y	N	Y
GEORGIA								
Mattingly	Y	Y	N	Y	Y	Y	Y	Y
Nunn	Y	Y	Y	N	N	Y	N	Y
HAWAII								
Inouye	N	N	Y	N	N	N	N	N
Matsunaga	N	N	Y	N	N	N	N	N
IDAHO								
McClure	Y	Y	N	Y	Y	Y	Y	Y
Symms	Y	Y	N	Y	Y	Y	Y	Y
ILLINOIS								
Dixon	Y	N	Y	N	N	Y	Y	Y
Simon	N	N	Y	N	N	N	N	N
INDIANA								
Lugar	Y	Y	N	Y	Y	Y	Y	Y
Quayle	Y	Y	N	Y	Y	Y	Y	Y
IOWA								
Grassley	Y	Y	N	Y	Y	N	Y	Y
Harkin	N	N	Y	N	N	N	N	N
KANSAS								
Dole	Y	Y	N	Y	Y	Y	Y	Y
Kassebaum	Y	Y	N	Y	Y	Y	Y	Y
KENTUCKY								
McConnell	Y	Y	N	Y	Y	Y	Y	Y
Ford	N	N	Y	N	Y	N	N	N
LOUISIANA								
Johnston	Y	N	Y	N	Y	Y	Y	Y
Long	Y	Y	N	Y	Y	Y	Y	Y
MAINE								
Cohen	N	Y	N	Y	Y	Y	Y	Y
Mitchell	N	N	Y	N	N	N	N	N
MARYLAND								
Mathias	N	N	N	Y	N	Y	N	N
Sarbanes	N	N	Y	N	N	N	N	N
MASSACHUSETTS								
Kennedy	N	N	Y	N	N	N	N	N
Kerry	N	N	Y	N	N	N	N	N
MICHIGAN								
Levin	N	N	Y	N	N	N	N	N
Riegle	N	N	Y	N	N	N	N	N
MINNESOTA								
Boschwitz	Y	Y	N	Y	Y	Y	Y	Y
Durenberger	N	Y	Y	Y	Y	N	Y	N
MISSISSIPPI								
Cochran	Y	Y	N	Y	Y	Y	Y	Y
Stennis	N	N	N	N	N	Y	N	Y
MISSOURI								
Danforth	Y	Y	N	Y	Y	Y	Y	Y
Eagleton	N	N	Y	N	N	?	N	N
MONTANA								
Baucus	N	N	Y	N	N	N	N	N
Melcher	N	N	Y	N	N	N	N	N
NEBRASKA								
Exon	N	N	Y	N	Y	N	N	N
Zorinsky	N	Y	Y	N	Y	N	N	N
NEVADA								
Hecht	Y	Y	N	Y	Y	Y	Y	Y
Laxalt	Y	Y	N	Y	Y	Y	Y	Y
NEW HAMPSHIRE								
Humphrey	Y	Y	N	Y	Y	Y	Y	Y
Rudman	?	Y	N	Y	Y	Y	Y	Y
NEW JERSEY								
Bradley	Y	Y	Y	Y	N	Y	N	Y
Lautenberg	N	N	Y	N	Y	N	N	N
NEW MEXICO								
Domenici	Y	Y	N	Y	Y	Y	Y	Y
Bingaman	N	N	Y	N	N	N	N	N
NEW YORK								
D'Amato	Y	Y	N	Y	Y	Y	Y	Y
Moynihan	N	N	Y	N	Y	Y	N	N
NORTH CAROLINA								
Broyhill	Y	Y	N	Y	Y	Y	Y	Y
Helms	Y	Y	N	Y	Y	Y	Y	Y
NORTH DAKOTA								
Andrews	Y	Y	Y	Y	Y	Y	Y	N
Burdick	N	N	Y	N	N	N	N	N
OHIO								
Glenn	N	N	Y	Y	Y	N	N	N
Metzenbaum	N	N	Y	N	N	N	N	N
OKLAHOMA								
Nickles	Y	Y	N	Y	Y	Y	Y	Y
Boren	Y	N	N	Y	Y	Y	N	Y
OREGON								
Hatfield	N	N	Y	N	N	N	N	N
Packwood	N	N	Y	Y	Y	N	N	N
PENNSYLVANIA								
Heinz	Y	Y	N	Y	Y	Y	Y	Y
Specter	N	Y	Y	N	N	N	N	N
RHODE ISLAND								
Chafee	N	Y	Y	Y	Y	Y	N	N
Pell	N	N	Y	N	N	N	N	N
SOUTH CAROLINA								
Thurmond	Y	Y	N	Y	Y	Y	Y	Y
Hollings	Y	Y	N	Y	Y	Y	Y	Y
SOUTH DAKOTA								
Abdnor	Y	Y	N	Y	Y	N	Y	N
Pressler	Y	Y	N	Y	Y	Y	Y	Y
TENNESSEE								
Gore	N	N	Y	N	N	N	N	N
Sasser	N	N	Y	N	N	N	N	N
TEXAS								
Gramm	Y	Y	N	Y	Y	Y	Y	Y
Bentsen	Y	N	N	Y	Y	Y	N	Y
UTAH								
Garn	Y	Y	N	Y	Y	Y	Y	Y
Hatch	Y	Y	N	Y	Y	Y	Y	Y
VERMONT								
Stafford	N	Y	N	Y	Y	N	Y	N
Leahy	N	N	Y	N	N	N	N	N
VIRGINIA								
Trible	Y	Y	N	Y	Y	Y	Y	Y
Warner	Y	Y	N	Y	Y	Y	Y	Y
WASHINGTON								
Evans	Y	Y	N	Y	Y	Y	Y	Y
Gorton	Y	Y	N	Y	Y	Y	Y	N
WEST VIRGINIA								
Byrd	N	N	Y	N	N	N	N	N
Rockefeller	N	N	Y	N	N	N	N	N
WISCONSIN								
Kasten	Y	Y	N	Y	Y	Y	Y	Y
Proxmire	N	N	Y	N	N	N	N	N
WYOMING								
Simpson	Y	Y	N	Y	Y	Y	Y	Y
Wallop	Y	Y	N	Y	Y	Y	Y	Y

KEY

Y Voted for (yea).
\# Paired for.
\+ Announced for.
N Voted against (nay).
X Paired against.
\- Announced against.
P Voted "present."
C Voted "present" to avoid possible conflict of interest.
? Did not vote or otherwise make a position known.

Democrats *Republicans*

ND - Northern Democrats SD - Southern Democrats (Southern states - Ala., Ark., Fla., Ga., Ky., La., Miss., N.C., Okla., S.C., Tenn., Texas, Va.)

222. HR 5052. Military Construction Appropriations, Fiscal 1987/Aid to Nicaraguan Rebels. Lugar, R-Ind., motion to table (kill) the Biden, D-Del., amendment to prohibit use of the funds in the bill for aid to the Nicaraguan "contra" guerrillas until the administration had begun direct negotiations with the Nicaraguan government with the aim of achieving an agreement on security and other issues. Motion agreed to 54-45: R 43-9; D 11-36 (ND 3-30, SD 8-6), Aug. 13, 1986. A "yea" was a vote supporting the president's position.

223. HR 5052. Military Construction Appropriations, Fiscal 1987/Aid to Nicaraguan Rebels. Lugar, R-Ind., motion to table (kill) the Byrd, D-W.Va., amendment to provide $450,000 through fiscal 1988 for aid to the Nicaraguan opposition newspaper *La Prensa*. Motion agreed to 57-43: R 50-3; D 7-40 (ND 2-31, SD 5-9), Aug. 13, 1986. A "yea" was a vote supporting the president's position.

224. HR 5052. Military Construction Appropriations, Fiscal 1987/Aid to Nicaraguan Rebels. Kerry, D-Mass., amendment to terminate aid in the bill for the Nicaraguan "contra" guerrillas if the countries of Central America signed a peace agreement containing the principles outlined in an April 1986 declaration by Costa Rica, El Salvador, Guatemala and Honduras. Rejected 46-54: R 6-47; D 40-7 (ND 33-0, SD 7-7), Aug. 13, 1986. A "nay" was a vote supporting the president's position.

225. HR 5052. Military Construction Appropriations, Fiscal 1987/Aid to Nicaraguan Rebels. Lugar, R-Ind., motion to table (kill) the Simon, D-Ill., amendment to require the president to give the comptroller general every 30 days a full accounting of the funds provided to the Nicaraguan "contra" guerrillas, and to require the comptroller general to analyze for Congress each presidential report. Motion agreed to 57-43: R 50-3; D 7-40 (ND 2-31, SD 5-9), Aug. 13, 1986. A "yea" was a vote supporting the president's position.

226. HR 5052. Military Construction Appropriations, Fiscal 1987/Aid to Nicaraguan Rebels. Lugar, R-Ind., motion to table (kill) the Simon, D-Ill., amendment to provide $50 million for drought relief and agricultural development in Africa. The money was to be taken from $300 million earmarked in the bill for economic aid to Central American countries. Motion agreed to 64-36: R 50-3; D 14-33 (ND 5-28, SD 9-5), Aug. 13, 1986. A "yea" was a vote supporting the president's position.

227. HR 5052. Military Construction Appropriations, Fiscal 1987/Aid to Nicaraguan Rebels. Lugar, R-Ind., motion to table (kill) the Harkin, D-Iowa, amendment to require that one-half of the $100 million intended in the bill for aid to Nicaraguan "contra" guerrillas be transferred to disaster relief for American farmers. Motion agreed to 58-41: R 46-7; D 12-34 (ND 4-28, SD 8-6), Aug. 13, 1986. A "yea" was a vote supporting the president's position.

228. HR 5052. Military Construction Appropriations, Fiscal 1987/Aid to Nicaraguan Rebels. Lugar, R-Ind., motion to table (kill) the Byrd, D-W.Va., amendment to require that any aid to the Nicaraguan "contra" guerrillas be specifically authorized by law, including any aid provided through the CIA contingency fund. Motion agreed to 52-48: R 47-6; D 5-42 (ND 1-32, SD 4-10), Aug. 13, 1986. A "yea" was a vote supporting the president's position.

229. HR 5052. Military Construction Appropriations, Fiscal 1987/Aid to Nicaraguan Rebels. Adoption of titles II and III of the bill, to provide $100 million in aid for the Nicaraguan "contra" guerrillas and $300 million for economic aid to the countries of Central America. Adopted 53-47: R 42-11; D 11-36 (ND 2-31, SD 9-5), Aug. 13, 1986. A "yea" was a vote supporting the president's position.

Corresponding to Congressional Record Votes 230, 231, 232, 233, 234, 235, 236, 237

	230	231	232	233	234	235	236	237
ALABAMA								
Denton	Y	Y	Y	Y	Y	Y	Y	Y
Heflin	Y	Y	Y	Y	Y	Y	N	N
ALASKA								
Murkowski	Y	N	Y	Y	Y	Y	Y	Y
Stevens	Y	N	Y	Y	Y	Y	Y	Y
ARIZONA								
Goldwater	Y	?	?	?	?	?	?	?
DeConcini	N	Y	Y	Y	N	Y	N	N
ARKANSAS								
Bumpers	N	Y	Y	Y	N	N	N	N
Pryor	N	Y	N	Y	N	N	N	N
CALIFORNIA								
Wilson	Y	N	Y	Y	Y	Y	Y	Y
Cranston	N	Y	N	Y	N	N	N	N
COLORADO								
Armstrong	Y	N	Y	Y	Y	Y	Y	Y
Hart	N	Y	N	Y	N	N	N	N
CONNECTICUT								
Weicker	N	Y	N	Y	N	Y	Y	N
Dodd	N	Y	N	Y	N	Y	N	N
DELAWARE								
Roth	Y	N	Y	Y	Y	Y	Y	N
Biden	N	Y	N	Y	N	N	N	N
FLORIDA								
Hawkins	Y	?	Y	Y	Y	Y	Y	Y
Chiles	Y	Y	N	Y	N	Y	N	N
GEORGIA								
Mattingly	Y	Y	Y	Y	Y	Y	Y	N
Nunn	Y	Y	N	Y	N	Y	N	N
HAWAII								
Inouye	N	Y	N	Y	N	N	N	N
Matsunaga	N	Y	N	Y	N	N	N	N
IDAHO								
McClure	Y	N	Y	Y	Y	Y	Y	Y
Symms	Y	N	Y	Y	Y	Y	Y	Y
ILLINOIS								
Dixon	Y	Y	N	Y	N	N	N	N
Simon	N	Y	N	Y	N	N	N	N
INDIANA								
Lugar	Y	N	Y	Y	Y	Y	Y	Y
Quayle	Y	N	Y	Y	Y	Y	Y	Y
IOWA								
Grassley	Y	Y	Y	Y	Y	Y	Y	Y
Harkin	N	Y	Y	Y	N	N	N	N
KANSAS								
Dole	Y	N	Y	Y	Y	Y	Y	Y
Kassebaum	Y	N	Y	Y	Y	Y	Y	N
KENTUCKY								
McConnell	Y	Y	Y	Y	Y	Y	Y	Y
Ford	N	Y	Y	Y	Y	Y	N	N
LOUISIANA								
Johnston	Y	Y	N	Y	N	Y	N	N
Long	Y	Y	Y	Y	N	Y	Y	N
MAINE								
Cohen	Y	Y	N	Y	Y	Y	Y	N
Mitchell	Y	Y	Y	Y	N	N	N	N
MARYLAND								
Mathias	N	N	N	Y	Y	Y	?	N
Sarbanes	N	Y	N	Y	N	N	N	N
MASSACHUSETTS								
Kennedy	N	Y	N	Y	N	N	N	N
Kerry	N	Y	N	Y	N	N	N	N
MICHIGAN								
Levin	N	Y	N	Y	N	N	N	N
Riegle	N	Y	N	Y	N	N	N	N
MINNESOTA								
Boschwitz	Y	N	Y	Y	Y	Y	Y	Y
Durenberger	N	N	Y	Y	Y	Y	Y	Y
MISSISSIPPI								
Cochran	Y	Y	Y	Y	Y	Y	Y	Y
Stennis	Y	Y	Y	Y	Y	?	?	?
MISSOURI								
Danforth	Y	Y	Y	Y	Y	Y	Y	Y
Eagleton	N	Y	Y	Y	N	N	N	N
MONTANA								
Baucus	N	Y	Y	Y	N	N	N	N
Melcher	N	Y	Y	Y	N	Y	N	N
NEBRASKA								
Exon	N	Y	Y	Y	N	Y	N	N
Zorinsky	N	Y	N	Y	Y	Y	N	N
NEVADA								
Hecht	Y	N	Y	Y	Y	Y	Y	Y
Laxalt	Y	N	Y	Y	Y	Y	Y	Y
NEW HAMPSHIRE								
Humphrey	Y	N	Y	Y	Y	Y	Y	Y
Rudman	Y	N	Y	Y	Y	Y	Y	Y
NEW JERSEY								
Bradley	Y	Y	N	Y	N	N	N	N
Lautenberg	Y	Y	N	Y	N	N	N	N
NEW MEXICO								
Domenici	Y	N	Y	Y	Y	Y	Y	Y
Bingaman	N	Y	Y	Y	N	N	N	N
NEW YORK								
D'Amato	Y	Y	N	Y	N	Y	Y	N
Moynihan	N	?	N	Y	N	N	N	N
NORTH CAROLINA								
Broyhill	Y	Y	Y	Y	Y	Y	Y	Y
Helms	Y	N	Y	Y	Y	Y	Y	Y
NORTH DAKOTA								
Andrews	Y	Y	Y	Y	Y	Y	Y	Y
Burdick	N	Y	Y	Y	N	N	N	N
OHIO								
Glenn	N	Y	N	Y	N	N	N	N
Metzenbaum	N	Y	N	Y	N	N	N	N
OKLAHOMA								
Nickles	Y	Y	Y	Y	Y	Y	Y	Y
Boren	Y	Y	Y	Y	Y	Y	N	N
OREGON								
Hatfield	N	N	Y	Y	N	Y	Y	Y
Packwood	N	Y	N	Y	N	Y	Y	Y
PENNSYLVANIA								
Heinz	Y	Y	N	Y	N	Y	Y	N
Specter	Y	Y	N	Y	N	N	N	N
RHODE ISLAND								
Chafee	Y	?	N	Y	Y	Y	Y	N
Pell	N	Y	N	Y	N	N	N	N
SOUTH CAROLINA								
Thurmond	Y	Y	Y	Y	Y	Y	Y	Y
Hollings	Y	Y	N	Y	N	N	Y	N
SOUTH DAKOTA								
Abdnor	Y	N	Y	Y	Y	Y	Y	Y
Pressler	Y	N	Y	Y	Y	Y	Y	Y
TENNESSEE								
Gore	N	Y	Y	Y	N	N	N	N
Sasser	N	Y	N	Y	N	Y	N	N
TEXAS								
Gramm	Y	N	Y	Y	Y	Y	Y	Y
Bentsen	Y	Y	N	Y	N	Y	N	N
UTAH								
Garn	Y	Y	Y	Y	Y	Y	Y	Y
Hatch	Y	N	Y	Y	Y	Y	Y	Y
VERMONT								
Stafford	Y	Y	Y	Y	Y	Y	Y	Y
Leahy	N	Y	N	Y	N	Y	N	N
VIRGINIA								
Trible	Y	Y	Y	Y	Y	Y	Y	Y
Warner	Y	Y	Y	Y	Y	Y	Y	Y
WASHINGTON								
Evans	N	N	N	Y	Y	Y	Y	Y
Gorton	N	N	Y	Y	Y	Y	Y	Y
WEST VIRGINIA								
Byrd	N	Y	N	Y	N	Y	N	N
Rockefeller	N	Y	N	Y	N	N	N	N
WISCONSIN								
Kasten	Y	Y	N	Y	Y	Y	N	Y
Proxmire	N	Y	N	Y	N	N	N	N
WYOMING								
Simpson	Y	N	Y	Y	Y	Y	Y	Y
Wallop	Y	N	Y	Y	Y	Y	Y	Y

KEY

- Y Voted for (yea).
- # Paired for.
- + Announced for.
- N Voted against (nay).
- X Paired against.
- - Announced against.
- P Voted "present."
- C Voted "present" to avoid possible conflict of interest.
- ? Did not vote or otherwise make a position known.

Democrats *Republicans*

ND - Northern Democrats SD - Southern Democrats (Southern states - Ala., Ark., Fla., Ga., Ky., La., Miss., N.C., Okla., S.C., Tenn., Texas, Va.)

230. HR 5052. Military Construction Appropriations, Fiscal 1987/Aid to Nicaraguan Rebels. Passage of the bill to appropriate $8.2 billion in fiscal 1987 for military construction programs of the Defense Department, to provide $100 million in military and non-military aid to the Nicaraguan "contra" guerrillas, and to provide $300 million in economic aid to the countries of Central America. Passed 59-41: R 46-7; D 13-34 (ND 4-29, SD 9-5), Aug. 13, 1986. A "yea" was a vote supporting the president's position.

231. S 2701. South Africa Sanctions. Cranston, D-Calif., amendment to impose a ban on the importation into the United States of South African textiles. Adopted 67-29: R 21-29; D 46-0 (ND 32-0, SD 14-0), Aug. 14, 1986. A "nay" was a vote supporting the president's position.

232. S 2701. South Africa Sanctions. Pressler, R-S.D., amendment to delete from the bill authority for the president to sell gold from U.S. stocks to affect the world price of gold. (Gold is South Africa's principal export.) Adopted 58-41: R 42-10; D 16-31 (ND 9-24, SD 7-7), Aug. 14, 1986.

233. S 2701. South Africa Sanctions. Kassebaum, R-Kan., amendment to delete from the bill a requirement that South African government officials may be granted visas for travel to the United States only on a case-by-case basis. Adopted 99-0: R 52-0; D 47-0 (ND 33-0, SD 14-0), Aug. 14, 1986.

234. S 2701. South Africa Sanctions. Lugar, R-Ind., motion to table (kill) the Kennedy, D-Mass., amendment to add the following sanctions: a ban on renewal of existing bank loans to South African businesses; a ban on the importation into the United States of South African agricultural products, coal and iron; and a ban on exports to South Africa of U.S. crude oil and petroleum products. Motion agreed to 51-48: R 46-6; D 5-42 (ND 1-32, SD 4-10), Aug. 14, 1986. A "yea" was a vote supporting the president's position.

235. S 2701. South Africa Sanctions. Helms, R-N.C., amendment to establish conditions on the U.S. insistence that the African National Congress and affiliated groups be included in any negotiations with the South African government. Adopted 67-31: R 51-1; D 16-30 (ND 7-26, SD 9-4), Aug. 14, 1986.

236. S 2701. South Africa Sanctions. Lugar, R-Ind., motion to table (kill) the Proxmire, D-Wis., amendment to require that the president's decisions to modify or terminate sanctions would not take effect until ratified by a joint resolution of Congress. Motion agreed to 51-46: R 49-2; D 2-44 (ND 0-33, SD 2-11), Aug. 14, 1986.

237. S 2701. South Africa Sanctions. Lugar, R-Ind., motion to table (kill) the Sarbanes, D-Md., amendment to make immediate a ban on flights to and from South Africa by U.S.-owned airlines. Motion rejected 42-56: R 42-10; D 0-46 (ND 0-33, SD 0-13), Aug. 14, 1986. (The Sarbanes amendment subsequently was adopted by voice vote.)

	238	239	240	241	242	243
ALABAMA						
Denton	Y	Y	Y	Y	N	Y
Heflin	Y	Y	N	Y	Y	N
ALASKA						
Murkowski	Y	N	Y	Y	N	Y
Stevens	Y	Y	Y	Y	N	Y
ARIZONA						
Goldwater	?	?	?	?	?	?
DeConcini	N	Y	N	N	Y	N
ARKANSAS						
Bumpers	N	N	N	N	Y	N
Pryor	N	N	N	N	Y	N
CALIFORNIA						
Wilson	Y	Y	Y	Y	N	Y
Cranston	N	N	N	N	Y	N
COLORADO						
Armstrong	Y	Y	Y	Y	N	Y
Hart	N	N	N	N	Y	N
CONNECTICUT						
Weicker	Y	N	N	Y	N	N
Dodd	N	N	N	N	Y	N
DELAWARE						
Roth	Y	Y	Y	Y	N	N
Biden	N	N	N	N	N	N
FLORIDA						
Hawkins	Y	Y	Y	Y	N	Y
Chiles	N	Y	N	Y	Y	N
GEORGIA						
Mattingly	Y	Y	N	Y	N	Y
Nunn	Y	N	N	Y	Y	N
HAWAII						
Inouye	N	N	N	N	Y	N
Matsunaga	N	N	N	Y	Y	N
IDAHO						
McClure	Y	Y	Y	Y	N	Y
Symms	Y	Y	Y	Y	N	Y
ILLINOIS						
Dixon	N	N	N	N	Y	N
Simon	N	N	N	N	Y	N
INDIANA						
Lugar	Y	N	Y	Y	N	N
Quayle	Y	Y	Y	Y	N	Y
IOWA						
Grassley	Y	Y	N	Y	N	Y
Harkin	N	N	N	N	Y	N
KANSAS						
Dole	Y	Y	Y	Y	N	N
Kassebaum	Y	N	Y	Y	N	N
KENTUCKY						
McConnell	Y	Y	Y	Y	N	N
Ford	Y	N	Y	Y	Y	N
LOUISIANA						
Johnston	N	N	N	Y	Y	N
Long	Y	N	N	Y	Y	N
MAINE						
Cohen	N	Y	Y	Y	N	Y
Mitchell	N	N	N	N	Y	N
MARYLAND						
Mathias	Y	N	N	Y	N	N
Sarbanes	N	N	N	N	Y	N
MASSACHUSETTS						
Kennedy	N	N	N	N	Y	N
Kerry	N	N	N	N	Y	N
MICHIGAN						
Levin	N	N	N	N	Y	N
Riegle	N	N	N	N	Y	N
MINNESOTA						
Boschwitz	Y	N	Y	Y	N	N
Durenberger	Y	N	Y	Y	N	Y
MISSISSIPPI						
Cochran	Y	N	Y	Y	N	Y
Stennis	Y	N	Y	N	Y	N
MISSOURI						
Danforth	Y	N	Y	Y	N	N
Eagleton	N	N	N	N	Y	N
MONTANA						
Baucus	N	N	N	Y	Y	N
Melcher	N	N	N	N	Y	N
NEBRASKA						
Exon	N	N	N	Y	Y	N
Zorinsky	Y	N	Y	Y	N	N
NEVADA						
Hecht	Y	Y	Y	Y	N	Y
Laxalt	Y	Y	Y	Y	N	Y
NEW HAMPSHIRE						
Humphrey	Y	Y	Y	Y	N	Y
Rudman	Y	Y	Y	Y	N	Y
NEW JERSEY						
Bradley	N	N	N	N	Y	N
Lautenberg	N	N	N	N	Y	N
NEW MEXICO						
Domenici	Y	Y	Y	Y	N	Y
Bingaman	N	N	N	Y	Y	N
NEW YORK						
D'Amato	N	Y	N	N	Y	Y
Moynihan	N	Y	N	N	Y	N
NORTH CAROLINA						
Broyhill	Y	Y	Y	Y	N	Y
Helms	Y	Y	Y	Y	N	Y
NORTH DAKOTA						
Andrews	Y	N	Y	Y	N	N
Burdick	N	N	N	N	Y	N
OHIO						
Glenn	N	N	N	N	Y	N
Metzenbaum	N	N	N	N	Y	N
OKLAHOMA						
Nickles	Y	N	Y	Y	N	Y
Boren	Y	N	N	Y	Y	N
OREGON						
Hatfield	Y	N	N	Y	N	N
Packwood	Y	Y	N	Y	N	Y
PENNSYLVANIA						
Heinz	N	Y	N	Y	N	N
Specter	N	N	N	N	N	N
RHODE ISLAND						
Chafee	Y	N	N	N	N	N
Pell	N	N	N	N	N	N
SOUTH CAROLINA						
Thurmond	Y	Y	Y	Y	N	Y
Hollings	N	Y	N	N	Y	N
SOUTH DAKOTA						
Abdnor	Y	N	Y	Y	N	Y
Pressler	Y	Y	Y	Y	N	Y
TENNESSEE						
Gore	N	N	N	Y	Y	N
Sasser	N	Y	N	Y	Y	N
TEXAS						
Gramm	Y	Y	Y	Y	N	Y
Bentsen	N	Y	N	N	Y	N
UTAH						
Garn	Y	Y	Y	Y	N	Y
Hatch	Y	Y	Y	Y	N	Y
VERMONT						
Stafford	Y	N	Y	Y	N	N
Leahy	N	N	N	N	Y	N
VIRGINIA						
Trible	Y	Y	Y	Y	N	Y
Warner	Y	Y	Y	Y	N	N
WASHINGTON						
Evans	Y	?	Y	Y	N	N
Gorton	Y	N	Y	Y	N	N
WEST VIRGINIA						
Byrd	N	N	N	N	Y	N
Rockefeller	N	N	N	Y	Y	N
WISCONSIN						
Kasten	Y	Y	N	Y	N	Y
Proxmire	N	N	N	N	Y	N
WYOMING						
Simpson	Y	Y	Y	Y	N	N
Wallop	Y	Y	Y	Y	N	Y

KEY

- Y Voted for (yea).
- # Paired for.
- + Announced for.
- N Voted against (nay).
- X Paired against.
- - Announced against.
- P Voted "present."
- C Voted "present" to avoid possible conflict of interest.
- ? Did not vote or otherwise make a position known.

Democrats ***Republicans***

ND - Northern Democrats SD - Southern Democrats (Southern states - Ala., Ark., Fla., Ga., Ky., La., Miss., N.C., Okla., S.C., Tenn., Texas, Va.)

238. S 2701. South Africa Sanctions. Lugar, R-Ind., motion to table (kill) the Biden, D-Del., amendment to impose additional sanctions after one year if the president reports to Congress that the South African government has not made sufficient progress toward eliminating apartheid. The sanctions would include banning the importation of South African iron, steel, agricultural products, food and diamonds. Motion agreed to 55-44: R 48-4; D 7-40 (ND 1-32, SD 6-8), Aug. 15, 1986.

239. S 2701. South Africa Sanctions. Wallop, R-Wyo., amendment to apply to the Soviet Union the same sanctions as were applied in the bill to South Africa. Rejected 41-57: R 34-17; D 7-40 (ND 2-31, SD 5-9), Aug. 15, 1986.

240. S 2701. South Africa Sanctions. Lugar, R-Ind., motion to table (kill) the Kennedy, D-Mass., amendment to add to the bill prohibitions on imports of South African agricultural products, iron and steel, and to prohibit exports to South Africa of crude oil and petroleum products. Motion rejected 44-55: R 41-11; D 3-44 (ND 1-32, SD 2-12), Aug. 15, 1986. (The Kennedy amendment subsequently was adopted by voice vote.)

241. S 2701. South Africa Sanctions. Lugar, R-Ind., motion to table (kill) the D'Amato, R-N.Y., amendment to prohibit the federal government from withholding aid to states and localities that have laws restricting contracts with South Africa. Motion agreed to 64-35: R 49-3; D 15-32 (ND 6-27, SD 9-5), Aug. 15, 1986.

242. S 2701. South Africa Sanctions. Byrd, D-W.Va., amendment to bar importation of South African uranium, coal and fluor spar, and to restructure the State Department's African Affairs bureau, with an assistant secretary to be responsible for West and Central African affairs and an assistant secretary to be responsible for South and East African affairs. Rejected 45-54: R 1-51; D 44-3 (ND 30-3, SD 14-0), Aug. 15, 1986.

243. S 2701. South Africa Sanctions. Humphrey, R-N.H., amendment to provide that restrictions in the bill on air transportation between South Africa and the United States would not take effect unless the same restrictions were applied to air transportation between the United States and the Soviet Union. Rejected 33-66: R 33-19; D 0-47 (ND 0-33, SD 0-14), Aug. 15, 1986.

CQ Senate Votes 244 - 249

Corresponding to Congressional Record Votes 244, 245, 246, 247, 248, 249

	244	245	246	247	248	249
ALABAMA						
Denton	Y	N	Y	Y	N	N
Heflin	Y	Y	Y	N	Y	Y
ALASKA						
Murkowski	Y	N	Y	Y	Y	Y
Stevens	Y	Y	Y	Y	N	Y
ARIZONA						
Goldwater	?	?	?	?	?	?
DeConcini	N	Y	N	N	Y	Y
ARKANSAS						
Bumpers	Y	Y	N	N	Y	Y
Pryor	Y	Y	N	N	Y	Y
CALIFORNIA						
Wilson	Y	N	Y	Y	Y	N
Cranston	N	Y	N	N	Y	Y
COLORADO						
Armstrong	Y	N	Y	Y	N	N
Hart	N	Y	N	N	Y	Y
CONNECTICUT						
Weicker	N	Y	N	N	Y	Y
Dodd	N	Y	N	N	Y	Y
DELAWARE						
Roth	Y	Y	Y	Y	N	N
Biden	N	Y	N	N	Y	Y
FLORIDA						
Hawkins	Y	Y	Y	Y	N	N
Chiles	Y	Y	N	N	Y	Y
GEORGIA						
Mattingly	Y	Y	Y	Y	Y	N
Nunn	Y	Y	N	N	Y	Y
HAWAII						
Inouye	N	Y	N	N	Y	Y
Matsunaga	N	Y	N	N	Y	Y
IDAHO						
McClure	Y	N	Y	Y	N	N
Symms	Y	N	Y	Y	N	N
ILLINOIS						
Dixon	N	Y	N	N	Y	Y
Simon	N	Y	N	N	Y	Y
INDIANA						
Lugar	Y	Y	Y	Y	Y	Y
Quayle	Y	N	Y	Y	Y	Y
IOWA						
Grassley	Y	Y	Y	Y	Y	N
Harkin	N	Y	N	N	Y	Y
KANSAS						
Dole	Y	Y	Y	Y	N	Y
Kassebaum	Y	Y	Y	Y	Y	Y
KENTUCKY						
McConnell	Y	Y	Y	Y	Y	Y
Ford	Y	Y	Y	Y	Y	Y
LOUISIANA						
Johnston	N	Y	N	N	Y	Y
Long	Y	Y	Y	Y	Y	Y
MAINE						
Cohen	Y	Y	N	N	Y	Y
Mitchell	N	Y	N	N	Y	Y
MARYLAND						
Mathias	Y	Y	N	N	Y	Y
Sarbanes	N	Y	N	N	Y	Y
MASSACHUSETTS						
Kennedy	N	Y	N	N	Y	Y
Kerry	N	Y	N	N	Y	Y
MICHIGAN						
Levin	N	Y	N	N	Y	Y
Riegle	N	Y	N	N	Y	Y
MINNESOTA						
Boschwitz	Y	N	Y	Y	N	Y
Durenberger	Y	Y	Y	Y	Y	Y
MISSISSIPPI						
Cochran	Y	Y	Y	Y	N	N
Stennis	?	Y	Y	Y	Y	Y
MISSOURI						
Danforth	Y	Y	Y	Y	Y	Y
Eagleton	N	Y	N	N	Y	Y
MONTANA						
Baucus	Y	Y	Y	N	Y	Y
Melcher	N	Y	Y	Y	Y	Y
NEBRASKA						
Exon	Y	Y	Y	N	Y	Y
Zorinsky	Y	Y	Y	N	Y	Y
NEVADA						
Hecht	Y	N	Y	Y	N	N
Laxalt	Y	Y	Y	Y	N	Y
NEW HAMPSHIRE						
Humphrey	Y	N	Y	Y	N	N
Rudman	Y	Y	Y	Y	N	N
NEW JERSEY						
Bradley	N	Y	N	N	Y	Y
Lautenberg	N	Y	N	N	Y	Y
NEW MEXICO						
Domenici	Y	Y	Y	Y	Y	N
Bingaman	Y	Y	N	N	Y	Y
NEW YORK						
D'Amato	N	Y	N	N	Y	Y
Moynihan	Y	Y	N	N	Y	Y
NORTH CAROLINA						
Broyhill	Y	N	Y	Y	N	N
Helms	Y	N	Y	Y	N	N
NORTH DAKOTA						
Andrews	Y	Y	Y	Y	Y	Y
Burdick	N	Y	Y	N	Y	Y
OHIO						
Glenn	Y	Y	N	N	Y	Y
Metzenbaum	N	Y	N	N	Y	Y
OKLAHOMA						
Nickles	Y	Y	Y	Y	N	N
Boren	Y	Y	Y	Y	Y	Y
OREGON						
Hatfield	Y	Y	Y	Y	Y	Y
Packwood	Y	Y	N	N	Y	Y
PENNSYLVANIA						
Heinz	Y	Y	N	Y	Y	Y
Specter	N	Y	N	N	Y	Y
RHODE ISLAND						
Chafee	Y	Y	N	N	Y	Y
Pell	N	Y	N	N	Y	Y
SOUTH CAROLINA						
Thurmond	Y	Y	Y	Y	N	N
Hollings	N	Y	N	N	Y	Y
SOUTH DAKOTA						
Abdnor	Y	Y	Y	Y	Y	N
Pressler	Y	N	Y	Y	N	N
TENNESSEE						
Gore	N	Y	N	N	Y	Y
Sasser	N	Y	Y	N	Y	Y
TEXAS						
Gramm	Y	Y	Y	Y	N	N
Bentsen	Y	Y	N	N	Y	Y
UTAH						
Garn	Y	N	Y	Y	N	Y
Hatch	Y	N	Y	Y	N	N
VERMONT						
Stafford	Y	Y	Y	Y	Y	Y
Leahy	N	Y	N	N	Y	Y
VIRGINIA						
Trible	Y	Y	Y	Y	Y	Y
Warner	Y	Y	Y	Y	N	Y
WASHINGTON						
Evans	Y	Y	Y	Y	Y	Y
Gorton	Y	N	Y	Y	N	Y
WEST VIRGINIA						
Byrd	Y	Y	N	N	Y	Y
Rockefeller	N	Y	N	N	Y	Y
WISCONSIN						
Kasten	Y	Y	Y	Y	Y	Y
Proxmire	N	Y	N	N	Y	Y
WYOMING						
Simpson	Y	N	Y	Y	N	N
Wallop	Y	N	Y	Y	N	N

KEY

- Y Voted for (yea).
- # Paired for.
- + Announced for.
- N Voted against (nay).
- X Paired against.
- - Announced against.
- P Voted "present."
- C Voted "present" to avoid possible conflict of interest.
- ? Did not vote or otherwise make a position known.

Democrats *Republicans*

ND - Northern Democrats SD - Southern Democrats (Southern states - Ala., Ark., Fla., Ga., Ky., La., Miss., N.C., Okla., S.C., Tenn., Texas, Va.)

244. S 2701. South Africa Sanctions. Lugar, R-Ind., motion to table (kill) the Cranston, D-Calif., amendment to prohibit all trade between the United States and South Africa (with the exception of exports of medical supplies and imports of strategic minerals certified by the president to be in short supply) and to prohibit U.S. businesses from holding any investments in South Africa. Motion agreed to 65-33: R 49-3; D 16-30 (ND 7-26, SD 9-4), Aug. 15, 1986.

245. S 2701. South Africa Sanctions. Lugar, R-Ind., motion to table (kill) the Boschwitz, R-Minn., amendment to provide humanitarian assistance to black South Africans who become unemployed as a result of U.S. sanctions, and to authorize the president to waive any sanctions in the bill if more than 40,000 black South African workers become unemployed as a result of the sanctions. Motion agreed to 81-18: R 34-18; D 47-0 (ND 33-0, SD 14-0), Aug. 15, 1986.

246. S 2701. South Africa Sanctions. Nickles, R-Okla., amendment to permit South Africa to receive U.S. agricultural export subsidies. Adopted 55-44: R 44-8; D 11-36 (ND 5-28, SD 6-8), Aug. 15, 1986.

247. S 2701. South Africa Sanctions. Nickles, R-Okla., motion to table (kill) the Lugar, R-Ind., motion to reconsider the vote by which the Nickles amendment *(vote 246, above)*, to permit South Africa to receive U.S. agricultural export subsidies, was adopted. Motion agreed to 50-49: R 45-7; D 5-42 (ND 1-32, SD 4-10), Aug. 15, 1986.

248. S 2701. South Africa Sanctions. Lugar, R-Ind., motion to table (kill) the Denton, R-Ala., amendment to provide that no future sanctions against South Africa contemplated by the bill would take effect until the president certified to Congress that the Soviet Union and its allies would not benefit from the sanctions, and until the president reported to Congress on the effect of those sanctions on the economy of the United States and on U.S. ability to obtain strategic minerals. Motion agreed to 73-26: R 26-26; D 47-0 (ND 33-0, SD 14-0), Aug. 15, 1986.

249. S 2701. South Africa Sanctions. Lugar, R-Ind., motion to table (kill) the Denton, R-Ala., amendment to prohibit U.S. foreign aid to any country that arrested or imprisoned black South African exiles for purposes other than immediate expulsion or for commission of activities that would not be criminal in the United States. Motion agreed to 75-24: R 28-24; D 47-0 (ND 33-0, SD 14-0), Aug. 15, 1986.

	250	251	252	253	254	255
ALABAMA						
Denton	N	N	N	Y	?	?
Heflin	N	Y	Y	N	N	?
ALASKA						
Murkowski	N	?	+	?	+	?
Stevens	N	Y	Y	N	Y	Y
ARIZONA						
Goldwater	?	?	-	?	?	?
DeConcini	Y	Y	Y	N	?	?
ARKANSAS						
Bumpers	Y	Y	Y	N	N	?
Pryor	Y	N	Y	?	?	?
CALIFORNIA						
Wilson	N	N	Y	N	N	Y
Cranston	Y	Y	Y	Y	N	N
COLORADO						
Armstrong	N	N	N	N	N	N
Hart	Y	Y	Y	Y	N	?
CONNECTICUT						
Weicker	Y	Y	Y	?	?	?
Dodd	Y	Y	Y	N	Y	Y
DELAWARE						
Roth	N	N	Y	Y	Y	Y
Biden	Y	Y	Y	N	Y	Y
FLORIDA						
Hawkins	N	N	Y	Y	N	N
Chiles	Y	Y	Y	N	Y	?
GEORGIA						
Mattingly	Y	N	Y	N	N	N
Nunn	Y	Y	Y	Y	N	N
HAWAII						
Inouye	Y	Y	Y	N	N	N
Matsunaga	Y	Y	Y	Y	N	N
IDAHO						
McClure	N	N	N	N	N	Y
Symms	N	N	N	N	N	Y
ILLINOIS						
Dixon	Y	Y	Y	N	Y	Y
Simon	Y	Y	Y	N	Y	Y
INDIANA						
Lugar	N	N	Y	N	Y	Y
Quayle	N	N	Y	N	?	?
IOWA						
Grassley	N	N	Y	N	N	N
Harkin	Y	Y	Y	Y	N	N
KANSAS						
Dole	N	N	Y	N	N	Y
Kassebaum	Y	Y	Y	N	Y	Y
KENTUCKY						
McConnell	N	N	Y	N	Y	Y
Ford	Y	N	Y	N	N	N
LOUISIANA						
Johnston	Y	Y	Y	Y	N	N
Long	Y	Y	Y	N	Y	Y
MAINE						
Cohen	Y	Y	Y	N	Y	?
Mitchell	Y	Y	Y	Y	N	N
MARYLAND						
Mathias	Y	Y	Y	Y	?	?
Sarbanes	Y	Y	Y	Y	N	N
MASSACHUSETTS						
Kennedy	Y	Y	Y	N	?	?
Kerry	Y	Y	Y	N	N	N
MICHIGAN						
Levin	Y	Y	Y	N	Y	Y
Riegle	Y	Y	Y	Y	N	N
MINNESOTA						
Boschwitz	N	N	Y	N	Y	Y
Durenberger	Y	Y	Y	N	?	?
MISSISSIPPI						
Cochran	N	N	Y	N	Y	?
Stennis	Y	?	Y	?	?	?
MISSOURI						
Danforth	Y	N	Y	N	Y	?
Eagleton	Y	Y	Y	?	?	?
MONTANA						
Baucus	Y	Y	Y	N	N	N
Melcher	Y	Y	Y	Y	N	N
NEBRASKA						
Exon	Y	N	Y	Y	N	N
Zorinsky	Y	N	Y	N	N	N
NEVADA						
Hecht	N	N	N	N	N	Y
Laxalt	Y	N	N	?	?	?
NEW HAMPSHIRE						
Humphrey	N	N	N	N	?	?
Rudman	N	N	N	N	Y	Y
NEW JERSEY						
Bradley	Y	Y	Y	Y	Y	Y
Lautenberg	Y	Y	Y	Y	N	N
NEW MEXICO						
Domenici	N	Y	Y	N	Y	Y
Bingaman	Y	Y	Y	Y	?	?
NEW YORK						
D'Amato	Y	Y	Y	N	Y	Y
Moynihan	Y	Y	Y	Y	N	N
NORTH CAROLINA						
Broyhill	N	N	N	N	N	Y
Helms	N	N	N	N	N	Y
NORTH DAKOTA						
Andrews	Y	Y	Y	Y	N	N
Burdick	Y	Y	Y	Y	N	N
OHIO						
Glenn	Y	Y	Y	Y	N	N
Metzenbaum	Y	Y	Y	Y	N	N
OKLAHOMA						
Nickles	N	N	Y	N	N	N
Boren	Y	Y	Y	N	Y	Y
OREGON						
Hatfield	Y	Y	Y	Y	?	?
Packwood	Y	?	Y	N	Y	Y
PENNSYLVANIA						
Heinz	N	N	Y	N	Y	Y
Specter	Y	Y	Y	N	Y	Y
RHODE ISLAND						
Chafee	Y	Y	Y	N	Y	Y
Pell	Y	N	Y	Y	N	N
SOUTH CAROLINA						
Thurmond	N	N	N	N	Y	Y
Hollings	Y	Y	Y	N	Y	Y
SOUTH DAKOTA						
Abdnor	N	N	Y	N	Y	Y
Pressler	N	N	N	N	N	N
TENNESSEE						
Gore	Y	Y	Y	Y	Y	Y
Sasser	Y	N	Y	Y	N	N
TEXAS						
Gramm	N	N	N	N	Y	?
Bentsen	Y	Y	Y	?	?	?
UTAH						
Garn	N	N	Y	N	Y	?
Hatch	N	N	Y	N	Y	Y
VERMONT						
Stafford	Y	Y	Y	N	?	?
Leahy	Y	Y	Y	N	N	N
VIRGINIA						
Trible	Y	N	Y	N	N	Y
Warner	N	N	Y	N	N	N
WASHINGTON						
Evans	Y	Y	Y	N	N	?
Gorton	Y	N	Y	N	Y	Y
WEST VIRGINIA						
Byrd	Y	N	Y	Y	N	N
Rockefeller	Y	Y	Y	Y	N	N
WISCONSIN						
Kasten	Y	Y	Y	N	N	N
Proxmire	Y	Y	Y	N	N	N
WYOMING						
Simpson	Y	Y	Y	N	Y	Y
Wallop	N	Y	N	N	?	?

KEY

- Y Voted for (yea).
- # Paired for.
- + Announced for.
- N Voted against (nay).
- X Paired against.
- - Announced against.
- P Voted "present."
- C Voted "present" to avoid possible conflict of interest.
- ? Did not vote or otherwise make a position known.

Democrats *Republicans*

ND - Northern Democrats SD - Southern Democrats (Southern states - Ala., Ark., Fla., Ga., Ky., La., Miss., N.C., Okla., S.C., Tenn., Texas, Va.)

250. S 2701. South Africa Sanctions. Dodd, D-Conn., motion to table (kill) the Pressler, R-S.D., amendment to delay implementation of a ban on imports of items produced by South African "parastatal" (quasi-governmental) organizations until the president reported to Congress on the employment costs in the United States, South Africa and southern Africa of such a ban. Motion agreed to 66-33: R 20-32; D 46-1 (ND 33-0, SD 13-1), Aug. 15, 1986.

251. S 2701. South Africa Sanctions. Dodd, D-Conn., motion to table (kill) the Dole, R-Kan., amendment to strike from the bill a ban on importation from South Africa of uranium and uranium ore. Motion agreed to 56-40: R 17-33; D 39-7 (ND 29-4, SD 10-3), Aug. 15, 1986.

252. HR 4868. South Africa Sanctions. Passage of the bill to impose economic and other sanctions against South Africa, including a ban on new U.S. investments in South Africa and prohibitions against importation of South African agricultural products, coal, uranium and steel. The bill also provided for modification or termination of the sanctions if South Africa met certain conditions, and gave authority to the president to impose new sanctions after a year if those conditions were not met. Passed 84-14: R 37-14; D 47-0 (ND 33-0, SD 14-0), Aug. 15, 1986. (The Senate had previously moved to strike the text of the House-passed bill and insert instead the text of S 2701, the Senate version of HR 4868.)

253. HR 5395. Temporary Debt Limit Increase. Moynihan, D-N.Y., motion to table (kill) the Gramm, R-Texas-Rudman, R-N.H.-Hollings, D-S.C., amendment to make changes in the Gramm-Rudman-Hollings anti-deficit law (PL 99-177) to reinstate for 1987 only the law's automatic spending cuts procedure (previously voided as a violation of the Constitution's separation-of-powers doctrine) by granting final authority for determining the automatic cuts to the director of the Office of Management and Budget, with certain limitations. The amendment also would change to the first Tuesday in February of each year the date in the Gramm-Rudman law by which the president is required to submit his budget request to Congress. Motion rejected 29-63: R 6-43; D 23-20 (ND 19-13, SD 4-7), Aug. 15, 1986. (The Gramm-Rudman-Hollings amendment later was adopted by voice vote.)

254. HR 5395. Temporary Debt Limit Increase. Passage of the bill to raise from \$2.079 trillion to \$2.111 trillion the ceiling on the federal debt. Rejected 34-47: R 23-18; D 11-29 (ND 6-23, SD 5-6), in the session that began Aug. 15, 1986. (The Senate, by voice vote, subsequently agreed to a Dole, R-Kan., motion to reconsider the vote by which the bill was rejected. The bill subsequently was passed on reconsideration *(see vote 255, below)*.)

255. HR 5395. Temporary Debt Limit Increase. Passage of the bill to raise from \$2.079 trillion to \$2.111 trillion the ceiling on the federal debt. Passed 36-35: R 26-9; D 10-26 (ND 6-22, SD 4-4), in the session that began Aug. 15, 1986.

CQ Senate Votes 256 - 260

Corresponding to Congressional Record Votes 256, 257, 258, 259, 260

	256	257	258	259	260
ALABAMA					
Denton	Y	Y	Y	N	Y
Heflin	Y	Y	Y	Y	Y
ALASKA					
Murkowski	+	+	?	N	Y
Stevens	Y	Y	Y	Y	Y
ARIZONA					
Goldwater	Y	Y	Y	N	N
DeConcini	Y	Y	N	N	Y
ARKANSAS					
Bumpers	+	+	?	N	Y
Pryor	Y	Y	N	N	Y
CALIFORNIA					
Wilson	Y	Y	Y	Y	Y
Cranston	Y	Y	N	N	Y
COLORADO					
Armstrong	Y	Y	N	N	N
Hart	Y	Y	N	N	Y
CONNECTICUT					
Weicker	Y	Y	Y	Y	Y
Dodd	Y	Y	N	Y	Y
DELAWARE					
Roth	Y	Y	N	N	N
Biden	Y	Y	N	N	Y
FLORIDA					
Hawkins	Y	Y	N	Y	Y
Chiles	Y	Y	N	N	Y
GEORGIA					
Mattingly	Y	Y	N	N	Y
Nunn	Y	Y	N	N	Y
HAWAII					
Inouye	Y	Y	N	Y	Y
Matsunaga	Y	Y	Y	N	Y
IDAHO					
McClure	Y	Y	Y	Y	Y
Symms	+	+	?	?	?
ILLINOIS					
Dixon	Y	Y	N	N	Y
Simon	Y	Y	N	N	Y
INDIANA					
Lugar	Y	Y	N	N	Y
Quayle	Y	Y	Y	N	Y
IOWA					
Grassley	Y	Y	Y	Y	Y
Harkin	Y	Y	N	Y	Y
KANSAS					
Dole	Y	Y	Y	Y	Y
Kassebaum	?	?	?	N	Y
KENTUCKY					
McConnell	Y	Y	Y	N	Y
Ford	Y	Y	Y	N	Y
LOUISIANA					
Johnston	Y	Y	Y	N	Y
Long	Y	Y	Y	N	+
MAINE					
Cohen	Y	Y	N	N	Y
Mitchell	Y	Y	N	N	Y
MARYLAND					
Mathias	Y	Y	Y	Y	Y
Sarbanes	Y	Y	N	Y	Y
MASSACHUSETTS					
Kennedy	Y	Y	N	Y	Y
Kerry	Y	Y	N	N	Y
MICHIGAN					
Levin	Y	Y	N	N	Y
Riegle	Y	Y	N	N	Y
MINNESOTA					
Boschwitz	Y	Y	Y	N	Y
Durenberger	Y	Y	Y	Y	Y
MISSISSIPPI					
Cochran	Y	Y	Y	N	Y
Stennis	Y	Y	Y	N	Y
MISSOURI					
Danforth	?	?	N	N	Y
Eagleton	Y	Y	N	N	Y
MONTANA					
Baucus	Y	Y	Y	N	Y
Melcher	Y	Y	Y	Y	Y
NEBRASKA					
Exon	Y	Y	N	N	N
Zorinsky	Y	Y	N	N	N
NEVADA					
Hecht	Y	Y	Y	N	N
Laxalt	Y	Y	Y	N	N
NEW HAMPSHIRE					
Humphrey	Y	Y	N	N	N
Rudman	+	+	?	Y	Y
NEW JERSEY					
Bradley	Y	Y	N	N	Y
Lautenberg	Y	Y	N	N	Y
NEW MEXICO					
Domenici	Y	Y	Y	N	Y
Bingaman	Y	Y	N	N	Y
NEW YORK					
D'Amato	Y	Y	Y	Y	Y
Moynihan	Y	Y	N	N	?
NORTH CAROLINA					
Broyhill	Y	Y	Y	N	Y
Helms	Y	Y	Y	N	N
NORTH DAKOTA					
Andrews	Y	Y	Y	Y	Y
Burdick	Y	Y	Y	Y	Y
OHIO					
Glenn	Y	Y	N	?	?
Metzenbaum	Y	Y	N	N	Y
OKLAHOMA					
Nickles	Y	Y	N	N	Y
Boren	Y	Y	N	N	Y
OREGON					
Hatfield	Y	Y	Y	Y	Y
Packwood	Y	Y	Y	Y	Y
PENNSYLVANIA					
Heinz	Y	Y	N	Y	Y
Specter	Y	Y	N	Y	Y
RHODE ISLAND					
Chafee	Y	Y	Y	N	Y
Pell	Y	Y	N	-	Y
SOUTH CAROLINA					
Thurmond	Y	Y	Y	Y	Y
Hollings	Y	Y	N	Y	Y
SOUTH DAKOTA					
Abdnor	Y	Y	Y	Y	Y
Pressler	Y	Y	N	N	Y
TENNESSEE					
Gore	Y	Y	N	Y	Y
Sasser	Y	Y	N	Y	Y
TEXAS					
Gramm	Y	Y	Y	N	N
Bentsen	Y	Y	N	N	Y
UTAH					
Garn	?	?	?	?	?
Hatch	Y	Y	Y	N	Y
VERMONT					
Stafford	Y	Y	N	N	Y
Leahy	Y	Y	N	N	Y
VIRGINIA					
Trible	Y	Y	N	N	Y
Warner	Y	Y	N	N	Y
WASHINGTON					
Evans	Y	Y	Y	N	Y
Gorton	Y	Y	Y	N	Y
WEST VIRGINIA					
Byrd	Y	Y	Y	N	Y
Rockefeller	Y	Y	Y	N	Y
WISCONSIN					
Kasten	Y	Y	N	N	Y
Proxmire	Y	Y	N	Y	N
WYOMING					
Simpson	Y	Y	Y	N	Y
Wallop	Y	Y	Y	N	N

KEY

- Y Voted for (yea).
- # Paired for.
- + Announced for.
- N Voted against (nay).
- X Paired against.
- \- Announced against.
- P Voted "present."
- C Voted "present" to avoid possible conflict of interest.
- ? Did not vote or otherwise make a position known.

Democrats *Republicans*

ND - Northern Democrats SD - Southern Democrats (Southern states - Ala., Ark., Fla., Ga., Ky., La., Miss., N.C., Okla., S.C., Tenn., Texas, Va.)

256. S Res 486. Daniloff Arrest. Adoption of the resolution to demand that the Soviet Union free Nicholas Daniloff, Moscow correspondent for *U.S. News & World Report*, who was being held on espionage charges. Adopted 93-0: R 47-0; D 46-0 (ND 33-0, SD 13-0), Sept. 9, 1986.

257. S Res 487. Terrorism in Pakistan and Turkey. Adoption of the resolution to condemn recent terrorist acts, including the hijacking of a Pan American World Airways plane in Karachi, Pakistan; the bombing of a Jewish synagogue in Istanbul, Turkey; and the kidnapping of Frank Herbert Reed and other Americans in Lebanon. Adopted 93-0: R 47-0; D 46-0 (ND 33-0, SD 13-0), Sept. 9, 1986.

258. HR 5234. Interior Appropriations, Fiscal 1987. McClure, R-Idaho, motion to table (kill) the Proxmire, D-Wis., amendment to cut by $90 million the amount appropriated in the bill for the National Forest Service road building program. The bill included $276,130,000 for the program, and President Reagan had requested $195,197,000. Motion rejected 43-51: R 32-16; D 11-35 (ND 6-27, SD 5-8), Sept. 9, 1986. (The Proxmire amendment Sept. 16 was modified *(see vote 261, p. 45-S)* and then adopted by voice vote.)

259. HR 5233. Labor, Health and Human Services, Education Appropriations, Fiscal 1987. Weicker, R-Conn., motion to table (kill) the Domenici, R-N.M., amendment to provide an additional $57 million for the Department of Education for math and science education. Motion rejected 30-66: R 18-33; D 12-33 (ND 8-23, SD 4-10), Sept. 10, 1986. (The Domenici amendment subsequently was adopted by voice vote.)

260. HR 5233. Labor, Health and Human Services, Education Appropriations, Fiscal 1987. Passage of the bill to provide $113,690,908,000 in fiscal 1987 funding (and advance fiscal 1988 and 1989 funding in some cases) for the Departments of Labor, Health and Human Services, and Education and related agencies. Passed 83-12: R 42-9; D 41-3 (ND 28-3, SD 13-0), Sept. 10, 1986. The president had requested $104,760,059,000 in fiscal 1987 and advance fiscal 1988 and 1989 funding.

	261	262	263	264	265	266	267
ALABAMA							
Denton	Y	N	N	Y	Y	Y	Y
Heflin	Y	N	Y	N	Y	Y	Y
ALASKA							
Murkowski	Y	Y	N	Y	Y	Y	Y
Stevens	Y	Y	Y	Y	Y	Y	Y
ARIZONA							
Goldwater	Y	Y	?	Y	Y	?	?
DeConcini	N	Y	N	Y	Y	Y	Y
ARKANSAS							
Bumpers	N	Y	Y	Y	Y	Y	Y
Pryor	N	Y	?	Y	N	Y	Y
CALIFORNIA							
Wilson	Y	Y	Y	Y	Y	Y	Y
Cranston	N	Y	Y	Y	N	N	Y
COLORADO							
Armstrong	Y	Y	N	N	Y	Y	Y
Hart	N	Y	Y	Y	N	N	Y
CONNECTICUT							
Weicker	Y	Y	Y	Y	Y	N	Y
Dodd	N	Y	Y	Y	N	N	Y
DELAWARE							
Roth	N	N	Y	N	Y	Y	Y
Biden	N	Y	Y	Y	N	N	Y
FLORIDA							
Hawkins	N	Y	N	Y	Y	Y	Y
Chiles	N	Y	Y	Y	Y	Y	Y
GEORGIA							
Mattingly	N	Y	N	Y	Y	Y	Y
Nunn	N	Y	Y	Y	Y	Y	Y
HAWAII							
Inouye	Y	Y	?	Y	N	N	Y
Matsunaga	Y	Y	Y	?	N	N	Y
IDAHO							
McClure	Y	Y	N	N	Y	Y	Y
Symms	Y	Y	N	N	Y	Y	Y
ILLINOIS							
Dixon	N	Y	Y	Y	N	Y	Y
Simon	N	Y	Y	Y	N	N	Y
INDIANA							
Lugar	N	Y	N	Y	Y	Y	Y
Quayle	Y	Y	N	Y	Y	Y	Y
IOWA							
Grassley	Y	Y	N	Y	Y	Y	Y
Harkin	N	Y	Y	Y	N	N	Y
KANSAS							
Dole	Y	Y	N	Y	Y	Y	Y
Kassebaum	Y	Y	Y	Y	Y	Y	Y
KENTUCKY							
McConnell	Y	Y	N	Y	Y	Y	Y
Ford	Y	Y	N	Y	Y	Y	Y
LOUISIANA							
Johnston	Y	Y	N	Y	N	Y	Y
Long	?	Y	N	Y	Y	Y	Y
MAINE							
Cohen	Y	Y	Y	Y	Y	Y	Y
Mitchell	Y	Y	Y	Y	N	N	Y
MARYLAND							
Mathias	Y	Y	Y	Y	Y	N	Y
Sarbanes	N	Y	Y	Y	N	N	Y
MASSACHUSETTS							
Kennedy	N	Y	?	Y	N	N	Y
Kerry	N	Y	Y	Y	N	N	Y
MICHIGAN							
Levin	N	Y	Y	Y	N	N	Y
Riegle	N	Y	Y	Y	N	N	Y
MINNESOTA							
Boschwitz	Y	Y	N	Y	Y	Y	Y
Durenberger	Y	Y	N	Y	Y	Y	Y
MISSISSIPPI							
Cochran	Y	Y	Y	Y	Y	Y	Y
Stennis	Y	Y	?	Y	Y	Y	Y
MISSOURI							
Danforth	N	Y	N	Y	Y	Y	Y
Eagleton	?	?	?	Y	N	N	Y
MONTANA							
Baucus	Y	Y	Y	Y	N	N	Y
Melcher	Y	Y	N	Y	N	N	Y
NEBRASKA							
Exon	N	N	N	Y	N	N	Y
Zorinsky	N	Y	N	N	Y	Y	Y
NEVADA							
Hecht	Y	Y	N	Y	Y	Y	Y
Laxalt	Y	Y	N	Y	Y	Y	Y
NEW HAMPSHIRE							
Humphrey	N	N	N	N	Y	Y	Y
Rudman	N	Y	Y	Y	Y	Y	Y
NEW JERSEY							
Bradley	N	Y	Y	Y	N	N	Y
Lautenberg	N	Y	Y	Y	N	N	Y
NEW MEXICO							
Domenici	Y	Y	N	Y	Y	Y	Y
Bingaman	N	Y	Y	Y	Y	N	Y
NEW YORK							
D'Amato	Y	Y	N	Y	Y	Y	Y
Moynihan	Y	Y	Y	Y	N	N	Y
NORTH CAROLINA							
Broyhill	Y	Y	N	Y	Y	Y	Y
Helms	Y	N	N	N	Y	Y	Y
NORTH DAKOTA							
Andrews	Y	Y	N	Y	Y	Y	Y
Burdick	Y	Y	Y	Y	N	N	Y
OHIO							
Glenn	N	Y	Y	Y	N	N	Y
Metzenbaum	N	Y	Y	Y	N	N	Y
OKLAHOMA							
Nickles	Y	Y	N	Y	Y	Y	Y
Boren	Y	Y	N	Y	Y	Y	Y
OREGON							
Hatfield	Y	Y	N	Y	Y	Y	Y
Packwood	Y	Y	Y	Y	Y	Y	Y
PENNSYLVANIA							
Heinz	N	Y	Y	Y	Y	Y	Y
Specter	?	Y	Y	Y	Y	Y	Y
RHODE ISLAND							
Chafee	Y	Y	Y	Y	Y	Y	Y
Pell	N	Y	Y	Y	Y	N	Y
SOUTH CAROLINA							
Thurmond	Y	Y	N	Y	Y	Y	Y
Hollings	N	Y	Y	Y	Y	Y	Y
SOUTH DAKOTA							
Abdnor	Y	Y	N	Y	Y	Y	Y
Pressler	Y	Y	N	Y	Y	Y	Y
TENNESSEE							
Gore	N	Y	Y	Y	N	N	Y
Sasser	N	Y	Y	Y	N	N	Y
TEXAS							
Gramm	Y	N	N	N	Y	Y	Y
Bentsen	N	Y	?	Y	Y	Y	Y
UTAH							
Garn	#	?	?	?	?	+	+
Hatch	Y	Y	N	Y	Y	Y	Y
VERMONT							
Stafford	N	Y	?	Y	Y	Y	Y
Leahy	N	Y	Y	Y	Y	N	Y
VIRGINIA							
Trible	N	Y	N	Y	Y	Y	Y
Warner	X	Y	Y	Y	Y	Y	Y
WASHINGTON							
Evans	Y	Y	Y	Y	Y	Y	Y
Gorton	Y	?	?	Y	Y	Y	Y
WEST VIRGINIA							
Byrd	Y	Y	Y	Y	N	N	Y
Rockefeller	Y	Y	Y	Y	N	N	Y
WISCONSIN							
Kasten	N	Y	N	Y	Y	Y	Y
Proxmire	N	N	N	N	Y	Y	Y
WYOMING							
Simpson	Y	Y	Y	Y	Y	Y	Y
Wallop	Y	Y	N	N	Y	Y	Y

KEY

- Y Voted for (yea).
- # Paired for.
- + Announced for.
- N Voted against (nay).
- X Paired against.
- - Announced against.
- P Voted "present."
- C Voted "present" to avoid possible conflict of interest.
- ? Did not vote or otherwise make a position known.

Democrats *Republicans*

ND - Northern Democrats SD - Southern Democrats (Southern states - Ala., Ark., Fla., Ga., Ky., La., Miss., N.C., Okla., S.C., Tenn., Texas, Va.)

261. HR 5234. Interior Appropriations, Fiscal 1987. McClure, R-Idaho, amendments to the Proxmire, D-Wis., amendment. The Proxmire amendment would have reduced by $90 million the amount appropriated for building roads in national forests. The McClure amendments restored all but $8 million and increased by $15 million the amount appropriated for land acquisition for national parks, wildlife refuges and forests. Adopted en bloc 53-42: R 39-11; D 14-31 (ND 9-23, SD 5-8), Sept. 16, 1986. (The Proxmire amendment, as amended by the McClure amendments, subsequently was adopted by voice vote.)

262. HR 5234. Interior Appropriations, Fiscal 1987. Passage of the bill to appropriate $8,041,481,000 in fiscal 1987 for the Department of Interior and related agencies. Passed 89-8: R 46-5; D 43-3 (ND 30-2, SD 13-1), Sept. 16, 1986. The president had requested $6,616,775,000 in new budget authority.

263. HR 5175. District of Columbia Appropriations, Fiscal 1987. Appropriations Committee amendment to prohibit federal funds in the bill from being used for abortions, except when the mother's life would be endangered if the fetus were carried to term, or in cases of rape or incest. The committee amendment replaced language that prohibited any funds in the bill — federal or District — from being used for abortions, except in cases endangering the mother's life. Adopted 48-42: R 16-33; D 32-9 (ND 25-5, SD 7-4), Sept. 16, 1986. (The bill subsequently was passed by voice vote. It provided $560,380,000 in federal funds and $3,009,098,000 in District funds in fiscal 1987. The president had requested $560,380,000 in federal funds and $2,989,598,000 in District funds.)

264. HR 5205. Transportation Appropriations, Fiscal 1987. Passage of the bill to appropriate $10,197,746,569 in fiscal 1987 for transportation programs. Passed 87-11: R 44-8; D 43-3 (ND 30-2, SD 13-1), Sept. 17, 1986. The president had requested $7,014,514,569 in new budget authority. A "nay" was a vote supporting the president's position.

265. Rehnquist Nomination. Dole, R-Kan., motion to invoke cloture (thus limiting debate) on President Reagan's nomination of Associate Justice William H. Rehnquist of Virginia to be chief justice of the United States. Motion agreed to 68-31: R 52-0; D 16-31 (ND 6-27, SD 10-4), Sept. 17, 1986. A three-fifths majority (60) of the total Senate is required to invoke cloture. A "yea" was a vote supporting the president's position.

266. Rehnquist Nomination. Confirmation of President Reagan's nomination of Associate Justice William H. Rehnquist of Virginia to be chief justice of the United States. Confirmed 65-33: R 49-2; D 16-31 (ND 4-29, SD 12-2), Sept. 17, 1986. A "yea" was a vote supporting the president's position.

267. Scalia Nomination. Confirmation of President Reagan's nomination of Antonin Scalia of Virginia to be an associate justice of the U.S. Supreme Court. Confirmed 98-0: R 51-0; D 47-0 (ND 33-0, SD 14-0), Sept. 17, 1986. A "yea" was a vote supporting the president's position.

CQ Senate Votes 268 - 275

Corresponding to Congressional Record Votes 268, 269, 270, 271, 272, 273, 274, 275

	268	269	270	271	272	273	274	275
ALABAMA								
Denton	Y	Y	Y	Y	Y	N	N	N
Heflin	Y	N	N	N	N	N	Y	N
ALASKA								
Murkowski	Y	N	N	Y	Y	Y	N	Y
Stevens	Y	N	Y	Y	C	Y	Y	Y
ARIZONA								
Goldwater	?	?	?	?	?	?	?	?
DeConcini	Y	Y	N	N	N	N	Y	Y
ARKANSAS								
Bumpers	Y	Y	N	N	N	N	Y	Y
Pryor	Y	Y	N	N	N	N	Y	Y
CALIFORNIA								
Wilson	Y	N	Y	Y	Y	Y	N	Y
Cranston	Y	Y	N	N	N	Y	Y	Y
COLORADO								
Armstrong	Y	N	Y	Y	Y	Y	N	Y
Hart	N	Y	N	?	N	?	Y	Y
CONNECTICUT								
Weicker	Y	Y	N	N	Y	N	N	Y
Dodd	Y	Y	N	Y	Y	N	Y	Y
DELAWARE								
Roth	Y	Y	Y	Y	N	Y	N	Y
Biden	Y	Y	N	N	N	Y	Y	Y
FLORIDA								
Hawkins	Y	Y	Y	N	Y	Y	N	N
Chiles	Y	Y	N	N	N	N	N	Y
GEORGIA								
Mattingly	Y	Y	Y	N	Y	Y	N	Y
Nunn	Y	Y	N	Y	N	N	N	Y
HAWAII								
Inouye	Y	Y	N	Y	Y	N	Y	Y
Matsunaga	?	?	?	?	?	?	?	?
IDAHO								
McClure	Y	N	N	N	Y	Y	N	N
Symms	Y	N	Y	Y	Y	Y	N	N
ILLINOIS								
Dixon	Y	Y	Y	Y	N	Y	Y	Y
Simon	Y	Y	Y	N	N	N	Y	Y
INDIANA								
Lugar	Y	Y	Y	Y	Y	N	N	N
Quayle	Y	Y	Y	Y	Y	Y	N	Y
IOWA								
Grassley	Y	Y	Y	Y	N	N	Y	Y
Harkin	N	Y	N	N	Y	N	Y	Y
KANSAS								
Dole	Y	Y	Y	Y	Y	N	Y	Y
Kassebaum	Y	Y	N	Y	Y	N	Y	Y
KENTUCKY								
McConnell	Y	Y	Y	Y	Y	Y	N	Y
Ford	Y	Y	N	N	Y	N	Y	Y
LOUISIANA								
Johnston	Y	Y	N	N	N	N	N	Y
Long	Y	N	N	Y	N	N	N	N
MAINE								
Cohen	Y	Y	N	Y	N	N	N	Y
Mitchell	Y	Y	N	N	N	N	Y	Y
MARYLAND								
Mathias	Y	N	N	N	Y	N	Y	Y
Sarbanes	Y	Y	N	N	N	N	Y	Y
MASSACHUSETTS								
Kennedy	Y	Y	Y	N	N	N	Y	Y
Kerry	Y	Y	N	N	N	Y	Y	Y
MICHIGAN								
Levin	Y	Y	N	N	N	N	Y	Y
Riegle	N	Y	N	N	N	Y	Y	Y
MINNESOTA								
Boschwitz	Y	Y	Y	Y	N	N	Y	Y
Durenberger	Y	N	N	Y	N	N	N	Y
MISSISSIPPI								
Cochran	Y	Y	N	Y	N	N	N	N
Stennis	Y	Y	N	N	N	N	N	N
MISSOURI								
Danforth	Y	Y	Y	Y	Y	Y	Y	Y
Eagleton	Y	Y	N	N	N	N	Y	Y
MONTANA								
Baucus	Y	Y	N	N	N	N	Y	Y
Melcher	Y	Y	N	N	N	N	Y	Y
NEBRASKA								
Exon	N	Y	Y	N	Y	N	N	Y
Zorinsky	Y	Y	Y	N	Y	N	N	Y
NEVADA								
Hecht	Y	Y	Y	Y	Y	Y	N	Y
Laxalt	Y	N	Y	?	Y	Y	N	Y
NEW HAMPSHIRE								
Humphrey	Y	N	Y	N	Y	N	N	Y
Rudman	Y	Y	Y	Y	Y	Y	N	Y
NEW JERSEY								
Bradley	N	N	N	N	N	Y	Y	Y
Lautenberg	Y	Y	N	Y	N	N	Y	Y
NEW MEXICO								
Domenici	Y	Y	N	N	N	N	N	Y
Bingaman	Y	Y	N	N	N	N	N	Y
NEW YORK								
D'Amato	Y	N	N	N	N	Y	Y	Y
Moynihan	N	Y	N	N	N	Y	Y	Y
NORTH CAROLINA								
Broyhill	Y	Y	Y	Y	Y	N	N	N
Helms	Y	N	Y	Y	Y	N	N	N
NORTH DAKOTA								
Andrews	N	Y	N	N	N	N	Y	Y
Burdick	N	Y	N	N	N	N	Y	Y
OHIO								
Glenn	N	Y	N	N	N	N	N	Y
Metzenbaum	N	Y	N	Y	N	N	N	Y
OKLAHOMA								
Nickles	Y	N	Y	Y	Y	N	N	Y
Boren	Y	?	?	?	?	?	?	?
OREGON								
Hatfield	Y	N	N	N	N	N	N	Y
Packwood	Y	Y	N	Y	N	N	Y	?
PENNSYLVANIA								
Heinz	Y	Y	N	Y	Y	Y	Y	Y
Specter	Y	Y	N	Y	Y	Y	Y	Y
RHODE ISLAND								
Chafee	Y	Y	Y	Y	Y	Y	N	Y
Pell	Y	Y	N	N	N	N	Y	Y
SOUTH CAROLINA								
Thurmond	Y	Y	N	N	N	Y	N	N
Hollings	Y	Y	N	N	N	N	N	N
SOUTH DAKOTA								
Abdnor	Y	N	N	Y	Y	Y	N	Y
Pressler	Y	Y	Y	Y	Y	N	Y	Y
TENNESSEE								
Gore	Y	Y	N	Y	N	N	Y	Y
Sasser	Y	Y	N	N	N	N	Y	Y
TEXAS								
Gramm	Y	Y	Y	Y	N	N	N	Y
Bentsen	Y	Y	N	Y	N	N	N	Y
UTAH								
Garn	?	?	?	?	?	?	?	?
Hatch	Y	N	N	Y	Y	Y	N	Y
VERMONT								
Stafford	Y	Y	N	Y	N	N	?	?
Leahy	Y	Y	N	N	N	N	Y	Y
VIRGINIA								
Trible	Y	Y	Y	Y	Y	N	N	Y
Warner	Y	Y	Y	Y	Y	Y	N	Y
WASHINGTON								
Evans	Y	Y	N	Y	Y	Y	N	Y
Gorton	Y	Y	N	Y	Y	Y	N	Y
WEST VIRGINIA								
Byrd	Y	Y	N	N	N	N	N	Y
Rockefeller	Y	Y	N	Y	Y	N	N	Y
WISCONSIN								
Kasten	Y	Y	Y	Y	Y	N	N	Y
Proxmire	Y	Y	N	N	N	N	N	Y
WYOMING								
Simpson	Y	Y	N	Y	Y	N	N	N
Wallop	Y	Y	Y	Y	Y	N	N	N

KEY

- Y Voted for (yea).
- # Paired for.
- + Announced for.
- N Voted against (nay).
- X Paired against.
- \- Announced against.
- P Voted "present."
- C Voted "present" to avoid possible conflict of interest.
- ? Did not vote or otherwise make a position known.

Democrats *Republicans*

ND - Northern Democrats SD - Southern Democrats (Southern states - Ala., Ark., Fla., Ga., Ky., La., Miss., N.C., Okla., S.C., Tenn., Texas, Va.)

268. S 2706. Omnibus Budget Reconciliation, Fiscal 1987. Domenici, R-N.M., motion to waive the germaneness requirement contained in the 1974 Congressional Budget and Impoundment Control Act (PL 93-344) with respect to the Domenici amendment to increase deficit reductions in the bill to $13.3 billion. Motion agreed to 87-10: R 50-1; D 37-9 (ND 23-9, SD 14-0), Sept. 19, 1986. A three-fifths majority (60) of the total Senate is required to waive the germaneness requirement contained in the budget act. (The Domenici amendment later was adopted by voice vote.)

269. S 2706. Omnibus Budget Reconciliation, Fiscal 1987. Domenici, R-N.M., motion to table (kill) the Stevens, R-Alaska, amendment to the Domenici amendment *(see vote 268, above)*, to strike a provision increasing from 10 percent to 25 percent the penalty for failure to pay income taxes. Motion agreed to 77-19: R 35-16; D 42-3 (ND 31-1, SD 11-2), Sept. 19, 1986. (The Domenici amendment later was adopted by voice vote.)

270. S 2706. Omnibus Budget Reconciliation, Fiscal 1987. Quayle, R-Ind., motion to waive the germaneness requirement contained in the 1974 Congressional Budget and Impoundment Control Act (PL 93-344) with respect to the Quayle amendment to the Domenici, R-N.M., amendment *(see vote 268, above)*, to expedite procedures for both chambers to vote on appropriations rescissions submitted by the president. Motion rejected 34-62: R 29-22; D 5-40 (ND 5-27, SD 0-13), Sept. 19, 1986. A three-fifths majority (60) of the total Senate is required to waive the germaneness requirement contained in the budget act. (The effect of the vote was to prevent consideration of the Quayle amendment. The Domenici amendment later was adopted by voice vote.)

271. S 2706. Omnibus Budget Reconciliation, Fiscal 1987. Trible, R-Va., motion to waive the germaneness requirement contained in the 1974 Congressional Budget and Impoundment Control Act (PL 93-344) with respect to the Trible amendment to the Domenici, R-N.M., amendment *(see vote 268, above)*, to lease Washington-Dulles International Airport and National Airport to a local authority. Motion rejected 49-45: R 39-11; D 10-34 (ND 6-25, SD 4-9), Sept. 19, 1986. A three-fifths majority (60) of the total Senate is required to waive the germaneness requirement contained in the budget act. (The effect of the vote was to prevent consideration of the Trible amendment. The Domenici amendment later was adopted by voice vote.)

272. S 2706. Omnibus Budget Reconciliation, Fiscal 1987. Kassebaum, R-Kan., motion to waive the germaneness requirement contained in the 1974 Congressional Budget and Impoundment Control Act (PL 93-344) with respect to the Kassebaum amendment to the Domenici, R-N.M., amendment *(see vote 268, above)*, to set federal liability standards for general aviation equipment manufacturers. Motion rejected 43-52: R 36-14; D 7-38 (ND 6-26, SD 1-12), Sept. 19, 1986. A three-fifths majority (60) of the total Senate is required to waive the germaneness requirement contained in the budget act. (The effect of the vote was to prevent consideration of the Kassebaum amendment. The Domenici amendment later was adopted by voice vote.)

273. S 2706. Omnibus Budget Reconciliation, Fiscal 1987. D'Amato, R-N.Y., amendment to the Domenici, R-N.M., amendment *(see vote 268, above)*, to delete a provision that would assess Federal Deposit Insurance Corporation fees on the foreign deposits of U.S. banks. Rejected 32-63: R 25-26; D 7-37 (ND 7-24, SD 0-13), Sept. 19, 1986. (The Domenici amendment later was adopted by voice vote.)

274. S 2706. Omnibus Budget Reconciliation, Fiscal 1987. Danforth, R-Mo., motion to waive the germaneness requirement contained in the 1974 Congressional Budget and Impoundment Control Act (PL 93-344) with respect to the Danforth amendment to the Domenici, R-N.M., amendment *(see vote 268, above)*, to preserve the seniority rights of airline employees in the case of a merger of companies. Motion rejected 43-52: R 13-37; D 30-15 (ND 24-8, SD 6-7), Sept. 19, 1986. A three-fifths majority (60) of the total Senate is required to waive the germaneness requirement contained in the budget act. (The effect of the vote was to prevent consideration of the Danforth amendment. The Domenici amendment later was adopted by voice vote.)

275. S 2706. Omnibus Budget Reconciliation, Fiscal 1987. Cohen, R-Maine, motion to waive the extraneous-matter limitation of the Consolidated Omnibus Budget Reconciliation Act of 1985 (PL 99-272) with respect to provisions in the bill establishing administrative procedures for claims against persons who make fraudulent claims against the government. Motion agreed to 79-15: R 38-11; D 41-4 (ND 32-0, SD 9-4), Sept. 19, 1986. A three-fifths majority (60) of the total Senate is required to waive the extraneous-matter limitation of the 1985 reconciliation act. (The effect of the vote was to keep the provisions in the bill.)

Corresponding to Congressional Record Votes 276, 277, 278, 279, 280, 281, 282, 283

	276	277	278	279	280	281	282	283
ALABAMA								
Denton	N	Y	N	N	N	Y	Y	Y
Heflin	N	Y	N	N	N	Y	Y	N
ALASKA								
Murkowski	N	Y	N	N	N	Y	Y	N
Stevens	N	Y	N	N	N	Y	?	N
ARIZONA								
Goldwater	?	?	?	N	N	Y	Y	?
DeConcini	Y	Y	N	N	N	N	Y	Y
ARKANSAS								
Bumpers	N	Y	N	N	N	N	Y	Y
Pryor	?	Y	N	N	N	Y	Y	Y
CALIFORNIA								
Wilson	N	Y	Y	N	N	Y	Y	Y
Cranston	N	Y	N	?	?	?	?	?
COLORADO								
Armstrong	N	Y	Y	N	N	Y	Y	Y
Hart	?	N	N	N	N	N	Y	N
CONNECTICUT								
Weicker	N	Y	N	N	Y	N	N	N
Dodd	N	Y	N	N	Y	N	N	N
DELAWARE								
Roth	N	Y	N	N	Y	N	N	Y
Biden	Y	Y	N	N	N	N	Y	N
FLORIDA								
Hawkins	N	Y	N	N	Y	N	N	Y
Chiles	N	Y	N	N	Y	N	N	Y
GEORGIA								
Mattingly	N	Y	N	N	Y	N	N	Y
Nunn	N	Y	N	N	N	N	Y	Y
HAWAII								
Inouye	Y	Y	N	?	?	?	?	N
Matsunaga	?	?	?	N	N	Y	Y	N
IDAHO								
McClure	N	Y	N	N	N	Y	Y	Y
Symms	N	Y	N	N	N	Y	Y	Y
ILLINOIS								
Dixon	Y	Y	N	N	Y	N	N	N
Simon	Y	Y	N	N	Y	N	N	N
INDIANA								
Lugar	N	Y	N	N	N	Y	Y	Y
Quayle	N	Y	N	N	N	N	?	Y
IOWA								
Grassley	N	Y	N	N	N	Y	Y	Y
Harkin	Y	N	N	N	N	N	Y	N
KANSAS								
Dole	N	Y	N	N	N	N	Y	Y
Kassebaum	N	Y	N	N	N	N	?	Y
KENTUCKY								
McConnell	N	Y	N	N	N	N	Y	Y
Ford	Y	Y	N	N	Y	N	Y	N
LOUISIANA								
Johnston	Y	Y	N	N	N	Y	Y	N
Long	N	Y	Y	N	N	Y	Y	N
MAINE								
Cohen	Y	Y	Y	N	Y	N	N	Y
Mitchell	Y	Y	N	N	Y	N	N	N
MARYLAND								
Mathias	N	Y	N	N	Y	N	N	N
Sarbanes	Y	Y	N	N	Y	N	N	N
MASSACHUSETTS								
Kennedy	Y	Y	N	N	N	N	Y	N
Kerry	Y	Y	N	N	N	N	Y	N
MICHIGAN								
Levin	Y	Y	N	N	Y	N	N	N
Riegle	Y	N	N	N	Y	N	Y	N
MINNESOTA								
Boschwitz	N	Y	N	N	Y	N	N	Y
Durenberger	Y	Y	N	N	N	N	Y	N
MISSISSIPPI								
Cochran	N	Y	N	N	N	Y	Y	Y
Stennis	N	Y	Y	N	N	N	Y	?
MISSOURI								
Danforth	N	Y	Y	N	Y	N	N	N
Eagleton	N	Y	N	N	Y	N	N	N
MONTANA								
Baucus	N	Y	N	N	N	Y	Y	N
Melcher	Y	Y	N	N	N	Y	Y	N
NEBRASKA								
Exon	Y	N	N	N	N	N	Y	Y
Zorinsky	Y	Y	N	N	N	N	?	Y
NEVADA								
Hecht	N	Y	Y	N	N	Y	Y	Y
Laxalt	N	Y	N	N	N	Y	Y	Y
NEW HAMPSHIRE								
Humphrey	N	Y	Y	N	N	Y	Y	Y
Rudman	N	Y	Y	N	N	Y	Y	Y
NEW JERSEY								
Bradley	Y	Y	N	N	Y	N	N	N
Lautenberg	Y	Y	N	N	Y	N	N	N
NEW MEXICO								
Domenici	N	Y	N	N	N	Y	Y	Y
Bingaman	Y	Y	N	N	N	Y	Y	N
NEW YORK								
D'Amato	N	Y	N	N	Y	N	N	N
Moynihan	N	N	N	N	Y	N	N	N
NORTH CAROLINA								
Broyhill	N	Y	N	N	N	Y	Y	Y
Helms	N	Y	Y	N	N	Y	Y	Y
NORTH DAKOTA								
Andrews	Y	Y	N	N	N	Y	Y	N
Burdick	N	Y	N	N	N	N	Y	N
OHIO								
Glenn	Y	N	N	N	Y	N	N	N
Metzenbaum	Y	N	N	?	Y	N	N	N
OKLAHOMA								
Nickles	N	Y	N	N	N	Y	Y	Y
Boren	?	?	?	N	N	Y	Y	Y
OREGON								
Hatfield	N	Y	N	N	Y	N	N	Y
Packwood	N	Y	N	N	N	N	Y	N
PENNSYLVANIA								
Heinz	N	Y	N	N	Y	N	N	N
Specter	Y	Y	N	N	Y	?	?	?
RHODE ISLAND								
Chafee	N	Y	N	N	Y	N	N	N
Pell	Y	Y	N	N	Y	N	N	N
SOUTH CAROLINA								
Thurmond	N	Y	N	N	N	Y	Y	Y
Hollings	N	Y	Y	N	Y	N	N	Y
SOUTH DAKOTA								
Abdnor	N	Y	N	N	N	Y	Y	Y
Pressler	N	Y	N	N	N	Y	Y	Y
TENNESSEE								
Gore	Y	Y	N	N	Y	N	N	N
Sasser	Y	Y	N	N	N	N	Y	N
TEXAS								
Gramm	N	Y	Y	N	N	Y	Y	Y
Bentsen	N	Y	N	N	N	N	Y	Y
UTAH								
Garn	?	?	?	?	?	?	?	?
Hatch	N	Y	Y	N	N	Y	Y	Y
VERMONT								
Stafford	?	?	?	N	Y	N	N	Y
Leahy	Y	Y	N	N	N	N	Y	N
VIRGINIA								
Trible	N	Y	N	N	Y	N	N	Y
Warner	Y	Y	N	N	Y	N	N	Y
WASHINGTON								
Evans	N	Y	N	N	Y	N	N	Y
Gorton	N	Y	N	N	Y	N	Y	Y
WEST VIRGINIA								
Byrd	N	Y	N	N	Y	N	N	N
Rockefeller	Y	Y	N	N	Y	N	N	N
WISCONSIN								
Kasten	N	Y	N	N	Y	N	N	Y
Proxmire	N	Y	Y	N	Y	N	N	N
WYOMING								
Simpson	N	Y	N	N	N	Y	Y	Y
Wallop	N	Y	Y	N	N	Y	Y	Y

KEY

- Y Voted for (yea).
- # Paired for.
- \+ Announced for.
- N Voted against (nay).
- X Paired against.
- \- Announced against.
- P Voted "present."
- C Voted "present" to avoid possible conflict of interest.
- ? Did not vote or otherwise make a position known.

Democrats *Republicans*

ND - Northern Democrats SD - Southern Democrats (Southern states - Ala., Ark., Fla., Ga., Ky., La., Miss., N.C., Okla., S.C., Tenn., Texas, Va.)

276. S 2706. Omnibus Budget Reconciliation, Fiscal 1987. Metzenbaum, D-Ohio, motion to waive the extraneous-matter limitation of the Consolidated Omnibus Budget Reconciliation Act of 1985 (PL 99-272) with respect to a section of the bill affecting state energy conservation programs. Motion rejected 32-61: R 5-45; D 27-16 (ND 23-8, SD 4-8), Sept. 19, 1986. A three-fifths majority (60) of the total Senate is required to waive the extraneous-matter limitation of the 1985 reconciliation act. (The effect of the vote was to strike the provision from the bill.)

277. S 2706. Omnibus Budget Reconciliation, Fiscal 1987. Passage of the bill to reduce the projected fiscal 1987 deficit by $13.3 billion. Passed 88-7: R 50-0; D 38-7 (ND 25-7, SD 13-0), Sept. 19, 1986.

278. S J Res 412. Sequestration Order. Passage of the joint resolution to affirm the Aug. 20, 1986, report of the Congressional Budget Office and the Office of Management and Budget setting out $19.4 billion in across-the-board spending cuts to bring the fiscal 1987 deficit into compliance with the target of $144 billion, as required by the Gramm-Rudman-Hollings anti-deficit law (PL 99-177). Rejected 15-80: R 11-39; D 4-41 (ND 1-31, SD 3-10), in the session that began Sept. 19, 1986. (A Dole, R-Kan., motion, to reconsider the vote by which the joint resolution was rejected, was left pending.)

279. S 2760. Product Liability Reform. Simpson, R-Wyo., motion to table (kill) the Kasten, R-Wis., motion to proceed to the consideration of the bill to make changes in product liability laws. Motion rejected 0-96: R 0-52; D 0-44 (ND 0-30, SD 0-14), Sept. 23, 1986.

280. S 2405. Omnibus Highway Authorization. Danforth, R-Mo., motion to table (kill) the Symms, R-Idaho, amendment to allow states to raise the speed limit to 65 mph on rural Interstate highways outside urbanized areas with populations of 50,000 or more. Motion rejected 40-57: R 19-33; D 21-24 (ND 17-14, SD 4-10), Sept. 23, 1986. (The Symms amendment later was adopted *(see vote 282, below)*.)

281. S 2405. Omnibus Highway Authorization. Hecht, R-Nev., amendment to the Symms, R-Idaho, amendment, to allow states to raise the speed limit to 65 mph on any federally funded rural highways outside urbanized areas with populations of 50,000 or more. Rejected 36-60: R 27-24; D 9-36 (ND 4-27, SD 5-9), Sept. 23, 1986. (The Symms amendment subsequently was adopted *(see vote 282, below)*.)

282. S 2405. Omnibus Highway Authorization. Symms, R-Idaho, amendment to allow states to raise the speed limit to 65 mph on rural Interstate highways outside urbanized areas with populations of 50,000 or more. Adopted 56-36: R 31-17; D 25-19 (ND 14-16, SD 11-3), Sept. 23, 1986.

283. S 2405. Omnibus Highway Authorization. Symms, R-Idaho, amendment to increase from $2,000 to $250,000 the minimum value of contracts covered by the 1931 Davis-Bacon Act, which requires contractors to pay the local prevailing wage. Adopted 49-46: R 39-11; D 10-35 (ND 3-29, SD 7-6), Sept. 23, 1986.

CQ Senate Votes 284 - 290

Corresponding to Congressional Record Votes 284, 285, 286, 287, 288, 289, 290

KEY

- Y Voted for (yea).
- # Paired for.
- + Announced for.
- N Voted against (nay).
- X Paired against.
- - Announced against.
- P Voted "present."
- C Voted "present" to avoid possible conflict of interest.
- ? Did not vote or otherwise make a position known.

Democrats ***Republicans***

	284	285	286	287	288	289	290
ALABAMA							
Denton	N	N	N	Y	Y	Y	N
Heflin	N	N	Y	Y	Y	Y	Y
ALASKA							
Murkowski	N	N	Y	Y	Y	Y	N
Stevens	N	N	Y	Y	Y	Y	N
ARIZONA							
Goldwater	?	Y	Y	?	Y	N	N
DeConcini	N	N	Y	N	Y	Y	N
ARKANSAS							
Bumpers	N	N	Y	Y	Y	N	Y
Pryor	N	N	N	N	Y	Y	Y
CALIFORNIA							
Wilson	N	Y	Y	Y	Y	Y	Y
Cranston	?	Y	Y	N	Y	Y	Y
COLORADO							
Armstrong	N	Y	Y	Y	Y	Y	Y
Hart	N	Y	Y	N	Y	N	N
CONNECTICUT							
Weicker	N	Y	Y	Y	Y	N	Y
Dodd	N	Y	Y	N	Y	N	Y
DELAWARE							
Roth	?	Y	Y	Y	Y	Y	Y
Biden	N	N	?	N	Y	N	Y
FLORIDA							
Hawkins	N	Y	N	Y	Y	Y	Y
Chiles	N	Y	Y	Y	Y	N	Y
GEORGIA							
Mattingly	N	N	Y	Y	Y	Y	Y
Nunn	N	Y	Y	Y	Y	N	Y
HAWAII							
Inouye	N	Y	Y	Y	Y	N	?
Matsunaga	N	?	Y	Y	Y	N	Y
IDAHO							
McClure	N	Y	Y	Y	Y	Y	Y
Symms	N	Y	N	Y	Y	Y	Y
ILLINOIS							
Dixon	N	N	Y	N	Y	Y	Y
Simon	N	Y	Y	N	Y	N	Y
INDIANA							
Lugar	N	Y	Y	Y	Y	N	Y
Quayle	N	Y	N	Y	Y	Y	Y
IOWA							
Grassley	N	N	Y	Y	Y	Y	N
Harkin	N	N	N	N	Y	N	Y
KANSAS							
Dole	N	Y	Y	Y	Y	Y	Y
Kassebaum	N	Y	N	Y	Y	Y	N
KENTUCKY							
McConnell	Y	N	Y	Y	Y	Y	Y
Ford	N	N	N	Y	Y	Y	Y
LOUISIANA							
Johnston	N	Y	Y	Y	Y	N	Y
Long	N	N	N	Y	Y	N	Y
MAINE							
Cohen	Y	N	Y	N	Y	N	Y
Mitchell	Y	N	Y	N	Y	N	Y
MARYLAND							
Mathias	N	Y	Y	Y	Y	N	Y
Sarbanes	N	N	Y	N	Y	N	Y
MASSACHUSETTS							
Kennedy	N	N	Y	N	Y	Y	Y
Kerry	N	Y	Y	N	Y	Y	Y
MICHIGAN							
Levin	N	N	N	N	Y	N	Y
Riegle	N	N	N	N	Y	N	Y
MINNESOTA							
Boschwitz	N	Y	Y	Y	Y	N	N
Durenberger	Y	Y	Y	Y	Y	N	N
MISSISSIPPI							
Cochran	N	N	Y	Y	Y	Y	Y
Stennis	?	N	Y	Y	Y	N	Y
MISSOURI							
Danforth	N	Y	Y	Y	Y	Y	Y
Eagleton	N	N	Y	N	Y	N	Y
MONTANA							
Baucus	N	Y	N	Y	Y	N	N
Melcher	N	N	Y	N	Y	N	Y
NEBRASKA							
Exon	N	Y	Y	Y	Y	N	Y
Zorinsky	Y	Y	Y	Y	Y	Y	Y
NEVADA							
Hecht	N	Y	N	Y	Y	Y	N
Laxalt	N	Y	Y	Y	Y	Y	N
NEW HAMPSHIRE							
Humphrey	Y	Y	Y	Y	Y	N	Y
Rudman	N	Y	Y	Y	Y	Y	Y
NEW JERSEY							
Bradley	N	Y	Y	N	Y	N	Y
Lautenberg	Y	Y	N	N	Y	N	Y
NEW MEXICO							
Domenici	N	N	Y	Y	Y	N	N
Bingaman	N	Y	Y	Y	Y	Y	Y
NEW YORK							
D'Amato	N	N	N	N	Y	Y	Y
Moynihan	N	Y	Y	N	Y	N	Y
NORTH CAROLINA							
Broyhill	N	N	Y	Y	Y	Y	Y
Helms	N	N	Y	Y	Y	Y	Y
NORTH DAKOTA							
Andrews	N	Y	Y	Y	Y	Y	N
Burdick	N	Y	N	Y	Y	Y	N
OHIO							
Glenn	N	N	N	N	Y	N	Y
Metzenbaum	N	?	?	?	Y	N	Y
OKLAHOMA							
Nickles	N	N	Y	Y	Y	Y	N
Boren	N	N	Y	Y	Y	N	N
OREGON							
Hatfield	N	Y	Y	Y	Y	Y	N
Packwood	N	Y	Y	Y	Y	Y	Y
PENNSYLVANIA							
Heinz	Y	N	N	Y	Y	Y	Y
Specter	?	N	N	N	Y	Y	Y
RHODE ISLAND							
Chafee	Y	Y	Y	N	Y	N	N
Pell	N	Y	Y	N	Y	Y	Y
SOUTH CAROLINA							
Thurmond	N	N	N	Y	Y	Y	N
Hollings	N	N	Y	N	Y	N	Y
SOUTH DAKOTA							
Abdnor	Y	N	N	Y	Y	Y	N
Pressler	N	N	N	Y	Y	Y	N
TENNESSEE							
Gore	N	Y	N	N	Y	N	Y
Sasser	N	N	N	Y	Y	Y	Y
TEXAS							
Gramm	N	Y	Y	Y	Y	Y	Y
Bentsen	N	Y	Y	Y	Y	N	Y
UTAH							
Garn	?	?	?	?	?	?	?
Hatch	N	Y	Y	Y	Y	Y	Y
VERMONT							
Stafford	Y	Y	Y	Y	Y	N	Y
Leahy	Y	Y	Y	N	Y	N	Y
VIRGINIA							
Trible	N	Y	Y	Y	Y	Y	N
Warner	N	Y	N	Y	Y	Y	Y
WASHINGTON							
Evans	Y	Y	Y	Y	Y	N	Y
Gorton	Y	Y	Y	Y	Y	Y	Y
WEST VIRGINIA							
Byrd	N	N	N	N	Y	N	Y
Rockefeller	N	Y	N	N	Y	N	?
WISCONSIN							
Kasten	N	Y	N	Y	Y	Y	Y
Proxmire	Y	Y	Y	N	Y	N	Y
WYOMING							
Simpson	Y	N	Y	Y	Y	Y	N
Wallop	N	Y	Y	Y	Y	Y	N

ND - Northern Democrats SD - Southern Democrats (Southern states - Ala., Ark., Fla., Ga., Ky., La., Miss., N.C., Okla., S.C., Tenn., Texas, Va.)

284. S 2405. Omnibus Highway Authorization. Stafford, R-Vt., motion to table (kill) the Inouye, D-Hawaii, amendment to exempt the H-3 Interstate highway project in Hawaii from a 1984 injunction issued on environmental grounds by the 9th U.S. Circuit Court of Appeals. Motion rejected 16-78: R 11-38; D 5-40 (ND 5-27, SD 0-13), Sept. 23, 1986. (The Inouye amendment subsequently was adopted by voice vote.)

285. S 2405. Omnibus Highway Authorization. Symms, R-Idaho, motion to table (kill) the Cochran, R-Miss., amendment to prohibit the use of imported cement and cement products on federally funded highway projects. Motion agreed to 56-41: R 33-19; D 23-22 (ND 18-13, SD 5-9), Sept. 24, 1986.

286. S 2405. Omnibus Highway Authorization. Domenici, R-N.M., motion to table (kill) the Specter, R-Pa., amendment to increase the limits on funds that could be obligated from the Highway Trust Fund from $12.3 billion to $14.2 billion in each of fiscal 1988-90. Motion agreed to 69-28: R 38-14; D 31-14 (ND 22-9, SD 9-5), Sept. 24, 1986.

287. S 2405. Omnibus Highway Authorization. Symms, R-Idaho, amendment to delete a provision allowing state and local governments to reject bids for work on federally funded highway projects by contractors doing business with South Africa. Adopted 65-32: R 47-4; D 18-28 (ND 7-25, SD 11-3), Sept. 24, 1986.

288. HR 3129. Omnibus Highway Authorization. Passage of the bill to authorize $52 billion for highway programs and $13 billion for mass transit programs in fiscal years 1987-90. Passed 99-0: R 52-0; D 47-0 (ND 33-0, SD 14-0), Sept. 24, 1986. (The Senate previously had moved to strike the text of the House-passed bill and insert the provisions of S 2405, the Senate version of the bill.)

289. S 2477. Intelligence Authorization, Fiscal 1987. Helms, R-N.C., amendment to require the CIA to report to Congress by March 1, 1987, on the role of Panama's armed forces in alleged human rights violations, drug trafficking and arms trade. Adopted 53-46: R 40-12; D 13-34 (ND 9-24, SD 4-10), Sept. 24, 1986. (The Senate subsequently moved to strike the text of HR 4759, the House-passed version of the bill, and insert the provisions of S 2477. The Senate then passed HR 4759 by voice vote.)

290. S 2045. Commodity Futures Trading Commission. Lugar, R-Ind., motion to table (kill) the Abdnor, R-S.D., amendment to ban trading in live-cattle futures and feeder-cattle futures. Motion agreed to 71-26: R 31-21; D 40-5 (ND 27-4, SD 13-1), Sept. 24, 1986.

	291	292	293	294	295
ALABAMA					
Denton	Y	?	?	N	Y
Heflin	Y	Y	Y	N	N
ALASKA					
Murkowski	Y	Y	Y	N	Y
Stevens	Y	Y	Y	Y	Y
ARIZONA					
Goldwater	Y	N	?	N	Y
DeConcini	Y	Y	Y	N	N
ARKANSAS					
Bumpers	Y	Y	Y	N	Y
Pryor	+	?	?	-	+
CALIFORNIA					
Wilson	Y	Y	Y	N	Y
Cranston	Y	Y	Y	N	N
COLORADO					
Armstrong	Y	Y	Y	N	Y
Hart	Y	Y	Y	N	N
CONNECTICUT					
Weicker	Y	N	N	N	Y
Dodd	Y	Y	Y	N	Y
DELAWARE					
Roth	Y	Y	Y	N	Y
Biden	Y	Y	Y	N	Y
FLORIDA					
Hawkins	Y	Y	Y	N	Y
Chiles	Y	Y	Y	N	Y
GEORGIA					
Mattingly	Y	Y	Y	N	Y
Nunn	Y	Y	Y	N	Y
HAWAII					
Inouye	Y	Y	Y	N	Y
Matsunaga	Y	Y	Y	N	Y
IDAHO					
McClure	Y	Y	Y	Y	Y
Symms	Y	Y	Y	?	?
ILLINOIS					
Dixon	Y	Y	Y	N	Y
Simon	Y	Y	Y	N	Y
INDIANA					
Lugar	Y	Y	Y	N	Y
Quayle	Y	N	N	N	Y

	291	292	293	294	295
IOWA					
Grassley	Y	Y	Y	N	Y
Harkin	Y	Y	Y	N	N
KANSAS					
Dole	Y	Y	Y	N	Y
Kassebaum	Y	Y	Y	N	Y
KENTUCKY					
McConnell	Y	Y	Y	N	Y
Ford	Y	Y	Y	N	Y
LOUISIANA					
Johnston	Y	N	Y	N	N
Long	Y	Y	Y	N	Y
MAINE					
Cohen	Y	Y	Y	N	Y
Mitchell	Y	Y	Y	N	Y
MARYLAND					
Mathias	Y	?	?	N	Y
Sarbanes	Y	Y	Y	N	Y
MASSACHUSETTS					
Kennedy	Y	Y	Y	N	Y
Kerry	Y	Y	Y	N	Y
MICHIGAN					
Levin	Y	?	Y	N	Y
Riegle	Y	Y	Y	N	Y
MINNESOTA					
Boschwitz	Y	Y	Y	N	Y
Durenberger	Y	Y	Y	N	Y
MISSISSIPPI					
Cochran	Y	Y	Y	N	Y
Stennis	N	Y	Y	N	N
MISSOURI					
Danforth	Y	Y	Y	N	Y
Eagleton	Y	Y	Y	N	Y
MONTANA					
Baucus	Y	Y	Y	N	N
Melcher	Y	Y	Y	N	N
NEBRASKA					
Exon	Y	Y	Y	N	Y
Zorinsky	Y	Y	Y	N	Y
NEVADA					
Hecht	Y	Y	Y	N	Y
Laxalt	Y	Y	Y	N	Y

	291	292	293	294	295
NEW HAMPSHIRE					
Humphrey	Y	Y	Y	N	Y
Rudman	Y	Y	Y	N	Y
NEW JERSEY					
Bradley	Y	Y	Y	N	Y
Lautenberg	Y	Y	Y	N	Y
NEW MEXICO					
Domenici	Y	Y	Y	N	Y
Bingaman	Y	Y	Y	N	Y
NEW YORK					
D'Amato	Y	Y	N	N	N
Moynihan	Y	Y	?	N	Y
NORTH CAROLINA					
Broyhill	Y	Y	Y	N	Y
Helms	Y	Y	Y	Y	Y
NORTH DAKOTA					
Andrews	Y	Y	Y	N	Y
Burdick	Y	Y	Y	N	Y
OHIO					
Glenn	Y	Y	Y	N	Y
Metzenbaum	Y	Y	Y	N	N
OKLAHOMA					
Nickles	Y	Y	N	N	Y
Boren	Y	Y	Y	N	Y
OREGON					
Hatfield	Y	Y	Y	N	Y
Packwood	Y	Y	Y	N	Y
PENNSYLVANIA					
Heinz	Y	Y	Y	N	Y
Specter	Y	Y	Y	N	Y
RHODE ISLAND					
Chafee	Y	Y	Y	N	Y
Pell	Y	Y	Y	N	Y
SOUTH CAROLINA					
Thurmond	Y	Y	Y	N	Y
Hollings	Y	Y	Y	N	N
SOUTH DAKOTA					
Abdnor	Y	Y	Y	N	Y
Pressler	Y	Y	Y	N	Y
TENNESSEE					
Gore	Y	Y	Y	N	Y
Sasser	Y	Y	Y	N	Y

KEY

- Y Voted for (yea).
- # Paired for.
- \+ Announced for.
- N Voted against (nay).
- X Paired against.
- \- Announced against.
- P Voted "present."
- C Voted "present" to avoid possible conflict of interest.
- ? Did not vote or otherwise make a position known.

Democrats *Republicans*

	291	292	293	294	295
TEXAS					
Gramm	Y	Y	Y	N	Y
Bentsen	Y	Y	Y	N	Y
UTAH					
Garn	?	?	?	?	?
Hatch	Y	Y	Y	Y	Y
VERMONT					
Stafford	Y	Y	?	N	Y
Leahy	Y	Y	Y	N	Y
VIRGINIA					
Trible	Y	Y	Y	N	Y
Warner	Y	Y	Y	N	Y
WASHINGTON					
Evans	Y	Y	Y	N	Y
Gorton	Y	Y	Y	N	Y
WEST VIRGINIA					
Byrd	Y	Y	Y	N	Y
Rockefeller	Y	Y	Y	N	Y
WISCONSIN					
Kasten	Y	Y	Y	N	Y
Proxmire	Y	N	N	N	Y
WYOMING					
Simpson	Y	Y	Y	N	N
Wallop	Y	Y	N	Y	Y

ND - Northern Democrats SD - Southern Democrats (Southern states - Ala., Ark., Fla., Ga., Ky., La., Miss., N.C., Okla., S.C., Tenn., Texas, Va.)

291. S 2760. Product Liability Reform. Kasten, R-Wis., motion to invoke cloture (thus limiting debate) on the Kasten motion to proceed to the consideration of the bill to regulate interstate commerce by providing for a uniform product liability law. Motion agreed to 97-1: R 52-0; D 45-1 (ND 33-0, SD 12-1), Sept. 25, 1986. A three-fifths majority (60) of the total Senate is required to invoke cloture. (The Kasten motion later was agreed to *(see vote 295, below).*)

292. Procedural Motion. Kasten, R-Wis., motion to instruct the sergeant-at-arms to request the attendance of absent senators. Motion agreed to 90-5: R 47-3; D 43-2 (ND 31-1, SD 12-1), Sept. 25, 1986.

293. Procedural Motion. Kasten, R-Wis., motion to instruct the sergeant-at-arms to request the attendance of absent senators. Motion agreed to 87-6: R 43-5; D 44-1 (ND 31-1, SD 13-0), Sept. 25, 1986.

294. S 2760. Product Liability Reform. Byrd, D-W.Va., appeal of the chair's ruling that Sen. Hollings had already delivered two speeches on the same subject. Ruling of the chair rejected 5-92: R 5-46; D 0-46 (ND 0-33, SD 0-13), Sept. 25, 1986. (Under Senate rules, a senator may deliver only two "speeches" on the same subject on the same legislative day. The effect of the vote was to establish a precedent that a procedural motion, in and of itself, does not constitute a speech.)

295. S 2760. Product Liability Reform. Kasten, R-Wis., motion to proceed to the consideration of the bill to regulate interstate commerce by providing for a uniform product liability law. Motion agreed to 84-13: R 49-2; D 35-11 (ND 26-7, SD 9-4), Sept. 25, 1986.

CQ Senate Votes 296 - 303

Corresponding to Congressional Record Votes 296, 297, 298, 299, 300, 301, 302, 303

	296	297	298	299	300	301	302	303
ALABAMA								
Denton	Y	Y	Y	Y	N	N	Y	N
Heflin	N	Y	Y	Y	N	Y	Y	Y
ALASKA								
Murkowski	Y	Y	Y	N	N	N	Y	N
Stevens	Y	Y	N	Y	N	N	Y	Y
ARIZONA								
Goldwater	Y	Y	Y	Y	?	N	Y	N
DeConcini	N	Y	Y	N	N	Y	Y	Y
ARKANSAS								
Bumpers	Y	Y	Y	Y	N	Y	Y	Y
Pryor	?	?	?	?	?	?	Y	Y
CALIFORNIA								
Wilson	Y	Y	Y	N	N	Y	Y	C
Cranston	Y	Y	N	Y	Y	?	Y	Y
COLORADO								
Armstrong	Y	Y	?	Y	N	N	Y	N
Hart	Y	Y	N	Y	Y	Y	Y	N
CONNECTICUT								
Weicker	N	N	N	Y	Y	N	Y	N
Dodd	N	Y	N	Y	N	Y	Y	N
DELAWARE								
Roth	N	Y	N	Y	N	N	Y	N
Biden	Y	Y	Y	Y	N	Y	Y	Y
FLORIDA								
Hawkins	Y	Y	Y	N	N	?	Y	Y
Chiles	N	Y	Y	Y	N	Y	Y	Y
GEORGIA								
Mattingly	Y	Y	Y	N	N	N	Y	Y
Nunn	N	Y	Y	Y	N	Y	Y	Y
HAWAII								
Inouye	N	Y	N	Y	Y	Y	Y	Y
Matsunaga	Y	Y	N	Y	Y	Y	Y	N
IDAHO								
McClure	Y	Y	Y	Y	N	N	Y	Y
Symms	Y	Y	Y	Y	N	N	Y	N
ILLINOIS								
Dixon	Y	Y	Y	N	N	N	Y	Y
Simon	-	?	?	?	?	Y	Y	Y
INDIANA								
Lugar	Y	Y	Y	Y	N	Y	Y	N
Quayle	Y	?	?	?	?	N	Y	N
IOWA								
Grassley	Y	Y	N	N	N	N	Y	Y
Harkin	Y	Y	N	Y	Y	Y	Y	N
KANSAS								
Dole	Y	Y	Y	Y	N	N	Y	Y
Kassebaum	Y	Y	Y	Y	N	Y	Y	N
KENTUCKY								
McConnell	Y	Y	Y	N	N	N	Y	Y
Ford	Y	Y	Y	Y	N	Y	Y	Y
LOUISIANA								
Johnston	Y	Y	Y	Y	N	Y	Y	Y
Long	Y	Y	Y	N	N	N	Y	Y
MAINE								
Cohen	Y	Y	Y	Y	Y	N	Y	Y
Mitchell	Y	Y	Y	Y	Y	Y	Y	Y
MARYLAND								
Mathias	Y	Y	N	Y	Y	Y	Y	Y
Sarbanes	Y	Y	Y	Y	Y	Y	Y	Y
MASSACHUSETTS								
Kennedy	Y	?	?	?	?	Y	Y	N
Kerry	Y	?	?	?	?	Y	Y	Y
MICHIGAN								
Levin	N	Y	N	Y	N	Y	Y	Y
Riegle	Y	Y	Y	N	N	Y	Y	Y
MINNESOTA								
Boschwitz	Y	Y	Y	Y	Y	N	Y	Y
Durenberger	Y	N	N	Y	Y	N	Y	N
MISSISSIPPI								
Cochran	Y	?	?	?	?	N	Y	N
Stennis	Y	N	Y	Y	Y	N	Y	N
MISSOURI								
Danforth	N	Y	Y	Y	Y	N	Y	Y
Eagleton	N	Y	N	Y	Y	Y	Y	Y
MONTANA								
Baucus	Y	Y	N	Y	N	Y	Y	Y
Melcher	N	Y	N	Y	Y	Y	N	Y
NEBRASKA								
Exon	N	Y	N	Y	N	Y	Y	Y
Zorinsky	Y	Y	Y	Y	N	N	Y	Y
NEVADA								
Hecht	Y	Y	Y	Y	N	N	Y	Y
Laxalt	Y	Y	N	Y	N	N	Y	Y
NEW HAMPSHIRE								
Humphrey	Y	Y	Y	Y	N	N	N	N
Rudman	Y	Y	Y	Y	N	N	Y	Y
NEW JERSEY								
Bradley	Y	Y	Y	Y	N	Y	Y	N
Lautenberg	Y	Y	Y	?	?	Y	Y	N
NEW MEXICO								
Domenici	Y	Y	Y	Y	N	N	Y	Y
Bingaman	Y	Y	N	Y	N	N	Y	N
NEW YORK								
D'Amato	Y	Y	Y	N	N	N	Y	N
Moynihan	Y	Y	Y	Y	N	Y	Y	N
NORTH CAROLINA								
Broyhill	Y	Y	Y	Y	N	?	Y	Y
Helms	N	Y	Y	Y	N	N	Y	N
NORTH DAKOTA								
Andrews	Y	Y	N	Y	Y	N	Y	Y
Burdick	Y	Y	N	N	Y	Y	Y	Y
OHIO								
Glenn	Y	Y	Y	Y	Y	Y	Y	N
Metzenbaum	Y	Y	N	Y	Y	Y	Y	N
OKLAHOMA								
Nickles	N	Y	Y	N	N	N	Y	Y
Boren	N	?	?	?	?	Y	Y	Y
OREGON								
Hatfield	Y	Y	Y	Y	Y	N	Y	N
Packwood	Y	Y	Y	Y	N	N	Y	N
PENNSYLVANIA								
Heinz	Y	Y	Y	Y	N	N	Y	N
Specter	Y	Y	N	Y	N	N	Y	N
RHODE ISLAND								
Chafee	Y	Y	Y	Y	Y	N	Y	N
Pell	Y	Y	N	Y	Y	Y	Y	N
SOUTH CAROLINA								
Thurmond	Y	Y	Y	Y	N	N	Y	N
Hollings	Y	Y	Y	Y	N	Y	Y	Y
SOUTH DAKOTA								
Abdnor	N	Y	N	N	N	N	Y	Y
Pressler	N	?	?	?	?	N	Y	Y
TENNESSEE								
Gore	Y	Y	Y	Y	N	Y	Y	Y
Sasser	N	Y	Y	Y	N	Y	Y	Y
TEXAS								
Gramm	Y	Y	Y	Y	N	N	Y	Y
Bentsen	Y	?	?	?	?	?	Y	?
UTAH								
Garn	-	?	?	?	?	?	+	?
Hatch	N	Y	Y	Y	N	N	Y	Y
VERMONT								
Stafford	Y	?	?	?	?	N	Y	N
Leahy	Y	Y	N	Y	N	Y	Y	Y
VIRGINIA								
Trible	Y	Y	Y	Y	N	N	Y	N
Warner	N	Y	N	Y	N	N	Y	N
WASHINGTON								
Evans	Y	N	N	Y	Y	N	Y	N
Gorton	Y	?	?	?	?	N	Y	N
WEST VIRGINIA								
Byrd	Y	Y	Y	Y	N	Y	Y	N
Rockefeller	Y	Y	Y	Y	N	Y	Y	N
WISCONSIN								
Kasten	Y	Y	Y	Y	N	N	Y	Y
Proxmire	Y	Y	N	Y	Y	Y	Y	Y
WYOMING								
Simpson	N	Y	Y	Y	N	N	Y	Y
Wallop	N	?	?	?	?	N	Y	Y

KEY

- Y Voted for (yea).
- # Paired for.
- + Announced for.
- N Voted against (nay).
- X Paired against.
- - Announced against.
- P Voted "present."
- C Voted "present" to avoid possible conflict of interest.
- ? Did not vote or otherwise make a position known.

Democrats *Republicans*

ND - Northern Democrats SD - Southern Democrats (Southern states - Ala., Ark., Fla., Ga., Ky., La., Miss., N.C., Okla., S.C., Tenn., Texas, Va.)

296. HR 3838. Tax Overhaul. Adoption of the conference report on the bill to revise the federal income tax system by reducing individual and corporate tax rates, eliminating or curtailing many deductions, credits and exclusions, repealing the investment tax credit, taxing capital gains as ordinary income and making other changes. Adopted 74-23: R 41-11; D 33-12 (ND 25-7, SD 8-5), Sept. 27, 1986. A "yea" was a vote supporting the president's position.

297. HR 5484. Omnibus Drug Bill. DeConcini, D-Ariz., amendment to the Dole, R-Kan.-Byrd, D-W.Va., substitute, to require the secretary of defense to inventory all military equipment, intelligence and personnel that could be used by civilian drug enforcement agencies and to devise a plan to lend such assets to such agencies. Adopted 83-4: R 43-3; D 40-1 (ND 30-0, SD 10-1), Sept. 27, 1986. (The Dole-Byrd substitute authorized about $1.4 billion for drug interdiction and enforcement, education, treatment and prevention programs. It later was adopted by voice vote.)

298. HR 5484. Omnibus Drug Bill. Moynihan, D-N.Y., amendment to the Dole, R-Kan.-Byrd, D-W.Va., substitute *(see vote 297, above)*, to express the sense of the Senate condemning the Aug. 30 arrest by the Soviet Union of *U.S. News and World Report* correspondent Nicholas Daniloff and urging the president to obtain Daniloff's prompt release before agreeing to a summit meeting with Soviet leader Mikhail S. Gorbachev. Adopted 57-29: R 33-12; D 24-17 (ND 13-17, SD 11-0), Sept. 27, 1986. (The Dole-Byrd substitute later was adopted by voice vote.)

299. HR 5484. Omnibus Drug Bill. Goldwater, R-Ariz., motion to table (kill) the Dixon, D-Ill., amendment to the Dole, R-Kan.-Byrd, D-W.Va., substitute *(see vote 297, above)*, to require the president, within 30 days of enactment, to deploy military personnel and equipment "to the extent possible" to combat drug smuggling, and within 45 days of enactment, to "substantially halt" drug smuggling across U.S. borders "to the extent possible." Motion agreed to 72-14: R 37-9; D 35-5 (ND 25-4, SD 10-1), Sept. 27, 1986. (The Dole-Byrd substitute later was adopted by voice vote.) A "yea" was a vote supporting the president's position.

300. HR 5484. Omnibus Drug Bill. Cohen, R-Maine, motion to table (kill) the Mattingly, R-Ga., amendment to the Dole, R-Kan.-Byrd, D-W.Va., substitute *(see vote 297, above)*, to authorize the death penalty for anyone who knowingly causes the death of another individual during the course of a continuing criminal enterprise. Motion rejected 25-60: R 10-35; D 15-25 (ND 14-15, SD 1-10), Sept. 27, 1986. (The Mattingly amendment subsequently was withdrawn. The effect of the vote was to express the sense of the Senate that should the bill go to conference, Senate conferees should accept House-passed language — identical to that in the Mattingly amendment — imposing the death penalty for certain offenses. The Dole-Byrd substitute subsequently was adopted by voice vote.)

301. H J Res 738. Continuing Appropriations, Fiscal 1987. Byrd, D-W.Va., amendment to provide $200 million in additional aid to the Philippines out of appropriations already programmed in the joint resolution. The amendment would have required that earmarked aid for Egypt and Israel be exempted from cuts made to increase aid to the Philippines. Rejected 43-51: R 4-46; D 39-5 (ND 29-3, SD 10-2), Sept. 29, 1986.

302. HR 5484. Omnibus Drug Bill. Passage of the bill to increase penalties for certain drug offenses and to authorize $1.4 billion for drug interdiction and enforcement, education, treatment and prevention programs. As amended by the Senate, the bill also reallocated certain U.S. sugar quotas; extended to homeless persons eligibility for federal welfare and health programs for the poor; prohibited "dial-a-porn" operations; required quality control testing of infant formula; mandated federal minimum standards for licensing of commercial truck and bus drivers and a reduction of highway funds to states that failed to comply with those standards; extended privacy protections to electronic communications; and banned manufacture, sale or possession of ballistic knives. Passed 97-2: R 51-1; D 46-1 (ND 32-1, SD 14-0), Sept. 30, 1986.

303. H J Res 738. Continuing Appropriations, Fiscal 1987. Hatfield, R-Ore., motion to table (kill) the Hatfield amendment to the Appropriations Committee amendment, to nullify provisions of the committee amendment granting antitrust protection to beer distributors. Motion agreed to 56-41: R 25-26; D 31-15 (ND 19-14, SD 12-1), Sept. 30, 1986. (The effect of the vote was to leave the antitrust protections in the committee amendment and demonstrate that the provisions' proponents did not have the 60 votes necessary to invoke cloture and halt a filibuster on the committee amendment. Hatfield later offered another amendment to strike the antitrust language, which was adopted by voice vote.)

	304	305	306	307	308
ALABAMA					
Denton	Y	N	N	N	N
Heflin	Y	Y	N	N	N
ALASKA					
Murkowski	N	N	N	N	N
Stevens	N	N	N	N	N
ARIZONA					
Goldwater	N	N	?	?	N
DeConcini	N	Y	Y	N	N
ARKANSAS					
Bumpers	Y	Y	Y	Y	N
Pryor	Y	Y	Y	Y	N
CALIFORNIA					
Wilson	N	N	N	N	N
Cranston	Y	Y	Y	Y	N
COLORADO					
Armstrong	N	N	N	N	N
Hart	Y	Y	Y	Y	Y
CONNECTICUT					
Weicker	N	N	N	N	N
Dodd	N	Y	Y	N	Y
DELAWARE					
Roth	N	N	N	N	Y
Biden	Y	Y	Y	Y	Y
FLORIDA					
Hawkins	N	N	N	N	N
Chiles	N	Y	N	N	N
GEORGIA					
Mattingly	Y	N	N	N	Y
Nunn	+	?	Y	N	Y
HAWAII					
Inouye	Y	Y	Y	Y	N
Matsunaga	Y	Y	Y	Y	N
IDAHO					
McClure	N	N	N	N	N
Symms	N	N	N	N	N
ILLINOIS					
Dixon	Y	Y	Y	Y	Y
Simon	Y	Y	Y	Y	Y
INDIANA					
Lugar	N	N	N	N	N
Quayle	N	N	N	N	N

	304	305	306	307	308
IOWA					
Grassley	Y	Y	N	N	Y
Harkin	Y	Y	Y	Y	Y
KANSAS					
Dole	N	N	N	N	N
Kassebaum	N	Y	N	N	N
KENTUCKY					
McConnell	N	N	N	N	N
Ford	Y	Y	Y	Y	Y
LOUISIANA					
Johnston	Y	N	Y	Y	N
Long	Y	N	N	N	N
MAINE					
Cohen	N	Y	Y	N	Y
Mitchell	N	Y	Y	N	Y
MARYLAND					
Mathias	N	N	N	N	N
Sarbanes	Y	Y	Y	Y	Y
MASSACHUSETTS					
Kennedy	Y	Y	Y	Y	Y
Kerry	N	Y	Y	Y	Y
MICHIGAN					
Levin	Y	Y	Y	Y	Y
Riegle	Y	Y	Y	Y	Y
MINNESOTA					
Boschwitz	N	N	N	N	Y
Durenberger	Y	N	N	N	Y
MISSISSIPPI					
Cochran	N	N	N	N	N
Stennis	N	N	N	N	N
MISSOURI					
Danforth	Y	Y	N	N	N
Eagleton	Y	Y	Y	Y	Y
MONTANA					
Baucus	Y	Y	N	N	Y
Melcher	Y	Y	Y	N	Y
NEBRASKA					
Exon	Y	Y	Y	N	N
Zorinsky	Y	Y	Y	N	N
NEVADA					
Hecht	N	N	N	N	N
Laxalt	N	N	N	N	N

	304	305	306	307	308
NEW HAMPSHIRE					
Humphrey	N	N	N	N	Y
Rudman	N	N	N	N	N
NEW JERSEY					
Bradley	N	Y	Y	Y	Y
Lautenberg	N	Y	Y	Y	Y
NEW MEXICO					
Domenici	N	N	N	N	N
Bingaman	N	Y	Y	N	Y
NEW YORK					
D'Amato	N	Y	N	Y	N
Moynihan	Y	Y	N	N	Y
NORTH CAROLINA					
Broyhill	N	N	N	N	Y
Helms	N	N	N	N	N
NORTH DAKOTA					
Andrews	Y	Y	N	N	Y
Burdick	Y	Y	Y	Y	Y
OHIO					
Glenn	Y	N	Y	Y	Y
Metzenbaum	N	Y	Y	Y	Y
OKLAHOMA					
Nickles	Y	N	N	N	Y
Boren	Y	Y	N	Y	N
OREGON					
Hatfield	N	N	N	N	N
Packwood	N	N	N	N	N
PENNSYLVANIA					
Heinz	N	N	N	N	Y
Specter	Y	Y	Y	Y	Y
RHODE ISLAND					
Chafee	N	N	N	N	Y
Pell	N	Y	Y	Y	Y
SOUTH CAROLINA					
Thurmond	N	N	N	N	N
Hollings	Y	Y	N	N	Y
SOUTH DAKOTA					
Abdnor	Y	N	N	N	Y
Pressler	Y	Y	N	N	Y
TENNESSEE					
Gore	Y	Y	Y	Y	N
Sasser	Y	Y	Y	Y	N

KEY

- Y Voted for (yea).
- # Paired for.
- + Announced for.
- N Voted against (nay).
- X Paired against.
- \- Announced against.
- P Voted "present."
- C Voted "present" to avoid possible conflict of interest.
- ? Did not vote or otherwise make a position known.

Democrats ***Republicans***

	304	305	306	307	308
TEXAS					
Gramm	N	N	N	N	N
Bentsen	Y	N	N	N	N
UTAH					
Garn	?	?	?	?	?
Hatch	N	N	N	N	N
VERMONT					
Stafford	N	N	N	N	N
Leahy	Y	Y	N	N	Y
VIRGINIA					
Trible	N	N	N	N	Y
Warner	N	N	N	N	N
WASHINGTON					
Evans	N	N	N	N	N
Gorton	N	N	N	N	N
WEST VIRGINIA					
Byrd	Y	Y	Y	Y	Y
Rockefeller	Y	Y	Y	Y	Y
WISCONSIN					
Kasten	Y	N	Y	N	Y
Proxmire	N	Y	Y	N	Y
WYOMING					
Simpson	N	N	N	N	N
Wallop	N	N	N	N	N

ND - Northern Democrats SD - Southern Democrats (Southern states - Ala., Ark., Fla., Ga., Ky., La., Miss., N.C., Okla., S.C., Tenn., Texas, Va.)

304. H J Res 738. Continuing Appropriations, Fiscal 1987. Boren, D-Okla., motion to waive the spending-allocation limitation contained in the 1985 Balanced Budget and Emergency Deficit Control Act (the Gramm-Rudman-Hollings anti-deficit law, PL 99-177) with respect to the Boren amendment to permit early repayment of Rural Electrification Administration loans, to require federal payments to cattle producers for economic loss caused by a dairy program in which whole herds are slaughtered to reduce milk production, to authorize a federal interest rate "buy-down" program for farm borrowers, and to revise school lunch and other feeding programs. Motion rejected 45-53: R 11-41; D 34-12 (ND 23-10, SD 11-2), Oct. 1, 1986. A three-fifths majority (60) of the total Senate is required to waive the spending-allocation limitation contained in Gramm-Rudman. (The effect of the vote was to prevent consideration of the Boren amendment.)

305. H J Res 738. Continuing Appropriations, Fiscal 1987. Judgment of the Senate whether the Danforth, R-Mo., amendment, to require seniority protection for airline employees when two airlines merge, was germane. Ruled non-germane 49-49: R 8-44; D 41-5 (ND 32-1, SD 9-4), Oct. 1, 1986.

306. H J Res 738. Continuing Appropriations, Fiscal 1987. Judgment of the Senate whether the Dixon, D-Ill., amendment, to authorize tenant managers in federally subsidized housing projects, was germane. Ruled non-germane 40-58: R 3-48; D 37-10 (ND 30-3, SD 7-7), Oct. 1, 1986.

307. H J Res 738. Continuing Appropriations, Fiscal 1987. Dixon, D-Ill., motion to waive the spending-allocation limitation contained in the 1985 Balanced Budget and Emergency Deficit Control Act (the Gramm-Rudman-Hollings anti-deficit law, PL 99-177) with respect to the Dixon amendment to restore $100 million to the teenage summer job program. Motion rejected 31-67: R 2-49; D 29-18 (ND 22-11, SD 7-7), Oct. 1, 1986. A three-fifths majority (60) of the total Senate is required to waive the spending-allocation limitation contained in Gramm-Rudman. (The effect of the vote was to prevent consideration of the Dixon amendment.)

308. H J Res 738. Continuing Appropriations, Fiscal 1987. Judgment of the Senate whether the Harkin, D-Iowa, amendment, to establish a $500,000 payment cap for a number of farm subsidy programs, was germane. Ruled non-germane 47-52: R 17-35; D 30-17 (ND 27-6, SD 3-11), Oct. 1, 1986.

CQ Senate Votes 309 - 316

Corresponding to Congressional Record Votes 309, 310, 311, 312, 313, 314, 315, 316

	309	310	311	312	313	314	315	316
ALABAMA								
Denton	Y	Y	N	Y	Y	Y	Y	N
Heflin	Y	N	Y	Y	Y	Y	Y	Y
ALASKA								
Murkowski	Y	Y	Y	Y	N	Y	Y	N
Stevens	Y	Y	N	N	N	N	N	N
ARIZONA								
Goldwater	Y	Y	N	N	N	?	N	N
DeConcini	Y	N	Y	N	N	Y	Y	Y
ARKANSAS								
Bumpers	N	N	Y	Y	N	Y	Y	Y
Pryor	N	N	Y	Y	N	Y	Y	Y
CALIFORNIA								
Wilson	Y	Y	Y	N	N	Y	Y	N
Cranston	N	N	Y	N	N	Y	N	Y
COLORADO								
Armstrong	Y	Y	N	C	Y	Y	Y	N
Hart	N	Y	Y	N	N	Y	N	Y
CONNECTICUT								
Weicker	N	Y	Y	N	N	N	N	N
Dodd	N	Y	Y	N	N	Y	N	Y
DELAWARE								
Roth	Y	Y	Y	N	N	Y	N	N
Biden	N	N	Y	Y	Y	Y	N	Y
FLORIDA								
Hawkins	Y	Y	Y	Y	Y	Y	Y	N
Chiles	Y	N	Y	Y	Y	Y	Y	Y
GEORGIA								
Mattingly	Y	Y	Y	Y	Y	Y	Y	N
Nunn	Y	N	Y	Y	Y	Y	N	Y
HAWAII								
Inouye	N	Y	Y	N	N	Y	N	Y
Matsunaga	N	N	Y	N	N	Y	N	Y
IDAHO								
McClure	Y	Y	N	N	Y	Y	Y	N
Symms	Y	Y	N	Y	Y	Y	Y	N
ILLINOIS								
Dixon	N	N	Y	Y	N	Y	Y	Y
Simon	N	N	Y	Y	N	Y	N	Y
INDIANA								
Lugar	Y	Y	Y	N	N	Y	N	N
Quayle	Y	Y	Y	N	Y	N	Y	N
IOWA								
Grassley	Y	N	Y	Y	Y	Y	Y	N
Harkin	N	N	Y	N	N	Y	N	Y
KANSAS								
Dole	Y	Y	N	N	Y	Y	N	N
Kassebaum	Y	Y	Y	N	N	Y	N	N
KENTUCKY								
McConnell	Y	Y	Y	Y	Y	Y	Y	N
Ford	N	N	Y	Y	Y	Y	Y	Y
LOUISIANA								
Johnston	Y	N	Y	Y	N	Y	N	N
Long	Y	N	Y	Y	N	Y	N	N
MAINE								
Cohen	Y	Y	Y	Y	N	Y	Y	N
Mitchell	N	N	Y	Y	N	Y	Y	Y
MARYLAND								
Mathias	N	?	Y	N	N	Y	N	N
Sarbanes	N	Y	Y	N	N	Y	N	Y
MASSACHUSETTS								
Kennedy	N	N	Y	N	N	Y	N	Y
Kerry	N	Y	Y	N	N	Y	N	Y
MICHIGAN								
Levin	?	N	Y	N	N	Y	N	Y
Riegle	N	N	Y	N	N	Y	N	Y
MINNESOTA								
Boschwitz	Y	Y	Y	N	N	Y	N	N
Durenberger	Y	Y	Y	N	Y	Y	N	N
MISSISSIPPI								
Cochran	Y	Y	N	N	N	Y	N	N
Stennis	Y	Y	Y	N	N	Y	N	N
MISSOURI								
Danforth	Y	Y	Y	N	N	Y	N	Y
Eagleton	N	N	Y	N	N	Y	Y	Y
MONTANA								
Baucus	N	N	Y	Y	N	Y	N	Y
Melcher	N	N	Y	N	N	Y	N	Y
NEBRASKA								
Exon	N	N	Y	Y	N	Y	N	Y
Zorinsky	Y	N	Y	Y	Y	Y	Y	Y
NEVADA								
Hecht	Y	Y	N	N	Y	Y	Y	N
Laxalt	Y	Y	N	N	Y	Y	N	N
NEW HAMPSHIRE								
Humphrey	Y	Y	N	N	Y	Y	Y	N
Rudman	Y	Y	N	N	Y	Y	Y	N
NEW JERSEY								
Bradley	N	Y	Y	N	N	Y	Y	?
Lautenberg	N	Y	Y	N	N	Y	N	Y
NEW MEXICO								
Domenici	Y	Y	Y	N	N	Y	N	N
Bingaman	N	N	Y	Y	N	Y	N	Y
NEW YORK								
D'Amato	N	Y	Y	Y	N	Y	Y	N
Moynihan	N	N	Y	Y	N	Y	N	Y
NORTH CAROLINA								
Broyhill	Y	Y	N	Y	Y	Y	Y	N
Helms	Y	Y	N	N	Y	Y	Y	N
NORTH DAKOTA								
Andrews	Y	Y	Y	N	Y	Y	Y	N
Burdick	N	N	Y	Y	N	Y	Y	Y
OHIO								
Glenn	N	N	Y	N	N	Y	N	N
Metzenbaum	N	N	Y	Y	N	Y	N	N
OKLAHOMA								
Nickles	Y	N	N	N	Y	Y	Y	N
Boren	Y	N	Y	N	Y	Y	N	Y
OREGON								
Hatfield	N	Y	Y	N	N	Y	N	N
Packwood	Y	N	Y	N	N	Y	N	N
PENNSYLVANIA								
Heinz	Y	Y	Y	N	N	Y	Y	Y
Specter	N	N	Y	Y	N	Y	Y	Y
RHODE ISLAND								
Chafee	N	Y	Y	N	N	Y	N	Y
Pell	N	N	Y	Y	N	Y	N	Y
SOUTH CAROLINA								
Thurmond	Y	Y	N	N	Y	Y	Y	N
Hollings	Y	N	Y	Y	N	Y	Y	Y
SOUTH DAKOTA								
Abdnor	Y	Y	Y	Y	Y	Y	Y	N
Pressler	Y	Y	N	Y	Y	Y	Y	N
TENNESSEE								
Gore	N	N	Y	Y	N	Y	N	Y
Sasser	N	N	Y	Y	N	Y	Y	Y
TEXAS								
Gramm	Y	Y	N	N	Y	Y	Y	N
Bentsen	Y	N	Y	Y	N	Y	Y	N
UTAH								
Garn	?	?	?	?	?	?	?	?
Hatch	Y	Y	N	N	Y	Y	Y	N
VERMONT								
Stafford	Y	Y	Y	N	N	Y	N	N
Leahy	N	N	Y	Y	N	Y	N	Y
VIRGINIA								
Trible	Y	Y	Y	Y	Y	Y	Y	Y
Warner	Y	Y	Y	N	N	Y	N	N
WASHINGTON								
Evans	Y	Y	Y	N	N	Y	N	N
Gorton	Y	Y	Y	Y	N	Y	N	N
WEST VIRGINIA								
Byrd	N	N	Y	Y	Y	Y	Y	Y
Rockefeller	N	N	Y	Y	N	Y	N	Y
WISCONSIN								
Kasten	Y	Y	Y	Y	N	Y	Y	N
Proxmire	N	N	Y	Y	N	N	N	Y
WYOMING								
Simpson	Y	Y	N	N	N	Y	N	N
Wallop	Y	Y	N	N	Y	N	Y	N

KEY

Y Voted for (yea).
\# Paired for.
\+ Announced for.
N Voted against (nay).
X Paired against.
\- Announced against.
P Voted "present."
C Voted "present" to avoid possible conflict of interest.
? Did not vote or otherwise make a position known.

Democrats *Republicans*

ND - Northern Democrats SD - Southern Democrats (Southern states - Ala., Ark., Fla., Ga., Ky., La., Miss., N.C., Okla., S.C., Tenn., Texas, Va.)

309. H J Res 738. Continuing Appropriations, Fiscal 1987. Dole, R-Kan., motion to table (kill) the Byrd, D-W.Va., amendment to increase aid to the Philippines by $200 million. Motion agreed to 57-41: R 46-6; D 11-35 (ND 2-30, SD 9-5), Oct. 2, 1986.

310. H J Res 738. Continuing Appropriations, Fiscal 1987. Kasten, R-Wis., motion to table (kill) the Bingaman, D-N.M., amendment to strike language permitting arms export loans to be converted to grants. Motion agreed to 55-43: R 47-4; D 8-39 (ND 7-26, SD 1-13), Oct. 2, 1986.

311. HR 4868. South Africa Sanctions. Passage, over President Reagan's Sept. 26 veto, of the bill to impose sanctions against South Africa. Among the sanctions imposed by the bill were bans on imports of South African iron, steel, sugar and other agricultural products. The bill also prohibited exports to South Africa of petroleum products, banned new U.S. investments there, and banned imports of South African uranium, coal and textiles. Passed (thus enacted into law) 78-21: R 31-21; D 47-0 (ND 33-0, SD 14-0), Oct. 2, 1986. A two-thirds majority of those present and voting (66 in this case) of both houses is required to override a veto. A "nay" was a vote supporting the president's position.

312. H J Res 738. Continuing Appropriations, Fiscal 1987. Judgment of the Senate whether the Gore, D-Tenn., amendment, to permit satellite dish owners to purchase transmitted programs, was germane. Ruled non-germane 44-54: R 16-35; D 28-19 (ND 16-17, SD 12-2), Oct. 2, 1986.

313. H J Res 738. Continuing Appropriations, Fiscal 1987. Judgment of the Senate whether the Helms, R-N.C., amendment, to bar the Health and Human Services Department from using funds to provide contraceptives to youths without parental consent, was germane. Ruled non-germane 34-65: R 26-26; D 8-39 (ND 3-30, SD 5-9), Oct. 2, 1986.

314. Procedural Motion. Hatfield, R-Ore., motion to instruct the sergeant-at-arms to request the attendance of absent senators. Motion agreed to 93-5: R 47-4; D 46-1 (ND 32-1, SD 14-0), Oct. 2, 1986.

315. H J Res 738. Continuing Appropriations, Fiscal 1987. Judgment of the Senate whether the Heinz, R-Pa., amendment, to withhold U.S. contributions to the United Nations until the president certifies that he has taken steps to combat spying there, was germane. Ruled non-germane 46-53: R 30-22; D 16-31 (ND 8-25, SD 8-6), Oct. 2, 1986.

316. H J Res 738. Continuing Appropriations, Fiscal 1987. Judgment of the Senate whether the Bumpers, D-Ark., amendment, to bar the Federal Energy Regulatory Commission from approving rates that include costs for certain closed nuclear power plants, was germane. Ruled non-germane 45-53: R 5-47; D 40-6 (ND 30-2, SD 10-4), Oct. 2, 1986.

	317	318	319	320	321	322	323	324
ALABAMA								
Denton	N	Y	Y	Y	N	Y	?	Y
Heflin	N	Y	N	Y	N	N	N	Y
ALASKA								
Murkowski	N	Y	Y	Y	N	N	Y	Y
Stevens	N	Y	Y	Y	N	N	N	N
ARIZONA								
Goldwater	N	?	?	?	?	?	N	?
DeConcini	Y	Y	Y	Y	N	Y	Y	N
ARKANSAS								
Bumpers	Y	Y	Y	Y	N	N	N	N
Pryor	Y	Y	Y	Y	N	N	N	Y
CALIFORNIA								
Wilson	N	N	Y	Y	N	Y	N	Y
Cranston	Y	?	?	?	?	?	N	N
COLORADO								
Armstrong	N	N	N	N	N	Y	Y	Y
Hart	Y	Y	Y	Y	?	?	N	N
CONNECTICUT								
Weicker	N	N	Y	N	N	N	N	N
Dodd	N	N	Y	Y	N	N	N	Y
DELAWARE								
Roth	N	N	Y	N	N	N	N	Y
Biden	Y	N	Y	Y	N	N	N	Y
FLORIDA								
Hawkins	N	N	Y	?	?	?	Y	Y
Chiles	Y	N	Y	Y	N	N	N	N
GEORGIA								
Mattingly	N	Y	Y	Y	N	Y	Y	N
Nunn	N	Y	Y	Y	N	N	N	Y
HAWAII								
Inouye	Y	Y	Y	Y	N	N	N	Y
Matsunaga	Y	N	Y	Y	N	N	N	Y
IDAHO								
McClure	N	Y	N	N	N	Y	Y	N
Symms	N	Y	Y	N	N	Y	Y	Y
ILLINOIS								
Dixon	Y	Y	N	Y	N	N	N	Y
Simon	Y	Y	Y	Y	N	N	N	N
INDIANA								
Lugar	N	N	N	Y	N	N	N	Y
Quayle	N	N	N	Y	N	Y	N	Y
IOWA								
Grassley	Y	Y	Y	N	N	Y	Y	Y
Harkin	Y	Y	Y	N	N	N	N	N
KANSAS								
Dole	N	N	Y	Y	N	Y	Y	Y
Kassebaum	N	N	N	N	N	N	N	Y
KENTUCKY								
McConnell	N	Y	Y	Y	N	Y	Y	Y
Ford	Y	Y	Y	Y	N	Y	Y	N
LOUISIANA								
Johnston	N	Y	Y	Y	N	N	Y	Y
Long	N	Y	N	Y	N	?	N	N
MAINE								
Cohen	N	N	Y	N	N	N	N	Y
Mitchell	Y	N	Y	N	N	N	N	N
MARYLAND								
Mathias	N	N	N	N	N	N	N	N
Sarbanes	Y	Y	Y	Y	N	N	N	N
MASSACHUSETTS								
Kennedy	Y	N	Y	Y	N	N	N	N
Kerry	Y	N	Y	Y	N	N	N	Y
MICHIGAN								
Levin	Y	Y	Y	Y	N	N	N	N
Riegle	Y	Y	Y	Y	N	N	N	N
MINNESOTA								
Boschwitz	N	N	Y	N	N	N	Y	Y
Durenberger	N	Y	Y	N	N	N	Y	Y
MISSISSIPPI								
Cochran	N	N	N	N	N	N	N	Y
Stennis	?	?	?	?	?	?	N	N
MISSOURI								
Danforth	N	N	Y	N	N	N	Y	Y
Eagleton	Y	Y	Y	Y	N	Y	N	N
MONTANA								
Baucus	Y	Y	Y	Y	N	N	N	N
Melcher	Y	Y	Y	Y	N	Y	Y	N
NEBRASKA								
Exon	Y	Y	N	Y	N	N	Y	Y
Zorinsky	Y	Y	Y	Y	N	Y	Y	N
NEVADA								
Hecht	N	N	N	N	N	N	Y	Y
Laxalt	N	N	N	Y	N	N	Y	Y
NEW HAMPSHIRE								
Humphrey	N	N	Y	N	N	Y	Y	N
Rudman	N	N	N	N	N	Y	N	Y
NEW JERSEY								
Bradley	Y	N	Y	N	N	N	N	N
Lautenberg	Y	N	Y	N	N	N	N	Y
NEW MEXICO								
Domenici	N	N	Y	Y	N	Y	N	Y
Bingaman	Y	N	Y	Y	N	N	N	N
NEW YORK								
D'Amato	N	N	Y	N	N	Y	Y	Y
Moynihan	N	N	Y	Y	N	N	N	Y
NORTH CAROLINA								
Broyhill	N	Y	Y	Y	N	Y	N	Y
Helms	N	N	N	Y	N	Y	Y	Y
NORTH DAKOTA								
Andrews	Y	Y	Y	N	N	Y	Y	Y
Burdick	Y	Y	Y	N	N	N	N	N
OHIO								
Glenn	N	N	Y	Y	N	N	N	N
Metzenbaum	Y	N	Y	Y	N	N	N	Y
OKLAHOMA								
Nickles	Y	Y	Y	Y	N	Y	Y	Y
Boren	Y	Y	Y	Y	N	N	N	Y
OREGON								
Hatfield	N	N	N	N	N	N	N	N
Packwood	N	N	Y	Y	?	N	N	Y
PENNSYLVANIA								
Heinz	Y	N	Y	Y	N	Y	N	Y
Specter	Y	Y	Y	Y	N	N	N	Y
RHODE ISLAND								
Chafee	N	N	Y	N	N	N	N	Y
Pell	Y	N	Y	N	N	N	N	Y
SOUTH CAROLINA								
Thurmond	N	Y	Y	Y	N	Y	Y	Y
Hollings	Y	Y	Y	Y	N	Y	N	N
SOUTH DAKOTA								
Abdnor	Y	Y	Y	Y	N	Y	Y	Y
Pressler	Y	Y	Y	Y	N	Y	Y	Y
TENNESSEE								
Gore	Y	Y	Y	Y	N	N	N	Y
Sasser	Y	Y	Y	Y	N	N	N	Y
TEXAS								
Gramm	N	N	N	N	N	Y	Y	Y
Bentsen	Y	N	Y	N	N	N	N	Y
UTAH								
Garn	?	?	?	?	?	?	?	?
Hatch	N	N	Y	Y	N	Y	Y	Y
VERMONT								
Stafford	N	N	?	?	?	?	N	N
Leahy	Y	Y	Y	Y	N	N	N	N
VIRGINIA								
Trible	N	Y	Y	Y	N	N	Y	Y
Warner	N	Y	Y	Y	N	N	N	Y
WASHINGTON								
Evans	Y	N	Y	N	N	N	N	Y
Gorton	Y	N	Y	N	N	N	N	Y
WEST VIRGINIA								
Byrd	Y	N	Y	Y	N	Y	N	N
Rockefeller	Y	N	Y	Y	N	N	N	Y
WISCONSIN								
Kasten	N	N	Y	Y	N	Y	Y	Y
Proxmire	Y	N	Y	N	N	N	Y	N
WYOMING								
Simpson	N	N	Y	N	N	N	N	Y
Wallop	N	N	Y	N	N	N	Y	Y

KEY

- Y Voted for (yea).
- # Paired for.
- + Announced for.
- N Voted against (nay).
- X Paired against.
- \- Announced against.
- P Voted "present."
- C Voted "present" to avoid possible conflict of interest.
- ? Did not vote or otherwise make a position known.

Democrats ***Republicans***

ND - Northern Democrats SD - Southern Democrats (Southern states - Ala., Ark., Fla., Ga., Ky., La., Miss., N.C., Okla., S.C., Tenn., Texas, Va.)

317. H J Res 738. Continuing Appropriations, Fiscal 1987. Judgment of the Senate whether the Leahy, D-Vt., amendment was germane. The amendment would have barred the use in Defense Department budget requests of special inflation indexes and expanded existing requirements for Defense Department reports to congressional committees on unused, appropriated funds. Ruled non-germane 48-50: R 9-43; D 39-7 (ND 30-3, SD 9-4), Oct. 2, 1986.

318. H J Res 738. Continuing Appropriations, Fiscal 1987. Abdnor, R-S.D., motion to waive the spending-allocation limitation contained in the 1985 Balanced Budget and Emergency Deficit Control Act (the Gramm-Rudman-Hollings anti-deficit law, PL 99-177) with respect to the Abdnor amendment to permit certain Rural Electrification Administration (REA) borrowers to make early repayments of principal due on their REA-guaranteed loans without penalty. Motion rejected 45-51: R 18-33; D 27-18 (ND 16-16, SD 11-2), in the session that began Oct. 2, 1986. A three-fifths majority (60) of the total Senate is required to waive the spending-allocation limitation contained in Gramm-Rudman. (The effect of the vote was to prevent consideration of the Abdnor amendment.)

319. H J Res 738. Continuing Appropriations, Fiscal 1987. Judgment of the Senate whether the Hawkins, R-Fla., amendment, to reauthorize federal child nutrition programs, permitting 1 percent growth over current services levels, as provided in the conference agreement on HR 7, was germane. Ruled germane 78-17: R 37-13; D 41-4 (ND 30-2, SD 11-2), in the session that began Oct. 2, 1986. (The Hawkins amendment subsequently was adopted by voice vote.)

320. H J Res 738. Continuing Appropriations, Fiscal 1987. Judgment of the Senate whether the Mattingly, R-Ga., amendment was germane. The amendment would make payments to farmers suffering drought, flood or other disaster damage; make the payments in the form of certificates of ownership of surplus commodity stocks held by the Commodity Credit Corporation; make comparable reductions in emergency disaster loans provided or guaranteed by the Agricultural Credit Insurance Fund; limit to $190 million the aggregate value of the CCC certificates; and limit to $100,000 the amount an individual producer could receive. Ruled germane 61-33: R 24-25; D 37-8 (ND 25-7, SD 12-1), in the session that began Oct. 2, 1986. (The Mattingly amendment subsequently was adopted by voice vote.)

321. H J Res 738. Continuing Appropriations, Fiscal 1987. Kennedy, D-Mass., motion to table (kill) the Kennedy amendment to express the sense of Congress that the United States should support Chile's National Accord for the Transition to Full Democracy. Motion rejected 0-92: R 0-48; D 0-44 (ND 0-31, SD 0-13), in the session that began Oct. 2, 1986. (Faced with a filibuster by Jesse Helms, R-N.C., Kennedy moved to table his amendment to show the depth of Senate support for it. Following the failure of the tabling motion, Kennedy withdrew the amendment.)

322. H J Res 738. Continuing Appropriations, Fiscal 1987. Judgment of the Senate whether the Kasten, R-Wis., amendment was germane. The amendment would have restricted U.S. contributions to the United Nations to the same amount as contributions from the Soviet Union, unless U.N. rules are changed to grant proportional voting, based on the size of a nation's contribution, on matters with budgetary consequences. Ruled non-germane 32-60: R 25-24; D 7-36 (ND 5-26, SD 2-10), in the session that began Oct. 2, 1986.

323. H J Res 738. Continuing Appropriations, Fiscal 1987. Judgment of the Senate whether the Humphrey, R-N.H., amendment, to deny tax-exempt and charitable-contribution-recipient status to organizations performing, financing or providing facilities for abortions, was germane. Ruled non-germane 34-64: R 27-24; D 7-40 (ND 5-28, SD 2-12), Oct. 3, 1986.

324. H J Res 738. Continuing Appropriations, Fiscal 1987. Judgment of the Senate whether the Warner, R-Va., amendment, to transfer from the federal government to a regional authority, by lease, Washington-Dulles International Airport and National Airport, was germane. Ruled germane 63-35: R 43-8; D 20-27 (ND 12-21, SD 8-6), Oct. 3, 1986. (The Warner amendment subsequently was adopted by voice vote.)

CQ Senate Votes 325 - 332

Corresponding to Congressional Record Votes 325, 326, 327, 328, 329, 330, 331, 332

	325	326	327	328	329	330	331	332
ALABAMA								
Denton	Y	Y	Y	Y	Y	N	?	?
Heflin	N	Y	N	N	Y	N	Y	Y
ALASKA								
Murkowski	Y	Y	Y	Y	Y	Y	?	?
Stevens	Y	Y	Y	Y	Y	Y	Y	Y
ARIZONA								
Goldwater	Y	Y	Y	?	?	?	Y	Y
DeConcini	N	Y	Y	N	Y	Y	Y	N
ARKANSAS								
Bumpers	N	Y	N	Y	Y	Y	Y	Y
Pryor	N	Y	N	Y	Y	Y	Y	N
CALIFORNIA								
Wilson	Y	Y	Y	Y	Y	Y	Y	Y
Cranston	N	N	Y	Y	Y	Y	Y	N
COLORADO								
Armstrong	Y	Y	Y	Y	Y	N	Y	Y
Hart	N	N	N	Y	Y	Y	Y	N
CONNECTICUT								
Weicker	Y	Y	N	Y	Y	Y	?	?
Dodd	N	Y	Y	Y	Y	Y	?	?
DELAWARE								
Roth	Y	Y	Y	Y	Y	N	Y	?
Biden	N	N	Y	?	+	?	?	?
FLORIDA								
Hawkins	Y	Y	Y	Y	Y	Y	+	?
Chiles	N	N	Y	Y	Y	Y	Y	Y
GEORGIA								
Mattingly	Y	Y	N	N	Y	Y	Y	Y
Nunn	N	N	Y	Y	Y	Y	Y	N
HAWAII								
Inouye	N	Y	Y	Y	Y	Y	?	?
Matsunaga	N	Y	Y	Y	Y	Y	Y	N
IDAHO								
McClure	Y	Y	Y	Y	N	Y	Y	Y
Symms	Y	Y	Y	Y	N	Y	+	?
ILLINOIS								
Dixon	N	Y	Y	Y	Y	Y	Y	Y
Simon	N	N	Y	Y	Y	Y	Y	N
INDIANA								
Lugar	Y	Y	Y	Y	Y	Y	Y	Y
Quayle	Y	Y	Y	Y	Y	Y	Y	Y
IOWA								
Grassley	Y	Y	Y	N	Y	N	Y	Y
Harkin	N	N	Y	Y	Y	Y	Y	N
KANSAS								
Dole	N	Y	Y	Y	Y	Y	Y	?
Kassebaum	Y	Y	Y	Y	Y	Y	Y	Y
KENTUCKY								
McConnell	Y	Y	Y	Y	Y	Y	Y	Y
Ford	N	Y	Y	Y	Y	Y	Y	Y
LOUISIANA								
Johnston	N	N	Y	Y	Y	Y	Y	#
Long	Y	Y	Y	Y	Y	Y	Y	Y
MAINE								
Cohen	Y	Y	Y	Y	Y	Y	Y	N
Mitchell	N	Y	Y	Y	Y	Y	Y	N
MARYLAND								
Mathias	?	?	?	?	?	?	Y	N
Sarbanes	N	N	Y	Y	Y	Y	Y	N
MASSACHUSETTS								
Kennedy	N	N	Y	Y	Y	Y	Y	N
Kerry	N	N	Y	Y	Y	Y	Y	N
MICHIGAN								
Levin	N	N	Y	Y	Y	Y	Y	N
Riegle	N	N	Y	Y	Y	Y	Y	N
MINNESOTA								
Boschwitz	Y	Y	Y	N	Y	Y	Y	N
Durenberger	Y	Y	Y	Y	Y	Y	Y	N
MISSISSIPPI								
Cochran	Y	Y	Y	Y	Y	Y	Y	Y
Stennis	Y	Y	Y	Y	Y	Y	Y	?
MISSOURI								
Danforth	N	Y	Y	Y	Y	Y	Y	?
Eagleton	N	N	Y	Y	Y	Y	Y	N
MONTANA								
Baucus	N	N	N	Y	Y	N	Y	N
Melcher	N	Y	N	Y	Y	Y	Y	Y
NEBRASKA								
Exon	N	Y	N	Y	Y	Y	Y	N
Zorinsky	N	Y	N	N	N	Y	Y	Y
NEVADA								
Hecht	Y	Y	Y	Y	Y	Y	Y	Y
Laxalt	Y	Y	Y	Y	Y	Y	?	?
NEW HAMPSHIRE								
Humphrey	Y	Y	Y	N	Y	N	Y	N
Rudman	Y	Y	Y	N	Y	Y	Y	N
NEW JERSEY								
Bradley	N	Y	Y	Y	Y	Y	Y	N
Lautenberg	N	N	Y	Y	Y	Y	?	X
NEW MEXICO								
Domenici	Y	Y	Y	Y	Y	Y	Y	Y
Bingaman	N	N	Y	Y	Y	N	Y	N
NEW YORK								
D'Amato	Y	Y	Y	Y	Y	Y	?	?
Moynihan	N	Y	Y	Y	Y	Y	?	?
NORTH CAROLINA								
Broyhill	Y	Y	N	Y	Y	N	+	+
Helms	Y	Y	N	N	N	N	Y	Y
NORTH DAKOTA								
Andrews	N	Y	Y	Y	Y	Y	Y	Y
Burdick	N	Y	N	Y	Y	Y	Y	N
OHIO								
Glenn	N	Y	Y	Y	Y	Y	?	Y
Metzenbaum	N	N	Y	Y	Y	Y	Y	N
OKLAHOMA								
Nickles	N	Y	N	N	N	Y	Y	Y
Boren	N	Y	N	Y	N	?	Y	Y
OREGON								
Hatfield	Y	Y	Y	Y	Y	Y	Y	N
Packwood	Y	Y	Y	Y	Y	Y	Y	N
PENNSYLVANIA								
Heinz	Y	Y	Y	Y	Y	Y	Y	?
Specter	Y	Y	Y	N	Y	Y	Y	N
RHODE ISLAND								
Chafee	Y	Y	Y	Y	Y	Y	Y	N
Pell	N	N	Y	Y	Y	Y	Y	N
SOUTH CAROLINA								
Thurmond	Y	Y	Y	Y	Y	Y	+	+
Hollings	N	N	N	Y	Y	Y	Y	N
SOUTH DAKOTA								
Abdnor	N	Y	Y	N	Y	Y	Y	Y
Pressler	N	Y	Y	N	Y	N	Y	Y
TENNESSEE								
Gore	N	N	Y	Y	Y	Y	Y	N
Sasser	N	Y	Y	Y	Y	Y	Y	N
TEXAS								
Gramm	Y	Y	N	Y	N	Y	Y	Y
Bentsen	N	Y	Y	Y	Y	Y	Y	Y
UTAH								
Garn	?	?	?	?	?	?	?	?
Hatch	Y	Y	Y	Y	Y	N	Y	Y
VERMONT								
Stafford	Y	Y	Y	Y	Y	Y	Y	N
Leahy	N	N	Y	Y	Y	Y	Y	N
VIRGINIA								
Trible	Y	Y	Y	Y	Y	Y	Y	N
Warner	Y	Y	Y	Y	Y	Y	Y	N
WASHINGTON								
Evans	Y	Y	Y	Y	Y	Y	Y	N
Gorton	Y	Y	Y	Y	Y	Y	Y	N
WEST VIRGINIA								
Byrd	N	Y	N	Y	Y	Y	Y	N
Rockefeller	N	N	Y	Y	Y	Y	Y	N
WISCONSIN								
Kasten	N	Y	Y	Y	Y	Y	Y	N
Proxmire	N	Y	N	Y	Y	N	N	N
WYOMING								
Simpson	Y	Y	Y	Y	Y	Y	Y	Y
Wallop	Y	Y	Y	N	N	Y	Y	Y

KEY

- Y Voted for (yea).
- # Paired for.
- + Announced for.
- N Voted against (nay).
- X Paired against.
- - Announced against.
- P Voted "present."
- C Voted "present" to avoid possible conflict of interest.
- ? Did not vote or otherwise make a position known.

Democrats *Republicans*

ND - Northern Democrats SD - Southern Democrats (Southern states - Ala., Ark., Fla., Ga., Ky., La., Miss., N.C., Okla., S.C., Tenn., Texas, Va.)

325. H J Res 738. Continuing Appropriations, Fiscal 1987. Hatfield, R-Ore., motion to table (kill) the Melcher, D-Mont., amendment to expand donations of U.S. surplus commodities to domestic food aid for the poor, and also to the Philippines and certain other nations. Motion rejected 46-52: R 44-7; D 2-45 (ND 0-33, SD 2-12), Oct. 3, 1986. (The Melcher amendment later was modified and adopted by voice vote.)

326. H J Res 738. Continuing Appropriations, Fiscal 1987. Judgment of the Senate to affirm the ruling of the chair that the Kennedy, D-Mass., amendment, to appropriate $29 million for health planning and to reduce by the same amount, through uniform percentage reductions of all programs and activities, the appropriation for the Public Health Service, involved a new appropriation for an unauthorized program, and was therefore not in order. Ruling of the chair upheld 75-23: R 51-0; D 24-23 (ND 15-18, SD 9-5), Oct. 3, 1986.

327. H J Res 738. Continuing Appropriations, Fiscal 1987. Hatfield, R-Ore., motion to table (kill) the Bumpers, D-Ark., amendment to bar funding for the National Endowment for Democracy. Motion agreed to 79-19: R 45-6; D 34-13 (ND 25-8, SD 9-5), Oct. 3, 1986.

328. H J Res 738. Continuing Appropriations, Fiscal 1987. Dole, R-Kan., amendment to appropriate an additional $200 million for economic aid for the Philippines and to reduce by $200 million other accounts included in the foreign affairs function of the fiscal 1987 budget resolution (S Con Res 120). Individual foreign aid accounts could not be reduced by more than 3 percent, in order to offset the additional $200 million provided for the Philippines. Adopted 82-14: R 39-11; D 43-3 (ND 30-2, SD 13-1), Oct. 3, 1986.

329. HR 2005. 'Superfund' Reauthorization. Adoption of the conference report on the bill to reauthorize the "superfund" hazardous-waste cleanup program for fiscal 1987-91 at a funding level of $8.5 billion and to establish a new program for cleanup of leaking underground storage tanks at $500,000. Adopted 88-8: R 44-6; D 44-2 (ND 31-1, SD 13-1), Oct. 3, 1986. A "nay" was a vote supporting the president's position.

330. H J Res 738. Continuing Appropriations, Fiscal 1987. Passage of the bill to appropriate $557,732,573,343 for programs covered by the 13 regular appropriations bills for fiscal 1987. The regular appropriations bills were included by reference in this measure. Passed 82-13: R 41-9; D 41-4 (ND 29-3, SD 12-1), Oct. 3, 1986.

331. HR 4613. Commodity Futures Trading Commission. Passage of the bill to reauthorize funding for the Commodity Futures Trading Commission through fiscal 1987-92 at such sums as deemed necessary, to ban off-exchange "leveraged" transactions in two years, to restructure sugar quotas for certain foreign countries and to improve grain quality standards for exports. Passed 83-1: R 43-0; D 40-1 (ND 26-1, SD 14-0), Oct. 6, 1986.

332. S 2792. Pesticide Control Reauthorization. Lugar, R-Ind., motion to table (kill) the Durenberger, R-Minn., amendment to strike provisions allowing federal regulations to preempt stricter, state-set standards (or "tolerances") for the amount of pesticide residues allowable on food products. Motion rejected 34-45: R 23-16; D 11-29 (ND 4-24, SD 7-5), Oct. 6, 1986. (The Durenberger amendment subsequently was adopted by voice vote. Later, the Senate moved to remove the text of HR 2482, the House-passed version of the bill, and insert the provisions of S 2792. Then, the Senate passed HR 2482 by voice vote.)

* Corresponding to Congressional Record Votes 333, 334, 335, 336, 337, 338, 339, 340, 341, 342, 343, 344

	333	334	335	336	337	338	339
ALABAMA							
Denton	?	?	Y	Y	Y	Y	Y
Heflin	N	N	Y	Y	P	Y	Y
ALASKA							
Murkowski	N	N	Y	Y	P	Y	Y
Stevens	N	N	P	P	P	P	Y
ARIZONA							
Goldwater	Y	Y	Y	Y	N	Y	Y
DeConcini	N	N	Y	Y	Y	Y	Y
ARKANSAS							
Bumpers	N	Y	Y	Y	Y	Y	Y
Pryor	Y	N	N	N	N	N	Y
CALIFORNIA							
Wilson	N	Y	Y	Y	Y	Y	Y
Cranston	N	N	Y	Y	P	Y	Y
COLORADO							
Armstrong	N	Y	Y	Y	P	Y	Y
Hart	Y	Y	Y	Y	P	Y	Y
CONNECTICUT							
Weicker	?	?	Y	Y	P	Y	Y
Dodd	N	Y	Y	Y	N	Y	Y
DELAWARE							
Roth	N	Y	Y	Y	Y	Y	Y
Biden	N	Y	Y	Y	P	Y	Y
FLORIDA							
Hawkins	?	?	Y	Y	N	Y	Y
Chiles	N	N	Y	Y	N	Y	Y
GEORGIA							
Mattingly	N	Y	Y	Y	P	Y	Y
Nunn	N	Y	Y	Y	P	Y	Y
HAWAII							
Inouye	N	N	Y	Y	P	Y	Y
Matsunaga	Y	N	Y	Y	N	Y	Y
IDAHO							
McClure	N	Y	Y	Y	N	Y	Y
Symms	?	?	?	?	?	?	?
ILLINOIS							
Dixon	N	Y	Y	Y	Y	Y	Y
Simon	Y	Y	Y	Y	Y	Y	Y
INDIANA							
Lugar	N	Y	Y	Y	Y	Y	Y
Quayle	N	Y	Y	Y	Y	Y	Y
IOWA							
Grassley	N	Y	Y	Y	Y	Y	Y
Harkin	N	Y	Y	Y	Y	Y	Y
KANSAS							
Dole	N	Y	Y	Y	P	Y	Y
Kassebaum	N	Y	Y	Y	Y	Y	Y
KENTUCKY							
McConnell	N	Y	Y	Y	P	Y	Y
Ford	N	Y	Y	Y	P	Y	Y
LOUISIANA							
Johnston	Y	Y	Y	Y	Y	Y	Y
Long	Y	N	N	N	Y	N	Y
MAINE							
Cohen	N	Y	Y	Y	P	Y	Y
Mitchell	N	Y	Y	Y	Y	Y	Y
MARYLAND							
Mathias	N	Y	Y	Y	P	Y	Y
Sarbanes	N	Y	Y	Y	P	Y	Y
MASSACHUSETTS							
Kennedy	N	Y	Y	Y	Y	Y	Y
Kerry	N	Y	Y	Y	P	Y	Y
MICHIGAN							
Levin	N	N	N	N	Y	Y	Y
Riegle	Y	N	Y	Y	Y	Y	Y
MINNESOTA							
Boschwitz	N	Y	Y	Y	Y	Y	Y
Durenberger	N	Y	Y	Y	Y	Y	Y
MISSISSIPPI							
Cochran	N	Y	Y	Y	Y	Y	Y
Stennis	?	Y	Y	Y	Y	Y	Y
MISSOURI							
Danforth	N	Y	Y	Y	Y	Y	Y
Eagleton	N	Y	Y	Y	Y	Y	Y
MONTANA							
Baucus	N	N	Y	Y	Y	Y	Y
Melcher	N	N	Y	Y	P	Y	Y
NEBRASKA							
Exon	N	N	Y	Y	Y	Y	Y
Zorinsky	N	Y	Y	Y	Y	Y	Y
NEVADA							
Hecht	N	N	N	Y	N	Y	Y
Laxalt	Y	N	N	Y	N	N	Y
NEW HAMPSHIRE							
Humphrey	N	N	Y	Y	P	Y	Y
Rudman	N	Y	Y	Y	P	Y	Y
NEW JERSEY							
Bradley	N	Y	Y	Y	Y	Y	Y
Lautenberg	N	Y	Y	Y	Y	Y	Y
NEW MEXICO							
Domenici	N	Y	Y	Y	P	Y	Y
Bingaman	N	N	N	N	Y	N	Y
NEW YORK							
D'Amato	N	N	Y	Y	P	Y	Y
Moynihan	N	N	Y	Y	P	Y	Y
NORTH CAROLINA							
Broyhill	N	Y	Y	Y	Y	Y	Y
Helms	Y	N	Y	Y	N	Y	Y
NORTH DAKOTA							
Andrews	?	?	Y	Y	P	Y	Y
Burdick	Y	N	Y	Y	P	Y	Y
OHIO							
Glenn	N	N	Y	Y	Y	Y	Y
Metzenbaum	Y	N	N	Y	Y	N	Y
OKLAHOMA							
Nickles	N	Y	Y	Y	Y	Y	Y
Boren	N	Y	Y	Y	Y	Y	Y
OREGON							
Hatfield	Y	N	N	N	Y	N	Y
Packwood	N	N	Y	Y	P	Y	Y
PENNSYLVANIA							
Heinz	N	-	Y	Y	N	Y	Y
Specter	?	Y	Y	Y	N	Y	Y
RHODE ISLAND							
Chafee	N	Y	Y	Y	N	Y	Y
Pell	Y	Y	Y	Y	N	Y	Y
SOUTH CAROLINA							
Thurmond	N	Y	Y	Y	P	Y	Y
Hollings	N	Y	Y	Y	Y	Y	Y
SOUTH DAKOTA							
Abdnor	N	Y	Y	Y	P	Y	Y
Pressler	N	Y	Y	Y	Y	Y	Y
TENNESSEE							
Gore	N	Y	Y	Y	P	Y	Y
Sasser	N	N	Y	Y	Y	Y	Y
TEXAS							
Gramm	N	Y	Y	Y	P	Y	Y
Bentsen	N	Y	Y	Y	Y	Y	Y
UTAH							
Garn	?	?	?	?	?	?	?
Hatch	Y	N	N	N	N	N	Y
VERMONT							
Stafford	N	Y	Y	Y	Y	Y	Y
Leahy	N	Y	Y	Y	Y	Y	Y
VIRGINIA							
Trible	N	Y	Y	Y	Y	Y	Y
Warner	Y	N	Y	Y	N	Y	Y
WASHINGTON							
Evans	Y	N	N	N	N	N	Y
Gorton	N	Y	Y	Y	P	Y	Y
WEST VIRGINIA							
Byrd	N	Y	Y	Y	P	Y	Y
Rockefeller	N	N	Y	Y	Y	Y	Y
WISCONSIN							
Kasten	N	Y	Y	Y	Y	Y	Y
Proxmire	N	Y	Y	Y	Y	Y	Y
WYOMING							
Simpson	N	Y	Y	Y	P	Y	Y
Wallop	N	Y	Y	Y	P	Y	Y

KEY

- Y Voted for (yea).
- # Paired for.
- + Announced for.
- N Voted against (nay).
- X Paired against.
- \- Announced against.
- P Voted "present."
- C Voted "present" to avoid possible conflict of interest.
- ? Did not vote or otherwise make a position known.

Democrats *Republicans*

ND - Northern Democrats SD - Southern Democrats (Southern states - Ala., Ark., Fla., Ga., Ky., La., Miss., N.C., Okla., S.C., Tenn., Texas, Va.)

* The *Congressional Record* vote number is different from the CQ vote number because the *Record* counts each treaty ratified when resolutions of ratification are adopted en bloc. CQ counts the one roll-call vote.

333. Claiborne Impeachment. Judge Claiborne's motion that the Senate establish "beyond a reasonable doubt" to be the standard of proof at the impeachment trial. Motion rejected 17-75: R 7-39; D 10-36 (ND 7-26, SD 3-10), Oct. 7, 1986.

334. Claiborne Impeachment. Dole, R-Kan., motion that the Senate not hear additional witnesses in the impeachment trial. Motion agreed to 61-32: R 34-12; D 27-20 (ND 18-15, SD 9-5), Oct. 8, 1986.

335. Claiborne Impeachment. Judgment of the Senate whether Judge Harry E. Claiborne was guilty as charged in the first article of impeachment, which alleged that Claiborne willfully under-reported his income by $18,741 in 1979. Adjudged guilty 87-10: R 45-5; D 42-5 (ND 30-3, SD 12-2), Oct. 9, 1986. A two-thirds majority of those present and voting (66 in this case) is required to adjudge a respondent guilty. A "Y" in the vote chart indicates a vote of "guilty"; an "N" indicates a vote of "not guilty."

336. Claiborne Impeachment. Judgment of the Senate whether Judge Harry E. Claiborne was guilty as charged in the second article of impeachment, which alleged that Claiborne willfully under-reported his income by $87,912 in 1980. Adjudged guilty 90-7: R 47-3; D 43-4 (ND 31-2, SD 12-2), Oct. 9, 1986. A two-thirds majority of those present and voting (66 in this case) is required to adjudge a respondent guilty. A "Y" in the vote chart indicates a vote of "guilty"; an "N" indicates a vote of "not guilty."

337. Claiborne Impeachment. Judgment of the Senate whether Judge Harry E. Claiborne was guilty as charged in the third article of impeachment, which alleged that Claiborne should be removed from office because of his 1984 conviction for tax fraud. Adjudged not guilty 46-17: R 18-12; D 28-5 (ND 20-3, SD 8-2), Oct. 9, 1986. (Thirty-five senators voted "present.") A two-thirds majority of those present and voting (66 in this case) is required to adjudge a respondent guilty. A "Y" in the vote chart indicates a vote of "guilty"; an "N" indicates a vote of "not guilty."

338. Claiborne Impeachment. Judgment of the Senate whether Judge Harry E. Claiborne was guilty as charged in the fourth article of impeachment, which alleged that Claiborne betrayed the trust of the people and brought disrepute on the federal judiciary. Adjudged guilty 89-8: R 46-4; D 43-4 (ND 31-2, SD 12-2), Oct. 9, 1986. A two-thirds majority of those present and voting (66 in this case) is required to adjudge a respondent guilty. A "Y" in the vote chart indicates a vote of "guilty"; an "N" indicates a vote of "not guilty."

339. Treaties. Adoption of the resolutions of ratification for: **Treaty Doc 98-9,** U.N. Convention on Contracts for the International Sale of Goods. **Treaty Doc 98-27,** Inter-American Convention on Letters Rogatory, With Protocol. **Treaty Doc 98-28,** Convention on Wetlands of International Importance. **Treaty Doc 98-29,** Request for Advice and Consent to Withdrawal of a Reservation Made to the 1975 Patent Cooperation Treaty. **Treaty Doc 97-12,** Inter-American Convention on Commercial Arbitration. **Treaty Doc 99-11,** Hague Convention on the Civil Aspects of International Child Abduction. Adopted en bloc 98-0: R 51-0; D 47-0 (ND 33-0, SD 14-0), Oct. 9, 1986. A two-thirds majority of those present and voting (66 in this case) is required for adoption of resolutions of ratification. A "yea" was a vote supporting the president's position.

CQ Senate Votes 340 - 347

* Corresponding to Congressional Record Votes 345, 346, 347, 348, 349, 350, 351, 352

	340	341	342	343	344	345	346	347
ALABAMA								
Denton	Y	Y	Y	N	N	Y	Y	Y
Heflin	Y	Y	Y	N	N	Y	Y	Y
ALASKA								
Murkowski	Y	Y	Y	Y	N	Y	Y	Y
Stevens	?	?	Y	Y	N	N	Y	Y
ARIZONA								
Goldwater	Y	Y	Y	Y	N	Y	Y	Y
DeConcini	N	Y	Y	N	Y	N	N	N
ARKANSAS								
Bumpers	N	Y	Y	Y	Y	Y	Y	N
Pryor	N	N	Y	Y	Y	Y	Y	N
CALIFORNIA								
Wilson	Y	Y	Y	Y	N	Y	N	Y
Cranston	N	Y	Y	Y	Y	Y	N	?
COLORADO								
Armstrong	Y	Y	Y	N	N	Y	Y	Y
Hart	N	N	?	?	Y	Y	Y	N
CONNECTICUT								
Weicker	Y	N	Y	Y	Y	N	Y	Y
Dodd	?	Y	Y	Y	Y	Y	N	Y
DELAWARE								
Roth	Y	Y	Y	Y	N	Y	Y	Y
Biden	?	N	Y	Y	Y	?	N	N
FLORIDA								
Hawkins	Y	Y	Y	Y	N	N	Y	Y
Chiles	N	Y	Y	Y	Y	N	Y	N
GEORGIA								
Mattingly	Y	Y	Y	Y	N	Y	Y	Y
Nunn	N	Y	Y	Y	Y	Y	Y	N
HAWAII								
Inouye	N	N	Y	Y	Y	Y	Y	N
Matsunaga	N	N	Y	Y	Y	N	N	N
IDAHO								
McClure	Y	Y	Y	N	N	N	Y	Y
Symms	?	+	+	-	-	-	?	?
ILLINOIS								
Dixon	N	Y	Y	Y	N	Y	N	N
Simon	N	N	Y	Y	Y	Y	N	N
INDIANA								
Lugar	Y	Y	Y	Y	N	Y	Y	Y
Quayle	Y	Y	Y	Y	N	Y	Y	Y
IOWA								
Grassley	Y	Y	Y	Y	Y	Y	Y	Y
Harkin	N	N	Y	Y	Y	Y	N	N
KANSAS								
Dole	Y	Y	Y	Y	N	Y	Y	Y
Kassebaum	Y	Y	Y	Y	N	Y	Y	Y
KENTUCKY								
McConnell	Y	Y	Y	Y	N	Y	Y	Y
Ford	N	Y	Y	Y	Y	Y	N	N
LOUISIANA								
Johnston	N	N	Y	Y	Y	N	Y	N
Long	N	N	Y	Y	N	Y	Y	N
MAINE								
Cohen	Y	N	Y	N	N	Y	Y	Y
Mitchell	N	N	Y	N	Y	Y	Y	N
MARYLAND								
Mathias	Y	N	Y	Y	N	N	Y	Y
Sarbanes	N	N	Y	Y	Y	N	N	N
MASSACHUSETTS								
Kennedy	N	N	Y	Y	Y	Y	N	N
Kerry	N	N	Y	Y	Y	Y	Y	N
MICHIGAN								
Levin	N	N	Y	Y	Y	Y	N	N
Riegle	N	Y	Y	Y	Y	N	N	N
MINNESOTA								
Boschwitz	Y	N	Y	Y	N	Y	Y	Y
Durenberger	Y	N	Y	Y	N	Y	N	N
MISSISSIPPI								
Cochran	Y	Y	Y	N	N	N	Y	Y
Stennis	?	N	Y	Y	Y	N	Y	Y
MISSOURI								
Danforth	Y	N	Y	Y	N	Y	Y	Y
Eagleton	N	N	Y	Y	Y	Y	Y	N
MONTANA								
Baucus	N	Y	Y	Y	Y	Y	Y	N
Melcher	N	Y	Y	Y	Y	Y	N	N
NEBRASKA								
Exon	N	Y	Y	Y	Y	Y	Y	Y
Zorinsky	N	Y	Y	N	N	Y	Y	Y
NEVADA								
Hecht	Y	Y	Y	N	N	Y	Y	Y
Laxalt	?	?	?	?	?	?	?	?
NEW HAMPSHIRE								
Humphrey	Y	N	Y	N	N	?	Y	Y
Rudman	Y	Y	Y	N	N	Y	Y	Y
NEW JERSEY								
Bradley	N	Y	Y	Y	Y	Y	Y	N
Lautenberg	N	Y	Y	Y	Y	N	Y	N
NEW MEXICO								
Domenici	Y	Y	Y	Y	N	Y	Y	Y
Bingaman	N	Y	Y	Y	Y	Y	Y	N
NEW YORK								
D'Amato	Y	Y	Y	Y	N	N	N	Y
Moynihan	N	N	Y	Y	Y	N	N	N
NORTH CAROLINA								
Broyhill	?	Y	Y	N	N	?	?	?
Helms	Y	Y	Y	N	N	Y	Y	Y
NORTH DAKOTA								
Andrews	?	?	Y	Y	N	N	Y	N
Burdick	N	N	Y	Y	Y	Y	N	N
OHIO								
Glenn	N	N	?	?	?	?	N	N
Metzenbaum	N	N	Y	Y	Y	Y	N	N
OKLAHOMA								
Nickles	Y	Y	Y	N	N	Y	Y	Y
Boren	N	Y	Y	Y	Y	Y	Y	N
OREGON								
Hatfield	Y	N	Y	Y	Y	N	Y	Y
Packwood	Y	Y	Y	Y	Y	N	Y	?
PENNSYLVANIA								
Heinz	Y	Y	Y	Y	Y	Y	N	?
Specter	?	Y	Y	Y	Y	?	N	N
RHODE ISLAND								
Chafee	Y	N	Y	Y	N	Y	Y	Y
Pell	N	Y	Y	Y	Y	+	?	?
SOUTH CAROLINA								
Thurmond	Y	Y	Y	Y	N	Y	Y	Y
Hollings	N	Y	Y	Y	N	Y	N	Y
SOUTH DAKOTA								
Abdnor	Y	Y	Y	N	N	Y	N	N
Pressler	Y	Y	Y	N	N	Y	Y	Y
TENNESSEE								
Gore	N	N	Y	Y	Y	N	N	N
Sasser	N	N	Y	Y	Y	N	N	N
TEXAS								
Gramm	Y	Y	Y	N	N	Y	Y	Y
Bentsen	N	N	Y	Y	N	Y	Y	N
UTAH								
Garn	?	Y	Y	N	N	Y	?	?
Hatch	Y	Y	Y	N	N	Y	Y	N
VERMONT								
Stafford	Y	N	Y	Y	N	Y	Y	Y
Leahy	?	N	Y	Y	Y	?	?	-
VIRGINIA								
Trible	Y	Y	Y	Y	N	Y	Y	Y
Warner	Y	Y	Y	Y	N	Y	Y	Y
WASHINGTON								
Evans	Y	N	Y	Y	N	Y	Y	Y
Gorton	Y	N	Y	Y	N	Y	Y	N
WEST VIRGINIA								
Byrd	N	Y	Y	Y	Y	Y	N	N
Rockefeller	N	N	Y	Y	Y	Y	N	N
WISCONSIN								
Kasten	Y	Y	Y	Y	Y	Y	N	Y
Proxmire	N	N	Y	Y	Y	Y	N	N
WYOMING								
Simpson	Y	Y	Y	Y	N	Y	Y	Y
Wallop	Y	Y	Y	N	N	+	Y	Y

KEY

- Y Voted for (yea).
- # Paired for.
- + Announced for.
- N Voted against (nay).
- X Paired against.
- \- Announced against.
- P Voted "present."
- C Voted "present" to avoid possible conflict of interest.
- ? Did not vote or otherwise make a position known.

Democrats *Republicans*

ND - Northern Democrats SD - Southern Democrats (Southern states - Ala., Ark., Fla., Ga., Ky., La., Miss., N.C., Okla., S.C., Tenn., Texas, Va.)

* The *Congressional Record* vote number is different from the CQ vote number because the *Record* counts each treaty ratified when resolutions of ratification are adopted en bloc. CQ counts the one roll-call vote.

340. Malone Nomination. Dole, R-Kan., motion that the Senate go into executive session to consider President Reagan's nomination of James L. Malone of Virginia to be ambassador to Belize. Motion agreed to 47-42: R 46-0; D 1-42 (ND 0-30, SD 1-12), Oct. 14, 1986. (The nomination later was set aside for the rest of the session.) A "yea" was a vote supporting the president's position.

341. HR 5484. Omnibus Drug Bill. Dole, R-Kan., motion to invoke cloture (thus limiting debate) on the Dole motion to concur in the House amendment to the Senate amendment to the bill to authorize $1.7 billion for drug interdiction, eradication, education and treatment efforts, and to increase penalties for certain drug offenses, with an amendment to make several modest changes from the House amendment. Motion rejected 58-38: R 37-12; D 21-26 (ND 14-19, SD 7-7), Oct. 15, 1986. A three-fifths majority (60) of the total Senate is required to invoke cloture. (Several members of both parties threatened a filibuster over a House provision authorizing the death penalty for certain drug-related murders. The provision subsequently was stricken from the bill by voice vote.)

342. S 1128. Clean Water Act Amendments. Adoption of the conference report on the bill to reauthorize and amend the Clean Water Act of 1972 (PL 92-500), to authorize $19.96 billion in appropriations in fiscal 1986-94 for controlling water pollution and for aiding local governments in building sewage treatment plants. Adopted (thus cleared for the president) 96-0: R 51-0; D 45-0 (ND 31-0, SD 14-0), Oct. 16, 1986. A "nay" was a vote supporting the president's position.

343. S 1200. Immigration Reform. Simpson, R-Wyo., motion to waive the prohibition, contained in the 1974 Congressional Budget and Impoundment Control Act (PL 93-344), on considering the conference report on the bill to overhaul the nation's immigration laws. The waiver was required because the bill would create a new entitlement through a program to grant legal status to possibly millions of people who can prove they were in the United States prior to Jan. 1, 1982. There was no provision in the budget for the expenditures associated with the legalization program. Motion agreed to 75-21: R 34-17; D 41-4 (ND 28-3, SD 13-1), Oct. 16, 1986.

344. S J Res 429. Report on U.S. Involvement in Aid to Nicaraguan Rebels. Passage of the joint resolution to require the president to report on all U.S. contacts with private individuals aiding the anti-government guerrillas in Nicaragua ("contras"). Rejected 47-50: R 7-44; D 40-6 (ND 30-2, SD 10-4), Oct. 16, 1986.

345. H J Res 738. Continuing Appropriations, Fiscal 1987. Judgment of the Senate whether the Goldwater, R-Ariz., amendment to the Abdnor, R-S.D., amendment (to the House amendment to the Senate amendment) was germane. The Goldwater amendment would virtually bar fiscal 1986 and fiscal 1987 Air Force spending for the T-46 trainer aircraft; the Abdnor amendment would eliminate from the legislation appropriations for certain proposed federal buildings and projects that had not been authorized by both chambers. Ruled germane 69-21: R 37-10; D 32-11 (ND 23-6, SD 9-5), Oct. 16, 1986.

346. H J Res 738. Continuing Appropriations, Fiscal 1987. Hatfield, R-Ore., motion to table (kill) the House amendment to the Senate amendment, to require that 50 percent of the materials and labor used in offshore oil-drilling rigs be American in origin. Motion agreed to 63-31: R 42-7; D 21-24 (ND 11-20, SD 10-4), Oct. 16, 1986. A "yea" was a vote supporting the president's position.

347. H J Res 738. Continuing Appropriations, Fiscal 1987. Hatfield, R-Ore., motion to table (kill) the Metzenbaum, D-Ohio, amendment (to the Abdnor, R-S.D., amendment to the House amendment to the Senate amendment *(see vote 345, above)*), to add to the continuing resolution the text of a bill (HR 5445) to curtail private lawsuits under a federal racketeering law. Motion agreed to 47-44: R 41-6; D 6-38 (ND 3-27, SD 3-11), in the session that began Oct. 16, 1986.

* Corresponding to Congressional Record Votes 353, 354, 355, 356, 357, 358, 359

	348	349	350	351	352	353	354
ALABAMA							
Denton	Y	N	N	Y	N	Y	Y
Heflin	N	Y	Y	Y	N	N	Y
ALASKA							
Murkowski	Y	Y	Y	Y	#	+	+
Stevens	Y	Y	Y	N	Y	Y	Y
ARIZONA							
Goldwater	Y	N	N	Y	?	?	?
DeConcini	N	Y	Y	N	-	?	?
ARKANSAS							
Bumpers	N	N	Y	Y	N	N	Y
Pryor	N	N	Y	Y	Y	N	Y
CALIFORNIA							
Wilson	Y	N	Y	Y	Y	Y	Y
Cranston	?	?	N	Y	Y	N	Y
COLORADO							
Armstrong	Y	N	N	Y	N	N	Y
Hart	N	Y	Y	Y	Y	Y	Y
CONNECTICUT							
Weicker	Y	Y	Y	Y	Y	?	?
Dodd	N	Y	Y	Y	Y	Y	Y
DELAWARE							
Roth	Y	N	Y	Y	Y	Y	Y
Biden	N	Y	Y	Y	Y	Y	Y
FLORIDA							
Hawkins	Y	Y	Y	Y	Y	Y	Y
Chiles	Y	Y	Y	Y	Y	Y	?
GEORGIA							
Mattingly	Y	N	Y	Y	Y	Y	Y
Nunn	N	N	Y	Y	Y	Y	Y
HAWAII							
Inouye	N	Y	N	Y	N	Y	Y
Matsunaga	N	Y	Y	Y	Y	Y	Y
IDAHO							
McClure	Y	Y	N	Y	N	N	Y
Symms	?	?	-	+	X	?	?
ILLINOIS							
Dixon	N	Y	Y	Y	Y	Y	Y
Simon	N	Y	Y	Y	Y	Y	Y
INDIANA							
Lugar	Y	N	Y	Y	Y	Y	Y
Quayle	Y	N	N	Y	Y	Y	Y
IOWA							
Grassley	Y	N	Y	Y	Y	N	Y
Harkin	N	N	Y	Y	Y	N	Y
KANSAS							
Dole	Y	N	Y	Y	Y	Y	Y
Kassebaum	Y	N	Y	Y	Y	Y	Y
KENTUCKY							
McConnell	Y	N	Y	Y	Y	Y	Y
Ford	N	N	Y	Y	N	Y	Y
LOUISIANA							
Johnston	N	Y	Y	Y	Y	Y	Y
Long	N	Y	Y	Y	Y	Y	Y
MAINE							
Cohen	Y	N	N	Y	N	Y	Y
Mitchell	N	N	N	Y	N	Y	Y
MARYLAND							
Mathias	Y	Y	Y	N	?	?	?
Sarbanes	N	Y	Y	N	Y	Y	Y
MASSACHUSETTS							
Kennedy	N	N	N	Y	N	Y	Y
Kerry	N	N	Y	Y	Y	N	Y
MICHIGAN							
Levin	N	N	Y	Y	Y	Y	Y
Riegle	N	N	Y	Y	N	N	Y
MINNESOTA							
Boschwitz	Y	N	Y	Y	Y	Y	Y
Durenberger	Y	N	Y	Y	Y	Y	Y
MISSISSIPPI							
Cochran	Y	Y	N	Y	N	Y	Y
Stennis	Y	Y	Y	Y	?	?	Y
MISSOURI							
Danforth	Y	N	Y	Y	Y	Y	Y
Eagleton	N	?	Y	Y	Y	Y	?
MONTANA							
Baucus	N	N	Y	Y	Y	N	Y
Melcher	N	N	Y	Y	Y	N	Y
NEBRASKA							
Exon	N	N	Y	Y	Y	N	Y
Zorinsky	Y	N	N	Y	N	N	Y
NEVADA							
Hecht	Y	N	N	Y	N	Y	Y
Laxalt	?	?	?	?	?	?	?
NEW HAMPSHIRE							
Humphrey	Y	N	N	Y	N	N	Y
Rudman	Y	N	N	Y	N	Y	Y
NEW JERSEY							
Bradley	N	Y	Y	Y	Y	Y	Y
Lautenberg	N	Y	Y	N	Y	Y	Y
NEW MEXICO							
Domenici	Y	N	Y	Y	N	Y	Y
Bingaman	N	N	Y	Y	Y	N	Y
NEW YORK							
D'Amato	Y	Y	Y	N	Y	Y	Y
Moynihan	N	Y	Y	N	Y	Y	Y
NORTH CAROLINA							
Broyhill	?	?	-	+	X	+	?
Helms	Y	N	N	Y	N	N	Y
NORTH DAKOTA							
Andrews	N	N	?	?	Y	Y	Y
Burdick	N	N	Y	Y	Y	Y	Y
OHIO							
Glenn	Y	N	+	+	+	N	Y
Metzenbaum	N	N	Y	Y	Y	N	Y
OKLAHOMA							
Nickles	N	N	N	Y	N	N	Y
Boren	N	N	?	?	?	?	?
OREGON							
Hatfield	Y	Y	Y	Y	Y	Y	Y
Packwood	?	?	Y	Y	Y	Y	Y
PENNSYLVANIA							
Heinz	N	N	Y	Y	Y	Y	Y
Specter	N	Y	Y	?	Y	?	Y
RHODE ISLAND							
Chafee	Y	N	Y	Y	Y	Y	Y
Pell	?	?	Y	Y	Y	Y	Y
SOUTH CAROLINA							
Thurmond	Y	N	Y	Y	Y	Y	Y
Hollings	N	N	Y	Y	Y	Y	Y
SOUTH DAKOTA							
Abdnor	N	N	N	Y	N	Y	Y
Pressler	N	N	N	Y	N	N	Y
TENNESSEE							
Gore	N	Y	Y	N	Y	Y	Y
Sasser	N	Y	Y	N	Y	Y	Y
TEXAS							
Gramm	Y	N	N	Y	N	Y	Y
Bentsen	N	N	Y	Y	Y	Y	Y
UTAH							
Garn	?	?	Y	Y	N	Y	Y
Hatch	Y	N	N	Y	N	N	Y
VERMONT							
Stafford	Y	N	Y	Y	Y	Y	Y
Leahy	?	?	?	?	+	?	?
VIRGINIA							
Trible	Y	N	?	Y	Y	Y	Y
Warner	Y	N	Y	Y	Y	N	Y
WASHINGTON							
Evans	Y	N	?	?	?	?	?
Gorton	Y	N	?	?	#	+	?
WEST VIRGINIA							
Byrd	N	N	Y	Y	Y	Y	Y
Rockefeller	N	N	Y	Y	Y	Y	Y
WISCONSIN							
Kasten	Y	N	Y	Y	Y	N	N
Proxmire	Y	N	Y	Y	Y	N	N
WYOMING							
Simpson	Y	N	Y	Y	Y	Y	Y
Wallop	Y	N	Y	Y	Y	Y	Y

KEY

- Y Voted for (yea).
- # Paired for.
- \+ Announced for.
- N Voted against (nay).
- X Paired against.
- \- Announced against.
- P Voted "present."
- C Voted "present" to avoid possible conflict of interest.
- ? Did not vote or otherwise make a position known.

Democrats ***Republicans***

ND - Northern Democrats SD - Southern Democrats (Southern states - Ala., Ark., Fla., Ga., Ky., La., Miss., N.C., Okla., S.C., Tenn., Texas, Va.)

* The *Congressional Record* vote number is different from the CQ vote number because the *Record* counts each treaty ratified when resolutions of ratification are adopted en bloc. CQ counts the one roll-call vote.

348. H J Res 738. Continuing Appropriations, Fiscal 1987. Hatfield, R-Ore., motion to table (kill) the Melcher, D-Mont., amendment (to the Abdnor, R-S.D., amendment to the House amendment to the Senate amendment), to increase by $50 million funding for the temporary emergency food assistance program (a surplus commodities distribution program). Motion agreed to 47-45: R 42-6; D 5-39 (ND 3-27, SD 2-12), in the session that began Oct. 16, 1986. (The Abdnor amendment would have eliminated appropriations for certain federal buildings or related projects that had not been authorized. The House amendment to the Senate amendment — which added money for federal buildings — had been reported in disagreement by conferees on the legislation.)

349. H J Res 738. Continuing Appropriations, Fiscal 1987. Hatfield, R-Ore., motion to table (kill) the Abdnor, R-S.D., amendment to the House amendment to the Senate amendment *(see vote 348, above)*, to eliminate appropriations for certain federal buildings or related projects that had not been authorized. Motion rejected 29-62: R 10-38; D 19-24 (ND 12-17, SD 7-7), in the session that began Oct. 16, 1986. (The intent of the motion was to kill an amendment by Barry Goldwater, R-Ariz. (to the Abdnor amendment), to bar funding for the T-46 Air Force trainer airplane.)

350. S 1200. Immigration Reform. Simpson, R-Wyo., motion to invoke cloture (thus limiting debate) on the conference report on the bill to overhaul the nation's immigration laws. Motion agreed to 69-21: R 30-16; D 39-5 (ND 26-5, SD 13-0), Oct. 17, 1986. A three-fifths majority (60) of the total Senate is required to invoke cloture.

351. H J Res 738. Continuing Appropriations, Fiscal 1987. Hatfield, R-Ore., motion to table (kill) the D'Amato, R-N.Y., motion to postpone until Dec. 29, 1986, consideration of the Goldwater, R-Ariz., amendment (to the Abdnor amendment to the House amendment to the Senate amendment *(see vote 348, above)*), to bar funding for the T-46 Air Force trainer airplane. Motion agreed to 81-9: R 43-3; D 38-6 (ND 27-4, SD 11-2), Oct. 17, 1986. (The Goldwater amendment later was modified and stripped from the Abdnor amendment, and then adopted by voice vote. Still later, the Abdnor amendment was tabled by voice vote.)

352. S 1200. Immigration Reform. Adoption of the conference report on the bill to overhaul the nation's immigration laws by creating new penalties against employers who knowingly hire illegal aliens; granting amnesty to illegal aliens who can prove they were in the country prior to Jan. 1, 1982; and creating a special farm worker program for Western agricultural growers. Adopted 63-24: R 29-16; D 34-8 (ND 25-5, SD 9-3), Oct. 17, 1986.

353. HR 5300. Omnibus Budget Reconciliation, Fiscal 1987. Adoption of the conference report on the bill to reduce the projected fiscal 1987 deficit by an estimated $11.7 billion. Adopted 61-25: R 33-10; D 28-15 (ND 19-12, SD 9-3), Oct. 17, 1986.

354. HR 6. Water Projects Authorization. Adoption of the conference report on the bill to authorize the Army Corps of Engineers to undertake various water resources development projects, at an estimated federal and non-federal cost of approximately $16.5 billion. Obligations from the amounts authorized to be appropriated in the bill are limited to $1.4 billion in fiscal 1987, $1.5 billion in 1988, $1.6 billion in 1989, $1.7 billion in 1990, and $1.8 billion in 1991. Adopted 84-2: R 43-1; D 41-1 (ND 29-1, SD 12-0), Oct. 17, 1986.

HOUSE ROLL-CALL VOTES

CQ

KEY

Y Voted for (yea).
\# Paired for.
\+ Announced for.
N Voted against (nay).
X Paired against.
\- Announced against.
P Voted "present."
C Voted "present" to avoid possible conflict of interest.
? Did not vote or otherwise make a position known.

Democrats ***Republicans***

1. Procedural Motion. Gingrich, R-Ga., motion to approve the House *Journal* of Wednesday, Jan. 22. Motion agreed to 223-87: R 48-78; D 175-9 (ND 116-7, SD 59-2), Jan. 23, 1986.

2. HR 2443. Expedited Funds Availability Act. Adoption of the rule (H Res 357) to provide for House floor consideration of the bill to limit the number of days a depository institution may restrict the availability of funds deposited in an account. Adopted 199-129: R 7-125; D 192-4 (ND 124-3, SD 68-1), Jan. 23, 1986.

3. HR 2443. Expedited Funds Availability Act. Wylie, R-Ohio, amendment to clarify the Federal Reserve Board's responsibility to prevent abuses of the check payments system. Rejected 21-289: R 20-101; D 1-188 (ND 1-127, SD 0-61), Jan. 23, 1986.

4. HR 2443. Expedited Funds Availability Act. Shumway, R-Calif., amendment to the Bartlett, R-Texas, amendment, to require depository institutions that are exempted from check-hold limits in cases where the institution has a reasonable doubt that a check might be bad to notify the customer by the end of the next business day. Adopted 156-146: R 111-8; D 45-138 (ND 21-102, SD 24-36), Jan. 23, 1986. (The Bartlett amendment, to exempt institutions from check-hold limits in cases where the institution has a reasonable doubt that a check might be bad, as amended by the Shumway amendment, subsequently was adopted by voice vote.)

5. HR 2443. Expedited Funds Availability Act. Shumway, R-Calif., substitute to replace the check-hold provisions with a requirement that the Federal Reserve Board within 18 months issue preliminary regulations to shorten the check-holding period, and within three years issue final regulations. Rejected 80-211: R 78-39; D 2-172 (ND 0-117, SD 2-55), Jan. 23, 1986.

6. HR 2443. Expedited Funds Availability Act. Passage of the bill to limit the number of days a depository institution may restrict the availability of funds deposited in an account. Passed 282-11: R 108-9; D 174-2 (ND 119-0, SD 55-2), Jan. 23, 1986.

	1	2	3	4	5	6
ALABAMA						
1 ***Callahan***	Y	N	N	Y	Y	Y
2 ***Dickinson***	?	N	?	?	?	?
3 Nichols	?	Y	N	N	N	Y
4 Bevill	?	?	?	?	?	?
5 Flippo	?	?	?	?	?	?
6 Erdreich	Y	Y	N	N	N	Y
7 Shelby	?	Y	N	N	N	Y
ALASKA						
AL ***Young***	?	?	?	?	?	?
ARIZONA						
1 ***McCain***	Y	N	N	Y	N	Y
2 Udall	Y	Y	N	N	N	Y
3 ***Stump***	Y	N	N	Y	Y	N
4 ***Rudd***	?	?	?	?	?	?
5 ***Kolbe***	N	N	N	Y	Y	Y
ARKANSAS						
1 Alexander	Y	Y	N	N	?	+
2 Robinson	Y	Y	N	N	N	?
3 ***Hammerschmidt***	?	?	?	?	?	?
4 Anthony	Y	Y	?	?	?	?
CALIFORNIA						
1 Bosco	Y	Y	N	N	N	Y
2 ***Chappie***	N	N	N	Y	Y	Y
3 Matsui	?	?	?	?	?	?
4 Fazio	Y	Y	N	N	N	Y
5 Burton	Y	Y	N	N	N	Y
6 Boxer	?	?	?	?	?	?
7 Miller	?	?	?	?	?	?
8 Dellums	Y	Y	N	N	N	Y
9 Stark	?	?	?	?	?	?
10 Edwards	Y	Y	N	N	N	Y
11 Lantos	?	?	?	?	?	?
12 ***Zschau***	N	N	N	Y	Y	N
13 Mineta	Y	Y	N	N	N	Y
14 ***Shumway***	Y	N	N	Y	Y	N
15 Coelho	?	?	?	?	?	?
16 Panetta	Y	Y	?	?	?	?
17 ***Pashayan***	?	?	?	?	?	?
18 Lehman	Y	Y	N	?	?	?
19 ***Lagomarsino***	N	N	N	Y	Y	Y
20 ***Thomas***	N	N	N	Y	Y	N
21 ***Fiedler***	?	?	?	?	?	?
22 ***Moorhead***	N	N	N	Y	Y	Y
23 Beilenson	Y	Y	N	N	N	Y
24 Waxman	Y	?	N	N	N	Y
25 Roybal	Y	Y	N	N	N	Y
26 Berman	Y	Y	N	N	N	Y
27 Levine	Y	Y	N	N	N	Y
28 Dixon	?	?	N	N	N	Y
29 Hawkins	Y	Y	N	N	N	Y
30 Martinez	Y	Y	N	N	N	Y
31 Dymally	Y	Y	N	N	N	Y
32 Anderson	P	Y	N	Y	N	Y
33 ***Dreier***	N	N	N	Y	Y	N
34 Torres	?	Y	N	N	N	Y
35 ***Lewis***	N	Y	?	?	?	?
36 Brown	?	?	?	?	?	?
37 ***McCandless***	N	N	N	Y	Y	Y
38 ***Dornan***	?	N	N	Y	Y	N
39 ***Dannemeyer***	N	N	N	Y	Y	Y
40 ***Badham***	N	N	N	?	?	?
41 ***Lowery***	N	N	?	?	?	?
42 ***Lungren***	?	N	N	Y	Y	Y
43 ***Packard***	?	?	?	?	?	?
44 Bates	Y	Y	N	N	N	Y
45 ***Hunter***	?	N	Y	Y	Y	Y
COLORADO						
1 Schroeder	N	N	N	N	-	+
2 Wirth	Y	Y	N	N	N	Y
3 ***Strang***	N	N	N	Y	N	Y
4 ***Brown***	N	N	N	Y	Y	Y
5 ***Kramer***	?	?	?	?	?	?
6 ***Schaefer***	N	N	N	Y	N	Y
CONNECTICUT						
1 Kennelly	Y	Y	N	N	N	Y
2 Gejdenson	Y	Y	N	N	N	Y
3 Morrison	Y	Y	N	N	?	?
4 ***McKinney***	Y	N	N	N	N	Y
5 ***Rowland***	Y	N	N	Y	N	Y
6 ***Johnson***	?	N	N	N	N	Y
DELAWARE						
AL Carper	Y	Y	N	Y	N	Y
FLORIDA						
1 Hutto	Y	Y	?	?	?	?
2 Fuqua	Y	Y	?	?	?	?
3 Bennett	Y	Y	N	N	N	Y
4 Chappell	?	?	?	?	?	?
5 ***McCollum***	Y	N	Y	Y	Y	Y
6 MacKay	+	+	-	-	-	+
7 Gibbons	Y	Y	N	N	N	Y
8 ***Young***	?	N	N	Y	Y	Y
9 ***Bilirakis***	N	N	N	Y	Y	Y
10 ***Ireland***	N	N	N	Y	Y	Y
11 Nelson	Y	Y	-	N	N	Y
12 ***Lewis***	+	X	-	+	+	+
13 ***Mack***	N	N	Y	Y	Y	N
14 Mica	?	#	?	?	?	?
15 ***Shaw***	N	N	N	Y	Y	Y
16 Smith	Y	Y	N	Y	N	Y
17 Lehman	Y	Y	N	N	N	Y
18 Pepper	Y	Y	N	N	N	Y
19 Fascell	Y	Y	N	N	N	Y
GEORGIA						
1 Thomas	Y	Y	N	N	N	Y
2 Hatcher	Y	Y	?	?	?	?
3 Ray	Y	Y	N	Y	N	Y
4 ***Swindall***	N	N	N	Y	N	Y
5 Fowler	?	?	?	?	?	?
6 ***Gingrich***	N	N	N	Y	Y	Y
7 Darden	Y	Y	N	N	N	Y
8 Rowland	Y	Y	N	N	N	Y
9 Jenkins	Y	Y	N	Y	N	Y
10 Barnard	Y	Y	N	N	N	Y
HAWAII						
1 Heftel	?	?	?	?	?	?
2 Akaka	?	?	?	?	?	?
IDAHO						
1 ***Craig***	Y	N	N	Y	Y	Y
2 Stallings	Y	Y	?	?	?	?
ILLINOIS						
1 Hayes	Y	Y	N	N	N	Y
2 Savage	?	?	?	?	?	?
3 Russo	Y	Y	N	N	N	Y
4 ***O'Brien***	?	?	?	?	?	?
5 Lipinski	Y	Y	N	N	N	Y
6 ***Hyde***	?	N	Y	Y	Y	Y
7 Collins	?	?	N	N	N	Y
8 Rostenkowski	Y	Y	?	?	?	?
9 Yates	Y	Y	N	N	N	Y
10 ***Porter***	Y	N	N	N	N	Y
11 Annunzio	Y	Y	N	N	N	Y
12 ***Crane***	?	?	?	?	?	?
13 ***Fawell***	N	N	Y	Y	Y	Y
14 ***Grotberg***	?	X	?	?	?	?
15 ***Madigan***	N	N	?	?	?	?
16 ***Martin***	?	?	N	Y	Y	Y
17 Evans	Y	Y	N	N	N	Y
18 ***Michel***	N	N	Y	Y	Y	Y
19 Bruce	Y	Y	N	Y	N	Y
20 Durbin	N	Y	N	Y	N	Y
21 Price	Y	Y	N	N	N	Y
22 Gray	?	?	?	?	?	?
INDIANA						
1 Visclosky	Y	Y	N	N	N	Y
2 Sharp	Y	Y	N	Y	N	Y
3 ***Hiler***	Y	N	N	Y	Y	Y
4 ***Coats***	Y	N	N	Y	Y	Y
5 ***Hillis***	?	?	?	?	?	?

ND - Northern Democrats SD - Southern Democrats

	1	2	3	4	5	6
6 ***Burton***	?	?	?	?	?	?
7 ***Myers***	Y	N	N	Y	Y	Y
8 McCloskey	?	Y	N	N	N	Y
9 Hamilton	Y	Y	N	Y	N	Y
10 Jacobs	N	N	N	N	N	Y
IOWA						
1 ***Leach***	N	N	Y	N	N	Y
2 ***Tauke***	N	N	N	Y	N	Y
3 ***Evans***	N	N	N	?	N	Y
4 Smith	Y	?	?	?	?	?
5 ***Lightfoot***	N	N	N	Y	Y	Y
6 Bedell	Y	Y	N	N	N	Y
KANSAS						
1 ***Roberts***	?	?	N	Y	N	Y
2 Slattery	Y	Y	N	Y	N	Y
3 ***Meyers***	N	Y	N	Y	N	Y
4 Glickman	Y	Y	N	Y	N	Y
5 ***Whittaker***	N	N	N	?	?	?
KENTUCKY						
1 Hubbard	Y	Y	N	N	N	Y
2 Natcher	Y	Y	N	Y	N	Y
3 Mazzoli	Y	Y	N	Y	N	Y
4 ***Snyder***	?	?	?	?	?	?
5 ***Rogers***	N	N	N	Y	Y	Y
6 ***Hopkins***	Y	N	N	Y	Y	Y
7 Perkins	P	Y	N	N	N	Y
LOUISIANA						
1 ***Livingston***	?	?	?	?	?	?
2 Boggs	Y	Y	N	N	N	Y
3 Tauzin	Y	Y	N	N	N	Y
4 Roemer	N	Y	N	N	N	Y
5 Huckaby	Y	Y	N	N	?	?
6 ***Moore***	?	?	?	?	?	?
7 Breaux	?	?	?	?	?	?
8 Long	?	?	?	?	?	?
MAINE						
1 ***McKernan***	N	N	N	Y	N	Y
2 ***Snowe***	N	N	N	Y	N	Y
MARYLAND						
1 Dyson	Y	Y	N	Y	N	Y
2 ***Bentley***	N	N	N	Y	Y	Y
3 Mikulski	?	?	?	?	?	?
4 ***Holt***	Y	N	Y	Y	Y	Y
5 Hoyer	Y	Y	N	N	?	Y
6 Byron	?	Y	?	?	?	?
7 Mitchell	N	Y	N	N	N	Y
8 Barnes	?	?	?	?	?	?
MASSACHUSETTS						
1 ***Conte***	N	N	N	N	N	Y
2 Boland	Y	?	N	N	N	Y
3 Early	Y	Y	N	N	N	Y
4 Frank	Y	Y	N	N	N	?
5 Atkins	Y	Y	N	N	N	Y
6 Mavroules	?	?	?	?	?	?
7 Markey	?	?	N	N	?	Y
8 O'Neill						
9 Moakley	?	?	?	?	?	?
10 Studds	?	?	?	?	?	?
11 Donnelly	?	?	?	?	?	?
MICHIGAN						
1 Conyers	Y	Y	N	N	N	Y
2 ***Pursell***	Y	N	N	Y	N	Y
3 Wolpe	Y	?	?	?	?	?
4 ***Siljander***	N	N	N	Y	Y	Y
5 ***Henry***	N	N	?	?	?	?
6 Carr	Y	Y	N	Y	N	Y
7 Kildee	Y	Y	N	N	N	Y
8 Traxler	Y	Y	N	N	N	Y
9 ***Vander Jagt***	Y	Y	Y	Y	Y	Y
10 ***Schuette***	N	N	N	Y	Y	Y
11 ***Davis***	N	N	N	Y	N	Y
12 Bonior	Y	Y	N	N	N	Y
13 Crockett	Y	Y	N	N	N	Y
14 Hertel	Y	Y	N	N	N	Y
15 Ford	?	?	N	N	N	Y
16 Dingell	Y	Y	N	N	N	Y
17 Levin	Y	Y	?	?	?	?
18 ***Broomfield***	?	?	?	?	?	?
MINNESOTA						
1 Penny	N	Y	N	N	N	Y
2 ***Weber***	?	X	?	?	?	?
3 ***Frenzel***	?	?	?	?	?	?
4 Vento	Y	Y	N	N	N	Y
5 Sabo	Y	Y	N	N	N	Y
6 Sikorski	N	Y	N	N	N	Y

	1	2	3	4	5	6
7 ***Stangeland***	?	?	?	?	?	?
8 Oberstar	Y	?	N	N	N	Y
MISSISSIPPI						
1 Whitten	Y	Y	N	Y	N	Y
2 ***Franklin***	Y	N	N	Y	Y	Y
3 Montgomery	Y	Y	N	Y	N	Y
4 Dowdy	?	?	?	?	?	?
5 ***Lott***	Y	N	N	Y	Y	Y
MISSOURI						
1 Clay	N	?	N	N	N	Y
2 Young	P	Y	N	N	N	Y
3 Gephardt	?	?	?	?	?	?
4 Skelton	Y	Y	N	N	N	Y
5 Wheat	Y	Y	N	N	N	Y
6 ***Coleman***	N	N	N	Y	N	Y
7 ***Taylor***	N	N	N	Y	?	?
8 ***Emerson***	N	N	N	Y	Y	Y
9 Volkmer	Y	Y	N	N	N	Y
MONTANA						
1 Williams	?	Y	N	Y	N	Y
2 ***Marlenee***	?	?	?	?	?	?
NEBRASKA						
1 ***Bereuter***	N	N	Y	Y	N	Y
2 ***Daub***	N	N	N	Y	Y	Y
3 ***Smith***	Y	N	N	Y	N	Y
NEVADA						
1 Reid	Y	Y	N	N	N	Y
2 ***Vucanovich***	N	N	N	Y	Y	Y
NEW HAMPSHIRE						
1 ***Smith***	N	N	N	Y	Y	Y
2 ***Gregg***	?	?	?	?	?	?
NEW JERSEY						
1 Florio	Y	Y	N	N	N	Y
2 Hughes	Y	Y	N	N	N	Y
3 Howard	Y	Y	N	?	?	?
4 ***Smith***	Y	Y	N	Y	N	Y
5 ***Roukema***	N	N	N	Y	N	Y
6 Dwyer	Y	Y	N	N	N	Y
7 ***Rinaldo***	Y	Y	?	?	?	?
8 Roe	?	?	?	?	?	?
9 Torricelli	Y	Y	N	N	N	Y
10 Rodino	Y	Y	N	N	N	Y
11 ***Gallo***	N	N	-	-	-	+
12 ***Courter***	N	N	N	Y	N	Y
13 ***Saxton***	Y	N	N	Y	N	Y
14 Guarini	?	Y	N	N	N	Y
NEW MEXICO						
1 ***Lujan***	Y	N	?	?	Y	Y
2 ***Skeen***	N	N	N	Y	Y	Y
3 Richardson	Y	Y	N	Y	N	Y
NEW YORK						
1 ***Carney***	?	?	?	?	?	?
2 Downey	?	Y	N	N	N	Y
3 Mrazek	Y	Y	N	N	?	Y
4 ***Lent***	N	N	N	Y	?	?
5 ***McGrath***	?	?	?	?	?	?
6 Addabbo	?	#	?	?	?	?
7 Ackerman	Y	Y	N	N	N	Y
8 Scheuer	Y	Y	N	N	N	Y
9 Manton	Y	Y	?	?	?	?
10 Schumer	Y	Y	N	N	N	Y
11 Towns	?	Y	N	N	N	Y
12 Owens	?	Y	N	N	N	Y
13 Solarz	Y	Y	N	N	?	?
14 ***Molinari***	N	N	N	Y	N	Y
15 ***Green***	Y	N	N	Y	N	Y
16 Rangel	Y	Y	N	N	N	Y
17 Weiss	Y	Y	N	N	N	Y
18 Garcia	?	#	?	?	?	?
19 Biaggi	Y	Y	N	N	N	Y
20 ***DioGuardi***	Y	N	N	Y	N	Y
21 ***Fish***	Y	N	?	?	?	?
22 ***Gilman***	Y	N	N	Y	N	Y
23 Stratton	Y	Y	Y	N	N	Y
24 ***Solomon***	N	N	?	?	?	?
25 ***Boehlert***	?	?	?	?	?	?
26 ***Martin***	Y	N	C	C	C	C
27 ***Wortley***	?	X	?	?	?	?
28 McHugh	Y	Y	N	N	N	Y
29 ***Horton***	Y	Y	N	N	N	Y
30 ***Eckert***	Y	N	N	Y	Y	Y
31 ***Kemp***	?	?	?	?	?	?
32 LaFalce	Y	Y	N	Y	N	Y
33 Nowak	Y	Y	N	N	N	Y
34 Lundine	?	?	?	?	?	?

	1	2	3	4	5	6
NORTH CAROLINA						
1 Jones	Y	Y	N	N	N	Y
2 Valentine	Y	Y	N	N	N	Y
3 Whitley	Y	Y	N	N	?	?
4 ***Cobey***	N	N	N	Y	Y	Y
5 Neal	Y	Y	N	Y	N	Y
6 ***Coble***	N	N	?	?	?	?
7 Rose	Y	Y	N	Y	?	?
8 Hefner	Y	Y	N	N	N	Y
9 ***McMillan***	Y	N	N	Y	Y	Y
10 ***Broyhill***	Y	N	N	Y	Y	Y
11 ***Hendon***	N	N	?	Y	Y	Y
NORTH DAKOTA						
AL Dorgan	?	?	?	?	?	?
OHIO						
1 Luken	Y	N	N	N	N	Y
2 ***Gradison***	Y	N	Y	Y	Y	Y
3 Hall	?	?	?	?	?	?
4 ***Oxley***	N	N	Y	Y	Y	Y
5 ***Latta***	N	N	Y	Y	Y	Y
6 ***McEwen***	Y	N	?	?	?	?
7 ***DeWine***	N	N	Y	Y	Y	Y
8 ***Kindness***	?	N	Y	Y	Y	Y
9 Kaptur	Y	Y	N	-	-	+
10 ***Miller***	?	?	?	?	?	?
11 Eckart	Y	Y	N	N	N	Y
12 ***Kasich***	Y	N	N	Y	Y	Y
13 Pease	Y	Y	N	N	N	Y
14 Seiberling	Y	Y	N	N	N	Y
15 ***Wylie***	Y	N	Y	Y	Y	Y
16 ***Regula***	N	N	?	?	?	?
17 Traficant	Y	Y	N	N	N	Y
18 Applegate	?	?	?	?	?	?
19 Feighan	Y	Y	N	Y	N	Y
20 Oakar	?	Y	?	?	?	?
21 Stokes	Y	Y	N	N	N	Y
OKLAHOMA						
1 Jones	?	?	?	?	?	?
2 Synar	Y	Y	-	-	-	+
3 Watkins	P	Y	N	Y	N	Y
4 McCurdy	Y	Y	N	Y	N	Y
5 ***Edwards***	N	N	N	Y	?	?
6 English	Y	Y	N	Y	N	Y
OREGON						
1 AuCoin	?	?	?	?	?	?
2 ***Smith, R.***	?	?	?	?	?	?
3 Wyden	Y	Y	N	N	N	Y
4 Weaver	Y	Y	N	N	N	Y
5 ***Smith, D.***	?	?	?	?	?	?
PENNSYLVANIA						
1 Foglietta	?	?	?	?	?	?
2 Gray	Y	?	?	?	?	?
3 Borski	Y	Y	N	N	N	Y
4 Kolter	P	Y	N	Y	N	Y
5 ***Schulze***	?	?	?	?	?	?
6 Yatron	Y	Y	N	Y	N	Y
7 Edgar	?	?	?	?	?	?
8 Kostmayer	Y	Y	N	Y	N	Y
9 ***Shuster***	Y	N	N	Y	?	?
10 ***McDade***	?	?	?	?	?	?
11 Kanjorski	Y	Y	N	?	?	?
12 Murtha	Y	Y	N	Y	N	Y
13 ***Coughlin***	N	N	N	Y	N	Y
14 Coyne	Y	Y	N	N	N	Y
15 ***Ritter***	?	X	?	?	?	?
16 ***Walker***	N	N	N	Y	Y	Y
17 ***Gekas***	N	Y	N	N	Y	Y
18 Walgren	?	Y	N	Y	N	Y
19 ***Goodling***	N	N	Y	Y	Y	Y
20 Gaydos	Y	Y	N	Y	N	Y
21 ***Ridge***	?	N	N	Y	N	Y
22 Murphy	?	?	?	?	?	?
23 ***Clinger***	+	+	-	+	-	+
RHODE ISLAND						
1 St Germain	Y	Y	N	N	N	Y
2 ***Schneider***	?	?	?	?	?	?
SOUTH CAROLINA						
1 ***Hartnett***	?	?	?	?	?	?
2 ***Spence***	N	N	N	Y	Y	Y
3 Derrick	Y	Y	N	N	N	Y
4 ***Campbell***	?	?	?	?	?	?
5 Spratt	Y	Y	N	Y	N	Y
6 Tallon	Y	Y	N	Y	N	Y
SOUTH DAKOTA						
AL Daschle	Y	Y	N	N	N	Y

	1	2	3	4	5	6
TENNESSEE						
1 ***Quillen***	?	?	?	?	?	?
2 ***Duncan***	Y	?	Y	Y	Y	Y
3 Lloyd	N	Y	N	Y	N	Y
4 Cooper	Y	Y	N	N	N	Y
5 Boner	Y	Y	N	N	N	Y
6 Gordon	Y	Y	N	N	N	Y
7 ***Sundquist***	N	N	N	Y	Y	Y
8 Jones	Y	Y	N	N	N	Y
9 Ford	Y	Y	?	?	?	?
TEXAS						
1 Chapman	Y	Y	N	Y	N	Y
2 Wilson	Y	Y	N	Y	N	Y
3 ***Bartlett***	N	N	N	Y	Y	N
4 Hall, R.	Y	N	N	Y	N	Y
5 Bryant	Y	Y	N	N	N	Y
6 ***Barton***	Y	N	N	Y	Y	Y
7 ***Archer***	?	?	?	?	?	?
8 ***Fields***	N	N	N	Y	Y	Y
9 Brooks	Y	Y	N	?	?	Y
10 Pickle	?	#	?	?	?	?
11 Leath	P	Y	N	?	Y	N
12 Wright	Y	Y	N	N	N	Y
13 ***Boulter***	?	?	N	Y	Y	Y
14 ***Sweeney***	?	?	?	?	?	?
15 de la Garza	?	?	?	?	?	?
16 Coleman	Y	Y	N	Y	N	Y
17 Stenholm	Y	Y	N	Y	Y	N
18 Leland	?	Y	N	N	N	Y
19 ***Combest***	Y	N	N	Y	Y	Y
20 Gonzalez	Y	Y	N	N	N	Y
21 ***Loeffler***	?	?	?	?	?	?
22 ***DeLay***	N	?	?	?	?	?
23 Bustamante	?	?	?	?	?	?
24 Frost	Y	Y	N	N	N	Y
25 Andrews	?	Y	N	Y	N	Y
26 ***Armey***	N	N	N	Y	Y	N
27 Ortiz	Y	Y	?	?	?	?
UTAH						
1 ***Hansen***	Y	N	N	Y	Y	Y
2 ***Monson***	?	?	?	?	?	?
3 ***Nielson***	Y	N	N	Y	Y	Y
VERMONT						
AL ***Jeffords***	Y	N	N	Y	N	Y
VIRGINIA						
1 ***Bateman***	Y	N	Y	Y	N	Y
2 ***Whitehurst***	Y	N	N	Y	Y	Y
3 ***Bliley***	N	?	?	?	?	?
4 Sisisky	Y	Y	N	N	N	Y
5 Daniel	Y	Y	N	Y	N	Y
6 Olin	?	Y	N	Y	N	Y
7 ***Slaughter***	N	?	?	?	?	?
8 ***Parris***	Y	N	Y	Y	Y	Y
9 Boucher	Y	Y	N	Y	N	Y
10 ***Wolf***	N	N	N	Y	N	Y
WASHINGTON						
1 ***Miller***	Y	N	N	Y	N	Y
2 Swift	Y	Y	N	N	N	Y
3 Bonker	?	?	?	?	?	?
4 ***Morrison***	Y	N	N	Y	N	Y
5 Foley	Y	Y	N	N	N	Y
6 Dicks	Y	Y	N	N	N	Y
7 Lowry	Y	Y	N	N	N	Y
8 ***Chandler***	N	N	N	Y	Y	Y
WEST VIRGINIA						
1 Mollohan	Y	Y	N	Y	N	Y
2 Staggers	Y	Y	N	N	N	Y
3 Wise	Y	Y	N	N	N	Y
4 Rahall	Y	Y	N	?	?	?
WISCONSIN						
1 Aspin	Y	Y	N	N	N	Y
2 Kastenmeier	Y	Y	N	N	N	Y
3 ***Gunderson***	N	N	N	Y	N	Y
4 Kleczka	Y	+	-	-	-	+
5 Moody	?	#	?	?	?	?
6 ***Petri***	N	N	N	N	N	Y
7 Obey	Y	Y	N	N	N	Y
8 ***Roth***	?	N	N	Y	Y	Y
9 ***Sensenbrenner***	N	N	N	Y	Y	Y
WYOMING						
AL ***Cheney***	?	?	?	?	?	?

Southern states - Ala., Ark., Fla., Ga., Ky., La., Miss., N.C., Okla., S.C., Tenn., Texas, Va.

* The *Congressional Record* vote number is different from the CQ vote number because the *Record* includes quorum calls in its tally. CQ does not publish quorum call votes.

7. HR 3525. Uniform Poll Closing. Passage of the bill to establish a single poll closing time throughout the continental United States for presidential elections. Passed 204-171: R 28-137; D 176-34 (ND 131-16, SD 45-18), Jan. 29, 1986.

8. HR 4055. Protection and Advocacy for the Mentally Ill. Adoption of the rule (H Res 360) to provide for House floor consideration of the bill to authorize aid to states for providing legal advocacy and protective services for the mentally ill. Adopted 240-134: R 34-125; D 206-9 (ND 141-3, SD 65-6), Jan. 30, 1986.

9. HR 4055. Protection and Advocacy for the Mentally Ill. Luken, D-Ohio, amendment to strike language that would have prevented the new aid for protection and advocacy programs for the mentally ill from going to certain states that have already established similar programs. Adopted 280-90: R 77-82; D 203-8 (ND 138-1, SD 65-7), Jan. 30, 1986.

10. HR 4055. Protection and Advocacy for the Mentally Ill. Passage of the bill to authorize $33 million over fiscal 1986-88 in aid to states for legal advocacy and protective services for the mentally ill. Passed 290-84: R 89-71; D 201-13 (ND 140-4, SD 61-9), Jan. 30, 1986.

KEY

Y Voted for (yea).
Paired for.
\+ Announced for.
N Voted against (nay).
X Paired against.
\- Announced against.
P Voted "present."
C Voted "present" to avoid possible conflict of interest.
? Did not vote or otherwise make a position known.

Democrats *Republicans*

	7	8	9	10
ALABAMA				
1 ***Callahan***	N	N	Y	Y
2 ***Dickinson***	N	?	N	N
3 Nichols	N	Y	N	N
4 Bevill	N	Y	?	Y
5 Flippo	?	?	Y	Y
6 Erdreich	N	Y	Y	Y
7 Shelby	N	Y	Y	Y
ALASKA				
AL ***Young***	Y	Y	Y	Y
ARIZONA				
1 ***McCain***	Y	Y	Y	Y
2 Udall	?	Y	Y	Y
3 ***Stump***	Y	N	N	N
4 ***Rudd***	N	N	N	N
5 ***Kolbe***	N	N	N	N
ARKANSAS				
1 Alexander	?	?	?	?
2 Robinson	Y	Y	Y	Y
3 ***Hammerschmidt***	N	N	N	Y
4 Anthony	?	Y	Y	Y
CALIFORNIA				
1 Bosco	Y	Y	Y	Y
2 ***Chappie***	N	N	N	N
3 Matsui	Y	Y	Y	Y
4 Fazio	Y	Y	Y	Y
5 Burton	#	?	?	?
6 Boxer	Y	Y	Y	Y
7 Miller	Y	Y	Y	Y
8 Dellums	Y	Y	Y	Y
9 Stark	Y	Y	Y	?
10 Edwards	Y	Y	Y	Y
11 Lantos	Y	Y	Y	Y
12 ***Zschau***	N	N	N	N
13 Mineta	Y	Y	Y	Y
14 ***Shumway***	N	N	N	N
15 Coelho	Y	Y	Y	Y
16 Panetta	Y	Y	Y	Y
17 ***Pashayan***	N	N	Y	Y
18 Lehman	Y	Y	Y	Y
19 ***Lagomarsino***	N	N	N	Y
20 ***Thomas***	Y	?	Y	Y
21 ***Fiedler***	N	N	N	N
22 ***Moorhead***	N	?	N	N
23 Beilenson	Y	Y	Y	Y
24 Waxman	Y	Y	Y	Y
25 Roybal	Y	Y	Y	Y
26 Berman	Y	Y	Y	Y
27 Levine	N	Y	Y	Y
28 Dixon	?	?	?	?
29 Hawkins	Y	Y	Y	Y
30 Martinez	Y	Y	Y	Y
31 Dymally	Y	Y	Y	Y
32 Anderson	Y	Y	Y	Y
33 ***Dreier***	N	N	N	N
34 Torres	Y	Y	Y	Y
35 ***Lewis***	Y	?	?	?
36 Brown	Y	Y	Y	Y
37 ***McCandless***	N	N	N	N
38 ***Dornan***	?	N	N	N
39 ***Dannemeyer***	Y	N	N	N
40 ***Badham***	N	N	N	N
41 ***Lowery***	Y	N	Y	Y
42 ***Lungren***	Y	N	N	N

	7	8	9	10
43 ***Packard***	N	N	Y	N
44 Bates	Y	Y	Y	Y
45 ***Hunter***	Y	?	N	Y
COLORADO				
1 Schroeder	N	Y	Y	Y
2 Wirth	Y	Y	Y	Y
3 ***Strang***	N	N	N	Y
4 ***Brown***	N	N	N	N
5 ***Kramer***	N	N	N	N
6 ***Schaefer***	N	N	N	N
CONNECTICUT				
1 Kennelly	Y	Y	Y	Y
2 Gejdenson	Y	?	Y	Y
3 Morrison	Y	Y	Y	Y
4 ***McKinney***	Y	Y	Y	Y
5 ***Rowland***	N	Y	Y	Y
6 ***Johnson***	Y	Y	N	Y
DELAWARE				
AL Carper	Y	Y	Y	Y
FLORIDA				
1 Hutto	Y	Y	Y	Y
2 Fuqua	Y	Y	Y	Y
3 Bennett	Y	Y	Y	Y
4 Chappell	Y	?	Y	Y
5 ***McCollum***	N	N	Y	Y
6 MacKay	Y	Y	Y	Y
7 Gibbons	Y	Y	Y	Y
8 ***Young***	Y	Y	Y	Y
9 ***Bilirakis***	N	N	Y	Y
10 ***Ireland***	Y	N	N	Y
11 Nelson	Y	Y	Y	Y
12 ***Lewis***	N	N	Y	Y
13 ***Mack***	N	N	N	Y
14 Mica	Y	Y	Y	Y
15 ***Shaw***	N	N	Y	Y
16 Smith	N	Y	Y	Y
17 Lehman	?	Y	Y	Y
18 Pepper	Y	Y	Y	Y
19 Fascell	?	Y	Y	Y
GEORGIA				
1 Thomas	N	Y	Y	Y
2 Hatcher	?	?	?	?
3 Ray	N	N	N	N
4 ***Swindall***	N	N	N	N
5 Fowler	?	?	?	?
6 ***Gingrich***	N	N	N	N
7 Darden	N	Y	Y	Y
8 Rowland	N	Y	Y	Y
9 Jenkins	N	Y	Y	Y
10 Barnard	Y	N	Y	?
HAWAII				
1 Heftel	Y	?	?	?
2 Akaka	Y	Y	Y	Y
IDAHO				
1 ***Craig***	N	?	N	N
2 Stallings	Y	N	?	Y
ILLINOIS				
1 Hayes	Y	Y	Y	Y
2 Savage	?	?	?	?
3 Russo	?	?	?	?
4 ***O'Brien***	X	?	?	?
5 Lipinski	Y	Y	Y	Y
6 ***Hyde***	N	N	N	N
7 Collins	#	+	+	+
8 Rostenkowski	?	?	?	?
9 Yates	Y	Y	Y	Y
10 ***Porter***	N	N	Y	?
11 Annunzio	Y	Y	Y	Y
12 ***Crane***	X	?	?	?
13 ***Fawell***	N	N	N	N
14 ***Grotberg***	X	?	?	?
15 ***Madigan***	N	N	N	N
16 ***Martin***	N	N	N	?
17 Evans	Y	Y	Y	Y
18 ***Michel***	N	N	N	Y
19 Bruce	N	Y	Y	Y
20 Durbin	N	Y	Y	Y
21 Price	Y	Y	Y	Y
22 Gray	?	?	?	?
INDIANA				
1 Visclosky	Y	Y	Y	Y
2 Sharp	Y	Y	Y	Y
3 ***Hiler***	N	N	N	N
4 ***Coats***	N	N	N	N
5 ***Hillis***	N	N	N	Y

ND - Northern Democrats SD - Southern Democrats

	7	8	9	10
6 ***Burton***	N	N	N	Y
7 ***Myers***	N	N	N	Y
8 McCloskey	Y	Y	Y	Y
9 Hamilton	Y	Y	Y	Y
10 Jacobs	Y	Y	Y	Y
IOWA				
1 ***Leach***	N	Y	?	Y
2 ***Tauke***	N	N	Y	Y
3 ***Evans***	N	Y	N	Y
4 Smith	Y	?	?	?
5 ***Lightfoot***	N	N	Y	Y
6 Bedell	N	Y	Y	Y
KANSAS				
1 ***Roberts***	N	N	N	N
2 Slattery	N	Y	Y	N
3 ***Meyers***	N	N	N	N
4 Glickman	N	Y	Y	N
5 ***Whittaker***	N	N	N	N
KENTUCKY				
1 Hubbard	Y	Y	N	N
2 Natcher	N	Y	Y	Y
3 Mazzoli	Y	Y	Y	N
4 ***Snyder***	?	?	?	?
5 ***Rogers***	N	N	?	Y
6 ***Hopkins***	Y	N	N	Y
7 Perkins	N	Y	Y	Y
LOUISIANA				
1 ***Livingston***	N	N	N	N
2 Boggs	Y	Y	Y	Y
3 Tauzin	Y	Y	Y	Y
4 Roemer	?	?	?	?
5 Huckaby	Y	Y	Y	?
6 ***Moore***	N	Y	N	N
7 Breaux	Y	Y	Y	Y
8 Long	?	?	?	?
MAINE				
1 ***McKernan***	N	N	Y	Y
2 ***Snowe***	N	Y	Y	Y
MARYLAND				
1 Dyson	Y	Y	Y	Y
2 ***Bentley***	?	N	Y	Y
3 Mikulski	Y	Y	Y	Y
4 ***Holt***	N	?	?	?
5 Hoyer	Y	Y	Y	Y
6 Byron	?	Y	Y	Y
7 Mitchell	Y	Y	Y	Y
8 Barnes	Y	Y	?	?
MASSACHUSETTS				
1 ***Conte***	N	Y	Y	Y
2 Boland	Y	Y	Y	Y
3 Early	?	?	?	?
4 Frank	?	Y	Y	Y
5 Atkins	Y	Y	Y	Y
6 Mavroules	Y	Y	Y	Y
7 Markey	Y	Y	Y	Y
8 O'Neill				
9 Moakley	?	Y	Y	Y
10 Studds	Y	Y	Y	Y
11 Donnelly	?	?	?	?
MICHIGAN				
1 Conyers	Y	?	?	Y
2 ***Pursell***	N	Y	Y	Y
3 Wolpe	Y	Y	Y	Y
4 ***Siljander***	?	N	Y	N
5 ***Henry***	N	Y	Y	Y
6 Carr	Y	Y	Y	Y
7 Kildee	Y	Y	Y	Y
8 Traxler	Y	Y	Y	Y
9 ***Vander Jagt***	N	N	?	Y
10 ***Schuette***	N	N	Y	Y
11 ***Davis***	N	Y	Y	Y
12 Bonior	Y	Y	Y	Y
13 Crockett	Y	?	Y	Y
14 Hertel	Y	Y	Y	Y
15 Ford	Y	Y	Y	Y
16 Dingell	Y	Y	?	Y
17 Levin	Y	Y	Y	Y
18 ***Broomfield***	N	Y	N	Y
MINNESOTA				
1 Penny	Y	Y	Y	N
2 ***Weber***	N	N	N	N
3 ***Frenzel***	N	N	Y	Y
4 Vento	Y	Y	Y	Y
5 Sabo	Y	Y	Y	Y
6 Sikorski	Y	Y	Y	Y
7 ***Stangeland***	N	?	Y	Y
8 Oberstar	Y	Y	Y	Y
MISSISSIPPI				
1 Whitten	?	Y	Y	Y
2 ***Franklin***	N	Y	N	N
3 Montgomery	N	Y	N	N
4 Dowdy	?	Y	Y	Y
5 ***Lott***	N	N	N	N
MISSOURI				
1 Clay	Y	Y	Y	Y
2 Young	?	Y	Y	Y
3 Gephardt	Y	Y	Y	Y
4 Skelton	Y	N	Y	N
5 Wheat	Y	Y	Y	Y
6 ***Coleman***	N	?	?	?
7 ***Taylor***	N	N	?	?
8 ***Emerson***	N	N	Y	Y
9 Volkmer	N	Y	Y	Y
MONTANA				
1 Williams	?	?	?	?
2 ***Marlenee***	?	?	?	?
NEBRASKA				
1 ***Bereuter***	Y	Y	Y	Y
2 ***Daub***	N	N	N	N
3 ***Smith***	Y	N	N	N
NEVADA				
1 Reid	Y	Y	Y	Y
2 ***Vucanovich***	Y	N	Y	N
NEW HAMPSHIRE				
1 ***Smith***	N	N	N	N
2 ***Gregg***	N	N	N	N
NEW JERSEY				
1 Florio	Y	?	Y	Y
2 Hughes	Y	N	N	Y
3 Howard	Y	Y	Y	Y
4 ***Smith***	N	Y	Y	Y
5 ***Roukema***	?	Y	Y	Y
6 Dwyer	Y	Y	Y	Y
7 ***Rinaldo***	N	Y	Y	Y
8 Roe	?	?	?	?
9 Torricelli	Y	?	?	?
10 Rodino	Y	Y	Y	Y
11 ***Gallo***	N	N	Y	Y
12 ***Courter***	Y	Y	Y	Y
13 ***Saxton***	N	N	Y	Y
14 Guarini	Y	Y	?	Y
NEW MEXICO				
1 ***Lujan***	N	N	Y	N
2 ***Skeen***	?	N	Y	N
3 Richardson	Y	Y	Y	Y
NEW YORK				
1 ***Carney***	N	N	Y	Y
2 Downey	Y	Y	Y	Y
3 Mrazek	Y	Y	?	Y
4 ***Lent***	Y	N	Y	Y
5 ***McGrath***	N	Y	Y	Y
6 Addabbo	#	?	?	?
7 Ackerman	Y	?	?	?
8 Scheuer	?	Y	Y	Y
9 Manton	Y	Y	Y	Y
10 Schumer	Y	Y	Y	Y
11 Towns	Y	Y	Y	Y
12 Owens	Y	Y	Y	Y
13 Solarz	Y	Y	Y	Y
14 ***Molinari***	N	N	Y	Y
15 ***Green***	N	Y	Y	Y
16 Rangel	Y	Y	Y	Y
17 Weiss	Y	Y	Y	Y
18 Garcia	Y	Y	Y	Y
19 Biaggi	Y	Y	Y	Y
20 ***DioGuardi***	N	Y	Y	Y
21 ***Fish***	Y	N	Y	Y
22 ***Gilman***	Y	Y	Y	Y
23 Stratton	Y	Y	Y	Y
24 ***Solomon***	N	N	?	?
25 ***Boehlert***	N	Y	Y	Y
26 ***Martin***	N	Y	Y	Y
27 ***Wortley***	N	N	Y	Y
28 McHugh	Y	Y	Y	Y
29 ***Horton***	Y	Y	Y	Y
30 ***Eckert***	N	?	?	?
31 ***Kemp***	X	N	Y	?
32 LaFalce	Y	?	?	?
33 Nowak	Y	Y	Y	Y
34 Lundine	Y	Y	Y	Y
NORTH CAROLINA				
1 Jones	Y	Y	Y	Y
2 Valentine	N	Y	Y	Y
3 Whitley	N	Y	Y	Y
4 ***Cobey***	N	N	Y	N
5 Neal	Y	Y	Y	Y
6 ***Coble***	N	N	Y	N
7 Rose	Y	Y	Y	Y
8 Hefner	Y	Y	Y	Y
9 ***McMillan***	N	N	Y	N
10 ***Broyhill***	N	N	Y	N
11 ***Hendon***	N	N	Y	Y
NORTH DAKOTA				
AL Dorgan	Y	Y	Y	Y
OHIO				
1 Luken	N	Y	Y	Y
2 ***Gradison***	N	N	Y	Y
3 Hall	N	Y	Y	Y
4 ***Oxley***	N	N	N	Y
5 ***Latta***	N	N	N	N
6 ***McEwen***	N	?	Y	N
7 ***DeWine***	N	N	Y	Y
8 ***Kindness***	N	N	Y	?
9 Kaptur	N	Y	Y	Y
10 ***Miller***	?	?	?	?
11 Eckart	Y	Y	Y	Y
12 ***Kasich***	N	N	Y	Y
13 Pease	Y	Y	Y	Y
14 Seiberling	?	?	?	?
15 ***Wylie***	N	N	Y	Y
16 ***Regula***	N	N	Y	Y
17 Traficant	Y	Y	Y	Y
18 Applegate	Y	Y	Y	Y
19 Feighan	Y	Y	Y	Y
20 Oakar	?	Y	Y	Y
21 Stokes	Y	Y	Y	Y
OKLAHOMA				
1 Jones	?	?	?	?
2 Synar	Y	Y	Y	Y
3 Watkins	Y	Y	Y	Y
4 McCurdy	Y	Y	Y	Y
5 ***Edwards***	N	N	N	N
6 English	Y	Y	Y	Y
OREGON				
1 AuCoin	Y	Y	Y	Y
2 ***Smith, R.***	?	?	?	?
3 Wyden	Y	Y	Y	Y
4 Weaver	Y	Y	Y	+
5 ***Smith, D.***	N	N	N	Y
PENNSYLVANIA				
1 Foglietta	Y	Y	Y	Y
2 Gray	Y	Y	Y	Y
3 Borski	N	Y	Y	Y
4 Kolter	Y	Y	Y	Y
5 ***Schulze***	N	N	N	Y
6 Yatron	Y	Y	Y	Y
7 Edgar	Y	Y	?	?
8 Kostmayer	Y	Y	Y	Y
9 ***Shuster***	N	N	Y	N
10 ***McDade***	?	?	?	?
11 Kanjorski	Y	Y	Y	Y
12 Murtha	?	Y	?	?
13 ***Coughlin***	N	N	N	Y
14 Coyne	Y	Y	Y	Y
15 ***Ritter***	N	N	N	N
16 ***Walker***	N	N	N	N
17 ***Gekas***	N	?	?	Y
18 Walgren	Y	Y	Y	Y
19 ***Goodling***	N	N	N	Y
20 Gaydos	Y	Y	Y	Y
21 ***Ridge***	Y	Y	Y	Y
22 Murphy	Y	Y	Y	Y
23 ***Clinger***	N	Y	N	Y
RHODE ISLAND				
1 St Germain	Y	Y	?	Y
2 ***Schneider***	N	Y	Y	Y
SOUTH CAROLINA				
1 ***Hartnett***	N	N	N	N
2 ***Spence***	N	N	Y	Y
3 Derrick	?	?	?	?
4 ***Campbell***	N	N	Y	Y
5 Spratt	Y	Y	Y	Y
6 Tallon	Y	Y	Y	Y
SOUTH DAKOTA				
AL Daschle	Y	Y	Y	Y
TENNESSEE				
1 ***Quillen***	?	?	?	?
2 ***Duncan***	N	N	N	Y
3 Lloyd	Y	N	Y	?
4 Cooper	Y	Y	Y	Y
5 Boner	Y	Y	Y	Y
6 Gordon	Y	Y	Y	Y
7 ***Sundquist***	Y	N	N	?
8 Jones	#	?	?	?
9 Ford	Y	Y	Y	Y
TEXAS				
1 Chapman	Y	Y	Y	Y
2 Wilson	Y	Y	Y	Y
3 ***Bartlett***	N	N	Y	N
4 Hall, R.	Y	Y	Y	Y
5 Bryant	Y	Y	Y	Y
6 ***Barton***	N	N	N	N
7 ***Archer***	N	N	N	N
8 ***Fields***	N	N	N	N
9 Brooks	Y	?	Y	Y
10 Pickle	Y	Y	Y	Y
11 Leath	?	N	N	N
12 Wright	?	Y	Y	?
13 ***Boulter***	N	N	Y	N
14 ***Sweeney***	N	N	?	N
15 de la Garza	?	Y	Y	Y
16 Coleman	Y	Y	Y	Y
17 Stenholm	Y	N	N	N
18 Leland	Y	Y	Y	Y
19 ***Combest***	N	N	Y	N
20 Gonzalez	Y	Y	Y	Y
21 ***Loeffler***	?	?	?	?
22 ***DeLay***	N	N	N	N
23 Bustamante	Y	Y	Y	Y
24 Frost	Y	Y	?	Y
25 Andrews	?	Y	Y	Y
26 ***Armey***	N	N	N	N
27 Ortiz	Y	Y	Y	Y
UTAH				
1 ***Hansen***	N	N	N	N
2 ***Monson***	N	N	N	N
3 ***Nielson***	N	N	Y	N
VERMONT				
AL ***Jeffords***	N	Y	Y	Y
VIRGINIA				
1 ***Bateman***	N	N	?	Y
2 ***Whitehurst***	N	N	N	N
3 ***Bliley***	N	N	N	N
4 Sisisky	N	Y	Y	Y
5 Daniel	N	Y	N	N
6 Olin	?	N	Y	N
7 ***Slaughter***	N	N	N	Y
8 ***Parris***	N	N	N	Y
9 Boucher	N	Y	Y	Y
10 ***Wolf***	N	N	N	Y
WASHINGTON				
1 ***Miller***	Y	N	Y	Y
2 Swift	Y	Y	Y	Y
3 Bonker	Y	Y	?	Y
4 ***Morrison***	Y	Y	Y	Y
5 Foley	?	Y	Y	Y
6 Dicks	Y	Y	Y	Y
7 Lowry	Y	Y	Y	Y
8 ***Chandler***	Y	Y	Y	Y
WEST VIRGINIA				
1 Mollohan	N	Y	Y	Y
2 Staggers	?	?	?	?
3 Wise	N	?	Y	Y
4 Rahall	N	Y	Y	Y
WISCONSIN				
1 Aspin	Y	Y	Y	Y
2 Kastenmeier	Y	Y	Y	Y
3 ***Gunderson***	Y	N	N	Y
4 Kleczka	Y	Y	Y	Y
5 Moody	Y	?	?	?
6 ***Petri***	N	N	N	N
7 Obey	N	?	?	?
8 ***Roth***	?	?	?	?
9 ***Sensenbrenner***	N	N	N	N
WYOMING				
AL ***Cheney***	N	N	N	N

Southern states - Ala., Ark., Fla., Ga., Ky., La., Miss., N.C., Okla., S.C., Tenn., Texas, Va.

* The *Congressional Record* vote number is different from the CQ vote number because the *Record* includes quorum calls in its tally. CQ does not publish quorum call votes.

11. S 2036. Technical Corrections to Farm Bill. De la Garza, D-Texas, motion to suspend the rules and pass the bill to amend the fiscal 1986-1990 farm programs reauthorization bill (PL 99-198) to clarify the agriculture secretary's authority to impose cross compliance in wheat and feed grain programs, and to specify the formula for wheat and feed grain bases for purposes of calculating price- and income-support payments. Motion agreed to 319-64: R 109-52; D 210-12 (ND 137-11, SD 73-1), Feb. 4, 1986. A two-thirds majority of those present and voting (256 in this case) is required for passage under suspension of the rules.

12. HR 3010. Health Planning. Passage of the bill to authorize $28.1 million in fiscal 1986 for aid to health planning agencies, which regulate the growth of hospitals and expensive medical services. Passed 390-3: R 165-1; D 225-2 (ND 150-2, SD 75-0), Feb. 4, 1986.

13. Procedural Motion. McCain, R-Ariz., motion to approve the House *Journal* of Tuesday, Feb. 4. Motion agreed to 227-170: R 6-160; D 221-10 (ND 150-5, SD 71-5), Feb. 5, 1986.

14. H Res 368. Committee Funds. Walker, R-Pa., motion to recommit the resolution to the House Administration Committee with instructions to report it back forthwith with an amendment directing each committee to study, prepare and publish alternative funding recommendations at least equal to the deficit-reduction levels set in the Gramm-Rudman-Hollings deficit-reduction law. Motion rejected 146-255: R 138-29; D 8-226 (ND 3-155, SD 5-71), Feb. 5, 1986.

15. H Res 368. Committee Funds. Adoption of the resolution to provide $43.6 million in funding for investigations and studies by standing and select committees of the House in the second session of the 99th Congress. Adopted 385-11: R 156-9; D 229-2 (ND 154-2, SD 75-0), Feb. 5, 1986.

16. HR 3456. Consumer Product Safety. Adoption of the rule (H Res 371) to provide for House floor consideration of the bill to authorize $36 million in fiscal year 1987 for the Consumer Product Safety Commission. Adopted 390-0: R 164-0; D 226-0 (ND 151-0, SD 75-0), Feb. 6, 1986.

17. S Con Res 107. Adjournment Resolution. Adoption of the concurrent resolution to provide for the adjournment of the House and Senate over the Presidents' Day recess. Adopted 208-179: R 15-147; D 193-32 (ND 135-15, SD 58-17), Feb. 6, 1986.

18. HR 3456. Consumer Product Safety. Dannemeyer, R-Calif., substitute for the Waxman, D-Calif., amendment, to authorize $33 million in each of fiscal years 1986-88 for the Consumer Product Safety Commission. The levels for 1987 and 1988 were those that the administration requested to comply with the Gramm-Rudman-Hollings deficit-reduction law. Rejected 189-200: R 154-11; D 35-189 (ND 8-140, SD 27-49), Feb. 6, 1986. (The Waxman amendment subsequently was adopted.) A "yea" was a vote supporting the president's position.

KEY

- Y Voted for (yea).
- # Paired for.
- + Announced for.
- N Voted against (nay).
- X Paired against.
- \- Announced against.
- P Voted "present."
- C Voted "present" to avoid possible conflict of interest.
- ? Did not vote or otherwise make a position known.

Democrats ***Republicans***

	11	12	13	14	15	16	17	18
ALABAMA								
1 ***Callahan***	Y	Y	?	?	?	Y	N	Y
2 ***Dickinson***	?	Y	N	N	Y	Y	Y	Y
3 Nichols	Y	Y	?	N	Y	Y	N	Y
4 Bevill	Y	Y	?	?	?	?	?	?
5 Flippo	Y	Y	Y	N	Y	Y	Y	Y
6 Erdreich	Y	Y	Y	N	Y	Y	N	Y
7 Shelby	Y	Y	Y	N	Y	?	Y	N
ALASKA								
AL ***Young***	Y	Y	N	N	Y	Y	N	Y
ARIZONA								
1 ***McCain***	Y	Y	N	Y	Y	Y	N	Y
2 Udall	Y	Y	Y	N	Y	Y	Y	N
3 ***Stump***	Y	Y	N	Y	Y	Y	N	Y
4 ***Rudd***	Y	Y	Y	N	Y	Y	Y	Y
5 ***Kolbe***	Y	Y	N	Y	Y	?	?	?
ARKANSAS								
1 Alexander	Y	Y	Y	N	Y	Y	Y	N
2 Robinson	Y	Y	Y	N	Y	Y	N	Y
3 ***Hammerschmidt***	Y	Y	N	N	Y	Y	N	Y
4 Anthony	Y	Y	?	N	Y	Y	Y	N
CALIFORNIA								
1 Bosco	Y	Y	Y	N	Y	?	?	?
2 ***Chappie***	N	Y	N	Y	Y	?	?	?
3 Matsui	Y	Y	Y	N	Y	Y	Y	N
4 Fazio	Y	Y	Y	N	Y	Y	Y	N
5 Burton	?	?	?	?	?	?	?	?
6 Boxer	Y	Y	Y	N	Y	Y	Y	N
7 Miller	Y	Y	?	N	Y	Y	?	N
8 Dellums	Y	Y	Y	N	Y	Y	Y	N
9 Stark	?	Y	Y	N	Y	?	?	?
10 Edwards	Y	Y	Y	N	Y	Y	Y	N
11 Lantos	Y	Y	Y	N	Y	Y	Y	N
12 ***Zschau***	N	Y	N	Y	Y	Y	N	Y
13 Mineta	Y	Y	Y	N	Y	Y	Y	N
14 ***Shumway***	N	Y	N	Y	Y	Y	N	Y
15 Coelho	?	?	Y	N	?	Y	Y	N
16 Panetta	Y	Y	Y	N	Y	Y	Y	N
17 ***Pashayan***	Y	Y	N	Y	Y	Y	N	Y
18 Lehman	Y	Y	Y	N	Y	Y	Y	N
19 ***Lagomarsino***	N	Y	N	Y	Y	Y	N	Y
20 ***Thomas***	Y	Y	N	Y	Y	Y	?	Y
21 ***Fiedler***	Y	Y	N	Y	Y	Y	N	?
22 ***Moorhead***	N	Y	N	Y	Y	Y	N	Y
23 Beilenson	Y	Y	Y	N	Y	Y	Y	N
24 Waxman	Y	Y	Y	N	Y	Y	Y	N
25 Roybal	Y	Y	Y	N	Y	Y	Y	N
26 Berman	Y	Y	Y	N	Y	Y	Y	N
27 Levine	Y	Y	Y	N	Y	Y	Y	N
28 Dixon	Y	Y	Y	N	Y	Y	Y	N
29 Hawkins	Y	Y	Y	N	Y	Y	Y	N
30 Martinez	Y	Y	Y	N	Y	Y	Y	N
31 Dymally	Y	Y	Y	N	Y	Y	Y	N
32 Anderson	N	Y	Y	N	Y	Y	N	N
33 ***Dreier***	N	Y	N	Y	Y	Y	N	Y
34 Torres	Y	Y	Y	N	Y	?	?	?
35 ***Lewis***	?	?	?	?	?	?	?	?
36 Brown	Y	Y	Y	?	?	Y	Y	N
37 ***McCandless***	N	Y	N	Y	Y	Y	N	Y
38 ***Dornan***	N	Y	N	Y	Y	Y	N	Y
39 ***Dannemeyer***	N	Y	N	?	?	Y	N	Y
40 ***Badham***	N	Y	N	N	Y	Y	Y	Y
41 ***Lowery***	N	Y	N	Y	Y	Y	N	Y
42 ***Lungren***	N	Y	N	Y	Y	Y	N	Y
43 ***Packard***	N	Y	N	Y	Y	Y	N	Y
44 Bates	N	Y	Y	N	Y	Y	Y	N
45 ***Hunter***	Y	Y	N	Y	Y	Y	N	Y
COLORADO								
1 Schroeder	N	Y	N	N	Y	Y	Y	N
2 Wirth	Y	Y	Y	N	Y	Y	N	N
3 ***Strang***	Y	Y	N	Y	Y	Y	N	Y
4 ***Brown***	Y	Y	N	Y	Y	Y	N	Y
5 ***Kramer***	Y	Y	N	Y	Y	Y	N	Y
6 ***Schaefer***	N	Y	N	Y	Y	Y	N	Y
CONNECTICUT								
1 Kennelly	Y	Y	Y	N	Y	Y	Y	N
2 Gejdenson	Y	Y	Y	N	Y	Y	Y	N
3 Morrison	Y	Y	Y	N	Y	Y	Y	N
4 ***McKinney***	Y	Y	N	N	Y	Y	N	N
5 ***Rowland***	Y	Y	N	Y	Y	Y	N	Y
6 ***Johnson***	Y	Y	N	Y	Y	Y	N	Y
DELAWARE								
AL Carper	Y	Y	Y	N	Y	Y	N	N
FLORIDA								
1 Hutto	Y	Y	Y	?	?	?	?	?
2 Fuqua	Y	Y	Y	N	Y	?	?	?
3 Bennett	Y	Y	Y	Y	Y	Y	Y	Y
4 Chappell	Y	Y	Y	N	Y	Y	Y	Y
5 ***McCollum***	N	Y	N	Y	Y	Y	N	Y
6 MacKay	?	Y	Y	N	Y	Y	Y	N
7 Gibbons	N	Y	Y	N	Y	Y	Y	N
8 ***Young***	Y	Y	N	Y	Y	Y	?	Y
9 ***Bilirakis***	N	Y	N	Y	Y	Y	N	Y
10 ***Ireland***	N	Y	?	?	?	Y	?	Y
11 Nelson	Y	Y	Y	N	Y	Y	Y	N
12 ***Lewis***	Y	Y	N	Y	Y	Y	N	Y
13 ***Mack***	N	Y	N	Y	N	Y	N	Y
14 Mica	Y	Y	Y	N	Y	Y	Y	N
15 ***Shaw***	Y	Y	N	Y	Y	Y	N	Y
16 Smith	Y	?	Y	N	Y	Y	Y	N
17 Lehman	Y	Y	Y	N	Y	Y	Y	N
18 Pepper	Y	Y	Y	X	+	Y	?	N
19 Fascell	Y	Y	Y	N	Y	Y	Y	N
GEORGIA								
1 Thomas	Y	Y	Y	N	Y	Y	Y	Y
2 Hatcher	Y	Y	Y	N	Y	Y	Y	N
3 Ray	Y	Y	N	N	Y	Y	Y	Y
4 ***Swindall***	Y	Y	N	Y	Y	?	N	Y
5 Fowler	?	?	?	?	?	?	?	?
6 ***Gingrich***	N	Y	N	Y	Y	Y	N	Y
7 Darden	Y	Y	Y	N	Y	Y	Y	Y
8 Rowland	Y	Y	Y	N	Y	Y	Y	Y
9 Jenkins	Y	Y	Y	N	Y	Y	Y	Y
10 Barnard	?	Y	Y	N	Y	Y	Y	Y
HAWAII								
1 Heftel	Y	Y	Y	N	N	?	Y	N
2 Akaka	Y	Y	Y	N	Y	Y	Y	N
IDAHO								
1 ***Craig***	Y	Y	N	Y	Y	Y	N	Y
2 Stallings	Y	Y	Y	N	Y	Y	N	Y
ILLINOIS								
1 Hayes	Y	Y	Y	N	Y	Y	Y	N
2 Savage	Y	Y	?	N	Y	?	Y	N
3 Russo	Y	Y	Y	N	Y	Y	Y	N
4 ***O'Brien***	X	?	?	?	?	?	?	#
5 Lipinski	Y	Y	Y	N	Y	Y	Y	N
6 ***Hyde***	Y	Y	N	Y	Y	Y	N	Y
7 Collins	+	+	+	X	+	?	?	?
8 Rostenkowski	?	?	?	?	?	?	?	?
9 Yates	N	Y	Y	N	Y	Y	Y	N
10 ***Porter***	Y	Y	N	Y	Y	Y	N	Y
11 Annunzio	Y	Y	Y	N	Y	Y	Y	N
12 ***Crane***	?	?	?	?	?	Y	Y	Y
13 ***Fawell***	N	Y	N	Y	Y	Y	N	Y
14 ***Grotberg***	?	?	?	?	?	?	?	?
15 ***Madigan***	Y	Y	N	N	Y	Y	N	Y
16 ***Martin***	Y	Y	N	Y	N	Y	N	Y
17 Evans	Y	Y	Y	N	Y	Y	Y	N
18 ***Michel***	?	Y	N	Y	Y	Y	N	Y
19 Bruce	Y	Y	Y	N	Y	Y	Y	N
20 Durbin	Y	Y	Y	N	Y	Y	Y	N
21 Price	Y	Y	Y	N	Y	Y	Y	N
22 Gray	?	?	Y	N	Y	Y	?	N
INDIANA								
1 Visclosky	Y	Y	Y	N	Y	Y	Y	N
2 Sharp	Y	Y	Y	N	Y	Y	N	N
3 ***Hiler***	Y	Y	N	Y	Y	Y	N	Y
4 ***Coats***	Y	Y	N	N	Y	Y	N	Y
5 ***Hillis***	Y	Y	N	Y	Y	Y	Y	Y

ND - Northern Democrats SD - Southern Democrats

* Corresponding to Congressional Record Votes 14, 15, 16, 17, 18, 19, 20, 21

	11	12	13	14	15	16	17	18
6 ***Burton***	Y	Y	N	Y	Y	Y	N	Y
7 ***Myers***	Y	Y	N	Y	Y	Y	Y	Y
8 McCloskey	Y	Y	Y	N	Y	Y	Y	N
9 Hamilton	Y	Y	Y	N	Y	Y	Y	Y
10 Jacobs	Y	Y	N	Y	N	Y	N	N
IOWA								
1 ***Leach***	Y	Y	N	Y	Y	Y	N	Y
2 ***Tauke***	Y	Y	N	Y	Y	?	N	Y
3 ***Evans***	Y	Y	N	Y	N	Y	N	Y
4 Smith	?	?	Y	N	Y	Y	Y	N
5 ***Lightfoot***	Y	Y	N	Y	Y	Y	N	Y
6 Bedell	Y	Y	Y	N	Y	?	Y	N
KANSAS								
1 ***Roberts***	Y	Y	N	Y	Y	Y	N	Y
2 Slattery	Y	Y	Y	N	Y	Y	N	N
3 ***Meyers***	N	Y	N	N	Y	Y	N	N
4 Glickman	?	?	Y	N	Y	Y	N	N
5 ***Whittaker***	Y	Y	N	Y	Y	Y	N	Y
KENTUCKY								
1 Hubbard	Y	Y	Y	N	Y	Y	N	Y
2 Natcher	Y	Y	Y	N	Y	Y	Y	N
3 Mazzoli	Y	Y	Y	N	Y	Y	Y	N
4 ***Snyder***	?	?	N	N	Y	Y	Y	Y
5 ***Rogers***	Y	Y	N	N	Y	Y	N	Y
6 ***Hopkins***	Y	Y	N	Y	Y	Y	N	Y
7 Perkins	Y	Y	Y	N	Y	Y	Y	N
LOUISIANA								
1 ***Livingston***	?	?	?	?	?	?	?	?
2 Boggs	Y	Y	Y	N	Y	Y	Y	N
3 Tauzin	Y	Y	N	Y	Y	Y	N	N
4 Roemer	Y	Y	N	Y	Y	Y	N	Y
5 Huckaby	Y	Y	Y	N	Y	Y	N	N
6 ***Moore***	?	?	?	?	?	?	?	?
7 Breaux	Y	Y	Y	N	Y	Y	Y	N
8 Long	?	?	Y	N	Y	Y	Y	N
MAINE								
1 ***McKernan***	Y	Y	N	Y	Y	Y	Y	Y
2 ***Snowe***	Y	Y	N	Y	Y	Y	N	Y
MARYLAND								
1 Dyson	Y	Y	Y	N	Y	Y	Y	Y
2 ***Bentley***	Y	Y	N	Y	Y	Y	N	Y
3 Mikulski	Y	Y	Y	N	Y	Y	Y	N
4 ***Holt***	N	Y	N	N	Y	Y	Y	Y
5 Hoyer	Y	Y	Y	N	Y	?	Y	N
6 Byron	Y	Y	?	?	?	Y	Y	N
7 Mitchell	Y	Y	Y	N	Y	Y	Y	N
8 Barnes	Y	Y	Y	N	Y	Y	Y	N
MASSACHUSETTS								
1 ***Conte***	N	Y	N	Y	Y	Y	N	N
2 Boland	?	Y	Y	N	Y	Y	Y	N
3 Early	Y	Y	?	?	?	?	?	?
4 Frank	N	Y	Y	N	Y	Y	Y	N
5 Atkins	Y	Y	Y	N	Y	Y	Y	N
6 Mavroules	?	?	Y	N	Y	Y	Y	N
7 Markey	?	Y	Y	N	Y	Y	Y	N
8 O'Neill								
9 Moakley	Y	Y	Y	N	Y	Y	Y	N
10 Studds	Y	Y	Y	N	Y	Y	Y	N
11 Donnelly	Y	Y	Y	N	Y	Y	Y	N
MICHIGAN								
1 Conyers	Y	Y	Y	N	Y	Y	Y	N
2 ***Pursell***	Y	Y	N	N	Y	Y	N	Y
3 Wolpe	Y	Y	Y	N	Y	Y	Y	?
4 ***Siljander***	Y	Y	N	Y	Y	?	?	?
5 ***Henry***	N	N	Y	N	Y	Y	N	N
6 Carr	Y	Y	Y	N	Y	Y	?	N
7 Kildee	Y	Y	Y	N	Y	Y	Y	N
8 Traxler	Y	Y	Y	N	Y	Y	Y	N
9 ***Vander Jagt***	Y	Y	N	Y	Y	Y	N	Y
10 ***Schuette***	Y	Y	N	Y	Y	Y	N	Y
11 ***Davis***	Y	Y	N	N	Y	Y	N	Y
12 Bonior	Y	Y	Y	N	Y	Y	Y	N
13 Crockett	Y	Y	Y	N	Y	Y	Y	?
14 Hertel	Y	Y	Y	N	Y	Y	Y	N
15 Ford	Y	Y	Y	N	Y	Y	Y	N
16 Dingell	Y	Y	Y	N	Y	Y	Y	?
17 Levin	Y	Y	Y	N	Y	Y	Y	N
18 ***Broomfield***	N	Y	N	N	Y	Y	N	Y
MINNESOTA								
1 Penny	Y	N	N	N	Y	Y	Y	Y
2 ***Weber***	Y	Y	N	Y	Y	Y	N	Y
3 ***Frenzel***	Y	Y	N	N	Y	Y	N	Y
4 Vento	Y	Y	Y	N	Y	Y	Y	N
5 Sabo	Y	N	Y	N	Y	Y	?	N
6 Sikorski	Y	Y	N	N	Y	Y	Y	N

	11	12	13	14	15	16	17	18
7 ***Stangeland***	?	Y	N	Y	Y	Y	N	Y
8 Oberstar	Y	Y	Y	N	Y	Y	Y	N
MISSISSIPPI								
1 Whitten	Y	Y	Y	N	?	Y	Y	N
2 ***Franklin***	?	Y	?	#	?	?	?	#
3 Montgomery	?	?	Y	N	Y	Y	Y	Y
4 Dowdy	?	?	Y	N	Y	Y	Y	N
5 ***Lott***	Y	Y	N	Y	Y	Y	N	Y
MISSOURI								
1 Clay	?	?	N	N	Y	Y	Y	N
2 Young	Y	Y	Y	N	Y	Y	Y	N
3 Gephardt	Y	Y	Y	N	Y	Y	Y	?
4 Skelton	Y	Y	Y	N	Y	Y	N	Y
5 Wheat	Y	Y	Y	N	Y	Y	Y	N
6 ***Coleman***	Y	Y	N	Y	Y	Y	N	Y
7 ***Taylor***	Y	Y	N	Y	Y	Y	N	Y
8 ***Emerson***	Y	Y	N	Y	Y	Y	N	Y
9 Volkmer	Y	Y	Y	N	Y	Y	Y	Y
MONTANA								
1 Williams	Y	Y	?	N	Y	?	N	N
2 ***Marlenee***	Y	Y	N	N	Y	Y	N	Y
NEBRASKA								
1 ***Bereuter***	Y	Y	N	Y	+	Y	N	N
2 ***Daub***	Y	Y	N	Y	Y	Y	N	Y
3 ***Smith***	Y	Y	?	?	?	Y	N	?
NEVADA								
1 Reid	Y	Y	Y	N	Y	Y	Y	N
2 ***Vucanovich***	Y	Y	N	Y	Y	Y	N	Y
NEW HAMPSHIRE								
1 ***Smith***	N	Y	N	Y	Y	Y	N	Y
2 ***Gregg***	?	Y	N	Y	Y	Y	N	Y
NEW JERSEY								
1 Florio	Y	Y	Y	N	Y	Y	Y	N
2 Hughes	N	Y	Y	N	Y	Y	N	N
3 Howard	Y	Y	Y	N	Y	Y	Y	N
4 ***Smith***	Y	Y	N	Y	Y	Y	N	N
5 ***Roukema***	Y	Y	N	N	Y	?	?	?
6 Dwyer	?	?	?	?	?	?	?	?
7 ***Rinaldo***	Y	Y	N	N	Y	Y	N	N
8 Roe	?	?	Y	N	Y	Y	Y	N
9 Torricelli	Y	Y	Y	N	Y	?	?	X
10 Rodino	Y	Y	Y	N	Y	Y	Y	N
11 ***Gallo***	Y	Y	N	Y	Y	Y	N	Y
12 ***Courter***	Y	Y	N	Y	Y	Y	N	Y
13 ***Saxton***	Y	Y	N	Y	Y	Y	N	Y
14 Guarini	Y	Y	Y	N	Y	Y	Y	N
NEW MEXICO								
1 ***Lujan***	Y	Y	N	Y	Y	Y	Y	Y
2 ***Skeen***	Y	Y	N	Y	Y	Y	N	Y
3 Richardson	Y	Y	Y	N	Y	Y	Y	N
NEW YORK								
1 ***Carney***	N	Y	N	Y	Y	Y	N	Y
2 Downey	N	Y	Y	N	Y	Y	Y	N
3 Mrazek	N	Y	Y	N	Y	Y	Y	N
4 ***Lent***	Y	Y	N	Y	Y	Y	N	Y
5 ***McGrath***	Y	Y	N	Y	Y	Y	N	Y
6 Addabbo	Y	Y	Y	N	Y	Y	Y	N
7 Ackerman	Y	Y	Y	N	Y	Y	Y	N
8 Scheuer	N	Y	Y	N	Y	Y	Y	N
9 Manton	Y	Y	Y	N	Y	Y	Y	N
10 Schumer	N	Y	?	?	?	Y	Y	N
11 Towns	Y	Y	Y	N	Y	Y	Y	N
12 Owens	Y	Y	Y	N	Y	Y	Y	N
13 Solarz	Y	Y	Y	N	Y	Y	Y	N
14 ***Molinari***	N	Y	N	Y	Y	Y	N	Y
15 ***Green***	N	Y	N	Y	Y	Y	N	N
16 Rangel	Y	Y	Y	N	Y	Y	Y	N
17 Weiss	Y	Y	Y	N	Y	Y	Y	N
18 Garcia	?	?	Y	N	Y	Y	Y	N
19 Biaggi	?	Y	Y	N	?	Y	Y	N
20 ***DioGuardi***	N	Y	N	Y	Y	Y	N	Y
21 ***Fish***	Y	Y	N	Y	Y	Y	N	N
22 ***Gilman***	Y	Y	N	Y	Y	Y	N	N
23 Stratton	?	?	?	?	?	?	?	?
24 ***Solomon***	N	Y	N	Y	Y	Y	N	Y
25 ***Boehlert***	Y	Y	N	Y	Y	Y	N	Y
26 ***Martin***	Y	Y	N	Y	Y	Y	Y	Y
27 ***Wortley***	Y	Y	N	Y	Y	Y	N	Y
28 McHugh	Y	Y	Y	N	Y	Y	?	N
29 ***Horton***	Y	Y	N	Y	Y	?	?	?
30 ***Eckert***	Y	Y	N	Y	Y	Y	N	Y
31 ***Kemp***	?	?	?	#	?	?	?	#
32 LaFalce	N	Y	Y	N	Y	Y	Y	N
33 Nowak	Y	?	Y	N	Y	Y	N	N
34 Lundine	Y	Y	Y	N	Y	Y	Y	N

	11	12	13	14	15	16	17	18
NORTH CAROLINA								
1 Jones	Y	Y	Y	N	Y	Y	Y	N
2 Valentine	Y	Y	Y	N	Y	Y	Y	Y
3 Whitley	Y	Y	Y	N	Y	Y	Y	Y
4 ***Cobey***	N	Y	N	Y	Y	Y	N	Y
5 Neal	Y	Y	Y	N	Y	Y	N	N
6 ***Coble***	N	Y	N	Y	Y	?	N	Y
7 Rose	Y	Y	Y	N	Y	Y	Y	Y
8 Hefner	Y	Y	Y	N	Y	Y	Y	N
9 ***McMillan***	?	?	N	Y	Y	Y	N	Y
10 ***Broyhill***	N	Y	?	Y	?	Y	N	Y
11 ***Hendon***	Y	Y	N	Y	Y	Y	N	Y
NORTH DAKOTA								
AL Dorgan	Y	Y	Y	N	Y	Y	Y	N
OHIO								
1 Luken	Y	Y	Y	N	Y	Y	Y	N
2 ***Gradison***	Y	Y	Y	N	Y	Y	N	Y
3 Hall	?	?	?	?	?	Y	Y	N
4 ***Oxley***	#	Y	N	Y	Y	Y	N	Y
5 ***Latta***	?	?	?	?	?	?	?	?
6 ***McEwen***	Y	Y	Y	Y	Y	Y	N	Y
7 ***DeWine***	Y	?	N	Y	Y	Y	N	Y
8 ***Kindness***	Y	Y	N	Y	Y	Y	?	?
9 Kaptur	Y	Y	Y	N	Y	Y	Y	N
10 ***Miller***	Y	Y	N	Y	N	Y	N	Y
11 Eckart	Y	Y	Y	N	Y	Y	Y	N
12 ***Kasich***	Y	Y	Y	Y	Y	Y	N	Y
13 Pease	Y	Y	Y	N	Y	Y	Y	N
14 Seiberling	Y	Y	?	N	Y	Y	Y	N
15 ***Wylie***	Y	Y	N	N	Y	Y	N	Y
16 ***Regula***	Y	Y	N	N	Y	Y	N	Y
17 Traficant	Y	Y	Y	N	Y	Y	Y	N
18 Applegate	Y	Y	Y	Y	Y	Y	Y	Y
19 Feighan	Y	Y	Y	N	Y	Y	Y	N
20 Oakar	Y	Y	Y	N	Y	Y	Y	N
21 Stokes	?	?	Y	N	Y	Y	Y	N
OKLAHOMA								
1 Jones	Y	Y	Y	N	Y	Y	N	N
2 Synar	Y	Y	Y	N	Y	Y	N	N
3 Watkins	Y	Y	Y	N	Y	Y	N	Y
4 McCurdy	Y	?	Y	N	Y	Y	N	N
5 ***Edwards***	Y	Y	N	Y	Y	Y	N	Y
6 English	Y	Y	Y	N	Y	Y	N	N
OREGON								
1 AuCoin	Y	Y	Y	Y	Y	Y	N	N
2 ***Smith, R.***	Y	Y	N	Y	Y	Y	N	Y
3 Wyden	Y	Y	Y	N	Y	Y	Y	N
4 Weaver	Y	Y	Y	N	Y	Y	Y	?
5 ***Smith, D.***	Y	Y	N	Y	Y	Y	N	Y
PENNSYLVANIA								
1 Foglietta	Y	Y	Y	N	Y	Y	Y	N
2 Gray	Y	Y	Y	N	Y	Y	Y	?
3 Borski	Y	Y	Y	N	Y	Y	Y	N
4 Kolter	Y	Y	Y	N	Y	Y	Y	N
5 ***Schulze***	?	?	?	?	?	Y	N	Y
6 Yatron	Y	Y	Y	N	Y	Y	N	N
7 Edgar	Y	Y	Y	N	Y	Y	Y	?
8 Kostmayer	?	Y	Y	N	Y	Y	N	N
9 ***Shuster***	Y	Y	N	Y	Y	Y	N	Y
10 ***McDade***	N	Y	N	Y	Y	Y	N	Y
11 Kanjorski	Y	Y	Y	N	Y	Y	Y	N
12 Murtha	?	?	?	?	?	?	?	?
13 ***Coughlin***	Y	Y	N	Y	Y	Y	N	Y
14 Coyne	Y	Y	Y	N	Y	Y	Y	N
15 ***Ritter***	N	Y	N	Y	Y	Y	N	Y
16 ***Walker***	N	Y	N	Y	N	Y	N	Y
17 ***Gekas***	N	Y	N	Y	Y	Y	N	Y
18 Walgren	Y	Y	Y	N	Y	?	?	?
19 ***Goodling***	Y	Y	N	Y	Y	Y	N	Y
20 Gaydos	Y	Y	Y	N	Y	Y	Y	N
21 ***Ridge***	Y	Y	N	N	Y	Y	N	Y
22 Murphy	Y	Y	Y	N	Y	Y	Y	N
23 ***Clinger***	Y	Y	N	N	Y	Y	N	Y
RHODE ISLAND								
1 St Germain	Y	Y	?	?	?	?	?	?
2 ***Schneider***	N	Y	N	Y	Y	Y	N	N
SOUTH CAROLINA								
1 ***Hartnett***	#	?	N	Y	Y	Y	Y	Y
2 ***Spence***	Y	Y	N	Y	Y	Y	N	Y
3 Derrick	Y	Y	Y	N	Y	Y	Y	N
4 ***Campbell***	Y	Y	?	Y	Y	Y	Y	Y
5 Spratt	Y	Y	Y	N	Y	Y	Y	N
6 Tallon	?	Y	Y	N	Y	Y	N	Y
SOUTH DAKOTA								
AL Daschle	Y	Y	Y	N	Y	Y	Y	N

	11	12	13	14	15	16	17	18
TENNESSEE								
1 ***Quillen***	Y	Y	N	N	Y	Y	Y	Y
2 ***Duncan***	Y	Y	N	N	Y	Y	N	Y
3 Lloyd	Y	Y	N	N	Y	Y	N	Y
4 Cooper	Y	Y	Y	N	Y	Y	Y	N
5 Boner	Y	Y	Y	N	Y	Y	Y	Y
6 Gordon	Y	Y	Y	N	Y	Y	Y	N
7 ***Sundquist***	Y	Y	N	Y	Y	Y	N	Y
8 Jones	Y	Y	Y	N	Y	Y	Y	N
9 Ford	Y	Y	Y	N	Y	Y	Y	N
TEXAS								
1 Chapman	Y	Y	Y	N	Y	Y	Y	N
2 Wilson	Y	Y	Y	N	Y	Y	Y	Y
3 ***Bartlett***	N	Y	N	Y	Y	Y	N	Y
4 Hall, R.	Y	Y	Y	Y	Y	Y	Y	N
5 Bryant	Y	Y	Y	N	Y	?	?	?
6 ***Barton***	Y	Y	N	Y	Y	Y	N	Y
7 ***Archer***	N	N	N	Y	Y	Y	N	Y
8 ***Fields***	N	Y	N	Y	Y	Y	N	Y
9 Brooks	Y	Y	Y	N	Y	Y	Y	N
10 Pickle	Y	Y	Y	N	Y	Y	Y	Y
11 Leath	Y	Y	?	?	?	Y	Y	Y
12 Wright	Y	Y	Y	N	Y	Y	Y	N
13 ***Boulter***	Y	Y	N	Y	Y	Y	N	Y
14 ***Sweeney***	?	?	N	Y	Y	Y	N	Y
15 de la Garza	Y	Y	Y	N	Y	Y	Y	N
16 Coleman	Y	Y	Y	N	Y	Y	N	N
17 Stenholm	Y	Y	N	Y	Y	Y	Y	Y
18 Leland	+	+	?	N	Y	?	?	X
19 ***Combest***	Y	Y	N	Y	Y	Y	N	Y
20 Gonzalez	Y	Y	Y	N	Y	Y	Y	N
21 ***Loeffler***	?	?	?	?	?	?	?	?
22 ***DeLay***	N	Y	Y	Y	Y	Y	N	Y
23 Bustamante	Y	Y	Y	?	?	Y	Y	N
24 Frost	Y	Y	Y	N	Y	Y	Y	N
25 Andrews	Y	Y	Y	N	Y	Y	Y	N
26 ***Armey***	N	Y	N	Y	N	Y	N	Y
27 Ortiz	Y	Y	Y	N	Y	Y	Y	N
UTAH								
1 ***Hansen***	N	Y	N	Y	Y	Y	N	Y
2 ***Monson***	N	Y	N	Y	Y	Y	N	Y
3 ***Nielson***	N	Y	N	Y	Y	Y	N	Y
VERMONT								
AL ***Jeffords***	Y	Y	Y	Y	Y	Y	N	Y
VIRGINIA								
1 ***Bateman***	Y	Y	N	Y	Y	Y	N	Y
2 ***Whitehurst***	Y	Y	N	N	Y	Y	Y	Y
3 ***Bliley***	N	Y	N	Y	Y	Y	N	Y
4 Sisisky	Y	Y	Y	N	Y	Y	Y	N
5 Daniel	Y	Y	Y	N	Y	Y	N	Y
6 Olin	Y	Y	Y	N	Y	Y	Y	N
7 ***Slaughter***	Y	Y	N	Y	Y	Y	N	Y
8 ***Parris***	?	?	N	Y	Y	?	?	Y
9 Boucher	Y	Y	Y	N	Y	Y	Y	N
10 ***Wolf***	Y	Y	N	Y	Y	Y	N	Y
WASHINGTON								
1 ***Miller***	N	Y	N	Y	N	Y	N	Y
2 Swift	Y	Y	Y	N	Y	Y	?	N
3 Bonker	Y	Y	Y	N	Y	Y	Y	X
4 ***Morrison***	Y	Y	N	N	Y	Y	N	Y
5 Foley	Y	Y	Y	N	Y	?	?	N
6 Dicks	Y	Y	Y	N	Y	Y	Y	N
7 Lowry	Y	Y	Y	N	Y	Y	Y	N
8 ***Chandler***	Y	Y	N	Y	Y	Y	N	Y
WEST VIRGINIA								
1 Mollohan	Y	Y	Y	N	Y	Y	Y	Y
2 Staggers	Y	Y	Y	N	Y	Y	Y	N
3 Wise	?	?	Y	N	Y	Y	Y	?
4 Rahall	Y	Y	Y	N	Y	Y	Y	N
WISCONSIN								
1 Aspin	Y	Y	Y	N	Y	Y	Y	N
2 Kastenmeier	Y	Y	Y	N	Y	Y	Y	N
3 ***Gunderson***	Y	Y	N	Y	Y	Y	N	Y
4 Kleczka	Y	Y	Y	N	Y	Y	Y	N
5 Moody	Y	Y	Y	N	Y	Y	Y	N
6 ***Petri***	N	Y	N	Y	N	Y	?	Y
7 Obey	Y	Y	Y	N	Y	Y	Y	N
8 ***Roth***	Y	Y	N	Y	Y	Y	N	Y
9 ***Sensenbrenner***	N	Y	N	Y	Y	Y	N	Y
WYOMING								
AL ***Cheney***	N	Y	N	Y	N	Y	N	Y

Southern states - Ala., Ark., Fla., Ga., Ky., La., Miss., N.C., Okla., S.C., Tenn., Texas, Va.

* The *Congressional Record* vote number is different from the CQ vote number because the *Record* includes quorum calls in its tally. CQ does not publish quorum call votes.

19. HR 3456. Consumer Product Safety. Waxman, D-Calif., amendment to reduce the period of authorization for the Consumer Product Safety Commission (CPSC) from three years to one, to authorize $36 million in fiscal 1987, and to direct the General Accounting Office to conduct a study of the structure and function of the CPSC. Adopted 385-2: R 162-0; D 223-2 (ND 153-0, SD 70-2), Feb. 6, 1986.

20. HR 3456. Consumer Product Safety. Dannemeyer, R-Calif., amendment to strike provisions extending the jurisdiction of the Consumer Product Safety Commission to fixed-site amusement parks and instead establish an 18-month study to determine if such jurisdiction is needed. Rejected 179-198: R 139-18; D 40-180 (ND 17-132, SD 23-48), Feb. 6, 1986.

21. HR 3456. Consumer Product Safety. Passage of the bill to authorize $36 million in fiscal year 1987 for the Consumer Product Safety Commission. Passed 298-81: R 81-74; D 217-7 (ND 150-1, SD 67-6), Feb. 6, 1986.

KEY

Y Voted for (yea).
Paired for.
+ Announced for.
N Voted against (nay).
X Paired against.
- Announced against.
P Voted "present."
C Voted "present" to avoid possible conflict of interest.
? Did not vote or otherwise make a position known.

Democrats ***Republicans***

	19	20	21
ALABAMA			
1 ***Callahan***	Y	Y	Y
2 ***Dickinson***	Y	Y	Y
3 Nichols	Y	Y	Y
4 Bevill	?	?	?
5 Flippo	Y	N	Y
6 Erdreich	Y	N	Y
7 Shelby	Y	Y	Y
ALASKA			
AL ***Young***	Y	Y	Y
ARIZONA			
1 ***McCain***	Y	Y	N
2 Udall	Y	Y	Y
3 ***Stump***	Y	Y	N
4 ***Rudd***	Y	Y	Y
5 ***Kolbe***	?	?	?
ARKANSAS			
1 Alexander	Y	N	Y
2 Robinson	Y	Y	N
3 ***Hammerschmidt***	Y	Y	N
4 Anthony	Y	N	Y
CALIFORNIA			
1 Bosco	?	?	?
2 ***Chappie***	?	?	?
3 Matsui	Y	N	Y
4 Fazio	Y	N	Y
5 Burton	?	?	?
6 Boxer	Y	N	Y
7 Miller	Y	N	Y
8 Dellums	Y	N	Y
9 Stark	?	?	?
10 Edwards	Y	N	Y
11 Lantos	Y	N	Y
12 ***Zschau***	Y	Y	Y
13 Mineta	Y	N	Y
14 ***Shumway***	Y	Y	N
15 Coelho	Y	?	Y
16 Panetta	Y	N	Y
17 ***Pashayan***	Y	Y	Y
18 Lehman	Y	N	Y
19 ***Lagomarsino***	Y	Y	Y
20 ***Thomas***	Y	Y	Y
21 ***Fiedler***	?	?	?
22 ***Moorhead***	Y	Y	N
23 Beilenson	Y	N	Y
24 Waxman	Y	N	Y
25 Roybal	Y	N	Y
26 Berman	Y	N	Y
27 Levine	Y	N	Y
28 Dixon	Y	N	Y
29 Hawkins	Y	N	Y
30 Martinez	Y	N	Y
31 Dymally	Y	N	Y
32 Anderson	Y	Y	Y
33 ***Dreier***	Y	Y	N
34 Torres	?	?	?
35 ***Lewis***	?	?	?
36 Brown	Y	N	Y
37 ***McCandless***	Y	Y	N
38 ***Dornan***	Y	Y	N
39 ***Dannemeyer***	Y	Y	N
40 ***Badham***	Y	Y	N
41 ***Lowery***	Y	Y	N
42 ***Lungren***	Y	Y	N
43 ***Packard***	Y	Y	N
44 Bates	Y	N	Y
45 ***Hunter***	Y	Y	N
COLORADO			
1 Schroeder	Y	N	Y
2 Wirth	Y	N	Y
3 ***Strang***	Y	Y	N
4 ***Brown***	Y	Y	N
5 ***Kramer***	Y	Y	N
6 ***Schaefer***	Y	Y	N
CONNECTICUT			
1 Kennelly	Y	N	Y
2 Gejdenson	Y	N	Y
3 Morrison	Y	N	Y
4 ***McKinney***	Y	Y	Y
5 ***Rowland***	Y	Y	Y
6 ***Johnson***	Y	Y	Y
DELAWARE			
AL Carper	Y	N	Y
FLORIDA			
1 Hutto	?	?	?
2 Fuqua	?	?	?
3 Bennett	Y	N	Y
4 Chappell	Y	N	Y
5 ***McCollum***	Y	Y	N
6 MacKay	Y	N	Y
7 Gibbons	Y	N	Y
8 ***Young***	Y	Y	Y
9 ***Bilirakis***	?	?	?
10 ***Ireland***	Y	Y	N
11 Nelson	Y	Y	Y
12 ***Lewis***	Y	Y	N
13 ***Mack***	Y	Y	N
14 Mica	Y	Y	Y
15 ***Shaw***	Y	Y	?
16 Smith	Y	N	Y
17 Lehman	Y	N	Y
18 Pepper	Y	?	Y
19 Fascell	Y	N	Y
GEORGIA			
1 Thomas	Y	N	Y
2 Hatcher	Y	N	Y
3 Ray	Y	N	Y
4 ***Swindall***	Y	Y	N
5 Fowler	?	?	?
6 ***Gingrich***	Y	Y	N
7 Darden	Y	Y	Y
8 Rowland	Y	N	Y
9 Jenkins	Y	N	Y
10 Barnard	?	?	#
HAWAII			
1 Heftel	Y	N	Y
2 Akaka	Y	?	#
IDAHO			
1 ***Craig***	Y	Y	N
2 Stallings	Y	Y	Y
ILLINOIS			
1 Hayes	Y	N	Y
2 Savage	Y	?	?
3 Russo	Y	N	Y
4 ***O'Brien***	?	?	X
5 Lipinski	Y	N	Y
6 ***Hyde***	Y	Y	?
7 Collins	?	X	?
8 Rostenkowski	?	?	?
9 Yates	Y	N	Y
10 ***Porter***	Y	Y	Y
11 Annunzio	Y	N	Y
12 ***Crane***	Y	Y	N
13 ***Fawell***	Y	Y	Y
14 ***Grotberg***	?	?	?
15 ***Madigan***	Y	?	?
16 ***Martin***	Y	Y	Y
17 Evans	Y	N	Y
18 ***Michel***	Y	?	?
19 Bruce	Y	N	Y
20 Durbin	Y	N	Y
21 Price	Y	N	Y
22 Gray	Y	N	Y
INDIANA			
1 Visclosky	Y	N	Y
2 Sharp	Y	N	Y
3 ***Hiler***	Y	Y	Y
4 ***Coats***	Y	Y	Y
5 ***Hillis***	Y	Y	Y

ND - Northern Democrats SD - Southern Democrats

	19	20	21
6 ***Burton***	Y	Y	N
7 ***Myers***	Y	Y	Y
8 McCloskey	Y	N	Y
9 Hamilton	Y	N	Y
10 Jacobs	Y	N	Y
IOWA			
1 ***Leach***	Y	N	Y
2 ***Tauke***	Y	N	Y
3 ***Evans***	Y	Y	N
4 Smith	Y	Y	Y
5 ***Lightfoot***	Y	Y	N
6 Bedell	Y	N	Y
KANSAS			
1 ***Roberts***	Y	Y	N
2 Slattery	Y	Y	Y
3 ***Meyers***	Y	Y	Y
4 Glickman	Y	N	Y
5 ***Whittaker***	Y	Y	N
KENTUCKY			
1 Hubbard	Y	Y	Y
2 Natcher	Y	Y	Y
3 Mazzoli	Y	N	Y
4 ***Snyder***	Y	Y	Y
5 ***Rogers***	Y	Y	Y
6 ***Hopkins***	Y	Y	Y
7 Perkins	N	N	Y
LOUISIANA			
1 ***Livingston***	?	?	?
2 Boggs	Y	N	Y
3 Tauzin	Y	N	Y
4 Roemer	Y	N	Y
5 Huckaby	Y	N	Y
6 ***Moore***	?	?	?
7 Breaux	?	N	Y
8 Long	?	N	Y
MAINE			
1 ***McKernan***	Y	Y	Y
2 ***Snowe***	Y	Y	Y
MARYLAND			
1 Dyson	Y	Y	Y
2 ***Bentley***	Y	Y	N
3 Mikulski	Y	N	Y
4 ***Holt***	Y	Y	N
5 Hoyer	Y	N	Y
6 Byron	Y	Y	Y
7 Mitchell	Y	N	Y
8 Barnes	Y	N	Y
MASSACHUSETTS			
1 ***Conte***	Y	N	Y
2 Boland	Y	?	Y
3 Early	?	?	?
4 Frank	Y	N	Y
5 Atkins	Y	N	Y
6 Mavroules	Y	Y	Y
7 Markey	Y	N	Y
8 O'Neill			
9 Moakley	Y	N	Y
10 Studds	Y	N	Y
11 Donnelly	Y	N	Y
MICHIGAN			
1 Conyers	Y	N	Y
2 ***Pursell***	?	?	?
3 Wolpe	Y	N	Y
4 ***Siljander***	?	?	?
5 ***Henry***	Y	N	Y
6 Carr	Y	N	Y
7 Kildee	Y	N	Y
8 Traxler	Y	N	Y
9 ***Vander Jagt***	Y	Y	Y
10 ***Schuette***	Y	Y	N
11 ***Davis***	Y	N	Y
12 Bonior	Y	?	?
13 Crockett	Y	N	Y
14 Hertel	Y	N	Y
15 Ford	Y	N	Y
16 Dingell	?	N	Y
17 Levin	Y	N	Y
18 ***Broomfield***	Y	Y	Y
MINNESOTA			
1 Penny	Y	Y	N
2 ***Weber***	Y	Y	N
3 ***Frenzel***	Y	Y	N
4 Vento	Y	N	Y
5 Sabo	Y	N	Y
6 Sikorski	Y	N	Y

	19	20	21
7 ***Stangeland***	Y	Y	N
8 Oberstar	Y	N	Y
MISSISSIPPI			
1 Whitten	Y	Y	Y
2 ***Franklin***	?	#	X
3 Montgomery	Y	Y	N
4 Dowdy	Y	N	Y
5 ***Lott***	Y	Y	N
MISSOURI			
1 Clay	Y	N	Y
2 Young	Y	Y	Y
3 Gephardt	?	?	?
4 Skelton	Y	N	Y
5 Wheat	Y	N	Y
6 ***Coleman***	Y	Y	Y
7 ***Taylor***	Y	Y	N
8 ***Emerson***	Y	Y	N
9 Volkmer	Y	N	Y
MONTANA			
1 Williams	Y	N	Y
2 ***Marlenee***	Y	Y	N
NEBRASKA			
1 ***Bereuter***	Y	N	Y
2 ***Daub***	Y	Y	N
3 ***Smith***	?	?	?
NEVADA			
1 Reid	Y	N	Y
2 ***Vucanovich***	Y	Y	N
NEW HAMPSHIRE			
1 ***Smith***	Y	Y	N
2 ***Gregg***	Y	Y	N
NEW JERSEY			
1 Florio	Y	N	Y
2 Hughes	Y	N	Y
3 Howard	Y	N	Y
4 ***Smith***	Y	N	Y
5 ***Roukema***	?	?	?
6 Dwyer	?	?	?
7 ***Rinaldo***	Y	N	Y
8 Roe	Y	N	Y
9 Torricelli	?	?	?
10 Rodino	Y	N	Y
11 ***Gallo***	Y	Y	Y
12 ***Courter***	Y	Y	Y
13 ***Saxton***	Y	Y	Y
14 Guarini	Y	N	Y
NEW MEXICO			
1 ***Lujan***	Y	Y	Y
2 ***Skeen***	Y	Y	Y
3 Richardson	Y	N	Y
NEW YORK			
1 ***Carney***	Y	Y	N
2 Downey	Y	N	Y
3 Mrazek	Y	N	Y
4 ***Lent***	Y	Y	Y
5 ***McGrath***	Y	Y	Y
6 Addabbo	Y	N	Y
7 Ackerman	Y	N	Y
8 Scheuer	Y	N	Y
9 Manton	Y	N	Y
10 Schumer	Y	N	Y
11 Towns	Y	N	Y
12 Owens	Y	N	Y
13 Solarz	Y	N	Y
14 ***Molinari***	Y	Y	Y
15 ***Green***	Y	N	Y
16 Rangel	Y	N	Y
17 Weiss	Y	N	Y
18 Garcia	Y	N	Y
19 Biaggi	Y	N	Y
20 ***DioGuardi***	Y	Y	Y
21 ***Fish***	Y	Y	Y
22 ***Gilman***	Y	N	Y
23 Stratton	?	?	?
24 ***Solomon***	Y	Y	N
25 ***Boehlert***	Y	N	Y
26 ***Martin***	Y	Y	Y
27 ***Wortley***	Y	Y	Y
28 McHugh	Y	N	Y
29 ***Horton***	?	?	?
30 ***Eckert***	Y	Y	N
31 ***Kemp***	?	?	?
32 LaFalce	Y	N	Y
33 Nowak	Y	Y	Y
34 Lundine	Y	N	Y

	19	20	21
NORTH CAROLINA			
1 Jones	Y	N	Y
2 Valentine	Y	N	Y
3 Whitley	Y	N	Y
4 ***Cobey***	Y	Y	N
5 Neal	Y	N	Y
6 ***Coble***	Y	Y	N
7 Rose	Y	N	Y
8 Hefner	Y	?	?
9 ***McMillan***	Y	Y	N
10 ***Broyhill***	Y	Y	Y
11 ***Hendon***	?	Y	Y
NORTH DAKOTA			
AL Dorgan	Y	N	Y
OHIO			
1 Luken	Y	N	Y
2 ***Gradison***	Y	Y	Y
3 Hall	Y	N	Y
4 ***Oxley***	Y	Y	Y
5 ***Latta***	?	?	?
6 ***McEwen***	Y	Y	Y
7 ***DeWine***	Y	Y	Y
8 ***Kindness***	Y	?	?
9 Kaptur	Y	N	Y
10 ***Miller***	Y	Y	Y
11 Eckart	Y	N	Y
12 ***Kasich***	Y	Y	Y
13 Pease	Y	N	Y
14 Seiberling	Y	N	Y
15 ***Wylie***	Y	N	Y
16 ***Regula***	Y	N	Y
17 Traficant	Y	N	Y
18 Applegate	Y	Y	Y
19 Feighan	Y	N	Y
20 Oakar	Y	N	Y
21 Stokes	Y	N	Y
OKLAHOMA			
1 Jones	Y	Y	Y
2 Synar	Y	N	Y
3 Watkins	Y	N	Y
4 McCurdy	Y	N	Y
5 ***Edwards***	Y	Y	N
6 English	Y	N	Y
OREGON			
1 AuCoin	Y	N	Y
2 ***Smith, R.***	Y	Y	N
3 Wyden	Y	N	Y
4 Weaver	?	?	?
5 ***Smith, D.***	Y	Y	N
PENNSYLVANIA			
1 Foglietta	Y	N	Y
2 Gray	Y	N	Y
3 Borski	Y	N	Y
4 Kolter	Y	Y	Y
5 ***Schulze***	Y	N	Y
6 Yatron	Y	Y	Y
7 Edgar	?	?	?
8 Kostmayer	Y	N	Y
9 ***Shuster***	Y	Y	N
10 ***McDade***	Y	N	Y
11 Kanjorski	Y	N	Y
12 Murtha	?	?	?
13 ***Coughlin***	Y	Y	Y
14 Coyne	Y	N	Y
15 ***Ritter***	Y	Y	N
16 ***Walker***	Y	Y	N
17 ***Gekas***	Y	Y	N
18 Walgren	?	?	?
19 ***Goodling***	Y	Y	Y
20 Gaydos	Y	Y	Y
21 ***Ridge***	Y	N	Y
22 Murphy	Y	N	Y
23 ***Clinger***	+	N	Y
RHODE ISLAND			
1 St Germain	?	?	?
2 ***Schneider***	Y	N	Y
SOUTH CAROLINA			
1 ***Hartnett***	Y	?	?
2 ***Spence***	Y	Y	Y
3 Derrick	Y	Y	Y
4 ***Campbell***	Y	?	?
5 Spratt	Y	Y	Y
6 Tallon	Y	Y	Y
SOUTH DAKOTA			
AL Daschle	Y	N	Y

	19	20	21
TENNESSEE			
1 ***Quillen***	Y	Y	Y
2 ***Duncan***	Y	Y	Y
3 Lloyd	Y	Y	N
4 Cooper	Y	N	Y
5 Boner	Y	Y	Y
6 Gordon	Y	Y	Y
7 ***Sundquist***	Y	Y	N
8 Jones	Y	Y	Y
9 Ford	Y	N	Y
TEXAS			
1 Chapman	Y	N	Y
2 Wilson	Y	Y	Y
3 ***Bartlett***	Y	Y	N
4 Hall, R.	Y	N	Y
5 Bryant	?	?	?
6 ***Barton***	Y	Y	N
7 ***Archer***	Y	Y	N
8 ***Fields***	Y	Y	Y
9 Brooks	Y	N	Y
10 Pickle	Y	Y	Y
11 Leath	Y	N	N
12 Wright	Y	N	Y
13 ***Boulter***	Y	Y	N
14 ***Sweeney***	Y	Y	N
15 de la Garza	Y	N	Y
16 Coleman	Y	N	Y
17 Stenholm	Y	?	?
18 Leland	?	?	?
19 ***Combest***	Y	Y	N
20 Gonzalez	N	P	Y
21 ***Loeffler***	?	?	?
22 ***DeLay***	Y	Y	N
23 Bustamante	Y	N	Y
24 Frost	Y	N	Y
25 Andrews	Y	N	Y
26 ***Armey***	Y	Y	N
27 Ortiz	Y	N	Y
UTAH			
1 ***Hansen***	Y	Y	N
2 ***Monson***	Y	Y	N
3 ***Nielson***	Y	Y	N
VERMONT			
AL ***Jeffords***	Y	Y	Y
VIRGINIA			
1 ***Bateman***	Y	Y	N
2 ***Whitehurst***	Y	Y	N
3 ***Bliley***	Y	Y	Y
4 Sisisky	Y	Y	Y
5 Daniel	Y	Y	N
6 Olin	Y	Y	N
7 ***Slaughter***	Y	Y	N
8 ***Parris***	Y	Y	N
9 Boucher	?	N	Y
10 ***Wolf***	Y	Y	Y
WASHINGTON			
1 ***Miller***	Y	Y	Y
2 Swift	Y	N	Y
3 Bonker	Y	N	Y
4 ***Morrison***	Y	Y	Y
5 Foley	Y	N	Y
6 Dicks	Y	N	Y
7 Lowry	Y	N	Y
8 ***Chandler***	Y	Y	Y
WEST VIRGINIA			
1 Mollohan	Y	Y	Y
2 Staggers	Y	Y	Y
3 Wise	Y	N	Y
4 Rahall	Y	N	Y
WISCONSIN			
1 Aspin	Y	N	Y
2 Kastenmeier	Y	N	Y
3 ***Gunderson***	Y	Y	Y
4 Kleczka	Y	N	Y
5 Moody	Y	N	Y
6 ***Petri***	Y	Y	Y
7 Obey	Y	N	Y
8 ***Roth***	Y	Y	Y
9 ***Sensenbrenner***	Y	?	?
WYOMING			
AL ***Cheney***	Y	?	?

Southern states - Ala., Ark., Fla., Ga., Ky., La., Miss., N.C., Okla., S.C., Tenn., Texas, Va.

* The *Congressional Record* vote number is different from the CQ vote number because the *Record* includes quorum calls in its tally. CQ does not publish quorum call votes.

22. HR 2418. Health Services Amendments. Waxman, D-Calif., motion to suspend the rules and pass the bill to reauthorize through fiscal 1988 federal aid for community and migrant health centers. Motion rejected 254-151: R 34-136; D 220-15 (ND 154-1, SD 66-14), Feb. 19, 1986. A two-thirds majority of those present and voting (270 in this case) is required for passage under suspension of the rules. A "nay" was a vote supporting the president's position.

23. HR 4130. Veterans' Home Loan Guarantees. Montgomery, D-Miss., motion to suspend the rules and pass the bill to raise the fiscal 1986 limit on veterans' home loan guarantees to $18.2 billion, from $11.5 billion, for purposes of implementing fiscal 1986 sequestration orders made by the president under the Gramm-Rudman-Hollings deficit-reduction law (PL 99-177). Motion agreed to 386-0: R 160-0; D 226-0 (ND 150-0, SD 76-0), Feb. 25, 1986. A two-thirds majority of those present and voting (258 in this case) is required for passage under suspension of the rules.

24. Procedural Motion. Russo, D-Ill., motion to approve the House *Journal* of Tuesday, Feb. 25. Motion agreed to 291-110: R 70-100; D 221-10 (ND 149-8, SD 72-2), Feb. 26, 1986.

25. H J Res 534. Commodity Credit Corporation Supplemental Appropriation, Fiscal 1986. Passage of the joint resolution to provide $5 billion in supplemental fiscal 1986 appropriations for the Commodity Credit Corporation. Passed 321-86: R 112-61; D 209-25 (ND 133-22, SD 76-3), Feb. 26, 1986.

26. H J Res 3. Nuclear Test Ban Negotiations. Adoption of the rule (H Res 281) to provide for House floor consideration of the joint resolution to call for a resumption of negotiations with the Soviet Union on a comprehensive ban on nuclear weapons tests. Adopted 263-152: R 31-145; D 232-7 (ND 159-1, SD 73-6), Feb. 26, 1986.

27. H J Res 3. Nuclear Test Ban Negotiations. Hyde, R-Ill., substitute to provide that negotiations on a comprehensive nuclear test ban be started only after deep reductions have been made in existing nuclear forces. Rejected 158-258: R 137-37; D 21-221 (ND 5-160, SD 16-61), Feb. 26, 1986. A "yea" was a vote supporting the president's position.

28. H J Res 3. Nuclear Test Ban Negotiations. Broomfield, R-Mich., motion to recommit the joint resolution to the Armed Services Committee with instructions to consider the impact of the joint resolution's enactment on the development of new strategic weapons systems such as the "Midgetman." Motion rejected 158-258: R 137-37; D 21-221 (ND 6-160, SD 15-61), Feb. 26, 1986. A "yea" was a vote supporting the president's position.

29. H J Res 3. Nuclear Test Ban Negotiations. Passage of the joint resolution to call for a resumption of negotiations with the Soviet Union on a comprehensive ban on nuclear weapons tests. Passed 268-148: R 49-126; D 219-22 (ND 160-6, SD 59-16), Feb. 26, 1986.

KEY

Y Voted for (yea).
Paired for.
+ Announced for.
N Voted against (nay).
X Paired against.
- Announced against.
P Voted "present."
C Voted "present" to avoid possible conflict of interest.
? Did not vote or otherwise make a position known.

Democrats *Republicans*

	22	23	24	25	26	27	28	29
ALABAMA								
1 *Callahan*	N	Y	Y	Y	N	Y	Y	N
2 *Dickinson*	N	Y	N	Y	N	Y	Y	N
3 Nichols	Y	Y	?	?	N	Y	Y	N
4 Bevill	Y	Y	Y	Y	Y	N	N	N
5 Flippo	Y	Y	Y	Y	Y	N	N	N
6 Erdreich	Y	Y	Y	Y	Y	N	N	Y
7 Shelby	Y	Y	Y	Y	Y	Y	Y	N
ALASKA								
AL *Young*	Y	Y	N	Y	N	Y	Y	N
ARIZONA								
1 *McCain*	N	Y	Y	Y	N	Y	Y	Y
2 Udall	Y	Y	Y	Y	Y	N	N	Y
3 *Stump*	N	Y	Y	Y	N	Y	Y	N
4 *Rudd*	N	Y	Y	Y	N	Y	Y	N
5 *Kolbe*	N	Y	N	Y	N	Y	Y	Y
ARKANSAS								
1 Alexander	Y	Y	Y	Y	Y	N	N	Y
2 Robinson	N	Y	Y	Y	Y	N	?	?
3 *Hammerschmidt*	N	Y	Y	Y	N	Y	Y	N
4 Anthony	Y	Y	Y	Y	Y	N	N	Y
CALIFORNIA								
1 Bosco	?	Y	Y	N	Y	N	N	Y
2 *Chappie*	?	Y	N	Y	N	Y	Y	N
3 Matsui	Y	Y	Y	Y	Y	N	N	Y
4 Fazio	Y	Y	Y	Y	Y	N	N	Y
5 Burton	?	Y	Y	Y	Y	N	N	Y
6 Boxer	Y	Y	Y	Y	Y	N	N	Y
7 Miller	Y	?	Y	?	Y	N	N	Y
8 Dellums	Y	?	Y	Y	Y	N	N	Y
9 Stark	Y	Y	Y	?	Y	N	N	Y
10 Edwards	Y	Y	Y	Y	Y	N	N	Y
11 Lantos	?	Y	Y	Y	Y	N	N	Y
12 *Zschau*	?	Y	N	?	N	Y	Y	N
13 Mineta	Y	?	Y	Y	Y	N	N	Y
14 *Shumway*	N	Y	Y	N	N	Y	Y	N
15 Coelho	Y	Y	Y	Y	Y	N	N	Y
16 Panetta	?	Y	Y	Y	Y	N	N	Y
17 *Pashayan*	Y	Y	Y	Y	N	Y	Y	N
18 Lehman	Y	Y	Y	Y	Y	N	N	Y
19 *Lagomarsino*	N	Y	N	Y	N	Y	Y	N
20 *Thomas*	N	Y	N	Y	N	Y	Y	N
21 *Fiedler*	N	Y	Y	Y	N	Y	Y	N
22 *Moorhead*	N	Y	N	N	N	Y	Y	N
23 Beilenson	Y	Y	Y	Y	Y	N	N	Y
24 Waxman	Y	Y	Y	Y	Y	N	N	Y
25 Roybal	Y	Y	Y	N	Y	N	N	Y
26 Berman	Y	Y	Y	Y	Y	N	N	Y
27 Levine	Y	Y	Y	Y	Y	N	N	Y
28 Dixon	Y	?	Y	Y	Y	N	N	Y
29 Hawkins	Y	Y	Y	Y	?	N	N	Y
30 Martinez	Y	Y	Y	Y	Y	N	N	Y
31 Dymally	Y	Y	Y	Y	Y	N	N	Y
32 Anderson	Y	Y	Y	N	Y	N	N	Y
33 *Dreier*	N	Y	N	N	N	Y	Y	N
34 Torres	Y	Y	Y	Y	Y	N	N	Y
35 *Lewis*	N	Y	N	Y	N	Y	Y	N
36 Brown	Y	Y	?	?	?	X	X	#
37 *McCandless*	N	Y	N	N	N	Y	Y	N
38 *Dornan*	N	Y	N	N	N	Y	Y	N
39 *Dannemeyer*	N	Y	N	N	N	Y	Y	N
40 *Badham*	N	Y	N	N	N	Y	Y	N
41 *Lowery*	N	Y	N	N	N	Y	Y	N
42 *Lungren*	N	Y	N	N	N	Y	Y	N
43 *Packard*	N	Y	Y	N	N	Y	Y	N
44 Bates	Y	Y	Y	N	Y	N	N	Y
45 *Hunter*	N	Y	N	Y	N	Y	Y	N
COLORADO								
1 Schroeder	Y	Y	N	Y	Y	N	N	Y
2 Wirth	Y	Y	Y	Y	Y	N	N	Y
3 *Strang*	N	Y	N	Y	N	Y	Y	N
4 *Brown*	N	Y	N	N	N	N	N	Y
5 *Kramer*	N	Y	N	Y	N	Y	Y	N
6 *Schaefer*	N	Y	Y	N	N	Y	Y	Y
CONNECTICUT								
1 Kennelly	Y	Y	Y	Y	Y	N	N	Y
2 Gejdenson	Y	Y	Y	Y	Y	N	N	Y
3 Morrison	Y	?	?	N	Y	N	N	Y
4 *McKinney*	Y	?	Y	Y	Y	N	N	Y
5 *Rowland*	Y	Y	N	Y	Y	Y	Y	Y
6 *Johnson*	Y	Y	?	Y	Y	N	N	Y
DELAWARE								
AL Carper	Y	Y	Y	N	Y	N	N	Y
FLORIDA								
1 Hutto	N	Y	Y	Y	N	Y	Y	N
2 Fuqua	Y	Y	?	Y	Y	N	N	Y
3 Bennett	Y	Y	Y	Y	Y	N	N	Y
4 Chappell	Y	Y	Y	Y	Y	?	?	?
5 *McCollum*	N	Y	N	N	N	Y	Y	N
6 MacKay	Y	Y	Y	Y	Y	N	N	Y
7 Gibbons	Y	Y	Y	N	Y	N	N	Y
8 *Young*	N	Y	N	N	N	Y	Y	N
9 *Bilirakis*	?	+	N	N	N	Y	Y	N
10 *Ireland*	N	Y	N	N	N	Y	Y	N
11 Nelson	Y	Y	Y	N	Y	N	N	Y
12 *Lewis*	N	Y	N	N	N	Y	Y	N
13 *Mack*	N	Y	N	N	N	Y	Y	N
14 Mica	Y	Y	Y	Y	Y	N	N	Y
15 *Shaw*	N	Y	N	N	N	Y	Y	N
16 Smith	Y	Y	P	Y	Y	N	N	Y
17 Lehman	Y	Y	Y	Y	Y	N	N	Y
18 Pepper	Y	Y	Y	Y	Y	N	N	Y
19 Fascell	Y	Y	Y	Y	Y	N	N	Y
GEORGIA								
1 Thomas	Y	Y	Y	Y	Y	N	N	Y
2 Hatcher	Y	Y	Y	Y	Y	N	N	Y
3 Ray	N	?	Y	Y	Y	Y	Y	N
4 *Swindall*	N	Y	N	Y	N	Y	Y	N
5 Fowler	Y	?	?	?	?	?	?	?
6 *Gingrich*	N	?	N	Y	N	Y	Y	N
7 Darden	Y	Y	Y	Y	Y	Y	Y	N
8 Rowland	Y	Y	Y	Y	Y	N	N	Y
9 Jenkins	Y	Y	Y	Y	Y	N	N	Y
10 Barnard	N	Y	Y	Y	Y	Y	Y	N
HAWAII								
1 Heftel	?	Y	?	Y	Y	N	N	Y
2 Akaka	Y	?	Y	Y	Y	N	N	Y
IDAHO								
1 *Craig*	N	Y	Y	Y	N	Y	Y	N
2 Stallings	Y	Y	Y	Y	Y	N	N	Y
ILLINOIS								
1 Hayes	Y	Y	Y	Y	Y	N	N	Y
2 Savage	Y	?	Y	Y	Y	N	N	Y
3 Russo	Y	Y	Y	Y	Y	N	N	Y
4 *O'Brien*	?	?	?	Y	Y	N	N	Y
5 Lipinski	Y	Y	Y	Y	Y	Y	Y	N
6 *Hyde*	N	Y	Y	N	N	Y	Y	N
7 Collins	?	?	?	?	?	X	X	#
8 Rostenkowski	Y	Y	Y	Y	Y	N	N	Y
9 Yates	Y	Y	?	?	?	N	N	Y
10 *Porter*	N	?	Y	N	N	N	N	Y
11 Annunzio	?	Y	?	?	Y	N	N	Y
12 *Crane*	N	Y	N	N	N	Y	Y	N
13 *Fawell*	N	Y	N	N	N	N	N	Y
14 *Grotberg*	?	?	?	?	?	?	?	?
15 *Madigan*	Y	?	N	Y	N	Y	Y	N
16 *Martin*	N	Y	N	Y	N	Y	Y	N
17 Evans	Y	Y	Y	Y	Y	N	N	Y
18 *Michel*	N	Y	N	Y	N	Y	Y	N
19 Bruce	Y	Y	Y	Y	Y	N	N	Y
20 Durbin	Y	Y	Y	Y	Y	N	N	Y
21 Price	Y	Y	?	?	?	N	N	Y
22 Gray	Y	Y	Y	Y	Y	N	N	Y
INDIANA								
1 Visclosky	Y	Y	Y	Y	Y	N	N	Y
2 Sharp	Y	Y	Y	Y	Y	N	N	Y
3 *Hiler*	N	Y	Y	Y	N	Y	Y	N
4 *Coats*	N	Y	Y	Y	N	Y	Y	N
5 *Hillis*	N	Y	Y	Y	N	Y	Y	N

ND - Northern Democrats SD - Southern Democrats

* Corresponding to Congressional Record Votes 26, 27, 28, 29, 30, 31, 32, 33

	22	23	24	25	26	27	28	29
6 ***Burton***	N	Y	N	Y	N	Y	Y	N
7 ***Myers***	N	Y	Y	Y	N	Y	Y	N
8 McCloskey	Y	Y	Y	Y	Y	N	N	Y
9 Hamilton	Y	Y	Y	Y	Y	N	N	Y
10 Jacobs	Y	Y	N	Y	Y	N	N	Y
IOWA								
1 ***Leach***	Y	Y	N	Y	Y	N	N	Y
2 ***Tauke***	Y	Y	Y	Y	Y	N	N	Y
3 ***Evans***	N	?	N	Y	Y	N	N	Y
4 Smith	Y	Y	Y	Y	Y	N	N	Y
5 ***Lightfoot***	N	Y	N	Y	Y	N	N	Y
6 Bedell	Y	Y	Y	Y	Y	N	N	Y
KANSAS								
1 ***Roberts***	N	Y	N	Y	N	N	N	Y
2 Slattery	Y	Y	Y	Y	Y	N	N	Y
3 ***Meyers***	Y	Y	N	Y	N	N	N	Y
4 Glickman	Y	Y	Y	Y	Y	N	N	Y
5 ***Whittaker***	Y	Y	N	Y	N	N	N	Y
KENTUCKY								
1 Hubbard	N	Y	Y	Y	N	Y	Y	N
2 Natcher	Y	Y	Y	Y	Y	N	N	Y
3 Mazzoli	Y	Y	Y	Y	Y	N	N	Y
4 ***Snyder***	N	Y	Y	N	N	Y	Y	N
5 ***Rogers***	N	Y	N	Y	N	Y	Y	N
6 ***Hopkins***	N	Y	Y	Y	N	Y	Y	Y
7 Perkins	Y	Y	Y	Y	Y	N	N	Y
LOUISIANA								
1 ***Livingston***	N	Y	N	Y	N	Y	Y	N
2 Boggs	Y	Y	Y	Y	Y	N	N	Y
3 Tauzin	N	Y	Y	Y	Y	N	N	Y
4 Roemer	N	Y	N	Y	Y	N	N	Y
5 Huckaby	Y	Y	Y	Y	Y	N	N	Y
6 ***Moore***	N	?	?	?	?	?	?	?
7 Breaux	Y	Y	Y	Y	Y	Y	Y	Y
8 Long	Y	Y	Y	Y	Y	N	N	Y
MAINE								
1 ***McKernan***	N	Y	N	Y	N	N	N	Y
2 ***Snowe***	Y	Y	N	Y	Y	N	N	Y
MARYLAND								
1 Dyson	Y	Y	N	Y	Y	Y	Y	N
2 ***Bentley***	?	+	?	+	?	#	#	X
3 Mikulski	Y	Y	Y	Y	Y	N	N	Y
4 ***Holt***	N	Y	Y	N	N	Y	Y	N
5 Hoyer	Y	Y	Y	Y	Y	N	N	Y
6 Byron	N	Y	Y	Y	Y	Y	Y	N
7 Mitchell	Y	Y	N	?	Y	N	N	Y
8 Barnes	Y	?	Y	Y	Y	N	N	Y
MASSACHUSETTS								
1 ***Conte***	Y	Y	N	Y	Y	N	N	Y
2 Boland	Y	Y	Y	Y	Y	N	N	Y
3 Early	?	Y	Y	Y	Y	N	N	Y
4 Frank	Y	Y	Y	N	Y	N	N	Y
5 Atkins	Y	Y	Y	Y	Y	N	N	Y
6 Mavroules	Y	Y	Y	Y	Y	N	N	Y
7 Markey	Y	Y	Y	N	Y	N	N	Y
8 O'Neill								
9 Moakley	?	?	?	?	?	X	X	#
10 Studds	Y	Y	Y	N	Y	N	N	Y
11 Donnelly	Y	Y	Y	Y	Y	N	N	Y
MICHIGAN								
1 Conyers	Y	Y	Y	Y	Y	N	N	Y
2 ***Pursell***	Y	Y	Y	Y	Y	N	N	Y
3 Wolpe	Y	Y	Y	Y	Y	N	N	Y
4 ***Siljander***	?	Y	Y	Y	N	Y	Y	N
5 ***Henry***	N	Y	N	Y	Y	N	N	Y
6 Carr	Y	Y	Y	Y	Y	N	N	Y
7 Kildee	Y	Y	Y	Y	Y	N	N	Y
8 Traxler	Y	?	Y	Y	Y	N	N	Y
9 ***Vander Jagt***	N	Y	N	Y	N	Y	Y	N
10 ***Schuette***	N	Y	N	Y	N	Y	Y	N
11 ***Davis***	Y	Y	Y	Y	Y	Y	N	Y
12 Bonior	Y	Y	Y	Y	Y	N	N	Y
13 Crockett	Y	?	?	?	?	N	N	Y
14 Hertel	Y	Y	Y	N	Y	N	N	Y
15 Ford	Y	Y	Y	Y	Y	N	N	Y
16 Dingell	Y	Y	Y	Y	?	N	N	Y
17 Levin	Y	Y	Y	Y	Y	N	N	Y
18 ***Broomfield***	Y	Y	Y	N	N	Y	Y	N
MINNESOTA								
1 Penny	Y	Y	N	N	Y	N	N	Y
2 ***Weber***	N	Y	N	Y	N	Y	Y	N
3 ***Frenzel***	N	Y	Y	N	N	N	Y	Y
4 Vento	Y	Y	Y	Y	Y	N	N	Y
5 Sabo	Y	Y	?	N	Y	N	N	Y
6 Sikorski	Y	Y	N	N	Y	N	N	Y
7 ***Stangeland***	N	Y	N	Y	N	Y	Y	N
8 Oberstar	Y	Y	Y	Y	Y	N	N	Y
MISSISSIPPI								
1 Whitten	Y	Y	Y	Y	Y	N	N	Y
2 ***Franklin***	N	Y	Y	Y	N	Y	Y	N
3 Montgomery	N	Y	Y	Y	Y	Y	Y	N
4 Dowdy	Y	Y	Y	Y	Y	N	N	Y
5 ***Lott***	N	Y	Y	Y	N	Y	Y	N
MISSOURI								
1 Clay	Y	Y	N	Y	?	N	N	Y
2 Young	Y	?	Y	?	Y	N	N	Y
3 Gephardt	Y	?	Y	Y	Y	N	N	Y
4 Skelton	Y	Y	Y	Y	Y	Y	Y	N
5 Wheat	Y	Y	Y	Y	Y	N	N	Y
6 ***Coleman***	N	Y	?	Y	N	Y	Y	N
7 ***Taylor***	N	Y	Y	Y	Y	Y	Y	N
8 ***Emerson***	N	Y	N	Y	N	Y	Y	N
9 Volkmer	Y	Y	Y	Y	Y	N	N	Y
MONTANA								
1 Williams	Y	Y	Y	Y	Y	N	N	Y
2 ***Marlenee***	N	Y	N	Y	N	Y	Y	N
NEBRASKA								
1 ***Bereuter***	N	Y	N	Y	N	Y	Y	N
2 ***Daub***	N	Y	N	Y	Y	Y	Y	N
3 ***Smith***	N	Y	Y	Y	N	Y	Y	N
NEVADA								
1 Reid	Y	Y	Y	Y	Y	N	Y	N
2 ***Vucanovich***	?	Y	N	N	N	Y	Y	N
NEW HAMPSHIRE								
1 ***Smith***	N	Y	N	N	N	Y	Y	N
2 ***Gregg***	N	Y	N	N	N	Y	Y	Y
NEW JERSEY								
1 Florio	Y	Y	Y	N	Y	N	N	Y
2 Hughes	Y	Y	Y	N	N	N	N	Y
3 Howard	Y	Y	Y	Y	Y	N	N	Y
4 ***Smith***	Y	Y	Y	Y	Y	N	N	Y
5 ***Roukema***	N	Y	N	N	N	Y	Y	N
6 Dwyer	Y	Y	Y	Y	Y	N	N	Y
7 ***Rinaldo***	Y	Y	Y	Y	Y	N	N	Y
8 Roe	Y	Y	Y	Y	Y	N	N	Y
9 Torricelli	Y	Y	Y	Y	Y	N	N	Y
10 Rodino	Y	Y	Y	Y	Y	N	N	Y
11 ***Gallo***	N	Y	N	N	Y	N	N	Y
12 ***Courter***	N	?	N	N	N	Y	Y	N
13 ***Saxton***	N	Y	Y	N	Y	N	N	Y
14 Guarini	?	Y	Y	Y	Y	N	N	Y
NEW MEXICO								
1 ***Lujan***	N	Y	Y	N	N	Y	Y	N
2 ***Skeen***	N	Y	N	Y	N	Y	Y	N
3 Richardson	Y	Y	Y	Y	Y	N	N	Y
NEW YORK								
1 ***Carney***	N	?	N	N	N	Y	Y	N
2 Downey	Y	Y	Y	N	Y	N	N	Y
3 Mrazek	Y	Y	Y	Y	Y	N	N	Y
4 ***Lent***	Y	Y	N	N	N	Y	Y	Y
5 ***McGrath***	Y	Y	N	N	N	N	N	Y
6 Addabbo	Y	Y	Y	Y	Y	N	N	Y
7 Ackerman	Y	Y	Y	Y	Y	N	N	Y
8 Scheuer	Y	Y	?	?	Y	N	N	Y
9 Manton	Y	Y	Y	Y	Y	N	N	Y
10 Schumer	Y	Y	Y	Y	Y	N	N	Y
11 Towns	Y	Y	Y	Y	Y	N	N	Y
12 Owens	Y	Y	Y	Y	Y	N	N	Y
13 Solarz	Y	Y	Y	Y	Y	N	N	Y
14 ***Molinari***	N	Y	N	N	N	Y	Y	N
15 ***Green***	Y	Y	Y	Y	Y	N	N	Y
16 Rangel	Y	Y	Y	Y	Y	N	N	Y
17 Weiss	Y	Y	Y	Y	Y	N	N	Y
18 Garcia	Y	Y	Y	Y	Y	N	N	Y
19 Biaggi	Y	Y	Y	Y	Y	N	N	Y
20 ***DioGuardi***	N	Y	Y	N	Y	N	N	Y
21 ***Fish***	Y	Y	Y	Y	N	N	N	Y
22 ***Gilman***	Y	Y	Y	Y	Y	N	N	Y
23 Stratton	Y	Y	Y	Y	Y	Y	Y	N
24 ***Solomon***	N	Y	?	?	?	#	#	X
25 ***Boehlert***	Y	Y	N	Y	Y	N	N	Y
26 ***Martin***	Y	?	Y	Y	N	Y	Y	N
27 ***Wortley***	N	Y	Y	Y	N	Y	Y	N
28 McHugh	Y	Y	Y	Y	Y	N	N	Y
29 ***Horton***	Y	Y	Y	Y	Y	N	N	Y
30 ***Eckert***	N	Y	Y	Y	N	Y	Y	N
31 ***Kemp***	N	Y	?	Y	N	Y	Y	N
32 LaFalce	Y	Y	Y	Y	Y	N	N	Y
33 Nowak	Y	Y	Y	Y	Y	N	N	Y
34 Lundine	?	Y	Y	?	?	N	N	Y
NORTH CAROLINA								
1 Jones	Y	Y	Y	Y	Y	N	N	Y
2 Valentine	Y	Y	Y	Y	Y	N	N	Y
3 Whitley	Y	Y	Y	Y	Y	N	N	Y
4 ***Cobey***	N	Y	N	Y	N	Y	Y	N
5 Neal	Y	Y	Y	Y	Y	N	N	Y
6 ***Coble***	N	Y	Y	Y	N	Y	Y	N
7 Rose	Y	Y	Y	Y	Y	N	N	Y
8 Hefner	Y	Y	Y	Y	Y	N	N	Y
9 ***McMillan***	N	Y	Y	Y	N	Y	Y	N
10 ***Broyhill***	Y	Y	Y	Y	N	+	+	N
11 ***Hendon***	N	Y	N	Y	N	Y	Y	N
NORTH DAKOTA								
AL Dorgan	Y	Y	Y	Y	Y	N	N	Y
OHIO								
1 Luken	Y	Y	Y	Y	Y	N	N	Y
2 ***Gradison***	N	Y	Y	Y	Y	Y	Y	N
3 Hall	Y	Y	Y	Y	Y	N	N	Y
4 ***Oxley***	N	Y	N	Y	N	Y	Y	N
5 ***Latta***	?	?	?	?	?	?	?	?
6 ***McEwen***	N	Y	Y	Y	N	Y	Y	N
7 ***DeWine***	N	Y	N	Y	N	Y	Y	N
8 ***Kindness***	N	Y	Y	Y	N	Y	Y	N
9 Kaptur	?	+	Y	Y	Y	N	N	Y
10 ***Miller***	N	Y	N	Y	N	Y	Y	N
11 Eckart	Y	Y	Y	Y	Y	N	N	Y
12 ***Kasich***	N	Y	Y	Y	N	Y	Y	N
13 Pease	Y	Y	Y	Y	Y	N	N	Y
14 Seiberling	Y	Y	?	Y	Y	N	N	Y
15 ***Wylie***	N	?	Y	?	N	Y	Y	Y
16 ***Regula***	N	Y	Y	Y	Y	Y	Y	Y
17 Traficant	Y	Y	Y	Y	Y	N	N	Y
18 Applegate	Y	Y	Y	Y	Y	N	N	Y
19 Feighan	Y	Y	Y	Y	Y	N	N	Y
20 Oakar	Y	Y	Y	Y	Y	?	?	+
21 Stokes	Y	?	Y	Y	Y	N	N	Y
OKLAHOMA								
1 Jones	N	?	?	Y	Y	N	N	Y
2 Synar	Y	Y	Y	Y	Y	N	N	Y
3 Watkins	Y	Y	Y	Y	Y	N	N	Y
4 McCurdy	Y	Y	Y	Y	Y	N	N	Y
5 ***Edwards***	N	Y	N	Y	N	Y	Y	N
6 English	Y	?	?	?	?	?	?	?
OREGON								
1 AuCoin	?	Y	Y	Y	Y	N	N	Y
2 ***Smith, R.***	N	Y	N	Y	N	?	?	?
3 Wyden	Y	Y	Y	N	Y	N	N	Y
4 Weaver	Y	Y	?	N	Y	N	N	Y
5 ***Smith, D.***	N	Y	N	N	N	Y	Y	N
PENNSYLVANIA								
1 Foglietta	Y	Y	Y	Y	Y	N	N	Y
2 Gray	Y	Y	Y	N	Y	N	N	Y
3 Borski	Y	?	Y	Y	Y	N	N	Y
4 Kolter	Y	Y	Y	Y	Y	N	N	Y
5 ***Schulze***	N	Y	Y	N	N	Y	Y	N
6 Yatron	Y	Y	Y	Y	Y	N	N	Y
7 Edgar	Y	?	Y	Y	Y	N	N	Y
8 Kostmayer	Y	Y	Y	Y	Y	N	N	Y
9 ***Shuster***	N	?	N	N	N	Y	Y	N
10 ***McDade***	Y	Y	Y	Y	Y	N	N	Y
11 Kanjorski	Y	Y	Y	Y	Y	N	N	Y
12 Murtha	Y	Y	Y	Y	Y	N	N	Y
13 ***Coughlin***	N	Y	N	N	Y	N	N	Y
14 Coyne	Y	Y	Y	Y	Y	N	N	Y
15 ***Ritter***	N	Y	Y	N	N	Y	Y	N
16 ***Walker***	N	Y	N	N	N	Y	Y	N
17 ***Gekas***	N	Y	N	Y	N	Y	Y	N
18 Walgren	Y	Y	Y	Y	Y	N	N	Y
19 ***Goodling***	N	Y	N	N	N	Y	Y	Y
20 Gaydos	Y	Y	Y	?	Y	N	N	Y
21 ***Ridge***	Y	Y	N	Y	Y	N	N	Y
22 Murphy	Y	Y	N	Y	Y	N	N	Y
23 ***Clinger***	Y	Y	Y	Y	N	Y	Y	N
RHODE ISLAND								
1 St Germain	Y	Y	Y	Y	Y	N	N	Y
2 ***Schneider***	Y	Y	Y	Y	Y	N	N	Y
SOUTH CAROLINA								
1 ***Hartnett***	N	Y	Y	Y	N	Y	Y	N
2 ***Spence***	N	Y	N	Y	N	Y	Y	N
3 Derrick	Y	Y	Y	Y	Y	?	?	?
4 ***Campbell***	N	?	?	?	N	Y	Y	N
5 Spratt	Y	Y	Y	Y	Y	N	N	Y
6 Tallon	Y	Y	Y	Y	Y	N	N	Y
SOUTH DAKOTA								
AL Daschle	Y	Y	Y	Y	Y	N	N	Y
TENNESSEE								
1 ***Quillen***	Y	Y	Y	Y	N	Y	Y	N
2 ***Duncan***	N	Y	Y	Y	N	Y	Y	N
3 Lloyd	N	Y	N	Y	N	Y	Y	N
4 Cooper	Y	Y	Y	Y	Y	N	N	Y
5 Boner	Y	Y	Y	Y	Y	N	N	Y
6 Gordon	Y	Y	Y	Y	Y	N	N	Y
7 ***Sundquist***	N	Y	N	Y	N	Y	Y	N
8 Jones	Y	Y	Y	Y	Y	N	N	Y
9 Ford	Y	Y	?	Y	Y	N	N	?
TEXAS								
1 Chapman	Y	Y	?	Y	Y	N	N	Y
2 Wilson	?	Y	Y	Y	Y	N	N	Y
3 ***Bartlett***	N	Y	N	N	N	Y	Y	N
4 Hall, R.	N	Y	Y	Y	N	Y	Y	N
5 Bryant	Y	Y	Y	Y	Y	N	N	Y
6 ***Barton***	N	Y	N	Y	N	Y	Y	N
7 ***Archer***	N	Y	Y	N	N	Y	Y	N
8 ***Fields***	N	Y	N	N	N	Y	Y	N
9 Brooks	?	?	Y	Y	Y	N	N	Y
10 Pickle	Y	Y	Y	Y	Y	N	N	Y
11 Leath	N	Y	Y	Y	Y	Y	Y	N
12 Wright	Y	Y	Y	Y	Y	N	N	Y
13 ***Boulter***	N	?	N	Y	N	Y	Y	N
14 ***Sweeney***	?	Y	Y	Y	N	Y	Y	N
15 de la Garza	Y	Y	Y	Y	Y	?	?	?
16 Coleman	Y	Y	Y	Y	Y	N	N	Y
17 Stenholm	N	Y	Y	Y	Y	Y	Y	N
18 Leland	Y	?	Y	Y	Y	N	N	Y
19 ***Combest***	N	Y	Y	Y	N	Y	Y	N
20 Gonzalez	Y	Y	Y	Y	Y	N	N	Y
21 ***Loeffler***	?	?	?	?	?	#	#	X
22 ***DeLay***	N	?	N	N	N	Y	Y	N
23 Bustamante	Y	Y	Y	Y	Y	N	N	Y
24 Frost	Y	Y	Y	Y	Y	N	N	Y
25 Andrews	Y	Y	Y	Y	Y	N	N	Y
26 ***Armey***	N	Y	N	N	N	Y	Y	N
27 Ortiz	Y	Y	Y	Y	Y	Y	N	Y
UTAH								
1 ***Hansen***	N	Y	Y	N	N	Y	Y	N
2 ***Monson***	N	Y	N	N	Y	Y	N	Y
3 ***Nielson***	N	Y	Y	Y	N	Y	Y	N
VERMONT								
AL ***Jeffords***	Y	?	Y	Y	N	N	N	Y
VIRGINIA								
1 ***Bateman***	N	Y	Y	Y	N	Y	Y	N
2 ***Whitehurst***	N	?	Y	N	N	Y	Y	N
3 ***Bliley***	N	Y	N	N	N	Y	Y	N
4 Sisisky	Y	Y	Y	Y	?	Y	Y	N
5 Daniel	N	Y	Y	N	N	Y	Y	N
6 Olin	Y	Y	Y	Y	Y	N	N	Y
7 ***Slaughter***	N	Y	N	Y	N	Y	Y	N
8 ***Parris***	N	Y	N	N	Y	Y	Y	N
9 Boucher	Y	Y	Y	Y	Y	N	N	Y
10 ***Wolf***	N	Y	N	N	N	Y	Y	N
WASHINGTON								
1 ***Miller***	N	Y	?	Y	N	Y	Y	N
2 Swift	Y	Y	Y	Y	Y	N	N	Y
3 Bonker	?	Y	Y	Y	Y	?	N	Y
4 ***Morrison***	Y	Y	Y	Y	N	Y	Y	N
5 Foley	Y	?	Y	Y	Y	N	N	Y
6 Dicks	Y	Y	Y	N	Y	N	N	Y
7 Lowry	Y	Y	Y	N	Y	N	N	Y
8 ***Chandler***	Y	Y	N	N	N	N	Y	N
WEST VIRGINIA								
1 Mollohan	Y	Y	Y	Y	Y	N	N	Y
2 Staggers	Y	?	Y	Y	Y	N	N	Y
3 Wise	Y	Y	Y	Y	Y	N	N	Y
4 Rahall	Y	Y	Y	Y	Y	N	N	Y
WISCONSIN								
1 Aspin	Y	Y	Y	?	Y	N	N	Y
2 Kastenmeier	?	Y	Y	Y	Y	N	N	Y
3 ***Gunderson***	N	Y	N	Y	N	N	N	Y
4 Kleczka	Y	Y	Y	Y	Y	N	N	Y
5 Moody	Y	Y	Y	Y	Y	N	N	Y
6 ***Petri***	N	Y	Y	N	N	Y	Y	Y
7 Obey	Y	Y	Y	N	Y	N	N	Y
8 ***Roth***	?	Y	N	Y	N	Y	Y	N
9 ***Sensenbrenner***	N	Y	N	N	N	Y	Y	N
WYOMING								
AL ***Cheney***	N	Y	N	N	N	Y	Y	N

Southern states - Ala., Ark., Fla., Ga., Ky., La., Miss., N.C., Okla., S.C., Tenn., Texas, Va.

* The *Congressional Record* vote number is different from the CQ vote number because the *Record* includes quorum calls in its tally. CQ does not publish quorum call votes.

30. H Res 384. Contempt of Congress. Adoption of the first part of the resolution to initiate contempt of Congress proceedings against Ralph Bernstein of New York for his refusal to testify before the House Foreign Affairs Subcommittee on Asian and Pacific Affairs. Adopted 352-34: R 132-31; D 220-3 (ND 151-2, SD 69-1), Feb. 27, 1986.

31. H Res 384. Contempt of Congress. Adoption of the second part of the resolution to initiate contempt of Congress proceedings against Joseph Bernstein of New York for his refusal to testify before the House Foreign Affairs Subcommittee on Asian and Pacific Affairs. Adopted 343-50: R 119-45; D 224-5 (ND 153-3, SD 71-2), Feb. 27, 1986.

32. HR 2418. Health Services Amendments. Adoption of the rule (H Res 289) to provide for House floor consideration of the bill to reauthorize through fiscal 1988 aid to community and migrant health centers. Adopted 412-0: R 173-0; D 239-0 (ND 160-0, SD 79-0), March 5, 1986.

33. HR 2418. Health Services Amendments. Dannemeyer, R-Calif., substitute for the Waxman, D-Calif., amendment, to freeze fiscal 1987 and 1988 authorizations at fiscal 1986 appropriations levels for community and migrant health centers and to retain authority for the optional primary care block grant, which states can choose to receive in lieu of categorical aid to their health clinics. Rejected 94-319: R 93-77; D 1-242 (ND 0-162, SD 1-80), March 5, 1986. (The Waxman amendment subsequently was adopted *(see vote 34, below)*.) A "yea" was a vote supporting the president's position.

34. HR 2418. Health Services Amendments. Waxman, D-Calif., amendment to freeze fiscal 1987 and 1988 authorizations at fiscal 1986 appropriations levels of $400 million a year for community health centers and $45 million for migrant health centers. Adopted 400-9: R 169-0; D 231-9 (ND 152-7, SD 79-2), March 5, 1986.

35. HR 2418. Health Services Amendments. Passage of the bill to reauthorize through fiscal 1988 aid to community and migrant health centers and to repeal authority for the optional primary care block grant. Passed 403-6: R 163-6; D 240-0 (ND 160-0, SD 80-0), March 5, 1986. A "nay" was a vote supporting the president's position.

36. HR 3128. Omnibus Budget Reconciliation, Fiscal 1986. Adoption of the rule (H Res 390) to provide for House floor consideration of the conference report on the bill, and to recede and concur in the Senate amendment to the House amendment to the Senate amendment thereto, with an amendment. Adopted 314-86: R 92-76; D 222-10 (ND 145-9, SD 77-1), March 6, 1986. (The effect of the vote was to return the conference report to the Senate, after again stripping off a provision imposing a new manufacturers' tax to pay for the "superfund" toxic-waste cleanup program, and amending several other provisions relating to, among other things, Medicare, the sharing of rents and royalties from offshore oil leases, and Trade Adjustment Assistance.) A "nay" was a vote supporting the president's position.

37. HR 4306. Corrections to 1985 Farm Bill. Adoption of the rule (H Res 391) to provide for House floor consideration of the bill to revise the terms of certain agriculture programs authorized in the 1985 farm bill, the Food Security Act (PL 99-198). Adopted 344-57: R 118-48; D 226-9 (ND 153-5, SD 73-4), March 6, 1986. (The House later passed HR 1614, a Senate-amended bill incorporating the terms of HR 4306 and other related agriculture provisions *(see vote 39, p. 14-H)*.)

KEY

- Y Voted for (yea).
- # Paired for.
- + Announced for.
- N Voted against (nay).
- X Paired against.
- \- Announced against.
- P Voted "present."
- C Voted "present" to avoid possible conflict of interest.
- ? Did not vote or otherwise make a position known.

Democrats *Republicans*

	30	31	32	33	34	35	36	37
ALABAMA								
1 *Callahan*	Y	Y	Y	Y	Y	Y	Y	Y
2 *Dickinson*	?	?	Y	Y	Y	Y	Y	Y
3 Nichols	Y	Y	Y	N	Y	Y	Y	Y
4 Bevill	Y	Y	Y	N	Y	Y	Y	Y
5 Flippo	Y	Y	Y	N	Y	Y	Y	Y
6 Erdreich	Y	Y	Y	N	Y	Y	Y	Y
7 Shelby	Y	Y	Y	N	Y	Y	Y	Y
ALASKA								
AL *Young*	Y	Y	Y	N	Y	Y	Y	Y
ARIZONA								
1 *McCain*	Y	Y	Y	Y	Y	Y	N	Y
2 Udall	Y	Y	Y	N	Y	Y	Y	Y
3 *Stump*	N	N	Y	Y	Y	Y	N	N
4 *Rudd*	N	N	?	?	?	?	?	?
5 *Kolbe*	Y	Y	Y	Y	Y	Y	Y	N
ARKANSAS								
1 Alexander	Y	Y	Y	N	Y	Y	Y	Y
2 Robinson	Y	Y	Y	N	Y	Y	Y	Y
3 *Hammerschmidt*	N	N	Y	Y	Y	Y	Y	Y
4 Anthony	Y	Y	Y	N	Y	Y	Y	Y
CALIFORNIA								
1 Bosco	Y	Y	Y	N	Y	Y	Y	Y
2 *Chappie*	?	Y	Y	Y	Y	Y	N	Y
3 Matsui	Y	Y	Y	N	Y	Y	Y	Y
4 Fazio	Y	Y	Y	N	Y	Y	Y	Y
5 Burton	Y	Y	Y	N	Y	Y	Y	Y
6 Boxer	Y	Y	Y	N	Y	Y	Y	Y
7 Miller	Y	Y	Y	N	Y	Y	Y	Y
8 Dellums	?	Y	?	N	Y	Y	Y	Y
9 Stark	Y	Y	Y	N	Y	Y	Y	Y
10 Edwards	Y	Y	Y	N	Y	Y	Y	Y
11 Lantos	Y	Y	Y	N	Y	Y	Y	Y
12 *Zschau*	Y	Y	?	?	?	?	X	?
13 Mineta	Y	Y	Y	N	Y	Y	?	?
14 *Shumway*	N	N	Y	Y	?	N	N	N
15 Coelho	Y	Y	Y	N	Y	Y	Y	Y
16 Panetta	Y	Y	Y	N	Y	Y	Y	Y
17 *Pashayan*	Y	Y	Y	N	Y	Y	N	Y
18 Lehman	?	N	Y	N	Y	Y	Y	Y
19 *Lagomarsino*	Y	Y	Y	Y	Y	Y	N	N
20 *Thomas*	Y	Y	Y	Y	Y	Y	N	Y
21 *Fiedler*	Y	Y	Y	Y	Y	Y	N	Y
22 *Moorhead*	N	N	Y	Y	Y	Y	N	N
23 Beilenson	Y	Y	Y	N	Y	Y	Y	Y
24 Waxman	?	?	Y	N	Y	Y	Y	Y
25 Roybal	Y	Y	Y	N	Y	Y	Y	?
26 Berman	Y	Y	Y	N	Y	Y	Y	Y
27 Levine	Y	Y	Y	N	Y	Y	+	?
28 Dixon	Y	Y	Y	N	Y	Y	Y	Y
29 Hawkins	Y	Y	Y	N	Y	Y	Y	Y
30 Martinez	Y	Y	?	?	?	?	Y	Y
31 Dymally	N	N	Y	N	Y	Y	Y	Y
32 Anderson	Y	Y	Y	N	Y	Y	Y	N
33 *Dreier*	?	?	Y	Y	Y	N	N	N
34 Torres	Y	Y	Y	N	Y	Y	Y	Y
35 *Lewis*	Y	Y	Y	Y	Y	Y	N	N
36 Brown	?	?	Y	N	Y	Y	Y	N
37 *McCandless*	Y	Y	Y	Y	Y	Y	N	N
38 *Dornan*	Y	Y	Y	?	?	Y	N	N
39 *Dannemeyer*	N	N	Y	Y	Y	N	N	N
40 *Badham*	N	N	Y	Y	Y	N	N	Y
41 *Lowery*	Y	Y	Y	Y	Y	Y	N	N
42 *Lungren*	Y	Y	Y	Y	Y	Y	N	N
43 *Packard*	N	N	Y	Y	Y	Y	N	N
44 Bates	Y	Y	Y	N	Y	Y	Y	Y
45 *Hunter*	N	N	Y	Y	Y	Y	N	?
COLORADO								
1 Schroeder	Y	Y	Y	N	Y	Y	Y	Y
2 Wirth	Y	Y	Y	N	Y	Y	Y	Y
3 *Strang*	Y	Y	Y	Y	Y	Y	Y	N
4 *Brown*	Y	Y	Y	Y	Y	Y	N	Y
5 *Kramer*	Y	Y	Y	Y	Y	Y	N	Y
6 *Schaefer*	Y	Y	Y	Y	Y	Y	N	Y
CONNECTICUT								
1 Kennelly	Y	Y	Y	N	Y	Y	Y	Y
2 Gejdenson	Y	Y	Y	N	Y	Y	Y	Y
3 Morrison	Y	Y	Y	N	Y	Y	Y	Y
4 *McKinney*	Y	Y	Y	N	Y	Y	Y	Y
5 *Rowland*	Y	Y	Y	N	Y	Y	Y	Y
6 *Johnson*	Y	Y	Y	N	Y	?	?	Y
DELAWARE								
AL Carper	Y	Y	Y	N	Y	?	Y	Y
FLORIDA								
1 Hutto	Y	Y	Y	N	Y	Y	Y	Y
2 Fuqua	Y	?	Y	N	Y	Y	Y	Y
3 Bennett	Y	Y	Y	N	Y	Y	Y	Y
4 Chappell	Y	Y	Y	N	Y	Y	?	?
5 *McCollum*	Y	N	Y	Y	Y	Y	Y	N
6 MacKay	Y	Y	Y	N	Y	Y	Y	Y
7 Gibbons	?	Y	Y	N	Y	Y	Y	Y
8 *Young*	Y	Y	Y	N	Y	Y	N	N
9 *Bilirakis*	Y	N	Y	Y	Y	Y	N	N
10 *Ireland*	Y	Y	Y	Y	Y	Y	N	N
11 Nelson	Y	Y	Y	N	Y	Y	Y	Y
12 *Lewis*	Y	Y	Y	Y	Y	Y	N	Y
13 *Mack*	Y	Y	Y	Y	Y	Y	N	N
14 Mica	?	?	Y	N	Y	Y	Y	Y
15 *Shaw*	Y	Y	Y	Y	Y	Y	N	N
16 Smith	Y	Y	Y	N	Y	Y	Y	Y
17 Lehman	Y	Y	Y	N	Y	Y	Y	Y
18 Pepper	Y	Y	Y	N	Y	Y	Y	Y
19 Fascell	Y	Y	Y	N	Y	Y	Y	Y
GEORGIA								
1 Thomas	Y	Y	Y	N	Y	Y	Y	Y
2 Hatcher	Y	Y	Y	N	Y	Y	Y	Y
3 Ray	Y	Y	Y	N	Y	Y	Y	?
4 *Swindall*	Y	Y	Y	Y	Y	Y	N	Y
5 Fowler	?	?	Y	N	Y	Y	Y	?
6 *Gingrich*	Y	Y	Y	Y	Y	Y	N	Y
7 Darden	Y	Y	Y	N	Y	Y	Y	Y
8 Rowland	Y	Y	Y	N	Y	Y	Y	Y
9 Jenkins	Y	Y	Y	N	Y	Y	Y	Y
10 Barnard	?	?	Y	N	Y	Y	?	?
HAWAII								
1 Heftel	Y	Y	Y	N	Y	Y	Y	Y
2 Akaka	Y	Y	Y	N	Y	Y	Y	Y
IDAHO								
1 *Craig*	Y	Y	Y	Y	Y	Y	N	Y
2 Stallings	Y	Y	Y	N	Y	Y	Y	Y
ILLINOIS								
1 Hayes	Y	Y	Y	N	Y	Y	Y	Y
2 Savage	Y	Y	Y	N	Y	Y	Y	Y
3 Russo	Y	Y	Y	N	Y	Y	Y	Y
4 *O'Brien*	?	?	?	Y	Y	Y	Y	?
5 Lipinski	Y	Y	Y	N	Y	Y	Y	Y
6 *Hyde*	Y	Y	Y	Y	Y	Y	N	Y
7 Collins	?	?	?	?	?	?	?	?
8 Rostenkowski	Y	Y	?	?	?	?	?	?
9 Yates	?	?	Y	N	Y	Y	N	Y
10 *Porter*	Y	Y	Y	N	Y	Y	N	Y
11 Annunzio	Y	Y	Y	N	Y	Y	Y	Y
12 *Crane*	N	N	Y	Y	Y	N	N	N
13 *Fawell*	Y	Y	Y	Y	Y	Y	N	N
14 *Grotberg*	?	?	?	?	?	?	?	?
15 *Madigan*	Y	Y	Y	Y	Y	?	N	Y
16 *Martin*	Y	Y	Y	Y	Y	Y	N	Y
17 Evans	Y	Y	Y	N	Y	Y	Y	Y
18 *Michel*	Y	Y	Y	?	?	Y	N	Y
19 Bruce	Y	Y	Y	N	Y	Y	Y	Y
20 Durbin	Y	Y	Y	N	Y	Y	Y	Y
21 Price	Y	Y	Y	N	Y	Y	Y	Y
22 Gray	Y	Y	Y	N	Y	Y	?	Y
INDIANA								
1 Visclosky	Y	Y	Y	N	Y	Y	Y	Y
2 Sharp	Y	Y	Y	N	Y	Y	N	Y
3 *Hiler*	Y	Y	Y	Y	Y	Y	N	Y
4 *Coats*	Y	Y	Y	N	Y	Y	N	Y
5 *Hillis*	Y	Y	Y	N	Y	Y	?	?

ND - Northern Democrats SD - Southern Democrats

* Corresponding to Congressional Record Votes 34, 35, 36, 38, 39, 40, 41, 42

	30	31	32	33	34	35	36	37
6 ***Burton***	N	N	Y	Y	Y	Y	N	Y
7 ***Myers***	N	N	Y	N	Y	Y	?	?
8 McCloskey	Y	Y	Y	N	Y	Y	Y	Y
9 Hamilton	Y	Y	Y	N	Y	Y	Y	Y
10 Jacobs	Y	Y	Y	N	Y	Y	Y	Y
IOWA								
1 ***Leach***	Y	Y	Y	N	Y	Y	Y	Y
2 ***Tauke***	Y	Y	Y	N	Y	Y	Y	Y
3 ***Evans***	N	N	?	N	Y	Y	?	Y
4 Smith	N	N	Y	N	?	Y	N	Y
5 ***Lightfoot***	N	Y	Y	N	Y	Y	Y	Y
6 Bedell	Y	Y	Y	N	Y	Y	Y	Y
KANSAS								
1 ***Roberts***	Y	Y	Y	N	Y	Y	Y	Y
2 Slattery	Y	Y	Y	N	Y	Y	Y	Y
3 ***Meyers***	Y	Y	Y	N	Y	Y	Y	N
4 Glickman	Y	Y	Y	N	Y	Y	Y	Y
5 ***Whittaker***	Y	Y	Y	N	Y	Y	Y	Y
KENTUCKY								
1 Hubbard	Y	Y	Y	N	Y	Y	Y	Y
2 Natcher	Y	Y	Y	N	Y	Y	Y	Y
3 Mazzoli	Y	Y	Y	N	Y	Y	Y	N
4 ***Snyder***	N	N	Y	Y	Y	Y	Y	Y
5 ***Rogers***	Y	Y	Y	N	Y	Y	Y	Y
6 ***Hopkins***	Y	Y	Y	Y	Y	Y	Y	Y
7 Perkins	Y	Y	Y	N	N	Y	Y	Y
LOUISIANA								
1 ***Livingston***	N	N	Y	Y	Y	Y	Y	Y
2 Boggs	Y	Y	Y	N	Y	Y	Y	Y
3 Tauzin	Y	Y	Y	N	Y	Y	Y	N
4 Roemer	Y	Y	Y	N	Y	Y	Y	N
5 Huckaby	Y	Y	Y	N	Y	Y	Y	Y
6 ***Moore***	?	?	Y	N	Y	Y	Y	Y
7 Breaux	Y	Y	Y	N	Y	Y	Y	Y
8 Long	Y	Y	Y	N	Y	Y	Y	Y
MAINE								
1 ***McKernan***	Y	Y	Y	N	Y	Y	Y	Y
2 ***Snowe***	Y	Y	Y	N	Y	Y	Y	Y
MARYLAND								
1 Dyson	Y	Y	Y	N	Y	Y	Y	Y
2 ***Bentley***	?	?	Y	N	Y	Y	Y	Y
3 Mikulski	Y	Y	Y	N	Y	Y	Y	Y
4 ***Holt***	N	N	Y	N	Y	Y	Y	Y
5 Hoyer	Y	Y	Y	N	Y	Y	Y	Y
6 Byron	Y	Y	Y	N	Y	Y	Y	Y
7 Mitchell	Y	Y	Y	N	Y	Y	N	Y
8 Barnes	Y	Y	Y	N	?	?	Y	Y
MASSACHUSETTS								
1 ***Conte***	Y	Y	Y	N	Y	Y	Y	Y
2 Boland	Y	?	Y	N	Y	Y	Y	Y
3 Early	?	?	Y	N	Y	Y	Y	N
4 Frank	Y	Y	Y	N	N	Y	Y	Y
5 Atkins	Y	Y	Y	N	Y	Y	Y	Y
6 Mavroules	Y	Y	Y	N	Y	Y	Y	Y
7 Markey	Y	Y	?	N	Y	Y	Y	Y
8 O'Neill								
9 Moakley	?	?	Y	N	Y	Y	Y	?
10 Studds	Y	Y	Y	N	N	Y	Y	Y
11 Donnelly	Y	Y	Y	N	N	Y	Y	Y
MICHIGAN								
1 Conyers	Y	Y	?	?	?	?	?	Y
2 ***Pursell***	Y	Y	Y	N	Y	Y	Y	Y
3 Wolpe	Y	Y	Y	N	Y	Y	Y	Y
4 ***Siljander***	Y	Y	Y	N	Y	Y	N	Y
5 ***Henry***	Y	Y	Y	N	Y	Y	Y	Y
6 Carr	Y	Y	Y	N	Y	Y	?	Y
7 Kildee	Y	Y	Y	N	Y	Y	Y	Y
8 Traxler	Y	Y	Y	N	Y	Y	?	Y
9 ***Vander Jagt***	Y	Y	Y	?	?	?	N	Y
10 ***Schuette***	Y	Y	Y	N	Y	Y	Y	Y
11 ***Davis***	Y	Y	Y	N	Y	Y	Y	Y
12 Bonior	Y	Y	Y	N	Y	Y	Y	Y
13 Crockett	?	?	Y	N	Y	Y	Y	Y
14 Hertel	Y	Y	Y	N	Y	Y	Y	Y
15 Ford	Y	Y	Y	N	Y	Y	Y	Y
16 Dingell	?	?	Y	N	?	Y	Y	Y
17 Levin	Y	Y	Y	N	Y	Y	Y	Y
18 ***Broomfield***	Y	Y	Y	Y	Y	Y	N	Y
MINNESOTA								
1 Penny	Y	Y	Y	N	Y	Y	Y	Y
2 ***Weber***	N	N	Y	Y	Y	Y	Y	Y
3 ***Frenzel***	Y	N	?	Y	Y	Y	N	Y
4 Vento	Y	Y	Y	N	Y	Y	Y	Y
5 Sabo	Y	Y	Y	N	Y	Y	Y	Y
6 Sikorski	Y	Y	Y	N	Y	Y	Y	Y

	30	31	32	33	34	35	36	37
7 ***Stangeland***	Y	Y	Y	Y	Y	Y	N	Y
8 Oberstar	Y	Y	Y	N	N	Y	Y	Y
MISSISSIPPI								
1 Whitten	Y	Y	Y	N	Y	Y	?	Y
2 ***Franklin***	N	N	Y	N	Y	Y	Y	Y
3 Montgomery	Y	Y	Y	N	Y	Y	Y	Y
4 Dowdy	Y	Y	Y	N	Y	Y	Y	Y
5 ***Lott***	N	N	Y	?	?	Y	Y	Y
MISSOURI								
1 Clay	Y	Y	Y	N	N	Y	Y	Y
2 Young	Y	Y	Y	N	Y	Y	Y	Y
3 Gephardt	?	?	Y	N	Y	Y	Y	Y
4 Skelton	?	?	Y	N	Y	Y	Y	Y
5 Wheat	Y	Y	Y	N	Y	Y	Y	Y
6 ***Coleman***	Y	Y	Y	N	Y	?	#	?
7 ***Taylor***	Y	N	Y	Y	Y	?	Y	Y
8 ***Emerson***	Y	Y	Y	N	Y	Y	Y	Y
9 Volkmer	?	?	Y	N	Y	Y	N	Y
MONTANA								
1 Williams	Y	Y	Y	N	N	Y	Y	Y
2 ***Marlenee***	N	N	Y	Y	Y	Y	N	Y
NEBRASKA								
1 ***Bereuter***	Y	Y	Y	Y	Y	Y	Y	Y
2 ***Daub***	Y	N	Y	Y	Y	Y	Y	N
3 ***Smith***	Y	Y	Y	Y	Y	Y	Y	Y
NEVADA								
1 Reid	Y	Y	Y	N	Y	Y	Y	Y
2 ***Vucanovich***	Y	Y	Y	Y	Y	Y	N	N
NEW HAMPSHIRE								
1 ***Smith***	Y	Y	Y	Y	Y	Y	N	N
2 ***Gregg***	Y	Y	Y	Y	Y	Y	N	Y
NEW JERSEY								
1 Florio	Y	Y	Y	N	Y	Y	N	Y
2 Hughes	Y	Y	Y	N	Y	Y	Y	Y
3 Howard	Y	Y	Y	N	Y	Y	Y	Y
4 ***Smith***	Y	Y	Y	N	Y	Y	Y	Y
5 ***Roukema***	Y	Y	Y	N	Y	Y	Y	Y
6 Dwyer	Y	Y	Y	N	Y	Y	Y	Y
7 ***Rinaldo***	Y	Y	Y	N	Y	Y	Y	Y
8 Roe	Y	Y	Y	N	Y	Y	Y	Y
9 Torricelli	Y	Y	Y	N	Y	Y	Y	Y
10 Rodino	Y	Y	Y	N	Y	Y	Y	Y
11 ***Gallo***	Y	Y	Y	N	Y	Y	Y	Y
12 ***Courter***	?	?	Y	N	Y	Y	Y	Y
13 ***Saxton***	Y	Y	Y	N	Y	Y	N	Y
14 Guarini	Y	Y	Y	N	Y	Y	Y	Y
NEW MEXICO								
1 ***Lujan***	Y	N	Y	Y	Y	Y	Y	Y
2 ***Skeen***	Y	N	Y	N	Y	Y	Y	Y
3 Richardson	Y	Y	Y	N	Y	Y	Y	Y
NEW YORK								
1 ***Carney***	Y	Y	Y	N	Y	Y	N	N
2 Downey	Y	Y	Y	N	Y	Y	Y	Y
3 Mrazek	Y	Y	Y	N	Y	Y	Y	Y
4 ***Lent***	Y	Y	Y	N	Y	Y	Y	Y
5 ***McGrath***	?	?	Y	N	Y	Y	N	N
6 Addabbo	?	Y	Y	N	Y	Y	?	?
7 Ackerman	Y	Y	?	?	?	?	?	?
8 Scheuer	Y	Y	Y	N	Y	Y	Y	Y
9 Manton	Y	Y	Y	N	Y	Y	Y	Y
10 Schumer	Y	Y	Y	N	Y	Y	Y	Y
11 Towns	Y	Y	Y	N	Y	Y	Y	Y
12 Owens	Y	Y	Y	N	Y	Y	Y	Y
13 Solarz	Y	Y	?	?	?	?	?	?
14 ***Molinari***	Y	N	Y	N	Y	Y	N	Y
15 ***Green***	Y	N	Y	N	Y	Y	Y	N
16 Rangel	Y	Y	Y	N	Y	Y	?	Y
17 Weiss	Y	Y	Y	N	N	Y	Y	Y
18 Garcia	Y	Y	Y	N	Y	Y	Y	Y
19 Biaggi	Y	Y	Y	N	Y	Y	Y	Y
20 ***DioGuardi***	Y	Y	Y	N	Y	Y	Y	N
21 ***Fish***	Y	Y	Y	N	Y	Y	Y	Y
22 ***Gilman***	Y	Y	Y	N	Y	Y	Y	Y
23 Stratton	Y	Y	Y	N	Y	Y	N	Y
24 ***Solomon***	?	?	Y	Y	Y	Y	N	Y
25 ***Boehlert***	Y	Y	Y	N	Y	Y	Y	Y
26 ***Martin***	Y	Y	Y	N	Y	Y	Y	Y
27 ***Wortley***	Y	N	Y	N	Y	Y	Y	Y
28 McHugh	Y	Y	Y	N	Y	Y	Y	Y
29 ***Horton***	Y	Y	Y	N	Y	Y	Y	Y
30 ***Eckert***	Y	Y	Y	Y	Y	Y	Y	Y
31 ***Kemp***	Y	Y	Y	Y	Y	Y	Y	Y
32 LaFalce	Y	Y	Y	N	Y	Y	Y	Y
33 Nowak	Y	Y	Y	N	Y	Y	Y	Y
34 Lundine	Y	Y	Y	N	Y	Y	Y	Y

	30	31	32	33	34	35	36	37
NORTH CAROLINA								
1 Jones	Y	Y	Y	N	Y	Y	Y	Y
2 Valentine	Y	Y	Y	N	Y	Y	Y	Y
3 Whitley	Y	Y	Y	N	Y	Y	Y	Y
4 ***Cobey***	Y	Y	Y	Y	Y	Y	Y	N
5 Neal	Y	Y	Y	N	Y	Y	Y	Y
6 ***Coble***	Y	Y	Y	Y	Y	Y	Y	N
7 Rose	Y	Y	Y	N	Y	Y	Y	Y
8 Hefner	Y	Y	Y	N	Y	Y	Y	Y
9 ***McMillan***	Y	Y	Y	N	Y	Y	Y	N
10 ***Broyhill***	Y	Y	Y	N	Y	Y	Y	N
11 ***Hendon***	Y	Y	Y	N	Y	Y	Y	Y
NORTH DAKOTA								
AL Dorgan	Y	Y	Y	N	Y	Y	Y	Y
OHIO								
1 Luken	Y	Y	Y	N	Y	Y	Y	Y
2 ***Gradison***	Y	Y	Y	Y	Y	Y	Y	Y
3 Hall	Y	Y	Y	N	Y	Y	Y	Y
4 ***Oxley***	Y	Y	Y	Y	Y	Y	N	Y
5 ***Latta***	?	?	?	?	?	?	?	?
6 ***McEwen***	?	?	Y	Y	Y	Y	N	Y
7 ***DeWine***	Y	Y	Y	Y	Y	Y	N	Y
8 ***Kindness***	N	N	Y	Y	Y	N	Y	Y
9 Kaptur	Y	Y	Y	N	Y	Y	Y	Y
10 ***Miller***	Y	Y	Y	Y	Y	Y	N	Y
11 Eckart	Y	Y	?	N	Y	Y	Y	Y
12 ***Kasich***	Y	Y	Y	N	Y	Y	Y	Y
13 Pease	Y	Y	Y	N	Y	Y	Y	Y
14 Seiberling	Y	Y	Y	N	Y	Y	Y	Y
15 ***Wylie***	Y	Y	Y	N	Y	Y	Y	Y
16 ***Regula***	Y	Y	Y	N	Y	Y	Y	Y
17 Traficant	Y	Y	Y	N	Y	Y	Y	Y
18 Applegate	Y	Y	Y	N	Y	Y	N	Y
19 Feighan	Y	Y	Y	N	Y	Y	Y	Y
20 Oakar	Y	Y	Y	N	Y	Y	Y	Y
21 Stokes	Y	Y	Y	N	Y	Y	Y	Y
OKLAHOMA								
1 Jones	Y	Y	?	?	?	?	Y	Y
2 Synar	Y	Y	Y	N	Y	Y	Y	Y
3 Watkins	?	?	Y	N	Y	Y	Y	Y
4 McCurdy	Y	Y	Y	N	Y	Y	Y	Y
5 ***Edwards***	Y	Y	Y	Y	Y	Y	Y	Y
6 English	?	?	Y	N	Y	Y	Y	Y
OREGON								
1 AuCoin	Y	Y	Y	N	Y	Y	Y	Y
2 ***Smith, R.***	?	?	Y	Y	Y	Y	N	Y
3 Wyden	Y	Y	Y	N	Y	Y	Y	Y
4 Weaver	Y	Y	Y	N	Y	Y	Y	Y
5 ***Smith, D.***	Y	Y	Y	Y	Y	Y	N	N
PENNSYLVANIA								
1 Foglietta	?	?	?	?	?	?	?	?
2 Gray	Y	Y	Y	N	Y	Y	Y	Y
3 Borski	Y	Y	Y	N	Y	Y	Y	Y
4 Kolter	Y	Y	Y	N	Y	Y	?	?
5 ***Schulze***	N	N	Y	Y	Y	Y	N	?
6 Yatron	Y	Y	Y	N	Y	Y	Y	Y
7 Edgar	Y	Y	Y	?	?	?	?	?
8 Kostmayer	Y	Y	Y	N	Y	Y	Y	Y
9 ***Shuster***	Y	N	Y	N	Y	Y	N	N
10 ***McDade***	Y	Y	Y	N	Y	Y	?	Y
11 Kanjorski	Y	Y	Y	N	Y	Y	N	Y
12 Murtha	Y	Y	Y	N	Y	Y	Y	Y
13 ***Coughlin***	Y	Y	Y	N	Y	Y	N	Y
14 Coyne	Y	Y	Y	N	Y	Y	Y	Y
15 ***Ritter***	Y	Y	Y	Y	Y	Y	N	Y
16 ***Walker***	Y	Y	Y	Y	Y	Y	N	N
17 ***Gekas***	Y	Y	Y	N	Y	Y	N	N
18 Walgren	Y	Y	Y	N	Y	Y	Y	Y
19 ***Goodling***	Y	N	Y	N	Y	Y	N	N
20 Gaydos	Y	Y	Y	N	Y	Y	Y	Y
21 ***Ridge***	Y	N	Y	N	Y	Y	Y	Y
22 Murphy	Y	Y	Y	N	Y	Y	Y	Y
23 ***Clinger***	Y	N	Y	N	Y	Y	Y	+
RHODE ISLAND								
1 St Germain	Y	Y	Y	N	Y	Y	Y	N
2 ***Schneider***	Y	Y	Y	N	Y	Y	Y	Y
SOUTH CAROLINA								
1 ***Hartnett***	?	?	Y	Y	Y	Y	?	?
2 ***Spence***	Y	Y	Y	Y	Y	Y	Y	Y
3 Derrick	Y	Y	Y	Y	Y	Y	Y	Y
4 ***Campbell***	?	?	Y	N	Y	Y	Y	?
5 Spratt	Y	Y	Y	N	Y	Y	Y	Y
6 Tallon	Y	Y	Y	N	Y	Y	Y	Y
SOUTH DAKOTA								
AL Daschle	Y	Y	Y	N	Y	Y	Y	Y

	30	31	32	33	34	35	36	37
TENNESSEE								
1 ***Quillen***	N	N	Y	N	Y	Y	Y	Y
2 ***Duncan***	Y	Y	Y	N	Y	Y	Y	Y
3 Lloyd	Y	Y	Y	N	Y	Y	N	Y
4 Cooper	Y	Y	?	N	Y	Y	Y	Y
5 Boner	Y	Y	Y	N	Y	?	Y	Y
6 Gordon	Y	Y	Y	N	Y	Y	Y	Y
7 ***Sundquist***	N	N	Y	Y	Y	Y	N	Y
8 Jones	Y	Y	Y	N	Y	Y	Y	Y
9 Ford	Y	Y	Y	N	Y	Y	Y	Y
TEXAS								
1 Chapman	Y	Y	Y	N	Y	Y	Y	Y
2 Wilson	?	?	Y	N	Y	Y	Y	Y
3 ***Bartlett***	N	N	Y	Y	Y	Y	Y	N
4 Hall, R.	Y	Y	Y	N	Y	Y	Y	Y
5 Bryant	?	Y	Y	N	Y	Y	Y	Y
6 ***Barton***	N	N	Y	Y	Y	Y	Y	Y
7 ***Archer***	Y	Y	Y	Y	Y	Y	Y	N
8 ***Fields***	Y	Y	Y	Y	Y	Y	Y	N
9 Brooks	?	Y	?	N	Y	Y	Y	Y
10 Pickle	Y	Y	Y	N	Y	Y	Y	Y
11 Leath	N	N	Y	N	Y	Y	Y	Y
12 Wright	Y	Y	Y	N	Y	Y	Y	?
13 ***Boulter***	Y	Y	Y	N	Y	Y	Y	Y
14 ***Sweeney***	?	?	Y	Y	Y	Y	Y	Y
15 de la Garza	?	?	Y	N	Y	Y	Y	Y
16 Coleman	Y	Y	Y	N	Y	Y	Y	Y
17 Stenholm	Y	Y	Y	N	Y	Y	Y	Y
18 Leland	Y	Y	Y	N	Y	Y	Y	Y
19 ***Combest***	N	N	Y	Y	Y	Y	Y	Y
20 Gonzalez	P	N	Y	N	N	Y	Y	Y
21 ***Loeffler***	?	?	?	?	?	?	Y	Y
22 ***DeLay***	?	?	Y	Y	Y	Y	N	N
23 Bustamante	Y	Y	Y	N	Y	Y	Y	Y
24 Frost	?	?	Y	N	Y	Y	Y	Y
25 Andrews	Y	Y	Y	N	Y	Y	Y	Y
26 ***Armey***	N	N	Y	Y	Y	Y	Y	N
27 Ortiz	Y	Y	Y	N	Y	Y	Y	Y
UTAH								
1 ***Hansen***	N	N	Y	Y	Y	Y	N	N
2 ***Monson***	N	N	?	?	?	?	?	?
3 ***Nielson***	Y	Y	Y	Y	Y	Y	Y	Y
VERMONT								
AL ***Jeffords***	Y	Y	Y	N	Y	Y	N	Y
VIRGINIA								
1 ***Bateman***	Y	Y	Y	N	Y	Y	Y	Y
2 ***Whitehurst***	Y	Y	Y	N	Y	Y	Y	Y
3 ***Bliley***	Y	Y	Y	Y	Y	Y	Y	N
4 Sisisky	Y	Y	Y	N	Y	Y	Y	Y
5 Daniel	Y	Y	Y	N	Y	Y	Y	Y
6 Olin	Y	Y	Y	N	Y	Y	Y	N
7 ***Slaughter***	Y	Y	Y	Y	Y	Y	?	?
8 ***Parris***	?	?	Y	Y	Y	Y	Y	N
9 Boucher	Y	Y	Y	N	Y	Y	?	Y
10 ***Wolf***	Y	Y	Y	N	Y	Y	Y	Y
WASHINGTON								
1 ***Miller***	Y	Y	Y	N	Y	Y	Y	Y
2 Swift	Y	Y	Y	N	Y	Y	Y	Y
3 Bonker	?	Y	Y	N	Y	Y	Y	Y
4 ***Morrison***	Y	Y	Y	N	Y	Y	N	Y
5 Foley	Y	Y	Y	N	Y	Y	Y	Y
6 Dicks	?	?	Y	N	Y	Y	Y	Y
7 Lowry	Y	Y	Y	N	Y	Y	Y	Y
8 ***Chandler***	Y	Y	Y	N	Y	Y	Y	Y
WEST VIRGINIA								
1 Mollohan	Y	Y	Y	N	Y	Y	?	Y
2 Staggers	Y	Y	Y	N	Y	Y	Y	N
3 Wise	Y	Y	Y	N	Y	Y	Y	Y
4 Rahall	Y	Y	Y	N	Y	Y	Y	Y
WISCONSIN								
1 Aspin	Y	Y	Y	N	Y	Y	Y	Y
2 Kastenmeier	Y	Y	Y	N	Y	Y	Y	Y
3 ***Gunderson***	Y	Y	Y	N	Y	Y	N	Y
4 Kleczka	Y	Y	Y	N	Y	Y	Y	Y
5 Moody	Y	Y	Y	N	Y	Y	Y	Y
6 ***Petri***	Y	Y	Y	Y	Y	Y	N	Y
7 Obey	Y	Y	Y	N	Y	Y	Y	Y
8 ***Roth***	Y	Y	Y	?	?	?	?	?
9 ***Sensenbrenner***	Y	N	Y	Y	Y	Y	Y	Y
WYOMING								
AL ***Cheney***	Y	Y	Y	?	?	?	N	N

Southern states - Ala., Ark., Fla., Ga., Ky., La., Miss., N.C., Okla., S.C., Tenn., Texas, Va.

* The *Congressional Record* vote number is different from the CQ vote number because the *Record* includes quorum calls in its tally. CQ does not publish quorum call votes.

38. HR 1614. Corrections to 1985 Farm Bill. Frank, D-Mass., amendment to the Senate amendment, to strike a provision to increase milk assessments on dairy farmers to meet deficit-reduction requirements. Rejected 120-267: R 57-104: D 63-163 (ND 44-109, SD 19-54), March 6, 1986.

39. HR 1614. Corrections to 1985 Farm Bill. De la Garza, D-Texas, motion to concur in the Senate amendments to increase milk assessments to meet deficit-reduction requirements, to limit planting of non-program crops on acres subsidized for program crops, to require distribution of government-owned commodities to compensate farmers for reductions in income subsidies caused by changing the yields-per-acre formula for program payments, and to reduce spending requirements for export programs. Motion agreed to (thus cleared for the president) 283-97: R 105-52; D 178-45 (ND 117-34, SD 61-11), March 6, 1986.

40. HR 1524. Employee Polygraph Protection. Young, R-Fla., substitute to allow polygraph (lie detector) testing by private employers as long as employers followed specified standards and told employees the test was voluntary. Rejected 173-241: R 130-44; D 43-197 (ND 4-157, SD 39-40), March 12, 1986. A "nay" was a vote supporting the president's position.

41. HR 1524. Employee Polygraph Protection. McCollum, R-Fla., amendment to allow polygraph (lie detector) testing of employees in financial institutions. Rejected 194-217: R 147-24; D 47-193 (ND 11-150, SD 36-43), March 12, 1986.

42. HR 1524. Employee Polygraph Protection. Passage of the bill to prohibit polygraph (lie detector) testing by private employers, with certain exceptions. Passed 236-173: R 39-132; D 197-41 (ND 156-5, SD 41-36), March 12, 1986. A "nay" was a vote supporting the president's position.

43. Procedural Motion. Strang, R-Colo., motion to approve the House *Journal* of Wednesday, March 12. Motion agreed to 266-132: R 49-118; D 217-14 (ND 144-10, SD 73-4), March 13, 1986.

44. H J Res 534. Commodity Credit Corporation Supplemental Appropriation, Fiscal 1986. Adoption of the rule (H Res 398) to waive points of order against House floor consideration of the conference report on the joint resolution to appropriate $5,000,000,000 for the Commodity Credit Corporation. Adopted 283-129: R 54-117; D 229-12 (ND 155-5, SD 74-7), March 13, 1986. A "nay" was a vote supporting the president's position.

45. H J Res 534. Commodity Credit Corporation Supplemental Appropriation, Fiscal 1986. Whitten, D-Miss., motion that the House recede from its disagreement with the Senate amendment and concur therein, with an amendment to specify the precedence of previous appropriations in establishing the fiscal 1986 budget level for Farmers Home Administration loans. Motion agreed to 272-141: R 67-105; D 205-36 (ND 135-26), SD 70-10), March 13, 1986. (The effect of the motion was to adopt the conference report on the joint resolution to appropriate $5,000,000,000 for the Commodity Credit Corporation, and send it back to the Senate with an amendment.) A "nay" was a vote supporting the president's position.

KEY

- Y Voted for (yea).
- # Paired for.
- + Announced for.
- N Voted against (nay).
- X Paired against.
- \- Announced against.
- P Voted "present."
- C Voted "present" to avoid possible conflict of interest.
- ? Did not vote or otherwise make a position known.

Democrats *Republicans*

	38	39	40	41	42	43	44	45
ALABAMA								
1 *Callahan*	N	Y	Y	Y	N	N	Y	Y
2 *Dickinson*	N	Y	Y	Y	Y	N	?	?
3 Nichols	?	?	Y	Y	Y	?	Y	Y
4 Bevill	N	Y	Y	N	Y	Y	Y	Y
5 Flippo	Y	Y	Y	N	Y	Y	Y	Y
6 Erdreich	N	Y	N	Y	Y	Y	Y	Y
7 Shelby	N	Y	N	N	Y	Y	Y	Y
ALASKA								
AL *Young*	N	Y	N	Y	Y	N	N	N
ARIZONA								
1 *McCain*	N	Y	Y	Y	N	N	Y	N
2 Udall	N	Y	N	N	Y	Y	Y	Y
3 *Stump*	N	Y	Y	Y	N	N	N	N
4 *Rudd*	?	?	#	?	X	?	?	?
5 *Kolbe*	Y	Y	Y	Y	N	N	N	N
ARKANSAS								
1 Alexander	N	Y	N	N	Y	Y	Y	Y
2 Robinson	N	Y	N	N	Y	Y	Y	Y
3 *Hammerschmidt*	N	Y	Y	Y	N	N	Y	Y
4 Anthony	N	Y	N	N	Y	?	Y	Y
CALIFORNIA								
1 Bosco	N	?	N	N	Y	Y	Y	Y
2 *Chappie*	N	?	Y	Y	N	N	N	N
3 Matsui	N	Y	N	N	Y	Y	Y	Y
4 Fazio	N	Y	N	N	Y	Y	Y	Y
5 Burton	N	Y	N	N	Y	Y	Y	Y
6 Boxer	N	Y	N	N	Y	Y	Y	Y
7 Miller	Y	Y	N	N	Y	Y	Y	?
8 Dellums	N	Y	N	N	Y	Y	Y	Y
9 Stark	Y	?	?	N	Y	Y	Y	N
10 Edwards	Y	Y	N	N	Y	Y	Y	Y
11 Lantos	Y	N	N	N	Y	Y	Y	Y
12 *Zschau*	?	?	N	Y	N	N	N	N
13 Mineta	?	?	N	N	Y	Y	Y	Y
14 *Shumway*	Y	N	Y	Y	N	Y	N	N
15 Coelho	N	Y	N	N	Y	Y	Y	Y
16 Panetta	N	Y	N	Y	Y	Y	Y	Y
17 *Pashayan*	N	Y	N	Y	Y	N	N	Y
18 Lehman	N	Y	N	N	Y	Y	Y	Y
19 *Lagomarsino*	Y	N	Y	Y	N	N	N	N
20 *Thomas*	Y	Y	Y	Y	N	N	N	N
21 *Fiedler*	N	?	Y	Y	N	N	N	N
22 *Moorhead*	Y	N	Y	Y	N	N	N	N
23 Beilenson	N	N	N	N	Y	Y	Y	Y
24 Waxman	Y	N	N	N	Y	Y	Y	Y
25 Roybal	N	Y	N	N	Y	Y	Y	Y
26 Berman	Y	N	N	N	Y	Y	Y	Y
27 Levine	?	?	N	N	Y	Y	Y	Y
28 Dixon	Y	N	N	N	Y	?	Y	Y
29 Hawkins	N	Y	N	N	Y	Y	Y	Y
30 Martinez	N	Y	N	N	Y	Y	Y	Y
31 Dymally	N	Y	X	N	Y	Y	Y	Y
32 Anderson	Y	N	Y	Y	N	Y	N	N
33 *Dreier*	Y	N	Y	Y	N	N	N	N
34 Torres	N	Y	N	N	Y	Y	Y	Y
35 *Lewis*	Y	?	Y	Y	N	N	N	N
36 Brown	Y	N	?	?	#	Y	?	Y
37 *McCandless*	N	?	Y	Y	N	N	N	N
38 *Dornan*	N	N	?	?	?	N	N	N
39 *Dannemeyer*	Y	N	Y	Y	N	N	N	N
40 *Badham*	Y	N	Y	Y	N	N	N	N
41 *Lowery*	Y	N	Y	Y	N	?	N	N
42 *Lungren*	Y	N	Y	Y	N	N	N	N
43 *Packard*	Y	N	Y	Y	N	N	N	N
44 Bates	Y	N	N	N	N	Y	Y	Y
45 *Hunter*	Y	Y	Y	Y	N	N	N	Y
COLORADO								
1 Schroeder	Y	N	N	Y	Y	N	N	N
2 Wirth	N	Y	N	N	Y	Y	Y	Y
3 *Strang*	N	Y	N	N	N	N	N	Y
4 *Brown*	Y	Y	Y	Y	N	N	N	N
5 *Kramer*	N	Y	Y	Y	N	N	N	N
6 *Schaefer*	N	N	Y	Y	N	N	N	N
CONNECTICUT								
1 Kennelly	Y	N	N	N	Y	Y	?	Y
2 Gejdenson	N	Y	N	N	Y	Y	Y	Y
3 Morrison	Y	N	N	N	Y	Y	Y	N
4 *McKinney*	N	Y	N	N	Y	Y	Y	Y
5 *Rowland*	N	Y	N	Y	Y	Y	N	N
6 *Johnson*	N	Y	N	N	Y	Y	N	Y
DELAWARE								
AL Carper	Y	Y	N	Y	Y	Y	Y	N
FLORIDA								
1 Hutto	Y	Y	Y	Y	N	Y	Y	Y
2 Fuqua	N	Y	Y	Y	N	Y	Y	Y
3 Bennett	N	Y	Y	Y	N	Y	Y	Y
4 Chappell	?	?	Y	Y	N	Y	Y	Y
5 *McCollum*	Y	N	Y	Y	N	Y	N	N
6 MacKay	Y	N	Y	Y	N	Y	Y	N
7 Gibbons	Y	N	N	N	N	Y	N	X
8 *Young*	Y	N	Y	Y	N	N	N	N
9 *Bilirakis*	N	Y	Y	Y	N	N	N	N
10 *Ireland*	N	Y	Y	Y	N	?	N	N
11 Nelson	Y	N	Y	Y	N	Y	Y	N
12 *Lewis*	N	Y	Y	Y	N	?	N	N
13 *Mack*	Y	N	Y	Y	N	N	N	N
14 Mica	N	Y	N	N	Y	Y	Y	Y
15 *Shaw*	Y	N	Y	Y	N	N	N	N
16 Smith	Y	N	N	N	Y	Y	N	N
17 Lehman	Y	N	N	N	Y	Y	Y	Y
18 Pepper	Y	Y	N	N	Y	Y	Y	Y
19 Fascell	Y	N	N	N	Y	Y	Y	Y
GEORGIA								
1 Thomas	N	Y	Y	Y	N	Y	Y	Y
2 Hatcher	N	Y	?	?	?	Y	Y	Y
3 Ray	?	?	Y	Y	N	Y	Y	Y
4 *Swindall*	Y	N	Y	Y	N	N	N	N
5 Fowler	?	?	Y	N	N	Y	Y	Y
6 *Gingrich*	N	Y	Y	Y	N	N	N	N
7 Darden	Y	Y	Y	Y	N	Y	Y	Y
8 Rowland	Y	Y	Y	Y	N	Y	Y	Y
9 Jenkins	Y	N	Y	N	N	Y	Y	N
10 Barnard	?	?	Y	Y	N	Y	N	N
HAWAII								
1 Heftel	N	Y	N	Y	Y	Y	Y	Y
2 Akaka	N	Y	N	N	Y	Y	Y	Y
IDAHO								
1 *Craig*	N	Y	Y	Y	N	N	N	N
2 Stallings	N	Y	N	N	Y	Y	Y	Y
ILLINOIS								
1 Hayes	N	Y	N	N	Y	Y	Y	Y
2 Savage	N	Y	N	N	Y	?	?	?
3 Russo	#	?	N	N	Y	Y	Y	N
4 *O'Brien*	X	?	N	Y	N	Y	Y	N
5 Lipinski	Y	N	N	N	Y	Y	Y	N
6 *Hyde*	N	Y	Y	Y	N	Y	N	N
7 Collins	?	?	X	?	#	?	?	#
8 Rostenkowski	?	?	N	N	Y	Y	Y	Y
9 Yates	Y	N	N	N	Y	Y	Y	N
10 *Porter*	?	?	Y	Y	N	Y	N	N
11 Annunzio	N	Y	N	N	Y	Y	Y	Y
12 *Crane*	Y	N	Y	Y	N	N	N	N
13 *Fawell*	Y	N	Y	Y	N	N	N	N
14 *Grotberg*	?	?	?	?	?	?	?	?
15 *Madigan*	N	Y	Y	?	?	?	?	?
16 *Martin*	N	Y	N	N	Y	N	N	Y
17 Evans	N	Y	N	N	Y	Y	Y	Y
18 *Michel*	N	Y	Y	Y	N	N	N	Y
19 Bruce	N	Y	N	N	Y	Y	Y	Y
20 Durbin	N	Y	N	N	Y	N	Y	Y
21 Price	?	?	N	N	Y	N	Y	Y
22 Gray	N	Y	N	N	Y	Y	Y	Y
INDIANA								
1 Visclosky	N	N	N	N	Y	Y	Y	Y
2 Sharp	N	Y	N	N	Y	Y	Y	Y
3 *Hiler*	Y	Y	Y	Y	N	N	Y	Y
4 *Coats*	Y	Y	N	Y	N	N	Y	Y
5 *Hillis*	?	?	Y	Y	N	Y	Y	Y

ND - Northern Democrats SD - Southern Democrats

* Corresponding to Congressional Record Votes 43, 44, 45, 46, 47, 48, 49, 50

	38	39	40	41	42	43	44	45
6 ***Burton***	N	Y	N	Y	N	N	Y	Y
7 ***Myers***	N	Y	Y	Y	N	Y	Y	Y
8 McCloskey	N	Y	N	N	Y	?	Y	Y
9 Hamilton	N	Y	N	N	Y	Y	Y	Y
10 Jacobs	Y	N	N	N	Y	N	N	N
IOWA								
1 ***Leach***	N	Y	N	N	Y	N	Y	Y
2 ***Tauke***	N	Y	N	N	Y	N	Y	Y
3 ***Evans***	N	Y	?	Y	N	N	Y	Y
4 Smith	N	Y	N	N	Y	Y	Y	Y
5 ***Lightfoot***	N	Y	Y	Y	N	N	Y	Y
6 Bedell	N	Y	N	N	Y	Y	Y	Y
KANSAS								
1 ***Roberts***	N	Y	Y	Y	N	N	Y	Y
2 Slattery	N	Y	N	N	Y	Y	N	N
3 ***Meyers***	Y	Y	N	Y	N	N	N	N
4 Glickman	N	Y	N	N	Y	Y	Y	Y
5 ***Whittaker***	N	Y	Y	Y	N	N	Y	Y
KENTUCKY								
1 Hubbard	N	Y	N	N	Y	Y	Y	Y
2 Natcher	N	Y	N	N	Y	Y	Y	Y
3 Mazzoli	Y	N	N	Y	Y	Y	Y	Y
4 ***Snyder***	N	Y	Y	Y	N	Y	Y	N
5 ***Rogers***	N	Y	Y	Y	N	N	N	Y
6 ***Hopkins***	N	Y	Y	Y	N	Y	N	N
7 Perkins	N	Y	N	N	Y	Y	Y	Y
LOUISIANA								
1 ***Livingston***	N	Y	Y	Y	N	Y	N	N
2 Boggs	N	Y	N	N	Y	Y	Y	Y
3 Tauzin	N	Y	Y	Y	Y	Y	Y	Y
4 Roemer	Y	Y	Y	Y	Y	N	N	Y
5 Huckaby	N	Y	Y	Y	N	Y	Y	Y
6 ***Moore***	N	Y	Y	Y	N	Y	Y	Y
7 Breaux	N	Y	N	N	Y	Y	Y	Y
8 Long	N	Y	N	N	Y	Y	Y	Y
MAINE								
1 ***McKernan***	N	Y	Y	Y	N	N	N	Y
2 ***Snowe***	N	Y	N	N	Y	N	Y	Y
MARYLAND								
1 Dyson	N	Y	N	N	Y	N	Y	Y
2 ***Bentley***	N	Y	Y	N	Y	N	N	N
3 Mikulski	N	Y	N	N	Y	Y	Y	Y
4 ***Holt***	N	N	Y	Y	N	Y	N	N
5 Hoyer	N	Y	N	N	Y	Y	Y	Y
6 Byron	N	Y	Y	Y	N	Y	Y	Y
7 Mitchell	N	Y	N	N	N	?	Y	Y
8 Barnes	N	Y	N	?	#	Y	Y	Y
MASSACHUSETTS								
1 ***Conte***	Y	N	N	N	Y	N	N	N
2 Boland	#	?	N	N	Y	Y	Y	Y
3 Early	Y	N	N	N	Y	Y	Y	Y
4 Frank	Y	N	N	N	Y	Y	Y	N
5 Atkins	Y	N	N	N	Y	Y	Y	Y
6 Mavroules	Y	N	N	N	Y	Y	Y	Y
7 Markey	Y	N	N	N	Y	Y	Y	Y
8 O'Neill								
9 Moakley	?	?	N	N	Y	Y	Y	Y
10 Studds	Y	N	N	N	Y	Y	Y	N
11 Donnelly	Y	N	N	N	Y	Y	Y	Y
MICHIGAN								
1 Conyers	N	Y	N	N	Y	Y	Y	Y
2 ***Pursell***	N	Y	N	Y	N	Y	N	N
3 Wolpe	N	Y	N	N	Y	Y	Y	Y
4 ***Siljander***	N	Y	Y	Y	N	N	Y	Y
5 ***Henry***	N	Y	Y	Y	N	N	N	N
6 Carr	N	Y	N	N	Y	Y	Y	Y
7 Kildee	N	Y	N	N	Y	Y	Y	Y
8 Traxler	N	Y	X	N	Y	Y	Y	Y
9 ***Vander Jagt***	?	?	Y	Y	N	N	N	N
10 ***Schuette***	N	Y	Y	Y	N	N	Y	Y
11 ***Davis***	N	Y	N	N	Y	N	Y	Y
12 Bonior	N	Y	N	N	Y	Y	Y	Y
13 Crockett	N	Y	N	N	Y	Y	Y	Y
14 Hertel	Y	N	N	N	Y	Y	Y	N
15 Ford	N	Y	N	N	Y	?	Y	Y
16 Dingell	N	Y	N	N	Y	Y	?	Y
17 Levin	N	Y	N	N	Y	Y	Y	Y
18 ***Broomfield***	Y	N	Y	Y	N	Y	N	N
MINNESOTA								
1 Penny	N	Y	N	N	Y	N	Y	N
2 ***Weber***	N	Y	N	N	Y	N	Y	Y
3 ***Frenzel***	N	Y	Y	Y	N	N	N	N
4 Vento	N	Y	N	N	Y	Y	Y	N
5 Sabo	N	N	N	N	Y	Y	Y	N
6 Sikorski	N	Y	N	N	Y	N	Y	Y

	38	39	40	41	42	43	44	45
7 ***Stangeland***	N	Y	N	Y	Y	N	Y	Y
8 Oberstar	N	Y	N	N	Y	Y	Y	Y
MISSISSIPPI								
1 Whitten	N	Y	Y	N	N	Y	Y	Y
2 ***Franklin***	N	Y	Y	Y	N	Y	Y	Y
3 Montgomery	N	Y	Y	Y	N	Y	Y	Y
4 Dowdy	N	?	Y	Y	N	Y	Y	Y
5 ***Lott***	N	Y	Y	Y	N	N	N	Y
MISSOURI								
1 Clay	N	Y	N	N	Y	N	Y	Y
2 Young	N	Y	N	N	Y	Y	Y	Y
3 Gephardt	?	Y	?	?	?	Y	Y	Y
4 Skelton	N	Y	N	N	Y	Y	Y	Y
5 Wheat	N	Y	N	N	Y	Y	Y	Y
6 ***Coleman***	?	?	Y	Y	N	N	Y	N
7 ***Taylor***	N	Y	#	?	X	?	?	?
8 ***Emerson***	N	Y	Y	Y	N	N	Y	Y
9 Volkmer	N	Y	N	N	Y	Y	Y	Y
MONTANA								
1 Williams	N	Y	N	N	Y	?	Y	?
2 ***Marlenee***	N	Y	Y	Y	N	N	Y	Y
NEBRASKA								
1 ***Bereuter***	N	Y	Y	Y	Y	N	Y	Y
2 ***Daub***	Y	Y	Y	Y	N	N	N	Y
3 ***Smith***	N	Y	Y	Y	N	Y	Y	Y
NEVADA								
1 Reid	N	Y	N	N	Y	Y	Y	Y
2 ***Vucanovich***	N	Y	Y	Y	N	N	N	N
NEW HAMPSHIRE								
1 ***Smith***	Y	N	Y	Y	N	N	N	N
2 ***Gregg***	Y	N	N	Y	Y	N	N	N
NEW JERSEY								
1 Florio	N	Y	N	N	Y	Y	Y	Y
2 Hughes	N	Y	N	Y	Y	Y	Y	N
3 Howard	Y	Y	N	N	Y	Y	Y	Y
4 ***Smith***	N	Y	N	N	Y	Y	Y	N
5 ***Roukema***	N	N	Y	Y	N	N	N	N
6 Dwyer	Y	N	N	N	Y	Y	Y	Y
7 ***Rinaldo***	Y	Y	N	N	Y	?	Y	N
8 Roe	N	Y	N	N	Y	Y	Y	Y
9 Torricelli	N	Y	N	Y	Y	Y	Y	Y
10 Rodino	N	Y	N	N	Y	Y	Y	Y
11 ***Gallo***	N	Y	N	Y	Y	N	N	N
12 ***Courter***	Y	N	N	N	Y	N	N	N
13 ***Saxton***	N	Y	N	Y	Y	N	N	N
14 Guarini	Y	Y	N	N	Y	Y	Y	Y
NEW MEXICO								
1 ***Lujan***	?	N	Y	Y	N	Y	Y	N
2 ***Skeen***	N	Y	Y	Y	N	N	Y	Y
3 Richardson	N	Y	N	N	Y	Y	Y	Y
NEW YORK								
1 ***Carney***	Y	N	Y	Y	N	N	N	N
2 Downey	Y	N	N	N	Y	Y	Y	Y
3 Mrazek	Y	N	N	N	Y	Y	Y	N
4 ***Lent***	N	N	Y	Y	?	N	N	N
5 ***McGrath***	Y	N	Y	Y	N	N	N	N
6 Addabbo	?	?	?	?	?	?	?	?
7 Ackerman	?	?	N	N	Y	Y	Y	Y
8 Scheuer	Y	Y	N	N	Y	Y	Y	N
9 Manton	N	Y	N	N	Y	Y	Y	Y
10 Schumer	Y	Y	N	N	Y	?	?	?
11 Towns	N	Y	N	?	?	?	?	?
12 Owens	Y	N	N	N	Y	Y	Y	Y
13 Solarz	?	?	N	N	Y	?	Y	Y
14 ***Molinari***	N	N	Y	Y	N	N	N	N
15 ***Green***	Y	N	N	Y	Y	Y	N	N
16 Rangel	Y	Y	N	N	Y	Y	Y	Y
17 Weiss	Y	N	N	N	N	Y	Y	N
18 Garcia	Y	N	N	N	Y	Y	Y	Y
19 Biaggi	N	Y	N	N	Y	Y	Y	Y
20 ***DioGuardi***	Y	N	Y	Y	N	?	N	N
21 ***Fish***	N	Y	Y	Y	N	Y	N	N
22 ***Gilman***	N	Y	N	N	Y	Y	Y	Y
23 Stratton	N	Y	Y	Y	N	Y	Y	Y
24 ***Solomon***	N	Y	Y	Y	N	N	N	N
25 ***Boehlert***	N	Y	N	N	Y	N	Y	Y
26 ***Martin***	N	Y	Y	Y	N	Y	Y	Y
27 ***Wortley***	N	Y	Y	Y	N	Y	Y	N
28 McHugh	N	Y	N	N	Y	Y	Y	Y
29 ***Horton***	N	Y	N	N	Y	Y	Y	Y
30 ***Eckert***	N	Y	Y	Y	N	Y	N	N
31 ***Kemp***	N	Y	N	N	Y	Y	Y	Y
32 LaFalce	N	Y	N	?	Y	Y	Y	Y
33 Nowak	Y	Y	N	N	Y	Y	Y	Y
34 Lundine	N	Y	N	N	Y	Y	Y	Y

	38	39	40	41	42	43	44	45
NORTH CAROLINA								
1 Jones	N	Y	Y	N	N	Y	Y	Y
2 Valentine	N	Y	Y	Y	N	Y	Y	Y
3 Whitley	N	Y	Y	Y	N	Y	Y	Y
4 ***Cobey***	Y	N	Y	Y	N	N	N	N
5 Neal	N	Y	N	N	Y	Y	Y	Y
6 ***Coble***	Y	N	Y	Y	N	N	N	Y
7 Rose	N	Y	Y	Y	N	Y	Y	Y
8 Hefner	N	Y	Y	N	N	Y	Y	Y
9 ***McMillan***	Y	N	Y	Y	N	N	N	Y
10 ***Broyhill***	Y	N	Y	?	N	Y	N	N
11 ***Hendon***	Y	N	Y	Y	N	N	Y	Y
NORTH DAKOTA								
AL Dorgan	N	Y	N	N	Y	Y	Y	Y
OHIO								
1 Luken	N	N	N	N	Y	Y	Y	N
2 ***Gradison***	N	Y	Y	Y	N	Y	?	Y
3 Hall	Y	Y	Y	Y	N	Y	Y	Y
4 ***Oxley***	N	Y	Y	Y	N	N	N	N
5 ***Latta***	?	?	?	?	?	?	?	N
6 ***McEwen***	?	?	Y	Y	N	Y	Y	Y
7 ***DeWine***	?	?	Y	Y	N	N	N	N
8 ***Kindness***	N	Y	Y	Y	?	?	?	?
9 Kaptur	N	Y	N	N	Y	Y	Y	Y
10 ***Miller***	N	Y	Y	Y	N	N	Y	Y
11 Eckart	N	Y	N	N	Y	Y	Y	Y
12 ***Kasich***	N	Y	N	Y	N	Y	N	Y
13 Pease	N	Y	N	N	Y	Y	Y	Y
14 Seiberling	Y	Y	N	N	Y	Y	Y	Y
15 ***Wylie***	N	Y	Y	?	?	?	?	?
16 ***Regula***	N	Y	Y	Y	Y	N	Y	N
17 Traficant	N	Y	N	N	Y	Y	Y	Y
18 Applegate	N	Y	N	N	Y	Y	Y	Y
19 Feighan	N	Y	N	N	Y	Y	Y	N
20 Oakar	?	?	N	N	Y	Y	Y	Y
21 Stokes	N	Y	N	N	Y	Y	Y	Y
OKLAHOMA								
1 Jones	N	Y	N	Y	Y	N	Y	Y
2 Synar	N	Y	N	N	Y	Y	Y	Y
3 Watkins	N	Y	N	Y	Y	Y	Y	Y
4 McCurdy	?	?	?	?	?	Y	Y	Y
5 ***Edwards***	N	Y	N	Y	N	N	Y	Y
6 English	N	Y	N	Y	Y	Y	Y	Y
OREGON								
1 AuCoin	N	Y	N	N	Y	N	Y	N
2 ***Smith, R.***	N	Y	Y	Y	N	N	N	Y
3 Wyden	N	Y	N	N	Y	Y	Y	N
4 Weaver	N	?	X	?	#	?	?	?
5 ***Smith, D.***	N	Y	Y	Y	N	N	N	?
PENNSYLVANIA								
1 Foglietta	?	?	N	N	Y	Y	Y	Y
2 Gray	N	Y	N	N	Y	Y	Y	Y
3 Borski	N	Y	N	N	Y	Y	Y	Y
4 Kolter	?	?	N	N	Y	Y	Y	Y
5 ***Schulze***	?	?	Y	Y	N	Y	N	Y
6 Yatron	N	Y	N	N	Y	Y	Y	Y
7 Edgar	?	?	N	N	?	?	?	?
8 Kostmayer	Y	N	N	N	Y	Y	Y	N
9 ***Shuster***	Y	N	Y	Y	N	N	N	N
10 ***McDade***	N	Y	N	N	Y	Y	Y	Y
11 Kanjorski	N	Y	N	N	Y	Y	Y	Y
12 Murtha	N	Y	N	N	Y	?	Y	Y
13 ***Coughlin***	Y	N	N	N	Y	N	N	N
14 Coyne	Y	N	N	N	Y	Y	Y	Y
15 ***Ritter***	Y	N	N	Y	Y	Y	N	N
16 ***Walker***	Y	N	Y	Y	N	N	N	N
17 ***Gekas***	N	N	Y	Y	Y	N	N	N
18 Walgren	Y	N	N	N	Y	Y	Y	Y
19 ***Goodling***	P	Y	Y	Y	N	N	N	N
20 Gaydos	N	Y	N	N	Y	?	Y	Y
21 ***Ridge***	N	Y	N	N	Y	N	N	N
22 Murphy	N	Y	N	N	Y	Y	Y	Y
23 ***Clinger***	-	+	N	N	Y	Y	Y	N
RHODE ISLAND								
1 St Germain	?	?	N	Y	Y	Y	Y	Y
2 ***Schneider***	N	Y	N	Y	Y	Y	N	N
SOUTH CAROLINA								
1 ***Hartnett***	?	?	Y	Y	N	Y	N	N
2 ***Spence***	Y	Y	Y	Y	N	N	Y	Y
3 Derrick	Y	Y	Y	Y	N	Y	Y	Y
4 ***Campbell***	?	?	#	?	X	?	?	?
5 Spratt	Y	Y	Y	N	N	Y	Y	Y
6 Tallon	N	Y	Y	Y	N	?	Y	Y
SOUTH DAKOTA								
AL Daschle	N	Y	N	N	Y	Y	Y	Y

	38	39	40	41	42	43	44	45
TENNESSEE								
1 ***Quillen***	N	?	N	Y	Y	Y	Y	Y
2 ***Duncan***	N	Y	Y	Y	N	Y	Y	Y
3 Lloyd	Y	N	Y	Y	N	N	Y	Y
4 Cooper	N	Y	N	N	Y	Y	Y	Y
5 Boner	N	Y	N	N	Y	Y	Y	Y
6 Gordon	N	Y	N	N	Y	Y	Y	Y
7 ***Sundquist***	N	Y	Y	Y	N	N	N	Y
8 Jones	N	Y	Y	Y	N	Y	Y	Y
9 Ford	N	Y	N	N	Y	Y	Y	Y
TEXAS								
1 Chapman	N	Y	Y	Y	N	Y	Y	Y
2 Wilson	N	Y	N	N	Y	?	?	?
3 ***Bartlett***	Y	N	Y	Y	N	N	N	N
4 Hall, R.	N	Y	?	?	?	N	N	Y
5 Bryant	N	Y	N	N	Y	Y	Y	Y
6 ***Barton***	Y	Y	Y	Y	N	N	N	Y
7 ***Archer***	Y	N	Y	Y	N	Y	N	N
8 ***Fields***	Y	N	Y	Y	N	N	N	N
9 Brooks	N	Y	N	N	Y	Y	Y	Y
10 Pickle	N	Y	Y	N	Y	Y	Y	Y
11 Leath	N	Y	Y	Y	N	Y	N	N
12 Wright	?	?	N	N	?	Y	Y	Y
13 ***Boulter***	N	Y	Y	Y	N	N	Y	Y
14 ***Sweeney***	N	Y	Y	Y	N	Y	N	Y
15 de la Garza	N	Y	N	Y	N	Y	Y	Y
16 Coleman	?	?	N	N	N	Y	Y	Y
17 Stenholm	N	Y	Y	Y	N	Y	N	N
18 Leland	N	Y	N	N	Y	?	Y	Y
19 ***Combest***	N	Y	Y	Y	N	Y	N	Y
20 Gonzalez	N	Y	N	N	Y	Y	Y	Y
21 ***Loeffler***	N	Y	#	?	X	?	?	?
22 ***DeLay***	Y	N	Y	Y	N	N	N	N
23 Bustamante	N	Y	N	N	Y	Y	Y	Y
24 Frost	N	Y	Y	Y	?	Y	Y	Y
25 Andrews	N	Y	N	N	Y	Y	Y	N
26 ***Armey***	Y	N	Y	Y	N	N	N	N
27 Ortiz	X	?	N	N	N	Y	Y	Y
UTAH								
1 ***Hansen***	N	Y	Y	Y	N	N	N	N
2 ***Monson***	?	?	Y	Y	N	N	N	N
3 ***Nielson***	Y	N	N	N	Y	N	N	Y
VERMONT								
AL ***Jeffords***	N	Y	N	?	Y	Y	Y	Y
VIRGINIA								
1 ***Bateman***	Y	Y	Y	Y	N	Y	N	N
2 ***Whitehurst***	?	?	Y	Y	N	N	N	N
3 ***Bliley***	Y	N	Y	Y	N	N	N	N
4 Sisisky	N	Y	Y	Y	N	Y	Y	Y
5 Daniel	N	N	Y	Y	N	Y	Y	N
6 Olin	Y	N	N	N	Y	Y	Y	N
7 ***Slaughter***	?	?	Y	Y	N	?	N	N
8 ***Parris***	Y	N	Y	Y	N	N	N	N
9 Boucher	Y	Y	N	N	Y	Y	Y	Y
10 ***Wolf***	Y	N	Y	Y	N	N	N	N
WASHINGTON								
1 ***Miller***	N	Y	N	N	Y	Y	N	N
2 Swift	N	Y	N	N	Y	Y	Y	Y
3 Bonker	N	Y	N	N	Y	Y	Y	Y
4 ***Morrison***	N	Y	Y	Y	N	Y	Y	Y
5 Foley	N	Y	N	N	Y	Y	Y	Y
6 Dicks	N	Y	N	N	Y	Y	Y	Y
7 Lowry	Y	Y	N	N	Y	N	N	N
8 ***Chandler***	N	Y	Y	Y	N	N	N	N
WEST VIRGINIA								
1 Mollohan	N	Y	N	N	Y	Y	Y	Y
2 Staggers	Y	Y	N	N	Y	Y	Y	Y
3 Wise	N	Y	N	N	Y	Y	Y	Y
4 Rahall	N	Y	N	N	Y	Y	Y	Y
WISCONSIN								
1 Aspin	N	Y	?	?	?	Y	Y	Y
2 Kastenmeier	N	Y	N	N	Y	Y	Y	Y
3 ***Gunderson***	N	Y	N	Y	N	N	Y	Y
4 Kleczka	N	Y	N	N	Y	?	Y	Y
5 Moody	N	Y	N	N	Y	Y	Y	Y
6 ***Petri***	N	Y	Y	Y	N	Y	N	Y
7 Obey	N	Y	N	N	Y	Y	Y	Y
8 ***Roth***	?	?	Y	Y	N	N	Y	Y
9 ***Sensenbrenner***	N	?	Y	Y	N	N	N	N
WYOMING								
AL ***Cheney***	Y	N	Y	Y	N	N	N	N

Southern states - Ala., Ark., Fla., Ga., Ky., La., Miss., N.C., Okla., S.C., Tenn., Texas, Va.

* The *Congressional Record* vote number is different from the CQ vote number because the *Record* includes quorum calls in its tally. CQ does not publish quorum call votes.

46. H Con Res 296. Budget Resolution, Fiscal 1987. Frost, D-Texas, motion to order the previous question (thus ending debate and the possibility of amendment) on the rule (H Res 397) to provide for House floor consideration of the concurrent resolution to set budget levels for the fiscal year ending Sept. 30, 1987, as calculated for the 1985 Balanced Budget and Emergency Deficit Control Act (PL 99-177), as follows: budget authority, $1,102 billion; outlays, $994 billion; revenues, $850.4 billion; and deficit, $143.6 billion. Motion agreed to 243-171: R 1-170; D 242-1 (ND 163-1, SD 79-0), March 13, 1986.

47. H Con Res 296. Budget Resolution, Fiscal 1987. Adoption of the rule (H Res 397) to provide for House floor consideration of the concurrent resolution to set budget levels for the fiscal year ending Sept. 30, 1987, as calculated for the 1985 Balanced Budget and Emergency Deficit Control Act (PL 99-177), as follows: budget authority, $1,102 billion; outlays, $994 billion; revenues, $850.4 billion; and deficit, $143.6 billion. Adopted 239-168: R 2-165; D 237-3 (ND 159-1, SD 78-2), March 13, 1986.

48. H Con Res 296. Budget Resolution, Fiscal 1987. Adoption of the concurrent resolution to set budget levels for the fiscal year ending Sept. 30, 1987, as calculated for the 1985 Balanced Budget and Emergency Deficit Control Act (PL 99-177), as follows: budget authority, $1,102 billion; outlays, $994 billion; revenues, $850.4 billion; and deficit, $143.6 billion. Rejected 12-312: R 12-74; D 0-238 (ND 0-162, SD 0-76), March 13, 1986. (This was the budget submitted to Congress by the president Feb. 5.) A "yea" was a vote supporting the president's position.

KEY

Y Voted for (yea).
Paired for.
+ Announced for.
N Voted against (nay).
X Paired against.
- Announced against.
P Voted "present."
C Voted "present" to avoid possible conflict of interest.
? Did not vote or otherwise make a position known.

Democrats *Republicans*

	46	47	48
ALABAMA			
1 ***Callahan***	N	N	P
2 ***Dickinson***	N	N	P
3 Nichols	Y	Y	N
4 Bevill	Y	Y	N
5 Flippo	Y	Y	N
6 Erdreich	Y	Y	N
7 Shelby	Y	Y	N
ALASKA			
AL ***Young***	N	N	N
ARIZONA			
1 ***McCain***	N	N	P
2 Udall	Y	Y	N
3 ***Stump***	N	N	P
4 ***Rudd***	X	X	#
5 ***Kolbe***	N	N	P
ARKANSAS			
1 Alexander	Y	Y	N
2 Robinson	Y	Y	N
3 ***Hammerschmidt***	N	N	N
4 Anthony	Y	Y	N
CALIFORNIA			
1 Bosco	Y	Y	N
2 ***Chappie***	N	N	P
3 Matsui	Y	Y	N
4 Fazio	Y	?	N
5 Burton	Y	Y	N
6 Boxer	Y	Y	N
7 Miller	Y	?	N
8 Dellums	Y	Y	N
9 Stark	Y	Y	?
10 Edwards	Y	Y	N
11 Lantos	Y	Y	N
12 ***Zschau***	N	N	P
13 Mineta	Y	Y	N
14 ***Shumway***	N	N	Y
15 Coelho	Y	Y	N
16 Panetta	Y	Y	N
17 ***Pashayan***	N	N	P
18 Lehman	Y	Y	N
19 ***Lagomarsino***	N	N	P
20 ***Thomas***	N	N	?
21 ***Fiedler***	N	N	P
22 ***Moorhead***	N	N	Y
23 Beilenson	Y	Y	?
24 Waxman	Y	Y	N
25 Roybal	Y	Y	N
26 Berman	Y	Y	N
27 Levine	Y	Y	N
28 Dixon	Y	Y	N
29 Hawkins	Y	Y	N
30 Martinez	Y	Y	N
31 Dymally	Y	Y	N
32 Anderson	Y	Y	N
33 ***Dreier***	N	N	P
34 Torres	Y	Y	N
35 ***Lewis***	N	N	P
36 Brown	Y	Y	N
37 ***McCandless***	N	?	P
38 ***Dornan***	N	N	P
39 ***Dannemeyer***	N	N	P
40 ***Badham***	N	N	Y
41 ***Lowery***	N	N	P
42 ***Lungren***	N	N	P
43 ***Packard***	N	N	P
44 Bates	Y	Y	N
45 ***Hunter***	N	N	P
COLORADO			
1 Schroeder	Y	Y	N
2 Wirth	Y	Y	N
3 ***Strang***	N	N	P
4 ***Brown***	N	N	N
5 ***Kramer***	N	N	P
6 ***Schaefer***	N	N	N
CONNECTICUT			
1 Kennelly	Y	Y	N
2 Gejdenson	Y	Y	N
3 Morrison	Y	Y	-
4 ***McKinney***	N	N	N
5 ***Rowland***	N	N	N
6 ***Johnson***	N	N	?
DELAWARE			
AL Carper	Y	Y	N
FLORIDA			
1 Hutto	Y	Y	P
2 Fuqua	Y	Y	N
3 Bennett	Y	Y	N
4 Chappell	#	#	?
5 ***McCollum***	N	N	P
6 MacKay	Y	Y	N
7 Gibbons	Y	Y	N
8 ***Young***	N	N	N
9 ***Bilirakis***	N	N	N
10 ***Ireland***	N	N	P
11 Nelson	Y	Y	N
12 ***Lewis***	N	N	P
13 ***Mack***	N	N	Y
14 Mica	Y	Y	N
15 ***Shaw***	N	N	P
16 Smith	Y	Y	N
17 Lehman	Y	Y	N
18 Pepper	Y	Y	N
19 Fascell	Y	Y	N
GEORGIA			
1 Thomas	Y	Y	N
2 Hatcher	Y	Y	N
3 Ray	Y	Y	N
4 ***Swindall***	N	N	N
5 Fowler	Y	Y	N
6 ***Gingrich***	N	N	P
7 Darden	Y	Y	N
8 Rowland	Y	Y	N
9 Jenkins	Y	Y	N
10 Barnard	Y	Y	?
HAWAII			
1 Heftel	Y	Y	N
2 Akaka	Y	Y	N
IDAHO			
1 ***Craig***	N	?	N
2 Stallings	Y	Y	N
ILLINOIS			
1 Hayes	Y	Y	N
2 Savage	Y	Y	N
3 Russo	Y	Y	N
4 ***O'Brien***	N	N	N
5 Lipinski	Y	Y	N
6 ***Hyde***	N	N	P
7 Collins	#	#	?
8 Rostenkowski	Y	Y	N
9 Yates	Y	Y	N
10 ***Porter***	N	N	N
11 Annunzio	Y	Y	N
12 ***Crane***	N	N	N
13 ***Fawell***	N	N	P
14 ***Grotberg***	?	?	?
15 ***Madigan***	?	?	?
16 ***Martin***	N	N	P
17 Evans	Y	Y	N
18 ***Michel***	N	N	?
19 Bruce	Y	Y	N
20 Durbin	Y	?	N
21 Price	Y	Y	N
22 Gray	Y	Y	N
INDIANA			
1 Visclosky	Y	Y	N
2 Sharp	Y	Y	N
3 ***Hiler***	N	N	N
4 ***Coats***	N	N	N
5 ***Hillis***	N	N	P

ND - Northern Democrats SD - Southern Democrats

* Corresponding to Congressional Record Votes 51, 52, 53

	46	47	48
6 ***Burton***	N	N	P
7 ***Myers***	N	N	N
8 McCloskey	Y	Y	N
9 Hamilton	Y	Y	N
10 Jacobs	N	N	N
IOWA			
1 ***Leach***	N	N	?
2 ***Tauke***	N	N	N
3 ***Evans***	N	N	N
4 Smith	Y	Y	N
5 ***Lightfoot***	N	N	N
6 Bedell	Y	Y	N
KANSAS			
1 ***Roberts***	N	N	N
2 Slattery	Y	Y	N
3 ***Meyers***	N	N	P
4 Glickman	Y	Y	N
5 ***Whittaker***	N	N	N
KENTUCKY			
1 Hubbard	Y	Y	N
2 Natcher	Y	Y	N
3 Mazzoli	Y	N	N
4 ***Snyder***	N	N	P
5 ***Rogers***	N	N	P
6 ***Hopkins***	N	Y	P
7 Perkins	Y	Y	N
LOUISIANA			
1 ***Livingston***	N	N	Y
2 Boggs	Y	Y	N
3 Tauzin	Y	Y	N
4 Roemer	Y	Y	N
5 Huckaby	#	#	?
6 ***Moore***	-	-	N
7 Breaux	Y	Y	N
8 Long	Y	Y	N
MAINE			
1 ***McKernan***	N	N	P
2 ***Snowe***	N	N	N
MARYLAND			
1 Dyson	Y	Y	N
2 ***Bentley***	N	N	P
3 Mikulski	Y	?	N
4 ***Holt***	N	N	P
5 Hoyer	Y	Y	N
6 Byron	Y	Y	N
7 Mitchell	Y	Y	N
8 Barnes	Y	Y	N
MASSACHUSETTS			
1 ***Conte***	N	N	N
2 Boland	Y	Y	N
3 Early	Y	Y	N
4 Frank	Y	Y	N
5 Atkins	Y	Y	N
6 Mavroules	Y	Y	N
7 Markey	Y	Y	N
8 O'Neill			
9 Moakley	Y	Y	N
10 Studds	Y	Y	N
11 Donnelly	Y	Y	N
MICHIGAN			
1 Conyers	Y	Y	N
2 ***Pursell***	N	N	N
3 Wolpe	Y	Y	N
4 ***Siljander***	N	N	P
5 ***Henry***	N	N	N
6 Carr	Y	Y	N
7 Kildee	Y	Y	N
8 Traxler	Y	Y	N
9 ***Vander Jagt***	N	N	P
10 ***Schuette***	N	N	N
11 ***Davis***	N	N	N
12 Bonior	Y	Y	N
13 Crockett	Y	Y	N
14 Hertel	Y	Y	N
15 Ford	Y	Y	N
16 Dingell	Y	Y	N
17 Levin	Y	Y	N
18 ***Broomfield***	N	N	P
MINNESOTA			
1 Penny	Y	Y	N
2 ***Weber***	N	N	N
3 ***Frenzel***	N	N	X
4 Vento	Y	Y	N
5 Sabo	Y	Y	N
6 Sikorski	Y	Y	N
7 ***Stangeland***	N	N	P
8 Oberstar	Y	Y	N
MISSISSIPPI			
1 Whitten	Y	Y	N
2 ***Franklin***	N	N	N
3 Montgomery	Y	Y	N
4 Dowdy	Y	Y	N
5 ***Lott***	N	N	P
MISSOURI			
1 Clay	Y	Y	N
2 Young	Y	Y	N
3 Gephardt	Y	Y	?
4 Skelton	Y	Y	N
5 Wheat	Y	Y	N
6 ***Coleman***	N	N	P
7 ***Taylor***	X	X	?
8 ***Emerson***	N	N	N
9 Volkmer	Y	Y	N
MONTANA			
1 Williams	Y	Y	N
2 ***Marlenee***	N	N	P
NEBRASKA			
1 ***Bereuter***	N	N	N
2 ***Daub***	N	N	N
3 ***Smith***	N	N	N
NEVADA			
1 Reid	Y	Y	N
2 ***Vucanovich***	N	N	P
NEW HAMPSHIRE			
1 ***Smith***	N	N	N
2 ***Gregg***	N	N	N
NEW JERSEY			
1 Florio	Y	Y	N
2 Hughes	Y	Y	N
3 Howard	Y	Y	N
4 ***Smith***	N	N	N
5 ***Roukema***	N	N	N
6 Dwyer	Y	Y	N
7 ***Rinaldo***	N	N	N
8 Roe	Y	Y	N
9 Torricelli	Y	Y	N
10 Rodino	Y	Y	N
11 ***Gallo***	N	N	P
12 ***Courter***	N	N	N
13 ***Saxton***	N	N	P
14 Guarini	Y	Y	N
NEW MEXICO			
1 ***Lujan***	N	N	Y
2 ***Skeen***	N	N	P
3 Richardson	Y	Y	N
NEW YORK			
1 ***Carney***	N	N	N
2 Downey	Y	Y	N
3 Mrazek	Y	Y	N
4 ***Lent***	N	N	N
5 ***McGrath***	N	N	N
6 Addabbo	?	?	?
7 Ackerman	Y	Y	N
8 Scheuer	Y	Y	N
9 Manton	Y	Y	N
10 Schumer	?	?	N
11 Towns	?	Y	N
12 Owens	Y	Y	N
13 Solarz	Y	Y	N
14 ***Molinari***	N	N	P
15 ***Green***	N	N	N
16 Rangel	Y	Y	N
17 Weiss	Y	Y	N
18 Garcia	Y	Y	N
19 Biaggi	Y	Y	N
20 ***DioGuardi***	N	N	N
21 ***Fish***	N	N	P
22 ***Gilman***	N	N	N
23 Stratton	Y	Y	N
24 ***Solomon***	N	N	N
25 ***Boehlert***	N	N	N
26 ***Martin***	?	?	?
27 ***Wortley***	N	N	N
28 McHugh	Y	Y	N
29 ***Horton***	N	N	N
30 ***Eckert***	Y	Y	N
31 ***Kemp***	N	?	P
32 LaFalce	Y	Y	N
33 Nowak	Y	Y	N
34 Lundine	Y	Y	N
NORTH CAROLINA			
1 Jones	Y	Y	N
2 Valentine	Y	Y	N
3 Whitley	Y	Y	N
4 ***Cobey***	N	N	N
5 Neal	Y	Y	N
6 ***Coble***	N	N	N
7 Rose	Y	Y	N
8 Hefner	Y	Y	N
9 ***McMillan***	N	N	P
10 ***Broyhill***	N	N	P
11 ***Hendon***	N	N	N
NORTH DAKOTA			
AL Dorgan	Y	Y	N
OHIO			
1 Luken	Y	Y	N
2 ***Gradison***	N	N	P
3 Hall	Y	Y	N
4 ***Oxley***	N	N	Y
5 ***Latta***	N	?	P
6 ***McEwen***	N	N	P
7 ***DeWine***	N	N	P
8 ***Kindness***	?	?	?
9 Kaptur	Y	Y	N
10 ***Miller***	N	N	P
11 Eckart	Y	Y	N
12 ***Kasich***	N	N	N
13 Pease	Y	Y	N
14 Seiberling	Y	Y	N
15 ***Wylie***	?	?	?
16 ***Regula***	N	N	N
17 Traficant	Y	Y	N
18 Applegate	Y	Y	N
19 Feighan	Y	Y	N
20 Oakar	Y	Y	N
21 Stokes	Y	Y	N
OKLAHOMA			
1 Jones	Y	Y	N
2 Synar	Y	Y	N
3 Watkins	Y	Y	N
4 McCurdy	Y	Y	N
5 ***Edwards***	N	N	P
6 English	Y	Y	N
OREGON			
1 AuCoin	Y	Y	N
2 ***Smith, R.***	N	N	N
3 Wyden	Y	Y	N
4 Weaver	?	?	?
5 ***Smith, D.***	?	?	?
PENNSYLVANIA			
1 Foglietta	Y	Y	N
2 Gray	Y	Y	N
3 Borski	Y	Y	N
4 Kolter	Y	Y	N
5 ***Schulze***	N	N	N
6 Yatron	Y	Y	N
7 Edgar	?	?	?
8 Kostmayer	Y	Y	N
9 ***Shuster***	N	N	?
10 ***McDade***	N	N	N
11 Kanjorski	Y	Y	N
12 Murtha	Y	Y	N
13 ***Coughlin***	N	N	?
14 Coyne	Y	Y	N
15 ***Ritter***	N	N	N
16 ***Walker***	N	N	P
17 ***Gekas***	N	N	P
18 Walgren	Y	Y	N
19 ***Goodling***	N	N	P
20 Gaydos	Y	?	N
21 ***Ridge***	N	N	N
22 Murphy	Y	Y	N
23 ***Clinger***	N	N	N
RHODE ISLAND			
1 St Germain	Y	Y	N
2 ***Schneider***	N	N	N
SOUTH CAROLINA			
1 ***Hartnett***	N	N	?
2 ***Spence***	N	N	N
3 Derrick	Y	Y	N
4 ***Campbell***	X	X	?
5 Spratt	Y	Y	N
6 Tallon	Y	Y	N
SOUTH DAKOTA			
AL Daschle	Y	Y	N
TENNESSEE			
1 ***Quillen***	N	N	Y
2 ***Duncan***	N	N	P
3 Lloyd	Y	Y	N
4 Cooper	Y	Y	N
5 Boner	Y	Y	N
6 Gordon	Y	Y	N
7 ***Sundquist***	N	N	P
8 Jones	Y	Y	N
9 Ford	Y	Y	N
TEXAS			
1 Chapman	Y	Y	N
2 Wilson	?	Y	N
3 ***Bartlett***	N	N	Y
4 Hall, R.	Y	N	N
5 Bryant	Y	Y	N
6 ***Barton***	N	N	Y
7 ***Archer***	N	N	P
8 ***Fields***	N	N	P
9 Brooks	Y	Y	N
10 Pickle	Y	Y	N
11 Leath	Y	Y	N
12 Wright	Y	Y	N
13 ***Boulter***	N	N	N
14 ***Sweeney***	N	N	N
15 de la Garza	Y	Y	N
16 Coleman	Y	Y	N
17 Stenholm	Y	Y	N
18 Leland	Y	Y	N
19 ***Combest***	N	N	N
20 Gonzalez	Y	Y	N
21 ***Loeffler***	?	?	?
22 ***DeLay***	N	N	P
23 Bustamante	Y	Y	?
24 Frost	Y	Y	N
25 Andrews	Y	Y	N
26 ***Armey***	N	N	Y
27 Ortiz	Y	Y	?
UTAH			
1 ***Hansen***	N	N	Y
2 ***Monson***	N	N	P
3 ***Nielson***	N	N	P
VERMONT			
AL ***Jeffords***	N	N	N
VIRGINIA			
1 ***Bateman***	N	N	P
2 ***Whitehurst***	N	N	?
3 ***Bliley***	N	N	P
4 Sisisky	Y	Y	N
5 Daniel	Y	Y	N
6 Olin	Y	Y	N
7 ***Slaughter***	N	N	P
8 ***Parris***	N	N	N
9 Boucher	Y	Y	N
10 ***Wolf***	N	N	N
WASHINGTON			
1 ***Miller***	N	N	N
2 Swift	Y	Y	N
3 Bonker	Y	Y	N
4 ***Morrison***	N	N	N
5 Foley	Y	Y	N
6 Dicks	Y	Y	N
7 Lowry	Y	Y	N
8 ***Chandler***	N	N	P
WEST VIRGINIA			
1 Mollohan	Y	Y	N
2 Staggers	Y	Y	N
3 Wise	Y	Y	N
4 Rahall	Y	Y	N
WISCONSIN			
1 Aspin	Y	Y	N
2 Kastenmeier	Y	Y	N
3 ***Gunderson***	N	N	P
4 Kleczka	Y	Y	N
5 Moody	Y	Y	N
6 ***Petri***	N	N	N
7 Obey	Y	Y	N
8 ***Roth***	N	N	P
9 ***Sensenbrenner***	N	N	N
WYOMING			
AL ***Cheney***	N	N	P

Southern states - Ala., Ark., Fla., Ga., Ky., La., Miss., N.C., Okla., S.C., Tenn., Texas, Va.

* The *Congressional Record* vote number is different from the CQ vote number because the *Record* includes quorum calls in its tally. CQ does not publish quorum call votes.

49. Procedural Motion. Lagomarsino, R-Calif., motion to approve the House *Journal* of Monday, March 17. Motion agreed to 268-113: R 58-105; D 210-8 (ND 140-7, SD 70-1), March 18, 1986.

50. HR 3128. Omnibus Budget Reconciliation, Fiscal 1986. Gray, D-Pa., motion to table (kill) the Martin, R-Ill., motion to concur in the Senate amendment making changes in the bill to reduce fiscal 1986 deficits. Motion agreed to 217-192: R 1-171; D 216-21 (ND 156-3, SD 60-18), March 18, 1986. (The Senate amendment was an amendment to the House amendment to the Senate amendment to the House amendment to the Senate amendment to the bill. The original Senate amendment was the conference agreement on the bill.) A "nay" was a vote supporting the president's position.

51. HR 3128. Omnibus Budget Reconciliation, Fiscal 1986. Gray, D-Pa., motion to table (kill) the Lott, R-Miss., motion to disagree to the Senate amendment *(see vote 50, above)* making changes in the deficit-reduction bill and request a conference thereon. Motion agreed to 223-186: R 0-172; D 223-14 (ND 158-1, SD 65-13), March 18, 1986.

52. HR 3128. Omnibus Budget Reconciliation, Fiscal 1986. Gray, D-Pa., motion to disagree to the Senate amendment *(see vote 50, above)* making changes in the deficit-reduction bill. Motion agreed to 331-76: R 97-74; D 234-2 (ND 156-2, SD 78-0), March 18, 1986.

53. HR 4151. Diplomatic Security. Walker, R-Pa., amendment to require Congress to authorize and appropriate funds on a regular basis for cash compensation to U.S. hostages rather than create an automatic entitlement to such funds. Rejected 144-252: R 110-57; D 34-195 (ND 20-133, SD 14-62), March 18, 1986.

54. HR 4151. Diplomatic Security. Passage of the bill to authorize $4.4 billion to bolster security at U.S. diplomatic missions and adopt other provisions aimed at combating international terrorism. Passed 389-7: R 163-4; D 226-3 (ND 151-3, SD 75-0), March 18, 1986. A "yea" was a vote supporting the president's position.

55. HR 2453. Older Americans Act. Adoption of the conference report on the bill to increase the amounts authorized for senior citizen nutrition programs from $120.8 million in fiscal 1985, $125.9 million in 1986 and $132 million in 1987 to $127.8 million in 1985 and $144 million in each of fiscal years 1986 and 1987. Adopted (thus cleared for the president) 344-0: R 137-0; D 207-0 (ND 136-0, SD 71-0), March 18, 1986.

56. Procedural Motion. Dreier, R-Calif., motion to approve the House *Journal* of Tuesday, March 18. Motion agreed to 265-119: R 57-112; D 208-7 (ND 138-5, SD 70-2), March 19, 1986.

KEY

Y Voted for (yea).
Paired for.
+ Announced for.
N Voted against (nay).
X Paired against.
- Announced against.
P Voted "present."
C Voted "present" to avoid possible conflict of interest.
? Did not vote or otherwise make a position known.

Democrats *Republicans*

	49	50	51	52	53	54	55	56
ALABAMA								
1 ***Callahan***	Y	N	N	Y	N	Y	Y	Y
2 ***Dickinson***	N	N	N	N	N	Y	Y	N
3 Nichols	Y	Y	Y	Y	N	Y	Y	Y
4 Bevill	Y	Y	Y	Y	N	Y	Y	Y
5 Flippo	Y	Y	Y	Y	?	?	?	Y
6 Erdreich	Y	N	Y	Y	N	Y	Y	Y
7 Shelby	Y	Y	Y	Y	N	Y	Y	Y
ALASKA								
AL ***Young***	N	N	N	Y	N	Y	Y	N
ARIZONA								
1 ***McCain***	Y	N	N	Y	Y	Y	Y	Y
2 Udall	Y	Y	Y	Y	N	Y	?	Y
3 ***Stump***	Y	N	N	N	Y	Y	Y	Y
4 ***Rudd***	Y	N	N	N	Y	Y	Y	Y
5 ***Kolbe***	N	N	N	Y	Y	Y	Y	N
ARKANSAS								
1 Alexander	Y	Y	Y	Y	?	?	?	Y
2 Robinson	Y	Y	Y	Y	N	Y	Y	Y
3 ***Hammerschmidt***	Y	N	N	Y	N	Y	Y	N
4 Anthony	Y	Y	Y	Y	?	?	Y	?
CALIFORNIA								
1 Bosco	Y	Y	Y	Y	N	Y	Y	Y
2 ***Chappie***	N	N	N	N	Y	Y	?	N
3 Matsui	Y	Y	Y	Y	N	Y	Y	Y
4 Fazio	Y	Y	Y	Y	Y	Y	Y	Y
5 Burton	Y	Y	Y	Y	N	Y	Y	Y
6 Boxer	Y	Y	Y	Y	N	Y	Y	Y
7 Miller	N	Y	Y	Y	N	Y	Y	Y
8 Dellums	Y	Y	Y	Y	N	Y	Y	Y
9 Stark	Y	Y	Y	Y	N	Y	Y	Y
10 Edwards	Y	Y	Y	Y	N	Y	?	Y
11 Lantos	Y	Y	Y	Y	N	Y	Y	Y
12 ***Zschau***	?	?	?	?	?	?	?	N
13 Mineta	Y	Y	Y	Y	N	Y	Y	Y
14 ***Shumway***	Y	N	N	N	Y	Y	Y	?
15 Coelho	Y	Y	Y	Y	N	Y	Y	Y
16 Panetta	Y	Y	Y	Y	Y	Y	Y	Y
17 ***Pashayan***	Y	N	N	N	?	?	?	N
18 Lehman	?	?	?	?	?	?	?	?
19 ***Lagomarsino***	N	N	N	N	N	Y	Y	N
20 ***Thomas***	N	N	N	N	N	Y	Y	N
21 ***Fiedler***	N	N	N	N	N	Y	Y	N
22 ***Moorhead***	N	N	N	N	Y	Y	Y	N
23 Beilenson	?	Y	Y	Y	N	Y	Y	Y
24 Waxman	Y	Y	Y	Y	N	Y	Y	Y
25 Roybal	Y	Y	Y	Y	N	Y	Y	Y
26 Berman	Y	Y	Y	Y	N	Y	Y	Y
27 Levine	Y	Y	Y	Y	N	Y	Y	Y
28 Dixon	Y	Y	Y	Y	N	Y	Y	Y
29 Hawkins	N	Y	Y	Y	N	Y	Y	Y
30 Martinez	Y	Y	Y	Y	N	Y	Y	Y
31 Dymally	Y	Y	Y	Y	N	Y	Y	Y
32 Anderson	Y	Y	Y	Y	N	Y	Y	Y
33 ***Dreier***	N	N	N	N	Y	Y	Y	N
34 Torres	Y	Y	Y	Y	N	Y	Y	Y
35 ***Lewis***	N	N	N	N	Y	Y	?	N
36 Brown	Y	Y	Y	Y	N	Y	Y	Y
37 ***McCandless***	N	N	N	N	Y	Y	Y	N
38 ***Dornan***	?	N	N	N	N	Y	Y	N
39 ***Dannemeyer***	N	N	N	N	Y	N	Y	N
40 ***Badham***	N	N	N	N	Y	Y	Y	Y
41 ***Lowery***	N	N	N	N	Y	Y	Y	?
42 ***Lungren***	N	N	N	N	N	Y	?	N
43 ***Packard***	Y	N	N	Y	Y	Y	Y	Y
44 Bates	Y	Y	Y	Y	N	Y	Y	Y
45 ***Hunter***	N	N	N	N	Y	Y	Y	N
COLORADO								
1 Schroeder	N	Y	Y	Y	N	Y	Y	N
2 Wirth	Y	Y	Y	Y	N	Y	Y	Y
3 ***Strang***	N	N	N	N	Y	Y	Y	N
4 ***Brown***	N	N	N	N	Y	N	Y	N
5 ***Kramer***	N	Y	N	Y	Y	Y	Y	N
6 ***Schaefer***	N	N	N	N	Y	Y	Y	N
CONNECTICUT								
1 Kennelly	Y	Y	Y	Y	N	Y	Y	?
2 Gejdenson	Y	Y	Y	Y	N	Y	Y	Y
3 Morrison	Y	Y	Y	Y	N	Y	Y	Y
4 ***McKinney***	Y	N	N	Y	N	Y	?	Y
5 ***Rowland***	Y	N	N	Y	N	Y	Y	Y
6 ***Johnson***	Y	N	N	Y	N	Y	Y	Y
DELAWARE								
AL Carper	Y	Y	Y	Y	N	Y	Y	?
FLORIDA								
1 Hutto	Y	Y	N	Y	N	Y	Y	Y
2 Fuqua	Y	Y	Y	Y	N	Y	Y	Y
3 Bennett	Y	Y	Y	Y	N	Y	Y	Y
4 Chappell	Y	Y	Y	Y	N	Y	?	Y
5 ***McCollum***	N	N	N	N	Y	Y	Y	Y
6 MacKay	Y	Y	Y	Y	N	Y	Y	Y
7 Gibbons	Y	Y	Y	Y	N	Y	Y	Y
8 ***Young***	N	N	N	Y	Y	Y	Y	N
9 ***Bilirakis***	N	N	N	N	Y	Y	Y	N
10 ***Ireland***	N	N	N	N	Y	Y	Y	N
11 Nelson	Y	Y	Y	Y	N	Y	Y	Y
12 ***Lewis***	N	N	N	N	Y	Y	Y	N
13 ***Mack***	N	N	N	N	Y	Y	Y	N
14 Mica	Y	Y	Y	Y	N	Y	Y	Y
15 ***Shaw***	N	N	N	N	Y	Y	Y	N
16 Smith	Y	Y	Y	Y	N	Y	Y	Y
17 Lehman	Y	Y	Y	Y	N	Y	Y	Y
18 Pepper	Y	Y	Y	Y	N	Y	+	+
19 Fascell	?	Y	Y	Y	N	Y	Y	Y
GEORGIA								
1 Thomas	Y	N	N	Y	N	Y	Y	Y
2 Hatcher	Y	N	N	Y	N	Y	Y	Y
3 Ray	Y	Y	Y	Y	N	Y	Y	Y
4 ***Swindall***	N	N	N	N	Y	Y	Y	N
5 Fowler	?	?	?	Y	N	Y	Y	Y
6 ***Gingrich***	N	N	N	N	?	?	?	?
7 Darden	Y	N	N	Y	N	Y	Y	Y
8 Rowland	Y	N	N	Y	N	Y	Y	Y
9 Jenkins	Y	N	Y	Y	Y	Y	Y	Y
10 Barnard	Y	Y	N	Y	Y	Y	Y	Y
HAWAII								
1 Heftel	Y	Y	Y	Y	N	Y	Y	?
2 Akaka	Y	Y	Y	Y	N	Y	Y	Y
IDAHO								
1 ***Craig***	N	N	N	N	N	Y	Y	N
2 Stallings	Y	Y	Y	Y	N	Y	Y	Y
ILLINOIS								
1 ***Hayes***	?	?	?	?	?	?	?	?
2 Savage	?	?	?	?	?	?	?	?
3 Russo	Y	Y	Y	Y	Y	Y	Y	Y
4 ***O'Brien***	Y	N	N	Y	?	?	?	?
5 Lipinski	?	?	?	?	?	?	?	?
6 ***Hyde***	Y	N	N	N	N	Y	Y	Y
7 Collins	?	?	?	?	?	?	?	?
8 Rostenkowski	?	?	?	?	?	?	?	?
9 Yates	Y	Y	Y	N	N	Y	Y	Y
10 ***Porter***	?	-	-	-	?	+	?	?
11 Annunzio	?	?	?	?	X	Y	Y	Y
12 ***Crane***	N	N	N	Y	N	Y	Y	N
13 ***Fawell***	N	N	N	N	Y	Y	Y	N
14 ***Grotberg***	?	?	?	?	?	?	?	?
15 ***Madigan***	?	?	?	?	?	?	?	?
16 ***Martin***	?	N	N	N	Y	Y	Y	N
17 Evans	Y	Y	Y	Y	N	Y	Y	Y
18 ***Michel***	N	N	N	N	Y	?	?	N
19 Bruce	Y	Y	Y	Y	N	Y	Y	Y
20 Durbin	N	Y	Y	Y	N	Y	Y	Y
21 Price	Y	Y	Y	Y	N	Y	Y	Y
22 Gray	Y	Y	Y	Y	N	Y	Y	Y
INDIANA								
1 Visclosky	Y	Y	Y	Y	N	Y	Y	Y
2 Sharp	Y	Y	Y	Y	N	Y	Y	Y
3 ***Hiler***	Y	N	N	N	N	Y	Y	N
4 ***Coats***	Y	N	N	Y	Y	Y	?	Y
5 ***Hillis***	Y	N	N	Y	Y	Y	Y	Y

ND - Northern Democrats SD - Southern Democrats

	49	50	51	52	53	54	55	56
6 ***Burton***	N	N	N	N	Y	Y	Y	N
7 ***Myers***	Y	N	N	Y	Y	Y	Y	Y
8 McCloskey	Y	Y	Y	Y	?	Y	?	Y
9 Hamilton	Y	Y	Y	Y	N	Y	Y	Y
10 Jacobs	N	Y	Y	Y	N	Y	?	N
IOWA								
1 ***Leach***	N	N	N	Y	N	Y	Y	N
2 ***Tauke***	?	N	N	Y	N	Y	Y	N
3 ***Evans***	N	N	N	Y	N	Y	Y	N
4 Smith	Y	Y	Y	N	N	Y	Y	Y
5 ***Lightfoot***	N	N	N	Y	Y	Y	Y	N
6 Bedell	Y	Y	Y	Y	N	Y	Y	Y
KANSAS								
1 ***Roberts***	N	N	N	Y	Y	Y	?	N
2 Slattery	Y	Y	Y	Y	Y	Y	Y	Y
3 ***Meyers***	Y	N	N	N	Y	Y	Y	N
4 Glickman	Y	Y	Y	Y	Y	Y	Y	Y
5 ***Whittaker***	N	N	N	Y	Y	Y	Y	N
KENTUCKY								
1 Hubbard	Y	N	N	Y	Y	Y	?	?
2 Natcher	Y	N	N	Y	N	Y	Y	Y
3 Mazzoli	Y	Y	Y	Y	-	+	+	Y
4 ***Snyder***	?	N	N	Y	N	Y	Y	Y
5 ***Rogers***	N	N	N	Y	Y	Y	Y	N
6 ***Hopkins***	N	N	N	Y	Y	Y	Y	Y
7 Perkins	Y	N	N	Y	N	Y	Y	Y
LOUISIANA								
1 ***Livingston***	Y	N	N	Y	Y	Y	Y	Y
2 Boggs	Y	Y	Y	Y	N	Y	Y	Y
3 Tauzin	Y	Y	Y	Y	Y	Y	Y	Y
4 Roemer	N	Y	Y	Y	Y	Y	Y	N
5 Huckaby	Y	Y	Y	Y	Y	Y	Y	Y
6 ***Moore***	Y	N	N	Y	Y	Y	Y	Y
7 Breaux	?	Y	Y	Y	Y	?	Y	Y
8 Long	Y	Y	Y	Y	N	Y	Y	Y
MAINE								
1 ***McKernan***	N	N	N	Y	N	Y	Y	N
2 ***Snowe***	Y	N	N	Y	N	Y	Y	N
MARYLAND								
1 Dyson	Y	Y	Y	Y	N	Y	Y	Y
2 ***Bentley***	N	N	N	Y	Y	Y	Y	N
3 Mikulski	Y	Y	Y	Y	N	Y	Y	?
4 ***Holt***	N	?	?	?	Y	Y	Y	P
5 Hoyer	Y	Y	Y	Y	N	Y	?	Y
6 Byron	Y	Y	Y	Y	?	Y	?	Y
7 Mitchell	Y	Y	Y	Y	N	Y	Y	N
8 Barnes	Y	Y	Y	Y	N	Y	Y	?
MASSACHUSETTS								
1 ***Conte***	N	N	N	Y	N	Y	Y	N
2 Boland	Y	Y	Y	Y	Y	Y	Y	Y
3 Early	Y	Y	Y	Y	Y	Y	Y	Y
4 Frank	Y	Y	Y	Y	N	Y	?	Y
5 Atkins	Y	Y	Y	Y	N	Y	Y	?
6 Mavroules	Y	Y	Y	Y	N	Y	?	Y
7 Markey	Y	Y	Y	Y	N	Y	Y	Y
8 O'Neill								
9 Moakley	Y	Y	Y	Y	N	Y	Y	Y
10 Studds	Y	Y	Y	Y	N	Y	Y	Y
11 Donnelly	Y	Y	Y	Y	N	Y	Y	Y
MICHIGAN								
1 Conyers	Y	Y	Y	Y	N	N	Y	Y
2 ***Pursell***	Y	N	N	Y	Y	Y	?	Y
3 Wolpe	Y	Y	Y	Y	Y	Y	Y	Y
4 ***Siljander***	?	N	N	N	N	Y	?	N
5 ***Henry***	N	N	N	Y	Y	Y	Y	N
6 Carr	?	Y	Y	Y	Y	Y	Y	Y
7 Kildee	Y	Y	Y	Y	N	Y	Y	Y
8 Traxler	Y	N	Y	Y	Y	Y	Y	Y
9 ***Vander Jagt***	N	N	N	N	Y	Y	?	?
10 ***Schuette***	N	N	N	Y	N	Y	Y	N
11 ***Davis***	N	N	N	Y	N	Y	?	Y
12 Bonior	Y	Y	Y	Y	N	Y	Y	Y
13 Crockett	Y	Y	Y	Y	N	Y	?	Y
14 Hertel	Y	Y	Y	Y	N	Y	Y	Y
15 Ford	?	Y	Y	Y	N	Y	Y	?
16 Dingell	?	Y	Y	Y	N	Y	Y	?
17 Levin	Y	Y	Y	Y	N	Y	Y	Y
18 ***Broomfield***	Y	N	N	N	N	Y	?	Y
MINNESOTA								
1 Penny	N	Y	Y	Y	N	Y	Y	N
2 ***Weber***	?	N	N	Y	Y	Y	Y	N
3 ***Frenzel***	N	N	N	N	Y	Y	Y	N
4 Vento	Y	Y	Y	Y	N	Y	Y	Y
5 Sabo	Y	Y	Y	Y	N	Y	Y	Y
6 Sikorski	N	Y	Y	Y	N	Y	Y	N

	49	50	51	52	53	54	55	56
7 ***Stangeland***	N	N	N	N	N	Y	Y	N
8 Oberstar	Y	Y	Y	Y	N	Y	Y	Y
MISSISSIPPI								
1 Whitten	Y	N	Y	Y	N	Y	Y	Y
2 ***Franklin***	Y	N	N	N	?	?	?	?
3 Montgomery	Y	N	N	Y	Y	Y	Y	Y
4 Dowdy	?	Y	Y	Y	N	Y	Y	Y
5 ***Lott***	Y	N	N	N	Y	Y	Y	N
MISSOURI								
1 Clay	?	?	?	?	?	?	?	?
2 Young	?	Y	Y	Y	N	Y	Y	Y
3 Gephardt	?	?	?	?	?	?	?	Y
4 Skelton	?	Y	Y	Y	N	Y	Y	Y
5 Wheat	Y	Y	Y	Y	N	Y	Y	Y
6 ***Coleman***	N	N	N	Y	N	Y	Y	N
7 ***Taylor***	Y	N	N	Y	Y	Y	Y	N
8 ***Emerson***	N	N	N	Y	N	Y	Y	N
9 Volkmer	Y	Y	Y	Y	N	Y	Y	Y
MONTANA								
1 Williams	?	Y	Y	Y	?	?	?	?
2 ***Marlenee***	N	N	N	N	Y	N	Y	Y
NEBRASKA								
1 ***Bereuter***	N	N	N	Y	N	Y	+	N
2 ***Daub***	N	N	N	Y	Y	Y	Y	N
3 ***Smith***	Y	N	N	Y	Y	Y	?	Y
NEVADA								
1 Reid	Y	Y	Y	Y	N	Y	Y	Y
2 ***Vucanovich***	N	N	N	N	Y	Y	?	N
NEW HAMPSHIRE								
1 ***Smith***	N	N	N	N	Y	Y	Y	N
2 ***Gregg***	N	N	N	N	N	Y	Y	N
NEW JERSEY								
1 Florio	Y	Y	Y	Y	Y	Y	?	Y
2 Hughes	Y	Y	Y	Y	Y	Y	Y	Y
3 Howard	Y	Y	Y	Y	N	Y	Y	Y
4 ***Smith***	Y	N	N	Y	N	Y	Y	Y
5 ***Roukema***	N	N	N	Y	N	Y	Y	N
6 Dwyer	Y	Y	Y	Y	N	Y	Y	Y
7 ***Rinaldo***	Y	N	N	Y	N	Y	Y	Y
8 Roe	Y	Y	Y	Y	N	Y	Y	Y
9 Torricelli	Y	Y	Y	Y	N	Y	Y	Y
10 Rodino	Y	Y	Y	Y	N	Y	Y	Y
11 ***Gallo***	N	N	N	Y	N	Y	Y	N
12 ***Courter***	N	N	N	Y	?	?	?	N
13 ***Saxton***	Y	N	N	Y	N	Y	Y	N
14 Guarini	Y	Y	Y	Y	N	Y	Y	Y
NEW MEXICO								
1 ***Lujan***	Y	N	N	Y	Y	Y	Y	Y
2 ***Skeen***	N	N	N	Y	Y	Y	Y	N
3 Richardson	Y	Y	Y	Y	N	Y	Y	Y
NEW YORK								
1 ***Carney***	N	N	N	N	Y	Y	Y	N
2 Downey	Y	Y	Y	Y	N	Y	Y	Y
3 Mrazek	Y	Y	Y	Y	N	?	Y	Y
4 ***Lent***	N	N	N	Y	Y	Y	Y	N
5 ***McGrath***	N	N	N	Y	Y	Y	Y	N
6 Addabbo	?	?	?	?	?	?	?	?
7 Ackerman	Y	Y	Y	Y	N	Y	Y	Y
8 Scheuer	Y	Y	Y	Y	N	Y	?	?
9 Manton	Y	Y	Y	Y	N	Y	?	Y
10 Schumer	Y	Y	Y	Y	N	Y	Y	Y
11 Towns	Y	Y	Y	Y	N	Y	?	Y
12 Owens	Y	Y	Y	Y	N	?	?	?
13 Solarz	Y	Y	Y	Y	?	?	?	?
14 ***Molinari***	N	N	N	Y	Y	Y	?	Y
15 ***Green***	Y	N	N	Y	Y	Y	?	Y
16 Rangel	Y	Y	Y	Y	N	Y	?	Y
17 Weiss	Y	Y	Y	Y	-	+	+	Y
18 Garcia	Y	Y	Y	Y	N	Y	Y	Y
19 Biaggi	Y	Y	Y	Y	N	Y	Y	Y
20 ***DioGuardi***	Y	N	N	Y	Y	Y	Y	Y
21 ***Fish***	Y	N	N	Y	?	?	?	Y
22 ***Gilman***	Y	N	N	Y	N	Y	Y	Y
23 Stratton	Y	Y	Y	Y	Y	Y	Y	Y
24 ***Solomon***	N	N	N	N	Y	Y	Y	N
25 ***Boehlert***	N	N	N	Y	N	Y	Y	N
26 ***Martin***	N	N	N	Y	N	Y	Y	N
27 ***Wortley***	Y	N	N	N	Y	Y	?	Y
28 McHugh	Y	Y	Y	Y	N	Y	Y	Y
29 ***Horton***	Y	N	N	Y	N	Y	Y	Y
30 ***Eckert***	Y	N	N	N	Y	Y	Y	Y
31 ***Kemp***	Y	N	N	N	Y	Y	Y	Y
32 LaFalce	Y	Y	Y	Y	Y	Y	Y	Y
33 Nowak	Y	Y	Y	Y	N	Y	Y	Y
34 Lundine	Y	Y	Y	Y	N	Y	Y	Y

	49	50	51	52	53	54	55	56
NORTH CAROLINA								
1 Jones	Y	N	Y	Y	N	Y	?	Y
2 Valentine	Y	Y	Y	Y	N	Y	Y	Y
3 Whitley	Y	Y	Y	Y	N	Y	Y	Y
4 ***Cobey***	N	N	N	Y	Y	Y	Y	N
5 Neal	Y	Y	Y	Y	N	Y	Y	Y
6 ***Coble***	N	N	N	Y	Y	Y	Y	N
7 Rose	Y	Y	Y	Y	N	Y	Y	Y
8 Hefner	Y	Y	Y	Y	N	Y	Y	P
9 ***McMillan***	Y	N	N	Y	N	Y	?	N
10 ***Broyhill***	Y	N	N	Y	Y	Y	Y	Y
11 ***Hendon***	N	N	N	Y	N	Y	Y	N
NORTH DAKOTA								
AL Dorgan	Y	Y	Y	Y	N	Y	Y	Y
OHIO								
1 Luken	Y	Y	Y	Y	N	Y	Y	Y
2 ***Gradison***	Y	N	N	N	N	Y	Y	Y
3 Hall	Y	Y	Y	Y	N	Y	Y	Y
4 ***Oxley***	?	?	?	?	#	?	?	N
5 ***Latta***	?	?	?	?	Y	Y	Y	N
6 ***McEwen***	Y	N	N	?	Y	Y	Y	Y
7 ***DeWine***	N	N	N	N	N	Y	Y	N
8 ***Kindness***	?	?	?	?	?	?	?	N
9 Kaptur	Y	Y	Y	Y	N	Y	Y	?
10 ***Miller***	N	N	N	N	Y	Y	Y	N
11 Eckart	Y	Y	Y	Y	N	Y	Y	Y
12 ***Kasich***	?	N	N	Y	N	Y	Y	Y
13 Pease	Y	N	Y	Y	N	Y	Y	Y
14 Seiberling	?	Y	Y	Y	N	Y	Y	Y
15 ***Wylie***	?	N	N	Y	Y	Y	Y	Y
16 ***Regula***	Y	N	N	Y	Y	Y	Y	Y
17 Traficant	Y	Y	Y	Y	N	Y	Y	Y
18 Applegate	Y	Y	Y	Y	Y	Y	Y	Y
19 Feighan	?	Y	Y	Y	N	Y	Y	?
20 Oakar	Y	Y	Y	Y	N	Y	Y	Y
21 Stokes	Y	Y	Y	Y	N	Y	Y	Y
OKLAHOMA								
1 Jones	Y	Y	Y	Y	Y	Y	Y	Y
2 Synar	?	?	?	?	?	?	?	Y
3 Watkins	Y	Y	Y	Y	N	Y	Y	Y
4 McCurdy	Y	Y	Y	Y	N	Y	Y	Y
5 ***Edwards***	N	N	N	N	?	Y	Y	N
6 English	Y	Y	N	Y	Y	Y	Y	Y
OREGON								
1 AuCoin	Y	Y	Y	Y	Y	Y	?	Y
2 ***Smith, R.***	N	N	N	Y	Y	Y	Y	N
3 Wyden	Y	N	N	Y	N	Y	Y	Y
4 Weaver	?	Y	Y	Y	Y	Y	Y	Y
5 ***Smith, D.***	?	?	?	?	Y	Y	Y	N
PENNSYLVANIA								
1 Foglietta	?	Y	Y	Y	N	Y	Y	Y
2 Gray	Y	Y	Y	Y	N	Y	Y	Y
3 Borski	Y	Y	Y	Y	N	Y	Y	Y
4 Kolter	Y	Y	Y	Y	Y	N	Y	Y
5 ***Schulze***	Y	N	N	N	Y	Y	Y	Y
6 Yatron	Y	Y	Y	Y	N	Y	Y	Y
7 Edgar	?	?	?	?	?	?	?	?
8 Kostmayer	Y	Y	Y	Y	N	Y	Y	Y
9 ***Shuster***	N	N	N	N	Y	Y	Y	N
10 ***McDade***	Y	N	N	Y	Y	Y	?	Y
11 Kanjorski	Y	Y	Y	Y	N	Y	Y	Y
12 Murtha	Y	Y	Y	Y	N	Y	?	Y
13 ***Coughlin***	N	N	N	N	Y	Y	Y	?
14 Coyne	Y	Y	Y	Y	N	Y	Y	Y
15 ***Ritter***	Y	N	N	Y	N	Y	Y	Y
16 ***Walker***	N	N	N	N	Y	Y	Y	N
17 ***Gekas***	N	N	N	N	Y	Y	Y	N
18 Walgren	Y	Y	Y	+	-	+	+	Y
19 ***Goodling***	N	N	N	Y	Y	Y	?	N
20 Gaydos	Y	Y	Y	Y	Y	N	Y	?
21 ***Ridge***	N	N	N	Y	Y	Y	Y	Y
22 Murphy	Y	Y	Y	Y	N	Y	Y	Y
23 ***Clinger***	Y	N	N	Y	N	Y	+	Y
RHODE ISLAND								
1 St Germain	?	Y	Y	Y	N	Y	Y	Y
2 ***Schneider***	Y	N	N	Y	Y	Y	Y	Y
SOUTH CAROLINA								
1 ***Hartnett***	N	N	N	Y	Y	Y	Y	Y
2 ***Spence***	?	N	N	Y	Y	Y	Y	N
3 Derrick	Y	Y	Y	?	N	Y	Y	Y
4 ***Campbell***	?	?	?	?	?	?	?	?
5 Spratt	Y	Y	Y	Y	N	Y	Y	Y
6 Tallon	?	?	?	?	N	Y	Y	Y
SOUTH DAKOTA								
AL Daschle	Y	Y	Y	Y	N	Y	Y	Y

	49	50	51	52	53	54	55	56
TENNESSEE								
1 ***Quillen***	Y	N	N	Y	N	Y	?	Y
2 ***Duncan***	Y	N	N	Y	N	Y	?	N
3 Lloyd	Y	N	N	Y	N	Y	Y	N
4 Cooper	Y	Y	Y	Y	N	Y	Y	Y
5 Boner	Y	Y	Y	Y	N	Y	Y	Y
6 Gordon	Y	Y	Y	Y	N	Y	Y	Y
7 ***Sundquist***	N	N	N	N	Y	Y	Y	N
8 Jones	Y	Y	Y	Y	N	Y	Y	Y
9 Ford	Y	Y	Y	Y	N	Y	?	Y
TEXAS								
1 Chapman	Y	Y	Y	Y	N	Y	Y	Y
2 Wilson	Y	?	?	?	?	?	?	?
3 ***Bartlett***	N	N	N	Y	Y	Y	Y	N
4 Hall, R.	Y	N	Y	Y	Y	Y	Y	Y
5 Bryant	?	Y	Y	Y	N	Y	?	Y
6 ***Barton***	N	N	N	Y	Y	Y	Y	N
7 ***Archer***	Y	N	N	Y	Y	Y	Y	Y
8 ***Fields***	N	N	N	Y	Y	Y	Y	N
9 Brooks	Y	N	Y	Y	N	Y	Y	Y
10 Pickle	?	Y	Y	Y	N	Y	Y	Y
11 Leath	Y	N	Y	Y	Y	Y	Y	?
12 Wright	?	Y	Y	Y	N	Y	Y	?
13 ***Boulter***	N	N	N	Y	Y	Y	Y	N
14 ***Sweeney***	?	N	N	Y	Y	Y	Y	Y
15 de la Garza	?	Y	Y	Y	N	Y	Y	Y
16 Coleman	Y	Y	Y	Y	N	Y	Y	Y
17 Stenholm	Y	N	Y	Y	Y	Y	Y	Y
18 Leland	?	Y	Y	Y	N	Y	Y	?
19 ***Combest***	Y	N	N	Y	Y	Y	Y	Y
20 Gonzalez	Y	Y	Y	Y	N	Y	Y	?
21 ***Loeffler***	N	N	N	Y	Y	Y	Y	?
22 ***DeLay***	N	N	N	N	Y	Y	Y	N
23 Bustamante	Y	Y	Y	Y	N	Y	Y	Y
24 Frost	Y	Y	Y	Y	N	Y	Y	?
25 Andrews	Y	Y	Y	Y	N	Y	Y	Y
26 ***Armey***	N	N	N	Y	Y	Y	Y	N
27 Ortiz	Y	Y	Y	Y	N	Y	Y	Y
UTAH								
1 ***Hansen***	N	N	N	N	Y	Y	?	N
2 ***Monson***	N	N	N	N	Y	N	?	N
3 ***Nielson***	Y	N	N	N	Y	Y	Y	N
VERMONT								
AL ***Jeffords***	Y	N	N	N	?	?	?	Y
VIRGINIA								
1 ***Bateman***	Y	N	N	N	Y	Y	Y	Y
2 ***Whitehurst***	N	N	N	Y	Y	Y	?	N
3 ***Bliley***	N	N	N	Y	N	Y	?	N
4 Sisisky	Y	Y	Y	Y	N	Y	Y	Y
5 Daniel	Y	N	N	Y	Y	Y	Y	Y
6 Olin	Y	Y	Y	Y	N	Y	Y	Y
7 ***Slaughter***	N	N	N	Y	N	Y	Y	N
8 ***Parris***	N	N	N	Y	N	Y	?	N
9 Boucher	Y	Y	Y	Y	N	Y	Y	Y
10 ***Wolf***	N	N	N	Y	N	Y	?	N
WASHINGTON								
1 ***Miller***	Y	N	N	Y	N	Y	Y	Y
2 Swift	Y	Y	Y	Y	N	Y	?	Y
3 Bonker	Y	Y	Y	Y	N	Y	Y	Y
4 ***Morrison***	N	N	N	Y	Y	Y	Y	Y
5 Foley	Y	Y	Y	Y	N	Y	Y	Y
6 Dicks	Y	Y	Y	Y	N	Y	?	Y
7 Lowry	Y	Y	Y	Y	N	Y	Y	Y
8 ***Chandler***	N	N	N	Y	Y	Y	Y	N
WEST VIRGINIA								
1 Mollohan	Y	Y	Y	Y	N	Y	Y	Y
2 Staggers	Y	Y	Y	Y	N	Y	Y	Y
3 Wise	Y	Y	Y	Y	N	Y	Y	Y
4 Rahall	Y	Y	Y	Y	N	Y	Y	Y
WISCONSIN								
1 Aspin	Y	Y	Y	Y	N	Y	Y	Y
2 Kastenmeier	Y	Y	Y	Y	N	Y	Y	Y
3 ***Gunderson***	N	N	N	N	Y	Y	Y	N
4 Kleczka	Y	Y	Y	Y	N	Y	Y	P
5 Moody	Y	Y	Y	Y	Y	Y	?	Y
6 ***Petri***	Y	N	N	N	N	Y	Y	Y
7 Obey	Y	Y	Y	Y	N	Y	Y	Y
8 ***Roth***	N	N	N	Y	Y	Y	?	N
9 ***Sensenbrenner***	N	N	N	N	Y	Y	Y	N
WYOMING								
AL ***Cheney***	N	N	N	N	N	Y	?	N

Southern states - Ala., Ark., Fla., Ga., Ky., La., Miss., N.C., Okla., S.C., Tenn., Texas, Va.

* The *Congressional Record* vote number is different from the CQ vote number because the *Record* includes quorum calls in its tally. CQ does not publish quorum call votes.

57. Procedural Motion. Vucanovich, R-Nev., motion to approve the House *Journal* of Wednesday, March 19. Motion agreed to 293-127: R 56-120; D 237-7 (ND 157-6, SD 80-1), March 20, 1986.

58. H J Res 540. Aid to Nicaraguan Rebels. Passage of the joint resolution to approve President Reagan's Feb. 25 request for $100 million in military and non-military aid to the "contra" guerrillas in Nicaragua, and to lift restrictions on CIA and Defense Department assistance to the contras. Rejected 210-222: R 164-16; D 46-206 (ND 7-163, SD 39-43), March 20, 1986. A "yea" was a vote supporting the president's position.

59. H J Res 534. Commodity Credit Corporation Supplemental Appropriation, Fiscal 1986. Adoption of the conference report on the joint resolution to provide an additional $5,000,000,000 in fiscal 1986 appropriations for the Commodity Credit Corporation. Adopted (thus cleared for the president) 352-71: R 127-50; D 225-21 (ND 148-17, SD 77-4), March 20, 1986.

60. HR 3128. Omnibus Budget Reconciliation, Fiscal 1986. Martin, R-Ill., motion that the House recede from its disagreement to the Senate amendment making changes in the bill to reduce fiscal 1986 deficits. Motion agreed to (thus cleared for the president) 230-154: R 146-21; D 84-133 (ND 27-115, SD 57-18), March 20, 1986. (The Senate amendment was an amendment to the House amendment to the Senate amendment to the House amendment to the Senate amendment to the bill. The original Senate amendment was the conference agreement on the bill.) A "yea" was a vote supporting the president's position.

61. H Con Res 304. Adjournment Resolution. Adoption of the concurrent resolution to provide for the adjournment of the House from March 25 to April 8, and of the Senate from March 26 or 27 to April 8. Adopted 170-158: R 6-130; D 164-28 (ND 115-14, SD 49-14), March 20, 1986.

KEY

Y Voted for (yea).
\# Paired for.
\+ Announced for.
N Voted against (nay).
X Paired against.
\- Announced against.
P Voted "present."
C Voted "present" to avoid possible conflict of interest.
? Did not vote or otherwise make a position known.

Democrats ***Republicans***

	57	58	59	60	61
ALABAMA					
1 ***Callahan***	Y	Y	Y	Y	N
2 ***Dickinson***	N	Y	Y	?	?
3 Nichols	Y	Y	N	Y	?
4 Bevill	Y	Y	Y	Y	Y
5 Flippo	Y	Y	Y	Y	Y
6 Erdreich	Y	Y	Y	Y	Y
7 Shelby	Y	Y	Y	Y	Y
ALASKA					
AL ***Young***	N	Y	Y	Y	Y
ARIZONA					
1 ***McCain***	Y	Y	Y	Y	N
2 Udall	Y	N	Y	N	Y
3 ***Stump***	N	Y	Y	Y	N
4 ***Rudd***	Y	Y	Y	Y	N
5 ***Kolbe***	N	Y	Y	Y	?
ARKANSAS					
1 Alexander	Y	N	Y	N	Y
2 Robinson	Y	Y	Y	N	Y
3 ***Hammerschmidt***	Y	Y	Y	Y	N
4 Anthony	Y	N	Y	N	N
CALIFORNIA					
1 Bosco	Y	N	Y	N	Y
2 ***Chappie***	N	Y	Y	Y	N
3 Matsui	Y	N	Y	N	Y
4 Fazio	Y	N	Y	N	Y
5 Burton	Y	N	Y	N	Y
6 Boxer	Y	N	Y	N	Y
7 Miller	Y	N	Y	N	Y
8 Dellums	Y	N	Y	N	Y
9 Stark	Y	N	N	N	?
10 Edwards	Y	N	Y	N	?
11 Lantos	Y	N	Y	N	Y
12 ***Zschau***	N	Y	N	Y	N
13 Mineta	Y	N	Y	N	Y
14 ***Shumway***	Y	Y	N	Y	N
15 Coelho	Y	N	Y	Y	Y
16 Panetta	Y	N	Y	N	Y
17 ***Pashayan***	N	Y	Y	Y	?
18 Lehman	Y	N	Y	N	Y
19 ***Lagomarsino***	N	Y	Y	Y	N
20 ***Thomas***	N	Y	N	Y	?
21 ***Fiedler***	N	Y	Y	Y	?
22 ***Moorhead***	N	Y	N	Y	N
23 Beilenson	Y	N	Y	N	Y
24 Waxman	Y	N	Y	N	?
25 Roybal	Y	N	Y	?	?
26 Berman	Y	N	Y	N	Y
27 Levine	Y	N	N	N	Y
28 Dixon	Y	N	Y	N	Y
29 Hawkins	Y	N	Y	N	?
30 Martinez	?	N	Y	N	Y
31 Dymally	Y	N	Y	X	?
32 Anderson	Y	N	N	N	N
33 ***Dreier***	N	Y	N	Y	?
34 Torres	Y	N	Y	N	Y
35 ***Lewis***	N	Y	Y	Y	N
36 Brown	?	N	Y	?	?
37 ***McCandless***	N	Y	N	N	N
38 ***Dornan***	N	Y	N	Y	N
39 ***Dannemeyer***	N	Y	N	Y	N
40 ***Badham***	N	Y	Y	Y	?
41 ***Lowery***	N	Y	N	Y	N
42 ***Lungren***	N	Y	N	Y	N
43 ***Packard***	Y	Y	N	Y	N
44 Bates	Y	N	Y	N	?
45 ***Hunter***	N	Y	Y	Y	N
COLORADO					
1 Schroeder	N	N	N	N	N
2 Wirth	Y	N	Y	?	?
3 ***Strang***	N	Y	Y	Y	N
4 ***Brown***	N	Y	N	Y	N
5 ***Kramer***	N	Y	Y	N	N
6 ***Schaefer***	N	Y	N	Y	N
CONNECTICUT					
1 Kennelly	Y	N	Y	?	?
2 Gejdenson	Y	N	Y	N	Y
3 Morrison	Y	N	N	N	Y
4 ***McKinney***	Y	N	Y	Y	?
5 ***Rowland***	Y	N	Y	Y	N
6 ***Johnson***	Y	Y	Y	Y	N
DELAWARE					
AL Carper	Y	N	N	Y	N
FLORIDA					
1 Hutto	Y	Y	Y	Y	?
2 Fuqua	Y	Y	Y	Y	?
3 Bennett	Y	Y	Y	N	Y
4 Chappell	Y	Y	Y	Y	Y
5 ***McCollum***	N	Y	N	Y	N
6 MacKay	Y	N	Y	N	Y
7 Gibbons	Y	Y	?	?	?
8 ***Young***	N	Y	Y	N	N
9 ***Bilirakis***	N	Y	N	Y	N
10 ***Ireland***	N	Y	N	Y	N
11 Nelson	Y	Y	N	Y	Y
12 ***Lewis***	N	Y	N	Y	N
13 ***Mack***	N	Y	N	Y	N
14 Mica	Y	Y	Y	N	Y
15 ***Shaw***	N	Y	Y	Y	?
16 Smith	Y	Y	Y	N	Y
17 Lehman	Y	N	Y	N	Y
18 Pepper	Y	Y	Y	N	Y
19 Fascell	Y	Y	Y	?	?
GEORGIA					
1 Thomas	Y	Y	Y	Y	Y
2 Hatcher	Y	Y	Y	Y	?
3 Ray	Y	N	Y	N	Y
4 ***Swindall***	N	Y	Y	Y	N
5 Fowler	Y	N	Y	?	?
6 ***Gingrich***	?	Y	N	Y	N
7 Darden	Y	Y	Y	Y	Y
8 Rowland	Y	Y	Y	Y	Y
9 Jenkins	Y	Y	Y	Y	Y
10 Barnard	Y	Y	Y	Y	Y
HAWAII					
1 Heftel	Y	N	Y	Y	Y
2 Akaka	Y	N	Y	N	Y
IDAHO					
1 ***Craig***	N	Y	Y	Y	N
2 Stallings	Y	N	Y	Y	N
ILLINOIS					
1 Hayes	Y	N	Y	N	Y
2 Savage	?	N	Y	N	Y
3 Russo	Y	N	N	N	Y
4 ***O'Brien***	Y	Y	Y	Y	Y
5 Lipinski	Y	Y	Y	?	?
6 ***Hyde***	Y	Y	Y	Y	N
7 Collins	?	N	?	N	Y
8 Rostenkowski	Y	N	Y	N	Y
9 Yates	Y	N	N	N	Y
10 ***Porter***	Y	Y	N	Y	N
11 Annunzio	Y	N	Y	?	?
12 ***Crane***	N	Y	N	Y	N
13 ***Fawell***	N	Y	N	Y	N
14 ***Grotberg***	?	?	?	?	?
15 ***Madigan***	N	Y	Y	Y	N
16 ***Martin***	N	Y	Y	Y	N
17 Evans	Y	N	Y	N	Y
18 ***Michel***	N	Y	Y	Y	N
19 Bruce	Y	N	Y	Y	N
20 Durbin	Y	N	Y	Y	Y
21 Price	Y	N	Y	N	Y
22 Gray	Y	N	Y	N	Y
INDIANA					
1 Visclosky	Y	N	Y	N	N
2 Sharp	Y	N	Y	N	?
3 ***Hiler***	N	Y	Y	Y	N
4 ***Coats***	Y	Y	Y	Y	N
5 ***Hillis***	Y	Y	Y	?	?

ND - Northern Democrats SD - Southern Democrats

* Corresponding to Congressional Record Votes 62, 64, 65, 66, 67

	57	58	59	60	61
6 ***Burton***	N	Y	Y	Y	N
7 ***Myers***	Y	Y	Y	Y	Y
8 McCloskey	Y	N	Y	Y	Y
9 Hamilton	Y	N	Y	Y	Y
10 Jacobs	N	N	Y	N	?
IOWA					
1 ***Leach***	N	N	Y	Y	?
2 ***Tauke***	N	N	Y	Y	N
3 ***Evans***	?	?	?	?	?
4 Smith	Y	N	Y	N	Y
5 ***Lightfoot***	N	N	Y	Y	N
6 Bedell	Y	N	Y	N	Y
KANSAS					
1 ***Roberts***	N	Y	Y	Y	N
2 Slattery	Y	N	Y	Y	N
3 ***Meyers***	N	Y	Y	Y	N
4 Glickman	Y	N	Y	Y	Y
5 ***Whittaker***	N	Y	Y	Y	?
KENTUCKY					
1 Hubbard	Y	N	Y	Y	N
2 Natcher	Y	N	Y	Y	Y
3 Mazzoli	Y	N	Y	Y	Y
4 ***Snyder***	Y	Y	Y	Y	Y
5 ***Rogers***	N	Y	Y	Y	N
6 ***Hopkins***	Y	N	Y	Y	N
7 Perkins	Y	N	Y	Y	Y
LOUISIANA					
1 ***Livingston***	Y	Y	Y	Y	N
2 Boggs	Y	N	Y	Y	Y
3 Tauzin	Y	Y	Y	Y	N
4 Roemer	N	Y	Y	Y	N
5 Huckaby	Y	Y	Y	Y	N
6 ***Moore***	Y	Y	Y	Y	?
7 Breaux	Y	Y	Y	Y	?
8 Long	Y	N	Y	?	?
MAINE					
1 ***McKernan***	N	Y	Y	Y	N
2 ***Snowe***	N	N	Y	Y	N
MARYLAND					
1 Dyson	Y	Y	Y	N	Y
2 ***Bentley***	N	Y	Y	N	N
3 Mikulski	Y	N	Y	N	N
4 ***Holt***	Y	Y	N	N	Y
5 Hoyer	Y	N	Y	N	Y
6 Byron	Y	Y	Y	N	Y
7 Mitchell	N	N	N	N	?
8 Barnes	Y	N	Y	N	Y
MASSACHUSETTS					
1 ***Conte***	N	N	Y	N	N
2 Boland	Y	N	Y	N	Y
3 Early	Y	N	Y	N	Y
4 Frank	Y	N	N	N	Y
5 Atkins	Y	N	Y	?	?
6 Mavroules	Y	N	?	N	Y
7 Markey	Y	N	Y	Y	?
8 O'Neill		N			
9 Moakley	Y	N	Y	N	Y
10 Studds	Y	N	N	N	Y
11 Donnelly	Y	N	Y	N	Y
MICHIGAN					
1 Conyers	Y	N	Y	N	Y
2 ***Pursell***	Y	Y	Y	?	?
3 Wolpe	Y	N	Y	N	Y
4 ***Siljander***	N	Y	Y	Y	N
5 ***Henry***	N	Y	Y	Y	?
6 Carr	Y	N	Y	Y	?
7 Kildee	Y	N	Y	N	Y
8 Traxler	Y	N	Y	?	?
9 ***Vander Jagt***	N	Y	Y	Y	?
10 ***Schuette***	N	Y	Y	Y	N
11 ***Davis***	Y	Y	Y	N	N
12 Bonior	Y	N	Y	N	Y
13 Crockett	Y	N	Y	?	?
14 Hertel	Y	N	N	N	Y
15 Ford	Y	N	Y	?	?
16 Dingell	Y	N	Y	N	Y
17 Levin	Y	N	Y	N	Y
18 ***Broomfield***	?	Y	Y	Y	?
MINNESOTA					
1 Penny	N	N	N	Y	Y
2 ***Weber***	N	Y	Y	Y	N
3 ***Frenzel***	N	N	N	Y	N
4 Vento	Y	N	Y	N	Y
5 Sabo	Y	N	Y	N	Y
6 Sikorski	N	N	Y	N	Y

	57	58	59	60	61
7 ***Stangeland***	N	Y	Y	Y	N
8 Oberstar	Y	N	Y	N	Y
MISSISSIPPI					
1 Whitten	Y	N	Y	Y	Y
2 ***Franklin***	Y	Y	Y	Y	N
3 Montgomery	Y	Y	Y	Y	Y
4 Dowdy	Y	Y	Y	?	?
5 ***Lott***	N	Y	Y	Y	N
MISSOURI					
1 Clay	N	N	Y	N	?
2 Young	Y	N	Y	N	Y
3 Gephardt	?	N	Y	?	?
4 Skelton	Y	Y	Y	?	?
5 Wheat	Y	N	Y	N	Y
6 ***Coleman***	N	Y	Y	Y	N
7 ***Taylor***	N	Y	Y	Y	?
8 ***Emerson***	N	Y	Y	Y	N
9 Volkmer	Y	N	Y	N	Y
MONTANA					
1 Williams	Y	N	Y	N	Y
2 ***Marlenee***	N	Y	Y	Y	N
NEBRASKA					
1 ***Bereuter***	N	Y	Y	Y	N
2 ***Daub***	N	Y	Y	Y	N
3 ***Smith***	Y	Y	Y	Y	N
NEVADA					
1 Reid	Y	N	Y	N	Y
2 ***Vucanovich***	N	Y	N	N	N
NEW HAMPSHIRE					
1 ***Smith***	N	Y	N	Y	N
2 ***Gregg***	N	Y	N	Y	?
NEW JERSEY					
1 Florio	Y	N	Y	N	?
2 Hughes	Y	N	Y	N	Y
3 Howard	Y	N	Y	N	Y
4 ***Smith***	Y	Y	Y	Y	N
5 ***Roukema***	N	Y	Y	Y	N
6 Dwyer	Y	N	Y	N	Y
7 ***Rinaldo***	Y	Y	Y	N	N
8 Roe	Y	N	Y	N	Y
9 Torricelli	Y	N	Y	N	Y
10 Rodino	Y	N	Y	N	Y
11 ***Gallo***	N	Y	N	Y	N
12 ***Courter***	N	Y	N	Y	N
13 ***Saxton***	N	Y	Y	N	N
14 Guarini	Y	N	Y	N	Y
NEW MEXICO					
1 ***Lujan***	Y	Y	Y	Y	N
2 ***Skeen***	N	Y	Y	Y	N
3 Richardson	Y	N	Y	Y	N
NEW YORK					
1 ***Carney***	N	Y	N	Y	N
2 Downey	Y	N	N	?	?
3 Mrazek	Y	N	Y	N	N
4 ***Lent***	N	Y	Y	Y	N
5 ***McGrath***	N	Y	N	?	?
6 Addabbo	?	?	?	?	?
7 Ackerman	Y	N	Y	?	?
8 Scheuer	?	N	Y	N	Y
9 Manton	Y	N	Y	N	Y
10 Schumer	Y	N	Y	?	?
11 Towns	Y	N	Y	N	Y
12 Owens	Y	N	Y	?	?
13 Solarz	Y	N	Y	N	Y
14 ***Molinari***	Y	Y	N	Y	?
15 ***Green***	Y	N	Y	Y	N
16 Rangel	Y	N	Y	N	Y
17 Weiss	Y	N	Y	?	?
18 Garcia	Y	N	Y	?	?
19 Biaggi	Y	N	Y	?	?
20 ***DioGuardi***	Y	Y	N	Y	?
21 ***Fish***	Y	Y	Y	?	?
22 ***Gilman***	Y	Y	Y	Y	?
23 Stratton	Y	Y	Y	Y	Y
24 ***Solomon***	N	Y	Y	Y	N
25 ***Boehlert***	N	N	Y	Y	N
26 ***Martin***	N	Y	Y	Y	N
27 ***Wortley***	Y	Y	Y	Y	N
28 McHugh	Y	N	Y	N	Y
29 ***Horton***	Y	N	Y	N	?
30 ***Eckert***	Y	Y	Y	Y	N
31 ***Kemp***	Y	Y	Y	?	?
32 LaFalce	Y	N	Y	N	Y
33 Nowak	Y	N	Y	N	Y
34 Lundine	Y	N	Y	N	?

	57	58	59	60	61
NORTH CAROLINA					
1 Jones	Y	N	Y	Y	Y
2 Valentine	Y	N	Y	Y	Y
3 Whitley	Y	N	Y	Y	Y
4 ***Cobey***	N	Y	Y	Y	N
5 Neal	Y	N	Y	Y	N
6 ***Coble***	N	Y	Y	Y	N
7 Rose	Y	N	Y	Y	?
8 Hefner	Y	N	Y	Y	Y
9 ***McMillan***	N	Y	Y	Y	N
10 ***Broyhill***	Y	Y	Y	Y	N
11 ***Hendon***	N	Y	Y	Y	N
NORTH DAKOTA					
AL Dorgan	Y	N	Y	N	Y
OHIO					
1 Luken	Y	N	N	Y	Y
2 ***Gradison***	Y	Y	Y	?	?
3 Hall	Y	N	Y	?	?
4 ***Oxley***	N	Y	Y	N	?
5 ***Latta***	N	Y	Y	Y	?
6 ***McEwen***	Y	Y	Y	N	N
7 ***DeWine***	N	Y	Y	Y	N
8 ***Kindness***	N	Y	Y	Y	?
9 Kaptur	Y	N	Y	N	Y
10 ***Miller***	N	Y	Y	N	N
11 Eckart	Y	N	Y	N	Y
12 ***Kasich***	Y	Y	Y	Y	N
13 Pease	Y	N	Y	Y	Y
14 Seiberling	Y	N	?	N	Y
15 ***Wylie***	Y	N	Y	?	?
16 ***Regula***	N	Y	Y	N	N
17 Traficant	Y	N	Y	N	N
18 Applegate	Y	N	Y	N	N
19 Feighan	Y	N	Y	N	Y
20 Oakar	Y	N	Y	N	Y
21 Stokes	Y	N	Y	N	Y
OKLAHOMA					
1 Jones	Y	Y	Y	Y	Y
2 Synar	Y	N	Y	N	N
3 Watkins	Y	Y	Y	Y	Y
4 McCurdy	Y	N	Y	Y	?
5 ***Edwards***	N	Y	Y	Y	N
6 English	Y	Y	Y	Y	Y
OREGON					
1 AuCoin	Y	N	?	Y	?
2 ***Smith, R.***	N	Y	Y	Y	?
3 Wyden	Y	N	Y	Y	N
4 Weaver	Y	N	N	N	?
5 ***Smith, D.***	N	Y	N	Y	N
PENNSYLVANIA					
1 Foglietta	Y	N	Y	?	?
2 Gray	Y	N	Y	N	?
3 Borski	Y	N	Y	N	Y
4 Kolter	Y	N	Y	N	Y
5 ***Schulze***	Y	Y	Y	N	?
6 Yatron	Y	N	Y	?	Y
7 Edgar	Y	N	Y	?	?
8 Kostmayer	Y	N	Y	?	Y
9 ***Shuster***	N	Y	Y	Y	N
10 ***McDade***	Y	Y	Y	N	Y
11 Kanjorski	Y	N	Y	N	Y
12 Murtha	Y	Y	Y	Y	Y
13 ***Coughlin***	N	Y	N	Y	N
14 Coyne	Y	N	Y	N	Y
15 ***Ritter***	Y	Y	Y	Y	N
16 ***Walker***	N	Y	N	Y	N
17 ***Gekas***	N	Y	N	Y	N
18 Walgren	Y	N	Y	?	Y
19 ***Goodling***	?	Y	N	Y	?
20 Gaydos	Y	Y	Y	N	Y
21 ***Ridge***	?	N	Y	Y	N
22 Murphy	Y	N	Y	N	Y
23 ***Clinger***	N	Y	Y	Y	N
RHODE ISLAND					
1 St Germain	Y	N	Y	N	Y
2 ***Schneider***	Y	N	Y	Y	N
SOUTH CAROLINA					
1 ***Hartnett***	N	Y	Y	?	?
2 ***Spence***	N	Y	Y	Y	N
3 Derrick	Y	N	Y	Y	Y
4 ***Campbell***	N	Y	Y	Y	N
5 Spratt	Y	N	Y	Y	Y
6 Tallon	Y	Y	Y	Y	N
SOUTH DAKOTA					
AL Daschle	Y	N	Y	N	Y

	57	58	59	60	61
TENNESSEE					
1 ***Quillen***	Y	Y	Y	Y	?
2 ***Duncan***	Y	Y	?	Y	N
3 Lloyd	Y	N	Y	N	N
4 Cooper	Y	N	Y	N	Y
5 Boner	Y	N	Y	N	N
6 Gordon	Y	N	Y	Y	Y
7 ***Sundquist***	N	Y	?	Y	N
8 Jones	Y	N	Y	N	Y
9 Ford	Y	N	Y	N	Y
TEXAS					
1 Chapman	?	N	Y	Y	Y
2 Wilson	Y	Y	Y	Y	?
3 ***Bartlett***	N	Y	N	Y	N
4 Hall, R.	Y	Y	Y	Y	N
5 Bryant	Y	N	Y	Y	N
6 ***Barton***	N	Y	Y	Y	N
7 ***Archer***	Y	Y	N	Y	?
8 ***Fields***	N	Y	N	Y	N
9 Brooks	Y	N	Y	Y	Y
10 Pickle	Y	N	Y	Y	?
11 Leath	Y	Y	Y	Y	?
12 Wright	Y	N	Y	?	?
13 ***Boulter***	N	Y	Y	Y	N
14 ***Sweeney***	Y	Y	Y	Y	N
15 de la Garza	Y	N	Y	Y	Y
16 Coleman	Y	N	Y	Y	N
17 Stenholm	Y	Y	Y	Y	N
18 Leland	Y	N	Y	N	Y
19 ***Combest***	Y	Y	Y	Y	N
20 Gonzalez	Y	N	Y	N	Y
21 ***Loeffler***	N	Y	?	#	?
22 ***DeLay***	N	Y	N	Y	N
23 Bustamante	Y	N	Y	?	?
24 Frost	Y	N	Y	Y	Y
25 Andrews	Y	N	Y	Y	?
26 ***Armey***	N	Y	N	Y	N
27 Ortiz	Y	Y	Y	Y	Y
UTAH					
1 ***Hansen***	Y	Y	N	Y	N
2 ***Monson***	N	Y	N	?	?
3 ***Nielson***	N	Y	Y	+	-
VERMONT					
AL ***Jeffords***	Y	N	Y	Y	?
VIRGINIA					
1 ***Bateman***	Y	Y	Y	Y	N
2 ***Whitehurst***	N	Y	Y	?	?
3 ***Bliley***	N	Y	Y	Y	N
4 Sisisky	Y	Y	Y	Y	?
5 Daniel	Y	Y	N	Y	Y
6 Olin	Y	N	N	Y	Y
7 ***Slaughter***	N	Y	Y	Y	N
8 ***Parris***	N	Y	Y	N	?
9 Boucher	Y	N	Y	Y	Y
10 ***Wolf***	N	Y	N	N	N
WASHINGTON					
1 ***Miller***	Y	Y	N	Y	N
2 Swift	Y	N	Y	N	Y
3 Bonker	Y	N	Y	Y	Y
4 ***Morrison***	Y	Y	Y	Y	N
5 Foley	Y	N	Y	N	Y
6 Dicks	Y	N	Y	Y	Y
7 Lowry	Y	N	N	N	Y
8 ***Chandler***	N	Y	N	Y	?
WEST VIRGINIA					
1 Mollohan	Y	N	Y	Y	Y
2 Staggers	Y	N	Y	N	Y
3 Wise	Y	N	Y	Y	N
4 Rahall	Y	N	Y	Y	Y
WISCONSIN					
1 Aspin	Y	N	Y	Y	Y
2 Kastenmeier	Y	N	Y	?	?
3 ***Gunderson***	N	Y	Y	N	N
4 Kleczka	Y	N	Y	Y	Y
5 Moody	Y	N	Y	N	Y
6 ***Petri***	Y	Y	Y	N	N
7 Obey	Y	N	Y	N	Y
8 ***Roth***	N	Y	Y	Y	N
9 ***Sensenbrenner***	N	Y	N	Y	N
WYOMING					
AL ***Cheney***	N	Y	N	Y	N

Southern states - Ala., Ark., Fla., Ga., Ky., La., Miss., N.C., Okla., S.C., Tenn., Texas, Va.

* The *Congressional Record* vote number is different from the CQ vote number because the *Record* includes quorum calls in its tally. CQ does not publish quorum call votes.

62. Procedural Motion. Barton, R-Texas, motion to approve the House *Journal* of Tuesday, April 8. Motion agreed to 269-103: R 57-94; D 212-9 (ND 143-7, SD 69-2), April 9, 1986.

63. HR 4332. Firearms Law Reform. Adoption of the rule (H Res 403) to provide for House floor consideration of the bill to revise the 1968 Gun Control Act. Adopted 410-2: R 172-1; D 238-1 (ND 162-1, SD 76-0), April 9, 1986.

64. HR 4332. Firearms Law Reform. Hughes, D-N.J., amendment to the Volkmer, D-Mo., substitute for the Judiciary Committee substitute, to continue the ban on interstate sales of handguns, bar interstate transportation of handguns, retain existing record-keeping requirements and ban silencers. Rejected 176-248: R 40-138; D 136-110 (ND 119-46, SD 17-64), April 9, 1986. (The Volkmer substitute later was adopted *(see vote 68, below)*, after which the Judiciary Committee substitute was adopted by voice vote.)

65. HR 4332. Firearms Law Reform. Hughes, D-N.J., amendment to the Volkmer, D-Mo., substitute for the Judiciary Committee substitute, to bar the interstate transportation of handguns. Rejected 177-242: R 40-136; D 137-106 (ND 115-48, SD 22-58), April 9, 1986.

66. HR 4332. Firearms Law Reform. Hughes, D-N.J., amendment to the Volkmer, D-Mo., substitute for the Judiciary Committee substitute, to retain the existing ban on interstate sales of handguns. Adopted 233-184: R 73-102; D 160-82 (ND 129-34, SD 31-48), April 10, 1986.

67. HR 4332. Firearms Law Reform. Hughes, D-N.J., motion that the Committee of the Whole rise. Motion rejected 124-298: R 8-168; D 116-130 (ND 104-62, SD 12-68), April 10, 1986. (The effect of the motion would have been to end debate on the bill.)

68. HR 4332. Firearms Law Reform. Volkmer, D-Mo., substitute for the Judiciary Committee substitute, to allow interstate sales of rifles and shotguns, to allow interstate transportation of all firearms, to ease record-keeping requirements for firearms transactions and to limit federal agents to one unannounced inspection per year of a gun dealer's premises. Adopted 286-136: R 158-18; D 128-118 (ND 60-106, SD 68-12), April 10, 1986. (The Judiciary Committee substitute, as amended by the Volkmer substitute, subsequently was adopted by voice vote.) A "yea" was a vote supporting the president's position.

69. HR 4332. Firearms Law Reform. Passage of the bill to revise the 1968 Gun Control Act to allow the interstate sales of rifles and shotguns and the interstate transportation of all types of firearms, to ease record-keeping requirements for firearms transactions and to limit federal agents to one unannounced inspection per year of a gun dealer's premises. Passed 292-130: R 161-15; D 131-115 (ND 62-103, SD 69-12), April 10, 1986. (The House subsequently moved to strike the language of S 49, the Senate-passed version of the bill, and insert instead the language of HR 4332.) A "yea" was a vote supporting the president's position.

KEY

- Y Voted for (yea).
- # Paired for.
- + Announced for.
- N Voted against (nay).
- X Paired against.
- \- Announced against.
- P Voted "present."
- C Voted "present" to avoid possible conflict of interest.
- ? Did not vote or otherwise make a position known.

Democrats ***Republicans***

	62	63	64	65	66	67	68	69
ALABAMA								
1 ***Callahan***	?	Y	N	N	N	N	Y	Y
2 ***Dickinson***	?	Y	N	N	N	N	Y	Y
3 Nichols	?	?	?	?	X	?	#	#
4 Bevill	Y	Y	N	N	N	N	Y	Y
5 Flippo	Y	Y	N	N	N	N	Y	Y
6 Erdreich	Y	Y	N	N	N	N	Y	Y
7 Shelby	?	Y	N	N	N	N	Y	Y
ALASKA								
AL ***Young***	N	Y	N	N	N	N	Y	Y
ARIZONA								
1 ***McCain***	Y	Y	N	N	N	N	Y	Y
2 Udall	Y	Y	N	Y	Y	Y	Y	Y
3 ***Stump***	?	Y	N	N	N	N	Y	Y
4 ***Rudd***	Y	Y	N	N	N	N	Y	Y
5 ***Kolbe***	N	?	N	N	N	N	Y	Y
ARKANSAS								
1 Alexander	Y	Y	N	N	N	N	Y	Y
2 Robinson	Y	Y	N	N	N	N	Y	Y
3 ***Hammerschmidt***	Y	Y	N	N	N	N	Y	Y
4 Anthony	Y	Y	Y	Y	Y	Y	Y	Y
CALIFORNIA								
1 Bosco	Y	Y	N	N	Y	N	Y	Y
2 ***Chappie***	N	Y	N	N	N	N	Y	Y
3 Matsui	Y	Y	Y	Y	Y	Y	N	N
4 Fazio	Y	Y	Y	Y	Y	Y	N	N
5 Burton	Y	Y	Y	Y	Y	Y	N	N
6 Boxer	Y	Y	Y	Y	Y	Y	N	N
7 Miller	Y	Y	Y	Y	Y	Y	N	N
8 Dellums	Y	Y	Y	Y	Y	Y	N	N
9 Stark	Y	Y	Y	Y	Y	Y	N	N
10 Edwards	Y	Y	Y	Y	Y	Y	N	N
11 Lantos	Y	Y	Y	Y	Y	N	N	Y
12 ***Zschau***	N	Y	Y	Y	Y	N	Y	Y
13 Mineta	Y	Y	Y	Y	Y	Y	N	N
14 ***Shumway***	Y	Y	N	N	N	N	Y	Y
15 Coelho	Y	Y	Y	N	Y	N	Y	Y
16 Panetta	Y	Y	Y	Y	Y	N	N	N
17 ***Pashayan***	N	Y	N	N	N	N	Y	Y
18 Lehman	Y	Y	Y	Y	Y	Y	Y	Y
19 ***Lagomarsino***	?	Y	N	N	N	N	Y	Y
20 ***Thomas***	?	Y	N	N	N	N	Y	Y
21 ***Fiedler***	N	Y	N	N	N	N	Y	Y
22 ***Moorhead***	N	Y	N	N	N	N	Y	Y
23 Beilenson	Y	Y	Y	Y	Y	Y	N	N
24 Waxman	Y	Y	Y	Y	Y	Y	N	N
25 Roybal	Y	Y	Y	Y	Y	Y	N	N
26 Berman	Y	Y	Y	Y	?	Y	N	N
27 Levine	Y	Y	Y	Y	Y	Y	N	N
28 Dixon	?	Y	Y	Y	Y	Y	N	N
29 Hawkins	?	Y	Y	Y	Y	Y	N	N
30 Martinez	?	?	?	?	Y	Y	N	N
31 Dymally	Y	Y	Y	Y	Y	Y	N	N
32 Anderson	Y	Y	Y	Y	Y	Y	Y	Y
33 ***Dreier***	N	Y	N	N	N	N	Y	Y
34 Torres	+	+	+	+	Y	Y	N	N
35 ***Lewis***	?	Y	N	N	N	N	Y	Y
36 Brown	Y	Y	Y	Y	Y	N	N	N
37 ***McCandless***	N	Y	N	N	Y	N	Y	Y
38 ***Dornan***	N	Y	N	N	N	N	Y	Y
39 ***Dannemeyer***	N	Y	N	N	N	N	Y	Y
40 ***Badham***	N	Y	N	N	N	N	Y	Y
41 ***Lowery***	?	Y	N	N	Y	N	Y	Y
42 ***Lungren***	?	Y	Y	Y	Y	N	Y	Y
43 ***Packard***	Y	Y	N	N	N	N	Y	Y
44 Bates	Y	Y	Y	Y	Y	Y	N	N
45 ***Hunter***	N	Y	N	N	N	N	Y	Y
COLORADO								
1 Schroeder	N	Y	Y	Y	Y	Y	N	N
2 Wirth	Y	Y	Y	Y	Y	N	Y	Y
3 ***Strang***	N	Y	N	N	N	N	Y	Y
4 ***Brown***	N	Y	N	N	N	N	Y	Y
5 ***Kramer***	N	Y	N	N	?	N	Y	Y
6 ***Schaefer***	N	Y	N	N	N	N	Y	Y
CONNECTICUT								
1 Kennelly	Y	Y	Y	Y	Y	Y	N	N
2 Gejdenson	Y	Y	Y	Y	Y	Y	N	N
3 Morrison	Y	Y	Y	Y	Y	Y	N	N
4 ***McKinney***	Y	Y	Y	Y	Y	Y	N	N
5 ***Rowland***	Y	Y	N	Y	Y	N	Y	Y
6 ***Johnson***	Y	Y	Y	Y	Y	N	Y	Y
DELAWARE								
AL Carper	Y	Y	Y	Y	Y	Y	N	N
FLORIDA								
1 Hutto	Y	Y	N	Y	Y	N	Y	Y
2 Fuqua	Y	Y	N	N	Y	N	Y	Y
3 Bennett	Y	Y	Y	Y	Y	Y	N	N
4 Chappell	Y	Y	N	N	N	N	Y	Y
5 ***McCollum***	Y	Y	N	N	Y	N	Y	Y
6 MacKay	Y	Y	N	N	Y	N	Y	Y
7 Gibbons	Y	Y	Y	Y	Y	Y	N	N
8 ***Young***	N	Y	N	Y	Y	N	Y	Y
9 ***Bilirakis***	N	Y	N	N	N	N	Y	Y
10 ***Ireland***	N	Y	N	N	?	?	#	#
11 Nelson	Y	Y	N	N	Y	N	Y	Y
12 ***Lewis***	-	+	N	N	Y	N	Y	Y
13 ***Mack***	N	Y	N	N	N	N	Y	Y
14 Mica	Y	?	Y	Y	Y	N	N	N
15 ***Shaw***	N	Y	N	N	Y	N	Y	Y
16 Smith	Y	Y	Y	Y	Y	Y	N	N
17 Lehman	Y	Y	Y	Y	Y	Y	N	N
18 Pepper	Y	Y	Y	Y	Y	N	N	N
19 Fascell	Y	Y	Y	Y	Y	Y	N	N
GEORGIA								
1 Thomas	Y	Y	N	N	N	N	Y	Y
2 Hatcher	Y	Y	Y	Y	Y	N	Y	Y
3 Ray	Y	Y	N	N	Y	N	Y	Y
4 ***Swindall***	N	Y	N	N	N	N	Y	Y
5 Fowler	?	Y	N	Y	Y	N	Y	Y
6 ***Gingrich***	N	Y	N	N	N	N	Y	Y
7 Darden	Y	Y	N	N	N	N	Y	Y
8 Rowland	Y	Y	N	N	Y	N	Y	Y
9 Jenkins	?	?	N	N	N	N	Y	Y
10 Barnard	Y	Y	N	N	Y	N	Y	Y
HAWAII								
1 Heftel	?	?	?	?	#	?	X	X
2 Akaka	Y	Y	Y	Y	Y	Y	N	N
IDAHO								
1 ***Craig***	Y	Y	N	N	N	N	Y	Y
2 Stallings	Y	Y	N	N	N	N	Y	Y
ILLINOIS								
1 Hayes	Y	Y	Y	Y	Y	Y	N	N
2 Savage	Y	Y	Y	Y	Y	Y	N	N
3 Russo	Y	Y	Y	Y	Y	Y	N	N
4 ***O'Brien***	?	?	?	?	?	?	?	?
5 Lipinski	Y	Y	Y	Y	Y	Y	N	N
6 ***Hyde***	Y	Y	Y	N	Y	N	Y	Y
7 Collins	Y	Y	Y	Y	Y	Y	N	N
8 Rostenkowski	Y	Y	Y	Y	Y	Y	N	N
9 Yates	Y	N	Y	Y	Y	Y	N	N
10 ***Porter***	Y	Y	Y	Y	Y	Y	N	N
11 Annunzio	Y	Y	Y	Y	Y	Y	N	N
12 ***Crane***	N	N	N	N	N	N	Y	Y
13 ***Fawell***	N	Y	Y	Y	Y	Y	N	N
14 ***Grotberg***	?	?	?	?	?	?	?	?
15 ***Madigan***	?	Y	N	Y	Y	N	Y	Y
16 ***Martin***	?	Y	Y	?	Y	N	Y	Y
17 Evans	Y	Y	Y	Y	Y	Y	N	N
18 ***Michel***	?	Y	N	N	Y	N	Y	Y
19 Bruce	Y	Y	N	N	N	N	Y	Y
20 Durbin	N	Y	Y	N	Y	Y	N	N
21 Price	Y	Y	N	Y	Y	Y	Y	Y
22 Gray	Y	Y	N	N	X	N	Y	Y
INDIANA								
1 Visclosky	Y	Y	Y	Y	Y	Y	N	N
2 Sharp	Y	Y	N	N	N	N	Y	Y
3 ***Hiler***	N	Y	N	N	Y	N	Y	Y
4 ***Coats***	N	Y	N	N	Y	N	Y	Y
5 ***Hillis***	Y	Y	Y	Y	Y	N	N	Y

ND - Northern Democrats SD - Southern Democrats

	62	63	64	65	66	67	68	69
6 ***Burton***	N	Y	N	N	N	N	Y	Y
7 ***Myers***	?	Y	N	N	Y	N	Y	Y
8 McCloskey	Y	Y	N	N	N	N	Y	Y
9 Hamilton	Y	Y	N	N	N	N	Y	Y
10 Jacobs	N	Y	Y	Y	Y	Y	N	N
IOWA								
1 ***Leach***	N	Y	Y	Y	Y	N	Y	Y
2 ***Tauke***	N	Y	Y	N	Y	N	Y	Y
3 ***Evans***	N	Y	N	N	Y	N	Y	Y
4 Smith	Y	Y	N	N	N	N	Y	Y
5 ***Lightfoot***	N	Y	N	N	N	N	Y	Y
6 Bedell	Y	Y	Y	Y	Y	N	N	N
KANSAS								
1 ***Roberts***	N	Y	N	N	N	N	Y	Y
2 Slattery	Y	Y	N	N	Y	N	Y	Y
3 ***Meyers***	Y	Y	Y	Y	Y	N	Y	Y
4 Glickman	Y	Y	N	N	Y	N	Y	Y
5 ***Whittaker***	N	Y	N	N	Y	N	Y	Y
KENTUCKY								
1 Hubbard	Y	Y	N	N	N	N	Y	Y
2 Natcher	Y	Y	N	N	N	N	Y	Y
3 Mazzoli	Y	Y	Y	Y	Y	N	N	Y
4 ***Snyder***	Y	Y	N	N	N	N	Y	Y
5 ***Rogers***	N	Y	N	N	N	N	Y	Y
6 ***Hopkins***	Y	Y	N	N	N	N	Y	Y
7 Perkins	Y	Y	N	N	N	N	Y	Y
LOUISIANA								
1 ***Livingston***	Y	Y	N	N	N	N	Y	Y
2 Boggs	Y	Y	N	Y	Y	N	?	Y
3 Tauzin	Y	Y	N	N	N	N	Y	Y
4 Roemer	N	?	N	N	Y	N	Y	Y
5 Huckaby	Y	Y	N	N	N	N	Y	Y
6 ***Moore***	Y	Y	N	N	N	N	Y	Y
7 Breaux	Y	Y	N	N	N	N	Y	Y
8 Long	Y	Y	N	N	Y	N	Y	Y
MAINE								
1 ***McKernan***	N	Y	N	N	N	N	Y	Y
2 ***Snowe***	N	Y	N	N	N	N	Y	Y
MARYLAND								
1 Dyson	N	Y	N	N	N	N	Y	Y
2 ***Bentley***	N	Y	N	N	Y	N	Y	Y
3 Mikulski	Y	Y	Y	Y	Y	Y	N	N
4 ***Holt***	Y	Y	N	N	N	N	Y	Y
5 Hoyer	Y	Y	Y	?	Y	Y	N	N
6 Byron	?	?	N	N	N	N	Y	Y
7 Mitchell	N	Y	Y	Y	Y	N	N	N
8 Barnes	Y	Y	Y	Y	Y	Y	N	N
MASSACHUSETTS								
1 ***Conte***	?	Y	Y	Y	Y	N	N	Y
2 Boland	Y	Y	Y	Y	Y	Y	N	N
3 Early	Y	Y	Y	Y	Y	Y	N	N
4 Frank	Y	Y	Y	Y	Y	Y	N	N
5 Atkins	Y	Y	Y	Y	Y	Y	N	N
6 Mavroules	Y	Y	Y	Y	Y	Y	N	N
7 Markey	Y	Y	Y	Y	Y	Y	N	N
8 O'Neill								
9 Moakley	Y	Y	Y	Y	Y	Y	N	N
10 Studds	Y	Y	Y	Y	Y	Y	N	N
11 Donnelly	Y	Y	Y	Y	Y	Y	N	N
MICHIGAN								
1 Conyers	Y	Y	Y	Y	Y	Y	N	N
2 ***Pursell***	Y	Y	Y	Y	Y	N	N	N
3 Wolpe	Y	Y	Y	Y	Y	Y	N	-
4 ***Siljander***	N	Y	N	N	N	N	Y	Y
5 ***Henry***	N	Y	Y	N	Y	Y	N	N
6 Carr	Y	Y	N	N	Y	N	Y	Y
7 Kildee	Y	Y	Y	Y	Y	Y	N	N
8 Traxler	Y	Y	N	N	N	N	Y	Y
9 ***Vander Jagt***	?	Y	N	N	N	N	Y	Y
10 ***Schuette***	N	Y	N	N	N	N	Y	Y
11 ***Davis***	Y	Y	N	N	N	N	Y	Y
12 Bonior	Y	Y	Y	Y	Y	Y	N	N
13 Crockett	Y	Y	Y	Y	Y	Y	N	N
14 Hertel	Y	Y	Y	Y	Y	Y	N	N
15 Ford	Y	Y	N	Y	Y	N	Y	Y
16 Dingell	?	Y	N	N	N	N	Y	Y
17 Levin	Y	Y	Y	Y	Y	Y	N	N
18 ***Broomfield***	?	Y	Y	Y	Y	Y	N	N
MINNESOTA								
1 Penny	N	Y	N	N	N	N	Y	Y
2 ***Weber***	N	Y	N	N	N	N	Y	Y
3 ***Frenzel***	Y	Y	Y	Y	Y	N	Y	Y
4 Vento	Y	Y	Y	Y	Y	Y	N	N
5 Sabo	Y	Y	Y	Y	Y	Y	N	N
6 Sikorski	N	Y	N	N	N	N	Y	Y

	62	63	64	65	66	67	68	69
7 ***Stangeland***	N	Y	N	N	N	N	Y	Y
8 Oberstar	Y	Y	N	N	N	N	Y	Y
MISSISSIPPI								
1 Whitten	Y	Y	N	N	N	N	Y	Y
2 ***Franklin***	Y	Y	N	N	N	N	Y	Y
3 Montgomery	Y	Y	N	N	N	N	Y	Y
4 Dowdy	Y	Y	N	N	N	N	Y	Y
5 ***Lott***	?	Y	N	N	N	N	Y	Y
MISSOURI								
1 Clay	?	?	Y	Y	Y	Y	N	N
2 Young	Y	Y	N	N	Y	N	Y	Y
3 Gephardt	?	Y	Y	?	#	?	X	X
4 Skelton	Y	Y	N	N	N	N	Y	Y
5 Wheat	Y	Y	Y	Y	Y	Y	N	N
6 ***Coleman***	Y	Y	Y	Y	Y	N	Y	Y
7 ***Taylor***	N	Y	N	N	N	N	Y	Y
8 ***Emerson***	N	Y	N	N	N	N	Y	Y
9 Volkmer	Y	Y	N	N	N	N	Y	Y
MONTANA								
1 Williams	Y	Y	N	N	N	N	Y	Y
2 ***Marlenee***	N	Y	N	N	N	N	Y	Y
NEBRASKA								
1 ***Bereuter***	N	Y	N	Y	Y	N	Y	Y
2 ***Daub***	N	Y	N	N	N	N	Y	Y
3 ***Smith***	Y	Y	N	N	N	N	Y	Y
NEVADA								
1 Reid	Y	Y	N	N	N	N	Y	Y
2 ***Vucanovich***	?	Y	N	N	N	N	Y	Y
NEW HAMPSHIRE								
1 ***Smith***	N	Y	N	N	N	N	Y	Y
2 ***Gregg***	N	Y	N	N	N	N	Y	Y
NEW JERSEY								
1 Florio	?	Y	Y	Y	Y	N	N	Y
2 Hughes	Y	Y	Y	Y	Y	Y	N	N
3 Howard	Y	Y	Y	Y	Y	Y	N	N
4 ***Smith***	Y	Y	Y	Y	Y	N	Y	Y
5 ***Roukema***	N	Y	Y	Y	Y	N	N	N
6 Dwyer	Y	Y	Y	Y	Y	Y	N	N
7 ***Rinaldo***	?	?	Y	Y	Y	N	N	Y
8 Roe	Y	Y	Y	Y	Y	Y	N	N
9 Torricelli	Y	Y	Y	Y	Y	Y	N	N
10 Rodino	Y	Y	Y	Y	Y	Y	N	N
11 ***Gallo***	N	Y	N	N	Y	N	Y	Y
12 ***Courter***	N	Y	Y	Y	Y	N	Y	Y
13 ***Saxton***	?	Y	Y	Y	Y	N	Y	Y
14 Guarini	?	Y	Y	Y	Y	Y	N	N
NEW MEXICO								
1 ***Lujan***	?	?	?	?	?	?	?	?
2 ***Skeen***	N	Y	N	N	N	N	Y	Y
3 Richardson	Y	Y	N	N	N	N	Y	Y
NEW YORK								
1 ***Carney***	N	Y	N	N	N	N	Y	Y
2 Downey	Y	Y	Y	Y	Y	Y	N	N
3 Mrazek	Y	Y	Y	Y	Y	Y	N	N
4 ***Lent***	N	Y	Y	Y	Y	N	Y	Y
5 ***McGrath***	N	Y	Y	Y	Y	N	Y	Y
6 Addabbo	?	?	?	?	?	?	?	?
7 Ackerman	Y	Y	Y	Y	Y	Y	N	N
8 Scheuer	Y	Y	Y	Y	Y	Y	N	N
9 Manton	Y	Y	Y	Y	Y	Y	N	N
10 Schumer	Y	Y	Y	Y	Y	Y	N	N
11 Towns	Y	Y	Y	Y	Y	Y	N	N
12 Owens	Y	Y	Y	Y	Y	Y	N	N
13 Solarz	Y	Y	Y	Y	Y	Y	N	N
14 ***Molinari***	N	Y	Y	Y	Y	N	Y	Y
15 ***Green***	Y	Y	Y	Y	Y	Y	N	N
16 Rangel	Y	Y	Y	Y	Y	Y	N	N
17 Weiss	Y	Y	Y	Y	Y	Y	N	N
18 Garcia	Y	Y	Y	Y	Y	Y	N	N
19 Biaggi	Y	Y	Y	Y	Y	Y	N	N
20 ***DioGuardi***	?	?	N	Y	Y	N	N	N
21 ***Fish***	Y	Y	N	N	Y	N	Y	Y
22 ***Gilman***	Y	Y	N	N	N	N	Y	Y
23 Stratton	Y	Y	Y	Y	Y	Y	N	N
24 ***Solomon***	N	Y	N	N	N	N	Y	Y
25 ***Boehlert***	N	Y	N	N	N	N	Y	Y
26 ***Martin***	Y	Y	N	?	N	N	Y	Y
27 ***Wortley***	Y	Y	N	N	N	N	Y	Y
28 McHugh	Y	Y	Y	Y	Y	N	N	N
29 ***Horton***	Y	Y	N	N	N	N	Y	Y
30 ***Eckert***	Y	Y	N	N	N	N	Y	Y
31 ***Kemp***	?	Y	N	N	N	N	Y	Y
32 LaFalce	Y	Y	Y	Y	Y	Y	N	N
33 Nowak	Y	Y	Y	Y	Y	Y	N	N
34 Lundine	?	Y	Y	N	Y	N	Y	Y

	62	63	64	65	66	67	68	69
NORTH CAROLINA								
1 Jones	?	Y	N	Y	Y	N	Y	Y
2 Valentine	Y	Y	N	N	N	N	Y	Y
3 Whitley	Y	Y	N	N	N	N	Y	Y
4 ***Cobey***	N	Y	N	N	N	N	Y	Y
5 Neal	?	Y	N	N	Y	N	Y	Y
6 ***Coble***	N	Y	N	N	N	N	Y	Y
7 Rose	Y	Y	N	Y	Y	N	Y	Y
8 Hefner	Y	Y	N	N	N	N	Y	Y
9 ***McMillan***	Y	Y	N	N	N	N	Y	Y
10 ***Broyhill***	Y	Y	N	N	N	N	Y	Y
11 ***Hendon***	N	Y	N	N	N	N	Y	Y
NORTH DAKOTA								
AL Dorgan	Y	Y	N	N	Y	N	Y	Y
OHIO								
1 Luken	Y	Y	N	N	N	N	Y	Y
2 ***Gradison***	Y	Y	Y	Y	Y	N	N	N
3 Hall	Y	Y	Y	Y	Y	N	N	N
4 ***Oxley***	N	Y	Y	Y	Y	N	Y	Y
5 ***Latta***	?	Y	N	N	N	N	Y	Y
6 ***McEwen***	Y	Y	N	N	N	N	Y	Y
7 ***DeWine***	N	Y	Y	N	Y	N	Y	Y
8 ***Kindness***	N	Y	N	N	Y	N	Y	Y
9 Kaptur	Y	Y	Y	Y	Y	Y	N	N
10 ***Miller***	N	Y	N	N	N	N	Y	Y
11 Eckart	Y	Y	Y	N	Y	N	Y	Y
12 ***Kasich***	Y	Y	N	N	Y	N	Y	Y
13 Pease	Y	Y	Y	Y	Y	N	Y	Y
14 Seiberling	?	Y	Y	Y	Y	Y	N	N
15 ***Wylie***	Y	Y	Y	Y	Y	N	N	N
16 ***Regula***	Y	Y	N	N	Y	N	Y	Y
17 Traficant	Y	Y	Y	Y	Y	Y	N	N
18 Applegate	Y	Y	Y	Y	Y	N	Y	Y
19 Feighan	Y	Y	Y	Y	Y	Y	N	N
20 Oakar	Y	Y	Y	Y	Y	Y	N	N
21 Stokes	?	?	?	?	#	?	X	X
OKLAHOMA								
1 Jones	Y	Y	N	N	N	N	Y	Y
2 Synar	Y	Y	Y	N	Y	N	Y	Y
3 Watkins	Y	Y	N	N	N	N	Y	Y
4 McCurdy	Y	Y	N	N	N	N	Y	Y
5 ***Edwards***	?	?	?	?	Y	N	Y	Y
6 English	Y	Y	N	N	N	N	Y	Y
OREGON								
1 AuCoin	?	Y	N	N	N	N	Y	Y
2 ***Smith, R.***	N	Y	N	N	N	N	Y	Y
3 Wyden	Y	Y	N	N	N	N	Y	Y
4 Weaver	Y	Y	N	N	N	N	Y	Y
5 ***Smith, D.***	N	Y	N	N	N	N	Y	Y
PENNSYLVANIA								
1 Foglietta	?	Y	Y	Y	Y	Y	N	N
2 Gray	Y	Y	Y	Y	?	Y	N	N
3 Borski	Y	Y	Y	Y	Y	Y	N	N
4 Kolter	Y	Y	N	N	N	N	Y	Y
5 ***Schulze***	Y	Y	N	N	X	?	#	#
6 Yatron	Y	Y	N	N	Y	N	Y	Y
7 Edgar	Y	Y	Y	Y	Y	Y	N	N
8 Kostmayer	?	Y	Y	N	Y	N	Y	Y
9 ***Shuster***	N	Y	N	N	N	N	Y	Y
10 ***McDade***	Y	Y	N	N	N	N	Y	Y
11 Kanjorski	Y	Y	N	N	N	N	Y	Y
12 Murtha	?	Y	N	N	N	N	Y	Y
13 ***Coughlin***	N	Y	Y	N	Y	N	N	N
14 Coyne	Y	Y	Y	Y	Y	Y	N	N
15 ***Ritter***	Y	Y	N	N	Y	N	Y	Y
16 ***Walker***	N	?	N	N	N	N	Y	Y
17 ***Gekas***	N	Y	N	N	Y	N	Y	Y
18 Walgren	Y	Y	Y	Y	Y	Y	N	N
19 ***Goodling***	N	Y	N	Y	Y	N	Y	Y
20 Gaydos	Y	Y	N	N	N	N	Y	Y
21 ***Ridge***	?	Y	N	Y	Y	N	Y	Y
22 Murphy	Y	Y	N	N	N	N	Y	Y
23 ***Clinger***	Y	Y	N	N	N	N	Y	Y
RHODE ISLAND								
1 St Germain	Y	Y	Y	Y	Y	Y	N	N
2 ***Schneider***	Y	Y	Y	Y	Y	N	N	N
SOUTH CAROLINA								
1 ***Hartnett***	Y	Y	N	N	N	N	Y	Y
2 ***Spence***	N	Y	N	N	N	N	Y	Y
3 Derrick	Y	Y	N	N	N	N	Y	Y
4 ***Campbell***	?	Y	N	N	N	N	Y	Y
5 Spratt	Y	Y	N	Y	N	Y	Y	Y
6 Tallon	Y	Y	N	N	N	N	Y	Y
SOUTH DAKOTA								
AL Daschle	Y	Y	N	N	N	N	Y	Y

	62	63	64	65	66	67	68	69
TENNESSEE								
1 ***Quillen***	Y	Y	N	N	N	N	Y	Y
2 ***Duncan***	Y	Y	N	N	N	N	Y	Y
3 Lloyd	N	Y	N	N	N	N	Y	Y
4 Cooper	Y	Y	N	N	N	Y	Y	Y
5 Boner	Y	Y	N	N	N	N	Y	Y
6 Gordon	Y	Y	N	N	N	Y	Y	Y
7 ***Sundquist***	N	Y	N	N	N	N	Y	Y
8 Jones	Y	Y	N	N	N	N	Y	Y
9 Ford	Y	Y	Y	Y	?	Y	Y	N
TEXAS								
1 Chapman	?	Y	N	N	N	N	Y	Y
2 Wilson	?	Y	N	N	?	N	Y	Y
3 ***Bartlett***	N	Y	N	N	N	N	Y	Y
4 Hall, R.	Y	Y	N	N	N	N	Y	Y
5 Bryant	?	Y	N	N	N	N	Y	Y
6 ***Barton***	N	Y	N	N	N	N	Y	Y
7 ***Archer***	Y	Y	N	N	N	N	Y	Y
8 ***Fields***	N	Y	N	N	N	N	Y	Y
9 Brooks	Y	Y	N	N	N	N	Y	Y
10 Pickle	Y	Y	N	Y	N	N	Y	Y
11 Leath	Y	Y	N	N	N	N	Y	Y
12 Wright	Y	Y	Y	Y	Y	?	N	N
13 ***Boulter***	Y	Y	N	N	-	-	+	+
14 ***Sweeney***	Y	Y	N	N	N	N	Y	Y
15 de la Garza	Y	?	N	N	Y	N	Y	Y
16 Coleman	Y	Y	N	N	N	N	Y	Y
17 Stenholm	Y	Y	Y	N	Y	N	Y	Y
18 Leland	?	Y	Y	Y	Y	Y	N	N
19 ***Combest***	Y	Y	N	N	N	N	Y	Y
20 Gonzalez	Y	Y	Y	Y	Y	Y	N	N
21 ***Loeffler***	N	Y	N	N	N	N	Y	Y
22 ***DeLay***	N	Y	N	N	N	N	Y	Y
23 Bustamante	Y	Y	N	?	N	N	Y	Y
24 Frost	Y	Y	Y	Y	Y	N	N	N
25 Andrews	Y	Y	N	N	N	N	Y	Y
26 ***Armey***	N	Y	N	N	N	N	Y	Y
27 Ortiz	Y	Y	N	N	N	N	Y	Y
UTAH								
1 ***Hansen***	N	Y	N	N	N	N	Y	Y
2 ***Monson***	N	Y	N	N	N	N	Y	Y
3 ***Nielson***	Y	Y	N	N	Y	N	Y	Y
VERMONT								
AL ***Jeffords***	Y	Y	Y	N	Y	N	Y	Y
VIRGINIA								
1 ***Bateman***	Y	Y	Y	Y	Y	N	Y	Y
2 ***Whitehurst***	N	Y	Y	Y	Y	Y	N	N
3 ***Bliley***	N	Y	N	N	N	N	Y	Y
4 Sisisky	Y	Y	N	N	N	N	Y	Y
5 Daniel	Y	Y	N	N	N	N	Y	Y
6 Olin	Y	?	N	N	N	N	Y	Y
7 ***Slaughter***	N	Y	Y	Y	Y	N	Y	Y
8 ***Parris***	N	Y	Y	N	Y	N	Y	Y
9 Boucher	?	Y	N	N	N	N	Y	Y
10 ***Wolf***	N	Y	Y	Y	Y	N	Y	Y
WASHINGTON								
1 ***Miller***	?	Y	Y	Y	Y	Y	N	N
2 Swift	Y	Y	N	N	Y	N	Y	Y
3 Bonker	?	Y	Y	Y	Y	N	Y	Y
4 ***Morrison***	Y	Y	N	N	Y	N	Y	Y
5 Foley	Y	Y	N	N	N	N	Y	Y
6 Dicks	Y	Y	Y	Y	Y	N	Y	Y
7 Lowry	Y	Y	Y	Y	Y	Y	N	N
8 ***Chandler***	N	Y	N	Y	Y	N	Y	Y
WEST VIRGINIA								
1 Mollohan	Y	Y	N	N	N	N	Y	Y
2 Staggers	Y	Y	N	N	N	N	Y	Y
3 Wise	Y	Y	N	N	N	N	Y	Y
4 Rahall	Y	Y	N	N	N	N	Y	Y
WISCONSIN								
1 Aspin	Y	Y	Y	Y	Y	Y	Y	Y
2 Kastenmeier	Y	Y	Y	Y	Y	Y	N	N
3 ***Gunderson***	N	Y	N	N	N	N	Y	Y
4 Kleczka	Y	Y	Y	Y	Y	Y	Y	Y
5 Moody	Y	Y	Y	Y	Y	Y	Y	Y
6 ***Petri***	Y	Y	N	N	Y	N	Y	Y
7 Obey	Y	Y	N	N	N	N	Y	Y
8 ***Roth***	N	Y	N	N	N	N	Y	Y
9 ***Sensenbrenner***	N	Y	N	N	Y	N	Y	Y
WYOMING								
AL ***Cheney***	?	Y	N	N	N	N	Y	Y

Southern states - Ala., Ark., Fla., Ga., Ky., La., Miss., N.C., Okla., S.C., Tenn., Texas, Va.

* The *Congressional Record* vote number is different from the CQ vote number because the *Record* includes quorum calls in its tally. CQ does not publish quorum call votes.

70. Procedural Motion. Sensenbrenner, R-Wis., motion to approve the House *Journal* of Monday, April 14. Motion agreed to 273-128: R 55-116; D 218-12 (ND 147-7, SD 71-5), April 15, 1986.

71. HR 4515. Aid to Nicaraguan Rebels/Urgent Supplemental Appropriations, Fiscal 1986. Bonior, D-Mich., motion to order the previous question (thus ending debate and the possibility of amendment) on the rule (H Res 415) to provide for House floor consideration of the bill to make supplemental appropriations for fiscal 1986 and to approve President Reagan's request for $100 million in aid to the Nicaraguan "contras." Motion agreed to 221-202: R 1-175; D 220-27 (ND 162-5, SD 58-22), April 15, 1986. A "nay" was a vote supporting the president's position.

72. HR 4515. Aid to Nicaraguan Rebels/Urgent Supplemental Appropriations, Fiscal 1986. Adoption of the rule (H Res 415) to provide for House floor consideration of the bill to make supplemental appropriations for fiscal 1986 and to approve President Reagan's request for $100 million in aid to the Nicaraguan "contras." Adopted 212-208: R 1-175; D 211-33 (ND 156-9, SD 55-24), April 15, 1986. A "nay" was a vote supporting the president's position.

73. Procedural Motion. Schuette, R-Mich., motion to approve the House *Journal* of Tuesday, April 15. Motion agreed to 244-134: R 41-123; D 203-11 (ND 135-8, SD 68-3), April 16, 1986.

74. H J Res 601. Aid to Nicaraguan Rebels. Hamilton, D-Ind., substitute to provide $27 million in humanitarian aid to Nicaraguan refugees. Adopted 361-66: R 177-1; D 184-65 (ND 154-14, SD 30-51), April 16, 1986. (Republicans voted "yea" on this amendment as a procedural move to prevent consideration of a subsequent amendment by Dave McCurdy, D-Okla.)

75. Procedural Motion. Clay, D-Mo., motion to approve the House *Journal* of Wednesday, April 16. Motion agreed to 281-116: R 61-107; D 220-9 (ND 146-6, SD 74-3), April 17, 1986.

76. HR 281. Construction Labor Law Amendments. Adoption of the rule (H Res 324) to provide for House floor consideration of the bill to prevent construction companies from circumventing labor laws to hire non-union workers. Adopted 379-38: R 139-34; D 240-4 (ND 167-0, SD 73-4), April 17, 1986.

77. HR 281. Construction Labor Law Amendments. Bartlett, R-Texas, amendment to narrow the definition of a "single employer" in the construction industry to cover companies and related entities only when there is a "substantial qualitative degree of interrelationship of operations." Rejected 165-247: R 138-31; D 27-216 (ND 1-167, SD 26-49), April 17, 1986.

KEY

- Y Voted for (yea).
- # Paired for.
- + Announced for.
- N Voted against (nay).
- X Paired against.
- - Announced against.
- P Voted "present."
- C Voted "present" to avoid possible conflict of interest.
- ? Did not vote or otherwise make a position known.

Democrats ***Republicans***

	70	71	72	73	74	75	76	77
ALABAMA								
1 ***Callahan***	Y	N	N	Y	Y	Y	Y	Y
2 ***Dickinson***	N	N	N	N	Y	N	?	Y
3 Nichols	?	?	?	?	?	?	?	?
4 Bevill	Y	Y	Y	Y	N	Y	Y	N
5 Flippo	Y	N	N	Y	N	Y	Y	N
6 Erdreich	Y	N	N	Y	N	Y	Y	N
7 Shelby	Y	N	N	Y	Y	Y	Y	N
ALASKA								
AL ***Young***	N	N	N	N	Y	N	Y	N
ARIZONA								
1 ***McCain***	N	N	N	N	Y	Y	Y	Y
2 Udall	Y	Y	Y	Y	Y	Y	Y	N
3 ***Stump***	N	N	N	N	Y	N	N	Y
4 ***Rudd***	Y	N	N	Y	Y	Y	N	Y
5 ***Kolbe***	N	N	N	N	Y	N	Y	Y
ARKANSAS								
1 Alexander	Y	Y	Y	Y	Y	Y	Y	N
2 Robinson	Y	N	Y	Y	N	Y	Y	N
3 ***Hammerschmidt***	Y	N	N	N	Y	Y	Y	Y
4 Anthony	Y	Y	Y	Y	Y	Y	Y	N
CALIFORNIA								
1 Bosco	Y	Y	Y	Y	Y	Y	Y	N
2 ***Chappie***	N	N	N	N	Y	N	Y	Y
3 Matsui	Y	Y	Y	Y	Y	Y	Y	N
4 Fazio	Y	Y	Y	?	Y	Y	Y	N
5 Burton	Y	Y	Y	Y	Y	Y	Y	N
6 Boxer	Y	Y	Y	Y	Y	Y	Y	N
7 Miller	Y	Y	Y	?	Y	Y	Y	N
8 Dellums	Y	Y	Y	?	Y	Y	Y	N
9 Stark	Y	Y	Y	?	Y	Y	?	N
10 Edwards	Y	Y	Y	Y	Y	Y	Y	N
11 Lantos	Y	Y	Y	Y	Y	Y	Y	N
12 ***Zschau***	N	N	N	N	Y	N	Y	Y
13 Mineta	Y	Y	Y	Y	Y	Y	Y	N
14 ***Shumway***	Y	N	N	Y	Y	Y	Y	Y
15 Coelho	Y	Y	Y	Y	Y	Y	Y	N
16 Panetta	Y	Y	Y	Y	Y	Y	Y	N
17 ***Pashayan***	N	N	N	N	Y	N	Y	Y
18 Lehman	Y	Y	Y	Y	Y	Y	Y	N
19 ***Lagomarsino***	N	N	N	N	Y	N	Y	Y
20 ***Thomas***	N	N	N	N	Y	N	Y	Y
21 ***Fiedler***	N	N	N	N	Y	N	Y	Y
22 ***Moorhead***	N	N	N	N	Y	N	Y	Y
23 Beilenson	Y	Y	Y	Y	Y	Y	Y	N
24 Waxman	Y	Y	Y	Y	Y	Y	Y	N
25 Roybal	Y	Y	Y	Y	Y	Y	Y	N
26 Berman	?	Y	Y	Y	Y	Y	Y	N
27 Levine	Y	Y	Y	Y	Y	Y	Y	N
28 Dixon	Y	Y	Y	?	Y	?	Y	N
29 Hawkins	Y	Y	Y	N	Y	N	Y	N
30 Martinez	Y	Y	Y	Y	Y	Y	Y	N
31 Dymally	Y	Y	Y	Y	Y	Y	Y	N
32 Anderson	Y	Y	Y	Y	Y	Y	Y	N
33 ***Dreier***	N	N	N	N	Y	N	N	Y
34 Torres	Y	Y	Y	Y	Y	Y	Y	N
35 ***Lewis***	N	N	N	N	Y	N	N	Y
36 Brown	Y	Y	Y	Y	Y	Y	Y	N
37 ***McCandless***	N	N	N	N	Y	N	N	Y
38 ***Dornan***	N	N	N	N	Y	N	Y	?
39 ***Dannemeyer***	N	N	N	N	Y	N	Y	Y
40 ***Badham***	N	N	N	N	Y	Y	N	Y
41 ***Lowery***	N	N	N	?	Y	N	?	?
42 ***Lungren***	N	N	N	N	Y	N	Y	Y
43 ***Packard***	Y	N	N	Y	Y	Y	Y	Y
44 Bates	Y	Y	Y	Y	Y	Y	Y	N
45 ***Hunter***	?	N	N	N	Y	N	N	Y
COLORADO								
1 Schroeder	N	Y	Y	N	Y	N	Y	N
2 Wirth	Y	Y	Y	Y	Y	Y	Y	N
3 ***Strang***	N	N	N	N	Y	Y	Y	Y
4 ***Brown***	N	N	N	N	Y	N	N	Y
5 ***Kramer***	N	N	N	N	Y	N	N	?
6 ***Schaefer***	N	N	N	N	Y	N	N	N
CONNECTICUT								
1 Kennelly	Y	Y	Y	Y	Y	Y	Y	N
2 Gejdenson	Y	Y	Y	Y	Y	Y	Y	N
3 Morrison	?	Y	Y	Y	Y	Y	Y	N
4 ***McKinney***	Y	N	N	Y	Y	?	Y	N
5 ***Rowland***	N	N	N	Y	Y	Y	Y	N
6 ***Johnson***	Y	N	N	Y	Y	Y	Y	N
DELAWARE								
AL Carper	Y	Y	Y	Y	Y	Y	Y	N
FLORIDA								
1 Hutto	Y	N	N	Y	N	Y	N	Y
2 Fuqua	Y	Y	Y	Y	N	Y	Y	N
3 Bennett	Y	N	N	Y	N	Y	Y	N
4 Chappell	Y	Y	Y	Y	N	Y	Y	Y
5 ***McCollum***	Y	N	N	Y	Y	N	N	Y
6 MacKay	N	Y	Y	Y	N	?	Y	N
7 Gibbons	Y	Y	?	P	N	Y	Y	Y
8 ***Young***	N	N	N	N	Y	N	Y	?
9 ***Bilirakis***	N	N	N	N	Y	N	Y	Y
10 ***Ireland***	N	N	N	N	Y	N	N	Y
11 Nelson	Y	Y	N	Y	N	Y	Y	Y
12 ***Lewis***	N	N	N	?	Y	N	Y	Y
13 ***Mack***	N	N	N	N	Y	N	Y	Y
14 Mica	Y	Y	Y	Y	N	Y	Y	N
15 ***Shaw***	N	N	N	N	Y	Y	Y	Y
16 Smith	Y	Y	Y	?	N	Y	Y	N
17 Lehman	Y	Y	Y	Y	Y	Y	Y	N
18 Pepper	Y	Y	Y	Y	N	Y	Y	N
19 Fascell	Y	N	N	Y	N	Y	Y	N
GEORGIA								
1 Thomas	Y	N	N	Y	N	Y	Y	N
2 Hatcher	Y	Y	Y	P	N	Y	Y	Y
3 Ray	Y	Y	N	Y	N	Y	Y	Y
4 ***Swindall***	N	N	N	N	Y	N	Y	+
5 Fowler	Y	Y	Y	Y	Y	Y	Y	N
6 ***Gingrich***	N	N	N	N	Y	?	Y	Y
7 Darden	Y	N	Y	Y	N	Y	Y	Y
8 Rowland	Y	N	N	Y	N	Y	Y	Y
9 Jenkins	Y	N	N	Y	N	Y	Y	Y
10 Barnard	Y	N	N	Y	N	Y	Y	N
HAWAII								
1 Heftel	Y	Y	Y	P	Y	?	Y	N
2 Akaka	Y	Y	Y	Y	Y	Y	Y	N
IDAHO								
1 ***Craig***	Y	N	N	N	Y	N	Y	Y
2 Stallings	Y	N	N	Y	Y	Y	Y	N
ILLINOIS								
1 Hayes	Y	Y	Y	Y	Y	Y	Y	N
2 Savage	?	Y	Y	?	Y	?	Y	N
3 Russo	Y	Y	Y	Y	Y	Y	Y	N
4 ***O'Brien***	?	?	?	?	?	?	?	?
5 Lipinski	Y	Y	Y	Y	N	Y	Y	N
6 ***Hyde***	Y	N	N	Y	Y	Y	Y	Y
7 Collins	Y	Y	Y	Y	Y	Y	Y	N
8 Rostenkowski	Y	Y	Y	P	Y	Y	Y	N
9 Yates	Y	Y	Y	Y	Y	Y	Y	N
10 ***Porter***	Y	Y	N	N	Y	N	Y	Y
11 Annunzio	Y	Y	Y	Y	Y	Y	Y	N
12 ***Crane***	N	N	N	N	Y	N	Y	Y
13 ***Fawell***	N	N	N	N	Y	N	Y	Y
14 ***Grotberg***	?	?	?	?	?	?	?	?
15 ***Madigan***	N	N	N	N	Y	N	Y	?
16 ***Martin***	N	N	N	N	Y	?	Y	Y
17 Evans	Y	Y	Y	Y	Y	Y	Y	N
18 ***Michel***	N	N	N	?	Y	Y	Y	Y
19 Bruce	Y	Y	Y	Y	Y	Y	Y	N
20 Durbin	Y	Y	Y	N	Y	Y	Y	N
21 Price	Y	Y	Y	Y	Y	Y	Y	N
22 Gray	Y	Y	Y	Y	Y	?	Y	N
INDIANA								
1 Visclosky	Y	Y	Y	Y	Y	Y	Y	N
2 Sharp	Y	Y	Y	Y	Y	Y	Y	N
3 ***Hiler***	N	N	N	N	Y	Y	Y	Y
4 ***Coats***	N	N	N	N	Y	N	Y	Y
5 ***Hillis***	?	?	?	Y	Y	Y	N	Y

ND - Northern Democrats SD - Southern Democrats

	70	71	72	73	74	75	76	77
6 **Burton**	N	N	N	N	Y	N	N	Y
7 **Myers**	Y	N	N	Y	Y	Y	Y	Y
8 McCloskey	Y	Y	Y	Y	Y	?	Y	N
9 Hamilton	Y	Y	Y	Y	Y	Y	Y	N
10 Jacobs	N	Y	Y	N	Y	N	Y	N
IOWA								
1 **Leach**	N	N	N	N	Y	N	Y	Y
2 **Tauke**	Y	N	N	N	Y	N	Y	Y
3 **Evans**	N	N	N	N	Y	?	Y	Y
4 Smith	Y	Y	Y	Y	N	Y	Y	N
5 **Lightfoot**	N	N	N	N	Y	N	Y	Y
6 Bedell	Y	Y	Y	Y	Y	Y	Y	N
KANSAS								
1 **Roberts**	N	N	N	N	Y	N	N	Y
2 Slattery	Y	Y	N	Y	Y	Y	Y	N
3 **Meyers**	N	N	N	N	Y	N	Y	Y
4 Glickman	Y	Y	Y	Y	Y	Y	Y	N
5 **Whittaker**	N	N	N	N	Y	N	N	Y
KENTUCKY								
1 Hubbard	Y	N	N	Y	Y	Y	Y	N
2 Natcher	Y	Y	Y	Y	Y	Y	Y	N
3 Mazzoli	Y	Y	Y	Y	N	Y	Y	Y
4 **Snyder**	Y	N	N	Y	Y	Y	N	Y
5 **Rogers**	N	N	N	N	Y	Y	Y	Y
6 **Hopkins**	Y	N	N	N	Y	Y	Y	Y
7 Perkins	Y	Y	Y	Y	N	Y	Y	N
LOUISIANA								
1 **Livingston**	Y	N	N	N	Y	N	Y	Y
2 Boggs	Y	Y	Y	Y	Y	Y	Y	N
3 Tauzin	Y	N	N	Y	N	Y	Y	Y
4 Roemer	N	N	N	N	N	N	Y	N
5 Huckaby	Y	Y	Y	Y	N	Y	Y	Y
6 **Moore**	Y	N	N	Y	Y	Y	Y	Y
7 Breaux	Y	N	N	Y	Y	Y	Y	N
8 Long	?	Y	Y	Y	Y	Y	Y	N
MAINE								
1 **McKernan**	N	N	N	N	Y	?	?	Y
2 **Snowe**	N	N	N	N	Y	N	Y	Y
MARYLAND								
1 Dyson	Y	N	N	Y	N	Y	Y	N
2 **Bentley**	N	N	N	N	Y	N	Y	N
3 Mikulski	Y	Y	Y	?	Y	Y	Y	N
4 **Holt**	?	N	N	Y	Y	Y	Y	Y
5 Hoyer	Y	Y	Y	Y	Y	Y	Y	N
6 Byron	Y	N	Y	Y	N	Y	Y	Y
7 Mitchell	N	Y	Y	?	Y	?	Y	N
8 Barnes	Y	Y	Y	Y	Y	Y	Y	N
MASSACHUSETTS								
1 **Conte**	N	N	N	Y	Y	N	Y	N
2 Boland	Y	Y	Y	Y	Y	Y	Y	N
3 Early	Y	Y	Y	Y	Y	Y	Y	N
4 Frank	Y	Y	Y	Y	Y	Y	Y	N
5 Atkins	?	Y	Y	?	Y	?	Y	N
6 Mavroules	Y	Y	Y	Y	Y	Y	Y	N
7 Markey	Y	Y	Y	Y	Y	?	Y	N
8 O'Neill								
9 Moakley	Y	Y	Y	Y	Y	Y	Y	N
10 Studds	Y	Y	Y	Y	Y	Y	Y	N
11 Donnelly	Y	Y	Y	Y	Y	Y	Y	N
MICHIGAN								
1 Conyers	Y	N	N	?	Y	Y	Y	N
2 **Pursell**	Y	N	N	Y	Y	Y	Y	Y
3 Wolpe	Y	Y	Y	Y	Y	Y	Y	N
4 **Siljander**	N	N	N	N	Y	N	Y	Y
5 **Henry**	N	N	N	N	Y	Y	Y	Y
6 Carr	Y	Y	Y	Y	Y	Y	Y	N
7 Kildee	Y	Y	Y	Y	Y	P	Y	N
8 Traxler	Y	Y	Y	Y	Y	Y	Y	N
9 **Vander Jagt**	N	N	N	N	Y	N	Y	Y
10 **Schuette**	N	N	N	N	Y	N	Y	Y
11 **Davis**	?	?	?	Y	Y	N	Y	?
12 Bonior	Y	Y	Y	Y	Y	Y	Y	N
13 Crockett	Y	Y	Y	Y	Y	Y	Y	N
14 Hertel	Y	Y	Y	Y	Y	Y	Y	N
15 Ford	Y	Y	Y	?	Y	Y	Y	N
16 Dingell	?	Y	?	?	Y	?	Y	N
17 Levin	Y	Y	Y	Y	Y	Y	Y	N
18 **Broomfield**	Y	N	N	Y	Y	?	N	Y
MINNESOTA								
1 Penny	N	Y	Y	N	Y	N	Y	N
2 **Weber**	?	N	N	N	Y	N	N	Y
3 **Frenzel**	Y	N	N	?	Y	N	Y	Y
4 Vento	Y	Y	Y	Y	Y	?	Y	N
5 Sabo	Y	Y	Y	Y	Y	Y	Y	N
6 Sikorski	N	Y	Y	N	Y	N	Y	N

	70	71	72	73	74	75	76	77
7 **Stangeland**	N	N	N	N	Y	N	Y	Y
8 Oberstar	Y	Y	Y	Y	Y	Y	Y	N
MISSISSIPPI								
1 Whitten	Y	Y	Y	Y	N	Y	Y	Y
2 **Franklin**	Y	N	N	N	Y	Y	Y	Y
3 Montgomery	Y	Y	Y	Y	N	Y	Y	Y
4 Dowdy	Y	Y	Y	Y	N	Y	Y	N
5 **Lott**	?	N	N	N	Y	Y	Y	Y
MISSOURI								
1 Clay	N	Y	Y	N	Y	N	Y	N
2 Young	Y	Y	Y	Y	Y	Y	Y	N
3 Gephardt	Y	Y	Y	Y	Y	?	?	?
4 Skelton	Y	Y	N	?	N	Y	Y	N
5 Wheat	Y	Y	Y	Y	Y	Y	Y	N
6 **Coleman**	N	N	N	N	Y	N	Y	Y
7 **Taylor**	N	N	N	Y	Y	Y	Y	Y
8 **Emerson**	N	N	N	N	Y	N	Y	Y
9 Volkmer	Y	Y	Y	Y	Y	Y	Y	N
MONTANA								
1 Williams	?	Y	Y	?	Y	Y	Y	N
2 **Marlenee**	N	N	N	?	Y	N	N	Y
NEBRASKA								
1 **Bereuter**	N	N	N	N	Y	N	Y	Y
2 **Daub**	N	N	N	N	Y	N	Y	Y
3 **Smith**	Y	N	N	Y	Y	Y	Y	Y
NEVADA								
1 Reid	Y	Y	N	Y	Y	Y	Y	N
2 **Vucanovich**	N	N	N	N	Y	N	Y	Y
NEW HAMPSHIRE								
1 **Smith**	N	N	N	N	Y	N	Y	Y
2 **Gregg**	N	N	N	N	Y	N	Y	Y
NEW JERSEY								
1 Florio	Y	Y	Y	Y	N	Y	Y	N
2 Hughes	Y	Y	N	Y	Y	Y	Y	N
3 Howard	Y	Y	Y	Y	Y	Y	Y	N
4 **Smith**	Y	N	N	?	Y	Y	Y	N
5 **Roukema**	N	N	N	N	Y	N	Y	Y
6 Dwyer	Y	Y	Y	Y	Y	Y	Y	N
7 **Rinaldo**	Y	N	N	?	Y	Y	Y	N
8 Roe	Y	Y	Y	Y	Y	Y	Y	N
9 Torricelli	Y	Y	N	Y	Y	Y	Y	N
10 Rodino	Y	Y	Y	?	Y	?	Y	N
11 **Gallo**	N	N	N	?	Y	N	Y	N
12 **Courter**	N	N	N	N	Y	N	Y	N
13 **Saxton**	N	N	N	N	Y	N	Y	N
14 Guarini	Y	Y	Y	?	Y	Y	Y	N
NEW MEXICO								
1 **Lujan**	?	?	?	?	?	?	?	?
2 **Skeen**	N	N	N	N	Y	N	Y	Y
3 Richardson	Y	Y	Y	Y	Y	Y	Y	N
NEW YORK								
1 **Carney**	N	N	N	N	Y	N	Y	Y
2 Downey	Y	Y	Y	Y	Y	Y	Y	N
3 Mrazek	Y	Y	Y	Y	Y	?	Y	N
4 **Lent**	N	N	N	N	Y	N	Y	N
5 **McGrath**	N	N	N	N	Y	N	Y	N
6 Vacancy *								
7 Ackerman	Y	Y	Y	Y	Y	Y	Y	N
8 Scheuer	Y	Y	?	?	Y	Y	Y	N
9 Manton	Y	Y	Y	Y	Y	Y	Y	N
10 Schumer	Y	Y	Y	Y	Y	Y	Y	N
11 Towns	?	?	?	?	Y	Y	Y	N
12 Owens	Y	Y	Y	Y	Y	Y	Y	N
13 Solarz	Y	Y	Y	Y	Y	Y	Y	N
14 **Molinari**	N	N	N	N	Y	N	Y	N
15 **Green**	Y	N	Y	Y	Y	Y	Y	Y
16 Rangel	Y	Y	Y	Y	Y	Y	Y	N
17 Weiss	Y	Y	Y	Y	Y	Y	Y	N
18 Garcia	Y	Y	Y	Y	Y	Y	Y	N
19 Biaggi	Y	Y	Y	?	Y	Y	Y	N
20 **DioGuardi**	Y	N	N	N	Y	Y	Y	N
21 **Fish**	Y	N	N	Y	Y	Y	Y	N
22 **Gilman**	Y	N	N	Y	Y	Y	Y	N
23 Stratton	Y	N	N	Y	Y	Y	Y	N
24 **Solomon**	N	N	N	N	Y	N	Y	Y
25 **Boehlert**	N	N	N	N	Y	N	Y	N
26 **Martin**	N	N	N	N	Y	N	Y	Y
27 **Wortley**	Y	N	N	N	Y	Y	Y	N
28 McHugh	Y	Y	Y	Y	Y	Y	Y	N
29 **Horton**	Y	N	N	Y	Y	Y	Y	N
30 **Eckert**	Y	N	N	Y	?	Y	Y	Y
31 **Kemp**	Y	N	N	?	Y	Y	Y	Y
32 LaFalce	Y	Y	Y	Y	Y	Y	Y	N
33 Nowak	Y	Y	Y	Y	Y	Y	Y	N
34 Lundine	?	Y	Y	Y	Y	Y	Y	N

	70	71	72	73	74	75	76	77
NORTH CAROLINA								
1 Jones	Y	Y	Y	Y	Y	Y	Y	N
2 Valentine	Y	Y	Y	Y	N	Y	Y	Y
3 Whitley	Y	Y	Y	Y	N	Y	Y	Y
4 **Cobey**	N	N	N	N	Y	N	N	Y
5 Neal	Y	Y	Y	Y	Y	Y	?	Y
6 **Coble**	N	N	N	N	Y	N	N	Y
7 Rose	Y	Y	Y	Y	Y	Y	?	N
8 Hefner	Y	Y	Y	Y	N	Y	Y	Y
9 **McMillan**	Y	N	N	N	Y	P	N	Y
10 **Broyhill**	Y	N	N	?	Y	Y	N	Y
11 **Hendon**	N	N	N	N	Y	N	N	Y
NORTH DAKOTA								
AL Dorgan	Y	Y	Y	Y	Y	Y	Y	N
OHIO								
1 Luken	Y	Y	Y	Y	Y	P	Y	N
2 **Gradison**	Y	N	N	Y	N	Y	Y	Y
3 Hall	Y	Y	Y	Y	N	Y	Y	N
4 **Oxley**	N	N	N	N	Y	N	Y	Y
5 **Latta**	N	N	N	N	Y	N	Y	Y
6 **McEwen**	Y	N	N	?	Y	Y	Y	Y
7 **DeWine**	N	N	N	N	Y	N	Y	Y
8 **Kindness**	N	N	N	N	Y	?	?	Y
9 Kaptur	Y	Y	Y	?	Y	Y	Y	N
10 **Miller**	N	N	N	N	Y	N	Y	Y
11 Eckart	Y	Y	Y	Y	Y	Y	Y	N
12 **Kasich**	Y	N	N	Y	Y	Y	Y	Y
13 Pease	Y	Y	Y	Y	Y	Y	Y	N
14 Seiberling	?	Y	Y	Y	Y	Y	Y	N
15 **Wylie**	Y	N	N	Y	Y	Y	Y	N
16 **Regula**	Y	N	N	Y	Y	Y	Y	N
17 Traficant	Y	Y	Y	Y	Y	Y	Y	N
18 Applegate	?	Y	Y	Y	Y	Y	Y	N
19 Feighan	Y	Y	Y	Y	Y	Y	Y	N
20 Oakar	Y	Y	Y	Y	Y	Y	Y	N
21 Stokes	Y	Y	Y	Y	Y	Y	Y	N
OKLAHOMA								
1 Jones	N	Y	Y	Y	N	Y	?	?
2 Synar	Y	Y	Y	Y	Y	Y	Y	N
3 Watkins	N	Y	Y	P	N	N	Y	Y
4 McCurdy	Y	Y	Y	Y	Y	Y	Y	N
5 **Edwards**	N	N	N	N	Y	Y	Y	Y
6 English	Y	Y	N	Y	N	Y	Y	Y
OREGON								
1 AuCoin	Y	Y	Y	Y	Y	Y	Y	N
2 **Smith, R.**	N	N	N	N	Y	N	Y	Y
3 Wyden	Y	Y	Y	Y	Y	Y	Y	N
4 Weaver	Y	Y	Y	Y	Y	Y	Y	N
5 **Smith, D.**	N	N	N	N	Y	Y	Y	Y
PENNSYLVANIA								
1 Foglietta	?	Y	Y	Y	Y	Y	Y	N
2 Gray	Y	Y	Y	Y	Y	?	Y	N
3 Borski	Y	Y	Y	Y	Y	Y	Y	N
4 Kolter	Y	Y	Y	Y	N	Y	Y	N
5 **Schulze**	Y	N	N	Y	Y	Y	Y	Y
6 Yatron	Y	Y	Y	Y	Y	Y	Y	N
7 Edgar	?	?	?	?	Y	?	Y	N
8 Kostmayer	Y	Y	Y	Y	Y	Y	Y	N
9 **Shuster**	N	N	N	N	Y	N	Y	Y
10 **McDade**	Y	N	N	Y	Y	Y	Y	N
11 Kanjorski	Y	Y	Y	Y	Y	Y	Y	N
12 Murtha	?	Y	Y	Y	N	Y	Y	N
13 **Coughlin**	N	N	N	N	Y	N	Y	N
14 Coyne	?	Y	Y	Y	Y	Y	Y	N
15 **Ritter**	Y	N	N	Y	Y	?	Y	N
16 **Walker**	N	N	N	N	Y	N	Y	Y
17 **Gekas**	N	N	N	N	Y	N	Y	Y
18 Walgren	Y	Y	Y	Y	N	Y	Y	N
19 **Goodling**	N	N	N	N	Y	N	Y	Y
20 Gaydos	?	Y	Y	?	N	Y	Y	N
21 **Ridge**	N	N	N	N	Y	N	Y	N
22 Murphy	Y	Y	Y	Y	N	Y	Y	N
23 **Clinger**	Y	N	N	N	Y	N	Y	N
RHODE ISLAND								
1 St Germain	Y	Y	Y	Y	Y	Y	Y	N
2 **Schneider**	N	N	N	Y	Y	Y	Y	N
SOUTH CAROLINA								
1 **Hartnett**	N	N	N	Y	Y	Y	N	Y
2 **Spence**	N	N	N	N	Y	N	Y	Y
3 Derrick	Y	Y	Y	?	Y	Y	Y	N
4 **Campbell**	N	N	N	?	Y	N	N	#
5 Spratt	Y	Y	Y	Y	N	Y	Y	N
6 Tallon	?	?	?	?	N	Y	Y	N
SOUTH DAKOTA								
AL Daschle	Y	Y	Y	Y	Y	Y	Y	N

	70	71	72	73	74	75	76	77
TENNESSEE								
1 **Quillen**	Y	N	N	N	Y	Y	Y	Y
2 **Duncan**	Y	N	N	N	Y	?	Y	Y
3 Lloyd	N	N	N	N	N	N	Y	?
4 Cooper	Y	Y	N	Y	Y	Y	Y	Y
5 Boner	Y	Y	Y	Y	Y	Y	Y	N
6 Gordon	Y	Y	Y	Y	Y	Y	Y	N
7 **Sundquist**	N	N	N	N	Y	N	Y	Y
8 Jones	?	Y	Y	Y	Y	Y	Y	?
9 Ford	Y	Y	Y	Y	Y	Y	Y	X
TEXAS								
1 Chapman	Y	Y	Y	?	N	Y	Y	N
2 Wilson	Y	Y	Y	Y	N	?	Y	N
3 **Bartlett**	N	N	N	N	Y	N	Y	Y
4 Hall, R.	Y	N	N	Y	N	Y	N	Y
5 Bryant	Y	Y	Y	Y	Y	Y	Y	N
6 **Barton**	N	N	N	N	Y	N	N	Y
7 **Archer**	Y	N	N	Y	Y	Y	N	Y
8 **Fields**	?	N	N	N	Y	N	N	Y
9 Brooks	Y	Y	Y	Y	Y	Y	Y	N
10 Pickle	Y	Y	Y	Y	N	Y	Y	N
11 Leath	Y	N	N	?	N	?	N	Y
12 Wright	?	Y	Y	Y	Y	Y	Y	N
13 **Boulter**	N	N	N	N	Y	N	?	Y
14 **Sweeney**	Y	N	N	?	Y	Y	Y	Y
15 de la Garza	Y	N	N	?	Y	Y	Y	N
16 Coleman	Y	Y	Y	Y	Y	Y	Y	N
17 Stenholm	Y	N	N	N	N	Y	N	Y
18 Leland	Y	Y	Y	?	Y	?	Y	N
19 **Combest**	Y	N	N	Y	Y	Y	Y	Y
20 Gonzalez	Y	Y	Y	Y	Y	Y	Y	N
21 **Loeffler**	?	?	?	N	Y	?	?	?
22 **DeLay**	N	N	N	N	Y	N	Y	Y
23 Bustamante	Y	Y	Y	Y	N	Y	?	?
24 Frost	Y	Y	Y	Y	Y	Y	Y	N
25 Andrews	Y	Y	Y	Y	N	Y	Y	N
26 **Armey**	N	N	N	N	Y	Y	N	Y
27 Ortiz	P	Y	Y	Y	N	Y	Y	N
UTAH								
1 **Hansen**	Y	N	N	N	Y	Y	N	Y
2 **Monson**	N	N	N	N	Y	N	N	Y
3 **Nielson**	N	N	N	N	Y	N	Y	Y
VERMONT								
AL **Jeffords**	Y	N	N	Y	Y	Y	Y	Y
VIRGINIA								
1 **Bateman**	Y	N	N	Y	Y	Y	Y	Y
2 **Whitehurst**	N	N	N	N	Y	N	Y	?
3 **Bliley**	N	N	N	N	Y	N	Y	Y
4 Sisisky	Y	Y	Y	Y	N	Y	Y	?
5 Daniel	Y	N	N	Y	N	Y	Y	Y
6 Olin	Y	Y	Y	Y	Y	Y	Y	N
7 **Slaughter**	N	N	N	N	Y	N	Y	Y
8 **Parris**	N	N	N	N	Y	N	Y	Y
9 Boucher	Y	Y	Y	Y	Y	Y	Y	N
10 **Wolf**	N	N	N	N	Y	N	Y	Y
WASHINGTON								
1 **Miller**	Y	N	N	Y	Y	Y	Y	N
2 Swift	Y	Y	Y	Y	Y	Y	Y	N
3 Bonker	Y	Y	Y	Y	Y	Y	Y	N
4 **Morrison**	Y	N	N	Y	Y	Y	Y	Y
5 Foley	Y	Y	Y	?	Y	Y	Y	N
6 Dicks	Y	Y	Y	Y	Y	Y	Y	N
7 Lowry	N	Y	Y	N	Y	Y	Y	N
8 **Chandler**	N	N	N	N	Y	N	Y	Y
WEST VIRGINIA								
1 Mollohan	Y	Y	Y	Y	N	Y	Y	N
2 Staggers	Y	Y	Y	Y	Y	Y	Y	N
3 Wise	Y	Y	Y	?	Y	Y	Y	N
4 Rahall	Y	Y	Y	Y	?	Y	Y	N
WISCONSIN								
1 Aspin	Y	Y	Y	Y	N	Y	Y	N
2 Kastenmeier	Y	Y	Y	Y	Y	Y	Y	N
3 **Gunderson**	Y	N	N	N	Y	N	Y	Y
4 Kleczka	Y	Y	Y	Y	Y	Y	Y	N
5 Moody	Y	Y	Y	Y	Y	Y	Y	N
6 **Petri**	Y	N	N	Y	Y	Y	Y	N
7 Obey	Y	Y	Y	Y	Y	Y	Y	N
8 **Roth**	N	N	N	N	Y	N	Y	Y
9 **Sensenbrenner**	N	N	N	?	Y	N	Y	Y
WYOMING								
AL **Cheney**	N	N	N	?	Y	N	Y	Y

** Rep. Joseph P. Addabbo, D-N.Y., died on April 10, 1986. The last vote for which he was eligible was CQ vote 69.*

Southern states - Ala., Ark., Fla., Ga., Ky., La., Miss., N.C., Okla., S.C., Tenn., Texas, Va.

* The *Congressional Record* vote number is different from the CQ vote number because the *Record* includes quorum calls in its tally. CQ does not publish quorum call votes.

78. HR 281. Construction Labor Law Amendments. Bartlett, R-Texas, amendment to let construction workers vote by secret ballot on whether or not they want to be represented by a union contract. Rejected 123-286: R 107-59; D 16-227 (ND 1-167, SD 15-60), April 17, 1986.

79. HR 281. Construction Labor Law Amendments. Armey, R-Texas, amendment to limit the compulsory payment of union dues to those workers who are a formal party to a pre-hire agreement between a union and a construction company, and to exempt employees who work for related subsidiaries. Rejected 121-283: R 106-60; D 15-223 (ND 1-164, SD 14-59), April 17, 1986.

80. HR 281. Construction Labor Law Amendments. Passage of the bill to bar construction companies from circumventing labor laws to hire non-union workers for construction projects. Passed 229-173: R 29-134; D 200-39 (ND 162-3, SD 38-36), April 17, 1986. A "nay" was a vote supporting the president's position.

81. HR 4392. Plague Control. Waxman, D-Calif., motion to suspend the rules and pass the bill to authorize $1 million in each of fiscal years 1987 and 1988 for grants to states for programs to control bubonic plague. Motion rejected 246-155: R 37-135; D 209-20 (ND 146-6, SD 63-14), April 22, 1986. A two-thirds majority of those present and voting (268 in this case) is required for passage under suspension of the rules. A "nay" was a vote supporting the president's position.

82. HR 4515. Urgent Supplemental Appropriations, Fiscal 1986. Adoption of the rule (H Res 425) to provide for House floor consideration of the bill to appropriate $1.7 billion in urgent supplemental funds for fiscal 1986. Rejected 187-220: R 8-160; D 179-60 (ND 131-30, SD 48-30), April 22, 1986.

83. HR 4420. Military Retirement Reform. Adoption of the rule (H Res 421) to provide for House floor consideration of the bill to reduce the annuities paid to military personnel who join the armed services after enactment of the bill and retire after less than 30 years of active service. Adopted 403-1: R 168-1; D 235-0 (ND 158-0, SD 77-0), April 22, 1986.

84. HR 4420. Military Retirement Reform. Montgomery, D-Miss., amendment to increase by $285 million the fiscal 1986 authorization for equipment for National Guard and reserve forces. Adopted 374-35: R 165-8; D 209-27 (ND 134-26, SD 75-1), April 22, 1986.

85. HR 4420. Military Retirement Reform. Passage of the bill to reduce the annuities paid to military personnel who join the armed services after enactment of the bill and retire after less than 30 years of active service. Passed 399-7: R 173-1; D 226-6 (ND 155-4, SD 71-2), April 22, 1986. A "nay" was a vote supporting the president's position.

KEY

Y Voted for (yea).
\# Paired for.
\+ Announced for.
N Voted against (nay).
X Paired against.
\- Announced against.
P Voted "present."
C Voted "present" to avoid possible conflict of interest.
? Did not vote or otherwise make a position known.

Democrats *Republicans*

	78	79	80	81	82	83	84	85
ALABAMA								
1 *Callahan*	Y	Y	N	N	N	Y	Y	Y
2 *Dickinson*	Y	?	?	N	N	Y	N	Y
3 Nichols	?	?	?	?	?	?	?	?
4 Bevill	N	N	Y	Y	Y	Y	Y	Y
5 Flippo	N	N	Y	Y	Y	Y	Y	Y
6 Erdreich	N	N	Y	Y	Y	Y	Y	Y
7 Shelby	N	N	Y	Y	Y	Y	Y	Y
ALASKA								
AL *Young*	N	N	Y	N	N	Y	Y	Y
ARIZONA								
1 *McCain*	N	Y	N	N	N	Y	Y	Y
2 Udall	N	N	Y	Y	Y	?	Y	Y
3 *Stump*	Y	Y	N	N	N	Y	Y	Y
4 *Rudd*	?	?	X	N	N	Y	Y	Y
5 *Kolbe*	N	Y	N	N	N	Y	Y	Y
ARKANSAS								
1 Alexander	N	N	Y	Y	Y	Y	?	?
2 Robinson	N	N	Y	Y	Y	Y	Y	?
3 *Hammerschmidt*	Y	Y	N	N	Y	Y	Y	Y
4 Anthony	Y	N	N	?	?	?	?	?
CALIFORNIA								
1 Bosco	N	?	Y	Y	Y	Y	Y	Y
2 *Chappie*	Y	Y	N	N	N	Y	Y	Y
3 Matsui	N	N	Y	Y	Y	Y	Y	Y
4 Fazio	N	N	Y	Y	Y	Y	Y	Y
5 Burton	N	N	Y	Y	Y	Y	Y	Y
6 Boxer	N	N	Y	Y	Y	Y	Y	Y
7 Miller	N	N	Y	Y	N	Y	N	Y
8 Dellums	N	N	Y	Y	Y	Y	N	Y
9 Stark	N	N	Y	Y	Y	Y	N	Y
10 Edwards	N	N	Y	Y	Y	Y	Y	Y
11 Lantos	N	N	Y	Y	Y	Y	Y	Y
12 *Zschau*	Y	Y	N	?	?	?	?	?
13 Mineta	N	N	Y	Y	Y	Y	Y	Y
14 *Shumway*	Y	Y	N	N	N	Y	Y	Y
15 Coelho	N	N	Y	Y	Y	Y	Y	Y
16 Panetta	N	N	Y	Y	N	Y	Y	Y
17 *Pashayan*	?	N	Y	Y	N	Y	Y	Y
18 Lehman	N	N	Y	Y	N	Y	Y	Y
19 *Lagomarsino*	N	Y	N	N	N	Y	Y	Y
20 *Thomas*	Y	Y	N	N	N	Y	Y	Y
21 *Fiedler*	Y	Y	N	?	?	?	?	?
22 *Moorhead*	N	Y	N	N	N	Y	Y	Y
23 Beilenson	N	N	Y	Y	Y	Y	N	Y
24 Waxman	N	N	Y	Y	Y	Y	Y	Y
25 Roybal	N	N	Y	Y	Y	Y	Y	Y
26 Berman	N	N	Y	Y	Y	Y	Y	Y
27 Levine	N	?	#	Y	Y	Y	Y	Y
28 Dixon	N	N	Y	Y	Y	Y	Y	Y
29 Hawkins	N	N	Y	Y	Y	Y	Y	Y
30 Martinez	N	N	Y	Y	N	Y	Y	Y
31 Dymally	N	N	Y	Y	Y	Y	Y	Y
32 Anderson	N	N	Y	Y	Y	Y	Y	Y
33 *Dreier*	Y	Y	N	N	N	Y	Y	Y
34 Torres	N	N	Y	Y	Y	Y	Y	Y
35 *Lewis*	Y	N	N	N	N	Y	Y	Y
36 Brown	N	N	Y	Y	Y	Y	N	Y
37 *McCandless*	Y	Y	N	N	N	Y	Y	Y
38 *Dornan*	Y	N	N	N	N	Y	Y	Y
39 *Dannemeyer*	Y	Y	N	N	N	Y	N	Y
40 *Badham*	Y	Y	N	N	N	Y	Y	Y
41 *Lowery*	?	?	?	N	N	Y	Y	Y
42 *Lungren*	Y	Y	N	N	N	Y	Y	Y
43 *Packard*	Y	Y	N	N	N	Y	Y	Y
44 Bates	N	N	Y	Y	N	Y	Y	Y
45 *Hunter*	Y	Y	N	?	N	Y	Y	Y
COLORADO								
1 Schroeder	N	N	Y	+	Y	Y	Y	Y
2 Wirth	N	N	Y	Y	N	?	Y	Y
3 *Strang*	Y	Y	N	Y	N	Y	Y	Y
4 *Brown*	Y	Y	N	N	N	Y	N	Y
5 *Kramer*	?	?	?	?	?	?	?	?
6 *Schaefer*	Y	Y	?	N	N	Y	Y	Y
CONNECTICUT								
1 Kennelly	N	N	Y	Y	Y	Y	Y	Y
2 Gejdenson	N	N	Y	Y	Y	Y	Y	Y
3 Morrison	N	N	Y	Y	Y	Y	Y	Y
4 *McKinney*	N	N	Y	Y	N	Y	Y	Y
5 *Rowland*	N	N	Y	N	N	Y	Y	Y
6 *Johnson*	N	N	Y	N	N	Y	Y	Y
DELAWARE								
AL Carper	N	N	Y	Y	Y	Y	Y	Y
FLORIDA								
1 Hutto	Y	Y	N	Y	N	Y	Y	Y
2 Fuqua	N	N	N	Y	Y	Y	Y	Y
3 Bennett	N	N	Y	Y	Y	Y	Y	N
4 Chappell	Y	Y	N	Y	Y	Y	Y	Y
5 *McCollum*	Y	Y	N	N	N	Y	Y	Y
6 MacKay	N	Y	N	Y	N	Y	Y	Y
7 Gibbons	N	N	N	Y	Y	Y	Y	Y
8 *Young*	?	?	?	Y	N	Y	Y	Y
9 *Bilirakis*	Y	Y	N	?	?	Y	Y	Y
10 *Ireland*	Y	Y	N	N	N	Y	Y	Y
11 Nelson	N	N	N	Y	Y	Y	Y	Y
12 *Lewis*	Y	Y	N	N	N	Y	Y	Y
13 *Mack*	Y	Y	N	N	N	Y	Y	Y
14 Mica	N	N	N	Y	Y	Y	Y	Y
15 *Shaw*	Y	Y	N	N	N	Y	Y	Y
16 Smith	N	N	Y	Y	Y	Y	?	Y
17 Lehman	N	N	Y	Y	Y	Y	Y	Y
18 Pepper	N	N	Y	Y	Y	Y	Y	Y
19 Fascell	N	N	Y	Y	Y	Y	Y	Y
GEORGIA								
1 Thomas	N	N	N	Y	N	Y	Y	Y
2 Hatcher	?	?	X	Y	N	Y	Y	Y
3 Ray	N	Y	N	N	N	Y	Y	Y
4 *Swindall*	Y	Y	N	N	N	Y	Y	Y
5 Fowler	N	N	N	Y	N	?	Y	Y
6 *Gingrich*	Y	Y	N	N	N	Y	Y	Y
7 Darden	N	?	?	Y	N	Y	Y	Y
8 Rowland	N	N	N	Y	N	Y	Y	Y
9 Jenkins	N	Y	N	Y	N	Y	Y	Y
10 Barnard	N	N	N	N	N	Y	Y	?
HAWAII								
1 Heftel	N	N	Y	?	?	?	?	?
2 Akaka	N	N	Y	#	?	?	?	?
IDAHO								
1 *Craig*	Y	Y	N	N	N	Y	Y	Y
2 Stallings	N	N	Y	N	N	Y	Y	Y
ILLINOIS								
1 Hayes	N	N	Y	Y	Y	Y	Y	Y
2 Savage	N	N	Y	Y	Y	Y	N	Y
3 Russo	N	N	Y	Y	N	Y	N	Y
4 *O'Brien*	?	?	X	Y	Y	Y	Y	Y
5 Lipinski	N	N	Y	Y	Y	Y	N	Y
6 *Hyde*	Y	Y	X	N	N	Y	Y	Y
7 Collins	N	N	Y	Y	Y	Y	Y	Y
8 Rostenkowski	N	N	Y	Y	Y	Y	Y	Y
9 Yates	N	N	Y	Y	Y	Y	N	Y
10 *Porter*	Y	Y	N	N	N	Y	Y	Y
11 Annunzio	N	N	Y	Y	Y	Y	Y	Y
12 *Crane*	?	?	?	N	N	N	N	Y
13 *Fawell*	Y	Y	N	N	N	Y	Y	Y
14 *Grotberg*	?	?	?	?	?	?	?	?
15 *Madigan*	N	Y	N	N	N	?	Y	Y
16 *Martin*	N	Y	N	N	N	Y	Y	Y
17 Evans	N	N	Y	?	Y	Y	Y	Y
18 *Michel*	Y	N	N	N	N	Y	Y	Y
19 Bruce	N	N	Y	Y	N	Y	Y	Y
20 Durbin	N	N	Y	Y	Y	Y	Y	Y
21 Price	N	N	Y	Y	Y	Y	Y	Y
22 Gray	N	N	Y	Y	Y	Y	Y	Y
INDIANA								
1 Visclosky	N	N	Y	Y	N	Y	Y	Y
2 Sharp	N	N	Y	Y	N	Y	Y	Y
3 *Hiler*	Y	N	N	N	N	Y	Y	Y
4 *Coats*	Y	N	N	N	N	Y	Y	Y
5 *Hillis*	Y	Y	N	N	N	Y	Y	Y

ND - Northern Democrats SD - Southern Democrats

* Corresponding to Congressional Record Votes 85, 86, 87, 88, 89, 90, 91, 92

	78	79	80	81	82	83	84	85
6 ***Burton***	Y	N	N	N	N	Y	Y	Y
7 ***Myers***	Y	N	N	Y	Y	Y	Y	Y
8 McCloskey	N	N	Y	Y	Y	?	Y	Y
9 Hamilton	N	N	N	Y	N	Y	Y	Y
10 Jacobs	N	N	Y	Y	N	Y	Y	Y
IOWA								
1 ***Leach***	N	Y	N	Y	N	Y	Y	Y
2 ***Tauke***	N	Y	N	N	N	Y	Y	Y
3 ***Evans***	?	?	?	N	N	Y	Y	Y
4 Smith	N	N	Y	Y	Y	Y	Y	Y
5 ***Lightfoot***	Y	Y	N	N	N	Y	Y	Y
6 Bedell	N	N	Y	Y	N	Y	Y	Y
KANSAS								
1 ***Roberts***	Y	Y	N	N	N	Y	?	Y
2 Slattery	N	N	Y	N	N	Y	Y	Y
3 ***Meyers***	Y	Y	N	N	N	Y	Y	Y
4 Glickman	N	N	Y	Y	N	Y	N	Y
5 ***Whittaker***	Y	Y	N	Y	N	Y	Y	Y
KENTUCKY								
1 Hubbard	N	N	Y	N	N	Y	Y	Y
2 Natcher	N	N	Y	Y	Y	Y	Y	Y
3 Mazzoli	N	N	N	N	Y	Y	Y	Y
4 ***Snyder***	Y	Y	N	N	N	Y	Y	Y
5 ***Rogers***	Y	Y	N	N	N	Y	Y	Y
6 ***Hopkins***	Y	Y	N	N	N	Y	Y	Y
7 Perkins	N	N	Y	Y	Y	Y	Y	Y
LOUISIANA								
1 ***Livingston***	Y	Y	N	N	N	Y	Y	Y
2 Boggs	N	N	Y	Y	Y	Y	Y	Y
3 Tauzin	Y	N	N	Y	N	Y	Y	Y
4 Roemer	Y	N	N	Y	N	Y	Y	Y
5 Huckaby	Y	N	N	Y	N	Y	Y	Y
6 ***Moore***	Y	Y	N	Y	N	Y	Y	Y
7 Breaux	N	N	Y	?	?	?	?	?
8 Long	N	N	Y	Y	Y	Y	Y	Y
MAINE								
1 ***McKernan***	?	N	N	Y	N	Y	Y	Y
2 ***Snowe***	N	N	N	Y	N	Y	Y	Y
MARYLAND								
1 Dyson	N	N	Y	N	N	Y	Y	Y
2 ***Bentley***	?	N	?	N	N	Y	Y	Y
3 Mikulski	N	N	Y	Y	Y	Y	Y	Y
4 ***Holt***	Y	Y	N	N	N	Y	Y	Y
5 Hoyer	N	N	Y	Y	Y	Y	Y	Y
6 Byron	Y	Y	N	Y	Y	Y	Y	Y
7 Mitchell	N	N	Y	Y	Y	Y	?	Y
8 Barnes	N	N	Y	Y	Y	Y	Y	?
MASSACHUSETTS								
1 ***Conte***	N	N	Y	Y	N	Y	Y	Y
2 Boland	N	N	Y	?	Y	Y	N	Y
3 Early	N	N	Y	?	?	?	?	?
4 Frank	N	N	Y	Y	Y	Y	Y	Y
5 Atkins	N	N	Y	Y	Y	Y	N	Y
6 Mavroules	N	N	Y	?	Y	Y	Y	Y
7 Markey	N	N	Y	Y	Y	Y	Y	Y
8 O'Neill								
9 Moakley	N	N	Y	Y	Y	Y	Y	Y
10 Studds	N	N	Y	Y	Y	Y	Y	Y
11 Donnelly	N	N	Y	Y	Y	Y	Y	Y
MICHIGAN								
1 Conyers	N	N	Y	Y	Y	Y	Y	Y
2 ***Pursell***	N	N	N	N	?	Y	Y	Y
3 Wolpe	N	N	Y	Y	Y	Y	Y	Y
4 ***Siljander***	Y	Y	N	N	N	Y	Y	Y
5 ***Henry***	N	N	N	N	N	Y	Y	Y
6 Carr	N	N	Y	Y	Y	Y	Y	Y
7 Kildee	N	N	Y	Y	Y	Y	Y	Y
8 Traxler	N	N	Y	Y	Y	Y	Y	Y
9 ***Vander Jagt***	N	Y	N	N	N	Y	Y	Y
10 ***Schuette***	N	N	N	N	N	Y	Y	Y
11 ***Davis***	?	?	#	Y	N	Y	Y	Y
12 Bonior	N	N	Y	Y	Y	Y	Y	Y
13 Crockett	N	N	Y	Y	Y	Y	N	Y
14 Hertel	N	N	Y	Y	Y	Y	Y	Y
15 Ford	N	N	Y	Y	Y	Y	N	Y
16 Dingell	N	N	Y	?	Y	Y	N	Y
17 Levin	N	N	Y	Y	Y	Y	Y	Y
18 ***Broomfield***	N	Y	N	Y	N	Y	Y	Y
MINNESOTA								
1 Penny	N	N	Y	N	N	Y	Y	Y
2 ***Weber***	Y	Y	N	N	N	Y	Y	Y
3 ***Frenzel***	Y	Y	N	N	N	Y	N	Y
4 Vento	N	N	Y	Y	Y	Y	Y	Y
5 Sabo	N	N	Y	Y	Y	Y	Y	Y
6 Sikorski	N	N	Y	Y	Y	Y	Y	Y

	78	79	80	81	82	83	84	85
7 ***Stangeland***	Y	Y	N	N	N	Y	Y	Y
8 Oberstar	N	N	Y	#	?	?	?	?
MISSISSIPPI								
1 Whitten	Y	N	Y	Y	Y	Y	Y	Y
2 ***Franklin***	Y	Y	N	N	N	Y	Y	Y
3 Montgomery	Y	Y	N	N	Y	Y	Y	Y
4 Dowdy	N	N	Y	Y	Y	Y	Y	Y
5 ***Lott***	Y	Y	N	N	N	Y	Y	Y
MISSOURI								
1 Clay	N	N	Y	Y	Y	Y	Y	Y
2 Young	N	N	Y	Y	Y	Y	Y	Y
3 Gephardt	?	?	#	?	?	?	?	?
4 Skelton	N	N	Y	Y	Y	Y	Y	Y
5 Wheat	N	N	Y	Y	Y	Y	Y	Y
6 ***Coleman***	Y	Y	N	Y	N	Y	Y	Y
7 ***Taylor***	Y	Y	N	N	Y	Y	Y	Y
8 ***Emerson***	Y	Y	N	N	N	Y	Y	Y
9 Volkmer	N	N	Y	Y	N	Y	Y	Y
MONTANA								
1 Williams	N	N	Y	Y	N	Y	Y	Y
2 ***Marlenee***	Y	Y	N	N	N	Y	Y	Y
NEBRASKA								
1 ***Bereuter***	Y	Y	N	N	N	Y	Y	Y
2 ***Daub***	N	Y	N	N	N	Y	Y	Y
3 ***Smith***	Y	Y	N	N	N	Y	Y	Y
NEVADA								
1 Reid	N	N	N	Y	N	Y	Y	Y
2 ***Vucanovich***	Y	Y	N	N	N	Y	Y	Y
NEW HAMPSHIRE								
1 ***Smith***	Y	Y	N	N	N	Y	Y	Y
2 ***Gregg***	N	N	N	N	N	Y	Y	Y
NEW JERSEY								
1 Florio	N	?	#	Y	Y	Y	Y	Y
2 Hughes	N	N	Y	Y	N	Y	Y	Y
3 Howard	N	N	Y	?	Y	Y	Y	Y
4 ***Smith***	N	N	Y	Y	N	Y	Y	Y
5 ***Roukema***	N	N	N	N	N	Y	Y	Y
6 Dwyer	N	N	Y	Y	Y	Y	Y	Y
7 ***Rinaldo***	N	N	Y	Y	N	Y	Y	Y
8 Roe	N	N	Y	Y	Y	Y	Y	Y
9 Torricelli	N	N	Y	?	Y	Y	Y	Y
10 Rodino	N	N	Y	Y	Y	Y	Y	Y
11 ***Gallo***	N	N	Y	N	N	Y	Y	Y
12 ***Courter***	N	N	Y	Y	N	Y	Y	Y
13 ***Saxton***	N	N	Y	N	N	Y	Y	Y
14 Guarini	N	N	Y	Y	Y	Y	Y	Y
NEW MEXICO								
1 ***Lujan***	?	?	?	?	?	?	?	?
2 ***Skeen***	Y	Y	N	Y	N	Y	Y	Y
3 Richardson	N	N	Y	Y	N	Y	Y	Y
NEW YORK								
1 ***Carney***	N	N	N	N	N	Y	Y	N
2 Downey	N	N	Y	Y	Y	Y	N	Y
3 Mrazek	N	N	Y	Y	Y	Y	Y	Y
4 ***Lent***	N	N	Y	N	N	Y	Y	Y
5 ***McGrath***	N	N	Y	N	N	Y	Y	Y
6 Vacancy								
7 Ackerman	N	N	Y	Y	Y	Y	Y	Y
8 Scheuer	N	N	Y	Y	Y	Y	N	Y
9 Manton	N	N	Y	?	Y	Y	Y	Y
10 Schumer	N	N	Y	Y	Y	Y	N	Y
11 Towns	N	N	Y	Y	Y	Y	Y	Y
12 Owens	N	N	Y	Y	Y	Y	N	Y
13 Solarz	N	N	Y	Y	Y	Y	N	Y
14 ***Molinari***	N	N	Y	N	N	Y	Y	Y
15 ***Green***	N	N	Y	N	Y	Y	Y	Y
16 Rangel	N	N	Y	Y	Y	Y	N	N
17 Weiss	N	N	Y	Y	Y	Y	N	N
18 Garcia	N	N	Y	Y	Y	Y	Y	?
19 Biaggi	N	N	Y	Y	Y	Y	Y	Y
20 ***DioGuardi***	N	N	Y	Y	N	Y	Y	Y
21 ***Fish***	N	N	Y	Y	N	Y	Y	Y
22 ***Gilman***	N	N	Y	Y	Y	Y	Y	Y
23 Stratton	N	N	Y	Y	N	Y	Y	Y
24 ***Solomon***	Y	?	N	N	N	Y	Y	Y
25 ***Boehlert***	N	N	N	N	N	Y	Y	Y
26 ***Martin***	N	N	Y	N	N	Y	?	Y
27 ***Wortley***	N	N	Y	N	N	Y	Y	Y
28 McHugh	N	N	Y	?	Y	Y	Y	Y
29 ***Horton***	N	N	Y	Y	N	Y	Y	Y
30 ***Eckert***	Y	Y	N	N	N	Y	Y	Y
31 ***Kemp***	N	N	Y	N	N	Y	Y	Y
32 LaFalce	N	N	Y	Y	Y	Y	Y	Y
33 Nowak	N	N	Y	Y	Y	Y	Y	Y
34 Lundine	N	N	Y	Y	Y	Y	Y	Y

	78	79	80	81	82	83	84	85
NORTH CAROLINA								
1 Jones	N	?	Y	Y	Y	Y	Y	Y
2 Valentine	Y	Y	N	Y	N	Y	Y	Y
3 Whitley	Y	Y	N	Y	N	Y	Y	Y
4 ***Cobey***	Y	Y	N	N	N	Y	Y	Y
5 Neal	N	N	N	Y	Y	Y	Y	Y
6 ***Coble***	Y	Y	N	N	N	Y	Y	Y
7 Rose	N	N	N	Y	N	Y	Y	Y
8 Hefner	Y	N	N	Y	Y	Y	Y	Y
9 ***McMillan***	Y	Y	N	N	N	Y	Y	Y
10 ***Broyhill***	Y	Y	N	N	N	Y	Y	Y
11 ***Hendon***	Y	Y	N	N	Y	Y	Y	Y
NORTH DAKOTA								
AL Dorgan	N	N	Y	Y	N	Y	N	Y
OHIO								
1 Luken	N	N	Y	Y	Y	Y	Y	Y
2 ***Gradison***	Y	N	N	Y	N	Y	Y	?
3 Hall	N	N	Y	Y	Y	Y	Y	Y
4 ***Oxley***	Y	Y	N	N	N	Y	Y	Y
5 ***Latta***	Y	N	N	Y	N	Y	Y	Y
6 ***McEwen***	N	Y	N	N	N	Y	Y	Y
7 ***DeWine***	Y	Y	N	N	N	Y	Y	Y
8 ***Kindness***	Y	Y	N	N	N	Y	Y	Y
9 Kaptur	N	N	Y	Y	N	Y	Y	Y
10 ***Miller***	N	Y	N	N	N	Y	Y	Y
11 Eckart	N	N	Y	Y	Y	Y	Y	Y
12 ***Kasich***	Y	N	N	N	N	Y	Y	Y
13 Pease	N	N	Y	Y	Y	Y	Y	Y
14 Seiberling	N	N	Y	Y	Y	Y	?	?
15 ***Wylie***	N	N	Y	N	N	Y	Y	Y
16 ***Regula***	N	N	Y	N	N	Y	Y	Y
17 Traficant	N	N	Y	Y	Y	Y	Y	Y
18 Applegate	N	N	Y	Y	Y	Y	Y	Y
19 Feighan	N	N	Y	Y	Y	Y	Y	Y
20 Oakar	N	N	Y	Y	Y	Y	Y	Y
21 Stokes	N	N	Y	Y	Y	Y	Y	Y
OKLAHOMA								
1 Jones	?	?	?	Y	Y	Y	Y	Y
2 Synar	N	N	N	Y	Y	Y	Y	Y
3 Watkins	N	N	N	Y	Y	Y	Y	Y
4 McCurdy	N	N	N	Y	N	Y	Y	?
5 ***Edwards***	Y	Y	N	N	?	?	Y	Y
6 English	N	Y	N	Y	N	Y	Y	Y
OREGON								
1 AuCoin	N	N	Y	Y	Y	Y	Y	Y
2 ***Smith, R.***	Y	Y	N	N	N	Y	N	Y
3 Wyden	N	N	Y	Y	Y	Y	Y	Y
4 Weaver	N	N	Y	Y	Y	Y	Y	Y
5 ***Smith, D.***	Y	?	?	N	N	Y	Y	Y
PENNSYLVANIA								
1 Foglietta	N	N	Y	?	?	Y	Y	Y
2 Gray	N	N	+	Y	Y	Y	Y	Y
3 Borski	N	N	Y	Y	Y	Y	Y	Y
4 Kolter	N	N	Y	Y	Y	Y	Y	N
5 ***Schulze***	Y	Y	N	Y	N	Y	Y	Y
6 Yatron	N	N	Y	Y	Y	Y	Y	Y
7 Edgar	N	N	Y	?	?	?	?	?
8 Kostmayer	N	N	Y	Y	Y	Y	Y	Y
9 ***Shuster***	Y	Y	N	N	N	Y	Y	Y
10 ***McDade***	N	N	Y	Y	Y	Y	Y	Y
11 Kanjorski	N	N	Y	Y	Y	Y	Y	Y
12 Murtha	N	N	Y	Y	Y	Y	Y	Y
13 ***Coughlin***	N	N	N	N	N	Y	Y	Y
14 Coyne	N	N	Y	?	?	?	?	?
15 ***Ritter***	N	N	N	N	N	Y	Y	Y
16 ***Walker***	Y	Y	N	N	N	Y	Y	Y
17 ***Gekas***	Y	Y	N	N	N	Y	Y	Y
18 Walgren	N	N	Y	Y	Y	Y	Y	Y
19 ***Goodling***	N	N	N	N	N	Y	Y	Y
20 Gaydos	N	N	Y	N	Y	Y	Y	N
21 ***Ridge***	N	N	Y	N	N	Y	Y	Y
22 Murphy	N	N	Y	Y	Y	Y	Y	Y
23 ***Clinger***	N	N	Y	N	N	Y	Y	Y
RHODE ISLAND								
1 St Germain	N	N	Y	Y	Y	Y	Y	Y
2 ***Schneider***	N	N	Y	N	N	Y	Y	Y
SOUTH CAROLINA								
1 ***Hartnett***	Y	Y	N	X	?	?	?	?
2 ***Spence***	Y	Y	N	Y	N	Y	Y	Y
3 Derrick	N	N	N	Y	Y	Y	Y	Y
4 ***Campbell***	?	?	X	N	N	Y	Y	Y
5 Spratt	N	N	N	Y	Y	Y	Y	Y
6 Tallon	N	N	Y	N	N	Y	Y	Y
SOUTH DAKOTA								
AL Daschle	N	N	Y	N	N	Y	Y	Y

	78	79	80	81	82	83	84	85
TENNESSEE								
1 ***Quillen***	Y	Y	N	N	N	Y	Y	Y
2 ***Duncan***	N	Y	N	N	N	Y	Y	Y
3 Lloyd	?	?	?	Y	N	Y	Y	Y
4 Cooper	N	N	N	Y	Y	Y	N	Y
5 Boner	N	N	Y	Y	Y	Y	Y	Y
6 Gordon	N	N	Y	Y	Y	Y	Y	Y
7 ***Sundquist***	N	Y	N	N	N	Y	Y	Y
8 Jones	?	?	?	N	N	Y	Y	Y
9 Ford	?	?	#	?	Y	Y	Y	Y
TEXAS								
1 Chapman	N	N	Y	Y	N	Y	Y	Y
2 Wilson	N	N	Y	?	?	?	?	?
3 ***Bartlett***	Y	Y	N	N	N	Y	Y	Y
4 Hall, R.	Y	Y	N	N	N	Y	Y	Y
5 Bryant	N	N	Y	Y	Y	Y	Y	Y
6 ***Barton***	Y	Y	N	N	N	Y	Y	Y
7 ***Archer***	Y	Y	N	N	?	?	Y	Y
8 ***Fields***	Y	Y	N	N	?	?	Y	Y
9 Brooks	N	N	Y	Y	Y	Y	Y	Y
10 Pickle	N	N	Y	N	Y	Y	Y	Y
11 Leath	Y	Y	N	N	N	Y	Y	Y
12 Wright	N	N	Y	Y	Y	Y	Y	Y
13 ***Boulter***	Y	Y	N	Y	N	Y	Y	Y
14 ***Sweeney***	Y	Y	N	?	N	Y	Y	Y
15 de la Garza	N	N	Y	Y	N	Y	Y	Y
16 Coleman	N	N	Y	Y	Y	Y	Y	Y
17 Stenholm	Y	Y	N	N	N	Y	Y	Y
18 Leland	N	N	Y	Y	Y	Y	Y	Y
19 ***Combest***	Y	Y	N	N	N	Y	Y	Y
20 Gonzalez	N	N	Y	Y	Y	Y	Y	N
21 ***Loeffler***	?	?	X	?	?	?	?	?
22 ***DeLay***	Y	Y	N	N	?	?	Y	Y
23 Bustamante	N	N	Y	Y	N	Y	Y	Y
24 Frost	N	N	Y	Y	Y	Y	Y	?
25 Andrews	N	N	Y	N	Y	Y	Y	Y
26 ***Armey***	Y	Y	N	N	N	Y	Y	Y
27 Ortiz	N	N	Y	Y	Y	Y	Y	Y
UTAH								
1 ***Hansen***	Y	Y	N	N	N	Y	Y	Y
2 ***Monson***	Y	Y	N	N	N	Y	N	Y
3 ***Nielson***	Y	N	N	N	N	Y	N	Y
VERMONT								
AL ***Jeffords***	N	N	N	Y	N	Y	Y	Y
VIRGINIA								
1 ***Bateman***	Y	Y	N	Y	N	Y	Y	Y
2 ***Whitehurst***	?	?	?	Y	N	Y	Y	Y
3 ***Bliley***	Y	Y	N	Y	N	Y	Y	Y
4 Sisisky	?	?	#	Y	Y	Y	Y	Y
5 Daniel	Y	Y	N	N	N	Y	Y	Y
6 Olin	N	Y	N	N	N	Y	Y	Y
7 ***Slaughter***	Y	Y	N	Y	N	Y	Y	Y
8 ***Parris***	Y	Y	?	N	N	Y	Y	Y
9 Boucher	N	N	Y	Y	Y	Y	Y	Y
10 ***Wolf***	Y	Y	N	Y	N	Y	Y	Y
WASHINGTON								
1 ***Miller***	N	N	Y	N	N	Y	Y	Y
2 Swift	N	N	Y	Y	Y	Y	Y	Y
3 Bonker	N	N	Y	Y	Y	Y	Y	Y
4 ***Morrison***	N	N	N	Y	N	Y	Y	Y
5 Foley	N	N	Y	Y	Y	Y	Y	Y
6 Dicks	N	N	Y	Y	N	Y	Y	Y
7 Lowry	N	N	Y	Y	Y	Y	N	Y
8 ***Chandler***	Y	N	N	N	N	Y	Y	Y
WEST VIRGINIA								
1 Mollohan	N	N	Y	Y	N	Y	Y	Y
2 Staggers	N	N	Y	Y	N	Y	Y	Y
3 Wise	N	N	Y	Y	Y	?	Y	Y
4 Rahall	N	N	Y	Y	Y	Y	Y	Y
WISCONSIN								
1 Aspin	N	N	Y	Y	Y	Y	N	Y
2 Kastenmeier	N	N	Y	Y	Y	Y	Y	Y
3 ***Gunderson***	N	N	N	N	N	Y	Y	Y
4 Kleczka	N	N	Y	Y	Y	Y	Y	Y
5 Moody	N	N	Y	Y	Y	Y	N	Y
6 ***Petri***	N	N	N	N	N	Y	Y	Y
7 Obey	N	N	Y	Y	Y	Y	Y	Y
8 ***Roth***	Y	N	N	Y	N	Y	Y	Y
9 ***Sensenbrenner***	N	N	N	N	N	Y	Y	Y
WYOMING								
AL ***Cheney***	Y	Y	N	N	?	?	Y	Y

Southern states - Ala., Ark., Fla., Ga., Ky., La., Miss., N.C., Okla., S.C., Tenn., Texas, Va.

* The *Congressional Record* vote number is different from the CQ vote number because the *Record* includes quorum calls in its tally. CQ does not publish quorum call votes.

86. Procedural Motion. Walker, R-Pa., motion to approve the House *Journal* of Tuesday, April 22. Motion agreed to 215-178: R 32-137; D 183-41 (ND 131-23, SD 52-18), April 23, 1986. (Walker sought to defeat the motion in protest of the April 22 approval by unanimous consent of H Res 427, which dropped a House rule limiting members' outside income to an amount equal to 30 percent of their annual salary.)

87. HR 1116. Garrison Diversion Unit. Bedell, D-Iowa, amendment to require farmers using irrigation water from the project to pay the full cost of water used to produce crops determined by the agriculture secretary to be in surplus. Rejected 199-203: R 92-76; D 107-127 (ND 81-80, SD 26-47), April 23, 1986.

88. HR 1116. Garrison Diversion Unit. Passage of the bill to reformulate the authorized design of the Garrison Diversion Unit of the Pick-Sloan Missouri Basin Program. Total cost to complete the project as reformulated is $1,177,480,910; the bill itself authorizes appropriations of $679,840,000. Passed 254-154: R 81-92; D 173-62 (ND 112-48, SD 61-14), April 23, 1986.

89. H Res 432. Members' Outside Income. Pepper, D-Fla., motion to consider the resolution to reinstate a House rule limiting members' outside income to an amount equal to 30 percent of their annual salary. Motion agreed to 333-68: R 134-35; D 199-33 (ND 137-21, SD 62-12), April 23, 1986. A two-thirds majority of those present and voting (268 in this case) is required to consider a privileged report from the Rules Committee on the same day it is presented to the House. (The resolution subsequently was adopted by voice vote, thus reversing the House's April 22 approval of H Res 427, which lifted the 30 percent limit on outside income.)

KEY

- Y Voted for (yea).
- # Paired for.
- + Announced for.
- N Voted against (nay).
- X Paired against.
- \- Announced against.
- P Voted "present."
- C Voted "present" to avoid possible conflict of interest.
- ? Did not vote or otherwise make a position known.

Democrats *Republicans*

	86	87	88	89
ALABAMA				
1 ***Callahan***	N	N	Y	Y
2 ***Dickinson***	Y	N	N	N
3 Nichols	?	?	?	?
4 Bevill	Y	N	Y	Y
5 Flippo	Y	N	Y	Y
6 Erdreich	N	Y	Y	Y
7 Shelby	?	N	Y	Y
ALASKA				
AL ***Young***	N	N	Y	N
ARIZONA				
1 ***McCain***	N	N	Y	Y
2 Udall	Y	N	Y	Y
3 ***Stump***	N	N	Y	Y
4 ***Rudd***	Y	N	Y	N
5 ***Kolbe***	N	N	Y	Y
ARKANSAS				
1 Alexander	Y	N	Y	N
2 Robinson	?	?	?	?
3 ***Hammerschmidt***	N	N	Y	N
4 Anthony	?	?	#	?
CALIFORNIA				
1 Bosco	Y	N	Y	?
2 ***Chappie***	N	N	N	Y
3 Matsui	Y	N	Y	Y
4 Fazio	Y	N	Y	Y
5 Burton	Y	N	Y	Y
6 Boxer	?	?	?	?
7 Miller	Y	N	Y	Y
8 Dellums	Y	N	N	Y
9 Stark	Y	Y	Y	N
10 Edwards	Y	Y	N	Y
11 Lantos	Y	N	Y	Y
12 ***Zschau***	?	?	X	?
13 Mineta	Y	N	Y	Y
14 ***Shumway***	Y	Y	N	N
15 Coelho	Y	N	Y	Y
16 Panetta	Y	N	Y	Y
17 ***Pashayan***	Y	N	Y	N
18 Lehman	Y	N	Y	N
19 ***Lagomarsino***	N	Y	N	Y
20 ***Thomas***	Y	N	Y	N
21 ***Fiedler***	?	?	?	?
22 ***Moorhead***	N	N	N	Y
23 Beilenson	Y	Y	N	Y
24 Waxman	Y	Y	Y	N
25 Roybal	Y	N	Y	Y
26 Berman	Y	Y	N	Y
27 Levine	Y	Y	Y	Y
28 Dixon	?	N	Y	Y
29 Hawkins	Y	N	Y	Y
30 Martinez	Y	N	Y	N
31 Dymally	Y	N	N	N
32 Anderson	Y	N	Y	Y
33 ***Dreier***	N	N	N	Y
34 Torres	Y	N	Y	Y
35 ***Lewis***	Y	N	Y	N
36 Brown	Y	N	Y	Y
37 ***McCandless***	N	N	Y	Y
38 ***Dornan***	N	N	N	Y
39 ***Dannemeyer***	N	Y	N	Y
40 ***Badham***	N	N	N	N
41 ***Lowery***	N	N	Y	Y
42 ***Lungren***	N	Y	N	Y
43 ***Packard***	N	N	Y	Y
44 Bates	Y	Y	N	Y
45 ***Hunter***	N	N	Y	Y
COLORADO				
1 Schroeder	Y	Y	N	Y
2 Wirth	N	?	?	?
3 ***Strang***	N	N	Y	Y
4 ***Brown***	N	N	Y	Y
5 ***Kramer***	N	N	Y	Y
6 ***Schaefer***	N	N	Y	Y
CONNECTICUT				
1 Kennelly	N	N	Y	Y
2 Gejdenson	Y	N	Y	Y
3 Morrison	Y	Y	N	Y
4 ***McKinney***	Y	N	Y	Y
5 ***Rowland***	N	N	Y	Y
6 ***Johnson***	N	?	Y	Y
DELAWARE				
AL Carper	Y	Y	N	Y
FLORIDA				
1 Hutto	N	N	Y	Y
2 Fuqua	Y	N	Y	Y
3 Bennett	Y	Y	Y	Y
4 Chappell	Y	?	Y	Y
5 ***McCollum***	N	Y	N	Y
6 MacKay	N	Y	Y	Y
7 Gibbons	Y	Y	Y	N
8 ***Young***	N	Y	Y	Y
9 ***Bilirakis***	N	Y	N	Y
10 ***Ireland***	N	N	Y	Y
11 Nelson	Y	Y	N	Y
12 ***Lewis***	N	N	Y	Y
13 ***Mack***	N	Y	N	Y
14 Mica	Y	N	Y	Y
15 ***Shaw***	N	Y	Y	?
16 Smith	Y	Y	Y	Y
17 Lehman	Y	N	Y	N
18 Pepper	?	N	Y	Y
19 Fascell	Y	N	Y	N
GEORGIA				
1 Thomas	Y	N	Y	Y
2 Hatcher	Y	Y	Y	Y
3 Ray	N	N	Y	Y
4 ***Swindall***	N	Y	Y	Y
5 Fowler	Y	Y	Y	Y
6 ***Gingrich***	N	Y	N	Y
7 Darden	Y	N	Y	Y
8 Rowland	Y	N	Y	Y
9 Jenkins	Y	Y	Y	Y
10 Barnard	Y	N	Y	Y
HAWAII				
1 Heftel	?	?	?	?
2 Akaka	?	?	?	?
IDAHO				
1 ***Craig***	N	N	N	Y
2 Stallings	Y	N	Y	Y
ILLINOIS				
1 Hayes	Y	Y	Y	Y
2 Savage	Y	Y	Y	Y
3 Russo	Y	N	Y	Y
4 ***O'Brien***	?	?	?	?
5 Lipinski	Y	N	Y	N
6 ***Hyde***	Y	N	Y	N
7 Collins	Y	Y	Y	Y
8 Rostenkowski	Y	N	Y	N
9 Yates	Y	Y	N	Y
10 ***Porter***	Y	Y	N	N
11 Annunzio	Y	N	Y	Y
12 ***Crane***	N	Y	N	N
13 ***Fawell***	N	Y	N	Y
14 ***Grotberg***	?	?	?	?
15 ***Madigan***	Y	N	N	N
16 ***Martin***	N	Y	N	Y
17 Evans	Y	Y	Y	Y
18 ***Michel***	?	?	?	?
19 Bruce	Y	N	Y	Y
20 Durbin	Y	N	Y	Y
21 Price	Y	N	Y	Y
22 Gray	?	N	Y	Y
INDIANA				
1 Visclosky	Y	Y	Y	Y
2 Sharp	N	Y	N	Y
3 ***Hiler***	N	Y	N	Y
4 ***Coats***	N	Y	N	Y
5 ***Hillis***	N	Y	N	N

ND - Northern Democrats SD - Southern Democrats

* Corresponding to Congressional Record Votes 93, 95, 96, 97

	86	87	88	89
6 ***Burton***	N	Y	N	N
7 ***Myers***	Y	N	Y	N
8 McCloskey	Y	Y	Y	Y
9 Hamilton	Y	Y	N	Y
10 Jacobs	N	Y	N	Y
IOWA				
1 ***Leach***	N	?	N	Y
2 ***Tauke***	N	Y	N	Y
3 ***Evans***	N	Y	N	Y
4 Smith	N	Y	N	Y
5 ***Lightfoot***	N	Y	N	Y
6 Bedell	N	Y	N	Y
KANSAS				
1 ***Roberts***	N	N	Y	Y
2 Slattery	?	Y	Y	Y
3 ***Meyers***	N	N	N	Y
4 Glickman	N	Y	Y	Y
5 ***Whittaker***	N	Y	Y	Y
KENTUCKY				
1 Hubbard	N	N	N	Y
2 Natcher	Y	N	Y	Y
3 Mazzoli	Y	N	Y	Y
4 ***Snyder***	Y	N	Y	N
5 ***Rogers***	N	N	Y	N
6 ***Hopkins***	N	N	Y	Y
7 Perkins	Y	N	Y	Y
LOUISIANA				
1 ***Livingston***	Y	N	N	N
2 Boggs	?	N	Y	Y
3 Tauzin	N	Y	N	Y
4 Roemer	N	Y	N	Y
5 Huckaby	N	Y	N	Y
6 ***Moore***	N	Y	N	Y
7 Breaux	N	?	?	Y
8 Long	Y	Y	N	Y
MAINE				
1 ***McKernan***	N	?	N	Y
2 ***Snowe***	N	Y	N	Y
MARYLAND				
1 Dyson	Y	Y	Y	Y
2 ***Bentley***	N	Y	Y	Y
3 Mikulski	?	Y	N	Y
4 ***Holt***	?	N	Y	Y
5 Hoyer	Y	N	Y	N
6 Byron	Y	N	Y	Y
7 Mitchell	?	Y	Y	Y
8 Barnes	Y	Y	N	Y
MASSACHUSETTS				
1 ***Conte***	N	Y	Y	Y
2 Boland	Y	N	Y	Y
3 Early	?	?	?	?
4 Frank	Y	Y	N	Y
5 Atkins	Y	Y	N	Y
6 Mavroules	Y	Y	Y	Y
7 Markey	Y	Y	N	Y
8 O'Neill				
9 Moakley	Y	Y	Y	Y
10 Studds	Y	Y	N	Y
11 Donnelly	Y	N	Y	Y
MICHIGAN				
1 Conyers	Y	Y	N	Y
2 ***Pursell***	N	Y	N	Y
3 Wolpe	N	Y	N	Y
4 ***Siljander***	N	Y	N	Y
5 ***Henry***	N	Y	N	Y
6 Carr	N	N	Y	Y
7 Kildee	Y	Y	N	Y
8 Traxler	Y	N	Y	Y
9 ***Vander Jagt***	?	Y	N	N
10 ***Schuette***	N	Y	N	Y
11 ***Davis***	N	N	Y	Y
12 Bonior	Y	N	Y	Y
13 Crockett	Y	Y	N	Y
14 Hertel	Y	Y	N	Y
15 Ford	Y	N	Y	N
16 Dingell	?	N	Y	N
17 Levin	Y	N	Y	Y
18 ***Broomfield***	N	Y	N	Y
MINNESOTA				
1 Penny	N	Y	N	Y
2 ***Weber***	N	Y	N	Y
3 ***Frenzel***	N	Y	N	N
4 Vento	Y	Y	N	Y
5 Sabo	Y	N	Y	Y
6 Sikorski	N	Y	N	Y

	86	87	88	89
7 ***Stangeland***	N	N	Y	Y
8 Oberstar	?	?	?	?
MISSISSIPPI				
1 Whitten	Y	N	Y	Y
2 ***Franklin***	Y	N	Y	N
3 Montgomery	Y	N	Y	N
4 Dowdy	Y	N	N	Y
5 ***Lott***	Y	N	Y	N
MISSOURI				
1 Clay	Y	Y	N	?
2 Young	Y	N	Y	Y
3 Gephardt	Y	N	Y	Y
4 Skelton	N	Y	Y	Y
5 Wheat	Y	Y	Y	Y
6 ***Coleman***	Y	Y	N	Y
7 ***Taylor***	Y	N	Y	N
8 ***Emerson***	N	N	Y	Y
9 Volkmer	N	Y	N	Y
MONTANA				
1 Williams	Y	N	Y	Y
2 ***Marlenee***	N	N	N	N
NEBRASKA				
1 ***Bereuter***	N	N	Y	Y
2 ***Daub***	N	N	Y	Y
3 ***Smith***	N	N	Y	Y
NEVADA				
1 Reid	Y	N	Y	Y
2 ***Vucanovich***	N	?	?	Y
NEW HAMPSHIRE				
1 ***Smith***	N	Y	N	Y
2 ***Gregg***	N	?	N	N
NEW JERSEY				
1 Florio	Y	Y	Y	Y
2 Hughes	N	Y	Y	Y
3 Howard	Y	N	Y	N
4 ***Smith***	N	Y	Y	Y
5 ***Roukema***	N	?	N	Y
6 Dwyer	Y	Y	Y	Y
7 ***Rinaldo***	Y	Y	Y	Y
8 Roe	Y	N	Y	Y
9 Torricelli	Y	N	Y	Y
10 Rodino	?	N	Y	Y
11 ***Gallo***	N	N	Y	Y
12 ***Courter***	N	Y	N	Y
13 ***Saxton***	N	Y	N	Y
14 Guarini	Y	N	Y	Y
NEW MEXICO				
1 ***Lujan***	?	?	?	?
2 ***Skeen***	Y	N	Y	N
3 Richardson	Y	N	Y	Y
NEW YORK				
1 ***Carney***	N	Y	Y	Y
2 Downey	Y	N	Y	Y
3 Mrazek	Y	Y	N	Y
4 ***Lent***	Y	Y	Y	Y
5 ***McGrath***	Y	Y	Y	N
6 Vacancy				
7 Ackerman	Y	Y	Y	?
8 Scheuer	Y	Y	N	Y
9 Manton	Y	N	?	N
10 Schumer	Y	N	Y	Y
11 Towns	Y	Y	Y	Y
12 Owens	Y	Y	N	Y
13 Solarz	Y	Y	Y	Y
14 ***Molinari***	N	Y	Y	N
15 ***Green***	Y	Y	Y	Y
16 Rangel	Y	Y	Y	N
17 Weiss	Y	Y	Y	Y
18 Garcia	Y	Y	Y	Y
19 Biaggi	Y	Y	Y	N
20 ***DioGuardi***	N	Y	N	Y
21 ***Fish***	Y	Y	Y	?
22 ***Gilman***	N	Y	Y	Y
23 Stratton	Y	Y	N	Y
24 ***Solomon***	N	Y	N	Y
25 ***Boehlert***	N	Y	N	Y
26 ***Martin***	N	Y	Y	?
27 ***Wortley***	N	Y	Y	Y
28 McHugh	Y	Y	Y	Y
29 ***Horton***	N	Y	Y	Y
30 ***Eckert***	N	Y	Y	Y
31 ***Kemp***	N	Y	Y	Y
32 LaFalce	?	Y	Y	Y
33 Nowak	Y	Y	Y	Y
34 Lundine	N	Y	Y	Y

	86	87	88	89
NORTH CAROLINA				
1 Jones	?	N	Y	N
2 Valentine	Y	N	Y	Y
3 Whitley	Y	N	Y	Y
4 ***Cobey***	N	Y	N	Y
5 Neal	Y	Y	N	Y
6 ***Coble***	N	Y	N	Y
7 Rose	Y	N	Y	Y
8 Hefner	Y	N	Y	N
9 ***McMillan***	N	Y	N	Y
10 ***Broyhill***	N	Y	N	Y
11 ***Hendon***	N	Y	N	Y
NORTH DAKOTA				
AL Dorgan	Y	N	Y	Y
OHIO				
1 Luken	Y	N	Y	Y
2 ***Gradison***	?	Y	Y	Y
3 Hall	Y	Y	N	Y
4 ***Oxley***	Y	N	N	Y
5 ***Latta***	N	?	?	Y
6 ***McEwen***	N	N	N	Y
7 ***DeWine***	N	Y	N	Y
8 ***Kindness***	N	N	Y	Y
9 Kaptur	Y	N	Y	Y
10 ***Miller***	N	Y	N	Y
11 Eckart	N	N	Y	Y
12 ***Kasich***	N	Y	N	Y
13 Pease	Y	Y	Y	Y
14 Seiberling	Y	Y	N	Y
15 ***Wylie***	N	N	Y	Y
16 ***Regula***	N	N	N	Y
17 Traficant	N	N	Y	Y
18 Applegate	Y	N	Y	Y
19 Feighan	Y	N	N	Y
20 Oakar	Y	N	Y	Y
21 Stokes	?	N	Y	?
OKLAHOMA				
1 Jones	N	N	Y	Y
2 Synar	?	N	Y	Y
3 Watkins	N	N	Y	Y
4 McCurdy	?	?	?	?
5 ***Edwards***	Y	Y	N	Y
6 English	N	Y	Y	Y
OREGON				
1 AuCoin	Y	Y	N	Y
2 ***Smith, R.***	N	N	Y	Y
3 Wyden	Y	N	N	Y
4 Weaver	Y	Y	N	Y
5 ***Smith, D.***	Y	N	Y	+
PENNSYLVANIA				
1 Foglietta	Y	Y	N	Y
2 Gray	Y	N	Y	Y
3 Borski	Y	N	Y	Y
4 Kolter	Y	Y	Y	N
5 ***Schulze***	Y	Y	N	N
6 Yatron	N	Y	Y	Y
7 Edgar	?	?	?	?
8 Kostmayer	N	Y	N	Y
9 ***Shuster***	N	N	Y	N
10 ***McDade***	N	Y	N	Y
11 Kanjorski	Y	Y	N	Y
12 Murtha	Y	N	Y	N
13 ***Coughlin***	N	Y	N	Y
14 Coyne	Y	N	Y	N
15 ***Ritter***	?	Y	N	Y
16 ***Walker***	N	Y	N	Y
17 ***Gekas***	N	Y	N	Y
18 Walgren	N	Y	Y	Y
19 ***Goodling***	N	Y	N	Y
20 Gaydos	Y	?	?	N
21 ***Ridge***	N	N	Y	?
22 Murphy	N	Y	Y	Y
23 ***Clinger***	N	N	Y	Y
RHODE ISLAND				
1 St Germain	Y	Y	Y	Y
2 ***Schneider***	Y	N	Y	Y
SOUTH CAROLINA				
1 ***Hartnett***	?	N	N	Y
2 ***Spence***	N	N	N	Y
3 Derrick	Y	Y	Y	Y
4 ***Campbell***	?	N	N	?
5 Spratt	Y	Y	N	Y
6 Tallon	Y	Y	N	Y
SOUTH DAKOTA				
AL Daschle	Y	N	Y	Y

	86	87	88	89
TENNESSEE				
1 ***Quillen***	Y	N	Y	N
2 ***Duncan***	Y	N	Y	N
3 Lloyd	N	N	Y	Y
4 Cooper	Y	Y	Y	Y
5 Boner	Y	N	N	Y
6 Gordon	Y	N	Y	Y
7 ***Sundquist***	N	N	N	Y
8 Jones	Y	N	N	?
9 Ford	Y	N	N	N
TEXAS				
1 Chapman	N	Y	Y	Y
2 Wilson	?	?	?	?
3 ***Bartlett***	N	Y	N	Y
4 Hall, R.	N	Y	Y	Y
5 Bryant	N	N	Y	Y
6 ***Barton***	N	Y	N	Y
7 ***Archer***	N	Y	N	Y
8 ***Fields***	N	Y	N	Y
9 Brooks	Y	Y	Y	?
10 Pickle	Y	Y	Y	Y
11 Leath	Y	N	Y	N
12 Wright	Y	?	Y	Y
13 ***Boulter***	N	Y	N	Y
14 ***Sweeney***	N	Y	N	Y
15 de la Garza	Y	N	Y	Y
16 Coleman	Y	N	Y	Y
17 Stenholm	N	Y	Y	Y
18 Leland	Y	N	Y	N
19 ***Combest***	N	Y	N	Y
20 Gonzalez	Y	Y	Y	Y
21 ***Loeffler***	?	?	?	?
22 ***DeLay***	Y	N	N	N
23 Bustamante	?	Y	Y	N
24 Frost	Y	N	Y	Y
25 Andrews	N	N	Y	Y
26 ***Armey***	N	Y	N	Y
27 Ortiz	?	?	?	?
UTAH				
1 ***Hansen***	N	Y	N	Y
2 ***Monson***	N	N	Y	N
3 ***Nielson***	N	N	Y	Y
VERMONT				
AL ***Jeffords***	N	Y	N	Y
VIRGINIA				
1 ***Bateman***	N	Y	Y	Y
2 ***Whitehurst***	N	N	N	Y
3 ***Bliley***	N	Y	N	Y
4 Sisisky	Y	N	Y	Y
5 Daniel	Y	N	N	N
6 Olin	Y	N	Y	Y
7 ***Slaughter***	N	N	N	Y
8 ***Parris***	N	Y	N	Y
9 Boucher	Y	N	Y	Y
10 ***Wolf***	N	N	N	Y
WASHINGTON				
1 ***Miller***	N	Y	N	Y
2 Swift	Y	N	Y	Y
3 Bonker	Y	Y	Y	Y
4 ***Morrison***	N	N	Y	Y
5 Foley	Y	N	Y	Y
6 Dicks	Y	N	Y	Y
7 Lowry	Y	N	N	Y
8 ***Chandler***	N	Y	N	Y
WEST VIRGINIA				
1 Mollohan	Y	N	Y	N
2 Staggers	N	N	Y	Y
3 Wise	N	N	Y	Y
4 Rahall	Y	N	Y	N
WISCONSIN				
1 Aspin	Y	N	Y	Y
2 Kastenmeier	Y	Y	N	Y
3 ***Gunderson***	N	Y	Y	Y
4 Kleczka	Y	N	Y	Y
5 Moody	Y	Y	N	N
6 ***Petri***	N	Y	Y	Y
7 Obey	Y	Y	N	Y
8 ***Roth***	N	Y	Y	Y
9 ***Sensenbrenner***	N	Y	Y	Y
WYOMING				
AL ***Cheney***	Y	N	Y	Y

Southern states - Ala., Ark., Fla., Ga., Ky., La., Miss., N.C., Okla., S.C., Tenn., Texas, Va.
* The *Congressional Record* vote number is different from the CQ vote number because the *Record* includes quorum calls in its tally. CQ does not publish quorum call votes.

90. HR 4600. Indian Health Care. Udall, D-Ariz., motion to suspend the rules and pass the bill to authorize $99 million in fiscal 1987-89 for health care programs under the 1976 Indian Health Care Improvement Act (PL 94-437). Motion rejected 263-141: R 40-129; D 223-12 (ND 155-4, SD 68-8), April 29, 1986. A two-thirds majority of those present and voting (270 in this case) is required for passage under suspension of the rules. A "nay" was a vote supporting the president's position.

91. HR 4421. Community Services Programs. Adoption of the rule (H Res 428) to provide for House floor consideration of the bill to reauthorize through fiscal 1990 the Head Start, Follow Through, Community Services Block Grant, Dependent Care and Community Food and Nutrition programs. Adopted 406-0: R 169-0; D 237-0 (ND 160-0, SD 77-0), April 29, 1986.

92. HR 4421. Community Services Programs. Tauke, R-Iowa, amendment to delete authorization for the Follow Through program. Rejected 161-245: R 140-27; D 21-218 (ND 5-158, SD 16-60), April 29, 1986. A "yea" was a vote supporting the president's position.

93. HR 4421. Community Services Programs. Walker, R-Pa., amendment to freeze the fiscal 1987 authorization for the Community Services Block Grant program at the fiscal 1986 outlay level of $370.3 million, instead of authorizing $390 million as provided in the bill. Rejected 140-267: R 124-45; D 16-222 (ND 5-157, SD 11-65), April 29, 1986.

94. HR 4421. Community Services Programs. Passage of the bill to reauthorize through fiscal 1990 the Head Start, Follow Through, Community Services Block Grant, Dependent Care and Community Food and Nutrition programs. Passed 377-33: R 137-33; D 240-0 (ND 163-0, SD 77-0), April 29, 1986. A "nay" was a vote supporting the president's position.

95. Procedural Motion. Sundquist, R-Tenn., motion to approve the House *Journal* of Tuesday, April 29. Motion agreed to 274-130: R 54-120; D 220-10 (ND 149-7, SD 71-3), April 30, 1986.

96. HR 3302. Nevada Wilderness Protection. Adoption of the rule (H Res 429) to provide for House floor consideration of the bill and to make in order a substitute consisting of the text of HR 4642, introduced by Harry Reid, D-Nev., to establish 11 wilderness areas totaling 592,000 acres and the 174,000-acre Great Basin National Park and Preserve in Nevada. Adopted 336-74: R 96-74; D 240-0 (ND 163-0, SD 77-0), April 30, 1986.

97. HR 3302. Nevada Wilderness Protection. Vucanovich, R-Nev., amendment to the Reid, D-Nev., substitute *(see vote 96, above)*, to strike from the bill the section establishing the 174,000-acre Great Basin National Park and Preserve in Nevada. Rejected 151-247: R 143-25; D 8-222 (ND 4-156, SD 4-66), April 30, 1986. (The Reid substitute subsequently was adopted by voice vote, after which the bill was passed by voice vote.) A "yea" was a vote supporting the president's position.

KEY

- Y Voted for (yea).
- # Paired for.
- + Announced for.
- N Voted against (nay).
- X Paired against.
- - Announced against.
- P Voted "present."
- C Voted "present" to avoid possible conflict of interest.
- ? Did not vote or otherwise make a position known.

Democrats ***Republicans***

	90	91	92	93	94	95	96	97
ALABAMA								
1 ***Callahan***	?	?	Y	Y	Y	Y	N	Y
2 ***Dickinson***	N	Y	Y	Y	Y	N	Y	Y
3 Nichols	?	?	?	?	?	?	?	?
4 Bevill	Y	Y	N	N	Y	Y	Y	N
5 Flippo	Y	Y	N	N	Y	Y	Y	N
6 Erdreich	Y	Y	N	N	Y	Y	Y	N
7 Shelby	Y	Y	N	N	Y	Y	Y	N
ALASKA								
AL ***Young***	Y	Y	Y	N	Y	N	Y	Y
ARIZONA								
1 ***McCain***	N	Y	Y	Y	Y	Y	N	Y
2 Udall	Y	Y	N	N	Y	Y	Y	N
3 ***Stump***	N	Y	Y	Y	N	N	N	Y
4 ***Rudd***	N	Y	Y	Y	N	Y	Y	Y
5 ***Kolbe***	N	Y	Y	Y	Y	N	Y	Y
ARKANSAS								
1 Alexander	Y	Y	N	N	Y	P	Y	N
2 Robinson	Y	Y	N	N	Y	Y	Y	?
3 ***Hammerschmidt***	N	Y	Y	Y	Y	?	N	Y
4 Anthony	Y	Y	N	N	Y	Y	Y	?
CALIFORNIA								
1 Bosco	Y	Y	N	N	Y	Y	Y	N
2 ***Chappie***	Y	?	N	N	Y	N	N	Y
3 Matsui	Y	Y	N	N	Y	?	Y	N
4 Fazio	Y	Y	N	N	Y	Y	Y	N
5 Burton	Y	Y	N	N	Y	Y	Y	N
6 Boxer	Y	Y	N	N	Y	Y	Y	N
7 Miller	Y	Y	N	N	Y	Y	Y	N
8 Dellums	Y	Y	N	N	Y	Y	Y	N
9 Stark	Y	Y	N	N	Y	Y	Y	N
10 Edwards	Y	Y	N	N	Y	Y	Y	N
11 Lantos	Y	Y	N	N	Y	Y	Y	N
12 ***Zschau***	N	Y	Y	Y	Y	N	N	Y
13 Mineta	Y	Y	N	N	Y	Y	Y	N
14 ***Shumway***	N	Y	Y	Y	N	Y	N	Y
15 Coelho	Y	Y	N	N	Y	Y	Y	N
16 Panetta	Y	Y	N	N	Y	Y	Y	N
17 ***Pashayan***	Y	Y	N	N	Y	N	N	Y
18 Lehman	Y	Y	N	N	Y	Y	Y	N
19 ***Lagomarsino***	N	Y	Y	Y	Y	N	N	Y
20 ***Thomas***	N	Y	Y	Y	Y	N	Y	Y
21 ***Fiedler***	?	?	?	?	?	?	?	?
22 ***Moorhead***	N	Y	Y	Y	N	N	N	?
23 Beilenson	Y	Y	N	N	Y	Y	Y	N
24 Waxman	Y	?	N	N	Y	Y	Y	N
25 Roybal	Y	Y	N	N	Y	Y	Y	N
26 Berman	Y	Y	?	N	Y	Y	Y	N
27 Levine	Y	Y	N	N	Y	Y	Y	N
28 Dixon	Y	Y	N	N	Y	Y	Y	N
29 Hawkins	Y	Y	N	N	Y	N	Y	?
30 Martinez	Y	Y	N	N	Y	Y	Y	N
31 Dymally	Y	Y	N	N	Y	Y	Y	N
32 Anderson	Y	Y	N	N	Y	Y	Y	N
33 ***Dreier***	N	Y	Y	Y	N	N	N	Y
34 Torres	Y	Y	N	N	Y	Y	Y	N
35 ***Lewis***	N	Y	Y	Y	Y	N	N	Y
36 Brown	Y	Y	N	N	Y	Y	Y	N
37 ***McCandless***	?	?	?	?	?	N	N	Y
38 ***Dornan***	N	Y	Y	Y	N	N	N	Y
39 ***Dannemeyer***	N	Y	Y	Y	N	N	N	Y
40 ***Badham***	?	?	?	?	?	?	?	?
41 ***Lowery***	N	Y	Y	N	Y	N	Y	Y
42 ***Lungren***	N	Y	Y	Y	N	N	N	Y
43 ***Packard***	N	Y	Y	N	Y	Y	N	Y
44 Bates	Y	Y	N	N	Y	Y	Y	N
45 ***Hunter***	Y	Y	Y	Y	Y	N	Y	Y
COLORADO								
1 Schroeder	Y	Y	N	N	Y	N	Y	N
2 Wirth	Y	Y	N	N	Y	Y	Y	N
3 ***Strang***	N	Y	?	Y	Y	N	N	Y
4 ***Brown***	?	Y	Y	Y	N	N	Y	Y
5 ***Kramer***	N	Y	Y	Y	Y	N	N	Y
6 ***Schaefer***	N	Y	Y	Y	N	N	N	Y
CONNECTICUT								
1 Kennelly	Y	Y	N	N	Y	Y	Y	N
2 Gejdenson	Y	Y	N	N	Y	Y	Y	N
3 Morrison	?	?	N	N	Y	Y	Y	N
4 ***McKinney***	N	Y	Y	N	Y	Y	Y	N
5 ***Rowland***	N	Y	Y	N	Y	Y	Y	N
6 ***Johnson***	Y	Y	Y	Y	Y	Y	Y	N
DELAWARE								
AL Carper	Y	Y	Y	Y	Y	Y	Y	N
FLORIDA								
1 Hutto	?	Y	Y	Y	Y	Y	Y	N
2 Fuqua	Y	Y	N	N	Y	Y	Y	N
3 Bennett	Y	Y	N	N	Y	Y	Y	N
4 Chappell	Y	Y	N	N	Y	Y	Y	N
5 ***McCollum***	N	Y	Y	Y	Y	Y	N	Y
6 MacKay	Y	Y	N	N	Y	Y	Y	N
7 Gibbons	Y	Y	N	N	Y	Y	Y	N
8 ***Young***	N	Y	Y	Y	Y	N	Y	Y
9 ***Bilirakis***	N	Y	Y	Y	Y	N	N	Y
10 ***Ireland***	N	Y	Y	Y	Y	N	N	Y
11 Nelson	Y	Y	N	Y	Y	Y	Y	N
12 ***Lewis***	Y	Y	Y	Y	Y	N	N	Y
13 ***Mack***	N	Y	Y	Y	N	N	N	Y
14 Mica	Y	Y	N	N	Y	Y	Y	?
15 ***Shaw***	N	Y	Y	Y	Y	N	N	Y
16 Smith	Y	Y	N	N	Y	Y	Y	N
17 Lehman	Y	Y	N	N	Y	Y	Y	?
18 Pepper	+	+	-	-	+	+	+	X
19 Fascell	Y	Y	N	N	Y	Y	Y	N
GEORGIA								
1 Thomas	Y	Y	N	Y	Y	Y	Y	N
2 Hatcher	Y	Y	N	N	Y	Y	Y	N
3 Ray	Y	Y	Y	Y	Y	Y	Y	N
4 ***Swindall***	N	Y	Y	Y	N	N	N	Y
5 Fowler	Y	Y	N	N	Y	?	Y	N
6 ***Gingrich***	N	Y	Y	Y	Y	N	N	Y
7 Darden	Y	Y	Y	+	Y	Y	Y	N
8 Rowland	Y	Y	N	N	Y	Y	Y	N
9 Jenkins	Y	Y	Y	N	Y	Y	Y	N
10 Barnard	Y	Y	Y	N	Y	Y	Y	N
HAWAII								
1 Heftel	Y	Y	N	N	Y	Y	Y	N
2 Akaka	Y	Y	N	N	Y	Y	Y	N
IDAHO								
1 ***Craig***	Y	Y	Y	Y	N	N	N	Y
2 Stallings	Y	Y	N	Y	Y	Y	Y	N
ILLINOIS								
1 Hayes	Y	Y	N	N	Y	Y	Y	N
2 Savage	Y	Y	N	N	Y	Y	Y	N
3 Russo	Y	Y	N	N	Y	Y	Y	N
4 ***O'Brien***	Y	Y	N	N	Y	Y	Y	Y
5 Lipinski	Y	Y	N	N	Y	Y	Y	N
6 ***Hyde***	N	Y	Y	Y	Y	Y	Y	Y
7 Collins	Y	Y	N	N	Y	Y	Y	N
8 Rostenkowski	Y	Y	N	N	Y	Y	Y	N
9 Yates	Y	Y	N	N	Y	Y	Y	N
10 ***Porter***	Y	Y	N	Y	Y	N	N	N
11 Annunzio	Y	Y	N	N	Y	Y	Y	N
12 ***Crane***	N	Y	Y	Y	N	N	N	?
13 ***Fawell***	N	Y	N	Y	Y	N	Y	N
14 ***Grotberg***	?	?	?	?	?	?	?	?
15 ***Madigan***	N	Y	Y	Y	Y	N	N	Y
16 ***Martin***	N	Y	Y	Y	Y	N	N	Y
17 Evans	Y	Y	N	N	Y	Y	Y	N
18 ***Michel***	N	Y	Y	Y	N	N	N	Y
19 Bruce	Y	Y	N	N	Y	Y	Y	N
20 Durbin	Y	Y	N	N	Y	Y	Y	N
21 Price	Y	Y	N	N	Y	Y	Y	N
22 Gray	Y	Y	N	N	Y	Y	Y	N
INDIANA								
1 Visclosky	Y	Y	N	N	Y	Y	Y	N
2 Sharp	Y	Y	N	N	Y	Y	Y	N
3 ***Hiler***	N	Y	Y	Y	Y	N	Y	Y
4 ***Coats***	N	Y	Y	Y	Y	N	Y	Y
5 ***Hillis***	N	Y	Y	Y	Y	Y	Y	Y

ND - Northern Democrats SD - Southern Democrats

* Corresponding to Congressional Record Votes 98, 99, 101, 103, 104, 105, 106, 107

	90	91	92	93	94	95	96	97
6 ***Burton***	N	Y	Y	Y	N	N	N	Y
7 ***Myers***	N	Y	Y	Y	Y	Y	Y	Y
8 McCloskey	Y	Y	N	N	Y	?	Y	N
9 Hamilton	Y	Y	N	N	Y	Y	Y	N
10 Jacobs	Y	Y	N	N	Y	N	Y	N
IOWA								
1 ***Leach***	Y	Y	Y	Y	Y	N	Y	N
2 ***Tauke***	Y	Y	Y	Y	Y	N	Y	Y
3 ***Evans***	Y	Y	N	Y	Y	N	Y	Y
4 Smith	Y	?	Y	N	Y	Y	Y	N
5 ***Lightfoot***	N	Y	Y	Y	Y	N	N	Y
6 Bedell	Y	Y	Y	N	Y	?	Y	N
KANSAS								
1 ***Roberts***	N	Y	Y	Y	N	N	?	Y
2 Slattery	Y	Y	N	Y	Y	Y	Y	N
3 ***Meyers***	N	Y	Y	Y	Y	N	Y	N
4 Glickman	?	Y	N	Y	Y	Y	Y	N
5 ***Whittaker***	N	Y	Y	N	Y	N	N	Y
KENTUCKY								
1 Hubbard	N	Y	N	Y	Y	Y	Y	N
2 Natcher	Y	Y	N	N	Y	Y	Y	N
3 Mazzoli	Y	Y	N	N	Y	Y	Y	N
4 ***Snyder***	N	Y	Y	Y	N	Y	Y	Y
5 ***Rogers***	N	Y	Y	Y	Y	N	N	Y
6 ***Hopkins***	N	Y	Y	Y	Y	Y	N	Y
7 Perkins	Y	Y	N	N	Y	Y	Y	N
LOUISIANA								
1 ***Livingston***	N	Y	Y	Y	Y	N	N	Y
2 Boggs	Y	Y	N	N	Y	Y	Y	N
3 Tauzin	Y	Y	N	N	Y	Y	Y	N
4 Roemer	N	Y	N	N	Y	N	Y	N
5 Huckaby	Y	Y	N	Y	Y	N	Y	N
6 ***Moore***	N	Y	Y	Y	Y	Y	Y	Y
7 Breaux	Y	Y	N	N	Y	Y	Y	?
8 Long	Y	Y	N	N	Y	Y	Y	N
MAINE								
1 ***McKernan***	?	?	?	N	Y	N	Y	Y
2 ***Snowe***	Y	Y	Y	N	Y	N	Y	Y
MARYLAND								
1 Dyson	N	Y	N	N	Y	Y	Y	N
2 ***Bentley***	Y	Y	N	N	Y	N	N	Y
3 Mikulski	Y	Y	N	N	Y	Y	Y	?
4 ***Holt***	N	Y	Y	Y	Y	Y	Y	Y
5 Hoyer	Y	Y	N	N	Y	Y	Y	N
6 Byron	Y	Y	Y	Y	Y	?	Y	N
7 Mitchell	Y	Y	N	N	Y	?	Y	?
8 Barnes	Y	Y	?	?	?	Y	Y	N
MASSACHUSETTS								
1 ***Conte***	Y	Y	N	N	Y	N	Y	N
2 Boland	Y	?	N	N	Y	Y	Y	N
3 Early	Y	Y	N	N	Y	Y	Y	N
4 Frank	Y	Y	N	N	Y	Y	Y	N
5 Atkins	Y	Y	N	N	Y	Y	?	N
6 Mavroules	Y	Y	N	N	Y	Y	Y	N
7 Markey	Y	Y	N	N	?	Y	Y	N
8 O'Neill								
9 Moakley	Y	Y	N	N	Y	Y	Y	N
10 Studds	Y	Y	N	N	Y	Y	Y	N
11 Donnelly	Y	Y	N	N	Y	Y	Y	N
MICHIGAN								
1 Conyers	Y	Y	N	N	Y	Y	Y	N
2 ***Pursell***	Y	Y	N	Y	Y	Y	Y	N
3 Wolpe	Y	Y	N	N	Y	Y	Y	N
4 ***Siljander***	N	Y	Y	Y	Y	Y	N	Y
5 ***Henry***	Y	Y	N	N	Y	N	Y	N
6 Carr	?	?	?	?	?	Y	Y	N
7 Kildee	Y	Y	N	N	Y	Y	Y	N
8 Traxler	Y	Y	N	N	Y	Y	Y	N
9 ***Vander Jagt***	Y	Y	Y	Y	Y	N	Y	Y
10 ***Schuette***	Y	Y	Y	Y	Y	N	Y	Y
11 ***Davis***	?	?	?	N	Y	Y	N	Y
12 Bonior	Y	Y	N	N	Y	Y	Y	N
13 Crockett	Y	Y	N	N	Y	Y	Y	N
14 Hertel	Y	Y	N	N	Y	Y	Y	N
15 Ford	Y	Y	N	N	Y	Y	Y	N
16 Dingell	Y	Y	N	N	Y	Y	Y	Y
17 Levin	Y	Y	N	N	Y	Y	Y	N
18 ***Broomfield***	N	Y	Y	Y	Y	Y	Y	Y
MINNESOTA								
1 Penny	Y	Y	Y	N	Y	N	Y	N
2 ***Weber***	N	Y	N	Y	Y	N	Y	N
3 ***Frenzel***	N	Y	Y	Y	Y	N	Y	Y
4 Vento	Y	Y	N	N	Y	Y	Y	N
5 Sabo	Y	Y	N	N	Y	Y	Y	N
6 Sikorski	Y	Y	N	N	Y	N	Y	N

	90	91	92	93	94	95	96	97
7 ***Stangeland***	Y	Y	Y	Y	Y	N	N	Y
8 Oberstar	Y	Y	N	N	Y	Y	Y	N
MISSISSIPPI								
1 Whitten	Y	Y	N	N	Y	Y	Y	N
2 ***Franklin***	?	?	?	?	?	?	?	?
3 Montgomery	Y	Y	Y	Y	Y	Y	Y	N
4 Dowdy	Y	Y	N	N	Y	Y	Y	N
5 ***Lott***	N	Y	Y	Y	N	N	N	Y
MISSOURI								
1 Clay	Y	Y	N	N	Y	N	Y	N
2 Young	Y	Y	N	N	Y	Y	Y	N
3 Gephardt	Y	Y	N	N	Y	Y	Y	N
4 Skelton	Y	Y	N	N	Y	Y	Y	N
5 Wheat	Y	Y	N	N	Y	Y	Y	N
6 ***Coleman***	N	Y	Y	Y	Y	N	Y	Y
7 ***Taylor***	N	Y	Y	Y	?	Y	Y	Y
8 ***Emerson***	N	Y	N	N	Y	N	N	Y
9 Volkmer	N	Y	N	N	Y	Y	Y	Y
MONTANA								
1 Williams	Y	Y	N	N	Y	Y	Y	N
2 ***Marlenee***	Y	Y	Y	Y	Y	N	N	Y
NEBRASKA								
1 ***Bereuter***	Y	Y	N	N	Y	N	Y	Y
2 ***Daub***	N	Y	Y	Y	Y	N	Y	Y
3 ***Smith***	N	Y	Y	Y	Y	Y	Y	Y
NEVADA								
1 Reid	Y	Y	N	N	Y	Y	Y	N
2 ***Vucanovich***	?	?	?	?	?	N	N	Y
NEW HAMPSHIRE								
1 ***Smith***	N	Y	Y	Y	Y	N	Y	Y
2 ***Gregg***	N	Y	Y	Y	Y	N	Y	N
NEW JERSEY								
1 Florio	Y	Y	N	N	Y	Y	Y	N
2 Hughes	N	Y	N	N	Y	Y	Y	N
3 Howard	Y	Y	N	N	Y	Y	Y	N
4 ***Smith***	N	Y	N	N	Y	N	Y	N
5 ***Roukema***	N	Y	Y	N	Y	N	Y	Y
6 Dwyer	Y	Y	N	N	Y	Y	Y	N
7 ***Rinaldo***	N	Y	N	N	Y	Y	Y	N
8 Roe	Y	Y	N	N	Y	Y	Y	N
9 Torricelli	Y	Y	N	N	Y	Y	Y	N
10 Rodino	Y	Y	N	N	Y	Y	Y	N
11 ***Gallo***	N	Y	Y	N	Y	N	N	Y
12 ***Courter***	N	Y	Y	N	Y	N	Y	Y
13 ***Saxton***	N	Y	Y	N	Y	N	N	Y
14 Guarini	Y	Y	N	N	Y	Y	Y	N
NEW MEXICO								
1 ***Lujan***	?	?	?	?	?	?	?	?
2 ***Skeen***	Y	Y	Y	N	Y	N	N	Y
3 Richardson	Y	Y	N	N	Y	Y	Y	N
NEW YORK								
1 ***Carney***	N	Y	Y	Y	Y	N	?	?
2 Downey	Y	Y	N	N	Y	Y	Y	N
3 Mrazek	?	Y	N	N	Y	Y	Y	N
4 ***Lent***	N	Y	Y	N	Y	N	Y	Y
5 ***McGrath***	N	Y	Y	N	Y	N	N	Y
6 Vacancy								
7 Ackerman	Y	Y	N	N	Y	Y	Y	N
8 Scheuer	Y	Y	N	N	Y	Y	Y	N
9 Manton	Y	Y	N	N	Y	Y	Y	N
10 Schumer	Y	Y	N	N	Y	Y	Y	N
11 Towns	Y	Y	N	N	Y	Y	Y	N
12 Owens	Y	Y	N	N	Y	Y	Y	N
13 Solarz	Y	Y	N	N	Y	P	Y	N
14 ***Molinari***	N	Y	?	N	Y	N	Y	Y
15 ***Green***	Y	Y	N	N	Y	Y	Y	N
16 Rangel	Y	Y	N	N	Y	Y	Y	N
17 Weiss	Y	Y	N	N	Y	Y	Y	N
18 Garcia	Y	Y	N	N	Y	Y	Y	N
19 Biaggi	Y	Y	N	N	Y	Y	Y	N
20 ***DioGuardi***	N	Y	Y	Y	Y	Y	Y	Y
21 ***Fish***	N	Y	N	N	Y	Y	Y	N
22 ***Gilman***	Y	Y	N	N	Y	Y	Y	N
23 Stratton	N	Y	N	N	Y	Y	Y	Y
24 ***Solomon***	N	Y	?	?	?	N	N	Y
25 ***Boehlert***	N	Y	Y	N	Y	N	Y	N
26 ***Martin***	Y	Y	N	N	Y	N	N	Y
27 ***Wortley***	Y	Y	Y	N	Y	Y	Y	Y
28 McHugh	Y	Y	N	N	Y	Y	Y	N
29 ***Horton***	Y	Y	N	N	Y	Y	Y	N
30 ***Eckert***	N	Y	Y	Y	Y	Y	Y	Y
31 ***Kemp***	N	Y	Y	?	Y	Y	Y	Y
32 LaFalce	Y	Y	N	N	Y	Y	Y	N
33 Nowak	Y	Y	N	N	Y	Y	Y	N
34 Lundine	Y	Y	N	?	Y	Y	Y	?

	90	91	92	93	94	95	96	97
NORTH CAROLINA								
1 Jones	Y	Y	N	N	Y	Y	Y	Y
2 Valentine	Y	Y	N	N	Y	Y	Y	N
3 Whitley	Y	Y	N	N	Y	Y	Y	N
4 ***Cobey***	N	Y	Y	Y	Y	N	N	Y
5 Neal	Y	Y	N	N	Y	Y	Y	N
6 ***Coble***	N	Y	Y	Y	Y	N	N	Y
7 Rose	Y	Y	N	N	Y	Y	Y	N
8 Hefner	Y	Y	N	N	Y	Y	Y	N
9 ***McMillan***	Y	Y	Y	N	Y	N	Y	Y
10 ***Broyhill***	Y	Y	Y	Y	Y	Y	Y	Y
11 ***Hendon***	Y	Y	N	Y	Y	N	N	Y
NORTH DAKOTA								
AL Dorgan	Y	Y	N	N	Y	Y	Y	N
OHIO								
1 Luken	Y	Y	N	N	Y	Y	Y	N
2 ***Gradison***	Y	Y	Y	Y	Y	Y	Y	Y
3 Hall	Y	Y	N	N	Y	Y	Y	N
4 ***Oxley***	N	Y	Y	Y	Y	N	Y	Y
5 ***Latta***	N	Y	Y	Y	Y	N	N	#
6 ***McEwen***	N	Y	Y	Y	Y	Y	Y	?
7 ***DeWine***	N	Y	Y	Y	Y	N	Y	Y
8 ***Kindness***	N	Y	Y	Y	Y	N	Y	Y
9 Kaptur	Y	Y	N	N	Y	Y	Y	N
10 ***Miller***	N	Y	Y	N	Y	N	Y	Y
11 Eckart	Y	Y	N	N	Y	Y	Y	N
12 ***Kasich***	N	Y	Y	Y	Y	Y	Y	Y
13 Pease	Y	Y	N	N	Y	Y	Y	N
14 Seiberling	Y	Y	N	N	Y	?	Y	N
15 ***Wylie***	N	Y	Y	Y	Y	Y	?	Y
16 ***Regula***	N	Y	Y	Y	Y	Y	Y	Y
17 Traficant	Y	Y	N	N	Y	Y	Y	N
18 Applegate	Y	Y	N	N	Y	Y	Y	Y
19 Feighan	Y	Y	N	N	Y	Y	Y	N
20 Oakar	Y	Y	N	N	Y	Y	Y	N
21 Stokes	Y	Y	N	N	Y	?	Y	N
OKLAHOMA								
1 Jones	Y	Y	Y	N	Y	Y	Y	N
2 Synar	Y	Y	Y	N	Y	Y	Y	N
3 Watkins	Y	Y	Y	N	Y	Y	Y	N
4 McCurdy	Y	Y	Y	N	Y	Y	Y	N
5 ***Edwards***	N	Y	Y	Y	Y	N	Y	Y
6 English	N	Y	Y	N	Y	Y	Y	N
OREGON								
1 AuCoin	?	?	N	N	Y	?	?	X
2 ***Smith, R.***	Y	Y	Y	Y	Y	N	N	Y
3 Wyden	Y	Y	N	N	Y	Y	Y	N
4 Weaver	?	?	?	?	?	?	?	?
5 ***Smith, D.***	N	Y	Y	?	Y	N	N	Y
PENNSYLVANIA								
1 Foglietta	Y	Y	N	N	Y	?	?	?
2 Gray	Y	Y	N	N	Y	Y	Y	N
3 Borski	Y	Y	N	N	Y	Y	Y	N
4 Kolter	Y	Y	N	N	Y	Y	Y	N
5 ***Schulze***	N	Y	Y	N	Y	Y	Y	Y
6 Yatron	Y	Y	N	N	Y	?	Y	N
7 Edgar	?	?	?	?	?	?	?	?
8 Kostmayer	Y	Y	N	N	Y	Y	Y	N
9 ***Shuster***	N	Y	Y	Y	N	N	N	Y
10 ***McDade***	?	?	?	?	?	?	?	?
11 Kanjorski	Y	Y	N	N	Y	Y	Y	N
12 Murtha	Y	Y	N	N	Y	Y	Y	N
13 ***Coughlin***	Y	Y	N	Y	Y	N	Y	N
14 Coyne	Y	Y	N	N	Y	Y	Y	N
15 ***Ritter***	N	Y	Y	Y	Y	Y	N	Y
16 ***Walker***	N	Y	Y	Y	N	N	N	Y
17 ***Gekas***	N	Y	Y	Y	N	N	N	Y
18 Walgren	Y	Y	N	N	Y	Y	Y	N
19 ***Goodling***	N	Y	Y	Y	Y	N	Y	Y
20 Gaydos	Y	Y	N	N	Y	Y	Y	N
21 ***Ridge***	N	Y	Y	Y	Y	N	Y	Y
22 Murphy	Y	Y	N	N	Y	Y	Y	N
23 ***Clinger***	N	Y	N	N	Y	Y	Y	Y
RHODE ISLAND								
1 St Germain	Y	Y	N	N	Y	Y	Y	N
2 ***Schneider***	Y	Y	N	N	Y	N	Y	N
SOUTH CAROLINA								
1 ***Hartnett***	N	Y	Y	Y	N	Y	Y	Y
2 ***Spence***	N	Y	Y	Y	Y	N	Y	Y
3 Derrick	Y	Y	N	N	Y	Y	Y	N
4 ***Campbell***	N	Y	?	?	?	Y	Y	Y
5 Spratt	Y	Y	N	N	Y	Y	Y	N
6 Tallon	Y	Y	N	N	Y	Y	Y	N
SOUTH DAKOTA								
AL Daschle	Y	Y	N	N	Y	Y	Y	N

	90	91	92	93	94	95	96	97
TENNESSEE								
1 ***Quillen***	N	Y	N	N	Y	Y	Y	Y
2 ***Duncan***	N	Y	N	N	Y	Y	Y	Y
3 Lloyd	N	Y	N	N	Y	N	Y	?
4 Cooper	Y	Y	N	N	Y	Y	Y	N
5 Boner	Y	Y	N	N	Y	Y	Y	N
6 Gordon	Y	Y	N	N	Y	Y	Y	N
7 ***Sundquist***	N	Y	Y	Y	Y	N	Y	Y
8 Jones	Y	Y	N	N	Y	?	?	?
9 Ford	Y	Y	N	N	Y	Y	Y	N
TEXAS								
1 Chapman	Y	Y	Y	N	Y	Y	Y	N
2 Wilson	Y	Y	N	N	Y	Y	Y	N
3 ***Bartlett***	N	Y	Y	Y	N	N	Y	Y
4 Hall, R.	Y	Y	Y	N	Y	Y	Y	?
5 Bryant	Y	Y	N	N	Y	Y	Y	N
6 ***Barton***	N	Y	Y	Y	Y	N	Y	Y
7 ***Archer***	N	Y	Y	Y	N	Y	N	Y
8 ***Fields***	N	Y	Y	Y	Y	N	N	Y
9 Brooks	Y	Y	N	N	Y	Y	Y	N
10 Pickle	?	?	?	?	?	?	?	?
11 Leath	N	Y	Y	Y	Y	Y	Y	Y
12 Wright	Y	Y	N	N	Y	Y	Y	N
13 ***Boulter***	N	Y	Y	Y	Y	N	Y	Y
14 ***Sweeney***	N	Y	Y	Y	Y	Y	Y	Y
15 de la Garza	Y	Y	N	N	Y	Y	Y	N
16 Coleman	Y	Y	N	N	Y	Y	Y	N
17 Stenholm	N	Y	N	Y	Y	Y	Y	Y
18 Leland	Y	Y	N	N	Y	Y	Y	N
19 ***Combest***	N	Y	Y	Y	N	Y	Y	Y
20 Gonzalez	Y	Y	N	N	Y	Y	Y	N
21 ***Loeffler***	?	?	?	?	?	?	?	?
22 ***DeLay***	N	Y	Y	Y	N	N	N	#
23 Bustamante	Y	Y	N	N	Y	Y	Y	N
24 Frost	?	?	?	?	?	Y	Y	N
25 Andrews	Y	Y	?	Y	Y	Y	Y	N
26 ***Armey***	N	Y	Y	Y	N	N	N	Y
27 Ortiz	?	?	?	?	?	?	?	X
UTAH								
1 ***Hansen***	N	Y	Y	Y	N	N	N	Y
2 ***Monson***	N	Y	Y	Y	N	N	N	Y
3 ***Nielson***	Y	Y	Y	Y	N	N	N	Y
VERMONT								
AL ***Jeffords***	Y	Y	Y	N	Y	Y	Y	Y
VIRGINIA								
1 ***Bateman***	N	Y	N	Y	Y	Y	?	#
2 ***Whitehurst***	N	Y	Y	Y	Y	N	Y	Y
3 ***Bliley***	N	Y	Y	Y	Y	N	N	Y
4 Sisisky	Y	Y	N	N	Y	Y	Y	N
5 Daniel	N	Y	Y	Y	Y	P	Y	N
6 Olin	N	Y	Y	N	Y	Y	Y	Y
7 ***Slaughter***	N	Y	Y	Y	Y	N	Y	Y
8 ***Parris***	N	Y	Y	N	Y	N	N	Y
9 Boucher	Y	Y	N	N	Y	Y	Y	N
10 ***Wolf***	N	Y	Y	Y	Y	N	Y	Y
WASHINGTON								
1 ***Miller***	Y	Y	Y	Y	Y	Y	Y	N
2 Swift	?	Y	N	N	Y	Y	Y	N
3 Bonker	Y	Y	N	N	Y	Y	?	N
4 ***Morrison***	N	Y	Y	N	Y	Y	?	N
5 Foley	?	Y	N	N	Y	Y	Y	N
6 Dicks	Y	Y	N	N	Y	Y	Y	N
7 Lowry	Y	Y	N	N	Y	N	Y	N
8 ***Chandler***	N	Y	Y	Y	Y	N	Y	Y
WEST VIRGINIA								
1 Mollohan	Y	Y	N	N	Y	Y	Y	N
2 Staggers	Y	Y	N	N	Y	Y	Y	N
3 Wise	?	?	?	?	?	Y	Y	N
4 Rahall	Y	Y	N	N	Y	Y	Y	N
WISCONSIN								
1 Aspin	Y	Y	N	?	Y	Y	Y	?
2 Kastenmeier	Y	Y	N	N	Y	Y	Y	N
3 ***Gunderson***	N	Y	Y	N	Y	N	Y	Y
4 Kleczka	Y	Y	N	N	Y	Y	Y	N
5 Moody	Y	Y	N	N	Y	Y	Y	N
6 ***Petri***	N	Y	Y	Y	Y	Y	Y	Y
7 Obey	Y	Y	N	N	Y	Y	Y	N
8 ***Roth***	Y	Y	Y	Y	Y	N	Y	Y
9 ***Sensenbrenner***	Y	Y	Y	Y	N	N	Y	N
WYOMING								
AL ***Cheney***	N	Y	Y	Y	N	N	N	Y

Southern states - Ala., Ark., Fla., Ga., Ky., La., Miss., N.C., Okla., S.C., Tenn., Texas, Va.

* The *Congressional Record* vote number is different from the CQ vote number because the *Record* includes quorum calls in its tally. CQ does not publish quorum call votes.

98. HR 4409. Panama Canal Commission Authorization, Fiscal 1987. Adoption of the rule (H Res 436) to provide for House floor consideration of and to waive points of order against the bill to authorize appropriations for fiscal year 1987 for the operation and maintenance of the Panama Canal. Adopted 338-56: R 115-53; D 223-3 (ND 157-3, SD 66-0), May 1, 1986.

99. HR 4409. Panama Canal Commission Authorization, Fiscal 1987. Passage of the bill to authorize appropriations of $437.3 million from the Panama Canal Commission Fund for fiscal year 1987 for the operation and maintenance of the Panama Canal. Passed 327-59: R 108-53; D 219-6 (ND 155-5, SD 64-1), May 1, 1986.

100. HR 4208. Coast Guard Authorization, Fiscal 1987. Passage of the bill to authorize $2.198 billion in fiscal 1987 funds for the U.S. Coast Guard, plus an estimated $354 million for retired pay. Passed 374-0: R 157-0; D 217-0 (ND 148-0, SD 69-0), May 6, 1986.

101. HR 4021. Rehabilitation Act Amendments. Williams, D-Mont., motion to suspend the rules and pass the bill to reauthorize federal aid for vocational rehabilitation of the handicapped through fiscal 1991. Motion agreed to 401-0: R 167-0; D 234-0 (ND 159-0, SD 75-0), May 7, 1986. A two-thirds majority of those present and voting (268 in this case) is required for passage under suspension of the rules.

102. H J Res 589. Saudi Arms Sale. Passage of the joint resolution to prohibit the administration's proposed $354 million sale of missiles to Saudi Arabia. Passed 356-62: R 131-45; D 225-17 (ND 155-8, SD 70-9), May 7, 1986. A "nay" was a vote supporting the president's position.

103. HR 4515. Urgent Supplemental Appropriations, Fiscal 1986. Adoption of the rule (H Res 448) to provide for House floor consideration of and to waive points of order against the bill to provide $1.7 billion in urgent supplemental appropriations for fiscal year 1986. Adopted 212-189: R 6-164; D 206-25 (ND 148-11, SD 58-14), May 8, 1986.

104. HR 4515. Urgent Supplemental Appropriations, Fiscal 1986. Walker, R-Pa., amendment to reduce funding for the Anglo-Irish economic support fund from $50 million to $20 million. Rejected 157-241: R 116-53; D 41-188 (ND 16-143, SD 25-45), May 8, 1986.

KEY

- Y Voted for (yea).
- # Paired for.
- + Announced for.
- N Voted against (nay).
- X Paired against.
- \- Announced against.
- P Voted "present."
- C Voted "present" to avoid possible conflict of interest.
- ? Did not vote or otherwise make a position known.

Democrats ***Republicans***

	98	99	100	101	102	103	104
ALABAMA							
1 ***Callahan***	Y	Y	Y	Y	Y	N	N
2 ***Dickinson***	Y	Y	Y	Y	N	N	Y
3 Nichols	?	?	?	?	?	Y	?
4 Bevill	Y	Y	Y	Y	Y	Y	N
5 Flippo	Y	Y	Y	Y	Y	Y	N
6 Erdreich	Y	Y	Y	Y	Y	Y	N
7 Shelby	Y	Y	Y	Y	Y	Y	N
ALASKA							
AL ***Young***	Y	Y	Y	Y	N	N	N
ARIZONA							
1 ***McCain***	N	N	Y	Y	Y	N	Y
2 Udall	Y	Y	Y	?	Y	Y	N
3 ***Stump***	N	N	Y	Y	N	N	Y
4 ***Rudd***	N	Y	Y	Y	N	N	Y
5 ***Kolbe***	Y	Y	Y	Y	Y	N	Y
ARKANSAS							
1 Alexander	Y	?	?	Y	Y	#	?
2 Robinson	?	?	Y	Y	Y	N	N
3 ***Hammerschmidt***	Y	Y	Y	Y	Y	Y	Y
4 Anthony	Y	Y	Y	Y	Y	N	N
CALIFORNIA							
1 Bosco	?	?	Y	Y	Y	Y	N
2 ***Chappie***	N	N	Y	Y	Y	N	Y
3 Matsui	Y	Y	Y	?	Y	Y	N
4 Fazio	Y	Y	Y	Y	Y	Y	N
5 Burton	Y	Y	Y	Y	Y	Y	N
6 Boxer	Y	Y	Y	Y	Y	?	?
7 Miller	Y	Y	Y	Y	Y	Y	N
8 Dellums	Y	Y	Y	Y	Y	Y	N
9 Stark	Y	Y	Y	Y	Y	Y	N
10 Edwards	Y	Y	Y	Y	Y	Y	N
11 Lantos	Y	Y	Y	Y	Y	Y	N
12 ***Zschau***	Y	Y	Y	Y	N	N	N
13 Mineta	Y	Y	Y	Y	Y	Y	N
14 ***Shumway***	N	Y	Y	Y	N	N	Y
15 Coelho	Y	Y	Y	Y	Y	Y	N
16 Panetta	Y	Y	Y	Y	Y	N	N
17 ***Pashayan***	Y	Y	Y	?	Y	N	Y
18 Lehman	Y	Y	?	?	+	Y	N
19 ***Lagomarsino***	Y	N	Y	Y	N	N	Y
20 ***Thomas***	Y	Y	Y	Y	N	N	Y
21 ***Fiedler***	?	?	Y	Y	Y	N	Y
22 ***Moorhead***	Y	Y	Y	Y	Y	N	Y
23 Beilenson	Y	Y	Y	Y	Y	Y	N
24 Waxman	Y	Y	Y	Y	Y	Y	N
25 Roybal	Y	?	?	Y	Y	Y	N
26 Berman	Y	Y	Y	Y	Y	Y	N
27 Levine	Y	Y	Y	Y	Y	Y	N
28 Dixon	Y	Y	Y	Y	Y	Y	N
29 Hawkins	Y	Y	Y	?	?	?	?
30 Martinez	Y	Y	Y	Y	Y	Y	N
31 Dymally	Y	Y	Y	Y	Y	Y	N
32 Anderson	Y	Y	Y	Y	Y	Y	N
33 ***Dreier***	N	N	Y	Y	Y	N	Y
34 Torres	Y	Y	Y	Y	Y	Y	N
35 ***Lewis***	Y	?	Y	Y	Y	?	Y
36 Brown	Y	Y	Y	Y	Y	Y	N
37 ***McCandless***	Y	N	Y	+	N	N	Y
38 ***Dornan***	N	N	Y	Y	Y	-	-
39 ***Dannemeyer***	N	N	Y	Y	N	N	Y
40 ***Badham***	N	N	?	?	X	X	?
41 ***Lowery***	Y	Y	Y	?	Y	N	N
42 ***Lungren***	Y	Y	Y	Y	N	N	Y
43 ***Packard***	Y	Y	Y	Y	N	N	Y
44 Bates	Y	Y	Y	Y	Y	N	Y
45 ***Hunter***	N	N	Y	Y	Y	N	Y
COLORADO							
1 Schroeder	Y	Y	Y	Y	Y	Y	Y
2 Wirth	Y	Y	Y	Y	Y	N	N
3 ***Strang***	N	Y	Y	Y	Y	N	Y
4 ***Brown***	N	N	Y	Y	Y	N	Y
5 ***Kramer***	N	N	?	Y	Y	N	Y
6 ***Schaefer***	N	N	?	Y	Y	?	Y
CONNECTICUT							
1 Kennelly	Y	Y	Y	Y	Y	Y	N
2 Gejdenson	Y	Y	Y	Y	Y	Y	N
3 Morrison	Y	Y	Y	+	Y	Y	N
4 ***McKinney***	Y	Y	Y	?	Y	N	N
5 ***Rowland***	N	Y	Y	Y	Y	N	N
6 ***Johnson***	Y	Y	Y	Y	Y	N	N
DELAWARE							
AL Carper	Y	Y	Y	Y	Y	Y	Y
FLORIDA							
1 Hutto	Y	Y	Y	Y	Y	N	Y
2 Fuqua	Y	Y	Y	Y	Y	?	?
3 Bennett	Y	Y	Y	Y	Y	Y	Y
4 Chappell	Y	Y	Y	Y	Y	Y	N
5 ***McCollum***	Y	Y	Y	Y	Y	N	Y
6 MacKay	Y	Y	Y	Y	N	?	N
7 Gibbons	Y	Y	Y	Y	Y	?	?
8 ***Young***	Y	Y	Y	Y	Y	N	Y
9 ***Bilirakis***	N	N	Y	Y	Y	N	Y
10 ***Ireland***	N	Y	Y	Y	Y	N	Y
11 Nelson	Y	Y	Y	Y	Y	Y	N
12 ***Lewis***	Y	Y	Y	Y	Y	N	Y
13 ***Mack***	?	N	Y	Y	Y	N	Y
14 Mica	Y	Y	Y	?	Y	Y	N
15 ***Shaw***	Y	Y	Y	Y	Y	N	Y
16 Smith	Y	Y	Y	Y	Y	Y	N
17 Lehman	Y	Y	Y	Y	Y	Y	N
18 Pepper	+	+	Y	Y	Y	+	-
19 Fascell	Y	Y	Y	Y	Y	Y	N
GEORGIA							
1 Thomas	Y	Y	Y	Y	Y	Y	N
2 Hatcher	?	?	Y	?	Y	?	?
3 Ray	Y	Y	Y	Y	N	N	Y
4 ***Swindall***	Y	N	Y	Y	Y	N	Y
5 Fowler	?	?	?	Y	Y	Y	Y
6 ***Gingrich***	Y	N	Y	Y	Y	N	Y
7 Darden	Y	Y	Y	Y	Y	Y	N
8 Rowland	Y	Y	Y	Y	Y	Y	N
9 Jenkins	Y	Y	?	Y	Y	Y	N
10 Barnard	Y	Y	Y	Y	Y	N	?
HAWAII							
1 Heftel	Y	Y	Y	Y	Y	Y	N
2 Akaka	Y	Y	Y	Y	Y	Y	N
IDAHO							
1 ***Craig***	N	N	Y	Y	Y	N	Y
2 Stallings	Y	Y	Y	Y	Y	Y	Y
ILLINOIS							
1 Hayes	?	?	Y	Y	Y	Y	N
2 Savage	?	?	?	Y	Y	Y	N
3 Russo	Y	Y	Y	Y	Y	Y	N
4 ***O'Brien***	Y	+	Y	Y	Y	N	N
5 Lipinski	Y	Y	Y	Y	N	Y	N
6 ***Hyde***	Y	Y	Y	Y	N	N	Y
7 Collins	Y	Y	Y	Y	Y	Y	N
8 Rostenkowski	Y	Y	Y	Y	Y	Y	N
9 Yates	Y	Y	Y	Y	Y	Y	N
10 ***Porter***	N	Y	Y	Y	Y	N	Y
11 Annunzio	Y	Y	Y	Y	Y	Y	N
12 ***Crane***	N	N	Y	Y	Y	N	Y
13 ***Fawell***	Y	Y	Y	Y	N	N	Y
14 ***Grotberg***	?	?	?	?	?	?	?
15 ***Madigan***	Y	Y	Y	Y	N	N	N
16 ***Martin***	Y	N	Y	Y	Y	N	Y
17 Evans	Y	Y	Y	Y	Y	Y	N
18 ***Michel***	Y	Y	Y	?	N	N	Y
19 Bruce	Y	Y	Y	Y	Y	Y	N
20 Durbin	Y	Y	Y	Y	Y	Y	N
21 Price	Y	Y	Y	Y	Y	Y	N
22 Gray	Y	Y	Y	Y	Y	Y	N
INDIANA							
1 Visclosky	Y	Y	Y	Y	Y	Y	N
2 Sharp	Y	Y	Y	Y	Y	?	?
3 ***Hiler***	Y	Y	Y	Y	N	N	Y
4 ***Coats***	Y	Y	Y	Y	Y	N	Y
5 ***Hillis***	Y	Y	Y	Y	N	N	Y

ND - Northern Democrats SD - Southern Democrats

* Corresponding to Congressional Record Votes 108, 109, 110, 111, 112, 113, 114

	98	99	100	101	102	103	104
6 ***Burton***	N	N	?	Y	Y	N	Y
7 ***Myers***	?	?	Y	Y	N	Y	N
8 McCloskey	Y	Y	Y	Y	Y	Y	N
9 Hamilton	Y	Y	Y	Y	N	Y	N
10 Jacobs	Y	Y	Y	Y	Y	N	N
IOWA							
1 ***Leach***	Y	Y	Y	Y	Y	N	N
2 ***Tauke***	Y	Y	Y	Y	N	N	Y
3 ***Evans***	?	N	?	?	Y	?	?
4 Smith	Y	Y	Y	Y	Y	Y	N
5 ***Lightfoot***	Y	N	Y	Y	Y	N	Y
6 Bedell	Y	Y	?	Y	Y	Y	?
KANSAS							
1 ***Roberts***	N	Y	Y	Y	Y	N	Y
2 Slattery	Y	Y	Y	Y	Y	Y	Y
3 ***Meyers***	N	Y	Y	Y	Y	N	Y
4 Glickman	Y	Y	Y	Y	Y	Y	Y
5 ***Whittaker***	N	Y	?	Y	Y	N	Y
KENTUCKY							
1 Hubbard	Y	Y	Y	Y	Y	N	Y
2 Natcher	Y	Y	Y	Y	Y	Y	N
3 Mazzoli	Y	Y	Y	Y	N	Y	N
4 ***Snyder***	Y	Y	?	Y	N	N	Y
5 ***Rogers***	Y	?	Y	Y	N	N	N
6 ***Hopkins***	Y	Y	Y	Y	N	N	Y
7 Perkins	Y	Y	Y	Y	Y	Y	N
LOUISIANA							
1 ***Livingston***	Y	Y	Y	Y	N	N	Y
2 Boggs	?	Y	Y	Y	Y	+	N
3 Tauzin	Y	Y	Y	Y	Y	Y	Y
4 Roemer	Y	Y	Y	Y	Y	N	Y
5 Huckaby	Y	Y	Y	Y	Y	Y	N
6 ***Moore***	Y	Y	Y	Y	Y	N	Y
7 Breaux	Y	Y	?	?	#	Y	Y
8 Long	Y	Y	Y	Y	Y	Y	N
MAINE							
1 ***McKernan***	Y	Y	Y	Y	Y	N	N
2 ***Snowe***	Y	Y	Y	Y	Y	N	N
MARYLAND							
1 Dyson	Y	Y	?	Y	Y	Y	Y
2 ***Bentley***	Y	Y	Y	Y	Y	N	N
3 Mikulski	Y	Y	Y	Y	Y	Y	N
4 ***Holt***	Y	Y	Y	Y	N	N	N
5 Hoyer	Y	Y	Y	Y	Y	Y	N
6 Byron	Y	Y	Y	Y	Y	Y	Y
7 Mitchell	Y	Y	Y	Y	Y	?	?
8 Barnes	Y	Y	Y	Y	Y	Y	N
MASSACHUSETTS							
1 ***Conte***	Y	Y	Y	Y	Y	Y	N
2 Boland	Y	Y	Y	Y	Y	Y	N
3 Early	Y	Y	Y	Y	Y	Y	N
4 Frank	Y	Y	Y	Y	Y	Y	N
5 Atkins	Y	Y	Y	Y	Y	Y	N
6 Mavroules	Y	Y	Y	Y	Y	Y	N
7 Markey	Y	Y	Y	Y	Y	Y	N
8 O'Neill							
9 Moakley	Y	Y	Y	Y	Y	Y	N
10 Studds	Y	Y	Y	Y	N	Y	N
11 Donnelly	Y	Y	?	+	+	?	?
MICHIGAN							
1 Conyers	?	?	Y	Y	N	Y	N
2 ***Pursell***	Y	Y	Y	Y	Y	N	N
3 Wolpe	Y	Y	Y	Y	Y	Y	N
4 ***Siljander***	Y	N	Y	Y	Y	N	Y
5 ***Henry***	Y	Y	Y	Y	Y	N	Y
6 Carr	Y	Y	Y	Y	Y	Y	Y
7 Kildee	Y	Y	Y	Y	Y	Y	N
8 Traxler	Y	Y	Y	Y	Y	Y	N
9 ***Vander Jagt***	Y	Y	Y	Y	Y	N	N
10 ***Schuette***	Y	N	Y	Y	Y	N	Y
11 ***Davis***	Y	?	Y	?	Y	N	Y
12 Bonior	?	Y	Y	Y	N	Y	N
13 Crockett	Y	Y	Y	Y	Y	Y	N
14 Hertel	Y	Y	Y	Y	Y	Y	N
15 Ford	Y	Y	Y	Y	Y	Y	N
16 Dingell	Y	Y	Y	Y	N	Y	N
17 Levin	Y	Y	Y	Y	Y	Y	N
18 ***Broomfield***	?	?	Y	Y	Y	N	N
MINNESOTA							
1 Penny	Y	Y	Y	Y	Y	Y	Y
2 ***Weber***	N	N	Y	Y	Y	N	Y
3 ***Frenzel***	N	Y	Y	Y	Y	N	Y
4 Vento	Y	Y	Y	Y	Y	Y	N
5 Sabo	Y	Y	Y	Y	Y	Y	N
6 Sikorski	Y	Y	Y	Y	Y	Y	N
7 ***Stangeland***	Y	?	Y	Y	N	N	Y
8 Oberstar	Y	Y	Y	Y	Y	Y	N
MISSISSIPPI							
1 Whitten	Y	Y	Y	Y	Y	Y	N
2 ***Franklin***	?	?	?	?	?	?	?
3 Montgomery	Y	Y	Y	Y	N	Y	Y
4 Dowdy	Y	?	Y	?	Y	?	?
5 ***Lott***	Y	Y	Y	Y	Y	N	Y
MISSOURI							
1 Clay	Y	Y	Y	Y	Y	Y	N
2 Young	Y	Y	?	Y	Y	Y	N
3 Gephardt	Y	Y	Y	Y	Y	?	?
4 Skelton	Y	Y	Y	Y	Y	?	?
5 Wheat	Y	Y	Y	Y	Y	Y	N
6 ***Coleman***	Y	Y	Y	Y	Y	N	Y
7 ***Taylor***	Y	Y	Y	Y	Y	Y	Y
8 ***Emerson***	Y	Y	Y	Y	Y	N	Y
9 Volkmer	Y	Y	Y	Y	Y	Y	Y
MONTANA							
1 Williams	N	N	Y	Y	Y	N	N
2 ***Marlenee***	N	N	Y	Y	N	N	Y
NEBRASKA							
1 ***Bereuter***	Y	Y	Y	Y	Y	N	Y
2 ***Daub***	N	Y	Y	Y	Y	N	Y
3 ***Smith***	Y	Y	Y	Y	Y	Y	Y
NEVADA							
1 Reid	Y	Y	Y	Y	Y	Y	N
2 ***Vucanovich***	N	N	?	Y	Y	N	Y
NEW HAMPSHIRE							
1 ***Smith***	N	N	Y	Y	Y	N	Y
2 ***Gregg***	Y	?	Y	Y	Y	N	Y
NEW JERSEY							
1 Florio	Y	Y	Y	Y	Y	Y	N
2 Hughes	Y	Y	Y	Y	Y	N	N
3 Howard	Y	Y	Y	Y	Y	Y	N
4 ***Smith***	Y	Y	Y	Y	Y	N	N
5 ***Roukema***	Y	Y	?	Y	Y	N	N
6 Dwyer	Y	Y	Y	Y	Y	Y	N
7 ***Rinaldo***	Y	Y	Y	Y	Y	N	N
8 Roe	Y	Y	Y	Y	Y	Y	N
9 Torricelli	Y	Y	Y	?	Y	Y	N
10 Rodino	?	Y	Y	Y	Y	Y	N
11 ***Gallo***	Y	Y	Y	Y	Y	N	N
12 ***Courter***	Y	Y	Y	Y	Y	N	N
13 ***Saxton***	Y	Y	Y	Y	Y	N	N
14 Guarini	Y	Y	Y	Y	Y	Y	N
NEW MEXICO							
1 ***Lujan***	?	?	?	?	?	?	?
2 ***Skeen***	Y	Y	Y	Y	Y	N	Y
3 Richardson	Y	Y	Y	Y	Y	Y	N
NEW YORK							
1 ***Carney***	Y	Y	Y	Y	Y	N	N
2 Downey	Y	Y	Y	Y	Y	Y	N
3 Mrazek	Y	Y	Y	Y	Y	Y	N
4 ***Lent***	Y	Y	?	Y	Y	N	?
5 ***McGrath***	Y	Y	?	Y	Y	N	?
6 Vacancy							
7 Ackerman	Y	Y	Y	Y	Y	Y	N
8 Scheuer	Y	Y	Y	Y	Y	Y	N
9 Manton	Y	Y	?	Y	Y	Y	N
10 Schumer	Y	Y	Y	Y	Y	Y	N
11 Towns	Y	Y	?	Y	Y	Y	N
12 Owens	Y	N	Y	Y	Y	Y	N
13 Solarz	Y	Y	Y	Y	Y	Y	N
14 ***Molinari***	Y	Y	Y	Y	Y	N	N
15 ***Green***	Y	Y	Y	Y	Y	Y	N
16 Rangel	Y	Y	?	Y	Y	Y	?
17 Weiss	Y	Y	Y	Y	Y	Y	N
18 Garcia	?	?	?	Y	Y	Y	N
19 Biaggi	Y	Y	Y	Y	Y	Y	N
20 ***DioGuardi***	Y	Y	Y	Y	Y	N	N
21 ***Fish***	Y	Y	?	Y	Y	N	N
22 ***Gilman***	Y	N	Y	Y	Y	N	N
23 Stratton	N	N	Y	Y	Y	Y	N
24 ***Solomon***	?	?	Y	Y	N	N	N
25 ***Boehlert***	Y	Y	Y	Y	Y	N	N
26 ***Martin***	Y	Y	Y	Y	Y	N	N
27 ***Wortley***	N	Y	Y	Y	Y	N	N
28 McHugh	Y	Y	Y	Y	Y	Y	N
29 ***Horton***	Y	Y	Y	Y	Y	N	N
30 ***Eckert***	Y	Y	Y	Y	Y	N	Y
31 ***Kemp***	Y	Y	?	Y	Y	N	N
32 LaFalce	Y	Y	Y	Y	Y	Y	N
33 Nowak	Y	Y	?	Y	Y	?	N
34 Lundine	Y	Y	Y	Y	Y	Y	N
NORTH CAROLINA							
1 Jones	Y	Y	?	?	?	?	?
2 Valentine	Y	Y	Y	Y	Y	Y	Y
3 Whitley	Y	?	Y	Y	Y	Y	N
4 ***Cobey***	N	N	?	Y	Y	N	Y
5 Neal	Y	Y	Y	Y	Y	Y	Y
6 ***Coble***	Y	N	Y	Y	Y	N	Y
7 Rose	?	?	Y	Y	N	Y	N
8 Hefner	Y	Y	Y	Y	Y	Y	N
9 ***McMillan***	Y	N	Y	Y	Y	N	Y
10 ***Broyhill***	Y	N	?	Y	Y	N	Y
11 ***Hendon***	N	N	Y	Y	Y	N	Y
NORTH DAKOTA							
AL Dorgan	Y	Y	Y	Y	Y	Y	N
OHIO							
1 Luken	Y	Y	?	Y	Y	Y	N
2 ***Gradison***	Y	Y	Y	Y	Y	N	Y
3 Hall	Y	Y	?	Y	Y	Y	N
4 ***Oxley***	N	N	?	Y	N	N	Y
5 ***Latta***	N	Y	Y	Y	N	N	Y
6 ***McEwen***	Y	N	Y	Y	Y	N	?
7 ***DeWine***	Y	Y	Y	Y	N	N	Y
8 ***Kindness***	N	Y	?	Y	Y	N	Y
9 Kaptur	Y	Y	?	Y	Y	Y	N
10 ***Miller***	N	N	Y	Y	N	N	Y
11 Eckart	Y	Y	Y	Y	-	Y	N
12 ***Kasich***	N	Y	Y	Y	Y	N	N
13 Pease	Y	Y	Y	Y	Y	Y	Y
14 Seiberling	Y	Y	Y	Y	Y	Y	N
15 ***Wylie***	Y	Y	Y	Y	Y	N	Y
16 ***Regula***	Y	N	Y	Y	Y	N	N
17 Traficant	Y	Y	?	Y	Y	N	N
18 Applegate	Y	N	Y	Y	Y	Y	Y
19 Feighan	Y	Y	Y	Y	Y	Y	N
20 Oakar	Y	Y	?	Y	Y	Y	N
21 Stokes	Y	Y	Y	Y	Y	Y	N
OKLAHOMA							
1 Jones	Y	Y	?	Y	Y	N	Y
2 Synar	Y	Y	Y	Y	Y	Y	Y
3 Watkins	Y	Y	?	Y	Y	Y	Y
4 McCurdy	Y	Y	Y	Y	Y	Y	Y
5 ***Edwards***	?	?	Y	Y	Y	N	Y
6 English	Y	Y	Y	Y	Y	Y	Y
OREGON							
1 AuCoin	Y	Y	Y	Y	Y	N	N
2 ***Smith, R.***	Y	Y	Y	Y	Y	N	Y
3 Wyden	Y	Y	Y	Y	Y	Y	N
4 Weaver	?	?	Y	Y	Y	Y	N
5 ***Smith, D.***	N	N	Y	Y	Y	N	Y
PENNSYLVANIA							
1 Foglietta	?	?	?	Y	Y	Y	N
2 Gray	Y	Y	Y	Y	Y	Y	N
3 Borski	Y	Y	Y	Y	Y	Y	N
4 Kolter	Y	Y	?	Y	Y	N	N
5 ***Schulze***	Y	Y	Y	Y	Y	N	N
6 Yatron	Y	Y	Y	Y	Y	Y	N
7 Edgar	Y	Y	?	?	?	?	?
8 Kostmayer	Y	Y	Y	Y	Y	Y	Y
9 ***Shuster***	Y	N	Y	Y	Y	N	Y
10 ***McDade***	?	?	?	Y	Y	N	N
11 Kanjorski	Y	Y	Y	Y	Y	Y	N
12 Murtha	Y	Y	Y	Y	Y	Y	N
13 ***Coughlin***	Y	Y	Y	Y	Y	N	N
14 Coyne	Y	Y	Y	Y	Y	Y	N
15 ***Ritter***	Y	?	?	Y	Y	N	Y
16 ***Walker***	N	N	Y	Y	Y	N	Y
17 ***Gekas***	N	N	Y	Y	Y	N	Y
18 Walgren	Y	Y	Y	Y	Y	Y	N
19 ***Goodling***	Y	Y	Y	Y	Y	N	Y
20 Gaydos	Y	Y	Y	Y	Y	Y	N
21 ***Ridge***	Y	Y	Y	?	N	N	Y
22 Murphy	Y	?	Y	?	?	N	Y
23 ***Clinger***	Y	Y	Y	Y	Y	N	N
RHODE ISLAND							
1 St Germain	Y	Y	Y	Y	Y	Y	N
2 ***Schneider***	Y	Y	Y	Y	Y	?	?
SOUTH CAROLINA							
1 ***Hartnett***	?	?	?	Y	N	?	?
2 ***Spence***	N	N	Y	Y	Y	N	N
3 Derrick	Y	Y	Y	Y	Y	Y	N
4 ***Campbell***	Y	N	Y	Y	Y	N	Y
5 Spratt	Y	Y	Y	Y	N	Y	N
6 Tallon	Y	Y	Y	Y	Y	Y	Y
SOUTH DAKOTA							
AL Daschle	Y	Y	Y	Y	Y	Y	N
TENNESSEE							
1 ***Quillen***	N	N	Y	?	?	?	?
2 ***Duncan***	Y	N	Y	Y	Y	N	N
3 Lloyd	?	?	Y	Y	Y	Y	Y
4 Cooper	Y	Y	Y	Y	N	Y	N
5 Boner	Y	Y	?	Y	Y	N	N
6 Gordon	+	Y	Y	Y	Y	N	N
7 ***Sundquist***	Y	N	Y	Y	Y	N	Y
8 Jones	?	?	Y	Y	N	Y	?
9 Ford	Y	Y	?	Y	Y	Y	N
TEXAS							
1 Chapman	Y	Y	Y	Y	Y	Y	Y
2 Wilson	Y	Y	?	Y	N	Y	?
3 ***Bartlett***	N	Y	Y	Y	N	N	Y
4 Hall, R.	Y	N	Y	Y	Y	N	Y
5 Bryant	Y	Y	Y	Y	Y	Y	N
6 ***Barton***	Y	Y	Y	Y	Y	N	Y
7 ***Archer***	N	Y	Y	Y	Y	N	Y
8 ***Fields***	Y	Y	Y	Y	Y	N	Y
9 Brooks	?	?	Y	Y	Y	Y	N
10 Pickle	?	?	Y	Y	Y	Y	Y
11 Leath	Y	Y	Y	Y	Y	N	Y
12 Wright	Y	Y	Y	Y	Y	Y	N
13 ***Boulter***	N	N	Y	Y	Y	N	Y
14 ***Sweeney***	Y	Y	?	Y	Y	N	Y
15 de la Garza	?	?	Y	Y	Y	Y	N
16 Coleman	Y	Y	Y	Y	Y	Y	N
17 Stenholm	?	Y	Y	Y	Y	N	Y
18 Leland	Y	Y	Y	Y	Y	Y	N
19 ***Combest***	Y	Y	Y	Y	N	N	Y
20 Gonzalez	Y	Y	Y	?	Y	Y	N
21 ***Loeffler***	?	?	?	?	?	?	?
22 ***DeLay***	N	N	Y	Y	Y	N	Y
23 Bustamante	Y	?	Y	Y	Y	Y	N
24 Frost	Y	Y	?	Y	Y	?	?
25 Andrews	?	?	Y	Y	Y	Y	Y
26 ***Armey***	Y	N	Y	Y	Y	N	Y
27 Ortiz	?	?	?	Y	Y	Y	N
UTAH							
1 ***Hansen***	Y	Y	Y	Y	N	N	Y
2 ***Monson***	N	Y	Y	Y	Y	N	Y
3 ***Nielson***	Y	Y	Y	Y	N	N	Y
VERMONT							
AL ***Jeffords***	Y	Y	Y	Y	N	N	N
VIRGINIA							
1 ***Bateman***	?	?	Y	?	Y	N	N
2 ***Whitehurst***	Y	Y	Y	Y	N	N	N
3 ***Bliley***	Y	?	Y	Y	Y	N	N
4 Sisisky	Y	Y	Y	Y	Y	Y	N
5 Daniel	Y	Y	Y	Y	Y	N	Y
6 Olin	Y	Y	Y	Y	Y	Y	N
7 ***Slaughter***	N	Y	Y	Y	N	N	Y
8 ***Parris***	Y	Y	Y	Y	Y	N	N
9 Boucher	Y	Y	Y	Y	Y	Y	N
10 ***Wolf***	Y	Y	Y	Y	Y	N	N
WASHINGTON							
1 ***Miller***	Y	Y	Y	Y	Y	N	Y
2 Swift	Y	Y	Y	Y	Y	Y	N
3 Bonker	Y	Y	Y	Y	N	?	Y
4 ***Morrison***	Y	Y	Y	Y	N	N	N
5 Foley	Y	Y	Y	Y	Y	Y	N
6 Dicks	Y	Y	Y	Y	Y	Y	N
7 Lowry	Y	Y	Y	Y	Y	Y	N
8 ***Chandler***	Y	?	Y	Y	N	N	Y
WEST VIRGINIA							
1 Mollohan	Y	Y	Y	Y	Y	Y	N
2 Staggers	Y	Y	Y	Y	Y	Y	N
3 Wise	Y	Y	Y	Y	Y	Y	N
4 Rahall	N	N	?	?	N	Y	N
WISCONSIN							
1 Aspin	Y	Y	Y	Y	Y	Y	N
2 Kastenmeier	Y	Y	Y	Y	Y	Y	N
3 ***Gunderson***	Y	Y	Y	Y	Y	N	Y
4 Kleczka	Y	Y	Y	Y	Y	Y	N
5 Moody	Y	Y	Y	Y	Y	Y	N
6 ***Petri***	N	Y	Y	Y	N	N	Y
7 Obey	Y	Y	Y	Y	Y	Y	N
8 ***Roth***	N	N	Y	Y	Y	N	Y
9 ***Sensenbrenner***	N	N	Y	Y	Y	N	Y
WYOMING							
AL ***Cheney***	N	Y	Y	Y	N	N	Y

Southern states - Ala., Ark., Fla., Ga., Ky., La., Miss., N.C., Okla., S.C., Tenn., Texas, Va.

* The *Congressional Record* vote number is different from the CQ vote number because the *Record* includes quorum calls in its tally. CQ does not publish quorum call votes.

105. HR 4515. Urgent Supplemental Appropriations, Fiscal 1986. Armey, R-Texas, amendment to delete language that would repeal the president's power to defer spending certain money appropriated by Congress. Rejected 163-224: R 143-19; D 20-205 (ND 8-148, SD 12-57), May 8, 1986.

106. HR 4515. Urgent Supplemental Appropriations, Fiscal 1986. Lott, R-Miss., amendment to limit language repealing the president's power to defer spending certain money appropriated by Congress exclusively to the bill, and no subsequent appropriations. Rejected 179-203: R 152-8; D 27-195 (ND 9-145, SD 18-50), May 8, 1986.

107. HR 4515. Urgent Supplemental Appropriations, Fiscal 1986. Pursell, R-Mich., motion to recommit the bill to the Appropriations Committee with instructions to report the bill back promptly, amended so that it does not add to the fiscal 1986 budget deficit. Motion rejected 168-212: R 145-14; D 23-198 (ND 8-148, SD 15-50), May 8, 1986.

108. HR 4515. Urgent Supplemental Appropriations, Fiscal 1986. Passage of the bill to provide $1.7 billion in urgent supplemental appropriations for fiscal year 1986. Passed 242-132: R 50-108; D 192-24 (ND 139-11, SD 53-13), May 8, 1986. A "nay" was a vote supporting the president's position.

109. Procedural Motion. Strang, R-Colo., motion to approve the House *Journal* of Monday, May 12. Motion agreed to 258-121: R 50-112; D 208-9 (ND 138-7, SD 70-2), May 13, 1986.

110. S 124. Safe Drinking Water. Adoption of the conference report on the bill to authorize appropriations to carry out the Safe Drinking Water Act of 1974 (PL 93-523) for fiscal 1987-91 — $170.15 million for fiscal 1987, $145.15 million for 1988, and $169.54 million annually for 1989-91 — and to amend certain provisions regulating drinking-water safety. Adopted 382-21: R 148-20; D 234-1 (ND 157-1, SD 77-0), May 13, 1986.

111. S 974. Protection and Advocacy for the Mentally Ill. Adoption of the conference report on the bill to authorize $31.53 million in fiscal 1986-88 for agencies that provide protection and advocacy services for the mentally ill. Adopted 383-21: R 150-21; D 233-0 (ND 156-0, SD 77-0), May 13, 1986.

112. HR 1. Housing Act. Adoption of the rule (H Res 450) to provide for House floor consideration of and to waive points of order against the bill to reauthorize housing programs for fiscal years 1986 and 1987. Adopted 257-149: R 33-139; D 224-10 (ND 154-2, SD 70-8), May 13, 1986.

KEY

- Y Voted for (yea).
- # Paired for.
- + Announced for.
- N Voted against (nay).
- X Paired against.
- \- Announced against.
- P Voted "present."
- C Voted "present" to avoid possible conflict of interest.
- ? Did not vote or otherwise make a position known.

Democrats ***Republicans***

	105	106	107	108	109	110	111	112
ALABAMA								
1 ***Callahan***	Y	Y	Y	N	Y	Y	Y	N
2 ***Dickinson***	Y	Y	Y	N	N	Y	Y	N
3 Nichols	?	?	?	?	?	Y	Y	?
4 Bevill	N	N	N	Y	Y	Y	Y	Y
5 Flippo	N	N	N	Y	?	?	?	Y
6 Erdreich	N	Y	N	Y	Y	Y	Y	Y
7 Shelby	N	N	N	Y	?	Y	Y	Y
ALASKA								
AL ***Young***	Y	Y	N	Y	N	Y	Y	N
ARIZONA								
1 ***McCain***	Y	Y	Y	N	Y	Y	Y	N
2 Udall	N	N	N	Y	Y	Y	Y	Y
3 ***Stump***	Y	Y	Y	N	N	N	Y	N
4 ***Rudd***	#	#	#	X	Y	N	Y	N
5 ***Kolbe***	Y	Y	Y	N	N	Y	Y	N
ARKANSAS								
1 Alexander	?	X	X	?	Y	Y	Y	Y
2 Robinson	N	N	X	#	?	?	?	?
3 ***Hammerschmidt***	Y	Y	N	Y	Y	N	Y	N
4 Anthony	N	N	N	Y	Y	Y	Y	Y
CALIFORNIA								
1 Bosco	?	?	?	?	Y	Y	Y	Y
2 ***Chappie***	Y	Y	Y	N	N	Y	Y	N
3 Matsui	N	N	N	Y	Y	Y	Y	Y
4 Fazio	N	N	N	Y	Y	Y	Y	Y
5 Burton	N	N	N	Y	?	Y	Y	?
6 Boxer	X	X	X	#	Y	Y	Y	Y
7 Miller	N	N	N	Y	Y	Y	?	Y
8 Dellums	N	N	N	Y	?	?	?	?
9 Stark	N	N	N	Y	Y	Y	Y	Y
10 Edwards	N	N	N	Y	Y	Y	Y	Y
11 Lantos	N	N	N	Y	?	?	?	?
12 ***Zschau***	Y	Y	Y	N	N	Y	Y	N
13 Mineta	N	N	N	Y	Y	Y	Y	Y
14 ***Shumway***	Y	Y	Y	N	Y	N	N	N
15 Coelho	N	N	N	Y	Y	Y	Y	Y
16 Panetta	N	N	N	?	Y	Y	Y	Y
17 ***Pashayan***	Y	Y	Y	Y	?	Y	Y	N
18 Lehman	N	?	N	Y	Y	Y	Y	Y
19 ***Lagomarsino***	Y	Y	Y	N	N	Y	Y	N
20 ***Thomas***	Y	Y	Y	N	?	Y	Y	N
21 ***Fiedler***	?	?	?	?	?	?	?	?
22 ***Moorhead***	Y	Y	Y	N	N	Y	N	N
23 Beilenson	N	N	N	Y	Y	Y	Y	Y
24 Waxman	N	N	N	Y	Y	Y	Y	Y
25 Roybal	N	N	N	Y	Y	Y	Y	Y
26 Berman	N	N	N	?	Y	Y	Y	Y
27 Levine	N	N	N	Y	Y	Y	Y	Y
28 Dixon	N	N	N	?	Y	Y	Y	Y
29 Hawkins	?	X	X	?	N	Y	Y	Y
30 Martinez	N	N	N	Y	Y	Y	Y	Y
31 Dymally	N	N	N	Y	Y	Y	Y	Y
32 Anderson	N	N	N	Y	Y	Y	Y	Y
33 ***Dreier***	Y	Y	Y	N	N	Y	N	N
34 Torres	N	N	N	Y	Y	Y	Y	Y
35 ***Lewis***	?	?	?	?	N	Y	Y	N
36 Brown	N	N	N	Y	?	Y	?	Y
37 ***McCandless***	Y	Y	Y	N	N	N	N	Y
38 ***Dornan***	+	+	+	-	N	Y	Y	N
39 ***Dannemeyer***	Y	Y	Y	N	N	N	N	N
40 ***Badham***	?	?	#	X	N	Y	Y	N
41 ***Lowery***	Y	Y	Y	N	N	Y	Y	N
42 ***Lungren***	Y	Y	Y	N	Y	N	N	N
43 ***Packard***	Y	Y	Y	N	Y	Y	N	N
44 Bates	N	N	Y	N	Y	Y	Y	Y
45 ***Hunter***	Y	Y	Y	N	?	?	Y	Y
COLORADO								
1 Schroeder	N	N	Y	N	N	Y	Y	+
2 Wirth	N	N	Y	N	Y	Y	Y	Y
3 ***Strang***	Y	Y	Y	Y	N	N	Y	N
4 ***Brown***	Y	Y	Y	N	N	Y	Y	N
5 ***Kramer***	Y	Y	?	?	N	N	N	N
6 ***Schaefer***	Y	#	#	X	N	Y	Y	N
CONNECTICUT								
1 Kennelly	N	N	N	Y	?	Y	Y	Y
2 Gejdenson	N	N	N	Y	Y	Y	Y	Y
3 Morrison	N	N	N	Y	?	Y	Y	Y
4 ***McKinney***	N	N	Y	Y	Y	Y	Y	Y
5 ***Rowland***	Y	Y	Y	N	Y	Y	Y	Y
6 ***Johnson***	Y	Y	Y	Y	Y	Y	Y	Y
DELAWARE								
AL Carper	N	N	N	Y	Y	Y	Y	Y
FLORIDA								
1 Hutto	N	Y	N	Y	Y	Y	Y	N
2 Fuqua	?	?	?	?	Y	Y	Y	Y
3 Bennett	N	N	N	Y	Y	Y	Y	Y
4 Chappell	N	N	N	Y	Y	Y	Y	Y
5 ***McCollum***	Y	Y	Y	N	Y	Y	Y	N
6 MacKay	N	N	P	Y	?	Y	Y	Y
7 Gibbons	X	X	X	#	Y	Y	Y	Y
8 ***Young***	Y	Y	Y	N	N	Y	Y	N
9 ***Bilirakis***	Y	Y	Y	N	N	Y	Y	N
10 ***Ireland***	Y	Y	Y	N	N	Y	Y	N
11 Nelson	N	N	N	Y	Y	Y	Y	Y
12 ***Lewis***	Y	Y	Y	N	N	Y	Y	N
13 ***Mack***	Y	Y	Y	N	N	Y	Y	N
14 Mica	N	N	N	Y	Y	Y	Y	Y
15 ***Shaw***	Y	Y	Y	N	N	Y	Y	N
16 Smith	N	N	N	Y	Y	Y	Y	Y
17 Lehman	N	N	N	Y	Y	Y	Y	Y
18 Pepper	X	X	X	+	Y	Y	Y	Y
19 Fascell	N	N	N	Y	Y	Y	Y	Y
GEORGIA								
1 Thomas	N	N	Y	N	Y	Y	Y	Y
2 Hatcher	?	?	?	?	Y	Y	Y	Y
3 Ray	Y	Y	Y	N	Y	Y	Y	Y
4 ***Swindall***	Y	Y	Y	N	N	Y	Y	N
5 Fowler	Y	Y	N	N	Y	Y	Y	Y
6 ***Gingrich***	Y	Y	Y	N	N	Y	Y	N
7 Darden	N	N	N	Y	Y	Y	Y	Y
8 Rowland	N	N	N	Y	Y	Y	Y	Y
9 Jenkins	N	N	N	Y	Y	Y	Y	Y
10 Barnard	N	N	Y	N	Y	Y	Y	Y
HAWAII								
1 Heftel	Y	Y	N	Y	?	Y	Y	Y
2 Akaka	N	N	N	Y	Y	Y	Y	Y
IDAHO								
1 ***Craig***	Y	Y	Y	N	N	N	N	N
2 Stallings	Y	Y	N	N	Y	N	Y	Y
ILLINOIS								
1 Hayes	N	N	N	Y	Y	Y	Y	Y
2 Savage	N	N	N	Y	?	Y	Y	Y
3 Russo	N	N	N	N	Y	Y	Y	Y
4 ***O'Brien***	N	N	N	Y	?	?	?	?
5 Lipinski	N	?	N	Y	Y	Y	Y	Y
6 ***Hyde***	Y	Y	Y	N	?	Y	Y	N
7 Collins	N	N	N	Y	Y	Y	Y	Y
8 Rostenkowski	N	N	N	Y	Y	Y	Y	Y
9 Yates	N	N	N	Y	Y	Y	Y	Y
10 ***Porter***	Y	Y	Y	N	Y	Y	Y	N
11 Annunzio	N	N	N	Y	Y	Y	Y	?
12 ***Crane***	Y	Y	Y	N	N	N	N	N
13 ***Fawell***	Y	Y	Y	Y	N	Y	Y	N
14 ***Grotberg***	?	?	?	?	?	?	?	?
15 ***Madigan***	Y	Y	Y	N	N	Y	Y	N
16 ***Martin***	Y	Y	Y	N	N	Y	Y	N
17 Evans	N	N	N	Y	Y	Y	Y	Y
18 ***Michel***	Y	Y	Y	Y	N	Y	Y	N
19 Bruce	N	N	N	Y	Y	Y	Y	Y
20 Durbin	N	N	N	Y	Y	Y	Y	Y
21 Price	N	N	N	Y	Y	Y	Y	Y
22 Gray	N	N	N	Y	Y	Y	Y	Y
INDIANA								
1 Visclosky	N	N	N	Y	Y	Y	Y	Y
2 Sharp	Y	Y	N	Y	Y	?	?	Y
3 ***Hiler***	#	#	#	X	N	Y	Y	N
4 ***Coats***	Y	Y	Y	N	N	Y	Y	N
5 ***Hillis***	Y	Y	Y	?	Y	Y	Y	N

ND - Northern Democrats SD - Southern Democrats

* Corresponding to Congressional Record Votes 115, 116, 117, 118, 119, 120, 121, 122

	105	106	107	108	109	110	111	112
6 ***Burton***	Y	Y	Y	N	?	Y	Y	N
7 ***Myers***	N	Y	Y	Y	Y	Y	Y	N
8 McCloskey	N	N	N	Y	Y	Y	Y	Y
9 Hamilton	Y	Y	N	Y	Y	Y	Y	Y
10 Jacobs	N	N	N	Y	N	Y	Y	N
IOWA								
1 ***Leach***	Y	Y	Y	N	N	?	?	?
2 ***Tauke***	Y	Y	Y	N	N	Y	Y	N
3 ***Evans***	?	?	?	?	N	Y	Y	N
4 Smith	N	N	N	Y	Y	Y	Y	Y
5 ***Lightfoot***	Y	Y	Y	N	Y	Y	Y	N
6 Bedell	N	N	N	Y	Y	Y	Y	Y
KANSAS								
1 ***Roberts***	Y	Y	Y	N	N	Y	Y	N
2 Slattery	Y	Y	N	N	Y	Y	Y	Y
3 ***Meyers***	Y	Y	Y	Y	N	Y	Y	N
4 Glickman	X	?	?	?	Y	Y	Y	Y
5 ***Whittaker***	Y	Y	Y	N	?	Y	Y	N
KENTUCKY								
1 Hubbard	Y	Y	Y	N	Y	Y	Y	Y
2 Natcher	N	N	N	Y	Y	Y	Y	Y
3 Mazzoli	N	N	N	Y	Y	Y	Y	Y
4 ***Snyder***	Y	Y	Y	N	?	Y	Y	N
5 ***Rogers***	Y	Y	Y	Y	N	Y	Y	N
6 ***Hopkins***	Y	Y	Y	N	N	Y	Y	N
7 Perkins	N	N	N	Y	Y	Y	Y	Y
LOUISIANA								
1 ***Livingston***	Y	Y	#	X	N	Y	N	N
2 Boggs	N	N	N	Y	Y	Y	Y	Y
3 Tauzin	Y	Y	Y	N	Y	Y	Y	Y
4 Roemer	Y	Y	Y	N	N	Y	Y	N
5 Huckaby	N	N	N	Y	Y	Y	Y	Y
6 ***Moore***	Y	Y	Y	N	Y	Y	Y	Y
7 Breaux	Y	Y	N	Y	Y	Y	Y	Y
8 Long	N	N	N	Y	?	Y	Y	Y
MAINE								
1 ***McKernan***	Y	Y	Y	Y	N	Y	Y	Y
2 ***Snowe***	N	Y	Y	Y	N	Y	Y	Y
MARYLAND								
1 Dyson	N	Y	Y	Y	N	Y	Y	Y
2 ***Bentley***	N	Y	Y	Y	N	Y	Y	N
3 Mikulski	N	N	N	Y	Y	Y	Y	Y
4 ***Holt***	Y	Y	Y	Y	?	?	?	?
5 Hoyer	N	N	N	Y	Y	Y	Y	Y
6 Byron	N	N	N	Y	Y	Y	Y	Y
7 Mitchell	?	X	?	?	?	Y	Y	Y
8 Barnes	N	N	N	Y	?	Y	Y	Y
MASSACHUSETTS								
1 ***Conte***	N	N	N	Y	N	Y	Y	Y
2 Boland	N	N	N	Y	Y	Y	Y	Y
3 Early	N	N	N	Y	Y	Y	Y	Y
4 Frank	N	N	N	Y	Y	Y	Y	Y
5 Atkins	N	N	N	?	Y	?	?	?
6 Mavroules	N	N	N	Y	Y	Y	Y	Y
7 Markey	N	N	N	Y	Y	Y	Y	Y
8 O'Neill								
9 Moakley	N	N	N	Y	Y	Y	Y	Y
10 Studds	N	N	N	Y	Y	Y	Y	Y
11 Donnelly	?	?	?	?	Y	Y	Y	Y
MICHIGAN								
1 Conyers	N	N	N	Y	Y	Y	Y	Y
2 ***Pursell***	N	Y	Y	N	Y	Y	Y	N
3 Wolpe	N	N	N	Y	Y	Y	Y	Y
4 ***Siljander***	Y	Y	Y	N	N	Y	Y	N
5 ***Henry***	Y	Y	Y	N	N	Y	Y	N
6 Carr	N	N	N	Y	Y	Y	Y	Y
7 Kildee	N	N	N	Y	Y	Y	Y	Y
8 Traxler	?	?	?	?	Y	Y	Y	Y
9 ***Vander Jagt***	Y	Y	Y	N	N	Y	Y	N
10 ***Schuette***	Y	Y	Y	Y	N	Y	Y	N
11 ***Davis***	Y	#	#	#	N	Y	Y	Y
12 Bonior	N	N	N	Y	?	Y	Y	Y
13 Crockett	N	N	N	Y	Y	Y	Y	Y
14 Hertel	N	N	N	Y	Y	Y	Y	Y
15 Ford	N	N	N	Y	Y	Y	Y	Y
16 Dingell	N	N	N	Y	Y	Y	Y	Y
17 Levin	N	N	N	Y	Y	Y	Y	Y
18 ***Broomfield***	Y	Y	Y	N	N	Y	Y	N
MINNESOTA								
1 Penny	Y	Y	Y	N	N	Y	Y	Y
2 ***Weber***	Y	Y	N	Y	N	Y	Y	N
3 ***Frenzel***	Y	Y	Y	N	?	Y	Y	N
4 Vento	N	N	N	Y	Y	Y	Y	Y
5 Sabo	N	N	N	Y	Y	Y	Y	Y
6 Sikorski	N	N	N	Y	N	Y	Y	Y

	105	106	107	108	109	110	111	112
7 ***Stangeland***	Y	Y	Y	Y	N	Y	Y	N
8 Oberstar	N	N	N	Y	Y	Y	Y	Y
MISSISSIPPI								
1 Whitten	N	N	N	Y	Y	Y	Y	Y
2 ***Franklin***	?	?	?	?	?	?	?	?
3 Montgomery	N	Y	Y	Y	Y	Y	Y	Y
4 Dowdy	?	?	?	?	?	Y	Y	Y
5 ***Lott***	Y	Y	Y	N	N	Y	Y	N
MISSOURI								
1 Clay	N	N	N	Y	N	Y	Y	Y
2 Young	N	N	N	Y	Y	Y	Y	Y
3 Gephardt	?	?	?	?	Y	Y	Y	Y
4 Skelton	X	?	X	#	Y	Y	Y	Y
5 Wheat	N	N	N	Y	Y	Y	Y	Y
6 ***Coleman***	Y	Y	Y	N	N	Y	Y	N
7 ***Taylor***	Y	Y	N	Y	Y	Y	Y	N
8 ***Emerson***	Y	Y	Y	Y	N	Y	Y	N
9 Volkmer	N	N	N	Y	Y	Y	Y	Y
MONTANA								
1 Williams	N	N	N	Y	Y	Y	Y	Y
2 ***Marlenee***	Y	Y	Y	N	N	N	N	N
NEBRASKA								
1 ***Bereuter***	Y	Y	Y	Y	-	+	+	+
2 ***Daub***	Y	Y	Y	N	?	?	?	?
3 ***Smith***	Y	Y	Y	Y	Y	Y	Y	N
NEVADA								
1 Reid	N	N	N	Y	Y	Y	Y	Y
2 ***Vucanovich***	Y	Y	Y	N	N	N	Y	N
NEW HAMPSHIRE								
1 ***Smith***	Y	Y	Y	N	N	Y	Y	N
2 ***Gregg***	Y	Y	Y	N	?	Y	Y	N
NEW JERSEY								
1 Florio	N	N	N	Y	Y	Y	Y	Y
2 Hughes	Y	Y	Y	N	Y	Y	Y	Y
3 Howard	N	N	N	Y	Y	Y	Y	Y
4 ***Smith***	N	Y	N	Y	Y	Y	Y	Y
5 ***Roukema***	Y	Y	Y	Y	N	Y	Y	Y
6 Dwyer	N	N	N	Y	Y	Y	Y	Y
7 ***Rinaldo***	N	N	N	Y	Y	Y	Y	Y
8 Roe	N	N	N	Y	?	Y	Y	Y
9 Torricelli	N	N	N	Y	Y	Y	Y	Y
10 Rodino	N	N	N	Y	?	Y	Y	Y
11 ***Gallo***	Y	Y	Y	N	N	Y	Y	N
12 ***Courter***	Y	Y	Y	N	N	?	Y	N
13 ***Saxton***	Y	Y	Y	Y	N	Y	Y	N
14 Guarini	N	N	N	Y	Y	Y	Y	Y
NEW MEXICO								
1 ***Lujan***	?	?	?	?	?	?	?	?
2 ***Skeen***	Y	Y	Y	Y	N	N	Y	N
3 Richardson	N	N	N	Y	Y	Y	Y	Y
NEW YORK								
1 ***Carney***	Y	Y	Y	N	N	Y	Y	N
2 Downey	N	N	N	Y	Y	Y	Y	Y
3 Mrazek	N	N	N	Y	Y	Y	Y	Y
4 ***Lent***	?	?	?	?	N	Y	Y	N
5 ***McGrath***	#	#	#	#	N	Y	Y	N
6 Vacancy								
7 Ackerman	N	N	N	Y	Y	?	?	?
8 Scheuer	N	?	?	?	?	?	?	?
9 Manton	X	X	X	?	Y	Y	Y	Y
10 Schumer	N	N	N	?	Y	Y	Y	Y
11 Towns	N	N	N	Y	Y	Y	Y	Y
12 Owens	N	N	N	Y	Y	Y	Y	Y
13 Solarz	N	N	N	Y	Y	Y	Y	Y
14 ***Molinari***	Y	Y	Y	N	N	Y	Y	Y
15 ***Green***	N	N	N	Y	Y	Y	Y	Y
16 Rangel	?	X	X	?	?	Y	Y	Y
17 Weiss	N	N	N	Y	Y	Y	Y	Y
18 Garcia	N	N	N	Y	Y	Y	Y	Y
19 Biaggi	N	N	N	Y	Y	Y	Y	Y
20 ***DioGuardi***	Y	Y	Y	N	Y	Y	Y	Y
21 ***Fish***	Y	Y	Y	Y	Y	Y	Y	Y
22 ***Gilman***	Y	Y	N	Y	Y	Y	Y	Y
23 Stratton	?	N	N	Y	Y	Y	Y	N
24 ***Solomon***	?	?	Y	N	N	Y	Y	N
25 ***Boehlert***	Y	Y	Y	Y	N	Y	Y	Y
26 ***Martin***	Y	Y	Y	Y	Y	Y	Y	N
27 ***Wortley***	Y	Y	Y	Y	?	?	Y	Y
28 McHugh	N	N	N	Y	Y	Y	Y	Y
29 ***Horton***	N	Y	N	Y	Y	?	Y	Y
30 ***Eckert***	Y	Y	Y	N	Y	Y	N	N
31 ***Kemp***	Y	Y	Y	N	Y	Y	Y	N
32 LaFalce	N	N	N	Y	Y	Y	Y	Y
33 Nowak	N	N	N	Y	Y	Y	Y	Y
34 Lundine	N	N	Y	Y	Y	Y	Y	Y

	105	106	107	108	109	110	111	112
NORTH CAROLINA								
1 Jones	?	?	?	#	Y	Y	Y	Y
2 Valentine	N	Y	N	Y	Y	Y	Y	Y
3 Whitley	N	?	?	?	Y	Y	Y	Y
4 ***Cobey***	Y	Y	Y	N	N	Y	Y	N
5 Neal	?	?	?	?	Y	Y	Y	Y
6 ***Coble***	Y	Y	Y	Y	N	Y	Y	Y
7 Rose	N	N	N	Y	Y	Y	Y	Y
8 Hefner	N	N	N	Y	?	Y	Y	Y
9 ***McMillan***	Y	Y	Y	Y	N	Y	Y	Y
10 ***Broyhill***	Y	Y	Y	N	Y	Y	Y	N
11 ***Hendon***	Y	Y	Y	Y	N	Y	?	N
NORTH DAKOTA								
AL Dorgan	Y	Y	N	N	Y	Y	Y	Y
OHIO								
1 Luken	N	N	N	Y	Y	Y	Y	?
2 ***Gradison***	Y	Y	Y	N	Y	Y	Y	N
3 Hall	N	N	N	N	Y	Y	Y	Y
4 ***Oxley***	Y	Y	Y	N	N	Y	N	N
5 ***Latta***	Y	Y	Y	N	N	Y	Y	N
6 ***McEwen***	?	?	?	?	Y	Y	Y	N
7 ***DeWine***	Y	Y	Y	N	N	Y	Y	N
8 ***Kindness***	Y	Y	Y	N	N	Y	Y	N
9 Kaptur	N	N	N	Y	Y	Y	Y	Y
10 ***Miller***	Y	Y	Y	N	N	Y	Y	N
11 Eckart	N	N	N	Y	Y	Y	Y	Y
12 ***Kasich***	Y	Y	Y	N	Y	Y	Y	N
13 Pease	N	N	N	Y	Y	Y	Y	Y
14 Seiberling	N	N	N	Y	?	Y	Y	Y
15 ***Wylie***	Y	Y	Y	N	Y	Y	Y	Y
16 ***Regula***	N	N	Y	N	N	Y	Y	N
17 Traficant	N	N	N	Y	Y	Y	Y	Y
18 Applegate	N	N	Y	Y	Y	Y	Y	Y
19 Feighan	N	N	N	Y	?	Y	Y	Y
20 Oakar	N	N	N	Y	Y	Y	Y	Y
21 Stokes	N	N	N	Y	Y	Y	Y	Y
OKLAHOMA								
1 Jones	Y	Y	Y	Y	Y	Y	Y	N
2 Synar	N	N	N	Y	Y	Y	Y	Y
3 Watkins	N	N	N	Y	?	?	?	?
4 McCurdy	N	N	Y	Y	Y	Y	Y	Y
5 ***Edwards***	N	Y	Y	N	N	Y	Y	N
6 English	N	N	Y	Y	Y	Y	Y	Y
OREGON								
1 AuCoin	N	N	N	Y	Y	Y	Y	Y
2 ***Smith, R.***	Y	Y	Y	N	N	N	Y	N
3 Wyden	N	N	N	Y	Y	Y	Y	Y
4 Weaver	N	N	N	Y	Y	Y	Y	Y
5 ***Smith, D.***	Y	Y	Y	N	N	Y	Y	N
PENNSYLVANIA								
1 Foglietta	N	N	N	Y	?	?	?	Y
2 Gray	N	N	N	Y	Y	Y	Y	Y
3 Borski	N	N	N	Y	Y	Y	Y	Y
4 Kolter	N	N	N	Y	Y	Y	Y	Y
5 ***Schulze***	Y	Y	Y	N	Y	Y	Y	N
6 Yatron	N	N	N	Y	Y	Y	Y	Y
7 Edgar	?	?	?	?	?	?	?	?
8 Kostmayer	N	N	N	Y	Y	Y	Y	Y
9 ***Shuster***	Y	Y	Y	N	?	?	?	?
10 ***McDade***	N	Y	Y	Y	Y	Y	Y	Y
11 Kanjorski	N	N	N	Y	Y	Y	Y	Y
12 Murtha	N	N	N	Y	Y	?	?	?
13 ***Coughlin***	Y	Y	Y	N	N	Y	Y	N
14 Coyne	N	N	N	Y	Y	Y	Y	Y
15 ***Ritter***	Y	Y	Y	N	Y	Y	Y	N
16 ***Walker***	Y	Y	Y	N	N	Y	Y	N
17 ***Gekas***	Y	Y	Y	N	N	Y	Y	N
18 Walgren	N	N	N	Y	Y	Y	Y	Y
19 ***Goodling***	Y	Y	Y	N	N	Y	Y	N
20 Gaydos	N	N	N	Y	Y	Y	Y	Y
21 ***Ridge***	Y	Y	Y	N	Y	Y	Y	Y
22 Murphy	N	N	N	Y	?	Y	Y	Y
23 ***Clinger***	N	Y	N	Y	N	Y	Y	Y
RHODE ISLAND								
1 St Germain	N	N	N	Y	Y	Y	Y	Y
2 ***Schneider***	N	N	Y	Y	Y	Y	Y	Y
SOUTH CAROLINA								
1 ***Hartnett***	#	#	#	X	N	Y	Y	N
2 ***Spence***	Y	Y	Y	N	Y	Y	Y	N
3 Derrick	N	N	N	Y	Y	Y	Y	Y
4 ***Campbell***	#	#	#	X	?	Y	Y	N
5 Spratt	N	N	N	Y	Y	Y	Y	Y
6 Tallon	N	N	N	Y	Y	Y	Y	Y
SOUTH DAKOTA								
AL Daschle	N	N	N	Y	Y	Y	Y	Y

	105	106	107	108	109	110	111	112
TENNESSEE								
1 ***Quillen***	?	?	?	?	Y	Y	Y	Y
2 ***Duncan***	Y	Y	Y	N	Y	Y	Y	Y
3 Lloyd	N	Y	Y	Y	N	Y	Y	N
4 Cooper	N	N	N	Y	Y	Y	Y	Y
5 Boner	N	N	N	Y	Y	Y	Y	Y
6 Gordon	Y	Y	N	Y	Y	Y	Y	Y
7 ***Sundquist***	Y	Y	Y	N	N	Y	Y	N
8 Jones	?	?	X	#	Y	Y	Y	Y
9 Ford	N	N	?	?	Y	Y	?	Y
TEXAS								
1 Chapman	N	N	Y	N	Y	Y	Y	Y
2 Wilson	N	N	N	Y	?	?	?	?
3 ***Bartlett***	Y	Y	Y	N	N	Y	Y	Y
4 Hall, R.	Y	Y	Y	N	Y	Y	Y	N
5 Bryant	N	N	N	Y	Y	Y	Y	Y
6 ***Barton***	Y	Y	Y	N	N	Y	Y	N
7 ***Archer***	Y	Y	Y	N	Y	Y	N	N
8 ***Fields***	Y	Y	Y	N	N	Y	N	N
9 Brooks	N	N	N	Y	Y	Y	Y	Y
10 Pickle	Y	Y	N	Y	Y	?	Y	Y
11 Leath	?	?	?	?	Y	Y	Y	N
12 Wright	?	?	?	?	Y	Y	Y	Y
13 ***Boulter***	Y	Y	N	Y	N	Y	Y	N
14 ***Sweeney***	Y	Y	Y	N	Y	Y	Y	N
15 de la Garza	N	N	N	Y	Y	Y	Y	Y
16 Coleman	N	N	N	Y	Y	Y	Y	Y
17 Stenholm	Y	Y	Y	N	Y	Y	Y	N
18 Leland	N	N	N	Y	Y	Y	Y	Y
19 ***Combest***	Y	Y	Y	N	Y	Y	Y	N
20 Gonzalez	N	N	N	Y	Y	Y	Y	Y
21 ***Loeffler***	?	?	?	?	N	Y	Y	N
22 ***DeLay***	Y	Y	Y	N	N	Y	Y	N
23 Bustamante	N	N	N	Y	Y	Y	Y	Y
24 Frost	?	?	?	?	Y	Y	Y	Y
25 Andrews	Y	Y	N	N	Y	Y	Y	Y
26 ***Armey***	Y	Y	Y	N	N	N	N	N
27 Ortiz	N	N	N	Y	Y	Y	Y	Y
UTAH								
1 ***Hansen***	Y	Y	Y	N	N	N	N	N
2 ***Monson***	#	#	#	X	N	N	N	N
3 ***Nielson***	Y	Y	Y	N	Y	N	N	N
VERMONT								
AL ***Jeffords***	N	Y	N	Y	Y	Y	Y	N
VIRGINIA								
1 ***Bateman***	Y	Y	Y	N	Y	Y	Y	N
2 ***Whitehurst***	?	?	?	?	N	Y	Y	N
3 ***Bliley***	Y	Y	Y	N	N	Y	Y	N
4 Sisisky	N	N	N	Y	Y	Y	Y	Y
5 Daniel	N	Y	Y	N	Y	Y	Y	Y
6 Olin	N	N	N	N	Y	Y	Y	N
7 ***Slaughter***	Y	Y	Y	N	N	Y	Y	N
8 ***Parris***	Y	Y	Y	Y	Y	Y	Y	Y
9 Boucher	N	N	N	Y	Y	Y	Y	Y
10 ***Wolf***	Y	Y	Y	Y	N	Y	Y	N
WASHINGTON								
1 ***Miller***	N	Y	Y	Y	Y	Y	Y	N
2 Swift	N	N	N	Y	?	Y	Y	Y
3 Bonker	N	N	N	Y	Y	Y	Y	Y
4 ***Morrison***	N	Y	Y	Y	Y	Y	Y	N
5 Foley	N	N	N	Y	Y	Y	Y	Y
6 Dicks	N	N	N	Y	Y	Y	Y	Y
7 Lowry	N	N	N	Y	Y	Y	Y	Y
8 ***Chandler***	Y	Y	Y	N	N	Y	Y	N
WEST VIRGINIA								
1 Mollohan	N	N	N	Y	?	?	?	?
2 Staggers	N	N	N	Y	?	?	?	?
3 Wise	N	N	N	Y	?	Y	Y	Y
4 Rahall	N	N	N	Y	Y	Y	Y	Y
WISCONSIN								
1 Aspin	N	N	N	Y	Y	Y	Y	Y
2 Kastenmeier	N	N	N	Y	Y	Y	Y	Y
3 ***Gunderson***	Y	Y	Y	N	N	Y	Y	N
4 Kleczka	N	N	N	Y	Y	Y	Y	Y
5 Moody	N	N	N	Y	Y	Y	Y	Y
6 ***Petri***	Y	Y	Y	N	Y	Y	Y	N
7 Obey	N	N	N	?	Y	Y	Y	Y
8 ***Roth***	Y	N	Y	N	N	Y	Y	Y
9 ***Sensenbrenner***	Y	Y	Y	N	N	Y	Y	N
WYOMING								
AL ***Cheney***	Y	Y	Y	N	N	N	N	N

Southern states - Ala., Ark., Fla., Ga., Ky., La., Miss., N.C., Okla., S.C., Tenn., Texas, Va.

* The *Congressional Record* vote number is different from the CQ vote number because the *Record* includes quorum calls in its tally. CQ does not publish quorum call votes.

113. H Con Res 310. Farm Credit System Loan Restructuring. De la Garza, D-Texas, motion to suspend the rules and adopt the concurrent resolution to urge the Farm Credit System to consider the restructuring of delinquent loans to farmers if the costs associated with foreclosure equal or exceed the costs of restructuring. Motion agreed to 407-0: R 169-0; D 238-0 (ND 158-0, SD 80-0), May 14, 1986. A two-thirds majority of those present and voting (272 in this case) is required for adoption under suspension of the rules.

114. H Con Res 337. Budget Resolution, Fiscal 1987. Dannemeyer, R-Calif., substitute to set budget targets for the fiscal year ending Sept. 30, 1987, as follows: budget authority, $1,086.8 billion; outlays, $971.1 billion; revenues, $844 billion; deficit, $127.1 billion. The substitute would allow federal programs to increase for inflation from fiscal 1986 levels, and would reduce outlays by selling new government bonds backed by gold at low interest rates. Rejected 73-338: R 70-103; D 3-235 (ND 2-158, SD 1-77), May 15, 1986.

115. H Con Res 337. Budget Resolution, Fiscal 1987. Leland, D-Texas, substitute to set budget targets for the fiscal year ending Sept. 30, 1987, as follows: budget authority, $1,088.7 billion; outlays, $1,011.9 billion; revenues, $868.1 billion; deficit, $143.8 billion. The substitute would reduce spending for defense and increase spending for social programs compared with the concurrent resolution. Rejected 61-359: R 0-176; D 61-183 (ND 54-110, SD 7-73), May 15, 1986.

116. H Con Res 337. Budget Resolution, Fiscal 1987. Latta, R-Ohio, substitute to set budget targets for the fiscal year ending Sept. 30, 1987, as follows: budget authority, $1,081.5 billion; outlays, $993.5 billion; revenues, $849.7 billion; deficit, $143.8 billion. The amendment would increase spending for defense, decrease spending for domestic programs and raise less in revenues compared with the concurrent resolution. Rejected 145-280: R 145-32; D 0-248 (ND 0-166, SD 0-82), May 15, 1986.

117. H Con Res 337. Budget Resolution, Fiscal 1987. Adoption of the concurrent resolution to set budget targets for the fiscal year ending Sept. 30, 1987, as follows: budget authority, $1,086.4 billion; outlays, $994.3 billion; revenues, $857.2 billion; deficit, $137.1 billion. Adopted 245-179: R 17-160; D 228-19 (ND 154-11, SD 74-8), May 15, 1986. A "nay" was a vote supporting the president's position.

KEY

- Y Voted for (yea).
- # Paired for.
- + Announced for.
- N Voted against (nay).
- X Paired against.
- - Announced against.
- P Voted "present."
- C Voted "present" to avoid possible conflict of interest.
- ? Did not vote or otherwise make a position known.

Democrats ***Republicans***

	113	114	115	116	117
ALABAMA					
1 ***Callahan***	Y	Y	N	Y	N
2 ***Dickinson***	Y	Y	N	N	N
3 Nichols	Y	N	N	N	Y
4 Bevill	Y	N	N	N	Y
5 Flippo	Y	N	N	N	Y
6 Erdreich	Y	N	N	N	Y
7 Shelby	Y	N	N	N	Y
ALASKA					
AL ***Young***	Y	Y	N	N	N
ARIZONA					
1 ***McCain***	Y	N	N	Y	N
2 Udall	Y	N	N	N	Y
3 ***Stump***	Y	Y	N	Y	N
4 ***Rudd***	Y	Y	N	Y	N
5 ***Kolbe***	Y	N	N	Y	N
ARKANSAS					
1 Alexander	Y	N	Y	N	Y
2 Robinson	Y	N	N	N	Y
3 ***Hammerschmidt***	Y	Y	N	Y	N
4 Anthony	Y	N	N	N	Y
CALIFORNIA					
1 Bosco	Y	N	N	N	Y
2 ***Chappie***	Y	Y	N	Y	N
3 Matsui	Y	N	N	N	Y
4 Fazio	Y	N	N	N	Y
5 Burton	Y	N	Y	N	Y
6 Boxer	Y	N	Y	N	Y
7 Miller	Y	N	Y	N	Y
8 Dellums	Y	N	Y	N	Y
9 Stark	Y	N	Y	N	N
10 Edwards	Y	N	Y	N	Y
11 Lantos	Y	N	N	N	Y
12 ***Zschau***	Y	?	N	Y	N
13 Mineta	Y	N	Y	N	Y
14 ***Shumway***	Y	Y	N	Y	N
15 Coelho	Y	N	N	N	Y
16 Panetta	Y	N	N	N	Y
17 ***Pashayan***	Y	N	N	Y	N
18 Lehman	Y	N	N	N	Y
19 ***Lagomarsino***	Y	Y	N	Y	N
20 ***Thomas***	Y	N	N	Y	N
21 ***Fiedler***	?	Y	N	Y	N
22 ***Moorhead***	Y	Y	N	Y	N
23 Beilenson	Y	N	Y	N	Y
24 Waxman	Y	N	Y	N	Y
25 Roybal	Y	N	Y	N	Y
26 Berman	Y	N	Y	N	Y
27 Levine	Y	N	N	N	Y
28 Dixon	?	N	Y	N	Y
29 Hawkins	Y	N	Y	N	Y
30 Martinez	Y	N	Y	N	Y
31 Dymally	Y	N	Y	N	Y
32 Anderson	Y	Y	N	N	Y
33 ***Dreier***	Y	Y	N	Y	N
34 Torres	Y	N	Y	N	Y
35 ***Lewis***	Y	Y	N	Y	N
36 Brown	Y	N	Y	N	Y
37 ***McCandless***	Y	Y	N	Y	N
38 ***Dornan***	Y	Y	N	Y	N
39 ***Dannemeyer***	Y	Y	N	Y	N
40 ***Badham***	Y	Y	N	Y	N
41 ***Lowery***	?	Y	N	Y	N
42 ***Lungren***	Y	Y	N	Y	N
43 ***Packard***	Y	Y	N	Y	N
44 Bates	Y	N	N	N	Y
45 ***Hunter***	Y	Y	?	Y	N
COLORADO					
1 Schroeder	Y	N	Y	N	Y
2 Wirth	?	N	N	N	N
3 ***Strang***	Y	Y	N	Y	N
4 ***Brown***	Y	N	N	Y	N
5 ***Kramer***	Y	N	N	N	N
6 ***Schaefer***	Y	N	N	N	N
CONNECTICUT					
1 Kennelly	Y	N	N	N	Y
2 Gejdenson	Y	N	N	N	Y
3 Morrison	Y	N	N	N	Y
4 ***McKinney***	?	N	N	Y	Y
5 ***Rowland***	Y	N	N	Y	N
6 ***Johnson***	Y	N	N	Y	N
DELAWARE					
AL Carper	Y	N	N	N	Y
FLORIDA					
1 Hutto	Y	N	N	N	N
2 Fuqua	Y	N	N	N	Y
3 Bennett	Y	N	N	N	N
4 Chappell	Y	N	N	N	Y
5 ***McCollum***	Y	N	N	N	N
6 MacKay	Y	N	?	N	Y
7 Gibbons	Y	N	N	N	Y
8 ***Young***	?	N	N	Y	N
9 ***Bilirakis***	Y	Y	N	N	N
10 ***Ireland***	Y	?	N	Y	N
11 Nelson	Y	N	N	N	Y
12 ***Lewis***	Y	N	N	Y	N
13 ***Mack***	Y	Y	N	Y	N
14 Mica	Y	N	N	N	Y
15 ***Shaw***	Y	N	N	Y	N
16 Smith	?	N	N	N	Y
17 Lehman	Y	N	Y	N	Y
18 Pepper	Y	N	N	N	Y
19 Fascell	Y	N	N	N	Y
GEORGIA					
1 Thomas	Y	N	N	N	Y
2 Hatcher	Y	N	N	N	Y
3 Ray	Y	N	N	N	Y
4 ***Swindall***	Y	N	N	Y	N
5 Fowler	Y	N	N	N	Y
6 ***Gingrich***	Y	N	N	Y	N
7 Darden	Y	N	N	N	Y
8 Rowland	Y	N	N	N	Y
9 Jenkins	Y	N	N	N	Y
10 Barnard	Y	?	N	N	Y
HAWAII					
1 Heftel	Y	?	?	?	?
2 Akaka	Y	N	Y	N	Y
IDAHO					
1 ***Craig***	Y	Y	N	Y	N
2 Stallings	Y	N	N	N	N
ILLINOIS					
1 Hayes	Y	N	Y	N	Y
2 Savage	Y	N	Y	N	Y
3 Russo	Y	N	N	N	Y
4 ***O'Brien***	Y	?	-	Y	Y
5 Lipinski	Y	N	N	N	Y
6 ***Hyde***	?	Y	N	Y	N
7 Collins	Y	N	Y	N	Y
8 Rostenkowski	Y	N	N	N	Y
9 Yates	Y	?	Y	N	N
10 ***Porter***	Y	N	N	N	N
11 Annunzio	Y	N	N	N	Y
12 ***Crane***	Y	Y	N	Y	N
13 ***Fawell***	Y	N	N	Y	N
14 ***Grotberg***	?	?	?	?	?
15 ***Madigan***	Y	N	N	Y	N
16 ***Martin***	Y	N	N	Y	N
17 Evans	Y	N	Y	N	Y
18 ***Michel***	Y	N	N	Y	N
19 Bruce	Y	N	N	N	Y
20 Durbin	Y	N	N	N	Y
21 Price	Y	N	N	N	Y
22 Gray	Y	N	N	N	Y
INDIANA					
1 Visclosky	Y	N	Y	N	Y
2 Sharp	Y	N	N	N	Y
3 ***Hiler***	Y	Y	N	Y	N
4 ***Coats***	Y	N	N	Y	N
5 ***Hillis***	Y	N	N	Y	N

ND - Northern Democrats SD - Southern Democrats

* Corresponding to Congressional Record Votes 123, 124, 126, 127, 128

	113	114	115	116	117
6 *Burton*	Y	Y	N	Y	N
7 *Myers*	Y	N	N	N	N
8 McCloskey	Y	N	N	N	N
9 Hamilton	Y	N	N	N	Y
10 Jacobs	Y	N	Y	N	Y
IOWA					
1 *Leach*	?	N	N	Y	N
2 *Tauke*	Y	N	N	Y	N
3 *Evans*	Y	N	N	Y	N
4 Smith	Y	N	N	N	Y
5 *Lightfoot*	Y	N	N	Y	N
6 Bedell	Y	N	Y	N	Y
KANSAS					
1 *Roberts*	Y	N	N	Y	N
2 Slattery	Y	N	N	N	Y
3 *Meyers*	Y	N	N	Y	N
4 Glickman	Y	N	N	N	Y
5 *Whittaker*	Y	N	N	Y	N
KENTUCKY					
1 Hubbard	Y	N	N	N	Y
2 Natcher	Y	N	N	N	Y
3 Mazzoli	Y	N	N	N	Y
4 *Snyder*	Y	N	N	Y	N
5 *Rogers*	Y	N	N	Y	N
6 *Hopkins*	Y	Y	N	Y	N
7 Perkins	Y	N	Y	N	Y
LOUISIANA					
1 *Livingston*	Y	Y	N	N	N
2 Boggs	Y	N	Y	N	Y
3 Tauzin	Y	N	N	N	Y
4 Roemer	C	N	N	N	Y
5 Huckaby	Y	N	N	N	Y
6 *Moore*	Y	N	N	Y	N
7 Breaux	Y	N	N	N	Y
8 Long	Y	N	N	N	Y
MAINE					
1 *McKernan*	Y	N	N	Y	N
2 *Snowe*	Y	N	N	Y	N
MARYLAND					
1 Dyson	Y	N	N	N	N
2 *Bentley*	Y	Y	N	Y	N
3 Mikulski	Y	?	Y	N	Y
4 *Holt*	Y	N	N	Y	N
5 Hoyer	Y	N	Y	N	Y
6 Byron	Y	N	N	N	N
7 Mitchell	Y	N	Y	N	Y
8 Barnes	?	N	Y	N	Y
MASSACHUSETTS					
1 *Conte*	Y	N	N	N	Y
2 Boland	?	N	N	N	Y
3 Early	Y	N	N	N	Y
4 Frank	Y	N	Y	N	Y
5 Atkins	Y	N	N	N	Y
6 Mavroules	Y	N	N	N	Y
7 Markey	Y	N	Y	N	Y
8 O'Neill					
9 Moakley	Y	N	N	N	Y
10 Studds	Y	N	N	N	Y
11 Donnelly	Y	N	N	N	Y
MICHIGAN					
1 Conyers	Y	?	Y	N	Y
2 *Pursell*	Y	Y	N	Y	N
3 Wolpe	Y	N	N	N	Y
4 *Siljander*	Y	Y	N	Y	N
5 *Henry*	Y	N	N	Y	N
6 Carr	Y	N	N	N	N
7 Kildee	Y	N	Y	N	Y
8 Traxler	Y	N	N	N	Y
9 *Vander Jagt*	Y	Y	N	Y	N
10 *Schuette*	Y	Y	N	Y	N
11 *Davis*	Y	N	N	Y	Y
12 Bonior	Y	N	Y	N	Y
13 Crockett	Y	N	Y	N	Y
14 Hertel	Y	N	N	N	Y
15 Ford	?	N	N	N	Y
16 Dingell	Y	N	N	N	Y
17 Levin	Y	N	N	N	Y
18 *Broomfield*	Y	N	N	Y	N
MINNESOTA					
1 Penny	Y	N	N	N	Y
2 *Weber*	Y	Y	N	Y	Y
3 *Frenzel*	?	N	N	Y	N
4 Vento	Y	N	N	N	Y
5 Sabo	Y	N	N	N	Y
6 Sikorski	Y	N	N	N	Y
7 *Stangeland*	Y	N	N	Y	Y
8 Oberstar	Y	N	N	N	Y
MISSISSIPPI					
1 Whitten	Y	N	N	N	Y
2 *Franklin*	?	?	?	?	?
3 Montgomery	Y	N	N	N	Y
4 Dowdy	Y	N	N	N	Y
5 *Lott*	Y	N	N	Y	N
MISSOURI					
1 Clay	Y	N	Y	N	Y
2 Young	Y	N	N	N	Y
3 Gephardt	Y	N	N	N	Y
4 Skelton	Y	N	N	N	Y
5 Wheat	Y	N	Y	N	Y
6 *Coleman*	Y	N	N	Y	N
7 *Taylor*	Y	Y	N	Y	N
8 *Emerson*	Y	Y	N	Y	N
9 Volkmer	Y	N	N	N	Y
MONTANA					
1 Williams	Y	N	N	N	Y
2 *Marlenee*	Y	Y	N	Y	N
NEBRASKA					
1 *Bereuter*	Y	N	N	N	Y
2 *Daub*	?	Y	N	Y	N
3 *Smith*	Y	N	N	Y	N
NEVADA					
1 Reid	Y	N	N	N	N
2 *Vucanovich*	Y	Y	N	N	N
NEW HAMPSHIRE					
1 *Smith*	Y	Y	N	Y	N
2 *Gregg*	Y	N	N	Y	N
NEW JERSEY					
1 Florio	Y	N	N	N	Y
2 Hughes	Y	N	N	N	Y
3 Howard	Y	N	N	N	Y
4 *Smith*	?	N	N	N	Y
5 *Roukema*	Y	N	N	Y	N
6 Dwyer	Y	N	N	N	Y
7 *Rinaldo*	Y	N	N	N	Y
8 Roe	Y	N	N	N	Y
9 Torricelli	Y	N	N	N	Y
10 Rodino	Y	N	Y	N	Y
11 *Gallo*	Y	N	N	Y	N
12 *Courter*	Y	Y	N	N	N
13 *Saxton*	Y	N	N	Y	N
14 Guarini	Y	N	N	N	Y
NEW MEXICO					
1 *Lujan*	?	?	?	?	?
2 *Skeen*	Y	Y	N	Y	N
3 Richardson	Y	N	N	N	Y
NEW YORK					
1 *Carney*	Y	Y	N	N	N
2 Downey	Y	N	N	N	Y
3 Mrazek	?	N	N	N	N
4 *Lent*	Y	N	N	Y	N
5 *McGrath*	Y	N	N	N	N
6 Vacancy					
7 Ackerman	Y	N	Y	N	Y
8 Scheuer	?	?	+	X	#
9 Manton	Y	N	N	N	Y
10 Schumer	Y	N	N	N	Y
11 Towns	Y	N	Y	N	Y
12 Owens	Y	N	Y	N	Y
13 Solarz	Y	N	N	N	N
14 *Molinari*	Y	N	N	Y	N
15 *Green*	Y	N	N	N	N
16 Rangel	Y	N	Y	N	Y
17 Weiss	Y	N	Y	N	Y
18 Garcia	?	N	Y	N	Y
19 Biaggi	Y	N	N	N	?
20 *DioGuardi*	Y	N	N	N	N
21 *Fish*	Y	N	N	Y	N
22 *Gilman*	Y	N	N	N	Y
23 Stratton	Y	Y	N	N	Y
24 *Solomon*	?	Y	N	N	N
25 *Boehlert*	Y	N	N	Y	N
26 *Martin*	Y	N	N	Y	N
27 *Wortley*	Y	N	N	Y	N
28 McHugh	Y	N	N	N	Y
29 *Horton*	Y	N	N	N	Y
30 *Eckert*	Y	N	N	N	N
31 *Kemp*	Y	Y	N	N	N
32 LaFalce	Y	N	N	N	Y
33 Nowak	Y	N	N	N	Y
34 Lundine	Y	N	N	N	Y
NORTH CAROLINA					
1 Jones	Y	N	N	N	Y
2 Valentine	Y	N	N	N	Y
3 Whitley	Y	N	N	N	Y
4 *Cobey*	Y	Y	N	Y	N
5 Neal	Y	N	N	N	Y
6 *Coble*	Y	N	N	Y	N
7 Rose	Y	N	N	N	Y
8 Hefner	Y	N	N	N	Y
9 *McMillan*	Y	N	N	Y	N
10 *Broyhill*	Y	Y	N	Y	N
11 *Hendon*	Y	?	?	?	?
NORTH DAKOTA					
AL Dorgan	Y	?	N	N	Y
OHIO					
1 Luken	Y	N	N	N	Y
2 *Gradison*	Y	N	N	Y	N
3 Hall	Y	N	N	N	Y
4 *Oxley*	Y	N	N	Y	N
5 *Latta*	Y	N	N	Y	N
6 *McEwen*	Y	?	N	Y	N
7 *DeWine*	Y	N	N	Y	N
8 *Kindness*	Y	N	N	Y	N
9 Kaptur	Y	N	N	N	Y
10 *Miller*	Y	Y	N	Y	N
11 Eckart	Y	N	N	N	Y
12 *Kasich*	Y	Y	N	Y	N
13 Pease	Y	N	N	N	Y
14 Seiberling	Y	N	N	N	Y
15 *Wylie*	Y	N	N	Y	N
16 *Regula*	Y	N	N	Y	N
17 Traficant	Y	N	Y	N	Y
18 Applegate	Y	N	N	N	Y
19 Feighan	Y	N	N	?	Y
20 Oakar	Y	N	Y	N	Y
21 Stokes	Y	N	Y	N	Y
OKLAHOMA					
1 Jones	Y	N	N	N	Y
2 Synar	Y	N	N	N	Y
3 Watkins	Y	N	N	N	Y
4 McCurdy	Y	N	N	N	N
5 *Edwards*	Y	N	N	Y	N
6 English	Y	N	N	N	N
OREGON					
1 AuCoin	Y	N	N	N	Y
2 *Smith, R.*	Y	N	N	N	N
3 Wyden	Y	N	N	N	Y
4 Weaver	Y	N	N	N	Y
5 *Smith, D.*	Y	N	N	Y	N
PENNSYLVANIA					
1 Foglietta	?	?	Y	N	Y
2 Gray	Y	N	P	N	Y
3 Borski	Y	N	N	N	Y
4 Kolter	Y	N	N	N	Y
5 *Schulze*	Y	N	N	Y	N
6 Yatron	Y	N	N	N	Y
7 Edgar	?	?	?	N	Y
8 Kostmayer	Y	N	N	N	Y
9 *Shuster*	Y	Y	N	Y	N
10 *McDade*	Y	N	N	N	N
11 Kanjorski	Y	N	N	N	Y
12 Murtha	Y	N	N	N	Y
13 *Coughlin*	Y	N	N	Y	Y
14 Coyne	Y	N	Y	N	Y
15 *Ritter*	Y	N	N	Y	N
16 *Walker*	Y	Y	N	Y	N
17 *Gekas*	Y	Y	N	Y	N
18 Walgren	Y	?	N	N	Y
19 *Goodling*	Y	N	N	#	X
20 Gaydos	Y	N	N	N	Y
21 *Ridge*	Y	N	N	Y	N
22 Murphy	Y	N	N	N	Y
23 *Clinger*	Y	N	N	N	N
RHODE ISLAND					
1 St Germain	Y	N	N	N	Y
2 *Schneider*	Y	?	N	N	Y
SOUTH CAROLINA					
1 *Hartnett*	Y	Y	N	Y	N
2 *Spence*	Y	N	N	Y	N
3 Derrick	Y	?	?	N	Y
4 *Campbell*	Y	N	N	Y	N
5 Spratt	Y	N	N	N	Y
6 Tallon	Y	N	N	N	Y
SOUTH DAKOTA					
AL Daschle	Y	N	N	N	Y
TENNESSEE					
1 *Quillen*	Y	Y	N	Y	N
2 *Duncan*	Y	Y	N	Y	N
3 Lloyd	Y	N	N	N	N
4 Cooper	Y	N	N	N	Y
5 Boner	Y	N	N	N	N
6 Gordon	Y	N	N	N	Y
7 *Sundquist*	Y	N	N	Y	N
8 Jones	Y	N	N	N	Y
9 Ford	Y	N	Y	N	Y
TEXAS					
1 Chapman	Y	N	N	N	Y
2 Wilson	Y	?	N	N	Y
3 *Bartlett*	Y	N	N	Y	N
4 Hall, R.	Y	N	N	N	N
5 Bryant	Y	N	N	N	Y
6 *Barton*	Y	Y	N	Y	N
7 *Archer*	Y	Y	N	Y	N
8 *Fields*	Y	Y	N	Y	N
9 Brooks	Y	N	N	N	Y
10 Pickle	Y	N	N	N	Y
11 Leath	Y	N	N	N	Y
12 Wright	Y	N	N	N	Y
13 *Boulter*	Y	N	N	Y	N
14 *Sweeney*	Y	N	N	Y	N
15 de la Garza	Y	?	N	N	Y
16 Coleman	Y	N	N	N	N
17 Stenholm	Y	N	N	N	Y
18 Leland	Y	N	Y	N	Y
19 *Combest*	Y	N	N	Y	N
20 Gonzalez	Y	N	Y	N	Y
21 *Loeffler*	Y	N	N	Y	N
22 *DeLay*	Y	Y	N	Y	N
23 Bustamante	Y	N	N	N	Y
24 Frost	Y	N	N	N	Y
25 Andrews	Y	N	N	N	Y
26 *Armey*	Y	Y	N	Y	N
27 Ortiz	Y	N	N	N	Y
UTAH					
1 *Hansen*	Y	Y	N	Y	N
2 *Monson*	Y	N	N	N	N
3 *Nielson*	Y	Y	N	Y	N
VERMONT					
AL *Jeffords*	Y	N	N	Y	Y
VIRGINIA					
1 *Bateman*	Y	N	N	Y	N
2 *Whitehurst*	Y	Y	N	Y	N
3 *Bliley*	Y	N	N	Y	Y
4 Sisisky	Y	N	N	N	Y
5 Daniel	Y	Y	N	N	Y
6 Olin	Y	N	N	N	Y
7 *Slaughter*	Y	N	N	Y	N
8 *Parris*	Y	Y	N	Y	N
9 Boucher	Y	N	N	N	Y
10 *Wolf*	Y	N	N	Y	N
WASHINGTON					
1 *Miller*	Y	N	N	Y	Y
2 Swift	Y	N	N	N	?
3 Bonker	Y	N	N	N	Y
4 *Morrison*	Y	N	N	N	Y
5 Foley	Y	N	?	N	Y
6 Dicks	Y	N	N	N	Y
7 Lowry	Y	N	Y	N	Y
8 *Chandler*	Y	N	N	Y	N
WEST VIRGINIA					
1 Mollohan	?	N	N	N	Y
2 Staggers	Y	N	N	N	Y
3 Wise	Y	N	N	N	Y
4 Rahall	Y	N	N	N	Y
WISCONSIN					
1 Aspin	Y	N	N	N	Y
2 Kastenmeier	Y	N	Y	N	Y
3 *Gunderson*	Y	N	N	Y	N
4 Kleczka	Y	N	N	N	Y
5 Moody	Y	N	Y	N	Y
6 *Petri*	Y	N	N	Y	N
7 Obey	Y	N	N	N	Y
8 *Roth*	Y	Y	N	Y	N
9 *Sensenbrenner*	Y	Y	N	Y	N
WYOMING					
AL *Cheney*	Y	Y	N	N	N

Southern states - Ala., Ark., Fla., Ga., Ky., La., Miss., N.C., Okla., S.C., Tenn., Texas, Va.

* The *Congressional Record* vote number is different from the CQ vote number because the *Record* includes quorum calls in its tally. CQ does not publish quorum call votes.

118. Procedural Motion. Daub, R-Neb., motion to approve the House *Journal* of Monday, May 19. Motion agreed to 215-99: R 45-90; D 170-9 (ND 115-6, SD 55-3), May 20, 1986.

119. S 2416. Veterans' Home Loan Guarantees. Montgomery, D-Miss., motion to suspend the rules and pass the bill to raise the fiscal 1986 VA mortgage guarantee cap from $17.4 billion to $38.3 billion to accommodate anticipated demand through the end of the fiscal year. Motion agreed to 398-0: R 169-0; D 229-0 (ND 153-0, SD 76-0), May 21, 1986. A two-thirds majority of those present and voting (266 in this case) is required for passage under suspension of the rules.

120. HR 4800. Omnibus Trade Bill. Crane, R-Ill., amendment to strike sections in the bill dealing with U.S. responses to foreign unfair trading practices. The amendment would have deleted export targeting provisions and a requirement that some countries reduce their trade surpluses with the United States. Rejected 137-276: R 130-44; D 7-232 (ND 6-152, SD 1-80), May 21, 1986. A "yea" was a vote supporting the president's position.

121. HR 4800. Omnibus Trade Bill. Frenzel, R-Minn., amendment to strike sections in the bill that address assistance to U.S. companies and workers harmed by import competition. The amendment would have deleted provisions that establish an adjustment trust fund, allow for industry adjustment plans and transfer authority from the president to the U.S. trade representative. Rejected 109-306: R 109-65; D 0-241 (ND 0-162, SD 0-79), May 21, 1986. A "yea" was a vote supporting the president's position.

122. HR 4800. Omnibus Trade Bill. Frenzel, R-Minn., amendment to strike sections in the bill dealing with anti-dumping enforcement and countervailing duties. The amendment would have deleted a provision allowing increased duties to foreign goods that use subsidized natural resources. It also would have eliminated the right for companies to file lawsuits to collect damages in dumping cases. Rejected 79-338: R 76-98; D 3-240 (ND 1-160, SD 2-80), May 21, 1986. A "yea" was a vote supporting the president's position.

123. HR 4800. Omnibus Trade Bill. AuCoin, D-Ore., amendment to express the sense of Congress that Japan should remove trading barriers to its semiconductor market and that the president should find Japan guilty of unfair trading practices. Adopted 408-5: R 170-5; D 238-0 (ND 159-0, SD 79-0), May 21, 1986.

124. HR 4800. Omnibus Trade Bill. Roth, R-Wis., amendment to strike sections of the bill easing restrictions on export controls affecting technology sales to foreign countries. The amendment would have eliminated a provision requiring the Commerce Department to reduce by 40 percent over the next three years a list of items that require export licenses because of possible military applications in communist countries. Rejected 181-238: R 133-42; D 48-196 (ND 14-150, SD 34-46), May 21, 1986. A "yea" was a vote supporting the president's position.

125. HR 4800. Omnibus Trade Bill. Bonker, D-Wash., amendment to strike a section of the bill authorizing a $300 million "war chest" to help finance foreign purchases of U.S. exports. The amendment instead would authorize so-called "tied-aid" credits to be funded from existing resources available to the Export-Import Bank and Agency for International Development. Adopted 248-166: R 62-110; D 186-56 (ND 124-37, SD 62-19), May 21, 1986. A "nay" was a vote supporting the president's position.

KEY

Y Voted for (yea).
Paired for.
+ Announced for.
N Voted against (nay).
X Paired against.
- Announced against.
P Voted "present."
C Voted "present" to avoid possible conflict of interest.
? Did not vote or otherwise make a position known.

Democrats ***Republicans***

	118	119	120	121	122	123	124	125
ALABAMA								
1 ***Callahan***	?	?	N	N	N	Y	Y	N
2 ***Dickinson***	N	Y	N	Y	N	Y	Y	N
3 Nichols	Y	Y	N	N	N	Y	Y	Y
4 Bevill	Y	Y	N	N	N	Y	Y	Y
5 Flippo	?	Y	N	N	N	Y	Y	Y
6 Erdreich	Y	Y	N	N	N	Y	Y	Y
7 Shelby	Y	Y	N	N	N	Y	?	Y
ALASKA								
AL ***Young***	N	Y	N	N	N	Y	Y	Y
ARIZONA								
1 ***McCain***	Y	Y	Y	N	Y	Y	Y	Y
2 Udall	Y	Y	N	N	N	Y	N	Y
3 ***Stump***	?	Y	Y	Y	Y	Y	Y	N
4 ***Rudd***	Y	Y	Y	N	N	N	?	X
5 ***Kolbe***	N	Y	Y	N	N	Y	Y	N
ARKANSAS								
1 Alexander	?	Y	N	?	N	Y	?	?
2 Robinson	?	Y	N	N	N	Y	Y	Y
3 ***Hammerschmidt***	Y	Y	Y	N	N	Y	Y	N
4 Anthony	Y	Y	N	N	N	Y	N	Y
CALIFORNIA								
1 Bosco	?	Y	N	N	N	Y	N	Y
2 ***Chappie***	N	Y	Y	Y	N	Y	Y	N
3 Matsui	Y	Y	N	N	N	Y	N	Y
4 Fazio	Y	Y	N	N	N	Y	N	Y
5 Burton	Y	Y	N	N	N	?	N	Y
6 Boxer	Y	Y	N	N	N	Y	N	?
7 Miller	Y	?	?	N	N	Y	N	Y
8 Dellums	?	Y	N	N	N	Y	N	Y
9 Stark	?	Y	N	N	N	Y	N	Y
10 Edwards	Y	Y	N	N	N	Y	N	Y
11 Lantos	Y	Y	N	N	N	Y	N	Y
12 ***Zschau***	?	?	#	?	#	?	?	?
13 Mineta	Y	Y	N	N	N	Y	N	Y
14 ***Shumway***	Y	Y	Y	Y	Y	Y	Y	N
15 Coelho	Y	Y	N	N	N	Y	N	Y
16 Panetta	Y	Y	N	N	N	Y	N	Y
17 ***Pashayan***	N	Y	N	N	N	Y	Y	Y
18 Lehman	Y	Y	N	N	N	Y	N	N
19 ***Lagomarsino***	N	Y	Y	Y	Y	Y	Y	N
20 ***Thomas***	N	Y	Y	Y	Y	Y	Y	N
21 ***Fiedler***	?	Y	Y	Y	N	Y	Y	N
22 ***Moorhead***	N	Y	Y	Y	Y	Y	Y	N
23 Beilenson	Y	Y	Y	N	N	Y	N	Y
24 Waxman	Y	Y	N	N	N	Y	N	Y
25 Roybal	?	Y	N	N	?	Y	N	Y
26 Berman	N	Y	N	N	N	Y	N	Y
27 Levine	Y	Y	Y	N	N	Y	N	Y
28 Dixon	Y	Y	N	N	N	Y	N	Y
29 Hawkins	Y	Y	N	N	N	Y	N	N
30 Martinez	Y	Y	?	N	N	Y	N	Y
31 Dymally	Y	Y	N	N	N	Y	N	Y
32 Anderson	Y	Y	N	N	N	Y	N	Y
33 ***Dreier***	?	Y	Y	Y	Y	Y	Y	N
34 Torres	Y	Y	N	N	N	Y	N	Y
35 ***Lewis***	N	Y	Y	Y	N	Y	Y	N
36 Brown	?	Y	N	N	N	Y	N	Y
37 ***McCandless***	?	Y	Y	Y	Y	Y	Y	N
38 ***Dornan***	?	Y	Y	Y	Y	Y	Y	N
39 ***Dannemeyer***	N	Y	Y	Y	Y	Y	Y	N
40 ***Badham***	?	?	?	?	?	?	?	?
41 ***Lowery***	N	Y	Y	Y	Y	Y	Y	N
42 ***Lungren***	N	Y	Y	Y	Y	Y	Y	N
43 ***Packard***	Y	Y	Y	Y	Y	Y	Y	N
44 Bates	Y	Y	N	N	N	Y	N	Y
45 ***Hunter***	N	Y	N	Y	N	Y	Y	N
COLORADO								
1 Schroeder	N	Y	N	N	N	Y	Y	Y
2 Wirth	Y	Y	N	N	N	Y	Y	Y
3 ***Strang***	N	Y	Y	Y	N	Y	Y	N
4 ***Brown***	N	Y	Y	Y	N	Y	Y	Y
5 ***Kramer***	N	Y	N	Y	N	Y	Y	N
6 ***Schaefer***	?	Y	Y	Y	Y	Y	N	N
CONNECTICUT								
1 Kennelly	Y	Y	N	N	N	Y	N	Y
2 Gejdenson	Y	Y	N	N	N	Y	N	Y
3 Morrison	?	Y	N	N	Y	Y	N	?
4 ***McKinney***	Y	Y	N	N	N	Y	N	Y
5 ***Rowland***	N	Y	Y	N	N	Y	N	Y
6 ***Johnson***	Y	Y	Y	N	Y	Y	N	Y
DELAWARE								
AL Carper	Y	Y	N	N	N	Y	N	N
FLORIDA								
1 Hutto	Y	Y	N	N	N	Y	Y	N
2 Fuqua	?	Y	N	N	N	Y	N	Y
3 Bennett	Y	Y	N	N	N	Y	Y	Y
4 Chappell	?	Y	N	N	N	Y	Y	N
5 ***McCollum***	N	Y	Y	Y	Y	?	Y	N
6 MacKay	?	+	N	N	N	Y	N	Y
7 Gibbons	Y	Y	N	N	N	Y	N	Y
8 ***Young***	?	Y	Y	Y	Y	Y	Y	N
9 ***Bilirakis***	N	Y	Y	Y	Y	Y	Y	N
10 ***Ireland***	?	Y	Y	Y	?	Y	Y	N
11 Nelson	Y	Y	N	N	N	Y	N	Y
12 ***Lewis***	N	Y	Y	Y	N	Y	Y	N
13 ***Mack***	?	Y	Y	Y	Y	Y	Y	N
14 Mica	?	Y	N	N	N	Y	N	Y
15 ***Shaw***	N	Y	Y	Y	Y	Y	Y	N
16 Smith	Y	Y	N	N	N	Y	N	Y
17 Lehman	Y	Y	N	N	N	Y	N	Y
18 Pepper	Y	Y	N	N	N	Y	Y	Y
19 Fascell	?	?	N	N	N	Y	N	Y
GEORGIA								
1 Thomas	Y	Y	N	N	N	Y	N	N
2 Hatcher	Y	Y	N	N	N	Y	N	Y
3 Ray	Y	Y	N	N	N	Y	Y	N
4 ***Swindall***	N	Y	Y	Y	Y	Y	Y	N
5 Fowler	?	Y	N	N	N	Y	Y	N
6 ***Gingrich***	?	Y	Y	Y	N	Y	Y	N
7 Darden	Y	Y	N	N	N	Y	Y	N
8 Rowland	Y	Y	N	N	N	Y	Y	N
9 Jenkins	Y	Y	N	N	N	Y	Y	N
10 Barnard	Y	Y	N	N	N	Y	N	N
HAWAII								
1 Heftel	?	?	?	?	?	?	?	?
2 Akaka	Y	Y	N	N	N	Y	N	Y
IDAHO								
1 ***Craig***	Y	Y	Y	N	N	Y	Y	N
2 Stallings	Y	Y	N	N	N	Y	N	Y
ILLINOIS								
1 Hayes	Y	Y	N	N	N	Y	N	Y
2 Savage	?	Y	N	N	N	Y	N	Y
3 Russo	Y	Y	N	N	N	Y	N	Y
4 ***O'Brien***	?	?	?	?	?	?	?	?
5 Lipinski	?	Y	N	N	N	Y	Y	N
6 ***Hyde***	Y	Y	Y	Y	N	Y	Y	Y
7 Collins	?	+	N	N	N	Y	N	Y
8 Rostenkowski	Y	Y	N	N	N	Y	N	Y
9 Yates	?	Y	N	N	N	Y	N	Y
10 ***Porter***	Y	Y	Y	Y	Y	Y	Y	N
11 Annunzio	Y	Y	N	N	N	Y	N	N
12 ***Crane***	N	Y	Y	Y	Y	Y	Y	N
13 ***Fawell***	N	Y	Y	Y	Y	Y	Y	N
14 ***Grotberg***	?	?	?	?	?	?	?	?
15 ***Madigan***	?	Y	Y	Y	Y	Y	Y	Y
16 ***Martin***	N	Y	N	Y	N	Y	Y	Y
17 Evans	Y	Y	N	N	N	Y	N	Y
18 ***Michel***	N	Y	Y	?	Y	Y	Y	?
19 Bruce	Y	Y	N	N	N	Y	N	Y
20 Durbin	Y	Y	N	N	N	Y	N	Y
21 Price	Y	Y	N	N	N	Y	N	N
22 Gray	Y	Y	N	N	N	Y	N	Y
INDIANA								
1 Visclosky	Y	Y	N	N	N	Y	N	Y
2 Sharp	Y	Y	N	N	N	Y	N	N
3 ***Hiler***	?	Y	Y	Y	Y	Y	Y	N
4 ***Coats***	N	?	Y	N	Y	Y	Y	N
5 ***Hillis***	?	Y	Y	N	N	Y	Y	N

ND - Northern Democrats SD - Southern Democrats

* Corresponding to Congressional Record Votes 129, 130, 131, 132, 133, 135, 136, 137

	118	119	120	121	122	123	124	125
6 ***Burton***	N	Y	Y	Y	N	Y	Y	Y
7 ***Myers***	Y	Y	Y	Y	N	Y	N	N
8 McCloskey	?	Y	N	N	N	Y	N	Y
9 Hamilton	Y	Y	Y	N	N	Y	N	Y
10 Jacobs	?	Y	N	N	P	Y	N	Y
IOWA								
1 ***Leach***	N	Y	Y	Y	Y	Y	Y	N
2 ***Tauke***	N	Y	Y	Y	Y	Y	N	Y
3 ***Evans***	N	Y	Y	Y	Y	Y	Y	N
4 Smith	?	?	?	?	?	?	?	?
5 ***Lightfoot***	N	Y	Y	Y	Y	N	Y	N
6 Bedell	Y	Y	N	N	N	Y	N	Y
KANSAS								
1 ***Roberts***	N	Y	Y	Y	Y	Y	Y	Y
2 Slattery	Y	?	N	N	N	Y	Y	Y
3 ***Meyers***	N	Y	Y	Y	Y	Y	Y	N
4 Glickman	Y	Y	N	N	N	Y	N	Y
5 ***Whittaker***	?	?	?	Y	Y	Y	Y	N
KENTUCKY								
1 Hubbard	?	Y	N	N	N	Y	N	N
2 Natcher	Y	Y	N	N	N	Y	N	Y
3 Mazzoli	Y	Y	Y	N	N	Y	N	N
4 ***Snyder***	?	Y	Y	N	N	Y	Y	N
5 ***Rogers***	N	Y	N	N	N	Y	Y	N
6 ***Hopkins***	?	Y	Y	N	N	Y	Y	N
7 Perkins	Y	Y	N	N	N	Y	N	N
LOUISIANA								
1 ***Livingston***	N	Y	N	Y	Y	Y	Y	Y
2 Boggs	Y	?	N	N	N	Y	Y	Y
3 Tauzin	Y	Y	N	N	N	Y	Y	Y
4 Roemer	N	Y	N	N	N	Y	Y	N
5 Huckaby	?	Y	N	N	N	Y	N	Y
6 ***Moore***	Y	Y	Y	Y	N	Y	Y	Y
7 Breaux	Y	?	N	N	N	Y	Y	Y
8 Long	?	Y	N	N	N	Y	N	Y
MAINE								
1 ***McKernan***	?	Y	N	N	N	Y	N	Y
2 ***Snowe***	N	Y	N	N	N	Y	Y	Y
MARYLAND								
1 Dyson	?	Y	N	N	N	Y	Y	N
2 ***Bentley***	?	Y	Y	N	N	Y	N	N
3 Mikulski	Y	Y	N	N	N	Y	N	Y
4 ***Holt***	?	Y	Y	Y	Y	?	?	?
5 Hoyer	Y	Y	N	N	N	Y	N	Y
6 Byron	?	Y	N	N	N	Y	Y	Y
7 Mitchell	N	Y	N	N	?	Y	N	Y
8 Barnes	?	Y	N	N	N	Y	N	Y
MASSACHUSETTS								
1 ***Conte***	N	Y	N	N	N	Y	N	N
2 Boland	Y	Y	N	N	N	Y	N	N
3 Early	Y	Y	N	N	N	Y	N	Y
4 Frank	Y	Y	N	N	N	?	N	N
5 Atkins	?	?	?	N	N	Y	N	Y
6 Mavroules	Y	Y	N	N	N	Y	N	Y
7 Markey	Y	?	?	N	N	Y	N	Y
8 O'Neill								
9 Moakley	Y	Y	N	N	N	Y	N	Y
10 Studds	Y	Y	N	N	N	Y	N	Y
11 Donnelly	?	Y	N	N	N	Y	N	Y
MICHIGAN								
1 Conyers	Y	Y	N	N	N	Y	N	Y
2 ***Pursell***	Y	Y	Y	?	Y	Y	N	Y
3 Wolpe	Y	Y	N	N	N	Y	N	Y
4 ***Siljander***	?	Y	Y	Y	Y	Y	Y	Y
5 ***Henry***	N	Y	N	N	N	Y	N	Y
6 Carr	Y	Y	N	N	N	Y	Y	Y
7 Kildee	Y	Y	N	N	N	Y	N	Y
8 Traxler	Y	Y	N	N	N	Y	N	N
9 ***Vander Jagt***	N	Y	Y	?	N	Y	N	?
10 ***Schuette***	N	Y	Y	Y	N	Y	Y	Y
11 ***Davis***	P	Y	X	N	N	Y	N	Y
12 Bonior	Y	Y	?	N	N	Y	N	Y
13 Crockett	Y	Y	N	N	N	Y	N	Y
14 Hertel	Y	Y	N	N	N	Y	N	Y
15 Ford	Y	Y	N	N	N	Y	N	N
16 Dingell	Y	Y	N	N	N	Y	N	Y
17 Levin	Y	Y	N	N	N	Y	N	N
18 ***Broomfield***	Y	?	Y	Y	Y	Y	Y	Y
MINNESOTA								
1 Penny	N	Y	Y	N	N	Y	N	Y
2 ***Weber***	?	Y	Y	Y	Y	Y	Y	Y
3 ***Frenzel***	N	Y	Y	Y	Y	N	N	Y
4 Vento	Y	Y	N	N	N	Y	N	N
5 Sabo	?	Y	N	N	N	Y	N	Y
6 Sikorski	N	Y	N	N	N	Y	N	Y

	118	119	120	121	122	123	124	125
7 ***Stangeland***	N	Y	Y	Y	Y	Y	Y	Y
8 Oberstar	Y	Y	N	N	N	Y	N	Y
MISSISSIPPI								
1 Whitten	?	Y	N	N	N	Y	Y	Y
2 ***Franklin***	Y	Y	N	N	?	Y	Y	N
3 Montgomery	Y	Y	N	N	N	Y	Y	Y
4 Dowdy	?	?	N	N	N	Y	N	Y
5 ***Lott***	N	Y	N	N	N	Y	Y	N
MISSOURI								
1 Clay	N	Y	N	N	N	Y	N	Y
2 Young	?	Y	N	N	N	Y	N	Y
3 Gephardt	Y	Y	N	N	X	?	?	#
4 Skelton	Y	Y	N	N	N	Y	N	Y
5 Wheat	?	Y	N	N	N	Y	N	Y
6 ***Coleman***	N	Y	Y	N	N	Y	Y	N
7 ***Taylor***	Y	Y	Y	N	N	Y	Y	N
8 ***Emerson***	N	Y	Y	N	Y	Y	Y	N
9 Volkmer	Y	Y	N	N	N	Y	N	N
MONTANA								
1 Williams	Y	Y	N	N	N	Y	N	Y
2 ***Marlenee***	?	Y	Y	Y	Y	Y	Y	Y
NEBRASKA								
1 ***Bereuter***	N	Y	Y	N	Y	Y	N	Y
2 ***Daub***	N	Y	Y	Y	Y	Y	Y	Y
3 ***Smith***	Y	Y	Y	Y	Y	Y	N	Y
NEVADA								
1 Reid	Y	Y	N	N	N	Y	N	Y
2 ***Vucanovich***	N	Y	Y	N	Y	Y	Y	N
NEW HAMPSHIRE								
1 ***Smith***	N	Y	Y	Y	Y	Y	Y	N
2 ***Gregg***	N	Y	Y	Y	Y	Y	N	Y
NEW JERSEY								
1 Florio	Y	Y	N	N	N	Y	N	Y
2 Hughes	Y	Y	Y	N	N	Y	N	Y
3 Howard	Y	Y	N	N	N	Y	N	Y
4 ***Smith***	Y	Y	N	N	N	Y	N	N
5 ***Roukema***	N	Y	N	Y	N	Y	Y	N
6 Dwyer	Y	Y	N	N	N	Y	N	Y
7 ***Rinaldo***	Y	?	N	N	N	Y	N	Y
8 Roe	Y	Y	N	N	N	Y	N	Y
9 Torricelli	Y	Y	N	N	N	Y	N	Y
10 Rodino	?	?	?	?	?	?	?	?
11 ***Gallo***	N	Y	Y	Y	N	Y	Y	N
12 ***Courter***	N	Y	Y	Y	N	Y	Y	N
13 ***Saxton***	N	Y	Y	Y	Y	Y	N	N
14 Guarini	Y	Y	N	N	N	Y	N	Y
NEW MEXICO								
1 ***Lujan***	?	?	?	?	?	?	?	?
2 ***Skeen***	N	Y	Y	N	N	Y	Y	Y
3 Richardson	Y	?	N	N	N	Y	N	Y
NEW YORK								
1 ***Carney***	?	Y	Y	Y	Y	Y	Y	N
2 Downey	Y	?	N	N	N	Y	N	Y
3 Mrazek	Y	?	?	?	N	Y	N	N
4 ***Lent***	?	Y	Y	Y	N	Y	Y	N
5 ***McGrath***	?	Y	Y	Y	N	Y	N	N
6 Vacancy								
7 Ackerman	?	Y	N	N	N	Y	N	Y
8 Scheuer	Y	Y	N	N	N	Y	N	Y
9 Manton	?	Y	N	N	N	Y	N	Y
10 Schumer	Y	Y	N	N	N	Y	N	N
11 Towns	Y	Y	N	N	N	Y	N	Y
12 Owens	?	Y	N	N	N	Y	N	Y
13 Solarz	Y	Y	N	N	N	Y	N	Y
14 ***Molinari***	N	Y	Y	Y	Y	Y	Y	N
15 ***Green***	Y	Y	Y	Y	Y	Y	N	Y
16 Rangel	Y	Y	N	N	N	Y	N	Y
17 Weiss	Y	Y	N	N	N	Y	N	Y
18 Garcia	?	?	N	N	N	Y	N	Y
19 Biaggi	Y	Y	N	N	N	Y	N	N
20 ***DioGuardi***	Y	Y	N	Y	Y	Y	N	Y
21 ***Fish***	Y	Y	Y	Y	Y	Y	N	Y
22 ***Gilman***	Y	Y	N	N	N	Y	Y	Y
23 Stratton	Y	Y	N	N	N	Y	Y	N
24 ***Solomon***	N	Y	Y	Y	N	Y	Y	N
25 ***Boehlert***	N	Y	N	N	N	Y	N	Y
26 ***Martin***	?	Y	N	N	N	Y	Y	N
27 ***Wortley***	N	Y	N	N	Y	Y	N	N
28 McHugh	Y	Y	N	N	N	Y	N	N
29 ***Horton***	Y	Y	N	N	N	Y	N	Y
30 ***Eckert***	Y	Y	Y	Y	Y	Y	Y	N
31 ***Kemp***	?	Y	Y	Y	Y	Y	Y	N
32 LaFalce	Y	Y	N	N	N	Y	N	N
33 Nowak	Y	Y	N	N	N	Y	N	N
34 Lundine	Y	Y	N	N	N	Y	N	N

	118	119	120	121	122	123	124	125
NORTH CAROLINA								
1 Jones	Y	Y	N	N	N	Y	N	Y
2 Valentine	Y	Y	N	N	N	Y	Y	Y
3 Whitley	?	Y	N	N	N	Y	Y	N
4 ***Cobey***	N	Y	N	N	N	Y	Y	Y
5 Neal	Y	?	N	N	N	?	Y	N
6 ***Coble***	N	Y	N	N	N	Y	Y	Y
7 Rose	Y	Y	N	?	N	Y	N	N
8 Hefner	Y	Y	N	?	N	Y	Y	Y
9 ***McMillan***	Y	Y	N	N	N	Y	Y	N
10 ***Broyhill***	Y	Y	N	N	N	Y	Y	N
11 ***Hendon***	N	Y	N	N	N	Y	Y	N
NORTH DAKOTA								
AL Dorgan	Y	Y	N	N	N	Y	Y	Y
OHIO								
1 Luken	Y	Y	N	N	N	Y	N	Y
2 ***Gradison***	Y	Y	Y	Y	Y	Y	N	Y
3 Hall	?	Y	N	N	N	?	Y	Y
4 ***Oxley***	N	Y	Y	Y	Y	Y	Y	Y
5 ***Latta***	N	Y	?	Y	N	Y	Y	N
6 ***McEwen***	Y	Y	N	N	N	Y	Y	N
7 ***DeWine***	N	Y	Y	N	N	Y	Y	N
8 ***Kindness***	N	Y	Y	Y	N	Y	N	N
9 Kaptur	Y	Y	N	N	N	Y	N	Y
10 ***Miller***	?	Y	Y	Y	Y	Y	Y	N
11 Eckart	Y	Y	N	N	N	Y	N	Y
12 ***Kasich***	Y	Y	Y	N	N	Y	Y	N
13 Pease	Y	Y	N	N	N	Y	N	Y
14 Seiberling	?	Y	N	N	N	Y	N	Y
15 ***Wylie***	Y	Y	Y	Y	Y	Y	Y	N
16 ***Regula***	Y	Y	N	N	N	Y	Y	N
17 Traficant	?	Y	N	N	N	Y	N	Y
18 Applegate	Y	Y	N	N	N	Y	N	N
19 Feighan	Y	Y	N	N	N	?	N	Y
20 Oakar	Y	Y	N	N	N	Y	N	N
21 Stokes	Y	Y	N	N	N	Y	N	Y
OKLAHOMA								
1 Jones	Y	Y	N	N	N	Y	Y	Y
2 Synar	?	Y	N	N	N	Y	N	Y
3 Watkins	Y	Y	N	N	N	Y	N	Y
4 McCurdy	Y	Y	N	N	N	Y	N	Y
5 ***Edwards***	N	Y	Y	Y	N	Y	Y	Y
6 English	?	Y	N	N	N	Y	Y	Y
OREGON								
1 AuCoin	?	Y	N	N	N	Y	N	Y
2 ***Smith, R.***	N	Y	Y	Y	N	Y	Y	Y
3 Wyden	?	Y	N	N	N	Y	N	Y
4 Weaver	?	Y	N	N	N	Y	N	Y
5 ***Smith, D.***	?	Y	Y	Y	N	Y	Y	N
PENNSYLVANIA								
1 Foglietta	?	?	?	?	?	?	?	?
2 Gray	Y	Y	N	?	N	?	N	?
3 Borski	?	Y	N	N	N	Y	N	Y
4 Kolter	?	Y	N	N	N	Y	N	N
5 ***Schulze***	?	Y	N	N	N	Y	Y	N
6 Yatron	?	Y	N	N	N	Y	N	Y
7 Edgar	?	?	N	N	N	Y	N	Y
8 Kostmayer	?	+	N	N	N	Y	N	N
9 ***Shuster***	?	Y	N	Y	N	Y	Y	N
10 ***McDade***	Y	Y	N	N	N	Y	N	Y
11 Kanjorski	?	Y	N	N	N	Y	N	N
12 Murtha	P	Y	N	N	N	Y	Y	N
13 ***Coughlin***	?	Y	N	N	Y	Y	N	N
14 Coyne	?	Y	N	N	N	Y	N	N
15 ***Ritter***	Y	Y	N	N	N	Y	Y	Y
16 ***Walker***	N	Y	Y	Y	N	Y	Y	N
17 ***Gekas***	N	Y	Y	N	N	Y	Y	N
18 Walgren	Y	Y	N	N	N	Y	N	N
19 ***Goodling***	N	Y	N	N	N	Y	Y	Y
20 Gaydos	?	?	?	?	N	Y	N	N
21 ***Ridge***	N	Y	N	N	N	Y	N	Y
22 Murphy	?	Y	N	N	N	Y	N	N
23 ***Clinger***	Y	Y	N	N	N	Y	N	Y
RHODE ISLAND								
1 St Germain	Y	Y	N	N	N	Y	N	N
2 ***Schneider***	?	Y	N	Y	Y	Y	N	Y
SOUTH CAROLINA								
1 ***Hartnett***	?	Y	Y	Y	N	N	Y	N
2 ***Spence***	N	Y	N	N	Y	Y	Y	N
3 Derrick	N	Y	N	N	N	Y	N	Y
4 ***Campbell***	N	Y	N	N	N	Y	Y	N
5 Spratt	Y	Y	N	N	N	Y	Y	Y
6 Tallon	Y	Y	N	N	N	Y	N	Y
SOUTH DAKOTA								
AL Daschle	Y	Y	N	N	N	Y	N	Y

	118	119	120	121	122	123	124	125
TENNESSEE								
1 ***Quillen***	?	Y	Y	N	N	Y	N	Y
2 ***Duncan***	Y	Y	Y	Y	N	Y	Y	N
3 Lloyd	N	Y	N	N	N	Y	Y	Y
4 Cooper	Y	Y	N	N	N	Y	Y	N
5 Boner	Y	Y	N	N	N	Y	N	Y
6 Gordon	P	Y	N	N	N	Y	Y	N
7 ***Sundquist***	N	Y	Y	N	N	Y	Y	N
8 Jones	Y	Y	N	N	N	Y	N	Y
9 Ford	?	Y	N	N	N	Y	N	Y
TEXAS								
1 Chapman	?	Y	N	N	N	Y	N	N
2 Wilson	Y	Y	N	N	N	Y	N	Y
3 ***Bartlett***	N	Y	Y	Y	N	Y	N	Y
4 Hall, R.	Y	Y	N	N	N	Y	N	Y
5 Bryant	?	Y	N	N	N	Y	N	Y
6 ***Barton***	N	Y	Y	Y	N	Y	Y	N
7 ***Archer***	Y	Y	Y	Y	Y	Y	Y	N
8 ***Fields***	N	Y	Y	Y	Y	Y	N	N
9 Brooks	Y	Y	N	N	N	Y	N	Y
10 Pickle	Y	Y	N	N	N	Y	N	Y
11 Leath	?	Y	N	N	N	Y	Y	Y
12 Wright	?	Y	N	N	N	Y	N	Y
13 ***Boulter***	?	Y	Y	N	N	Y	Y	Y
14 ***Sweeney***	?	Y	Y	Y	N	Y	Y	N
15 de la Garza	Y	Y	N	N	N	Y	N	Y
16 Coleman	Y	Y	N	N	Y	Y	N	Y
17 Stenholm	Y	Y	N	N	N	Y	Y	Y
18 Leland	Y	Y	N	N	N	Y	N	Y
19 ***Combest***	Y	Y	Y	N	N	Y	Y	N
20 Gonzalez	Y	Y	N	N	N	Y	N	Y
21 ***Loeffler***	N	Y	Y	Y	N	Y	Y	N
22 ***DeLay***	N	Y	Y	Y	Y	Y	Y	N
23 Bustamante	Y	Y	N	N	Y	?	N	Y
24 Frost	Y	Y	N	N	N	Y	N	Y
25 Andrews	Y	Y	N	N	N	Y	N	Y
26 ***Armey***	?	?	Y	Y	Y	Y	Y	Y
27 Ortiz	?	Y	N	N	N	?	N	Y
UTAH								
1 ***Hansen***	Y	Y	Y	Y	?	Y	Y	N
2 ***Monson***	N	Y	Y	Y	Y	Y	Y	N
3 ***Nielson***	Y	Y	Y	Y	Y	Y	Y	N
VERMONT								
AL ***Jeffords***	Y	Y	Y	N	Y	Y	N	Y
VIRGINIA								
1 ***Bateman***	Y	Y	Y	N	N	Y	Y	N
2 ***Whitehurst***	?	?	Y	Y	Y	N	N	N
3 ***Bliley***	N	Y	Y	Y	N	Y	Y	N
4 Sisisky	Y	Y	N	N	N	Y	Y	Y
5 Daniel	Y	Y	?	N	N	Y	Y	Y
6 Olin	Y	Y	N	N	N	Y	N	Y
7 ***Slaughter***	N	Y	Y	Y	N	Y	Y	?
8 ***Parris***	N	Y	Y	Y	N	Y	Y	N
9 Boucher	Y	Y	N	N	N	Y	N	Y
10 ***Wolf***	N	Y	Y	Y	N	Y	Y	Y
WASHINGTON								
1 ***Miller***	Y	Y	Y	Y	N	Y	N	Y
2 Swift	?	Y	N	N	N	Y	N	Y
3 Bonker	Y	Y	N	N	N	Y	N	Y
4 ***Morrison***	Y	Y	Y	Y	N	Y	N	Y
5 Foley	?	Y	N	N	N	Y	N	Y
6 Dicks	?	Y	N	N	N	Y	N	Y
7 Lowry	Y	Y	N	N	N	Y	N	Y
8 ***Chandler***	?	Y	Y	Y	N	Y	N	Y
WEST VIRGINIA								
1 Mollohan	Y	Y	N	N	N	Y	N	Y
2 Staggers	Y	Y	N	N	N	Y	Y	Y
3 Wise	?	Y	N	N	N	Y	N	Y
4 Rahall	Y	Y	N	N	N	Y	N	Y
WISCONSIN								
1 Aspin	Y	Y	N	N	N	Y	Y	Y
2 Kastenmeier	Y	Y	N	N	N	Y	N	N
3 ***Gunderson***	N	Y	N	N	N	Y	Y	N
4 Kleczka	Y	Y	N	N	N	Y	N	N
5 Moody	Y	Y	N	N	N	Y	N	Y
6 ***Petri***	Y	Y	Y	Y	N	Y	Y	Y
7 Obey	Y	Y	N	N	N	Y	N	Y
8 ***Roth***	N	Y	Y	N	N	Y	Y	Y
9 ***Sensenbrenner***	N	?	Y	Y	N	Y	Y	N
WYOMING								
AL ***Cheney***	N	Y	Y	Y	Y	Y	Y	N

Southern states - Ala., Ark., Fla., Ga., Ky., La., Miss., N.C., Okla., S.C., Tenn., Texas, Va.

* The *Congressional Record* vote number is different from the CQ vote number because the *Record* includes quorum calls in its tally. CQ does not publish quorum call votes.

126. HR 4800. Omnibus Trade Bill. Wylie, R-Ohio, amendment to strike sections of the bill linking U.S. trade policy with international exchange rates and Third World debt and creating an industrial competitiveness council to devise strategies to make U.S. firms more competitive. Rejected 188-221: R 165-4; D 23-217 (ND 7-153, SD 16-64), May 21, 1986. A "yea" was a vote supporting the president's position.

127. HR 4800. Omnibus Trade Bill. Michel, R-Ill., substitute to replace the bill with alternative legislation that addresses a variety of trade issues, but does not go as far as the bill in areas such as limiting presidential discretion and ordering mandatory retaliation against other countries. Rejected 145-265: R 144-26; D 1-239 (ND 1-160, SD 0-79), May 22, 1986.

128. HR 4800. Omnibus Trade Bill. Passage of the bill to revise U.S. trade laws by emphasizing retaliation against other countries that fail to allow U.S. goods into their markets. Other sections of the bill ease restrictions on U.S. technology exports, link trade policy with international exchange rates and Third World debt, increase funds for job training and education programs, reauthorize the Export-Import Bank and increase the role of the Agriculture Department in trade matters affecting farmers. Passed 295-115: R 59-111; D 236-4 (ND 158-4, SD 78-0), May 22, 1986. A "nay" was a vote supporting the president's position.

KEY

- Y Voted for (yea).
- # Paired for.
- + Announced for.
- N Voted against (nay).
- X Paired against.
- - Announced against.
- P Voted "present."
- C Voted "present" to avoid possible conflict of interest.
- ? Did not vote or otherwise make a position known.

Democrats *Republicans*

	126	127	128
ALABAMA			
1 ***Callahan***	Y	Y	N
2 ***Dickinson***	Y	Y	Y
3 Nichols	Y	N	Y
4 Bevill	N	N	Y
5 Flippo	N	N	Y
6 Erdreich	N	N	Y
7 Shelby	N	N	Y
ALASKA			
AL ***Young***	Y	?	?
ARIZONA			
1 ***McCain***	Y	Y	N
2 Udall	N	N	Y
3 ***Stump***	Y	Y	N
4 ***Rudd***	?	#	?
5 ***Kolbe***	Y	Y	N
ARKANSAS			
1 Alexander	?	X	#
2 Robinson	Y	N	Y
3 ***Hammerschmidt***	Y	Y	Y
4 Anthony	?	N	Y
CALIFORNIA			
1 Bosco	N	N	Y
2 ***Chappie***	Y	?	?
3 Matsui	N	N	Y
4 Fazio	N	N	Y
5 Burton	N	N	Y
6 Boxer	?	X	#
7 Miller	N	N	Y
8 Dellums	N	N	Y
9 Stark	N	N	Y
10 Edwards	N	N	Y
11 Lantos	N	N	Y
12 ***Zschau***	#	#	X
13 Mineta	N	N	Y
14 ***Shumway***	Y	Y	N
15 Coelho	N	N	Y
16 Panetta	N	N	Y
17 ***Pashayan***	Y	N	Y
18 Lehman	N	N	Y
19 ***Lagomarsino***	Y	Y	N
20 ***Thomas***	Y	Y	N
21 ***Fiedler***	Y	Y	N
22 ***Moorhead***	Y	Y	N
23 Beilenson	N	N	N
24 Waxman	N	N	Y
25 Roybal	N	N	Y
26 Berman	N	N	Y
27 Levine	N	N	Y
28 Dixon	N	N	Y
29 Hawkins	N	N	Y
30 Martinez	N	N	Y
31 Dymally	N	N	Y
32 Anderson	N	N	Y
33 ***Dreier***	Y	Y	N
34 Torres	N	N	Y
35 ***Lewis***	Y	Y	N
36 Brown	N	N	Y
37 ***McCandless***	Y	Y	N
38 ***Dornan***	Y	Y	N
39 ***Dannemeyer***	Y	Y	N
40 ***Badham***	#	#	X
41 ***Lowery***	Y	Y	N
42 ***Lungren***	Y	Y	N
43 ***Packard***	Y	Y	N
44 Bates	N	N	Y
45 ***Hunter***	Y	Y	N
COLORADO			
1 Schroeder	N	N	Y
2 Wirth	N	N	Y
3 ***Strang***	Y	Y	N
4 ***Brown***	Y	Y	N
5 ***Kramer***	Y	Y	Y
6 ***Schaefer***	Y	Y	N
CONNECTICUT			
1 Kennelly	N	N	Y
2 Gejdenson	N	N	Y
3 Morrison	X	N	Y
4 ***McKinney***	Y	N	Y
5 ***Rowland***	Y	Y	Y
6 ***Johnson***	N	N	Y
DELAWARE			
AL Carper	N	N	Y
FLORIDA			
1 Hutto	Y	N	Y
2 Fuqua	N	N	Y
3 Bennett	N	N	Y
4 Chappell	N	N	Y
5 ***McCollum***	Y	Y	N
6 MacKay	N	N	Y
7 Gibbons	N	N	Y
8 ***Young***	Y	Y	N
9 ***Bilirakis***	Y	Y	N
10 ***Ireland***	Y	Y	N
11 Nelson	N	N	Y
12 ***Lewis***	Y	Y	N
13 ***Mack***	Y	Y	N
14 Mica	N	N	Y
15 ***Shaw***	Y	Y	N
16 Smith	N	N	Y
17 Lehman	N	N	C
18 Pepper	N	N	Y
19 Fascell	N	N	Y
GEORGIA			
1 Thomas	N	N	Y
2 Hatcher	N	N	Y
3 Ray	Y	N	Y
4 ***Swindall***	Y	Y	N
5 Fowler	N	N	Y
6 ***Gingrich***	Y	Y	N
7 Darden	N	N	Y
8 Rowland	N	N	Y
9 Jenkins	N	N	Y
10 Barnard	N	N	Y
HAWAII			
1 Heftel	?	?	?
2 Akaka	N	N	Y
IDAHO			
1 ***Craig***	Y	Y	Y
2 Stallings	Y	N	Y
ILLINOIS			
1 Hayes	N	N	Y
2 Savage	N	N	Y
3 Russo	N	N	Y
4 ***O'Brien***	?	?	?
5 Lipinski	N	N	Y
6 ***Hyde***	Y	Y	N
7 Collins	N	N	Y
8 Rostenkowski	N	N	Y
9 Yates	N	?	?
10 ***Porter***	Y	Y	N
11 Annunzio	N	N	Y
12 ***Crane***	Y	Y	N
13 ***Fawell***	Y	Y	N
14 ***Grotberg***	?	?	?
15 ***Madigan***	Y	Y	N
16 ***Martin***	Y	Y	N
17 Evans	N	N	Y
18 ***Michel***	Y	Y	N
19 Bruce	N	N	Y
20 Durbin	N	N	Y
21 Price	N	N	Y
22 Gray	N	N	Y
INDIANA			
1 Visclosky	N	N	Y
2 Sharp	N	N	Y
3 ***Hiler***	Y	Y	N
4 ***Coats***	Y	Y	N
5 ***Hillis***	Y	Y	Y

ND - Northern Democrats SD - Southern Democrats

* Corresponding to Congressional Record Votes 138, 140, 141

	126	127	128
6 ***Burton***	Y	Y	N
7 ***Myers***	Y	Y	N
8 McCloskey	N	N	Y
9 Hamilton	Y	N	Y
10 Jacobs	N	N	Y
IOWA			
1 ***Leach***	Y	Y	N
2 ***Tauke***	Y	Y	N
3 ***Evans***	?	?	X
4 Smith	?	?	?
5 ***Lightfoot***	Y	Y	N
6 Bedell	N	N	Y
KANSAS			
1 ***Roberts***	Y	Y	N
2 Slattery	Y	N	Y
3 ***Meyers***	Y	Y	N
4 Glickman	Y	N	Y
5 ***Whittaker***	Y	Y	N
KENTUCKY			
1 Hubbard	N	N	Y
2 Natcher	N	N	Y
3 Mazzoli	N	N	Y
4 ***Snyder***	Y	Y	N
5 ***Rogers***	Y	Y	Y
6 ***Hopkins***	Y	Y	N
7 Perkins	N	N	Y
LOUISIANA			
1 ***Livingston***	Y	Y	N
2 Boggs	N	N	Y
3 Tauzin	N	N	Y
4 Roemer	N	N	Y
5 Huckaby	N	N	Y
6 ***Moore***	Y	N	Y
7 Breaux	N	N	Y
8 Long	N	N	Y
MAINE			
1 ***McKernan***	Y	N	Y
2 ***Snowe***	Y	N	Y
MARYLAND			
1 Dyson	N	N	Y
2 ***Bentley***	Y	Y	Y
3 Mikulski	N	N	Y
4 ***Holt***	?	#	X
5 Hoyer	N	N	Y
6 Byron	N	N	Y
7 Mitchell	N	N	Y
8 Barnes	N	N	Y
MASSACHUSETTS			
1 ***Conte***	?	N	Y
2 Boland	N	N	Y
3 Early	N	N	Y
4 Frank	N	N	Y
5 Atkins	N	N	Y
6 Mavroules	N	N	Y
7 Markey	N	N	Y
8 O'Neill			
9 Moakley	N	N	Y
10 Studds	N	N	Y
11 Donnelly	N	N	Y
MICHIGAN			
1 Conyers	N	N	Y
2 ***Pursell***	Y	Y	N
3 Wolpe	N	N	Y
4 ***Siljander***	Y	Y	N
5 ***Henry***	Y	N	Y
6 Carr	N	N	Y
7 Kildee	N	N	Y
8 Traxler	N	N	Y
9 ***Vander Jagt***	?	Y	N
10 ***Schuette***	Y	Y	Y
11 ***Davis***	Y	N	Y
12 Bonior	N	N	Y
13 Crockett	N	?	Y
14 Hertel	N	N	Y
15 Ford	N	N	Y
16 Dingell	N	N	Y
17 Levin	N	N	Y
18 ***Broomfield***	Y	Y	N
MINNESOTA			
1 Penny	N	N	Y
2 ***Weber***	Y	Y	N
3 ***Frenzel***	Y	Y	N
4 Vento	N	N	Y
5 Sabo	N	N	Y
6 Sikorski	N	N	Y

	126	127	128
7 ***Stangeland***	Y	Y	N
8 Oberstar	N	N	Y
MISSISSIPPI			
1 Whitten	Y	N	Y
2 ***Franklin***	Y	Y	Y
3 Montgomery	Y	N	Y
4 Dowdy	N	N	Y
5 ***Lott***	Y	Y	Y
MISSOURI			
1 Clay	N	N	Y
2 Young	N	N	Y
3 Gephardt	X	N	Y
4 Skelton	N	N	Y
5 Wheat	N	N	Y
6 ***Coleman***	Y	Y	Y
7 ***Taylor***	Y	Y	Y
8 ***Emerson***	Y	Y	Y
9 Volkmer	Y	N	Y
MONTANA			
1 Williams	N	N	Y
2 ***Marlenee***	?	Y	N
NEBRASKA			
1 ***Bereuter***	Y	Y	N
2 ***Daub***	Y	Y	N
3 ***Smith***	Y	Y	N
NEVADA			
1 Reid	N	N	Y
2 ***Vucanovich***	Y	Y	N
NEW HAMPSHIRE			
1 ***Smith***	Y	Y	N
2 ***Gregg***	Y	Y	N
NEW JERSEY			
1 Florio	N	N	Y
2 Hughes	Y	N	Y
3 Howard	N	N	Y
4 ***Smith***	Y	N	Y
5 ***Roukema***	Y	Y	Y
6 Dwyer	N	N	Y
7 ***Rinaldo***	Y	N	Y
8 Roe	N	N	Y
9 Torricelli	N	N	Y
10 Rodino	?	X	#
11 ***Gallo***	Y	Y	N
12 ***Courter***	Y	Y	N
13 ***Saxton***	Y	Y	N
14 Guarini	N	N	Y
NEW MEXICO			
1 ***Lujan***	?	?	?
2 ***Skeen***	Y	Y	N
3 Richardson	N	N	Y
NEW YORK			
1 ***Carney***	?	?	?
2 Downey	N	N	Y
3 Mrazek	N	N	N
4 ***Lent***	Y	Y	N
5 ***McGrath***	Y	Y	N
6 Vacancy			
7 Ackerman	N	N	Y
8 Scheuer	N	N	Y
9 Manton	N	N	Y
10 Schumer	N	N	Y
11 Towns	N	N	Y
12 Owens	N	N	Y
13 Solarz	N	N	Y
14 ***Molinari***	Y	Y	N
15 ***Green***	Y	Y	N
16 Rangel	N	N	Y
17 Weiss	N	N	Y
18 Garcia	N	N	Y
19 Biaggi	N	N	Y
20 ***DioGuardi***	Y	Y	Y
21 ***Fish***	Y	Y	N
22 ***Gilman***	Y	N	Y
23 Stratton	N	N	Y
24 ***Solomon***	Y	Y	N
25 ***Boehlert***	Y	N	Y
26 ***Martin***	?	Y	Y
27 ***Wortley***	Y	Y	N
28 McHugh	N	N	N
29 ***Horton***	Y	N	Y
30 ***Eckert***	Y	Y	N
31 ***Kemp***	Y	N	N
32 LaFalce	N	N	Y
33 Nowak	N	Y	Y
34 Lundine	N	N	Y

	126	127	128
NORTH CAROLINA			
1 Jones	N	N	Y
2 Valentine	Y	N	Y
3 Whitley	N	N	Y
4 ***Cobey***	Y	Y	Y
5 Neal	Y	N	Y
6 ***Coble***	Y	Y	Y
7 Rose	N	N	Y
8 Hefner	N	N	Y
9 ***McMillan***	Y	Y	Y
10 ***Broyhill***	Y	Y	Y
11 ***Hendon***	Y	Y	Y
NORTH DAKOTA			
AL Dorgan	N	N	Y
OHIO			
1 Luken	N	N	Y
2 ***Gradison***	Y	Y	N
3 Hall	?	N	Y
4 ***Oxley***	Y	Y	N
5 ***Latta***	Y	Y	Y
6 ***McEwen***	Y	Y	Y
7 ***DeWine***	Y	Y	N
8 ***Kindness***	Y	Y	Y
9 Kaptur	N	N	Y
10 ***Miller***	Y	Y	N
11 Eckart	N	N	Y
12 ***Kasich***	Y	Y	Y
13 Pease	N	N	Y
14 Seiberling	N	N	Y
15 ***Wylie***	Y	Y	N
16 ***Regula***	Y	N	Y
17 Traficant	N	N	Y
18 Applegate	N	N	Y
19 Feighan	N	N	Y
20 Oakar	N	N	Y
21 Stokes	N	N	Y
OKLAHOMA			
1 Jones	Y	N	Y
2 Synar	N	N	Y
3 Watkins	Y	N	Y
4 McCurdy	Y	N	Y
5 ***Edwards***	Y	Y	N
6 English	Y	N	Y
OREGON			
1 AuCoin	Y	N	Y
2 ***Smith, R.***	Y	N	N
3 Wyden	?	N	Y
4 Weaver	N	N	Y
5 ***Smith, D.***	Y	Y	N
PENNSYLVANIA			
1 Foglietta	?	N	Y
2 Gray	N	N	Y
3 Borski	N	N	Y
4 Kolter	N	N	Y
5 ***Schulze***	Y	Y	Y
6 Yatron	N	N	Y
7 Edgar	N	N	Y
8 Kostmayer	N	N	Y
9 ***Shuster***	N	N	Y
10 ***McDade***	N	N	Y
11 Kanjorski	N	N	Y
12 Murtha	N	N	Y
13 ***Coughlin***	Y	Y	Y
14 Coyne	N	N	Y
15 ***Ritter***	Y	N	Y
16 ***Walker***	Y	Y	N
17 ***Gekas***	Y	Y	N
18 Walgren	N	N	Y
19 ***Goodling***	Y	Y	Y
20 Gaydos	N	N	Y
21 ***Ridge***	Y	N	Y
22 Murphy	N	N	Y
23 ***Clinger***	Y	N	Y
RHODE ISLAND			
1 St Germain	N	N	Y
2 ***Schneider***	Y	Y	Y
SOUTH CAROLINA			
1 ***Hartnett***	Y	Y	N
2 ***Spence***	Y	Y	Y
3 Derrick	N	N	Y
4 ***Campbell***	Y	Y	Y
5 Spratt	N	N	Y
6 Tallon	Y	N	Y
SOUTH DAKOTA			
AL Daschle	N	N	Y

	126	127	128
TENNESSEE			
1 ***Quillen***	Y	Y	Y
2 ***Duncan***	Y	Y	N
3 Lloyd	N	N	Y
4 Cooper	N	N	Y
5 Boner	N	N	Y
6 Gordon	N	N	Y
7 ***Sundquist***	Y	Y	Y
8 Jones	N	N	Y
9 Ford	N	N	Y
TEXAS			
1 Chapman	N	N	Y
2 Wilson	N	N	Y
3 ***Bartlett***	Y	Y	N
4 Hall, R.	N	N	Y
5 Bryant	N	N	Y
6 ***Barton***	Y	Y	N
7 ***Archer***	Y	Y	N
8 ***Fields***	Y	Y	N
9 Brooks	N	N	Y
10 Pickle	N	N	Y
11 Leath	Y	X	#
12 Wright	N	N	Y
13 ***Boulter***	Y	Y	Y
14 ***Sweeney***	N	N	Y
15 de la Garza	N	?	?
16 Coleman	N	N	Y
17 Stenholm	Y	N	Y
18 Leland	N	N	Y
19 ***Combest***	Y	Y	Y
20 Gonzalez	N	N	Y
21 ***Loeffler***	Y	Y	N
22 ***DeLay***	Y	Y	N
23 Bustamante	N	N	Y
24 Frost	N	N	Y
25 Andrews	N	N	Y
26 ***Armey***	Y	Y	N
27 Ortiz	N	N	Y
UTAH			
1 ***Hansen***	Y	#	X
2 ***Monson***	Y	Y	N
3 ***Nielson***	Y	Y	N
VERMONT			
AL ***Jeffords***	Y	N	Y
VIRGINIA			
1 ***Bateman***	Y	Y	N
2 ***Whitehurst***	Y	Y	N
3 ***Bliley***	Y	Y	N
4 Sisisky	N	N	Y
5 Daniel	Y	N	Y
6 Olin	N	N	Y
7 ***Slaughter***	Y	Y	N
8 ***Parris***	Y	Y	N
9 Boucher	N	N	Y
10 ***Wolf***	Y	Y	N
WASHINGTON			
1 ***Miller***	Y	Y	N
2 Swift	N	N	Y
3 Bonker	N	N	Y
4 ***Morrison***	Y	Y	N
5 Foley	N	N	Y
6 Dicks	N	N	Y
7 Lowry	N	N	N
8 ***Chandler***	Y	Y	N
WEST VIRGINIA			
1 Mollohan	N	N	Y
2 Staggers	N	N	Y
3 Wise	N	N	Y
4 Rahall	N	X	#
WISCONSIN			
1 Aspin	N	?	?
2 Kastenmeier	N	N	Y
3 ***Gunderson***	Y	N	Y
4 Kleczka	N	N	Y
5 Moody	N	N	Y
6 ***Petri***	Y	N	N
7 Obey	N	N	Y
8 ***Roth***	Y	Y	N
9 ***Sensenbrenner***	Y	Y	N
WYOMING			
AL ***Cheney***	Y	Y	N

Southern states - Ala., Ark., Fla., Ga., Ky., La., Miss., N.C., Okla., S.C., Tenn., Texas, Va.

* The *Congressional Record* vote number is different from the CQ vote number because the *Record* includes quorum calls in its tally. CQ does not publish quorum call votes.

129. HR 1. Housing Act of 1986. Bereuter, R-Neb., amendment to the Gonzalez, D-Texas, substitute, to change the selection criteria for Urban Development Action Grants (UDAG) from 65 percent on the basis of such factors as economic distress and 35 percent on the project quality to 50-50, and to give additional consideration to applications from areas that have not received UDAG aid on or after Dec. 21, 1983. Rejected 142-238: R 117-43; D 25-195 (ND 9-148, SD 16-47), June 4, 1986. (The Gonzalez substitute, which contains the text of HR 4746, would authorize and revise federal housing programs for fiscal 1986 and 1987.)

130. HR 1. Housing Act of 1986. Hiler, R-Ind., amendment to the Gonzalez, D-Texas, substitute *(see vote 129)*, to eliminate the UDAG program. Rejected 93-289: R 83-77; D 10-212 (ND 3-152, SD 7-60), June 4, 1986. A "yea" was a vote supporting the president's position.

131. Procedural Motion. McKernan, R-Maine, motion to approve the House *Journal* of Wednesday, June 4. Motion agreed to 263-115: R 52-108; D 211-7 (ND 141-5, SD 70-2), June 5, 1986.

132. HR 1. Housing Act of 1986. Kolbe, R-Ariz., amendment to the Gonzalez, D-Texas, substitute *(see vote 129)*, to delete special interest provisions in the bill benefiting public housing projects in Pittsburgh, Boston and Port Arthur, Texas. Rejected 162-245: R 148-20; D 14-225 (ND 8-152, SD 6-73), June 5, 1986.

133. HR 1. Housing Act of 1986. Wylie, R-Ohio, amendment to the Gonzalez, D-Texas, substitute *(see vote 129)*, to terminate the federal crime insurance program. Rejected 176-219: R 141-27; D 35-192 (ND 18-137, SD 17-55), June 5, 1986.

134. HR 1. Housing Act of 1986. Bartlett, R-Texas, amendment to the Gonzalez, D-Texas, substitute *(see vote 129)*, to limit the obligation of funds for new construction of public housing units to repair and renovation of existing units, except in limited circumstances. Adopted 223-180: R 148-19; D 75-161 (ND 35-125, SD 40-36), June 5, 1986.

135. HR 4116. VISTA Reauthorization. Adoption of the rule (H Res 463) to provide for House floor consideration of the bill to reauthorize for three years anti-poverty programs under the Domestic Volunteer Service Act of 1973 (PL 93-113). Adopted 395-1: R 161-1; D 234-0 (ND 160-0, SD 74-0), June 5, 1986.

136. HR 4784. Washington, D.C., Homeless Shelter. DioGuardi, R-N.Y., amendment to prohibit political activities on property whose jurisdiction would be transferred from the federal government to the District of Columbia government under the bill. Rejected 181-182: R 152-2; D 29-180 (ND 12-132, SD 17-48), June 5, 1986.

KEY

- Y Voted for (yea).
- # Paired for.
- + Announced for.
- N Voted against (nay).
- X Paired against.
- - Announced against.
- P Voted "present."
- C Voted "present" to avoid possible conflict of interest.
- ? Did not vote or otherwise make a position known.

Democrats ***Republicans***

	129	130	131	132	133	134	135	136
ALABAMA								
1 ***Callahan***	Y	Y	Y	Y	N	Y	Y	Y
2 ***Dickinson***	Y	Y	N	Y	Y	Y	Y	Y
3 Nichols	N	N	?	N	N	Y	Y	?
4 Bevill	N	N	Y	N	N	Y	Y	N
5 Flippo	N	N	Y	Y	N	N	Y	N
6 Erdreich	N	N	Y	N	N	N	Y	N
7 Shelby	?	?	?	N	N	N	Y	N
ALASKA								
AL ***Young***	Y	N	N	Y	Y	Y	Y	Y
ARIZONA								
1 ***McCain***	Y	N	N	Y	Y	Y	Y	Y
2 Udall	N	N	Y	N	?	N	Y	N
3 ***Stump***	Y	Y	N	Y	Y	?	?	?
4 ***Rudd***	Y	Y	Y	Y	Y	Y	Y	Y
5 ***Kolbe***	Y	Y	N	Y	Y	Y	Y	Y
ARKANSAS								
1 Alexander	N	N	Y	N	N	N	Y	N
2 Robinson	Y	N	Y	N	Y	Y	Y	Y
3 ***Hammerschmidt***	Y	N	N	N	Y	Y	Y	Y
4 Anthony	?	N	?	N	N	Y	Y	N
CALIFORNIA								
1 Bosco	N	N	Y	N	N	N	Y	N
2 ***Chappie***	?	?	?	?	?	?	?	?
3 Matsui	N	N	Y	N	N	N	Y	N
4 Fazio	Y	N	Y	N	N	N	Y	N
5 Burton	N	N	Y	N	N	N	Y	N
6 Boxer	N	N	Y	N	N	N	Y	N
7 Miller	?	?	?	?	?	?	?	?
8 Dellums	?	?	?	?	X	X	?	?
9 Stark	N	N	Y	N	N	N	Y	N
10 Edwards	N	N	Y	N	N	N	Y	N
11 Lantos	N	N	Y	N	N	N	Y	N
12 ***Zschau***	?	?	?	?	?	?	?	?
13 Mineta	N	N	Y	N	N	N	Y	N
14 ***Shumway***	Y	Y	Y	Y	Y	Y	Y	Y
15 Coelho	N	N	Y	N	N	?	?	?
16 Panetta	Y	N	Y	N	N	N	Y	?
17 ***Pashayan***	Y	Y	N	Y	Y	Y	Y	Y
18 Lehman	?	?	Y	N	N	N	Y	?
19 ***Lagomarsino***	Y	Y	N	Y	Y	Y	Y	Y
20 ***Thomas***	Y	Y	N	Y	Y	Y	Y	Y
21 ***Fiedler***	?	?	?	?	?	?	?	?
22 ***Moorhead***	Y	Y	N	Y	Y	Y	Y	Y
23 Beilenson	Y	N	Y	N	N	Y	Y	N
24 Waxman	N	N	Y	N	N	N	Y	N
25 Roybal	N	N	Y	N	N	N	?	?
26 Berman	Y	N	Y	N	N	N	Y	?
27 Levine	N	N	Y	N	N	?	Y	N
28 Dixon	?	?	?	N	N	N	Y	N
29 Hawkins	X	?	?	X	?	?	?	?
30 Martinez	N	N	Y	N	N	N	Y	N
31 Dymally	?	?	P	N	N	N	Y	N
32 Anderson	N	N	Y	N	N	N	Y	N
33 ***Dreier***	Y	Y	N	Y	Y	Y	Y	Y
34 Torres	N	N	?	N	N	N	Y	N
35 ***Lewis***	?	?	N	Y	Y	Y	Y	Y
36 Brown	N	?	Y	N	N	N	Y	?
37 ***McCandless***	Y	Y	N	Y	Y	Y	Y	Y
38 ***Dornan***	Y	Y	N	Y	Y	Y	Y	Y
39 ***Dannemeyer***	Y	Y	N	Y	Y	Y	Y	Y
40 ***Badham***	#	#	?	#	#	?	?	?
41 ***Lowery***	?	?	N	Y	Y	Y	Y	Y
42 ***Lungren***	Y	Y	N	Y	Y	Y	Y	Y
43 ***Packard***	Y	Y	Y	Y	Y	Y	Y	Y
44 Bates	N	N	Y	N	N	N	Y	N
45 ***Hunter***	Y	Y	?	?	Y	Y	Y	Y
COLORADO								
1 Schroeder	N	N	N	N	N	N	Y	N
2 Wirth	N	N	Y	N	N	N	Y	N
3 ***Strang***	Y	Y	N	Y	Y	Y	Y	?
4 ***Brown***	Y	Y	N	Y	Y	Y	Y	Y
5 ***Kramer***	?	?	?	?	?	?	?	?
6 ***Schaefer***	Y	Y	N	Y	Y	Y	Y	Y
CONNECTICUT								
1 Kennelly	N	N	Y	N	N	N	Y	N
2 Gejdenson	N	N	Y	N	N	N	Y	N
3 Morrison	N	N	Y	N	N	N	Y	N
4 ***McKinney***	N	N	Y	N	N	N	Y	Y
5 ***Rowland***	N	N	N	Y	Y	N	Y	Y
6 ***Johnson***	N	N	Y	Y	N	N	Y	?
DELAWARE								
AL Carper	N	N	Y	Y	Y	Y	Y	N
FLORIDA								
1 Hutto	N	N	Y	N	Y	Y	Y	Y
2 Fuqua	N	N	Y	N	N	N	Y	?
3 Bennett	N	N	Y	N	N	N	Y	Y
4 Chappell	N	N	Y	N	?	N	Y	N
5 ***McCollum***	Y	Y	N	Y	Y	Y	Y	Y
6 MacKay	Y	Y	Y	Y	N	Y	+	-
7 Gibbons	N	Y	Y	Y	N	Y	Y	?
8 ***Young***	?	?	N	Y	Y	Y	Y	Y
9 ***Bilirakis***	Y	Y	N	Y	Y	N	Y	Y
10 ***Ireland***	Y	N	N	Y	Y	Y	Y	Y
11 Nelson	#	N	Y	N	N	Y	Y	N
12 ***Lewis***	Y	N	N	Y	Y	N	Y	Y
13 ***Mack***	?	?	N	Y	Y	Y	Y	Y
14 Mica	Y	N	Y	N	N	N	Y	N
15 ***Shaw***	Y	N	N	Y	Y	Y	Y	Y
16 Smith	N	N	Y	N	N	N	Y	?
17 Lehman	N	N	Y	N	N	N	Y	N
18 Pepper	-	N	Y	N	N	N	Y	N
19 Fascell	N	N	Y	N	N	N	Y	N
GEORGIA								
1 Thomas	N	N	Y	N	N	Y	Y	Y
2 Hatcher	Y	N	Y	N	N	N	Y	?
3 Ray	?	?	Y	N	N	Y	Y	Y
4 ***Swindall***	Y	Y	N	Y	Y	Y	Y	Y
5 Fowler	N	N	Y	N	N	Y	Y	N
6 ***Gingrich***	Y	Y	?	Y	Y	Y	Y	Y
7 Darden	N	Y	Y	N	Y	Y	Y	Y
8 Rowland	Y	N	Y	N	N	N	Y	Y
9 Jenkins	N	N	Y	N	Y	Y	Y	Y
10 Barnard	N	N	Y	N	Y	Y	Y	?
HAWAII								
1 Heftel	?	?	?	?	?	?	?	?
2 Akaka	N	N	Y	N	N	N	Y	?
IDAHO								
1 ***Craig***	Y	Y	?	Y	Y	Y	Y	Y
2 Stallings	Y	N	Y	Y	Y	N	Y	Y
ILLINOIS								
1 Hayes	N	N	Y	N	N	N	Y	N
2 Savage	N	N	Y	N	N	N	Y	N
3 Russo	N	N	Y	N	N	Y	Y	N
4 ***O'Brien***	?	?	?	?	?	?	?	?
5 Lipinski	N	N	Y	N	N	Y	Y	N
6 ***Hyde***	Y	Y	?	?	Y	Y	Y	Y
7 Collins	N	N	Y	N	N	N	Y	N
8 Rostenkowski	N	N	Y	N	N	Y	Y	N
9 Yates	N	N	Y	N	N	N	Y	N
10 ***Porter***	Y	N	N	Y	Y	Y	Y	Y
11 Annunzio	N	N	Y	N	N	Y	Y	N
12 ***Crane***	Y	Y	N	Y	Y	Y	N	Y
13 ***Fawell***	Y	Y	N	Y	Y	Y	Y	Y
14 ***Grotberg***	?	?	?	?	?	?	?	?
15 ***Madigan***	Y	N	N	N	Y	Y	Y	Y
16 ***Martin***	N	Y	N	Y	Y	Y	Y	Y
17 Evans	N	N	Y	N	N	N	Y	N
18 ***Michel***	Y	N	Y	Y	Y	Y	Y	Y
19 Bruce	N	N	Y	N	N	N	Y	N
20 Durbin	Y	N	Y	N	N	N	Y	N
21 Price	N	N	Y	N	N	N	Y	N
22 Gray	N	N	Y	N	N	N	Y	N
INDIANA								
1 Visclosky	N	N	Y	N	N	N	Y	N
2 Sharp	N	N	Y	Y	N	Y	Y	N
3 ***Hiler***	Y	Y	N	Y	Y	Y	Y	Y
4 ***Coats***	Y	Y	Y	Y	Y	Y	Y	Y
5 ***Hillis***	Y	Y	Y	Y	Y	Y	?	?

ND - Northern Democrats SD - Southern Democrats

* Corresponding to Congressional Record Votes 142, 143, 144, 145, 147, 149, 150, 151

	129	130	131	132	133	134	135	136
6 ***Burton***	Y	Y	N	Y	Y	Y	Y	Y
7 ***Myers***	Y	Y	Y	Y	Y	Y	Y	Y
8 McCloskey	N	N	Y	N	N	Y	Y	N
9 Hamilton	N	N	Y	N	N	Y	Y	N
10 Jacobs	Y	N	N	Y	Y	Y	Y	Y
IOWA								
1 ***Leach***	Y	Y	N	Y	Y	Y	Y	Y
2 ***Tauke***	Y	Y	N	Y	Y	Y	Y	Y
3 ***Evans***	Y	N	N	Y	?	Y	?	Y
4 Smith	N	N	Y	N	N	Y	Y	N
5 ***Lightfoot***	Y	N	N	Y	Y	Y	Y	Y
6 Bedell	Y	N	Y	N	N	Y	Y	N
KANSAS								
1 ***Roberts***	Y	Y	N	Y	Y	Y	Y	Y
2 Slattery	N	N	Y	Y	Y	Y	Y	N
3 ***Meyers***	Y	N	N	Y	Y	Y	Y	Y
4 Glickman	N	N	Y	N	Y	Y	Y	N
5 ***Whittaker***	Y	Y	N	Y	Y	Y	Y	Y
KENTUCKY								
1 Hubbard	N	N	Y	N	Y	N	Y	Y
2 Natcher	N	N	Y	N	N	Y	Y	N
3 Mazzoli	N	N	Y	N	N	N	Y	Y
4 ***Snyder***	Y	N	Y	Y	Y	Y	Y	Y
5 ***Rogers***	Y	N	N	Y	Y	Y	Y	Y
6 ***Hopkins***	Y	Y	Y	Y	Y	Y	Y	Y
7 Perkins	N	N	Y	N	N	N	Y	N
LOUISIANA								
1 ***Livingston***	Y	N	Y	Y	Y	Y	Y	Y
2 Boggs	N	N	?	N	N	N	Y	N
3 Tauzin	Y	N	Y	N	Y	Y	Y	N
4 Roemer	Y	N	N	N	Y	Y	Y	N
5 Huckaby	Y	N	Y	N	Y	Y	Y	N
6 ***Moore***	Y	N	Y	Y	Y	Y	Y	Y
7 Breaux	?	?	?	?	?	?	?	?
8 Long	N	N	Y	N	N	N	Y	N
MAINE								
1 ***McKernan***	N	N	N	Y	Y	N	Y	Y
2 ***Snowe***	?	?	N	Y	Y	N	Y	Y
MARYLAND								
1 Dyson	N	Y	?	N	Y	Y	Y	Y
2 ***Bentley***	N	N	?	Y	Y	Y	Y	Y
3 Mikulski	N	N	Y	N	Y	N	Y	N
4 ***Holt***	?	?	Y	Y	Y	Y	Y	Y
5 Hoyer	N	N	Y	N	?	N	Y	N
6 Byron	?	N	Y	N	Y	Y	Y	Y
7 Mitchell	N	N	?	N	N	N	Y	N
8 Barnes	N	?	Y	N	Y	N	Y	N
MASSACHUSETTS								
1 ***Conte***	N	N	N	N	N	N	Y	Y
2 Boland	N	N	Y	N	N	N	Y	?
3 Early	N	N	Y	N	N	N	Y	?
4 Frank	N	N	Y	N	N	N	Y	N
5 Atkins	N	N	Y	N	Y	N	Y	N
6 Mavroules	N	N	Y	N	N	N	Y	?
7 Markey	N	N	Y	N	N	N	Y	N
8 O'Neill								
9 Moakley	N	N	Y	N	N	N	Y	N
10 Studds	N	N	Y	N	N	N	Y	N
11 Donnelly	N	N	Y	N	N	N	Y	Y
MICHIGAN								
1 Conyers	N	N	Y	N	N	N	Y	N
2 ***Pursell***	N	N	Y	Y	Y	Y	Y	Y
3 Wolpe	N	N	Y	N	Y	N	Y	N
4 ***Siljander***	N	Y	N	Y	Y	Y	Y	Y
5 ***Henry***	N	N	N	Y	Y	Y	?	?
6 Carr	N	N	Y	N	Y	Y	Y	N
7 Kildee	N	N	Y	N	N	N	Y	N
8 Traxler	N	N	?	N	N	N	Y	N
9 ***Vander Jagt***	N	N	N	Y	Y	Y	Y	Y
10 ***Schuette***	N	N	N	Y	Y	Y	Y	Y
11 ***Davis***	X	X	?	?	?	?	?	?
12 Bonior	N	N	Y	?	N	N	Y	N
13 Crockett	N	N	Y	N	N	N	Y	N
14 Hertel	N	N	Y	N	N	N	Y	N
15 Ford	N	N	Y	N	N	N	Y	N
16 Dingell	N	?	Y	N	N	N	Y	N
17 Levin	N	N	Y	N	N	N	Y	N
18 ***Broomfield***	N	N	Y	Y	Y	Y	Y	?
MINNESOTA								
1 Penny	N	Y	N	Y	Y	Y	Y	N
2 ***Weber***	Y	Y	N	Y	Y	Y	Y	Y
3 ***Frenzel***	Y	Y	N	Y	Y	Y	Y	Y
4 Vento	N	N	Y	N	N	N	Y	N
5 Sabo	N	N	Y	N	N	N	Y	N
6 Sikorski	N	N	N	N	N	N	Y	N

	129	130	131	132	133	134	135	136
7 ***Stangeland***	Y	N	?	Y	Y	Y	Y	?
8 Oberstar	N	N	Y	N	N	N	Y	N
MISSISSIPPI								
1 Whitten	?	?	Y	N	Y	Y	?	N
2 ***Franklin***	Y	N	Y	Y	Y	Y	Y	Y
3 Montgomery	Y	N	Y	N	Y	Y	Y	Y
4 Dowdy	N	N	Y	N	N	Y	Y	?
5 ***Lott***	Y	Y	N	Y	Y	Y	Y	?
MISSOURI								
1 Clay	N	N	N	N	N	N	Y	?
2 Young	N	N	Y	N	N	Y	Y	Y
3 Gephardt	N	N	Y	N	N	N	Y	?
4 Skelton	N	N	Y	N	N	N	Y	?
5 Wheat	N	N	Y	N	N	N	Y	N
6 ***Coleman***	Y	N	N	Y	Y	Y	Y	Y
7 ***Taylor***	Y	Y	Y	Y	Y	Y	Y	Y
8 ***Emerson***	Y	N	N	Y	Y	Y	Y	Y
9 Volkmer	N	N	Y	Y	Y	Y	Y	Y
MONTANA								
1 Williams	?	?	?	N	N	N	Y	N
2 ***Marlenee***	Y	Y	N	Y	Y	Y	Y	Y
NEBRASKA								
1 ***Bereuter***	Y	N	N	Y	Y	Y	Y	Y
2 ***Daub***	Y	Y	N	Y	Y	Y	Y	Y
3 ***Smith***	Y	Y	Y	Y	Y	Y	Y	Y
NEVADA								
1 Reid	N	N	Y	Y	N	N	Y	N
2 ***Vucanovich***	Y	Y	N	Y	Y	Y	Y	Y
NEW HAMPSHIRE								
1 ***Smith***	Y	Y	N	Y	Y	Y	Y	Y
2 ***Gregg***	Y	Y	N	Y	Y	Y	Y	Y
NEW JERSEY								
1 Florio	N	N	Y	N	N	N	Y	N
2 Hughes	N	N	Y	N	Y	Y	Y	Y
3 Howard	N	N	?	N	N	N	Y	N
4 ***Smith***	N	N	Y	Y	N	Y	Y	Y
5 ***Roukema***	N	N	N	Y	Y	Y	Y	Y
6 Dwyer	N	N	Y	N	N	N	Y	N
7 ***Rinaldo***	N	N	Y	Y	N	N	Y	Y
8 Roe	N	N	Y	N	?	N	Y	N
9 Torricelli	N	N	Y	N	?	?	?	?
10 Rodino	?	?	?	?	?	N	Y	N
11 ***Gallo***	N	N	N	Y	N	Y	Y	Y
12 ***Courter***	N	N	?	Y	N	Y	Y	Y
13 ***Saxton***	N	N	N	Y	N	Y	Y	Y
14 Guarini	N	N	Y	N	N	N	Y	Y
NEW MEXICO								
1 ***Lujan***	Y	Y	Y	Y	Y	Y	?	Y
2 ***Skeen***	Y	Y	N	Y	Y	Y	Y	Y
3 Richardson	N	N	Y	N	N	N	Y	N
NEW YORK								
1 ***Carney***	?	?	N	N	Y	Y	Y	Y
2 Downey	N	N	Y	N	N	N	Y	N
3 Mrazek	N	N	Y	N	N	N	Y	N
4 ***Lent***	N	N	Y	Y	N	N	Y	Y
5 ***McGrath***	N	N	N	N	N	N	Y	Y
6 Vacancy								
7 Ackerman	N	N	Y	N	N	N	Y	N
8 Scheuer	N	N	Y	N	N	N	Y	N
9 Manton	N	N	Y	N	N	N	Y	N
10 Schumer	N	N	Y	N	N	N	Y	N
11 Towns	N	N	Y	N	N	N	Y	N
12 Owens	N	N	Y	N	N	N	Y	N
13 Solarz	N	N	Y	N	N	N	Y	N
14 ***Molinari***	N	N	N	Y	N	Y	Y	?
15 ***Green***	N	N	Y	N	N	N	Y	Y
16 Rangel	N	N	Y	N	?	N	Y	N
17 Weiss	N	N	Y	N	N	N	Y	N
18 Garcia	N	N	Y	N	N	N	Y	N
19 Biaggi	N	N	Y	N	N	N	Y	?
20 ***DioGuardi***	N	N	N	N	N	N	Y	Y
21 ***Fish***	N	N	Y	Y	N	N	Y	Y
22 ***Gilman***	N	N	Y	Y	N	-	Y	Y
23 Stratton	N	N	Y	N	N	N	Y	Y
24 ***Solomon***	N	N	N	Y	N	Y	Y	Y
25 ***Boehlert***	N	N	N	Y	N	N	Y	Y
26 ***Martin***	N	N	N	Y	?	Y	Y	Y
27 ***Wortley***	N	N	Y	N	N	Y	Y	Y
28 McHugh	N	N	Y	N	N	N	Y	N
29 ***Horton***	N	N	Y	N	N	N	Y	N
30 ***Eckert***	Y	Y	Y	Y	Y	Y	Y	Y
31 ***Kemp***	N	Y	Y	Y	N	Y	Y	Y
32 LaFalce	N	N	Y	N	N	N	Y	?
33 Nowak	N	N	Y	N	N	N	Y	N
34 Lundine	N	N	?	?	?	?	?	?

	129	130	131	132	133	134	135	136
NORTH CAROLINA								
1 Jones	N	N	Y	N	N	N	Y	N
2 Valentine	N	N	Y	N	N	Y	Y	?
3 Whitley	N	N	Y	N	N	N	Y	Y
4 ***Cobey***	?	?	N	Y	Y	Y	Y	Y
5 Neal	?	N	Y	N	N	N	Y	N
6 ***Coble***	?	?	N	Y	Y	Y	Y	Y
7 Rose	N	N	Y	N	?	?	?	?
8 Hefner	N	N	Y	N	N	N	Y	N
9 ***McMillan***	Y	Y	Y	Y	Y	Y	Y	Y
10 ***Broyhill***	?	?	Y	Y	Y	Y	Y	Y
11 ***Hendon***	Y	N	N	Y	Y	Y	Y	Y
NORTH DAKOTA								
AL Dorgan	N	Y	Y	N	N	Y	Y	N
OHIO								
1 Luken	N	N	Y	N	Y	N	Y	N
2 ***Gradison***	Y	Y	Y	Y	Y	Y	Y	Y
3 Hall	N	N	Y	N	Y	Y	Y	N
4 ***Oxley***	N	Y	N	Y	Y	Y	?	?
5 ***Latta***	Y	Y	Y	Y	Y	Y	Y	Y
6 ***McEwen***	N	N	Y	Y	Y	Y	Y	Y
7 ***DeWine***	N	Y	N	Y	Y	Y	Y	Y
8 ***Kindness***	N	Y	?	Y	Y	Y	Y	Y
9 Kaptur	N	N	Y	N	N	N	Y	?
10 ***Miller***	Y	Y	N	Y	Y	Y	Y	Y
11 Eckart	N	N	Y	N	N	Y	Y	N
12 ***Kasich***	Y	Y	?	Y	Y	Y	Y	Y
13 Pease	N	N	Y	N	Y	Y	Y	N
14 Seiberling	N	N	?	N	N	Y	Y	N
15 ***Wylie***	Y	Y	Y	Y	Y	Y	?	?
16 ***Regula***	N	N	Y	Y	Y	Y	Y	Y
17 Traficant	N	N	Y	N	N	N	Y	Y
18 Applegate	N	N	?	N	N	Y	Y	Y
19 Feighan	N	N	Y	N	N	N	Y	N
20 Oakar	N	N	Y	N	N	N	Y	N
21 Stokes	N	N	Y	N	N	N	Y	N
OKLAHOMA								
1 Jones	Y	N	Y	N	N	Y	Y	N
2 Synar	Y	N	Y	Y	N	Y	Y	?
3 Watkins	Y	N	Y	N	N	Y	Y	N
4 McCurdy	?	?	Y	N	N	Y	Y	N
5 ***Edwards***	Y	N	N	Y	Y	Y	Y	Y
6 English	Y	N	Y	N	N	Y	Y	N
OREGON								
1 AuCoin	N	N	?	N	N	N	Y	N
2 ***Smith, R.***	Y	N	N	?	Y	Y	Y	Y
3 Wyden	N	N	Y	N	N	N	Y	N
4 Weaver	N	N	?	N	N	N	Y	N
5 ***Smith, D.***	Y	Y	N	Y	Y	Y	Y	Y
PENNSYLVANIA								
1 Foglietta	N	N	Y	N	N	N	Y	N
2 Gray	N	N	Y	N	N	N	Y	N
3 Borski	N	N	Y	N	N	N	Y	N
4 Kolter	N	N	Y	N	N	N	Y	N
5 ***Schulze***	Y	N	?	?	?	?	?	?
6 Yatron	N	N	Y	N	N	N	Y	N
7 Edgar	N	N	?	N	N	N	Y	N
8 Kostmayer	N	N	Y	N	N	N	Y	N
9 ***Shuster***	Y	N	N	Y	Y	Y	Y	Y
10 ***McDade***	?	N	Y	Y	Y	N	Y	Y
11 Kanjorski	N	N	Y	N	N	N	Y	N
12 Murtha	N	N	Y	N	N	N	Y	N
13 ***Coughlin***	N	N	?	Y	N	Y	Y	?
14 Coyne	N	N	Y	N	N	N	Y	N
15 ***Ritter***	Y	N	Y	Y	Y	Y	Y	Y
16 ***Walker***	Y	Y	N	Y	Y	Y	Y	Y
17 ***Gekas***	N	N	N	N	N	N	Y	Y
18 Walgren	-	-	?	-	-	Y	Y	N
19 ***Goodling***	Y	N	N	Y	Y	Y	Y	Y
20 Gaydos	N	N	Y	N	?	N	Y	N
21 ***Ridge***	N	N	N	N	N	Y	Y	Y
22 Murphy	N	N	Y	N	N	Y	Y	?
23 ***Clinger***	N	N	N	N	N	Y	Y	Y
RHODE ISLAND								
1 St Germain	N	N	P	N	N	N	Y	N
2 ***Schneider***	N	N	Y	Y	N	N	Y	Y
SOUTH CAROLINA								
1 ***Hartnett***	?	?	?	?	?	?	?	?
2 ***Spence***	Y	N	Y	Y	Y	Y	Y	Y
3 Derrick	N	N	Y	N	N	N	Y	N
4 ***Campbell***	#	?	?	?	?	?	?	?
5 Spratt	?	?	Y	N	N	N	Y	N
6 Tallon	?	?	Y	N	Y	N	Y	Y
SOUTH DAKOTA								
AL Daschle	N	N	Y	N	N	Y	Y	N

	129	130	131	132	133	134	135	136
TENNESSEE								
1 ***Quillen***	Y	Y	Y	N	Y	Y	Y	N
2 ***Duncan***	Y	N	Y	Y	Y	Y	Y	Y
3 Lloyd	Y	N	N	Y	?	?	?	?
4 Cooper	?	?	Y	N	N	N	Y	N
5 Boner	N	N	Y	N	?	N	Y	N
6 Gordon	N	N	Y	N	N	Y	Y	N
7 ***Sundquist***	Y	N	N	Y	Y	Y	Y	Y
8 Jones	N	N	Y	N	N	Y	Y	N
9 Ford	N	N	?	N	N	N	Y	N
TEXAS								
1 Chapman	?	?	Y	N	N	Y	Y	N
2 Wilson	?	?	?	?	?	?	?	?
3 ***Bartlett***	Y	Y	N	Y	Y	Y	Y	Y
4 Hall, R.	Y	Y	?	N	Y	Y	Y	Y
5 Bryant	N	N	Y	N	N	Y	Y	N
6 ***Barton***	Y	Y	N	N	Y	Y	Y	Y
7 ***Archer***	Y	Y	Y	Y	Y	Y	Y	Y
8 ***Fields***	Y	Y	N	N	Y	Y	Y	Y
9 Brooks	N	N	Y	N	N	?	Y	N
10 Pickle	N	N	?	?	?	#	?	?
11 Leath	Y	Y	Y	N	Y	Y	Y	N
12 Wright	N	?	Y	N	?	N	Y	N
13 ***Boulter***	Y	Y	N	N	Y	Y	Y	Y
14 ***Sweeney***	Y	N	Y	Y	Y	Y	?	?
15 de la Garza	N	N	Y	N	?	N	Y	?
16 Coleman	X	?	Y	N	N	N	Y	N
17 Stenholm	?	Y	Y	Y	Y	Y	Y	Y
18 Leland	N	N	?	N	N	N	Y	N
19 ***Combest***	Y	Y	Y	N	Y	Y	Y	Y
20 Gonzalez	N	N	Y	N	N	N	Y	N
21 ***Loeffler***	Y	Y	N	N	Y	Y	Y	Y
22 ***DeLay***	Y	Y	N	N	Y	Y	Y	Y
23 Bustamante	?	?	Y	N	?	N	Y	N
24 Frost	N	N	Y	N	N	Y	Y	N
25 Andrews	?	?	Y	N	N	Y	Y	N
26 ***Armey***	Y	Y	N	Y	Y	Y	Y	Y
27 Ortiz	N	N	Y	N	N	N	Y	N
UTAH								
1 ***Hansen***	Y	N	N	Y	Y	Y	Y	?
2 ***Monson***	Y	Y	?	Y	Y	Y	Y	?
3 ***Nielson***	Y	Y	N	Y	Y	Y	Y	Y
VERMONT								
AL ***Jeffords***	Y	N	Y	Y	N	Y	Y	Y
VIRGINIA								
1 ***Bateman***	Y	N	Y	Y	Y	Y	Y	Y
2 ***Whitehurst***	N	N	Y	Y	Y	?	?	?
3 ***Bliley***	Y	N	N	Y	Y	Y	Y	Y
4 Sisisky	N	N	Y	N	N	Y	?	?
5 Daniel	N	Y	Y	N	Y	Y	Y	Y
6 Olin	N	N	Y	N	Y	Y	Y	Y
7 ***Slaughter***	Y	Y	N	Y	Y	Y	Y	Y
8 ***Parris***	Y	?	N	Y	Y	Y	Y	Y
9 Boucher	?	?	Y	N	N	Y	Y	N
10 ***Wolf***	Y	Y	N	Y	Y	Y	Y	Y
WASHINGTON								
1 ***Miller***	Y	Y	Y	Y	Y	Y	Y	Y
2 Swift	N	N	Y	N	N	N	Y	N
3 Bonker	N	N	P	N	N	N	Y	N
4 ***Morrison***	Y	N	N	Y	Y	?	Y	Y
5 Foley	N	N	Y	N	N	N	Y	N
6 Dicks	N	N	Y	N	N	N	Y	N
7 Lowry	Y	N	Y	N	N	N	Y	N
8 ***Chandler***	?	?	N	Y	?	Y	Y	Y
WEST VIRGINIA								
1 Mollohan	?	?	?	?	?	?	?	?
2 Staggers	N	N	Y	N	N	N	Y	N
3 Wise	N	N	Y	N	N	N	Y	?
4 Rahall	N	N	Y	N	N	N	Y	N
WISCONSIN								
1 Aspin	N	N	Y	N	N	Y	Y	N
2 Kastenmeier	N	N	Y	N	N	N	Y	N
3 ***Gunderson***	Y	N	N	Y	Y	Y	Y	Y
4 Kleczka	N	N	Y	N	N	N	Y	N
5 Moody	N	N	Y	N	N	N	Y	N
6 ***Petri***	Y	Y	Y	Y	Y	Y	Y	Y
7 Obey	N	N	Y	N	N	N	Y	N
8 ***Roth***	Y	N	N	Y	Y	Y	Y	Y
9 ***Sensenbrenner***	Y	Y	N	Y	Y	Y	Y	Y
WYOMING								
AL ***Cheney***	Y	Y	N	Y	Y	Y	Y	?

Southern states - Ala., Ark., Fla., Ga., Ky., La., Miss., N.C., Okla., S.C., Tenn., Texas, Va.

* The *Congressional Record* vote number is different from the CQ vote number because the *Record* includes quorum calls in its tally. CQ does not publish quorum call votes.

137. HR 4784. Washington, D.C., Homeless Shelter. Passage of the bill to transfer jurisdiction of property from the federal government to the District of Columbia government for use as a shelter for homeless individuals. Passed 242-116: R 47-105; D 195-11 (ND 139-4, SD 56-7), June 5, 1986.

138. Procedural Motion. Sensenbrenner, R-Wis., motion to approve the House *Journal* of Tuesday, June 10. Motion agreed to 261-109: R 57-102; D 204-7 (ND 139-6, SD 65-1), June 11, 1986.

139. HR 2591. Congressional Gold Medals. Annunzio, D-Ill., motion to suspend the rules and pass the bill to award gold medals to Jan Scruggs, Robert Doubek and John Wheeler, founders of the Vietnam Veterans Memorial Fund, in recognition of their efforts to erect the memorial. Motion rejected 224-186: R 32-138; D 192-48 (ND 145-18, SD 47-30), June 11, 1986. A two-thirds majority of those present and voting (274 in this case) is required for passage under suspension of the rules.

140. HR 1. Housing Act of 1986. Gray, D-Ill., amendment to the Gonzalez, D-Texas, substitute, to reduce the rent for elderly tenants of subsidized housing from 30 percent of adjusted gross income to 25 percent. Adopted 277-137: R 50-121; D 227-16 (ND 159-7, SD 68-9), June 11, 1986. (The Gonzalez substitute, which contains the text of HR 4746, would authorize and revise federal housing programs for fiscal 1986 and 1987.)

141. HR 1. Housing Act of 1986. McCollum, R-Fla., amendment to the Gonzalez, D-Texas, substitute *(see vote 140)*, to strike the Nehemiah program providing aid to help first-time owners buy homes. Rejected 123-300: R 108-67; D 15-233 (ND 5-163, SD 10-70), June 11, 1986.

142. HR 1. Housing Act of 1986. Fauntroy, D-D.C., amendment to the Gonzalez, D-Texas, substitute *(see vote 140)*, to authorize for fiscal 1987 a total of $1.5 million to assist up to 15 public housing authorities in encouraging and establishing tenant management programs. Adopted 419-1: R 174-0; D 245-1 (ND 166-0, SD 79-1), June 11, 1986.

143. HR 1. Housing Act of 1986. Kemp, R-N.Y., amendment to the Gonzalez, D-Texas, substitute *(see vote 140)*, to allow public housing tenants to buy their dwellings for 25 percent of the market value with a low-interest loan from a public housing authority. Adopted 238-176: R 164-9; D 74-167 (ND 40-124, SD 34-43), June 11, 1986.

KEY

Y Voted for (yea).
\# Paired for.
\+ Announced for.
N Voted against (nay).
X Paired against.
\- Announced against.
P Voted "present."
C Voted "present" to avoid possible conflict of interest.
? Did not vote or otherwise make a position known.

Democrats ***Republicans***

	137	138	139	140	141	142	143
ALABAMA							
1 ***Callahan***	N	Y	N	N	Y	Y	Y
2 ***Dickinson***	N	N	N	N	Y	?	Y
3 Nichols	?	?	N	N	Y	Y	Y
4 Bevill	Y	?	N	Y	Y	Y	Y
5 Flippo	Y	Y	N	Y	Y	Y	Y
6 Erdreich	Y	Y	N	Y	N	Y	Y
7 Shelby	Y	?	N	Y	N	Y	Y
ALASKA							
AL ***Young***	N	N	N	Y	Y	Y	Y
ARIZONA							
1 ***McCain***	Y	Y	N	N	Y	Y	Y
2 Udall	Y	Y	Y	Y	N	Y	N
3 ***Stump***	?	N	N	N	Y	Y	Y
4 ***Rudd***	N	Y	N	N	Y	Y	Y
5 ***Kolbe***	Y	N	Y	N	Y	Y	Y
ARKANSAS							
1 Alexander	?	Y	Y	Y	N	Y	N
2 Robinson	N	Y	N	Y	Y	Y	N
3 ***Hammerschmidt***	N	Y	N	Y	Y	Y	Y
4 Anthony	Y	Y	N	Y	N	Y	N
CALIFORNIA							
1 Bosco	Y	Y	Y	Y	N	Y	Y
2 ***Chappie***	?	N	N	N	Y	Y	Y
3 Matsui	Y	?	Y	Y	N	Y	N
4 Fazio	Y	Y	Y	Y	N	Y	N
5 Burton	Y	Y	Y	Y	N	Y	N
6 Boxer	Y	Y	Y	Y	N	Y	N
7 Miller	?	Y	Y	Y	N	Y	N
8 Dellums	#	Y	Y	Y	N	Y	N
9 Stark	Y	Y	Y	Y	N	Y	N
10 Edwards	Y	Y	Y	Y	N	Y	N
11 Lantos	Y	Y	N	Y	N	Y	N
12 ***Zschau***	?	?	N	N	N	Y	Y
13 Mineta	Y	Y	Y	Y	N	Y	N
14 ***Shumway***	N	Y	N	N	Y	Y	Y
15 Coelho	?	Y	Y	Y	N	Y	N
16 Panetta	Y	Y	Y	Y	N	Y	Y
17 ***Pashayan***	Y	N	Y	Y	N	Y	Y
18 Lehman	?	Y	Y	Y	N	Y	N
19 ***Lagomarsino***	N	N	N	N	Y	Y	Y
20 ***Thomas***	N	N	N	N	Y	Y	Y
21 ***Fiedler***	?	N	N	Y	Y	Y	Y
22 ***Moorhead***	N	N	N	N	Y	Y	Y
23 Beilenson	Y	Y	Y	Y	N	Y	N
24 Waxman	Y	Y	Y	Y	N	Y	N
25 Roybal	?	Y	Y	Y	N	Y	N
26 Berman	?	Y	Y	Y	N	Y	N
27 Levine	Y	Y	Y	Y	N	Y	N
28 Dixon	Y	?	?	Y	N	Y	N
29 Hawkins	?	P	Y	Y	N	Y	N
30 Martinez	Y	?	Y	Y	N	Y	N
31 Dymally	Y	Y	Y	Y	N	Y	N
32 Anderson	Y	Y	Y	Y	N	Y	Y
33 ***Dreier***	N	N	N	N	Y	Y	Y
34 Torres	Y	Y	Y	Y	N	Y	N
35 ***Lewis***	Y	N	N	N	Y	Y	Y
36 Brown	?	Y	Y	Y	N	Y	N
37 ***McCandless***	N	N	N	N	Y	Y	Y
38 ***Dornan***	N	N	N	N	Y	Y	Y
39 ***Dannemeyer***	N	N	N	N	Y	Y	Y
40 ***Badham***	X	N	N	N	Y	Y	Y
41 ***Lowery***	N	?	?	N	N	Y	Y
42 ***Lungren***	N	Y	N	N	N	Y	Y
43 ***Packard***	N	Y	N	N	Y	Y	Y
44 Bates	Y	Y	Y	Y	N	Y	N
45 ***Hunter***	N	N	N	Y	N	Y	Y
COLORADO							
1 Schroeder	Y	N	Y	Y	N	Y	N
2 Wirth	Y	Y	Y	Y	N	Y	Y
3 ***Strang***	?	N	Y	N	Y	Y	Y
4 ***Brown***	N	N	N	N	Y	Y	Y
5 ***Kramer***	?	N	N	N	Y	Y	Y
6 ***Schaefer***	N	N	N	N	Y	Y	Y
CONNECTICUT							
1 Kennelly	Y	Y	Y	Y	N	Y	N
2 Gejdenson	Y	Y	Y	Y	N	Y	N
3 Morrison	Y	Y	Y	Y	N	Y	N
4 ***McKinney***	Y	Y	Y	N	N	Y	Y
5 ***Rowland***	Y	N	Y	Y	N	Y	Y
6 ***Johnson***	?	Y	N	N	N	Y	N
DELAWARE							
AL Carper	Y	Y	N	N	N	Y	Y
FLORIDA							
1 Hutto	Y	Y	N	Y	N	Y	Y
2 Fuqua	?	Y	N	Y	N	Y	Y
3 Bennett	Y	Y	Y	Y	N	Y	N
4 Chappell	?	?	N	Y	N	Y	N
5 ***McCollum***	N	Y	Y	Y	Y	Y	Y
6 MacKay	+	Y	Y	Y	N	N	N
7 Gibbons	?	Y	Y	Y	N	Y	Y
8 ***Young***	N	N	N	Y	Y	Y	Y
9 ***Bilirakis***	N	N	Y	Y	Y	Y	Y
10 ***Ireland***	N	N	N	N	Y	Y	Y
11 Nelson	Y	Y	Y	Y	N	Y	Y
12 ***Lewis***	N	N	N	Y	Y	Y	Y
13 ***Mack***	N	N	Y	?	N	Y	Y
14 Mica	Y	Y	Y	Y	Y	Y	N
15 ***Shaw***	N	?	N	Y	Y	Y	Y
16 Smith	Y	Y	Y	Y	N	Y	N
17 Lehman	Y	Y	Y	Y	N	Y	N
18 Pepper	Y	Y	N	Y	N	Y	N
19 Fascell	Y	Y	Y	Y	N	?	N
GEORGIA							
1 Thomas	Y	Y	Y	Y	N	Y	N
2 Hatcher	?	Y	N	Y	N	Y	N
3 Ray	Y	Y	N	N	N	Y	Y
4 ***Swindall***	N	N	N	N	Y	Y	+
5 Fowler	Y	?	Y	Y	N	Y	?
6 ***Gingrich***	N	N	N	N	N	Y	Y
7 Darden	Y	Y	Y	N	N	Y	N
8 Rowland	Y	Y	N	Y	N	Y	N
9 Jenkins	Y	Y	Y	N	N	Y	N
10 Barnard	?	?	?	N	N	Y	N
HAWAII							
1 Heftel	?	?	Y	Y	N	Y	?
2 Akaka	#	Y	Y	Y	N	Y	N
IDAHO							
1 ***Craig***	N	N	-	N	N	Y	Y
2 Stallings	Y	Y	Y	Y	N	Y	Y
ILLINOIS							
1 Hayes	Y	Y	Y	Y	N	Y	N
2 Savage	Y	Y	Y	Y	N	Y	N
3 Russo	Y	Y	Y	Y	N	Y	Y
4 ***O'Brien***	?	?	?	?	?	?	?
5 Lipinski	Y	?	Y	Y	N	Y	Y
6 ***Hyde***	N	N	N	N	Y	Y	Y
7 Collins	Y	Y	Y	Y	N	Y	N
8 Rostenkowski	Y	Y	Y	Y	N	Y	N
9 Yates	Y	?	Y	Y	N	Y	N
10 ***Porter***	Y	Y	N	N	N	Y	Y
11 Annunzio	Y	Y	Y	Y	N	Y	N
12 ***Crane***	N	N	N	N	Y	Y	Y
13 ***Fawell***	N	N	Y	N	Y	Y	Y
14 ***Grotberg***	?	?	?	?	?	?	?
15 ***Madigan***	N	N	N	Y	N	Y	Y
16 ***Martin***	N	N	N	N	N	Y	Y
17 Evans	Y	Y	Y	Y	N	Y	N
18 ***Michel***	N	?	N	N	Y	Y	Y
19 Bruce	Y	Y	Y	N	N	Y	N
20 Durbin	Y	Y	Y	Y	N	Y	Y
21 Price	Y	Y	Y	Y	N	Y	N
22 Gray	Y	Y	Y	Y	N	Y	N
INDIANA							
1 Visclosky	Y	Y	Y	Y	N	Y	N
2 Sharp	Y	?	Y	Y	N	Y	Y
3 ***Hiler***	N	N	N	N	Y	Y	Y
4 ***Coats***	N	Y	N	N	N	Y	Y
5 ***Hillis***	?	?	?	?	N	Y	Y

ND - Northern Democrats SD - Southern Democrats

* Corresponding to Congressional Record Votes 152, 153, 154, 155, 156, 158, 159

	137	138	139	140	141	142	143
6 ***Burton***	N	?	?	N	Y	Y	Y
7 ***Myers***	N	Y	N	Y	Y	Y	Y
8 McCloskey	Y	Y	Y	Y	N	Y	Y
9 Hamilton	Y	Y	Y	Y	N	Y	Y
10 Jacobs	Y	N	Y	Y	N	Y	N
IOWA							
1 ***Leach***	Y	N	Y	N	Y	Y	Y
2 ***Tauke***	N	N	N	N	N	Y	Y
3 ***Evans***	N	N	N	N	Y	Y	Y
4 Smith	Y	Y	N	Y	N	Y	N
5 ***Lightfoot***	N	N	N	N	Y	Y	Y
6 Bedell	Y	Y	N	N	N	Y	N
KANSAS							
1 ***Roberts***	N	N	N	N	Y	Y	Y
2 Slattery	Y	Y	Y	N	N	Y	Y
3 ***Meyers***	N	N	Y	N	Y	Y	N
4 Glickman	Y	Y	Y	Y	N	Y	Y
5 ***Whittaker***	N	N	N	N	Y	Y	Y
KENTUCKY							
1 Hubbard	N	Y	N	Y	N	Y	Y
2 Natcher	Y	Y	Y	Y	N	Y	Y
3 Mazzoli	Y	Y	N	Y	N	Y	Y
4 ***Snyder***	N	?	?	?	Y	Y	Y
5 ***Rogers***	N	N	N	Y	Y	Y	Y
6 ***Hopkins***	N	Y	N	Y	Y	Y	Y
7 Perkins	Y	Y	Y	Y	N	Y	N
LOUISIANA							
1 ***Livingston***	N	Y	N	N	Y	Y	Y
2 Boggs	Y	?	Y	Y	N	Y	N
3 Tauzin	Y	Y	N	Y	N	Y	Y
4 Roemer	Y	Y	Y	Y	N	Y	Y
5 Huckaby	Y	Y	N	Y	N	Y	N
6 ***Moore***	N	?	?	?	?	?	?
7 Breaux	?	?	?	#	X	?	?
8 Long	Y	Y	Y	Y	N	Y	N
MAINE							
1 ***McKernan***	Y	?	?	?	N	Y	Y
2 ***Snowe***	Y	Y	Y	Y	N	Y	Y
MARYLAND							
1 Dyson	N	Y	Y	Y	N	Y	Y
2 ***Bentley***	N	N	Y	Y	N	Y	Y
3 Mikulski	Y	Y	Y	Y	N	Y	N
4 ***Holt***	N	Y	N	Y	Y	Y	Y
5 Hoyer	Y	Y	Y	Y	N	Y	N
6 Byron	N	N	Y	N	Y	Y	Y
7 Mitchell	Y	?	Y	Y	N	Y	N
8 Barnes	Y	Y	Y	Y	N	Y	?
MASSACHUSETTS							
1 ***Conte***	Y	N	Y	Y	N	Y	N
2 Boland	?	Y	Y	Y	N	Y	N
3 Early	?	Y	Y	Y	N	Y	N
4 Frank	Y	Y	Y	Y	N	Y	N
5 Atkins	Y	Y	Y	Y	N	Y	N
6 Mavroules	?	Y	Y	Y	N	Y	Y
7 Markey	Y	Y	Y	Y	N	Y	N
8 O'Neill							
9 Moakley	Y	Y	N	Y	N	Y	N
10 Studds	Y	Y	Y	Y	N	Y	N
11 Donnelly	Y	Y	Y	Y	N	Y	N
MICHIGAN							
1 Conyers	Y	?	?	?	N	Y	N
2 ***Pursell***	?	Y	Y	N	N	Y	Y
3 Wolpe	Y	Y	Y	Y	N	Y	N
4 ***Siljander***	N	?	N	N	Y	Y	Y
5 ***Henry***	?	N	Y	N	Y	Y	Y
6 Carr	Y	?	Y	Y	Y	Y	Y
7 Kildee	Y	Y	Y	Y	N	Y	N
8 Traxler	?	Y	Y	Y	N	Y	N
9 ***Vander Jagt***	N	N	N	N	Y	Y	Y
10 ***Schuette***	Y	N	N	N	Y	Y	Y
11 ***Davis***	?	?	?	?	?	?	?
12 Bonior	Y	Y	Y	Y	N	Y	N
13 Crockett	Y	Y	Y	Y	N	Y	N
14 Hertel	Y	Y	Y	Y	N	Y	N
15 Ford	Y	?	Y	Y	N	Y	N
16 Dingell	Y	?	?	Y	N	Y	N
17 Levin	Y	Y	Y	Y	N	Y	N
18 ***Broomfield***	?	Y	N	N	Y	Y	Y
MINNESOTA							
1 Penny	Y	N	Y	N	Y	Y	Y
2 ***Weber***	N	N	N	N	N	Y	Y
3 ***Frenzel***	N	N	N	N	Y	Y	N
4 Vento	Y	Y	Y	Y	N	?	N
5 Sabo	Y	Y	Y	Y	N	Y	N
6 Sikorski	Y	N	Y	Y	N	Y	N
7 ***Stangeland***	?	N	N	Y	Y	Y	Y
8 Oberstar	Y	Y	Y	Y	N	Y	N
MISSISSIPPI							
1 Whitten	Y	Y	Y	Y	N	Y	Y
2 ***Franklin***	?	Y	N	N	Y	Y	Y
3 Montgomery	N	Y	N	Y	Y	Y	Y
4 Dowdy	?	?	?	?	N	Y	N
5 ***Lott***	?	N	Y	N	Y	Y	Y
MISSOURI							
1 Clay	?	N	Y	Y	N	Y	N
2 Young	N	Y	Y	Y	N	Y	Y
3 Gephardt	?	Y	Y	Y	N	?	?
4 Skelton	?	Y	N	N	N	Y	N
5 Wheat	Y	Y	Y	Y	N	Y	N
6 ***Coleman***	N	N	Y	N	Y	Y	Y
7 ***Taylor***	?	Y	N	N	Y	Y	Y
8 ***Emerson***	N	N	N	Y	Y	Y	Y
9 Volkmer	N	Y	Y	Y	N	Y	Y
MONTANA							
1 Williams	Y	Y	Y	Y	N	Y	N
2 ***Marlenee***	N	N	N	N	Y	Y	Y
NEBRASKA							
1 ***Bereuter***	N	N	N	N	N	Y	Y
2 ***Daub***	N	N	N	N	Y	Y	Y
3 ***Smith***	N	Y	N	Y	Y	Y	Y
NEVADA							
1 Reid	Y	Y	Y	Y	N	Y	Y
2 ***Vucanovich***	N	N	Y	N	N	Y	Y
NEW HAMPSHIRE							
1 ***Smith***	N	N	N	N	N	Y	Y
2 ***Gregg***	N	N	N	N	N	Y	Y
NEW JERSEY							
1 Florio	Y	Y	Y	Y	N	Y	Y
2 Hughes	Y	Y	Y	Y	N	Y	Y
3 Howard	Y	Y	Y	Y	N	Y	N
4 ***Smith***	Y	Y	N	Y	N	Y	Y
5 ***Roukema***	Y	?	N	N	N	Y	Y
6 Dwyer	Y	Y	Y	Y	N	Y	N
7 ***Rinaldo***	Y	Y	Y	Y	N	Y	Y
8 Roe	Y	Y	Y	Y	N	Y	Y
9 Torricelli	#	Y	Y	Y	N	Y	N
10 Rodino	Y	?	?	?	?	?	?
11 ***Gallo***	Y	N	N	N	N	Y	Y
12 ***Courter***	Y	N	N	N	N	Y	Y
13 ***Saxton***	Y	?	Y	N	N	Y	Y
14 Guarini	Y	Y	Y	Y	N	Y	Y
NEW MEXICO							
1 ***Lujan***	N	Y	N	N	Y	Y	Y
2 ***Skeen***	N	N	N	N	Y	Y	Y
3 Richardson	Y	Y	Y	Y	N	Y	N
NEW YORK							
1 ***Carney***	N	N	N	N	Y	Y	?
2 Downey	Y	?	?	Y	N	Y	?
3 Mrazek	Y	Y	N	Y	N	Y	N
4 ***Lent***	Y	N	N	Y	N	Y	N
5 ***McGrath***	Y	N	N	Y	N	Y	N
6 Vacancy							
7 Ackerman	Y	Y	Y	Y	N	Y	N
8 Scheuer	?	Y	Y	Y	N	Y	N
9 Manton	Y	Y	Y	Y	N	Y	N
10 Schumer	Y	Y	Y	Y	N	Y	N
11 Towns	Y	?	Y	Y	N	Y	N
12 Owens	Y	Y	Y	Y	N	Y	N
13 Solarz	Y	Y	N	Y	N	Y	N
14 ***Molinari***	?	N	N	N	N	Y	N
15 ***Green***	Y	Y	N	N	N	Y	N
16 Rangel	Y	Y	Y	Y	N	Y	N
17 Weiss	Y	Y	Y	Y	N	Y	N
18 Garcia	Y	Y	Y	Y	N	Y	N
19 Biaggi	?	Y	Y	Y	N	Y	N
20 ***DioGuardi***	Y	?	Y	Y	N	Y	Y
21 ***Fish***	Y	Y	Y	Y	N	Y	Y
22 ***Gilman***	Y	Y	Y	Y	N	Y	Y
23 Stratton	Y	Y	N	Y	N	Y	Y
24 ***Solomon***	N	N	N	Y	N	Y	Y
25 ***Boehlert***	Y	N	N	Y	N	Y	Y
26 ***Martin***	N	N	N	Y	N	Y	Y
27 ***Wortley***	Y	Y	N	Y	N	Y	Y
28 McHugh	Y	Y	Y	Y	N	Y	N
29 ***Horton***	Y	Y	N	Y	N	Y	Y
30 ***Eckert***	N	Y	N	N	N	Y	Y
31 ***Kemp***	Y	Y	N	Y	N	Y	Y
32 LaFalce	?	Y	N	N	N	Y	Y
33 Nowak	Y	Y	Y	Y	N	Y	Y
34 Lundine	?	Y	Y	Y	N	Y	N
NORTH CAROLINA							
1 Jones	N	?	Y	Y	N	Y	N
2 Valentine	?	Y	N	Y	N	Y	Y
3 Whitley	?	Y	N	Y	N	Y	N
4 ***Cobey***	N	N	N	N	N	Y	Y
5 Neal	Y	?	Y	Y	N	Y	N
6 ***Coble***	N	N	N	N	Y	Y	Y
7 Rose	?	?	Y	Y	N	Y	?
8 Hefner	Y	Y	Y	Y	N	Y	Y
9 ***McMillan***	Y	Y	N	N	N	Y	Y
10 ***Broyhill***	N	Y	N	N	Y	Y	Y
11 ***Hendon***	Y	N	N	N	N	Y	Y
NORTH DAKOTA							
AL Dorgan	Y	Y	Y	Y	N	Y	Y
OHIO							
1 Luken	Y	Y	Y	Y	N	Y	Y
2 ***Gradison***	Y	Y	N	N	N	Y	N
3 Hall	Y	Y	Y	Y	Y	Y	N
4 ***Oxley***	X	?	N	N	Y	Y	Y
5 ***Latta***	N	N	N	N	Y	Y	Y
6 ***McEwen***	Y	Y	Y	Y	N	Y	Y
7 ***DeWine***	Y	N	N	N	Y	Y	Y
8 ***Kindness***	N	N	N	N	N	Y	Y
9 Kaptur	#	?	Y	Y	N	Y	N
10 ***Miller***	N	N	N	N	Y	Y	Y
11 Eckart	Y	Y	Y	Y	N	Y	N
12 ***Kasich***	Y	?	Y	N	Y	Y	Y
13 Pease	Y	Y	Y	Y	N	Y	N
14 Seiberling	Y	Y	Y	Y	N	Y	N
15 ***Wylie***	?	Y	N	N	Y	Y	Y
16 ***Regula***	N	Y	Y	Y	Y	Y	Y
17 Traficant	Y	Y	Y	Y	N	Y	N
18 Applegate	Y	Y	N	Y	N	Y	Y
19 Feighan	Y	Y	Y	Y	N	Y	N
20 Oakar	Y	Y	Y	Y	N	Y	N
21 Stokes	Y	Y	Y	Y	N	Y	N
OKLAHOMA							
1 Jones	Y	Y	Y	Y	N	Y	N
2 Synar	?	Y	Y	Y	N	Y	N
3 Watkins	Y	Y	Y	Y	N	Y	N
4 McCurdy	Y	?	Y	Y	N	Y	N
5 ***Edwards***	N	N	N	N	Y	Y	Y
6 English	Y	Y	Y	Y	N	Y	N
OREGON							
1 AuCoin	Y	Y	Y	Y	N	Y	N
2 ***Smith, R.***	Y	N	N	N	Y	Y	Y
3 Wyden	Y	Y	Y	Y	N	Y	N
4 Weaver	Y	Y	Y	Y	N	Y	N
5 ***Smith, D.***	N	N	N	N	Y	Y	Y
PENNSYLVANIA							
1 Foglietta	Y	?	Y	Y	N	Y	N
2 Gray	Y	Y	Y	Y	N	Y	N
3 Borski	Y	Y	Y	Y	N	Y	Y
4 Kolter	Y	?	Y	Y	N	Y	N
5 ***Schulze***	?	Y	N	Y	Y	Y	Y
6 Yatron	Y	Y	Y	Y	N	Y	Y
7 Edgar	Y	Y	Y	Y	N	Y	N
8 Kostmayer	Y	Y	Y	Y	N	Y	Y
9 ***Shuster***	N	N	N	N	Y	Y	Y
10 ***McDade***	Y	Y	N	Y	N	Y	Y
11 Kanjorski	Y	Y	Y	Y	N	Y	N
12 Murtha	Y	Y	Y	Y	Y	Y	N
13 ***Coughlin***	?	N	Y	Y	N	Y	Y
14 Coyne	Y	Y	N	Y	N	Y	N
15 ***Ritter***	N	Y	N	N	N	Y	Y
16 ***Walker***	N	N	N	N	N	Y	Y
17 ***Gekas***	N	N	N	Y	N	Y	Y
18 Walgren	Y	Y	Y	Y	N	Y	N
19 ***Goodling***	Y	N	N	Y	Y	Y	Y
20 Gaydos	Y	Y	Y	Y	N	Y	Y
21 ***Ridge***	N	N	N	N	N	Y	Y
22 Murphy	?	Y	N	Y	N	Y	Y
23 ***Clinger***	N	Y	N	Y	Y	Y	Y
RHODE ISLAND							
1 St Germain	Y	Y	N	Y	N	Y	N
2 ***Schneider***	Y	Y	N	Y	N	Y	Y
SOUTH CAROLINA							
1 ***Hartnett***	?	?	?	X	#	?	?
2 ***Spence***	N	Y	Y	Y	Y	Y	Y
3 Derrick	Y	Y	N	Y	N	Y	N
4 ***Campbell***	?	?	?	?	?	?	?
5 Spratt	Y	Y	Y	Y	N	Y	?
6 Tallon	Y	?	?	?	N	Y	N
SOUTH DAKOTA							
AL Daschle	Y	Y	Y	Y	N	Y	Y
TENNESSEE							
1 ***Quillen***	Y	Y	N	Y	Y	Y	Y
2 ***Duncan***	Y	Y	N	Y	Y	Y	Y
3 Lloyd	?	N	Y	Y	Y	Y	?
4 Cooper	Y	Y	N	N	N	Y	N
5 Boner	Y	Y	N	Y	N	Y	Y
6 Gordon	Y	Y	Y	Y	N	Y	Y
7 ***Sundquist***	N	N	N	N	Y	Y	Y
8 Jones	Y	Y	Y	Y	Y	Y	N
9 Ford	Y	Y	Y	Y	N	Y	Y
TEXAS							
1 Chapman	Y	Y	Y	Y	N	Y	Y
2 Wilson	?	?	?	Y	N	Y	Y
3 ***Bartlett***	N	N	N	N	N	Y	Y
4 Hall, R.	N	Y	Y	Y	N	Y	Y
5 Bryant	Y	Y	Y	Y	N	Y	N
6 ***Barton***	N	N	N	N	Y	Y	Y
7 ***Archer***	N	Y	N	N	Y	Y	Y
8 ***Fields***	N	Y	N	N	Y	Y	Y
9 Brooks	Y	Y	Y	Y	N	Y	Y
10 Pickle	?	Y	Y	N	N	Y	Y
11 Leath	Y	Y	N	Y	N	Y	Y
12 Wright	Y	Y	Y	Y	N	Y	Y
13 ***Boulter***	N	N	N	N	Y	Y	Y
14 ***Sweeney***	N	Y	N	N	N	Y	Y
15 de la Garza	?	Y	N	Y	N	Y	N
16 Coleman	Y	Y	N	Y	N	Y	N
17 Stenholm	N	Y	N	N	Y	Y	Y
18 Leland	Y	?	Y	Y	N	Y	N
19 ***Combest***	N	Y	N	N	Y	Y	Y
20 Gonzalez	Y	Y	Y	P	N	Y	N
21 ***Loeffler***	N	P	N	N	Y	Y	Y
22 ***DeLay***	N	?	N	N	Y	Y	Y
23 Bustamante	Y	Y	Y	Y	N	Y	N
24 Frost	Y	Y	Y	Y	N	Y	Y
25 Andrews	Y	Y	Y	Y	N	Y	Y
26 ***Armey***	N	N	N	N	N	Y	Y
27 Ortiz	Y	Y	Y	Y	N	Y	N
UTAH							
1 ***Hansen***	?	N	N	N	Y	Y	Y
2 ***Monson***	X	N	N	N	Y	Y	Y
3 ***Nielson***	N	Y	Y	N	Y	Y	Y
VERMONT							
AL ***Jeffords***	Y	Y	Y	Y	N	Y	Y
VIRGINIA							
1 ***Bateman***	N	Y	N	N	Y	Y	Y
2 ***Whitehurst***	?	N	N	N	Y	Y	Y
3 ***Bliley***	Y	N	N	N	N	Y	Y
4 Sisisky	?	Y	N	Y	N	Y	Y
5 Daniel	N	Y	N	N	Y	Y	Y
6 Olin	Y	Y	Y	Y	N	Y	N
7 ***Slaughter***	N	N	N	N	Y	Y	Y
8 ***Parris***	N	N	N	Y	N	Y	Y
9 Boucher	Y	Y	Y	?	?	Y	N
10 ***Wolf***	Y	N	N	Y	N	Y	Y
WASHINGTON							
1 ***Miller***	Y	Y	N	N	Y	Y	Y
2 Swift	Y	Y	?	Y	N	Y	N
3 Bonker	Y	Y	N	Y	N	Y	N
4 ***Morrison***	Y	Y	N	N	Y	Y	Y
5 Foley	Y	Y	Y	?	N	Y	N
6 Dicks	Y	?	Y	Y	N	Y	Y
7 Lowry	Y	N	Y	Y	N	Y	N
8 ***Chandler***	Y	?	N	N	?	?	?
WEST VIRGINIA							
1 Mollohan	?	?	Y	Y	N	Y	N
2 Staggers	Y	P	Y	Y	N	Y	N
3 Wise	?	Y	Y	Y	N	Y	N
4 Rahall	Y	Y	Y	Y	N	Y	N
WISCONSIN							
1 Aspin	Y	?	N	Y	N	Y	N
2 Kastenmeier	Y	Y	Y	Y	N	Y	Y
3 ***Gunderson***	Y	N	Y	N	Y	Y	Y
4 Kleczka	Y	Y	Y	Y	N	Y	N
5 Moody	Y	?	N	Y	N	Y	N
6 ***Petri***	N	Y	N	N	Y	Y	Y
7 Obey	Y	Y	Y	Y	N	Y	N
8 ***Roth***	N	Y	N	N	Y	Y	Y
9 ***Sensenbrenner***	N	N	N	N	Y	Y	Y
WYOMING							
AL ***Cheney***	X	N	N	?	Y	Y	Y

Southern states - Ala., Ark., Fla., Ga., Ky., La., Miss., N.C., Okla., S.C., Tenn., Texas, Va.

* The *Congressional Record* vote number is different from the CQ vote number because the *Record* includes quorum calls in its tally. CQ does not publish quorum call votes.

144. Procedural Motion. Bartlett, R-Texas, motion to approve the House *Journal* of Wednesday, June 11. Motion agreed to 268-118: R 55-109; D 213-9 (ND 142-7, SD 71-2), June 12, 1986.

145. HR 4515. Urgent Supplemental Appropriations, Fiscal 1986. Lightfoot, R-Iowa, motion to instruct the House conferees to accept the higher appropriation amount provided by the Senate for the Commodity Credit Corporation. Motion rejected 169-247: R 150-25; D 19-222 (ND 11-154, SD 8-68), June 12, 1986.

146. HR 1. Housing Act of 1986. Garcia, D-N.Y., amendment to the Gonzalez, D-Texas, substitute, to designate 100 enterprise zones to encourage development in blighted areas. The amendment provides for 33 of the enterprise zones to be located in rural areas. Adopted 366-32: R 169-0; D 197-32 (ND 129-26, SD 68-6), June 12, 1986. (The Gonzalez substitute, which contains the text of HR 4746, would authorize and revise federal housing programs for fiscal 1986 and 1987; it later was adopted by voice vote.)

147. HR 1. Housing Act of 1986. Wylie, R-Ohio, substitute for the Gonzalez, D-Texas, substitute *(see vote 146)*, to limit the housing authorization to $11.2 billion by eliminating several housing programs. Rejected 131-262: R 121-48; D 10-214 (ND 2-149, SD 8-65), June 12, 1986. (The Gonzalez substitute subsequently was adopted by voice vote.)

148. HR 1. Housing Act of 1986. Wylie, R-Ohio, motion to recommit the bill to the Banking, Finance and Urban Affairs Committee with instructions to report the bill back with amendments to freeze the fiscal 1987 housing authorization level at the fiscal 1986 appropriation level. Motion rejected 160-224: R 142-23; D 18-201 (ND 8-139, SD 10-62), June 12, 1986.

149. HR 1. Housing Act of 1986. Passage of the bill to reauthorize federal housing and community development programs for fiscal 1986 and 1987. Passed 340-36: R 128-35; D 212-1 (ND 143-1, SD 69-0), June 12, 1986.

KEY

- Y Voted for (yea).
- # Paired for.
- + Announced for.
- N Voted against (nay).
- X Paired against.
- \- Announced against.
- P Voted "present."
- C Voted "present" to avoid possible conflict of interest.
- ? Did not vote or otherwise make a position known.

Democrats *Republicans*

	144	145	146	147	148	149
ALABAMA						
1 ***Callahan***	Y	Y	Y	Y	Y	Y
2 ***Dickinson***	N	Y	Y	Y	Y	Y
3 Nichols	?	N	Y	Y	N	Y
4 Bevill	Y	N	Y	Y	Y	Y
5 Flippo	Y	N	Y	?	?	?
6 Erdreich	Y	N	Y	N	N	Y
7 Shelby	?	N	Y	N	N	Y
ALASKA						
AL ***Young***	N	Y	Y	?	?	?
ARIZONA						
1 ***McCain***	Y	Y	Y	Y	Y	Y
2 Udall	Y	N	Y	N	N	Y
3 ***Stump***	N	N	Y	Y	Y	?
4 ***Rudd***	Y	N	Y	Y	Y	N
5 ***Kolbe***	N	Y	Y	Y	Y	Y
ARKANSAS						
1 Alexander	Y	N	Y	N	N	Y
2 Robinson	Y	N	Y	N	N	Y
3 ***Hammerschmidt***	Y	N	Y	Y	Y	Y
4 Anthony	Y	N	?	N	N	Y
CALIFORNIA						
1 Bosco	Y	N	?	?	?	?
2 ***Chappie***	N	Y	Y	Y	Y	Y
3 Matsui	Y	N	N	N	N	Y
4 Fazio	Y	N	Y	N	N	Y
5 Burton	Y	N	Y	N	N	Y
6 Boxer	Y	N	N	?	?	?
7 Miller	Y	N	N	?	?	?
8 Dellums	Y	N	Y	N	N	Y
9 Stark	Y	N	?	?	?	?
10 Edwards	Y	N	Y	N	N	Y
11 Lantos	Y	N	Y	N	N	Y
12 ***Zschau***	N	Y	?	Y	Y	Y
13 Mineta	Y	N	?	N	N	Y
14 ***Shumway***	Y	Y	Y	Y	Y	N
15 Coelho	Y	N	?	N	N	Y
16 Panetta	Y	N	N	N	N	Y
17 ***Pashayan***	N	Y	Y	Y	Y	Y
18 Lehman	Y	N	Y	?	?	?
19 ***Lagomarsino***	N	Y	Y	Y	Y	Y
20 ***Thomas***	?	Y	Y	Y	#	?
21 ***Fiedler***	N	Y	Y	Y	Y	?
22 ***Moorhead***	N	Y	Y	Y	Y	N
23 Beilenson	?	N	N	N	N	Y
24 Waxman	Y	N	Y	N	N	Y
25 Roybal	Y	N	Y	N	?	?
26 Berman	Y	N	Y	N	N	Y
27 Levine	Y	N	Y	N	N	Y
28 Dixon	?	N	Y	N	N	Y
29 Hawkins	N	N	Y	N	N	Y
30 Martinez	Y	N	N	N	N	Y
31 Dymally	Y	N	Y	N	N	Y
32 Anderson	Y	N	Y	N	N	Y
33 ***Dreier***	N	Y	Y	Y	Y	N
34 Torres	+	N	Y	N	N	Y
35 ***Lewis***	N	Y	Y	#	#	?
36 Brown	Y	N	Y	N	N	Y
37 ***McCandless***	N	Y	Y	Y	Y	N
38 ***Dornan***	?	Y	Y	Y	Y	Y
39 ***Dannemeyer***	N	Y	Y	Y	Y	N
40 ***Badham***	N	Y	Y	?	?	?
41 ***Lowery***	?	?	?	?	#	?
42 ***Lungren***	N	Y	Y	Y	Y	N
43 ***Packard***	Y	Y	Y	Y	Y	Y
44 Bates	Y	N	Y	N	N	Y
45 ***Hunter***	N	Y	Y	Y	Y	Y
COLORADO						
1 Schroeder	?	N	Y	N	-	+
2 Wirth	Y	Y	Y	?	?	?
3 ***Strang***	N	Y	Y	Y	Y	Y
4 ***Brown***	N	N	Y	Y	Y	N
5 ***Kramer***	N	Y	Y	Y	Y	Y
6 ***Schaefer***	N	Y	Y	Y	Y	Y
CONNECTICUT						
1 Kennelly	Y	N	Y	N	?	?
2 Gejdenson	Y	N	Y	N	N	Y
3 Morrison	Y	N	N	N	N	Y
4 ***McKinney***	Y	Y	Y	N	N	Y
5 ***Rowland***	N	Y	Y	N	Y	Y
6 ***Johnson***	Y	Y	Y	N	N	Y
DELAWARE						
AL Carper	Y	N	Y	N	N	Y
FLORIDA						
1 Hutto	Y	N	Y	Y	Y	Y
2 Fuqua	Y	N	Y	N	N	Y
3 Bennett	Y	N	N	N	Y	Y
4 Chappell	Y	N	Y	N	N	Y
5 ***McCollum***	Y	Y	Y	Y	Y	N
6 MacKay	Y	N	Y	N	N	Y
7 Gibbons	Y	N	N	N	Y	Y
8 ***Young***	N	N	Y	Y	Y	Y
9 ***Bilirakis***	N	Y	Y	N	Y	Y
10 ***Ireland***	N	Y	Y	Y	Y	N
11 Nelson	Y	N	Y	N	Y	Y
12 ***Lewis***	N	Y	Y	N	Y	Y
13 ***Mack***	N	Y	Y	Y	Y	Y
14 Mica	Y	N	Y	N	N	Y
15 ***Shaw***	?	Y	Y	Y	Y	Y
16 Smith	Y	N	Y	N	N	Y
17 Lehman	Y	N	Y	N	N	+
18 Pepper	Y	N	Y	N	N	Y
19 Fascell	Y	N	Y	N	N	Y
GEORGIA						
1 Thomas	Y	N	Y	N	N	Y
2 Hatcher	Y	N	Y	N	N	?
3 Ray	Y	N	Y	N	Y	Y
4 ***Swindall***	N	Y	Y	Y	Y	Y
5 Fowler	?	?	?	?	?	?
6 ***Gingrich***	N	Y	Y	Y	Y	Y
7 Darden	Y	N	Y	Y	Y	Y
8 Rowland	Y	N	Y	N	N	Y
9 Jenkins	Y	N	N	Y	N	Y
10 Barnard	Y	N	Y	Y	N	Y
HAWAII						
1 Heftel	Y	N	Y	N	N	Y
2 Akaka	Y	N	Y	N	N	Y
IDAHO						
1 ***Craig***	N	Y	Y	Y	Y	N
2 Stallings	Y	Y	Y	N	Y	Y
ILLINOIS						
1 Hayes	Y	N	N	N	N	Y
2 Savage	Y	N	N	N	N	Y
3 Russo	Y	N	N	N	N	Y
4 ***O'Brien***	?	?	?	?	#	?
5 Lipinski	P	N	Y	N	N	Y
6 ***Hyde***	N	Y	Y	Y	Y	N
7 Collins	Y	N	Y	N	N	Y
8 Rostenkowski	Y	N	N	N	N	Y
9 Yates	Y	N	N	N	N	Y
10 ***Porter***	Y	Y	Y	Y	Y	Y
11 Annunzio	Y	N	Y	N	N	Y
12 ***Crane***	N	N	Y	Y	Y	N
13 ***Fawell***	N	N	Y	Y	Y	N
14 ***Grotberg***	?	?	?	?	?	?
15 ***Madigan***	N	Y	Y	N	Y	Y
16 ***Martin***	N	Y	Y	Y	Y	N
17 Evans	Y	N	N	N	N	?
18 ***Michel***	?	Y	Y	Y	Y	N
19 Bruce	Y	N	Y	N	N	Y
20 Durbin	Y	N	Y	N	N	Y
21 Price	Y	N	Y	N	N	Y
22 Gray	?	Y	Y	N	N	Y
INDIANA						
1 Visclosky	Y	N	Y	N	N	Y
2 Sharp	Y	N	?	N	N	Y
3 ***Hiler***	N	Y	Y	Y	Y	Y
4 ***Coats***	N	Y	Y	Y	Y	Y
5 ***Hillis***	Y	Y	Y	?	?	?

ND - Northern Democrats SD - Southern Democrats

	144	145	146	147	148	149
6 ***Burton***	N	Y	Y	Y	Y	Y
7 ***Myers***	Y	N	Y	Y	Y	Y
8 McCloskey	Y	N	Y	N	N	Y
9 Hamilton	Y	N	Y	N	Y	Y
10 Jacobs	N	N	Y	N	N	Y
IOWA						
1 ***Leach***	N	Y	Y	Y	Y	Y
2 ***Tauke***	N	Y	Y	Y	Y	Y
3 ***Evans***	N	Y	?	Y	Y	Y
4 Smith	Y	N	Y	N	N	Y
5 ***Lightfoot***	N	Y	Y	Y	Y	Y
6 Bedell	Y	N	Y	N	Y	Y
KANSAS						
1 ***Roberts***	N	Y	Y	Y	Y	N
2 Slattery	Y	Y	Y	N	N	Y
3 ***Meyers***	N	Y	Y	Y	Y	Y
4 Glickman	Y	Y	Y	N	N	Y
5 ***Whittaker***	N	Y	Y	Y	Y	N
KENTUCKY						
1 Hubbard	Y	Y	Y	?	?	?
2 Natcher	Y	N	Y	N	N	Y
3 Mazzoli	Y	N	Y	N	N	Y
4 ***Snyder***	Y	N	Y	Y	Y	Y
5 ***Rogers***	N	N	Y	N	Y	Y
6 ***Hopkins***	Y	Y	Y	Y	Y	Y
7 Perkins	Y	N	Y	N	N	Y
LOUISIANA						
1 ***Livingston***	Y	Y	Y	Y	Y	Y
2 Boggs	Y	N	Y	N	N	+
3 Tauzin	Y	Y	Y	N	N	Y
4 Roemer	N	Y	Y	N	N	Y
5 Huckaby	Y	Y	Y	N	N	Y
6 ***Moore***	?	#	?	?	?	?
7 Breaux	?	?	?	?	X	?
8 Long	Y	Y	Y	N	?	?
MAINE						
1 ***McKernan***	N	Y	Y	N	Y	Y
2 ***Snowe***	N	Y	Y	N	Y	Y
MARYLAND						
1 Dyson	N	N	Y	N	N	Y
2 ***Bentley***	N	Y	Y	Y	N	Y
3 Mikulski	Y	N	Y	N	N	Y
4 ***Holt***	Y	N	Y	Y	Y	Y
5 Hoyer	?	N	Y	N	N	Y
6 Byron	Y	N	Y	N	Y	Y
7 Mitchell	?	?	N	N	N	Y
8 Barnes	Y	N	Y	N	N	Y
MASSACHUSETTS						
1 ***Conte***	N	Y	Y	N	N	Y
2 Boland	Y	N	Y	N	?	?
3 Early	Y	N	Y	?	?	?
4 Frank	Y	N	Y	N	N	Y
5 Atkins	Y	N	Y	N	N	Y
6 Mavroules	?	N	Y	N	N	Y
7 Markey	Y	N	?	N	N	Y
8 O'Neill						
9 Moakley	Y	N	Y	X	X	?
10 Studds	Y	N	Y	N	N	Y
11 Donnelly	Y	N	Y	N	?	Y
MICHIGAN						
1 Conyers	Y	N	N	N	N	Y
2 ***Pursell***	Y	Y	Y	Y	Y	Y
3 Wolpe	Y	Y	Y	N	N	Y
4 ***Siljander***	N	Y	Y	Y	Y	Y
5 ***Henry***	N	Y	Y	Y	Y	Y
6 Carr	P	Y	Y	Y	Y	Y
7 Kildee	Y	N	N	N	N	Y
8 Traxler	?	N	Y	N	N	?
9 ***Vander Jagt***	N	Y	Y	Y	Y	Y
10 ***Schuette***	N	Y	Y	N	N	Y
11 ***Davis***	?	?	?	?	?	?
12 Bonior	?	N	N	N	N	Y
13 Crockett	Y	N	N	N	N	Y
14 Hertel	Y	N	N	N	N	Y
15 Ford	Y	N	N	N	N	Y
16 Dingell	Y	N	N	N	N	Y
17 Levin	Y	N	Y	N	N	Y
18 ***Broomfield***	Y	N	Y	Y	Y	Y
MINNESOTA						
1 Penny	N	N	Y	Y	Y	Y
2 ***Weber***	N	Y	Y	Y	Y	Y
3 ***Frenzel***	N	Y	?	Y	Y	N
4 Vento	Y	N	Y	N	N	Y
5 Sabo	Y	N	Y	N	N	?
6 Sikorski	N	N	Y	N	N	Y
7 ***Stangeland***	N	Y	Y	N	N	Y
8 Oberstar	Y	N	N	N	N	Y
MISSISSIPPI						
1 Whitten	Y	N	?	N	N	Y
2 ***Franklin***	Y	Y	Y	N	Y	Y
3 Montgomery	Y	N	Y	Y	Y	Y
4 Dowdy	Y	N	Y	?	?	?
5 ***Lott***	Y	Y	Y	Y	Y	Y
MISSOURI						
1 Clay	N	N	Y	N	N	Y
2 Young	Y	N	Y	?	X	?
3 Gephardt	?	?	?	?	?	?
4 Skelton	Y	Y	Y	?	N	Y
5 Wheat	Y	N	Y	N	N	Y
6 ***Coleman***	N	Y	Y	N	Y	Y
7 ***Taylor***	Y	Y	Y	Y	Y	Y
8 ***Emerson***	N	Y	Y	N	Y	Y
9 Volkmer	Y	Y	Y	N	N	Y
MONTANA						
1 Williams	Y	N	Y	N	N	Y
2 ***Marlenee***	?	Y	Y	?	?	?
NEBRASKA						
1 ***Bereuter***	N	Y	Y	Y	Y	Y
2 ***Daub***	N	Y	Y	Y	Y	Y
3 ***Smith***	Y	Y	Y	Y	#	?
NEVADA						
1 Reid	Y	N	Y	N	N	Y
2 ***Vucanovich***	N	N	Y	Y	Y	N
NEW HAMPSHIRE						
1 ***Smith***	N	N	Y	Y	Y	N
2 ***Gregg***	N	N	Y	Y	Y	N
NEW JERSEY						
1 Florio	Y	N	Y	N	N	Y
2 Hughes	Y	N	Y	N	Y	Y
3 Howard	Y	N	Y	N	N	Y
4 ***Smith***	Y	N	Y	N	N	Y
5 ***Roukema***	N	Y	Y	Y	Y	Y
6 Dwyer	Y	N	Y	N	N	Y
7 ***Rinaldo***	Y	N	Y	N	N	Y
8 Roe	Y	N	Y	N	N	Y
9 Torricelli	Y	N	Y	N	N	Y
10 Rodino	?	?	?	N	N	Y
11 ***Gallo***	N	Y	Y	N	N	Y
12 ***Courter***	N	Y	Y	N	N	Y
13 ***Saxton***	N	Y	Y	N	N	Y
14 Guarini	?	N	Y	N	N	Y
NEW MEXICO						
1 ***Lujan***	Y	Y	Y	Y	Y	Y
2 ***Skeen***	N	Y	Y	Y	Y	Y
3 Richardson	Y	N	Y	N	N	Y
NEW YORK						
1 ***Carney***	N	N	Y	?	Y	Y
2 Downey	Y	N	Y	N	N	Y
3 Mrazek	Y	N	Y	N	N	Y
4 ***Lent***	N	N	Y	N	Y	Y
5 ***McGrath***	N	N	Y	N	Y	Y
6 Vacancy						
7 Ackerman	Y	N	Y	N	N	Y
8 Scheuer	Y	N	Y	N	N	Y
9 Manton	Y	N	Y	N	N	Y
10 Schumer	Y	N	Y	N	N	Y
11 Towns	?	N	Y	N	N	Y
12 Owens	Y	N	Y	N	N	Y
13 Solarz	Y	N	?	N	N	Y
14 ***Molinari***	N	Y	Y	N	N	Y
15 ***Green***	Y	N	Y	N	N	Y
16 Rangel	Y	N	Y	N	N	Y
17 Weiss	Y	N	Y	N	N	Y
18 Garcia	Y	N	Y	N	N	Y
19 Biaggi	Y	N	Y	N	N	Y
20 ***DioGuardi***	N	Y	Y	N	N	Y
21 ***Fish***	Y	Y	Y	N	?	Y
22 ***Gilman***	Y	Y	Y	N	N	Y
23 Stratton	Y	N	Y	N	N	Y
24 ***Solomon***	N	Y	Y	Y	Y	Y
25 ***Boehlert***	N	Y	Y	N	N	Y
26 ***Martin***	Y	Y	Y	N	X	?
27 ***Wortley***	Y	Y	Y	N	Y	Y
28 McHugh	Y	N	N	N	N	Y
29 ***Horton***	Y	Y	Y	N	N	Y
30 ***Eckert***	Y	Y	Y	Y	Y	Y
31 ***Kemp***	Y	Y	Y	Y	N	Y
32 LaFalce	Y	N	N	N	N	Y
33 Nowak	Y	N	Y	?	?	?
34 Lundine	Y	N	Y	?	?	?
NORTH CAROLINA						
1 Jones	?	N	Y	N	N	Y
2 Valentine	Y	N	Y	N	N	Y
3 Whitley	Y	N	Y	N	N	Y
4 ***Cobey***	N	Y	Y	Y	Y	Y
5 Neal	Y	N	Y	N	N	Y
6 ***Coble***	N	Y	Y	Y	Y	Y
7 Rose	Y	N	Y	N	N	Y
8 Hefner	Y	N	Y	N	N	Y
9 ***McMillan***	Y	Y	Y	N	Y	Y
10 ***Broyhill***	?	Y	Y	Y	Y	Y
11 ***Hendon***	N	Y	Y	N	Y	Y
NORTH DAKOTA						
AL Dorgan	Y	N	Y	N	N	Y
OHIO						
1 Luken	Y	N	?	?	?	?
2 ***Gradison***	Y	Y	Y	Y	Y	Y
3 Hall	Y	N	Y	N	N	N
4 ***Oxley***	N	Y	Y	Y	Y	N
5 ***Latta***	N	Y	?	Y	Y	Y
6 ***McEwen***	Y	Y	Y	Y	Y	Y
7 ***DeWine***	N	Y	Y	Y	Y	Y
8 ***Kindness***	N	Y	Y	Y	Y	Y
9 Kaptur	Y	N	Y	N	N	Y
10 ***Miller***	N	Y	Y	Y	Y	Y
11 Eckart	Y	N	Y	N	N	Y
12 ***Kasich***	Y	Y	Y	Y	Y	Y
13 Pease	Y	N	N	N	N	Y
14 Seiberling	Y	N	Y	N	N	Y
15 ***Wylie***	Y	Y	Y	Y	Y	N
16 ***Regula***	Y	Y	Y	N	Y	Y
17 Traficant	Y	N	Y	N	N	Y
18 Applegate	Y	Y	Y	N	N	Y
19 Feighan	Y	N	Y	N	N	Y
20 Oakar	Y	N	Y	N	N	Y
21 Stokes	Y	N	Y	N	N	Y
OKLAHOMA						
1 Jones	Y	Y	Y	?	?	?
2 Synar	Y	N	Y	N	N	Y
3 Watkins	Y	N	Y	N	N	Y
4 McCurdy	Y	N	Y	N	N	Y
5 ***Edwards***	N	Y	?	Y	Y	N
6 English	Y	Y	Y	N	N	Y
OREGON						
1 AuCoin	?	N	Y	N	N	Y
2 ***Smith, R.***	N	Y	Y	Y	Y	Y
3 Wyden	Y	N	Y	N	N	Y
4 Weaver	Y	N	Y	N	N	Y
5 ***Smith, D.***	N	Y	Y	Y	Y	N
PENNSYLVANIA						
1 Foglietta	?	X	?	X	X	?
2 Gray	Y	N	Y	N	N	Y
3 Borski	Y	N	Y	N	N	Y
4 Kolter	Y	N	Y	N	N	Y
5 ***Schulze***	Y	Y	Y	N	Y	Y
6 Yatron	Y	N	Y	N	N	Y
7 Edgar	Y	N	Y	N	N	Y
8 Kostmayer	Y	N	Y	N	N	Y
9 ***Shuster***	N	Y	Y	Y	Y	N
10 ***McDade***	?	Y	Y	N	N	Y
11 Kanjorski	Y	N	Y	N	N	Y
12 Murtha	Y	N	Y	N	N	Y
13 ***Coughlin***	N	N	Y	N	Y	Y
14 Coyne	Y	N	Y	N	N	Y
15 ***Ritter***	Y	Y	Y	N	Y	Y
16 ***Walker***	N	Y	Y	Y	Y	Y
17 ***Gekas***	N	N	Y	N	N	Y
18 Walgren	Y	N	?	?	?	?
19 ***Goodling***	Y	Y	Y	Y	Y	Y
20 Gaydos	Y	N	Y	N	N	Y
21 ***Ridge***	N	Y	Y	N	N	Y
22 Murphy	Y	N	Y	N	N	Y
23 ***Clinger***	N	Y	Y	N	N	+
RHODE ISLAND						
1 St Germain	Y	N	Y	N	N	Y
2 ***Schneider***	Y	Y	Y	N	N	Y
SOUTH CAROLINA						
1 ***Hartnett***	?	#	?	#	#	?
2 ***Spence***	Y	Y	Y	Y	Y	Y
3 Derrick	Y	N	Y	N	N	Y
4 ***Campbell***	?	Y	Y	Y	Y	Y
5 Spratt	?	?	?	?	?	?
6 Tallon	Y	N	Y	N	N	Y
SOUTH DAKOTA						
AL Daschle	Y	Y	Y	N	Y	Y
TENNESSEE						
1 ***Quillen***	Y	Y	Y	Y	Y	Y
2 ***Duncan***	Y	Y	Y	N	Y	Y
3 Lloyd	N	N	Y	N	N	Y
4 Cooper	Y	N	Y	N	N	Y
5 Boner	Y	N	?	?	X	?
6 Gordon	Y	N	Y	N	N	Y
7 ***Sundquist***	?	Y	Y	Y	Y	Y
8 Jones	Y	N	Y	N	N	Y
9 Ford	?	X	?	?	X	?
TEXAS						
1 Chapman	Y	N	Y	N	N	Y
2 Wilson	?	?	Y	N	N	Y
3 ***Bartlett***	Y	Y	Y	Y	Y	Y
4 Hall, R.	Y	Y	Y	N	N	Y
5 Bryant	Y	N	Y	N	N	Y
6 ***Barton***	N	Y	Y	Y	Y	Y
7 ***Archer***	Y	N	Y	Y	Y	N
8 ***Fields***	N	Y	Y	Y	Y	N
9 Brooks	Y	N	Y	N	N	Y
10 Pickle	Y	N	N	N	N	Y
11 Leath	Y	N	N	N	N	Y
12 Wright	?	N	Y	N	N	Y
13 ***Boulter***	N	Y	Y	Y	Y	N
14 ***Sweeney***	Y	Y	Y	Y	Y	Y
15 de la Garza	Y	N	Y	N	N	Y
16 Coleman	Y	?	Y	N	N	Y
17 Stenholm	Y	N	Y	N	N	Y
18 Leland	Y	N	+	N	N	Y
19 ***Combest***	Y	Y	Y	Y	Y	Y
20 Gonzalez	Y	N	Y	N	N	Y
21 ***Loeffler***	N	Y	Y	Y	Y	Y
22 ***DeLay***	N	Y	Y	Y	Y	N
23 Bustamante	Y	N	Y	N	N	Y
24 Frost	Y	N	Y	N	N	Y
25 Andrews	Y	N	Y	N	N	Y
26 ***Armey***	N	Y	Y	Y	Y	Y
27 Ortiz	Y	N	Y	N	N	Y
UTAH						
1 ***Hansen***	Y	Y	Y	Y	Y	N
2 ***Monson***	N	Y	Y	Y	#	?
3 ***Nielson***	N	Y	Y	Y	Y	N
VERMONT						
AL ***Jeffords***	Y	Y	Y	N	Y	Y
VIRGINIA						
1 ***Bateman***	Y	N	Y	N	Y	Y
2 ***Whitehurst***	?	Y	Y	N	Y	Y
3 ***Bliley***	N	Y	Y	Y	Y	Y
4 Sisisky	Y	N	Y	N	N	Y
5 Daniel	Y	N	Y	Y	Y	Y
6 Olin	Y	N	N	N	Y	Y
7 ***Slaughter***	N	Y	Y	Y	Y	Y
8 ***Parris***	N	Y	?	Y	Y	Y
9 Boucher	Y	N	Y	N	N	Y
10 ***Wolf***	N	Y	Y	Y	Y	Y
WASHINGTON						
1 ***Miller***	Y	Y	Y	Y	Y	Y
2 Swift	Y	N	Y	N	N	Y
3 Bonker	Y	N	Y	N	N	Y
4 ***Morrison***	Y	Y	Y	N	Y	Y
5 Foley	Y	N	Y	N	N	Y
6 Dicks	?	N	Y	N	N	Y
7 Lowry	N	N	N	N	N	Y
8 ***Chandler***	?	?	?	?	?	?
WEST VIRGINIA						
1 Mollohan	Y	N	?	?	?	?
2 Staggers	Y	N	Y	N	N	Y
3 Wise	Y	N	Y	N	N	Y
4 Rahall	Y	N	Y	N	N	Y
WISCONSIN						
1 Aspin	?	N	Y	N	N	?
2 Kastenmeier	Y	N	Y	N	N	Y
3 ***Gunderson***	N	Y	Y	Y	Y	Y
4 Kleczka	Y	N	Y	N	N	Y
5 Moody	Y	N	?	?	?	?
6 ***Petri***	?	Y	Y	Y	Y	Y
7 Obey	Y	N	Y	N	N	Y
8 ***Roth***	N	Y	Y	N	Y	Y
9 ***Sensenbrenner***	N	Y	Y	Y	Y	N
WYOMING						
AL ***Cheney***	N	Y	Y	Y	Y	N

Southern states - Ala., Ark., Fla., Ga., Ky., La., Miss., N.C., Okla., S.C., Tenn., Texas, Va.

* The *Congressional Record* vote number is different from the CQ vote number because the *Record* includes quorum calls in its tally. CQ does not publish quorum call votes.

150. HR 4841. Vocational Education Act. Perkins, D-Ky., motion to suspend the rules and pass the bill to revise the formulas for allocating aid to states under the Vocational Education Act. Motion agreed to 402-1: R 171-0; D 231-1 (ND 157-1, SD 74-0), June 17, 1986. A two-thirds majority of those present and voting (269 in this case) is required for passage under suspension of the rules.

151. HR 2798. Veterans' Employment Rights. Montgomery, D-Miss., motion to suspend the rules and pass the bill to prohibit hiring discrimination against a member of the National Guard or the reserves. Motion agreed to 409-0: R 170-0; D 239-0 (ND 164-0, SD 75-0), June 17, 1986. A two-thirds majority of those present and voting (273 in this case) is required for passage under suspension of the rules.

152. HR 4384. Veterans' Readjustment Appointment Authority. Montgomery, D-Miss., motion to suspend the rules and pass the bill to extend the "veterans' readjustment appointment" program allowing federal agencies to hire Vietnam War-era veterans without requiring them to compete on civil service exams. Motion agreed to 413-0: R 173-0; D 240-0 (ND 164-0, SD 76-0), June 17, 1986. A two-thirds majority of those present and voting (276 in this case) is required for passage under suspension of the rules.

153. HR 4259. Gettysburg National Military Park. Vento, D-Minn., motion to suspend the rules and pass the bill to authorize the secretary of the interior to accept on behalf of the United States the donation by the Gettysburg Battlefield Preservation Association of approximately 31 acres of land, known as the Taney Farm, as part of the Gettysburg National Military Park in Pennsylvania. Motion rejected 264-146: R 45-127; D 219-19 (ND 153-9, SD 66-10), June 17, 1986. A two-thirds majority of those present and voting (274 in this case) is required for passage under suspension of the rules.

154. HR 4116. VISTA Reauthorization. Tauke, R-Iowa, amendment to reduce fiscal 1987 authorization levels for programs in the bill to the fiscal 1986 appropriations level. Rejected 189-221: R 156-15; D 33-206 (ND 10-154, SD 23-52), June 17, 1986. A "yea" was a vote supporting the president's position.

155. HR 4116. VISTA Reauthorization. Martin, R-Ill., amendment to freeze the VISTA service year funding floor at 2,400 for fiscal 1987-89. The funding floor mandates the number of hours for which funding must be made available to VISTA before money can be spent on other programs contained in the same title of the bill. Rejected 204-208: R 171-2; D 33-206 (ND 10-152, SD 23-54), June 17, 1986. A "yea" was a vote supporting the president's position.

156. HR 4116. VISTA Reauthorization. Passage of the bill to reauthorize for three years programs under the Domestic Volunteer Services Act, including Volunteers in Service to America (VISTA), and Older American volunteer programs. The legislation authorizes a total of $561.3 million for the programs. Passed 360-52: R 123-49; D 237-3 (ND 164-0, SD 73-3), June 17, 1986. A "nay" was a vote supporting the president's position.

157. HR 4175. Maritime Authorizations, Fiscal 1987. Adoption of the rule (H Res 473) to provide for House floor consideration of the bill to authorize $400.1 million in fiscal 1987 appropriations for maritime programs, including $388.2 million for the Maritime Administration and $11.9 million for the Federal Maritime Commission. Adopted 393-5: R 164-5; D 229-0 (ND 154-0, SD 75-0), June 17, 1986.

KEY

Y Voted for (yea).
\# Paired for.
\+ Announced for.
N Voted against (nay).
X Paired against.
\- Announced against.
P Voted "present."
C Voted "present" to avoid possible conflict of interest.
? Did not vote or otherwise make a position known.

Democrats *Republicans*

	150	151	152	153	154	155	156	157
ALABAMA								
1 *Callahan*	Y	Y	Y	N	Y	Y	Y	Y
2 *Dickinson*	Y	Y	Y	N	Y	Y	Y	Y
3 Nichols	Y	Y	Y	N	N	Y	Y	Y
4 Bevill	Y	Y	Y	Y	N	N	Y	Y
5 Flippo	Y	Y	Y	Y	N	N	Y	Y
6 Erdreich	Y	Y	Y	Y	N	N	Y	Y
7 Shelby	Y	Y	Y	N	N	N	Y	Y
ALASKA								
AL *Young*	Y	Y	Y	N	N	Y	Y	Y
ARIZONA								
1 *McCain*	Y	Y	Y	Y	Y	Y	Y	Y
2 Udall	Y	Y	Y	N	N	N	Y	Y
3 *Stump*	Y	Y	Y	N	Y	Y	N	Y
4 *Rudd*	Y	Y	Y	N	Y	Y	N	Y
5 *Kolbe*	Y	Y	Y	Y	Y	Y	N	Y
ARKANSAS								
1 Alexander	Y	Y	Y	Y	N	N	Y	Y
2 Robinson	Y	Y	Y	Y	N	N	Y	Y
3 *Hammerschmidt*	Y	Y	Y	N	Y	Y	Y	Y
4 Anthony	Y	?	Y	Y	N	N	Y	Y
CALIFORNIA								
1 Bosco	?	Y	Y	?	N	?	Y	Y
2 *Chappie*	Y	Y	Y	N	Y	Y	N	Y
3 Matsui	?	?	Y	Y	N	N	Y	Y
4 Fazio	Y	Y	Y	Y	N	N	Y	Y
5 Burton	Y	Y	Y	Y	N	N	Y	Y
6 Boxer	Y	Y	Y	Y	N	N	Y	Y
7 Miller	Y	Y	Y	Y	N	N	Y	Y
8 Dellums	Y	Y	Y	Y	N	N	Y	Y
9 Stark	Y	Y	Y	Y	N	N	Y	Y
10 Edwards	Y	Y	Y	Y	N	N	Y	Y
11 Lantos	Y	Y	Y	Y	N	N	Y	Y
12 *Zschau*	Y	Y	Y	Y	Y	Y	Y	Y
13 Mineta	Y	Y	Y	Y	N	N	Y	Y
14 *Shumway*	Y	Y	Y	N	Y	Y	N	Y
15 Coelho	Y	Y	Y	Y	?	N	Y	Y
16 Panetta	Y	Y	Y	Y	N	N	Y	Y
17 *Pashayan*	Y	Y	Y	N	Y	Y	Y	Y
18 Lehman	Y	Y	Y	Y	N	N	Y	Y
19 *Lagomarsino*	Y	Y	Y	Y	Y	Y	Y	Y
20 *Thomas*	Y	Y	Y	N	Y	Y	Y	Y
21 *Fiedler*	Y	Y	Y	N	Y	Y	Y	Y
22 *Moorhead*	Y	Y	Y	N	Y	Y	Y	Y
23 Beilenson	Y	Y	Y	Y	N	N	Y	Y
24 Waxman	Y	Y	Y	Y	N	N	Y	Y
25 Roybal	Y	Y	Y	Y	N	N	Y	Y
26 Berman	Y	Y	Y	Y	N	N	Y	?
27 Levine	Y	Y	Y	Y	N	N	Y	Y
28 Dixon	Y	Y	Y	Y	N	N	Y	Y
29 Hawkins	Y	Y	Y	N	N	N	Y	Y
30 Martinez	Y	Y	Y	Y	N	N	Y	Y
31 Dymally	?	?	?	?	N	N	Y	Y
32 Anderson	Y	Y	Y	Y	N	N	Y	Y
33 *Dreier*	Y	Y	Y	N	Y	Y	N	Y
34 Torres	Y	Y	Y	Y	N	N	Y	Y
35 *Lewis*	Y	Y	Y	N	Y	Y	N	Y
36 Brown	Y	Y	Y	Y	N	N	Y	?
37 *McCandless*	Y	Y	Y	N	Y	Y	Y	Y
38 *Dornan*	Y	?	Y	N	Y	Y	N	Y
39 *Dannemeyer*	Y	Y	Y	N	Y	Y	N	Y
40 *Badham*	Y	Y	Y	N	Y	Y	N	Y
41 *Lowery*	Y	Y	Y	Y	Y	Y	Y	Y
42 *Lungren*	Y	Y	Y	N	Y	Y	N	Y
43 *Packard*	Y	Y	Y	N	Y	Y	N	Y
44 Bates	Y	Y	Y	Y	N	N	Y	Y
45 *Hunter*	Y	Y	Y	N	Y	Y	N	Y
COLORADO								
1 Schroeder	Y	Y	Y	Y	N	N	Y	Y
2 Wirth	Y	Y	Y	Y	N	N	Y	Y
3 *Strang*	Y	Y	Y	Y	Y	Y	N	Y
4 *Brown*	Y	Y	Y	N	Y	Y	N	Y
5 *Kramer*	Y	Y	Y	N	Y	Y	Y	Y
6 *Schaefer*	Y	Y	Y	N	Y	Y	N	Y
CONNECTICUT								
1 Kennelly	Y	Y	Y	Y	N	N	Y	Y
2 Gejdenson	Y	Y	Y	Y	N	N	Y	Y
3 Morrison	Y	Y	Y	Y	N	N	Y	Y
4 *McKinney*	Y	Y	Y	N	Y	Y	Y	Y
5 *Rowland*	Y	Y	Y	N	Y	Y	Y	Y
6 *Johnson*	Y	Y	Y	N	Y	Y	Y	Y
DELAWARE								
AL Carper	Y	Y	Y	Y	Y	Y	Y	Y
FLORIDA								
1 Hutto	Y	Y	Y	Y	N	Y	Y	Y
2 Fuqua	?	?	?	?	?	?	?	?
3 Bennett	Y	Y	Y	Y	N	Y	Y	Y
4 Chappell	Y	Y	Y	N	N	Y	Y	Y
5 *McCollum*	Y	Y	Y	N	Y	Y	Y	Y
6 MacKay	Y	Y	Y	Y	N	N	Y	Y
7 Gibbons	Y	Y	Y	Y	Y	N	Y	Y
8 *Young*	Y	Y	Y	N	Y	Y	Y	Y
9 *Bilirakis*	Y	Y	Y	Y	Y	Y	Y	Y
10 *Ireland*	Y	Y	Y	N	Y	Y	Y	Y
11 Nelson	Y	Y	Y	Y	N	Y	Y	Y
12 *Lewis*	Y	Y	Y	N	Y	Y	Y	Y
13 *Mack*	Y	Y	Y	N	Y	Y	?	Y
14 Mica	Y	Y	Y	Y	N	N	Y	Y
15 *Shaw*	Y	Y	Y	N	Y	Y	Y	Y
16 Smith	Y	Y	Y	Y	Y	N	Y	Y
17 Lehman	Y	Y	Y	Y	N	N	Y	Y
18 Pepper	Y	Y	Y	Y	N	N	Y	Y
19 Fascell	?	Y	Y	Y	N	N	Y	Y
GEORGIA								
1 Thomas	Y	Y	Y	Y	Y	Y	Y	Y
2 Hatcher	Y	Y	Y	Y	N	N	Y	Y
3 Ray	Y	Y	Y	Y	Y	Y	N	Y
4 *Swindall*	Y	Y	Y	N	Y	Y	N	Y
5 Fowler	?	?	?	?	?	?	?	Y
6 *Gingrich*	?	?	?	?	Y	Y	Y	Y
7 Darden	Y	Y	Y	Y	Y	Y	Y	Y
8 Rowland	Y	Y	Y	Y	Y	Y	Y	Y
9 Jenkins	Y	Y	Y	Y	Y	N	Y	Y
10 Barnard	Y	Y	Y	Y	Y	Y	N	Y
HAWAII								
1 Heftel	Y	Y	Y	Y	N	N	Y	Y
2 Akaka	Y	Y	Y	Y	N	N	Y	Y
IDAHO								
1 *Craig*	Y	Y	Y	N	Y	Y	N	Y
2 Stallings	Y	Y	Y	Y	Y	Y	Y	Y
ILLINOIS								
1 Hayes	Y	Y	Y	N	N	N	Y	Y
2 Savage	Y	Y	Y	Y	N	N	Y	Y
3 Russo	Y	Y	Y	Y	N	N	Y	Y
4 *O'Brien*	?	?	?	?	?	?	?	?
5 Lipinski	Y	Y	Y	Y	N	N	Y	Y
6 *Hyde*	Y	Y	Y	N	Y	Y	Y	Y
7 Collins	Y	Y	Y	Y	N	N	Y	Y
8 Rostenkowski	Y	Y	Y	Y	N	N	Y	Y
9 Yates	Y	Y	Y	Y	N	N	Y	Y
10 *Porter*	Y	Y	Y	Y	Y	Y	Y	Y
11 Annunzio	Y	Y	Y	Y	N	N	Y	Y
12 *Crane*	Y	Y	Y	N	Y	Y	N	N
13 *Fawell*	Y	Y	Y	N	Y	Y	Y	Y
14 *Grotberg*	?	?	?	?	?	?	?	?
15 *Madigan*	Y	Y	Y	Y	Y	Y	Y	Y
16 *Martin*	Y	Y	Y	N	Y	Y	N	Y
17 Evans	Y	Y	Y	Y	N	N	Y	Y
18 *Michel*	Y	Y	Y	?	Y	Y	N	Y
19 Bruce	Y	Y	Y	Y	N	N	Y	Y
20 Durbin	Y	Y	Y	Y	N	N	Y	Y
21 Price	Y	Y	Y	Y	N	N	Y	Y
22 Gray	Y	Y	Y	Y	N	N	Y	Y
INDIANA								
1 Visclosky	Y	Y	Y	Y	N	N	Y	Y
2 Sharp	Y	Y	Y	Y	Y	Y	Y	Y
3 *Hiler*	Y	Y	Y	Y	Y	Y	Y	Y
4 *Coats*	Y	Y	Y	N	Y	Y	Y	?
5 *Hillis*	?	?	?	?	?	?	?	?

ND - Northern Democrats SD - Southern Democrats

* Corresponding to Congressional Record Votes 168, 169, 170, 171, 172, 173, 174, 175

	150	151	152	153	154	155	156	157
6 ***Burton***	Y	Y	Y	N	Y	Y	N	Y
7 ***Myers***	Y	Y	Y	N	Y	Y	Y	Y
8 McCloskey	Y	Y	Y	Y	N	N	Y	Y
9 Hamilton	Y	Y	Y	Y	Y	N	Y	Y
10 Jacobs	Y	Y	Y	Y	N	N	Y	Y
IOWA								
1 ***Leach***	Y	Y	Y	Y	Y	Y	Y	Y
2 ***Tauke***	Y	Y	Y	N	Y	Y	Y	Y
3 ***Evans***	Y	Y	Y	N	Y	Y	Y	Y
4 Smith	Y	Y	Y	Y	N	N	Y	Y
5 ***Lightfoot***	Y	Y	Y	N	Y	Y	Y	Y
6 Bedell	Y	Y	Y	Y	N	N	Y	Y
KANSAS								
1 ***Roberts***	Y	Y	Y	N	Y	Y	Y	Y
2 Slattery	Y	Y	Y	Y	Y	N	Y	Y
3 ***Meyers***	Y	Y	Y	Y	Y	Y	Y	Y
4 Glickman	Y	Y	Y	Y	N	N	Y	Y
5 ***Whittaker***	Y	Y	Y	N	Y	Y	Y	Y
KENTUCKY								
1 Hubbard	Y	Y	Y	Y	Y	Y	Y	Y
2 Natcher	Y	Y	Y	Y	N	N	Y	Y
3 Mazzoli	Y	Y	Y	N	N	Y	Y	Y
4 ***Snyder***	Y	Y	Y	N	Y	Y	Y	Y
5 ***Rogers***	Y	Y	Y	N	Y	Y	Y	Y
6 ***Hopkins***	Y	Y	Y	N	Y	Y	Y	Y
7 Perkins	Y	Y	Y	N	N	N	Y	Y
LOUISIANA								
1 ***Livingston***	Y	Y	Y	N	Y	Y	N	Y
2 Boggs	Y	Y	Y	Y	N	N	Y	Y
3 Tauzin	Y	Y	Y	Y	N	N	Y	Y
4 Roemer	Y	Y	Y	Y	N	N	Y	Y
5 Huckaby	Y	Y	Y	Y	Y	N	Y	Y
6 ***Moore***	Y	Y	Y	N	Y	Y	Y	Y
7 Breaux	?	?	?	?	?	?	?	?
8 Long	Y	Y	Y	Y	N	N	Y	Y
MAINE								
1 ***McKernan***	Y	Y	Y	N	Y	Y	Y	Y
2 ***Snowe***	Y	Y	Y	Y	Y	Y	Y	Y
MARYLAND								
1 Dyson	Y	Y	Y	N	N	Y	Y	Y
2 ***Bentley***	Y	Y	Y	N	N	Y	Y	Y
3 Mikulski	Y	Y	Y	Y	N	N	Y	Y
4 ***Holt***	Y	Y	Y	N	Y	Y	Y	Y
5 Hoyer	Y	Y	Y	Y	N	N	Y	Y
6 Byron	Y	Y	Y	N	Y	Y	Y	Y
7 Mitchell	Y	Y	Y	Y	N	N	Y	Y
8 Barnes	Y	Y	Y	Y	N	N	Y	Y
MASSACHUSETTS								
1 ***Conte***	Y	Y	Y	Y	N	N	Y	Y
2 Boland	Y	Y	Y	Y	N	N	Y	?
3 Early	Y	Y	Y	Y	N	N	Y	Y
4 Frank	Y	Y	Y	Y	N	N	Y	Y
5 Atkins	Y	Y	Y	Y	N	N	Y	Y
6 Mavroules	?	Y	Y	Y	N	N	Y	Y
7 Markey	Y	Y	Y	Y	N	N	Y	?
8 O'Neill								
9 Moakley	Y	Y	Y	Y	N	N	Y	Y
10 Studds	Y	Y	Y	Y	N	N	Y	Y
11 Donnelly	Y	Y	Y	Y	N	N	Y	Y
MICHIGAN								
1 Conyers	Y	Y	Y	?	N	?	Y	Y
2 ***Pursell***	Y	Y	Y	Y	Y	Y	Y	Y
3 Wolpe	Y	Y	Y	Y	N	N	Y	Y
4 ***Siljander***	Y	Y	Y	Y	Y	Y	Y	Y
5 ***Henry***	Y	Y	Y	Y	Y	Y	Y	Y
6 Carr	Y	Y	Y	Y	N	Y	Y	Y
7 Kildee	Y	Y	Y	Y	N	N	Y	Y
8 Traxler	Y	Y	Y	Y	N	N	Y	Y
9 ***Vander Jagt***	?	?	?	?	?	?	?	?
10 ***Schuette***	Y	Y	Y	N	Y	Y	Y	Y
11 ***Davis***	?	?	?	?	?	?	?	?
12 Bonior	Y	Y	Y	Y	N	N	Y	Y
13 Crockett	Y	Y	Y	Y	N	N	Y	Y
14 Hertel	Y	Y	Y	Y	N	N	Y	Y
15 Ford	Y	Y	Y	N	N	N	Y	Y
16 Dingell	?	Y	Y	Y	N	N	Y	Y
17 Levin	Y	Y	Y	Y	N	N	Y	Y
18 ***Broomfield***	Y	Y	Y	N	Y	Y	Y	Y
MINNESOTA								
1 Penny	Y	Y	Y	Y	Y	Y	Y	Y
2 ***Weber***	Y	Y	Y	Y	Y	Y	N	?
3 ***Frenzel***	Y	Y	Y	N	Y	Y	N	N
4 Vento	Y	Y	Y	Y	Y	N	Y	Y
5 Sabo	Y	Y	Y	Y	N	N	Y	?
6 Sikorski	Y	Y	Y	Y	N	N	Y	Y

	150	151	152	153	154	155	156	157
7 ***Stangeland***	Y	Y	Y	N	Y	Y	Y	Y
8 Oberstar	Y	Y	Y	Y	N	N	Y	Y
MISSISSIPPI								
1 Whitten	Y	Y	Y	Y	N	N	Y	Y
2 ***Franklin***	Y	Y	Y	N	?	Y	Y	Y
3 Montgomery	Y	Y	Y	N	Y	N	Y	Y
4 Dowdy	?	?	?	?	?	?	?	?
5 ***Lott***	Y	Y	Y	N	Y	Y	Y	Y
MISSOURI								
1 Clay	Y	Y	Y	Y	N	N	Y	Y
2 Young	Y	Y	Y	Y	N	N	Y	Y
3 Gephardt	?	?	?	?	?	?	?	?
4 Skelton	Y	Y	Y	Y	N	N	Y	Y
5 Wheat	Y	Y	Y	Y	N	N	Y	Y
6 ***Coleman***	Y	Y	Y	N	Y	Y	Y	Y
7 ***Taylor***	Y	Y	Y	N	Y	Y	Y	Y
8 ***Emerson***	Y	Y	Y	N	Y	Y	Y	Y
9 Volkmer	Y	Y	Y	Y	N	Y	Y	Y
MONTANA								
1 Williams	Y	Y	Y	Y	N	N	Y	Y
2 ***Marlenee***	Y	Y	Y	N	Y	Y	N	N
NEBRASKA								
1 ***Bereuter***	Y	Y	Y	Y	Y	Y	Y	Y
2 ***Daub***	Y	Y	Y	N	Y	Y	Y	Y
3 ***Smith***	Y	?	Y	N	Y	Y	Y	Y
NEVADA								
1 Reid	Y	Y	Y	Y	N	N	Y	Y
2 ***Vucanovich***	Y	Y	Y	N	Y	Y	Y	Y
NEW HAMPSHIRE								
1 ***Smith***	Y	Y	Y	Y	Y	Y	Y	Y
2 ***Gregg***	Y	Y	Y	Y	Y	Y	N	Y
NEW JERSEY								
1 Florio	Y	Y	Y	Y	N	N	Y	Y
2 Hughes	Y	Y	Y	Y	N	N	Y	Y
3 Howard	Y	Y	Y	N	N	N	Y	Y
4 ***Smith***	Y	Y	Y	Y	N	Y	Y	Y
5 ***Roukema***	Y	Y	Y	N	Y	Y	Y	?
6 Dwyer	Y	Y	Y	Y	N	N	Y	Y
7 ***Rinaldo***	Y	Y	Y	Y	N	N	Y	Y
8 Roe	Y	Y	Y	Y	N	N	Y	Y
9 Torricelli	Y	Y	Y	Y	N	N	Y	Y
10 Rodino	Y	Y	Y	Y	N	N	Y	Y
11 ***Gallo***	Y	Y	Y	Y	N	Y	Y	Y
12 ***Courter***	Y	Y	Y	Y	Y	Y	Y	Y
13 ***Saxton***	Y	Y	Y	Y	Y	Y	Y	Y
14 Guarini	Y	Y	Y	Y	N	N	Y	Y
NEW MEXICO								
1 ***Lujan***	Y	Y	Y	Y	Y	Y	Y	Y
2 ***Skeen***	Y	Y	Y	N	Y	Y	N	Y
3 Richardson	Y	Y	Y	Y	N	N	Y	Y
NEW YORK								
1 ***Carney***	?	?	?	?	?	?	?	?
2 Downey	Y	Y	Y	Y	N	N	Y	?
3 Mrazek	Y	Y	Y	Y	N	N	Y	?
4 ***Lent***	Y	Y	Y	Y	Y	Y	Y	Y
5 ***McGrath***	Y	Y	Y	N	Y	Y	Y	Y
6 Vacancy								
7 Ackerman	Y	Y	Y	Y	N	N	Y	Y
8 Scheuer	?	Y	Y	Y	N	N	Y	Y
9 Manton	Y	Y	Y	Y	N	N	Y	Y
10 Schumer	Y	Y	Y	Y	N	N	Y	Y
11 Towns	Y	Y	Y	N	N	N	Y	Y
12 Owens	Y	Y	Y	N	N	N	Y	Y
13 Solarz	Y	Y	Y	Y	N	N	Y	Y
14 ***Molinari***	Y	Y	Y	N	Y	Y	Y	Y
15 ***Green***	Y	Y	Y	Y	Y	Y	Y	Y
16 Rangel	?	?	?	?	?	?	?	?
17 Weiss	Y	Y	Y	Y	N	N	Y	Y
18 Garcia	Y	Y	Y	Y	N	N	Y	Y
19 Biaggi	Y	Y	Y	Y	N	N	Y	Y
20 ***DioGuardi***	Y	Y	Y	N	Y	Y	Y	Y
21 ***Fish***	Y	Y	Y	N	Y	Y	Y	Y
22 ***Gilman***	Y	Y	Y	N	N	Y	Y	Y
23 Stratton	Y	Y	Y	Y	Y	Y	Y	Y
24 ***Solomon***	Y	Y	Y	N	Y	Y	Y	Y
25 ***Boehlert***	Y	Y	Y	Y	N	Y	Y	Y
26 ***Martin***	Y	Y	Y	N	Y	Y	Y	Y
27 ***Wortley***	Y	Y	Y	N	Y	Y	Y	Y
28 McHugh	Y	Y	Y	Y	N	N	Y	Y
29 ***Horton***	Y	Y	Y	N	N	?	Y	Y
30 ***Eckert***	Y	Y	Y	Y	Y	Y	N	Y
31 ***Kemp***	?	Y	Y	N	Y	Y	Y	Y
32 LaFalce	Y	Y	Y	Y	N	N	Y	Y
33 Nowak	Y	Y	Y	Y	N	N	Y	Y
34 Lundine	?	?	?	?	?	?	?	?

	150	151	152	153	154	155	156	157
NORTH CAROLINA								
1 Jones	Y	Y	Y	Y	N	N	Y	Y
2 Valentine	Y	Y	Y	N	N	Y	Y	Y
3 Whitley	Y	Y	Y	Y	N	N	Y	Y
4 ***Cobey***	Y	Y	Y	Y	Y	Y	N	N
5 Neal	Y	Y	Y	Y	N	N	Y	Y
6 ***Coble***	Y	Y	Y	Y	Y	Y	N	Y
7 Rose	Y	Y	Y	Y	N	?	?	?
8 Hefner	Y	Y	Y	Y	N	N	Y	Y
9 ***McMillan***	Y	Y	Y	N	Y	Y	Y	Y
10 ***Broyhill***	Y	Y	Y	Y	Y	Y	N	Y
11 ***Hendon***	Y	Y	Y	Y	Y	Y	Y	Y
NORTH DAKOTA								
AL Dorgan	+	Y	Y	Y	N	N	Y	Y
OHIO								
1 Luken	Y	Y	Y	Y	N	N	Y	Y
2 ***Gradison***	Y	Y	Y	N	Y	Y	Y	Y
3 Hall	Y	Y	Y	Y	N	N	Y	Y
4 ***Oxley***	Y	Y	Y	N	Y	Y	Y	?
5 ***Latta***	Y	Y	Y	N	Y	Y	Y	Y
6 ***McEwen***	Y	Y	Y	N	Y	Y	Y	Y
7 ***DeWine***	Y	Y	Y	Y	Y	Y	Y	Y
8 ***Kindness***	Y	Y	Y	N	Y	Y	Y	Y
9 Kaptur	Y	Y	Y	P	N	N	Y	Y
10 ***Miller***	Y	Y	Y	N	Y	Y	Y	Y
11 Eckart	Y	Y	Y	Y	N	N	Y	Y
12 ***Kasich***	Y	Y	Y	N	Y	Y	Y	Y
13 Pease	Y	Y	Y	Y	N	N	Y	Y
14 Seiberling	Y	Y	Y	Y	?	?	Y	Y
15 ***Wylie***	Y	Y	Y	N	Y	Y	Y	Y
16 ***Regula***	Y	Y	Y	N	Y	Y	Y	Y
17 Traficant	Y	Y	Y	Y	N	N	Y	Y
18 Applegate	Y	Y	Y	Y	N	N	Y	Y
19 Feighan	Y	Y	Y	Y	N	N	Y	Y
20 Oakar	Y	Y	Y	Y	N	N	Y	Y
21 Stokes	Y	Y	Y	Y	N	N	Y	Y
OKLAHOMA								
1 Jones	Y	Y	Y	Y	Y	Y	Y	?
2 Synar	Y	Y	Y	Y	Y	N	Y	Y
3 Watkins	Y	Y	Y	Y	Y	N	Y	Y
4 McCurdy	Y	Y	Y	Y	Y	N	Y	Y
5 ***Edwards***	Y	Y	Y	N	Y	Y	?	Y
6 English	Y	Y	Y	Y	Y	Y	Y	Y
OREGON								
1 AuCoin	Y	Y	Y	Y	N	Y	+	Y
2 ***Smith, R.***	Y	Y	Y	N	Y	Y	N	Y
3 Wyden	Y	Y	Y	Y	N	N	Y	Y
4 Weaver	Y	Y	Y	Y	N	N	Y	?
5 ***Smith, D.***	Y	Y	Y	N	Y	Y	N	Y
PENNSYLVANIA								
1 Foglietta	Y	Y	Y	Y	N	N	Y	Y
2 Gray	Y	Y	Y	Y	N	?	Y	Y
3 Borski	Y	Y	Y	Y	N	N	Y	Y
4 Kolter	Y	Y	Y	Y	N	N	Y	Y
5 ***Schulze***	Y	Y	Y	Y	N	Y	Y	Y
6 Yatron	Y	Y	Y	Y	N	N	Y	Y
7 Edgar	?	Y	Y	Y	Y	N	Y	Y
8 Kostmayer	Y	Y	Y	Y	N	N	Y	Y
9 ***Shuster***	Y	Y	Y	N	Y	Y	N	Y
10 ***McDade***	Y	Y	Y	N	N	Y	Y	Y
11 Kanjorski	Y	Y	Y	Y	N	N	Y	Y
12 Murtha	Y	Y	Y	Y	N	N	Y	Y
13 ***Coughlin***	Y	Y	Y	Y	?	Y	Y	Y
14 Coyne	Y	Y	Y	Y	N	N	Y	Y
15 ***Ritter***	Y	Y	Y	Y	Y	Y	Y	Y
16 ***Walker***	Y	Y	Y	N	Y	Y	N	Y
17 ***Gekas***	Y	Y	Y	N	Y	Y	N	Y
18 Walgren	Y	Y	Y	Y	N	N	Y	Y
19 ***Goodling***	Y	Y	Y	N	Y	Y	Y	Y
20 Gaydos	Y	Y	Y	Y	N	N	Y	Y
21 ***Ridge***	Y	Y	Y	N	Y	Y	Y	Y
22 Murphy	Y	Y	Y	Y	N	N	Y	Y
23 ***Clinger***	Y	Y	Y	N	N	Y	Y	Y
RHODE ISLAND								
1 St Germain	N	Y	Y	Y	N	N	Y	Y
2 ***Schneider***	Y	Y	Y	N	Y	Y	Y	Y
SOUTH CAROLINA								
1 ***Hartnett***	Y	Y	Y	N	Y	Y	Y	Y
2 ***Spence***	Y	Y	Y	N	Y	Y	Y	Y
3 Derrick	Y	Y	Y	Y	N	N	Y	Y
4 ***Campbell***	?	?	?	?	?	?	?	?
5 Spratt	Y	Y	Y	Y	N	Y	Y	Y
6 Tallon	Y	Y	Y	Y	N	N	Y	Y
SOUTH DAKOTA								
AL Daschle	Y	Y	Y	Y	N	N	Y	Y

	150	151	152	153	154	155	156	157
TENNESSEE								
1 ***Quillen***	Y	Y	Y	N	N	Y	Y	Y
2 ***Duncan***	Y	Y	Y	N	N	Y	Y	Y
3 Lloyd	Y	Y	Y	N	N	N	Y	Y
4 Cooper	?	Y	Y	Y	N	N	Y	Y
5 Boner	Y	Y	Y	Y	?	N	?	?
6 Gordon	Y	Y	Y	Y	N	N	Y	Y
7 ***Sundquist***	Y	Y	Y	N	Y	Y	Y	Y
8 Jones	Y	Y	Y	N	N	N	Y	Y
9 Ford	?	?	?	?	?	N	Y	Y
TEXAS								
1 Chapman	Y	Y	Y	Y	Y	Y	Y	Y
2 Wilson	Y	Y	Y	Y	N	N	Y	Y
3 ***Bartlett***	Y	Y	Y	N	Y	Y	N	N
4 Hall, R.	Y	Y	Y	Y	N	N	Y	Y
5 Bryant	Y	Y	Y	Y	N	N	Y	Y
6 ***Barton***	Y	Y	Y	N	Y	Y	Y	Y
7 ***Archer***	Y	Y	Y	N	Y	Y	N	Y
8 ***Fields***	Y	Y	Y	N	Y	Y	N	Y
9 Brooks	Y	Y	Y	Y	N	N	Y	Y
10 Pickle	Y	Y	Y	Y	Y	Y	Y	Y
11 Leath	Y	Y	Y	Y	Y	Y	Y	Y
12 Wright	Y	Y	Y	Y	N	N	Y	Y
13 ***Boulter***	Y	Y	Y	N	Y	Y	Y	Y
14 ***Sweeney***	Y	Y	Y	Y	Y	N	Y	Y
15 de la Garza	?	?	?	?	?	N	Y	Y
16 Coleman	Y	Y	Y	Y	Y	Y	Y	Y
17 Stenholm	Y	Y	Y	Y	Y	Y	N	Y
18 Leland	Y	Y	Y	Y	N	N	Y	Y
19 ***Combest***	Y	Y	Y	Y	Y	Y	Y	Y
20 Gonzalez	Y	Y	Y	Y	N	N	Y	Y
21 ***Loeffler***	Y	Y	Y	N	Y	Y	Y	?
22 ***DeLay***	Y	Y	Y	N	Y	Y	N	Y
23 Bustamante	Y	Y	Y	Y	N	N	Y	Y
24 Frost	Y	Y	Y	Y	N	N	Y	Y
25 Andrews	Y	Y	Y	Y	Y	N	Y	Y
26 ***Armey***	Y	Y	Y	N	Y	Y	N	Y
27 Ortiz	Y	Y	Y	Y	N	N	Y	Y
UTAH								
1 ***Hansen***	Y	Y	Y	N	Y	Y	N	Y
2 ***Monson***	Y	Y	Y	N	Y	Y	N	Y
3 ***Nielson***	Y	Y	Y	N	Y	Y	Y	Y
VERMONT								
AL ***Jeffords***	Y	Y	Y	N	Y	Y	Y	Y
VIRGINIA								
1 ***Bateman***	Y	Y	Y	Y	Y	Y	Y	Y
2 ***Whitehurst***	Y	Y	Y	Y	Y	Y	Y	Y
3 ***Bliley***	Y	Y	Y	Y	Y	Y	N	Y
4 Sisisky	Y	Y	Y	Y	N	N	Y	?
5 Daniel	Y	Y	Y	N	N	Y	Y	Y
6 Olin	Y	Y	Y	Y	Y	Y	Y	Y
7 ***Slaughter***	Y	Y	Y	N	Y	Y	N	Y
8 ***Parris***	Y	Y	Y	N	Y	Y	Y	Y
9 Boucher	Y	Y	Y	Y	N	N	Y	Y
10 ***Wolf***	Y	Y	Y	N	Y	Y	Y	Y
WASHINGTON								
1 ***Miller***	Y	Y	Y	Y	Y	Y	Y	Y
2 Swift	Y	Y	Y	Y	N	N	Y	Y
3 Bonker	Y	Y	?	Y	N	N	Y	Y
4 ***Morrison***	Y	Y	Y	N	N	Y	Y	Y
5 Foley	Y	Y	Y	Y	N	N	Y	Y
6 Dicks	Y	Y	Y	Y	N	N	Y	?
7 Lowry	Y	Y	Y	Y	N	N	Y	Y
8 ***Chandler***	?	?	?	?	?	?	?	?
WEST VIRGINIA								
1 Mollohan	Y	Y	Y	Y	N	N	Y	Y
2 Staggers	Y	Y	Y	Y	N	N	Y	?
3 Wise	Y	Y	Y	Y	N	N	Y	Y
4 Rahall	Y	Y	Y	Y	N	N	?	?
WISCONSIN								
1 Aspin	Y	Y	Y	Y	N	N	Y	Y
2 Kastenmeier	Y	Y	Y	Y	N	N	Y	Y
3 ***Gunderson***	Y	Y	Y	N	Y	Y	Y	Y
4 Kleczka	Y	Y	Y	Y	N	N	Y	Y
5 Moody	Y	Y	Y	Y	N	N	Y	?
6 ***Petri***	Y	Y	Y	N	Y	Y	Y	Y
7 Obey	Y	Y	Y	Y	N	N	Y	Y
8 ***Roth***	?	?	Y	N	Y	Y	Y	Y
9 ***Sensenbrenner***	Y	Y	Y	N	Y	Y	N	Y
WYOMING								
AL ***Cheney***	Y	Y	Y	N	?	Y	N	Y

Southern states - Ala., Ark., Fla., Ga., Ky., La., Miss., N.C., Okla., S.C., Tenn., Texas, Va.

* The *Congressional Record* vote number is different from the CQ vote number because the *Record* includes quorum calls in its tally. CQ does not publish quorum call votes.

158. HR 4175. Maritime Authorizations, Fiscal 1987. Passage of the bill to authorize $400.1 million in fiscal 1987 appropriations for maritime programs, including $388.2 million for the Maritime Administration and $11.9 million for the Federal Maritime Commission. Passed 367-29: R 141-26; D 226-3 (ND 154-3, SD 72-0), June 17, 1986.

159. HR 4868. South Africa Sanctions. Adoption of the rule (H Res 478) to provide for House floor consideration of the bill to impose economic sanctions against South Africa. Adopted 286-127: R 48-123; D 238-4 (ND 166-1, SD 72-3), June 18, 1986.

160. HR 4868. South Africa Sanctions. Burton, R-Ind., amendment to prohibit any funds authorized in the legislation from going to the African National Congress if any members of the group's governing body belong to the South African Communist Party. Adopted 365-49: R 173-0; D 192-49 (ND 118-44, SD 74-5), June 18, 1986.

161. HR 4868. South Africa Sanctions. Burton, R-Ind., amendment to exempt from the bill's sanctions companies that comply with the Sullivan principles relating to anti-discrimination in the work place. Rejected 150-268: R 138-35; D 12-233 (ND 5-160, SD 7-73), June 18, 1986. (A Dellums, D-Calif., substitute, to establish a comprehensive trade embargo on South Africa and to require all U.S. companies there to leave within 180 days of enactment, was adopted later by voice vote, after which the bill was passed by voice vote.)

162. Procedural Motion. Ridge, R-Pa., motion to approve the House *Journal* of Wednesday, June 18. Motion agreed to 260-137: R 45-123; D 215-14 (ND 147-7, SD 68-7), June 19, 1986.

163. H Con Res 350. Adherence to SALT II Agreements. Adoption of the rule (H Res 479) to provide for House floor consideration of the concurrent resolution to call on President Reagan to continue to comply with the nuclear arms limits in the unratified SALT II treaty. Adopted 341-74: R 107-69; D 234-5 (ND 158-2, SD 76-3), June 19, 1986.

164. H Con Res 350. Adherence to SALT II Agreements. Broomfield, R-Mich., amendment to provide that the United States should abide by all provisions of the SALT II nuclear arms treaty as long as the Soviet Union does likewise. Rejected 187-222: R 152-15; D 35-207 (ND 7-158, SD 28-49), June 19, 1986. A "yea" was a vote supporting the president's position.

165. H Con Res 350. Adherence to SALT II Agreements. Broomfield, R-Mich., motion to recommit the concurrent resolution to the Foreign Affairs Committee with instructions to report it back to the House forthwith with an amendment expressing the support of the House for U.S. efforts to negotiate a new arms reduction agreement with weapons ceilings lower than those of the SALT II treaty. Motion agreed to 406-0: R 167-0; D 239-0 (ND 164-0, SD 75-0), June 19, 1986. (The concurrent resolution subsequently was reported back to the House and adopted.)

KEY

- Y Voted for (yea).
- # Paired for.
- \+ Announced for.
- N Voted against (nay).
- X Paired against.
- \- Announced against.
- P Voted "present."
- C Voted "present" to avoid possible conflict of interest.
- ? Did not vote or otherwise make a position known.

Democrats *Republicans*

	158	159	160	161	162	163	164	165
ALABAMA								
1 *Callahan*	Y	N	Y	Y	Y	Y	Y	Y
2 *Dickinson*	Y	N	Y	Y	N	N	Y	Y
3 Nichols	Y	Y	Y	N	Y	Y	Y	Y
4 Bevill	Y	Y	Y	N	Y	Y	N	Y
5 Flippo	Y	Y	Y	N	Y	Y	Y	Y
6 Erdreich	Y	Y	Y	N	Y	Y	Y	Y
7 Shelby	Y	Y	Y	N	Y	Y	Y	Y
ALASKA								
AL *Young*	Y	N	Y	N	N	Y	Y	Y
ARIZONA								
1 *McCain*	Y	N	Y	Y	N	Y	Y	Y
2 Udall	Y	Y	Y	N	?	Y	N	Y
3 *Stump*	N	N	Y	Y	N	N	Y	Y
4 *Rudd*	Y	N	Y	Y	Y	N	?	?
5 *Kolbe*	Y	N	Y	Y	N	Y	Y	Y
ARKANSAS								
1 Alexander	Y	Y	Y	N	Y	Y	N	Y
2 Robinson	Y	Y	Y	N	Y	Y	N	Y
3 *Hammerschmidt*	Y	N	Y	Y	Y	Y	Y	Y
4 Anthony	Y	Y	Y	N	P	Y	X	?
CALIFORNIA								
1 Bosco	Y	Y	Y	N	Y	Y	N	Y
2 *Chappie*	Y	N	Y	Y	N	Y	Y	Y
3 Matsui	Y	Y	N	N	Y	Y	N	Y
4 Fazio	Y	Y	N	N	Y	Y	N	Y
5 Burton	Y	Y	N	N	Y	Y	X	?
6 Boxer	Y	?	N	N	Y	Y	N	Y
7 Miller	Y	Y	Y	N	P	?	N	Y
8 Dellums	Y	Y	N	N	Y	Y	N	Y
9 Stark	Y	Y	N	N	Y	Y	N	Y
10 Edwards	Y	Y	N	N	Y	Y	N	Y
11 Lantos	Y	Y	Y	N	Y	Y	N	Y
12 *Zschau*	Y	Y	Y	Y	N	Y	Y	Y
13 Mineta	Y	Y	N	N	Y	Y	N	Y
14 *Shumway*	Y	N	Y	Y	Y	N	Y	Y
15 Coelho	Y	Y	Y	N	Y	Y	N	Y
16 Panetta	Y	Y	Y	N	Y	Y	N	Y
17 *Pashayan*	Y	N	Y	Y	N	Y	Y	Y
18 Lehman	Y	Y	Y	N	Y	Y	N	Y
19 *Lagomarsino*	Y	N	Y	Y	N	N	Y	Y
20 *Thomas*	Y	N	Y	Y	?	N	N	Y
21 *Fiedler*	Y	N	Y	Y	N	Y	Y	Y
22 *Moorhead*	Y	N	Y	Y	N	N	Y	Y
23 Beilenson	Y	Y	N	N	Y	Y	N	Y
24 Waxman	Y	Y	Y	N	Y	?	N	Y
25 Roybal	Y	Y	N	?	Y	Y	N	Y
26 Berman	?	Y	Y	N	Y	Y	N	Y
27 Levine	Y	Y	Y	N	Y	Y	N	Y
28 Dixon	Y	Y	Y	Y	Y	Y	N	Y
29 Hawkins	Y	Y	N	N	N	Y	N	Y
30 Martinez	Y	Y	Y	N	Y	Y	N	Y
31 Dymally	Y	Y	N	N	Y	Y	N	Y
32 Anderson	Y	Y	Y	N	Y	Y	N	Y
33 *Dreier*	N	N	Y	Y	N	N	Y	Y
34 Torres	Y	Y	Y	N	Y	Y	N	Y
35 *Lewis*	Y	N	Y	Y	N	N	?	?
36 Brown	?	Y	Y	N	Y	Y	N	Y
37 *McCandless*	Y	N	Y	Y	N	N	Y	Y
38 *Dornan*	Y	N	Y	Y	Y	N	Y	Y
39 *Dannemeyer*	N	N	Y	Y	?	N	Y	Y
40 *Badham*	Y	N	Y	Y	N	N	#	?
41 *Lowery*	Y	N	Y	Y	N	N	Y	Y
42 *Lungren*	N	N	Y	Y	N	N	Y	Y
43 *Packard*	Y	N	Y	Y	Y	Y	Y	Y
44 Bates	Y	Y	Y	N	Y	Y	N	Y
45 *Hunter*	Y	N	Y	Y	N	N	Y	Y
COLORADO								
1 Schroeder	Y	Y	Y	N	N	Y	N	Y
2 Wirth	Y	Y	Y	N	Y	Y	N	Y
3 *Strang*	N	N	Y	Y	N	Y	Y	Y
4 *Brown*	N	N	Y	Y	N	N	Y	Y
5 *Kramer*	Y	N	Y	Y	N	N	Y	Y
6 *Schaefer*	Y	N	Y	Y	N	N	Y	Y
CONNECTICUT								
1 Kennelly	Y	Y	Y	N	Y	Y	N	Y
2 Gejdenson	Y	Y	Y	N	Y	Y	N	Y
3 Morrison	Y	Y	N	N	Y	Y	N	Y
4 *McKinney*	Y	Y	Y	N	?	?	X	?
5 *Rowland*	Y	N	Y	Y	N	Y	Y	Y
6 *Johnson*	Y	N	Y	Y	Y	N	N	Y
DELAWARE								
AL Carper	Y	Y	Y	N	Y	Y	N	Y
FLORIDA								
1 Hutto	Y	Y	Y	Y	Y	Y	Y	Y
2 Fuqua	?	?	?	?	?	?	?	?
3 Bennett	Y	Y	Y	N	Y	Y	N	Y
4 Chappell	Y	Y	Y	Y	Y	Y	Y	Y
5 *McCollum*	Y	N	Y	Y	Y	Y	Y	Y
6 MacKay	Y	Y	Y	N	Y	Y	N	Y
7 Gibbons	Y	Y	Y	N	Y	Y	N	Y
8 *Young*	Y	Y	Y	Y	N	Y	Y	Y
9 *Bilirakis*	Y	N	Y	Y	N	Y	Y	Y
10 *Ireland*	Y	N	Y	Y	N	Y	Y	Y
11 Nelson	Y	Y	Y	N	Y	Y	Y	Y
12 *Lewis*	Y	Y	Y	Y	N	Y	Y	Y
13 *Mack*	?	N	Y	Y	N	N	Y	Y
14 Mica	Y	Y	Y	N	Y	Y	N	Y
15 *Shaw*	Y	N	Y	Y	N	N	Y	Y
16 Smith	?	Y	Y	N	Y	Y	N	Y
17 Lehman	Y	Y	N	N	Y	Y	N	Y
18 Pepper	Y	Y	Y	N	+	Y	N	Y
19 Fascell	Y	Y	Y	N	Y	Y	N	Y
GEORGIA								
1 Thomas	Y	Y	Y	N	Y	Y	Y	Y
2 Hatcher	Y	Y	Y	N	Y	Y	?	?
3 Ray	Y	Y	Y	N	Y	Y	Y	Y
4 *Swindall*	N	N	Y	Y	N	Y	Y	Y
5 Fowler	?	?	Y	N	Y	Y	N	Y
6 *Gingrich*	Y	N	Y	Y	N	N	Y	Y
7 Darden	Y	Y	Y	N	Y	Y	Y	Y
8 Rowland	Y	Y	Y	N	Y	Y	Y	Y
9 Jenkins	Y	Y	Y	N	Y	Y	Y	Y
10 Barnard	Y	Y	Y	N	Y	Y	Y	Y
HAWAII								
1 Heftel	?	Y	Y	N	?	Y	N	Y
2 Akaka	Y	Y	N	N	Y	Y	N	Y
IDAHO								
1 *Craig*	N	N	Y	Y	N	N	Y	Y
2 Stallings	Y	Y	Y	N	Y	Y	Y	Y
ILLINOIS								
1 Hayes	Y	Y	N	N	Y	Y	N	Y
2 Savage	Y	Y	N	N	Y	Y	N	Y
3 Russo	Y	Y	Y	N	Y	Y	N	Y
4 *O'Brien*	?	?	?	?	?	?	?	?
5 Lipinski	Y	Y	Y	N	Y	Y	Y	Y
6 *Hyde*	Y	N	Y	Y	N	Y	Y	Y
7 Collins	?	Y	N	N	Y	?	N	Y
8 Rostenkowski	Y	Y	Y	N	Y	Y	?	?
9 Yates	N	Y	N	N	Y	Y	N	Y
10 *Porter*	Y	N	Y	Y	N	N	Y	Y
11 Annunzio	Y	Y	Y	N	Y	Y	N	Y
12 *Crane*	N	N	Y	Y	N	N	Y	Y
13 *Fawell*	Y	Y	Y	Y	N	Y	Y	Y
14 *Grotberg*	?	?	?	?	?	?	?	?
15 *Madigan*	Y	N	Y	Y	Y	Y	Y	Y
16 *Martin*	Y	N	Y	N	N	Y	Y	Y
17 Evans	Y	Y	N	N	Y	Y	N	Y
18 *Michel*	N	N	Y	Y	N	Y	Y	Y
19 Bruce	Y	Y	Y	N	Y	Y	N	Y
20 Durbin	Y	Y	Y	N	Y	Y	N	Y
21 Price	Y	Y	Y	N	Y	Y	N	Y
22 Gray	Y	Y	Y	N	Y	Y	N	Y
INDIANA								
1 Visclosky	Y	Y	Y	N	Y	Y	N	Y
2 Sharp	Y	Y	Y	N	Y	Y	N	Y
3 *Hiler*	Y	N	Y	Y	N	Y	Y	Y
4 *Coats*	?	N	Y	Y	N	Y	Y	Y
5 *Hillis*	?	N	Y	Y	Y	Y	?	?

ND - Northern Democrats SD - Southern Democrats

* Corresponding to Congressional Record Votes 176, 177, 179, 180, 181, 182, 184, 185

	158	159	160	161	162	163	164	165
6 ***Burton***	N	N	Y	Y	N	N	Y	Y
7 ***Myers***	Y	N	Y	Y	Y	Y	Y	Y
8 McCloskey	Y	Y	Y	N	Y	Y	N	Y
9 Hamilton	Y	Y	Y	N	Y	Y	N	Y
10 Jacobs	N	N	Y	N	N	N	N	Y
IOWA								
1 ***Leach***	Y	Y	Y	N	N	Y	N	Y
2 ***Tauke***	Y	N	Y	Y	N	N	N	Y
3 ***Evans***	?	Y	Y	Y	N	Y	Y	Y
4 Smith	Y	Y	Y	N	Y	Y	N	Y
5 ***Lightfoot***	Y	N	Y	Y	N	Y	Y	Y
6 Bedell	Y	Y	Y	N	Y	Y	N	Y
KANSAS								
1 ***Roberts***	Y	N	Y	Y	N	N	Y	Y
2 Slattery	Y	Y	Y	N	Y	Y	N	Y
3 ***Meyers***	Y	N	Y	Y	N	Y	Y	Y
4 Glickman	Y	Y	Y	N	Y	Y	N	Y
5 ***Whittaker***	Y	N	Y	Y	N	Y	Y	Y
KENTUCKY								
1 Hubbard	Y	Y	Y	N	Y	Y	Y	Y
2 Natcher	Y	Y	Y	N	Y	Y	N	Y
3 Mazzoli	Y	Y	Y	N	Y	Y	Y	Y
4 ***Snyder***	Y	N	Y	Y	N	Y	Y	Y
5 ***Rogers***	Y	N	Y	Y	N	Y	Y	Y
6 ***Hopkins***	Y	N	Y	Y	N	N	Y	Y
7 Perkins	Y	Y	N	N	Y	Y	N	Y
LOUISIANA								
1 ***Livingston***	Y	N	Y	Y	N	N	Y	Y
2 Boggs	Y	Y	Y	N	Y	Y	N	Y
3 Tauzin	Y	Y	Y	N	Y	N	Y	Y
4 Roemer	Y	Y	Y	N	N	Y	Y	Y
5 Huckaby	Y	?	Y	N	Y	Y	X	?
6 ***Moore***	Y	N	Y	Y	Y	N	Y	Y
7 Breaux	?	Y	?	N	?	?	?	?
8 Long	Y	Y	Y	N	Y	Y	N	Y
MAINE								
1 ***McKernan***	Y	N	Y	N	N	N	N	Y
2 ***Snowe***	Y	Y	Y	N	N	Y	N	Y
MARYLAND								
1 Dyson	Y	Y	Y	N	Y	Y	Y	Y
2 ***Bentley***	Y	?	Y	Y	?	Y	Y	Y
3 Mikulski	Y	Y	N	N	Y	Y	N	Y
4 ***Holt***	Y	Y	Y	Y	N	Y	Y	Y
5 Hoyer	Y	Y	N	N	Y	Y	N	Y
6 Byron	Y	Y	Y	Y	Y	Y	N	Y
7 Mitchell	Y	Y	N	N	N	Y	N	Y
8 Barnes	Y	Y	N	N	?	?	N	Y
MASSACHUSETTS								
1 ***Conte***	Y	Y	Y	N	N	Y	N	Y
2 Boland	?	Y	Y	N	Y	Y	N	Y
3 Early	Y	Y	Y	N	Y	Y	N	Y
4 Frank	Y	Y	N	N	Y	Y	N	Y
5 Atkins	Y	Y	Y	N	Y	Y	N	Y
6 Mavroules	Y	Y	Y	N	Y	Y	N	Y
7 Markey	Y	Y	N	N	Y	Y	N	Y
8 O'Neill								
9 Moakley	Y	Y	Y	N	Y	Y	N	Y
10 Studds	Y	Y	N	N	Y	Y	N	Y
11 Donnelly	Y	Y	Y	N	Y	Y	N	Y
MICHIGAN								
1 Conyers	Y	Y	N	N	?	Y	N	Y
2 ***Pursell***	Y	Y	Y	N	Y	Y	Y	Y
3 Wolpe	Y	Y	Y	N	Y	Y	N	Y
4 ***Siljander***	Y	N	Y	Y	N	Y	Y	Y
5 ***Henry***	Y	Y	Y	N	N	Y	N	Y
6 Carr	Y	Y	Y	N	Y	Y	N	Y
7 Kildee	Y	Y	Y	N	Y	Y	N	Y
8 Traxler	Y	Y	Y	N	Y	Y	N	Y
9 ***Vander Jagt***	?	?	?	?	N	Y	Y	Y
10 ***Schuette***	Y	Y	Y	Y	N	Y	Y	Y
11 ***Davis***	?	?	?	?	?	Y	?	?
12 Bonior	?	Y	N	N	Y	Y	N	Y
13 Crockett	Y	Y	N	N	Y	Y	N	Y
14 Hertel	Y	Y	Y	N	Y	Y	N	Y
15 Ford	Y	Y	Y	N	Y	Y	N	Y
16 Dingell	Y	Y	Y	N	?	?	N	Y
17 Levin	Y	Y	Y	N	Y	Y	N	Y
18 ***Broomfield***	Y	Y	Y	Y	Y	Y	Y	Y
MINNESOTA								
1 Penny	Y	Y	Y	N	N	Y	N	Y
2 ***Weber***	N	Y	Y	N	N	Y	Y	Y
3 ***Frenzel***	N	Y	Y	Y	N	Y	Y	Y
4 Vento	Y	Y	Y	N	Y	Y	N	Y
5 Sabo	Y	Y	Y	N	Y	Y	N	Y
6 Sikorski	Y	Y	Y	N	N	Y	N	Y
7 ***Stangeland***	?	N	Y	Y	N	Y	Y	Y
8 Oberstar	Y	Y	Y	N	?	Y	N	Y
MISSISSIPPI								
1 Whitten	Y	Y	Y	Y	Y	Y	N	Y
2 ***Franklin***	Y	Y	Y	Y	Y	Y	Y	Y
3 Montgomery	Y	Y	Y	Y	Y	Y	Y	Y
4 Dowdy	?	?	?	?	?	?	N	Y
5 ***Lott***	Y	N	Y	Y	N	Y	Y	Y
MISSOURI								
1 Clay	Y	Y	N	N	N	Y	N	Y
2 Young	Y	Y	Y	N	Y	Y	N	Y
3 Gephardt	?	Y	Y	N	Y	Y	N	Y
4 Skelton	Y	Y	Y	N	Y	Y	Y	Y
5 Wheat	Y	Y	N	N	Y	Y	N	Y
6 ***Coleman***	Y	N	Y	Y	N	N	Y	Y
7 ***Taylor***	Y	N	Y	Y	Y	Y	Y	Y
8 ***Emerson***	Y	N	Y	Y	N	Y	Y	Y
9 Volkmer	Y	Y	Y	N	Y	Y	N	Y
MONTANA								
1 Williams	Y	Y	Y	N	?	Y	N	Y
2 ***Marlenee***	N	N	Y	Y	?	N	Y	Y
NEBRASKA								
1 ***Bereuter***	Y	Y	Y	Y	N	N	Y	Y
2 ***Daub***	Y	N	Y	Y	N	N	Y	Y
3 ***Smith***	Y	N	Y	Y	Y	Y	Y	Y
NEVADA								
1 Reid	Y	Y	Y	N	Y	Y	N	Y
2 ***Vucanovich***	Y	N	Y	Y	N	N	Y	Y
NEW HAMPSHIRE								
1 ***Smith***	Y	N	Y	Y	N	N	Y	Y
2 ***Gregg***	N	Y	Y	Y	N	Y	Y	Y
NEW JERSEY								
1 Florio	Y	Y	Y	N	Y	Y	N	Y
2 Hughes	Y	Y	Y	N	Y	Y	N	Y
3 Howard	Y	Y	N	N	Y	Y	N	Y
4 ***Smith***	Y	Y	Y	N	Y	Y	Y	Y
5 ***Roukema***	Y	N	Y	N	N	Y	N	Y
6 Dwyer	Y	Y	Y	N	Y	Y	N	Y
7 ***Rinaldo***	Y	Y	Y	N	Y	Y	Y	Y
8 Roe	Y	Y	Y	N	Y	Y	N	Y
9 Torricelli	Y	Y	Y	N	Y	Y	N	Y
10 Rodino	Y	Y	N	N	Y	Y	X	?
11 ***Gallo***	Y	N	Y	Y	N	Y	Y	Y
12 ***Courter***	Y	Y	Y	N	N	N	Y	Y
13 ***Saxton***	Y	Y	Y	Y	N	Y	Y	Y
14 Guarini	Y	Y	?	N	Y	?	N	Y
NEW MEXICO								
1 ***Lujan***	Y	N	Y	Y	Y	N	Y	Y
2 ***Skeen***	Y	N	Y	Y	N	Y	Y	Y
3 Richardson	Y	Y	Y	N	Y	Y	N	Y
NEW YORK								
1 ***Carney***	?	N	Y	Y	N	N	Y	Y
2 Downey	Y	Y	Y	N	?	Y	N	Y
3 Mrazek	Y	Y	Y	N	Y	Y	N	Y
4 ***Lent***	Y	N	Y	N	N	Y	Y	Y
5 ***McGrath***	Y	?	Y	N	N	Y	Y	Y
6 Vacancy								
7 Ackerman	Y	Y	N	N	?	Y	N	Y
8 Scheuer	Y	Y	Y	N	Y	Y	N	Y
9 Manton	Y	Y	Y	N	Y	Y	N	Y
10 Schumer	?	Y	Y	N	?	?	N	Y
11 Towns	Y	Y	N	N	Y	Y	N	Y
12 Owens	Y	Y	N	N	?	Y	N	Y
13 Solarz	Y	Y	Y	N	Y	Y	N	Y
14 ***Molinari***	Y	N	Y	N	N	Y	Y	Y
15 ***Green***	Y	N	Y	N	Y	Y	N	Y
16 Rangel	Y	Y	?	?	Y	Y	X	?
17 Weiss	Y	Y	N	N	Y	Y	N	Y
18 Garcia	Y	?	N	N	?	?	N	Y
19 Biaggi	Y	Y	Y	N	Y	Y	N	Y
20 ***DioGuardi***	Y	Y	Y	N	N	Y	Y	Y
21 ***Fish***	Y	Y	Y	N	Y	Y	N	Y
22 ***Gilman***	Y	Y	Y	N	Y	Y	Y	Y
23 Stratton	Y	Y	Y	Y	Y	N	Y	Y
24 ***Solomon***	Y	N	Y	Y	N	N	Y	Y
25 ***Boehlert***	Y	Y	Y	N	N	N	Y	Y
26 ***Martin***	Y	Y	Y	N	Y	Y	#	?
27 ***Wortley***	Y	N	Y	N	Y	Y	Y	Y
28 McHugh	Y	Y	Y	N	Y	Y	N	Y
29 ***Horton***	Y	Y	Y	N	Y	Y	#	?
30 ***Eckert***	N	N	Y	Y	Y	Y	Y	Y
31 ***Kemp***	Y	Y	Y	Y	Y	N	Y	Y
32 LaFalce	Y	Y	Y	N	Y	Y	N	Y
33 Nowak	Y	Y	Y	N	Y	Y	N	Y
34 Lundine	?	Y	?	?	Y	Y	N	?
NORTH CAROLINA								
1 Jones	Y	Y	Y	N	?	Y	N	Y
2 Valentine	Y	Y	Y	N	Y	Y	Y	Y
3 Whitley	Y	Y	Y	N	Y	Y	N	Y
4 ***Cobey***	N	N	Y	Y	N	N	Y	Y
5 Neal	Y	Y	Y	N	Y	Y	N	Y
6 ***Coble***	N	N	Y	Y	N	N	Y	Y
7 Rose	?	Y	Y	N	Y	Y	N	Y
8 Hefner	Y	Y	Y	N	Y	Y	N	Y
9 ***McMillan***	Y	N	Y	Y	N	Y	Y	Y
10 ***Broyhill***	Y	?	Y	Y	Y	Y	Y	Y
11 ***Hendon***	Y	N	Y	Y	Y	N	Y	Y
NORTH DAKOTA								
AL Dorgan	Y	Y	Y	N	Y	Y	N	Y
OHIO								
1 Luken	Y	Y	Y	N	Y	Y	N	Y
2 ***Gradison***	Y	Y	Y	N	Y	Y	Y	Y
3 Hall	Y	Y	Y	N	Y	Y	N	Y
4 ***Oxley***	Y	N	Y	Y	N	Y	Y	Y
5 ***Latta***	?	Y	?	?	N	Y	Y	Y
6 ***McEwen***	Y	N	Y	Y	Y	Y	Y	Y
7 ***DeWine***	Y	N	Y	Y	N	N	Y	Y
8 ***Kindness***	Y	Y	Y	Y	N	N	Y	Y
9 Kaptur	Y	Y	Y	N	?	Y	N	Y
10 ***Miller***	Y	Y	Y	Y	N	Y	Y	Y
11 Eckart	Y	Y	Y	N	Y	Y	N	Y
12 ***Kasich***	Y	N	Y	Y	?	Y	Y	Y
13 Pease	Y	Y	Y	N	Y	Y	N	Y
14 Seiberling	Y	Y	Y	N	?	Y	N	Y
15 ***Wylie***	Y	Y	Y	N	Y	Y	Y	Y
16 ***Regula***	Y	Y	Y	Y	Y	Y	Y	Y
17 Traficant	Y	Y	Y	N	Y	Y	N	Y
18 Applegate	Y	Y	Y	Y	Y	Y	N	Y
19 Feighan	Y	Y	Y	N	Y	?	N	Y
20 Oakar	Y	Y	Y	N	Y	Y	N	Y
21 Stokes	Y	Y	N	N	Y	Y	N	Y
OKLAHOMA								
1 Jones	?	Y	Y	N	N	Y	N	Y
2 Synar	Y	Y	Y	N	N	Y	N	Y
3 Watkins	Y	Y	Y	N	Y	Y	N	Y
4 McCurdy	Y	Y	Y	N	N	Y	N	Y
5 ***Edwards***	?	Y	Y	Y	N	Y	Y	Y
6 English	Y	Y	Y	N	Y	Y	Y	Y
OREGON								
1 AuCoin	Y	Y	?	N	Y	Y	N	Y
2 ***Smith, R.***	Y	N	Y	Y	N	Y	Y	Y
3 Wyden	Y	Y	Y	N	Y	Y	N	Y
4 Weaver	?	Y	?	N	Y	Y	N	Y
5 ***Smith, D.***	N	N	Y	Y	N	?	Y	Y
PENNSYLVANIA								
1 Foglietta	Y	Y	N	N	Y	Y	N	Y
2 Gray	?	Y	N	N	Y	Y	N	Y
3 Borski	Y	Y	Y	N	Y	Y	N	Y
4 Kolter	Y	Y	Y	?	Y	Y	N	Y
5 ***Schulze***	Y	N	Y	N	Y	Y	Y	Y
6 Yatron	Y	Y	Y	N	Y	Y	N	Y
7 Edgar	Y	Y	Y	N	Y	Y	N	Y
8 Kostmayer	Y	Y	Y	N	Y	Y	N	Y
9 ***Shuster***	Y	N	Y	Y	N	N	Y	Y
10 ***McDade***	Y	Y	Y	N	Y	Y	Y	Y
11 Kanjorski	Y	Y	Y	N	Y	Y	N	Y
12 Murtha	Y	Y	Y	N	Y	Y	Y	Y
13 ***Coughlin***	Y	Y	Y	N	N	Y	N	Y
14 Coyne	Y	Y	?	N	Y	Y	N	Y
15 ***Ritter***	?	Y	Y	Y	N	Y	Y	Y
16 ***Walker***	Y	N	Y	Y	N	N	Y	Y
17 ***Gekas***	Y	Y	Y	Y	N	N	Y	Y
18 Walgren	Y	Y	Y	N	Y	Y	N	Y
19 ***Goodling***	Y	Y	Y	N	N	Y	Y	Y
20 Gaydos	Y	Y	Y	N	Y	Y	Y	Y
21 ***Ridge***	Y	N	Y	Y	N	N	Y	Y
22 Murphy	Y	Y	Y	Y	Y	Y	N	Y
23 ***Clinger***	Y	N	Y	Y	Y	Y	Y	Y
RHODE ISLAND								
1 St Germain	Y	Y	N	N	Y	Y	N	Y
2 ***Schneider***	Y	?	?	?	?	Y	N	Y
SOUTH CAROLINA								
1 ***Hartnett***	Y	N	Y	?	Y	N	#	?
2 ***Spence***	Y	N	Y	Y	Y	Y	Y	Y
3 Derrick	?	Y	Y	N	Y	Y	N	?
4 ***Campbell***	?	?	Y	Y	?	Y	#	?
5 Spratt	Y	Y	Y	N	Y	Y	N	Y
6 Tallon	Y	Y	Y	N	Y	Y	Y	Y
SOUTH DAKOTA								
AL Daschle	Y	Y	Y	N	Y	Y	N	Y
TENNESSEE								
1 ***Quillen***	Y	Y	Y	Y	N	N	Y	Y
2 ***Duncan***	Y	Y	Y	Y	Y	Y	Y	Y
3 Lloyd	Y	Y	Y	N	N	Y	Y	Y
4 Cooper	Y	Y	Y	N	Y	Y	N	Y
5 Boner	?	?	Y	N	Y	Y	N	Y
6 Gordon	Y	Y	Y	N	Y	Y	N	Y
7 ***Sundquist***	Y	N	Y	Y	N	Y	Y	Y
8 Jones	Y	Y	Y	N	Y	Y	N	Y
9 Ford	Y	Y	N	N	?	Y	N	Y
TEXAS								
1 Chapman	Y	?	Y	N	Y	Y	N	Y
2 Wilson	Y	?	Y	N	Y	Y	N	Y
3 ***Bartlett***	N	N	Y	Y	N	N	Y	Y
4 Hall, R.	Y	N	Y	Y	N	N	Y	Y
5 Bryant	Y	Y	Y	N	Y	Y	N	Y
6 ***Barton***	N	N	Y	Y	N	N	?	?
7 ***Archer***	Y	N	Y	Y	Y	N	Y	Y
8 ***Fields***	Y	N	Y	Y	N	N	Y	Y
9 Brooks	Y	Y	Y	N	Y	Y	N	Y
10 Pickle	Y	Y	Y	N	Y	Y	Y	Y
11 Leath	Y	N	Y	Y	Y	Y	Y	Y
12 Wright	Y	Y	Y	N	Y	Y	N	Y
13 ***Boulter***	N	N	Y	Y	N	N	Y	Y
14 ***Sweeney***	Y	Y	Y	Y	?	Y	Y	Y
15 de la Garza	Y	Y	Y	N	Y	Y	N	Y
16 Coleman	Y	Y	Y	N	Y	Y	N	Y
17 Stenholm	Y	N	Y	Y	N	N	Y	Y
18 Leland	Y	Y	N	N	Y	Y	N	Y
19 ***Combest***	Y	N	Y	Y	N	N	Y	Y
20 Gonzalez	Y	Y	N	N	Y	Y	N	Y
21 ***Loeffler***	N	N	Y	Y	N	N	Y	Y
22 ***DeLay***	Y	N	Y	Y	N	N	Y	Y
23 Bustamante	Y	Y	Y	N	Y	Y	N	?
24 Frost	Y	Y	Y	N	Y	Y	N	Y
25 Andrews	Y	Y	Y	N	Y	Y	N	Y
26 ***Armey***	N	N	Y	Y	N	N	Y	Y
27 Ortiz	Y	Y	Y	N	Y	Y	N	Y
UTAH								
1 ***Hansen***	Y	N	Y	Y	N	N	Y	Y
2 ***Monson***	N	N	Y	Y	N	Y	Y	Y
3 ***Nielson***	Y	N	Y	Y	N	Y	Y	Y
VERMONT								
AL ***Jeffords***	Y	Y	Y	N	Y	Y	N	Y
VIRGINIA								
1 ***Bateman***	Y	N	Y	Y	Y	N	Y	Y
2 ***Whitehurst***	Y	N	?	Y	N	Y	Y	Y
3 ***Bliley***	Y	N	Y	N	N	Y	Y	Y
4 Sisisky	?	Y	Y	N	Y	Y	Y	Y
5 Daniel	Y	Y	Y	N	Y	Y	Y	Y
6 Olin	Y	Y	Y	N	Y	Y	N	Y
7 ***Slaughter***	Y	N	Y	Y	N	N	Y	Y
8 ***Parris***	Y	N	Y	Y	N	N	Y	Y
9 Boucher	Y	Y	Y	N	Y	Y	N	Y
10 ***Wolf***	Y	N	Y	Y	N	Y	Y	Y
WASHINGTON								
1 ***Miller***	Y	Y	Y	N	Y	Y	Y	Y
2 Swift	Y	Y	Y	N	Y	Y	N	Y
3 Bonker	Y	Y	Y	N	Y	Y	N	Y
4 ***Morrison***	Y	N	Y	Y	Y	Y	Y	Y
5 Foley	Y	Y	?	N	Y	Y	N	Y
6 Dicks	Y	Y	Y	N	Y	Y	N	Y
7 Lowry	Y	Y	N	N	Y	Y	N	Y
8 ***Chandler***	?	?	?	?	?	?	?	?
WEST VIRGINIA								
1 Mollohan	Y	Y	Y	N	Y	Y	N	Y
2 Staggers	Y	Y	Y	N	Y	Y	N	Y
3 Wise	Y	Y	Y	N	Y	Y	N	Y
4 Rahall	?	Y	N	N	Y	Y	N	Y
WISCONSIN								
1 Aspin	Y	Y	Y	N	Y	Y	N	Y
2 Kastenmeier	N	Y	Y	N	Y	Y	N	Y
3 ***Gunderson***	Y	N	Y	Y	N	N	Y	Y
4 Kleczka	Y	Y	Y	N	Y	Y	N	Y
5 Moody	Y	Y	Y	N	Y	Y	N	Y
6 ***Petri***	Y	Y	Y	Y	N	Y	Y	Y
7 Obey	Y	Y	Y	N	Y	Y	N	Y
8 ***Roth***	Y	N	Y	Y	N	Y	Y	Y
9 ***Sensenbrenner***	Y	N	Y	N	N	Y	Y	Y
WYOMING								
AL ***Cheney***	N	?	?	?	?	?	#	?

Southern states - Ala., Ark., Fla., Ga., Ky., La., Miss., N.C., Okla., S.C., Tenn., Texas, Va.

* The *Congressional Record* vote number is different from the CQ vote number because the *Record* includes quorum calls in its tally. CQ does not publish quorum call votes.

166. H Con Res 350. Adherence to SALT II Agreements. Adoption of the concurrent resolution to urge President Reagan not to disregard certain weapons limits set by the unratified strategic arms limitation treaty (SALT II). Adopted 256-145: R 37-128; D 219-17 (ND 156-4, SD 63-13), June 19, 1986. A "nay" was a vote supporting the president's position.

167. Procedural Motion. McCandless, R-Calif., motion to approve the House *Journal* of Monday, June 23. Motion agreed to 261-120: R 49-112; D 212-8 (ND 145-6, SD 67-2), June 24, 1986.

168. H Con Res 345. Democracy in South Korea. Solarz, D-N.Y., motion to suspend the rules and adopt the concurrent resolution to express the sense of Congress regarding democracy in South Korea and calling for a dialogue between the government and the democratic opposition. Motion agreed to 414-0: R 172-0; D 242-0 (ND 164-0, SD 78-0), June 24, 1986. A two-thirds majority of those present and voting (276 in this case) is required for adoption under suspension of the rules.

169. H Con Res 347. Human Rights in North Korea. Solarz, D-N.Y., motion to suspend the rules and adopt the concurrent resolution to express the sense of Congress that North Korea should take steps to reduce tensions on the Korean peninsula and cease its abuse of human rights. Motion agreed to 403-0: R 169-0; D 234-0 (ND 160-0, SD 74-0), June 24, 1986. A two-thirds majority of those present and voting (269 in this case) is required for adoption under suspension of the rules.

170. S J Res 361. Chilean Tall Ship. Barnes, D-Md., motion to suspend the rules and pass the joint resolution to disinvite the Chilean tall ship *Esmeralda* from the July 4 Statue of Liberty celebration because of its use for the torture of 112 political prisoners in 1973. Motion rejected 194-223: R 27-148; D 167-75 (ND 136-28, SD 31-47), June 24, 1986. A two-thirds majority of those present and voting (278 in this case) is required for passage under suspension of the rules.

171. HR 4060. Civil Service Retirees' COLA. Oakar, D-Ohio, motion to suspend the rules and pass the bill to guarantee a cost-of-living adjustment (COLA) to civil service retirees in January 1987. Motion agreed to 396-19: R 159-16; D 237-3 (ND 163-0, SD 74-3), June 24, 1986. A two-thirds majority of those present and voting (277 in this case) is required for passage under suspension of the rules.

172. HR 3559. Bicentennial Commission on the Constitution. Garcia, D-N.Y., motion to suspend the rules and pass the bill to make some changes in the law that established the Commission on the Bicentennial of the Constitution. Motion agreed to 409-7: R 167-7; D 242-0 (ND 164-0, SD 78-0), June 24, 1986. A two-thirds majority of those present and voting (278 in this case) is required for passage under suspension of the rules.

173. HR 4252. Federal Fire Protection. Walgren, D-Pa., motion to suspend the rules and pass the bill to authorize $18.3 million in fiscal 1987 for U.S. fire prevention and control programs under the Federal Emergency Management Agency. Motion agreed to 386-28: R 145-28; D 241-0 (ND 163-0, SD 78-0), June 24, 1986. A two-thirds majority of those present and voting (276 in this case) is required for passage under suspension of the rules. (The House subsequently passed S 2180, the Senate-passed version of HR 4252, which also contained provisions extending daylight-saving time from the last Sunday in April to the first Sunday in April. That action cleared the bill for the president.)

KEY

- Y Voted for (yea).
- # Paired for.
- + Announced for.
- N Voted against (nay).
- X Paired against.
- \- Announced against.
- P Voted "present."
- C Voted "present" to avoid possible conflict of interest.
- ? Did not vote or otherwise make a position known.

Democrats ***Republicans***

	166	167	168	169	170	171	172	173
ALABAMA								
1 ***Callahan***	N	N	Y	Y	N	Y	Y	Y
2 ***Dickinson***	N	N	Y	Y	N	Y	Y	Y
3 Nichols	N	?	?	?	?	?	?	?
4 Bevill	Y	Y	Y	Y	N	Y	Y	Y
5 Flippo	Y	Y	Y	Y	N	Y	Y	Y
6 Erdreich	Y	Y	Y	Y	N	Y	Y	Y
7 Shelby	N	Y	Y	Y	N	Y	Y	Y
ALASKA								
AL ***Young***	N	N	Y	Y	N	Y	Y	Y
ARIZONA								
1 ***McCain***	N	N	Y	Y	N	Y	Y	Y
2 Udall	Y	Y	Y	Y	Y	Y	Y	Y
3 ***Stump***	N	N	Y	Y	N	Y	Y	N
4 ***Rudd***	X	Y	Y	Y	N	Y	Y	Y
5 ***Kolbe***	Y	N	Y	Y	N	Y	Y	Y
ARKANSAS								
1 Alexander	Y	Y	Y	Y	Y	Y	Y	Y
2 Robinson	Y	Y	Y	?	N	Y	Y	Y
3 ***Hammerschmidt***	N	N	Y	Y	N	Y	Y	Y
4 Anthony	#	Y	Y	Y	N	Y	Y	Y
CALIFORNIA								
1 Bosco	Y	Y	Y	Y	N	Y	Y	Y
2 ***Chappie***	N	N	Y	Y	N	Y	Y	Y
3 Matsui	Y	Y	Y	Y	Y	Y	Y	Y
4 Fazio	Y	Y	Y	Y	Y	Y	Y	Y
5 Burton	#	Y	Y	Y	Y	?	Y	Y
6 Boxer	Y	Y	Y	Y	Y	Y	Y	Y
7 Miller	Y	Y	Y	Y	Y	Y	Y	Y
8 Dellums	Y	Y	Y	Y	Y	Y	Y	Y
9 Stark	Y	Y	Y	Y	Y	Y	Y	Y
10 Edwards	Y	Y	Y	Y	Y	Y	Y	Y
11 Lantos	Y	Y	Y	Y	Y	Y	Y	Y
12 ***Zschau***	Y	N	Y	Y	Y	Y	Y	Y
13 Mineta	Y	Y	Y	Y	Y	Y	Y	Y
14 ***Shumway***	N	?	?	?	?	?	?	?
15 Coelho	Y	Y	Y	Y	Y	Y	Y	Y
16 Panetta	Y	Y	Y	Y	Y	Y	Y	Y
17 ***Pashayan***	N	N	Y	Y	N	Y	Y	Y
18 Lehman	Y	?	Y	Y	Y	Y	Y	Y
19 ***Lagomarsino***	N	N	Y	Y	N	Y	Y	Y
20 ***Thomas***	N	N	Y	Y	N	Y	Y	Y
21 ***Fiedler***	N	N	Y	Y	N	Y	Y	Y
22 ***Moorhead***	N	N	Y	Y	N	Y	Y	Y
23 Beilenson	Y	Y	Y	Y	Y	Y	Y	Y
24 Waxman	Y	Y	Y	Y	Y	Y	Y	Y
25 Roybal	?	Y	Y	Y	N	Y	Y	Y
26 Berman	Y	Y	Y	Y	Y	Y	Y	Y
27 Levine	Y	Y	Y	Y	Y	Y	Y	Y
28 Dixon	Y	Y	Y	?	Y	Y	Y	Y
29 Hawkins	Y	N	Y	Y	Y	Y	Y	Y
30 Martinez	Y	Y	Y	Y	Y	Y	Y	Y
31 Dymally	Y	Y	Y	Y	Y	Y	Y	Y
32 Anderson	Y	Y	Y	Y	Y	Y	Y	Y
33 ***Dreier***	N	N	Y	Y	N	Y	Y	Y
34 Torres	Y	Y	Y	Y	Y	Y	Y	Y
35 ***Lewis***	X	N	Y	Y	N	Y	Y	Y
36 Brown	Y	Y	Y	Y	Y	Y	Y	Y
37 ***McCandless***	N	N	Y	Y	N	Y	Y	N
38 ***Dornan***	N	?	Y	Y	Y	Y	Y	Y
39 ***Dannemeyer***	N	N	Y	Y	N	N	Y	N
40 ***Badham***	X	N	Y	Y	N	Y	Y	N
41 ***Lowery***	N	N	Y	Y	N	Y	Y	Y
42 ***Lungren***	N	N	Y	Y	N	Y	Y	Y
43 ***Packard***	N	Y	Y	Y	N	Y	Y	N
44 Bates	Y	Y	Y	Y	Y	Y	Y	Y
45 ***Hunter***	N	N	Y	Y	N	Y	Y	Y
COLORADO								
1 Schroeder	Y	N	Y	Y	Y	Y	Y	Y
2 Wirth	Y	Y	Y	Y	Y	Y	Y	Y
3 ***Strang***	N	N	Y	Y	N	Y	Y	Y
4 ***Brown***	Y	N	Y	Y	N	N	N	N
5 ***Kramer***	N	N	Y	Y	Y	Y	Y	Y
6 ***Schaefer***	N	Y	Y	Y	N	Y	Y	Y
CONNECTICUT								
1 Kennelly	Y	Y	Y	Y	Y	Y	Y	Y
2 Gejdenson	Y	?	Y	Y	Y	Y	Y	Y
3 Morrison	Y	Y	Y	Y	Y	Y	Y	Y
4 ***McKinney***	#	Y	Y	Y	Y	Y	Y	Y
5 ***Rowland***	N	N	Y	Y	N	Y	Y	Y
6 ***Johnson***	Y	?	?	Y	N	Y	Y	Y
DELAWARE								
AL Carper	Y	Y	Y	Y	Y	Y	Y	Y
FLORIDA								
1 Hutto	N	Y	Y	Y	N	Y	Y	Y
2 Fuqua	?	Y	Y	Y	N	Y	Y	Y
3 Bennett	Y	Y	Y	Y	N	Y	Y	Y
4 Chappell	Y	?	Y	Y	N	Y	Y	Y
5 ***McCollum***	N	N	Y	Y	N	Y	Y	Y
6 MacKay	Y	Y	Y	Y	Y	Y	Y	Y
7 Gibbons	Y	Y	Y	Y	Y	Y	Y	Y
8 ***Young***	N	?	Y	Y	N	Y	Y	Y
9 ***Bilirakis***	N	N	Y	Y	N	Y	Y	Y
10 ***Ireland***	N	N	Y	Y	N	Y	Y	Y
11 Nelson	Y	Y	Y	Y	N	Y	Y	Y
12 ***Lewis***	N	N	Y	Y	N	Y	Y	Y
13 ***Mack***	N	?	Y	Y	N	Y	N	N
14 Mica	Y	Y	Y	Y	N	Y	Y	Y
15 ***Shaw***	N	N	Y	Y	N	Y	Y	Y
16 Smith	Y	Y	Y	Y	Y	Y	Y	Y
17 Lehman	Y	Y	Y	Y	Y	Y	Y	Y
18 Pepper	Y	Y	Y	Y	Y	Y	Y	Y
19 Fascell	Y	Y	Y	Y	Y	Y	Y	Y
GEORGIA								
1 Thomas	Y	Y	Y	Y	N	Y	Y	Y
2 Hatcher	?	Y	Y	Y	N	Y	Y	Y
3 Ray	N	Y	Y	Y	N	N	Y	Y
4 ***Swindall***	N	N	Y	Y	N	Y	Y	Y
5 Fowler	Y	?	?	?	?	?	?	?
6 ***Gingrich***	N	N	Y	Y	N	Y	Y	Y
7 Darden	Y	Y	Y	Y	N	Y	Y	Y
8 Rowland	Y	Y	Y	Y	N	Y	Y	Y
9 Jenkins	Y	Y	Y	Y	N	Y	Y	Y
10 Barnard	Y	Y	Y	Y	N	Y	Y	Y
HAWAII								
1 Heftel	Y	?	Y	Y	Y	Y	Y	Y
2 Akaka	Y	Y	Y	Y	N	Y	Y	Y
IDAHO								
1 ***Craig***	N	?	?	?	?	?	?	?
2 Stallings	N	Y	Y	Y	N	Y	Y	Y
ILLINOIS								
1 Hayes	Y	Y	Y	Y	Y	Y	Y	Y
2 Savage	Y	Y	Y	?	Y	Y	Y	Y
3 Russo	Y	Y	Y	Y	Y	Y	Y	Y
4 ***O'Brien***	?	?	?	?	?	?	?	?
5 Lipinski	Y	Y	Y	Y	N	Y	Y	Y
6 ***Hyde***	N	?	Y	Y	N	Y	Y	Y
7 Collins	Y	?	?	?	?	?	?	?
8 Rostenkowski	?	Y	Y	Y	N	Y	Y	Y
9 Yates	Y	Y	Y	Y	Y	Y	Y	Y
10 ***Porter***	Y	Y	Y	Y	Y	N	Y	?
11 Annunzio	Y	Y	Y	Y	N	Y	Y	Y
12 ***Crane***	N	N	Y	Y	N	N	Y	?
13 ***Fawell***	Y	N	Y	Y	N	N	Y	Y
14 ***Grotberg***	?	?	?	?	?	?	?	?
15 ***Madigan***	N	N	Y	Y	N	Y	Y	Y
16 ***Martin***	N	N	Y	Y	N	Y	Y	Y
17 Evans	Y	Y	Y	Y	Y	Y	Y	Y
18 ***Michel***	N	?	Y	?	N	Y	Y	Y
19 Bruce	Y	Y	Y	Y	Y	Y	Y	Y
20 Durbin	Y	Y	Y	Y	Y	Y	Y	Y
21 Price	Y	Y	Y	Y	N	Y	Y	Y
22 Gray	Y	Y	Y	Y	Y	Y	Y	Y
INDIANA								
1 Visclosky	Y	Y	Y	Y	Y	Y	Y	Y
2 Sharp	Y	Y	Y	Y	Y	Y	Y	Y
3 ***Hiler***	N	N	Y	Y	N	Y	Y	Y
4 ***Coats***	N	Y	Y	Y	N	Y	Y	Y
5 ***Hillis***	?	Y	Y	Y	N	Y	Y	Y

ND - Northern Democrats SD - Southern Democrats

* Corresponding to Congressional Record Votes 186, 187, 188, 189, 190, 191, 192, 193

	166	167	168	169	170	171	172	173
6 ***Burton***	N	N	Y	Y	N	Y	Y	Y
7 ***Myers***	N	Y	Y	Y	N	Y	Y	Y
8 McCloskey	Y	Y	Y	Y	Y	Y	Y	Y
9 Hamilton	Y	Y	Y	Y	Y	Y	Y	Y
10 Jacobs	Y	N	Y	Y	Y	Y	Y	Y
IOWA								
1 ***Leach***	Y	N	Y	Y	Y	Y	Y	Y
2 ***Tauke***	Y	N	Y	Y	N	Y	Y	N
3 ***Evans***	Y	N	Y	Y	N	Y	Y	Y
4 Smith	Y	Y	Y	Y	N	Y	Y	Y
5 ***Lightfoot***	Y	N	Y	Y	N	Y	Y	Y
6 Bedell	Y	Y	Y	Y	Y	Y	Y	Y
KANSAS								
1 ***Roberts***	N	N	Y	Y	N	Y	Y	Y
2 Slattery	Y	Y	Y	Y	Y	Y	Y	Y
3 ***Meyers***	Y	N	Y	Y	Y	Y	Y	Y
4 Glickman	Y	Y	Y	Y	N	Y	Y	Y
5 ***Whittaker***	N	N	Y	Y	N	Y	Y	Y
KENTUCKY								
1 Hubbard	Y	Y	Y	Y	N	Y	Y	Y
2 Natcher	Y	Y	Y	Y	N	Y	Y	Y
3 Mazzoli	N	Y	Y	Y	N	Y	Y	Y
4 ***Snyder***	N	Y	Y	Y	N	Y	Y	Y
5 ***Rogers***	N	N	Y	Y	N	Y	Y	Y
6 ***Hopkins***	N	N	Y	Y	N	Y	Y	Y
7 Perkins	Y	Y	Y	Y	Y	Y	Y	Y
LOUISIANA								
1 ***Livingston***	N	?	Y	Y	N	Y	Y	Y
2 Boggs	Y	Y	Y	Y	N	Y	Y	Y
3 Tauzin	N	Y	Y	Y	N	Y	Y	Y
4 Roemer	N	Y	Y	Y	N	Y	Y	Y
5 Huckaby	#	N	Y	Y	N	Y	Y	Y
6 ***Moore***	N	Y	Y	Y	N	Y	Y	Y
7 Breaux	?	?	?	?	?	?	?	?
8 Long	Y	Y	Y	Y	Y	Y	Y	Y
MAINE								
1 ***McKernan***	Y	N	Y	Y	Y	Y	Y	Y
2 ***Snowe***	Y	N	Y	Y	Y	Y	Y	Y
MARYLAND								
1 Dyson	N	Y	Y	Y	N	Y	Y	Y
2 ***Bentley***	N	?	?	?	?	?	?	?
3 Mikulski	Y	Y	Y	Y	Y	Y	Y	Y
4 ***Holt***	N	N	Y	?	N	Y	Y	Y
5 Hoyer	Y	Y	Y	Y	Y	Y	Y	Y
6 Byron	Y	Y	Y	Y	N	Y	Y	Y
7 Mitchell	Y	?	Y	Y	Y	Y	Y	Y
8 Barnes	Y	Y	Y	Y	Y	Y	Y	Y
MASSACHUSETTS								
1 ***Conte***	Y	N	Y	Y	Y	Y	Y	Y
2 Boland	Y	Y	Y	Y	Y	Y	Y	Y
3 Early	Y	Y	Y	Y	Y	Y	Y	Y
4 Frank	Y	Y	Y	Y	Y	Y	Y	Y
5 Atkins	Y	?	Y	Y	Y	Y	Y	Y
6 Mavroules	Y	?	Y	Y	N	Y	Y	Y
7 Markey	Y	Y	Y	Y	Y	Y	Y	Y
8 O'Neill								
9 Moakley	Y	Y	Y	Y	Y	Y	Y	Y
10 Studds	Y	Y	Y	Y	Y	Y	Y	Y
11 Donnelly	Y	Y	Y	Y	N	Y	Y	Y
MICHIGAN								
1 Conyers	Y	Y	Y	Y	N	Y	Y	Y
2 ***Pursell***	Y	Y	Y	Y	N	Y	Y	Y
3 Wolpe	Y	Y	Y	Y	Y	Y	Y	Y
4 ***Siljander***	N	Y	Y	Y	N	Y	Y	Y
5 ***Henry***	Y	N	Y	Y	Y	Y	Y	Y
6 Carr	Y	Y	Y	Y	N	Y	Y	Y
7 Kildee	Y	Y	Y	Y	Y	Y	Y	Y
8 Traxler	Y	Y	Y	Y	Y	Y	Y	Y
9 ***Vander Jagt***	N	N	Y	Y	N	Y	Y	Y
10 ***Schuette***	N	N	Y	Y	N	Y	Y	Y
11 ***Davis***	?	Y	Y	?	N	Y	Y	Y
12 Bonior	Y	Y	Y	Y	Y	Y	Y	Y
13 Crockett	?	Y	Y	Y	Y	Y	Y	Y
14 Hertel	Y	Y	Y	Y	Y	Y	Y	Y
15 Ford	Y	Y	Y	Y	N	Y	Y	Y
16 Dingell	Y	?	Y	Y	N	Y	Y	Y
17 Levin	Y	Y	Y	Y	Y	Y	Y	Y
18 ***Broomfield***	N	Y	Y	Y	N	Y	Y	Y
MINNESOTA								
1 Penny	Y	N	Y	Y	Y	Y	Y	Y
2 ***Weber***	N	N	Y	Y	N	Y	Y	Y
3 ***Frenzel***	Y	N	Y	Y	Y	N	Y	Y
4 Vento	Y	Y	Y	Y	Y	Y	Y	Y
5 Sabo	Y	Y	Y	Y	Y	Y	Y	Y
6 Sikorski	Y	?	?	?	?	?	?	?

	166	167	168	169	170	171	172	173
7 ***Stangeland***	Y	?	Y	Y	N	Y	Y	Y
8 Oberstar	Y	Y	Y	Y	Y	Y	Y	Y
MISSISSIPPI								
1 Whitten	Y	Y	Y	Y	N	?	Y	Y
2 ***Franklin***	N	?	Y	Y	N	Y	Y	Y
3 Montgomery	N	Y	Y	Y	N	Y	Y	Y
4 Dowdy	Y	?	?	?	?	?	?	?
5 ***Lott***	N	N	Y	Y	N	Y	Y	Y
MISSOURI								
1 Clay	Y	N	Y	Y	Y	Y	Y	Y
2 Young	Y	Y	Y	Y	N	Y	Y	Y
3 Gephardt	Y	Y	Y	Y	Y	Y	Y	Y
4 Skelton	N	Y	Y	Y	Y	Y	Y	Y
5 Wheat	Y	Y	Y	Y	Y	Y	Y	Y
6 ***Coleman***	N	N	Y	Y	N	Y	Y	Y
7 ***Taylor***	N	Y	Y	Y	N	Y	Y	Y
8 ***Emerson***	N	N	Y	Y	N	Y	Y	Y
9 Volkmer	Y	Y	Y	Y	N	Y	Y	Y
MONTANA								
1 Williams	Y	Y	Y	Y	Y	Y	Y	Y
2 ***Marlenee***	N	N	Y	Y	N	Y	Y	N
NEBRASKA								
1 ***Bereuter***	N	N	Y	Y	N	Y	Y	Y
2 ***Daub***	N	N	Y	Y	N	Y	Y	N
3 ***Smith***	N	Y	Y	Y	N	Y	Y	N
NEVADA								
1 Reid	Y	Y	Y	Y	Y	Y	Y	Y
2 ***Vucanovich***	N	N	Y	Y	N	Y	Y	Y
NEW HAMPSHIRE								
1 ***Smith***	N	N	Y	Y	N	Y	Y	Y
2 ***Gregg***	N	?	Y	Y	N	N	Y	N
NEW JERSEY								
1 Florio	Y	Y	Y	Y	Y	Y	Y	Y
2 Hughes	Y	Y	Y	Y	Y	Y	Y	Y
3 Howard	Y	Y	Y	Y	Y	Y	Y	Y
4 ***Smith***	Y	Y	Y	Y	Y	Y	Y	Y
5 ***Roukema***	Y	N	?	Y	Y	Y	Y	Y
6 Dwyer	Y	Y	Y	Y	Y	Y	Y	Y
7 ***Rinaldo***	Y	Y	Y	Y	Y	Y	Y	Y
8 Roe	Y	Y	Y	Y	Y	Y	Y	Y
9 Torricelli	Y	Y	Y	Y	Y	Y	Y	Y
10 Rodino	#	?	?	?	?	?	?	?
11 ***Gallo***	N	N	Y	Y	N	Y	Y	Y
12 ***Courter***	N	N	Y	Y	N	Y	Y	Y
13 ***Saxton***	Y	N	Y	?	Y	Y	Y	Y
14 Guarini	Y	Y	Y	Y	N	Y	Y	Y
NEW MEXICO								
1 ***Lujan***	N	Y	Y	Y	N	Y	Y	N
2 ***Skeen***	N	N	Y	Y	N	Y	Y	Y
3 Richardson	Y	Y	Y	Y	Y	Y	Y	Y
NEW YORK								
1 ***Carney***	N	N	Y	Y	N	Y	Y	Y
2 Downey	Y	Y	Y	Y	Y	Y	Y	Y
3 Mrazek	Y	Y	Y	?	Y	Y	Y	Y
4 ***Lent***	N	N	Y	Y	N	Y	Y	Y
5 ***McGrath***	N	N	Y	Y	Y	Y	Y	Y
6 Vacancy								
7 Ackerman	Y	Y	Y	Y	Y	Y	Y	Y
8 Scheuer	Y	Y	Y	Y	Y	Y	Y	Y
9 Manton	Y	Y	Y	Y	Y	Y	Y	Y
10 Schumer	Y	?	Y	Y	Y	Y	Y	Y
11 Towns	Y	?	Y	Y	Y	Y	Y	Y
12 Owens	Y	?	Y	Y	Y	Y	Y	Y
13 Solarz	Y	Y	Y	Y	Y	Y	Y	Y
14 ***Molinari***	N	N	Y	Y	N	Y	Y	Y
15 ***Green***	Y	Y	Y	Y	Y	Y	Y	Y
16 Rangel	#	Y	Y	Y	Y	Y	Y	Y
17 Weiss	Y	Y	Y	Y	Y	Y	Y	Y
18 Garcia	Y	?	Y	Y	Y	Y	Y	Y
19 Biaggi	Y	?	Y	Y	N	Y	Y	Y
20 ***DioGuardi***	Y	N	Y	Y	N	Y	Y	Y
21 ***Fish***	Y	Y	Y	Y	Y	Y	?	Y
22 ***Gilman***	N	Y	Y	Y	Y	Y	Y	Y
23 Stratton	N	Y	Y	?	N	Y	Y	Y
24 ***Solomon***	N	N	Y	Y	N	Y	Y	Y
25 ***Boehlert***	Y	N	Y	Y	N	Y	Y	Y
26 ***Martin***	X	Y	Y	Y	N	Y	Y	Y
27 ***Wortley***	N	Y	Y	Y	N	Y	Y	Y
28 McHugh	Y	Y	Y	Y	Y	Y	Y	Y
29 ***Horton***	#	?	Y	Y	N	Y	Y	Y
30 ***Eckert***	N	?	?	?	?	?	?	?
31 ***Kemp***	N	Y	Y	Y	N	Y	Y	Y
32 LaFalce	Y	Y	Y	Y	N	Y	Y	Y
33 Nowak	Y	Y	Y	Y	Y	Y	Y	Y
34 Lundine	?	Y	Y	Y	Y	Y	Y	?

	166	167	168	169	170	171	172	173
NORTH CAROLINA								
1 Jones	Y	Y	Y	Y	Y	Y	Y	Y
2 Valentine	N	Y	Y	Y	N	Y	Y	Y
3 Whitley	Y	Y	Y	Y	N	Y	Y	Y
4 ***Cobey***	N	N	Y	Y	N	Y	N	Y
5 Neal	Y	Y	Y	Y	Y	Y	Y	Y
6 ***Coble***	N	N	Y	Y	N	Y	N	Y
7 Rose	Y	Y	Y	Y	N	Y	Y	Y
8 Hefner	Y	Y	Y	?	N	Y	Y	Y
9 ***McMillan***	N	Y	Y	?	N	Y	Y	Y
10 ***Broyhill***	N	Y	Y	Y	N	Y	Y	Y
11 ***Hendon***	N	N	Y	Y	N	Y	Y	Y
NORTH DAKOTA								
AL Dorgan	Y	Y	Y	Y	Y	Y	Y	Y
OHIO								
1 Luken	Y	?	?	?	?	+	?	?
2 ***Gradison***	N	Y	Y	Y	N	N	Y	Y
3 Hall	Y	Y	Y	Y	Y	Y	Y	Y
4 ***Oxley***	N	N	Y	Y	N	Y	Y	N
5 ***Latta***	N	N	Y	Y	N	Y	Y	N
6 ***McEwen***	N	Y	Y	Y	N	Y	Y	Y
7 ***DeWine***	N	N	Y	Y	N	Y	Y	Y
8 ***Kindness***	N	Y	Y	Y	N	Y	Y	Y
9 Kaptur	Y	Y	Y	Y	Y	Y	Y	Y
10 ***Miller***	N	N	Y	Y	N	Y	Y	N
11 Eckart	Y	Y	Y	Y	Y	Y	Y	Y
12 ***Kasich***	N	Y	Y	Y	N	Y	Y	Y
13 Pease	Y	Y	Y	Y	Y	Y	Y	Y
14 Seiberling	Y	Y	Y	Y	Y	Y	Y	Y
15 ***Wylie***	Y	Y	Y	Y	N	Y	Y	Y
16 ***Regula***	Y	Y	Y	Y	N	Y	Y	Y
17 Traficant	Y	Y	Y	Y	Y	Y	Y	Y
18 Applegate	Y	Y	Y	Y	Y	Y	Y	Y
19 Feighan	Y	Y	Y	Y	Y	Y	Y	Y
20 Oakar	Y	Y	Y	Y	Y	Y	Y	Y
21 Stokes	Y	Y	Y	Y	Y	Y	Y	Y
OKLAHOMA								
1 Jones	Y	Y	Y	Y	Y	Y	Y	Y
2 Synar	Y	Y	Y	Y	Y	Y	Y	Y
3 Watkins	Y	Y	Y	Y	Y	Y	Y	Y
4 McCurdy	Y	Y	Y	Y	Y	Y	Y	Y
5 ***Edwards***	N	N	Y	Y	N	Y	Y	Y
6 English	Y	Y	Y	Y	Y	Y	Y	Y
OREGON								
1 AuCoin	Y	Y	Y	Y	Y	Y	Y	Y
2 ***Smith, R.***	N	N	Y	Y	N	Y	Y	Y
3 Wyden	Y	Y	Y	Y	Y	Y	Y	Y
4 Weaver	?	?	?	?	?	?	?	?
5 ***Smith, D.***	N	N	Y	Y	N	N	Y	N
PENNSYLVANIA								
1 Foglietta	Y	Y	Y	Y	Y	Y	Y	Y
2 Gray	?	Y	Y	Y	Y	Y	Y	Y
3 Borski	Y	Y	Y	Y	Y	Y	Y	Y
4 Kolter	Y	Y	Y	Y	Y	Y	Y	Y
5 ***Schulze***	Y	Y	Y	Y	N	Y	Y	Y
6 Yatron	Y	Y	Y	Y	Y	Y	Y	Y
7 Edgar	Y	?	Y	Y	Y	Y	Y	Y
8 Kostmayer	Y	Y	Y	Y	Y	Y	Y	Y
9 ***Shuster***	N	N	Y	Y	N	Y	Y	Y
10 ***McDade***	Y	Y	Y	?	Y	Y	Y	Y
11 Kanjorski	Y	Y	Y	Y	N	Y	Y	Y
12 Murtha	Y	Y	Y	Y	N	Y	Y	Y
13 ***Coughlin***	Y	N	Y	Y	Y	Y	Y	Y
14 Coyne	Y	Y	Y	Y	Y	Y	Y	Y
15 ***Ritter***	N	Y	Y	Y	N	Y	Y	Y
16 ***Walker***	N	N	Y	Y	N	N	N	N
17 ***Gekas***	N	N	Y	Y	N	Y	Y	N
18 Walgren	Y	Y	Y	Y	Y	Y	Y	Y
19 ***Goodling***	Y	N	Y	Y	N	Y	Y	Y
20 Gaydos	Y	Y	Y	Y	N	Y	Y	Y
21 ***Ridge***	Y	?	Y	Y	N	Y	Y	Y
22 Murphy	Y	Y	Y	Y	N	Y	Y	Y
23 ***Clinger***	Y	Y	Y	Y	N	Y	Y	Y
RHODE ISLAND								
1 St Germain	Y	Y	Y	Y	Y	Y	Y	Y
2 ***Schneider***	Y	Y	Y	Y	Y	Y	Y	Y
SOUTH CAROLINA								
1 ***Hartnett***	X	N	Y	Y	N	Y	Y	N
2 ***Spence***	N	Y	Y	Y	N	Y	Y	Y
3 Derrick	Y	Y	Y	Y	Y	Y	Y	Y
4 ***Campbell***	X	?	?	?	?	?	?	?
5 Spratt	Y	Y	Y	Y	Y	Y	Y	Y
6 Tallon	Y	P	Y	Y	N	Y	Y	Y
SOUTH DAKOTA								
AL Daschle	Y	Y	Y	Y	Y	Y	Y	Y

	166	167	168	169	170	171	172	173
TENNESSEE								
1 ***Quillen***	N	Y	Y	Y	N	Y	Y	Y
2 ***Duncan***	N	Y	Y	Y	N	Y	Y	Y
3 Lloyd	N	N	Y	Y	N	Y	Y	Y
4 Cooper	Y	Y	Y	Y	Y	N	Y	Y
5 Boner	Y	Y	Y	Y	Y	Y	Y	Y
6 Gordon	Y	Y	Y	Y	Y	Y	Y	Y
7 ***Sundquist***	N	N	Y	Y	N	Y	Y	Y
8 Jones	Y	?	Y	Y	N	Y	Y	Y
9 Ford	Y	?	Y	Y	Y	Y	Y	Y
TEXAS								
1 Chapman	Y	?	Y	Y	Y	Y	Y	Y
2 Wilson	Y	Y	Y	?	N	Y	Y	Y
3 ***Bartlett***	N	N	Y	Y	Y	N	Y	N
4 Hall, R.	N	Y	Y	Y	N	Y	Y	Y
5 Bryant	Y	P	Y	Y	Y	Y	Y	Y
6 ***Barton***	?	N	Y	Y	N	N	N	N
7 ***Archer***	N	Y	Y	Y	N	Y	Y	Y
8 ***Fields***	N	N	Y	Y	N	Y	Y	Y
9 Brooks	Y	Y	Y	Y	N	Y	Y	Y
10 Pickle	Y	Y	Y	?	Y	Y	Y	Y
11 Leath	Y	?	Y	Y	N	Y	Y	Y
12 Wright	Y	Y	Y	Y	N	Y	Y	Y
13 ***Boulter***	N	N	Y	Y	N	Y	Y	Y
14 ***Sweeney***	?	Y	Y	Y	N	Y	Y	Y
15 de la Garza	Y	Y	Y	Y	N	Y	Y	Y
16 Coleman	Y	Y	Y	Y	Y	Y	Y	Y
17 Stenholm	N	Y	Y	Y	N	N	Y	Y
18 Leland	Y	?	Y	Y	Y	Y	Y	Y
19 ***Combest***	N	Y	Y	Y	N	Y	Y	Y
20 Gonzalez	Y	Y	Y	Y	Y	Y	Y	Y
21 ***Loeffler***	N	N	Y	Y	N	Y	Y	Y
22 ***DeLay***	N	N	Y	Y	N	N	Y	N
23 Bustamante	?	Y	Y	Y	N	Y	Y	Y
24 Frost	Y	Y	Y	Y	Y	Y	Y	Y
25 Andrews	Y	Y	Y	Y	N	Y	Y	Y
26 ***Armey***	N	N	Y	Y	N	N	Y	N
27 Ortiz	Y	Y	Y	Y	N	Y	Y	Y
UTAH								
1 ***Hansen***	N	N	Y	Y	N	Y	Y	N
2 ***Monson***	?	N	Y	Y	N	N	N	N
3 ***Nielson***	N	Y	Y	Y	N	Y	Y	N
VERMONT								
AL ***Jeffords***	Y	Y	Y	Y	Y	Y	Y	Y
VIRGINIA								
1 ***Bateman***	N	Y	Y	Y	N	Y	Y	Y
2 ***Whitehurst***	N	N	Y	Y	N	Y	Y	Y
3 ***Bliley***	N	N	Y	Y	N	Y	Y	Y
4 Sisisky	Y	Y	Y	Y	Y	Y	Y	Y
5 Daniel	N	?	Y	Y	N	Y	Y	Y
6 Olin	Y	Y	Y	Y	N	Y	Y	Y
7 ***Slaughter***	N	N	Y	Y	N	Y	Y	Y
8 ***Parris***	N	N	?	Y	N	Y	Y	Y
9 Boucher	Y	Y	Y	Y	Y	Y	Y	Y
10 ***Wolf***	N	N	Y	Y	N	Y	Y	Y
WASHINGTON								
1 ***Miller***	N	?	Y	Y	N	Y	Y	Y
2 Swift	Y	Y	Y	Y	Y	Y	Y	Y
3 Bonker	Y	Y	Y	Y	Y	Y	Y	Y
4 ***Morrison***	N	Y	Y	Y	Y	Y	Y	Y
5 Foley	Y	Y	Y	Y	Y	Y	Y	Y
6 Dicks	Y	Y	Y	Y	Y	Y	Y	Y
7 Lowry	Y	N	Y	Y	Y	Y	Y	Y
8 ***Chandler***	?	N	Y	Y	Y	Y	Y	Y
WEST VIRGINIA								
1 Mollohan	Y	Y	Y	Y	Y	Y	Y	Y
2 Staggers	Y	Y	Y	Y	Y	Y	Y	Y
3 Wise	Y	Y	Y	Y	Y	Y	Y	Y
4 Rahall	Y	Y	Y	Y	Y	Y	Y	Y
WISCONSIN								
1 Aspin	Y	Y	Y	Y	Y	Y	Y	Y
2 Kastenmeier	Y	Y	Y	Y	Y	Y	Y	Y
3 ***Gunderson***	Y	N	Y	Y	N	Y	Y	Y
4 Kleczka	Y	Y	Y	Y	Y	Y	Y	Y
5 Moody	Y	Y	Y	Y	Y	Y	Y	Y
6 ***Petri***	N	Y	Y	Y	N	Y	Y	Y
7 Obey	Y	Y	Y	Y	Y	Y	Y	Y
8 ***Roth***	N	?	Y	Y	N	Y	Y	Y
9 ***Sensenbrenner***	N	N	Y	Y	N	N	Y	Y
WYOMING								
AL ***Cheney***	X	N	Y	Y	N	Y	Y	N

Southern states - Ala., Ark., Fla., Ga., Ky., La., Miss., N.C., Okla., S.C., Tenn., Texas, Va.

* The *Congressional Record* vote number is different from the CQ vote number because the *Record* includes quorum calls in its tally. CQ does not publish quorum call votes.

174. HR 4515. Urgent Supplemental Appropriations, Fiscal 1986. Adoption of the conference report on the bill to appropriate $1,698,120,000 for various government programs for fiscal 1986. Adopted 355-52: R 133-39; D 222-13 (ND 151-8, SD 71-5), June 24, 1986.

175. Procedural Motion. Sundquist, R-Tenn., motion to approve the House *Journal* of Tuesday, June 24. Motion agreed to 273-119: R 57-113; D 216-6 (ND 146-5, SD 70-1), June 25, 1986.

176. HR 5052. Military Construction Appropriations, Fiscal 1987/Aid to Nicaraguan Rebels. Adoption of the rule (H Res 481) to provide for House floor consideration of the bill to appropriate funds for military construction projects in fiscal 1987, with amendments dealing with aid to the "contra" rebels in Nicaragua. Adopted 279-148: R 153-26; D 126-122 (ND 58-108, SD 68-14), June 25, 1986.

177. HR 5052. Military Construction Appropriations, Fiscal 1987/Aid to Nicaraguan Rebels. Hertel, D-Mich., amendment to drop from the bill $138 million for new naval bases in New York and Washington state. Adopted 241-190: R 89-91; D 152-99 (ND 128-41, SD 24-58), June 25, 1986. A "nay" was a vote supporting the president's position.

178. HR 5052. Military Construction Appropriations, Fiscal 1987/Aid to Nicaraguan Rebels. Edwards, R-Okla., substitute for title II of the bill, to provide $70 million in military aid and $30 million in non-military aid to the "contra" guerrillas in Nicaragua and $300 million in economic aid to Costa Rica, El Salvador, Guatemala and Honduras. Adopted 221-209: R 170-11; D 51-198 (ND 8-159, SD 43-39), June 25, 1986. A "yea" was a vote supporting the president's position.

179. HR 5052. Military Construction Appropriations, Fiscal 1987/Aid to Nicaraguan Rebels. Hamilton, D-Ind., substitute for title II of the bill as amended by the Edwards, R-Okla., substitute *(see vote 178, above)*, to provide $27 million for Nicaraguan refugees and $5 million to promote peace negotiations in Central America. Rejected 183-245: R 7-173; D 176-72 (ND 152-15, SD 24-57), June 25, 1986. A "nay" was a vote supporting the president's position.

180. HR 5052. Military Construction Appropriations, Fiscal 1987/Aid to Nicaraguan Rebels. Barnes, D-Md., amendment to title II of the bill as amended by the Edwards, R-Okla., substitute *(see vote 178, above)*, to prohibit obligation of aid to the Nicaraguan "contras" until the president provided a full accounting to Congress of $27 million in previously appropriated non-military aid. Rejected 198-225: R 7-171; D 191-54 (ND 154-10, SD 37-44), June 25, 1986. A "nay" was a vote supporting the president's position.

181. HR 5052. Military Construction Appropriations, Fiscal 1987/Aid to Nicaraguan Rebels. Mrazek, D-N.Y., amendment to title II of the bill as amended by the Edwards, R-Okla., substitute *(see vote 178, above)*, to prohibit U.S. government personnel from providing training or other services to the Nicaraguan "contras" in Honduras or Costa Rica within 20 miles of the border with Nicaragua. Adopted 215-212: R 23-156; D 192-56 (ND 160-6, SD 32-50), June 25, 1986. A "nay" was a vote supporting the president's position.

KEY

Y Voted for (yea).
\# Paired for.
\+ Announced for.
N Voted against (nay).
X Paired against.
\- Announced against.
P Voted "present."
C Voted "present" to avoid possible conflict of interest.
? Did not vote or otherwise make a position known.

Democrats ***Republicans***

	174	175	176	177	178	179	180	181
ALABAMA								
1 ***Callahan***	Y	Y	Y	N	Y	N	N	N
2 ***Dickinson***	Y	N	Y	N	Y	N	N	N
3 Nichols	X	Y	Y	N	Y	N	N	N
4 Bevill	Y	?	Y	N	Y	N	Y	N
5 Flippo	Y	Y	Y	N	Y	N	Y	N
6 Erdreich	Y	Y	Y	N	Y	N	Y	N
7 Shelby	Y	?	Y	N	Y	N	N	N
ALASKA								
AL ***Young***	Y	N	Y	N	Y	N	N	N
ARIZONA								
1 ***McCain***	Y	N	Y	Y	Y	N	N	N
2 Udall	Y	Y	Y	Y	N	Y	?	Y
3 ***Stump***	N	N	N	N	Y	N	N	N
4 ***Rudd***	Y	Y	Y	N	Y	N	N	N
5 ***Kolbe***	Y	N	Y	Y	Y	N	N	N
ARKANSAS								
1 Alexander	Y	Y	N	N	N	Y	Y	Y
2 Robinson	Y	Y	Y	N	Y	N	N	N
3 ***Hammerschmidt***	Y	Y	Y	N	Y	N	N	N
4 Anthony	Y	Y	Y	N	N	N	Y	Y
CALIFORNIA								
1 Bosco	Y	Y	N	Y	N	Y	Y	?
2 ***Chappie***	Y	N	Y	Y	Y	N	N	N
3 Matsui	Y	Y	Y	N	N	Y	Y	Y
4 Fazio	Y	Y	Y	Y	N	Y	Y	Y
5 Burton	Y	?	N	Y	N	Y	Y	Y
6 Boxer	Y	Y	N	Y	N	Y	Y	Y
7 Miller	?	Y	N	Y	N	Y	Y	Y
8 Dellums	Y	Y	N	Y	N	Y	Y	Y
9 Stark	Y	Y	?	Y	N	Y	Y	Y
10 Edwards	Y	Y	N	Y	N	Y	Y	Y
11 Lantos	Y	Y	Y	Y	N	Y	Y	Y
12 ***Zschau***	Y	N	Y	Y	Y	N	N	N
13 Mineta	Y	Y	N	Y	N	Y	Y	Y
14 ***Shumway***	?	Y	N	Y	Y	N	N	N
15 Coelho	Y	Y	Y	Y	N	Y	Y	Y
16 Panetta	Y	Y	N	Y	N	Y	Y	Y
17 ***Pashayan***	Y	N	Y	Y	Y	N	N	N
18 Lehman	Y	Y	N	Y	N	Y	Y	Y
19 ***Lagomarsino***	Y	N	Y	Y	Y	N	N	N
20 ***Thomas***	Y	?	Y	Y	Y	N	N	N
21 ***Fiedler***	Y	N	Y	Y	Y	N	N	N
22 ***Moorhead***	N	N	Y	Y	Y	N	N	N
23 Beilenson	Y	Y	Y	Y	N	Y	Y	Y
24 Waxman	Y	Y	N	Y	N	Y	Y	Y
25 Roybal	Y	Y	N	Y	N	Y	Y	Y
26 Berman	Y	?	N	N	N	Y	Y	Y
27 Levine	Y	Y	N	Y	N	Y	Y	Y
28 Dixon	Y	?	N	Y	N	Y	Y	Y
29 Hawkins	Y	Y	N	Y	?	Y	Y	Y
30 Martinez	Y	Y	N	Y	N	Y	Y	Y
31 Dymally	Y	Y	N	Y	N	Y	Y	Y
32 Anderson	Y	Y	N	Y	N	Y	Y	Y
33 ***Dreier***	N	N	Y	Y	Y	N	N	N
34 Torres	Y	Y	N	Y	N	Y	Y	Y
35 ***Lewis***	Y	N	N	Y	Y	N	N	N
36 Brown	Y	Y	?	Y	N	Y	Y	Y
37 ***McCandless***	N	N	Y	Y	Y	N	N	N
38 ***Dornan***	N	N	Y	N	Y	N	N	N
39 ***Dannemeyer***	N	N	Y	Y	Y	N	N	N
40 ***Badham***	Y	N	Y	Y	Y	N	N	N
41 ***Lowery***	Y	N	Y	Y	Y	N	N	N
42 ***Lungren***	N	N	Y	Y	Y	N	N	N
43 ***Packard***	N	Y	Y	Y	Y	N	N	N
44 Bates	Y	Y	N	Y	N	Y	Y	Y
45 ***Hunter***	Y	Y	N	Y	Y	N	N	N
COLORADO								
1 Schroeder	N	N	N	Y	N	Y	Y	Y
2 Wirth	N	Y	N	Y	N	Y	Y	Y
3 ***Strang***	Y	N	Y	N	Y	N	N	N
4 ***Brown***	N	N	N	Y	Y	N	N	Y
5 ***Kramer***	Y	N	Y	N	Y	N	N	N
6 ***Schaefer***	N	N	Y	Y	Y	N	N	N
CONNECTICUT								
1 Kennelly	Y	Y	N	N	N	Y	Y	Y
2 Gejdenson	Y	Y	N	Y	N	Y	Y	Y
3 Morrison	Y	Y	N	Y	N	Y	Y	Y
4 ***McKinney***	?	Y	N	N	N	N	Y	Y
5 ***Rowland***	Y	N	Y	N	Y	N	N	N
6 ***Johnson***	Y	Y	Y	N	Y	N	N	N
DELAWARE								
AL Carper	Y	Y	Y	Y	N	N	Y	Y
FLORIDA								
1 Hutto	Y	Y	Y	N	Y	N	N	N
2 Fuqua	Y	Y	Y	N	Y	N	N	N
3 Bennett	Y	Y	Y	N	Y	N	N	Y
4 Chappell	Y	Y	Y	N	Y	N	N	N
5 ***McCollum***	N	N	Y	N	Y	N	N	N
6 MacKay	Y	Y	Y	Y	N	N	N	Y
7 Gibbons	Y	Y	Y	N	Y	N	N	N
8 ***Young***	Y	N	Y	N	Y	N	N	N
9 ***Bilirakis***	N	N	Y	N	Y	N	N	N
10 ***Ireland***	Y	?	Y	N	Y	N	N	N
11 Nelson	Y	Y	Y	N	Y	N	N	N
12 ***Lewis***	N	N	Y	N	Y	N	N	N
13 ***Mack***	N	N	Y	N	Y	N	N	N
14 Mica	Y	Y	Y	N	Y	N	Y	Y
15 ***Shaw***	Y	N	Y	N	Y	N	N	N
16 Smith	Y	?	Y	N	Y	N	N	Y
17 Lehman	Y	Y	N	N	N	Y	Y	Y
18 Pepper	Y	Y	Y	N	Y	N	N	N
19 Fascell	Y	Y	Y	N	Y	N	N	N
GEORGIA								
1 Thomas	Y	?	Y	Y	Y	N	N	N
2 Hatcher	Y	?	Y	Y	Y	N	N	N
3 Ray	N	Y	Y	Y	Y	N	N	N
4 ***Swindall***	N	N	Y	Y	Y	N	N	N
5 Fowler	?	?	Y	Y	N	Y	Y	N
6 ***Gingrich***	Y	N	N	Y	Y	N	N	N
7 Darden	Y	Y	Y	N	Y	N	N	N
8 Rowland	Y	Y	Y	Y	Y	N	N	N
9 Jenkins	Y	?	Y	Y	Y	N	N	N
10 Barnard	Y	Y	Y	N	Y	N	N	N
HAWAII								
1 Heftel	Y	Y	Y	Y	N	Y	?	Y
2 Akaka	Y	Y	Y	Y	N	Y	Y	Y
IDAHO								
1 ***Craig***	N	N	Y	N	Y	N	N	N
2 Stallings	Y	?	Y	N	N	N	Y	Y
ILLINOIS								
1 Hayes	Y	Y	N	Y	N	Y	Y	Y
2 Savage	Y	Y	N	Y	N	Y	Y	Y
3 Russo	N	Y	N	Y	N	Y	Y	Y
4 ***O'Brien***	?	?	?	?	Y	?	?	?
5 Lipinski	Y	Y	Y	Y	Y	N	N	Y
6 ***Hyde***	Y	?	Y	Y	Y	N	N	N
7 Collins	?	Y	N	Y	N	Y	Y	Y
8 Rostenkowski	Y	Y	Y	Y	N	Y	Y	Y
9 Yates	Y	Y	N	Y	N	Y	Y	Y
10 ***Porter***	Y	Y	N	Y	Y	N	N	N
11 Annunzio	Y	Y	N	Y	N	Y	Y	Y
12 ***Crane***	N	N	N	N	Y	N	N	N
13 ***Fawell***	Y	N	Y	Y	Y	N	N	N
14 ***Grotberg***	?	?	?	?	?	?	?	?
15 ***Madigan***	Y	N	Y	Y	Y	N	N	N
16 ***Martin***	Y	N	Y	Y	Y	N	N	N
17 Evans	Y	Y	N	Y	N	Y	Y	Y
18 ***Michel***	Y	N	Y	Y	Y	N	N	N
19 Bruce	Y	Y	N	Y	N	Y	Y	Y
20 Durbin	Y	Y	N	Y	N	Y	Y	Y
21 Price	Y	Y	Y	Y	N	Y	Y	Y
22 Gray	Y	Y	N	Y	N	Y	Y	Y
INDIANA								
1 Visclosky	Y	Y	N	Y	N	Y	Y	Y
2 Sharp	Y	Y	N	Y	N	Y	Y	Y
3 ***Hiler***	Y	N	Y	N	Y	N	N	N
4 ***Coats***	Y	Y	Y	Y	Y	N	N	N
5 ***Hillis***	Y	Y	Y	Y	Y	N	N	N

ND - Northern Democrats SD - Southern Democrats

* Corresponding to Congressional Record Votes 194, 195, 196, 197, 199, 200, 201, 202

	174	175	176	177	178	179	180	181
6 ***Burton***	N	N	Y	N	Y	N	N	N
7 ***Myers***	Y	Y	Y	N	Y	N	N	Y
8 McCloskey	Y	?	N	Y	N	Y	Y	Y
9 Hamilton	Y	Y	N	Y	N	Y	Y	Y
10 Jacobs	Y	N	N	Y	N	Y	Y	Y
IOWA								
1 ***Leach***	Y	N	N	Y	N	Y	Y	Y
2 ***Tauke***	Y	N	N	Y	N	Y	N	N
3 ***Evans***	Y	?	Y	N	Y	N	N	N
4 Smith	Y	Y	Y	Y	N	Y	Y	Y
5 ***Lightfoot***	Y	N	Y	Y	N	N	N	N
6 Bedell	Y	Y	Y	Y	N	Y	Y	Y
KANSAS								
1 ***Roberts***	Y	N	Y	Y	Y	N	N	N
2 Slattery	Y	Y	Y	Y	N	Y	Y	Y
3 ***Meyers***	Y	N	Y	Y	Y	N	N	Y
4 Glickman	Y	Y	N	Y	N	Y	Y	Y
5 ***Whittaker***	Y	N	Y	Y	Y	N	N	N
KENTUCKY								
1 Hubbard	Y	Y	Y	N	Y	N	N	N
2 Natcher	Y	Y	Y	N	N	N	N	N
3 Mazzoli	Y	Y	Y	N	N	N	N	N
4 ***Snyder***	Y	Y	Y	N	Y	N	N	N
5 ***Rogers***	Y	N	N	N	Y	N	N	N
6 ***Hopkins***	Y	Y	N	N	Y	N	N	N
7 Perkins	Y	Y	N	Y	N	N	N	Y
LOUISIANA								
1 ***Livingston***	Y	N	Y	N	Y	N	N	N
2 Boggs	Y	Y	Y	N	N	?	Y	Y
3 Tauzin	Y	Y	Y	N	Y	N	N	N
4 Roemer	N	Y	Y	N	Y	N	N	N
5 Huckaby	?	Y	Y	N	Y	N	N	N
6 ***Moore***	Y	Y	N	N	Y	N	N	N
7 Breaux	?	Y	Y	N	Y	N	N	N
8 Long	Y	Y	N	N	N	Y	Y	Y
MAINE								
1 ***McKernan***	Y	N	Y	Y	Y	N	N	Y
2 ***Snowe***	Y	Y	Y	N	Y	N	N	Y
MARYLAND								
1 Dyson	Y	Y	Y	Y	Y	N	N	N
2 ***Bentley***	?	N	Y	N	Y	N	N	N
3 Mikulski	Y	Y	N	Y	N	Y	Y	Y
4 ***Holt***	Y	N	Y	N	Y	N	N	N
5 Hoyer	Y	Y	Y	N	N	Y	Y	Y
6 Byron	Y	Y	Y	Y	Y	N	N	N
7 Mitchell	Y	?	N	Y	N	Y	Y	Y
8 Barnes	Y	Y	Y	Y	N	Y	Y	Y
MASSACHUSETTS								
1 ***Conte***	Y	N	N	N	N	Y	Y	Y
2 Boland	Y	Y	Y	Y	N	Y	Y	Y
3 Early	Y	Y	N	Y	N	Y	Y	Y
4 Frank	Y	Y	Y	Y	N	Y	Y	Y
5 Atkins	Y	Y	Y	Y	N	Y	Y	Y
6 Mavroules	Y	Y	Y	Y	N	Y	Y	Y
7 Markey	Y	Y	N	Y	N	Y	Y	Y
8 O'Neill								Y
9 Moakley	Y	Y	Y	Y	N	Y	Y	Y
10 Studds	Y	Y	N	Y	N	Y	Y	Y
11 Donnelly	N	Y	N	Y	N	Y	Y	Y
MICHIGAN								
1 Conyers	Y	Y	N	Y	N	Y	Y	Y
2 ***Pursell***	Y	Y	Y	Y	Y	N	N	Y
3 Wolpe	?	Y	N	Y	N	Y	Y	Y
4 ***Siljander***	Y	Y	Y	Y	Y	N	N	N
5 ***Henry***	Y	N	Y	Y	Y	N	N	Y
6 Carr	Y	Y	N	Y	N	Y	Y	Y
7 Kildee	Y	Y	N	Y	N	Y	Y	Y
8 Traxler	Y	Y	Y	Y	N	Y	Y	Y
9 ***Vander Jagt***	Y	N	Y	Y	Y	N	N	N
10 ***Schuette***	Y	N	Y	Y	Y	N	N	N
11 ***Davis***	Y	N	N	N	Y	N	?	?
12 Bonior	Y	Y	Y	Y	N	Y	Y	Y
13 Crockett	Y	Y	N	Y	N	Y	Y	Y
14 Hertel	N	Y	N	Y	N	Y	Y	Y
15 Ford	Y	?	N	Y	N	Y	Y	Y
16 Dingell	Y	?	Y	Y	N	Y	Y	Y
17 Levin	Y	Y	N	Y	N	Y	Y	Y
18 ***Broomfield***	Y	Y	N	Y	Y	N	N	N
MINNESOTA								
1 Penny	N	N	Y	Y	N	Y	Y	Y
2 ***Weber***	Y	N	Y	Y	Y	N	N	N
3 ***Frenzel***	N	N	Y	Y	Y	N	N	N
4 Vento	Y	Y	N	Y	N	Y	Y	Y
5 Sabo	Y	Y	N	Y	N	Y	Y	Y
6 Sikorski	#	N	N	Y	N	Y	Y	Y
7 ***Stangeland***	Y	N	Y	Y	Y	N	N	N
8 Oberstar	Y	Y	N	Y	N	Y	Y	Y
MISSISSIPPI								
1 Whitten	Y	Y	Y	N	N	N	N	Y
2 ***Franklin***	?	Y	Y	N	Y	N	N	N
3 Montgomery	Y	Y	Y	N	Y	N	N	N
4 Dowdy	?	?	Y	N	Y	N	N	N
5 ***Lott***	N	N	Y	N	Y	N	N	N
MISSOURI								
1 Clay	Y	N	N	Y	N	Y	Y	Y
2 Young	Y	Y	N	N	N	Y	Y	Y
3 Gephardt	?	Y	Y	Y	N	Y	Y	Y
4 Skelton	Y	Y	Y	N	Y	N	N	N
5 Wheat	Y	Y	N	Y	N	Y	Y	Y
6 ***Coleman***	Y	N	Y	Y	Y	N	N	N
7 ***Taylor***	Y	Y	Y	N	Y	N	N	N
8 ***Emerson***	Y	N	Y	N	Y	N	N	N
9 Volkmer	Y	Y	N	Y	N	Y	Y	Y
MONTANA								
1 Williams	Y	?	N	Y	N	Y	Y	Y
2 ***Marlenee***	Y	N	Y	Y	Y	N	N	N
NEBRASKA								
1 ***Bereuter***	Y	N	N	Y	Y	N	N	Y
2 ***Daub***	Y	N	N	Y	Y	N	N	N
3 ***Smith***	Y	Y	Y	Y	Y	N	N	Y
NEVADA								
1 Reid	Y	Y	N	Y	N	Y	Y	Y
2 ***Vucanovich***	N	N	Y	Y	Y	N	N	N
NEW HAMPSHIRE								
1 ***Smith***	N	N	Y	Y	Y	N	N	N
2 ***Gregg***	N	N	Y	N	Y	N	N	N
NEW JERSEY								
1 Florio	Y	Y	Y	N	N	N	Y	Y
2 Hughes	N	Y	N	Y	N	Y	Y	Y
3 Howard	Y	Y	N	N	N	Y	Y	Y
4 ***Smith***	Y	Y	Y	N	Y	N	N	N
5 ***Roukema***	Y	N	Y	N	Y	N	N	Y
6 Dwyer	Y	Y	Y	N	N	Y	Y	Y
7 ***Rinaldo***	Y	Y	Y	N	Y	N	N	N
8 Roe	Y	Y	N	N	N	Y	Y	Y
9 Torricelli	Y	Y	Y	N	N	Y	Y	Y
10 Rodino	?	Y	N	N	N	Y	Y	Y
11 ***Gallo***	Y	N	Y	N	Y	N	N	N
12 ***Courter***	Y	N	Y	N	Y	N	N	N
13 ***Saxton***	Y	N	Y	Y	Y	N	N	N
14 Guarini	Y	Y	Y	N	N	N	Y	Y
NEW MEXICO								
1 ***Lujan***	?	Y	Y	Y	Y	N	N	N
2 ***Skeen***	Y	N	Y	Y	Y	N	N	N
3 Richardson	Y	Y	Y	N	N	Y	Y	Y
NEW YORK								
1 ***Carney***	Y	N	Y	N	Y	N	N	N
2 Downey	Y	Y	N	N	N	Y	Y	Y
3 Mrazek	Y	Y	Y	N	N	Y	Y	Y
4 ***Lent***	Y	N	Y	N	Y	N	?	N
5 ***McGrath***	Y	?	Y	N	Y	N	N	N
6 Vacancy								
7 Ackerman	Y	Y	N	Y	N	Y	Y	Y
8 Scheuer	Y	Y	N	N	N	Y	Y	Y
9 Manton	Y	Y	Y	N	N	Y	?	?
10 Schumer	Y	Y	N	Y	N	Y	Y	Y
11 Towns	Y	?	?	Y	N	Y	Y	Y
12 Owens	?	?	N	Y	N	Y	Y	Y
13 Solarz	Y	Y	Y	Y	N	Y	Y	Y
14 ***Molinari***	Y	N	Y	N	Y	N	N	N
15 ***Green***	Y	Y	N	N	N	Y	Y	N
16 Rangel	Y	Y	N	Y	N	Y	Y	Y
17 Weiss	Y	Y	N	Y	N	Y	Y	Y
18 Garcia	Y	?	N	Y	N	Y	Y	Y
19 Biaggi	Y	Y	Y	N	Y	N	N	Y
20 ***DioGuardi***	Y	Y	Y	N	Y	N	N	N
21 ***Fish***	Y	Y	Y	N	Y	N	N	Y
22 ***Gilman***	Y	Y	Y	N	Y	N	N	Y
23 Stratton	Y	Y	Y	N	Y	N	N	N
24 ***Solomon***	N	N	Y	N	Y	N	N	N
25 ***Boehlert***	Y	N	N	N	N	Y	N	Y
26 ***Martin***	Y	Y	Y	N	Y	N	N	N
27 ***Wortley***	Y	Y	Y	N	Y	N	N	N
28 McHugh	Y	Y	N	N	N	Y	Y	Y
29 ***Horton***	Y	Y	Y	N	N	N	N	Y
30 ***Eckert***	?	?	Y	N	Y	N	N	N
31 ***Kemp***	?	Y	Y	N	Y	N	N	N
32 LaFalce	?	Y	Y	N	N	Y	Y	Y
33 Nowak	Y	Y	Y	N	N	Y	Y	Y
34 Lundine	Y	Y	Y	N	N	?	?	?
NORTH CAROLINA								
1 Jones	Y	P	Y	N	N	Y	Y	N
2 Valentine	Y	Y	Y	Y	N	Y	?	N
3 Whitley	Y	Y	Y	Y	N	N	Y	Y
4 ***Cobey***	Y	N	Y	N	Y	N	N	N
5 Neal	Y	Y	Y	Y	N	Y	Y	Y
6 ***Coble***	Y	N	Y	Y	Y	N	N	N
7 Rose	Y	Y	N	Y	N	Y	Y	Y
8 Hefner	Y	Y	Y	N	N	Y	Y	Y
9 ***McMillan***	Y	Y	Y	Y	Y	N	N	N
10 ***Broyhill***	Y	Y	Y	Y	Y	N	N	N
11 ***Hendon***	Y	?	N	Y	Y	N	N	N
NORTH DAKOTA								
AL Dorgan	Y	Y	N	Y	N	Y	Y	Y
OHIO								
1 Luken	?	Y	N	Y	N	Y	Y	Y
2 ***Gradison***	Y	Y	Y	Y	Y	N	N	Y
3 Hall	N	Y	N	Y	N	Y	Y	Y
4 ***Oxley***	Y	N	Y	Y	Y	N	N	N
5 ***Latta***	Y	N	Y	Y	Y	N	N	N
6 ***McEwen***	Y	Y	Y	N	Y	N	N	N
7 ***DeWine***	N	N	Y	Y	Y	N	N	N
8 ***Kindness***	Y	N	Y	Y	Y	N	N	N
9 Kaptur	Y	Y	N	Y	N	Y	Y	Y
10 ***Miller***	Y	N	Y	N	Y	N	N	N
11 Eckart	Y	Y	N	Y	N	Y	Y	Y
12 ***Kasich***	Y	Y	Y	Y	Y	N	N	N
13 Pease	Y	Y	N	Y	N	Y	Y	Y
14 Seiberling	Y	Y	N	Y	N	Y	Y	Y
15 ***Wylie***	Y	Y	Y	Y	Y	N	N	N
16 ***Regula***	Y	Y	Y	Y	Y	N	N	Y
17 Traficant	Y	Y	N	Y	N	Y	Y	Y
18 Applegate	Y	Y	N	Y	N	Y	Y	Y
19 Feighan	Y	Y	N	Y	N	Y	Y	Y
20 Oakar	Y	?	N	Y	N	Y	Y	Y
21 Stokes	Y	Y	N	Y	N	Y	Y	Y
OKLAHOMA								
1 Jones	Y	Y	N	N	Y	N	Y	Y
2 Synar	Y	Y	N	Y	N	Y	Y	Y
3 Watkins	Y	?	N	N	Y	N	Y	Y
4 McCurdy	Y	Y	Y	Y	N	N	Y	N
5 ***Edwards***	Y	N	Y	N	Y	N	N	N
6 English	Y	Y	N	Y	Y	N	Y	N
OREGON								
1 AuCoin	Y	?	Y	Y	N	Y	Y	Y
2 ***Smith, R.***	Y	N	Y	Y	Y	N	N	N
3 Wyden	Y	Y	N	Y	N	Y	Y	Y
4 Weaver	?	Y	N	Y	N	Y	Y	Y
5 ***Smith, D.***	N	N	Y	Y	Y	N	N	N
PENNSYLVANIA								
1 Foglietta	Y	Y	N	N	N	Y	Y	Y
2 Gray	Y	Y	N	Y	N	Y	Y	Y
3 Borski	Y	Y	N	N	N	Y	Y	Y
4 Kolter	Y	Y	Y	N	N	N	N	Y
5 ***Schulze***	Y	Y	Y	Y	Y	N	N	N
6 Yatron	Y	Y	Y	Y	N	Y	Y	Y
7 Edgar	Y	Y	N	N	N	Y	Y	Y
8 Kostmayer	Y	Y	Y	Y	N	Y	Y	Y
9 ***Shuster***	N	N	Y	N	Y	N	N	N
10 ***McDade***	Y	Y	Y	Y	Y	N	N	N
11 Kanjorski	Y	Y	Y	N	N	Y	Y	Y
12 Murtha	Y	Y	Y	N	Y	N	N	Y
13 ***Coughlin***	Y	N	Y	N	Y	N	Y	Y
14 Coyne	Y	Y	Y	Y	N	Y	Y	Y
15 ***Ritter***	Y	Y	Y	Y	Y	N	N	N
16 ***Walker***	N	N	Y	Y	Y	N	N	N
17 ***Gekas***	Y	N	Y	Y	Y	N	N	N
18 Walgren	Y	Y	Y	Y	N	Y	Y	Y
19 ***Goodling***	N	?	Y	Y	Y	N	N	Y
20 Gaydos	Y	Y	Y	N	?	?	?	?
21 ***Ridge***	Y	?	N	Y	N	N	N	N
22 Murphy	Y	Y	N	Y	N	N	Y	Y
23 ***Clinger***	Y	Y	Y	Y	Y	N	N	N
RHODE ISLAND								
1 St Germain	Y	Y	N	N	N	Y	Y	Y
2 ***Schneider***	Y	Y	N	Y	N	Y	Y	Y
SOUTH CAROLINA								
1 ***Hartnett***	Y	N	N	N	Y	N	N	N
2 ***Spence***	Y	Y	Y	N	Y	N	N	N
3 Derrick	Y	Y	Y	Y	N	Y	Y	Y
4 ***Campbell***	?	?	Y	N	Y	N	N	N
5 Spratt	Y	Y	Y	Y	N	N	Y	N
6 Tallon	Y	Y	Y	N	Y	N	N	N
SOUTH DAKOTA								
AL Daschle	Y	?	Y	Y	N	Y	Y	Y
TENNESSEE								
1 ***Quillen***	Y	Y	Y	Y	Y	N	N	N
2 ***Duncan***	Y	Y	Y	N	Y	N	N	N
3 Lloyd	Y	N	Y	N	Y	N	N	N
4 Cooper	Y	Y	Y	N	N	N	Y	N
5 Boner	Y	Y	Y	N	N	N	Y	Y
6 Gordon	Y	Y	Y	Y	N	Y	Y	Y
7 ***Sundquist***	Y	N	Y	N	Y	N	N	N
8 Jones	Y	Y	N	N	N	Y	Y	Y
9 Ford	Y	Y	Y	Y	N	Y	Y	Y
TEXAS								
1 Chapman	Y	Y	Y	N	N	N	N	Y
2 Wilson	?	?	Y	N	Y	N	N	N
3 ***Bartlett***	N	N	Y	N	Y	N	N	N
4 Hall, R.	N	Y	N	N	Y	N	N	N
5 Bryant	Y	Y	Y	N	N	Y	Y	Y
6 ***Barton***	Y	N	Y	N	Y	N	N	N
7 ***Archer***	N	Y	Y	N	Y	N	N	N
8 ***Fields***	N	N	Y	N	Y	N	N	N
9 Brooks	Y	Y	Y	N	N	Y	Y	Y
10 Pickle	Y	Y	Y	N	N	N	N	N
11 Leath	N	Y	Y	N	Y	N	N	N
12 Wright	Y	Y	Y	N	N	Y	Y	Y
13 ***Boulter***	Y	N	Y	N	Y	N	N	N
14 ***Sweeney***	Y	Y	Y	N	Y	N	N	N
15 de la Garza	Y	Y	Y	N	N	Y	Y	N
16 Coleman	Y	Y	N	N	N	Y	Y	Y
17 Stenholm	N	Y	Y	N	Y	N	N	N
18 Leland	Y	Y	N	Y	N	Y	Y	Y
19 ***Combest***	Y	Y	Y	N	Y	N	N	N
20 Gonzalez	Y	Y	N	N	N	Y	Y	Y
21 ***Loeffler***	N	N	Y	N	Y	N	N	N
22 ***DeLay***	N	N	Y	N	Y	N	N	N
23 Bustamante	Y	Y	Y	N	N	N	N	N
24 Frost	Y	Y	Y	N	N	Y	Y	N
25 Andrews	Y	Y	Y	N	N	N	N	N
26 ***Armey***	N	N	Y	N	Y	N	N	N
27 Ortiz	Y	Y	Y	N	Y	N	N	N
UTAH								
1 ***Hansen***	Y	N	Y	N	Y	N	N	N
2 ***Monson***	N	N	Y	Y	Y	N	N	N
3 ***Nielson***	N	N	Y	Y	Y	N	N	N
VERMONT								
AL ***Jeffords***	Y	Y	N	N	N	Y	Y	Y
VIRGINIA								
1 ***Bateman***	Y	Y	Y	Y	Y	N	N	N
2 ***Whitehurst***	Y	N	?	Y	Y	N	N	N
3 ***Bliley***	Y	N	Y	Y	Y	N	N	N
4 Sisisky	Y	Y	Y	Y	Y	N	N	N
5 Daniel	Y	Y	Y	Y	Y	N	N	N
6 Olin	Y	Y	Y	Y	N	Y	Y	Y
7 ***Slaughter***	Y	N	Y	Y	Y	N	N	N
8 ***Parris***	Y	N	Y	Y	Y	N	N	N
9 Boucher	Y	Y	Y	Y	N	Y	Y	Y
10 ***Wolf***	Y	N	Y	Y	Y	N	N	N
WASHINGTON								
1 ***Miller***	Y	Y	Y	N	Y	N	N	N
2 Swift	Y	Y	N	N	N	Y	Y	Y
3 Bonker	Y	?	N	N	N	Y	Y	Y
4 ***Morrison***	Y	Y	Y	N	Y	N	N	N
5 Foley	Y	?	Y	N	N	Y	Y	Y
6 Dicks	Y	Y	N	N	N	Y	Y	Y
7 Lowry	Y	Y	N	Y	N	Y	Y	Y
8 ***Chandler***	Y	N	Y	N	Y	N	N	N
WEST VIRGINIA								
1 Mollohan	Y	Y	Y	N	N	N	N	N
2 Staggers	Y	Y	N	N	N	Y	Y	Y
3 Wise	Y	Y	N	N	N	Y	Y	Y
4 Rahall	Y	Y	N	N	N	Y	Y	Y
WISCONSIN								
1 Aspin	Y	Y	Y	Y	Y	N	N	N
2 Kastenmeier	Y	Y	N	Y	N	Y	Y	Y
3 ***Gunderson***	Y	N	Y	Y	Y	N	N	N
4 Kleczka	Y	Y	N	Y	N	Y	Y	Y
5 Moody	Y	?	N	Y	N	Y	Y	Y
6 ***Petri***	Y	Y	Y	N	Y	N	N	N
7 Obey	Y	Y	N	Y	N	Y	Y	Y
8 ***Roth***	Y	Y	Y	N	Y	N	N	N
9 ***Sensenbrenner***	N	N	Y	N	Y	N	N	N
WYOMING								
AL ***Cheney***	N	N	Y	N	Y	N	N	N

Southern states - Ala., Ark., Fla., Ga., Ky., La., Miss., N.C., Okla., S.C., Tenn., Texas, Va.

* The *Congressional Record* vote number is different from the CQ vote number because the *Record* includes quorum calls in its tally. CQ does not publish quorum call votes.

182. HR 5052. Military Construction Appropriations, Fiscal 1987/Aid to Nicaraguan Rebels. Passage of the bill to appropriate $8,390,301,000 for military construction projects in fiscal 1987, and to provide $70 million in military aid and $30 million in non-military aid to the "contra" guerrillas in Nicaragua and $300 million in economic aid to Costa Rica, El Salvador, Guatemala and Honduras. Passed 249-174: R 165-13; D 84-161 (ND 22-142, SD 62-19), June 25, 1986. The president had requested $10,520,200,000 for military construction appropriations.

183. H Con Res 364. Adjournment Resolution. Adoption of the concurrent resolution to provide for adjournment of the House and Senate from June 26 or 27 until July 14. Adopted 215-189: R 19-154; D 196-35 (ND 136-19, SD 60-16), June 26, 1986.

184. HR 2436. Nutrition Monitoring and Research. Adoption of the rule (H Res 484) to provide for House floor consideration of the bill to establish an interagency board to coordinate national nutritional monitoring and research, and to require implementation of a 10-year comprehensive plan to assess and report, on a continuing basis, the nutritional status of the population and trends relating to it. Adopted 395-4: R 166-3; D 229-1 (ND 155-0, SD 74-1), June 26, 1986.

185. HR 4184. National Science Foundation Authorization, Fiscal 1987. Passage of the bill to authorize $1.7 billion for the National Science Foundation for fiscal 1987. Passed 405-2: R 167-2; D 238-0 (ND 161-0, SD 77-0), June 26, 1986.

186. HR 2436. Nutrition Monitoring and Research. Monson, R-Utah, amendments to remove from the bill a requirement for a program of competitive grants and matching grants to state and local governments for research on development of uniform nutritional assessment standards and monitoring techniques. Rejected en bloc 84-312: R 81-88; D 3-224 (ND 0-153, SD 3-71), June 26, 1986.

187. HR 2436. Nutrition Monitoring and Research. Barton, R-Texas, amendment to remove from the bill language specifying the members to be appointed by the president to an advisory council to monitor national nutrition. Rejected 157-231: R 155-10; D 2-221 (ND 0-149, SD 2-72), June 26, 1986.

188. HR 2436. Nutrition Monitoring and Research. Passage of the bill to establish an interagency board to coordinate national nutritional monitoring and research, and to require implementation of a 10-year comprehensive plan to assess and report, on a continuing basis, the nutritional status of the population and trends relating to it. Passed 305-85: R 79-83; D 226-2 (ND 154-0, SD 72-2), June 26, 1986.

189. S Con Res 120. Budget Resolution, Fiscal 1987. Gray, D-Pa., motion that the House recede from its amendment and concur in the concurrent resolution, with an amendment setting fiscal 1987 budget totals as follows: budget authority, $1.093 trillion; outlays, $995.0 billion; revenues, $852.4 billion; deficit, $142.6 billion. Motion agreed to 333-43: R 134-24; D 199-19 (ND 133-13, SD 66-6), June 26, 1986. (The effect of the vote was to adopt the conference agreement on the fiscal 1987 budget resolution.)

KEY

- Y Voted for (yea).
- # Paired for.
- + Announced for.
- N Voted against (nay).
- X Paired against.
- \- Announced against.
- P Voted "present."
- C Voted "present" to avoid possible conflict of interest.
- ? Did not vote or otherwise make a position known.

Democrats ***Republicans***

	182	183	184	185	186	187	188	189
ALABAMA								
1 ***Callahan***	Y	N	Y	Y	Y	Y	N	Y
2 ***Dickinson***	Y	Y	Y	Y	N	Y	N	Y
3 Nichols	Y	Y	Y	Y	?	?	?	?
4 Bevill	Y	Y	Y	Y	N	N	Y	Y
5 Flippo	Y	Y	Y	Y	N	N	Y	?
6 Erdreich	Y	N	Y	Y	N	N	Y	Y
7 Shelby	Y	Y	Y	Y	N	N	Y	Y
ALASKA								
AL ***Young***	Y	Y	Y	Y	N	Y	Y	Y
ARIZONA								
1 ***McCain***	Y	N	Y	Y	N	Y	Y	Y
2 Udall	N	Y	Y	Y	N	N	Y	Y
3 ***Stump***	Y	N	N	N	Y	Y	N	N
4 ***Rudd***	Y	Y	Y	Y	?	?	?	?
5 ***Kolbe***	Y	N	Y	Y	Y	Y	Y	Y
ARKANSAS								
1 Alexander	N	Y	Y	Y	N	N	Y	Y
2 Robinson	Y	N	Y	Y	N	N	Y	Y
3 ***Hammerschmidt***	Y	N	Y	Y	N	Y	Y	Y
4 Anthony	N	Y	Y	Y	N	N	Y	Y
CALIFORNIA								
1 Bosco	?	Y	Y	Y	N	N	Y	Y
2 ***Chappie***	Y	?	?	?	?	?	?	?
3 Matsui	N	Y	Y	Y	N	N	Y	Y
4 Fazio	N	Y	Y	Y	N	N	Y	Y
5 Burton	N	Y	Y	Y	?	N	Y	Y
6 Boxer	N	Y	Y	Y	N	N	Y	Y
7 Miller	N	Y	Y	Y	N	N	Y	Y
8 Dellums	N	Y	Y	Y	N	N	Y	N
9 Stark	N	Y	Y	?	N	N	Y	Y
10 Edwards	N	Y	Y	Y	N	N	Y	Y
11 Lantos	Y	Y	Y	Y	N	N	Y	Y
12 ***Zschau***	Y	N	Y	Y	N	Y	Y	Y
13 Mineta	N	Y	Y	Y	N	N	Y	Y
14 ***Shumway***	Y	N	Y	Y	Y	Y	N	N
15 Coelho	N	Y	Y	Y	N	N	Y	Y
16 Panetta	N	Y	Y	Y	N	N	Y	Y
17 ***Pashayan***	Y	N	Y	Y	N	Y	Y	Y
18 Lehman	N	Y	Y	Y	?	N	Y	Y
19 ***Lagomarsino***	Y	N	Y	Y	Y	Y	N	Y
20 ***Thomas***	Y	N	Y	Y	N	Y	Y	Y
21 ***Fiedler***	Y	N	Y	Y	Y	Y	N	Y
22 ***Moorhead***	Y	N	Y	Y	Y	Y	N	Y
23 Beilenson	N	Y	Y	Y	?	?	?	?
24 Waxman	N	Y	Y	Y	N	N	Y	Y
25 Roybal	N	Y	Y	Y	N	N	Y	Y
26 Berman	N	Y	Y	Y	N	N	Y	Y
27 Levine	N	Y	Y	Y	N	N	Y	Y
28 Dixon	N	Y	Y	Y	N	N	Y	?
29 Hawkins	N	Y	Y	Y	N	N	Y	Y
30 Martinez	N	Y	Y	Y	N	?	Y	Y
31 Dymally	N	Y	Y	Y	N	N	Y	Y
32 Anderson	N	N	Y	Y	N	N	Y	Y
33 ***Dreier***	Y	N	Y	Y	Y	Y	N	N
34 Torres	N	Y	Y	Y	N	N	Y	Y
35 ***Lewis***	Y	?	?	?	?	?	?	?
36 Brown	N	?	Y	Y	N	N	Y	Y
37 ***McCandless***	Y	N	Y	Y	Y	?	?	?
38 ***Dornan***	Y	N	Y	Y	Y	?	?	?
39 ***Dannemeyer***	Y	N	N	Y	Y	Y	N	N
40 ***Badham***	Y	N	Y	Y	Y	Y	N	Y
41 ***Lowery***	Y	N	Y	Y	N	Y	Y	Y
42 ***Lungren***	Y	N	Y	Y	Y	Y	N	Y
43 ***Packard***	Y	N	Y	Y	Y	Y	N	Y
44 Bates	N	N	Y	Y	N	N	Y	Y
45 ***Hunter***	Y	N	Y	Y	Y	Y	N	N
COLORADO								
1 Schroeder	N	N	Y	Y	N	N	Y	Y
2 Wirth	N	N	Y	?	?	?	?	Y
3 ***Strang***	Y	N	Y	Y	Y	Y	N	Y
4 ***Brown***	Y	N	Y	Y	Y	Y	N	N
5 ***Kramer***	Y	N	Y	Y	Y	Y	N	N
6 ***Schaefer***	Y	N	Y	Y	Y	Y	N	N
CONNECTICUT								
1 Kennelly	N	Y	Y	Y	N	N	Y	Y
2 Gejdenson	N	Y	Y	Y	N	N	Y	Y
3 Morrison	N	Y	Y	Y	N	N	Y	Y
4 ***McKinney***	N	Y	?	Y	?	?	?	?
5 ***Rowland***	Y	N	Y	Y	N	N	Y	Y
6 ***Johnson***	Y	N	Y	Y	N	N	Y	Y
DELAWARE								
AL Carper	Y	N	Y	Y	N	N	Y	Y
FLORIDA								
1 Hutto	Y	Y	Y	Y	N	N	Y	Y
2 Fuqua	Y	?	?	?	?	?	?	?
3 Bennett	Y	Y	Y	Y	N	N	Y	Y
4 Chappell	Y	Y	Y	Y	N	N	Y	Y
5 ***McCollum***	Y	N	Y	Y	Y	Y	N	N
6 MacKay	Y	N	Y	Y	N	N	Y	Y
7 Gibbons	Y	Y	Y	Y	N	N	Y	?
8 ***Young***	Y	N	Y	Y	N	Y	N	Y
9 ***Bilirakis***	Y	N	Y	Y	N	Y	Y	Y
10 ***Ireland***	Y	N	Y	Y	Y	Y	N	Y
11 Nelson	Y	Y	Y	Y	N	N	Y	Y
12 ***Lewis***	Y	N	Y	Y	N	Y	Y	Y
13 ***Mack***	Y	N	Y	Y	Y	Y	N	Y
14 Mica	Y	Y	Y	Y	N	N	Y	Y
15 ***Shaw***	Y	N	Y	Y	N	Y	Y	?
16 Smith	Y	Y	Y	Y	N	N	Y	Y
17 Lehman	N	Y	Y	Y	N	N	Y	Y
18 Pepper	Y	Y	Y	Y	N	N	Y	Y
19 Fascell	Y	Y	Y	Y	?	N	Y	Y
GEORGIA								
1 Thomas	Y	Y	Y	Y	N	N	Y	Y
2 Hatcher	Y	Y	Y	Y	N	N	Y	Y
3 Ray	Y	Y	Y	Y	Y	N	N	Y
4 ***Swindall***	Y	N	Y	Y	Y	Y	N	Y
5 Fowler	Y	N	Y	Y	N	N	Y	?
6 ***Gingrich***	Y	N	Y	Y	Y	Y	N	Y
7 Darden	Y	N	Y	Y	N	N	Y	Y
8 Rowland	Y	Y	Y	Y	N	N	Y	Y
9 Jenkins	Y	Y	Y	Y	N	N	Y	Y
10 Barnard	Y	N	Y	Y	N	N	Y	Y
HAWAII								
1 Heftel	Y	?	Y	Y	N	?	Y	?
2 Akaka	N	Y	Y	Y	N	N	Y	Y
IDAHO								
1 ***Craig***	Y	N	Y	Y	Y	Y	Y	Y
2 Stallings	Y	N	Y	Y	N	N	Y	Y
ILLINOIS								
1 Hayes	N	Y	Y	Y	N	N	Y	Y
2 Savage	N	?	?	?	?	?	?	?
3 Russo	N	Y	Y	Y	N	N	Y	Y
4 ***O'Brien***	?	?	?	?	?	?	?	?
5 Lipinski	Y	Y	Y	Y	N	?	?	?
6 ***Hyde***	Y	?	Y	Y	Y	Y	?	?
7 Collins	N	Y	Y	Y	N	N	Y	Y
8 Rostenkowski	?	Y	Y	Y	?	?	?	?
9 Yates	N	Y	Y	Y	N	N	Y	?
10 ***Porter***	Y	N	Y	Y	Y	Y	N	N
11 Annunzio	N	Y	Y	Y	N	N	Y	?
12 ***Crane***	Y	N	Y	N	Y	Y	N	N
13 ***Fawell***	Y	N	Y	Y	Y	Y	Y	Y
14 ***Grotberg***	?	?	?	?	?	?	?	?
15 ***Madigan***	Y	N	Y	Y	N	Y	?	?
16 ***Martin***	Y	N	Y	Y	Y	Y	Y	Y
17 Evans	N	Y	Y	Y	N	N	Y	Y
18 ***Michel***	Y	Y	Y	Y	N	Y	Y	Y
19 Bruce	N	N	Y	Y	N	N	Y	Y
20 Durbin	N	Y	Y	Y	N	N	Y	Y
21 Price	Y	Y	Y	Y	N	N	Y	?
22 Gray	N	Y	Y	Y	N	N	Y	Y
INDIANA								
1 Visclosky	N	Y	Y	Y	N	N	Y	Y
2 Sharp	N	N	Y	Y	N	N	Y	Y
3 ***Hiler***	Y	N	Y	Y	Y	Y	N	Y
4 ***Coats***	Y	N	Y	Y	N	Y	N	Y
5 ***Hillis***	Y	Y	Y	Y	N	Y	N	?

ND - Northern Democrats SD - Southern Democrats

* Corresponding to Congressional Record Votes 203, 204, 205, 206, 208, 209, 210, 211

	182	183	184	185	186	187	188	189
6 ***Burton***	Y	N	Y	Y	Y	Y	N	Y
7 ***Myers***	Y	Y	Y	Y	N	Y	N	N
8 McCloskey	N	Y	Y	Y	N	N	Y	Y
9 Hamilton	N	Y	Y	Y	N	N	Y	Y
10 Jacobs	N	N	?	Y	N	N	Y	N
IOWA								
1 ***Leach***	N	N	Y	Y	N	?	?	Y
2 ***Tauke***	N	N	Y	Y	N	Y	N	Y
3 ***Evans***	N	N	?	Y	N	Y	N	Y
4 Smith	N	Y	Y	Y	?	N	Y	N
5 ***Lightfoot***	N	N	Y	Y	N	Y	N	Y
6 Bedell	N	Y	Y	?	N	N	Y	?
KANSAS								
1 ***Roberts***	Y	N	Y	Y	N	Y	Y	Y
2 Slattery	Y	N	Y	Y	N	N	Y	Y
3 ***Meyers***	Y	N	Y	Y	Y	Y	Y	Y
4 Glickman	Y	Y	Y	Y	N	N	Y	Y
5 ***Whittaker***	Y	N	Y	Y	Y	Y	Y	Y
KENTUCKY								
1 Hubbard	Y	N	Y	Y	N	Y	Y	Y
2 Natcher	N	Y	Y	Y	N	N	Y	Y
3 Mazzoli	Y	Y	Y	Y	N	N	Y	Y
4 ***Snyder***	Y	?	?	?	?	?	?	?
5 ***Rogers***	Y	N	Y	Y	N	Y	Y	Y
6 ***Hopkins***	Y	N	Y	Y	N	Y	N	Y
7 Perkins	N	Y	Y	Y	N	N	Y	Y
LOUISIANA								
1 ***Livingston***	Y	N	Y	Y	N	Y	N	Y
2 Boggs	Y	Y	Y	Y	N	N	Y	Y
3 Tauzin	Y	Y	Y	Y	N	N	Y	Y
4 Roemer	Y	Y	Y	Y	N	N	Y	Y
5 Huckaby	Y	Y	Y	Y	N	N	Y	Y
6 ***Moore***	Y	N	Y	Y	N	?	?	?
7 Breaux	Y	?	?	?	?	?	?	?
8 Long	Y	Y	Y	Y	N	N	Y	Y
MAINE								
1 ***McKernan***	Y	N	Y	?	N	N	Y	Y
2 ***Snowe***	Y	N	Y	Y	N	N	Y	Y
MARYLAND								
1 Dyson	Y	Y	Y	Y	N	N	Y	Y
2 ***Bentley***	Y	N	Y	Y	N	Y	Y	Y
3 Mikulski	N	Y	Y	Y	N	N	Y	Y
4 ***Holt***	Y	Y	Y	Y	Y	Y	N	Y
5 Hoyer	N	Y	Y	Y	N	N	Y	Y
6 Byron	Y	Y	Y	Y	N	N	Y	Y
7 Mitchell	N	?	?	Y	N	?	Y	N
8 Barnes	N	?	?	Y	N	?	?	?
MASSACHUSETTS								
1 ***Conte***	N	N	Y	Y	N	N	Y	Y
2 Boland	N	Y	Y	Y	?	?	?	?
3 Early	N	Y	Y	Y	?	?	?	?
4 Frank	N	Y	Y	Y	N	N	Y	Y
5 Atkins	N	Y	?	Y	N	N	Y	Y
6 Mavroules	N	Y	?	Y	N	?	Y	Y
7 Markey	Y	Y	Y	Y	N	N	?	Y
8 O'Neill								
9 Moakley	N	Y	Y	Y	N	N	Y	Y
10 Studds	N	Y	Y	Y	N	N	Y	Y
11 Donnelly	N	Y	Y	Y	N	N	Y	?
MICHIGAN								
1 Conyers	N	Y	Y	Y	N	N	Y	Y
2 ***Pursell***	Y	N	Y	Y	N	Y	Y	Y
3 Wolpe	N	Y	Y	Y	N	N	Y	Y
4 ***Siljander***	Y	N	Y	Y	Y	Y	N	Y
5 ***Henry***	Y	N	Y	Y	N	Y	Y	Y
6 Carr	N	N	Y	Y	N	N	Y	N
7 Kildee	N	Y	Y	Y	N	N	Y	Y
8 Traxler	N	Y	Y	Y	N	N	Y	Y
9 ***Vander Jagt***	Y	N	Y	Y	N	Y	N	Y
10 ***Schuette***	Y	N	Y	Y	N	Y	Y	Y
11 ***Davis***	?	N	Y	Y	N	?	?	?
12 Bonior	N	Y	Y	Y	N	N	Y	Y
13 Crockett	N	Y	Y	Y	N	N	Y	Y
14 Hertel	N	Y	Y	Y	N	N	Y	Y
15 Ford	N	Y	Y	Y	N	N	Y	Y
16 Dingell	N	Y	Y	Y	N	N	Y	Y
17 Levin	N	Y	Y	Y	N	N	Y	Y
18 ***Broomfield***	Y	N	Y	Y	Y	Y	N	Y
MINNESOTA								
1 Penny	N	Y	Y	Y	N	N	Y	Y
2 ***Weber***	Y	N	Y	Y	Y	Y	N	Y
3 ***Frenzel***	Y	N	Y	Y	Y	Y	Y	Y
4 Vento	N	Y	Y	Y	N	N	Y	Y
5 Sabo	N	Y	Y	Y	N	?	?	Y
6 Sikorski	N	Y	Y	Y	N	N	Y	Y

	182	183	184	185	186	187	188	189
7 ***Stangeland***	Y	N	Y	Y	N	Y	N	Y
8 Oberstar	N	Y	Y	Y	N	N	Y	Y
MISSISSIPPI								
1 Whitten	N	Y	N	Y	N	N	Y	Y
2 ***Franklin***	Y	N	Y	Y	N	Y	Y	Y
3 Montgomery	Y	Y	Y	Y	Y	N	?	Y
4 Dowdy	Y	Y	Y	Y	N	N	Y	Y
5 ***Lott***	Y	N	Y	Y	Y	Y	N	Y
MISSOURI								
1 Clay	N	Y	Y	Y	N	N	Y	Y
2 Young	Y	Y	Y	Y	N	N	Y	Y
3 Gephardt	N	Y	Y	Y	N	N	Y	Y
4 Skelton	Y	Y	Y	Y	?	?	?	?
5 Wheat	N	Y	Y	Y	N	N	Y	Y
6 ***Coleman***	Y	N	Y	Y	N	Y	Y	Y
7 ***Taylor***	Y	Y	Y	Y	N	Y	Y	Y
8 ***Emerson***	Y	N	Y	Y	N	Y	Y	Y
9 Volkmer	N	Y	Y	Y	N	N	Y	Y
MONTANA								
1 Williams	N	N	Y	Y	N	N	Y	Y
2 ***Marlenee***	Y	N	Y	Y	Y	Y	N	Y
NEBRASKA								
1 ***Bereuter***	Y	N	Y	Y	N	Y	Y	Y
2 ***Daub***	Y	N	Y	Y	Y	Y	N	Y
3 ***Smith***	Y	N	Y	Y	Y	Y	Y	Y
NEVADA								
1 Reid	N	Y	Y	Y	N	N	Y	Y
2 ***Vucanovich***	Y	N	Y	Y	N	Y	N	N
NEW HAMPSHIRE								
1 ***Smith***	Y	N	Y	Y	Y	Y	N	Y
2 ***Gregg***	Y	N	Y	Y	Y	Y	N	N
NEW JERSEY								
1 Florio	Y	Y	Y	Y	?	?	?	?
2 Hughes	N	N	Y	Y	N	N	Y	Y
3 Howard	N	?	Y	Y	N	N	Y	Y
4 ***Smith***	Y	Y	Y	Y	N	Y	Y	Y
5 ***Roukema***	Y	N	Y	Y	N	Y	Y	Y
6 Dwyer	N	Y	Y	Y	N	N	Y	Y
7 ***Rinaldo***	Y	N	Y	Y	N	Y	Y	Y
8 Roe	N	Y	Y	Y	N	N	Y	?
9 Torricelli	N	Y	Y	Y	N	N	Y	Y
10 Rodino	N	Y	Y	Y	N	N	Y	Y
11 ***Gallo***	Y	N	Y	Y	N	Y	Y	Y
12 ***Courter***	Y	N	Y	Y	N	Y	Y	N
13 ***Saxton***	Y	N	Y	Y	N	Y	Y	Y
14 Guarini	Y	Y	Y	Y	N	N	Y	Y
NEW MEXICO								
1 ***Lujan***	Y	N	Y	Y	Y	Y	Y	Y
2 ***Skeen***	Y	N	Y	Y	Y	Y	N	Y
3 Richardson	Y	Y	Y	Y	N	N	Y	Y
NEW YORK								
1 ***Carney***	Y	Y	Y	Y	N	Y	N	N
2 Downey	N	Y	Y	Y	N	N	Y	Y
3 Mrazek	N	N	?	Y	N	Y	Y	N
4 ***Lent***	Y	N	?	Y	N	Y	Y	Y
5 ***McGrath***	Y	N	Y	Y	N	Y	Y	Y
6 Vacancy								
7 Ackerman	N	Y	Y	Y	N	N	Y	Y
8 Scheuer	N	Y	Y	Y	N	N	Y	Y
9 Manton	?	Y	Y	Y	N	N	Y	Y
10 Schumer	N	Y	Y	Y	N	N	Y	Y
11 Towns	N	Y	Y	Y	N	N	Y	Y
12 Owens	N	Y	Y	Y	N	N	Y	Y
13 Solarz	N	Y	Y	Y	N	N	Y	Y
14 ***Molinari***	Y	N	Y	Y	N	Y	N	Y
15 ***Green***	N	N	Y	Y	N	N	Y	N
16 Rangel	N	Y	Y	Y	N	N	Y	Y
17 Weiss	N	Y	Y	Y	N	N	Y	Y
18 Garcia	N	?	?	?	?	N	Y	N
19 Biaggi	Y	Y	Y	Y	N	N	Y	Y
20 ***DioGuardi***	Y	N	Y	Y	N	N	Y	Y
21 ***Fish***	?	Y	Y	?	?	?	?	?
22 ***Gilman***	Y	N	Y	Y	N	N	Y	Y
23 Stratton	Y	Y	Y	Y	N	N	Y	Y
24 ***Solomon***	Y	N	Y	Y	Y	Y	N	?
25 ***Boehlert***	N	N	Y	Y	N	Y	Y	Y
26 ***Martin***	Y	Y	Y	Y	N	Y	Y	Y
27 ***Wortley***	Y	N	Y	Y	N	Y	Y	Y
28 McHugh	N	?	?	Y	N	N	Y	Y
29 ***Horton***	N	Y	Y	?	N	N	Y	Y
30 ***Eckert***	Y	N	Y	Y	Y	Y	N	Y
31 ***Kemp***	Y	N	Y	?	?	?	?	?
32 LaFalce	N	Y	Y	Y	N	N	Y	N
33 Nowak	N	Y	Y	Y	N	N	Y	N
34 Lundine	?	?	?	?	?	?	?	?

	182	183	184	185	186	187	188	189
NORTH CAROLINA								
1 Jones	N	Y	Y	Y	N	N	Y	?
2 Valentine	Y	Y	Y	Y	N	N	Y	Y
3 Whitley	N	Y	Y	Y	?	N	Y	Y
4 ***Cobey***	Y	N	Y	Y	N	Y	Y	Y
5 Neal	N	N	Y	Y	N	N	Y	Y
6 ***Coble***	Y	N	Y	Y	Y	Y	N	Y
7 Rose	N	Y	Y	Y	N	?	Y	Y
8 Hefner	Y	Y	Y	Y	N	N	Y	Y
9 ***McMillan***	Y	N	Y	Y	Y	Y	Y	Y
10 ***Broyhill***	Y	?	Y	Y	Y	Y	Y	Y
11 ***Hendon***	Y	N	Y	Y	N	Y	Y	Y
NORTH DAKOTA								
AL Dorgan	N	N	Y	Y	?	?	Y	N
OHIO								
1 Luken	N	Y	Y	Y	N	N	Y	Y
2 ***Gradison***	Y	N	Y	Y	Y	Y	N	Y
3 Hall	N	Y	Y	Y	N	N	Y	?
4 ***Oxley***	Y	N	Y	Y	Y	Y	N	Y
5 ***Latta***	Y	N	?	Y	N	Y	Y	Y
6 ***McEwen***	Y	N	Y	Y	?	Y	N	Y
7 ***DeWine***	Y	N	Y	Y	Y	Y	N	Y
8 ***Kindness***	Y	N	Y	Y	Y	Y	N	Y
9 Kaptur	N	Y	Y	Y	N	N	Y	Y
10 ***Miller***	Y	N	Y	Y	Y	Y	N	Y
11 Eckart	N	Y	Y	Y	N	N	Y	Y
12 ***Kasich***	Y	N	Y	Y	Y	Y	Y	Y
13 Pease	N	Y	Y	Y	N	N	Y	Y
14 Seiberling	N	Y	Y	Y	N	?	Y	Y
15 ***Wylie***	Y	N	Y	Y	N	Y	Y	Y
16 ***Regula***	Y	N	Y	Y	N	Y	Y	Y
17 Traficant	N	N	Y	Y	N	N	Y	Y
18 Applegate	N	Y	Y	Y	N	N	Y	Y
19 Feighan	N	N	Y	Y	N	N	Y	Y
20 Oakar	N	?	?	Y	N	N	Y	Y
21 Stokes	N	Y	Y	Y	N	N	Y	Y
OKLAHOMA								
1 Jones	Y	Y	Y	Y	N	N	Y	Y
2 Synar	N	N	Y	Y	N	N	Y	Y
3 Watkins	Y	Y	Y	Y	N	N	Y	N
4 McCurdy	Y	Y	Y	Y	N	N	Y	Y
5 ***Edwards***	Y	?	?	Y	N	N	N	Y
6 English	Y	Y	Y	Y	N	N	Y	N
OREGON								
1 AuCoin	N	?	Y	Y	N	N	Y	N
2 ***Smith, R.***	Y	N	Y	Y	Y	Y	Y	N
3 Wyden	N	Y	Y	Y	N	N	Y	Y
4 Weaver	N	?	?	?	?	?	?	?
5 ***Smith, D.***	Y	N	Y	Y	Y	Y	N	Y
PENNSYLVANIA								
1 Foglietta	N	Y	Y	Y	N	N	Y	?
2 Gray	N	Y	Y	Y	N	N	Y	Y
3 Borski	N	Y	Y	Y	N	N	Y	Y
4 Kolter	N	Y	Y	Y	N	N	Y	Y
5 ***Schulze***	Y	Y	Y	Y	Y	Y	Y	?
6 Yatron	N	N	Y	Y	N	N	Y	Y
7 Edgar	N	?	?	?	?	?	?	Y
8 Kostmayer	N	Y	Y	Y	N	N	Y	Y
9 ***Shuster***	Y	N	Y	Y	N	Y	N	?
10 ***McDade***	Y	N	Y	Y	?	Y	Y	Y
11 Kanjorski	Y	Y	Y	Y	N	N	Y	Y
12 Murtha	Y	Y	Y	Y	N	N	Y	Y
13 ***Coughlin***	Y	N	Y	Y	N	Y	Y	Y
14 Coyne	N	Y	Y	Y	N	N	Y	Y
15 ***Ritter***	Y	N	Y	Y	N	Y	Y	Y
16 ***Walker***	Y	N	Y	Y	Y	Y	N	Y
17 ***Gekas***	Y	N	Y	Y	N	Y	Y	Y
18 Walgren	N	Y	Y	Y	N	N	Y	Y
19 ***Goodling***	Y	N	Y	Y	N	Y	Y	Y
20 Gaydos	?	Y	Y	Y	N	N	Y	N
21 ***Ridge***	N	Y	Y	Y	N	Y	Y	N
22 Murphy	N	Y	Y	Y	N	N	Y	Y
23 ***Clinger***	Y	-	+	Y	N	Y	Y	Y
RHODE ISLAND								
1 St Germain	N	?	Y	Y	N	N	Y	Y
2 ***Schneider***	N	Y	Y	Y	N	Y	?	Y
SOUTH CAROLINA								
1 ***Hartnett***	Y	N	Y	?	?	?	?	?
2 ***Spence***	Y	N	Y	Y	N	Y	Y	N
3 Derrick	N	Y	Y	Y	N	N	Y	Y
4 ***Campbell***	Y	N	Y	?	?	?	?	?
5 Spratt	Y	Y	Y	Y	N	N	Y	Y
6 Tallon	Y	N	Y	Y	N	N	Y	Y
SOUTH DAKOTA								
AL Daschle	N	Y	Y	Y	N	N	Y	N

	182	183	184	185	186	187	188	189
TENNESSEE								
1 ***Quillen***	Y	Y	N	Y	N	?	?	?
2 ***Duncan***	Y	N	Y	Y	N	Y	Y	Y
3 Lloyd	Y	N	Y	Y	N	N	Y	N
4 Cooper	Y	Y	Y	Y	N	N	Y	Y
5 Boner	N	N	Y	Y	N	N	Y	Y
6 Gordon	N	N	Y	Y	N	N	Y	Y
7 ***Sundquist***	Y	N	Y	Y	N	Y	Y	Y
8 Jones	Y	Y	Y	Y	N	N	Y	Y
9 Ford	N	Y	Y	Y	N	N	Y	Y
TEXAS								
1 Chapman	Y	Y	Y	Y	N	N	Y	Y
2 Wilson	Y	?	?	Y	N	N	Y	Y
3 ***Bartlett***	Y	N	Y	Y	Y	Y	N	Y
4 Hall, R.	Y	N	Y	Y	N	Y	Y	N
5 Bryant	Y	N	Y	Y	N	N	Y	Y
6 ***Barton***	Y	N	Y	Y	Y	Y	N	Y
7 ***Archer***	Y	N	Y	Y	Y	Y	N	Y
8 ***Fields***	Y	N	Y	Y	Y	Y	N	Y
9 Brooks	N	Y	Y	Y	N	?	?	Y
10 Pickle	Y	?	?	?	?	?	?	?
11 Leath	Y	Y	Y	Y	N	N	Y	Y
12 Wright	N	Y	Y	Y	N	N	Y	Y
13 ***Boulter***	Y	N	Y	Y	Y	Y	N	Y
14 ***Sweeney***	Y	N	Y	Y	N	Y	Y	Y
15 de la Garza	Y	?	?	?	?	?	?	?
16 Coleman	N	Y	Y	Y	N	N	Y	N
17 Stenholm	Y	N	Y	Y	N	N	N	Y
18 Leland	N	Y	Y	Y	N	N	Y	Y
19 ***Combest***	Y	N	Y	Y	Y	Y	N	Y
20 Gonzalez	Y	Y	Y	Y	N	N	Y	N
21 ***Loeffler***	Y	N	Y	Y	Y	Y	N	?
22 ***DeLay***	Y	N	Y	Y	Y	Y	N	Y
23 Bustamante	Y	Y	Y	Y	N	N	Y	Y
24 Frost	Y	?	?	?	?	?	?	?
25 Andrews	Y	Y	?	Y	N	N	Y	Y
26 ***Armey***	Y	N	Y	Y	Y	Y	N	N
27 Ortiz	Y	Y	Y	Y	N	N	Y	Y
UTAH								
1 ***Hansen***	Y	N	Y	Y	Y	Y	N	Y
2 ***Monson***	Y	N	Y	Y	Y	Y	N	N
3 ***Nielson***	Y	N	Y	Y	Y	Y	N	Y
VERMONT								
AL ***Jeffords***	N	N	Y	Y	N	Y	Y	Y
VIRGINIA								
1 ***Bateman***	Y	N	Y	Y	Y	Y	Y	Y
2 ***Whitehurst***	Y	Y	Y	Y	Y	Y	N	Y
3 ***Bliley***	Y	N	Y	Y	Y	Y	N	Y
4 Sisisky	Y	Y	Y	Y	N	N	Y	Y
5 Daniel	?	Y	Y	Y	Y	N	Y	Y
6 Olin	Y	Y	Y	Y	N	N	Y	Y
7 ***Slaughter***	Y	N	Y	Y	Y	Y	N	Y
8 ***Parris***	Y	N	?	P	Y	Y	N	Y
9 Boucher	Y	Y	Y	Y	N	N	Y	Y
10 ***Wolf***	Y	N	Y	Y	N	Y	Y	Y
WASHINGTON								
1 ***Miller***	Y	N	Y	Y	N	Y	Y	Y
2 Swift	N	Y	Y	Y	N	N	Y	Y
3 Bonker	N	Y	?	Y	N	N	Y	Y
4 ***Morrison***	Y	N	Y	Y	N	Y	Y	Y
5 Foley	N	Y	Y	Y	N	N	Y	Y
6 Dicks	N	Y	Y	Y	N	N	Y	?
7 Lowry	N	Y	Y	Y	N	N	Y	Y
8 ***Chandler***	Y	N	?	?	Y	Y	N	Y
WEST VIRGINIA								
1 Mollohan	Y	Y	Y	Y	N	N	Y	Y
2 Staggers	N	Y	Y	Y	N	N	Y	Y
3 Wise	N	N	Y	Y	N	N	Y	Y
4 Rahall	N	Y	Y	Y	N	N	Y	Y
WISCONSIN								
1 Aspin	Y	Y	Y	Y	N	N	Y	?
2 Kastenmeier	N	Y	Y	Y	N	N	Y	Y
3 ***Gunderson***	Y	N	Y	Y	N	N	Y	Y
4 Kleczka	N	Y	Y	Y	N	N	Y	Y
5 Moody	N	Y	Y	Y	N	N	Y	Y
6 ***Petri***	Y	N	Y	Y	N	Y	Y	N
7 Obey	N	Y	Y	Y	N	N	Y	Y
8 ***Roth***	Y	N	Y	Y	Y	Y	N	N
9 ***Sensenbrenner***	N	N	Y	Y	Y	Y	N	Y
WYOMING								
AL ***Cheney***	Y	N	Y	Y	Y	Y	N	Y

Southern states - Ala., Ark., Fla., Ga., Ky., La., Miss., N.C., Okla., S.C., Tenn., Texas, Va.

* The *Congressional Record* vote number is different from the CQ vote number because the *Record* includes quorum calls in its tally. CQ does not publish quorum call votes.

190. HR 4510. Export-Import Bank. Adoption of the rule (H Res 472) to provide for House floor consideration of the bill to authorize operations in fiscal years 1987-88 by the Export-Import Bank. Adopted 365-9: R 150-9; D 215-0 (ND 144-0, SD 71-0), July 15, 1986.

191. HR 4510. Export-Import Bank. Neal, D-N.C., amendment to the Rahall, D-W.Va., amendment, to allow Export-Import Bank loans in cases where the foreign manufacturer could obtain financing elsewhere. Adopted 307-87: R 144-21; D 163-66 (ND 108-48, SD 55-18), July 15, 1986. (The Rahall amendment would have banned all Export-Import Bank loans for foreign industries whose products or commodities compete with U.S.-made items. The Rahall amendment, as amended by the Neal amendment, subsequently was adopted by voice vote. Later, the bill was passed by voice vote.)

192. HR 4259. Gettysburg National Military Park. Adoption of the rule (H Res 483) to provide for House floor consideration of the bill to authorize donation of certain non-federal lands for inclusion within the Gettysburg National Military Park. Adopted 398-2: R 168-2; D 230-0 (ND 156-0, SD 74-0), July 16, 1986.

193. HR 4259. Gettysburg National Military Park. Passage of the bill to authorize donation to the federal government of a 31-acre land parcel known as the Taney Farm within the boundaries of the Gettysburg National Military Park. Passed 408-1: R 171-1; D 237-0 (ND 160-0, SD 77-0), July 16, 1986. A "yea" was a vote supporting the president's position.

194. HR 4613. Commodity Futures Trading Commission. Adoption of the rule (H Res 474) to provide for House floor consideration of the bill to reauthorize appropriations and make revisions in the Commodity Exchange Act. Adopted 404-0: R 171-0; D 233-0 (ND 159-0, SD 74-0), July 16, 1986.

195. HR 4613. Commodity Futures Trading Commission. Glickman, D-Kan., amendment to require that leverage contracts on precious metals be regulated in the same manner as futures contracts on precious metals. Adopted 219-193: R 62-112; D 157-81 (ND 121-41, SD 36-40), July 16, 1986. (The Glickman amendment subsequently was rejected after the House rose from the Committee of the Whole *(see vote 198, p. 60-H)*.) A "nay" was a vote supporting the president's position.

196. HR 4613. Commodity Futures Trading Commission. Watkins, D-Okla., amendment to end authority for futures trading in live cattle by December 1987 unless a majority of cattlemen approve such markets in a referendum. Rejected 142-265: R 28-143; D 114-122 (ND 92-67, SD 22-55), July 16, 1986.

197. HR 4613. Commodity Futures Trading Commission. Jones, D-Okla., amendment to direct the House Agriculture Committee to study the economic purpose of trading in cattle futures, whether such trading is being manipulated, and the economic effects on cattlemen and beef producers. Adopted 406-1: R 171-1; D 235-0 (ND 158-0, SD 77-0), July 16, 1986.

[1] *Rep. Cecil Heftel, D-Hawaii, resigned July 11, 1986, to run for governor of Hawaii. The last vote for which he was eligible was CQ vote 189.*

[2] *Rep. James T. Broyhill, R-N.C., resigned July 13, 1986, to fill the vacant seat resulting from the June 29 death of Sen. John P. East. The last House vote for which he was eligible was CQ vote 189.*

KEY

Y Voted for (yea).
Paired for.
+ Announced for.
N Voted against (nay).
X Paired against.
- Announced against.
P Voted "present."
C Voted "present" to avoid possible conflict of interest.
? Did not vote or otherwise make a position known.

Democrats ***Republicans***

	190	191	192	193	194	195	196	197
ALABAMA								
1 ***Callahan***	Y	Y	Y	Y	Y	N	N	Y
2 ***Dickinson***	Y	Y	Y	Y	Y	Y	N	Y
3 Nichols	Y	Y	Y	Y	Y	N	N	Y
4 Bevill	Y	N	Y	Y	Y	N	Y	Y
5 Flippo	Y	Y	Y	Y	Y	N	?	Y
6 Erdreich	Y	N	Y	Y	Y	Y	N	Y
7 Shelby	Y	N	Y	Y	Y	Y	N	Y
ALASKA								
AL ***Young***	Y	Y	Y	Y	Y	N	N	Y
ARIZONA								
1 ***McCain***	Y	Y	Y	Y	Y	N	N	Y
2 Udall	Y	N	?	Y	Y	Y	N	Y
3 ***Stump***	Y	Y	Y	Y	Y	N	Y	Y
4 ***Rudd***	Y	Y	Y	Y	Y	N	Y	Y
5 ***Kolbe***	Y	Y	Y	Y	Y	N	N	Y
ARKANSAS								
1 Alexander	Y	Y	Y	Y	Y	N	N	Y
2 Robinson	Y	N	Y	Y	Y	N	N	Y
3 ***Hammerschmidt***	Y	Y	Y	Y	Y	Y	Y	Y
4 Anthony	Y	Y	Y	Y	Y	Y	N	Y
CALIFORNIA								
1 Bosco	Y	Y	Y	Y	Y	N	N	Y
2 ***Chappie***	?	?	?	?	?	?	?	?
3 Matsui	?	Y	Y	Y	Y	N	Y	Y
4 Fazio	Y	Y	Y	Y	Y	N	N	Y
5 Burton	Y	Y	Y	Y	Y	N	Y	Y
6 Boxer	Y	Y	Y	Y	Y	N	Y	Y
7 Miller	?	Y	Y	Y	?	Y	Y	Y
8 Dellums	Y	N	Y	Y	Y	Y	Y	Y
9 Stark	Y	?	Y	Y	Y	Y	Y	Y
10 Edwards	Y	Y	Y	Y	Y	Y	C	Y
11 Lantos	Y	Y	Y	Y	Y	N	Y	Y
12 ***Zschau***	Y	Y	Y	Y	Y	N	N	Y
13 Mineta	Y	?	Y	Y	Y	N	Y	Y
14 ***Shumway***	Y	N	Y	Y	Y	N	Y	Y
15 Coelho	Y	Y	Y	Y	Y	N	N	Y
16 Panetta	Y	Y	Y	Y	Y	N	N	Y
17 ***Pashayan***	Y	N	Y	Y	Y	N	N	Y
18 Lehman	Y	Y	Y	Y	Y	Y	N	Y
19 ***Lagomarsino***	Y	Y	Y	Y	Y	N	N	Y
20 ***Thomas***	Y	Y	Y	Y	Y	N	Y	Y
21 ***Fiedler***	?	?	?	?	?	?	?	?
22 ***Moorhead***	Y	Y	Y	Y	Y	N	N	Y
23 Beilenson	Y	Y	Y	Y	Y	Y	N	Y
24 Waxman	Y	Y	Y	Y	?	Y	Y	Y
25 Roybal	Y	N	Y	Y	Y	?	Y	Y
26 Berman	Y	Y	Y	Y	Y	Y	N	Y
27 Levine	Y	Y	Y	Y	Y	Y	N	Y
28 Dixon	Y	Y	Y	Y	Y	N	Y	Y
29 Hawkins	Y	N	Y	Y	Y	N	Y	Y
30 Martinez	?	Y	Y	Y	Y	N	Y	Y
31 Dymally	?	?	Y	Y	Y	N	Y	Y
32 Anderson	Y	N	Y	Y	Y	N	Y	Y
33 ***Dreier***	Y	Y	Y	Y	Y	N	N	Y
34 Torres	Y	N	Y	Y	Y	N	Y	Y
35 ***Lewis***	Y	Y	Y	Y	Y	N	Y	Y
36 Brown	Y	Y	Y	Y	?	N	N	Y
37 ***McCandless***	?	Y	Y	Y	Y	N	N	Y
38 ***Dornan***	Y	Y	Y	Y	Y	N	N	Y
39 ***Dannemeyer***	Y	Y	Y	Y	Y	N	N	Y
40 ***Badham***	Y	Y	Y	Y	Y	N	Y	Y
41 ***Lowery***	Y	Y	Y	Y	Y	N	N	Y
42 ***Lungren***	Y	Y	Y	Y	Y	N	N	Y
43 ***Packard***	Y	Y	Y	Y	Y	N	N	Y
44 Bates	Y	Y	Y	Y	Y	N	Y	Y
45 ***Hunter***	Y	Y	Y	Y	Y	N	Y	Y
COLORADO								
1 Schroeder	Y	Y	Y	Y	Y	Y	Y	Y
2 Wirth	Y	Y	Y	Y	Y	Y	Y	Y
3 ***Strang***	Y	Y	Y	Y	Y	Y	N	Y
4 ***Brown***	N	N	Y	Y	Y	N	N	Y
5 ***Kramer***	Y	Y	Y	Y	Y	N	Y	Y
6 ***Schaefer***	Y	Y	Y	Y	Y	N	N	Y
CONNECTICUT								
1 Kennelly	Y	Y	Y	Y	Y	Y	N	Y
2 Gejdenson	Y	Y	Y	Y	Y	Y	N	Y
3 Morrison	Y	Y	Y	Y	Y	Y	N	Y
4 ***McKinney***	Y	Y	Y	Y	Y	N	N	Y
5 ***Rowland***	Y	Y	Y	Y	Y	Y	N	Y
6 ***Johnson***	Y	Y	Y	Y	Y	Y	N	Y
DELAWARE								
AL Carper	Y	Y	Y	Y	Y	Y	N	Y
FLORIDA								
1 Hutto	Y	Y	Y	Y	Y	Y	N	Y
2 Fuqua	Y	Y	Y	Y	Y	N	N	Y
3 Bennett	Y	Y	Y	Y	Y	Y	Y	Y
4 Chappell	?	Y	Y	Y	Y	?	Y	Y
5 ***McCollum***	Y	Y	Y	Y	Y	N	N	Y
6 MacKay	Y	Y	Y	Y	Y	Y	Y	Y
7 Gibbons	Y	Y	Y	Y	Y	Y	N	Y
8 ***Young***	?	?	Y	Y	Y	Y	N	Y
9 ***Bilirakis***	?	?	Y	Y	Y	N	N	Y
10 ***Ireland***	Y	Y	Y	Y	Y	N	N	Y
11 Nelson	Y	Y	Y	Y	Y	Y	N	Y
12 ***Lewis***	Y	Y	Y	Y	Y	N	N	Y
13 ***Mack***	N	N	Y	Y	Y	N	N	Y
14 Mica	Y	Y	Y	Y	Y	Y	N	Y
15 ***Shaw***	Y	Y	Y	Y	Y	Y	N	Y
16 Smith	Y	Y	Y	Y	Y	Y	N	?
17 Lehman	Y	Y	Y	Y	Y	N	N	Y
18 Pepper	Y	Y	Y	Y	Y	N	N	Y
19 Fascell	Y	Y	Y	Y	Y	Y	N	Y
GEORGIA								
1 Thomas	Y	Y	Y	Y	Y	N	N	Y
2 Hatcher	?	N	Y	Y	Y	N	N	Y
3 Ray	?	Y	Y	Y	Y	Y	N	Y
4 ***Swindall***	Y	Y	Y	Y	Y	N	N	Y
5 Fowler	?	?	?	?	?	Y	N	Y
6 ***Gingrich***	Y	Y	Y	?	?	Y	N	Y
7 Darden	Y	Y	Y	Y	Y	N	Y	Y
8 Rowland	Y	Y	Y	Y	Y	N	N	Y
9 Jenkins	Y	N	Y	Y	Y	Y	Y	Y
10 Barnard	?	?	?	?	?	?	?	?
HAWAII								
1 Vacancy [1]								
2 Akaka	Y	Y	Y	Y	Y	Y	Y	Y
IDAHO								
1 ***Craig***	Y	N	Y	Y	Y	N	Y	Y
2 Stallings	Y	Y	Y	Y	Y	N	N	Y
ILLINOIS								
1 Hayes	Y	N	Y	Y	?	Y	Y	Y
2 Savage	?	N	Y	Y	Y	Y	Y	Y
3 Russo	Y	N	Y	Y	Y	Y	Y	Y
4 ***O'Brien***	?	?	?	?	?	?	?	?
5 Lipinski	Y	Y	Y	Y	Y	N	Y	Y
6 ***Hyde***	Y	Y	N	Y	Y	N	N	Y
7 Collins	?	?	Y	Y	Y	Y	N	Y
8 Rostenkowski	Y	Y	Y	Y	Y	N	Y	Y
9 Yates	Y	Y	Y	Y	Y	Y	Y	Y
10 ***Porter***	Y	Y	Y	Y	Y	N	N	Y
11 Annunzio	Y	Y	Y	Y	Y	N	Y	Y
12 ***Crane***	N	Y	Y	Y	Y	N	N	N
13 ***Fawell***	Y	Y	Y	Y	Y	N	N	Y
14 ***Grotberg***	?	?	?	?	?	?	?	?
15 ***Madigan***	Y	Y	Y	Y	Y	N	N	Y
16 ***Martin***	Y	Y	Y	Y	Y	N	N	Y
17 Evans	Y	Y	Y	Y	Y	Y	Y	Y
18 ***Michel***	Y	Y	Y	Y	Y	N	?	Y
19 Bruce	Y	Y	Y	Y	Y	N	N	Y
20 Durbin	Y	Y	Y	Y	Y	N	N	Y
21 Price	Y	Y	Y	Y	Y	N	Y	Y
22 Gray	Y	N	Y	Y	Y	N	Y	Y
INDIANA								
1 Visclosky	Y	N	Y	Y	Y	Y	N	Y
2 Sharp	Y	Y	Y	Y	Y	Y	Y	Y
3 ***Hiler***	Y	Y	Y	Y	Y	N	N	Y
4 ***Coats***	Y	Y	Y	Y	Y	Y	N	Y
5 ***Hillis***	?	?	Y	Y	Y	N	N	Y

ND - Northern Democrats SD - Southern Democrats

* Corresponding to Congressional Record Votes 212, 213, 214, 215, 216, 217, 218, 219

	190	191	192	193	194	195	196	197
6 ***Burton***	Y	Y	Y	Y	Y	N	N	Y
7 ***Myers***	Y	Y	Y	Y	Y	N	Y	Y
8 McCloskey	Y	N	Y	Y	Y	N	N	Y
9 Hamilton	Y	Y	Y	Y	Y	Y	N	Y
10 Jacobs	Y	Y	Y	Y	Y	Y	Y	Y
IOWA								
1 ***Leach***	Y	Y	Y	Y	Y	Y	C	Y
2 ***Tauke***	?	Y	Y	Y	Y	Y	Y	Y
3 ***Evans***	Y	Y	Y	Y	?	?	?	?
4 Smith	Y	Y	Y	Y	Y	Y	Y	Y
5 ***Lightfoot***	Y	Y	Y	Y	Y	N	Y	Y
6 Bedell	Y	Y	Y	Y	Y	N	Y	Y
KANSAS								
1 ***Roberts***	Y	Y	Y	Y	Y	Y	N	Y
2 Slattery	Y	Y	Y	Y	Y	Y	N	Y
3 ***Meyers***	Y	Y	Y	Y	Y	Y	N	Y
4 Glickman	Y	Y	Y	Y	Y	Y	N	Y
5 ***Whittaker***	?	?	Y	Y	Y	Y	N	Y
KENTUCKY								
1 Hubbard	Y	N	Y	Y	Y	N	N	Y
2 Natcher	Y	Y	Y	Y	Y	Y	Y	Y
3 Mazzoli	Y	Y	Y	Y	Y	N	N	Y
4 ***Snyder***	Y	Y	Y	Y	Y	Y	Y	Y
5 ***Rogers***	Y	N	Y	Y	Y	N	N	Y
6 ***Hopkins***	Y	Y	Y	Y	Y	N	N	?
7 Perkins	Y	N	Y	Y	Y	N	Y	Y
LOUISIANA								
1 ***Livingston***	Y	Y	Y	Y	Y	N	N	Y
2 Boggs	Y	Y	Y	Y	Y	N	N	Y
3 Tauzin	Y	N	Y	Y	Y	N	N	Y
4 Roemer	Y	N	Y	Y	Y	Y	Y	Y
5 Huckaby	Y	Y	Y	Y	Y	N	N	Y
6 ***Moore***	?	?	?	?	?	?	?	?
7 Breaux	?	?	?	?	?	?	?	?
8 Long	Y	Y	Y	Y	Y	N	N	Y
MAINE								
1 ***McKernan***	Y	Y	Y	Y	Y	N	Y	Y
2 ***Snowe***	Y	Y	Y	Y	Y	N	Y	Y
MARYLAND								
1 Dyson	Y	Y	Y	Y	Y	N	N	Y
2 ***Bentley***	N	N	Y	Y	Y	N	Y	Y
3 Mikulski	Y	N	?	Y	Y	Y	N	Y
4 ***Holt***	Y	?	Y	Y	Y	Y	N	Y
5 Hoyer	Y	Y	?	Y	Y	N	N	Y
6 Byron	Y	Y	Y	Y	Y	Y	N	Y
7 Mitchell	Y	Y	?	?	?	?	?	?
8 Barnes	?	Y	?	?	?	?	?	?
MASSACHUSETTS								
1 ***Conte***	Y	Y	Y	Y	Y	Y	N	Y
2 Boland	Y	Y	Y	Y	Y	Y	N	Y
3 Early	Y	Y	Y	Y	Y	Y	Y	Y
4 Frank	Y	Y	Y	Y	Y	N	Y	Y
5 Atkins	Y	Y	Y	Y	Y	Y	N	Y
6 Mavroules	Y	Y	Y	Y	Y	Y	?	Y
7 Markey	Y	Y	Y	Y	Y	Y	Y	Y
8 O'Neill								
9 Moakley	Y	Y	Y	Y	Y	N	N	Y
10 Studds	Y	Y	Y	Y	Y	Y	Y	Y
11 Donnelly	Y	Y	Y	Y	Y	Y	Y	Y
MICHIGAN								
1 Conyers	?	?	Y	Y	Y	Y	Y	Y
2 ***Pursell***	Y	Y	Y	Y	Y	N	N	Y
3 Wolpe	Y	Y	Y	Y	Y	Y	Y	Y
4 ***Siljander***	Y	Y	Y	Y	Y	N	N	Y
5 ***Henry***	Y	Y	Y	Y	Y	Y	N	Y
6 Carr	Y	Y	Y	Y	Y	N	N	Y
7 Kildee	Y	N	Y	Y	Y	Y	Y	Y
8 Traxler	Y	Y	Y	Y	Y	Y	Y	Y
9 ***Vander Jagt***	Y	Y	Y	Y	Y	Y	N	Y
10 ***Schuette***	Y	Y	Y	Y	Y	N	N	Y
11 ***Davis***	?	Y	Y	Y	Y	Y	N	Y
12 Bonior	?	Y	Y	Y	Y	?	?	?
13 Crockett	Y	Y	Y	Y	Y	Y	Y	?
14 Hertel	Y	N	Y	Y	Y	Y	Y	Y
15 Ford	Y	N	?	Y	Y	Y	Y	Y
16 Dingell	?	N	Y	Y	Y	Y	Y	Y
17 Levin	Y	N	Y	Y	Y	Y	N	Y
18 ***Broomfield***	Y	Y	Y	Y	Y	N	N	Y
MINNESOTA								
1 Penny	Y	Y	Y	Y	Y	N	Y	Y
2 ***Weber***	Y	Y	Y	Y	Y	N	Y	Y
3 ***Frenzel***	Y	Y	Y	Y	Y	Y	N	Y
4 Vento	Y	Y	Y	Y	Y	Y	Y	Y
5 Sabo	Y	Y	Y	Y	Y	Y	Y	Y
6 Sikorski	Y	N	Y	Y	Y	Y	Y	Y

	190	191	192	193	194	195	196	197
7 ***Stangeland***	Y	Y	Y	Y	Y	N	N	Y
8 Oberstar	Y	N	Y	Y	Y	Y	Y	Y
MISSISSIPPI								
1 Whitten	Y	Y	Y	Y	?	Y	Y	Y
2 ***Franklin***	?	Y	Y	Y	Y	N	N	Y
3 Montgomery	Y	Y	Y	Y	?	Y	N	Y
4 Dowdy	Y	N	Y	Y	Y	Y	N	Y
5 ***Lott***	Y	Y	Y	Y	Y	N	N	Y
MISSOURI								
1 Clay	Y	Y	Y	Y	Y	Y	Y	Y
2 Young	Y	Y	Y	Y	Y	Y	Y	Y
3 Gephardt	Y	Y	Y	Y	Y	Y	N	Y
4 Skelton	?	Y	Y	Y	Y	Y	Y	Y
5 Wheat	Y	Y	Y	Y	Y	N	N	Y
6 ***Coleman***	Y	Y	Y	Y	Y	N	N	Y
7 ***Taylor***	Y	Y	Y	Y	Y	Y	Y	Y
8 ***Emerson***	Y	N	Y	Y	Y	N	Y	Y
9 Volkmer	?	Y	Y	Y	Y	Y	Y	Y
MONTANA								
1 Williams	Y	N	?	Y	Y	Y	Y	Y
2 ***Marlenee***	?	?	Y	Y	Y	N	Y	Y
NEBRASKA								
1 ***Bereuter***	Y	Y	Y	Y	Y	Y	N	Y
2 ***Daub***	?	Y	Y	Y	Y	N	Y	Y
3 ***Smith***	Y	Y	Y	Y	Y	N	Y	Y
NEVADA								
1 Reid	Y	Y	Y	Y	Y	Y	Y	Y
2 ***Vucanovich***	Y	N	Y	Y	Y	Y	N	Y
NEW HAMPSHIRE								
1 ***Smith***	N	Y	Y	Y	Y	N	N	Y
2 ***Gregg***	Y	Y	Y	Y	Y	N	N	Y
NEW JERSEY								
1 Florio	?	?	Y	Y	Y	Y	Y	Y
2 Hughes	Y	Y	Y	Y	Y	Y	Y	Y
3 Howard	Y	N	Y	Y	Y	N	Y	Y
4 ***Smith***	?	Y	Y	Y	Y	N	N	Y
5 ***Roukema***	Y	Y	Y	Y	Y	Y	N	Y
6 Dwyer	Y	N	Y	Y	Y	Y	Y	Y
7 ***Rinaldo***	Y	Y	Y	Y	Y	Y	N	Y
8 Roe	Y	N	Y	Y	Y	N	Y	Y
9 Torricelli	?	Y	?	?	?	?	?	?
10 Rodino	Y	Y	Y	Y	Y	Y	Y	Y
11 ***Gallo***	Y	Y	Y	Y	Y	N	N	Y
12 ***Courter***	Y	Y	Y	Y	Y	N	N	Y
13 ***Saxton***	Y	Y	Y	Y	Y	N	Y	Y
14 Guarini	Y	Y	?	Y	Y	Y	Y	Y
NEW MEXICO								
1 ***Lujan***	Y	Y	Y	Y	Y	N	N	Y
2 ***Skeen***	Y	Y	Y	Y	Y	N	N	Y
3 Richardson	Y	N	Y	Y	Y	Y	Y	Y
NEW YORK								
1 ***Carney***	?	?	Y	Y	Y	Y	N	Y
2 Downey	?	?	Y	Y	Y	Y	Y	Y
3 Mrazek	Y	Y	Y	Y	Y	Y	Y	Y
4 ***Lent***	Y	Y	Y	Y	Y	Y	N	Y
5 ***McGrath***	Y	Y	Y	Y	Y	Y	N	Y
6 Vacancy								
7 Ackerman	?	?	?	?	Y	Y	Y	?
8 Scheuer	Y	Y	Y	Y	Y	Y	Y	Y
9 Manton	Y	Y	Y	Y	Y	Y	N	Y
10 Schumer	Y	Y	Y	Y	Y	Y	Y	Y
11 Towns	Y	N	Y	Y	Y	Y	N	Y
12 Owens	Y	N	Y	Y	Y	Y	Y	Y
13 Solarz	Y	Y	Y	Y	Y	Y	N	Y
14 ***Molinari***	Y	N	Y	Y	Y	Y	N	Y
15 ***Green***	Y	Y	Y	Y	Y	Y	N	Y
16 Rangel	Y	Y	Y	Y	Y	Y	?	Y
17 Weiss	Y	Y	Y	Y	Y	Y	Y	Y
18 Garcia	Y	N	Y	Y	Y	Y	Y	Y
19 Biaggi	?	N	Y	Y	Y	Y	Y	Y
20 ***DioGuardi***	Y	Y	Y	Y	Y	Y	N	Y
21 ***Fish***	Y	Y	Y	Y	Y	Y	N	Y
22 ***Gilman***	Y	Y	Y	Y	Y	Y	N	Y
23 Stratton	Y	Y	Y	Y	Y	N	N	Y
24 ***Solomon***	Y	N	Y	Y	Y	N	N	Y
25 ***Boehlert***	Y	Y	Y	Y	Y	N	N	Y
26 ***Martin***	Y	Y	Y	Y	Y	Y	N	Y
27 ***Wortley***	Y	Y	Y	Y	Y	Y	N	Y
28 McHugh	Y	Y	Y	Y	Y	Y	Y	Y
29 ***Horton***	Y	Y	Y	Y	Y	Y	N	Y
30 ***Eckert***	Y	Y	Y	Y	Y	N	N	Y
31 ***Kemp***	Y	Y	?	Y	Y	Y	N	Y
32 LaFalce	Y	Y	Y	?	Y	Y	N	Y
33 Nowak	Y	Y	Y	Y	Y	Y	N	Y
34 Lundine	Y	Y	Y	Y	Y	Y	?	?

	190	191	192	193	194	195	196	197
NORTH CAROLINA								
1 Jones	?	?	?	?	?	?	?	?
2 Valentine	Y	Y	Y	Y	Y	N	N	Y
3 Whitley	Y	Y	Y	Y	Y	N	N	Y
4 ***Cobey***	N	Y	Y	Y	Y	Y	N	Y
5 Neal	Y	Y	Y	Y	Y	Y	Y	Y
6 ***Coble***	Y	Y	Y	Y	Y	N	N	Y
7 Rose	Y	Y	Y	Y	Y	Y	N	Y
8 Hefner	Y	Y	Y	Y	Y	N	Y	Y
9 ***McMillan***	Y	Y	Y	Y	Y	N	N	Y
10 Vacancy [2]								
11 ***Hendon***	Y	Y	Y	Y	Y	N	N	Y
NORTH DAKOTA								
AL Dorgan	Y	Y	Y	?	Y	Y	Y	Y
OHIO								
1 Luken	Y	Y	Y	Y	Y	Y	N	Y
2 ***Gradison***	Y	Y	Y	Y	Y	Y	N	Y
3 Hall	Y	Y	Y	Y	?	Y	N	Y
4 ***Oxley***	Y	Y	Y	Y	Y	N	N	Y
5 ***Latta***	Y	Y	Y	Y	Y	N	N	Y
6 ***McEwen***	N	N	Y	Y	Y	N	N	Y
7 ***DeWine***	Y	Y	Y	Y	Y	N	N	Y
8 ***Kindness***	Y	Y	Y	Y	Y	N	N	Y
9 Kaptur	Y	N	Y	Y	Y	Y	N	Y
10 ***Miller***	Y	N	Y	Y	Y	Y	N	Y
11 Eckart	Y	N	Y	Y	Y	Y	N	Y
12 ***Kasich***	Y	Y	Y	Y	Y	N	N	Y
13 Pease	Y	Y	Y	Y	Y	Y	N	Y
14 Seiberling	Y	N	Y	Y	Y	Y	N	?
15 ***Wylie***	Y	Y	Y	Y	Y	Y	N	Y
16 ***Regula***	Y	N	Y	Y	Y	N	N	Y
17 Traficant	?	?	Y	Y	Y	Y	Y	Y
18 Applegate	Y	N	Y	Y	Y	Y	Y	Y
19 Feighan	Y	N	Y	Y	Y	Y	N	Y
20 Oakar	Y	N	Y	Y	Y	Y	Y	Y
21 Stokes	Y	Y	Y	Y	Y	Y	Y	Y
OKLAHOMA								
1 Jones	?	?	Y	Y	Y	Y	Y	Y
2 Synar	Y	Y	Y	Y	Y	Y	N	Y
3 Watkins	Y	Y	Y	Y	Y	Y	Y	Y
4 McCurdy	Y	Y	Y	Y	Y	Y	Y	Y
5 ***Edwards***	?	?	Y	Y	Y	Y	Y	Y
6 English	Y	Y	Y	Y	Y	Y	Y	Y
OREGON								
1 AuCoin	?	?	Y	Y	Y	N	N	Y
2 ***Smith, R.***	Y	Y	Y	Y	Y	Y	N	Y
3 Wyden	Y	Y	Y	Y	Y	Y	N	Y
4 Weaver	?	?	?	?	?	?	?	?
5 ***Smith, D.***	Y	Y	Y	Y	Y	N	N	Y
PENNSYLVANIA								
1 Foglietta	Y	N	Y	Y	Y	Y	Y	Y
2 Gray	?	N	Y	Y	Y	Y	Y	Y
3 Borski	?	N	Y	Y	Y	N	Y	Y
4 Kolter	Y	N	Y	Y	Y	Y	N	Y
5 ***Schulze***	Y	N	Y	Y	Y	N	N	Y
6 Yatron	Y	N	Y	Y	Y	Y	Y	Y
7 Edgar	Y	Y	Y	Y	Y	Y	N	Y
8 Kostmayer	Y	Y	Y	Y	Y	Y	N	Y
9 ***Shuster***	Y	Y	Y	Y	Y	Y	N	Y
10 ***McDade***	Y	Y	Y	Y	Y	N	N	Y
11 Kanjorski	Y	N	Y	Y	Y	Y	Y	Y
12 Murtha	Y	N	Y	Y	Y	N	Y	Y
13 ***Coughlin***	Y	Y	Y	Y	Y	Y	N	?
14 Coyne	Y	Y	Y	Y	Y	Y	Y	Y
15 ***Ritter***	Y	Y	Y	Y	Y	Y	N	Y
16 ***Walker***	N	N	Y	Y	Y	N	N	Y
17 ***Gekas***	N	N	Y	Y	Y	N	N	Y
18 Walgren	Y	Y	Y	Y	Y	Y	N	Y
19 ***Goodling***	Y	Y	Y	Y	Y	N	Y	Y
20 Gaydos	Y	N	Y	Y	Y	N	N	Y
21 ***Ridge***	Y	Y	Y	Y	Y	Y	N	Y
22 Murphy	Y	N	Y	Y	Y	Y	Y	Y
23 ***Clinger***	Y	N	Y	Y	Y	N	N	Y
RHODE ISLAND								
1 St Germain	Y	Y	Y	Y	Y	Y	Y	Y
2 ***Schneider***	Y	Y	Y	Y	Y	Y	N	Y
SOUTH CAROLINA								
1 ***Hartnett***	Y	Y	Y	Y	Y	N	N	Y
2 ***Spence***	Y	Y	Y	Y	Y	N	N	Y
3 Derrick	Y	Y	Y	Y	Y	N	N	Y
4 ***Campbell***	?	?	?	?	?	N	N	Y
5 Spratt	Y	?	Y	Y	Y	Y	N	Y
6 Tallon	Y	N	Y	Y	Y	N	N	Y
SOUTH DAKOTA								
AL Daschle	Y	Y	Y	Y	Y	Y	Y	Y

	190	191	192	193	194	195	196	197
TENNESSEE								
1 ***Quillen***	Y	N	Y	Y	Y	N	N	Y
2 ***Duncan***	Y	Y	Y	Y	Y	N	N	Y
3 Lloyd	Y	Y	Y	Y	Y	N	N	Y
4 Cooper	Y	Y	Y	Y	Y	Y	N	Y
5 Boner	?	?	Y	Y	Y	N	N	Y
6 Gordon	Y	Y	Y	Y	Y	N	N	Y
7 ***Sundquist***	Y	Y	Y	Y	Y	N	N	Y
8 Jones	Y	N	Y	Y	Y	N	N	Y
9 Ford	Y	Y	?	Y	Y	Y	N	Y
TEXAS								
1 Chapman	Y	Y	?	Y	Y	N	N	Y
2 Wilson	Y	Y	Y	Y	Y	?	N	Y
3 ***Bartlett***	Y	Y	Y	Y	Y	Y	N	Y
4 Hall, R.	Y	N	Y	Y	Y	Y	Y	Y
5 Bryant	Y	N	Y	Y	Y	Y	N	Y
6 ***Barton***	Y	Y	Y	Y	Y	Y	N	Y
7 ***Archer***	Y	Y	Y	Y	Y	N	N	Y
8 ***Fields***	?	?	N	N	Y	N	N	Y
9 Brooks	Y	Y	Y	Y	Y	N	N	Y
10 Pickle	Y	Y	Y	Y	Y	N	N	Y
11 Leath	Y	Y	Y	Y	Y	N	N	Y
12 Wright	Y	Y	Y	Y	?	N	Y	Y
13 ***Boulter***	Y	N	Y	Y	Y	Y	N	Y
14 ***Sweeney***	?	Y	Y	?	Y	N	?	Y
15 de la Garza	?	?	?	Y	Y	N	N	Y
16 Coleman	Y	Y	Y	Y	Y	N	N	Y
17 Stenholm	Y	N	Y	Y	Y	Y	N	Y
18 Leland	?	?	?	?	?	?	?	?
19 ***Combest***	Y	Y	Y	Y	Y	N	N	Y
20 Gonzalez	Y	N	Y	Y	Y	Y	Y	Y
21 ***Loeffler***	Y	Y	Y	Y	Y	Y	N	Y
22 ***DeLay***	Y	Y	Y	Y	Y	N	N	Y
23 Bustamante	Y	Y	Y	Y	Y	N	N	Y
24 Frost	Y	N	Y	Y	Y	N	N	Y
25 Andrews	Y	Y	Y	Y	Y	N	N	Y
26 ***Armey***	Y	Y	Y	Y	Y	N	N	Y
27 Ortiz	Y	Y	Y	Y	Y	N	N	Y
UTAH								
1 ***Hansen***	Y	Y	Y	Y	Y	Y	N	Y
2 ***Monson***	Y	N	Y	Y	Y	Y	N	Y
3 ***Nielson***	Y	Y	Y	Y	Y	Y	N	Y
VERMONT								
AL ***Jeffords***	Y	Y	Y	Y	Y	N	N	Y
VIRGINIA								
1 ***Bateman***	Y	Y	Y	Y	Y	N	Y	Y
2 ***Whitehurst***	?	?	?	?	?	?	?	?
3 ***Bliley***	Y	Y	Y	Y	Y	Y	N	Y
4 Sisisky	Y	Y	Y	Y	Y	Y	Y	Y
5 Daniel	Y	Y	Y	Y	Y	Y	Y	Y
6 Olin	Y	Y	Y	Y	Y	N	N	Y
7 ***Slaughter***	Y	Y	Y	Y	Y	N	N	Y
8 ***Parris***	Y	Y	?	Y	Y	N	Y	Y
9 Boucher	Y	Y	Y	Y	Y	Y	Y	Y
10 ***Wolf***	Y	Y	?	Y	Y	N	N	Y
WASHINGTON								
1 ***Miller***	Y	Y	Y	Y	Y	Y	N	Y
2 Swift	Y	Y	Y	Y	Y	Y	N	Y
3 Bonker	Y	Y	Y	Y	Y	Y	N	?
4 ***Morrison***	Y	Y	?	Y	Y	Y	N	Y
5 Foley	Y	Y	Y	Y	Y	N	N	Y
6 Dicks	Y	Y	Y	Y	Y	Y	N	Y
7 Lowry	Y	Y	Y	Y	Y	Y	Y	Y
8 ***Chandler***	Y	Y	Y	Y	Y	Y	N	Y
WEST VIRGINIA								
1 Mollohan	?	N	Y	Y	Y	Y	N	Y
2 Staggers	Y	N	Y	Y	Y	Y	N	Y
3 Wise	Y	N	Y	Y	Y	Y	N	Y
4 Rahall	Y	N	Y	Y	Y	Y	N	Y
WISCONSIN								
1 Aspin	?	?	?	?	Y	Y	N	Y
2 Kastenmeier	Y	Y	Y	Y	Y	Y	N	Y
3 ***Gunderson***	Y	Y	Y	Y	Y	Y	N	Y
4 Kleczka	Y	Y	Y	Y	Y	Y	N	Y
5 Moody	Y	Y	Y	Y	Y	Y	N	Y
6 ***Petri***	Y	Y	Y	Y	Y	Y	N	Y
7 Obey	Y	Y	Y	Y	Y	Y	N	Y
8 ***Roth***	Y	Y	Y	Y	?	N	N	Y
9 ***Sensenbrenner***	Y	Y	Y	Y	Y	N	N	Y
WYOMING								
AL ***Cheney***	Y	Y	Y	Y	Y	N	N	Y

Southern states - Ala., Ark., Fla., Ga., Ky., La., Miss., N.C., Okla., S.C., Tenn., Texas, Va.

* The *Congressional Record* vote number is different from the CQ vote number because the *Record* includes quorum calls in its tally. CQ does not publish quorum call votes.

198. HR 4613. Commodity Futures Trading Commission. Glickman, D-Kan., amendment to require that leverage contracts on precious metals be regulated in the same manner as futures contracts on precious metals. Rejected 192-218: R 53-119; D 139-99 (ND 103-57, SD 36-42), July 16, 1986. (The Glickman amendment had been previously adopted in the Committee of the Whole *(see vote 195, p. 58-H).*) A "nay" was a vote supporting the president's position.

199. HR 4613. Commodity Futures Trading Commission. Passage of the bill to reauthorize appropriations and make revisions in the Commodity Exchange Act. Passed 401-7: R 164-6; D 237-1 (ND 160-0, SD 77-1), July 16, 1986.

200. HR 3838. Tax Overhaul. Duncan, R-Tenn., motion to instruct House conferees on the bill to insist that the conference agreement contain marginal (top effective) tax rates no higher than those in the Senate bill; treat low- and middle-income families fairly, which requires granting $2,000 personal exemptions to taxpayers who itemize deductions, as well as to those who do not; retain the House position on deductions for Individual Retirement Accounts to the extent necessary to preserve retirement savings incentives for low- and middle-income taxpayers; and prevent a net increase in taxes. Motion agreed to 338-61: R 170-0; D 168-61 (ND 104-52, SD 64-9), July 16, 1986.

201. HR 5161. Commerce, Justice, State and the Judiciary Appropriations, Fiscal 1987. Adoption of the rule (H Res 493) to waive certain points of order against the bill to provide approximately $12.2 billion in fiscal year 1987 funding for the Commerce, Justice and State departments and the federal judiciary, and related agencies. Adopted 237-160: R 31-138; D 206-22 (ND 143-9, SD 63-13), July 17, 1986.

202. H J Res 672. Sequestration Order. Passage of the joint resolution to ratify and affirm the Jan. 15, 1986, report of the Congressional Budget Office (CBO) and the Office of Management and Budget (OMB) setting forth $11.7 billion in spending reductions for fiscal 1986. Passed 339-72: R 156-15; D 183-57 (ND 112-50, SD 71-7), July 17, 1986. (A separate resolution, H Con Res 368, authorized the text of the resolution to be corrected, in the enrollment process, to reflect technical modifications in the spending-reduction order, made by the General Accounting Office and by legislation after OMB and CBO completed their version. As provided in the rule (H Res 495) for consideration of H J Res 672, H Con Res 368 was considered to have been adopted once the joint resolution was passed.) A "yea" was a vote supporting the president's position.

203. HR 5161. Commerce, Justice, State and the Judiciary Appropriations, Fiscal 1987. Monson, R-Utah, amendment to delete $190 million for the Economic Development Administration. Rejected 108-302: R 96-73; D 12-229 (ND 5-158, SD 7-71), July 17, 1986.

204. HR 5161. Commerce, Justice, State and the Judiciary Appropriations, Fiscal 1987. Walker, R-Pa., amendment to cut $50 million from the Economic Development Administration. Rejected 150-256: R 121-46; D 29-210 (ND 15-147, SD 14-63), July 17, 1986.

205. HR 5161. Commerce, Justice, State and the Judiciary Appropriations, Fiscal 1987. Combest, R-Texas, amendment to delete $305.5 million for the Legal Services Corporation. Rejected 103-278: R 93-69; D 10-209 (ND 1-145, SD 9-64), July 17, 1986.

KEY

Y Voted for (yea).
\# Paired for.
\+ Announced for.
N Voted against (nay).
X Paired against.
\- Announced against.
P Voted "present."
C Voted "present" to avoid possible conflict of interest.
? Did not vote or otherwise make a position known.

Democrats *Republicans*

	198	199	200	201	202	203	204	205
ALABAMA								
1 *Callahan*	N	Y	Y	N	Y	Y	Y	Y
2 *Dickinson*	N	Y	Y	Y	Y	N	Y	N
3 Nichols	N	Y	Y	Y	Y	N	N	N
4 Bevill	N	Y	Y	Y	Y	N	N	N
5 Flippo	N	Y	Y	Y	Y	N	N	N
6 Erdreich	Y	Y	Y	Y	Y	N	N	N
7 Shelby	N	Y	Y	Y	Y	N	N	N
ALASKA								
AL *Young*	N	Y	Y	N	Y	N	N	Y
ARIZONA								
1 *McCain*	N	Y	Y	N	N	Y	Y	N
2 Udall	Y	Y	Y	Y	Y	N	N	N
3 *Stump*	N	Y	Y	N	Y	Y	Y	Y
4 *Rudd*	N	Y	Y	Y	Y	N	Y	Y
5 *Kolbe*	N	Y	Y	N	Y	Y	Y	N
ARKANSAS								
1 Alexander	N	Y	Y	Y	N	N	N	N
2 Robinson	N	Y	Y	Y	Y	N	N	Y
3 *Hammerschmidt*	Y	Y	Y	N	Y	N	N	Y
4 Anthony	Y	Y	Y	Y	Y	N	N	N
CALIFORNIA								
1 Bosco	N	Y	?	Y	Y	N	N	?
2 *Chappie*	?	?	?	?	?	?	?	?
3 Matsui	Y	Y	Y	Y	Y	N	N	N
4 Fazio	N	Y	?	Y	Y	N	N	N
5 Burton	Y	Y	Y	Y	Y	N	N	?
6 Boxer	N	Y	Y	Y	Y	N	N	?
7 Miller	N	Y	Y	Y	Y	N	N	?
8 Dellums	Y	Y	N	Y	N	N	?	N
9 Stark	Y	Y	Y	Y	Y	N	N	N
10 Edwards	Y	Y	Y	Y	Y	N	N	N
11 Lantos	N	Y	Y	Y	Y	N	N	N
12 *Zschau*	N	Y	Y	N	Y	Y	Y	N
13 Mineta	N	Y	Y	Y	Y	N	N	N
14 *Shumway*	N	Y	Y	N	Y	Y	Y	Y
15 Coelho	N	Y	Y	Y	Y	N	N	N
16 Panetta	N	Y	N	N	Y	N	N	?
17 *Pashayan*	N	Y	Y	N	Y	N	Y	N
18 Lehman	N	Y	Y	Y	Y	N	N	?
19 *Lagomarsino*	N	Y	Y	N	Y	Y	Y	Y
20 *Thomas*	N	Y	Y	N	Y	Y	Y	Y
21 *Fiedler*	?	?	?	?	?	?	?	?
22 *Moorhead*	N	Y	Y	N	Y	Y	Y	Y
23 Beilenson	Y	Y	N	Y	Y	N	N	N
24 Waxman	Y	Y	N	?	N	?	N	N
25 Roybal	N	Y	N	Y	N	N	N	?
26 Berman	N	Y	N	Y	Y	N	N	?
27 Levine	Y	Y	N	Y	Y	N	N	N
28 Dixon	N	Y	N	Y	N	N	N	N
29 Hawkins	N	Y	N	Y	N	N	N	?
30 Martinez	N	Y	Y	Y	N	N	N	?
31 Dymally	N	Y	N	Y	N	N	N	?
32 Anderson	N	Y	N	Y	N	N	N	N
33 *Dreier*	N	Y	Y	N	Y	Y	Y	Y
34 Torres	N	Y	Y	?	Y	N	N	N
35 *Lewis*	N	Y	Y	N	Y	Y	#	#
36 Brown	N	Y	?	Y	Y	N	N	N
37 *McCandless*	N	Y	Y	N	Y	Y	Y	Y
38 *Dornan*	N	Y	Y	N	Y	Y	Y	Y
39 *Dannemeyer*	N	Y	Y	N	Y	Y	Y	Y
40 *Badham*	N	Y	Y	N	Y	Y	Y	Y
41 *Lowery*	N	Y	Y	N	Y	Y	Y	Y
42 *Lungren*	N	Y	Y	N	Y	Y	Y	Y
43 *Packard*	N	Y	Y	N	Y	Y	Y	Y
44 Bates	N	Y	Y	Y	Y	Y	Y	N
45 *Hunter*	N	Y	Y	N	Y	Y	Y	N
COLORADO								
1 Schroeder	Y	Y	Y	N	Y	N	N	N
2 Wirth	Y	Y	Y	N	Y	N	?	?
3 *Strang*	Y	Y	Y	N	Y	N	Y	Y
4 *Brown*	N	N	Y	N	Y	Y	Y	Y
5 *Kramer*	N	Y	Y	N	Y	Y	Y	N
6 *Schaefer*	N	Y	Y	N	N	Y	Y	Y
CONNECTICUT								
1 Kennelly	Y	Y	Y	Y	Y	N	N	N
2 Gejdenson	Y	Y	Y	Y	Y	N	N	N
3 Morrison	Y	Y	N	Y	Y	N	N	N
4 *McKinney*	N	Y	Y	Y	Y	N	N	N
5 *Rowland*	Y	Y	Y	Y	Y	N	N	N
6 *Johnson*	Y	Y	Y	N	Y	N	N	N
DELAWARE								
AL Carper	Y	Y	Y	Y	Y	Y	Y	N
FLORIDA								
1 Hutto	N	Y	Y	N	Y	N	Y	Y
2 Fuqua	Y	Y	Y	Y	Y	N	N	N
3 Bennett	Y	Y	Y	Y	Y	Y	Y	N
4 Chappell	Y	Y	Y	Y	Y	N	N	N
5 *McCollum*	N	Y	Y	N	Y	Y	Y	N
6 MacKay	Y	Y	Y	N	Y	Y	Y	N
7 Gibbons	Y	Y	N	N	Y	Y	Y	N
8 *Young*	N	Y	Y	N	N	Y	Y	Y
9 *Bilirakis*	N	Y	Y	N	N	Y	Y	Y
10 *Ireland*	N	Y	Y	N	Y	Y	Y	Y
11 Nelson	Y	Y	Y	Y	Y	Y	Y	N
12 *Lewis*	N	Y	Y	N	Y	Y	Y	Y
13 *Mack*	N	Y	Y	N	Y	Y	Y	Y
14 Mica	Y	Y	Y	Y	Y	N	N	N
15 *Shaw*	Y	Y	Y	N	Y	Y	Y	Y
16 Smith	Y	Y	Y	Y	Y	N	N	N
17 Lehman	N	Y	N	Y	Y	N	N	N
18 Pepper	N	Y	N	Y	Y	N	N	N
19 Fascell	Y	Y	N	Y	Y	N	N	N
GEORGIA								
1 Thomas	N	Y	Y	Y	Y	N	N	N
2 Hatcher	N	Y	Y	Y	Y	N	N	?
3 Ray	Y	Y	Y	?	Y	Y	Y	N
4 *Swindall*	N	Y	Y	N	Y	Y	Y	Y
5 Fowler	Y	Y	Y	Y	Y	?	?	?
6 *Gingrich*	N	Y	Y	N	Y	Y	Y	Y
7 Darden	N	Y	Y	Y	Y	N	Y	Y
8 Rowland	N	Y	Y	Y	Y	N	N	N
9 Jenkins	Y	Y	Y	Y	Y	N	N	N
10 Barnard	?	?	?	Y	Y	N	?	?
HAWAII								
1 Vacancy								
2 Akaka	N	Y	Y	Y	Y	N	N	N
IDAHO								
1 *Craig*	N	Y	Y	N	Y	N	Y	Y
2 Stallings	N	Y	Y	N	Y	N	Y	N
ILLINOIS								
1 Hayes	N	Y	N	Y	N	N	N	?
2 Savage	N	Y	N	Y	N	N	N	?
3 Russo	Y	Y	Y	Y	Y	N	N	N
4 *O'Brien*	?	?	?	?	?	?	?	?
5 Lipinski	N	Y	Y	Y	Y	N	N	N
6 *Hyde*	N	Y	Y	N	Y	Y	Y	Y
7 Collins	N	Y	Y	Y	N	N	N	?
8 Rostenkowski	N	Y	Y	Y	Y	N	N	N
9 Yates	Y	Y	N	Y	Y	N	N	N
10 *Porter*	N	Y	Y	N	Y	Y	Y	N
11 Annunzio	N	Y	Y	Y	Y	N	N	N
12 *Crane*	N	N	Y	N	Y	Y	Y	Y
13 *Fawell*	N	Y	Y	N	Y	Y	Y	N
14 *Grotberg*	?	?	?	?	?	?	?	?
15 *Madigan*	N	Y	Y	N	Y	?	?	?
16 *Martin*	N	Y	Y	N	Y	Y	Y	N
17 Evans	Y	Y	Y	Y	N	N	N	N
18 *Michel*	N	Y	Y	N	Y	N	Y	Y
19 Bruce	N	Y	Y	Y	Y	N	N	N
20 Durbin	N	Y	Y	Y	Y	N	N	N
21 Price	N	Y	Y	Y	Y	N	N	N
22 Gray	N	Y	Y	Y	Y	N	N	N
INDIANA								
1 Visclosky	Y	Y	N	Y	Y	N	N	N
2 Sharp	Y	Y	Y	Y	Y	N	N	N
3 *Hiler*	N	Y	Y	N	Y	Y	Y	Y
4 *Coats*	Y	Y	Y	N	Y	N	Y	Y
5 *Hillis*	N	Y	Y	Y	Y	Y	Y	Y

ND - Northern Democrats SD - Southern Democrats

* Corresponding to Congressional Record Votes 220, 221, 222, 223, 224, 225, 226, 227

	198	199	200	201	202	203	204	205
6 ***Burton***	N	Y	Y	N	Y	Y	Y	Y
7 ***Myers***	N	Y	?	Y	N	N	N	Y
8 McCloskey	N	Y	Y	Y	Y	N	N	N
9 Hamilton	Y	Y	Y	Y	Y	N	N	N
10 Jacobs	N	Y	N	N	Y	N	N	N
IOWA								
1 ***Leach***	Y	Y	Y	N	Y	Y	Y	N
2 ***Tauke***	Y	Y	Y	N	Y	Y	Y	N
3 ***Evans***	?	?	?	?	?	?	?	?
4 Smith	Y	Y	Y	Y	N	N	N	N
5 ***Lightfoot***	N	Y	Y	N	Y	N	N	Y
6 Bedell	N	Y	N	Y	Y	N	N	N
KANSAS								
1 ***Roberts***	Y	Y	Y	N	Y	Y	Y	Y
2 Slattery	Y	Y	Y	N	Y	Y	Y	N
3 ***Meyers***	Y	Y	Y	N	Y	Y	Y	N
4 Glickman	Y	Y	Y	N	Y	N	Y	N
5 ***Whittaker***	Y	Y	Y	N	Y	N	N	Y
KENTUCKY								
1 Hubbard	N	Y	Y	N	Y	N	N	N
2 Natcher	Y	Y	Y	Y	Y	N	N	N
3 Mazzoli	N	Y	Y	Y	Y	N	N	N
4 ***Snyder***	Y	Y	Y	Y	Y	Y	Y	Y
5 ***Rogers***	N	Y	Y	N	Y	N	N	Y
6 ***Hopkins***	N	Y	Y	N	Y	Y	Y	N
7 Perkins	N	Y	N	Y	N	N	N	N
LOUISIANA								
1 ***Livingston***	N	Y	Y	N	Y	Y	N	N
2 Boggs	N	Y	Y	Y	N	N	N	N
3 Tauzin	N	Y	Y	N	Y	N	Y	N
4 Roemer	Y	Y	Y	N	Y	N	Y	N
5 Huckaby	N	Y	Y	N	Y	?	?	?
6 ***Moore***	?	?	?	?	?	?	?	?
7 Breaux	?	?	?	?	?	?	?	?
8 Long	N	Y	?	Y	Y	N	N	N
MAINE								
1 ***McKernan***	Y	Y	Y	N	Y	N	N	N
2 ***Snowe***	Y	Y	Y	N	Y	N	N	N
MARYLAND								
1 Dyson	N	Y	Y	Y	Y	N	Y	Y
2 ***Bentley***	N	Y	Y	N	Y	N	N	Y
3 Mikulski	Y	Y	Y	Y	Y	N	N	N
4 ***Holt***	N	Y	Y	Y	N	N	Y	?
5 Hoyer	N	Y	N	Y	Y	N	N	N
6 Byron	Y	Y	Y	Y	Y	?	?	?
7 Mitchell	?	?	?	?	?	N	N	N
8 Barnes	?	?	?	?	X	?	?	X
MASSACHUSETTS								
1 ***Conte***	Y	Y	Y	Y	N	N	N	N
2 Boland	Y	Y	Y	Y	Y	N	N	?
3 Early	Y	Y	N	?	N	N	N	N
4 Frank	N	Y	N	Y	N	N	N	N
5 Atkins	N	Y	N	Y	Y	Y	N	N
6 Mavroules	Y	Y	Y	Y	Y	N	N	N
7 Markey	Y	Y	N	Y	N	N	N	N
8 O'Neill								
9 Moakley	N	Y	Y	Y	N	N	N	N
10 Studds	Y	Y	N	Y	N	N	N	N
11 Donnelly	Y	Y	N	?	N	N	N	N
MICHIGAN								
1 Conyers	Y	Y	N	Y	N	N	N	N
2 ***Pursell***	N	Y	Y	Y	Y	N	Y	N
3 Wolpe	Y	Y	Y	Y	Y	N	N	N
4 ***Siljander***	N	Y	Y	N	Y	Y	Y	Y
5 ***Henry***	Y	Y	Y	N	Y	N	N	N
6 Carr	N	Y	Y	?	N	N	Y	N
7 Kildee	Y	Y	Y	Y	N	N	N	N
8 Traxler	Y	Y	Y	Y	N	N	N	N
9 ***Vander Jagt***	N	Y	?	N	Y	N	Y	N
10 ***Schuette***	N	Y	Y	N	Y	?	X	X
11 ***Davis***	N	Y	Y	N	Y	N	N	N
12 Bonior	?	?	?	?	?	?	?	?
13 Crockett	?	?	?	?	?	N	N	N
14 Hertel	Y	Y	Y	Y	Y	N	N	N
15 Ford	Y	Y	Y	?	Y	N	N	N
16 Dingell	Y	Y	Y	Y	Y	N	N	N
17 Levin	Y	Y	Y	Y	Y	N	N	N
18 ***Broomfield***	N	Y	Y	N	Y	N	Y	N
MINNESOTA								
1 Penny	N	Y	Y	Y	Y	N	Y	N
2 ***Weber***	N	Y	Y	N	N	Y	Y	Y
3 ***Frenzel***	Y	Y	Y	N	Y	Y	Y	N
4 Vento	Y	Y	Y	Y	Y	N	N	N
5 Sabo	Y	Y	N	Y	Y	N	N	N
6 Sikorski	Y	Y	Y	Y	Y	N	N	N

	198	199	200	201	202	203	204	205
7 ***Stangeland***	N	Y	Y	Y	Y	N	N	Y
8 Oberstar	Y	Y	N	Y	Y	N	N	N
MISSISSIPPI								
1 Whitten	Y	Y	?	Y	Y	N	N	N
2 ***Franklin***	N	Y	Y	N	Y	N	N	Y
3 Montgomery	Y	Y	Y	Y	Y	N	N	Y
4 Dowdy	N	Y	?	Y	N	N	N	N
5 ***Lott***	N	Y	Y	N	Y	N	Y	Y
MISSOURI								
1 Clay	Y	Y	N	Y	N	N	N	?
2 Young	Y	Y	Y	Y	Y	N	N	N
3 Gephardt	Y	Y	Y	Y	Y	N	N	N
4 Skelton	Y	Y	Y	Y	Y	N	N	N
5 Wheat	Y	Y	N	Y	N	N	N	N
6 ***Coleman***	N	Y	Y	N	Y	N	Y	N
7 ***Taylor***	Y	Y	Y	N	Y	N	Y	Y
8 ***Emerson***	N	Y	Y	N	Y	N	N	N
9 Volkmer	Y	Y	Y	Y	Y	N	N	N
MONTANA								
1 Williams	Y	Y	N	Y	N	N	N	N
2 ***Marlenee***	N	N	Y	N	Y	Y	Y	Y
NEBRASKA								
1 ***Bereuter***	Y	+	Y	N	Y	Y	Y	N
2 ***Daub***	N	Y	Y	N	Y	Y	Y	Y
3 ***Smith***	N	Y	Y	Y	Y	Y	Y	?
NEVADA								
1 Reid	Y	Y	Y	Y	Y	N	N	N
2 ***Vucanovich***	Y	Y	Y	Y	Y	Y	Y	Y
NEW HAMPSHIRE								
1 ***Smith***	N	Y	Y	N	Y	Y	Y	Y
2 ***Gregg***	Y	Y	Y	N	Y	Y	Y	Y
NEW JERSEY								
1 Florio	Y	Y	Y	Y	N	N	N	N
2 Hughes	Y	Y	Y	Y	N	N	Y	N
3 Howard	N	Y	Y	Y	Y	N	N	N
4 ***Smith***	N	Y	Y	?	Y	N	N	N
5 ***Roukema***	Y	Y	Y	N	Y	N	Y	N
6 Dwyer	Y	Y	Y	Y	Y	N	N	N
7 ***Rinaldo***	Y	Y	Y	Y	N	N	N	N
8 Roe	N	Y	Y	Y	Y	N	N	N
9 Torricelli	?	?	?	Y	Y	N	N	N
10 Rodino	Y	Y	N	Y	N	N	N	N
11 ***Gallo***	N	Y	Y	N	Y	N	N	N
12 ***Courter***	N	Y	Y	N	Y	N	N	N
13 ***Saxton***	N	Y	Y	N	Y	N	N	N
14 Guarini	Y	Y	N	Y	Y	N	N	N
NEW MEXICO								
1 ***Lujan***	N	Y	Y	N	Y	N	Y	N
2 ***Skeen***	N	Y	Y	N	Y	N	Y	Y
3 Richardson	Y	Y	Y	Y	Y	N	N	N
NEW YORK								
1 ***Carney***	Y	Y	Y	N	Y	Y	Y	Y
2 Downey	Y	Y	Y	Y	N	N	N	N
3 Mrazek	Y	Y	Y	Y	Y	N	Y	N
4 ***Lent***	Y	Y	Y	N	Y	N	Y	Y
5 ***McGrath***	Y	Y	Y	N	Y	Y	Y	Y
6 Vacancy								
7 Ackerman	?	?	?	Y	N	N	N	N
8 Scheuer	Y	Y	N	Y	Y	N	N	N
9 Manton	Y	Y	Y	Y	Y	N	N	N
10 Schumer	Y	Y	Y	Y	N	N	N	N
11 Towns	N	Y	N	Y	N	N	N	N
12 Owens	Y	Y	Y	Y	N	N	N	N
13 Solarz	Y	Y	N	Y	Y	N	N	N
14 ***Molinari***	Y	Y	Y	N	Y	Y	Y	Y
15 ***Green***	Y	Y	Y	Y	Y	N	N	N
16 Rangel	Y	Y	N	Y	N	N	N	N
17 Weiss	Y	Y	N	Y	N	N	N	N
18 Garcia	Y	Y	N	Y	N	N	N	N
19 Biaggi	Y	Y	Y	?	N	N	N	N
20 ***DioGuardi***	Y	Y	Y	N	Y	Y	Y	N
21 ***Fish***	Y	Y	Y	N	N	N	N	N
22 ***Gilman***	Y	Y	Y	Y	N	N	N	N
23 Stratton	Y	Y	N	Y	Y	N	N	?
24 ***Solomon***	N	N	Y	N	Y	N	Y	Y
25 ***Boehlert***	N	Y	Y	N	Y	N	N	N
26 ***Martin***	Y	Y	Y	N	Y	N	N	?
27 ***Wortley***	N	Y	Y	N	Y	N	N	N
28 McHugh	Y	Y	N	Y	Y	N	N	N
29 ***Horton***	Y	Y	Y	Y	N	N	N	N
30 ***Eckert***	Y	Y	Y	N	Y	Y	Y	Y
31 ***Kemp***	Y	Y	Y	Y	Y	N	Y	?
32 LaFalce	Y	Y	N	Y	Y	N	N	N
33 Nowak	Y	Y	Y	Y	Y	N	N	N
34 Lundine	?	?	?	?	?	?	?	?

	198	199	200	201	202	203	204	205
NORTH CAROLINA								
1 Jones	?	?	?	?	#	?	?	?
2 Valentine	N	Y	Y	N	Y	N	Y	Y
3 Whitley	N	Y	Y	Y	Y	N	N	N
4 ***Cobey***	Y	Y	Y	N	Y	Y	Y	Y
5 Neal	Y	Y	Y	N	Y	N	N	N
6 ***Coble***	N	Y	Y	N	Y	N	Y	Y
7 Rose	Y	Y	Y	Y	Y	N	N	N
8 Hefner	N	Y	Y	Y	Y	N	N	N
9 ***McMillan***	N	Y	Y	N	Y	N	Y	N
10 Vacancy								
11 ***Hendon***	N	Y	Y	N	Y	N	Y	Y
NORTH DAKOTA								
AL Dorgan	Y	Y	N	Y	Y	Y	Y	N
OHIO								
1 Luken	N	Y	Y	Y	Y	N	Y	N
2 ***Gradison***	Y	Y	Y	N	Y	Y	Y	N
3 Hall	N	Y	Y	Y	Y	N	Y	N
4 ***Oxley***	N	Y	Y	Y	Y	Y	Y	Y
5 ***Latta***	N	Y	Y	?	?	Y	Y	Y
6 ***McEwen***	?	?	?	?	?	?	?	?
7 ***DeWine***	N	Y	Y	N	Y	Y	Y	N
8 ***Kindness***	N	Y	Y	N	Y	N	Y	N
9 Kaptur	Y	Y	Y	Y	Y	N	N	N
10 ***Miller***	N	Y	Y	Y	Y	N	Y	Y
11 Eckart	Y	Y	Y	Y	Y	N	N	N
12 ***Kasich***	N	Y	Y	N	Y	Y	Y	Y
13 Pease	Y	Y	Y	Y	Y	N	N	N
14 Seiberling	Y	Y	N	Y	Y	N	N	N
15 ***Wylie***	Y	Y	Y	N	Y	Y	Y	N
16 ***Regula***	N	Y	Y	Y	Y	N	N	N
17 Traficant	Y	Y	Y	N	N	N	N	N
18 Applegate	Y	Y	Y	Y	Y	N	N	N
19 Feighan	Y	Y	Y	?	Y	N	N	N
20 Oakar	N	Y	N	Y	Y	N	N	N
21 Stokes	Y	Y	N	Y	N	N	N	N
OKLAHOMA								
1 Jones	Y	Y	Y	Y	Y	N	N	N
2 Synar	Y	Y	Y	Y	Y	N	N	N
3 Watkins	Y	N	Y	Y	Y	N	N	N
4 McCurdy	Y	Y	Y	Y	Y	N	N	N
5 ***Edwards***	Y	Y	Y	N	Y	N	Y	N
6 English	Y	Y	Y	Y	Y	N	Y	N
OREGON								
1 AuCoin	N	Y	Y	Y	Y	N	N	N
2 ***Smith, R.***	Y	Y	Y	N	Y	N	N	Y
3 Wyden	Y	Y	Y	Y	Y	N	N	N
4 Weaver	?	?	?	Y	N	N	N	N
5 ***Smith, D.***	N	Y	Y	N	Y	Y	Y	Y
PENNSYLVANIA								
1 Foglietta	Y	Y	Y	Y	Y	N	Y	N
2 Gray	Y	Y	N	Y	Y	N	N	N
3 Borski	N	Y	N	Y	Y	N	N	N
4 Kolter	N	Y	Y	Y	N	N	N	N
5 ***Schulze***	N	Y	Y	N	Y	Y	Y	N
6 Yatron	Y	Y	Y	Y	Y	N	N	N
7 Edgar	Y	Y	Y	?	?	N	N	N
8 Kostmayer	Y	Y	Y	Y	Y	N	N	N
9 ***Shuster***	N	Y	Y	N	Y	N	N	Y
10 ***McDade***	N	Y	Y	Y	Y	N	N	N
11 Kanjorski	Y	Y	Y	Y	N	N	N	N
12 Murtha	N	Y	?	Y	Y	N	N	N
13 ***Coughlin***	?	?	?	Y	Y	Y	Y	N
14 Coyne	Y	Y	N	Y	N	N	N	N
15 ***Ritter***	N	Y	Y	Y	Y	N	N	Y
16 ***Walker***	N	N	Y	N	Y	Y	Y	Y
17 ***Gekas***	N	Y	Y	N	Y	N	N	N
18 Walgren	Y	Y	Y	Y	Y	N	Y	N
19 ***Goodling***	N	Y	Y	N	Y	N	Y	N
20 Gaydos	N	Y	Y	Y	Y	N	N	N
21 ***Ridge***	Y	Y	Y	?	Y	N	N	N
22 Murphy	N	Y	Y	Y	N	N	N	N
23 ***Clinger***	N	Y	Y	Y	Y	N	N	N
RHODE ISLAND								
1 St Germain	Y	Y	Y	Y	Y	N	N	N
2 ***Schneider***	Y	Y	Y	Y	Y	N	N	N
SOUTH CAROLINA								
1 ***Hartnett***	N	Y	Y	N	?	?	?	?
2 ***Spence***	N	Y	Y	N	N	N	N	N
3 Derrick	N	Y	Y	Y	Y	N	N	Y
4 ***Campbell***	N	Y	Y	?	N	?	?	?
5 Spratt	Y	Y	Y	Y	Y	N	N	N
6 Tallon	N	Y	Y	Y	N	N	N	N
SOUTH DAKOTA								
AL Daschle	Y	Y	Y	N	Y	N	N	N

	198	199	200	201	202	203	204	205
TENNESSEE								
1 ***Quillen***	N	Y	Y	Y	Y	N	N	N
2 ***Duncan***	N	Y	Y	Y	Y	N	N	N
3 Lloyd	N	Y	Y	N	Y	N	N	N
4 Cooper	Y	Y	Y	Y	Y	N	N	N
5 Boner	N	Y	Y	Y	Y	N	N	?
6 Gordon	N	Y	Y	Y	Y	N	N	N
7 ***Sundquist***	N	?	Y	Y	Y	Y	Y	N
8 Jones	N	Y	Y	Y	Y	N	N	N
9 Ford	N	Y	N	?	N	N	N	N
TEXAS								
1 Chapman	N	Y	Y	Y	Y	N	N	N
2 Wilson	N	Y	Y	Y	Y	N	N	N
3 ***Bartlett***	Y	Y	Y	N	Y	Y	Y	Y
4 Hall, R.	Y	Y	Y	N	Y	N	Y	Y
5 Bryant	Y	Y	Y	Y	Y	N	N	N
6 ***Barton***	Y	Y	Y	N	Y	Y	Y	Y
7 ***Archer***	N	Y	Y	N	Y	Y	Y	Y
8 ***Fields***	Y	Y	Y	N	Y	Y	Y	Y
9 Brooks	N	Y	N	Y	Y	N	N	N
10 Pickle	N	Y	Y	Y	Y	N	N	N
11 Leath	Y	Y	Y	Y	Y	N	N	N
12 Wright	Y	Y	N	Y	Y	N	N	N
13 ***Boulter***	Y	Y	Y	N	Y	Y	?	Y
14 ***Sweeney***	N	Y	Y	Y	Y	Y	Y	Y
15 de la Garza	N	Y	?	?	?	N	N	N
16 Coleman	N	Y	Y	Y	Y	N	N	N
17 Stenholm	Y	Y	Y	N	Y	Y	Y	Y
18 Leland	?	?	?	?	?	N	N	N
19 ***Combest***	N	Y	Y	N	Y	Y	Y	Y
20 Gonzalez	Y	Y	N	Y	N	N	N	N
21 ***Loeffler***	N	Y	Y	N	Y	Y	Y	?
22 ***DeLay***	Y	Y	Y	N	Y	Y	Y	Y
23 Bustamante	N	Y	Y	Y	Y	N	N	N
24 Frost	N	Y	?	Y	Y	N	N	?
25 Andrews	N	Y	Y	Y	Y	N	N	N
26 ***Armey***	N	Y	Y	N	Y	Y	Y	Y
27 Ortiz	N	Y	Y	Y	Y	N	N	?
UTAH								
1 ***Hansen***	Y	Y	Y	N	Y	Y	Y	Y
2 ***Monson***	N	Y	Y	N	Y	Y	Y	#
3 ***Nielson***	Y	Y	Y	N	Y	Y	Y	Y
VERMONT								
AL ***Jeffords***	N	Y	Y	N	Y	N	N	N
VIRGINIA								
1 ***Bateman***	N	Y	Y	N	Y	N	Y	Y
2 ***Whitehurst***	?	?	?	?	?	?	?	?
3 ***Bliley***	Y	Y	Y	N	Y	Y	Y	Y
4 Sisisky	Y	Y	Y	Y	Y	N	N	N
5 Daniel	Y	Y	Y	N	Y	Y	Y	Y
6 Olin	N	Y	Y	Y	Y	N	N	N
7 ***Slaughter***	N	Y	Y	N	Y	Y	Y	Y
8 ***Parris***	N	Y	Y	N	Y	Y	Y	Y
9 Boucher	Y	Y	Y	Y	Y	N	N	N
10 ***Wolf***	N	Y	Y	Y	N	Y	Y	Y
WASHINGTON								
1 ***Miller***	Y	Y	Y	N	Y	Y	Y	N
2 Swift	Y	Y	Y	Y	Y	N	N	N
3 Bonker	Y	Y	Y	?	Y	N	N	N
4 ***Morrison***	Y	Y	Y	N	Y	N	N	N
5 Foley	N	Y	Y	Y	Y	N	N	N
6 Dicks	Y	Y	Y	Y	Y	N	N	N
7 Lowry	Y	Y	Y	Y	N	N	N	N
8 ***Chandler***	Y	Y	Y	N	Y	Y	Y	N
WEST VIRGINIA								
1 Mollohan	N	Y	Y	Y	N	N	N	N
2 Staggers	Y	Y	Y	Y	N	N	N	N
3 Wise	N	Y	Y	Y	N	N	N	N
4 Rahall	N	Y	N	Y	N	N	N	N
WISCONSIN								
1 Aspin	Y	Y	Y	Y	Y	N	N	N
2 Kastenmeier	Y	Y	Y	Y	Y	N	N	N
3 ***Gunderson***	Y	Y	Y	N	Y	N	N	N
4 Kleczka	Y	Y	Y	?	Y	N	N	N
5 Moody	Y	Y	N	Y	Y	N	N	N
6 ***Petri***	Y	Y	Y	N	Y	Y	Y	Y
7 Obey	Y	Y	N	Y	Y	N	N	N
8 ***Roth***	N	Y	Y	N	Y	Y	Y	Y
9 ***Sensenbrenner***	N	Y	Y	N	Y	Y	Y	Y
WYOMING								
AL ***Cheney***	N	N	Y	N	Y	Y	Y	Y

Southern states - Ala., Ark., Fla., Ga., Ky., La., Miss., N.C., Okla., S.C., Tenn., Texas, Va.

* The *Congressional Record* vote number is different from the CQ vote number because the *Record* includes quorum calls in its tally. CQ does not publish quorum call votes.

206. HR 5161. Commerce, Justice, State and the Judiciary Appropriations, Fiscal 1987. Combest, R-Texas, amendment to reduce the appropriation of the Legal Services Corporation by $25 million, from $305.5 million to $280.5 million. Rejected 161-204: R 132-23; D 29-181 (ND 6-134, SD 23-47), July 17, 1986.

207. HR 5161. Commerce, Justice, State and the Judiciary Appropriations, Fiscal 1987. Hiler, R-Ind., amendment to delete funding for the Small Business Administration direct loan program, except for $39 million in loans for minority enterprises and $15 million for the handicapped assistance loan program. Rejected 118-243: R 103-47; D 15-196 (ND 5-136, SD 10-60), July 17, 1986.

208. HR 5161. Commerce, Justice, State and the Judiciary Appropriations, Fiscal 1987. Conyers, D-Mich., amendment to delete $17.5 million for the National Endowment for Democracy, which was established in 1983 to provide money for private organizations to set up programs in foreign countries about the American political system. Rejected 121-228: R 32-116; D 89-112 (ND 69-67, SD 20-45), July 17, 1986.

209. HR 5161. Commerce, Justice, State and the Judiciary Appropriations, Fiscal 1987. Frenzel, R-Minn., amendment to cut all discretionary funding in the bill, except for the FBI and the Drug Enforcement Administration, by 5.03 percent. Adopted 213-125: R 129-15; D 84-110 (ND 44-86, SD 40-24), July 17, 1986.

210. HR 5161. Commerce, Justice, State and the Judiciary Appropriations, Fiscal 1987. Smith, D-Iowa, motion that the Committee of the Whole rise and report the bill back to the House. Motion rejected 148-189: R 25-119; D 123-70 (ND 88-41, SD 35-29), July 17, 1986. (The effect of the vote was to allow consideration of amendments limiting spending on the appropriations bill, in this case the Dornan, R-Calif., amendment to bar the federal prison system from using money to pay for abortions for female inmates or for providing facilities for abortion, unless the life of the pregnant woman would be endangered by carrying the fetus to term. Such amendments are in order only following a defeated motion to rise and report. The Dornan amendment subsequently was adopted by voice vote.)

211. HR 5161. Commerce, Justice, State and the Judiciary Appropriations, Fiscal 1987. Passage of the bill to provide $12,311,620,000 for the Commerce, Justice and State departments, the federal judiciary and related agencies. Passed 269-66: R 90-54; D 179-12 (ND 120-8, SD 59-4), July 17, 1986. The president had requested $15,957,736,000 in new budget authority.

212. H Res 461. Claiborne Impeachment. Adoption of the resolution to impeach Judge Harry E. Claiborne of the U.S. District Court for the District of Nevada. Adopted 406-0: R 171-0; D 235-0 (ND 160-0, SD 75-0), July 22, 1986.

213. HR 5050. Social Security Reform. Jones, D-Okla., motion to suspend the rules and pass the bill to make the Social Security Administration an independent agency; prohibit the government from redeeming Social Security Trust Fund investments to fund continued government spending when the debt ceiling has been reached; and to make various improvements in the management of Social Security. Motion agreed to 401-0: R 169-0; D 232-0 (ND 159-0, SD 73-0), July 22, 1986. A two-thirds majority of those present and voting (268 in this case) is required for passage under suspension of the rules.

KEY

Y Voted for (yea).
Paired for.
+ Announced for.
N Voted against (nay).
X Paired against.
- Announced against.
P Voted "present."
C Voted "present" to avoid possible conflict of interest.
? Did not vote or otherwise make a position known.

Democrats ***Republicans***

	206	207	208	209	210	211	212	213
ALABAMA								
1 ***Callahan***	Y	Y	N	Y	N	Y	Y	Y
2 ***Dickinson***	Y	Y	N	Y	Y	Y	Y	Y
3 Nichols	Y	N	N	Y	N	Y	Y	Y
4 Bevill	N	N	N	N	N	Y	Y	Y
5 Flippo	N	N	N	Y	N	Y	Y	Y
6 Erdreich	N	N	N	Y	N	Y	Y	Y
7 Shelby	N	N	N	Y	N	Y	Y	Y
ALASKA								
AL ***Young***	Y	N	N	Y	N	Y	Y	Y
ARIZONA								
1 ***McCain***	?	#	X	#	?	?	Y	Y
2 Udall	N	N	Y	N	Y	Y	Y	?
3 ***Stump***	Y	Y	N	Y	N	N	Y	Y
4 ***Rudd***	Y	?	?	?	?	Y	Y	Y
5 ***Kolbe***	Y	Y	N	Y	Y	Y	Y	Y
ARKANSAS								
1 Alexander	N	N	N	N	Y	Y	Y	Y
2 Robinson	Y	N	N	Y	N	Y	Y	Y
3 ***Hammerschmidt***	Y	Y	Y	Y	N	Y	Y	Y
4 Anthony	N	N	Y	N	Y	Y	Y	Y
CALIFORNIA								
1 Bosco	?	?	?	?	?	?	Y	Y
2 ***Chappie***	?	?	?	?	?	?	Y	Y
3 Matsui	N	N	N	N	Y	Y	Y	Y
4 Fazio	N	N	N	N	Y	Y	Y	Y
5 Burton	?	?	?	X	?	?	Y	Y
6 Boxer	?	?	?	?	?	?	Y	Y
7 Miller	?	?	?	?	?	?	Y	Y
8 Dellums	N	N	Y	N	Y	Y	Y	Y
9 Stark	?	N	Y	N	Y	Y	Y	Y
10 Edwards	N	N	Y	N	Y	N	Y	Y
11 Lantos	N	N	N	N	Y	Y	Y	Y
12 ***Zschau***	Y	Y	N	Y	N	Y	Y	Y
13 Mineta	N	N	N	N	Y	Y	Y	Y
14 ***Shumway***	Y	Y	N	Y	N	N	Y	Y
15 Coelho	N	N	?	?	Y	Y	Y	Y
16 Panetta	?	?	?	?	?	?	Y	Y
17 ***Pashayan***	Y	N	N	Y	N	Y	Y	Y
18 Lehman	?	?	?	?	?	?	?	?
19 ***Lagomarsino***	Y	Y	N	Y	N	N	Y	Y
20 ***Thomas***	Y	Y	N	Y	Y	Y	Y	Y
21 ***Fiedler***	?	?	?	?	?	?	Y	Y
22 ***Moorhead***	Y	Y	N	Y	N	N	Y	Y
23 Beilenson	N	N	Y	N	?	?	Y	Y
24 Waxman	N	N	N	?	?	Y	Y	Y
25 Roybal	?	?	?	?	?	?	Y	Y
26 Berman	?	?	?	?	?	?	Y	Y
27 Levine	N	N	?	?	?	?	Y	Y
28 Dixon	N	N	N	N	Y	Y	Y	Y
29 Hawkins	?	?	#	X	?	?	Y	Y
30 Martinez	?	?	?	?	?	?	Y	Y
31 Dymally	N	N	Y	N	Y	N	Y	Y
32 Anderson	?	N	N	N	Y	Y	Y	Y
33 ***Dreier***	Y	Y	?	#	?	X	Y	Y
34 Torres	N	N	Y	N	Y	Y	Y	Y
35 ***Lewis***	?	?	?	?	?	?	Y	Y
36 Brown	N	N	Y	N	Y	Y	Y	Y
37 ***McCandless***	Y	Y	N	Y	Y	N	Y	Y
38 ***Dornan***	Y	Y	N	Y	N	Y	Y	Y
39 ***Dannemeyer***	Y	Y	Y	Y	N	N	Y	Y
40 ***Badham***	Y	Y	N	Y	N	N	Y	Y
41 ***Lowery***	Y	Y	N	Y	N	Y	Y	Y
42 ***Lungren***	Y	Y	N	Y	N	N	Y	Y
43 ***Packard***	Y	Y	N	Y	N	N	Y	Y
44 Bates	Y	N	Y	Y	Y	Y	Y	Y
45 ***Hunter***	?	N	N	Y	N	Y	Y	Y
COLORADO								
1 Schroeder	N	N	Y	Y	Y	N	Y	Y
2 Wirth	?	?	?	?	?	?	Y	Y
3 ***Strang***	Y	Y	N	Y	N	N	Y	Y
4 ***Brown***	Y	Y	Y	Y	N	N	Y	Y
5 ***Kramer***	Y	Y	?	?	?	?	Y	Y
6 ***Schaefer***	Y	Y	Y	Y	N	N	Y	Y
CONNECTICUT								
1 Kennelly	N	N	Y	?	?	?	Y	Y
2 Gejdenson	N	N	N	N	Y	Y	Y	Y
3 Morrison	N	N	Y	N	Y	Y	Y	Y
4 ***McKinney***	N	N	N	Y	Y	Y	Y	?
5 ***Rowland***	Y	Y	N	Y	N	Y	Y	Y
6 ***Johnson***	N	N	N	Y	?	?	Y	Y
DELAWARE								
AL Carper	N	N	N	Y	N	Y	Y	Y
FLORIDA								
1 Hutto	Y	Y	N	Y	N	Y	Y	Y
2 Fuqua	N	N	N	N	Y	Y	Y	Y
3 Bennett	N	N	N	Y	N	Y	Y	Y
4 Chappell	N	N	N	N	N	Y	Y	Y
5 ***McCollum***	Y	Y	N	N	N	Y	Y	Y
6 MacKay	N	Y	N	Y	Y	Y	Y	Y
7 Gibbons	N	?	?	?	?	?	Y	Y
8 ***Young***	Y	N	Y	?	?	?	Y	Y
9 ***Bilirakis***	Y	N	N	Y	N	Y	Y	Y
10 ***Ireland***	Y	Y	N	Y	N	Y	Y	Y
11 Nelson	Y	N	N	Y	N	Y	Y	Y
12 ***Lewis***	Y	Y	N	Y	N	Y	Y	Y
13 ***Mack***	Y	Y	N	Y	N	N	Y	Y
14 Mica	N	N	N	Y	?	?	Y	Y
15 ***Shaw***	?	?	#	?	?	#	Y	Y
16 Smith	Y	N	?	?	?	?	Y	Y
17 Lehman	N	N	?	N	Y	Y	Y	Y
18 Pepper	N	N	N	N	Y	Y	Y	Y
19 Fascell	N	N	N	N	Y	Y	Y	Y
GEORGIA								
1 Thomas	Y	N	N	Y	Y	Y	Y	Y
2 Hatcher	?	?	?	?	?	?	Y	Y
3 Ray	N	Y	Y	#	N	Y	Y	Y
4 ***Swindall***	Y	Y	N	Y	N	N	Y	Y
5 Fowler	?	?	?	?	?	?	?	?
6 ***Gingrich***	Y	Y	N	Y	N	N	Y	Y
7 Darden	Y	Y	N	Y	N	Y	Y	Y
8 Rowland	Y	N	N	Y	Y	Y	Y	Y
9 Jenkins	?	N	Y	Y	Y	Y	Y	Y
10 Barnard	?	?	?	?	?	?	Y	?
HAWAII								
1 Vacancy								
2 Akaka	N	N	Y	N	Y	Y	+	+
IDAHO								
1 ***Craig***	Y	Y	N	Y	N	N	Y	Y
2 Stallings	Y	N	Y	Y	N	Y	Y	Y
ILLINOIS								
1 Hayes	?	?	?	X	?	?	Y	Y
2 Savage	?	?	?	?	?	?	Y	Y
3 Russo	N	N	N	Y	N	N	Y	Y
4 Vacancy *								
5 Lipinski	?	?	?	?	?	?	Y	Y
6 ***Hyde***	Y	N	N	Y	N	Y	Y	Y
7 Collins	?	?	?	X	?	?	Y	Y
8 Rostenkowski	N	N	N	Y	N	Y	Y	Y
9 Yates	N	N	Y	N	Y	Y	Y	Y
10 ***Porter***	Y	Y	N	Y	N	N	Y	Y
11 Annunzio	N	N	N	Y	N	Y	Y	Y
12 ***Crane***	?	?	?	?	?	?	Y	Y
13 ***Fawell***	Y	Y	N	Y	Y	Y	Y	Y
14 ***Grotberg***	?	?	?	?	?	?	?	?
15 ***Madigan***	?	?	?	?	?	?	Y	Y
16 ***Martin***	Y	Y	N	Y	Y	N	Y	Y
17 Evans	N	N	Y	N	Y	Y	Y	Y
18 ***Michel***	Y	?	?	?	?	?	Y	Y
19 Bruce	N	N	N	Y	N	Y	Y	Y
20 Durbin	N	N	Y	N	N	Y	Y	Y
21 Price	N	N	N	N	N	Y	Y	Y
22 Gray	N	N	N	N	N	Y	Y	Y
INDIANA								
1 Visclosky	N	N	Y	Y	Y	Y	Y	Y
2 Sharp	N	N	N	Y	Y	Y	Y	Y
3 ***Hiler***	Y	Y	Y	Y	N	N	Y	Y
4 ***Coats***	Y	Y	Y	Y	N	Y	Y	Y
5 ***Hillis***	?	?	?	?	?	?	Y	?

ND - Northern Democrats SD - Southern Democrats

* Corresponding to Congressional Record Votes 228, 229, 230, 231, 232, 233, 234, 235

	206	207	208	209	210	211	212	213
6 ***Burton***	Y	Y	N	Y	N	N	Y	Y
7 ***Myers***	Y	N	N	N	Y	Y	Y	Y
8 McCloskey	N	N	Y	Y	N	Y	Y	Y
9 Hamilton	N	N	Y	Y	N	Y	Y	Y
10 Jacobs	N	N	Y	Y	Y	Y	Y	Y
IOWA								
1 ***Leach***	N	N	Y	Y	N	Y	Y	Y
2 ***Tauke***	Y	Y	Y	Y	N	N	Y	Y
3 ***Evans***	?	?	?	?	?	?	Y	Y
4 Smith	N	N	N	N	Y	Y	Y	Y
5 ***Lightfoot***	Y	Y	N	Y	N	Y	Y	Y
6 Bedell	N	N	N	Y	Y	Y	Y	Y
KANSAS								
1 ***Roberts***	Y	Y	N	Y	N	Y	Y	Y
2 Slattery	N	Y	N	Y	N	Y	Y	Y
3 ***Meyers***	Y	Y	N	Y	Y	Y	Y	Y
4 Glickman	N	N	N	Y	Y	Y	Y	Y
5 ***Whittaker***	Y	Y	N	Y	Y	Y	Y	Y
KENTUCKY								
1 Hubbard	N	N	N	Y	N	N	Y	Y
2 Natcher	N	N	N	N	Y	Y	Y	Y
3 Mazzoli	N	N	Y	N	N	Y	Y	Y
4 ***Snyder***	Y	?	?	?	?	?	Y	Y
5 ***Rogers***	Y	Y	N	N	N	Y	Y	Y
6 ***Hopkins***	Y	Y	N	Y	N	N	Y	Y
7 Perkins	N	N	Y	N	N	Y	Y	Y
LOUISIANA								
1 ***Livingston***	Y	Y	N	N	N	Y	Y	Y
2 Boggs	N	N	X	?	?	?	Y	Y
3 Tauzin	Y	N	N	Y	N	Y	Y	Y
4 Roemer	Y	N	N	Y	N	Y	Y	Y
5 Huckaby	?	?	?	?	?	?	?	?
6 ***Moore***	?	?	?	?	?	?	Y	Y
7 Breaux	?	?	?	?	?	?	?	?
8 Long	N	N	N	Y	N	Y	?	?
MAINE								
1 ***McKernan***	N	N	N	Y	Y	Y	Y	Y
2 ***Snowe***	N	N	N	Y	Y	Y	Y	Y
MARYLAND								
1 Dyson	Y	Y	Y	Y	N	Y	Y	Y
2 ***Bentley***	Y	N	N	Y	N	Y	Y	Y
3 Mikulski	N	N	Y	N	Y	Y	Y	Y
4 ***Holt***	?	?	?	?	?	?	?	?
5 Hoyer	N	N	N	N	Y	Y	Y	Y
6 Byron	?	?	?	?	?	?	Y	Y
7 Mitchell	N	N	Y	N	Y	Y	Y	Y
8 Barnes	?	?	?	?	?	?	?	?
MASSACHUSETTS								
1 ***Conte***	N	N	N	N	N	Y	Y	Y
2 Boland	?	?	?	?	?	?	Y	Y
3 Early	N	N	N	N	Y	Y	Y	Y
4 Frank	N	N	Y	N	Y	Y	Y	Y
5 Atkins	N	Y	N	N	?	?	Y	Y
6 Mavroules	N	N	N	N	N	Y	Y	Y
7 Markey	?	N	Y	N	Y	Y	Y	Y
8 O'Neill								
9 Moakley	N	N	N	N	N	Y	Y	Y
10 Studds	N	N	Y	N	Y	Y	Y	Y
11 Donnelly	N	N	Y	N	N	Y	Y	Y
MICHIGAN								
1 Conyers	N	N	Y	N	Y	N	?	?
2 ***Pursell***	N	N	N	Y	Y	Y	Y	Y
3 Wolpe	N	N	Y	Y	Y	Y	Y	Y
4 ***Siljander***	Y	Y	N	?	N	N	Y	Y
5 ***Henry***	Y	Y	N	Y	N	Y	Y	Y
6 Carr	N	Y	N	N	Y	Y	Y	Y
7 Kildee	N	N	N	N	N	Y	Y	Y
8 Traxler	N	N	N	N	N	Y	Y	Y
9 ***Vander Jagt***	Y	Y	N	Y	N	?	Y	Y
10 ***Schuette***	?	?	?	#	?	?	Y	Y
11 ***Davis***	Y	N	N	Y	N	Y	Y	Y
12 Bonior	?	?	?	?	?	?	Y	Y
13 Crockett	N	N	Y	N	Y	?	Y	Y
14 Hertel	N	N	Y	N	Y	Y	Y	Y
15 Ford	N	N	Y	?	?	?	Y	Y
16 Dingell	N	N	Y	N	Y	Y	Y	Y
17 Levin	N	N	N	N	Y	Y	Y	Y
18 ***Broomfield***	Y	Y	N	Y	N	Y	Y	Y
MINNESOTA								
1 Penny	N	Y	N	Y	N	Y	Y	Y
2 ***Weber***	Y	N	N	Y	N	N	Y	Y
3 ***Frenzel***	N	Y	Y	Y	Y	N	Y	Y
4 Vento	N	N	Y	Y	N	Y	Y	Y
5 Sabo	N	N	Y	N	Y	Y	Y	Y
6 Sikorski	N	N	N	N	N	Y	Y	Y

	206	207	208	209	210	211	212	213
7 ***Stangeland***	Y	N	N	Y	N	Y	?	?
8 Oberstar	N	N	Y	N	N	Y	Y	Y
MISSISSIPPI								
1 Whitten	N	N	N	N	Y	Y	Y	Y
2 ***Franklin***	Y	N	N	Y	N	Y	Y	Y
3 Montgomery	Y	N	N	Y	N	Y	Y	Y
4 Dowdy	N	N	?	?	?	?	Y	Y
5 ***Lott***	?	?	?	?	?	?	Y	Y
MISSOURI								
1 Clay	?	?	?	?	?	?	Y	Y
2 Young	N	?	?	?	?	#	Y	Y
3 Gephardt	N	N	N	N	Y	Y	Y	Y
4 Skelton	N	N	N	Y	N	Y	Y	Y
5 Wheat	N	N	Y	N	Y	Y	Y	Y
6 ***Coleman***	Y	N	N	Y	N	Y	?	?
7 ***Taylor***	Y	Y	Y	Y	N	Y	Y	Y
8 ***Emerson***	Y	N	Y	Y	N	Y	Y	Y
9 Volkmer	N	N	Y	Y	N	Y	Y	Y
MONTANA								
1 Williams	N	N	Y	N	Y	Y	Y	Y
2 ***Marlenee***	Y	Y	Y	Y	N	N	Y	Y
NEBRASKA								
1 ***Bereuter***	Y	N	N	Y	N	Y	Y	Y
2 ***Daub***	Y	Y	Y	Y	N	Y	Y	Y
3 ***Smith***	?	?	?	?	?	?	Y	Y
NEVADA								
1 Reid	N	N	N	Y	N	Y	Y	Y
2 ***Vucanovich***	Y	N	N	Y	N	Y	Y	Y
NEW HAMPSHIRE								
1 ***Smith***	Y	Y	N	Y	N	N	Y	Y
2 ***Gregg***	Y	Y	Y	Y	N	N	Y	?
NEW JERSEY								
1 Florio	?	?	?	?	?	?	Y	Y
2 Hughes	N	N	Y	N	Y	Y	Y	Y
3 Howard	N	N	N	N	Y	Y	Y	Y
4 ***Smith***	N	N	N	N	N	Y	Y	Y
5 ***Roukema***	Y	Y	Y	Y	Y	Y	Y	Y
6 Dwyer	N	N	N	N	Y	Y	Y	Y
7 ***Rinaldo***	N	N	N	N	N	Y	Y	Y
8 Roe	N	N	N	N	N	Y	Y	Y
9 Torricelli	?	N	?	?	?	?	Y	Y
10 Rodino	N	N	N	N	Y	Y	Y	Y
11 ***Gallo***	N	Y	N	Y	Y	Y	Y	Y
12 ***Courter***	N	N	N	Y	N	Y	Y	Y
13 ***Saxton***	Y	Y	N	Y	N	Y	Y	Y
14 Guarini	N	N	N	N	Y	Y	Y	Y
NEW MEXICO								
1 ***Lujan***	Y	N	N	Y	N	N	Y	Y
2 ***Skeen***	Y	N	Y	Y	N	Y	Y	Y
3 Richardson	N	N	N	Y	Y	Y	+	+
NEW YORK								
1 ***Carney***	Y	N	Y	Y	N	Y	?	?
2 Downey	N	N	Y	N	Y	Y	Y	Y
3 Mrazek	N	N	N	N	Y	Y	Y	Y
4 ***Lent***	Y	Y	N	?	?	?	?	Y
5 ***McGrath***	Y	Y	Y	Y	N	Y	Y	Y
6 Vacancy								
7 Ackerman	N	N	?	?	?	?	Y	Y
8 Scheuer	N	N	N	N	Y	N	Y	Y
9 Manton	N	N	N	N	N	Y	Y	Y
10 Schumer	N	N	N	N	Y	Y	Y	Y
11 Towns	?	?	?	?	?	?	Y	?
12 Owens	N	N	Y	N	Y	Y	Y	Y
13 Solarz	N	N	N	N	Y	Y	Y	Y
14 ***Molinari***	Y	N	N	Y	N	Y	Y	Y
15 ***Green***	N	N	N	N	Y	Y	Y	Y
16 Rangel	N	?	Y	N	Y	N	Y	Y
17 Weiss	N	N	Y	N	Y	N	Y	Y
18 Garcia	N	?	?	?	?	?	Y	Y
19 Biaggi	N	N	N	?	?	?	Y	Y
20 ***DioGuardi***	Y	Y	N	Y	N	Y	Y	Y
21 ***Fish***	?	N	N	N	N	Y	Y	Y
22 ***Gilman***	N	N	N	N	N	Y	Y	Y
23 Stratton	N	N	N	Y	Y	Y	Y	Y
24 ***Solomon***	Y	N	N	Y	N	N	Y	Y
25 ***Boehlert***	N	Y	N	Y	Y	Y	Y	Y
26 ***Martin***	?	?	?	?	?	?	Y	Y
27 ***Wortley***	Y	Y	N	?	?	?	Y	Y
28 McHugh	N	N	N	N	N	Y	Y	Y
29 ***Horton***	N	N	N	Y	Y	Y	Y	Y
30 ***Eckert***	Y	Y	N	Y	N	Y	Y	Y
31 ***Kemp***	?	?	?	?	?	?	?	?
32 LaFalce	Y	N	?	?	?	?	Y	Y
33 Nowak	N	N	N	N	Y	Y	Y	Y
34 Lundine	?	?	?	?	?	?	?	?

	206	207	208	209	210	211	212	213
NORTH CAROLINA								
1 Jones	?	?	?	?	?	?	Y	Y
2 Valentine	Y	N	N	Y	N	Y	Y	Y
3 Whitley	Y	N	N	?	?	?	Y	Y
4 ***Cobey***	Y	Y	N	Y	N	N	Y	Y
5 Neal	N	N	N	Y	Y	Y	Y	Y
6 ***Coble***	Y	Y	N	Y	N	Y	Y	Y
7 Rose	N	N	N	Y	Y	Y	Y	Y
8 Hefner	N	N	Y	N	Y	Y	Y	Y
9 ***McMillan***	Y	Y	N	Y	N	Y	Y	Y
10 Vacancy								
11 ***Hendon***	Y	Y	N	Y	N	Y	Y	Y
NORTH DAKOTA								
AL Dorgan	N	N	Y	Y	N	Y	Y	Y
OHIO								
1 Luken	N	N	Y	Y	N	Y	Y	Y
2 ***Gradison***	N	N	N	Y	N	Y	Y	Y
3 Hall	Y	N	Y	Y	N	Y	Y	Y
4 ***Oxley***	Y	Y	N	Y	N	Y	Y	Y
5 ***Latta***	Y	Y	N	Y	N	N	Y	Y
6 ***McEwen***	?	?	?	?	?	?	Y	Y
7 ***DeWine***	Y	Y	N	Y	N	Y	Y	Y
8 ***Kindness***	Y	Y	Y	Y	N	Y	Y	Y
9 Kaptur	N	N	Y	Y	Y	Y	Y	Y
10 ***Miller***	Y	Y	Y	Y	N	Y	Y	Y
11 Eckart	N	N	Y	Y	N	Y	Y	Y
12 ***Kasich***	Y	Y	N	Y	N	Y	Y	Y
13 Pease	N	N	Y	N	Y	Y	Y	Y
14 Seiberling	N	N	Y	N	Y	Y	Y	Y
15 ***Wylie***	Y	Y	Y	Y	N	Y	Y	Y
16 ***Regula***	Y	N	N	N	N	Y	Y	Y
17 Traficant	N	N	N	N	Y	Y	Y	Y
18 Applegate	Y	N	N	Y	N	Y	Y	Y
19 Feighan	N	N	N	Y	Y	Y	Y	Y
20 Oakar	N	N	Y	N	Y	Y	Y	Y
21 Stokes	N	N	Y	N	Y	Y	Y	Y
OKLAHOMA								
1 Jones	N	N	N	Y	N	Y	Y	Y
2 Synar	N	Y	Y	N	Y	Y	Y	Y
3 Watkins	N	N	N	N	Y	Y	Y	Y
4 McCurdy	N	N	N	Y	Y	Y	Y	Y
5 ***Edwards***	Y	N	N	Y	N	Y	Y	Y
6 English	N	N	N	Y	N	N	Y	Y
OREGON								
1 AuCoin	N	N	N	N	Y	Y	Y	Y
2 ***Smith, R.***	Y	Y	N	Y	N	Y	Y	Y
3 Wyden	N	N	Y	N	Y	Y	Y	Y
4 Weaver	N	N	Y	Y	Y	?	Y	Y
5 ***Smith, D.***	Y	Y	Y	Y	N	N	Y	Y
PENNSYLVANIA								
1 Foglietta	?	?	?	?	?	?	Y	Y
2 Gray	N	N	Y	N	Y	Y	?	Y
3 Borski	N	N	N	Y	N	Y	Y	Y
4 Kolter	N	N	N	Y	N	Y	Y	Y
5 ***Schulze***	Y	Y	N	Y	N	N	Y	Y
6 Yatron	N	N	N	Y	N	Y	Y	Y
7 Edgar	N	N	Y	N	Y	Y	?	?
8 Kostmayer	N	N	N	N	Y	Y	Y	Y
9 ***Shuster***	Y	Y	Y	Y	N	N	Y	Y
10 ***McDade***	N	N	N	N	N	Y	Y	Y
11 Kanjorski	N	N	Y	Y	N	Y	Y	Y
12 Murtha	N	N	N	?	?	?	Y	Y
13 ***Coughlin***	N	N	N	Y	Y	Y	Y	Y
14 Coyne	N	N	N	N	Y	Y	Y	Y
15 ***Ritter***	Y	?	N	Y	N	Y	Y	Y
16 ***Walker***	Y	Y	N	Y	N	N	Y	Y
17 ***Gekas***	Y	N	N	Y	N	Y	Y	Y
18 Walgren	N	N	Y	Y	Y	Y	Y	Y
19 ***Goodling***	N	N	N	Y	N	Y	+	+
20 Gaydos	N	N	N	?	?	?	Y	Y
21 ***Ridge***	Y	Y	N	Y	N	Y	Y	Y
22 Murphy	N	N	N	Y	Y	Y	Y	Y
23 ***Clinger***	N	N	N	N	N	Y	Y	Y
RHODE ISLAND								
1 St Germain	N	N	N	Y	N	Y	Y	Y
2 ***Schneider***	N	?	?	?	?	#	Y	Y
SOUTH CAROLINA								
1 ***Hartnett***	?	?	?	?	?	?	?	?
2 ***Spence***	Y	N	N	Y	N	N	Y	Y
3 Derrick	Y	N	N	N	Y	Y	Y	Y
4 ***Campbell***	?	?	?	?	?	X	Y	Y
5 Spratt	N	Y	N	Y	Y	Y	Y	Y
6 Tallon	Y	N	Y	Y	N	Y	Y	Y
SOUTH DAKOTA								
AL Daschle	N	N	Y	Y	Y	Y	Y	Y

	206	207	208	209	210	211	212	213
TENNESSEE								
1 ***Quillen***	Y	?	?	?	?	?	Y	Y
2 ***Duncan***	Y	N	N	Y	N	Y	Y	Y
3 Lloyd	N	N	N	Y	N	Y	Y	Y
4 Cooper	N	N	N	Y	Y	Y	Y	Y
5 Boner	?	?	?	?	?	?	?	?
6 Gordon	N	N	N	Y	Y	Y	Y	Y
7 ***Sundquist***	Y	N	Y	Y	N	Y	Y	Y
8 Jones	Y	N	Y	Y	Y	Y	?	?
9 Ford	N	N	Y	N	Y	Y	?	?
TEXAS								
1 Chapman	?	?	?	?	?	?	Y	Y
2 Wilson	N	Y	?	?	?	?	Y	Y
3 ***Bartlett***	Y	Y	N	Y	N	N	Y	Y
4 Hall, R.	Y	Y	Y	Y	N	N	Y	Y
5 Bryant	N	N	N	N	N	Y	Y	Y
6 ***Barton***	Y	Y	N	Y	N	N	Y	Y
7 ***Archer***	Y	Y	Y	Y	N	N	Y	Y
8 ***Fields***	Y	Y	Y	Y	N	N	Y	Y
9 Brooks	N	N	N	N	Y	Y	Y	Y
10 Pickle	Y	N	Y	Y	Y	Y	Y	Y
11 Leath	Y	N	Y	Y	Y	?	Y	Y
12 Wright	N	N	N	N	Y	Y	Y	Y
13 ***Boulter***	Y	Y	N	Y	N	N	Y	Y
14 ***Sweeney***	Y	Y	N	Y	N	N	Y	Y
15 de la Garza	Y	N	N	N	N	Y	Y	Y
16 Coleman	N	N	N	Y	Y	Y	Y	Y
17 Stenholm	Y	Y	Y	Y	N	N	Y	Y
18 Leland	N	N	Y	N	Y	Y	Y	Y
19 ***Combest***	Y	Y	N	Y	N	N	Y	Y
20 Gonzalez	N	N	Y	N	Y	Y	Y	Y
21 ***Loeffler***	?	?	?	?	?	?	Y	Y
22 ***DeLay***	Y	Y	N	Y	N	N	Y	Y
23 Bustamante	?	?	?	?	?	?	Y	Y
24 Frost	?	?	?	?	?	?	Y	?
25 Andrews	Y	N	N	Y	Y	Y	Y	Y
26 ***Armey***	Y	Y	N	Y	N	N	Y	Y
27 Ortiz	?	X	?	X	?	?	Y	Y
UTAH								
1 ***Hansen***	Y	Y	Y	Y	N	N	Y	Y
2 ***Monson***	?	?	?	#	?	X	Y	Y
3 ***Nielson***	Y	Y	Y	Y	N	N	Y	Y
VERMONT								
AL ***Jeffords***	N	Y	N	Y	Y	Y	Y	Y
VIRGINIA								
1 ***Bateman***	Y	Y	N	Y	N	Y	Y	Y
2 ***Whitehurst***	?	?	?	?	?	?	Y	Y
3 ***Bliley***	Y	Y	N	Y	N	Y	Y	Y
4 Sisisky	N	N	Y	Y	Y	Y	Y	Y
5 Daniel	Y	N	Y	Y	N	Y	Y	Y
6 Olin	N	Y	Y	Y	Y	Y	Y	Y
7 ***Slaughter***	Y	Y	N	Y	N	N	Y	Y
8 ***Parris***	Y	N	?	?	?	?	Y	Y
9 Boucher	N	N	Y	N	Y	Y	Y	Y
10 ***Wolf***	Y	Y	N	N	N	Y	Y	Y
WASHINGTON								
1 ***Miller***	Y	Y	N	Y	Y	N	Y	Y
2 Swift	N	N	Y	N	Y	Y	Y	Y
3 Bonker	N	N	N	N	Y	Y	Y	Y
4 ***Morrison***	Y	Y	N	N	Y	Y	Y	Y
5 Foley	N	N	N	N	Y	Y	Y	Y
6 Dicks	N	N	N	N	Y	Y	Y	Y
7 Lowry	N	N	Y	N	Y	Y	Y	Y
8 ***Chandler***	Y	Y	Y	Y	Y	Y	Y	Y
WEST VIRGINIA								
1 Mollohan	N	N	N	N	N	Y	Y	Y
2 Staggers	N	N	N	N	Y	Y	Y	Y
3 Wise	N	N	Y	Y	Y	Y	Y	Y
4 Rahall	N	N	Y	N	Y	Y	Y	Y
WISCONSIN								
1 Aspin	N	N	?	?	?	?	Y	Y
2 Kastenmeier	N	N	Y	N	Y	Y	Y	Y
3 ***Gunderson***	Y	Y	N	Y	N	Y	Y	Y
4 Kleczka	N	N	Y	N	Y	Y	Y	Y
5 Moody	N	N	Y	N	Y	Y	Y	Y
6 ***Petri***	Y	Y	Y	Y	N	N	Y	Y
7 Obey	N	N	Y	N	Y	Y	Y	Y
8 ***Roth***	Y	?	?	?	?	?	Y	Y
9 ***Sensenbrenner***	Y	Y	Y	Y	N	N	Y	Y
WYOMING								
AL ***Cheney***	Y	Y	N	Y	N	N	Y	Y

**Rep. George M. O'Brien, R-Ill., died on July 17, 1986. The last vote for which he was eligible was CQ vote 205.*

Southern states - Ala., Ark., Fla., Ga., Ky., La., Miss., N.C., Okla., S.C., Tenn., Texas, Va.

* The *Congressional Record* vote number is different from the CQ vote number because the *Record* includes quorum calls in its tally. CQ does not publish quorum call votes.

214. HR 5162. Energy and Water Appropriations, Fiscal 1987. Adoption of the rule (H Res 494) to waive points of order against the bill to make $15.55 billion in appropriations for energy and water development in fiscal 1987. Adopted 365-46: R 129-42; D 236-4 (ND 158-3, SD 78-1), July 23, 1986.

215. HR 5162. Energy and Water Appropriations, Fiscal 1987. Petri, R-Wis., amendment to reduce appropriations in the bill by $83,700,000, eliminating funds for continued construction of the Bonneville Unit of the Central Utah Project. Rejected 149-262: R 58-115; D 91-147 (ND 79-84, SD 12-63), July 23, 1986. A "nay" was a vote supporting the president's position.

216. HR 5162. Energy and Water Appropriations, Fiscal 1987. Walker, R-Pa., amendment to reduce appropriations in the bill by $69,700,000, eliminating funds for construction of eight research facilities under the Energy Department that had not been authorized by Congress. Rejected 106-315: R 87-90; D 19-225 (ND 14-152, SD 5-73), July 23, 1986.

217. HR 5162. Energy and Water Appropriations, Fiscal 1987. Weaver, D-Ore., amendment to reduce appropriations in the bill from the Nuclear Waste Disposal Fund by $291,200,000, which would be used for study of potential nuclear-waste repository sites in Washington state, Nevada and Texas. Rejected 68-351: R 19-158: D 49-193 (ND 33-130, SD 16-63), July 23, 1986. A "nay" was a vote supporting the president's position.

218. HR 5162. Energy and Water Appropriations, Fiscal 1987. Markey, D-Mass., amendment to transfer $16.25 million out of the appropriations account for nuclear weapons operating expenses into the accounts for nuclear test ban verification research and nuclear safeguards. Rejected 152-263: R 20-156; D 132-107 (ND 121-41, SD 11-66), July 23, 1986.

219. HR 5162. Energy and Water Appropriations, Fiscal 1987. Armey, R-Texas, amendment to reduce appropriations for the Appalachian Regional Commission (ARC) by $53,500,000. (The bill provided $105,000,000 for the ARC; the president had requested no funds for the agency.) Rejected 102-309: R 95-78; D 7-231 (ND 6-155, SD 1-76), July 23, 1986.

220. HR 5162. Energy and Water Appropriations, Fiscal 1987. Schroeder, D-Colo., amendment to reduce the appropriation for the Tennessee Valley Authority (TVA) by $355,200. The amount for TVA funding was equivalent to annual payments under a personal services contract to retired Adm. Steven A. White, for management of TVA's nuclear power plants. Rejected 131-273: R 26-141; D 105-132 (ND 92-69, SD 13-63), July 23, 1986.

221. HR 5162. Energy and Water Appropriations, Fiscal 1987. Frenzel, R-Minn., amendment to apply an across-the-board reduction of 4.62 percent to each amount appropriated in the bill. Rejected 167-241: R 116-57; D 51-184 (ND 33-125, SD 18-59), July 23, 1986. A "nay" was a vote supporting the president's position.

KEY

Y Voted for (yea).
\# Paired for.
\+ Announced for.
N Voted against (nay).
X Paired against.
\- Announced against.
P Voted "present."
C Voted "present" to avoid possible conflict of interest.
? Did not vote or otherwise make a position known.

Democrats ***Republicans***

	214	215	216	217	218	219	220	221
ALABAMA								
1 ***Callahan***	Y	N	N	N	N	N	N	N
2 ***Dickinson***	Y	N	Y	N	N	N	N	Y
3 Nichols	Y	N	N	N	N	N	N	N
4 Bevill	Y	N	N	N	N	N	N	N
5 Flippo	Y	N	N	N	N	N	N	N
6 Erdreich	Y	N	N	N	N	N	N	N
7 Shelby	Y	?	N	N	N	N	N	N
ALASKA								
AL ***Young***	Y	N	N	N	N	N	N	N
ARIZONA								
1 ***McCain***	Y	N	Y	N	N	Y	N	N
2 Udall	Y	N	N	N	Y	N	Y	N
3 ***Stump***	Y	N	Y	N	N	Y	N	Y
4 ***Rudd***	Y	N	N	N	N	N	N	N
5 ***Kolbe***	Y	N	Y	N	N	Y	N	Y
ARKANSAS								
1 Alexander	Y	N	N	N	N	N	N	N
2 Robinson	Y	Y	N	N	N	N	N	N
3 ***Hammerschmidt***	Y	N	N	N	N	N	N	N
4 Anthony	Y	N	N	N	N	N	N	N
CALIFORNIA								
1 Bosco	Y	Y	N	N	Y	N	N	N
2 ***Chappie***	Y	N	Y	Y	N	Y	Y	Y
3 Matsui	Y	N	N	N	Y	N	N	N
4 Fazio	Y	N	N	N	N	N	Y	N
5 Burton	Y	N	N	N	Y	N	Y	N
6 Boxer	Y	Y	N	Y	Y	N	Y	N
7 Miller	Y	N	Y	Y	Y	N	Y	?
8 Dellums	Y	Y	N	Y	Y	N	Y	N
9 Stark	Y	Y	N	N	Y	N	Y	N
10 Edwards	Y	Y	N	N	Y	N	Y	N
11 Lantos	Y	N	N	N	Y	N	N	N
12 ***Zschau***	Y	?	Y	N	N	Y	Y	Y
13 Mineta	Y	N	N	N	Y	N	N	N
14 ***Shumway***	N	N	Y	N	N	Y	N	Y
15 Coelho	Y	N	N	N	N	N	N	N
16 Panetta	Y	Y	N	N	Y	N	N	Y
17 ***Pashayan***	Y	N	N	N	N	Y	N	N
18 Lehman	Y	N	N	N	Y	N	Y	N
19 ***Lagomarsino***	Y	N	Y	N	N	Y	N	Y
20 ***Thomas***	Y	N	N	N	N	N	N	Y
21 ***Fiedler***	Y	N	Y	N	N	Y	?	Y
22 ***Moorhead***	Y	N	Y	N	N	Y	N	Y
23 Beilenson	Y	Y	Y	N	Y	N	N	N
24 Waxman	Y	Y	N	Y	Y	N	Y	N
25 Roybal	Y	N	N	N	N	N	Y	N
26 Berman	Y	Y	N	N	Y	N	Y	N
27 Levine	Y	Y	N	Y	Y	N	N	N
28 Dixon	?	N	N	N	N	N	N	N
29 Hawkins	Y	N	N	N	Y	N	Y	N
30 Martinez	Y	N	N	N	N	N	N	N
31 Dymally	Y	N	N	Y	Y	N	Y	N
32 Anderson	Y	N	N	N	N	N	N	N
33 ***Dreier***	N	Y	Y	N	N	Y	N	Y
34 Torres	Y	N	N	N	Y	N	Y	N
35 ***Lewis***	N	N	Y	N	N	?	?	N
36 Brown	Y	N	N	N	Y	N	N	N
37 ***McCandless***	+	N	N	N	N	N	N	N
38 ***Dornan***	Y	N	Y	N	N	Y	N	Y
39 ***Dannemeyer***	N	Y	Y	N	N	Y	Y	Y
40 ***Badham***	Y	N	Y	N	N	Y	?	Y
41 ***Lowery***	Y	N	N	N	N	N	N	N
42 ***Lungren***	N	N	Y	N	N	Y	Y	Y
43 ***Packard***	Y	N	N	N	N	Y	N	Y
44 Bates	Y	Y	Y	Y	Y	N	Y	Y
45 ***Hunter***	Y	N	Y	N	N	Y	N	Y
COLORADO								
1 Schroeder	N	Y	N	N	Y	N	Y	Y
2 Wirth	Y	N	N	N	Y	N	Y	Y
3 ***Strang***	Y	N	N	N	N	N	N	N
4 ***Brown***	N	N	Y	N	Y	Y	Y	Y
5 ***Kramer***	Y	N	Y	Y	N	Y	Y	Y
6 ***Schaefer***	Y	N	Y	Y	N	Y	N	N
CONNECTICUT								
1 Kennelly	Y	N	N	N	Y	N	Y	Y
2 Gejdenson	Y	Y	N	N	Y	N	Y	Y
3 Morrison	Y	Y	N	N	Y	N	Y	Y
4 ***McKinney***	Y	N	N	N	Y	N	N	Y
5 ***Rowland***	Y	Y	Y	N	N	Y	N	Y
6 ***Johnson***	Y	N	N	N	Y	N	N	Y
DELAWARE								
AL Carper	Y	Y	Y	N	Y	Y	N	N
FLORIDA								
1 Hutto	Y	N	N	N	N	N	N	Y
2 Fuqua	Y	N	N	N	N	N	N	N
3 Bennett	Y	N	N	N	N	N	Y	N
4 Chappell	Y	N	N	N	N	N	N	N
5 ***McCollum***	N	Y	Y	N	N	Y	N	N
6 MacKay	Y	Y	Y	N	Y	N	N	Y
7 Gibbons	Y	N	N	N	N	N	N	Y
8 ***Young***	Y	Y	N	N	N	Y	N	N
9 ***Bilirakis***	N	N	Y	N	N	Y	N	Y
10 ***Ireland***	N	N	Y	N	N	Y	N	Y
11 Nelson	Y	N	N	N	N	N	N	N
12 ***Lewis***	Y	N	N	N	N	Y	N	N
13 ***Mack***	N	Y	Y	N	N	Y	?	Y
14 Mica	Y	N	N	N	N	N	N	N
15 ***Shaw***	Y	Y	N	N	N	Y	N	N
16 Smith	Y	Y	N	N	N	N	Y	N
17 Lehman	Y	N	N	N	N	N	Y	N
18 Pepper	Y	N	N	N	N	-	N	N
19 Fascell	Y	N	N	N	Y	N	Y	N
GEORGIA								
1 Thomas	Y	N	N	N	N	N	N	N
2 Hatcher	Y	N	N	N	N	N	N	N
3 Ray	Y	N	N	N	N	N	Y	Y
4 ***Swindall***	N	N	N	N	N	Y	N	Y
5 Fowler	Y	N	?	N	?	?	?	?
6 ***Gingrich***	N	Y	Y	N	N	Y	?	Y
7 Darden	Y	N	N	N	N	N	N	Y
8 Rowland	Y	N	N	N	N	N	N	N
9 Jenkins	Y	N	N	N	N	N	N	N
10 Barnard	Y	N	N	N	N	N	N	Y
HAWAII								
1 Vacancy								
2 Akaka	?	?	N	N	N	N	N	N
IDAHO								
1 ***Craig***	N	N	Y	Y	N	Y	N	Y
2 Stallings	Y	N	N	Y	N	Y	N	Y
ILLINOIS								
1 Hayes	Y	N	N	N	Y	N	Y	N
2 Savage	Y	N	N	N	Y	N	Y	N
3 Russo	Y	Y	N	N	Y	N	N	Y
4 Vacancy								
5 Lipinski	Y	N	N	N	N	N	N	N
6 ***Hyde***	N	Y	Y	N	N	Y	N	Y
7 Collins	Y	Y	N	N	Y	N	Y	N
8 Rostenkowski	Y	?	N	N	N	N	N	N
9 Yates	Y	Y	N	N	Y	N	Y	N
10 ***Porter***	Y	Y	Y	N	N	Y	Y	Y
11 Annunzio	Y	N	N	N	Y	N	N	N
12 ***Crane***	N	Y	Y	N	N	Y	Y	Y
13 ***Fawell***	N	Y	Y	N	Y	Y	N	Y
14 ***Grotberg***	?	?	?	?	?	?	?	?
15 ***Madigan***	Y	N	N	N	N	Y	N	Y
16 ***Martin***	N	N	Y	N	N	Y	Y	Y
17 Evans	Y	Y	N	N	Y	N	Y	N
18 ***Michel***	Y	N	N	N	N	Y	N	Y
19 Bruce	Y	Y	N	N	Y	N	Y	Y
20 Durbin	Y	Y	N	N	Y	N	Y	N
21 Price	Y	N	N	N	N	N	N	N
22 Gray	Y	N	N	N	N	N	N	N
INDIANA								
1 Visclosky	Y	Y	N	N	Y	N	Y	Y
2 Sharp	Y	Y	N	N	Y	Y	Y	Y
3 ***Hiler***	Y	Y	N	N	N	Y	N	Y
4 ***Coats***	Y	Y	N	N	N	Y	N	Y
5 ***Hillis***	Y	Y	N	N	N	N	N	Y

ND - Northern Democrats SD - Southern Democrats

* Corresponding to Congressional Record Votes 236, 238, 239, 240, 241, 242, 243, 244

	214	215	216	217	218	219	220	221
6 ***Burton***	Y	Y	N	N	N	Y	N	Y
7 ***Myers***	Y	N	N	N	N	N	N	N
8 McCloskey	Y	Y	N	N	Y	N	Y	Y
9 Hamilton	Y	Y	N	N	Y	N	Y	Y
10 Jacobs	Y	Y	Y	N	Y	N	Y	Y
IOWA								
1 ***Leach***	Y	Y	N	N	Y	Y	Y	Y
2 ***Tauke***	Y	N	N	N	N	Y	N	Y
3 ***Evans***	?	N	N	N	N	N	N	Y
4 Smith	Y	N	N	N	N	N	N	N
5 ***Lightfoot***	Y	N	N	N	N	N	N	Y
6 Bedell	Y	Y	N	Y	Y	N	Y	Y
KANSAS								
1 ***Roberts***	N	N	N	N	N	Y	Y	Y
2 Slattery	N	Y	N	N	N	Y	Y	Y
3 ***Meyers***	Y	?	Y	N	Y	Y	Y	Y
4 Glickman	Y	Y	N	N	Y	Y	Y	Y
5 ***Whittaker***	N	N	N	N	N	Y	Y	N
KENTUCKY								
1 Hubbard	Y	N	Y	N	N	N	N	Y
2 Natcher	Y	N	N	N	N	N	N	N
3 Mazzoli	Y	N	N	N	N	N	N	N
4 ***Snyder***	Y	N	N	N	N	Y	N	N
5 ***Rogers***	Y	N	N	N	N	N	N	N
6 ***Hopkins***	Y	N	Y	N	N	Y	N	Y
7 Perkins	Y	N	N	N	N	N	N	N
LOUISIANA								
1 ***Livingston***	Y	N	N	N	N	Y	N	N
2 Boggs	Y	N	N	N	N	N	N	N
3 Tauzin	Y	N	N	N	N	N	N	Y
4 Roemer	Y	N	N	N	Y	Y	Y	Y
5 Huckaby	Y	N	N	N	N	N	N	N
6 ***Moore***	?	?	?	?	?	?	?	?
7 Breaux	?	?	N	N	N	N	?	?
8 Long	?	?	?	N	Y	N	N	N
MAINE								
1 ***McKernan***	N	N	N	N	N	N	Y	Y
2 ***Snowe***	Y	N	N	N	Y	N	Y	Y
MARYLAND								
1 Dyson	Y	N	N	N	N	N	N	N
2 ***Bentley***	Y	N	Y	N	N	N	N	N
3 Mikulski	Y	Y	N	Y	Y	?	?	N
4 ***Holt***	N	N	N	N	N	N	N	N
5 Hoyer	Y	N	N	N	N	N	Y	N
6 Byron	Y	N	N	N	N	N	N	N
7 Mitchell	Y	N	N	Y	?	?	?	?
8 Barnes	Y	Y	N	?	?	?	?	?
MASSACHUSETTS								
1 ***Conte***	Y	Y	N	N	Y	N	Y	N
2 Boland	Y	N	N	N	Y	N	N	N
3 Early	Y	Y	N	N	Y	N	N	N
4 Frank	Y	Y	N	N	Y	N	Y	N
5 Atkins	Y	Y	N	N	Y	N	Y	N
6 Mavroules	Y	N	N	N	Y	N	Y	N
7 Markey	Y	Y	N	Y	Y	N	Y	N
8 O'Neill								
9 Moakley	Y	Y	N	N	Y	N	Y	N
10 Studds	Y	Y	N	N	Y	N	Y	N
11 Donnelly	Y	Y	N	N	Y	N	Y	N
MICHIGAN								
1 Conyers	Y	Y	N	Y	Y	?	Y	?
2 ***Pursell***	Y	N	N	N	N	N	N	Y
3 Wolpe	Y	Y	Y	N	Y	N	Y	Y
4 ***Siljander***	Y	Y	Y	N	N	?	N	Y
5 ***Henry***	Y	Y	Y	N	Y	Y	N	Y
6 Carr	Y	Y	N	N	N	Y	N	N
7 Kildee	Y	Y	N	N	Y	N	Y	N
8 Traxler	Y	N	N	N	N	N	N	N
9 ***Vander Jagt***	Y	Y	Y	N	N	Y	N	N
10 ***Schuette***	Y	Y	N	N	N	Y	N	Y
11 ***Davis***	Y	N	N	N	N	N	N	?
12 Bonior	Y	Y	N	N	Y	N	Y	N
13 Crockett	Y	N	N	Y	Y	N	Y	N
14 Hertel	Y	Y	Y	N	Y	N	Y	Y
15 Ford	Y	Y	N	N	Y	N	Y	N
16 Dingell	Y	N	N	N	?	N	Y	N
17 Levin	Y	Y	N	N	Y	N	N	Y
18 ***Broomfield***	Y	Y	N	N	N	Y	N	Y
MINNESOTA								
1 Penny	Y	Y	N	N	Y	N	N	Y
2 ***Weber***	N	Y	Y	N	N	Y	N	Y
3 ***Frenzel***	N	Y	Y	N	N	Y	N	Y
4 Vento	Y	Y	N	N	Y	N	Y	Y
5 Sabo	Y	N	N	N	Y	N	N	N
6 Sikorski	Y	Y	Y	N	Y	N	Y	Y
7 ***Stangeland***	Y	N	N	N	N	N	N	N
8 Oberstar	Y	N	N	N	Y	N	N	N
MISSISSIPPI								
1 Whitten	Y	N	N	N	N	N	N	N
2 ***Franklin***	Y	N	N	N	N	N	N	Y
3 Montgomery	Y	N	Y	N	N	N	N	N
4 Dowdy	Y	N	N	N	N	N	N	N
5 ***Lott***	Y	N	Y	N	N	N	N	N
MISSOURI								
1 Clay	Y	N	N	Y	Y	N	Y	N
2 Young	Y	N	N	N	N	N	N	N
3 Gephardt	Y	N	N	N	N	N	N	N
4 Skelton	Y	N	N	N	N	N	Y	N
5 Wheat	Y	Y	N	N	Y	N	Y	N
6 ***Coleman***	Y	N	N	N	N	?	?	?
7 ***Taylor***	Y	N	Y	N	N	Y	N	N
8 ***Emerson***	Y	N	N	N	N	N	N	N
9 Volkmer	Y	N	N	N	N	N	Y	N
MONTANA								
1 Williams	Y	N	N	Y	Y	N	?	?
2 ***Marlenee***	N	N	Y	N	?	Y	N	Y
NEBRASKA								
1 ***Bereuter***	Y	N	Y	N	N	Y	N	Y
2 ***Daub***	Y	N	Y	N	Y	Y	N	Y
3 ***Smith***	Y	N	N	N	N	N	N	N
NEVADA								
1 Reid	Y	Y	N	Y	N	N	N	N
2 ***Vucanovich***	N	N	Y	Y	N	N	N	N
NEW HAMPSHIRE								
1 ***Smith***	N	Y	Y	N	N	Y	Y	Y
2 ***Gregg***	N	Y	Y	N	N	Y	Y	Y
NEW JERSEY								
1 Florio	Y	Y	N	Y	Y	N	Y	N
2 Hughes	Y	N	N	N	N	N	Y	N
3 Howard	Y	N	N	N	Y	N	N	N
4 ***Smith***	Y	N	N	N	N	N	N	Y
5 ***Roukema***	Y	Y	N	N	N	N	N	Y
6 Dwyer	Y	N	N	N	Y	N	N	N
7 ***Rinaldo***	Y	N	Y	N	N	N	N	Y
8 Roe	Y	N	N	N	N	N	N	N
9 Torricelli	Y	N	N	N	Y	N	Y	N
10 Rodino	Y	N	N	N	Y	N	N	N
11 ***Gallo***	Y	N	Y	N	N	N	N	Y
12 ***Courter***	Y	N	Y	N	N	N	N	Y
13 ***Saxton***	Y	N	Y	N	N	N	N	Y
14 Guarini	Y	N	N	N	Y	N	Y	N
NEW MEXICO								
1 ***Lujan***	Y	N	N	N	N	N	N	Y
2 ***Skeen***	Y	N	N	N	N	N	N	N
3 Richardson	Y	Y	N	N	N	N	N	N
NEW YORK								
1 ***Carney***	?	?	N	N	N	N	N	N
2 Downey	Y	Y	N	N	Y	N	Y	N
3 Mrazek	Y	Y	N	N	Y	N	Y	N
4 ***Lent***	Y	?	N	N	N	N	N	Y
5 ***McGrath***	?	Y	N	N	N	Y	N	Y
6 Vacancy								
7 Ackerman	Y	Y	N	N	Y	N	Y	N
8 Scheuer	Y	N	N	N	Y	N	N	N
9 Manton	?	N	N	N	N	N	N	N
10 Schumer	Y	Y	N	N	Y	N	Y	Y
11 Towns	Y	N	N	N	Y	N	Y	N
12 Owens	?	Y	N	Y	Y	N	Y	N
13 Solarz	Y	N	N	Y	Y	N	N	N
14 ***Molinari***	Y	N	N	N	N	N	N	Y
15 ***Green***	Y	Y	N	N	Y	N	N	N
16 Rangel	Y	N	N	N	Y	N	Y	N
17 Weiss	Y	Y	N	Y	Y	N	Y	Y
18 Garcia	Y	N	N	N	Y	N	Y	?
19 Biaggi	Y	N	N	N	Y	N	N	N
20 ***DioGuardi***	Y	N	Y	N	N	Y	N	Y
21 ***Fish***	Y	Y	N	N	N	N	N	Y
22 ***Gilman***	Y	Y	N	N	N	N	N	N
23 Stratton	Y	Y	N	N	N	N	N	N
24 ***Solomon***	N	Y	Y	N	N	Y	N	Y
25 ***Boehlert***	Y	Y	N	N	N	N	N	N
26 ***Martin***	Y	N	N	N	N	N	N	N
27 ***Wortley***	Y	Y	N	N	N	N	N	N
28 McHugh	Y	N	N	N	N	N	N	N
29 ***Horton***	Y	N	N	N	N	N	N	N
30 ***Eckert***	N	Y	Y	N	N	Y	N	Y
31 ***Kemp***	Y	N	N	N	N	Y	N	N
32 LaFalce	Y	N	Y	N	Y	N	Y	Y
33 Nowak	Y	N	N	N	Y	N	Y	N
34 Lundine	?	?	?	?	?	?	?	?
NORTH CAROLINA								
1 Jones	Y	?	N	N	N	N	N	N
2 Valentine	Y	N	N	N	N	N	N	N
3 Whitley	Y	N	N	N	N	N	N	N
4 ***Cobey***	Y	N	N	N	N	Y	N	Y
5 Neal	Y	Y	N	N	Y	N	N	Y
6 ***Coble***	Y	N	N	N	N	N	N	N
7 Rose	Y	N	N	N	N	N	N	N
8 Hefner	Y	N	N	N	N	N	N	N
9 ***McMillan***	Y	N	N	N	N	N	N	Y
10 Vacancy								
11 ***Hendon***	Y	N	N	N	N	N	N	N
NORTH DAKOTA								
AL Dorgan	Y	N	Y	N	Y	N	N	N
OHIO								
1 Luken	Y	N	N	Y	Y	N	N	N
2 ***Gradison***	Y	N	Y	N	N	Y	N	Y
3 Hall	Y	Y	Y	Y	Y	N	Y	Y
4 ***Oxley***	Y	Y	Y	N	N	Y	N	Y
5 ***Latta***	Y	Y	Y	N	Y	Y	N	Y
6 ***McEwen***	Y	N	N	N	N	N	N	N
7 ***DeWine***	Y	Y	Y	N	N	N	N	Y
8 ***Kindness***	Y	Y	Y	N	N	N	?	Y
9 Kaptur	Y	N	N	N	N	N	N	N
10 ***Miller***	Y	N	N	N	N	N	N	Y
11 Eckart	Y	Y	N	N	Y	N	Y	N
12 ***Kasich***	Y	Y	Y	N	N	N	Y	Y
13 Pease	Y	N	N	N	Y	N	N	N
14 Seiberling	?	Y	Y	Y	Y	N	Y	N
15 ***Wylie***	Y	Y	N	N	N	N	N	Y
16 ***Regula***	Y	Y	N	N	N	N	N	N
17 Traficant	Y	N	N	Y	Y	N	Y	N
18 Applegate	Y	N	N	N	N	N	N	N
19 Feighan	Y	Y	N	N	Y	N	Y	N
20 Oakar	Y	N	N	N	Y	N	N	N
21 Stokes	Y	Y	N	N	Y	N	N	N
OKLAHOMA								
1 Jones	Y	Y	N	Y	N	N	N	N
2 Synar	Y	N	N	N	Y	N	N	N
3 Watkins	Y	N	N	N	N	N	N	N
4 McCurdy	Y	N	N	N	Y	N	N	N
5 ***Edwards***	Y	N	N	N	N	N	N	N
6 English	Y	N	N	Y	N	N	N	N
OREGON								
1 AuCoin	Y	N	N	Y	Y	N	Y	N
2 ***Smith, R.***	Y	N	N	Y	N	N	N	Y
3 Wyden	Y	N	N	Y	Y	N	Y	N
4 Weaver	Y	Y	Y	Y	Y	N	Y	Y
5 ***Smith, D.***	N	N	Y	Y	N	Y	N	Y
PENNSYLVANIA								
1 Foglietta	Y	Y	N	N	Y	N	Y	N
2 Gray	Y	N	N	?	?	?	?	?
3 Borski	?	?	X	?	Y	N	Y	N
4 Kolter	Y	N	N	N	Y	N	N	N
5 ***Schulze***	Y	N	Y	N	N	Y	N	Y
6 Yatron	Y	Y	N	N	N	N	Y	N
7 Edgar	Y	Y	N	?	?	?	?	?
8 Kostmayer	Y	Y	N	N	Y	N	Y	Y
9 ***Shuster***	Y	N	Y	N	N	N	N	Y
10 ***McDade***	Y	N	N	N	N	N	?	N
11 Kanjorski	Y	Y	N	N	N	N	N	Y
12 Murtha	Y	N	N	N	N	N	N	N
13 ***Coughlin***	Y	Y	N	N	Y	N	N	Y
14 Coyne	Y	N	N	N	Y	N	Y	N
15 ***Ritter***	?	Y	Y	N	N	N	Y	Y
16 ***Walker***	N	Y	Y	N	N	Y	Y	Y
17 ***Gekas***	Y	N	Y	N	N	N	N	Y
18 Walgren	Y	Y	N	N	Y	N	Y	Y
19 ***Goodling***	N	N	Y	N	Y	N	N	Y
20 Gaydos	Y	N	N	N	N	N	N	N
21 ***Ridge***	Y	Y	N	N	Y	N	N	N
22 Murphy	Y	Y	N	N	N	N	Y	N
23 ***Clinger***	Y	N	N	N	N	N	N	N
RHODE ISLAND								
1 St Germain	Y	N	N	N	Y	N	N	N
2 ***Schneider***	Y	Y	N	N	Y	N	N	Y
SOUTH CAROLINA								
1 ***Hartnett***	?	?	#	?	?	?	?	?
2 ***Spence***	Y	N	N	N	N	?	?	?
3 Derrick	Y	N	N	N	N	N	N	N
4 ***Campbell***	Y	N	N	N	N	N	?	?
5 Spratt	Y	Y	N	N	Y	N	N	Y
6 Tallon	Y	N	N	N	N	N	Y	N
SOUTH DAKOTA								
AL Daschle	Y	Y	N	N	Y	N	N	N
TENNESSEE								
1 ***Quillen***	Y	N	N	N	N	N	N	Y
2 ***Duncan***	Y	N	N	N	N	N	N	N
3 Lloyd	Y	N	N	N	N	N	N	N
4 Cooper	Y	N	N	N	N	N	N	N
5 Boner	Y	N	N	N	N	N	N	N
6 Gordon	Y	N	N	N	N	N	N	N
7 ***Sundquist***	Y	N	N	N	N	Y	N	N
8 Jones	?	?	?	?	?	?	?	?
9 Ford	Y	N	N	N	Y	N	N	N
TEXAS								
1 Chapman	Y	N	N	Y	N	N	N	N
2 Wilson	Y	N	N	Y	N	N	N	N
3 ***Bartlett***	N	Y	Y	Y	N	Y	N	Y
4 Hall, R.	Y	N	N	Y	N	N	N	Y
5 Bryant	Y	Y	N	Y	N	N	Y	Y
6 ***Barton***	Y	Y	Y	N	N	Y	N	Y
7 ***Archer***	N	Y	Y	Y	N	Y	N	Y
8 ***Fields***	N	N	Y	Y	N	Y	N	Y
9 Brooks	Y	?	?	?	?	?	?	?
10 Pickle	Y	N	N	Y	N	N	N	N
11 Leath	Y	N	N	Y	N	N	N	N
12 Wright	Y	N	N	Y	N	N	?	N
13 ***Boulter***	Y	N	Y	Y	N	Y	N	N
14 ***Sweeney***	Y	N	Y	Y	N	Y	N	Y
15 de la Garza	Y	?	N	Y	N	N	Y	N
16 Coleman	Y	Y	N	Y	N	N	N	N
17 Stenholm	N	N	N	Y	N	N	Y	Y
18 Leland	Y	N	N	Y	Y	N	Y	N
19 ***Combest***	N	N	Y	Y	N	Y	N	Y
20 Gonzalez	Y	N	N	Y	Y	N	Y	N
21 ***Loeffler***	N	N	Y	Y	N	Y	N	Y
22 ***DeLay***	N	N	Y	Y	N	Y	N	N
23 Bustamante	Y	N	N	N	N	N	N	N
24 Frost	Y	N	N	?	?	?	?	?
25 Andrews	Y	Y	N	Y	N	N	N	Y
26 ***Armey***	N	Y	Y	Y	N	Y	N	Y
27 Ortiz	Y	N	N	Y	N	N	N	N
UTAH								
1 ***Hansen***	Y	N	Y	N	N	Y	N	Y
2 ***Monson***	N	N	Y	N	Y	Y	N	Y
3 ***Nielson***	Y	N	N	N	N	Y	Y	Y
VERMONT								
AL ***Jeffords***	Y	Y	N	N	Y	N	N	Y
VIRGINIA								
1 ***Bateman***	Y	N	N	N	N	N	N	N
2 ***Whitehurst***	Y	N	Y	N	N	N	N	Y
3 ***Bliley***	Y	N	N	N	N	N	N	N
4 Sisisky	Y	Y	N	N	N	N	Y	Y
5 Daniel	Y	Y	Y	N	N	N	N	N
6 Olin	Y	Y	Y	N	N	N	N	Y
7 ***Slaughter***	Y	N	Y	N	N	N	N	Y
8 ***Parris***	Y	N	Y	N	N	N	Y	N
9 Boucher	Y	N	N	N	?	N	N	N
10 ***Wolf***	Y	N	N	N	N	Y	N	N
WASHINGTON								
1 ***Miller***	Y	Y	Y	Y	Y	Y	N	Y
2 Swift	Y	N	N	Y	Y	N	N	N
3 Bonker	Y	N	N	Y	N	N	N	N
4 ***Morrison***	Y	N	N	Y	N	Y	N	N
5 Foley	Y	N	N	Y	N	N	N	N
6 Dicks	Y	N	N	Y	N	N	N	N
7 Lowry	N	Y	N	Y	Y	N	Y	N
8 ***Chandler***	Y	N	Y	Y	N	N	N	Y
WEST VIRGINIA								
1 Mollohan	Y	N	N	N	N	N	N	N
2 Staggers	Y	Y	Y	N	Y	N	N	N
3 Wise	Y	Y	N	N	Y	N	N	N
4 Rahall	Y	N	N	N	Y	N	N	N
WISCONSIN								
1 Aspin	Y	?	N	N	Y	N	Y	Y
2 Kastenmeier	Y	Y	N	N	Y	N	Y	N
3 ***Gunderson***	Y	N	N	N	N	Y	N	N
4 Kleczka	Y	N	N	N	Y	N	Y	N
5 Moody	Y	Y	N	N	Y	N	N	N
6 ***Petri***	N	Y	N	Y	Y	Y	Y	Y
7 Obey	Y	N	N	Y	N	N	N	?
8 ***Roth***	?	Y	Y	N	N	Y	Y	Y
9 ***Sensenbrenner***	N	Y	Y	N	N	Y	Y	Y
WYOMING								
AL ***Cheney***	Y	N	N	N	N	Y	N	Y

Southern states - Ala., Ark., Fla., Ga., Ky., La., Miss., N.C., Okla., S.C., Tenn., Texas, Va.

* The *Congressional Record* vote number is different from the CQ vote number because the *Record* includes quorum calls in its tally. CQ does not publish quorum call votes.

222. HR 5162. Energy and Water Appropriations, Fiscal 1987. Passage of the bill to appropriate $15,548,000,000 in fiscal 1987 for energy and water development programs. Passed 329-82: R 119-55; D 210-27 (ND 138-22, SD 72-5), July 23, 1986. The president had requested $15,867,643,000 in new budget authority.

223. HR 5177. Agriculture Appropriations, Fiscal 1987. Adoption of the rule (H Res 504) to waive points of order against the bill to appropriate $45.25 billion in fiscal 1987 for the Agriculture Department and related agencies. Adopted 364-48: R 128-43; D 236-5 (ND 162-1, SD 74-4), July 24, 1986.

224. HR 5205. Transportation Appropriations, Fiscal 1987. Adoption of the rule (H Res 507) to waive points of order against the bill to provide $10.28 billion in fiscal 1987 for transportation programs. Adopted 315-98: R 80-91; D 235-7 (ND 158-4, SD 77-3), July 24, 1986.

225. HR 5175. District of Columbia Appropriations, Fiscal 1987. Frenzel, R-Minn., amendment to reduce the federal payment to the District from $425,000,000 to $414,147,000. Adopted 230-176: R 153-19; D 77-157 (ND 37-122, SD 40-35), July 24, 1986.

226. HR 5175. District of Columbia Appropriations, Fiscal 1987. Walker, R-Pa., amendments to transfer $1 million in the District budget from the Arts and Humanities Commission to the District police department. Rejected en bloc 183-229: R 146-28; D 37-201 (ND 15-148, SD 22-53), July 24, 1986.

227. HR 5175. District of Columbia Appropriations, Fiscal 1987. Dixon, D-Calif., motion that the Committee of the Whole rise and report the bill back to the House. Motion agreed to 241-173: R 23-152; D 218-21 (ND 156-7, SD 62-14), July 24, 1986. (The effect of the vote was to prevent consideration of amendments limiting spending on the appropriations bill, in this case the Dannemeyer, R-Calif., amendment to kill a District law barring insurers from refusing coverage to persons who test positive for acquired immune deficiency syndrome (AIDS). Such amendments are in order only following a defeated motion to rise and report.)

228. HR 5175. District of Columbia Appropriations, Fiscal 1987. Passage of the bill to provide $530,027,000 in federal funds and $2,989,598,000 in District funds in fiscal 1987. Passed 296-117: R 76-97; D 220-20 (ND 154-9, SD 66-11), July 24, 1986. The president had requested new budget authority of $560,380,000 in federal funds and $2,989,598,000 in District funds.

229. HR 5177. Agriculture Appropriations, Fiscal 1987. Morrison, D-Conn., amendment to reduce each appropriation not required to be appropriated or otherwise made available by previously enacted law by 0.896 percent. Rejected 175-205: R 103-57; D 72-148 (ND 45-106, SD 27-42), July 24, 1986.

KEY

Y Voted for (yea).
\# Paired for.
\+ Announced for.
N Voted against (nay).
X Paired against.
\- Announced against.
P Voted "present."
C Voted "present" to avoid possible conflict of interest.
? Did not vote or otherwise make a position known.

Democrats ***Republicans***

	222	223	224	225	226	227	228	229
ALABAMA								
1 ***Callahan***	Y	N	N	Y	Y	N	Y	Y
2 ***Dickinson***	Y	N	N	Y	Y	N	N	N
3 Nichols	Y	Y	Y	Y	Y	Y	N	Y
4 Bevill	Y	Y	Y	N	N	Y	Y	N
5 Flippo	Y	Y	Y	N	N	Y	Y	N
6 Erdreich	Y	Y	Y	N	N	N	Y	Y
7 Shelby	Y	Y	Y	Y	N	N	N	N
ALASKA								
AL ***Young***	Y	N	Y	N	Y	N	N	Y
ARIZONA								
1 ***McCain***	Y	Y	N	Y	Y	N	Y	Y
2 Udall	?	Y	Y	N	N	Y	Y	N
3 ***Stump***	Y	N	N	Y	Y	N	N	Y
4 ***Rudd***	Y	Y	N	Y	Y	N	N	N
5 ***Kolbe***	Y	Y	N	Y	Y	Y	Y	Y
ARKANSAS								
1 Alexander	Y	Y	Y	N	N	Y	Y	N
2 Robinson	Y	Y	Y	Y	Y	N	Y	N
3 ***Hammerschmidt***	Y	Y	Y	Y	Y	N	N	N
4 Anthony	Y	Y	Y	Y	N	Y	Y	N
CALIFORNIA								
1 Bosco	Y	Y	Y	Y	N	Y	Y	Y
2 ***Chappie***	Y	?	?	?	?	?	?	?
3 Matsui	Y	Y	Y	N	N	Y	Y	N
4 Fazio	Y	Y	Y	N	N	Y	Y	N
5 Burton	Y	Y	Y	N	N	Y	Y	N
6 Boxer	Y	Y	Y	N	N	Y	Y	N
7 Miller	?	Y	Y	N	N	Y	Y	N
8 Dellums	Y	Y	Y	N	N	Y	Y	N
9 Stark	Y	Y	Y	?	N	Y	Y	N
10 Edwards	Y	Y	Y	N	N	Y	Y	N
11 Lantos	Y	Y	Y	N	N	Y	Y	?
12 ***Zschau***	Y	Y	?	Y	Y	N	Y	Y
13 Mineta	Y	Y	Y	N	N	Y	Y	N
14 ***Shumway***	N	N	N	Y	Y	N	N	Y
15 Coelho	Y	Y	Y	N	N	Y	Y	N
16 Panetta	Y	Y	Y	N	N	Y	Y	N
17 ***Pashayan***	Y	Y	N	Y	Y	N	Y	N
18 Lehman	Y	Y	Y	Y	N	Y	Y	N
19 ***Lagomarsino***	Y	Y	N	Y	Y	N	N	Y
20 ***Thomas***	Y	Y	N	Y	Y	N	Y	Y
21 ***Fiedler***	Y	Y	N	Y	Y	N	Y	Y
22 ***Moorhead***	N	Y	Y	Y	Y	N	N	Y
23 Beilenson	Y	Y	Y	N	N	Y	Y	N
24 Waxman	Y	Y	N	N	N	Y	Y	N
25 Roybal	Y	Y	Y	N	N	Y	Y	N
26 Berman	Y	Y	Y	N	N	Y	Y	N
27 Levine	Y	?	Y	N	N	Y	Y	N
28 Dixon	Y	Y	Y	N	N	Y	Y	N
29 Hawkins	Y	Y	Y	N	N	Y	Y	N
30 Martinez	Y	Y	Y	N	N	Y	Y	N
31 Dymally	Y	Y	Y	N	N	Y	Y	N
32 Anderson	Y	Y	Y	Y	N	Y	Y	Y
33 ***Dreier***	N	N	N	Y	Y	N	N	Y
34 Torres	Y	Y	Y	N	N	Y	Y	N
35 ***Lewis***	Y	Y	N	N	Y	N	Y	N
36 Brown	Y	Y	Y	N	N	Y	Y	N
37 ***McCandless***	Y	N	N	Y	Y	N	Y	?
38 ***Dornan***	Y	Y	N	Y	Y	N	N	?
39 ***Dannemeyer***	Y	N	N	Y	Y	N	N	Y
40 ***Badham***	N	N	N	Y	Y	N	N	Y
41 ***Lowery***	Y	Y	Y	N	N	N	Y	N
42 ***Lungren***	Y	N	N	Y	Y	N	N	Y
43 ***Packard***	Y	Y	Y	Y	Y	N	Y	?
44 Bates	N	Y	Y	Y	N	Y	Y	Y
45 ***Hunter***	Y	Y	N	Y	Y	N	N	Y
COLORADO								
1 Schroeder	N	Y	Y	Y	N	Y	N	N
2 Wirth	Y	Y	Y	Y	N	Y	N	?
3 ***Strang***	Y	N	N	Y	Y	N	Y	Y
4 ***Brown***	N	N	N	Y	Y	N	N	Y
5 ***Kramer***	Y	Y	N	Y	Y	N	N	Y
6 ***Schaefer***	N	Y	N	Y	Y	N	N	Y
CONNECTICUT								
1 Kennelly	Y	Y	Y	Y	N	Y	Y	Y
2 Gejdenson	Y	Y	Y	N	N	Y	Y	Y
3 Morrison	N	Y	Y	Y	N	Y	Y	Y
4 ***McKinney***	Y	Y	Y	Y	N	Y	Y	?
5 ***Rowland***	Y	Y	Y	Y	Y	N	N	Y
6 ***Johnson***	Y	Y	Y	Y	N	Y	Y	Y
DELAWARE								
AL Carper	Y	Y	Y	Y	N	Y	Y	Y
FLORIDA								
1 Hutto	Y	Y	Y	Y	Y	N	N	Y
2 Fuqua	Y	Y	Y	N	N	?	?	?
3 Bennett	Y	Y	Y	Y	Y	Y	Y	Y
4 Chappell	Y	Y	Y	N	N	N	Y	N
5 ***McCollum***	Y	N	N	Y	Y	N	Y	Y
6 MacKay	N	N	N	Y	N	Y	Y	Y
7 Gibbons	Y	Y	Y	Y	Y	Y	Y	Y
8 ***Young***	Y	Y	N	N	Y	N	Y	Y
9 ***Bilirakis***	Y	Y	N	Y	Y	N	Y	Y
10 ***Ireland***	Y	?	?	Y	Y	N	N	Y
11 Nelson	Y	Y	Y	Y	Y	N	Y	Y
12 ***Lewis***	Y	Y	N	Y	Y	N	N	N
13 ***Mack***	N	N	N	Y	Y	N	N	Y
14 Mica	Y	Y	Y	Y	N	Y	N	Y
15 ***Shaw***	Y	N	N	Y	Y	N	N	?
16 Smith	Y	Y	Y	Y	Y	Y	Y	Y
17 Lehman	Y	Y	Y	N	N	Y	Y	N
18 Pepper	Y	Y	Y	N	N	Y	Y	N
19 Fascell	Y	Y	Y	N	?	Y	Y	N
GEORGIA								
1 Thomas	Y	Y	Y	Y	N	Y	Y	N
2 Hatcher	Y	Y	Y	?	N	Y	Y	N
3 Ray	N	Y	Y	Y	N	N	Y	Y
4 ***Swindall***	N	Y	N	Y	Y	N	N	Y
5 Fowler	?	?	?	?	?	?	?	?
6 ***Gingrich***	N	N	N	Y	Y	N	Y	Y
7 Darden	Y	Y	Y	Y	Y	Y	Y	Y
8 Rowland	Y	Y	Y	Y	N	Y	Y	N
9 Jenkins	Y	Y	Y	Y	N	Y	Y	?
10 Barnard	Y	N	Y	Y	N	Y	Y	Y
HAWAII								
1 Vacancy								
2 Akaka	Y	Y	Y	N	N	Y	Y	N
IDAHO								
1 ***Craig***	N	N	N	Y	Y	N	Y	Y
2 Stallings	Y	Y	Y	Y	Y	Y	Y	Y
ILLINOIS								
1 Hayes	N	Y	Y	N	N	Y	Y	N
2 Savage	N	?	Y	N	N	Y	Y	?
3 Russo	Y	Y	Y	N	N	N	Y	Y
4 Vacancy								
5 Lipinski	Y	Y	Y	N	Y	Y	Y	?
6 ***Hyde***	N	N	N	Y	N	N	Y	Y
7 Collins	Y	Y	Y	?	N	Y	Y	N
8 Rostenkowski	Y	Y	Y	Y	N	Y	Y	Y
9 Yates	Y	Y	Y	N	N	Y	Y	N
10 ***Porter***	Y	N	N	Y	Y	N	Y	Y
11 Annunzio	Y	Y	Y	N	N	Y	Y	Y
12 ***Crane***	N	N	N	Y	Y	N	N	Y
13 ***Fawell***	N	N	N	N	Y	N	N	Y
14 ***Grotberg***	?	?	?	?	?	?	?	?
15 ***Madigan***	N	Y	N	Y	Y	N	N	N
16 ***Martin***	N	N	N	Y	Y	N	N	Y
17 Evans	Y	Y	Y	N	N	Y	Y	N
18 ***Michel***	N	Y	Y	N	?	N	Y	Y
19 Bruce	Y	Y	Y	Y	Y	Y	Y	N
20 Durbin	Y	Y	Y	N	N	Y	Y	N
21 Price	Y	Y	Y	N	N	Y	Y	N
22 Gray	Y	Y	Y	N	N	Y	Y	N
INDIANA								
1 Visclosky	Y	Y	Y	Y	N	Y	Y	Y
2 Sharp	N	Y	Y	Y	Y	N	Y	N
3 ***Hiler***	N	Y	N	Y	Y	N	N	Y
4 ***Coats***	N	Y	N	Y	Y	N	N	Y
5 ***Hillis***	Y	Y	Y	Y	Y	N	Y	?

ND - Northern Democrats SD - Southern Democrats

* Corresponding to Congressional Record Votes 245, 246, 247, 248, 249, 250, 251, 252

	222	223	224	225	226	227	228	229
6 ***Burton***	N	Y	Y	Y	Y	N	N	Y
7 ***Myers***	Y	Y	Y	N	Y	Y	Y	N
8 McCloskey	Y	Y	?	Y	N	N	Y	Y
9 Hamilton	Y	Y	Y	Y	N	Y	Y	Y
10 Jacobs	N	Y	Y	Y	N	Y	Y	Y
IOWA								
1 ***Leach***	N	Y	N	Y	N	Y	N	N
2 ***Tauke***	N	Y	N	Y	N	N	N	N
3 ***Evans***	N	Y	Y	Y	Y	N	N	Y
4 Smith	Y	Y	Y	N	N	Y	Y	N
5 ***Lightfoot***	Y	Y	N	Y	Y	N	N	N
6 Bedell	Y	Y	Y	N	N	Y	Y	N
KANSAS								
1 ***Roberts***	N	Y	N	Y	Y	N	N	Y
2 Slattery	N	Y	Y	Y	N	N	Y	Y
3 ***Meyers***	Y	Y	Y	Y	N	N	N	Y
4 Glickman	N	Y	Y	Y	N	N	Y	Y
5 ***Whittaker***	Y	Y	Y	Y	Y	N	N	Y
KENTUCKY								
1 Hubbard	Y	Y	Y	Y	Y	N	N	Y
2 Natcher	Y	Y	Y	N	N	Y	Y	N
3 Mazzoli	Y	Y	Y	N	N	N	Y	N
4 ***Snyder***	Y	Y	Y	Y	Y	N	N	?
5 ***Rogers***	Y	Y	Y	Y	Y	N	N	N
6 ***Hopkins***	Y	Y	Y	Y	Y	N	N	Y
7 Perkins	Y	Y	Y	N	N	Y	Y	N
LOUISIANA								
1 ***Livingston***	Y	Y	Y	Y	Y	N	N	N
2 Boggs	Y	Y	Y	N	N	Y	Y	N
3 Tauzin	Y	Y	Y	Y	Y	Y	Y	Y
4 Roemer	Y	Y	Y	Y	Y	Y	Y	Y
5 Huckaby	Y	Y	N	?	?	?	?	?
6 ***Moore***	?	Y	Y	Y	Y	N	Y	?
7 Breaux	?	Y	Y	Y	?	Y	Y	?
8 Long	Y	Y	Y	N	N	Y	Y	N
MAINE								
1 ***McKernan***	Y	Y	Y	Y	Y	N	Y	Y
2 ***Snowe***	Y	Y	Y	Y	Y	N	Y	N
MARYLAND								
1 Dyson	Y	Y	Y	Y	Y	Y	Y	Y
2 ***Bentley***	Y	Y	Y	Y	Y	Y	Y	N
3 Mikulski	Y	Y	Y	N	X	?	?	?
4 ***Holt***	Y	Y	N	N	Y	N	Y	N
5 Hoyer	Y	Y	Y	N	N	Y	Y	N
6 Byron	Y	Y	Y	Y	Y	Y	Y	Y
7 Mitchell	?	Y	Y	N	N	Y	Y	?
8 Barnes	?	Y	Y	N	N	Y	Y	?
MASSACHUSETTS								
1 ***Conte***	Y	Y	Y	N	N	Y	Y	N
2 Boland	Y	Y	?	N	N	Y	Y	?
3 Early	Y	Y	Y	N	N	Y	Y	?
4 Frank	Y	Y	Y	N	N	Y	Y	Y
5 Atkins	Y	Y	Y	N	N	Y	Y	Y
6 Mavroules	Y	Y	Y	N	N	Y	Y	Y
7 Markey	Y	Y	Y	N	N	Y	Y	Y
8 O'Neill								
9 Moakley	Y	Y	Y	N	N	Y	Y	N
10 Studds	N	Y	Y	N	N	Y	Y	N
11 Donnelly	Y	Y	Y	N	N	Y	Y	N
MICHIGAN								
1 Conyers	N	Y	Y	N	N	Y	Y	N
2 ***Pursell***	N	Y	Y	Y	Y	N	Y	Y
3 Wolpe	N	Y	Y	Y	N	Y	Y	N
4 ***Siljander***	N	Y	Y	Y	Y	N	N	Y
5 ***Henry***	N	Y	N	Y	Y	N	N	Y
6 Carr	Y	Y	Y	N	N	Y	Y	N
7 Kildee	Y	Y	Y	N	N	Y	Y	N
8 Traxler	Y	Y	Y	N	N	Y	Y	N
9 ***Vander Jagt***	Y	Y	Y	Y	Y	N	Y	Y
10 ***Schuette***	Y	Y	Y	Y	Y	N	N	N
11 ***Davis***	Y	Y	Y	Y	Y	N	Y	N
12 Bonior	N	Y	Y	N	N	Y	Y	N
13 Crockett	N	Y	Y	N	N	Y	Y	N
14 Hertel	N	Y	Y	N	N	Y	Y	N
15 Ford	Y	?	?	?	N	Y	Y	N
16 Dingell	Y	Y	Y	?	N	Y	Y	N
17 Levin	Y	Y	Y	N	N	Y	Y	Y
18 ***Broomfield***	Y	Y	Y	Y	Y	N	N	Y
MINNESOTA								
1 Penny	Y	Y	N	Y	N	Y	Y	Y
2 ***Weber***	N	Y	N	Y	Y	N	N	N
3 ***Frenzel***	N	N	N	Y	N	Y	Y	Y
4 Vento	N	Y	Y	N	N	Y	Y	Y
5 Sabo	Y	Y	Y	N	N	Y	Y	N
6 Sikorski	N	Y	Y	N	N	N	Y	N
7 ***Stangeland***	Y	Y	Y	Y	Y	N	Y	N
8 Oberstar	Y	?	?	N	N	Y	Y	N
MISSISSIPPI								
1 Whitten	Y	Y	Y	N	N	Y	Y	N
2 ***Franklin***	Y	Y	Y	Y	Y	N	Y	N
3 Montgomery	Y	Y	Y	Y	Y	N	N	N
4 Dowdy	Y	Y	Y	N	N	Y	Y	N
5 ***Lott***	Y	Y	N	Y	Y	N	N	Y
MISSOURI								
1 Clay	Y	Y	Y	N	N	Y	Y	N
2 Young	Y	Y	Y	N	N	?	?	?
3 Gephardt	Y	Y	Y	N	N	Y	Y	?
4 Skelton	Y	Y	Y	N	N	Y	Y	N
5 Wheat	Y	Y	Y	N	N	Y	Y	N
6 ***Coleman***	?	Y	Y	Y	Y	N	N	N
7 ***Taylor***	Y	Y	Y	N	Y	N	N	N
8 ***Emerson***	Y	Y	Y	Y	Y	N	N	N
9 Volkmer	Y	Y	Y	Y	Y	Y	N	N
MONTANA								
1 Williams	Y	Y	Y	?	N	Y	N	N
2 ***Marlenee***	Y	N	N	Y	Y	N	N	?
NEBRASKA								
1 ***Bereuter***	Y	Y	Y	Y	N	N	Y	N
2 ***Daub***	Y	Y	Y	Y	Y	N	N	N
3 ***Smith***	Y	Y	Y	Y	Y	Y	Y	N
NEVADA								
1 Reid	Y	Y	Y	Y	N	Y	Y	Y
2 ***Vucanovich***	Y	Y	N	Y	Y	N	N	Y
NEW HAMPSHIRE								
1 ***Smith***	N	N	N	Y	Y	N	N	Y
2 ***Gregg***	N	N	N	Y	Y	N	N	Y
NEW JERSEY								
1 Florio	Y	Y	Y	N	N	Y	Y	N
2 Hughes	Y	Y	Y	Y	Y	Y	Y	Y
3 Howard	Y	Y	Y	N	N	Y	Y	N
4 ***Smith***	Y	Y	Y	Y	Y	N	Y	Y
5 ***Roukema***	Y	Y	Y	Y	Y	N	Y	Y
6 Dwyer	Y	Y	Y	N	N	Y	Y	N
7 ***Rinaldo***	Y	Y	Y	Y	Y	N	N	Y
8 Roe	Y	Y	Y	N	N	Y	Y	N
9 Torricelli	Y	Y	Y	Y	Y	Y	Y	N
10 Rodino	Y	Y	Y	N	N	Y	Y	N
11 ***Gallo***	Y	Y	Y	Y	Y	Y	N	Y
12 ***Courter***	Y	Y	Y	Y	Y	N	N	Y
13 ***Saxton***	Y	Y	Y	Y	Y	N	Y	Y
14 Guarini	Y	Y	Y	N	Y	Y	Y	N
NEW MEXICO								
1 ***Lujan***	Y	Y	Y	Y	Y	N	N	Y
2 ***Skeen***	Y	Y	Y	Y	Y	N	Y	N
3 Richardson	Y	Y	Y	N	N	Y	Y	Y
NEW YORK								
1 ***Carney***	Y	?	?	Y	Y	N	N	Y
2 Downey	Y	Y	Y	N	N	Y	Y	N
3 Mrazek	Y	Y	Y	N	N	Y	Y	N
4 ***Lent***	Y	Y	Y	Y	Y	N	N	Y
5 ***McGrath***	Y	Y	Y	Y	Y	N	N	Y
6 Vacancy								
7 Ackerman	N	Y	Y	N	N	Y	Y	N
8 Scheuer	Y	Y	Y	N	N	Y	N	N
9 Manton	Y	Y	Y	N	N	Y	Y	N
10 Schumer	Y	?	?	?	?	?	?	?
11 Towns	Y	Y	Y	N	N	Y	Y	N
12 Owens	Y	Y	Y	N	N	Y	Y	?
13 Solarz	Y	Y	Y	N	N	Y	Y	N
14 ***Molinari***	Y	Y	Y	Y	Y	N	Y	Y
15 ***Green***	Y	Y	Y	N	N	Y	Y	Y
16 Rangel	Y	Y	Y	N	N	Y	Y	N
17 Weiss	N	Y	Y	N	N	Y	N	N
18 Garcia	?	Y	Y	N	N	Y	Y	N
19 Biaggi	Y	Y	Y	N	N	Y	Y	N
20 ***DioGuardi***	Y	Y	Y	Y	Y	N	N	Y
21 ***Fish***	Y	Y	Y	Y	N	N	Y	N
22 ***Gilman***	Y	Y	Y	N	N	N	?	N
23 Stratton	Y	Y	N	Y	N	Y	Y	N
24 ***Solomon***	N	N	N	Y	Y	N	N	N
25 ***Boehlert***	Y	Y	Y	Y	N	N	Y	Y
26 ***Martin***	Y	Y	Y	Y	Y	N	Y	?
27 ***Wortley***	Y	Y	Y	Y	Y	N	Y	N
28 McHugh	Y	Y	Y	N	N	Y	Y	N
29 ***Horton***	Y	Y	Y	N	N	Y	Y	?
30 ***Eckert***	N	N	N	Y	Y	N	Y	Y
31 ***Kemp***	Y	?	Y	Y	Y	N	Y	Y
32 LaFalce	Y	Y	Y	N	N	Y	Y	Y
33 Nowak	Y	Y	Y	N	N	Y	Y	N
34 Lundine	?	Y	Y	?	?	?	?	?
NORTH CAROLINA								
1 Jones	Y	Y	Y	N	N	Y	Y	N
2 Valentine	Y	Y	Y	Y	Y	Y	Y	N
3 Whitley	Y	Y	Y	N	N	Y	Y	N
4 ***Cobey***	Y	N	N	Y	Y	N	N	N
5 Neal	Y	Y	Y	Y	Y	Y	Y	N
6 ***Coble***	Y	Y	N	Y	Y	N	N	N
7 Rose	Y	Y	Y	N	N	Y	Y	?
8 Hefner	Y	Y	Y	N	N	Y	Y	N
9 ***McMillan***	Y	Y	Y	Y	?	?	?	?
10 Vacancy								
11 ***Hendon***	Y	Y	N	Y	Y	N	N	N
NORTH DAKOTA								
AL Dorgan	Y	Y	Y	Y	N	Y	Y	N
OHIO								
1 Luken	Y	Y	Y	N	N	Y	Y	Y
2 ***Gradison***	N	Y	N	Y	N	Y	Y	Y
3 Hall	Y	Y	Y	Y	N	N	Y	Y
4 ***Oxley***	N	N	N	Y	Y	N	N	Y
5 ***Latta***	N	Y	N	Y	Y	N	N	N
6 ***McEwen***	Y	Y	Y	Y	Y	N	N	N
7 ***DeWine***	N	Y	N	Y	Y	N	N	Y
8 ***Kindness***	N	Y	N	Y	Y	N	N	N
9 Kaptur	Y	Y	Y	N	N	Y	Y	N
10 ***Miller***	Y	Y	Y	Y	Y	N	N	Y
11 Eckart	Y	Y	Y	Y	Y	Y	N	N
12 ***Kasich***	N	Y	N	Y	Y	N	Y	Y
13 Pease	Y	Y	Y	N	N	Y	Y	N
14 Seiberling	Y	Y	Y	N	N	Y	Y	Y
15 ***Wylie***	N	Y	Y	Y	Y	N	Y	Y
16 ***Regula***	Y	Y	Y	Y	Y	N	Y	Y
17 Traficant	Y	Y	Y	N	N	Y	Y	N
18 Applegate	Y	Y	Y	N	N	Y	Y	N
19 Feighan	Y	Y	Y	N	N	Y	Y	Y
20 Oakar	Y	Y	Y	N	N	Y	Y	N
21 Stokes	Y	Y	Y	N	N	Y	Y	N
OKLAHOMA								
1 Jones	Y	Y	Y	Y	Y	Y	N	N
2 Synar	Y	Y	Y	N	N	Y	Y	N
3 Watkins	Y	Y	Y	N	Y	Y	Y	N
4 McCurdy	Y	Y	Y	Y	Y	Y	Y	Y
5 ***Edwards***	Y	Y	Y	Y	Y	N	N	N
6 English	Y	Y	Y	Y	Y	Y	N	N
OREGON								
1 AuCoin	Y	Y	Y	N	N	Y	N	N
2 ***Smith, R.***	Y	Y	N	Y	Y	N	N	Y
3 Wyden	Y	Y	Y	Y	N	Y	Y	Y
4 Weaver	N	Y	Y	Y	N	Y	N	Y
5 ***Smith, D.***	N	N	N	Y	Y	N	?	?
PENNSYLVANIA								
1 Foglietta	Y	Y	Y	N	N	Y	Y	N
2 Gray	?	Y	Y	N	N	Y	Y	Y
3 Borski	Y	Y	Y	N	N	Y	Y	Y
4 Kolter	Y	Y	Y	N	Y	Y	Y	N
5 ***Schulze***	N	?	?	?	Y	N	N	Y
6 Yatron	Y	Y	Y	N	Y	Y	Y	N
7 Edgar	?	Y	Y	N	N	Y	Y	N
8 Kostmayer	Y	Y	Y	Y	N	Y	Y	Y
9 ***Shuster***	Y	Y	N	Y	Y	N	N	Y
10 ***McDade***	Y	Y	Y	N	N	Y	Y	N
11 Kanjorski	Y	Y	Y	N	N	Y	Y	N
12 Murtha	Y	Y	Y	N	N	Y	Y	N
13 ***Coughlin***	Y	Y	Y	N	N	Y	Y	Y
14 Coyne	Y	Y	Y	N	N	Y	Y	N
15 ***Ritter***	N	Y	Y	Y	Y	N	N	Y
16 ***Walker***	N	N	N	Y	Y	N	N	Y
17 ***Gekas***	Y	N	Y	N	Y	N	Y	N
18 Walgren	Y	Y	Y	N	Y	Y	Y	Y
19 ***Goodling***	N	Y	Y	N	Y	N	Y	Y
20 Gaydos	Y	Y	Y	Y	N	Y	Y	N
21 ***Ridge***	Y	N	Y	Y	Y	N	Y	Y
22 Murphy	Y	Y	Y	N	Y	Y	Y	Y
23 ***Clinger***	Y	Y	Y	Y	Y	Y	Y	N
RHODE ISLAND								
1 St Germain	Y	Y	Y	N	N	Y	Y	Y
2 ***Schneider***	Y	Y	Y	Y	N	Y	Y	Y
SOUTH CAROLINA								
1 ***Hartnett***	?	?	?	?	#	?	?	?
2 ***Spence***	?	?	?	?	Y	N	Y	N
3 Derrick	Y	Y	Y	Y	N	Y	Y	N
4 ***Campbell***	?	?	?	?	?	?	?	?
5 Spratt	Y	Y	Y	Y	N	Y	Y	N
6 Tallon	Y	Y	Y	Y	N	Y	Y	?
SOUTH DAKOTA								
AL Daschle	Y	Y	Y	Y	N	Y	Y	N
TENNESSEE								
1 ***Quillen***	Y	Y	Y	Y	Y	N	N	N
2 ***Duncan***	Y	Y	Y	Y	Y	Y	N	N
3 Lloyd	Y	Y	Y	Y	Y	N	N	N
4 Cooper	Y	Y	Y	N	N	Y	Y	Y
5 Boner	Y	Y	Y	?	?	?	?	?
6 Gordon	Y	Y	Y	N	N	Y	Y	Y
7 ***Sundquist***	Y	Y	N	Y	Y	N	N	N
8 Jones	?	?	?	?	?	?	?	?
9 Ford	Y	Y	Y	?	N	Y	Y	N
TEXAS								
1 Chapman	Y	Y	Y	Y	N	Y	Y	Y
2 Wilson	Y	Y	Y	N	N	Y	Y	N
3 ***Bartlett***	N	N	N	Y	Y	N	N	Y
4 Hall, R.	N	Y	N	Y	Y	N	N	?
5 Bryant	Y	Y	Y	N	Y	Y	Y	Y
6 ***Barton***	N	N	N	Y	Y	N	N	N
7 ***Archer***	N	N	N	Y	Y	N	N	Y
8 ***Fields***	Y	N	N	Y	Y	N	N	Y
9 Brooks	?	Y	Y	Y	N	Y	Y	N
10 Pickle	Y	?	Y	Y	N	Y	Y	N
11 Leath	Y	N	Y	N	N	Y	Y	Y
12 Wright	Y	Y	Y	?	?	Y	Y	?
13 ***Boulter***	Y	Y	N	Y	Y	N	N	N
14 ***Sweeney***	Y	Y	N	Y	Y	N	Y	N
15 de la Garza	Y	Y	Y	N	N	Y	Y	N
16 Coleman	Y	Y	Y	N	N	Y	Y	N
17 Stenholm	N	N	Y	Y	Y	N	N	Y
18 Leland	Y	Y	Y	N	N	Y	Y	N
19 ***Combest***	Y	Y	N	Y	Y	N	Y	N
20 Gonzalez	Y	Y	Y	N	N	Y	Y	N
21 ***Loeffler***	Y	Y	Y	?	Y	N	N	N
22 ***DeLay***	Y	N	N	Y	Y	N	N	Y
23 Bustamante	Y	Y	Y	N	N	Y	Y	N
24 Frost	?	?	Y	N	N	Y	Y	Y
25 Andrews	Y	Y	Y	Y	N	Y	Y	Y
26 ***Armey***	N	N	N	Y	Y	N	N	Y
27 Ortiz	Y	Y	Y	N	N	Y	Y	?
UTAH								
1 ***Hansen***	Y	Y	N	Y	Y	N	N	?
2 ***Monson***	Y	N	N	Y	Y	N	N	?
3 ***Nielson***	Y	Y	N	Y	Y	N	Y	Y
VERMONT								
AL ***Jeffords***	N	Y	Y	Y	N	Y	Y	N
VIRGINIA								
1 ***Bateman***	Y	Y	N	Y	N	N	Y	N
2 ***Whitehurst***	Y	Y	N	Y	N	Y	Y	?
3 ***Bliley***	Y	Y	N	Y	N	N	Y	Y
4 Sisisky	Y	Y	Y	Y	N	Y	Y	Y
5 Daniel	Y	Y	Y	Y	N	N	Y	Y
6 Olin	N	Y	Y	Y	N	Y	Y	Y
7 ***Slaughter***	N	Y	N	?	Y	N	Y	Y
8 ***Parris***	Y	Y	N	N	Y	N	Y	Y
9 Boucher	Y	Y	Y	N	N	?	Y	?
10 ***Wolf***	Y	Y	Y	N	N	N	Y	Y
WASHINGTON								
1 ***Miller***	N	N	N	Y	N	Y	Y	Y
2 Swift	Y	Y	Y	N	N	Y	Y	N
3 Bonker	Y	Y	?	?	?	?	?	?
4 ***Morrison***	Y	Y	Y	Y	N	N	N	N
5 Foley	Y	Y	Y	N	N	Y	Y	N
6 Dicks	Y	Y	Y	N	N	Y	Y	N
7 Lowry	N	N	N	N	N	Y	Y	?
8 ***Chandler***	N	Y	Y	Y	N	Y	Y	Y
WEST VIRGINIA								
1 Mollohan	Y	Y	Y	N	N	Y	Y	N
2 Staggers	Y	Y	Y	N	N	Y	Y	N
3 Wise	Y	Y	Y	N	N	Y	Y	N
4 Rahall	Y	Y	Y	N	N	Y	Y	N
WISCONSIN								
1 Aspin	Y	Y	Y	N	?	Y	Y	Y
2 Kastenmeier	Y	Y	Y	?	N	Y	Y	N
3 ***Gunderson***	Y	Y	Y	Y	Y	Y	N	N
4 Kleczka	Y	Y	Y	N	N	Y	Y	?
5 Moody	N	Y	Y	N	N	Y	Y	Y
6 ***Petri***	N	Y	N	Y	Y	N	N	Y
7 Obey	Y	Y	Y	N	N	Y	Y	N
8 ***Roth***	N	Y	N	Y	Y	N	Y	N
9 ***Sensenbrenner***	N	Y	N	Y	Y	N	N	Y
WYOMING								
AL ***Cheney***	Y	N	N	Y	N	N	N	Y

Southern states - Ala., Ark., Fla., Ga., Ky., La., Miss., N.C., Okla., S.C., Tenn., Texas, Va.

* The *Congressional Record* vote number is different from the CQ vote number because the *Record* includes quorum calls in its tally. CQ does not publish quorum call votes.

230. HR 5177. Agriculture Appropriations, Fiscal 1987. Passage of the bill to appropriate $45,249,103,000 for the Department of Agriculture and related agencies in fiscal 1987. Passed 329-49: R 126-35; D 203-14 (ND 137-11, SD 66-3), July 24, 1986. The president had requested $45,255,332,000 in total budget authority.

231. Procedural Motion. Sensenbrenner, R-Wis., motion to approve the House *Journal* of Monday, July 28. Motion agreed to 270-117: R 54-109; D 216-8 (ND 144-7, SD 72-1), July 29, 1986.

232. H Res 475. Romania Trade. Gibbons, D-Fla., motion to table (kill) the Crane, R-Ill., motion to discharge the Ways and Means Committee from consideration of the resolution to express the House's disapproval of President Reagan's decision to continue special trade privileges for Romania by renewing most-favored-nation status for that country. Motion agreed to 216-190: R 41-130; D 175-60 (ND 132-25, SD 43-35), July 29, 1986. (The effect of the Crane motion would have been to place the House on record against President Reagan's decision to continue the special trade privileges for Romania.) A "yea" was a vote supporting the president's position.

233. HR 5203. Legislative Branch Appropriations, Fiscal 1987. Cobey, R-N.C., amendment to reduce funding for House committee staff from $48,000,000 to $43,691,000. Rejected 172-237: R 144-25; D 28-212 (ND 12-150, SD 16-62), July 29, 1986.

234. HR 5203. Legislative Branch Appropriations, Fiscal 1987. Swindall, R-Ga., amendment to cut funding for House office buildings by $91,450 to phase out the jobs of 14 automatic-elevator operators. Rejected 168-238: R 130-41; D 38-197 (ND 15-146, SD 23-51), July 29, 1986.

235. HR 5203. Legislative Branch Appropriations, Fiscal 1987. Frenzel, R-Minn., amendment to reduce most accounts in the bill by 3.51 percent, bringing spending approximately to fiscal 1986 levels. Rejected 199-209: R 156-14; D 43-195 (ND 20-142, SD 23-53), July 29, 1986.

236. HR 5203. Legislative Branch Appropriations, Fiscal 1987. Passage of the bill to provide $1,305,264,000 in fiscal 1987 appropriations for the operations of the House of Representatives and other legislative agencies. Passed 266-146: R 45-127; D 221-19 (ND 152-9, SD 69-10), July 29, 1986.

237. Procedural Motion. Fields, R-Texas, motion to approve the House *Journal* of Tuesday, July 29. Motion agreed to 269-129: R 48-119; D 221-10 (ND 151-6, SD 70-4), July 30, 1986.

KEY

Y Voted for (yea).
Paired for.
+ Announced for.
N Voted against (nay).
X Paired against.
- Announced against.
P Voted "present."
C Voted "present" to avoid possible conflict of interest.
? Did not vote or otherwise make a position known.

Democrats *Republicans*

	230	231	232	233	234	235	236	237
ALABAMA								
1 ***Callahan***	Y	Y	N	Y	Y	Y	Y	Y
2 ***Dickinson***	Y	N	N	Y	N	Y	Y	N
3 Nichols	Y	Y	N	N	N	Y	Y	Y
4 Bevill	Y	Y	N	N	N	N	Y	Y
5 Flippo	Y	Y	Y	?	N	N	Y	Y
6 Erdreich	Y	Y	N	Y	Y	Y	N	Y
7 Shelby	Y	Y	Y	N	N	N	Y	?
ALASKA								
AL ***Young***	Y	Y	N	N	N	N	Y	N
ARIZONA								
1 ***McCain***	Y	Y	N	Y	Y	Y	N	Y
2 Udall	Y	Y	?	N	N	N	Y	Y
3 ***Stump***	N	N	N	Y	Y	Y	N	N
4 ***Rudd***	Y	Y	N	N	N	N	Y	Y
5 ***Kolbe***	Y	N	N	Y	Y	Y	N	N
ARKANSAS								
1 Alexander	Y	Y	N	N	N	N	Y	Y
2 Robinson	Y	?	N	Y	Y	Y	N	Y
3 ***Hammerschmidt***	Y	Y	N	Y	N	Y	N	Y
4 Anthony	Y	Y	Y	N	N	N	Y	Y
CALIFORNIA								
1 Bosco	Y	Y	Y	N	?	N	Y	Y
2 ***Chappie***	?	N	N	Y	N	Y	N	N
3 Matsui	Y	Y	Y	N	N	N	Y	Y
4 Fazio	Y	Y	Y	N	N	N	Y	Y
5 Burton	Y	Y	Y	N	N	N	Y	Y
6 Boxer	Y	Y	Y	N	N	N	Y	Y
7 Miller	N	Y	Y	N	N	N	Y	Y
8 Dellums	Y	Y	Y	N	N	N	Y	Y
9 Stark	?	Y	Y	N	N	N	Y	Y
10 Edwards	Y	Y	Y	N	N	N	Y	Y
11 Lantos	?	Y	Y	N	N	N	Y	Y
12 ***Zschau***	Y	N	Y	Y	Y	Y	N	N
13 Mineta	Y	Y	Y	N	N	N	Y	Y
14 ***Shumway***	N	Y	N	Y	Y	Y	N	Y
15 Coelho	Y	?	?	N	N	N	Y	Y
16 Panetta	Y	Y	Y	N	N	N	Y	Y
17 ***Pashayan***	Y	N	N	N	Y	Y	N	N
18 Lehman	Y	Y	Y	N	N	N	Y	Y
19 ***Lagomarsino***	N	N	N	Y	Y	Y	N	N
20 ***Thomas***	Y	N	Y	Y	Y	?	N	N
21 ***Fiedler***	Y	N	N	Y	Y	Y	N	N
22 ***Moorhead***	N	N	N	Y	Y	Y	N	N
23 Beilenson	Y	Y	Y	N	N	N	Y	Y
24 Waxman	Y	Y	Y	N	N	N	Y	Y
25 Roybal	Y	Y	N	N	N	N	Y	Y
26 Berman	Y	Y	Y	N	N	N	Y	Y
27 Levine	Y	Y	Y	N	N	N	Y	Y
28 Dixon	Y	?	Y	N	N	N	Y	Y
29 Hawkins	Y	Y	Y	N	N	N	Y	N
30 Martinez	Y	?	Y	N	N	N	Y	Y
31 Dymally	Y	Y	Y	N	N	N	Y	Y
32 Anderson	N	Y	Y	N	N	N	Y	Y
33 ***Dreier***	N	N	N	Y	Y	Y	N	N
34 Torres	Y	Y	Y	N	N	N	Y	Y
35 ***Lewis***	Y	N	N	N	N	N	Y	N
36 Brown	Y	Y	Y	N	N	N	Y	Y
37 ***McCandless***	?	N	N	Y	Y	Y	N	N
38 ***Dornan***	?	N	N	Y	Y	Y	N	Y
39 ***Dannemeyer***	N	N	N	Y	Y	Y	N	N
40 ***Badham***	Y	N	N	Y	Y	Y	N	N
41 ***Lowery***	Y	P	N	Y	N	N	Y	N
42 ***Lungren***	N	N	N	Y	Y	Y	N	N
43 ***Packard***	?	N	N	Y	Y	Y	N	N
44 Bates	N	Y	Y	N	N	Y	Y	Y
45 ***Hunter***	Y	N	N	Y	Y	Y	N	N
COLORADO								
1 Schroeder	N	N	Y	N	Y	N	Y	N
2 Wirth	?	Y	Y	N	Y	Y	N	?
3 ***Strang***	Y	N	N	Y	Y	Y	N	N
4 ***Brown***	N	N	N	Y	Y	Y	N	N
5 ***Kramer***	Y	N	N	Y	Y	Y	N	N
6 ***Schaefer***	N	N	N	Y	Y	Y	N	N
CONNECTICUT								
1 Kennelly	Y	Y	Y	N	N	N	Y	Y
2 Gejdenson	Y	Y	Y	N	N	N	Y	Y
3 Morrison	N	Y	Y	N	N	N	Y	Y
4 ***McKinney***	Y	Y	Y	N	N	N	Y	?
5 ***Rowland***	Y	N	Y	Y	Y	Y	N	N
6 ***Johnson***	Y	Y	Y	Y	Y	Y	N	Y
DELAWARE								
AL Carper	Y	Y	Y	N	Y	Y	Y	Y
FLORIDA								
1 Hutto	Y	Y	N	Y	N	Y	Y	Y
2 Fuqua	?	Y	Y	N	N	N	Y	Y
3 Bennett	Y	Y	Y	Y	Y	Y	Y	Y
4 Chappell	Y	Y	Y	N	N	N	Y	Y
5 ***McCollum***	N	N	Y	Y	N	Y	N	Y
6 MacKay	Y	?	Y	N	Y	Y	Y	Y
7 Gibbons	N	Y	Y	N	Y	Y	Y	P
8 ***Young***	N	N	N	Y	Y	Y	Y	N
9 ***Bilirakis***	Y	N	N	Y	Y	Y	N	N
10 ***Ireland***	N	N	N	Y	Y	?	N	N
11 Nelson	N	Y	N	N	Y	Y	Y	Y
12 ***Lewis***	Y	N	X	Y	Y	Y	N	N
13 ***Mack***	N	N	N	Y	Y	Y	N	N
14 Mica	Y	P	Y	N	N	N	Y	Y
15 ***Shaw***	?	N	Y	Y	Y	Y	N	N
16 Smith	Y	Y	Y	N	?	N	Y	Y
17 Lehman	Y	Y	Y	N	N	N	Y	Y
18 Pepper	Y	Y	Y	N	N	N	Y	Y
19 Fascell	Y	Y	Y	N	N	N	Y	Y
GEORGIA								
1 Thomas	Y	Y	Y	N	Y	N	Y	Y
2 Hatcher	Y	Y	Y	N	N	N	Y	Y
3 Ray	Y	Y	N	Y	Y	Y	N	Y
4 ***Swindall***	N	N	N	Y	Y	Y	N	N
5 Fowler	?	?	?	?	?	?	?	?
6 ***Gingrich***	Y	N	N	?	Y	Y	N	N
7 Darden	Y	Y	N	Y	Y	N	Y	Y
8 Rowland	Y	Y	Y	N	N	N	Y	Y
9 Jenkins	?	Y	N	N	Y	N	Y	Y
10 Barnard	Y	?	#	?	?	X	#	Y
HAWAII								
1 Vacancy								
2 Akaka	Y	Y	N	N	N	N	Y	Y
IDAHO								
1 ***Craig***	Y	N	Y	Y	Y	Y	N	N
2 Stallings	Y	Y	Y	Y	Y	Y	Y	Y
ILLINOIS								
1 Hayes	Y	Y	Y	N	N	N	Y	?
2 Savage	?	Y	Y	N	N	N	Y	Y
3 Russo	N	Y	Y	N	N	N	Y	Y
4 Vacancy								
5 Lipinski	?	Y	Y	N	N	N	Y	Y
6 ***Hyde***	Y	N	N	Y	Y	Y	N	Y
7 Collins	Y	?	?	?	?	?	?	Y
8 Rostenkowski	Y	Y	Y	N	N	N	Y	Y
9 Yates	?	Y	Y	N	N	N	Y	Y
10 ***Porter***	Y	Y	N	Y	N	Y	Y	N
11 Annunzio	Y	Y	Y	N	N	N	Y	Y
12 ***Crane***	N	N	N	Y	Y	Y	N	N
13 ***Fawell***	N	N	N	Y	Y	Y	N	N
14 ***Grotberg***	?	?	?	?	?	?	?	?
15 ***Madigan***	Y	N	N	N	Y	Y	Y	N
16 ***Martin***	Y	Y	Y	Y	Y	Y	N	N
17 Evans	Y	Y	Y	N	N	N	Y	Y
18 ***Michel***	Y	N	Y	Y	Y	Y	Y	N
19 Bruce	Y	Y	Y	N	N	N	Y	Y
20 Durbin	Y	Y	N	N	N	N	Y	Y
21 Price	Y	Y	Y	N	N	N	Y	Y
22 Gray	Y	Y	Y	N	N	N	Y	Y
INDIANA								
1 Visclosky	Y	Y	Y	N	N	N	Y	Y
2 Sharp	Y	Y	Y	Y	N	Y	N	Y
3 ***Hiler***	Y	N	N	Y	Y	Y	N	N
4 ***Coats***	Y	N	N	Y	Y	Y	N	N
5 ***Hillis***	?	?	Y	N	Y	Y	Y	Y

ND - Northern Democrats SD - Southern Democrats

* Corresponding to Congressional Record Votes 253, 254, 255, 256, 257, 259, 260, 261

	230	231	232	233	234	235	236	237
6 ***Burton***	Y	N	N	Y	Y	Y	N	N
7 ***Myers***	Y	Y	N	N	N	N	Y	Y
8 McCloskey	Y	Y	N	Y	N	Y	Y	Y
9 Hamilton	Y	Y	Y	N	Y	Y	Y	Y
10 Jacobs	N	N	Y	Y	N	Y	N	N
IOWA								
1 ***Leach***	Y	N	Y	Y	Y	Y	N	N
2 ***Tauke***	Y	N	Y	Y	Y	Y	N	N
3 ***Evans***	Y	N	Y	Y	N	Y	N	N
4 Smith	Y	Y	Y	N	N	N	Y	Y
5 ***Lightfoot***	Y	N	Y	Y	Y	Y	N	N
6 Bedell	Y	Y	Y	Y	N	Y	Y	Y
KANSAS								
1 ***Roberts***	Y	N	Y	Y	Y	Y	N	N
2 Slattery	Y	Y	Y	Y	Y	Y	N	Y
3 ***Meyers***	Y	N	Y	Y	N	Y	N	N
4 Glickman	Y	Y	Y	N	Y	Y	N	Y
5 ***Whittaker***	Y	Y	N	Y	Y	Y	N	N
KENTUCKY								
1 Hubbard	Y	Y	N	N	Y	Y	N	Y
2 Natcher	Y	Y	Y	N	N	N	Y	Y
3 Mazzoli	Y	Y	Y	N	N	N	Y	Y
4 ***Snyder***	?	Y	N	N	N	Y	N	Y
5 ***Rogers***	Y	N	N	Y	Y	Y	Y	N
6 ***Hopkins***	Y	N	N	Y	Y	Y	N	N
7 Perkins	Y	Y	Y	N	N	N	Y	Y
LOUISIANA								
1 ***Livingston***	Y	N	N	N	Y	N	Y	N
2 Boggs	Y	Y	N	N	N	N	Y	Y
3 Tauzin	Y	Y	N	Y	Y	Y	Y	Y
4 Roemer	Y	Y	N	Y	?	?	N	N
5 Huckaby	?	Y	N	Y	Y	Y	Y	Y
6 ***Moore***	?	?	?	?	?	?	?	?
7 Breaux	?	?	N	Y	?	?	?	?
8 Long	Y	Y	Y	N	N	N	Y	Y
MAINE								
1 ***McKernan***	Y	N	N	Y	N	Y	N	N
2 ***Snowe***	Y	N	N	Y	Y	Y	Y	N
MARYLAND								
1 Dyson	Y	?	N	N	Y	N	Y	Y
2 ***Bentley***	Y	?	N	Y	N	Y	Y	N
3 Mikulski	?	Y	Y	N	N	N	Y	?
4 ***Holt***	Y	N	N	Y	N	Y	Y	N
5 Hoyer	Y	Y	Y	N	N	N	Y	Y
6 Byron	Y	Y	N	N	Y	Y	Y	Y
7 Mitchell	?	N	Y	N	N	N	Y	?
8 Barnes	?	?	?	?	?	?	?	?
MASSACHUSETTS								
1 ***Conte***	Y	N	Y	Y	Y	N	Y	N
2 Boland	?	Y	Y	N	N	N	Y	Y
3 Early	?	Y	N	N	N	N	Y	Y
4 Frank	?	Y	Y	N	N	N	Y	Y
5 Atkins	Y	Y	Y	N	N	N	Y	Y
6 Mavroules	Y	?	Y	N	N	N	Y	Y
7 Markey	Y	Y	Y	N	N	N	Y	Y
8 O'Neill								
9 Moakley	Y	?	?	N	N	N	Y	?
10 Studds	Y	Y	Y	N	N	N	Y	Y
11 Donnelly	Y	Y	Y	N	N	N	Y	Y
MICHIGAN								
1 Conyers	Y	Y	Y	N	N	N	Y	Y
2 ***Pursell***	Y	Y	N	Y	Y	Y	N	Y
3 Wolpe	Y	Y	Y	N	Y	N	Y	Y
4 ***Siljander***	Y	Y	N	Y	Y	Y	N	Y
5 ***Henry***	Y	N	N	Y	Y	Y	N	N
6 Carr	Y	Y	N	N	N	N	Y	Y
7 Kildee	Y	Y	Y	N	N	N	Y	Y
8 Traxler	Y	Y	N	N	N	N	Y	Y
9 ***Vander Jagt***	Y	Y	Y	Y	Y	Y	Y	N
10 ***Schuette***	Y	N	N	Y	Y	Y	N	N
11 ***Davis***	Y	Y	N	N	N	Y	Y	Y
12 Bonior	Y	Y	Y	N	N	N	Y	Y
13 Crockett	Y	?	?	?	?	?	?	?
14 Hertel	N	Y	N	N	N	N	Y	Y
15 Ford	Y	Y	Y	N	N	N	Y	Y
16 Dingell	Y	Y	Y	N	N	N	?	?
17 Levin	Y	Y	Y	N	N	N	Y	Y
18 ***Broomfield***	N	Y	N	N	N	Y	N	Y
MINNESOTA								
1 Penny	Y	N	Y	Y	N	Y	N	N
2 ***Weber***	Y	N	Y	Y	Y	Y	N	N
3 ***Frenzel***	N	Y	Y	Y	Y	Y	N	N
4 Vento	Y	Y	Y	N	N	N	Y	Y
5 Sabo	Y	Y	Y	N	N	N	Y	Y
6 Sikorski	Y	N	Y	N	N	Y	Y	N

	230	231	232	233	234	235	236	237
7 ***Stangeland***	Y	?	Y	N	N	Y	N	N
8 Oberstar	Y	Y	Y	N	N	N	Y	Y
MISSISSIPPI								
1 Whitten	Y	Y	Y	N	N	N	Y	Y
2 ***Franklin***	Y	?	N	Y	N	Y	Y	Y
3 Montgomery	Y	Y	N	N	Y	N	Y	Y
4 Dowdy	Y	Y	Y	N	N	N	Y	Y
5 ***Lott***	Y	N	N	Y	Y	Y	N	N
MISSOURI								
1 Clay	Y	N	Y	N	N	N	Y	N
2 Young	?	Y	N	N	N	N	Y	Y
3 Gephardt	?	Y	Y	N	N	N	Y	Y
4 Skelton	Y	Y	Y	N	N	N	Y	Y
5 Wheat	Y	Y	Y	N	N	N	Y	Y
6 ***Coleman***	Y	N	Y	Y	Y	Y	N	N
7 ***Taylor***	Y	Y	N	N	N	Y	N	Y
8 ***Emerson***	Y	N	N	Y	Y	Y	N	N
9 Volkmer	Y	Y	N	Y	Y	N	Y	Y
MONTANA								
1 Williams	Y	?	Y	N	N	N	Y	Y
2 ***Marlenee***	?	?	?	?	?	?	?	?
NEBRASKA								
1 ***Bereuter***	Y	N	Y	Y	Y	Y	N	N
2 ***Daub***	Y	N	N	Y	Y	Y	N	N
3 ***Smith***	Y	Y	Y	Y	Y	Y	N	Y
NEVADA								
1 Reid	Y	Y	N	N	N	N	Y	Y
2 ***Vucanovich***	Y	N	N	Y	N	Y	N	N
NEW HAMPSHIRE								
1 ***Smith***	N	N	N	Y	Y	Y	N	N
2 ***Gregg***	N	N	N	Y	Y	Y	N	N
NEW JERSEY								
1 Florio	Y	Y	Y	N	N	N	Y	Y
2 Hughes	N	Y	Y	N	N	N	N	Y
3 Howard	Y	Y	Y	N	N	N	Y	Y
4 ***Smith***	Y	Y	N	N	Y	Y	Y	Y
5 ***Roukema***	Y	N	Y	Y	Y	Y	N	N
6 Dwyer	Y	Y	N	N	N	N	Y	Y
7 ***Rinaldo***	Y	Y	N	N	Y	Y	N	Y
8 Roe	Y	Y	Y	N	N	N	Y	Y
9 Torricelli	Y	Y	Y	Y	Y	N	Y	Y
10 Rodino	Y	Y	Y	N	N	N	Y	Y
11 ***Gallo***	Y	N	N	Y	Y	Y	N	N
12 ***Courter***	Y	N	N	Y	Y	Y	N	N
13 ***Saxton***	Y	N	N	Y	Y	Y	N	N
14 Guarini	Y	N	Y	N	N	N	Y	Y
NEW MEXICO								
1 ***Lujan***	Y	Y	N	Y	N	Y	N	Y
2 ***Skeen***	Y	N	N	Y	N	N	Y	N
3 Richardson	Y	Y	Y	N	N	N	Y	Y
NEW YORK								
1 ***Carney***	N	?	?	?	?	?	?	?
2 Downey	Y	Y	Y	N	N	N	Y	Y
3 Mrazek	Y	Y	N	N	N	N	Y	Y
4 ***Lent***	Y	N	Y	N	Y	Y	Y	N
5 ***McGrath***	N	N	N	N	N	Y	Y	N
6 Waldon *			Y	-	N	N	Y	Y
7 Ackerman	Y	Y	Y	N	N	N	Y	Y
8 Scheuer	Y	Y	Y	N	N	N	Y	Y
9 Manton	Y	Y	Y	N	N	N	Y	Y
10 Schumer	?	Y	Y	N	N	N	Y	Y
11 Towns	Y	Y	?	N	N	N	Y	?
12 Owens	?	Y	Y	N	N	N	Y	Y
13 Solarz	Y	Y	Y	N	N	N	Y	Y
14 ***Molinari***	Y	N	N	N	N	Y	Y	N
15 ***Green***	Y	?	N	N	N	N	Y	Y
16 Rangel	Y	Y	Y	N	N	N	Y	Y
17 Weiss	Y	Y	Y	N	N	N	Y	Y
18 Garcia	Y	?	Y	N	N	N	Y	Y
19 Biaggi	Y	Y	Y	N	N	N	Y	Y
20 ***DioGuardi***	Y	Y	N	?	Y	Y	N	Y
21 ***Fish***	Y	Y	N	Y	N	Y	Y	Y
22 ***Gilman***	Y	Y	Y	Y	Y	Y	Y	Y
23 Stratton	Y	Y	Y	N	N	N	Y	Y
24 ***Solomon***	Y	N	Y	Y	Y	Y	N	N
25 ***Boehlert***	Y	N	N	Y	N	Y	N	N
26 ***Martin***	?	Y	N	?	Y	Y	Y	Y
27 ***Wortley***	Y	Y	N	Y	?	Y	Y	Y
28 McHugh	Y	Y	Y	N	N	N	Y	Y
29 ***Horton***	?	Y	Y	N	N	N	Y	Y
30 ***Eckert***	Y	Y	N	Y	Y	Y	N	?
31 ***Kemp***	Y	P	N	Y	N	Y	N	?
32 LaFalce	Y	Y	Y	N	N	N	Y	Y
33 Nowak	Y	Y	N	N	N	N	Y	Y
34 Lundine	?	Y	Y	N	?	N	Y	Y

	230	231	232	233	234	235	236	237
NORTH CAROLINA								
1 Jones	Y	Y	Y	N	N	N	Y	?
2 Valentine	Y	Y	N	Y	Y	Y	Y	Y
3 Whitley	Y	Y	N	N	N	N	Y	Y
4 ***Cobey***	Y	N	N	Y	Y	Y	N	N
5 Neal	Y	Y	N	N	N	N	Y	Y
6 ***Coble***	Y	N	N	Y	Y	Y	N	N
7 Rose	?	Y	N	N	N	N	Y	Y
8 Hefner	Y	Y	N	N	N	N	Y	Y
9 ***McMillan***	#	Y	N	Y	Y	Y	N	N
10 Vacancy								
11 ***Hendon***	Y	Y	N	Y	Y	Y	N	?
NORTH DAKOTA								
AL Dorgan	Y	Y	Y	N	N	N	N	Y
OHIO								
1 Luken	N	Y	Y	N	Y	N	Y	Y
2 ***Gradison***	N	Y	Y	Y	Y	Y	N	Y
3 Hall	Y	Y	N	N	N	N	Y	Y
4 ***Oxley***	Y	N	N	Y	Y	Y	N	N
5 ***Latta***	Y	Y	N	Y	Y	Y	N	Y
6 ***McEwen***	Y	Y	N	Y	Y	Y	N	Y
7 ***DeWine***	Y	N	N	Y	Y	Y	N	N
8 ***Kindness***	Y	N	N	Y	Y	Y	N	N
9 Kaptur	Y	Y	Y	N	N	N	Y	Y
10 ***Miller***	Y	N	N	Y	Y	Y	N	N
11 Eckart	Y	Y	N	N	N	N	Y	Y
12 ***Kasich***	Y	?	N	Y	Y	Y	N	Y
13 Pease	Y	Y	N	Y	Y	N	Y	Y
14 Seiberling	Y	Y	Y	N	N	N	Y	Y
15 ***Wylie***	Y	?	Y	Y	Y	Y	N	Y
16 ***Regula***	Y	Y	N	Y	N	Y	N	Y
17 Traficant	Y	Y	Y	N	N	N	Y	Y
18 Applegate	Y	Y	N	Y	N	N	Y	Y
19 Feighan	Y	?	?	?	?	?	?	?
20 Oakar	Y	?	Y	N	N	N	Y	?
21 Stokes	Y	Y	Y	N	N	N	Y	Y
OKLAHOMA								
1 Jones	Y	Y	Y	N	Y	Y	N	N
2 Synar	Y	Y	Y	N	N	N	Y	Y
3 Watkins	Y	Y	N	N	N	N	Y	Y
4 McCurdy	Y	Y	N	N	N	Y	Y	Y
5 ***Edwards***	Y	N	N	Y	Y	Y	Y	Y
6 English	Y	Y	Y	N	N	Y	Y	Y
OREGON								
1 AuCoin	Y	Y	Y	N	N	N	Y	Y
2 ***Smith, R.***	Y	N	N	Y	Y	Y	N	N
3 Wyden	Y	Y	Y	N	N	N	N	Y
4 Weaver	N	?	?	?	?	N	Y	Y
5 ***Smith, D.***	?	N	N	Y	Y	Y	N	N
PENNSYLVANIA								
1 Foglietta	Y	?	?	N	N	N	Y	Y
2 Gray	Y	Y	Y	N	N	N	Y	Y
3 Borski	Y	Y	Y	N	N	N	Y	Y
4 Kolter	Y	Y	Y	N	N	N	Y	Y
5 ***Schulze***	Y	Y	N	Y	Y	Y	N	Y
6 Yatron	Y	Y	N	N	N	N	Y	Y
7 Edgar	Y	Y	Y	?	?	?	?	Y
8 Kostmayer	Y	?	?	N	N	N	Y	Y
9 ***Shuster***	Y	N	N	Y	Y	Y	N	N
10 ***McDade***	Y	Y	N	N	Y	N	Y	Y
11 Kanjorski	Y	Y	N	N	Y	Y	Y	Y
12 Murtha	Y	Y	N	N	N	N	Y	Y
13 ***Coughlin***	Y	N	N	Y	N	Y	Y	N
14 Coyne	Y	Y	Y	N	N	N	Y	Y
15 ***Ritter***	Y	Y	N	Y	Y	Y	N	?
16 ***Walker***	N	N	N	Y	Y	Y	N	N
17 ***Gekas***	Y	N	N	Y	Y	Y	N	N
18 Walgren	Y	Y	N	Y	N	Y	Y	Y
19 ***Goodling***	Y	N	N	Y	Y	Y	N	N
20 Gaydos	Y	Y	N	N	N	N	Y	Y
21 ***Ridge***	Y	N	N	Y	Y	Y	N	N
22 Murphy	Y	Y	N	N	N	N	Y	Y
23 ***Clinger***	Y	Y	Y	N	Y	N	N	N
RHODE ISLAND								
1 St Germain	Y	Y	Y	N	N	N	Y	Y
2 ***Schneider***	Y	Y	Y	Y	Y	Y	Y	Y
SOUTH CAROLINA								
1 ***Hartnett***	?	?	?	?	?	?	?	?
2 ***Spence***	Y	Y	N	Y	N	Y	N	Y
3 Derrick	Y	Y	?	N	Y	N	Y	Y
4 ***Campbell***	?	?	?	?	?	#	X	?
5 Spratt	Y	Y	N	N	Y	N	Y	Y
6 Tallon	?	?	N	Y	Y	N	Y	Y
SOUTH DAKOTA								
AL Daschle	Y	Y	Y	Y	N	Y	Y	Y

	230	231	232	233	234	235	236	237
TENNESSEE								
1 ***Quillen***	Y	Y	N	N	N	Y	Y	N
2 ***Duncan***	Y	Y	N	Y	N	Y	Y	Y
3 Lloyd	Y	N	N	Y	Y	Y	Y	N
4 Cooper	Y	Y	Y	N	N	Y	Y	?
5 Boner	?	Y	N	N	N	N	Y	Y
6 Gordon	Y	Y	Y	N	N	N	Y	Y
7 ***Sundquist***	Y	N	N	Y	Y	Y	N	N
8 Jones	?	Y	Y	N	N	N	Y	Y
9 Ford	Y	?	?	N	N	N	Y	Y
TEXAS								
1 Chapman	Y	Y	N	N	N	N	Y	Y
2 Wilson	Y	?	Y	N	N	N	Y	Y
3 ***Bartlett***	N	N	N	Y	Y	Y	N	N
4 Hall, R.	?	Y	N	Y	Y	Y	N	Y
5 Bryant	Y	Y	N	N	N	N	Y	Y
6 ***Barton***	Y	N	N	Y	Y	Y	N	N
7 ***Archer***	N	Y	Y	Y	Y	Y	N	Y
8 ***Fields***	N	N	N	Y	Y	Y	N	N
9 Brooks	Y	Y	Y	N	N	N	Y	?
10 Pickle	Y	Y	Y	N	N	N	Y	Y
11 Leath	Y	Y	N	N	?	?	Y	Y
12 Wright	?	Y	Y	N	N	N	Y	Y
13 ***Boulter***	Y	N	N	Y	Y	Y	N	N
14 ***Sweeney***	Y	Y	N	Y	Y	Y	N	Y
15 de la Garza	Y	Y	Y	N	N	N	Y	Y
16 Coleman	Y	Y	N	N	N	N	Y	Y
17 Stenholm	Y	Y	N	Y	?	?	N	N
18 Leland	Y	Y	Y	-	N	N	Y	Y
19 ***Combest***	Y	Y	Y	Y	Y	Y	N	Y
20 Gonzalez	Y	Y	Y	N	N	N	Y	Y
21 ***Loeffler***	Y	N	Y	Y	Y	Y	Y	N
22 ***DeLay***	N	N	N	Y	Y	Y	N	N
23 Bustamante	Y	Y	Y	N	N	N	Y	Y
24 Frost	Y	Y	Y	N	N	N	Y	?
25 Andrews	Y	Y	Y	N	?	Y	Y	Y
26 ***Armey***	N	N	N	Y	Y	Y	N	N
27 Ortiz	?	Y	Y	N	N	N	Y	Y
UTAH								
1 ***Hansen***	?	N	N	Y	Y	Y	N	N
2 ***Monson***	X	N	N	Y	Y	Y	N	N
3 ***Nielson***	N	Y	N	Y	Y	Y	N	N
VERMONT								
AL ***Jeffords***	Y	Y	Y	N	N	N	Y	Y
VIRGINIA								
1 ***Bateman***	Y	Y	Y	Y	N	Y	Y	Y
2 ***Whitehurst***	?	N	Y	Y	N	Y	Y	N
3 ***Bliley***	N	N	N	Y	Y	Y	Y	N
4 Sisisky	Y	Y	Y	N	N	N	Y	Y
5 Daniel	Y	Y	N	Y	Y	Y	Y	Y
6 Olin	N	Y	Y	N	Y	Y	N	Y
7 ***Slaughter***	Y	N	N	Y	Y	Y	N	N
8 ***Parris***	Y	?	?	?	?	?	?	N
9 Boucher	?	Y	Y	N	N	N	Y	Y
10 ***Wolf***	Y	N	N	Y	Y	N	Y	N
WASHINGTON								
1 ***Miller***	N	Y	N	Y	Y	Y	N	Y
2 Swift	Y	Y	Y	N	N	N	Y	Y
3 Bonker	?	Y	Y	N	N	?	Y	Y
4 ***Morrison***	Y	Y	N	Y	Y	Y	N	?
5 Foley	Y	Y	Y	N	N	N	Y	Y
6 Dicks	Y	Y	Y	N	N	N	Y	Y
7 Lowry	?	Y	Y	N	N	N	Y	Y
8 ***Chandler***	Y	N	N	Y	Y	Y	N	N
WEST VIRGINIA								
1 Mollohan	Y	?	?	N	N	N	Y	?
2 Staggers	Y	Y	Y	N	N	N	Y	Y
3 Wise	Y	Y	Y	N	N	N	Y	Y
4 Rahall	Y	Y	Y	N	N	?	?	Y
WISCONSIN								
1 Aspin	Y	Y	Y	N	N	N	?	Y
2 Kastenmeier	Y	Y	Y	N	N	N	Y	Y
3 ***Gunderson***	Y	-	+	+	-	+	-	-
4 Kleczka	?	Y	Y	N	N	N	Y	Y
5 Moody	Y	Y	Y	N	N	N	Y	Y
6 ***Petri***	N	Y	Y	Y	Y	Y	N	Y
7 Obey	Y	Y	Y	N	N	N	Y	Y
8 ***Roth***	Y	N	N	Y	Y	Y	N	N
9 ***Sensenbrenner***	N	N	N	Y	Y	Y	N	N
WYOMING								
AL ***Cheney***	N	N	N	Y	Y	Y	N	N

**Rep. Alton R. Waldon Jr., D-N.Y., was sworn in on July 29, 1986. The first vote for which he was eligible was CQ vote 232.*

Southern states - Ala., Ark., Fla., Ga., Ky., La., Miss., N.C., Okla., S.C., Tenn., Texas, Va.

* The *Congressional Record* vote number is different from the CQ vote number because the *Record* includes quorum calls in its tally. CQ does not publish quorum call votes.

238. HR 5205. Transportation Appropriations, Fiscal 1987. Walker, R-Pa., amendment to delete $315,000 from the Office of the Secretary of Transportation that was to be used for the enforcement of the 55 mph speed limit. Rejected 115-299: R 85-88; D 30-211 (ND 15-146, SD 15-65), July 30, 1986. (Walker had sought to offer two amendments en bloc that would have deleted the $315,000 and shifted it to the Coast Guard for efforts to combat the flow of illegal drugs into the United States. That move was blocked. Walker then offered the deleting amendment by itself *(this vote)*, but did not have an opportunity to offer the second amendment because the first one was rejected.)

239. HR 5205. Transportation Appropriations, Fiscal 1987. Armey, R-Texas, amendments to remove $43 million from capital construction funds for two Washington, D.C., metropolitan airports, $61.3 million from funding for Amtrak and $21.7 million from funding for the Washington, D.C., mass transit rail construction program. Rejected en bloc 77-344: R 67-107; D 10-237 (ND 1-166, SD 9-71), July 30, 1986.

240. HR 5205. Transportation Appropriations, Fiscal 1987. Walker, R-Pa., amendment to remove $20 million in funding for the National Highway Transportation Safety Administration for the enforcement of the 55 mph speed limit. Rejected 118-303: R 88-87; D 30-216 (ND 16-151, SD 14-65), July 30, 1986.

241. HR 5205. Transportation Appropriations, Fiscal 1987. Brown, R-Colo., amendment to reduce Amtrak funding by $22.3 million to $590.7 million, the amount of funding appropriated in fiscal 1986. Rejected 169-248: R 125-48; D 44-200 (ND 7-159, SD 37-41), July 30, 1986.

242. HR 5205. Transportation Appropriations, Fiscal 1987. Molinari, R-N.Y., amendment to strike language that would allow the New York Metropolitan Transportation Authority to eliminate one-way toll collections on the Verrazano-Narrows Bridge connecting Staten Island and Brooklyn, N.Y., if it determines that such collections have resulted in traffic problems or loss of revenues. Rejected 168-253: R 117-58; D 51-195 (ND 27-139, SD 24-56), July 30, 1986.

243. HR 5205. Transportation Appropriations, Fiscal 1987. Molinari, R-N.Y., amendment to require the rehiring in each of fiscal years 1987 and 1988 of at least 500 air traffic controllers who were fired during the 1981 air traffic controllers' strike. Rejected 193-226: R 21-154; D 172-72 (ND 149-16, SD 23-56), July 30, 1986.

244. HR 5205. Transportation Appropriations, Fiscal 1987. Traficant, D-Ohio, amendment to ban the purchase of any non-domestic goods or services with funds made available by the bill. Rejected 133-281: R 26-146; D 107-135 (ND 73-92, SD 34-43), July 30, 1986.

245. HR 5205. Transportation Appropriations, Fiscal 1987. Armey, R-Texas, amendment to cut all discretionary spending in the bill by 1.23 percent, or $313 million. Rejected 143-270: R 122-50; D 21-220 (ND 9-154, SD 12-66), July 30, 1986.

KEY

Y Voted for (yea).
\# Paired for.
\+ Announced for.
N Voted against (nay).
X Paired against.
\- Announced against.
P Voted "present."
C Voted "present" to avoid possible conflict of interest.
? Did not vote or otherwise make a position known.

Democrats ***Republicans***

	238	239	240	241	242	243	244	245
ALABAMA								
1 ***Callahan***	Y	Y	Y	Y	Y	N	N	Y
2 ***Dickinson***	N	N	N	Y	Y	N	N	N
3 Nichols	N	N	N	Y	Y	N	Y	Y
4 Bevill	N	N	N	N	N	N	Y	N
5 Flippo	N	N	N	Y	Y	N	Y	N
6 Erdreich	Y	N	Y	N	Y	N	Y	N
7 Shelby	Y	N	Y	N	N	N	Y	N
ALASKA								
AL ***Young***	N	N	N	Y	N	N	N	N
ARIZONA								
1 ***McCain***	Y	N	Y	Y	Y	N	N	Y
2 Udall	N	N	N	N	N	Y	N	N
3 ***Stump***	Y	Y	Y	Y	Y	N	N	Y
4 ***Rudd***	Y	N	Y	N	Y	N	N	Y
5 ***Kolbe***	Y	Y	Y	Y	N	N	N	Y
ARKANSAS								
1 Alexander	N	N	N	N	N	Y	Y	N
2 Robinson	N	N	N	N	N	N	Y	N
3 ***Hammerschmidt***	N	N	N	Y	Y	N	N	N
4 Anthony	?	N	N	N	N	N	N	N
CALIFORNIA								
1 Bosco	N	N	N	N	Y	Y	N	N
2 ***Chappie***	Y	N	Y	Y	Y	N	N	Y
3 Matsui	N	N	N	N	N	N	N	N
4 Fazio	N	N	N	N	Y	Y	N	N
5 Burton	N	N	N	N	N	Y	N	N
6 Boxer	N	N	N	N	N	Y	N	N
7 Miller	N	N	N	N	N	Y	N	N
8 Dellums	N	N	N	N	N	Y	N	N
9 Stark	N	N	N	N	N	Y	N	N
10 Edwards	N	N	N	N	N	Y	N	N
11 Lantos	N	N	N	N	N	Y	N	N
12 ***Zschau***	Y	Y	Y	Y	Y	N	N	Y
13 Mineta	N	N	N	N	N	N	N	N
14 ***Shumway***	Y	Y	Y	Y	Y	N	N	Y
15 Coelho	N	N	N	N	N	Y	N	N
16 Panetta	N	N	N	N	N	Y	N	N
17 ***Pashayan***	Y	N	Y	N	Y	?	?	?
18 Lehman	N	N	N	N	N	Y	N	N
19 ***Lagomarsino***	Y	Y	Y	Y	Y	N	N	Y
20 ***Thomas***	Y	Y	Y	N	Y	N	N	Y
21 ***Fiedler***	Y	Y	N	Y	Y	N	?	?
22 ***Moorhead***	Y	Y	Y	Y	Y	N	N	Y
23 Beilenson	N	N	N	N	N	Y	N	N
24 Waxman	?	N	N	N	N	Y	N	N
25 Roybal	N	N	N	N	N	N	N	N
26 Berman	N	N	N	N	N	Y	N	N
27 Levine	N	N	N	N	N	Y	N	N
28 Dixon	N	N	N	N	N	Y	N	N
29 Hawkins	N	N	N	N	N	Y	Y	N
30 Martinez	N	N	N	N	N	Y	Y	N
31 Dymally	N	N	N	N	N	Y	Y	N
32 Anderson	N	N	N	N	Y	Y	N	N
33 ***Dreier***	Y	Y	Y	Y	Y	N	N	Y
34 Torres	N	N	N	N	Y	Y	Y	N
35 ***Lewis***	N	N	N	N	N	N	N	N
36 Brown	N	N	N	N	N	Y	Y	N
37 ***McCandless***	Y	Y	Y	Y	N	N	N	Y
38 ***Dornan***	Y	N	Y	Y	N	N	N	Y
39 ***Dannemeyer***	Y	Y	Y	Y	Y	N	N	Y
40 ***Badham***	N	N	N	Y	Y	N	N	Y
41 ***Lowery***	N	N	N	Y	N	N	N	N
42 ***Lungren***	Y	N	Y	Y	N	N	N	Y
43 ***Packard***	N	N	N	Y	Y	N	N	Y
44 Bates	N	Y	Y	N	N	Y	N	N
45 ***Hunter***	Y	Y	Y	Y	Y	N	Y	Y
COLORADO								
1 Schroeder	Y	N	N	N	N	Y	N	N
2 Wirth	Y	N	N	N	N	Y	N	N
3 ***Strang***	Y	Y	Y	Y	Y	N	N	Y
4 ***Brown***	Y	Y	Y	Y	Y	N	N	Y
5 ***Kramer***	Y	Y	Y	Y	Y	N	N	Y
6 ***Schaefer***	Y	N	Y	N	N	N	N	N
CONNECTICUT								
1 Kennelly	N	N	N	N	N	Y	N	N
2 Gejdenson	N	N	N	N	N	Y	N	N
3 Morrison	N	N	N	N	N	Y	N	N
4 ***McKinney***	?	?	?	?	Y	N	N	N
5 ***Rowland***	N	N	N	N	Y	N	N	N
6 ***Johnson***	N	N	N	N	Y	Y	N	N
DELAWARE								
AL Carper	N	N	N	N	N	Y	N	Y
FLORIDA								
1 Hutto	N	N	N	Y	Y	N	N	Y
2 Fuqua	N	N	N	N	N	N	N	N
3 Bennett	N	N	N	N	N	N	Y	N
4 Chappell	N	N	N	N	Y	N	N	N
5 ***McCollum***	Y	N	Y	Y	Y	N	N	Y
6 MacKay	N	N	N	Y	N	Y	?	?
7 Gibbons	N	N	N	Y	N	N	N	N
8 ***Young***	Y	N	Y	Y	Y	N	N	Y
9 ***Bilirakis***	Y	Y	Y	Y	Y	N	N	Y
10 ***Ireland***	N	N	N	Y	Y	N	N	Y
11 Nelson	N	N	N	Y	N	N	N	N
12 ***Lewis***	N	N	N	Y	Y	N	N	N
13 ***Mack***	Y	Y	Y	Y	Y	N	N	Y
14 Mica	N	N	N	Y	N	N	Y	N
15 ***Shaw***	Y	N	Y	Y	Y	N	N	Y
16 Smith	N	N	N	N	N	Y	N	N
17 Lehman	N	N	N	N	N	N	N	N
18 Pepper	N	N	N	N	N	Y	Y	N
19 Fascell	N	N	N	N	N	Y	N	N
GEORGIA								
1 Thomas	N	N	N	Y	Y	N	N	N
2 Hatcher	N	N	N	N	N	N	N	N
3 Ray	N	Y	N	Y	Y	N	N	Y
4 ***Swindall***	Y	Y	Y	Y	Y	N	N	Y
5 Fowler	?	?	?	?	?	?	?	?
6 ***Gingrich***	Y	?	Y	Y	Y	N	N	Y
7 Darden	Y	N	N	Y	Y	N	N	N
8 Rowland	N	N	N	Y	Y	N	N	N
9 Jenkins	N	N	N	Y	Y	N	Y	N
10 Barnard	N	N	N	Y	Y	N	N	N
HAWAII								
1 Vacancy								
2 Akaka	N	N	N	N	N	Y	N	N
IDAHO								
1 ***Craig***	Y	Y	Y	Y	Y	N	N	Y
2 Stallings	N	N	N	Y	N	Y	N	N
ILLINOIS								
1 Hayes	N	N	N	N	N	Y	Y	N
2 Savage	N	N	N	N	N	Y	Y	N
3 Russo	N	N	N	N	N	Y	Y	N
4 Vacancy								
5 Lipinski	N	N	N	N	N	Y	Y	N
6 ***Hyde***	N	N	Y	Y	Y	N	N	Y
7 Collins	N	N	N	N	N	Y	Y	N
8 Rostenkowski	N	N	N	N	N	Y	N	N
9 Yates	N	N	N	N	N	Y	N	N
10 ***Porter***	N	Y	Y	Y	Y	N	N	Y
11 Annunzio	N	N	N	N	Y	Y	Y	N
12 ***Crane***	Y	N	Y	Y	Y	N	N	Y
13 ***Fawell***	N	N	N	Y	N	N	N	Y
14 ***Grotberg***	?	?	?	?	?	?	?	?
15 ***Madigan***	Y	N	Y	N	N	N	N	N
16 ***Martin***	N	Y	N	?	Y	N	N	Y
17 Evans	N	N	N	N	N	Y	N	N
18 ***Michel***	Y	Y	Y	Y	Y	Y	N	Y
19 Bruce	N	N	N	N	N	Y	N	N
20 Durbin	N	N	N	N	N	Y	N	N
21 Price	N	N	N	N	N	Y	Y	N
22 Gray	N	N	N	N	Y	Y	Y	N
INDIANA								
1 Visclosky	N	N	N	N	N	Y	Y	N
2 Sharp	?	N	N	N	N	N	Y	Y
3 ***Hiler***	N	Y	N	Y	Y	N	N	Y
4 ***Coats***	N	N	N	Y	Y	N	N	Y
5 ***Hillis***	N	N	N	N	N	N	N	Y

ND - Northern Democrats SD - Southern Democrats

* Corresponding to Congressional Record Votes 262, 263, 264, 265, 266, 267, 268, 269

	238	239	240	241	242	243	244	245
6 ***Burton***	Y	N	Y	Y	Y	N	N	Y
7 ***Myers***	N	N	N	N	N	N	N	N
8 McCloskey	N	N	N	N	N	Y	?	Y
9 Hamilton	Y	N	N	N	N	Y	N	Y
10 Jacobs	N	N	N	N	N	Y	Y	N
IOWA								
1 ***Leach***	N	N	Y	N	N	N	N	Y
2 ***Tauke***	N	Y	N	Y	N	N	N	Y
3 ***Evans***	Y	N	N	Y	Y	N	N	Y
4 Smith	N	N	N	N	N	Y	N	N
5 ***Lightfoot***	N	N	N	Y	Y	N	N	Y
6 Bedell	?	?	?	?	?	?	?	?
KANSAS								
1 ***Roberts***	Y	N	Y	Y	Y	N	N	Y
2 Slattery	Y	N	Y	Y	N	N	N	N
3 ***Meyers***	N	N	N	Y	Y	N	N	Y
4 Glickman	Y	N	Y	Y	N	N	N	N
5 ***Whittaker***	Y	N	Y	Y	Y	N	N	N
KENTUCKY								
1 Hubbard	N	Y	N	Y	N	N	Y	Y
2 Natcher	N	N	N	N	N	Y	Y	N
3 Mazzoli	N	N	N	N	Y	N	N	N
4 ***Snyder***	N	N	N	Y	Y	N	Y	Y
5 ***Rogers***	N	N	N	Y	Y	N	Y	N
6 ***Hopkins***	N	N	Y	Y	Y	N	N	Y
7 Perkins	N	N	N	N	Y	Y	Y	N
LOUISIANA								
1 ***Livingston***	Y	Y	N	N	N	N	N	N
2 Boggs	N	N	N	N	N	Y	N	N
3 Tauzin	Y	Y	Y	Y	N	N	N	Y
4 Roemer	Y	Y	Y	Y	Y	N	N	Y
5 Huckaby	Y	Y	Y	Y	N	N	N	Y
6 ***Moore***	?	?	?	?	?	?	?	?
7 Breaux	Y	?	?	?	N	?	?	?
8 Long	N	N	N	N	N	Y	N	N
MAINE								
1 ***McKernan***	Y	N	Y	Y	N	N	N	Y
2 ***Snowe***	N	N	N	Y	N	Y	N	N
MARYLAND								
1 Dyson	Y	N	N	Y	N	N	N	Y
2 ***Bentley***	Y	N	N	N	Y	Y	Y	N
3 Mikulski	?	N	N	N	N	Y	Y	N
4 ***Holt***	N	N	N	N	N	N	N	N
5 Hoyer	N	N	N	N	N	Y	N	N
6 Byron	N	N	N	N	Y	N	N	N
7 Mitchell	N	N	N	N	N	Y	Y	N
8 Barnes	N	N	N	?	?	?	?	?
MASSACHUSETTS								
1 ***Conte***	N	N	N	N	N	Y	Y	N
2 Boland	N	N	N	N	N	Y	N	N
3 Early	N	N	N	N	N	Y	N	N
4 Frank	Y	N	Y	N	N	Y	N	N
5 Atkins	N	N	N	N	N	Y	N	N
6 Mavroules	N	N	N	N	Y	Y	Y	N
7 Markey	N	N	N	N	N	Y	N	N
8 O'Neill								
9 Moakley	N	N	N	N	N	Y	Y	N
10 Studds	N	N	N	N	N	Y	N	N
11 Donnelly	N	N	N	N	N	Y	Y	N
MICHIGAN								
1 Conyers	N	N	N	N	Y	Y	Y	N
2 ***Pursell***	N	N	N	N	N	N	N	N
3 Wolpe	N	N	N	N	N	Y	Y	N
4 ***Siljander***	N	Y	N	Y	Y	N	N	Y
5 ***Henry***	N	N	N	N	Y	N	N	Y
6 Carr	N	N	N	N	N	N	Y	N
7 Kildee	N	N	N	N	N	Y	Y	N
8 Traxler	Y	N	N	N	N	Y	Y	N
9 ***Vander Jagt***	N	N	Y	Y	Y	N	N	Y
10 ***Schuette***	N	Y	N	Y	Y	N	N	Y
11 ***Davis***	N	N	N	Y	N	Y	Y	N
12 Bonior	N	N	N	N	N	Y	Y	N
13 Crockett	N	N	N	N	N	Y	Y	N
14 Hertel	N	N	N	N	N	Y	Y	N
15 Ford	N	N	N	N	Y	Y	Y	N
16 Dingell	N	N	N	N	Y	Y	Y	N
17 Levin	N	N	N	N	N	Y	N	N
18 ***Broomfield***	N	Y	Y	Y	N	N	N	Y
MINNESOTA								
1 Penny	N	N	Y	Y	N	Y	N	Y
2 ***Weber***	Y	Y	Y	Y	N	N	N	Y
3 ***Frenzel***	?	Y	Y	Y	Y	N	N	Y
4 Vento	N	N	N	N	N	Y	N	N
5 Sabo	N	N	N	N	N	Y	N	N
6 Sikorski	N	N	N	N	Y	Y	Y	N

	238	239	240	241	242	243	244	245
7 ***Stangeland***	N	N	N	Y	Y	N	N	Y
8 Oberstar	N	N	N	N	Y	Y	Y	N
MISSISSIPPI								
1 Whitten	N	N	N	N	N	N	N	N
2 ***Franklin***	Y	Y	Y	Y	Y	N	N	Y
3 Montgomery	N	Y	N	Y	Y	N	N	N
4 Dowdy	N	N	N	N	N	Y	Y	N
5 ***Lott***	N	Y	Y	Y	N	N	N	Y
MISSOURI								
1 Clay	N	N	N	N	N	Y	Y	N
2 Young	N	N	N	N	N	Y	Y	N
3 Gephardt	N	N	N	N	N	Y	N	N
4 Skelton	N	N	N	N	Y	N	N	Y
5 Wheat	N	N	N	N	N	Y	N	N
6 ***Coleman***	N	N	N	Y	Y	N	Y	N
7 ***Taylor***	N	N	N	N	Y	N	Y	N
8 ***Emerson***	N	N	N	N	Y	N	Y	N
9 Volkmer	N	N	N	N	N	N	Y	N
MONTANA								
1 Williams	Y	N	Y	N	N	Y	N	N
2 ***Marlenee***	Y	N	N	N	N	N	N	N
NEBRASKA								
1 ***Bereuter***	N	N	N	N	N	N	N	N
2 ***Daub***	Y	Y	Y	Y	Y	N	N	Y
3 ***Smith***	Y	Y	Y	Y	Y	N	N	Y
NEVADA								
1 Reid	Y	N	Y	N	N	Y	N	N
2 ***Vucanovich***	Y	N	Y	Y	N	N	N	N
NEW HAMPSHIRE								
1 ***Smith***	Y	Y	Y	Y	N	N	N	Y
2 ***Gregg***	N	Y	Y	Y	Y	N	N	Y
NEW JERSEY								
1 Florio	N	N	N	N	N	Y	Y	N
2 Hughes	N	N	Y	N	N	Y	N	N
3 Howard	N	N	N	N	Y	Y	Y	N
4 ***Smith***	N	N	N	N	Y	Y	Y	N
5 ***Roukema***	N	N	N	Y	N	Y	N	Y
6 Dwyer	N	N	N	N	Y	Y	N	N
7 ***Rinaldo***	N	N	N	N	N	Y	Y	N
8 Roe	N	N	N	N	?	Y	N	N
9 Torricelli	N	N	N	N	N	Y	N	N
10 Rodino	N	N	N	N	N	Y	N	N
11 ***Gallo***	N	N	N	N	N	N	N	Y
12 ***Courter***	N	N	N	N	N	N	N	?
13 ***Saxton***	N	N	N	N	N	N	N	Y
14 Guarini	N	N	N	N	N	Y	N	N
NEW MEXICO								
1 ***Lujan***	Y	Y	Y	Y	Y	N	Y	Y
2 ***Skeen***	N	N	Y	Y	N	N	N	N
3 Richardson	Y	N	Y	N	N	Y	N	N
NEW YORK								
1 ***Carney***	?	?	?	?	?	?	?	?
2 Downey	N	N	N	N	N	Y	N	N
3 Mrazek	N	N	N	N	N	Y	N	N
4 ***Lent***	N	N	N	N	Y	N	N	N
5 ***McGrath***	N	N	N	N	Y	Y	N	N
6 Waldon	N	N	N	N	N	Y	Y	N
7 Ackerman	N	N	N	N	N	Y	Y	N
8 Scheuer	N	N	N	N	N	Y	N	N
9 Manton	N	N	N	N	N	Y	Y	N
10 Schumer	N	N	N	N	N	Y	Y	N
11 Towns	N	N	N	N	N	Y	Y	N
12 Owens	N	N	N	N	N	Y	Y	N
13 Solarz	N	N	N	N	N	Y	N	N
14 ***Molinari***	N	N	N	N	Y	Y	N	N
15 ***Green***	N	N	N	N	N	N	N	N
16 Rangel	N	N	N	N	N	Y	Y	N
17 Weiss	N	N	N	N	N	Y	N	N
18 Garcia	N	N	N	N	N	Y	Y	N
19 Biaggi	N	N	Y	N	N	Y	Y	N
20 ***DioGuardi***	N	N	N	Y	Y	Y	N	N
21 ***Fish***	N	N	N	N	Y	Y	N	N
22 ***Gilman***	N	N	N	N	Y	Y	Y	N
23 Stratton	N	N	N	N	Y	N	N	N
24 ***Solomon***	Y	Y	Y	Y	Y	N	Y	Y
25 ***Boehlert***	N	N	N	N	Y	Y	N	Y
26 ***Martin***	N	N	N	N	Y	N	N	N
27 ***Wortley***	N	N	N	N	Y	Y	N	Y
28 McHugh	N	N	N	N	N	Y	N	N
29 ***Horton***	N	N	N	N	Y	Y	N	N
30 ***Eckert***	N	Y	N	Y	N	N	Y	Y
31 ***Kemp***	Y	N	Y	Y	Y	N	N	Y
32 LaFalce	N	N	N	?	N	Y	N	N
33 Nowak	N	N	N	N	Y	?	Y	N
34 Lundine	?	N	N	N	N	?	?	?

	238	239	240	241	242	243	244	245
NORTH CAROLINA								
1 Jones	N	N	N	N	N	N	Y	N
2 Valentine	N	N	N	Y	N	N	?	N
3 Whitley	N	N	N	Y	N	N	Y	N
4 ***Cobey***	Y	Y	Y	Y	Y	N	N	Y
5 Neal	N	N	N	Y	N	N	Y	N
6 ***Coble***	Y	Y	Y	Y	Y	N	Y	Y
7 Rose	Y	N	N	?	Y	N	Y	N
8 Hefner	N	N	N	N	N	N	Y	N
9 ***McMillan***	Y	N	Y	Y	Y	N	N	Y
10 Vacancy								
11 ***Hendon***	Y	N	Y	Y	Y	N	Y	Y
NORTH DAKOTA								
AL Dorgan	N	?	N	N	N	N	N	N
OHIO								
1 Luken	N	N	N	N	N	Y	Y	N
2 ***Gradison***	N	Y	N	Y	N	N	N	Y
3 Hall	N	N	?	Y	Y	Y	Y	Y
4 ***Oxley***	Y	Y	Y	Y	N	N	N	Y
5 ***Latta***	N	Y	Y	Y	N	N	Y	Y
6 ***McEwen***	N	N	N	N	Y	N	Y	Y
7 ***DeWine***	N	N	N	N	Y	N	N	Y
8 ***Kindness***	Y	Y	Y	Y	N	N	Y	Y
9 Kaptur	N	N	N	N	N	Y	Y	N
10 ***Miller***	Y	Y	N	Y	Y	N	Y	Y
11 Eckart	N	N	N	N	N	Y	Y	N
12 ***Kasich***	Y	Y	Y	Y	Y	N	N	Y
13 Pease	N	N	N	N	N	Y	N	N
14 Seiberling	N	N	Y	N	N	Y	Y	N
15 ***Wylie***	N	N	N	Y	N	N	N	Y
16 ***Regula***	N	N	N	N	N	N	Y	N
17 Traficant	N	N	N	N	N	Y	Y	N
18 Applegate	Y	N	N	N	N	Y	Y	N
19 Feighan	N	N	N	N	N	Y	Y	N
20 Oakar	?	N	N	N	N	Y	Y	N
21 Stokes	N	N	N	N	N	Y	Y	N
OKLAHOMA								
1 Jones	Y	N	Y	Y	N	N	N	N
2 Synar	N	N	N	Y	N	N	N	N
3 Watkins	N	N	N	Y	N	N	N	N
4 McCurdy	N	N	N	Y	N	N	N	N
5 ***Edwards***	Y	N	Y	Y	Y	N	N	N
6 English	Y	N	Y	Y	N	N	N	N
OREGON								
1 AuCoin	N	N	N	N	N	Y	N	N
2 ***Smith, R.***	Y	N	Y	Y	Y	N	N	Y
3 Wyden	N	N	N	N	Y	Y	N	N
4 Weaver	N	N	Y	N	N	Y	Y	N
5 ***Smith, D.***	Y	Y	N	Y	Y	N	N	Y
PENNSYLVANIA								
1 Foglietta	N	N	Y	N	N	Y	Y	N
2 Gray	N	N	N	N	N	Y	N	?
3 Borski	N	N	N	N	N	Y	N	N
4 Kolter	N	N	N	N	Y	Y	Y	N
5 ***Schulze***	N	N	N	Y	Y	N	N	Y
6 Yatron	N	N	N	N	N	Y	Y	N
7 Edgar	N	N	N	N	N	Y	Y	?
8 Kostmayer	N	N	N	N	N	Y	N	N
9 ***Shuster***	N	N	N	Y	Y	N	Y	Y
10 ***McDade***	N	N	N	Y	Y	Y	Y	N
11 Kanjorski	?	N	N	N	Y	Y	Y	N
12 Murtha	N	N	N	N	N	Y	Y	N
13 ***Coughlin***	N	N	N	N	N	N	N	N
14 Coyne	N	N	N	N	N	Y	Y	N
15 ***Ritter***	N	N	N	Y	Y	N	Y	Y
16 ***Walker***	Y	Y	Y	Y	Y	N	N	Y
17 ***Gekas***	Y	N	N	N	N	N	N	Y
18 Walgren	N	N	N	N	N	Y	Y	N
19 ***Goodling***	N	N	N	Y	Y	N	Y	Y
20 Gaydos	N	N	N	N	N	Y	Y	N
21 ***Ridge***	N	N	N	Y	Y	N	N	N
22 Murphy	Y	N	Y	N	Y	Y	Y	N
23 ***Clinger***	N	N	N	N	Y	N	N	Y
RHODE ISLAND								
1 St Germain	Y	N	Y	N	N	Y	N	N
2 ***Schneider***	N	N	N	N	Y	Y	N	Y
SOUTH CAROLINA								
1 ***Hartnett***	Y	Y	Y	Y	Y	N	?	Y
2 ***Spence***	N	N	N	Y	Y	N	N	Y
3 Derrick	N	N	N	N	Y	N	Y	Y
4 ***Campbell***	?	N	Y	?	?	N	?	?
5 Spratt	N	N	N	Y	N	Y	N	N
6 Tallon	Y	N	N	N	Y	N	Y	N
SOUTH DAKOTA								
AL Daschle	Y	N	Y	Y	N	N	N	Y

	238	239	240	241	242	243	244	245
TENNESSEE								
1 ***Quillen***	N	N	N	Y	N	N	N	N
2 ***Duncan***	N	N	N	Y	Y	N	N	N
3 Lloyd	Y	N	Y	Y	Y	N	N	Y
4 Cooper	N	N	N	Y	N	N	N	N
5 Boner	N	N	N	N	?	Y	N	N
6 Gordon	N	N	N	Y	N	Y	N	N
7 ***Sundquist***	Y	Y	N	Y	Y	N	N	Y
8 Jones	N	N	N	N	N	N	Y	N
9 Ford	N	N	N	?	N	Y	Y	N
TEXAS								
1 Chapman	N	N	N	N	N	N	Y	N
2 Wilson	N	N	N	N	N	Y	Y	N
3 ***Bartlett***	Y	Y	Y	Y	N	N	N	Y
4 Hall, R.	Y	Y	Y	Y	Y	N	Y	Y
5 Bryant	N	N	N	N	N	Y	Y	N
6 ***Barton***	Y	Y	Y	Y	Y	N	N	Y
7 ***Archer***	Y	N	Y	Y	Y	N	N	Y
8 ***Fields***	Y	N	Y	Y	N	N	N	Y
9 Brooks	N	N	N	N	N	Y	N	N
10 Pickle	N	N	Y	Y	Y	N	N	N
11 Leath	Y	N	Y	N	N	N	Y	N
12 Wright	N	N	N	N	N	?	N	N
13 ***Boulter***	Y	Y	Y	Y	Y	N	N	Y
14 ***Sweeney***	Y	Y	Y	Y	Y	N	N	Y
15 de la Garza	N	N	N	N	N	N	?	?
16 Coleman	N	N	N	N	N	Y	Y	N
17 Stenholm	Y	Y	Y	Y	Y	N	N	Y
18 Leland	N	N	N	N	N	Y	Y	N
19 ***Combest***	Y	Y	Y	Y	N	N	N	Y
20 Gonzalez	N	N	N	N	N	Y	Y	N
21 ***Loeffler***	Y	N	Y	Y	N	N	N	Y
22 ***DeLay***	N	Y	Y	Y	N	N	N	Y
23 Bustamante	N	N	N	N	N	Y	N	N
24 Frost	N	N	Y	Y	N	Y	Y	N
25 Andrews	N	N	N	Y	N	N	N	N
26 ***Armey***	Y	Y	Y	Y	N	N	N	Y
27 Ortiz	N	N	N	N	Y	N	N	N
UTAH								
1 ***Hansen***	Y	Y	Y	Y	Y	N	N	Y
2 ***Monson***	Y	Y	Y	Y	Y	N	N	Y
3 ***Nielson***	Y	Y	Y	Y	Y	N	N	Y
VERMONT								
AL ***Jeffords***	N	N	N	N	N	Y	N	N
VIRGINIA								
1 ***Bateman***	N	N	N	Y	N	N	N	N
2 ***Whitehurst***	N	N	N	Y	N	N	N	Y
3 ***Bliley***	Y	N	Y	Y	Y	N	N	Y
4 Sisisky	N	N	N	N	N	N	N	N
5 Daniel	N	Y	Y	Y	Y	N	Y	Y
6 Olin	N	N	N	Y	N	N	N	N
7 ***Slaughter***	Y	N	Y	N	Y	N	N	Y
8 ***Parris***	N	N	N	N	Y	N	N	N
9 Boucher	N	N	?	N	N	Y	N	N
10 ***Wolf***	N	N	N	N	Y	N	N	N
WASHINGTON								
1 ***Miller***	N	Y	N	Y	N	N	N	Y
2 Swift	N	N	N	N	Y	Y	N	N
3 Bonker	?	N	N	N	N	N	N	?
4 ***Morrison***	Y	N	N	N	Y	N	N	Y
5 Foley	N	N	N	N	N	Y	N	N
6 Dicks	N	N	N	N	N	N	N	N
7 Lowry	N	N	N	N	N	Y	N	N
8 ***Chandler***	N	N	N	Y	N	Y	N	Y
WEST VIRGINIA								
1 Mollohan	N	N	N	N	N	Y	Y	N
2 Staggers	N	N	N	N	N	Y	Y	N
3 Wise	N	N	N	N	Y	Y	Y	N
4 Rahall	N	N	N	N	Y	Y	Y	N
WISCONSIN								
1 Aspin	N	N	N	N	N	Y	N	N
2 Kastenmeier	N	N	N	N	N	Y	N	N
3 ***Gunderson***	-	-	-	+	-	+	-	+
4 Kleczka	N	N	N	N	N	Y	N	N
5 Moody	N	N	N	N	Y	Y	N	N
6 ***Petri***	Y	Y	Y	Y	Y	N	N	Y
7 Obey	N	N	N	N	N	Y	N	N
8 ***Roth***	Y	Y	Y	Y	N	N	N	Y
9 ***Sensenbrenner***	Y	Y	Y	Y	N	N	N	Y
WYOMING								
AL ***Cheney***	Y	Y	Y	Y	Y	N	N	Y

Southern states - Ala., Ark., Fla., Ga., Ky., La., Miss., N.C., Okla., S.C., Tenn., Texas, Va.

* The *Congressional Record* vote number is different from the CQ vote number because the *Record* includes quorum calls in its tally. CQ does not publish quorum call votes.

246. HR 5205. Transportation Appropriations, Fiscal 1987. Passage of the bill to appropriate $10,284,900,569 in fiscal 1987 for transportation programs. Passed 329-87: R 93-80; D 236-7 (ND 163-2, SD 73-5), July 30, 1986. The president had requested $7,014,514,569 in new budget authority. A "nay" was a vote supporting the president's position.

247. Procedural Motion. Bilirakis, R-Fla., motion to approve the House *Journal* of Wednesday, July 30. Motion agreed to 263-131: R 54-119; D 209-12 (ND 143-9, SD 66-3), July 31, 1986.

248. HR 5233. Labor, Health and Human Services, Education Appropriations, Fiscal 1987. Frenzel, R-Minn., substitute for the Michel, R-Ill., amendment, to reduce each discretionary item in the bill by 9.14 percent, cutting a total of $2.276 billion from the bill. Rejected 99-321: R 88-89; D 11-232 (ND 0-164, SD 11-68), July 31, 1986. (The Michel amendment, to cap at 3 percent all increases in the bill for discretionary programs, subsequently was rejected *(see vote 249, below).*)

249. HR 5233. Labor, Health and Human Services, Education Appropriations, Fiscal 1987. Michel, R-Ill., amendment to cap increases for programs in the bill at 3 percent over available fiscal 1986 funding, resulting in a reduction of approximately $1.6 billion from the bill's total. Rejected 164-253: R 137-40; D 27-213 (ND 5-157, SD 22-56), July 31, 1986.

250. HR 5233. Labor, Health and Human Services, Education Appropriations, Fiscal 1987. Passage of the bill to appropriate $90,897,951,000 in fiscal 1987 funding and $12,812,065,000 in advance fiscal 1988 and 1989 funding for the Departments of Labor, Health and Human Services, Education and related agencies. Passed 328-86: R 94-79; D 234-7 (ND 161-1, SD 73-6), July 31, 1986. The president had requested $85,016,-700,000 for fiscal 1987 and $12,728,065,000 in advance fiscal 1988 and 1989 funding. A "nay" was a vote supporting the president's position.

251. HR 5234. Interior Appropriations, Fiscal 1987. Adoption of the rule (H Res 516) to waive points of order against the bill to make $8.19 billion in appropriations for the Department of the Interior and related agencies in fiscal 1987. Adopted 315-93: R 84-89; D 231-4 (ND 156-1, SD 75-3), July 31, 1986.

252. HR 5234. Interior Appropriations, Fiscal 1987. Passage of the bill to appropriate $8,190,146,000 for the Department of the Interior and related agencies in 1987. Passed 359-51: R 123-50; D 236-1 (ND 159-1, 77-0), July 31, 1986. The president had requested $6,616,975,000 in new budget authority. A "nay" was a vote supporting the president's position.

253. S J Res 371. Helsinki Human Rights Day. Passage of the joint resolution to designate Aug. 1, 1986, as "Helsinki Human Rights Day," commemorating the 11th anniversary of the signing of the Final Act of the Conference on Security and Cooperation in Europe, also known as the Helsinki Accords. Passed 389-1: R 164-1; D 225-0 (ND 150-0, SD 75-0), July 31, 1986.

KEY

Y Voted for (yea).
\# Paired for.
\+ Announced for.
N Voted against (nay).
X Paired against.
\- Announced against.
P Voted "present."
C Voted "present" to avoid possible conflict of interest.
? Did not vote or otherwise make a position known.

Democrats *Republicans*

	246	247	248	249	250	251	252	253
ALABAMA								
1 ***Callahan***	Y	?	Y	Y	?	N	Y	Y
2 ***Dickinson***	Y	N	N	Y	Y	Y	Y	Y
3 Nichols	Y	?	N	Y	Y	Y	Y	Y
4 Bevill	Y	Y	N	N	Y	Y	?	?
5 Flippo	Y	Y	N	N	Y	Y	Y	Y
6 Erdreich	Y	Y	N	N	Y	Y	Y	Y
7 Shelby	Y	?	N	N	Y	Y	Y	Y
ALASKA								
AL ***Young***	Y	N	N	Y	Y	Y	Y	Y
ARIZONA								
1 ***McCain***	Y	Y	N	N	Y	Y	Y	Y
2 Udall	Y	Y	N	N	Y	Y	Y	Y
3 ***Stump***	N	N	Y	Y	N	N	N	Y
4 ***Rudd***	N	Y	N	N	Y	Y	?	?
5 ***Kolbe***	N	N	Y	Y	Y	Y	Y	Y
ARKANSAS								
1 Alexander	Y	Y	N	N	Y	Y	Y	Y
2 Robinson	Y	Y	N	N	Y	Y	Y	Y
3 ***Hammerschmidt***	Y	Y	N	Y	Y	Y	Y	Y
4 Anthony	Y	Y	N	?	Y	Y	Y	Y
CALIFORNIA								
1 Bosco	Y	Y	N	N	Y	Y	Y	Y
2 ***Chappie***	N	N	Y	Y	N	N	N	Y
3 Matsui	Y	Y	N	N	Y	Y	Y	Y
4 Fazio	Y	Y	N	N	Y	Y	Y	Y
5 Burton	Y	Y	N	N	Y	Y	Y	Y
6 Boxer	Y	Y	N	N	Y	Y	Y	?
7 Miller	Y	Y	N	N	Y	Y	Y	Y
8 Dellums	Y	Y	N	N	Y	Y	Y	Y
9 Stark	Y	?	?	N	Y	Y	Y	Y
10 Edwards	Y	Y	N	N	Y	Y	Y	Y
11 Lantos	Y	Y	N	N	Y	Y	Y	Y
12 ***Zschau***	Y	N	N	N	Y	?	Y	Y
13 Mineta	Y	Y	N	N	Y	Y	Y	Y
14 ***Shumway***	N	Y	Y	Y	N	N	N	Y
15 Coelho	Y	Y	N	N	Y	Y	Y	Y
16 Panetta	Y	?	N	N	Y	Y	Y	Y
17 ***Pashayan***	Y	N	N	Y	Y	Y	Y	Y
18 Lehman	Y	Y	N	N	Y	Y	Y	Y
19 ***Lagomarsino***	N	N	N	Y	N	N	N	Y
20 ***Thomas***	N	N	Y	Y	N	Y	N	Y
21 ***Fiedler***	?	N	Y	Y	N	N	N	Y
22 ***Moorhead***	N	N	Y	Y	N	Y	N	Y
23 Beilenson	Y	Y	N	N	Y	Y	Y	Y
24 Waxman	Y	N	N	N	Y	?	Y	Y
25 Roybal	Y	Y	N	N	Y	Y	Y	?
26 Berman	Y	Y	N	N	Y	Y	Y	Y
27 Levine	Y	Y	N	N	Y	Y	Y	Y
28 Dixon	Y	?	N	N	Y	Y	Y	Y
29 Hawkins	Y	N	N	N	Y	Y	Y	Y
30 Martinez	Y	Y	N	N	Y	Y	Y	Y
31 Dymally	Y	Y	N	N	Y	Y	Y	?
32 Anderson	Y	Y	N	N	Y	Y	Y	Y
33 ***Dreier***	N	N	Y	Y	N	N	N	Y
34 Torres	Y	?	N	N	Y	Y	Y	Y
35 ***Lewis***	Y	N	N	Y	Y	N	Y	Y
36 Brown	Y	Y	N	N	Y	Y	?	?
37 ***McCandless***	N	N	Y	Y	N	N	Y	Y
38 ***Dornan***	N	N	Y	Y	N	N	N	Y
39 ***Dannemeyer***	N	N	Y	Y	N	N	N	Y
40 ***Badham***	N	N	Y	Y	N	N	?	?
41 ***Lowery***	Y	N	N	Y	Y	Y	Y	Y
42 ***Lungren***	N	N	Y	Y	N	N	N	Y
43 ***Packard***	N	N	Y	Y	N	N	Y	Y
44 Bates	Y	Y	N	N	Y	Y	Y	Y
45 ***Hunter***	N	N	Y	Y	N	N	N	Y
COLORADO								
1 Schroeder	Y	N	N	N	Y	Y	Y	Y
2 Wirth	Y	Y	N	N	Y	Y	Y	Y
3 ***Strang***	N	N	Y	Y	N	N	N	Y
4 ***Brown***	N	N	Y	Y	N	N	N	Y
5 ***Kramer***	Y	N	Y	Y	N	Y	Y	Y
6 ***Schaefer***	Y	Y	Y	Y	N	N	N	Y
CONNECTICUT								
1 Kennelly	Y	Y	N	N	Y	Y	Y	Y
2 Gejdenson	Y	Y	N	N	Y	Y	Y	Y
3 Morrison	Y	Y	N	N	Y	Y	Y	Y
4 ***McKinney***	Y	Y	N	N	Y	Y	Y	Y
5 ***Rowland***	Y	N	N	N	Y	Y	Y	Y
6 ***Johnson***	Y	Y	N	Y	Y	Y	Y	Y
DELAWARE								
AL Carper	Y	Y	N	N	Y	Y	Y	Y
FLORIDA								
1 Hutto	Y	Y	Y	Y	Y	Y	Y	Y
2 Fuqua	Y	Y	N	N	Y	Y	Y	Y
3 Bennett	Y	Y	N	Y	Y	Y	Y	Y
4 Chappell	Y	?	N	N	Y	Y	Y	Y
5 ***McCollum***	Y	N	Y	Y	N	N	N	Y
6 MacKay	?	?	N	N	Y	Y	Y	Y
7 Gibbons	Y	Y	Y	Y	Y	Y	Y	Y
8 ***Young***	Y	N	N	N	Y	N	Y	Y
9 ***Bilirakis***	Y	N	N	N	Y	N	N	Y
10 ***Ireland***	N	N	Y	Y	N	N	N	Y
11 Nelson	Y	Y	N	N	Y	Y	Y	Y
12 ***Lewis***	Y	N	N	N	Y	N	Y	Y
13 ***Mack***	N	N	Y	Y	N	N	N	Y
14 Mica	Y	Y	N	N	Y	Y	Y	Y
15 ***Shaw***	Y	N	N	N	Y	N	Y	Y
16 Smith	Y	Y	N	N	Y	Y	Y	Y
17 Lehman	Y	Y	N	N	Y	Y	Y	Y
18 Pepper	Y	Y	N	N	Y	Y	Y	Y
19 Fascell	Y	Y	N	N	Y	Y	Y	Y
GEORGIA								
1 Thomas	Y	Y	N	N	Y	Y	Y	Y
2 Hatcher	Y	Y	N	N	Y	Y	Y	Y
3 Ray	N	Y	Y	Y	N	Y	Y	Y
4 ***Swindall***	N	N	Y	Y	N	N	Y	Y
5 Fowler	?	?	?	?	?	?	?	?
6 ***Gingrich***	N	N	Y	Y	?	N	Y	Y
7 Darden	Y	Y	N	Y	Y	Y	Y	Y
8 Rowland	Y	Y	N	N	Y	Y	Y	Y
9 Jenkins	Y	Y	N	N	Y	Y	Y	Y
10 Barnard	Y	Y	Y	Y	Y	Y	Y	Y
HAWAII								
1 Vacancy								
2 Akaka	Y	Y	N	N	Y	Y	Y	Y
IDAHO								
1 ***Craig***	N	N	Y	Y	N	Y	Y	Y
2 Stallings	Y	Y	N	Y	Y	Y	Y	Y
ILLINOIS								
1 Hayes	Y	Y	N	N	Y	Y	Y	Y
2 Savage	Y	Y	N	N	Y	Y	Y	Y
3 Russo	Y	Y	N	N	Y	Y	Y	Y
4 Vacancy								
5 Lipinski	Y	Y	N	N	Y	Y	Y	Y
6 ***Hyde***	N	N	N	Y	Y	N	Y	Y
7 Collins	Y	?	N	N	Y	Y	Y	Y
8 Rostenkowski	Y	Y	N	N	Y	Y	Y	Y
9 Yates	Y	Y	N	N	Y	Y	Y	Y
10 ***Porter***	Y	Y	Y	Y	Y	N	Y	Y
11 Annunzio	Y	Y	N	N	Y	Y	Y	Y
12 ***Crane***	N	N	Y	Y	N	N	N	N
13 ***Fawell***	N	N	Y	Y	Y	Y	Y	Y
14 ***Grotberg***	?	?	?	?	?	?	?	?
15 ***Madigan***	Y	N	N	Y	N	N	Y	Y
16 ***Martin***	N	N	Y	Y	N	N	N	Y
17 Evans	Y	Y	N	N	Y	Y	Y	Y
18 ***Michel***	Y	N	Y	Y	N	N	Y	Y
19 Bruce	Y	Y	N	N	Y	Y	Y	Y
20 Durbin	Y	Y	N	N	Y	Y	Y	Y
21 Price	Y	Y	N	N	Y	Y	Y	Y
22 Gray	Y	?	N	N	Y	Y	Y	Y
INDIANA								
1 Visclosky	Y	Y	N	N	Y	Y	Y	Y
2 Sharp	Y	Y	N	N	Y	Y	Y	Y
3 ***Hiler***	N	N	Y	Y	N	N	Y	Y
4 ***Coats***	N	N	Y	Y	Y	Y	Y	Y
5 ***Hillis***	Y	Y	N	N	Y	Y	Y	?

ND - Northern Democrats SD - Southern Democrats

* Corresponding to Congressional Record Votes 270, 271, 272, 273, 274, 275, 276, 277

	246	247	248	249	250	251	252	253
6 ***Burton***	N	N	Y	Y	N	N	N	Y
7 ***Myers***	Y	Y	N	N	Y	Y	Y	Y
8 McCloskey	Y	Y	N	N	Y	Y	Y	Y
9 Hamilton	Y	Y	N	Y	Y	Y	Y	Y
10 Jacobs	Y	N	N	Y	Y	Y	N	Y
IOWA								
1 ***Leach***	N	N	N	Y	N	N	Y	Y
2 ***Tauke***	N	N	N	Y	N	Y	N	Y
3 ***Evans***	N	N	N	Y	Y	?	N	Y
4 Smith	Y	Y	N	N	Y	Y	Y	Y
5 ***Lightfoot***	N	N	N	Y	N	N	N	Y
6 Bedell	?	?	?	?	?	?	?	?
KANSAS								
1 ***Roberts***	N	N	Y	Y	N	N	Y	Y
2 Slattery	Y	?	N	Y	Y	Y	Y	Y
3 ***Meyers***	N	N	Y	Y	Y	N	Y	Y
4 Glickman	Y	Y	N	N	Y	Y	Y	Y
5 ***Whittaker***	N	N	Y	Y	Y	Y	Y	Y
KENTUCKY								
1 Hubbard	N	Y	N	N	Y	Y	Y	Y
2 Natcher	Y	Y	N	N	Y	Y	Y	Y
3 Mazzoli	Y	Y	N	N	Y	Y	Y	Y
4 ***Snyder***	Y	Y	N	N	Y	Y	Y	Y
5 ***Rogers***	Y	N	N	N	Y	Y	Y	Y
6 ***Hopkins***	N	N	Y	Y	Y	N	Y	Y
7 Perkins	Y	Y	N	N	Y	Y	Y	Y
LOUISIANA								
1 ***Livingston***	Y	Y	N	Y	Y	Y	Y	Y
2 Boggs	Y	Y	N	N	Y	Y	Y	Y
3 Tauzin	Y	Y	Y	Y	Y	Y	Y	Y
4 Roemer	Y	N	Y	Y	Y	N	Y	Y
5 Huckaby	Y	Y	Y	Y	N	Y	Y	Y
6 ***Moore***	?	?	?	?	?	?	?	?
7 Breaux	?	?	?	?	?	?	?	?
8 Long	Y	Y	N	N	Y	Y	Y	Y
MAINE								
1 ***McKernan***	Y	N	N	Y	Y	Y	Y	Y
2 ***Snowe***	Y	Y	N	Y	Y	Y	Y	Y
MARYLAND								
1 Dyson	Y	N	N	N	Y	Y	Y	Y
2 ***Bentley***	Y	N	N	Y	Y	N	Y	Y
3 Mikulski	Y	?	N	N	Y	Y	Y	Y
4 ***Holt***	Y	N	N	Y	N	N	Y	Y
5 Hoyer	Y	Y	N	N	Y	Y	Y	Y
6 Byron	Y	Y	N	N	Y	Y	Y	Y
7 Mitchell	Y	?	N	N	Y	?	?	?
8 Barnes	?	?	?	?	?	?	?	?
MASSACHUSETTS								
1 ***Conte***	Y	N	N	N	Y	Y	Y	Y
2 Boland	Y	Y	N	N	Y	Y	Y	Y
3 Early	Y	Y	N	N	Y	Y	Y	Y
4 Frank	Y	Y	N	N	Y	Y	Y	Y
5 Atkins	Y	Y	N	N	Y	Y	Y	Y
6 Mavroules	Y	Y	N	N	Y	?	Y	Y
7 Markey	Y	Y	N	N	Y	Y	Y	Y
8 O'Neill								
9 Moakley	Y	Y	N	N	Y	Y	Y	Y
10 Studds	Y	Y	N	N	Y	Y	Y	Y
11 Donnelly	Y	Y	N	N	Y	Y	Y	Y
MICHIGAN								
1 Conyers	Y	Y	N	?	?	?	?	?
2 ***Pursell***	Y	Y	N	N	Y	N	Y	?
3 Wolpe	Y	Y	N	N	Y	Y	Y	Y
4 ***Siljander***	N	Y	Y	Y	N	N	N	Y
5 ***Henry***	Y	N	N	Y	Y	N	Y	Y
6 Carr	Y	Y	N	N	Y	Y	Y	Y
7 Kildee	Y	Y	N	N	Y	Y	Y	Y
8 Traxler	Y	Y	N	N	Y	Y	Y	Y
9 ***Vander Jagt***	Y	N	Y	Y	Y	N	Y	Y
10 ***Schuette***	Y	N	N	Y	Y	Y	Y	Y
11 ***Davis***	Y	Y	N	N	Y	Y	Y	Y
12 Bonior	Y	Y	N	N	Y	Y	Y	Y
13 Crockett	Y	Y	N	N	Y	Y	Y	Y
14 Hertel	N	Y	N	N	Y	Y	Y	Y
15 Ford	Y	Y	N	N	Y	Y	Y	?
16 Dingell	Y	?	N	N	Y	Y	Y	Y
17 Levin	Y	Y	N	N	Y	Y	Y	Y
18 ***Broomfield***	Y	Y	N	Y	Y	N	Y	?
MINNESOTA								
1 Penny	N	N	N	Y	Y	Y	Y	Y
2 ***Weber***	N	N	Y	Y	N	N	N	Y
3 ***Frenzel***	N	N	Y	Y	N	N	N	Y
4 Vento	Y	Y	N	N	Y	Y	Y	Y
5 Sabo	Y	Y	N	N	Y	Y	Y	Y
6 Sikorski	Y	N	N	N	Y	Y	Y	Y
7 ***Stangeland***	Y	N	Y	Y	Y	Y	Y	Y
8 Oberstar	Y	Y	N	N	Y	Y	Y	Y
MISSISSIPPI								
1 Whitten	Y	Y	N	N	Y	?	Y	Y
2 ***Franklin***	Y	Y	N	Y	Y	Y	N	Y
3 Montgomery	Y	Y	Y	Y	Y	Y	Y	Y
4 Dowdy	Y	Y	N	N	Y	Y	Y	Y
5 ***Lott***	N	N	Y	Y	N	N	N	Y
MISSOURI								
1 Clay	Y	?	?	?	?	?	?	?
2 Young	Y	Y	N	N	Y	Y	Y	Y
3 Gephardt	Y	Y	N	N	Y	Y	Y	?
4 Skelton	Y	Y	N	N	Y	Y	?	?
5 Wheat	Y	Y	N	N	Y	Y	Y	Y
6 ***Coleman***	Y	N	N	Y	Y	Y	Y	Y
7 ***Taylor***	Y	Y	N	Y	Y	Y	Y	Y
8 ***Emerson***	Y	N	N	Y	Y	Y	Y	Y
9 Volkmer	Y	Y	N	N	Y	Y	Y	Y
MONTANA								
1 Williams	Y	Y	N	?	Y	?	Y	Y
2 ***Marlenee***	N	N	N	Y	N	Y	Y	Y
NEBRASKA								
1 ***Bereuter***	Y	N	N	Y	Y	N	Y	Y
2 ***Daub***	N	N	N	Y	Y	N	Y	Y
3 ***Smith***	Y	Y	N	N	Y	Y	Y	Y
NEVADA								
1 Reid	Y	Y	N	N	Y	Y	Y	Y
2 ***Vucanovich***	Y	N	N	Y	N	Y	Y	Y
NEW HAMPSHIRE								
1 ***Smith***	N	N	Y	Y	N	N	N	Y
2 ***Gregg***	N	N	Y	Y	N	N	N	Y
NEW JERSEY								
1 Florio	Y	Y	N	N	Y	Y	Y	Y
2 Hughes	Y	Y	N	N	N	Y	Y	Y
3 Howard	Y	Y	N	N	Y	Y	Y	Y
4 ***Smith***	Y	Y	N	N	Y	Y	Y	Y
5 ***Roukema***	Y	N	N	Y	Y	Y	Y	Y
6 Dwyer	Y	Y	N	N	Y	Y	Y	Y
7 ***Rinaldo***	Y	Y	N	N	Y	Y	Y	Y
8 Roe	Y	Y	N	N	Y	Y	Y	?
9 Torricelli	Y	Y	N	N	Y	Y	Y	Y
10 Rodino	Y	Y	N	N	Y	Y	Y	Y
11 ***Gallo***	Y	N	N	N	Y	N	Y	Y
12 ***Courter***	Y	N	N	N	Y	N	Y	Y
13 ***Saxton***	Y	N	N	N	Y	N	Y	Y
14 Guarini	Y	Y	N	N	Y	Y	Y	Y
NEW MEXICO								
1 ***Lujan***	N	Y	Y	Y	N	Y	N	Y
2 ***Skeen***	Y	N	N	Y	Y	Y	Y	Y
3 Richardson	Y	Y	N	N	Y	Y	Y	Y
NEW YORK								
1 ***Carney***	?	?	?	?	?	?	?	?
2 Downey	Y	Y	N	N	Y	Y	Y	Y
3 Mrazek	Y	Y	N	N	Y	Y	Y	Y
4 ***Lent***	Y	N	N	Y	Y	Y	Y	Y
5 ***McGrath***	Y	N	N	Y	Y	Y	Y	Y
6 Waldon	Y	Y	N	?	?	?	Y	Y
7 Ackerman	Y	Y	N	N	Y	Y	Y	?
8 Scheuer	Y	Y	N	N	Y	Y	Y	Y
9 Manton	Y	Y	N	N	Y	Y	Y	Y
10 Schumer	Y	Y	N	N	Y	Y	Y	Y
11 Towns	Y	?	N	N	Y	Y	Y	Y
12 Owens	Y	Y	N	N	Y	Y	Y	Y
13 Solarz	Y	Y	N	N	Y	Y	Y	Y
14 ***Molinari***	Y	N	Y	Y	N	Y	Y	Y
15 ***Green***	Y	Y	N	N	Y	Y	Y	Y
16 Rangel	Y	Y	N	N	Y	Y	Y	Y
17 Weiss	Y	Y	N	N	Y	Y	Y	Y
18 Garcia	Y	Y	N	N	Y	Y	Y	?
19 Biaggi	Y	Y	N	N	Y	Y	Y	Y
20 ***DioGuardi***	Y	Y	N	Y	Y	Y	Y	Y
21 ***Fish***	?	Y	N	Y	Y	Y	Y	Y
22 ***Gilman***	Y	Y	N	N	Y	Y	Y	Y
23 Stratton	Y	Y	N	N	Y	Y	Y	Y
24 ***Solomon***	N	N	Y	Y	N	N	N	Y
25 ***Boehlert***	Y	N	N	N	Y	Y	Y	Y
26 ***Martin***	Y	Y	N	Y	Y	Y	Y	Y
27 ***Wortley***	Y	Y	N	Y	Y	Y	Y	Y
28 McHugh	Y	Y	N	N	Y	Y	Y	Y
29 ***Horton***	Y	Y	N	N	Y	Y	Y	?
30 ***Eckert***	N	?	Y	Y	N	N	N	Y
31 ***Kemp***	Y	Y	Y	Y	?	Y	Y	Y
32 LaFalce	Y	Y	N	N	Y	Y	Y	Y
33 Nowak	Y	Y	N	N	Y	Y	Y	Y
34 Lundine	?	?	?	?	?	?	?	?
NORTH CAROLINA								
1 Jones	Y	?	N	N	Y	Y	Y	Y
2 Valentine	Y	Y	N	N	Y	Y	Y	Y
3 Whitley	Y	Y	N	N	Y	Y	Y	Y
4 ***Cobey***	Y	N	N	Y	Y	N	Y	Y
5 Neal	Y	?	N	N	Y	Y	Y	Y
6 ***Coble***	Y	N	Y	Y	Y	Y	Y	Y
7 Rose	Y	Y	N	N	Y	Y	Y	Y
8 Hefner	Y	Y	N	N	Y	Y	Y	Y
9 ***McMillan***	Y	Y	Y	Y	Y	Y	Y	Y
10 Vacancy								
11 ***Hendon***	Y	N	N	N	Y	Y	Y	Y
NORTH DAKOTA								
AL Dorgan	Y	Y	N	N	Y	Y	Y	Y
OHIO								
1 Luken	Y	Y	N	N	Y	Y	Y	Y
2 ***Gradison***	N	Y	Y	Y	N	Y	Y	Y
3 Hall	Y	Y	N	N	Y	Y	Y	Y
4 ***Oxley***	N	N	Y	Y	N	N	Y	Y
5 ***Latta***	N	N	Y	Y	N	N	Y	Y
6 ***McEwen***	?	Y	Y	Y	N	Y	Y	Y
7 ***DeWine***	N	N	N	Y	N	N	Y	Y
8 ***Kindness***	N	N	Y	Y	N	N	Y	Y
9 Kaptur	Y	Y	N	N	Y	Y	Y	Y
10 ***Miller***	N	N	Y	Y	N	Y	Y	Y
11 Eckart	Y	Y	N	N	Y	Y	Y	Y
12 ***Kasich***	Y	Y	Y	Y	Y	N	Y	Y
13 Pease	Y	Y	N	N	Y	Y	Y	Y
14 Seiberling	Y	?	N	N	Y	Y	Y	Y
15 ***Wylie***	N	Y	N	N	Y	Y	Y	Y
16 ***Regula***	Y	Y	N	Y	Y	Y	Y	Y
17 Traficant	Y	Y	N	N	Y	Y	Y	Y
18 Applegate	Y	Y	N	N	Y	Y	Y	Y
19 Feighan	Y	Y	N	N	Y	Y	Y	Y
20 Oakar	Y	Y	N	N	Y	Y	Y	Y
21 Stokes	Y	Y	N	N	Y	Y	Y	Y
OKLAHOMA								
1 Jones	Y	N	N	Y	Y	Y	Y	Y
2 Synar	Y	Y	N	N	Y	Y	Y	Y
3 Watkins	Y	Y	N	N	Y	Y	Y	Y
4 McCurdy	Y	?	N	Y	Y	Y	Y	Y
5 ***Edwards***	Y	Y	Y	Y	N	N	Y	Y
6 English	Y	Y	N	Y	Y	Y	?	?
OREGON								
1 AuCoin	Y	Y	N	N	Y	Y	Y	Y
2 ***Smith, R.***	Y	N	Y	Y	N	Y	Y	Y
3 Wyden	Y	Y	N	N	Y	Y	Y	Y
4 Weaver	Y	Y	N	N	Y	Y	Y	Y
5 ***Smith, D.***	N	N	Y	Y	N	N	N	Y
PENNSYLVANIA								
1 Foglietta	Y	Y	N	N	Y	Y	Y	?
2 Gray	Y	Y	N	N	Y	Y	Y	Y
3 Borski	Y	Y	N	N	Y	Y	Y	Y
4 Kolter	Y	Y	N	N	Y	Y	Y	Y
5 ***Schulze***	Y	Y	N	Y	Y	Y	Y	Y
6 Yatron	Y	Y	N	N	Y	Y	Y	Y
7 Edgar	?	Y	N	N	Y	?	?	?
8 Kostmayer	Y	Y	N	N	Y	Y	Y	Y
9 ***Shuster***	N	N	Y	Y	N	N	N	Y
10 ***McDade***	Y	Y	N	N	Y	Y	Y	Y
11 Kanjorski	Y	Y	N	N	Y	Y	Y	Y
12 Murtha	Y	Y	N	N	Y	Y	Y	Y
13 ***Coughlin***	Y	N	N	N	Y	Y	Y	Y
14 Coyne	Y	Y	N	N	Y	?	Y	Y
15 ***Ritter***	Y	Y	Y	Y	Y	Y	N	Y
16 ***Walker***	N	N	Y	Y	N	N	N	Y
17 ***Gekas***	Y	N	Y	Y	N	N	N	Y
18 Walgren	Y	Y	N	N	Y	Y	Y	Y
19 ***Goodling***	Y	N	N	N	Y	Y	Y	?
20 Gaydos	Y	Y	N	N	Y	Y	Y	Y
21 ***Ridge***	Y	N	N	Y	Y	N	Y	Y
22 Murphy	Y	Y	N	N	Y	Y	Y	Y
23 ***Clinger***	Y	Y	N	N	Y	Y	Y	Y
RHODE ISLAND								
1 St Germain	Y	N	N	N	Y	Y	Y	Y
2 ***Schneider***	Y	Y	N	N	Y	Y	Y	Y
SOUTH CAROLINA								
1 ***Hartnett***	N	Y	Y	Y	?	?	?	?
2 ***Spence***	N	Y	Y	N	Y	Y	Y	Y
3 Derrick	Y	Y	N	N	Y	Y	Y	Y
4 ***Campbell***	N	?	N	N	Y	?	?	?
5 Spratt	Y	Y	N	N	Y	Y	Y	Y
6 Tallon	Y	Y	N	N	Y	Y	Y	Y
SOUTH DAKOTA								
AL Daschle	Y	Y	N	N	Y	Y	Y	Y
TENNESSEE								
1 ***Quillen***	Y	Y	N	Y	Y	Y	Y	Y
2 ***Duncan***	Y	Y	Y	Y	Y	Y	Y	Y
3 Lloyd	Y	N	N	Y	Y	Y	Y	Y
4 Cooper	Y	Y	Y	Y	Y	Y	Y	Y
5 Boner	Y	Y	?	?	?	?	?	?
6 Gordon	Y	?	N	N	Y	Y	Y	Y
7 ***Sundquist***	Y	N	Y	Y	Y	N	Y	Y
8 Jones	Y	Y	N	N	Y	Y	Y	Y
9 Ford	Y	?	N	N	Y	Y	Y	?
TEXAS								
1 Chapman	Y	Y	N	N	Y	Y	Y	Y
2 Wilson	Y	?	N	N	Y	Y	Y	Y
3 ***Bartlett***	N	N	Y	Y	N	N	N	Y
4 Hall, R.	N	Y	Y	Y	N	N	Y	Y
5 Bryant	Y	Y	N	N	Y	Y	Y	Y
6 ***Barton***	N	N	Y	Y	N	Y	Y	Y
7 ***Archer***	N	Y	Y	Y	N	N	Y	Y
8 ***Fields***	N	N	Y	Y	N	N	N	Y
9 Brooks	Y	Y	N	N	Y	Y	Y	Y
10 Pickle	Y	?	N	Y	Y	Y	Y	Y
11 Leath	Y	Y	N	N	Y	Y	Y	Y
12 Wright	Y	Y	N	N	Y	Y	Y	Y
13 ***Boulter***	N	N	Y	Y	N	N	Y	Y
14 ***Sweeney***	N	?	Y	Y	N	Y	Y	?
15 de la Garza	?	Y	N	N	Y	Y	Y	Y
16 Coleman	Y	Y	N	N	Y	Y	Y	Y
17 Stenholm	N	Y	Y	Y	N	N	Y	Y
18 Leland	Y	Y	N	N	Y	Y	Y	Y
19 ***Combest***	N	Y	Y	Y	N	N	Y	Y
20 Gonzalez	N	Y	N	N	Y	Y	Y	Y
21 ***Loeffler***	Y	N	Y	Y	Y	Y	Y	Y
22 ***DeLay***	N	N	Y	Y	N	N	N	Y
23 Bustamante	Y	Y	N	N	Y	Y	Y	Y
24 Frost	Y	Y	N	N	Y	Y	Y	Y
25 Andrews	Y	Y	N	Y	Y	Y	Y	Y
26 ***Armey***	N	N	Y	Y	N	N	N	Y
27 Ortiz	Y	Y	N	N	Y	Y	Y	Y
UTAH								
1 ***Hansen***	N	N	Y	Y	N	Y	N	Y
2 ***Monson***	N	N	Y	Y	N	N	N	Y
3 ***Nielson***	N	N	Y	Y	N	Y	Y	Y
VERMONT								
AL ***Jeffords***	Y	Y	N	N	Y	Y	Y	Y
VIRGINIA								
1 ***Bateman***	Y	Y	N	Y	Y	Y	Y	Y
2 ***Whitehurst***	N	N	N	Y	N	Y	Y	?
3 ***Bliley***	Y	N	N	Y	N	N	Y	Y
4 Sisisky	Y	Y	N	N	Y	Y	Y	Y
5 Daniel	Y	Y	N	Y	N	Y	Y	Y
6 Olin	Y	Y	N	Y	N	Y	Y	Y
7 ***Slaughter***	N	N	Y	Y	N	N	N	Y
8 ***Parris***	Y	N	N	Y	Y	Y	Y	?
9 Boucher	Y	Y	N	N	Y	Y	Y	?
10 ***Wolf***	Y	N	N	N	Y	Y	Y	Y
WASHINGTON								
1 ***Miller***	N	Y	N	Y	Y	N	Y	Y
2 Swift	Y	Y	N	N	Y	Y	Y	Y
3 Bonker	Y	Y	N	N	?	Y	Y	?
4 ***Morrison***	Y	Y	N	N	Y	Y	Y	Y
5 Foley	Y	Y	N	N	Y	Y	Y	Y
6 Dicks	Y	Y	N	N	Y	Y	Y	Y
7 Lowry	Y	N	N	N	Y	N	Y	Y
8 ***Chandler***	Y	N	N	N	Y	Y	Y	Y
WEST VIRGINIA								
1 Mollohan	Y	Y	N	N	Y	Y	Y	Y
2 Staggers	Y	Y	N	N	Y	Y	Y	Y
3 Wise	Y	Y	N	N	Y	Y	Y	Y
4 Rahall	Y	Y	N	N	Y	Y	Y	Y
WISCONSIN								
1 Aspin	Y	Y	N	N	Y	Y	Y	Y
2 Kastenmeier	Y	Y	N	N	Y	Y	Y	Y
3 ***Gunderson***	+	N	N	N	Y	N	Y	Y
4 Kleczka	Y	?	N	N	Y	Y	Y	Y
5 Moody	Y	Y	N	N	Y	Y	Y	Y
6 ***Petri***	N	Y	Y	Y	N	N	N	Y
7 Obey	Y	Y	N	N	Y	Y	Y	Y
8 ***Roth***	Y	N	N	Y	N	N	Y	Y
9 ***Sensenbrenner***	N	N	Y	Y	N	N	N	Y
WYOMING								
AL ***Cheney***	N	N	Y	Y	N	N	N	Y

Southern states - Ala., Ark., Fla., Ga., Ky., La., Miss., N.C., Okla., S.C., Tenn., Texas, Va.

* The *Congressional Record* vote number is different from the CQ vote number because the *Record* includes quorum calls in its tally. CQ does not publish quorum call votes.

254. HR 4428. Defense Authorization, Fiscal 1987. Adoption of the rule (H Res 523) to provide for House floor consideration of the bill to authorize funds for military programs in the Departments of Defense and Energy in fiscal 1987. Adopted 245-122: R 49-109; D 196-13 (ND 139-4, SD 57-9), Aug. 1, 1986.

255. HR 5294. Treasury, Postal Service and General Government Appropriations, Fiscal 1987. Adoption of the rule (H Res 521) to waive points of order against the bill to provide $13,794,437,000 in fiscal 1987 appropriations for the Treasury Department, U.S. Postal Service, Executive Office of the President and other agencies. Adopted 278-92: R 72-89; D 206-3 (ND 144-1, SD 62-2), Aug. 1, 1986.

256. HR 5294. Treasury, Postal Service and General Government Appropriations, Fiscal 1987. Walker, R-Pa., amendments to add $3 million to the U.S. Customs Service, taking the money away from the office of the Treasury secretary. Adopted en bloc 254-109: R 130-29; D 124-80 (ND 81-61, SD 43-19), Aug. 1, 1986. (The Walker amendments were again adopted after the House rose from the Committee of the Whole *(see vote 270, p. 78-H)*.)

257. HR 4428. Defense Authorization, Fiscal 1987. Nichols, D-Ala., amendment to reorganize the Pentagon, shifting power from the separate services to the commanders in chief (CINCs) who would be responsible for combat operations in wartime. Adopted 406-4: R 170-1; D 236-3 (ND 158-2, SD 78-1), Aug. 5, 1986.

258. HR 4428. Defense Authorization, Fiscal 1987. Courter, R-N.J., amendment to the Mavroules, D-Mass., amendment, to delete a provision in the Mavroules amendment that would make corporate executives criminally liable if claims were submitted to the Pentagon for unallowable costs. Rejected 157-251: R 130-45; D 27-206 (ND 3-153, SD 24-53), Aug. 5, 1986. (The Mavroules amendment, to change the way the Pentagon buys its weapons and to create the position of acquisitions chief, later was adopted *(see vote 261, below)*.)

259. HR 4428. Defense Authorization, Fiscal 1987. Traficant, D-Ohio, amendment to the Mavroules, D-Mass., amendment, to require the Pentagon to buy U.S.-built goods rather than competing foreign-built goods if the price of the U.S. items is not more than 5 percent higher than the foreign items. Adopted 241-163: R 74-100; D 167-63 (ND 115-39, SD 52-24), Aug. 5, 1986. (The Mavroules amendment later was adopted *(see vote 261, below)*.)

260. HR 4428. Defense Authorization, Fiscal 1987. Courter, R-N.J., substitute for the Mavroules, D-Mass., amendment, to change the Pentagon's weapons procurement procedures. Rejected 164-245: R 138-37; D 26-208 (ND 4-153, SD 22-55), Aug. 5, 1986. (The Mavroules amendment subsequently was adopted *(see vote 261, below)*.)

261. HR 4428. Defense Authorization, Fiscal 1987. Mavroules, D-Mass., amendment to change the way the Pentagon buys its weapons and to create the position of acquisitions chief. Adopted 347-60: R 119-54; D 228-6 (ND 156-1, SD 72-5), Aug. 5, 1986.

KEY

- Y Voted for (yea).
- # Paired for.
- + Announced for.
- N Voted against (nay).
- X Paired against.
- \- Announced against.
- P Voted "present."
- C Voted "present" to avoid possible conflict of interest.
- ? Did not vote or otherwise make a position known.

Democrats *Republicans*

	254	255	256	257	258	259	260	261
ALABAMA								
1 ***Callahan***	N	Y	Y	Y	Y	Y	Y	N
2 ***Dickinson***	Y	Y	N	Y	Y	N	Y	N
3 Nichols	Y	?	N	Y	Y	Y	Y	Y
4 Bevill	?	?	?	Y	Y	Y	Y	Y
5 Flippo	Y	Y	N	Y	Y	Y	N	Y
6 Erdreich	Y	Y	Y	Y	N	Y	N	Y
7 Shelby	?	?	?	Y	Y	Y	N	Y
ALASKA								
AL ***Young***	Y	Y	N	Y	Y	Y	N	Y
ARIZONA								
1 ***McCain***	N	N	Y	Y	N	N	Y	Y
2 Udall	Y	Y	N	Y	N	N	N	Y
3 ***Stump***	N	N	Y	Y	Y	N	Y	N
4 ***Rudd***	?	?	?	Y	Y	N	Y	N
5 ***Kolbe***	N	N	Y	Y	Y	N	Y	Y
ARKANSAS								
1 Alexander	Y	Y	N	Y	N	Y	N	Y
2 Robinson	Y	Y	Y	Y	N	Y	N	Y
3 ***Hammerschmidt***	N	Y	N	Y	Y	N	Y	N
4 Anthony	Y	Y	Y	Y	N	N	N	Y
CALIFORNIA								
1 Bosco	Y	Y	N	Y	N	?	?	Y
2 ***Chappie***	N	N	Y	Y	Y	N	Y	N
3 Matsui	Y	Y	N	Y	N	N	N	Y
4 Fazio	Y	Y	?	Y	N	N	N	Y
5 Burton	Y	Y	N	Y	N	Y	N	Y
6 Boxer	?	?	?	Y	N	Y	N	Y
7 Miller	Y	Y	N	?	N	Y	N	Y
8 Dellums	Y	Y	N	Y	N	N	N	Y
9 Stark	Y	Y	N	Y	N	N	N	Y
10 Edwards	Y	Y	N	Y	N	Y	N	Y
11 Lantos	?	?	?	?	N	Y	N	Y
12 ***Zschau***	?	?	?	Y	Y	N	Y	N
13 Mineta	Y	Y	N	Y	N	N	N	Y
14 ***Shumway***	N	N	Y	Y	Y	N	Y	N
15 Coelho	?	?	?	Y	N	Y	N	Y
16 Panetta	Y	Y	N	Y	N	N	N	Y
17 ***Pashayan***	Y	Y	Y	Y	Y	Y	Y	Y
18 Lehman	Y	Y	Y	Y	N	Y	N	Y
19 ***Lagomarsino***	N	N	N	Y	Y	N	Y	Y
20 ***Thomas***	N	N	N	Y	Y	N	Y	Y
21 ***Fiedler***	N	N	Y	Y	Y	N	Y	Y
22 ***Moorhead***	N	N	Y	Y	Y	N	Y	N
23 Beilenson	Y	Y	N	Y	N	N	N	Y
24 Waxman	Y	?	N	Y	N	?	N	Y
25 Roybal	Y	Y	N	Y	N	N	N	Y
26 Berman	?	?	?	Y	N	?	N	Y
27 Levine	Y	Y	Y	Y	N	N	N	Y
28 Dixon	?	?	N	Y	N	Y	N	Y
29 Hawkins	Y	Y	N	Y	N	Y	N	Y
30 Martinez	Y	Y	N	Y	N	Y	N	Y
31 Dymally	?	?	N	Y	N	Y	N	Y
32 Anderson	Y	Y	Y	Y	?	Y	N	Y
33 ***Dreier***	N	N	Y	Y	Y	N	Y	N
34 Torres	Y	Y	N	Y	N	Y	N	Y
35 ***Lewis***	N	N	Y	Y	Y	N	Y	N
36 Brown	?	?	N	Y	?	?	?	?
37 ***McCandless***	N	N	Y	Y	N	N	Y	Y
38 ***Dornan***	N	?	Y	Y	Y	N	Y	N
39 ***Dannemeyer***	Y	N	Y	Y	Y	N	Y	N
40 ***Badham***	?	?	?	Y	Y	N	Y	N
41 ***Lowery***	N	Y	N	Y	Y	N	Y	Y
42 ***Lungren***	N	N	Y	Y	Y	N	Y	N
43 ***Packard***	N	N	Y	Y	Y	N	Y	N
44 Bates	Y	Y	Y	Y	N	Y	N	Y
45 ***Hunter***	N	N	Y	Y	Y	Y	Y	N
COLORADO								
1 Schroeder	Y	Y	?	Y	N	N	N	Y
2 Wirth	?	?	?	Y	N	Y	N	Y
3 ***Strang***	N	N	?	Y	Y	N	Y	Y
4 ***Brown***	N	N	Y	Y	Y	N	Y	Y
5 ***Kramer***	N	N	Y	Y	Y	N	Y	Y
6 ***Schaefer***	N	N	Y	Y	Y	Y	Y	Y
CONNECTICUT								
1 Kennelly	Y	Y	Y	Y	N	Y	N	Y
2 Gejdenson	Y	Y	?	Y	N	Y	N	Y
3 Morrison	#	Y	N	Y	N	Y	N	Y
4 ***McKinney***	Y	Y	N	Y	N	Y	N	Y
5 ***Rowland***	Y	Y	Y	Y	Y	Y	Y	Y
6 ***Johnson***	N	Y	Y	Y	Y	Y	Y	Y
DELAWARE								
AL Carper	Y	Y	Y	Y	N	Y	N	Y
FLORIDA								
1 Hutto	N	Y	Y	Y	Y	N	Y	Y
2 Fuqua	Y	Y	Y	Y	Y	N	Y	Y
3 Bennett	Y	Y	Y	Y	N	Y	N	Y
4 Chappell	?	Y	?	Y	N	N	N	N
5 ***McCollum***	N	N	Y	Y	Y	N	Y	Y
6 MacKay	Y	Y	Y	Y	N	N	N	Y
7 Gibbons	Y	Y	N	Y	N	N	N	Y
8 ***Young***	N	Y	Y	Y	Y	N	N	N
9 ***Bilirakis***	N	Y	Y	Y	N	N	N	Y
10 ***Ireland***	Y	N	Y	Y	Y	?	Y	Y
11 Nelson	Y	Y	Y	Y	N	Y	N	Y
12 ***Lewis***	Y	Y	Y	Y	N	N	Y	Y
13 ***Mack***	N	N	Y	Y	Y	N	Y	N
14 Mica	Y	?	?	Y	Y	N	N	Y
15 ***Shaw***	N	N	Y	Y	Y	N	Y	Y
16 Smith	Y	Y	Y	Y	N	Y	N	Y
17 Lehman	Y	Y	N	Y	N	N	N	Y
18 Pepper	Y	Y	N	Y	X	?	?	#
19 Fascell	Y	?	Y	Y	N	N	N	Y
GEORGIA								
1 Thomas	Y	Y	Y	Y	Y	N	Y	Y
2 Hatcher	Y	Y	N	Y	Y	N	Y	Y
3 Ray	Y	Y	Y	Y	Y	N	Y	Y
4 ***Swindall***	N	Y	Y	Y	Y	N	Y	Y
5 Fowler	?	?	?	?	?	?	?	?
6 ***Gingrich***	N	?	Y	Y	Y	N	Y	N
7 Darden	Y	Y	Y	Y	Y	N	Y	Y
8 Rowland	Y	Y	Y	Y	Y	N	Y	Y
9 Jenkins	Y	Y	Y	Y	Y	Y	Y	Y
10 Barnard	Y	Y	Y	Y	Y	N	Y	Y
HAWAII								
1 Vacancy								
2 Akaka	Y	Y	N	Y	N	Y	N	Y
IDAHO								
1 ***Craig***	Y	N	Y	Y	Y	Y	Y	Y
2 Stallings	Y	Y	Y	Y	N	Y	N	Y
ILLINOIS								
1 Hayes	Y	Y	N	Y	N	Y	N	Y
2 Savage	Y	Y	N	Y	N	Y	N	Y
3 Russo	Y	Y	Y	Y	N	Y	N	Y
4 Vacancy								
5 Lipinski	Y	Y	Y	Y	N	Y	N	Y
6 ***Hyde***	N	N	N	Y	Y	N	Y	N
7 Collins	Y	Y	N	Y	N	Y	N	Y
8 Rostenkowski	Y	Y	N	Y	N	Y	N	Y
9 Yates	Y	Y	N	Y	N	N	N	Y
10 ***Porter***	N	N	Y	Y	N	N	Y	Y
11 Annunzio	?	?	?	Y	N	Y	N	Y
12 ***Crane***	N	N	Y	Y	Y	N	Y	N
13 ***Fawell***	N	N	Y	Y	Y	N	Y	Y
14 ***Grotberg***	?	?	?	?	?	?	?	?
15 ***Madigan***	Y	N	Y	Y	Y	Y	Y	Y
16 ***Martin***	N	N	Y	Y	Y	Y	Y	Y
17 Evans	Y	Y	N	Y	N	Y	N	Y
18 ***Michel***	Y	N	Y	Y	Y	N	Y	Y
19 Bruce	Y	Y	Y	Y	N	Y	N	Y
20 Durbin	Y	Y	Y	Y	N	Y	N	Y
21 Price	Y	Y	Y	Y	N	Y	N	Y
22 Gray	Y	Y	Y	Y	N	Y	N	Y
INDIANA								
1 Visclosky	Y	Y	Y	Y	N	Y	N	Y
2 Sharp	Y	Y	Y	?	N	Y	N	Y
3 ***Hiler***	N	N	N	Y	Y	N	Y	Y
4 ***Coats***	N	N	N	Y	Y	Y	Y	Y
5 ***Hillis***	?	?	?	?	?	?	?	?

ND - Northern Democrats SD - Southern Democrats

* Corresponding to Congressional Record Votes 278, 279, 280, 281, 282, 283, 284, 285

	254	255	256	257	258	259	260	261
6 ***Burton***	N	N	Y	Y	Y	N	Y	N
7 ***Myers***	N	Y	N	Y	Y	Y	Y	Y
8 McCloskey	Y	Y	Y	Y	N	Y	N	Y
9 Hamilton	Y	?	Y	Y	N	Y	N	Y
10 Jacobs	Y	Y	Y	Y	N	Y	N	Y
IOWA								
1 ***Leach***	N	Y	Y	Y	N	N	N	Y
2 ***Tauke***	N	Y	N	Y	Y	Y	Y	Y
3 ***Evans***	?	N	Y	Y	Y	N	Y	Y
4 Smith	N	Y	N	Y	N	Y	N	Y
5 ***Lightfoot***	?	N	Y	Y	Y	Y	Y	Y
6 Bedell	?	?	?	Y	N	Y	N	Y
KANSAS								
1 ***Roberts***	N	N	Y	Y	N	N	Y	Y
2 Slattery	Y	Y	Y	Y	N	N	N	Y
3 ***Meyers***	N	N	Y	Y	N	N	N	Y
4 Glickman	Y	Y	Y	Y	N	N	N	Y
5 ***Whittaker***	N	N	Y	Y	N	Y	Y	Y
KENTUCKY								
1 Hubbard	N	Y	Y	Y	N	Y	N	Y
2 Natcher	Y	Y	N	Y	N	Y	Y	Y
3 Mazzoli	Y	Y	N	Y	N	Y	N	Y
4 ***Snyder***	Y	Y	N	Y	Y	N	Y	Y
5 ***Rogers***	N	Y	N	Y	Y	Y	Y	Y
6 ***Hopkins***	N	N	Y	Y	Y	Y	Y	N
7 Perkins	Y	Y	N	Y	N	Y	N	Y
LOUISIANA								
1 ***Livingston***	?	?	?	Y	Y	N	Y	N
2 Boggs	Y	Y	N	Y	N	?	N	Y
3 Tauzin	N	Y	Y	Y	N	Y	N	Y
4 Roemer	N	N	Y	Y	N	Y	N	Y
5 Huckaby	Y	Y	Y	Y	N	Y	N	Y
6 ***Moore***	?	?	?	?	?	?	?	?
7 Breaux	?	?	?	Y	?	?	?	?
8 Long	Y	Y	N	?	?	?	?	?
MAINE								
1 ***McKernan***	N	N	Y	Y	Y	Y	N	Y
2 ***Snowe***	Y	Y	Y	Y	N	Y	N	Y
MARYLAND								
1 Dyson	?	Y	Y	Y	?	?	Y	Y
2 ***Bentley***	N	Y	Y	Y	Y	Y	Y	Y
3 Mikulski	?	?	?	Y	N	Y	N	Y
4 ***Holt***	Y	N	N	Y	Y	N	Y	N
5 Hoyer	Y	Y	N	Y	N	N	N	Y
6 Byron	Y	Y	Y	Y	N	N	Y	Y
7 Mitchell	Y	Y	N	Y	N	Y	N	Y
8 Barnes	?	?	?	+	-	+	-	+
MASSACHUSETTS								
1 ***Conte***	Y	Y	N	Y	N	Y	N	Y
2 Boland	Y	Y	?	Y	N	Y	N	Y
3 Early	?	?	?	Y	N	N	N	Y
4 Frank	Y	Y	Y	Y	N	N	N	Y
5 Atkins	Y	Y	N	Y	N	N	N	Y
6 Mavroules	Y	Y	Y	Y	N	N	N	Y
7 Markey	Y	Y	?	Y	N	N	N	Y
8 O'Neill								
9 Moakley	Y	Y	Y	Y	N	Y	N	Y
10 Studds	Y	Y	N	Y	N	N	N	Y
11 Donnelly	Y	Y	Y	Y	N	Y	N	Y
MICHIGAN								
1 Conyers	?	?	?	?	?	?	?	?
2 ***Pursell***	N	Y	Y	Y	N	Y	N	Y
3 Wolpe	Y	Y	Y	Y	N	Y	N	Y
4 ***Siljander***	N	N	Y	?	#	?	?	X
5 ***Henry***	N	N	Y	Y	N	Y	N	Y
6 Carr	Y	Y	N	Y	N	Y	N	Y
7 Kildee	Y	Y	Y	Y	N	Y	N	Y
8 Traxler	Y	Y	Y	Y	N	Y	N	Y
9 ***Vander Jagt***	Y	N	Y	Y	Y	Y	Y	Y
10 ***Schuette***	N	Y	Y	Y	N	Y	N	Y
11 ***Davis***	N	Y	N	Y	Y	Y	Y	Y
12 Bonior	Y	Y	?	Y	N	Y	N	Y
13 Crockett	N	Y	N	?	?	?	?	?
14 Hertel	Y	Y	Y	Y	N	Y	?	?
15 Ford	?	Y	N	Y	N	Y	N	Y
16 Dingell	Y	Y	?	Y	N	Y	N	Y
17 Levin	Y	Y	Y	Y	N	Y	N	Y
18 ***Broomfield***	N	N	Y	Y	Y	N	Y	Y
MINNESOTA								
1 Penny	Y	Y	Y	Y	N	Y	N	Y
2 ***Weber***	N	N	Y	Y	Y	N	N	Y
3 ***Frenzel***	N	N	N	Y	Y	N	N	Y
4 Vento	Y	Y	N	Y	N	Y	N	Y
5 Sabo	Y	Y	N	Y	N	Y	N	Y
6 Sikorski	Y	Y	Y	Y	N	Y	N	Y
7 ***Stangeland***	Y	N	N	Y	N	N	Y	Y
8 Oberstar	Y	Y	N	Y	N	Y	N	Y
MISSISSIPPI								
1 Whitten	Y	Y	N	Y	N	Y	Y	Y
2 ***Franklin***	N	Y	Y	Y	Y	Y	Y	N
3 Montgomery	N	Y	Y	Y	Y	N	Y	N
4 Dowdy	?	?	?	Y	N	Y	N	Y
5 ***Lott***	N	N	Y	Y	Y	N	Y	N
MISSOURI								
1 Clay	?	?	?	?	?	?	?	?
2 Young	Y	Y	N	Y	Y	Y	N	Y
3 Gephardt	Y	Y	Y	Y	N	Y	N	Y
4 Skelton	?	?	?	Y	N	N	N	Y
5 Wheat	Y	Y	N	Y	N	Y	N	Y
6 ***Coleman***	N	Y	Y	Y	Y	N	Y	Y
7 ***Taylor***	Y	Y	Y	?	Y	N	Y	N
8 ***Emerson***	N	N	Y	Y	Y	Y	Y	Y
9 Volkmer	Y	Y	?	Y	N	Y	N	Y
MONTANA								
1 Williams	?	?	?	Y	N	Y	N	Y
2 ***Marlenee***	N	N	Y	Y	N	N	Y	N
NEBRASKA								
1 ***Bereuter***	N	Y	Y	Y	Y	N	Y	Y
2 ***Daub***	N	N	Y	Y	Y	N	Y	Y
3 ***Smith***	Y	Y	Y	Y	Y	N	Y	Y
NEVADA								
1 Reid	Y	Y	Y	Y	N	Y	N	Y
2 ***Vucanovich***	N	N	Y	Y	Y	N	Y	N
NEW HAMPSHIRE								
1 ***Smith***	N	N	Y	Y	Y	N	Y	Y
2 ***Gregg***	N	N	Y	Y	Y	N	Y	Y
NEW JERSEY								
1 Florio	Y	Y	Y	Y	N	Y	N	Y
2 Hughes	Y	Y	Y	Y	N	Y	N	Y
3 Howard	Y	Y	N	?	?	?	?	?
4 ***Smith***	Y	Y	Y	Y	N	Y	N	Y
5 ***Roukema***	Y	Y	Y	Y	N	Y	N	Y
6 Dwyer	Y	Y	Y	Y	N	?	N	Y
7 ***Rinaldo***	Y	Y	Y	Y	N	Y	N	Y
8 Roe	Y	Y	Y	Y	N	Y	N	Y
9 Torricelli	Y	Y	Y	Y	N	Y	N	Y
10 Rodino	Y	Y	N	Y	N	Y	N	Y
11 ***Gallo***	N	Y	Y	Y	N	N	Y	Y
12 ***Courter***	N	N	Y	Y	Y	N	Y	N
13 ***Saxton***	N	Y	Y	Y	N	N	N	Y
14 Guarini	Y	Y	Y	Y	N	N	N	Y
NEW MEXICO								
1 ***Lujan***	Y	Y	Y	Y	Y	Y	Y	Y
2 ***Skeen***	N	Y	N	Y	Y	N	Y	Y
3 Richardson	Y	Y	Y	Y	N	Y	N	Y
NEW YORK								
1 ***Carney***	?	?	?	N	Y	N	Y	N
2 Downey	Y	Y	Y	Y	N	N	N	Y
3 Mrazek	Y	Y	N	Y	N	Y	N	Y
4 ***Lent***	N	Y	Y	Y	N	Y	Y	Y
5 ***McGrath***	N	Y	Y	?	N	N	Y	Y
6 Waldon	Y	Y	N	Y	N	Y	N	Y
7 Ackerman	Y	Y	Y	Y	N	Y	N	Y
8 Scheuer	Y	?	Y	Y	N	Y	N	Y
9 Manton	Y	Y	Y	?	?	?	?	?
10 Schumer	Y	Y	N	Y	N	N	N	Y
11 Towns	?	?	?	Y	X	?	?	#
12 Owens	Y	Y	Y	Y	N	Y	N	Y
13 Solarz	Y	Y	N	Y	N	N	N	Y
14 ***Molinari***	Y	Y	Y	Y	Y	N	N	Y
15 ***Green***	N	Y	N	Y	Y	N	N	Y
16 Rangel	Y	Y	N	Y	N	Y	N	Y
17 Weiss	Y	Y	Y	Y	N	N	N	Y
18 Garcia	Y	Y	Y	Y	N	Y	N	Y
19 Biaggi	?	?	?	Y	N	Y	N	Y
20 ***DioGuardi***	Y	Y	Y	Y	Y	Y	Y	Y
21 ***Fish***	Y	Y	N	Y	N	Y	N	Y
22 ***Gilman***	Y	Y	Y	Y	N	Y	N	+
23 Stratton	N	Y	N	N	Y	Y	Y	N
24 ***Solomon***	N	N	Y	Y	Y	Y	Y	N
25 ***Boehlert***	N	Y	N	Y	N	Y	N	Y
26 ***Martin***	Y	Y	?	Y	Y	N	Y	N
27 ***Wortley***	N	Y	Y	Y	Y	Y	Y	Y
28 McHugh	Y	Y	N	Y	N	N	N	Y
29 ***Horton***	Y	Y	?	Y	N	Y	N	Y
30 ***Eckert***	N	N	N	Y	Y	N	Y	Y
31 ***Kemp***	?	?	?	Y	Y	N	Y	N
32 LaFalce	N	Y	Y	Y	N	N	N	Y
33 Nowak	Y	Y	Y	Y	N	Y	N	Y
34 Lundine	?	?	?	Y	?	?	?	?
NORTH CAROLINA								
1 Jones	Y	Y	N	Y	N	Y	N	Y
2 Valentine	Y	Y	Y	Y	N	Y	N	Y
3 Whitley	Y	Y	?	Y	N	Y	Y	Y
4 ***Cobey***	N	N	Y	Y	Y	Y	Y	Y
5 Neal	?	?	Y	Y	N	Y	N	Y
6 ***Coble***	?	N	Y	Y	Y	Y	Y	Y
7 Rose	Y	Y	Y	Y	N	Y	N	Y
8 Hefner	Y	Y	Y	Y	N	Y	N	Y
9 ***McMillan***	N	Y	Y	Y	Y	Y	Y	Y
10 Vacancy								
11 ***Hendon***	Y	Y	Y	Y	N	Y	Y	Y
NORTH DAKOTA								
AL Dorgan	Y	Y	Y	Y	N	Y	N	Y
OHIO								
1 Luken	Y	Y	Y	Y	N	Y	N	Y
2 ***Gradison***	Y	Y	Y	Y	N	N	N	Y
3 Hall	Y	Y	Y	Y	N	Y	N	Y
4 ***Oxley***	N	N	Y	?	Y	N	Y	Y
5 ***Latta***	Y	N	Y	Y	N	Y	Y	Y
6 ***McEwen***	Y	Y	Y	Y	Y	Y	Y	N
7 ***DeWine***	N	N	Y	Y	Y	N	Y	Y
8 ***Kindness***	Y	Y	Y	Y	Y	Y	Y	N
9 Kaptur	Y	Y	Y	Y	N	Y	N	Y
10 ***Miller***	N	Y	Y	Y	Y	Y	Y	Y
11 Eckart	Y	Y	Y	Y	N	Y	N	Y
12 ***Kasich***	Y	N	Y	Y	Y	Y	Y	Y
13 Pease	Y	Y	Y	Y	N	Y	N	Y
14 Seiberling	Y	Y	Y	Y	N	Y	N	Y
15 ***Wylie***	?	?	?	Y	N	Y	Y	Y
16 ***Regula***	Y	Y	Y	Y	Y	Y	Y	Y
17 Traficant	Y	Y	Y	Y	N	Y	N	Y
18 Applegate	Y	Y	Y	Y	N	Y	N	Y
19 Feighan	Y	Y	Y	Y	N	Y	N	Y
20 Oakar	?	Y	N	Y	N	Y	N	Y
21 Stokes	Y	Y	N	Y	N	Y	N	Y
OKLAHOMA								
1 Jones	Y	Y	Y	Y	N	N	N	Y
2 Synar	Y	Y	N	Y	N	N	N	Y
3 Watkins	Y	Y	Y	Y	N	Y	N	Y
4 McCurdy	Y	Y	Y	Y	N	N	N	Y
5 ***Edwards***	?	Y	Y	Y	Y	N	Y	Y
6 English	?	?	?	Y	N	N	N	Y
OREGON								
1 AuCoin	Y	Y	Y	Y	N	N	N	Y
2 ***Smith, R.***	N	N	?	Y	Y	Y	Y	Y
3 Wyden	Y	Y	Y	Y	N	N	N	Y
4 Weaver	Y	Y	Y	N	N	Y	N	?
5 ***Smith, D.***	?	?	?	Y	N	Y	N	Y
PENNSYLVANIA								
1 Foglietta	Y	Y	Y	Y	N	Y	N	Y
2 Gray	Y	Y	?	Y	N	Y	N	Y
3 Borski	Y	Y	Y	Y	N	Y	N	Y
4 Kolter	Y	Y	N	Y	N	Y	N	Y
5 ***Schulze***	N	Y	Y	Y	Y	Y	Y	?
6 Yatron	Y	Y	Y	Y	N	Y	N	Y
7 Edgar	?	?	?	Y	?	?	?	?
8 Kostmayer	Y	Y	Y	Y	N	Y	N	Y
9 ***Shuster***	N	N	Y	Y	Y	Y	Y	Y
10 ***McDade***	Y	Y	N	Y	N	Y	N	Y
11 Kanjorski	Y	Y	Y	Y	N	Y	N	Y
12 Murtha	Y	Y	N	Y	N	Y	N	Y
13 ***Coughlin***	Y	Y	Y	Y	N	Y	N	Y
14 Coyne	Y	Y	N	Y	N	Y	N	Y
15 ***Ritter***	Y	Y	Y	Y	Y	Y	Y	Y
16 ***Walker***	N	N	Y	Y	Y	Y	Y	Y
17 ***Gekas***	N	N	Y	Y	N	Y	Y	Y
18 Walgren	Y	Y	Y	Y	-	Y	N	Y
19 ***Goodling***	Y	Y	Y	Y	N	Y	Y	Y
20 Gaydos	Y	Y	N	Y	N	Y	N	Y
21 ***Ridge***	N	N	Y	Y	N	Y	N	Y
22 Murphy	Y	Y	N	Y	N	Y	N	Y
23 ***Clinger***	Y	Y	N	Y	Y	Y	N	Y
RHODE ISLAND								
1 St Germain	Y	Y	Y	Y	N	Y	N	Y
2 ***Schneider***	Y	Y	Y	Y	Y	Y	N	Y
SOUTH CAROLINA								
1 ***Hartnett***	?	?	?	?	Y	N	Y	N
2 ***Spence***	N	N	Y	Y	Y	Y	Y	N
3 Derrick	Y	Y	Y	Y	N	Y	N	Y
4 ***Campbell***	?	?	?	Y	#	?	?	X
5 Spratt	Y	Y	Y	Y	Y	Y	Y	Y
6 Tallon	Y	Y	?	Y	N	Y	N	Y
SOUTH DAKOTA								
AL Daschle	Y	Y	Y	Y	N	Y	N	Y
TENNESSEE								
1 ***Quillen***	Y	N	?	Y	Y	Y	Y	Y
2 ***Duncan***	Y	Y	N	Y	Y	Y	Y	Y
3 Lloyd	Y	Y	?	Y	N	Y	N	Y
4 Cooper	?	?	?	Y	N	N	N	Y
5 Boner	?	?	?	Y	N	Y	N	Y
6 Gordon	Y	Y	?	Y	N	Y	N	Y
7 ***Sundquist***	N	Y	Y	Y	Y	N	Y	Y
8 Jones	Y	Y	Y	Y	N	Y	N	Y
9 Ford	?	?	?	?	?	?	?	?
TEXAS								
1 Chapman	Y	Y	Y	Y	N	Y	N	Y
2 Wilson	Y	Y	Y	Y	Y	N	Y	N
3 ***Bartlett***	X	N	Y	Y	Y	N	Y	N
4 Hall, R.	N	Y	Y	Y	Y	Y	Y	N
5 Bryant	?	?	?	Y	N	Y	N	Y
6 ***Barton***	N	N	Y	Y	Y	N	Y	N
7 ***Archer***	N	N	Y	Y	Y	N	Y	Y
8 ***Fields***	N	N	Y	Y	Y	N	Y	Y
9 Brooks	Y	Y	Y	Y	N	Y	N	Y
10 Pickle	Y	Y	N	Y	N	Y	N	Y
11 Leath	?	?	?	Y	N	Y	N	Y
12 Wright	Y	Y	Y	Y	N	Y	N	Y
13 ***Boulter***	N	N	Y	Y	Y	N	Y	Y
14 ***Sweeney***	N	N	Y	Y	Y	N	Y	Y
15 de la Garza	Y	Y	?	Y	N	Y	Y	Y
16 Coleman	Y	Y	Y	Y	Y	Y	Y	Y
17 Stenholm	N	N	Y	Y	Y	N	N	Y
18 Leland	Y	Y	N	Y	N	Y	N	Y
19 ***Combest***	Y	N	Y	Y	Y	N	Y	N
20 Gonzalez	N	Y	N	N	N	Y	N	Y
21 ***Loeffler***	Y	Y	Y	Y	Y	N	Y	N
22 ***DeLay***	N	N	Y	Y	Y	N	Y	N
23 Bustamante	Y	Y	Y	Y	N	Y	N	Y
24 Frost	?	?	?	Y	N	Y	N	Y
25 Andrews	Y	Y	Y	Y	N	Y	N	Y
26 ***Armey***	N	N	Y	Y	Y	N	Y	N
27 Ortiz	Y	Y	Y	Y	N	Y	N	Y
UTAH								
1 ***Hansen***	?	?	?	Y	Y	N	Y	N
2 ***Monson***	N	N	Y	Y	Y	N	Y	N
3 ***Nielson***	N	Y	Y	Y	N	N	Y	Y
VERMONT								
AL ***Jeffords***	N	Y	Y	Y	N	Y	N	Y
VIRGINIA								
1 ***Bateman***	Y	Y	Y	Y	Y	N	Y	N
2 ***Whitehurst***	?	?	?	Y	Y	N	Y	N
3 ***Bliley***	N	N	Y	Y	Y	N	Y	N
4 Sisisky	?	?	N	Y	Y	N	N	Y
5 Daniel	N	Y	Y	Y	Y	Y	Y	N
6 Olin	Y	Y	Y	Y	Y	Y	Y	Y
7 ***Slaughter***	N	N	Y	Y	Y	N	Y	N
8 ***Parris***	?	?	N	Y	Y	Y	Y	N
9 Boucher	?	?	?	Y	Y	Y	N	Y
10 ***Wolf***	?	?	N	Y	Y	N	Y	Y
WASHINGTON								
1 ***Miller***	N	N	Y	Y	Y	N	Y	Y
2 Swift	Y	Y	Y	Y	N	N	N	Y
3 Bonker	?	Y	N	Y	N	N	N	Y
4 ***Morrison***	Y	Y	?	Y	Y	Y	Y	Y
5 Foley	Y	Y	N	Y	N	N	N	Y
6 Dicks	Y	Y	Y	Y	N	N	N	Y
7 Lowry	Y	N	Y	Y	N	N	N	Y
8 ***Chandler***	Y	Y	Y	?	Y	N	N	Y
WEST VIRGINIA								
1 Mollohan	Y	Y	Y	Y	N	Y	N	Y
2 Staggers	Y	Y	Y	Y	N	Y	N	Y
3 Wise	Y	Y	Y	Y	N	Y	N	Y
4 Rahall	Y	Y	Y	Y	N	Y	N	Y
WISCONSIN								
1 Aspin	Y	Y	Y	Y	N	N	N	Y
2 Kastenmeier	Y	Y	N	Y	N	N	N	Y
3 ***Gunderson***	N	Y	Y	Y	N	Y	N	Y
4 Kleczka	Y	Y	Y	Y	Y	Y	N	Y
5 Moody	Y	Y	N	Y	N	Y	N	Y
6 ***Petri***	N	N	Y	Y	Y	N	Y	Y
7 Obey	Y	Y	N	Y	N	Y	N	Y
8 ***Roth***	N	Y	Y	Y	N	Y	N	Y
9 ***Sensenbrenner***	N	N	Y	Y	N	Y	N	Y
WYOMING								
AL ***Cheney***	N	N	Y	Y	Y	N	Y	N

Southern states - Ala., Ark., Fla., Ga., Ky., La., Miss., N.C., Okla., S.C., Tenn., Texas, Va.

* The *Congressional Record* vote number is different from the CQ vote number because the *Record* includes quorum calls in its tally. CQ does not publish quorum call votes.

262. HR 4333. Improved Benefits for Former Prisoners of War. Montgomery, D-Miss., motion to suspend the rules and pass the bill to improve health benefits for former prisoners of war. Motion agreed to 413-0: R 173-0; D 240-0 (ND 162-0, SD 78-0), Aug. 6, 1986. A two-thirds majority of those present and voting (276 in this case) is required for passage under suspension of the rules.

263. HR 4623. Veterans' Health Care Amendments. Montgomery, D-Miss., motion to suspend the rules and pass the bill to improve readjustment counseling for Vietnam-era veterans. Motion agreed to 418-0: R 174-0; D 244-0 (ND 165-0, SD 79-0), Aug. 6, 1986. A two-thirds majority of those present and voting (279 in this case) is required for passage under suspension of the rules.

264. HR 5288. Emergency Drought Relief. De la Garza, D-Texas, motion to suspend the rules and pass the bill to authorize $530 million in fiscal 1986 disaster aid for drought-stricken farmers. Motion agreed to 418-0: R 173-0; D 245-0 (ND 166-0, SD 79-0), Aug. 6, 1986. A two-thirds majority of those present and voting (279 in this case) is required for passage under suspension of the rules. A "yea" was a vote supporting the president's position.

265. HR 1562. Textile Import Quotas. Passage, over President Reagan's Dec. 17, 1985, veto, of the bill to place import restrictions on textile and apparel goods. Rejected 276-149: R 71-106; D 205-43 (ND 132-36, SD 73-7), Aug. 6, 1986. A two-thirds majority of those present and voting (284 in this case) of both houses is required to override a veto. A "nay" was a vote supporting the president's position.

266. HR 5294. Treasury, Postal Service and General Government Appropriations, Fiscal 1987. Skeen, R-N.M., substitute for the Jacobs, D-Ind., amendment, to cut $58,000 from allowances to former U.S. presidents for office expenses. The Jacobs amendment would have reduced the account by $958,000. Adopted 356-61: R 168-6; D 188-55 (ND 116-51, SD 72-4), Aug. 6, 1986. (The Jacobs amendment, as amended by the Skeen substitute, subsequently was adopted *(see vote 267, below)*.)

267. HR 5294. Treasury, Postal Service and General Government Appropriations, Fiscal 1987. Jacobs, D-Ind., amendment, as amended by the Skeen, R-N.M., substitute *(see vote 266, above)*, to cut $58,000 from allowances to former U.S. presidents for office expenses. Adopted 405-1: R 169-1; D 236-0 (ND 161-0, SD 75-0), Aug. 6, 1986.

268. HR 5294. Treasury, Postal Service and General Government Appropriations, Fiscal 1987. Morrison, D-Conn., amendment to cut about $143 million from the bill by reducing the budgets of various agencies by 9.75 percent, but exempting other agencies such as the Internal Revenue Service, Customs Service, Postal Service and Bureau of Alcohol, Tobacco and Firearms. Adopted 269-152: R 145-31; D 124-121 (ND 74-95, SD 50-26), Aug. 6, 1986.

269. HR 5294. Treasury, Postal Service and General Government Appropriations, Fiscal 1987. Roybal, D-Calif., motion that the Committee of the Whole rise and report the bill back to the House. Motion agreed to 249-168: R 29-146; D 220-22 (ND 163-4, SD 57-18), Aug. 6, 1986. (The effect of the vote was to prevent consideration of amendments limiting spending on the appropriations bill, in this case the Cobey, R-N.C., amendment to require the Federal Election Commission to uphold recent Supreme Court rulings regarding the use of union dues for political purposes. Such amendments are in order only following a defeated motion to rise and report.)

KEY

Y Voted for (yea).
\# Paired for.
\+ Announced for.
N Voted against (nay).
X Paired against.
\- Announced against.
P Voted "present."
C Voted "present" to avoid possible conflict of interest.
? Did not vote or otherwise make a position known.

Democrats ***Republicans***

	262	263	264	265	266	267	268	269
ALABAMA								
1 ***Callahan***	Y	Y	Y	Y	Y	Y	Y	N
2 ***Dickinson***	Y	?	Y	Y	Y	Y	Y	N
3 Nichols	Y	Y	Y	Y	Y	?	Y	N
4 Bevill	Y	Y	Y	Y	Y	Y	N	Y
5 Flippo	Y	Y	Y	Y	Y	Y	N	Y
6 Erdreich	Y	Y	Y	Y	Y	Y	Y	Y
7 Shelby	Y	Y	Y	Y	Y	Y	Y	Y
ALASKA								
AL ***Young***	Y	Y	Y	N	Y	Y	N	Y
ARIZONA								
1 ***McCain***	C	Y	Y	N	Y	Y	Y	N
2 Udall	Y	Y	Y	Y	N	Y	N	Y
3 ***Stump***	Y	Y	Y	N	Y	Y	Y	N
4 ***Rudd***	Y	Y	Y	N	Y	Y	N	N
5 ***Kolbe***	Y	Y	Y	N	Y	Y	Y	N
ARKANSAS								
1 Alexander	Y	Y	Y	Y	Y	Y	N	Y
2 Robinson	Y	Y	Y	Y	Y	Y	Y	Y
3 ***Hammerschmidt***	Y	Y	Y	Y	Y	Y	Y	N
4 Anthony	Y	Y	Y	Y	Y	Y	Y	Y
CALIFORNIA								
1 Bosco	Y	Y	Y	Y	Y	Y	N	Y
2 ***Chappie***	Y	Y	Y	N	Y	Y	Y	N
3 Matsui	Y	Y	Y	N	Y	Y	N	Y
4 Fazio	?	Y	Y	Y	Y	Y	N	Y
5 Burton	Y	Y	Y	Y	N	Y	N	Y
6 Boxer	Y	Y	Y	Y	N	Y	Y	Y
7 Miller	Y	Y	Y	N	N	Y	Y	Y
8 Dellums	Y	Y	Y	Y	?	Y	N	Y
9 Stark	Y	Y	Y	N	N	Y	N	Y
10 Edwards	Y	Y	Y	Y	Y	Y	N	Y
11 Lantos	Y	Y	Y	Y	Y	Y	Y	Y
12 ***Zschau***	Y	Y	Y	N	Y	Y	Y	N
13 Mineta	Y	Y	Y	N	Y	Y	N	Y
14 ***Shumway***	Y	Y	Y	N	Y	Y	Y	N
15 Coelho	Y	Y	Y	Y	N	Y	N	Y
16 Panetta	Y	Y	Y	N	Y	Y	Y	Y
17 ***Pashayan***	Y	Y	Y	Y	Y	Y	Y	N
18 Lehman	Y	Y	Y	Y	Y	Y	Y	Y
19 ***Lagomarsino***	Y	Y	Y	N	Y	Y	N	N
20 ***Thomas***	Y	Y	Y	Y	Y	Y	Y	N
21 ***Fiedler***	Y	Y	Y	N	Y	Y	Y	N
22 ***Moorhead***	Y	Y	Y	N	Y	Y	Y	N
23 Beilenson	Y	Y	Y	N	Y	Y	N	Y
24 Waxman	Y	Y	Y	N	N	Y	N	Y
25 Roybal	Y	Y	Y	Y	Y	Y	N	Y
26 Berman	Y	Y	Y	N	Y	Y	N	Y
27 Levine	Y	Y	Y	N	N	Y	N	Y
28 Dixon	Y	Y	Y	Y	Y	Y	N	Y
29 Hawkins	?	Y	Y	Y	Y	Y	N	Y
30 Martinez	Y	Y	Y	Y	Y	Y	N	Y
31 Dymally	?	Y	Y	Y	Y	Y	N	Y
32 Anderson	Y	Y	Y	N	Y	Y	N	Y
33 ***Dreier***	Y	Y	Y	N	Y	Y	Y	N
34 Torres	Y	Y	Y	Y	Y	+	N	Y
35 ***Lewis***	Y	Y	Y	N	Y	Y	N	N
36 Brown	Y	Y	Y	Y	Y	Y	N	Y
37 ***McCandless***	Y	Y	Y	N	Y	Y	Y	N
38 ***Dornan***	Y	Y	Y	N	Y	Y	N	N
39 ***Dannemeyer***	Y	Y	Y	N	N	Y	Y	N
40 ***Badham***	Y	Y	Y	N	N	Y	Y	N
41 ***Lowery***	Y	Y	Y	N	Y	Y	N	N
42 ***Lungren***	Y	Y	Y	N	Y	Y	Y	N
43 ***Packard***	Y	Y	Y	N	Y	Y	Y	N
44 Bates	Y	Y	Y	Y	Y	Y	Y	Y
45 ***Hunter***	Y	Y	Y	Y	Y	Y	Y	N
COLORADO								
1 Schroeder	Y	Y	Y	Y	Y	Y	Y	Y
2 Wirth	Y	Y	Y	N	Y	Y	Y	Y
3 ***Strang***	Y	Y	Y	N	Y	Y	Y	N
4 ***Brown***	Y	Y	Y	N	N	Y	Y	N
5 ***Kramer***	Y	Y	Y	N	Y	Y	Y	N
6 ***Schaefer***	Y	Y	Y	N	Y	Y	Y	N
CONNECTICUT								
1 Kennelly	Y	Y	Y	Y	N	Y	Y	Y
2 Gejdenson	Y	Y	Y	Y	Y	Y	Y	Y
3 Morrison	Y	Y	Y	Y	N	Y	Y	Y
4 ***McKinney***	Y	Y	Y	Y	Y	Y	Y	Y
5 ***Rowland***	Y	Y	Y	N	Y	Y	Y	Y
6 ***Johnson***	Y	Y	Y	N	Y	Y	Y	Y
DELAWARE								
AL Carper	Y	Y	Y	Y	N	Y	Y	N
FLORIDA								
1 Hutto	Y	Y	Y	Y	Y	Y	Y	N
2 Fuqua	Y	Y	Y	Y	Y	Y	Y	Y
3 Bennett	Y	Y	Y	N	N	Y	Y	Y
4 Chappell	Y	Y	Y	Y	Y	Y	N	Y
5 ***McCollum***	Y	Y	Y	N	Y	Y	Y	N
6 MacKay	Y	Y	Y	N	Y	Y	Y	Y
7 Gibbons	Y	Y	Y	N	Y	Y	Y	Y
8 ***Young***	Y	Y	Y	N	Y	Y	Y	N
9 ***Bilirakis***	Y	Y	Y	Y	Y	Y	N	N
10 ***Ireland***	Y	Y	Y	N	Y	Y	Y	N
11 Nelson	Y	Y	Y	N	Y	Y	Y	Y
12 ***Lewis***	Y	Y	Y	N	Y	Y	Y	N
13 ***Mack***	Y	Y	Y	N	Y	Y	Y	N
14 Mica	?	Y	Y	N	Y	Y	Y	Y
15 ***Shaw***	Y	Y	Y	N	Y	Y	Y	N
16 Smith	Y	Y	Y	Y	Y	Y	?	Y
17 Lehman	Y	Y	Y	Y	Y	Y	N	Y
18 Pepper	?	?	?	#	?	?	?	?
19 Fascell	Y	Y	Y	Y	Y	Y	N	Y
GEORGIA								
1 Thomas	Y	Y	Y	Y	Y	Y	Y	N
2 Hatcher	Y	Y	Y	Y	Y	Y	Y	Y
3 Ray	Y	Y	Y	Y	Y	Y	Y	N
4 ***Swindall***	Y	Y	Y	Y	Y	Y	Y	N
5 Fowler	Y	Y	Y	Y	?	?	?	?
6 ***Gingrich***	Y	Y	Y	Y	Y	Y	Y	N
7 Darden	Y	Y	Y	Y	Y	Y	Y	N
8 Rowland	Y	Y	Y	Y	Y	Y	Y	N
9 Jenkins	Y	Y	Y	Y	Y	Y	Y	N
10 Barnard	Y	Y	Y	Y	Y	Y	Y	N
HAWAII								
1 Vacancy								
2 Akaka	Y	Y	Y	N	Y	Y	N	Y
IDAHO								
1 ***Craig***	Y	Y	Y	N	Y	Y	Y	N
2 Stallings	Y	Y	Y	N	Y	Y	Y	N
ILLINOIS								
1 Hayes	Y	Y	Y	Y	N	Y	N	Y
2 Savage	Y	Y	Y	Y	Y	Y	N	Y
3 Russo	Y	Y	Y	Y	Y	Y	Y	N
4 Vacancy								
5 Lipinski	Y	Y	Y	Y	Y	Y	Y	Y
6 ***Hyde***	Y	Y	Y	N	Y	Y	N	N
7 Collins	Y	Y	Y	Y	Y	Y	N	Y
8 Rostenkowski	Y	Y	Y	N	Y	Y	Y	Y
9 Yates	Y	Y	Y	Y	Y	Y	N	Y
10 ***Porter***	Y	Y	Y	N	Y	Y	Y	N
11 Annunzio	Y	Y	Y	Y	Y	Y	Y	Y
12 ***Crane***	Y	Y	Y	N	Y	Y	Y	N
13 ***Fawell***	Y	Y	Y	N	Y	Y	Y	N
14 ***Grotberg***	?	?	?	?	?	?	?	?
15 ***Madigan***	Y	Y	Y	N	Y	?	Y	N
16 ***Martin***	Y	Y	Y	N	Y	Y	Y	N
17 Evans	Y	Y	Y	Y	N	Y	Y	Y
18 ***Michel***	Y	Y	Y	N	Y	Y	Y	N
19 Bruce	Y	Y	Y	Y	Y	Y	Y	Y
20 Durbin	Y	Y	Y	Y	N	Y	N	Y
21 Price	Y	Y	Y	Y	N	Y	Y	Y
22 Gray	Y	Y	Y	Y	N	Y	Y	Y
INDIANA								
1 Visclosky	Y	Y	Y	Y	N	Y	N	Y
2 Sharp	Y	Y	Y	Y	N	Y	Y	Y
3 ***Hiler***	Y	Y	Y	N	Y	Y	Y	N
4 ***Coats***	Y	Y	Y	N	Y	Y	Y	N
5 ***Hillis***	Y	Y	Y	Y	Y	Y	Y	N

ND - Northern Democrats SD - Southern Democrats

* Corresponding to Congressional Record Votes 286, 287, 288, 290, 291, 292, 293, 294

	262	263	264	265	266	267	268	269
6 ***Burton***	Y	Y	Y	N	Y	Y	N	N
7 ***Myers***	Y	Y	Y	N	Y	Y	N	Y
8 McCloskey	Y	Y	Y	Y	N	Y	Y	Y
9 Hamilton	Y	Y	Y	N	N	Y	Y	Y
10 Jacobs	Y	Y	Y	Y	N	Y	Y	Y
IOWA								
1 ***Leach***	Y	Y	Y	N	Y	Y	Y	N
2 ***Tauke***	Y	Y	Y	N	Y	Y	Y	N
3 ***Evans***	Y	Y	Y	N	Y	Y	Y	N
4 Smith	Y	Y	Y	N	Y	Y	N	Y
5 ***Lightfoot***	Y	Y	Y	N	Y	Y	Y	N
6 Bedell	Y	Y	Y	C	Y	Y	Y	Y
KANSAS								
1 ***Roberts***	Y	Y	Y	N	Y	Y	Y	N
2 Slattery	Y	Y	Y	N	N	Y	Y	Y
3 ***Meyers***	Y	Y	Y	N	Y	Y	Y	N
4 Glickman	Y	Y	Y	N	N	Y	Y	Y
5 ***Whittaker***	Y	Y	Y	N	Y	Y	Y	N
KENTUCKY								
1 Hubbard	Y	Y	Y	Y	Y	Y	Y	Y
2 Natcher	Y	Y	Y	Y	Y	Y	N	Y
3 Mazzoli	Y	Y	Y	N	Y	Y	N	Y
4 ***Snyder***	Y	Y	Y	N	Y	Y	N	N
5 ***Rogers***	Y	Y	Y	Y	Y	Y	Y	N
6 ***Hopkins***	Y	Y	Y	Y	Y	Y	Y	N
7 Perkins	Y	Y	Y	Y	Y	Y	N	Y
LOUISIANA								
1 ***Livingston***	Y	Y	Y	N	Y	Y	Y	N
2 Boggs	Y	Y	Y	Y	Y	Y	N	Y
3 Tauzin	Y	Y	Y	Y	Y	Y	Y	Y
4 Roemer	Y	Y	Y	Y	Y	Y	Y	N
5 Huckaby	Y	Y	Y	Y	?	?	Y	N
6 ***Moore***	?	?	?	?	?	?	?	?
7 Breaux	Y	Y	Y	Y	?	?	?	?
8 Long	?	?	?	#	?	?	?	?
MAINE								
1 ***McKernan***	Y	Y	Y	Y	Y	Y	Y	N
2 ***Snowe***	Y	Y	Y	Y	Y	Y	Y	N
MARYLAND								
1 Dyson	Y	Y	Y	Y	N	Y	Y	Y
2 ***Bentley***	Y	Y	Y	Y	Y	Y	N	Y
3 Mikulski	Y	Y	Y	Y	Y	Y	N	Y
4 ***Holt***	Y	Y	Y	N	Y	Y	N	N
5 Hoyer	Y	Y	Y	Y	Y	Y	N	Y
6 Byron	Y	Y	Y	Y	Y	Y	Y	N
7 Mitchell	Y	Y	Y	Y	N	Y	N	Y
8 Barnes	Y	Y	Y	Y	Y	Y	N	Y
MASSACHUSETTS								
1 ***Conte***	Y	Y	Y	Y	Y	Y	N	Y
2 Boland	Y	Y	Y	Y	Y	Y	N	Y
3 Early	Y	Y	Y	Y	Y	Y	N	Y
4 Frank	Y	Y	?	Y	N	Y	N	Y
5 Atkins	Y	Y	Y	Y	N	Y	N	Y
6 Mavroules	Y	Y	Y	Y	Y	Y	N	Y
7 Markey	Y	Y	Y	Y	Y	?	N	Y
8 O'Neill				Y				
9 Moakley	Y	Y	Y	Y	Y	Y	N	Y
10 Studds	Y	Y	Y	Y	Y	Y	N	Y
11 Donnelly	Y	Y	Y	Y	Y	Y	Y	Y
MICHIGAN								
1 Conyers	?	?	Y	Y	N	Y	N	Y
2 ***Pursell***	Y	Y	Y	N	Y	Y	Y	Y
3 Wolpe	Y	Y	Y	Y	N	Y	Y	Y
4 ***Siljander***	?	?	?	?	?	?	?	?
5 ***Henry***	Y	Y	Y	Y	Y	Y	Y	N
6 Carr	Y	Y	Y	Y	Y	Y	N	Y
7 Kildee	Y	Y	Y	Y	Y	Y	N	Y
8 Traxler	Y	Y	Y	Y	Y	Y	Y	Y
9 ***Vander Jagt***	Y	Y	?	N	Y	?	Y	N
10 ***Schuette***	Y	Y	Y	Y	Y	Y	N	N
11 ***Davis***	Y	Y	Y	Y	Y	Y	Y	Y
12 Bonior	Y	Y	Y	Y	Y	Y	N	Y
13 Crockett	Y	Y	Y	Y	N	Y	Y	Y
14 Hertel	?	?	?	Y	Y	Y	Y	Y
15 Ford	Y	Y	Y	Y	Y	Y	N	Y
16 Dingell	Y	Y	Y	Y	Y	Y	N	?
17 Levin	Y	Y	Y	Y	N	Y	Y	Y
18 ***Broomfield***	Y	Y	Y	N	Y	Y	Y	N
MINNESOTA								
1 Penny	Y	Y	Y	N	Y	Y	Y	Y
2 ***Weber***	Y	Y	Y	N	Y	Y	Y	N
3 ***Frenzel***	Y	Y	Y	N	Y	?	Y	N
4 Vento	Y	Y	Y	Y	Y	Y	N	Y
5 Sabo	Y	Y	Y	Y	Y	Y	N	Y
6 Sikorski	Y	Y	Y	Y	N	Y	Y	Y

	262	263	264	265	266	267	268	269
7 ***Stangeland***	Y	Y	Y	N	Y	Y	Y	N
8 Oberstar	Y	Y	Y	Y	Y	Y	N	Y
MISSISSIPPI								
1 Whitten	Y	Y	Y	Y	Y	Y	N	?
2 ***Franklin***	?	Y	Y	Y	Y	Y	Y	N
3 Montgomery	Y	Y	Y	Y	Y	Y	Y	N
4 Dowdy	Y	Y	Y	Y	Y	Y	N	Y
5 ***Lott***	Y	Y	Y	Y	Y	Y	Y	N
MISSOURI								
1 Clay	?	?	?	Y	Y	Y	N	?
2 Young	Y	Y	Y	Y	Y	Y	N	Y
3 Gephardt	Y	Y	Y	Y	Y	Y	N	Y
4 Skelton	Y	Y	Y	Y	Y	Y	Y	Y
5 Wheat	Y	Y	Y	Y	Y	Y	Y	Y
6 ***Coleman***	Y	Y	Y	Y	Y	?	N	N
7 ***Taylor***	Y	Y	Y	Y	Y	Y	Y	N
8 ***Emerson***	Y	Y	Y	Y	Y	Y	Y	N
9 Volkmer	Y	Y	Y	Y	Y	Y	Y	Y
MONTANA								
1 Williams	?	Y	Y	Y	N	?	N	Y
2 ***Marlenee***	Y	Y	Y	N	Y	Y	Y	N
NEBRASKA								
1 ***Bereuter***	Y	Y	Y	N	Y	Y	Y	N
2 ***Daub***	Y	Y	Y	N	Y	Y	Y	N
3 ***Smith***	Y	Y	Y	N	Y	Y	Y	N
NEVADA								
1 Reid	Y	Y	Y	Y	Y	Y	Y	Y
2 ***Vucanovich***	Y	Y	Y	N	Y	Y	Y	N
NEW HAMPSHIRE								
1 ***Smith***	Y	Y	Y	Y	Y	Y	Y	N
2 ***Gregg***	Y	Y	Y	Y	Y	Y	Y	N
NEW JERSEY								
1 Florio	Y	Y	Y	Y	Y	Y	N	Y
2 Hughes	Y	Y	Y	Y	Y	Y	Y	Y
3 Howard	Y	Y	Y	Y	Y	Y	N	Y
4 ***Smith***	Y	Y	Y	Y	Y	Y	N	Y
5 ***Roukema***	?	Y	Y	Y	Y	Y	Y	Y
6 Dwyer	Y	Y	Y	Y	Y	Y	N	Y
7 ***Rinaldo***	Y	Y	Y	Y	Y	Y	N	Y
8 Roe	Y	Y	Y	Y	Y	Y	N	Y
9 Torricelli	Y	Y	Y	Y	Y	Y	N	Y
10 Rodino	Y	Y	Y	Y	Y	Y	N	Y
11 ***Gallo***	Y	Y	Y	N	Y	Y	Y	Y
12 ***Courter***	?	?	?	N	Y	Y	Y	Y
13 ***Saxton***	Y	Y	Y	N	Y	Y	Y	Y
14 Guarini	Y	Y	Y	Y	Y	Y	N	Y
NEW MEXICO								
1 ***Lujan***	Y	Y	Y	N	Y	Y	Y	N
2 ***Skeen***	Y	Y	Y	Y	Y	Y	N	N
3 Richardson	Y	Y	Y	Y	Y	Y	Y	Y
NEW YORK								
1 ***Carney***	Y	?	Y	N	Y	Y	Y	N
2 Downey	Y	Y	Y	N	Y	Y	Y	Y
3 Mrazek	Y	Y	Y	Y	Y	Y	N	Y
4 ***Lent***	Y	Y	Y	N	Y	Y	Y	N
5 ***McGrath***	Y	Y	Y	Y	?	Y	Y	N
6 Waldon	Y	Y	Y	Y	Y	Y	Y	Y
7 Ackerman	Y	Y	Y	Y	N	Y	N	Y
8 Scheuer	Y	Y	Y	Y	N	Y	N	Y
9 Manton	Y	Y	Y	Y	Y	Y	N	Y
10 Schumer	Y	Y	Y	N	Y	Y	Y	Y
11 Towns	Y	Y	Y	Y	N	Y	N	Y
12 Owens	Y	Y	Y	Y	N	Y	Y	Y
13 Solarz	Y	Y	Y	N	Y	?	N	Y
14 ***Molinari***	Y	Y	Y	Y	Y	Y	N	N
15 ***Green***	Y	Y	Y	N	Y	Y	N	Y
16 Rangel	Y	Y	Y	Y	N	Y	N	Y
17 Weiss	Y	Y	Y	Y	Y	Y	N	Y
18 Garcia	Y	Y	Y	Y	N	Y	N	Y
19 Biaggi	Y	Y	Y	Y	Y	?	N	Y
20 ***DioGuardi***	Y	Y	Y	Y	Y	Y	Y	N
21 ***Fish***	Y	Y	Y	Y	Y	Y	Y	N
22 ***Gilman***	Y	Y	Y	Y	Y	Y	N	N
23 Stratton	Y	Y	Y	Y	Y	Y	N	Y
24 ***Solomon***	Y	Y	Y	Y	Y	Y	Y	N
25 ***Boehlert***	Y	Y	Y	Y	Y	Y	Y	Y
26 ***Martin***	Y	Y	Y	Y	Y	Y	Y	?
27 ***Wortley***	Y	Y	Y	N	Y	Y	Y	Y
28 McHugh	Y	Y	Y	N	Y	Y	N	Y
29 ***Horton***	Y	Y	Y	Y	?	Y	N	Y
30 ***Eckert***	Y	Y	Y	N	Y	Y	Y	N
31 ***Kemp***	Y	Y	Y	N	Y	Y	Y	N
32 LaFalce	Y	Y	Y	Y	Y	Y	N	Y
33 Nowak	Y	Y	Y	Y	Y	Y	Y	Y
34 Lundine	Y	Y	Y	Y	Y	Y	Y	Y

	262	263	264	265	266	267	268	269
NORTH CAROLINA								
1 Jones	Y	Y	Y	Y	Y	Y	Y	Y
2 Valentine	+	+	+	Y	Y	Y	Y	N
3 Whitley	Y	Y	Y	Y	Y	Y	Y	Y
4 ***Cobey***	Y	Y	Y	Y	Y	Y	Y	N
5 Neal	Y	Y	Y	Y	Y	Y	Y	Y
6 ***Coble***	Y	Y	Y	Y	N	Y	Y	N
7 Rose	Y	Y	Y	Y	Y	Y	N	Y
8 Hefner	Y	Y	Y	Y	Y	Y	Y	Y
9 ***McMillan***	Y	Y	Y	Y	Y	Y	Y	N
10 Vacancy								
11 ***Hendon***	Y	Y	+	Y	Y	Y	Y	N
NORTH DAKOTA								
AL Dorgan	Y	Y	Y	N	N	Y	Y	Y
OHIO								
1 Luken	Y	Y	Y	N	Y	Y	N	Y
2 ***Gradison***	Y	Y	Y	N	Y	Y	Y	N
3 Hall	Y	Y	Y	Y	Y	Y	Y	Y
4 ***Oxley***	Y	Y	Y	N	Y	Y	Y	N
5 ***Latta***	Y	Y	Y	N	Y	Y	Y	N
6 ***McEwen***	Y	Y	Y	N	Y	Y	Y	N
7 ***DeWine***	Y	Y	Y	N	Y	Y	Y	N
8 ***Kindness***	Y	Y	Y	Y	Y	Y	Y	N
9 Kaptur	Y	Y	Y	Y	Y	Y	Y	Y
10 ***Miller***	Y	Y	Y	Y	Y	Y	N	N
11 Eckart	Y	Y	Y	Y	Y	?	N	Y
12 ***Kasich***	Y	Y	Y	N	Y	?	Y	N
13 Pease	Y	Y	Y	N	N	Y	Y	Y
14 Seiberling	Y	Y	Y	N	Y	Y	N	Y
15 ***Wylie***	Y	Y	Y	N	Y	Y	Y	N
16 ***Regula***	Y	Y	Y	Y	Y	Y	N	Y
17 Traficant	Y	Y	Y	Y	Y	Y	N	Y
18 Applegate	Y	Y	Y	Y	Y	Y	N	Y
19 Feighan	Y	Y	Y	Y	Y	Y	Y	Y
20 Oakar	Y	Y	Y	Y	Y	Y	N	Y
21 Stokes	Y	Y	Y	Y	Y	?	N	Y
OKLAHOMA								
1 Jones	Y	Y	Y	Y	Y	Y	Y	Y
2 Synar	Y	Y	Y	Y	Y	Y	N	Y
3 Watkins	Y	Y	Y	Y	Y	Y	N	Y
4 McCurdy	Y	Y	Y	Y	Y	Y	Y	Y
5 ***Edwards***	Y	Y	Y	N	Y	Y	Y	N
6 English	Y	Y	Y	Y	Y	Y	Y	Y
OREGON								
1 AuCoin	Y	Y	Y	N	Y	Y	Y	Y
2 ***Smith, R.***	Y	Y	Y	N	Y	Y	Y	N
3 Wyden	Y	Y	Y	N	Y	Y	Y	Y
4 Weaver	Y	Y	Y	Y	N	Y	Y	Y
5 ***Smith, D.***	Y	Y	Y	Y	Y	Y	Y	N
PENNSYLVANIA								
1 Foglietta	Y	Y	Y	Y	Y	Y	N	Y
2 Gray	Y	Y	Y	Y	Y	Y	Y	Y
3 Borski	Y	Y	Y	Y	Y	Y	Y	Y
4 Kolter	Y	Y	Y	Y	?	Y	Y	Y
5 ***Schulze***	Y	Y	Y	Y	N	Y	Y	N
6 Yatron	Y	Y	Y	Y	Y	Y	Y	Y
7 Edgar	Y	Y	Y	Y	Y	Y	N	Y
8 Kostmayer	Y	Y	Y	Y	Y	Y	Y	Y
9 ***Shuster***	Y	Y	Y	Y	Y	Y	Y	N
10 ***McDade***	Y	Y	Y	Y	Y	Y	N	Y
11 Kanjorski	Y	Y	Y	Y	Y	Y	N	Y
12 Murtha	Y	Y	Y	Y	Y	Y	N	Y
13 ***Coughlin***	Y	Y	Y	Y	Y	Y	Y	N
14 Coyne	Y	Y	Y	Y	N	Y	N	Y
15 ***Ritter***	Y	Y	Y	Y	Y	Y	Y	Y
16 ***Walker***	Y	Y	Y	N	Y	Y	Y	N
17 ***Gekas***	Y	Y	Y	N	Y	Y	Y	N
18 Walgren	Y	Y	Y	Y	N	Y	Y	Y
19 ***Goodling***	Y	Y	Y	Y	Y	Y	Y	N
20 Gaydos	Y	Y	Y	Y	Y	?	N	Y
21 ***Ridge***	Y	Y	Y	Y	Y	Y	Y	N
22 Murphy	Y	Y	Y	Y	N	Y	N	Y
23 ***Clinger***	Y	Y	Y	Y	Y	Y	Y	Y
RHODE ISLAND								
1 St Germain	Y	Y	Y	Y	Y	Y	Y	Y
2 ***Schneider***	Y	Y	Y	Y	Y	?	Y	Y
SOUTH CAROLINA								
1 ***Hartnett***	Y	Y	Y	Y	Y	Y	Y	N
2 ***Spence***	Y	Y	Y	Y	Y	Y	Y	N
3 Derrick	Y	Y	Y	Y	Y	Y	N	N
4 ***Campbell***	Y	Y	Y	Y	Y	Y	Y	N
5 Spratt	Y	Y	Y	Y	Y	Y	Y	Y
6 Tallon	Y	Y	Y	Y	Y	Y	Y	Y
SOUTH DAKOTA								
AL Daschle	Y	Y	Y	N	N	Y	Y	Y

	262	263	264	265	266	267	268	269
TENNESSEE								
1 ***Quillen***	Y	Y	Y	Y	Y	N	N	N
2 ***Duncan***	Y	Y	?	Y	Y	Y	N	N
3 Lloyd	Y	Y	Y	Y	Y	Y	Y	N
4 Cooper	Y	Y	Y	Y	Y	Y	Y	Y
5 Boner	Y	Y	Y	Y	N	Y	N	Y
6 Gordon	Y	Y	Y	Y	Y	Y	Y	Y
7 ***Sundquist***	Y	Y	Y	Y	Y	Y	Y	N
8 Jones	Y	Y	Y	Y	Y	Y	Y	Y
9 Ford	Y	Y	Y	Y	?	?	?	?
TEXAS								
1 Chapman	Y	Y	Y	Y	Y	Y	Y	Y
2 Wilson	Y	Y	Y	Y	Y	Y	N	Y
3 ***Bartlett***	Y	Y	Y	N	Y	Y	Y	N
4 Hall, R.	Y	Y	Y	Y	Y	Y	Y	N
5 Bryant	Y	Y	Y	Y	N	Y	Y	Y
6 ***Barton***	Y	Y	Y	N	Y	Y	Y	N
7 ***Archer***	Y	Y	Y	N	Y	Y	Y	N
8 ***Fields***	Y	Y	Y	N	Y	Y	Y	N
9 Brooks	Y	Y	Y	Y	Y	Y	Y	Y
10 Pickle	Y	Y	Y	N	Y	Y	Y	N
11 Leath	Y	Y	Y	Y	Y	Y	Y	Y
12 Wright	Y	Y	Y	Y	Y	Y	N	Y
13 ***Boulter***	Y	Y	Y	N	Y	Y	Y	N
14 ***Sweeney***	Y	Y	Y	Y	?	?	?	?
15 de la Garza	Y	Y	Y	Y	Y	Y	N	Y
16 Coleman	Y	Y	Y	Y	Y	Y	N	Y
17 Stenholm	Y	Y	Y	Y	Y	Y	Y	N
18 Leland	Y	Y	Y	Y	N	Y	N	Y
19 ***Combest***	Y	Y	Y	Y	Y	Y	Y	N
20 Gonzalez	Y	Y	Y	Y	Y	Y	N	Y
21 ***Loeffler***	Y	Y	Y	Y	Y	Y	Y	N
22 ***DeLay***	Y	Y	Y	N	Y	Y	Y	N
23 Bustamante	Y	Y	Y	Y	Y	Y	N	Y
24 Frost	Y	Y	Y	Y	Y	Y	Y	?
25 Andrews	Y	Y	Y	Y	Y	Y	Y	Y
26 ***Armey***	Y	Y	Y	N	Y	Y	Y	N
27 Ortiz	Y	Y	Y	Y	Y	Y	N	Y
UTAH								
1 ***Hansen***	Y	Y	Y	N	Y	Y	Y	N
2 ***Monson***	Y	Y	Y	N	N	Y	Y	N
3 ***Nielson***	Y	Y	Y	N	Y	Y	Y	N
VERMONT								
AL ***Jeffords***	Y	Y	Y	Y	Y	Y	Y	Y
VIRGINIA								
1 ***Bateman***	Y	Y	Y	N	Y	Y	Y	N
2 ***Whitehurst***	Y	Y	Y	N	Y	Y	Y	N
3 ***Bliley***	Y	Y	Y	Y	Y	Y	Y	N
4 Sisisky	Y	Y	Y	Y	Y	Y	Y	Y
5 Daniel	Y	Y	Y	Y	Y	Y	Y	N
6 Olin	Y	Y	Y	Y	Y	Y	Y	Y
7 ***Slaughter***	Y	Y	Y	Y	Y	Y	Y	N
8 ***Parris***	Y	Y	Y	Y	Y	Y	N	N
9 Boucher	Y	Y	Y	Y	Y	Y	N	Y
10 ***Wolf***	Y	Y	Y	N	Y	Y	N	N
WASHINGTON								
1 ***Miller***	Y	Y	Y	N	Y	Y	Y	Y
2 Swift	Y	Y	Y	N	Y	Y	N	Y
3 Bonker	Y	Y	Y	N	Y	Y	Y	Y
4 ***Morrison***	Y	Y	Y	N	Y	Y	Y	Y
5 Foley	Y	Y	Y	X	Y	Y	Y	Y
6 Dicks	Y	Y	Y	N	Y	Y	N	Y
7 Lowry	Y	Y	Y	N	Y	Y	N	Y
8 ***Chandler***	Y	Y	Y	N	Y	Y	Y	Y
WEST VIRGINIA								
1 Mollohan	Y	Y	Y	Y	Y	Y	N	Y
2 Staggers	Y	Y	Y	Y	N	Y	Y	Y
3 Wise	Y	Y	Y	Y	N	Y	Y	Y
4 Rahall	Y	Y	Y	Y	Y	Y	N	Y
WISCONSIN								
1 Aspin	Y	Y	Y	Y	N	Y	Y	Y
2 Kastenmeier	Y	Y	Y	Y	Y	Y	Y	Y
3 ***Gunderson***	Y	Y	Y	Y	Y	Y	Y	Y
4 Kleczka	Y	Y	Y	N	N	Y	Y	Y
5 Moody	Y	?	Y	Y	N	Y	Y	Y
6 ***Petri***	Y	Y	Y	N	Y	Y	Y	N
7 Obey	Y	Y	Y	Y	Y	Y	N	Y
8 ***Roth***	Y	Y	Y	N	Y	Y	Y	N
9 ***Sensenbrenner***	Y	Y	Y	N	Y	Y	Y	N
WYOMING								
AL ***Cheney***	Y	Y	Y	N	Y	Y	Y	N

Southern states - Ala., Ark., Fla., Ga., Ky., La., Miss., N.C., Okla., S.C., Tenn., Texas, Va.

* The *Congressional Record* vote number is different from the CQ vote number because the *Record* includes quorum calls in its tally. CQ does not publish quorum call votes.

270. HR 5294. Treasury, Postal Service and General Government Appropriations, Fiscal 1987. Walker, R-Pa., amendments to transfer $3 million from the Treasury secretary's office to the U.S. Customs Service. Adopted en bloc 387-30: R 163-13; D 224-17 (ND 151-16, SD 73-1), Aug. 6, 1986. (The Walker amendments had been previously adopted in the Committee of the Whole *(see vote 256, p. 74-H)*.)

271. HR 5294. Treasury, Postal Service and General Government Appropriations, Fiscal 1987. Passage of the bill to appropriate $13,651,810,000 in fiscal 1987 for the Treasury Department, Executive Office of the President, U.S. Postal Service and independent agencies. Passed 302-118: R 76-100; D 226-18 (ND 160-8, SD 66-10), Aug. 6, 1986. The president had requested $12,856,230,000 in new budget authority.

272. HR 3129. Omnibus Highway Authorization. Adoption of the rule (H Res 513) to provide for House floor consideration of and to waive points of order against the bill to authorize spending for fiscal years 1987-81 for highway and mass transit programs. Adopted 302-102: R 74-96; D 228-6 (ND 157-1, SD 71-5), Aug. 6, 1986.

273. HR 3129. Omnibus Highway Authorization. McCurdy, D-Okla., amendment to establish a five-year test program permitting states to raise the speed limit from 55 mph to 65 mph on rural sections of the Interstate system. Rejected 198-218: R 117-57; D 81-161 (ND 45-120, SD 36-41), Aug. 6, 1986.

274. HR 3129. Omnibus Highway Authorization. Bentley, R-Md., amendment to exclude all foreign cement material and finished cement from being used in public construction projects financed by the bill. Adopted 300-102: R 118-51; D 182-51 (ND 114-44, SD 68-7), Aug. 6, 1986.

275. HR 3129. Omnibus Highway Authorization. Shuster, R-Pa., substitute for the Shaw, R-Fla., amendment, to place restrictions on billboards on federal highways. The Shuster substitute would freeze the total number of billboards on federal highways while continuing the policy of reimbursing the billboard industry with federal funds for billboards that are taken down. The Shaw amendment would not have required cash compensation for billboards that are removed. Adopted 251-159: R 104-68; D 147-91 (ND 87-76, SD 60-15), Aug. 7, 1986. (The Shaw amendment, as amended by the Shuster substitute, subsequently was adopted *(see vote 276, below)*.)

276. HR 3129. Omnibus Highway Authorization. Shaw, R-Fla., amendment, as amended by the Shuster, R-Pa., substitute *(see vote 275, above)*, to place restrictions on billboards on federal highways. Adopted 385-28: R 149-25; D 236-3 (ND 163-0, SD 73-3), Aug. 7, 1986.

277. HR 3129. Omnibus Highway Authorization. Waxman, D-Calif., amendment to strike funding for the Los Angeles mass transit rail project. Adopted 210-201: R 120-53; D 90-148 (ND 57-107, SD 33-41), Aug. 7, 1986. (The Waxman amendment was rejected Aug. 15 after the House rose from the Committee of the Whole *(see vote 329, p. 92-H)*.)

KEY

- Y Voted for (yea).
- # Paired for.
- + Announced for.
- N Voted against (nay).
- X Paired against.
- \- Announced against.
- P Voted "present."
- C Voted "present" to avoid possible conflict of interest.
- ? Did not vote or otherwise make a position known.

Democrats ***Republicans***

	270	271	272	273	274	275	276	277
ALABAMA								
1 ***Callahan***	Y	Y	Y	N	Y	Y	Y	N
2 ***Dickinson***	Y	N	N	Y	Y	Y	Y	Y
3 Nichols	Y	Y	Y	N	Y	Y	Y	Y
4 Bevill	Y	Y	Y	Y	Y	Y	Y	Y
5 Flippo	?	Y	Y	Y	?	Y	Y	N
6 Erdreich	Y	Y	Y	Y	Y	Y	Y	Y
7 Shelby	Y	Y	Y	?	?	Y	Y	Y
ALASKA								
AL ***Young***	Y	Y	Y	Y	Y	Y	Y	N
ARIZONA								
1 ***McCain***	Y	Y	Y	+	?	Y	Y	Y
2 Udall	Y	Y	Y	Y	N	N	Y	N
3 ***Stump***	Y	N	N	Y	N	Y	N	Y
4 ***Rudd***	Y	Y	N	Y	N	Y	Y	Y
5 ***Kolbe***	Y	Y	N	Y	Y	N	Y	N
ARKANSAS								
1 Alexander	Y	Y	Y	N	Y	Y	Y	N
2 Robinson	Y	Y	Y	N	Y	Y	Y	N
3 ***Hammerschmidt***	Y	N	Y	N	Y	Y	Y	N
4 Anthony	Y	Y	Y	N	N	Y	Y	N
CALIFORNIA								
1 Bosco	Y	Y	Y	N	Y	Y	?	?
2 ***Chappie***	Y	N	N	Y	Y	Y	Y	N
3 Matsui	Y	Y	Y	N	N	N	Y	Y
4 Fazio	Y	Y	Y	Y	Y	Y	Y	N
5 Burton	Y	Y	Y	N	N	N	Y	N
6 Boxer	Y	Y	Y	N	Y	N	Y	N
7 Miller	Y	Y	?	Y	N	N	Y	N
8 Dellums	Y	Y	Y	N	Y	N	Y	N
9 Stark	N	Y	Y	Y	?	?	Y	N
10 Edwards	Y	Y	Y	N	N	N	Y	N
11 Lantos	Y	Y	Y	N	Y	Y	Y	Y
12 ***Zschau***	Y	Y	N	Y	N	N	Y	N
13 Mineta	Y	Y	Y	N	Y	Y	Y	N
14 ***Shumway***	Y	N	Y	Y	N	Y	Y	Y
15 Coelho	Y	Y	?	Y	Y	?	Y	N
16 Panetta	Y	Y	Y	Y	Y	N	Y	N
17 ***Pashayan***	Y	N	Y	N	Y	Y	N	N
18 Lehman	Y	Y	Y	Y	Y	Y	Y	N
19 ***Lagomarsino***	Y	N	N	Y	N	N	Y	Y
20 ***Thomas***	N	N	N	Y	N	Y	Y	N
21 ***Fiedler***	Y	Y	N	Y	Y	N	N	Y
22 ***Moorhead***	Y	N	N	Y	Y	Y	Y	N
23 Beilenson	N	Y	Y	N	N	N	Y	N
24 Waxman	Y	Y	Y	N	N	N	Y	Y
25 Roybal	N	Y	Y	Y	N	Y	Y	N
26 Berman	Y	Y	Y	N	N	N	Y	Y
27 Levine	Y	Y	Y	N	N	N	Y	Y
28 Dixon	Y	Y	Y	N	Y	Y	Y	N
29 Hawkins	Y	Y	Y	N	Y	Y	Y	N
30 Martinez	Y	Y	Y	N	Y	Y	Y	Y
31 Dymally	Y	Y	Y	N	N	N	Y	N
32 Anderson	Y	Y	Y	N	N	Y	Y	N
33 ***Dreier***	Y	N	N	Y	N	Y	Y	N
34 Torres	Y	Y	Y	N	Y	Y	Y	N
35 ***Lewis***	Y	Y	N	Y	N	Y	Y	X
36 Brown	Y	Y	Y	N	N	?	?	N
37 ***McCandless***	Y	N	Y	Y	Y	Y	Y	N
38 ***Dornan***	Y	N	N	Y	Y	Y	Y	N
39 ***Dannemeyer***	Y	N	N	Y	N	N	Y	N
40 ***Badham***	Y	N	Y	Y	Y	Y	Y	Y
41 ***Lowery***	N	Y	Y	Y	Y	N	Y	N
42 ***Lungren***	Y	N	N	Y	N	N	Y	Y
43 ***Packard***	Y	N	Y	N	N	Y	Y	N
44 Bates	Y	Y	?	N	Y	N	Y	N
45 ***Hunter***	Y	N	N	N	Y	N	Y	N
COLORADO								
1 Schroeder	Y	N	Y	Y	Y	N	Y	Y
2 Wirth	Y	Y	Y	Y	Y	N	Y	Y
3 ***Strang***	Y	N	N	Y	Y	N	Y	Y
4 ***Brown***	Y	N	N	Y	N	Y	Y	Y
5 ***Kramer***	Y	N	N	Y	Y	N	Y	Y
6 ***Schaefer***	Y	N	N	Y	Y	Y	Y	Y
CONNECTICUT								
1 Kennelly	Y	Y	Y	N	Y	N	Y	Y
2 Gejdenson	Y	Y	Y	N	Y	N	Y	Y
3 Morrison	N	Y	Y	N	Y	Y	Y	Y
4 ***McKinney***	Y	Y	Y	Y	Y	N	Y	Y
5 ***Rowland***	Y	Y	Y	N	Y	Y	Y	Y
6 ***Johnson***	Y	Y	Y	N	Y	Y	Y	Y
DELAWARE								
AL Carper	Y	Y	Y	N	N	N	Y	Y
FLORIDA								
1 Hutto	Y	Y	Y	N	N	N	Y	Y
2 Fuqua	Y	Y	Y	Y	Y	Y	Y	N
3 Bennett	Y	Y	Y	N	Y	N	Y	N
4 Chappell	Y	Y	Y	Y	Y	?	Y	N
5 ***McCollum***	Y	N	N	Y	N	N	Y	N
6 MacKay	Y	Y	Y	N	N	N	Y	Y
7 Gibbons	Y	Y	Y	N	N	Y	Y	Y
8 ***Young***	Y	Y	Y	Y	Y	N	Y	Y
9 ***Bilirakis***	Y	Y	N	Y	Y	N	Y	Y
10 ***Ireland***	Y	Y	N	Y	N	N	Y	Y
11 Nelson	Y	Y	Y	N	Y	N	Y	Y
12 ***Lewis***	Y	Y	N	Y	Y	N	Y	Y
13 ***Mack***	Y	N	N	Y	N	Y	Y	Y
14 Mica	Y	Y	Y	N	Y	N	Y	N
15 ***Shaw***	Y	Y	Y	Y	N	N	Y	Y
16 Smith	Y	Y	Y	N	Y	N	Y	Y
17 Lehman	Y	Y	Y	N	Y	Y	Y	N
18 Pepper	?	?	Y	N	Y	Y	Y	N
19 Fascell	Y	Y	Y	N	Y	N	Y	N
GEORGIA								
1 Thomas	Y	Y	Y	N	Y	Y	Y	N
2 Hatcher	Y	Y	Y	Y	Y	Y	Y	N
3 Ray	Y	N	Y	N	Y	Y	Y	N
4 ***Swindall***	Y	N	N	Y	Y	Y	Y	Y
5 Fowler	?	?	?	?	?	?	?	?
6 ***Gingrich***	Y	N	N	Y	Y	Y	Y	Y
7 Darden	Y	Y	Y	Y	Y	Y	Y	N
8 Rowland	Y	Y	Y	N	Y	Y	Y	N
9 Jenkins	Y	Y	N	Y	?	Y	Y	N
10 Barnard	Y	Y	N	Y	Y	Y	Y	N
HAWAII								
1 Vacancy								
2 Akaka	N	Y	Y	N	N	Y	Y	N
IDAHO								
1 ***Craig***	Y	N	N	Y	Y	Y	N	Y
2 Stallings	Y	Y	Y	Y	Y	Y	Y	Y
ILLINOIS								
1 Hayes	Y	Y	Y	Y	Y	Y	Y	N
2 Savage	Y	Y	Y	N	Y	Y	Y	N
3 Russo	Y	Y	?	N	?	Y	Y	Y
4 Vacancy								
5 Lipinski	Y	Y	Y	N	Y	Y	Y	N
6 ***Hyde***	Y	N	Y	Y	Y	N	Y	N
7 Collins	Y	Y	Y	Y	Y	Y	Y	N
8 Rostenkowski	Y	Y	Y	N	?	Y	Y	N
9 Yates	N	Y	Y	N	N	N	Y	N
10 ***Porter***	Y	Y	N	Y	N	N	Y	Y
11 Annunzio	Y	Y	Y	N	Y	Y	Y	N
12 ***Crane***	Y	N	N	Y	N	Y	N	Y
13 ***Fawell***	Y	N	Y	N	N	N	Y	N
14 ***Grotberg***	?	?	?	?	?	?	?	?
15 ***Madigan***	Y	N	N	Y	Y	Y	Y	Y
16 ***Martin***	Y	N	N	N	Y	N	Y	#
17 Evans	Y	Y	Y	N	Y	N	Y	Y
18 ***Michel***	Y	Y	Y	Y	Y	?	Y	Y
19 Bruce	Y	Y	Y	N	Y	N	Y	Y
20 Durbin	Y	Y	Y	Y	Y	N	Y	N
21 Price	Y	Y	Y	Y	Y	N	Y	N
22 Gray	Y	Y	Y	Y	Y	Y	Y	N
INDIANA								
1 Visclosky	Y	Y	Y	N	Y	Y	Y	N
2 Sharp	Y	Y	Y	Y	Y	N	Y	Y
3 ***Hiler***	N	N	N	Y	Y	Y	Y	Y
4 ***Coats***	Y	N	N	Y	Y	Y	Y	Y
5 ***Hillis***	Y	Y	Y	?	?	?	?	?

ND - Northern Democrats SD - Southern Democrats

* Corresponding to Congressional Record Votes 295, 296, 297, 298, 299, 301, 302, 304

	270	271	272	273	274	275	276	277
6 ***Burton***	Y	N	N	Y	Y	Y	N	Y
7 ***Myers***	Y	Y	Y	Y	Y	Y	N	N
8 McCloskey	Y	Y	Y	Y	Y	Y	Y	Y
9 Hamilton	Y	Y	Y	Y	Y	Y	Y	Y
10 Jacobs	Y	N	Y	N	Y	N	Y	Y
IOWA								
1 ***Leach***	Y	Y	Y	N	N	N	Y	Y
2 ***Tauke***	N	N	N	Y	Y	Y	Y	Y
3 ***Evans***	Y	N	N	Y	N	N	N	Y
4 Smith	Y	Y	Y	Y	Y	Y	Y	N
5 ***Lightfoot***	Y	N	Y	Y	Y	Y	Y	N
6 Bedell	Y	Y	Y	N	Y	Y	Y	Y
KANSAS								
1 ***Roberts***	Y	N	N	Y	N	N	Y	Y
2 Slattery	Y	N	?	Y	N	Y	Y	Y
3 ***Meyers***	Y	N	N	N	Y	N	Y	Y
4 Glickman	Y	Y	Y	Y	N	Y	Y	Y
5 ***Whittaker***	Y	N	N	Y	Y	N	Y	Y
KENTUCKY								
1 Hubbard	Y	N	Y	Y	Y	Y	Y	Y
2 Natcher	Y	Y	Y	N	Y	Y	Y	N
3 Mazzoli	Y	Y	Y	N	N	Y	Y	Y
4 ***Snyder***	Y	Y	Y	N	Y	Y	Y	N
5 ***Rogers***	Y	Y	Y	N	Y	Y	Y	N
6 ***Hopkins***	Y	N	Y	Y	Y	Y	Y	Y
7 Perkins	Y	Y	Y	N	Y	Y	Y	N
LOUISIANA								
1 ***Livingston***	Y	Y	N	Y	Y	Y	Y	Y
2 Boggs	Y	Y	Y	N	Y	Y	Y	Y
3 Tauzin	Y	Y	Y	Y	Y	Y	Y	Y
4 Roemer	Y	N	Y	Y	Y	Y	Y	Y
5 Huckaby	Y	N	Y	Y	Y	Y	Y	Y
6 ***Moore***	?	?	?	?	?	?	?	?
7 Breaux	?	?	?	?	?	?	?	?
8 Long	?	?	?	?	?	?	?	?
MAINE								
1 ***McKernan***	Y	Y	N	Y	Y	N	Y	Y
2 ***Snowe***	Y	Y	N	N	Y	N	Y	Y
MARYLAND								
1 Dyson	Y	Y	Y	Y	Y	N	Y	N
2 ***Bentley***	Y	Y	Y	N	Y	Y	Y	Y
3 Mikulski	Y	Y	Y	N	Y	Y	Y	Y
4 ***Holt***	Y	N	?	?	?	?	?	?
5 Hoyer	N	Y	Y	N	N	N	Y	N
6 Byron	Y	Y	Y	N	Y	N	Y	N
7 Mitchell	Y	Y	Y	?	?	?	?	N
8 Barnes	Y	Y	Y	N	Y	-	+	-
MASSACHUSETTS								
1 ***Conte***	Y	Y	Y	N	Y	N	Y	N
2 Boland	Y	Y	Y	N	N	N	Y	N
3 Early	N	Y	Y	N	N	N	Y	N
4 Frank	Y	Y	Y	Y	Y	N	Y	Y
5 Atkins	Y	Y	Y	N	N	N	Y	Y
6 Mavroules	Y	Y	?	N	?	N	Y	N
7 Markey	Y	Y	Y	N	Y	N	Y	Y
8 O'Neill								
9 Moakley	Y	Y	?	N	Y	N	Y	N
10 Studds	N	Y	Y	N	N	N	Y	Y
11 Donnelly	Y	Y	Y	N	Y	N	Y	N
MICHIGAN								
1 Conyers	N	Y	Y	N	N	N	Y	N
2 ***Pursell***	Y	Y	Y	N	N	Y	Y	Y
3 Wolpe	Y	Y	Y	N	Y	N	Y	Y
4 ***Siljander***	?	?	N	Y	Y	Y	Y	Y
5 ***Henry***	Y	N	N	Y	Y	N	Y	Y
6 Carr	Y	Y	Y	Y	Y	Y	Y	N
7 Kildee	Y	Y	Y	N	Y	N	Y	N
8 Traxler	Y	N	Y	Y	Y	N	Y	N
9 ***Vander Jagt***	Y	N	N	Y	Y	N	Y	Y
10 ***Schuette***	Y	Y	Y	N	Y	Y	Y	Y
11 ***Davis***	Y	Y	Y	Y	Y	?	Y	N
12 Bonior	Y	Y	Y	?	?	N	Y	N
13 Crockett	Y	Y	Y	Y	Y	Y	Y	N
14 Hertel	Y	Y	Y	N	Y	N	Y	Y
15 Ford	N	Y	Y	?	?	N	Y	N
16 Dingell	?	?	?	N	Y	Y	Y	N
17 Levin	Y	Y	Y	N	Y	N	Y	Y
18 ***Broomfield***	Y	N	N	N	Y	N	Y	Y
MINNESOTA								
1 Penny	Y	Y	Y	N	Y	Y	Y	Y
2 ***Weber***	Y	N	N	Y	N	Y	Y	Y
3 ***Frenzel***	N	N	Y	Y	N	Y	Y	Y
4 Vento	Y	Y	Y	N	Y	N	Y	N
5 Sabo	Y	Y	?	N	Y	Y	Y	N
6 Sikorski	Y	Y	Y	N	Y	Y	Y	Y
7 ***Stangeland***	Y	N	Y	N	N	Y	Y	N
8 Oberstar	Y	Y	Y	N	Y	Y	Y	N
MISSISSIPPI								
1 Whitten	Y	Y	Y	N	Y	Y	Y	N
2 ***Franklin***	Y	N	Y	Y	Y	Y	Y	Y
3 Montgomery	Y	Y	Y	N	Y	Y	Y	Y
4 Dowdy	Y	Y	Y	N	Y	Y	Y	Y
5 ***Lott***	Y	N	N	Y	?	Y	Y	Y
MISSOURI								
1 Clay	Y	Y	Y	N	Y	N	Y	N
2 Young	Y	Y	Y	N	Y	Y	Y	N
3 Gephardt	Y	Y	Y	N	Y	Y	Y	N
4 Skelton	Y	Y	Y	Y	Y	Y	Y	N
5 Wheat	Y	Y	Y	N	Y	N	Y	N
6 ***Coleman***	Y	Y	Y	Y	Y	Y	Y	Y
7 ***Taylor***	Y	N	Y	N	Y	Y	Y	N
8 ***Emerson***	Y	Y	Y	Y	Y	Y	Y	Y
9 Volkmer	Y	Y	Y	N	Y	Y	Y	N
MONTANA								
1 Williams	N	Y	Y	Y	Y	Y	Y	N
2 ***Marlenee***	Y	N	N	Y	Y	N	N	Y
NEBRASKA								
1 ***Bereuter***	Y	N	N	Y	N	N	Y	Y
2 ***Daub***	Y	N	N	Y	N	N	Y	Y
3 ***Smith***	Y	Y	N	Y	N	N	Y	Y
NEVADA								
1 Reid	Y	Y	Y	Y	Y	Y	Y	Y
2 ***Vucanovich***	Y	N	N	Y	Y	Y	Y	Y
NEW HAMPSHIRE								
1 ***Smith***	Y	N	N	Y	Y	N	Y	Y
2 ***Gregg***	Y	N	?	Y	Y	N	Y	Y
NEW JERSEY								
1 Florio	Y	Y	Y	N	Y	Y	Y	Y
2 Hughes	Y	N	Y	N	N	Y	Y	N
3 Howard	N	Y	Y	N	Y	Y	Y	N
4 ***Smith***	Y	Y	Y	N	Y	Y	Y	Y
5 ***Roukema***	Y	Y	Y	N	Y	Y	Y	N
6 Dwyer	Y	Y	Y	N	Y	Y	Y	N
7 ***Rinaldo***	Y	Y	Y	N	Y	Y	Y	Y
8 Roe	Y	Y	Y	N	Y	Y	Y	N
9 Torricelli	Y	Y	Y	N	Y	Y	Y	N
10 Rodino	Y	Y	Y	N	Y	Y	?	N
11 ***Gallo***	Y	Y	Y	N	Y	Y	Y	N
12 ***Courter***	Y	Y	N	N	N	Y	Y	Y
13 ***Saxton***	Y	Y	Y	N	Y	Y	Y	Y
14 Guarini	Y	Y	Y	N	N	Y	Y	N
NEW MEXICO								
1 ***Lujan***	Y	Y	Y	Y	Y	Y	Y	Y
2 ***Skeen***	N	Y	Y	Y	Y	Y	Y	N
3 Richardson	Y	Y	Y	Y	?	Y	Y	N
NEW YORK								
1 ***Carney***	Y	N	N	Y	N	Y	N	Y
2 Downey	Y	Y	?	N	N	N	Y	Y
3 Mrazek	Y	Y	Y	Y	Y	N	Y	N
4 ***Lent***	Y	Y	N	N	Y	Y	Y	N
5 ***McGrath***	Y	Y	N	N	Y	Y	Y	Y
6 Waldon	Y	Y	Y	N	Y	Y	Y	N
7 Ackerman	Y	Y	Y	N	Y	Y	Y	N
8 Scheuer	Y	Y	Y	N	N	N	Y	Y
9 Manton	Y	Y	Y	N	Y	Y	Y	N
10 Schumer	Y	Y	Y	N	N	N	Y	Y
11 Towns	Y	Y	Y	N	Y	Y	Y	N
12 Owens	Y	Y	Y	N	Y	N	Y	N
13 Solarz	Y	Y	Y	N	N	N	Y	Y
14 ***Molinari***	Y	N	N	N	Y	N	Y	Y
15 ***Green***	N	Y	Y	N	N	N	Y	Y
16 Rangel	N	Y	Y	N	N	Y	N	N
17 Weiss	Y	Y	Y	N	N	N	Y	Y
18 Garcia	Y	Y	Y	?	?	N	Y	N
19 Biaggi	Y	Y	Y	Y	?	N	Y	Y
20 ***DioGuardi***	Y	Y	Y	N	Y	N	Y	Y
21 ***Fish***	N	Y	N	N	Y	Y	Y	N
22 ***Gilman***	Y	Y	Y	N	Y	N	Y	N
23 Stratton	Y	Y	Y	Y	Y	Y	Y	N
24 ***Solomon***	Y	N	N	Y	Y	Y	Y	?
25 ***Boehlert***	Y	Y	Y	N	Y	Y	Y	Y
26 ***Martin***	Y	Y	Y	Y	Y	Y	Y	N
27 ***Wortley***	Y	Y	Y	N	Y	Y	Y	N
28 McHugh	Y	Y	Y	N	N	Y	Y	N
29 ***Horton***	Y	Y	Y	Y	Y	Y	Y	N
30 ***Eckert***	N	N	N	Y	N	Y	Y	Y
31 ***Kemp***	Y	N	Y	Y	N	Y	Y	Y
32 LaFalce	Y	Y	Y	N	N	Y	Y	N
33 Nowak	Y	Y	Y	N	Y	Y	Y	N
34 Lundine	Y	Y	Y	N	Y	Y	Y	?
NORTH CAROLINA								
1 Jones	Y	Y	Y	N	Y	Y	Y	N
2 Valentine	Y	Y	Y	N	Y	N	Y	N
3 Whitley	Y	Y	Y	N	Y	Y	Y	N
4 ***Cobey***	Y	Y	N	Y	N	Y	Y	Y
5 Neal	Y	N	Y	Y	Y	Y	Y	Y
6 ***Coble***	Y	Y	?	Y	Y	Y	Y	Y
7 Rose	Y	Y	Y	Y	Y	Y	Y	N
8 Hefner	Y	Y	Y	N	Y	Y	Y	N
9 ***McMillan***	Y	Y	N	Y	N	Y	Y	Y
10 Vacancy								
11 ***Hendon***	Y	N	Y	Y	Y	Y	Y	Y
NORTH DAKOTA								
AL Dorgan	Y	Y	?	Y	Y	N	Y	Y
OHIO								
1 Luken	Y	Y	Y	Y	Y	Y	Y	Y
2 ***Gradison***	Y	N	Y	Y	?	Y	Y	Y
3 Hall	Y	Y	Y	Y	Y	Y	Y	Y
4 ***Oxley***	Y	N	?	Y	Y	Y	Y	Y
5 ***Latta***	Y	N	Y	N	Y	Y	Y	Y
6 ***McEwen***	Y	N	Y	Y	Y	Y	Y	N
7 ***DeWine***	Y	N	N	N	Y	N	Y	Y
8 ***Kindness***	Y	N	N	Y	Y	N	Y	Y
9 Kaptur	Y	Y	Y	N	Y	Y	Y	N
10 ***Miller***	Y	Y	Y	Y	Y	N	Y	Y
11 Eckart	Y	Y	Y	N	Y	Y	Y	Y
12 ***Kasich***	Y	N	N	Y	Y	N	Y	Y
13 Pease	Y	Y	Y	N	N	N	Y	N
14 Seiberling	Y	Y	Y	N	N	N	Y	N
15 ***Wylie***	Y	N	Y	N	N	N	Y	Y
16 ***Regula***	Y	Y	Y	N	Y	N	Y	Y
17 Traficant	Y	Y	Y	N	Y	Y	Y	N
18 Applegate	Y	Y	Y	N	Y	?	Y	N
19 Feighan	Y	Y	Y	N	Y	Y	Y	Y
20 Oakar	Y	Y	Y	N	Y	N	Y	N
21 Stokes	Y	Y	Y	N	Y	N	Y	N
OKLAHOMA								
1 Jones	Y	N	Y	Y	Y	Y	Y	Y
2 Synar	N	Y	Y	N	N	N	Y	Y
3 Watkins	Y	Y	?	Y	Y	Y	Y	Y
4 McCurdy	Y	Y	Y	Y	Y	Y	Y	Y
5 ***Edwards***	Y	N	N	Y	Y	Y	Y	Y
6 English	Y	Y	Y	Y	Y	Y	Y	Y
OREGON								
1 AuCoin	Y	N	Y	N	N	N	Y	Y
2 ***Smith, R.***	Y	N	N	Y	Y	Y	Y	Y
3 Wyden	Y	N	Y	Y	Y	N	Y	Y
4 Weaver	Y	N	Y	Y	Y	N	Y	Y
5 ***Smith, D.***	Y	N	N	Y	Y	Y	N	Y
PENNSYLVANIA								
1 Foglietta	Y	Y	Y	N	Y	Y	Y	Y
2 Gray	Y	Y	Y	N	Y	Y	Y	N
3 Borski	Y	Y	Y	N	Y	Y	Y	N
4 Kolter	Y	Y	Y	N	Y	Y	Y	N
5 ***Schulze***	Y	N	Y	N	?	Y	Y	Y
6 Yatron	Y	Y	Y	N	Y	Y	Y	Y
7 Edgar	Y	Y	Y	N	Y	Y	Y	?
8 Kostmayer	Y	Y	Y	N	N	N	Y	Y
9 ***Shuster***	Y	N	Y	N	Y	Y	Y	N
10 ***McDade***	N	Y	?	N	Y	Y	Y	N
11 Kanjorski	Y	Y	Y	Y	Y	Y	Y	N
12 Murtha	Y	Y	Y	N	Y	Y	Y	N
13 ***Coughlin***	Y	Y	Y	N	Y	N	Y	Y
14 Coyne	N	Y	N	N	Y	Y	Y	N
15 ***Ritter***	Y	N	Y	Y	Y	Y	Y	Y
16 ***Walker***	Y	N	N	Y	Y	N	Y	Y
17 ***Gekas***	Y	N	N	N	Y	Y	Y	Y
18 Walgren	Y	Y	Y	N	Y	N	Y	Y
19 ***Goodling***	Y	Y	Y	N	Y	Y	Y	Y
20 Gaydos	Y	Y	Y	N	Y	Y	Y	N
21 ***Ridge***	Y	Y	?	N	Y	Y	Y	Y
22 Murphy	Y	Y	Y	N	Y	Y	Y	N
23 ***Clinger***	N	Y	Y	N	+	Y	Y	N
RHODE ISLAND								
1 St Germain	Y	Y	Y	N	?	N	Y	N
2 ***Schneider***	Y	Y	N	N	Y	N	Y	Y
SOUTH CAROLINA								
1 ***Hartnett***	Y	N	N	Y	Y	Y	Y	N
2 ***Spence***	Y	N	N	Y	Y	N	N	N
3 Derrick	Y	Y	Y	N	Y	N	N	N
4 ***Campbell***	Y	N	Y	Y	Y	?	?	Y
5 Spratt	Y	Y	Y	N	Y	Y	Y	Y
6 Tallon	Y	Y	Y	Y	Y	Y	Y	Y
SOUTH DAKOTA								
AL Daschle	Y	Y	Y	Y	Y	Y	Y	N
TENNESSEE								
1 ***Quillen***	Y	N	Y	N	Y	Y	Y	N
2 ***Duncan***	Y	Y	Y	N	Y	N	Y	Y
3 Lloyd	Y	Y	Y	Y	Y	Y	Y	?
4 Cooper	Y	Y	Y	Y	Y	N	Y	Y
5 Boner	Y	Y	Y	Y	Y	?	?	?
6 Gordon	Y	Y	Y	Y	Y	?	?	?
7 ***Sundquist***	Y	Y	Y	N	Y	Y	Y	N
8 Jones	Y	Y	Y	Y	Y	Y	Y	N
9 Ford	?	?	?	?	?	?	?	?
TEXAS								
1 Chapman	Y	Y	Y	N	Y	Y	Y	N
2 Wilson	Y	Y	Y	N	Y	Y	Y	N
3 ***Bartlett***	Y	N	N	Y	N	N	N	Y
4 Hall, R.	Y	N	N	Y	Y	N	N	Y
5 Bryant	Y	Y	Y	N	Y	Y	Y	Y
6 ***Barton***	Y	N	N	Y	Y	N	N	Y
7 ***Archer***	Y	N	N	Y	N	Y	Y	N
8 ***Fields***	Y	N	?	Y	N	C	C	N
9 Brooks	Y	Y	Y	N	Y	Y	Y	N
10 Pickle	Y	Y	Y	Y	Y	N	Y	N
11 Leath	Y	Y	Y	Y	Y	Y	Y	N
12 Wright	Y	Y	Y	N	Y	Y	Y	N
13 ***Boulter***	Y	Y	N	Y	N	Y	N	N
14 ***Sweeney***	?	?	?	?	?	N	Y	Y
15 de la Garza	Y	Y	Y	Y	Y	Y	Y	N
16 Coleman	Y	Y	Y	Y	Y	Y	Y	N
17 Stenholm	Y	N	N	Y	Y	Y	Y	Y
18 Leland	Y	Y	Y	Y	Y	Y	Y	N
19 ***Combest***	Y	N	N	Y	N	N	N	Y
20 Gonzalez	P	Y	Y	N	Y	Y	Y	N
21 ***Loeffler***	Y	Y	N	Y	?	Y	Y	Y
22 ***DeLay***	Y	N	N	Y	N	Y	N	N
23 Bustamante	Y	Y	Y	Y	Y	Y	Y	N
24 Frost	?	?	?	N	Y	Y	Y	N
25 Andrews	Y	Y	Y	N	Y	N	Y	Y
26 ***Armey***	Y	N	N	Y	N	N	N	Y
27 Ortiz	Y	Y	Y	Y	Y	Y	Y	N
UTAH								
1 ***Hansen***	Y	Y	N	Y	N	Y	N	Y
2 ***Monson***	Y	N	Y	Y	N	Y	N	N
3 ***Nielson***	Y	N	N	Y	N	Y	N	Y
VERMONT								
AL ***Jeffords***	Y	Y	Y	N	N	N	Y	Y
VIRGINIA								
1 ***Bateman***	Y	Y	N	Y	Y	Y	Y	N
2 ***Whitehurst***	Y	N	N	N	Y	Y	Y	Y
3 ***Bliley***	Y	N	N	Y	Y	Y	N	Y
4 Sisisky	Y	Y	Y	Y	Y	Y	Y	Y
5 Daniel	Y	N	N	N	Y	Y	N	Y
6 Olin	Y	N	Y	N	Y	N	Y	Y
7 ***Slaughter***	Y	N	N	N	Y	Y	Y	N
8 ***Parris***	N	Y	Y	Y	Y	Y	Y	N
9 Boucher	Y	Y	Y	Y	N	Y	Y	?
10 ***Wolf***	N	Y	Y	N	Y	N	Y	N
WASHINGTON								
1 ***Miller***	Y	N	N	N	N	N	Y	Y
2 Swift	Y	Y	Y	N	N	Y	Y	Y
3 Bonker	?	Y	Y	Y	N	N	Y	N
4 ***Morrison***	Y	Y	Y	Y	N	N	Y	Y
5 Foley	Y	Y	Y	N	N	N	Y	?
6 Dicks	Y	Y	Y	Y	N	Y	Y	N
7 Lowry	Y	Y	Y	N	N	N	Y	N
8 ***Chandler***	Y	Y	Y	Y	N	N	Y	Y
WEST VIRGINIA								
1 Mollohan	Y	Y	Y	N	N	N	Y	N
2 Staggers	Y	Y	Y	N	Y	Y	Y	N
3 Wise	Y	Y	Y	N	Y	Y	Y	N
4 Rahall	Y	Y	Y	N	Y	Y	Y	N
WISCONSIN								
1 Aspin	Y	Y	Y	Y	Y	N	Y	Y
2 Kastenmeier	Y	Y	Y	Y	Y	N	Y	N
3 ***Gunderson***	Y	N	N	Y	Y	N	Y	Y
4 Kleczka	Y	Y	Y	N	Y	Y	Y	Y
5 Moody	N	Y	Y	N	N	Y	?	Y
6 ***Petri***	Y	N	N	Y	N	N	N	Y
7 Obey	Y	Y	Y	N	Y	Y	Y	N
8 ***Roth***	Y	Y	N	Y	Y	N	N	Y
9 ***Sensenbrenner***	Y	N	N	Y	Y	N	Y	Y
WYOMING								
AL ***Cheney***	Y	N	N	Y	Y	N	N	Y

Southern states - Ala., Ark., Fla., Ga., Ky., La., Miss., N.C., Okla., S.C., Tenn., Texas, Va.

* The *Congressional Record* vote number is different from the CQ vote number because the *Record* includes quorum calls in its tally. CQ does not publish quorum call votes.

278. HR 5081. Philippines Aid. Adoption of the rule (H Res 526) to provide for House floor consideration of the bill to authorize $250 million in fiscal 1986 appropriations for the Philippines. The bill also includes fiscal 1987 authorizations for Haiti, international narcotics control and other programs. Adopted 303-96: R 78-88; D 225-8 (ND 157-3, SD 68-5), Aug. 7, 1986.

279. HR 5081. Philippines Aid. Solomon, R-N.Y., amendment to the Leach, R-Iowa, amendment, to delete the $250 million authorization for the Philippines. Rejected 195-203: R 130-37; D 65-166 (ND 25-135, SD 40-31), Aug. 7, 1986. (The Leach amendment, to reduce the $250 million authorization for the Philippines by $50 million and eliminate a requirement that the money be used solely for general budgetary support, subsequently was adopted *(see vote 280, below).*)

280. HR 5081. Philippines Aid. Leach, R-Iowa, amendment to reduce the $250 million authorization for the Philippines by $50 million and eliminate a requirement that the money be used solely for general budgetary support. Adopted 320-76: R 166-0; D 154-76 (ND 97-63, SD 57-13), Aug. 7, 1986.

281. HR 5081. Philippines Aid. Passage of the bill to authorize fiscal 1986 spending of $200 million for assistance to the Philippines, and fiscal 1987 spending of $108 million for Haiti, $65.4 million for international narcotics control, $75 million for child health programs and $18.2 million for an inspector general at the Agency for International Development. Passed 219-178: R 46-120; D 173-58 (ND 140-21, SD 33-37), Aug. 7, 1986.

282. HR 4428. Defense Authorization, Fiscal 1987. Pepper, D-Fla., motion to consider the rule (H Res 531) to provide for House floor consideration of the bill to authorize funds for military programs of the Departments of Defense and Energy in fiscal 1987. Motion agreed to 276-118: R 61-105; D 215-13 (ND 148-11, SD 67-2), Aug. 7, 1986. A two-thirds majority of those present and voting (263 in this case) is required to consider a privileged report from the Rules Committee on the same day it is presented to the House.

283. HR 4428. Defense Authorization, Fiscal 1987. Adoption of the rule (H Res 531) to provide for House floor consideration of the bill to authorize funds for military programs of the Departments of Defense and Energy in fiscal 1987. Adopted 261-117: R 56-108; D 205-9 (ND 141-8, SD 64-1), Aug. 7, 1986.

284. Procedural Motion. Smith, R-N.H., motion to approve the House *Journal* of Thursday, Aug. 7. Motion agreed to 246-127: R 44-118; D 202-9 (ND 135-9, SD 67-0), Aug. 8, 1986.

285. HR 4428. Defense Authorization, Fiscal 1987. Spratt, D-S.C., amendment to reduce the total national defense budget for fiscal 1987 to $285 billion in budget authority and $279 billion in outlays. Adopted 245-156: R 37-130; D 208-26 (ND 152-7, SD 56-19), Aug. 8, 1986.

KEY

- Y Voted for (yea).
- # Paired for.
- + Announced for.
- N Voted against (nay).
- X Paired against.
- - Announced against.
- P Voted "present."
- C Voted "present" to avoid possible conflict of interest.
- ? Did not vote or otherwise make a position known.

Democrats ***Republicans***

	278	279	280	281	282	283	284	285
ALABAMA								
1 ***Callahan***	Y	Y	Y	N	N	Y	Y	N
2 ***Dickinson***	N	Y	Y	N	Y	Y	N	N
3 Nichols	Y	Y	Y	N	Y	?	Y	N
4 Bevill	Y	Y	Y	N	Y	Y	Y	Y
5 Flippo	Y	N	Y	N	Y	Y	Y	Y
6 Erdreich	Y	Y	Y	N	Y	Y	Y	Y
7 Shelby	Y	Y	Y	N	Y	Y	Y	N
ALASKA								
AL ***Young***	N	Y	Y	N	N	N	N	N
ARIZONA								
1 ***McCain***	Y	N	Y	Y	N	N	N	N
2 Udall	Y	N	Y	Y	Y	Y	Y	?
3 ***Stump***	N	Y	Y	N	N	N	N	N
4 ***Rudd***	Y	?	?	?	?	N	N	N
5 ***Kolbe***	N	Y	Y	N	N	N	N	N
ARKANSAS								
1 Alexander	Y	Y	Y	N	Y	Y	?	Y
2 Robinson	Y	Y	Y	N	N	Y	Y	N
3 ***Hammerschmidt***	N	Y	Y	N	N	N	Y	N
4 Anthony	Y	Y	Y	N	Y	Y	Y	Y
CALIFORNIA								
1 Bosco	?	?	?	?	?	?	Y	Y
2 ***Chappie***	N	Y	Y	N	N	N	N	N
3 Matsui	Y	N	N	Y	Y	Y	Y	Y
4 Fazio	Y	N	N	Y	Y	Y	Y	Y
5 Burton	Y	N	N	Y	Y	Y	Y	Y
6 Boxer	Y	N	N	Y	Y	Y	Y	Y
7 Miller	Y	N	N	Y	Y	Y	Y	Y
8 Dellums	Y	N	N	Y	Y	Y	Y	Y
9 Stark	Y	N	N	Y	Y	Y	Y	Y
10 Edwards	Y	?	N	Y	Y	Y	Y	Y
11 Lantos	Y	N	Y	Y	Y	Y	Y	Y
12 ***Zschau***	Y	N	Y	Y	Y	Y	N	Y
13 Mineta	Y	N	N	Y	Y	Y	Y	Y
14 ***Shumway***	Y	Y	Y	N	N	N	Y	N
15 Coelho	Y	?	?	?	Y	Y	?	Y
16 Panetta	Y	N	Y	Y	Y	Y	Y	Y
17 ***Pashayan***	Y	N	Y	Y	Y	Y	N	N
18 Lehman	Y	N	Y	Y	Y	Y	Y	Y
19 ***Lagomarsino***	N	N	Y	Y	Y	Y	N	N
20 ***Thomas***	N	Y	Y	Y	N	N	N	N
21 ***Fiedler***	N	Y	Y	N	N	?	N	N
22 ***Moorhead***	N	Y	Y	N	Y	Y	N	N
23 Beilenson	Y	Y	Y	N	Y	Y	Y	Y
24 Waxman	?	N	N	Y	?	?	Y	Y
25 Roybal	Y	N	N	Y	Y	Y	Y	Y
26 Berman	Y	N	N	Y	Y	Y	Y	Y
27 Levine	Y	N	N	Y	Y	?	Y	Y
28 Dixon	Y	N	N	Y	Y	Y	?	Y
29 Hawkins	Y	N	N	Y	Y	Y	N	Y
30 Martinez	Y	?	X	Y	Y	?	Y	Y
31 Dymally	Y	N	N	Y	Y	Y	Y	Y
32 Anderson	Y	N	N	Y	Y	Y	Y	N
33 ***Dreier***	N	Y	Y	N	N	N	N	N
34 Torres	Y	N	N	Y	Y	Y	Y	+
35 ***Lewis***	?	?	?	?	?	?	?	?
36 Brown	Y	N	N	Y	Y	Y	?	?
37 ***McCandless***	N	Y	Y	N	Y	N	N	N
38 ***Dornan***	Y	N	Y	Y	Y	N	N	N
39 ***Dannemeyer***	N	Y	Y	N	N	Y	N	N
40 ***Badham***	N	Y	Y	N	Y	Y	N	N
41 ***Lowery***	Y	N	Y	Y	Y	Y	N	N
42 ***Lungren***	N	#	#	X	?	?	?	X
43 ***Packard***	Y	N	Y	Y	Y	N	N	N
44 Bates	?	N	Y	Y	Y	Y	?	Y
45 ***Hunter***	N	Y	Y	N	N	N	Y	N
COLORADO								
1 Schroeder	Y	N	Y	Y	Y	Y	N	Y
2 Wirth	Y	N	Y	Y	Y	Y	Y	Y
3 ***Strang***	N	Y	Y	N	Y	N	N	N
4 ***Brown***	N	Y	Y	N	N	N	N	Y
5 ***Kramer***	Y	Y	Y	N	N	N	N	N
6 ***Schaefer***	N	Y	Y	N	N	N	N	N
CONNECTICUT								
1 Kennelly	Y	N	Y	Y	Y	Y	Y	Y
2 Gejdenson	Y	N	Y	Y	Y	Y	Y	Y
3 Morrison	Y	N	N	Y	Y	Y	Y	Y
4 ***McKinney***	Y	N	Y	Y	N	Y	Y	Y
5 ***Rowland***	N	Y	Y	N	Y	Y	N	N
6 ***Johnson***	Y	N	Y	Y	Y	Y	Y	N
DELAWARE								
AL Carper	Y	Y	Y	N	Y	Y	Y	Y
FLORIDA								
1 Hutto	Y	Y	Y	N	Y	Y	Y	N
2 Fuqua	Y	N	Y	Y	?	?	Y	Y
3 Bennett	Y	N	N	Y	Y	Y	Y	N
4 Chappell	Y	Y	Y	Y	Y	Y	?	N
5 ***McCollum***	N	Y	Y	N	N	N	N	N
6 MacKay	Y	N	Y	Y	Y	Y	?	Y
7 Gibbons	Y	N	Y	Y	Y	Y	Y	N
8 ***Young***	Y	Y	Y	N	N	N	N	N
9 ***Bilirakis***	N	Y	Y	N	Y	N	N	N
10 ***Ireland***	N	Y	Y	N	N	N	N	N
11 Nelson	Y	Y	Y	N	Y	Y	Y	N
12 ***Lewis***	N	Y	Y	N	Y	N	N	N
13 ***Mack***	N	Y	Y	N	N	N	N	N
14 Mica	Y	N	Y	Y	Y	Y	Y	Y
15 ***Shaw***	N	Y	Y	N	N	N	N	N
16 Smith	Y	N	Y	Y	Y	Y	Y	Y
17 Lehman	Y	N	N	Y	Y	Y	Y	Y
18 Pepper	Y	N	N	Y	Y	Y	Y	Y
19 Fascell	Y	N	N	Y	Y	Y	Y	Y
GEORGIA								
1 Thomas	Y	Y	Y	N	Y	Y	Y	Y
2 Hatcher	Y	N	Y	Y	Y	Y	Y	Y
3 Ray	Y	Y	Y	N	Y	Y	Y	Y
4 ***Swindall***	N	Y	Y	N	N	N	N	N
5 Fowler	?	?	?	?	?	?	?	?
6 ***Gingrich***	Y	N	Y	Y	N	N	N	N
7 Darden	Y	Y	Y	N	Y	Y	Y	N
8 Rowland	Y	Y	Y	N	Y	Y	Y	Y
9 Jenkins	Y	Y	Y	N	Y	Y	?	Y
10 Barnard	?	?	?	?	?	?	Y	N
HAWAII								
1 Vacancy								
2 Akaka	Y	N	N	Y	Y	Y	Y	?
IDAHO								
1 ***Craig***	N	Y	Y	N	N	N	N	N
2 Stallings	Y	N	Y	Y	Y	Y	Y	Y
ILLINOIS								
1 Hayes	Y	N	Y	Y	Y	Y	N	Y
2 Savage	Y	N	Y	Y	Y	Y	Y	Y
3 Russo	Y	Y	Y	N	Y	Y	Y	Y
4 Vacancy								
5 Lipinski	Y	N	Y	Y	Y	Y	P	Y
6 ***Hyde***	Y	N	Y	Y	Y	N	N	N
7 Collins	Y	N	Y	Y	Y	Y	Y	Y
8 Rostenkowski	Y	N	?	Y	Y	Y	Y	Y
9 Yates	Y	N	Y	Y	Y	?	Y	Y
10 ***Porter***	N	Y	Y	Y	Y	N	Y	Y
11 Annunzio	Y	N	Y	Y	Y	?	Y	Y
12 ***Crane***	N	Y	Y	N	Y	N	N	N
13 ***Fawell***	Y	Y	Y	N	N	Y	N	Y
14 ***Grotberg***	?	?	?	?	?	?	?	?
15 ***Madigan***	N	Y	Y	N	N	Y	N	N
16 ***Martin***	N	Y	Y	N	N	N	N	N
17 Evans	Y	N	Y	Y	Y	Y	Y	Y
18 ***Michel***	N	Y	Y	Y	Y	Y	N	N
19 Bruce	Y	N	Y	Y	Y	Y	Y	Y
20 Durbin	Y	N	Y	Y	Y	Y	Y	Y
21 Price	Y	N	Y	Y	Y	Y	Y	Y
22 Gray	Y	Y	Y	Y	?	?	Y	Y
INDIANA								
1 Visclosky	Y	N	Y	Y	Y	Y	Y	Y
2 Sharp	Y	N	Y	Y	Y	Y	Y	Y
3 ***Hiler***	Y	Y	Y	N	N	N	N	N
4 ***Coats***	N	Y	Y	N	N	Y	N	N
5 ***Hillis***	?	?	?	?	?	?	?	?

ND - Northern Democrats SD - Southern Democrats

* Corresponding to Congressional Record Votes 305, 306, 307, 308, 309, 310, 311, 312

	278	279	280	281	282	283	284	285
6 ***Burton***	N	Y	Y	N	N	N	N	N
7 ***Myers***	Y	Y	Y	N	N	N	Y	N
8 McCloskey	Y	N	Y	Y	Y	Y	Y	Y
9 Hamilton	Y	N	Y	Y	Y	Y	Y	Y
10 Jacobs	Y	Y	Y	N	Y	N	N	N
IOWA								
1 ***Leach***	Y	N	Y	Y	Y	Y	Y	Y
2 ***Tauke***	N	N	Y	N	N	N	N	Y
3 ***Evans***	N	?	?	N	N	N	N	Y
4 Smith	Y	N	Y	Y	N	N	Y	Y
5 ***Lightfoot***	N	Y	Y	N	N	N	N	Y
6 Bedell	Y	N	Y	Y	Y	Y	Y	Y
KANSAS								
1 ***Roberts***	?	Y	Y	N	N	N	N	Y
2 Slattery	Y	Y	Y	Y	Y	Y	Y	Y
3 ***Meyers***	Y	Y	Y	Y	N	N	N	Y
4 Glickman	Y	N	Y	Y	Y	Y	Y	Y
5 ***Whittaker***	Y	Y	Y	N	N	N	N	N
KENTUCKY								
1 Hubbard	N	Y	Y	N	Y	Y	Y	Y
2 Natcher	Y	N	Y	Y	Y	Y	Y	Y
3 Mazzoli	Y	Y	Y	Y	Y	Y	Y	Y
4 ***Snyder***	N	?	?	?	?	?	?	?
5 ***Rogers***	N	Y	Y	N	Y	Y	N	N
6 ***Hopkins***	N	Y	Y	N	Y	N	N	N
7 Perkins	Y	Y	Y	N	Y	Y	Y	Y
LOUISIANA								
1 ***Livingston***	Y	Y	Y	Y	Y	N	N	N
2 Boggs	Y	N	N	Y	Y	Y	Y	Y
3 Tauzin	N	Y	Y	N	Y	Y	Y	Y
4 Roemer	N	Y	Y	N	Y	Y	Y	Y
5 Huckaby	Y	?	?	?	?	?	?	?
6 ***Moore***	?	?	?	?	?	?	?	?
7 Breaux	?	?	?	?	?	?	?	?
8 Long	?	?	?	?	?	?	?	?
MAINE								
1 ***McKernan***	?	N	Y	Y	N	N	N	N
2 ***Snowe***	Y	N	Y	Y	N	Y	N	Y
MARYLAND								
1 Dyson	Y	Y	Y	N	Y	Y	?	N
2 ***Bentley***	Y	X	#	?	?	?	N	N
3 Mikulski	Y	?	?	?	?	?	?	Y
4 ***Holt***	?	?	?	?	?	?	?	?
5 Hoyer	Y	N	N	Y	Y	Y	Y	Y
6 Byron	Y	N	Y	Y	Y	Y	Y	Y
7 Mitchell	Y	N	N	Y	Y	Y	N	Y
8 Barnes	+	-	-	+	+	+	+	#
MASSACHUSETTS								
1 ***Conte***	Y	N	Y	Y	Y	Y	N	Y
2 Boland	Y	N	Y	Y	Y	Y	?	Y
3 Early	Y	Y	Y	Y	Y	Y	Y	Y
4 Frank	Y	N	N	Y	Y	Y	Y	Y
5 Atkins	Y	N	N	Y	Y	Y	Y	Y
6 Mavroules	Y	N	N	Y	Y	Y	Y	Y
7 Markey	Y	N	N	Y	Y	Y	Y	Y
8 O'Neill								
9 Moakley	Y	N	Y	Y	Y	Y	Y	?
10 Studds	Y	N	N	Y	Y	Y	Y	Y
11 Donnelly	Y	N	N	Y	Y	?	?	?
MICHIGAN								
1 Conyers	Y	N	N	?	?	?	?	?
2 ***Pursell***	Y	Y	Y	N	N	N	Y	N
3 Wolpe	Y	N	Y	Y	Y	Y	Y	Y
4 ***Siljander***	Y	N	Y	Y	N	N	Y	N
5 ***Henry***	Y	Y	Y	N	N	N	N	N
6 Carr	?	Y	Y	N	Y	Y	Y	Y
7 Kildee	Y	N	Y	Y	Y	Y	P	Y
8 Traxler	Y	Y	Y	N	Y	Y	Y	Y
9 ***Vander Jagt***	Y	Y	Y	N	N	Y	N	N
10 ***Schuette***	Y	Y	Y	N	N	N	N	N
11 ***Davis***	?	Y	Y	N	Y	Y	Y	N
12 Bonior	Y	N	N	Y	Y	Y	Y	Y
13 Crockett	Y	N	N	Y	Y	Y	Y	Y
14 Hertel	Y	N	Y	Y	Y	Y	Y	Y
15 Ford	Y	N	N	Y	Y	Y	Y	Y
16 Dingell	Y	N	Y	Y	Y	Y	Y	Y
17 Levin	Y	N	Y	Y	Y	Y	Y	Y
18 ***Broomfield***	Y	N	Y	Y	N	N	Y	N
MINNESOTA								
1 Penny	Y	N	Y	Y	Y	Y	N	Y
2 ***Weber***	Y	N	Y	Y	N	N	N	Y
3 ***Frenzel***	N	N	Y	Y	Y	Y	N	Y
4 Vento	Y	N	Y	Y	Y	Y	?	Y
5 Sabo	?	N	N	Y	Y	Y	Y	Y
6 Sikorski	Y	N	Y	Y	Y	Y	N	Y

	278	279	280	281	282	283	284	285
7 ***Stangeland***	N	N	Y	Y	N	N	?	Y
8 Oberstar	Y	N	Y	Y	Y	Y	Y	Y
MISSISSIPPI								
1 Whitten	Y	Y	Y	N	Y	Y	Y	Y
2 ***Franklin***	Y	Y	Y	N	N	N	Y	Y
3 Montgomery	Y	Y	Y	N	Y	Y	Y	N
4 Dowdy	Y	Y	Y	N	Y	Y	Y	N
5 ***Lott***	Y	Y	Y	N	Y	N	N	N
MISSOURI								
1 Clay	Y	N	N	Y	Y	Y	N	Y
2 Young	Y	N	N	Y	Y	?	Y	Y
3 Gephardt	Y	N	Y	Y	Y	Y	?	Y
4 Skelton	Y	Y	Y	N	Y	Y	Y	N
5 Wheat	Y	N	Y	Y	Y	Y	Y	Y
6 ***Coleman***	N	Y	Y	N	Y	N	N	N
7 ***Taylor***	N	Y	Y	N	Y	N	Y	N
8 ***Emerson***	N	Y	Y	N	Y	N	N	N
9 Volkmer	Y	Y	Y	N	Y	Y	Y	Y
MONTANA								
1 Williams	Y	N	Y	Y	Y	Y	?	Y
2 ***Marlenee***	N	Y	Y	?	N	N	?	N
NEBRASKA								
1 ***Bereuter***	N	Y	Y	N	N	N	N	Y
2 ***Daub***	N	Y	Y	N	N	N	N	N
3 ***Smith***	Y	Y	Y	N	N	Y	Y	Y
NEVADA								
1 Reid	Y	N	Y	Y	Y	Y	Y	Y
2 ***Vucanovich***	N	Y	Y	N	Y	N	N	N
NEW HAMPSHIRE								
1 ***Smith***	N	Y	Y	N	N	N	N	N
2 ***Gregg***	Y	Y	Y	N	N	N	N	N
NEW JERSEY								
1 Florio	Y	N	Y	Y	Y	Y	Y	Y
2 Hughes	Y	N	Y	N	N	N	Y	Y
3 Howard	Y	N	N	Y	Y	Y	Y	Y
4 ***Smith***	Y	N	Y	Y	Y	Y	?	Y
5 ***Roukema***	Y	Y	Y	N	Y	Y	N	Y
6 Dwyer	Y	N	N	Y	Y	Y	Y	Y
7 ***Rinaldo***	Y	N	Y	Y	Y	Y	Y	Y
8 Roe	Y	N	Y	Y	Y	Y	Y	Y
9 Torricelli	Y	N	N	Y	N	Y	Y	Y
10 Rodino	Y	N	N	Y	Y	Y	Y	Y
11 ***Gallo***	N	N	Y	Y	N	N	N	N
12 ***Courter***	N	Y	Y	N	N	N	N	N
13 ***Saxton***	Y	Y	Y	Y	N	N	N	N
14 Guarini	Y	N	N	Y	Y	Y	Y	Y
NEW MEXICO								
1 ***Lujan***	Y	Y	Y	N	Y	N	Y	Y
2 ***Skeen***	Y	Y	Y	N	Y	N	N	N
3 Richardson	Y	N	Y	Y	Y	Y	Y	Y
NEW YORK								
1 ***Carney***	N	N	Y	Y	N	N	?	N
2 Downey	Y	N	Y	Y	Y	Y	?	Y
3 Mrazek	Y	N	Y	Y	Y	?	Y	Y
4 ***Lent***	N	Y	Y	N	N	Y	?	?
5 ***McGrath***	N	Y	Y	N	N	Y	N	N
6 Waldon	Y	N	N	Y	Y	Y	Y	Y
7 Ackerman	Y	N	N	Y	Y	Y	Y	Y
8 Scheuer	Y	N	N	Y	Y	Y	Y	Y
9 Manton	Y	N	N	Y	Y	Y	Y	Y
10 Schumer	Y	N	N	Y	Y	Y	Y	Y
11 Towns	Y	N	N	Y	Y	Y	Y	Y
12 Owens	Y	N	N	Y	Y	Y	Y	Y
13 Solarz	Y	N	N	Y	Y	?	Y	Y
14 ***Molinari***	N	Y	Y	N	N	N	N	N
15 ***Green***	?	N	Y	Y	N	N	Y	Y
16 Rangel	Y	N	Y	Y	Y	Y	Y	Y
17 Weiss	Y	N	N	Y	Y	Y	Y	Y
18 Garcia	Y	N	Y	Y	Y	Y	Y	Y
19 Biaggi	Y	N	Y	Y	?	Y	Y	Y
20 ***DioGuardi***	Y	Y	Y	Y	N	N	N	Y
21 ***Fish***	Y	N	Y	Y	?	?	Y	N
22 ***Gilman***	Y	N	Y	Y	Y	Y	Y	N
23 Stratton	N	Y	Y	N	N	N	Y	N
24 ***Solomon***	N	Y	Y	N	N	N	N	N
25 ***Boehlert***	Y	Y	Y	Y	N	N	N	N
26 ***Martin***	Y	Y	Y	N	Y	Y	N	N
27 ***Wortley***	Y	Y	Y	N	N	N	Y	N
28 McHugh	Y	N	N	Y	Y	?	?	Y
29 ***Horton***	Y	N	Y	Y	Y	Y	Y	N
30 ***Eckert***	Y	N	Y	Y	N	N	Y	N
31 ***Kemp***	Y	?	?	#	?	?	Y	N
32 LaFalce	Y	N	Y	Y	Y	Y	?	?
33 Nowak	Y	N	Y	Y	Y	Y	Y	Y
34 Lundine	?	?	?	?	?	?	?	?

	278	279	280	281	282	283	284	285
NORTH CAROLINA								
1 Jones	Y	Y	Y	N	Y	?	Y	Y
2 Valentine	Y	Y	Y	N	Y	Y	Y	Y
3 Whitley	Y	N	Y	Y	Y	Y	Y	Y
4 ***Cobey***	N	Y	Y	N	N	N	N	N
5 Neal	Y	Y	Y	N	Y	Y	Y	Y
6 ***Coble***	N	Y	Y	N	N	Y	N	N
7 Rose	Y	N	Y	Y	Y	Y	Y	Y
8 Hefner	Y	N	Y	N	Y	Y	Y	Y
9 ***McMillan***	Y	Y	Y	Y	Y	Y	N	N
10 Vacancy								
11 ***Hendon***	N	Y	Y	N	Y	Y	N	N
NORTH DAKOTA								
AL Dorgan	Y	Y	Y	N	Y	Y	Y	Y
OHIO								
1 Luken	Y	N	Y	Y	Y	Y	Y	Y
2 ***Gradison***	Y	Y	Y	Y	N	N	Y	N
3 Hall	Y	N	N	Y	Y	?	?	Y
4 ***Oxley***	N	Y	Y	N	N	N	N	N
5 ***Latta***	N	Y	Y	N	Y	Y	N	N
6 ***McEwen***	N	Y	Y	N	N	N	Y	N
7 ***DeWine***	Y	N	Y	Y	N	N	N	?
8 ***Kindness***	N	Y	Y	N	N	N	N	N
9 Kaptur	Y	N	Y	Y	Y	Y	Y	Y
10 ***Miller***	Y	Y	Y	N	Y	Y	N	N
11 Eckart	Y	Y	Y	N	Y	Y	Y	Y
12 ***Kasich***	Y	Y	Y	N	Y	Y	Y	N
13 Pease	Y	Y	Y	N	Y	Y	Y	Y
14 Seiberling	Y	N	Y	Y	Y	Y	Y	Y
15 ***Wylie***	N	Y	Y	N	Y	Y	Y	N
16 ***Regula***	N	Y	Y	N	N	Y	Y	N
17 Traficant	Y	Y	Y	N	N	N	Y	Y
18 Applegate	Y	Y	Y	N	N	Y	Y	Y
19 Feighan	Y	N	N	Y	Y	Y	Y	Y
20 Oakar	Y	N	Y	Y	Y	Y	Y	Y
21 Stokes	Y	N	N	Y	Y	Y	Y	Y
OKLAHOMA								
1 Jones	Y	Y	Y	N	Y	Y	Y	Y
2 Synar	Y	N	N	Y	Y	Y	Y	Y
3 Watkins	Y	Y	Y	N	Y	Y	Y	Y
4 McCurdy	Y	N	N	Y	Y	Y	Y	Y
5 ***Edwards***	Y	Y	Y	N	Y	Y	Y	N
6 English	Y	Y	Y	N	Y	Y	Y	Y
OREGON								
1 AuCoin	Y	N	Y	Y	Y	Y	?	Y
2 ***Smith, R.***	?	Y	Y	N	N	N	N	Y
3 Wyden	Y	Y	Y	Y	Y	Y	Y	Y
4 Weaver	Y	N	Y	Y	Y	?	Y	Y
5 ***Smith, D.***	Y	Y	Y	N	Y	N	N	N
PENNSYLVANIA								
1 Foglietta	Y	N	N	Y	Y	Y	Y	Y
2 Gray	Y	N	N	Y	?	?	Y	Y
3 Borski	Y	N	Y	Y	Y	Y	Y	Y
4 Kolter	Y	N	Y	?	N	N	Y	Y
5 ***Schulze***	Y	Y	Y	N	N	Y	Y	N
6 Yatron	Y	N	Y	Y	Y	Y	Y	Y
7 Edgar	?	?	?	?	?	?	?	Y
8 Kostmayer	Y	N	N	Y	Y	Y	Y	Y
9 ***Shuster***	N	Y	Y	N	N	?	N	N
10 ***McDade***	Y	Y	Y	Y	Y	Y	?	Y
11 Kanjorski	Y	Y	Y	N	N	Y	Y	Y
12 Murtha	Y	N	N	Y	Y	Y	Y	N
13 ***Coughlin***	Y	N	Y	Y	N	N	N	Y
14 Coyne	Y	N	N	Y	N	Y	Y	Y
15 ***Ritter***	Y	Y	Y	N	Y	Y	Y	Y
16 ***Walker***	Y	Y	Y	N	N	N	N	N
17 ***Gekas***	Y	Y	Y	N	N	N	N	N
18 Walgren	Y	Y	Y	Y	Y	Y	Y	Y
19 ***Goodling***	Y	Y	Y	N	Y	Y	N	Y
20 Gaydos	N	N	Y	N	N	N	Y	Y
21 ***Ridge***	N	Y	Y	N	N	N	N	N
22 Murphy	N	Y	Y	N	N	N	Y	Y
23 ***Clinger***	Y	Y	Y	N	N	N	N	N
RHODE ISLAND								
1 St Germain	Y	N	N	Y	Y	Y	Y	Y
2 ***Schneider***	Y	N	Y	Y	Y	Y	Y	?
SOUTH CAROLINA								
1 ***Hartnett***	N	?	?	?	?	?	?	?
2 ***Spence***	N	Y	Y	N	Y	N	Y	N
3 Derrick	Y	N	N	Y	Y	Y	Y	Y
4 ***Campbell***	?	?	?	?	?	?	?	X
5 Spratt	Y	N	N	Y	Y	Y	Y	Y
6 Tallon	Y	Y	Y	Y	Y	Y	Y	Y
SOUTH DAKOTA								
AL Daschle	Y	Y	Y	N	Y	Y	Y	Y

	278	279	280	281	282	283	284	285
TENNESSEE								
1 ***Quillen***	Y	Y	Y	N	Y	Y	Y	N
2 ***Duncan***	Y	Y	Y	N	Y	Y	Y	N
3 Lloyd	?	Y	Y	N	Y	Y	Y	N
4 Cooper	Y	?	?	?	?	?	?	Y
5 Boner	?	?	?	?	?	?	?	?
6 Gordon	?	?	?	?	?	?	?	Y
7 ***Sundquist***	Y	Y	Y	N	N	N	N	N
8 Jones	Y	?	?	?	?	?	?	?
9 Ford	?	?	?	?	?	?	?	#
TEXAS								
1 Chapman	Y	Y	Y	N	Y	Y	?	Y
2 Wilson	Y	N	Y	Y	Y	Y	?	N
3 ***Bartlett***	N	Y	Y	N	N	N	N	Y
4 Hall, R.	N	Y	Y	N	Y	Y	Y	Y
5 Bryant	Y	N	Y	Y	Y	Y	Y	Y
6 ***Barton***	N	Y	Y	N	N	N	N	N
7 ***Archer***	N	Y	Y	N	N	N	Y	N
8 ***Fields***	?	Y	Y	N	N	N	N	N
9 Brooks	Y	Y	?	?	?	Y	Y	Y
10 Pickle	Y	Y	Y	Y	Y	Y	Y	N
11 Leath	Y	N	N	Y	Y	Y	Y	Y
12 Wright	?	?	?	?	?	?	Y	Y
13 ***Boulter***	N	Y	Y	N	N	N	N	N
14 ***Sweeney***	N	Y	Y	N	N	N	?	N
15 de la Garza	Y	N	N	Y	Y	Y	Y	N
16 Coleman	Y	Y	Y	N	Y	Y	Y	N
17 Stenholm	N	Y	Y	N	N	N	Y	Y
18 Leland	Y	N	N	Y	Y	Y	Y	Y
19 ***Combest***	N	Y	Y	N	N	N	Y	N
20 Gonzalez	Y	N	N	Y	Y	Y	Y	N
21 ***Loeffler***	N	Y	Y	N	Y	N	N	N
22 ***DeLay***	N	Y	Y	N	N	N	?	N
23 Bustamante	Y	N	Y	Y	Y	Y	Y	Y
24 Frost	Y	N	Y	Y	Y	?	Y	Y
25 Andrews	Y	Y	Y	N	Y	?	Y	Y
26 ***Armey***	N	Y	Y	N	N	N	N	Y
27 Ortiz	Y	N	Y	Y	Y	Y	Y	N
UTAH								
1 ***Hansen***	N	Y	Y	N	N	N	N	N
2 ***Monson***	N	Y	Y	N	N	Y	N	Y
3 ***Nielson***	N	Y	Y	N	N	N	N	N
VERMONT								
AL ***Jeffords***	Y	N	Y	Y	Y	Y	Y	Y
VIRGINIA								
1 ***Bateman***	Y	Y	Y	N	N	N	Y	N
2 ***Whitehurst***	N	Y	Y	N	N	Y	Y	N
3 ***Bliley***	Y	Y	Y	N	N	Y	N	N
4 Sisisky	Y	N	Y	Y	Y	Y	Y	Y
5 Daniel	Y	Y	Y	N	Y	Y	Y	Y
6 Olin	Y	Y	Y	N	Y	Y	Y	Y
7 ***Slaughter***	Y	Y	Y	N	Y	Y	N	N
8 ***Parris***	Y	Y	Y	N	N	?	Y	N
9 Boucher	Y	N	Y	Y	Y	?	Y	Y
10 ***Wolf***	Y	Y	Y	N	N	N	N	N
WASHINGTON								
1 ***Miller***	Y	N	X	+	-	-	+	+
2 Swift	Y	N	Y	Y	Y	Y	Y	Y
3 Bonker	Y	?	?	Y	Y	Y	Y	Y
4 ***Morrison***	?	N	Y	Y	N	N	Y	N
5 Foley	Y	N	Y	Y	Y	Y	?	Y
6 Dicks	Y	N	Y	Y	Y	Y	Y	Y
7 Lowry	Y	N	N	Y	Y	Y	N	Y
8 ***Chandler***	?	N	Y	Y	Y	N	N	N
WEST VIRGINIA								
1 Mollohan	Y	N	Y	Y	Y	Y	Y	N
2 Staggers	?	Y	Y	Y	Y	Y	Y	Y
3 Wise	Y	N	Y	Y	Y	Y	Y	Y
4 Rahall	Y	N	Y	Y	Y	Y	Y	Y
WISCONSIN								
1 Aspin	Y	N	Y	Y	Y	Y	Y	Y
2 Kastenmeier	Y	N	Y	Y	Y	Y	Y	Y
3 ***Gunderson***	N	Y	Y	N	Y	Y	N	Y
4 Kleczka	Y	Y	Y	N	Y	Y	?	Y
5 Moody	Y	N	N	Y	Y	Y	Y	Y
6 ***Petri***	N	Y	Y	N	Y	Y	N	Y
7 Obey	Y	N	N	Y	Y	Y	?	Y
8 ***Roth***	N	Y	Y	N	N	N	N	Y
9 ***Sensenbrenner***	Y	Y	Y	N	N	N	N	N
WYOMING								
AL ***Cheney***	N	Y	Y	N	Y	N	N	N

Southern states - Ala., Ark., Fla., Ga., Ky., La., Miss., N.C., Okla., S.C., Tenn., Texas, Va.

* The *Congressional Record* vote number is different from the CQ vote number because the *Record* includes quorum calls in its tally. CQ does not publish quorum call votes.

286. HR 4428. Defense Authorization, Fiscal 1987. Dickinson, R-Ala., amendment to reduce outlays for the total national defense budget in fiscal 1987 to $279 billion while keeping the associated new budget authority at $292 billion, the amount in the bill as reported by the Armed Services Committee. Rejected 181-224: R 145-23; D 36-201 (ND 9-154, SD 27-47), Aug. 8, 1986.

287. HR 4428. Defense Authorization, Fiscal 1987. Aspin, D-Wis., amendment to bar tests between Jan. 1, 1987, and Sept. 30, 1987, of nuclear weapons with an explosive power greater than 1 kiloton, provided the Soviet Union conducts no nuclear tests in the meantime and provided the United States and Soviet Union agree to permit equipment to be placed in their territory to monitor compliance with the ban. Adopted 234-155: R 34-124; D 200-31 (ND 152-8, SD 48-23), Aug. 8, 1986. A "nay" was a vote supporting the president's position.

288. HR 4428. Defense Authorization, Fiscal 1987. Bennett, D-Fla., amendment to delete $1.1 billion for 12 MX missiles and add $250 million for various conventional weapons. Rejected 178-210: R 23-144; D 155-66 (ND 129-18, SD 26-48), Aug. 11, 1986.

289. HR 4428. Defense Authorization, Fiscal 1987. Bennett, D-Fla., amendment to delete $1.1 billion for 12 MX missiles and add $550 million for various conventional weapons. Rejected 179-217: R 24-144; D 155-73 (ND 134-18, SD 21-55), Aug. 11, 1986.

290. HR 4428. Defense Authorization, Fiscal 1987. Dickinson, R-Ala., substitute for the Spratt, D-S.C., amendment, to bar the use of any funds to purchase T-46 trainer planes. Rejected 125-277: R 88-81; D 37-196 (ND 23-133, SD 14-63), Aug. 11, 1986. (The Spratt amendment, to bar the purchase of any training plane until a competition was conducted between the T-46 and modified versions of the existing T-37 trainer, subsequently was rejected *(see vote 291, below).*)

291. HR 4428. Defense Authorization, Fiscal 1987. Spratt, D-S.C., amendment to bar the purchase of any training plane until a competition was conducted between the T-46 and modified versions of the existing T-37 trainer. Rejected 190-213: R 110-60; D 80-153 (ND 43-113, SD 37-40), Aug. 11, 1986.

292. HR 4428. Defense Authorization, Fiscal 1987. Byron, D-Md., substitute for the Levine, D-Calif., amendment, to permit production of only 336 Bradley troop carriers (of 593 authorized by the bill) until the Army conducts certain tests of the effect of Soviet weapons on the vehicle. Rejected 179-223: R 35-134; D 144-89 (ND 120-36, SD 24-53), Aug. 11, 1986. (The Levine amendment, to bar production of all 593 Bradley vehicles until the tests were conducted, subsequently was rejected *(see vote 293, below).*)

293. HR 4428. Defense Authorization, Fiscal 1987. Levine, D-Calif., amendment to bar production of 593 Bradley troop carriers authorized by the bill until the Army conducts certain tests of the effect of Soviet weapons on the vehicle. Rejected 123-277: R 18-151; D 105-126 (ND 93-62, SD 12-64), Aug. 11, 1986. A "nay" was a vote supporting the president's position.

KEY

Y Voted for (yea).
\# Paired for.
\+ Announced for.
N Voted against (nay).
X Paired against.
\- Announced against.
P Voted "present."
C Voted "present" to avoid possible conflict of interest.
? Did not vote or otherwise make a position known.

Democrats *Republicans*

	286	287	288	289	290	291	292	293
ALABAMA								
1 *Callahan*	Y	N	N	N	Y	N	N	N
2 *Dickinson*	Y	N	N	N	Y	Y	N	N
3 Nichols	Y	N	N	N	Y	Y	N	N
4 Bevill	Y	N	N	N	Y	Y	N	N
5 Flippo	Y	Y	?	?	?	?	?	?
6 Erdreich	Y	Y	N	N	Y	Y	N	N
7 Shelby	?	X	N	N	Y	Y	N	X
ALASKA								
AL *Young*	Y	N	N	N	N	Y	N	N
ARIZONA								
1 *McCain*	Y	N	N	N	N	N	Y	Y
2 Udall	N	Y	Y	Y	N	N	N	N
3 *Stump*	Y	N	N	N	N	N	N	N
4 *Rudd*	Y	N	N	N	N	N	N	N
5 *Kolbe*	Y	N	N	N	N	N	Y	Y
ARKANSAS								
1 Alexander	N	Y	?	N	N	Y	Y	Y
2 Robinson	Y	N	N	N	Y	Y	N	N
3 *Hammerschmidt*	Y	N	N	N	N	Y	N	N
4 Anthony	N	Y	Y	Y	Y	Y	Y	Y
CALIFORNIA								
1 Bosco	N	Y	Y	Y	Y	Y	Y	Y
2 *Chappie*	Y	N	N	N	N	N	N	N
3 Matsui	N	Y	Y	Y	N	N	Y	Y
4 Fazio	N	Y	N	N	N	N	Y	Y
5 Burton	N	Y	?	?	?	?	?	?
6 Boxer	N	Y	Y	Y	N	N	Y	Y
7 Miller	N	Y	#	Y	N	N	Y	Y
8 Dellums	N	Y	Y	Y	N	N	Y	Y
9 Stark	N	Y	Y	Y	N	N	Y	Y
10 Edwards	N	Y	Y	Y	N	N	N	N
11 Lantos	N	Y	Y	Y	N	Y	N	N
12 *Zschau*	Y	?	?	?	?	?	?	?
13 Mineta	N	Y	Y	Y	N	Y	N	N
14 *Shumway*	Y	N	N	N	N	N	N	N
15 Coelho	N	Y	Y	Y	N	N	?	?
16 Panetta	N	Y	Y	Y	N	N	N	N
17 *Pashayan*	Y	N	N	N	N	Y	Y	N
18 Lehman	N	Y	Y	Y	N	N	Y	N
19 *Lagomarsino*	Y	N	N	N	N	Y	N	N
20 *Thomas*	Y	N	N	N	Y	Y	Y	N
21 *Fiedler*	Y	N	N	N	Y	Y	N	N
22 *Moorhead*	Y	N	N	N	N	N	N	N
23 Beilenson	N	Y	Y	Y	Y	Y	Y	Y
24 Waxman	N	Y	Y	Y	N	N	Y	?
25 Roybal	N	Y	?	Y	N	N	N	N
26 Berman	N	Y	Y	Y	N	N	Y	Y
27 Levine	N	Y	Y	Y	N	Y	Y	Y
28 Dixon	N	Y	?	?	?	?	?	#
29 Hawkins	N	Y	Y	Y	N	N	Y	Y
30 Martinez	N	Y	?	?	N	N	Y	Y
31 Dymally	N	Y	Y	Y	N	N	Y	Y
32 Anderson	N	Y	N	N	N	N	Y	N
33 *Dreier*	Y	N	N	N	N	N	N	N
34 Torres	N	Y	Y	Y	N	N	Y	Y
35 *Lewis*	?	?	X	X	#	#	X	X
36 Brown	N	Y	Y	Y	Y	Y	Y	N
37 *McCandless*	Y	N	N	N	N	Y	N	N
38 *Dornan*	Y	N	N	N	N	N	N	N
39 *Dannemeyer*	Y	N	N	N	N	N	Y	N
40 *Badham*	Y	X	N	N	N	N	N	N
41 *Lowery*	Y	N	N	N	N	N	N	N
42 *Lungren*	#	X	N	N	N	Y	Y	N
43 *Packard*	Y	N	N	N	N	N	N	N
44 Bates	N	Y	Y	Y	Y	Y	Y	Y
45 *Hunter*	Y	N	N	N	Y	Y	N	N
COLORADO								
1 Schroeder	N	Y	Y	Y	Y	Y	Y	N
2 Wirth	N	Y	Y	Y	Y	Y	Y	N
3 *Strang*	Y	N	N	N	Y	Y	Y	N
4 *Brown*	Y	Y	N	N	Y	Y	N	N
5 *Kramer*	Y	Y	N	N	N	Y	N	N
6 *Schaefer*	Y	N	N	N	N	N	N	N
CONNECTICUT								
1 Kennelly	N	Y	Y	Y	N	Y	Y	N
2 Gejdenson	N	Y	Y	Y	N	Y	Y	Y
3 Morrison	N	Y	#	#	?	?	#	#
4 *McKinney*	N	Y	Y	Y	N	N	Y	Y
5 *Rowland*	Y	Y	N	N	N	N	Y	N
6 *Johnson*	Y	Y	Y	Y	Y	Y	Y	N
DELAWARE								
AL Carper	N	Y	Y	Y	N	Y	Y	N
FLORIDA								
1 Hutto	Y	N	N	N	N	N	N	N
2 Fuqua	N	Y	N	N	N	N	N	N
3 Bennett	Y	Y	Y	Y	N	N	Y	Y
4 Chappell	Y	N	N	N	N	N	N	N
5 *McCollum*	Y	N	N	N	Y	Y	N	N
6 MacKay	N	Y	Y	Y	N	Y	N	N
7 Gibbons	Y	Y	Y	Y	N	N	N	N
8 *Young*	Y	N	N	N	N	N	N	N
9 *Bilirakis*	Y	N	N	N	N	Y	N	N
10 *Ireland*	Y	N	N	N	N	N	N	N
11 Nelson	Y	N	N	N	Y	Y	N	N
12 *Lewis*	Y	N	N	N	N	N	Y	N
13 *Mack*	Y	N	N	N	N	N	N	N
14 Mica	N	Y	Y	N	N	N	N	N
15 *Shaw*	Y	X	N	N	N	Y	N	N
16 Smith	N	Y	Y	Y	N	N	Y	Y
17 Lehman	N	Y	Y	Y	N	N	Y	N
18 Pepper	N	Y	X	X	N	N	N	N
19 Fascell	N	Y	Y	Y	N	N	Y	Y
GEORGIA								
1 Thomas	N	Y	N	N	N	N	N	N
2 Hatcher	N	Y	N	N	N	N	N	N
3 Ray	N	N	N	N	N	N	N	N
4 *Swindall*	Y	N	N	N	Y	Y	N	N
5 Fowler	?	?	?	?	?	?	?	?
6 *Gingrich*	Y	N	N	N	Y	Y	N	N
7 Darden	Y	N	X	X	?	?	X	X
8 Rowland	N	Y	N	N	N	N	N	N
9 Jenkins	N	Y	?	?	?	?	?	?
10 Barnard	Y	Y	N	N	N	N	N	N
HAWAII								
1 Vacancy								
2 Akaka	N	Y	Y	Y	N	N	N	N
IDAHO								
1 *Craig*	Y	N	N	N	Y	Y	N	N
2 Stallings	N	Y	Y	Y	N	Y	N	N
ILLINOIS								
1 Hayes	N	Y	Y	Y	N	N	Y	Y
2 Savage	N	Y	?	#	N	N	Y	Y
3 Russo	N	Y	Y	Y	N	N	Y	Y
4 Vacancy								
5 Lipinski	N	N	N	N	N	Y	Y	N
6 *Hyde*	Y	N	N	N	Y	Y	N	N
7 Collins	N	Y	Y	Y	N	N	Y	Y
8 Rostenkowski	N	?	Y	Y	N	N	Y	Y
9 Yates	N	Y	+	Y	N	N	Y	Y
10 *Porter*	N	Y	N	N	N	N	N	N
11 Annunzio	N	Y	Y	Y	N	N	Y	N
12 *Crane*	Y	N	N	N	N	Y	N	N
13 *Fawell*	N	Y	N	N	Y	Y	N	N
14 *Grotberg*	?	?	?	?	?	?	?	?
15 *Madigan*	Y	?	N	N	N	N	N	N
16 *Martin*	Y	N	N	N	Y	Y	Y	N
17 Evans	N	Y	?	Y	N	N	Y	Y
18 *Michel*	Y	N	N	N	Y	Y	N	N
19 Bruce	N	Y	Y	Y	N	Y	Y	Y
20 Durbin	N	#	Y	Y	N	Y	Y	Y
21 Price	N	Y	N	Y	N	N	Y	N
22 Gray	N	Y	Y	Y	N	N	N	N
INDIANA								
1 Visclosky	N	Y	Y	Y	Y	N	N	Y
2 Sharp	N	Y	Y	Y	Y	Y	N	N
3 *Hiler*	Y	N	N	N	Y	Y	N	N
4 *Coats*	Y	N	N	N	Y	Y	N	N
5 *Hillis*	?	?	?	?	?	?	?	?

ND - Northern Democrats SD - Southern Democrats

* Corresponding to Congressional Record Votes 313, 314, 316, 317, 318, 319, 320, 321

	286	287	288	289	290	291	292	293
6 *Burton*	Y	N	N	N	Y	Y	N	N
7 *Myers*	Y	?	N	N	N	N	N	N
8 McCloskey	Y	Y	Y	Y	N	N	Y	Y
9 Hamilton	N	Y	Y	Y	Y	Y	N	N
10 Jacobs	N	Y	Y	Y	N	Y	Y	Y
IOWA								
1 *Leach*	N	Y	Y	Y	Y	Y	Y	Y
2 *Tauke*	N	Y	Y	Y	Y	Y	N	N
3 *Evans*	Y	Y	Y	Y	N	N	N	N
4 Smith	N	Y	?	?	?	?	Y	Y
5 *Lightfoot*	Y	Y	Y	Y	N	Y	N	N
6 Bedell	N	Y	Y	Y	Y	Y	Y	Y
KANSAS								
1 *Roberts*	N	N	N	?	Y	Y	N	N
2 Slattery	N	Y	Y	Y	Y	Y	N	N
3 *Meyers*	N	Y	N	N	Y	Y	N	N
4 Glickman	N	Y	Y	Y	Y	Y	Y	N
5 *Whittaker*	Y	N	N	N	Y	Y	N	N
KENTUCKY								
1 Hubbard	Y	Y	N	N	N	N	N	N
2 Natcher	N	Y	N	N	N	N	N	N
3 Mazzoli	N	?	Y	Y	Y	Y	N	N
4 *Snyder*	?	?	N	N	Y	Y	N	N
5 *Rogers*	Y	N	N	N	Y	Y	N	N
6 *Hopkins*	Y	Y	N	N	Y	Y	N	N
7 Perkins	N	Y	Y	Y	Y	Y	Y	Y
LOUISIANA								
1 *Livingston*	Y	N	N	N	Y	Y	N	N
2 Boggs	Y	Y	N	N	N	N	N	N
3 Tauzin	N	N	N	N	N	Y	N	N
4 Roemer	N	Y	N	N	N	N	N	N
5 Huckaby	?	?	N	N	Y	Y	N	N
6 *Moore*	?	?	?	?	?	?	?	?
7 Breaux	?	?	?	?	?	?	?	?
8 Long	X	?	Y	Y	N	Y	Y	N
MAINE								
1 *McKernan*	Y	Y	N	N	N	Y	Y	N
2 *Snowe*	N	Y	N	N	N	Y	Y	N
MARYLAND								
1 Dyson	N	N	N	N	N	N	N	N
2 *Bentley*	Y	N	N	N	N	N	N	N
3 Mikulski	N	Y	#	#	?	?	?	?
4 *Holt*	?	?	X	?	?	?	?	?
5 Hoyer	N	Y	N	N	N	N	Y	N
6 Byron	Y	N	N	N	N	N	N	N
7 Mitchell	?	#	Y	Y	N	Y	#	#
8 Barnes	X	#	Y	Y	N	N	Y	Y
MASSACHUSETTS								
1 *Conte*	N	Y	+	Y	N	N	N	N
2 Boland	N	Y	Y	Y	N	N	N	N
3 Early	N	Y	Y	Y	N	N	Y	Y
4 Frank	N	Y	Y	Y	N	N	Y	Y
5 Atkins	N	Y	Y	Y	N	N	Y	Y
6 Mavroules	N	Y	Y	Y	N	N	N	N
7 Markey	N	Y	Y	Y	N	N	Y	Y
8 O'Neill								
9 Moakley	N	Y	Y	Y	N	N	Y	Y
10 Studds	N	Y	Y	Y	N	N	Y	Y
11 Donnelly	?	#	Y	Y	N	N	Y	Y
MICHIGAN								
1 Conyers	?	?	Y	Y	N	N	Y	Y
2 *Pursell*	Y	Y	N	N	N	N	N	N
3 Wolpe	N	Y	Y	Y	Y	Y	Y	Y
4 *Siljander*	Y	N	N	N	Y	Y	N	N
5 *Henry*	N	Y	Y	Y	N	N	N	N
6 Carr	N	Y	Y	Y	Y	Y	Y	N
7 Kildee	N	Y	Y	Y	N	N	Y	Y
8 Traxler	N	Y	Y	Y	N	N	N	N
9 *Vander Jagt*	Y	N	?	?	?	?	?	?
10 *Schuette*	Y	N	N	N	Y	Y	N	N
11 *Davis*	Y	N	N	N	N	N	N	N
12 Bonior	N	Y	Y	Y	N	N	Y	Y
13 Crockett	N	Y	#	#	N	N	Y	Y
14 Hertel	N	Y	Y	Y	N	N	Y	Y
15 Ford	N	Y	Y	Y	N	N	Y	Y
16 Dingell	N	Y	Y	Y	N	N	N	N
17 Levin	N	Y	?	Y	N	N	Y	Y
18 *Broomfield*	Y	N	N	N	Y	Y	N	N
MINNESOTA								
1 Penny	N	Y	Y	Y	N	Y	N	N
2 *Weber*	N	N	N	N	Y	Y	N	N
3 *Frenzel*	N	Y	N	N	Y	Y	N	N
4 Vento	N	Y	Y	Y	N	N	Y	Y
5 Sabo	N	Y	Y	Y	N	N	N	N
6 Sikorski	N	Y	Y	Y	N	N	N	N
7 *Stangeland*	Y	N	N	N	Y	Y	N	N
8 Oberstar	N	Y	Y	Y	N	N	Y	Y
MISSISSIPPI								
1 Whitten	N	N	N	N	N	N	N	N
2 *Franklin*	Y	X	N	N	Y	Y	N	N
3 Montgomery	Y	N	N	N	N	N	N	N
4 Dowdy	Y	Y	N	N	N	N	N	N
5 *Lott*	Y	N	N	N	Y	Y	N	N
MISSOURI								
1 Clay	N	Y	?	?	?	?	?	?
2 Young	N	Y	Y	Y	N	N	N	N
3 Gephardt	N	Y	Y	Y	N	N	Y	Y
4 Skelton	Y	N	N	N	N	N	Y	N
5 Wheat	N	Y	Y	Y	Y	Y	Y	Y
6 *Coleman*	Y	N	N	N	Y	Y	Y	N
7 *Taylor*	Y	N	X	X	N	Y	N	N
8 *Emerson*	Y	N	N	N	N	Y	N	N
9 Volkmer	N	Y	Y	Y	N	N	Y	N
MONTANA								
1 Williams	N	Y	Y	N	Y	Y	Y	Y
2 *Marlenee*	Y	N	N	N	Y	Y	N	N
NEBRASKA								
1 *Bereuter*	N	N	Y	Y	Y	Y	N	Y
2 *Daub*	Y	N	N	N	Y	Y	N	N
3 *Smith*	N	X	Y	Y	Y	Y	Y	Y
NEVADA								
1 Reid	N	N	N	N	Y	Y	Y	Y
2 *Vucanovich*	Y	N	N	N	N	N	N	N
NEW HAMPSHIRE								
1 *Smith*	Y	N	N	N	Y	Y	N	N
2 *Gregg*	N	Y	N	N	Y	Y	N	N
NEW JERSEY								
1 Florio	N	Y	Y	Y	N	N	Y	Y
2 Hughes	N	Y	Y	Y	N	N	Y	N
3 Howard	N	Y	Y	Y	N	N	N	N
4 *Smith*	N	Y	Y	Y	N	Y	Y	Y
5 *Roukema*	N	N	Y	Y	N	N	Y	N
6 Dwyer	N	Y	Y	Y	N	N	Y	Y
7 *Rinaldo*	Y	N	N	N	N	N	N	N
8 Roe	N	Y	Y	Y	N	N	Y	N
9 Torricelli	N	Y	Y	Y	Y	Y	Y	Y
10 Rodino	N	Y	Y	Y	N	N	Y	Y
11 *Gallo*	Y	N	N	N	N	N	N	N
12 *Courter*	Y	N	N	N	Y	Y	?	N
13 *Saxton*	Y	N	N	N	N	N	N	N
14 Guarini	Y	Y	N	N	N	Y	Y	N
NEW MEXICO								
1 *Lujan*	Y	N	N	N	Y	N	N	N
2 *Skeen*	Y	N	N	N	Y	Y	N	N
3 Richardson	N	Y	Y	Y	N	N	N	N
NEW YORK								
1 *Carney*	Y	N	N	N	N	N	N	N
2 Downey	N	Y	Y	Y	N	N	N	N
3 Mrazek	N	Y	Y	Y	N	N	Y	Y
4 *Lent*	?	?	N	N	N	N	N	N
5 *McGrath*	Y	N	N	N	N	N	N	N
6 Waldon	N	Y	Y	Y	N	N	Y	Y
7 Ackerman	N	Y	Y	Y	N	N	Y	Y
8 Scheuer	N	Y	Y	Y	N	N	Y	Y
9 Manton	N	Y	Y	Y	N	N	Y	Y
10 Schumer	N	Y	Y	Y	N	N	Y	N
11 Towns	N	Y	Y	Y	N	N	Y	Y
12 Owens	N	Y	Y	Y	N	N	Y	Y
13 Solarz	N	Y	Y	Y	N	N	Y	Y
14 *Molinari*	Y	N	N	N	N	N	N	N
15 *Green*	N	Y	Y	Y	N	N	Y	Y
16 Rangel	N	Y	Y	Y	N	N	Y	N
17 Weiss	N	Y	+	+	-	-	+	+
18 Garcia	N	Y	#	Y	N	N	Y	Y
19 Biaggi	N	Y	Y	Y	N	N	N	N
20 *DioGuardi*	Y	Y	Y	N	N	N	N	N
21 *Fish*	Y	Y	N	N	N	N	N	N
22 *Gilman*	Y	Y	N	N	N	N	N	?
23 Stratton	Y	N	N	N	N	N	N	N
24 *Solomon*	Y	N	N	N	N	N	N	N
25 *Boehlert*	Y	Y	Y	Y	N	N	N	N
26 *Martin*	Y	N	N	N	N	N	N	N
27 *Wortley*	Y	N	N	N	N	N	N	N
28 McHugh	N	Y	Y	Y	N	N	Y	Y
29 *Horton*	Y	Y	?	?	?	?	?	?
30 *Eckert*	Y	N	N	N	N	N	N	N
31 *Kemp*	Y	N	N	N	N	N	N	N
32 LaFalce	X	#	#	#	?	?	#	#
33 Nowak	N	Y	Y	Y	N	N	Y	Y
34 Lundine	?	?	?	?	?	?	?	?
NORTH CAROLINA								
1 Jones	N	Y	Y	N	N	N	N	N
2 Valentine	N	N	N	N	Y	Y	N	N
3 Whitley	N	Y	N	N	N	Y	Y	N
4 *Cobey*	Y	N	N	N	Y	Y	N	N
5 Neal	N	Y	N	N	N	Y	N	N
6 *Coble*	Y	N	N	N	Y	Y	N	N
7 Rose	N	Y	N	N	N	Y	N	N
8 Hefner	N	Y	N	N	N	Y	N	N
9 *McMillan*	Y	N	N	N	N	Y	N	N
10 Vacancy								
11 *Hendon*	Y	N	N	N	Y	Y	Y	Y
NORTH DAKOTA								
AL Dorgan	N	Y	Y	Y	N	Y	Y	Y
OHIO								
1 Luken	N	Y	?	?	?	?	?	?
2 *Gradison*	Y	N	Y	Y	Y	Y	Y	Y
3 Hall	N	Y	Y	Y	N	N	Y	Y
4 *Oxley*	Y	N	N	N	Y	Y	N	N
5 *Latta*	Y	N	N	N	Y	Y	N	N
6 *McEwen*	Y	?	N	N	Y	Y	N	N
7 *DeWine*	#	?	N	N	Y	Y	N	N
8 *Kindness*	Y	?	N	N	Y	Y	N	N
9 Kaptur	N	#	Y	N	N	N	Y	N
10 *Miller*	Y	N	N	N	Y	Y	N	N
11 Eckart	N	Y	Y	Y	N	N	N	N
12 *Kasich*	Y	N	N	N	Y	Y	Y	N
13 Pease	N	Y	Y	Y	Y	Y	Y	Y
14 Seiberling	N	Y	Y	Y	N	N	Y	Y
15 *Wylie*	Y	N	N	N	Y	Y	N	N
16 *Regula*	Y	N	N	N	Y	Y	N	N
17 Traficant	N	Y	Y	Y	N	N	Y	Y
18 Applegate	N	Y	Y	N	Y	Y	N	N
19 Feighan	N	Y	Y	Y	N	N	Y	Y
20 Oakar	N	Y	Y	Y	N	N	Y	Y
21 Stokes	N	Y	Y	Y	N	N	Y	Y
OKLAHOMA								
1 Jones	Y	?	Y	Y	N	Y	N	N
2 Synar	N	Y	Y	Y	N	Y	Y	Y
3 Watkins	Y	?	Y	Y	N	Y	N	N
4 McCurdy	N	N	N	N	N	Y	Y	N
5 *Edwards*	Y	N	N	N	Y	Y	N	N
6 English	Y	N	N	N	N	N	Y	N
OREGON								
1 AuCoin	N	Y	Y	Y	N	N	Y	N
2 *Smith, R.*	Y	N	N	N	Y	Y	Y	Y
3 Wyden	N	Y	Y	Y	N	N	Y	Y
4 Weaver	N	Y	Y	Y	N	Y	Y	Y
5 *Smith, D.*	Y	N	N	N	Y	Y	Y	Y
PENNSYLVANIA								
1 Foglietta	N	Y	Y	Y	N	N	Y	Y
2 Gray	N	Y	?	?	N	N	Y	Y
3 Borski	N	Y	Y	Y	Y	Y	Y	Y
4 Kolter	N	Y	Y	Y	N	N	Y	N
5 *Schulze*	Y	N	N	N	Y	Y	Y	Y
6 Yatron	Y	Y	N	N	N	N	N	N
7 Edgar	N	Y	?	?	?	?	?	?
8 Kostmayer	N	Y	Y	Y	N	Y	Y	Y
9 *Shuster*	Y	N	N	N	Y	Y	N	N
10 *McDade*	Y	N	N	N	N	N	N	N
11 Kanjorski	N	Y	Y	Y	N	N	Y	N
12 Murtha	N	N	N	N	N	N	N	N
13 *Coughlin*	N	Y	N	N	Y	Y	Y	N
14 Coyne	N	Y	Y	Y	N	N	Y	Y
15 *Ritter*	Y	N	?	N	?	Y	N	N
16 *Walker*	Y	N	N	N	Y	Y	Y	N
17 *Gekas*	Y	N	N	N	N	Y	N	N
18 Walgren	N	Y	Y	Y	N	N	N	N
19 *Goodling*	Y	Y	Y	Y	Y	Y	N	N
20 Gaydos	Y	Y	N	Y	N	Y	Y	N
21 *Ridge*	Y	Y	Y	Y	N	N	Y	Y
22 Murphy	N	Y	?	?	?	?	?	?
23 *Clinger*	Y	N	N	N	Y	Y	N	N
RHODE ISLAND								
1 St Germain	N	Y	Y	Y	N	N	Y	Y
2 *Schneider*	N	Y	Y	Y	N	N	N	N
SOUTH CAROLINA								
1 *Hartnett*	?	?	?	?	?	?	?	?
2 *Spence*	Y	N	N	N	N	N	N	N
3 Derrick	N	Y	Y	Y	Y	Y	N	N
4 *Campbell*	#	X	X	X	X	X	X	X
5 Spratt	N	Y	N	N	N	Y	Y	N
6 Tallon	N	Y	N	N	N	Y	N	N
SOUTH DAKOTA								
AL Daschle	N	Y	Y	Y	Y	Y	Y	Y
TENNESSEE								
1 *Quillen*	Y	?	N	N	Y	Y	N	N
2 *Duncan*	Y	N	N	N	N	Y	N	N
3 Lloyd	Y	N	N	N	N	N	N	N
4 Cooper	N	Y	Y	N	Y	Y	Y	Y
5 Boner	?	?	?	N	N	N	Y	N
6 Gordon	N	Y	Y	Y	N	Y	Y	N
7 *Sundquist*	Y	N	N	N	N	N	N	N
8 Jones	?	?	N	N	N	Y	Y	N
9 Ford	?	#	Y	Y	N	N	Y	Y
TEXAS								
1 Chapman	N	Y	N	N	N	Y	N	N
2 Wilson	Y	N	N	N	N	N	N	N
3 *Bartlett*	Y	N	N	N	Y	Y	N	N
4 Hall, R.	Y	N	N	N	N	Y	N	N
5 Bryant	N	Y	Y	Y	N	Y	Y	N
6 *Barton*	Y	N	N	N	Y	Y	N	N
7 *Archer*	Y	N	N	N	Y	Y	N	N
8 *Fields*	Y	N	N	N	Y	Y	N	N
9 Brooks	N	Y	Y	N	N	N	Y	Y
10 Pickle	Y	Y	N	N	N	N	N	N
11 Leath	N	Y	N	N	N	N	N	N
12 Wright	N	Y	N	N	N	N	N	N
13 *Boulter*	Y	N	N	N	Y	Y	Y	N
14 *Sweeney*	Y	N	N	N	N	Y	N	N
15 de la Garza	Y	N	N	N	N	N	N	N
16 Coleman	Y	Y	Y	N	N	N	N	N
17 Stenholm	N	N	N	N	N	Y	N	N
18 Leland	N	Y	Y	Y	N	N	Y	Y
19 *Combest*	Y	N	N	N	N	Y	N	N
20 Gonzalez	N	Y	Y	Y	N	N	Y	N
21 *Loeffler*	Y	N	N	N	Y	Y	N	N
22 *DeLay*	Y	N	N	N	Y	Y	N	N
23 Bustamante	N	N	N	N	N	N	Y	Y
24 Frost	N	Y	N	N	N	Y	N	N
25 Andrews	N	Y	N	N	N	Y	N	N
26 *Armey*	Y	N	N	N	Y	Y	N	N
27 Ortiz	Y	N	N	N	N	N	N	N
UTAH								
1 *Hansen*	Y	N	N	N	Y	Y	N	N
2 *Monson*	Y	N	N	N	Y	Y	N	N
3 *Nielson*	Y	N	N	N	Y	Y	N	N
VERMONT								
AL *Jeffords*	N	Y	Y	Y	N	Y	Y	Y
VIRGINIA								
1 *Bateman*	Y	N	N	N	N	Y	N	N
2 *Whitehurst*	Y	N	N	N	N	N	N	N
3 *Bliley*	Y	N	N	N	N	N	N	N
4 Sisisky	N	N	N	N	N	N	N	N
5 Daniel	Y	N	N	N	N	N	N	N
6 Olin	N	Y	Y	Y	Y	Y	N	N
7 *Slaughter*	Y	N	N	N	Y	Y	N	N
8 *Parris*	Y	N	N	N	N	N	N	N
9 Boucher	N	Y	Y	Y	N	Y	Y	N
10 *Wolf*	Y	N	N	N	Y	Y	N	N
WASHINGTON								
1 *Miller*	-	-	Y	Y	Y	Y	Y	Y
2 Swift	N	Y	Y	Y	N	Y	Y	Y
3 Bonker	N	Y	Y	Y	Y	Y	Y	Y
4 *Morrison*	Y	N	N	N	N	N	N	N
5 Foley	N	Y	N	?	N	N	Y	Y
6 Dicks	Y	Y	N	N	?	?	N	N
7 Lowry	N	Y	Y	Y	N	N	Y	Y
8 *Chandler*	Y	N	N	N	Y	Y	Y	Y
WEST VIRGINIA								
1 Mollohan	Y	N	N	N	N	N	N	N
2 Staggers	N	Y	Y	Y	N	N	Y	Y
3 Wise	N	Y	Y	Y	N	N	N	N
4 Rahall	N	Y	Y	Y	N	N	Y	Y
WISCONSIN								
1 Aspin	N	Y	N	N	N	N	Y	N
2 Kastenmeier	N	Y	Y	Y	N	N	Y	Y
3 *Gunderson*	N	Y	N	N	Y	Y	Y	Y
4 Kleczka	N	Y	Y	Y	N	N	N	N
5 Moody	N	Y	Y	Y	N	N	Y	Y
6 *Petri*	N	N	Y	Y	Y	Y	N	N
7 Obey	N	Y	Y	Y	N	N	Y	Y
8 *Roth*	Y	N	Y	Y	N	N	N	N
9 *Sensenbrenner*	Y	N	Y	Y	Y	Y	Y	N
WYOMING								
AL *Cheney*	Y	N	N	N	Y	Y	N	N

Southern states - Ala., Ark., Fla., Ga., Ky., La., Miss., N.C., Okla., S.C., Tenn., Texas, Va.

* The *Congressional Record* vote number is different from the CQ vote number because the *Record* includes quorum calls in its tally. CQ does not publish quorum call votes.

294. HR 4428. Defense Authorization, Fiscal 1987. Gejdenson, D-Conn., amendment to add $1.5 billion to purchase a Trident missile-launching submarine. Rejected 188-211: R 22-146; D 166-65 (ND 122-35, SD 44-30), Aug. 11, 1986.

295. HR 4428. Defense Authorization, Fiscal 1987. Garcia, D-N.Y., amendment to require that 5 percent of the funds authorized by the bill for procurement be spent in enterprise zones designated by the secretary of housing and urban development. Rejected 120-279: R 10-159; D 110-120 (ND 89-68, SD 21-52), Aug. 11, 1986.

296. HR 4428. Defense Authorization, Fiscal 1987. Weiss, D-N.Y., amendment to use all funds for procurement of Trident II missiles to procure instead Trident I missiles. Rejected 94-306: R 3-166; D 91-140 (ND 85-72, SD 6-68), Aug. 11, 1986. A "nay" was a vote supporting the president's position.

297. HR 4428. Defense Authorization, Fiscal 1987. Dornan, R-Calif., amendment to increase from $3.4 billion to $4.8 billion the amount authorized for research on the strategic defense initiative, or "star wars." Rejected 94-324: R 82-93; D 12-231 (ND 2-162, SD 10-69), Aug. 12, 1986.

298. HR 4428. Defense Authorization, Fiscal 1987. Dellums, D-Calif., amendment to reduce from $3.4 billion to $1 billion the amount authorized for research on the strategic defense initiative, or "star wars." Rejected 114-302: R 1-173; D 113-129 (ND 104-59, SD 9-70), Aug. 12, 1986. A "nay" was a vote supporting the president's position.

299. HR 4428. Defense Authorization, Fiscal 1987. Badham, R-Calif., amendment to reduce from $3.4 billion to $3.25 billion the amount authorized for research on the strategic defense initiative, or "star wars." Rejected 196-218: R 150-25; D 46-193 (ND 17-144, SD 29-49), Aug. 12, 1986. A "yea" was a vote supporting the president's position.

300. HR 4428. Defense Authorization, Fiscal 1987. Bennett, D-Fla., amendment to decrease from $3.4 billion to $2.85 billion the amount authorized for research on the strategic defense initiative, or "star wars." Adopted 239-176: R 33-142; D 206-34 (ND 154-8, SD 52-26), Aug. 12, 1986. A "nay" was a vote supporting the president's position.

301. HR 4428. Defense Authorization, Fiscal 1987. Broomfield, R-Mich., amendment to prohibit the use of funds to deploy any weapons inconsistent with the SALT II arms control treaty at such time as the Soviet Union comes into full compliance with the treaty. Rejected 199-214: R 162-13; D 37-201 (ND 8-153, SD 29-48), Aug. 12, 1986. A "yea" was a vote supporting the president's position.

KEY

- Y Voted for (yea).
- # Paired for.
- \+ Announced for.
- N Voted against (nay).
- X Paired against.
- \- Announced against.
- P Voted "present."
- C Voted "present" to avoid possible conflict of interest.
- ? Did not vote or otherwise make a position known.

Democrats ***Republicans***

	294	295	296	297	298	299	300	301
ALABAMA								
1 ***Callahan***	N	N	N	Y	N	Y	N	Y
2 ***Dickinson***	N	N	N	Y	N	Y	N	Y
3 Nichols	N	N	N	Y	N	Y	N	Y
4 Bevill	N	N	N	Y	N	Y	N	Y
5 Flippo	?	?	?	Y	N	Y	?	?
6 Erdreich	N	Y	N	N	N	Y	N	Y
7 Shelby	X	?	?	Y	N	Y	N	Y
ALASKA								
AL ***Young***	N	N	N	N	N	Y	N	Y
ARIZONA								
1 ***McCain***	N	N	N	Y	N	Y	N	Y
2 Udall	Y	Y	N	N	Y	N	Y	N
3 ***Stump***	N	N	N	Y	N	Y	N	Y
4 ***Rudd***	N	N	N	Y	N	Y	N	Y
5 ***Kolbe***	N	N	N	N	N	Y	N	Y
ARKANSAS								
1 Alexander	N	N	N	N	N	?	Y	N
2 Robinson	Y	N	N	Y	N	Y	N	Y
3 ***Hammerschmidt***	N	N	N	Y	N	Y	N	Y
4 Anthony	?	N	N	N	N	N	Y	N
CALIFORNIA								
1 Bosco	N	N	Y	N	N	N	Y	N
2 ***Chappie***	N	N	N	Y	N	Y	N	Y
3 Matsui	Y	N	Y	N	Y	N	Y	N
4 Fazio	Y	N	N	N	N	N	Y	N
5 Burton	?	?	?	?	?	?	?	X
6 Boxer	Y	N	Y	N	Y	N	Y	N
7 Miller	Y	N	Y	N	Y	N	Y	N
8 Dellums	N	N	Y	N	Y	N	Y	N
9 Stark	Y	N	Y	N	Y	N	Y	N
10 Edwards	Y	Y	Y	N	Y	N	Y	N
11 Lantos	Y	N	N	N	N	N	Y	N
12 ***Zschau***	?	?	?	N	N	Y	N	Y
13 Mineta	Y	Y	N	N	Y	N	Y	N
14 ***Shumway***	N	N	N	Y	N	Y	N	Y
15 Coelho	Y	N	N	N	N	N	Y	N
16 Panetta	Y	N	Y	N	Y	N	Y	N
17 ***Pashayan***	N	N	N	N	N	Y	N	Y
18 Lehman	Y	N	N	N	Y	N	Y	N
19 ***Lagomarsino***	N	N	N	Y	N	Y	N	Y
20 ***Thomas***	N	N	N	N	N	Y	N	Y
21 ***Fiedler***	N	N	N	Y	N	Y	N	Y
22 ***Moorhead***	N	N	N	Y	N	Y	N	Y
23 Beilenson	Y	N	Y	N	Y	N	Y	N
24 Waxman	Y	Y	Y	N	Y	N	Y	N
25 Roybal	Y	Y	Y	N	Y	N	Y	N
26 Berman	Y	N	Y	N	Y	N	Y	N
27 Levine	Y	N	Y	N	Y	N	Y	?
28 Dixon	#	?	?	?	?	?	?	?
29 Hawkins	Y	Y	Y	N	Y	N	Y	N
30 Martinez	Y	Y	Y	N	N	N	Y	N
31 Dymally	Y	Y	Y	N	Y	N	Y	N
32 Anderson	N	Y	N	N	Y	N	Y	N
33 ***Dreier***	N	N	N	Y	N	Y	N	Y
34 Torres	Y	Y	Y	N	Y	N	Y	-
35 ***Lewis***	X	?	?	#	X	?	X	#
36 Brown	Y	Y	Y	N	Y	Y	Y	N
37 ***McCandless***	N	N	N	N	N	Y	N	Y
38 ***Dornan***	N	N	N	Y	N	Y	N	Y
39 ***Dannemeyer***	N	N	N	Y	N	Y	N	Y
40 ***Badham***	N	N	N	Y	N	Y	N	Y
41 ***Lowery***	Y	N	N	Y	N	Y	N	Y
42 ***Lungren***	N	N	N	Y	N	Y	N	Y
43 ***Packard***	N	N	N	Y	N	Y	N	Y
44 Bates	N	N	N	N	Y	N	Y	N
45 ***Hunter***	N	N	N	Y	N	Y	N	Y
COLORADO								
1 Schroeder	N	Y	N	N	Y	N	Y	N
2 Wirth	Y	N	N	N	N	N	Y	N
3 ***Strang***	N	N	N	Y	N	Y	N	Y
4 ***Brown***	N	N	N	N	N	Y	Y	Y
5 ***Kramer***	Y	N	N	Y	N	N	N	Y
6 ***Schaefer***	N	N	N	N	N	N	N	Y
CONNECTICUT								
1 Kennelly	Y	N	Y	N	N	N	Y	N
2 Gejdenson	Y	Y	Y	N	Y	N	Y	N
3 Morrison	#	X	?	X	#	?	#	X
4 ***McKinney***	Y	Y	Y	N	N	N	Y	N
5 ***Rowland***	Y	N	N	N	N	Y	N	Y
6 ***Johnson***	+	N	N	N	N	Y	N	N
DELAWARE								
AL Carper	Y	Y	N	N	N	N	Y	N
FLORIDA								
1 Hutto	Y	N	N	Y	N	Y	N	Y
2 Fuqua	N	N	N	N	N	Y	N	Y
3 Bennett	Y	Y	N	N	N	N	Y	N
4 Chappell	N	N	N	N	N	Y	N	N
5 ***McCollum***	N	N	N	Y	N	Y	N	Y
6 MacKay	Y	N	N	N	N	N	Y	N
7 Gibbons	?	N	N	N	N	N	Y	N
8 ***Young***	Y	N	N	Y	N	Y	N	Y
9 ***Bilirakis***	N	N	N	N	N	Y	N	Y
10 ***Ireland***	N	N	N	Y	N	Y	N	Y
11 Nelson	Y	N	N	Y	N	N	N	Y
12 ***Lewis***	N	N	N	N	N	Y	N	Y
13 ***Mack***	N	N	N	Y	N	Y	N	Y
14 Mica	Y	Y	N	N	N	N	Y	N
15 ***Shaw***	N	N	N	N	N	Y	N	Y
16 Smith	Y	N	N	N	N	N	Y	N
17 Lehman	Y	Y	Y	N	Y	N	Y	N
18 Pepper	Y	Y	N	N	N	N	Y	N
19 Fascell	Y	Y	N	N	N	N	Y	N
GEORGIA								
1 Thomas	Y	N	N	N	N	Y	N	Y
2 Hatcher	N	N	N	N	N	Y	Y	Y
3 Ray	N	N	N	N	N	N	Y	Y
4 ***Swindall***	N	N	N	Y	N	Y	N	Y
5 Fowler	?	?	?	?	?	?	?	?
6 ***Gingrich***	N	N	N	Y	N	Y	N	Y
7 Darden	#	?	X	N	N	N	N	Y
8 Rowland	Y	N	N	N	N	N	Y	Y
9 Jenkins	?	?	?	?	?	?	?	?
10 Barnard	Y	N	N	Y	N	Y	N	Y
HAWAII								
1 Vacancy								
2 Akaka	N	Y	N	N	N	N	Y	N
IDAHO								
1 ***Craig***	N	N	N	Y	N	Y	N	Y
2 Stallings	Y	N	N	N	N	N	Y	N
ILLINOIS								
1 Hayes	Y	Y	Y	N	Y	N	Y	N
2 Savage	N	Y	Y	N	Y	N	Y	N
3 Russo	N	N	Y	N	Y	N	Y	N
4 Vacancy								
5 Lipinski	N	Y	N	N	N	Y	N	Y
6 ***Hyde***	N	N	N	Y	N	Y	N	Y
7 Collins	N	Y	Y	N	Y	N	Y	N
8 Rostenkowski	Y	N	N	N	N	N	Y	N
9 Yates	X	?	?	N	Y	N	Y	?
10 ***Porter***	N	N	N	N	N	Y	Y	Y
11 Annunzio	Y	Y	N	N	N	Y	Y	N
12 ***Crane***	N	N	N	Y	N	Y	N	Y
13 ***Fawell***	N	N	N	N	N	Y	Y	Y
14 ***Grotberg***	?	?	?	?	?	?	?	?
15 ***Madigan***	N	N	N	N	N	Y	N	Y
16 ***Martin***	N	Y	N	N	N	Y	N	Y
17 Evans	N	N	Y	N	Y	N	Y	N
18 ***Michel***	N	N	N	Y	N	Y	N	Y
19 Bruce	Y	Y	Y	N	Y	N	Y	N
20 Durbin	Y	Y	Y	N	Y	N	Y	N
21 Price	Y	N	N	N	N	N	Y	N
22 Gray	Y	Y	N	N	N	Y	N	N
INDIANA								
1 Visclosky	Y	Y	N	N	N	N	Y	N
2 Sharp	Y	N	N	N	N	N	Y	N
3 ***Hiler***	Y	N	N	Y	N	Y	N	Y
4 ***Coats***	Y	N	N	N	N	Y	N	Y
5 ***Hillis***	?	?	?	?	?	?	?	?

ND - Northern Democrats SD - Southern Democrats

* Corresponding to Congressional Record Votes 322, 323, 324, 325, 326, 327, 328, 329

	294	295	296	297	298	299	300	301
6 ***Burton***	N	N	N	Y	N	Y	N	Y
7 ***Myers***	N	N	N	Y	N	Y	N	Y
8 McCloskey	Y	N	N	N	N	N	Y	N
9 Hamilton	Y	N	N	N	N	N	Y	N
10 Jacobs	Y	Y	N	N	Y	N	Y	N
IOWA								
1 ***Leach***	N	N	N	N	Y	N	Y	N
2 ***Tauke***	N	N	N	N	N	Y	Y	Y
3 ***Evans***	N	N	N	N	N	Y	Y	Y
4 Smith	N	N	N	N	N	N	Y	N
5 ***Lightfoot***	N	N	N	N	N	Y	N	Y
6 Bedell	N	N	Y	N	Y	N	Y	N
KANSAS								
1 ***Roberts***	N	N	N	N	N	Y	Y	Y
2 Slattery	Y	N	N	N	N	N	Y	N
3 ***Meyers***	N	N	N	N	N	Y	Y	Y
4 Glickman	Y	N	N	N	Y	N	Y	N
5 ***Whittaker***	N	N	N	N	N	Y	N	Y
KENTUCKY								
1 Hubbard	N	N	N	N	N	N	Y	Y
2 Natcher	Y	Y	N	N	N	N	Y	N
3 Mazzoli	N	N	N	N	N	N	Y	Y
4 ***Snyder***	N	N	N	Y	N	Y	N	Y
5 ***Rogers***	N	N	N	N	N	Y	N	Y
6 ***Hopkins***	N	N	N	N	N	Y	N	Y
7 Perkins	Y	Y	N	N	Y	N	Y	N
LOUISIANA								
1 ***Livingston***	Y	N	N	Y	N	Y	N	Y
2 Boggs	Y	Y	Y	N	N	Y	Y	N
3 Tauzin	N	N	N	N	N	Y	N	Y
4 Roemer	N	N	N	N	N	Y	N	Y
5 Huckaby	N	N	N	N	N	Y	N	N
6 ***Moore***	?	?	?	?	?	?	?	?
7 Breaux	?	?	?	?	?	?	?	?
8 Long	Y	N	Y	N	Y	N	Y	N
MAINE								
1 ***McKernan***	N	N	N	N	N	N	Y	N
2 ***Snowe***	N	N	N	N	N	N	Y	Y
MARYLAND								
1 Dyson	Y	Y	N	N	N	N	Y	Y
2 ***Bentley***	N	N	N	N	N	Y	N	Y
3 Mikulski	?	?	?	N	Y	?	?	N
4 ***Holt***	?	?	?	Y	N	Y	N	Y
5 Hoyer	Y	Y	N	N	Y	N	Y	N
6 Byron	Y	N	N	N	N	Y	Y	Y
7 Mitchell	X	?	?	X	#	X	?	?
8 Barnes	Y	Y	Y	N	Y	?	#	N
MASSACHUSETTS								
1 ***Conte***	Y	N	Y	N	N	N	Y	N
2 Boland	Y	N	N	N	N	N	Y	N
3 Early	Y	N	Y	N	N	N	Y	N
4 Frank	Y	N	Y	N	Y	N	Y	N
5 Atkins	Y	Y	Y	N	Y	N	Y	N
6 Mavroules	Y	N	Y	N	Y	N	Y	N
7 Markey	Y	N	Y	N	Y	N	Y	N
8 O'Neill								
9 Moakley	Y	N	Y	N	Y	N	Y	N
10 Studds	Y	N	Y	N	Y	N	Y	N
11 Donnelly	Y	Y	N	N	N	N	Y	Y
MICHIGAN								
1 Conyers	Y	N	Y	N	Y	N	Y	N
2 ***Pursell***	N	N	N	N	N	N	Y	Y
3 Wolpe	Y	N	Y	N	Y	N	Y	N
4 ***Siljander***	N	N	N	Y	N	Y	N	Y
5 ***Henry***	N	N	N	N	N	N	Y	N
6 Carr	N	N	Y	N	Y	N	Y	N
7 Kildee	N	N	Y	N	Y	N	Y	N
8 Traxler	Y	N	Y	N	Y	N	Y	N
9 ***Vander Jagt***	?	?	?	Y	N	N	N	Y
10 ***Schuette***	N	N	N	N	N	Y	N	Y
11 ***Davis***	N	Y	N	N	N	Y	N	Y
12 Bonior	Y	N	Y	N	Y	N	Y	N
13 Crockett	N	Y	Y	N	Y	N	Y	N
14 Hertel	Y	N	N	N	N	N	Y	N
15 Ford	Y	N	Y	N	Y	Y	Y	N
16 Dingell	Y	N	N	N	Y	N	Y	N
17 Levin	Y	Y	N	N	N	N	Y	N
18 ***Broomfield***	N	N	N	Y	N	Y	N	Y
MINNESOTA								
1 Penny	Y	N	Y	N	Y	N	Y	N
2 ***Weber***	N	N	N	Y	N	Y	N	Y
3 ***Frenzel***	N	N	N	N	N	N	Y	Y
4 Vento	N	N	Y	N	Y	N	Y	N
5 Sabo	Y	N	Y	N	Y	N	Y	N
6 Sikorski	Y	Y	Y	N	Y	N	Y	N

	294	295	296	297	298	299	300	301
7 ***Stangeland***	N	N	N	N	N	Y	N	Y
8 Oberstar	Y	N	Y	N	Y	N	Y	N
MISSISSIPPI								
1 Whitten	Y	Y	N	N	N	N	Y	N
2 ***Franklin***	N	Y	N	Y	N	Y	N	Y
3 Montgomery	N	N	N	N	N	Y	N	Y
4 Dowdy	Y	N	N	N	N	N	Y	N
5 ***Lott***	N	N	?	Y	N	Y	N	Y
MISSOURI								
1 Clay	?	?	?	?	?	?	?	?
2 Young	Y	Y	N	N	N	N	Y	N
3 Gephardt	Y	Y	N	N	N	N	Y	N
4 Skelton	Y	N	N	N	N	Y	N	Y
5 Wheat	Y	Y	Y	N	Y	N	Y	N
6 ***Coleman***	N	N	N	Y	N	Y	N	Y
7 ***Taylor***	N	N	N	Y	N	Y	N	Y
8 ***Emerson***	N	Y	N	Y	N	Y	N	Y
9 Volkmer	Y	N	N	N	N	N	Y	N
MONTANA								
1 Williams	Y	Y	Y	N	Y	N	Y	N
2 ***Marlenee***	N	N	N	Y	N	Y	Y	Y
NEBRASKA								
1 ***Bereuter***	N	N	N	N	N	Y	Y	Y
2 ***Daub***	N	N	N	N	N	Y	N	Y
3 ***Smith***	N	N	N	N	N	Y	Y	Y
NEVADA								
1 Reid	Y	Y	N	Y	N	N	N	N
2 ***Vucanovich***	N	N	N	Y	N	Y	N	Y
NEW HAMPSHIRE								
1 ***Smith***	N	N	N	Y	N	Y	N	Y
2 ***Gregg***	N	N	N	N	N	Y	N	Y
NEW JERSEY								
1 Florio	Y	Y	N	N	N	N	Y	N
2 Hughes	Y	N	N	N	N	N	Y	N
3 Howard	Y	Y	N	N	Y	N	Y	N
4 ***Smith***	N	N	N	N	N	Y	N	Y
5 ***Roukema***	N	N	N	N	N	N	Y	Y
6 Dwyer	Y	Y	N	N	N	N	Y	N
7 ***Rinaldo***	N	N	N	N	N	Y	N	Y
8 Roe	Y	Y	N	N	Y	N	Y	N
9 Torricelli	Y	Y	N	N	N	N	Y	N
10 Rodino	Y	Y	Y	N	Y	N	Y	N
11 ***Gallo***	N	N	N	N	N	Y	N	Y
12 ***Courter***	N	N	N	Y	N	Y	N	Y
13 ***Saxton***	N	N	N	N	N	Y	N	Y
14 Guarini	Y	Y	N	N	N	N	Y	N
NEW MEXICO								
1 ***Lujan***	N	Y	N	N	N	Y	N	Y
2 ***Skeen***	Y	N	N	N	N	Y	N	Y
3 Richardson	Y	Y	N	N	N	Y	N	N
NEW YORK								
1 ***Carney***	N	N	N	Y	N	N	N	Y
2 Downey	Y	N	Y	N	Y	N	Y	N
3 Mrazek	Y	Y	Y	N	Y	?	Y	N
4 ***Lent***	N	N	N	N	N	Y	N	Y
5 ***McGrath***	Y	N	N	N	N	Y	Y	Y
6 Waldon	N	Y	Y	N	Y	N	Y	N
7 Ackerman	Y	Y	N	N	Y	N	Y	N
8 Scheuer	Y	Y	Y	N	Y	N	Y	N
9 Manton	Y	Y	N	N	N	N	Y	N
10 Schumer	Y	Y	Y	N	N	N	Y	N
11 Towns	N	Y	Y	N	Y	N	Y	N
12 Owens	Y	Y	Y	N	Y	N	Y	N
13 Solarz	Y	N	Y	N	Y	Y	Y	N
14 ***Molinari***	N	Y	N	N	N	N	Y	Y
15 ***Green***	N	N	N	N	N	N	Y	N
16 Rangel	N	Y	Y	N	Y	N	Y	N
17 Weiss	-	Y	Y	N	Y	N	Y	N
18 Garcia	Y	Y	Y	N	Y	N	Y	N
19 Biaggi	Y	Y	N	N	N	N	Y	N
20 ***DioGuardi***	Y	N	N	N	N	Y	N	Y
21 ***Fish***	N	N	N	N	N	N	Y	N
22 ***Gilman***	Y	N	N	N	N	N	Y	Y
23 Stratton	Y	Y	N	Y	N	Y	N	Y
24 ***Solomon***	Y	N	N	Y	N	Y	N	Y
25 ***Boehlert***	N	N	N	N	N	Y	N	N
26 ***Martin***	N	N	N	N	N	Y	N	Y
27 ***Wortley***	N	Y	N	N	N	Y	N	Y
28 McHugh	Y	N	Y	N	Y	N	Y	N
29 ***Horton***	?	?	?	N	N	N	Y	N
30 ***Eckert***	N	N	N	Y	N	Y	N	Y
31 ***Kemp***	N	N	N	Y	N	N	N	Y
32 LaFalce	#	?	#	N	Y	N	Y	N
33 Nowak	Y	Y	Y	N	Y	N	Y	N
34 Lundine	?	?	?	N	Y	N	Y	N

	294	295	296	297	298	299	300	301
NORTH CAROLINA								
1 Jones	Y	?	?	N	N	N	Y	?
2 Valentine	N	N	N	N	N	N	Y	Y
3 Whitley	N	N	N	N	N	N	Y	N
4 ***Cobey***	N	N	N	Y	N	Y	N	Y
5 Neal	Y	?	N	N	N	N	Y	N
6 ***Coble***	N	N	N	N	N	Y	Y	Y
7 Rose	N	N	N	N	N	N	Y	N
8 Hefner	Y	N	N	N	N	N	Y	N
9 ***McMillan***	N	N	N	N	N	Y	N	Y
10 Vacancy								
11 ***Hendon***	N	N	N	Y	N	Y	N	Y
NORTH DAKOTA								
AL Dorgan	N	N	N	N	Y	N	Y	N
OHIO								
1 Luken	?	?	?	N	Y	N	Y	N
2 ***Gradison***	N	N	N	N	N	N	N	Y
3 Hall	Y	Y	N	N	Y	N	Y	N
4 ***Oxley***	N	N	N	N	N	Y	N	Y
5 ***Latta***	N	N	N	Y	N	Y	N	Y
6 ***McEwen***	N	N	N	Y	N	Y	N	Y
7 ***DeWine***	N	N	N	Y	N	Y	N	Y
8 ***Kindness***	N	?	N	N	N	Y	N	Y
9 Kaptur	Y	Y	N	N	N	N	Y	N
10 ***Miller***	N	N	N	N	N	Y	N	Y
11 Eckart	Y	Y	N	N	N	N	Y	N
12 ***Kasich***	N	N	N	Y	N	Y	N	Y
13 Pease	N	N	N	N	Y	N	Y	N
14 Seiberling	N	Y	Y	N	Y	N	Y	N
15 ***Wylie***	N	N	N	N	N	Y	N	Y
16 ***Regula***	N	N	N	N	N	N	Y	Y
17 Traficant	Y	Y	Y	N	Y	N	Y	N
18 Applegate	Y	Y	N	N	N	Y	Y	N
19 Feighan	Y	Y	Y	N	Y	N	Y	N
20 Oakar	Y	Y	Y	N	Y	N	Y	N
21 Stokes	N	Y	Y	N	Y	N	Y	N
OKLAHOMA								
1 Jones	Y	N	N	N	N	N	Y	N
2 Synar	Y	N	N	N	Y	N	Y	N
3 Watkins	Y	Y	N	N	N	N	Y	N
4 McCurdy	Y	N	N	N	N	Y	Y	N
5 ***Edwards***	Y	N	N	Y	N	Y	N	Y
6 English	Y	N	N	N	N	Y	Y	Y
OREGON								
1 AuCoin	N	N	Y	N	Y	N	Y	N
2 ***Smith, R.***	N	N	N	N	?	Y	Y	Y
3 Wyden	Y	N	N	N	Y	N	Y	N
4 Weaver	N	?	?	N	Y	N	Y	N
5 ***Smith, D.***	N	N	N	N	N	Y	N	Y
PENNSYLVANIA								
1 Foglietta	Y	Y	Y	N	Y	N	Y	N
2 Gray	Y	Y	Y	N	Y	N	Y	N
3 Borski	Y	Y	N	N	N	N	Y	N
4 Kolter	N	Y	N	N	N	N	Y	N
5 ***Schulze***	N	Y	N	N	N	Y	N	Y
6 Yatron	Y	Y	N	N	N	Y	Y	N
7 Edgar	?	?	?	N	Y	N	Y	N
8 Kostmayer	Y	Y	Y	N	Y	N	Y	N
9 ***Shuster***	N	N	N	Y	N	Y	N	Y
10 ***McDade***	N	Y	N	N	N	Y	N	Y
11 Kanjorski	Y	Y	N	N	N	N	Y	N
12 Murtha	Y	Y	N	N	N	Y	N	Y
13 ***Coughlin***	N	N	N	N	N	Y	Y	Y
14 Coyne	N	Y	Y	N	Y	N	Y	N
15 ***Ritter***	N	N	N	N	N	Y	N	Y
16 ***Walker***	N	N	N	Y	N	Y	N	Y
17 ***Gekas***	N	N	N	Y	N	Y	N	Y
18 Walgren	N	Y	Y	N	Y	N	Y	N
19 ***Goodling***	N	N	N	N	N	Y	N	Y
20 Gaydos	Y	Y	N	N	N	N	Y	N
21 ***Ridge***	Y	N	N	N	N	N	Y	N
22 Murphy	N	N	Y	N	N	N	Y	N
23 ***Clinger***	N	N	N	N	N	Y	N	Y
RHODE ISLAND								
1 St Germain	Y	N	N	N	Y	N	Y	N
2 ***Schneider***	Y	N	Y	N	N	N	Y	N
SOUTH CAROLINA								
1 ***Hartnett***	?	?	?	Y	N	Y	N	Y
2 ***Spence***	Y	N	N	Y	N	Y	N	Y
3 Derrick	Y	N	N	N	N	N	Y	N
4 ***Campbell***	?	?	?	#	X	#	X	#
5 Spratt	Y	N	N	N	N	N	Y	N
6 Tallon	N	N	N	N	N	N	Y	Y
SOUTH DAKOTA								
AL Daschle	Y	N	Y	N	Y	N	Y	N

	294	295	296	297	298	299	300	301
TENNESSEE								
1 ***Quillen***	?	N	N	Y	N	Y	N	Y
2 ***Duncan***	N	N	N	Y	N	Y	N	Y
3 Lloyd	N	N	N	N	N	Y	N	Y
4 Cooper	Y	N	N	N	N	N	Y	N
5 Boner	Y	N	N	N	N	Y	N	N
6 Gordon	Y	N	N	N	N	N	Y	N
7 ***Sundquist***	N	N	N	N	N	Y	N	Y
8 Jones	N	N	N	N	N	Y	N	N
9 Ford	N	Y	Y	N	Y	N	Y	N
TEXAS								
1 Chapman	N	N	N	N	N	N	Y	N
2 Wilson	Y	N	N	Y	N	Y	N	Y
3 ***Bartlett***	N	N	N	Y	N	Y	N	Y
4 Hall, R.	N	N	N	Y	N	Y	N	Y
5 Bryant	Y	Y	N	N	Y	N	Y	N
6 ***Barton***	N	N	N	Y	N	Y	N	Y
7 ***Archer***	N	N	N	Y	N	Y	N	Y
8 ***Fields***	N	N	N	Y	N	Y	N	Y
9 Brooks	Y	Y	N	N	Y	N	Y	N
10 Pickle	N	N	N	N	N	N	N	Y
11 Leath	N	N	N	N	N	N	Y	N
12 Wright	Y	N	N	N	N	N	Y	N
13 ***Boulter***	N	N	N	Y	N	Y	N	Y
14 ***Sweeney***	N	N	N	Y	N	Y	N	Y
15 de la Garza	Y	#	?	N	N	N	Y	N
16 Coleman	Y	Y	N	N	N	N	N	N
17 Stenholm	N	N	N	N	N	Y	Y	Y
18 Leland	Y	Y	Y	N	Y	N	Y	N
19 ***Combest***	N	N	N	Y	N	Y	N	Y
20 Gonzalez	N	Y	Y	N	Y	N	Y	N
21 ***Loeffler***	N	N	N	Y	N	Y	N	Y
22 ***DeLay***	N	N	N	Y	N	Y	N	Y
23 Bustamante	Y	Y	N	N	N	N	Y	N
24 Frost	Y	Y	N	N	N	N	Y	N
25 Andrews	N	N	N	N	N	N	N	N
26 ***Armey***	N	N	N	Y	N	Y	N	Y
27 Ortiz	Y	Y	N	N	N	N	Y	N
UTAH								
1 ***Hansen***	N	N	N	Y	N	Y	N	Y
2 ***Monson***	N	N	N	N	N	Y	N	Y
3 ***Nielson***	N	N	N	N	N	Y	N	Y
VERMONT								
AL ***Jeffords***	Y	N	N	N	N	N	Y	N
VIRGINIA								
1 ***Bateman***	N	N	N	N	N	Y	N	Y
2 ***Whitehurst***	N	N	N	Y	N	Y	N	Y
3 ***Bliley***	N	N	N	N	N	Y	N	Y
4 Sisisky	Y	Y	N	N	N	Y	N	Y
5 Daniel	N	N	N	N	N	Y	N	Y
6 Olin	N	N	N	N	N	Y	Y	N
7 ***Slaughter***	N	N	N	N	N	Y	N	Y
8 ***Parris***	N	N	N	N	N	Y	N	Y
9 Boucher	Y	N	N	N	N	Y	Y	N
10 ***Wolf***	N	N	N	N	N	Y	N	Y
WASHINGTON								
1 ***Miller***	N	N	N	N	N	Y	N	Y
2 Swift	Y	Y	Y	N	Y	N	Y	N
3 Bonker	Y	N	N	N	Y	N	Y	N
4 ***Morrison***	Y	N	N	N	N	Y	N	Y
5 Foley	Y	Y	N	N	?	N	Y	N
6 Dicks	Y	N	N	N	N	Y	Y	N
7 Lowry	N	N	Y	N	Y	N	Y	N
8 ***Chandler***	N	N	N	N	N	N	Y	Y
WEST VIRGINIA								
1 Mollohan	Y	Y	N	N	N	Y	Y	Y
2 Staggers	Y	Y	Y	N	Y	N	Y	N
3 Wise	Y	Y	N	N	N	N	Y	N
4 Rahall	N	Y	Y	N	Y	N	Y	N
WISCONSIN								
1 Aspin	Y	N	N	N	N	N	Y	N
2 Kastenmeier	N	Y	Y	N	Y	N	Y	N
3 ***Gunderson***	Y	N	N	N	N	N	Y	Y
4 Kleczka	N	Y	N	N	N	N	Y	N
5 Moody	Y	Y	Y	N	Y	N	Y	N
6 ***Petri***	N	N	N	N	N	N	Y	Y
7 Obey	N	N	Y	N	Y	N	Y	N
8 ***Roth***	N	N	N	Y	N	Y	N	Y
9 ***Sensenbrenner***	N	N	N	N	N	Y	N	Y
WYOMING								
AL ***Cheney***	Y	N	N	Y	N	Y	N	Y

Southern states - Ala., Ark., Fla., Ga., Ky., La., Miss., N.C., Okla., S.C., Tenn., Texas, Va.

* The *Congressional Record* vote number is different from the CQ vote number because the *Record* includes quorum calls in its tally. CQ does not publish quorum call votes.

302. HR 4428. Defense Authorization, Fiscal 1987. Dicks, D-Wash., amendment to prohibit the use of funds to deploy any weapons inconsistent with certain limits contained in the SALT II arms control treaty, provided the Soviet Union continues to observe those limits. Adopted 225-186: R 19-154; D 206-32 (ND 155-6, SD 51-26), Aug. 12, 1986.

303. Procedural Motion. Bliley, R-Va., motion to approve the House *Journal* of Tuesday, Aug. 12. Motion agreed to 252-138: R 41-129; D 211-9 (ND 143-7, SD 68-2), Aug. 13, 1986.

304. H Res 373. South African Negotiations. Wolpe, D-Mich., motion to suspend the rules and adopt the resolution to express the sense of the House that the president should urge the South African government to engage in political negotiations with that country's black majority; grant immediately unconditional freedom to Nelson Mandela and other political prisoners; and recognize the African National Congress as a legitimate representative for the black majority. Motion rejected 245-177: R 30-145; D 215-32 (ND 157-10, SD 58-22), Aug. 13, 1986. A two-thirds majority of those present and voting (282 in this case) is required for adoption under suspension of the rules.

305. HR 2631. Atmospheric Pollution Research. Whitley, D-N.C., motion to suspend the rules and pass the bill to provide for a 10-year program under the Department of Agriculture to study the effects of atmospheric pollution on the health and productivity of forest ecosystems. The bill authorized no new appropriations. Motion agreed to 416-4: R 172-4; D 244-0 (ND 167-0, SD 77-0), Aug. 13, 1986. A two-thirds majority of those present and voting (280 in this case) is required for passage under suspension of the rules.

306. HR 4260. Small Business Innovation Programs. Mavroules, D-Mass., motion to suspend the rules and pass the bill to provide the Small Business Administration continuing authority to administer small business innovation research programs. Motion agreed to 421-1: R 174-1; D 247-0 (ND 167-0, SD 80-0), Aug. 13, 1986. A two-thirds majority of those present and voting (282 in this case) is required for passage under suspension of the rules.

307. HR 2889. Computer Security Act. Fuqua, D-Fla., motion to suspend the rules and pass the bill to provide for a computer security research program within the National Bureau of Standards to improve the security and privacy of sensitive information in federal computer systems. Motion rejected 217-206: R 15-161; D 202-45 (ND 149-18, SD 53-27), Aug. 13, 1986. A two-thirds majority of those present and voting (282 in this case) is required for passage under suspension of the rules.

308. HR 5013. Fishing Vessel Liability and Safety. Jones, D-N.C., motion to suspend the rules and pass the bill to establish guidelines for damage awards in actions for personal injury incurred by seamen on fishing industry vessels and to require additional safety regulations for fishing industry vessels. Motion rejected 181-241: R 106-70; D 75-171 (ND 48-118, SD 27-53), Aug. 13, 1986. A two-thirds majority of those present and voting (282 in this case) is required for passage under suspension of the rules.

309. HR 4428. Defense Authorization, Fiscal 1987. Brown, D-Calif., amendment to bar tests against an object in space of the anti-satellite (ASAT) missile provided the Soviet Union abstains from testing its own version of the weapon. Adopted 222-197: R 28-148; D 194-49 (ND 153-10, SD 41-39), Aug. 13, 1986. A "nay" was a vote supporting the president's position.

KEY

- Y Voted for (yea).
- # Paired for.
- + Announced for.
- N Voted against (nay).
- X Paired against.
- - Announced against.
- P Voted "present."
- C Voted "present" to avoid possible conflict of interest.
- ? Did not vote or otherwise make a position known.

Democrats *Republicans*

	302	303	304	305	306	307	308	309
ALABAMA								
1 *Callahan*	N	N	N	Y	Y	N	N	N
2 *Dickinson*	N	N	N	N	Y	N	Y	N
3 Nichols	N	Y	N	Y	Y	N	N	N
4 Bevill	N	Y	Y	Y	Y	N	N	N
5 Flippo	?	?	?	?	?	?	?	?
6 Erdreich	Y	Y	Y	Y	Y	N	N	N
7 Shelby	N	Y	Y	Y	Y	N	N	N
ALASKA								
AL *Young*	N	N	N	Y	Y	N	Y	N
ARIZONA								
1 *McCain*	N	N	N	Y	Y	N	Y	N
2 Udall	Y	Y	Y	Y	Y	N	N	Y
3 *Stump*	N	N	N	N	Y	N	N	N
4 *Rudd*	N	Y	N	Y	Y	N	N	N
5 *Kolbe*	N	N	N	Y	Y	N	Y	N
ARKANSAS								
1 Alexander	Y	Y	Y	Y	Y	Y	N	Y
2 Robinson	N	Y	N	Y	Y	N	N	N
3 *Hammerschmidt*	N	Y	N	Y	Y	N	N	N
4 Anthony	Y	Y	Y	Y	Y	Y	N	Y
CALIFORNIA								
1 Bosco	Y	Y	Y	Y	Y	Y	Y	Y
2 *Chappie*	N	N	N	Y	Y	N	N	N
3 Matsui	Y	Y	Y	Y	Y	Y	N	Y
4 Fazio	Y	Y	Y	Y	Y	Y	N	Y
5 Burton	?	?	?	?	?	?	?	?
6 Boxer	Y	Y	Y	Y	Y	Y	Y	Y
7 Miller	Y	Y	Y	Y	Y	Y	N	Y
8 Dellums	Y	Y	Y	Y	Y	Y	N	Y
9 Stark	Y	Y	Y	Y	Y	Y	Y	?
10 Edwards	Y	Y	Y	Y	Y	Y	N	Y
11 Lantos	Y	Y	Y	Y	Y	Y	N	Y
12 *Zschau*	N	?	Y	Y	Y	N	Y	Y
13 Mineta	Y	Y	Y	Y	Y	Y	N	Y
14 *Shumway*	N	Y	N	Y	Y	N	Y	N
15 Coelho	Y	Y	Y	Y	Y	Y	N	Y
16 Panetta	Y	Y	Y	Y	Y	Y	Y	Y
17 *Pashayan*	N	N	N	Y	Y	N	N	N
18 Lehman	Y	Y	Y	Y	Y	Y	Y	Y
19 *Lagomarsino*	N	N	N	Y	Y	N	Y	N
20 *Thomas*	N	N	N	Y	Y	N	Y	N
21 *Fiedler*	N	N	N	Y	Y	N	Y	N
22 *Moorhead*	N	N	N	Y	Y	N	N	N
23 Beilenson	Y	Y	Y	Y	Y	Y	Y	Y
24 Waxman	Y	Y	Y	Y	Y	Y	N	Y
25 Roybal	Y	Y	Y	Y	Y	Y	N	Y
26 Berman	Y	Y	Y	Y	Y	Y	N	Y
27 Levine	Y	Y	Y	Y	Y	Y	N	Y
28 Dixon	?	?	Y	Y	Y	Y	Y	Y
29 Hawkins	Y	?	Y	Y	Y	Y	N	Y
30 Martinez	Y	Y	Y	Y	Y	Y	Y	Y
31 Dymally	Y	Y	Y	Y	Y	Y	N	Y
32 Anderson	Y	Y	Y	Y	Y	Y	Y	Y
33 *Dreier*	N	N	N	Y	Y	N	N	N
34 Torres	+	Y	Y	Y	Y	Y	N	Y
35 *Lewis*	X	N	N	Y	Y	N	Y	N
36 Brown	Y	Y	Y	Y	Y	Y	Y	Y
37 *McCandless*	N	N	N	Y	Y	Y	N	N
38 *Dornan*	N	N	N	Y	Y	N	Y	N
39 *Dannemeyer*	N	N	N	Y	Y	N	Y	N
40 *Badham*	N	N	N	Y	Y	N	N	N
41 *Lowery*	N	N	N	Y	Y	N	Y	N
42 *Lungren*	N	N	N	Y	Y	N	Y	N
43 *Packard*	N	N	N	Y	Y	N	Y	N
44 Bates	Y	Y	Y	Y	Y	Y	Y	Y
45 *Hunter*	N	N	N	Y	Y	N	Y	N
COLORADO								
1 Schroeder	Y	N	Y	Y	Y	Y	N	Y
2 Wirth	Y	Y	Y	Y	Y	Y	N	Y
3 *Strang*	N	N	N	Y	Y	N	Y	N
4 *Brown*	N	N	N	Y	Y	N	Y	N
5 *Kramer*	N	N	N	Y	Y	N	Y	N
6 *Schaefer*	N	N	N	Y	Y	N	N	N
CONNECTICUT								
1 Kennelly	Y	Y	Y	Y	Y	Y	N	Y
2 Gejdenson	Y	Y	Y	Y	Y	Y	Y	Y
3 Morrison	#	?	?	?	?	?	?	#
4 *McKinney*	?	Y	Y	Y	Y	N	Y	Y
5 *Rowland*	N	N	N	Y	Y	N	Y	N
6 *Johnson*	Y	Y	N	Y	Y	Y	Y	Y
DELAWARE								
AL Carper	Y	Y	Y	Y	Y	Y	Y	Y
FLORIDA								
1 Hutto	N	Y	N	Y	Y	N	Y	N
2 Fuqua	Y	Y	Y	Y	Y	Y	Y	N
3 Bennett	Y	Y	N	Y	Y	Y	Y	Y
4 Chappell	Y	Y	N	Y	Y	Y	Y	N
5 *McCollum*	N	Y	N	Y	Y	N	N	N
6 MacKay	Y	Y	Y	Y	Y	Y	N	Y
7 Gibbons	Y	?	Y	Y	Y	Y	N	Y
8 *Young*	N	N	N	Y	Y	N	N	N
9 *Bilirakis*	N	N	N	Y	Y	N	Y	N
10 *Ireland*	N	N	N	Y	Y	N	N	N
11 Nelson	N	Y	N	Y	Y	Y	Y	N
12 *Lewis*	N	N	N	Y	Y	N	N	N
13 *Mack*	N	N	N	Y	Y	N	N	N
14 Mica	Y	Y	N	Y	Y	Y	N	Y
15 *Shaw*	N	N	N	Y	Y	N	Y	N
16 Smith	Y	P	Y	Y	Y	Y	N	Y
17 Lehman	Y	Y	Y	Y	Y	Y	Y	Y
18 Pepper	Y	Y	Y	Y	Y	Y	N	Y
19 Fascell	Y	Y	Y	Y	Y	Y	Y	Y
GEORGIA								
1 Thomas	N	Y	N	Y	Y	Y	Y	N
2 Hatcher	N	Y	N	Y	Y	Y	N	N
3 Ray	N	P	Y	Y	Y	N	N	N
4 *Swindall*	N	N	N	Y	Y	N	N	N
5 Fowler	?	?	?	?	?	?	?	?
6 *Gingrich*	?	N	N	Y	Y	N	N	N
7 Darden	N	Y	N	Y	Y	Y	N	N
8 Rowland	N	Y	N	Y	Y	N	Y	N
9 Jenkins	?	Y	N	Y	Y	N	N	N
10 Barnard	N	Y	N	Y	Y	Y	N	N
HAWAII								
1 Vacancy								
2 Akaka	Y	Y	Y	Y	Y	Y	Y	Y
IDAHO								
1 *Craig*	N	N	N	Y	Y	N	Y	N
2 Stallings	Y	Y	N	Y	Y	Y	N	Y
ILLINOIS								
1 Hayes	Y	Y	Y	Y	Y	Y	N	Y
2 Savage	Y	Y	Y	Y	Y	Y	N	?
3 Russo	Y	Y	N	Y	Y	Y	N	Y
4 Vacancy								
5 Lipinski	Y	Y	N	Y	Y	N	Y	N
6 *Hyde*	N	N	N	Y	Y	N	N	N
7 Collins	Y	Y	Y	Y	Y	Y	N	Y
8 Rostenkowski	Y	Y	Y	Y	Y	Y	N	Y
9 Yates	#	Y	Y	Y	Y	Y	N	Y
10 *Porter*	N	N	N	Y	Y	N	N	Y
11 Annunzio	Y	Y	Y	Y	Y	Y	N	Y
12 *Crane*	N	N	N	N	N	N	N	N
13 *Fawell*	N	N	Y	Y	Y	N	N	N
14 *Grotberg*	?	?	?	?	?	?	?	?
15 *Madigan*	N	N	N	Y	Y	N	N	N
16 *Martin*	N	N	N	Y	Y	N	Y	N
17 Evans	Y	Y	Y	Y	Y	Y	N	Y
18 *Michel*	N	N	N	Y	Y	N	N	N
19 Bruce	Y	Y	Y	Y	Y	Y	N	Y
20 Durbin	Y	Y	Y	Y	Y	Y	N	Y
21 Price	Y	Y	Y	Y	Y	N	N	Y
22 Gray	Y	?	Y	Y	Y	Y	Y	Y
INDIANA								
1 Visclosky	Y	Y	Y	Y	Y	Y	N	Y
2 Sharp	Y	?	Y	Y	Y	Y	N	Y
3 *Hiler*	N	Y	N	Y	Y	N	Y	N
4 *Coats*	N	N	N	Y	Y	Y	N	N
5 *Hillis*	?	?	?	?	?	?	?	?

ND - Northern Democrats SD - Southern Democrats

* Corresponding to Congressional Record Votes 330, 331, 332, 333, 334, 335, 336, 337

	302	303	304	305	306	307	308	309
6 ***Burton***	N	N	N	Y	Y	N	N	N
7 ***Myers***	N	Y	N	Y	Y	N	Y	N
8 McCloskey	Y	Y	Y	Y	Y	Y	N	Y
9 Hamilton	Y	Y	Y	Y	Y	N	N	Y
10 Jacobs	Y	N	Y	Y	Y	Y	N	Y
IOWA								
1 ***Leach***	Y	N	Y	Y	Y	N	N	Y
2 ***Tauke***	Y	N	N	Y	Y	N	N	Y
3 ***Evans***	N	N	N	Y	Y	N	N	Y
4 Smith	Y	Y	Y	Y	Y	N	N	Y
5 ***Lightfoot***	N	N	N	Y	Y	N	Y	N
6 Bedell	Y	Y	Y	Y	Y	Y	Y	Y
KANSAS								
1 ***Roberts***	N	N	N	Y	Y	Y	Y	N
2 Slattery	Y	Y	Y	Y	Y	Y	N	Y
3 ***Meyers***	N	N	N	Y	Y	Y	Y	Y
4 Glickman	Y	Y	Y	Y	Y	Y	N	Y
5 ***Whittaker***	N	N	N	Y	Y	Y	Y	N
KENTUCKY								
1 Hubbard	N	Y	N	Y	Y	N	N	N
2 Natcher	Y	Y	Y	Y	Y	Y	Y	Y
3 Mazzoli	N	Y	Y	Y	Y	Y	N	Y
4 ***Snyder***	N	Y	N	Y	Y	N	N	N
5 ***Rogers***	N	N	N	Y	Y	N	N	N
6 ***Hopkins***	N	N	N	Y	Y	N	N	N
7 Perkins	Y	Y	Y	Y	Y	Y	N	Y
LOUISIANA								
1 ***Livingston***	N	N	N	Y	Y	N	N	N
2 Boggs	Y	?	Y	Y	Y	Y	N	Y
3 Tauzin	N	Y	Y	Y	Y	N	N	N
4 Roemer	N	Y	Y	Y	Y	N	N	N
5 Huckaby	Y	Y	Y	Y	Y	N	N	N
6 ***Moore***	?	?	?	?	?	?	?	?
7 Breaux	?	?	Y	Y	Y	N	N	N
8 Long	Y	Y	Y	Y	Y	Y	N	Y
MAINE								
1 ***McKernan***	Y	N	Y	Y	Y	N	Y	Y
2 ***Snowe***	Y	N	Y	Y	Y	N	Y	Y
MARYLAND								
1 Dyson	N	Y	N	Y	Y	N	Y	N
2 ***Bentley***	N	N	N	Y	Y	N	Y	N
3 Mikulski	Y	?	Y	Y	Y	Y	?	Y
4 ***Holt***	N	N	N	Y	Y	N	Y	N
5 Hoyer	Y	Y	Y	Y	Y	Y	N	Y
6 Byron	N	Y	N	Y	Y	N	Y	N
7 Mitchell	?	N	Y	Y	Y	Y	Y	Y
8 Barnes	Y	Y	Y	Y	Y	Y	Y	Y
MASSACHUSETTS								
1 ***Conte***	Y	N	Y	Y	Y	N	Y	Y
2 Boland	Y	Y	Y	Y	Y	N	Y	+
3 Early	Y	Y	Y	Y	Y	Y	Y	Y
4 Frank	Y	Y	Y	Y	Y	Y	Y	Y
5 Atkins	Y	Y	Y	Y	Y	Y	Y	Y
6 Mavroules	Y	Y	Y	Y	Y	Y	Y	Y
7 Markey	Y	Y	Y	Y	Y	Y	Y	Y
8 O'Neill								
9 Moakley	Y	Y	Y	Y	Y	Y	Y	Y
10 Studds	Y	Y	Y	Y	Y	Y	Y	Y
11 Donnelly	Y	Y	Y	Y	Y	Y	Y	N
MICHIGAN								
1 Conyers	Y	Y	Y	Y	Y	Y	N	Y
2 ***Pursell***	Y	Y	Y	Y	Y	N	Y	Y
3 Wolpe	Y	Y	Y	Y	Y	Y	N	Y
4 ***Siljander***	N	?	N	Y	Y	N	Y	N
5 ***Henry***	Y	N	Y	Y	Y	N	Y	N
6 Carr	Y	Y	Y	Y	Y	Y	N	Y
7 Kildee	Y	P	Y	Y	Y	Y	N	Y
8 Traxler	Y	Y	Y	Y	Y	Y	N	Y
9 ***Vander Jagt***	N	N	N	Y	Y	N	N	N
10 ***Schuette***	N	N	Y	Y	Y	N	Y	N
11 ***Davis***	Y	Y	Y	Y	Y	Y	Y	N
12 Bonior	Y	?	Y	Y	Y	Y	N	Y
13 Crockett	Y	Y	Y	Y	Y	Y	N	Y
14 Hertel	Y	Y	Y	Y	Y	Y	N	Y
15 Ford	Y	Y	Y	Y	Y	Y	N	Y
16 Dingell	Y	Y	Y	Y	Y	Y	N	Y
17 Levin	Y	Y	Y	Y	Y	Y	N	Y
18 ***Broomfield***	N	Y	N	Y	Y	N	Y	N
MINNESOTA								
1 Penny	Y	N	Y	Y	Y	Y	N	Y
2 ***Weber***	N	N	N	Y	Y	N	N	N
3 ***Frenzel***	Y	N	N	Y	Y	Y	Y	Y
4 Vento	Y	Y	Y	Y	Y	Y	N	Y
5 Sabo	Y	Y	Y	Y	Y	Y	Y	Y
6 Sikorski	Y	N	Y	Y	Y	Y	N	Y

	302	303	304	305	306	307	308	309
7 ***Stangeland***	N	N	N	Y	Y	N	Y	N
8 Oberstar	Y	Y	Y	Y	Y	Y	Y	Y
MISSISSIPPI								
1 Whitten	Y	Y	Y	?	Y	Y	Y	Y
2 ***Franklin***	N	N	Y	Y	Y	N	N	N
3 Montgomery	N	Y	N	Y	Y	N	N	N
4 Dowdy	Y	Y	Y	Y	Y	N	N	Y
5 ***Lott***	N	N	N	Y	Y	N	N	N
MISSOURI								
1 Clay	?	N	Y	Y	Y	Y	N	Y
2 Young	Y	Y	Y	Y	Y	N	N	N
3 Gephardt	Y	Y	Y	Y	Y	N	N	Y
4 Skelton	N	Y	N	Y	Y	N	N	N
5 Wheat	Y	?	Y	Y	Y	Y	N	Y
6 ***Coleman***	N	N	N	Y	Y	N	N	N
7 ***Taylor***	N	N	N	Y	Y	N	Y	N
8 ***Emerson***	N	N	N	Y	Y	N	Y	N
9 Volkmer	Y	Y	N	Y	Y	N	N	Y
MONTANA								
1 Williams	Y	?	Y	Y	Y	Y	N	Y
2 ***Marlenee***	N	N	N	Y	Y	N	Y	N
NEBRASKA								
1 ***Bereuter***	N	N	Y	Y	Y	N	N	N
2 ***Daub***	N	N	N	Y	Y	N	N	N
3 ***Smith***	N	Y	N	Y	Y	N	N	N
NEVADA								
1 Reid	Y	Y	Y	Y	Y	Y	N	Y
2 ***Vucanovich***	N	N	N	Y	Y	N	Y	N
NEW HAMPSHIRE								
1 ***Smith***	N	N	N	Y	Y	N	Y	N
2 ***Gregg***	N	N	N	Y	Y	N	Y	N
NEW JERSEY								
1 Florio	Y	Y	Y	Y	Y	Y	N	Y
2 Hughes	Y	Y	Y	Y	Y	Y	N	Y
3 Howard	Y	Y	Y	Y	Y	Y	N	Y
4 ***Smith***	N	Y	N	Y	Y	N	Y	N
5 ***Roukema***	N	N	N	Y	Y	N	Y	Y
6 Dwyer	Y	Y	Y	Y	Y	Y	Y	Y
7 ***Rinaldo***	N	Y	Y	Y	Y	N	N	N
8 Roe	Y	Y	Y	Y	Y	Y	N	Y
9 Torricelli	Y	Y	Y	Y	Y	Y	N	Y
10 Rodino	Y	Y	Y	Y	Y	Y	N	Y
11 ***Gallo***	N	N	N	Y	Y	N	Y	N
12 ***Courter***	N	N	N	Y	Y	Y	Y	N
13 ***Saxton***	N	N	Y	Y	Y	N	Y	N
14 Guarini	Y	Y	Y	Y	Y	Y	N	Y
NEW MEXICO								
1 ***Lujan***	N	Y	N	Y	Y	N	Y	N
2 ***Skeen***	N	N	N	Y	Y	N	Y	N
3 Richardson	Y	Y	Y	Y	Y	Y	N	Y
NEW YORK								
1 ***Carney***	N	?	N	Y	Y	N	Y	N
2 Downey	Y	?	Y	Y	Y	Y	Y	Y
3 Mrazek	Y	Y	N	Y	Y	N	Y	Y
4 ***Lent***	N	N	N	Y	Y	N	Y	N
5 ***McGrath***	N	N	N	Y	Y	N	N	N
6 Waldon	Y	P	Y	Y	Y	Y	N	Y
7 Ackerman	Y	Y	Y	Y	Y	Y	N	Y
8 Scheuer	Y	Y	Y	Y	Y	Y	Y	Y
9 Manton	Y	Y	Y	Y	Y	Y	N	Y
10 Schumer	Y	Y	Y	Y	Y	Y	N	Y
11 Towns	Y	Y	Y	Y	Y	Y	N	Y
12 Owens	Y	?	Y	Y	Y	Y	N	Y
13 Solarz	Y	Y	Y	Y	Y	Y	N	Y
14 ***Molinari***	N	N	N	Y	Y	N	Y	N
15 ***Green***	Y	Y	Y	Y	Y	Y	Y	Y
16 Rangel	Y	Y	Y	Y	Y	Y	N	Y
17 Weiss	Y	Y	Y	Y	Y	Y	N	Y
18 Garcia	Y	Y	Y	Y	Y	Y	N	Y
19 Biaggi	Y	Y	Y	Y	Y	Y	Y	Y
20 ***DioGuardi***	N	N	Y	Y	Y	Y	Y	N
21 ***Fish***	Y	N	Y	Y	Y	Y	Y	Y
22 ***Gilman***	N	Y	Y	Y	Y	N	N	N
23 Stratton	N	Y	N	Y	Y	N	N	N
24 ***Solomon***	N	N	N	Y	Y	N	Y	N
25 ***Boehlert***	Y	N	N	Y	Y	N	Y	Y
26 ***Martin***	N	Y	N	Y	Y	N	Y	N
27 ***Wortley***	N	Y	N	Y	Y	N	Y	N
28 McHugh	Y	Y	Y	Y	Y	N	N	Y
29 ***Horton***	Y	Y	Y	Y	Y	Y	Y	Y
30 ***Eckert***	N	Y	N	Y	Y	Y	Y	N
31 ***Kemp***	N	?	N	Y	Y	N	N	N
32 LaFalce	Y	Y	Y	Y	Y	Y	N	?
33 Nowak	Y	?	Y	Y	Y	Y	N	Y
34 Lundine	Y	Y	Y	Y	Y	Y	Y	Y

	302	303	304	305	306	307	308	309
NORTH CAROLINA								
1 Jones	?	Y	Y	Y	Y	Y	Y	Y
2 Valentine	N	Y	Y	Y	Y	Y	Y	N
3 Whitley	Y	Y	Y	Y	Y	Y	Y	Y
4 ***Cobey***	N	N	N	Y	Y	N	N	N
5 Neal	Y	Y	Y	Y	Y	Y	N	Y
6 ***Coble***	N	N	N	Y	Y	N	N	N
7 Rose	Y	Y	Y	Y	Y	Y	Y	Y
8 Hefner	Y	Y	Y	Y	Y	Y	Y	Y
9 ***McMillan***	N	N	N	Y	Y	N	Y	N
10 Vacancy								
11 ***Hendon***	N	N	N	Y	Y	N	Y	N
NORTH DAKOTA								
AL Dorgan	Y	Y	Y	Y	Y	Y	N	Y
OHIO								
1 Luken	Y	Y	Y	Y	Y	Y	N	Y
2 ***Gradison***	N	Y	N	Y	Y	N	N	Y
3 Hall	Y	?	Y	Y	Y	Y	N	Y
4 ***Oxley***	N	N	N	Y	Y	N	N	N
5 ***Latta***	N	Y	?	Y	?	N	N	N
6 ***McEwen***	N	Y	N	Y	Y	N	Y	N
7 ***DeWine***	N	N	N	Y	Y	N	N	N
8 ***Kindness***	N	N	N	Y	Y	N	N	N
9 Kaptur	Y	Y	Y	Y	Y	Y	N	Y
10 ***Miller***	N	N	N	Y	Y	N	Y	N
11 Eckart	Y	N	Y	Y	Y	Y	Y	Y
12 ***Kasich***	N	Y	N	Y	Y	N	N	N
13 Pease	Y	Y	Y	Y	Y	Y	Y	Y
14 Seiberling	Y	?	Y	Y	Y	Y	Y	Y
15 ***Wylie***	N	Y	N	Y	Y	N	N	N
16 ***Regula***	N	Y	N	Y	Y	N	N	Y
17 Traficant	Y	Y	Y	Y	Y	Y	Y	Y
18 Applegate	Y	Y	Y	Y	Y	N	Y	N
19 Feighan	Y	Y	Y	Y	Y	Y	N	Y
20 Oakar	Y	Y	Y	Y	Y	Y	N	Y
21 Stokes	Y	Y	Y	Y	Y	N	N	Y
OKLAHOMA								
1 Jones	Y	Y	N	Y	Y	N	N	Y
2 Synar	Y	Y	Y	Y	Y	Y	N	Y
3 Watkins	Y	Y	N	?	Y	N	N	Y
4 McCurdy	Y	Y	Y	Y	Y	N	N	Y
5 ***Edwards***	N	N	N	Y	Y	N	N	N
6 English	Y	Y	Y	Y	Y	Y	N	N
OREGON								
1 AuCoin	Y	Y	Y	Y	Y	Y	Y	Y
2 ***Smith, R.***	N	N	N	Y	Y	N	Y	N
3 Wyden	Y	Y	Y	Y	Y	Y	N	Y
4 Weaver	Y	?	Y	Y	Y	Y	N	Y
5 ***Smith, D.***	N	N	N	Y	Y	N	Y	N
PENNSYLVANIA								
1 Foglietta	Y	Y	Y	Y	Y	Y	N	Y
2 Gray	Y	Y	Y	Y	Y	Y	N	Y
3 Borski	Y	Y	Y	Y	Y	Y	Y	Y
4 Kolter	Y	Y	Y	Y	Y	Y	Y	Y
5 ***Schulze***	N	Y	Y	Y	Y	N	Y	N
6 Yatron	Y	Y	Y	Y	Y	Y	N	Y
7 Edgar	Y	Y	Y	Y	Y	Y	N	Y
8 Kostmayer	Y	Y	Y	Y	Y	Y	N	Y
9 ***Shuster***	N	N	N	Y	Y	N	Y	N
10 ***McDade***	Y	Y	Y	Y	Y	N	N	N
11 Kanjorski	Y	Y	Y	Y	Y	Y	N	Y
12 Murtha	N	Y	Y	Y	Y	Y	N	N
13 ***Coughlin***	Y	N	N	Y	Y	N	Y	Y
14 Coyne	Y	Y	Y	Y	Y	Y	Y	Y
15 ***Ritter***	N	Y	N	Y	Y	N	Y	N
16 ***Walker***	N	N	N	Y	Y	N	N	N
17 ***Gekas***	N	N	N	Y	Y	N	N	N
18 Walgren	Y	Y	Y	Y	Y	Y	N	Y
19 ***Goodling***	N	N	N	Y	Y	N	Y	N
20 Gaydos	Y	Y	Y	Y	Y	Y	Y	Y
21 ***Ridge***	N	N	Y	Y	Y	N	N	Y
22 Murphy	Y	Y	Y	Y	Y	Y	N	Y
23 ***Clinger***	Y	N	Y	Y	Y	N	N	Y
RHODE ISLAND								
1 St Germain	Y	Y	Y	Y	Y	Y	N	Y
2 ***Schneider***	Y	P	Y	Y	Y	N	Y	Y
SOUTH CAROLINA								
1 ***Hartnett***	N	N	N	Y	Y	N	Y	N
2 ***Spence***	N	N	N	Y	Y	N	Y	N
3 Derrick	Y	N	N	Y	Y	Y	N	Y
4 ***Campbell***	X	?	?	?	?	?	?	X
5 Spratt	Y	Y	Y	Y	Y	Y	Y	Y
6 Tallon	N	Y	Y	Y	Y	N	Y	N
SOUTH DAKOTA								
AL Daschle	Y	Y	Y	Y	Y	Y	N	Y

	302	303	304	305	306	307	308	309
TENNESSEE								
1 ***Quillen***	N	N	N	Y	Y	N	N	N
2 ***Duncan***	N	N	N	Y	Y	N	N	N
3 Lloyd	N	?	Y	Y	Y	N	N	N
4 Cooper	Y	Y	Y	Y	Y	N	Y	Y
5 Boner	Y	Y	Y	Y	Y	N	N	Y
6 Gordon	Y	Y	Y	Y	Y	Y	N	Y
7 ***Sundquist***	N	N	N	Y	Y	N	N	N
8 Jones	Y	Y	Y	Y	Y	Y	N	Y
9 Ford	Y	?	Y	Y	Y	Y	N	Y
TEXAS								
1 Chapman	Y	Y	N	Y	Y	Y	N	N
2 Wilson	N	N	Y	Y	Y	N	Y	N
3 ***Bartlett***	N	N	N	Y	Y	N	Y	N
4 Hall, R.	N	Y	N	Y	Y	Y	N	N
5 Bryant	Y	Y	Y	Y	Y	Y	N	Y
6 ***Barton***	N	N	N	Y	Y	N	Y	N
7 ***Archer***	N	Y	N	Y	Y	N	Y	N
8 ***Fields***	N	Y	N	Y	Y	N	N	N
9 Brooks	Y	?	Y	Y	Y	Y	N	Y
10 Pickle	N	Y	Y	Y	Y	Y	N	Y
11 Leath	Y	Y	Y	Y	Y	Y	Y	N
12 Wright	Y	Y	Y	?	Y	Y	Y	N
13 ***Boulter***	N	N	N	Y	Y	N	Y	N
14 ***Sweeney***	N	?	N	Y	Y	N	Y	N
15 de la Garza	Y	?	Y	Y	Y	Y	Y	N
16 Coleman	Y	Y	Y	Y	Y	Y	Y	N
17 Stenholm	N	Y	N	Y	Y	Y	Y	N
18 Leland	Y	Y	Y	Y	Y	Y	N	Y
19 ***Combest***	N	Y	N	Y	Y	N	N	N
20 Gonzalez	Y	Y	Y	Y	Y	Y	N	Y
21 ***Loeffler***	N	N	N	Y	Y	N	N	N
22 ***DeLay***	N	N	N	N	Y	N	Y	N
23 Bustamante	Y	Y	Y	Y	Y	Y	N	Y
24 Frost	Y	?	Y	Y	Y	Y	N	N
25 Andrews	Y	Y	Y	Y	Y	Y	N	N
26 ***Armey***	N	N	N	Y	Y	N	Y	N
27 Ortiz	Y	Y	Y	Y	Y	Y	Y	N
UTAH								
1 ***Hansen***	N	Y	N	Y	Y	N	N	N
2 ***Monson***	N	N	N	Y	Y	N	Y	N
3 ***Nielson***	N	N	N	Y	Y	N	Y	N
VERMONT								
AL ***Jeffords***	Y	Y	Y	Y	Y	Y	Y	Y
VIRGINIA								
1 ***Bateman***	N	Y	N	Y	Y	N	Y	N
2 ***Whitehurst***	N	N	N	Y	Y	N	Y	N
3 ***Bliley***	N	N	Y	Y	Y	N	Y	N
4 Sisisky	N	Y	Y	Y	Y	N	Y	N
5 Daniel	N	Y	N	Y	Y	N	Y	N
6 Olin	Y	Y	Y	Y	Y	N	N	Y
7 ***Slaughter***	N	N	N	Y	Y	N	Y	N
8 ***Parris***	N	N	N	Y	Y	N	Y	N
9 Boucher	Y	Y	Y	Y	Y	Y	N	Y
10 ***Wolf***	N	N	N	Y	Y	N	Y	N
WASHINGTON								
1 ***Miller***	N	Y	N	Y	Y	N	Y	Y
2 Swift	Y	Y	Y	Y	Y	Y	N	Y
3 Bonker	Y	?	N	Y	Y	Y	N	Y
4 ***Morrison***	N	Y	N	Y	Y	N	Y	N
5 Foley	Y	Y	Y	Y	Y	Y	N	Y
6 Dicks	Y	Y	Y	Y	Y	Y	N	Y
7 Lowry	Y	Y	Y	Y	Y	Y	N	Y
8 ***Chandler***	N	N	N	Y	Y	N	Y	Y
WEST VIRGINIA								
1 Mollohan	N	Y	Y	Y	Y	Y	N	N
2 Staggers	Y	Y	Y	Y	Y	Y	N	Y
3 Wise	Y	Y	Y	Y	Y	Y	N	Y
4 Rahall	Y	Y	Y	Y	Y	Y	N	Y
WISCONSIN								
1 Aspin	Y	Y	Y	Y	Y	N	N	Y
2 Kastenmeier	Y	Y	Y	Y	Y	Y	N	Y
3 ***Gunderson***	N	N	Y	Y	Y	N	Y	Y
4 Kleczka	Y	Y	Y	Y	Y	Y	N	Y
5 Moody	+	Y	Y	Y	Y	Y	N	Y
6 ***Petri***	N	Y	Y	Y	Y	N	N	N
7 Obey	Y	Y	Y	Y	Y	Y	N	Y
8 ***Roth***	N	N	N	Y	Y	N	Y	N
9 ***Sensenbrenner***	N	N	Y	Y	Y	N	N	N
WYOMING								
AL ***Cheney***	N	N	N	Y	Y	N	N	N

Southern states - Ala., Ark., Fla., Ga., Ky., La., Miss., N.C., Okla., S.C., Tenn., Texas, Va.

* The *Congressional Record* vote number is different from the CQ vote number because the *Record* includes quorum calls in its tally. CQ does not publish quorum call votes.

310. HR 4428. Defense Authorization, Fiscal 1987. Dellums, D-Calif., amendment to reduce total defense outlays for fiscal 1987 to $255.4 billion. Rejected 56-365: R 0-176; D 56-189 (ND 51-116, SD 5-73), Aug. 13, 1986. A "nay" was a vote supporting the president's position.

311. HR 4428. Defense Authorization, Fiscal 1987. Porter, R-Ill., amendment to prohibit the production of binary chemical weapons before Oct. 1, 1987. Adopted 210-209: R 38-137; D 172-72 (ND 142-23, SD 30-49), Aug. 13, 1986. A "nay" was a vote supporting the president's position.

312. HR 4428. Defense Authorization, Fiscal 1987. Courter, R-N.J., amendment to require the secretary of defense to reorient the strategic defense initiative ("star wars") to develop an anti-missile defense that could be deployed quickly and would be consistent with the 1972 treaty limiting anti-missile defenses. Rejected 124-293: R 115-59; D 9-234 (ND 3-162, SD 6-72), Aug. 13, 1986.

313. HR 4428. Defense Authorization, Fiscal 1987. Broomfield, R-Mich., amendment to increase by $3 million the amount earmarked for Air Force research and to earmark $9.85 million for development of technologies that could be used to verify nuclear weapons treaties. Adopted 411-0: R 171-0; D 240-0 (ND 162-0, SD 78-0), Aug. 13, 1986.

314. HR 4428. Defense Authorization, Fiscal 1987. Dornan, R-Calif., amendment to require that the conventional defense initiative be administered by the office administering the strategic defense initiative, or "star wars." Rejected 89-309: R 86-82; D 3-227 (ND 1-156, SD 2-71), Aug. 13, 1986.

315. HR 4428. Defense Authorization, Fiscal 1987. Schroeder, D-Colo., amendment to require the withdrawal over a five-year period of one-half the U.S. ground troops currently stationed in Europe and one-third of the U.S. ground troops currently stationed elsewhere abroad and to demobilize half the forces withdrawn. Rejected 90-322: R 14-159; D 76-163 (ND 65-98, SD 11-65), Aug. 13, 1986. A "nay" was a vote supporting the president's position.

KEY

Y Voted for (yea).
Paired for.
+ Announced for.
N Voted against (nay).
X Paired against.
- Announced against.
P Voted "present."
C Voted "present" to avoid possible conflict of interest.
? Did not vote or otherwise make a position known.

Democrats ***Republicans***

	310	311	312	313	314	315
ALABAMA						
1 ***Callahan***	N	N	N	Y	Y	N
2 ***Dickinson***	N	N	N	Y	Y	N
3 Nichols	N	N	N	Y	N	N
4 Bevill	N	N	N	Y	N	N
5 Flippo	?	?	?	?	?	?
6 Erdreich	N	Y	N	Y	N	N
7 Shelby	N	N	N	Y	N	N
ALASKA						
AL ***Young***	N	N	Y	Y	N	N
ARIZONA						
1 ***McCain***	N	N	N	Y	Y	N
2 Udall	N	Y	N	Y	N	Y
3 ***Stump***	N	N	Y	Y	N	N
4 ***Rudd***	N	N	Y	Y	N	N
5 ***Kolbe***	N	Y	Y	Y	N	N
ARKANSAS						
1 Alexander	N	N	N	Y	X	Y
2 Robinson	N	N	Y	Y	Y	Y
3 ***Hammerschmidt***	N	N	Y	Y	Y	N
4 Anthony	N	N	N	Y	?	N
CALIFORNIA						
1 Bosco	N	N	N	?	N	?
2 ***Chappie***	N	N	Y	Y	Y	N
3 Matsui	N	Y	N	Y	N	N
4 Fazio	N	N	N	Y	N	N
5 Burton	?	?	?	?	?	?
6 Boxer	Y	Y	N	Y	N	Y
7 Miller	Y	Y	N	Y	N	Y
8 Dellums	Y	Y	N	Y	N	Y
9 Stark	Y	Y	N	Y	?	Y
10 Edwards	Y	Y	N	Y	N	Y
11 Lantos	N	Y	N	Y	N	N
12 ***Zschau***	N	N	N	Y	N	N
13 Mineta	N	Y	N	Y	N	Y
14 ***Shumway***	N	N	Y	Y	Y	N
15 Coelho	N	Y	N	Y	X	Y
16 Panetta	N	Y	N	Y	N	N
17 ***Pashayan***	N	N	Y	Y	N	N
18 Lehman	N	Y	N	Y	N	N
19 ***Lagomarsino***	N	N	N	Y	Y	N
20 ***Thomas***	N	N	Y	Y	Y	N
21 ***Fiedler***	N	N	Y	Y	?	N
22 ***Moorhead***	N	N	Y	Y	Y	N
23 Beilenson	Y	Y	N	Y	N	Y
24 Waxman	Y	Y	N	Y	?	N
25 Roybal	Y	Y	N	Y	N	Y
26 Berman	Y	Y	N	Y	N	Y
27 Levine	N	Y	N	Y	?	Y
28 Dixon	Y	Y	N	Y	N	Y
29 Hawkins	N	Y	N	?	N	Y
30 Martinez	N	Y	N	Y	N	Y
31 Dymally	Y	Y	N	Y	N	Y
32 Anderson	N	Y	N	Y	N	Y
33 ***Dreier***	N	N	Y	Y	Y	N
34 Torres	N	Y	N	Y	N	Y
35 ***Lewis***	N	N	Y	Y	?	N
36 Brown	N	Y	N	Y	N	Y
37 ***McCandless***	N	N	Y	Y	Y	N
38 ***Dornan***	N	N	Y	Y	Y	N
39 ***Dannemeyer***	N	N	Y	Y	Y	N
40 ***Badham***	N	N	N	Y	?	N
41 ***Lowery***	N	N	Y	Y	Y	N
42 ***Lungren***	N	N	Y	Y	Y	N
43 ***Packard***	N	N	Y	Y	Y	N
44 Bates	N	Y	N	Y	N	Y
45 ***Hunter***	N	N	Y	Y	Y	N
COLORADO						
1 Schroeder	Y	Y	N	Y	N	Y
2 Wirth	N	Y	N	Y	N	N
3 ***Strang***	N	N	N	Y	Y	Y
4 ***Brown***	N	Y	Y	Y	Y	Y
5 ***Kramer***	N	N	N	Y	N	N
6 ***Schaefer***	N	N	Y	Y	N	N
CONNECTICUT						
1 Kennelly	N	Y	N	Y	N	N
2 Gejdenson	N	Y	N	Y	N	N
3 Morrison	?	?	?	?	?	?
4 ***McKinney***	N	Y	N	Y	N	N
5 ***Rowland***	N	N	Y	Y	Y	N
6 ***Johnson***	N	N	N	Y	N	N
DELAWARE						
AL Carper	N	N	N	Y	N	N
FLORIDA						
1 Hutto	N	N	N	Y	N	N
2 Fuqua	N	N	N	Y	N	N
3 Bennett	N	Y	N	Y	N	N
4 Chappell	N	N	N	Y	N	N
5 ***McCollum***	N	N	Y	Y	N	N
6 MacKay	N	Y	N	Y	N	N
7 Gibbons	N	N	N	Y	N	N
8 ***Young***	N	N	Y	Y	N	N
9 ***Bilirakis***	N	N	Y	Y	N	N
10 ***Ireland***	N	N	Y	Y	Y	?
11 Nelson	N	N	N	Y	N	N
12 ***Lewis***	N	Y	Y	Y	N	N
13 ***Mack***	N	N	Y	Y	Y	N
14 Mica	N	Y	N	Y	N	N
15 ***Shaw***	N	N	N	Y	N	N
16 Smith	N	Y	N	Y	N	N
17 Lehman	Y	Y	N	Y	N	Y
18 Pepper	N	Y	N	Y	N	N
19 Fascell	N	Y	N	Y	N	N
GEORGIA						
1 Thomas	N	N	N	Y	N	N
2 Hatcher	N	N	N	Y	N	?
3 Ray	N	N	N	Y	N	N
4 ***Swindall***	N	N	Y	Y	Y	N
5 Fowler	?	?	?	?	?	?
6 ***Gingrich***	N	N	Y	Y	Y	N
7 Darden	N	N	N	Y	N	N
8 Rowland	N	N	N	Y	N	N
9 Jenkins	N	Y	N	Y	?	N
10 Barnard	N	N	N	Y	N	N
HAWAII						
1 Vacancy						
2 Akaka	N	Y	N	Y	N	N
IDAHO						
1 ***Craig***	N	N	Y	Y	N	N
2 Stallings	N	Y	Y	Y	N	N
ILLINOIS						
1 Hayes	Y	Y	N	Y	N	Y
2 Savage	Y	Y	N	Y	N	Y
3 Russo	N	Y	N	Y	N	N
4 Vacancy						
5 Lipinski	N	N	N	Y	N	N
6 ***Hyde***	N	N	Y	Y	Y	N
7 Collins	Y	Y	N	Y	N	Y
8 Rostenkowski	N	Y	N	Y	N	N
9 Yates	Y	Y	N	Y	?	?
10 ***Porter***	N	Y	N	Y	N	N
11 Annunzio	N	Y	N	Y	N	N
12 ***Crane***	N	N	Y	Y	Y	N
13 ***Fawell***	N	N	N	Y	N	N
14 ***Grotberg***	?	?	?	?	?	?
15 ***Madigan***	N	N	Y	Y	N	N
16 ***Martin***	N	Y	Y	Y	N	Y
17 Evans	N	Y	N	Y	N	Y
18 ***Michel***	N	N	Y	Y	Y	N
19 Bruce	N	Y	N	Y	N	Y
20 Durbin	N	Y	N	Y	N	Y
21 Price	N	N	N	Y	N	N
22 Gray	N	N	N	Y	N	N
INDIANA						
1 Visclosky	N	Y	N	Y	N	N
2 Sharp	N	?	?	Y	N	N
3 ***Hiler***	N	N	Y	Y	N	N
4 ***Coats***	N	Y	Y	Y	N	N
5 ***Hillis***	?	?	?	?	?	?

ND - Northern Democrats SD - Southern Democrats

* Corresponding to Congressional Record Votes 338, 339, 340, 341, 342, 343

	310	311	312	313	314	315
6 ***Burton***	N	N	Y	Y	Y	N
7 ***Myers***	N	N	Y	Y	N	N
8 McCloskey	N	N	N	Y	N	N
9 Hamilton	N	N	N	Y	N	N
10 Jacobs	N	Y	N	Y	N	Y
IOWA						
1 ***Leach***	N	Y	N	Y	N	N
2 ***Tauke***	N	Y	Y	Y	N	Y
3 ***Evans***	N	N	Y	Y	Y	N
4 Smith	N	Y	N	Y	N	N
5 ***Lightfoot***	N	N	N	Y	N	N
6 Bedell	Y	Y	N	Y	N	Y
KANSAS						
1 ***Roberts***	N	N	N	Y	N	N
2 Slattery	N	N	N	?	N	N
3 ***Meyers***	N	Y	N	Y	N	N
4 Glickman	N	N	N	?	N	N
5 ***Whittaker***	N	N	N	Y	Y	N
KENTUCKY						
1 Hubbard	N	N	Y	Y	N	N
2 Natcher	N	Y	N	Y	N	N
3 Mazzoli	N	Y	N	Y	N	N
4 ***Snyder***	N	N	N	Y	Y	N
5 ***Rogers***	N	N	Y	Y	Y	N
6 ***Hopkins***	N	N	Y	Y	N	N
7 Perkins	Y	Y	N	Y	N	N
LOUISIANA						
1 ***Livingston***	N	N	Y	Y	Y	N
2 Boggs	N	Y	N	Y	?	?
3 Tauzin	N	N	Y	Y	N	N
4 Roemer	N	N	Y	Y	N	N
5 Huckaby	N	Y	N	Y	N	N
6 ***Moore***	?	?	?	?	?	?
7 Breaux	?	?	?	?	?	?
8 Long	N	Y	N	Y	N	Y
MAINE						
1 ***McKernan***	N	Y	N	Y	N	N
2 ***Snowe***	N	Y	N	Y	N	N
MARYLAND						
1 Dyson	N	N	N	Y	N	N
2 ***Bentley***	N	N	N	Y	N	N
3 Mikulski	N	Y	N	Y	?	?
4 ***Holt***	N	N	N	Y	N	N
5 Hoyer	N	Y	N	Y	N	N
6 Byron	N	N	N	Y	N	N
7 Mitchell	Y	Y	N	Y	N	Y
8 Barnes	N	Y	N	?	?	N
MASSACHUSETTS						
1 ***Conte***	N	Y	N	Y	N	N
2 Boland	N	Y	N	Y	N	N
3 Early	N	Y	N	Y	N	Y
4 Frank	Y	Y	N	Y	N	Y
5 Atkins	N	Y	N	Y	N	Y
6 Mavroules	N	Y	N	Y	N	N
7 Markey	Y	Y	N	Y	N	Y
8 O'Neill						
9 Moakley	N	Y	N	Y	N	N
10 Studds	Y	Y	N	Y	N	Y
11 Donnelly	N	Y	N	Y	N	Y
MICHIGAN						
1 Conyers	Y	Y	N	Y	N	Y
2 ***Pursell***	N	Y	Y	Y	N	N
3 Wolpe	N	Y	N	Y	N	N
4 ***Siljander***	N	N	Y	Y	Y	N
5 ***Henry***	N	Y	N	Y	N	N
6 Carr	N	Y	N	Y	N	N
7 Kildee	Y	Y	N	Y	N	N
8 Traxler	N	Y	N	Y	?	N
9 ***Vander Jagt***	N	N	N	Y	Y	N
10 ***Schuette***	N	N	N	Y	Y	N
11 ***Davis***	N	N	N	Y	Y	N
12 Bonior	Y	Y	N	Y	N	Y
13 Crockett	Y	Y	N	Y	N	Y
14 Hertel	N	Y	N	Y	N	N
15 Ford	Y	?	N	Y	N	N
16 Dingell	N	N	N	Y	N	N
17 Levin	N	Y	N	Y	N	N
18 ***Broomfield***	N	N	Y	Y	Y	N
MINNESOTA						
1 Penny	N	Y	N	Y	N	N
2 ***Weber***	N	Y	Y	Y	Y	N
3 ***Frenzel***	N	N	?	Y	N	N
4 Vento	N	Y	N	Y	N	N
5 Sabo	Y	Y	N	Y	N	N
6 Sikorski	N	Y	N	Y	N	Y
7 ***Stangeland***	N	N	Y	?	N	N
8 Oberstar	Y	Y	N	Y	N	N
MISSISSIPPI						
1 Whitten	N	Y	N	Y	N	?
2 ***Franklin***	N	N	Y	Y	Y	N
3 Montgomery	N	N	N	Y	N	N
4 Dowdy	N	N	N	Y	N	N
5 ***Lott***	N	N	Y	Y	N	?
MISSOURI						
1 Clay	Y	Y	N	Y	N	Y
2 Young	N	N	N	Y	N	N
3 Gephardt	N	Y	N	Y	N	N
4 Skelton	N	N	N	Y	N	N
5 Wheat	Y	Y	N	Y	N	Y
6 ***Coleman***	N	N	Y	Y	N	N
7 ***Taylor***	N	N	Y	Y	Y	N
8 ***Emerson***	N	N	Y	Y	N	N
9 Volkmer	N	N	N	Y	N	N
MONTANA						
1 Williams	Y	Y	N	Y	?	N
2 ***Marlenee***	N	N	Y	Y	Y	N
NEBRASKA						
1 ***Bereuter***	N	N	Y	Y	N	N
2 ***Daub***	N	N	Y	Y	N	N
3 ***Smith***	N	N	Y	Y	N	N
NEVADA						
1 Reid	N	Y	N	Y	N	N
2 ***Vucanovich***	N	N	Y	Y	N	N
NEW HAMPSHIRE						
1 ***Smith***	N	N	Y	Y	Y	N
2 ***Gregg***	N	Y	Y	Y	Y	N
NEW JERSEY						
1 Florio	N	Y	N	Y	N	Y
2 Hughes	N	Y	N	Y	N	N
3 Howard	N	Y	N	Y	N	N
4 ***Smith***	N	Y	Y	Y	N	N
5 ***Roukema***	N	Y	N	Y	N	N
6 Dwyer	N	Y	N	Y	N	N
7 ***Rinaldo***	N	Y	Y	Y	N	N
8 Roe	N	Y	N	Y	N	N
9 Torricelli	N	Y	N	Y	N	N
10 Rodino	Y	Y	N	Y	N	Y
11 ***Gallo***	N	N	Y	Y	Y	N
12 ***Courter***	N	N	Y	Y	Y	N
13 ***Saxton***	N	N	N	Y	N	N
14 Guarini	N	Y	N	Y	N	N
NEW MEXICO						
1 ***Lujan***	N	N	Y	Y	Y	N
2 ***Skeen***	N	N	Y	Y	Y	N
3 Richardson	N	Y	N	Y	N	N
NEW YORK						
1 ***Carney***	N	N	Y	Y	N	Y
2 Downey	N	Y	N	Y	N	N
3 Mrazek	N	Y	N	Y	N	Y
4 ***Lent***	N	N	N	Y	Y	N
5 ***McGrath***	N	Y	N	Y	N	N
6 Waldon	Y	Y	N	Y	N	N
7 Ackerman	Y	Y	N	Y	N	N
8 Scheuer	Y	Y	Y	Y	N	Y
9 Manton	N	Y	N	Y	N	N
10 Schumer	N	Y	N	Y	N	N
11 Towns	Y	Y	N	Y	N	Y
12 Owens	Y	Y	N	Y	N	Y
13 Solarz	N	Y	N	Y	N	N
14 ***Molinari***	N	Y	Y	Y	Y	N
15 ***Green***	N	Y	N	Y	N	N
16 Rangel	Y	Y	N	Y	N	Y
17 Weiss	Y	Y	N	Y	N	N
18 Garcia	Y	Y	N	Y	N	N
19 Biaggi	N	Y	N	Y	N	N
20 ***DioGuardi***	N	N	Y	Y	N	N
21 ***Fish***	N	Y	N	Y	N	N
22 ***Gilman***	N	N	N	Y	Y	N
23 Stratton	N	N	Y	Y	Y	N
24 ***Solomon***	N	N	Y	Y	Y	N
25 ***Boehlert***	N	N	N	Y	N	N
26 ***Martin***	N	N	N	Y	N	N
27 ***Wortley***	N	Y	N	Y	N	N
28 McHugh	N	Y	N	Y	N	N
29 ***Horton***	N	Y	N	Y	N	N
30 ***Eckert***	N	N	Y	Y	Y	Y
31 ***Kemp***	N	N	Y	Y	Y	N
32 LaFalce	N	Y	N	Y	N	N
33 Nowak	N	Y	N	Y	N	N
34 Lundine	Y	Y	N	Y	N	Y
NORTH CAROLINA						
1 Jones	N	N	N	Y	N	N
2 Valentine	N	N	N	Y	N	N
3 Whitley	N	N	N	Y	N	N
4 ***Cobey***	N	N	Y	Y	Y	N
5 Neal	N	N	N	Y	N	N
6 ***Coble***	N	Y	Y	Y	Y	N
7 Rose	N	N	N	Y	N	N
8 Hefner	N	N	N	Y	N	N
9 ***McMillan***	N	N	N	Y	Y	N
10 Vacancy						
11 ***Hendon***	N	N	Y	Y	Y	N
NORTH DAKOTA						
AL Dorgan	N	Y	N	Y	N	Y
OHIO						
1 Luken	N	Y	N	Y	N	N
2 ***Gradison***	N	Y	Y	Y	N	N
3 Hall	N	Y	N	Y	N	N
4 ***Oxley***	N	N	Y	?	#	N
5 ***Latta***	N	N	Y	Y	Y	N
6 ***McEwen***	N	N	Y	Y	Y	Y
7 ***DeWine***	N	N	Y	Y	Y	N
8 ***Kindness***	N	N	Y	Y	Y	N
9 Kaptur	N	Y	N	Y	N	N
10 ***Miller***	N	N	Y	Y	Y	N
11 Eckart	N	Y	N	Y	N	Y
12 ***Kasich***	N	N	Y	Y	Y	N
13 Pease	N	Y	N	Y	N	N
14 Seiberling	Y	Y	?	Y	N	N
15 ***Wylie***	N	N	N	Y	N	N
16 ***Regula***	N	Y	N	Y	Y	N
17 Traficant	Y	Y	N	Y	N	Y
18 Applegate	N	Y	N	Y	N	Y
19 Feighan	N	Y	N	Y	N	N
20 Oakar	Y	Y	N	Y	N	Y
21 Stokes	Y	Y	N	Y	N	Y
OKLAHOMA						
1 Jones	N	N	N	Y	N	N
2 Synar	N	Y	N	Y	N	N
3 Watkins	N	N	N	Y	?	N
4 McCurdy	N	N	N	Y	N	N
5 ***Edwards***	N	N	Y	?	N	N
6 English	N	N	N	Y	N	N
OREGON						
1 AuCoin	N	Y	N	Y	N	N
2 ***Smith, R.***	N	Y	Y	Y	Y	N
3 Wyden	N	Y	N	Y	N	N
4 Weaver	Y	Y	N	Y	N	Y
5 ***Smith, D.***	N	N	Y	Y	N	Y
PENNSYLVANIA						
1 Foglietta	N	Y	N	Y	N	N
2 Gray	Y	Y	N	Y	?	Y
3 Borski	N	Y	N	Y	N	N
4 Kolter	N	Y	N	Y	N	N
5 ***Schulze***	N	N	N	Y	?	N
6 Yatron	N	Y	N	Y	N	N
7 Edgar	N	Y	N	Y	N	N
8 Kostmayer	N	Y	N	Y	N	Y
9 ***Shuster***	N	N	Y	Y	Y	Y
10 ***McDade***	N	N	N	Y	?	N
11 Kanjorski	N	Y	N	Y	N	N
12 Murtha	N	N	N	Y	N	N
13 ***Coughlin***	N	Y	N	Y	N	N
14 Coyne	Y	Y	N	Y	N	N
15 ***Ritter***	N	N	Y	Y	N	N
16 ***Walker***	N	N	Y	Y	Y	N
17 ***Gekas***	N	N	Y	Y	Y	N
18 Walgren	N	Y	N	Y	N	Y
19 ***Goodling***	N	Y	Y	Y	N	N
20 Gaydos	N	N	N	Y	N	N
21 ***Ridge***	N	N	N	Y	N	N
22 Murphy	N	N	N	Y	N	Y
23 ***Clinger***	N	Y	N	Y	N	N
RHODE ISLAND						
1 St Germain	N	Y	N	Y	N	N
2 ***Schneider***	N	Y	N	Y	N	N
SOUTH CAROLINA						
1 ***Hartnett***	N	?	?	?	?	?
2 ***Spence***	N	N	Y	Y	Y	N
3 Derrick	N	Y	N	Y	N	N
4 ***Campbell***	?	?	?	?	#	?
5 Spratt	N	N	N	Y	N	N
6 Tallon	N	N	N	Y	N	N
SOUTH DAKOTA						
AL Daschle	N	Y	N	Y	N	N
TENNESSEE						
1 ***Quillen***	N	N	Y	Y	N	N
2 ***Duncan***	N	N	Y	Y	Y	N
3 Lloyd	N	N	N	Y	N	N
4 Cooper	N	Y	N	Y	N	N
5 Boner	N	N	N	?	N	N
6 Gordon	N	Y	N	Y	N	N
7 ***Sundquist***	N	N	Y	Y	Y	N
8 Jones	N	N	N	Y	N	N
9 Ford	Y	Y	N	Y	N	Y
TEXAS						
1 Chapman	N	N	N	Y	N	N
2 Wilson	?	N	Y	Y	N	N
3 ***Bartlett***	N	N	Y	Y	Y	N
4 Hall, R.	N	N	N	Y	Y	Y
5 Bryant	N	Y	N	Y	N	Y
6 ***Barton***	N	N	Y	Y	Y	N
7 ***Archer***	N	N	Y	Y	Y	N
8 ***Fields***	N	N	Y	Y	Y	N
9 Brooks	N	Y	?	Y	N	N
10 Pickle	N	Y	N	Y	N	N
11 Leath	N	N	N	Y	N	N
12 Wright	N	Y	N	Y	N	N
13 ***Boulter***	N	N	Y	Y	Y	Y
14 ***Sweeney***	N	N	N	Y	N	N
15 de la Garza	N	N	N	Y	N	Y
16 Coleman	N	N	N	Y	N	N
17 Stenholm	N	N	Y	Y	N	Y
18 Leland	Y	Y	N	Y	N	Y
19 ***Combest***	N	N	Y	Y	Y	N
20 Gonzalez	Y	Y	N	Y	N	Y
21 ***Loeffler***	N	N	Y	?	?	N
22 ***DeLay***	N	N	Y	Y	Y	Y
23 Bustamante	N	N	N	Y	?	N
24 Frost	N	Y	N	Y	N	N
25 Andrews	N	N	N	Y	N	N
26 ***Armey***	N	N	Y	Y	Y	N
27 Ortiz	N	N	N	Y	N	N
UTAH						
1 ***Hansen***	N	N	Y	Y	Y	N
2 ***Monson***	N	N	Y	Y	Y	N
3 ***Nielson***	N	N	N	Y	N	Y
VERMONT						
AL ***Jeffords***	N	Y	N	Y	N	N
VIRGINIA						
1 ***Bateman***	N	N	N	Y	N	N
2 ***Whitehurst***	N	N	N	Y	N	N
3 ***Bliley***	N	N	N	Y	N	N
4 Sisisky	N	N	N	Y	N	N
5 Daniel	N	N	N	Y	N	N
6 Olin	N	Y	N	Y	N	N
7 ***Slaughter***	N	N	Y	Y	Y	N
8 ***Parris***	N	N	N	Y	N	N
9 Boucher	N	Y	N	Y	N	N
10 ***Wolf***	N	N	Y	Y	N	N
WASHINGTON						
1 ***Miller***	N	Y	Y	Y	Y	N
2 Swift	N	Y	N	Y	N	N
3 Bonker	N	Y	N	Y	N	N
4 ***Morrison***	N	N	Y	Y	N	N
5 Foley	N	Y	N	Y	N	N
6 Dicks	N	N	N	Y	N	N
7 Lowry	Y	Y	N	Y	N	Y
8 ***Chandler***	N	N	N	Y	Y	N
WEST VIRGINIA						
1 Mollohan	N	N	N	Y	N	N
2 Staggers	N	Y	N	Y	N	Y
3 Wise	N	Y	N	Y	N	N
4 Rahall	N	Y	N	Y	N	?
WISCONSIN						
1 Aspin	N	N	N	Y	N	N
2 Kastenmeier	Y	Y	N	Y	N	Y
3 ***Gunderson***	N	Y	N	Y	N	N
4 Kleczka	N	Y	N	Y	N	N
5 Moody	Y	Y	N	Y	N	Y
6 ***Petri***	N	N	N	Y	N	Y
7 Obey	N	Y	N	Y	N	Y
8 ***Roth***	N	N	Y	Y	N	N
9 ***Sensenbrenner***	N	Y	N	Y	N	Y
WYOMING						
AL ***Cheney***	N	N	Y	Y	Y	N

Southern states - Ala., Ark., Fla., Ga., Ky., La., Miss., N.C., Okla., S.C., Tenn., Texas, Va.

* The *Congressional Record* vote number is different from the CQ vote number because the *Record* includes quorum calls in its tally. CQ does not publish quorum call votes.

316. HR 4428. Defense Authorization, Fiscal 1987. Robinson, D-Ark., amendment to require the Defense Department to buy alcoholic beverages for military installations from suppliers located in the same state as the installation. Rejected 149-265: R 55-118; D 94-147 (ND 62-104, SD 32-43), Aug. 14, 1986.

317. HR 4428. Defense Authorization, Fiscal 1987. Kaptur, D-Ohio, amendment to require the Defense Department to spend at least $10 million in fiscal 1987 on cargo transportation on the Great Lakes. Rejected 165-256: R 47-128; D 118-128 (ND 96-71, SD 22-57), Aug. 14, 1986.

318. HR 4428. Defense Authorization, Fiscal 1987. Montgomery, D-Miss., amendment to prevent governors from blocking overseas training programs for National Guard troops because of objections to the location, purpose, type or schedule of the programs. Adopted 261-159: R 164-10; D 97-149 (ND 35-133, SD 62-16), Aug. 14, 1986.

319. HR 4428. Defense Authorization, Fiscal 1987. Hunter, R-Calif., amendment to direct the Navy to perform overhauls of aircraft carriers at installations on the same coast as the carrier's home port. Rejected 69-350: R 43-131; D 26-219 (ND 26-140, SD 0-79), Aug. 14, 1986.

320. HR 5395. Temporary Debt Limit Increase. Pepper, D-Fla., motion to order the previous question (thus ending debate and the possibility of amendment) on the rule (H Res 534) to provide for House floor consideration of the bill to raise the ceiling on the federal debt to $2.152 trillion, from $2.079 trillion. The increase would be enough, under current estimates, to last through Sept. 25, 1986. Motion agreed to 244-178: R 0-176; D 244-2 (ND 166-2, SD 78-0), Aug. 14, 1986. (The rule subsequently was adopted by voice vote.)

321. HR 5395. Temporary Debt Limit Increase. Passage of the bill to increase the ceiling on the federal debt to $2.152 trillion, from $2.079 trillion. The increase would be enough, under current estimates, to last through Sept. 25, 1986. Passed 216-199: R 19-155; D 197-44 (ND 141-25, SD 56-19), Aug. 14, 1986.

322. HR 4428. Defense Authorization, Fiscal 1987. Solomon, R-N.Y., amendment to bar anyone from performing services under a Pentagon contract who is required to register with the Selective Service but has not registered. Adopted 284-120: R 164-6; D 120-114 (ND 62-100, SD 58-14), Aug. 14, 1986.

323. HR 4428. Defense Authorization, Fiscal 1987. Savage, D-Ill., amendment to increase from 5 percent to 10 percent the proportion of Pentagon contracts that must go to minority-controlled businesses. Adopted 259-135: R 57-108; D 202-27 (ND 147-12, SD 55-15), Aug. 14, 1986.

KEY

Y Voted for (yea).
\# Paired for.
\+ Announced for.
N Voted against (nay).
X Paired against.
\- Announced against.
P Voted "present."
C Voted "present" to avoid possible conflict of interest.
? Did not vote or otherwise make a position known.

Democrats ***Republicans***

	316	317	318	319	320	321	322	323
ALABAMA								
1 ***Callahan***	Y	N	Y	N	N	N	Y	N
2 ***Dickinson***	N	N	Y	N	N	N	Y	N
3 Nichols	N	N	Y	N	Y	Y	Y	N
4 Bevill	Y	N	Y	N	Y	Y	Y	Y
5 Flippo	?	?	?	?	?	?	?	?
6 Erdreich	Y	N	Y	N	Y	Y	?	?
7 Shelby	Y	N	Y	N	?	?	?	?
ALASKA								
AL ***Young***	N	N	Y	Y	N	N	Y	Y
ARIZONA								
1 ***McCain***	C	N	Y	N	N	N	Y	Y
2 Udall	Y	Y	N	N	Y	Y	N	Y
3 ***Stump***	Y	N	Y	N	N	N	Y	N
4 ***Rudd***	N	N	Y	N	N	N	Y	N
5 ***Kolbe***	N	N	Y	N	N	N	Y	Y
ARKANSAS								
1 Alexander	N	N	Y	N	Y	Y	Y	Y
2 Robinson	Y	N	Y	N	Y	N	Y	Y
3 ***Hammerschmidt***	Y	N	Y	?	N	N	Y	Y
4 Anthony	Y	N	?	N	Y	Y	Y	Y
CALIFORNIA								
1 Bosco	N	N	N	Y	Y	?	N	Y
2 ***Chappie***	Y	N	Y	Y	N	N	Y	N
3 Matsui	Y	N	N	Y	Y	Y	N	Y
4 Fazio	Y	N	N	Y	Y	Y	Y	Y
5 Burton	Y	Y	N	Y	Y	Y	?	?
6 Boxer	Y	Y	N	Y	Y	Y	N	Y
7 Miller	N	Y	N	Y	Y	Y	N	Y
8 Dellums	N	Y	N	Y	Y	Y	N	Y
9 Stark	N	Y	N	Y	Y	Y	N	Y
10 Edwards	N	Y	N	N	Y	Y	N	Y
11 Lantos	N	N	N	Y	Y	Y	Y	Y
12 ***Zschau***	N	N	N	Y	N	N	?	?
13 Mineta	N	N	N	N	Y	Y	N	Y
14 ***Shumway***	N	N	Y	Y	N	N	Y	N
15 Coelho	Y	Y	N	N	Y	Y	Y	Y
16 Panetta	N	N	N	Y	Y	Y	N	Y
17 ***Pashayan***	N	N	Y	Y	N	N	Y	Y
18 Lehman	N	Y	N	Y	Y	Y	N	Y
19 ***Lagomarsino***	P	N	Y	Y	N	N	Y	N
20 ***Thomas***	N	N	Y	Y	N	N	Y	N
21 ***Fiedler***	N	N	Y	Y	N	N	Y	N
22 ***Moorhead***	N	N	Y	Y	N	N	Y	N
23 Beilenson	N	N	N	N	Y	Y	N	Y
24 Waxman	N	Y	N	?	Y	Y	N	Y
25 Roybal	N	N	N	Y	Y	Y	N	Y
26 Berman	N	N	N	N	Y	Y	N	Y
27 Levine	Y	Y	N	N	Y	Y	N	Y
28 Dixon	N	Y	N	Y	Y	Y	N	Y
29 Hawkins	N	Y	N	N	Y	Y	N	Y
30 Martinez	Y	Y	N	N	Y	Y	N	Y
31 Dymally	?	N	N	Y	Y	Y	N	Y
32 Anderson	N	N	N	Y	Y	N	N	Y
33 ***Dreier***	N	N	Y	Y	N	N	Y	N
34 Torres	Y	N	N	Y	Y	Y	N	Y
35 ***Lewis***	Y	Y	Y	Y	N	N	Y	N
36 Brown	N	Y	N	N	Y	Y	N	Y
37 ***McCandless***	N	N	Y	Y	N	N	Y	N
38 ***Dornan***	Y	N	Y	Y	N	N	Y	N
39 ***Dannemeyer***	Y	N	Y	Y	N	N	Y	N
40 ***Badham***	N	N	Y	Y	N	N	Y	Y
41 ***Lowery***	N	N	N	Y	N	N	?	?
42 ***Lungren***	N	N	Y	Y	N	N	Y	N
43 ***Packard***	N	N	Y	Y	N	N	Y	N
44 Bates	N	N	N	Y	Y	N	Y	Y
45 ***Hunter***	Y	N	Y	Y	N	N	Y	Y
COLORADO								
1 Schroeder	N	N	N	N	Y	Y	N	Y
2 Wirth	N	N	N	N	Y	Y	N	Y
3 ***Strang***	Y	N	Y	N	N	N	Y	Y
4 ***Brown***	N	N	N	Y	N	N	Y	N
5 ***Kramer***	N	N	Y	N	N	N	Y	N
6 ***Schaefer***	N	N	Y	Y	N	N	Y	?
CONNECTICUT								
1 Kennelly	N	Y	N	N	Y	Y	Y	Y
2 Gejdenson	Y	Y	N	N	Y	N	Y	Y
3 Morrison	?	?	?	?	?	?	?	?
4 ***McKinney***	N	N	N	N	N	Y	N	Y
5 ***Rowland***	N	Y	Y	N	N	N	Y	N
6 ***Johnson***	N	Y	Y	N	N	Y	Y	N
DELAWARE								
AL Carper	Y	N	Y	N	Y	Y	Y	Y
FLORIDA								
1 Hutto	P	N	Y	N	Y	N	Y	N
2 Fuqua	N	N	Y	N	Y	?	?	?
3 Bennett	N	N	Y	N	Y	Y	Y	Y
4 Chappell	N	N	Y	N	Y	N	?	?
5 ***McCollum***	N	N	Y	N	N	N	Y	N
6 MacKay	N	N	Y	N	Y	Y	Y	Y
7 Gibbons	N	N	Y	N	Y	Y	Y	N
8 ***Young***	N	N	N	Y	N	N	Y	N
9 ***Bilirakis***	N	N	Y	N	N	N	Y	Y
10 ***Ireland***	N	N	Y	N	N	N	Y	?
11 Nelson	N	N	Y	N	Y	Y	Y	N
12 ***Lewis***	N	N	Y	N	N	N	Y	Y
13 ***Mack***	N	N	Y	N	N	N	Y	N
14 Mica	N	N	Y	N	Y	Y	Y	Y
15 ***Shaw***	N	N	Y	N	N	N	Y	N
16 Smith	Y	N	N	N	Y	Y	Y	Y
17 Lehman	N	Y	N	N	Y	?	N	Y
18 Pepper	Y	N	Y	N	Y	Y	N	Y
19 Fascell	N	N	Y	N	Y	Y	N	Y
GEORGIA								
1 Thomas	Y	N	Y	N	Y	Y	Y	N
2 Hatcher	N	N	Y	N	Y	Y	Y	Y
3 Ray	N	N	Y	N	Y	N	Y	N
4 ***Swindall***	N	N	Y	N	N	N	Y	N
5 Fowler	?	?	?	?	?	?	?	?
6 ***Gingrich***	N	N	Y	N	N	N	Y	N
7 Darden	N	Y	Y	N	Y	Y	Y	N
8 Rowland	N	Y	Y	N	Y	Y	Y	N
9 Jenkins	N	N	Y	N	Y	Y	Y	N
10 Barnard	Y	N	Y	N	Y	Y	Y	N
HAWAII								
1 Vacancy								
2 Akaka	Y	N	Y	N	Y	N	N	Y
IDAHO								
1 ***Craig***	Y	N	N	N	N	N	Y	Y
2 Stallings	N	N	N	N	Y	Y	Y	Y
ILLINOIS								
1 Hayes	N	Y	N	N	Y	Y	N	Y
2 Savage	Y	Y	N	N	Y	Y	N	Y
3 Russo	N	Y	N	N	Y	Y	Y	Y
4 Vacancy								
5 Lipinski	N	Y	Y	N	Y	Y	Y	N
6 ***Hyde***	N	Y	Y	N	N	N	Y	Y
7 Collins	N	Y	N	N	Y	Y	N	Y
8 Rostenkowski	N	Y	N	?	Y	Y	Y	Y
9 Yates	N	Y	N	N	Y	Y	?	?
10 ***Porter***	N	Y	Y	N	N	N	Y	N
11 Annunzio	N	Y	Y	N	Y	Y	Y	Y
12 ***Crane***	N	N	Y	N	N	N	Y	N
13 ***Fawell***	N	Y	Y	Y	N	N	Y	N
14 ***Grotberg***	?	?	?	?	?	?	?	?
15 ***Madigan***	N	N	Y	N	N	N	Y	Y
16 ***Martin***	Y	Y	Y	N	N	N	Y	Y
17 Evans	Y	Y	N	N	Y	Y	N	Y
18 ***Michel***	Y	Y	Y	N	N	Y	Y	N
19 Bruce	N	Y	N	N	Y	N	Y	Y
20 Durbin	Y	Y	N	N	Y	Y	N	Y
21 Price	N	Y	Y	N	Y	Y	Y	Y
22 Gray	Y	Y	Y	N	Y	Y	Y	Y
INDIANA								
1 Visclosky	N	Y	N	N	Y	Y	N	Y
2 Sharp	N	Y	N	N	Y	Y	Y	Y
3 ***Hiler***	Y	Y	Y	N	N	N	Y	N
4 ***Coats***	N	Y	Y	N	N	N	Y	N
5 ***Hillis***	Y	Y	Y	N	N	?	?	?

ND - Northern Democrats SD - Southern Democrats

* Corresponding to Congressional Record Votes 345, 346, 347, 348, 349, 350, 351, 352

	316	317	318	319	320	321	322	323
6 ***Burton***	Y	Y	Y	Y	N	N	Y	N
7 ***Myers***	Y	Y	Y	N	N	N	Y	N
8 McCloskey	N	Y	N	N	Y	Y	Y	Y
9 Hamilton	N	Y	N	N	Y	Y	Y	Y
10 Jacobs	N	Y	N	N	N	N	Y	Y
IOWA								
1 ***Leach***	N	N	Y	N	N	N	Y	N
2 ***Tauke***	N	N	N	N	N	N	Y	N
3 ***Evans***	N	N	Y	N	N	N	?	?
4 Smith	N	N	Y	N	Y	Y	N	Y
5 ***Lightfoot***	N	N	Y	N	N	N	Y	Y
6 Bedell	N	N	N	N	Y	Y	N	Y
KANSAS								
1 ***Roberts***	Y	N	Y	N	N	N	Y	N
2 Slattery	Y	N	Y	N	Y	Y	Y	Y
3 ***Meyers***	Y	N	Y	N	N	N	Y	N
4 Glickman	Y	N	Y	N	Y	Y	Y	Y
5 ***Whittaker***	Y	N	Y	N	N	N	Y	N
KENTUCKY								
1 Hubbard	N	N	Y	N	Y	N	Y	Y
2 Natcher	N	Y	N	N	Y	Y	N	Y
3 Mazzoli	N	N	Y	N	Y	Y	Y	N
4 ***Snyder***	N	N	Y	N	N	N	Y	N
5 ***Rogers***	N	N	Y	N	N	N	Y	N
6 ***Hopkins***	N	N	Y	N	N	N	Y	Y
7 Perkins	N	Y	N	N	Y	Y	N	Y
LOUISIANA								
1 ***Livingston***	N	N	Y	N	N	N	Y	Y
2 Boggs	Y	N	Y	N	Y	Y	N	Y
3 Tauzin	Y	N	Y	N	Y	N	Y	Y
4 Roemer	Y	N	Y	N	Y	N	Y	Y
5 Huckaby	N	N	Y	N	Y	N	Y	Y
6 ***Moore***	?	?	?	?	?	?	?	?
7 Breaux	?	?	?	?	?	?	?	?
8 Long	N	N	N	N	Y	Y	N	?
MAINE								
1 ***McKernan***	Y	N	N	N	N	N	Y	Y
2 ***Snowe***	N	N	Y	N	N	N	Y	Y
MARYLAND								
1 Dyson	Y	N	N	N	Y	N	Y	Y
2 ***Bentley***	Y	N	Y	N	N	N	Y	Y
3 Mikulski	Y	N	N	N	Y	Y	?	?
4 ***Holt***	Y	N	Y	N	N	N	Y	N
5 Hoyer	Y	N	N	N	Y	Y	N	Y
6 Byron	N	N	Y	N	Y	N	Y	N
7 Mitchell	N	N	N	N	Y	Y	N	Y
8 Barnes	Y	N	N	N	Y	Y	N	Y
MASSACHUSETTS								
1 ***Conte***	N	Y	N	N	N	Y	N	Y
2 Boland	N	N	N	N	Y	Y	N	Y
3 Early	N	N	N	N	Y	Y	N	N
4 Frank	N	N	N	N	Y	Y	N	Y
5 Atkins	Y	Y	N	N	Y	Y	N	Y
6 Mavroules	N	N	Y	N	Y	Y	N	Y
7 Markey	N	N	N	N	Y	Y	N	Y
8 O'Neill								
9 Moakley	N	N	N	N	Y	Y	N	Y
10 Studds	N	N	N	N	Y	Y	N	Y
11 Donnelly	Y	N	N	N	Y	Y	N	N
MICHIGAN								
1 Conyers	N	Y	N	N	Y	?	N	Y
2 ***Pursell***	N	Y	Y	N	N	N	Y	N
3 Wolpe	Y	Y	N	N	Y	Y	N	Y
4 ***Siljander***	N	Y	Y	N	N	N	Y	Y
5 ***Henry***	Y	Y	Y	N	N	N	Y	N
6 Carr	Y	Y	Y	N	Y	N	N	N
7 Kildee	N	Y	N	N	Y	Y	N	Y
8 Traxler	Y	Y	N	N	Y	Y	N	Y
9 ***Vander Jagt***	N	Y	Y	N	N	?	Y	N
10 ***Schuette***	Y	Y	Y	N	N	N	Y	N
11 ***Davis***	Y	Y	Y	N	N	N	Y	N
12 Bonior	Y	Y	N	N	Y	Y	Y	Y
13 Crockett	Y	Y	N	N	N	N	N	Y
14 Hertel	Y	Y	N	N	Y	N	Y	N
15 Ford	Y	Y	N	N	Y	N	N	Y
16 Dingell	N	?	N	N	Y	Y	Y	N
17 Levin	N	Y	N	N	Y	Y	N	Y
18 ***Broomfield***	N	Y	Y	N	N	N	Y	Y
MINNESOTA								
1 Penny	Y	Y	Y	N	Y	Y	Y	Y
2 ***Weber***	N	Y	Y	N	N	N	Y	N
3 ***Frenzel***	N	Y	Y	N	N	N	Y	N
4 Vento	Y	Y	Y	N	Y	Y	N	Y
5 Sabo	N	Y	N	N	Y	Y	N	Y
6 Sikorski	N	Y	N	N	Y	Y	N	Y

	316	317	318	319	320	321	322	323
7 ***Stangeland***	Y	Y	Y	N	N	N	Y	N
8 Oberstar	N	Y	N	N	Y	Y	N	Y
MISSISSIPPI								
1 Whitten	N	Y	N	N	Y	Y	N	Y
2 ***Franklin***	Y	N	Y	N	N	N	Y	N
3 Montgomery	N	Y	Y	N	Y	Y	Y	N
4 Dowdy	N	N	Y	N	Y	Y	Y	Y
5 ***Lott***	Y	N	Y	N	N	Y	?	?
MISSOURI								
1 Clay	N	Y	N	N	Y	Y	N	Y
2 Young	N	Y	Y	N	Y	Y	Y	Y
3 Gephardt	N	Y	Y	N	Y	Y	Y	Y
4 Skelton	Y	Y	Y	N	Y	Y	Y	Y
5 Wheat	N	Y	N	N	Y	Y	N	Y
6 ***Coleman***	N	N	Y	N	N	N	Y	N
7 ***Taylor***	Y	N	Y	N	N	N	Y	N
8 ***Emerson***	Y	N	Y	N	N	N	Y	N
9 Volkmer	N	Y	Y	N	Y	Y	Y	Y
MONTANA								
1 Williams	Y	Y	N	Y	Y	Y	N	Y
2 ***Marlenee***	N	N	Y	N	N	N	Y	N
NEBRASKA								
1 ***Bereuter***	Y	N	Y	Y	N	N	Y	N
2 ***Daub***	Y	N	Y	N	N	N	Y	Y
3 ***Smith***	Y	N	Y	N	N	N	Y	N
NEVADA								
1 Reid	Y	N	N	N	Y	Y	Y	Y
2 ***Vucanovich***	N	N	Y	Y	N	N	Y	Y
NEW HAMPSHIRE								
1 ***Smith***	N	N	Y	N	N	N	Y	N
2 ***Gregg***	N	N	Y	N	N	N	Y	N
NEW JERSEY								
1 Florio	Y	N	Y	N	Y	N	Y	?
2 Hughes	Y	N	Y	N	Y	N	Y	Y
3 Howard	N	N	N	N	Y	Y	N	Y
4 ***Smith***	Y	N	Y	N	N	Y	Y	Y
5 ***Roukema***	N	N	Y	N	N	N	Y	N
6 Dwyer	N	N	N	N	Y	Y	Y	Y
7 ***Rinaldo***	Y	N	Y	N	N	N	Y	Y
8 Roe	N	N	Y	N	Y	Y	Y	Y
9 Torricelli	N	N	Y	N	Y	N	Y	Y
10 Rodino	N	N	N	N	Y	Y	N	Y
11 ***Gallo***	N	N	Y	N	N	N	Y	N
12 ***Courter***	N	N	Y	N	N	N	Y	Y
13 ***Saxton***	N	N	Y	N	N	N	Y	Y
14 Guarini	N	Y	N	N	Y	Y	Y	Y
NEW MEXICO								
1 ***Lujan***	Y	N	Y	Y	N	N	Y	Y
2 ***Skeen***	Y	N	Y	N	N	N	Y	Y
3 Richardson	Y	Y	Y	N	Y	Y	Y	Y
NEW YORK								
1 ***Carney***	N	N	Y	N	N	N	Y	N
2 Downey	N	N	Y	N	Y	Y	N	Y
3 Mrazek	N	N	N	N	Y	Y	N	?
4 ***Lent***	N	N	?	N	N	N	Y	N
5 ***McGrath***	N	N	Y	N	N	N	Y	N
6 Waldon	N	N	N	Y	Y	Y	Y	Y
7 Ackerman	N	N	N	N	Y	Y	N	Y
8 Scheuer	N	N	N	N	Y	Y	N	Y
9 Manton	N	N	N	N	Y	Y	?	Y
10 Schumer	N	N	N	N	Y	Y	N	Y
11 Towns	Y	N	N	N	Y	Y	N	Y
12 Owens	N	N	N	N	Y	Y	N	Y
13 Solarz	N	N	Y	N	Y	Y	N	Y
14 ***Molinari***	N	N	Y	N	N	N	Y	N
15 ***Green***	N	N	Y	N	N	Y	N	Y
16 Rangel	N	Y	N	N	Y	Y	N	Y
17 Weiss	N	N	N	N	Y	Y	N	Y
18 Garcia	N	Y	N	N	Y	Y	?	?
19 Biaggi	Y	N	N	N	Y	Y	Y	Y
20 ***DioGuardi***	N	N	Y	N	N	N	Y	Y
21 ***Fish***	N	Y	Y	N	N	N	N	Y
22 ***Gilman***	N	Y	Y	N	N	N	Y	Y
23 Stratton	N	Y	Y	N	Y	Y	Y	Y
24 ***Solomon***	N	Y	Y	N	N	N	Y	N
25 ***Boehlert***	N	Y	Y	N	N	Y	Y	N
26 ***Martin***	N	Y	Y	N	N	N	Y	N
27 ***Wortley***	N	Y	Y	N	N	N	Y	N
28 McHugh	N	Y	N	N	Y	Y	N	N
29 ***Horton***	N	Y	Y	N	N	Y	Y	Y
30 ***Eckert***	N	N	Y	Y	N	Y	Y	N
31 ***Kemp***	N	Y	Y	N	N	Y	Y	?
32 LaFalce	N	Y	Y	N	Y	Y	Y	N
33 Nowak	Y	Y	N	N	Y	Y	N	Y
34 Lundine	N	Y	N	N	Y	Y	N	?

	316	317	318	319	320	321	322	323
NORTH CAROLINA								
1 Jones	N	Y	Y	N	Y	Y	Y	Y
2 Valentine	N	Y	Y	N	Y	Y	Y	Y
3 Whitley	Y	Y	Y	N	Y	?	Y	Y
4 ***Cobey***	Y	N	Y	N	N	N	Y	N
5 Neal	N	N	N	N	Y	N	?	Y
6 ***Coble***	N	N	N	Y	N	N	Y	N
7 Rose	Y	Y	Y	N	Y	Y	Y	Y
8 Hefner	Y	Y	Y	N	Y	Y	Y	Y
9 ***McMillan***	Y	N	Y	N	N	N	Y	N
10 Vacancy								
11 ***Hendon***	N	N	Y	N	N	N	Y	Y
NORTH DAKOTA								
AL Dorgan	Y	N	N	N	Y	N	Y	N
OHIO								
1 Luken	Y	Y	Y	Y	Y	Y	Y	Y
2 ***Gradison***	N	N	Y	N	N	Y	Y	N
3 Hall	N	Y	N	N	Y	Y	N	Y
4 ***Oxley***	N	Y	Y	N	N	N	Y	N
5 ***Latta***	N	Y	Y	N	N	N	Y	Y
6 ***McEwen***	N	Y	Y	Y	N	N	Y	Y
7 ***DeWine***	Y	Y	Y	N	N	N	Y	N
8 ***Kindness***	?	?	?	?	N	N	Y	Y
9 Kaptur	N	Y	N	N	Y	Y	?	?
10 ***Miller***	N	Y	Y	N	N	N	Y	N
11 Eckart	Y	Y	N	N	Y	N	Y	Y
12 ***Kasich***	N	Y	Y	Y	N	N	Y	Y
13 Pease	N	Y	N	N	Y	Y	N	Y
14 Seiberling	Y	Y	N	N	Y	Y	N	Y
15 ***Wylie***	N	Y	Y	N	N	N	Y	Y
16 ***Regula***	Y	Y	Y	N	N	N	Y	Y
17 Traficant	Y	Y	N	N	Y	N	N	Y
18 Applegate	Y	Y	N	N	Y	Y	Y	Y
19 Feighan	Y	Y	N	N	Y	Y	Y	Y
20 Oakar	Y	Y	N	N	Y	Y	N	Y
21 Stokes	N	Y	N	N	Y	Y	N	Y
OKLAHOMA								
1 Jones	Y	N	Y	N	Y	N	Y	Y
2 Synar	Y	N	N	N	Y	Y	N	N
3 Watkins	Y	N	Y	N	Y	N	Y	Y
4 McCurdy	Y	N	Y	N	Y	Y	Y	Y
5 ***Edwards***	Y	N	Y	N	N	N	Y	Y
6 English	?	N	Y	N	Y	N	Y	Y
OREGON								
1 AuCoin	N	N	N	Y	Y	N	Y	Y
2 ***Smith, R.***	N	N	Y	N	N	N	Y	N
3 Wyden	N	N	N	Y	Y	N	Y	Y
4 Weaver	Y	N	N	Y	Y	N	N	Y
5 ***Smith, D.***	N	N	Y	Y	N	N	Y	N
PENNSYLVANIA								
1 Foglietta	N	N	N	N	Y	Y	N	Y
2 Gray	N	N	N	N	Y	Y	N	Y
3 Borski	N	N	N	N	Y	Y	N	Y
4 Kolter	Y	N	Y	N	Y	N	Y	Y
5 ***Schulze***	N	N	Y	N	N	N	Y	Y
6 Yatron	Y	Y	N	N	Y	N	Y	Y
7 Edgar	?	Y	N	N	Y	Y	N	Y
8 Kostmayer	N	N	N	N	Y	Y	N	Y
9 ***Shuster***	N	N	Y	N	N	N	Y	?
10 ***McDade***	N	Y	Y	N	N	Y	?	?
11 Kanjorski	Y	Y	N	N	Y	Y	Y	N
12 Murtha	N	Y	Y	N	Y	Y	Y	?
13 ***Coughlin***	N	N	Y	N	N	N	Y	Y
14 Coyne	N	Y	N	N	Y	Y	N	Y
15 ***Ritter***	N	N	Y	N	N	N	Y	N
16 ***Walker***	N	N	Y	N	N	N	Y	Y
17 ***Gekas***	N	N	Y	N	N	Y	Y	Y
18 Walgren	Y	Y	N	N	Y	Y	N	Y
19 ***Goodling***	N	N	Y	N	N	N	Y	Y
20 Gaydos	Y	Y	Y	N	Y	Y	Y	Y
21 ***Ridge***	N	Y	Y	N	N	N	Y	N
22 Murphy	Y	N	N	N	Y	N	Y	Y
23 ***Clinger***	Y	Y	Y	N	N	N	Y	N
RHODE ISLAND								
1 St Germain	N	Y	N	N	Y	Y	Y	Y
2 ***Schneider***	N	N	Y	N	N	N	Y	Y
SOUTH CAROLINA								
1 ***Hartnett***	?	?	?	?	?	?	?	?
2 ***Spence***	Y	N	Y	N	N	N	Y	N
3 Derrick	Y	N	N	N	Y	Y	Y	Y
4 ***Campbell***	?	?	?	?	?	?	?	?
5 Spratt	N	N	Y	N	Y	Y	Y	Y
6 Tallon	Y	N	Y	N	Y	N	Y	Y
SOUTH DAKOTA								
AL Daschle	Y	Y	N	N	Y	N	Y	Y

	316	317	318	319	320	321	322	323
TENNESSEE								
1 ***Quillen***	Y	N	Y	N	N	N	Y	N
2 ***Duncan***	N	N	Y	N	N	Y	Y	?
3 Lloyd	N	N	Y	N	Y	N	Y	Y
4 Cooper	N	Y	Y	N	Y	Y	Y	N
5 Boner	Y	N	Y	N	Y	N	Y	Y
6 Gordon	N	Y	Y	N	Y	Y	Y	N
7 ***Sundquist***	N	N	Y	N	N	N	Y	N
8 Jones	Y	N	N	N	Y	N	Y	Y
9 Ford	?	Y	N	N	Y	Y	N	Y
TEXAS								
1 Chapman	N	N	Y	N	Y	Y	Y	Y
2 Wilson	N	N	Y	N	Y	Y	Y	?
3 ***Bartlett***	N	N	Y	Y	N	N	Y	N
4 Hall, R.	Y	N	Y	N	Y	Y	Y	Y
5 Bryant	N	Y	Y	N	Y	N	Y	Y
6 ***Barton***	Y	N	Y	Y	N	N	Y	N
7 ***Archer***	Y	N	Y	N	N	N	Y	N
8 ***Fields***	Y	N	Y	N	N	N	Y	N
9 Brooks	Y	N	Y	N	Y	Y	Y	Y
10 Pickle	Y	N	Y	N	Y	Y	Y	Y
11 Leath	N	N	Y	N	Y	Y	Y	Y
12 Wright	Y	Y	Y	N	Y	Y	Y	Y
13 ***Boulter***	Y	N	Y	Y	N	N	Y	Y
14 ***Sweeney***	N	N	Y	N	N	N	Y	N
15 de la Garza	N	N	Y	N	Y	Y	Y	Y
16 Coleman	Y	Y	Y	N	Y	Y	Y	?
17 Stenholm	N	N	Y	N	Y	Y	Y	Y
18 Leland	Y	Y	N	N	Y	Y	N	Y
19 ***Combest***	Y	N	Y	N	N	N	Y	N
20 Gonzalez	N	N	N	N	Y	Y	N	Y
21 ***Loeffler***	Y	N	Y	N	N	N	Y	N
22 ***DeLay***	Y	N	Y	Y	N	N	Y	N
23 Bustamante	Y	Y	Y	N	Y	Y	N	Y
24 Frost	Y	N	N	N	Y	Y	?	?
25 Andrews	N	N	Y	N	Y	Y	Y	Y
26 ***Armey***	N	N	Y	Y	N	N	Y	N
27 Ortiz	Y	N	Y	N	Y	Y	N	Y
UTAH								
1 ***Hansen***	N	N	Y	N	N	N	Y	N
2 ***Monson***	N	N	Y	Y	N	N	Y	N
3 ***Nielson***	N	N	Y	Y	N	N	Y	N
VERMONT								
AL ***Jeffords***	N	N	N	N	N	Y	N	Y
VIRGINIA								
1 ***Bateman***	N	N	Y	N	N	Y	N	Y
2 ***Whitehurst***	N	N	Y	N	N	Y	Y	N
3 ***Bliley***	N	N	Y	N	N	N	Y	Y
4 Sisisky	C	N	Y	N	Y	Y	Y	Y
5 Daniel	N	Y	Y	N	Y	N	Y	Y
6 Olin	N	Y	N	N	Y	Y	Y	Y
7 ***Slaughter***	N	N	Y	N	N	N	Y	N
8 ***Parris***	N	N	Y	N	N	N	Y	N
9 Boucher	N	N	N	N	Y	N	?	?
10 ***Wolf***	N	N	Y	N	N	Y	Y	N
WASHINGTON								
1 ***Miller***	N	N	Y	Y	N	N	Y	N
2 Swift	N	N	N	Y	Y	Y	N	Y
3 Bonker	N	N	Y	N	Y	Y	N	Y
4 ***Morrison***	Y	N	Y	Y	N	N	Y	N
5 Foley	N	Y	N	N	Y	Y	N	Y
6 Dicks	N	N	N	Y	Y	Y	N	Y
7 Lowry	N	N	N	Y	Y	Y	N	Y
8 ***Chandler***	N	N	Y	Y	N	N	Y	N
WEST VIRGINIA								
1 Mollohan	N	N	Y	N	Y	Y	Y	Y
2 Staggers	N	Y	N	N	Y	Y	Y	Y
3 Wise	N	Y	N	N	Y	Y	Y	Y
4 Rahall	N	Y	Y	N	Y	Y	Y	Y
WISCONSIN								
1 Aspin	N	Y	Y	N	Y	Y	N	Y
2 Kastenmeier	Y	Y	N	N	Y	Y	N	Y
3 ***Gunderson***	N	Y	Y	N	N	N	Y	Y
4 Kleczka	Y	Y	N	N	Y	Y	N	Y
5 Moody	Y	Y	N	N	Y	Y	N	Y
6 ***Petri***	N	Y	Y	N	N	N	Y	N
7 Obey	Y	Y	N	N	Y	Y	N	N
8 ***Roth***	N	Y	Y	Y	N	N	Y	Y
9 ***Sensenbrenner***	Y	Y	Y	Y	N	N	Y	N
WYOMING								
AL ***Cheney***	Y	N	Y	N	N	N	Y	N

Southern states - Ala., Ark., Fla., Ga., Ky., La., Miss., N.C., Okla., S.C., Tenn., Texas, Va.

* The *Congressional Record* vote number is different from the CQ vote number because the *Record* includes quorum calls in its tally. CQ does not publish quorum call votes.

324. HR 4428. Defense Authorization, Fiscal 1987. Dickinson, R-Ala., substitute for the Hawkins, D-Calif., amendment, to raise from $2,000 to $250,000 the value below which construction contracts for military facilities would be exempt from the requirements of the Davis-Bacon Act, which mandates that the local prevailing wage be paid to construction workers on federal projects. Rejected 167-244: R 134-35; D 33-209 (ND 3-162, SD 30-47), Aug. 15, 1986. (The Hawkins amendment, to raise from $2,000 to $25,000 the value below which contracts would be exempt from Davis-Bacon requirements, subsequently was adopted *(see vote 325, below).*)

325. HR 4428. Defense Authorization, Fiscal 1987. Hawkins, D-Calif., amendment to raise from $2,000 to $25,000 the value below which construction contracts for military facilities would be exempt from the requirements of the Davis-Bacon Act *(see vote 324, above).* Adopted 406-5: R 169-1; D 237-4 (ND 162-3, SD 75-1), Aug. 15, 1986.

326. HR 4428. Defense Authorization, Fiscal 1987. Solomon, R-N.Y., amendment to exempt from the provisions of the previously adopted Solomon amendment *(vote 322, p. 90-H)* persons who have been honorably discharged from the armed services or who are permanently handicapped. That Solomon amendment barred from performing services under a Pentagon contract anyone required by law to register with the Selective Service who has not done so. Adopted 408-0: R 169-0; D 239-0 (ND 162-0, SD 77-0), Aug. 15, 1986.

327. HR 4428. Defense Authorization, Fiscal 1987. Dickinson, R-Ala., motion to recommit the bill to the Armed Services Committee with instructions to delete four amendments relating to arms control and add provisions expanding the role of military units in stopping drug smuggling. Motion rejected 163-247: R 138-30; D 25-217 (ND 6-158, SD 19-59), Aug. 15, 1986. A "yea" was a vote supporting the president's position.

328. HR 4428. Defense Authorization, Fiscal 1987. Passage of the bill to authorize $212 billion for military programs of the Departments of Defense and Energy in fiscal 1987. Passed 255-152: R 23-145; D 232-7 (ND 157-5, SD 75-2), Aug. 15, 1986.

329. HR 3129. Omnibus Highway Authorization. Waxman, D-Calif., amendment to strike funding for the Los Angeles mass transit rail project. Rejected 153-231: R 86-78; D 67-153 (ND 45-105, SD 22-48), Aug. 15, 1986. (The Waxman amendment had previously been adopted in the Committee of the Whole *(see vote 277, p. 78-H).*)

330. HR 3129. Omnibus Highway Authorization. McEwen, R-Ohio, motion to recommit the bill to the Public Works and Transportation Committee with instructions to add a provision that would exempt the Highway Trust Fund from the Gramm-Rudman-Hollings anti-deficit law (PL 99-177). Motion rejected 171-214: R 104-60; D 67-154 (ND 40-109, SD 27-45), Aug. 15, 1986.

331. HR 3129. Omnibus Highway Authorization. Passage of the bill to authorize $13.9 billion annually in fiscal years 1987-91 for highway and mass transit programs. Passed 345-34: R 136-27; D 209-7 (ND 140-5, SD 69-2), Aug. 15, 1986.

KEY

Y Voted for (yea).
Paired for.
+ Announced for.
N Voted against (nay).
X Paired against.
- Announced against.
P Voted "present."
C Voted "present" to avoid possible conflict of interest.
? Did not vote or otherwise make a position known.

Democrats ***Republicans***

	324	325	326	327	328	329	330	331
ALABAMA								
1 ***Callahan***	Y	Y	Y	Y	N	N	Y	Y
2 ***Dickinson***	Y	Y	Y	Y	N	Y	Y	Y
3 Nichols	Y	Y	Y	Y	Y	N	N	Y
4 Bevill	N	Y	Y	Y	Y	N	N	Y
5 Flippo	?	?	?	?	?	?	?	?
6 Erdreich	?	?	?	?	?	?	?	?
7 Shelby	N	Y	Y	Y	N	Y	N	Y
ALASKA								
AL ***Young***	N	Y	Y	Y	N	N	Y	Y
ARIZONA								
1 ***McCain***	Y	Y	Y	Y	N	Y	N	Y
2 Udall	N	Y	Y	N	?	?	?	?
3 ***Stump***	Y	Y	Y	Y	N	Y	Y	N
4 ***Rudd***	Y	Y	Y	Y	N	?	?	?
5 ***Kolbe***	Y	Y	Y	Y	N	N	N	Y
ARKANSAS								
1 Alexander	N	Y	Y	N	Y	N	Y	Y
2 Robinson	N	Y	Y	Y	Y	N	Y	Y
3 ***Hammerschmidt***	Y	Y	Y	Y	N	N	Y	Y
4 Anthony	Y	Y	Y	N	Y	N	Y	Y
CALIFORNIA								
1 Bosco	N	Y	Y	N	Y	N	Y	Y
2 ***Chappie***	#	?	?	#	X	?	?	?
3 Matsui	N	Y	Y	N	Y	N	N	Y
4 Fazio	N	Y	Y	N	Y	N	N	Y
5 Burton	N	Y	?	?	?	?	?	?
6 Boxer	N	Y	Y	N	Y	N	Y	Y
7 Miller	N	N	Y	N	Y	N	N	?
8 Dellums	N	N	Y	N	N	N	N	Y
9 Stark	N	Y	Y	N	Y	N	N	Y
10 Edwards	N	Y	Y	N	Y	N	N	Y
11 Lantos	N	Y	Y	N	Y	N	N	Y
12 ***Zschau***	?	?	?	?	?	?	?	?
13 Mineta	N	Y	Y	N	Y	N	Y	Y
14 ***Shumway***	Y	Y	Y	Y	N	Y	Y	N
15 Coelho	N	Y	Y	N	Y	N	Y	Y
16 Panetta	N	Y	Y	N	Y	N	N	Y
17 ***Pashayan***	N	Y	Y	Y	N	N	Y	Y
18 Lehman	N	Y	Y	N	Y	N	N	Y
19 ***Lagomarsino***	Y	Y	Y	Y	N	Y	Y	Y
20 ***Thomas***	#	?	?	?	?	?	?	?
21 ***Fiedler***	Y	Y	Y	Y	N	Y	N	N
22 ***Moorhead***	Y	Y	Y	Y	N	N	Y	N
23 Beilenson	Y	Y	Y	N	Y	N	N	Y
24 Waxman	N	Y	?	N	Y	Y	N	N
25 Roybal	N	Y	Y	N	N	N	N	Y
26 Berman	N	Y	Y	N	Y	Y	N	Y
27 Levine	N	Y	Y	N	Y	Y	N	Y
28 Dixon	N	Y	Y	N	Y	N	N	Y
29 Hawkins	N	Y	Y	N	Y	N	N	Y
30 Martinez	X	?	?	X	#	#	?	?
31 Dymally	N	Y	Y	N	Y	N	N	Y
32 Anderson	N	Y	Y	N	?	N	Y	Y
33 ***Dreier***	Y	Y	Y	Y	N	N	Y	N
34 Torres	N	Y	Y	N	Y	N	N	Y
35 ***Lewis***	N	Y	Y	Y	N	N	N	Y
36 Brown	N	Y	Y	N	Y	N	Y	?
37 ***McCandless***	Y	Y	?	#	X	?	?	?
38 ***Dornan***	Y	Y	Y	Y	N	N	Y	Y
39 ***Dannemeyer***	+	+	+	+	-	-	+	-
40 ***Badham***	Y	Y	Y	Y	?	N	Y	Y
41 ***Lowery***	Y	Y	Y	Y	N	N	N	Y
42 ***Lungren***	Y	Y	Y	Y	N	Y	N	N
43 ***Packard***	Y	Y	Y	Y	N	N	Y	Y
44 Bates	N	Y	Y	N	Y	N	N	Y
45 ***Hunter***	Y	Y	Y	Y	N	N	Y	Y
COLORADO								
1 Schroeder	N	Y	Y	N	Y	N	N	Y
2 Wirih	N	Y	Y	N	Y	Y	Y	Y
3 ***Strang***	Y	Y	Y	Y	N	N	Y	Y
4 ***Brown***	Y	Y	Y	N	N	Y	Y	N
5 ***Kramer***	Y	Y	Y	Y	N	Y	N	N
6 ***Schaefer***	Y	Y	Y	Y	N	Y	Y	N
CONNECTICUT								
1 Kennelly	N	Y	Y	N	Y	Y	N	Y
2 Gejdenson	N	Y	Y	N	Y	Y	N	Y
3 Morrison	X	?	?	X	#	?	?	?
4 ***McKinney***	N	Y	Y	N	Y	Y	N	Y
5 ***Rowland***	N	Y	Y	Y	N	N	Y	Y
6 ***Johnson***	N	Y	Y	N	Y	N	Y	Y
DELAWARE								
AL Carper	N	Y	Y	N	Y	Y	N	Y
FLORIDA								
1 Hutto	Y	Y	Y	Y	Y	N	N	Y
2 Fuqua	?	?	?	?	?	?	?	?
3 Bennett	N	Y	Y	N	Y	N	Y	Y
4 Chappell	N	Y	Y	N	Y	N	Y	Y
5 ***McCollum***	Y	Y	Y	Y	N	N	Y	Y
6 MacKay	Y	Y	Y	N	Y	Y	N	?
7 Gibbons	Y	Y	Y	N	Y	N	N	Y
8 ***Young***	Y	Y	Y	Y	N	?	?	?
9 ***Bilirakis***	Y	Y	Y	Y	N	Y	Y	Y
10 ***Ireland***	Y	Y	Y	Y	N	Y	Y	N
11 Nelson	Y	Y	Y	Y	Y	N	N	Y
12 ***Lewis***	Y	Y	Y	Y	N	N	Y	Y
13 ***Mack***	Y	Y	Y	Y	N	Y	N	N
14 Mica	N	Y	Y	N	Y	N	N	Y
15 ***Shaw***	Y	Y	Y	Y	N	N	Y	Y
16 Smith	N	Y	?	N	Y	Y	N	Y
17 Lehman	N	Y	Y	N	Y	N	N	N
18 Pepper	N	Y	Y	N	Y	Y	Y	Y
19 Fascell	N	Y	Y	N	Y	N	Y	Y
GEORGIA								
1 Thomas	N	Y	Y	N	Y	N	Y	Y
2 Hatcher	Y	Y	Y	N	?	?	?	?
3 Ray	Y	Y	Y	Y	Y	N	Y	Y
4 ***Swindall***	Y	Y	Y	Y	N	N	Y	Y
5 Fowler	?	?	Y	N	Y	?	?	?
6 ***Gingrich***	Y	Y	Y	Y	N	N	Y	Y
7 Darden	Y	Y	Y	Y	Y	N	Y	Y
8 Rowland	N	Y	Y	N	Y	Y	Y	Y
9 Jenkins	Y	Y	Y	N	Y	N	N	Y
10 Barnard	Y	Y	Y	Y	Y	N	Y	Y
HAWAII								
1 Vacancy								
2 Akaka	N	Y	Y	N	Y	N	N	Y
IDAHO								
1 ***Craig***	Y	Y	Y	Y	N	Y	Y	Y
2 Stallings	Y	Y	Y	N	Y	?	?	?
ILLINOIS								
1 Hayes	N	Y	Y	N	Y	N	N	Y
2 Savage	N	Y	Y	N	Y	N	Y	Y
3 Russo	N	Y	Y	N	Y	Y	N	Y
4 Vacancy								
5 Lipinski	N	Y	Y	Y	Y	N	Y	Y
6 ***Hyde***	Y	Y	Y	Y	N	N	Y	Y
7 Collins	N	Y	Y	N	Y	N	N	Y
8 Rostenkowski	N	Y	Y	N	Y	N	N	Y
9 Yates	N	Y	Y	N	Y	N	N	Y
10 ***Porter***	Y	Y	Y	N	Y	N	N	Y
11 Annunzio	N	Y	Y	N	Y	N	N	Y
12 ***Crane***	Y	Y	Y	Y	N	Y	Y	N
13 ***Fawell***	N	Y	Y	Y	Y	N	Y	Y
14 ***Grotberg***	?	?	?	?	?	?	?	?
15 ***Madigan***	N	Y	Y	Y	N	Y	Y	Y
16 ***Martin***	Y	Y	Y	N	N	Y	N	Y
17 Evans	N	Y	Y	N	Y	Y	N	Y
18 ***Michel***	Y	Y	Y	Y	N	N	N	Y
19 Bruce	N	Y	Y	N	Y	Y	N	Y
20 Durbin	N	Y	Y	N	Y	N	N	Y
21 Price	N	Y	Y	N	Y	N	N	Y
22 Gray	N	Y	Y	N	Y	N	Y	Y
INDIANA								
1 Visclosky	N	Y	Y	N	Y	N	Y	Y
2 Sharp	N	Y	Y	N	Y	Y	N	Y
3 ***Hiler***	Y	Y	Y	Y	N	Y	N	Y
4 ***Coats***	Y	Y	Y	Y	N	Y	Y	Y
5 ***Hillis***	?	?	?	?	?	?	?	?

ND - Northern Democrats SD - Southern Democrats

* Corresponding to Congressional Record Votes 354, 355, 356, 357, 358, 359, 360, 361

	324	325	326	327	328	329	330	331
6 ***Burton***	N	Y	Y	Y	N	N	Y	Y
7 ***Myers***	Y	Y	Y	Y	N	N	Y	Y
8 McCloskey	N	Y	Y	N	Y	Y	N	Y
9 Hamilton	N	Y	Y	N	Y	N	N	Y
10 Jacobs	N	Y	Y	N	Y	Y	Y	N
IOWA								
1 ***Leach***	Y	Y	Y	N	Y	Y	N	Y
2 ***Tauke***	Y	Y	Y	N	N	Y	Y	Y
3 ***Evans***	?	?	?	?	?	?	?	?
4 Smith	N	Y	Y	N	N	N	Y	Y
5 ***Lightfoot***	Y	Y	Y	N	N	N	Y	Y
6 Bedell	?	?	?	?	?	?	?	?
KANSAS								
1 ***Roberts***	Y	Y	Y	Y	N	Y	Y	Y
2 Slattery	N	Y	Y	N	Y	Y	N	Y
3 ***Meyers***	Y	Y	Y	N	N	Y	N	Y
4 Glickman	N	Y	Y	N	Y	Y	Y	Y
5 ***Whittaker***	Y	Y	Y	Y	N	Y	N	Y
KENTUCKY								
1 Hubbard	N	Y	Y	Y	Y	Y	N	N
2 Natcher	N	Y	Y	N	Y	N	N	Y
3 Mazzoli	N	Y	Y	N	Y	Y	N	Y
4 ***Snyder***	Y	Y	Y	Y	N	N	Y	Y
5 ***Rogers***	Y	Y	Y	Y	N	N	Y	Y
6 ***Hopkins***	Y	Y	Y	Y	N	?	Y	Y
7 Perkins	N	N	Y	N	Y	N	Y	Y
LOUISIANA								
1 ***Livingston***	Y	Y	Y	Y	N	Y	N	Y
2 Boggs	N	Y	Y	N	Y	N	N	Y
3 Tauzin	Y	Y	Y	Y	Y	Y	N	Y
4 Roemer	Y	Y	Y	Y	Y	Y	Y	Y
5 Huckaby	Y	Y	Y	N	Y	N	Y	Y
6 ***Moore***	?	?	?	?	?	?	?	?
7 Breaux	?	?	?	?	?	?	?	?
8 Long	N	Y	Y	N	Y	Y	Y	Y
MAINE								
1 ***McKernan***	Y	Y	Y	N	Y	Y	N	Y
2 ***Snowe***	Y	Y	Y	N	Y	Y	N	Y
MARYLAND								
1 Dyson	N	Y	Y	Y	Y	N	N	Y
2 ***Bentley***	?	Y	Y	Y	N	N	Y	Y
3 Mikulski	N	Y	Y	N	Y	Y	N	Y
4 ***Holt***	Y	Y	Y	Y	N	N	Y	Y
5 Hoyer	N	Y	Y	N	Y	N	N	Y
6 Byron	Y	Y	Y	Y	Y	N	N	Y
7 Mitchell	N	Y	Y	N	Y	N	N	Y
8 Barnes	N	Y	Y	N	Y	N	N	Y
MASSACHUSETTS								
1 ***Conte***	N	Y	Y	N	Y	N	N	Y
2 Boland	N	Y	Y	N	Y	?	N	Y
3 Early	N	Y	Y	N	Y	N	N	Y
4 Frank	N	Y	Y	N	Y	Y	Y	Y
5 Atkins	N	Y	Y	N	Y	N	Y	Y
6 Mavroules	N	Y	Y	N	Y	N	N	Y
7 Markey	N	Y	Y	N	Y	Y	N	Y
8 O'Neill								
9 Moakley	N	Y	Y	N	Y	X	?	?
10 Studds	N	Y	Y	N	Y	?	?	?
11 Donnelly	N	Y	Y	N	Y	?	?	?
MICHIGAN								
1 Conyers	N	Y	Y	N	Y	?	?	?
2 ***Pursell***	Y	Y	Y	N	Y	Y	N	Y
3 Wolpe	N	Y	Y	N	Y	Y	N	Y
4 ***Siljander***	Y	Y	Y	Y	N	Y	Y	N
5 ***Henry***	Y	Y	Y	N	Y	Y	N	N
6 Carr	N	Y	Y	N	Y	N	N	Y
7 Kildee	N	Y	Y	N	Y	N	N	Y
8 Traxler	N	Y	Y	N	Y	?	?	?
9 ***Vander Jagt***	Y	Y	Y	Y	N	Y	N	Y
10 ***Schuette***	Y	Y	Y	Y	N	Y	Y	Y
11 ***Davis***	N	Y	Y	Y	N	N	N	Y
12 Bonior	N	Y	Y	N	Y	N	N	Y
13 Crockett	N	Y	Y	N	N	?	?	?
14 Hertel	N	Y	Y	N	Y	Y	N	Y
15 Ford	N	Y	Y	N	Y	?	?	?
16 Dingell	N	Y	Y	N	Y	N	N	Y
17 Levin	N	Y	Y	N	Y	Y	N	Y
18 ***Broomfield***	Y	Y	Y	Y	N	Y	Y	Y
MINNESOTA								
1 Penny	N	Y	Y	N	Y	Y	N	Y
2 ***Weber***	Y	Y	Y	N	N	Y	Y	Y
3 ***Frenzel***	Y	Y	Y	Y	N	Y	N	Y
4 Vento	N	Y	Y	N	Y	N	N	Y
5 Sabo	N	Y	Y	N	Y	N	N	Y
6 Sikorski	N	Y	Y	N	Y	Y	N	Y
7 ***Stangeland***	Y	Y	Y	Y	N	N	Y	Y
8 Oberstar	N	Y	Y	N	Y	N	Y	Y
MISSISSIPPI								
1 Whitten	N	Y	Y	N	Y	N	N	Y
2 ***Franklin***	Y	Y	Y	?	N	N	N	Y
3 Montgomery	Y	Y	Y	Y	Y	Y	Y	Y
4 Dowdy	N	Y	Y	N	Y	?	?	?
5 ***Lott***	Y	Y	Y	Y	N	N	Y	Y
MISSOURI								
1 Clay	N	Y	Y	N	Y	N	N	Y
2 Young	N	Y	Y	N	Y	N	Y	Y
3 Gephardt	N	Y	Y	N	Y	N	N	Y
4 Skelton	N	Y	Y	N	Y	N	Y	Y
5 Wheat	N	Y	Y	N	Y	N	N	Y
6 ***Coleman***	Y	Y	Y	Y	N	Y	Y	Y
7 ***Taylor***	Y	Y	Y	Y	N	N	Y	Y
8 ***Emerson***	Y	Y	Y	Y	N	N	Y	Y
9 Volkmer	N	Y	Y	N	Y	N	Y	Y
MONTANA								
1 Williams	N	Y	Y	N	Y	N	N	Y
2 ***Marlenee***	Y	Y	Y	Y	N	Y	Y	N
NEBRASKA								
1 ***Bereuter***	Y	Y	Y	Y	N	N	Y	Y
2 ***Daub***	N	Y	Y	Y	N	Y	Y	N
3 ***Smith***	Y	Y	Y	Y	N	Y	N	N
NEVADA								
1 Reid	N	Y	Y	N	Y	Y	Y	Y
2 ***Vucanovich***	Y	Y	Y	Y	N	Y	Y	Y
NEW HAMPSHIRE								
1 ***Smith***	Y	Y	Y	Y	N	Y	N	Y
2 ***Gregg***	Y	Y	Y	Y	N	Y	N	Y
NEW JERSEY								
1 Florio	N	Y	Y	N	Y	Y	Y	Y
2 Hughes	N	Y	Y	N	Y	N	N	Y
3 Howard	N	Y	Y	N	Y	N	Y	Y
4 ***Smith***	N	Y	Y	N	Y	Y	Y	Y
5 ***Roukema***	Y	Y	Y	N	Y	N	N	Y
6 Dwyer	N	Y	Y	N	Y	N	N	Y
7 ***Rinaldo***	N	Y	Y	Y	Y	Y	Y	Y
8 Roe	N	Y	Y	N	Y	N	Y	Y
9 Torricelli	N	Y	Y	N	Y	N	Y	Y
10 Rodino	N	Y	Y	N	Y	N	Y	Y
11 ***Gallo***	N	Y	Y	Y	N	N	Y	Y
12 ***Courter***	N	Y	Y	Y	N	Y	Y	Y
13 ***Saxton***	N	Y	Y	Y	N	N	N	Y
14 Guarini	N	Y	Y	N	Y	N	N	Y
NEW MEXICO								
1 ***Lujan***	Y	Y	Y	Y	N	N	Y	Y
2 ***Skeen***	Y	Y	Y	Y	N	N	Y	Y
3 Richardson	N	Y	Y	N	Y	Y	N	Y
NEW YORK								
1 ***Carney***	Y	Y	Y	Y	N	Y	Y	Y
2 Downey	N	Y	Y	N	Y	Y	N	Y
3 Mrazek	N	Y	Y	N	Y	N	N	Y
4 ***Lent***	N	Y	Y	Y	N	N	N	Y
5 ***McGrath***	N	Y	Y	Y	N	N	N	Y
6 Waldon	N	Y	Y	N	Y	N	N	Y
7 Ackerman	N	Y	Y	N	Y	N	N	Y
8 Scheuer	N	Y	Y	N	Y	Y	N	Y
9 Manton	N	Y	Y	N	Y	N	N	Y
10 Schumer	N	Y	Y	N	Y	Y	N	Y
11 Towns	N	Y	Y	N	Y	N	Y	Y
12 Owens	N	Y	Y	N	Y	N	N	Y
13 Solarz	N	Y	Y	N	Y	Y	N	Y
14 ***Molinari***	Y	Y	Y	Y	N	N	Y	Y
15 ***Green***	N	Y	Y	N	Y	Y	N	Y
16 Rangel	N	Y	Y	N	Y	N	N	Y
17 Weiss	N	Y	Y	N	Y	Y	N	Y
18 Garcia	?	?	?	X	#	?	?	?
19 Biaggi	N	Y	Y	N	Y	N	?	?
20 ***DioGuardi***	N	Y	Y	Y	N	Y	Y	Y
21 ***Fish***	N	Y	Y	N	Y	N	N	Y
22 ***Gilman***	N	Y	Y	Y	N	N	Y	Y
23 Stratton	N	Y	Y	Y	Y	Y	Y	Y
24 ***Solomon***	Y	Y	Y	Y	N	Y	Y	N
25 ***Boehlert***	N	Y	Y	N	Y	Y	Y	Y
26 ***Martin***	Y	Y	Y	Y	N	N	Y	Y
27 ***Wortley***	N	Y	Y	Y	N	N	Y	Y
28 McHugh	N	Y	?	N	Y	N	N	Y
29 ***Horton***	N	Y	Y	N	Y	?	?	?
30 ***Eckert***	Y	Y	Y	Y	N	Y	N	?
31 ***Kemp***	N	Y	Y	Y	N	N	N	Y
32 LaFalce	N	Y	Y	N	Y	N	Y	Y
33 Nowak	N	Y	Y	N	Y	N	Y	Y
34 Lundine	N	Y	Y	N	Y	N	N	Y
NORTH CAROLINA								
1 Jones	N	Y	Y	N	Y	N	Y	Y
2 Valentine	Y	Y	Y	N	Y	N	Y	Y
3 Whitley	Y	Y	Y	N	Y	N	N	Y
4 ***Cobey***	Y	Y	Y	Y	N	Y	Y	Y
5 Neal	Y	Y	Y	N	Y	Y	N	Y
6 ***Coble***	Y	Y	Y	Y	N	Y	N	Y
7 Rose	N	Y	Y	N	Y	?	?	?
8 Hefner	Y	Y	Y	N	Y	N	N	Y
9 ***McMillan***	Y	Y	Y	Y	N	Y	N	Y
10 Vacancy								
11 ***Hendon***	Y	Y	Y	Y	N	Y	N	Y
NORTH DAKOTA								
AL Dorgan	N	Y	Y	N	Y	Y	N	N
OHIO								
1 Luken	N	Y	Y	N	Y	Y	?	?
2 ***Gradison***	Y	Y	Y	Y	N	Y	N	Y
3 Hall	N	Y	Y	N	Y	N	N	?
4 ***Oxley***	Y	Y	Y	Y	N	N	N	Y
5 ***Latta***	Y	Y	Y	Y	N	N	N	Y
6 ***McEwen***	Y	Y	Y	Y	N	N	Y	N
7 ***DeWine***	Y	Y	Y	Y	N	Y	Y	Y
8 ***Kindness***	Y	Y	Y	Y	N	Y	Y	Y
9 Kaptur	N	Y	Y	N	Y	?	?	?
10 ***Miller***	Y	Y	Y	Y	N	Y	N	Y
11 Eckart	N	Y	Y	N	Y	Y	N	Y
12 ***Kasich***	Y	Y	Y	Y	N	Y	N	Y
13 Pease	N	Y	Y	N	Y	N	N	Y
14 Seiberling	N	Y	Y	N	Y	N	N	Y
15 ***Wylie***	N	Y	Y	Y	N	Y	N	Y
16 ***Regula***	N	Y	Y	Y	N	Y	N	Y
17 Traficant	N	Y	Y	N	Y	N	Y	Y
18 Applegate	N	Y	Y	N	Y	?	?	?
19 Feighan	N	Y	Y	N	Y	Y	N	Y
20 Oakar	N	Y	Y	N	Y	Y	N	Y
21 Stokes	N	Y	Y	N	Y	N	N	Y
OKLAHOMA								
1 Jones	N	Y	Y	N	Y	?	?	?
2 Synar	N	Y	Y	N	Y	Y	N	Y
3 Watkins	Y	Y	Y	N	Y	N	N	Y
4 McCurdy	Y	Y	Y	N	Y	Y	N	Y
5 ***Edwards***	Y	Y	Y	Y	N	Y	N	Y
6 English	Y	Y	Y	N	Y	Y	N	Y
OREGON								
1 AuCoin	N	Y	Y	N	Y	N	N	Y
2 ***Smith, R.***	Y	Y	Y	Y	N	Y	Y	Y
3 Wyden	N	Y	Y	N	Y	Y	N	Y
4 Weaver	N	Y	Y	N	Y	Y	N	?
5 ***Smith, D.***	Y	Y	Y	Y	N	Y	Y	N
PENNSYLVANIA								
1 Foglietta	N	N	Y	N	Y	Y	N	Y
2 Gray	N	Y	Y	N	Y	N	N	Y
3 Borski	N	Y	Y	N	Y	N	Y	Y
4 Kolter	N	Y	Y	N	Y	N	Y	Y
5 ***Schulze***	N	Y	Y	Y	N	N	Y	Y
6 Yatron	N	Y	Y	N	Y	N	N	Y
7 Edgar	N	Y	Y	N	Y	N	Y	Y
8 Kostmayer	N	Y	Y	N	Y	Y	N	Y
9 ***Shuster***	Y	Y	Y	Y	N	N	Y	Y
10 ***McDade***	N	Y	Y	Y	N	N	N	Y
11 Kanjorski	N	Y	Y	N	Y	N	N	Y
12 Murtha	N	Y	Y	Y	Y	N	N	Y
13 ***Coughlin***	N	Y	Y	N	Y	Y	N	Y
14 Coyne	N	Y	Y	N	Y	N	N	Y
15 ***Ritter***	Y	Y	Y	Y	N	Y	Y	Y
16 ***Walker***	Y	Y	Y	Y	N	Y	N	Y
17 ***Gekas***	Y	Y	Y	Y	N	Y	Y	Y
18 Walgren	N	Y	Y	N	Y	Y	N	Y
19 ***Goodling***	Y	Y	Y	N	N	N	N	Y
20 Gaydos	N	Y	Y	N	Y	?	?	?
21 ***Ridge***	N	Y	Y	N	Y	Y	Y	Y
22 Murphy	N	Y	Y	N	Y	N	Y	Y
23 ***Clinger***	N	Y	Y	N	Y	N	Y	Y
RHODE ISLAND								
1 St Germain	N	Y	Y	N	Y	N	N	Y
2 ***Schneider***	N	Y	Y	N	Y	Y	N	Y
SOUTH CAROLINA								
1 ***Hartnett***	?	?	?	#	X	?	?	?
2 ***Spence***	Y	Y	Y	Y	N	N	N	Y
3 Derrick	Y	Y	Y	N	Y	N	N	Y
4 ***Campbell***	?	?	?	?	?	?	?	?
5 Spratt	Y	Y	Y	N	Y	?	N	Y
6 Tallon	N	Y	Y	N	Y	N	Y	Y
SOUTH DAKOTA								
AL Daschle	N	Y	Y	N	Y	N	N	Y
TENNESSEE								
1 ***Quillen***	Y	Y	Y	Y	N	N	Y	Y
2 ***Duncan***	Y	Y	Y	Y	N	N	Y	Y
3 Lloyd	N	Y	Y	Y	Y	N	Y	Y
4 Cooper	N	Y	Y	N	Y	Y	N	Y
5 Boner	N	Y	Y	N	Y	N	N	Y
6 Gordon	N	Y	Y	N	Y	Y	N	Y
7 ***Sundquist***	Y	Y	Y	Y	N	N	Y	Y
8 Jones	N	Y	Y	N	Y	Y	N	Y
9 Ford	N	Y	Y	N	Y	N	N	Y
TEXAS								
1 Chapman	N	Y	Y	N	Y	N	Y	Y
2 Wilson	N	Y	Y	N	Y	N	N	Y
3 ***Bartlett***	Y	Y	Y	Y	N	Y	Y	N
4 Hall, R.	Y	Y	Y	Y	N	Y	N	Y
5 Bryant	N	Y	Y	Y	Y	Y	N	Y
6 ***Barton***	Y	Y	Y	Y	N	Y	Y	Y
7 ***Archer***	Y	Y	Y	Y	N	N	Y	N
8 ***Fields***	Y	Y	Y	Y	N	N	Y	Y
9 Brooks	N	Y	Y	N	Y	N	N	Y
10 Pickle	N	Y	Y	N	Y	N	N	Y
11 Leath	Y	Y	Y	N	Y	N	Y	Y
12 Wright	N	Y	Y	N	Y	N	Y	Y
13 ***Boulter***	Y	Y	Y	Y	N	N	Y	Y
14 ***Sweeney***	Y	Y	Y	Y	N	N	Y	Y
15 de la Garza	N	Y	Y	N	Y	Y	N	Y
16 Coleman	Y	Y	Y	N	Y	N	N	Y
17 Stenholm	Y	Y	Y	Y	Y	Y	Y	Y
18 Leland	N	Y	Y	N	Y	N	N	Y
19 ***Combest***	Y	Y	Y	Y	N	Y	Y	Y
20 Gonzalez	N	Y	Y	N	Y	N	N	Y
21 ***Loeffler***	Y	Y	Y	Y	N	Y	N	Y
22 ***DeLay***	Y	N	Y	Y	N	N	Y	Y
23 Bustamante	N	Y	Y	N	Y	N	N	Y
24 Frost	N	Y	Y	N	Y	?	?	?
25 Andrews	Y	Y	Y	N	Y	N	N	Y
26 ***Armey***	Y	Y	Y	Y	N	Y	Y	N
27 Ortiz	N	Y	Y	N	Y	N	N	Y
UTAH								
1 ***Hansen***	Y	Y	Y	Y	N	Y	?	?
2 ***Monson***	Y	Y	Y	Y	N	N	Y	Y
3 ***Nielson***	Y	Y	Y	Y	N	Y	Y	Y
VERMONT								
AL ***Jeffords***	Y	Y	Y	N	Y	N	Y	Y
VIRGINIA								
1 ***Bateman***	Y	Y	Y	Y	N	N	Y	Y
2 ***Whitehurst***	Y	Y	Y	Y	N	?	?	?
3 ***Bliley***	Y	Y	Y	Y	N	N	Y	Y
4 Sisisky	N	Y	Y	Y	Y	N	Y	Y
5 Daniel	Y	?	Y	Y	Y	N	Y	Y
6 Olin	N	Y	Y	N	Y	N	N	Y
7 ***Slaughter***	Y	Y	Y	Y	N	N	Y	Y
8 ***Parris***	Y	Y	Y	Y	N	N	Y	Y
9 Boucher	N	Y	Y	N	Y	?	N	Y
10 ***Wolf***	Y	Y	Y	Y	N	N	N	Y
WASHINGTON								
1 ***Miller***	Y	Y	Y	Y	N	Y	N	Y
2 Swift	N	Y	Y	N	Y	N	N	Y
3 Bonker	N	Y	Y	N	Y	N	N	Y
4 ***Morrison***	Y	Y	Y	Y	N	Y	Y	Y
5 Foley	N	Y	Y	N	Y	Y	N	Y
6 Dicks	N	Y	Y	N	Y	N	N	Y
7 Lowry	N	Y	Y	N	Y	N	N	Y
8 ***Chandler***	Y	Y	Y	Y	N	Y	Y	Y
WEST VIRGINIA								
1 Mollohan	N	Y	Y	Y	Y	N	N	Y
2 Staggers	N	Y	Y	N	Y	N	Y	Y
3 Wise	N	Y	Y	N	Y	N	Y	Y
4 Rahall	N	Y	Y	N	Y	N	Y	Y
WISCONSIN								
1 Aspin	N	Y	Y	N	Y	?	?	?
2 Kastenmeier	N	Y	Y	N	N	N	N	N
3 ***Gunderson***	Y	Y	Y	N	N	N	Y	N
4 Kleczka	N	Y	Y	N	Y	Y	Y	Y
5 Moody	N	Y	Y	N	Y	Y	Y	Y
6 ***Petri***	Y	Y	Y	Y	N	Y	Y	Y
7 Obey	N	Y	Y	N	Y	N	N	N
8 ***Roth***	Y	Y	Y	Y	N	N	N	N
9 ***Sensenbrenner***	Y	Y	Y	N	N	Y	N	N
WYOMING								
AL ***Cheney***	Y	Y	Y	Y	N	Y	N	N

Southern states - Ala., Ark., Fla., Ga., Ky., La., Miss., N.C., Okla., S.C., Tenn., Texas, Va.

* The *Congressional Record* vote number is different from the CQ vote number because the *Record* includes quorum calls in its tally. CQ does not publish quorum call votes.

332. HR 5395. Temporary Debt Limit Increase. Foley, D-Wash., motion to concur in the Senate amendment raising from $2.079 trillion to $2.111 trillion the ceiling on the federal debt and to disagree to the Senate amendment to make changes in the Gramm-Rudman-Hollings anti-deficit law (PL 99-177) to reinstate, for 1987 only, the law's automatic spending cuts procedure (previously voided as a violation of the Constitution's separation-of-powers doctrine) by granting final authority for determining the automatic cuts to the director of the Office of Management and Budget, with certain limitations. The amendment also would change to the first Tuesday in February of each year the date in the Gramm-Rudman law by which the president is required to submit his budget request to Congress. Motion agreed to 175-133: R 21-119; D 154-14 (ND 108-6, SD 46-8), in the session that began Aug. 15, 1986.

333. HR 5395. Temporary Debt Limit Increase. Daschle, D-S.D., motion to table (kill) the Foley, D-Wash., motion to reconsider the vote by which the Foley motion *(vote 332, above)* was agreed to. Motion agreed to 193-102: R 37-98; D 156-4 (ND 107-2, SD 49-2), in the session that began Aug. 15, 1986.

334. Procedural Motion. Foley, D-Wash., motion to adjourn. Motion agreed to 202-91: R 49-83; D 153-8 (ND 107-2, SD 46-6), in the session that began Aug. 15, 1986.

KEY

Y Voted for (yea).
\# Paired for.
\+ Announced for.
N Voted against (nay).
X Paired against.
\- Announced against.
P Voted "present."
C Voted "present" to avoid possible conflict of interest.
? Did not vote or otherwise make a position known.

Democrats ***Republicans***

	332	333	334
ALABAMA			
1 ***Callahan***	N	N	N
2 ***Dickinson***	?	?	?
3 Nichols	?	?	?
4 Bevill	?	?	?
5 Flippo	?	?	?
6 Erdreich	?	?	?
7 Shelby	N	N	Y
ALASKA			
AL ***Young***	N	N	Y
ARIZONA			
1 ***McCain***	Y	Y	N
2 Udall	?	?	?
3 ***Stump***	N	N	N
4 ***Rudd***	?	?	?
5 ***Kolbe***	N	N	N
ARKANSAS			
1 Alexander	?	?	?
2 Robinson	N	Y	N
3 ***Hammerschmidt***	N	N	N
4 Anthony	?	?	?
CALIFORNIA			
1 Bosco	?	?	?
2 ***Chappie***	?	?	?
3 Matsui	Y	Y	Y
4 Fazio	Y	Y	Y
5 Burton	?	?	?
6 Boxer	Y	Y	Y
7 Miller	Y	Y	Y
8 Dellums	Y	Y	Y
9 Stark	Y	Y	Y
10 Edwards	?	?	?
11 Lantos	?	?	?
12 ***Zschau***	?	?	?
13 Mineta	Y	Y	Y
14 ***Shumway***	Y	Y	Y
15 Coelho	Y	Y	Y
16 Panetta	Y	Y	Y
17 ***Pashayan***	N	Y	Y
18 Lehman	Y	?	?
19 ***Lagomarsino***	N	N	N
20 ***Thomas***	?	?	?
21 ***Fiedler***	?	?	?
22 ***Moorhead***	N	N	N
23 Beilenson	?	?	?
24 Waxman	?	?	?
25 Roybal	Y	Y	Y
26 Berman	Y	Y	Y
27 Levine	?	?	?
28 Dixon	?	?	?
29 Hawkins	?	?	?
30 Martinez	#	?	?
31 Dymally	?	?	?
32 Anderson	Y	Y	Y
33 ***Dreier***	N	N	N
34 Torres	Y	Y	Y
35 ***Lewis***	?	?	?
36 Brown	?	?	?
37 ***McCandless***	X	?	?
38 ***Dornan***	N	N	N
39 ***Dannemeyer***	-	-	-
40 ***Badham***	?	?	?
41 ***Lowery***	N	Y	Y
42 ***Lungren***	N	N	N
43 ***Packard***	N	?	?
44 Bates	Y	Y	Y
45 ***Hunter***	N	N	N
COLORADO			
1 Schroeder	?	?	?
2 Wirth	N	N	Y
3 ***Strang***	N	N	N
4 ***Brown***	N	N	N
5 ***Kramer***	N	N	N
6 ***Schaefer***	N	N	N
CONNECTICUT			
1 Kennelly	Y	Y	Y
2 Gejdenson	Y	Y	Y
3 Morrison	?	?	?
4 ***McKinney***	Y	Y	Y
5 ***Rowland***	N	Y	N
6 ***Johnson***	N	N	Y
DELAWARE			
AL Carper	N	Y	Y
FLORIDA			
1 Hutto	Y	Y	Y
2 Fuqua	?	?	?
3 Bennett	Y	Y	Y
4 Chappell	?	?	Y
5 ***McCollum***	?	?	?
6 MacKay	Y	?	?
7 Gibbons	?	?	?
8 ***Young***	?	?	?
9 ***Bilirakis***	Y	?	?
10 ***Ireland***	N	?	?
11 Nelson	Y	Y	Y
12 ***Lewis***	N	N	Y
13 ***Mack***	N	N	N
14 Mica	?	?	?
15 ***Shaw***	N	N	Y
16 Smith	Y	Y	Y
17 Lehman	?	?	?
18 Pepper	Y	?	+
19 Fascell	?	?	?
GEORGIA			
1 Thomas	Y	Y	Y
2 Hatcher	?	?	?
3 Ray	N	Y	Y
4 ***Swindall***	N	N	N
5 Fowler	?	?	?
6 ***Gingrich***	N	N	N
7 Darden	Y	Y	Y
8 Rowland	Y	Y	Y
9 Jenkins	Y	Y	Y
10 Barnard	Y	Y	Y
HAWAII			
1 Vacancy			
2 Akaka	Y	Y	Y
IDAHO			
1 ***Craig***	?	?	?
2 Stallings	?	?	?
ILLINOIS			
1 Hayes	Y	Y	Y
2 Savage	?	?	?
3 Russo	Y	Y	Y
4 Vacancy			
5 Lipinski	Y	Y	Y
6 ***Hyde***	?	?	?
7 Collins	Y	Y	Y
8 Rostenkowski	Y	Y	Y
9 Yates	?	?	?
10 ***Porter***	?	?	?
11 Annunzio	Y	Y	Y
12 ***Crane***	N	Y	N
13 ***Fawell***	N	Y	Y
14 ***Grotberg***	?	?	?
15 ***Madigan***	N	N	Y
16 ***Martin***	N	N	Y
17 Evans	Y	Y	Y
18 ***Michel***	N	Y	Y
19 Bruce	Y	Y	Y
20 Durbin	Y	Y	Y
21 Price	?	?	?
22 Gray	Y	Y	Y
INDIANA			
1 Visclosky	Y	Y	Y
2 Sharp	Y	Y	Y
3 ***Hiler***	N	N	N
4 ***Coats***	N	N	N
5 ***Hillis***	?	?	?

ND - Northern Democrats SD - Southern Democrats

* Corresponding to Congressional Record Votes 362, 363, 364

	332	333	334
6 ***Burton***	N	N	N
7 ***Myers***	Y	Y	Y
8 McCloskey	Y	Y	Y
9 Hamilton	Y	Y	Y
10 Jacobs	N	Y	N
IOWA			
1 ***Leach***	Y	Y	N
2 ***Tauke***	N	Y	Y
3 ***Evans***	?	?	?
4 Smith	Y	Y	Y
5 ***Lightfoot***	N	Y	Y
6 Bedell	?	?	?
KANSAS			
1 ***Roberts***	Y	Y	Y
2 Slattery	Y	Y	Y
3 ***Meyers***	N	N	Y
4 Glickman	Y	Y	Y
5 ***Whittaker***	N	Y	Y
KENTUCKY			
1 Hubbard	N	Y	Y
2 Natcher	Y	Y	Y
3 Mazzoli	?	?	?
4 ***Snyder***	?	?	?
5 ***Rogers***	N	N	N
6 ***Hopkins***	N	N	N
7 Perkins	Y	Y	Y
LOUISIANA			
1 ***Livingston***	N	N	Y
2 Boggs	Y	Y	Y
3 Tauzin	Y	Y	Y
4 Roemer	Y	Y	N
5 Huckaby	N	Y	Y
6 ***Moore***	?	?	?
7 Breaux	?	?	?
8 Long	?	?	?
MAINE			
1 ***McKernan***	N	N	Y
2 ***Snowe***	N	N	Y
MARYLAND			
1 Dyson	Y	Y	Y
2 ***Bentley***	Y	Y	Y
3 Mikulski	?	?	?
4 ***Holt***	Y	Y	Y
5 Hoyer	Y	Y	Y
6 Byron	N	Y	Y
7 Mitchell	?	?	?
8 Barnes	?	?	?
MASSACHUSETTS			
1 ***Conte***	Y	Y	N
2 Boland	Y	?	?
3 Early	?	?	?
4 Frank	Y	Y	Y
5 Atkins	?	?	?
6 Mavroules	?	?	?
7 Markey	?	?	?
8 O'Neill			
9 Moakley	?	?	?
10 Studds	?	?	?
11 Donnelly	?	?	?
MICHIGAN			
1 Conyers	?	?	?
2 ***Pursell***	N	?	?
3 Wolpe	Y	Y	Y
4 ***Siljander***	?	?	?
5 ***Henry***	N	N	N
6 Carr	Y	Y	Y
7 Kildee	Y	Y	Y
8 Traxler	?	?	?
9 ***Vander Jagt***	N	N	N
10 ***Schuette***	N	N	N
11 ***Davis***	?	?	?
12 Bonior	Y	?	?
13 Crockett	?	?	?
14 Hertel	?	?	?
15 Ford	?	?	?
16 Dingell	Y	Y	Y
17 Levin	Y	Y	Y
18 ***Broomfield***	?	?	?
MINNESOTA			
1 Penny	Y	Y	Y
2 ***Weber***	N	N	N
3 ***Frenzel***	N	N	N
4 Vento	Y	Y	Y
5 Sabo	Y	Y	Y
6 Sikorski	Y	Y	Y

	332	333	334
7 ***Stangeland***	N	N	Y
8 Oberstar	Y	Y	Y
MISSISSIPPI			
1 Whitten	Y	?	?
2 ***Franklin***	?	?	?
3 Montgomery	?	?	?
4 Dowdy	?	?	?
5 ***Lott***	?	?	?
MISSOURI			
1 Clay	Y	Y	Y
2 Young	Y	Y	Y
3 Gephardt	Y	Y	Y
4 Skelton	Y	Y	Y
5 Wheat	Y	Y	Y
6 ***Coleman***	?	?	?
7 ***Taylor***	N	N	Y
8 ***Emerson***	N	N	N
9 Volkmer	Y	Y	Y
MONTANA			
1 Williams	Y	Y	N
2 ***Marlenee***	Y	N	N
NEBRASKA			
1 ***Bereuter***	N	N	N
2 ***Daub***	N	N	N
3 ***Smith***	N	N	N
NEVADA			
1 Reid	Y	Y	Y
2 ***Vucanovich***	N	N	N
NEW HAMPSHIRE			
1 ***Smith***	N	N	N
2 ***Gregg***	N	N	N
NEW JERSEY			
1 Florio	?	?	?
2 Hughes	Y	Y	Y
3 Howard	Y	Y	Y
4 ***Smith***	Y	Y	Y
5 ***Roukema***	N	Y	Y
6 Dwyer	Y	Y	Y
7 ***Rinaldo***	Y	Y	N
8 Roe	Y	Y	Y
9 Torricelli	Y	?	?
10 Rodino	?	?	?
11 ***Gallo***	N	N	Y
12 ***Courter***	N	N	N
13 ***Saxton***	N	N	N
14 Guarini	Y	Y	Y
NEW MEXICO			
1 ***Lujan***	?	?	?
2 ***Skeen***	N	N	Y
3 Richardson	Y	Y	Y
NEW YORK			
1 ***Carney***	N	N	N
2 Downey	Y	?	?
3 Mrazek	?	?	?
4 ***Lent***	?	?	?
5 ***McGrath***	Y	Y	Y
6 Waldon	Y	Y	Y
7 Ackerman	?	?	?
8 Scheuer	Y	Y	Y
9 Manton	Y	Y	Y
10 Schumer	Y	Y	Y
11 Towns	?	?	?
12 Owens	?	?	?
13 Solarz	?	?	?
14 ***Molinari***	N	N	N
15 ***Green***	N	N	Y
16 Rangel	Y	Y	Y
17 Weiss	Y	Y	Y
18 Garcia	?	?	?
19 Biaggi	?	?	?
20 ***DioGuardi***	N	N	N
21 ***Fish***	?	?	?
22 ***Gilman***	Y	Y	N
23 Stratton	Y	Y	Y
24 ***Solomon***	N	N	N
25 ***Boehlert***	N	Y	N
26 ***Martin***	?	?	?
27 ***Wortley***	N	N	Y
28 McHugh	Y	Y	Y
29 ***Horton***	?	?	?
30 ***Eckert***	Y	?	?
31 ***Kemp***	?	?	?
32 LaFalce	Y	Y	Y
33 Nowak	Y	Y	Y
34 Lundine	Y	Y	Y

	332	333	334
NORTH CAROLINA			
1 Jones	?	?	?
2 Valentine	?	?	?
3 Whitley	Y	Y	Y
4 ***Cobey***	N	N	N
5 Neal	Y	Y	N
6 ***Coble***	N	N	N
7 Rose	?	?	?
8 Hefner	?	Y	Y
9 ***McMillan***	N	N	N
10 Vacancy			
11 ***Hendon***	N	N	N
NORTH DAKOTA			
AL Dorgan	?	Y	Y
OHIO			
1 Luken	?	?	?
2 ***Gradison***	?	?	?
3 Hall	?	?	?
4 ***Oxley***	N	N	?
5 ***Latta***	N	N	N
6 ***McEwen***	N	N	N
7 ***DeWine***	Y	Y	N
8 ***Kindness***	N	Y	N
9 Kaptur	?	?	?
10 ***Miller***	N	N	N
11 Eckart	Y	Y	Y
12 ***Kasich***	N	N	N
13 Pease	Y	Y	Y
14 Seiberling	Y	Y	Y
15 ***Wylie***	N	Y	Y
16 ***Regula***	N	N	Y
17 Traficant	Y	Y	Y
18 Applegate	?	?	?
19 Feighan	Y	Y	Y
20 Oakar	Y	Y	Y
21 Stokes	Y	?	?
OKLAHOMA			
1 Jones	?	?	?
2 Synar	Y	Y	N
3 Watkins	Y	Y	Y
4 McCurdy	?	?	?
5 ***Edwards***	N	N	Y
6 English	N	Y	Y
OREGON			
1 AuCoin	N	N	Y
2 ***Smith, R.***	N	N	N
3 Wyden	Y	Y	Y
4 Weaver	?	?	?
5 ***Smith, D.***	N	N	N
PENNSYLVANIA			
1 Foglietta	?	?	?
2 Gray	Y	Y	Y
3 Borski	Y	Y	Y
4 Kolter	Y	Y	Y
5 ***Schulze***	N	N	Y
6 Yatron	?	?	?
7 Edgar	Y	Y	Y
8 Kostmayer	Y	Y	Y
9 ***Shuster***	?	?	?
10 ***McDade***	?	?	?
11 Kanjorski	Y	Y	Y
12 Murtha	Y	Y	Y
13 ***Coughlin***	N	N	N
14 Coyne	Y	Y	Y
15 ***Ritter***	N	N	Y
16 ***Walker***	N	N	N
17 ***Gekas***	N	?	?
18 Walgren	N	Y	Y
19 ***Goodling***	N	N	N
20 Gaydos	?	?	?
21 ***Ridge***	N	N	N
22 Murphy	Y	Y	Y
23 ***Clinger***	N	N	N
RHODE ISLAND			
1 St Germain	Y	Y	Y
2 ***Schneider***	N	N	Y
SOUTH CAROLINA			
1 ***Hartnett***	?	?	?
2 ***Spence***	N	N	N
3 Derrick	Y	Y	Y
4 ***Campbell***	?	?	?
5 Spratt	Y	Y	Y
6 Tallon	Y	Y	Y
SOUTH DAKOTA			
AL Daschle	Y	Y	Y

	332	333	334
TENNESSEE			
1 ***Quillen***	N	Y	Y
2 ***Duncan***	N	N	Y
3 Lloyd	Y	Y	N
4 Cooper	Y	Y	Y
5 Boner	?	?	?
6 Gordon	Y	Y	Y
7 ***Sundquist***	N	N	N
8 Jones	Y	Y	Y
9 Ford	Y	Y	Y
TEXAS			
1 Chapman	Y	Y	Y
2 Wilson	Y	Y	Y
3 ***Bartlett***	N	N	N
4 Hall, R.	Y	Y	Y
5 Bryant	Y	Y	N
6 ***Barton***	N	N	N
7 ***Archer***	N	N	N
8 ***Fields***	N	N	N
9 Brooks	Y	Y	Y
10 Pickle	N	N	Y
11 Leath	?	?	?
12 Wright	Y	Y	Y
13 ***Boulter***	N	N	N
14 ***Sweeney***	N	N	N
15 de la Garza	Y	?	?
16 Coleman	Y	Y	Y
17 Stenholm	Y	Y	Y
18 Leland	Y	Y	Y
19 ***Combest***	N	Y	N
20 Gonzalez	Y	Y	Y
21 ***Loeffler***	?	N	Y
22 ***DeLay***	N	N	N
23 Bustamante	Y	Y	Y
24 Frost	Y	Y	Y
25 Andrews	Y	Y	Y
26 ***Armey***	N	N	N
27 Ortiz	Y	Y	Y
UTAH			
1 ***Hansen***	?	?	?
2 ***Monson***	N	N	Y
3 ***Nielson***	N	N	N
VERMONT			
AL ***Jeffords***	Y	Y	N
VIRGINIA			
1 ***Bateman***	Y	Y	P
2 ***Whitehurst***	?	?	?
3 ***Bliley***	N	N	Y
4 Sisisky	Y	Y	Y
5 Daniel	N	Y	Y
6 Olin	Y	Y	Y
7 ***Slaughter***	N	N	Y
8 ***Parris***	Y	Y	N
9 Boucher	?	?	?
10 ***Wolf***	Y	Y	Y
WASHINGTON			
1 ***Miller***	N	Y	Y
2 Swift	Y	Y	Y
3 Bonker	?	?	?
4 ***Morrison***	N	Y	?
5 Foley	Y	Y	Y
6 Dicks	Y	Y	Y
7 Lowry	Y	Y	Y
8 ***Chandler***	N	Y	Y
WEST VIRGINIA			
1 Mollohan	Y	Y	Y
2 Staggers	Y	Y	Y
3 Wise	Y	Y	Y
4 Rahall	Y	Y	Y
WISCONSIN			
1 Aspin	?	?	?
2 Kastenmeier	Y	Y	Y
3 ***Gunderson***	N	N	N
4 Kleczka	Y	Y	Y
5 Moody	Y	Y	Y
6 ***Petri***	N	N	Y
7 Obey	Y	Y	Y
8 ***Roth***	N	N	N
9 ***Sensenbrenner***	N	N	N
WYOMING			
AL ***Cheney***	N	Y	Y

Southern states - Ala., Ark., Fla., Ga., Ky., La., Miss., N.C., Okla., S.C., Tenn., Texas, Va.

* The *Congressional Record* vote number is different from the CQ vote number because the *Record* includes quorum calls in its tally. CQ does not publish quorum call votes.

335. H Res 542. Daniloff Arrest. Adoption of the resolution to demand that the Soviet Union free Nicholas Daniloff, Moscow correspondent for *U.S. News & World Report*, who was being held on espionage charges. Adopted 394-0: R 165-0; D 229-0 (ND 151-0, SD 78-0), Sept. 10, 1986.

336. HR 5484. Omnibus Drug Bill. Adoption of the rule (H Res 541) to provide for House floor consideration of the bill to authorize more than $6 billion over three years for improved federal drug eradication, enforcement, interdiction, education, treatment and prevention efforts. Adopted 382-19: R 164-4; D 218-15 (ND 140-15, SD 78-0), Sept. 10, 1986.

337. HR 5484. Omnibus Drug Bill. Hunter, R-Calif., amendment to the Bennett, D-Fla., amendment, to require that the president deploy the armed forces to halt substantially, within 45 days, the unlawful entry of aircraft and vessels carrying narcotics. Adopted 237-177: R 145-29; D 92-148 (ND 55-108, SD 37-40), Sept. 11, 1986. (The Bennett amendment, to allow the use of members of the armed services to assist drug enforcement officials outside the United States, as amended by the Hunter amendment, subsequently was adopted *(see vote 338, below)*.) A "nay" was a vote supporting the president's position.

338. HR 5484. Omnibus Drug Bill. Bennett, D-Fla., amendment, as amended by the Hunter, R-Calif., amendment *(see vote 337, above)*, to allow the use of members of the armed services to assist drug enforcement officials outside the United States, and to require that the president deploy the armed forces to halt substantially, within 45 days, the unlawful entry of aircraft and vessels carrying narcotics. Adopted 359-52: R 170-2; D 189-50 (ND 117-46, SD 72-4), Sept. 11, 1986. A "nay" was a vote supporting the president's position.

339. HR 5484. Omnibus Drug Bill. Crane, R-Ill., amendment to reduce authorization levels in the bill for the U.S. Customs Service and to spread additional authorizations over three years. Rejected 12-395: R 11-161; D 1-234 (ND 0-157, SD 1-77), Sept. 11, 1986.

340. HR 5484. Omnibus Drug Bill. Kramer, R-Colo., amendment to impose a mandatory life sentence for a person aged 21 or older convicted of a second offense of selling a controlled substance to a person under age 21. Adopted 355-54: R 172-1; D 183-53 (ND 112-48, SD 71-5), Sept. 11, 1986.

341. HR 5484. Omnibus Drug Bill. Rangel, D-N.Y., amendment to increase authorization levels for grants to state and local law enforcement agencies to $660 million for fiscal 1987 and to $695 million for fiscal 1988; to reduce the state matching requirement from 50 percent to 10 percent; and to permit the use of grant funds for non-federal prison construction. Adopted 242-171: R 53-120; D 189-51 (ND 131-32, SD 58-19), Sept. 11, 1986.

342. HR 5484. Omnibus Drug Bill. McCollum, R-Fla., amendment to remove the monetary cap for state prison industry contracts with the federal government. Rejected 72-339: R 56-117; D 16-222 (ND 10-151, SD 6-71), Sept. 11, 1986.

KEY

- Y Voted for (yea).
- # Paired for.
- + Announced for.
- N Voted against (nay).
- X Paired against.
- - Announced against.
- P Voted "present."
- C Voted "present" to avoid possible conflict of interest.
- ? Did not vote or otherwise make a position known.

Democrats ***Republicans***

	335	336	337	338	339	340	341	342
ALABAMA								
1 ***Callahan***	Y	Y	Y	?	N	Y	N	Y
2 ***Dickinson***	Y	Y	N	N	N	Y	N	Y
3 Nichols	Y	Y	N	Y	N	Y	Y	N
4 Bevill	Y	Y	N	Y	N	Y	Y	N
5 Flippo	Y	Y	N	?	N	Y	Y	N
6 Erdreich	Y	Y	Y	Y	N	Y	Y	N
7 Shelby	?	Y	Y	Y	Y	Y	Y	N
ALASKA								
AL ***Young***	?	?	?	?	?	?	?	?
ARIZONA								
1 ***McCain***	Y	Y	Y	Y	N	Y	N	N
2 Udall	?	?	N	Y	N	N	Y	N
3 ***Stump***	Y	Y	Y	Y	N	Y	N	N
4 ***Rudd***	?	?	?	?	?	?	?	?
5 ***Kolbe***	Y	Y	Y	Y	N	Y	N	Y
ARKANSAS								
1 Alexander	Y	Y	N	Y	N	Y	Y	N
2 Robinson	Y	Y	Y	Y	N	Y	Y	N
3 ***Hammerschmidt***	Y	Y	Y	Y	N	Y	Y	N
4 Anthony	Y	Y	N	Y	N	Y	Y	Y
CALIFORNIA								
1 Bosco	Y	?	N	N	N	N	N	N
2 ***Chappie***	?	?	?	?	?	?	?	?
3 Matsui	Y	Y	N	Y	N	Y	Y	N
4 Fazio	Y	Y	N	Y	N	Y	N	N
5 Burton	?	?	?	?	?	?	?	?
6 Boxer	Y	N	N	Y	N	N	Y	N
7 Miller	?	Y	N	Y	N	Y	Y	N
8 Dellums	Y	N	N	N	N	N	Y	N
9 Stark	Y	Y	N	N	?	N	Y	N
10 Edwards	Y	N	N	N	N	N	Y	N
11 Lantos	Y	Y	Y	Y	N	Y	Y	N
12 ***Zschau***	Y	Y	Y	Y	N	Y	N	N
13 Mineta	Y	Y	N	N	N	Y	Y	N
14 ***Shumway***	?	Y	Y	Y	N	Y	N	Y
15 Coelho	Y	Y	N	Y	N	Y	Y	N
16 Panetta	Y	Y	N	N	N	Y	N	N
17 ***Pashayan***	Y	Y	Y	Y	N	Y	Y	N
18 Lehman	Y	Y	Y	Y	N	Y	Y	N
19 ***Lagomarsino***	Y	Y	Y	Y	N	Y	N	N
20 ***Thomas***	Y	Y	Y	Y	N	Y	N	N
21 ***Fiedler***	Y	Y	Y	Y	N	Y	N	Y
22 ***Moorhead***	Y	Y	Y	Y	N	Y	N	N
23 Beilenson	Y	N	N	N	N	N	N	N
24 Waxman	Y	Y	Y	Y	N	N	Y	N
25 Roybal	Y	?	N	N	N	N	Y	N
26 Berman	Y	N	N	N	N	Y	Y	N
27 Levine	Y	N	N	Y	N	Y	Y	N
28 Dixon	?	Y	N	N	N	Y	Y	N
29 Hawkins	Y	Y	N	N	N	N	Y	N
30 Martinez	Y	Y	N	Y	N	Y	Y	N
31 Dymally	Y	Y	N	N	N	N	Y	N
32 Anderson	Y	Y	Y	Y	N	Y	Y	N
33 ***Dreier***	Y	Y	Y	Y	N	Y	N	Y
34 Torres	Y	Y	N	Y	N	Y	Y	N
35 ***Lewis***	Y	Y	Y	Y	N	Y	N	N
36 Brown	Y	Y	N	Y	?	?	Y	N
37 ***McCandless***	Y	Y	Y	Y	Y	Y	N	Y
38 ***Dornan***	+	Y	Y	Y	N	Y	Y	N
39 ***Dannemeyer***	Y	N	Y	Y	Y	Y	N	Y
40 ***Badham***	Y	Y	Y	Y	N	Y	N	Y
41 ***Lowery***	Y	Y	Y	Y	N	Y	N	Y
42 ***Lungren***	Y	Y	N	Y	N	Y	N	Y
43 ***Packard***	Y	Y	Y	Y	N	Y	N	Y
44 Bates	Y	Y	Y	Y	N	Y	Y	N
45 ***Hunter***	Y	Y	Y	Y	N	Y	?	Y
COLORADO								
1 Schroeder	Y	N	N	Y	N	Y	Y	N
2 Wirth	Y	Y	N	Y	N	Y	Y	N
3 ***Strang***	Y	Y	Y	Y	N	Y	?	N
4 ***Brown***	Y	N	Y	Y	Y	Y	N	Y
5 ***Kramer***	Y	Y	Y	Y	N	Y	N	Y
6 ***Schaefer***	Y	N	Y	Y	N	Y	N	N
CONNECTICUT								
1 Kennelly	Y	Y	N	Y	N	Y	Y	N
2 Gejdenson	Y	Y	N	Y	N	Y	Y	N
3 Morrison	Y	Y	N	N	N	N	Y	N
4 ***McKinney***	Y	Y	Y	Y	N	Y	Y	N
5 ***Rowland***	Y	Y	Y	Y	N	Y	Y	Y
6 ***Johnson***	Y	Y	N	Y	N	Y	Y	N
DELAWARE								
AL Carper	Y	Y	Y	Y	N	Y	N	Y
FLORIDA								
1 Hutto	Y	Y	N	Y	N	Y	N	N
2 Fuqua	Y	Y	N	Y	N	Y	N	N
3 Bennett	Y	Y	Y	Y	N	Y	Y	N
4 Chappell	Y	Y	N	Y	N	Y	N	N
5 ***McCollum***	Y	Y	N	Y	N	Y	N	Y
6 MacKay	Y	Y	Y	Y	N	Y	Y	Y
7 Gibbons	Y	Y	N	Y	N	Y	Y	N
8 ***Young***	Y	Y	N	Y	N	Y	Y	N
9 ***Bilirakis***	Y	Y	Y	Y	N	Y	N	Y
10 ***Ireland***	Y	Y	Y	Y	N	Y	N	N
11 Nelson	Y	Y	+	Y	N	Y	Y	Y
12 ***Lewis***	Y	Y	Y	Y	N	Y	Y	N
13 ***Mack***	Y	Y	Y	Y	N	Y	N	N
14 Mica	Y	Y	Y	Y	N	Y	Y	N
15 ***Shaw***	Y	Y	Y	Y	N	Y	N	Y
16 Smith	Y	Y	Y	Y	N	Y	Y	N
17 Lehman	Y	Y	N	N	N	N	N	Y
18 Pepper	Y	Y	N	Y	N	Y	Y	N
19 Fascell	Y	Y	N	Y	N	Y	Y	N
GEORGIA								
1 Thomas	Y	Y	Y	Y	N	Y	Y	N
2 Hatcher	Y	Y	Y	Y	N	Y	Y	N
3 Ray	Y	Y	N	N	N	Y	N	N
4 ***Swindall***	Y	Y	Y	Y	N	Y	N	N
5 Fowler	?	?	?	?	?	Y	Y	N
6 ***Gingrich***	Y	Y	Y	Y	N	Y	N	N
7 Darden	Y	Y	Y	Y	N	Y	N	N
8 Rowland	Y	Y	Y	Y	N	Y	Y	N
9 Jenkins	Y	Y	Y	Y	N	Y	N	N
10 Barnard	Y	Y	Y	Y	N	Y	N	Y
HAWAII								
1 Vacancy								
2 Akaka	Y	Y	N	Y	N	Y	Y	N
IDAHO								
1 ***Craig***	Y	Y	Y	Y	N	Y	Y	N
2 Stallings	Y	Y	Y	Y	N	Y	N	N
ILLINOIS								
1 Hayes	Y	Y	N	Y	N	N	Y	N
2 Savage	?	?	N	N	N	N	Y	N
3 Russo	Y	Y	Y	Y	N	Y	N	N
4 Vacancy								
5 Lipinski	Y	Y	Y	Y	N	Y	Y	N
6 ***Hyde***	Y	Y	Y	Y	N	Y	N	Y
7 Collins	Y	Y	N	N	N	N	Y	N
8 Rostenkowski	?	?	?	?	N	Y	Y	N
9 Yates	Y	Y	N	N	N	N	Y	N
10 ***Porter***	?	Y	Y	Y	Y	Y	N	?
11 Annunzio	Y	Y	Y	Y	N	Y	Y	N
12 ***Crane***	Y	N	Y	Y	Y	Y	N	Y
13 ***Fawell***	Y	Y	Y	Y	N	Y	N	Y
14 ***Grotberg***	?	?	?	?	?	?	?	?
15 ***Madigan***	Y	Y	Y	Y	N	Y	N	N
16 ***Martin***	Y	Y	Y	Y	N	Y	N	N
17 Evans	Y	Y	N	Y	N	N	Y	N
18 ***Michel***	Y	Y	Y	Y	N	Y	N	N
19 Bruce	Y	Y	N	Y	N	Y	Y	N
20 Durbin	Y	Y	N	Y	N	Y	Y	Y
21 Price	Y	Y	N	Y	N	Y	Y	N
22 Gray	Y	Y	N	Y	N	Y	Y	Y
INDIANA								
1 Visclosky	Y	N	N	N	N	N	Y	N
2 Sharp	Y	Y	N	Y	N	Y	Y	N
3 ***Hiler***	Y	Y	Y	Y	N	Y	N	N
4 ***Coats***	Y	Y	Y	?	N	Y	N	Y
5 ***Hillis***	Y	Y	N	Y	N	Y	Y	Y

ND - Northern Democrats SD - Southern Democrats

* Corresponding to Congressional Record Votes 365, 366, 367, 368, 369, 370, 371, 372

	335	336	337	338	339	340	341	342
6 ***Burton***	Y	Y	Y	Y	N	Y	N	N
7 ***Myers***	Y	Y	N	Y	N	Y	N	N
8 McCloskey	Y	Y	Y	Y	N	Y	Y	N
9 Hamilton	Y	Y	N	Y	N	Y	Y	N
10 Jacobs	Y	Y	Y	Y	N	Y	Y	N
IOWA								
1 ***Leach***	Y	Y	N	Y	N	Y	N	N
2 ***Tauke***	Y	Y	Y	Y	N	Y	N	N
3 ***Evans***	Y	Y	Y	Y	N	Y	N	N
4 Smith	Y	Y	Y	Y	N	Y	N	N
5 ***Lightfoot***	Y	Y	Y	Y	N	Y	N	N
6 Bedell	Y	Y	N	N	N	Y	N	N
KANSAS								
1 ***Roberts***	Y	Y	Y	Y	N	Y	N	N
2 Slattery	Y	Y	Y	Y	N	Y	N	Y
3 ***Meyers***	Y	Y	Y	Y	N	Y	N	N
4 Glickman	Y	Y	N	N	N	Y	N	Y
5 ***Whittaker***	Y	Y	Y	Y	N	Y	N	Y
KENTUCKY								
1 Hubbard	Y	Y	Y	Y	N	Y	Y	N
2 Natcher	Y	Y	Y	Y	N	Y	Y	N
3 Mazzoli	Y	Y	N	Y	N	Y	Y	N
4 ***Snyder***	Y	Y	Y	Y	N	Y	N	N
5 ***Rogers***	Y	Y	Y	Y	N	Y	N	N
6 ***Hopkins***	Y	Y	Y	Y	?	Y	Y	N
7 Perkins	Y	Y	Y	Y	N	Y	Y	N
LOUISIANA								
1 ***Livingston***	Y	Y	Y	Y	N	Y	N	Y
2 Boggs	Y	Y	Y	?	N	Y	Y	N
3 Tauzin	Y	Y	Y	Y	N	Y	Y	N
4 Roemer	Y	Y	Y	Y	N	Y	Y	N
5 Huckaby	Y	Y	?	?	?	?	?	?
6 ***Moore***	?	Y	Y	Y	N	Y	Y	N
7 Breaux	?	?	?	?	?	?	?	?
8 Long	Y	Y	N	Y	N	N	Y	N
MAINE								
1 ***McKernan***	Y	Y	Y	Y	N	Y	Y	N
2 ***Snowe***	Y	Y	Y	Y	N	Y	Y	N
MARYLAND								
1 Dyson	Y	Y	Y	Y	N	Y	Y	N
2 ***Bentley***	Y	Y	Y	Y	N	Y	Y	N
3 Mikulski	?	Y	N	Y	N	Y	Y	?
4 ***Holt***	Y	Y	?	?	?	Y	N	Y
5 Hoyer	Y	Y	N	N	N	Y	Y	N
6 Byron	?	Y	N	Y	N	Y	Y	N
7 Mitchell	?	Y	N	N	N	?	Y	N
8 Barnes	?	Y	N	N	N	N	Y	N
MASSACHUSETTS								
1 ***Conte***	Y	Y	N	Y	N	Y	N	N
2 Boland	Y	Y	N	Y	N	Y	Y	N
3 Early	Y	Y	Y	Y	N	N	N	N
4 Frank	Y	Y	N	N	N	Y	Y	N
5 Atkins	Y	Y	N	N	N	Y	N	N
6 Mavroules	Y	Y	N	Y	N	Y	Y	N
7 Markey	Y	Y	?	?	?	?	?	?
8 O'Neill								
9 Moakley	Y	Y	N	Y	?	Y	Y	N
10 Studds	Y	Y	N	N	N	N	Y	N
11 Donnelly	Y	Y	Y	Y	N	Y	Y	N
MICHIGAN								
1 Conyers	?	?	N	N	?	N	Y	Y
2 ***Pursell***	Y	Y	N	Y	N	Y	Y	N
3 Wolpe	Y	Y	N	N	N	Y	Y	N
4 ***Siljander***	Y	Y	Y	Y	N	Y	N	N
5 ***Henry***	Y	Y	Y	Y	N	Y	Y	Y
6 Carr	Y	Y	Y	Y	N	Y	Y	N
7 Kildee	Y	Y	N	Y	N	Y	Y	N
8 Traxler	Y	Y	N	Y	N	Y	Y	N
9 ***Vander Jagt***	Y	Y	Y	Y	N	Y	Y	Y
10 ***Schuette***	Y	Y	Y	Y	N	Y	Y	N
11 ***Davis***	Y	Y	Y	Y	N	Y	N	N
12 Bonior	Y	Y	N	N	N	Y	Y	N
13 Crockett	?	Y	N	N	N	N	Y	N
14 Hertel	Y	Y	Y	Y	N	Y	Y	Y
15 Ford	Y	Y	N	Y	N	Y	Y	N
16 Dingell	Y	Y	N	Y	N	Y	Y	N
17 Levin	Y	Y	N	Y	N	Y	Y	N
18 ***Broomfield***	Y	Y	Y	Y	N	Y	Y	N
MINNESOTA								
1 Penny	Y	Y	Y	Y	N	Y	N	N
2 ***Weber***	Y	Y	Y	Y	N	Y	N	N
3 ***Frenzel***	Y	Y	Y	Y	Y	Y	N	N
4 Vento	Y	Y	N	Y	N	N	Y	N
5 Sabo	Y	N	N	N	N	N	N	N
6 Sikorski	Y	Y	?	?	?	?	?	?
7 ***Stangeland***	?	?	Y	Y	N	Y	N	Y
8 Oberstar	Y	Y	N	Y	N	N	N	N
MISSISSIPPI								
1 Whitten	Y	Y	?	?	?	?	?	?
2 ***Franklin***	Y	Y	Y	Y	N	Y	N	N
3 Montgomery	Y	Y	N	Y	N	Y	N	N
4 Dowdy	Y	Y	Y	Y	N	Y	Y	N
5 ***Lott***	Y	Y	Y	Y	N	Y	N	N
MISSOURI								
1 Clay	Y	N	N	N	N	N	Y	N
2 Young	Y	Y	N	Y	N	Y	Y	N
3 Gephardt	Y	Y	N	Y	N	Y	Y	N
4 Skelton	Y	Y	N	Y	N	Y	Y	N
5 Wheat	Y	N	N	N	N	Y	Y	N
6 ***Coleman***	Y	Y	Y	Y	N	Y	Y	N
7 ***Taylor***	Y	Y	Y	Y	N	Y	Y	N
8 ***Emerson***	Y	Y	Y	Y	N	Y	Y	N
9 Volkmer	Y	Y	Y	Y	N	Y	Y	N
MONTANA								
1 Williams	Y	?	N	Y	N	N	N	?
2 ***Marlenee***	Y	Y	Y	Y	N	Y	N	N
NEBRASKA								
1 ***Bereuter***	Y	Y	N	Y	N	Y	N	N
2 ***Daub***	Y	Y	N	Y	N	Y	N	N
3 ***Smith***	Y	Y	Y	Y	N	Y	N	N
NEVADA								
1 Reid	Y	Y	Y	Y	N	Y	Y	N
2 ***Vucanovich***	Y	Y	Y	Y	N	Y	N	Y
NEW HAMPSHIRE								
1 ***Smith***	Y	Y	Y	Y	N	Y	N	Y
2 ***Gregg***	Y	Y	Y	Y	N	Y	N	Y
NEW JERSEY								
1 Florio	Y	Y	Y	Y	N	Y	Y	N
2 Hughes	Y	N	N	Y	N	N	N	Y
3 Howard	Y	Y	Y	Y	N	Y	Y	N
4 ***Smith***	Y	Y	Y	Y	N	Y	Y	N
5 ***Roukema***	Y	Y	Y	Y	N	Y	N	N
6 Dwyer	Y	Y	Y	Y	N	Y	Y	N
7 ***Rinaldo***	Y	Y	Y	Y	N	Y	Y	N
8 Roe	Y	Y	Y	Y	N	Y	Y	N
9 Torricelli	Y	Y	Y	Y	N	Y	Y	N
10 Rodino	Y	Y	N	N	N	N	Y	N
11 ***Gallo***	Y	Y	Y	Y	N	Y	Y	N
12 ***Courter***	?	Y	Y	Y	N	Y	Y	N
13 ***Saxton***	Y	Y	Y	Y	N	Y	Y	N
14 Guarini	Y	Y	Y	Y	N	Y	Y	N
NEW MEXICO								
1 ***Lujan***	Y	Y	Y	Y	N	Y	N	Y
2 ***Skeen***	Y	Y	Y	Y	N	Y	N	N
3 Richardson	Y	Y	Y	Y	N	Y	Y	N
NEW YORK								
1 ***Carney***	Y	?	N	Y	N	Y	N	Y
2 Downey	Y	Y	N	Y	N	Y	Y	N
3 Mrazek	Y	Y	N	Y	N	Y	Y	N
4 ***Lent***	Y	Y	Y	Y	N	Y	Y	N
5 ***McGrath***	Y	?	Y	Y	N	Y	Y	N
6 Waldon	?	?	N	Y	N	Y	Y	N
7 Ackerman	Y	Y	N	Y	?	?	?	?
8 Scheuer	Y	Y	N	Y	N	N	Y	N
9 Manton	Y	Y	Y	Y	N	Y	Y	N
10 Schumer	Y	Y	Y	Y	N	Y	Y	N
11 Towns	Y	Y	N	N	N	N	Y	N
12 Owens	?	?	N	Y	N	Y	Y	N
13 Solarz	Y	Y	N	Y	N	N	Y	N
14 ***Molinari***	Y	Y	Y	Y	N	Y	Y	N
15 ***Green***	Y	Y	N	N	N	Y	Y	N
16 Rangel	Y	Y	N	Y	N	N	Y	N
17 Weiss	Y	N	N	N	N	N	Y	N
18 Garcia	Y	Y	N	Y	N	N	Y	N
19 Biaggi	Y	?	Y	Y	N	Y	Y	N
20 ***DioGuardi***	Y	Y	Y	Y	N	Y	Y	N
21 ***Fish***	Y	Y	N	Y	N	Y	N	Y
22 ***Gilman***	Y	Y	N	Y	N	Y	Y	N
23 Stratton	?	?	?	?	?	?	#	?
24 ***Solomon***	Y	Y	Y	Y	N	Y	Y	N
25 ***Boehlert***	Y	Y	Y	Y	N	Y	N	N
26 ***Martin***	Y	Y	Y	Y	N	Y	Y	N
27 ***Wortley***	Y	Y	Y	Y	N	Y	Y	N
28 McHugh	Y	Y	Y	Y	N	N	Y	N
29 ***Horton***	Y	Y	N	Y	N	Y	Y	N
30 ***Eckert***	Y	Y	Y	Y	N	Y	N	N
31 ***Kemp***	Y	Y	Y	Y	N	Y	Y	N
32 LaFalce	Y	Y	Y	Y	N	N	Y	N
33 Nowak	Y	Y	Y	Y	N	Y	Y	N
34 Lundine	Y	Y	Y	Y	N	Y	Y	N
NORTH CAROLINA								
1 Jones	Y	Y	N	Y	N	Y	Y	N
2 Valentine	Y	Y	N	Y	N	Y	N	N
3 Whitley	Y	Y	N	Y	N	Y	Y	N
4 ***Cobey***	Y	Y	Y	Y	N	Y	N	N
5 Neal	Y	Y	N	Y	N	Y	Y	N
6 ***Coble***	Y	Y	Y	Y	N	Y	N	N
7 Rose	Y	Y	N	Y	N	Y	Y	N
8 Hefner	Y	Y	N	Y	N	Y	Y	N
9 ***McMillan***	Y	Y	Y	Y	N	Y	Y	N
10 Vacancy								
11 ***Hendon***	Y	?	Y	Y	N	Y	Y	N
NORTH DAKOTA								
AL Dorgan	Y	Y	N	Y	N	Y	N	N
OHIO								
1 Luken	Y	Y	Y	Y	N	Y	Y	N
2 ***Gradison***	Y	Y	Y	Y	N	Y	N	Y
3 Hall	Y	Y	Y	Y	N	Y	N	Y
4 ***Oxley***	Y	Y	N	Y	N	Y	N	Y
5 ***Latta***	Y	Y	Y	Y	N	Y	N	N
6 ***McEwen***	Y	Y	N	Y	N	Y	N	Y
7 ***DeWine***	Y	Y	Y	Y	N	Y	N	Y
8 ***Kindness***	Y	Y	Y	Y	N	Y	Y	Y
9 Kaptur	Y	Y	Y	Y	N	Y	N	N
10 ***Miller***	Y	Y	Y	Y	N	Y	N	Y
11 Eckart	Y	Y	Y	Y	N	Y	Y	N
12 ***Kasich***	Y	Y	Y	Y	N	Y	N	Y
13 Pease	Y	Y	N	N	N	N	N	N
14 Seiberling	?	Y	N	N	N	Y	Y	N
15 ***Wylie***	Y	Y	Y	Y	N	Y	N	N
16 ***Regula***	Y	Y	Y	Y	N	Y	N	N
17 Traficant	Y	Y	Y	Y	N	Y	Y	N
18 Applegate	Y	Y	Y	Y	N	Y	Y	Y
19 Feighan	Y	Y	N	Y	N	Y	Y	N
20 Oakar	Y	Y	N	Y	N	Y	Y	N
21 Stokes	Y	N	N	N	N	N	N	N
OKLAHOMA								
1 Jones	Y	Y	Y	Y	N	Y	Y	N
2 Synar	Y	Y	N	N	N	-	-	-
3 Watkins	Y	Y	Y	Y	N	?	Y	N
4 McCurdy	Y	Y	Y	Y	N	Y	Y	N
5 ***Edwards***	Y	Y	Y	Y	N	Y	Y	N
6 English	Y	Y	N	Y	N	Y	Y	N
OREGON								
1 AuCoin	Y	Y	N	N	N	Y	N	N
2 ***Smith, R.***	Y	Y	Y	Y	N	Y	Y	N
3 Wyden	Y	Y	Y	Y	N	Y	Y	N
4 Weaver	?	?	?	?	?	?	?	?
5 ***Smith, D.***	Y	Y	Y	Y	N	Y	N	N
PENNSYLVANIA								
1 Foglietta	Y	Y	N	Y	N	Y	Y	N
2 Gray	Y	Y	N	Y	?	Y	Y	N
3 Borski	Y	Y	N	Y	N	Y	Y	N
4 Kolter	Y	Y	Y	Y	N	Y	Y	N
5 ***Schulze***	Y	Y	Y	Y	N	Y	Y	N
6 Yatron	Y	Y	Y	Y	N	Y	Y	N
7 Edgar	Y	Y	N	Y	N	Y	Y	N
8 Kostmayer	Y	Y	N	Y	N	Y	N	N
9 ***Shuster***	Y	Y	Y	Y	N	Y	N	N
10 ***McDade***	Y	Y	N	Y	N	Y	Y	N
11 Kanjorski	Y	Y	Y	Y	N	Y	Y	N
12 Murtha	Y	Y	N	Y	N	N	Y	N
13 ***Coughlin***	Y	Y	N	Y	N	Y	Y	N
14 Coyne	Y	Y	N	Y	N	Y	Y	N
15 ***Ritter***	Y	Y	Y	Y	N	Y	N	N
16 ***Walker***	Y	Y	Y	Y	Y	Y	N	Y
17 ***Gekas***	Y	Y	Y	Y	Y	Y	N	Y
18 Walgren	Y	Y	Y	Y	N	Y	Y	N
19 ***Goodling***	Y	?	Y	Y	N	Y	N	Y
20 Gaydos	Y	Y	Y	Y	?	?	Y	N
21 ***Ridge***	Y	Y	Y	Y	N	Y	N	N
22 Murphy	Y	Y	Y	Y	N	Y	N	N
23 ***Clinger***	Y	Y	Y	Y	N	Y	N	Y
RHODE ISLAND								
1 St Germain	Y	Y	Y	Y	N	Y	Y	N
2 ***Schneider***	Y	Y	N	Y	?	?	N	N
SOUTH CAROLINA								
1 ***Hartnett***	?	?	Y	Y	N	Y	N	N
2 ***Spence***	Y	Y	Y	Y	N	?	N	N
3 Derrick	Y	Y	N	Y	N	Y	N	N
4 ***Campbell***	?	?	?	?	?	?	X	?
5 Spratt	Y	Y	N	Y	N	Y	N	N
6 Tallon	Y	Y	Y	Y	N	Y	N	N
SOUTH DAKOTA								
AL Daschle	Y	Y	Y	Y	N	Y	Y	N
TENNESSEE								
1 ***Quillen***	Y	Y	Y	Y	N	Y	Y	N
2 ***Duncan***	Y	Y	Y	Y	N	Y	Y	?
3 Lloyd	Y	Y	Y	Y	N	Y	Y	N
4 Cooper	Y	Y	N	Y	N	Y	Y	N
5 Boner	Y	Y	Y	Y	N	?	?	N
6 Gordon	Y	Y	N	Y	N	Y	Y	Y
7 ***Sundquist***	Y	Y	Y	Y	N	Y	N	N
8 Jones	Y	Y	N	Y	N	Y	Y	N
9 Ford	Y	Y	N	Y	N	Y	Y	N
TEXAS								
1 Chapman	Y	Y	Y	Y	N	Y	Y	N
2 Wilson	Y	Y	Y	Y	N	Y	Y	?
3 ***Bartlett***	Y	Y	Y	Y	N	Y	N	Y
4 Hall, R.	Y	Y	Y	Y	N	Y	Y	N
5 Bryant	Y	Y	Y	Y	N	Y	Y	N
6 ***Barton***	Y	Y	Y	Y	N	Y	N	N
7 ***Archer***	Y	Y	Y	Y	N	Y	N	Y
8 ***Fields***	Y	Y	Y	Y	N	Y	N	Y
9 Brooks	Y	Y	N	Y	N	Y	Y	N
10 Pickle	Y	Y	Y	Y	N	Y	N	N
11 Leath	Y	?	N	Y	N	Y	Y	N
12 Wright	Y	Y	N	Y	N	Y	Y	N
13 ***Boulter***	Y	Y	Y	Y	N	Y	N	Y
14 ***Sweeney***	Y	Y	Y	Y	N	Y	N	N
15 de la Garza	?	?	Y	Y	N	Y	Y	N
16 Coleman	Y	Y	Y	Y	N	Y	Y	N
17 Stenholm	Y	Y	Y	Y	N	Y	N	N
18 Leland	Y	Y	N	Y	N	N	Y	N
19 ***Combest***	Y	Y	Y	Y	N	Y	N	N
20 Gonzalez	Y	Y	N	N	N	N	N	N
21 ***Loeffler***	Y	Y	Y	Y	N	Y	N	N
22 ***DeLay***	Y	Y	Y	Y	N	Y	N	N
23 Bustamante	Y	Y	N	Y	N	Y	Y	N
24 Frost	Y	Y	Y	Y	N	N	Y	N
25 Andrews	Y	Y	Y	Y	N	Y	Y	N
26 ***Armey***	Y	Y	Y	Y	N	Y	N	N
27 Ortiz	Y	Y	Y	Y	N	Y	Y	N
UTAH								
1 ***Hansen***	Y	Y	N	Y	N	Y	N	N
2 ***Monson***	Y	Y	Y	Y	Y	Y	N	Y
3 ***Nielson***	Y	Y	N	Y	Y	Y	N	Y
VERMONT								
AL ***Jeffords***	?	?	N	Y	N	Y	Y	N
VIRGINIA								
1 ***Bateman***	Y	Y	N	Y	N	Y	N	N
2 ***Whitehurst***	Y	Y	N	Y	N	Y	N	N
3 ***Bliley***	Y	Y	Y	Y	N	Y	N	N
4 Sisisky	Y	Y	N	Y	N	Y	N	N
5 Daniel	Y	Y	N	Y	N	Y	N	N
6 Olin	Y	Y	N	Y	N	Y	N	N
7 ***Slaughter***	Y	Y	Y	Y	N	Y	N	N
8 ***Parris***	Y	Y	Y	Y	N	Y	Y	N
9 Boucher	Y	Y	N	Y	N	Y	Y	N
10 ***Wolf***	Y	Y	Y	Y	N	Y	Y	Y
WASHINGTON								
1 ***Miller***	Y	Y	Y	Y	N	Y	N	N
2 Swift	Y	Y	N	N	N	N	Y	N
3 Bonker	Y	?	N	Y	N	N	N	N
4 ***Morrison***	Y	Y	Y	Y	N	Y	Y	Y
5 Foley	Y	Y	N	N	N	N	Y	N
6 Dicks	Y	Y	N	Y	N	Y	Y	N
7 Lowry	Y	Y	N	N	N	N	N	N
8 ***Chandler***	Y	Y	N	Y	N	N	N	Y
WEST VIRGINIA								
1 Mollohan	Y	Y	Y	Y	N	Y	Y	N
2 Staggers	Y	Y	Y	Y	N	Y	N	N
3 Wise	Y	Y	Y	Y	N	Y	Y	N
4 Rahall	Y	Y	Y	Y	N	Y	Y	N
WISCONSIN								
1 Aspin	Y	Y	N	N	N	Y	Y	N
2 Kastenmeier	Y	N	N	N	N	N	N	N
3 ***Gunderson***	Y	Y	Y	Y	N	Y	N	N
4 Kleczka	?	Y	N	Y	N	Y	N	N
5 Moody	Y	Y	N	N	N	N	Y	N
6 ***Petri***	Y	Y	Y	Y	N	Y	N	N
7 Obey	Y	Y	N	N	N	N	N	N
8 ***Roth***	+	Y	Y	Y	N	Y	N	N
9 ***Sensenbrenner***	?	Y	Y	Y	N	Y	N	N
WYOMING								
AL ***Cheney***	Y	Y	N	Y	Y	Y	N	N

Southern states - Ala., Ark., Fla., Ga., Ky., La., Miss., N.C., Okla., S.C., Tenn., Texas, Va.
* The *Congressional Record* vote number is different from the CQ vote number because the *Record* includes quorum calls in its tally. CQ does not publish quorum call votes.

343. HR 5484. Omnibus Drug Bill. Lungren, R-Calif., amendment to permit the introduction in court of evidence obtained in a warrantless search if the search or seizure was undertaken "in a reasonable, good faith belief that it was in conformity with the Fourth Amendment to the Constitution." Adopted 259-153: R 163-8; D 96-145 (ND 38-127, SD 58-18), Sept. 11, 1986.

344. HR 5484. Omnibus Drug Bill. Gekas, R-Pa., amendment to authorize imposition of the death penalty on anyone who knowingly causes the death of another individual during the course of a continuing criminal enterprise. Adopted 296-112: R 160-10; D 136-102 (ND 69-93, SD 67-9), Sept. 11, 1986.

345. HR 5484. Omnibus Drug Bill. Bennett, D-Fla., amendment to mandate the transfer from state and local jails to federal prisons of deportable aliens convicted of a crime. Rejected 198-206: R 92-77; D 106-129 (ND 60-100, SD 46-29), Sept. 11, 1986.

346. HR 5484. Omnibus Drug Bill. Chandler, R-Wash., amendment to delete the requirement that 10 percent of funds allocated for grants for drug abuse education be earmarked for institutions of higher education. Rejected 170-231: R 125-46; D 45-185 (ND 30-128, SD 15-57), Sept. 11, 1986.

347. HR 5484. Omnibus Drug Bill. Bilirakis, R-Fla., amendment to strike the provision authorizing $650,000 for an Advisory Commission on the Comprehensive Education of Intercollegiate Athletes. Rejected 165-245: R 128-44; D 37-201 (ND 18-144, SD 19-57), Sept. 11, 1986.

348. HR 5484. Omnibus Drug Bill. Passage of the bill to authorize more than $6 billion for fiscal 1987, 1988 and 1989 for improved federal drug eradication, enforcement, interdiction, education, treatment and prevention efforts. Passed 392-16: R 170-1; D 222-15 (ND 146-14, SD 76-1), Sept. 11, 1986.

349. Procedural Motion. Broomfield, R-Mich., motion to approve the House *Journal* of Thursday, Sept. 11. Motion agreed to 232-53: R 71-45; D 161-8 (ND 105-8, SD 56-0), Sept. 12, 1986.

350. HR 4868. South Africa Sanctions. Adoption of the rule (H Res 548) to provide for House floor consideration of the bill to set policy goals and impose a series of economic sanctions on South Africa. Adopted 292-92: R 72-90; D 220-2 (ND 151-0, SD 69-2), Sept. 12, 1986. A "nay" was a vote supporting the president's position.

KEY

- Y Voted for (yea).
- # Paired for.
- + Announced for.
- N Voted against (nay).
- X Paired against.
- \- Announced against.
- P Voted "present."
- C Voted "present" to avoid possible conflict of interest.
- ? Did not vote or otherwise make a position known.

Democrats ***Republicans***

	343	344	345	346	347	348	349	350
ALABAMA								
1 ***Callahan***	Y	Y	Y	Y	Y	Y	Y	N
2 ***Dickinson***	Y	Y	Y	Y	Y	Y	?	N
3 Nichols	Y	Y	Y	N	Y	Y	Y	Y
4 Bevill	Y	Y	N	N	Y	Y	Y	Y
5 Flippo	Y	Y	N	N	Y	Y	Y	Y
6 Erdreich	Y	Y	N	N	Y	Y	Y	Y
7 Shelby	Y	Y	N	N	Y	Y	Y	Y
ALASKA								
AL ***Young***	?	?	?	?	?	?	?	?
ARIZONA								
1 ***McCain***	Y	Y	N	Y	Y	Y	Y	Y
2 Udall	N	N	N	N	N	Y	?	Y
3 ***Stump***	Y	Y	N	Y	N	Y	N	N
4 ***Rudd***	?	?	?	?	?	?	?	?
5 ***Kolbe***	Y	Y	Y	Y	Y	Y	N	Y
ARKANSAS								
1 Alexander	Y	Y	N	N	N	Y	Y	Y
2 Robinson	Y	Y	Y	Y	N	Y	Y	Y
3 ***Hammerschmidt***	Y	Y	N	Y	N	Y	Y	N
4 Anthony	Y	Y	Y	N	N	Y	?	Y
CALIFORNIA								
1 Bosco	N	Y	N	N	N	Y	?	Y
2 ***Chappie***	?	?	?	?	?	?	?	?
3 Matsui	N	N	N	N	N	Y	Y	Y
4 Fazio	N	N	N	Y	N	Y	Y	Y
5 Burton	?	?	?	?	?	?	?	?
6 Boxer	N	Y	Y	Y	N	Y	?	?
7 Miller	N	N	Y	Y	N	Y	Y	Y
8 Dellums	N	N	N	N	N	N	P	Y
9 Stark	N	N	N	?	N	Y	?	Y
10 Edwards	N	N	N	N	N	N	Y	Y
11 Lantos	Y	Y	N	Y	N	Y	Y	Y
12 ***Zschau***	Y	Y	Y	Y	Y	Y	N	Y
13 Mineta	N	N	N	N	N	Y	P	Y
14 ***Shumway***	Y	Y	N	Y	Y	Y	Y	N
15 Coelho	Y	Y	Y	N	N	Y	?	?
16 Panetta	N	Y	N	N	N	Y	Y	Y
17 ***Pashayan***	Y	Y	Y	Y	N	Y	?	N
18 Lehman	N	Y	Y	N	N	Y	?	Y
19 ***Lagomarsino***	Y	Y	Y	Y	Y	Y	N	N
20 ***Thomas***	Y	Y	Y	Y	Y	Y	?	?
21 ***Fiedler***	Y	Y	Y	N	N	Y	N	N
22 ***Moorhead***	Y	Y	N	Y	Y	Y	N	N
23 Beilenson	N	Y	N	Y	N	Y	?	Y
24 Waxman	N	N	N	N	N	Y	?	?
25 Roybal	N	N	N	?	N	N	Y	Y
26 Berman	N	N	N	N	N	Y	Y	Y
27 Levine	N	N	N	N	N	Y	Y	Y
28 Dixon	N	N	N	N	N	Y	?	Y
29 Hawkins	N	N	Y	N	N	Y	N	Y
30 Martinez	Y	Y	N	N	N	Y	Y	Y
31 Dymally	N	N	N	N	N	Y	Y	Y
32 Anderson	Y	Y	Y	N	N	Y	Y	Y
33 ***Dreier***	Y	Y	Y	Y	Y	Y	Y	N
34 Torres	N	Y	N	N	N	Y	Y	Y
35 ***Lewis***	Y	Y	Y	Y	Y	Y	Y	Y
36 Brown	N	N	Y	N	N	Y	?	?
37 ***McCandless***	Y	Y	Y	Y	Y	Y	N	N
38 ***Dornan***	Y	Y	Y	Y	Y	Y	Y	N
39 ***Dannemeyer***	Y	Y	Y	Y	Y	Y	N	N
40 ***Badham***	Y	Y	Y	Y	Y	Y	N	N
41 ***Lowery***	Y	Y	Y	Y	Y	Y	?	N
42 ***Lungren***	Y	Y	N	Y	Y	Y	Y	Y
43 ***Packard***	Y	Y	Y	Y	Y	Y	Y	N
44 Bates	N	N	Y	N	N	Y	Y	Y
45 ***Hunter***	Y	Y	Y	Y	Y	Y	?	N
COLORADO								
1 Schroeder	N	N	-	-	-	-	-	+
2 Wirth	N	N	N	N	N	Y	?	Y
3 ***Strang***	Y	Y	Y	Y	Y	Y	Y	N
4 ***Brown***	Y	Y	Y	Y	Y	Y	N	Y
5 ***Kramer***	Y	Y	N	Y	Y	Y	N	N
6 ***Schaefer***	Y	Y	Y	Y	N	Y	Y	N
CONNECTICUT								
1 Kennelly	N	N	Y	N	N	Y	Y	Y
2 Gejdenson	N	N	Y	N	N	Y	Y	Y
3 Morrison	N	N	N	Y	N	Y	?	Y
4 ***McKinney***	N	N	Y	N	N	Y	?	?
5 ***Rowland***	Y	Y	Y	Y	N	Y	Y	Y
6 ***Johnson***	Y	Y	Y	N	Y	Y	Y	N
DELAWARE								
AL Carper	Y	Y	N	Y	Y	Y	Y	Y
FLORIDA								
1 Hutto	Y	Y	Y	N	N	Y	Y	Y
2 Fuqua	Y	Y	Y	?	N	Y	Y	Y
3 Bennett	Y	Y	Y	N	N	Y	Y	Y
4 Chappell	Y	Y	Y	N	Y	Y	?	Y
5 ***McCollum***	Y	Y	Y	Y	Y	Y	Y	Y
6 MacKay	Y	Y	Y	Y	N	Y	?	Y
7 Gibbons	Y	Y	Y	N	Y	Y	Y	Y
8 ***Young***	Y	Y	Y	Y	Y	Y	Y	Y
9 ***Bilirakis***	Y	Y	Y	Y	Y	Y	?	N
10 ***Ireland***	Y	Y	Y	Y	Y	Y	Y	Y
11 Nelson	Y	Y	Y	Y	N	Y	Y	Y
12 ***Lewis***	Y	Y	Y	Y	Y	Y	N	N
13 ***Mack***	Y	Y	Y	Y	Y	Y	N	N
14 Mica	Y	Y	Y	Y	N	Y	Y	Y
15 ***Shaw***	Y	Y	Y	Y	Y	Y	Y	N
16 Smith	Y	Y	Y	N	N	Y	Y	Y
17 Lehman	N	N	Y	?	N	Y	Y	Y
18 Pepper	N	N	Y	N	N	Y	+	+
19 Fascell	Y	Y	Y	N	N	Y	Y	Y
GEORGIA								
1 Thomas	Y	Y	N	N	N	Y	Y	Y
2 Hatcher	Y	Y	Y	N	N	Y	?	Y
3 Ray	Y	Y	Y	N	Y	Y	?	Y
4 ***Swindall***	Y	Y	Y	Y	Y	Y	N	N
5 Fowler	Y	Y	Y	Y	N	Y	?	Y
6 ***Gingrich***	Y	Y	Y	Y	Y	Y	?	N
7 Darden	Y	Y	N	N	N	Y	Y	Y
8 Rowland	Y	Y	Y	N	N	Y	Y	Y
9 Jenkins	Y	Y	N	N	N	Y	Y	Y
10 Barnard	Y	Y	N	N	N	Y	Y	Y
HAWAII								
1 Vacancy								
2 Akaka	N	N	Y	N	N	Y	Y	Y
IDAHO								
1 ***Craig***	Y	Y	N	N	Y	Y	Y	N
2 Stallings	Y	Y	N	Y	Y	Y	?	Y
ILLINOIS								
1 Hayes	N	N	Y	N	N	Y	N	Y
2 Savage	N	N	N	N	N	N	Y	Y
3 Russo	Y	Y	Y	Y	N	Y	Y	Y
4 Vacancy								
5 Lipinski	Y	Y	N	N	N	Y	Y	Y
6 ***Hyde***	Y	Y	N	Y	N	Y	Y	N
7 Collins	N	N	Y	N	N	Y	Y	Y
8 Rostenkowski	Y	Y	N	Y	N	Y	Y	Y
9 Yates	N	N	N	N	N	Y	?	Y
10 ***Porter***	Y	Y	N	N	Y	Y	?	N
11 Annunzio	N	Y	N	N	N	Y	Y	Y
12 ***Crane***	Y	Y	Y	Y	Y	N	?	N
13 ***Fawell***	Y	Y	Y	Y	Y	Y	N	N
14 ***Grotberg***	?	?	?	?	?	?	?	?
15 ***Madigan***	Y	Y	N	N	N	Y	N	N
16 ***Martin***	Y	Y	N	Y	N	Y	?	Y
17 Evans	N	N	Y	N	N	Y	Y	Y
18 ***Michel***	Y	Y	N	N	Y	Y	Y	N
19 Bruce	N	Y	N	N	N	Y	Y	Y
20 Durbin	Y	Y	Y	N	N	Y	Y	Y
21 Price	N	Y	N	N	N	Y	?	Y
22 Gray	N	Y	N	N	N	Y	?	Y
INDIANA								
1 Visclosky	N	N	N	N	N	Y	Y	Y
2 Sharp	N	N	N	N	N	Y	Y	Y
3 ***Hiler***	Y	Y	N	Y	Y	Y	Y	N
4 ***Coats***	Y	Y	N	Y	Y	Y	Y	Y
5 ***Hillis***	Y	Y	N	Y	Y	Y	Y	Y

ND - Northern Democrats SD - Southern Democrats

* Corresponding to Congressional Record Votes 373, 374, 375, 376, 377, 378, 379, 380

	343	344	345	346	347	348	349	350
6 ***Burton***	Y	Y	Y	Y	Y	Y	?	N
7 ***Myers***	Y	Y	N	N	N	Y	Y	N
8 McCloskey	N	Y	Y	N	N	Y	?	Y
9 Hamilton	N	N	N	N	N	Y	Y	Y
10 Jacobs	N	N	N	N	Y	Y	N	Y
IOWA								
1 ***Leach***	N	N	N	Y	Y	Y	?	Y
2 ***Tauke***	Y	N	N	Y	Y	Y	N	Y
3 ***Evans***	Y	Y	N	N	N	Y	N	Y
4 Smith	Y	N	N	N	N	?	Y	Y
5 ***Lightfoot***	Y	Y	N	Y	Y	Y	Y	N
6 Bedell	N	N	N	N	Y	Y	Y	Y
KANSAS								
1 ***Roberts***	Y	Y	Y	Y	Y	Y	?	Y
2 Slattery	N	Y	N	Y	N	Y	?	Y
3 ***Meyers***	Y	Y	Y	N	Y	Y	?	Y
4 Glickman	N	Y	N	N	N	Y	Y	Y
5 ***Whittaker***	Y	Y	Y	Y	Y	Y	N	Y
KENTUCKY								
1 Hubbard	Y	Y	N	Y	N	Y	Y	Y
2 Natcher	Y	Y	N	N	N	Y	Y	Y
3 Mazzoli	Y	Y	N	N	N	Y	Y	Y
4 ***Snyder***	Y	?	?	?	?	?	?	?
5 ***Rogers***	Y	Y	N	Y	N	Y	Y	N
6 ***Hopkins***	Y	Y	N	Y	N	Y	Y	Y
7 Perkins	N	Y	N	N	N	Y	Y	Y
LOUISIANA								
1 ***Livingston***	Y	Y	N	Y	Y	Y	?	?
2 Boggs	N	N	Y	N	N	Y	?	Y
3 Tauzin	Y	Y	Y	N	Y	Y	Y	Y
4 Roemer	Y	Y	Y	Y	Y	Y	Y	Y
5 Huckaby	?	?	?	?	?	?	?	?
6 ***Moore***	Y	Y	Y	Y	Y	Y	?	Y
7 Breaux	?	?	?	?	?	?	?	?
8 Long	N	N	Y	N	N	Y	Y	Y
MAINE								
1 ***McKernan***	Y	Y	N	Y	N	Y	?	Y
2 ***Snowe***	Y	Y	N	Y	N	Y	Y	Y
MARYLAND								
1 Dyson	Y	Y	Y	N	N	Y	?	Y
2 ***Bentley***	Y	Y	N	N	N	Y	?	N
3 Mikulski	Y	N	Y	N	N	Y	?	Y
4 ***Holt***	Y	Y	N	Y	Y	Y	N	N
5 Hoyer	N	N	N	N	N	Y	Y	Y
6 Byron	Y	Y	N	Y	N	Y	Y	Y
7 Mitchell	N	N	N	N	N	N	?	Y
8 Barnes	N	N	N	N	N	Y	Y	Y
MASSACHUSETTS								
1 ***Conte***	N	Y	N	N	N	Y	?	Y
2 Boland	N	Y	Y	N	N	Y	Y	Y
3 Early	N	Y	N	Y	Y	Y	Y	Y
4 Frank	N	N	N	Y	Y	N	Y	Y
5 Atkins	N	N	N	N	N	Y	?	?
6 Mavroules	N	Y	N	N	N	Y	?	Y
7 Markey	?	?	?	?	?	?	?	?
8 O'Neill								
9 Moakley	N	Y	N	N	N	Y	Y	Y
10 Studds	N	N	N	N	N	Y	Y	Y
11 Donnelly	N	Y	N	N	N	Y	?	Y
MICHIGAN								
1 Conyers	N	X	N	N	Y	N	Y	Y
2 ***Pursell***	Y	Y	N	N	Y	Y	?	Y
3 Wolpe	N	N	N	N	N	Y	Y	Y
4 ***Siljander***	Y	Y	N	Y	Y	Y	?	N
5 ***Henry***	Y	Y	N	N	Y	Y	?	Y
6 Carr	Y	Y	Y	N	Y	Y	Y	Y
7 Kildee	N	N	N	N	N	Y	Y	Y
8 Traxler	N	N	N	Y	N	Y	?	Y
9 ***Vander Jagt***	Y	Y	N	Y	Y	Y	?	N
10 ***Schuette***	Y	Y	N	N	Y	Y	N	Y
11 ***Davis***	Y	Y	Y	N	N	Y	?	Y
12 Bonior	N	N	N	N	N	Y	Y	Y
13 Crockett	N	N	N	N	Y	N	?	Y
14 Hertel	N	N	N	N	N	Y	Y	Y
15 Ford	N	N	N	N	N	Y	?	?
16 Dingell	N	Y	N	N	N	Y	Y	Y
17 Levin	N	N	N	N	N	Y	Y	Y
18 ***Broomfield***	Y	Y	N	Y	N	Y	Y	N
MINNESOTA								
1 Penny	Y	N	N	Y	Y	Y	N	Y
2 ***Weber***	Y	N	N	Y	Y	Y	?	Y
3 ***Frenzel***	Y	Y	N	Y	Y	Y	Y	Y
4 Vento	N	N	N	N	N	Y	Y	Y
5 Sabo	N	N	Y	N	N	N	N	Y
6 Sikorski	N	N	N	Y	N	Y	N	Y
7 ***Stangeland***	Y	Y	?	Y	Y	Y	?	Y
8 Oberstar	N	N	N	N	N	Y	Y	Y
MISSISSIPPI								
1 Whitten	?	?	?	?	?	?	Y	Y
2 ***Franklin***	Y	Y	N	Y	Y	Y	Y	Y
3 Montgomery	Y	Y	N	N	Y	Y	Y	Y
4 Dowdy	Y	Y	N	N	N	Y	Y	Y
5 ***Lott***	Y	Y	N	Y	Y	Y	?	N
MISSOURI								
1 Clay	N	N	N	N	N	N	N	Y
2 Young	Y	Y	N	N	N	Y	Y	Y
3 Gephardt	N	?	?	?	?	?	?	?
4 Skelton	Y	Y	N	Y	N	Y	Y	Y
5 Wheat	N	N	Y	N	N	Y	Y	Y
6 ***Coleman***	Y	Y	N	Y	Y	Y	?	N
7 ***Taylor***	Y	Y	N	Y	N	Y	?	N
8 ***Emerson***	Y	Y	Y	Y	Y	Y	Y	N
9 Volkmer	Y	Y	N	N	N	Y	Y	Y
MONTANA								
1 Williams	N	N	?	N	N	Y	?	?
2 ***Marlenee***	Y	Y	N	Y	Y	Y	?	N
NEBRASKA								
1 ***Bereuter***	Y	Y	N	Y	Y	Y	N	Y
2 ***Daub***	Y	Y	Y	N	Y	Y	Y	N
3 ***Smith***	Y	Y	N	N	Y	Y	Y	Y
NEVADA								
1 Reid	Y	Y	Y	N	N	Y	Y	Y
2 ***Vucanovich***	Y	Y	Y	Y	Y	Y	?	N
NEW HAMPSHIRE								
1 ***Smith***	Y	Y	Y	Y	Y	Y	N	N
2 ***Gregg***	Y	N	?	Y	Y	Y	N	Y
NEW JERSEY								
1 Florio	N	Y	Y	N	N	Y	?	Y
2 Hughes	Y	Y	N	N	N	Y	Y	Y
3 Howard	N	Y	N	N	N	Y	Y	Y
4 ***Smith***	Y	N	Y	N	N	Y	Y	Y
5 ***Roukema***	Y	N	Y	N	N	Y	?	Y
6 Dwyer	N	Y	Y	N	N	Y	Y	Y
7 ***Rinaldo***	Y	Y	Y	N	Y	Y	?	Y
8 Roe	Y	Y	Y	N	N	Y	Y	Y
9 Torricelli	N	Y	N	Y	N	Y	Y	Y
10 Rodino	N	N	N	Y	N	Y	P	Y
11 ***Gallo***	Y	Y	N	N	N	Y	N	Y
12 ***Courter***	Y	Y	Y	N	N	Y	?	Y
13 ***Saxton***	Y	Y	N	N	N	Y	Y	Y
14 Guarini	Y	Y	N	N	N	Y	?	Y
NEW MEXICO								
1 ***Lujan***	Y	Y	Y	Y	Y	Y	?	Y
2 ***Skeen***	Y	Y	Y	Y	Y	Y	?	N
3 Richardson	Y	Y	Y	Y	N	Y	Y	Y
NEW YORK								
1 ***Carney***	Y	?	?	?	?	?	?	?
2 Downey	N	N	Y	N	N	Y	Y	Y
3 Mrazek	N	N	Y	Y	N	Y	Y	Y
4 ***Lent***	Y	Y	N	Y	Y	Y	N	Y
5 ***McGrath***	Y	Y	Y	N	N	Y	?	Y
6 Waldon	N	N	Y	N	N	Y	Y	Y
7 Ackerman	?	?	?	?	?	?	?	?
8 Scheuer	N	N	N	N	N	Y	?	Y
9 Manton	Y	Y	Y	N	N	Y	Y	Y
10 Schumer	N	N	Y	Y	N	Y	Y	Y
11 Towns	N	N	Y	N	N	Y	?	?
12 Owens	N	N	Y	N	N	Y	?	?
13 Solarz	N	N	Y	N	N	Y	?	Y
14 ***Molinari***	Y	Y	Y	Y	Y	Y	N	N
15 ***Green***	N	Y	Y	Y	Y	Y	Y	Y
16 Rangel	N	N	Y	N	N	Y	?	Y
17 Weiss	N	N	Y	N	N	N	Y	Y
18 Garcia	N	N	Y	N	N	Y	Y	Y
19 Biaggi	N	Y	Y	N	N	Y	Y	Y
20 ***DioGuardi***	Y	Y	Y	Y	N	Y	?	Y
21 ***Fish***	Y	Y	Y	Y	N	Y	?	Y
22 ***Gilman***	Y	Y	Y	N	N	Y	+	+
23 Stratton	?	?	?	?	?	?	?	?
24 ***Solomon***	Y	Y	Y	N	N	Y	N	N
25 ***Boehlert***	Y	Y	Y	N	Y	Y	?	Y
26 ***Martin***	Y	Y	Y	Y	N	Y	Y	Y
27 ***Wortley***	Y	+	Y	Y	N	Y	Y	Y
28 McHugh	N	N	N	N	N	Y	?	Y
29 ***Horton***	N	Y	Y	N	N	Y	Y	Y
30 ***Eckert***	Y	Y	N	N	Y	+	?	N
31 ***Kemp***	Y	Y	Y	N	N	Y	?	Y
32 LaFalce	N	N	Y	N	N	Y	Y	Y
33 Nowak	N	N	Y	N	N	Y	Y	Y
34 Lundine	N	N	N	N	N	Y	?	?
NORTH CAROLINA								
1 Jones	Y	Y	N	N	N	Y	?	Y
2 Valentine	Y	Y	Y	N	N	Y	?	Y
3 Whitley	Y	Y	N	N	Y	Y	Y	Y
4 ***Cobey***	Y	Y	N	Y	Y	Y	N	?
5 Neal	?	Y	N	N	N	Y	?	Y
6 ***Coble***	Y	Y	N	Y	Y	Y	Y	N
7 Rose	Y	Y	N	N	Y	Y	?	Y
8 Hefner	Y	Y	N	N	N	Y	Y	Y
9 ***McMillan***	Y	Y	N	N	N	Y	Y	Y
10 Vacancy								
11 ***Hendon***	Y	Y	N	Y	N	Y	Y	N
NORTH DAKOTA								
AL Dorgan	Y	Y	N	N	N	+	Y	Y
OHIO								
1 Luken	Y	N	N	N	N	Y	N	Y
2 ***Gradison***	Y	Y	N	N	Y	Y	Y	Y
3 Hall	N	Y	N	Y	N	Y	?	Y
4 ***Oxley***	Y	Y	Y	Y	Y	Y	?	N
5 ***Latta***	Y	Y	N	N	Y	Y	Y	Y
6 ***McEwen***	Y	Y	Y	Y	Y	Y	Y	Y
7 ***DeWine***	Y	Y	N	Y	N	Y	N	N
8 ***Kindness***	Y	Y	N	N	Y	Y	N	Y
9 Kaptur	N	Y	N	N	N	Y	?	Y
10 ***Miller***	Y	Y	N	N	Y	Y	Y	N
11 Eckart	N	Y	Y	Y	N	Y	Y	Y
12 ***Kasich***	Y	Y	Y	Y	Y	Y	Y	Y
13 Pease	N	Y	N	Y	N	Y	Y	Y
14 Seiberling	N	N	?	N	N	Y	?	Y
15 ***Wylie***	Y	Y	N	Y	N	Y	Y	Y
16 ***Regula***	Y	Y	N	N	Y	Y	Y	Y
17 Traficant	Y	Y	Y	N	N	Y	Y	Y
18 Applegate	Y	Y	Y	Y	N	Y	Y	Y
19 Feighan	N	N	Y	Y	N	Y	Y	Y
20 Oakar	N	Y	Y	N	N	Y	?	Y
21 Stokes	N	N	N	N	N	N	Y	Y
OKLAHOMA								
1 Jones	Y	Y	Y	N	Y	Y	?	?
2 Synar	-	-	-	-	+	+	+	+
3 Watkins	Y	Y	Y	Y	N	Y	Y	Y
4 McCurdy	Y	Y	Y	N	Y	Y	Y	Y
5 ***Edwards***	Y	Y	Y	Y	N	Y	?	N
6 English	Y	Y	Y	N	Y	Y	Y	Y
OREGON								
1 AuCoin	N	N	N	N	N	Y	?	Y
2 ***Smith, R.***	Y	Y	Y	Y	Y	Y	?	N
3 Wyden	N	Y	N	N	N	Y	Y	Y
4 Weaver	N	N	N	N	N	N	Y	Y
5 ***Smith, D.***	Y	Y	N	Y	Y	Y	Y	N
PENNSYLVANIA								
1 Foglietta	N	Y	Y	N	N	Y	Y	Y
2 Gray	N	Y	N	?	N	Y	Y	Y
3 Borski	Y	Y	Y	N	Y	Y	Y	Y
4 Kolter	Y	Y	N	N	Y	Y	Y	Y
5 ***Schulze***	?	?	?	N	Y	Y	Y	Y
6 Yatron	Y	Y	Y	Y	Y	Y	Y	Y
7 Edgar	N	N	N	N	N	Y	Y	Y
8 Kostmayer	N	N	Y	N	N	Y	Y	Y
9 ***Shuster***	Y	Y	N	Y	Y	Y	N	N
10 ***McDade***	?	#	?	?	?	?	?	?
11 Kanjorski	Y	Y	N	N	Y	Y	Y	Y
12 Murtha	N	Y	Y	N	Y	Y	Y	Y
13 ***Coughlin***	Y	Y	Y	N	N	Y	N	Y
14 Coyne	N	N	N	N	N	Y	?	Y
15 ***Ritter***	Y	Y	Y	Y	N	Y	Y	N
16 ***Walker***	Y	Y	Y	Y	Y	Y	Y	N
17 ***Gekas***	Y	Y	Y	Y	Y	Y	N	N
18 Walgren	Y	Y	Y	N	N	Y	Y	Y
19 ***Goodling***	Y	N	N	N	Y	Y	N	?
20 Gaydos	Y	Y	Y	N	Y	Y	Y	Y
21 ***Ridge***	N	Y	N	Y	Y	Y	?	N
22 Murphy	N	Y	N	N	Y	Y	Y	Y
23 ***Clinger***	Y	Y	N	N	Y	Y	Y	Y
RHODE ISLAND								
1 St Germain	N	Y	N	N	N	Y	?	?
2 ***Schneider***	N	N	Y	Y	Y	Y	Y	Y
SOUTH CAROLINA								
1 ***Hartnett***	?	?	?	?	?	?	?	?
2 ***Spence***	Y	Y	Y	Y	Y	Y	Y	N
3 Derrick	N	Y	N	N	N	Y	Y	Y
4 ***Campbell***	?	Y	Y	Y	Y	Y	?	?
5 Spratt	N	Y	N	N	N	Y	Y	Y
6 Tallon	Y	Y	?	?	?	Y	Y	Y
SOUTH DAKOTA								
AL Daschle	Y	Y	N	N	N	Y	Y	Y
TENNESSEE								
1 ***Quillen***	Y	Y	N	Y	Y	Y	Y	N
2 ***Duncan***	Y	Y	N	Y	Y	Y	N	Y
3 Lloyd	Y	Y	N	N	N	Y	Y	Y
4 Cooper	N	N	Y	N	N	Y	Y	Y
5 Boner	Y	Y	Y	N	N	Y	?	?
6 Gordon	N	N	N	N	N	Y	Y	Y
7 ***Sundquist***	Y	Y	N	Y	Y	Y	N	N
8 Jones	Y	Y	Y	N	N	Y	Y	Y
9 Ford	N	N	Y	Y	N	Y	Y	Y
TEXAS								
1 Chapman	Y	Y	Y	N	N	Y	?	?
2 Wilson	N	Y	Y	N	N	Y	?	Y
3 ***Bartlett***	Y	Y	Y	Y	Y	Y	N	N
4 Hall, R.	Y	Y	Y	Y	N	Y	Y	N
5 Bryant	Y	Y	Y	N	N	Y	P	Y
6 ***Barton***	Y	Y	Y	N	Y	Y	?	N
7 ***Archer***	Y	Y	Y	Y	Y	Y	Y	N
8 ***Fields***	Y	Y	Y	Y	Y	Y	N	N
9 Brooks	N	Y	N	N	N	Y	?	?
10 Pickle	Y	Y	Y	N	N	Y	Y	Y
11 Leath	Y	Y	Y	N	Y	Y	?	Y
12 Wright	N	Y	Y	N	N	Y	Y	Y
13 ***Boulter***	Y	Y	Y	Y	Y	Y	?	N
14 ***Sweeney***	Y	Y	Y	Y	Y	Y	Y	N
15 de la Garza	Y	Y	Y	Y	N	Y	Y	Y
16 Coleman	Y	Y	N	N	N	Y	Y	?
17 Stenholm	Y	Y	Y	Y	Y	Y	Y	N
18 Leland	N	N	N	N	N	Y	?	Y
19 ***Combest***	Y	Y	Y	Y	Y	Y	Y	N
20 Gonzalez	N	N	N	N	N	N	Y	Y
21 ***Loeffler***	Y	Y	Y	Y	Y	Y	?	?
22 ***DeLay***	Y	Y	Y	Y	Y	Y	Y	N
23 Bustamante	N	Y	Y	Y	N	Y	?	Y
24 Frost	Y	Y	Y	?	N	Y	?	?
25 Andrews	Y	Y	Y	N	N	Y	Y	Y
26 ***Armey***	Y	Y	Y	Y	Y	Y	N	N
27 Ortiz	N	Y	Y	N	N	Y	Y	Y
UTAH								
1 ***Hansen***	Y	Y	N	Y	Y	Y	N	N
2 ***Monson***	Y	Y	N	N	Y	Y	N	N
3 ***Nielson***	Y	Y	N	Y	Y	Y	N	N
VERMONT								
AL ***Jeffords***	N	Y	N	N	N	Y	Y	Y
VIRGINIA								
1 ***Bateman***	Y	Y	Y	Y	Y	Y	Y	N
2 ***Whitehurst***	Y	Y	N	Y	Y	Y	?	?
3 ***Bliley***	Y	Y	Y	Y	Y	Y	Y	Y
4 Sisisky	Y	Y	N	N	N	Y	Y	Y
5 Daniel	Y	Y	Y	Y	Y	Y	Y	Y
6 Olin	N	?	?	?	Y	Y	Y	Y
7 ***Slaughter***	Y	Y	N	Y	Y	Y	Y	N
8 ***Parris***	Y	Y	N	Y	Y	Y	Y	N
9 Boucher	?	?	?	?	?	?	?	?
10 ***Wolf***	Y	Y	N	Y	N	Y	?	N
WASHINGTON								
1 ***Miller***	Y	N	Y	Y	Y	Y	Y	Y
2 Swift	N	N	Y	N	N	Y	?	Y
3 Bonker	N	N	N	?	N	Y	Y	Y
4 ***Morrison***	Y	Y	Y	Y	Y	Y	Y	Y
5 Foley	N	Y	N	N	N	Y	Y	Y
6 Dicks	N	Y	N	N	Y	Y	Y	Y
7 Lowry	N	N	Y	N	N	N	Y	Y
8 ***Chandler***	Y	Y	Y	Y	N	Y	N	Y
WEST VIRGINIA								
1 Mollohan	Y	N	Y	N	N	Y	Y	Y
2 Staggers	N	N	N	N	N	Y	Y	Y
3 Wise	N	N	N	Y	N	Y	Y	Y
4 Rahall	Y	N	Y	N	N	Y	Y	Y
WISCONSIN								
1 Aspin	N	N	N	N	N	Y	?	Y
2 Kastenmeier	N	N	N	N	N	Y	?	Y
3 ***Gunderson***	Y	Y	Y	N	Y	Y	?	Y
4 Kleczka	N	N	Y	N	N	Y	Y	Y
5 Moody	N	N	Y	N	N	Y	Y	Y
6 ***Petri***	Y	Y	N	Y	Y	Y	Y	N
7 Obey	N	?	?	?	?	?	Y	Y
8 ***Roth***	Y	Y	Y	Y	Y	Y	N	Y
9 ***Sensenbrenner***	Y	Y	N	Y	Y	Y	Y	Y
WYOMING								
AL ***Cheney***	+	Y	Y	?	Y	Y	?	N

Southern states - Ala., Ark., Fla., Ga., Ky., La., Miss., N.C., Okla., S.C., Tenn., Texas, Va.

* The *Congressional Record* vote number is different from the CQ vote number because the *Record* includes quorum calls in its tally. CQ does not publish quorum call votes.

351. HR 4868. South Africa Sanctions. Fascell, D-Fla., motion to concur in the Senate amendment to the bill to set policy goals to encourage South Africa to end its racial apartheid system and impose economic sanctions, among them barring importation of South African coal, steel and agricultural products, ending U.S. landing rights for South African airliners, and — with some exceptions — barring new U.S. loans to South African businesses or the South African government. Motion agreed to (thus cleared for the president) 308-77: R 90-73; D 218-4 (ND 150-0, SD 68-4), Sept. 12, 1986. A "nay" was a vote supporting the president's position.

352. HR 5313. Housing and Urban Development/Independent Agencies Appropriations, Fiscal 1987. Beilenson, D-Calif., motion to order the previous question (thus ending debate and the possibility of amendment) on the rule (H Res 532) to waive points of order against the bill to appropriate $54 billion for the Department of Housing and Urban Development and 17 independent agencies. Motion agreed to 226-137: R 30-127; D 196-10 (ND 133-6, SD 63-4), Sept. 12, 1986. (The rule subsequently was adopted by voice vote.)

353. HR 5313. Housing and Urban Development/Independent Agencies Appropriations, Fiscal 1987. Passage of the bill to appropriate $54,006,168,700 for the Department of Housing and Urban Development and 17 independent agencies. Passed 295-46: R 106-41; D 189-5 (ND 129-4, SD 60-1), Sept. 12, 1986. The president had requested $46,519,488,000 in new budget authority.

354. HR 4421. Human Services Reauthorization. Adoption of the conference report on the bill to authorize $15.79 billion for fiscal 1987-90 for the Head Start, Follow Through, Dependent Care, Community Services Block Grant, Community Food and Nutrition, Low Income Home Energy Assistance, and Child Development Associate Scholarship Assistance programs. Adopted 375-27: R 137-27; D 238-0 (ND 160-0, SD 78-0), Sept. 16, 1986.

355. HR 4838. Airline Employee Protection. Mineta, D-Calif., motion to suspend the rules and pass the bill to require the secretary of transportation to impose labor protective conditions in airline merger cases to ensure that the merger is fair to employees. Protection would not be imposed if the secretary determines that the projected cost of such protection would exceed the projected financial benefits of the transaction. Motion agreed to 329-72: R 97-68; D 232-4 (ND 160-0, SD 72-4), Sept. 16, 1986. A two-thirds majority of those present and voting (268 in this case) is required for passage under suspension of the rules.

356. HR 4759. Intelligence Authorization, Fiscal 1987. Stump, R-Ariz., amendment to strike a section of the bill restricting covert military aid to UNITA rebels in Angola. Adopted 229-186: R 166-7; D 63-179 (ND 16-148, SD 47-31), Sept. 17, 1986. (The bill, to authorize fiscal 1987 funds for the CIA and other federal intelligence agencies, subsequently was passed by voice vote. Most of the authorization levels contained in the bill were classified.) A "yea" was a vote supporting the president's position.

357. HR 2482. Pesticide Control Reauthorization. Adoption of the rule (H Res 536) to provide for House floor consideration of the bill to amend and authorize funds for the Federal Insecticide, Fungicide and Rodenticide Act (PL 92-516) in fiscal 1987-91. Adopted 390-15: R 155-15; D 235-0 (ND 160-0, SD 75-0), Sept. 17, 1986.

KEY

- Y Voted for (yea).
- # Paired for.
- + Announced for.
- N Voted against (nay).
- X Paired against.
- - Announced against.
- P Voted "present."
- C Voted "present" to avoid possible conflict of interest.
- ? Did not vote or otherwise make a position known.

Democrats *Republicans*

	351	352	353	354	355	356	357
ALABAMA							
1 ***Callahan***	N	N	Y	Y	Y	Y	Y
2 ***Dickinson***	N	N	Y	Y	Y	Y	Y
3 Nichols	Y	Y	Y	Y	Y	Y	?
4 Bevill	Y	Y	Y	Y	Y	N	Y
5 Flippo	Y	Y	Y	?	?	?	?
6 Erdreich	Y	Y	Y	Y	Y	Y	Y
7 Shelby	Y	?	?	Y	Y	Y	Y
ALASKA							
AL ***Young***	?	?	?	Y	Y	Y	Y
ARIZONA							
1 ***McCain***	Y	N	Y	Y	Y	Y	Y
2 Udall	Y	?	Y	Y	Y	N	Y
3 ***Stump***	N	N	N	N	N	Y	Y
4 ***Rudd***	?	?	?	N	N	Y	Y
5 ***Kolbe***	Y	N	?	Y	Y	Y	Y
ARKANSAS							
1 Alexander	Y	Y	Y	Y	Y	N	Y
2 Robinson	Y	Y	Y	Y	Y	Y	Y
3 ***Hammerschmidt***	N	Y	Y	Y	Y	Y	Y
4 Anthony	Y	Y	Y	Y	Y	Y	Y
CALIFORNIA							
1 Bosco	Y	Y	Y	Y	Y	N	Y
2 ***Chappie***	?	?	?	Y	Y	Y	Y
3 Matsui	Y	Y	Y	Y	Y	N	Y
4 Fazio	Y	Y	Y	Y	Y	N	Y
5 Burton	?	?	?	?	?	?	?
6 Boxer	?	?	?	Y	Y	N	Y
7 Miller	Y	Y	?	Y	Y	N	Y
8 Dellums	Y	Y	Y	Y	Y	N	Y
9 Stark	Y	?	Y	Y	Y	N	Y
10 Edwards	Y	Y	Y	Y	Y	N	Y
11 Lantos	Y	Y	Y	Y	Y	Y	Y
12 ***Zschau***	Y	N	?	?	?	?	?
13 Mineta	Y	Y	Y	Y	Y	N	Y
14 ***Shumway***	N	N	N	N	N	Y	Y
15 Coelho	?	?	?	?	?	N	Y
16 Panetta	Y	Y	?	Y	Y	N	Y
17 ***Pashayan***	Y	Y	Y	Y	Y	Y	Y
18 Lehman	Y	Y	?	Y	Y	N	Y
19 ***Lagomarsino***	Y	N	Y	Y	N	Y	Y
20 ***Thomas***	?	?	?	?	?	Y	Y
21 ***Fiedler***	Y	N	Y	Y	Y	Y	Y
22 ***Moorhead***	N	N	N	Y	N	Y	Y
23 Beilenson	Y	Y	Y	Y	Y	N	Y
24 Waxman	Y	Y	Y	Y	Y	N	Y
25 Roybal	Y	?	Y	Y	Y	N	Y
26 Berman	Y	Y	Y	Y	Y	N	Y
27 Levine	Y	Y	Y	Y	Y	N	Y
28 Dixon	Y	Y	Y	Y	Y	N	Y
29 Hawkins	Y	?	Y	Y	Y	N	Y
30 Martinez	Y	?	Y	Y	Y	N	Y
31 Dymally	Y	Y	Y	Y	Y	N	Y
32 Anderson	Y	Y	Y	Y	Y	N	Y
33 ***Dreier***	N	N	N	N	N	Y	N
34 Torres	Y	+	+	Y	Y	N	Y
35 ***Lewis***	Y	Y	Y	Y	Y	Y	Y
36 Brown	?	?	?	Y	Y	N	Y
37 ***McCandless***	N	N	N	N	N	Y	Y
38 ***Dornan***	N	N	Y	Y	Y	Y	Y
39 ***Dannemeyer***	N	N	N	N	N	Y	Y
40 ***Badham***	N	N	N	N	N	Y	Y
41 ***Lowery***	Y	N	Y	Y	Y	Y	Y
42 ***Lungren***	N	N	N	X	X	Y	Y
43 ***Packard***	N	N	Y	Y	Y	Y	Y
44 Bates	Y	Y	Y	Y	Y	N	Y
45 ***Hunter***	N	N	Y	Y	N	Y	Y
COLORADO							
1 Schroeder	+	+	+	Y	Y	N	Y
2 Wirth	Y	Y	?	?	#	N	Y
3 ***Strang***	N	N	N	Y	N	Y	N
4 ***Brown***	Y	N	N	N	N	Y	N
5 ***Kramer***	N	N	Y	Y	N	Y	Y
6 ***Schaefer***	N	N	N	Y	N	Y	N
CONNECTICUT							
1 Kennelly	Y	?	?	Y	Y	N	Y
2 Gejdenson	Y	Y	Y	?	?	N	Y
3 Morrison	Y	Y	Y	Y	Y	N	Y
4 ***McKinney***	#	#	?	Y	Y	N	Y
5 ***Rowland***	Y	N	Y	Y	Y	Y	Y
6 ***Johnson***	Y	N	Y	Y	Y	Y	Y
DELAWARE							
AL Carper	Y	Y	Y	Y	Y	Y	Y
FLORIDA							
1 Hutto	Y	Y	?	Y	Y	Y	Y
2 Fuqua	Y	Y	Y	Y	?	Y	Y
3 Bennett	Y	Y	Y	Y	Y	N	Y
4 Chappell	Y	Y	Y	Y	Y	Y	Y
5 ***McCollum***	N	N	N	Y	Y	Y	N
6 MacKay	Y	Y	Y	Y	Y	Y	Y
7 Gibbons	Y	?	Y	Y	Y	N	Y
8 ***Young***	N	N	Y	Y	Y	Y	Y
9 ***Bilirakis***	N	N	Y	Y	Y	Y	N
10 ***Ireland***	Y	N	Y	Y	N	Y	Y
11 Nelson	Y	Y	Y	Y	Y	Y	Y
12 ***Lewis***	Y	N	Y	Y	Y	#	+
13 ***Mack***	N	?	Y	N	N	Y	Y
14 Mica	Y	Y	Y	Y	Y	Y	Y
15 ***Shaw***	N	N	Y	Y	N	Y	Y
16 Smith	Y	Y	?	Y	Y	Y	?
17 Lehman	Y	Y	Y	Y	Y	N	Y
18 Pepper	+	+	+	Y	Y	Y	Y
19 Fascell	Y	Y	Y	Y	Y	Y	Y
GEORGIA							
1 Thomas	Y	Y	Y	Y	Y	Y	Y
2 Hatcher	Y	Y	Y	Y	N	Y	Y
3 Ray	Y	Y	Y	Y	N	Y	Y
4 ***Swindall***	N	N	Y	N	Y	Y	Y
5 Fowler	Y	?	?	Y	Y	?	?
6 ***Gingrich***	Y	N	Y	Y	Y	Y	Y
7 Darden	Y	Y	Y	Y	Y	Y	Y
8 Rowland	Y	Y	Y	Y	Y	Y	Y
9 Jenkins	Y	Y	?	Y	Y	Y	Y
10 Barnard	Y	Y	Y	Y	Y	Y	Y
HAWAII							
1 Vacancy							
2 Akaka	Y	Y	Y	Y	Y	N	Y
IDAHO							
1 ***Craig***	N	N	Y	Y	N	Y	Y
2 Stallings	Y	Y	Y	Y	Y	Y	Y
ILLINOIS							
1 Hayes	Y	Y	Y	Y	Y	N	Y
2 Savage	Y	Y	Y	Y	Y	N	Y
3 Russo	Y	Y	N	Y	Y	N	Y
4 Vacancy							
5 Lipinski	Y	Y	Y	Y	Y	Y	Y
6 ***Hyde***	N	N	Y	Y	Y	Y	?
7 Collins	Y	Y	Y	Y	Y	N	Y
8 Rostenkowski	Y	Y	Y	Y	Y	N	Y
9 Yates	Y	Y	?	Y	Y	N	Y
10 ***Porter***	N	N	Y	Y	N	Y	Y
11 Annunzio	Y	Y	Y	Y	Y	N	Y
12 ***Crane***	N	N	N	N	N	Y	N
13 ***Fawell***	Y	N	N	Y	N	Y	Y
14 ***Grotberg***	?	?	?	?	?	?	?
15 ***Madigan***	Y	N	?	Y	Y	Y	Y
16 ***Martin***	Y	N	Y	Y	N	Y	Y
17 Evans	Y	Y	Y	Y	Y	N	Y
18 ***Michel***	?	?	?	Y	Y	Y	Y
19 Bruce	Y	Y	Y	Y	Y	N	Y
20 Durbin	Y	Y	Y	Y	Y	N	Y
21 Price	Y	Y	Y	Y	Y	N	Y
22 Gray	Y	Y	Y	#	?	N	Y
INDIANA							
1 Visclosky	Y	Y	Y	Y	Y	N	Y
2 Sharp	Y	N	?	Y	Y	N	Y
3 ***Hiler***	Y	N	N	Y	N	Y	Y
4 ***Coats***	Y	N	Y	Y	N	Y	Y
5 ***Hillis***	Y	N	?	Y	Y	Y	Y

ND - Northern Democrats SD - Southern Democrats

* Corresponding to Congressional Record Votes 381, 382, 383, 384, 385, 387, 388

	351	352	353	354	355	356	357
6 ***Burton***	N	N	N	N	N	Y	N
7 ***Myers***	N	Y	Y	Y	Y	Y	Y
8 McCloskey	Y	Y	Y	Y	Y	N	Y
9 Hamilton	Y	Y	Y	Y	Y	N	Y
10 Jacobs	Y	N	Y	Y	Y	N	Y
IOWA							
1 ***Leach***	Y	N	Y	Y	Y	N	Y
2 ***Tauke***	Y	N	Y	N	N	Y	Y
3 ***Evans***	Y	N	N	Y	N	Y	Y
4 Smith	Y	Y	Y	Y	Y	N	Y
5 ***Lightfoot***	Y	N	Y	Y	N	Y	Y
6 Bedell	Y	Y	Y	Y	Y	N	Y
KANSAS							
1 ***Roberts***	Y	N	N	N	N	Y	Y
2 Slattery	Y	?	Y	Y	Y	N	Y
3 ***Meyers***	Y	N	Y	Y	Y	Y	Y
4 Glickman	Y	Y	Y	Y	Y	Y	Y
5 ***Whittaker***	N	N	Y	Y	N	Y	Y
KENTUCKY							
1 Hubbard	Y	Y	Y	Y	Y	Y	Y
2 Natcher	Y	Y	Y	Y	Y	Y	Y
3 Mazzoli	Y	N	+	Y	Y	N	Y
4 ***Snyder***	?	?	?	Y	Y	Y	Y
5 ***Rogers***	N	N	Y	Y	Y	Y	Y
6 ***Hopkins***	Y	N	Y	Y	N	Y	Y
7 Perkins	Y	Y	Y	Y	Y	N	Y
LOUISIANA							
1 ***Livingston***	?	?	?	Y	Y	Y	Y
2 Boggs	Y	Y	Y	Y	Y	Y	Y
3 Tauzin	Y	N	Y	Y	Y	Y	Y
4 Roemer	Y	N	Y	Y	Y	N	Y
5 Huckaby	?	?	?	Y	Y	Y	Y
6 ***Moore***	?	?	?	?	?	?	?
7 Breaux	?	?	?	?	?	?	?
8 Long	Y	Y	Y	Y	Y	N	Y
MAINE							
1 ***McKernan***	Y	N	Y	?	?	Y	Y
2 ***Snowe***	Y	N	?	Y	Y	Y	Y
MARYLAND							
1 Dyson	Y	Y	Y	Y	Y	Y	Y
2 ***Bentley***	Y	Y	Y	Y	Y	Y	Y
3 Mikulski	Y	Y	Y	Y	Y	N	Y
4 ***Holt***	N	N	Y	Y	Y	Y	Y
5 Hoyer	Y	Y	Y	Y	Y	N	Y
6 Byron	Y	Y	Y	Y	Y	Y	Y
7 Mitchell	Y	Y	Y	Y	Y	N	Y
8 Barnes	Y	Y	Y	Y	Y	N	Y
MASSACHUSETTS							
1 ***Conte***	Y	Y	Y	Y	Y	N	Y
2 Boland	Y	Y	Y	?	?	X	?
3 Early	?	?	?	Y	Y	N	Y
4 Frank	Y	Y	Y	Y	Y	N	Y
5 Atkins	?	?	?	?	?	N	Y
6 Mavroules	Y	Y	Y	Y	Y	N	Y
7 Markey	?	?	?	Y	Y	N	Y
8 O'Neill							
9 Moakley	Y	?	?	Y	Y	N	Y
10 Studds	Y	Y	Y	Y	Y	N	Y
11 Donnelly	Y	Y	Y	Y	Y	N	Y
MICHIGAN							
1 Conyers	Y	Y	?	Y	Y	N	?
2 ***Pursell***	Y	N	Y	Y	Y	Y	Y
3 Wolpe	Y	Y	?	Y	Y	N	Y
4 ***Siljander***	N	?	N	Y	N	Y	Y
5 ***Henry***	Y	N	Y	Y	N	Y	Y
6 Carr	Y	Y	Y	Y	Y	N	Y
7 Kildee	Y	Y	Y	Y	Y	N	Y
8 Traxler	Y	Y	?	Y	Y	N	Y
9 ***Vander Jagt***	N	N	Y	Y	Y	Y	Y
10 ***Schuette***	Y	X	+	Y	Y	Y	Y
11 ***Davis***	Y	Y	Y	Y	Y	Y	Y
12 Bonior	Y	Y	Y	Y	Y	N	?
13 Crockett	?	?	?	Y	Y	N	Y
14 Hertel	Y	N	Y	Y	Y	N	Y
15 Ford	Y	Y	Y	Y	Y	N	Y
16 Dingell	Y	Y	Y	Y	Y	N	Y
17 Levin	Y	Y	Y	Y	Y	N	Y
18 ***Broomfield***	Y	N	?	Y	N	Y	?
MINNESOTA							
1 Penny	Y	N	Y	Y	Y	N	Y
2 ***Weber***	Y	N	Y	Y	Y	Y	Y
3 ***Frenzel***	Y	N	N	?	?	Y	Y
4 Vento	Y	Y	Y	Y	Y	N	Y
5 Sabo	Y	Y	Y	Y	Y	N	Y
6 Sikorski	Y	Y	Y	Y	Y	N	Y
7 ***Stangeland***	Y	N	Y	Y	Y	Y	Y
8 Oberstar	Y	Y	Y	Y	Y	N	Y
MISSISSIPPI							
1 Whitten	Y	Y	Y	Y	?	Y	Y
2 ***Franklin***	Y	N	?	Y	N	Y	Y
3 Montgomery	N	Y	Y	Y	Y	Y	Y
4 Dowdy	Y	Y	Y	Y	Y	N	Y
5 ***Lott***	N	N	N	N	Y	Y	Y
MISSOURI							
1 Clay	Y	Y	Y	Y	Y	X	?
2 Young	Y	Y	Y	Y	Y	N	Y
3 Gephardt	?	?	?	Y	Y	N	Y
4 Skelton	Y	Y	Y	Y	Y	Y	Y
5 Wheat	Y	Y	Y	Y	Y	N	Y
6 ***Coleman***	Y	Y	Y	Y	Y	Y	Y
7 ***Taylor***	N	Y	Y	Y	Y	Y	Y
8 ***Emerson***	N	N	Y	Y	Y	Y	Y
9 Volkmer	Y	Y	Y	Y	Y	Y	Y
MONTANA							
1 Williams	Y	Y	Y	Y	Y	N	?
2 ***Marlenee***	N	N	N	N	N	Y	Y
NEBRASKA							
1 ***Bereuter***	Y	N	Y	Y	Y	Y	Y
2 ***Daub***	Y	X	?	Y	N	Y	Y
3 ***Smith***	Y	N	Y	Y	N	Y	Y
NEVADA							
1 Reid	Y	Y	?	Y	Y	N	Y
2 ***Vucanovich***	Y	N	Y	Y	Y	Y	Y
NEW HAMPSHIRE							
1 ***Smith***	N	N	Y	N	N	Y	N
2 ***Gregg***	Y	?	?	N	N	Y	Y
NEW JERSEY							
1 Florio	Y	Y	Y	Y	Y	N	Y
2 Hughes	Y	Y	N	Y	Y	N	Y
3 Howard	Y	Y	Y	Y	Y	N	Y
4 ***Smith***	Y	Y	Y	Y	Y	Y	Y
5 ***Roukema***	Y	Y	Y	Y	Y	Y	Y
6 Dwyer	Y	Y	Y	Y	Y	N	Y
7 ***Rinaldo***	Y	Y	Y	Y	Y	Y	Y
8 Roe	Y	Y	Y	Y	Y	?	Y
9 Torricelli	Y	Y	Y	Y	Y	N	Y
10 Rodino	Y	Y	Y	Y	Y	N	?
11 ***Gallo***	Y	N	Y	Y	Y	Y	Y
12 ***Courter***	Y	N	Y	Y	Y	Y	Y
13 ***Saxton***	Y	N	Y	Y	Y	Y	Y
14 Guarini	Y	Y	Y	Y	Y	N	Y
NEW MEXICO							
1 ***Lujan***	Y	N	Y	Y	Y	Y	Y
2 ***Skeen***	N	N	Y	Y	Y	Y	Y
3 Richardson	Y	Y	Y	Y	Y	N	Y
NEW YORK							
1 ***Carney***	?	?	?	?	?	Y	Y
2 Downey	Y	Y	Y	Y	Y	N	Y
3 Mrazek	?	Y	Y	Y	Y	N	Y
4 ***Lent***	Y	N	Y	Y	Y	Y	Y
5 ***McGrath***	Y	Y	Y	?	?	Y	Y
6 Waldon	Y	Y	Y	Y	Y	N	Y
7 Ackerman	?	?	?	Y	Y	N	Y
8 Scheuer	Y	?	Y	Y	Y	N	Y
9 Manton	Y	Y	Y	Y	Y	N	Y
10 Schumer	Y	Y	Y	Y	Y	N	Y
11 Towns	?	?	?	Y	Y	N	Y
12 Owens	?	?	?	Y	Y	N	Y
13 Solarz	Y	Y	Y	Y	Y	N	Y
14 ***Molinari***	Y	Y	Y	Y	Y	Y	Y
15 ***Green***	Y	Y	Y	Y	Y	Y	Y
16 Rangel	#	?	?	Y	Y	N	Y
17 Weiss	Y	Y	Y	Y	Y	N	Y
18 Garcia	Y	Y	?	Y	Y	N	Y
19 Biaggi	Y	Y	Y	Y	Y	Y	Y
20 ***DioGuardi***	Y	Y	Y	Y	Y	Y	Y
21 ***Fish***	Y	Y	Y	Y	Y	N	?
22 ***Gilman***	Y	Y	Y	Y	Y	Y	Y
23 Stratton	+	?	?	Y	Y	Y	Y
24 ***Solomon***	N	N	N	Y	Y	Y	Y
25 ***Boehlert***	Y	Y	Y	Y	Y	Y	Y
26 ***Martin***	Y	N	?	Y	Y	Y	Y
27 ***Wortley***	Y	N	Y	Y	Y	Y	Y
28 McHugh	Y	Y	Y	Y	Y	N	Y
29 ***Horton***	Y	Y	?	Y	Y	N	Y
30 ***Eckert***	N	N	N	N	N	Y	Y
31 ***Kemp***	N	?	?	?	?	Y	Y
32 LaFalce	Y	Y	Y	Y	Y	N	Y
33 Nowak	Y	Y	Y	Y	Y	N	Y
34 Lundine	?	?	?	Y	Y	N	Y
NORTH CAROLINA							
1 Jones	Y	Y	Y	Y	Y	N	Y
2 Valentine	Y	Y	Y	Y	Y	Y	Y
3 Whitley	Y	Y	?	Y	Y	N	Y
4 ***Cobey***	N	N	Y	Y	N	Y	Y
5 Neal	Y	Y	Y	Y	Y	N	Y
6 ***Coble***	N	N	Y	Y	N	Y	Y
7 Rose	Y	Y	Y	Y	Y	N	Y
8 Hefner	Y	Y	Y	Y	Y	Y	?
9 ***McMillan***	Y	Y	Y	Y	N	Y	Y
10 Vacancy							
11 ***Hendon***	N	N	Y	Y	Y	Y	Y
NORTH DAKOTA							
AL Dorgan	Y	N	Y	Y	Y	N	Y
OHIO							
1 Luken	Y	Y	Y	Y	Y	N	Y
2 ***Gradison***	Y	N	N	Y	N	Y	Y
3 Hall	Y	Y	Y	Y	Y	N	Y
4 ***Oxley***	N	N	N	Y	N	Y	Y
5 ***Latta***	N	N	N	Y	Y	Y	Y
6 ***McEwen***	N	N	?	Y	Y	Y	Y
7 ***DeWine***	Y	N	N	Y	N	Y	Y
8 ***Kindness***	N	N	N	?	?	#	?
9 Kaptur	Y	Y	Y	Y	Y	N	Y
10 ***Miller***	N	N	Y	Y	Y	Y	Y
11 Eckart	Y	Y	Y	Y	Y	N	Y
12 ***Kasich***	Y	N	Y	Y	Y	Y	Y
13 Pease	Y	Y	Y	Y	Y	N	Y
14 Seiberling	Y	Y	Y	Y	Y	N	Y
15 ***Wylie***	Y	Y	?	Y	Y	Y	Y
16 ***Regula***	Y	N	Y	Y	Y	Y	Y
17 Traficant	Y	Y	P	Y	Y	N	Y
18 Applegate	Y	Y	Y	Y	Y	N	Y
19 Feighan	Y	Y	Y	Y	Y	N	Y
20 Oakar	Y	Y	?	Y	Y	N	Y
21 Stokes	Y	Y	Y	Y	Y	N	Y
OKLAHOMA							
1 Jones	?	?	?	Y	Y	Y	Y
2 Synar	+	+	+	Y	Y	N	Y
3 Watkins	Y	Y	?	Y	Y	Y	Y
4 McCurdy	Y	Y	Y	Y	Y	Y	Y
5 ***Edwards***	Y	Y	Y	Y	N	Y	Y
6 English	Y	Y	Y	Y	Y	Y	Y
OREGON							
1 AuCoin	Y	Y	N	Y	Y	N	Y
2 ***Smith, R.***	N	Y	Y	Y	N	Y	Y
3 Wyden	Y	Y	Y	Y	Y	N	Y
4 Weaver	Y	Y	Y	Y	Y	N	?
5 ***Smith, D.***	N	N	N	Y	N	Y	Y
PENNSYLVANIA							
1 Foglietta	Y	Y	Y	Y	Y	N	Y
2 Gray	Y	Y	Y	Y	Y	N	Y
3 Borski	Y	Y	Y	Y	Y	N	Y
4 Kolter	Y	Y	Y	Y	Y	N	Y
5 ***Schulze***	Y	Y	Y	Y	Y	Y	Y
6 Yatron	Y	Y	Y	Y	Y	Y	Y
7 Edgar	Y	Y	Y	Y	Y	N	Y
8 Kostmayer	Y	N	Y	Y	Y	N	Y
9 ***Shuster***	N	N	N	Y	N	Y	Y
10 ***McDade***	?	#	?	Y	Y	Y	Y
11 Kanjorski	Y	Y	Y	Y	Y	Y	Y
12 Murtha	Y	?	?	Y	Y	Y	Y
13 ***Coughlin***	Y	Y	Y	Y	Y	Y	Y
14 Coyne	Y	Y	Y	Y	Y	N	Y
15 ***Ritter***	N	N	Y	Y	N	Y	Y
16 ***Walker***	Y	N	Y	Y	Y	Y	N
17 ***Gekas***	Y	N	Y	Y	Y	Y	N
18 Walgren	Y	Y	Y	Y	Y	N	Y
19 ***Goodling***	Y	N	Y	Y	Y	Y	Y
20 Gaydos	Y	Y	Y	Y	Y	Y	Y
21 ***Ridge***	Y	N	Y	Y	Y	Y	Y
22 Murphy	Y	?	?	Y	Y	N	Y
23 ***Clinger***	Y	N	Y	Y	Y	Y	Y
RHODE ISLAND							
1 St Germain	?	?	?	Y	Y	N	Y
2 ***Schneider***	Y	Y	Y	Y	Y	N	Y
SOUTH CAROLINA							
1 ***Hartnett***	?	?	?	?	?	#	?
2 ***Spence***	N	N	Y	Y	Y	Y	Y
3 Derrick	Y	Y	Y	Y	Y	N	Y
4 ***Campbell***	?	?	?	?	?	#	?
5 Spratt	Y	Y	Y	Y	Y	N	Y
6 Tallon	Y	?	?	Y	Y	Y	Y
SOUTH DAKOTA							
AL Daschle	Y	Y	Y	Y	Y	N	Y
TENNESSEE							
1 ***Quillen***	N	Y	?	Y	Y	Y	Y
2 ***Duncan***	Y	Y	Y	Y	Y	Y	Y
3 Lloyd	Y	Y	?	Y	Y	Y	Y
4 Cooper	Y	Y	Y	Y	Y	N	Y
5 Boner	?	?	?	Y	Y	N	Y
6 Gordon	Y	Y	Y	Y	Y	N	Y
7 ***Sundquist***	N	N	N	Y	Y	Y	Y
8 Jones	Y	Y	Y	Y	Y	N	Y
9 Ford	Y	?	Y	?	?	X	?
TEXAS							
1 Chapman	Y	Y	?	Y	Y	Y	Y
2 Wilson	Y	Y	Y	Y	Y	Y	Y
3 ***Bartlett***	N	N	Y	N	N	Y	Y
4 Hall, R.	N	N	Y	Y	Y	Y	Y
5 Bryant	Y	Y	Y	Y	Y	Y	Y
6 ***Barton***	N	N	Y	Y	N	Y	Y
7 ***Archer***	N	N	N	N	N	Y	Y
8 ***Fields***	N	N	Y	?	?	Y	Y
9 Brooks	?	?	?	Y	Y	N	Y
10 Pickle	Y	Y	Y	Y	Y	Y	Y
11 Leath	Y	Y	Y	Y	Y	N	Y
12 Wright	?	?	?	Y	Y	N	Y
13 ***Boulter***	N	N	Y	Y	N	Y	Y
14 ***Sweeney***	N	N	Y	Y	N	Y	Y
15 de la Garza	Y	Y	Y	Y	Y	N	Y
16 Coleman	Y	Y	Y	Y	Y	N	Y
17 Stenholm	N	Y	N	Y	N	Y	Y
18 Leland	Y	Y	Y	Y	Y	N	Y
19 ***Combest***	N	N	N	N	N	Y	Y
20 Gonzalez	Y	Y	Y	Y	Y	N	Y
21 ***Loeffler***	X	?	?	Y	N	Y	Y
22 ***DeLay***	N	N	N	N	N	Y	N
23 Bustamante	Y	Y	Y	Y	Y	Y	Y
24 Frost	?	?	?	Y	Y	Y	Y
25 Andrews	Y	Y	Y	Y	Y	Y	Y
26 ***Armey***	N	N	N	N	N	Y	N
27 Ortiz	Y	Y	Y	Y	Y	Y	Y
UTAH							
1 ***Hansen***	X	?	?	Y	N	Y	Y
2 ***Monson***	N	N	N	?	N	Y	N
3 ***Nielson***	N	N	N	N	N	Y	N
VERMONT							
AL ***Jeffords***	Y	Y	Y	Y	Y	N	Y
VIRGINIA							
1 ***Bateman***	Y	N	Y	Y	Y	Y	Y
2 ***Whitehurst***	?	?	?	Y	Y	Y	Y
3 ***Bliley***	Y	N	Y	?	?	Y	Y
4 Sisisky	Y	Y	Y	?	?	N	Y
5 Daniel	N	Y	Y	Y	N	Y	Y
6 Olin	Y	Y	Y	Y	Y	N	Y
7 ***Slaughter***	N	N	Y	Y	Y	Y	Y
8 ***Parris***	N	N	Y	Y	Y	Y	Y
9 Boucher	?	?	?	Y	Y	N	Y
10 ***Wolf***	Y	N	Y	Y	Y	Y	Y
WASHINGTON							
1 ***Miller***	Y	N	Y	Y	Y	Y	Y
2 Swift	Y	Y	Y	Y	Y	N	Y
3 Bonker	Y	Y	?	?	#	X	?
4 ***Morrison***	Y	N	Y	Y	N	Y	Y
5 Foley	Y	Y	Y	Y	Y	N	Y
6 Dicks	Y	Y	Y	Y	Y	N	Y
7 Lowry	Y	Y	Y	Y	Y	N	Y
8 ***Chandler***	Y	N	Y	Y	Y	Y	Y
WEST VIRGINIA							
1 Mollohan	Y	Y	Y	Y	Y	Y	Y
2 Staggers	Y	Y	Y	Y	Y	N	Y
3 Wise	Y	Y	Y	Y	Y	N	Y
4 Rahall	Y	Y	Y	Y	Y	N	Y
WISCONSIN							
1 Aspin	?	?	Y	Y	Y	N	Y
2 Kastenmeier	Y	Y	Y	Y	Y	N	Y
3 ***Gunderson***	Y	N	Y	Y	Y	Y	Y
4 Kleczka	Y	Y	Y	?	?	N	Y
5 Moody	Y	Y	N	Y	Y	N	Y
6 ***Petri***	Y	N	N	Y	N	Y	Y
7 Obey	Y	Y	Y	Y	Y	N	Y
8 ***Roth***	N	N	Y	Y	Y	Y	Y
9 ***Sensenbrenner***	Y	N	N	N	N	Y	Y
WYOMING							
AL ***Cheney***	N	N	N	N	N	Y	Y

Southern states - Ala., Ark., Fla., Ga., Ky., La., Miss., N.C., Okla., S.C., Tenn., Texas, Va.

* The *Congressional Record* vote number is different from the CQ vote number because the *Record* includes quorum calls in its tally. CQ does not publish quorum call votes.

358. S 2638. Defense Authorization, Fiscal 1987. Aspin, D-Wis., motion that meetings of the conference committee on the bill be closed to the public. Motion agreed to 391-2: R 164-0; D 227-2 (ND 153-1, SD 74-1), Sept. 18, 1986.

359. HR 4430. Minimum Altitude for Aircraft Over National Parks. Passage of the bill to restrict overflights of certain national parks pending a three-year study on potential safety and environmental hazards. Passed 378-12: R 152-12; D 226-0 (ND 154-0, SD 72-0), Sept. 18, 1986.

360. H J Res 732. Philippines Assistance. Passage of the joint resolution to provide $200 million in supplemental economic aid to the Philippines in fiscal 1986. Passed 203-197: R 53-114; D 150-83 (ND 120-39, SD 30-44), Sept. 18, 1986.

KEY

Y Voted for (yea).
\# Paired for.
\+ Announced for.
N Voted against (nay).
X Paired against.
\- Announced against.
P Voted "present."
C Voted "present" to avoid possible conflict of interest.
? Did not vote or otherwise make a position known.

Democrats ***Republicans***

	358	359	360
ALABAMA			
1 ***Callahan***	?	?	?
2 ***Dickinson***	?	?	?
3 Nichols	Y	Y	N
4 Bevill	Y	Y	N
5 Flippo	Y	?	N
6 Erdreich	Y	Y	N
7 Shelby	Y	Y	N
ALASKA			
AL ***Young***	Y	Y	N
ARIZONA			
1 ***McCain***	Y	Y	N
2 Udall	Y	Y	Y
3 ***Stump***	Y	N	N
4 ***Rudd***	Y	N	N
5 ***Kolbe***	Y	Y	N
ARKANSAS			
1 Alexander	Y	Y	N
2 Robinson	Y	Y	Y
3 ***Hammerschmidt***	Y	N	N
4 Anthony	Y	Y	N
CALIFORNIA			
1 Bosco	Y	Y	N
2 ***Chappie***	Y	Y	N
3 Matsui	Y	Y	Y
4 Fazio	Y	Y	Y
5 Burton	?	?	?
6 Boxer	Y	Y	Y
7 Miller	Y	Y	Y
8 Dellums	?	?	#
9 Stark	Y	?	Y
10 Edwards	Y	Y	Y
11 Lantos	Y	Y	Y
12 ***Zschau***	Y	Y	Y
13 Mineta	Y	Y	Y
14 ***Shumway***	Y	Y	N
15 Coelho	Y	Y	Y
16 Panetta	Y	Y	N
17 ***Pashayan***	Y	Y	Y
18 Lehman	Y	Y	Y
19 ***Lagomarsino***	Y	Y	Y
20 ***Thomas***	Y	Y	Y
21 ***Fiedler***	Y	Y	N
22 ***Moorhead***	Y	Y	N
23 Beilenson	Y	Y	Y
24 Waxman	Y	Y	Y
25 Roybal	Y	Y	Y
26 Berman	Y	Y	Y
27 Levine	Y	Y	Y
28 Dixon	Y	Y	Y
29 Hawkins	Y	Y	Y
30 Martinez	Y	Y	N
31 Dymally	Y	Y	Y
32 Anderson	Y	Y	Y
33 ***Dreier***	Y	Y	N
34 Torres	Y	Y	Y
35 ***Lewis***	Y	Y	Y
36 Brown	Y	Y	Y
37 ***McCandless***	Y	Y	N
38 ***Dornan***	Y	N	Y
39 ***Dannemeyer***	Y	Y	N
40 ***Badham***	Y	Y	N
41 ***Lowery***	Y	Y	Y
42 ***Lungren***	Y	Y	N

	358	359	360
43 ***Packard***	Y	Y	N
44 Bates	Y	Y	Y
45 ***Hunter***	Y	Y	Y
COLORADO			
1 Schroeder	Y	Y	Y
2 Wirth	Y	Y	Y
3 ***Strang***	Y	Y	N
4 ***Brown***	Y	Y	N
5 ***Kramer***	Y	Y	N
6 ***Schaefer***	?	?	?
CONNECTICUT			
1 Kennelly	Y	Y	Y
2 Gejdenson	Y	Y	Y
3 Morrison	Y	Y	Y
4 ***McKinney***	Y	Y	Y
5 ***Rowland***	Y	Y	N
6 ***Johnson***	Y	Y	Y
DELAWARE			
AL Carper	Y	Y	N
FLORIDA			
1 Hutto	Y	Y	N
2 Fuqua	Y	?	Y
3 Bennett	Y	Y	Y
4 Chappell	Y	?	Y
5 ***McCollum***	Y	Y	N
6 MacKay	Y	Y	Y
7 Gibbons	Y	Y	Y
8 ***Young***	Y	Y	N
9 ***Bilirakis***	Y	Y	N
10 ***Ireland***	?	?	?
11 Nelson	Y	Y	N
12 ***Lewis***	Y	N	N
13 ***Mack***	Y	Y	N
14 Mica	Y	Y	Y
15 ***Shaw***	Y	Y	N
16 Smith	Y	Y	Y
17 Lehman	Y	Y	Y
18 Pepper	Y	Y	Y
19 Fascell	Y	Y	Y
GEORGIA			
1 Thomas	Y	Y	N
2 Hatcher	Y	Y	Y
3 Ray	Y	Y	N
4 ***Swindall***	Y	Y	N
5 Fowler	?	?	?
6 ***Gingrich***	Y	Y	Y
7 Darden	Y	Y	N
8 Rowland	Y	Y	N
9 Jenkins	Y	Y	N
10 Barnard	Y	?	X
HAWAII			
1 Vacancy			
2 Akaka	Y	Y	N
IDAHO			
1 ***Craig***	Y	Y	N
2 Stallings	Y	Y	N
ILLINOIS			
1 Hayes	Y	Y	Y
2 Savage	?	?	Y
3 Russo	Y	Y	N
4 Vacancy			
5 Lipinski	Y	Y	Y
6 ***Hyde***	Y	Y	Y
7 Collins	Y	Y	Y
8 Rostenkowski	Y	Y	Y
9 Yates	Y	Y	Y
10 ***Porter***	Y	Y	N
11 Annunzio	Y	Y	Y
12 ***Crane***	Y	N	N
13 ***Fawell***	Y	Y	N
14 ***Grotberg***	?	?	?
15 ***Madigan***	Y	Y	N
16 ***Martin***	Y	Y	N
17 Evans	Y	Y	Y
18 ***Michel***	Y	?	Y
19 Bruce	Y	Y	Y
20 Durbin	Y	Y	Y
21 Price	Y	Y	Y
22 Gray	Y	Y	N
INDIANA			
1 Visclosky	Y	Y	N
2 Sharp	Y	Y	Y
3 ***Hiler***	Y	Y	N
4 ***Coats***	Y	Y	N
5 ***Hillis***	Y	Y	Y

ND - Northern Democrats SD - Southern Democrats

* Corresponding to Congressional Record Votes 389, 390, 391

	358	359	360
6 ***Burton***	Y	Y	N
7 ***Myers***	Y	Y	N
8 McCloskey	Y	Y	N
9 Hamilton	Y	Y	N
10 Jacobs	Y	Y	N
IOWA			
1 ***Leach***	Y	Y	Y
2 ***Tauke***	Y	Y	Y
3 ***Evans***	Y	Y	Y
4 Smith	Y	Y	N
5 ***Lightfoot***	Y	Y	N
6 Bedell	Y	Y	Y
KANSAS			
1 ***Roberts***	Y	Y	N
2 Slattery	Y	Y	Y
3 ***Meyers***	Y	Y	Y
4 Glickman	Y	Y	N
5 ***Whittaker***	Y	Y	N
KENTUCKY			
1 Hubbard	Y	Y	N
2 Natcher	Y	Y	Y
3 Mazzoli	Y	Y	N
4 ***Snyder***	Y	Y	N
5 ***Rogers***	Y	Y	N
6 ***Hopkins***	Y	Y	N
7 Perkins	Y	Y	N
LOUISIANA			
1 ***Livingston***	?	?	?
2 Boggs	Y	Y	Y
3 Tauzin	Y	Y	N
4 Roemer	Y	Y	N
5 Huckaby	Y	Y	N
6 ***Moore***	?	?	?
7 Breaux	?	?	?
8 Long	Y	Y	Y
MAINE			
1 ***McKernan***	Y	Y	Y
2 ***Snowe***	Y	Y	Y
MARYLAND			
1 Dyson	Y	Y	N
2 ***Bentley***	Y	Y	N
3 Mikulski	Y	Y	Y
4 ***Holt***	Y	Y	N
5 Hoyer	Y	Y	Y
6 Byron	Y	Y	N
7 Mitchell	Y	Y	Y
8 Barnes	Y	Y	Y
MASSACHUSETTS			
1 ***Conte***	Y	Y	Y
2 Boland	?	?	?
3 Early	?	?	?
4 Frank	Y	Y	Y
5 Atkins	Y	Y	Y
6 Mavroules	Y	Y	Y
7 Markey	Y	Y	Y
8 O'Neill			
9 Moakley	Y	Y	Y
10 Studds	Y	Y	Y
11 Donnelly	Y	Y	Y
MICHIGAN			
1 Conyers	Y	Y	?
2 ***Pursell***	?	Y	Y
3 Wolpe	Y	?	Y
4 ***Siljander***	Y	Y	Y
5 ***Henry***	Y	Y	N
6 Carr	Y	Y	N
7 Kildee	Y	Y	Y
8 Traxler	?	Y	N
9 ***Vander Jagt***	Y	Y	Y
10 ***Schuette***	?	?	?
11 ***Davis***	Y	Y	N
12 Bonior	Y	Y	Y
13 Crockett	Y	Y	Y
14 Hertel	Y	Y	Y
15 Ford	Y	Y	Y
16 Dingell	Y	Y	Y
17 Levin	Y	Y	Y
18 ***Broomfield***	Y	Y	Y
MINNESOTA			
1 Penny	Y	Y	Y
2 ***Weber***	Y	Y	Y
3 ***Frenzel***	Y	Y	N
4 Vento	Y	Y	Y
5 Sabo	Y	Y	Y
6 Sikorski	Y	Y	Y
7 ***Stangeland***	Y	Y	N
8 Oberstar	Y	Y	Y
MISSISSIPPI			
1 Whitten	Y	Y	N
2 ***Franklin***	Y	Y	N
3 Montgomery	?	Y	N
4 Dowdy	Y	Y	N
5 ***Lott***	Y	Y	Y
MISSOURI			
1 Clay	Y	Y	N
2 Young	Y	Y	N
3 Gephardt	Y	Y	Y
4 Skelton	Y	Y	N
5 Wheat	Y	Y	Y
6 ***Coleman***	Y	Y	N
7 ***Taylor***	Y	Y	N
8 ***Emerson***	Y	Y	N
9 Volkmer	Y	Y	N
MONTANA			
1 Williams	?	Y	Y
2 ***Marlenee***	Y	N	N
NEBRASKA			
1 ***Bereuter***	Y	Y	N
2 ***Daub***	Y	Y	N
3 ***Smith***	Y	Y	N
NEVADA			
1 Reid	Y	Y	N
2 ***Vucanovich***	Y	Y	Y
NEW HAMPSHIRE			
1 ***Smith***	Y	Y	N
2 ***Gregg***	Y	Y	N
NEW JERSEY			
1 Florio	Y	Y	Y
2 Hughes	Y	Y	N
3 Howard	Y	Y	Y
4 ***Smith***	Y	Y	Y
5 ***Roukema***	Y	Y	N
6 Dwyer	Y	Y	Y
7 ***Rinaldo***	Y	Y	N
8 Roe	Y	Y	Y
9 Torricelli	Y	Y	Y
10 Rodino	Y	Y	Y
11 ***Gallo***	Y	Y	Y
12 ***Courter***	Y	Y	N
13 ***Saxton***	Y	Y	N
14 Guarini	Y	Y	Y
NEW MEXICO			
1 ***Lujan***	?	Y	N
2 ***Skeen***	Y	Y	N
3 Richardson	Y	Y	Y
NEW YORK			
1 ***Carney***	?	N	N
2 Downey	Y	Y	Y
3 Mrazek	?	?	Y
4 ***Lent***	Y	Y	Y
5 ***McGrath***	Y	Y	Y
6 Waldon	?	?	?
7 Ackerman	Y	Y	Y
8 Scheuer	Y	Y	Y
9 Manton	Y	Y	Y
10 Schumer	Y	Y	Y
11 Towns	Y	Y	Y
12 Owens	?	?	Y
13 Solarz	Y	Y	Y
14 ***Molinari***	Y	Y	Y
15 ***Green***	Y	Y	Y
16 Rangel	?	?	?
17 Weiss	Y	Y	Y
18 Garcia	Y	Y	Y
19 Biaggi	Y	Y	Y
20 ***DioGuardi***	Y	Y	Y
21 ***Fish***	?	Y	Y
22 ***Gilman***	Y	Y	Y
23 Stratton	?	?	?
24 ***Solomon***	Y	Y	N
25 ***Boehlert***	Y	Y	Y
26 ***Martin***	Y	Y	Y
27 ***Wortley***	Y	Y	Y
28 McHugh	Y	Y	Y
29 ***Horton***	Y	Y	Y
30 ***Eckert***	Y	Y	Y
31 ***Kemp***	Y	Y	Y
32 LaFalce	Y	Y	Y
33 Nowak	Y	Y	Y
34 Lundine	Y	Y	Y
NORTH CAROLINA			
1 Jones	Y	Y	N
2 Valentine	Y	Y	N
3 Whitley	Y	Y	Y
4 ***Cobey***	Y	Y	N
5 Neal	Y	Y	Y
6 ***Coble***	Y	Y	N
7 Rose	?	?	?
8 Hefner	Y	Y	N
9 ***McMillan***	Y	Y	N
10 Vacancy			
11 ***Hendon***	Y	Y	N
NORTH DAKOTA			
AL Dorgan	Y	Y	N
OHIO			
1 Luken	Y	Y	N
2 ***Gradison***	Y	Y	N
3 Hall	Y	Y	Y
4 ***Oxley***	Y	Y	N
5 ***Latta***	Y	Y	N
6 ***McEwen***	Y	Y	N
7 ***DeWine***	Y	Y	Y
8 ***Kindness***	?	?	?
9 Kaptur	Y	Y	Y
10 ***Miller***	Y	N	N
11 Eckart	Y	Y	N
12 ***Kasich***	Y	Y	N
13 Pease	Y	Y	N
14 Seiberling	Y	Y	Y
15 ***Wylie***	Y	Y	N
16 ***Regula***	Y	Y	N
17 Traficant	Y	Y	N
18 Applegate	Y	Y	N
19 Feighan	Y	Y	Y
20 Oakar	Y	Y	Y
21 Stokes	?	?	?
OKLAHOMA			
1 Jones	Y	Y	N
2 Synar	Y	Y	Y
3 Watkins	Y	Y	N
4 McCurdy	Y	Y	Y
5 ***Edwards***	Y	Y	Y
6 English	Y	Y	N
OREGON			
1 AuCoin	Y	Y	Y
2 ***Smith, R.***	Y	Y	N
3 Wyden	Y	Y	N
4 Weaver	Y	Y	Y
5 ***Smith, D.***	Y	N	N
PENNSYLVANIA			
1 Foglietta	Y	Y	Y
2 Gray	Y	Y	Y
3 Borski	Y	Y	Y
4 Kolter	Y	Y	Y
5 ***Schulze***	Y	Y	N
6 Yatron	Y	Y	N
7 Edgar	?	Y	Y
8 Kostmayer	Y	Y	Y
9 ***Shuster***	Y	Y	N
10 ***McDade***	Y	Y	Y
11 Kanjorski	Y	Y	N
12 Murtha	Y	?	Y
13 ***Coughlin***	Y	?	Y
14 Coyne	Y	Y	Y
15 ***Ritter***	Y	?	N
16 ***Walker***	Y	Y	N
17 ***Gekas***	Y	Y	N
18 Walgren	Y	Y	Y
19 ***Goodling***	Y	Y	N
20 Gaydos	Y	Y	N
21 ***Ridge***	Y	Y	N
22 Murphy	Y	Y	N
23 ***Clinger***	Y	Y	N
RHODE ISLAND			
1 St Germain	Y	Y	N
2 ***Schneider***	Y	Y	N
SOUTH CAROLINA			
1 ***Hartnett***	?	?	?
2 ***Spence***	Y	Y	N
3 Derrick	Y	Y	Y
4 ***Campbell***	?	?	?
5 Spratt	Y	Y	Y
6 Tallon	Y	Y	N
SOUTH DAKOTA			
AL Daschle	Y	Y	N
TENNESSEE			
1 ***Quillen***	Y	Y	N
2 ***Duncan***	Y	Y	N
3 Lloyd	Y	Y	N
4 Cooper	Y	Y	Y
5 Boner	Y	Y	N
6 Gordon	Y	Y	N
7 ***Sundquist***	Y	Y	N
8 Jones	Y	Y	N
9 Ford	?	?	?
TEXAS			
1 Chapman	Y	Y	N
2 Wilson	?	?	?
3 ***Bartlett***	Y	Y	N
4 Hall, R.	Y	Y	N
5 Bryant	Y	Y	Y
6 ***Barton***	Y	Y	N
7 ***Archer***	Y	Y	N
8 ***Fields***	Y	Y	N
9 Brooks	Y	Y	N
10 Pickle	Y	Y	N
11 Leath	Y	Y	Y
12 Wright	Y	Y	Y
13 ***Boulter***	Y	Y	N
14 ***Sweeney***	?	?	?
15 de la Garza	Y	Y	Y
16 Coleman	Y	Y	N
17 Stenholm	Y	Y	N
18 Leland	?	?	?
19 ***Combest***	Y	Y	N
20 Gonzalez	N	Y	P
21 ***Loeffler***	Y	Y	N
22 ***DeLay***	Y	N	N
23 Bustamante	Y	Y	Y
24 Frost	Y	Y	Y
25 Andrews	Y	Y	N
26 ***Armey***	Y	N	N
27 Ortiz	Y	Y	Y
UTAH			
1 ***Hansen***	Y	Y	N
2 ***Monson***	Y	Y	N
3 ***Nielson***	Y	Y	N
VERMONT			
AL ***Jeffords***	Y	Y	Y
VIRGINIA			
1 ***Bateman***	Y	Y	N
2 ***Whitehurst***	Y	?	N
3 ***Bliley***	Y	Y	N
4 Sisisky	Y	Y	N
5 Daniel	Y	Y	N
6 Olin	Y	Y	N
7 ***Slaughter***	Y	Y	N
8 ***Parris***	Y	Y	N
9 Boucher	Y	Y	Y
10 ***Wolf***	Y	Y	Y
WASHINGTON			
1 ***Miller***	Y	Y	Y
2 Swift	?	?	?
3 Bonker	Y	Y	Y
4 ***Morrison***	Y	Y	Y
5 Foley	Y	Y	Y
6 Dicks	Y	Y	Y
7 Lowry	N	Y	Y
8 ***Chandler***	Y	Y	Y
WEST VIRGINIA			
1 Mollohan	Y	Y	Y
2 Staggers	Y	Y	Y
3 Wise	Y	Y	Y
4 Rahall	Y	Y	N
WISCONSIN			
1 Aspin	Y	Y	Y
2 Kastenmeier	Y	Y	Y
3 ***Gunderson***	Y	Y	Y
4 Kleczka	Y	Y	N
5 Moody	Y	Y	Y
6 ***Petri***	Y	Y	N
7 Obey	Y	Y	Y
8 ***Roth***	Y	Y	N
9 ***Sensenbrenner***	Y	Y	N
WYOMING			
AL ***Cheney***	Y	Y	?

Southern states - Ala., Ark., Fla., Ga., Ky., La., Miss., N.C., Okla., S.C., Tenn., Texas, Va.

* The *Congressional Record* vote number is different from the CQ vote number because the *Record* includes quorum calls in its tally. CQ does not publish quorum call votes.

361. HR 1426. Indian Health Care. Adoption of the rule (H Res 528) to provide for House floor consideration of the bill to authorize over $200 million in fiscal 1987-90 for health care programs for American Indians. Adopted 385-1: R 162-1; D 223-0 (ND 149-0, SD 74-0), Sept. 18, 1986.

362. HR 1426. Indian Health Care. McCain, R-Ariz., amendment to strike a section that specified certain California Indian tribes not recognized as tribes by the federal government as eligible for Indian health services. Adopted 206-180: R 150-10; D 56-170 (ND 21-130, SD 35-40), Sept. 18, 1986. A "yea" was a vote supporting the president's position.

363. HR 1426. Indian Health Care. Nielson, R-Utah, substitute to authorize $99 million in fiscal 1987-89 for Indian health care programs. Rejected 127-253: R 111-48; D 16-205 (ND 3-144, SD 13-61), Sept. 18, 1986.

364. HR 1426. Indian Health Care. Passage of the bill to authorize over $200 million in fiscal 1987-90 for health care programs for American Indians. Passed 308-70: R 95-60; D 213-10 (ND 148-2, SD 65-8), Sept. 18, 1986.

365. HR 2482. Pesticide Control Reauthorization. Panetta, D-Calif., amendment to the Roberts, R-Kan., amendment. The Panetta amendment would have given the Environmental Protection Agency (EPA) more discretion than did the Roberts amendment in setting uniform national standards for pesticide residues on foods, and would have shifted the burden onto EPA to prove the standards necessary to prevent disruption of commerce. It also would have required EPA to respond to comments submitted during rulemaking procedures to set the standards. Rejected 157-183: R 22-118; D 135-65 (ND 111-25, SD 24-40), Sept. 19, 1986. (The Roberts amendment subsequently was adopted *(see vote 366, below).*)

366. HR 2482. Pesticide Control Reauthorization. Roberts, R-Kan., amendment to require the Environmental Protection Agency to issue uniform national standards for residues of pesticides on food products. Adopted 214-121: R 115-24; D 99-97 (ND 45-90, SD 54-7), Sept. 19, 1986.

367. HR 2482. Pesticide Control Reauthorization. Passage of the bill to amend and reauthorize the Federal Insecticide, Fungicide and Rodenticide Act (PL 92-516) for fiscal years 1987-91, at the following levels: $87 million for 1987; $96 million for 1988; $101 million for 1989; $107 million for 1990; and $116 million for 1991. Passed 329-4: R 134-3; D 195-1 (ND 134-1, SD 61-0), Sept. 19, 1986.

368. HR 5369. Asbestos Information. Florio, D-N.J., motion to suspend the rules and pass the bill to require manufacturers of asbestos products to submit information on them to the Environmental Protection Agency and to require building owners to inspect and sample asbestos in their buildings before filing lawsuits against asbestos manufacturers. Motion agreed to 390-4: R 163-0; D 227-4 (ND 155-3, SD 72-1), Sept. 23, 1986. A two-thirds majority of those present and voting (263 in this case) is required for passage under suspension of the rules.

KEY

Y Voted for (yea).
\# Paired for.
\+ Announced for.
N Voted against (nay).
X Paired against.
\- Announced against.
P Voted "present."
C Voted "present" to avoid possible conflict of interest.
? Did not vote or otherwise make a position known.

Democrats ***Republicans***

	361	362	363	364	365	366	367	368
ALABAMA								
1 ***Callahan***	?	?	?	?	N	Y	Y	Y
2 ***Dickinson***	?	?	?	?	?	?	?	Y
3 Nichols	Y	Y	Y	Y	N	Y	Y	Y
4 Bevill	Y	Y	Y	Y	N	Y	Y	Y
5 Flippo	Y	Y	Y	Y	N	Y	Y	Y
6 Erdreich	Y	N	Y	Y	N	Y	Y	Y
7 Shelby	Y	N	?	Y	N	Y	Y	Y
ALASKA								
AL ***Young***	Y	Y	N	Y	N	Y	Y	Y
ARIZONA								
1 ***McCain***	Y	Y	N	Y	Y	N	Y	Y
2 Udall	Y	N	N	Y	?	?	?	Y
3 ***Stump***	Y	Y	Y	N	N	Y	Y	Y
4 ***Rudd***	Y	?	?	?	?	?	?	Y
5 ***Kolbe***	Y	Y	Y	Y	?	?	?	Y
ARKANSAS								
1 Alexander	Y	N	N	Y	N	Y	Y	Y
2 Robinson	Y	Y	Y	N	N	Y	Y	Y
3 ***Hammerschmidt***	Y	Y	N	Y	N	Y	?	Y
4 Anthony	Y	N	N	Y	N	Y	Y	Y
CALIFORNIA								
1 Bosco	Y	N	N	Y	Y	Y	Y	Y
2 ***Chappie***	Y	Y	Y	Y	N	Y	Y	?
3 Matsui	Y	N	N	Y	Y	N	Y	Y
4 Fazio	Y	N	N	Y	?	?	?	Y
5 Burton	?	?	?	?	?	?	?	?
6 Boxer	Y	N	N	Y	Y	N	Y	?
7 Miller	Y	N	N	Y	Y	?	?	Y
8 Dellums	?	X	X	#	Y	N	Y	Y
9 Stark	Y	N	?	?	Y	N	Y	Y
10 Edwards	Y	N	N	Y	Y	N	Y	Y
11 Lantos	Y	N	N	Y	Y	N	Y	Y
12 ***Zschau***	Y	Y	Y	Y	?	?	?	?
13 Mineta	Y	N	N	Y	Y	N	Y	Y
14 ***Shumway***	Y	N	Y	?	N	Y	Y	Y
15 Coelho	Y	N	N	Y	N	Y	Y	?
16 Panetta	Y	N	N	Y	Y	Y	Y	N
17 ***Pashayan***	Y	N	N	Y	N	Y	Y	Y
18 Lehman	Y	N	N	Y	N	Y	Y	Y
19 ***Lagomarsino***	Y	Y	N	Y	N	Y	Y	Y
20 ***Thomas***	Y	Y	Y	Y	?	?	?	Y
21 ***Fiedler***	?	Y	N	Y	N	Y	Y	Y
22 ***Moorhead***	Y	Y	Y	N	N	Y	Y	Y
23 Beilenson	Y	N	N	Y	Y	N	Y	Y
24 Waxman	Y	N	N	Y	Y	N	Y	Y
25 Roybal	Y	N	N	Y	Y	N	Y	Y
26 Berman	Y	N	N	Y	Y	N	Y	Y
27 Levine	Y	N	N	Y	Y	N	Y	Y
28 Dixon	Y	?	?	?	?	X	?	?
29 Hawkins	?	X	?	?	?	X	?	Y
30 Martinez	Y	N	N	Y	Y	N	Y	Y
31 Dymally	Y	N	N	Y	?	?	?	Y
32 Anderson	Y	N	N	Y	Y	N	Y	Y
33 ***Dreier***	Y	Y	Y	N	N	Y	Y	Y
34 Torres	Y	N	N	Y	Y	?	?	Y
35 ***Lewis***	Y	?	?	?	?	?	?	Y
36 Brown	Y	N	N	Y	?	?	?	Y
37 ***McCandless***	Y	Y	Y	N	N	Y	N	Y
38 ***Dornan***	Y	Y	Y	N	N	Y	Y	Y
39 ***Dannemeyer***	Y	Y	Y	N	-	+	+	Y
40 ***Badham***	Y	Y	Y	N	?	?	?	Y
41 ***Lowery***	Y	Y	Y	N	N	Y	Y	Y
42 ***Lungren***	Y	Y	Y	N	N	Y	Y	Y
43 ***Packard***	Y	Y	?	?	?	#	?	Y
44 Bates	Y	N	N	Y	Y	N	Y	Y
45 ***Hunter***	Y	Y	Y	Y	N	?	Y	Y
COLORADO								
1 Schroeder	Y	N	N	Y	Y	N	Y	Y
2 Wirth	?	N	N	Y	?	?	?	Y
3 ***Strang***	Y	Y	N	Y	N	Y	Y	Y
4 ***Brown***	Y	Y	Y	N	N	Y	Y	Y
5 ***Kramer***	Y	Y	N	Y	N	Y	Y	Y
6 ***Schaefer***	?	?	?	?	?	?	?	Y
CONNECTICUT								
1 Kennelly	Y	N	N	Y	Y	N	Y	Y
2 Gejdenson	Y	N	N	Y	Y	Y	Y	Y
3 Morrison	Y	N	N	Y	Y	N	Y	Y
4 ***McKinney***	Y	N	N	Y	N	Y	Y	Y
5 ***Rowland***	Y	Y	Y	Y	N	Y	Y	Y
6 ***Johnson***	Y	?	Y	N	N	Y	Y	Y
DELAWARE								
AL Carper	Y	Y	N	Y	Y	Y	Y	Y
FLORIDA								
1 Hutto	Y	Y	N	Y	Y	Y	Y	Y
2 Fuqua	Y	Y	N	Y	?	?	?	Y
3 Bennett	Y	N	N	Y	N	Y	Y	Y
4 Chappell	Y	Y	N	Y	?	?	?	Y
5 ***McCollum***	Y	Y	N	Y	N	Y	Y	Y
6 MacKay	Y	N	N	Y	N	Y	Y	Y
7 Gibbons	Y	N	N	Y	?	?	?	?
8 ***Young***	Y	Y	Y	Y	N	Y	Y	Y
9 ***Bilirakis***	Y	Y	Y	Y	N	Y	Y	Y
10 ***Ireland***	?	?	?	?	?	#	?	Y
11 Nelson	Y	N	N	Y	N	Y	Y	Y
12 ***Lewis***	Y	Y	N	Y	-	#	+	Y
13 ***Mack***	Y	Y	Y	N	N	Y	Y	Y
14 Mica	Y	Y	N	Y	Y	Y	Y	Y
15 ***Shaw***	Y	Y	Y	Y	N	Y	Y	Y
16 Smith	Y	N	N	Y	Y	N	Y	Y
17 Lehman	Y	?	?	?	?	?	+	Y
18 Pepper	Y	N	N	Y	Y	Y	Y	Y
19 Fascell	Y	N	N	Y	Y	N	Y	Y
GEORGIA								
1 Thomas	Y	N	N	Y	N	Y	Y	Y
2 Hatcher	Y	N	N	Y	N	Y	Y	?
3 Ray	Y	Y	Y	N	N	Y	Y	Y
4 ***Swindall***	Y	Y	Y	N	N	Y	Y	Y
5 Fowler	?	?	?	?	?	?	?	?
6 ***Gingrich***	Y	Y	Y	Y	?	?	Y	?
7 Darden	Y	N	N	Y	N	Y	Y	Y
8 Rowland	Y	N	N	Y	N	Y	Y	Y
9 Jenkins	Y	Y	N	Y	N	Y	Y	Y
10 Barnard	?	#	?	?	X	?	?	Y
HAWAII								
1 Abercrombie *								Y
2 Akaka	Y	N	N	Y	?	?	?	Y
IDAHO								
1 ***Craig***	Y	Y	Y	N	N	Y	Y	Y
2 Stallings	Y	Y	N	Y	N	Y	Y	Y
ILLINOIS								
1 Hayes	Y	N	N	Y	Y	N	Y	Y
2 Savage	Y	N	N	Y	Y	N	Y	Y
3 Russo	Y	?	?	?	#	?	?	Y
4 Vacancy								
5 Lipinski	Y	N	N	Y	Y	Y	Y	Y
6 ***Hyde***	?	?	Y	N	N	N	Y	Y
7 Collins	Y	N	N	Y	Y	N	Y	Y
8 Rostenkowski	Y	N	N	Y	?	?	?	Y
9 Yates	Y	N	N	Y	Y	N	Y	Y
10 ***Porter***	Y	Y	Y	Y	N	N	Y	Y
11 Annunzio	Y	N	N	Y	Y	Y	Y	Y
12 ***Crane***	N	Y	Y	N	N	Y	N	Y
13 ***Fawell***	Y	Y	Y	N	N	N	Y	Y
14 ***Grotberg***	?	?	?	?	?	?	?	?
15 ***Madigan***	Y	Y	Y	N	?	?	?	Y
16 ***Martin***	Y	Y	Y	N	N	Y	Y	Y
17 Evans	Y	N	N	Y	Y	N	Y	Y
18 ***Michel***	Y	Y	Y	N	N	Y	Y	Y
19 Bruce	Y	N	N	Y	Y	N	Y	Y
20 Durbin	Y	N	N	Y	Y	Y	Y	N
21 Price	Y	N	N	Y	Y	Y	Y	Y
22 Gray	Y	N	N	Y	Y	Y	Y	Y
INDIANA								
1 Visclosky	Y	N	N	Y	N	Y	Y	Y
2 Sharp	Y	Y	N	Y	Y	Y	Y	Y
3 ***Hiler***	Y	Y	Y	Y	?	?	?	Y
4 ***Coats***	Y	Y	Y	Y	N	Y	Y	Y
5 ***Hillis***	Y	Y	Y	N	?	?	?	Y

ND - Northern Democrats SD - Southern Democrats

* Corresponding to Congressional Record Votes 392, 394, 395, 396, 398, 399, 400, 401

	361	362	363	364	365	366	367	368
6 ***Burton***	Y	Y	Y	N	N	Y	Y	Y
7 ***Myers***	Y	Y	Y	Y	N	Y	Y	Y
8 McCloskey	Y	Y	N	Y	N	Y	Y	Y
9 Hamilton	Y	Y	N	Y	N	Y	Y	Y
10 Jacobs	Y	?	N	Y	Y	N	Y	Y
IOWA								
1 ***Leach***	Y	Y	Y	N	N	Y	Y	Y
2 ***Tauke***	Y	Y	Y	N	N	Y	Y	Y
3 ***Evans***	Y	Y	N	Y	N	Y	Y	Y
4 Smith	Y	N	N	Y	N	Y	Y	Y
5 ***Lightfoot***	Y	Y	Y	N	N	Y	Y	Y
6 Bedell	Y	N	N	Y	Y	Y	Y	Y
KANSAS								
1 ***Roberts***	Y	Y	Y	Y	N	Y	Y	Y
2 Slattery	Y	Y	N	Y	N	Y	Y	Y
3 ***Meyers***	Y	Y	N	Y	Y	N	Y	Y
4 Glickman	Y	Y	N	Y	N	Y	Y	Y
5 ***Whittaker***	Y	Y	N	Y	N	Y	Y	Y
KENTUCKY								
1 Hubbard	Y	Y	Y	N	N	Y	Y	Y
2 Natcher	Y	N	N	Y	N	Y	Y	Y
3 Mazzoli	Y	N	N	Y	N	Y	Y	Y
4 ***Snyder***	Y	Y	Y	N	N	Y	Y	Y
5 ***Rogers***	Y	Y	Y	N	N	Y	Y	Y
6 ***Hopkins***	Y	Y	Y	N	N	Y	Y	Y
7 Perkins	Y	N	N	Y	N	Y	Y	Y
LOUISIANA								
1 ***Livingston***	?	?	?	?	N	Y	Y	Y
2 Boggs	Y	N	N	Y	Y	Y	Y	?
3 Tauzin	Y	Y	N	Y	N	Y	Y	Y
4 Roemer	Y	Y	Y	N	Y	N	Y	Y
5 Huckaby	Y	Y	N	Y	Y	Y	Y	Y
6 ***Moore***	?	?	?	?	?	?	?	?
7 Breaux	?	?	?	?	?	?	?	?
8 Long	Y	N	N	Y	Y	Y	Y	Y
MAINE								
1 ***McKernan***	Y	Y	N	Y	Y	N	Y	Y
2 ***Snowe***	Y	Y	N	Y	Y	N	Y	Y
MARYLAND								
1 Dyson	Y	Y	N	N	N	Y	Y	Y
2 ***Bentley***	Y	Y	Y	Y	N	Y	Y	Y
3 Mikulski	Y	N	N	Y	?	?	?	?
4 ***Holt***	Y	Y	Y	N	N	Y	Y	?
5 Hoyer	Y	N	N	Y	Y	N	Y	Y
6 Byron	Y	Y	Y	N	N	Y	Y	Y
7 Mitchell	?	N	N	Y	Y	N	Y	Y
8 Barnes	Y	N	N	Y	Y	N	Y	Y
MASSACHUSETTS								
1 ***Conte***	Y	N	N	Y	Y	N	Y	Y
2 Boland	?	?	?	?	?	?	?	?
3 Early	?	?	?	?	?	?	?	Y
4 Frank	Y	N	N	Y	Y	N	Y	Y
5 Atkins	Y	N	N	Y	Y	N	Y	Y
6 Mavroules	Y	N	N	Y	Y	N	Y	Y
7 Markey	Y	N	N	Y	Y	N	Y	?
8 O'Neill								
9 Moakley	Y	N	N	Y	Y	N	Y	Y
10 Studds	Y	N	N	Y	?	?	?	Y
11 Donnelly	Y	N	N	Y	Y	Y	Y	Y
MICHIGAN								
1 Conyers	?	?	?	?	?	?	?	?
2 ***Pursell***	Y	Y	N	Y	N	Y	Y	Y
3 Wolpe	?	N	N	Y	Y	N	Y	Y
4 ***Siljander***	Y	Y	Y	Y	?	?	?	Y
5 ***Henry***	Y	Y	Y	N	N	Y	Y	Y
6 Carr	Y	N	Y	Y	N	Y	Y	Y
7 Kildee	Y	N	N	Y	Y	N	Y	Y
8 Traxler	Y	?	N	Y	?	?	?	Y
9 ***Vander Jagt***	Y	Y	Y	Y	N	Y	Y	Y
10 ***Schuette***	?	?	?	?	?	?	?	Y
11 ***Davis***	Y	N	N	Y	N	Y	Y	Y
12 Bonior	Y	N	?	Y	Y	N	Y	Y
13 Crockett	Y	N	?	?	?	?	?	Y
14 Hertel	?	?	?	?	Y	N	Y	Y
15 Ford	Y	N	N	Y	Y	N	Y	Y
16 Dingell	Y	Y	?	?	Y	?	Y	Y
17 Levin	Y	N	N	Y	Y	N	Y	Y
18 ***Broomfield***	Y	N	Y	Y	N	Y	Y	Y
MINNESOTA								
1 Penny	Y	Y	N	Y	N	N	Y	Y
2 ***Weber***	Y	Y	Y	Y	N	Y	Y	Y
3 ***Frenzel***	Y	Y	Y	Y	N	Y	Y	Y
4 Vento	Y	N	N	Y	Y	N	Y	Y
5 Sabo	Y	N	N	Y	Y	N	Y	Y
6 Sikorski	Y	N	N	Y	Y	N	Y	Y

	361	362	363	364	365	366	367	368
7 ***Stangeland***	Y	Y	Y	Y	?	?	?	Y
8 Oberstar	Y	N	N	Y	Y	N	Y	Y
MISSISSIPPI								
1 Whitten	Y	N	N	Y	N	Y	Y	Y
2 ***Franklin***	Y	Y	Y	Y	?	?	?	Y
3 Montgomery	Y	Y	N	Y	N	Y	Y	Y
4 Dowdy	Y	N	N	?	?	?	?	Y
5 ***Lott***	Y	Y	Y	N	?	?	?	Y
MISSOURI								
1 Clay	Y	N	N	Y	?	?	?	Y
2 Young	Y	N	N	Y	N	Y	Y	Y
3 Gephardt	Y	N	?	?	?	?	?	Y
4 Skelton	Y	Y	N	Y	N	Y	Y	Y
5 Wheat	Y	N	N	Y	Y	N	Y	Y
6 ***Coleman***	Y	Y	Y	Y	N	Y	Y	Y
7 ***Taylor***	Y	Y	Y	Y	N	Y	Y	?
8 ***Emerson***	Y	Y	Y	Y	N	Y	Y	Y
9 Volkmer	Y	N	N	Y	N	Y	Y	Y
MONTANA								
1 Williams	?	Y	N	Y	N	Y	Y	Y
2 ***Marlenee***	Y	Y	N	?	N	Y	N	Y
NEBRASKA								
1 ***Bereuter***	Y	Y	N	Y	N	Y	Y	Y
2 ***Daub***	Y	Y	?	N	N	Y	?	Y
3 ***Smith***	Y	Y	Y	N	N	Y	Y	Y
NEVADA								
1 Reid	Y	N	N	Y	Y	N	Y	Y
2 ***Vucanovich***	Y	Y	Y	Y	N	Y	Y	?
NEW HAMPSHIRE								
1 ***Smith***	Y	Y	Y	N	Y	Y	Y	Y
2 ***Gregg***	Y	Y	Y	N	?	?	?	Y
NEW JERSEY								
1 Florio	?	N	N	Y	Y	N	Y	Y
2 Hughes	Y	N	N	Y	Y	N	Y	Y
3 Howard	Y	N	N	Y	Y	N	Y	Y
4 ***Smith***	Y	Y	N	Y	Y	N	Y	Y
5 ***Roukema***	Y	Y	Y	P	Y	N	Y	Y
6 Dwyer	Y	N	N	Y	Y	N	Y	Y
7 ***Rinaldo***	Y	Y	Y	Y	Y	N	Y	Y
8 Roe	Y	N	N	Y	Y	N	Y	Y
9 Torricelli	Y	N	N	Y	Y	N	Y	Y
10 Rodino	?	?	N	Y	Y	N	Y	Y
11 ***Gallo***	Y	Y	Y	Y	Y	N	Y	Y
12 ***Courter***	Y	Y	Y	Y	Y	N	Y	Y
13 ***Saxton***	Y	Y	Y	Y	Y	N	Y	Y
14 Guarini	Y	N	N	Y	Y	N	Y	Y
NEW MEXICO								
1 ***Lujan***	Y	Y	Y	Y	N	Y	Y	Y
2 ***Skeen***	Y	Y	N	Y	N	Y	Y	?
3 Richardson	Y	N	N	Y	?	?	?	Y
NEW YORK								
1 ***Carney***	Y	Y	N	Y	Y	N	Y	Y
2 Downey	Y	N	N	Y	Y	N	?	Y
3 Mrazek	Y	N	N	Y	?	?	?	Y
4 ***Lent***	Y	Y	Y	?	?	?	?	Y
5 ***McGrath***	Y	Y	Y	Y	N	N	Y	?
6 Waldon	?	?	?	?	?	?	?	Y
7 Ackerman	Y	N	N	Y	Y	N	Y	Y
8 Scheuer	Y	N	N	Y	Y	N	Y	Y
9 Manton	Y	?	?	?	N	Y	Y	Y
10 Schumer	Y	N	N	Y	Y	N	Y	Y
11 Towns	Y	N	N	Y	Y	N	Y	Y
12 Owens	Y	N	N	Y	Y	N	Y	Y
13 Solarz	Y	N	N	Y	Y	N	Y	Y
14 ***Molinari***	Y	Y	N	Y	Y	N	Y	Y
15 ***Green***	Y	Y	N	Y	Y	N	Y	Y
16 Rangel	?	?	?	?	Y	N	Y	Y
17 Weiss	Y	N	N	Y	+	N	Y	Y
18 Garcia	Y	N	N	Y	?	?	?	Y
19 Biaggi	Y	N	N	Y	?	?	?	Y
20 ***DioGuardi***	Y	Y	Y	Y	N	Y	Y	Y
21 ***Fish***	Y	Y	N	Y	Y	N	Y	Y
22 ***Gilman***	Y	Y	N	Y	N	Y	Y	Y
23 Stratton	?	?	?	?	?	?	?	Y
24 ***Solomon***	Y	Y	Y	N	N	Y	Y	Y
25 ***Boehlert***	Y	Y	N	Y	Y	N	Y	Y
26 ***Martin***	Y	Y	N	Y	N	Y	Y	Y
27 ***Wortley***	Y	Y	N	Y	N	Y	?	Y
28 McHugh	Y	N	N	Y	Y	Y	Y	Y
29 ***Horton***	Y	Y	N	Y	N	Y	Y	Y
30 ***Eckert***	Y	Y	Y	N	N	Y	Y	Y
31 ***Kemp***	Y	?	?	?	?	?	?	Y
32 LaFalce	Y	N	N	Y	Y	N	Y	Y
33 Nowak	Y	N	?	Y	Y	N	Y	Y
34 Lundine	Y	Y	N	Y	Y	N	Y	Y

	361	362	363	364	365	366	367	368
NORTH CAROLINA								
1 Jones	Y	Y	N	Y	N	Y	Y	Y
2 Valentine	Y	Y	N	Y	N	Y	Y	Y
3 Whitley	Y	Y	N	Y	?	?	?	Y
4 ***Cobey***	Y	Y	Y	N	?	?	?	Y
5 Neal	?	Y	N	Y	Y	Y	Y	Y
6 ***Coble***	Y	Y	Y	Y	Y	Y	Y	Y
7 Rose	Y	Y	N	Y	Y	Y	Y	Y
8 Hefner	Y	N	N	Y	?	?	?	Y
9 ***McMillan***	Y	Y	N	Y	N	Y	Y	Y
10 Vacancy								
11 ***Hendon***	Y	Y	N	Y	N	Y	Y	Y
NORTH DAKOTA								
AL Dorgan	Y	Y	N	Y	Y	Y	Y	Y
OHIO								
1 Luken	Y	N	N	Y	N	Y	Y	Y
2 ***Gradison***	Y	Y	N	Y	?	?	?	Y
3 Hall	Y	N	N	Y	Y	N	Y	Y
4 ***Oxley***	Y	Y	Y	N	N	Y	Y	Y
5 ***Latta***	?	Y	Y	N	?	?	?	?
6 ***McEwen***	?	Y	Y	N	N	Y	Y	Y
7 ***DeWine***	Y	Y	N	Y	N	Y	Y	Y
8 ***Kindness***	?	?	?	?	?	?	?	?
9 Kaptur	Y	N	N	Y	N	Y	Y	?
10 ***Miller***	Y	Y	Y	N	N	Y	Y	Y
11 Eckart	Y	N	N	Y	Y	N	Y	Y
12 ***Kasich***	Y	Y	Y	Y	N	Y	Y	Y
13 Pease	Y	N	N	Y	Y	N	Y	Y
14 Seiberling	Y	N	N	Y	Y	N	Y	Y
15 ***Wylie***	Y	Y	Y	Y	N	Y	Y	Y
16 ***Regula***	Y	Y	Y	Y	N	Y	Y	Y
17 Traficant	Y	N	N	Y	Y	Y	Y	Y
18 Applegate	Y	N	?	Y	N	Y	Y	Y
19 Feighan	Y	N	N	Y	Y	N	Y	Y
20 Oakar	Y	N	N	Y	?	?	?	?
21 Stokes	?	?	?	?	?	?	?	Y
OKLAHOMA								
1 Jones	Y	Y	N	Y	?	?	?	+
2 Synar	Y	Y	N	Y	Y	N	Y	Y
3 Watkins	Y	Y	N	Y	N	?	?	Y
4 McCurdy	Y	Y	N	Y	N	Y	Y	Y
5 ***Edwards***	Y	Y	Y	Y	N	Y	Y	Y
6 English	Y	Y	N	Y	N	Y	Y	Y
OREGON								
1 AuCoin	Y	N	N	Y	Y	N	Y	Y
2 ***Smith, R.***	Y	Y	N	Y	N	Y	Y	Y
3 Wyden	Y	N	N	Y	Y	N	Y	Y
4 Weaver	Y	N	N	Y	Y	N	Y	N
5 ***Smith, D.***	Y	Y	Y	N	N	Y	Y	Y
PENNSYLVANIA								
1 Foglietta	Y	N	N	Y	Y	N	Y	?
2 Gray	Y	Y	N	Y	Y	N	Y	Y
3 Borski	Y	N	N	Y	Y	N	Y	Y
4 Kolter	Y	N	N	Y	N	Y	Y	Y
5 ***Schulze***	Y	Y	Y	Y	?	?	?	Y
6 Yatron	Y	?	?	?	?	?	?	Y
7 Edgar	Y	N	N	Y	?	?	?	?
8 Kostmayer	Y	N	N	Y	Y	N	Y	Y
9 ***Shuster***	Y	Y	Y	N	N	Y	Y	Y
10 ***McDade***	Y	Y	Y	Y	N	Y	Y	Y
11 Kanjorski	Y	N	N	Y	N	Y	Y	Y
12 Murtha	Y	N	N	Y	Y	Y	Y	Y
13 ***Coughlin***	Y	Y	Y	Y	Y	N	Y	Y
14 Coyne	Y	N	N	Y	Y	N	Y	Y
15 ***Ritter***	Y	N	Y	N	N	Y	Y	Y
16 ***Walker***	Y	Y	Y	N	N	Y	Y	Y
17 ***Gekas***	Y	Y	Y	N	N	Y	Y	Y
18 Walgren	Y	N	N	Y	Y	N	Y	Y
19 ***Goodling***	Y	Y	Y	N	N	Y	Y	Y
20 Gaydos	Y	N	N	Y	Y	Y	Y	Y
21 ***Ridge***	Y	Y	N	Y	N	Y	Y	Y
22 Murphy	Y	Y	Y	N	Y	Y	Y	Y
23 ***Clinger***	Y	Y	Y	Y	N	Y	Y	+
RHODE ISLAND								
1 St Germain	Y	N	N	Y	Y	N	Y	Y
2 ***Schneider***	Y	Y	N	Y	Y	N	Y	Y
SOUTH CAROLINA								
1 ***Hartnett***	?	?	?	?	?	?	?	?
2 ***Spence***	Y	Y	Y	N	Y	Y	Y	Y
3 Derrick	Y	N	N	Y	Y	Y	Y	Y
4 ***Campbell***	?	#	#	X	?	X	?	?
5 Spratt	Y	N	N	Y	Y	Y	Y	Y
6 Tallon	Y	Y	N	Y	?	?	?	Y
SOUTH DAKOTA								
AL Daschle	Y	Y	N	Y	Y	N	Y	Y

	361	362	363	364	365	366	367	368
TENNESSEE								
1 ***Quillen***	Y	?	?	?	?	?	?	Y
2 ***Duncan***	Y	Y	Y	Y	N	Y	Y	Y
3 Lloyd	Y	Y	Y	Y	N	Y	Y	Y
4 Cooper	Y	N	N	Y	?	?	?	Y
5 Boner	Y	N	N	Y	Y	?	?	Y
6 Gordon	Y	N	N	Y	N	Y	Y	Y
7 ***Sundquist***	Y	Y	Y	Y	N	Y	Y	Y
8 Jones	Y	Y	N	Y	N	Y	Y	Y
9 Ford	?	?	?	?	?	?	?	?
TEXAS								
1 Chapman	Y	Y	Y	?	Y	Y	Y	Y
2 Wilson	?	?	?	?	?	?	?	P
3 ***Bartlett***	Y	Y	Y	N	N	Y	Y	Y
4 Hall, R.	Y	Y	Y	N	N	?	?	Y
5 Bryant	Y	N	N	Y	Y	Y	Y	Y
6 ***Barton***	Y	Y	Y	?	?	?	?	Y
7 ***Archer***	Y	Y	Y	N	N	Y	Y	Y
8 ***Fields***	Y	Y	Y	N	N	Y	Y	Y
9 Brooks	Y	Y	N	Y	Y	Y	Y	Y
10 Pickle	Y	Y	N	Y	Y	Y	Y	Y
11 Leath	Y	N	N	Y	N	Y	Y	Y
12 Wright	Y	N	N	Y	N	Y	Y	?
13 ***Boulter***	Y	Y	Y	N	N	Y	Y	Y
14 ***Sweeney***	?	?	?	?	N	Y	Y	Y
15 de la Garza	Y	N	N	Y	N	Y	Y	Y
16 Coleman	Y	N	N	Y	Y	Y	Y	Y
17 Stenholm	Y	Y	Y	N	N	Y	Y	Y
18 Leland	?	?	?	?	Y	N	Y	Y
19 ***Combest***	Y	Y	Y	N	N	Y	Y	Y
20 Gonzalez	Y	N	N	Y	Y	N	Y	Y
21 ***Loeffler***	Y	Y	Y	N	?	?	?	Y
22 ***DeLay***	Y	Y	Y	N	N	Y	Y	Y
23 Bustamante	Y	N	N	Y	?	?	?	Y
24 Frost	Y	Y	N	Y	Y	Y	Y	Y
25 Andrews	Y	N	N	Y	N	Y	Y	Y
26 ***Armey***	Y	Y	Y	N	N	Y	Y	?
27 Ortiz	Y	N	N	Y	?	?	?	Y
UTAH								
1 ***Hansen***	Y	N	Y	N	?	?	?	?
2 ***Monson***	Y	N	?	?	?	?	?	Y
3 ***Nielson***	Y	N	Y	N	N	Y	Y	Y
VERMONT								
AL ***Jeffords***	Y	Y	N	Y	Y	N	?	Y
VIRGINIA								
1 ***Bateman***	Y	Y	Y	Y	N	Y	Y	Y
2 ***Whitehurst***	Y	?	?	?	?	?	?	Y
3 ***Bliley***	Y	Y	Y	Y	N	Y	Y	Y
4 Sisisky	Y	N	N	Y	N	Y	Y	N
5 Daniel	Y	Y	Y	N	N	Y	Y	Y
6 Olin	Y	N	N	N	Y	N	Y	Y
7 ***Slaughter***	Y	Y	Y	N	N	Y	Y	Y
8 ***Parris***	Y	Y	Y	Y	N	Y	Y	Y
9 Boucher	?	N	N	Y	?	?	?	Y
10 ***Wolf***	Y	Y	N	Y	N	Y	Y	Y
WASHINGTON								
1 ***Miller***	Y	Y	N	Y	Y	N	Y	Y
2 Swift	?	N	N	Y	Y	N	Y	Y
3 Bonker	Y	Y	N	Y	Y	Y	Y	Y
4 ***Morrison***	Y	Y	N	Y	N	Y	Y	Y
5 Foley	Y	N	N	Y	Y	Y	Y	Y
6 Dicks	Y	N	N	Y	Y	Y	Y	Y
7 Lowry	Y	N	N	Y	Y	N	Y	Y
8 ***Chandler***	Y	Y	N	Y	N	Y	Y	Y
WEST VIRGINIA								
1 Mollohan	?	N	N	Y	N	Y	Y	Y
2 Staggers	Y	N	N	Y	Y	N	Y	Y
3 Wise	Y	N	N	Y	Y	N	Y	Y
4 Rahall	Y	N	N	Y	Y	Y	Y	Y
WISCONSIN								
1 Aspin	Y	N	N	Y	?	?	?	Y
2 Kastenmeier	?	N	N	Y	Y	N	Y	Y
3 ***Gunderson***	Y	Y	N	Y	N	Y	Y	Y
4 Kleczka	Y	N	N	Y	Y	N	N	Y
5 Moody	Y	N	N	Y	?	N	Y	Y
6 ***Petri***	Y	Y	N	Y	N	Y	Y	Y
7 Obey	Y	Y	N	Y	Y	N	Y	Y
8 ***Roth***	Y	Y	N	Y	N	Y	Y	Y
9 ***Sensenbrenner***	Y	Y	Y	N	N	Y	Y	Y
WYOMING								
AL ***Cheney***	?	?	?	?	?	?	?	Y

**Rep. Neil Abercrombie, D-Hawaii, was sworn in on Sept. 23, 1986. The first vote for which he was eligible was CQ vote 368.*

Southern states - Ala., Ark., Fla., Ga., Ky., La., Miss., N.C., Okla., S.C., Tenn., Texas, Va.

* The *Congressional Record* vote number is different from the CQ vote number because the *Record* includes quorum calls in its tally. CQ does not publish quorum call votes.

369. HR 4216. Gila Bend Indian Reservation Lands. Udall, D-Ariz., motion to suspend the rules and pass the bill to provide for the replacement of lands of the Gila Bend Indian Reservation in southwestern Arizona. Motion agreed to 258-127: R 61-100; D 197-27 (ND 142-9, SD 55-18), Sept. 23, 1986. A two-thirds majority of those present and voting (257 in this case) is required for passage under suspension of the rules. A "nay" was a vote supporting the president's position.

370. HR 4154. Age Discrimination in Employment. Adoption of the rule (H Res 554) to provide for House floor consideration of the bill to ban mandatory retirement plans for most public and private sector workers. Adopted 335-66: R 100-65; D 235-1 (ND 158-1, SD 77-0), Sept. 23, 1986.

371. HR 4154. Age Discrimination in Employment. Murphy, D-Pa., amendment to exempt from the bill's provisions state and local jurisdictions that want to use age as a criterion in hiring or retiring firefighters and law enforcement officials. Adopted 291-103: R 135-30; D 156-73 (ND 100-53, SD 56-20), Sept. 23, 1986.

372. HR 4154. Age Discrimination in Employment. Passage of the bill to amend the 1967 Age Discrimination in Employment Act so that persons aged 70 and over would be protected from age discrimination in hiring, firing, promotions and salary, which would have the effect of banning mandatory retirement plans for most public and private sector workers. Passed 394-0: R 164-0; D 230-0 (ND 154-0, SD 76-0), Sept. 23, 1986. A "yea" was a vote supporting the president's position.

373. HR 5300. Omnibus Budget Reconciliation, Fiscal 1987. Derrick, D-S.C., motion to order the previous question (thus ending debate and the possibility of amendment) on the rule (H Res 558) to provide for House floor consideration of the bill to reduce the projected fiscal 1987 deficit by $15.2 billion. Motion agreed to 216-196: R 1-168; D 215-28 (ND 154-10, SD 61-18), Sept. 24, 1986. (The rule subsequently was adopted *(see vote 374, below)*.)

374. HR 5300. Omnibus Budget Reconciliation, Fiscal 1987. Adoption of the rule (H Res 558) to provide for House floor consideration of the bill to reduce the projected fiscal 1987 deficit by $15.2 billion. Adopted 255-157: R 38-129; D 217-28 (ND 153-12, SD 64-16), Sept. 24, 1986.

375. HR 5300. Omnibus Budget Reconciliation, Fiscal 1987. Passage of the bill to reduce the projected fiscal 1987 deficit by $15.2 billion. Passed 309-106: R 99-71; D 210-35 (ND 151-14, SD 59-21), Sept. 24, 1986.

376. S 1965. Higher Education Reauthorization. Adoption of the conference report on the bill to reauthorize aid to colleges and needy students through fiscal 1991, authorizing $10.2 billion in fiscal 1987. Adopted 385-25: R 146-24; D 239-1 (ND 162-0, SD 77-1), Sept. 24, 1986.

KEY

Y Voted for (yea).
Paired for.
+ Announced for.
N Voted against (nay).
X Paired against.
- Announced against.
P Voted "present."
C Voted "present" to avoid possible conflict of interest.
? Did not vote or otherwise make a position known.

Democrats ***Republicans***

	369	370	371	372	373	374	375	376
ALABAMA								
1 ***Callahan***	N	N	Y	Y	N	N	N	Y
2 ***Dickinson***	N	N	Y	Y	N	N	N	N
3 Nichols	N	Y	Y	Y	Y	Y	N	Y
4 Bevill	N	Y	N	Y	Y	Y	Y	Y
5 Flippo	Y	?	Y	Y	Y	Y	Y	Y
6 Erdreich	Y	Y	Y	Y	Y	Y	Y	Y
7 Shelby	N	Y	Y	Y	Y	Y	N	Y
ALASKA								
AL ***Young***	Y	Y	Y	Y	N	N	Y	Y
ARIZONA								
1 ***McCain***	Y	?	?	?	N	N	Y	Y
2 Udall	Y	Y	N	Y	Y	Y	Y	Y
3 ***Stump***	N	N	Y	Y	N	N	N	N
4 ***Rudd***	Y	Y	N	Y	N	Y	N	N
5 ***Kolbe***	Y	N	Y	Y	N	N	Y	Y
ARKANSAS								
1 Alexander	Y	Y	N	Y	Y	Y	Y	?
2 Robinson	N	Y	Y	Y	N	N	N	Y
3 ***Hammerschmidt***	N	Y	Y	Y	N	N	N	Y
4 Anthony	Y	Y	Y	Y	Y	Y	Y	Y
CALIFORNIA								
1 Bosco	Y	Y	N	Y	Y	N	Y	Y
2 ***Chappie***	?	?	?	?	?	?	?	?
3 Matsui	Y	Y	Y	Y	Y	Y	Y	Y
4 Fazio	Y	Y	Y	Y	Y	Y	Y	Y
5 Burton	?	?	?	?	?	?	?	?
6 Boxer	?	?	?	?	Y	Y	Y	Y
7 Miller	Y	Y	Y	Y	Y	Y	Y	Y
8 Dellums	Y	Y	N	Y	Y	Y	Y	Y
9 Stark	Y	Y	Y	Y	Y	Y	Y	Y
10 Edwards	Y	Y	N	Y	Y	Y	Y	Y
11 Lantos	Y	Y	N	Y	Y	Y	Y	Y
12 ***Zschau***	?	?	?	?	?	?	?	?
13 Mineta	?	Y	Y	Y	Y	Y	Y	Y
14 ***Shumway***	N	N	Y	Y	N	N	N	N
15 Coelho	?	?	?	?	Y	Y	Y	Y
16 Panetta	Y	Y	Y	Y	Y	Y	Y	Y
17 ***Pashayan***	Y	Y	Y	Y	N	Y	Y	Y
18 Lehman	Y	Y	N	Y	Y	Y	Y	Y
19 ***Lagomarsino***	Y	N	Y	Y	N	N	Y	Y
20 ***Thomas***	N	Y	Y	Y	N	N	N	Y
21 ***Fiedler***	N	N	Y	Y	N	N	N	Y
22 ***Moorhead***	N	Y	Y	Y	N	N	N	Y
23 Beilenson	Y	Y	N	Y	Y	Y	N	Y
24 Waxman	Y	Y	N	Y	Y	Y	Y	?
25 Roybal	Y	Y	N	Y	Y	Y	Y	Y
26 Berman	Y	Y	N	Y	?	Y	Y	Y
27 Levine	Y	Y	Y	Y	Y	Y	Y	Y
28 Dixon	?	?	?	?	Y	Y	Y	Y
29 Hawkins	?	Y	N	Y	Y	Y	Y	Y
30 Martinez	?	Y	N	Y	Y	Y	Y	Y
31 Dymally	Y	Y	N	Y	Y	Y	Y	Y
32 Anderson	Y	Y	N	Y	N	N	N	Y
33 ***Dreier***	N	N	Y	Y	N	N	N	N
34 Torres	Y	Y	Y	Y	Y	Y	Y	Y
35 ***Lewis***	Y	Y	Y	Y	N	N	Y	Y
36 Brown	Y	Y	Y	Y	Y	Y	Y	Y
37 ***McCandless***	Y	Y	Y	Y	N	N	N	N
38 ***Dornan***	N	Y	?	?	N	N	N	Y
39 ***Dannemeyer***	N	N	Y	Y	N	N	N	N
40 ***Badham***	N	N	Y	Y	N	N	N	Y
41 ***Lowery***	Y	Y	Y	Y	N	N	Y	Y
42 ***Lungren***	N	?	Y	Y	N	N	N	N
43 ***Packard***	Y	Y	Y	Y	N	N	N	Y
44 Bates	Y	Y	Y	Y	Y	Y	Y	Y
45 ***Hunter***	Y	?	Y	Y	N	N	N	Y
COLORADO								
1 Schroeder	Y	Y	Y	Y	Y	Y	Y	Y
2 Wirth	Y	Y	?	Y	Y	Y	Y	Y
3 ***Strang***	Y	N	Y	Y	N	N	Y	Y
4 ***Brown***	N	N	Y	Y	N	N	N	Y
5 ***Kramer***	Y	Y	N	Y	N	N	N	Y
6 ***Schaefer***	N	N	Y	Y	N	N	N	N
CONNECTICUT								
1 Kennelly	Y	Y	Y	Y	Y	Y	Y	Y
2 Gejdenson	Y	Y	N	Y	Y	Y	Y	Y
3 Morrison	Y	Y	Y	Y	Y	Y	N	Y
4 ***McKinney***	N	N	Y	Y	Y	Y	Y	Y
5 ***Rowland***	N	Y	Y	Y	N	Y	Y	Y
6 ***Johnson***	Y	Y	Y	Y	N	Y	Y	Y
DELAWARE								
AL Carper	Y	Y	Y	Y	Y	N	N	Y
FLORIDA								
1 Hutto	N	Y	Y	Y	N	N	N	Y
2 Fuqua	Y	Y	Y	Y	Y	Y	Y	Y
3 Bennett	Y	Y	N	Y	Y	Y	Y	Y
4 Chappell	Y	Y	N	Y	Y	Y	Y	Y
5 ***McCollum***	N	N	Y	Y	N	N	Y	Y
6 MacKay	Y	Y	N	Y	Y	Y	Y	Y
7 Gibbons	Y	Y	Y	Y	Y	Y	Y	Y
8 ***Young***	N	Y	Y	Y	?	?	?	?
9 ***Bilirakis***	N	Y	Y	Y	N	N	Y	Y
10 ***Ireland***	N	N	Y	Y	N	N	N	Y
11 Nelson	Y	Y	Y	Y	N	Y	N	Y
12 ***Lewis***	Y	Y	Y	Y	N	N	Y	Y
13 ***Mack***	N	N	Y	Y	N	N	Y	N
14 Mica	Y	Y	N	Y	Y	Y	Y	Y
15 ***Shaw***	N	N	Y	Y	N	N	N	Y
16 Smith	Y	Y	N	Y	Y	Y	Y	Y
17 Lehman	Y	Y	N	Y	Y	Y	Y	Y
18 Pepper	Y	Y	N	Y	Y	Y	Y	Y
19 Fascell	Y	Y	?	?	Y	Y	Y	Y
GEORGIA								
1 Thomas	Y	Y	Y	Y	N	Y	Y	Y
2 Hatcher	?	?	?	?	Y	Y	Y	Y
3 Ray	Y	Y	Y	Y	N	N	N	Y
4 ***Swindall***	N	N	Y	Y	N	N	N	N
5 Fowler	?	?	?	?	?	?	?	?
6 ***Gingrich***	N	N	Y	Y	N	N	N	Y
7 Darden	Y	Y	Y	Y	N	N	Y	Y
8 Rowland	Y	Y	Y	Y	Y	Y	Y	Y
9 Jenkins	Y	Y	Y	Y	Y	Y	Y	Y
10 Barnard	N	Y	Y	Y	N	N	Y	Y
HAWAII								
1 Abercrombie	+	Y	Y	Y	Y	Y	Y	Y
2 Akaka	Y	Y	N	Y	Y	Y	Y	Y
IDAHO								
1 ***Craig***	N	N	Y	Y	N	N	N	Y
2 Stallings	Y	Y	Y	Y	Y	Y	N	Y
ILLINOIS								
1 Hayes	Y	Y	N	Y	Y	Y	Y	Y
2 Savage	Y	Y	N	Y	Y	Y	Y	Y
3 Russo	Y	Y	Y	Y	Y	Y	Y	Y
4 Vacancy								
5 Lipinski	Y	Y	Y	Y	Y	Y	Y	Y
6 ***Hyde***	Y	?	Y	Y	N	N	N	Y
7 Collins	Y	Y	N	Y	Y	Y	Y	Y
8 Rostenkowski	Y	Y	Y	Y	Y	Y	Y	Y
9 Yates	Y	Y	N	Y	Y	Y	Y	Y
10 ***Porter***	Y	Y	Y	Y	N	N	N	Y
11 Annunzio	Y	Y	Y	Y	Y	Y	Y	Y
12 ***Crane***	Y	N	Y	Y	N	N	N	N
13 ***Fawell***	N	N	Y	Y	N	N	N	Y
14 ***Grotberg***	?	?	?	?	?	?	?	?
15 ***Madigan***	N	N	N	Y	N	N	Y	Y
16 ***Martin***	N	N	N	Y	N	Y	Y	Y
17 Evans	Y	Y	N	Y	Y	Y	Y	Y
18 ***Michel***	Y	Y	?	?	N	Y	Y	N
19 Bruce	Y	Y	Y	Y	Y	Y	Y	Y
20 Durbin	Y	Y	N	Y	Y	Y	Y	Y
21 Price	Y	Y	Y	Y	Y	Y	Y	Y
22 Gray	Y	Y	Y	Y	Y	Y	Y	Y
INDIANA								
1 Visclosky	Y	Y	Y	Y	Y	Y	Y	Y
2 Sharp	Y	Y	?	?	Y	Y	Y	Y
3 ***Hiler***	Y	Y	Y	Y	N	N	N	Y
4 ***Coats***	Y	Y	N	Y	N	N	Y	Y
5 ***Hillis***	Y	Y	N	Y	?	?	N	Y

ND - Northern Democrats SD - Southern Democrats

* Corresponding to Congressional Record Votes 402, 403, 404, 405, 406, 407, 408, 409

	369	370	371	372	373	374	375	376
6 ***Burton***	N	N	Y	Y	N	N	N	N
7 ***Myers***	Y	Y	N	Y	N	N	N	Y
8 McCloskey	Y	Y	Y	Y	Y	Y	Y	Y
9 Hamilton	Y	Y	Y	Y	Y	Y	Y	Y
10 Jacobs	Y	N	Y	Y	N	N	Y	Y
IOWA								
1 ***Leach***	Y	N	N	Y	N	N	N	Y
2 ***Tauke***	Y	N	N	Y	N	N	N	Y
3 ***Evans***	N	N	Y	Y	N	N	N	Y
4 Smith	Y	Y	N	Y	Y	N	N	Y
5 ***Lightfoot***	N	N	Y	Y	N	N	N	Y
6 Bedell	Y	Y	Y	Y	Y	Y	Y	Y
KANSAS								
1 ***Roberts***	N	Y	Y	Y	N	N	N	Y
2 Slattery	Y	Y	Y	Y	Y	Y	Y	Y
3 ***Meyers***	N	Y	Y	Y	N	N	Y	Y
4 Glickman	Y	Y	Y	Y	Y	Y	Y	Y
5 ***Whittaker***	N	Y	?	?	N	Y	Y	Y
KENTUCKY								
1 Hubbard	N	Y	Y	Y	N	N	N	Y
2 Natcher	Y	Y	N	Y	Y	Y	Y	Y
3 Mazzoli	Y	Y	Y	Y	Y	Y	Y	Y
4 ***Snyder***	N	Y	Y	Y	N	N	N	Y
5 ***Rogers***	N	Y	Y	Y	N	N	N	Y
6 ***Hopkins***	N	N	Y	Y	N	N	N	Y
7 Perkins	Y	Y	N	Y	Y	Y	Y	Y
LOUISIANA								
1 ***Livingston***	N	Y	Y	Y	N	N	N	Y
2 Boggs	Y	Y	Y	Y	Y	Y	Y	Y
3 Tauzin	Y	Y	Y	Y	N	N	N	Y
4 Roemer	N	Y	Y	Y	N	N	N	Y
5 Huckaby	Y	Y	Y	Y	N	N	N	Y
6 ***Moore***	?	?	?	?	?	?	?	?
7 Breaux	?	?	?	?	?	?	?	?
8 Long	Y	Y	Y	Y	Y	Y	Y	Y
MAINE								
1 ***McKernan***	Y	Y	Y	Y	N	N	Y	Y
2 ***Snowe***	Y	Y	N	Y	N	N	Y	Y
MARYLAND								
1 Dyson	N	Y	Y	Y	N	Y	Y	Y
2 ***Bentley***	Y	Y	Y	Y	N	Y	Y	Y
3 Mikulski	?	Y	?	?	Y	Y	Y	Y
4 ***Holt***	?	?	?	?	N	N	Y	Y
5 Hoyer	Y	Y	Y	Y	Y	Y	Y	Y
6 Byron	N	Y	Y	Y	N	N	N	Y
7 Mitchell	Y	Y	N	Y	Y	Y	Y	Y
8 Barnes	Y	Y	Y	Y	Y	Y	N	Y
MASSACHUSETTS								
1 ***Conte***	Y	Y	N	Y	N	Y	Y	Y
2 Boland	?	?	?	?	?	?	?	?
3 Early	Y	Y	Y	Y	N	N	N	Y
4 Frank	Y	Y	N	Y	Y	Y	Y	?
5 Atkins	Y	Y	Y	Y	Y	Y	Y	Y
6 Mavroules	Y	Y	Y	Y	Y	Y	Y	Y
7 Markey	?	?	N	Y	Y	Y	Y	Y
8 O'Neill								
9 Moakley	Y	Y	?	?	Y	Y	Y	Y
10 Studds	Y	Y	N	Y	Y	Y	Y	Y
11 Donnelly	Y	Y	Y	Y	Y	Y	Y	Y
MICHIGAN								
1 Conyers	?	?	?	?	?	?	?	?
2 ***Pursell***	Y	Y	Y	Y	N	Y	Y	Y
3 Wolpe	Y	Y	Y	Y	Y	Y	Y	Y
4 ***Siljander***	N	N	Y	Y	N	N	N	Y
5 ***Henry***	N	Y	Y	Y	N	N	Y	Y
6 Carr	Y	Y	Y	Y	Y	Y	N	Y
7 Kildee	Y	Y	N	Y	Y	Y	Y	Y
8 Traxler	Y	Y	Y	Y	Y	Y	N	Y
9 ***Vander Jagt***	N	?	Y	Y	N	N	N	Y
10 ***Schuette***	N	Y	Y	Y	N	N	Y	Y
11 ***Davis***	Y	Y	Y	Y	N	Y	Y	Y
12 Bonior	Y	Y	N	Y	Y	Y	Y	Y
13 Crockett	Y	Y	N	Y	Y	Y	Y	Y
14 Hertel	Y	Y	Y	Y	Y	Y	Y	Y
15 Ford	Y	Y	Y	Y	Y	Y	Y	Y
16 Dingell	Y	Y	Y	Y	Y	Y	Y	?
17 Levin	Y	Y	Y	Y	Y	Y	Y	Y
18 ***Broomfield***	N	Y	Y	Y	?	?	?	?
MINNESOTA								
1 Penny	Y	Y	Y	Y	Y	Y	N	Y
2 ***Weber***	N	Y	Y	Y	N	N	Y	Y
3 ***Frenzel***	N	N	?	?	?	?	N	Y
4 Vento	Y	Y	N	Y	Y	Y	Y	Y
5 Sabo	Y	Y	Y	Y	Y	Y	Y	Y
6 Sikorski	Y	Y	Y	Y	Y	Y	Y	Y
7 ***Stangeland***	?	Y	Y	Y	N	N	Y	Y
8 Oberstar	Y	Y	?	?	Y	Y	Y	Y
MISSISSIPPI								
1 Whitten	Y	Y	N	Y	?	N	N	Y
2 ***Franklin***	Y	N	Y	Y	N	?	Y	Y
3 Montgomery	N	Y	Y	Y	Y	Y	Y	Y
4 Dowdy	Y	Y	N	Y	Y	Y	Y	Y
5 ***Lott***	N	N	Y	Y	N	Y	Y	Y
MISSOURI								
1 Clay	Y	Y	?	?	Y	Y	Y	Y
2 Young	Y	Y	Y	Y	Y	Y	Y	Y
3 Gephardt	Y	Y	?	?	Y	Y	Y	Y
4 Skelton	N	Y	Y	Y	Y	Y	Y	Y
5 Wheat	Y	Y	N	Y	Y	Y	Y	Y
6 ***Coleman***	N	Y	Y	Y	N	N	Y	Y
7 ***Taylor***	?	?	Y	Y	N	Y	Y	Y
8 ***Emerson***	N	Y	Y	Y	N	Y	Y	Y
9 Volkmer	Y	Y	Y	Y	Y	Y	Y	Y
MONTANA								
1 Williams	Y	Y	N	Y	Y	Y	Y	Y
2 ***Marlenee***	Y	N	Y	Y	N	N	N	Y
NEBRASKA								
1 ***Bereuter***	Y	Y	Y	Y	N	N	Y	Y
2 ***Daub***	N	Y	N	Y	N	N	Y	Y
3 ***Smith***	N	Y	N	Y	N	N	Y	Y
NEVADA								
1 Reid	Y	Y	N	Y	Y	Y	Y	Y
2 ***Vucanovich***	?	Y	Y	Y	N	N	N	Y
NEW HAMPSHIRE								
1 ***Smith***	N	N	N	Y	N	N	N	N
2 ***Gregg***	N	N	N	Y	N	N	N	N
NEW JERSEY								
1 Florio	Y	Y	Y	Y	Y	Y	Y	Y
2 Hughes	Y	Y	Y	Y	N	N	Y	Y
3 Howard	Y	Y	Y	Y	N	N	Y	Y
4 ***Smith***	Y	Y	Y	Y	N	Y	Y	Y
5 ***Roukema***	N	Y	Y	Y	N	N	Y	Y
6 Dwyer	Y	Y	Y	Y	Y	Y	Y	Y
7 ***Rinaldo***	N	Y	Y	Y	N	Y	Y	Y
8 Roe	Y	Y	Y	Y	Y	N	Y	Y
9 Torricelli	Y	Y	Y	?	Y	Y	Y	Y
10 Rodino	Y	?	Y	Y	Y	Y	Y	Y
11 ***Gallo***	N	Y	Y	Y	N	N	Y	Y
12 ***Courter***	N	N	Y	Y	N	N	Y	Y
13 ***Saxton***	N	Y	Y	Y	N	N	Y	Y
14 Guarini	Y	Y	Y	Y	Y	Y	Y	Y
NEW MEXICO								
1 ***Lujan***	Y	Y	Y	Y	N	Y	Y	Y
2 ***Skeen***	?	Y	Y	Y	N	Y	Y	Y
3 Richardson	Y	Y	Y	Y	Y	Y	Y	Y
NEW YORK								
1 ***Carney***	N	N	Y	Y	N	N	?	Y
2 Downey	Y	Y	N	Y	Y	Y	Y	Y
3 Mrazek	Y	Y	Y	Y	Y	Y	Y	Y
4 ***Lent***	Y	Y	Y	Y	N	Y	Y	Y
5 ***McGrath***	?	Y	Y	Y	N	Y	Y	Y
6 Waldon	Y	Y	Y	Y	Y	Y	Y	Y
7 Ackerman	Y	Y	N	Y	Y	Y	Y	Y
8 Scheuer	Y	Y	Y	Y	Y	Y	+	Y
9 Manton	Y	Y	N	Y	Y	Y	#	?
10 Schumer	?	Y	N	Y	Y	Y	Y	Y
11 Towns	Y	Y	N	Y	Y	Y	Y	Y
12 Owens	Y	Y	Y	Y	Y	Y	Y	Y
13 Solarz	Y	Y	N	Y	Y	Y	Y	Y
14 ***Molinari***	N	Y	Y	Y	N	N	Y	Y
15 ***Green***	Y	Y	Y	Y	N	N	Y	Y
16 Rangel	Y	Y	N	Y	Y	Y	Y	Y
17 Weiss	Y	Y	N	Y	Y	Y	Y	Y
18 Garcia	Y	Y	N	Y	Y	Y	Y	Y
19 Biaggi	N	Y	N	Y	?	?	Y	Y
20 ***DioGuardi***	N	Y	Y	Y	N	Y	Y	Y
21 ***Fish***	Y	Y	Y	Y	N	Y	Y	Y
22 ***Gilman***	+	Y	Y	Y	N	Y	Y	Y
23 Stratton	N	Y	Y	Y	Y	Y	Y	Y
24 ***Solomon***	N	Y	N	Y	N	N	Y	Y
25 ***Boehlert***	Y	Y	Y	Y	N	N	Y	Y
26 ***Martin***	Y	Y	Y	Y	N	N	Y	?
27 ***Wortley***	N	Y	Y	Y	N	N	Y	Y
28 McHugh	Y	Y	Y	Y	Y	?	Y	Y
29 ***Horton***	Y	Y	Y	Y	N	Y	Y	Y
30 ***Eckert***	N	?	?	?	N	N	Y	Y
31 ***Kemp***	Y	Y	Y	Y	N	N	N	Y
32 LaFalce	Y	Y	Y	Y	N	N	Y	Y
33 Nowak	Y	Y	Y	Y	N	Y	Y	Y
34 Lundine	Y	Y	Y	Y	?	Y	Y	Y
NORTH CAROLINA								
1 Jones	Y	Y	Y	Y	Y	Y	Y	Y
2 Valentine	Y	Y	N	Y	Y	Y	Y	Y
3 Whitley	Y	Y	Y	Y	Y	Y	Y	Y
4 ***Cobey***	N	Y	N	Y	N	N	Y	Y
5 Neal	Y	Y	Y	Y	Y	Y	Y	Y
6 ***Coble***	N	Y	N	Y	N	N	Y	Y
7 Rose	Y	Y	Y	Y	Y	Y	Y	Y
8 Hefner	Y	Y	Y	Y	Y	Y	Y	Y
9 ***McMillan***	?	Y	Y	Y	N	Y	Y	Y
10 Vacancy								
11 ***Hendon***	Y	Y	N	Y	N	Y	Y	Y
NORTH DAKOTA								
AL Dorgan	Y	Y	Y	Y	Y	Y	Y	Y
OHIO								
1 Luken	Y	Y	Y	Y	Y	Y	Y	Y
2 ***Gradison***	N	Y	N	Y	N	N	N	Y
3 Hall	Y	Y	Y	Y	Y	Y	Y	Y
4 ***Oxley***	N	Y	Y	Y	N	?	N	Y
5 ***Latta***	?	Y	Y	Y	N	Y	Y	Y
6 ***McEwen***	N	Y	N	Y	N	N	?	?
7 ***DeWine***	Y	N	Y	Y	N	N	N	Y
8 ***Kindness***	?	?	?	?	?	?	X	?
9 Kaptur	?	?	?	?	Y	Y	Y	Y
10 ***Miller***	N	Y	Y	Y	N	N	Y	Y
11 Eckart	Y	Y	Y	Y	Y	Y	Y	Y
12 ***Kasich***	N	Y	Y	Y	N	N	Y	Y
13 Pease	Y	Y	Y	Y	Y	Y	Y	Y
14 Seiberling	Y	Y	Y	Y	Y	Y	Y	Y
15 ***Wylie***	Y	Y	Y	Y	N	N	Y	Y
16 ***Regula***	N	Y	Y	Y	N	N	N	Y
17 Traficant	Y	Y	N	Y	N	N	Y	Y
18 Applegate	Y	Y	Y	Y	Y	Y	Y	Y
19 Feighan	Y	Y	Y	Y	Y	Y	Y	Y
20 Oakar	?	?	?	?	Y	Y	Y	Y
21 Stokes	Y	Y	N	Y	Y	Y	Y	Y
OKLAHOMA								
1 Jones	+	Y	N	Y	N	N	N	Y
2 Synar	Y	Y	N	Y	Y	Y	Y	Y
3 Watkins	Y	Y	?	Y	Y	Y	N	Y
4 McCurdy	Y	Y	Y	Y	Y	Y	Y	?
5 ***Edwards***	N	N	Y	Y	N	N	N	Y
6 English	Y	Y	Y	?	N	Y	N	Y
OREGON								
1 AuCoin	N	Y	N	Y	Y	Y	Y	Y
2 ***Smith, R.***	N	Y	Y	Y	N	N	Y	Y
3 Wyden	Y	Y	N	Y	Y	Y	Y	Y
4 Weaver	Y	Y	N	Y	Y	Y	Y	Y
5 ***Smith, D.***	N	N	Y	Y	N	N	N	N
PENNSYLVANIA								
1 Foglietta	?	?	?	?	Y	Y	Y	Y
2 Gray	Y	Y	N	Y	Y	Y	Y	Y
3 Borski	Y	Y	Y	Y	Y	Y	Y	Y
4 Kolter	?	Y	Y	Y	Y	Y	Y	Y
5 ***Schulze***	Y	Y	?	?	N	N	N	Y
6 Yatron	N	Y	Y	Y	Y	Y	Y	Y
7 Edgar	?	Y	Y	Y	Y	Y	Y	?
8 Kostmayer	Y	Y	Y	Y	Y	Y	Y	Y
9 ***Shuster***	N	N	Y	Y	N	Y	Y	Y
10 ***McDade***	N	Y	Y	Y	N	Y	Y	Y
11 Kanjorski	N	Y	Y	Y	Y	Y	Y	Y
12 Murtha	?	Y	Y	Y	Y	Y	Y	Y
13 ***Coughlin***	N	Y	Y	Y	N	Y	Y	Y
14 Coyne	Y	Y	Y	Y	Y	Y	Y	Y
15 ***Ritter***	N	Y	Y	Y	N	N	Y	Y
16 ***Walker***	N	N	Y	Y	N	N	N	Y
17 ***Gekas***	N	N	Y	Y	N	N	N	Y
18 Walgren	Y	Y	Y	Y	Y	Y	Y	Y
19 ***Goodling***	N	Y	Y	Y	N	Y	N	Y
20 Gaydos	N	Y	Y	Y	Y	Y	Y	Y
21 ***Ridge***	Y	N	Y	Y	N	N	N	Y
22 Murphy	Y	Y	Y	Y	Y	Y	Y	Y
23 ***Clinger***	-	Y	Y	Y	N	N	Y	Y
RHODE ISLAND								
1 St Germain	Y	Y	Y	Y	Y	Y	Y	Y
2 ***Schneider***	Y	Y	N	Y	N	N	Y	Y
SOUTH CAROLINA								
1 ***Hartnett***	?	?	?	?	?	?	N	Y
2 ***Spence***	Y	Y	Y	Y	N	N	Y	Y
3 Derrick	Y	Y	Y	Y	Y	Y	Y	Y
4 ***Campbell***	?	?	?	?	?	?	?	?
5 Spratt	Y	Y	Y	Y	Y	Y	Y	Y
6 Tallon	N	Y	N	Y	Y	Y	Y	Y
SOUTH DAKOTA								
AL Daschle	Y	Y	Y	Y	Y	Y	Y	Y
TENNESSEE								
1 ***Quillen***	Y	Y	Y	Y	N	Y	Y	Y
2 ***Duncan***	N	Y	Y	Y	N	Y	N	Y
3 Lloyd	N	Y	Y	Y	N	N	Y	Y
4 Cooper	Y	Y	Y	Y	Y	Y	Y	Y
5 Boner	Y	Y	Y	Y	Y	Y	Y	Y
6 Gordon	Y	Y	Y	Y	Y	Y	Y	Y
7 ***Sundquist***	N	N	Y	Y	N	N	Y	Y
8 Jones	Y	Y	Y	Y	Y	Y	Y	Y
9 Ford	?	Y	Y	Y	Y	Y	Y	Y
TEXAS								
1 Chapman	N	Y	Y	Y	Y	Y	Y	Y
2 Wilson	Y	Y	Y	Y	Y	Y	Y	Y
3 ***Bartlett***	N	N	N	Y	N	N	Y	N
4 Hall, R.	N	Y	Y	Y	N	N	N	Y
5 Bryant	?	Y	Y	Y	Y	Y	Y	Y
6 ***Barton***	N	N	Y	Y	N	N	N	Y
7 ***Archer***	N	N	Y	Y	N	N	N	N
8 ***Fields***	N	N	Y	Y	N	N	Y	N
9 Brooks	Y	Y	Y	Y	Y	Y	Y	Y
10 Pickle	Y	Y	Y	Y	N	Y	N	Y
11 Leath	N	Y	Y	Y	N	N	Y	Y
12 Wright	?	?	?	?	Y	Y	N	Y
13 ***Boulter***	N	N	Y	Y	N	N	Y	N
14 ***Sweeney***	N	Y	Y	Y	N	N	Y	Y
15 de la Garza	Y	Y	Y	Y	Y	Y	Y	Y
16 Coleman	Y	Y	N	Y	Y	N	N	Y
17 Stenholm	N	Y	Y	Y	N	N	N	N
18 Leland	?	Y	N	Y	Y	Y	Y	Y
19 ***Combest***	N	N	Y	Y	N	N	Y	Y
20 Gonzalez	P	Y	N	Y	Y	Y	Y	Y
21 ***Loeffler***	Y	N	Y	Y	N	Y	Y	Y
22 ***DeLay***	N	N	N	Y	N	N	N	N
23 Bustamante	Y	Y	Y	Y	Y	Y	Y	Y
24 Frost	Y	Y	Y	Y	Y	Y	Y	Y
25 Andrews	N	Y	Y	Y	Y	Y	Y	Y
26 ***Armey***	?	N	N	Y	N	N	N	N
27 Ortiz	Y	Y	Y	Y	Y	Y	Y	Y
UTAH								
1 ***Hansen***	?	N	Y	Y	N	N	N	Y
2 ***Monson***	N	N	Y	Y	N	N	N	Y
3 ***Nielson***	N	N	Y	Y	N	N	N	Y
VERMONT								
AL ***Jeffords***	Y	N	N	Y	N	N	Y	Y
VIRGINIA								
1 ***Bateman***	Y	N	Y	Y	N	N	Y	Y
2 ***Whitehurst***	N	N	Y	?	N	N	Y	Y
3 ***Bliley***	N	N	Y	Y	N	Y	Y	Y
4 Sisisky	N	Y	Y	Y	Y	Y	Y	Y
5 Daniel	N	Y	Y	Y	Y	Y	N	Y
6 Olin	Y	Y	Y	Y	Y	Y	N	Y
7 ***Slaughter***	N	Y	Y	Y	N	N	Y	Y
8 ***Parris***	Y	Y	Y	Y	N	N	Y	Y
9 Boucher	Y	Y	Y	Y	Y	Y	Y	Y
10 ***Wolf***	Y	Y	Y	Y	N	Y	Y	Y
WASHINGTON								
1 ***Miller***	Y	Y	N	Y	N	Y	Y	Y
2 Swift	Y	Y	Y	Y	Y	Y	N	Y
3 Bonker	Y	Y	Y	Y	Y	Y	Y	Y
4 ***Morrison***	Y	Y	Y	Y	N	N	Y	Y
5 Foley	Y	Y	Y	Y	Y	Y	Y	Y
6 Dicks	Y	Y	N	Y	Y	Y	Y	Y
7 Lowry	Y	Y	Y	Y	Y	Y	Y	Y
8 ***Chandler***	N	Y	Y	Y	N	N	N	Y
WEST VIRGINIA								
1 Mollohan	Y	Y	Y	Y	Y	Y	Y	Y
2 Staggers	Y	Y	Y	Y	Y	Y	Y	Y
3 Wise	Y	Y	Y	Y	Y	Y	Y	Y
4 Rahall	Y	Y	Y	Y	Y	Y	Y	Y
WISCONSIN								
1 Aspin	Y	Y	N	Y	Y	Y	Y	Y
2 Kastenmeier	Y	Y	Y	Y	Y	Y	Y	Y
3 ***Gunderson***	Y	Y	N	Y	N	N	Y	Y
4 Kleczka	Y	Y	Y	Y	Y	Y	Y	Y
5 Moody	Y	Y	N	Y	Y	Y	Y	Y
6 ***Petri***	N	Y	N	Y	N	N	N	Y
7 Obey	Y	Y	?	Y	Y	Y	Y	Y
8 ***Roth***	Y	Y	Y	Y	N	N	Y	Y
9 ***Sensenbrenner***	N	Y	N	Y	N	N	Y	Y
WYOMING								
AL ***Cheney***	Y	N	Y	Y	N	N	Y	N

Southern states - Ala., Ark., Fla., Ga., Ky., La., Miss., N.C., Okla., S.C., Tenn., Texas, Va.

* The *Congressional Record* vote number is different from the CQ vote number because the *Record* includes quorum calls in its tally. CQ does not publish quorum call votes.

377. Procedural Motion. Russo, D-Ill., motion to approve the House *Journal* of Wednesday, Sept. 24. Motion agreed to 271-120: R 54-110; D 217-10 (ND 145-7, SD 72-3), Sept. 25, 1986.

378. HR 3838. Tax Overhaul. Archer, R-Texas, motion to recommit the conference report to the conference committee. Motion rejected 160-268: R 86-92; D 74-176 (ND 35-133, SD 39-43), Sept. 25, 1986. (The intent of the motion was to kill the bill.) A "nay" was a vote supporting the president's position.

379. HR 3838. Tax Overhaul. Adoption of the conference report on the bill to revise the federal income tax system by reducing individual and corporate tax rates, eliminating or curtailing many deductions, credits and exclusions, repealing the investment tax credit, taxing capital gains as regular income and making other changes. Adopted 292-136: R 116-62; D 176-74 (ND 132-36, SD 44-38), Sept. 25, 1986. A "yea" was a vote supporting the president's position.

380. HR 5495. National Aeronautics and Space Administration Authorization, Fiscal 1987. Passage of the bill to authorize $7.7 billion in fiscal 1987 for the National Aeronautics and Space Administration. Passed 407-8: R 172-1; D 235-7 (ND 156-7, SD 79-0), Sept. 25, 1986.

381. H J Res 738. Continuing Appropriations, Fiscal 1987. Derrick, D-S.C., motion to order the previous question (thus ending debate and the possibility of amendment) on the rule (H Res 560) to provide for House floor consideration of the joint resolution to appropriate $561.9 billion in budget authority for all government programs funded by regular fiscal 1987 appropriations bills, with the funds to be available through Sept. 30, 1987. The measure included several policy changes, including bans on nuclear testing and nerve gas production, a requirement that President Reagan observe portions of the SALT II arms control agreement he has repudiated, and a new $250,000 limit on farm program payments. Motion agreed to 268-150: R 64-112; D 204-38 (ND 138-23, SD 66-15), Sept. 25, 1986. (The rule subsequently was adopted *(see vote 382, below).*)

382. H J Res 738. Continuing Appropriations, Fiscal 1987. Adoption of the rule (H Res 560) to provide for House floor consideration of the joint resolution to appropriate $561.9 billion in budget authority for all government programs funded by regular fiscal 1987 appropriations bills, with the funds to be available through Sept. 30, 1987. The measure included several policy changes, including bans on nuclear testing and nerve gas production, a requirement that President Reagan observe portions of the SALT II arms control agreement he has repudiated, and a new $250,000 limit on farm program payments. Adopted 216-202: R 72-104; D 144-98 (ND 94-67, SD 50-31), Sept. 25, 1986.

383. H J Res 738. Continuing Appropriations, Fiscal 1987. Passage of the joint resolution to appropriate $561.9 billion in budget authority for all government programs funded by regular fiscal 1987 appropriations bills, with the funds to be available through Sept. 30, 1987. The measure included several policy changes, including bans on nuclear testing and nerve gas production, a requirement that President Reagan observe portions of the SALT II arms control agreement he has repudiated, and a new $250,000 limit on farm program payments. Passed 201-200: R 15-157; D 186-43 (ND 127-25, SD 59-18), Sept. 25, 1986. A "nay" was a vote supporting the president's position.

KEY

- Y Voted for (yea).
- # Paired for.
- + Announced for.
- N Voted against (nay).
- X Paired against.
- \- Announced against.
- P Voted "present."
- C Voted "present" to avoid possible conflict of interest.
- ? Did not vote or otherwise make a position known.

Democrats ***Republicans***

	377	378	379	380	381	382	383
ALABAMA							
1 ***Callahan***	Y	N	Y	Y	N	N	N
2 ***Dickinson***	N	Y	Y	Y	Y	Y	N
3 Nichols	Y	Y	Y	Y	Y	N	Y
4 Bevill	Y	Y	Y	Y	Y	N	Y
5 Flippo	Y	N	Y	Y	Y	N	Y
6 Erdreich	Y	Y	Y	Y	Y	N	N
7 Shelby	Y	Y	Y	Y	N	N	N
ALASKA							
AL ***Young***	N	Y	N	Y	N	N	N
ARIZONA							
1 ***McCain***	Y	N	Y	Y	Y	Y	N
2 Udall	Y	N	Y	Y	Y	Y	?
3 ***Stump***	N	Y	Y	Y	Y	Y	N
4 ***Rudd***	N	Y	Y	Y	Y	Y	N
5 ***Kolbe***	N	N	Y	Y	Y	N	N
ARKANSAS							
1 Alexander	Y	N	Y	Y	Y	N	#
2 Robinson	Y	Y	N	Y	N	N	N
3 ***Hammerschmidt***	N	N	N	Y	N	N	N
4 Anthony	Y	N	Y	Y	Y	N	Y
CALIFORNIA							
1 Bosco	Y	N	N	Y	?	?	Y
2 ***Chappie***	N	Y	N	Y	Y	N	N
3 Matsui	Y	N	Y	Y	Y	Y	Y
4 Fazio	Y	Y	N	Y	Y	Y	Y
5 Burton	?	?	?	?	?	?	?
6 Boxer	Y	N	Y	Y	Y	N	Y
7 Miller	Y	N	Y	Y	Y	Y	Y
8 Dellums	Y	N	Y	N	Y	N	Y
9 Stark	?	N	Y	N	Y	Y	Y
10 Edwards	Y	N	Y	Y	Y	Y	Y
11 Lantos	Y	N	Y	Y	Y	N	Y
12 ***Zschau***	N	N	Y	Y	N	N	N
13 Mineta	Y	N	Y	Y	Y	N	Y
14 ***Shumway***	Y	Y	N	Y	N	N	N
15 Coelho	Y	N	Y	Y	Y	Y	Y
16 Panetta	Y	N	Y	Y	Y	N	Y
17 ***Pashayan***	P	Y	Y	Y	Y	Y	N
18 Lehman	Y	N	N	Y	Y	Y	Y
19 ***Lagomarsino***	N	N	Y	Y	N	Y	N
20 ***Thomas***	N	Y	N	?	N	Y	N
21 ***Fiedler***	N	Y	Y	Y	N	N	N
22 ***Moorhead***	N	Y	N	Y	N	N	N
23 Beilenson	Y	N	Y	N	Y	Y	Y
24 Waxman	Y	N	Y	Y	Y	Y	Y
25 Roybal	Y	N	Y	Y	Y	Y	Y
26 Berman	Y	N	Y	Y	Y	Y	Y
27 Levine	Y	N	Y	Y	Y	Y	Y
28 Dixon	?	Y	N	Y	Y	Y	Y
29 Hawkins	Y	N	Y	Y	Y	Y	Y
30 Martinez	Y	N	Y	Y	?	?	X
31 Dymally	Y	N	N	Y	Y	Y	Y
32 Anderson	Y	Y	Y	Y	Y	N	Y
33 ***Dreier***	N	Y	N	Y	N	N	N
34 Torres	Y	N	Y	Y	Y	Y	Y
35 ***Lewis***	N	N	Y	Y	N	Y	N
36 Brown	Y	Y	Y	Y	Y	Y	Y
37 ***McCandless***	N	Y	N	Y	Y	Y	N
38 ***Dornan***	N	Y	Y	Y	N	Y	N
39 ***Dannemeyer***	N	Y	N	Y	N	Y	N
40 ***Badham***	N	Y	N	Y	N	N	-
41 ***Lowery***	?	N	Y	Y	Y	Y	N
42 ***Lungren***	Y	N	Y	Y	N	Y	N
43 ***Packard***	N	N	Y	Y	N	N	N
44 Bates	Y	N	Y	Y	Y	N	N
45 ***Hunter***	N	N	Y	Y	Y	Y	N
COLORADO							
1 Schroeder	N	N	N	Y	N	N	Y
2 Wirth	Y	N	Y	Y	Y	Y	Y
3 ***Strang***	N	Y	Y	Y	N	Y	N
4 ***Brown***	N	Y	Y	Y	N	N	N
5 ***Kramer***	N	Y	Y	Y	Y	N	N
6 ***Schaefer***	N	Y	N	Y	Y	Y	N
CONNECTICUT							
1 Kennelly	Y	N	Y	Y	Y	Y	Y
2 Gejdenson	Y	N	N	Y	Y	Y	Y
3 Morrison	Y	N	Y	Y	Y	Y	Y
4 ***McKinney***	Y	N	N	Y	Y	Y	Y
5 ***Rowland***	N	N	Y	Y	Y	Y	N
6 ***Johnson***	Y	N	Y	Y	Y	Y	N
DELAWARE							
AL Carper	Y	N	Y	Y	Y	Y	Y
FLORIDA							
1 Hutto	Y	Y	N	Y	Y	N	Y
2 Fuqua	Y	N	Y	Y	Y	Y	Y
3 Bennett	Y	N	Y	Y	Y	Y	Y
4 Chappell	P	N	N	Y	Y	Y	Y
5 ***McCollum***	N	N	Y	Y	N	Y	N
6 MacKay	?	N	Y	Y	Y	Y	Y
7 Gibbons	Y	N	Y	Y	Y	Y	Y
8 ***Young***	?	N	Y	Y	Y	N	N
9 ***Bilirakis***	N	N	Y	Y	N	N	N
10 ***Ireland***	N	N	Y	Y	N	N	N
11 Nelson	Y	N	Y	Y	Y	Y	Y
12 ***Lewis***	N	Y	N	Y	N	N	N
13 ***Mack***	N	N	Y	Y	Y	Y	N
14 Mica	Y	Y	N	Y	Y	Y	Y
15 ***Shaw***	N	N	Y	Y	N	N	N
16 Smith	Y	Y	Y	+	Y	Y	Y
17 Lehman	Y	N	Y	Y	Y	Y	Y
18 Pepper	Y	N	Y	+	Y	Y	+
19 Fascell	Y	N	Y	Y	Y	Y	Y
GEORGIA							
1 Thomas	Y	Y	N	Y	Y	Y	Y
2 Hatcher	Y	N	Y	Y	Y	Y	Y
3 Ray	Y	Y	N	Y	Y	Y	Y
4 ***Swindall***	N	Y	N	Y	N	Y	N
5 Fowler	Y	N	Y	Y	N	N	Y
6 ***Gingrich***	N	N	Y	Y	N	N	N
7 Darden	Y	Y	N	Y	Y	Y	N
8 Rowland	Y	Y	N	Y	Y	Y	Y
9 Jenkins	Y	N	Y	Y	Y	Y	Y
10 Barnard	Y	N	Y	Y	Y	Y	N
HAWAII							
1 Abercrombie	Y	N	Y	Y	Y	N	Y
2 Akaka	Y	Y	N	Y	Y	Y	Y
IDAHO							
1 ***Craig***	?	Y	N	Y	N	N	N
2 Stallings	Y	Y	Y	Y	N	N	N
ILLINOIS							
1 Hayes	Y	Y	Y	Y	Y	N	Y
2 Savage	?	N	Y	Y	N	N	Y
3 Russo	Y	N	Y	Y	N	N	N
4 Vacancy							
5 Lipinski	Y	N	Y	Y	N	N	Y
6 ***Hyde***	Y	N	Y	Y	N	N	N
7 Collins	Y	N	Y	Y	Y	N	Y
8 Rostenkowski	Y	N	Y	Y	?	?	?
9 Yates	Y	N	Y	Y	Y	N	Y
10 ***Porter***	N	N	Y	Y	Y	N	N
11 Annunzio	Y	N	Y	Y	Y	Y	Y
12 ***Crane***	N	Y	N	?	N	N	N
13 ***Fawell***	N	N	Y	Y	Y	Y	N
14 ***Grotberg***	?	?	?	?	?	?	?
15 ***Madigan***	?	Y	N	Y	Y	N	?
16 ***Martin***	N	N	Y	Y	Y	Y	N
17 Evans	Y	N	Y	Y	Y	N	Y
18 ***Michel***	Y	N	Y	Y	Y	Y	N
19 Bruce	Y	N	N	Y	Y	N	N
20 Durbin	Y	N	Y	Y	Y	N	Y
21 Price	Y	N	Y	Y	Y	Y	Y
22 Gray	Y	N	Y	Y	Y	Y	Y
INDIANA							
1 Visclosky	Y	N	Y	Y	Y	N	Y
2 Sharp	Y	Y	Y	Y	Y	Y	Y
3 ***Hiler***	N	N	Y	Y	Y	Y	N
4 ***Coats***	N	N	Y	Y	Y	Y	N
5 ***Hillis***	Y	N	Y	Y	Y	Y	N

ND - Northern Democrats SD - Southern Democrats

* Corresponding to Congressional Record Votes 410, 412, 413, 414, 415, 416, 417

	377	378	379	380	381	382	383
6 ***Burton***	N	Y	N	Y	N	N	N
7 ***Myers***	Y	Y	N	Y	Y	Y	Y
8 McCloskey	Y	N	Y	Y	Y	Y	Y
9 Hamilton	Y	N	Y	Y	Y	N	N
10 Jacobs	N	Y	N	N	N	N	?
IOWA							
1 ***Leach***	N	N	Y	Y	N	N	N
2 ***Tauke***	N	Y	Y	Y	N	Y	N
3 ***Evans***	N	N	Y	Y	Y	Y	N
4 Smith	Y	N	Y	Y	Y	Y	Y
5 ***Lightfoot***	N	N	Y	Y	N	N	N
6 Bedell	Y	N	Y	Y	Y	Y	Y
KANSAS							
1 ***Roberts***	N	Y	N	Y	N	N	N
2 Slattery	Y	N	Y	Y	Y	Y	N
3 ***Meyers***	Y	N	Y	Y	Y	Y	N
4 Glickman	Y	N	Y	Y	Y	Y	N
5 ***Whittaker***	N	Y	N	Y	Y	Y	N
KENTUCKY							
1 Hubbard	Y	Y	N	Y	N	N	N
2 Natcher	Y	N	Y	Y	Y	N	Y
3 Mazzoli	Y	N	Y	Y	N	N	N
4 ***Snyder***	Y	N	Y	Y	Y	Y	N
5 ***Rogers***	Y	Y	Y	Y	N	N	Y
6 ***Hopkins***	Y	Y	Y	Y	N	N	N
7 Perkins	Y	Y	N	Y	N	N	Y
LOUISIANA							
1 ***Livingston***	N	N	Y	Y	N	N	N
2 Boggs	Y	Y	Y	Y	N	N	Y
3 Tauzin	Y	N	Y	Y	N	N	Y
4 Roemer	N	N	Y	Y	Y	N	N
5 Huckaby	Y	N	Y	Y	Y	N	N
6 ***Moore***	?	Y	Y	?	?	?	?
7 Breaux	?	Y	Y	?	?	?	X
8 Long	P	N	Y	Y	Y	N	Y
MAINE							
1 ***McKernan***	N	N	Y	Y	N	N	N
2 ***Snowe***	N	N	Y	Y	N	N	N
MARYLAND							
1 Dyson	?	Y	N	Y	Y	N	N
2 ***Bentley***	?	Y	N	Y	N	N	N
3 Mikulski	Y	Y	Y	Y	N	N	Y
4 ***Holt***	Y	Y	N	Y	Y	Y	N
5 Hoyer	?	Y	N	Y	Y	Y	Y
6 Byron	Y	N	Y	Y	Y	N	N
7 Mitchell	N	Y	N	Y	Y	N	Y
8 Barnes	Y	Y	N	Y	Y	N	N
MASSACHUSETTS							
1 ***Conte***	N	N	Y	Y	Y	N	Y
2 Boland	?	N	Y	Y	Y	Y	Y
3 Early	Y	N	Y	Y	Y	Y	Y
4 Frank	Y	N	Y	Y	Y	Y	Y
5 Atkins	Y	N	Y	Y	Y	Y	Y
6 Mavroules	Y	N	Y	Y	Y	Y	Y
7 Markey	Y	N	Y	Y	Y	Y	Y
8 O'Neill							
9 Moakley	Y	N	Y	Y	Y	Y	Y
10 Studds	Y	N	Y	Y	Y	Y	Y
11 Donnelly	Y	N	Y	Y	Y	Y	Y
MICHIGAN							
1 Conyers	?	Y	N	N	N	N	N
2 ***Pursell***	Y	N	Y	Y	N	N	?
3 Wolpe	Y	N	Y	Y	Y	N	Y
4 ***Siljander***	N	N	Y	Y	Y	N	N
5 ***Henry***	N	N	Y	N	N	N	N
6 Carr	Y	Y	N	Y	Y	Y	Y
7 Kildee	Y	N	Y	Y	Y	N	Y
8 Traxler	Y	N	Y	Y	N	N	Y
9 ***Vander Jagt***	N	N	Y	Y	N	N	N
10 ***Schuette***	N	Y	Y	Y	N	N	N
11 ***Davis***	Y	N	Y	Y	Y	Y	Y
12 Bonior	Y	N	Y	Y	Y	Y	N
13 Crockett	?	N	Y	Y	?	?	X
14 Hertel	Y	Y	N	Y	N	N	N
15 Ford	?	Y	N	Y	Y	Y	Y
16 Dingell	?	N	N	Y	Y	Y	Y
17 Levin	Y	N	Y	Y	Y	Y	Y
18 ***Broomfield***	Y	Y	Y	Y	N	N	N
MINNESOTA							
1 Penny	N	N	Y	Y	Y	Y	Y
2 ***Weber***	N	N	Y	Y	N	N	N
3 ***Frenzel***	N	Y	N	Y	Y	Y	N
4 Vento	Y	N	Y	Y	Y	Y	Y
5 Sabo	Y	N	Y	Y	Y	Y	Y
6 Sikorski	N	N	Y	Y	Y	Y	Y
7 ***Stangeland***	N	Y	Y	Y	N	N	N
8 Oberstar	Y	N	Y	Y	Y	Y	Y
MISSISSIPPI							
1 Whitten	Y	N	Y	Y	Y	N	Y
2 ***Franklin***	?	N	Y	Y	N	N	N
3 Montgomery	Y	Y	N	Y	Y	Y	Y
4 Dowdy	Y	Y	N	Y	Y	N	Y
5 ***Lott***	N	N	Y	Y	Y	Y	N
MISSOURI							
1 Clay	P	Y	N	Y	Y	Y	Y
2 Young	Y	N	Y	Y	N	N	Y
3 Gephardt	?	N	Y	?	?	?	?
4 Skelton	Y	N	Y	Y	Y	N	?
5 Wheat	Y	N	Y	Y	Y	Y	Y
6 ***Coleman***	N	Y	N	Y	N	Y	N
7 ***Taylor***	Y	Y	N	Y	N	Y	N
8 ***Emerson***	N	Y	Y	Y	N	N	N
9 Volkmer	Y	N	Y	Y	N	Y	N
MONTANA							
1 Williams	Y	Y	N	Y	Y	Y	Y
2 ***Marlenee***	N	Y	N	Y	N	N	N
NEBRASKA							
1 ***Bereuter***	N	N	Y	Y	N	N	N
2 ***Daub***	Y	N	Y	Y	N	N	N
3 ***Smith***	Y	N	Y	Y	N	N	Y
NEVADA							
1 Reid	Y	N	Y	Y	Y	N	N
2 ***Vucanovich***	N	Y	N	Y	N	N	N
NEW HAMPSHIRE							
1 ***Smith***	N	N	Y	Y	N	N	N
2 ***Gregg***	N	N	Y	Y	Y	Y	N
NEW JERSEY							
1 Florio	Y	N	Y	Y	Y	Y	Y
2 Hughes	Y	Y	Y	Y	Y	Y	N
3 Howard	Y	N	Y	Y	Y	Y	Y
4 ***Smith***	Y	N	Y	Y	Y	N	Y
5 ***Roukema***	N	N	Y	Y	Y	Y	N
6 Dwyer	Y	N	Y	Y	Y	Y	Y
7 ***Rinaldo***	Y	?	?	?	N	N	Y
8 Roe	Y	N	Y	Y	Y	N	Y
9 Torricelli	Y	N	Y	Y	Y	Y	Y
10 Rodino	Y	N	Y	Y	Y	Y	Y
11 ***Gallo***	N	N	Y	Y	N	N	N
12 ***Courter***	N	N	Y	Y	N	Y	N
13 ***Saxton***	N	N	Y	Y	N	N	N
14 Guarini	Y	N	Y	Y	Y	N	#
NEW MEXICO							
1 ***Lujan***	Y	N	Y	Y	Y	Y	N
2 ***Skeen***	N	N	Y	Y	Y	Y	N
3 Richardson	Y	N	Y	Y	Y	Y	Y
NEW YORK							
1 ***Carney***	?	Y	N	Y	Y	N	N
2 Downey	Y	N	Y	Y	Y	Y	Y
3 Mrazek	Y	N	N	Y	Y	Y	Y
4 ***Lent***	N	Y	N	Y	N	N	N
5 ***McGrath***	N	N	Y	Y	N	N	N
6 Waldon	?	Y	N	Y	Y	Y	Y
7 Ackerman	Y	Y	N	Y	Y	Y	Y
8 Scheuer	Y	N	Y	Y	Y	N	Y
9 Manton	Y	N	N	Y	Y	Y	Y
10 Schumer	Y	N	Y	Y	Y	N	Y
11 Towns	Y	N	Y	Y	Y	N	Y
12 Owens	Y	N	Y	Y	Y	Y	Y
13 Solarz	Y	N	Y	Y	Y	N	Y
14 ***Molinari***	N	Y	N	Y	Y	Y	N
15 ***Green***	Y	Y	N	Y	Y	N	Y
16 Rangel	?	N	Y	Y	Y	Y	Y
17 Weiss	Y	Y	N	N	Y	N	Y
18 Garcia	Y	N	Y	Y	?	?	?
19 Biaggi	Y	Y	Y	?	?	?	?
20 ***DioGuardi***	Y	N	Y	Y	N	N	N
21 ***Fish***	Y	N	Y	Y	N	Y	Y
22 ***Gilman***	Y	Y	N	Y	N	N	Y
23 Stratton	Y	N	Y	Y	Y	Y	Y
24 ***Solomon***	N	N	Y	Y	N	N	N
25 ***Boehlert***	N	N	Y	Y	N	N	N
26 ***Martin***	N	Y	N	Y	N	N	N
27 ***Wortley***	Y	N	Y	Y	N	N	N
28 McHugh	Y	N	Y	Y	Y	N	Y
29 ***Horton***	Y	Y	N	Y	N	N	N
30 ***Eckert***	Y	N	Y	Y	Y	Y	N
31 ***Kemp***	Y	N	Y	Y	N	N	N
32 LaFalce	Y	N	Y	?	Y	Y	Y
33 Nowak	Y	N	Y	Y	Y	N	Y
34 Lundine	Y	N	Y	Y	Y	N	Y
NORTH CAROLINA							
1 Jones	Y	N	Y	Y	N	N	N
2 Valentine	Y	N	Y	Y	Y	Y	Y
3 Whitley	Y	N	N	Y	Y	Y	Y
4 ***Cobey***	N	N	Y	Y	N	N	N
5 Neal	Y	N	Y	Y	Y	Y	N
6 ***Coble***	N	Y	Y	Y	N	Y	N
7 Rose	Y	N	Y	Y	Y	Y	Y
8 Hefner	Y	N	Y	Y	Y	Y	Y
9 ***McMillan***	N	N	Y	Y	Y	Y	N
10 Vacancy							
11 ***Hendon***	N	N	Y	Y	N	N	N
NORTH DAKOTA							
AL Dorgan	Y	N	Y	Y	Y	N	N
OHIO							
1 Luken	Y	N	Y	Y	Y	Y	Y
2 ***Gradison***	Y	N	Y	Y	Y	Y	N
3 Hall	Y	Y	N	?	Y	Y	Y
4 ***Oxley***	N	N	Y	Y	Y	Y	N
5 ***Latta***	Y	N	Y	Y	N	N	N
6 ***McEwen***	Y	N	Y	Y	N	N	N
7 ***DeWine***	N	N	Y	Y	N	Y	N
8 ***Kindness***	N	Y	N	Y	N	N	N
9 Kaptur	Y	N	N	Y	Y	Y	Y
10 ***Miller***	N	Y	N	Y	N	N	N
11 Eckart	Y	N	Y	Y	Y	N	N
12 ***Kasich***	Y	N	Y	Y	N	N	N
13 Pease	Y	N	Y	Y	Y	Y	Y
14 Seiberling	Y	N	Y	Y	Y	Y	Y
15 ***Wylie***	Y	N	Y	Y	N	N	N
16 ***Regula***	Y	Y	N	Y	N	N	N
17 Traficant	Y	Y	Y	Y	N	N	Y
18 Applegate	Y	Y	N	Y	N	N	?
19 Feighan	Y	N	Y	Y	Y	N	?
20 Oakar	Y	N	Y	Y	Y	N	Y
21 Stokes	?	?	?	?	?	?	#
OKLAHOMA							
1 Jones	Y	Y	N	Y	N	N	N
2 Synar	Y	Y	N	Y	Y	N	N
3 Watkins	Y	Y	N	Y	Y	Y	Y
4 McCurdy	Y	Y	N	Y	Y	Y	Y
5 ***Edwards***	?	Y	N	Y	Y	N	N
6 English	Y	Y	N	Y	N	N	N
OREGON							
1 AuCoin	Y	N	Y	Y	Y	Y	Y
2 ***Smith, R.***	N	Y	Y	Y	N	N	N
3 Wyden	Y	N	Y	Y	Y	Y	N
4 Weaver	Y	N	N	N	Y	N	?
5 ***Smith, D.***	N	Y	N	Y	Y	Y	N
PENNSYLVANIA							
1 Foglietta	Y	N	Y	Y	N	N	Y
2 Gray	Y	N	Y	Y	Y	Y	Y
3 Borski	Y	N	Y	Y	Y	Y	Y
4 Kolter	Y	Y	N	Y	N	N	N
5 ***Schulze***	Y	N	Y	Y	N	N	N
6 Yatron	Y	Y	Y	Y	N	N	Y
7 Edgar	N	N	Y	Y	N	N	Y
8 Kostmayer	Y	N	Y	Y	Y	Y	Y
9 ***Shuster***	N	Y	N	Y	N	N	N
10 ***McDade***	Y	N	Y	?	Y	Y	Y
11 Kanjorski	Y	Y	Y	Y	N	N	Y
12 Murtha	Y	N	Y	Y	Y	Y	Y
13 ***Coughlin***	N	N	Y	Y	N	Y	N
14 Coyne	Y	N	Y	Y	Y	Y	Y
15 ***Ritter***	Y	N	Y	Y	N	N	N
16 ***Walker***	N	N	Y	Y	N	N	N
17 ***Gekas***	N	Y	N	Y	N	N	N
18 Walgren	Y	N	Y	Y	N	Y	?
19 ***Goodling***	N	Y	Y	Y	Y	Y	N
20 Gaydos	?	N	Y	?	N	N	Y
21 ***Ridge***	N	N	Y	Y	N	N	N
22 Murphy	Y	N	N	Y	N	N	N
23 ***Clinger***	Y	Y	Y	Y	N	N	N
RHODE ISLAND							
1 St Germain	Y	N	Y	Y	Y	N	N
2 ***Schneider***	Y	N	Y	Y	N	N	Y
SOUTH CAROLINA							
1 ***Hartnett***	Y	Y	N	Y	?	?	?
2 ***Spence***	Y	Y	N	Y	N	N	N
3 Derrick	Y	N	Y	Y	Y	Y	Y
4 ***Campbell***	?	Y	Y	?	?	?	?
5 Spratt	Y	N	Y	Y	Y	Y	Y
6 Tallon	Y	Y	N	Y	Y	N	Y
SOUTH DAKOTA							
AL Daschle	Y	Y	N	Y	Y	N	N
TENNESSEE							
1 ***Quillen***	Y	N	Y	Y	Y	Y	N
2 ***Duncan***	Y	N	Y	Y	Y	N	N
3 Lloyd	N	Y	Y	Y	N	N	N
4 Cooper	Y	N	Y	Y	Y	Y	Y
5 Boner	Y	Y	Y	Y	Y	N	Y
6 Gordon	Y	Y	N	Y	Y	Y	?
7 ***Sundquist***	N	Y	N	Y	Y	N	N
8 Jones	Y	N	Y	Y	Y	Y	Y
9 Ford	?	N	Y	Y	Y	N	?
TEXAS							
1 Chapman	Y	Y	N	Y	Y	Y	Y
2 Wilson	?	N	Y	Y	Y	Y	Y
3 ***Bartlett***	N	Y	N	Y	N	Y	N
4 Hall, R.	Y	Y	N	Y	N	N	N
5 Bryant	Y	Y	N	Y	Y	Y	Y
6 ***Barton***	N	Y	Y	Y	N	N	N
7 ***Archer***	Y	Y	N	Y	Y	Y	N
8 ***Fields***	N	Y	N	Y	N	N	N
9 Brooks	Y	Y	N	Y	Y	Y	Y
10 Pickle	Y	N	Y	Y	Y	Y	Y
11 Leath	Y	N	N	Y	Y	Y	Y
12 Wright	Y	Y	N	Y	Y	Y	Y
13 ***Boulter***	N	Y	Y	Y	N	Y	N
14 ***Sweeney***	?	Y	N	Y	N	Y	N
15 de la Garza	Y	N	N	Y	Y	Y	Y
16 Coleman	?	Y	N	Y	Y	Y	Y
17 Stenholm	N	Y	N	Y	Y	Y	N
18 Leland	Y	Y	N	Y	Y	Y	Y
19 ***Combest***	Y	Y	N	Y	N	N	N
20 Gonzalez	Y	Y	N	Y	N	N	Y
21 ***Loeffler***	N	Y	N	Y	Y	Y	N
22 ***DeLay***	N	Y	N	Y	N	Y	N
23 Bustamante	Y	Y	N	Y	Y	Y	Y
24 Frost	Y	Y	N	Y	Y	Y	Y
25 Andrews	Y	N	Y	Y	Y	Y	Y
26 ***Armey***	N	Y	Y	Y	N	N	N
27 Ortiz	Y	Y	N	Y	Y	Y	Y
UTAH							
1 ***Hansen***	N	Y	N	Y	Y	N	N
2 ***Monson***	N	Y	N	Y	N	N	N
3 ***Nielson***	N	Y	N	Y	N	N	N
VERMONT							
AL ***Jeffords***	Y	N	Y	Y	N	N	Y
VIRGINIA							
1 ***Bateman***	Y	Y	N	Y	Y	Y	N
2 ***Whitehurst***	?	Y	N	Y	Y	Y	?
3 ***Bliley***	N	N	Y	Y	N	Y	N
4 Sisisky	Y	N	N	Y	Y	Y	Y
5 Daniel	Y	N	N	Y	N	Y	N
6 Olin	Y	N	N	Y	Y	Y	Y
7 ***Slaughter***	N	N	Y	Y	Y	Y	N
8 ***Parris***	P	Y	N	Y	N	Y	N
9 Boucher	Y	N	N	Y	Y	Y	Y
10 ***Wolf***	N	Y	N	Y	Y	Y	N
WASHINGTON							
1 ***Miller***	Y	N	Y	Y	N	N	N
2 Swift	Y	Y	N	Y	Y	Y	?
3 Bonker	?	N	N	Y	Y	Y	Y
4 ***Morrison***	Y	Y	Y	Y	N	N	Y
5 Foley	Y	N	Y	Y	Y	Y	Y
6 Dicks	Y	N	Y	Y	Y	Y	Y
7 Lowry	N	Y	N	Y	Y	Y	Y
8 ***Chandler***	?	Y	N	Y	Y	Y	N
WEST VIRGINIA							
1 Mollohan	Y	N	Y	Y	Y	N	Y
2 Staggers	Y	N	Y	Y	Y	N	Y
3 Wise	Y	N	Y	Y	N	N	Y
4 Rahall	Y	N	Y	Y	Y	N	Y
WISCONSIN							
1 Aspin	Y	N	Y	Y	Y	Y	Y
2 Kastenmeier	Y	N	Y	Y	N	N	+
3 ***Gunderson***	N	N	Y	Y	N	N	N
4 Kleczka	Y	Y	Y	Y	Y	Y	Y
5 Moody	Y	N	Y	Y	Y	N	N
6 ***Petri***	Y	N	Y	Y	N	N	N
7 Obey	Y	N	Y	Y	Y	Y	Y
8 ***Roth***	N	N	Y	Y	N	N	N
9 ***Sensenbrenner***	N	Y	N	Y	N	N	N
WYOMING							
AL ***Cheney***	N	Y	N	Y	Y	Y	N

Southern states - Ala., Ark., Fla., Ga., Ky., La., Miss., N.C., Okla., S.C., Tenn., Texas, Va.

* The *Congressional Record* vote number is different from the CQ vote number because the *Record* includes quorum calls in its tally. CQ does not publish quorum call votes.

384. HR 3810. Immigration Reform. Beilenson, D-Calif., motion to order the previous question (thus ending debate and the possibility of amendment) on the rule (H Res 559) to provide for House floor consideration of the bill to revise the nation's immigration laws. Motion agreed to 196-189: R 10-149; D 186-40 (ND 137-15, SD 49-25), Sept. 26, 1986. (The rule subsequently was rejected *(see vote 385, below)*.)

385. HR 3810. Immigration Reform. Adoption of the rule (H Res 559) to provide for House floor consideration of the bill to revise the nation's immigration laws by creating a system of penalties against employers who knowingly hire illegal aliens, establishing a program to give legal status to illegal aliens already in the United States who meet certain conditions, and granting permanent resident status to foreigners who could prove they worked at least 60 days in American agriculture between May 1985 and May 1986. Rejected 180-202: R 13-145; D 167-57 (ND 130-22, SD 37-35), Sept. 26, 1986.

386. HR 5559. Immigration and Nationality Laws. Mazzoli, D-Ky., motion to suspend the rules and pass the bill to permit a limited number of lay workers into the United States to work for non-profit religious organizations. Motion rejected 81-308: R 3-160; D 78-148 (ND 70-87, SD 8-61), Sept. 29, 1986. A two-thirds majority of those present and voting (260 in this case) is required for passage under suspension of the rules.

387. HR 5560. Child Sexual Abuse and Pornography. Hughes, D-N.J., motion to suspend the rules and pass the bill to bar the production and use of advertisements for child pornography or solicitations for child pornography. Motion agreed to 390-0: R 162-0; D 228-0 (ND 157-0, SD 71-0), Sept. 29, 1986. A two-thirds majority of those present and voting (260 in this case) is required for passage under suspension of the rules.

388. HR 5564. Housing Act Amendments. Lundine, D-N.Y., motion to suspend the rules and pass the bill to ensure that Federal Housing Administration single-family mortgage insurance remain available for properties located within the Seneca Indian reservation in Salamanca, N.Y., after 99-year leases on the land expire in 1991. Motion agreed to 277-112: R 58-102; D 219-10 (ND 155-3, SD 64-7), Sept. 29, 1986. A two-thirds majority of those present and voting (260 in this case) is required for passage under suspension of the rules.

389. HR 4917. Depository Institution Examination Improvement. St Germain, D-R.I., motion to suspend the rules and pass the bill to improve compensation and training for federal bank examiners, and to exempt federal bank regulatory agencies from automatic budget cuts under the Gramm-Rudman-Hollings anti-deficit law (PL 99-177). Motion agreed to 342-49: R 143-18; D 199-31 (ND 139-19, SD 60-12), Sept. 29, 1986. A two-thirds majority of those present and voting (261 in this case) is required for passage under suspension of the rules.

390. HR 4868. South African Sanctions. Passage, over President Reagan's Sept. 26 veto, of the bill to impose economic sanctions against South Africa. Passed 313-83: R 81-79; D 232-4 (ND 163-0, SD 69-4), Sept. 29, 1986. A two-thirds majority of those present and voting (264 in this case) of both houses is required to override a veto. A "nay" was a vote supporting the president's position.

391. H J Res 743. Interim Continuing Appropriations, Fiscal 1987. Passage of the joint resolution to provide continued spending authority for all government programs subject to regular appropriations from Oct. 1 through Oct. 8, 1986. The resolution provided that funding would be provided at the following levels, depending on the status of individual appropriations bills: the lower of appropriations for fiscal 1986 or of amounts in House-passed bills; the lower of amounts in House- or Senate-passed bills; or the amounts in conference agreements. Passed 315-101: R 88-82; D 227-19 (ND 156-12, SD 71-7), Sept. 30, 1986.

KEY

- Y Voted for (yea).
- # Paired for.
- + Announced for.
- N Voted against (nay).
- X Paired against.
- \- Announced against.
- P Voted "present."
- C Voted "present" to avoid possible conflict of interest.
- ? Did not vote or otherwise make a position known.

Democrats ***Republicans***

	384	385	386	387	388	389	390	391
ALABAMA								
1 ***Callahan***	N	N	N	Y	N	Y	N	N
2 ***Dickinson***	N	N	N	Y	N	Y	N	Y
3 Nichols	N	N	N	Y	Y	Y	Y	Y
4 Bevill	N	N	?	Y	N	N	Y	Y
5 Flippo	N	N	N	Y	Y	Y	Y	Y
6 Erdreich	N	N	N	Y	Y	Y	Y	Y
7 Shelby	N	N	N	Y	Y	Y	Y	N
ALASKA								
AL ***Young***	N	N	N	Y	Y	Y	Y	Y
ARIZONA								
1 ***McCain***	N	N	N	Y	Y	Y	Y	N
2 Udall	Y	Y	Y	Y	Y	Y	Y	Y
3 ***Stump***	N	N	N	Y	N	Y	N	N
4 ***Rudd***	N	N	N	Y	N	N	N	?
5 ***Kolbe***	N	N	N	Y	Y	Y	Y	Y
ARKANSAS								
1 Alexander	Y	?	Y	Y	Y	N	Y	Y
2 Robinson	N	N	N	Y	N	Y	Y	Y
3 ***Hammerschmidt***	?	?	N	Y	N	N	N	Y
4 Anthony	Y	Y	?	?	?	X	#	Y
CALIFORNIA								
1 Bosco	Y	Y	?	?	Y	Y	Y	Y
2 ***Chappie***	?	?	N	Y	N	Y	N	N
3 Matsui	Y	Y	Y	Y	Y	Y	Y	Y
4 Fazio	Y	Y	Y	Y	Y	N	Y	Y
5 Burton	?	?	?	?	?	?	?	?
6 Boxer	Y	Y	N	Y	Y	Y	Y	Y
7 Miller	Y	Y	?	?	?	?	?	Y
8 Dellums	Y	Y	N	Y	Y	Y	Y	Y
9 Stark	Y	Y	Y	Y	Y	Y	Y	Y
10 Edwards	Y	Y	Y	Y	Y	Y	Y	Y
11 Lantos	?	?	?	?	?	Y	Y	Y
12 ***Zschau***	?	?	?	?	?	?	?	N
13 Mineta	Y	Y	Y	Y	Y	Y	Y	Y
14 ***Shumway***	N	N	N	Y	N	Y	N	N
15 Coelho	Y	Y	Y	Y	Y	Y	Y	Y
16 Panetta	Y	Y	?	?	?	?	#	Y
17 ***Pashayan***	Y	Y	N	Y	N	Y	Y	Y
18 Lehman	Y	Y	N	Y	Y	Y	Y	Y
19 ***Lagomarsino***	N	N	N	Y	N	Y	Y	Y
20 ***Thomas***	N	N	?	?	?	?	?	N
21 ***Fiedler***	N	N	?	?	?	?	?	N
22 ***Moorhead***	N	N	N	Y	N	Y	N	N
23 Beilenson	Y	Y	Y	Y	Y	Y	Y	Y
24 Waxman	?	#	Y	Y	Y	Y	Y	Y
25 Roybal	Y	N	N	Y	Y	N	Y	Y
26 Berman	Y	Y	Y	Y	Y	Y	Y	Y
27 Levine	Y	Y	N	Y	Y	Y	Y	Y
28 Dixon	Y	Y	N	Y	Y	Y	Y	Y
29 Hawkins	Y	Y	N	Y	Y	Y	Y	Y
30 Martinez	?	#	?	Y	Y	Y	Y	Y
31 Dymally	Y	Y	Y	Y	Y	Y	Y	Y
32 Anderson	N	N	Y	Y	Y	Y	Y	Y
33 ***Dreier***	Y	N	N	Y	N	Y	N	N
34 Torres	Y	Y	Y	Y	Y	Y	Y	Y
35 ***Lewis***	N	N	N	Y	Y	Y	N	Y
36 Brown	Y	Y	Y	Y	Y	Y	Y	Y
37 ***McCandless***	N	N	N	Y	Y	Y	N	N
38 ***Dornan***	N	N	N	Y	Y	Y	N	N
39 ***Dannemeyer***	N	N	N	Y	N	N	N	N
40 ***Badham***	N	N	?	?	?	?	-	N
41 ***Lowery***	N	N	N	Y	N	Y	Y	Y
42 ***Lungren***	N	N	Y	Y	N	Y	N	N
43 ***Packard***	Y	Y	N	Y	N	Y	N	N
44 Bates	Y	Y	Y	Y	Y	?	Y	N
45 ***Hunter***	N	N	N	Y	N	Y	N	N
COLORADO								
1 Schroeder	N	Y	N	Y	Y	Y	Y	N
2 Wirth	N	N	N	Y	Y	Y	Y	Y
3 ***Strang***	N	N	N	Y	Y	Y	N	N
4 ***Brown***	N	N	N	Y	Y	N	Y	N
5 ***Kramer***	?	X	N	Y	?	?	?	N
6 ***Schaefer***	N	N	N	Y	N	Y	N	N
CONNECTICUT								
1 Kennelly	Y	Y	N	Y	Y	Y	Y	Y
2 Gejdenson	Y	Y	N	Y	Y	Y	Y	Y
3 Morrison	Y	Y	Y	Y	Y	Y	Y	Y
4 ***McKinney***	Y	Y	N	Y	Y	Y	Y	Y
5 ***Rowland***	N	N	N	Y	Y	Y	Y	Y
6 ***Johnson***	N	N	N	Y	N	Y	Y	Y
DELAWARE								
AL Carper	Y	Y	N	Y	Y	Y	Y	Y
FLORIDA								
1 Hutto	N	Y	N	Y	Y	Y	N	Y
2 Fuqua	Y	Y	N	Y	Y	Y	Y	Y
3 Bennett	Y	Y	N	Y	Y	Y	Y	Y
4 Chappell	?	?	N	Y	Y	Y	Y	Y
5 ***McCollum***	N	N	N	Y	Y	Y	N	Y
6 MacKay	Y	Y	N	Y	Y	Y	Y	Y
7 Gibbons	?	?	N	Y	Y	Y	Y	Y
8 ***Young***	N	N	N	Y	N	N	N	Y
9 ***Bilirakis***	N	N	N	Y	N	Y	N	Y
10 ***Ireland***	N	N	N	Y	N	Y	Y	Y
11 Nelson	Y	Y	N	Y	Y	Y	Y	Y
12 ***Lewis***	N	N	N	Y	N	Y	Y	?
13 ***Mack***	N	N	N	Y	N	Y	N	N
14 Mica	Y	N	N	Y	Y	Y	Y	Y
15 ***Shaw***	N	N	N	Y	N	Y	N	Y
16 Smith	Y	Y	N	Y	Y	Y	Y	Y
17 Lehman	Y	Y	N	Y	Y	Y	Y	Y
18 Pepper	Y	Y	N	Y	Y	Y	Y	Y
19 Fascell	Y	Y	N	Y	Y	Y	Y	Y
GEORGIA								
1 Thomas	Y	Y	N	Y	Y	Y	Y	Y
2 Hatcher	Y	Y	?	?	?	?	?	?
3 Ray	N	N	N	Y	Y	Y	Y	N
4 ***Swindall***	N	N	N	Y	N	Y	N	N
5 Fowler	?	?	?	?	?	?	?	?
6 ***Gingrich***	N	N	N	Y	Y	Y	Y	N
7 Darden	Y	N	N	Y	Y	Y	Y	Y
8 Rowland	Y	N	N	Y	Y	Y	Y	Y
9 Jenkins	Y	N	N	Y	Y	Y	Y	Y
10 Barnard	Y	N	N	Y	Y	Y	Y	Y
HAWAII								
1 Abercrombie	Y	Y	Y	Y	Y	Y	Y	Y
2 Akaka	Y	Y	N	Y	Y	N	Y	Y
IDAHO								
1 ***Craig***	?	X	?	?	?	Y	N	N
2 Stallings	Y	Y	N	Y	Y	Y	Y	N
ILLINOIS								
1 Hayes	Y	Y	Y	Y	Y	Y	Y	Y
2 Savage	?	?	Y	Y	Y	Y	Y	Y
3 Russo	Y	?	N	Y	Y	Y	Y	Y
4 Vacancy								
5 Lipinski	Y	N	N	Y	Y	Y	Y	Y
6 ***Hyde***	N	N	N	Y	N	Y	N	Y
7 Collins	Y	Y	N	Y	Y	Y	Y	Y
8 Rostenkowski	Y	Y	?	?	?	?	?	Y
9 Yates	Y	Y	N	Y	Y	N	Y	Y
10 ***Porter***	N	N	N	Y	Y	Y	N	N
11 Annunzio	Y	Y	N	Y	Y	Y	Y	Y
12 ***Crane***	N	N	N	Y	N	Y	N	N
13 ***Fawell***	N	N	N	Y	N	Y	Y	N
14 ***Grotberg***	?	?	?	?	?	?	?	?
15 ***Madigan***	N	N	N	Y	Y	Y	Y	Y
16 ***Martin***	N	N	N	Y	N	Y	Y	Y
17 Evans	Y	Y	N	Y	Y	Y	Y	Y
18 ***Michel***	N	N	N	Y	N	Y	N	Y
19 Bruce	Y	Y	N	Y	Y	Y	Y	N
20 Durbin	Y	Y	Y	Y	Y	Y	Y	Y
21 Price	Y	Y	N	Y	Y	Y	Y	Y
22 Gray	Y	Y	N	Y	Y	Y	Y	Y
INDIANA								
1 Visclosky	Y	Y	Y	Y	Y	Y	Y	Y
2 Sharp	Y	Y	N	Y	Y	Y	Y	Y
3 ***Hiler***	N	N	N	Y	N	Y	Y	N
4 ***Coats***	N	N	N	Y	N	Y	Y	N
5 ***Hillis***	?	?	N	Y	Y	Y	Y	Y

ND - Northern Democrats SD - Southern Democrats

* Corresponding to Congressional Record Votes 419, 420, 421, 422, 423, 424, 425, 426

	384	385	386	387	388	389	390	391
6 *Burton*	N	N	N	Y	N	Y	N	N
7 *Myers*	N	N	N	Y	N	Y	N	Y
8 McCloskey	Y	Y	N	Y	Y	Y	Y	Y
9 Hamilton	Y	Y	Y	Y	Y	Y	Y	Y
10 Jacobs	N	N	Y	Y	Y	Y	Y	N
IOWA								
1 *Leach*	N	N	N	Y	N	Y	Y	N
2 *Tauke*	N	N	N	Y	N	Y	Y	N
3 *Evans*	Y	N	N	Y	N	Y	Y	N
4 Smith	Y	N	N	Y	Y	N	Y	Y
5 *Lightfoot*	N	N	N	Y	N	Y	Y	N
6 Bedell	Y	Y	N	Y	Y	Y	Y	Y
KANSAS								
1 *Roberts*	N	?	N	Y	N	Y	Y	N
2 Slattery	Y	Y	N	Y	Y	Y	Y	Y
3 *Meyers*	N	N	N	Y	N	Y	Y	Y
4 Glickman	Y	Y	N	Y	Y	Y	Y	Y
5 *Whittaker*	N	N	N	Y	N	Y	N	N
KENTUCKY								
1 Hubbard	N	N	N	Y	N	Y	Y	N
2 Natcher	Y	Y	N	Y	Y	N	Y	Y
3 Mazzoli	Y	Y	Y	Y	Y	Y	Y	Y
4 *Snyder*	N	N	N	Y	N	Y	N	Y
5 *Rogers*	N	N	N	Y	N	Y	N	Y
6 *Hopkins*	N	N	N	Y	N	Y	Y	N
7 Perkins	Y	Y	N	Y	Y	N	Y	Y
LOUISIANA								
1 *Livingston*	N	N	N	Y	N	N	N	Y
2 Boggs	N	Y	N	Y	Y	N	Y	Y
3 Tauzin	N	N	N	Y	Y	Y	Y	Y
4 Roemer	Y	Y	N	Y	Y	Y	Y	N
5 Huckaby	?	?	?	?	?	?	?	Y
6 *Moore*	?	?	?	?	?	?	?	?
7 Breaux	?	?	?	?	?	?	?	?
8 Long	Y	Y	N	Y	Y	Y	Y	Y
MAINE								
1 *McKernan*	N	N	N	Y	Y	Y	Y	N
2 *Snowe*	N	N	N	Y	Y	Y	Y	N
MARYLAND								
1 Dyson	Y	Y	N	Y	N	Y	Y	Y
2 *Bentley*	N	N	N	Y	N	Y	Y	Y
3 Mikulski	?	?	N	Y	Y	Y	Y	Y
4 *Holt*	N	N	N	Y	N	Y	N	?
5 Hoyer	Y	Y	Y	Y	Y	Y	Y	Y
6 Byron	N	N	N	Y	N	Y	Y	N
7 Mitchell	?	#	Y	Y	Y	Y	Y	Y
8 Barnes	Y	Y	Y	Y	Y	Y	Y	Y
MASSACHUSETTS								
1 *Conte*	N	Y	N	Y	Y	Y	Y	Y
2 Boland	Y	Y	N	Y	Y	N	Y	Y
3 Early	Y	Y	N	Y	Y	N	Y	Y
4 Frank	Y	Y	Y	Y	Y	Y	Y	Y
5 Atkins	Y	Y	Y	Y	Y	Y	Y	Y
6 Mavroules	Y	Y	Y	Y	Y	Y	Y	Y
7 Markey	Y	Y	Y	Y	Y	Y	Y	Y
8 O'Neill							Y	
9 Moakley	Y	Y	Y	Y	Y	Y	Y	Y
10 Studds	Y	Y	Y	Y	Y	Y	Y	Y
11 Donnelly	Y	Y	Y	Y	Y	Y	Y	Y
MICHIGAN								
1 Conyers	Y	Y	N	?	?	Y	Y	Y
2 *Pursell*	N	N	N	Y	Y	Y	Y	Y
3 Wolpe	?	#	N	Y	Y	Y	Y	Y
4 *Siljander*	N	N	?	?	?	?	?	N
5 *Henry*	N	N	N	Y	N	Y	Y	N
6 Carr	Y	N	N	Y	Y	N	Y	Y
7 Kildee	Y	Y	Y	Y	Y	Y	Y	Y
8 Traxler	?	?	N	Y	Y	N	Y	Y
9 *Vander Jagt*	N	N	N	?	?	?	?	Y
10 *Schuette*	N	N	N	Y	Y	Y	Y	Y
11 *Davis*	N	N	N	Y	Y	Y	Y	Y
12 Bonior	Y	Y	Y	Y	Y	Y	Y	Y
13 Crockett	?	?	N	Y	Y	Y	Y	Y
14 Hertel	Y	Y	N	Y	Y	Y	Y	N
15 Ford	Y	Y	Y	Y	Y	Y	Y	Y
16 Dingell	?	Y	N	Y	Y	N	Y	Y
17 Levin	Y	Y	Y	Y	Y	N	Y	Y
18 *Broomfield*	N	N	N	Y	N	Y	N	N
MINNESOTA								
1 Penny	Y	Y	N	Y	Y	Y	Y	N
2 *Weber*	N	N	N	Y	Y	N	Y	N
3 *Frenzel*	N	N	N	Y	N	Y	Y	N
4 Vento	Y	Y	Y	Y	Y	N	Y	Y
5 Sabo	Y	Y	Y	Y	Y	Y	Y	Y
6 Sikorski	Y	Y	Y	Y	Y	Y	Y	Y
7 *Stangeland*	N	N	N	Y	Y	Y	?	?
8 Oberstar	Y	Y	Y	Y	Y	Y	Y	Y
MISSISSIPPI								
1 Whitten	Y	N	N	Y	Y	N	Y	Y
2 *Franklin*	N	N	N	Y	N	Y	Y	Y
3 Montgomery	N	N	N	Y	Y	Y	N	Y
4 Dowdy	N	N	N	Y	Y	Y	Y	Y
5 *Lott*	N	N	N	Y	N	Y	N	Y
MISSOURI								
1 Clay	Y	Y	Y	Y	Y	Y	Y	Y
2 Young	Y	Y	N	Y	Y	Y	Y	Y
3 Gephardt	?	?	N	Y	Y	Y	Y	Y
4 Skelton	Y	Y	?	?	?	?	?	Y
5 Wheat	Y	Y	Y	Y	Y	Y	Y	Y
6 *Coleman*	N	N	?	?	?	?	?	Y
7 *Taylor*	N	N	N	Y	N	Y	N	Y
8 *Emerson*	N	N	N	Y	N	Y	N	Y
9 Volkmer	N	Y	N	Y	Y	Y	Y	Y
MONTANA								
1 Williams	?	?	Y	Y	Y	N	Y	Y
2 *Marlenee*	N	N	N	Y	N	Y	N	N
NEBRASKA								
1 *Bereuter*	N	N	N	Y	Y	Y	Y	Y
2 *Daub*	N	N	N	Y	N	Y	Y	Y
3 *Smith*	N	N	N	Y	N	Y	Y	Y
NEVADA								
1 Reid	Y	Y	N	Y	Y	Y	Y	Y
2 *Vucanovich*	N	N	N	Y	N	Y	N	Y
NEW HAMPSHIRE								
1 *Smith*	N	N	N	Y	N	Y	N	N
2 *Gregg*	?	?	?	?	?	?	?	N
NEW JERSEY								
1 Florio	Y	Y	N	Y	Y	Y	Y	Y
2 Hughes	?	N	N	Y	Y	Y	Y	Y
3 Howard	Y	Y	N	Y	Y	Y	Y	Y
4 *Smith*	N	N	N	Y	Y	Y	Y	Y
5 *Roukema*	N	N	N	Y	Y	Y	Y	Y
6 Dwyer	Y	Y	N	Y	Y	Y	Y	Y
7 *Rinaldo*	N	N	N	Y	N	Y	Y	Y
8 Roe	N	N	N	Y	Y	Y	Y	Y
9 Torricelli	N	N	N	Y	Y	Y	Y	Y
10 Rodino	Y	Y	Y	Y	Y	#	Y	Y
11 *Gallo*	N	N	N	Y	Y	Y	Y	Y
12 *Courter*	N	N	N	Y	N	Y	Y	N
13 *Saxton*	N	N	N	Y	N	Y	Y	Y
14 Guarini	Y	Y	N	Y	Y	Y	Y	Y
NEW MEXICO								
1 *Lujan*	N	N	N	Y	N	N	Y	Y
2 *Skeen*	N	N	N	Y	Y	N	N	Y
3 Richardson	Y	Y	?	?	?	?	Y	Y
NEW YORK								
1 *Carney*	N	N	N	Y	Y	Y	Y	Y
2 Downey	Y	Y	N	Y	Y	Y	Y	Y
3 Mrazek	Y	Y	N	Y	Y	Y	Y	Y
4 *Lent*	N	N	N	Y	Y	Y	Y	Y
5 *McGrath*	N	N	N	Y	Y	Y	Y	Y
6 Waldon	Y	Y	Y	Y	Y	Y	Y	Y
7 Ackerman	Y	Y	Y	Y	Y	Y	Y	N
8 Scheuer	N	N	N	Y	Y	Y	Y	Y
9 Manton	Y	Y	Y	Y	Y	Y	Y	Y
10 Schumer	Y	Y	N	Y	Y	Y	Y	Y
11 Towns	Y	Y	Y	Y	Y	Y	Y	Y
12 Owens	Y	Y	Y	Y	Y	Y	Y	Y
13 Solarz	Y	Y	Y	Y	Y	Y	Y	Y
14 *Molinari*	N	N	N	Y	N	Y	Y	N
15 *Green*	Y	Y	N	Y	N	N	Y	Y
16 Rangel	Y	Y	Y	Y	Y	Y	Y	Y
17 Weiss	Y	Y	Y	Y	Y	Y	Y	Y
18 Garcia	Y	Y	Y	Y	Y	Y	Y	Y
19 Biaggi	?	?	N	Y	Y	Y	Y	Y
20 *DioGuardi*	N	Y	N	Y	Y	Y	Y	Y
21 *Fish*	Y	Y	Y	Y	Y	Y	Y	Y
22 *Gilman*	Y	Y	N	Y	Y	Y	Y	Y
23 Stratton	Y	Y	N	Y	N	Y	Y	Y
24 *Solomon*	N	N	N	Y	N	Y	N	N
25 *Boehlert*	N	N	N	Y	Y	Y	Y	Y
26 *Martin*	N	N	?	?	?	?	?	Y
27 *Wortley*	?	X	N	Y	Y	Y	Y	Y
28 McHugh	Y	Y	Y	Y	Y	Y	Y	Y
29 *Horton*	N	N	N	Y	Y	Y	Y	Y
30 *Eckert*	N	N	N	Y	Y	Y	N	N
31 *Kemp*	N	N	N	Y	Y	N	N	Y
32 LaFalce	Y	Y	Y	Y	Y	Y	Y	Y
33 Nowak	Y	Y	Y	Y	Y	Y	Y	Y
34 Lundine	?	?	Y	Y	Y	Y	Y	Y
NORTH CAROLINA								
1 Jones	Y	Y	?	?	?	#	?	Y
2 Valentine	Y	N	N	Y	Y	Y	Y	Y
3 Whitley	?	?	N	Y	Y	Y	Y	Y
4 *Cobey*	N	N	N	Y	N	Y	N	N
5 Neal	N	N	?	?	?	?	Y	Y
6 *Coble*	N	N	N	Y	N	Y	N	Y
7 Rose	Y	Y	?	?	?	?	?	Y
8 Hefner	Y	N	?	?	?	Y	Y	Y
9 *McMillan*	N	N	N	Y	Y	Y	N	Y
10 Vacancy								
11 *Hendon*	N	N	N	Y	N	Y	N	Y
NORTH DAKOTA								
AL Dorgan	Y	?	N	Y	Y	Y	Y	Y
OHIO								
1 Luken	Y	Y	N	Y	Y	Y	Y	Y
2 *Gradison*	N	N	N	Y	N	Y	Y	Y
3 Hall	Y	Y	N	Y	Y	Y	Y	N
4 *Oxley*	N	N	?	?	?	?	X	N
5 *Latta*	?	?	N	Y	N	Y	N	Y
6 *McEwen*	N	N	N	Y	N	Y	N	N
7 *DeWine*	N	N	N	Y	N	Y	N	N
8 *Kindness*	?	X	?	?	?	?	?	X
9 Kaptur	Y	Y	N	Y	Y	Y	Y	Y
10 *Miller*	N	N	N	Y	N	N	N	Y
11 Eckart	Y	Y	N	Y	Y	Y	Y	N
12 *Kasich*	N	N	N	Y	Y	Y	Y	N
13 Pease	Y	N	?	?	?	?	Y	Y
14 Seiberling	Y	Y	Y	Y	Y	Y	Y	Y
15 *Wylie*	N	N	N	Y	Y	Y	Y	Y
16 *Regula*	?	?	N	Y	Y	Y	Y	Y
17 Traficant	Y	N	N	Y	Y	Y	Y	Y
18 Applegate	N	N	N	Y	Y	Y	Y	Y
19 Feighan	Y	Y	N	Y	Y	Y	Y	Y
20 Oakar	Y	Y	Y	Y	Y	Y	Y	Y
21 Stokes	?	#	Y	Y	Y	Y	Y	Y
OKLAHOMA								
1 Jones	?	?	N	Y	Y	N	Y	Y
2 Synar	Y	Y	Y	Y	Y	N	Y	Y
3 Watkins	N	N	N	Y	Y	N	Y	Y
4 McCurdy	Y	Y	N	Y	Y	N	Y	Y
5 *Edwards*	?	?	?	?	?	?	?	N
6 English	N	N	N	Y	Y	N	Y	Y
OREGON								
1 AuCoin	Y	Y	N	Y	Y	Y	Y	Y
2 *Smith, R.*	Y	Y	N	Y	Y	Y	N	N
3 Wyden	Y	Y	N	Y	Y	Y	Y	Y
4 Weaver	Y	Y	?	?	?	?	?	Y
5 *Smith, D.*	N	N	N	Y	N	Y	N	N
PENNSYLVANIA								
1 Foglietta	Y	Y	Y	Y	Y	Y	Y	Y
2 Gray	Y	Y	N	Y	Y	N	Y	Y
3 Borski	Y	Y	N	Y	Y	Y	Y	Y
4 Kolter	N	N	N	Y	Y	Y	Y	Y
5 *Schulze*	N	N	N	Y	N	N	Y	N
6 Yatron	N	N	N	Y	Y	Y	Y	Y
7 Edgar	?	?	N	Y	Y	Y	Y	?
8 Kostmayer	Y	Y	Y	Y	Y	Y	Y	Y
9 *Shuster*	N	N	N	Y	N	Y	N	N
10 *McDade*	?	?	N	Y	Y	N	?	Y
11 Kanjorski	Y	N	N	Y	Y	Y	Y	Y
12 Murtha	Y	Y	N	Y	Y	N	Y	Y
13 *Coughlin*	N	N	N	Y	Y	Y	Y	Y
14 Coyne	Y	Y	Y	Y	Y	Y	Y	Y
15 *Ritter*	N	N	N	Y	N	Y	N	Y
16 *Walker*	N	N	N	Y	N	Y	Y	N
17 *Gekas*	N	N	N	Y	N	N	Y	N
18 Walgren	Y	N	N	Y	Y	Y	Y	Y
19 *Goodling*	N	N	N	Y	N	N	Y	Y
20 Gaydos	Y	N	?	?	?	?	?	Y
21 *Ridge*	N	N	N	Y	Y	Y	Y	Y
22 Murphy	N	N	N	Y	Y	Y	Y	Y
23 *Clinger*	N	N	N	Y	Y	Y	Y	Y
RHODE ISLAND								
1 St Germain	Y	Y	N	Y	Y	Y	Y	Y
2 *Schneider*	-	-	-	+	+	+	+	Y
SOUTH CAROLINA								
1 *Hartnett*	?	?	?	?	?	?	?	?
2 *Spence*	N	N	N	Y	?	Y	N	N
3 Derrick	?	?	?	?	?	?	?	Y
4 *Campbell*	?	?	?	?	?	?	?	?
5 Spratt	Y	Y	N	Y	Y	Y	Y	Y
6 Tallon	Y	N	N	Y	Y	Y	Y	Y
SOUTH DAKOTA								
AL Daschle	Y	Y	N	Y	Y	N	Y	N
TENNESSEE								
1 *Quillen*	N	Y	N	Y	Y	Y	N	Y
2 *Duncan*	N	N	N	Y	Y	Y	Y	Y
3 Lloyd	N	N	N	Y	N	Y	Y	Y
4 Cooper	Y	Y	Y	Y	Y	Y	Y	Y
5 Boner	Y	N	N	Y	Y	Y	Y	Y
6 Gordon	Y	Y	N	Y	Y	Y	Y	Y
7 *Sundquist*	N	N	N	Y	N	Y	N	Y
8 Jones	Y	Y	N	Y	Y	Y	Y	Y
9 Ford	Y	N	Y	Y	Y	Y	Y	Y
TEXAS								
1 Chapman	N	N	N	Y	Y	Y	Y	Y
2 Wilson	N	N	Y	Y	Y	Y	Y	Y
3 *Bartlett*	N	N	N	Y	Y	Y	N	Y
4 Hall, R.	N	N	N	Y	N	Y	?	N
5 Bryant	Y	Y	N	Y	Y	Y	Y	Y
6 *Barton*	N	N	N	Y	N	Y	N	N
7 *Archer*	N	N	N	Y	Y	Y	N	N
8 *Fields*	N	N	N	Y	N	Y	N	N
9 Brooks	N	N	N	Y	Y	Y	Y	Y
10 Pickle	N	N	N	Y	Y	Y	Y	Y
11 Leath	Y	Y	N	Y	Y	Y	Y	Y
12 Wright	Y	Y	?	Y	Y	Y	Y	#
13 *Boulter*	N	N	N	Y	N	N	N	N
14 *Sweeney*	N	N	N	Y	Y	Y	N	N
15 de la Garza	Y	?	N	Y	Y	Y	Y	Y
16 Coleman	Y	Y	N	Y	Y	Y	Y	Y
17 Stenholm	N	N	N	Y	N	Y	N	N
18 Leland	Y	Y	Y	Y	Y	Y	Y	Y
19 *Combest*	N	N	N	Y	N	Y	N	N
20 Gonzalez	N	N	N	Y	Y	N	Y	N
21 *Loeffler*	N	N	N	Y	N	N	N	Y
22 *DeLay*	N	N	N	Y	N	Y	N	N
23 Bustamante	Y	Y	?	?	?	?	Y	Y
24 Frost	Y	N	N	Y	Y	Y	Y	Y
25 Andrews	N	N	N	Y	Y	Y	Y	Y
26 *Armey*	N	N	N	Y	N	?	N	N
27 Ortiz	Y	Y	N	Y	Y	Y	Y	Y
UTAH								
1 *Hansen*	?	?	N	Y	N	Y	N	N
2 *Monson*	?	?	N	Y	N	Y	N	N
3 *Nielson*	N	Y	N	Y	N	Y	N	N
VERMONT								
AL *Jeffords*	N	N	N	Y	Y	Y	Y	Y
VIRGINIA								
1 *Bateman*	N	N	N	Y	N	Y	Y	Y
2 *Whitehurst*	N	N	N	Y	N	Y	Y	?
3 *Bliley*	N	N	Y	Y	N	Y	Y	Y
4 Sisisky	Y	Y	N	Y	Y	Y	Y	Y
5 Daniel	Y	Y	N	Y	N	Y	N	Y
6 Olin	Y	Y	N	Y	Y	Y	Y	Y
7 *Slaughter*	N	N	N	Y	N	Y	N	Y
8 *Parris*	?	X	N	Y	N	Y	N	Y
9 Boucher	Y	Y	Y	Y	Y	Y	Y	Y
10 *Wolf*	N	N	N	Y	N	Y	Y	Y
WASHINGTON								
1 *Miller*	N	N	N	Y	Y	Y	Y	Y
2 Swift	Y	Y	N	Y	Y	Y	Y	Y
3 Bonker	Y	Y	?	?	?	?	?	Y
4 *Morrison*	Y	Y	N	Y	N	Y	Y	Y
5 Foley	Y	Y	Y	Y	Y	Y	Y	Y
6 Dicks	Y	Y	N	Y	Y	N	Y	Y
7 Lowry	Y	Y	Y	Y	Y	N	Y	Y
8 *Chandler*	N	Y	N	Y	Y	Y	Y	N
WEST VIRGINIA								
1 Mollohan	Y	Y	N	Y	Y	Y	Y	Y
2 Staggers	N	Y	Y	Y	Y	Y	Y	Y
3 Wise	Y	Y	N	Y	Y	Y	Y	Y
4 Rahall	Y	Y	N	Y	Y	N	Y	Y
WISCONSIN								
1 Aspin	Y	Y	N	Y	Y	Y	Y	Y
2 Kastenmeier	Y	Y	Y	Y	Y	Y	Y	Y
3 *Gunderson*	N	N	N	Y	Y	Y	Y	N
4 Kleczka	N	N	N	Y	Y	Y	Y	Y
5 Moody	Y	Y	Y	Y	Y	Y	Y	Y
6 *Petri*	N	N	N	Y	N	Y	Y	N
7 Obey	Y	Y	Y	Y	Y	Y	Y	Y
8 *Roth*	N	N	N	Y	Y	Y	N	N
9 *Sensenbrenner*	N	N	N	Y	N	Y	Y	N
WYOMING								
AL *Cheney*	N	N	N	Y	N	Y	N	N

Southern states - Ala., Ark., Fla., Ga., Ky., La., Miss., N.C., Okla., S.C., Tenn., Texas, Va.

* The *Congressional Record* vote number is different from the CQ vote number because the *Record* includes quorum calls in its tally. CQ does not publish quorum call votes.

392. Procedural Motion. Lungren, R-Calif., motion to approve the House *Journal* of Tuesday, Sept. 30. Motion agreed to 284-115: R 59-107; D 225-8 (ND 150-8, SD 75-0), Oct. 1, 1986.

393. HR 2348. Department of Justice Authorization, Fiscal 1986/Immigration Reform. Lott, R-Miss., motion to order the previous question (thus ending debate and the possibility of amendment) on the rule (H Res 215) to provide for House floor consideration of the bill. Lott's hope was to defeat the previous question, which would have allowed him to amend the rule. He had announced that he wanted to alter the rule to provide for consideration of a bill overhauling the nation's immigration laws (HR 3810). A rule for that bill had been rejected Sept. 26 *(see vote 385, p. 110-H)*. Motion agreed to 235-177: R 5-167; D 230-10 (ND 160-3, SD 70-7), Oct. 1, 1986.

394. Procedural Motion. Gekas, R-Pa., motion to approve the House *Journal* of Wednesday, Oct. 1. Motion agreed to 247-122: R 47-115; D 200-7 (ND 134-6, SD 66-1), Oct. 2, 1986.

395. HR 4116. VISTA Reauthorization. Adoption of the rule (H Res 568) to waive points of order against the conference report on the bill to authorize for three years anti-poverty volunteer programs administered by the ACTION agency. Adopted 265-141: R 28-141; D 237-0 (ND 158-0, SD 79-0), Oct. 2, 1986.

396. HR 4021. Rehabilitation Act Amendments. Adoption of the rule (H Res 569) to waive points of order against the conference report on the bill to renew vocational rehabilitation programs for the handicapped through fiscal 1991, authorizing about $1.4 billion in fiscal 1987. Adopted 258-143: R 27-142; D 231-1 (ND 157-0, SD 74-1), Oct. 2, 1986.

397. HR 4116. VISTA Reauthorization. Adoption of the conference report on the bill to reauthorize for three years anti-poverty volunteer programs administered by the ACTION agency. The bill authorized $99.39 million for Volunteers in Service to America (VISTA), $380.03 million for Older American Volunteer Programs and $75.94 million for administrative expenses for ACTION. Adopted 366-33: R 135-33; D 231-0 (ND 155-0, SD 76-0), Oct. 2, 1986.

398. HR 4021. Rehabilitation Act Amendments. Adoption of the conference report on the bill to renew vocational rehabilitation programs for the handicapped through fiscal 1991, authorizing about $1.4 billion in fiscal 1987. Adopted 408-0: R 171-0; D 237-0 (ND 158-0, SD 79-0), Oct. 2, 1986.

KEY

- Y Voted for (yea).
- # Paired for.
- + Announced for.
- N Voted against (nay).
- X Paired against.
- - Announced against.
- P Voted "present."
- C Voted "present" to avoid possible conflict of interest.
- ? Did not vote or otherwise make a position known.

Democrats ***Republicans***

	392	393	394	395	396	397	398
ALABAMA							
1 ***Callahan***	Y	?	Y	Y	N	Y	Y
2 ***Dickinson***	N	N	N	N	N	Y	Y
3 Nichols	?	Y	?	Y	Y	Y	Y
4 Bevill	Y	Y	Y	Y	Y	Y	Y
5 Flippo	Y	Y	Y	Y	Y	Y	Y
6 Erdreich	Y	N	Y	Y	Y	Y	Y
7 Shelby	Y	N	Y	Y	Y	Y	Y
ALASKA							
AL ***Young***	N	N	N	N	N	Y	Y
ARIZONA							
1 ***McCain***	Y	N	N	N	N	Y	Y
2 Udall	Y	Y	?	Y	Y	Y	Y
3 ***Stump***	N	N	N	N	N	N	Y
4 ***Rudd***	Y	N	Y	N	N	N	Y
5 ***Kolbe***	N	N	N	N	N	N	Y
ARKANSAS							
1 Alexander	Y	Y	Y	Y	Y	Y	Y
2 Robinson	Y	Y	Y	Y	N	Y	Y
3 ***Hammerschmidt***	Y	N	Y	N	N	Y	Y
4 Anthony	Y	Y	?	Y	Y	Y	Y
CALIFORNIA							
1 Bosco	Y	Y	Y	Y	Y	Y	?
2 ***Chappie***	N	N	N	N	N	N	Y
3 Matsui	Y	?	Y	Y	Y	Y	Y
4 Fazio	Y	Y	Y	Y	Y	Y	Y
5 Burton	?	?	?	?	?	?	?
6 Boxer	Y	Y	Y	Y	Y	Y	Y
7 Miller	Y	Y	Y	Y	Y	Y	Y
8 Dellums	?	Y	Y	Y	Y	?	Y
9 Stark	?	Y	Y	Y	Y	Y	Y
10 Edwards	Y	Y	Y	Y	Y	Y	Y
11 Lantos	Y	Y	Y	Y	Y	Y	Y
12 ***Zschau***	N	N	?	Y	?	?	?
13 Mineta	Y	Y	Y	Y	Y	Y	Y
14 ***Shumway***	Y	N	Y	N	N	N	Y
15 Coelho	Y	Y	Y	Y	Y	Y	Y
16 Panetta	Y	Y	Y	Y	Y	Y	Y
17 ***Pashayan***	Y	N	Y	N	N	Y	Y
18 Lehman	Y	Y	Y	Y	Y	Y	Y
19 ***Lagomarsino***	N	N	N	N	N	Y	Y
20 ***Thomas***	N	N	N	N	N	Y	Y
21 ***Fiedler***	?	N	N	N	N	Y	Y
22 ***Moorhead***	N	N	N	N	N	Y	Y
23 Beilenson	Y	Y	Y	Y	Y	Y	Y
24 Waxman	Y	Y	?	Y	Y	Y	?
25 Roybal	Y	Y	Y	Y	Y	Y	Y
26 Berman	Y	Y	Y	Y	Y	Y	Y
27 Levine	Y	Y	Y	Y	Y	Y	Y
28 Dixon	Y	Y	?	Y	Y	Y	Y
29 Hawkins	N	Y	N	Y	Y	Y	Y
30 Martinez	Y	Y	Y	Y	Y	Y	Y
31 Dymally	Y	Y	?	Y	Y	Y	Y
32 Anderson	Y	Y	Y	Y	Y	Y	Y
33 ***Dreier***	N	N	N	N	N	N	Y
34 Torres	Y	Y	N	Y	Y	Y	Y
35 ***Lewis***	N	N	N	N	N	N	Y
36 Brown	Y	?	Y	Y	Y	Y	Y
37 ***McCandless***	N	N	N	N	N	Y	Y
38 ***Dornan***	N	N	N	N	N	Y	Y
39 ***Dannemeyer***	N	N	N	N	N	N	Y
40 ***Badham***	N	N	N	N	N	N	Y
41 ***Lowery***	N	N	?	N	N	Y	Y
42 ***Lungren***	N	N	N	N	N	Y	Y
43 ***Packard***	N	N	N	N	N	Y	Y
44 Bates	Y	Y	?	Y	Y	Y	Y
45 ***Hunter***	N	N	N	N	N	N	Y
COLORADO							
1 Schroeder	N	Y	N	Y	Y	Y	Y
2 Wirth	Y	Y	Y	Y	Y	Y	Y
3 ***Strang***	N	N	N	N	N	Y	Y
4 ***Brown***	N	N	N	N	N	N	Y
5 ***Kramer***	N	N	N	N	N	Y	Y
6 ***Schaefer***	N	N	N	N	N	N	Y
CONNECTICUT							
1 Kennelly	Y	Y	Y	Y	Y	Y	Y
2 Gejdenson	Y	Y	?	Y	Y	Y	Y
3 Morrison	Y	Y	Y	Y	Y	Y	Y
4 ***McKinney***	Y	N	Y	Y	Y	Y	Y
5 ***Rowland***	N	N	N	Y	Y	Y	Y
6 ***Johnson***	Y	N	Y	Y	Y	Y	Y
DELAWARE							
AL Carper	Y	Y	Y	Y	Y	Y	Y
FLORIDA							
1 Hutto	Y	Y	P	Y	Y	Y	Y
2 Fuqua	Y	?	Y	Y	Y	Y	Y
3 Bennett	Y	Y	Y	Y	Y	Y	Y
4 Chappell	Y	Y	Y	Y	Y	?	Y
5 ***McCollum***	N	N	?	?	?	?	?
6 MacKay	Y	Y	Y	Y	Y	Y	Y
7 Gibbons	Y	Y	Y	Y	Y	Y	Y
8 ***Young***	Y	N	N	N	N	?	Y
9 ***Bilirakis***	N	N	N	Y	N	Y	Y
10 ***Ireland***	N	N	N	N	N	Y	Y
11 Nelson	Y	Y	Y	Y	Y	Y	Y
12 ***Lewis***	N	N	N	N	N	Y	Y
13 ***Mack***	N	N	N	N	N	Y	Y
14 Mica	Y	Y	Y	Y	Y	Y	Y
15 ***Shaw***	N	N	N	N	N	Y	Y
16 Smith	Y	Y	Y	Y	Y	Y	Y
17 Lehman	Y	Y	Y	Y	Y	Y	Y
18 Pepper	Y	Y	Y	Y	Y	Y	Y
19 Fascell	Y	Y	?	Y	Y	Y	Y
GEORGIA							
1 Thomas	Y	Y	Y	Y	Y	Y	Y
2 Hatcher	Y	Y	Y	Y	Y	Y	Y
3 Ray	Y	N	Y	Y	Y	Y	Y
4 ***Swindall***	N	N	?	?	?	?	?
5 Fowler	?	?	?	Y	?	?	?
6 ***Gingrich***	?	N	N	N	N	Y	Y
7 Darden	Y	Y	Y	Y	Y	Y	Y
8 Rowland	Y	Y	Y	Y	Y	Y	Y
9 Jenkins	?	Y	?	Y	Y	Y	Y
10 Barnard	Y	Y	Y	Y	Y	Y	Y
HAWAII							
1 Abercrombie	Y	Y	Y	Y	Y	Y	Y
2 Akaka	Y	Y	Y	Y	Y	Y	Y
IDAHO							
1 ***Craig***	N	N	N	N	N	N	Y
2 Stallings	Y	Y	Y	Y	Y	Y	Y
ILLINOIS							
1 Hayes	Y	Y	Y	Y	Y	Y	Y
2 Savage	Y	Y	Y	Y	Y	Y	Y
3 Russo	Y	Y	Y	Y	Y	Y	Y
4 Vacancy							
5 Lipinski	Y	Y	Y	Y	Y	Y	Y
6 ***Hyde***	Y	N	Y	N	N	Y	Y
7 Collins	Y	Y	Y	Y	Y	Y	Y
8 Rostenkowski	Y	Y	?	Y	Y	Y	Y
9 Yates	Y	Y	Y	Y	Y	Y	Y
10 ***Porter***	N	N	Y	N	N	Y	Y
11 Annunzio	Y	Y	Y	Y	Y	Y	Y
12 ***Crane***	N	N	?	N	N	N	Y
13 ***Fawell***	N	N	N	N	N	Y	Y
14 ***Grotberg***	?	?	?	?	?	?	?
15 ***Madigan***	Y	N	N	N	N	Y	Y
16 ***Martin***	N	N	N	N	N	Y	Y
17 Evans	Y	Y	Y	Y	Y	Y	Y
18 ***Michel***	Y	N	N	N	N	Y	Y
19 Bruce	Y	Y	Y	Y	Y	Y	Y
20 Durbin	Y	Y	Y	Y	Y	Y	Y
21 Price	Y	Y	Y	Y	Y	Y	Y
22 Gray	Y	Y	?	Y	Y	Y	Y
INDIANA							
1 Visclosky	Y	Y	Y	Y	Y	Y	Y
2 Sharp	Y	Y	Y	Y	Y	Y	Y
3 ***Hiler***	N	N	N	N	N	Y	Y
4 ***Coats***	N	N	N	N	N	Y	Y
5 ***Hillis***	Y	Y	Y	N	?	Y	Y

ND - Northern Democrats SD - Southern Democrats

* Corresponding to Congressional Record Votes 427, 428, 429, 430, 431, 432, 433

	392	393	394	395	396	397	398
6 ***Burton***	N	N	N	N	N	N	Y
7 ***Myers***	Y	?	Y	N	Y	Y	Y
8 McCloskey	Y	Y	Y	Y	Y	Y	Y
9 Hamilton	Y	Y	Y	Y	Y	Y	Y
10 Jacobs	N	Y	N	Y	Y	Y	Y
IOWA							
1 ***Leach***	N	N	N	N	N	Y	Y
2 ***Tauke***	N	N	N	N	N	Y	Y
3 ***Evans***	N	N	N	N	N	Y	Y
4 Smith	Y	Y	Y	Y	Y	Y	Y
5 ***Lightfoot***	N	N	N	N	N	Y	Y
6 Bedell	Y	?	Y	Y	Y	Y	Y
KANSAS							
1 ***Roberts***	N	N	N	N	N	N	Y
2 Slattery	Y	Y	Y	Y	Y	Y	Y
3 ***Meyers***	N	N	N	Y	N	Y	Y
4 Glickman	Y	Y	Y	Y	?	Y	Y
5 ***Whittaker***	N	N	N	N	N	Y	Y
KENTUCKY							
1 Hubbard	Y	Y	Y	Y	Y	Y	Y
2 Natcher	Y	Y	Y	Y	Y	Y	Y
3 Mazzoli	Y	Y	Y	Y	Y	Y	Y
4 ***Snyder***	Y	N	Y	N	N	Y	Y
5 ***Rogers***	N	N	N	N	N	Y	Y
6 ***Hopkins***	N	N	N	N	N	Y	Y
7 Perkins	Y	Y	Y	Y	Y	Y	Y
LOUISIANA							
1 ***Livingston***	N	N	N	N	N	Y	Y
2 Boggs	Y	Y	?	Y	Y	Y	Y
3 Tauzin	Y	Y	Y	Y	Y	Y	Y
4 Roemer	Y	N	N	Y	Y	Y	Y
5 Huckaby	Y	Y	Y	Y	Y	Y	Y
6 ***Moore***	?	?	?	?	?	?	?
7 Breaux	?	?	?	?	?	?	?
8 Long	Y	Y	Y	?	Y	Y	Y
MAINE							
1 ***McKernan***	N	N	N	N	N	Y	Y
2 ***Snowe***	N	N	N	N	N	Y	Y
MARYLAND							
1 Dyson	Y	Y	?	Y	Y	Y	Y
2 ***Bentley***	N	N	N	N	Y	Y	Y
3 Mikulski	?	?	Y	Y	?	?	?
4 ***Holt***	N	N	N	?	Y	Y	Y
5 Hoyer	Y	Y	Y	Y	Y	Y	Y
6 Byron	Y	N	Y	Y	Y	Y	Y
7 Mitchell	N	Y	?	?	?	?	?
8 Barnes	Y	Y	Y	Y	Y	Y	Y
MASSACHUSETTS							
1 ***Conte***	?	N	N	Y	Y	Y	Y
2 Boland	Y	Y	Y	Y	Y	Y	Y
3 Early	Y	Y	Y	Y	Y	Y	Y
4 Frank	Y	Y	?	Y	Y	Y	Y
5 Atkins	Y	Y	?	Y	?	?	?
6 Mavroules	Y	Y	?	Y	Y	Y	Y
7 Markey	?	Y	Y	Y	Y	Y	Y
8 O'Neill							
9 Moakley	Y	Y	Y	Y	Y	Y	Y
10 Studds	Y	Y	Y	Y	Y	Y	Y
11 Donnelly	Y	Y	Y	Y	Y	Y	Y
MICHIGAN							
1 Conyers	Y	Y	?	?	?	?	?
2 ***Pursell***	Y	N	Y	N	Y	Y	Y
3 Wolpe	Y	Y	Y	Y	Y	Y	Y
4 ***Siljander***	?	N	?	?	N	Y	Y
5 ***Henry***	N	N	N	N	N	Y	Y
6 Carr	Y	Y	Y	Y	Y	Y	Y
7 Kildee	Y	Y	Y	Y	Y	Y	Y
8 Traxler	Y	N	?	?	?	?	?
9 ***Vander Jagt***	N	N	N	N	N	Y	Y
10 ***Schuette***	N	N	N	N	Y	Y	Y
11 ***Davis***	Y	?	Y	Y	Y	Y	Y
12 Bonior	Y	Y	Y	Y	Y	Y	Y
13 Crockett	Y	Y	?	Y	Y	Y	Y
14 Hertel	Y	Y	Y	Y	Y	Y	Y
15 Ford	Y	Y	?	?	?	Y	Y
16 Dingell	?	Y	?	Y	Y	Y	Y
17 Levin	Y	Y	Y	Y	Y	Y	Y
18 ***Broomfield***	Y	N	Y	N	N	Y	Y
MINNESOTA							
1 Penny	N	Y	N	Y	Y	Y	Y
2 ***Weber***	N	N	N	N	N	Y	Y
3 ***Frenzel***	N	N	N	?	N	N	Y
4 Vento	Y	Y	Y	Y	Y	Y	Y
5 Sabo	Y	Y	Y	Y	Y	Y	Y
6 Sikorski	N	Y	N	Y	Y	Y	Y

	392	393	394	395	396	397	398
7 ***Stangeland***	?	N	N	N	?	?	Y
8 Oberstar	Y	Y	Y	Y	Y	Y	Y
MISSISSIPPI							
1 Whitten	Y	Y	Y	Y	Y	Y	Y
2 ***Franklin***	Y	N	Y	N	N	Y	Y
3 Montgomery	Y	Y	Y	Y	Y	Y	Y
4 Dowdy	Y	Y	Y	Y	Y	Y	Y
5 ***Lott***	Y	N	N	N	N	Y	Y
MISSOURI							
1 Clay	N	Y	?	?	?	?	?
2 Young	Y	Y	Y	Y	Y	Y	Y
3 Gephardt	Y	Y	Y	Y	Y	?	Y
4 Skelton	Y	Y	Y	Y	Y	Y	Y
5 Wheat	Y	Y	Y	Y	Y	Y	Y
6 ***Coleman***	Y	N	?	N	Y	Y	Y
7 ***Taylor***	Y	N	Y	N	N	Y	Y
8 ***Emerson***	N	N	N	N	N	Y	Y
9 Volkmer	Y	Y	Y	Y	Y	Y	Y
MONTANA							
1 Williams	?	Y	Y	Y	Y	Y	Y
2 ***Marlenee***	Y	N	N	N	N	N	Y
NEBRASKA							
1 ***Bereuter***	N	N	N	N	N	Y	Y
2 ***Daub***	N	N	N	N	N	Y	Y
3 ***Smith***	Y	N	Y	N	N	Y	Y
NEVADA							
1 Reid	Y	Y	Y	Y	Y	Y	Y
2 ***Vucanovich***	?	N	N	N	N	Y	Y
NEW HAMPSHIRE							
1 ***Smith***	N	N	N	N	N	Y	Y
2 ***Gregg***	N	N	N	N	N	N	Y
NEW JERSEY							
1 Florio	Y	Y	Y	Y	Y	Y	Y
2 Hughes	Y	Y	Y	Y	Y	Y	Y
3 Howard	Y	Y	Y	Y	Y	?	Y
4 ***Smith***	Y	N	Y	Y	Y	Y	Y
5 ***Roukema***	N	N	N	N	N	Y	Y
6 Dwyer	Y	Y	Y	Y	Y	Y	Y
7 ***Rinaldo***	Y	N	Y	Y	Y	Y	Y
8 Roe	Y	Y	Y	Y	Y	Y	Y
9 Torricelli	Y	Y	Y	Y	Y	Y	Y
10 Rodino	Y	Y	Y	Y	Y	Y	Y
11 ***Gallo***	N	N	N	N	N	Y	Y
12 ***Courter***	N	N	N	N	N	Y	Y
13 ***Saxton***	N	N	N	N	N	Y	Y
14 Guarini	Y	Y	Y	Y	Y	Y	Y
NEW MEXICO							
1 ***Lujan***	Y	N	Y	N	N	Y	Y
2 ***Skeen***	N	N	N	N	N	Y	Y
3 Richardson	Y	Y	Y	Y	Y	Y	Y
NEW YORK							
1 ***Carney***	N	N	?	?	N	Y	Y
2 Downey	Y	Y	Y	Y	Y	Y	Y
3 Mrazek	?	?	Y	Y	Y	?	?
4 ***Lent***	N	N	N	N	N	Y	Y
5 ***McGrath***	N	N	N	N	N	Y	Y
6 Waldon	Y	Y	?	?	?	?	?
7 Ackerman	Y	Y	Y	Y	Y	Y	Y
8 Scheuer	Y	Y	Y	Y	Y	Y	Y
9 Manton	Y	Y	Y	Y	Y	Y	Y
10 Schumer	Y	Y	Y	Y	Y	Y	Y
11 Towns	?	Y	Y	Y	Y	Y	Y
12 Owens	Y	Y	Y	Y	Y	Y	Y
13 Solarz	Y	Y	Y	Y	Y	Y	Y
14 ***Molinari***	N	N	N	N	N	Y	Y
15 ***Green***	Y	N	P	Y	Y	Y	Y
16 Rangel	?	Y	Y	Y	Y	Y	Y
17 Weiss	Y	Y	Y	Y	Y	Y	Y
18 Garcia	Y	Y	?	?	?	?	Y
19 Biaggi	Y	Y	Y	Y	Y	Y	Y
20 ***DioGuardi***	Y	N	Y	N	N	Y	Y
21 ***Fish***	Y	N	Y	N	N	Y	Y
22 ***Gilman***	Y	N	Y	Y	Y	Y	Y
23 Stratton	Y	Y	?	?	Y	Y	Y
24 ***Solomon***	N	N	N	Y	Y	Y	Y
25 ***Boehlert***	N	N	N	N	N	Y	Y
26 ***Martin***	Y	N	Y	N	?	?	?
27 ***Wortley***	Y	?	Y	N	N	Y	Y
28 McHugh	Y	Y	?	Y	Y	Y	Y
29 ***Horton***	Y	N	Y	Y	Y	Y	Y
30 ***Eckert***	?	N	?	N	N	Y	Y
31 ***Kemp***	Y	N	Y	N	Y	Y	Y
32 LaFalce	Y	Y	?	Y	Y	Y	Y
33 Nowak	Y	Y	Y	Y	Y	Y	Y
34 Lundine	Y	Y	?	Y	Y	Y	Y

	392	393	394	395	396	397	398
NORTH CAROLINA							
1 Jones	Y	Y	Y	Y	Y	Y	Y
2 Valentine	Y	Y	Y	Y	Y	Y	Y
3 Whitley	Y	?	Y	Y	Y	Y	Y
4 ***Cobey***	N	N	N	N	N	Y	Y
5 Neal	Y	Y	?	Y	Y	Y	Y
6 ***Coble***	N	N	N	Y	N	Y	Y
7 Rose	Y	Y	Y	Y	Y	Y	Y
8 Hefner	Y	Y	Y	Y	Y	Y	Y
9 ***McMillan***	Y	N	N	Y	N	Y	Y
10 Vacancy							
11 ***Hendon***	?	N	N	Y	Y	Y	Y
NORTH DAKOTA							
AL Dorgan	Y	Y	Y	Y	Y	Y	Y
OHIO							
1 Luken	Y	Y	Y	Y	Y	Y	Y
2 ***Gradison***	Y	N	Y	N	Y	Y	Y
3 Hall	Y	Y	Y	Y	Y	Y	Y
4 ***Oxley***	N	N	N	N	N	Y	Y
5 ***Latta***	N	N	N	Y	N	Y	Y
6 ***McEwen***	Y	N	?	N	N	Y	Y
7 ***DeWine***	N	N	?	?	?	?	?
8 ***Kindness***	N	N	N	N	N	Y	Y
9 Kaptur	Y	Y	Y	Y	Y	Y	Y
10 ***Miller***	N	N	N	N	N	Y	Y
11 Eckart	Y	Y	Y	Y	Y	Y	Y
12 ***Kasich***	Y	N	Y	N	N	Y	Y
13 Pease	Y	Y	Y	Y	Y	Y	Y
14 Seiberling	Y	Y	Y	Y	Y	Y	Y
15 ***Wylie***	Y	N	Y	N	N	Y	Y
16 ***Regula***	Y	N	N	N	Y	Y	Y
17 Traficant	Y	Y	Y	Y	Y	Y	Y
18 Applegate	?	N	Y	Y	Y	Y	Y
19 Feighan	Y	Y	Y	Y	Y	Y	Y
20 Oakar	Y	Y	Y	Y	Y	Y	Y
21 Stokes	Y	?	?	Y	Y	Y	Y
OKLAHOMA							
1 Jones	Y	Y	Y	Y	Y	Y	Y
2 Synar	Y	Y	Y	Y	Y	Y	Y
3 Watkins	Y	Y	Y	Y	Y	Y	Y
4 McCurdy	Y	Y	?	Y	Y	Y	Y
5 ***Edwards***	Y	N	Y	N	N	Y	Y
6 English	Y	Y	Y	Y	Y	Y	Y
OREGON							
1 AuCoin	Y	Y	?	Y	Y	Y	Y
2 ***Smith, R.***	N	N	N	N	Y	Y	Y
3 Wyden	Y	Y	Y	Y	Y	Y	Y
4 Weaver	Y	Y	Y	Y	Y	Y	Y
5 ***Smith, D.***	N	N	N	N	N	N	Y
PENNSYLVANIA							
1 Foglietta	Y	Y	Y	?	?	Y	Y
2 Gray	?	Y	Y	Y	Y	Y	Y
3 Borski	Y	Y	Y	Y	Y	Y	Y
4 Kolter	Y	Y	Y	Y	Y	Y	Y
5 ***Schulze***	Y	N	Y	N	N	Y	Y
6 Yatron	Y	Y	Y	Y	?	?	Y
7 Edgar	N	Y	?	?	Y	Y	Y
8 Kostmayer	Y	Y	Y	Y	Y	Y	Y
9 ***Shuster***	N	N	N	N	N	N	Y
10 ***McDade***	Y	N	Y	Y	N	Y	Y
11 Kanjorski	Y	Y	Y	Y	Y	Y	Y
12 Murtha	Y	Y	Y	Y	Y	Y	Y
13 ***Coughlin***	N	N	N	Y	Y	Y	Y
14 Coyne	Y	Y	Y	Y	Y	Y	Y
15 ***Ritter***	?	N	?	N	N	Y	Y
16 ***Walker***	N	N	N	N	N	N	Y
17 ***Gekas***	N	N	N	N	N	N	Y
18 Walgren	Y	Y	Y	Y	Y	Y	Y
19 ***Goodling***	N	N	N	N	N	Y	Y
20 Gaydos	Y	Y	Y	Y	Y	Y	Y
21 ***Ridge***	?	N	N	N	N	Y	Y
22 Murphy	Y	Y	Y	Y	Y	Y	Y
23 ***Clinger***	Y	N	Y	Y	N	Y	Y
RHODE ISLAND							
1 St Germain	Y	Y	Y	Y	Y	Y	Y
2 ***Schneider***	Y	N	Y	N	N	Y	Y
SOUTH CAROLINA							
1 ***Hartnett***	?	?	?	?	?	?	?
2 ***Spence***	Y	N	N	N	Y	Y	Y
3 Derrick	?	Y	Y	Y	Y	Y	Y
4 ***Campbell***	?	?	?	?	?	?	?
5 Spratt	Y	Y	Y	Y	Y	Y	Y
6 Tallon	Y	Y	Y	Y	Y	Y	Y
SOUTH DAKOTA							
AL Daschle	Y	Y	Y	Y	Y	Y	Y

	392	393	394	395	396	397	398
TENNESSEE							
1 ***Quillen***	Y	N	Y	Y	Y	Y	Y
2 ***Duncan***	Y	N	Y	N	Y	?	Y
3 Lloyd	?	N	Y	Y	Y	Y	Y
4 Cooper	Y	Y	Y	Y	Y	Y	Y
5 Boner	Y	Y	Y	Y	Y	Y	Y
6 Gordon	Y	Y	?	Y	Y	Y	Y
7 ***Sundquist***	N	N	N	N	N	Y	Y
8 Jones	Y	Y	Y	Y	Y	Y	Y
9 Ford	Y	Y	?	?	Y	Y	Y
TEXAS							
1 Chapman	Y	Y	?	Y	Y	Y	Y
2 Wilson	Y	Y	Y	Y	Y	Y	Y
3 ***Bartlett***	Y	N	N	N	N	N	Y
4 Hall, R.	Y	N	Y	Y	Y	Y	Y
5 Bryant	Y	Y	Y	Y	Y	Y	Y
6 ***Barton***	N	Y	N	N	N	N	Y
7 ***Archer***	Y	N	Y	N	N	N	Y
8 ***Fields***	N	Y	N	N	N	N	Y
9 Brooks	Y	Y	?	Y	Y	Y	Y
10 Pickle	Y	Y	Y	Y	Y	Y	Y
11 Leath	Y	Y	Y	Y	?	Y	Y
12 Wright	?	?	Y	Y	Y	Y	Y
13 ***Boulter***	N	N	N	N	N	Y	Y
14 ***Sweeney***	Y	Y	Y	N	N	Y	Y
15 de la Garza	Y	Y	Y	Y	?	?	?
16 Coleman	Y	Y	Y	Y	Y	Y	Y
17 Stenholm	Y	N	Y	Y	Y	Y	Y
18 Leland	Y	Y	?	Y	Y	Y	Y
19 ***Combest***	Y	N	Y	N	N	Y	Y
20 Gonzalez	Y	Y	Y	Y	Y	Y	Y
21 ***Loeffler***	N	Y	N	N	N	Y	Y
22 ***DeLay***	N	N	N	N	N	N	Y
23 Bustamante	Y	Y	Y	Y	Y	Y	Y
24 Frost	Y	Y	Y	Y	?	?	Y
25 Andrews	Y	Y	Y	Y	Y	Y	Y
26 ***Armey***	N	N	N	N	N	N	Y
27 Ortiz	Y	Y	Y	Y	Y	Y	Y
UTAH							
1 ***Hansen***	N	N	N	N	N	N	Y
2 ***Monson***	N	N	N	N	N	N	Y
3 ***Nielson***	Y	N	Y	N	N	Y	Y
VERMONT							
AL ***Jeffords***	Y	N	Y	Y	N	Y	Y
VIRGINIA							
1 ***Bateman***	Y	N	Y	N	N	Y	Y
2 ***Whitehurst***	N	N	?	N	N	Y	Y
3 ***Bliley***	N	N	N	N	N	Y	Y
4 Sisisky	Y	Y	Y	Y	Y	Y	Y
5 Daniel	Y	Y	Y	Y	Y	Y	Y
6 Olin	Y	Y	Y	Y	?	?	Y
7 ***Slaughter***	N	N	N	N	N	Y	Y
8 ***Parris***	Y	N	N	Y	Y	Y	Y
9 Boucher	Y	Y	Y	Y	?	Y	Y
10 ***Wolf***	N	N	N	N	N	Y	Y
WASHINGTON							
1 ***Miller***	Y	N	Y	N	N	Y	Y
2 Swift	Y	Y	Y	Y	Y	Y	Y
3 Bonker	Y	Y	Y	Y	Y	Y	Y
4 ***Morrison***	Y	N	Y	Y	N	Y	Y
5 Foley	Y	Y	Y	Y	Y	?	Y
6 Dicks	Y	Y	Y	Y	Y	Y	Y
7 Lowry	Y	Y	Y	Y	Y	Y	Y
8 ***Chandler***	N	N	N	N	N	Y	Y
WEST VIRGINIA							
1 Mollohan	Y	Y	Y	Y	Y	Y	Y
2 Staggers	Y	Y	Y	Y	Y	Y	Y
3 Wise	Y	Y	Y	Y	Y	Y	?
4 Rahall	Y	Y	Y	Y	Y	Y	Y
WISCONSIN							
1 Aspin	Y	Y	Y	Y	Y	Y	Y
2 Kastenmeier	Y	Y	Y	Y	Y	Y	Y
3 ***Gunderson***	N	N	N	Y	N	Y	Y
4 Kleczka	Y	Y	?	?	Y	Y	Y
5 Moody	Y	Y	Y	Y	Y	Y	Y
6 ***Petri***	N	N	Y	Y	N	Y	Y
7 Obey	Y	Y	Y	Y	Y	Y	Y
8 ***Roth***	N	N	N	N	N	Y	Y
9 ***Sensenbrenner***	N	N	N	N	N	N	Y
WYOMING							
AL ***Cheney***	N	N	N	N	N	N	Y

Southern states - Ala., Ark., Fla., Ga., Ky., La., Miss., N.C., Okla., S.C., Tenn., Texas, Va.

* The *Congressional Record* vote number is different from the CQ vote number because the *Record* includes quorum calls in its tally. CQ does not publish quorum call votes.

399. HR 5445. Civil RICO. Conyers, D-Mich., demand for a second on the Boucher, D-Va., motion to suspend the rules and pass the bill to curtail private lawsuits under a federal anti-racketeering law. Second ordered 371-28: R 166-2; D 205-26 (ND 135-23, SD 70-3), Oct. 7, 1986. (The bill later was passed by voice vote.)

400. S 2880. H-3 Interstate Transfer Deadline Extension. Howard, D-N.J., motion to suspend the rules and pass the bill to provide for a temporary extension of the Interstate transfer deadline for the H-3 Interstate highway construction project in Hawaii. Motion rejected 264-147: R 60-112; D 204-35 (ND 141-21, SD 63-14), Oct. 7, 1986. A two-thirds majority of those present and voting (274 in this case) is required for passage under suspension of the rules.

401. HR 5215. Salinity Research Laboratory Construction. De la Garza, D-Texas, motion to suspend the rules and pass the bill to authorize the secretary of agriculture, through the Agriculture Research Service, to construct a salinity laboratory in Riverside, Calif. Motion agreed to 326-85: R 94-78; D 232-7 (ND 159-3, SD 73-4), Oct. 7, 1986. A two-thirds majority of those present and voting (274 in this case) is required for passage under suspension of the rules.

402. HR 2868. Gay Head Indian Land Claims. Passage of the bill to settle land claims of the Wampanoag Indians in the town of Gay Head, Mass., on the western portion of Martha's Vineyard Island, and to authorize $1.5 million for a fund within the Treasury to settle the claims, to be matched by $1.5 million from the commonwealth of Massachusetts. The settlement would become effective only if the secretary of the interior grants federal recognition to the Wampanoag Indian Tribe of Gay Head. Passed 217-172: R 23-139; D 194-33 (ND 141-13, SD 53-20), Oct. 7, 1986.

403. Procedural Motion. Sensenbrenner, R-Wis., motion to approve the House *Journal* of Tuesday, Oct. 7. Motion agreed to 260-116: R 51-108; D 209-8 (ND 139-6, SD 70-2), Oct. 8, 1986.

404. HR 5484. Omnibus Drug Bill. Adoption of the rule (H Res 576) to provide for House floor consideration of the House amendment to the Senate amendment to the bill to authorize $1.708 billion for fiscal 1987 for drug interdiction, eradication, prevention, education and treatment efforts, as well as for grants to states and localities for drug enforcement, and to set increased penalties for drug offenses. The rule was drafted so that its adoption constituted adoption of the House amendment. Adopted 391-23: R 175-0; D 216-23 (ND 143-22, SD 73-1), Oct. 8, 1986.

405. HR 2005. 'Superfund' Reauthorization. Derrick, D-S.C., motion to order the previous question (thus ending debate and the possibility of amendment) on the rule (H Res 577) to waive points of order against House floor consideration of the conference report on the bill to reauthorize the "superfund" hazardous-waste cleanup fund. Motion agreed to 311-104: R 89-86; D 222-18 (ND 151-14, SD 71-4), Oct. 8, 1986. (The effect of the motion was to preclude a possible action to divide the superfund legislation into two bills, thus averting a possible presidential veto of the entire bill because of objections to the funding provisions. The rule subsequently was adopted *(see vote 406, below).*)

406. HR 2005. 'Superfund' Reauthorization. Adoption of the rule (H Res 577) to waive points of order against House floor consideration of the conference report on the bill to reauthorize the "superfund" hazardous-waste cleanup program for fiscal 1987-91 at a funding level of $8.5 billion, and to establish a new program for cleanup of leaking underground storage tanks at a funding level of $500,000. Adopted 339-74: R 108-64; D 231-10 (ND 163-3, SD 68-7), Oct. 8, 1986.

KEY

- Y Voted for (yea).
- # Paired for.
- \+ Announced for.
- N Voted against (nay).
- X Paired against.
- \- Announced against.
- P Voted "present."
- C Voted "present" to avoid possible conflict of interest.
- ? Did not vote or otherwise make a position known.

Democrats *Republicans*

	399	400	401	402	403	404	405	406
ALABAMA								
1 ***Callahan***	Y	Y	N	N	Y	Y	N	N
2 ***Dickinson***	Y	Y	N	N	N	Y	N	Y
3 Nichols	?	Y	Y	Y	Y	Y	Y	Y
4 Bevill	Y	Y	Y	Y	Y	Y	Y	Y
5 Flippo	Y	Y	Y	Y	Y	Y	Y	Y
6 Erdreich	Y	Y	Y	Y	Y	Y	Y	Y
7 Shelby	Y	Y	N	Y	Y	Y	Y	N
ALASKA								
AL ***Young***	Y	Y	Y	Y	N	Y	N	N
ARIZONA								
1 ***McCain***	Y	N	N	Y	Y	Y	Y	Y
2 Udall	Y	Y	Y	Y	Y	Y	Y	Y
3 ***Stump***	Y	N	N	N	N	Y	N	N
4 ***Rudd***	Y	N	N	N	Y	Y	N	N
5 ***Kolbe***	Y	N	N	N	N	Y	Y	Y
ARKANSAS								
1 Alexander	Y	Y	Y	Y	?	Y	Y	Y
2 Robinson	Y	Y	N	N	Y	Y	N	N
3 ***Hammerschmidt***	Y	Y	Y	N	Y	Y	N	N
4 Anthony	Y	Y	Y	Y	Y	Y	Y	Y
CALIFORNIA								
1 Bosco	Y	Y	Y	Y	Y	Y	Y	Y
2 ***Chappie***	Y	N	Y	N	N	Y	N	N
3 Matsui	Y	Y	Y	Y	Y	Y	Y	Y
4 Fazio	Y	Y	Y	Y	Y	Y	Y	Y
5 Burton	?	?	?	?	?	?	?	?
6 Boxer	Y	Y	Y	Y	Y	Y	Y	Y
7 Miller	Y	Y	Y	Y	Y	Y	Y	Y
8 Dellums	Y	Y	Y	Y	Y	N	Y	Y
9 Stark	Y	Y	Y	Y	?	Y	Y	Y
10 Edwards	N	Y	Y	Y	Y	N	Y	Y
11 Lantos	Y	Y	Y	Y	?	Y	Y	Y
12 ***Zschau***	Y	N	Y	N	N	Y	Y	Y
13 Mineta	Y	Y	Y	Y	Y	Y	Y	Y
14 ***Shumway***	Y	N	Y	N	Y	Y	N	N
15 Coelho	Y	Y	Y	Y	Y	Y	Y	Y
16 Panetta	Y	Y	Y	Y	Y	Y	Y	Y
17 ***Pashayan***	Y	Y	Y	?	N	Y	Y	?
18 Lehman	Y	Y	Y	Y	Y	Y	Y	Y
19 ***Lagomarsino***	Y	N	Y	N	N	Y	Y	Y
20 ***Thomas***	Y	N	Y	N	N	Y	Y	Y
21 ***Fiedler***	Y	N	Y	N	N	Y	N	Y
22 ***Moorhead***	Y	N	Y	N	N	Y	N	Y
23 Beilenson	Y	N	Y	Y	Y	Y	Y	Y
24 Waxman	Y	N	Y	Y	Y	Y	Y	Y
25 Roybal	Y	Y	Y	Y	Y	N	Y	Y
26 Berman	Y	Y	Y	Y	Y	Y	Y	Y
27 Levine	Y	Y	Y	Y	Y	Y	Y	Y
28 Dixon	N	Y	Y	Y	Y	Y	Y	Y
29 Hawkins	N	Y	Y	Y	N	Y	Y	Y
30 Martinez	Y	Y	Y	Y	Y	+	Y	Y
31 Dymally	N	Y	Y	Y	Y	Y	Y	Y
32 Anderson	Y	Y	Y	Y	Y	N	N	Y
33 ***Dreier***	Y	N	Y	N	N	Y	N	Y
34 Torres	Y	Y	Y	Y	Y	Y	Y	Y
35 ***Lewis***	Y	Y	Y	N	N	Y	N	N
36 Brown	Y	Y	Y	Y	Y	Y	Y	Y
37 ***McCandless***	Y	Y	Y	N	N	Y	N	N
38 ***Dornan***	Y	N	Y	N	Y	Y	N	Y
39 ***Dannemeyer***	?	?	?	?	N	Y	N	N
40 ***Badham***	Y	N	Y	N	N	Y	N	N
41 ***Lowery***	Y	N	Y	N	?	Y	N	Y
42 ***Lungren***	Y	N	Y	N	Y	Y	N	N
43 ***Packard***	Y	Y	Y	N	Y	Y	N	N
44 Bates	Y	N	Y	Y	Y	Y	Y	Y
45 ***Hunter***	Y	N	Y	N	N	Y	N	?
COLORADO								
1 Schroeder	Y	N	Y	Y	N	Y	Y	Y
2 Wirth	Y	N	Y	Y	Y	Y	Y	Y
3 ***Strang***	Y	N	N	N	N	Y	N	N
4 ***Brown***	Y	N	N	N	N	Y	N	N
5 ***Kramer***	Y	N	Y	N	N	Y	Y	Y
6 ***Schaefer***	Y	N	N	?	N	Y	Y	Y
CONNECTICUT								
1 Kennelly	?	?	?	?	Y	Y	Y	Y
2 Gejdenson	N	Y	Y	Y	Y	Y	N	Y
3 Morrison	Y	Y	Y	Y	Y	Y	Y	Y
4 ***McKinney***	Y	Y	Y	Y	Y	Y	Y	Y
5 ***Rowland***	Y	N	Y	Y	N	Y	Y	Y
6 ***Johnson***	Y	Y	Y	Y	Y	Y	Y	Y
DELAWARE								
AL Carper	Y	Y	Y	Y	Y	Y	Y	Y
FLORIDA								
1 Hutto	Y	Y	Y	N	Y	Y	Y	Y
2 Fuqua	Y	Y	Y	Y	Y	Y	Y	Y
3 Bennett	Y	Y	Y	Y	Y	Y	Y	Y
4 Chappell	Y	Y	Y	N	Y	?	Y	Y
5 ***McCollum***	Y	N	N	N	Y	Y	N	Y
6 MacKay	?	Y	Y	Y	Y	Y	Y	Y
7 Gibbons	Y	Y	Y	Y	?	Y	Y	Y
8 ***Young***	Y	Y	Y	N	N	Y	Y	Y
9 ***Bilirakis***	Y	N	N	N	N	Y	Y	Y
10 ***Ireland***	Y	Y	Y	N	N	Y	N	N
11 Nelson	Y	Y	Y	N	Y	Y	Y	Y
12 ***Lewis***	Y	N	N	N	N	Y	N	N
13 ***Mack***	Y	N	N	N	N	Y	N	N
14 Mica	Y	Y	Y	?	Y	Y	Y	Y
15 ***Shaw***	Y	Y	N	N	N	Y	N	N
16 Smith	Y	Y	Y	Y	Y	Y	Y	Y
17 Lehman	?	Y	Y	?	Y	Y	Y	Y
18 Pepper	Y	Y	Y	Y	Y	Y	Y	Y
19 Fascell	Y	Y	Y	Y	Y	Y	Y	Y
GEORGIA								
1 Thomas	Y	Y	Y	Y	Y	Y	Y	Y
2 Hatcher	Y	Y	Y	Y	Y	Y	Y	Y
3 Ray	Y	N	Y	Y	Y	Y	Y	Y
4 ***Swindall***	Y	N	N	N	N	Y	N	N
5 Fowler	?	?	?	?	?	?	?	?
6 ***Gingrich***	Y	Y	Y	N	N	Y	?	Y
7 Darden	Y	Y	Y	Y	Y	Y	Y	Y
8 Rowland	Y	Y	Y	Y	Y	Y	Y	Y
9 Jenkins	Y	Y	Y	N	Y	Y	Y	Y
10 Barnard	?	#	?	?	?	?	?	?
HAWAII								
1 Abercrombie	Y	Y	Y	Y	Y	Y	Y	Y
2 Akaka	Y	Y	Y	Y	Y	Y	Y	Y
IDAHO								
1 ***Craig***	Y	N	N	N	N	Y	Y	Y
2 Stallings	Y	N	Y	N	Y	Y	Y	Y
ILLINOIS								
1 Hayes	N	Y	Y	Y	?	N	Y	Y
2 Savage	N	Y	Y	Y	?	N	Y	Y
3 Russo	Y	Y	Y	Y	Y	Y	Y	Y
4 Vacancy								
5 Lipinski	Y	Y	Y	Y	Y	Y	Y	Y
6 ***Hyde***	?	N	N	?	Y	Y	N	Y
7 Collins	N	Y	Y	Y	Y	N	Y	Y
8 Rostenkowski	Y	Y	Y	Y	Y	Y	Y	Y
9 Yates	Y	Y	Y	Y	Y	Y	Y	Y
10 ***Porter***	N	N	N	N	?	Y	N	N
11 Annunzio	Y	Y	Y	Y	Y	Y	Y	Y
12 ***Crane***	N	N	N	N	?	Y	N	N
13 ***Fawell***	Y	N	N	N	N	Y	Y	Y
14 ***Grotberg***	?	?	?	?	?	?	?	?
15 ***Madigan***	Y	N	Y	N	N	Y	Y	Y
16 ***Martin***	Y	N	N	N	N	Y	N	Y
17 Evans	Y	Y	Y	Y	Y	Y	Y	Y
18 ***Michel***	Y	N	Y	N	N	Y	N	Y
19 Bruce	Y	Y	Y	Y	Y	Y	Y	Y
20 Durbin	Y	Y	Y	Y	Y	Y	Y	Y
21 Price	Y	Y	Y	Y	Y	Y	Y	Y
22 Gray	Y	Y	Y	Y	?	Y	Y	Y
INDIANA								
1 Visclosky	Y	Y	Y	Y	Y	Y	Y	Y
2 Sharp	Y	Y	Y	?	Y	Y	Y	Y
3 ***Hiler***	Y	N	N	N	N	Y	N	N
4 ***Coats***	Y	N	N	N	N	Y	N	N
5 ***Hillis***	Y	Y	Y	N	Y	Y	Y	Y

ND - Northern Democrats SD - Southern Democrats

* Corresponding to Congressional Record Votes 434, 435, 436, 437, 438, 439, 440, 441

	399	400	401	402	403	404	405	406
6 ***Burton***	Y	N	N	N	N	Y	N	N
7 ***Myers***	Y	Y	Y	N	Y	Y	N	N
8 McCloskey	Y	Y	?	Y	Y	Y	Y	Y
9 Hamilton	Y	Y	Y	Y	Y	Y	Y	Y
10 Jacobs	Y	N	Y	Y	N	Y	?	Y
IOWA								
1 ***Leach***	Y	N	N	N	N	Y	Y	Y
2 ***Tauke***	Y	N	N	N	N	Y	N	N
3 ***Evans***	Y	Y	Y	N	N	Y	N	Y
4 Smith	Y	Y	Y	Y	Y	Y	Y	Y
5 ***Lightfoot***	Y	N	N	N	N	Y	N	N
6 Bedell	Y	Y	Y	Y	Y	N	Y	Y
KANSAS								
1 ***Roberts***	Y	N	Y	N	N	Y	N	Y
2 Slattery	Y	N	Y	N	Y	Y	Y	Y
3 ***Meyers***	Y	N	N	N	N	Y	Y	Y
4 Glickman	Y	N	Y	N	Y	Y	Y	Y
5 ***Whittaker***	Y	Y	Y	N	N	Y	Y	Y
KENTUCKY								
1 Hubbard	Y	N	N	N	Y	Y	Y	Y
2 Natcher	Y	Y	Y	Y	Y	Y	Y	Y
3 Mazzoli	Y	Y	Y	Y	Y	Y	Y	Y
4 ***Snyder***	Y	Y	Y	N	Y	Y	Y	Y
5 ***Rogers***	Y	Y	Y	N	N	Y	Y	Y
6 ***Hopkins***	Y	N	N	N	N	Y	N	Y
7 Perkins	Y	Y	Y	Y	Y	Y	Y	Y
LOUISIANA								
1 ***Livingston***	Y	N	N	N	P	Y	Y	Y
2 Boggs	Y	Y	Y	Y	?	Y	Y	Y
3 Tauzin	Y	N	Y	Y	Y	Y	Y	Y
4 Roemer	?	?	?	?	?	?	?	?
5 Huckaby	Y	N	Y	Y	Y	Y	Y	Y
6 ***Moore***	?	?	?	?	?	?	?	?
7 Breaux	?	?	?	?	?	?	?	?
8 Long	Y	Y	Y	Y	Y	Y	Y	Y
MAINE								
1 ***McKernan***	Y	Y	Y	Y	?	Y	N	N
2 ***Snowe***	Y	Y	Y	Y	N	Y	N	N
MARYLAND								
1 Dyson	Y	Y	Y	N	?	Y	N	Y
2 ***Bentley***	Y	Y	Y	N	?	Y	Y	Y
3 Mikulski	Y	Y	Y	?	?	Y	Y	Y
4 ***Holt***	Y	N	N	N	N	Y	N	Y
5 Hoyer	?	Y	Y	Y	Y	Y	Y	Y
6 Byron	Y	N	Y	N	Y	Y	N	Y
7 Mitchell	N	Y	Y	Y	?	N	?	Y
8 Barnes	Y	Y	Y	Y	Y	?	Y	Y
MASSACHUSETTS								
1 ***Conte***	Y	Y	Y	Y	N	Y	N	Y
2 Boland	Y	?	?	?	Y	Y	Y	Y
3 Early	Y	Y	Y	Y	Y	Y	N	Y
4 Frank	Y	Y	Y	Y	Y	N	N	Y
5 Atkins	Y	Y	Y	Y	Y	Y	Y	Y
6 Mavroules	?	Y	Y	Y	Y	Y	N	Y
7 Markey	Y	Y	Y	Y	Y	Y	N	Y
8 O'Neill								
9 Moakley	Y	Y	Y	Y	Y	Y	Y	Y
10 Studds	Y	Y	Y	Y	Y	Y	Y	Y
11 Donnelly	Y	Y	Y	Y	Y	Y	N	N
MICHIGAN								
1 Conyers	N	Y	Y	Y	Y	N	Y	Y
2 ***Pursell***	Y	N	Y	N	Y	Y	N	Y
3 Wolpe	N	Y	Y	Y	Y	Y	N	Y
4 ***Siljander***	Y	N	N	N	?	Y	N	N
5 ***Henry***	Y	N	N	N	N	Y	Y	Y
6 Carr	N	Y	Y	N	Y	Y	N	Y
7 Kildee	Y	Y	Y	Y	Y	N	Y	Y
8 Traxler	Y	Y	Y	Y	Y	Y	Y	Y
9 ***Vander Jagt***	Y	Y	Y	Y	?	Y	N	N
10 ***Schuette***	Y	N	Y	N	N	Y	Y	Y
11 ***Davis***	Y	Y	Y	Y	Y	Y	Y	?
12 Bonior	N	Y	Y	Y	Y	Y	Y	Y
13 Crockett	N	Y	Y	Y	Y	N	Y	Y
14 Hertel	Y	N	Y	Y	Y	Y	N	Y
15 Ford	N	Y	Y	Y	?	Y	Y	Y
16 Dingell	N	?	?	N	?	Y	Y	Y
17 Levin	N	Y	Y	Y	Y	Y	Y	Y
18 ***Broomfield***	Y	N	N	?	Y	Y	Y	Y
MINNESOTA								
1 Penny	Y	Y	Y	Y	N	Y	Y	Y
2 ***Weber***	Y	N	Y	N	N	Y	Y	Y
3 ***Frenzel***	Y	N	N	N	N	Y	Y	Y
4 Vento	Y	Y	Y	Y	Y	Y	Y	Y
5 Sabo	Y	Y	Y	Y	Y	N	Y	Y
6 Sikorski	Y	Y	Y	Y	N	Y	Y	Y

	399	400	401	402	403	404	405	406
7 ***Stangeland***	Y	Y	Y	?	N	Y	Y	Y
8 Oberstar	Y	Y	Y	Y	?	Y	Y	Y
MISSISSIPPI								
1 Whitten	Y	Y	Y	N	Y	Y	Y	Y
2 ***Franklin***	Y	N	Y	N	Y	Y	N	N
3 Montgomery	Y	Y	Y	N	Y	Y	Y	Y
4 Dowdy	Y	Y	Y	Y	Y	Y	Y	Y
5 ***Lott***	Y	N	N	N	N	Y	N	N
MISSOURI								
1 Clay	N	Y	Y	?	N	N	Y	Y
2 Young	Y	Y	Y	Y	Y	Y	Y	Y
3 Gephardt	Y	Y	Y	Y	Y	Y	Y	Y
4 Skelton	Y	Y	Y	N	Y	Y	Y	Y
5 Wheat	N	Y	Y	Y	Y	N	Y	Y
6 ***Coleman***	Y	Y	N	N	N	Y	Y	Y
7 ***Taylor***	Y	Y	Y	N	Y	Y	N	N
8 ***Emerson***	Y	Y	Y	N	N	Y	Y	Y
9 Volkmer	Y	Y	Y	?	?	Y	Y	Y
MONTANA								
1 Williams	?	N	Y	Y	?	Y	Y	Y
2 ***Marlenee***	Y	N	Y	N	N	Y	N	N
NEBRASKA								
1 ***Bereuter***	Y	N	Y	N	N	Y	N	Y
2 ***Daub***	Y	N	Y	N	N	Y	N	N
3 ***Smith***	Y	N	Y	N	?	Y	N	N
NEVADA								
1 Reid	Y	N	Y	Y	Y	Y	Y	Y
2 ***Vucanovich***	Y	N	Y	N	N	Y	Y	Y
NEW HAMPSHIRE								
1 ***Smith***	Y	N	N	N	N	Y	N	N
2 ***Gregg***	Y	N	N	N	N	Y	N	N
NEW JERSEY								
1 Florio	Y	Y	Y	Y	Y	Y	Y	Y
2 Hughes	Y	Y	Y	?	Y	Y	Y	Y
3 Howard	Y	Y	Y	Y	Y	Y	Y	Y
4 ***Smith***	Y	Y	Y	N	Y	Y	Y	Y
5 ***Roukema***	Y	Y	Y	N	N	Y	Y	Y
6 Dwyer	Y	Y	Y	Y	Y	Y	Y	Y
7 ***Rinaldo***	Y	Y	Y	N	?	Y	Y	Y
8 Roe	Y	Y	Y	Y	Y	Y	Y	Y
9 Torricelli	Y	Y	Y	?	?	Y	Y	Y
10 Rodino	?	?	?	?	Y	N	Y	Y
11 ***Gallo***	Y	Y	Y	N	N	Y	Y	Y
12 ***Courter***	Y	Y	Y	N	N	Y	Y	Y
13 ***Saxton***	Y	Y	Y	N	N	Y	Y	Y
14 Guarini	Y	Y	Y	Y	Y	Y	Y	Y
NEW MEXICO								
1 ***Lujan***	Y	N	Y	N	Y	Y	N	N
2 ***Skeen***	Y	N	Y	N	N	Y	N	N
3 Richardson	Y	Y	Y	Y	Y	Y	Y	Y
NEW YORK								
1 ***Carney***	?	N	N	Y	?	?	?	?
2 Downey	Y	Y	Y	N	Y	Y	Y	Y
3 Mrazek	Y	Y	Y	Y	Y	Y	Y	Y
4 ***Lent***	Y	Y	Y	N	N	Y	Y	Y
5 ***McGrath***	Y	Y	Y	N	N	Y	Y	Y
6 Waldon	Y	Y	Y	Y	Y	Y	Y	Y
7 Ackerman	Y	Y	Y	Y	Y	N	Y	Y
8 Scheuer	Y	Y	Y	Y	Y	Y	Y	?
9 Manton	Y	Y	Y	Y	?	Y	Y	Y
10 Schumer	Y	Y	Y	Y	Y	Y	Y	Y
11 Towns	N	Y	Y	Y	Y	Y	Y	Y
12 Owens	Y	Y	Y	?	?	Y	Y	Y
13 Solarz	Y	Y	Y	Y	Y	Y	Y	Y
14 ***Molinari***	Y	Y	Y	N	N	Y	Y	Y
15 ***Green***	Y	Y	Y	Y	Y	Y	Y	Y
16 Rangel	N	Y	Y	Y	Y	Y	Y	Y
17 Weiss	?	?	?	?	?	?	?	?
18 Garcia	Y	Y	Y	Y	?	Y	Y	Y
19 Biaggi	Y	Y	Y	Y	Y	Y	Y	Y
20 ***DioGuardi***	Y	Y	Y	N	Y	Y	Y	Y
21 ***Fish***	?	N	Y	?	Y	Y	Y	Y
22 ***Gilman***	Y	Y	Y	Y	Y	Y	Y	Y
23 Stratton	Y	Y	Y	Y	Y	Y	Y	Y
24 ***Solomon***	Y	N	N	N	N	Y	Y	Y
25 ***Boehlert***	Y	Y	Y	Y	N	Y	Y	Y
26 ***Martin***	Y	Y	Y	Y	N	Y	Y	Y
27 ***Wortley***	?	Y	Y	Y	Y	Y	Y	Y
28 McHugh	Y	Y	Y	Y	Y	Y	Y	Y
29 ***Horton***	Y	Y	Y	Y	Y	Y	Y	Y
30 ***Eckert***	Y	N	N	Y	Y	Y	Y	Y
31 ***Kemp***	Y	N	Y	?	Y	Y	N	N
32 LaFalce	Y	Y	Y	Y	Y	Y	Y	Y
33 Nowak	Y	Y	Y	Y	Y	Y	Y	Y
34 Lundine	Y	Y	Y	Y	?	N	Y	Y

	399	400	401	402	403	404	405	406
NORTH CAROLINA								
1 Jones	Y	Y	Y	Y	Y	Y	Y	Y
2 Valentine	Y	Y	Y	N	Y	Y	Y	Y
3 Whitley	Y	Y	Y	Y	Y	Y	Y	Y
4 ***Cobey***	Y	N	N	N	N	Y	Y	Y
5 Neal	Y	Y	Y	Y	?	Y	Y	Y
6 ***Coble***	Y	N	N	N	N	Y	Y	Y
7 Rose	Y	Y	Y	?	Y	?	?	?
8 Hefner	Y	Y	Y	N	Y	Y	Y	Y
9 ***McMillan***	Y	N	N	N	N	Y	Y	Y
10 Vacancy								
11 ***Hendon***	Y	N	N	N	?	Y	Y	Y
NORTH DAKOTA								
AL Dorgan	Y	Y	Y	Y	Y	Y	Y	Y
OHIO								
1 Luken	Y	Y	Y	Y	Y	Y	Y	Y
2 ***Gradison***	Y	N	N	N	N	Y	Y	Y
3 Hall	Y	Y	Y	Y	Y	Y	Y	Y
4 ***Oxley***	Y	N	Y	N	N	Y	Y	Y
5 ***Latta***	Y	Y	N	N	N	Y	N	N
6 ***McEwen***	Y	Y	N	N	N	Y	N	N
7 ***DeWine***	Y	N	N	?	N	Y	Y	Y
8 ***Kindness***	?	?	?	?	?	?	?	?
9 Kaptur	Y	Y	Y	Y	Y	Y	Y	Y
10 ***Miller***	Y	N	N	N	N	Y	N	N
11 Eckart	Y	N	Y	N	Y	Y	Y	Y
12 ***Kasich***	Y	N	Y	N	?	Y	Y	Y
13 Pease	Y	N	Y	Y	Y	Y	Y	Y
14 Seiberling	N	Y	Y	Y	?	Y	Y	Y
15 ***Wylie***	Y	N	N	N	Y	Y	Y	Y
16 ***Regula***	Y	Y	Y	N	Y	Y	Y	Y
17 Traficant	Y	Y	Y	Y	Y	Y	Y	Y
18 Applegate	Y	Y	Y	Y	Y	Y	N	N
19 Feighan	Y	Y	Y	Y	Y	Y	Y	Y
20 Oakar	?	Y	Y	Y	Y	Y	Y	Y
21 Stokes	?	#	?	?	Y	N	Y	Y
OKLAHOMA								
1 Jones	?	X	?	?	?	?	?	?
2 Synar	Y	N	Y	Y	Y	Y	Y	Y
3 Watkins	Y	N	N	Y	Y	Y	Y	N
4 McCurdy	Y	N	Y	N	Y	Y	Y	Y
5 ***Edwards***	Y	N	Y	N	?	Y	N	N
6 English	Y	N	Y	N	Y	Y	N	N
OREGON								
1 AuCoin	Y	Y	Y	Y	Y	Y	Y	Y
2 ***Smith, R.***	Y	N	Y	?	N	Y	N	N
3 Wyden	Y	Y	Y	Y	Y	Y	Y	Y
4 Weaver	Y	Y	Y	?	Y	N	Y	Y
5 ***Smith, D.***	Y	N	N	N	N	Y	N	N
PENNSYLVANIA								
1 Foglietta	N	Y	Y	Y	Y	Y	Y	Y
2 Gray	?	Y	Y	Y	?	Y	Y	Y
3 Borski	Y	Y	Y	Y	?	Y	Y	Y
4 Kolter	Y	Y	Y	Y	Y	Y	Y	Y
5 ***Schulze***	Y	N	N	N	Y	Y	N	Y
6 Yatron	Y	N	Y	Y	Y	Y	Y	Y
7 Edgar	Y	Y	Y	Y	Y	Y	Y	Y
8 Kostmayer	Y	N	Y	Y	Y	Y	Y	Y
9 ***Shuster***	Y	Y	N	N	N	Y	N	N
10 ***McDade***	Y	Y	Y	N	Y	Y	Y	Y
11 Kanjorski	?	Y	Y	Y	?	Y	Y	Y
12 Murtha	Y	Y	Y	Y	Y	Y	Y	Y
13 ***Coughlin***	Y	N	N	N	N	Y	Y	Y
14 Coyne	Y	Y	Y	Y	Y	Y	Y	Y
15 ***Ritter***	?	?	?	N	?	Y	Y	Y
16 ***Walker***	Y	N	N	N	N	Y	N	N
17 ***Gekas***	Y	N	N	N	N	Y	Y	Y
18 Walgren	Y	Y	Y	?	Y	Y	Y	Y
19 ***Goodling***	Y	Y	Y	N	?	Y	Y	Y
20 Gaydos	Y	Y	Y	N	Y	Y	Y	Y
21 ***Ridge***	Y	N	Y	Y	N	Y	Y	Y
22 Murphy	Y	N	N	Y	Y	Y	Y	Y
23 ***Clinger***	Y	Y	Y	N	Y	Y	Y	Y
RHODE ISLAND								
1 St Germain	?	Y	Y	Y	Y	Y	N	N
2 ***Schneider***	Y	N	Y	Y	?	?	Y	Y
SOUTH CAROLINA								
1 ***Hartnett***	Y	N	N	N	Y	Y	N	?
2 ***Spence***	Y	Y	Y	N	Y	Y	N	N
3 Derrick	Y	Y	Y	Y	Y	Y	Y	Y
4 ***Campbell***	?	?	?	?	?	Y	Y	Y
5 Spratt	Y	Y	Y	Y	Y	Y	Y	Y
6 Tallon	Y	N	Y	N	Y	Y	Y	Y
SOUTH DAKOTA								
AL Daschle	Y	N	Y	Y	Y	Y	Y	Y

	399	400	401	402	403	404	405	406
TENNESSEE								
1 ***Quillen***	Y	N	N	Y	Y	Y	Y	Y
2 ***Duncan***	Y	Y	Y	N	Y	Y	N	N
3 Lloyd	?	Y	Y	N	N	Y	N	N
4 Cooper	Y	Y	Y	Y	Y	Y	Y	Y
5 Boner	Y	Y	Y	Y	Y	Y	Y	Y
6 Gordon	Y	Y	Y	Y	Y	Y	Y	Y
7 ***Sundquist***	Y	?	?	?	N	Y	Y	N
8 Jones	Y	Y	Y	Y	Y	Y	Y	Y
9 Ford	N	Y	Y	?	Y	Y	Y	Y
TEXAS								
1 Chapman	Y	N	Y	N	?	Y	Y	Y
2 Wilson	Y	Y	Y	Y	Y	Y	Y	Y
3 ***Bartlett***	Y	N	N	N	N	Y	Y	Y
4 Hall, R.	Y	N	Y	N	Y	Y	Y	Y
5 Bryant	Y	N	Y	Y	Y	Y	Y	Y
6 ***Barton***	Y	N	N	N	N	Y	Y	Y
7 ***Archer***	Y	N	N	N	N	Y	N	N
8 ***Fields***	Y	N	N	N	N	Y	Y	Y
9 Brooks	Y	Y	Y	Y	Y	Y	Y	Y
10 Pickle	Y	Y	Y	Y	Y	Y	Y	Y
11 Leath	Y	Y	Y	Y	Y	Y	Y	Y
12 Wright	Y	Y	Y	Y	Y	Y	Y	Y
13 ***Boulter***	Y	N	Y	N	N	Y	Y	Y
14 ***Sweeney***	Y	N	N	N	Y	Y	Y	Y
15 de la Garza	Y	Y	Y	Y	Y	Y	Y	Y
16 Coleman	Y	N	Y	Y	Y	Y	Y	Y
17 Stenholm	Y	N	Y	N	N	Y	Y	Y
18 Leland	N	Y	Y	Y	Y	Y	Y	Y
19 ***Combest***	Y	N	Y	N	Y	Y	N	N
20 Gonzalez	N	Y	Y	Y	Y	N	N	N
21 ***Loeffler***	Y	N	Y	N	N	Y	Y	Y
22 ***DeLay***	Y	N	N	N	N	Y	N	N
23 Bustamante	Y	Y	Y	Y	Y	Y	Y	?
24 Frost	Y	Y	Y	Y	Y	Y	Y	Y
25 Andrews	Y	Y	Y	Y	Y	Y	Y	Y
26 ***Armey***	Y	N	N	N	N	Y	N	N
27 Ortiz	Y	Y	Y	Y	Y	Y	Y	Y
UTAH								
1 ***Hansen***	?	?	?	?	Y	Y	N	N
2 ***Monson***	Y	N	N	N	N	Y	Y	Y
3 ***Nielson***	Y	N	N	N	Y	Y	Y	Y
VERMONT								
AL ***Jeffords***	Y	Y	Y	Y	Y	Y	N	N
VIRGINIA								
1 ***Bateman***	Y	Y	Y	?	Y	Y	N	Y
2 ***Whitehurst***	?	Y	N	Y	Y	Y	N	N
3 ***Bliley***	Y	Y	N	?	N	Y	Y	Y
4 Sisisky	Y	Y	Y	N	Y	Y	Y	Y
5 Daniel	Y	Y	Y	N	Y	Y	Y	N
6 Olin	Y	Y	Y	N	Y	Y	Y	Y
7 ***Slaughter***	Y	N	N	N	N	Y	Y	Y
8 ***Parris***	Y	N	Y	N	Y	Y	N	Y
9 Boucher	Y	Y	Y	Y	Y	?	?	Y
10 ***Wolf***	Y	Y	Y	N	N	Y	N	Y
WASHINGTON								
1 ***Miller***	Y	N	N	Y	Y	Y	Y	Y
2 Swift	Y	Y	Y	Y	Y	Y	Y	Y
3 Bonker	Y	Y	Y	Y	Y	Y	Y	Y
4 ***Morrison***	Y	N	Y	N	Y	Y	Y	Y
5 Foley	Y	?	Y	Y	Y	Y	Y	?
6 Dicks	Y	Y	Y	Y	Y	Y	Y	Y
7 Lowry	Y	Y	Y	Y	Y	N	Y	Y
8 ***Chandler***	Y	N	Y	N	N	Y	Y	Y
WEST VIRGINIA								
1 Mollohan	Y	Y	Y	Y	Y	Y	Y	Y
2 Staggers	Y	Y	Y	N	Y	Y	Y	Y
3 Wise	Y	Y	Y	Y	Y	Y	Y	Y
4 Rahall	Y	Y	N	Y	Y	Y	Y	Y
WISCONSIN								
1 Aspin	Y	Y	Y	Y	Y	Y	Y	Y
2 Kastenmeier	Y	Y	Y	?	Y	Y	Y	Y
3 ***Gunderson***	Y	N	N	N	N	Y	Y	Y
4 Kleczka	Y	N	N	N	+	+	+	Y
5 Moody	Y	Y	Y	Y	Y	Y	Y	Y
6 ***Petri***	Y	N	N	N	Y	Y	N	N
7 Obey	Y	N	Y	Y	Y	Y	Y	Y
8 ***Roth***	Y	N	N	N	N	Y	Y	Y
9 ***Sensenbrenner***	Y	N	N	N	N	Y	N	N
WYOMING								
AL ***Cheney***	Y	N	N	N	N	Y	N	N

Southern states - Ala., Ark., Fla., Ga., Ky., La., Miss., N.C., Okla., S.C., Tenn., Texas, Va.

* The *Congressional Record* vote number is different from the CQ vote number because the *Record* includes quorum calls in its tally. CQ does not publish quorum call votes.

407. H J Res 748. Further Interim Continuing Appropriations, Fiscal 1987. Passage of the joint resolution to appropriate funds through Oct. 10, 1986, for programs covered by the 13 regular appropriations bills, with spending at various rates determined by the status of individual bills at the time H J Res 748 was passed. Funding for the Departments of Housing and Urban Development, Labor, Health and Human Services, Education and Transportation, and for legislative branch programs would be at levels set by conference agreements on fiscal 1987 appropriations bills; for others, spending would be at fiscal 1986 levels or at levels contained in the House- or the Senate-passed 1987 bill, whichever was lowest. The measure also included a repeal of a prohibition on rehiring air traffic controllers fired in a 1981 labor dispute. Passed 264-151: R 44-130; D 220-21 (ND 150-15, SD 70-6), Oct. 8, 1986. A "nay" was a vote supporting the president's position.

408. HR 2005. 'Superfund' Reauthorization. Adoption of the conference report on the bill to reauthorize the "superfund" hazardous-waste cleanup program for fiscal 1987-91 at a funding level of $8.5 billion, and to establish a new program for cleanup of leaking underground storage tanks at $500,000. Adopted 386-27: R 147-26; D 239-1 (ND 165-0, SD 74-1), Oct. 8, 1986. A "nay" was a vote supporting the president's position.

409. H J Res 750. Further Interim Continuing Appropriations, Fiscal 1987. Passage of the joint resolution appropriating funds through Oct. 10, 1986, for programs covered by the 13 regular appropriations bills, at various rates determined by the status of the individual bills at the time H J Res 750 was passed. Funding for the Departments of Housing and Urban Development, Labor, Health and Human Services, Education and Transportation, and for legislative branch programs would be at levels set by conference agreements on fiscal 1987 appropriations bills; for others, spending would be at fiscal 1986 levels or at levels contained in the House- or Senate-passed 1987 bill, whichever was lowest. Passed 255-150: R 48-125; D 207-25 (ND 138-19, SD 69-6), Oct. 8, 1986. (Following White House threats to veto H J Res 748 because of its air traffic control provision *(see vote 407, above)*, the House passed H J Res 750, which did not include that provision.)

410. Procedural Motion. Nielson, R-Utah, motion to approve the House *Journal* of Wednesday, Oct. 8. Motion agreed to 256-117: R 48-108; D 208-9 (ND 139-7, SD 69-2), Oct. 9, 1986.

411. Procedural Motion. Gonzalez, D-Texas, motion to adjourn. Motion rejected 18-387: R 10-158; D 8-229 (ND 5-159, SD 3-70), Oct. 9, 1986. (The intent of the motion was to delay consideration of the immigration reform bill.)

412. HR 3810. Immigration Reform. Beilenson, D-Calif., motion to order the previous question (thus ending debate and the possibility of amendment) on the rule (H Res 580) to provide for House floor consideration of and to waive points of order against the bill to revise the nation's immigration laws. Motion agreed to 299-103: R 92-76; D 207-27 (ND 143-18, SD 64-9), Oct. 9, 1986.

413. HR 3810. Immigration Reform. Adoption of the rule (H Res 580) to provide for House floor consideration of and to waive points of order against the bill to revise the nation's immigration laws. Adopted 278-129: R 88-81; D 190-48 (ND 130-33, SD 60-15), Oct. 9, 1986.

414. HR 3810. Immigration Reform. Ford, D-Mich., amendment to strike provisions that exempt employers from penalties in cases where an employee is referred for employment by a state employment agency, as long as the employer retains documentation certifying that the employment agency checked the applicant's legal status. Rejected 55-342: R 1-166; D 54-176 (ND 48-109, SD 6-67), Oct. 9, 1986.

KEY

- Y Voted for (yea).
- # Paired for.
- + Announced for.
- N Voted against (nay).
- X Paired against.
- \- Announced against.
- P Voted "present."
- C Voted "present" to avoid possible conflict of interest.
- ? Did not vote or otherwise make a position known.

Democrats ***Republicans***

	407	408	409	410	411	412	413	414
ALABAMA								
1 ***Callahan***	N	N	N	Y	N	N	N	N
2 ***Dickinson***	N	N	N	N	N	Y	Y	N
3 Nichols	Y	Y	Y	Y	N	Y	Y	N
4 Bevill	Y	Y	Y	Y	N	Y	Y	N
5 Flippo	Y	Y	Y	?	?	?	?	?
6 Erdreich	Y	Y	Y	Y	N	Y	Y	N
7 Shelby	N	Y	N	Y	N	N	N	N
ALASKA								
AL ***Young***	Y	N	Y	N	N	Y	N	N
ARIZONA								
1 ***McCain***	N	Y	N	Y	N	N	N	N
2 Udall	?	Y	Y	?	N	Y	Y	N
3 ***Stump***	N	N	N	N	Y	N	N	N
4 ***Rudd***	N	N	Y	?	?	?	?	?
5 ***Kolbe***	N	Y	N	N	N	N	N	N
ARKANSAS								
1 Alexander	Y	Y	Y	Y	N	Y	Y	N
2 Robinson	Y	N	N	Y	N	N	N	N
3 ***Hammerschmidt***	Y	N	N	N	N	Y	Y	N
4 Anthony	Y	Y	Y	Y	N	Y	Y	?
CALIFORNIA								
1 Bosco	Y	Y	Y	Y	N	Y	Y	N
2 ***Chappie***	N	Y	N	N	Y	Y	N	N
3 Matsui	Y	Y	Y	Y	N	Y	Y	N
4 Fazio	Y	Y	Y	Y	N	Y	Y	N
5 Burton	?	?	?	?	?	?	?	?
6 Boxer	Y	Y	Y	Y	N	Y	Y	Y
7 Miller	Y	Y	Y	Y	N	Y	Y	Y
8 Dellums	Y	Y	Y	Y	N	N	N	Y
9 Stark	Y	?	?	?	N	Y	?	Y
10 Edwards	Y	Y	Y	Y	N	Y	N	Y
11 Lantos	Y	Y	Y	Y	N	Y	Y	N
12 ***Zschau***	N	Y	N	N	N	Y	Y	N
13 Mineta	Y	Y	Y	Y	N	Y	Y	Y
14 ***Shumway***	N	Y	N	Y	N	Y	N	N
15 Coelho	Y	Y	Y	Y	N	Y	Y	N
16 Panetta	Y	Y	Y	Y	N	Y	Y	N
17 ***Pashayan***	N	Y	N	N	N	Y	Y	N
18 Lehman	Y	Y	Y	Y	N	Y	Y	N
19 ***Lagomarsino***	N	Y	N	N	N	Y	Y	N
20 ***Thomas***	N	Y	N	N	N	Y	Y	N
21 ***Fiedler***	N	Y	N	?	N	N	N	N
22 ***Moorhead***	N	Y	N	N	N	Y	Y	N
23 Beilenson	Y	Y	Y	Y	N	Y	Y	N
24 Waxman	Y	Y	Y	Y	N	Y	Y	N
25 Roybal	Y	Y	Y	Y	Y	N	N	N
26 Berman	Y	Y	Y	Y	N	Y	Y	Y
27 Levine	Y	Y	Y	Y	N	Y	Y	N
28 Dixon	Y	Y	Y	?	N	N	N	N
29 Hawkins	Y	Y	#	N	N	N	N	Y
30 Martinez	Y	Y	N	Y	N	?	N	Y
31 Dymally	Y	Y	Y	Y	N	N	N	Y
32 Anderson	Y	Y	Y	Y	N	N	?	N
33 ***Dreier***	N	Y	N	N	N	Y	Y	N
34 Torres	Y	Y	Y	Y	N	Y	Y	N
35 ***Lewis***	N	Y	N	N	N	Y	N	N
36 Brown	Y	Y	Y	Y	N	Y	Y	Y
37 ***McCandless***	N	Y	N	N	N	Y	Y	N
38 ***Dornan***	N	Y	N	Y	N	Y	Y	N
39 ***Dannemeyer***	N	Y	N	N	N	Y	Y	N
40 ***Badham***	N	Y	N	N	N	Y	Y	N
41 ***Lowery***	N	Y	N	?	N	Y	Y	N
42 ***Lungren***	N	Y	N	N	N	Y	Y	N
43 ***Packard***	N	Y	N	N	N	Y	Y	N
44 Bates	N	Y	N	Y	N	Y	Y	N
45 ***Hunter***	N	Y	N	N	N	N	N	?
COLORADO								
1 Schroeder	N	Y	N	Y	N	N	N	N
2 Wirth	N	Y	N	Y	N	N	N	N
3 ***Strang***	N	Y	N	N	N	N	N	N
4 ***Brown***	N	Y	N	N	N	N	N	N
5 ***Kramer***	N	Y	N	N	N	N	N	N
6 ***Schaefer***	N	Y	N	N	N	Y	Y	N
CONNECTICUT								
1 Kennelly	Y	Y	Y	Y	N	Y	Y	N
2 Gejdenson	Y	Y	Y	Y	N	Y	Y	N
3 Morrison	Y	Y	Y	Y	N	Y	Y	Y
4 ***McKinney***	Y	Y	Y	Y	N	Y	Y	N
5 ***Rowland***	Y	Y	Y	N	N	Y	Y	N
6 ***Johnson***	N	Y	Y	Y	N	Y	Y	N
DELAWARE								
AL Carper	Y	Y	Y	?	N	Y	Y	Y
FLORIDA								
1 Hutto	Y	Y	Y	Y	N	Y	Y	N
2 Fuqua	Y	Y	Y	Y	N	Y	Y	N
3 Bennett	Y	Y	Y	Y	N	Y	Y	Y
4 Chappell	Y	Y	Y	Y	N	Y	Y	N
5 ***McCollum***	N	Y	N	Y	N	N	Y	N
6 MacKay	Y	Y	Y	Y	?	Y	Y	N
7 Gibbons	Y	Y	Y	Y	N	Y	Y	N
8 ***Young***	Y	Y	Y	N	N	N	N	N
9 ***Bilirakis***	N	Y	N	N	N	N	Y	N
10 ***Ireland***	N	Y	N	N	N	Y	N	N
11 Nelson	Y	Y	Y	Y	N	Y	Y	N
12 ***Lewis***	N	Y	N	N	N	N	Y	N
13 ***Mack***	N	N	N	?	N	N	N	N
14 Mica	Y	Y	Y	Y	N	?	N	N
15 ***Shaw***	N	Y	N	N	N	Y	Y	N
16 Smith	Y	Y	Y	Y	N	Y	Y	N
17 Lehman	Y	Y	Y	Y	N	Y	Y	Y
18 Pepper	Y	Y	Y	Y	N	Y	Y	N
19 Fascell	Y	Y	Y	Y	N	Y	Y	N
GEORGIA								
1 Thomas	Y	Y	Y	Y	N	Y	Y	N
2 Hatcher	Y	Y	Y	Y	N	Y	Y	N
3 Ray	N	Y	N	Y	N	Y	Y	N
4 ***Swindall***	N	Y	N	N	N	N	N	N
5 Fowler	?	?	?	?	?	?	?	?
6 ***Gingrich***	N	Y	N	N	N	Y	Y	?
7 Darden	Y	Y	Y	Y	N	Y	Y	N
8 Rowland	Y	Y	Y	Y	N	Y	Y	N
9 Jenkins	Y	Y	Y	Y	N	Y	Y	N
10 Barnard	?	?	?	?	?	?	?	X
HAWAII								
1 Abercrombie	Y	Y	Y	Y	N	Y	Y	N
2 Akaka	Y	Y	Y	Y	N	Y	N	Y
IDAHO								
1 ***Craig***	N	Y	N	N	N	N	N	N
2 Stallings	N	Y	N	Y	N	Y	Y	N
ILLINOIS								
1 Hayes	Y	Y	Y	N	N	N	N	Y
2 Savage	Y	Y	Y	?	N	N	N	Y
3 Russo	N	Y	N	Y	N	Y	Y	?
4 Vacancy								
5 Lipinski	Y	Y	Y	Y	N	Y	Y	N
6 ***Hyde***	N	Y	N	Y	N	N	N	N
7 Collins	Y	Y	Y	Y	N	Y	Y	Y
8 Rostenkowski	Y	Y	Y	Y	N	Y	Y	N
9 Yates	Y	Y	?	Y	N	Y	N	Y
10 ***Porter***	N	Y	N	N	N	N	N	N
11 Annunzio	Y	Y	Y	Y	N	Y	Y	N
12 ***Crane***	N	N	N	?	Y	N	N	N
13 ***Fawell***	N	Y	N	N	N	N	Y	N
14 ***Grotberg***	?	?	?	?	?	?	?	?
15 ***Madigan***	N	Y	N	N	N	Y	N	N
16 ***Martin***	N	Y	N	N	N	Y	Y	N
17 Evans	Y	Y	Y	Y	N	Y	N	N
18 ***Michel***	N	Y	N	N	N	Y	Y	N
19 Bruce	N	Y	N	Y	N	Y	Y	Y
20 Durbin	Y	Y	Y	Y	N	Y	Y	N
21 Price	Y	Y	Y	Y	N	Y	Y	Y
22 Gray	Y	Y	Y	?	N	Y	Y	N
INDIANA								
1 Visclosky	Y	Y	Y	Y	N	Y	Y	N
2 Sharp	Y	Y	Y	Y	N	Y	Y	N
3 ***Hiler***	N	Y	N	N	N	N	Y	N
4 ***Coats***	N	Y	N	N	N	Y	Y	N
5 ***Hillis***	Y	Y	Y	?	N	Y	Y	N

ND - Northern Democrats SD - Southern Democrats

* Corresponding to Congressional Record Votes 442, 443, 444, 445, 446, 447, 448, 450

	407	408	409	410	411	412	413	414
6 ***Burton***	N	N	N	N	N	N	N	N
7 ***Myers***	Y	Y	Y	Y	N	Y	Y	N
8 McCloskey	Y	Y	Y	Y	N	Y	Y	?
9 Hamilton	Y	Y	Y	Y	N	Y	Y	N
10 Jacobs	Y	Y	Y	N	N	N	N	N
IOWA								
1 ***Leach***	N	Y	N	N	N	Y	Y	Y
2 ***Tauke***	N	+	X	?	?	?	?	?
3 ***Evans***	N	Y	N	?	N	Y	Y	N
4 Smith	Y	Y	Y	Y	N	Y	Y	N
5 ***Lightfoot***	N	N	N	N	N	N	N	N
6 Bedell	Y	Y	Y	Y	N	Y	Y	N
KANSAS								
1 ***Roberts***	N	N	N	N	N	N	N	N
2 Slattery	N	Y	N	Y	N	Y	Y	N
3 ***Meyers***	N	Y	N	N	N	N	N	N
4 Glickman	Y	Y	Y	Y	N	Y	Y	N
5 ***Whittaker***	N	Y	N	N	N	Y	N	N
KENTUCKY								
1 Hubbard	N	Y	N	Y	N	N	N	N
2 Natcher	Y	Y	Y	Y	N	Y	Y	N
3 Mazzoli	Y	Y	Y	Y	N	Y	Y	N
4 ***Snyder***	Y	Y	Y	Y	N	Y	Y	N
5 ***Rogers***	Y	Y	Y	N	N	Y	Y	N
6 ***Hopkins***	N	Y	N	N	N	N	N	N
7 Perkins	Y	Y	Y	Y	Y	Y	Y	Y
LOUISIANA								
1 ***Livingston***	Y	Y	Y	N	N	Y	Y	N
2 Boggs	Y	Y	Y	Y	N	Y	Y	Y
3 Tauzin	Y	Y	Y	Y	N	Y	Y	N
4 Roemer	?	?	?	?	?	?	?	N
5 Huckaby	Y	Y	Y	Y	N	Y	Y	N
6 ***Moore***	?	?	?	?	?	?	?	?
7 Breaux	?	?	?	?	?	?	?	?
8 Long	Y	Y	Y	Y	N	Y	Y	N
MAINE								
1 ***McKernan***	N	Y	N	?	N	Y	N	N
2 ***Snowe***	N	Y	N	N	N	Y	N	N
MARYLAND								
1 Dyson	N	Y	Y	Y	N	Y	Y	N
2 ***Bentley***	Y	Y	Y	N	N	Y	N	N
3 Mikulski	Y	Y	Y	Y	N	Y	Y	N
4 ***Holt***	Y	Y	Y	?	N	Y	Y	N
5 Hoyer	Y	Y	Y	Y	N	Y	Y	Y
6 Byron	N	Y	N	?	N	Y	Y	N
7 Mitchell	Y	Y	?	N	N	?	Y	Y
8 Barnes	Y	Y	Y	Y	?	Y	Y	Y
MASSACHUSETTS								
1 ***Conte***	Y	Y	Y	N	N	Y	Y	N
2 Boland	Y	Y	Y	Y	N	?	?	?
3 Early	Y	Y	Y	Y	N	Y	Y	N
4 Frank	Y	Y	Y	Y	N	Y	Y	N
5 Atkins	Y	Y	Y	Y	N	Y	Y	Y
6 Mavroules	Y	Y	Y	?	N	?	Y	N
7 Markey	Y	Y	Y	Y	N	Y	Y	N
8 O'Neill								
9 Moakley	Y	Y	Y	Y	N	Y	Y	N
10 Studds	Y	Y	Y	Y	N	Y	Y	N
11 Donnelly	Y	Y	Y	Y	N	Y	Y	N
MICHIGAN								
1 Conyers	Y	Y	N	?	Y	N	N	?
2 ***Pursell***	N	Y	N	Y	N	Y	Y	N
3 Wolpe	Y	Y	Y	Y	N	Y	Y	Y
4 ***Siljander***	N	Y	N	Y	Y	Y	N	N
5 ***Henry***	N	Y	N	N	N	Y	Y	N
6 Carr	Y	Y	Y	Y	N	Y	N	N
7 Kildee	Y	Y	Y	Y	N	Y	Y	N
8 Traxler	Y	Y	Y	Y	N	Y	Y	?
9 ***Vander Jagt***	Y	Y	Y	N	N	N	Y	N
10 ***Schuette***	Y	Y	Y	N	N	N	N	N
11 ***Davis***	Y	Y	Y	Y	N	N	Y	N
12 Bonior	?	Y	Y	Y	N	Y	Y	Y
13 Crockett	Y	Y	Y	Y	N	N	N	Y
14 Hertel	Y	Y	N	Y	N	Y	Y	Y
15 Ford	Y	Y	N	?	N	Y	Y	Y
16 Dingell	Y	Y	Y	?	N	Y	Y	Y
17 Levin	Y	Y	Y	Y	N	Y	Y	Y
18 ***Broomfield***	N	Y	N	Y	N	N	Y	N
MINNESOTA								
1 Penny	N	Y	N	N	N	Y	Y	N
2 ***Weber***	N	Y	N	N	N	N	N	N
3 ***Frenzel***	N	Y	N	Y	N	Y	Y	N
4 Vento	Y	Y	Y	Y	N	Y	Y	Y
5 Sabo	Y	Y	Y	Y	N	Y	Y	N
6 Sikorski	Y	Y	N	N	N	Y	Y	Y

	407	408	409	410	411	412	413	414
7 ***Stangeland***	N	Y	N	?	N	Y	Y	N
8 Oberstar	Y	Y	Y	Y	N	Y	Y	N
MISSISSIPPI								
1 Whitten	Y	Y	Y	Y	N	Y	Y	N
2 ***Franklin***	Y	Y	Y	N	N	N	N	N
3 Montgomery	Y	Y	Y	Y	N	Y	Y	N
4 Dowdy	Y	Y	Y	Y	N	Y	Y	N
5 ***Lott***	N	N	N	N	N	Y	Y	N
MISSOURI								
1 Clay	Y	Y	N	P	N	Y	Y	Y
2 Young	Y	Y	Y	Y	N	Y	Y	Y
3 Gephardt	?	?	?	?	?	?	?	?
4 Skelton	Y	Y	Y	Y	N	Y	Y	N
5 Wheat	Y	Y	Y	Y	N	Y	Y	N
6 ***Coleman***	N	Y	N	N	N	?	Y	N
7 ***Taylor***	N	N	N	Y	N	Y	N	N
8 ***Emerson***	Y	Y	N	N	N	N	N	N
9 Volkmer	Y	Y	Y	Y	N	Y	Y	N
MONTANA								
1 Williams	Y	Y	Y	?	N	Y	Y	N
2 ***Marlenee***	N	N	N	?	N	N	N	N
NEBRASKA								
1 ***Bereuter***	N	Y	N	N	N	N	N	N
2 ***Daub***	N	N	N	N	N	N	N	N
3 ***Smith***	Y	Y	?	Y	?	?	?	N
NEVADA								
1 Reid	Y	Y	Y	Y	N	Y	Y	N
2 ***Vucanovich***	Y	Y	Y	N	N	Y	Y	N
NEW HAMPSHIRE								
1 ***Smith***	N	Y	N	N	N	N	N	N
2 ***Gregg***	N	Y	N	N	N	N	N	N
NEW JERSEY								
1 Florio	Y	Y	Y	Y	N	Y	Y	Y
2 Hughes	Y	Y	Y	Y	N	Y	N	N
3 Howard	Y	Y	Y	Y	N	Y	Y	N
4 ***Smith***	Y	Y	Y	Y	N	Y	Y	N
5 ***Roukema***	N	Y	N	N	N	N	N	N
6 Dwyer	Y	Y	Y	Y	N	Y	Y	N
7 ***Rinaldo***	Y	Y	Y	Y	N	Y	Y	N
8 Roe	Y	Y	Y	Y	N	Y	Y	N
9 Torricelli	Y	Y	Y	Y	N	Y	Y	N
10 Rodino	Y	Y	Y	Y	N	Y	Y	N
11 ***Gallo***	N	Y	N	N	N	N	N	N
12 ***Courter***	N	Y	N	N	N	N	N	N
13 ***Saxton***	Y	Y	Y	N	N	N	N	N
14 Guarini	Y	Y	Y	Y	N	Y	Y	N
NEW MEXICO								
1 ***Lujan***	N	Y	N	Y	Y	N	N	N
2 ***Skeen***	Y	N	Y	N	Y	N	N	N
3 Richardson	Y	Y	Y	Y	N	Y	Y	N
NEW YORK								
1 ***Carney***	X	Y	N	?	N	Y	Y	N
2 Downey	Y	Y	Y	?	N	Y	?	N
3 Mrazek	Y	Y	Y	Y	N	Y	Y	N
4 ***Lent***	N	Y	N	N	N	N	N	N
5 ***McGrath***	N	Y	N	N	N	N	N	N
6 Waldon	Y	Y	Y	Y	N	Y	Y	N
7 Ackerman	Y	Y	Y	Y	N	Y	Y	N
8 Scheuer	Y	Y	Y	Y	N	Y	Y	Y
9 Manton	Y	Y	?	Y	N	Y	Y	N
10 Schumer	Y	Y	Y	Y	N	Y	Y	N
11 Towns	Y	Y	Y	?	N	N	N	N
12 Owens	Y	Y	Y	?	?	N	N	Y
13 Solarz	Y	Y	Y	Y	N	Y	Y	Y
14 ***Molinari***	N	Y	N	N	N	N	N	N
15 ***Green***	Y	Y	Y	Y	N	Y	Y	N
16 Rangel	Y	Y	Y	Y	Y	Y	Y	Y
17 Weiss	#	?	?	?	?	?	#	#
18 Garcia	Y	Y	Y	Y	N	Y	Y	N
19 Biaggi	Y	Y	Y	Y	N	Y	N	Y
20 ***DioGuardi***	Y	Y	Y	Y	N	Y	Y	N
21 ***Fish***	Y	Y	Y	Y	N	Y	Y	N
22 ***Gilman***	N	Y	N	Y	N	Y	Y	N
23 Stratton	Y	Y	Y	Y	N	Y	Y	N
24 ***Solomon***	N	Y	N	N	N	N	Y	N
25 ***Boehlert***	N	Y	N	N	N	Y	Y	N
26 ***Martin***	Y	Y	N	N	?	Y	Y	N
27 ***Wortley***	Y	Y	Y	Y	N	Y	Y	N
28 McHugh	Y	Y	Y	Y	N	Y	Y	N
29 ***Horton***	Y	Y	Y	Y	N	N	Y	N
30 ***Eckert***	N	Y	N	Y	N	Y	Y	N
31 ***Kemp***	N	N	N	Y	N	N	N	N
32 LaFalce	Y	Y	?	Y	N	Y	Y	N
33 Nowak	Y	Y	Y	Y	N	Y	N	N
34 Lundine	Y	Y	?	?	N	?	Y	N

	407	408	409	410	411	412	413	414
NORTH CAROLINA								
1 Jones	Y	Y	Y	Y	N	Y	Y	N
2 Valentine	Y	Y	Y	Y	N	Y	Y	N
3 Whitley	Y	Y	Y	Y	?	Y	Y	N
4 ***Cobey***	N	Y	N	N	N	N	N	N
5 Neal	Y	Y	Y	?	N	Y	Y	N
6 ***Coble***	N	Y	N	N	N	N	N	N
7 Rose	?	?	?	?	?	?	Y	N
8 Hefner	Y	Y	Y	Y	N	?	?	?
9 ***McMillan***	Y	Y	Y	N	N	Y	N	N
10 Vacancy								
11 ***Hendon***	Y	Y	Y	N	N	N	N	N
NORTH DAKOTA								
AL Dorgan	Y	Y	Y	Y	N	Y	Y	N
OHIO								
1 Luken	Y	Y	Y	Y	N	Y	Y	N
2 ***Gradison***	Y	Y	Y	Y	N	Y	Y	N
3 Hall	N	Y	N	Y	N	Y	Y	N
4 ***Oxley***	N	Y	N	N	N	Y	Y	N
5 ***Latta***	N	Y	N	N	N	N	N	N
6 ***McEwen***	N	Y	N	Y	Y	N	N	?
7 ***DeWine***	N	Y	N	N	N	N	N	N
8 ***Kindness***	?	?	?	?	?	?	?	?
9 Kaptur	Y	Y	Y	Y	N	Y	Y	?
10 ***Miller***	Y	Y	Y	N	N	N	?	N
11 Eckart	N	Y	N	Y	N	Y	Y	N
12 ***Kasich***	N	Y	N	?	N	Y	Y	N
13 Pease	Y	Y	Y	Y	N	Y	Y	N
14 Seiberling	Y	Y	Y	?	N	Y	Y	N
15 ***Wylie***	N	Y	Y	Y	N	Y	Y	N
16 ***Regula***	N	Y	N	Y	N	Y	Y	N
17 Traficant	Y	Y	Y	Y	Y	N	N	N
18 Applegate	Y	Y	Y	Y	N	N	N	N
19 Feighan	Y	Y	Y	Y	N	Y	Y	N
20 Oakar	Y	Y	Y	Y	N	Y	Y	Y
21 Stokes	Y	Y	N	Y	N	Y	Y	Y
OKLAHOMA								
1 Jones	?	#	?	?	N	N	N	N
2 Synar	Y	Y	Y	Y	N	Y	Y	Y
3 Watkins	Y	Y	Y	Y	N	Y	N	N
4 McCurdy	Y	Y	Y	Y	N	Y	Y	?
5 ***Edwards***	N	N	N	Y	N	Y	Y	N
6 English	Y	X	Y	Y	N	Y	N	N
OREGON								
1 AuCoin	Y	Y	Y	Y	N	Y	Y	N
2 ***Smith, R.***	N	Y	N	N	N	Y	Y	N
3 Wyden	Y	Y	Y	Y	N	Y	Y	N
4 Weaver	Y	Y	Y	Y	N	Y	Y	Y
5 ***Smith, D.***	N	N	N	N	N	N	N	N
PENNSYLVANIA								
1 Foglietta	N	Y	Y	Y	N	Y	Y	N
2 Gray	Y	Y	Y	Y	N	Y	Y	Y
3 Borski	Y	?	?	Y	N	Y	Y	N
4 Kolter	Y	Y	Y	Y	N	Y	N	N
5 ***Schulze***	N	Y	N	Y	N	Y	Y	N
6 Yatron	Y	Y	Y	Y	N	Y	N	N
7 Edgar	N	Y	?	?	?	?	Y	?
8 Kostmayer	Y	Y	Y	Y	N	Y	Y	N
9 ***Shuster***	N	N	N	N	N	Y	Y	N
10 ***McDade***	Y	Y	Y	Y	N	Y	Y	N
11 Kanjorski	Y	Y	Y	?	N	N	N	N
12 Murtha	Y	Y	Y	Y	N	Y	Y	?
13 ***Coughlin***	Y	Y	Y	?	N	Y	Y	N
14 Coyne	Y	Y	Y	Y	N	Y	Y	N
15 ***Ritter***	N	+	Y	?	N	N	?	N
16 ***Walker***	N	N	N	N	N	N	N	N
17 ***Gekas***	N	Y	N	N	N	Y	Y	N
18 Walgren	Y	Y	Y	Y	N	Y	N	N
19 ***Goodling***	N	Y	Y	Y	N	Y	Y	N
20 Gaydos	Y	Y	Y	Y	N	Y	N	N
21 ***Ridge***	N	Y	N	N	N	N	N	N
22 Murphy	Y	Y	Y	Y	Y	Y	N	Y
23 ***Clinger***	Y	Y	Y	N	-	Y	Y	N
RHODE ISLAND								
1 St Germain	Y	Y	Y	Y	N	Y	Y	N
2 ***Schneider***	Y	Y	Y	Y	N	Y	Y	?
SOUTH CAROLINA								
1 ***Hartnett***	?	?	?	?	?	?	?	?
2 ***Spence***	N	Y	N	Y	N	Y	N	N
3 Derrick	Y	Y	Y	Y	N	Y	Y	N
4 ***Campbell***	?	?	?	?	?	?	X	?
5 Spratt	Y	Y	Y	Y	N	Y	Y	N
6 Tallon	Y	Y	Y	Y	N	Y	Y	N
SOUTH DAKOTA								
AL Daschle	N	Y	N	Y	N	Y	Y	N

	407	408	409	410	411	412	413	414
TENNESSEE								
1 ***Quillen***	N	Y	N	Y	N	Y	Y	N
2 ***Duncan***	N	Y	N	Y	N	Y	Y	N
3 Lloyd	Y	Y	Y	N	N	N	N	N
4 Cooper	Y	Y	Y	Y	N	Y	Y	N
5 Boner	Y	Y	Y	Y	N	Y	Y	N
6 Gordon	Y	Y	Y	Y	N	Y	Y	N
7 ***Sundquist***	N	Y	N	N	N	N	N	N
8 Jones	Y	Y	Y	Y	N	Y	N	N
9 Ford	N	Y	Y	?	N	Y	Y	Y
TEXAS								
1 Chapman	Y	Y	Y	Y	N	Y	Y	N
2 Wilson	Y	Y	Y	?	N	Y	Y	N
3 ***Bartlett***	N	Y	N	N	Y	N	N	N
4 Hall, R.	Y	Y	N	Y	N	Y	Y	N
5 Bryant	Y	Y	Y	Y	N	Y	Y	N
6 ***Barton***	N	Y	N	N	N	N	N	N
7 ***Archer***	N	N	N	Y	N	N	N	N
8 ***Fields***	N	Y	N	N	N	N	N	N
9 Brooks	Y	Y	Y	?	?	?	?	?
10 Pickle	Y	Y	Y	Y	N	N	N	N
11 Leath	Y	Y	Y	Y	N	Y	Y	N
12 Wright	Y	Y	Y	Y	N	Y	Y	?
13 ***Boulter***	N	Y	Y	Y	N	?	N	N
14 ***Sweeney***	N	Y	Y	Y	N	N	N	N
15 de la Garza	Y	Y	Y	Y	N	Y	N	N
16 Coleman	Y	Y	Y	Y	Y	N	N	N
17 Stenholm	N	Y	N	Y	Y	N	Y	N
18 Leland	Y	Y	Y	Y	N	N	N	N
19 ***Combest***	N	N	N	Y	N	N	N	N
20 Gonzalez	N	Y	P	N	Y	N	N	N
21 ***Loeffler***	Y	Y	Y	N	Y	N	N	?
22 ***DeLay***	N	N	N	?	N	N	N	N
23 Bustamante	Y	Y	Y	Y	N	Y	Y	N
24 Frost	Y	Y	Y	Y	N	Y	Y	N
25 Andrews	Y	Y	Y	Y	N	Y	N	N
26 ***Armey***	N	N	N	N	N	N	N	N
27 Ortiz	Y	Y	Y	Y	N	Y	Y	N
UTAH								
1 ***Hansen***	N	Y	N	N	N	Y	N	N
2 ***Monson***	N	Y	N	N	N	N	N	N
3 ***Nielson***	N	Y	N	N	N	Y	Y	N
VERMONT								
AL ***Jeffords***	Y	Y	Y	Y	N	Y	Y	N
VIRGINIA								
1 ***Bateman***	Y	Y	Y	?	?	?	?	?
2 ***Whitehurst***	N	Y	Y	?	N	Y	Y	N
3 ***Bliley***	Y	Y	Y	N	?	?	N	N
4 Sisisky	Y	Y	Y	Y	N	Y	Y	N
5 Daniel	Y	Y	Y	Y	N	Y	Y	N
6 Olin	Y	Y	Y	Y	N	Y	Y	N
7 ***Slaughter***	N	Y	N	N	N	N	N	N
8 ***Parris***	Y	Y	Y	N	N	Y	Y	N
9 Boucher	Y	Y	Y	Y	N	Y	Y	N
10 ***Wolf***	Y	Y	Y	N	N	Y	Y	N
WASHINGTON								
1 ***Miller***	N	Y	N	Y	N	Y	Y	N
2 Swift	Y	Y	Y	?	N	Y	Y	N
3 Bonker	Y	Y	?	Y	N	Y	Y	N
4 ***Morrison***	N	Y	N	Y	N	Y	Y	N
5 Foley	Y	Y	Y	Y	N	Y	Y	?
6 Dicks	Y	Y	Y	Y	N	Y	Y	N
7 Lowry	Y	Y	Y	N	N	Y	Y	N
8 ***Chandler***	N	Y	N	N	N	Y	Y	N
WEST VIRGINIA								
1 Mollohan	Y	Y	Y	Y	N	Y	Y	N
2 Staggers	Y	Y	Y	Y	N	Y	N	N
3 Wise	Y	Y	Y	Y	N	Y	Y	N
4 Rahall	Y	Y	Y	Y	N	Y	Y	Y
WISCONSIN								
1 Aspin	Y	Y	Y	Y	N	Y	Y	?
2 Kastenmeier	Y	Y	Y	Y	N	Y	Y	Y
3 ***Gunderson***	N	Y	N	N	N	Y	Y	N
4 Kleczka	Y	Y	Y	Y	N	Y	N	N
5 Moody	Y	Y	Y	Y	N	Y	Y	N
6 ***Petri***	N	Y	N	Y	N	N	N	N
7 Obey	Y	Y	Y	Y	N	Y	Y	N
8 ***Roth***	N	Y	N	N	N	N	N	N
9 ***Sensenbrenner***	N	Y	N	N	Y	N	N	N
WYOMING								
AL ***Cheney***	N	N	N	N	N	N	Y	N

Southern states - Ala., Ark., Fla., Ga., Ky., La., Miss., N.C., Okla., S.C., Tenn., Texas, Va.

* The *Congressional Record* vote number is different from the CQ vote number because the *Record* includes quorum calls in its tally. CQ does not publish quorum call votes.

415. HR 3810. Immigration Reform. Bartlett, R-Texas, amendment to allow only civil rather than criminal penalties for engaging in a pattern or practice of knowingly hiring illegal aliens. Rejected 137-264: R 71-97; D 66-167 (ND 48-110, SD 18-57), Oct. 9, 1986.

416. HR 3810. Immigration Reform. Sensenbrenner, R-Wis., amendment to strike provisions barring discrimination based on citizenship status and setting up a special office within the Justice Department to investigate bias claims. Rejected 140-260: R 115-54; D 25-206 (ND 5-151, SD 20-55), Oct. 9, 1986. A "yea" was a vote supporting the president's position.

417. HR 3810. Immigration Reform. De la Garza, D-Texas, amendment to require Immigration and Naturalization Service employees to obtain warrants before searching open fields for violations of immigration laws. Adopted 221-170: R 85-79; D 136-91 (ND 98-58, SD 38-33), Oct. 9, 1986. A "nay" was a vote supporting the president's position.

418. HR 3810. Immigration Reform. Gonzalez, D-Texas, amendment to assure that a family containing at least one member eligible for housing assistance could receive assistance without regard to legal status of other family members. Rejected 73-310: R 5-157; D 68-153 (ND 56-94, SD 12-59), Oct. 9, 1986.

419. HR 3810. Immigration Reform. McCollum, R-Fla., amendment to strike the program that would grant legal status to millions of illegal aliens already in the country who could meet certain conditions. Rejected 192-199: R 124-40; D 68-159 (ND 21-131, SD 47-28), Oct. 9, 1986.

420. HR 3810. Immigration Reform. Fish, R-N.Y., amendment to strike provisions that would provide temporary legal status to Salvadorans and Nicaraguans already in the United States. Rejected 197-199: R 145-22; D 52-177 (ND 12-143, SD 40-34), Oct. 9, 1986.

421. HR 3810. Immigration Reform. Passage of the bill to overhaul the nation's immigration laws by creating a new system of penalties against employers who knowingly hire illegal aliens, providing legal status to millions of illegal aliens already in the United States, and creating a special program for foreigners to gain legal status if they have a history of working in U.S. agriculture. Passed 230-166: R 62-105; D 168-61 (ND 126-29, SD 42-32), Oct. 9, 1986. (The House subsequently moved to strike the provisions of S 1200, the Senate-passed version of the bill, and insert the provisions of HR 3810. The House then passed S 1200 by voice vote.)

422. H J Res 751. Further Interim Continuing Appropriations, Fiscal 1987. Adoption of the rule (H Res 583) to provide for House floor consideration of the joint resolution to appropriate funds through Oct. 15, 1986, for programs covered by the 13 regular appropriations bills, at various rates determined by the status of the individual bills at the time H J Res 751 was passed. Funding for the Departments of Housing and Urban Development, Labor, Health and Human Services, Education and Transportation, and for legislative branch programs would be at levels set by conference agreements on fiscal 1987 appropriations bills; for others, spending would be at fiscal 1986 levels or at levels contained in the House- or Senate-passed 1987 bill, whichever was lowest. Adopted 265-115: R 51-110; D 214-5 (ND 149-1, SD 65-4), Oct. 10, 1986.

KEY

- Y Voted for (yea).
- # Paired for.
- + Announced for.
- N Voted against (nay).
- X Paired against.
- - Announced against.
- P Voted "present."
- C Voted "present" to avoid possible conflict of interest.
- ? Did not vote or otherwise make a position known.

Democrats *Republicans*

	415	416	417	418	419	420	421	422
ALABAMA								
1 *Callahan*	Y	Y	Y	N	Y	Y	N	N
2 *Dickinson*	N	N	N	N	Y	Y	N	N
3 Nichols	N	Y	N	N	Y	?	X	?
4 Bevill	N	N	N	N	Y	Y	N	Y
5 Flippo	N	N	N	N	Y	Y	N	Y
6 Erdreich	N	N	N	N	Y	Y	N	Y
7 Shelby	N	N	N	N	Y	Y	N	Y
ALASKA								
AL *Young*	Y	N	Y	Y	Y	Y	N	Y
ARIZONA								
1 *McCain*	Y	N	Y	N	N	Y	N	?
2 Udall	Y	N	Y	Y	N	N	Y	Y
3 *Stump*	Y	Y	Y	N	Y	Y	N	N
4 *Rudd*	?	?	?	?	?	?	?	?
5 *Kolbe*	Y	N	Y	N	Y	Y	N	?
ARKANSAS								
1 Alexander	N	N	N	N	N	N	Y	Y
2 Robinson	N	Y	N	N	Y	Y	N	Y
3 *Hammerschmidt*	N	Y	Y	N	Y	Y	N	N
4 Anthony	Y	N	N	N	N	Y	Y	Y
CALIFORNIA								
1 Bosco	?	N	Y	N	?	N	Y	Y
2 *Chappie*	Y	Y	Y	N	?	Y	N	N
3 Matsui	Y	N	Y	N	N	N	Y	Y
4 Fazio	Y	N	Y	Y	N	N	Y	Y
5 Burton	?	?	?	?	?	?	?	?
6 Boxer	N	N	Y	?	N	N	Y	Y
7 Miller	N	N	Y	?	N	N	Y	Y
8 Dellums	Y	N	Y	Y	N	N	N	Y
9 Stark	N	N	N	?	N	N	Y	Y
10 Edwards	Y	N	Y	Y	N	N	N	Y
11 Lantos	N	N	Y	N	N	N	Y	Y
12 *Zschau*	N	N	Y	N	N	N	Y	?
13 Mineta	N	N	Y	Y	N	N	Y	Y
14 *Shumway*	Y	Y	Y	N	Y	Y	N	N
15 Coelho	N	N	Y	N	N	N	Y	Y
16 Panetta	N	N	Y	N	N	N	Y	Y
17 *Pashayan*	Y	N	Y	N	?	Y	Y	N
18 Lehman	Y	N	Y	N	N	N	Y	Y
19 *Lagomarsino*	Y	N	Y	N	N	Y	Y	N
20 *Thomas*	N	N	Y	N	N	Y	N	N
21 *Fiedler*	N	Y	Y	N	Y	Y	N	N
22 *Moorhead*	N	Y	Y	N	Y	Y	Y	Y
23 Beilenson	N	N	Y	N	N	N	Y	Y
24 Waxman	N	N	Y	N	N	N	Y	Y
25 Roybal	Y	N	Y	Y	N	N	N	Y
26 Berman	N	N	Y	Y	N	N	Y	Y
27 Levine	N	N	Y	Y	N	N	Y	Y
28 Dixon	N	N	Y	N	N	N	Y	?
29 Hawkins	Y	N	Y	Y	N	N	N	Y
30 Martinez	Y	N	Y	Y	N	N	N	Y
31 Dymally	Y	N	Y	Y	N	N	N	Y
32 Anderson	N	N	Y	N	N	N	Y	Y
33 *Dreier*	N	Y	Y	N	Y	Y	N	N
34 Torres	Y	N	Y	Y	N	N	Y	Y
35 *Lewis*	N	Y	Y	N	N	Y	Y	N
36 Brown	Y	N	Y	Y	N	N	Y	Y
37 *McCandless*	Y	Y	Y	N	Y	Y	Y	N
38 *Dornan*	N	N	Y	N	N	Y	Y	N
39 *Dannemeyer*	Y	N	Y	N	Y	Y	Y	N
40 *Badham*	N	Y	Y	N	N	Y	Y	N
41 *Lowery*	N	Y	Y	N	N	Y	Y	N
42 *Lungren*	N	Y	Y	N	N	Y	Y	N
43 *Packard*	N	Y	Y	N	N	Y	Y	N
44 Bates	N	N	Y	N	N	N	Y	Y
45 *Hunter*	Y	Y	N	N	Y	Y	N	N
COLORADO								
1 Schroeder	N	N	Y	Y	Y	N	N	Y
2 Wirth	N	N	Y	N	N	N	N	?
3 *Strang*	Y	Y	Y	N	Y	Y	Y	N
4 *Brown*	Y	Y	Y	N	Y	Y	N	N
5 *Kramer*	Y	N	Y	N	Y	Y	N	N
6 *Schaefer*	N	Y	Y	N	Y	Y	Y	N
CONNECTICUT								
1 Kennelly	Y	N	N	N	N	N	Y	Y
2 Gejdenson	Y	N	Y	N	N	N	Y	Y
3 Morrison	N	N	Y	Y	N	N	Y	Y
4 *McKinney*	N	N	N	Y	N	N	Y	Y
5 *Rowland*	Y	Y	N	N	N	Y	Y	Y
6 *Johnson*	Y	N	N	N	N	Y	Y	Y
DELAWARE								
AL Carper	N	N	N	N	N	N	Y	Y
FLORIDA								
1 Hutto	N	Y	N	N	Y	Y	Y	Y
2 Fuqua	N	N	Y	N	Y	Y	Y	?
3 Bennett	N	N	N	N	Y	Y	Y	Y
4 Chappell	N	N	?	N	Y	Y	Y	Y
5 *McCollum*	N	Y	N	N	Y	Y	N	Y
6 MacKay	N	N	N	N	Y	N	Y	Y
7 Gibbons	Y	N	Y	N	N	Y	Y	Y
8 *Young*	N	Y	Y	N	Y	Y	N	Y
9 *Bilirakis*	Y	N	Y	N	Y	Y	N	N
10 *Ireland*	?	Y	?	N	Y	Y	N	N
11 Nelson	N	N	N	N	Y	Y	Y	Y
12 *Lewis*	N	Y	Y	N	Y	Y	N	N
13 *Mack*	N	Y	Y	N	Y	Y	N	N
14 Mica	N	N	X	X	Y	Y	Y	Y
15 *Shaw*	N	Y	N	N	Y	Y	Y	N
16 Smith	N	N	N	N	N	N	Y	Y
17 Lehman	N	N	Y	?	N	N	Y	Y
18 Pepper	N	N	Y	Y	N	N	Y	Y
19 Fascell	N	N	Y	Y	N	N	Y	Y
GEORGIA								
1 Thomas	N	Y	Y	N	Y	Y	Y	Y
2 Hatcher	Y	Y	Y	N	Y	Y	Y	Y
3 Ray	N	Y	Y	N	Y	Y	N	Y
4 *Swindall*	N	Y	N	N	Y	Y	N	N
5 Fowler	?	?	?	?	?	?	?	?
6 *Gingrich*	N	Y	Y	N	N	Y	Y	N
7 Darden	N	Y	N	N	Y	N	Y	Y
8 Rowland	N	N	N	N	Y	N	Y	Y
9 Jenkins	N	Y	N	N	Y	Y	Y	Y
10 Barnard	X	X	#	#	#	?	X	Y
HAWAII								
1 Abercrombie	N	N	Y	N	N	N	Y	Y
2 Akaka	Y	N	Y	Y	N	N	N	Y
IDAHO								
1 *Craig*	Y	Y	Y	N	Y	Y	N	N
2 Stallings	Y	Y	Y	N	Y	Y	Y	Y
ILLINOIS								
1 Hayes	Y	N	N	Y	N	N	N	Y
2 Savage	Y	N	Y	Y	N	N	N	Y
3 Russo	?	?	?	?	?	?	?	?
4 Vacancy								
5 Lipinski	N	N	N	N	N	Y	Y	Y
6 *Hyde*	N	N	N	N	Y	Y	N	N
7 Collins	N	N	N	Y	N	N	Y	Y
8 Rostenkowski	N	N	Y	N	N	N	Y	Y
9 Yates	N	N	?	?	?	?	?	Y
10 *Porter*	N	Y	N	N	Y	Y	Y	Y
11 Annunzio	N	N	Y	N	N	N	Y	Y
12 *Crane*	Y	Y	Y	N	Y	Y	N	N
13 *Fawell*	N	Y	N	N	Y	Y	N	N
14 *Grotberg*	?	?	?	?	?	?	?	?
15 *Madigan*	N	Y	Y	N	Y	Y	N	N
16 *Martin*	N	Y	Y	N	Y	Y	Y	Y
17 Evans	Y	N	Y	Y	N	N	N	Y
18 *Michel*	N	N	N	N	N	Y	Y	Y
19 Bruce	Y	N	Y	N	N	N	Y	Y
20 Durbin	Y	N	Y	N	N	N	Y	Y
21 Price	N	N	Y	N	N	N	Y	Y
22 Gray	Y	N	Y	Y	N	N	Y	Y
INDIANA								
1 Visclosky	Y	N	N	Y	N	N	Y	Y
2 Sharp	N	N	N	N	N	N	Y	Y
3 *Hiler*	Y	Y	N	N	Y	Y	N	N
4 *Coats*	N	Y	N	N	Y	Y	N	N
5 *Hillis*	N	Y	?	?	?	?	?	?

ND - Northern Democrats SD - Southern Democrats

* Corresponding to Congressional Record Votes 451, 452, 453, 454, 455, 456, 457, 458

	415	416	417	418	419	420	421	422
6 ***Burton***	Y	Y	Y	N	Y	Y	N	N
7 ***Myers***	N	N	N	N	Y	Y	N	Y
8 McCloskey	N	N	N	N	Y	N	Y	Y
9 Hamilton	N	N	N	N	N	N	Y	Y
10 Jacobs	Y	N	N	N	Y	N	N	Y
IOWA								
1 ***Leach***	N	N	N	N	N	N	Y	N
2 ***Tauke***	?	?	?	?	?	?	?	?
3 ***Evans***	N	N	Y	N	N	Y	Y	N
4 Smith	N	N	Y	N	N	Y	Y	Y
5 ***Lightfoot***	Y	Y	N	N	Y	N	Y	N
6 Bedell	N	N	Y	N	N	N	Y	Y
KANSAS								
1 ***Roberts***	Y	Y	Y	N	Y	Y	N	N
2 Slattery	N	N	Y	N	N	N	Y	Y
3 ***Meyers***	N	N	N	N	Y	Y	N	N
4 Glickman	N	N	Y	N	N	Y	Y	Y
5 ***Whittaker***	N	Y	N	N	Y	Y	N	N
KENTUCKY								
1 Hubbard	N	N	Y	N	Y	Y	N	N
2 Natcher	N	N	Y	N	N	Y	Y	Y
3 Mazzoli	N	N	Y	N	N	Y	Y	Y
4 ***Snyder***	N	Y	N	N	Y	Y	N	?
5 ***Rogers***	N	Y	N	N	Y	Y	Y	Y
6 ***Hopkins***	N	N	N	N	Y	Y	N	N
7 Perkins	N	N	Y	Y	N	N	Y	Y
LOUISIANA								
1 ***Livingston***	N	Y	N	N	Y	Y	Y	N
2 Boggs	Y	N	?	Y	N	N	Y	Y
3 Tauzin	N	Y	N	N	Y	Y	N	Y
4 Roemer	N	N	N	N	Y	Y	N	N
5 Huckaby	Y	Y	Y	N	Y	Y	Y	Y
6 ***Moore***	?	?	?	?	?	?	?	?
7 Breaux	?	?	?	?	?	?	?	?
8 Long	N	N	Y	?	N	N	Y	Y
MAINE								
1 ***McKernan***	N	N	Y	N	N	N	Y	N
2 ***Snowe***	N	N	Y	N	Y	N	Y	N
MARYLAND								
1 Dyson	N	Y	Y	N	Y	Y	Y	Y
2 ***Bentley***	N	Y	N	N	Y	N	N	?
3 Mikulski	N	N	Y	N	N	N	Y	Y
4 ***Holt***	N	Y	N	N	Y	Y	N	?
5 Hoyer	N	N	N	N	Y	N	Y	Y
6 Byron	N	N	N	N	Y	Y	Y	Y
7 Mitchell	Y	?	?	?	?	?	X	?
8 Barnes	N	N	Y	N	N	N	Y	Y
MASSACHUSETTS								
1 ***Conte***	N	N	N	N	N	N	Y	Y
2 Boland	?	?	?	?	?	?	#	?
3 Early	N	N	N	N	N	N	Y	?
4 Frank	N	N	N	Y	N	N	Y	Y
5 Atkins	N	N	N	N	N	N	Y	Y
6 Mavroules	N	N	N	N	N	N	Y	Y
7 Markey	N	N	?	?	?	N	Y	Y
8 O'Neill						N		
9 Moakley	N	N	N	N	N	N	Y	Y
10 Studds	N	N	Y	Y	N	N	Y	Y
11 Donnelly	N	N	N	N	N	N	Y	Y
MICHIGAN								
1 Conyers	?	?	?	?	X	?	X	?
2 ***Pursell***	N	N	N	N	Y	Y	N	N
3 Wolpe	Y	N	Y	Y	N	N	Y	Y
4 ***Siljander***	N	Y	N	N	Y	Y	N	N
5 ***Henry***	N	N	N	N	N	Y	Y	N
6 Carr	N	Y	Y	N	Y	N	N	Y
7 Kildee	Y	N	Y	Y	N	N	Y	Y
8 Traxler	?	?	?	?	?	?	?	?
9 ***Vander Jagt***	Y	Y	Y	N	Y	Y	N	N
10 ***Schuette***	Y	Y	Y	N	Y	Y	N	Y
11 ***Davis***	N	Y	Y	N	N	Y	Y	N
12 Bonior	N	N	Y	Y	N	N	Y	Y
13 Crockett	N	?	?	?	?	?	?	Y
14 Hertel	Y	N	Y	Y	N	N	Y	Y
15 Ford	Y	N	N	N	?	N	Y	Y
16 Dingell	N	N	Y	Y	N	Y	Y	Y
17 Levin	Y	N	Y	N	N	Y	Y	Y
18 ***Broomfield***	N	Y	N	N	Y	Y	N	N
MINNESOTA								
1 Penny	N	N	Y	N	N	N	Y	Y
2 ***Weber***	N	Y	Y	N	N	Y	Y	?
3 ***Frenzel***	N	N	N	N	Y	Y	Y	N
4 Vento	N	N	N	Y	N	N	Y	Y
5 Sabo	N	N	N	Y	N	N	Y	Y
6 Sikorski	N	N	N	N	N	N	N	Y
7 ***Stangeland***	N	N	Y	N	Y	Y	Y	N
8 Oberstar	N	N	N	N	N	N	Y	Y
MISSISSIPPI								
1 Whitten	N	N	Y	N	N	N	N	Y
2 ***Franklin***	Y	Y	N	N	Y	Y	N	N
3 Montgomery	N	Y	N	N	Y	Y	N	Y
4 Dowdy	Y	Y	N	N	Y	Y	N	Y
5 ***Lott***	N	Y	N	N	Y	Y	Y	N
MISSOURI								
1 Clay	N	N	Y	Y	N	N	Y	Y
2 Young	N	N	N	Y	N	N	Y	Y
3 Gephardt	#	?	?	?	X	?	#	Y
4 Skelton	N	Y	N	N	Y	Y	N	Y
5 Wheat	N	N	Y	N	N	N	Y	Y
6 ***Coleman***	N	Y	Y	N	Y	Y	Y	N
7 ***Taylor***	N	Y	Y	N	Y	Y	N	Y
8 ***Emerson***	Y	Y	Y	N	Y	Y	N	Y
9 Volkmer	N	Y	N	N	Y	N	N	Y
MONTANA								
1 Williams	Y	N	Y	Y	N	N	Y	?
2 ***Marlenee***	Y	Y	Y	N	N	Y	N	N
NEBRASKA								
1 ***Bereuter***	N	N	N	N	Y	Y	N	N
2 ***Daub***	N	N	N	N	Y	Y	N	N
3 ***Smith***	Y	Y	?	?	?	Y	Y	Y
NEVADA								
1 Reid	Y	N	N	N	Y	N	N	Y
2 ***Vucanovich***	Y	Y	N	N	Y	Y	Y	N
NEW HAMPSHIRE								
1 ***Smith***	N	Y	N	N	Y	Y	N	N
2 ***Gregg***	N	Y	N	N	Y	Y	N	N
NEW JERSEY								
1 Florio	N	N	N	N	N	N	Y	Y
2 Hughes	N	N	N	N	N	N	N	Y
3 Howard	N	N	Y	Y	N	N	Y	Y
4 ***Smith***	N	N	N	N	N	N	Y	Y
5 ***Roukema***	N	Y	N	?	Y	Y	N	Y
6 Dwyer	N	N	N	N	N	N	Y	Y
7 ***Rinaldo***	Y	N	N	N	N	N	N	Y
8 Roe	N	N	N	N	N	N	Y	Y
9 Torricelli	N	N	N	N	N	N	Y	Y
10 Rodino	N	N	Y	Y	N	N	Y	Y
11 ***Gallo***	Y	N	N	N	Y	Y	N	N
12 ***Courter***	Y	N	N	N	N	Y	N	N
13 ***Saxton***	Y	N	Y	N	Y	Y	N	N
14 Guarini	Y	N	N	Y	N	N	N	Y
NEW MEXICO								
1 ***Lujan***	Y	N	Y	N	Y	Y	Y	Y
2 ***Skeen***	Y	N	Y	N	Y	Y	N	Y
3 Richardson	Y	N	Y	Y	N	N	Y	Y
NEW YORK								
1 ***Carney***	N	Y	N	?	Y	Y	N	N
2 Downey	Y	N	Y	N	N	N	Y	Y
3 Mrazek	N	N	Y	N	N	N	Y	Y
4 ***Lent***	N	N	N	N	Y	Y	N	N
5 ***McGrath***	N	Y	N	N	Y	N	N	N
6 Waldon	N	N	Y	Y	N	N	Y	Y
7 Ackerman	N	N	N	Y	N	N	Y	Y
8 Scheuer	N	N	N	N	N	N	Y	Y
9 Manton	N	N	Y	N	N	N	Y	Y
10 Schumer	N	N	Y	N	N,	N	Y	Y
11 Towns	Y	N	Y	Y	N	N	N	Y
12 Owens	Y	?	N	Y	N	N	Y	?
13 Solarz	N	?	?	#	?	?	#	Y
14 ***Molinari***	Y	Y	N	N	Y	Y	N	N
15 ***Green***	N	N	N	Y	N	Y	Y	Y
16 Rangel	Y	N	Y	Y	N	N	Y	Y
17 Weiss	?	?	?	?	?	X	?	?
18 Garcia	Y	N	Y	Y	N	N	N	Y
19 Biaggi	N	N	N	N	N	N	Y	Y
20 ***DioGuardi***	N	N	N	N	Y	Y	Y	Y
21 ***Fish***	N	N	N	N	N	Y	Y	Y
22 ***Gilman***	N	N	N	N	N	N	Y	Y
23 Stratton	N	N	N	N	Y	Y	Y	Y
24 ***Solomon***	Y	Y	?	?	?	?	-	N
25 ***Boehlert***	N	N	N	N	N	N	Y	N
26 ***Martin***	Y	Y	N	N	Y	Y	N	Y
27 ***Wortley***	N	N	N	Y	Y	N	Y	Y
28 McHugh	N	N	N	N	N	N	Y	Y
29 ***Horton***	Y	N	Y	N	Y	N	N	Y
30 ***Eckert***	N	Y	N	N	Y	Y	N	Y
31 ***Kemp***	Y	N	Y	N	N	Y	N	N
32 LaFalce	N	N	N	N	N	Y	Y	Y
33 Nowak	N	N	N	N	N	N	Y	Y
34 Lundine	N	N	Y	Y	N	N	Y	?
NORTH CAROLINA								
1 Jones	N	N	Y	N	N	Y	N	Y
2 Valentine	N	Y	N	N	Y	Y	N	Y
3 Whitley	N	N	Y	N	Y	Y	N	Y
4 ***Cobey***	N	Y	Y	N	Y	Y	N	N
5 Neal	N	N	Y	N	Y	N	Y	Y
6 ***Coble***	Y	Y	Y	N	Y	Y	N	N
7 Rose	N	N	Y	N	Y	N	Y	Y
8 Hefner	?	?	?	?	?	?	?	Y
9 ***McMillan***	N	Y	N	N	Y	Y	Y	N
10 Vacancy								
11 ***Hendon***	Y	Y	N	N	Y	N	N	N
NORTH DAKOTA								
AL Dorgan	N	N	N	N	N	N	Y	Y
OHIO								
1 Luken	N	N	Y	N	N	N	Y	Y
2 ***Gradison***	N	Y	N	N	Y	N	N	Y
3 Hall	Y	N	Y	N	N	?	?	?
4 ***Oxley***	Y	Y	N	N	N	Y	N	N
5 ***Latta***	Y	Y	Y	N	Y	Y	N	Y
6 ***McEwen***	?	#	?	X	#	#	#	N
7 ***DeWine***	Y	Y	N	N	N	Y	Y	N
8 ***Kindness***	?	?	?	?	?	?	?	?
9 Kaptur	?	?	?	?	?	?	?	?
10 ***Miller***	N	Y	N	N	Y	Y	N	Y
11 Eckart	Y	N	Y	N	N	N	Y	Y
12 ***Kasich***	Y	Y	?	N	Y	Y	N	N
13 Pease	N	N	N	N	N	N	Y	Y
14 Seiberling	N	N	Y	Y	N	N	Y	?
15 ***Wylie***	N	Y	N	N	Y	Y	N	Y
16 ***Regula***	N	Y	N	N	Y	N	N	Y
17 Traficant	N	N	Y	N	Y	Y	N	Y
18 Applegate	N	N	N	N	Y	Y	N	Y
19 Feighan	N	N	N	N	N	N	Y	Y
20 Oakar	Y	N	Y	Y	N	N	Y	Y
21 Stokes	N	N	Y	Y	N	N	Y	?
OKLAHOMA								
1 Jones	N	N	Y	N	Y	N	Y	?
2 Synar	N	N	N	N	N	N	Y	Y
3 Watkins	N	N	Y	N	Y	N	N	Y
4 McCurdy	?	?	?	?	?	?	?	?
5 ***Edwards***	?	?	?	?	?	?	?	?
6 English	N	N	Y	N	Y	Y	N	Y
OREGON								
1 AuCoin	Y	N	Y	N	N	N	Y	Y
2 ***Smith, R.***	Y	Y	Y	N	Y	Y	N	N
3 Wyden	Y	N	Y	N	N	N	Y	Y
4 Weaver	N	N	Y	?	?	?	?	Y
5 ***Smith, D.***	Y	Y	Y	N	Y	Y	N	N
PENNSYLVANIA								
1 Foglietta	N	N	Y	Y	N	N	Y	Y
2 Gray	?	?	Y	Y	N	N	Y	Y
3 Borski	N	N	Y	N	N	N	Y	Y
4 Kolter	N	N	N	N	Y	N	N	Y
5 ***Schulze***	N	?	?	?	?	?	?	?
6 Yatron	N	N	N	N	Y	?	N	Y
7 Edgar	?	?	?	?	?	?	?	?
8 Kostmayer	N	N	Y	N	N	N	Y	?
9 ***Shuster***	N	Y	N	N	Y	Y	N	N
10 ***McDade***	N	N	Y	N	Y	N	Y	Y
11 Kanjorski	N	N	N	Y	Y	N	Y	Y
12 Murtha	N	N	Y	N	N	N	Y	Y
13 ***Coughlin***	N	Y	N	N	N	N	Y	Y
14 Coyne	N	N	N	Y	N	N	Y	Y
15 ***Ritter***	N	Y	Y	N	Y	Y	N	Y
16 ***Walker***	N	Y	Y	N	Y	Y	N	N
17 ***Gekas***	N	Y	N	N	Y	Y	N	N
18 Walgren	N	N	N	N	N	N	Y	Y
19 ***Goodling***	Y	Y	Y	N	Y	Y	Y	Y
20 Gaydos	N	N	Y	N	N	N	N	Y
21 ***Ridge***	N	N	Y	N	Y	Y	Y	Y
22 Murphy	N	N	N	N	Y	N	N	Y
23 ***Clinger***	N	N	Y	N	N	N	Y	Y
RHODE ISLAND								
1 St Germain	N	N	N	N	N	N	Y	Y
2 ***Schneider***	?	?	?	?	?	?	?	Y
SOUTH CAROLINA								
1 ***Hartnett***	?	?	?	?	?	?	?	?
2 ***Spence***	N	Y	N	N	Y	Y	N	N
3 Derrick	N	Y	Y	N	N	N	Y	Y
4 ***Campbell***	?	?	?	?	?	?	?	?
5 Spratt	N	N	Y	N	N	N	Y	Y
6 Tallon	N	Y	N	N	Y	Y	N	Y
SOUTH DAKOTA								
AL Daschle	N	N	Y	N	Y	N	Y	Y
TENNESSEE								
1 ***Quillen***	Y	N	N	?	Y	Y	Y	Y
2 ***Duncan***	N	Y	N	N	Y	Y	N	N
3 Lloyd	N	N	Y	N	Y	Y	N	N
4 Cooper	N	N	N	N	N	Y	Y	Y
5 Boner	N	N	N	N	Y	Y	N	Y
6 Gordon	Y	N	N	N	Y	Y	N	Y
7 ***Sundquist***	N	Y	N	N	Y	Y	N	N
8 Jones	N	N	Y	N	Y	Y	N	Y
9 Ford	N	N	Y	Y	N	N	Y	Y
TEXAS								
1 Chapman	Y	Y	N	N	Y	N	N	Y
2 Wilson	N	N	N	N	Y	Y	Y	?
3 ***Bartlett***	Y	N	Y	N	Y	Y	N	?
4 Hall, R.	N	Y	Y	N	Y	Y	N	Y
5 Bryant	N	N	N	N	Y	N	Y	Y
6 ***Barton***	Y	Y	N	N	Y	Y	N	N
7 ***Archer***	Y	Y	Y	N	Y	Y	N	N
8 ***Fields***	Y	Y	Y	N	Y	Y	N	N
9 Brooks	?	?	?	?	?	?	?	?
10 Pickle	Y	Y	Y	N	N	N	Y	Y
11 Leath	Y	N	?	?	Y	Y	N	Y
12 Wright	N	N	Y	Y	N	N	Y	Y
13 ***Boulter***	Y	Y	Y	N	Y	Y	N	Y
14 ***Sweeney***	Y	Y	Y	N	Y	Y	N	N
15 de la Garza	Y	N	Y	Y	N	N	N	Y
16 Coleman	Y	N	Y	Y	Y	N	N	Y
17 Stenholm	Y	Y	Y	N	Y	Y	N	Y
18 Leland	Y	N	Y	Y	N	N	N	+
19 ***Combest***	Y	Y	Y	N	Y	Y	N	N
20 Gonzalez	Y	N	Y	Y	N	N	N	N
21 ***Loeffler***	Y	Y	Y	N	Y	Y	N	Y
22 ***DeLay***	Y	Y	Y	N	Y	Y	N	N
23 Bustamante	Y	N	N	Y	N	N	Y	Y
24 Frost	N	N	N	N	Y	N	Y	Y
25 Andrews	Y	N	N	N	Y	N	N	?
26 ***Armey***	Y	Y	Y	N	Y	Y	N	N
27 Ortiz	Y	N	N	Y	N	N	Y	Y
UTAH								
1 ***Hansen***	Y	Y	Y	N	Y	Y	N	N
2 ***Monson***	Y	Y	Y	N	Y	Y	Y	N
3 ***Nielson***	Y	Y	Y	N	Y	Y	Y	N
VERMONT								
AL ***Jeffords***	N	Y	N	?	N	N	Y	N
VIRGINIA								
1 ***Bateman***	?	Y	N	N	Y	Y	N	Y
2 ***Whitehurst***	N	Y	Y	N	Y	Y	N	?
3 ***Bliley***	Y	Y	Y	N	Y	Y	N	Y
4 Sisisky	N	N	Y	N	N	N	Y	Y
5 Daniel	?	?	?	?	?	?	?	?
6 Olin	N	Y	Y	N	Y	Y	N	?
7 ***Slaughter***	Y	Y	Y	N	Y	Y	N	Y
8 ***Parris***	Y	Y	N	N	Y	Y	N	Y
9 Boucher	N	N	Y	N	N	N	Y	?
10 ***Wolf***	N	Y	N	N	Y	Y	N	Y
WASHINGTON								
1 ***Miller***	N	N	N	N	N	Y	Y	N
2 Swift	Y	N	Y	Y	N	N	Y	Y
3 Bonker	N	N	Y	N	N	N	Y	Y
4 ***Morrison***	Y	N	Y	Y	N	Y	Y	N
5 Foley	N	N	Y	N	N	N	Y	Y
6 Dicks	?	N	Y	?	N	N	Y	Y
7 Lowry	Y	N	Y	Y	N	N	Y	N
8 ***Chandler***	N	N	Y	N	N	Y	Y	N
WEST VIRGINIA								
1 Mollohan	Y	N	N	N	Y	N	Y	Y
2 Staggers	N	N	N	N	Y	N	Y	Y
3 Wise	N	N	N	N	Y	N	Y	Y
4 Rahall	Y	N	N	N	N	N	Y	?
WISCONSIN								
1 Aspin	N	N	N	N	N	N	Y	Y
2 Kastenmeier	N	N	Y	Y	N	N	Y	Y
3 ***Gunderson***	Y	Y	Y	N	N	Y	Y	N
4 Kleczka	N	N	Y	N	N	N	N	Y
5 Moody	N	N	Y	?	?	N	Y	Y
6 ***Petri***	N	Y	N	N	Y	Y	N	N
7 Obey	N	N	Y	N	N	N	Y	Y
8 ***Roth***	N	Y	N	N	Y	Y	N	Y
9 ***Sensenbrenner***	N	Y	N	N	Y	Y	N	N
WYOMING								
AL ***Cheney***	Y	Y	Y	N	Y	Y	Y	N

Southern states - Ala., Ark., Fla., Ga., Ky., La., Miss., N.C., Okla., S.C., Tenn., Texas, Va.

* The *Congressional Record* vote number is different from the CQ vote number because the *Record* includes quorum calls in its tally. CQ does not publish quorum call votes.

423. H J Res 751. Further Interim Continuing Appropriations, Fiscal 1987. Lewis, R-Calif., motion to recommit the joint resolution to the Appropriations Committee with instructions to change the date through which the resolution would be effective from Oct. 15, 1986, to Oct. 11, 1986. Motion rejected 158-222: R 146-14; D 12-208 (ND 4-148, SD 8-60), Oct. 10, 1986.

424. H J Res 751. Further Interim Continuing Appropriations, Fiscal 1987. Passage of the joint resolution to provide funds through Oct. 15, 1986, for programs covered by the 13 regular appropriations bills, at various rates determined by the status of the individual bills at the time H J Res 751 was passed. Funding for the Departments of Housing and Urban Development, Labor, Health and Human Services, Education and Transportation, and for legislative branch programs would be at levels set by conference agreements on fiscal 1987 appropriations bills; for others, spending would be at fiscal 1986 levels or at levels contained in the House- or Senate-passed 1987 bill, whichever was lowest. Passed 235-143: R 36-122; D 199-21 (ND 138-13, SD 61-8), Oct. 10, 1986.

425. S 2245. Export Administration Act. Mica, D-Fla., motion to suspend the rules and pass the bill to authorize President Reagan's request of $123.9 million in each of fiscal 1987 and 1988 for export promotion activities of the Commerce Department. The measure also authorized $35.9 million in each of those fiscal years for export control functions of the Commerce Department. Motion agreed to 366-0: R 155-0; D 211-0 (ND 139-0, SD 72-0), Oct. 14, 1986. A two-thirds majority of those present and voting (244 in this case) is required for passage under suspension of the rules.

426. S 2216. Constitution Day. Garcia, D-N.Y., motion to suspend the rules and pass the bill to designate the bicentennial of the signing of the Constitution, Sept. 17, 1987, a legal public holiday. Motion rejected 130-240: R 14-143; D 116-97 (ND 86-55, SD 30-42), Oct. 14, 1986. A two-thirds majority of those present and voting (247 in this case) is required for passage under suspension of the rules.

427. HR 3113. California Water and Small Reclamation. Miller, D-Calif., motion to suspend the rules and adopt the conference report on the bill to implement a federal-state agreement for coordinated operation of the Bureau of Reclamation's Central Valley Project and California's State Water Project. The bill also changed the bureau's program of grants and loans for the construction of small irrigation projects. Motion agreed to 359-10: R 145-10; D 214-0 (ND 143-0, SD 71-0), Oct. 14, 1986. A two-thirds majority of those present and voting (246 in this case) is required for adoption under suspension of the rules.

428. HR 4613. Commodity Futures Trading Commission. Madigan, R-Ill., motion to delete a provision from the conference report on the bill that would require the agriculture secretary to make all final income subsidy payments for the 1986 wheat crop in November 1986, instead of making partial payments in November 1986 and June 1987. Motion rejected 162-239: R 109-59; D 53-180 (ND 44-117, SD 9-63), Oct. 15, 1986.

429. HR 4613. Commodity Futures Trading Commission. Whitley, D-N.C., motion to delete a provision from the conference report on the bill that would require the U.S. Forest Service to convey without fee a parcel of land to the Nebraska Games and Parks Commission for use as camping and parking facilities by Chadron State Park. Motion agreed to 274-130: R 57-111; D 217-19 (ND 152-13, SD 65-6), Oct. 15, 1986.

430. S 2638. Defense Authorization, Fiscal 1987. Adoption of the rule (H Res 591) to waive points of order against House floor consideration of the conference report on the bill to authorize $217.4 billion in fiscal 1987 for defense programs of the Departments of Defense and Energy. Adopted 250-159: R 19-148; D 231-11 (ND 157-10, SD 74-1), Oct. 15, 1986.

KEY

- Y Voted for (yea).
- # Paired for.
- + Announced for.
- N Voted against (nay).
- X Paired against.
- - Announced against.
- P Voted "present."
- C Voted "present" to avoid possible conflict of interest.
- ? Did not vote or otherwise make a position known.

Democrats ***Republicans***

	423	424	425	426	427	428	429	430
ALABAMA								
1 ***Callahan***	Y	N	Y	N	Y	Y	N	N
2 ***Dickinson***	Y	N	?	?	?	N	N	N
3 Nichols	?	?	?	?	?	?	?	?
4 Bevill	N	Y	Y	Y	Y	N	N	Y
5 Flippo	N	Y	Y	Y	Y	N	Y	Y
6 Erdreich	N	Y	Y	N	Y	N	Y	Y
7 Shelby	N	N	Y	N	Y	N	N	N
ALASKA								
AL ***Young***	N	Y	Y	N	Y	N	N	Y
ARIZONA								
1 ***McCain***	?	?	Y	N	Y	Y	N	N
2 Udall	N	Y	Y	N	Y	N	Y	Y
3 ***Stump***	Y	N	Y	N	Y	Y	N	N
4 ***Rudd***	?	?	?	?	?	?	?	?
5 ***Kolbe***	?	?	Y	N	Y	Y	N	N
ARKANSAS								
1 Alexander	N	Y	Y	Y	Y	N	Y	Y
2 Robinson	Y	N	Y	N	Y	N	Y	Y
3 ***Hammerschmidt***	Y	N	Y	N	Y	N	N	N
4 Anthony	N	Y	Y	N	Y	N	Y	Y
CALIFORNIA								
1 Bosco	N	Y	Y	Y	Y	N	Y	Y
2 ***Chappie***	Y	N	Y	N	Y	Y	Y	N
3 Matsui	N	Y	Y	Y	Y	N	Y	Y
4 Fazio	N	Y	?	?	?	N	Y	Y
5 Burton	?	?	?	?	?	N	Y	Y
6 Boxer	N	Y	?	?	?	N	Y	Y
7 Miller	N	Y	Y	Y	Y	Y	Y	Y
8 Dellums	N	Y	Y	Y	Y	N	Y	Y
9 Stark	N	Y	Y	N	Y	N	Y	Y
10 Edwards	N	Y	Y	Y	Y	N	Y	Y
11 Lantos	N	Y	Y	Y	Y	N	Y	Y
12 ***Zschau***	?	?	?	?	?	Y	N	N
13 Mineta	N	Y	Y	Y	Y	N	Y	Y
14 ***Shumway***	Y	N	Y	N	Y	Y	Y	N
15 Coelho	N	Y	Y	Y	Y	N	Y	Y
16 Panetta	N	Y	Y	N	Y	Y	Y	Y
17 ***Pashayan***	Y	N	Y	N	Y	N	Y	N
18 Lehman	N	Y	?	?	?	N	Y	Y
19 ***Lagomarsino***	Y	N	Y	N	Y	Y	N	N
20 ***Thomas***	Y	N	Y	N	Y	Y	N	N
21 ***Fiedler***	Y	N	Y	N	Y	N	N	N
22 ***Moorhead***	Y	N	Y	N	Y	N	N	N
23 Beilenson	N	Y	Y	Y	Y	Y	Y	Y
24 Waxman	N	Y	Y	Y	Y	Y	Y	Y
25 Roybal	N	Y	Y	Y	Y	N	Y	Y
26 Berman	Y	Y	Y	Y	Y	Y	Y	Y
27 Levine	N	Y	Y	Y	Y	N	Y	Y
28 Dixon	N	Y	Y	Y	Y	N	Y	Y
29 Hawkins	N	Y	Y	Y	Y	N	Y	Y
30 Martinez	?	Y	Y	Y	Y	N	Y	Y
31 Dymally	N	Y	Y	Y	Y	N	Y	Y
32 Anderson	N	Y	Y	Y	Y	Y	N	Y
33 ***Dreier***	Y	N	Y	N	Y	Y	Y	N
34 Torres	N	Y	Y	Y	Y	N	Y	Y
35 ***Lewis***	Y	N	Y	N	Y	N	N	N
36 Brown	N	Y	Y	Y	Y	N	Y	Y
37 ***McCandless***	Y	N	Y	N	Y	Y	Y	N
38 ***Dornan***	Y	N	Y	N	Y	Y	N	N
39 ***Dannemeyer***	Y	N	Y	N	Y	Y	Y	N
40 ***Badham***	Y	N	Y	N	Y	?	?	?
41 ***Lowery***	Y	N	Y	N	Y	N	N	N
42 ***Lungren***	Y	N	Y	N	Y	Y	N	N
43 ***Packard***	Y	N	Y	N	Y	Y	Y	N
44 Bates	N	N	Y	N	Y	Y	Y	Y
45 ***Hunter***	Y	N	Y	N	Y	N	N	N
COLORADO								
1 Schroeder	N	N	?	?	?	Y	Y	N
2 Wirth	Y	N	Y	N	Y	N	Y	Y
3 ***Strang***	Y	N	Y	N	Y	N	N	N
4 ***Brown***	Y	N	Y	N	Y	Y	N	N
5 ***Kramer***	Y	N	Y	N	Y	N	Y	N
6 ***Schaefer***	Y	N	Y	N	Y	N	N	N
CONNECTICUT								
1 Kennelly	N	Y	?	?	Y	Y	Y	Y
2 Gejdenson	N	Y	Y	Y	Y	N	Y	Y
3 Morrison	N	Y	?	?	Y	N	Y	N
4 ***McKinney***	Y	Y	?	?	?	Y	Y	Y
5 ***Rowland***	Y	N	Y	Y	Y	Y	Y	N
6 ***Johnson***	Y	N	Y	N	Y	Y	Y	Y
DELAWARE								
AL Carper	N	Y	Y	N	Y	Y	Y	Y
FLORIDA								
1 Hutto	N	Y	Y	N	Y	N	Y	Y
2 Fuqua	?	?	Y	Y	Y	N	Y	Y
3 Bennett	N	Y	Y	Y	Y	N	Y	Y
4 Chappell	N	Y	Y	Y	Y	Y	Y	Y
5 ***McCollum***	?	?	Y	N	Y	Y	N	N
6 MacKay	?	?	?	?	?	?	?	?
7 Gibbons	N	Y	Y	N	Y	Y	Y	Y
8 ***Young***	Y	Y	Y	N	Y	Y	N	N
9 ***Bilirakis***	Y	N	Y	N	Y	Y	N	N
10 ***Ireland***	Y	N	Y	N	Y	Y	N	N
11 Nelson	N	Y	Y	N	Y	Y	Y	Y
12 ***Lewis***	Y	N	Y	N	Y	N	N	N
13 ***Mack***	Y	N	Y	N	Y	Y	N	N
14 Mica	N	Y	Y	Y	Y	N	Y	Y
15 ***Shaw***	Y	N	Y	N	Y	Y	Y	N
16 Smith	N	Y	Y	Y	Y	N	Y	Y
17 Lehman	N	Y	Y	Y	Y	N	Y	Y
18 Pepper	N	Y	Y	Y	Y	N	Y	Y
19 Fascell	N	Y	Y	?	?	N	Y	Y
GEORGIA								
1 Thomas	N	Y	Y	N	Y	N	Y	Y
2 Hatcher	N	Y	?	N	Y	N	Y	Y
3 Ray	Y	N	Y	Y	Y	N	Y	Y
4 ***Swindall***	Y	N	Y	N	Y	N	Y	N
5 Fowler	?	?	?	?	?	?	?	?
6 ***Gingrich***	Y	N	Y	N	Y	Y	?	N
7 Darden	N	Y	Y	N	Y	N	Y	Y
8 Rowland	N	Y	Y	Y	Y	N	Y	Y
9 Jenkins	N	Y	Y	N	Y	N	Y	Y
10 Barnard	N	Y	?	?	?	N	Y	Y
HAWAII								
1 Abercrombie	N	Y	Y	Y	Y	N	Y	Y
2 Akaka	N	Y	Y	Y	Y	N	Y	Y
IDAHO								
1 ***Craig***	Y	N	Y	N	Y	?	N	N
2 Stallings	N	N	?	?	?	N	Y	Y
ILLINOIS								
1 Hayes	N	Y	Y	Y	Y	Y	Y	Y
2 Savage	N	Y	Y	Y	Y	N	Y	Y
3 Russo	?	?	?	?	?	N	Y	Y
4 Vacancy								
5 Lipinski	?	?	Y	N	Y	Y	Y	Y
6 ***Hyde***	N	N	Y	N	Y	Y	N	N
7 Collins	N	Y	?	?	?	N	Y	Y
8 Rostenkowski	N	Y	Y	Y	Y	N	Y	Y
9 Yates	N	Y	Y	N	Y	?	Y	N
10 ***Porter***	Y	N	Y	Y	Y	Y	N	N
11 Annunzio	N	Y	Y	N	Y	N	Y	Y
12 ***Crane***	N	N	?	?	?	Y	Y	N
13 ***Fawell***	Y	N	Y	N	N	Y	N	N
14 ***Grotberg***	?	?	?	?	?	?	?	?
15 ***Madigan***	Y	Y	Y	Y	Y	Y	N	N
16 ***Martin***	Y	N	Y	N	N	Y	N	N
17 Evans	N	Y	Y	Y	Y	Y	Y	Y
18 ***Michel***	Y	N	Y	N	Y	Y	N	N
19 Bruce	N	N	Y	N	Y	Y	Y	Y
20 Durbin	N	Y	Y	N	Y	Y	N	Y
21 Price	?	?	Y	Y	Y	Y	Y	Y
22 Gray	N	Y	?	N	Y	Y	Y	Y
INDIANA								
1 Visclosky	N	Y	Y	N	Y	Y	Y	Y
2 Sharp	N	Y	Y	N	Y	Y	Y	Y
3 ***Hiler***	Y	N	Y	N	Y	Y	N	N
4 ***Coats***	Y	N	Y	N	Y	Y	N	N
5 ***Hillis***	?	?	Y	N	Y	N	N	Y

ND - Northern Democrats SD - Southern Democrats

* Corresponding to Congressional Record Votes 459, 460, 461, 462, 463, 464, 465, 466

	423	424	425	426	427	428	429	430
6 ***Burton***	Y	N	Y	N	Y	Y	N	N
7 ***Myers***	N	Y	Y	N	Y	Y	N	N
8 McCloskey	N	Y	Y	Y	Y	Y	Y	Y
9 Hamilton	N	Y	Y	N	Y	Y	Y	Y
10 Jacobs	N	Y	Y	N	Y	Y	Y	N
IOWA								
1 ***Leach***	Y	N	Y	N	N	Y	N	N
2 ***Tauke***	?	?	Y	N	Y	Y	N	N
3 ***Evans***	Y	N	?	?	?	N	N	N
4 Smith	N	Y	Y	Y	Y	N	N	N
5 ***Lightfoot***	N	N	Y	N	N	Y	N	N
6 Bedell	N	Y	Y	N	Y	N	N	Y
KANSAS								
1 ***Roberts***	Y	N	Y	N	Y	N	N	N
2 Slattery	N	N	Y	N	Y	N	Y	Y
3 ***Meyers***	Y	N	Y	N	Y	N	N	N
4 Glickman	N	Y	Y	N	Y	N	Y	Y
5 ***Whittaker***	Y	N	Y	N	Y	N	N	N
KENTUCKY								
1 Hubbard	N	N	Y	N	Y	Y	N	Y
2 Natcher	N	Y	Y	Y	Y	N	Y	Y
3 Mazzoli	N	Y	Y	Y	Y	N	Y	Y
4 ***Snyder***	?	?	Y	N	Y	Y	Y	N
5 ***Rogers***	Y	Y	Y	N	Y	Y	Y	Y
6 ***Hopkins***	Y	N	Y	N	Y	Y	N	Y
7 Perkins	N	Y	Y	Y	Y	N	Y	Y
LOUISIANA								
1 ***Livingston***	Y	N	Y	N	Y	Y	N	Y
2 Boggs	N	Y	Y	Y	Y	Y	N	Y
3 Tauzin	Y	Y	Y	Y	Y	N	Y	Y
4 Roemer	N	Y	Y	N	Y	N	Y	Y
5 Huckaby	N	Y	Y	N	Y	N	Y	Y
6 ***Moore***	?	?	?	?	?	?	?	?
7 Breaux	?	?	?	?	?	?	?	?
8 Long	N	Y	?	?	?	?	?	?
MAINE								
1 ***McKernan***	Y	N	?	?	?	Y	Y	N
2 ***Snowe***	Y	N	Y	N	Y	Y	Y	N
MARYLAND								
1 Dyson	N	Y	Y	N	Y	N	Y	Y
2 ***Bentley***	?	?	Y	N	Y	N	N	Y
3 Mikulski	N	Y	?	?	?	?	?	Y
4 ***Holt***	?	?	Y	N	Y	Y	N	?
5 Hoyer	N	Y	Y	Y	Y	N	Y	Y
6 Byron	N	N	Y	N	Y	N	Y	Y
7 Mitchell	?	?	Y	Y	N	Y	Y	Y
8 Barnes	N	Y	Y	Y	Y	N	Y	Y
MASSACHUSETTS								
1 ***Conte***	Y	Y	Y	Y	Y	Y	Y	Y
2 Boland	?	?	Y	Y	Y	?	Y	Y
3 Early	?	?	Y	N	Y	Y	Y	Y
4 Frank	N	Y	Y	N	Y	Y	Y	Y
5 Atkins	N	Y	Y	N	Y	Y	Y	Y
6 Mavroules	N	Y	Y	Y	Y	N	Y	Y
7 Markey	N	Y	Y	Y	Y	Y	Y	Y
8 O'Neill								
9 Moakley	N	?	Y	Y	Y	N	Y	Y
10 Studds	N	Y	?	?	?	N	Y	Y
11 Donnelly	N	Y	?	N	Y	N	Y	Y
MICHIGAN								
1 Conyers	?	?	?	?	?	N	Y	Y
2 ***Pursell***	Y	N	Y	N	Y	Y	Y	N
3 Wolpe	N	Y	Y	N	Y	N	Y	Y
4 ***Siljander***	Y	N	Y	N	Y	N	N	?
5 ***Henry***	Y	N	Y	N	Y	Y	Y	N
6 Carr	N	Y	Y	N	Y	Y	N	Y
7 Kildee	N	Y	Y	Y	Y	N	Y	Y
8 Traxler	?	?	Y	Y	Y	N	Y	Y
9 ***Vander Jagt***	Y	Y	?	?	?	N	N	N
10 ***Schuette***	N	Y	Y	N	Y	Y	Y	N
11 ***Davis***	Y	N	?	?	?	Y	N	N
12 Bonior	N	Y	Y	Y	Y	N	Y	Y
13 Crockett	N	N	Y	Y	Y	N	Y	Y
14 Hertel	N	Y	Y	Y	Y	N	Y	Y
15 Ford	N	Y	Y	Y	Y	N	Y	Y
16 Dingell	N	Y	?	Y	Y	N	Y	Y
17 Levin	N	Y	Y	Y	Y	N	Y	Y
18 ***Broomfield***	N	N	Y	N	Y	Y	N	N
MINNESOTA								
1 Penny	N	N	Y	Y	Y	N	Y	N
2 ***Weber***	Y	N	Y	N	Y	N	Y	N
3 ***Frenzel***	Y	N	Y	N	Y	N	Y	N
4 Vento	N	Y	Y	Y	Y	Y	Y	Y
5 Sabo	N	Y	Y	N	Y	N	N	Y
6 Sikorski	N	N	Y	Y	Y	Y	Y	Y

	423	424	425	426	427	428	429	430
7 ***Stangeland***	Y	N	Y	N	Y	N	Y	?
8 Oberstar	N	Y	Y	N	Y	Y	Y	Y
MISSISSIPPI								
1 Whitten	N	Y	Y	N	Y	N	Y	Y
2 ***Franklin***	Y	N	?	?	?	?	?	N
3 Montgomery	N	Y	Y	N	Y	Y	Y	Y
4 Dowdy	N	Y	Y	N	Y	N	Y	Y
5 ***Lott***	Y	N	Y	N	?	Y	N	N
MISSOURI								
1 Clay	N	Y	Y	Y	Y	N	Y	Y
2 Young	N	Y	Y	Y	Y	N	Y	Y
3 Gephardt	N	Y	?	?	?	?	?	?
4 Skelton	N	Y	Y	N	Y	N	Y	Y
5 Wheat	N	Y	Y	Y	Y	N	Y	Y
6 ***Coleman***	Y	N	Y	N	Y	Y	N	N
7 ***Taylor***	Y	Y	Y	N	Y	N	N	N
8 ***Emerson***	Y	N	Y	N	Y	N	N	N
9 Volkmer	N	Y	Y	N	Y	N	Y	Y
MONTANA								
1 Williams	N	Y	Y	Y	Y	Y	Y	Y
2 ***Marlenee***	Y	N	?	?	?	N	N	N
NEBRASKA								
1 ***Bereuter***	Y	N	Y	N	Y	N	N	N
2 ***Daub***	Y	N	Y	N	Y	N	N	N
3 ***Smith***	N	Y	Y	N	Y	N	N	N
NEVADA								
1 Reid	N	Y	Y	N	Y	Y	Y	Y
2 ***Vucanovich***	Y	N	Y	N	Y	Y	N	N
NEW HAMPSHIRE								
1 ***Smith***	Y	N	Y	N	Y	Y	N	N
2 ***Gregg***	Y	N	Y	N	Y	Y	N	N
NEW JERSEY								
1 Florio	N	Y	Y	N	Y	Y	Y	Y
2 Hughes	N	Y	Y	N	Y	Y	Y	N
3 Howard	N	Y	?	?	?	N	Y	Y
4 ***Smith***	Y	Y	Y	N	Y	N	Y	N
5 ***Roukema***	Y	N	Y	N	Y	Y	Y	Y
6 Dwyer	N	Y	Y	Y	Y	N	Y	Y
7 ***Rinaldo***	Y	Y	Y	N	Y	N	Y	N
8 Roe	N	Y	Y	Y	Y	N	Y	Y
9 Torricelli	N	Y	Y	N	Y	N	Y	Y
10 Rodino	N	Y	Y	Y	Y	?	Y	Y
11 ***Gallo***	Y	N	Y	N	Y	Y	Y	N
12 ***Courter***	Y	N	Y	Y	Y	Y	Y	N
13 ***Saxton***	Y	Y	Y	N	Y	Y	Y	N
14 Guarini	N	Y	?	?	?	Y	Y	Y
NEW MEXICO								
1 ***Lujan***	Y	?	Y	N	Y	Y	N	N
2 ***Skeen***	Y	Y	Y	N	Y	Y	N	N
3 Richardson	N	Y	Y	N	Y	N	Y	Y
NEW YORK								
1 ***Carney***	Y	N	Y	N	Y	?	?	?
2 Downey	N	Y	?	?	?	N	Y	Y
3 Mrazek	N	Y	Y	N	Y	N	Y	Y
4 ***Lent***	Y	N	Y	N	Y	N	N	N
5 ***McGrath***	Y	N	Y	N	Y	N	N	N
6 Waldon	N	Y	?	?	?	N	Y	Y
7 Ackerman	N	Y	Y	Y	Y	N	Y	Y
8 Scheuer	N	Y	Y	Y	Y	Y	Y	Y
9 Manton	N	Y	?	?	?	Y	Y	Y
10 Schumer	N	Y	Y	N	Y	Y	Y	Y
11 Towns	N	Y	Y	Y	Y	X	?	Y
12 Owens	?	?	?	?	?	N	Y	Y
13 Solarz	N	Y	Y	Y	Y	N	Y	Y
14 ***Molinari***	Y	N	Y	N	Y	N	N	N
15 ***Green***	Y	Y	Y	N	Y	Y	Y	N
16 Rangel	N	Y	Y	Y	Y	N	Y	Y
17 Weiss	?	?	?	?	?	?	?	?
18 Garcia	N	Y	Y	Y	Y	N	Y	Y
19 Biaggi	N	Y	?	?	?	N	Y	Y
20 ***DioGuardi***	Y	Y	?	?	?	Y	Y	N
21 ***Fish***	Y	Y	Y	N	Y	Y	Y	Y
22 ***Gilman***	Y	N	Y	N	Y	Y	Y	Y
23 Stratton	Y	Y	Y	N	Y	N	N	Y
24 ***Solomon***	Y	N	Y	N	Y	Y	Y	N
25 ***Boehlert***	Y	N	?	?	?	Y	Y	N
26 ***Martin***	Y	N	Y	N	?	Y	Y	N
27 ***Wortley***	Y	N	?	N	Y	Y	Y	N
28 McHugh	N	Y	Y	N	Y	N	Y	Y
29 ***Horton***	N	Y	Y	Y	Y	N	Y	Y
30 ***Eckert***	Y	N	Y	N	Y	Y	N	N
31 ***Kemp***	Y	N	?	?	?	Y	N	Y
32 LaFalce	N	Y	Y	Y	Y	N	Y	Y
33 Nowak	N	Y	Y	Y	Y	N	Y	Y
34 Lundine	N	Y	?	?	?	?	?	?

	423	424	425	426	427	428	429	430
NORTH CAROLINA								
1 Jones	N	Y	Y	Y	Y	N	Y	Y
2 Valentine	N	Y	Y	N	Y	N	Y	Y
3 Whitley	N	Y	Y	N	Y	N	Y	Y
4 ***Cobey***	Y	N	Y	N	Y	Y	Y	N
5 Neal	N	Y	Y	N	Y	N	Y	Y
6 ***Coble***	Y	N	Y	N	Y	Y	Y	N
7 Rose	N	Y	Y	N	Y	N	Y	Y
8 Hefner	N	Y	?	?	?	N	Y	Y
9 ***McMillan***	Y	Y	Y	N	Y	Y	Y	N
10 Vacancy								
11 ***Hendon***	Y	Y	Y	N	Y	N	N	N
NORTH DAKOTA								
AL Dorgan	N	Y	Y	N	Y	N	Y	Y
OHIO								
1 Luken	N	Y	?	?	?	N	Y	Y
2 ***Gradison***	Y	Y	Y	N	Y	Y	Y	Y
3 Hall	?	?	Y	N	Y	N	Y	Y
4 ***Oxley***	N	N	Y	N	Y	Y	N	N
5 ***Latta***	?	?	Y	N	Y	N	N	N
6 ***McEwen***	Y	N	Y	N	Y	N	N	N
7 ***DeWine***	Y	N	Y	N	Y	N	N	N
8 ***Kindness***	?	?	?	?	?	?	?	?
9 Kaptur	?	?	Y	Y	Y	N	Y	Y
10 ***Miller***	N	Y	Y	N	Y	N	N	N
11 Eckart	N	N	Y	N	Y	N	Y	Y
12 ***Kasich***	N	N	Y	N	Y	Y	N	N
13 Pease	N	Y	Y	N	Y	N	Y	Y
14 Seiberling	N	Y	Y	Y	Y	N	N	Y
15 ***Wylie***	N	N	Y	N	Y	N	N	N
16 ***Regula***	Y	N	Y	N	Y	N	N	N
17 Traficant	N	N	Y	N	Y	N	Y	N
18 Applegate	N	Y	Y	Y	Y	N	N	Y
19 Feighan	N	Y	Y	N	Y	N	Y	Y
20 Oakar	N	Y	Y	Y	Y	N	Y	Y
21 Stokes	?	?	Y	Y	Y	N	N	Y
OKLAHOMA								
1 Jones	?	?	?	?	?	?	?	?
2 Synar	N	Y	Y	Y	Y	N	Y	Y
3 Watkins	N	Y	Y	Y	?	N	Y	Y
4 McCurdy	?	?	Y	N	Y	N	Y	Y
5 ***Edwards***	?	?	Y	N	Y	N	N	N
6 English	N	Y	Y	N	Y	N	N	Y
OREGON								
1 AuCoin	N	Y	Y	Y	Y	N	Y	Y
2 ***Smith, R.***	Y	N	Y	N	Y	N	Y	Y
3 Wyden	N	Y	Y	N	Y	N	Y	Y
4 Weaver	N	Y	Y	Y	Y	N	Y	Y
5 ***Smith, D.***	Y	N	Y	N	Y	Y	N	N
PENNSYLVANIA								
1 Foglietta	N	Y	?	?	?	N	Y	Y
2 Gray	N	Y	Y	Y	Y	N	Y	Y
3 Borski	N	Y	Y	Y	Y	N	Y	Y
4 Kolter	N	Y	Y	Y	Y	N	Y	Y
5 ***Schulze***	?	?	?	Y	Y	Y	N	N
6 Yatron	N	Y	Y	Y	Y	N	Y	Y
7 Edgar	?	?	?	?	?	?	Y	Y
8 Kostmayer	?	?	Y	Y	Y	N	N	Y
9 ***Shuster***	Y	N	Y	Y	Y	N	N	N
10 ***McDade***	Y	Y	Y	N	Y	Y	N	Y
11 Kanjorski	N	Y	Y	N	Y	N	Y	N
12 Murtha	N	Y	Y	N	Y	N	Y	Y
13 ***Coughlin***	Y	N	Y	Y	Y	Y	N	N
14 Coyne	N	Y	Y	Y	Y	N	Y	Y
15 ***Ritter***	Y	Y	Y	Y	Y	Y	N	N
16 ***Walker***	Y	N	Y	N	Y	Y	N	N
17 ***Gekas***	Y	N	Y	N	Y	Y	N	N
18 Walgren	N	Y	Y	Y	Y	N	Y	Y
19 ***Goodling***	N	Y	Y	N	Y	Y	N	?
20 Gaydos	N	Y	Y	Y	Y	N	Y	Y
21 ***Ridge***	Y	N	Y	N	Y	Y	N	N
22 Murphy	N	Y	Y	Y	Y	N	Y	Y
23 ***Clinger***	Y	N	?	?	?	Y	Y	N
RHODE ISLAND								
1 St Germain	N	Y	Y	Y	Y	Y	Y	Y
2 ***Schneider***	Y	Y	Y	N	Y	#	?	N
SOUTH CAROLINA								
1 ***Hartnett***	?	?	?	?	?	?	?	?
2 ***Spence***	Y	N	Y	N	Y	N	N	N
3 Derrick	N	Y	Y	N	Y	N	Y	Y
4 ***Campbell***	?	?	?	?	?	?	?	?
5 Spratt	N	Y	Y	Y	Y	N	Y	Y
6 Tallon	N	Y	Y	N	Y	N	Y	Y
SOUTH DAKOTA								
AL Daschle	N	N	Y	N	Y	N	Y	Y

	423	424	425	426	427	428	429	430
TENNESSEE								
1 ***Quillen***	Y	Y	?	?	?	Y	N	N
2 ***Duncan***	Y	N	Y	N	Y	Y	N	N
3 Lloyd	Y	Y	Y	N	Y	N	N	Y
4 Cooper	N	Y	Y	Y	Y	N	Y	Y
5 Boner	N	Y	Y	N	Y	N	Y	Y
6 Gordon	N	Y	Y	N	Y	N	Y	Y
7 ***Sundquist***	Y	N	?	?	?	N	N	N
8 Jones	N	Y	Y	N	Y	N	Y	Y
9 Ford	N	Y	Y	Y	Y	?	?	Y
TEXAS								
1 Chapman	N	Y	Y	N	Y	N	Y	Y
2 Wilson	?	?	Y	N	Y	N	Y	Y
3 ***Bartlett***	?	?	Y	N	N	N	N	N
4 Hall, R.	Y	N	Y	N	Y	N	Y	Y
5 Bryant	N	Y	Y	N	Y	N	Y	Y
6 ***Barton***	Y	N	Y	N	Y	N	Y	N
7 ***Archer***	Y	N	Y	N	Y	Y	Y	N
8 ***Fields***	Y	N	Y	N	Y	N	N	N
9 Brooks	?	?	?	?	?	?	?	?
10 Pickle	Y	N	Y	N	Y	?	?	Y
11 Leath	N	Y	Y	Y	Y	?	?	Y
12 Wright	N	Y	Y	Y	Y	N	Y	Y
13 ***Boulter***	Y	Y	Y	N	Y	N	N	N
14 ***Sweeney***	Y	?	Y	N	Y	N	N	N
15 de la Garza	N	Y	Y	Y	Y	N	Y	Y
16 Coleman	N	Y	Y	N	Y	N	Y	Y
17 Stenholm	Y	N	Y	N	Y	N	Y	Y
18 Leland	-	Y	Y	Y	Y	N	Y	Y
19 ***Combest***	Y	N	Y	N	N	N	N	N
20 Gonzalez	N	Y	Y	Y	Y	N	P	Y
21 ***Loeffler***	Y	Y	Y	N	Y	N	N	N
22 ***DeLay***	Y	N	Y	N	Y	?	?	?
23 Bustamante	N	Y	Y	N	Y	N	Y	Y
24 Frost	N	Y	Y	N	Y	N	Y	Y
25 Andrews	?	?	Y	N	Y	N	Y	Y
26 ***Armey***	Y	N	Y	N	Y	Y	Y	N
27 Ortiz	N	Y	Y	N	Y	N	Y	Y
UTAH								
1 ***Hansen***	Y	N	?	?	?	Y	N	N
2 ***Monson***	Y	N	Y	N	Y	Y	N	N
3 ***Nielson***	Y	N	Y	N	Y	Y	N	N
VERMONT								
AL ***Jeffords***	Y	Y	Y	N	N	Y	Y	N
VIRGINIA								
1 ***Bateman***	Y	Y	Y	N	Y	Y	N	Y
2 ***Whitehurst***	?	?	Y	N	Y	Y	N	Y
3 ***Bliley***	Y	Y	Y	N	Y	Y	N	N
4 Sisisky	N	Y	Y	Y	Y	N	Y	Y
5 Daniel	?	?	Y	Y	Y	Y	Y	Y
6 Olin	?	?	Y	N	Y	Y	Y	Y
7 ***Slaughter***	Y	Y	Y	Y	Y	Y	N	N
8 ***Parris***	Y	Y	Y	Y	Y	Y	Y	N
9 Boucher	?	?	Y	N	Y	Y	Y	Y
10 ***Wolf***	Y	Y	Y	Y	Y	Y	N	N
WASHINGTON								
1 ***Miller***	Y	N	Y	N	Y	Y	Y	N
2 Swift	N	Y	Y	Y	Y	N	Y	Y
3 Bonker	N	Y	?	?	?	N	Y	Y
4 ***Morrison***	Y	N	Y	N	Y	N	Y	N
5 Foley	N	Y	Y	?	Y	N	Y	Y
6 Dicks	N	?	Y	N	Y	N	N	Y
7 Lowry	Y	Y	Y	Y	Y	N	Y	Y
8 ***Chandler***	Y	N	Y	N	Y	N	N	N
WEST VIRGINIA								
1 Mollohan	N	Y	Y	Y	Y	N	Y	Y
2 Staggers	N	Y	Y	N	Y	N	Y	Y
3 Wise	N	Y	Y	N	Y	N	Y	Y
4 Rahall	?	?	Y	Y	Y	N	Y	Y
WISCONSIN								
1 Aspin	N	Y	Y	N	Y	Y	Y	Y
2 Kastenmeier	N	Y	Y	Y	?	Y	Y	N
3 ***Gunderson***	Y	N	Y	N	N	Y	Y	N
4 Kleczka	N	Y	?	?	?	Y	Y	Y
5 Moody	N	Y	Y	N	Y	N	Y	Y
6 ***Petri***	Y	N	Y	N	Y	N	Y	Y
7 Obey	N	Y	Y	N	Y	Y	Y	Y
8 ***Roth***	Y	N	Y	N	N	Y	Y	N
9 ***Sensenbrenner***	Y	N	Y	N	Y	Y	Y	N
WYOMING								
AL ***Cheney***	Y	N	Y	N	Y	N	N	N

Southern states - Ala., Ark., Fla., Ga., Ky., La., Miss., N.C., Okla., S.C., Tenn., Texas, Va.

* The *Congressional Record* vote number is different from the CQ vote number because the *Record* includes quorum calls in its tally. CQ does not publish quorum call votes.

431. S 2638. Defense Authorization, Fiscal 1987. Adoption of the conference report on the bill to authorize $217.4 billion in fiscal 1987 for defense programs of the Departments of Defense and Energy. Adopted 283-128: R 121-47; D 162-81 (ND 90-77, SD 72-4), Oct. 15, 1986.

432. S 1200. Immigration Reform. Adoption of the rule (H Res 592) to waive points of order against House floor consideration of the conference report on the bill to overhaul the nation's immigration laws. Adopted 274-132: R 70-99; D 204-33 (ND 141-21, SD 63-12), Oct. 15, 1986.

433. S 1200. Immigration Reform. Adoption of the conference report on the bill to overhaul the nation's immigration laws by penalizing employers who knowingly hire illegal aliens, providing legal status to millions of illegal aliens already in the country, and setting up a new program to grant legal status to foreign farm workers with a history of working in American agriculture. Adopted 238-173: R 77-93; D 161-80 (ND 123-42, SD 38-38), Oct. 15, 1986.

434. S 1128. Clean Water Act Amendments. Adoption of the conference report on the bill to reauthorize and amend the Clean Water Act of 1972 (PL 92-500), to authorize funds for controlling water pollution and for aiding local governments in building sewage treatment plants. Adopted 408-0: R 166-0; D 242-0 (ND 166-0, SD 76-0), Oct. 15, 1986. A "nay" was a vote supporting the president's position.

435. H J Res 738. Continuing Appropriations, Fiscal 1987. Adoption of the rule (H Res 593) to waive points of order against House floor consideration of the conference report on the joint resolution to appropriate $575.9 billion for programs covered by the 13 regular appropriations bills for fiscal 1987. Adopted 281-122: R 62-106; D 219-16 (ND 150-9, SD 69-7), Oct. 15, 1986.

436. H J Res 738. Continuing Appropriations, Fiscal 1987. Adoption of the conference report on the joint resolution to appropriate $575.9 billion for programs covered by the 13 regular appropriations bills for fiscal 1987. Adopted 235-172: R 79-90; D 156-82 (ND 94-69, SD 62-13), Oct. 15, 1986.

437. H J Res 738. Continuing Appropriations, Fiscal 1987. Whitten, D-Miss., motion that the House recede from its disagreement and concur in the Senate amendment, with an amendment to allow work on certain federal buildings not previously authorized and to restrict to Alaska the effect of a provision that would limit future Rural Electrification Administration-backed loans to cooperatives choosing to refinance their current REA loans. Motion agreed to 301-106: R 68-102; D 233-4 (ND 159-2, SD 74-2), Oct. 15, 1986.

438. H J Res 738. Continuing Appropriations, Fiscal 1987. Lowry, D-Wash., motion that the House recede from its disagreement and concur in the Senate amendment to drop House language requiring imported wine, beer and distilled spirits to be certified as meeting U.S. purity standards. Motion agreed to 297-113: R 129-43; D 168-70 (ND 108-54, SD 60-16), Oct. 15, 1986.

KEY

Y Voted for (yea).
Paired for.
\+ Announced for.
N Voted against (nay).
X Paired against.
\- Announced against.
P Voted "present."
C Voted "present" to avoid possible conflict of interest.
? Did not vote or otherwise make a position known.

Democrats ***Republicans***

	431	432	433	434	435	436	437	438
ALABAMA								
1 ***Callahan***	Y	N	N	Y	N	N	N	Y
2 ***Dickinson***	N	N	N	Y	N	N	N	N
3 Nichols	#	?	?	?	?	#	?	?
4 Bevill	Y	Y	N	Y	Y	Y	Y	Y
5 Flippo	Y	Y	N	Y	Y	N	Y	Y
6 Erdreich	Y	Y	N	Y	N	N	Y	Y
7 Shelby	N	N	N	Y	N	N	Y	Y
ALASKA								
AL ***Young***	Y	N	N	Y	N	Y	Y	Y
ARIZONA								
1 ***McCain***	Y	N	N	?	?	?	?	?
2 Udall	Y	Y	Y	Y	Y	Y	Y	Y
3 ***Stump***	N	N	N	Y	N	N	N	Y
4 ***Rudd***	?	?	?	?	?	?	?	?
5 ***Kolbe***	Y	N	N	Y	N	N	N	Y
ARKANSAS								
1 Alexander	Y	Y	Y	Y	Y	Y	Y	Y
2 Robinson	Y	N	N	Y	N	N	N	Y
3 ***Hammerschmidt***	Y	Y	N	Y	N	Y	Y	N
4 Anthony	Y	Y	Y	Y	Y	Y	Y	Y
CALIFORNIA								
1 Bosco	N	Y	Y	Y	Y	Y	Y	Y
2 ***Chappie***	Y	N	N	Y	N	Y	N	Y
3 Matsui	?	Y	Y	Y	Y	N	Y	Y
4 Fazio	Y	Y	Y	Y	Y	Y	Y	N
5 Burton	N	Y	N	Y	?	?	?	?
6 Boxer	N	Y	N	Y	Y	N	Y	N
7 Miller	N	Y	Y	Y	Y	N	Y	N
8 Dellums	N	N	N	Y	Y	N	Y	N
9 Stark	N	Y	Y	Y	?	N	Y	?
10 Edwards	N	N	N	Y	Y	N	Y	N
11 Lantos	Y	Y	Y	Y	Y	Y	Y	N
12 ***Zschau***	Y	Y	Y	Y	N	N	N	N
13 Mineta	N	Y	N	Y	Y	N	Y	N
14 ***Shumway***	N	N	Y	Y	N	N	N	Y
15 Coelho	Y	Y	Y	Y	Y	Y	Y	N
16 Panetta	N	Y	Y	Y	Y	N	Y	N
17 ***Pashayan***	Y	Y	Y	Y	Y	Y	Y	N
18 Lehman	N	Y	Y	Y	Y	Y	Y	N
19 ***Lagomarsino***	Y	Y	Y	Y	N	N	N	N
20 ***Thomas***	N	Y	Y	Y	N	N	N	N
21 ***Fiedler***	Y	N	N	Y	N	N	Y	Y
22 ***Moorhead***	Y	Y	Y	Y	N	N	N	N
23 Beilenson	N	Y	Y	Y	Y	Y	Y	Y
24 Waxman	N	Y	Y	Y	?	Y	Y	Y
25 Roybal	N	N	N	Y	Y	Y	Y	N
26 Berman	N	Y	Y	Y	Y	Y	Y	Y
27 Levine	Y	Y	Y	Y	Y	Y	Y	N
28 Dixon	N	Y	Y	Y	Y	Y	Y	N
29 Hawkins	Y	N	N	Y	Y	Y	Y	N
30 Martinez	Y	N	N	Y	Y	Y	Y	N
31 Dymally	N	Y	N	Y	Y	N	Y	Y
32 Anderson	Y	Y	Y	Y	Y	Y	Y	N
33 ***Dreier***	N	N	N	Y	N	N	N	Y
34 Torres	Y	Y	Y	Y	Y	N	Y	Y
35 ***Lewis***	Y	N	Y	Y	N	N	Y	N
36 Brown	Y	Y	Y	Y	Y	Y	Y	N
37 ***McCandless***	N	Y	Y	Y	N	N	N	Y
38 ***Dornan***	N	N	Y	Y	N	N	N	Y
39 ***Dannemeyer***	Y	N	Y	Y	N	N	N	Y
40 ***Badham***	?	?	+	?	N	N	N	N
41 ***Lowery***	Y	Y	Y	Y	Y	Y	Y	N
42 ***Lungren***	Y	Y	Y	Y	N	N	N	Y
43 ***Packard***	Y	Y	Y	Y	N	N	N	Y
44 Bates	Y	Y	Y	Y	Y	N	?	Y
45 ***Hunter***	N	N	N	Y	N	N	Y	N
COLORADO								
1 Schroeder	N	N	N	Y	Y	N	N	Y
2 Wirth	Y	N	N	Y	Y	Y	Y	Y
3 ***Strang***	Y	N	Y	Y	N	N	Y	Y
4 ***Brown***	N	N	N	Y	N	N	N	Y
5 ***Kramer***	Y	N	N	?	N	N	N	Y
6 ***Schaefer***	N	N	Y	Y	N	N	N	Y
CONNECTICUT								
1 Kennelly	Y	Y	Y	Y	Y	Y	Y	Y
2 Gejdenson	Y	Y	Y	Y	Y	Y	Y	Y
3 Morrison	N	Y	Y	Y	Y	Y	Y	Y
4 ***McKinney***	Y	Y	Y	Y	Y	Y	Y	Y
5 ***Rowland***	Y	Y	Y	Y	Y	Y	Y	Y
6 ***Johnson***	Y	Y	Y	Y	N	Y	Y	Y
DELAWARE								
AL Carper	Y	Y	Y	Y	Y	Y	Y	Y
FLORIDA								
1 Hutto	Y	Y	Y	Y	Y	Y	Y	N
2 Fuqua	Y	Y	Y	Y	Y	Y	Y	Y
3 Bennett	Y	Y	Y	Y	Y	Y	Y	Y
4 Chappell	Y	Y	N	Y	Y	Y	Y	Y
5 ***McCollum***	Y	N	Y	Y	N	N	N	Y
6 MacKay	Y	Y	Y	Y	Y	Y	Y	Y
7 Gibbons	Y	Y	Y	Y	Y	Y	Y	Y
8 ***Young***	N	N	N	Y	N	Y	N	Y
9 ***Bilirakis***	N	N	N	Y	N	Y	N	Y
10 ***Ireland***	N	N	Y	Y	N	Y	N	Y
11 Nelson	Y	Y	Y	Y	Y	Y	Y	Y
12 ***Lewis***	Y	N	N	Y	N	N	N	Y
13 ***Mack***	Y	N	N	Y	N	N	Y	Y
14 Mica	Y	Y	Y	Y	Y	Y	Y	Y
15 ***Shaw***	Y	Y	Y	Y	N	N	Y	Y
16 Smith	Y	Y	Y	Y	Y	Y	Y	N
17 Lehman	N	Y	Y	Y	Y	Y	Y	N
18 Pepper	Y	Y	Y	Y	Y	Y	Y	Y
19 Fascell	Y	Y	Y	Y	Y	Y	Y	N
GEORGIA								
1 Thomas	Y	Y	Y	Y	Y	Y	Y	N
2 Hatcher	Y	Y	Y	Y	Y	Y	Y	Y
3 Ray	Y	Y	N	Y	Y	N	N	Y
4 ***Swindall***	N	N	N	Y	N	N	N	Y
5 Fowler	?	?	?	?	?	?	?	?
6 ***Gingrich***	N	Y	Y	Y	N	N	N	Y
7 Darden	Y	Y	Y	Y	Y	Y	Y	N
8 Rowland	Y	Y	N	Y	Y	Y	Y	N
9 Jenkins	Y	Y	N	Y	Y	Y	Y	N
10 Barnard	Y	Y	N	Y	Y	Y	Y	N
HAWAII								
1 Abercrombie	Y	Y	Y	Y	Y	N	Y	Y
2 Akaka	Y	N	N	Y	Y	Y	Y	N
IDAHO								
1 ***Craig***	Y	N	N	Y	N	N	N	Y
2 Stallings	Y	Y	Y	Y	Y	N	Y	Y
ILLINOIS								
1 Hayes	N	N	N	Y	Y	N	Y	Y
2 Savage	N	N	N	Y	Y	N	Y	N
3 Russo	N	Y	N	Y	Y	N	Y	Y
4 Vacancy								
5 Lipinski	Y	Y	Y	Y	Y	Y	Y	Y
6 ***Hyde***	Y	N	N	Y	Y	Y	N	Y
7 Collins	Y	Y	Y	Y	Y	N	Y	Y
8 Rostenkowski	N	Y	Y	Y	Y	Y	Y	Y
9 Yates	N	Y	Y	Y	Y	Y	Y	Y
10 ***Porter***	N	N	N	Y	N	N	N	Y
11 Annunzio	Y	Y	Y	Y	Y	Y	Y	Y
12 ***Crane***	Y	N	N	Y	N	N	N	Y
13 ***Fawell***	Y	N	N	Y	N	N	N	Y
14 ***Grotberg***	?	?	?	?	?	?	?	?
15 ***Madigan***	Y	N	N	Y	N	Y	Y	Y
16 ***Martin***	Y	Y	Y	Y	N	N	Y	Y
17 Evans	N	N	N	Y	Y	N	Y	N
18 ***Michel***	Y	Y	Y	Y	Y	Y	Y	N
19 Bruce	N	Y	Y	Y	Y	N	Y	N
20 Durbin	N	Y	Y	Y	Y	Y	Y	N
21 Price	Y	Y	Y	Y	Y	Y	Y	Y
22 Gray	Y	Y	Y	Y	Y	Y	Y	N
INDIANA								
1 Visclosky	Y	Y	N	Y	Y	N	Y	Y
2 Sharp	Y	Y	Y	Y	Y	N	Y	Y
3 ***Hiler***	Y	Y	N	Y	N	N	N	Y
4 ***Coats***	Y	Y	N	Y	Y	N	N	Y
5 ***Hillis***	Y	Y	Y	Y	Y	Y	N	Y

ND - Northern Democrats SD - Southern Democrats

* Corresponding to Congressional Record Votes 467, 468, 469, 470, 471, 472, 473, 474

	431	432	433	434	435	436	437	438
6 ***Burton***	Y	N	N	Y	N	N	N	Y
7 ***Myers***	Y	Y	N	Y	Y	Y	Y	Y
8 McCloskey	Y	Y	Y	Y	Y	Y	Y	N
9 Hamilton	Y	Y	Y	Y	Y	N	Y	N
10 Jacobs	Y	N	N	Y	N	N	Y	Y
IOWA								
1 ***Leach***	N	Y	Y	Y	N	N	N	Y
2 ***Tauke***	N	N	Y	Y	N	N	N	Y
3 ***Evans***	N	N	Y	Y	N	N	Y	Y
4 Smith	N	Y	Y	Y	Y	Y	Y	Y
5 ***Lightfoot***	N	N	Y	Y	N	N	Y	Y
6 Bedell	N	Y	Y	Y	Y	N	Y	Y
KANSAS								
1 ***Roberts***	Y	N	N	Y	N	N	Y	Y
2 Slattery	Y	Y	Y	Y	Y	N	Y	Y
3 ***Meyers***	Y	N	N	Y	Y	N	Y	Y
4 Glickman	Y	Y	Y	Y	Y	N	Y	Y
5 ***Whittaker***	Y	N	N	Y	N	N	N	Y
KENTUCKY								
1 Hubbard	Y	Y	N	Y	N	N	Y	Y
2 Natcher	Y	Y	Y	Y	Y	Y	Y	Y
3 Mazzoli	Y	Y	Y	Y	Y	Y	Y	Y
4 ***Snyder***	Y	N	N	Y	Y	Y	Y	Y
5 ***Rogers***	Y	Y	Y	Y	Y	Y	Y	Y
6 ***Hopkins***	Y	Y	N	Y	N	N	Y	Y
7 Perkins	N	Y	Y	Y	Y	Y	Y	Y
LOUISIANA								
1 ***Livingston***	Y	Y	Y	Y	Y	Y	Y	N
2 Boggs	Y	Y	N	Y	Y	Y	Y	Y
3 Tauzin	Y	Y	N	Y	Y	Y	Y	Y
4 Roemer	Y	N	N	Y	Y	Y	Y	Y
5 Huckaby	Y	Y	Y	Y	Y	Y	Y	Y
6 ***Moore***	?	?	?	?	?	?	?	?
7 Breaux	?	?	?	?	?	?	?	?
8 Long	?	?	?	?	?	?	?	?
MAINE								
1 ***McKernan***	Y	N	Y	Y	Y	Y	N	Y
2 ***Snowe***	Y	N	Y	Y	Y	Y	N	Y
MARYLAND								
1 Dyson	Y	Y	N	Y	Y	N	Y	Y
2 ***Bentley***	Y	N	N	Y	Y	Y	N	N
3 Mikulski	Y	Y	Y	Y	Y	Y	Y	Y
4 ***Holt***	?	N	N	Y	Y	Y	Y	Y
5 Hoyer	Y	Y	Y	Y	Y	Y	Y	N
6 Byron	Y	Y	Y	Y	Y	N	Y	Y
7 Mitchell	N	?	Y	Y	Y	Y	Y	Y
8 Barnes	N	Y	Y	Y	Y	N	Y	Y
MASSACHUSETTS								
1 ***Conte***	N	Y	Y	Y	Y	Y	Y	N
2 Boland	Y	Y	Y	Y	Y	Y	Y	Y
3 Early	N	Y	Y	Y	Y	Y	Y	Y
4 Frank	N	Y	Y	Y	Y	N	Y	Y
5 Atkins	N	Y	Y	Y	Y	N	Y	Y
6 Mavroules	Y	?	Y	Y	Y	N	Y	Y
7 Markey	N	Y	Y	Y	Y	N	Y	N
8 O'Neill								
9 Moakley	Y	Y	Y	Y	N	Y	Y	Y
10 Studds	N	Y	Y	Y	Y	N	Y	Y
11 Donnelly	Y	Y	Y	Y	Y	Y	Y	Y
MICHIGAN								
1 Conyers	N	?	X	?	?	?	?	?
2 ***Pursell***	N	Y	N	Y	Y	Y	N	N
3 Wolpe	Y	Y	Y	Y	Y	Y	Y	Y
4 ***Siljander***	Y	N	N	Y	N	N	N	Y
5 ***Henry***	N	Y	Y	Y	N	N	N	Y
6 Carr	Y	N	N	Y	Y	Y	Y	N
7 Kildee	N	Y	Y	Y	Y	Y	Y	N
8 Traxler	Y	?	Y	Y	Y	Y	Y	N
9 ***Vander Jagt***	Y	N	N	Y	N	Y	N	Y
10 ***Schuette***	Y	N	N	Y	Y	Y	Y	N
11 ***Davis***	Y	Y	Y	Y	Y	Y	N	Y
12 Bonior	N	Y	Y	Y	?	N	Y	N
13 Crockett	N	Y	N	Y	N	N	Y	?
14 Hertel	Y	N	N	Y	N	N	Y	Y
15 Ford	N	Y	Y	Y	N	Y	Y	N
16 Dingell	Y	Y	Y	Y	Y	Y	Y	N
17 Levin	Y	Y	Y	Y	Y	Y	Y	Y
18 ***Broomfield***	Y	N	N	Y	N	N	N	Y
MINNESOTA								
1 Penny	N	Y	Y	Y	Y	N	Y	Y
2 ***Weber***	Y	Y	Y	Y	N	N	Y	Y
3 ***Frenzel***	N	Y	Y	Y	N	N	N	Y
4 Vento	N	Y	Y	Y	Y	N	Y	Y
5 Sabo	Y	Y	Y	Y	Y	Y	Y	Y
6 Sikorski	N	Y	Y	Y	Y	N	Y	Y
7 ***Stangeland***	Y	Y	Y	Y	N	Y	Y	Y
8 Oberstar	Y	Y	Y	Y	Y	Y	Y	Y
MISSISSIPPI								
1 Whitten	Y	Y	N	Y	Y	Y	Y	Y
2 ***Franklin***	Y	N	N	Y	Y	N	N	Y
3 Montgomery	Y	Y	Y	Y	Y	Y	Y	Y
4 Dowdy	Y	Y	Y	Y	Y	Y	Y	Y
5 ***Lott***	Y	Y	Y	Y	Y	Y	N	N
MISSOURI								
1 Clay	N	Y	Y	Y	Y	N	Y	Y
2 Young	Y	Y	Y	Y	Y	Y	Y	N
3 Gephardt	Y	Y	Y	Y	Y	Y	Y	Y
4 Skelton	Y	Y	N	Y	Y	Y	Y	Y
5 Wheat	N	Y	Y	Y	Y	N	Y	Y
6 ***Coleman***	Y	Y	Y	Y	N	Y	Y	Y
7 ***Taylor***	Y	Y	N	Y	Y	Y	Y	N
8 ***Emerson***	Y	N	N	Y	N	Y	Y	Y
9 Volkmer	Y	Y	Y	Y	Y	Y	Y	Y
MONTANA								
1 Williams	N	Y	Y	Y	Y	Y	Y	Y
2 ***Marlenee***	Y	N	N	Y	N	N	N	Y
NEBRASKA								
1 ***Bereuter***	N	Y	Y	Y	N	N	Y	Y
2 ***Daub***	Y	N	N	Y	N	Y	Y	Y
3 ***Smith***	Y	Y	Y	Y	Y	Y	Y	Y
NEVADA								
1 Reid	Y	N	N	Y	Y	N	Y	Y
2 ***Vucanovich***	N	N	Y	Y	N	N	N	Y
NEW HAMPSHIRE								
1 ***Smith***	N	N	N	Y	N	N	N	Y
2 ***Gregg***	Y	N	N	Y	N	N	N	Y
NEW JERSEY								
1 Florio	Y	Y	Y	Y	Y	N	Y	Y
2 Hughes	Y	N	N	Y	Y	N	Y	Y
3 Howard	Y	Y	Y	Y	Y	Y	Y	Y
4 ***Smith***	Y	Y	Y	Y	Y	Y	N	Y
5 ***Roukema***	Y	Y	N	Y	Y	Y	N	Y
6 Dwyer	Y	Y	Y	Y	Y	Y	Y	N
7 ***Rinaldo***	Y	N	N	Y	Y	Y	N	Y
8 Roe	Y	Y	Y	Y	Y	Y	Y	N
9 Torricelli	N	Y	Y	Y	Y	Y	Y	N
10 Rodino	N	Y	Y	Y	Y	N	Y	Y
11 ***Gallo***	Y	N	N	Y	N	Y	N	Y
12 ***Courter***	Y	N	N	Y	N	Y	N	Y
13 ***Saxton***	Y	N	N	Y	N	N	N	Y
14 Guarini	Y	Y	N	Y	Y	Y	Y	Y
NEW MEXICO								
1 ***Lujan***	Y	N	N	Y	N	N	Y	N
2 ***Skeen***	Y	N	N	Y	N	Y	Y	Y
3 Richardson	Y	Y	Y	Y	Y	Y	Y	Y
NEW YORK								
1 ***Carney***	?	?	N	Y	?	N	N	N
2 Downey	Y	Y	Y	Y	Y	Y	Y	N
3 Mrazek	Y	Y	Y	Y	Y	Y	Y	N
4 ***Lent***	Y	?	N	Y	Y	Y	N	N
5 ***McGrath***	Y	N	N	Y	N	Y	Y	N
6 Waldon	Y	Y	Y	Y	Y	Y	Y	N
7 Ackerman	N	Y	Y	Y	Y	Y	Y	N
8 Scheuer	Y	Y	Y	Y	Y	Y	Y	N
9 Manton	Y	Y	Y	Y	Y	Y	Y	Y
10 Schumer	Y	Y	Y	Y	Y	Y	Y	N
11 Towns	N	Y	N	Y	Y	N	Y	Y
12 Owens	Y	Y	Y	Y	Y	N	Y	N
13 Solarz	Y	Y	Y	Y	Y	Y	Y	N
14 ***Molinari***	Y	N	N	Y	N	Y	N	Y
15 ***Green***	N	Y	Y	Y	Y	Y	Y	Y
16 Rangel	N	Y	N	Y	Y	N	Y	Y
17 Weiss	X	?	?	?	?	?	?	?
18 Garcia	N	Y	N	Y	Y	N	Y	Y
19 Biaggi	N	Y	N	Y	Y	Y	Y	Y
20 ***DioGuardi***	Y	Y	Y	Y	N	Y	N	N
21 ***Fish***	Y	Y	Y	Y	Y	Y	N	N
22 ***Gilman***	Y	Y	Y	Y	Y	Y	N	N
23 Stratton	Y	N	N	Y	Y	Y	Y	N
24 ***Solomon***	Y	N	N	Y	N	N	N	N
25 ***Boehlert***	Y	Y	Y	Y	Y	Y	N	N
26 ***Martin***	Y	N	N	Y	Y	Y	?	N
27 ***Wortley***	Y	Y	Y	Y	Y	Y	Y	N
28 McHugh	Y	Y	Y	Y	Y	Y	Y	N
29 ***Horton***	Y	Y	N	Y	Y	Y	Y	N
30 ***Eckert***	Y	N	Y	?	N	N	N	N
31 ***Kemp***	N	Y	N	Y	Y	Y	N	N
32 LaFalce	N	Y	Y	Y	Y	N	N	N
33 Nowak	N	Y	Y	Y	Y	Y	Y	N
34 Lundine	?	?	?	?	?	?	?	?
NORTH CAROLINA								
1 Jones	Y	Y	N	Y	Y	Y	Y	Y
2 Valentine	Y	Y	N	Y	Y	Y	Y	Y
3 Whitley	Y	Y	N	Y	Y	Y	Y	N
4 ***Cobey***	Y	N	N	Y	N	N	N	Y
5 Neal	Y	Y	N	Y	Y	N	Y	Y
6 ***Coble***	Y	N	N	Y	Y	Y	N	Y
7 Rose	Y	Y	Y	Y	Y	Y	Y	N
8 Hefner	Y	Y	Y	Y	Y	Y	Y	Y
9 ***McMillan***	Y	Y	Y	Y	Y	Y	N	Y
10 Vacancy								
11 ***Hendon***	Y	N	N	Y	Y	N	Y	Y
NORTH DAKOTA								
AL Dorgan	N	Y	Y	Y	Y	N	Y	Y
OHIO								
1 Luken	Y	Y	Y	Y	Y	Y	Y	Y
2 ***Gradison***	Y	Y	N	Y	N	N	N	Y
3 Hall	Y	Y	N	Y	Y	Y	Y	Y
4 ***Oxley***	Y	Y	Y	+	+	X	+	Y
5 ***Latta***	?	?	?	?	?	?	N	N
6 ***McEwen***	?	?	?	?	?	?	Y	Y
7 ***DeWine***	Y	Y	Y	Y	N	N	N	Y
8 ***Kindness***	?	?	?	?	?	?	?	?
9 Kaptur	Y	Y	N	Y	Y	Y	Y	Y
10 ***Miller***	N	N	N	Y	Y	Y	Y	N
11 Eckart	Y	Y	Y	Y	N	N	Y	Y
12 ***Kasich***	N	N	Y	Y	N	N	Y	Y
13 Pease	N	Y	Y	Y	Y	Y	Y	Y
14 Seiberling	N	Y	Y	Y	Y	N	Y	Y
15 ***Wylie***	Y	N	Y	Y	Y	Y	Y	Y
16 ***Regula***	N	N	N	Y	Y	Y	Y	Y
17 Traficant	N	N	N	Y	N	N	Y	Y
18 Applegate	N	Y	N	Y	Y	N	Y	Y
19 Feighan	Y	Y	Y	Y	Y	N	Y	N
20 Oakar	Y	Y	N	Y	Y	Y	Y	Y
21 Stokes	N	Y	Y	Y	Y	Y	Y	Y
OKLAHOMA								
1 Jones	?	?	?	?	?	?	?	?
2 Synar	Y	Y	Y	Y	Y	N	Y	Y
3 Watkins	Y	Y	N	Y	Y	Y	Y	Y
4 McCurdy	Y	Y	Y	Y	Y	Y	Y	Y
5 ***Edwards***	Y	Y	N	Y	N	Y	Y	Y
6 English	Y	Y	N	Y	Y	N	Y	Y
OREGON								
1 AuCoin	N	Y	Y	Y	Y	Y	Y	Y
2 ***Smith, R.***	N	N	N	Y	N	N	N	Y
3 Wyden	N	N	Y	Y	Y	Y	Y	Y
4 Weaver	N	?	?	Y	Y	N	Y	Y
5 ***Smith, D.***	N	N	N	Y	N	N	N	Y
PENNSYLVANIA								
1 Foglietta	N	Y	Y	Y	?	N	?	Y
2 Gray	N	Y	Y	Y	?	#	Y	Y
3 Borski	Y	Y	Y	Y	Y	Y	Y	Y
4 Kolter	Y	Y	N	Y	Y	N	Y	Y
5 ***Schulze***	Y	N	Y	Y	N	N	N	Y
6 Yatron	Y	Y	N	Y	Y	N	Y	Y
7 Edgar	N	Y	Y	Y	?	?	Y	Y
8 Kostmayer	N	Y	Y	Y	Y	N	Y	Y
9 ***Shuster***	N	N	N	Y	N	N	Y	Y
10 ***McDade***	N	Y	Y	Y	Y	Y	Y	Y
11 Kanjorski	Y	Y	Y	Y	Y	Y	Y	Y
12 Murtha	Y	Y	Y	Y	Y	Y	Y	Y
13 ***Coughlin***	N	Y	Y	Y	Y	Y	N	Y
14 Coyne	N	Y	Y	Y	Y	N	Y	Y
15 ***Ritter***	Y	N	N	Y	N	Y	N	Y
16 ***Walker***	N	N	Y	Y	N	N	N	Y
17 ***Gekas***	N	N	N	Y	N	N	N	Y
18 Walgren	Y	Y	Y	Y	Y	Y	Y	Y
19 ***Goodling***	Y	Y	Y	Y	Y	N	Y	Y
20 Gaydos	Y	Y	N	Y	Y	Y	Y	Y
21 ***Ridge***	Y	Y	Y	Y	N	N	N	Y
22 Murphy	Y	Y	N	Y	Y	N	Y	Y
23 ***Clinger***	N	Y	Y	Y	N	N	Y	Y
RHODE ISLAND								
1 St Germain	N	?	#	?	?	X	?	?
2 ***Schneider***	N	Y	Y	Y	N	N	N	Y
SOUTH CAROLINA								
1 ***Hartnett***	?	?	?	?	?	?	?	?
2 ***Spence***	Y	N	N	Y	N	N	Y	Y
3 Derrick	Y	Y	Y	Y	Y	Y	Y	Y
4 ***Campbell***	?	?	?	?	?	#	?	?
5 Spratt	Y	Y	Y	Y	Y	Y	Y	Y
6 Tallon	Y	N	N	Y	Y	N	Y	Y
SOUTH DAKOTA								
AL Daschle	N	Y	Y	Y	Y	N	?	N
TENNESSEE								
1 ***Quillen***	Y	Y	Y	Y	Y	Y	Y	N
2 ***Duncan***	Y	N	N	Y	Y	Y	Y	Y
3 Lloyd	Y	N	N	Y	N	N	Y	Y
4 Cooper	Y	Y	Y	Y	Y	Y	Y	Y
5 Boner	Y	Y	N	Y	Y	Y	Y	Y
6 Gordon	Y	Y	N	Y	Y	Y	Y	Y
7 ***Sundquist***	Y	N	N	Y	Y	Y	Y	Y
8 Jones	Y	Y	N	Y	Y	Y	Y	Y
9 Ford	Y	Y	Y	Y	Y	Y	Y	Y
TEXAS								
1 Chapman	Y	Y	N	Y	Y	Y	Y	Y
2 Wilson	Y	?	Y	Y	Y	Y	Y	N
3 ***Bartlett***	Y	N	N	Y	Y	Y	N	N
4 Hall, R.	Y	N	N	Y	N	Y	Y	Y
5 Bryant	Y	Y	Y	Y	Y	Y	Y	N
6 ***Barton***	Y	N	N	Y	N	N	N	Y
7 ***Archer***	Y	N	N	Y	N	N	Y	Y
8 ***Fields***	Y	N	N	Y	N	N	N	Y
9 Brooks	?	?	X	?	?	?	?	?
10 Pickle	Y	Y	Y	Y	Y	Y	Y	Y
11 Leath	Y	Y	N	Y	Y	Y	Y	Y
12 Wright	Y	Y	Y	Y	Y	Y	Y	N
13 ***Boulter***	Y	N	N	Y	Y	Y	Y	Y
14 ***Sweeney***	Y	N	N	Y	Y	Y	N	Y
15 de la Garza	Y	N	N	Y	Y	?	Y	Y
16 Coleman	Y	N	N	Y	Y	Y	Y	N
17 Stenholm	Y	N	N	Y	Y	Y	Y	Y
18 Leland	N	N	N	Y	Y	N	Y	Y
19 ***Combest***	Y	N	N	Y	N	N	Y	Y
20 Gonzalez	Y	N	N	Y	N	N	Y	Y
21 ***Loeffler***	Y	N	N	Y	Y	Y	Y	N
22 ***DeLay***	?	N	N	Y	N	N	N	N
23 Bustamante	Y	Y	Y	Y	Y	Y	Y	Y
24 Frost	Y	Y	N	Y	Y	Y	Y	Y
25 Andrews	Y	Y	N	Y	Y	Y	Y	N
26 ***Armey***	Y	N	N	Y	N	N	N	Y
27 Ortiz	Y	N	Y	Y	Y	Y	Y	Y
UTAH								
1 ***Hansen***	N	N	#	?	?	X	?	?
2 ***Monson***	N	Y	Y	Y	N	N	N	N
3 ***Nielson***	Y	Y	Y	Y	N	N	N	Y
VERMONT								
AL ***Jeffords***	Y	Y	Y	Y	Y	Y	Y	Y
VIRGINIA								
1 ***Bateman***	Y	Y	N	Y	Y	Y	N	N
2 ***Whitehurst***	Y	Y	Y	Y	Y	Y	Y	Y
3 ***Bliley***	Y	N	N	Y	Y	Y	N	Y
4 Sisisky	Y	Y	Y	Y	Y	Y	Y	Y
5 Daniel	Y	Y	N	Y	Y	Y	Y	Y
6 Olin	Y	Y	N	Y	Y	Y	Y	Y
7 ***Slaughter***	Y	N	N	Y	Y	Y	Y	N
8 ***Parris***	Y	Y	N	Y	Y	Y	Y	Y
9 Boucher	Y	Y	Y	Y	Y	Y	Y	Y
10 ***Wolf***	Y	Y	Y	Y	Y	Y	N	Y
WASHINGTON								
1 ***Miller***	Y	Y	Y	Y	N	N	N	Y
2 Swift	Y	Y	Y	Y	Y	Y	?	Y
3 Bonker	Y	Y	Y	Y	Y	Y	Y	Y
4 ***Morrison***	Y	Y	Y	Y	Y	Y	Y	Y
5 Foley	Y	Y	Y	Y	Y	Y	Y	Y
6 Dicks	Y	Y	Y	Y	Y	Y	Y	Y
7 Lowry	N	N	Y	Y	Y	N	Y	Y
8 ***Chandler***	Y	Y	Y	Y	N	Y	Y	Y
WEST VIRGINIA								
1 Mollohan	Y	Y	Y	Y	Y	Y	Y	Y
2 Staggers	Y	N	N	Y	Y	Y	Y	Y
3 Wise	Y	Y	Y	Y	Y	Y	Y	Y
4 Rahall	N	Y	Y	Y	Y	Y	Y	Y
WISCONSIN								
1 Aspin	Y	Y	Y	Y	Y	Y	Y	?
2 Kastenmeier	N	Y	Y	Y	Y	N	Y	Y
3 ***Gunderson***	N	Y	Y	Y	N	N	Y	Y
4 Kleczka	N	Y	N	Y	Y	N	Y	N
5 Moody	N	Y	Y	Y	N	N	Y	Y
6 ***Petri***	N	N	N	Y	N	N	N	Y
7 Obey	N	Y	Y	Y	Y	Y	Y	N
8 ***Roth***	Y	N	Y	Y	N	N	N	Y
9 ***Sensenbrenner***	N	N	N	Y	N	N	N	N
WYOMING								
AL ***Cheney***	N	N	Y	Y	Y	Y	N	Y

Southern states - Ala., Ark., Fla., Ga., Ky., La., Miss., N.C., Okla., S.C., Tenn., Texas, Va.

* The *Congressional Record* vote number is different from the CQ vote number because the *Record* includes quorum calls in its tally. CQ does not publish quorum call votes.

439. H J Res 738. Continuing Appropriations, Fiscal 1987. Regula, R-Ohio, motion that the House recede from its disagreement and concur in the Senate amendment, with an amendment to require that 50 percent of labor and materials used in offshore drilling rigs be American in origin. Motion agreed to 264-133: R 79-88; D 185-45 (ND 128-28, SD 57-17), in the session that began Oct. 15, 1986.

440. H J Res 738. Continuing Appropriations, Fiscal 1987. Lehman, D-Fla., motion that the House recede from its disagreement and concur in the Senate amendment, with an amendment to allow for the transfer of Washington-Dulles International Airport and National Airport from the federal government to a regional authority. Motion agreed to 250-135: R 138-25; D 112-110 (ND 67-80, SD 45-30), in the session that began Oct. 15, 1986.

441. H J Res 753. Further Interim Continuing Appropriations, Fiscal 1987. Passage of the joint resolution to provide funds through Oct. 16, 1986, for programs covered by the 13 regular appropriations bills, at various rates determined by the status of the individual bills at the time H J Res 753 was passed. Funding for the Departments of Housing and Urban Development, Labor, Health and Human Services, Education and Transportation, and for legislative branch programs would be at levels set by conference agreements on fiscal 1987 appropriations bills; for others, spending would be at fiscal 1986 levels or at levels contained in the House- or Senate-passed 1987 bill, whichever was lowest. Passed 260-97: R 71-82; D 189-15 (ND 125-9, SD 64-6), in the session that began Oct. 15, 1986.

442. Procedural Motion. Porter, R-Ill., motion to approve the House *Journal* of Wednesday, Oct. 15. Motion agreed to 237-120: R 41-112; D 196-8 (ND 131-6, SD 65-2), Oct. 16, 1986.

443. HR 5705. Columbia River Gorge. Adoption of the rule (H Res 596) to provide for House floor consideration of the bill to protect and enhance the resources of the Columbia River Gorge, along the border of Oregon and Washington. Adopted 252-138: R 30-132; D 222-6 (ND 156-2, SD 66-4), Oct. 16, 1986.

444. HR 5705. Columbia River Gorge. Robert F. Smith, R-Ore., substitute to establish a scenic area commission and provide for expanded local control of the scenic area. Rejected 111-272: R 100-56; D 11-216 (ND 4-154, SD 7-62), Oct. 16, 1986.

445. HR 5705. Columbia River Gorge. Passage of the bill to protect and enhance the resources of the Columbia River Gorge, along the border of Oregon and Washington. Passed 290-91: R 75-84; D 215-7 (ND 154-2, SD 61-5), Oct. 16, 1986.

446. S 2127. Boxing Commission. Adoption of the rule (H Res 595) to provide for House floor consideration of the bill to establish a U.S. Boxing Commission to oversee and regulate the sport of boxing. Adopted 337-28: R 128-26; D 209-2 (ND 145-1, SD 64-1), Oct. 16, 1986. (The bill later was passed by voice vote.)

KEY

Y Voted for (yea).
Paired for.
+ Announced for.
N Voted against (nay).
X Paired against.
- Announced against.
P Voted "present."
C Voted "present" to avoid possible conflict of interest.
? Did not vote or otherwise make a position known.

Democrats ***Republicans***

	439	440	441	442	443	444	445	446
ALABAMA								
1 ***Callahan***	Y	Y	N	N	N	Y	N	Y
2 ***Dickinson***	N	Y	Y	N	N	Y	Y	N
3 Nichols	?	?	?	?	?	?	?	?
4 Bevill	Y	N	?	?	Y	N	Y	Y
5 Flippo	Y	N	Y	Y	Y	N	Y	Y
6 Erdreich	Y	Y	Y	Y	Y	N	Y	Y
7 Shelby	Y	N	N	Y	Y	N	Y	Y
ALASKA								
AL ***Young***	Y	Y	Y	N	N	Y	N	Y
ARIZONA								
1 ***McCain***	?	?	?	?	?	?	?	?
2 Udall	N	N	Y	Y	Y	N	Y	Y
3 ***Stump***	N	Y	N	N	N	Y	N	N
4 ***Rudd***	?	?	?	?	?	?	?	?
5 ***Kolbe***	N	Y	N	N	N	Y	N	Y
ARKANSAS								
1 Alexander	Y	Y	Y	Y	Y	N	Y	Y
2 Robinson	Y	N	N	Y	N	N	N	Y
3 ***Hammerschmidt***	Y	Y	Y	Y	N	Y	N	Y
4 Anthony	N	Y	Y	Y	Y	N	Y	Y
CALIFORNIA								
1 Bosco	Y	N	?	Y	Y	N	Y	Y
2 ***Chappie***	Y	Y	N	N	N	Y	N	Y
3 Matsui	N	Y	Y	Y	Y	N	Y	Y
4 Fazio	Y	Y	Y	Y	Y	N	Y	Y
5 Burton	?	?	?	Y	Y	N	Y	?
6 Boxer	Y	N	Y	Y	Y	N	Y	Y
7 Miller	Y	?	?	Y	Y	N	Y	Y
8 Dellums	Y	?	Y	?	Y	N	Y	Y
9 Stark	Y	N	Y	Y	Y	N	Y	?
10 Edwards	Y	N	Y	Y	Y	N	Y	Y
11 Lantos	Y	Y	Y	Y	Y	N	Y	Y
12 ***Zschau***	N	Y	N	?	N	N	Y	Y
13 Mineta	N	Y	Y	Y	Y	N	Y	Y
14 ***Shumway***	N	Y	N	Y	N	Y	N	Y
15 Coelho	Y	N	Y	Y	Y	N	Y	Y
16 Panetta	Y	Y	Y	Y	Y	Y	Y	Y
17 ***Pashayan***	Y	N	Y	N	N	Y	N	Y
18 Lehman	Y	N	Y	Y	Y	N	Y	Y
19 ***Lagomarsino***	N	Y	N	N	N	Y	N	Y
20 ***Thomas***	N	Y	N	N	N	Y	N	Y
21 ***Fiedler***	?	?	?	?	?	?	?	?
22 ***Moorhead***	N	Y	N	N	N	Y	N	Y
23 Beilenson	N	Y	Y	Y	Y	N	Y	Y
24 Waxman	?	?	?	?	Y	N	Y	Y
25 Roybal	Y	Y	Y	Y	Y	N	Y	Y
26 Berman	N	Y	Y	Y	Y	N	?	Y
27 Levine	Y	?	?	Y	Y	N	Y	Y
28 Dixon	Y	Y	?	Y	Y	N	Y	Y
29 Hawkins	Y	?	?	Y	Y	N	Y	Y
30 Martinez	Y	N	Y	Y	Y	N	Y	Y
31 Dymally	Y	Y	Y	Y	Y	N	Y	Y
32 Anderson	Y	N	Y	Y	Y	?	Y	Y
33 ***Dreier***	N	Y	N	N	N	Y	N	Y
34 Torres	Y	Y	Y	Y	Y	?	Y	Y
35 ***Lewis***	N	Y	N	N	N	Y	N	N
36 Brown	Y	Y	?	Y	Y	N	Y	?
37 ***McCandless***	N	Y	N	N	N	Y	N	N
38 ***Dornan***	N	Y	N	Y	N	Y	N	N
39 ***Dannemeyer***	N	Y	N	N	N	Y	N	Y
40 ***Badham***	N	Y	N	N	N	Y	N	Y
41 ***Lowery***	Y	Y	Y	N	N	Y	Y	Y
42 ***Lungren***	N	Y	N	Y	N	Y	N	Y
43 ***Packard***	N	Y	N	N	N	Y	N	Y
44 Bates	N	Y	N	Y	Y	N	Y	Y
45 ***Hunter***	Y	Y	N	N	N	Y	N	N
COLORADO								
1 Schroeder	N	N	Y	N	Y	N	Y	Y
2 Wirth	Y	Y	?	Y	Y	N	Y	Y
3 ***Strang***	Y	Y	N	?	N	Y	N	Y
4 ***Brown***	N	Y	N	N	N	Y	N	Y
5 ***Kramer***	Y	Y	N	N	N	Y	N	Y
6 ***Schaefer***	Y	Y	N	N	N	N	N	N
CONNECTICUT								
1 Kennelly	Y	Y	Y	Y	Y	N	Y	?
2 Gejdenson	Y	N	Y	Y	Y	N	Y	Y
3 Morrison	Y	Y	Y	Y	Y	N	Y	Y
4 ***McKinney***	Y	Y	Y	?	?	N	Y	Y
5 ***Rowland***	Y	Y	N	?	Y	N	Y	Y
6 ***Johnson***	Y	Y	Y	Y	Y	N	Y	Y
DELAWARE								
AL Carper	Y	Y	Y	Y	Y	N	Y	Y
FLORIDA								
1 Hutto	N	Y	Y	Y	Y	N	Y	Y
2 Fuqua	Y	Y	?	Y	Y	N	Y	Y
3 Bennett	Y	N	Y	Y	Y	N	Y	Y
4 Chappell	Y	N	Y	Y	Y	N	Y	?
5 ***McCollum***	N	Y	Y	N	N	?	Y	Y
6 MacKay	N	N	Y	Y	Y	N	Y	?
7 Gibbons	N	N	Y	Y	Y	N	Y	Y
8 ***Young***	Y	Y	Y	N	N	N	Y	N
9 ***Bilirakis***	N	Y	N	N	N	Y	N	N
10 ***Ireland***	N	Y	Y	N	N	N	Y	Y
11 Nelson	Y	Y	Y	Y	Y	N	Y	Y
12 ***Lewis***	N	Y	N	N	N	Y	Y	Y
13 ***Mack***	N	Y	N	N	N	Y	N	N
14 Mica	N	N	Y	Y	Y	N	Y	Y
15 ***Shaw***	N	Y	Y	N	N	Y	N	Y
16 Smith	Y	Y	Y	Y	Y	N	Y	Y
17 Lehman	N	Y	Y	Y	Y	N	Y	Y
18 Pepper	Y	N	Y	Y	Y	N	Y	Y
19 Fascell	N	Y	Y	Y	Y	N	?	Y
GEORGIA								
1 Thomas	Y	Y	Y	Y	Y	N	Y	Y
2 Hatcher	Y	Y	Y	Y	Y	Y	Y	Y
3 Ray	Y	Y	N	Y	N	Y	N	Y
4 ***Swindall***	N	Y	N	N	N	Y	N	Y
5 Fowler	?	?	?	Y	Y	N	?	Y
6 ***Gingrich***	Y	Y	?	?	Y	N	Y	?
7 Darden	Y	Y	Y	Y	Y	N	Y	Y
8 Rowland	Y	Y	Y	Y	Y	N	Y	Y
9 Jenkins	Y	N	Y	Y	Y	N	Y	Y
10 Barnard	Y	Y	Y	Y	Y	N	Y	Y
HAWAII								
1 Abercrombie	Y	N	Y	Y	Y	N	Y	Y
2 Akaka	Y	Y	Y	Y	Y	N	Y	Y
IDAHO								
1 ***Craig***	N	Y	N	N	N	Y	N	Y
2 Stallings	N	Y	N	Y	Y	N	Y	Y
ILLINOIS								
1 Hayes	Y	N	Y	Y	#	X	#	?
2 Savage	Y	N	Y	Y	Y	N	Y	Y
3 Russo	Y	N	N	Y	Y	N	Y	Y
4 Vacancy								
5 Lipinski	Y	N	Y	Y	Y	N	Y	Y
6 ***Hyde***	N	Y	?	Y	N	?	?	?
7 Collins	Y	N	Y	Y	Y	N	Y	Y
8 Rostenkowski	Y	Y	Y	Y	Y	N	Y	?
9 Yates	Y	N	?	Y	Y	N	?	Y
10 ***Porter***	N	Y	N	N	N	N	Y	Y
11 Annunzio	Y	N	Y	Y	Y	N	Y	Y
12 ***Crane***	N	Y	N	N	N	N	N	Y
13 ***Fawell***	N	Y	N	N	Y	N	N	Y
14 ***Grotberg***	?	?	?	?	?	?	?	?
15 ***Madigan***	Y	Y	Y	N	Y	Y	Y	Y
16 ***Martin***	Y	Y	Y	N	N	Y	N	Y
17 Evans	Y	N	Y	Y	Y	N	Y	Y
18 ***Michel***	N	Y	Y	Y	N	Y	N	Y
19 Bruce	Y	N	N	Y	Y	N	Y	Y
20 Durbin	Y	Y	Y	Y	Y	N	Y	Y
21 Price	Y	N	Y	Y	Y	N	Y	Y
22 Gray	Y	Y	Y	Y	Y	N	Y	Y
INDIANA								
1 Visclosky	Y	N	Y	Y	Y	N	Y	Y
2 Sharp	Y	Y	Y	Y	Y	N	Y	Y
3 ***Hiler***	N	Y	N	N	N	Y	Y	Y
4 ***Coats***	N	Y	N	N	N	?	Y	Y
5 ***Hillis***	N	Y	?	Y	N	Y	Y	?

ND - Northern Democrats SD - Southern Democrats

* Corresponding to Congressional Record Votes 475, 476, 477, 478, 479, 481, 482, 483

	439	440	441	442	443	444	445	446
6 ***Burton***	N	Y	N	N	N	Y	N	N
7 ***Myers***	Y	N	Y	Y	Y	N	Y	Y
8 McCloskey	Y	Y	Y	Y	Y	N	Y	Y
9 Hamilton	Y	Y	Y	Y	Y	N	Y	Y
10 Jacobs	Y	Y	Y	N	N	N	N	Y
IOWA								
1 ***Leach***	N	Y	N	N	Y	N	Y	Y
2 ***Tauke***	N	Y	N	N	N	N	Y	Y
3 ***Evans***	N	Y	N	?	N	Y	N	Y
4 Smith	N	N	Y	Y	Y	N	Y	Y
5 ***Lightfoot***	N	Y	N	N	N	Y	N	Y
6 Bedell	N	N	Y	?	Y	N	Y	Y
KANSAS								
1 ***Roberts***	N	Y	N	N	N	Y	N	Y
2 Slattery	Y	Y	N	Y	Y	N	Y	Y
3 ***Meyers***	N	Y	N	N	Y	N	Y	Y
4 Glickman	Y	Y	Y	Y	Y	N	Y	Y
5 ***Whittaker***	N	Y	N	N	N	Y	N	Y
KENTUCKY								
1 Hubbard	Y	N	N	Y	Y	N	Y	Y
2 Natcher	Y	N	Y	Y	Y	N	Y	Y
3 Mazzoli	N	N	Y	Y	Y	Y	Y	Y
4 ***Snyder***	Y	N	Y	Y	N	Y	N	?
5 ***Rogers***	Y	N	Y	N	N	Y	N	Y
6 ***Hopkins***	?	Y	N	N	N	?	N	Y
7 Perkins	Y	N	Y	Y	Y	N	Y	Y
LOUISIANA								
1 ***Livingston***	Y	Y	Y	Y	N	Y	N	Y
2 Boggs	Y	Y	Y	Y	Y	N	Y	Y
3 Tauzin	Y	Y	Y	Y	Y	N	Y	Y
4 Roemer	Y	Y	N	N	Y	N	Y	Y
5 Huckaby	Y	Y	Y	?	Y	Y	Y	N
6 ***Moore***	?	?	?	?	?	?	?	?
7 Breaux	?	?	?	?	?	?	?	?
8 Long	?	?	?	?	Y	N	Y	Y
MAINE								
1 ***McKernan***	Y	N	Y	N	N	N	Y	Y
2 ***Snowe***	Y	N	Y	N	N	N	Y	Y
MARYLAND								
1 Dyson	Y	N	Y	Y	Y	N	Y	Y
2 ***Bentley***	Y	Y	Y	N	N	Y	N	Y
3 Mikulski	Y	Y	?	?	Y	N	Y	?
4 ***Holt***	N	Y	Y	Y	N	Y	?	?
5 Hoyer	N	Y	Y	Y	Y	N	Y	Y
6 Byron	Y	N	N	?	Y	N	Y	Y
7 Mitchell	Y	Y	?	N	?	?	?	?
8 Barnes	Y	Y	Y	Y	Y	N	Y	Y
MASSACHUSETTS								
1 ***Conte***	Y	Y	Y	N	Y	N	Y	Y
2 Boland	Y	N	Y	Y	Y	N	Y	Y
3 Early	N	N	Y	Y	Y	N	Y	Y
4 Frank	N	N	Y	Y	Y	N	Y	N
5 Atkins	N	N	Y	?	Y	N	Y	Y
6 Mavroules	Y	N	Y	Y	Y	N	Y	?
7 Markey	N	N	Y	?	Y	N	Y	Y
8 O'Neill								
9 Moakley	Y	N	Y	Y	Y	N	Y	Y
10 Studds	Y	Y	?	Y	Y	N	Y	Y
11 Donnelly	Y	Y	Y	Y	Y	N	Y	Y
MICHIGAN								
1 Conyers	?	?	?	?	?	N	Y	?
2 ***Pursell***	N	?	?	N	Y	N	Y	Y
3 Wolpe	Y	N	Y	Y	Y	N	Y	Y
4 ***Siljander***	N	?	?	N	N	Y	N	Y
5 ***Henry***	Y	Y	N	N	Y	N	Y	Y
6 Carr	Y	N	Y	Y	Y	N	Y	Y
7 Kildee	Y	Y	Y	Y	Y	N	Y	Y
8 Traxler	?	?	?	Y	Y	N	Y	Y
9 ***Vander Jagt***	N	Y	?	N	N	N	N	Y
10 ***Schuette***	Y	Y	Y	N	N	Y	N	Y
11 ***Davis***	Y	Y	Y	?	?	?	?	?
12 Bonior	Y	N	?	Y	Y	N	Y	Y
13 Crockett	?	?	?	P	Y	N	Y	?
14 Hertel	Y	N	N	Y	Y	N	Y	Y
15 Ford	Y	N	Y	?	Y	N	Y	Y
16 Dingell	Y	?	?	?	Y	N	Y	Y
17 Levin	Y	N	Y	Y	Y	N	Y	Y
18 ***Broomfield***	Y	?	?	Y	N	?	?	?
MINNESOTA								
1 Penny	N	Y	N	N	Y	N	Y	Y
2 ***Weber***	N	Y	N	N	N	N	Y	N
3 ***Frenzel***	N	Y	N	N	N	N	Y	Y
4 Vento	Y	N	Y	Y	Y	N	Y	Y
5 Sabo	Y	N	Y	Y	Y	N	Y	Y
6 Sikorski	Y	Y	Y	N	Y	N	Y	Y

	439	440	441	442	443	444	445	446
7 ***Stangeland***	N	N	Y	N	N	Y	N	N
8 Oberstar	Y	N	Y	Y	Y	N	Y	Y
MISSISSIPPI								
1 Whitten	Y	N	Y	?	?	?	?	?
2 ***Franklin***	Y	Y	N	N	N	Y	N	Y
3 Montgomery	Y	Y	?	Y	Y	N	Y	Y
4 Dowdy	Y	N	Y	Y	Y	N	Y	Y
5 ***Lott***	Y	Y	N	?	N	?	N	N
MISSOURI								
1 Clay	Y	N	Y	N	Y	N	Y	Y
2 Young	Y	Y	Y	Y	Y	N	Y	Y
3 Gephardt	Y	?	?	?	?	N	?	?
4 Skelton	Y	?	?	Y	Y	N	Y	Y
5 Wheat	Y	Y	Y	Y	Y	N	Y	Y
6 ***Coleman***	Y	N	Y	N	N	Y	Y	Y
7 ***Taylor***	Y	N	N	N	N	Y	N	Y
8 ***Emerson***	Y	N	Y	N	N	Y	N	Y
9 Volkmer	Y	N	Y	Y	Y	N	Y	Y
MONTANA								
1 Williams	?	?	?	?	N	N	Y	Y
2 ***Marlenee***	N	N	N	?	N	Y	N	N
NEBRASKA								
1 ***Bereuter***	N	Y	N	N	N	N	Y	Y
2 ***Daub***	Y	Y	Y	N	N	Y	N	Y
3 ***Smith***	N	Y	Y	Y	N	Y	N	Y
NEVADA								
1 Reid	Y	N	Y	Y	Y	N	Y	Y
2 ***Vucanovich***	N	Y	Y	?	N	N	N	N
NEW HAMPSHIRE								
1 ***Smith***	Y	Y	N	N	N	Y	Y	Y
2 ***Gregg***	N	Y	N	N	N	Y	Y	N
NEW JERSEY								
1 Florio	?	?	?	?	Y	N	Y	Y
2 Hughes	Y	N	Y	?	Y	N	Y	Y
3 Howard	Y	N	Y	Y	Y	N	Y	Y
4 ***Smith***	Y	Y	Y	?	Y	N	Y	Y
5 ***Roukema***	Y	Y	Y	N	N	N	Y	Y
6 Dwyer	Y	Y	Y	Y	Y	N	Y	Y
7 ***Rinaldo***	Y	N	Y	?	Y	N	Y	Y
8 Roe	?	?	?	Y	Y	N	Y	Y
9 Torricelli	Y	N	Y	?	Y	N	Y	Y
10 Rodino	N	Y	?	?	Y	N	Y	Y
11 ***Gallo***	Y	Y	Y	N	Y	?	Y	Y
12 ***Courter***	N	Y	N	N	N	N	Y	Y
13 ***Saxton***	N	Y	Y	N	Y	N	Y	Y
14 Guarini	N	N	Y	Y	Y	N	Y	Y
NEW MEXICO								
1 ***Lujan***	Y	N	N	Y	N	Y	N	Y
2 ***Skeen***	Y	Y	Y	N	N	Y	N	Y
3 Richardson	Y	Y	Y	Y	Y	N	Y	Y
NEW YORK								
1 ***Carney***	Y	N	N	?	Y	?	?	?
2 Downey	Y	N	Y	Y	Y	N	Y	Y
3 Mrazek	Y	Y	Y	?	Y	N	Y	Y
4 ***Lent***	N	N	Y	N	N	Y	Y	Y
5 ***McGrath***	?	?	?	N	?	?	?	?
6 Waldon	Y	Y	Y	?	Y	N	Y	?
7 Ackerman	Y	N	Y	Y	Y	N	Y	Y
8 Scheuer	N	N	Y	Y	Y	N	Y	Y
9 Manton	Y	Y	Y	Y	Y	?	?	?
10 Schumer	Y	N	Y	Y	Y	N	Y	Y
11 Towns	Y	N	Y	?	?	N	Y	Y
12 Owens	Y	N	Y	Y	Y	N	Y	Y
13 Solarz	N	N	?	Y	Y	N	Y	?
14 ***Molinari***	N	Y	Y	N	N	Y	Y	Y
15 ***Green***	N	Y	Y	Y	Y	N	Y	Y
16 Rangel	Y	N	Y	Y	Y	N	Y	Y
17 Weiss	?	?	?	?	?	?	?	?
18 Garcia	Y	N	?	?	Y	N	Y	Y
19 Biaggi	Y	N	Y	Y	Y	N	?	?
20 ***DioGuardi***	N	Y	Y	Y	N	N	Y	Y
21 ***Fish***	?	?	?	Y	Y	N	Y	Y
22 ***Gilman***	Y	Y	Y	Y	Y	N	Y	Y
23 Stratton	Y	N	Y	Y	Y	Y	Y	Y
24 ***Solomon***	Y	N	N	N	N	N	Y	Y
25 ***Boehlert***	Y	Y	Y	N	N	N	Y	Y
26 ***Martin***	Y	Y	Y	N	?	?	?	?
27 ***Wortley***	Y	Y	Y	Y	Y	N	Y	Y
28 McHugh	N	N	Y	Y	Y	N	Y	Y
29 ***Horton***	Y	N	Y	Y	Y	N	Y	Y
30 ***Eckert***	N	Y	Y	Y	N	Y	N	Y
31 ***Kemp***	N	?	?	?	?	?	?	?
32 LaFalce	N	Y	Y	Y	Y	N	Y	Y
33 Nowak	Y	Y	Y	Y	Y	N	Y	Y
34 Lundine	?	?	?	?	?	?	?	?

	439	440	441	442	443	444	445	446
NORTH CAROLINA								
1 Jones	Y	Y	Y	Y	Y	N	Y	Y
2 Valentine	Y	Y	Y	Y	Y	N	Y	Y
3 Whitley	Y	N	Y	Y	Y	N	Y	Y
4 ***Cobey***	Y	Y	N	N	N	Y	N	Y
5 Neal	?	N	Y	?	Y	N	Y	Y
6 ***Coble***	Y	Y	Y	N	Y	Y	Y	Y
7 Rose	Y	N	Y	Y	Y	N	?	?
8 Hefner	Y	N	Y	?	?	?	?	?
9 ***McMillan***	Y	Y	Y	N	Y	N	Y	Y
10 Vacancy								
11 ***Hendon***	Y	N	Y	N	N	Y	Y	N
NORTH DAKOTA								
AL Dorgan	Y	N	Y	Y	Y	N	Y	Y
OHIO								
1 Luken	Y	N	?	Y	Y	N	Y	Y
2 ***Gradison***	N	Y	?	Y	N	Y	N	Y
3 Hall	?	?	?	Y	Y	N	Y	Y
4 ***Oxley***	N	Y	N	N	N	Y	N	N
5 ***Latta***	N	Y	N	N	N	Y	N	Y
6 ***McEwen***	Y	?	N	Y	N	N	Y	Y
7 ***DeWine***	N	Y	N	N	N	Y	Y	Y
8 ***Kindness***	?	?	?	?	?	?	?	?
9 Kaptur	?	?	?	+	+	-	+	+
10 ***Miller***	Y	N	Y	N	N	Y	N	Y
11 Eckart	Y	Y	N	Y	Y	N	Y	Y
12 ***Kasich***	Y	N	N	Y	N	Y	N	Y
13 Pease	Y	Y	Y	Y	Y	N	Y	Y
14 Seiberling	Y	Y	Y	Y	Y	N	Y	?
15 ***Wylie***	Y	Y	Y	Y	N	N	Y	Y
16 ***Regula***	Y	Y	Y	Y	N	N	Y	Y
17 Traficant	Y	Y	Y	Y	Y	Y	Y	Y
18 Applegate	Y	Y	Y	Y	Y	Y	N	Y
19 Feighan	Y	N	Y	Y	Y	N	Y	Y
20 Oakar	Y	N	Y	?	Y	N	Y	Y
21 Stokes	Y	N	?	?	Y	N	Y	Y
OKLAHOMA								
1 Jones	?	?	?	?	?	?	?	?
2 Synar	N	Y	Y	Y	Y	N	Y	Y
3 Watkins	N	N	Y	Y	Y	N	Y	Y
4 McCurdy	N	Y	Y	Y	Y	N	Y	Y
5 ***Edwards***	N	Y	Y	?	N	Y	N	Y
6 English	N	N	Y	Y	Y	N	Y	Y
OREGON								
1 AuCoin	N	Y	Y	Y	Y	N	Y	Y
2 ***Smith, R.***	N	Y	?	N	N	Y	N	Y
3 Wyden	N	Y	Y	Y	Y	N	Y	Y
4 Weaver	Y	?	?	Y	Y	N	Y	Y
5 ***Smith, D.***	N	Y	N	N	N	N	N	N
PENNSYLVANIA								
1 Foglietta	Y	Y	Y	Y	Y	N	Y	Y
2 Gray	Y	Y	Y	Y	Y	?	?	?
3 Borski	Y	N	Y	Y	Y	N	Y	Y
4 Kolter	Y	N	Y	Y	Y	N	Y	?
5 ***Schulze***	Y	N	?	Y	N	Y	Y	Y
6 Yatron	Y	Y	Y	Y	Y	N	Y	Y
7 Edgar	Y	Y	Y	?	Y	N	Y	Y
8 Kostmayer	Y	Y	Y	?	?	?	?	Y
9 ***Shuster***	?	?	?	N	N	Y	N	N
10 ***McDade***	Y	Y	?	Y	Y	N	Y	Y
11 Kanjorski	Y	N	Y	?	Y	N	Y	Y
12 Murtha	Y	?	?	?	?	?	?	?
13 ***Coughlin***	Y	Y	Y	N	N	N	Y	Y
14 Coyne	Y	Y	Y	Y	Y	N	Y	Y
15 ***Ritter***	Y	Y	Y	Y	Y	N	Y	Y
16 ***Walker***	Y	Y	N	N	N	Y	N	Y
17 ***Gekas***	Y	Y	N	N	N	Y	N	Y
18 Walgren	Y	Y	Y	?	Y	N	Y	Y
19 ***Goodling***	Y	Y	Y	N	N	Y	Y	Y
20 Gaydos	Y	Y	Y	Y	Y	N	Y	Y
21 ***Ridge***	Y	Y	N	N	N	N	?	?
22 Murphy	Y	N	Y	Y	Y	N	Y	Y
23 ***Clinger***	Y	Y	?	Y	Y	N	Y	Y
RHODE ISLAND								
1 St Germain	?	?	?	Y	Y	N	Y	Y
2 ***Schneider***	Y	Y	Y	N	N	N	Y	Y
SOUTH CAROLINA								
1 ***Hartnett***	?	?	?	?	?	?	?	?
2 ***Spence***	Y	N	Y	Y	N	N	Y	Y
3 Derrick	Y	N	Y	Y	?	?	?	?
4 ***Campbell***	?	?	?	?	?	?	?	?
5 Spratt	Y	N	Y	Y	Y	N	Y	Y
6 Tallon	N	Y	Y	Y	N	?	?	?
SOUTH DAKOTA								
AL Daschle	Y	N	Y	Y	Y	N	Y	Y

	439	440	441	442	443	444	445	446
TENNESSEE								
1 ***Quillen***	Y	N	Y	Y	N	Y	N	N
2 ***Duncan***	Y	N	Y	Y	N	Y	Y	Y
3 Lloyd	Y	N	Y	?	Y	N	Y	?
4 Cooper	N	Y	Y	Y	?	?	?	?
5 Boner	Y	N	Y	Y	Y	?	?	?
6 Gordon	Y	N	Y	Y	Y	N	Y	Y
7 ***Sundquist***	Y	N	N	N	N	Y	N	Y
8 Jones	Y	N	Y	?	?	?	?	?
9 Ford	Y	N	Y	Y	Y	N	Y	Y
TEXAS								
1 Chapman	Y	Y	Y	Y	Y	N	Y	Y
2 Wilson	Y	Y	Y	Y	Y	N	Y	Y
3 ***Bartlett***	N	Y	N	N	?	Y	N	Y
4 Hall, R.	Y	Y	Y	Y	Y	N	Y	Y
5 Bryant	Y	Y	Y	Y	Y	N	Y	Y
6 ***Barton***	N	Y	N	N	?	?	X	?
7 ***Archer***	N	Y	N	?	?	?	?	?
8 ***Fields***	N	Y	N	N	N	Y	N	Y
9 Brooks	?	?	?	?	?	?	?	?
10 Pickle	N	Y	?	?	?	?	?	?
11 Leath	?	?	?	Y	?	N	Y	Y
12 Wright	Y	Y	Y	Y	?	N	Y	Y
13 ***Boulter***	N	Y	Y	Y	N	Y	N	Y
14 ***Sweeney***	N	Y	N	?	?	?	?	?
15 de la Garza	Y	Y	Y	?	Y	?	?	?
16 Coleman	Y	Y	Y	Y	Y	N	Y	Y
17 Stenholm	N	Y	N	N	Y	Y	N	Y
18 Leland	Y	Y	Y	?	Y	N	Y	Y
19 ***Combest***	N	Y	N	N	N	Y	N	N
20 Gonzalez	Y	Y	Y	Y	Y	N	Y	Y
21 ***Loeffler***	N	Y	Y	N	N	Y	N	N
22 ***DeLay***	N	Y	N	?	N	Y	N	?
23 Bustamante	Y	Y	Y	Y	Y	N	Y	Y
24 Frost	Y	Y	Y	Y	Y	N	Y	Y
25 Andrews	Y	Y	Y	Y	Y	N	Y	Y
26 ***Armey***	N	Y	N	N	N	Y	N	Y
27 Ortiz	N	Y	Y	Y	Y	N	Y	Y
UTAH								
1 ***Hansen***	?	?	?	?	X	#	X	?
2 ***Monson***	N	Y	N	N	N	Y	N	N
3 ***Nielson***	N	Y	N	N	N	Y	N	Y
VERMONT								
AL ***Jeffords***	Y	Y	?	Y	N	N	Y	Y
VIRGINIA								
1 ***Bateman***	Y	Y	Y	Y	N	Y	Y	Y
2 ***Whitehurst***	Y	Y	?	N	N	Y	Y	?
3 ***Bliley***	N	Y	Y	N	N	Y	Y	Y
4 Sisisky	Y	Y	Y	Y	Y	N	Y	Y
5 Daniel	Y	Y	Y	Y	Y	Y	N	Y
6 Olin	Y	Y	?	Y	N	Y	N	Y
7 ***Slaughter***	N	Y	Y	N	N	Y	N	Y
8 ***Parris***	Y	Y	Y	Y	N	Y	N	Y
9 Boucher	Y	Y	Y	Y	Y	N	Y	Y
10 ***Wolf***	N	Y	Y	N	N	Y	Y	Y
WASHINGTON								
1 ***Miller***	N	Y	N	Y	Y	N	Y	Y
2 Swift	Y	Y	Y	Y	Y	N	Y	Y
3 Bonker	N	Y	Y	Y	?	N	Y	Y
4 ***Morrison***	N	Y	Y	Y	Y	N	Y	Y
5 Foley	N	Y	Y	Y	Y	N	Y	Y
6 Dicks	Y	Y	Y	?	Y	N	Y	Y
7 Lowry	N	N	Y	Y	Y	N	Y	Y
8 ***Chandler***	N	Y	Y	N	Y	N	Y	Y
WEST VIRGINIA								
1 Mollohan	Y	Y	Y	Y	Y	N	Y	Y
2 Staggers	Y	N	Y	Y	Y	N	Y	Y
3 Wise	Y	N	Y	Y	Y	N	Y	Y
4 Rahall	Y	N	Y	Y	Y	N	Y	Y
WISCONSIN								
1 Aspin	?	?	?	Y	Y	N	Y	Y
2 Kastenmeier	Y	N	Y	Y	Y	N	Y	Y
3 ***Gunderson***	Y	Y	N	N	N	N	Y	Y
4 Kleczka	Y	N	Y	?	Y	N	Y	Y
5 Moody	N	N	Y	Y	?	?	#	?
6 ***Petri***	N	Y	N	N	N	Y	Y	Y
7 Obey	Y	N	Y	Y	Y	N	Y	Y
8 ***Roth***	Y	Y	N	N	Y	N	Y	Y
9 ***Sensenbrenner***	N	Y	N	N	N	Y	Y	Y
WYOMING								
AL ***Cheney***	Y	Y	Y	Y	N	Y	N	N

Southern states - Ala., Ark., Fla., Ga., Ky., La., Miss., N.C., Okla., S.C., Tenn., Texas, Va.

* The *Congressional Record* vote number is different from the CQ vote number because the *Record* includes quorum calls in its tally. CQ does not publish quorum call votes.

447. Procedural Motion. Brown, R-Colo., motion to approve the House *Journal* of Thursday, Oct. 16. Motion agreed to 226-113: R 40-107; D 186-6 (ND 128-5, SD 58-1), Oct. 17, 1986.

448. HR 5484. Omnibus Drug Bill. Adoption of the rule (H Res 597) to provide for concurring in the Senate amendment to the House amendment to the Senate amendment to the bill to authorize $1.7 billion for federal drug interdiction, enforcement, education, treatment and rehabilitation efforts, with an amendment to make modest changes in the bill. By adopting the rule, the House was considered to have concurred in the Senate amendment, with its own amendment, and also to have adopted a concurrent resolution (H Con Res 415) directing the clerk of the House to add a death penalty provision to the bill. The Senate then agreed to the House amendment, but did not act on the concurrent resolution, effectively killing the death penalty provision. Adopted 378-16: R 164-0; D 214-16 (ND 143-15, SD 71-1), Oct. 17, 1986.

449. HR 6. Water Projects Authorization. Adoption of the rule (H Res 587) to waive points of order against House floor consideration of the conference report on the bill to authorize the Army Corps of Engineers to undertake various water resources development projects. Adopted 375-5: R 154-5; D 221-0 (ND 152-0, SD 69-0), Oct. 17, 1986.

450. HR 5300. Omnibus Budget Reconciliation, Fiscal 1987. Adoption of the conference report on the bill to reduce the projected fiscal 1987 deficit by an estimated $11.7 billion. Adopted 305-70: R 112-51; D 193-19 (ND 137-11, SD 56-8), Oct. 17, 1986.

451. HR 6. Water Projects Authorization. Adoption of the conference report on the bill to authorize the Army Corps of Engineers to undertake various water resources development projects, at an estimated federal and non-federal cost of approximately $16.5 billion. Obligations from the amounts authorized to be appropriated in the bill are limited to $1.4 billion in fiscal 1987, $1.5 billion in 1988, $1.6 billion in 1989, $1.7 billion in 1990, and $1.8 billion in 1991. Adopted 329-11: R 143-8; D 186-3 (ND 126-1, SD 60-2), Oct. 17, 1986.

KEY

Y Voted for (yea).
Paired for.
+ Announced for.
N Voted against (nay).
X Paired against.
- Announced against.
P Voted "present."
C Voted "present" to avoid possible conflict of interest.
? Did not vote or otherwise make a position known.

Democrats *Republicans*

	447	448	449	450	451
ALABAMA					
1 ***Callahan***	N	Y	Y	Y	Y
2 ***Dickinson***	N	Y	Y	Y	?
3 Nichols	?	?	?	?	?
4 Bevill	Y	Y	Y	Y	Y
5 Flippo	Y	Y	Y	Y	Y
6 Erdreich	Y	Y	Y	Y	Y
7 Shelby	Y	Y	Y	Y	Y
ALASKA					
AL ***Young***	N	Y	Y	Y	Y
ARIZONA					
1 ***McCain***	?	?	?	?	?
2 Udall	?	Y	Y	Y	Y
3 ***Stump***	N	Y	Y	N	Y
4 ***Rudd***	?	?	?	?	?
5 ***Kolbe***	N	Y	Y	N	?
ARKANSAS					
1 Alexander	Y	?	?	?	?
2 Robinson	Y	Y	Y	N	Y
3 ***Hammerschmidt***	Y	Y	Y	Y	Y
4 Anthony	Y	Y	Y	Y	Y
CALIFORNIA					
1 Bosco	Y	Y	?	Y	Y
2 ***Chappie***	N	Y	Y	N	Y
3 Matsui	Y	Y	Y	Y	Y
4 Fazio	Y	Y	Y	Y	Y
5 Burton	?	?	?	?	?
6 Boxer	?	?	?	?	?
7 Miller	Y	Y	Y	Y	?
8 Dellums	Y	N	Y	Y	Y
9 Stark	Y	Y	Y	Y	Y
10 Edwards	Y	N	Y	Y	Y
11 Lantos	Y	Y	Y	Y	Y
12 ***Zschau***	N	Y	Y	Y	Y
13 Mineta	Y	?	?	#	?
14 ***Shumway***	Y	Y	Y	N	Y
15 Coelho	Y	Y	Y	Y	Y
16 Panetta	Y	Y	Y	Y	?
17 ***Pashayan***	N	Y	Y	Y	Y
18 Lehman	Y	Y	Y	Y	Y
19 ***Lagomarsino***	N	Y	Y	Y	Y
20 ***Thomas***	N	Y	Y	N	Y
21 ***Fiedler***	N	Y	Y	N	Y
22 ***Moorhead***	N	Y	Y	N	Y
23 Beilenson	Y	Y	Y	N	Y
24 Waxman	Y	Y	Y	Y	Y
25 Roybal	Y	Y	Y	Y	Y
26 Berman	Y	Y	Y	Y	?
27 Levine	Y	Y	Y	Y	Y
28 Dixon	?	Y	Y	Y	Y
29 Hawkins	Y	Y	Y	Y	?
30 Martinez	?	Y	Y	Y	Y
31 Dymally	Y	Y	Y	Y	Y
32 Anderson	Y	Y	Y	N	Y
33 ***Dreier***	N	Y	Y	N	Y
34 Torres	?	Y	Y	Y	Y
35 ***Lewis***	N	Y	Y	Y	Y
36 Brown	?	?	?	?	?
37 ***McCandless***	N	Y	Y	N	Y
38 ***Dornan***	N	Y	Y	Y	Y
39 ***Dannemeyer***	N	Y	Y	N	Y
40 ***Badham***	N	Y	Y	Y	Y
41 ***Lowery***	?	Y	Y	Y	Y
42 ***Lungren***	N	Y	Y	N	Y
43 ***Packard***	N	Y	Y	N	Y
44 Bates	Y	Y	Y	Y	Y
45 ***Hunter***	?	Y	Y	N	Y
COLORADO					
1 Schroeder	N	Y	Y	N	?
2 Wirth	?	Y	Y	Y	Y
3 ***Strang***	N	Y	Y	Y	Y
4 ***Brown***	N	Y	Y	N	N
5 ***Kramer***	N	Y	Y	N	Y
6 ***Schaefer***	?	?	?	?	Y
CONNECTICUT					
1 Kennelly	Y	Y	Y	Y	Y
2 Gejdenson	Y	Y	Y	Y	Y
3 Morrison	Y	Y	Y	Y	Y
4 ***McKinney***	Y	Y	Y	Y	Y
5 ***Rowland***	N	Y	Y	Y	Y
6 ***Johnson***	Y	Y	Y	Y	Y
DELAWARE					
AL Carper	Y	Y	Y	Y	Y
FLORIDA					
1 Hutto	Y	Y	Y	Y	?
2 Fuqua	Y	Y	Y	Y	Y
3 Bennett	Y	Y	Y	Y	Y
4 Chappell	Y	Y	Y	Y	Y
5 ***McCollum***	Y	Y	Y	Y	Y
6 MacKay	Y	Y	Y	Y	Y
7 Gibbons	Y	Y	Y	Y	Y
8 ***Young***	N	Y	Y	Y	?
9 ***Bilirakis***	N	Y	Y	Y	?
10 ***Ireland***	N	Y	Y	N	Y
11 Nelson	Y	Y	Y	Y	Y
12 ***Lewis***	N	Y	Y	Y	Y
13 ***Mack***	N	Y	Y	N	N
14 Mica	Y	Y	?	Y	Y
15 ***Shaw***	N	Y	Y	Y	Y
16 Smith	Y	Y	Y	Y	Y
17 Lehman	Y	Y	Y	Y	Y
18 Pepper	Y	Y	Y	Y	Y
19 Fascell	Y	Y	Y	Y	Y
GEORGIA					
1 Thomas	Y	Y	Y	Y	Y
2 Hatcher	Y	Y	Y	Y	?
3 Ray	Y	Y	Y	N	Y
4 ***Swindall***	N	Y	Y	N	Y
5 Fowler	Y	Y	Y	?	?
6 ***Gingrich***	?	Y	Y	N	Y
7 Darden	Y	Y	Y	Y	Y
8 Rowland	Y	Y	Y	Y	Y
9 Jenkins	Y	Y	Y	Y	Y
10 Barnard	Y	Y	Y	N	Y
HAWAII					
1 Abercrombie	Y	N	Y	Y	Y
2 Akaka	Y	Y	Y	Y	Y
IDAHO					
1 ***Craig***	N	Y	Y	N	?
2 Stallings	Y	Y	Y	Y	Y
ILLINOIS					
1 Hayes	Y	N	Y	X	?
2 Savage	?	Y	Y	Y	?
3 Russo	Y	Y	Y	?	?
4 Vacancy					
5 Lipinski	Y	Y	Y	?	?
6 ***Hyde***	Y	Y	Y	Y	Y
7 Collins	Y	Y	Y	Y	Y
8 Rostenkowski	Y	Y	Y	Y	?
9 Yates	Y	Y	Y	Y	Y
10 ***Porter***	N	Y	Y	N	Y
11 Annunzio	Y	Y	Y	Y	Y
12 ***Crane***	?	?	N	?	N
13 ***Fawell***	N	Y	N	N	N
14 ***Grotberg***	?	?	?	?	?
15 ***Madigan***	N	Y	Y	Y	Y
16 ***Martin***	N	Y	Y	Y	Y
17 Evans	Y	Y	Y	Y	Y
18 ***Michel***	Y	Y	?	Y	Y
19 Bruce	Y	Y	Y	Y	Y
20 Durbin	Y	Y	Y	Y	Y
21 Price	Y	Y	Y	Y	Y
22 Gray	?	Y	Y	Y	Y
INDIANA					
1 Visclosky	Y	Y	Y	Y	Y
2 Sharp	Y	Y	Y	Y	Y
3 ***Hiler***	N	Y	Y	N	Y
4 ***Coats***	?	?	?	?	?
5 ***Hillis***	?	?	?	?	?

ND - Northern Democrats SD - Southern Democrats

	447	448	449	450	451
6 ***Burton***	N	Y	Y	N	?
7 ***Myers***	Y	Y	Y	N	?
8 McCloskey	Y	Y	Y	Y	Y
9 Hamilton	Y	Y	Y	Y	Y
10 Jacobs	N	Y	Y	Y	N
IOWA					
1 ***Leach***	N	Y	Y	Y	Y
2 ***Tauke***	N	Y	Y	Y	Y
3 ***Evans***	N	Y	Y	N	Y
4 Smith	Y	Y	Y	Y	Y
5 ***Lightfoot***	N	Y	Y	Y	Y
6 Bedell	Y	Y	Y	Y	Y
KANSAS					
1 ***Roberts***	N	Y	Y	Y	Y
2 Slattery	Y	Y	Y	Y	Y
3 ***Meyers***	N	Y	Y	Y	Y
4 Glickman	Y	Y	Y	Y	Y
5 ***Whittaker***	N	Y	Y	Y	Y
KENTUCKY					
1 Hubbard	Y	Y	Y	N	Y
2 Natcher	Y	Y	Y	Y	Y
3 Mazzoli	Y	Y	Y	Y	Y
4 ***Snyder***	Y	Y	Y	Y	Y
5 ***Rogers***	N	Y	Y	Y	Y
6 ***Hopkins***	Y	Y	Y	Y	Y
7 Perkins	Y	Y	Y	Y	N
LOUISIANA					
1 ***Livingston***	Y	Y	Y	N	Y
2 Boggs	?	Y	Y	Y	Y
3 Tauzin	Y	Y	Y	Y	Y
4 Roemer	N	Y	Y	N	Y
5 Huckaby	Y	Y	Y	Y	Y
6 ***Moore***	?	?	?	?	?
7 Breaux	?	?	?	?	?
8 Long	Y	Y	Y	?	Y
MAINE					
1 ***McKernan***	N	Y	Y	Y	Y
2 ***Snowe***	N	Y	Y	Y	Y
MARYLAND					
1 Dyson	N	Y	Y	Y	Y
2 ***Bentley***	?	Y	Y	Y	Y
3 Mikulski	?	Y	Y	Y	Y
4 ***Holt***	N	Y	Y	Y	Y
5 Hoyer	Y	N	Y	Y	Y
6 Byron	Y	Y	Y	Y	Y
7 Mitchell	?	Y	?	?	?
8 Barnes	?	Y	Y	Y	Y
MASSACHUSETTS					
1 ***Conte***	N	Y	Y	Y	Y
2 Boland	Y	Y	Y	Y	Y
3 Early	Y	Y	Y	Y	Y
4 Frank	Y	N	?	N	Y
5 Atkins	Y	Y	Y	?	?
6 Mavroules	?	Y	Y	Y	Y
7 Markey	Y	N	Y	Y	Y
8 O'Neill					
9 Moakley	Y	Y	Y	Y	?
10 Studds	Y	Y	Y	Y	?
11 Donnelly	Y	Y	Y	Y	Y
MICHIGAN					
1 Conyers	Y	N	Y	N	?
2 ***Pursell***	N	Y	Y	Y	Y
3 Wolpe	Y	Y	Y	Y	Y
4 ***Siljander***	?	Y	?	N	?
5 ***Henry***	N	Y	Y	N	?
6 Carr	Y	Y	Y	Y	Y
7 Kildee	Y	N	Y	Y	Y
8 Traxler	?	Y	Y	Y	?
9 ***Vander Jagt***	N	Y	Y	Y	Y
10 ***Schuette***	N	Y	Y	Y	Y
11 ***Davis***	?	Y	Y	Y	Y
12 Bonior	Y	Y	?	Y	Y
13 Crockett	Y	N	Y	N	?
14 Hertel	Y	Y	Y	Y	Y
15 Ford	?	Y	Y	Y	Y
16 Dingell	?	Y	Y	Y	Y
17 Levin	Y	Y	Y	Y	Y
18 ***Broomfield***	?	?	?	?	?
MINNESOTA					
1 Penny	N	Y	Y	N	Y
2 ***Weber***	N	Y	Y	Y	Y
3 ***Frenzel***	N	Y	Y	N	Y
4 Vento	?	Y	Y	Y	Y
5 Sabo	Y	N	Y	Y	Y
6 Sikorski	N	Y	Y	Y	Y
7 ***Stangeland***	?	Y	Y	Y	Y
8 Oberstar	?	Y	Y	Y	Y
MISSISSIPPI					
1 Whitten	?	Y	Y	Y	Y
2 ***Franklin***	N	Y	N	Y	N
3 Montgomery	Y	Y	Y	?	?
4 Dowdy	Y	Y	Y	Y	Y
5 ***Lott***	?	?	?	?	?
MISSOURI					
1 Clay	?	N	Y	Y	?
2 Young	Y	Y	Y	Y	Y
3 Gephardt	?	?	?	?	?
4 Skelton	Y	Y	Y	Y	Y
5 Wheat	Y	N	Y	Y	Y
6 ***Coleman***	N	Y	Y	Y	Y
7 ***Taylor***	Y	Y	Y	Y	Y
8 ***Emerson***	N	Y	Y	Y	Y
9 Volkmer	Y	Y	Y	?	?
MONTANA					
1 Williams	?	Y	Y	Y	Y
2 ***Marlenee***	N	Y	Y	N	Y
NEBRASKA					
1 ***Bereuter***	N	Y	Y	Y	Y
2 ***Daub***	N	Y	?	Y	Y
3 ***Smith***	Y	Y	Y	Y	Y
NEVADA					
1 Reid	Y	Y	Y	Y	Y
2 ***Vucanovich***	?	Y	Y	Y	Y
NEW HAMPSHIRE					
1 ***Smith***	N	Y	Y	N	Y
2 ***Gregg***	N	Y	Y	N	?
NEW JERSEY					
1 Florio	Y	Y	Y	N	Y
2 Hughes	Y	Y	Y	?	?
3 Howard	Y	Y	Y	Y	Y
4 ***Smith***	Y	Y	Y	Y	Y
5 ***Roukema***	N	Y	Y	Y	Y
6 Dwyer	Y	Y	Y	Y	Y
7 ***Rinaldo***	?	Y	Y	Y	Y
8 Roe	Y	Y	Y	Y	Y
9 Torricelli	Y	Y	Y	Y	?
10 Rodino	Y	Y	Y	Y	Y
11 ***Gallo***	N	Y	Y	Y	Y
12 ***Courter***	N	Y	Y	Y	Y
13 ***Saxton***	N	Y	Y	Y	Y
14 Guarini	Y	Y	Y	Y	Y
NEW MEXICO					
1 ***Lujan***	Y	Y	Y	N	?
2 ***Skeen***	N	Y	Y	Y	Y
3 Richardson	Y	Y	?	?	?
NEW YORK					
1 ***Carney***	N	Y	Y	N	Y
2 Downey	Y	Y	Y	Y	Y
3 Mrazek	Y	Y	Y	Y	Y
4 ***Lent***	N	Y	Y	Y	Y
5 ***McGrath***	?	?	?	#	?
6 Waldon	?	Y	Y	Y	?
7 Ackerman	Y	Y	?	?	?
8 Scheuer	Y	Y	Y	Y	Y
9 Manton	Y	Y	Y	Y	Y
10 Schumer	Y	Y	Y	Y	?
11 Towns	Y	?	Y	Y	Y
12 Owens	?	?	?	?	?
13 Solarz	Y	Y	Y	Y	?
14 ***Molinari***	N	Y	?	Y	Y
15 ***Green***	Y	Y	Y	Y	Y
16 Rangel	Y	Y	Y	Y	Y
17 Weiss	?	?	?	?	?
18 Garcia	Y	Y	Y	Y	?
19 Biaggi	?	?	?	?	?
20 ***DioGuardi***	?	?	?	?	?
21 ***Fish***	Y	Y	Y	Y	Y
22 ***Gilman***	Y	Y	Y	Y	Y
23 Stratton	Y	Y	Y	?	Y
24 ***Solomon***	N	Y	N	Y	N
25 ***Boehlert***	N	Y	Y	Y	Y
26 ***Martin***	N	Y	Y	Y	Y
27 ***Wortley***	Y	Y	Y	Y	Y
28 McHugh	?	Y	Y	Y	Y
29 ***Horton***	Y	Y	Y	Y	Y
30 ***Eckert***	Y	Y	Y	Y	Y
31 ***Kemp***	?	Y	Y	Y	Y
32 LaFalce	Y	Y	Y	Y	?
33 Nowak	Y	Y	Y	Y	Y
34 Lundine	?	?	?	?	?
NORTH CAROLINA					
1 Jones	Y	Y	Y	Y	Y
2 Valentine	Y	Y	Y	Y	Y
3 Whitley	Y	Y	Y	Y	Y
4 ***Cobey***	N	Y	Y	Y	Y
5 Neal	?	Y	Y	Y	Y
6 ***Coble***	N	Y	Y	Y	Y
7 Rose	?	?	?	?	?
8 Hefner	?	?	?	?	?
9 ***McMillan***	N	Y	Y	Y	Y
10 Vacancy					
11 ***Hendon***	N	Y	Y	Y	Y
NORTH DAKOTA					
AL Dorgan	Y	Y	Y	N	Y
OHIO					
1 Luken	Y	Y	Y	Y	Y
2 ***Gradison***	Y	Y	Y	?	?
3 Hall	Y	Y	Y	Y	Y
4 ***Oxley***	N	Y	Y	Y	?
5 ***Latta***	N	Y	Y	Y	Y
6 ***McEwen***	Y	Y	Y	N	Y
7 ***DeWine***	N	Y	Y	N	Y
8 ***Kindness***	N	Y	Y	Y	Y
9 Kaptur	?	?	?	?	?
10 ***Miller***	N	Y	Y	N	Y
11 Eckart	Y	Y	Y	N	Y
12 ***Kasich***	?	Y	Y	Y	Y
13 Pease	Y	Y	Y	Y	Y
14 Seiberling	?	Y	Y	Y	Y
15 ***Wylie***	Y	Y	Y	Y	Y
16 ***Regula***	Y	Y	Y	?	Y
17 Traficant	Y	Y	Y	Y	Y
18 Applegate	Y	Y	Y	Y	Y
19 Feighan	Y	Y	Y	Y	Y
20 Oakar	Y	Y	Y	Y	Y
21 Stokes	Y	N	Y	Y	Y
OKLAHOMA					
1 Jones	?	?	?	?	?
2 Synar	Y	Y	Y	Y	Y
3 Watkins	Y	Y	Y	Y	Y
4 McCurdy	?	Y	Y	?	?
5 ***Edwards***	?	Y	?	N	Y
6 English	Y	Y	Y	N	Y
OREGON					
1 AuCoin	Y	Y	Y	Y	Y
2 ***Smith, R.***	N	Y	Y	Y	Y
3 Wyden	Y	Y	Y	Y	Y
4 Weaver	?	?	?	?	?
5 ***Smith, D.***	N	Y	Y	N	Y
PENNSYLVANIA					
1 Foglietta	Y	Y	?	Y	?
2 Gray	Y	Y	Y	Y	Y
3 Borski	Y	Y	Y	Y	Y
4 Kolter	Y	Y	Y	Y	Y
5 ***Schulze***	Y	Y	Y	N	Y
6 Yatron	Y	Y	Y	Y	Y
7 Edgar	Y	Y	Y	Y	Y
8 Kostmayer	Y	Y	Y	Y	Y
9 ***Shuster***	N	Y	Y	N	Y
10 ***McDade***	Y	Y	Y	Y	Y
11 Kanjorski	?	Y	Y	Y	Y
12 Murtha	?	Y	Y	Y	Y
13 ***Coughlin***	N	Y	Y	Y	Y
14 Coyne	Y	Y	Y	Y	Y
15 ***Ritter***	?	Y	Y	Y	Y
16 ***Walker***	N	Y	N	N	N
17 ***Gekas***	N	Y	Y	Y	Y
18 Walgren	?	Y	Y	Y	Y
19 ***Goodling***	?	Y	Y	Y	Y
20 Gaydos	Y	Y	Y	Y	?
21 ***Ridge***	N	Y	Y	N	Y
22 Murphy	Y	Y	Y	Y	Y
23 ***Clinger***	Y	Y	Y	Y	Y
RHODE ISLAND					
1 St Germain	?	Y	Y	?	?
2 ***Schneider***	?	Y	Y	Y	Y
SOUTH CAROLINA					
1 ***Hartnett***	?	?	?	?	?
2 ***Spence***	Y	Y	Y	Y	Y
3 Derrick	?	Y	Y	Y	Y
4 ***Campbell***	?	?	?	?	?
5 Spratt	Y	Y	Y	?	?
6 Tallon	?	Y	Y	Y	Y
SOUTH DAKOTA					
AL Daschle	Y	Y	Y	N	Y
TENNESSEE					
1 ***Quillen***	Y	Y	Y	Y	?
2 ***Duncan***	Y	Y	Y	Y	Y
3 Lloyd	Y	Y	Y	Y	Y
4 Cooper	Y	Y	Y	Y	Y
5 Boner	?	Y	Y	Y	Y
6 Gordon	?	Y	Y	Y	Y
7 ***Sundquist***	N	Y	Y	Y	Y
8 Jones	?	Y	Y	Y	N
9 Ford	?	Y	Y	N	Y
TEXAS					
1 Chapman	?	Y	Y	Y	?
2 Wilson	?	Y	Y	?	?
3 ***Bartlett***	N	Y	Y	Y	Y
4 Hall, R.	Y	Y	Y	Y	Y
5 Bryant	?	Y	Y	Y	Y
6 ***Barton***	?	Y	Y	Y	Y
7 ***Archer***	?	?	?	?	?
8 ***Fields***	N	Y	Y	Y	Y
9 Brooks	?	?	?	?	?
10 Pickle	?	?	?	?	?
11 Leath	?	?	?	?	?
12 Wright	Y	Y	Y	?	?
13 ***Boulter***	N	Y	Y	Y	Y
14 ***Sweeney***	?	Y	Y	Y	Y
15 de la Garza	?	?	?	?	?
16 Coleman	Y	Y	Y	Y	Y
17 Stenholm	Y	Y	Y	Y	Y
18 Leland	Y	Y	?	Y	Y
19 ***Combest***	N	Y	Y	Y	Y
20 Gonzalez	Y	N	Y	N	Y
21 ***Loeffler***	?	?	?	?	?
22 ***DeLay***	N	Y	Y	N	Y
23 Bustamante	Y	Y	Y	Y	Y
24 Frost	?	Y	Y	Y	Y
25 Andrews	Y	Y	Y	Y	Y
26 ***Armey***	N	Y	Y	N	N
27 Ortiz	Y	Y	Y	Y	Y
UTAH					
1 ***Hansen***	?	?	?	X	?
2 ***Monson***	N	Y	Y	N	Y
3 ***Nielson***	N	Y	Y	N	Y
VERMONT					
AL ***Jeffords***	Y	Y	Y	Y	Y
VIRGINIA					
1 ***Bateman***	Y	Y	Y	Y	Y
2 ***Whitehurst***	Y	Y	Y	Y	Y
3 ***Bliley***	N	Y	Y	Y	Y
4 Sisisky	Y	Y	Y	Y	Y
5 Daniel	Y	Y	Y	?	?
6 Olin	Y	Y	Y	Y	Y
7 ***Slaughter***	Y	Y	Y	Y	Y
8 ***Parris***	N	Y	Y	Y	Y
9 Boucher	Y	Y	?	Y	Y
10 ***Wolf***	N	Y	Y	Y	Y
WASHINGTON					
1 ***Miller***	Y	Y	Y	Y	Y
2 Swift	Y	Y	Y	Y	Y
3 Bonker	Y	Y	Y	Y	Y
4 ***Morrison***	Y	Y	Y	Y	Y
5 Foley	Y	Y	Y	Y	Y
6 Dicks	Y	Y	Y	Y	Y
7 Lowry	Y	N	Y	Y	Y
8 ***Chandler***	N	Y	Y	N	Y
WEST VIRGINIA					
1 Mollohan	Y	Y	Y	Y	Y
2 Staggers	Y	Y	Y	Y	Y
3 Wise	Y	Y	Y	Y	Y
4 Rahall	Y	Y	Y	Y	Y
WISCONSIN					
1 Aspin	?	Y	Y	Y	?
2 Kastenmeier	Y	Y	Y	Y	Y
3 ***Gunderson***	N	Y	Y	Y	Y
4 Kleczka	Y	Y	Y	Y	Y
5 Moody	?	Y	Y	Y	Y
6 ***Petri***	Y	Y	Y	N	Y
7 Obey	Y	Y	Y	Y	Y
8 ***Roth***	Y	Y	Y	Y	Y
9 ***Sensenbrenner***	N	Y	Y	Y	Y
WYOMING					
AL ***Cheney***	N	Y	Y	N	Y

Southern states - Ala., Ark., Fla., Ga., Ky., La., Miss., N.C., Okla., S.C., Tenn., Texas, Va.

* The *Congressional Record* vote number is different from the CQ vote number because the *Record* includes quorum calls in its tally. CQ does not publish quorum call votes.

INDEXES

Roll Call Votes

General Index

CQ

In the index for 1986 roll call votes, numbers followed by the letter S refer to votes taken in the Senate; numbers followed by the letter H refer to votes taken in the House. The numbers are the page numbers for the Senate and House voting charts in this volume. Numbers followed by the letter C refer to Congressional Quarterly's annual voting studies. The number indicates the page of one of the five voting studies in which that vote is analyzed or discussed.

General Index

A

B

D

F

G

H

J

K

L

M

O

Q

R

S

X, Y, Z